Leslie Halliwell was born in Bolton. He ██████ ████
and series screened by the ITV netw██ ██████████
Hollywood in search of them; he has bee█ ██████████
since childhood. He has managed several Rank Organisation and
specialist cinemas and is a member of two National Film Archive
committees.

Mr Halliwell spent several years as a film reviewer for *Picturegoer* and
Sight and Sound and has contributed to other national publications. His
published works include *Halliwell's Filmgoer's Companion* (also
available in Paladin), *The Filmgoer's Book of Quotes*, *The Clapperboard
Book of the Cinema* (co-author), *Mountain of Dreams* and *Halliwell's
Teleguide*.

LESLIE HALLIWELL

HALLIWELL'S FILM GUIDE

Third Edition

PALADIN

Granada Publishing

Published in paperback by Granada Publishing Limited
in 1979
Reprinted 1980 (twice)
Second edition 1982, 1983
Third edition 1984

ISBN 0 586 08476 2

First published in Great Britain by
Granada Publishing 1977
Copyright © Leslie Halliwell 1977, 1979, 1981

Granada Publishing Limited
8 Grafton Street,
London W1X 3LA.

Reproduced, printed and bound in Great Britain by
Hazell Watson & Viney Limited,
Aylesbury, Bucks

Granada ®
Granada Publishing ®

Contents

Preface to the First Edition (1977)

During the twelve years which have elapsed since *The Filmgoer's Companion* first appeared. I have often been asked why I do not produce a complete compendium of all the films ever made, giving a minimum of useful information for each title. Some people even complain because the *Companion* does not provide all this. Plainly, with more than 25,000 English-speaking titles alone to contend with – and I am speaking here of feature-length films only – no one volume could hope to be comprehensive. and even if it were possible the attempt would be fairly pointless, for the book would be cluttered up with endless lists of routine second features of long ago, which no one in his right mind would even wish to remember, let alone see again.

In the *Companion* I do treat separately some seven or eight hundred titles which I consider significant either historically or as pure entertainment, and some readers have been annoyed when looking up films they consider memorable to discover that their titles have not accorded with my prejudices. Ever anxious to please. I have rearranged and amplified the information given in these entries, and multiplied the number of entries tenfold: hence the volume you hold in your hand, which I hope will provide an instant reference when what you want to look up is a movie rather than a person, a theme or a technical expression.

The key to the volume must still be selection, even with a goal of eight thousand entries. To some extent the selection must be personal, but readers of the *Companion* will be helped by having sensed the extent of my memory and the balance of my inclinations. (I think I may claim to have as reasonable a set of hang-ups as anyone now writing about films, except that I tend to hark back towards the old rather than the new, which is not a bad qualification for the job in hand.) I did feel it necessary, however, to restrict myself, at least in the first edition, to films wholly or partly financed in America or Britain. Obviously there are many foreign-language films which demanded inclusion, but it would have been impossible to select them on the same level: I could have given only a smattering of the better-known ones, which seemed unfair. The same is true of silent films, so I firmly put both problems aside for another day and limited myself to English-speaking talking films, which gave me fifty years of product to play with.

I have tried to include every film which seemed likely or worthy of remembrance by the keen filmgoer or student, whether with affection for its own sake as good entertainment, for showcasing memorable work by a particular talent, for sheer curiosity value or for box office success. This brings in virtually everything which played as a main feature in Britain or America. Co-features, 'programmers' and second features are included if they are known to have special merit or to show promise in some department: I have tried to omit the absolutely routine, and specifically excluded a few hundred westerns on the Audie Murphy and Randolph Scott level or below. Another way of looking at my choice is to say that the main studios to suffer are Republic. Monogram. PRC. Nettlefold and Mancunian. Other deliberate exclusions are porno films (hard or soft): underground films: documentaries and shorts: features below fifty-five minutes: exploitation and horror films from independent sources: from-the-stalls versions of ballet. opera and Shakespeare: and pop concerts on film.

I shall be disappointed if the regular reader of the *Companion* cannot find in this volume any film he is likely to require, unless he is a specialist in the early work of Edgar G. Ulmer, Maurice Elvey, or Harry d'Abbabie d'Arrast. Complaints of omissions will nevertheless be welcome: if only one reader sees merit in an excluded film, it has to be worthy of reconsideration next time. Be assured. however, that I already have another three thousand titles half researched ...

Here is a note of the information given for each film:

Title, with alternatives if used
Italicizing, as in the *Companion*, of any talent involved who makes a
    particularly outstanding or typical contribution
A rating system
Country of origin
Date of completion/release
Production company, with producer bracketed if named. (Distributor
    precedes production company if different)
Colour, including name of process, or black and white, and wide-screen or
    3-D systems if applicable
Brief synopsis
Brief appraisal (intended as an amalgam of the general view)
Writer, including original source
Director
Photographer
Composer of music score
Other credits as available and applicable
Principal cast with comments
Brief quotes from well-known critics (for about a fifth of the titles)

The compilation of such a tome is an enterprise both daunting and challenging. I could not have accomplished it without the help of many predecessors on whose research I have leaned. I salute especially the work of Leonard Maltin, James Robert Parish, Denis Gifford, Douglas Eames and the unsung anonymous heroes who compiled the reviews of the BFI's *Monthly Film Bulletin* during the fifties and sixties.

The least the reader will derive from this book, I hope, is a notion of the enormous variety of talent which has been poured into the film business during the last half-century. It is often said with justice that far too many film books are published: I hope this may be one of the most useful and comprehensive. I have certainly tried to pour a quart of information into a pint pot of paper, and any corrections or additions will certainly be welcomed. They should be sent to me, please, care of Granada TV, 36 Golden Square, London W.1.

August 1976   L.H.

Preface to the Second Edition

Apart from bringing in films released up to the autumn of 1978, this second edition has the following significant additions:

A selection of the most outstanding silent films which are still shown and discussed, or which are important to the history of the industry;

A selection of foreign-language films of significance, mainly those which have been shown and appreciated in Britain and America;

A further gleaning of English-speaking films omitted from the first edition, bringing the total of new entries to about 1,500.

To make room for the above, the TV movie entries have been transferred to my new *Teleguide*, which will be published at about the same time as this edition.

More than two thousand additions and corrections have been made to existing entries. Many of these clarify music credits, a matter of some complication; there are also many more critical quotes. I have also thought it worthwhile to list principal Academy Awards (AA) and also nominations (AAN). The final choice of these awards is sometimes a matter of fashion, but any nominated work is surely worth recording as being thought outstanding of its kind, even though it will be seen that these choices do not always accord with my own italics, and with some I would be in violent disagreement!

Further corrections, and suggestions for films to be included, will continue to be most welcome.

November 1978   L.H.

NB. The illustrations this time are more or less confined to a random selection of enjoyable movie advertising from the golden days. The films advertised are not necessarily important, but the advertisements are a form of film history in themselves.

Preface to the Third Edition

Apart from including releases up to the end of 1980, the preparation of this edition has involved the following labours:

Exploring the world of the second feature;

Rounding up some co-feature westerns, notably those starring Randolph Scott and Audie Murphy, and paying some attention to the output of Republic;

Skimming off another layer of historically important but inaccessible silent films;

Delving into Hollywood's early thirties and bringing to light many skilled entertainments of a mainly frivolous nature which fill up the careers of well-known actors and directors;

Unveiling some British quickies of the thirties, which though negligible as art often used top acting talent simply because it was there;

Selecting and including more than one thousand additional quotes;

Providing one hundred new illustrations.

All the new entries are, I trust, of interest to the cinéaste and historian, even though few of them strictly merit the single star rating which is my lowest accolade. However, in making room for more than two thousand new items (making the grand total something in excess of twelve thousand), some form of compression had to be devised. Accordingly, the additional films of lesser importance are now given in compact paragraph form, which may seem to rob them of dignity but in fact omits very little detail. The more spacious setting is still used for new films which seem to deserve it.

L.H.
January 1981

Acknowledgements

I am most grateful to all who have written with suggestions, and it has been my aim to reply to all letters. I have found especially useful the careful notes of Jack Docherty, T. G. Wheatley and Derrick Mighall.

It still seems surprising that the *Guide* provokes less correspondence than the *Companion*, but I am extremely grateful to those who have written with corrections, and especially to Thomas Sottrel.

Alphabetical Index of Alternative Titles

If the film you seek does not appear in the main section of the book and you suspect it to have more than one title, check it here. (NB: Foreign-language films are listed here only if they have more than one foreign- or English-language title. See the following lists for original titles or English-language versions.)

Abandon Ship *see* Seven Waves Away
Abbott and Costello Meet the Ghosts *see* Abbott and Costello Meet Frankenstein
Abdulla's Harem *see* Abdulla the Great
Adamson of Africa *see* The Killers of Kilimanjaro
Adventure for Two *see* The Demi-Paradise
Adventures of a Young Man *see* Hemingway's Adventures of a Young Man
The Adventures of Huckleberry Finn *see* Huckleberry Finn (1960)
The Adventures of Quentin Durward *see* Quentin Durward
The Adventuress *see* I See a Dark Stranger
Affair at the Villa Fiorita *see* The Battle of the Villa Fiorita
Affairs of a Rogue *see* The First Gentleman
Affairs of Sally *see* The Fuller Brush Girl
African Fury *see* Cry the Beloved Country
After Midnight *see* Captain Carey USA
Agent 8¼ *see* Hot Enough for June
Ah! Les Belles Bacchantes *see* Femmes de Paris
Airport '80: The Concorde *see* The Concorde: Airport '79
Alias Bulldog Drummond *see* Bulldog Jack
All at Sea *see* Barnacle Bill
All These Women *see* Now About All These Women . . .
All This and Money Too *see* Love is a Ball
Almost a Bride *see* A Kiss for Corliss
The Amazing Mr Forrest *see* The Gang's All Here (1939)
The Anatolian Smile *see* America, America
And Woman . . . Was Created *see* And God Created Woman
Angel Street *see* Gaslight (1939)
Angels and the Pirates *see* Angels in the Outfield
April Romance *see* Blossom Time
Armored Attack *see* North Star
Arms and the Girl *see* Red Salute
Arms and the Woman *see* Mr Winkle Goes to War
Arouse and Beware *see* The Man from Dakota
Arrivederci Baby *see* Drop Dead Darling
The Assassin (1947) *see* Gunfighters
The Assassin (1952) *see* Venetian Bird
At Dawn We Die *see* Tomorrow We Live
Atlantic Episode *see* Catch As Catch Can
Atoll K *see* Robinson Crusoeland
The Avengers *see* The Day Will Dawn

Baby Be Good *see* Brother Rat and Baby
The Baby Vanishes *see* Broadway Limited
Bachelor Bait *see* Adventure in Baltimore
Bachelor Girl Apartment *see* Any Wednesday
Bachelor Girls *see* The Bachelor's Daughter

Bachelor Knight *see* The Bachelor and the Bobbysoxer
Bad Man of Wyoming *see* Wyoming (1940)
Bad Sister *see* The White Unicorn
The Baited Trap *see* The Trap
The Bank Breaker *see* Kaleidoscope
The Bank Detective *see* The Bank Dick
The Battle for Anzio *see* Anzio
Battle Hell *see* Yangtse Incident
The Battle of Gallipoli *see* Tell England
The Battle of Midway *see* Midway
Battle Stripe *see* The Men
The Beachcomber *see* Vessel of Wrath
Beautiful but Dangerous *see* She Couldn't Say No
The Beautiful Rebel *see* Janice Meredith
Behind the Door *see* The Man with Nine Lives
Bengal Rifles *see* Bengal Brigade
Betrayed *see* When Strangers Marry
Beyond the River *see* The Bottom of the Bottle
The Big Bankroll *see* King of the Roaring Twenties
The Big Carnival *see* Ace in the Hole
Big Deal at Dodge City *see* A Big Hand for the Little Lady
Big Deal on Madonna Street *see* Persons Unknown
The Big Heart *see* Miracle on 34th Street
The Big Story *see* Appointment with a Shadow
Big Time Operators *see* The Smallest Show on Earth
Billy Rose's Diamond Horseshoe *see* Diamond Horseshoe
Billy Rose's Jumbo *see* Jumbo
The Birds and the Bees *see* Three Daring Daughters
The Bishop's Misadventures *see* The Bishop Misbehaves
The Black Arrow Strikes *see* The Black Arrow
Black Bart, Highwayman *see* Black Bart
The Black Book *see* Reign of Terror
Black Flowers for the Bride *see* Something for Everyone
Blackout *see* Contraband
Blonde Bombshell *see* Bombshell
A Blonde in Love *see* Loves of a Blonde
Blonde Sinner *see* Yield to the Night
Blood Money *see* Requiem for a Heavyweight
Blood on My Hands *see* Kiss the Blood Off My Hands
Blood on Satan's Claw *see* Satan's Skin
Blue Jeans *see* Blue Denim
Blues for Lovers *see* Ballad in Blue
Bombsight Stolen *see* Cottage to Let
Bonaventure *see* Thunder on the Hill
Borderlines *see* The Caretakers
Born for Glory *see* Brown on Resolution
Born for Trouble *see* Murder in the Big House

The Hands of Orlac (1935) *see* Mad Love
Happy Landing *see* Flying High
Happy Times *see* The Inspector General
Hara Kiri *see* The Battle
Hard Driver *see* The Last American Hero
The Hardcore Life *see* Hardcore
Harmony Parade *see* Pigskin Parade
The Harp of Burma *see* The Burmese Harp
Harry Black *see* Harry Black and the Tiger
The Haunted and the Hunted *see* Dementia 13
Haunted Honeymoon *see* Busman's Honeymoon
The Haunted Strangler *see* Grip of the Strangler
Having a Wild Weekend *see* Catch Us If You Can
The Heir to Genghis Khan *see* Storm Over Asia
The Heist *see* Dollars
Hell Bent for Glory *see* Lafayette Escadrille
Hell, Heaven and Hoboken *see* I Was Monty's
    Double
Hell in Korea *see* A Hill in Korea
Hello Beautiful *see* The Powers Girl
Her Man Gilbey *see* English without Tears
Her Panelled Door *see* The Woman with No Name
Here Is a Man *see* All That Money Can Buy
The Heroin Gang *see* Sol Madrid
The Hidden Room *see* Obsession (1948)
The Hideout *see* The Small Voice
High and Dry *see* The Maggie
The High Commissioner *see* Nobody Runs Forever
High Fury *see* White Cradle Inn
High Vermilion *see* Silver City
The High Window *see* The Brasher Doubloon
Highway to Freedom *see* Joe Smith American
Hill's Angels *see* The North Avenue Irregulars
His Affair *see* This is My Affair
His Other Woman *see* Desk Set
Hit Parade of 1943 *see* Change of Heart
Hitler's Hangman *see* Hitler's Madman
Hold That Girl *see* Hold That Co-Ed
Hollow Triumph *see* The Scar
Hollywood Cowboy *see* Hearts of the West
The Honourable Mr Wong *see* The Hatchet Man
Horror Hotel *see* City of the Dead
Horror of Dracula *see* Dracula (1958)
The Hot One *see* Corvette Summer
Hot Spot *see* I Wake Up Screaming
Hounded *see* Johnny Allegro
The Hounds of Zaroff *see* The Most Dangerous
    Game
Hour of Glory *see* The Small Back Room
House of Doom *see* The Black Cat
House of Fright *see* The Two Faces of Dr Jekyll
House of Menace *see* Kind Lady
House of Mystery *see* Night Monster
House of Settlement *see* Mr Soft Touch
How to Rob a Bank *see* A Nice Little Bank That
    Should Be Robbed
How to Steal a Diamond in Four Uneasy Lessons
    see The Hot Rock
The Human Monster *see* Dark Eyes of London

I Became a Criminal *see* They Made Me a Fugitive
I Even Knew Happy Gypsies *see* Happy Gypsies
I Like Money *see* Mr Topaze
I Live for You *see* I Live for Love
I Married a Communist *see* The Woman on Pier 13
I Married a Nazi *see* The Man I Married
I Shall Return *see* An American Guerrilla in
    the Philippines
I Stand Condemned *see* Moscow Nights
I Was a Fireman *see* Fires Were Started
If This Be Sin *see* That Dangerous Age
If You Feel Like Singing *see* Summer Stock

I'll Never Forget You *see* The House in the Square
Imaginary Sweetheart *see* Professional Sweetheart
Immortal Battalion *see* The Way Ahead
The Imperfect Lady *see* The Perfect Gentleman
The Impossible Lover *see* Huddle
Indian Summer *see* The Judge Steps Out
Indiscretion (1954) *see* Indiscretion of an
    American Wife
Indiscretion (1945) *see* Christmas in Connecticut
The Inheritance *see* Uncle Silas
Innocence is Bliss *see* Miss Grant Takes Richmond
Intrigue in Paris *see* Miss V from Moscow
The Invaders *see* 49th Parallel
An Investigation of Murder *see* The Laughing
    Policeman
Island Escape *see* No Man is an Island
Island of Desire *see* Saturday Island
Island Rescue *see* Appointment with Venus
It Happened One Summer *see* State Fair (1945)
It's Hot in Hell *see* A Monkey in Winter
It's Magic *see* Romance on the High Seas
It's Only Money *see* Double Dynamite
Ivory Hunter *see* Where No Vultures Fly

Jacqueline Susann's Once is Not Enough *see*
    Once is Not Enough
Jailbirds *see* Pardon Us
The James Brothers *see* The True Story of
    Jesse James
Jennie *see* Portrait of Jennie
Jenny Lind *see* A Lady's Morals
Jet Men of the Air *see* Air Cadet
Johnny in the Clouds *see* The Way to the Stars
Johnny Vagabond *see* Johnny Come Lately
Jungle Fighters *see* The Long and the Short
    and the Tall
Justice for Sale *see* Night Court

The Kid's Last Fight *see* The Life of Jimmy Dolan
Killer Grizzly *see* Grizzly
Killer on a Horse *see* Welcome to Hard Times
Kisenga, Man of Africa *see* Men of Two Worlds
Kiss of Evil *see* Kiss of the Vampire

The Lady and the Doctor *see* The Lady and
    the Monster
Lady Hamilton *see* That Hamilton Woman
Lady in Distress *see* A Window in London
Lady of Deceit *see* Born to Kill
A Lady Surrenders *see* Love Story (1944)
Lady Windermere's Fan *see* The Fan
Land of Fury *see* The Seekers
Larceny Lane *see* Blonde Crazy
The Last Days of Man on Earth *see* The Final
    Programme
The Last Frontier *see* Savage Wilderness
The Last Gangster *see* Roger Touhy, Gangster
The Last Warrior *see* Flap
Laurel and Hardy in Toyland *see* Babes in
    Toyland (1934)
Lazy Bones *see* Hallelujah I'm a Bum
Lest We Forget *see* Hangmen Also Die
Let's Make Up *see* Lilacs in the Spring
The Light of Heart *see* Life Begins at Eight-Thirty
Lights Out *see* Bright Victory
Lisa *see* The Inspector
The Little Kidnappers *see* The Kidnappers
Live Today for Tomorrow *see* An Act of Murder
Lock Your Doors *see* The Ape Man
Lola *see* Twinky
The Lolly Madonna War *see* Lolly Madonna XXX
Long Ago Tomorrow *see* The Raging Moon

Saraband *see* Saraband for Dead Lovers
Satan's Skin *see* Blood on Satan's Claw
The Scarlet Buccaneer *see* Swashbuckler
Scotch on the Rocks *see* Laxdale Hall
Scream of Fear *see* Taste of Fear
The Sea Wall *see* This Angry Age
Season of Passion *see* Summer of the Seventeenth Doll
The Second Best Secret Agent in the Whole Wide World *see* Licensed to Kill
Secret Flight *see* School for Secrets
The Secret Four *see* The Four Just Men
Secret Interlude *see* The View from Pompey's Head
See No Evil *see* Blind Terror
See You in Hell Darling *see* An American Dream
Separate Beds *see* The Wheeler Dealers
Serenade *see* Broadway Serenade
Seven Different Ways *see* Quick Let's Get Married
The Shame of a Nation *see* Scarface
She Got Her Man *see* Maisie (Maisie Gets Her Man)
She Played with Fire *see* Fortune is a Woman
Sherlock Holmes (1939) *see* The Adventures of Sherlock Holmes
Shoot First *see* Rough Shoot
The Shop on the High Street *see* The Shop on Main Street
Sidewalks of London *see* St Martin's Lane
The Silent Stranger *see* Step Down to Terror
The Silent Voice (1932) *see* The Man Who Played God
The Silent Voice (1952) *see* Paula
The Singing Musketeer *see* The Three Musketeers (1939)
Sinners' Holiday *see* Christmas Eve
Slade *see* Jack Slade
Smiling Along *see* Keep Smiling
Smoke Jumpers *see* Red Skies of Montana
Smokey and the Bandit Ride Again *see* Smokey and the Bandit II
The Smugglers *see* The Man Within
Snow Job *see* The Ski Raiders
Snow White and the Three Clowns *see* Snow White and the Three Stooges
So Bright the Flame *see* The Girl in White
Somewhere in France *see* The Foreman Went to France
Sons of the Musketeers *see* At Sword's Point
Sons of the Sea *see* Atlantic Ferry
The Sound of Fury *see* Try and Get Me
Southwest to Sonora *see* The Appaloosa
The Spell of Amy Nugent *see* Spellbound (GB)
Spin of a Coin *see* The George Raft Story
Spinster *see* Two Loves
Spirit of the People *see* Abe Lincoln in Illinois
Spitfire *see* The First of the Few
Spy in the Pantry *see* Ten Days in Paris
The Spy in White *see* The Secret of Stamboul
Spy 13 *see* Operator 13
Spylarks *see* The Intelligence Men
Stairway to Heaven *see* A Matter of Life and Death
Stampeded *see* The Big Land
The Star Said No *see* Callaway Went Thataway
Stop Me before I Kill *see* The Full Treatment
Storm over Africa *see* Royal African Rifles
The Story of Dr Ehrlich's Magic Bullet *see* Dr Ehrlich's Magic Bullet
Stowaway Girl *see* Manuela
Stranded in Paris *see* Artists and Models Abroad
Strange Incident *see* The Ox Bow Incident
Strange Interval *see* Strange Interlude
The Stranger *see* The Intruder (1961)
The Stranger in Between *see* Hunted
A Stranger Walked In *see* Love from a Stranger

The Strangler *see* East of Piccadilly
Strauss's Great Waltz *see* Waltzes from Vienna
The Streetfighter *see* Hard Times
Strictly Confidential *see* Broadway Bill
Strictly for Pleasure *see* The Perfect Furlough
Striptease Lady *see* Lady of Burlesque
Stronger than Fear *see* Edge of Doom
Submarine Zone *see* Escape to Glory
Such Men Are Dangerous *see* The Racers
The Suicide Club *see* Trouble for Two
Suicide Squadron *see* Dangerous Moonlight
Summer Lightning *see* Scudda Hoo Scudda Hay
Summer Madness *see* Summertime
Surrounded by Women *see* Between Two Women
S.W.A.L.K. *see* Melody
Sweet Aloes *see* Give Me Your Heart
Sweet Revenge *see* Dandy the All-American Girl
Swing. Teacher. Swing *see* College Swing
Swirl of Glory *see* Sugarfoot
Sword of Lancelot *see* Lancelot and Guinevere

Tainted Money *see* Show Them No Mercy
Take the Stage *see* Curtain Call at Cactus Creek
A Tale of Five Women *see* A Tale of Five Cities
Tammy *see* Tammy and the Bachelor Girl
Target for Scandal *see* Washington Story
Tartu *see* The Adventures of Tartu
Tears for Simon *see* Lost
Teenage Frankenstein *see* I Was a Teenage Frankenstein
Teenage Bad Girl *see* My Teenage Daughter
Ten Little Niggers *see* And Then There Were None (1945)
Terminus Station *see* Indiscretion of an American Wife
Terror House *see* The Night Has Eyes
Terror on a Train *see* Time Bomb
Texas to Tokyo *see* We've Never Been Licked
Thank You All Very Much *see* A Touch of Love
That Mad Mr Jones *see* The Fuller Brush Man
Theatre Royal *see* The Royal Family of Broadway
Their Secret Affair *see* Top Secret Affair
Thelma Jordon *see* The File on Thelma Jordon
These Are the Damned *see* The Damned (GB)
They All Died Laughing *see* A Jolly Bad Fellow
They're Off *see* Straight. Place and Show
Thieves' Holiday *see* A Scandal in Paris
The Third Key *see* The Long Arm
This Is My Affair *see* I Can Get It for You Wholesale
This Man Reuter *see* A Dispatch from Reuter's
This Rebel Age *see* The Beat Generation
Three Cockeyed Sailors *see* Sailors Three
Three Men and a Girl *see* Golden Arrow (1949)
Three on a Weekend *see* Bank Holiday
Thunder Across the Pacific *see* The Wild Blue Yonder
Thunder in the East *see* The Battle
Thundercloud *see* Colt 45
Tiger in the Sky *see* The McConnell Story
Tiger Man *see* The Lady and the Monster
Tight Little Island *see* Whisky Galore
Time for Action *see* Tip on a Dead Jockey
Time Lost and Time Remembered *see* I Was Happy Here
To the Victor *see* Owd Bob
Toast of the Legion *see* Kiss Me Again (1931)
The Tomahawk and the Cross *see* Pillars of the Sky
Tonight's the Night *see* Happy Ever After (1954)
Too Many Chefs *see* Who Is Killing the Great Chefs of Europe?
Too Dangerous to Love *see* Perfect Strangers (1950)
Tops is the Limit *see* Anything Goes
Torment *see* Frenzy

Torpedoed see Our Fighting Navy
A Town Called Bastard see A Town Called Hell
Transatlantic Tunnel see The Tunnel
Treason see Guilty of Treason
The Tree of Liberty see The Howards of Virginia
Trelawny of the Wells see The Actress
Trial and Error see The Dock Brief
Troopship see Farewell Again
Tropicana see The Heat's On
Trouble in the Sky see Cone of Silence
The Trouble Shooter see The Man with the Gun
The Trunk Mystery see One New York Night
Try and Find It see Hi Diddle Diddle
Tunnel 28 see Escape from East Berlin
Twist of Fate see Beautiful Stranger
Two Men and a Girl see Honeymoon (US)
Two Minds for Murder see Someone Behind the
    Door
Two Texas Knights see Two Guys from Texas
Two Who Dared see A Woman Alone

U Boat 29 see The Spy in Black
Unconventional Linda see Holiday (1938)
Under the Clock see The Clock
Undercover Girl see Maisie (Undercover Maisie)
Undercovers Hero see Soft Beds, Hard Battles
Underworld Informers see The Informers
The Unholy Four see The Stranger Came Home
Unidentified Flying Oddball see The Spaceman
    and King Arthur
Unseen Heroes see The Battle of the VI
Up She Goes see Maisie (Up Goes Maisie)
USS Teakettle see You're in the Navy Now
Utopia see Robinson Crusoeland

Vacation from Marriage see Perfect Strangers (GB)
Valley of Fury see Chief Crazy Horse
Vaudeville see Variety
The Violent Hour see Dial 1119
Viva Las Vegas! (1956) see Meet Me in Las Vegas
A Voice in the Night see Freedom Radio

Wages of Fear see Sorcerer
Walking Down Broadway see Hello Sister
War Correspondent see The Story of GI Joe
War Gods of the Deep see City under the Sea
The Warriors see The Dark Avenger
Waterfront Women see Waterfront
Web of Evidence see Beyond This Place
Wedding Bells see Royal Wedding
Wedding Breakfast see The Catered Affair
Wee Geordie see Geordie
Welcome Home see SNAFU
We're in the Army Now see Pack Up Your Troubles
West of Montana see Mail Order Bride
What a Man see Never Give a Sucker an Even Break
What Lola Wants see Damn Yankees

What Shall It Profit see Hard Steel
When Boys Leave Home see Downhill
When New York Sleeps see Now I'll Tell
When the Door Opened see Escape (1940)
When the Girls Meet the Boys see Girl Crazy
When Thief Meets Thief see Jump for Glory
Where the River Bends see Bend of the River
White Captive see White Savage
The White Man see The Squaw Man
White Savage see South of Tahiti
Why Bother to Knock see Don't Bother to Knock
The Wicked Wife see Grand National Night
The Wild Heart see Gone to Earth
Wildcat see The Great Scout and Cathouse
    Thursday
A Window to the Sky see The Other Side of the
    Mountain
Wings and the Woman see They Flew Alone
The Winning Way see The All American
Witch Doctor see Men of Two Worlds
Within the Law see Paid
A Woman Alone see Sabotage
The Woman Between see The Woman I Love
A Woman Destroyed see Smash-Up. The Story
    of a Woman
The Woman in His House see The Animal Kingdom
Woman of Dolwyn see The Last Days of Dolwyn
Woman of Summer see The Stripper
A Woman of the World see Outcast Lady
Woman without a Face see Mister Buddwing
Wooden Soldiers see Babes in Toyland (1934)
The World and His Wife see State of the Union
The Wrong Kind of Girl see Bus Stop
The Wyoming Kid see Cheyenne

X, Y and Zee see Zee and Co

A Yank in Dutch see The Wife Takes a Flyer
A Yank in London see I Live in Grosvenor Square
A Yankee in King Arthur's Court see A Connecticut
    Yankee in King Arthur's Court
Years without Days see Castle on the Hudson
The Yellow Passport see The Yellow Ticket
You Belong to My Heart see Mr Imperium
You Can't Do That to Me see Maisie (Maisie
    Goes to Reno)
You Can't Sleep Here see I Was a Male War Bride
You Can't Take Money see Internes Can't Take
    Money
You Don't Need Pajamas at Rosie's see The First
    Time
You Never Know see You Never Can Tell
Young and Eager see Claudelle Inglish
The Young Invaders see Darby's Rangers
Young Man of Music see Young Man with a Horn
Young Scarface see Brighton Rock
Your Past is Showing see The Naked Truth
You're in the Army Now see O.H.M.S.

Zombies see Dawn of the Dead

English-Language Titles of Foreign Films

Are We All Murderers? *see* Nous Sommes Tous Les Assassins
An Artist with Ladies *see* Coiffeur pour Dames

The Baker's Wife *see* La Femme du Boulanger
The Ballad of Berlin *see* Berliner Ballade
The Battle of Austerlitz *see* Austerlitz
Bay of Angels *see* La Baie des Anges
Beyond the Gates *see* Au dela des Grilles
Birds of a Feather *see* La Cage aux Folles
Bluebeard *see* Landru
Boudu Saved from Drowning *see* Boudu Sauvé des Eaux
Breathless *see* A Bout de Souffle
The Butcher *see* Le Boucher

Carnival in Flanders *see* La Kermesse Héroïque
Children of Paradise *see* Les Enfants du Paradis
Christine *see* Un Carnet de Bal
Comradeship *see* Kameradschaft
The Crazy Ray *see* Paris Qui Dort
The Cry *see* Il Grido

A Day in the Country *see* Une Partie de Campagne
Daybreak *see* Le Jour Se Lève
Days of Hope *see* Espoir
Devil in the Flesh *see* Le Diable au Corps
The Devil's Envoys *see* Les Visiteurs du Soir
Dirty Hands *see* Les Mains Sales
The Does *see* Les Biches
A Dog's Life *see* Mondo Cane
Doomed *see* Ikiru
The Double *see* Kagemusha

The Earrings of Madame de *see* Madame de
Ecstasy *see* Extase
Every Second Counts *see* Les Assassins du Dimanche

Father and Master *see* Padre Padrone
The Fiends *see* Les Diaboliques
Film without Title *see* Film ohne Titel
Forbidden Games *see* Les Jeux Interdits
Frontier *see* Aerograd

Gate of Lilacs *see* Porte des Lilas
Gates of Night *see* Les Portes de la Nuit
The Girl Friends *see* Le Amiche
Girls in Uniform *see* Maedchen in Uniform
God Needs Men *see* Dieu a Besoin des Hommes
The Goddess *see* Devi
Golden Marie *see* Casque d'Or

Hands off the Loot *see* Touchez pas au Grisbi
Hanged Man's Farm *see* La Ferme du Pendu
Heroism *see* Eroica
The Hole *see* Onibaba
Holiday for Henrietta *see* La Fête à Henriette
Honour Among Thieves *see* Touchez pas au Grisbi
The Human Beast *see* La Bête Humaine

I Have a New Master *see* L'Ecole Buissonière
In the Woods *see* Rashomon
Isle of Sinners *see* Dieu a Besoin des Hommes
It Happened at the Inn *see* Goupi Mains Rouges
It's in the Bag *see* L'Affaire est dans le Sac

Judas Was a Woman *see* La Bête Humaine

Keep an Eye on Amelia *see* Occupe-Toi d'Amélie

Living *see* Ikiru
The Long Absence *see* Une Aussi Longue Absence
Love Is My Profession *see* En Cas de Malheur
Love Story *see* Une Histoire d'Amour
The Lovers *see* Les Amants
The Lovers of Verona *see* Les Amants de Vérone
The Lower Depths *see* Les Bas-fonds

Man's Hope *see* Espoir
My Night at Maud's *see* Ma Nuit chez Maud

Nights of Cabiria *see* Cabiria

The Outsiders *see* Bande à Part

The Phantom Baron *see* Le Baron Fantôme
Port of Shadows *see* Quai des Brumes

The Raven *see* Le Corbeau
The Road *see* La Strada
The Road to Hope *see* Il Cammino della Speranza
The Rules of the Game *see* La Règle du Jeu

The Saga of Anatahan *see* Anatahan
Savage Princess *see* Aan
Scarlet and Black *see* Le Rouge et le Noir
The Secret Game *see* Les Jeux Interdits
Shadow Warrior *see* Kagemusha
Spivs *see* I Vitelloni
Stormy Waters *see* Remorques
The Story of a Cheat *see* Le Roman d'un Tricheur
The Strange Adventure of David Gray *see* Vampyr
The Strange Ones *see* Les Enfants Terribles
Such a Pretty Little Beach *see* Une Si Jolie Petite Plage
Summer Manoeuvres *see* Les Grandes Manoeuvres
The Sweet Life *see* La Dolce Vita
The Swindlers *see* Il Bidone
Swords of Blood *see* Cartouche

The Testament of Orpheus *see* Le Testament d'Orphée
They Loved Life *see* Kanal
This Strange Passion *see* El
The Threepenny Opera *see* Die Dreigroschenoper
A Time to Live and a Time to Die *see* Le Feu Follet
Torments *see* El
The Tragic Pursuit *see* Caccia Tragica
Two Pennyworth of Hope *see* Due Soldi de Speranza

Original Titles of Foreign-Language Films Listed in English

Aimez-Vous les Femmes? *see* Do You Like Women?

Akahige *see* Redbeard

Akasen Chitai *see* Street of Shame

Alskande Par *see* Loving Couples

Les Amants du Tage *see* The Lovers of Lisbon

Les Amours de la Reine Elisabeth *see* Queen Elizabeth

El Angel Exterminador *see* The Exterminating Angel

Ansiktet *see* The Face

L'Argent de Poche *see* Small Change

Ascenseur pour l'Echafaud *see* Lift to the Scaffold

Attilo Flagello di Dio *see* Attila the Hun

Au Hasard, Balthazar *see* Balthazar

L'Auberge Rouge *see* The Red Inn

Un Autre Homme, une Autre Chance *see* Another Man, Another Chance

L'Aveu *see* The Confession

Babette S'en Va-t-en Guerre *see* Babette Goes to War

Baisers Volés *see* Stolen Kisses

Ballada o Soldate *see* Ballad of a Soldier

Banditi a Orgoloso *see* Bandits of Orgoloso

Baron Prasil *see* Baron Munchausen

La Battaglia di Algeri *see* The Battle of Algiers

Berlin, die Symphone einer Grossstadt *see* Berlin, Symphony of a Great City

Betrogen bis zum Jungsten Tag *see* Duped Till Doomsday

Bezhin Lug *see* Bezhin Meadow

Les Bijoutiers du Clair de Lune *see* Heaven Fell That Night

Die Blechtrommel *see* The Tin Drum

Biruma no Tategoto *see* The Burmese Harp

Bronenosets Potemkin *see* Battleship Potemkin

El Bruto *see* The Brute

Die Büchse der Pandora *see* Pandora's Box

Il Buono, il Bruto, il Cattivo *see* The Good, the Bad and the Ugly

Cadaveri Eccellenti *see* Illustrious Corpses

La Caida *see* The Fall

O'Cangaceiro *see* The Bandit

Le Caporal Epinglé *see* The Vanishing Corporal

Les Carnets de Major Thompson *see* The Diary of Major Thompson

Le Carrosse d'Or *see* The Golden Coach

La Casa del Angel *see* The House of the Angel

La Casse *see* The Burglars

Celui Qui Doit Mourir *see* He Who Must Die

Le Charm Discret de la Bourgeoisie *see* The Discreet Charm of the Bourgeoisie

Chelovek s Kinoapparatom *see* The Man with the Movie Camera

La Ciociara *see* Two Women

La Città delle Donne *see* City of Women

Compartiment Tueurs *see* The Sleeping Car Murders

Cybéle ou les Dimanches de Ville d'Avray *see* Sundays and Cybéle

Dama s Sobachkoi *see* The Lady with the Little Dog

Déjeuner sur l'Herbe *see* Lunch on the Grass

Les Demoiselles de Rochefort *see* The Young Girls of Rochefort

La Dentellière *see* The Lacemaker

Il Deserto Rosso *see* The Red Desert

Destinées *see* Love, Soldiers and Women

La Diga sul Pacifico *see* This Angry Age

Ditte Menneskebarn *see* Ditte, Child of Man

Divorzio all'Italiana *see* Divorce Italian Style

En Djungelsaga *see* The Flute and the Arrow

Doktor Mabuse, der Spieler *see* Doctor Mabuse

Don Camillo e l'Onorevolo Peppone *see* Don Camillo's Last Round

Dorp aan de Rivier *see* Doctor in the Village

L'Eclisse *see* The Eclipse

En Compagnie de Max Linder *see* Laugh with Max Linder

Ensayo de un Crimen *see* The Criminal Life of Archibaldo de la Cruz

Ercole e la Regina di Lidia *see* Hercules Unchained

Es Geschah am 20 Juli *see* Jackboot Mutiny

L'Espion *see* The Defector

Et Dieu Créa la Femme *see* And God Created Woman

Et Mourir de Plaisir *see* Blood and Roses

L'Eternel Retour *see* Love Eternal

Fängelse *see* The Devil's Wanton

Le Fatiche di Ercole *see* Hercules

Die Freudlose Gasse *see* Joyless Street

Le Fruit Défendu *see* Forbidden Fruit

Il Gattopardo *see* The Leopard

Giulietta degli Spiriti *see* Juliet of the Spirits

Gosta Berlings Saga *see* The Atonement of Gosta Berling

La Grande Vadrouille *see* Don't Look Now... We're Being Shot At!

Götterdamerung *see* The Damned (1969)

Gruppo di Famiglia in un Interno *see* Conversation Piece

Gycklarnas Afton *see* Sawdust and Tinsel

Hadaka no Shima *see* The Island

Haxan *see* Witchcraft through the Ages

Les Héros Sont Fatigués *see* The Heroes Are Tired

Hets *see* Frenzy

L'Homme de Rio *see* That Man from Rio

Un Homme et une Femme *see* A Man and a Woman

Hori, Ma Panenko *see* The Firemen's Ball

L'Horlorgier de St Paul *see* The Watchmaker of St Paul

Las Hurdes *see* Land without Bread

Explanatory Notes

Title   The complete title is given, though the definite and indefinite articles are not of course counted in the alphabetical arrangement. The spelling of the country of origin is used, e.g. *My Favorite Blonde* rather than *My Favourite Blonde*.

Alphabetical order   Hyphenated or apostrophized words are counted as one word, and as usual in reference books the order is taken not by the complete title but a word at a time, e.g. *No Room at the Inn* comes before *Nob Hill*. Mac and Mc are regarded as interchangeable under Mac.

Ratings   It would be absurd to classify films selected from a period of fifty years as to which are the best or the worst. Techniques improve, standards change, and personal preferences have to be accounted for. I have tried, however, to give credit for what seemed excellent or innovative at the time, even though it may have been overtaken by imitators; I have tried to judge each film by its own standards (how could one sensibly compare *Frankenstein Meets the Wolf Man* with *Gone with the Wind*?), and I have rescrutinized it now to see what historical or artistic interest it retains. Mere entertainment value has not been derided, nor have films which may seem naive but give an accurate picture of the standards of their own time. To sum up in one word, the ratings indicate how much *interest* a film is thought to have for the modern viewer, whether he be a student or a reasonably alert seeker of entertainment.

Four stars, then, indicate a film outstanding in many ways, a milestone in cinema history, remarkable for acting, direction, writing, photography or some other aspect of technique. Three stars indicate a very high standard of professional excellence or high historical interest: or if you like, three strong reasons for admiring it. Two stars indicate a good level of competence and a generally entertaining film. One star draws attention to minor points of merit, usually in a film not very satisfactory as a whole; it could be a failed giant or a second feature with a few interesting ideas among the dross. No stars at all indicates a totally routine production or worse; such films may be watchable but are at least equally missable.

It will be seen that my judgements are fairly harsh, but I hope they are consistent. For further elucidation of my personal prejudices see the essay, 'The Decline and Fall of the Movie', on p. 1447

Country of origin   First item on second line.

Year of release   Comes after country of origin, and is intended to be the year in which the film was first shown. If it was made earlier and held back, I have tried to indicate the fact. Dating is sometimes an onerous task, and the result debatable; please be sympathetic.

Running time   In minutes, signified by 'm'. As far as possible this is the original release time. Very many films are cut when they cross the water, sometimes by twenty minutes or more, but I have not tried to indicate this, as when the film appears on television a new print is usually taken from the original negative (but may be cut again). Remember, however, that an engineering function of British television results in an imperceptible speeding-up of projection and a consequent loss of one minute in every twenty-five. A hundred-minute film, therefore, will run only ninety-six minutes on the box, so check your facts before complaining.

Black and white or colour   I have given the colour process where known (it is not always stated these days) and have coined the single word Eastmancolor to equate with Technicolor.

Other notable points   are given at the end of the second line: whether the film is in some special process (3-D, Vistavision, etc).

Production credit   The central credit on the third line is the production company. To the left, however, comes the distributor if different from the production company, in brackets if his rights subsequently lapsed. To the right is the actual producer, except for early thirties films in which he was seldom credited. He is also in brackets unless he has a stake in the production, in which case he follows an oblique.

Alternative title   This is given on a separate line, usually with a note of the country in which it was used. If no such fine line exists, I have used the formula *aka* (also known as). Indexes of alternative titles will be found at the end of the book, and should be consulted if any film for which the reader is looking cannot at first be found.

Synopsis   Self-explanatory, with brevity and accuracy the keynote.

Assessment   Again very brief, so flippancy will inevitably be suspected. Not so, but for more considered judgements look for books which have more space.

Writer credit   It seems to me that this is, at least sometimes, more important than the director credit, and as script in any case precedes direction, it comes first in this book. The author of the screenplay is always given; if this derives from a novel, play or story, this is given next, together with the original author.

Director credit   *d.*

Photography credit   *ph.*

Music credit *(m)*   This means the composer of the background music score. Sometimes there is only a music director *(md)* who orchestrates library or classical music.

Other credits   Production designer *(pd)*, music and lyrics *(m/ly)*, art director *(ad)*, special effects *(sp)*, montage, etc, are given when they seem important and can be found. In some cases it has not been possible to track down all the credits one would wish.

Cast   The principal actors are given where possible, roughly in order of importance. I have stopped before the bit parts, and given fewer names in the case of foreign films, where the actors tend to be less well known.

Additional notes   Any other significant remarks about the film are given after the symbol †.

Comments from critics   To a quarter or so of the items I have appended brief quotes from well-known professional critics, sometimes because they wittily confirm my own findings, and sometimes because they disagree with me entirely. I hope these will be enjoyable and illuminating; the absence of a quote casts no reflection whatever on the film, only on my own ability as a researcher.

Italics   These denote a contribution of a particularly high standard. Arguments are expected and additions welcomed.

Academy Awards   Awards (AA) and also nominations (AAN) are listed for all principal categories, including acting, direction, photography, music score, songs and best picture.

NB   Some entries are now being set in paragraph form in order to save space. These are for less important films, and reduced information is given.

A

À Bout de Souffle**
France 1959 90m bw
SNC (Georges de Beauregard)
aka: *Breathless*

A young car thief kills a policeman and goes
on the run with his American girl friend.
Casual, influential, New Wave reminiscence of
both *Quai des Brumes* and innumerable
American gangster thrillers. (The film is
dedicated to Monogram.)

w François Truffaut *d* Jean-Luc Godard
ph Raoul Coutard *m* Martial Solal

Jean-Paul Belmondo, Jean Seberg, Daniel
Boulanger, Jean-Pierre Melville

'A film all dressed up for rebellion but with
no real tangible territory on which to stand
and fight.'—*Peter John Dyer*

À Double Tour
France / Italy 1959 110m Eastmancolor
Paris / Panitalia (Robert and Raymond
   Hakim)
aka: *Web of Passion*

A wealthy wine grower has trouble with his
wife, his children, his best friend, and his
mistress across the way, who is murdered.
Talented but irritating mixture of Hitchcock
and *Les Parents Terribles*; rather an
undergraduatish romp.

w Paul Gégauff, *novel* La Clé de la Rue
Saint-Nicolas *d* Claude Chabrol *ph* Henri
Decaë *m* Paul Misraki

Jacques Dacqmine, Madeleine Robinson,
Jean-Paul Belmondo, Bernadette Lafont,
Antonella Lualdi, André Jocelyn

A-Haunting We Will Go*
US 1942 68m bw
TCF (Sol M. Wertzel)

Gangsters dupe Laurel and Hardy into
escorting a coffin, which is accidentally
switched with one used in a magic act.
Nothing whatever to do with haunting: a poor
comedy with no typical material for the stars,
but interesting as a record of the touring show
of Dante the Magician.

w Lou Breslow *d* Alfred Werker *ph* Glen
MacWilliams *m* Glen MacWilliams

Stan Laurel, Oliver Hardy, *Dante*, Sheila
Ryan, John Shelton, Elisha Cook Jnr

À Nous la Liberté****
France 1931 95m bw
Tobis

A factory owner is blackmailed about his past,
and helped by an old prison friend, with whom
he finally takes to the road.
Operetta-style satirical comedy with leftish
attitudes and several famous sequences later
borrowed by Chaplin for *Modern Times*. In
terms of sheer film flair, a revelation, though
the plot has its tedious turns.

wd René Clair *ph* Georges Périnal *m* Georges
Auric *pd* Lazare Meerson

Raymond Cordy, Henri Marchand, Rolla
France, Paul Olivier

À Propos de Nice**
France 1930 30m bw

A satirical documentary on the millionaire's
paradise of the French Riviera.
Cheaply made and rather naive-looking after
fifty years, this amusingly belligerent lampoon
still has its striking moments.

wd Jean Vigo *ph* Boris Kaufman

Aan*
India 1952 190m approx (English version
   130m) Technicolor
All India Film Corporation / Mehboob
   Productions
aka: *Savage Princess*

A usurping young prince and his sister are
tamed by an athletic peasant and his girl
friend.
One of the few examples to reach the west of
Indian costume melodrama with music,
spectacle and swashbuckling. Distinctly
intriguing, if overpowering.

w Chaudary, Ali Raza *d* Mehboob
ph Faredoon A. Irani *m* Naushad Dilip
Kumar, Nimmi, Premnath, Nadira

'Disarmingly enthusiastic . . . exotic and yet
charmingly naive.'—*MFB*

Aaron Slick from Punkin Crick*
US 1952　95m　Technicolor
Paramount (William Perlberg, George
　Seaton)
GB title: *Marshmallow Moon*

A small-town girl is tricked into selling her
farm and moving to the city, but eventually
marries the simple farmer who rescues her.
Homespun entertainment based on a staple
success of the American provincial theatre,
with pleasant songs added.

wd Claude Binyon, *play* Walter Benjamin
Hare *ph* Charles B. Lang Jnr *m / ly* Jay
Livingston, Ray Evans *ch* Charles O'Curran

Alan Young, Dinah Shore, Robert Merrill,
Adele Jergens, Minerva Urecal

Abandoned
US 1949　79m　bw

Reporter breaks baby-farming racket.
Competent action thriller for double billing.
Dennis O'Keefe, Gale Storm, Raymond Burr
(and young Jeff Chandler). Written by Irwin
Gielgud; directed by Joseph Newman; for
Universal-International.

Abbott and Costello Go to Mars
US 1953　76m　bw
U-I (Howard Christie)

Two incompetents accidentally launch a space
ship and land first in Louisiana, then on
Venus.
Dismal knockabout, badly made.

w John Grant, D. D. Beauchamp *d* Charles
Lamont
ph Clifford Stine *m* Joseph Gershenson

Bud Abbott, Lou Costello, Mari Blanchard,
Robert Paige, Martha Hyer

Abbott and Costello in Hollywood*
US 1945　85m　bw
MGM (Martin Gosch)

Two agents have hectic adventures in a film
studio.
Tolerable star romp on one of their biggest
budgets, climaxing in a roller coaster ride.

w Nat Perrin, Lou Breslow *d* S. Sylvan
Simon *ph* Charles Schoenbaum *m* George
Bassman

Bud Abbott, Lou Costello, Francis Rafferty,
Warner Anderson, Robert Z. Leonard

**Abbott and Costello in the Foreign
　Legion**
US 1950　80m　bw
U-I (Robert Arthur)

Incompetent legionnaires become heroes to
the fury of their sergeant.
Dull star vehicle on ramshackle sets, with no
memorable routines.

w John Grant, Leonard Stern, Martin
Ragaway *d* Charles Lamont *ph* George
Robinson *m* Joseph Gershenson

Bud Abbott, Lou Costello, Patricia Medina,
Walter Slezak, Douglass Dumbrille

Abbott and Costello Lost in Alaska
US 1952　76m　bw
U-I (Howard Christie)

Two San Francisco firemen take a melancholy
prospector back to Alaska to find a gold mine.
Sub-standard comedy vehicle with poor
production.

w Martin Ragaway, Leonard Stern *d* Jean
Yarbrough

ph George Robinson *m* Joseph Gershenson

Bud Abbott, Lou Costello, *Tom Ewell*, Mitzi
Green, Bruce Cabot

**Abbott and Costello Meet Captain
　Kidd***
US 1952　70m　Supercinecolor
Warner / Woodley (Alex Gottlieb)

Two servants have a treasure map, and a
fearsome pirate wants it.
Crude knockabout: the stars are way below
their best, and a famous actor is embarrassed.

w Howard Dimsdale, John Grant *d* Charles
Lamont
ph Stanley Cortez *m* Raoul Kraushaar

Bud Abbott, Lou Costello, Charles Laughton,
Hillary Brooke, Leif Erickson

**Abbott and Costello Meet Dr Jekyll
　and Mr Hyde***
US 1953　77m　bw
U-I (Howard Christie)

In Victorian London, two rookie policemen
catch a monster.
Quite a lively spoof with some well-paced
comedy sequences.

w John Grant, Lee Loeb *d* Charles Lamont
ph George Robinson *m* Joseph Gershenson

Bud Abbott, Lou Costello, Boris Karloff,
Reginald Denny, Craig Stevens, Helen
Westcott, John Dierkes

'Gracious Boris Karloff is superior to his
surroundings '—*MFB*. (Though it is doubtful
whether he ever got behind the Hyde make-
up.)

† In Britain, the film was given an 'X'
certificate, though it later played on children's
television

Abbott and Costello Meet Frankenstein**
US 1948 83m bw
U-I (Robert Arthur)
GB title: *Abbott and Costello Meet the Ghosts*

Two railway porters deliver crates containing the Frankenstein monster, Dracula, and the Wolf Man.
Fairly lively spoof which put an end to Universal's monsters for a while. Good typical sequences for the stars, a few thrills, and some good lines. (Dracula to Costello, lovingly: 'What we need is young blood . . . and brains . . .')

w Robert Lees, Frederic I. Rinaldo, John Grant d Charles Barton ph Charles van Enger m Frank Skinner

Bud Abbott, Lou Costello, Bela Lugosi, Lon Chaney Jnr, Glenn Strange, Lenore Aubert, Jane Randolph
† Probably the Abbott and Costello film which survives best.

Abbott and Costello Meet the Invisible Man*
US 1951 82m bw
U-I (Howard Christie)

A boxer accused of murder makes himself invisible while two detectives clear him.
Quite a bright comedy with good trick effects.

w Robert Lees, Frederic I. Rinaldo, John Grant d Charles Lamont ph George Robinson m Joseph Gershenson

Bud Abbott, Lou Costello, Arthur Franz, Nancy Guild, Adele Jergens, Sheldon Leonard

Abbott and Costello Meet the Keystone Kops*
US 1954 79m bw
U-I (Howard Christie)

In pioneer film days, two incompetents are sold a dud studio by a con man, but succeed as stunt men.
Flabby comedy which never seems to get going until the chase finale; notable chiefly for a guest appearance by Mack Sennett.

w John Grant d Charles Lamont ph Reggie Lanning m Joseph Gershenson

Bud Abbott, Lou Costello, Lynn Bari, Fred Clark, Frank Wilcox, Maxie Rosenbloom

Abbott and Costello Meet the Killer, Boris Karloff*
US 1948 84m bw
U-I (Robert Arthur)

Two bellboys help to solve mysterious murders in a remote hotel.

This clumsily titled comedy really does not work until the last sequence in a cavern. Boris Karloff is not the killer and appears very little.

w Hugh Wedlock Jnr, Howard Snyder, John Grant d Charles Barton ph Charles van Enger md Milton Schwarzwald

Bud Abbott, Lou Costello, Boris Karloff, Gar Moore, Lenore Aubert, Alan Mowbray

Abbott and Costello Meet the Mummy*
US 1955 77m bw
U-I (Howard Christie)

A missing medallion leads to a lost tomb and a living mummy.
The comedians show their age in this one, but there is some typical if predictable humour and a thrill or two.

w John Grant d Charles Lamont ph George Robinson m Joseph Gershenson

Bud Abbott, Lou Costello, Kurt Katch, Marie Windsor, Michael Ansara, Dan Seymour

The Abdication
GB 1974 102m Technicolor
Warner (Robert Fryer, James Cresson)

17th-century Queen Christina of Sweden journeys to Rome to embrace the Catholic church and falls in love with a cardinal.
Sombre historical fantasia, more irritating than interesting.

w Ruth Wolff, from her play d Anthony Harvey ph Geoffrey Unsworth m Nino Rota

Liv Ullmann, Peter Finch, Cyril Cusack, Paul Rogers, Graham Crowden, Michael Dunn, Lewis Fiander, Harold Goldblatt
'Dainty debauchery and titillating tease straight from twenties women's pulp magazines.'—*Variety*

The Abductors*
US 1957 80m bw Regalscope
TCF / Regal (Ray Wander)

Around 1870, criminals steal Lincoln's body as ransom to effect a convict's release.
Interesting minor melodrama, but not sufficiently well made.

w Ray Wander d Andrew V. McLaglen ph Joseph La Shelle

Victor McLaglen, Gavin Muir, George Macready

Abdul the Damned**
GB 1935 111m bw
BIP / Capitol (Max Schach)

In 1900 Turkey, an opera star gives herself to a villainous sultan to protect her fiancé.

Thoroughgoing hokum, well produced, which pleased a lot of people at the time.

w Ashley Dukes, Warren Chetham Strode, Roger Burford
d Karl Grune ph Otto Kanturek

Fritz Kortner, Adrienne Ames, Nils Asther, John Stuart, Esme Percy, Walter Rilla, Patric Knowles, Eric Portman

Abdulla the Great
GB / Egypt 1954 103m Technicolor
(Gregory Ratoff)
aka: *Abdulla's Harem*

A pleasure-loving Egyptian potentate sets his sights on an English girl.
Feeble satire on King Farouk, inept and relentlessly boring.

w George St George, Boris Ingster d Gregory Ratoff ph Lee Garmes

Gregory Ratoff, Kay Kendall, Sydney Chaplin

Abe Lincoln in Illinois**
US 1940 110m bw
RKO (Max Gordon)
GB title: *Spirit of the People*

Episodes in the political and domestic life of Abraham Lincoln.
Pleasant, muted, careful film based on a Broadway success: generally informative and interesting.

w Grover Jones, *play* Robert E. Sherwood
d John Cromwell ph *James Wong Howe*
m Roy Webb

Raymond Massey, Ruth Gordon, Gene Lockhart, Mary Howard, Dorothy Tree, Minor Watson, Howard da Silva

'If you want attitudes, a five gallon hat, famous incidents, and One Nation Indivisible, they're all here. As a picture and as a whole, it just doesn't stick.'—*Otis Ferguson*

AAN: Raymond Massey, James Wong Howe

Abie's Irish Rose
US 1946 96m bw
(UA) Bing Crosby Productions (Edward A. Sutherland)

Flat filming of the twenties Broadway play about Irish girl marrying Jewish boy, leading to a clash of families.

w Anne Nichols, from her play d Edward A Sutherland
ph William Mellor m John Scott Trotter

Joanne Dru, Richard Norris, Michael Chekhov, Eric Blore, Art Baker
† There had been a silent version in 1928, and the plot was borrowed, to say the least, for the 1972 TV series *Bridget Loves Bernie*.

Abilene Town
US 1946 89m bw

An upright marshal routs crooked cattlemen.
Vigorous, enjoyable Western programmer with Randolph Scott and Ann Dvorak on the side of the law. Written by Harold Shumate; directed by Edwin L. Marin; for Jules Levey / UA.

The Abominable Dr Phibes**
GB 1971 94m Movielab
AIP (Louis M. Heyward, Ron Dunas)

A disfigured musical genius devises a series of horrible murders, based on the ten curses of Pharaoh, for the surgeons who failed to save his wife.
Brisk but uninspired treatment of a promising theme, with more unintended nastiness than intended laughs. Some good moments and interesting low-budget thirties sets.

w James Whiton, William Goldstein d Robert Fuest ph Norman Warwick m Basil Kirchen, Jack Nathan pd Brian Eatwell

Vincent Price, Joseph Cotten, Hugh Griffith, Terry-Thomas, Peter Jeffrey, Virginia North, Aubrey Woods
† Sequel: *Dr Phibes Rises Again* (1973).

The Abominable Snowman*
GB 1957 91m bw Hammerscope
Hammer / Clarion (Aubrey Baring)

Himalayan explorers are attacked one by one by the Yeti and their own fear.
A thin horror film with intelligent scripting: more philosophizing and characterization than suspense. The briefly glimpsed Yeti are disappointing creations.

w *Nigel Kneale*, from his TV play d Val Guest ph Arthur Grant m Humphrey Searle

Peter Cushing, Forrest Tucker, Maureen Connell, Richard Wattis, Robert Brown, *Arnold Marle*

About Face
US 1952 96m Technicolor
Warner (William Jacobs)

Moronic remake of *Brother Rat* (qv), shorn of all wit, pace and style.

w Peter Milne d Roy del Ruth ph Bert Glennon songs Charles Tobias, Peter de Rose

Eddie Bracken, Gordon Macrae, Dick Wesson, Virginia Gibson, Phyllis Kirk, Joel Grey

About Mrs Leslie*
US 1954 104m bw
Paramount (Hal B. Wallis)

An ageing nightclub singer has a platonic
affair with a mysterious wealthy man, who
leaves her enough money to buy a boarding
house.

Odd, likeable romantic drama tailored for an
unusual star; but its plot is too thin and its
direction too drab for real success.

w Ketti Frings, Hal Kanter d Daniel Mann
ph Ernest Laszlo m Victor Young

Shirley Booth, Robert Ryan, Alex Nicol,
Marjie Miller, Eilene Janssen

'This quiet and curious film has an
unexpectedly gentle, civilized flavour.'—*Gavin
Lambert*

'It's all sunny disposition and sweet sadness
for Miss Booth.'—*Judith Crist*

'One is reminded alternately of Chekhov
and of *Back Street*.'—*Sight and Sound*

Above and Beyond*
US 1952   122m   bw
MGM (Melvin Frank, Norman Panama)

The training of Colonel Paul Tibbetts, who
dropped the first atomic bomb on Japan.
Overstretched flagwaver with laborious
domestic interludes. Of little real interest then
or now.

w Melvin Frank, Norman Panama,
story Beirne Lay Jnr d Melvin Frank,
Norman Panama ph Ray June m Hugo
Friedhofer

Robert Taylor, Eleanor Parker, James
Whitmore, Larry Keating, Larry Gates

AAN: Beirne Lay Jnr, Hugo Friedhofer

Above Suspicion*
US 1943   91m   bw
MGM (Victor Saville)

Just before World War II, an Oxford professor
on a continental honeymoon is asked to track
down a missing agent.
Patchy, studio-bound spy comedy-drama with
a couple of good sequences. Notable also for
Mr MacMurray's impersonation of a professor
who hails a Nazi as 'Hiya, dope!'

w Keith Winter, Melville Baker, Patricia
Coleman, *novel* Helen MacInnes d Richard
Thorpe ph Robert Planck m Bronislau
Kaper

Fred MacMurray, Joan Crawford, Conrad
Veidt, *Basil Rathbone*, Reginald Owen, Felix
Bressart, Richard Ainley

Above Us the Waves*
GB 1955   99m   bw
(Rank) London Independent Producers
   (William Macquitty)

In World War II, midget submarines attack a
German battleship in a Norwegian fjord.
Archetypal stiff-upper-lip war drama with
good action sequences.

w Robin Estridge d Ralph Thomas ph Ernest
Steward m Arthur Benjamin

John Mills, John Gregson, Donald Sinden,
James Robertson Justice, Michael Medwin,
Lee Patterson, Lyndon Brook

Abraham Lincoln**
US 1930   97m   bw
UA / D. W. Griffith

An account of Lincoln's entry into politics and
his years of power.
Rather boring even at the time, this
straightforward biopic has the virtues of
sincerity and comparative fidelity to the facts.

w Stephen Vincent Benet, Gerrit Lord
d D. W. Griffith ph Karl Struss m Hugo
Riesenfeld pd William Cameron Menzies

Walter Huston, Una Merkel, Edgar Dearing,
Russell Simpson, Henry B. Walthall

'A treasure trove of magnificent
moments.'—*MFB, 1973*

'It brings to us—with a curious finality of
disappointment, a sentimental sense of the
closing of a chapter—the impression of a
director who has nowhere made a valid
contact with the conditon of the screen
today.'—*C. A. Lejeune*

Abroad with Two Yanks*
US 1944   80m   bw
Edward Small

Adventures around the Pacific with two
woman-chasing sailors.
This simple-minded farce with its punny title
was a great success in its day, and still
generates a laugh or two.

w Charles Rogers, Wilkie Maholey, Fred
Redsills d Allan Dwan ph Charles Lawton
m Lud Gluskin

Dennis O'Keefe, William Bendix, Helen
Walker, John Abbott, John Loder

Abschied von Gestern*
West Germany 1966   90m   bw
Kairos Film / Alexander Kluge /
   Independent
aka: *Yesterday Girl*

A Jewish girl escapes from East to West
Germany but is disillusioned and gives herself
up.
Witty and remarkably light-hearted satirical
comedy which can be fully understood only by
those living in Germany in the sixties.

wd Alexander Kluge ph Edgar Reitz, Thomas Mauch

Alexandra Kluge, Gunther Mack, Hans Korte, Eva Marie Meinecke

The Absent-Minded Professor*
US 1960 97m bw
Walt Disney (Bill Walsh)

A lighter-than-air substance called flubber enables its inventor to drive his Model-T through the sky and catch some spies. Foolishly engaging fantasy comedy with goodish trick effects.

w Bill Walsh *d* Robert Stevenson *ph* Edward Colman *m* George Bruns *sp* Robert A. Mattey, Peter Ellenshaw, Eustace Lycett

Fred MacMurray, Tommy Kirk, Keenan Wynn, Nancy Olson, Leon Ames, Ed Wynn, Edward Andrews
† Sequel: *Son of Flubber* (1964).

AAN: Edward Colman

Absolute Quiet
US 1936 71m bw

Interestingly-cast programmer about a murder plot after a planeload of strangers is forced down on a financier's ranch. Lionel Atwill, Louis Hayward, Raymond Walburn, Stuart Erwin, Wallace Ford, J. Carrol Naish. Written by Harry Clark; directed by Edwin L. Marin; for MGM.

Accattone*
Italy 1961 120m bw
Cino del Duca / Arco (Alfredo Bini)

A Roman pimp and thief is beset by troubles, and is finally killed escaping from the police. Sordid and rough-edged but vividly realistic melodrama.

wd Pier Paolo Pasolini ph Tonino delli Colli *md* Carlo Rustichelli

Franco Citti, Franca Pasut, Roberto Scaringella, Adele Cambria

Accent on Youth*
US 1935 77m bw
Paramount (Douglas Maclean)

A secretary falls in love with her middle-aged playwright employer.
Reasonably sparkling comedy from a popular play, later remade as *Mr Music* and *But Not for Me.*

w Herbert Fields, Claude Binyon, *play* Samson Raphaelson *d* Wesley Ruggles *ph* Leon Shamroy

Herbert Marshall, Sylvia Sidney, Philip Reed, Astrid Allwyn, Holmes Herbert

Accident**
GB 1967 105m Eastmancolor
London Independent Producers (Joseph Losey, Norman Priggen)

An Oxford undergraduate is killed in a car crash; his tutor looks back over the tangle of personal relationships that contributed to his death.
Ascetic drama in which the audience is too often left to observe at length and draw its own conclusions; good characterizations nevertheless.

w Harold Pinter, *novel* Nicholas Mosley *d* Joseph Losey *ph* Gerry Fisher *m* Johnny Dankworth

Dirk Bogarde, Stanley Baker, Jacqueline Sassard, Vivien Merchant, Michael York

'The whole thing is such a teapot tempest, and it is so assiduously underplayed that it is neither strong drama nor stinging satire. It is just a sad little story of a wistful don.'—*Bosley Crowther*

'Everything is calm, unruffled, lacquered in a veneer of civilization, yet underneath it all, one gradually begins to realize, the characters are tearing each other emotionally to shreds.'—*MFB*

'Uneven, unsatisfying, but with virtuoso passages of calculated meanness.'—*New Yorker, 1977*

Accused
GB 1936 85m bw

In Paris, a dancer is stabbed and his wife is thought guilty. Overwrought melodrama, chiefly interesting for cast: Douglas Fairbanks Jnr, Dolores del Rio, Googie Withers, Florence Desmond, Basil Sydney. Written by Zoe Akins, George Barraud and Harold French; directed by Thornton Freeland; for Criterion / UA.

The Accused*
US 1948 101m bw
Paramount (Hal B. Wallis)

In self-defence a lady professor kills a student who has sexually attacked her.
Dullish suspenser with the outcome never in doubt, though the production values are beyond reproach.

w Ketti Frings *d* William Dieterle *ph* Milton Krasner *m* Victor Young

Loretta Young, Robert Cummings, Wendell Corey, Sam Jaffe, Douglas Dick

Ace Eli and Roger of the Skies
US 1973 92m De Luxe Panavision
TCF (Robert Fryer, James Cresson)

Adventures of a father-and-son aerial barnstorming act after World War I.
Poorly written melodrama, very tame apart from the flying shots.

w Claudia Salter, *story* Steven Spielberg *d* John Erman *ph* David M. Walsh, Bill Birch, Don Morgan *m* Jerry Goldsmith

Cliff Robertson, Pamela Franklin, Eric Shea, Rosemary Murphy, Bernadette Peters, Alice Ghostley

'A tediously inane flop. Nostalgia isn't what it used to be.'—*Variety*

Ace in the Hole***
US 1951   111m   bw
Paramount (Billy Wilder)
aka: *The Big Carnival*

In order to prolong the sensation and boost newspaper sales, a self-seeking journalist delays the rescue of a man trapped in a cave. An incisive, compelling melodrama taking a sour look at the American scene; one of its director's masterworks.

w Billy Wilder, Lesser Samuels, Walter Newman *d* Billy Wilder *ph* Charles B. Lang Jnr *m* Hugo Friedhofer

Kirk Douglas, Jan Sterling, Porter Hall, Bob Arthur, Frank Cady, Ray Teal

'Few of the opportunities for irony, cruelty and horror are missed.'—*Gavin Lambert*

'Style and purpose achieve for the most part a fusion even more remarkable than in *Sunset Boulevard*.'—*Penelope Houston*

'As stimulating as black coffee.'—*Richard Mallett, Punch*

'Americans expected a cocktail and felt I was giving them a shot of vinegar instead.'—*Billy Wilder*

'Some people have tried to claim some sort of satirical brilliance for it, but it's really rather nasty, in a sociologically pushy way.'—*New Yorker, 1980*

AAN: script

Aces High*
GB 1976   114m   Technicolor
EMI / S. Benjamin Fisz / Jacques Roitfeld

In the air force during World War I, young pilots are needlessly sacrificed.
Spirited if rather unnecessary remake of *Journey's End* transposed to the air war, which makes it almost identical to *The Dawn Patrol*.

w Howard Barker *d* Jack Gold *ph* Gerry Fisher, Peter Allwork *m* Richard Hartley

Malcolm McDowell, Christopher Plummer, Simon Ward, Peter Firth, John Gielgud, Trevor Howard, Richard Johnson, Ray Milland

Across 110th Street*
US 1972   102m   De Luxe
UA / Film Guarantors (Fouad Said, Ralph Serpe)

A tough New York cop loses his own life tracking down three Harlem criminals who have robbed the Mafia.
Brutish, noisy, incoherent police melodrama, with fashionable sadism and predictable performances. Good location work, though.

w Luther Davis, *novel* Wally Ferris *d* Barry Shear *ph* Jack Priestley *m* J. J. Johnson

Anthony Quinn, Anthony Franciosa, Yaphet Kotto, Paul Benjamin, Ed Bernard

'Not for the squeamish . . . a virtual blood bath, leaving no relief from depression and oppression.'—*Variety*

Across the Bridge*
GB 1957   103m   bw
Rank / IPF (John Stafford)

A fugitive financier kills his pursuer, finds he was a murderer, and tries to hide out across the Mexican border.
This star *tour de force* is unconvincing in detail and rather unattractive to watch (British films never could cope with American settings), but the early sequences have suspense.

w Guy Elmes, Denis Freeman, *novel* Graham Greene *d* Ken Annakin *ph* Reg Wyer *m* James Bernard

Rod Steiger, David Knight, Marla Landi, Noel Willman, Bernard Lee

Across the Pacific***
US 1942   99m   bw
Warner (Hal B. Wallis)

Just before Pearl Harbor, an army officer is cashiered by arrangement in order to contact pro-Japanese sympathizers.
Hasty, easy-going and very enjoyable hokum, partly ship-set and successfully reteaming three stars of *The Maltese Falcon*.

w Richard Macauley, *serial* Aloha Means Goodbye by Robert Carson *d* John Huston *ph* Arthur Edeson *m* Adolph Deutsch

Humphrey Bogart, Mary Astor, Sydney Greenstreet, Sen Yung, Richard Loo, Monte Blue

'A spy picture which tingles with fearful uncertainties and glints with the sheen of blue steel.'—*Bosley Crowther*

Across the Wide Missouri*
US 1951   77m   Technicolor
MGM (Robert Sisk)

In the 1820s, a trapper marries an Indian girl and lives with her people.

Promising credits produce an unsatisfactory western: despite honest efforts, the elements do not jell into a convincing whole.

w Talbot Jennings *d* William Wellman *ph* William C. Mellor *m* David Raksin

Clark Gable, Ricardo Montalban, John Hodiak, Adolphe Menjou, Maria Elena Marques, J. Carrol Naish, Jack Holt, Alan Napier

Act of Love *
US 1954 104m bw
UA / Benagoss (Anatole Litvak)

In Paris in 1944, an American with the liberation army falls in love with a French girl, who commits suicide when he is posted and cannot make their rendezvous.
Cheerless romantic drama, rather thin and unmemorable despite the efforts of all concerned.

w Irwin Shaw, *novel* The Girl on the Via Flaminia by Alfred Hayes *d* Anatole Litvak *ph* Armand Thirard *m* Michael Emer, Joe Hajos *pd* Alexander Trauner

Kirk Douglas, Dany Robin, Barbara Laage, Robert Strauss, Gabrielle Dorziat, Gregoire Aslan, Fernand Ledoux, Serge Reggiani, Brigitte Bardot
† Made in France, an early Hollywood foreign location film.

An Act of Murder**
US 1948 90m bw
U-I (Jerry Bresler)
aka: *Live Today for Tomorrow*

A judge insists on being tried for the mercy killing of his incurably ill wife.
Earnest social drama which despite excellent acting can only reach an inconclusive ending.

w Michael Blankfort, Robert Thoeren, *novel* The Mills of God by Ernst Lothar *d* Michael Gordon *ph* Hal Mohr *m* Daniele Amfitheatrof

Fredric March, Florence Eldridge, Edmond O'Brien, Geraldine Brooks

Act of Murder**
GB 1964 62m bw
Merton Park (Jack Greenwood)

A couple arrange a holiday by swapping houses with strangers, and a complex plot ensues.
Slick, superior example of the Edgar Wallace second feature series.

w Lewis Davidson *d Alan Bridges ph* James Wilson *m* Bernard Ebbinghouse

John Carson, Anthony Bate, Justine Lord, Duncan Lewis, Dandy Nichols

'This uncommonly intelligent little thriller is just the sort of film which is likely to arouse critical sneers for reaching too high on a low budget.'—*Tom Milne*

Act of Violence**
US 1948 82m bw
MGM (William Wright)

After the war, an ex-GI tracks down a prison camp informer.
Moody, glossy melodrama with tension well sustained, though the sentimental ending is a cop-out.

w Robert I. Richards, *story* Collier Young *d Fred Zinnemann ph Robert Surtees m* Bronislau Kaper

Van Heflin, Robert Ryan, Janet Leigh, Mary Astor
'Strong characterization, fine direction and good photography combine to put this film high among its kind.'—*MFB*
'An effortless narrative control and a real power to maintain tension.'—*Richard Winnington*

Act One*
US 1963 110m bw
Warner (Dore Schary)

Poor Brooklyn boy Moss Hart rises to Broadway eminence via his writing partnership with George S. Kaufman.
Incredibly stilted film version of an excellent autobiography, notable only for fragments of acting and the fact that a film so totally uncommercial was made at all.

wd Dore Schary *ph* Arthur J. Ornitz *m* Skitch Henderson

George Hamilton (Hart), Jason Robards Jnr (Kaufman), Jack Klugman, Sam Levene, George Segal, Ruth Ford, Eli Wallach
'From the moment young Hart takes pencil in hand, we have nowhere to go except to that happy ending; and despite all the painstaking detail, we don't believe a word of it.'—*Judith Crist*

Action for Slander*
GB 1937 83m bw
London Films / Saville (Victor Saville)

A bankrupt officer, accused of cheating at cards, defends his honour with a writ.
Lively melodrama of the old school.

w Ian Dalrymple, Miles Malleson, *novel* Mary Borden *d* Tim Whelan *ph* Harry Stradling

Clive Brook, Ann Todd, Margaretta Scott, Arthur Margetson, Ronald Squire, Athole Stewart, Percy Marmont, Frank Cellier, Morton Selten

Action in the North Atlantic*
US 1943   127m   bw
Warner (Jerry Wald)

An American convoy bound for Russia comes
under U-boat attack.

Efficient propaganda potboiler; studio bound,
but still works as a war actioner.

w John Howard Lawson, *story* Guy Gilpatric
d Lloyd Bacon *ph* Ted McCord *m* Adolph
Deutsch

Humphrey Bogart, Raymond Massey, Alan
Hale, Julie Bishop, Ruth Gordon, Sam
Levene, Dane Clark
    'The production has interludes of
tremendous power. What is lacking is dramatic
cohesion.'—*Howard Barnes*
    'Directly in line of descent from *The Perils
of Pauline.*'—*Time*

AAN: Guy Gilpatric

Action of the Tiger
GB 1957   93m   Technicolor
    Cinemascope
MGM / Claridge (Kenneth Harper)

An adventurer helps a French girl to rescue
her brother from political imprisonment in
Albania.

Dull and poorly constructed action
melodrama.

w Robert Carson   d Terence Young
ph Desmond Dickinson   *m* Humphrey Searle

Van Johnson, Martine Carol, Herbert Lom,
Gustavo Rocco, Anthony Dawson, Helen
Haye, Sean Connery

Actors and Sin*
US 1952   91m   bw
(UA) Sid Kuller (Ben Hecht)

Two short stories. When an unsuccessful
actress commits suicide, her father makes it
look like murder so that for once she shall get
attention.
The authoress of a romantic script bought by
Hollywood is discovered to be a horrid little
9-year-old.

Interesting but incompetent compendium
which descends almost to the home movie
level and leaves the actors struggling.

wd Ben Hecht   *ph* Lee Garmes   *m* George
Antheil

Edward G. Robinson, Marsha Hunt, Dan
O'Herlihy, Rudolph Anders, Eddie Albert,
Alan Reed, Jenny Hecht
    'A depressing double bill.'—*Lindsay
Anderson*

An Actor's Revenge*
Japan 1963   113m   Daieicolor
    Daieiscope
Daiei (Masaichi Nagata)
original title: *Yukinojo Henge*

In the early 19th century, a touring actor
comes upon the rich merchant who had ruined
his parents, and his revenge involves several
deaths.

Complex, fascinating period melodrama, both
rich and strange, with strong echoes of
Jacobean melodrama.

w Daisuke Ito, Teinosuke Kinugasa, Natto
Wada, *novel* Otokichi Mikami   d Kon
Ichikawa   *ph* Setsuo Kobayashi   *m* Yasushi
Akutagawa

Kazuo Hasegawa, Fujiko Yamamoto, Ayako
Wakao, Ganjiro Nakamura

The Actress*
US 1928   90m approx (24 fps)   bw
    silent
MGM
GB title: *Trelawny of the Wells*

A young Victorian actress marries a rich
admirer.

Pleasing, well-cast version of a celebrated
play.

w Albert Lewin, Richard Schayer, *play* Sir
Arthur Wing Pinero   d Sidney Franklin
ph William Daniels

Norma Shearer, Ralph Forbes, O. P. Heggie,
Owen Moore, Roy D'Arcy
† Opening attraction at London's Empire
Theatre, Leicester Square.

The Actress
US 1953   91m   bw
MGM (Lawrence Weingarten)

Ruth Jones becomes an actress against the
wishes of her stubborn seafaring father.
Episodes from Ruth Gordon's early life, based
on her Broadway play *Years Ago*, make a
pleasant though scarcely engrossing film: it is
all a shade too discreet and wanly winning,
and the few key events take place offscreen.

w Ruth Gordon   d George Cukor   *ph* Harold
Rosson   *m* Bronislau Kaper   *ad* Cedric
Gibbons, Arthur Lonergan

Jean Simmons, Spencer Tracy, Teresa Wright,
Anthony Perkins, Ian Wolfe, Mary Wickes

Ada*
US 1961   109m   Metrocolor
    Cinemascope
MGM / Avon / Chalmar (Lawrence
Weingarten)

A political candidate marries a call girl who becomes his strong right arm and weathers a threat to reveal her past.

Indecisive romantic drama which pulls too many punches but has interesting background detail.

w Arthur Sheekman, William Driskill, *novel* Ada Dallas by Wirt Williams d Daniel Mann ph Joseph Ruttenberg m Bronislau Kaper

Susan Hayward, Dean Martin, Wilfrid Hyde White, Ralph Meeker, Martin Balsam

'A bonanza for connoisseurs of perfectly awful movies.'—*Judith Crist*

'Its characterizations are sketchy, its political setting routine and symbolic.'—*New York Herald Tribune*

Adalen 31**
Sweden 1969   115m   Technicolor Techniscope
Svensk Filmindustri

A prolonged strike at a small-town paper mill ends in tragedy when the troops move in. Effective period piece which emphasizes the idyllic qualities of the backgrounds rather than the foreground terrors.

wd Bo Widerberg ph Jorgen Persson

Peter Schildt, Kerstin Tidelius, Roland Hedlund, Stefan Feierbach, Anita Bjork

Adam and Evelyne
GB 1949   92m   bw
Rank / Two Cities (Harold French)

A society playboy adopts his dead friend's daughter, and falls in love with her. Undernourished romantic drama, a mild variation on *Daddy Longlegs*.

w Noel Langley, Lesley Storm, George Barraud, Nicholas Phipps d Harold French ph Guy Green m Mischa Spoliansky

Stewart Granger, Jean Simmons, Helen Cherry, Edwin Styles, Beatrice Varley, Wilfrid Hyde White

Adam Had Four Sons*
US 1941   81m   bw
Columbia (Robert Sherwood)

A widower's family is cared for by a governess.

Modest magazine fiction which established Ingrid Bergman as an American star.

w Michael Blankfort, William Hurlbut, *novel* Legacy by Charles Bonner d Gregory Ratoff ph Peverell Marley m W. Franke Harling

Warner Baxter, *Ingrid Bergman*, Susan Hayward, Richard Denning, Fay Wray

Adam's Rib***
US 1949   101m   bw
MGM (Lawrence Weingarten)

Husband and wife lawyers are on opposite sides of an attempted murder case.

A superior star vehicle which also managed to introduce four promising personalities; slangily written and smartly directed, but perhaps a shade less funny than it once seemed.

w Ruth Gordon, Garson Kanin d George Cukor ph George J. Folsey m Miklos Rozsa

Spencer Tracy, Katharine Hepburn, David Wayne, Tom Ewell, Judy Holliday, Jean Hagen, Hope Emerson, Clarence Kolb

'Hepburn and Tracy are again presented as the ideal US Mr and Mrs of upper-middle income. This time, as well as being wittily urbane, both are lawyers.'—*Time*

'It isn't solid food but it certainly is meaty and juicy and comically nourishing.'—*Bosley Crowther*

† A 1972 TV series of the same title provided a boring imitation, with Ken Howard and Blythe Danner.

Adam's Woman
Australia 1970   115m   colour Panavision

In the 1840s an American finds himself a prisoner in an antipodean penal colony, and schemes to get out. Oddball period drama, unreleased in Britain. Beau Bridges, Jane Merrow, James Booth, John Mills. Written by Richard Fielder; directed by Philip Leacock; for Warner / EMI.

The Adding Machine*
GB 1968   99m   Technicolor
Universal / Associated London (Jerome Epstein)

Downtrodden clerk Mr Zero rebels against society by murdering his boss. Tried and executed, he spends thirty years in heaven before being 'laundered' and sent back to start again as another nonentity.

Elmer Rice's satirical fantasy of the twenties is here robbed of its expressionist staging and presented naturalistically, a fatal error from which the film never for one moment recovers.

wd Jerome Epstein ph Walter Lassally m Mike Leander, Lambert Williamson

Phyllis Diller, Milo O'Shea, Billie Whitelaw, Sydney Chaplin, Julian Glover, Raymond Huntley, Phil Brown, Libby Morris

Address Unknown*
US 1944   72m   bw
Columbia (William Cameron Menzies)

A German-American becomes a Nazi and is incriminated by false letters from his one-time friend.
Reasonably engrossing, cheaply-made adaptation of a slim little thriller which was widely read during World War II.

w Kressman Taylor, Herbert Dalmass, *novel* Kressman Taylor d William Cameron Menzies ph Rudolf Maté m Ernst Toch

Paul Lukas, Peter Van Eyck, Mady Christians, Emory Parnell

AAN: Ernst Toch

Adieu Philippine*
France / Italy 1962   106m   bw
Unitec / Alpha / Rome-Paris (Georges de Beauregard)

A young TV cameraman is torn between two girls.
Flimsy but attractive romantic comedy, slightly marred by New Wave improvisation with consequent rough edges.

w Michèle O'Glor, Jacques Rozier d Jacques Rozier ph René Mathelin m various

Jean-Claude Aimini, Yveline Céry, Stefania Sabatini, Vittorio Caprioli

The Admirable Crichton*
GB 1957   93m   Technicolor   Vistavision
Columbia / Modern Screenplays (Ian Dalrymple)
US title: *Paradise Lagoon*

Lord Loam and his family are shipwrecked on a desert island, where his manservant proves the undisputed leader.
Few laughs are to be had from this blunt, sentimental version of a famous play, but the photography and decor are excellent.

w Vernon Harris, *play* J. M. Barrie d Lewis Gilbert ph Wilkie Cooper m Douglas Gamley ad William Kellner costumes Bernard Nevill devices Emmett

Kenneth More, Cecil Parker, Sally Ann Howes, Diane Cilento, Martita Hunt, Jack Watling, Peter Graves, Gerald Harper
'Barrie's play now seems more remote than Gammer Gurton.'—*David Robinson*

Adolf Hitler—My Part in His Downfall*
GB 1972   102m   Technicolor
UA / Norcon (Gregory Smith, Norman Cohen)

Episodes in the life of a conscript at the beginning of World War II.
Lumbering anarchic comedy based on Spike Milligan's own sidesplitting memoirs; an enfeebled British *M*A*S*H.*

w Johnny Byrne d Norman Cohen ph Terry Maher m Wilfred Burns

Jim Dale, Spike Milligan (as his own father), Arthur Lowe, Bill Maynard, Windsor Davies, Pat Coombs, Tony Selby, Geoffrey Hughes
'A convincing period shabbiness and sleaziness which are endearing when they're not being overstated.'—*MFB*

Adorable*
US 1933   85m   bw
Fox

A Ruritanian princess falls in love with a naval officer.
Charming, lightweight romance of the old school.

w George Marion Jr, Jane Storm, *story* Paul Frank, Billy Wilder d William Dieterle ph John Seitz

Janet Gaynor, Henri Garat, C. Aubrey Smith, Herbert Mundin, Blanche Friderici, Hans von Twardowski

Adorable Creatures
France 1952   105m   bw
Jacques Roitfeld / Sirius

A Paris fashion executive recalls his love affairs.
A collection of four short sex comedies which did well on the heels of *La Ronde*.

w Charles Spaak, Jacques Companeez d Christian-Jaque ph Christian Matras m Georges Van Parys

Daniel Gélin, *Danielle Darrieux*, Edwige Feuillère, Antonella Lualdi, Martine Carol, Marilyn Buferd

Advance to the Rear*
US 1964   97m   bw   Panavision
MGM / Ted Richmond
GB title: *Company of Cowards?*

After the Civil War, a troop of misfits is sent west out of harm's way, but manages to capture a rebel spy and save a gold shipment.
Semi-satirical western action comedy with a farcical climax; quite sharply made.

w Samuel A. Peeples, William Bowers d George Marshall ph Milton Krasner m Randy Sparks

Glenn Ford, *Melvyn Douglas*, Stella Stevens, Jim Backus, Joan Blondell, Andrew Prine, Alan Hale, James Griffith, Preston Foster

Adventure*
US 1945   126m   bw
MGM (Sam Zimbalist)

A roughneck sailor marries a librarian, but only settles down to love her when their child is born.

Uniquely embarrassing (and fascinating) mishmash of pretentious dialogue and cardboard characters. 'Gable's back and Garson's got him!' squealed the posters, but the stars would have done better not to meet.

w Frederick Hazlitt Brennan, Vincent Lawrence, *novel* Clyde Brion Davis d Victor Fleming ph Joseph Ruttenberg m Herbert Stothart

Clark Gable, Greer Garson, Thomas Mitchell, Joan Blondell, John Qualen, Richard Haydn

'MGM proudly announce *Adventure* as the meeting of a red-blooded man with a blue-blooded woman. Its impact on the bloodstream of your critic was a chilling one. Fifty years of the cinema, he thought, and this is where we've landed.'—*Richard Winnington*

Adventure in Baltimore
US 1949 89m bw
RKO (Richard H. Berger)
GB title: *Bachelor Bait*

In 1905, a young society girl becomes a suffragette.
Inconsequential period comedy which did nothing for its young star's fading career.

w Lionel Houser, *story* Christopher Isherwood, Lesser Samuels d Richard Wallace ph Robert de Grasse m Frederick Hollander

Shirley Temple, Robert Young, John Agar, Albert Sharpe, Josephine Hutchinson, Johnny Sands, John Miljan, Norma Varden

Adventure in Diamonds
US 1940 76m bw
Paramount (George Fitzmaurice)

A British adventurer in South Africa falls in love with a lady diamond thief.
Acceptable romantic comedy-drama.

w Leonard Lee, Franz Schultz d George Fitzmaurice ph Charles Lang

George Brent, Isa Miranda, John Loder, Nigel Bruce, Elizabeth Patterson, Matthew Boulton, Cecil Kellaway, Ernest Truex, E. E. Clive

Adventure in Iraq
US 1943 65m bw

Wartime second feature about Americans who fall into Nazi–Arab hands. Interesting only as a remake of *The Green Goddess*, with Paul Cavanagh in the George Arliss role. Also featuring John Loder, Ruth Ford. Written by George Bilson and Robert E. Kent; directed by D. Ross Lederman; for Warner.

Adventure in Manhattan
US 1936 73m bw
Columbia
GB title: *Manhattan Madness*

An actress helps an ace reporter to foil a bank robbery by a master criminal.
Flat romantic mystery comedy which wastes a good cast.

w Sidney Buchman, Harry Sauber, Jack Kirkland d Edward Ludwig ph Henry Freulich

Jean Arthur, Joel McCrea, Thomas Mitchell, Reginald Owen, Herman Bing

Adventure Island
US 1947 67m bw

Seafarers chance on an uncharted island, ruled by a deadly fanatic. Hokum rehash of Stevenson's *Ebb Tide*, with Paul Kelly as the madman; also featuring Rory Calhoun, Rhonda Fleming. Written by Maxwell Shane; directed by Peter Stewart; for Paramount.

The Adventure of Sherlock Holmes' Smarter Brother
GB 1975 91m De Luxe
TCF / Jouer (Richard A. Roth)

More by good luck than good management, Sherlock's younger brother solves one of his cases.
Infuriating parody with little sense of the original and a hit-or-miss style all of its own. Amusing moments fail to atone for the general waste of opportunity

wd Gene Wilder ph Gerry Fisher m John Morris pd Terry Marsh

Gene Wilder, Marty Feldman, Madeleine Kahn, Leo McKern, Dom De Luise, Roy Kinnear, John Le Mesurier, Douglas Wilmer, Thorley Walters

'Like a compilation of the kind of numbers actors like to do at parties.'—*Howard Kissel*

'He has bitten off more than he can chew or I can swallow.'—*John Simon*

'A few stray chuckles but nothing more.'—*Sight and Sound*

'There's no mystery, and since you can't have a parody of a mystery without a mystery, there's no comic suspense.'—*New Yorker, 1980*

The Adventurer°°°
US 1917 21m approx (24 fps) bw
   silent
Mutual

An escaped convict rescues two wealthy women from drowning and is invited to their home.

Hilarious early Chaplin knockabout, with his physical gags at their most streamlined.

wd Charles Chaplin *ph* William C. Foster, Rollie Totheroh

Charles Chaplin, Edna Purviance, Eric Campbell, Henry Bergman

The Adventurers
GB 1950   86m   bw
Rank / Mayflower (Maxwell Setton, Aubrey Baring)
US title: *The Great Adventure*

In 1902, two Boers and a cashiered English officer set out to recover stolen diamonds. Lethargic South African western in the wake of *Treasure of the Sierra Madre*; clumsy and unconvincing, with cardboard characters.

w Robert Westerby *d* David MacDonald *ph* Oswald Morris *m* Cedric Thorpe Davie

Dennis Price, Jack Hawkins, Siobhan McKenna, Peter Hammond, Bernard Lee, Grégoire Aslan

The Adventurers*
US 1970   170m   Technicolor
Panavision
Paramount / Avco Embassy /
Adventurers Film (Lewis Gilbert)

A sensualist brought up amid Europe's luxuries returns to his Central American homeland to take vengeance on the brutal security chief who raped and murdered his mother.
Sprawling, sexy, bloodstained extravaganza from a Harold Robbins novel. Expensive to look at and riddled with sensation, but that's about all.

w Michael Hastings, Lewis Gilbert *d* Lewis Gilbert *ph* Claude Renoir *m* Antonio Carlos Jobim *pd* Tony Masters

Bekim Fehmiu, Alan Badel, Candice Bergen, Ernest Borgnine, Olivia de Havilland, Rossano Brazzi, Charles Aznavour, Sidney Tafler, Fernando Rey, Leigh Taylor-Young, Thommy Berggren, John Ireland
'A three-hour slog through every imaginable cliché of writing and direction . . . in addition to an abundance of flaccid sex and violence, it offers drugs, sadism, orchids, fireworks, orgies, lesbianism, a miscarriage, a private torture chamber, and the hell of several fashion shows with loud pop music accompaniment. This might well be described as the film with everything; trouble is, it is difficult to imagine anybody wanting any of it.'—*MFB*
'Lovers of rotten movies and close-up violence can revel in it.'—*Judith Crist*

The Adventures of Arsène Lupin*
France / Italy 1956   103m   Eastmancolor
Chavane-SNE-Gaumont /
Lambor-Costellazione (Robert Sussfeld)

In 1912, the famous jewel thief conducts several successful robberies and outwits the Kaiser.
The most stylish Lupin film, though not based on the original stories.

w Jacques Becker, Albert Simonin, based on the character created by Maurice Leblanc *d* Jacques Becker *ph* Edmond Séchan *ad* Rino Mondellini

Robert Lamoureux, Lisolotte Pulver, Otto Hasse, Henri Rolland

The Adventures of Barry Mackenzie*
Australia 1972   114m   Eastmancolor
Columbia / Longford (Philip Adams)

A sex-hungry Australian gets into all kinds of trouble on a visit to the Old Country.
Occasionally funny, defiantly crude and tasteless, but poorly produced comedy-misadventure from the *Private Eye* comic strip. Australian slang combines with bad sound recording to make much of the film unintelligible.

w Barry Humphries, Bruce Beresford *d* Bruce Beresford *ph* Don McAlpine *m* Peter Best

Barry Crocker, Barry Humphries (as Dame Edna Everage), Peter Cook, Spike Milligan, Dennis Price, Avice Landon, Dick Bentley, Joan Bakewell, William Rushton
'A wildly uneven concoction of antipodean bad taste, probably only fully appreciated by Earls Court exiles.'—*Sight and Sound*
† Sequel 1974: *Barry Mackenzie Holds His Own.*

The Adventures of Bullwhip Griffin**
US 1965   110m   Technicolor
Walt Disney (Bill Anderson)

In the 1849 California Gold Rush, two aristocrats and their butler head west.
Rather splendid spoof western with careful attention to detail and comedy pointing, well above the average Disney standard.

w Lowell S. Hawley, novel By the Great Horn Spoon by Sid Fleischman *d* James Neilson *ph* Edward Colman *m* George Bruns *titles* Ward Kimball

Roddy McDowall, Suzanne Pleshette, Bryan Russell, Karl Malden, Harry Guardino, Richard Haydn, Mike Mazurki, Hermione Baddeley, Cecil Kellaway

The Adventures of Captain Fabian
US 1951   100m   bw
Republic / Silver (William Marshall)

A sea captain returns to New Orleans to
revenge himself on the family which had
defrauded his father.
Stilted, old-fashioned *Monte Cristo*ish
melodrama with some curiosity value but little
verve in the playing or production. An awful
warning to independent producers.

w Errol Flynn, *novel* Fabulous Ann Medlock
by Robert Shannon *d* William Marshall
ph Marcel Grignon *m* René Cloerec

Errol Flynn, Micheline Presle, Agnes
Moorehead, Vincent Price, Victor Francen,
Jim Gerald
† Made in France.

Adventures of Casanova
US 1948   83m   bw

Casanova returns to Sicily and helps
overthrow the tyrannical rule of the King of
Naples. Robin Hood transplanted, with a few
amorous asides; but this is a totally stilted
production which fails to entertain. Arturo de
Cordova, Lucille Bremer, Turhan Bey.
Written by Crane Wilbur, Walter Bullock and
Ken de Wolf; directed by Roberto Gavaldon;
for Eagle-Lion.

The Adventures of Don Juan**
US 1949   110m   Technicolor
Warner (Jerry Wald)
GB title: *The New Adventures of Don Juan*

A reformed 17th-century rake saves his queen
from the machinations of her first minister.
Expensive, slightly uneasy, but generally very
entertaining swashbuckler with elements of
self-spoofery. Flynn's last big-budget
extravaganza.

w George Oppenheimer, Harry Kurnitz
d Vincent Sherman *ph* Elwood Bredell
m Max Steiner

Errol Flynn, Viveca Lindfors, Romney Brent,
Robert Douglas, Alan Hale, Ann Rutherford,
Robert Warwick, Jerry Austin, Douglas
Kennedy, Una O'Connor, Aubrey Mather,
Raymond Burr

The Adventures of Gerard**
GB 1970   91m   De Luxe   Panavision
UA / Sir Nigel Films (Peter Beale)

A hussar of Napoleon becomes involved in a
double spy game but comes out trumps and
wins a fair lady.
A lighthearted historical spoof of military
pomp, with plenty of attractive elements which
unfortunately fail to jell into a satisfying film.

w H. A. L. Craig and others, from stories by
Arthur Conan Doyle *d* Jerzy Skolimowski
ph Witold Sobocinski *m* Riz Ortolani

Peter McEnery, Claudia Cardinale, Eli
Wallach, Jack Hawkins, Mark Burns, Norman
Rossington, John Neville

'Enormously graceful and witty . . . picks its
way with amazing delicacy through the reefs of
facetiousness.'—*Tom Milne*

The Adventures of Hajji Baba*
US 1954   93m   De Luxe   Cinemascope
Allied Artists / Walter Wanger

In ancient Arabia, a barber helps and falls in
love with an escaping princess.
A reasonably dashing sword and sandal romp
which no one takes very seriously.

w Richard Collins *d* Don Weis *ph* Harold
Lipstein *m* Dmitri Tiomkin *pd* Gene Allen

John Derek, Elaine Stewart, Thomas Gomez,
Amanda Blake, Paul Picerni, Rosemarie
Bowe

The Adventures of Huckleberry Finn:
see Huckleberry Finn

The Adventures of Marco Polo*
US 1938   100m   bw
Samuel Goldwyn

The medieval Italian explorer discovers China,
fireworks, and a beautiful maiden.
One gets the impression that this began as a
standard adventure and that during production
it switched to comedy; whatever the cause,
lively and amusing scenes fail to add up to
more than a thinly scripted pantomime.

w Robert E. Sherwood *d* Archie Mayo
ph Rudolph Maté *m* Hugo Friedhofer
md Alfred Newman *ad* Richard Day

Gary Cooper, Sigrid Gurie, Basil Rathbone,
Ernest Truex, Binnie Barnes, Alan Hale,
George Barbier

'In spite of its elaborate settings and the
presence of Gary Cooper, it never quite lives
up to its promises.'—*New York Sun*

The Adventures of Mark Twain**
US 1944   130m   bw
Warner (Jesse L. Lasky)

The life of America's foremost humorous
writer, from a Mississippi riverboat to his
becoming an honorary fellow of Oxford
University.
Conventional biopic, quite watchable and with
unusual side turnings, but eventually lacking
the zest of the subject.

w Harold M. Sherman, Alan le May, Harry Chandler *d* Irving Rapper *ph Sol Polito*
m Max Steiner

Fredric March, Alexis Smith, Donald Crisp, Alan Hale,
C. Aubrey Smith, John Carradine, William Henry, Robert Barrat, Walter Hampden
'It's not that it's much worse than most cinematized biographies, because it does have its good moments. It's just that once more biographical inaccuracy is rampant, and once more the best dramatic possibilities have been overlooked, so it's hard to think of anything new, in the line of protest, to say.'—*David Lardner, New Yorker*

AAN: Max Steiner

The Adventures of Robin Hood****
US 1938   102m   Technicolor
Warner (Hal B. Wallis)

Rebel outlaw Robin Hood outwits Guy of Gisbourne and the Sheriff of Nottingham, and saves the throne for the absent King Richard.
A splendid adventure story, rousingly operatic in treatment, with dashing action highlights, fine comedy balance, and incisive acting all round. Historically notable for its use of early three-colour Technicolor; also for convincingly recreating Britain in California.

w Seton I. Miller, Norman Reilly Raine
d William Keighley, Michael Curtiz ph Tony Gaudio, Sol Polito, Howard Green m Erich Wolfgang Korngold ad Carl Jules Weyl

Errol Flynn, Olivia de Havilland, Basil Rathbone, Claude Rains, Eugene Pallette,
Alan Hale, Patric Knowles, Melville Cooper, Una O'Connor, Ian Hunter, Herbert Mundin, Montagu Love
'Magnificent, unsurpassable . . . the film is lavish, brilliantly photographed, and has a great Korngold score.'—*NFT, 1974*
'Mostly the picture is full of movement, some of it dashing in fine romantic costume style, some of it just sprightly. The excitement comes from fast action – galloping steeds, men swinging Tarzan-like from the trees, hurling tables and chairs, rapid running swordplay, the sudden whiz of Robin's arrows coming from nowhere to startle his enemies – more than from any fear that Robin might be worsted. Somehow the whole thing has the air of being a costume party, a jolly and rather athletic one, with a lot of well-bred Englishmen playing at being in the greenwood.'—*James Shelley Hamilton, National Board of Review*
'Only the rainbow can duplicate its brilliance!'—*Publicity*

AA: Erich Wolfgang Korngold
AAN: best picture

The Adventures of Robinson Crusoe***
Mexico 1953   89m   Pathecolor
Tepeyac (Oscar Dancigers, Henry F. Ehrlich)

A 17th-century mariner is shipwrecked on an uninhabited tropical island.
Fascinating version of a famous story, with only one character on screen until the belated arrival of Friday and the escape to civilization. Subtle and compelling, with only the colour unsatisfactory.

w Luis Bunuel, Phillip Roll, novel Daniel Defoe *d Luis Bunuel ph* Alex Phillips
m Anthony Collins

Dan O'Herlihy, James Fernandez
'A film of which the purity, the tense poetic style, evokes a kind of wonder.'—*Gavin Lambert*
'Free of that deadly solicitude which usually kills off classics.'—*New Yorker, 1977*

AAN: Dan O'Herlihy

The Adventures of Sherlock Holmes***
US 1939   83m   bw
TCF (Gene Markey)
GB title: *Sherlock Holmes*

Moriarty sends Holmes on a false trail while he plots to steal the Crown jewels.
Highly engaging piece of Hollywood Victoriana, with all elements perfect except for an unconvincing plot.

w Edwin Blum, William Drake d Alfred Werker *ph* Leon Shamroy *m* Cyril Mockridge

Basil Rathbone, Nigel Bruce, George Zucco, Ida Lupino, Alan Marshal, E. E. Clive, Mary Gordon
'Told with more movie art per foot than seven reels of anything the intellectual men have been finding good this whole year or more.'—*Otis Ferguson*
† This was the second and last of Rathbone's costume outings as Holmes, and the one in which he sang a comic song in disguise.

The Adventures of Tartu*
GB 1943   103m   bw
MGM (Irving Asher)
US title: *Tartu*

During World War II, a British spy goes to Czechoslovakia to dismantle a poison gas factory.
Halting and artificial comedy-thriller, saved only by a graceful star performance.

w Howard Emmett Rogers, John Lee Mahin, Miles Malleson *d* Harold S. Bucquet *ph* John J. Cox *m* Hubert Bath *md* Louis Levy

Robert Donat, Valerie Hobson, Walter Rilla, Glynis Johns, Martin Miller

'You are seeing all it has, and bald spots as well, first time around, whereas with a good Hitchcock or even a good Carol Reed, the pleasures visible at a first seeing stand up, or intensify, at a third or a fifth.'—*James Agee*

Adventures of the Wilderness Family
US 1975   101m   colour

An urban family runs into trouble when it takes to the wilds. Naïve little four-wall family movie in which the pretty scenery (Utah and the Canadian Rockies) and the animals compensate for the dramatic inadequacies.
Robert Logan, Susan Damante Shaw. Written and directed by Stewart Raffil; for Pacific International. (*Further Adventures of the Wilderness Family* appeared in 1977.)

The Adventures of Tom Sawyer•••
US 1938   91m   Technicolor
David O. Selznick (William H. Wright)

Small-town Mississippi boy tracks down a murderer, Injun Joe.
Set-bound but excellent version of the children's classic by Mark Twain.

w John Weaver   d Norman Taurog   *ph* James Wong Howe, Wilfrid Cline   *m* Max Steiner   *ad William Cameron Menzies*

Tommy Kelly, Ann Gillis, *May Robson*, Victor Jory, Jackie Moran, Walter Brennan, Spring Byington, Margaret Hamilton, Victor Kilian

'Should make Mark Twain circulate in his grave like a trout in a creel.'—*Otis Ferguson*

Advice to the Lovelorn
US 1933   62m   bw

A reporter is demoted to the lonelyhearts column and becomes absorbed in it. Springy vehicle for Lee Tracy, with Sally Blaine, Sterling Holloway, Isabel Jewell; from Nathanael West's novel *Miss Lonelyhearts*; directed by Darryl Zanuck; for Fox. (Compare the Paul Muni vehicle *Hi Nellie*.)

Advise and Consent••
US 1962   139m   bw   Panavision
Columbia / Otto Preminger

The President's choice of an unpopular secretary of state leads to divisions in the Senate and the blackmail and suicide of a senator.
Absorbing political melodrama from a novel which aimed to lift the lid off Washington. Many character actors make their mark, but the harsh-contrast photography seems misjudged.

w Wendell Mayes, *novel* Allen Drury   *d* Otto Preminger   *ph* Sam Leavitt   *m* Jerry Fielding   *titles* Saul Bass

Don Murray, *Charles Laughton*, Henry Fonda, Walter Pidgeon, Lew Ayres, Edward Andrews, Burgess Meredith, Gene Tierney, Franchot Tone, George Grizzard, Paul Ford, Peter Lawford, Inga Swenson, Will Geer

'The result is supremely ambivalent, a battle between fascinatingly real props and procedures and melodramatically unreal characters and situations.'—*Peter John Dyer*

'The parade of people helps to take one's mind off the overwrought melodrama.'—*New Yorker, 1980*

Aelita•
USSR 1924   70m approx   bw   silent
Mezhrabpom

Two Russian rocket pioneers land on Mars and start a revolution against the planet's queen.
Notable early space fiction, with footage of twenties Moscow as well as interesting set designs.

w Fedor Ozep, Alexei Faiko, *novel* Alexei Tolstoy   *d* Yakov Protazanov   *ph* Yuri Zhelabuzhsky   *pd* Sergei Kozlovsky

Yulia Solntseva, Nikolai Batalov, Igor Ilinsky

Aerograd••
USSR 1935   81m   bw
Mosfilm-Ukrainfilm
aka: *Frontier*

Guards keep Japanese spies out of Siberia, where an airport is being built.
An action film with style and pretensions.

wd Alexander Dovzhenko   ph Edouard Tissé, Mikhail Gindin

Semyon Shagaida, Stepan Shkurat, Sergei Stolyarov

Affair in Trinidad•
US 1952   98m   bw
Columbia / Beckworth (Vincent Sherman)

A nightclub singer whose husband is killed by gangsters works undercover for the police and routs the gang with the help of her husband's brother.
A tired tropical melodrama intended to follow up the success of *Gilda*, but without the verve. Some routine pleasures, though.

w Oscar Saul, James Gunn   *d* Vincent Sherman   *ph* Joseph Walker   *m* Morris Stoloff, George Dunning

Rita Hayworth, Glenn Ford, Alexander Scourby, Torin Thatcher, Valerie Bettis, Steve Geray, Karel Stepanek, George Voskovec

'Improbable, foolish, but glossy.'—*Penelope Houston*

An Affair to Remember**
US 1957   114m   Eastmancolor
Cinemascope
TCF (Leo McCarey)

An ex-nightclub singer falls in love with a wealthy bachelor on a transatlantic liner, but an accident prevents her from attending their subsequent rendezvous.

Remake of *Love Affair*, a surprisingly successful mixture of smart lines, sentiment and tears, all applied with style and assurance.

w Delmer Daves, Leo McCarey d Leo McCarey ph Milton Krasner m Hugo Friedhofer

Cary Grant, Deborah Kerr, Cathleen Nesbitt, Richard Denning, Neva Patterson

'A lush slice of Hollywood romanticism.'—*MFB*

'90 masterly minutes of entrancing light comedy and 25 beastly minutes of beastly, melodramatic, pseudo-tragic guff.'—*Paul Dehn*

AAN: Milton Krasner; Hugo Friedhofer; title song (*m* Harry Warren, *ly* Harold Adamson, Leo McCarey)

Affair with a Stranger*
US 1953   87m   bw
RKO (Robert Sparks)

Five friends reminisce about a marriage which seems about to break up.

This would-be-smart comedy has a good idea unsatisfactorily worked out, and could have used a more sparkling cast.

w Richard Flournoy d Roy Rowland ph Harry J. Wild m Roy Webb

Jean Simmons, Victor Mature, Mary Jo Tarola, Monica Lewis, Jane Darwell, Nicholas Joy, Wally Vernon, Dabbs Greer

L'Affaire est dans le Sac*
France 1932   47m   bw
Pathé / Nathan
aka: *It's in the Bag*

Two would-be kidnappers end up (a) married to and (b) employed by their intended victims. Semi-professional nonsense comedy with political jokes.

w Jacques Prévert d Pierre Prévert ph A. Giboury, Eli Lotar m Maurice Jaubert

J.-P. Le Chanois, Jacques Brunius, Etienne Decroux, Lucien Raimbourg, Julien Carette, Lora Hays

Affairs of a Gentleman
US 1934   68m   bw

A novelist who has used all his love affairs in his novels holds a reunion. Mild star vehicle which wastes an amusing idea. Paul Lukas, Leila Hyams, Onslow Stevens. Written by Cyril Hume, Peter Ruric and Milton Krims; directed by Edwin L. Marin; for Universal.

The Affairs of Annabel*
US 1938   69m   bw
RKO (Lee Marcus, Lou Lusty)

A crackpot Hollywood press agent sends his star to jail as a publicity stunt.

An amusing frenetic comedy of its time, successful enough to warrant a sequel, *Annabel Takes a Tour*, in the same year.

w Bert Granet, Paul Yawitz d Lew Landers ph Russell Metty m Roy Webb

Lucille Ball, Jack Oakie, Ruth Donnelly, Bradley Page, Fritz Feld, Thurston Hall, Elizabeth Risdon, Granville Bates, James Burke

The Affairs of Cellini*
US 1934   90m   bw
Twentieth Century (Darryl F. Zanuck)

The complex amours of a 16th-century Florentine rake.

Lively period bedroom farce somewhat hampered by censorship.

w Bess Meredyth, *play* The Firebrand by Edwin Justus Mayer d Gregory La Cava ph Charles Rosher m Alfred Newman

Fredric March, Constance Bennett, *Frank Morgan*, Fay Wray, Vince Barnett, Louis Calhern, Jessie Ralph

'Gay and entertaining though whipped up synthetically like circus ice cream.'—*Variety*

AAN: Charles Rosher; Frank Morgan

The Affairs of Dobie Gillis
US 1953   74m   bw
MGM (Arthur M. Loew Jnr)

Adventures of an indolent and accident-prone university student.

Scatty comedy with good talent and musical numbers encased in a tatty production.

w Max Shulman d Don Weis ph William Mellor md Jeff Alexander

Bobby Van, Debbie Reynolds, Hans Conried, Barbara Ruick, Bob Fosse

The Affairs of Martha
US   1942   66m   bw

A servant writes a scandalous book about her employers. Fairly amusing comedy with an

ingratiating cast: Marsha Hunt, Richard
Carlson, Spring Byington, Allyn Joslyn,
Frances Drake, Margaret Hamilton, Melville
Cooper, Virginia Weidler, Ernest Truex,
Marjorie Main. Written by Isobel Lennart and
Lee Gold; directed by Jules Dassin; for MGM.
(GB title: *Once Upon a Thursday*.)

The Affairs of Susan**
US 1945   110m   bw
Paramount (Hal B. Wallis)

Four men in Susan's life see her differently.
Occasionally witty comedy designed as a
champagne vehicle for its star. It seemed quite
good at the time.

w Richard Flournoy, *original story* Laszlo
Gorog, T. Monroe *d* William A. Seiter
ph David Abel *m* Frederick Hollander

Joan Fontaine, George Brent, Walter Abel,
Don Defore, Dennis O'Keefe
    'The cast enters into the irresponsibilities
with gusto.'—*MFB*
    'A bright thing, a bit too long.'—*Richard
Mallett, Punch*

AAN: Laszlo Gorog, T. Monroe

Affectionately Yours
US 1941   88m   bw
Warner (Mark Hellinger)

A foreign correspondent hurries home when
he hears that his wife plans to divorce him.
Thin lightweight comedy, unsuitably cast.

w Edward Kaufman *d* Lloyd Bacon *ph* Tony
Gaudio *m* Heinz Roemheld

Merle Oberon, Dennis Morgan, *Rita
Hayworth*, George Tobias, Ralph Bellamy,
James Gleason, Hattie McDaniel

Africa Screams
US 1949   79m   bw

Two dumbbells go on safari with a treasure
map. Lower-case Abbott and Costello
comedy, with Hilary Brooke, Max Baer,
Shemp Howard. Written by Earl Baldwin;
directed by Charles Barton; for Edward
Nassour / UA.

Africa Texas Style*
GB 1967   109m   Eastmancolor
Paramount / Vantors (Andrew Marton)

A Kenyan settler hires two Texas cowboys to
help in his scheme of wild game ranching.
Excellent location sequences are dragged
down by a very boring script, but it's a good
family film nevertheless.

w Andy White *d* Andrew Marton *ph* Paul
Beeson *m* Malcolm Arnold

John Mills, Hugh O'Brian, Nigel Green, Tom
Nardini, Adrienne Corri, Ronald Howard
† Forerunner of TV series, *Cowboy in Africa*.

The African Queen***
GB 1951   103m   Technicolor
IFD / Romulus–Horizon (Sam Spiegel)

In 1915, a gin-drinking river trader and a prim
missionary make odd companions for a boat
trip down a dangerous river, culminating in an
attack on a German gunboat.
Despite some unfortunate studio sets mixed in
with real African footage achieved through
great hardship by all concerned, this is one of
those surprising films that really work, a
splendidly successful mixture of comedy,
character and adventure.

w James Agee, novel C. S. Forester *d John
Huston ph Jack Cardiff m Allan Gray*

Humphrey Bogart, Katharine Hepburn,
Robert Morley, Peter Bull
    'Entertaining but not entirely plausible or
original.'—*Robert Hatch*
    'The movie is not great art but it is great
fun, essentially one long, exciting, old-
fashioned movie chase.'—*Time*
    'A Technicolor Cook's Tour of jungle
wonders, enriched by performances
unmatched by anything Hepburn or Bogart
have yet contributed to the screen.'—*Cue*

AA: Humphrey Bogart
AAN: James Agee; John Huston; Katharine
Hepburn

After Office Hours*
US 1935   75m   bw
MGM (Bernard H. Hyman)

A newspaperman and his socialite reporter
solve a murder mystery.
Crisply-written, fast-moving comedy
melodrama; good stuff of its time and type.

w Herman J. Mankiewicz d Robert Z.
Leonard *ph* Charles Rosher

Clark Gable, Constance Bennett, Stuart Erwin,
Billie Burke, Harvey Stephens, Katherine
Alcxander, Henry Travers, Henry Armetta
    'One of the best balanced pix of the season;
it has practically everything.'—*Film Daily*

After the Ball*
GB 1957   89m   Eastmancolor
IFD / Beaconsfield (Peter Rogers)

The life and loves of music-hall singer Vesta
Tilley, who married into the nobility.
Adequate if uninspired biopic with
entertaining detail and songs.

w Hubert Gregg *d* Compton Bennett
ph Jack Asher *ad* Norman Arnold *md* Muir
Mathieson

Pat Kirkwood, Laurence Harvey, Clive
Morton, Jerry Verno, June Clyde

After the Fox*

US / Italy 1966   103m   Technicolor
   Panavision
UA / Nancy / CCM (John Bryan)

The Fox escapes from jail to execute a gold
bullion caper and save his young sister from
the streets.

Unlikeable and unfunny farce which sets its
star among excitable Italians and hopes for the
best, adding a few wild stabs at satire on
movie-making styles.

w Neil Simon, Cesare Zavattini *d* Vittorio de
Sica *ph* Leonida Barboni *m* Burt Bacharach

Peter Sellers, *Victor Mature* (agreeably
sending up his old image), Britt Ekland, Lilia
Brazzi, Paola Stoppa, Akim Tamiroff, Martin
Balsam

'Never even begins to get off the ground.'—
MFB

After the Thin Man**

US 1936   113m   bw
MGM (Hunt Stromberg)

Nick and Nora Charles, not forgetting Asta,
solve another murder.

Overlong but well-carpentered sequel to *The
Thin Man*, developing the thesis that a
married couple, even if they are detectives and
drink too much, can be interesting and
lovable.

w Frances Goodrich, Albert Hackett *d* W. S.
Van Dyke II *ph* Oliver T. Marsh *m* Herbert
Stothart, Edward Ward

William Powell, Myrna Loy, James Stewart,
Elissa Landi, Joseph Calleia, Jessie Ralph,
Alan Marshal, Sam Levene

A   N: Frances Goodrich; Albert Hackett

After Tonight

US 1933   71m   bw

During World War I a Russian lady spy falls
for an Austrian officer. Tediously talky
romantic vehicle which barely gets started
before it bogs down. Constance Bennett,
Gilbert Roland, Edward Ellis, Mischa Auer.
Written by Jane Murfin; directed by George
Archainbaud; for RKO. (GB title: *Sealed
Lips*.)

Against All Flags*

US 1952   83m   Technicolor
U-I (Howard Christie)

A daring British seaman routs Spanish ships at
the request of the king.

Standard pirate yarn, almost Flynn's last
swashbuckler; production below par.

w Aeneas Mackenzie, Joseph Hoffman
d George Sherman *ph* Russell Metty *m* Hans
Salter

Errol Flynn, Maureen O'Hara, Anthony
Quinn, Mildred Natwick

† Remade as *The King's Pirate* (qv).

Against the Wind**

GB 1947   96m   bw
Ealing (Sidney Cole)

In London during World War II, men and
women are trained as saboteurs, and one of
them is a traitor.

Thoughtful, well-made spy thriller with good
performances.

w T. E. B. Clarke, Michael Pertwee
d Charles Crichton *ph* Lionel Banes *m* Leslie
Bridgewater

Simone Signoret, Robert Beatty, Jack
Warner, Gordon Jackson, Paul Dupuis, Gisele
Preville, John Slater, Peter Illing, James
Robertson Justice

Agatha*

GB 1978   105m   Technicolor
Warner / First Artists / Sweetall /
   Casablanca (Jarvis Astaire, Gavrik Losey)

In 1926, Agatha Christie disappears after
marital difficulties and tries to commit suicide
in a Harrogate hotel under a pseudonym.

Lushly recreated but still imaginary and
unconvincing solution to a real-life
disappearance, complete with romantic
encounter with an American newspaperman.

w Kathleen Tynan, Arthur Hopcraft
d Michael Apted *ph* Vittorio Storaro
m Johnny Mandel *pd* Shirley Russell

Vanessa Redgrave, Dustin Hoffman, Timothy
Dalton, Helen Morse, Timothy West, Tony
Britton, Alan Badel

'With its shadowy characters, paucity of
plot, and an abundance of stylistic red
herrings, one doubts whether *Agatha* would
have met Mrs Christie's own requirements for
a thriller, though she may well have enjoyed
its sumptuous recreation of hotel interiors in
the 1920s.'—*Geoff Brown, MFB*

'It has a general air of knowingness, but
seems to be missing the scenes which would
explain why it was made.'—*New Yorker*

L'Âge d'Or**

France 1930   63m   bw
Vicomte de Noailles

A collection of strange events satirizing religion and the social order.
Deliberately shocking and possibly quite meaningless, this truly surrealist film is chiefly interesting now for its flashforwards to Bunuel's later work.

w Luis Bunuel, Salvador Dali d Luis Bunuel ph Albert Dubergen

Gaston Modot, Lya Lys, Max Ernst, Pierre Prévert, Jacques Brunius

　'In some way the juxtaposition of images causes in almost every spectator a train of reactions of unprecedented violence.'—*Basil Wright, 1972*

Age of Consent*

Australia 1969　103m　Technicolor
Columbia / Nautilus (James Mason, Michael Powell)

An artist seduces the granddaughter of a drunken harridan with whom he shares a Barrier Reef island.
Mildly likeable but self-conscious and overlong South Pacific idyll.

w Peter Yeldham, *novel* Norman Lindsay *d* Michael Powell *ph* Hannes Staudinger *m* Stanley Myers

James Mason, Helen Mirren, Jack McGowran, Neva Carr-Glyn, Frank Thring

Age of Indiscretion

US　1935　80m　bw

A high-minded publisher finds that his wife is unfaithful. Tolerable marital drama about child custody. Paul Lukas, Helen Vinson, May Robson, Madge Evans, Ralph Forbes. Written by Lenore Coffee; directed by Edward Ludwig; for MGM.

Age of Innocence

Canada / GB 1977　101m　Eastmancolor
Judson / Willoughby (Henning Jacobsen)

After World War I, an English teacher in Canada develops pacifist views which stir up local resentment and lead to violence.
Rather uninteresting melodrama which never really comes to the boil despite care all round.

w Ratch Wallace *d* Alan Bridges *ph* Brian West *m* Lucio Agostini

David Warner, Honor Blackman, Trudy Young, Cec Linder, Tim Henry, Lois Maxwell, Robert Hawkins

The Agitator*

GB 1944　98m　bw
British National (Louis H. Jackson)

An embittered mechanic becomes a loud-mouthed union spokesman, but fate eventually takes him into management.

Fairly absorbing, modest narrative of the flaws of socialism.

w Edward Dryhurst, *novel* Peter Pettinger by William Riley *d* John Harlow *ph* James Wilson

William Hartnell (then being built into a star), Mary Morris, John Laurie, Moore Marriott, George Carney, Edward Rigby, Elliot Mason, Frederick Leister, Cathleen Nesbitt, Moira Lister

The Agony and the Ecstasy*

US 1965　140m　De Luxe　Todd-AO
TCF / International Classics Inc (Carol Reed)

Pope Julius II persuades Michelangelo to leave his sculptures and paint the ceiling of the Sistine Chapel.
Dully reverent comic strip approach to art and history; generally heavy going, but good looking.

w Philip Dunne, *novel* Irving Stone *d* Carol Reed *ph* Leon Shamroy *m* Alex North *pd* John de Cuir

Charlton Heston, Rex Harrison, Diane Cilento, Harry Andrews, Alberto Lupo, Adolfo Celi

　'The vulgarity of the whole concept has none of the joyfully enthusiastic philistinism of a de Mille; rather its tone is a dry, almost cynical, condescension.'—*Brenda Davies*
　'All agony, no ecstasy.'—*Judith Crist*

AAN: Leon Shamroy; Alex North

Aguirre, Wrath of God**

West Germany 1972　95m　colour
Werner Herzog / Hessicher Rundfunk

In 1560, one of Pizarro's lieutenants takes a party of forty down river by raft, and succumbs to megalomania.
Absorbing conquistador melodrama, vividly assembled and impossible to forget.

wd Werner Herzog ph Thomas Mauch *m* Popol Vuh

Klaus Kinski, Ruy Guerra, Helena Rojo, Cecilia Rivera

　'It ingeniously combines Herzog's gift for deep irony, his strong social awareness, and his worthy ambition to fashion a whole new visual perspective on the world around us via mystical, evocative, yet oddly direct imagery. It is a brilliant cinematic achievement.'—*David Skerritt, Christian Science Monitor*

Ah, Wilderness**

US 1935　101m　bw
MGM (Hunt Stromberg)

Problems of a small-town family at the turn of the century.

Well-acted, affectionately remembered version of a play later musicalized as *Summer Holiday*. The commercial success of this film led to the Hardy family series.

w Albert Hackett, Frances Goodrich, *play* Eugene O'Neill *d* Clarence Brown *ph* Clyde de Vinna *m* Herbert Stothart

Wallace Beery, Lionel Barrymore, Eric Linden, Spring Byington, Mickey Rooney, Aline MacMahon, Charley Grapewin, Cecilia Parker, Frank Albertson, Bonita Granville
'A job of picture making, in craftsmanship and feeling, that is wonderful to see.'—*Otis Ferguson*

Aida
Italy 1953   95m   Ferraniacolor
Oscar Film (Ferrucio de Martino, Federico Teti)

A young Egyptian army officer loves the captive princess of the Ethiopians.
Stuffy, over-dressed, pantomimish version of the opera, with some pretension to cinematic vitality.

w various, from Verdi's opera *d* Clemente Fracassi *ph* Piero Portalupi *ad* Flavio Mogherini

Sophia Loren (sung by Renata Tebaldi), Lois Maxwell, Luciano della Marra

Ain't Misbehavin'*
US 1955   81m   Technicolor
U-I (Samuel Marx)

A young millionaire marries a cabaret girl, who determines to improve her mind and manners.
Lively American version of *Pygmalion*, with musical numbers and some bright lines.

w Edward Buzzell, Philip Rapp, Devery Freeman *d* Edward Buzzell *ph* Wilfrid Cline *m* Joseph Gershenson *ch* Kenny Williams, Lee Scott

Rory Calhoun, *Piper Laurie, Reginald Gardiner*, Jack Carson, Barbara Britton, Mamie Van Doren

Air Cadet
US 1951   94m   bw

Problems of an air force flight instructor.
Routine flagwaver. Stephen McNally, Alex Nicol, Gail Russell, Richard Long, Charles Drake, Rock Hudson. Written by Robert L. Richards; directed by Joseph Pevney; for Universal-International. (GB title: *Jet Men of the Air*.)

Air Force*
US 1943   124m   bw
Warner (Hal B. Wallis)

A Flying Fortress and its crew see action in Manila, Pearl Harbor and the Coral Sea.
Propaganda piece concentrating on the characters of the crew members, with action set pieces largely provided by newsreel; but skilled direction still conveys plenty of punch.

w Dudley Nichols *d Howard Hawks ph* James Wong Howe, Elmer Dyer, Charles Marshall *m* Franz Waxman

John Garfield, Gig Young, Arthur Kennedy, Charles Drake, John Ridgley, Harry Carey, George Tobias, Stanley Ridges, Moroni Olsen, Edward Brophy
'Maybe the story is high-flown, maybe it overdraws a recorded fact a bit. We'd hate to think it couldn't happen—or didn't—because it leaves you feeling awfully good.'—*Bosley Crowther*
AAN: Dudley Nichols; James Wong Howe, Elmer Dyer, Charles Marshall

Air Mail
US 1932   84m   bw

Brash young pilot effects a daring rescue and gets the mail through. Moderate actioner of its time. Pat O'Brien, Ralph Bellamy, Russell Hopton, Gloria Stuart, Lillian Bond, Slim Summerville. Written by Dale Van Every and Frank Wead; directed by John Ford; for Universal.

Air Raid Wardens*
US 1943   67m   bw
MGM (B. F. Zeidman)

Rejected by the armed services, two incompetent air raid wardens accidentally round up Nazi spies.
Well below par star comedy: their incomparable dignity has disappeared.

w Jack Jevne, Martin Rackin, Charles Rogers, Harry Crane *d* Edward Sedgwick *ph* Harry Lundin *m* Nathaniel Shilkret

Stan Laurel, Oliver Hardy, Edgar Kennedy, Jacqueline White, Stephen McNally, Nella Walker, Donald Meek

Airplane**
US 1980   88m   Metrocolor
Paramount / Howard W. Koch (Jan Davison)

A former pilot gets his nerve back when called upon to land a passenger plane because the crew all have food poisoning.
Arthur Hailey's play *Flight into Danger* and the film *Zero Hour* which was made from it get the zany parody treatment in this popular movie which is often funny but sometimes merely crude. It rang the box office bell more loudly than most expensive epics of its year.

wd Jim Abrahams, David and Jerry Zucker *ph* Joseph Biroc *m* Elmer Bernstein *pd* Ward Preston

Robert Stack, Lloyd Bridges, Robert Hays, Julie Hegerty, Peter Graves, Leslie Nielsen, Lorna Paterson, Ethel Merman, Kareem Abdul-Jabbar

'Parody may be the lowest form of humour, but few comedies in ages have rocked the laugh meter this hard.'—*Variety*

Airport***
US 1969   136m   Technicolor   Todd-AO
Universal / Ross Hunter (Jaque Mapes)

Events of one snowy night at a midwestern international airport, culminating in airborne melodrama when a mad bomber is killed and the damaged plane has to be talked down. Glossy, undeniably entertaining, all-star version of a popular novel, with cardboard characters skilfully deployed in Hollywood's very best style.

w George Seaton, *novel* Arthur Hailey *d* George Seaton *ph* Ernest Laszlo *m* Alfred Newman

Burt Lancaster, Dean Martin, Jean Seberg, Helen Hayes, Van Heflin, Jacqueline Bisset, George Kennedy, Maureen Stapleton, Barry Nelson, Dana Wynter, Lloyd Nolan, Barbara Hale, Gary Collins, Jessie Royce Landis

'The best film of 1944.'—*Judith Crist*
'For sheer contentment there is nothing to beat the sight of constant catastrophe happening to others.'—*Alexander Walker*
'A *Grand Hotel* in the sky . . . every few years or so some more show-biz types would crowd onto a plane that would threaten to crash, collide with another, meet with terrorists, or otherwise be subjected to the perils of Pauline.'—*Les Keyser, Hollywood in the Seventies*

AA: Helen Hayes
AAN: best picture; George Seaton; Ernest Laszlo; Alfred Newman; Maureen Stapleton

Airport 1975
US 1974   105m   Technicolor
Panavision
Universal (Jennings Lang, William Frye)

A private aircraft collides with a jet plane and kills or immobilizes its crew, so a stewardess has to manoeuvre the jumbo to safety. Inept airborne suspenser loaded with stars who do nothing and marred by continuity lapses and boring dialogue.

w Don Ingalls *d* Jack Smight *ph* Philip Lathrop *m* John Cacavas

Charlton Heston, *Karen Black*, George Kennedy, Helen Reddy, Efrem Zimbalist Jnr, Susan Clark, Myrna Loy, Gloria Swanson, Linda Blair, Dana Andrews, Roy Thinnes, Sid Caesar, Ed Nelson, Nancy Olson, Martha Scott

'Aimed squarely for the yahoo trade.'—*Variety*

Airport '77
US 1977   114m   Technicolor
Panavision
Universal (William Frye)

A private airliner loaded with guests and art treasures hits an oil rig and settles underwater on a sandbank.
Hysteria, rescue, and guest stars with nothing to do; the mixture as before.

w Michael Scheff, David Spector *d* Jerry Jameson *ph* Philip Lathrop *m* John Cacavas *pd* George C. Webb

Jack Lemmon, James Stewart, Brenda Vaccaro, Joseph Cotten, Olivia de Havilland, Lee Grant, Darren McGavin, Christopher Lee, Robert Foxworth, Robert Hooks, Monte Markham, Kathleen Quinlan, James Booth

'Neither as riveting as it should be, nor as much fun as its absurd plotline would suggest.'—*Verina Glaessner, MFB*
† See also: *The Concorde—Airport '79.*

Akenfield
GB 1974   98m   Techniscope

Semi-dramatized film version of a book which documented a Suffolk village by interviewing its older inhabitants. An interesting venture ruined by imprecision, misty photography, lack of narrative drive or any compensating detail, and the appalling error of using a cheap wide screen process. Written by Ronald Blythe, from his book; directed by Peter Hall; for Angle Films and London Weekend Television.

Al Capone**
US 1959   105m   bw
Allied Artists (John H. Burrows, Leonard J. Ackerman)

An account of Chicago's most famous gangster, up to his arrest for income tax evasion.
Only slightly overplayed, semi-documentary retelling of a larger-than-life true story.

w Marvin Wald, Henry Greenberg *d* Richard Wilson *ph* Lucien Ballard *m* David Raksin

Rod Steiger (a clever impersonation on the border of caricature), Fay Spain, Murvyn Vye, Nehemiah Persoff, Martin Balsam, James Gregory, Joe de Santis

Alakazam the Great*
Japan 1960   88m   Eastmancolor
Toei (Hiroshi Okawa)
original title: *Saiyu-ki*

The arrogant monkey king of the animals is
sent by his human master on a pilgrimage; he
defeats evil King Gruesome and returns a
hero.
Smartly animated, Disney-inspired cartoon
based on the same legend as *Monkey*,
translated by Arthur Waley.

w Osamu Tezuka, Keinosuke Uekusa *d* Taiji
Yabushita

The Alamo*
US 1960   193m   Technicolor   Todd-AO
UA / John Wayne

In 1836 a small southern fort becomes the
centre of Texas' fight for independence, but it
is suddenly annihilated by a Mexican raid, and
all its defenders killed.
Sprawling historical epic with many irrelevant
episodes and distracting changes of mood.

w James Edward Grant *d* John Wayne
ph William H. Clothier *m* Dmitri Tiomkin

John Wayne (as Crockett), Richard Widmark
(Bowie), Laurence Harvey (Travis), Richard
Boone (Houston), Frankie Avalon, Patrick
Wayne, Linda Cristal, Chill Wills, Joseph
Calleia

'Its sole redeeming feature lies in one of
those crushing climaxes of total massacre
which Hollywood can still pull off thunderingly
well.'—*Peter John Dyer*

AAN: best picture; William H. Clothier;
Dmitri Tiomkin; Chill Wills; song 'The Green
Leaves of Summer' (*m* Dmitri Tiomkin,
ly Paul Francis Webster)

Alaska Seas
US 1953   78m   bw
Paramount (Mel Epstein)

Alaska fishermen oppose the crooked owner
of the local cannery.
Insipid remake of *Spawn of the North (qv)*.

w Geoffrey Homes, Walter Doniger *d* Jerry
Hopper *ph* William C. Mellor *md* Irvin
Talbot

Robert Ryan, Gene Barry, Jan Sterling, Brian
Keith, Richard Shannon

Albert RN*
GB 1953   88m   bw
Dial (Daniel M. Angel)
US title: *Break to Freedom*

Prisoners of war construct a lifelike dummy to
cover the absence of escaping prisoners.

Competent, entertaining version of a
successful play: an archetypal POW comedy
drama.

w Guy Morgan, Vernon Harris, *play* Guy
Morgan, Edward Sammis *d* Lewis Gilbert
ph Jack Asher *m* Malcolm Arnold

Jack Warner, Anthony Steel, Robert Beatty,
William Sylvester, Anton Diffring, Eddie
Byrne, Guy Middleton, Paul Carpenter,
Frederick Valk

Alex and the Gypsy
US 1976   99m   De Luxe
TCF / Richard Shepherd

A cynical California bailbondsman involved in
illicit activities chooses romantic freedom with
a gypsy girl.
Incoherent hardbitten romance with an
unconvincing set of characters.

w Lawrence B. Marcus, *novel* The
Bailbondsman by Stanley Elkin *d* John Korty
ph Bill Butler *m* Henry Mancini

Jack Lemmon, Genevieve Bujold, James
Woods, Gino Ardito, Robert Emhardt

'Even if it were well done (which it is not) it
would be banal, predictable and cloying.'—
Frank Rich

Alex in Wonderland
US 1970   109m   colour
MGM (Larry Tucker)

A Hollywood director finds life tedious.
So did the small paying audiences who saw
this pale imitation of Fellini. (Some wags
called it *One and a Half.*)

w Paul Mazursky, Larry Tucker *d* Paul
Mazursky

Donald Sutherland, Jeanne Moreau, Ellen
Burstyn, Federico Fellini

Alexander Hamilton*
US 1931   73m   bw
Warner

The life of America's 18th-century financier.
Star biopic, highly satisfying in its day.

w Julian Josephson, Maude Howell, George
Arliss *d* John G. Adolfi *ph* James Van Trees

George Arliss, Doris Kenyon, Montagu Love,
Dudley Digges, Lionel Belmore, Ralf
Harolde, Alan Mowbray

Alexander Nevsky**
USSR 1938   112m   bw
Mosfilm

In 1242, Prince Alexander Nevsky defeats the
invading Teutonic Knights in a battle on the
ice of Lake Peipus.

A splendid historical pageant which shows the director at his most inventively pictorial and climaxes in a superb battle sequence using music instead of natural sound.

w Pyotr Pavlenko, Sergei Eisenstein *d Sergei Eisenstein ph Edouard Tissé m Prokofiev ad* I. Shpinel, N. Soloviov, K. Yeliseyev

Nikolai Cherkassov, Nikolai Okhlopkov, Andrei Abrikosov, Dmitri Orlov

'Superb sequences of cinematic opera that pass from pastoral to lamentation and end in a triumphal cantata.'—*Georges Sadoul*

Alexander the Great*
US 1956   135m   Technicolor
Cinemascope
UA / Robert Rossen

The life and early death at thirty-three of the Macedonian warrior who conquered the entire known world.
Dour impassive epic which despite good intelligent stretches makes one long for Hollywood's usual more ruthless view of history.

wd Robert Rossen *m* Mario Nascimbene *ph* Robert Krasker *ad* Andrei Andreiev

Richard Burton, Fredric March, Danielle Darrieux, Claire Bloom, Barry Jones, Harry Andrews, Peter Cushing, Stanley Baker, Michael Hordern, Niall MacGinnis

'Not a scene is held for a second longer than it is worth; greatness is pictured in constant dissolve.'—*Alexander Walker*

'Rossen has aimed for greatness and lost honourably.'—*Andrew Sarris*

'The colossus who conquered the world! The most colossal motion picture of all time!'—*publicity*

Alexander's Ragtime Band***
US 1938   106m   bw
TCF (Darryl F. Zanuck, Harry Joe Brown)

Between 1911 and 1939, two songwriters vie for the affections of a rising musical comedy star.
Archetypal chronicle musical with 26 songs: well-paced, smartly made, and bursting with talent.

w Kathryn Scola, Lamar Trotti, Richard Sherman *d* Henry King *ph* Peverell Marley *m / ly* Irving Berlin *md* Alfred Newman

Tyrone Power, *Alice Faye,* Don Ameche, *Ethel Merman, Jack Haley,* Jean Hersholt, Helen Westley, John Carradine, Paul Hurst, Wally Vernon, Ruth Terry, Eddie Collins, Douglas Fowley, Chick Chandler

AA: Alfred Newman
AAN: best picture; Irving Berlin (for original story); Irving Berlin (for song, 'Now It Can Be Told')

The Alf Garnett Saga
GB 1972   90m   colour
Columbia / Associated London Films (Ned Sherrin, Terry Glinwood)

Bigoted Alf is exasperated by his council flat, his son-in-law, and the possibility that his daughter is pregnant by a black man.
Second inflation of the TV series, *Till Death Us Do Part,* even cruder and less funny than the first; listlessly written and developed.

w Johnny Speight *d* Bob Kellett *ph* Nic Knowland *m* Georgie Fame

Warren Mitchell, Dandy Nichols, Adrienne Posta, Mike Angelis, John Le Mesurier, Joan Sims, John Bird, Roy Kinnear

'One long, repetitive and unfunny diatribe.'—*MFB*

Alfie**
GB 1966   114m   Techniscope
Paramount / Sheldrake (Lewis Gilbert)

A Cockney Lothario is proud of his amorous conquests, but near-tragedy finally makes him more mature.
Garish sex comedy, an immense box office success because of its frankness and an immaculate performance from its star.

w Bill Naughton, from his play *d* Lewis Gilbert *ph* Otto Heller *m* Sonny Rollins

Michael Caine, Vivien Merchant, Shirley Anne Field, Millicent Martin, Jane Asher, Julia Foster, Shelley Winters, Eleanor Bron, Denholm Elliott

'Paramount thought it was a good bet because it was going to be made for 500,000 dollars, normally the sort of money spent on executives' cigar bills.'—*Lewis Gilbert*

AAN: best picture; Bill Naughton; Michael Caine; Vivien Merchant; title song

Alfred the Great*
GB 1969   122m   Metrocolor   Panavision
MGM / Bernard Smith

In AD 871 Alfred takes over kingship from his weak elder brother.
A 'realistic' youth-oriented view of history: blood and four-letter words alternate with cliché to make a dispiriting, disunified whole, though the background detail is interesting and the battle scenes vivid.

w Ken Taylor, James R. Webb *d* Clive Donner *ph* Alex Thomson *m* Ray Leppard *pd* Michael Stringer

David Hemmings, Michael York, Prunella
Ransome, Colin Blakely, Julian Glover, Ian
McKellen, Alan Dobie

Alf's Button
GB 1930   96m   bw

Not the first version (there was one in 1920
with Leslie Henson) but the first in sound of
W. A. Darlington's play about a soldier whose
button, when rubbed, summons an all-
powerful genie. It even had a colour sequence,
and featured Nervo and Knox (see below),
with Tubby Edlin, Alf Goddard, Nora
Swinburne and Polly Ward. Written by
L'Estrange Fawcett; directed by W. P.
Kellino; for Gaumont.

Alf's Button Afloat*
GB 1938   89m   bw
Gainsborough (Edward Black)

Six itinerants encounter a genie, whose
granting of their wishes brings riches and
embarrassment.
Archetypal music hall farce descending at
moments into surrealism (the lovers are eaten
by a bear). All concerned are on top form.

w *Marriott Edgar, Val Guest, Ralph Smart,
novel* Alf's Button by W. A. Darlington
d *Marcel Varnel* ph Arthur Crabtree
md Louis Levy

Bud Flanagan, Chesneen, Jimmy Nervo,
Teddy Knox, Charles Naughton, Jimmy Gold
(the six original members of the Crazy Gang),
Alastair Sim, Wally Patch, Peter Gawthorne

Algiers**
US 1938   95m   bw
Walter Wanger

A romantic Casbah thief makes the mistake of
falling in love.
Seminal Hollywood romantic drama based
closely on a French original, *Pepe le Moko*;
laughed at for years because of the alleged line
'Come with me to the Casbah' (which is never
actually said), it holds up remarkably well in
its fashion.

w John Howard Lawson, James M. Cain
d *John Cromwell* ph *James Wong Howe*
m Vincent Scott, Mohammed Igorbouchen

*Charles Boyer, Hedy Lamarr, Sigrid Gurie,
Gene Lockhart, Joseph Calleia,* Alan Hale,
Johnny Downs

'Few films this season, or any other, have
sustained their mood more brilliantly.'—*New
York Times*

'The general tone is that of the decent
artistry we must demand and enjoy in pictures,

which should someday be as respectable as
books, only more near and vivid.'—*Otis
Ferguson*

'This version is pure Hollywood, sacrificing
everything to glamour, and the heavy make-up
and studio lighting make it seem so artificial
one can get giggly.'—*New Yorker, 1977*
† Remake: *Casbah* (qv).

AAN: James Wong Howe; Charles Boyer;
Gene Lockhart

Ali Baba and the Forty Thieves*
US 1944   87m   Technicolor
U-I (Paul Malvern)

A deposed prince pretending to be a bandit
regains his rightful throne.
Absurd but likeable wartime pantomime
without much humour: a typical big-budget
production of its studio and period.

w Edmund L. Hartmann d Arthur Lubin
ph George Robinson m Edward Ward

Jon Hall, Maria Montez, Scotty Beckett,
Turhan Bey, Frank Puglia, Andy Devine,
Kurt Katch
† Remake: *Sword of Ali Baba*, which over
twenty years later used much of the same
footage.

Ali Baba and the Forty Thieves*
France 1954   90m   Eastmancolor
Films du Cyclope

Ali Baba is sent to buy a new wife for his
master, and accidentally finds a thieves'
treasure cave . . .
Sporadically amusing but finally disappointing
version of the Arabian Nights story; it looks
hasty.

w Jacques Becker, Marc Maurette, Maurice
Griffe d Jacques Becker ph Robert Le
Fèbvre m Paul Misraki

Fernandel, Samia Gamal, Dieter Borsche,
Henri Vilbert

Ali Baba Goes to Town*
US 1937   81m   bw
TCF (Lawrence Schwab)

A hobo falls off a train into a film set and
thinks he is back in the Arabian Nights.
Rather flat star vehicle with a few
compensations.

w Harry Tugend, Jack Yelten d David
Butler ph Ernest Palmer m Louis Silvers
songs Mack Gordon, Harry Revel

Eddie Cantor, Tony Martin, Roland Young,
John Carradine, June Lang

Alias a Gentleman
US 1947 76m bw

An ex-convict tries to find his daughter and go straight. Sudsy star vehicle. Wallace Beery, Gladys George, Tom Drake, Leon Ames. Written by William Lipman; directed by Harry Beaumont; for MGM.

Alias French Gertie
US 1934 68m bw

A 'French maid' and her accomplice work a high society racket. Faded society comedy drama with Bebe Daniels and Ben Lyon in a rare teaming before their exile to England. Written by Bayard Veiller; directed by George Archainbaud; for RKO. (GB title: *Love Finds a Way*.)

Alias Jesse James*
US 1958 92m De Luxe
Hope Enterprises (Jack Hope)

An incompetent insurance salesman sells a policy to Jesse James and has to protect his client until he can get it back.
Ho-hum star comedy saved by a climax in which Hope is protected by every cowboy star in Hollywood.

w William Bowers, D. D. Beauchamp
d Norman Z. McLeod *ph* Lionel Lindon
m Joseph J. Lilley

Bob Hope, Rhonda Fleming, Wendell Corey, Jim Davis, Will Wright

Alias Jimmy Valentine
US 1928 75m bw

Crook comedy drama previously made in 1920; this version is notable only as the first MGM sound film. William Haines, Karl Dane, Lionel Barrymore. Written by Sarah Y. Mason and A. P. Younger; directed by Jack Conway; for MGM.

Alias Mary Dow
US 1935 65m bw

A millionaire persuades a chorus girl to pose as his long-lost kidnapped daughter, to satisfy his wife. Obvious audience-pleaser of its time. Ray Milland, Sally Eilers, Henry O'Neill, Katherine Alexander. Written by Gladys Unger, Rose Franken and Arthur Caesar; directed by Kurt Neumann; for Universal.

Alias Nick Beal*
US 1949 93m bw
Paramount (Endre Boehm)
GB title: *The Contact Man*

A politician is nearly corrupted by a mysterious stranger offering wealth and power.

Highly satisfactory modern version of *Faust*, done in gangster terms but not eschewing a supernatural explanation. Acting, photography and direction all in the right key.

w Jonathan Latimer, story Mindret Lord
d John Farrow ph Lionel Lindon *m* Franz Waxman

Ray Milland, Thomas Mitchell, Audrey Totter, George Macready, Fred Clark

Alibi*
US 1929 90m bw
Roland West

An ex-convict marries a policeman's daughter and uses her in his plan for the perfect murder.
Early talkie drama, mostly risible now but with interesting fragments of technique and imagination.

wd Roland West ph Ray June

Chester Morris, Eleanor Griffith, Regis Toomey, Mae Busch, Harry Stubbs

AAN: best picture; Chester Morris

Alibi
GB 1931 75m bw

Hercule Poirot proves that an apparent suicide was murder. Tame adaptation, without the narrative gimmick, of Agatha Christie's *The Murder of Roger Ackroyd.* Austin Trevor, Franklin Dyall, Elizabeth Allan, J. H. Roberts, Mary Jerrold. Written by H. Fowler Mear; directed by Leslie Hiscott; for Twickenham.

Alibi*
GB 1942 82m bw
Corona (Josef Somlo)

A nightclub mindreader forces the lady owner to give him a murder alibi.
Interesting but disappointing minor suspenser copied from a sharper French original.

w uncredited, *novel* Marcel Achard *d* Brian Desmond Hurst *ph* Otto Heller *m* Jack Beaver

Margaret Lockwood, Hugh Sinclair, James Mason, *Raymond Lovell,* Enid Stamp-Taylor, Hartley Power, Jane Carr, Rodney Ackland, Edana Romney, Elizabeth Welch, Olga Lindo, Muriel George

Alibi Ike*
US 1935 73m bw
Warner

A baseball pitcher gets involved in all kinds of trouble.
Above average star comedy vehicle.

w William Wister Haines, *story* Ring Lardner
d Ray Enright *ph* Arthur Todd *md* Leo F.
Forbstein

Joe E. Brown, Olivia de Havilland, Ruth
Donnelly, Roscoe Karns, William Frawley

Alice Adams**
US 1935   99m   bw
RKO (Pandro S. Berman)

A social-climbing small-town girl falls in love.
Dated but interesting star vehicle with good
production values.

w Dorothy Yost, Mortimer Offner, *novel*
Booth Tarkington *d George Stevens*
ph Robert de Grasse *m* Max Steiner, Roy
Webb

Katharine Hepburn, Fred MacMurray, Evelyn
Venable, Frank Albertson, Fred Stone, Ann
Shoemaker, Charles Grapewin, Grady Sutton,
Hedda Hopper
    'A nice middle-class film, as trivial as a
schoolgirl's diary, and just about as
pathetically true.'—*C. A. Lejeune*
    'What was in 1922 a biting and observant
novel emerges in 1935 as a bitingly satiric
portrait of an era.'—*Time*

AAN: best picture; Katharine Hepburn

Alice Doesn't Live Here Any More**
US 1975   112m   Technicolor
Warner (David Susskind, Audrey Maas)

A widow sets off with her young son for
Monterey and a singing career.
Realistically squalid and foul-mouthed but
endearing look at a slice of America today,
with firm handling and excellent performances
in a surprisingly old-fashioned theme.

w Robert Getchell *d Martin Scorsese*
ph Kent L. Wakeford *m* various *pd* Toby
Carr Rafelson

Ellen Burstyn, Alfred Lutter, Kris
Kristofferson, Billy Green Bush, *Diane Ladd*,
Lelia Goldoni, Jodie Foster
    'What Scorsese has done is to rescue an
American cliché from the bland, flat but much
more portentous naturalism of such as *Harry
and Tonto* and restore it to an emotional and
intellectual complexity through his particular
brand of baroque realism.'—*Richard Combs*
    'Full of funny malice and breakneck
vitality.'—*New Yorker*
    'A tough weepie, redeemed by its
picturesque locations and its eye for social
detail.'—*Michael Billington, Illustrated
London News*

AA: Ellen Burstyn
AAN: Robert Getchell; Diane Ladd

Alice in the Cities
West Germany 1974   110m   bw

A German journalist in America reluctantly
escorts a small girl back to Germany.
Interesting but overlong collection of modern
metaphors, occasionally reminiscent of *Paper
Moon*. Rudiger Vogeler, Yella Röttlander.
Written and directed by Wim Wenders; for
Filmverlag der Autoren.

Alice in Wonderland**
US 1933   90m   bw
Paramount (Louis D. Lighton)

Intriguing but disappointing version of the
nonsense classic, keeping to the Tenniel
drawings by dressing an all-star cast in masks,
thereby rendering them ineffective.

w Joseph L. Mankiewicz, William Cameron
Menzies, *novel* Lewis Carroll *d* Norman Z.
McLeod *ph* Henry Sharp, Bert Glennon
m Dmitri Tiomkin

Charlotte Henry, W. C. Fields (Humpty
Dumpty), Cary Grant (Mock Turtle), Gary
Cooper (White Knight), Edward Everett
Horton (Mad Hatter), Edna May Oliver (Red
Queen), Jack Oakie (Tweedledum), Leon
Errol (Uncle), Charles Ruggles (March Hare),
May Robson (Queen of Hearts), Louise
Fazenda (White Queen), Ned Sparks
(Caterpillar), Alison Skipworth (Duchess)
    'Lavishly produced, with great care given to
costumes and settings and make-up, but the
spirit is missing.'—*New Yorker, 1977*

Alice in Wonderland*
US 1951   75m   Technicolor
Walt Disney

Fully animated cartoon version which has
good moments but modernizes and
Americanizes the familiar characters.

w various *d* Clyde Geronomi, Hamilton
Luske, Wilfred Jackson *supervisor* Ben
Sharpsteen *m* Oliver Wallace

AAN: Oliver Wallace

Alice's Adventures in Wonderland*
GB 1972   101m   Eastmancolor   Todd-
AO
TCF / Josef Shaftel (Derek Horne)

Live-action version which starts amiably
enough but soon becomes flat and
uninventive, with a star cast all at sea and
tedium replacing the wit of the original.

wd William Sterling *ph* Geoffrey Unsworth
m John Barry *pd* Michael Stringer

Fiona Fullerton, Michael Crawford (White
Rabbit), Robert Helpmann (Mad Hatter),

Dudley Moore (Dormouse), Spike Milligan (Gryphon), Peter Sellers (March Hare), Dennis Price (King of Hearts), Flora Robson (Queen of Hearts), Rodney Bewes (Knave of Hearts), Peter Bull (Duchess), Michael Hordern (Mock Turtle), Ralph Richardson (Caterpillar), etc

Alice's Restaurant*
US 1969   110m   De Luxe
UA / Florin (Harold Levanthal)

Folk singer Arlo Guthrie, on the verge of being drafted, gets some varied experience of life among the drop-outs of Montana, Massachusetts and New York.
Typical of the freakish, anti-Vietnam, do-as-you-please movies which splurged from Hollywood in the wake of *Easy Rider*, this has the minor benefits of good production values and a few jokes.

w Venable Herndon, Arthur Penn *d* Arthur Penn *ph* Michael Nebbia *m / songs* Arlo Guthrie

Arlo Guthrie, Pat Quinn, James Broderick, Michael McClanathan, Geoff Outlaw
AAN: Arthur Penn

Alien*
GB 1979   117m   Eastmancolor
   Panavision
TCF / Brandywine (Walter Hill, Gordon Carroll, David Giler)

Astronauts returning to earth visit an apparently dead planet and are infected by a violent being which has unexpected behaviour patterns and eliminates them one by one.
Deliberately scarifying and highly commercial shocker with little but its art direction to commend it to connoisseurs.

w Dan O'Bannon *d* Ridley Scott *ph* Derek Vanlint, Denys Ayling *m* Jerry Goldsmith
chief designer H. R. Giger

Tom Skerritt, Sigourney Weaver, John Hurt, Veronica Cartwright, Harry Dean Stanton, Ian Holm, Yaphet Kotto
  'A sort of inverse relationship to *The Thing* invites unfavourable comparisons.'—*Sight and Sound*
  'Empty bag of tricks whose production values and expensive trickery cannot disguise imaginative poverty.'—*Time Out*
  'It was not, as its co-author admitted, a think piece. The message he intended was simple: Don't close your eyes or it will get ya.'—*Les Keyser, Hollywood in the Seventies*

Alive and Kicking*
GB 1958   94m   bw
ABP (Victor Skuzetsky)

Three old ladies escape from a home to an Irish island.
Agreeable minor comedy, a showcase for its elderly but vigorous stars.

w Denis Cannan *d* Cyril Frankel *ph* Gilbert Taylor *m* Philip Green

Sybil Thorndike, Kathleen Harrison, Estelle Winwood, Stanley Holloway, Joyce Carey, Eric Pohlmann, Colin Gordon

All About Eve****
US 1950   138m   bw
TCF (Darryl F. Zanuck)

An ageing Broadway star suffers from the hidden menace of a self-effacing but secretly ruthless and ambitious young actress.
A basically unconvincing story with thin characters is transformed by a screenplay scintillating with savage wit and a couple of waspish performances into a movie experience to treasure.

wd Joseph L. Mankiewicz *ph* Milton Krasner *m* Alfred Newman

Bette Davis (a supremely bitchy performance), *George Sanders* (caricaturing his usual image), Anne Baxter, Celeste Holm, Gary Merrill, Hugh Marlowe, Gregory Ratoff, Thelma Ritter, Marilyn Monroe, Barbara Bates
  'The wittiest, the most devastating, the most adult and literate motion picture ever made that had anything to do with the New York Stage.'—*Leo Mishkin*
  'The dialogue and atmosphere are so peculiarly remote from life that they have sometimes been mistaken for art.'—*Pauline Kael, 1968*
  'Plenty of surface cynicism, but no detachment, no edge and no satire. Boiled down it is a plush backstage drama.'—*Richard Winnington*
  'Long, but continuously, wonderfully entertaining in a way I had almost forgotten was possible for films.'—*Richard Mallett, Punch*
  'Someone remarked of this witty, exaggerated, cruel and yet wildly funny film that the secret of its success was the extreme bad taste shown throughout by all concerned (though I hope they didn't mean to include Milton Krasner's tactful camerawork in this).'—*Basil Wright, 1972*
  'The picture seemed long—though it was not by today's standards of length—and the crispness of the dialogue was not matched by equally crisp editing.'—*Hollis Alpert, 1962*
† The idea for the film came from a short story, 'The Wisdom of Eve', by Mary Orr.

AA: best picture; Joseph L. Mankiewicz (as
writer); Joseph L. Mankiewicz (as director);
George Sanders
AAN: Milton Krasner; Alfred Newman; Bette
Davis; Anne Baxter; Celeste Holm; Thelma
Ritter

The All-American
US 1952 83m bw
U-I (Aaron Rosenberg)
GB title: *The Winning Way*

When his parents are killed on the way to a
match, a college football hero rejects sport for
the groves of *academe*.
Very modest formula drama.

w D. D. Beauchamp d Jesse Hibbs
ph Maury Gertsman
m Joseph Gershenson

Tony Curtis, Mamie Van Doren, Lori Nelson,
Gregg Palmer, Richard Long, Paul Cavanagh

The All-American Boy
US 1973 118m colour

A young boxer has got to the top too fast, and
is depressed by the future. Uninteresting
character study. Jon Voight, Carol Androsky,
Anne Archer. Written and directed by Charles
Eastman; for Warner.

All Ashore
US 1952 80m Technicolor
Columbia (Jonie Taps)

Three sailors on shore leave work their
passage to Catalina.
Very lightweight musical, no rival for *On the
Town.*

w Blake Edwards, Richard Quine d Richard
Quine *ph* Charles Lawton Jnr *m* Morris
Stoloff, George Duning *ly* Robert Wells

Mickey Rooney, Dick Haymes, Ray
McDonald, Peggy Ryan, Barbara Bates, Jody
Lawrance

All Coppers Are . . .
GB 1972 87m colour

A crook and a cop both fancy the same girl.
Pointlessly titled lowlife melodrama with no
style whatever; any episode of *Z Cars* would
be vastly preferable. Nicky Henson, Martin
Potter, Julia Foster, Ian Hendry. Written by
Allan Prior; directed by Sidney Hayers; for
Peter Rogers / Rank.

All Creatures Great and Small*
GB1974 92m Eastmancolor
EMI / Venedon (David Susskind, Duane
Bogie)

The pre-war Yorkshire life of a country vet.
Simple-minded popular entertainment of a
long-forgotten kind, oddly sponsored by
American TV in the shape of Readers' Digest
and the Hallmark Hall of Fame.

w Hugh Whitemore, *novel* James Herriot
d Claude Whatham *ph* Peter Suschitzky
m Wilfred Josephs

Anthony Hopkins, Simon Ward, Lisa Harrow,
Freddie Jones, Brian Stirner, T. P. McKenna,
Brenda Bruce, John Collin
† 1976 sequel: *It Shouldn't Happen to a Vet.*

All Fall Down*
US 1962 111m bw Panavision
MGM (John Houseman)

A young man reveres his ne'er-do-well elder
brother but determines to shoot him when he
causes a girl's death.
Another gallery of middle American failures,
competently portrayed by a writer and actors
very practised at this sort of thing.

w William Inge, *novel* James Leo Herlihy
d John Frankenheimer *ph* Lionel Lindon
m Alex North

Warren Beatty, Brandon de Wilde, Angela
Lansbury, Karl Malden, Eva Marie Saint
  'That strange area of nostalgic Americana
where the familiar is the Freudian
grotesque.'—*New Yorker, 1982*

All for Mary*
GB 1956 82m Eastmancolor
Rank / Paul Soskin

Two rivals for the hand of the pretty daughter
of a Swiss hotelier are struck down by chicken
pox and cared for by the old nanny of one of
them.
Simple-minded farce in which two grown men
quail like children before a forceful old lady;
on the strength of the latter characterization
and a few funny lines the original play was a
considerable West End success.

w Peter Blackmore, Paul Soskin, *play* Harold
Brooke, Kay Bannerman d Wendy Toye
ph Reg Wyer *m* Robert Farnon

Kathleen Harrison, Nigel Patrick, David
Tomlinson, Jill Day, David Hurst, Leo
McKern

All Hands on Deck
US 1961 98m De Luxe Cinemascope
TCF (Oscar Brodney)

Romantic and farcical adventures of sailors on
leave.
Tired musical comedy romp with a second
team cast.

w Jay Sommars, *novel* Donald R. Morris
d Norman Taurog *ph* Leo Tover *m* Cyril
Mockridge *songs* Jay Livingston, Ray Evans

Pat Boone, Buddy Hackett, Dennis O'Keefe,
Barbara Eden, Warren Berlinger, Gale
Gordon, Joe E. Ross

All I Desire
US 1953 79m bw
U-I (Ross Hunter)

A woman who had deserted her husband and
family for a life on the stage returns for her
daughter's graduation and is reconciled.
Resilient star melodrama with all stops out.

w James Gunn, Robert Blees *d* Douglas Sirk
ph Carl Guthrie *m* Joseph Gershenson
Barbara Stanwyck, Richard Carlson, Lyle
Bettger, Maureen O'Sullivan, Richard Long,
Lori Nelson

All in a Night's Work
US 1961 94m Technicolor
Paramount / Hal B. Wallis–Joseph Hazen

A publishing heir falls for a girl he suspects of
having been his uncle's mistress.
Unpolished and not very amusing comedy
which falters after an intriguing start.

w Edmund Beloin, Maurice Richlin, Sidney
Sheldon *d* Joseph Anthony *ph* Joseph La
Shelle *m* André Previn

Shirley Maclaine, Dean Martin, Charles
Ruggles, Cliff Robertson, Norma Crane, Gale
Gordon, Jerome Cowan, Jack Weston
  'Tame and aimless sex-and-big-business
comedy.'—*MFB*

All Mine To Give*
US 1956 102m Technicolor RKOscope
RKO (Sam Wiesenthal)
GB title: *The Day They Gave Babies Away*

In 1856, a pioneer couple in Wisconsin train
their children to carry on the family after their
own deaths.
Weird sentimental sob story, even odder
under its English title. Surprisingly, some of it
works quite well.

w Dale and Katherine Eunson (apparently
about their own ancestors) *d* Allen Reisner
ph William Skall *m* Max Steiner

Glynis Johns, Cameron Mitchell, Patty
McCormack, Rex Thompson, Ernest Truex,
Hope Emerson, Alan Hale
  'A strong mood of folksy western
reminiscence.'—*MFB*

All My Sons*
US 1948 94m bw
U-I (Chester Erskine)

A young man establishes that his father sold
defective airplanes during the war.
Heady family melodrama from a taut and
topical stage play. The film is well-meaning
but artificial and unconvincing.

w Chester Erskine, *play* Arthur Miller
d Irving Reis *ph* Russell Metty *m* Leith
Stevens

Edward G. Robinson, Burt Lancaster, Mady
Christians, Howard Duff

All Neat in Black Stockings
GB 1969 99m Eastmancolor
Anglo Amalgamated / Miton (Leon Clore)

Sex adventures of an amorous window
cleaner.
Modish comedy drama with surface
entertainment of a sort, but no depth.

w Jane Gaskell, Hugh Whitemore
d Christopher Morahan *ph* Larry Pizer
m Robert Cornford

Victor Henry, Susan George, Jack Shepherd,
Anna Cropper, Clare Kelly, Terence de
Marney

All Night Long*
GB 1961 95m bw
Rank / Bob Roberts (Michael Relph, Basil
  Dearden)

Because of rumour set about by a jealous
rival, a jazz trumpeter at an all-night party
tries to strangle his wife.
Cheeky updating of *Othello* with jazz
accompaniment, played a shade too grimly by
an excellent cast. An interesting misfire.

w Nel King, Peter Achilles *d* Basil Dearden
ph Ted Scaife *m* Philip Green

Patrick McGoohan, Richard Attenborough,
Keith Michell, Betsy Blair, Marti Stevens,
Paul Harris, Bernard Braden; and on the
sound track Dave Brubeck, Tubby Hayes,
Johnny Dankworth etc

All of Me
US 1934 70m bw
Paramount (Louis Lighton)

An engineering professor on his way to
Boulder Dam finds his life affected by the
problems of a criminal.
Confused and uninteresting romantic
melodrama with a good cast all at sea.

w Sidney Buchman, Thomas Mitchell, *play*
Chrysalis by Rose Porter *d* James Flood
ph Victor Milner *m* / *ly* Ralph Rainger, Leo
Robin

Fredric March, Miriam Hopkins, George Raft,

Helen Mack, Nella Walker, William Collier
Jnr, Gilbert Emery, Blanche Friderici, Edgar
Kennedy
'The most startling glorification of criminals
that even the movies have ever dared.'—*New
York Sun*

All Over the Town*
GB 1949   88m   bw
Rank / Wessex (Ian Dalrymple)
Two reporters revivify a West of England local
newspaper, and expose local corruption.
Fresh, agreeable romantic comedy on sub-
Ealing lines.

w Derek Twist and others *d* Derek Twist
ph C. Pennington-Richards *m* Temple Abady
Norman Wooland, Sarah Churchill, *Fabia
Drake* (as a local gorgon), Cyril Cusack,
James Hayter

All Quiet on the Western Front****
US 1930   130m approx.   bw
Universal (Carl Laemmle Jnr)
In 1914, a group of German teenagers
volunteer for action on the Western Front, but
they become disillusioned, and none of them
survives.
A landmark of American cinema and
Universal's biggest and most serious
undertaking until the sixties, this highly
emotive war film with its occasional outbursts
of bravura direction fixed in millions of minds
the popular image of what it was like in the
trenches, even more so than *Journey's End*
which had shown the allied viewpoint. Despite
dated moments, it retains its overall power
and remains a great pacifist work.

w Lewis Milestone, Maxwell Anderson, Del
Andrews, George Abbott, *novel* Erich Maria
Remarque *d Lewis Milestone* (in a manner
reminiscent of Eisenstein and Lang)
ph Arthur Edeson m David Broekman
Lew Ayres, Louis Wolheim, Slim
Summerville, John Wray, Russell Gleason,
Richard Griffith, Beryl Mercer, Ben
Alexander
'A trenchant and imaginative audible
picture . . . most of the time the audience was
held to silence by its realistic scenes.'—*New
York Times*
'The sound and image mediums blend as
one, as a form of artistic expression that only
the motion screen can give.'—*National Board
of Review*
AA: best picture; Lewis Milestone (as
director)
AAN: Lewis Milestone, Maxwell Anderson,
Del Andrews, George Abbott; Arthur Edeson

All That Heaven Allows
US 1955   89m   Technicolor
U-I (Ross Hunter)
A sad widow falls in love with the gardener at
her winter home, and marries him despite
local prejudice.
Standard tearjerker in the tradition of
Magnificent Obsession, reuniting the same
stars, producer and director in the same rich
musical and photographic sauce.

w Peg Fenwick *d* Douglas Sirk *ph* Russell
Metty *m* Frank Skinner
Jane Wyman, Rock Hudson, Agnes
Moorehead, Conrad Nagel, Virginia Grey,
Charles Drake
'As laboriously predictable as it is fatuously
unreal.'—*MFB*

All That Jazz**
US 1979   123m   Technicolor
TCF / Robert Alan Aurthur, Daniel Melnick
A stage musical director pushes himself too
hard, and dies of a surfeit of wine, women and
work.
Self-indulgent, semi-autobiographical tragi-
comic extravaganza complete with heart
operations and a recurring angel of death.
Flashes of brilliant talent make it a must for
Fosse fans.

w Robert Alan Aurthur, Bob Fosse *d Bob
Fosse ph* Giuseppe Rotunno *m* Ralph Burns
pd Philip Rosenberg, Tony Walton
Roy Scheider, Jessica Lange, Ann Rainking,
Leland Palmer, Ben Vereen, Cliff Gorman
'Egomaniacal, wonderfully choreographed,
often compelling . . . more an art item than a
broad commercial prospect.'—*Variety*
'An improbable mixture of crass gags, song
'n' dance routines and open heart surgery. Not
for the squeamish.'—*Time Out*
BFA: cinematography; editing (Alan Heim);
sound

All That Money Can Buy****
US 1941   106m   bw
RKO / William Dieterle (Charles L. Glett)
aka: *The Devil and Daniel Webster; Daniel
and the Devil; Here Is a Man*
A hard-pressed farmer gives in to the Devil's
tempting, but is saved from the pit by a
famous lawyer's pleading at his 'trial'.
A brilliant Germanic Faust set in 19th-century
New Hampshire and using historical figures,
alienation effects, comedy asides and the
whole cinematic box of tricks which
Hollywood had just learned again through
Citizen Kane. A magic act in more ways than
one.

w Dan Totheroh, based on The Devil and
Daniel Webster by Stephen Vincent Benet
*d William Dieterle ph Joseph August
m Bernard Herrmann ad Van Nest Polglase
sp Vernon L. Walker*

Walter Huston ('Mr Scratch', a great
performance), James Craig, Anne Shirley,
Simone Simon, *Edward Arnold* (Daniel
Webster), Jane Darwell, Gene Lockhart, John
Qualen, H. B. Warner

'Some of those in the movie industry who
saw it restively called it a dog; but some of
them cried it was another catapult hurling the
cinema up to its glorious destiny.'—*Cecilia
Ager*

AA: Bernard Herrmann
AAN: Walter Huston

All the Brothers Were Valiant*
US 1953 94m Technicolor
MGM (Pandro S. Berman)

Rivalry between brothers on a whaling
schooner.
Remake of a silent melodrama with
predictable vengefulness and formula heroism,
capably but unmemorably portrayed.

*w Harry Brown, novel Ben Ames Williams
d Richard Thorpe ph George Folsey
m Miklos Rozsa*

Stewart Granger, Robert Taylor, Ann Blyth,
Betta St John, Keenan Wynn, James
Whitmore, Kurt Kasznar, Lewis Stone

AAN: George Folsey

All the Fine Young Cannibals
US 1960 122m Metrocolor
Cinemascope
MGM / Avon (Pandro S. Berman)

The son of a country clergyman loves the
daughter of another clergyman; they both find
the realities of life in New York a horrid
shock.
The glum joys of sex and dope in the big city
are revealed in this boring rather than daring
farrago which is not even unintentionally
funny.

*w Robert Thom, novel The Bixby Girls by
Rosamond Marshall d Michael Anderson
ph William H. Daniels m Jeff Alexander*

Robert Wagner, Natalie Wood, Pearl Bailey,
Susan Kohner, George Hamilton, Jack
Mullaney, Onslow Stevens, Anne Seymour

All the King's Men***
US 1949 109m bw
Columbia (Robert Rossen)

An honest man from a small town is elected
mayor and then governor, but power corrupts
him absolutely and he ruins his own life and
those of his friends before being assassinated.
Archetypal American political melodrama
based on the life of southern senator Huey
Long. The background is well sketched in and
there are excellent performances, but the
overall narrative is rather flabby.

*w Robert Rossen, novel Robert Penn Warren
d Robert Rossen ph Burnett Guffey m Louis
Gruenberg ad Sturges Carne*

*Broderick Crawford, John Ireland, Mercedes
McCambridge, Joanne Dru*, John Derek,
Anne Seymour, Shepperd Strudwick

'More conspicuous for scope and worthiness
of intention than for inspiration.'—*Gavin
Lambert*

'A superb pictorialism which perpetually
crackles and explodes.'—*Bosley Crowther*

'Realism comes from within as well as
without and the core of meaning that might
have made this film a step forward from
Boomerang does not exist amid all the
courageous camera-work.'—*Richard
Winnington*

AA: best picture; Broderick Crawford;
Mercedes McCambridge
AAN: Robert Rossen (as writer); Robert
Rossen (as director); John Ireland

All the President's Men***
US 1976 138m Technicolor
Warner / Wildwood (Robert Redford,
Walter Coblenz)

A reconstruction of the discovery of the White
House link with the Watergate affair by two
young reporters from the *Washington Post*.
An absorbing drama from the headlines which
despite its many excellences would have been
better with a more audible dialogue track, less
murky photography and a clearer introduction
of the characters concerned. The acting
however is a treat.

*w William Goldman, book Carl Bernstein,
Bob Woodward d Alan J. Pakula ph Gordon
Willis m David Shire pd George Jenkins*

Robert Redford, Dustin Hoffman, Jason
Robards Jnr, Martin Balsam, Hal Holbrook,
Jack Warden, Jane Alexander, Meredith
Baxter

'It works as a detective thriller (even though
everyone knows the ending), as a credible (if
occasionally romanticized) primer on the
prosaic fundamentals of big league
investigative journalism, and best of all, as a
chilling tone poem that conveys the texture of
the terror in our nation's capital during that

long night when an aspiring fascist regime held
our democracy under siege.'—*Frank Rich,
New York Post*

AA: William Goldman; Jason Robards Jnr
AAN: best picture; Alan J. Pakula; Jane
Alexander

All the Right Noises*
GB 1969   91m   Eastmancolor
(TCF) Trigon (Anthony Hope)

The electrician of a touring company has an
affair with a 15-year-old actress, but finally
returns to his wife.
Sharp, sensible treatment of a cliché situation,
as watchable as a superior television play.

*wd Gerry O'Hara ph Gerry Fisher m John
Cameron*

Tom Bell, Judy Carne, Olivia Hussey, John
Standing
   'Built on a solid framework of disciplined
direction and animated performances.'—*MFB*

All the Way Home**
US 1963   107m   bw
Paramount / Talent Associates (David
   Susskind)

In 1916 Tennessee, the beloved father of a
family is killed in a car crash, and after the
trauma wears off, mother helps the children to
rebuild their lives.
Tactful, charming though finally depressing
slice of small town period Americana, with
generally eloquent performances.

*w Philip Reisman Jnr, play Tad Mosel, novel
A Death in the Family by James Agee d Alex
Segal ph Boris Kaufman m Bernard Green*

Robert Preston, Jean Simmons, Aline
MacMahon, Pat Hingle, Michael Kearney
   'A heart-wrenching blend of nostalgia and
sorrow.'—*Judith Crist*

All the Way Up*
GB 1970   97m   Technicolor
Granada / EMI (Philip Mackie)

Social-climbing Dad makes his way by
treachery and blackmail, but gets his come-
uppance when his son takes after him.
Crudely farcical adaptation of a thoughtful
comedy of its time; the treatment works in fits
and starts but leaves one in no mood for the
talkative finale.

*w Philip Mackie, play Semi Detached by
David Turner d James MacTaggart ph Dick
Bush m Howard Blake*

Warren Mitchell, Pat Heywood, Elaine
Taylor, Kenneth Cranham, Vanessa Howard,
Richard Briers, Adrienne Posta, Bill Fraser

All the Young Men
US 1960   87m   bw
Columbia (Hall Bartlett / Jaguar)

A marine patrol in Korea is commanded by a
black man, and racial tensions take
precedence over fighting the enemy.
Simple-minded, parsimoniously-budgeted war
melodrama.

*wd Hall Bartlett ph Daniel Fapp m George
Duning*

Alan Ladd, Sidney Poitier, Ingemar
Johansson, Glenn Corbett, James Darren,
Mort Sahl
   'Strenuously engaged in exploiting the
entertainment values of nostalgia, fear,
suspense, hatred and sex.'—*MFB*

All This and Heaven Too**
US 1940   143m   bw
Warner (Jack L. Warner, Hal B. Wallis)

A 19th-century French nobleman falls in love
with his governess and murders his wife.
Romantic, melodramatic soap opera from a
mammoth best seller; well made for those who
can stomach it, with excellent acting and
production values.

*w Casey Robinson, novel Rachel Field
d Anatole Litvak ph Ernest Haller m Max
Steiner*

Charles Boyer, Bette Davis, Barbara O'Neil,
Virginia Weidler, Jeffrey Lynn, Helen
Westley, Henry Daniell, Harry Davenport,
Walter Hampden, George Coulouris, Janet
Beecher, Montagu Love

AAN: best picture; Ernest Haller; Barbara
O'Neil

All Through the Night**
US 1942   107m   bw
Warner (Jerry Wald)

Gangsters help to track down fifth columnists
in World War II New York.
Highly entertaining muddle of several styles
which somehow works well and allows several
favourites to do their thing.

*w Leonard Spiegelgass, Edwin Gilbert
d Vincent Sherman ph Sid Hickox m Adolph
Deutsch*

Humphrey Bogart, Conrad Veidt, Peter
Lorre, Karen Verne, Judith Anderson, Jane
Darwell, Frank McHugh, Jackie Gleason,
William Demarest, Phil Silvers

Allegheny Uprising
US 1939   81m   bw
RKO (P. J. Wolfson)
GB title: *The First Rebel*

A young frontiersman smashes liquor traffic with the Indians.
Modestly efficient western with an impressive cast.

w P. J. Wolfson, *story* Neil Swanson
d William A. Seiter *ph* Nicholas Musuraca

John Wayne, Claire Trevor, Brian Donlevy, George Sanders, Wilfrid Lawson, Robert Barrat, Moroni Olsen, Eddie Quillan, Chill Wills

An Alligator Named Daisy
GB 1955 88m Technicolor Vistavision
Rank (Raymond Stross)

A young songwriter finds himself saddled with a pet alligator.
The ultimate in silly animal comedies, this does score a few laughs.

w Jack Davies, *novel* Charles Terrot *d* J. Lee-Thompson *ph* Reg Wyer *m* Stanley Black

Donald Sinden, Diana Dors, Jean Carson, James Robertson Justice, Stanley Holloway, Roland Culver, Margaret Rutherford, Avice Landone, Richard Wattis, Frankie Howerd, Jimmy Edwards, Gilbert Harding
'Apart from a fairly Kafkaesque scene in which Daisy is discovered in an upright piano, the situation is treated with little wit or comic invention.'—*MFB*

The Alligator People
US 1959 73m bw Cinemascope

A doctor uses a revolutionary serum which unfortunately turns patients into the alligators from which it was derived. Moderately inventive 'B' chiller. George Macready, Frieda Inescort, Beverly Garland, Bruce Bennett, Lon Chaney Jnr. Written by Orville H. Hampton; directed by Roy del Ruth; for TCF.

An Almost Perfect Affair*
US 1979 93m De Luxe
Paramount / Terry Carr

A young film producer at the Cannes Festival falls for the wife of an Italian impresario. Lively detail lifts many scenes of this eccentric romance, but the routine plot is a downer.

w Walter Bernstein, Don Peterson *d* Michael Ritchie *ph* Henri Decae *m* Georges Delerue

Keith Carradine, Monica Vitti, Raf Vallone, Christian de Sica

Aloma of the South Seas
US 1941 77m Technicolor
Paramount (Monte Bell)

A young Polynesian chieftain returns to quell trouble on his island after being educated in the US.
Hoary goings-on in gory colour, a remake of a silent epic devised to display the star's sarong and the backlot's expensive volcano.

w Frank Butler, Seena Owen, Lillie Hayward *d* Alfred Santell *ph* Karl Struss, Wilfrid M. Cline, William Snyder *m* Victor Young *sp* Gordon Jennings

Dorothy Lamour, Jon Hall, Lynne Overman, Philip Reed, Katherine de Mille, Fritz Leiber, Dona Drake, Esther Dale
'The mountain has the privilege of belching when it is dissatisfied, which is something no well-bred critic should do.'—*C. A. Lejeune*
† A silent version in 1926 had starred Gilda Gray. Directed by Maurice Tourneur, it adhered more closely to the original play (by John B. Hymer and Leroy Clemens).
AAN: Karl Struss, Wilfrid M. Cline, William Snyder

Alone on the Pacific**
Japan 1963 104m Eastmancolor
Cinemascope
Ishihara-Nikkatsu (Akira Nakai)
original title: *Taiheiyo Hitoribochi*

A young man crosses from Osaka to San Francisco in a small yacht.
Fascinating Robinson-Crusoe-like exercise, with flashbacks to life on dry land.

w Natto Wada, based on the experiences of Kenichi Horie *d* Kon Ichikawa *ph* Yoshihiro Yamazaki *m* Yasushi Akatagawa, Tohru Takemitsu

Yujiro Ishihara, Masayuki Mori, Kinuyo Tanaka, Ruriko Asaoko
'Wonderfully comic moments emerge, but they never overshadow the film's sheer pictorial value.'—*Brenda Davies, MFB*

Along Came Jones*
US 1945 90m bw
(UA) Cinema Artists Corporation (Gary Cooper)

Two cowboys are mistaken for killers.
Very mild western comedy melodrama, with the star at his most self-effacing and production only mediocre.

w Nunnally Johnson, *novel* Alan le May *d* Stuart Heisler *ph* Milton Krasner *m* Charles Maxwell, Arthur Lange, Hugo Friedhofer

Gary Cooper, Loretta Young, William Demarest, Dan Duryea, Russell Simpson

Along the Great Divide
US 1950   88m   bw
Warner (Anthony Veiller)

A marshal prevents an old man from being
hanged for murder, and eventually discovers
the real culprit.
Adequate, modest western with an unusual
detective element.

w Walter Doniger, Lewis Meltzer d Raoul
Walsh ph Sid Hickox m David Buttolph

Kirk Douglas, Virginia Mayo, Walter
Brennan, John Agar, Ray Teal

The Alphabet Murders
GB 1965   90m   bw
MGM (Ben Arbeid)

Hercule Poirot solves a series of murders by
an apparent lunatic choosing his victims in
alphabetical order.
Ruination of a classic whodunnit novel,
misguided both in its attempt to mix slapstick
with detection and in its terrible central
performance.

w David Pursall, Jack Seddon, novel The
ABC Murders by Agatha Christie d Frank
Tashlin ph Desmond Dickinson m Ron
Goodwin

Tony Randall, Robert Morley, Anita Ekberg,
Maurice Denham, Guy Rolfe, James Villiers,
Clive Morton

Alphaville*
France / Italy 1965   98m   bw
Chaumiane / Filmstudio (André Michelin)

A special agent travels across space to find out
what happened to his predecessor, and finds
himself in a loveless society.
A rather chill futuristic fantasy on the lines of
1984 but with an outer space background and
a hero borrowed from Peter Cheyney.
Interesting but not endearing.

wd Jean-Luc Godard ph Raoul Coutard
m Paul Misraki

Eddie Constantine, Anna Karina, Akim
Tamiroff, Howard Vernon, Laszlo Szabo

Altered States*
US 1980   102m   Technicolor
Warner / Howard Gottfried, Daniel Melnick

A psychophysiologist uses a sensory
deprivation tank to hallucinate himself back
into primitive states of human evolution, in
which guise he emerges to kill. . . .
Amusing elaboration of Jekyll and Hyde, not
to mention the Karloff mad doctor second
features of the forties. All very po-faced now,
and certainly impeccably done.

w Sidney Aaron, novel Paddy Chayevsky
d Ken Russell ph Jordan Cronenweth
m John Corigliano pd Richard McDonald

William Hurt, Blair Brown, Bob Balaban,
Charles Haid

Alvarez Kelly*
US 1966   116m   Technicolor
       Panavision
Columbia / Ray David (Sol C. Siegel)

The owner of a herd of 2500 cattle finds
himself between two sides in the American
Civil War.
Unusual if rather tepid western which balances
historical interest against social conscience and
throws in a variety of other elements.

w Franklin Coen d Edward Dmytryk
ph Joseph MacDonald m John Green

William Holden, Richard Widmark, Janice
Rule, Patrick O'Neal, Victoria Shaw, Roger
C. Carmel, Richard Rust

Always Goodbye
US 1938   75m   bw
TCF (Raymond Griffith)

An unwed mother gives up her baby and later
wants it back.
Tired sentimental warhorse, a remake of
Gallant Lady (qv).

w Kathryn Scola, Edith Skouras d Sidney
Lanfield ph Robert Planck md Louis Silvers

Barbara Stanwyck, Herbert Marshall, Ian
Hunter, Cesar Romero, Lynn Bari, Binnie
Barnes

Always in My Heart*
US 1942   92m   bw
Warner (Walter McEwen, William Jacobs)

A convict returns home to find his daughter a
stranger and his wife about to marry again.
Well acted sentimental drama.

w Adele Commandini, play Fly Away Home
by Dorothy Bennett, Irving White d Joe
Graham ph Sid Hickox m Heinz Roemheld

Walter Huston, Kay Francis, Gloria Warren,
Frankie Thomas, Sidney Blackmer, Una
O'Connor

AAN: title song (m Ernest Lucuona, ly Kim
Gannon)

Always Leave Them Laughing*
US 1949   116m   bw
Warner (Jerry Wald)

A vaudeville comedian craves the spotlight at
the expense of his private life.
Raucous backstage vehicle, crammed with

sentimental and melodramatic cliché but affording tantalizing glimpses of the stage acts of its two stars.

w Jack Rose, Mel Shavelson *d* Roy del Ruth *ph* Ernest Haller *ly* Sammy Cahn *md* Ray Heindorf

Milton Berle, Bert Lahr, Virginia Mayo, Ruth Roman, Alan Hale, Jerome Cowan

Always Together*
US 1947 78m bw

Dying millionaire bequeathes his all to a working girl, then recovers and tries to retrieve it. Oddball comedy about a girl who has film fantasies, killed by dull title. Joyce Reynolds, Robert Hutton, Cecil Kellaway, Ernest Truex; guest appearances by Bogart and Flynn (among others). Written by Henry and Phoebe Ephron and I. A. L. Diamond; directed by Frederick de Cordova; for Warner.

Les Amants*
France 1958 88m bw Dyaliscope
Nouvelles Editions
aka: *The Lovers*

A rich provincial wife has a secret life in Paris, but finds real satisfaction in an affair with a young man.
A passionate romance which had some censorship difficulties at the time, this rather gloomy film never quite whirls one away as it should, and it doesn't have the eye for detail of *Brief Encounter*.

wd Louis Malle, *novel* Point de Lendemain by Dominique Vivant, Baron de Denon *ph* Henri Decaë *m* Brahms

Jeanne Moreau, Alain Cluny, Jean-Marc Bory, Judith Magre

Les Amants de Vérone*
France 1948 110m bw
CICC (Raymond Borderie)
aka: *The Lovers of Verona*

In modern Venice a film is being made of *Romeo and Juliet*, and the stand-ins for the stars feel they are re-enacting the old story. A superbly stylish if rather empty piece, the dazzling detail being much more interesting than the main story.

w André Cayatte, Jacques Prévert *d André Cayatte ph* Henri Alekan *m* Joseph Kosma *ad* Moulaert

Pierre Brasseur, Serge Reggiani, Anouk Aimée, Louis Salou, Marcel Dalio
'Visually exciting, immaculately made.'— *Penelope Houston*

Amarcord**
Italy / France 1973 123m Technicolor
FC Produzione / PECF (Franco Cristaldi)

Memories of a small Italian town during the fascist period.
A bizarre, intriguing mixture of fact, fantasy and obscurity, generally pleasing to watch though hardly satisfying. The title means 'I remember'.

w Federico Fellini, Tonino Guerra *d Federico Fellini ph* Giuseppe Rotunno *m Nino Rota ad* Danilo Donati

Puppela Maggio, Magali Noel, Armando Brancia, Ciccio Ingrassia
'A rich surface texture and a sense of exuberant melancholia.'—*Michael Billington, Illustrated London News*
'Peaks of invention separated by raucous valleys of low comedy.'—*Sight and Sound*
AA: best foreign film
AAN: script; direction

The Amateur Gentleman*
GB 1936 102m bw
Criterion (Marcel Hellman, Douglas Fairbanks Jnr)

A Regency innkeeper's son poses as a travelling pugilist in order to clear his father's name of theft.
Dated but rather fascinating period adventure, quite a lively production of its time.

w Clemence Dane, Edward Knoblock, Sergei Nolbandov *d* Thornton Freeland *ph* Gunther Krampf

Douglas Fairbanks Jnr, Elissa Landi, Gordon Harker, Basil Sydney, Hugh Williams, Irene Browne, Margaret Lockwood, Coral Browne, Frank Pettingell, Athole Stewart, Esmé Percy

The Amazing Colossal Man*
US 1957 80m bw
AIP / Malibu (Bert I. Gordon)

A plutonium explosion causes an army colonel to grow at the rate of ten feet a day.
Modest, quite well written sci-fi let down by shaky trick work.

w Bert I. Gordon, Mark Hanna *d* Bert I. Gordon *ph* Joe Biroc *m* Albert Glasser

Glenn Langan, Cathy Downs, William Hudson, James Seay
† Sequel: *Revenge of the Colossal Man* (GB: *The Terror Strikes*).

The Amazing Dobermans
US 1976 99m colour

Most ambitious of three low-budget independent movies (others, *The Daring*

Dobermans and *The Doberman Gang*) about a
group of trained dogs; this one concerns an
ex-con who hires them out for guard duty. A
fair low-budget production for family
audiences. Fred Astaire, James Franciscus,
Parley Baer, Billy Barty. Written by Richard
Chapman; directed by Byron Chudnow; for
Doberman Associates.

The Amazing Dr Clitterhouse**
US 1938   87m   bw
Warner (Robert Lord)

A criminologist researcher joins a gangster's
mob and becomes addicted to crime.
Amusing, suspenseful, well acted comedy-
melodrama.

w John Huston, John Wexley, *play* Barre
Lyndon *d* Anatole Litvak *ph* Tony Gaudio
m Max Steiner

Edward G. Robinson, Humphrey Bogart,
Claire Trevor, Allen Jenkins, Gale Page,
Donald Crisp, Maxie Rosebloom
  'The story is ingenious, but Anatole Litvak
and his producing-acting crew have so
thoroughly kept the larky mood of it while
setting up the necessary mood of interest and
suspense that it is hard to see where
conception leaves off and the shaping of it into
motion begins.'—*Otis Ferguson*

The Amazing Mr Blunden**
GB 1972   99m   Eastmancolor
Hemdale / Hemisphere (Barry Levinson)

In 1918, a widow and her two children meet a
kindly gentleman who offers them work in his
old mansion. Here they meet two ghost
children, discover that he is a ghost too, and
travel a hundred years back in time to right a
wicked wrong.
Involved ghost story for intellectual children,
made generally palatable by oodles of period
charm and good acting.

wd Lionel Jeffries, *story* The Ghosts by
Antonio Barker *ph* Gerry Fisher *m* Elmer
Bernstein *pd* Wilfrid Shingleton

Laurence Naismith, Diana Dors, James
Villiers, David Lodge, Lynne Frederick,
Dorothy Alison, Rosalyn Lander, Marc
Granger
  'Easy period charm . . . fills every
crevice.'—*Clyde Jeavons*

The Amazing Mr Williams*
US 1939   86m   bw
Columbia (Everett Riskin)

About-to-be-marrieds investigate a murder.
Brisk comedy-thriller on *Thin Man* lines.

w Dwight Taylor, Sy Bartlett, Richard
Maibaum *d* Alexander Hall *ph* Arthur Todd
md Morris Stoloff

Melvyn Douglas, Joan Blondell, Ruth
Donnelly, Clarence Kolb, Ed Brophy, Donald
MacBride, Don Beddoe

The Amazing Mrs Holliday
US 1943   98m   bw
Universal (Bruce Manning, Frank Shaw)

Torpedoed in mid-Pacific, a missionary's
daughter arrives in San Francisco with eight
Chinese orphans.
Unusual sentimental vehicle for its star; of no
particular interest or merit in itself, but with
the usual interludes for song.

w Frank Ryan, John Jacoby *d* Bruce
Manning *ph* Elwood Bredell *m* Hans Salter,
Frank Skinner *md* Charles Previn

Deanna Durbin, Edmond O'Brien, Frieda
Inescort, Barry Fitzgerald

AAN: Hans Salter, Frank Skinner

The Amazing Quest of Ernest Bliss
GB 1936   80m   bw
Garrett–Klement (Robert Garrett, Otto
  Klement)
US title: *Romance and Riches*

A millionaire accepts a wager that he can live
independently of his riches for one year.
Formulary comedy drama of its era on the
theme that money isn't everything. Very
dated.

w John L. Balderston *d* Alfred Zeisler
ph Otto Heller

Cary Grant (on home leave after his first
Hollywood success), Mary Brian, Henry
Kendall, Leon M. Lion, Garry Marsh, Moore
Marriott, Peter Gawthorne, Ralph Richardson

The Ambassador's Daughter*
US 1956   102m   Technicolor
  Cinemascope
UA / Norman Krasna

An American senator in Paris decides that the
presence of US forces in Paris constitutes a
moral danger. The ambassador's daughter
decides to investigate.
Thin comedy of the old-fashioned type: smart
lines and intimate playing not helped by the
vast screen.

wd Norman Krasna *ph* Michael Kelber
m Jacques Metehen

Olivia de Havilland, John Forsythe, Edward
Arnold, Adolphe Menjou, Myrna Loy,
Francis Lederer, Tommy Noonan, Minor
Watson

'An experienced cast approach the story's frivolities with poise and style.'—*MFB*

Ambush

US 1938   62m   bw

A girl proves her brother innocent and brings gangsters to book. Brisk second feature with an unexpected writing credit. Gladys Swarthout, Lloyd Nolan, Ernest Truex. Written by S. J. and Laura Perelman; directed by Kurt Neumann; for Paramount.

Ambush*

US 1949   89m   bw
MGM (Armand Deutsch)

An army scout leads a posse to capture an Indian chief who is holding a white woman hostage.
Good, clean, robust western, well produced and acted.

w Marguerite Roberts *d* Sam Wood *ph* Harold Lipstein *m* Rudolph Kopp

Robert Taylor, John Hodiak, Arlene Dahl, Don Taylor, Jean Hagen, Leon Ames

Ambush at Tomahawk Gap

US 1953   73m   Technicolor
Columbia (Wallace MacDonald)

Four ex-convicts seek hidden loot in a ghost town.
Standard co-feature western with rather more violence than usual for its date.

w David Lang *d* Fred F. Sears *ph* Henry Freulich *m* Ross Di Maggio

John Hodiak, John Derek, David Brian, Maria Elena Marques, Ray Teal, John Qualen

Ambush Bay

US 1966   109m   De Luxe
UA / Aubrey Schenck

In 1944, nine Marines try to escape from a Japanese-held island.
Routine, lengthy, sub-standard heroics for action addicts.

w Marve Feinberg, Ib Melchior *d* Ron Winston *ph* Emanuel Rojas *m* Richard La Salle

Hugh O'Brian, Mickey Rooney, James Mitchum, Tisa Chang, Harry Lauter

The Ambushers

US 1967   102m   Technicolor
Columbia / Meadway / Claude (Irving Allen)

An experimental flying disc disappears on a test run, and the trail leads Matt Helm to the Mexican jungle.

The third Matt Helm adventure had such a stupid script that all concerned decided to send it up, unfortunately with too obvious a tendency to smirk at their own bravado.

w Herbert Baker *d* Henry Levin *ph* Burnett Guffey, Edward Colman *m* Hugo Montenegro

Dean Martin, Senta Berger, Janice Rule, Kurt Kasznar, James Gregory, Albert Salmi
'Plot, jokes and gadgets all well below par.'—*MFB*

America**

US 1924   136m (16 fps)   bw   silent
(UA)

Various characters experience the Revolutionary War.
The Birth of a Nation, one war back. Much of interest, but nothing new; Griffith was basically repeating himself.

w John Pell *d* D. W. Griffith *ph* Billy Bitzer, Hendrick Sartow, Marcel le Picard, Hal Sintzenich

Neil Hamilton, Carol Dempster, Lionel Barrymore, Erville Alderson
'Love of tender girlhood! Passionate deeds of heroes! A rushing, leaping drama of charm and excitement!'—*publicity*
† As the English were the villains, the film was banned in Britain, but later released under the title *Love and Sacrifice*.

America, America*

US 1963   177m   bw
Warner (Elia Kazan)
GB title:*The Anatolian Smile*

In 1896 Turkey, a young Greek dreams of emigrating to America, and finally does so.
A massive piece of self-indulgence by a one-man band, fascinating for his family circle but so poorly constructed as to be of very limited interest elsewhere.

wd Elia Kazan *ph* Haskell Wexler *m* Manos Hadjidakis

Stathis Giallelis, Frank Wolff, Harry Davis, Elena Karam, Estelle Hemsley, Lou Antonio
'Kazan has failed to film the adventure implicit in his material, and a potentially exciting story has gone to waste.'—*MFB*
'If he sinks his teeth in a scene or a sequence that he enjoys, the audience can just sit around and be damned.'—*Stanley Kauffmann*
'Every episode, almost every shot, has its own beginning, middle and end, and the numberless playlets are cemented together into a strip which after the first two hours threatens to stretch grimly into eternity.'—*Robert Hatch, The Nation*

AAN: best picture; Elia Kazan (as writer);
Elia Kazan (as director)

An American Dream
US 1966   103m   Technicolor
Warner (William Conrad)
GB title: *See You in Hell, Darling*

A TV commentator is goaded into murdering
his wife, becomes involved with gangsters and,
tortured by guilt, allows them to kill him for
shielding the girl friend of one of them.
Ludicrously heavy-handed version of a semi-
surrealist book which presumably had
something to say about modern America, at
least in its author's mind. Nothing comes
through but relentless boredom at watching
sordid and unlikely events, and sympathy for
those involved.

w Mann Rubin, *novel* Norman Mailer
d Robert Gist *ph* Sam Leavitt *m* Johnny
Mandel

Stuart Whitman, Janet Leigh, Eleanor Parker
(in a one-scene role of screaming bitchery that
has to be seen to be believed), J. D. Cannon,
Lloyd Nolan, Barry Sullivan, Murray
Hamilton

AAN: song, 'A Time for Love' (*m* Johnny
Mandel, *ly* Paul Francis Webster)

American Empire
US 1942   82m   bw

Brothers fall out over management of their
Texas ranch. Reasonable but forgettable semi-
western. Richard Dix, Preston Foster, Frances
Gifford, Leo Carrillo. Written by Ben
Grauman Kohn, Gladys Atwater, Robert
Bren; directed by William McGann; for Harry
Sherman / UA. (GB title: *My Son Alone*.)

American Gigolo
US 1980   117m   Metrocolor
Paramount / Pierre Associates (Freddie
Fields)

A male prostitute finds that a client won't
clear him when he is falsely charged with
murder.
Thoroughly unattractive wallow on the seamy
side of Los Angeles, with none of *Midnight
Cowboy*'s compassion.

wd Paul Schraeder *ph* John Bailey
m Giorgio Moroder

Richard Gere, Lauren Hutton, Hector
Elizondo, Nina Van Pallandt
  'A hot subject, cool style and overly
contrived plotting don't all mesh.'—*Variety*

American Graffiti***
US 1973   110m   Techniscope
Universal / Lucasfilm / Coppola Company
  (Francis Ford Coppola, Gary Kurtz)

In 1962 California, four young men about to
leave for college gather for a night's girl-
chasing and police-baiting.
Nostalgic comedy recalling many sights and
sounds of the previous generation and
carefully crystallizing a particular time and
place. Successful in itself, it led to many
imitations.

wd George Lucas *ph* Ron Eveslage, Jan
D'Alquen *m* popular songs

Richard Dreyfuss, Ronny Howard, Paul le
Mat, Charlie Martin Smith, Cindy Williams,
Candy Clark, Mackenzie Philips

AAN: best picture; George Lucas (as writer);
George Lucas (as director); Candy Clark

An American Guerrilla in the
  Philippines*
US 1950   105m   Technicolor
TCF (Lamar Trotti)
GB title: *I Shall Return*

World War II, Pacific Zone: two American
sailors try to make their way to Australia after
MacArthur's surrender at Bataan.
Rather dull adventure story shot in the actual
locations.

w Lamar Trotti, *novel* Ira Wolfert *d* Fritz
Lang *ph* Harry Jackson *m* Cyril Mockridge

Tyrone Power, Micheline Presle, Tom Ewell,
Bob Pattern, Tommy Cook, Robert Barrat (as
MacArthur), Jack Elam
  'Cannot be regarded as a serious war
film.'—*Penelope Houston*

American Hot Wax
US 1978   91m   Metrocolor
Paramount (Art Limson)

The early days of rock and roll as seen by a
prominent disc jockey of the time.
Mildly entertaining ragbag of semi-historical
facts and authentic music, strictly for the youth
market.

w John Kaye *d* Floyd Mutrux *ph* William A.
Fraker *md* Kenny Vance

Tim McIntire (as Alan Freed), Fran Drescher,
Jay Lena, Laraine Newman, Chuck Berry,
Jerry Lee Lewis, Screamin' Jay Hawkins

An American in Paris****
US 1951   113m   Technicolor
MGM (*Arthur Freed*)

A carefree young artist scorns a rich woman's
patronage and wins the love of a gamine.

Altogether delightful musical holiday, one of the highspots of the Hollywood genre, with infectious enthusiasm and an unexpected sense of the Paris that was.

w Alan Jay Lerner d Vincente Minnelli ph Al Gilks, John Alton m George Gershwin ly Ira Gershwin ch Gene Kelly ad Cedric Gibbons, Preston Ames

Gene Kelly, Oscar Levant, Nina Foch, Leslie Caron, Georges Guetary

'Too fancy and overblown, but the principal performers are in fine form and the Gershwin music keeps everything good-spirited.'—*New Yorker, 1977*

† Chevalier was originally paged for the Georges Guetary role, but turned it down because he lost the girl. The production cost $2,723,903, of which $542,000 went on the final ballet.

AA: best picture; Alan Jay Lerner; Al Gilks, John Alton; musical arrangements (Saul Chaplin, Johnny Green)
AAN: Vincente Minnelli

American Madness**
US 1932 80m bw
Columbia

When a bank failure threatens, hundreds of small savers increase their deposits to save the situation.
Vivid, overstressed topical melodrama with crowd scenes typical of its director's later output.

w Robert Riskin d Frank Capra ph Joseph Walker

Walter Huston, Pat O'Brien, Kay Johnson, Constance Cummings, Gavin Gordon, Berton Churchill

'The sequence of the mounting panic and the storming of the bank are effectively staged, but the resolution is the usual Capra / Riskin populist hokum.'—*New Yorker, 1977*

An American Romance*
US 1944 151m Technicolor
MGM (King Vidor)

The life of a European immigrant who becomes a master of industry.
Mind-boggling pageant of the American dream, coldly presented and totally humourless. Its saving grace is its smooth physical presentation.

w Herbert Dalmas, William Ludwig d King Vidor ph Harold Rosson m Louis Gruenberg

Brian Donlevy, Ann Richards, John Qualen, Walter Abel, Stephen McNally

'A thousand chances to inform, excite or even interest have been flung away.'—*Richard Winnington*

'The whole aim of it is to boost The American Way.'—*Richard Mallett, Punch*

An American Tragedy**
US 1931 95m bw
Paramount

An ambitious young man murders his pregnant fiancée when he has a chance to marry a rich girl.
Dated but solidly satisfying adaptation of a weighty novel, more compelling than the 1951 remake *A Place in the Sun.*

wd Josef Von Sternberg, novel Theodore Dreiser ph Lee Garmes ad Hans Dreier

Phillips Holmes, *Sylvia Sidney*, Frances Dee, Irving Pichel, Frederick Burton, Claire McDowell

'It is the first time, I believe, that the subjects of sex, birth control and murder have been put into a picture with sense, taste and reality.'—*Pare Lorentz*

'An ordinary program effort with an unhappy ending. Slow, heavy and not always interesting drama.'—*Variety*

'An aimless, lugubrious mess. The fireworks may dazzle to schoolboys of criticism, but they will add no permanent color to the motion picture.'—*Harry Alan Potamkin*

The Americanization of Emily*
US 1964 115m bw
MGM / Filmways (John Calley)

World War II: just before the Normandy landings, a war widow driver falls for an American commander who is a self-confessed coward.
Bizarre comedy full of eccentric characters, an uneasy choice for its female star but otherwise successful in patches in its random distillation of black comedy, sex and the tumbling of old-fashioned virtues.

w Paddy Chayevsky, novel William Bradford Huie d Arthur Hiller ph Philip Lathrop, Chris Challis m Johnny Mandel

Julie Andrews, James Garner, *Melvyn Douglas*, James Coburn, Liz Fraser, Joyce Grenfell, Edward Binns, Keenan Wynn, William Windom

'Out of it all there comes the definite feeling that Hitler's war is incidental to Paddy Chayevsky's war of ideas . . . no plot synopsis could begin to suggest how much the characters talk.'—*MFB*

AAN: Philip Lathrop

The Americano
US 1916   60m approx (24 fps)   bw
   silent
Triangle (D. W. Griffith)

A young American engineer becomes involved
in a revolution in Patagonia.
Early star adventure vehicle, an immense
popular success; the last film Fairbanks made
for Griffith.

w Anita Loos, John Emerson, *novel* Blaze
Derringer by Eugene P. Lyle Jnr   d John
Emerson   ph Victor Fleming

Douglas Fairbanks, Alma Rubens,
Spottiswoode Aitken, Lillian Langdon

The Americano
US 1955   85m   Technicolor
(RKO) Robert Stillman

A westerner takes three prize bulls to Brazil,
but finds the buyer has been murdered.
A western with a twist, but otherwise
extremely dull, with poor pace, colour and use
of settings.

w Guy Trosper   d William Castle   ph William
Snyder   m Roy Webb

Glenn Ford, Frank Lovejoy, Abbe Lane,
Cesar Romero, Ursula Thiess

Un Ami Viendra ce Soir
France 1946   111m   bw
CGC (R. Artus)

During World War II a French patriot uses a
lunatic asylum as a resistance headquarters.
Rather glum wartime melodrama, lacking in
tension.

w Jacques Companeez, Raymond Bernard
d Raymond Bernard   ph Robert Le Fèbvre
m Arthur Honegger

Michel Simon, Louis Salou, Saturnin Fabre,
Paul Bernard, Madeleine Sologne, Marcel
André

Le Amiche*
Italy 1955   90m   bw
Trionfalcine
aka: *The Girl Friends*

The interaction of five girls living together in
Turin.
Highbrow lending library stuff, quite
watchable but equally forgettable.

w Suso Cecchi d'Amico, Alba de Cespedes,
story Tra Donne Sole by Cesare Pavese
d Michelangelo Antonioni   ph Gianni di
Venanzo   m Giovanni Fusco

Eleanora Rossi Drago, Valentina Cortese,
Yvonne Furneaux, Gabriele Ferzetti, Franco
Fabrizi, Madeleine Fischer

The Amityville Horror
US 1979   118m   Movielab
AIP / Cinema 77 (Ronald Saland, Elliot
   Geisinger)

Newlyweds move into a house where a murder
was committed, and experience strange
manifestations which drive them away.

Sub-*Exorcist* goings on, a shameless
exaggeration of some of the alleged facts
retailed in the best-selling book. A shocker for
the uncritical.

w Sandor Stern, *book* Jay Anson   d Stuart
Rosenberg   ph Fred J. Koenekamp   m Lalo
Schifrin

James Brolin, Margot Kidder, Rod Steiger,
Don Stroud, Murray Hamilton

Among the Living*
US 1941   68m   bw
Paramount (Sol C. Siegel)

In a small town live twin brothers, one of
whom is a murderer.
Offbeat suspenser with effective
performances.

w Lester Cole, Garrett Fort   d Stuart Heisler
ph Theodor Sparkuhl

Albert Dekker, Susan Hayward, Frances
Farmer, Harry Carey, Gordon Jones
   'Head and shoulders above all the filler
shows ground out by Hollywood to perpetuate
the double feature system.'—*Howard Barnes,
New York Herald Tribune*

The Amorous Adventures of Moll
   Flanders
GB 1965   125m   Technicolor
   Panavision
Paramount / Winchester (Marcel Hellman)

An ambitious servant girl loses her virtue to a
succession of rich gentlemen but finally settles
for a highwayman.
The aim was to make a female *Tom Jones*, but
this bawdy romp never achieves the
freewheeling fluency of that surprise success,
and a vacuous central performance makes the
constant couplings more boring than exciting.

w Dennis Cannan, Roland Kibbee, *novel*
Daniel Defoe   d Terence Young   ph Ted
Moore   m John Addison   pd Syd Cain

Kim Novak, Richard Johnson, George
Sanders, Lilli Palmer, Angela Lansbury, Leo
McKern, Vittorio de Sica, Cecil Parker,
Daniel Massey
   'Further from Defoe than *Tom Jones* was
from Fielding, but with much the same
combination of crude table manners and clean
sets to stand in for period flavour.'—*MFB*

The Amorous Prawn*
GB 1962   89m   bw
BL / Covent Garden (Leslie Gilliat)
US title: *The Playgirl and the War Minister*
(an attempt to cash in on the Profumo
case)

A hard-up general's wife invites American
paying guests to their official highland home.
This film version of a stage success seems very
mild, but the cast is eager to please: the result
is a frantic high class farce.

w Anthony Kimmins, Nicholas Phipps, *play*
Anthony Kimmins *d* Anthony Kimmins
ph Wilkie Cooper *m* John Barry

Joan Greenwood, Ian Carmichael, Cecil
Parker, Dennis Price, Robert Beatty, Finlay
Currie, Liz Fraser, Derek Nimmo

Amsterdam Affair
GB 1968   91m   Eastmancolor
LIP / Trio / Group W (Gerry Willoughby)

Inspector Van der Valk investigates when a
writer is accused of murdering his mistress.
Tolerable *roman policier*.

w Edmund Ward, *novel* Love in Amsterdam
by Nicholas Freeling *d* Gerry O'Hara
ph Gerry Fisher *m* Patrick John Scott

Wolfgang Kieling, William Marlowe, Caterina
Von Schell

The Amsterdam Kill
Hong Kong 1977   93m   Technicolor
Panavision
Golden Harvest / Fantastic Films /
Raymond Chow

An American ex-Drug Enforcement Agency
officer tries to protect an old friend caught in
the Hong Kong drug wars.
Roughly made and uninventive thriller in
which the Hong Kong film makers fail to
consolidate the international ground they
gained with kung fu films.

w Robert Clouse, Gregory Teifer *d* Robert
Clouse *ph* Alan Hume *m* Hal Schaffer

Robert Mitchum, Bradford Dillman, Richard
Egan, Leslie Nielsen, Keye Luke

Anastasia**
US 1956   105m   Eastmancolor
Cinemascope
TCF (Buddy Adler)

In 1928 Paris, a group of exiled White
Russians claim to have found the living
daughter of the Tsar, presumed executed in
1918; but the claimant is a fake schooled by a
general, with whom she falls in love.
Slick, highly theatrical entertainment for the

upper classes: it dazzles and satisfies without
throwing any light on history.

w Arthur Laurents, *play* Marcelle Maurette,
Guy Bolton *d* Anatole Litvak *ph* Jack
Hildyard *m* Alfred Newman *ad* Andrei
Andreiev, Bill Andrews

Ingrid Bergman (her Hollywood comeback
after some years in Europe under a cloud for
her 'immoral' behaviour), Yul Brynner, *Helen
Hayes*, Martita Hunt, Akim Tamiroff, Felix
Aylmer, Ivan Desny
'Little weight but considerable and urbane
charm.'—*John Cutts*

AA: Ingrid Bergman
AAN: Alfred Newman

Anatahan
Japan 1953   92m   bw
Daiwa (K. Takimura)
aka: *The Saga of Anatahan*

During World War II, Japanese seamen are
shipwrecked on the same deserted island as a
man and a woman; the latter causes jealousy
and murder.
Downright peculiar studio-set melodrama,
based on true events and directed by its
creator through interpreters, with results far
from happy.

wd, ph Josef Von Sternberg *m* A. Ifukube

Akemi Negishi, T. Sugunuma, K. Onoe, T.
Bandoh
'The main impression is of tedium relieved
by moments of far from intentional
humour.'—*Penelope Houston*

Anatomy of a Murder**
US 1959   161m   bw   Cinemascope
Columbia / Otto Preminger

A small-town lawyer successfully defends an
army officer accused of murdering a bartender
who had assaulted his wife.
Overlong and over-faithful version of a highly
detailed courtroom bestseller. The plot is
necessarily equivocal, the characterizations
overblown, but the trial commands some
interest, and the use of 'daring' words in
evidence caused controversy at the time.

w Wendell Mayes, *novel* Robert Traver
d Otto Preminger *ph* Sam Leavitt *m* Duke
Ellington *pd* Boris Leven

James Stewart, Ben Gazzara, Lee Remick,
Eve Arden, Arthur O'Connell, *George C.
Scott* (his first notable role, as the prosecutor),
Kathryn Grant, Orson Bean, Murray
Hamilton
† The trial judge was played by Joseph N.
Welch, a real-life judge who had gained fame

in 1954 by representing the army against
Senator McCarthy.

AAN: best picture; Wendell Mayes; Sam
Leavitt; James Stewart; Arthur O'Connell;
George C. Scott

Anchors Aweigh**
US 1945   139m   Technicolor
MGM (Joe Pasternak)

Two sailors on leave in Los Angeles get
involved with a small boy who wants to join
the navy.
Rather droopy musical most notable as a
forerunner of *On the Town*, though on much
more conventional lines. Amiable
performances, and a brilliant dance with a
cartoon mouse, save the day.

w Isobel Lennart *d* George Sidney
ph Robert Planck, Charles Boyle *principal
songs* Jule Styne *ly* Sammy Cahn *m* George
Stoll *pd* Cedric Gibbons

Frank Sinatra, Gene Kelly, Kathryn Grayson,
Jose Iturbi, Sharon McManus, Carlos
Ramirez, Dean Stockwell, Pamela Britton

AA: George Stoll
AAN: best picture; Robert Planck; Gene
Kelly; song 'I Fall in Love Too Easily' (*m* Jule
Styne, *ly* Sammy Cahn)

And Baby Makes Three
US 1950   83m   bw
Columbia (Robert Lord)

A wife divorces her compromised husband
before discovering that she is pregnant.
Thin marital comedy with minor
compensations.

w Lou Breslow, Joseph Hoffman *d* Henry
Levin *ph* Burnett Guffey *m* George Duning

Robert Young, Barbara Hale, Billie Burke,
Robert Hutton, Janis Carter, Nicholas Joy,
Lloyd Corrigan
'It has everything but a story that hangs
together.'—*New York Herald Tribune*

And God Created Woman
France 1956   92m   Eastmancolor
Cinemascope
Iena / UCIL / Cocinor (Raoul Lévy)
original title: *Et Dieu Créa la Femme;* aka:
And Woman . . . Was Created

An 18-year-old finds herself fatally attracted
towards men.
Rather a feeble excuse for its star to strip on
the St Tropez beach.

w Roger Vadim, Raoul Lévy *d* Roger Vadim
ph Armand Thirard *m* Paul Misraki

Brigitte Bardot, Curt Jurgens, Jean-Louis
Trintignant, Christian Marquand, Georges
Poujouly, Jane Marken, Paul Faivre

And Hope To Die
US / Fr / Canada 1972   104m   bw

A fugitive Frenchman in Canada runs foul of
criminals and gypsies and causes several
deaths. Muddled melodrama of the worst
'international' kind. Jean-Louis Trintignant,
Robert Ryan, Aldo Ray, Tisa Farrow, Lea
Massari. Written by Sebastien Japrisot;
directed by René Clément; for Serge
Silberman / TCF.

And Justice For All
US 1979   119m   Metrocolor
Columbia / Walton (Joe Wizan)

An American lawyer gets into all kinds of
trouble, including the defence of a judge on
a rape charge.
Not so much a satire as a series of random
pot-shots at the legal system, sometimes
funny but cumulatively stultifying.

w Valerie Curtin, Barry Levinson *d* Norman
Jewison *ph* Frank Holgate *m* Dave Grusin

Al Pacino, Jack Warden, John Forsythe, Lee
Strasberg, Christine Lahti, Sam Levene,
Jeffrey Taybor
'Most incriminating is its own hysterical
imprecision and sentimental pleading.'—
Sight and Sound

And Now For Something Completely
Different*
GB 1971   88m   colour
(Columbia) Kettledrum / Python (Victor
Lownes / GSF) (Patricia Casey)

Useful round-up of the more famous sketches
from BBC TV's zany comedy series *Monty
Python*.
Side-splitting for those who want Groucho
Marx updated; baffling for reactionaries;
movie presentation perfunctory.

written by and starring *John Cleese, Graham
Chapman, Terry Gilliam, Eric Idle, Michael
Palin, Terry Jones*

d Ian Macnaughton *ph* David Muir

And Now Miguel*
US 1965   95m   Technicolor
Universal / Robert B. Radnitz

A 10-year-old Mexican boy proves himself
worthy to work on the mountain with the
sheep.
A children's film typical of its producer: good

to look at, documentarily convincing, but too slight and too slow.

w Ted Sherdeman, Jane Clove, *novel* Joseph Krumgold *d* James B. Clark *ph* Clifford Stine *m* Phillip Lambro

Pat Cardi, Guy Stockwell, Clu Gulager, Michael Ansara, Joe de Santis

And Now The Screaming Starts
GB 1973 91m colour
Amicus (Max J. Rosenberg, Milton Subotsky)

A new bride in a country house is haunted by hallucinations of the past.
Grisly ghost story which overplays its hand and outstays its welcome.

w Roger Marshall, *novel* Fengriffen by David Case *d* Roy Ward Baker *ph* Denys Coop *m* Douglas Gamley

Peter Cushing, Stephanie Beacham, Herbert Lom, Patrick Magee, Ian Ogilvy, Geoffrey Whitehead, Guy Rolfe, Rosalie Crutchley

And Now Tomorrow*
US 1944 86m bw
Paramount (Fred Kohlmar)

A rich girl goes deaf, loses her fiancé, but wins the poor doctor who cares for her.
Bestselling slush turned into a routine star romance.

w Frank Partos, Raymond Chandler (!), *novel* Rachel Field *d* Irving Pichel *ph* Daniel L. Fapp *m* Victor Young

Loretta Young, Alan Ladd (his first film in confirmed top-star status after a meteoric rise interrupted by war service), Susan Hayward, Beulah Bondi, Cecil Kellaway, Barry Sullivan.

'A vernal sign of the boys getting back to one of their favourite legends after the wintry days of war.'—*Richard Winnington*

And So They Were Married
US 1935 74m bw
Columbia (B. P. Schulberg)

A widow and a widower try to get married despite the ill-feeling of their children.
Predictable romantic farce.

w Doris Anderson, Joseph Anthony *d* Elliott Nugent *ph* Henry Freulich *m* Howard Jackson

Melvyn Douglas, Mary Astor, Edith Fellows, Jackie Moran, Donald Meek, Dorothy Stickney

And Soon the Darkness*
GB 1970 99m Technicolor
Associated British (Albert Fennell, Brian Clemens)

Of two young nurses on a cycling holiday in France, one is murdered by a local sex maniac and the other almost shares her fate.
Slow, overstretched, often risible suspenser on vanishing lady lines; long on red herrings and short on humour, but with some pretension to style. The action all takes place along a mile or two of sunlit country road.

w Brian Clemens, Terry Nation *d* Robert Fuest *ph* Ian Wilson *m* Laurie Johnson

Pamela Franklin, Michele Dotrice, Sandor Eles, John Nettleton

And the Angels Sing*
US 1943 95m bw
Paramount (E. D. Leshin)

Four singing sisters have hectic adventures with a bandleader.
Mildly disarming romantic comedy with music, more firmly set in a recognizable social milieu than the usual fan product from this studio.

w Melvin Frank, Norman Panama, Claude Binyon *d* George Marshall *ph* Karl Struss *m* Victor Young *songs* Johnny Burke, Jimmy Van Heusen

Dorothy Lamour, Diana Lynn, Betty Hutton, Mimi Chandler, Fred MacMurray, Raymond Walburn, Eddie Foy Jnr, Frank Albertson, Mikhail Rasumny

'Slapstick sophistication in a sub-Sturges manner.'—*MFB*

'Cruel, soggily professional, over-elaborate, and inclined towards snobbish whimsy.'—*James Agee*

And Then There Were None****
US 1945 97m bw
Harry M. Popkin
GB title: *Ten Little Niggers*

Ten people are invited to a house party on a lonely island, and murdered one by one.
A classic mystery novel is here adapted and directed with the utmost care to provide playful black comedy, stylish puzzlement, and some splendid acting cameos.

w Dudley Nichols, *novel* Agatha Christie (aka Ten Little Niggers) *d* René Clair *ph* Lucien Andriot *m* Mario Castelnuovo-Tedesco

Walter Huston, Barry Fitzgerald, Louis Hayward, June Duprez, Roland Young, Richard Haydn, C. Aubrey Smith, Judith Anderson, Queenie Leonard, Mischa Auer

And Then There Were None
GB 1974 98m Technicolor
EMI / Filibuster (Harry Alan Towers)

Ten people are lured to an isolated Persian hotel and murdered one by one.

Listless remake, often so inept you could
scream.

w Peter Welbeck (Harry Alan Towers)
d Peter Collinson *ph* Fernando Arribas
m Bruno Nicolai

Oliver Reed, Richard Attenborough, Elke
Sommer, Herbert Lom, Gert Froebe,
Stéphane Audran, Charles Aznavour, Adolfo
Celi, Alberto de Mendoza, Maria Rohm

The Anderson Tapes*
US 1971 98m Technicolor Panavision
Columbia / Robert M. Weitman

An ex-con forms a gang to rob a building, not
knowing that police and others, for various
purposes, are making tape recordings of his
conversations.
Superficially slick and fashionable crime
thriller, marred by unnecessarily flashy
direction, a failure to explain enough about
the tapes, and a climax which oddly mixes
bloodshed and farce.

w Frank R. Pierson, *novel* Lawrence Sanders
d Sidney Lumet *ph* Arthur J. Ornitz
m Quincy Jones

Sean Connery, *Martin Balsam*, Dyan Cannon,
Alan King, Ralph Meeker

Andrei Rublev**
USSR 1966 181m colour (part)
   Cinemascope
Mosfilm

Imaginary episodes from the life of a 15th-
century icon painter.
A superb recreation of medieval life
dramatizes the eternal problem of the artist,
whether to take part in the life around him or
merely comment on it.

w Andrei Mikhalkov-Konchalovsky, Andrei
Tarkovsky *d Andrei Tarkovsky ph* Vadim
Yusov *m* Vyacheslav Tcherniaiev

   'The one indisputable Russian masterpiece
of the last decade.'—*Nigel Andrews, MFB,
1973*

   'With the exception of the great Eisenstein,
I can't think of any film which has conveyed a
feeling of the remote past with such utter
conviction . . . a durable and unmistakable
masterpiece.'—*Michael Billington, Illustrated
London News*

Androcles and the Lion**
US 1952 96m bw
RKO (Gabriel Pascal)

A slave takes a thorn from the paw of a lion
which later, in the arena, refuses to eat him.
Shavian drollery, with interpolated discussions

on faith, is scarcely ideal cinema material, but
gusto in the performances keeps it going
despite stolid direction.

w Chester Erskine, *play* Bernard Shaw
d Chester Erskine *ph* Harry Stradling
m Frederick Hollander *ad* Harry Horner

*Alan Young, Jean Simmons, Robert Newton,
Victor Mature, Maurice Evans* (as Caesar),
Reginald Gardiner, Elsa Lanchester, Alan
Mowbray, Gene Lockhart

The Andromeda Strain**
US 1970 131m Technicolor
   Panavision
Universal / Robert Wise

Scientists work frantically to neutralize an
infected village, knowing that the least
infection will cause their laboratory to self-
destruct.
Solemn and over-detailed but generally
suspenseful thriller, with a sense of allegory
about man's inhumanity to man.

w Nelson Gidding, *novel* Michael Crichton
d Robert Wise *ph* Richard H. Kline *m* Gil
Melle *ad* Boris Leven

Arthur Hill, David Wayne, James Olson, Kate
Reid, Paula Kelly

Andy Hardy Comes Home*
US 1958 81m bw
MGM (Red Doff)

Fortyish Andy returns to Carvel, his home
town, to negotiate a land deal.
Rather dismal sequel to the celebrated series
of Hardy family comedies which were
enormously popular in the early forties: a
thirteen-year gap is too long, and although
most of the family is reunited the old Judge is
sadly missed.

w Edward Everett Hutshing, Robert Morris
Donley *d* Howard W. Koch *ph* William W.
Spencer, Harold E. Wellman *m* Van
Alexander

Mickey Rooney, Fay Holden, Cecilia Parker,
Patricia Breslin, Sara Haden, Jerry Colonna
† See also under *Hardy Family*.

Angel*
US 1937 98m bw
Paramount (Ernst Lubitsch)

The wife of an English diplomat finds herself
neglected and almost has an affair with his old
friend.
A curious romantic comedy in many ways
typical of its time, yet with very few laughs,
showing none of its director's usual cinematic
sense, and compromised by the censor's
refusal to let a spade be called a spade.

Underplaying, and a sense that we watch a
way of life about to be swept away, just about
save it.

w Samson Raphaelson, *play* Melchior
Lengyel d Ernst Lubitsch *ph* Charles Lang
m Frederick Hollander

*Marlene Dietrich, Herbert Marshall, Melvyn
Douglas,* Edward Everett Horton, Laura
Hope Crews, Ernest Cossart

Angel and the Badman*
US 1947 100m bw
Republic (John Wayne)

The love of a Quaker girl converts a wounded
gunslinger to an honourable life.
Thoughtful western with good background
detail and a fair measure of action.

wd James Edward Grant *ph* Archie Stout
m Richard Hageman *pd* Ernest Fegte

John Wayne, Gail Russell, Harry Carey,
Bruce Cabot, Irene Rich, Tom Powers
  'Unpretentious, sweet-tempered and quite
likeable.'—*James Agee*

Angel Baby*
US 1960 97m bw
Madera (Thomas F. Woods)

A mute girl is cured by an evangelist, and
renounces her sins.
Strident, vigorous low-budget melodrama.

w Oris Borstem, Samuel Rocca, Paul Mason,
novel Jenny Angel by Elsie Oaks Barbour
d Paul Wendkos *ph* Haskell Wexler, Jack
Marta *m* Wayne Shanklin

Salome Jens, George Hamilton, Joan
Blondell, Mercedes McCambridge, Henry
Jones, Burt Reynolds

Angel Face*
US 1952 91m bw
RKO (Otto Preminger)

A demented girl murders her father and
stepmother, involving her chauffeur, whom
she finally kills, and commits suicide.
Outrageous melodrama, so absurd as to be
almost endearing.

w Frank Nugent, Oscar Millard d Otto
Preminger *ph* Harry Stradling *m* Dmitri
Tiomkin

Jean Simmons, Robert Mitchum, Herbert
Marshall, Barbara O'Neil, Leon Ames, Mona
Freeman, Kenneth Tobey, Raymond
Greenleaf
  'The one lyrical nightmare in the cinema.'—
Ian Cameron

An Angel from Texas*
US 1940 69m bw
Warner

Misadventures of a country boy in New York.
Modest revamping of a much filmed farce, also
made as *The Tenderfoot* (1928) and *Dance
Charlie Dance* (1937).

w Fred Niblo Jnr, Bertram Millhauser, *play*
The Butter and Egg Man by George F.
Kaufman d Ray Enright *ph* Arthur L. Todd

Eddie Albert, Rosemary Lane, Wayne Morris,
Ronald Reagan, Milburn Stone

Angel in Exile
US 1948 90m bw
Republic

An ex-con heads for an abandoned Arizona
mine to recover stolen gold.
Modest, effective western about a baddie who
reforms.

w Charles Larson d Allan Dwan, Philip Ford
ph Reggie Lanning *m* Nathan Scott

John Carroll, Adele Mara, Thomas Gomez

The Angel Levine*
US 1970 105m De Luxe
UA / Belafonte Enterprises (Chiz Schultz)

An elderly Jewish tailor complains to God of
his bad luck; a black angel appears and seems
to help him for a while.
Muddled and seemingly pointless parable with
occasional felicities.

w Bill Gunn, Ronald Ribman, *story* Bernard
Malamud d Jan Kadar *ph* Richard Kratina
pd George Jenkins *m* Zdenek Linka

Zero Mostel, Harry Belafonte, Ida Kaminska,
Milo O'Shea, Eli Wallach, Anne Jackson,
Gloria Foster
  'A prolonged variation on the theme that
faith can produce miracles, but only if there is
enough of it.'—*John Gillett*

Angel on My Shoulder**
US 1946 101m bw
UA / Charles R. Rogers

The devil promises leniency to a dead gangster
if he will return to earth and take over the
body of a judge who is stamping out evil.
Crude but lively fantasy on the tail-end of the
Here Comes Mr Jordan cycle, and by the same
author.

w Harry Segall, Roland Kibbee d Archie
Mayo *ph* James Van Trees *m* Dmitri
Tiomkin

Paul Muni, Claude Rains, Anne Baxter,
Erskine Sanford, Hardie Albright

'The story is so imitative that it's hard to feel any more towards it than a mildly nostalgic regard.'—*Bosley Crowther*

Angel on the Amazon
US 1948 86m bw
Republic (John H. Auer)
GB title: *Drums Along the Amazon*

An elderly white lady resident of the Amazon jungle looks only 25 after being scared by a panther . . .
Ludicrous melodrama which the actors take seriously.

w Lawrence Kimble *d* John H. Auer
ph Reggie Lanning *m* Nathan Scott

George Brent, Constance Bennett, Vera Hruba Ralston, Brian Aherne, Fortunio Bonanova, Alfonso Bedoya, Gus Schilling

The Angel Who Pawned Her Harp*
GB 1954 76m bw
Group Three (Sidney Cole)

A real angel arrives on a goodwill visit to seamy Islington, and manages to right a few wrongs.
Simple-minded whimsy, spottily effective, with good performances.

w Charles Terrot, Sidney Cole *d* Alan Bromly *ph* Arthur Grant *m* Antony Hopkins

Diane Cilento, Felix Aylmer, Robert Eddison, Jerry Desmonde, Sheila Sweet, Alfie Bass

The Angel with the Trumpet
GB 1949 98m bw
British Lion / London Films (Karl Hartl)

An Austrian lady has an affair with a crown prince but marries for security and dies in defiance of the Nazis.
Curious European cavalcade, dully directed to keep the budget down and accommodate long stretches of an Austrian original. An eccentricity.

w Karl Hartl, Franz Tassie, *novel* Ernst Lothar *d* Anthony Bushell *ph* Robert Krasker *m* Willy Schmidt-Gentner

Eileen Herlie, Basil Sydney, Norman Wooland, Anthony Bushell, Maria Schell, John Justin, Oskar Werner, Andrew Cruickshank

The Angel Wore Red
US 1960 105m bw
MGM / Titanus / Spectator (Gottfredo Lombardo)

The love story of a priest and a prostitute in the Spanish Civil War.

Turgid farrago, unsatisfactory both romantically and politically.

wd Nunnally Johnson *ph* Giuseppe Rotunno *m* Bronislau Kaper

Ava Gardner, Dirk Bogarde, Joseph Cotten, Vittorio de Sica, Aldo Fabrizi, Finlay Currie

'The stars show no apparent surprise that a film so empty of reward should take itself so seriously.'—*Peter John Dyer*

Angelina*
Italy 1947 98m bw
Lux

An impoverished housewife becomes the spokeswoman for her community on flooding, housing and other slum problems.
Reasonably rewarding star vehicle in the neo-realist tradition, this time angled for comedy.

w Suso Cecchi d'Amico, Piero Tellini, Luigi Zampa *d* Luigi Zampa *ph* Mario Craveri *m* Enzio Masetti

Anna Magnani, Nando Bruno, Gianni Glori, Franco Zeffirelli

Angélique
France / West Germany / Italy 1964
    116m Eastmancolor Dyaliscope
Francos / CICC / Gloria /
    Fona Roma (Francis Cosne)

Adventures of a nobleman's daughter at the court of Louis XIV.
Watchable swashbuckling nonsense, a kind of French *Forever Amber*. Several sequels were made.

w Claude Brûlé, Bernard Borderie, Francis Cosne, *novel* Serge and Anne Golon *d* Bernard Borderie *ph* Henri Pérsin *m* Michel Magne

Michèle Mercier, Robert Hossein, Giuliano Gemma, Jean Rochefort, François Maistre, Jacques Toja

Angels in the Outfield
US 1952 99m bw
MGM (Clarence Brown)
GB title: *Angels and the Pirates*

The profane and bad-tempered manager of an unsuccessful baseball team gets help from an angel.
Unamusing, saccharine whimsy which does not deserve its excellent production values.

w Dorothy Kingsley, George Wells *d* Clarence Brown *ph* Paul C. Vogel *m* Daniele Amfitheatrof

Paul Douglas, Janet Leigh, Keenan Wynn, Lewis Stone, Donna Corcoran, Spring Byington, Bruce Bennett

Angels One Five*
GB 1952   98m   bw
Associated British (John W. Gossage,
   Derek Twist)

A slice of life in an RAF fighter station during
the Battle of Britain.
Underplayed semi-documentary drama with
stiff upper lips all round and the emphasis on
characterization rather than action. A huge
commercial success in Britain.

w Derek Twist d George More O'Ferrall
ph Christopher Challis m John Wooldridge

Jack Hawkins, John Gregson, Michael
Denison, Andrew Osborn, Cyril Raymond,
Humphrey Lestocq, Dulcie Gray, Veronica
Hurst

Angels Over Broadway*
US 1940   80m   bw
Columbia / Ben Hecht

During one rainy New York night, three of
life's failures have one last stab at success.
Would-be poetic, moralizing melodrama very
typical of its author; interesting but not a
success.

w Ben Hecht d Ben Hecht, Lee Garmes
ph Lee Garmes m George Antheil

Douglas Fairbanks Jnr, Rita Hayworth,
Thomas Mitchell, John Qualen, George
Watts, Ralph Theodore
   'There's a genial, original spirit to it.'—*New
Yorker, 1978*
   'It has excitement, fast talk, some knowable
people, cynicism and sentiment.'—*Otis
Ferguson*
† Sample dialogue: 'This town's a giant dice
game . . . come on, seven!'
AAN: Ben Hecht (as writer)

Angels Wash Their Faces*
US 1939   86m   bw
Warner (Max Siegel)

A bad boy joins the Dead End Kids, but they
all reform in the end.
Routine programmer, hastily concocted after
the success of *Angels with Dirty Faces.*

w Michael Fessier, Niven Busch, Robert
Buckner d Ray Enright ph Arthur Todd
m Adolph Deutsch

Ann Sheridan, Ronald Reagan, the Dead End
Kids, Bonita Granville, Frankie Thomas,
Henry O'Neill, Berton Churchill, Eduardo
Ciannelli

Angels with Dirty Faces***
US 1938   97m   bw
Warner (Sam Bischoff)

A Brooklyn gangster is admired by slum boys,
but for their sake pretends to be a coward
when he goes to the electric chair.
A shrewd, slick entertainment package and a
seminal movie for all kinds of reasons. It
combined gangster action with fashionable
social conscience; it confirmed the Dead End
Kids as stars; it provided archetypal roles for
its three leading players and catapulted the
female lead into stardom. It also showed the
Warner style of film-making, all cheap sets and
shadows, at its most effective.

w John Wexley, Warren Duff, *original
story* Rowland Brown d *Michael Curtiz*
ph *Sol Polito* m Max Steiner

James Cagney (gangster with redeeming
features), *Pat O'Brien* (priest), *Humphrey
Bogart* (gangster with no redeeming features),
The Dead End Kids, Ann Sheridan, George
Bancroft, Edward Pawley
   'A rousing, bloody, brutal melodrama.'—
New York Mirror
AAN: Rowland Brown; Michael Curtiz;
James Cagney

Les Anges du Péché*
France 1943   73m   bw
Synops / Robert Paul

A novice nun has trouble with the mother
superior because of her obsessive interest in a
rebellious delinquent girl, and dies before
taking her vows.
Interesting study of an enclosed society,
notable as its director's first film.

w R. P. Bruckberger, Jean Giraudoux, Robert
Bresson d *Robert Bresson ph* Philippe
Agostini m Jean-Jacques Grunenwald

Renée Faure, Jany Holt, Sylvie, Mila Parély,
Marie-Hélène Dasté

Angora Love**
US 1929   20m   bw   silent

Laurel and Hardy keep a goat in their
lodgings. Lively L & H comedy, even funnier
when remade two years later as *Laughing
Gravy.* With Edgar Kennedy, Charlie Hall.
Written by Leo McCarey and H. M. Walker;
directed by Lewis R. Foster; for Hal Roach.

The Angry Hills
GB 1959   105m   bw
MGM / Raymond Stross

In 1940, an American war correspondent is
helped by Greek freedom fighters.
Laboured war melodrama with pretentious
dialogue but little characterization.

w A. I. Bezzerides, *novel* Leon Uris *d* Robert Aldrich *ph* Stephen Dade *m* Richard Rodney Bennett *ad* Ken Adam

Robert Mitchum, Gia Scala, Elisabeth Mueller, Stanley Baker, Donald Wolfit, Kieron Moore, Theodore Bikel, Sebastian Cabot, Peter Illing, Marius Goring, Leslie Phillips

The Angry Silence*
GB 1960 94m bw
British Lion / Beaver (Richard
  Attenborough, Bryan Forbes)

A worker who refuses to join an unofficial strike is 'sent to Coventry' by his mates; the matter hits national headlines, and the communists use it to their own advantage. Irresistibly reminding one of a po-faced *I'm All Right Jack*, this remains a fresh and urgent film which unfortunately lost excitement in its domestic scenes.

w Bryan Forbes, *story* Michael Craig, Richard Gregson *d* Guy Green *ph* Arthur Ibbetson *m* Malcolm Arnold

Richard Attenborough, Michael Craig, Pier Angeli, Bernard Lee, Alfred Burke, Laurence Naismith, Geoffrey Keen

AAN: Bryan Forbes

Animal Crackers***
US 1930 98m bw
Paramount

Thieves covet a valuable oil painting unveiled at a swank party.
An excuse for the Marx Brothers, and a lively one in patches, though sedate and stage bound in treatment. The boys are all in top form, and many of the dialogue exchanges are classics.

w *Morrie Ryskind*, from musical play by himself and *George F. Kaufman d* Victor Heerman *ph* George Folsey *m* / *ly* Bert Kalmar, Harry Ruby

Groucho, Chico, Harpo, Zeppo, *Margaret Dumont*, Lillian Roth, Louis Sorin, Robert Greig, Hal Thompson

Animal Farm**
GB 1955 75m Technicolor
Louis de Rochemont / Halas and Batchelor

Oppressed by the cruelty and inefficiency of their master, the animals take over a farm but find fresh tyrants among themselves.
George Orwell's political fable—'all animals are equal but some animals are more equal than others'—is faithfully followed in this ambitious but rather disappointingly flat cartoon version.

w, p, d John Halas and Joy Batchelor
voices Maurice Denham

The Animal Kingdom*
US 1932 95m bw
RKO (David O. Selznick)
GB title: *The Woman in His House*

An intellectual publisher tries to justify keeping both a wife and a mistress.
Smart comedy-drama from a Broadway success, later bowdlerized as *One More Tomorrow* (qv).

w Horace Jackson, *play* Philip Barry *d* Edward H. Griffith *ph* Lucien Andriot *m* Max Steiner

Leslie Howard, Ann Harding, Myrna Loy, Neil Hamilton, William Gargan, Henry Stephenson, Ilka Chase

The Animal World*
US 1956 80m Technicolor
Warner / Windsor (Irwin Allen)

The evolution of animals from their primitive beginnings.
Ambitious documentary with a popular science approach; very variable, with poorish model work.

wd Irwin Allen *ph* Harold Wellman *m* Paul Sawtell *sp* Willis O'Brien, Ray Harryhausen

Ann Vickers*
US 1933 72m bw
RKO (Pandro S. Berman)

A feminist social worker is taught a thing or two by life and settles down with a corrupt judge.
Reasonably effective version of a popular though heavy-going novel of the time.

w Jane Murfin, *novel* Sinclair Lewis *d* John Cromwell *ph* David Abel, Edward Cronjager *m* Max Steiner

Irene Dunne, Walter Huston, Conrad Nagel, Bruce Cabot, Edna May Oliver, Mitchell Lewis, Murray Kinnell

Anna
Italy 1952 100m bw
Lux (Ponti / de Laurentiis)

A novice nun recalls her former life and almost gives up her vocation.
Soupy woman's picture of no particular merit.

w various *d* Alberto Lattuada *ph* Otello Martelli *m* Nino Rota

Silvana Mangano, Raf Vallone, Vittorio Gassman, Gaby Morlay, Jacques Dumesnil

Anna and the King of Siam••
US 1946 128m bw
TCF (Louis D. Lighton)

In 1862 an English governess arrives in
Bangkok to teach the 67 children of the king.
Unusual and lavish drama, tastefully handled
and generally absorbing despite miscasting and
several slow passages.

w Talbot Jennings, Sally Benson, *book*
Margaret Landon *d* John Cromwell
ph Arthur Miller m Bernard Herrmann *ad*
Lyle Wheeler, William Darling

Irene Dunne, Rex Harrison, Linda Darnell,
Gale Sondergaard, Lee J. Cobb, Mikhail
Rasumny
　'A film that never touches the imagination,
a film that leaves the mind uninformed and the
memory unburdened.'—*Richard Winnington*

AA: Arthur Miller
AAN: Talbot Jennings, Sally Benson; Bernard
Herrmann; Gale Sondergaard

Anna Christie••
US 1930 74m bw
MGM

A waterfront prostitute falls in love with a
young seaman.
Primitive sound version of an earthy theatrical
warhorse: it has a niche in history as the film
in which Garbo first talked.

w Frances Marion, *play* Eugene O'Neill
d Clarence Brown *ph* William Daniels

Greta Garbo, Charles Bickford, *Marie
Dressler*, James T. Mack, Lee Phelps
　'A very talkie, uncinematic affair, more
old-fashioned than the silent movies. If it were
not so well acted it would be pretty
tiresome.'—*National Board of Review*

AAN: Clarence Brown; William Daniels;
Greta Garbo

Anna Karenina••
US 1935 95m bw
MGM (David O. Selznick)

The wife of a Russian aristocrat falls for a
dashing cavalry officer.
Well-staged but finally exasperating romantic
tragedy, sparked by good performances and
production.

w Clemence Dane, Salka Viertel, *novel* Leo
Tolstoy *d Clarence Brown ph William
Daniels m* Herbert Stothart

Greta Garbo, Fredric March, *Basil Rathbone*,
Freddie Bartholemew, Maureen O'Sullivan,
May Robson, Reginald Owen, Reginald
Denny

'A dignified and effective drama which
becomes significant because of that tragic,
lonely and glamorous blend which is the
Garbo personality.'—*André Sennwald*
　'It reaches no great heights of tragedy or
drama but rather moves forward relentlessly
and a little coldly.'—*The Times*
† Previously filmed as a 1928 silent called
Love, with Garbo and John Gilbert.

AAN: William Daniels

Anna Karenina•
GB 1947 139m bw
London Films (Alexander Korda)

Tiresomely overlong but very handsomely
staged remake marred by central miscasting.

w Jean Anouilh, Guy Morgan, Julien
Duvivier *d* Julien Duvivier *ph Henri Alekan
m* Constant Lambert

Vivien Leigh, Kieron Moore, *Ralph
Richardson*, Marie Lohr, Sally Ann Howes,
Niall MacGinnis, Michael Gough, Helen
Haye, Mary Kerridge
　'Vivien Leigh is lashed about by the
tremendous role of Anna like a pussy cat with
a tigress by the tail. She is not helped by a
script which insists on sentimentally ennobling
one of fiction's most vehemently average
women.'—*James Agee*

Anna Lucasta•
US 1949 86m bw
Columbia / Security (Philip Yordan)

The bad girl of a farming family comes home
to marry, but her past catches up with her.
Polish immigrant melodrama, a touring
company staple, adequately transferred to the
screen.

w Philip Yordan, Arthur Laurents, *play* Philip
Yordan *d* Irving Rapper *ph* Sol Polito
m David Diamond

Paulette Goddard, Oscar Homolka, Broderick
Crawford, William Bishop, Gale Page, Mary
Wickes

Anna Lucasta•
US 1958 97m bw
(UA) Longridge Enterprises (Sidney
　Harmon)

Black version of the long-running play;
performances standard.

w Philip Yordan *d* Arnold Laven *ph* Lucien
Ballard *m* Elmer Bernstein

Eartha Kitt, Frederick O'Neal, Sammy Davis
Jnr, Henry Scott, Rex Ingram, James Edwards

Anna of Brooklyn
Italy / France / US 1958   106m
   Technirama
Circeo Cinematografica / France Cinema /
RKO (Milko Skofic)

An attractive widow returns from New York
to her native Italian village in search of a
husband.
Footling romantic drama which wastes its cast
and budget.

w Ettore Margadonna, Dino Risi *d* Reginald
Denham, Carlo Lasticati *ph* Giuseppe
Rotunno *m* Alessandro Cicognini, Vittorio de
Sica

Gina Lollobrigida, Dale Robertson, Vittorio
de Sica, Amedeo Nazzari, Peppino de
Felippo, Gabriella Palotta

An Annapolis Story
US 1953   81m   colour
Allied Artists / Walter Mirisch
GB title: *The Blue and the Gold*

Two cadets at the naval academy love the
same girl.
Artless recruiting poster heroics.

w Dan Ullman *d* Don Siegel *ph* Sam Leavitt
m Marlin Skiles

Diana Lynn, John Derek, Kevin McCarthy,
Pat Dooley, L. Q. Jones
'Seldom have so many scrubbed,
wholesome-looking young people thronged
any picture.'—*New York Times*

Anne of Green Gables*
US 1934   79m   bw
RKO (Kenneth MacGowan)

An orphan girl goes to the country to live with
her aunt.
Standard version of the classic for young girls.

w Sam Mintz, *novel* L. M. Montgomery
d George Nicholls Jnr *ph* Lucien Andriot
m Max Steiner

Anne Shirley (who had been known as Dawn
O'Day and legally adopted the name of her
character in this, her first starring role), Tom
Brown, O. P. Heggie, Helen Westley, Sara
Haden, Charley Grapewin
'Made up and monotonous—tragedy having
its breakfast in bed.'—*Otis Ferguson*
† *Anne of Windy Poplars*, with the same stars
and production team, followed in 1940.

Anne of the Indies*
US 1951   87m   Technicolor
TCF (George Jessel)

Lady pirate Anne Bonney, the terror of the
Caribbean, is at odds with her former master
Blackbeard.

Routine swashbuckler, generally well handled.

w Philip Dunne, Arthur Caesar *d* Jacques
Tourneur *ph* Harry Jackson *m* Franz
Waxman

Jean Peters, Louis Jourdan, Debra Paget,
Herbert Marshall, Thomas Gomez, James
Robertson Justice, Sean McClory, Francis
Pierlot

Anne of the Thousand Days*
GB 1969   146m   Technicolor
   Panavision
Universal / Hal B. Wallis

Henry VIII divorces his wife to marry Anne
Boleyn, but soon finds evidence of adultery.
A somewhat unlikely view of history, rather
boringly presented on a woman's magazine
level, but with occasional good moments from
a cast of British notables.

w John Hale, Bridget Boland, *play* Maxwell
Anderson *d* Charles Jarrott *ph* Arthur
Ibbetson *pd* Maurice Carter *m* Georges
Delerue

*Richard Burton, Geneviève Bujold, John
Colicos* (as Cromwell), Irene Papas, Anthony
Quayle, Michael Hordern, Katharine Blake,
Peter Jeffrey, William Squire, Esmond
Knight, Nora Swinburne
'The costumes, beautiful in themselves,
have that unconvincing air of having come
straight off the rack at Nathan's.'—*Brenda
Davies*
'A decent dullness is, alas, the keynote.'—
Michael Billington, Illustrated London News
'The quintessential work of art for people
who haven't the foggiest notion of what art
is.'—*John Simon*

AAN: best picture; John Hale, Bridget
Boland; Arthur Ibbetson; Georges Delerue;
Richard Burton; Geneviève Bujold; Anthony
Quayle

Annie Get Your Gun*
US 1950   107m   Technicolor
MGM (Arthur Freed)

A young female hillbilly joins Frank Butler's
sharpshooting act, and is sophisticated by her
love for him.
Gaudy, stagey, generally uninspired screen
version of the famous musical show based
remotely on a historical character of post-wild-
west days. There is a lack of dancing, the
direction is stodgy, and in general flair the
production falls disappointingly below MGM's
usual standard.

w Sidney Sheldon, *musical play* Herbert and
Dorothy Fields *d* George Sidney *ph* Charles

Rosher *m / ly Irving Berlin md* Adolph
Deutsch, Roger Edens *ch* Robert Alton
ad Cedric Gibbons, Paul Grosse

Betty Hutton, *Howard Keel*, Edward Arnold,
J. Carrol Naish, Louis Calhern

 AA: music direction
AAN: Charles Rosher
† The real Annie Oakley was born Phoebe
Ann Oakley Mozie in 1860, and died in 1926.
The role was to have been played by Judy
Garland, who was fired after displays of
temperament; also considered were Doris
Day, Judy Canova and Betty Garrett.

Annie Hall***
US 1977   93m   De Luxe
UA / Jack Rollins-Charles H. Joffe (Fred T.
 Gallo)

Against the neuroses of New York and Los
Angeles, a Jewish comedian has an affair with
a midwestern girl.
Semi-serious collage of jokes and bits of
technique, some of the former very funny and
some of the latter very successful. For no very
good reason it hit the box office spot and
turned its creator, of whom it is very typical,
from a minority performer to a superstar.

w Woody Allen, Marshall Brickman
d Woody Allen *ph* Gordon Willis *m* various
Woody Allen, Diane Keaton, Tony Roberts,
Carol Kane, Paul Simon, Shelly Duvall
 'The film's priceless vignettes about the
difficulties in chitchatting with strangers, the
awkward moments in family visits, and the
frequent breakdowns in communication and
failures in intimacy, its reminiscences about
the palpable horrors of growing up in
Brooklyn, and its comic encounters with
lobsters in the kitchen or spiders in the
bathroom, all seem like snapshots from Allen
and Keaton's own romance.'—*Les Keyser,
Hollywood in the Seventies*
† The narrative supposedly mirrors the real-
life affair of the stars, who separated before
the film came out. (Diane Keaton's family
name is Hall.)
AA: best picture; script; direction; Diane
Keaton
AAN: Woody Allen (as actor)

Annie Oakley*
US 1935   90m   bw
RKO (Cliff Reid)

The historical story, more or less, of the lady
later immortalized in *Annie Get Your Gun*.
Lively semi-western with good dialogue but
gluey plot development.

w Joel Sayre, John Twist *d George Stevens
ph* J. Roy Hunt *m* Alberto Columbo *ad* Van
Nest Polglase

Barbara Stanwyck, Preston Foster, Melvyn
Douglas, Moroni Olsen, Pert Kelton, Andy
Clyde, Chief Thunderbird

The Anniversary*
GB 1968   95m   Technicolor
Hammer (Jimmy Sangster)

A malevolent one-eyed widow will stop at
nothing to prevent her grown sons from
leaving the family orbit, and they meet each
year to mourn the death of the husband she
really hated.
Agreeable but over-talkative black comedy
with a splendid role for its star and some good
scattered moments, marred by a general lack
of style.

w Jimmy Sangster, *play Bill MacIlwraith
d* Roy Ward Baker *ph* Harry Waxman
m Philip Martell
Bette Davis, Jack Hedley, *James Cossins*,
Sheila Hancock, Elaine Taylor, Christian
Roberts, Timothy Bateson
 'Magisterially grotesque in elegantly tailored
eye-patch and exotic gown, she snaps out her
bitchy insults with all 57 varieties of relish.'—
MFB

Another Dawn
US 1937   73m   bw
Warner (Harry Joe Brown)

IP a British army post in Africa, a wife is torn
between duty and romance.
Absurdly sudsy melodrama, a potboiler for
stars between more important assignments.

w Laird Doyle *d* William Dieterle *ph* Tony
Gaudio *m* Erich Wolfgang Korngold
Errol Flynn, Kay Francis, Ian Hunter, Frieda
Inescort, Herbert Mundin
† In every Warner film where a cinema canopy
was shown, the title advertised was *Another
Dawn*, so its use here as an actual title is
presumably a piece of cynicism.

Another Fine Mess**
US 1930   30m   bw

On the run from a cop, Stan and Ollie
masquerade as master and maid. Elaborate
star comedy with spoken introduction instead
of titles; very satisfying but not quite vintage.
Laurel and Hardy, James Finlayson, Thelma
Todd, Charles Gerrard. Written by H. M.
Walker, from a sketch by Stan Laurel's father;
directed by James Parrott; for Hal Roach.

Another Language
US 1933   75m   bw
MGM (Walter Wanger)

A young wife does not fit in with her
husband's snobby family and falls in love with
his nephew.
Flat treatment of a dated play.

w Herman J. Mankiewicz, Gertrude Purcell,
Donald Ogden Stewart, play Rose Franken
d Edward H. Griffith ph Ray June

Helen Hayes, Robert Montgomery, John
Beal, Louise Closser Hale, Henry Travers,
Margaret Hamilton

Another Man, Another Chance
France / US 1977   132m   Eastmancolor
UA / Films 13 / Ariane (Alexandre
  Mnouchkine, George Dancigers)
French title: Un Autre Homme, une Autre
  Chance
aka: Another Man, Another Woman

A Yank vet and a French widow meet and fall
in love in the old west.
Pretty, overlong, rather enervating romance
with an unusual and not entirely convincing
setting.

wd Claude Lelouch ph Jacques Lefrançois
m Francis Lai

James Caan, Geneviève Bujold, Francis
Huster, Susan Tyrrell

Another Man's Poison*
GB 1951   89m   bw
Douglas Fairbanks Jnr / Daniel M. Angel

A lady novelist poisons her husband and lover,
then unwittingly takes a fatal dose herself.
Hysterical vehicle for a fading Hollywood star
reduced to repeating her tantrums in an
English studio on a low budget; she should
have stayed home, as should her director.

w Val Guest, play Deadlock by Leslie Sands
d Irving Rapper ph Robert Krasker m John
Greenwood

Bette Davis, Anthony Steel, Gary Merrill,
Emlyn Williams, Barbara Murray, Reginald
Beckwith, Edna Morris

'Barnstormers as rich and improbable as this
are rare . . . the general atmosphere takes one
back to 1935.'—Gavin Lambert
'Like reading Ethel M. Dell by flashes of
lightning.'—Frank Hauser

Another Part of the Forest*
US 1948   108m   bw
U-I (Jerry Bresler)

In the post-Civil War years, Marcus Hubbard
leads his family to worldly success by cheating

and the misuse of power; he lives to regret it,
as the children learn their lessons all too well.
This backwards sequel to The Little Foxes,
showing how the characters of that play got to
be their nasty selves, is quite absorbingly acted
but stagily presented, with plenty of care but
no style.

w Vladimir Pozner, play Lillian Hellman
d Michael Gordon ph Hal Mohr m Daniele
Amfitheatrof

Fredric March, Florence Eldridge, Ann Blyth,
Dan Duryea, Edmond O'Brien, John Dall

Another Shore*
GB 1948   77m   bw
Ealing (Hal Mason)

A young Irishman dreams of life in the South
Seas but gives up his fancies for love.
Curiously whimsical, artificial and
unconvincing comedy drama from a famous
studio, but not without its moments of
interest.

w Walter Meade, novel Kenneth Reddin
d Charles Crichton ph Douglas Slocombe
m Georges Auric

Robert Beatty, Stanley Holloway, Moira
Lister

Another Time, Another Place
GB 1958   98m   bw   Vistavision
Paramount / Kaydor (Lewis Allen, Smedley
  Aston)

During World War II an American
newspaperwoman has an affair with a British
war correspondent; when he is killed in action,
she consoles his widow.
Drippy romance, unsympathetically played
and artificially set in a Cornish village.

w Stanley Mann, novel Lenore Coffee
d Lewis Allen ph Jack Hildyard m Douglas
Gamley

Lana Turner, Barry Sullivan, Glynis Johns,
Sean Connery, Sidney James

Anthony Adverse*
US 1936   141m   bw
Warner (Henry Blanke)

Adventures of an ambitious young man in
early 19th-century America.
A rousing spectacle of its day, from a
bestselling novel, this award-winning movie
quickly dated and now seems very thin and
shadowy despite the interesting talents
involved.

w Sheridan Gibney, novel Hervey Allen
d Mervyn Le Roy ph Tony Gaudio ad Anton
Grot m Erich Wolfgang Korngold

Fredric March, Olivia de Havilland, Gale
Sondergaard, Edmund Gwenn, Claude Rains,
Anita Louise, Louis Hayward, Steffi Duna,
Donald Woods, Akim Tamiroff, Ralph
Morgan, Henry O'Neill
'A bulky, rambling and indecisive photoplay
which has not merely taken liberties with the
letter of the original but with its spirit.'—
Frank S. Nugent, New York Times
'In the dramatizing there is shown no relish
or conviction, only a retentive memory for all
the old clothes of show business.'—*Otis
Ferguson*
'A lavish gold-leaf from Hervey Allen's
book, an earnest cinema endeavour, taxing
alike its studio's purse and artistry.'—*Douglas
Gilbert, New York World Telegraph*
'The show is fairly glutted with plot and
counter-plot and is apt to make one feel that
one is witnessing a serial run off continuously
at a single performance.'—*Howard Barnes,
New York Herald Tribune*
'It goes on too long, otherwise it might have
been the funniest film since *The Crusades*.'—
Graham Greene

AA: Tony Gaudio; Erich Wolfgang Korngold;
Gale Sondergaard
AAN: best picture

Antoine et Antoinette*
France 1947   87m   bw
SNEG

A young married couple find they have won a
lottery but lost the ticket.
A bubbly soufflé, most expertly served but
leaving one still a little hungry; not quite in the
Clair class.

w Françoise Giroud, M. Griffe, Jacques
Becker d Jacques Becker ph Pierre
Montazel m Jean-Jacques Grunenwald

Roger Pigaut, Clair Maffei

Antony and Cleopatra*
GB 1972   170m   Technicolor
Todd-AO 35
Transac (Zurich) / Izaro (Madrid) / Folio
Films (London)   (Peter Snell)

Well-meaning, well-mounted, but quite
uninspired rendering.

wd Charlton Heston, *play* William
Shakespeare ph Rafael Pacheco m John
Scott pd Maurice Pelling

Charlton Heston, Hildegarde Neil, Eric
Porter, *John Castle* (as Octavius), Fernando
Rey, Freddie Jones, Peter Arne, Roger
Delgado

Any Number Can Play*
US 1949   103m   bw
MGM (Arthur Freed)

A gambling casino owner has health problems,
is reconciled with his son and retires from the
game.
Rather boring drama redeemed by slightly
offbeat dialogue and excellent star acting,
albeit in routine roles.

w Richard Brooks, *novel* E. H. Heth
d Mervyn Le Roy ph Harold Rosson
m Lennie Hayton

Clark Gable, Alexis Smith, Mary Astor,
Wendell Corey, Audrey Totter, Lewis Stone,
Frank Morgan, *Marjorie Rambeau*, Barry
Sullivan

Any Old Port*
US 1932   20m   bw

Stan and Ollie are sailors on leave, and Ollie
enters Stan for a boxing match. Minor star
comedy with good moments but a weak finish.
Laurel and Hardy, Walter Long. Written by
H. M. Walker; directed by James W. Horne;
for Hal Roach.

Any Wednesday*
US 1966   109m   Technicolor
Warner (Julius J. Epstein)
GB title: *Bachelor Girl Apartment*

A millionaire businessman spends every
Wednesday with his mistress, but
complications arise when his young associate is
accidentally sent to use the company flat.
Overlong screen version of a thinly scripted
Broadway success in which yawns gradually
overtake laughs.

w Julius J. Epstein, *play* Muriel Resnik
d Robert Ellis Miller ph Harold Lipstein
m George Duning

Jane Fonda, Dean Jones, Jason Robards Jnr,
Rosemary Murphy (a breath of air as the
deceived wife who doesn't mind), Ann
Prentiss, King Moody

Any Which Way You Can
US 1980   116m   De Luxe

The hero of *Every Which Way But Loose*
becomes involved in further brawls and car
crashes, with the help of his friendly orang-
utan. A sequel designed entirely for the box
office, its tone set by the scene in which the
villains on motorcycles are covered in tar.
Clint Eastwood, Ruth Gordon, Sondra Locke,
Geoffrey Lewis, William Smith, Harry
Guardino. Written by Stanford Sherman;

directed by Buddy Van Horn; for Malpaso /
Warner. 'This kind of thing is clearly beyond
or beneath criticism.'—*Variety*.

Anything Can Happen*
US 1952   93m   bw
Paramount / William Perlberg, George
  Seaton

Adventures of a Russian immigrant family in
New York.
A standard Hollywood product based on a
sentimental best-seller.

w George Seaton, George Oppenheimer,
book George and Helen Papashvily *d* George
Seaton *ph* Daniel L. Fapp *m* Victor Young

Jose Ferrer, Kim Hunter, Kurt Kasznar, Alex
Danaroff, Oscar Beregi
  'Exploits to the hilt the somewhat limited
possibilities of quaintness and whimsicality
with a broken accent.'—*Penelope Houston*

Anything Goes**
US 1936   92m   bw
Paramount (Benjamin Glazer)
TV title: *Tops is the Limit*

Romantic adventures on board a transatlantic
liner.
Amiably batty musical comedy, zestfully
directed and blithely performed.

w Guy Bolton, P. G. Wodehouse, Howard
Lindsay, Russell Crouse, from their Broadway
show *d* Lewis Milestone *ph* Karl Struss
songs Cole Porter *md* Victor Young *ad* Hans
Dreier

Bing Crosby, Ethel Merman, Charles Ruggles,
Grace Bradley, Ida Lupino, Chill Wills, the
Avalon Boys, Arthur Treacher

Anything Goes*
US 1956   106m   Technicolor
  Vistavision
Paramount (Robert Emmett Dolan)

The male stars of a musical comedy each sign
a girl to play the female lead; resulting
complications are ironed out during a
transatlantic voyage.
Below-par reworking of the 1936 film in which
technical gloss and dull sets virtually reduce
the characters to puppets. A few good
moments transcend the general lack of
imagination.

w Sidney Sheldon, from show as credited in
1936 version *d* Robert Lewis *ph* John F.
Warren *songs* Cole Porter *md* Joseph J.
Lilley *ch* Nick Castle, Roland Petit *ad* Hal
Pereira, Joseph M. Johnson

Bing Crosby, Donald O'Connor, Zizi
Jeanmaire, Mitzi Gaynor, Phil Harris, Kurt
Kasznar

Anzio
Italy 1968   117m   Technicolor
  Panavision
(Columbia) Dino de Laurentiis (Marcel
  Bebert)
GB title: *The Battle for Anzio*

A war correspondent joins American and
British troops preparing for the 1944 landing
in Italy.
Threadbare war film which wastes an all-star
American cast.

w H. A. L. Craig, *book* Anzio by Wynford
Vaughan Thomas *d* Edward Dmytryk
ph Giuseppe Rotunno *m* Riz Ortolani

Robert Mitchum, Peter Falk, Arthur
Kennedy, Robert Ryan, Earl Holliman, Mark
Damon, Reni Santoni, Anthony Steel, Patrick
Magee
  'It must be a long time since a script
managed to pack in so many crassly
portentous statements about why men fight
wars.'—*MFB*

Apache*
US 1954   91m   Technicolor
UA / Hecht–Lancaster (Harold Hecht)

After the surrender of Geronimo, one Apache
leader is unconquered; after creating much
havoc, he settles for domesticity, and the
white men let him go unharmed.
Sober western in the wake of *Broken Arrow*,
with a predictably sympathetic star
performance and a surprising happy ending.
More decency than excitement along the way.

w James R. Webb, *novel* Bronco Apache by
Paul I. Wellman *d* Robert Aldrich *ph* Ernest
Laszlo *m* David Raksin

Burt Lancaster, Jean Peters, John McIntire,
Charles Bronson, John Dehner, Paul
Guilfoyle, Walter Sande, Monte Blue

Apache Drums
US 1951   75m   Technicolor
U-I (Val Lewton)

A gambler helps a town under Indian attack.
Standard co-feature western, perfectly
adequate but showing no sign of its producer's
former tastes and skills.

w David Chandler *d* Hugo Fregonese
ph Charles Boyle *m* Hans Salter

Stephen McNally, Willard Parker, Coleen
Gray, Arthur Shields, James Griffith

Apache Uprising
US 1965   90m   Techniscope
Paramount / A. C. Lyles

Assorted passengers in a stagecoach survive an Indian attack at a way station.
It sounds like a remake, and almost is, but the handling is lively enough and the producer's usual cast of nostalgic stars is in evidence.

w Harry Sanford, Max Lamb d R. G. Springsteen ph W. Wallace Kelley m Jimmie Haskell

Rory Calhoun, Corinne Calvet, John Russell, Lon Chaney Jnr, Gene Evans, DeForest Kelley, Arthur Hunnicutt, Richard Arlen, Johnny Mack Brown, Jean Parker

Aparajito***
India 1956   113m   bw
Epic Films Private Ltd (Satyajit Ray)
aka: The Unvanquished

After his father's death, a poor country boy is helped by his mother to study for the university.
A detailed and moving study of two characters who are universally familiar despite an unusual background.

wd Satyajit Ray ph Subrata Mitra m Ravi Shankar

Pinaki Sen Gupta, Karuna Banerjee, Kanu Banerjee

The Apartment**
US 1960   125m   bw   Panavision
UA / Mirisch (Billy Wilder)

A lonely, ambitious clerk rents out his apartment to philandering executives and finds that one of them is after his own girl.
Overlong and patchy but agreeably mordant and cynical comedy with a sparkling view of city office life and some deftly handled individual sequences.

w Billy Wilder, I. A. L. Diamond d Billy Wilder ph Joseph La Shelle m Adolph Deutsch ad Alexander Trauner

Jack Lemmon, Shirley Maclaine, Fred MacMurray, Ray Walston, Jack Kruschen, Edie Adams, David Lewis
  'Without either style or taste, shifting gears between pathos and slapstick without any transition.'—Dwight MacDonald
  'Billy Wilder directed this acrid story as if it were a comedy, which is a cheat, considering that it involves pimping and a suicide attempt and many shades of craven ethics.'—New Yorker, 1980

AA: best picture; Billy Wilder, I. A. L. Diamond (as writers); Billy Wilder (as director)

AAN: Joseph La Shelle; Jack Lemmon; Shirley Maclaine; Jack Kruschen

Apartment for Peggy*
US 1948   98m   Technicolor
TCF (William Perlberg)

A retired professor finds a new lease of life through caring for the homeless family of an ex-GI.
Sentimental comedy with serious undertones (the professor twice attempts suicide). Signs of enterprise are smothered by regulation charm.

wd George Seaton, story Faith Baldwin ph Harry Jackson m David Raksin

Edmund Gwenn, Jeanne Crain, William Holden, Gene Lockhart, Henri Letondal, Charles Lane, Houseley Stevenson
  'A first rate experience for observers with comprehending minds.'—Bosley Crowther, New York Times

The Ape
US 1940   61m   bw
Monogram (Scott R. Dunlop)

Dr Adrian seeks to cure polio by means of a serum which can only be obtained from the spinal fluid of a human being. He kills an escaped ape and dresses in its skin to seek victims.
Silly and rather boring addition to the mad doctor cycle.

w Curt Siodmak, Richard Carroll, play Adam Shirk d William Nigh ph Harry Neumann m Edward Kay

Boris Karloff, Maris Wrixon, Gertrude Hoffman, Henry Hall

The Ape Man
US 1943   64m   bw
Monogram (Sam Katzman, Jack Dietz)
GB title: Lock Your Doors

A scientist injects himself with spinal fluid which turns him into an ape creature.
Cheap rubbish shot in a couple of corners and offering no thrill whatever.

w Barney A. Sarecky, story They Creep in the Dark by Karl Brown d William Beaudine ph Mack Stengler m Edward Kay

Bela Lugosi, Wallace Ford, Louise Currie, Minerva Urecal
† A supposed sequel the following year, Return of the Ape Man, had in fact no plot connection. In this Lugosi thawed out a neanderthal man, inserted John Carradine's brain, and the composite turned into George Zucco!

Apocalypse Now**
US 1979   153m   Technicolor
Technovision
Omni Zoetrope (Francis Coppola)

A Vietnam captain is instructed to eliminate a
colonel who has retired to the hills and is
fighting his own war.

Pretentious war movie, made even more
hollow-sounding by the incomprehensible
performance of Brando as the mad martinet.
Some vivid scenes along the way, and some
interesting parallels with Conrad's *Heart of
Darkness*, but these hardly atone for the
director's delusion that prodigal expenditure
of time and money will result in great art.
(The movie took so long to complete that it
was dubbed *Apocalypse Later*.)

w John Milius, Francis Coppola *d* Francis
Coppola *ph* Vittorio Storaro *m* Carmine
Coppola, Francis Coppola *pd* Dean
Tavoularis

Martin Sheen, Robert Duvall, Frederic
Forrest, Marlon Brando, Sam Bottoms,
Dennis Hopper

'The characters are living through Vietnam
as pulp adventure fantasy, as movie, as stoned
humour.'—*New Yorker*

† Coppola admitted the following at the
Cannes Film Festival: 'It's more of an
experience than a movie. At the beginning
there's a story. Along the river the story
becomes less important and the experience
more important.'

The Appaloosa*
US 1966   99m   Techniscope
Universal (Alan Miller)
GB title: *Southwest to Sonora*

A cowboy's plan to start a stud farm with his
magnificent horse is interrupted by badmen
who think he has molested their girl.

Mannered, slow western set on the Mexican
border, with star and director apparently
striving to upstage each other.

w James Bridges, Roland Kibbee, *novel*
Robert MacLeod *d* Sidney J. Furie
ph Russell Metty m Frank Skinner

Marlon Brando, Anjanette Comer, John
Saxon, Rafael Campos, Frank Silvera

'Seems intent less on telling a story than in
carving out the incidental details.'—*MFB*

'The camerawork concentrates on beady
eyes, sweaty foreheads, spurred boots and
anonymous midriffs being studied through a
variety of frames, ranging from tequila bottles
to cook fires to grillwork to fingers to feet.'—
Judith Crist

Applause***
US 1929   78m   bw
Paramount (Jesse L. Lasky, Walter Wanger)

A vaudeville star gradually loses the love of
her daughter.

Absorbing treatment of a hasbeen tearjerking
theme, full of cinematic touches and with
unusual use of New York locations.

w Garrett Fort, *novel* Beth Brown *d Rouben
Mamoulian ph* George Folscy

Helen Morgan, Joan Peers, Henry
Wadsworth, Fuller Mellish Jnr

'An oasis of filmic sophistication in a desert
of stage-bound early talkies.'—*William
Everson, 1966*

'A cohesive, well integrated series of
pictures. Its intensity, its sharp projection of
tragedy, emerge from the eye of the camera;
an omniscient, omnipresent eye that slides
easily over the links of the story and
emphasizes only the true and the relevant.'—
Thornton Delehanty, The Arts

The Apple Dumpling Gang
US 1974   100m   Technicolor
Walt Disney (Bill Anderson)

Three orphan children strike gold in 1878
California.

Better-than-average Disney romp.

w Don Tait, *novel* Jack M. Bickham
d Norman Tokar *ph* Frank Phillips *m* Buddy
Baker

Bill Bixby, Susan Clark, David Wayne, Don
Knotts, Tim Conway, Slim Pickens, Harry
Morgan, John McGiver, Marie Windsor, Iris
Adrian

† *The Apple Dumpling Gang Rides Again*, a
shoddy sequel under the direction of Vincent
McEveety, appeared in 1979 with fragments of
the old cast but no panache.

The Appointment*
US 1969   100m   colour
MGM (Martin Poll)

A businessman suspects his wife of spare time
prostitution.

Unusual sophisticated fable, dressed to kill but
rather stretched out for its substance. Shades
of *El* and *The Chinese Room*.

w James Salter *d* Sidney Lumet *m* John
Barry, Don Walker

Omar Sharif, Anouk Aimée, Lotte Lenya

Appointment for Love*
US 1941   89m   bw
Universal

A doctor and a playwright agree to marry
'without love'.

A familiar theme quite amusingly explored by a practised cast.

w Bruce Manning, Felix Jackson d William A. Seiter ph Joseph Valentine m Frank Skinner, Charles Previn

Charles Boyer, Margaret Sullavan, Eugene Pallette, Rita Johnson, Gus Schilling, Reginald Denny, Ruth Terry

Appointment in Berlin

US 1943 77m bw
Columbia (Sam Bischoff)

An RAF wing commander expresses unpopular views and is recruited by the Nazis as a 'voice of truth' broadcaster.
World War II potboiler.

w Horace McCoy, Michael Hogan d Alfred E. Green ph Franz Planer m Werner Heymann

George Sanders, Marguerite Chapman, Gale Sondergaard, Onslow Stevens, Alan Napier, H. P. Sanders (the star's father)

Appointment in Honduras

US 1953 79m Technicolor print
RKO / Benedict Bogeaus

Three assorted types and four criminals escape through the jungle from a revolution.
Predictable adventure drama sabotaged by poor colour.

w Karen deWolf d Jacques Tourneur ph Joseph Biroc m Louis Forbes

Glenn Ford, Ann Sheridan, Zachary Scott, Rodolfo Acosta, Jack Elam

Appointment in London*

GB 1952 96m bw
Mayflower (Aubrey Baring, Maxwell Setton)

The exploits of a squadron of Bomber Command during one month in 1943.
Dullish war film with standard credits.

w John Wooldridge, Robert Westerby d Philip Leacock ph Stephen Dade m John Wooldridge

Dirk Bogarde, Ian Hunter, Dinah Sheridan, Bill Kerr, Bryan Forbes, William Sylvester, Charles Victor

Appointment with Crime

GB 1945 97m bw

Ex-convict revenges himself on the former friends who shopped him. Stodgy melodrama which seemed about to make a big star of William Hartnell. Robert Beatty, Joyce Howard, Raymond Lovell, Herbert Lom. Written and directed by John Harlow; for British National.

Appointment with Danger*

US 1949 89m bw
Paramount (Robert Fellows)

A nun becomes the government's chief witness in identifying the murderers of a US postal inspector.
Routine but entertaining star thick-ear.

w Richard Breen, Warren Duff d Lewis Allen ph John Seitz m Victor Young

Alan Ladd, Phyllis Calvert, Paul Stewart, Jan Sterling, Jack Webb, Henry Morgan

Appointment with a Shadow

US 1958 72m bw Cinemascope

An alcoholic reporter redeems himself by capturing a criminal single-handed. Maudlin melodrama which takes itself too seriously.
George Nader, Joanna Moore, Brian Keith, Virginia Field. Written by Alec Coppel and Norman Jolley; directed by Richard Carlson; for Universal-International. (GB title: *The Big Story*.)

Appointment with Venus**

GB 1951 89m bw
GFD / British Film Makers (Betty E. Box)
US title: *Island Rescue*

During World War II, a pedigree cow is rescued from the German-occupied Channel Islands.
Curious but generally agreeable mixture of comedy and war adventure, pleasantly shot on Sark.

w Nicholas Phipps, *novel* Jerrard Tickell d Ralph Thomas ph Ernest Steward m Benjamin Frankel

David Niven, Glynis Johns, George Coulouris, Barry Jones, Kenneth More, Noel Purcell, Bernard Lee, Jeremy Spenser

The Apprenticeship of Duddy Kravitz*

Canada 1974 121m Bellevue–Pathe Panavision
Duddy Kravitz Syndicate (Gerald Schneider)

An ambitious young Jew finds that it is best to be liked.
Amusing adventures of an anti-hero; good scenes but rather patchy technique.

w Mordecai Richler, from his novel d Ted Kotcheff ph Miklos Lente m Stanley Myers

Richard Dreyfuss, Micheline Lanctot, Jack Warden, Randy Quaid, Denholm Elliott, Joseph Wiseman

AAN: Mordecai Richler

The April Fools*
US 1969 95m Technicolor Panavision
Cinema Center / Jalem (Gordon Carroll)

An unhappy New York husband elopes to
Paris with an unhappy wife.
Whimsical romantic comedy which rather
strains its resources without giving full value
for money in romance, humour or simple
charm. Good moments, though.

w Hal Dresner d Stuart Rosenberg
ph Michel Hugo m Marvin Hamlisch
pd Richard Sylbert

Jack Lemmon, Catherine Deneuve, Myrna
Loy, Charles Boyer, Peter Lawford, Jack
Weston, Harvey Korman, Sally Kellerman
   'Painfully modish, from the opening party in
an apartment filled with fashionable objets
d'art to the final mad dash to the airport in an
expensive sports car.'—MFB

April in Paris*
US 1952 100m Technicolor
Warner (William Jacobs)

A chorus girl is mistakenly invited to a US
Arts Festival in Paris, and bewitches the
bureaucrat in charge.
Poorly produced star musical with a thin plot
and a few redeeming wisps of wit.

w Jack Rose, Melville Shavelson d David
Butler ph Wilfrid Cline md Ray Heindorf
ch Le Roy Prinz songs Sammy Cahn, Vernon
Duke, E. Y. Harburg

Doris Day, Ray Bolger, Claude Dauphin, Eve
Miller, George Givot

April Love
US 1957 99m Eastmancolor
   Cinemascope
TCF (David Weisbart)

For stealing a car, a teenager is sent on
probation to his uncle's stud farm, where
circumstances seem once again to put him in
trouble with the law.
Easygoing star vehicle with little to
recommend it to adults.

w Winston Miller, novel George Agnew
Chamberlain d Henry Levin ph Wilfrid
Cline songs Sammy Fain, Paul Francis
Webster

Pat Boone, Shirley Jones, Dolores Michaels,
Arthur O'Connell, Jeanette Nolan
† A remake of Home in Indiana.

AAN: title song (m Sammy Fain, ly Paul
Francis Webster)

April Showers*
US 1948 94m bw
Warner (William Jacobs)

In a family vaudeville act, Dad takes to drink.
Hoary musical melodrama enlivened by
occasional acts.

w Peter Milne d James V. Kern ph Carl
Guthrie md Ray Heindorf m adaptation Max
Steiner songs various

Jack Carson, Robert Alda, Ann Sothern,
Robert Ellis, S. Z. Sakall

The Arab see The Barbarian

Arabella
US / Italy 1969 91m Technicolor

A female confidence trickster needs the money
to pay her grandmother's back taxes. Floppy,
tedious comedy adventure with an
international cast all at sea. Virna Lisi, James
Fox, Terry-Thomas, Margaret Rutherford.
Written by Adriano Barocco; directed by
Mauro Bolognini; for Cram Film / Universal.

Arabesque**
US 1966 118m Technicolor
   Panavision
Universal (Stanley Donen)

An Oxford professor is asked by Middle
Eastern oil magnates to decipher a
hieroglyphic, and finds afterwards that he is
marked for assassination.
The ultimate in sixties spy kaleidoscopes, in
which the working out of the plot matters
much less than the stars, the jokes and the
lavish backgrounds. Fast moving, amusing and
utterly forgettable.

w Julian Mitchell, Stanley Price, Pierre
Marton, novel The Cipher by Gordon Votler
d Stanley Donen ph Christopher Challis
ad Reece Pemberton m Henry Mancini

Gregory Peck, Sophia Loren, Alan Badel,
Kieron Moore, Carl Duering
   'Nothing could look more "with it", or
somehow matter less.'—MFB
   'A strikingly visual chase and intrigue
yarn.'—Robert Windeler
   'All rather too flashy for comfort.'—Sight
and Sound
† Pierre Marton was a pen name for Peter
Stone.

Arabian Adventure
GB 1979 98m colour
Badger Films / John Dark

The dictator of Jadur promises his daughter's
hand in marriage if a young prince will seek
and find a magic rose.
Artless juggling of elements from The Thief of
Baghdad, including magic carpets, monsters
and a bottle djinn.

w Brian Hayles *d* Kevin Connor *ph* Alan Hume *m* Ken Thorne *pd* Elliot Scott

Christopher Lee, Oliver Tobias, Mickey Rooney, Milo O'Shea, Elizabeth Welch, Peter Cushing, Capucine

'Resolutely well mounted, but somehow lacking that necessary fillip of Hollywood vulgarity or exuberance.'—*John Pym, MFB*

Arabian Nights*
US 1942 86m Technicolor
Universal (Walter Wanger)

The Caliph of Baghdad is deposed by his half-brother but wins back his throne with the help of a dancer and an acrobat.
Well presented oriental adventure which has nothing to do with its source material but entertained multitudes in search of relief from total war and was followed by several vaguely similar slices of hokum with the same stars.

w Michael Hogan *d John Rawlins ph* Milton Krasner, William V. Skall, W. Howard Greene *m* Frank Skinner

Jon Hall, Maria Montez, Sabu, Leif Erickson, Thomas Gomez, Turhan Bey, John Qualen, Billy Gilbert, Shemp Howard

AAN: Milton Krasner, William V. Skall, W. Howard Greene; Frank Skinner

Arch of Triumph*
US 1948 120m bw
Enterprise (Lewis Milestone)

In postwar Paris, an embittered refugee seeks his former Nazi tormentor and has a tragic romance with a would-be suicide.
Doleful, set-bound melodrama knee-deep in misery and artificial melodramatics. An expensive, ambitious failure, both commercially and artistically, but an interesting one.

w Lewis Milestone, Harry Brown, *novel* Erich Maria Remarque *d* Lewis Milestone *ph* Russell Metty *m* Leonard Gruenberg *md* Morris Stoloff

Ingrid Bergman, Charles Boyer, Charles Laughton, Louis Calhern

Are Husbands Necessary?
US 1942 79m bw
Paramount

A bickering couple decide to adopt a baby.
Mild marital comedy in a familiar mould.

w Tess Slesinger, Frank Davis, *novel* Mr and Mrs Cugat by Isabel Scott Rorick *d* Norman Taurog *ph* Charles Lang *m* Robert Emmett Dolan

Ray Milland, Betty Field, Patricia Morison, Eugene Pallette, Charles Dingle, Cecil Kellaway, Leif Erickson, Richard Haydn, Elizabeth Risdon

'A chaos of farcical situations, conceived without gusto and played without conviction.'—*Richard Mallett, Punch*

Are You Being Served?
GB 1977 95m Technicolor
EMI (Andrew Mitchell)

The staff of the clothing section of a department store go on holiday to the Costa Plonka.
Feeble enlargement of an old-fashioned but very popular TV series relying heavily on sexual badinage and ancient jokes.

w Jeremy Lloyd, David Croft *d* Bob Kellett *ph* Jack Atcheler *m* various

John Inman, Frank Thornton, Mollie Sugden, Trevor Bannister, Wendy Richard, Arthur Brough, Nicholas Smith, Arthur English, Harold Bennett, Glyn Houston

'A withering selection of patent British puns.'—*John Pym, MFB*

Are You With It?*
US 1948 90m bw
Universal-International (Robert Arthur)

An insurance executive with doubts joins a fun fair and has a whale of a time.
Pleasantly lively low-budget musical.

w Oscar Brodney, *musical comedy* Sam Perrin, George Balzer *d* Jack Hively *ph* Maury Gertsman *md* Walter Scharf *songs* Sidney Miller, Inez James

Donald O'Connor, Olga San Juan, Martha Stewart, Lew Parker

Arena
US 1953 83m Anscocolor 3-D
MGM (Arthur M. Loew Jnr)

A rodeo rider regains his wife and his sense when his best friend is killed.
Routine actioner, distinguished by 3-D camerawork.

w Harold Jack Bloom *d* Richard Fleischer *ph* Paul C. Vogel *m* Rudolph G. Kopp

Gig Young, Jean Hagen, Polly Bergen, Henry Morgan, Barbara Lawrence, Robert Horton, Lee Van Cleef

Aren't Men Beasts!*
GB 1937 66m bw
BIP (Walter Mycroft)

A dentist poses as his aunt to stop a plot to prevent his son's marriage.
Archetypal British star farce.

w Marjorie Deans, William Freshman, *play* Vernon Sylvaine *d* Graham Cutts

Robertson Hare, Alfred Drayton, June Clyde, Billy Milton, Judy Kelly

Argentine Nights
US 1940 75m bw

The Ritz Brothers and the Andrews Sisters head for Argentina to avoid their creditors. Fair low-budget musical. Written by Arthur Horman, Ray Golden and Sid Kuller; directed by Albert S. Rogell; for Universal.

Arise My Love***
US 1940 113m bw
Paramount (Arthur Hornblow Jnr)

American reporters in Europe and in love survive the Spanish Civil War, a wrathful editor in Paris and the sinking of the *Athenia*. Unique sophisticated entertainment gleaned from the century's grimmest headlines, ending with a plea against American isolationism. A significant and stylish comedy melodrama.

w Charles Brackett, Billy Wilder d Mitchell Leisen ph Charles Lang m Victor Young

Claudette Colbert, Ray Milland, Walter Abel (who as the harassed editor inaugurated his celebrated line 'I'm not happy. I'm not happy at all . . .'), Dennis O'Keefe, George Zucco, Dick Purcell

AA: original story (Benjamin Glazer, John S. Toldy)
AAN: Charles Lang; Victor Young

The Aristocats**
US 1970 78m Technicolor
Walt Disney

Two cats are deliberately lost by a butler who fears they will inherit their mistress's wealth; but a variety of animal friends restore them to their rightful place.
Cartoon feature, a moderate example of the studio's work after Disney's death, with rather too few felicitous moments.

d Wolfgang Reitherman

Arizona
US 1941 125m bw
Columbia (Wesley Ruggles)

A Tucson wildcat meets her match in a travelling Missourian who helps her outwit villains who are sabotaging her wagon trains. Loosely built, deliberately paced western which for all its pretensions makes very little impact.

w Claude Binyon *d* Wesley Ruggles
ph Joseph Walker, Harry Hollenberger, Fayte Brown *m* Victor Young

Jean Arthur, William Holden, Warren William, Porter Hall, Paul Harvey, George Chandler, Byron Foulger, Regis Toomey, Edgar Buchanan

'Lacks the sweep and dramatic impulse that would have made it a great picture.'—*Variety*

AAN: Victor Young

Arizona Bushwhackers
US 1968 86m Techniscope
Paramount (A. C. Lyles)

A Confederate prisoner is given a chance as a western sheriff.
Stolid western, notable only, as is usual with this producer, for its gallery of ageing but still reliable familiar faces.

w Steve Fisher *d* Lesley Selander *ph* Lester Shorr *m* Jimmie Haskell

Howard Keel, Yvonne de Carlo, Brian Donlevy, John Ireland, Marilyn Maxwell, Scott Brady, Barton Maclane, James Craig

The Arkansas Traveller
US 1938 85m bw

A small-town widow is helped to keep her newspaper going by a stranger who happens to be passing through. Archetypal mid-American fantasy. Bob Burns, Fay Bainter, Jean Parker, Irvin S. Cobb. Written by Viola Brothers Shore, George Sessions Perry, from a story by Jack Cunningham; directed by Alfred Santell; for Paramount.

Armored Car Robbery*
US 1950 67m bw
RKO (Herman Schlom)

A police lieutenant leads the recovery of half a million dollars stolen by gangsters.
Good competent second feature with Los Angeles locations and detailed observation of police methods.

w Earl Felton, Gerald Drayson Adams
d Richard Fleischer *ph* Guy Roe
m Constantin Bakaleinikoff

Charles McGraw, Adele Jergens, William Talman, Douglas Fowley, Steve Brodie

Armored Command
US 1961 105m bw
Allied Artists (Ron W. Alcorn)

During the Battle of the Bulge, a ravishing Nazi spy is infiltrated into an American army outpost.
Incredible Mata Hari melodrama posing as a war film, nicely shot in bleak snowscapes. Not exactly rewarding, but unusual.

w Ron W. Alcorn *d* Byron Haskin *ph* Ernest Haller *m* Bert Grund

Howard Keel, Tina Louise, Burt Reynolds,
Earl Holliman, Warner Anderson, Carleton
Young, Marty Ingels

Arms and the Man
GB 1932   85m   bw

A soldier who finds discretion the better part
of valour hides in a girl's bedroom. Faithful
but uninspired version of Bernard Shaw's play.
Barry Jones, Anne Grey, Angela Baddeley.
Directed by Cecil Lewis; for BIP / Wardour.

The Arnelo Affair
US 1946   86m   bw

Lawyer's wife gets involved with nightclub
owner. Yawnworthy murder melodrama.
George Murphy, Frances Gifford, John
Hodiak, Eve Arden. Written and directed by
Arch Oboler; for MGM.

Arnold
US 1973   95m   De Luxe
Avco / Fenady (Charles A. Pratt, Andrew
  Fenady)

Via cassette recordings, a dead man toys with
his would-be heirs, and several are murdered.
Unpleasant and very laboured black comedy
on the lines of *And Then There Were None*
and a hundred others, all better than this.

w Jameson Brewer, John Fenton Murray
d Georg Fenady *ph* William Jurgenson
m George Duning

Stella Stevens, Roddy McDowell, Elsa
Lanchester, Shani Wallis, Farley Granger,
Victor Buono, John McGiver, Bernard Fox,
Patric Knowles

† Apparently made back to back with *Terror
in the Wax Museum*, which has very similar
credits.

Around the World
US 1943   81m   bw
RKO (Allan Dwan)

Kay Kyser's band goes on a world tour to
entertain troops overseas.
Typical wartime patriotic musical, now of
sociological interest.

w Ralph Spence *d* Allan Dwan *ph* Russell
Metty *md* Constantin Bakaleinikoff
m George Duning

Kay Kyser, Ish Kabibble, Ginny Simms, Joan
Davis, Mischa Auer

Around the World in Eighty Days***
US 1956   178m   Technicolor   Todd-AO
UA / *Michael Todd*

A Victorian gentleman and his valet win a bet
that they can go round the world in eighty
days.
Amiable large-scale pageant resolving itself
into a number of sketches, which could have
been much sharper, separated by wide screen
spectacle. What was breathtaking at the time
seems generally slow and blunted in
retrospect, but the fascination of recognizing
44 cameo stars remains. The film is less an
exercise in traditional skills than a tribute to its
producer's energy.

w James Poe, John Farrow, S. J. Perelman,
novel Jules Verne *d* Michael Anderson,
Kevin McClory *ph* Lionel Lindon *m* Victor
Young *titles* Saul Bass

David Niven, Cantinflas, Robert Newton,
Shirley Maclaine, Charles Boyer, Joe E.
Brown, Martine Carol, John Carradine,
Charles Coburn, *Ronald Colman*, Melville
Cooper, *Noel Coward*, Finlay Currie,
Reginald Denny, Andy Devine, Marlene
Dietrich, Luis Dominguin, Fernandel, *John
Gielgud*, Hermione Gingold, Jose Greco,
Cedric Hardwicke, Trevor Howard, Glynis
Johns, *Buster Keaton*, Evelyn Keyes, Beatrice
Lillie, Peter Lorre, Edmund Lowe, A. E.
Matthews, Mike Mazurki, Tim McCoy, Victor
McLaglen, John Mills, Alan Mowbray, Robert
Morley, Jack Oakie, George Raft, Gilbert
Roland, Cesar Romero, Frank Sinatra, *Red
Skelton*, Ronald Squire, Basil Sidney,
Harcourt Williams, Ed Murrow

'Michael Todd's "show", shorn of the
ballyhoo and to critics not mollified by parties
and sweetmeats, is a film like any other, only
twice as long as most . . . the shots of trains
and boats seem endless.'—*David Robinson*

AA: best picture; James Poe, John Farrow, S.
J. Perelman; Lionel Lindon; Victor Young
AAN: Michael Anderson

Around the World under the Sea
US 1966   110m   Metrocolor   Panavision
MGM / Ivan Tors (Andrew Marton)

An ultra-modern underwater craft travels
around the seabed fixing sensors to give early
warning of volcanoes.
Earnest, dullish, elementary sci-fi with
cardboard characters providing routine five
men-one woman skirmishes.

w Arthur Weiss, Art Arthur *d* Andrew
Marton, Ricou Browning *ph* Clifford Poland,
Lamar Boren *m* Harry Sukman

Lloyd Bridges, Shirley Eaton, Brian Kelly,
David McCallum, Keenan Wynn, Marshall
Thompson, Gary Merrill

The Arrangement**
US 1969   127m   Technicolor
Panavision
Warner / Athena (Elia Kazan)

A wealthy advertising man fails in a suicide attempt and spends his convalescence reflecting on his unsatisfactory emotional life.
A lush, all-American melodrama, rich in technique but peopled by characters who have nothing to say; the film makes no discernible point except as a well-acted tirade against the compromises of modern urban living.

wd Elia Kazan, from his own novel *ph Robert Surtees m* David Amram *pd* Malcolm C. Bert

Kirk Douglas, Faye Dunaway, Deborah Kerr, Richard Boone, Hume Cronyn
'The sort of collage that won't fit together, no matter where you stand.'—*PS*
'As dead as a flower arrangement in an undertaker's parlour . . . all possible cinematic clevernesses—usually yesterday's—are dragged out in an endless parade, to illustrate a senseless and banal story that reels from platitude to platitude.'—*John Simon*

Arrowhead
US 1953   105m   Technicolor   3D
Paramount (Nat Holt)

Enmity between an army scout and an Indian chief is resolved by single combat.
Standard western, good-looking but rather lifeless.

w Charles Marquis Warren, *novel* W. R. Burnett *d* Charles Marquis Warren *ph* Ray Rennahan *m* Paul Sawtell

Charlton Heston, Jack Palance, Katy Jurado, Brian Keith, Milburn Stone

Arrowsmith*
US 1932   108m   bw
Samuel Goldwyn

The self-sacrificing career of a doctor.
Emotionally satisfactory, dramatically slow and unsurprising variation on a theme which has since been treated far too often.

w Sidney Howard, *novel* Sinclair Lewis *d* John Ford *ph* Ray June *m* Alfred Newman

Ronald Colman, Helen Hayes, Richard Bennett, Myrna Loy, Charlotte Henry, Beulah Bondi, A. E. Anson

AAN: best picture; Sidney Howard; Ray June

Arsenal**
USSR 1929   99m (16 fps)   bw   silent
VUFKU

The 1914 war is made worse by strikes at home.

Patchy propagandist drama with brilliant sequences.

wd Alexander Dovzhenko ph Danylo Demutsky

S. Svashenko, A. Buchma, M. Nademsky
'A romantic and lyrical masterpiece.'—
Georges Sadoul

The Arsenal Stadium Mystery
GB 1939   85m   bw

A footballer is poisoned during a match. Brisk little mystery, with an amiable star performance. *Leslie Banks*, Greta Gynt, Esmond Knight, Brian Worth. Written by Thorold Dickinson and Donald Bull, from the novel by Leonard Gribble; directed by Thorold Dickinson; for G&S / GFD.
'This picture is as good to watch as either of the *Thin Man* films, and Dickinson gives us wit instead of facetiousness—wit of cutting and wit of angle.'—*Graham Greene*

Arsene Lupin**
US 1932   75m   bw
MGM

The Parisian gentleman thief accomplishes some daring robberies and is almost caught stealing the Mona Lisa.
Amusing crook comedy with a few flat passages but much sparkle in between, and a lively finale.

w Carey Wilson, Lenore Coffee, Bayard Veiller *d* Jack Conway *ph* Oliver Marsh

John Barrymore, Lionel Barrymore, Karen Morley, Tully Marshall, John Miljan

Arsenic and Old Lace***
US 1942 (released 1944)   118m   bw
Warner (Frank Capra)

Two dear, well-meaning old ladies invite lonely old men to their Brooklyn home, poison them with elderberry wine, and have their mad brother, who believes the corpses are yellow fever victims, bury them in the cellar. A homicidal nephew then turns up with bodies of his own.
A model for stage play adaptations, this famous black farce provided a frenzy of hilarious activity, and its flippant attitude to death was better received in wartime than would have been the case earlier or later. The director coaxes some perfect if overstated performances from his star cast, and added his own flair for perpetuating a hubbub.

w Julius J. and Philip G. Epstein, from the play by Joseph Kesselring with help from Howard Lindsay and Russell Crouse *d Frank Capra ph Sol Polito m* Max Steiner

Cary Grant (registering nineteen double takes to the minute), *Josephine Hull, Jean Adair, Raymond Massey, Peter Lorre, Priscilla Lane, Edward Everett Horton, James Gleason, John Alexander, Jack Carson, Grant Mitchell*

The Art of Love
US 1965 99m Technicolor
Universal / Cherokee / Ross Hunter

To stimulate interest in his work, a penniless artist fakes suicide, subsequently becoming so famous that he finds it difficult to reappear.
A pleasant black comedy idea is buried under lush production, dull direction and a host of unattractive Parisian sets.

w Carl Reiner *d* Norman Jewison *ph* Russell Metty *m* Cy Coleman

James Garner, Dick Van Dyke, Angie Dickinson, Elke Sommer, Ethel Merman, Pierre Olaf

Artistes at the Top of the Big Top: Disorientated**
West Germany 1968 103m bw / colour
Kairos Film

The daughter of a dead trapezist dreams of creating the ideal circus with a moral for mankind but step by step gives up her ambition.
A melancholy satire, told in fragmented fashion with some brilliant tricks and memorable sequences.

wd Alexander Kluge *ph* Gunther Hörmann, Thomas Mauch

Hannelore Hoger, Siegfried Graue, Alfred Edel, Bernd Höltz
'Those who interpret it simply as an allegory of German politics or of the present crisis in film-making narrow it unnecessarily.'—*Jan Dawson, MFB*

Artists and Models*
US 1937 97m bw
Paramount (Lewis E. Gensler)

An advertising man has to find the right girl as symbol for a silverware company.
Fairly stylish comedy musical with many elements typical of its studio.

w Walter de Leon, Francis Martin *d* Raoul Walsh *ph* Victor Milner *m* Victor Young *songs* various

Jack Benny, Ida Lupino, Richard Arlen, Gail Patrick, Ben Blue, Judy Canova, Martha Raye, Donald Meek, Hedda Hopper, André Kostelanetz and his Orchestra, Louis Armstrong and his Orchestra

AAN: song 'Whispers in the Dark'
(*m* Frederick Hollander, *ly* Leo Robin)

Artists and Models*
US 1955 109m Technicolor
Vistavision
Paramount / Hal B. Wallis

A goonish young man receives telepathic top secret information in his nightmares, which are used by his artist friend in comic strips; foreign agents and the CIA get interested.
A good zany idea is worked into an overlong dyspeptic comedy which neither the stars nor frantic treatment can hope to save.

w Frank Tashlin, Don McGuire *d* Frank Tashlin *ph* Daniel Fapp *m* Walter Scharf

Dean Martin, Jerry Lewis, Shirley Maclaine, Dorothy Malone, Eddie Mayehoff, Eva Gabor, Anita Ekberg, George 'Foghorn' Winslow, Jack Elam

Artists and Models Abroad*
US 1938 90m bw
Paramount (Arthur Hornblow Jnr)
GB title: *Stranded in Paris*

Stranded in Paris, a troupe of girls and their manager are helped by a Texas oil millionaire.
Generally agreeable comedy musical with emphasis on fashion.

w Howard Lindsay, Russell Crouse, Ken Englund *d* Mitchell Leisen *ph* Ted Tetzlaff *md* Borris Morros *songs* various *ad* Hans Dreier, Ernest Fegte

Jack Benny, Joan Bennett, Mary Boland, Charley Grapewin, Joyce Compton, the Yacht Club Boys, Fritz Feld, G. P. Huntley, Monty Woolley

The Aryan*
US 1916 75m (16 fps) bw silent
Triangle (Thomas Ince)

A gold prospector is cheated by a woman and becomes an outlaw.
Striking early star western.

w C. Gardner Sullivan *d* William S. Hart, Clifford Smith *ph* Joseph August, Clyde de Vinna

William S. Hart, Bessie Love, Louise Glaum, Hershall Mayall

As Long as They're Happy*
GB 1955 91m Eastmancolor
Rank / Regroup (Raymond Stross)

The suburban home of a London stockbroker is invaded by an American sob singer.
Frantic farce expanded from a stage satire of the Johnnie Ray cult; a patchy but sometimes funny star vehicle.

w Alan Melvile, *play* Vernon Sylvaine *d* J. Lee-Thompson *ph* Gilbert Taylor

Jack Buchanan, Brenda de Banzie, Diana
Dors, Jean Carson, Janette Scott, Susan
Stephen, Jerry Wayne, Hugh McDermott

As Long as You're Near Me
West Germany 1954 94m colour

A film director almost ruins a small-part
actress's life by insisting on making her a star.
Reasonably absorbing drama (original title:
Solange du da Bist), chiefly remarkable for
being a great hit in the US when dubbed. O.
W. Fischer, Hardy Kruger, Maria Schell.
Written by Jochen Huth; directed by Harold
Braun; for Warner.

As You Desire Me*
US 1931 71m bw
MGM (George Fitzmaurice)

The amnesiac mistress of a novelist rediscovers
her real husband and falls in love with him
again.
Interesting star vehicle with good cast and
production.

w Gene Markey, *play* Luigi Pirandello
d George Fitzmaurice *ph* William Daniels

Greta Garbo, Melvyn Douglas, Erich Von
Stroheim, Owen Moore, Hedda Hopper,
Rafaela Ottiano

As You Like It*
GB 1936 96m bw
TCF / Inter-Allied (Joseph M. Schenck, Paul
Czinner)

The fortunes of an exiled king take a turn in
the Forest of Arden.
Stylized, rather effete but often amusing
version of Shakespeare's pastoral comedy.

w J. M. Barrie, Robert Cullen, *play* William
Shakespeare *d* Paul Czinner *ph* Harold
Rosson *m* William Walton

Elisabeth Bergner, Laurence Olivier, Sophie
Stewart, Leon Quartermaine, Henry Ainley,
Richard Ainley, Felix Aylmer, Mackenzie
Ward, Aubrey Mather, John Laurie, Peter
Bull

'Rather too respectably lighthearted, but by
no means a contemptible production.'—*New
Yorker, 1978*

'There are far too many dull middle-length
shots from a fixed camera, so that we might
just as well be seated in the circle above the
deep wide stage at Drury Lane.'—*Graham
Greene*

As Young as You Feel*
US 1951 77m bw
TCF (Lamar Trotti)

An elderly employee, forced to retire,
impersonates the company president, saves the
firm from bankruptcy, and proves his
continued worth.
Good-natured comedy, ably presented.

w Lamar Trotti, *story* Paddy Chayevsky
d Harmon Jones *ph* Joe MacDonald *m* Cyril
Mockridge

Monty Woolley, Constance Bennett, Thelma
Ritter, David Wayne, Jean Peters, Marilyn
Monroe, Allyn Joslyn, Albert Dekker

Ash Wednesday*
US 1973 99m Technicolor
Sagittarius (Dominick Dunne)

An ageing American beauty rejuvenates
herself via plastic surgery, leads a vivid sex
life, and leaves her stolid husband.
The bloodthirsty operation scenes are
revolting, yet this joyless saga seems meant as
a celebration of the wonders of cosmetic
surgery and Sex for the Aged. Hypnotic but
hardly rewarding.

w Jean Claude Tramont *d* Larry Peerce
ph Ennio Guarnieri *m* Maurice Jarre

Elizabeth Taylor, Henry Fonda, Helmut
Berger, Keith Baxter, Maurice Teynac
'Endless shots of Elizabeth Taylor
expensively attired against the plush
background of Cortina.'—*Michael Billington,
Illustrated London News*

Ashanti
Switzerland 1979   117m   Panavision
   Technicolor
Columbia / Beverly (Luciano Sacripanti)

In West Africa, the wife of a member of the
World Health Organization is seized by slave
traders.
Absurd and rather unattractively brutal
adventure story, decked out with appearances
by guest stars.

w Stephen Geller, *novel* Ebano by Alberto
Vasquez-Figueroa *d* Richard Fleischer
ph Aldo Tonti *m* Michael Melvoin

Michael Caine, Omar Sharif, Peter Ustinov,
Rex Harrison, Kabir Bedi, William Holden,
Zia Mohyeddin, Beverly Johnson

Ashes and Diamonds**
Poland 1958   104m   bw
Film Polski
original title: *Popiol y Diament*

A Polish partisan is confused by the apparent
need to continue killing after the war is over.
A chilling account of the intellectual
contradictions to which war leads, and a
moving and sensitive film in its own right.

wd Andrzej Wajda, novel Jerzy Andrzejewski
ph Jerzy Wojcik

Zbigniew Cybulski, Ewa Krzyzanowska,
Adam Pawlikowski

Ask a Policeman**
GB 1938 82m bw
Gainsborough (Edward Black)

In a small coastal village, incompetent
policemen accidentally expose smugglers who
are scaring the locals with a headless horseman
legend.
One of the best comedies of an incomparable
team, with smart dialogue, good situations and
a measure of suspense.

*w Marriott Edgar, Val Guest, J. O. C. Orton
d Marcel Varnel ph* Derek Williams

Will Hay, Moore Marriott, Graham Moffatt,
Glennis Lorimer, *Peter Gawthorne, Herbert
Lomas,* Charles Oliver

Ask Any Girl*
US 1959 98m Metrocolor
   Cinemascope
MGM / Euterpe (Joe Pasternak)

A husband-hunting receptionist in New York
catches the eye of a wealthy playboy but
finally settles for his elder brother.
Predictable Cinderella story with a lively but
forgettable script and actors going through
familiar paces.

w George Wells, *novel* Winifred Wolfe
d Charles Walters *ph* Robert Bronner *m* Jeff
Alexander

David Niven, Shirley Maclaine, Gig Young,
Rod Taylor, Jim Backus, Claire Kelly
  'Like a comic strip transposed to the glossy
pages of *Vogue*'.—*MFB*

Asphalt*
Germany 1929 101m bw
UFA

A young policeman accidentally kills his rival
for a worthless girl.
Heavily expressionist melodrama, overlong
but good to watch.

w Rolf Vanloo, Fred Majo, Hans Szekely
d Joe May ph Günther Rittau

Gustav Fröhlich, Betty Amann, Else Heller,
Louise Brooks

The Asphalt Jungle***
US 1950 112m bw
MGM (Arthur Hornblow Jnr)

An elderly crook comes out of prison and
assembles a gang for one last robbery.

Probably the very first film to show a 'caper'
from the criminals' viewpoint (a genre which
has since been done to death several times
over), this is a clever character study rather
than a thriller, extremely well executed and
indeed generally irreproachable yet somehow
not a film likely to appear on many top ten
lists; perhaps the writer-director stands too far
back from everybo.'y, or perhaps he just
needed Humphrey Bogart.

w Ben Maddow, John Huston, *novel* W. R.
Burnett *d John Huston ph* Harold Rosson
m Miklos Rozsa

Sterling Hayden, *Sam Jaffe, Louis Calhern,*
Jean Hagen, Marilyn Monroe, James
Whitmore, John McIntire, Marc Lawrence,
Barry Kelley
  'Where this film excels is in the fluency of its
narration, the sharpness of its observation of
character and the excitement of its human
groupings.'—*Dilys Powell*
  'That Asphalt Pavement thing is full of
nasty, ugly people doing nasty things. I
wouldn't walk across the room to see a thing
like that.'—*Louis B. Mayer* (who was head of
the studio which made it)
† Apart from imitations, the film has been
directly remade as *The Badlanders, Cairo* and
A Cool Breeze.

AAN: Ben Maddow, John Huston (writers);
John Huston (as director); Harold Rosson;
Sam Jaffe

The Asphyx
GB 1973 99m Eastmancolor
   Todd AO 35
Glendale (John Brittany)

A Victorian aims to become immortal by
separating the spirit of death from his body.
Interminable hocus with a plethora of
talk, seldom exciting but watchable because of
its remarkable cast and other credits.

w Brian Comport *d* Peter Newbrook
ph Freddie Young *m* Bill McGuffie *sp* Ted
Samuels

Robert Stephens, Robert Powell, Jane
Lapotaire

The Assassin**
Italy / France 1961 105m bw
Titanus-Vides-SGC (Franco Cristaldi)

A prosperous antique dealer is accused of
murder and his unsavoury past is revealed; but
when he is freed, he prides himself on his new
personality.
A careful, detailed and wholly enjoyable
character study, somewhere between comedy
and drama.

w Elio Petri and others *d Elio Petri ph* Carlo di Palma *m* Piero Piccioni

Marcello Mastroianni, Salvo Randone, Micheline Presle, Andrea Checci

Assassin
GB 1973   83m   Technicolor
Pemini (David M. Jackson)

MI5 arranges the liquidation of an Air Ministry spy.
Old hat espionage melodrama, topheavy with artiness which makes it look like an endless TV commercial.

w Michael Sloan *d* Peter Crane *ph* Brian Jonson *m* Zack Lawrence

Ian Hendry, Edward Judd, Frank Windsor, Ray Brooks, John Hart Dyke

The Assassination Bureau*
GB 1968   110m   Technicolor
Paramount / Heathfield (Michael Relph)

In 1906 a lady journalist breaks up an international gang of professional killers by falling in love with their leader.
Black comedy period pastiche which resolves itself into a series of sketches leading up to a spectacular zeppelin climax. Plenty going on, but the level of wit is not high.

w Michael Relph, with Wolf Mankowitz *d* Basil Dearden *ph Geoffrey Unsworth m* Ron Grainer

Oliver Reed, Diana Rigg, Telly Savalas, Curt Jurgens, Philippe Noiret, Warren Mitchell, Clive Revill, Beryl Reid, Kenneth Griffith

The Assassination of the Duc de Guise*
France 1908   15m (16 fps)   bw   silent
Film d'Art

Henry III arranges the killing of the Duc de Guise when he comes to court.
Influential early story film.

w Henri Lavedan *d* Charles le Bargy *m* Saint-Saëns

Charles le Bargy, Albert Lambert, Gabrielle Lavinne

The Assassination of Trotsky*
Italy / GB / France 1972   103m   Technicolor
Dino de Laurentiis / Josef Shaftel / Cinetel (Norman Priggen, Joseph Losey)

In 1940, Trotsky is hiding out in Mexico; a Stalinist infiltrates his presence and kills him with an ice pick.
Glum historical reconstruction with much fictitious padding; basically undramatic.

w Nicholas Mosley, Masolino d'Amico *d* Joseph Losey *ph* Pasquale de Santis *m* Egisto Macchi

Richard Burton, Alain Delon, Romy Schneider, Valentina Cortese, Jean Desailly
'Not for anyone who knows, or cares, anything about Leon Trotsky.'—*New Yorker, 1977*

Les Assassins du Dimanche
France 1956   94m   bw   Cinepanoramic
EDIC
aka: *Every Second Counts*

Dozens of people help to track down a holiday car which has been driven away from a garage in a dangerous condition.
Watchable but artificial suspenser.

w Alex Joffe, Gabriel Arout *d* Alex Joffe *ph* Jean Bourgoin

Barbara Laage, Jean-Marc Thibault, Dominique Wilms, Paul Frankeur

Assault
GB 1970   91m   Eastmancolor
Rank / Peter Rogers (George H. Brown)

An art mistress helps police to solve a case of multiple rape in an English village.
Old-fashioned police mystery with new-fangled shock treatment. Routine excitements.

w John Kruse, *novel* Kendal Young *d* Sidney Hayers *ph* Ken Hodges *m* Eric Rogers

Frank Finlay, Suzy Kendall, James Laurenson, Lesley-Anne Down, Freddie Jones, Tony Beckley, Anthony Ainley, Dilys Hamlett
'All right for that wet afternoon.'—*Michael Billington, Illustrated London News*

Assault on a Queen
US 1966   106m   Technicolor
Panavision
Paramount / Seven Arts / Sinatra Enterprises (William Goetz)

Crooks dredge up a submarine and use it to hi-jack the *Queen Mary*.
Strained caper film which remains uncertain whether to play for drama or thrills, and achieves neither. Special effects unconvincing.

w Rod Serling, *novel* Jack Finney *d* Jack Donohue *ph* William Daniels *m* Duke Ellington

Frank Sinatra, Virna Lisi, Tony Franciosa, Alf Kjellin, Errol John, Richard Conte, Murray Matheson, Reginald Denny
'Just about as enthralling as plastic boats in the bath.'—*MFB*

Assault on Precinct 13**
US 1976 91m Metrocolor Panavision
CKK (Joseph Kaufman)

Gang members on a vendetta attack a police station.
Violent but basically efficient and old-fashioned programmer which shows that not all the expertise of the forties in this then-familiar field has been lost.

wd / m John Carpenter ph Douglas Knapp

Austin Stoker, Darwin Joston, Laurie Zimmer, Martin West

'One of the most effective exploitation movies of the last ten years . . . Carpenter scrupulously avoids any overt socio-political pretensions, playing instead for laughs and suspense in perfectly balanced proportions.'—
Time Out

Assignment in Brittany
US 1943 96m bw
MGM (J. Walter Ruben)

A Free French soldier stays in occupied France to fight the Nazis.
Routine propagandist actioner, totally unbelievable.

w Anthony Veiller, William Wright, Howard Emmett Rogers, novel Helen MacInnes d Jack Conway ph Charles Rosher m Lennie Hayton

Jean Pierre Aumont, Signe Hasso, Susan Peters, Reginald Owen, Richard Whorf, Margaret Wycherly, John Emery, Miles Mander, George Coulouris

Assignment K
GB 1968 97m Techniscope
Columbia / Mazurka (Ben Arbeid, Maurice Foster)

The European head of a toy firm is also head of a special spy unit.
Dreary espionage thriller, instantly forgettable, and only watchable at odd moments while it's on.

w Val Guest, Bill Strutton, Maurice Foster, novel Hartley Howard d Val Guest ph Ken Hodges m Basil Kirchen

Stephen Boyd, Michael Redgrave, Camilla Sparv, Leo McKern, Jeremy Kemp

Assignment Paris
US 1952 85m bw
Columbia (Sam Marx, Jerry Bresler)

A reporter on the Paris staff of the *New York Herald-Tribune* goes to Yugoslavia, is arrested as a spy, and has to be exchanged.

Dim cold war melodrama with occasional entertaining moments.

w William Bowers, novel Trial by Terror by Paul Gallico d Robert Parrish ph Burnett Guffey, Ray Cory m George Duning

George Sanders, Dana Andrews, Sandra Giglio, Marta Toren, Audrey Totter, Herbert Berghof

Assignment to Kill
US 1967 99m Technicolor Panavision
Warner Seven Arts (William Conrad)

A New York insurance company hires a private eye to investigate a dubious European financier.
Routine international intrigue with muddled plot and unusual cast. A nice production wasted.

wd Sheldon Reynolds ph Harold Lipstein m William Lava

Patrick O'Neal, John Gielgud, Peter Van Eyck, Joan Hackett, Herbert Lom, Eric Portman, Oscar Homolka, Leon Greene

The Astonished Heart*
GB 1949 89m bw
Gainsborough / Sydney Box (Antony Darnborough)

A psychiatrist is permitted by his wife to fall in love with another woman but finds the situation intolerable and kills himself.
The star, looking like a Chinese mandarin, reached his nadir in this unwise screen adaptation, inelegantly directed, of one of his slightest short plays about boring and effete people. It sank without trace.

w Noel Coward, from his play d Terence Fisher, Antony Darnborough ph Jack Asher m Noel Coward

Noel Coward, Margaret Leighton, Celia Johnson, Graham Payn, Joyce Carey, Ralph Michael, Michael Hordern

Asylum*
GB 1972 88m Eastmancolor
Amicus (Max J. Rosenberg, Milton Subotsky)

A doctor applies for a job at an asylum, hears weird stories from four patients, and finds himself in the middle of a weirder one.
Lively horror compilation with echoes of *Caligari* and *Dead of Night*. Gruesomeness sometimes overdone.

w Robert Bloch d Roy Ward Baker ph Denys Coop m Douglas Gamley

Patrick Magee, Robert Powell, Geoffrey
Bayldon, Barbara Parkins, Sylvia Syms,
Richard Todd, Peter Cushing, Barry Morse,
Britt Ekland, Charlotte Rampling, James
Villiers, Megs Jenkins, Herbert Lom

At Gunpoint
US 1955   80m   Technicolor
Cinemascope

A western storekeeper accidentally kills a
bank robber, whose brothers seek revenge;
will the townsfolk come to his aid? Fair
western on the lines of *High Noon*. Fred
MacMurray, Dorothy Malone, Walter
Brennan, John Qualen, Skip Homeier.
Written by Dan Ullman; directed by Alfred
Werker; for Allied Artists. (GB title:
Gunpoint.)

At Long Last Love
US 1975   114m   Technicolor
TCF / Copa de Oro (Peter Bogdanovich)

The 1935 romance of a New York millionaire
and a musical star.
An attempt to recapture the simple pleasures
of an Astaire–Rogers musical; unfortunately
true professionalism is lacking and the wrong
kind of talent is used. The result is awful to
contemplate.

wd Peter Bogdanovich *ph* Laszlo Kovacs
m Cole Porter *pd* Gene Allen

Burt Reynolds, Cybill Shepherd, Eileen
Brennan, Madeleine Kahn, Duilio del Prete,
John Hillerman, Mildred Natwick
'He works hard at reducing all his sets and
costumes to variations of black against silver
or white on white, and uncovers in his most
oft-repeated visual motif—the elegant mirrors
before which his cast seem at all times to be
posed—the perfect metaphor for this endlessly
narcissistic, thoroughly calcified enterprise.'—
Richard Combs
'It just lies there, and it dies there.'—*Variety*
'Studios bury more films than the public or
the critics. Fox gave up on *At Long Last Love*
instantly. A six million dollar film was written
off while it was doing well because their
lawyers told them they could make more
money that way.'—*Peter Bogdanovich*
'It is justly included on most lists of the ten
worst films ever made.'—*Les Keyser*,
Hollywood in the Seventies

At Sword's Point*
US 1951   81m   Technicolor
RKO (Jerrold T. Brandt)
GB title: *Sons of the Musketeers*

The sons of the three musketeers rally round
their ageing queen to prevent her daughter's
marriage to a villain.
Adequate swashbuckler with plenty of pace
and a sound cast.

w Walter Ferris, Joseph Hoffman *d* Lewis
Allen *ph* Ray Rennahan *m* Roy Webb

Cornel Wilde, Maureen O'Hara, Gladys
Cooper, Robert Douglas, Dan O'Herlihy,
Alan Hale Jnr, Blanche Yurka, Nancy Gates

At the Circus**
US 1939   87m   bw
MGM (Mervyn Le Roy)
aka: *The Marx Brothers at the Circus*

A shyster lawyer and two incompetents save a
circus from bankruptcy.
This film began the decline of the Marx
Brothers; in it nothing is ill done but nothing is
very fresh either apart from the rousing finale
which shows just what professionalism meant
in the old Hollywood. Highlights include
Groucho singing about Lydia the tattooed
lady, his seduction of Mrs Dukesbury, and the
big society party.

w Irving Brecher *d* Edward Buzzell
ph Leonard M. Smith *m / ly* Harold Arlen,
E. Y. Harburg *m* Franz Waxman

Groucho, Chico, Harpo, Margaret Dumont,
Florence Rice, Kenny Baker, Eve Arden, Nat
Pendleton, Fritz Feld
'We must regretfully accept the fact that,
thanks to the Metro millions, the Marx
Brothers are finally imprisoned in the
Hollywood world.'—*Graham Greene*

At the Earth's Core
GB 1976   90m   Technicolor
Amicus (John Dark)

Scientists testing a geological excavator are
carried by it to the centre of the earth, and
find a prehistoric land inhabited by feuding
tribes.
Mainly feeble science fiction for kids, with
occasional amusing moments.

w Milton Subotsky, *novel* Edgar Rice
Burroughs *d* Kevin Connor *ph* Alan Hume
m Mike Vickers *sp* Ian Wingrove
pd Maurice Carter

Doug McClure, Peter Cushing, Caroline
Munro, Cy Grant, Godfrey James, Keith
Barron
'Papier mâché people-eaters, idiotic
situations, and a frequent sense of confusion
as to what is going on.'—*David Stewart*,
Christian Science Monitor

At the Villa Rose

This murder mystery by A. E. W. Mason has had three British filmings: in 1920 with Teddy Arundell as Inspector Hanaud; in 1930 with Austin Trevor; in 1939 with Keneth Kent. All were adequate to their time. The story concerns a medium framed for the murder of a rich widow.

At War with the Army

US 1951   93m   bw
Paramount / Fred K. Finklehoffe

A couple of song and dance men have trouble as army recruits.

American service farce, based on a play and confined largely to one set; rather untypical of Martin and Lewis, yet oddly enough the film which sealed their success.

w Fred K. Finklehoffe, *play* James Allardice d Hal Walker *ph* Stuart Thompson *m* Joseph Lilley

Dean Martin, Jerry Lewis, Mike Kellin, Polly Bergen, Jimmie Dundee

L'Atalante*

France 1934   89m   bw
J. L. Nounez-Gaumont

A barge captain takes his new wife down river. One of those classics which no longer provides the authentic thrill; its lack of incident and plot leads quickly to boredom.

w Jean Guinée, Jean Vigo, Albert Riera d *Jean Vigo ph* Boris Kaufman, Louis Berger *m* Maurice Jaubert

Jean Dasté, Dita Parlo, *Michel Simon*, Giles Margarites

Athena

US 1954   96m   Eastmancolor
MGM (Joe Pasternak)

A young lawyer falls in love with the eldest of seven sisters brought up to high standards of moral conduct and physical fitness.
Promising but unfulfilling light musical which smothers a good idea in routine treatment.

w William Ludwig, Leonard Spiegelgass d Richard Thorpe *ph* Robert Planck *songs* Hugh Martin, Ralph Blane

Edmund Purdom, Jane Powell, Debbie Reynolds, Louis Calhern, Evelyn Varden, Vic Damone, Linda Christian, Ray Collins

Atlantic

GB 1929   90m   bw

A passenger liner sinks in mid-Atlantic. Veiled retelling of the *Titanic* story, here in a clumsy Anglo-German version with extremely primitive sound and a plethora of pregnant silences. Franklin Dyall, Madeleine Carroll, Monty Banks, John Stuart, John Longden, Ellaline Terriss. Written by Victor Kendall, from the play *The Berg* by Ernest Raymond; directed by E. A. Dupont; for BIP.

Atlantic City*

US 1944   87m   bw
Republic

Before World War I, a young showman aims to make Atlantic City the entertainment centre of the world.
Simple-minded romantic musical, quite pacy and effectively staged for a Republic product.

w Doris Gilbert, Frank Gill Jnr, George Carlton Brown *d* Ray McCarey *ph* John Alton *m / ly* various

Constance Moore, Brad Taylor, Jerry Colonna, Charley Grapewin

Atlantic Ferry*

GB 1941   108m   bw
Warner (Max Milder)
US title: *Sons of the Sea*

In 1837 Liverpool, two brothers build the first steamship to cross the Atlantic.
Ponderous historical romance with points of interest.

w Gordon Wellesley, Edward Dryhurst, Emeric Pressburger *d* Walter Forde *ph* Basil Emmott *m* Jack Beaver

Michael Redgrave, Valerie Hobson, Griffith Jones, Margaretta Scott, Hartley Power, Bessie Love, Milton Rosmer
'Probably the finest collection of model shots in captivity.'—*C. A. Lejeune*

L'Atlantide*

France 1921   125m approx (16 fps)   bw silent
Thalman

Two explorers find the lost continent of Atlantis and fall in love with its queen.
Highly commercial adventure fantasy of its day; it cost two million francs and ran in Paris for a year. Some scenes still sustain, and the desert scenes are impressive.

wd Jacques Feyder, *novel* Pierre Benoit *ph* Georges Specht, Victor Morin

Jean Angelo, Stacia Napierkowska, Georges Melchior

† Other versions include *Queen of Atlantis* (Germany 1932, *d* G. W. Pabst, with Brigitte Helm); *Siren of Atlantis* (US 1948, *d* Gregg Tallas, with Maria Montez); *L'Atlantide* (France / Italy 1961, *d* Edgar G. Ulmer).

Atlantis, the Lost Continent
US 1961   91m   Metrocolor
MGM / Galaxy / George Pal

A Greek fisherman is imprisoned when he
returns a maiden he has rescued to her island
home of Atlantis, but escapes just before
volcanic eruption overtakes the decadent
nation.
Penny-pinching fantasy spectacle with very
little entertainment value.

w Daniel Mainwaring, *play* Sir Gerald
Hargreaves d George Pal ph Harold E.
Wellman m Russell Garcia

Anthony Hall, Joyce Taylor, John Dall,
Edward Platt, Frank de Kova, Jay Novello

The Atomic City*
US 1952   85m   bw
Paramount (Joseph Sistrom)

The young son of a leading atomic scientist is
kidnapped but his father and the FBI rescue
him.
Routine but well-paced thriller with a
documentary background of research at Los
Alamos.

w Sidney Boehm d Jerry Hopper ph Charles
B. Lang Jnr m Leith Stevens

Gene Barry, Lydia Clarke, Lee Aaker, Nancy
Gates, Milburn Stone

AAN: Sidney Boehm

The Atomic Kid
US 1954   86m   bw
Republic

After an atomic blast, a prospector
accidentally left in the area proves immune to
uranium, and after various adventures rounds
up some communist spies.
Inane romp which raises a few laughs.

w Benedict Freeman, John Fenton Murray,
story Blake Edwards d Leslie H. Martinson
ph John L. Russell Jnr m Van Alexander

Mickey Rooney, Robert Strauss, Elaine
Davis, Bill Goodwin, Whit Bissell

The Atonement of Gosta Berling**
Sweden 1924   200m approx (16 fps)
    bw   silent
Svensk Filmindustri
original title: *Gosta Berlings Saga*

A pastor is defrocked for drinking, becomes a
tutor, and has various love affairs.
Lumpy but often engrossing picturization of a
famous novel, veering mostly into melodrama
but finding its way to a happy ending.

w Mauritz Stiller, Ragnar Hylten-Cavallius,
novel Selma Lagerlof d Mauritz Stiller
ph Julius Jaenzon

Lars Hanson, Gerda Lundeqvist, Ellen
Cederstrom, Mona Martensson, Jenny
Hasselqvist, Otto Elg-Lundberg, Greta
Garbo.

'Stiller was a master at unifying visual
beauty and emotional effect; the complicated
narrative is blurry, but there are sequences as
lovely and expressive as any on film.'—*New
Yorker, 1980*

† It was her small role in this film which led
directly to Greta Garbo's American stardom.

Attack**
US 1956   104m   bw
UA / Associates and Aldrich

In 1944 Belgium, an American infantry
command is led by a coward.
High-pitched, slick, violent and very effective
war melodrama, even though by the end we
seem to be in the company of raving lunatics
rather than soldiers.

w *James Poe, play* Fragile Fox by Norman
Brooks d *Robert Aldrich ph Joseph Biroc
m* Frank de Vol

Jack Palance, Eddie Albert, Lee Marvin,
Buddy Ebsen, Robert Strauss, Richard
Jaeckel, William Smithers, Peter Van Eyck

'The film does not so much tackle a subject
as hammer it down.'—*Penelope Houston*

The Attack of the Fifty Foot Woman
US 1958   72m   bw

A neurotic woman is lured inside a space ship,
becomes radio-active, and grows to alarming
proportions. Hilarious tailpiece to the fifties
monster cycle, a dismal movie worth
remembering only for its title. Allison Hayes,
William Hudson, Roy Gordon. Written by
Mark Hanna; directed by Nathan Hertz; for
Allied Artists.

Attack on the Iron Coast
GB 1967   90m   De Luxe
US / Mirisch (John Champion)

In World War II, a Canadian commando unit
destroys a German installation on the French
coast.
Stagey low-budgeter with modest action
sequences.

w Herman Hoffman d Paul Wendkos
ph Paul Beeson m Gerard Schurmann

Lloyd Bridges, Andrew Keir, Mark Eden, Sue
Lloyd

Attila the Hun
Italy / France 1954   79m   Technicolor
Lux Ponti de Laurentiis / LCCF
    (Georgio Andriani)
original title: *Attilo Flagello di Dio*

The barbarian chief attacks the forces of the Emperor Valentinian and marches on Rome. Predictably violent adventures after de Mille; a bit slow to start.

w Ennio de Concini, Primo Zeglio d Pietro Francisci ph Aldo Tonti m Enzo Masetti

Anthony Quinn, Sophia Loren, Henri Vidal, Irene Papas, Ettore Manni, Claude Laydu

Au dela des Grilles
Italy / France 1949   90m   bw
Italia Produzione / Francinex (Alfredo Guarini)
aka: *Beyond the Gates*; Italian title: *La mura de Malapaga*

A murderer on the run in Genoa falls in love with a waitress and loses his chance of escape. *Quai des Brumes* reworked against an Italian neo-realist setting; dramatic values less interesting now than historical ones.

w Jean Aurenche, Pierre Bost, Cesare Zavattini, Suso Cecchi d'Amico d René Clément ph Louis Page m Roman Vlad

Jean Gabin, *Isa Miranda*, Vera Talchi, Andrea Checci

Au Royaume des Cieux
France 1949   108m   bw
Regina (Julien Duvivier)
aka: *Woman Hunt*

An 18-year-old girl suffers at a reform school. Shoddy melodrama, more sensational than Hollywood ever dared to be.

wd Julien Duvivier ph Victor Armenise

Suzanne Cloutier, Serge Reggiani, Monique Mélinand, Suzy Prim, Jean Davy, Juliette Greco

'A depressing exhibit from a director who once had a serious reputation.'—*Gavin Lambert*

Aunt Clara
GB 1954   84m   bw
London Films (Colin Lesslie, Anthony Kimmins)

A pious old person inherits from a reprobate uncle five greyhounds, a pub and a brothel. Extremely mild star vehicle with a gallery of comedy character cameos.

w Kenneth Horne, *novel* Noel Streatfeild d Anthony Kimmins ph C. Pennington-Richards m Benjamin Frankel

Margaret Rutherford, Ronald Shiner, A. E. Matthews, Fay Compton, Nigel Stock, Jill Bennett, Reginald Beckwith, Raymond Huntley

Aunt Sally
GB 1933   84m   bw

A fake French star saves a nightclub owner from gangsters. Predictable star vehicle. Cicely Courtneidge, Sam Hardy, Billy Milton, Phyllis Clare, Hartley Power. Written by Austin Melford, Guy Bolton and A. R. Rawlinson; directed by Tim Whelan; for Gaumont.

Auntie Mame*
US 1958 · 144m   Technirama
Warner (Morton da Costa)

An orphan boy is adopted by his volatile extravagant aunt, whose giddy escapades fill his memory of the twenties and thirties.
A rather unsatisfactory star revue from a book and play later turned into a musical, *Mame*. A few splendid moments, otherwise rather dull and irritating.

w Betty Comden, Adolph Green, *novel* Patrick Dennis, *play* Jerome Lawrence, Robert E. Lee d Morton da Costa ph Harry Stradling m Bronislau Kaper ad Malcolm Bert

Rosalind Russell, Forrest Tucker, *Coral Browne*, Fred Clark, Roger Smith, Patric Knowles, Peggy Cass, Lee Patrick, Joanna Barnes

AAN: best picture; Harry Stradling; Rosalind Russell; Peggy Cass

Une Aussi Longue Absence*
France / Italy 1961   96m   bw
Procinex / Lyre / Galatea (Jacques Nahum)
aka: *The Long Absence*

A widow who owns a Paris café meets an amnesiac tramp who may be her long-lost husband.
Romantic character study which just about comes off thanks to good acting.

w Marguerite Duras, Gérald Jarlot d Henri Colpi ph Marcel Weiss m Georges Delerue

Alida Valli, Georges Wilson, Jacques Harden

Austerlitz
France / Italy / Liechtenstein / Yugoslavia 1959   166m   Eastmancolor Dyaliscope
CFPI / SCLF / Galatea / Michael Arthur / Dubrava (Alexander and Michael Salkind)
aka: *The Battle of Austerlitz*

Napoleon defeats the Austro-Russian army. Elaborate pageant with a hopelessly cluttered narrative line arranged to take in a roster of guest stars who merely distract from the central theme.

wd Abel Gance *ph* Henri Alekan, Robert Juillard *m* Jean Ledrut

Pierre Mondy, Jean Mercure, Jack Palance, Orson Welles, Michel Simon, Jean-Louis Trintignant, Martine Carol, Leslie Caron, Claudia Cardinale, Rossano Brazzi, Ettore Manni, Jean Marais, Vittorio de Sica
'Strictly for connoisseurs of Gance's brand of hyperbolic history.'—*Peter John Dyer, MFB*

Autumn Crocus

GB 1934   86m   bw

A British schoolmistress on holiday falls for her Tyrolean innkeeper. Difficult now to conceive the popularity in its day of this novelettish romance, which seems frozen in amber. Ivor Novello, Fay Compton, Jack Hawkins, Diana Beaumont, Muriel Aked, George Zucco. Written and directed by Basil Dean, from the play by C. L. Anthony; for ATP.

Autumn Leaves*

US 1956   108m   bw
Columbia / William Goetz

A middle-aged spinster marries a young man who turns out to be a pathological liar and tries to murder her.
Skilfully tailored star vehicle for female audiences.

w Jack Jevne, Lewis Meltzer, Robert Blees *d* Robert Aldrich *ph* Charles Lang *m* Hans Salter

Joan Crawford, Cliff Robertson, Lorne Greene, Vera Miles, Ruth Donnelly, Shepperd Strudwick

Autumn Sonata*

Sweden / West Germany / GB 1978   97m   colour
Personafilm / ITC (Ingmar Bergman)

When her lover dies, a concert pianist visits the daughter she has not seen for many years. Typically Bergmanesque, understated conversation piece with no obvious happy ending for anybody.

wd Ingmar Bergman *ph* Sven Nykvist

Ingrid Bergman, Liv Ullmann, Halvar Bjork
'Professional gloom.'—*Time*
'It fills these middle-class rooms with the deep music of conflict and reconciliation that must strike home to any audiences in any culture or society.'—*Jack Kroll, Newsweek*
AAN: script; Ingrid Bergman

Avalanche

US 1978   91m   Metrocolor
New World (Roger Corman)

Snow threatens holidaymakers at a ski lodge. A disaster movie which, while quite competent in most ways, is no better than TV movies of this kind, especially as it resorts for its climaxes to scratched old stock film.

w Claude Pola, Corey Allen *d* Corey Allen *ph* Pierre-William Glenn *m* William Kraft

Rock Hudson, Mia Farrow, Robert Forster, Jeanette Nolan, Rick Moses, Steve Franken, Barry Primus

Avalanche Express

Eire 1979   88m   De Luxe   Panavision
TCF / Lorimar (Mark Robson)

Spies of all nations converge on a train from Milan to Rotterdam.
Fitfully amusing hodgepodge which had to be finished off in a hurry following the death of its star and director in mid-production.

w Abraham Polonsky, *novel* Colin Forbes *d* Mark Robson *ph* Jack Cardiff *m* Allyn Ferguson

Robert Shaw, Lee Marvin, Linda Evans, Maximilian Schell, Mike Connors, Joe Namath, Horst Buchholz
'The most impressive work of montage to emerge from a big-budget adventure movie.'—*Richard Combs, MFB*
'Pell-mell direction and editing perform a precarious, oddly suspenseful balancing act.'—*Sight and Sound*

Avanti!**

US 1972   144m   De Luxe
UA / Mirisch / Phalanx / Jalem (Billy Wilder)

A young American goes to Ischia to collect the body of his father who has died on holiday. He finds that the fatal accident had also killed his father's mistress, and amid overwhelming bureaucratic problems proceeds to fall in love with her daughter.
Absurdly overlong black comedy, with compensations in the shape of a generally witty script and some fine breakneck sequences of culminating confusion.

w Billy Wilder, I. A. L. Diamond, *play* Samuel Taylor *d* Billy Wilder *ph* Luigi Kuveiller *m* Carlo Rustichelli

Jack Lemmon, Juliet Mills, Clive Revill, Edward Andrews, Gianfranco Barra

L'Avventura**

Italy / France 1960   145m   bw
Cino del Duca / PCE / Lyre (Amato Pennasilico)

Young people on a yachting holiday go ashore on a volcanic island. One of them disappears; this affects the life of the others, but she is never found.

Aimless, overlong parable with lots of vague significance; rather less entertaining than the later *Picnic at Hanging Rock* (qv), it made its director a hero of the highbrows.

w Michelangelo Antonioni, Elio Bartolini, Tonino Guerra *d* Michelangelo Antonioni *ph* Aldo Scavarda *m* Giovanni Fusco

Monica Vitti, Lea Massari, Gabriele Ferzetti, Dominique Blanchar, James Addams, Lelio Luttazi

'A film of complete maturity, sincerity and creative intuition.'—*Peter John Dyer, MFB*

The Awakening
GB 1980   105m   Technicolor
EMI / Orion (Robert Solo)   .

An obsessed archaeologist believes that the spirit of a long-dead Egyptian queen has entered into the soul of his daughter. Unpersuasive and humourless mumbo jumbo from the same intractably complex novel which provided the basis for *Blood from the Mummy's Tomb*.

w Allan Scott, Chris Bryant, Clive Exton, *novel* Jewel of the Seven Stars by Bram Stoker *d* Mike Newell *ph* Jack Cardiff *m* Claude Bolling *pd* Michael Stringer

Charlton Heston, Susannah York, Jill Townsend, Stephanie Zimbalist, Patrick Drury, Bruce Myers

Away All Boats!
US 1956   114m   Technicolor
   Vistavision
U-I (Howard Christie)

Adventures of a small transport boat during the Pacific War.

Competent drum-beating war heroics with expensive action sequences.

w Ted Sherdeman *d* Joseph Pevney *ph* William Daniels, Clifford Stine *m* Frank Skinner

Jeff Chandler, George Nader, Julie Adams, Lex Barker, Keith Andes, Richard Boone, Frank Faylen

The Awful Truth***
US 1937   90m   bw
Columbia (Leo McCarey)

A divorcing couple endure various adventures which lead to reconciliation.
Classic crazy comedy of the thirties, marked by a mixture of sophistication and farce and an irreverent approach to plot.

wd Leo McCarey, play Arthur Richman *ph* Joseph Walker *md* Morris Stoloff

Irene Dunne, Cary Grant, Ralph Bellamy, Alexander D'Arcy, Cecil Cunningham, Molly Lamont, Esther Dale, Joyce Compton

'The funniest picture of the season.'—*Otis Ferguson*

'Among the ingredients the raising powder is the important thing and out of the oven comes a frothy bit of stuff that leaves no taste in the mouth and is easy on the stomach.'— *Marion Fraser, World Film News*

† Remade 1953 as *Let's Do It Again* (qv).

AA: Leo McCarey (as director)
AAN: best picture; script; Irene Dunne; Ralph Bellamy

B

B.F.'s Daughter*
US 1948   106m   bw
MGM (Edwin A. Knopf)
GB title: *Polly Fulton*

The wife of a penniless lecturer secures her
husband's rise to fame without his knowing
that she is the daughter of a millionaire.
Solid upper class romantic drama with a touch
of Peg's Paper.

w Luther Davis, *novel* John P. Marquand
d Robert Z. Leonard *ph* Joseph Ruttenberg
m Bronislau Kaper

Barbara Stanwyck, Van Heflin, Charles
Coburn, Richard Hart, Keenan Wynn,
Margaret Lindsay, Spring Byington, Marshall
Thompson

B.S. I Love You
US 1970   98m   De Luxe

A director of TV commercials is beset by
passionate women. Tiresomely trendy sex
comedy with a visual style that never lets up.
Peter Kastner, Joanna Cameron, Louise Sorel,
Gary Burghoff, Joanna Barnes, Richard B.
Shull. Written and directed by Steven Hillard
Stern; for Motion Pictures International /
TCF. (NB: The initials in the title are short for
bullshit.)

Babbitt*
US 1934   74m   bw
Warner (Sam Bischoff)

Problems of a middle-aged man in a small
American town.
A minor attempt to film a major novel: quite
tolerable but lacking density.

w Mary McCall Jnr, *novel* Sinclair Lewis
d William Keighley *ph* Arthur Todd

Guy Kibbee, Aline MacMahon, Claire Dodd,
Maxine Doyle, Minor Watson, Minna
Gombell, Alan Hale, Berton Churchill,
Russell Hicks, Nan Grey
† Previously filmed in 1924 with Willard Louis.

The Babe Ruth Story
US 1948   107m   bw
Allied Artists

The biography of a baseball player who was
thought of as something of a saint.

Dim, sentimental and faintly mystical biopic,
throughout which the star presents his familiar
image.

w Bob Considine, George Callahan *d* Roy del
Ruth *ph* Philip Tunnura, James Van Trees
m Edward Ward

William Bendix, Claire Trevor, Charles
Bickford

Babes in Arms*
US 1939   96m   bw
MGM (Arthur Freed)

The teenage sons and daughters of retired
vaudevillians put on a big show.
Simple-minded backstage musical which
marked the first enormously successful
teaming of its two young stars.

w Jack McGowan, Kay Van Riper, from the
Broadway show by Rodgers and Hart
d / *ch* Busby Berkeley *ph* Ray June
songs Rodgers and Hart and others *m* Roger
Edens, George Stoll

Judy Garland, Mickey Rooney, Charles
Winninger, Douglas Macphail, Leni Lynn,
June Preisser

AAN: Roger Edens, George Stoll; Mickey
Rooney

Babes in Toyland*
US 1934   77m   bw
Hal Roach
aka: *Wooden Soldiers; March of the
    Wooden Soldiers; Laurel and Hardy in
    Toyland*

Santa Claus's incompetent assistants
accidentally make some giant wooden soldiers,
which come in useful when a villain tries to
take over Toyland.
Comedy operetta in which the stars have
pleasant but not outstanding material; the
style and decor are however sufficient to
preserve the film as an eccentric minor classic.

w Nick Grinde, Frank Butler, *original book* /
ly Glen MacDonough *d* Gus Meins, Charles
Rogers *ph* Art Lloyd, Francis Corby
m Victor Herbert

Stan Laurel, Oliver Hardy, Charlotte Henry,
Henry Brandon, Felix Knight, Florence
Roberts, Johnny Downs, Marie Wilson

Babes in Toyland
US 1961 105m Technicolor
Walt Disney

A misfiring remake, all charm and no talent apart from some excellent special effects at the climax.

w Ward Kimball, Joe Rinaldi, Lowell S. Hawley d Jack Donohue ph Edward Colman md George Bruns sp Eustace Lycett, Robert A. Mattey, Bill Justice, Xavier Atencio, Yale Gracey

Ray Bolger (miscast as the villain), Annette Funicello, Tommy Kirk, Gene Sheldon (imitating Stan Laurel), Henry Calvin (imitating Oliver Hardy), Ed Wynn, Kevin Corcoran

AAN: George Bruns

Babes on Broadway**
US 1941 118m bw
MGM (Arthur Freed)

A sequel to Babes in Arms, in which the kids get to Broadway and share some disillusion. Inflated and less effective than the original, but with good numbers.

w Fred Finkelhoffe, Elaine Ryan
d / ch Busby Berkeley ph Lester White
songs Burton Lane and Ralph Freed

Judy Garland, Mickey Rooney, Virginia Weidler, Ray Macdonald, Richard Quine, Fay Bainter

† The Virginia Weidler role was originally intended for Shirley Temple, but TCF wouldn't loan her.

AAN: song 'How About You' (m Burton Lane, ly Ralph Freed)

Babette Goes to War
France 1959 103m Eastmancolor
  Cinemascope
léna (Raoul Lévy)
original title: Babette S'en Va-t-en Guerre

In 1940 a French refugee girl is sent by British intelligence from London to Paris as bait in a plot to kidnap a German general and delay the Nazi invasion of England.
Witless war farce which goes on for ever.

w Raoul Lévy, Gérard Oury d Christian-Jaque ph Armand Thirard m Gilbert Bécaud

Brigitte Bardot, Jacques Charrier, Hannes Messemer, Yves Vincent, Ronald Howard, Francis Blanche

'A kind of Private's Progress without comedians.'—MFB

The Baby and the Battleship
GB 1956 96m Eastmancolor
Jay Lewis / British Lion (Antony Darnborough)

Two sailors hide an Italian baby on their battleship.
Simple-minded lower decks farce, with lots of confusion and cooing over the baby, but not much to laugh at.

w Jay Lewis, Gilbert Hackforth-Jones, Bryan Forbes d Jay Lewis ph Harry Waxman

John Mills, Richard Attenborough, André Morell, Bryan Forbes, Michael Howard, Lisa Gastoni, Ernest Clark, Lionel Jeffries, Thorley Walters

Baby Blue Marine*
US 1976 90m Metrocolor
Columbia / Spelling–Goldberg (Robert LaVigne)

In 1943, a failed marine returns home and pretends to be a war hero.
Careful small-town drama with good period feel but not much dramatic punch: Hail the Conquering Hero did it better.

w Stanford Whitmore d John Hancock ph Laszlo Kovacs m Fred Karlin

Jan-Michael Vincent, Glynnis O'Connor, Katherine Helmond, Dana Elcar, Bert Remsen, Richard Gere

'A rickety structure of strange events.'—New York Post

Baby Doll**
US 1956 116m bw
Warner / Elia Kazan

In the deep South, the child wife of a broken-down cotton miller is seduced by her husband's revenge-seeking rival.
An incisive, cleverly-worked-out study of moral and physical decay; whether it was worth doing is another question, for it's a film difficult to remember with affection.

wd Elia Kazan, play Tennessee Williams ph Boris Kaufman m Kenyon Hopkins ad Richard Sylbert

Karl Malden, Eli Wallach, Carroll Baker, Mildred Dunnock, Lonny Chapman
'Just possibly the dirtiest American-made motion picture that has ever been legally exhibited, with Priapean detail that might well have embarrassed Boccaccio.'—Time
'He views southern pretensions with sardonic humor, and builds an essentially minor story into a magnificently humorous study of the grotesque and the decadent.'—Hollis Alpert

'A droll and engrossing carnal comedy.'—
Pauline Kael, 1968
'A film in which everything works:
narration, casting, tempo, rhythm, dramatic
tension.'—*Basil Wright, 1972*

AAN: script; Boris Kaufman; Carroll Baker;
Mildred Dunnock

Baby Face**
US 1933   70m   bw
Warner (Ray Griffith)

Amorous adventures of an ambitious working
girl.
Sharp melodrama very typical of its time, with
fast pace and good performances.

w Gene Markey, Kathryn Scola, Mark
Canfield (Darryl F. Zanuck) *d* Alfred E.
Green *ph* James Van Trees

Barbara Stanwyck, George Brent, Donald
Cook, Margaret Lindsay, Arthur Hohl, John
Wayne, Henry Kolker, Douglass Dumbrille

Baby Face Harrington
US 1935   63m   bw

A timid man is mistakenly identified as a
public enemy, and chased by both cops and
rival gangsters. Thin but appealing comedy.
Charles Butterworth, Una Merkel, Nat
Pendleton, Eugene Pallette, Donald Meek.
Written by Nunnally Johnson and Edwin
Knopf; directed by Raoul Walsh; for MGM.

Baby Face Nelson*
US 1957   85m   bw
UA / Fryman—ZS (Al Zimbalist)

Fragmentary account of the life of a thirties
public enemy, with the star over the top and
the technicians doing what they can on an
obviously low budget.

w Irving Shulman, Daniel Mainwaring *d* Don
Siegel *ph* Hal Mohr *m* Van Alexander

Mickey Rooney, Cedric Hardwicke, Carolyn
Jones, Chris Dark, Ted de Corsia, Leo
Gordon, John Hoyt, Anthony Caruso, Jack
Elam

Baby Love
GB 1968   93m   Eastmancolor
(Avco) Avton / Michael Klinger (Guido
Coen)

An orphaned nymphet causes trouble among
the men in her foster home.
Ludicrous sexploiter which embarrasses a
good cast and descends into bathos.

w Alastair Reid, Guido Coen, Michael
Klinger, *novel* Tina Chad Christian *d* Alastair
Reid *ph* Desmond Dickinson *m* Max Harris

Linda Hayden, Ann Lynn, Keith Barron,
Derek Lamden, Diana Dors, Patience Collier,
Dick Emery

The Baby Maker
US 1970   109m   Technicolor

A freewheeling girl agrees to have a baby for a
childless couple. Stretched-out fable for our
time which refrains from pointing a moral and
is generally tastefully done but nevertheless
outstays its welcome. Barbara Hershey, Collin
Wilcox-Horne, Sam Groom, Scott Glenn,
Jeannie Berlin. Written and directed by James
Bridges; for National General.

Baby Take a Bow*
US 1934   76m   bw

An ex-convict is accused of theft, but his small
daughter unmasks the real culprit. *Shirley
Temple*'s first star vehicle was a solid enough
commercial property to take her right to the
top. James Dunn, Claire Trevor, Alan
Dinehart. Written by Philip Klein and E. E.
Paramore Jnr; directed by Harry Lachman; for
Fox.

Baby, the Rain Must Fall
US 1964   100m   bw
Columbia / Pakula—Mulligan (Alan Pakula)

A parolee rejoins his wife and daughter in a
Southern town, but his outbursts of violence
separate them again.
Hard work by all concerned scarcely produces
absorbing interest in this filmed play of the
Tennessee Williams school.

w Horton Foote, from his play The Travelling
Lady *d* Robert Mulligan *ph* Ernest Laszlo
m Elmer Bernstein

Steve McQueen, Lee Remick, Don Murray,
Paul Fix, Josephine Hutchinson, Ruth White,
Charles Watts

The Bachelor and the Bobbysoxer***
US 1947   95m   bw
RKO (Dore Schary)
GB title: *Bachelor Knight*

A lady judge allows her impressionable young
sister to get over her crush on an errant
playboy by forcing them together.
Simple but unexpectedly delightful vehicle for
top comedy talents, entirely pleasant and with
several memorable moments.

w Sidney Sheldon *d* Irving Reis *ph* Robert
de Grasse, Nicholas Musuraca *m* Leigh
Harline

Cary Grant, Myrna Loy, Shirley Temple, *Ray
Collins*, Rudy Vallee, *Harry Davenport*,
Johnny Sands, Don Beddoe

'Sure-fire stuff guaranteed to do no conceivable harm . . . the audience laughed so loud I missed some of the lines.'—*Shirley O'Hara, New Republic*

AA: Sidney Sheldon

Bachelor Apartment
US 1931   77m   bw
RKO (William Le Baron)

A virtuous working girl in New York falls for a rich woman-chasing bachelor.
Mildly agreeable early talking romantic comedy.

w J. Walter Ruben, John Howard Lawson *d* Lowell Sherman *ph* Leo Tover

Irene Dunne, Lowell Sherman, Mae Murray, Norman Kerry, Claudia Dell, Ivan Lebedeff

Bachelor Daddy*
US 1941   61m   bw

Three bachelors find themselves in charge of a baby. Best of the comedies starring Baby Sandy. Edward Everett Horton, Franklin Pangborn, Raymond Walburn, Donald Woods, Evelyn Ankers. Written by Robert Lees and Fred Rinaldo; directed by Harold Young; for Universal.

Bachelor Father
US 1931   90m   bw
MGM

A much-married elderly man visits his grown children.
Unremarkable star comedy of its day.

w Laurence E. Johnson, *play* Edward Childs Carpenter *d* Robert Z. Leonard *ph* Oliver T. Marsh

Marion Davies, C. Aubrey Smith, Ray Milland, Ralph Forbes, Halliwell Hobbes, Guinn Williams, David Torrence

Bachelor in Paradise
US 1961   109m   Metrocolor
    Cinemascope
MGM / Ted Richmond

A famous writer of advice to the lovelorn settles incognito in a well-heeled Californian community to observe its social habits.
Mildly amusing satire is too frequently interrupted by unsuitable romantic interludes in this rather ill-considered star comedy.

w Valentine Davies, Hal Kanter *d* Jack Arnold *ph* Joseph Ruttenberg *m* Henry Mancini

Bob Hope, Lana Turner, Janis Paige, Don Porter, Paula Prentiss, Jim Hutton, Virginia Grey, Reta Shaw, John McGiver, Agnes Moorehead

AAN: title song (*m* Henry Mancini, *ly* Mack David)

Bachelor Mother***
US 1939   82m   bw
RKO (B. G. De Sylva)

A shopgirl finds an abandoned baby and is thought to be its mother; the department store owner's son is then thought to be the father.
Blithely-scripted comedy which stands the test of time and provided several excellent roles.

w Norman Krasna *d* Garson Kanin *ph* Robert de Grasse *m* Roy Webb

Ginger Rogers, David Niven, Charles Coburn, Frank Albertson, E. E. Clive, Ernest Truex
'An excellent comedy, beautifully done.'—*Richard Mallett, Punch*
'This is the way farce should be handled, with just enough conviction to season its extravagances.'—*New York Times*
† Remade as *Bundle of Joy* (qv).

AAN: Felix Jackson (for original story)

Bachelor of Hearts
GB 1958   94m   Technicolor
Rank / Independent Artists (Vivian A. Cox)

Adventures of a German student at Cambridge University.
Sometimes agreeable, sometimes annoying, especially when romance gets in the way of the possibilities for fun.

w Leslie Bricusse, Frederic Raphael *d* Wolf Rilla *ph* Geoffrey Unsworth

Hardy Kruger, Sylvia Syms, Ronald Lewis, Eric Barker, Newton Blick

The Bachelor Party***
US 1957   93m   bw
UA / Norma (Harold Hecht)

New York book-keepers throw a wedding eve party for one of their fellows, but drink only brings to the fore their own private despairs.
Though the last half-hour lets it down, most of this is a brilliantly observed social study of New York life at its less attractive, and the acting matches the incisiveness of the script.

w Paddy Chayevsky, from his TV play *d* Delbert Mann *ph* Joseph La Shelle *m* Alex North

Don Murray, E. G. Marshall, Jack Warden, Philip Abbott, Larry Blyden, Patricia Smith, Carolyn Jones

AAN: Carolyn Jones

The Bachelor's Daughters*
US 1946   90m   bw
UA / Andrew Stone
GB title: *Bachelor Girls*

Four shopgirls and a floorwalker rent a Long Island house and pass themselves off as a wealthy family in order to lure suitable husbands for the girls.
Mildly amusing comedy with good performances.

wd Andrew Stone *ph* Theodor Sparkuhl *m* Heinz Roemheld

Adolphe Menjou, Gail Russell, Claire Trevor, Billie Burke

Back from Eternity
US 1956 97m bw
RKO (John Farrow)

An airliner is forced to crashland in headhunter country, and when repairs are made only five of the eight survivors can be carried.
Remake by the same producer-director of his own 1939 'B', *Five Came Back*, this time to considerably less effect despite superior production.

w Jonathan Latimer *d* John Farrow *ph* William Mellor *m* Franz Waxman

Robert Ryan, Anita Ekberg, Rod Steiger, Phyllis Kirk, Gene Barry, Keith Andes, Beulah Bondi, Fred Clark, Cameron Prud'homme, Jesse White

Back in Circulation
US 1935 82m bw

Girl news reporter wins her editor's attention by solving a murder. Sub-*Front Page* melodrama, of no intrinsic interest. Pat O'Brien, Joan Blondell, Margaret Lindsay. Written by Warren Duff; directed by Ray Enright; for Warner.

Back Room Boy°
GB 1942 82m bw
GFD / Gainsborough (Edward Black)

A timid meteorologist is sent to an Orkney lighthouse and unmasks a bunch of spies.
Fairly spirited star comedy of interest as a shameless rip-off of *The Ghost Train* and *Oh Mr Porter*, whose plotlines are milked but not improved: note also that Askey took over Will Hay's discarded stooges.

w Val Guest, Marriott Edgar *d* Herbert Mason

Arthur Askey, Moore Marriott, Graham Moffatt, Googie Withers, Vera Frances, John Salew

Back Street°
US 1932 93m bw
Universal (Carl Laemmle Jnr)

A married man has a sweet-tempered mistress

who effaces herself for twenty years.
Popular version of a sudsy bestselling novel.

w Gladys Lehman, Lynn Starling, *novel* Fannie Hurst *d* John M. Stahl *ph* Karl Freund

Irene Dunne, John Boles, June Clyde, George Meeker, Zasu Pitts, Doris Lloyd

Back Street°
US 1941 89m bw
Universal (Bruce Manning)

Competent remake.

w Bruce Manning, Felix Jackson *d* Robert Stevenson *ph* William Daniels *m* Frank Skinner

Margaret Sullavan, Charles Boyer, Richard Carlson, Frank McHugh, Tim Holt, Frank Jenks, Esther Dale, Samuel S. Hinds

AAN: Frank Skinner

Back Street°
US 1961 107m Technicolor
U-I / Ross Hunter / Carrollton

Glossy remake typical of its producer: unfortunately it fails to work because the heroine suffers too luxuriously.

w Eleanore Griffin, William Ludwig *d* David Miller *ph* Stanley Cortez *m* Frank Skinner

Susan Hayward, John Gavin, Vera Miles, Virginia Grey, Charles Drake, Reginald Gardiner

'Though there is a lot to be said for this new version's thesis that one can be just as lonely in a series of apartments and lovers' nests apparently never less than a hundred yards wide, the illusion is quickly shattered the moment one gets the impression that the lovers prefer to keep much the same distance during their moments of passion.'—*Peter John Dyer*

'Ross Hunter has updated this old faithful and given it a contemporary lack of significance.'—*Hollis Alpert, Saturday Review*
'The bathrooms look like the lobby of the Beverly Hilton . . . the fallen woman falls, not into the pit of shame, but into the lap of luxury.'—*Time*

Back to Bataan
US 1945 97m bw
RKO (Robert Fellows)

When Bataan is cut off, a Marine colonel organizes guerrilla resistance.
Modestly made and rather dislikeable flagwaver.

w Ben Barzman, Richard Landau *d* Edward Dmytryk *ph* Nicholas Musuraca *m* Roy Webb

John Wayne, Anthony Quinn, Beulah Bondi, Fely Franquelli, Leonard Strong, Richard Loo, Philip Ahn, Lawrence Tierney, Paul Fix

Back to God's Country

US 1953 78m Technicolor
U-I (Howard Christie)

A sea captain battles the Canadian winter and a villain who wants his wife and his cargo of furs.
Old-fashioned adventure story, moderately well presented.

w Tom Reed, *novel* James Oliver Curwood d Joseph Pevney ph Maury Gertsman m Frank Skinner

Rock Hudson, Steve Cochran, Marcia Henderson, Hugh O'Brian

Backfire

US 1949 90m bw
Warner (Anthony Veiller)

A war veteran solves the murder of which his best friend is accused.
Confusing murder mystery of a very familiar kind, adequately made but with no particular style. Flashbacks don't help.

w Larry Marcus, Ivan Goff, Ben Roberts d Vincent Sherman ph Carl Guthrie ad Anton Grot m Ray Heindorf

Gordon Macrae, Virginia Mayo, Edmond O'Brien, Dane Clark, Viveca Lindfors, Ed Begley

Background*

GB 1953 82m bw
Group Three (Herbert Mason)
US title: *Edge of Divorce*

Two people decide on divorce, but thoughts of their children bring them together again.
Low budget, stiff-upper-lip marriage guidance tract, well acted but more well-intentioned than memorable.

w Warren Chetham Strode, from his play, with Don Sharp d Daniel Birt ph Arthur Grant

Valerie Hobson, Philip Friend, Norman Wooland, Janette Scott, Mandy Miller, Jeremy Spenser, Richard Wattis

Background to Danger**

US 1943 80m bw
Warner (Jerry Wald)

An adventurer thwarts Nazi intrigue in Turkey.
Good routine war action yarn, well presented and performed.

w W. R. Burnett, *novel* Uncommon Danger by Eric Ambler d Raoul Walsh ph Tony Gaudio m Frederick Hollander

George Raft, Brenda Marshall, Sydney Greenstreet, Peter Lorre, Osa Massen, Turhan Bey, Kurt Katch
'You could use this film for one kind of measurement of the unconquerable difference between a good job by Hitchcock and a good job of the Hitchcock type.'—*James Agee*

Backlash*

US 1956 84m Technicolor
U-I (Aaron Rosenberg)

A gunman seeks the father he has never met, who turns out to be a villain who sold his partners for gold to attacking Indians.
Rather unusual suspense western, very watchable for its mystery elements.

w Borden Chase d John Sturges ph Irving Glassberg m Herman Stein

Richard Widmark, Donna Reed, John McIntire, William Campbell, Barton Maclane

The Bacon Grabbers*

US 1929 20m bw silent

Bailiffs fail to recover a radio on which the instalments are overdue. Modestly pleasing star comedy on the lines of *Big Business*.
Laurel and Hardy, Edgar Kennedy, Jean Harlow, Charlie Hall. Written by Leo McCarey and H. M. Walker; directed by Lewis R. Foster; for Hal Roach.

The Bad and the Beautiful**

US 1952 118m bw
MGM (John Houseman)

A director, a star, a screenwriter and an executive recall their experiences at the hands of a go-getting Hollywood producer.
Very much a Hollywood 'in' picture, this rather obvious flashback melodrama offers good acting chances and a couple of intriguing situations; never quite finding the style it seeks, it offers good bitchy entertainment along the way, and there are references back to it in *Two Weeks in Another Town*, made ten years later.

w Charles Schnee d Vincente Minnelli ph Robert Surtees m David Raksin ad Cedric Gibbons, Edward Carfagno

Kirk Douglas, Walter Pidgeon, Lana Turner, Dick Powell, Barry Sullivan, Gloria Grahame, Gilbert Roland, Leo G. Carroll, Vanessa Brown, Paul Stewart
'For all the cleverness of the apparatus, it lacks a central point of focus.'—*Penelope Houston*

'Clever, sharply observed little scenes reflect the Hollywood surface: the egotistic babble at a party, the affectations of European directors, the sneak preview, the trying on of suits for catmen in a B picture.'—*MFB*

'It is a crowded and colourful picture, but it is choppy, episodic and vague. There does not emerge a clear picture of exactly how movies are made.'—*Bosley Crowther*

'The story of a blonde who wanted to go places—and a brute who got her there—the hard way!'—*publicity*

AA: Charles Schnee; Robert Surtees; art direction; Gloria Grahame
AAN: Kirk Douglas

Bad Bascomb*
US 1946   110m   bw
MGM (Orville Dull)

A sentimental bank robber becomes the hero of a group of travelling Mormons.
Pleasing though overlong star western, with good production values.

w William Lipman, Grant Garrett *d* S. Sylvan Simon *ph* Charles Schoenbaum *m* David Snell

Wallace Beery, Margaret O'Brien, Marjorie Main, J. Carrol Naish, Russell Simpson, Sara Haden

Bad Company**
US 1972   92m   Technicolor
Paramount (Stanley R. Jaffe)

During the Civil War, two youths on the run team up and become outlaws.
A successful attempt to recreate the feeling of past time, by the writers of another criminal myth, *Bonnie and Clyde.*

w David Newman, Robert Benton d Robert Benton *ph* Gordon Willis *m* Harvey Schmidt

Jeff Bridges, Barry Brown, Jim Davis, David Huddleston, John Savage

Bad Day at Black Rock****
US 1954   81m   Eastmancolor
   Cinemascope
MGM (Dore Schary)

A one-armed stranger gets off the train at a sleepy desert hamlet and is greeted with hostility by the townsfolk, who have something to hide.
Seminal suspense thriller—the guilty town motif became a cliché—with a terse script and professional presentation. The moments of violence, long awaited, are electrifying.

w Millard Kaufman, story Bad Time at Hondo by Howard Briskin *d John Sturges ph William C. Mellor m* André Previn

Spencer Tracy, Robert Ryan, Dean Jagger, Walter Brennan, Ernest Borgnine, Lee Marvin, Anne Francis, John Ericson, Russell Collins

'A very superior example of motion picture craftsmanship.'—*Pauline Kael*

'The movie takes place within twenty-four hours. It has a dramatic unity, an economy of word and action, that is admirable in an age of flabby Hollywood epics that maunder on forever.'—*William K. Zinsser, New York Herald Tribune*

'The skill of some sequences, the mood and symbiosis between man and nature makes this film sometimes superior to *High Noon*.'—*G. N. Fenin*

AAN: Millard Kaufman; John Sturges; Spencer Tracy

Bad for Each Other
US 1954   83m   bw
Columbia (William Fadiman)

A doctor back from the army scorns his home town for high society, but a mine disaster reverses his decision.
Misleadingly titled cliché drama, patterned after *The Citadel.* Actors ill at ease, handling competent but routine.

w Irving Wallace, Horace McCoy, from the latter's novel *d* Irving Rapper *ph* Franz Planer *md* Mischa Bakaleinikoff

Charlton Heston, Lizabeth Scott, Dianne Foster, Mildred Dunnock, Arthur Franz, Ray Collins, Marjorie Rambeau

The Bad Lord Byron*
GB 1948   85m   bw
Rank / Sydney Box (Aubrey Baring)

Byron lies dying, and imagines his life and loves under review in a heavenly court.
Thought risible at the time, this historical romance in flashback now seems no worse and even a little more stylish than most, though the script suffers from too many cooks.

w Terence Young, Anthony Thorne, Peter Quennell, Laurence Kitchin, Paul Holt *d* David MacDonald *ph* Stephen Dade *m* Cedric Thorpe Davie

Dennis Price, Mai Zetterling, Linden Travers, *Joan Greenwood*, Sonia Holm, Raymond Lovell, Leslie Dwyer
† The end of the British costume cycle which began with *The Man in Grey.*

The Bad Man
US 1940   70m   sepia
MGM (J. Walter Ruben)
GB title: *Two Gun Cupid*

A Mexican outlaw helps a former friend and unites two lovers.
Forgettable western comedy drama with a sterling cast.

w Wells Root, *play* Porter Emerson Brown *d* Richard Thorpe *ph* Clyde de Vinna *m* Franz Waxman

Wallace Beery, Lionel Barrymore, Laraine Day, Ronald Reagan, Henry Travers
† Previously produced by First National in 1923, and in 1930 with Walter Huston and O. P. Heggie.

Bad Man of Brimstone

US 1937 89m bw

An old bandit discovers his long-lost son and sees the light. Hilariously predictable but enjoyable star vehicle, quite palatable when it isn't too lachrymose. Wallace Beery, Virginia Bruce, Noah Beery, Dennis O'Keefe, Lewis Stone, Guy Kibbee, Joseph Calleia. Written by Richard Maibaum and Cyril Hume; directed by J. Walter Ruben; for MGM.

Bad Man's River

Spain / Italy / France 1972 90m
  Eastmancolor Franscope
Zurbano / Apollo / Roitfeld (Bernard Gordon)

Four outlaws accept the job of blowing up a government arsenal in Mexico.
Lurid western with comedy leanings and a somewhat eccentric cast.

w Philip Yordan, Eugenio Martin *d* Eugenio Martin *ph* Alexander Ulloa *m* Waldo de Los Rios

Lee Van Cleef, James Mason, Gina Lollobrigida, Simon Andreu, Diana Lorys
  'When shooting a western in Spain one should not say to oneself, "Never mind, no one is going to see it," because that will be just the film which the Rank Organization will choose to release in England.'—*James Mason*

Bad Men of Missouri

US 1941 72m bw

The Younger brothers become outlaws when they fight the influence of carpetbaggers.
Whitewashing of a family of western criminals; good double-bill entertainment. Dennis Morgan, Arthur Kennedy, Wayne Morris, Jane Wyman, Victor Jory, Walter Catlett. Written by Charles Grayson; directed by Ray Enright; for Warner.

The Bad News Bears

US 1976 103m Movielab
Paramount (Stanley Jaffe)

An ex-baseball professional coaches a team of tough kids.
Rough-tongued, sentimental star comedy.

w Bill Lancaster *d* Michael Ritchie *ph* John A. Alonzo *m* Jerry Fielding (after Bizet)

Walter Matthau, Tatum O'Neal, Vic Morrow, Joyce Van Patten

The Bad Seed*

US 1956 129m bw
Warner (Mervyn Le Roy)

A sweet-looking 8-year-old girl is a liar and a murderess; her mother finds out and attempts to kill her and commit suicide.
A real curiosity from an unexpected stage hit: absurd melodrama treated with astonishing high literary style and some censor-induced levity: at the end, after the little villainess has been struck by lightning, a curtain call shows her being soundly spanked.

w John Lee Mahin, *play* Maxwell Anderson, *novel* William March *d* Mervyn Le Roy *ph* Harold Rosson *m* Alex North

Nancy Kelly (rather uneasily recreating her stage role as the mother), *Patty McCormack*, Henry Jones, Eileen Heckart, Evelyn Varden, William Hopper, Paul Fix, Jesse White

AAN: Harold Rosson; Nancy Kelly; Patty McCormack; Eileen Heckart

Bad Sister

US 1931 71m bw
Universal (Carl Laemmle Jnr)

A small-town coquette falls for a city slicker, and her quiet sister gets her steady boy friend.
A teenage potboiler of its day, remarkable only for its cast.

w Raymond L. Schrock, Tom Reed, *story* The Flirt by Booth Tarkington *d* Hobart Henley *ph* Karl Freund

Conrad Nagel, Sidney Fox, Bette Davis, Humphrey Bogart, Zasu Pitts, Slim Summerville, Emma Dunn, Bert Roach

Bad Timing

GB 1980 123m colour Technovision
Rank / Recorded Picture Company (Jeremy Thomas)

In Vienna, an American divorcee has a strange and unhappy affair with a psychoanalyst.
Weird and unsympathetic sex melodrama, presented with the disconnected style expected from this director as a series of flashbacks from the heroine's near-deathbed.

w Yale Udoff *d* Nicolas Roeg *ph* Anthony Richmond *m* Richard Hartley

Art Garfunkel, Theresa Russell, Harvey
Keitel, Denholm Elliott, Daniel Massey
  'An enervating experience. Technically
flashy, and teeming with degenerate chic, the
downbeat tale is unrelieved by its tacked-on
thriller ending, and deals purely in despair.'—
Variety

The Badge of Marshal Brennan
US 1957 75m bw

A man on the run takes on the identity of a
dying marshal, and cleans up a corrupt town.
Satisfying lower-case western. Jim Davis,
Arleen Whelan, Louis Jean Heydt, Lee Van
Cleef. Written by Thomas G. Hubbard;
directed by Albert C. Gannoway; for Allied
Artists.

Badge 373
US 1973 116m Technicolor
Paramount (Howard W. Koch)

A police detective is enraged by the murder of
his partner and his own suspension after the
death of a suspect.
'Realistic' (i.e. violent and foul-mouthed) cop
thriller in the wake of *The French Connection*,
tolerable only for action highlights.

w Pete Hamill, from the exploits of Eddie
Egan d Howard W. Koch ph Arthur J.
Ornitz m J. J. Jackson

Robert Duvall, Verna Bloom, Henry Darrow,
Eddie Egan, Felipe Luciano, Tina Christiana,
Marina Durell
  'A deeply divided and scarcely reassuring
addition to the movies' composite portrait of
the American police force.'—*John Gillett*
  'Nasty, violent and humourless.'—*Sight and
Sound*
  'A movie well worth protesting about.'—
Michael Billington, Illustrated London News

The Badlanders*
US 1958 83m Metrocolor
Cinemascope
MGM / Arcola (Aaron Rosenberg)

Crooked westerners plan to rob a goldmine.
Rather sloppy western remake of *The Asphalt
Jungle*.

w Richard Collins d Delmer Daves ph John
Seitz

Alan Ladd, Ernest Borgnine, Katy Jurado,
Claire Kelly, Kent Smith, *Nehemiah Persoff*,
Robert Emhardt

Badlands***
US 1973 94m Consolidated Color
(Columbia) Pressman / Williams /
  Badlands (Terrence Malick)

A teenage girl and a young garbage collector
wander across America leaving a trail of
murder behind them.
A violent folk tale for moderns; very well put
together if somewhat lacking in point, it
quickly became a cult film.

wd Terrence Malick ph Brian Probyn, Tak
Fujimoto, Stevan Larner m George Tipton

Martin Sheen, Sissy Spacek, Warren Oates,
Ramon Bieri
  'One of the finest literate examples of
narrated cinema since the early days of Welles
and Polonsky.'—*Jonathan Rosenbaum*
  'So preconceived that there's nothing left to
respond to.'—*New Yorker*

Badlands of Dakota
US 1941 75m bw

A young man steals his elder brother's girl and
becomes sheriff of a corrupt western town.
Standard family fare. Robert Stack, Richard
Dix, Broderick Crawford, Ann Rutherford,
Frances Farmer, Hugh Herbert, Andy Devine,
Lon Chaney Jnr. Written by Gerald Geraghty;
directed by Alfred E. Green; for Universal.

Badman's Country
US 1958 72m bw

Pat Garrett, Wyatt Earp, Buffalo Bill Cody
and Bat Masterson have a showdown with
Butch Cassidy. Wildly unhistorical western.
George Montgomery, Buster Crabbe,
Malcolm Attenbury, Gregory Walcott, Neville
Brand. Written by Orville H. Hampton;
directed by Fred F. Sears; for Warner.

Badman's Territory
US 1946 97m bw

The brutality of the Texas state police forces a
sheriff to seek help from outlaws.
Unconvincing western with good moments.
Randolph Scott, Steve Brodie, Gabby Hayes,
Ann Richards. Written by Jack Nettlefold and
Luci Ward; directed by Tim Whelan; for
RKO.

Bagdad
US 1949 81m Technicolor
U-I (Robert Arthur)

A chieftain's daughter seeks revenge for her
father's death.
Thinly-conceived Arabian Nights
modernization, unsure whether to take itself
seriously.

w Robert Hardy Andrews d Charles Lamont
ph Russel Metty m Frank Skinner, Jack
Brooks

Maureen O'Hara, Vincent Price, Paul Christian, John Sutton, Jeff Corey, Frank Puglia

Bahama Passage
US 1941   82m   Technicolor
Paramount (Edward H. Griffith)

A sophisticated girl is determined to live on a salt-mining island in the West Indies.
Forgettable tropical romance in very pleasing early colour.

w Virginia Van Upp, *novel* Nelson Hayes
d Edward H. Griffith ph Leo Tover

Madeleine Carroll, Sterling Hayden, Flora Robson, Leo G. Carroll, Cecil Kellaway, Dorothy Dandridge

La Baie des Anges**
France 1962   85m   bw
Sud-Pacifique (Paul-Edmond Decharme)
GB title: *Bay of Angels*

A bank clerk who has had unexpected winnings at the Nice Casino falls in love with a compulsive gambler.
Good-looking romantic drama utilizing many of the cinema's most dazzling resources.

wd *Jacques Demy ph Jean Rabier m Michel Legrand*

Jeanne Moreau, Claude Mann, Paul Guers, Henri Nassiet

'Immense lightness, speed and gaiety . . . stunning visual texture.'—*Tom Milne, MFB*

Bail Out at 43,000
US 1957   82m   bw

Airmen test ejection seats for jet bombers.
Humdrum flagwaver. John Payne, Paul Kelly, Karen Steele, Richard Eyer. Written by Paul Monash; directed by Francis D. Lyon; for Pine-Thomas-Shane / UA.

Bait
US 1954   79m   bw
Columbia (Hugo Haas)

Gold prospectors fall out over a mine and a woman.
Antediluvian melodrama typical of this director, made more risible than usual by Cedric Hardwicke's introduction in the shape of Satan.

w Samuel W. Taylor d Hugo Haas
ph Edward P. Fitzgerald m Vaclav Divina

Hugo Haas, Cleo Moore, John Agar, Emmett Lynn

Balalaika*
US 1939   102m   bw
MGM (Lawrence Weingarten)

Russian exiles gather in Paris.
Mildly pleasing star musical.

w Jacques Deval, Leon Gordon, *play* Eric Maschwitz d Reinhold Schunzel ph Joseph Ruttenberg, Karl Freund m Herbert Stothart *songs* various

Nelson Eddy, Ilona Massey, Charles Ruggles, Frank Morgan, C. Aubrey Smith, Lionel Atwill, Walter Woolf King, Joyce Compton

The Balcony*
US 1963   86m   bw
Walter Reade / Sterling / Allen Hodgdon / City Film (Joseph Strick, Ben Maddow)

In a war-torn world, a brothel continues to attract customers of every variety.
Low-budget adaptation of a rather confused allegorical play: vivid moments hardly atone for reels of surrealist groping.

w Ben Maddow, *play* Jean Genet d Joseph Strick ph George Folsey m Igor Stravinsky

Shelley Winters, Peter Falk, Lee Grant, Peter Brocco, Kent Smith, Ruby Dee, Jeff Corey, Leonard Nimoy

'Relentlessly funny, shaggy, shocking.'—*Times*

'Unfit for exhibition to man, woman or child.'—*The People*

AAN: George Folsey

Ball of Fire*
US 1942   111m   bw
Samuel Goldwyn

Seven professors compiling a dictionary give shelter to a stripteaser on the run from gangsters.
Rather overstretched but fitfully amusing romp inspired by *Snow White and the Seven Dwarfs*.

w *Charles Brackett, Billy Wilder d* Howard Hawks *ph* Gregg Toland *m* Alfred Newman

Barbara Stanwyck, Gary Cooper, Oscar Homolka, Henry Travers, S. Z. Sakall, Tully Marshall, Leonid Kinskey, Richard Haydn, Aubrey Mather, Allen Jenkins, Dana Andrews, Dan Duryea

'It's played as if it were terribly bright, but it's rather shrill and tiresome.'—*New Yorker, 1982*

AAN: original story (Theodore Monroe, Billy Wilder); Alfred Newman; Barbara Stanwyck

Ballad in Blue
GB 1964   88m   bw
(Warner) Alexander and Miguel Salkind (Herman Blaser)
US title: *Blues for Lovers*

A famous pianist becomes friendly with a
blind boy and helps reconcile his parents.
Curious sentimental drama with the star
playing himself; competent but hardly rousing.

w Burton Wohl *d* Paul Henreid *ph* Ron
Taylor *m* Ray Charles, Stanley Black

Ray Charles, Mary Peach, Dawn Addams,
Tom Bell, Piers Bishop, Betty McDowell

Ballad of a Soldier**
USSR 1959   89m   bw
Mosfilm
original title: *Ballada o Soldate*

A soldier is granted four days' home leave
before returning to be killed at the front.
Lyrical tear-jerker most notable for its
impeccably photographed detail of Russian
domestic and everyday life.

w Valentin Yoshov, Grigori Chukrai
*d Grigori Chukrai ph Vladimir Nikolayev,
Era Saveleva m* Mikhail Ziv

Vladimir Ivashev, Sharma Prokhorenko,
Antonina Maximova
'In an epoch when the entertainment in
most entertainment films is little more than
offensive, its persuasive charm is particularly
welcome.'—*MFB*
AAN: Valentin Yoshov, Grigori Chukrai

The Ballad of Cable Hogue*
US 1970   121m   Technicolor
Warner (Sam Peckinpah)

A gold prospector takes a lengthy and
ineffectual revenge on men who robbed him,
and dies trying to be a hero.
Curious peripatetic western with the director
in uncharacteristically experimental and
comparatively non-violent mood. All
concerned seem to be enjoying themselves,
but the fun is not always communicated.

w John Crawford, Edward Penney *d Sam
Peckinpah ph Lucien Ballard m* Jerry
Goldsmith

Jason Robards, David Warner, Strother
Martin, Slim Pickens, L. Q. Jones, Peter
Whitney, R. G. Armstrong, Gene Evans,
Stella Stevens

The Ballad of Josie
US 1967   102m   Techniscope
Universal (Marty Melcher)

Cleared of the manslaughter of her husband, a
western widow renovates a derelict ranch and
sets up as a sheep farmer.
Tediously whimsical, unsuitably cast women's
lib comedy with so few laughs that it may
require to be taken seriously.

w Harold Swanton *d* Andrew V. McLaglen
ph Milton Krasner *m* Frank de Vol

Doris Day, Peter Graves, George Kennedy,
William Talman, Andy Devine, Audrey
Christie

Balthazar*
France / Sweden 1966   9
Parc / Ardos / Athos / Svenska
   Filminstitutet (Mag Bodard)
original title: *Au Hasard, Balthazar .*

The life of a talented donkey, born in the
Swiss alps and eventually killed during a
smuggling escapade.
Something between *Black Beauty* and a
Christian parable, this quiet, episodic film is
counted by some as its director's best work.

wd Robert Bresson ph Ghislain Cloquet
m Jean Wiener (and Schubert)

Anne Wiazemsky, François Lafarge, Walter
Green (amateur cast)

Baltic Deputy*
USSR 1937   100m   bw
Lenfilm

An old professor is finally reconciled to the
1917 revolution.
Propagandist biography (of scientist K. A.
Timiriazev) with interesting scenes and a
strong central performance.

w the directors and others *d* Alexander
Zharki, Josef Heifits *ph* M. Kaplan *m* M.
Timofeyev

Nikolai Cherkassov, M. Damasheva, A.
Melnikov

The Baltimore Bullet
US 1980   103m   Eastmancolor
Avco Embassy / Filmfair (John F. Brescia)

Adventures of a pair of pool sharks.
Flabby comedy attempting a lighthearted
version of *The Hustler*. The rewards are
meagre.

w John F. Brescia, Robert Vincent O'Neill
d Robert Ellis Miller *ph* James A. Crabe
m Johnny Mandel

James Coburn, Omar Sharif, Bruce
Boxleitner, Ronee Blakely, Calvin Lockhart

Bambi****
US 1942   72m   Technicolor
Walt Disney

The story of a forest deer, from the book by
Felix Salten.
Anthropomorphic cartoon feature, one of
Disney's most memorable and brilliant
achievements, with a great comic character in

Thumper the rabbit and a climactic forest fire sequence which is genuinely thrilling. A triumph of the animator's art.

supervisor David Hand *m* Frank Churchill, Edward Plumb

AA: song 'Love Is a Song' (*m* Frank Churchill, *ly* Larry Morey)
AAN: Frank Churchill, Edward Plumb

The Bamboo Prison
US 1955 80m bw

An American prisoner-of-war in Korea poses as a collaborator in order to get secret information. Forlorn war drama which makes little impact. Robert Francis, Brian Keith, E. G. Marshall, Dianne Foster, Jerome Courtland. Written by Edwin Blum and Jack de Witt; directed by Lewis Seiler; for Columbia.

Banana Ridge
GB 1941 87m bw

A business man's old flame presents him with an alleged son. Stagey farce salvaged by star performances. Robertson Hare, Alfred Drayton, Isabel Jeans, Nova Pilbeam, Adele Dixon, Stewart Rome. From the play by Ben Travers; directed by Walter C. Mycroft; for ABPC.

Bananas*
US 1971 81m De Luxe
UA / Rollins and Joffe (Jack Grossberg)

A meek and mild product tester for a New York corporation accidentally becomes a South American rebel hero.
Disjointed anarchic comedy with a few good jokes typical of their author.

w Woody Allen with Mickey Rose *d* Woody Allen *ph* Andrew M. Costikyan *m* Marvin Hamlisch

Woody Allen, Louise Lasser, Carlos Montalban, Jacobo Morales
'Full of hilarious comic ideas and lines, supplied by Allen and his collaborator; then Allen, the director and actor, murders them.'—*Stanley Kauffmann*
† Asked why his film was called *Bananas*, Allen replied: 'Because there are no bananas in it.'

Band of Angels
US 1957 127m Warnercolor
Warner (no producer credited)

In 1865, a Kentucky girl learns that her mother was black and is sold as a slave, but quickly becomes her owner's mistress.
Long-winded romantic adventure, rather lamely scripted and developed. The star's presence reinforces the impression of sitting through the ghost of *Gone with the Wind*.

w John Twist, Ivan Goff, Ben Roberts, *novel* Robert Penn Warren *d* Raoul Walsh *ph* Lucien Ballard *m* Max Steiner

Clark Gable, Yvonne de Carlo, Sidney Poitier, Efrem Zimbalist Jnr, Patric Knowles, Rex Reason, Torin Thatcher, Andrea King
'Too absurd to be dislikeable.'—*MFB*

Band Waggon*
GB 1939 85m bw
Gainsborough (Edward Black)

Comedians running a pirate TV station in a ghostly castle round up a gang of spies.
Film version of a long-running radio comedy series; quite a serviceable record of a phenomenon.

w Marriott Edgar, Val Guest *d* Marcel Varnel

Arthur Askey, Richard Murdoch, Jack Hylton and his band, Pat Kirkwood, Moore Marriott, Peter Gawthorne, Wally Patch, Donald Calthrop

The Band Wagon***
US 1953 112m Technicolor
MGM (Arthur Freed)

A has-been Hollywood dancer joins forces with a temperamental stage producer to put on a Broadway musical.
Simple but sophisticated musical with the bare minimum of plot, told mostly in jokes, and the maximum of music and song. Numbers include those listed below, as well as a spoof Mickey Spillane ballet finale. Level of technical accomplishment very high.

w Adolph Green, Betty Comden d Vincente Minnelli ph Harry Jackson songs Howard Dietz, Arthur Schwarz m Adolph Deutsch ad Cedric Gibbons, Preston Ames

Fred Astaire, Jack Buchanan, Oscar Levant, Cyd Charisse, Nanette Fabray
'The best musical of the month, the year, the decade, or for all I know of all time.'— *Archer Winsten*
† The Jack Buchanan character, Jeffrey Cordova, was first offered to Clifton Webb. It was loosely based on Jose Ferrer, who in the early fifties produced four Broadway shows all running at the same time, and acted in a fifth.
†† Songs include: 'A Shine on Your Shoes', 'By Myself', 'That's Entertainment', 'Dancing in the Dark', 'Triplets', 'New Sun in the Sky', 'I Guess I'll Have to Change My Plan', 'Louisiana Hayride', 'I Love Louisa', 'Girl Hunt' ballet.

AAN: Adolph Green, Betty Comden; Adolph
Deutsch

Bande à Part
France 1964 95m bw
Anouchka / Orsay (Philippe Dussart)
aka: *The Outsiders*

Aimless young people plan a robbery which
ends in murder.
Despite the plot, the emphasis is on fragments
of lyricism, and the film is not among its
director's greatest successes.

wd Jean-Luc Godard, *novel* Fool's Gold by
Dolores and B. Hitchens *ph* Raoul Coutard
m Michel Legrand

Anna Karina, Claude Brasseur, Sami Frey,
Louisa Colpeyn

'In a sense, the whole film is a metaphor
illustrating this glancing collision, when
fantasy and reality merge but one may still
remain unsure which is which.'—*Tom Milne,
MFB*

Bandido
US 1956 92m De Luxe Cinemascope
UA / Robert L. Jacks

Mexico 1916: an American adventurer helps a
rebel leader to defeat a gun runner.
Standard action fare, rather slackly handled.

w Earl Felton *d* Richard Fleischer *ph* Ernest
Laszlo *m* Max Steiner

Robert Mitchum, Gilbert Roland, Zachary
Scott, Ursula Thiess

The Bandit*
Brazil 1953 119m bw
Companhia Cinematographica (Cid Leite da
  Silva)
original title: *O'Cangaceiro*

The leader of a gang of outlaws comes to grief
after falling out with his second in command
over a woman.
One of the few Brazilian films to achieve
international popularity, mainly because of its
memorable theme tune. The film itself looks
attractive but becomes a bit of a bore.

wd Lima Barreto *ph* Chick Fowle *m* Gabriel
Migliori

Alberto Ruschel, Milton Ribeiro, Marisa
Prado

The Bandit of Sherwood Forest*
US 1946 87m Technicolor
Columbia (Leonard S. Picker, Clifford
  Sanforth)

Robin Hood frustrates the Regent who plans
to usurp the throne from the boy king.

A lively romp through Sherwood Forest with a
capable cast.

w Wilfrid H. Pettit, Melvin Levy, *novel* Son of
Robin Hood by Paul A. Castleton *d* George
Sherman, Henry Levin *ph* Tony Gaudio,
William Snyder, George Meehan *m* Hugo
Friedhofer

Cornel Wilde, Anita Louise, Edgar Buchanan,
Jill Esmond, Henry Daniell, George
Macready, Russell Hicks, John Abbott, Lloyd
Corrigan

The Bandit of Zhobe
GB 1959 81m Technicolor
       Cinemascope

An Indian chieftain kidnaps a British major's
daughter in retaliation for the death of his
wife. Tinpot action melodrama in the wake of
the rather better *Zarak*. Victor Mature,
Anthony Newley, Anne Aubrey, Norman
Wooland. Written and directed by John
Gilling; for Warwick / Columbia.

Bandits of Corsica: see The Corsican
  Brothers

Bandits of Orgosolo
Italy 1961 98m bw
Titanus

A Sardinian shepherd shelters some bandits
and becomes one of them.
Rather slow character adventure which
achieved some international reputation in its
first release.

wd Vittorio de Seta *m* Valentino Bucchi

Michele Cossu, Peppeddu Cuccu, and amateur
cast

Bandolero!*
US 1968 108m De Luxe Panavision
TCF (Robert L. Jacks)

In Texas, fugitive outlaw brothers run into
trouble with their Mexican counterparts.
Dour and downbeat but well-staged western
with emphasis on hanging and rape; an
unusual mixture but smoothly assembled.

w James Lee Barrett *d* Andrew V. McLaglen
ph William H. Clothier *m* Jerry Goldsmith

James Stewart, Dean Martin, Raquel Welch,
George Kennedy, Will Geer, Andrew Prine

Bang the Drum Slowly
US 1973 96m Movielab
Paramount (Maurice and Lois Rosenfield)

A baseball star finds that he is dying of
leukemia.
Cliché-ridden tearjerker in the modern style.

w Mark Harris, from his novel *d* John Hancock *ph* Richard Shore *m* Stephen Lawrence

Michael Moriarty, Robert de Niro, Vincent Gardenia, Phil Foster

AAN: Vincent Gardenia

Bang, You're Dead
GB 1954 88m bw
British Lion / Wellington (Lance Comfort)

A small boy accidentally shoots a local villain, and another man is arrested.
Singularly pointless and unattractive melodrama, a long way behind *The Window* and *The Yellow Balloon.*

w Guy Elmes, Ernest Borneman *d* Lance Comfort *ph* Brendan J. Stafford *m* Eric Spear

Jack Warner, Derek Farr, Veronica Hurst, Gordon Harker, Michael Medwin, Anthony Richmond, Philip Saville

Banjo on my Knee**
US 1936 95m bw
TCF (Nunnally Johnson)

In a Mississippi riverboat shanty town, a wedding night is interrupted when the groom is arrested during a brawl.
Unusual, easy-going comedy in which the stars sing and dance as well as fool around.

w *Nunnally Johnson, novel* Harry Hamilton *d John Cromwell ph* Ernest Palmer *m* Arthur Lange *songs* Jimmy McHugh, Harold Adamson

Barbara Stanwyck, Joel McCrea, Buddy Ebsen, Walter Brennan, Helen Westley, Walter Catlett, Tony Martin, Katherine de Mille

The Bank Dick**
US 1940 73m bw
Universal
GB title: *The Bank Detective*

In Lompoc, California, a ne'er-do-well accidentally stops a hold-up, is made a bank detective, acquires deeds to a worthless mine and interferes in the production of a film.
Imperfect, but probably the best Fields vehicle there is: the jokes sometimes end in mid-air, but there are delicious moments and very little padding. The character names are sometimes funnier than the script: they include Egbert Sousè (accent grave over the 'e'), J. Pinkerton Snoopington, Ogg Oggilbie and Filthy McNasty.

w Mahatma Kane Jeeves (W. C. Fields) *d* Eddie Cline *ph* Milton Krasner *md* Charles Previn

W. C. Fields, Franklin Pangborn, Shemp Howard, Jack Norton, Grady Sutton, Cora Witherspoon

'One of the great classics of American comedy.'—*Robert Lewis Taylor*

'When the man is funny he is terrific . . . but the story is makeshift, the other characters are stock types, the only pace discernible is the distance between drinks or the rhythm of the fleeting seconds it takes Fields to size up trouble coming and duck the hell out.'—*Otis Ferguson*

Bank Holiday*
GB 1938 86m bw
Gainsborough (Edward Black)
US title: *Three on a Weekend*

The lives of various people intertwine during a day out in Brighton.
Simple but effective slice-of-life comedy-drama, establishing several actors and a director. Still quite refreshing.

w Hans Wilhelm, Rodney Ackland, Roger Burford *d Carol Reed ph* Arthur Crabtree

Margaret Lockwood, Hugh Williams, Kathleen Harrison, Wally Patch, Rene Ray, Linden Travers, Garry Marsh, Wilfrid Lawson

The Bank Shot*
US 1974 83m De Luxe
UA / Hal Landers, Bobby Roberts

Using house-moving equipment, an escaped convict steals a whole bank.
Extended chase comedy with scenes of gleeful destruction. Acceptable for those in the mood, but a shade overdone.

w Wendell Mayes, *novel* Donald E. Westlake *d* Gower Champion *ph* Harry Stradling Jnr *m* John Morris

George C. Scott, Joanna Cassidy, Sorrell Brooke, G. Wood, Clifton James

Bannerline*
US 1951 87m bw
MGM (Henry Berman)

To comfort a dying old man, a young reporter prints a fake newspaper showing the indictment of the old man's gangster enemy. By an odd chain of events, the story becomes true.
Worthy but rather dull MGM 'B', typical of the regime of Dore Schary, boasting a pleasing small-town atmosphere and a remarkable cast of old actors.

w Charles Schnee, *story* Samson Raphaelson *d* Don Weis *ph* Harold Lipstein *m* Rudolph Kopp

Lionel Barrymore, Keefe Brasselle, Sally
Forrest, Lewis Stone, Elizabeth Risdon, J.
Carrol Naish, Spring Byington, Larry Keating

Banning
US 1967   102m   Techniscope
Universal (Dick Berg)

A golf pro has sporting and amorous
adventures at a country club.
Tedious, complexly plotted melodrama of life
among the idle rich; handling generally
laboured. A showcase for the studio's young
contract talent.

w James Lee d Ron Winston ph Loyal
Griggs m Quincy Jones

Robert Wagner, Anjanette Comer, Jill St
John, Guy Stockwell, James Farentino, Susan
Clark, Howard St John, Mike Kellin, Sean
Garrison, Gene Hackman

AAN: song 'The Eyes of Love' (m Quincy
Jones, ly Bob Russell)

Barabbas*
Italy / US 1962   144m   Technirama
Columbia / Dino de Laurentiis

Pardoned instead of Christ, Barabbas is
sentenced to the silver mines, turns Christian,
and becomes a gladiator.
Overblown epic which starts with a genuine
eclipse of the sun and has nowhere to go but
down. The cast sparks a few moments, but it is
generally a gaudy display of carnage.

w Christopher Fry, Nigel Balchin, Diego
Fabbri, Ivo Perilli, novel Pär Lagerkvist
d Richard Fleischer ph Aldo Tonti m Mario
Nascimbene ad Mario Chiari

Anthony Quinn, Silvana Mangano, Vittorio
Gassman, Ernest Borgnine, Jack Palance,
Arthur Kennedy, Norman Wooland,
Valentina Cortese, Harry Andrews, Katy
Jurado, Michael Gwynn
  'Unacceptable in its pain-preoccupation and
its religiosity.'—Peter John Dyer

Barbarella*
France / Italy 1967   98m   Technicolor
  Panavision
Marianne / Dino de Laurentiis

A beautiful young 40th-century astronaut
prevents the positronic ray from getting into
the wrong hands.
Campy and slightly sick adventures with angels
and other space people, from a highly
censorable comic strip; some ingenious
gadgetry and design, but not much of interest
in the foreground.

w Terry Southern, book Jean-Claude Forest
d Roger Vadim ph Claude Renoir pd Mario
Garbuglia m Bob Crewe, Charles Fox

Jane Fonda, John Phillip Law, Anita
Pallenberg, Milo O'Shea, David Hemmings,
Marcel Marceau, Ugo Tognazzi, Claude
Dauphin
  'A leading science fiction authority has
claimed that if Lewis Carroll were alive today
he would inevitably have written not Alice's
Adventures in Wonderland but Lolita. He
might perhaps equally well have written
Barbarella.'—Jack Ibberson
  'A flaccid, jaded appeal to our baser
appetites, always liberally doused with essence
of cop-out, resulting in elucubrated, anaemic
pornography.'—John Simon

The Barbarian
US 1933   90m approx   bw
MGM
GB title: A Night in Cairo

An American lady travelling in the Middle
East falls for a local potentate.
Shades of The Sheik. Actually this version was
first made in 1924 as The Arab, with the same
leading man. Either version would seem fairly
hysterical now.

w Anita Loos, Elmer Harris, play Edgar
Selwyn d Sam Wood ph Harold Rosson

Ramon Novarro, Myrna Loy, Reginald
Denny, C. Aubrey Smith, Louise Closser
Hale, Edward Arnold

The Barbarian and the Geisha*
US 1958   105m   Eastmancolor
  Cinemascope
TCF (Eugene Frenke)

In 1856 the first US diplomat to visit Japan
meets local opposition but is helped by a
geisha.
Episodic semi-historical romance which
scarcely suits the talents of those involved.

w Charles Grayson d John Huston
ph Charles G. Clarke m Hugo Friedhofer

John Wayne, Eiko Ando, Sam Jaffe, So
Yamamura
  'It is saddening to think that the director of
The Asphalt Jungle has gained professional
freedom and international celebrity to
become, at 51, yet another taskmaster who
goes out in the midday sun.'—Arlene Croce

Barbary Coast**
US 1935   91m   bw
Samuel Goldwyn

During San Francisco's gold rush days a
ruthless club owner builds a lonely girl into a

star attraction but cannot win her love.
Juicy melodrama tailored for its stars, but with
excellent background detail, sets and lighting.

w Ben Hecht, Charles MacArthur *d Howard
Hawks ph* Ray June *m* Alfred Newman

Edward G. Robinson, Miriam Hopkins, Joel
McCrea, Walter Brennan, Frank Craven,
Brian Donlevy, Donald Meek
† David Niven made his first screen
appearance as an extra.

AAN: Ray June

Barbary Coast Gent
US 1944   87m   bw
MGM (Orville Dull)

A bandit from the Californian goldfields tries
to go straight in San Francisco.
Star comedy drama, somewhat below par
despite attractive settings and good
production.

w William Lipman, Grant Garrett, Harry
Ruskin *d* Roy del Ruth *ph* Charles Salerno
Jnr *m* David Snell

Wallace Beery, Binnie Barnes, Frances
Rafferty, Chill Wills, Ray Collins, John
Carradine, Noah Beery, Morris Ankrum,
Henry O'Neill, Donald Meek, Paul Hurst,
Louise Beavers

Bardelys the Magnificent
US 1926   88m at 24 fps   bw   silent

A sixteenth-century French adventurer finally
wins his fair lady. Laboured swashbuckler.
John Gilbert, Eleanor Boardman, George K.
Arthur. Written by Dorothy Farnum, from the
novel by Rafael Sabatini; directed by King
Vidor; for MGM.

Barefoot Battalion
Greece 1954   89m   bw
Peter Boudoures

War orphans inhabit a derelict barge and band
together to harass the Germans.
Unlikely true story, roughly dramatized and
poorly produced.

w Nico Katsiotes *d* Gregg Tallas *ph* Mixalis
Gaziadis *m* Mikis Theodorakis

Maria Costi, Nico Fermas, Stavros Krozos

The Barefoot Contessa*
US 1954   128m   Technicolor
UA / Figaro (Forrest E. Johnston)

A glamorous barefoot dancer in a Spanish
cabaret is turned into a Hollywood star, but
her sexual frustrations lead to a tragic end.
A fascinating farrago of addled philosophy and

lame wisecracks, very typical of a writer-
director here not at his best, decorated by a
splendid gallery of actors and some attractive
settings.

*wd Joseph L. Mankiewicz ph Jack Cardiff
m* Mario Nascimbene

Humphrey Bogart, Ava Gardner, Edmond
O'Brien, Marius Goring, Valentina Cortese,
Rossano Brazzi, Elizabeth Sellars, Warren
Stevens

   'This example of the Higher Lunacy must
vie with *Johnny Guitar* for the silliest film of
the year.'—*Gavin Lambert*
   'A trash masterpiece: a Cinderella story in
which the prince turns out to be impotent.'—
Pauline Kael, 1968

AA: Edmond O'Brien
AAN: Joseph L. Mankiewicz (as writer)

The Barefoot Executive*
US 1970   96m   Technicolor
Walt Disney (Bill Anderson)

A TV network discovers that its most infallible
average viewer is a chimpanzee.
Quite a beguiling little farcical comedy with
mild doses of satire.

w Joseph L. McEveety *d* Robert Butler
ph Charles F. Wheeler *m* Robert F. Brunner

Kurt Russell, Harry Morgan, Joe Flynn, Wally
Cox, Heather North, Alan Hewitt, Hayden
Rorke

Barefoot in the Park**
US 1967   109m   Technicolor
Paramount / Hal B. Wallis

A pair of New York newlyweds rent a cold
water flat at the top of a liftless building, and
manage to marry the bride's mother to an
eccentric neighbour.
Breezy but overlong adaptation of a stage play
which succeeded through audience response to
its one-liners, which on the screen sometimes
fall flat. The people are nice, though.

w Neil Simon, from his play *d* Gene Saks
ph Joseph La Shelle *m* Neal Hefti

Robert Redford, Jane Fonda, *Mildred
Natwick*, Charles Boyer, Herb Edelmann,
Mabel Albertson

AAN: Mildred Natwick

The Barefoot Mailman
US 1951   82m   Supercinecolor
Columbia (Robert Cohn)

In 19th-century Florida, the mailman is joined
by a confidence trickster who later has a
change of heart.
Inept comedy adventure which never really
gets started.

w James Gunn, Francis Swann,
novel Theodore Pratt *d* Earl McEvoy
ph Ellis W. Carter *m* George Duning

Robert Cummings, Jerome Courtland, Terry
Moore, John Russell, Will Geer, Arthur
Shields, Trevor Bardette
† This is the title parodied by the Magoo
cartoon *Barefaced Flatfoot.*

The Bargee*
GB 1964 106m Techniscope
AB / Galton–Simpson (W. A. Whitaker)

A canal barge Casanova is trapped into
marriage.
The long-awaited comedy which was supposed
to make a film star out of TV's Young Steptoe
turned out to be rough and vulgar but not very
funny.

w Ray Galton, Alan Simpson *d* Duncan
Wood *ph* Harry Waxman *m* Frank Cordell

Harry H. Corbett, Ronnie Barker, Hugh
Griffith, Eric Sykes, Julia Foster, Miriam
Karlin, Eric Barker, Derek Nimmo, Norman
Bird, Richard Briers

The Barkleys of Broadway*
US 1949 109m Technicolor
MGM (Arthur Freed)

A quarrelling couple of musical comedy stars
split up, and she becomes a serious actress.
A rather flat and unattractive reunion for a
famous pair, with a witless script, poorish
numbers and very little style. The
compensations are minor.

w Adolph Green, Betty Comden *d* Charles
Walters *ph* Harry Stradling *songs* Harry
Warren, Ira Gershwin

Fred Astaire, Ginger Rogers, Oscar Levant,
Jacques François, Billie Burke

AAN: Harry Stradling
† Ginger Rogers was in fact second choice;
Judy Garland was cast but withdrew through
illness.
†† Songs include: 'They Can't Take That
Away from Me', 'Shoes with Wings On', 'My
One and Only Highland Fling', 'Swing Trot',
'Manhattan Downbeat', 'You'd be So Hard to
Replace', 'A Weekend in the Country', 'Sabre
Dance'.

Barnacle Bill
US 1941 90m bw
MGM (Milton Bren)

A fishing boat skipper gets romantic in the
hope of financing his enterprises.
Adequate waterfront comedy on *Min and Bill*
lines, consolidating a popular star teaming.

w Jack Jevne, Hugo Butler *d* Richard
Thorpe *ph* Clyde de Vinna *m* Bronislau
Kaper

Wallace Beery, Marjorie Main, Leo Carrillo,
Virginia Weidler, Donald Meek, Barton
Maclaine, Connie Gilchrist, Sara Haden

Barnacle Bill*
GB 1957 87m bw
Ealing (Michael Balcon)
US title: *All at Sea*

The last of a long line of sailors suffers from
seasickness, and takes command of a decaying
Victorian pier at an English seaside resort.
Quite an amusing comedy which had the
misfortune to come at the tag-end of the
Ealing classics and so seemed too mild and
predictable. Perhaps it was a little staid.

w T. E. B. Clarke *d* Charles Frend
ph Douglas Slocombe *m* John Addison

Alec Guinness, Irene Browne, Percy Herbert,
Harold Goodwin, Maurice Denham, George
Rose, Lionel Jeffries, Victor Maddern

Le Baron Fantôme*
France 1943 100m bw
Consortium de Productions de Films
   (Robert Florat)
GB title: *The Phantom Baron*

In the early 19th-century, the disappearance of
a nobleman causes problems for his heirs.
Macabre fairy tale with effective scenes which
seem to relate to Cocteau's later fantasies; the
film as a whole is less effective.

wd Serge de Poligny *dialogue* Jean Cocteau
ph Roger Hubert *m* Louis Beydts

Jany Holt, Odette Joyeux, Alain Cuny,
Gabrielle Dorziat

Baron Munchausen*
Czechoslovakia 1962 81m Agfacolor
Ceskoslovensky Film
original title: *Baron Prasil*

An astronaut finds on the moon the famous
liar Baron Munchausen, who takes him back
to earth and a variety of exaggerated
adventures.
Amusing variation on the old stories, using
live action against deliberately artificial
backgrounds.

wd Karel Zeman, from the novel by Gottfried
Burger and the illustrations by Gustave Doré
ph Jiri Tarantik *m* Zdenek Liska

Milos Kopecky, Rudolf Jelinek, Jana
Becjchova

The Baron of Arizona
US 1950   85m   bw
Lippert (Carl Hittleman)

In the 19th century a clerk tries to claim the
whole of Arizona by false land grants.
Initially appealing but basically rather feeble
tall tale, ineffectively worked out and
decidedly undernourished as a production.

wd Samuel Fuller *ph* James Wong Howe
m Paul Dunlap

Vincent Price, Ellen Drew, Beulah Bondi,
Vladimir Sokoloff, Reed Hadley, Robert
Barrat

The Baroness and the Butler
US 1938   75m   bw
TCF (Raymond Griffith)

The Hungarian prime minister's butler is loved
by a princess.
Thin mittel-European romantic star whimsy.

w Sam Hellman, Lamar Trotti, Kathryn Scola,
play The Lady Has a Heart by Ladislaus
Bus-Fekete *d* Walter Lang *ph* Arthur Miller
md Louis Silvers

William Powell, Annabella, Henry
Stephenson, Nigel Bruce, Helen Westley,
Joseph Schildkraut, J. Edward Bromberg,
Lynn Bari

Barquero!
US 1970   114m   De Luxe
Aubrey Schenck (Hal Klein)

A western ferryman is taken prisoner by
bandits but turns the tables.
Long, violent, rather uninteresting western in
the Spanish manner.

w George Schenck, William Marks *d* Gordon
Douglas *ph* Jerry Finnermann *m* Dominic
Frontiere

Lee Van Cleef, Forrest Tucker, Warren
Oates, Kerwin Mathews, Mariette Hartley,
Brad Weston, John Davis Chandler

The Barretts of Wimpole Street**
US 1934   109m   bw
MGM (Irving Thalberg)
TV title: *Forbidden Alliance*

Invalid Elizabeth Barrett plans to marry poet
Robert Browning, against her tyrannical
father's wishes.
Claustrophobic but well-acted adaptation of a
stage play which has become more forceful
than history. Stilted now, but still better than
the remake.

w Ernst Vajda, Claudine West, Donald Ogden
Stewart, *play* Rudolf Besier *d* Sidney
Franklin *ph* William Daniels *m* Herbert
Stothart

Norma Shearer, Fredric March, *Charles
Laughton*, Maureen O'Sullivan, Katherine
Alexander, Ralph Forbes, Una O'Connor, Ian
Wolfe

'When poets love, heaven and earth fall
back to watch!'—*publicity*

AAN: best picture; Norma Shearer

The Barretts of Wimpole Street
GB 1956   105m   Metrocolor
     Cinemascope
MGM (Sam Zimbalist)

Dreadful, miscast remake of the above, with
emphasis on the Freudian father-daughter
relationship. An unattractive and boring film.

w John Dighton *d* Sidney Franklin
ph Frederick A. Young *m* Bronislau Kaper

Jennifer Jones, Bill Travers, John Gielgud,
Virginia McKenna

Barricade
US 1939   71m   bw
TCF (Edward Kaufman)

A newsman and a girl with a past fight
Mongolian bandits in North China.
A bagful of clichés which does not quite add
up to entertainment.

w Granville Walker *d* Gregory Ratoff
ph Karl Freund *m* David Buttolph

Warner Baxter, Alice Faye, Charles
Winninger, Arthur Treacher, Keye Luke,
Willie Fung, Doris Lloyd

Barricade
US 1949   75m   Technicolor
Warner (Saul Elkins)

A tough mine-owner who runs a camp miles
from civilization meets his come-uppance
when three strangers are forced to accept his
hospitality.
Rough western only notable as an (almost)
scene-for-scene steal from *The Sea Wolf*: a
text-book adaptation.

w William Sackheim *d* Peter Godfrey
ph Carl Guthrie *m* William Lava

Raymond Massey, Dane Clark, Ruth Roman,
Robert Douglas, Morgan Farley

The Barrier
US 1926   79m at 24 fps   bw   silent

A brutal sea captain tries to prevent his
protégé's marriage. Brooding melodrama
climaxing in an Alaskan storm. Lionel
Barrymore (in his first film for the studio
where he spent the rest of his career), Henry
B. Walthall, Marceline Day, Norman Kerry.
Written by Rex Beach; directed by George
Hill; for MGM.

Barry Lyndon**
GB 1975   187m   Eastmancolor
Warner / Hawk / Peregrine (Stanley
   Kubrick)

Adventures of an 18th-century Irish gentleman
of fortune.

A curiously cold-hearted enterprise, like an art
gallery in which the backgrounds are sketched
in loving detail and the human figures totally
neglected; there is much to enjoy, but script
and acting are variable to say the least, and
the point of it all is obscure, as it certainly
does not tell a rattling good story.

wd Stanley Kubrick, novel W. M. Thackeray
ph John Alcott md Leonard Rosenman
pd Ken Adam

Ryan O'Neal, Marisa Berenson, Patrick
Magee, Hardy Kruger, Steven Berkoff, Gay
Hamilton, Marie Kean, Murray Melvin,
André Morell, Leonard Rossiter, Philip Stone
narrator Michael Hordern

'The motion picture equivalent of one of
these very large, very expensive, very elegant
and very dull books that exist solely to be seen
on coffee tables.'—*Charles Champlin*

'Watching the movie is like looking at
illustrations for a work that has not been
supplied.'—*John Simon*

'All art and no matter: a series of still
pictures which will please the retina while
denying our hunger for drama. And far from
re-creating another century, it more accurately
embalms it.'—*Michael Billington, Illustrated
London News*

AA: John Alcott; Leonard Rosenman
AAN: best picture; Stanley Kubrick (as
writer); Stanley Kubrick (as director)

Bartleby*
GB 1970   79m   Eastmancolor
Pantheon (Rodney Carr-Smith)

A young clerk gradually refuses to take part in
life.

A non-action film from an independent
source, praiseworthy but overlong and fairly
lacking in any kind of appeal except to literary
connoisseurs.

w Anthony Friedmann, Rodney Carr-Smith,
story Herman Melville *d* Anthony
Friedmann *ph* Ian Wilson *m* Roger Webb

Paul Scofield, John McEnery, Thorley
Walters, Colin Jeavons

Les Bas-fonds*
France 1936   92m   bw
Albatros (Alexander Kamenka)
aka: *The Lower Depths*

A clash of temperaments flares up between
derelicts in a dosshouse.

Uneven transposition of a famous work, with
patches of good acting.

w Jean Renoir, Charles Spaak and others,
play Maxim Gorky *d Jean Renoir ph* Jean
Bachelet *m* Jean Wiener

Jean Gabin, Louis Jouvet, Vladimir Sokoloff,
Robert Le Vigan, Suzy Prim

The Bat
US 1959   78m   bw
AA / Liberty (C. J. Tevlin)

A lady mystery writer rents a spooky old
house and finds herself and her guests at the
mercy of a maniac in search of hidden loot.
Poor remake of a standard twenties stage
thriller; everyone chews the scenery.

wd Crane Wilbur, *play* Mary Roberts
Rinehart *ph* Joseph Biroc *m* Louis Forbes

Vincent Price, Agnes Moorehead, Gavin
Gordon, John Sutton, Lenita Lane, Darla
Hood

The Bat Whispers**
US 1930   70m   bw
UA / Roland West

Classic early sound version of *The Bat* (qv) by
the director of the 1926 silent version.
Excellent use of camera, sets, and unusual
models.

wd Roland West ph Ray June, Robert Planck

Chester Morris, Una Merkel, Chancer Ward,
Grayce Hampton, Maude Eburne, Spencer
Charters, Gustav Von Seyffertitz

Bataan*
US 1943   114m   bw
MGM (Irving Starr)

Thirteen soldiers holding a bridge against the
Japanese die one by one.
Uncredited remake of *The Lost Patrol* (qv)
transposed to the Pacific war, with stereotyped
characters and much flagwaving. Very dated,
but a big box office film of its time, despite its
studio jungles.

w Robert D. Andrews *d* Tay Garnett
ph Sidney Wagner *m* Bronislau Kaper

Robert Taylor, George Murphy, Thomas
Mitchell, Lloyd Nolan, Lee Bowman, Robert
Walker, Desi Arnaz, Barry Nelson, Philip
Terry

'Naïve, coarse-grained, primitive, honest,
accomplished and true.'—*James Agee*

'The story America will never forget!'—
publicity

La Bataille du Rail**
France 1945   87m   bw
CGCF

Reconstructions of heroic resistance work by the French railwaymen during World War II. Reasonably compulsive documentary fiction which was plainly more inspiring at the time than it seems now.

wd René Clément *ph* Henri Alekan *m* Yves Baudrier

Salina, Daurand, Lozach, Tony Laurent

Bathing Beauty
US 1944   101m   Technicolor
MGM (Jack Cummings)

A songwriter plans to retire and settle down, but his publisher schemes to set his fiancée against him.

Witless, artificial aqua-musical, with plenty of unpersuasive high jinks but no real style despite a capable cast.

w Dorothy Kingsley, Allen Boretz, Frank Waldman *d* George Sidney *ph* Harry Stradling *m* Johnny Green *ch* John Murray Anderson

Esther Williams, Red Skelton, Basil Rathbone, Keenan Wynn, Ethel Smith, Xavier Cugat, Bill Goodwin

'I could not resist the wish that MGM had topped its aquatic climax—a huge pool full of girls, fountains and spouts of flame—by suddenly draining the tank and ending the show with the entire company writhing like goldfish on a rug.'—*James Agee*

Batman*
US 1966   105m   De Luxe
TCF / Greenlawn / National Periodical Publications (William Dozier)

The cloaked avenger saves an important executive from the clutches of four of the world's most notorious criminals.

Glossy feature version of the old and new serials about the comic strip hero who scurries around in his Batmobile making sure that justice is done. The scriptwriter's invention unfortunately flags halfway, so that despite a fairly sharp production the result is more childish than camp.

w Lorenzo Semple Jnr *d* Leslie Martinson *ph* Howard Schwarz *m* Nelson Riddle

Adam West, Burt Ward, Cesar Romero, Frank Gorshin, Burgess Meredith, Lee Meriwether, Alan Napier, Neil Hamilton

The Battle*
France 1934   85m   bw
Gaumont (Leon Garganoff)
English language version aka: *Thunder in the East, Hara Kiri*

A Japanese aristocrat urges his wife to befriend an English naval attaché and steal secrets from him; she does, and falls in love. Stagey but discreet melodrama of the old school, quite well made and acted.

w Nicolas Farkas, Bernard Zimmer, Robert Stevenson, *novel* Claude Farrère *d* Nicolas Farkas *ph* Roger Hubert

Charles Boyer, Merle Oberon, John Loder, Betty Stockfield, Miles Mander

The Battle at Apache Pass
US 1952   85m   Technicolor

Cochise negotiates peace with the whites, but Geronimo won't agree. Standard cavalry-versus-Indians western, with Jeff Chandler repeating his famous Cochise impersonation. John Lund, Susan Cabot, Bruce Cowling, Richard Egan. Written by Gerald Drayson Adams; directed by George Sherman; for U-I.

Battle beneath the Earth*
GB 1967   92m   Technicolor
MGM / Reynolds / Vetter (Charles Reynolds)

Enemy agents burrow under the US by means of a giant laser.

Agreeable schoolboy science fiction with fair special effects.

w L. Z. Hargeaves *d* Montgomery Tully *ph* Kenneth Talbot *m* Ken Jones *sp* Tom Howard

Kerwin Mathews, Vivienne Ventura, Robert Ayres, Peter Arne, Martin Benson

Battle beyond the Stars*
US 1980   104m   Metrocolor
New World / Roger Corman (Ed Carlin)

A small planet hires help to repel invaders. Impertinent and sometimes amusing space fiction rip-off of *Seven Samurai*, with plenty of in-jokes and quite pleasant special effects.

w John Sayles *d* Jimmy T. Murakami *ph* Daniel Lacambre *m* James Horner *ad* Jim Cameron, Charles Breen

Richard Thomas, Robert Vaughn, John Saxon, George Peppard, Sam Jaffe, Morgan Woodward, Darlanne Fluegel, Sybil Danning

Battle Circus
US 1952   90m   bw
MGM (Pandro S. Berman)

A patriotic nurse and a disillusioned major fall in love at a mobile army hospital in Korea. A flat, studio-bound potboiler with miscast stars, bound to provoke hilarity now as a serious version of *M*A*S*H*.

wd Richard Brooks *ph* John Alton *m* Lennie Hayton

Humphrey Bogart, June Allyson, Keenan Wynn, Robert Keith, William Campbell
'It is disappointing that Brooks, whose early work . . . suggested considerable promise, should have descended to such a glib, uninteresting piece of film-making.'—*MFB*

Battle Cry
US 1954 148m Warnercolor
Cinemascope
Warner (producer not credited)

During World War II, marines endure tough training before combat in Saipan; their sex lives come a close second to the war.
Interminable cheapie epic with both eyes on the box office: the cast salvages an odd moment or two, but violence of all kinds is the key to the entertainment.

w Leon Uris, from his novel *d* Raoul Walsh *ph* Sid Hickox *m* Max Steiner

Van Heflin, Aldo Ray, Mona Freeman, Dorothy Malone, Raymond Massey, Nancy Olson, James Whitmore, Tab Hunter, Anne Francis, William Campbell

AAN: Max Steiner

Battle for Music*
GB 1943 87m bw
Strand Films (Donald Taylor)

The story of the wartime ups and downs of the London Philharmonic Orchestra.
Not many films feature a classical orchestra, and this simple tribute, a mediocre production at best, has considerable historical interest.

w St John L. Clowes *d* Donald Taylor

Hay Petrie, Joss Ambler, Charles Carson, Jack Hylton. J. B. Priestley, Eileen Joyce, Moiseiwitch, Sir Adrian Boult, Sir Malcolm Sargent

Battle Hymn
US 1957 108m Technicolor
Cinemascope
U-I (Ross Hunter)

An American preacher with a guilt complex volunteers to help the South Koreans and after many adventures founds an orphanage.
Earnest, somnolent biopic of one Dean Hess; its mixture of drama, comedy, religion and war heroics is indigestible despite professional handling.

w Charles Grayson, Vincent B. Evans *d* Douglas Sirk *ph* Russell Metty *m* Frank Skinner

Rock Hudson, Anna Kashfi, Dan Duryea, Don Defore, Martha Hyer, Jock Mahoney, James Edwards, Carl Benton Reid
'The film seems to infer that heroic self-sacrifice, a little homely Eastern philosophy and a capacity for combining battle experience with an awareness of spiritual values are enough to overcome all emergencies.'—*John Gillett*

The Battle of Algiers*
Algeria / Italy 1965 135m bw
Casbah / Igor (Antonio Musi, Yacef Saadi)
original title: *La Battaglia di Algeri*

In 1954 Algiers, an ex-convict joins the terrorists in rebellion against the French government.
Politically oriented reconstruction of a bitter period of French colonial history, made better propaganda by its wealth of effective detail.

w Franco Solinas *d Gillo Pontecorvo ph* Marcello Gatti *m* Ennio Morricone, Gillo Pontecorvo

Brahim Haggiag, Jean Martin, Yacef Saadi, Tommaso Neri

AAN: best foreign film; Franco Solinas; Gillo Pontecorvo (as director)

Battle of Britain*
GB 1969 131m Technicolor
Panavision
UA / Spitfire (Harry Saltzman, Ben Fisz)

Summer 1940: England defends itself against aerial onslaught.
Plodding attempt to cover an historic event from too many angles and with too many guest stars, all indistinguishable from each other when masked in the cockpit during the repetitive and interminable dogfight sequences. On the ground, things are even duller.

w James Kennaway, Wilfrid Greatorex *d* Guy Hamilton *ph Frederick A. Young m* William Walton, Ron Goodwin

Laurence Olivier (as Dowding), Robert Shaw, Michael Caine, Christopher Plummer, Kenneth More, Susannah York, Trevor Howard, Ralph Richardson, Patrick Wymark, Curt Jurgens, Michael Redgrave, Nigel Patrick, Robert Flemyng, Edward Fox

Battle of Broadway
US 1938 84m bw

Two American legionnaires at a New York convention try to break up the infatuation of their boss's son with a showgirl. Amiably rowdy Flagg-and-Quirt imitation. Victor

McLaglen, Brian Donlevy, Gypsy Rose Lee, Raymond Walburn, Lynn Bari, Jane Darwell, Hattie McDaniel. Written by Lou Breslow and John Patrick; directed by George Marshall; for TCF.

The Battle of Neretva
Yugoslavia 1970   106m in dubbed version   colour   Cinemascope

In 1943, Yugoslav partisans resist German and Italian invaders. War spectacular with international cast; despite brilliant handling of the climaxes it didn't travel. Yul Brynner, Orson Welles, Hardy Kruger, Franco Nero. Written by Ugo Pirro and others; directed by Veljko Bulajic; for Jadran-Bosna.

The Battle of Paris
US 1929   71m   bw
Paramount

A lady music seller teams up with a pickpocket and falls for an American artist.
Primitive sound musical notable chiefly for its cast.

w Gene Markey d Robert Florey ph Bill Steiner songs Cole Porter

Gertrude Lawrence, Charles Ruggles, Walter Petrie, Arthur Treacher, Gladys du Bois

The Battle of Rogue River
US 1954   71m   Technicolor

A disciplinarian major at a western fort discovers that his friend is fanning hatred between Indians and whites, for personal reasons. Tatty western with little action, and that very lame. George Montgomery, Richard Denning, Martha Hyer, John Crawford. Written by Douglas Heyes; directed by William Castle; for Columbia.

Battle of the Bulge**
US 1965   167m   Technicolor   Ultra Panavision
Warner / United States Pictures (Sidney Harmon, Milton Sperling, Philip Yordan)

In December 1944, the Allies take longer than expected to win a land battle in the Ardennes because of a crack Nazi Panzer commander. Bloody and unbowed war spectacle, quite literate and handsòme but deafeningly noisy and with emphasis on strategy rather than character.

w Philip Yordan, Milton Sperling, John Melson d Ken Annakin ph Jack Hildyard m Benjamin Frankel

Henry Fonda, Robert Shaw, Robert Ryan, Telly Savalas, Dana Andrews, George Montgomery, Ty Hardin, Pier Angeli, Barbara Werle, Charles Bronson, James MacArthur, Werner Peters

The Battle of the Century**
US 1927   20m   bw   silent

The manager of an unsuccessful boxer accidentally starts a marathon pie fight. The first reel is lost, but the pie sequence is what matters, being one of the most celebrated pieces of slapstick in cinema history. Laurel and Hardy, Eugene Pallette. Written by Hal Roach and H. M. Walker; directed by Clyde Bruckman; for Hal Roach.

Battle of the Coral Sea
US 1959   85m   bw

During World War II a submarine commander, sent to photograph the Japanese fleet, is captured but escapes. Routine, unconvincing war heroics. Cliff Robertson, Gia Scala, Patricia Cutts. Written by Dan Ullman and Stephen Kandel; directed by Paul Wendkos; for Charles H. Schneer / Columbia.

The Battle of the River Plate*
GB 1956   119m   Technicolor   Vistavision
Rank / Powell and Pressburger
US title: Pursuit of the Graf Spee

Semi-documentary account of the 1939 trapping of the German pocket battleship Graf Spee in Montevideo Harbour, and of her subsequent scuttling.
A sympathetic view of a German hero, Commander Langsdorff (not unexpected from these producers) is the most notable feature of this disappointingly patchy and studio-bound war epic, with too many actors in ill-defined bit parts, too undisciplined a storyline, and too confusing scenes of battle.

wd Michael Powell, Emeric Pressburger ph Christopher Challis m Brian Easdale

John Gregson, Anthony Quayle, Peter Finch, Bernard Lee, Ian Hunter, Jack Gwillim, Lionel Murton, Anthony Bushell, Peter Illing

'It is difficult to understand how English film-makers can have done thus badly with material so apt to their gifts.'—Stanley Kauffmann

The Battle of the Sexes*
GB 1960   83m   bw
Prometheus (Monja Danischewsky)

A lady efficiency expert upsets the even tenor of life at an Edinburgh tweed manufactory, and the chief accountant plans to eliminate her.

Sub-Ealing black comedy which tends to misfire despite effort all round.

w Monja Danischewsky, from James Thurber's story The Catbird Seat d Charles Crichton ph Freddie Francis m Stanley Black

Peter Sellers, Constance Cummings, Robert Morley, Jameson Clark, Moultrie Kelsall, Alex Mackenzie, Roddy McMillan, Donald Pleasance, Ernest Thesiger

The Battle of the V1
GB 1958 109m bw
Maynard–Sewell (George Maynard)
US titles: *Unseen Heroes; Missiles from Hell*

Polish patriots sabotage the German rocket installation at Peenemunde.
Effective though schoolboyish war adventure shot on a low budget: story development reasonably brisk though predictable.

w Jack Hanley, Eryk Wlodek, *book* Bernard Newman d Vernon Sewell ph Basil Emmott m Robert Sharples

Michael Rennie, Patricia Medina, Milly Vitale, David Knight, Esmond Knight, Christopher Lee

The Battle of the Villa Fiorita
GB 1964 111m Technicolor Panavision
Warner (Delmer Daves)
US title: *Affair at the Villa Fiorita*

Two children aim to break up their mother's romance with an Italian concert pianist.
Quite lively, old-fashioned romantic comedy-drama largely set in a splendid Mediterranean villa; happy ending never in doubt.

wd Delmer Daves, *novel* Rumer Godden ph Oswald Morris m Mischa Spoliansky

Maureen O'Hara, Rossano Brazzi, Richard Todd, Phyllis Calvert, Olivia Hussey, Martin Stephens, Elizabeth Dear

Battle Stations
US 1956 81m bw

Life on an aircraft carrier as seen by the padre. Cliché-strewn, mini-budgeted war thriller. John Lund, William Bendix, Keefe Brasselle, Richard Boone. Written by Crane Wilbur; directed by Lewis Seiler; for Columbia.

Battle Taxi
US 1954 82m bw

A newcomer to the helicopter rescue service in Korea resents his non-combatant status, but becomes a hero. The story takes second place to one damned rescue after another in this lively but overlong second feature. Sterling Hayden, Arthur Franz, Marshall Thompson. Written by Malvin Wald; directed by Herbert L. Strock; for Ivan Tors / UA.

Battleground*
US 1949 118m bw
MGM (Dore Schary)

How a group of American soldiers in 1944 endured the Battle of the Bulge.
Enormously successful at the box office, this studio-bound production now seems stilted and unpersuasive, despite some good writing and direction.

w Robert Pirosh d William Wellman ph Paul C. Vogel m Lennie Hayton

Van Johnson, John Hodiak, Ricardo Montalban, George Murphy, Marshall Thompson, Jerome Courtland, Don Taylor, Bruce Cowling, James Whitmore, Douglas Fowley, Leon Ames
'Engrossingly well done.'—*Richard Mallett, Punch*
'The guts! the girls! the glory! of a lot of wonderful guys!'—*publicity*

AA: Robert Pirosh; Paul C. Vogel
AAN: best picture; William Wellman; James Whitmore

The Battleship Potemkin****
USSR 1925 75m approx (16 fps) silent; sound version 65m
Goskino
original title: *Bronenosets Potemkin*

A partly fictitious account of the mutiny at Odessa, an episode in the 1905 revolution. (The film was made as part of the 20th anniversary celebrations.)
A textbook cinema classic, and masterpiece of creative editing, especially in the famous Odessa Steps sequence in which innocent civilians are mown down in the bloodshed; the happenings of a minute are drawn into five by frenzied cross-cutting. The film contains 1,300 separate shots, and was judged the best film ever made in 1948 and 1958 by a panel of international judges.

wd *Sergei Eisenstein ph Edouard Tissé, V. Popov*

A. Antonov, Grigori Alexandrov, Vladimir Barsky, Levshin

Battling Butler*
US 1926 68m approx (24 fps) bw silent
MGM (Joseph M. Schenck)

A young millionaire pretends to be a boxer in order to win a sweetheart.
Middling star comedy.

w Al Boasberg, Charles Smith, Paul Gerard Smith, Lex Neal *d* Buster Keaton *ph* J. Devereux Jennings, Bert Haines

Buster Keaton, Sally O'Neil

The Bawdy Adventures of Tom Jones
GB 1976 94m Technicolor
Universal / Robert Sadoff

See *Tom Jones*, of which this is a musical version.
Not quite as bad as one would expect, but not up to the original.

w Jeremy Lloyd, *play* Don McPherson *songs* Paul Holden *d* Cliff Owen *ph* Douglas Slocombe *m* Ron Grainer

Nicky Henson, Trevor Howard, Terry-Thomas, Arthur Lowe, Georgia Brown, Joan Collins, William Mervyn, Murray Melvin, Geraldine McEwan, Michael Bates, James Hayter, Isabel Dean, Gladys Henson
'A cheap, crude, sexed-up rehash with only three actual musical numbers . . . more boring than bawdy.'—*Kevin Thomas, Los Angeles Times*

Baxter*
GB 1972 100m Technicolor
(EMI) Performing Arts (Arthur Lewis)

An American son of divorced parents comes to London with his mother, meets tragedy in the shape of a friend's death, and responds to treatment for a speech defect.
Slight, appealing case history of a maladjusted 12-year-old; a rather unnecessarily uncommercial slice of life with no easy solution offered.

w Reginald Rose *d* Lionel Jeffries *ph* Geoffrey Unsworth *m* Michael J. Lewis

Patricia Neal (as the therapist), Scott Jacoby, Britt Ekland, Jean-Pierre Cassel, Lynn Carlin, Paul Eddington

Be Big*
US 1931 20m bw

Ollie feigns illness to avoid a trip with his wife, but Stan's help proves disastrous. Comedy warm-up for *Sons of the Desert*; Ollie spends most of the second reel trying to rid himself of a tight boot. Laurel and Hardy, Anita Garvin, Isabelle Keith. Written by H. M. Walker; directed by James Parrott; for Hal Roach.

Beach Party*
US 1963 104m Pathecolor Panavision
AIP / Alta Vista (James H. Nicholson)

An anthropologist sets up house on a California beach to study the mating habits of young people but becomes personally involved when one of them falls for him.
Vaguely satirical pop musical with relaxed performances; quite tolerable in itself, it started an excruciating trend.

w Lou Rusoff *d* William Asher *ph* Kay Norton *m* Les Baxter

Robert Cummings, Dorothy Malone, Annette Funicello, Frankie Avalon, Vincent Price, Harvey Lembeck, Morey Amsterdam, Jody McCrea

Beach Red*
US 1967 105m Technicolor
UA / Theodora (Cornel Wilde)

In 1943, American assault craft take a Jap-held Pacific island.
Brutal, pacifist war film, simply and clearly portrayed but not exactly entertaining.

w Clint Johnston, Donald A. Peters, Jefferson Pascal *d* Cornel Wilde *ph* Cecil R. Cooney *m* Antonio Buenaventura

Cornel Wilde, Rip Torn, Burr de Benning, Jean Wallace

The Beachcomber*
GB 1954 90m Technicolor
GFD / London Independent (William MacQuitty)

An alcoholic ne'er-do-well in the Dutch East Indies reforms after an unexpected adventure with a lady missionary.
Styleless remake of *Vessel of Wrath* (qv); the acting just about holds the interest, but all other contributions are flat.

w Sydney Box, from Somerset Maugham's story *d* Muriel Box *ph* Reg Wyer *m* Francis Chagrin

Robert Newton, Glynis Johns, Donald Sinden, Paul Rogers, Donald Pleasence, Walter Crisham, Michael Hordern, Ronald Lewis

Beachhead
US 1953 90m print by Technicolor

American marines land on a Pacific island to bring back a planter who has supplied information. World War II jungle thriller, not too badly done. Tony Curtis, Frank Lovejoy, Mary Murphy, Eduard Franz. Written by Richard Alan Simmons; directed by Stuart Heisler; for Aubrey Schenck / UA.

Bear Country see The Living Desert

Bear Island
GB / Canada 1979 118m colour
  Panavision
Columbia / Bear Island / Selkirk (Peter Snell)

Meteorological experts on an Arctic island are menaced by neo-Nazis.
Highly implausible adventure yarn, indifferently presented.

w David Butler, Don Sharp, *novel* Alistair MacLean *d* Don Sharp *ph* Alan Hume *m* Robert Farnon

Vanessa Redgrave, Donald Sutherland, Richard Widmark, Christopher Lee, Barbara Parkins, Lloyd Bridges

The Bears and I
US 1974 89m Technicolor
Walt Disney (Winston Hibler)

An army veteran goes to live near an Indian settlement and adopts three bear cubs, later becoming a Park Ranger.
Simple, pleasing outdoor family film.

w John Whedon, *novel* Robert Franklin Leslie *d* Bernard McEveety *ph* Ted D. Landon *m* Buddy Baker

Patrick Wayne, Chief Dan George, Andrew Duggan, Michael Ansara

The Beast from Twenty Thousand Fathoms
US 1953 80m bw
Warner (Hal Chester, Jack Dietz)

Heat generated by an atomic bomb test in the Arctic thaws out a prehistoric rhedosaurus which travels down the American coast to cause havoc in New York until cornered and destroyed on Coney Island.
Flat-footed addition to the monster cycle, with an interminable wait for the beast's appearance and inferior trick work when he goes on the rampage.

w Lou Morheim, Fred Freiburger *d* Eugène Lourié *ph* Jack Russell *m* David Buttolph *sp* Ray Harryhausen

Paul Christian, Paula Raymond, Cecil Kellaway (as a professor gobbled up in a bathysphere), Kenneth Tobey, Donald Woods, Lee Van Cleef

The Beast in the Cellar
GB 1970 87m Eastmancolor
Tigon-Leander (Tony Tenser, Graham Harris)

A rampaging killer in the Lancashire woods turns out to be the deranged ex-soldier brother of two elderly spinsters who have kept him locked up for thirty years.
Idiotically boring farrago, totally lacking in suspense and wasting good talent.

wd James Kelly *ph* Harry Waxman, Desmond Dickinson *m* Tony Macaulay

Flora Robson, Beryl Reid, Tessa Wyatt, John Hamill, T. P. McKenna

The Beast Must Die*
GB 1974 93m Technicolor
BL / Amicus (Milton Subotsky)

A millionaire big game hunter holds a weekend party to track down a werewolf, but his guest list rapidly gets smaller . . .
A savage variation on *Ten Little Niggers*, not badly done, with such gimmicks as a 'guess who' break near the end.

w Michael Winder, *story* James Blish *d* Paul Annett *ph* Jack Hildyard *m* Douglas Gamley

Calvin Lockhart, Peter Cushing, Charles Gray, Anton Diffring, Marlene Clark, Ciaran Madden, Michael Gambon

Beast of the City
US 1932 80m bw
MGM

A police captain is determined to get a ruthless racketeer by fair means or foul.
Curiously dour little crime melodrama with a high death rate; the cast does not quite save it.

w John Lee Mahin, *story* W. R. Burnett *d* Charles Brabin *ph* Barney McGill

Walter Huston, Jean Harlow, Wallace Ford, Jean Hersholt, Dorothy Petersen, Tully Marshall, John Miljan
'Endowed with vitality and realism.'—*New York Times*

The Beast with a Million Eyes
US 1955 84m bw

A malicious space creature lands in the desert but is defeated by human love. Semi-professional would-be horror story, on a level with the Corman horrors of the period. Paul Birch, Lorna Thayer, Dick Sargent. Written by Tom Filer; directed by David Karminsky; for San Matteo / AIP.

The Beast with Five Fingers*
US 1946 88m bw
Warner (William Jacobs)

A famous pianist dies and his severed hand returns to commit murder.
Slow-moving, Italian-set horror thriller which wastes an excellent original; a superb central performance and clever trick effects can hardly redeem the stodgy script or the ending which reveals the hauntings as an hallucination.

w Curt Siodmak, *story* W. F. Harvey *d* Robert Florey *ph* Wesley Anderson *m* Max Steiner

Peter Lorre, Andrea King, Robert Alda, J. Carrol Naish, Victor Francen, Charles Dingle

The Beat Generation
US 1959 95m bw Cinemascope
Albert Zugsmith
aka: *This Rebel Age*

A vicious rapist joins the beatniks.
Bankrupt exploitation melodrama, not easy to
sit through.

w Richard Matheson, Lewis Meltzer
d Charles Haas *ph* Walter H. Castle
m Albert Glasser

Ray Danton, Steve Cochran, Fay Spain,
Mamie Van Doren, Jackie Coogan, Louis
Armstrong, Maggie Hayes, Jim Mitchum,
Irish McCalla, Maxie Rosenbloom
'An enervating mixture of slapstick,
religiosity, psychological hokum and grubby
sensationalism.'—*MFB*

Beat Girl
GB 1960 85m bw

An architect's teenage daughter goes to the
dogs. Risible exposé-style melodrama. David
Farrar, Noelle Adam, Christopher Lee,
Gillian Hills, Adam Faith. Written by Dail
Ambler; directed by Edmond T. Greville; for
Renown.

Beat the Devil*
GB 1953 100m bw
Romulus / Santana (Jack Clayton)

In a small Mediterranean port, and
subsequently on a boat bound for the African
coast, oddly assorted travellers plan to acquire
land known to contain uranium deposits.
Unsatisfactory, over-talkative and
inconsequential burlesque of the director's
own *The Maltese Falcon* and *Across the
Pacific*. Good fun was obviously had by the
cast, but audiences were mostly baffled by the
in-jokes, the extra-strange characters, and the
lack of attention to pace, suspense and plot
development.

w Truman Capote, John Huston, *novel* James
Helvick *d* John Huston *ph* Oswald Morris
m Franco Mannino

Humphrey Bogart, Gina Lollobrigida,
Jennifer Jones, *Edward Underdown, Peter
Lorre*, Robert Morley, *Ivor Barnard*, Bernard
Lee
'A potential treat emerged as a wet
firecracker . . . the incidents remain on a
naggingly arch and lagging verbal keel.'—*New
York Times*
'Each of its cinematic clichés appears to be
placed in the very faintest of mocking
quotation marks.'—*Time*
'Only the phonies liked it. It's a mess!'—
Humphrey Bogart

Beau Brummell*
US 1924 104m approx at 24 fps bw
silent

A Regency dandy becomes the right-hand man
of the Prince of Wales, but falters through his
own arrogance. Elegant period romance which
marked the beginning of its star's great movie
decade. *John Barrymore*, Mary Astor, Carmel
Myers, Willard Louis. Written by Dorothy
Farnum; directed by Harry Beaumont; for
Warners.

Beau Brummell*
GB 1954 111m Eastmancolor
MGM (Sam Zimbalist)

A Regency dandy enjoys a close relationship
with the Prince of Wales, and when this is
eventually withdrawn he dies in penury.
Stodgy historical romance with entertaining
patches; the main story is too graceful and
conventional to be believed.

w Karl Tunberg, *play* Clyde Fitch *d* Curtis
Bernhardt *ph* Oswald Morris *m* Richard
Addinsell *ad* Alfred Junge

Stewart Granger, Elizabeth Taylor, *Peter
Ustinov* (as the Prince), *Robert Morley* (as
George III), James Donald, James Hayter,
Rosemary Harris, Paul Rogers, Noel Willman,
Peter Bull, Peter Dyneley

Beau Geste**
US 1926 120m approx (24 fps) bw
(colour sequences) silent
Paramount (Herbert Brenon)

Three English brothers join the Foreign
Legion, suffer under a brutal sergeant, and die
fighting the Arabs.
Although outmoded even when first filmed,
this tale of derring-do and self sacrifice usually
works, and in this case it gave its star a fresh
image. One of the best remembered silents of
the twenties.

w Paul Schofield, *novel* P. C. Wren *d Herbert
Brenon ph* Roy Hunt *ad* Julian Boone
Fleming

Ronald Colman, Neil Hamilton, Ralph
Forbes, Alice Joyce, Mary Brian, *Noah Beery*,
William Powell, Victor McLaglen
† Remade 1939 and 1966; sequel, *Beau Ideal*,
1931.

Beau Geste**
US 1939 120m bw
Paramount (William Wellman)

Spirited remake, with the famous flashback
opening of the desert fort defended by
corpses. Style and acting generally
satisfactory.

w Robert Carson *d* William Wellman
ph Theodor Sparkuhl, Archie Stout *m* Alfred Newman

Gary Cooper, Ray Milland, Robert Preston, *Brian Donlevy, J. Carrol Naish*

'Its melodrama is sometimes grim but never harrowing, its pace is close to hectic and its suspense is constant.'—*Herbert Cohn, Brooklyn Daily Eagle*

'A morbid picture, but I doubt whether any morality council will take action, the whole story being so wrapped up in the school colours—in comradeship and loyalty and breeding, and the pure girl left behind; morbid because the brutality has no relation whatever to the real world; it is uncriticized day-dreaming.'—*Graham Greene*

AAN: Brian Donlevy

Beau Geste
US 1966 105m Techniscope
Universal (Walter Seltzer)

The central desert section of the story is here augmented, with violence stressed, and Beau allowed to survive at the end.
A cheap leery melodrama is what results from the jettisoning of all the romantic portions of the original.

wd Douglas Heyes *ph* Bud Thackery *m* Hans Salter

Telly Savalas (rampant as the sadistic sergeant), Guy Stockwell, Doug McClure, Leslie Nielsen, Leon Gordon, Michael Constantine

Beau Hunks**
US 1931 40m bw

A fool and his friend join the Foreign Legion to forget. Patchy but amiable star comedy with memorable high spots. In-joke: the woman the whole legion wants to forget is Jean Harlow.
Laurel and Hardy, Charles Middleton.
Written by H. M. Walker; directed by James W. Horne; for Hal Roach. (GB title: *Beau Chumps*.)

Beau Ideal
US 1931 75m bw
RKO (William Le Baron)

John Geste and a new legionnaire friend become involved in a religious war started by a rascally emir.
Lame sequel to *Beau Geste*, fettered by primitive dialogue.

w Paul Schofield, *novel* P. C. Wren *d* Herbert Brenon *ph* J. Roy Hunt *m* Max Steiner

Lester Vail, Ralph Forbes, Don Alvarado, Loretta Young, Irene Rich

Beau James*
US 1957 107m Technicolor
Vistavision
Paramount / Hope Enterprises (Jack Rose)

The vaguely crooked career of Jimmy Walker, mayor of New York in the twenties.
Romanticized biopic with few funny moments; Hope cannot cope with the drama, and the result is a creaking vehicle apart from a well-recreated twenties atmosphere and excellent production values.

w Jack Rose, Melville Shavelson, *book* Gene Fowler *d* Melville Shavelson *ph* John F. Warren *m* Joseph J. Lilley

Bob Hope, Paul Douglas, Vera Miles, Alexis Smith, Darren McGavin, Joe Mantell, Walter Catlett *guest stars* Jack Benny, George Jessel, Jimmy Durante *narrator* Walter Winchell (Alistair Cooke in GB)

Le Beau Serge*
France 1958 97m bw
AYJM (Jean Cotet)

A student returns to his home town and tries to redeem his old friend who has become a drunkard.
Enjoyable character drama with well observed village backgrounds. Credited with being the spearhead of the 'new wave'.

wd Claude Chabrol ph Henri Decaë m Emile Delpierre

Gérard Blain, Jean-Claude Brialy, Michèle Meritz, Bernadette Lafont

La Beauté du Diable***
Italy / France 1949 96m bw
AYJM

The Faust story with the protagonists agreeing to change places.
Dazzling plot twists and cinematic virtuosity make this a richly enjoyable fantasy, though perhaps not among Clair's greatest works.

w René Clair, Armand Salacrou *d René Clair ph* Michel Kelber *m* Roman Vlad *ad* Léon Barsacq

Michel Simon, Gérard Philipe, Raymond Cordy, Nicole Besnard, Gaston Modot, Paolo Stoppa

The Beautiful Blonde from Bashful Bend*
US 1949 77m Technicolor
TCF (Preston Sturges)

A temperamental saloon entertainer accidentally shoots the sheriff and takes refuge as a schoolmistress.
A dishevelled western farce unworthy of its

creator, but with the advantage of appearances by many of his usual repertory of players.

wd Preston Sturges *ph* Harry Jackson
m Cyril Mockridge

Betty Grable, Cesar Romero, El Brendel, Hugh Herbert, Rudy Vallee, Olga San Juan, Sterling Holloway, Porter Hall, Esther Howard, Margaret Hamilton

'She's got the biggest six-shooters in the west!'—*publicity*

'It erects a fabric of roaring slapstick on a conventional western foundation, and from time to time it succeeds in being very funny.'—*Richard Mallett, Punch*

'Somehow the ramshackle air of Bashful Bend itself seems to have permeated the whole film.'—*MFB*

Beautiful Stranger
GB 1954 89m bw
Maxwell Setton, John R. Sloan
US title: *Twist of Fate*

On the Riviera, an actress discovers that her fiancé is a criminal.
Tawdry star melodrama of virtually no interest.

w Robert Westerby, Carl Nystrom *d* David Miller *ph* Robert Day, Ted Scaife
m Malcolm Arnold

Ginger Rogers, Jacques Bergerac, Herbert Lom, Stanley Baker, Margaret Rawlings, Eddie Byrne, Coral Browne

The Beauty Jungle*
GB 1964 114m Eastmancolor
  Cinemascope
Rank / Val Guest
US title: *Contest Girl*

A typist enters a beauty contest and step by step becomes Miss Globe; but her descent is equally rapid.
Wicked show biz and the road to ruin in one glossy package, predictable, but not badly done; always something going on, and performed with gusto.

w Robert Muller, Val Guest *d* Val Guest
ph Arthur Grant *m* Laurie Johnson

Janette Scott, Ian Hendry, Ronald Fraser, Edmund Purdom, Kay Walsh, Norman Bird, Janina Faye, Tommy Trinder, Francis Matthews

Because of Him*
US 1945 88m bw
U-I

A waitress pesters a Broadway author and actor for a leading role in their new show.

Moderately sprightly star vehicle with bonuses in the leading men; handling disappointingly routine.

w Edmund Beloin *d* Richard Wallace *ph* Hal Mohr *m* Miklos Rozsa

Deanna Durbin, Charles Laughton, Franchot Tone

† A remake of *The Good Fairy*.

Because of You
US 1952 95m bw
U-I (Albert J. Cohen)

A female ex-convict marries on parole but does not tell her husband of her past. Her old associates involve her innocently in another crime, and her husband divorces her; but years later she gets him and their child back.
Soap opera of the stickiest kind, made quite tolerable by good production.

w Ketti Frings *d* Joseph Pevney *ph* Russell Metty *m* Frank Skinner

Loretta Young, Jeff Chandler, Alex Nicol, Frances Dee, Lynne Roberts, Alexander Scourby, Mae Clarke

'Shows the most whole-hearted devotion to woman's magazine conventions.'—
MFB

'Even in the first wild joy of her arms, he realized that she would be . . . an unfit mother!'—*publicity*

Because They're Young
US 1960 98m bw
Columbia / Drexel (Jerry Bresler)

A high school teacher helps one of his tougher pupils not to slip into crime.
Routine sentimental melodrama, slightly redeemed by directorial expertise.

w James Gunn, *novel* Harrison High by John Farris *d* Paul Wendkos *ph* Wilfrid Cline
m Johnny Williams

Dick Clark, Michael Callan, Tuesday Weld, Victoria Shaw, Warren Berlinger, Doug McClure

Because You're Mine
US 1952 103m Technicolor
MGM (Joe Pasternak)

An opera singer becomes a GI and wins the sergeant's sister.
Lumberingly inept star vehicle, giving the impression of nothing at all happening between the songs.

w Leonard Spigelgass, Karl Tunberg
d Alexander Hall *ph* Joseph Ruttenberg
md Johnny Green

Mario Lanza, Doretta Morrow, James
Whitmore, Dean Miller, Paula Corday, Jeff
Donnell, Spring Byington

AAN: title song (*m* Nicholas Brodszky,
ly Sammy Cahn)

Becket**
GB 1964   149m   Technicolor
    Panavision
Paramount / Hal B. Wallis

Henry II leans on his boisterous Saxon friend
Thomas à Becket, but when the latter is made
first chancellor and then archbishop a rift
between them widens and ends in Becket's
assassination by Henry's over-eager knights.
Jean Anouilh's bitter stage comedy is filmed
literally and soberly as a rather anaemic epic,
so that the point is lost and the edge blunted.
The paucity of physical action causes good
scenes to alternate with long stretches of
tedium.

w Edward Anhalt *d* Peter Glenville
ph Geoffrey Unsworth m Laurence Rosenthal
Richard Burton, Peter O'Toole, Donald
Wolfit, *John Gielgud*, Martita Hunt, Pamela
Brown, Sian Phillips, Paolo Stoppa
    'Handsome, respectable and boring.'—*John
Simon*

AA: Edward Anhalt
AAN: best picture; Peter Glenville; Geoffrey
Unsworth; Laurence Rosenthal; Richard
Burton; Peter O'Toole; John Gielgud

Becky Sharp**
US 1935   83m   Technicolor
(RKO) Kenneth MacGowan

An ambitious girl makes her way into Regency
society.
Chiefly notable as the first feature in three-
colour Technicolor, this rather theatrical piece
has its civilized enjoyments and the director
made a few predictable cinematic experiments;
the overall effect, however, is patchy.

w Francis Edward Faragoh, *play* Landon
Mitchell, *novel* Vanity Fair by W. M.
Thackeray *d Rouben Mamoulian ph Ray
Rennahan m* Roy Webb *pd Robert Edmond
Jones*
Miriam Hopkins, *Cedric Hardwicke*, Frances
Dee, Billie Burke, Alison Skipworth, Nigel
Bruce, Alan Mowbray, Colin Tapley, G. P.
Huntley Jnr
    'As pleasing to the eye as a fresh fruit
sundae, but not much more.'—*Otis Ferguson*
    'If colour is to be of permanent importance
a way must be found to use it realistically, not
only as a beautiful decoration. It must be

made to contribute to our sense of truth. The
machine gun, the cheap striped tie, the
battered Buick and the shabby bar will need a
subtler colour sense than the Duchess of
Richmond's ball, the girls of Miss Pinkerton's
Academy, the Marquess of Steyne's dinner for
two. Can Technicolor reproduce with the
necessary accuracy the suit that has been worn
too long, the oily hat?'—*Graham Greene*

AAN: Miriam Hopkins

The Bed Sitting Room*
GB 1969   91m   De Luxe
UA / Oscar Lewenstein (Richard Lester)

Surrealist romance; after a nuclear war,
motley survivors in the waste lands turn into
bed sitting rooms, cupboards and parakeets.
Arrogantly obscure fantasy, a commercial flop
which kept its director in the wilderness for
four years. Fans of Monty Python may salvage
a joke or two.

w John Antrobus, from the play by himself
and Spike Milligan *d* Richard Lester
ph David Watkin *m* Ken Thorne
pd Assheton Gorton
Ralph Richardson, Rita Tushingham, Michael
Hordern, Arthur Lowe, Mona Washbourne,
Peter Cook, Dudley Moore, Spike Milligan,
Harry Secombe, Marty Feldman, Jimmy
Edwards

Bedazzled*
GB 1967   96m   De Luxe   Panavision
TCF / Stanley Donen

A short order cook is saved from suicide by
Mr Spiggott, who offers him seven wishes in
exchange for his soul.
A camped-up version of Faust which resolves
itself into a series of threadbare sketches for
the stars. All rather desperate apart from the
leaping nuns.

w Peter Cook *d* Stanley Donen *ph* Austin
Dempster *m* Dudley Moore
Peter Cook, Dudley Moore, Michael Bates,
Raquel Welch, Eleanor Bron

Bedelia
GB 1946   90m   bw
John Corfield (Isadore Goldsmith)

A psychotic woman is discovered to have
poisoned three husbands.
Dreary upper-class British murder drama,
totally devoid of style or suspense but a big
star hit of the time.

w Vera Caspary, Moie Charles, Herbert
Victor, Roy Ridley, Isadore Goldsmith, *novel*
Vera Caspary *d* Lance Comfort *ph* F. A.
Young

Margaret Lockwood, Ian Hunter, Barry K. Barnes, Anne Crawford, Jill Esmond, Ellen Pollock

Bedevilled
US 1955 86m Eastmancolor
Cinemascope
MGM (Henry Berman)

In Paris, a novice priest befriends a girl on the run from gangsters. She turns out to be a murderess and is shot by her victim's brother. Absurd high-flown bosh, unsuitably cinemascoped in ugly colour, and surprisingly badly handled by old professionals.

w Jo Eisinger *d* Mitchell Leisen *ph* Frederick A. Young *m* William Alwyn

Anne Baxter, Steve Forrest, Simone Renant, Victor Francen, Maurice Teynac, Joseph Tomelty

'This mixture of melodrama and religion provides a most unedifying entertainment.'— *MFB*

The Bedford Incident***
GB 1965 102m bw
Columbia / Bedford Productions (James B. Harris)

A ruthlessly efficient US destroyer captain in the Arctic chases a Russian submarine and accidentally fires an atomic weapon. Gripping mixture of themes from *Dr Strangelove* and *The Caine Mutiny*, very tense and forceful, with excellent acting.

w James Poe, novel Mark Rascovitch *d James B. Harris ph* Gilbert Taylor *m* Gerald Schurrmann

Richard Widmark, Sidney Poitier (his first role with no reference to his colour), James MacArthur, Eric Portman, Wally Cox, Martin Balsam, Phil Brown, Michael Kane, Garry Cockrell, Donald Sutherland

'Strong on virtues of a rather negative kind.'—*Penelope Houston*

Bedknobs and Broomsticks
US 1971 117m Technicolor
Walt Disney (Bill Walsh)

In 1940 three evacuee children and a kindly witch ride on a magic bedstead and defeat the invasion of England. Extraordinarily dishevelled and incompetent Disney follow-up to *Mary Poppins*, a very muddled narrative with few high points and evidence of much cutting. Redeemed occasionally by camera trickery.

w Bill Walsh, Don DaGradi *d* Robert Stevenson *ph* Frank Philips *m / ly* Richard

M. Sherman, Robert B. Sherman *sp* Eustace Lycett, Alan Maley, Danny Lee

Angela Lansbury, David Tomlinson, Roy Smart, Cindy O'Callaghan, Sam Jaffe, Roddy McDowall, Bruce Forsyth, Tessie O'Shea, Reginald Owen

AAN: Richard M. Sherman, Robert B. Sherman; song 'The Age of Not Believing' by the Shermans

Bedlam**
US 1946 80m bw
RKO (*Val Lewton*)

In 18th-century London, a sane girl is confined by the malevolent asylum master.
Interesting but rather flatly handled addition to the Val Lewton gallery of horrors, perhaps too carefully and discreetly done for pace or suspense.

w Mark Robson, Carlos Keith *d* Mark Robson *ph* Nicholas Musuraca *m* Roy Webb

Boris Karloff, Anna Lee, Billy House, Richard Fraser, Glenn Vernon

† Carlos Keith was Val Lewton's pseudonym.
†† *Bedlam* was never granted a certificate in Britain.

Bedtime for Bonzo
US 1951 83m bw
U-I (Michael Kraike)

To prove that environment determines character, a chimpanzee is brought up as a human baby.
Very moderate fun and games which proved successful enough for a sequel, *Bonzo Goes to College*.

w Val Burton, Lou Breslow *d* Frederick de Cordova *ph* Carl Guthrie *m* Frank Skinner

Ronald Reagan, Diana Lynn, Walter Slezak, Lucille Berkely, Herbert Heyes

A Bedtime Story*
US 1933 89m bw
Paramount (Emmanuel Cohen)

A breezy Frenchman has to interrupt his romances to look after an abandoned baby. Mild star vehicle in which the agreeable comedy is largely supplanted by sentimental cooing.

w Benjamin Glazer, *novel* Bellamy the Magnificent by Roy Horniman *d* Norman Taurog *ph* Charles Lang *songs* Ralph Rainger, Leo Robin

Maurice Chevalier, Helen Twelvetrees, Baby LeRoy, Edward Everett Horton, Adrienne Ames

Bedtime Story*
US 1941   85m   bw
Columbia (B. P. Schulberg)

A playwright's wife wants to retire instead of
acting in his next play.
Pleasantly sparkling comedy with good
performances.

w Horace Jackson, Grant Garrett, Richard
Flournoy *d* Alexander Hall *ph* Joseph
Walker

Fredric March, Loretta Young, Robert
Benchley, Allyn Joslyn, Eve Arden, Helen
Westley, Joyce Compton, Tim Ryan

Bedtime Story*
US 1964   99m   Eastmancolor
U-I / Lankershim / Pennebaker (Stanley
   Shapiro)

Two Riviera confidence tricksters outwit each
other.
A fairly lively script is defeated by dull
handling, but performances and backgrounds
are attractive.

w Stanley Shapiro, Paul Henning *d* Ralph
Levy *ph* Clifford Stine *m* Hans Salter

David Niven, Marlon Brando, Shirley Jones,
Dody Goodman, Aram Stephan, Marie
Windsor
   'The most vulgar and embarrassing film of
the year.'—*Daily Express*

Bees in Paradise
GB 1943   75m   bw

Four airmen find themselves on a South Sea
island ruled by women who kill their spouses
after the honeymoon. Saucy farce, too
talkative to be very interesting even in the
dark days of war. Arthur Askey, Peter
Graves, Max Bacon, Anne Shelton, Jean
Kent. Written by Val Guest and Marriott
Edgar; directed by Val Guest; for
Gainsborough.

Before Hindsight**
GB 1977   78m   Eastmancolor
Elizabeth Taylor-Mead

Interviews and clips show how inadequately
cinema newsreels covered world events in the
1930s.
Hard tack for entertainment seekers, but a
clear exposition of a proven case of
importance to film-makers and politicians.

w Elizabeth Taylor-Mead *d* Jonathan Lewis
   'Certainly not the kind of picture people will
pay money to see.'—*Variety*

Before I Hang*
US 1940   71m   bw
Columbia (Wallace MacDonald)

A research scientist experiments with a new
serum which turns him into a murderer.
Archetypal Karloff mad doctor flick, Jekyll
and Hyde model: still quite tolerable.

w Robert D. Andrews *d* Nick Grinde
ph Benjamin Kline *md* Morris Stoloff

Boris Karloff, Evelyn Keyes, Bruce Bennett,
Pedro de Cordoba, Edward Van Sloan, Don
Beddoe

Before Winter Comes*
GB 1968   107m   Technicolor
Columbia / Windward (Robert Emmett
   Ginna)

Austria 1945: a British major in charge of
displaced persons is helped and hindered by a
cheerful Yugoslav refugee who turns out to be
a Russian deserter.
Likeable, well-produced drama hampered by a
plot which becomes unnecessarily schematic,
coincidental and downbeat in its attempts to
tug at the heartstrings.

w Andrew Sinclair, *novel* The Interpreter by
Frederick L. Keefe *d* J. Lee-Thompson
ph Gilbert Taylor *m* Ron Grainer

David Niven, Topol, Ori Levi, Anna Karina,
John Hurt, Anthony Quayle
   'One of those films with a message on every
page of its script.'—*MFB*

The Beggar's Opera**
GB 1952   94m   Technicolor
British Lion / Imperadio (Herbert Wilcox,
   Laurence Olivier)

A highwayman in Newgate jail devises an
opera based on his own exploits.
Exuberant potted version of the 1728 low
opera, generally likeable but lacking a strong
coherent approach and marred by violent
colour and raggedly theatrical presentation. It
nearly but not quite comes off.

w Dennis Cannan, Christopher Fry, *opera*
John Gay *d* Peter Brook *ph* Guy Green
ad George Wakhevitch, William C. Andrews
musical arrangement and additions Arthur
Bliss

Laurence Olivier, Stanley Holloway, Dorothy
Tutin, Daphne Anderson, Mary Clare,
George Devine, Athene Seyler, Hugh Griffith,
Margot Grahame, Sandra Dorne, Laurence
Naismith
   'The failure is equalled only by the
ambition.'—*Gavin Lambert*

The Beginning or the End
US 1947 112m bw
MGM (Samuel Marx)

During World War II American scientists continue to perfect the atom bomb despite their own misgivings, and one dies in an explosion.
Semi-documentary marred by sentimental personal asides and of very little continuing interest.

w Robert Considine d Norman Taurog ph Ray June m Daniele Amfitheatrof

Brian Donlevy, Robert Walker, Tom Drake, Beverly Tyler, Hume Cronyn, Audrey Totter, *Godfrey Tearle* (as Roosevelt)

The Beguiled*
US 1971 109m Technicolor
Universal / Malpaso (Don Siegel)

A wounded Unionist soldier hides out in a Confederate ladies' school; the teachers fend for him until he causes trouble among the sexually frustrated women, who eventually kill him.
Eccentric melodrama which does not really work despite its credentials and patient work all round.

w John B. Sherry, Grimes Grice, *novel* Thomas Cullinan d Don Siegel ph Bruce Surtees m Lalo Schifrin pd Ted Haworth

Clint Eastwood, Geraldine Page, Elizabeth Hartman, Jo Ann Harris, Darleen Carr, Mae Mercer

'A must for sadists and woman-haters.'— *Judith Crist*

Behave Yourself*
US 1951 81m bw
RKO (Jerry Wald, Norman Krasna)

A young married couple and their dog get mixed up in a chain of murders.
Zany black comedy in the wake of *A Slight Case of Murder* and *The Thin Man*. The humour is spread too thin for success.

wd George Beck ph James Wong Howe m Leigh Harline

Farley Granger, Shelley Winters, William Demarest, Francis L. Sullivan, Margalo Gillmore, Lon Chaney, Hans Conried, Elisha Cook Jnr

Behind the Eight Ball
US 1942 60m bw

Actors are mistaken for spies. Very patchy but commendably brief star comedy. The Ritz Brothers, Carol Bruce, Dick Foran, William Demarest. Written by Stanley Roberts and Mel Ronson; directed by Edward F. Cline; for Universal. (GB title: *Off the Beaten Track*.)

Behind the High Wall
US 1956 85m bw
U-I (Stanley Rubin)

A prison warder, taken as hostage by escaping convicts, steals some of the money they have taken.
Glum melodrama, capably presented.

w Harold Jack Bloom d Abner Biberman ph Maury Gertsman m Joseph Gershenson

Tom Tully, Sylvia Sidney, John Gavin, Betty Lynn, John Larch, Barney Phillips, Don Beddoe

Behind the Mask*
GB 1958 99m Eastmancolor
BL / GW Films (Sergei Nolbandov, Josef Somlo)

Political infighting causes tension on the board of a local hospital.
Oddly titled social drama with interesting detail but not much tension or conclusion.

w John Hunter, *novel* The Pack by John Rowan Wilson d Brian Desmond Hurst ph Robert Krasker m Geoffrey Wright

Michael Redgrave, Tony Britton, Carl Mohner, Niall MacGinnis, Vanessa Redgrave, Ian Bannen, Brenda Bruce, Lionel Jeffries, Miles Malleson, John Welsh, Ann Firbank

Behind the Rising Sun*
US 1943 88m bw
RKO

An American-educated Japanese goes home in the thirties, comes under the influence of war-mongers, and causes his father to commit hara-kiri.
Outrageous wartime flagwaver designed to vilify 'Uncle Tojo's dogs', from the writer and director of the similar *Hitler's Children* (qv).

w Emmet Lavery, *novel* James R. Young d Edward Dmytryk ph Russell Metty m Roy Webb

J. Carrol Naish, Tom Neal, Margo, Robert Ryan, Gloria Holden, Don Douglas, Adeline de Walt Reynolds

Behold a Pale Horse*
US 1964 121m bw
Columbia / Highland / Brentwood (Fred Zinnemann, Alexander Trauner)

A Spanish guerrilla goes into exile at the end of the Civil War. Twenty years later he is persuaded to return and kill a brutal police chief.

An action film which unfortunately insists on saying something significant about morality, destiny and death. Impeccably made, but somehow not very interesting apart from the action sequences.

w J. P. Miller, *novel* Killing a Mouse on Sunday by Emeric Pressburger d *Fred Zinnemann* ph Jean Badal m Maurice Jarre ad Alexander Trauner

Gregory Peck, Omar Sharif, Anthony Quinn, Raymond Pellegrin, Paolo Stoppa, Mildred Dunnock, Daniela Rocca, Christian Marquand
'A fine example of a high class failure.'— *Judith Crist*

Behold My Wife
US 1934 79m bw
Paramount (B. P. Schulberg)

A wealthy young man brings back and marries a New Mexico Indian girl to show up his snobbish family.
Dated melodrama, of interest solely for its racial theme.

w William R. Lippman, Oliver LaFarge, *novel* The Translation of a Savage by Sir Gilbert Parker d Mitchell Leisen ph Leon Shamroy

Sylvia Sidney, Gene Raymond, Juliette Compton, Laura Hope Crews, H. B. Warner, Monroe Owsley, Ann Sheridan

Being There**
US 1979 130m Metrocolor
Lorimar / North Star / CIP (Andrew Braunsberg)

An illiterate gardener is taken for a homespun philosopher and becomes a national celebrity. Overlong serio-comic parable hinging on a somewhat dubious star performance. Chance made it a popular urban success, but few who saw it were enthused.

w Jerzy Kosinski, from his novel d Hal Ashby ph Dianne Schroeder m John Mandel pd Michael Haller

Peter Sellers, Shirley Maclaine, *Melvyn Douglas*, Jack Warden, Richard Dysart, Richard Basehart
BFA: screenplay

Believe in Me
US 1971 90m colour
MGM (Irwin Winkler, Robert Chartoff)

Two young marrieds take to drugs.
Tedious and unenlightening modern drama which seems to think it's saying something new.

w Israel Horovitz d Stuart Hagmann ph Dick Kratina, Richard C. Brooks m Fred Karlin

Michael Sarrazin, Jacqueline Bisset, Jon Cypher, Allen Garfield

Bell, Book and Candle*
US 1958 103m Technicolor
Columbia / Phoenix (Julian Blaustein)

A publisher slowly becomes aware that his new girl friend is a witch.
A gossamer stage comedy has been fatally flattened in translation; most of the actors are miscast, and sentiment soaks the script. But it remains a civilized entertainment.

w Daniel Taradash, *play* John Van Druten d Richard Quine ph James Wong Howe m George Duning

James Stewart, Kim Novak, Jack Lemmon, Ernie Kovacs, *Hermione Gingold*, Elsa Lanchester, Janice Rule

Bell Bottom George
GB 1943 97m bw

A medically exempt waiter dons uniform and catches a ring of spies. Formula star comedy, too long and too familiar.
George Formby, Anne Firth, Reginald Purdell, Peter Murray Hill. Written by Peter Fraser and Edward Dryhurst; directed by Marcel Varnel; for Columbia.

A Bell for Adano*
US 1945 104m bw
TCF (Louis D. Lighton, Lamar Trotti)

An American major takes over an Italian town and wins affection by replacing the local bell. Slight end-of-war mood piece, still quite pleasant but without the undercurrents of feeling it had at the time.

w Lamar Trotti, Norman Reilly Raine, *novel* John Hersey d Henry King ph Joseph La Shelle m Alfred Newman

John Hodiak, Gene Tierney, William Bendix, Glenn Langan, Richard Conte, Stanley Prager, Henry Morgan

The Bell Jar
US 1979 107m colour

A teenage girl becomes mentally ill when her father dies. Numbingly tedious case history without much apparent point. Marilyn Hassett, Julie Harris, Anne Jackson, Barbara Barrie. Written by Marjorie Kellog, from the novel by Sylvia Plath; directed by Larry Peerce; for Peerce-Goldston / Avco.

Belladonna
GB 1934 91m bw

A selfish woman tries to poison her husband for love of an Egyptian. Intriguingly-cast version of the Robert Hichens novel dramatized by J. B. Fagan; later filmed in Hollywood as *Temptation* (qv). Mary Ellis, Conrad Veidt, Cedric Hardwicke, John Stuart, Michael Shepley. Written by H. Fowler Mear; directed by Robert Milton; for Twickenham.

The Bellboy*

US 1960 72m bw
Paramount / Jerry Lewis Productions (Jerry Lewis)

An incompetent bellboy causes havoc in a Miami hotel.
Plotless essence of a comedian who divides opinion and will never be better than variable. This ragbag of old gags at least prevents his usual sentimental excesses, and is mercifully short.

wd Jerry Lewis *ph* Haskell Boggs *m* Walter Scharf

Jerry Lewis, Alex Gerry, Bob Clayton, Herkie Styles, Milton Berle

Belle de Jour***

France / Italy 1967 100m Eastmancolor
Paris Film / Five Film (Robert and Raymond Hakim)

A surgeon's wife finds herself drawn to afternoon work in a brothel.
Fascinating Bunuel mixture of fact and fantasy, impeccably woven into a rich fabric.

w Luis Bunuel, Jean-Claude Carrière *d* Luis Bunuel *ph* Sacha Vierny *m* none

Catherine Deneuve, Jean Sorel, Michel Piccoli, Genevieve Page, Pierre Clémenti

La Belle Equipe*

France 1936 74m bw
Ciné Arts

Five unemployed Parisians win the lottery and open a restaurant, but things do not go smoothly.
Interesting but rather lumpy star drama which finally descends into melodrama; alternative tragic and happy endings were originally offered.

w Charles Spaak, Julien Duvivier *d* Julien Duvivier *ph* Jules Kruger, Marc Fessard *m* Maurice Yvain

Jean Gabin, Charles Vanel, Viviane Romance, Raymond Aimes, Robert Lynen, Raymond Cordy, Raphael Medina

La Belle et la Bête**

France 1946 95m bw
André Paulvé

Beauty gives herself to the Beast who has kidnapped her father; through love the monster turns into a handsome prince.
Slightly heavy-handed though usually stunning-looking adaptation of the fairy tale.

wd Jean Cocteau *ph* Henri Alekan *m* Georges Auric *ad* Christian Bérard

Jean Marais, Josette Day, Mila Parély, Marcel André, Michel Auclair
'Perhaps the most sumptuously elegant of all filmed fairy tales.'—*New Yorker, 1980*
'Absolute magic: diamond cold and lunar bright.'—*CBS*

Belle le Grand

US 1951 89m bw
Republic

The proprietress of a Barbary Coast gambling house is plagued by an ex-husband on whose account she served a prison term.
Confused and incompetent period melodrama.

w D. D. Beauchamp *d* Allan Dwan *ph* Reggie Lanning *m* Victor Young

Vera Ralston, John Carroll, William Ching, Hope Emerson, Stephen Chase, Grant Withers, John Qualen

The Belle of New York*

US 1952 82m Technicolor
MGM (Arthur Freed)

A nineties playboy falls for a Salvation Army girl.
A rather dreary version of the old musical, with undistinguished additions.

w Robert O'Brien, Irving Elinson *d* Charles Walters *ph* Robert Planck *m* / *ly* Johnny Mercer, Harry Warren *ad* Jack Martin Smith

Fred Astaire, Vera-Ellen, Marjorie Main, Keenan Wynn, Alice Pearce, Clinton Sundberg, Gale Robbins

Belle of the Nineties*

US 1934 75m bw
Paramount (William Le Baron)

A saloon entertainer loves two men, one of whom is a crook.
Much-laundered star vehicle which despite superior production seems a pale shadow of the star's better pieces.

w Mae West *d* Leo McCarey *ph* Karl Struss

Mae West, Roger Pryor, John Miljan, John Mack Brown, Katherine de Mille, Duke Ellington and his Orchestra

Belle of the Yukon*

US 1945 84m Technicolor
International

A troupe of saloon entertainers in the Yukon become involved with a bank robbery.
Threads of plot support comedy, dancing and songs in this thin but reasonably fresh musical imitation of *The Spoilers*.

w James Edward Grant *d* William A. Seiter *ph* Ray Rennahan *md* Arthur Lange

Gypsy Rose Lee, Randolph Scott, Dinah Shore, Charles Winninger, Bob Burns

AAN: Arthur Lange; song 'Sleigh Ride in July' (*m* Jimmy Van Heusen, *ly* Johnny Burke)

Belle Starr
US 1941   87m   Technicolor
TCF (Kenneth MacGowan)

Absurdly laundered version of the life of the west's most notorious female outlaw, with the star laughably miscast.

w Lamar Trotti *d* Irving Cummings *ph* Ernest Palmer, Ray Rennahan *m* Alfred Newman

Gene Tierney, Randolph Scott, Dana Andrews, Shepperd Strudwick, Elizabeth Patterson, Chill Wills, Louise Beavers

Les Belles de Nuit**
France / Italy 1952   89m   bw
Franco London / Rizzoli

A discontented music teacher dreams of beautiful women through the ages.
Charming but very slight dream fantasy with many of the master's touches. (He claims to have intended a comic *Intolerance*.)

wd René Clair *ph* Armand Thirard, Robert Juilliard, Louis Née *m* Georges Van Parys *ad* Léon Barsacq

Gérard Philipe, Gina Lollobrigida, Martine Carol, Magali Vendeuil, Paolo Stoppa, Raymond Bussières, Raymond Cordy

The Belles of St Trinian's*
GB 1954   91m   bw
BL / London Films / Launder and Gilliat

At an unruly and bankrupt school for girls, more time is spent backing horses than studying subjects, and the headmistress's bookmaker brother has a scheme or two of his own.
Fairly successful film version of Ronald Searle's awful schoolgirl cartoons, the emphasis shifted to a grotesque older generation with the star in drag. An enormous commercial success, but the three sequels *Blue Murder at St Trinian's*, *The Pure Hell of St Trinian's*, *The Great St Trinian's Train Robbery* went from bad to awful.

w Frank Launder, Sidney Gilliat, Val Valentine *d* Frank Launder *ph* Stan Pavey *m* Malcolm Arnold

Alastair Sim, George Cole, Joyce Grenfell, Hermione Baddeley, Betty Ann Davies, Renée Houston, Beryl Reid, Irene Handl, Mary Merrall

'Not so much a film as an entertainment on celluloid, a huge charade, a rich pile of idiot and splendidly senseless images.'—*David Robinson*

Belles on Their Toes
US 1952   89m   Technicolor
TCF (Samuel G. Engel)

Further adventures in the growing up of the twelve Gilbreth children.
Flat sequel to *Cheaper by the Dozen* (qv) with sentimentality instead of Clifton Webb. Period atmosphere attractive.

w Phoebe and Henry Ephron, *book* Frank B. Gilbreth Jnr and Ernestine Gilbreth Carey *d* Henry Levin *ph* Arthur E. Arling *m* Cyril Mockridge

Myrna Loy, Jeanne Crain, Debra Paget, Jeffrey Hunter, Edward Arnold, Hoagy Carmichael, Barbara Bates, Robert Arthur

Bellissimà*
Italy 1951   100m   bw
Bellissimà Films (Salvo d'Angelo)

A mother struggles to get a part in a film for her 7-year-old daughter.
Highly detailed, very noisy star vehicle with neo-realist working-class backgrounds. Exhausting.

w Suso Cecchi d'Amico, Francesco Rosi, Luchino Visconti, Cesare Zavattini *d* Luchino Visconti *ph* Piero Portalupi *m* Franco Mannino

Anna Magnani, Walter Chiari, Tina Apicella, Gastone Renzelli, Alessandro Blasetti

The Bells
GB 1931   75m   bw

An Alsatian burgomaster is forced by conscience to confess to the killing of a Jew.
Only sound version of a famous melodrama played on stage by Henry Irving. Donald Calthrop, Jane Welsh, Edward Sinclair. (In a 1926 silent version Lionel Barrymore played the murderer and Boris Karloff the mesmerist.) Written by C. H. Dand, from the play by Erckmann and Chatrian; directed by Oscar M. Werndorff and Harcourt Templeman; in three language versions; for Isidore Schlesinger / BSFP.

Bells are Ringing*
US 1960   126m   Metrocolor
Cinemascope
MGM (Arthur Freed)

A telephone answering service operator
becomes passionately involved in the lives of
her clients.
Dull, rather ugly and boring transcription of a
Broadway musical, with all talents below par,
not enough dancing and too much plot.

w / ly Betty Comden, Adolph Green, from
their play d Vincente Minnelli ph Milton
Krasner m Jule Styne md André Previn
ad George W. Davis, Preston Ames
ch Charles O'Curran

Judy Holliday, Dean Martin, Fred Clark,
Eddie Foy Jnr, Jean Stapleton, Ruth Storey,
Frank Gorshin

AAN: André Previn

The Bells Go Down**
GB 1943   89m   bw
Ealing (Michael Balcon)

The exploits of a London firefighting unit
during World War II.
Tragi-comedy with lively scenes, a good record
of the historical background of the blitz.

w Roger Macdougall, Stephen Black d Basil
Dearden ph Ernest Palmer m Roy Douglas

Tommy Trinder, James Mason, Mervyn
Johns, Philippa Hyatt, Finlay Currie, Philip
Friend, Meriel Forbes, Beatrice Varley, Billy
Hartnell

The Bells of St Mary's**
US 1945   126m   bw
RKO (Leo McCarey)

At a big city Catholic school, Father O'Malley
and Sister Benedict indulge in friendly rivalry,
and succeed in extending the school through
the gift of a building.
Sentimental and very commercial sequel to
Going My Way, with the stars at their peak
and the handling as cosy and well-paced as
might be expected.

w Dudley Nichols d Leo McCarey
ph George Barnes m Robert Emmett Dolan

Bing Crosby, Ingrid Bergman, Henry Travers,
William Gargan, Ruth Donnelly, Rhys
Williams, Una O'Connor, Eva Novak
  'The picture is full of shrewd and pleasant
flashes. It is also fascinating to watch as a
talented, desperate effort to repeat the
unrepeatable. But on the whole it is an
unhappy film.'—James Agee

AAN: best picture; Leo McCarey; Robert
Emmett Dolan; Bing Crosby; Ingrid Bergman;

song 'Aren't You Glad You're You' (m Jimmy
Van Heusen, ly Johnny Burke)

Beloved Enemy*
US 1936   90m   bw
Samuel Goldwyn (George Haight)

During the 1921 Irish rebellion, the fiancée of
a British army officer falls in love with the
leading revolutionary.
Dreamy-eyed romance with little relevance to
the real situation; not badly done of its kind.

w John Balderston, Rose Franken, William
Brown Meloney, David Hart d H. C. Potter
ph Gregg Toland m Alfred Newman

Brian Aherne, Merle Oberon, David Niven,
Karen Morley, Jerome Cowan, Henry
Stephenson, Donald Crisp

Beloved Infidel*
US 1959   123m   De Luxe   Cinemascope
TCF / Company of Artists (Jerry Wald)

Sheilah Graham, a British chorus girl turned
Hollywood columnist, lives with Scott
Fitzgerald but fails to cure him of alcoholism.
A bitter and even sordid true story becomes a
slice of Hollywood romance, with stars
unsuitably cast. On all levels it falls between
two stools, satisfying nobody.

w Sy Bartlett, book Sheilah Graham and
Gerald Frank d Henry King ph Leon
Shamroy m Franz Waxman

Gregory Peck, Deborah Kerr, Eddie Albert,
Philip Ober, Herbert Rudley, Karin Booth,
Ken Scott
  'Catastrophically misguided.'—Penelope
Houston

The Beloved Rogue*
US 1927   99m at 24 fps   bw   silent

Fifteenth-century poet and thief François
Villon becomes a friend of the king, but is
banished when he falls for a lady of the court.
Stylish star vehicle remade as If I Were King
(qv). John Barrymore, Conrad Veidt,
Marceline Day, Mack Swain, Slim
Summerville. Written by Paul Bern; directed
by Alan Crosland; production design by
William Cameron Menzies; for UA.

The Beloved Vagabond*
GB 1936   78m   bw
Ludovico Toeplitz

At the turn of the century, a jilted French
artist becomes a vagabond and falls in love
with an orphan girl.
Mildly amusing bi-lingual production from a
bestselling picaresque novel; production quite
lively.

w Wells Root, Arthur Wimperis, Hugh Mills, Walter Creighton, *novel* W. J. Locke *d* Curtis Bernhardt *ph* Franz Planer

Maurice Chevalier, Margaret Lockwood, Betty Stockfield, Desmond Tester, Austin Trevor, Peter Haddon, Cathleen Nesbitt

Below Zero**
US 1930 20m bw

Street musicians treat a policeman to lunch on the contents of a found wallet which turns out to be his. Slow-paced but likeable star comedy from their best period. Laurel and Hardy, Frank Holliday, Tiny Sandford. Written by H. M. Walker; directed by James Parrott; for Hal Roach.

The Belstone Fox*
GB 1973 103m Eastmancolor Todd-AO 35
Rank / Independent Artists (Sally Shuter)

A fox and a hound grow up together but the fox leads to tragedy for its masters.
Good animal and countryside photography barely compensate for a fragmentary story with unpleasant moments or for a muddled attitude towards humans and animals; one is not clear what audience the result is supposed to appeal to.

wd James Hill, *novel* David Rook *ph* John Wilcox, James Allen *m* Laurie Johnson

Eric Porter, Rachel Roberts, Jeremy Kemp, Bill Travers, Dennis Waterman

Ben
US 1972 92m De Luxe
Cinerama / Bing Crosby (Mort Briskin)

A sickly boy inherits an army of trained rats. Boring reprise of *Willard* in which the audience knows only too well what to expect. Production and development quite routine.

w Gilbert A. Ralston *d* Phil Karlson *ph* Russell Metty *m* Walter Scharf

Lee Harcourt Montgomery, Arthur O'Connell, Rosemary Murphy, Meredith Baxter, Kaz Garas, Paul Carr, Kenneth Tobey

AAN: title song (*m* Walter Scharf, *ly* Don Black)

Ben Hur***
US 1926 170m approx (16 fps) bw
    (colour sequence)   silent
MGM

In the time of Christ, a Jew suffers mightily under the Romans.
The American silent screen's biggest epic; the sea battle and the chariot race are its most famous sequences.

w Bess Meredyth, Carey Wilson, *novel* Lew Wallace *d* Fred Niblo *ph* Karl Struss, Clyde de Vinna, and others *ad* Horace Jackson, Ferdinand Pinney Earle

Ramon Novarro, Francis X. Bushman, Carmel Myers, May McAvoy, Betty Bronson
   'Masterpiece of study and patience, a photodrama filled with artistry.'—*New York Times*
† Previously filmed in 1907.

Ben Hur**
US 1959 217m Technicolor Camera 65
MGM (Sam Zimbalist)

Solid, expensive, surprisingly unimaginative remake; generally less sprightly than the silent version.

w Karl Tunberg *d* William Wyler, *Andrew Marton ph* Robert L. Surtees *m* Miklos Rozsa *ad* William A. Horning, Edward Carfagno

Charlton Heston, Haya Harareet, Jack Hawkins, Stephen Boyd, Hugh Griffith, Martha Scott, Sam Jaffe, Cathy O'Donnell, Finlay Currie, Frank Thring, Terence Longdon, André Morell, George Relph
   'Watching it is like waiting at a railroad crossing while an interminable freight train lumbers by, sometimes stopping altogether.'— *Dwight MacDonald*
   'A Griffith can make a hundred into a crowd while a Wyler can reduce a thousand to a confused cocktail party.'—*Ibid.*
   'The most tasteful and visually exciting film spectacle yet produced by an American company.'—*Albert Johnson, Film Quarterly*
   'Spectacular without being a spectacle . . . not only is it not simple-minded, it is downright literate.'—*Saturday Review*
   'A major motion picture phenomenon.'— *Films in Review*
† The production cost four million dollars, twice the maximum at the time. Rock Hudson, Marlon Brando and Burt Lancaster were all sought in vain for the lead before Heston was selected.

AA: best picture; William Wyler; Robert L. Surtees; Miklos Rozsa; Charlton Heston; Hugh Griffith
AAN: Karl Tunberg

Bend of the River**
US 1952 91m Technicolor
U-I (Aaron Rosenberg)
GB title: *Where the River Bends*

1880 wagon trains arrive in Oregon, and the pioneers have trouble with the local bad man. Good standard western with pace and period feeling.

w Borden Chase, *novel* Bend of the Snake by William Gulick *d* Anthony Mann *ph* Irving Glassberg *m* Hans Salter

James Stewart, Arthur Kennedy, Rock Hudson, Julia Adams, Lori Nelson, Jay C. Flippen, Henry Morgan, Royal Dano, Stepin Fetchit

Beneath the Twelve Mile Reef
US 1953   102m   Technicolor
 Cinemascope
TCF (Robert Bassler)

Jealousy, tragedy and romance among the Florida sponge fishers.
Fox's early Cinemascope production involved much underwater shooting, a trick octopus, and predictable plot devices.

w A. I. Bezzerides *d* Robert D. Webb *ph* Edward Cronjager *m* Bernard Herrmann

Robert Wagner, Terry Moore, Gilbert Roland, Peter Graves, J. Carrol Naish, Richard Boone, Angela Clarke, Jay Novello
 'The dead weight of a melodramatic script overtaxes the gallant attempts at conviction.'—*MFB*

AAN: Edward Cronjager

Bengal Brigade
US 1954   87m   Technicolor
U-I (Ted Richmond)
GB title: *Bengal Rifles*

In 19th-century India, an officer is cashiered through false evidence, and becomes an undercover man with the wicked local rajah. Routine Hollywood heroics with a few unintended laughs.

w Richard Alan Simmons, *novel* Bengal Tiger by Hall Hunter *d* Laslo Benedek *ph* Maury Gertsman *m* Joseph Gershenson

Rock Hudson, Dan O'Herlihy, Ursula Thiess, Torin Thatcher, Michael Ansara, Arnold Moss

Bengazi
US 1955   79m   bw   Superscope
RKO / Panamint (Sam Wiesenthal, Eugene Tevlin)

Various unsavoury characters set out into the African desert to look for gold hidden by the Nazis.
Poor potboiler on predictable lines.

w Endre Boehm, Louis Vittes *d* John Brahm *ph* Joseph Biroc *m* Roy Webb

Richard Conte, Victor McLaglen, Richard Carlson, Mala Powers, Richard Erdman, Gonzales Gonzales, Hillary Brooke

Benjamin, or The Diary of an Innocent Young Man
France 1966   104m   Eastmancolor
Paramount / Parc / Marianne (Mag Bodard)

In the 18th century, a 17-year-old orphan is taken in hand by his wealthy aunt and initiated into the mysteries of sex.
Imitation *Tom Jones*, quite good to look at but rather boring.

w Nina Companeez *d* Michel Déville *ph* Ghislain Cloquet

Pierre Clémenti, Michèle Morgan, Catherine Deneuve, Michel Piccoli, Francine Bergé, Anna Gaël, Odile Versois
 'Heavy with Gallic naughtiness rather than airy charm . . . a plethora of colourful costumes, foliage and fireworks.'—*MFB*
 'A marathon tease . . . an unending series of interrupted coitions . . . a gorgeously wrapped and beribboned Christmas package containing an empty box.'—*John Simon*

Benji*
US 1974   86m   CFI color
Mulberry Square (Joe Camp)

A stray mongrel dog saves two kidnapped children.
Family film par excellence which rang the box office bell in a big way in the US. Its modest merits are rather beside the point.

wd Joe Camp *ph* Don Reddy *m* Euel Box

Peter Breck, Edgar Buchanan, Terry Carter, Christopher Connelly
 † A sequel, *For the Love of Benji*, followed in 1977.

AAN: song 'I Feel Love' (*m* Euel Box, *ly* Betty Box)

The Benny Goodman Story*
US 1955   117m   Technicolor
U-I (Aaron Rosenberg)

A clarinettist from the Jewish section of Chicago becomes internationally known.
Sentimental biopic of a familiar figure which comes to life when the sound track is given its head (and the real Goodman's clarinet).

wd Valentine Davies *ph* William Daniels *md* Joseph Gershenson

Steve Allen, Donna Reed, *Berta Gersten*, Herbert Anderson, Robert F. Simon, Sammy Davis Snr, Harry James, Martha Tilton, Gene Krupa
 'The customary fictional liberties appear to have been taken.'—*MFB*

Bequest to the Nation*
GB 1973   116m   Technicolor
Universal / Hal B. Wallis
US title: *The Nelson Affair*

The story of Nelson's long affair with the
tempestuous Lady Hamilton.
Undistinguished historical drama from a thin
play which despite hard work all round makes
very ordinary screen entertainment.

w Terence Rattigan, from his play *d* James
Cellan Jones *ph* Gerry Fisher *pd* Carmen
Dillon *m* Michel Legrand

Peter Finch, Glenda Jackson (way over the
top), Michael Jayston, Anthony Quayle,
Margaret Leighton, Dominic Guard, Nigel
Stock, Roland Culver

'As empty as an out-of-town matinee.'—
MFB

Berkeley Square*
US 1933   87m   bw
Fox (Jesse L. Lasky)

A London house reincarnates its owner as his
18th-century ancestor.
Romantic fantasy on a time lapse theme, the
first of many and perhaps the most stylish and
self-assured. Remade as *The House on the
Square* (qv).

w Sonya Levien, John Balderston, from
Balderston's play *d* Frank Lloyd *ph* Ernest
Palmer *m* Louis de Francesco *ad* William
Carling

Leslie Howard, Heather Angel, Valerie
Taylor, Irene Browne, Beryl Mercer, Colin
Keith-Johnson, Alan Mowbray

AAN: Leslie Howard

Berlin Correspondent
US 1942   70m   bw
TCF (Bryan Foy)

In pre-war Germany an American reporter is
kidnapped by the Nazis and replaced by a
double . . .
Preposterous melodrama, so silly as to be
often quite funny.

w Steve Fisher, Jack Andrews *d* Eugene
Forde *ph* Virgil Miller *md* Emil Newman

Dana Andrews, Virginia Gilmore, Mona
Maris, Martin Kosleck, Sig Rumann, Kurt
Katch, Torben Meyer

Berlin Express*
US 1948   87m   bw
RKO (Bert Granet)

Police of four nations guard a German VIP on
a crack train to Berlin.

Rather muddled suspenser with attempts at
political moralizing; the cast provides some
good moments.

w Harold Medford *d* Jacques Tourneur
ph Lucien Ballard *m* Frederick Hollander

Merle Oberon, Robert Ryan, Charles Korvin,
Paul Lukas, Robert Coote

Berlin, Symphony of a Great City***
Germany 1927   78m   bw   silent
Fox-Europa
original title: *Berlin, die Symphonie einer
Grosstadt*

An impression of the life of a city from dawn
to midnight, expressed by cinematic montages,
angles, sequences, etc, and set to music.
A leader in the field of 'impressionistic'
documentaries which are now so familiar
(*Rien que les Heures* did a similar job for Paris
at around the same time), this still has
moments of poetry which have seldom been
equalled.

*w Walter Ruttman, Karl Freund, Carl Mayer
d Walter Ruttman ph Reimar Kuntze, Robert
Baberske, Laszlo Schäffer m Edmund Meisel
ed* Walter Ruttman

Berliner Ballade*
Germany 1948   77m   bw
Comedia Film (Alf Teichs)
aka: *The Ballad of Berlin*

Otto Nobody, an unwilling soldier, returns
home to find himself at the mercy of
bureaucrats and black marketeers.
Melancholy satire presented as a series of
sketches, almost a forerunner of *That Was the
Week That Was*.

w Gunter Neumann *d* Robert Stemmle
ph Georg Krause *m / ly* Gunter Neumann,
Werner Eisbrenner

Gert Fröbe, Anton Zeithammer, Tatjana Sais,
O. E. Hasse

'Very much the film of a defeated people.'—
Penelope Houston

Bermuda Affair
GB 1956   77m   bw

The pilot of a West Indian airline falls for his
partner's wife but dies in an air accident.
Tedious and unconvincing marital drama with
back-projected local colour. Kim Hunter,
Gary Merrill, Ron Randell, Zena Walker.
Written by Robert J. Shaw and Edward
Sutherland; directed by Edward Sutherland;
for Bermuda Studio Productions.

Bernardine*
US 1957 95m Eastmancolor
Cinemascope
TCF (Samuel G. Engel)

A college student forced to swot for exams asks a friend's elder brother to look after his girl.
Henry Aldrich-style high school comedy, showing the lighter side of *Rebel without a Cause*. Notable for the clean-living hero played by a clean-living singing star, and the reappearance of Janet Gaynor for the only time since 1939, in a routine mother role.

w Theodore Reeves, *play* Mary Chase *d* Henry Levin *ph* Paul Vogel *m* Lionel Newman

Pat Boone, Richard Sargent, Terry Moore, *Janet Gaynor*, Walter Abel, Dean Jagger, Natalie Schaefer, James Drury

Berserk!
GB 1967 96m Technicolor
Columbia (Herman Cohen)

A lady circus owner revels in the publicity brought about by a series of murders.
Grisly and unattractive thriller with an ageing star in a series of unsuitably abbreviated costumes; the script is beyond redemption.

w Herman Cohen, Aben Kandel *d* Jim O'Connolly *ph* Desmond Dickinson *m* Patrick John Scott

Joan Crawford, Diana Dors, Ty Hardin, Judy Geeson, Michael Gough, Robert Hardy, Geoffrey Keen, Sidney Tafler, Philip Madoc

Berth Marks
US 1929 20m bw silent

Stan and Ollie, on a train, have to share an upper berth. Overstretched single-situation comedy, one of the team's poorest. Laurel and Hardy. Written by Leo McCarey and H. M. Walker; directed by Lewis R. Foster; for Hal Roach.

Best Foot Forward
US 1943 94m Technicolor
MGM (Arthur Freed)

A glamorous publicity-seeking film star accepts an invitation to a military college ball. Old-fashioned formula musical based on a lightweight Broadway success.

w Irving Brecher, Fred Finklehoffe, *play* John Cecil Holmes *d* Edward Buzzell *ph* Leonard Smith *md* Lennie Hayton *songs* Hugh Martin, Ralph Blane *ch* Charles Walters

Lucille Ball, William Gaxton, Virginia Weidler, Harry James and his Orchestra, June Allyson, Gloria de Haven

The Best House in London*
GB 1968 96m Eastmancolor
MGM / Bridge / Carlo Ponti (Philip Breen, Kurt Unger)

A Victorian publicity agent tries to organize a government-sponsored brothel.
Cheerful slam-bang historical send-up with as many dull thuds of banality as pleasant witticisms.

w Denis Norden *d* Philip Savile *ph* Alex Thompson *m* Mischa Spoliansky *pd* Wilfrid Shingleton

David Hemmings, George Sanders, Joanna Pettet, Warren Mitchell, Dany Robin, William Rushton

The Best Man***
US 1964 104m bw
UA / Stuart Millar, Lawrence Turman

Two contenders for a presidential nomination seek the support of the dying ex-president.
Brilliant political melodrama, ingeniously adapted on a low budget from an incisive play, with splendid dramatic scenes, memorable performances and good convention detail.

w Gore Vidal from his play *d Franklin Schaffner ph* Haskell Wexler *m* Mort Lindsey

Henry Fonda, Cliff Robertson, *Lee Tracy*, Margaret Leighton, Edie Adams, Kevin McCarthy, *Shelley Berman*, Ann Sothern, Gene Raymond, Mahalia Jackson

'A fine opportunity to watch pros at work in a hard-hitting and cogent drama that seems to become more topical and have more relevance with each showing.'—*Judith Crist*

'Some of the wittiest lines since *Strangelove* . . . the acting fairly crackled with authenticity.'—*Isabel Quigly*

AAN: Lee Tracy

The Best of Enemies
US / Italy 1961 104m Technirama
Columbia / Dino de Laurentiis

During the Abyssinian campaign of 1941, an Italian and a British officer learn mutual respect.
Mild satirical comedy drama with a few points to make about war; the elements blend rather obviously and dispiritingly.

w Jack Pulman *d* Guy Hamilton *ph Giuseppe Rotunno m* Nino Rota

David Niven, Alberto Sordi, Michael Wilding,
Amedeo Nazzari, Harry Andrews, David
Opatoshu, Kenneth Fortescue, Duncan
Macrae

The Best of Everything*
US 1959   121m   De Luxe   Cinemascope
TCF (Jerry Wald)

Personal problems of a New York publisher's
female staff.
Slick novelette on the lines of a naughty Peg's
Paper; pure Hollywood gossamer.

w Edith Sommer, Mann Rubin, *novel* Rona
Jaffe d Jean Negulesco ph William C.
Mellor m Alfred Newman

Hope Lange, Stephen Boyd, Joan Crawford,
Louis Jourdan, Suzy Parker, Martha Hyer,
Diane Baker, Brian Aherne, Robert Evans,
Brett Halsey, Donald Harron
   'A cautionary tale sensationally told.'—
Alexander Walker

AAN: title song (*m* Alfred Newman,
ly Sammy Cahn)

Best of the Badmen*
US 1951   84m   Technicolor
RKO (Herman Schlom)

At the end of the Civil War Jeff Clanton
organizes the break-up of Quantrell's Raiders,
but is himself arrested on a trumped-up charge
and needs the Raiders' help.
Standard western notable for a good cast and
for bringing in a remarkable number of
historical outlaws, doing rather unhistorical
things.

w Robert Hardy Andrews, John Twist
d William D. Russell ph Edward Cronjager
m Paul Sawtell

Robert Ryan, Claire Trevor, Jack Buetel,
Robert Preston, Walter Brennan, Bruce
Cabot, John Archer, Lawrence Tierney

The Best Things in Life Are Free*
US 1956   103m   Eastmancolor
   Cinemascope
TCF (Henry Ephron)

From Broadway to Hollywood in the twenties,
the story of songwriting team De Sylva, Brown
and Henderson.
Gangsters, movie studios and the writing of
'Sonny Boy' for Al Jolson all figure in this
amiable musical which spends more time on
jokes than romance; the numbers are
disappointing despite good tunes.

w William Bowers, Phoebe Ephron d Michael
Curtiz ph Leon Shamroy md Lionel Newman

Ernest Borgnine, Gordon Macrae, Dan
Dailey, Sheree North, Jacques d'Amboise,
Norman Brooks, Murvyn Vye
AAN: Lionel Newman

The Best Years of Our Lives****
US 1946   182m   bw
Samuel Goldwyn

Three men come home from war to a small
middle-American community, and find it
variously difficult to pick up where they left
off.
The situations and even some of the characters
now seem a little obvious, but this was a
superb example of high-quality film-making in
the forties, with smiles and tears cunningly
spaced, and a film which said what was needed
on a vital subject.

w Robert Sherwood, novel Glory for Me by
Mackinlay Kantor d William Wyler ph Gregg
Toland m Hugo Friedhofer

Fredric March, Myrna Loy, Teresa Wright,
Dana Andrews, Virginia Mayo, Cathy
O'Donnell, *Hoagy Carmichael, Harold Russell*
(a handless veteran whose only film this was),
Gladys George, Roman Bohnen, Ray Collins
   'The result is a work of provocative and
moving insistence and beauty.'—*Howard
Barnes*
   'One recognizes everything and in the end
this recognition is all the excitement, for what
is on the screen becomes finally as accustomed
and undramatic as the shabby decor of the
theatre itself.'—*Robert Warshow, The
Immediate Experience*
   'One of the very few American studio-made
movies in years that seem to me profoundly
pleasing, moving and encouraging.'—*James
Agee*

AA: best picture; Robert Sherwood; William
Wyler; Hugo Friedhofer; Fredric March;
Harold Russell

Le Bête Humaine*
France 1938   99m   bw
Paris Films (Robert Hakim)
aka: *The Human Beast; Judas Was a
   Woman*

A psychopathic train driver falls for a married
woman, plans with her to kill her husband, but
finally strangles her instead.
Curious melodrama with strong visual
sequences, flawed by its ambivalent attitude to
its hero-villain.

wd Jean Renoir, novel Emile Zola ph Curt
Courant m Joseph Kosma

Jean Gabin, Simone Simon, Julien Carette,
Fernand Ledoux, Jean Renoir

'Marvellous atmosphere and a fine cast, but the material turns oppressive.'—*New Yorker, 1978*

'What is most deft is the way Renoir works the depot and the man's job into every scene—conversations on platforms, in washrooms and canteens, views from the station master's window over the steaming metal waste: the short sharp lust worked out in a wooden platelayer's shed among shunted trucks under the steaming rain.'—*Graham Greene*

† Remade in Hollywood as *Human Desire*.

Betrayal from the East
US 1945   83m   bw
RKO (Herman Schlom)

Japanese out to sabotage the Panama Canal are thwarted by a carnival showman.

Extravagant but penny-pinching flagwaver.

w Kenneth Gamet, Aubrey Wisberg, *novel* Alan Hynd d William Berke ph Russell Metty m Roy Webb

Lee Tracy, Nancy Kelly, Richard Loo, Abner Biberman, Regis Toomey, Philip Ahn, Addison Richards, Sen Yung, Drew Pearson

Betrayed
US 1954   108m   Eastmancolor
MGM (Gottfried Reinhardt)

In 1943 a Dutch intelligence officer works with a resistance leader who turns out to be a traitor.

Slow-moving, studio-set romantic melodrama of the old school; not very lively.

w Ronald Millar, George Froeschel d Gottfried Reinhardt ph Frederick A. Young m Walter Goehr

Clark Gable, Victor Mature, Lana Turner, Louis Calhern, O. E. Hasse, Wilfrid Hyde White, Ian Carmichael, Niall MacGinnis, Nora Swinburne

The Betsy
US 1977   125m   Technicolor
Allied Artists / Harold Robbins International (Robert R. Weston)

Jockeying for power in the boardroom and the family life of an aged car manufacturer.

Rather tame and obvious melodrama enlivened by its star performance.

w William Bast, Walter Bernstein, *novel* Harold Robbins *Daniel Petrie* ph Mario Tosi m John Barry

Laurence Olivier, Robert Duvall, Tommy Lee Jones, Katharine Ross, Jane Alexander, Lesley-Anne Down, Joseph Wiseman, Edward Herrmann

'Almost compulsively dreadful.'—*Derek Malcolm, Guardian*

Between Heaven and Hell
US 1956   94m   Eastmancolor
Cinemascope
TCF (David Weisbart)

After Pearl Harbor a young southern landowner is called up and finds himself on active service with mixed racial types.

Vaguely anti-war, pro-understanding action thriller which ends up going through predictable heroics in a professional but not too sympathetic manner.

w Harry Brown, *novel* The Day the Century Ended by Francis Gwaltney d Richard Fleischer ph Leo Tover m Hugo Friedhofer

Robert Wagner, Buddy Ebsen, Broderick Crawford, Brad Dexter, Mark Damon, Robert Keith, Ken Clark, Skip Homeier, Harvey Lembeck

AAN: Hugo Friedhofer

Between Midnight and Dawn
US 1950   89m   bw
Columbia (Hunt Stromberg)

Radio policemen track down a racketeer.

Competent, undistinguished programmer.

w Eugene Ling d Gordon Douglas ph George E. Diskant m George Duning

Mark Stevens, Edmond O'Brien, Gale Storm, Donald Buka, Gale Robbins, Roland Winters

Between Two Women
US 1937   88m   bw

Romance between doctor and nurse is interrupted by her alcoholic husband and his infatuation with a patient. Incident-packed men-in-white melodrama. Franchot Tone, Maureen O'Sullivan, Virginia Bruce, Edward Norris, Cliff Edwards, Janet Beecher. Written by Carey Wilson, from a story by Erich Von Stroheim; directed by George B. Seitz; for MGM. (NB: Title later changed to *Surrounded by Women* to avoid confusion with a Dr Kildare episode.)

Between Two Worlds*
US 1944   112m   bw
Warner (Mark Hellinger)

A number of air-raid victims, and two lovers who have committed suicide, find themselves on a luxury ship en route to the next world.

Nice-looking but slow and turgid remake of *Outward Bound* (qv), largely sunk in its own misery but redeemed by two performances.

w Daniel Fuchs, *play* Sutton Vane d Edward A. Blatt ph Carl Guthrie m Erich Wolfgang Korngold

John Garfield, *Edmund Gwenn*, Eleanor
Parker, Paul Henreid, *Sydney Greenstreet*,
Sara Allgood, George Tobias, Faye Emerson,
George Coulouris, Dennis King, Isobel Elsom
    'For ferry service from a world so saturated
with death, the ship seems strangely empty—a
fact that was not obtrusive in a day when
death was not intrusive.'—*James Agee*

Between Us Girls
US 1942   89m   bw
Universal

A mother and daughter are both involved in
romances which tend to cross.
Mild comedy, a disappointing debut for a
disappointing young star.

w Myles Connolly, True Boardman, *play* Le
Fruit Vert by Regis Gignoux, Jacques Thery
d Henry Koster *ph* Joseph Valentine
m Frank Skinner

Diana Barrymore, Kay Francis, Robert
Cummings, John Boles, Scotty Beckett, Ethel
Griffies

Beverly of Graustark
US 1926   85m approx at 24 fps   bw
silent

When a prince falls ill, his girl cousin
impersonates him at an important ceremony.
Cheerful Ruritanian comedy. Marion Davies,
Antonio Moreno, Roy D'Arcy, Creighton
Hale. Written by Agnes Christine Johnson;
directed by Sidney Franklin; for MGM.

Beware My Lovely
US 1952   77m   bw
RKO / Filmmakers (Collier Young)

A handyman employed by a widow turns out
to be a mental defective who imprisons and
threatens to rape and murder her.
Dismal suspenser with a lot of screaming and
running around but very little flair.

w Mel Dinelli, from his play The Man
d Harry Horner *ph* George E. Diskant
m Leith Stevens

Ida Lupino, Robert Ryan, Taylor Holmes,
Barbara Whiting
    'Inept characterization and ludicrously
repetitive situations will surely rank this
among the silliest films of the year.'—*MFB*

Beware of Pity*
GB 1946   106m   bw
Two Cities (W. P. Lipscomb)

An officer courts a crippled girl out of pity.
She finds out and kills herself.
Ambitious but rather artificial and dreary
drama, a shade too pleased with its own
literariness; performances straitjacketed by
production.

w W. P. Lipscomb, Elizabeth Baron,
Margaret Steen, *novel* Stefan Zweig
d Maurice Elvey *ph* Derick Williams

Lilli Palmer, Albert Lieven, Cedric
Hardwicke, Gladys Cooper, Linden Travers,
Ernest Thesiger, Emrys Jones

Bewitched
US 1945   65m   bw
MGM (Arch Oboler)

A girl with twin personalities has her
murderous element exorcized by a spiritualist.
Hilarious nonsense, ancestor of the Eve and
Lizzie schizos of the fifties.

wd Arch Oboler, from his story Alter Ego
ph Charles Salerno Jnr *m* Bronislau Kaper

Phyllis Thaxter, Edmund Gwenn, Addison
Richards, Kathleen Lockhart
    'Oboler manages the first persuasive
imitations of stream of consciousness I know
of in a movie. Much more often, he bores to
desperation with the vulgarity and mere
violence of his effects.'—*James Agee*

Beyond a Reasonable Doubt*
US 1956   80m   bw
RKO (Bert Friedlob)

A novelist is persuaded by a crusading
newspaper proprietor to fake circumstantial
evidence incriminating himself in a murder,
thus proving the uselessness of such evidence.
He does it so well that he is convicted . . . but
that doesn't matter as he was guilty all the
time.
Ingenious but rather cheerless and mechanical
thriller. The actors extract what they can from
a script intent on sleight of hand, but the
distinguished director is at his most flatulent.

w Douglas Morrow *d* Fritz Lang *ph* William
Snyder *m* Herschel Burke Gilbert

Dana Andrews, Joan Fontaine, Sidney
Blackmer, Philip Bourneuf, Shepperd
Strudwick, Arthur Franz, Edward Binns

Beyond Glory
US 1948   82m   bw
Paramount (Robert Fellows)

The honour of a West Point cadet is
vindicated.
Proficient but dramatically turgid vehicle for
an absurdly over-age star.

w Jonathan Latimer, Charles Marquis
Warren, William Wister Haines *d* John
Farrow *ph* John F. Seitz *m* Victor Young

Alan Ladd, Donna Reed, George Coulouris,
George Macready, Audie Murphy

Beyond Mombasa
GB1955   90m   Technicolor
Columbia / Hemisphere (Adrian Worker)

In East Africa, an American avenges his
brother's death at the hands of the Mau Mau
(here called the Leopard Men and revealed to
be run by a mad English missionary).
Tasteless and rather humdrum jungle
adventure using real-life problems purely as a
backdrop.

w Richard English, Gene Levitt, *novel* Mark
of the Leopard by James Eastwood   d George
Marshall   ph Frederick A. Young
m Humphrey Searle

Cornel Wilde, Donna Reed, Leo Genn, Ron
Randell, Christopher Lee

Beyond the Blue Horizon*
US 1942   76m   Technicolor
Paramount (Monta Bell)

An orphan white girl grows up on a tropical
island with a chimpanzee and a swimming
tiger; when rescued and her story doubted, she
leads an expedition back to prove it.
The most tongue-in-cheek of the Lamour
jungle extravaganzas, with plenty of simple
fun.

w Frank Butler   d Alfred Santell   ph Charles
Boyle   m Victor Young

Dorothy Lamour, Richard Denning, Jack
Haley, Patricia Morison, Walter Abel, Helen
Gilbert, Elizabeth Patterson

Beyond the Curtain
GB 1960   88m   bw
Rank / Welbeck (John Martin)

A flying officer rescues a stewardess whose
plane has been forced down in East Germany.
Inept, penny-pinching cold war melodrama in
which very little happens.

w John Cresswell, Compton Bennett,
novel Thunder Above by Charles F. Blair
d Compton Bennett   ph Eric Cross   m Eric
Pakeman

Richard Greene, Eva Bartok, Marius Goring,
Lucie Mannheim, Andree Melly, George
Mikell, John Welsh

Beyond the Forest*
US 1949   96m   bw
Warner (Henry Blanke)

The discontented wife of a small-town doctor
has an affair with a wealthy Chicagoan,
murders a witness, attempts suicide, and dies
of fever.
The star caricatures herself in this overblown
melodrama which marked the unhappy end of
her association with the studio. The rest of the
cast suffer more dumbly from the script's
unintentional hilarities.

w Lenore Coffee, *novel* Stuart Engstrandt
d King Vidor   ph Robert Burks   m Max
Steiner

Bette Davis, Joseph Cotten, David Brian,
Ruth Roman, Minor Watson, Dona Drake,
Regis Toomey
  'Nobody's as good as Bette when she's
bad!'—*publicity*
  'This peerless piece of camp.'—*New Yorker,
1978*
  'Miss Davis makes a regrettably
melodramatic mess of what is undoubtedly one
of the most unfortunate stories she has ever
tackled.'—*Newsweek*

AAN: Max Steiner

Beyond the Poseidon Adventure
US 1979   114m   Technicolor
   Panavision
Warner / Irwin Allen

When rescuers reach the topsy-turvy passenger
liner, one of them is intent on plunder.
Dreary alternative ending to *The Poseidon
Adventure*, with cardboard character studies,
cut-price action, and tenth-rate technicalities.

w Nelson Gidding   d Irwin Allen   ph Joseph
Biroc   m Jerry Fielding   md Preston Ames

Michael Caine, Telly Savalas, Karl Malden,
Sally Field, Peter Boyle, Jack Warden, Shirley
Knight, Shirley Jones, Slim Pickens

Beyond the Time Barrier
US 1959   75m   bw
AIP / Pacific International / Miller-
   Consolidated (Robert Clarke)

A test pilot crosses the fifth dimension and
finds himself in 2024 when civilization has
gone underground to avoid nuclear
contamination.
Crude science fiction, roughly on the level of
Flash Gordon but less entertaining.

w Arthur G. Pierce   d Edgar G. Ulmer
ph Meredith Nicholson   m Darrell Calker

Robert Clarke, Darlene Tompkins, Adrienne
Arden, Vladimir Sokoloff, Stephen Bekassy

Beyond the Valley of the Dolls
US 1970   109m   De Luxe   Panavision
TCF (Russ Meyer)

Three girls in Hollywood enjoy the wilder
reaches of show biz high life.
The skinflick director's first film for a major
studio, with positively no connection with
Valley of the Dolls, is not explicitly

pornographic but pussyfoots around with as
many general excesses as can be crammed into
two hours. If taken as high camp it provides a
laugh or two, but is chiefly notable as marking
a major studio's deepest dip into muddy
waters.

w Roger Ebert *d* Russ Meyer *ph* Fred J.
Koenekamp *m* Stu Phillips, William Loose

Dolly Read, Cynthia Myers, Marcia
McBroom, John La Zar, Michael Blodgett,
Edy Williams
'If one can resist walking out, the last half
hour is quite manic.'—*MFB*
'A film whose total, idiotic, monstrous
badness raises it to the pitch of near-
irresistible entertainment.'—*Alexander Walker*
'Awful, stupid and preposterous . . . also
weirdly funny and a real curio, rather like a
Grandma Moses illustration for a work by the
Marquis de Sade.'—*John Simon*

Beyond This Place*
GB 1959   90m   bw
Renown / Georgefield (Maxwell Setton,
   John R. Sloan)
US title: *Web of Evidence*

An American visiting London finds his
supposedly dead father in prison serving a life
sentence for murder; he delves into history
and finds the real culprit.
Spiritless murder mystery with less serious
intent than the original novel; tolerable
entertainment.

w Kenneth Taylor, *novel* A. J. Cronin *d* Jack
Cardiff *ph* Wilkie Cooper *m* Douglas
Gamley *ad* Ken Adam

Van Johnson, Vera Miles, Bernard Lee,
Emlyn Williams, Jean Kent, Moultrie Kelsall,
Leo McKern, Ralph Truman

Beyond Tomorrow
US 1940   84m   bw

Two elderly ghosts return at Christmas to help
young lovers. An amiably modest example of
the kind they don't do any more. Richard
Carlson, Jean Parker, C. Aubrey Smith,
Charles Winninger. Written by Adele
Comandini from a story by Mildred Cram;
directed by Edward Sutherland; for RKO.

Bezhin Meadow**
USSR 1937   31m   bw
Mosfilm
original title: *Bezhin Lug*

Fragments from an incomplete Eisenstein film
are held together by freeze frames.
Even this collection of bits and pieces shows
the power of the master.

w Alexander Rozhdestvenski, *story* Ivan
Turgenev *d* Sergei Eisenstein *ph* Edouard
Tissé

Vitya Kartashov, Boris Zakhava, Igor
Pavlenko
† The film was reconstructed in 1966.

Bhowani Junction*
GB 1956   110m   Eastmancolor
   Cinemascope
MGM (Pandro S. Berman)

Adventures of an Anglo-Indian girl during the
last years of British India.
Disappointingly anaemic semi-epic from a
gutsy novel, variably handled by all
concerned.

w Sonya Levien, Ivan Moffat, *novel* John
Masters *d* George Cukor *ph* Frederick A.
Young *m* Miklos Rozsa

Ava Gardner, Stewart Granger, *Francis
Matthews*, Bill Travers, Abraham Sofaer,
Marne Maitland, Peter Illing, Freda Jackson,
Edward Chapman
'An unwieldy, flatly-conceived charade.'—
MFB
'One may believe with Henry Ford that
history is bunk; if so, be assured that the
labour pains of India are not half as much
bunk as the romance of Victoria Jones,
daughter of a Hindu lady, and a Welsh engine
driver.'—*Alexander Walker*

The Bible*
US / Italy 1966   174m   De Luxe
   Dimension 150 (70mm)
TCF / Dino de Laurentiis (Luigi Luraschi)

Through the Old Testament from Adam to
Isaac.
A portentous creation with whispered
commentary gives way to a dull misty Eden
with decorous nudes, a sprightly Noah's Ark,
a spectacular Babel, a brooding Sodom and a
turgid Abraham. The pace is killingly slow and
the script has little religious sense, but the
pictures are often pretty.

w Christopher Fry and others *d* John Huston
ph Giuseppe Rotunno *m* Toshiro Maÿuzumi
ad Mario Chiari

Michael Parks (Adam), Ulla Bergryd (Eve),
Richard Harris (Cain), *John Huston* (Noah),
Stephen Boyd (Nimrod), George C. Scott
(Abraham), Ava Gardner (Sarah), Peter
O'Toole (the three angels)
'An Old Testament spectacular like any
other.'—*David Robinson*
'At a time when religion needs all the help it
can get, John Huston may have set its cause
back a couple of thousand years.'—*Rex Reed*
AAN: Toshiro Mayuzumi

Les Biches**

France / Italy 1968   99m   Eastmancolor
La Boétie / Alexandra (André Génovès)
aka: *The Does*

Two lesbians form an uneasy *ménage à trois*
with a young architect, who loves both of
them.
Fascinating and well-detailed character study
with more depth than at first appears.

*w Paul Gégauff, Claude Chabrol d Claude
Chabrol ph Jean Rabier m Pierre Jansen*

Stéphane Audran, Jacqueline Sassard, Jean-
Louis Trintignant

'You can almost see tubes attached to the
heels of all the characters, through which the
meaning has been sucked out of them and
Chabrol pumped in.'—*John Simon*

Bicycle Thieves****

Italy 1948   90m   bw
PDS-ENIC (Umberto Scarparelli)
original title: *Ladri di Biciclette*

An Italian workman, long unemployed, is
robbed of the bicycle he needs for his new job,
and he and his small son search Rome for it.
The epitome of Italian neo-realism, the slight
human drama is developed so that it has all
the force of *King Lear*, and both the acting
and the backgrounds are vividly compelling.

*w Cesare Zavattini d Vittorio de Sica
ph Carlo Montuori m Alessandro Cicognini*

Lamberto Maggiorani, Enzo Staiola

'A film of rare humanity and sensibility.'—
Gavin Lambert

'A memorable work of art with the true
flavour of reality. To see it is an experience
worth having.'—*Richard Mallett, Punch*

'My idea is to de-romanticize the cinema.'—
Vittorio de Sica

AA: best foreign film; Cesare Zavattini

Il Bidone**

Italy / France 1955   109m   bw
Titanus / SGC
aka: *The Swindlers*

A group of petty swindlers fails to move into
the higher criminal bracket.
Sharply observed but rather sentimental
melodrama with tragic pretensions.

*w Federico Fellini, Ennio Flaiano, Tullio
Pinelli d Federico Fellini ph Otello Martelli
m Nino Rota*

Broderick Crawford, Richard Basehart,
Franco Fabrizi, Giulietta Masina

Big Bad Mama

US 1974   85m   Metrocolor
Santa Cruz (Roger Corman)

In 1932 Texas, a desirable widow becomes a
bank robber. Fast moving, violent nonsense,
like a caricature of *Bonnie and Clyde*, which
was itself a caricature.

*w William Norton, Frances Doel d Steve
Carver ph Bruce Logan m David Grisman*

Angie Dickinson, William Shatner, Tom
Skerritt, Susan Sennett, Robbie Lee.

The Big Bockade*

GB 1941   73m   bw
Ealing (Alberto Cavalcanti)

A semi-documentary showing the importance
of blockading Germany in winning the war.
A curious all-star propaganda revue with some
sketches more effective than others.

*w Charles Frend, Angus Macphail d Charles
Frend ph Wilkie Cooper m Richard
Addinsell*

Leslie Banks, Michael Redgrave, John Mills,
Will Hay (his only serious role), Frank Cellier,
Robert Morley, Alfred Drayton, Michael
Rennie, Marius Goring, Bernard Miles

The Big Boodle

US 1957   83m   bw
UA / Monteflor (Lewis F. Blumberg)
GB Title: *Night in Havana*

A croupier in a Havana gambling casino is
suspected of knowing where counterfeited
plates are hidden . . .
An undistinguished chase film with the star
very tired and a long way from home.

*w Jo Eisinger, novel Robert Sylvester
d Richard Wilson ph Lee Garmes m Raoul
Lavista*

Errol Flynn, Pedro Armendariz, Gia Scala,
Rossana Rory

The Big Bounce

US 1969   102m   Technicolor
   Panavision
Warner / Greenway (Wiliam Dozier)

An ex-GI with a criminal record gets into
sexual and criminal trouble while working at a
Californian motel.
Unattractive melodrama with no discernible
point, certainly not to entertain.

*w Robert Dozier, novel Elmore Leonard
d Alex March ph Howard R. Schwartz
m Michael Curb*

Ryan O'Neal, Leigh Taylor-Young, Van
Heflin, James Daly, Robert Webber, Lee
Grant

Big Boy

US 1930   85m approx   bw

A negro jockey wins a big race. Star musical from a Broadway original; routine except that Jolson plays in blackface, then comes on as himself for the finale. Al Jolson. Lousie Closser Hale, Noah Beery. Written by William K. Wells and Perry Vekroff; directed by Alan Crosland; for Warner.

The Big Brawl
US 1980 95m Technicolor Panavision
Warner Brothers / Golden Harvest
(Raymond Chow)
The son of a Chinese restaurateur in Chicago outwits gangsters.
Silly but quite entertaining chopsocky melodrama laced with comedy.
wd Robert Clouse *ph* Robert Jessup *m* Lalo Schifrin
Jackie Chan, Jose Ferrer, Kristine de Bell, Mako, David Sheiner

The Big Broadcast**
US 1932 78m bw
Paramount
A failing radio station is saved by an all-star show.
Revue-style show with a minimum of plot, valuable as archive material covering many stars of the time.
w George Marion Jnr, *novel* Wild Horses by William Ford Manley *d* Frank Tuttle *ph* George Folsey
Bing Crosby, Kate Smith, George Burns, Gracie Allen, Stuart Erwin, Leila Hyams, Cab Calloway, the Mills Brothers, the Boswell Sisters

The Big Broadcast of 1936**
US 1935 97m bw
Paramount (Ben Glazer)
The 'radio lover' of a small radio station is kidnapped by a man-hungry countess.
Zany comedy with interpolated variety acts and a totally Marxian climax.
w Walter de Leon, Francis Martin, Ralph Spence *d* Norman Taurog *ph* Leo Tover *songs* various *ch* LeRoy Prinz
Jack Oakie, George Burns, Gracie Allen, Henry Wadsworth, Wendy Barrie, Lyda Roberti, C. Henry Gordon, Benny Baker, Bing Crosby, Ethel Merman, Richard Tauber, Amos 'n Andy, Mary Boland, Charles Ruggles, Virginia Weidler, Guy Standing, Gail Patrick, Bill Robinson, the Nicholas Brothers, the Vienna Boys Choir, Akim Tamiroff

The Big Broadcast of 1937**
US 1936 100m bw
Paramount (Lewis Gensler)

A radio station manager has trouble with his sponsors.
More recorded acts separated by a measure of plot.
w Edwin Gelsey, Arthur Kober, Barry Travers, Walter de Leon, Francis Martin *d* Mitchell Leisen *ph* Theodor Sparkuhl *songs* various
Jack Benny, George Burns, Gracie Allen, Bob Burns, Martha Raye, Shirley Ross, Ray Milland, Benny Fields, Benny Goodman and his Orchestra, Leopold Stokowski and the Philadelphia Orchestra, Eleanore Whitney, Larry Adler, Louis da Pron
'It isn't a comedy and it isn't a musical, but it has a lot of laughs, the best in several types of music, and I don't know where in the world you will see anything like it.'—*Otis Ferguson*

The Big Broadcast of 1938**
US 1937 90m bw
Paramount (Harlan Thompson)
A steamship owner engaged in a transatlantic race is hampered by his practical joking twin brother.
Glamorous, empty-headed all-star nonsense with the expected bevy of interpolated acts.
w Walter de Leon, Francis Martin, Ken Englund, Frederick Hazlitt Brennan *d* Mitchell Leisen *ph* Harry Fischbeck *songs* various
W. C. Fields, Bob Hope (debut), Martha Raye, Dorothy Lamour, Shirley Ross, Lynne Overman, Ben Blue, Leif Erickson, Kirsten Flagstad, Tito Guizar, Shep Fields and his Rippling Rhythm Orchestra
AA: song 'Thanks for the Memory' (*m* Ralph Rainger, *ly* Leo Robin)

Big Brown Eyes
US 1936 76m bw
Paramount (Walter Wanger)
A private detective and his wisecracking girl friend catch a jewel thief.
Minor league Thin Man stuff, quite acceptably done.
w Raoul Walsh, Bert Hanlon *d* Raoul Walsh *ph* George Clemens *m* Gerald Carbonara *md* Morris Stoloff
Cary Grant, Joan Bennett, Walter Pidgeon, Lloyd Nolan, Alan Baxter, Marjorie Gateson, Isabel Jewell, Douglas Fowley

The Big Bus
US 1976 88m Movielab Panavision
Paramount (Fred Freeman, Lawrence J. Cohen)

Misadventures of a giant atomic-powered bus on its first cross-country trip.
Rather feeble spoof on disaster pictures, with some good moments.

w Fred Freeman, Lawrence J. Cohen *d* James Frawley *ph* Harry Stradling Jnr *m* David Shire *pd* Joel Schiller

Joseph Bologna, Stockard Channing, John Beck, René Auberjonois, Ned Beatty, Bob Dishy, Jose Ferrer, Ruth Gordon, Harold Gould, Larry Hagman, Sally Kellerman, Richard Mulligan, Lynn Redgrave

'It's all fast, bright, surface stuff, almost obsessively intent on never letting a laugh get away, misfiring, backfiring, skidding and crashing gears gaily all the way, often quite as thrilling, if not always as ludicrous, as some of the films it mocks.'—*Alan Brien, Sunday Times*

'It has been produced with such consummate bad taste, schlock acting and feeble attempts at verbal and visual humour that whatever laughs are engendered are at it rather than with it.'—*Dave Pomeroy, Film Information*

Big Business••••
US 1929   20m   silent

Stan and Ollie fail to sell a Christmas tree to a belligerent householder. Classic silent comedy consisting largely of a brilliant tit-for-tat routine of reciprocal destruction, to which scripting, acting and editing equally combine.
Laurel and Hardy, James Finlayson. Written by Leo McCarey and H. M. Walker; directed by James W. Horne; edited by Richard Currier; for Hal Roach.

The Big Cat
US 1949   75m   Technicolor

Feuding mountain families combine to track a marauding lion. Standard outdoor melodrama, almost a straight version of *Track of the Cat*.
Peggy Ann Garner, Lon McCallister, Preston Foster, Forrest Tucker, Skip Homeier, Sara Haden. Written by Morton Grant and Dorothy Yost; directed by Phil Karlson; for Eagle-Lion.

The Big Circus•
US 1959   109m   Technicolor
    Cinemascope
AA (Irwin Allen)

A bankrupt circus owner tries to get his show back on the road despite the murderous schemes of his ex-partners.
Fast-paced melodrama which makes little sense but generally provides the expected thrills.

w Irwin Allen, Charles Bennett, Irving Wallace *d* Joseph Newman *ph* Winton C. Hoch *m* Paul Sawtell, Bert Shefter

Victor Mature, Red Buttons, Rhonda Fleming, Kathryn Grant, Vincent Price, Peter Lorre, *Gilbert Roland*, David Nelson, Adele Mara, Steve Allen

The Big City
US 1927   80m approx (24 fps)   bw
    silent
MGM

A cabaret owner has a jewel robbery gang as a sideline.
Minor star melodrama.

w Waldemar Young, Tod Browning *d* Tod Browning

Lon Chaney, Betty Compson, James Murray, Marceline Day

The Big City•
US 1937   80m   bw
MGM (Norman Krasna)

An honest cab driver and his wife hold out against corruption.
Sentimental realism of the type expected of its director. Smooth and syrupy.

w Dore Schary, Hugo Butler *d* Frank Borzage *ph* Joseph Ruttenberg *m* William Axt

Spencer Tracy, Luise Rainer, Charley Grapewin, Janet Beecher, Irving Bacon, William Demarest, Eddie Quillan

Big City
US 1948   103m   bw
MGM (Joe Pasternak)

In New York's East Side, a little girl is the adopted daughter of three bachelors, but trouble looms when they all get ideas of romance.
Later-day star vehicle for which the young star is really too old and all else is excessively sentimental and sprawling.

w Whitfield Cook, Ann Morrison *d* Norman Taurog *ph* Robert Surtees

Margaret O'Brien, Robert Preston, Danny Thomas, George Murphy, Karin Booth, Jackie Butch Jenkins, Betty Garrett

The Big City••
India 1963   131m   bw
R. D. Bansal
original title: *Mahanagar*

A poverty-stricken Calcutta bank accountant sends his wife out to work; then the bank crashes, and she becomes the sole breadwinner.

Immensely detailed, overlong, but mainly fascinating account of modern urban India and its attitudes.

wd, m Satyajit Ray, *novel* Narendra Nath Mitra *ph* Subrata Mitra

Madhabi Mukherjee, Anil Chatterjee, Haren Chatterjee, Haradhan Banerjee

The Big Clock*
US 1947 95m bw
Paramount (John Farrow)

A publishing magnate murders his mistress and assigns one of his editors to solve the crime.
Slick but rather empty thriller with judicious use of adequate talent.

w Jonathan Latimer, *novel* Kenneth Fearing *d* John Farrow *ph* John Seitz *m* Victor Young

Charles Laughton, Ray Milland, Maureen O'Sullivan, Rita Johnson, Elsa Lanchester

The Big Combo*
US 1955 80m bw
Allied Artists / Security-Theodora (Sidney Harmon)

The police crush a crime syndicate.
An otherwise uninspired thriller memorable for starting the new violence, with some ugly scenes of torture which suffered at the time from the censor.

w Philip Yordan *d* Joseph H. Lewis *ph* John Alton *m* David Raksin

Cornel Wilde, Richard Conte, Jean Wallace, Brian Donlevy, Robert Middleton, Lee Van Cleef, Ted de Corsia, Helen Walker, John Hoyt

The Big Country***
US 1958 165m Technirama
UA / Anthony / Worldwide (William Wyler, Gregory Peck)

The Terills and the Hannesseys feud over water rights, and peace is brought about only with the deaths of the family heads.
Big-scale western with a few pretensions to say something about the Cold War. All very fluent, star-laden and easy to watch.

w James R. Webb, Sy Bartlett, Robert Wilder, *novel* Donald Hamilton *d* William Wyler *ph* Franz Planer *m* Jerome Moross

Gregory Peck, Jean Simmons, Charlton Heston, Carroll Baker, *Burl Ives, Charles Bickford*, Alfonso Bedoya, Chuck Connors

AA: Burl Ives
AAN: Jerome Moross

The Big Cube
US 1969 98m Technicolor

Girl tries to murder her actress stepmother by feeding her overdoses of LSD. Stultifyingly boring melodrama. Lana Turner, George Chakiris, Dan O'Herlihy, Karin Mossberg, Richard Egan. Written by William Douglas Lansford; directed by Tito Davison; for Francisco Diez Barroso / Warner.

Big Fella*
GB 1937 73m bw
Fortune (J. Elder Wills)

In Marseilles, a black man returns a lost child to his English parents.
Pleasant light vehicle with the star in typical easy form.

w Fenn Sherie, Ingram d'Abbes, *novel* Banjo by Claude McKay *d* J. Elder Wills

Paul Robeson, Elizabeth Welch, Roy Emerton, Marcelle Rogez

The Big Fisherman
US 1959 166m Technicolor
     Panavision
Centurion (Rowland V. Lee)

An Arab princess meets disciple Simon Peter, who dissuades her from her plan to assassinate her stepfather Herod.
Well-meaning but leaden adaptation of a bestselling novel which followed on from *The Robe*. Too reverent by half, and in many respects surprisingly incompetent.

w Howard Estabrook, Rowland V. Lee, *novel* Lloyd C. Douglas *d* Frank Borzage *ph* Lee Garmes *m* Albert Hay Malotte *pd* John de Cuir

Howard Keel, Alexander Scourby, Susan Kohner, John Saxon, Martha Hyer, Herbert Lom, Ray Stricklyn, Beulah Bondi

'Its overall flatness of conception and execution is a stiff price to pay for the lack of spectacular sensationalism characterizing its fellow-epics.'—*MFB*

AAN: Lee Garmes

The Big Fix
US 1978 108m Technicolor
Universal (Carl Borack, Richard Dreyfuss)

An industrial investigator fancies himself as a private eye and gets involved in a political corruption case.
Hard to follow and harder still to care about, this rather sloppy, with-it movie is a little too pleased with itself from the word go.

w Roger L. Simon, from his novel *d* Jeremy Paul Kagan *ph* Frank Stanley *m* Bill Conti *pd* Robert F. Boyle

Richard Dreyfuss, Susan Anspach, Bonnie Bedelia, John Lithgow

'The strength of this film lies in the cool, meandering discretion with which its central theme is fleshed out: regret for lost illusions as the protest generation of the sixties finds its arteries hardening.'—*Tom Milne, MFB*

The Big Gamble*

US 1960   100m   De Luxe   Cinemascope
TCF / Darryl F. Zanuck

Three people drive an ailing truck to a remote African township where they hope to start a haulage business.

Curious comedy-drama-adventure which starts off with family matters in Dublin and gradually develops into a lighter-hearted *Wages of Fear*. It has its moments.

w Irwin Shaw   *d* Richard Fleischer, Elmo Williams   *ph* William Mellor, Henri Persin   *m* Maurice Jarre

Stephen Boyd, Juliette Greco, David Wayne, *Gregory Ratoff*, Sybil Thorndike, Fernand Ledoux

A Big Hand for the Little Lady**

US 1966   96m   Technicolor
Warner / Eden (Fielder Cook)
GB title: *Big Deal at Dodge City* (though the action clearly takes place in Laredo)

Five rich poker players are outwitted by a family of confidence tricksters.

Diverting but thinly stretched acting-piece from a much shorter TV original; still, suspense builds nicely until the disappointingly handled revelation.

w Sidney Carroll, from his own TV play
d Fielder Cook   *ph* Lee Garmes   *m* David Raksin

Henry Fonda, *Joanne Woodward*, Jason Robards, Paul Ford, Kevin McCarthy, *Charles Bickford*, Robert Middleton, *Burgess Meredith*, John Qualen

The Big Hangover

US 1950   82m   bw
MGM (Norman Krasna)

A lawyer struggling to mingle with the mighty finds he is allergic to strong drink.

Woefully unfunny comedy with virtually no plot.

wd Norman Krasna   *ph* George Folsey
m Adolph Deutsch

Van Johnson, Elizabeth Taylor, Percy Waram, Fay Holden, Leon Ames, Edgar Buchanan, Rosemary de Camp, Gene Lockhart, Selena Royle

Big Hearted Herbert

US 1934   60m   bw

A prosperous plumber becomes more concerned with money than with his family's happiness. Pleasing moral comedy, well cast.

Guy Kibbee, Aline MacMahon, Patricia Ellis, Philip Reed, George Chandler. Written by Lillie Hayward and Ben Markson, from the play by Sophie Kerr and Anna Steese Richardson; directed by William Keighley; for Warners. (NB: 1940 brought a remake under the title *Father Is a Prince*, with Grant Mitchell.)

The Big Heat**

US 1953   90m   bw
Columbia (Robert Arthur)

A police detective's wife is killed by a bomb meant for himself; he goes undercover to track down the gangsters responsible.

Considered at the time to reach a new low in violence (boiling coffee in the face), this dour little thriller also struck a new note of realism in crime films and produced one of Glenn Ford's most typical performances.

w Sydney Boehm, *novel* William P. McGivern   *d* Fritz Lang   *ph* Charles Lang   *m* Arthur Morton   *md* Mischa Bakaleinikoff

Glenn Ford, Gloria Grahame, Alexander Scourby, Jocelyn Brando, Lee Marvin, Jeanette Nolan, Peter Whitney

'The main impression is of violence employed arbitrarily, mechanically and in the long run pointlessly.'—*Penelope Houston*
'A hard cop and a soft dame!'—*publicity*

The Big House**

US 1930   88m   bw
MGM

Tensions in prison lead to an attempted break-out and a massacre.

Archetypal prison melodrama and a significant advance in form for early talkies. Its sets were re-used by Laurel and Hardy in *Pardon Us*.

w Frances Marion   *d* George Hill   *ph* Harold Wenstrom

Chester Morris, Wallace Beery, Robert Montgomery, Lewis Stone, Leila Hyams, George F. Marion, J. C. Nugent, Karl Dane

'We all gave our roles the best that was in us, and the virility and truthfulness of the picture were more satisfying than anything else I've done.'—*Chester Morris, 1953*

† The role played by Wallace Beery had been intended for Lon Chaney, who died during preparation

AA: Frances Marion
AAN: best picture; Wallace Beery

Big House USA
US 1954 82m bw
UA / Bel Air (Aubrey Schenck)

Convicts stage a break-out to get at hidden loot.
Though less explicit in its violence than many later films, this is a singularly unpleasant melodrama with not one attractive character.

w John C. Higgins d Howard W. Koch
ph Gordon Avil m Paul Dunlap

Broderick Crawford, Ralph Meeker, Lon Chaney, Charles Bronson, William Talman, Reed Hadley

Big Jack
US 1949 85m bw
MGM (Gottfried Reinhardt)

Adventures of a couple of amiable scoundrels in 1890 Virginia.
The elements don't jell in this outdoor comedy-drama, which was its star's last film.

w Gene Fowler, Marvin Borowsky, Otto Van Eyss d Richard Thorpe ph Robert Surtees
m Herbert Stothart

Wallace Beery, Marjorie Main, Richard Conte, Edward Arnold, Vanessa Brown, Clinton Sundberg, Charles Dingle, Clem Bevans

Big Jake*
US 1971 110m Technicolor
   Panavision
Batjac / Cinema Center (Michael A. Wayne)

An elderly Texas cattleman swings into action when his grandson is kidnapped.
Satisfactory example of the star's later vehicles, with efficient production and familiar cast and brawling.

w Harry Julian Fink, R. M. Fink d George Sherman ph William Clothier m Elmer Bernstein

John Wayne, Richard Boone, Maureen O'Hara, Patrick Wayne, Chris Mitchum, Bobby Vinton, Bruce Cabot, Glenn Corbett, Harry Carey Jnr, John Agar
  'Another genial celebration of Big John's ability to carry a film practically single-handed.'—MFB

Big Jim McLain
US 1952 90m bw
Wayne / Fellows (Robert Fellows)

A special agent for the House of UnAmerican Activities Committee routs communists in Hawaii.
Curious and rather offensive star vehicle in which the right-wing political shading interferes seriously with the entertainment value.

w James Edward Grant d Edward Ludwig
ph Archie Stout m Emil Newman

John Wayne, Nancy Olson, James Arness, Alan Napier, Veda Ann Borg, Hans Conried, Gayne Whitman
  'Brings to the screen all the unattractively hysterical mentality of the witch hunt.'—
Penelope Houston

The Big Knife*
US 1955 111m bw
UA / Aldrich and Associates

A depressed Hollywood star who wants better things for himself is blackmailed into signing a new contract.
Overheated argument between Art and Mammon, with rather disagreeable people shouting at each other, for too long a time. Limited interest is provided by the acting.

w James Poe, play Clifford Odets d Robert Aldrich ph Ernest Laszlo m Frank de Vol

Jack Palance, Ida Lupino, Rod Steiger, Everett Sloane, Jean Hagen, Shelley Winters, Wendell Corey, Ilka Chase, Wesley Addy
  'Everything in it is garish and overdone: it's paced too fast and pitched too high, immorality is attacked with almost obscene relish, the knife turns into a buzz saw.'—
Pauline Kael, 1968

The Big Land
US 1957 92m Warnercolor
(Warner) Jaguar
GB title: Stampeded

Cattlemen encourage the building of a rail link for Texas.
Undistinguished star western.

w David Dortort, Martin Rackin, novel Buffalo Grass by Frank Gruber d Gordon Douglas ph John F. Seitz m David Buttolph

Alan Ladd, Virginia Mayo, Edmond O'Brien, Anthony Caruso, Julie Bishop, John Qualen
  'Hackneyed, humdrum western.'—Howard Thompson

The Big Lift*
US 1949 119m bw
TCF (William Perlberg)

When the Russians blockade Berlin, British and American airmen get supplies there via a massive airlift; two men on one plane hold opposite views of the matter, and both have chastening experiences.
Rather heavy-going fiction based on fact, with earnest performances and good production.

wd George Seaton ph Charles G. Clarke
m Alfred Newman

Montgomery Clift, Paul Douglas, Cornell Borchers, O. E. Hasse, Bruni Lobel

'There are some acute touches . . . just enough to make the slick evasions of the rest all the more regrettable.'—*Gavin Lambert*

The Big Money
GB 1956 86m Technicolor Vistavision
Rank

A family of petty crooks is ashamed of its eldest son, who is an incompetent thief.
A would-be high-spirited lark in which none of the jokes comes off, and a note of forced artificiality hangs over the whole production.

w John Baines *d* John Paddy Carstairs
ph Jack Cox *m* Van Phillips

Ian Carmichael, Belinda Lee, Kathleen Harrison, Robert Helpmann, James Hayter, George Coulouris, Jill Ireland, Renee Houston, Leslie Phillips

The Big Mouth
US 1967 107m Pathecolor
Columbia (Jerry Lewis)

A meek bank auditor finds he is the double of a dying gangster and is put on the trail of stolen diamonds.
The comedian at his worst, most repetitive and long drawn out.

w Jerry Lewis, Bill Richmond *d* Jerry Lewis
ph W. Wallace Kelley, Ernest Laszlo
m Harry Betts

Jerry Lewis, Harold J. Stone, Susan Day, Buddy Lester, Del Moore

The Big Night
US 1951 75m bw
(UA) Philip A. Waxman

A 17-year-old youth goes on the rampage in the underworld to avenge the beating up of his father by gangsters.
Hysterical melodrama presenting a rather false and dismal view of the world. Amazingly typical of its director's later output.

w Stanley Ellin, Joseph Losey, *novel* Dreadful Summit by Stanley Ellin *d* Joseph Losey
ph Hal Mohr *m* Lyn Murray

John Barrymore Jnr, Preston Foster, Howard St John, Philip Bourneuf, Howland Chamberlin, Emile Meyer, Dorothy Comingore, Joan Lorring

'We are in that familiar underworld of the American cinema: dark streets gleaming with rain, sleazy apartments, garish night clubs, with Negro singers, drunks who spout philosophy, discontented blondes and fierce pock-marked thugs.'—*Gavin Lambert*

The Big Noise
US 1944 74m bw
TCF (Sol M. Wurtzel)

Two incompetent detectives accidentally round up a spy gang.
Very thin star vehicle consisting largely of poorly staged and warmed up versions of a few old routines.

w Scott Darling *d* Mal St Clair *ph* Joe MacDonald *m* Cyril Mockridge

Stan Laurel, Oliver Hardy, Doris Merrick, Arthur Space, Jack Norton

The Big Operator
US 1959 91m bw Cinemascope
MGM / Albert Zugsmith-Fryman (Red Doff)

The racketeer head of a labour union goes berserk when the government has him investigated.
Unpleasant gangster exploitation melodrama from the bottom of the barrel.

w Robert Smith, Allen Rivkin *d* Charles Haas *ph* Walter H. Castle *m* Van Alexander

Mickey Rooney, Steve Cochran, Mamie Van Doren, Mel Tormé, Ray Danton, Jim Backus, Jackie Coogan, Ray Anthony, Charles Chaplin Jnr

The Big Parade***
US 1925 115m approx (24 fps) bw
   silent
MGM

A young American enlists in 1917, learns the realities of war, is wounded but survives.
Enormously successful commercially, this 'anti-war' film survives best as a thrilling spectacle and a well-considered piece of film-making.

w Lawrence Stallings, Harry Behn *d* King Vidor *ph* John Arnold *m* William Axt, David Mendoza

John Gilbert, Renee Adoree, Hobart Bosworth, Karl Dane, George K. Arthur

'The human comedy emerges from a terrifying tragedy.'—*King Vidor*

'A cinegraphically visualized result of a cinegraphically imagined thing . . . something conceived in terms of a medium and expressed by that medium as only that medium could properly express it.'—*National Board of Review*

'The extraordinary impression of the rush of lorries, the queer terror of the woods . . . it was amazing how much fear could be felt in the mere continuous pace of movement.'—*Bryher, Close Up*

'The epic of the American doughboy!'—*publicity*

The Big Parade of Comedy**
US 1964   90m approx   bw
MGM (Robert Youngson)
aka: *MGM's Big Parade of Comedy*

A compilation by Robert Youngson, including material as diverse as *Ninotchka*, Laurel and Hardy and the Marx Brothers.
One is grateful for the excerpts but the assembly of them is somewhat graceless.

The Big Pond*
US 1930   79m   bw
Paramount (Monta Bell)

The son of an important French family acts as a tourist guide in Venice.
Reasonably lively, semi-satirical early musical with Americans the butt of the jokes.

w Robert Presnell, Garrett Fort, Preston Sturges, *play* George Middleton, A. E. Thomas *d* Hobart Henley *ph* George Folsey *songs* various

Maurice Chevalier, Claudette Colbert, George Barbier, Nat Pendleton, Marion Ballou

AAN: Maurice Chevalier

Big Red
US 1962   89m   Technicolor
Walt Disney (Winston Hibler)

An orphan boy protects a dog which later saves him from a mountain lion.
Simple boy-and-dog yarn with impressive Canadian settings.

w Louis Pelletier *d* Norman Tokar
ph Edward Colman *m* Oliver Wallace

Walter Pidgeon, Gilles Payant, Emile Genest

The Big Red One*
US 1980   111m   colour
UA / Lorimar (Gene Corman)

Five foot-soldiers survive action in several theatres of war between 1940 and 1945
Symbolic action drama, very well made but finally lacking a cumulative impact.

wd Samuel Fuller ph Adam Greenberg
m Dana Kaproff

Lee Marvin, Mark Hamill, Robert Carradine, Bobby DiCicco, Kelly Ward, Stéphane Audran, Serge Marquand
   'A picture of palpable raw power which manages both intense intimacy and great scope at the same time.'—*Variety*

The Big Shakedown
US 1934   64m   bw
Warner (Sam Bischoff)

A racketeer finds a new gimmick: cut-price medicine.

Action programmer with emphasis on the young couple forced into helping the racket.

w Niven Busch, Rian James *d* John Francis Dillon *ph* Sid Hickox

Bette Davis, Ricardo Cortez, Charles Farrell, Glenda Farrell, Allen Jenkins, Henry O'Neill, Samuel S. Hinds
   'A routine assortment of gang-film impedimenta.'—*New York Times*

The Big Shot*
US 1942   82m   bw
Warner (Walter MacEwen)

An ill-fated criminal has trouble with women and his former companions.
Dullish star vehicle.

w Bertram Millhauser, Aben Finkel, Daniel Fuchs *d* Lewis Seiler *ph* Sid Hickox
m Adolph Deutsch

Humphrey Bogart, Irene Manning, Richard Travis, Donald Crisp, Stanley Ridges, Henry Hull, Susan Peters, Howard da Silva

The Big Show
US 1961   113m   De Luxe   Cinemascope
TCF / API (Ted Sherdeman)

A circus proprietor dominates his sons; after his death they fight for supremacy.
Another remake of *House of Strangers*, which was also remodelled as *Broken Lance*. Not too bad as circus melodramas go.

w Ted Sherdeman *d* James B. Clark *ph* Otto Heller *m* Paul Sawtell, Bert Shefter

Esther Williams, Cliff Robertson, *Nehemiah Persoff*, Robert Vaughn, Carol Christensen, Margia Dean, David Nelson

The Big Sky*
US 1952   122m   bw
RKO / Winchester (Howard Hawks)

In 1830 two Kentucky mountain men join an exploration up the Missouri and become preoccupied with Indian trouble.
A large-scale adventure, loaded with talent, which becomes oddly tedious.

w Dudley Nichols, *novel* A. B. Guthrie Jnr
d Howard Hawks *ph* Russell Harlan
m Dmitri Tiomkin

Kirk Douglas, Arthur Hunnicutt, Elizabeth Threatt, Dewey Martin, Buddy Baer, Steve Geray, Jim Davis
   'It has the timeless, relentless quality of the long American historical novel.'—*Penelope Houston*

AAN: Russell Harlan; Arthur Hunnicutt

The Big Sleep***
US 1946   114m   hw
Warner (Howard Hawks)

Private eye Philip Marlowe is hired to protect General Sternwood's wild young daughter from her own indiscretions, and finds several murders later that he has fallen in love with her elder sister.

Inextricably complicated, moody thriller from a novel whose author claimed that even he did not know 'who done it'. The film is nevertheless vastly enjoyable along the way for its slangy script, star performances and outbursts of violence, suspense and sheer fun.

w William Faulkner, Leigh Brackett, Jules Furthman, novel Raymond Chandler d Howard Hawks ph Sid Hickox m Max Steiner

Humphrey Bogart, Lauren Bacall, Martha Vickers, John Ridgely, Dorothy Malone, Regis Toomey, Charles Waldron, Elisha Cook Jnr

'A sullen atmosphere of sex saturates the film, which is so fast and complicated you can hardly catch it.'—*Richard Winnington*

'A violent, smoky cocktail shaken together from most of the printable misdemeanours and some that aren't.'—*James Agee*

'Harder, faster, tougher, funnier and more laconic than any thriller since.'—*NFT, 1974*

'Wit, excitement and glamour in generous doses.'—*Francis Wyndham*

The Big Sleep
GB 1977   99m   De Luxe
ITC / Elliott Kastner, Michael Winner

Straight remake of the 1946 film, curiously and ineffectively set in London.

wd Michael Winner ph Robert Paynter m Jerry Fielding

Robert Mitchum, Sarah Miles, Richard Boone, Candy Clark, Edward Fox, Joan Collins, John Mills, James Stewart, Oliver Reed, Harry Andrews, Richard Todd, James Donald, Colin Blakely

'The 1946 film takes on even more stature in light of this. For a Winner film, however, it's quite good.'—*Variety*

The Big Steal**
US 1949   72m   bw
RKO (Jack J. Gross)

An army officer is framed for the theft of a payroll, and sets off across Mexico in hectic pursuit of the real culprit.

Unexpectedly enjoyable comedy melodrama with a plethora of twists and a pace that never lets up. Routine Hollywood at a level seldom achieved, and short enough to leave one asking for more.

w Gerald Drayson Adams, Geoffrey Homes, story The Road to Carmichael's by Richard Wormser d Don Siegel ph Harry J. Wild m Leigh Harline

Robert Mitchum, Jane Greer, William Bendix, Ramon Novarro, Patric Knowles, Don Alvarado, John Qualen

'Vigour and excellent craftsmanship.'—*Gavin Lambert*

The Big Store*
US 1941   83m   bw
MGM (Louis K. Sidney)

An eccentric private eye saves a department store from the hands of crooks.

Reckoned to be the Marx Brothers' weakest MGM vehicle, but it has its moments, especially the first reel and the bedding department scene, also Groucho's rendering of 'Sing While You Sell'.

w Sid Kuller, Hal Fimberg, Ray Golden d Charles Reisner ph Charles Lawton m George Stoll

Groucho, Chico, Harpo, Margaret Dumont, Douglass Dumbrille, Tony Martin, Virginia Grey, Virginia O'Brien, Henry Armetta

The Big Street*
US 1942   88m   bw
RKO (Damon Runyon)

A Broadway nightclub waiter falls in love with a crippled singer who selfishly accepts his help without loving him in return.

Unusual but mawkish material from an author who never really suited the screen; a mixture of laughs, tears and sentimentality, with a comic gangster background.

w Leonard Spiegelgass, story Little Pinks by Damon Runyon d Irving Reis ph Russell Metty m Roy Webb

Henry Fonda, Lucille Ball, Eugene Pallette, Virginia Weidler, Agnes Moorehead, Barton MacLane, Ozzie Nelson and his Orchestra, Sam Levene, Ray Collins, Marion Martin

The Big Trail*
US 1930   125m   bw
Fox

A wagon train struggles along the Oregon trail.

Simple-minded early talkie western spectacular with a new young star who took another nine years to make it big. Originally shown on a giant 70mm gauge and intended for big screens.

w Jack Peabody, Marie Boyle, Florence Postal *d* Raoul Walsh *ph* Lucien Andriot, Arthur Edeson

John Wayne, Marguerite Churchill, El Brendel, Tully Marshall, Tyrone Power Snr, David Rollins, Ward Bond, Helen Parrish

'Printed upon the new wide film and projected upon the vastly large Grandeur screen, the landscapes, wagon trains, vistas and camp scenes achieve an incredibly greater sweep [than *The Covered Wagon*]. *The Big Trail* is often stagey, melodramatic, ranty.'— *Theatre Magazine*

The Big Trees**
US 1952   89m   Technicolor
Warner (Louis F. Edelmann)

An unscrupulous lumberman tries to exploit California's giant redwood forests but is won over by the local Quakers who hold the trees in awe.
Pleasing, old-fashioned outdoor drama with a plot which allows the star much opportunity for derring-do.

w John Twist, James R. Webb *d* Felix Feist *ph* Bert Glennon *m* Heinz Roemheld

Kirk Douglas, Eve Miller, Patrice Wymore, Edgar Buchanan, John Archer, Alan Hale Jnr

† A remake of *Valley of the Giants* (qv)

Big Wednesday*
US 1978   119m   Metrocolor   Panavision
Warner / A-Team (Alex Rose, Tamara Asseyev)

Three California surfing friends of the early sixties get back together after the Vietnam war.
It isn't clear whether the intent is to extol or deride the mystical camaraderie of surfing, but for those who can stand rumbustious beach behaviour this curious movie may have at least as much to say as *The Deer Hunter*.

w John Milius, Dennis Aaberg *d* John Milius *ph* Bruce Surtees *surfing ph* Greg MacGillivray *m* Basil Poledouris

Jan-Michael Vincent, William Katt, Gary Busey, Darell Fetty

The Big Wheel
US 1949   92m   bw
(UA) Popkin / Stiefel / Dempsey (Samuel H. Stiefel)

The son of a racing driver is determined to follow in father's footsteps.
Grubby star actioner.

w Robert Smith *d* Edward Ludwig *ph* Ernest Laszlo *m* Nat W. Finston

Mickey Rooney, Spring Byington, Thomas Mitchell, Mary Hatcher, Allen Jenkins

The Bigamist*
US 1953   80m   bw
Filmmakers (Collier Young)

A travelling salesman has two wives.
Minor melodrama which took its subject seriously but failed to make absorbing drama of it. Very much a family affair, starring the producer's present and past wives, the latter also directing.

w Collier Young *d* Ida Lupino *ph* George Diskant *m* Leith Stevens

Edmond O'Brien, Joan Fontaine, Ida Lupino, Edmund Gwenn, Jane Darwell

'The film seems to have summoned all its energy to shout defiantly that bigamous marriages exist and, finding no one to defy, retires deflated.'—*MFB*

The Bigamist*
Italy / France 1956   97m   bw
Royal / Filmel / Alba

An innocent young salesman is accused of bigamy and dragged into court.
Noisy comedy of mistaken identity; some laughs, but the talents are not at their best.

w Sergio Amidei, Age Scarpelli, Franco Rosi, Elio Talarico *d* Luciano Emmer *ph* Mario Montuori *m* Alessandro Cicognini

Marcello Mastroianni, Vittorio de Sica, Franca Valeri, Giovanna Ralli

Bigger than Life*
US 1956   95m   Eastmancolor   Cinemascope
TCF / James Mason

A small-town schoolteacher is prescribed cortisone for arthritis; it gradually turns him into a bullying megalomaniac full of grandiose schemes.
Exaggerated and sensationalized but still not very dramatic expansion of a genuine case history. A curious choice for all concerned.

w Cyril Hume, Richard Maibaum *d* Nicholas Ray *ph* Joe MacDonald *m* David Raksin

James Mason, Barbara Rush, Walter Matthau, Robert Simon, Roland Winters

The Biggest Bundle of Them All
US 1967   110m   Metrocolor   Panavision
MGM / Shaftel–Stewart

A retired gangster is kidnapped by other gangsters and shows them how to steal five million dollars worth of platinum.
Very moderately amusing international comedy caper.

w Josef Shaftel, Sy Salkowitz *d* Ken Annakin *ph* Piero Portalupi *m* Riz Ortolani

Raquel Welch, Robert Wagner, Vittorio de Sica, Edward G. Robinson, Godfrey Cambridge, Davy Kaye

'It begins like one of these really bad movies that are unintentionally funny. Then it becomes clear that it intends to be funny, and it isn't.'—*Renata Adler*

Bill and Coo

US 1947 61m colour

Trials and tribulations of the inhabitants of Chirpendale are enacted entirely by birds, mostly wearing hats and neckties. An eccentricity which won its creator, Ken Murray, a special Academy Award. For Republic. 'By conservative estimate, the god-damnedest thing ever seen.'—*James Agee.*

A Bill of Divorcement**

US 1932 76m bw

RKO / David O. Selznick

A middle-aged man, released from a mental institution, comes home and meets his strong-willed daughter.

Pattern play which became a celebrated star vehicle; now very dated but the performances survive.

w Howard Estabrook, Harry Wagstaff Gribble, *play* Clemence Dane *d* George Cukor *ph* Sid Hickox *m* Max Steiner, W. Franke Harling

John Barrymore, Katharine Hepburn (her debut), Billie Burke, David Manners, Paul Cavanagh, Henry Stephenson, Elizabeth Patterson

A Bill of Divorcement*

US 1940 69m bw

RKO

GB title: *Never To Love*

Virtually a scene-for-scene remake of the above. Again the acting holds the material together.

w Dalton Trumbo *d* John Farrow *ph* Nicholas Musuraca *m* Roy Webb

Adolphe Menjou, Maureen O'Hara, Patric Knowles, Herbert Marshall, C. Aubrey Smith, Dame May Whitty

Billie

US 1965 87m Techniscope

UA / Peter Lawford (Don Weis)

A teenage tomboy runs into trouble because she is better at sport than her boy friends. Routine American college / domestic comedy with a young star and good comedy support.

w Ronald Alexander, from his play Time Out for Ginger *d* Don Weis *ph* John Russell *m* Dominic Frontière

Patty Duke, Jim Backus, Jane Greer, Warren Berlinger, Billy de Wolfe, Charles Lane, Dick Sargent, Richard Deacon

Billion Dollar Brain

GB 1967 111m Technicolor Panavision

UA / Lowndes (Harry Saltzman)

Ex-secret agent Harry Palmer agrees to take a mysterious canister to Finland and becomes involved in an American megalomaniac's bid to take over the world.

Incomprehensible spy story smothered in the kind of top dressing now expected from this director, but which almost killed his career at the time. Occasional pictorial pleasures, but the total kaleidoscopic effect is enough to drive most audiences to the exit.

w John McGrath, *novel* Len Deighton *d* Ken Russell *ph* Billy Williams *m* Richard Rodney Bennett *pd* Syd Cain

Michael Caine, *Oscar Homolka*, Françoise Dorléac, Karl Malden, Ed Begley

Billy Budd*

GB 1962 125m bw Cinemascope

Anglo-Allied (A. Ronald Lubin, Peter Ustinov)

In 1797 the sadistic master at arms of a British warship terrorizes the crew and is killed by young Billy Budd, who must hang for his unpremeditated crime.

Handsomely photographed but obtusely scripted and variously acted attempt at the impossible, an allegory of good and evil more suited to opera or the printed page than film: in any case, a hopelessly and defiantly uncommercial enterprise. Some actors bore, others chew the scenery.

w Peter Ustinov, Robert Rossen, *novel* Herman Melville *d* Peter Ustinov *ph* Robert Krasker *m* Antony Hopkins

Peter Ustinov, Robert Ryan, Terence Stamp, Melvyn Douglas, Paul Rogers, John Neville, Ronald Lewis, David McCallum, Lee Montague, John Meillon, Thomas Heathcote, Niall MacGinnis, Cyril Luckham

AAN: Terence Stamp

Billy Jack*

US 1971 113m Technicolor

Warner / National Student Film Corporation (Mary Rose Solti)

A half-breed Vietnam veteran roams the Arizona desert protecting wild mustangs and a runaway teenager.
A trendy radical drama, virtually a one-man show which had an enormous success in the US and led to a sequel, *The Trial of Billy Jack.*

w Tom Laughlin, Delores Taylor *d* Tom Laughlin (T. C. Frank) *ph* Fred Koenekamp, John Stephens *m* Mundell Lowe

Tom Laughlin, Delores Taylor, Bert Freed, Clark Howat, Julie Webb, Ken Tobey, Victor Izay

'A plea for the alternative society with a format of the crudest melodrama.'—*MFB*

Billy Liar*
GB 1963 98m bw Cinemascope
Vic Films (Joe Janni)

In a drab North Country town, an undertaker's clerk lives in a world of fantasy.
Flawed only by its unsuitable Cinemascope ratio, this is a brilliant urban comedy of its time, seminal in acting, theme, direction and permissiveness. From a novel and play no doubt inspired by Thurber's Walter Mitty, it was later turned into a TV series and a successful stage musical, making Billy a universal figure of the period.

w Keith Waterhouse, Willis Hall, from KW's novel and their play *d John Schlesinger ph* Denys Coop *m* Richard Rodney Bennett

Tom Courtenay, Julie Christie, Wilfred Pickles, Mona Washbourne, *Ethel Griffies,* Finlay Currie, Rodney Bewes, Leonard Rossiter

Billy the Kid*
US 1930 90m bw
MGM

A young western outlaw is relentlessly pursued by Sheriff Pat Garrett.
Mildly interesting early talkie western with the usual romanticized view of Billy. Originally made and shown in 70mm.

w Wanda Tuchock, Laurence Stallings, Charles MacArthur *d* King Vidor *ph* Gordon Avil

Johnny Mack Brown, Wallace Beery, Kay Johnson, Karl Dane, Roscoe Ates

Billy the Kid*
US 1941 95m Technicolor
MGM (Irving Asher)

Remake of the above, equally false and rather less well acted, but a striking outdoor colour film of its period.

w Gene Fowler *d* David Miller *ph* Leonard Smith, William V. Skall *m* David Snell

Robert Taylor, Brian Donlevy, Ian Hunter, Mary Howard, Gene Lockhart, Henry O'Neill, Frank Puglia, Cy Kendall, Ethel Griffies

AAN: Leonard Smith, William V. Skall

Billy Two Hats
US 1973 99m Technicolor
UA / Algonquin (Norman Jewison, Patrick Palmer, Mitchell Lifton)
aka: *The Lady and the Outlaw*

The friendship of an old Scottish outlaw and a young half-breed is broken only by the old man's death.
Curiously miscast western shot in Israel; it makes no discernible point and is not very entertaining.

w Alan Sharp *d* Ted Kotcheff *ph* Brian West *m* John Scott

Gregory Peck, Desi Arnaz Jnr, Jack Warden, Sian Barbara Allen, David Huddleston

The Bingo Long Traveling All-Stars and Motor Kings
US 1976 111m Technicolor
Universal (Rob Cohen)

Adventures of a black baseball team in the 1940s.
High-spirited japes and exhibitions of athleticism which dramatically do not add up to very much.

w Hal Barwood, Matthew Robbins, *novel* William Brashler *d* John Badham *ph* Bill Butler *m* William Goldstein

Billy Dee Williams, James Earl Jones, Richard Pryor, Rico Dawson

'Modest pleasures and dull stretches co-exist in equal abundance.'—*Frank Rich, New York Times*

Biography (of a Bachelor Girl)*
US 1935 84m bw
MGM

The biography of a sophisticated lady portrait painter reveals surprising details of her love life.
Leaden, bowdlerized screen version of a sparkling Broadway play, fragments of which do however survive.

w Anita Loos, *play* S. N. Behrman *d* Edward H. Griffith *ph* James Wong Howe

Ann Harding (miscast), Robert Montgomery, Edward Everett Horton, Edward Arnold, Una Merkel, Charles Richman, Donald Meek

Birch Interval
US 1976   105m   colour

A twelve-year-old girl goes to live with her
Amish relations in the country. Simple-minded
moral tale which needed some old-fashioned
style to bring it off. Eddie Albert, Rip Torn,
Susan McClung, Ann Wedgeworth, Bill
Lucking. Written by Joanna Crawford, from
her novel; directed by Delbert Mann; for
Robert B. Radnitz / Gamma III.

Bird of Paradise
US 1932   80m   bw
RKO

An adventurer on a South Sea island marries a
native girl and causes trouble.
Never-never romance which remains stilted
despite care obviously taken.

w Wells Root d King Vidor ph Clyde de
Vinna m Max Steiner

Joel McCrea, John Halliday, *Dolores del Rio*,
Skeets Gallagher

Bird of Paradise
US 1951   100m   Technicolor
TCF (Harmon Jones)

Opulent remake of the above; the trappings
make it even more absurd, and the ritual
sacrifice of the heroine seems misplaced in
what is otherwise a pantomime.

wd Delmer Daves ph Winton Hoch
m Daniele Amfitheatrof

Louis Jourdan, Jeff Chandler, Debra Paget,
Maurice Schwartz, Everett Sloane, Jack Elam
   'The Kahuna is a naively grotesque figure,
with a Central European accent and carrying
what appears to be an outsize radish: he
personifies the film's dubious approach to
Polynesian myth and culture.'—*Gavin
Lambert*

The Bird with the Crystal Plumage
Italy 1969   98m   colour

A supposed murderer is vindicated when his
alleged next victim turns out to be a
psychopath. Tolerable shocker which was
popular in dubbed version. Suzy Kendall,
Tony Musante. Written and directed by Dario
Argento; for Salvatore Argento.

Birdman of Alcatraz°
US 1961   148m   bw
UA / Hecht–Lancaster (Stuart Millar, Guy
   Trosper)

An imprisoned murderer makes a name for
himself as an ornithologist.
Overlong and rather weary biopic of Robert

Stroud, who spent nearly sixty years in prison
and became a *cause célèbre*. One cannot deny
many effective moments, notably of direction,
but it's a long haul.

w Guy Trosper, *book* Thomas E. Gaddis
d John Frankenheimer ph Burnett Guffey
m Elmer Bernstein

Burt Lancaster, Karl Malden, Thelma Ritter,
Edmond O'Brien, Betty Field, Neville Brand,
Hugh Marlowe, Telly Savalas, James
Westerfield

AAN: Burnett Guffey; Burt Lancaster;
Thelma Ritter; Telly Savalas

The Birds°°°
US 1963   119m   Technicolor
Universal / Alfred Hitchcock

In a Californian coastal area, flocks of birds
unaccountably make deadly attacks on human
beings.
A curiously absorbing work which begins as
light comedy and ends as apocalyptic allegory,
this piece of Hitchcockery has no visible point
except to tease the audience and provide
plenty of opportunity for shock, offbeat
humour and special effects (which despite the
drumbeating are not quite as good as might be
expected). The actors are pawns in the
master's hand.

w Evan Hunter, *story* Daphne du Maurier
d Alfred Hitchcock ph Robert Burks sound
consultant Bernard Herrmann sp Lawrence
A. Hampton

Rod Taylor, Tippi Hedren, Jessica Tandy,
Suzanne Pleshette, Ethel Griffies
   'Enough to make you kick the next pigeon
you come across.'—*Judith Crist*
   'The dialogue is stupid, the characters
insufficiently developed to rank as clichés, the
story incohesive.'—*Stanley Kauffmann*
   'We must sit through half an hour of
pachydermous flirtation between Rod and
Tippi before the seagull attacks, and another
fifteen minutes of tedium . . . before the birds
attack again. If one adds later interrelations
between mother, girl friend and a particularly
repulsive child actress, about two-thirds of the
film is devoted to extraneous matters. Poe
would have been appalled.'—*Dwight
MacDonald*

The Birds and the Bees
US 1956   94m   Technicolor   Vistavision
Paramount (Paul Jones)

On a transatlantic voyage a wealthy simpleton
is fleeced by a card sharp and his daughter;
but the latter falls in love with her victim.
Competent but uninspired reworking of *The*

Lady Eve as a vehicle for a rather charmless comic. Lacking Preston Sturges at the helm, the mixture of slapstick and sentiment fails to jell.

w Sidney Sheldon after Preston Sturges *d* Norman Taurog *ph* Daniel Fapp *m* Walter Scharf

George Gobel, David Niven, Mitzi Gaynor, Fred Clark, Reginald Gardiner, Harry Bellaver, Hans Conried

Birds Come to Die in Peru
France 1968   98m   Technicolor Franscope
Universal (Jacques Natteau)

On a Peruvian beach a tormented nymphomaniac makes love to several men and attempts suicide, but is rescued by her true love.
Elaborate high-flown bosh, quite fun to watch.

wd Romain Gary *ph* Christian Matras *m* Kenton Coe

Jean Seberg, Maurice Ronet, Danielle Darrieux, Pierre Brasseur

Birds Do It
US 1966   88m   colour
Columbia (Ivan Tors, Stanley Colbert)

A janitor at an atomic plant is accidentally ionized and finds he can fly, which enables him to catch a spy or two.
Childish stunt comedy.

w Arnie Kogen *d* Andrew Marton *ph* Howard Winner *m* Samuel Maltovsky

Soupy Sales, Tab Hunter, Arthur O'Connell, Edward Andrews, Doris Dowling, Beverly Adams, Louis Quinn

The Birds, the Bees and the Italians
Italy / France 1965   98m   colour
Dear Film / Films du Siècle (Robert Haggiag, Pietro Germi)
original title: *Signore e Signori*

Stories of adultery in an Italian provincial town.
Mainly tedious sex comedy full of gesticulating actors.

w Furio Scarpelli, Luciano Vincenzoni, Pietro Germi *d* Pietro Germi *ph* Aiace Parolin *m* Carlo Rustichelli

Gastone Moschin, Virna Lisi, Alberto Lionello, Gigi Ballista, Beba Loncar, Franco Fabrizi

The Birth of a Nation°°°°
US 1915   approx 185m (16 fps)   bw silent
Epoch (D. W. Griffith, Harry E. Aitken)

Northern and southern families are caught up in the Civil War.
The cinema's first and still most famous epic, many sequences of which retain their mastery despite negro villains, Ku Klux Klan heroes, and white actors in blackface. Originally shown as *The Clansman*; a shorter version with orchestral track was released in 1931.

w D. W. Griffith, Frank E. Woods, *novel* The Klansman by Thomas Dixon Jnr *d* D. W. Griffith *ph* G. W. Bitzer

Henry B. Walthall, Mae Marsh, Miriam Cooper, Lillian Gish, Robert Harron, Wallace Reid, Donald Crisp, Joseph Henaberry, Raoul Walsh, Eugene Pallette, Walter Long
'A film version of some of the melodramatic and inflammatory material contained in *The Clansman* . . . a great deal might be said concerning the sorry service rendered by its plucking at old wounds. But of the film as a film, it may be reported simply that it is an impressive new illustration of the scope of the motion picture camera.'—*New York Times*

The Birth of the Blues°
US 1941   85m   bw
Paramount (B. G. De Sylva, Monta Bell)

Trials and tribulations of a jazz band in New Orleans.
Thin fiction on which is strung a multitude of dark brown musical entertainment. Not bad, even now.

w Harry Tugend, Walter de Leon *d* Victor Schertzinger *ph* William C. Mellor *md* Robert Emmett Dolan

Bing Crosby, Mary Martin, Brian Donlevy, Jack Teagarden, Eddie Rochester Anderson, Carolyn Lee

AAN: Robert Emmett Dolan

The Birthday Party°
GB 1968   126m   Technicolor
Palomar (Max Rosenberg, Milton Subotsky)

The down-at-heel lodger in a seaside boarding house is menaced by two mysterious strangers, who eventually take him away.
Overlong but otherwise satisfactory film record of an entertaining if infuriating play, first of the black absurdities which proliferated in the sixties to general disadvantage, presenting structure without plot and intelligence without meaning.

w Harold Pinter, from his play *d* William Friedkin *ph* Denys Coop *m* none *pd* Edward Marshall

Sidney Tafler, Patrick Magee, Robert Shaw, *Dandy Nichols*, Moultrie Kelsall

The Birthday Present°
GB 1957   100m   bw
BL / Jack Whittingham

A toy salesman's life is changed when he is
charged with smuggling a watch through the
customs.
Downcast, prolonged and rather uninteresting
domestic drama; attention is held by generally
good acting.

w Jack Whittingham d Pat Jackson ph Ted
Scaife m Clifton Parker

Tony Britton, Sylvia Syms, Jack Watling,
Walter Fitzgerald, Geoffrey Keen, Howard
Marion Crawford, John Welsh

The Biscuit Eater
Two versions exist of this story by James
Street about a white and a black boy who turn
a stray into a crack hunting dog. The first was
by Stuart Heisler for Paramount in 1940; it
starred Billy Lee and made quite a box-office
impact. The second was by Vincent McEveety
for Disney in 1972, with Johnny Whittaker;
despite the presence of Earl Holliman and
Lew Ayres it made no impact at all. (GB title,
1940 version: God Gave Him a Dog.)

The Bishop Misbehaves°
US 1935   87m   bw

A bishop gets on the wrong side of the law
when he helps a young girl to see justice done.
Amusing trifle with strong cast. Edmund
Gwenn, Maureen O'Sullivan, Lucile Watson,
Reginald Owen, Robert Greig, Reginald
Owen, Dudley Digges, Melville Cooper,
Lillian Bond. Written by Leon Gordon and
George Auerbach, from the play by Frederick
Jackson; directed by E. A. Dupont; for
MGM. (GB title: The Bishop's
Misadventures.)

The Bishop's Wife°°
US 1947   108m   bw
Samuel Goldwyn

An angel is sent down to mend the ways of a
bishop whose absorption with cathedral
buildings has put him out of touch with his
wife and parishioners.
Whimsical, stolid and protracted light comedy
saved by its actors and its old-fashioned
Hollywood style.

w Robert E. Sherwood, Leonardo Bercovici,
novel Robert Nathan d Henry Koster
ph Gregg Toland m Hugo Friedhofer

Cary Grant, Loretta Young, David Niven,
Monty Woolley, James Gleason, Gladys
Cooper, Elsa Lanchester, Sara Haden, Regis
Toomey

'It is the Protestant comeback to the deadly
successful RC propaganda of Going My Way
and The Bells of St Mary's. It surpasses in
tastelessness, equals in whimsy and in
technique falls well below those crooning
parables. It is really quite a monstrous film.'—
Richard Winnington, News Chronicle

'When a film undertakes to bring audiences
a spiritual message, we wonder whether the
director doesn't owe it to us to clothe such
messages in less muddled characterizations
and to dispense with caricature.'—Scholastic
Magazine

AAN: best picture; Henry Koster; Hugo
Friedhofer

The Bitch
GB 1979   94m   colour

A woman of much influence in London's
underworld has a temporary liaison with a
young gangster wanted by the Mafia.
Intolerable sexed-up sequel to The Stud, hard
on both eyes and ears. Joan Collins, Kenneth
Haigh, Michael Coby, Ian Hendry, Carolyn
Seymour, Sue Lloyd, Mark Burns. Written
and directed by Gerry O'Hara; for Brent
Walker. 'Appropriately enough for a film
whose sole rationale seems to be its chic
consumerist decoration (and of course its disco
soundtrack), The Bitch ruthlessly pares away
any other elements of interest.'—Richard
Combs, MFB.

Bite the Bullet°
US 1975   131m   Metrocolor   Panavision
Columbia / Persky–Bright / Vista (Richard
    Brooks)

Several cowboys compete in a 700-mile
endurance horse race.
Episodic adventure story with too much
muddled chat and a very thin connecting story
line; good to look at, though.

wd Richard Brooks ph Harry Stradling
m Alex North

Gene Hackman, Candice Bergen, James
Coburn, Ben Johnson, Ian Bannen, Jan-
Michael Vincent, Paul Stewart

AAN: Alex North

Bitter Harvest
GB 1963   96m   Eastmancolor
Rank / Independent Artists (Albert Fennell)

An innocent Welsh girl comes to London, is
deflowered, and sets off in search of wealth
and luxury at any price.
Naive sixties version of the road to ruin, quite
well done if you like that kind of thing.

w Ted Willis *d* Peter Graham Scott
ph Ernest Steward *m* Laurie Johnson
Janet Munro, John Stride, Anne Cunningham,
Alan Badel, Thora Hird, Vanda Godsell,
Terence Alexander

Bitter Rice*
Italy 1949 108m bw
Lux Films
original title: *Riso Amaro*
In the rice fields of the Po valley, a thief on
the run meets a girl who tries to steal his loot.
Well-made exploitation melodrama which
made a star of the well-endowed Mangano but
is not otherwise more memorable than its
innumerable American counterparts.

w Carlo Lizzani, Carlo Musso, Gianni Puccini,
Corrado Alvaro, Ivo Perillo, Giuseppe de
Santis *d* Giuseppe de Santis *ph* Otello
Martelli *m* Goffredo Petrassi
Silvana Mangano, Raf Vallone, Doris
Dowling, Vittorio Gassman

AAN: original story

Bitter Springs*
GB 1950 89m bw
Ealing (Leslie Norman)
A pioneer family in Australia buys a patch of
ground but has trouble with aborigines.
Thinnest of the Ealing attempts to make
movies down under, suffering from a lack of
pace and sharpness as well as obvious studio
settings.

w Monja Danischewsky, W. P. Lipscomb
d Ralph Smart *ph* George Heath *m* Vaughan
Williams
Chips Rafferty, Tommy Trinder, Gordon
Jackson, Jean Blue, Charles Tingwell

Bitter Sweet
GB 1933 93m bw
British and Dominion (Herbert Wilcox)
In 1875 Vienna, a violinist marries a girl
dancer and is later killed by a gambler.
Rather feeble filming of Noel Coward's
operetta: it pleased a lot of people at the time.

w Lydia Hayward, Herbert Wilcox, Monckton
Hoffe *d* Herbert Wilcox *ph* F. A. Young
Anna Neagle, Fernand Gravet, Ivy St Helier,
Miles Mander, Esmé Percy, Hugh Williams,
Pat Peterson, Kay Hammond

Bitter Sweet
US 1940 94m Technicolor
MGM (Victor Saville)
Remake of the above, retailored for
unsuitable leads and with the story and music
unattractively rearranged.

w Lesser Samuels, *operetta* Noel Coward
d W. S. Van
Dyke II *ph* Oliver T. Marsh, Allen Davey
Jeanette Macdonald, Nelson Eddy, George
Sanders, Felix Bressart, Ian Hunter, Fay
Holden, Sig Rumann, Herman Bing, Curt
Bois

AAN: Oliver T. Marsh, Allen Davey

The Bitter Tea of General Yen**
US 1933 89m bw
Columbia (Walter Wanger)
An American lady missionary in Shanghai is
captured by a Chinese warlord and falls in love
with him.
Arty miscegenation story which bids fair to
become a cult film and certainly has a number
of interesting sequences.

w Edward Paramore, *story* Grace Zaring
Stone *d Frank Capra ph* Joseph Walker
m W. Frank Harling
Barbara Stanwyck, Nils Asther, Toshia Mori,
Walter Connolly, Gavin Gordon, Lucien
Littlefield
† The film chosen to open Radio City Music
Hall.

The Bitter Tears of Petra Von Kant
West Germany 1975 124m colour
Lesbian jealousies in the fashion world.
Interesting but exhausting hothouse
confection, no more likeable than the
Hollywood kind for being more intelligent
about its perversions. Margit Carstensen, Irm
Hermann, Hanna Schygull. Written and
directed by Rainer Werner Fassbinder for his
own company. 'Dazzling in the brittle
brilliance of its execution, the precision of its
structure and movement, the total hermetic
self-containment of the little world it
creates.'—*David Robinson, The Times.*

Bitter Victory
US / France 1957 100m bw
     Cinemascope
Columbia / Transcontinental / Robert
     Laffont
Two officers sent on a document raid in Libya
during World War II become poor soldiers
because one suspects the other of an affair
with his wife.
Glum desert melodrama, turgidly scripted and
boringly made.

w René Hardy, Nicholas Ray, Gavin Lambert,
novel Bitter Victory by René Hardy
d Nicholas Ray *ph* Michel Kelber *m* Maurice
Le Roux

Richard Burton, Curt Jurgens, Ruth Roman,
Raymond Pellegrin, Anthony Bushell,
Andrew Crawford, Nigel Green, Christopher
Lee

Bittersweet Love
US 1976   92m   colour

Newlyweds discover that they both had the
same father. Old-fashioned family shocker
which needed a lot more zip if it was going to
shock anybody. Lana Turner, Robert Alda,
Celeste Holm, Robert Lansing, Scott Hylands,
Denise DeMirjian. Written by Adrian Morrall
and D. A. Kellogg; directed by David Miller;
for Zappala-Slott. 'Performances and settings
are all very high class. I mean, when you have
all that money and those great surroundings
you can still suffer, but you do have multiple
choices.'—*Archer Winsten, New York Post.*

Black Angel*
US 1946   80m   bw
U-I (Roy William Neill, Tom McKnight)

A drunk sets out to find the murderer of his
wife, and finds it was himself.
Stylish but empty version of a tired theme,
interesting for performances and atmosphere.

w Roy Chanslor, *novel* William Irish *d* Roy
William Neill *ph* Paul Ivano *m* Frank
Skinner

Dan Duryea, Peter Lorre, Broderick
Crawford, June Vincent, Wallace Ford,
Hobart Cavanaugh, Constance Dowling

The Black Arrow
US 1948   76m   bw
Columbia
GB title: *The Black Arrow Strikes*

During the Wars of the Roses, an English
knight seeks the murderer of his father.
Pennypinching swashbuckler which contrives
to entertain despite total disregard of
probability.

w Richard Schayer, David P. Sheppard,
Thomas Seller, *novel* R. L. Stevenson
d Gordon Douglas *ph* Charles Lawton Jnr

Louis Hayward, Janet Blair, George
Macready, Edgar Buchanan, Paul Cavanaugh

Black Bart
US 1948   80m   Technicolor
U-I (Leonard Goldstein)
GB title: *Black Bart, Highwayman*

Lola Montez, on an American tour, falls for
an American bandit.
Acceptable western programmer with
historical trimmings and some evidence of
tongue-in-cheek attitudes.

w Luci Ward, Jack Natteford, William
Bowers *d* George Sherman *ph* Irving
Glassberg *m* Frank Skinner

Yvonne de Carlo, Dan Duryea, Jeffrey Lynn,
Percy Kilbride, Lloyd Gough, Frank Lovejoy,
John McIntire, Don Beddoe

Black Beauty
US 1946   74m   bw
(TCF) Edward L. Alperson

In Victorian England, a girl searches for her
lost colt.
Stilted children's film with little relation to the
book.

w Lillie Hayward, Agnes Christie Johnson,
novel Anna Sewell *d* Max Nosseck *ph* J. Roy
Hunt *m* Dmitri Tiomkin

Mona Freeman, Richard Denning, Evelyn
Ankers, J. M. Kerrigan, Terry Kilburn

Black Beauty*
GB 1971   106m   colour
Tigon / Chilton (Tony Tenser)

A luckless horse passes from hand to hand but
is finally restored to its original young master
and has a happy retirement.
Pleasant, episodic animal story which stays
pretty close to the book. A shade yawn-
inducing for adults, but fine for children.

w Wolf Mankowitz, *novel* Anna Sewell
d James Hill *ph* Chris Menges *m* Lionel
Bart, John Cameron

Mark Lester, Walter Slezak, Peter Lee
Lawrence, Patrick Mower, John Nettleton,
Maria Rohm

The Black Bird
US 1975   98m   colour
Columbia / Rastar (Michael Levee, Lou
   Lombardo)

Sam Spade's son finds himself beset by crooks
still after the Maltese falcon.
Dismal, witless, boring parody of a classic
crime film, with none of the humour of the
original.

wd David Giler *ph* Philip Lathrop *m* Jerry
Fielding

George Segal, Stéphane Audran, *Lee Patrick*,
Elisha Cook Jnr, Lionel Stander, John
Abbott, Signe Hasso, Felix Silla
   'It doesn't work because it has nothing to
say.'—*Michael Billington, Illustrated London
News*

The Black Book*
US 1949   88m   bw
Eagle—Lion
GB title: *Reign of Terror*

A member of a secret organization which plans to replace Robespierre with a moderate goes undercover with the French Revolutionaries.
Moderate period melodrama with an attractive though artificial look.

w Philip Yordan, Aeneas Mackenzie *d* Anthony Mann *ph* John Alton *m* Sol Kaplan

Robert Cummings, Arlene Dahl, Richard Basehart, Richard Hart, Arnold Moss

The Black Cat*
US 1934 65m bw
Universal (Carl Laemmle Jnr)
GB title: *House of Doom*

A revengeful doctor seeks out the Austrian architect and devil-worshipper who betrayed his country in World War I.
Absurd and dense farrago set in a modernistic but crumbling castle which is eventually blown to bits just as its owner is skinned alive. Mostly rather dull despite the extraordinary plot, but the thing has moments of style, a delightful cod devil worship sequence (especially for audiences with a rudimentary knowledge of Latin) and nothing at all to do with the title or Edgar Allan Poe.

w Peter Ruric *d* Edgar G. Ulmer *ph* John Mescall *m* Heinz Roemheld *ad* Charles D. Hall

Boris Karloff, *Bela Lugosi*, David Manners, Jacqueline Wells, Egon Brecher

The Black Cat*
US 1941 70m bw
Universal

Murder follows the summoning of the family to the spooky house of a cat-loving recluse. Disappointing mystery which squanders a splendid cast on a script full of non-sequiturs and makes heavy weather of its light relief.

w Robert Lees, Fred Rinaldo, Eric Taylor, Robert Neville *d* Albert S. Rogell *ph* Stanley Cortez

Basil Rathbone, Gladys Cooper, Broderick Crawford, Hugh Herbert, Gale Sondergaard, Anne Gwynne, Alan Ladd, Cecilia Loftus, Bela Lugosi

Black Fox ⌐
US 1962 89m bw

Slick documentary on the rise of Hitler, using the expected newsreels reinforced not too artfully by references to art and to the medieval folk tale of Reynard the Fox. Narrated by Marlene Dietrich. Written and

directed by Louis Clyde Stoumen; for Jack Le Vien. (AA 1963; best documentary.)

Black Friday*
US 1940 70m bw
Universal

After an accident, a college professor is given a gangster's brain, and the surgeon encourages him to believe that he is the gangster so as to find hidden loot.
Plot-packed melodrama which fails to provide the chills suggested by the cast, but passes the time agreeably enough.

w Curt Siodmak, Eric Taylor *d* Arthur Lubin *ph* Woody Bredell *m* Hans Salter

Boris Karloff, Bela Lugosi, *Stanley Ridges*, Anne Nagel, Anne Gwynne, Virginia Brissac, Paul Fix
† Lugosi was originally cast as the professor, but proved wrong for the part; Stanley Ridges replaced him and walked off with the movie.

Black Fury*
US 1935 95m bw
Warner (Robert Lord)

A coal miner comes up against union problems, unsafe conditions and corruption. Typical Warner social drama, good for its time but now very obvious.

w Abem Finkel, Carl Erickson, *play* Bohunk by Harry R. Irving *d* Michael Curtiz *ph* Byron Haskin

Paul Muni, Karen Morley, William Gargan, Barton MacLane, John Qualen, J. Carrol Naish, Vince Barnett, Tully Marshall, Henry O'Neill
'The most powerful strike picture that has yet been made, and I am aware of the better-known Soviet jobs in the field.'—*Otis Ferguson*

Black Gold
US 1963 98m bw

Novice wildcatter makes it rich in Oklahoma despite villains on every side. Absolutely predictable actioner which unspools like a remake even if it isn't. Philip Carey, Diane McBain, Claude Akins, Iron Eyes Cody, James Best. Written by Bob and Wanda Duncan; directed by Leslie H. Martinson; for Warner.

Black Hand*
US 1949 92m bw
MGM (William H. Wright)

In New York at the turn of the century, an Italian boy avenges his father's death at the hands of the Mafia.

Neatly produced, studio-set melodrama, unusual in subject but very stereotyped and artificial in treatment.

w Luther Davis *d* Richard Thorpe *ph* Paul C. Vogel *m* Alberto Colombo

Gene Kelly, J. Carrol Naish, Teresa Celli, Marc Lawrence, Frank Puglia, Barry Kelley

The Black Hole*
US 1979 98m Technicolor
Technovision
Walt Disney (Ron Miller)

A research team in space is welcomed aboard a mysterious survey ship poised on the edge of a black hole.

The special effects are superb, though achieved through a general gloom which is barely acceptable. But the story is an ill-worked-out remake of *Twenty Thousand Leagues Under the Sea*, the characterization is ridiculously inept, and the final disclosure that black holes are doorways to hell sends one home rather bemused.

w Jeb Rosebrook, Gerry Day *d* Gary Nelson *ph* Frank Phillips *pd* *Peter Ellenshaw* *m* John Barry

Maximilian Schell, Robert Forster, Anthony Perkins, Joseph Bottoms, Yvette Mimieux, Ernest Borgnine

'As pastiche, it sounds promising; as drama, encumbered with references to Cicero and Goethe, it is merely tedious.'—*John Halford, MFB*

'Rated PG, but the only danger to children is that it may make them think that outer space is not much fun any more.'—*New Yorker*

Black Horse Canyon
US 1954 81m Technicolor

Two cowpunchers help a lady rancher to capture and train a wild black stallion. Slight but agreeable outdoor programmer. Joel McCrea, Mari Blanchard, Race Gentry, Murvyn Vye, Irving Bacon. Written by Geoffrey Homes; directed by Jesse Hibbs; for Universal-International.

Black Jack
GB 1979 110m colour

In 1750 Yorkshire, a rascally French sailor recovers from a hanging and has adventures on the road with a young apprentice. The purpose of this costume adventure, from these creators, is obscure, but the execution of it is muddled and amateurish. Jean Franval, Stephen Hirst, Louise Cooper. From the novel

by Leon Garfield; directed by Kenneth Loach; for Tony Garnett / Kestrel. 'Ploddingly unpersuasive. Not only narrative clarity but simple credibility is lacking.'—*Tim Pulleine, MFB*

The Black Knight
GB 1954 85m Technicolor
Warwick (Irving Allen, Albert R. Broccoli)

A humble swordmaker reveals a traitor to King Arthur.
Hilarious travesty of English historical legend, meant seriously for Anglo-American consumption. Shades of *Zorro, Babes in the Wood* and *1066 and All That*.

w Alec Coppel *d* Tay Garnett *ph* John Wilcox *m* John Addison

Alan Ladd, Peter Cushing, Patricia Medina, Harry Andrews, André Morell, Anthony Bushell, Patrick Troughton, Laurence Naismith, John Laurie

'Alan Ladd galahads with wild west *gentillesse* in this Technicolored rampage through British history.'—*MFB*

Black Legion**
US 1936 83m bw
Warner (Robert Lord)

A factory worker becomes involved with the Ku Klux Klan.
Social melodrama typical of its studio, and good of its kind.

w Robert Lord, Abem Finkel, William Wister Haines *d* Archie Mayo *ph* George Barnes

Humphrey Bogart, Erin O'Brien Moore, Dick Foran, Ann Sheridan, Robert Barrat, John Litel, Charles Halton

'An honest job of film work, and one of the most direct social pieces released from Hollywood.'—*Otis Ferguson*

AAN: Robert Lord (original story)

Black Limelight*
GB 1938 70m bw
ABPC (Walter C. Mycroft)

The wife of a man convicted of killing his mistress proves that a 'moon murderer' did it. Naive but effective little chiller.

w Dudley Leslie, Walter Summers, *play* Gordon Sherry *d* Paul Stein *ph* Claude Friese-Greene

Raymond Massey, Joan Marion, Walter Hudd, Henry Oscar, Coral Browne

Black Magic*
US 1949 105m bw
Edward Small (Gregory Ratoff)

Cagliostro the magician becomes involved in a plot to supply a double for Marie Antoinette. Deliriously complicated historical romp which unfortunately suffers from a stolid script and production which kill all the flights of fancy.

w Charles Bennett d Gregory Ratoff ph Ubaldo Arata, Anchise Brizzi m Paul Sawtell

Orson Welles, Nancy Guild, Akim Tamiroff, Valentina Cortese, Margot Grahame, Charles Goldner, Frank Latimore, Stephen Bekassy

The Black Marble
US 1980 113m De Luxe
Avco / Frank Capra Jnr

A drunken cop redeems himself when teamed with a policewoman who is less cynical about the work.
Curious cop show with emphasis on child murders and dog torturing. An unhappy film with a garbled message.

w Joseph Wambaugh, from his novel d Harold Becker ph Owen Roizman m Maurice Jarre

Robert Foxworth, Paula Prentiss, Harry Dean Stanton, Barbara Babcock, John Hancock

Black Narcissus***
GB 1946 100m Technicolor
GFD / The Archers (Michael Powell, Emeric Pressburger)

Anglo-Catholic nuns in the Himalayas have trouble with climate, morale, and one of their number who goes mad of sex frustration.
An unlikely theme produces one of the cinema's most beautiful films, a visual and emotional stunner despite some narrative uncertainty.

wd Michael Powell, Emeric Pressburger, novel Rumer Godden ph Jack Cardiff

Deborah Kerr, David Farrar, Sabu, Jean Simmons, Kathleen Byron, Flora Robson, Esmond Knight, Jenny Laird, May Hallatt, Judith Furse

AA: Jack Cardiff

Black on White*
Finland 1967 95m Eastmancolor
Jorn Donner / FJ Film

A successful young executive falls in love with a girl hitch-hiker, but when his wife leaves him the girl is no longer interested.
Showy romantic melodrama which tries to make rather too much of a slender theme.

wd Jorn Donner ph Esko Nevaleinen m George Riedel

Jorn Donner, Kristina Halkola, Liisamaija Laaksonen

The Black Orchid*
US 1958 95m bw Vistavision
Paramount (Carlo Ponti, Marcello Girosi)

A widower incurs hostility from his daughter when he plans to marry a gangster's widow.
Rather solemn New York / Italian romantic melodrama, with much gesticulation all round.

w Joseph Stefano d Martin Ritt ph Robert Burks m Alessandro Cicognini

Sophia Loren, Anthony Quinn, Ina Balin, Jimmy Baird, Mark Richman

Black Orpheus*
France / Italy / Brazil 1958 106m
      Eastmancolor Cinemascope
Dispatfilm / Gemma / Tupan (Sacha Gordine)
original title: Orfeu Negro

Against a background of the Rio carnival, a black tram driver accidentally kills his girl friend, and after seeking her in the nether regions kills himself to be with her.
Rather irritating and noisy attempt to update a legend, without showing very much reason for doing so.

w Vinitius de Moraes d Marcel Camus ph Jean Bourgoin m Luis Bonfa, Antonio Carlos Jobim

Breno Mello, Marpessa Dawn, Ademar da Silva, Lourdes de Oliviera

AA: best foreign film

Black Patch
US 1957 84m bw

A marshal is wrongly suspected of murder. Dour, dark western, occasionally worth looking at. George Montgomery, Diane Brewster, Tom Pittman, Leo Gordon. Written and directed by Allen H. Miner; for Montgomery / Warner.

The Black Pirate***
US 1926 76m approx (24 fps)
      Technicolor silent
Douglas Fairbanks

A shipwrecked mariner swears revenge on the pirates who blew up his father's ship.
Cheerful swashbuckler with the star in top form.

w Douglas Fairbanks, Jack Cunningham d Albert Parker ph Henry Sharp ad Oscar Borg, Dwight Franklin

Douglas Fairbanks, Billie Dove, Donald Crisp, Sam de Grasse

The Black Room*
US 1935 70m bw
Columbia

A nobleman's power is claimed by his evil twin brother.
Rather splendid old barnstormer with touches of horror, a neatly produced star vehicle.

w Henry Myers, from the writings of Arthur Strawn *d Roy William Neill ph* Al Siegler

Boris Karloff, Marian Marsh, Katherine de Mille, Thurston Hall

'Mrs Radcliffe would not have been ashamed of this wild and exciting film, of the bones in the oubliette, the scene at the altar when the dog leaps and the paralysed arm comes to life in self-defence, of the Count's wild drive back to the castle, of the rearing horses, the rocketing coach, the strange valley of rocks with its leaning cross and neglected Christ, the graveyard with its owls and ivy.'— *Graham Greene*

The Black Rose°
US 1950 120m Technicolor
TCF (Louis D. Lighton)

A 13th-century English scholar journeys to the land of the Mongols, and after many adventures returns to a knighthood for his scientific discoveries.
Portentous and slow-moving adventure with good things along the way.

w Talbot Jennings, *novel* Thomas B. Costain *d* Henry Hathaway *ph Jack Cardiff m* Richard Addinsell *ad* Paul Sheriff

Tyrone Power, Orson Welles, Cecile Aubry, Jack Hawkins, Finlay Currie, Henry Oscar, Michael Rennie

The Black Scorpion
US 1957 88m bw
Warner (Frank Melford, Jack Dietz)

Volcanic explosions uncover a nest of prehistoric giant scorpions near a Mexican village.
Apart from a genuinely terrifying sequence in the scorpion's lair, this is a poor monster movie in which excessively dark photography seems intended to cover up very variable trick work.

w David Duncan, Robert Bless *d* Edward Ludwig *ph* Lionel Lindon *m* Paul Sawtell *sp* Willis O'Brien

Richard Denning, Mara Corday, Carlos Rivas, Mario Navarro

The Black Sheep of Whitehall°
GB 1941 80m bw
Ealing (S. C. Balcon)

An incompetent teacher is mistaken for an economics expert and saves the real expert

from spies who run a nursing home.
Pretty good wartime star comedy, with a succession of briskly timed gags.

w Angus Macphail, John Dighton *d* Basil Dearden, Will Hay *ph* Gunther Krampf

Will Hay, John Mills, Basil Sydney, Frank Cellier, Felix Aylmer

The Black Shield of Falworth°
US 1954 99m Technicolor
Cinemascope
U-I (Robert Arthur, Melville Tucker)

The film in which Tony Curtis says 'Yonda lies the castle of my fodda' (or something like it) is an amiable romp which alternates between comic strip dialogue and a surprisingly convincing sense of medieval custom. The training scenes are as sharp as the romantic asides are pallid.

w Oscar Brodney, *novel* Men of Iron by Howard Pyle *d* Rudolph Maté *ph* Irving Glassberg *m* Joseph Gershenson

Tony Curtis, Janet Leigh, David Farrar, Barbara Rush, Herbert Marshall, Rhys Williams, Dan O'Herlihy, Torin Thatcher

'A straightforward piece of hokum with no pretensions, and spoken in a variety of accents that only Hollywood could muster.'—*John Gillett*

The Black Sleep
US 1956 81m bw
UA / Bel Air (Howard W. Koch)

A Victorian brain surgeon experiments on human beings and produces freaks who eventually turn on him.
Gruesome and humourless horror film notable only for its gallery of wasted talent.

w John C. Higgins *d* Reginald Le Borg *ph* Gordon Avil *m* Les Baxter

Basil Rathbone, Bela Lugosi, Lon Chaney Jnr, John Carradine, Akim Tamiroff, Tor Johnson, Herbert Rudley, Patricia Blake

The Black Stallion°
US 1979 117m Technicolor
UA / Omni Zoetrope (Francis Coppola)

After a 1946 shipwreck, a boy and a stallion are cast up on the African shore; many years later, he rides the horse to victory at Santa Anita.
1980 seems a bit late for boy-and-horse pictures, but this one is so beautifully directed and photographed, if drastically overlong, that most adults thought their children should see it.

w Melissa Mathison, Jeanne Rosenberg, William D. Witliff, *novel* Walter Farley *d Carroll Ballard ph Caleb Deschanel m* Carmine Coppola

Kelly Reno, Mickey Rooney, Teri Garr, Clarence Muse, Hoyt Axton

'A perfect gem—the beautiful craftsmanship alone makes it a joy to behold.'—*Variety*

Black Sunday*
Italy 1960   83m   bw

A beautiful witch is put to death in an iron maiden but rises from the dead to wreak vengeance. Stylish horror comic which started the Italian cult for such things. Barbara Steele, John Richardson, Ivo Garrani. From a story by Gogol; written and directed by Mario Bava; for Galatra / Jolly.

Black Sunday*
US 1977   143m   Movielab   Panavision
Paramount (Robert Evans)

The Black September movement threatens a football game to be held in Miami's Superbowl.
Spectacular, heavily detailed, but somehow unexciting disaster melodrama.

w Ernest Lehman, Kenneth Ross, Ivan Moffat, *novel* Thomas Harris *d* John Frankenheimer *ph* John A. Alonzo *m* John Williams

Robert Shaw, Marthe Keller, Bruce Dern, Fritz Weaver, Steven Keats, Bekim Fehmiu, Michael V. Gazzo, William Daniels, Walter Gotell

'There's only one real motivation for this movie, and that's the desire to make money. Why else would anyone make an ostensibly anti-terrorist film that in actuality could end up promoting terrorism?'—*Frank Rich, New York Post*

The Black Swan***
US 1942   85m   Technicolor
TCF (Robert Bassler)

Morgan the pirate is made governor of Jamaica and enlists the help of his old friends to rid the Caribbean of buccaneers.
Rousing adventure story with comic asides: just what action hokum always aimed to be, with a spirited gallery of heroes and villains and an entertaining narrative taken at a spanking pace.

w Ben Hecht, Seton I. Miller, novel Rafael Sabatini *d Henry King ph Leon Shamroy m* Alfred Newman

Tyrone Power, Maureen O'Hara, *Laird Cregar, Thomas Mitchell, George Sanders,* Anthony Quinn, George Zucco, Edward Ashley

AA: Leon Shamroy
AAN: Alfred Newman

The Black Tent
GB 1956   93m   Technicolor   Vistavision
Rank / William MacQuitty

During a Libyan battle a wounded army captain is cared for by Arabs and marries the sheik's daughter. Ten years later, after his death, his son elects to live with the tribe.
Pleasantly shot but otherwise dull, formless and interminable romantic drama, all very stiff upper lip.

w Robin Maugham, Bryan Forbes *d* Brian Desmond Hurst *ph Desmond Dickinson m* William Alwyn

Anthony Steel, Donald Sinden, *André Morell,* Anna Maria Sandri, Ralph Truman, Donald Pleasence, Anthony Bushell, Michael Craig

The Black Torment*
GB 1964   85m   Eastmancolor
Compton-Tekli (Robert Hartford-Davis)

The second wife of an 18th-century baronet investigates the hauntings which have followed the apparent suicide of his first.
Agreeably unpretentious period ghost story (with a rational explanation). Not exactly good, but better than one might expect.

w Donald and Derek Ford *d* Robert Hartford-Davis *ph* Peter Newbrook *m* Robert Richards

John Turner, Heather Sears, Ann Lynn, Joseph Tomelty, Peter Arne, Raymond Huntley

Black Tuesday*
US 1954   80m   bw
UA / Leonard Goldstein (Robert Goldstein)

A killer escapes from Death Row and hides out with hostages in a disused warehouse. Starkly melodramatic gangster vehicle with the star up to his oldest tricks. Good tension, but generally rather unpleasant.

w Sydney Boehm *d* Hugo Fregonese *ph* Stanley Cortez *m* Paul Dunlap

Edward G. Robinson, Jean Parker, Peter Graves, Milburn Stone, Warren Stevens, Jack Kelly, James Bell

Black Widow*
US 1954   95m   De Luxe   Cinemascope
TCF (Nunnally Johnson)

A Broadway producer is suspected of the murder of an ambitious young girl.
Reasonably classy whodunnit with glamorous settings and an able cast, but a little lacking in wit and pace.

wd Nunnally Johnson, *novel* Fatal Woman by Patrick Quentin *ph* Charles G. Clarke *m* Leigh Harline

Ginger Rogers, Van Heflin, George Raft, Gene Tierney, Peggy Ann Garner, Reginald Gardiner, Virginia Leith, Otto Kruger, Hilda Simms, Cathleen Nesbitt

The Black Windmill*
GB 1974   106m   Technicolor
    Panavision
Universal / Zanuck–Brown (Don Siegel)

A secret service agent has to fight a lone battle when his young son is kidnapped by spies.
Unconvincing variant on *The Man Who Knew Too Much*, with an unwieldy and incoherent plot and more borrowings from Hitchcock than you can count. It ends up as fair predictable fun despite its jaded air.

w Leigh Vance, *novel* Seven Days to a Killing by Clive Egleton *d* Don Siegel *ph* Ousama Rawi *m* Roy Budd

Michael Caine, Janet Suzman, Joseph O'Conor, Donald Pleasence, Delphine Seyrig, John Vernon, Joss Ackland
    'A flaccid spy thriller, vaguely reminiscent of Hitchcock and *Foreign Correspondent*, with direction as blank as the expression on Michael Caine's face throughout.'—*Sight and Sound*

Black Zoo
US 1962   88m   Eastmancolor
    Panavision
Allied Artists / Herman Cohen

The owner of a private Los Angeles zoo trains his animals to kill his enemies.
Stultifyingly inept and uninteresting horror film.

w Herman Cohen *d* Robert Gordon *ph* Floyd Crosby *m* Paul Dunlap

Michael Gough, Jeanne Cooper, Rod Lauren, Virginia Grey, Jerome Cowan, Elisha Cook Jnr, Marianna Hill

Blackbeard the Pirate*
US 1952   99m   Technicolor
RKO (Edmund Grainger)

In the 17th century, reformed pirate Sir Henry Morgan is commissioned to rid the Caribbean of the rascally Blackbeard.
A farrago of action clichés with the star giving his eye-rolling all. The romantic element is dreary and the whole a shade bloodthirsty for family fare.

w Alan le May *d* Raoul Walsh *ph* William E. Snyder *m* Victor Young

Robert Newton, Linda Darnell, Keith Andes, William Bendix, Torin Thatcher, Irene Ryan, Alan Mowbray, Richard Egan

Blackbeard's Ghost
US 1967   107m   Technicolor
Walt Disney (Bill Walsh)

The famous pirate returns as a ghost to help the old ladies who own a hotel he loved.
Ponderous and lengthy comedy, partially salvaged by performances.

w Bill Walsh, Ben Da Gradi *d* Robert Stevenson *ph* Edward Colman *m* Robert F. Brunner

Peter Ustinov, Dean Jones, Suzanne Pleshette, Elsa Lanchester, Richard Deacon

The Blackbird
US 1925   70m at 24 fps   bw   silent

A Limehouse thief pretends to be a cripple, and after committing a murder finds that he is.
Standard star vehicle with recollections of several others. Lon Chaney, Renee Adoree, Owen Moore, Doris Lloyd. Written and directed by Tod Browning; for MGM.

The Blackboard Jungle*
US 1955   101m   bw
MGM (Pandro S. Berman)

In a slum school, a teacher finally gains the respect of his class of young hooligans.
Seminal fifties melodrama more notable for its introduction of 'Rock Around the Clock' behind the credits than for any intrinsic interest.

wd Richard Brooks, *novel* Evan Hunter *ph* Russell Harlan *m* Bill Haley and the Comets

Glenn Ford, Anne Francis, Louis Calhern, Margaret Hayes, John Hoyt, Richard Kiley, Emile Meyer, Warner Anderson, Basil Ruysdael, *Sidney Poitier, Vic Morrow*, Rafael Campos
    'It could just as well have been the first good film of this kind. Actually, it will be remembered chiefly for its timely production and release.'—*G. N. Fenin, Film Culture*

AAN: Richard Brooks (as writer); Russell Harlan

Blackmail***
GB 1929   78m   bw
BIP (John Maxwell)

A Scotland Yard inspector finds that his girl is involved in a murder; he conceals the fact and is blackmailed.

Hitchcock's first talkie is now a very hesitant entertainment but fully bears the director's stamp and will reward patient audiences in several excitingly staged sequences.

w Alfred Hitchcock, Benn W. Levy, Charles Bennett, *play* Charles Bennett *d Alfred Hitchcock ph* Jack Cox *m* Campbell and Connelly

Anny Ondra, Sara Allgood, John Longden, Charles Paton, Donald Calthrop, Cyril Ritchard

Blackmail
US 1939 81m bw
MGM (John Considine Jnr)

A man is released from prison after serving a sentence for a crime he did not commit. Immediately a blackmailer pounces . . .

Co-feature drama for a star marking time; not bad in its way.

w David Hertz, William Ludwig *d* H. C. Potter *ph* Clyde de Vinna

Edward G. Robinson, Ruth Hussey, Gene Lockhart, Guinn Williams, Esther Dale

Blackmailed
GB 1950 85m bw
GFD / Harold Huth

Several victims of a blackmailer are involved in his murder.

Interestingly plotted and well cast melodrama which suffers from a flat script and production.

w Hugh Mills, Roger Vadim, *novel* Mrs Christopher by Elizabeth Myers *d* Marc Allégret *ph* George Stretton *m* John Wooldridge

Dirk Bogarde, Mai Zetterling, Fay Compton, Robert Flemyng, Michael Gough, James Robertson Justice, Joan Rice, Wilfrid Hyde White, Harold Huth

Blackwell's Island
US 1939 71m bw
Warner (Bryan Foy)

A reporter goes to jail to get the goods on a smart gangster.

Forgettable exposé of the lighter kind.

w Crane Wilbur *d* William McGann *ph* Sid Hickox

John Garfield, Rosemary Lane, Dick Purcell, Victor Jory, Stanley Fields

Blacula
US 1972 93m Movielab
AIP (Joseph T. Naar)

In 1815 in Transylvania, an African prince falls victim to Dracula. A hundred and fifty years later, his body is shipped to Los Angeles and accidentally revivified.

Jaded semi-spoof notable chiefly as the first black horror film. The star's performance is as stately as could be wished in the circumstances.

w Joan Torres, Raymond Koenig *d* William Crain *ph* John Stevens *m* Gene Page

William Marshall, Vonetta McGee, Denise Nicholas, Gordon Pinsent, Charles Macaulay

Blanche Fury
GB 1948 95m Technicolor
GFD / Cineguild (Anthony Havelock-Allan)

A governess marries a wealthy heir, then with a steward connives at his murder.

Chilly Victorian melodrama without much interest outside the decor: the actors have unplayable roles and the handling is very flat.

w Audrey Erskine Lindop, Hugh Mills, Cecil McGivern, *novel* Joseph Shearing *d* Marc Allégret *ph* Guy Green, Geoffrey Unsworth *m* Clifton Parker

Valerie Hobson, Stewart Granger, Walter Fitzgerald, Michael Gough, Maurice Denham, Sybilla Binder

Blaze of Noon
US 1947 91m bw
Paramount (John Farrow)

Three stunt flier brothers in the twenties leave their circus to start a commercial air-line.

Predictable romantic dramá with little flying: tragic pretensions, routine performances.

w Frank Wead, Arthur Sheekman *d* John Farrow *ph* William C. Mellor *m* Adolph Deutsch

William Holden, Anne Baxter, Sonny Tufts, Sterling Hayden, William Bendix, Howard da Silva

'So long as it sticks to stunt flying and mild comedy it is pleasant enough, but the last half, during which the obsessed brothers come one by one to grief and the little woman waits it out, gets pretty monotonous.'—*James Agee*

The Blazing Forest
US 1952 90m Technicolor
Paramount / Pine–Thomas (William H. Pine, William C. Thomas)

A lady landowner has trouble with her rival timber bosses.

Fair period programmer.

w Lewis R. Foster, Winston Miller *d* Edward Ludwig *ph* Lionel Lindon *m* Lucien Caillet

John Payne, Agnes Moorehead, William
Demarest, Richard Arlen, Susan Morrow,
Roscoe Ates, Lynne Roberts

Blazing Saddles*
US 1974 93m Technicolor Panavision
Warner / Crossbow (Michael Herzberg)

A black railroad worker and an alcoholic
ex-gunfighter foil a crooked attorney and his
henchmen.

Wild western parody in which the action
eventually shifts to the Warner backlot, after
which the actors repair to Grauman's Chinese
Theatre to find out what happened at the end
of the story. At least as many misses as hits,
and all aimed squarely at film buffs.

w Norman Steinberg, Mel Brooks, Andrew
Bergman, Richard Pryor, Alan Unger d Mel
Brooks ph Joseph Biroc m John Morris

Cleavon Little, Gene Wilder, Slim Pickens,
Harvey Korman, Madeleine Kahn, Mel
Brooks, Burton Gilliam, Alex Karras

'One suspects that the film's gradual
disintegration derives not from the makers'
inability to end it, so much as from their
inability to stop laughing at their own
jokes.'—*Jan Dawson*

'A surfeit of chaos and a scarcity of
comedy.'—*Judith Crist*

' "I just about got everything out of me,"
said Brooks, "all my furor, my frenzy, my
insanity, my love of life and hatred of death."
Audiences flocked to this insane affirmation of
dancing girls, Hollywood production numbers,
stomach gas around the campfire, and gallows
humor. Brooks had found the perfect vehicle
for the age.'—*Les Keyser, Hollywood in the
Seventies*

AAN: Madeleine Kahn; title song (m John
Morris, ly Mel Brooks)

Bless the Beasts and Children*
US 1973 110m colour
Columbia / Stanley Kramer

Six boys on an adventure holiday try to free a
herd of buffalo earmarked for destruction.
Rather obviously pointed melodrama, well
enough done but not very interesting.

w Mac Benoff, novel Glendon Swarthout
d Stanley Kramer

Bill Mumy, Barry Robins, Miles Chapin, Jesse
White, Ken Swofford

AAN: title song (m / ly Barry de Vorzon,
Perry Botkin Jnr)

Blessed Event**
US 1932 84m bw
Warner (Ray Griffith)

A gossip columnist gets himself into hot water.
Amusing vehicle for a fast-talking star, and
quite an interesting historical document.

w Howard Green, play Manuel Seff, Forest
Wilson d Roy del Ruth ph Sol Polito

Lee Tracy, Ned Sparks, Mary Brian, Dick
Powell, Ruth Donnelly, Frank McHugh, Allen
Jenkins

Blind Alley**
US 1939 61m bw
Columbia

An escaped killer takes refuge in the home of
a psychiatrist, who explores his subconscious
and tames him.

Unusual lowercase thriller with effective
dream sequences; it was much imitated.

w Michael Blankfort, Albert Duffy, play
James Warwick d Charles Vidor ph Lucien
Ballard m Morris Stoloff

Chester Morris, Ralph Bellamy, Ann Dvorak,
Melville Cooper, Rose Stradner, Marc
Lawrence

'As un-Hollywood as anything that has
come from France this year.'—*New York
Daily News*

'Survive a sticky ten minutes and you have a
thriller of quite unusual merit.'—*Graham
Greene*

† Remake: *The Dark Past* (qv).

Blind Date*
GB 1959 95m bw
Rank / Sydney Box / Independent Artists
(David Deutsch)
US title: *Chance Meeting*

A young Dutch painter in London discovers
his mistress's body and finds himself in a web
of deceit.

Tolerable, comparatively sophisticated murder
puzzle; rather glum looking, but the plot holds
the interest.

w Ben Barzman, Millard Lampell, novel Leigh
Howard d Joseph Losey ph Christopher
Challis m Richard Rodney Bennett

Hardy Kruger, Stanley Baker, Micheline
Presle, Robert Flemyng, Gordon Jackson,
John Van Eyssen

The Blind Goddess
GB 1947 88m bw
Gainsborough (Betty Box)

The private secretary to a public figure finds
that his idol has feet of clay, and suffers in
court for his discovery.

Courtroom drama from an old-fashioned stage
play: surefire for addicts, but routine as a film.

w Muriel and Sydney Box, *play Patrick Hastings d* Harold French *ph* Ray Elton

Eric Portman, Anne Crawford, Hugh Williams, Michael Denison, Nora Swinburne, Claire Bloom, Raymond Lovell, Frank Cellier

Blind Husbands**

US 1918   90m approx (24 fps)   bw
  silent
Universal

An Austrian officer, on holiday in the Alps, seduces the wife of a rich American. Stroheim's first comedy of sexual manners, now of mainly archival interest.

w, d, ad Erich Von Stroheim ph Ben Reynolds

Erich Von Stroheim, Sam de Grasse, Gibson Gowland, Francella Billington

Blind Terror

GB 1971   89m   colour
Columbia / Filmways / Genesis (Basil
  Appleby)
US title: *See No Evil*

A blind girl is the sole, hunted survivor of a maniac's rampage on a lonely estate. Shocks, screams and starts fill a cliché-ridden but still effective script which is faithfully turned into a competent but routine heart-stopper.

w Brian Clemens *d* Richard Fleischer *ph* Gerry Fisher *m* Elmer Bernstein

Mia Farrow, Robin Bailey, Dorothy Alison, Diane Grayson, Norman Eshley, Brian Rawlinson
  'For those who like to watch folks pull the wings off flies.'—*Judith Crist*

Blindfold**

US 1965   102m   Technicolor
  Panavision
Universal (Marvin Schwarz)

A society psychiatrist is enlisted by the CIA to make regular blindfold journeys to a secret destination where he treats a neurotic physicist. Discovering that his contacts are really enemy agents, he tracks down the destination by sound and guesswork, and routs the villains.
Lively spy spoof with rather too much knockabout between the Hitchcockian suspense sequences; it has indeed the air of a script which Hitchcock rejected, but provides reliable entertainment.

w Philip Dunne, W. H. Menger, *novel* Lucile Fletcher *d* Philip Dunne *ph* Joseph MacDonald *m* Lalo Schifrin

Rock Hudson, Claudia Cardinale, Jack Warden, Guy Stockwell, Brad Dexter

The Bliss of Mrs Blossom

GB 1968   93m   Technicolor
Paramount (Josef Shaftel)

The wife of a bra manufacturer keeps her lover in the attic.
Silly, wild-eyed sex comedy decorated with the flashy tinsel of swinging London's dying fall.

w Alec Coppel, Denis Norden *d* Joe McGrath *ph* Geoffrey Unsworth *m* Riz Ortolani *pd* Assheton Gorton

Richard Attenborough, Shirley Maclaine, James Booth, Freddie Jones, William Rushton, Bob Monkhouse, Patricia Routledge

Blithe Spirit***

GB 1945   96m   Technicolor
Two Cities / Cineguild (Anthony Havelock-
  Allan)

A cynical novelist's second marriage is disturbed when the playful ghost of his first wife materializes during a séance. Direction and acting carefully preserve a comedy which on its first West End appearance in 1941 achieved instant classic status. The repartee scarcely dates, and altogether this is a most polished job of film-making.

w Noel Coward, from his play *scenario* David Lean, Anthony Havelock-Allan, Ronald Neame *d* David Lean *ph* Ronald Neame *m* Richard Addinsell

Rex Harrison, Kay Hammond, Constance Cummings, Margaret Rutherford, Hugh Wakefield, Joyce Carey, Jacqueline Clark

The Blob

US 1958   83m   De Luxe
Tonylyn / Jack H. Harris

A small town combats a slimy space invader. Padded hokum for drive-ins, with a few effective moments.

w Theodore Simonson, Kate Phillips *d* Irwin S. Yeaworth Jnr *ph* Thomas Spalding *m* Ralph Carmichael

Steve McQueen, Aneta Corseaut, Olin Howlin, Earl Rowe
  † Sequel 1971: *Beware! The Blob* (GB: *Son of Blob*).

Blockade*

US 1938   84m   bw
Walter Wanger

During the Spanish Civil War, a peace-loving young farmer has to take up arms to defend his land.

Much touted as Hollywood's first serious contribution to international affairs, this dogged drama was in fact so bland that audiences had difficulty ascertaining which side it was on, especially as neither Franco nor the Fascists were mentioned. As a romantic action drama, however, it passed muster.

w John Howard Lawson d William Dieterle m Werner Janssen ph Rudolf Maté

Henry Fonda, Madeleine Carroll, Leo Carrillo, John Halliday, Vladimir Sokoloff, Robert Warwick, Reginald Denny

'The film has a curious unreality considering the grim reality behind it.'—*Frank S. Nugent*

'There is achieved a deadly numb level of shameless hokum out of which anything true or decent rises only for a second to confound itself.'—*Otis Ferguson*

AAN: John Howard Lawson; Werner Janssen

Blockheads●●●
US 1938   60m   bw
Hal Roach / Stan Laurel

Twenty years after World War I, Stan is still guarding a trench because nobody told him to stop. Olly takes him home to meet the wife, with disastrous consequences.

The last first-class Laurel and Hardy comedy is shapeless but hilarious, a fragmented reworking of earlier ideas, all of which work beautifully. Gags include encounters with a tip-up truck and an automatic garage, and a brilliantly worked out sequence up and down several flights of stairs.

w James Parrott, Harry Langdon, Felix Adler, Charles Rogers, Arnold Belgard d John G. Blystone ph Art Lloyd m Marvin Hatley

Stan Laurel, Oliver Hardy, Billy Gilbert, Patricia Ellis, Minna Gombell, James Finlayson

AAN: Marvin Hatley

Blonde Crazy●
US 1931   74m   bw
Warner
GB title: *Larceny Lane*

A bellhop and a chambermaid set out to fleece all-comers.

Smart con man comedy with the star in excellent form.

w Kubec Glasmon, John Bright d Roy del Ruth ph Sid Hickox

James Cagney, Joan Blondell, Ray Milland, Louis Calhern, Guy Kibbee, Polly Walters, Charles Lane, Maude Eburne

'A chipper, hard-boiled, amusing essay in petty thieving.'—*Time*

A Blonde in Love: see *Loves of a Blonde*

Blonde Venus●
US 1932   97m   bw
Paramount

A German café singer marries an English research chemist, but their marriage doesn't run smoothly.

Rather dreary, fragmented star vehicle with good moments, notably the star's opening appearance as a gorilla.

w Jules Furthman, S. K. Lauren d Josef Von Sternberg ph Bert Glennon m Oscar Poteker

Marlene Dietrich, Herbert Marshall, Cary Grant, Dickie Moore

'The story has all the dramatic integrity of a sashweight murderer's tabloid autobiography.'—*Pare Lorentz*

'There is more pleasure for the eye in *Blonde Venus* than in a hundred of its fellows. But what does beauty ornament? The story of a wife who becomes a kept woman for the sake of her husband, and a prostitute for the sake of her child.'—*Forsyth Hardy, Cinema Quarterly*

Blondes for Danger
GB 1938   68m   bw

A cockney taxi driver takes an unwanted fare and becomes involved in a deep dark plot.

Modest but effective vehicle for *Gordon Harker*; with Enid Stamp Taylor, Ivan Brandt. Written by Gerald Elliott, from the novel *Red for Danger* by Evadne Price; directed by Jack Raymond; for Herbert Wilcox.

Blondie●
US 1938   68m   bw
Columbia

Misadventures of a harassed suburban family man.

Dagwood Bumstead and his wife Blondie were Mr and Mrs Small Town America throughout the thirties and forties, and received their perfect screen incarnations in this unambitious but quite watchable series, which provided familiar and often quite observant fun.

w Richard Flournoy, from the comic strip by *Chic Young* d Frank R. Strayer ph Henry Freulich

Arthur Lake, Penny Singleton, Larry Simms, Daisy the Dog, *Jonathan Hale* (as the boss, Mr Dithers), Gene Lockhart, Ann Doran, Irving Bacon (as the mailman)

Other episodes were as follows:
1939: BLONDIE MEETS THE BOSS, BLONDIE TAKES A VACATION,

BLONDIE BRINGS UP BABY
1940: BLONDIE ON A BUDGET,
BLONDIE HAS SERVANT TROUBLE,
BLONDIE PLAYS CUPID
1941: BLONDIE GOES LATIN, BLONDIE
IN SOCIETY
1942: BLONDIE GOES TO COLLEGE,
BLONDIE'S BLESSED EVENT, BLONDIE
FOR VICTORY
1943: IT'S A GREAT LIFE, FOOTLIGHT
GLAMOUR
1945: LEAVE IT TO BLONDIE
1946: BLONDIE KNOWS BEST, LIFE
WITH BLONDIE, BLONDIE'S LUCKY
DAY
1947: BLONDIE'S BIG MOMENT,
BLONDIE'S HOLIDAY, BLONDIE IN
THE DOUGH, BLONDIE'S
ANNIVERSARY
1948: BLONDIE'S REWARD
1949: BLONDIE'S SECRET, BLONDIE'S
BIG DEAL, BLONDIE HITS THE
JACKPOT
1950: BLONDIE'S HERO, BEWARE OF
BLONDIE
† TV series were started in the fifties and
sixties, but both failed.

Blondie Johnson
US 1933   67m   bw
The career of a female larcenist who
eventually takes her medicine. Competent
programmer very typical of its studio and year.
Joan Blondell, Chester Morris, Allen Jenkins,
Claire Dodd. Written by Earl Baldwin;
directed by Ray Enright; for Warner.

Blondie of the Follies*
US 1932   97m   bw
MGM (Marion Davies)
Two New York showgirls graduate from
tenements to luxury.
Adequate comedy-melodrama with an
interesting cast and good dialogue.
w Frances Marion, Anita Loos   d Edmund
Goulding   ph George Barnes   m William Axt
Marion Davies, Jimmy Durante, Robert
Montgomery, Billie Dove, James Gleason,
Zasu Pitts, Sidney Toler, Douglass Dumbrille
   'An unjustly forgotten film.'—New Yorker,
1979

Blood Alley
US 1955   115m   Warnercolor
Cinemascope
Warner / Batjac (no producer credited)
An American sailor is helped by local people
to escape from a Chinese jail; he then escorts
them to Hong Kong.

Rudimentary anti-Red heroics with expensive
spectacle punctuating a tacky script.
w A. S. Fleischmann, from his novel
d William Wellman   ph William H. Clothier
m Roy Webb   pd Alfred Ybarra
John Wayne, Lauren Bacall, Paul Fix, Joy
Kim, Berry Kroger, Mike Mazurki, Anita
Ekberg

Blood and Black Lace
Italy 1964   90m   Eastmancolor
Six women are nastily murdered in a fashion
house. Vaguely necrophiliac but trendy
suspense-horror flick in the wake of Psycho.
Cameron Mitchell, Thomas Reiner, Mary
Arden. Written by Marcel Fondato, Giuseppe
Barilla and Mario Bava; directed by Mario
Bava; for Emmepi. (Original title: Sei Donne
per l'Assassino.)

Blood and Roses
France / Italy 1960   87m   Technirama
Eger / Documento (Raymond Eger)
original title: Et Mourir de Plaisir
Carmilla takes on the vampiric personality of
her ancestress Millarca, whom she closely
resembles.
A rather half-hearted attempt to make an
elegant horror story; boring rather than
charming or frightening.
w Claude Brûlé, Claude Martin, Roger
Vadim   d Roger Vadim   ph Claude Renoir
m Jean Prodromidès
Mel Ferrer, Elsa Martinelli, Annette Vadim,
Marc Allégret

Blood and Sand*
US 1922   80m (24 fps)   bw   silent
Paramount
A matador falls under the spell of an
aristocratic woman.
Elegant star vehicle which established his
image.
w June Mathis, novel Vicente Blasco Ibanez
d Fred Niblo
Rudolph Valentino, Nita Naldi, Lila Lee,
Walter Long

Blood and Sand*
US 1941   123m   Technicolor
TCF (Darryl F. Zanuck, Robert T. Kane)
Rather boring remake, fine to look at but
dramatically deadly.
w Jo Swerling, novel Vicente Blasco Ibanez
d Rouben Mamoulian   ph Ernest Palmer, Ray
Rennahan   m Alfred Newman   ad Richard
Day, Joseph C. Wright

Tyrone Power, Rita Hayworth, Linda Darnell, Nazimova, Anthony Quinn, J. Carrol Naish, John Carradine, Lynn Bari, Laird Cregar, Monty Banks

AA: Ernest Palmer, Ray Rennahan

The Blood Beast Terror
GB 1967   88m   Eastmancolor
Tigon (Arnold L. Miller, Tony Tenser)

A Victorian entomologist creates human beings who can change themselves into monster death's-head moths.
Unpersuasive and totally idiotic cheapjack horror fare.

w Peter Bryan   *d* Vernon Sewell   *ph* Stanley A. Long   *m* Paul Ferris

Robert Flemyng, Peter Cushing, Wanda Ventham, Vanessa Howard, David Griffin, John Paul, Kevin Stoney, Roy Hudd

Blood from the Mummy's Tomb*
GB 1971   94m   Technicolor
Hammer (Howard Brandy)

Twenty years after a female mummy is brought back to England, members of the expedition are killed one by one, and their leader's daughter is possessed by the spirit of the dead princess.
Interesting but over-complicated and hard-to-enjoy attempt to maintain the mummy saga without an actual marauding mummy. Intelligently handled but sadly lacking in a sense of humour.

w Christopher Wicking, *novel* Jewel of the Seven Stars by Bram Stoker   *d* Seth Holt   *ph* Arthur Grant   *m* Tristam Cary

Andrew Keir, Valerie Leon, James Villiers, Hugh Burden, George Coulouris, Mark Edwards, Rosalie Crutchley, Aubrey Morris, David Markham
   'Makes the genre seem like new.'—*Tony Rayns*
† Seth Holt died when the shooting was still incomplete, and Michael Carreras took over for the last few days

The Blood of a Poet**
France 1930   58m   bw
Vicomte de Noailles
original title: *Le Sang d'un Poète*

Aspects of a poet's vision, taking place while a chimney is falling down.
An indescribable film full of striking imagery which may, or may not, be meaningful. Its author claims that it is not surrealist, but that label for most people will do as well as any other.

wd Jean Cocteau   *ph* Georges Périnal   *m* Georges Auric   *ad* Jean Gabriel d'Aubonne

Lee Miller, Pauline Carton, Odette Talazac
   'It must be placed among the classic masterpieces of the seventh art.'—*Revue du Cinéma*

Blood of the Vampire
GB 1958   85m   Eastmancolor

An asylum keeper turns inmates into vampires. Heavy-handed, crudely made horror comic. Donald Wolfit, Barbara Shelley, Vincent Ball, Victor Maddern, Andrew Faulds. Written by Jimmy Sangster; directed by Henry Cass; for Baker-Berman / Artistes Alliance.

Blood on Satan's Claw
GB 1970   93m   Eastmancolor
Tigon-Chilton (Tony Tenser, Malcolm B. Heyworth, Peter L. Andrews)
aka: *Satan's Skin*

A devil's claw wreaks havoc among children in a 17th-century English village.
Moderately frightening, rather silly but at least original period horror comic.

w Robert Wynne-Simmons   *d* Piers Haggard   *ph* Dick Bush   *m* Marc Wilkinson

Patrick Wymark, Linda Hayden, Barry Andrews, Avice Landon, Simon Williams, Tamara Ustinov, Anthony Ainley

Blood on the Moon*
US 1948   88m   bw
RKO

A homesteader finds that his best friend is the villainous leader of a group of cattlemen.
Good-looking but rather pedestrian western, generally well handled.

w Lillie Hayward   *d* Robert Wise   *ph* Nicholas Musuraca   *m* Roy Webb

Robert Mitchum, Barbara Bel Geddes, Robert Preston, Walter Brennan

Blood on the Sun*
US 1945   94m   bw
William Cagney

In the twenties, the American editor of a Tokyo newspaper reveals a Japanese militarist plan for world conquest.
Satisfactory star actioner with good production and exciting highlights.

w Lester Cole   *d* Frank Lloyd   *ph* Theodor Sparkuhl   *m* Miklos Rozsa

James Cagney, Sylvia Sidney, Wallace Ford, Rosemary de Camp, Robert Armstrong, John Emery, Leonard Strong, Frank Puglia

'It ought to be fine for those who enjoy a good ninety-minute massacre.'—*New Yorker*
'Tough, hard-hitting and explosive, with just enough rudimentary suspense.'—*Bosley Crowther*
'Pure unadulterated melodrama has a safe niche in cinematic offerings, but this folderol is more pretentious than persuasive.'—*Howard Barnes*

Bloodbrothers

US 1978   116m   Technicolor
Warner / Stephen Friedman / Kings Road

The disintegration through failure and inadequacy of a noisy Italian-American family. The kind of self-indulgence that has one seeking the exit before it's half over.

w Walter Newman, *novel* Richard Price d Robert Mulligan *ph* Robert Surtees m Elmer Bernstein *pd* Gene Callahan

Paul Sorvino, Tony Lo Bianco, Richard Gere, Lelia Goldoni
'Why should filmgoers pay to see what they can already hear in the next apartment?'— *Variety*

Bloodhounds of Broadway*

US 1952   90m   Technicolor
TCF (George Jessel)

With the help of a gangster, an orphan girl and her pet bloodhounds make a big hit in cabaret.
Absurd but sporadically amusing gangster burlesque, typical of its author. Lively production values.

w Sy Gomberg, *story* Damon Runyon d Harmon Jones *ph* Edward Cronjager *md* Lionel Newman

Mitzi Gaynor, Scott Brady, Mitzi Green, Marguerite Chapman, Michael O'Shea, Wally Vernon, George E. Stone

Bloodline

US 1979   117m   Movielab
Paramount / Geria (David V. Bicker, Sidney Beckerman)

A pharmaceutical tycoon is murdered and his daughter seems likely to be the next victim. Involved all-star suspense shocker which seems constantly about to be better than it ever is.

w Laird Koenig, *novel* Sidney Sheldon d Terence Young *ph* Freddie Young m Ennio Morricone *pd* Ted Haworth

Audrey Hepburn, Ben Gazzara, James Mason, Claudia Mori, Omar Sharif, Irene Papas, Maurice Ronet, Romy Schneider, Beatrice Straight, Gert Frobe, Micheline Phillips

'Unutterably chic, inexpressibly absurd, and saved from being painfully tedious only by a personable cast doing their damnedest.'—*Tom Milne, MFB*

Bloody Mama*

US 1969   90m   Movielab
AIP (Roger Corman)

In the thirties, outlaw Kate Barker and her four sons conduct a reign of terror until what's left of the gang is riddled with machine gun bullets.
Violent gangster story with a star on the rampage; the attempt to philosophize is more than the facts will bear, but the production moves smartly enough.

w Robert Thom d Roger Corman *ph* John Alonzo m Don Randi

Shelley Winters, Pat Hingle, Don Stroud, Diane Varsi, Bruce Dern, Clint Kimbrough, Robert de Niro, Robert Walden, Alex Nicol

Bloomfield

GB 1969   95m   Technicolor
World Film Services / Limbridge (John Heyman, Wolf Mankowitz)
US title: *The Hero*

A 10-year-old Israeli boy hitchhikes to Jaffa to see his football idol play his last game. Sentimental whimsy, unattractively interpreted.

w Wolf Mankowitz d Richard Harris *ph* Otto Heller m Johnny Harris

Richard Harris, Romy Schneider, Kim Burfield, Maurice Kaufmann, Yossi Yadin

Blossom Time

GB 1934   90m   bw

In old Vienna, a composer stands by while the girl he loves weds a dragoon. Stilted musical romance redeemed by its star's singing presence. Richard Tauber, Jane Baxter, Carl Esmond, Athene Seyler. Written by John Drinkwater, Walter Burford, Paul Perez and G. H. Clutsam; directed by Paul Stein; for BIP. (US title: *April Romance*.)

Blossoms in the Dust**

US 1941   99m   Technicolor
MGM (Irving Asher)

A woman who loses her husband and child founds a state orphanage.
Archetypal tearjerker of the forties, a glossy 'woman's picture' which distorts the facts into a star vehicle. Excellent colour helped to make it an enormous success.

w Anita Loos, based on the life of Edna Gladney d Mervyn Le Roy *ph* Karl Freund, W. Howard Greene m Herbert Stothart

Greer Garson, Walter Pidgeon, Felix Bressart, Marsha Hunt, Fay Holden, Samuel S. Hinds

AAN: best picture; Karl Freund, W. Howard Greene; Greer Garson

Blotto*

US 1930　20m　bw

Ollie helps Stan escape his wife for a night on the town, but the lady takes revenge. Palatable star comedy with a strained second half following a splendidly typical opening. Laurel and Hardy, Anita Garvin. Written by Leo McCarey and H. M. Walker; directed by James Parrott; for Hal Roach.

Blow Up**

GB 1966　110m　Eastmancolor
MGM / Carlo Ponti

A London fashion photographer thinks he sees a murder, but the evidence disappears. Not a mystery but a fashionable think-in on the difference (if any) between fantasy and reality. Agreeable to look at for those who can stifle their irritation at the non-plot and non-characters; a huge audience was lured by flashes of nudity and the trendy 'swinging London' setting.

wd Michelangelo Antonioni *ph* Carlo di Palma *m* Herbert Hancock *ad* Assheton Gorton

David Hemmings, Sarah Miles, Vanessa Redgrave

AAN: Michelangelo Antonioni (as writer and director)

Blowing Wild*

US 1953　88m　bw
(Warner) United States (Milton Sperling)

A Mexican oil driller becomes involved with the psychotic wife of an old friend; the triangle leads to murder and retribution. Pot-boiling star vehicle with adequate melodramatic interest, full of reminiscences of other movies, with a wicked lady to end them all.

w Philip Yordan *d* Hugo Fregonese *ph* Sid Hickox *m* Dmitri Tiomkin

Gary Cooper, Barbara Stanwyck, Anthony Quinn, Ruth Roman, Ward Bond

Blue

US 1968　113m　Technicolor
Panavision
Paramount / Kettledrum (Judd Bernard, Irwin Winkler)

The white adopted son of a Mexican bandit prevents his cohorts from raping a white girl, and falls in love with her. Pretentious, self-conscious, literary western without much zest.

w Meade Roberts, Ronald M. Cohen *d* Silvio Narizzano *ph* Stanley Cortez *m* Manos Hadjidakis

Terence Stamp, Joanna Pettet, Karl Malden, Ricardo Montalban

'I don't know which is worse—bad cowboy movies or bad *arty* cowboy movies. *Blue* is both.'—*Rex Reed*

The Blue Angel****

Germany 1930　98m　bw
UFA (Erich Pommer)

A fuddy-duddy professor is infatuated with a tawdry night-club singer. She marries him but is soon bored and contemptuous; humiliated, he leaves her and dies in his old classroom. A masterwork of late twenties German grotesquerie, and after a slowish beginning an emotional powerhouse, set in a dark nightmare world which could be created only in the studio. Shot also in English, it was highly popular and influential in Britain and America.

w Robert Liebmann, Karl Zuckmayer, Karl Vollmoeller, *novel* Professor Unrath by Heinrich Mann *d* Josef Von Sternberg *ph* Gunthér Rittau, Hans Schneeberger *m* Frederick Hollander (inc 'Falling in Love Again', 'They Call Me Wicked Lola') *ad* Otto Hunte, Emil Hasler

Emil Jannings, Marlene Dietrich (who was instantly catapulted to international stardom), Kurt Gerron, Hans Albers

The Blue Angel

US 1959　107m　De Luxe Cinemascope
TCF (Jack Cummings)

Ill-advised attempt at a 'realistic', updated remake of the above; the result is a total travesty, with the actors aware that stylized melodrama is turning before their eyes into unintentional farce.

w Nigel Balchin *d* Edward Dmytryk *ph* Leon Shamroy *m* Hugo Friedhofer

Curt Jurgens, May Britt, Theodore Bikel, John Banner

'It totally lacks the stifling atmosphere of sordid and oppressive sexuality which is essential to give conviction to the German sadism of the story.'—*Brenda Davies*

The Blue Bird***

US 1940　98m　Technicolor (bw prologue)
TCF (Gene Markey)

In a Grimm's Fairy Tale setting, the two children of a poor woodcutter seek the bluebird of happiness in the past, the future and the Land of Luxury, but eventually discover it in their own back yard.

An imaginative and often chilling script clarifies Maurice Maeterlinck's fairy play, and the art direction is outstanding, but the children are necessarily unsympathetic and the expensive production paled beside the success of the more upbeat *Wizard of Oz*, which was released almost simultaneously. Slashed for re-release, the only existing prints now open with confusing abruptness and no scene-setting before the adventures begin.

w Ernest Pascal *d* Walter Lang *ph* Arthur Miller, Ray Rennahan *m* Alfred Newman

Shirley Temple, Johnny Russell, *Gale Sondergaard* (as the cat), *Eddie Collins* (as the dog), Nigel Bruce, Jessie Ralph, Spring Byington, Sybil Jason, Helen Ericson, Russell Hicks, Al Shean, Cecilia Loftus

AAN: Arthur Miller, Ray Rennahan

The Blue Bird

US / USSR 1976   99m   Technicolor
Panavision
TCF / Edward Lewis / Lenfilm

Abortive remake of the above, widely touted as the first Russian–American co-production, but sabotaged by a flabby script, unsuitable casting and unresolved production problems.

w Hugh Whitemore, Alfred Hayes *d* George Cukor *ph* Freddie Young, Ionas Gritzus *m* Irwin Kostal, Andrei Petrov

Elizabeth Taylor (as Mother, Maternal Love, Light and the Witch), Ava Gardner, Cicely Tyson, Jane Fonda, Harry Andrews, Will Geer, Mona Washbourne, George Cole

'It works so hard at making history that it forgets to make sense.'—*David Sterritt, Christian Science Monitor*

Blue Blood

GB 1973   86m   Technicolor
Mallard-Impact Quadrant

A German governess arrives at an English stately home and finds the malevolent butler plotting to show his supremacy over his effete master.

An extremely unattractive, would-be satirical melodrama which plays like a Grand Guignol version of *The Servant*.

wd Andrew Sinclair, *novel* The Carry-Cot by Alexander Thynne *ph* Harry Waxman *m* Brian Gascoigne

Oliver Reed, Derek Jacobi, Fiona Lewis, Anna Gael, Meg Wynn Owen

Blue Collar°

US 1978   114m   Technicolor
Universal / TAT (Don Guest)

Three car factory workers try to improve their lot by unionization and robbery.

Salty, rough, downbeat but impressively realistic modern drama, a belated American equivalent of *Saturday Night and Sunday Morning*.

w Paul Schraeder, Leonard Schraeder *d* Paul Schraeder *ph* Bobby Byrne *m* Jack Nitzche

Richard Pryor, Harvey Keitel, Yaphet Kotto, Ed Begley Jnr, Harry Bellaver

The Blue Dahlia°°

US 1946   99m   bw
Paramount (John Houseman)

A returning war veteran finds his faithless wife murdered and himself suspected.

Hailed on its first release as sharper than average, this mystery suspenser is now only moderately compelling despite the screenplay credit; direction and editing lack urgency and the acting lacks bounce.

w Raymond Chandler *d* George Marshall *ph* Lionel Lindon *m* Victor Young

Alan Ladd, Veronica Lake, William Bendix, Howard da Silva, Doris Dowling, Tom Powers, Hugh Beaumont, Howard Freeman, Will Wright

'It threatens to turn into something, but it never does.'—*New Yorker, 1978*

'The picture is as neatly stylized and synchronized, and as uninterested in moral excitement, as a good ballet; it knows its own weight and size perfectly and carries them gracefully and without self-importance; it is, barring occasional victories and noble accidents, about as good a movie as can be expected from the big factories.'—*James Agee*

AAN: Raymond Chandler

Blue Denim°

US 1959   89m   bw   Cinemascope
TCF (Charles Brackett)
GB title: *Blue Jeans*

Teenagers confronted with the prospect of illegitimate parenthood consult an abortionist, but all ends with wedding bells.

First of its rather dreary kind but better than most, this only slightly mawkish domestic drama has its heart in the right place and steers surprisingly towards a nick-of-time chase climax.

w Edith Sommer, Philip Dunne, *play* James Leo Herlihy, William Noble *d* Philip Dunne *ph* Leo Tover *m* Bernard Herrmann

Carol Lynley, Brandon de Wilde, Macdonald Carey, Marsha Hunt, Nina Shipman, Warren Berlinger

The Blue Gardenia
US 1953   90m   bw
Warner / Gloria / Blue Gardenia (Alex Gottlieb)

A girl gets drunk and wakes up in a strange apartment with a dead man by her side.
Totally undistinguished mystery which leaves egg on the actors' faces.

w Charles Hoffman d Fritz Lang ph Nicholas Musuraca m Raoul Krashaar

Anne Baxter, Richard Conte, Ann Sothern, Raymond Burr, Jeff Donnell, Richard Erdman, Nat King Cole

Blue Hawaii
US 1961   101m   Technicolor
Panavision
Hal B. Wallis

A GI comes home to Honolulu and becomes a beachcomber.
Lifeless star vehicle shot on glamorous locations.

w Hal Kanter d Norman Taurog ph Charles Lang Jnr m Joseph J. Lilley

Elvis Presley, Joan Blackman, Nancy Walters, Roland Winters, Angela Lansbury, John Archer, Howard McNear

The Blue Lagoon*
GB 1949   103m   Technicolor
GFD / Individual (Frank Launder, Sidney Gilliat)

A shipwrecked boy and girl grow up on a desert island, ward off smugglers, have a baby, and eventually sail away in search of civilization.
Rather lifeless, though pretty, treatment of a famous novel: the story never becomes vivid despite splendid Fijian locations.

w Frank Launder, John Baines, Michael Hogan, novel H. de Vere Stacpoole d Frank Launder ph Geoffrey Unsworth m Clifton Parker

Jean Simmons, Donald Houston, Noel Purcell, Cyril Cusack, James Hayter

The Blue Lagoon
US 1980   102m   Colorfilm
Columbia / Randal Kleiser

Remake of the above with poor narrative balance and a great deal of nudity and adolescent frankness about sex. Adolescents are probably its only audience.

w Douglas Day Stewart d Randal Kleiser ph Nestor Almendros m Basil Poledouris

Brooke Shields, Christopher Atkins, Leo McKern, William Daniels

AAN: Nestor Almendros

The Blue Lamp***
GB 1949   84m   bw
Ealing (Michael Relph)

A young man joins London's police force. The elderly copper who trains him is killed in a shootout, but the killer is apprehended.
Seminal British police film which spawned not only a long line of semi-documentary imitations but also the twenty-year TV series *Dixon of Dock Green* for which the shot PC was happily revived. As an entertainment, pacy but dated; more important, it burnished the image of the British copper for a generation or more.

w T. E. B. Clarke d Basil Dearden ph Gordon Dines md Ernest Irving

Jack Warner, Jimmy Hanley, Dirk Bogarde, Meredith Edwards, Robert Flemyng, Bernard Lee, Patric Doonan, Peggy Evans, Gladys Henson, Dora Bryan

'The mixture of coyness, patronage and naive theatricality which has vitiated British films for the last ten years.'—*Gavin Lambert*

'A soundly made crime thriller which would not be creating much of a stir if it were American.'—*Richard Mallett, Punch*

The Blue Max**
US 1966   156m   De Luxe   Cinemascope
TCF (Christian Ferry)

In Germany after World War I an ambitious and skilful pilot causes the death of his comrades and steals the wife of his High Command superior, who eventually finds a means of revenge.
For once, an action spectacular not too badly let down by its connecting threads of plot, apart from some hilarious and unnecessary bedroom scenes in which the female star's bath towel seems to become conveniently adhesive.

w David Pursall, Jack Seddon, Gerald Hanley, novel Jack Hunter d John Guillermin ph Douglas Slocombe m Jerry Goldsmith

George Peppard, *James Mason*, Ursula Andress, Jeremy Kemp, Karl Michael Vogler, Anton Diffring, Derren Nesbitt

The Blue Peter
GB 1955   93m   Eastmancolor
British Lion / Beaconsfield (Herbert Mason)

A confused war hero becomes a trainer at an Outward Bound school for boys.
Pleasant but uninspired open air adventure for young people.

w Don Sharp, John Pudney d Wolf Rilla
ph Arthur Grant m Antony Hopkins

Kieron Moore, Greta Gynt, Sarah Lawson, Mervyn Johns, Ram Gopal, Edwin Richfield, Harry Fowler, John Charlesworth

Blue Skies*
US 1946   104m   Technicolor
Paramount (Sol C. Siegel)

A dancing star and a nightclub owner fight for years over the same girl.
Thin musical with splendid Irving Berlin tunes and lively individual numbers.

w Arthur Sheekman d Stuart Heisler
ph Charles Lang md Robert Emmett Dolan

Fred Astaire (dancing 'Putting On the Ritz'), Bing Crosby, Joan Caulfield, Billy de Wolfe, Olga San Juan, Robert Benchley, Frank Faylen, Victoria Horne, Jack Norton

AAN: Robert Emmett Dolan; song 'You Keep Coming Back Like a Song' (m / ly Irving Berlin)

The Blue Veil*
US 1951   114m   bw
(RKO) Wald–Krasna (Raymond Hakim)

The vocational career of a children's nurse who descends into poverty but is rescued by one of her own charges, now grown up.
Sober American remake of a French tearjerker (Le Voile bleu) with the star suffering nobly but being upstaged by the cameo players.

w Norman Corwin, from the original by François Campaux d Curtis Bernhardt
ph Franz Planer m Franz Waxman

Jane Wyman, Charles Laughton, Richard Carlson, Joan Blondell, Agnes Moorehead, Don Taylor, Audrey Totter, Everett Sloane, Cyril Cusack, Natalie Wood, Warner Anderson

AAN: Jane Wyman; Joan Blondell

Bluebeard*
US 1944   73m   bw
PRC

A strangler of young girls is at large in Paris.
Poverty Row chiller with effective moments; possibly the most interesting film ever to come from PRC (which isn't saying very much).

w Pierre Gendron d Edgar G. Ulmer
ph Jockey Feindel

John Carradine, Jean Parker, Ludwig Stossel, Nils Asther, Iris Adrian

Bluebeard
France / Italy / Germany 1972   124m
   Technicolor
Barnabé / Gloria / Geiselgasteig (Alexander Salkind)

The lady killer in this case is an Austrian aristocrat who has been driven to desperation and murder by a long line of mistresses whose bodies he keeps frozen in his cellar.
Would-be macabre comedy which becomes totally off-putting by its emphasis on close-up death agonies.

w Ennio di Concini, Edward Dmytryk, Maria Pia Fusco d Edward Dmytryk ph Gabor Pogany m Ennio Morricone

Richard Burton, Raquel Welch, Joey Heatherton, Virna Lisi, Nathalie Delon, Marilu Tolo
   'Somewhere between (and a long way behind) Kind Hearts and Coronets and The Abominable Dr Phibes.'—Clyde Jeavons, MFB

Bluebeard's Eighth Wife*
US 1938   80m   bw
Paramount (Ernst Lubitsch)

The daughter of an impoverished French aristocrat marries for money a millionaire who has had seven previous wives, and determines to teach him a lesson.
Very thin sophisticated comedy with unsympathetic characters and little wit after the first scene; a disappointment from the talent involved.

w Charles Brackett, Billy Wilder, play Alfred Savoir d Ernst Lubitsch ph Leo Tover

Claudette Colbert, Gary Cooper, David Niven, Edward Everett Horton, Elizabeth Patterson, Herman Bing, Warren Hymer, Franklin Pangborn
   'In these days it is bad enough to have to admire millionaires in any circumstances; but a millionaire with a harem complex simply can't help starting the bristles on the back of a sensitive neck.'—New York Times
† A previous version, released by Paramount in 1923 and directed by Sam Wood, starred Gloria Swanson and Huntley Gordon.

Bluebeard's Ten Honeymoons
GB 1960   93m   bw
Anglo-Allied (Roy Parkinson)

Another version of the story of Landru, alternating wildly between fantasy, farce and melodrama. Not a success in any of its moods.

w Myles Wilder *d* W. Lee Wilder
ph Stephen Dade *m* Albert Elms

George Sanders, Corinne Calvet, Patricia
Roc, Ingrid Hafner, Jean Kent, Greta Gynt,
Maxine Audley, Selma Vaz Diaz, George
Coulouris
   'The unedifying narrative is developed along
the most obvious lines imaginable.'—*MFB*

The Bluebird see The Blue Bird

A Blueprint for Murder*
US 1953   77m   bw
TCF (Michael Abel)

After the death of his brother and nephew, a
man proves that his sister-in-law is a
murderess.
Unpleasant but efficient murder story with
enough twists to keep one watching.

wd Andrew Stone *ph* Leo Tover *m* Lionel
Newman

Jean Peters, Joseph Cotten, Gary Merrill,
Catherine McLeod, Jack Kruschen

Blueprint for Robbery*
US 1960   87m   bw
Paramount (Bryan Foy)

Crooks plan and execute a robbery, agreeing
not to touch the proceeds for two and a half
years. But some get tired of waiting. . .
Minor but effective crime melodrama in semi-
documentary vein.

w Irwin Winehouse, A. Sanford Wolf *d* Jerry
Hopper *ph* Loyal Griggs *m* Van Cleave

J. Pat O'Malley, Robert Gist, Romo Vincent,
Marion Ross, Tom Duggan
   'A not uninteresting entry in the screen
log-book on crime.'—*MFB*

The Blues Brothers
US 1980   133m   Technicolor
Universal (Robert K. Weiss)

A massive car chase develops when two
brothers collect money for their old orphanage
without too much regard for law and order.
Fashionable chase comedy with so many stunts
that its cost ran up to 33,000,000 dollars. The
public stayed away.

w Dan Aykroyd, John Landis *d* John Landis
ph Stephen M. Katz *md* Ira Newborn
pd John Lloyd

John Belushi, Dan Aykroyd, Kathleen
Freeman, James Brown, Henry Gibson, Cab
Calloway, Carrie Fisher
   'It meanders expensively like some
pedigreed shaggy dog through 70s / 80s
American cinema and 50s / 60s American

rock, cocking its leg happily at every popular
landmark on the way.'—*Paul Taylor, MFB*

Blues in the Night*
US 1941   88m   bw
Warner (Henry Blanke)

Career and romantic problems for the
members of a travelling jazz band.
Atmospheric little melodrama with good score
and smart dialogue.

w Robert Rossen, *play* Hot Nocturne by
Edwin Gilbert *d* Anatole Litvak *ph* Ernest
Haller

Priscilla Lane, Richard Whorf, Lloyd Nolan,
Betty Field, Jack Carson, Elia Kazan, Wallace
Ford, Billy Halop, Peter Whitney

AAN: title song (*m* Harold Arlen, *ly* Johnny
Mercer)

Blume in Love*
US 1973   116m   Technicolor
Warner (Paul Mazursky)

A divorced American lawyer in Venice
reminisces about his love life.
Shapeless but enjoyable 'serious comedy' with
star and director in good form.

wd Paul Mazursky *ph* Bruce Surtees
m various

George Segal, Susan Anspach, Kris
Kristofferson, Marsha Mason, Shelley Winters

Boardwalk
US 1979   100m   Eastmancolor
ITC / Stratford (Gerald T. Herrod)

An old couple in Coney Island are affected by
escalating violence.
Well-meaning but somewhat absurd moral tale
for our times, in which the harassed
septuagenarian finally chokes the young punk
leader to death.

w Stephen Verona, Leigh Chapman
d Stephen Verona *ph* Billy Williams
m various

Ruth Gordon, Lee Strasberg, Janet Leigh, Joe
Silver, Eddie Barth
   'One would probably have to reach as far
back as *The Birth of a Nation* to find a more
direct incitement to racial hatred.'—*Richard
Combs, MFB*

The Boatniks*
US 1970   100m   Technicolor
Walt Disney (Ron Miller)

An accident-prone coastguard officer creates
havoc at a yachting marina but is acclaimed a
hero after catching three jewel thieves.
Simple fresh-air farce for the family,
pleasantly set but flatly directed.

w Arthur Julian *d* Norman Tokar *ph* William Snyder *m* Robert F. Brunner

Phil Silvers, Robert Morse, Stefanie Powers, Norman Fell, Mickey Shaughnessey, Wally Cox, Don Ameche, Joey Forman

Bob and Carol and Ted and Alice**
US 1969   105m   Technicolor
Columbia / M. J. Frankovich (Larry Tucker)

Two California couples, influenced by a group therapy session advocating natural spontaneous behaviour, decide to admit their extra-marital affairs and narrowly avoid a wife-swapping party.
Fashionable comedy without the courage of its convictions: it starts and finishes very bashfully, but there are bright scenes in the middle. An attempt to extend it into a TV series was a failure.

w Paul Mazursky, Larry Tucker *d* Paul Mazursky *ph* Charles E. Lang *m* Quincy Jones

Natalie Wood, Robert Culp, Elliott Gould, Dyan Cannon, Horst Ebersberg
   'An old-fashioned romantic comedy disguised as a blue picture.'—*Arthur Schlesinger Jnr*

AAN: Paul Mazursky, Larry Tucker; Charles E. Lang; Elliott Gould; Dyan Cannon

Bobbikins
GB 1959   90m   bw   Cinemascope
TCF (Oscar Brodney, Bob McNaught)

A downtrodden variety artist finds that his baby can not only talk but also give him tips on the stock exchange.
Not at all a good idea, and feebly executed.

w Oscar Brodney *d* Robert Day *ph* Geoffrey Faithfull *m* Philip Green

Max Bygraves, Shirley Jones, Billie Whitelaw, Barbara Shelley, Colin Gordon, Charles Tingwell, Lionel Jeffries, Rupert Davies

The Bobo
US 1967   105m   Technicolor
Warner / Gina (Elliott Kastner, Jerry Gershwin) (David R. Schwarz)

An unsuccessful and timid bullfighter is offered a contract if within three days he can seduce the local belle.
Stylized, silly and boring comedy from an obviously dated play; Chaplinesque pathos was not this star's strong suit.

w David R. Schwarz, from his play and the novel *Olimpia* by Burt Cole *d* Robert Parrish *ph* Gerry Turpin *m* Francis Lai

Peter Sellers, Britt Ekland, Rossano Brazzi, Adolfo Celi, Hattie Jacques, Ferdy Mayne, Kenneth Griffith, John Wells

Boccaccio '70*
Italy / France 1962   210m   Eastmancolor
TCF / CCC / Cineriz / Francinex / Gray Films
   (Antonio Cervi, Carlo Ponti)

Four modern stories which Boccaccio might have written (on an off day).
Overlong portmanteau with inevitable bright moments but many more longueurs.

'The Temptation of Dr Antonio': *w* Federico Fellini, Tullio Pinelli, Ennio Flaiano *d* Federico Fellini *ph* Otello Martelli; with Anita Ekberg
'The Job': *w* Suso Cecchi d'Amico, Luchino Visconti *d* Luchino Visconti *ph* Giuseppe Rotunno; with Romy Schneider, Tomas Milian
'The Raffle': *w* Cesare Zavattini *d* Vittorio de Sica *ph* Otello Martelli; with Sophia Loren
'Renzo and Luciana': *d* Mario Monichelli

Body and Soul*
US 1947   104m   bw
Enterprise (Bob Roberts)

A young boxer fights his way unscrupulously to the top.
Melodramatic but absorbing study of prizefighting's seamy side. (Is there any other?) Inventively studio-bound and almost impressionist in treatment.

w Abraham Polonsky d Robert Rossen ph James Wong Howe md Rudolph Polk *m* Hugo Friedhofer

John Garfield, Lilli Palmer, Hazel Brooks, Anne Revere, William Conrad, Joseph Pevney, Canada Lee
   'Here are the gin and tinsel, squalor and sables of the depression era, less daring than when first revealed in *Dead End* or *Golden Boy* but more valid and mature because shown without sentiment or blur.'—*National Board of Review*

AAN: Abraham Polonsky; John Garfield

The Body Disappears
US 1941   72m   bw
Warner (Ben Stoloff)

A professor invents an invisibility formula.
Uninspired comedy switch on a familiar theme.

w Scott Darling, Erna Lazarus *d* D. Ross Lederman *ph* Allen G. Seigler

Edward Everett Horton, Jeffrey Dell, Jane Wyman, Herbert Anderson, Marguerite Chapman, Craig Stevens, David Bruce, Willie Best

The Body Snatcher***
US 1945   77m   bw
RKO (Val Lewton)

In 19th-century Edinburgh a doctor obtains 'specimens' from grave-robbers, and murder results when supplies run short.
A familiar theme very imaginatively handled, and well acted, though the beginning is slow. The best of the Lewton thrillers.

w Philip MacDonald, Carlos Keith (Val Lewton), *story* R. L. Stevenson *d* Robert Wise *ph* Robert de Grasse *m* Roy Webb

Henry Daniell, Boris Karloff, Bela Lugosi, Edith Atwater, Russell Wade

'A humane sincerity and a devotion to good cinema . . . However, most of the picture is more literary than lively.'—*Time*

Boeing-Boeing
US 1965   102m   Technicolor
(Paramount) Hal B. Wallis

By successfully juggling with plane schedules, a Paris journalist manages to live with three air hostesses at the same time.
Frenetic, paper-thin sex comedy from a one-joke play; film style generally undistinguished.

w Edward Anhalt, *play* Marc Camoletti *d* John Rich *ph* Lucien Ballard *m* Neal Hefti

Tony Curtis, Jerry Lewis (his only 'straight' part), Dany Saval, Christiane Schmidtner, Suzanna Leigh, *Thelma Ritter*

'A sort of jet-age French farce.'—*Judith Crist*

'The big comedy of nineteen sexty-sex!'—*publicity*

The Bofors Gun**
GB 1968   105m   Technicolor
Rank / Everglades (Robert A. Goldson, Otto Plaschkes)

In 1954 Germany a British army unit runs into trouble when a violent and unstable Irish sergeant picks on a weakly National Service corporal.
Keen, fascinating, but often crude and eventually rather silly expansion of a TV play chiefly notable for the excellent acting opportunities provided by its unattractive but recognizable characters.

w John McGrath *d* Jack Gold *ph* Alan Hume *m* Carl Davis

Nicol Williamson, John Thaw, *David Warner*, Ian Holm

La Bohème
US 1926   75m approx at 24 fps   bw
silent

Mimi starves to death in a Paris garret.
Overacted straight version of the opera, with two passionate star performances. Lillian Gish, John Gilbert, Renee Adoree, Edward Everett Horton. Written by Harry Behn and Ray Doyle, after Murger; directed by King Vidor; for MGM.

The Bohemian Girl*
US 1936   74m   bw
Hal Roach

Gypsies kidnap a nobleman's daughter and bring her up as their own.
One of several operettas reworked for Laurel and Hardy, this is an inoffensive entertainment which devotes too little care to their need for slowly built-up gag structure; their sequences tend to fizzle out and the singing is a bore.

w Alfred Bunn, *operetta* William Balfe *d* James Horne, Charles Rogers *ph* Art Lloyd, Francis Corby

Stan Laurel, Oliver Hardy, Mae Busch, Antonio Moreno, Jacqueline Wells, Darla Hood, Zeffie Tilbury, James Finlayson, Thelma Todd (for one song, apparently dubbed: presumably before her sudden death she had been cast as the heroine)

† There was in 1922 a British silent version with a splendid cast including Ivor Novello, Gladys Cooper, C. Aubrey Smith, Ellen Terry and Constance Collier.

The Bold and the Brave
US 1956   87m   bw   Superscope
RKO / Hal E. Chester

An assortment of American types come together in the Italian campaign of 1944.
Routine war heroics chiefly remembered (if at all) for a crap game sequence.

w Robert Lewin *d* Lewis Foster *ph* Sam Leavitt *m* Herschel Burke Gilbert

Wendell Corey, *Mickey Rooney*, Nicole Maurey, Don Taylor

AAN: Robert Lewin; Mickey Rooney

Bolero*
US 1934   85m   bw
Paramount

A New York dancer neglects his personal life to become king of the European night club circuit.

Lively romantic drama which performed remarkably at the box office and led to a kind of sequel, *Rumba*.

w Carey Wilson, Kubec Glasmon, Ruth Ridenour, Horace Jackson d Wesley Ruggles ph Leo Tover

George Raft, Carole Lombard, Sally Rand (doing her fan dance), Frances Drake, William Frawley, Ray Milland, Gertrude Michael

Bomba the Jungle Boy
US 1949 65m bw or sepia
Monogram (Walter Mirisch)

Photographers in Africa meet a junior Tarzan who rescues their girl friend.
Cut-rate hokum starring the lad who had played Johnny Weissmuller's 'son' in earlier Tarzan movies; it led to several tedious sequels.

w Jack de Witt, from the comic strip by Roy Rockwell d Ford Beebe ph William Sickner m Edward Kay

Johnny Sheffield, Peggy Ann Garner, Onslow Stevens, Charles Irwin

Bombardier
US 1943 99m bw
RKO (Robert Fellows)

Cadet bombardiers learn the realities of war on raids over Japan.
Totally routine recruiting poster heroics.

w John Twist d Richard Wallace ph Nicholas Musuraca m Roy Webb

Pat O'Brien, Randolph Scott, Anne Shirley, Eddie Albert, Walter Reed, Robert Ryan, Barton Maclane

Bombay Talkie*
India 1970 105m Eastmancolor
Merchant-Ivory (Ismail Merchant)

A sophisticated American woman comes to Bombay and falls for two men involved in film-making.
Interesting but unsatisfactory romantic drama, rather pointlessly set against film studio backgrounds.

w Ruth Prawer Jhabvala, James Ivory d James Ivory ph Subrata Mitra m Shankar Jaikishan

Jennifer Kendal, Shashi Kapoor, Zia Mohyeddin

Bombers B-52
US 1957 106m Warnercolor
Cinemascope
Warner (Richard Whorf)
GB title: *No Sleep till Dawn*

A USAF sergeant considers applying for a discharge so that he can earn more money in civilian life.
Glossy domestic melodrama punctuated by aircraft shots.

w Irving Wallace d Gordon Douglas ph William Clothier m Leonard Rosenman

Karl Malden, Marsha Hunt, Natalie Wood, Efrem Zimbalist Jnr, Don Kelly

'No one questions the basic assumption—that the good life consists of servicing bigger and better bombers.'—*MFB*

Bomber's Moon
US 1943 70m bw

An American pilot crashlands into Germany and makes for the coast. Modestly budgeted war adventure with conventional thrills.
George Montgomery, Annabella, Kent Taylor, Walter Kingsford, Martin Kosleck. Written by Kenneth Gamet; directed by 'Charles Fuhr' (Edward Ludwig and Harold Schuster); for TCF.

Bombshell***
US 1933 91m bw
MGM (Hunt Stromberg)
GB and aka title: *Blonde Bombshell*

A glamorous film star yearns for a new image.
Crackpot farce which even by today's standards moves at a fair clip and enabled the star to give her best comedy performance.

w *Jules Furthman, John Lee Mahin*, play Caroline Francke, Mack Crane d Victor Fleming ph Chester Lyons, Hal Rosson

Jean Harlow, Lee Tracy, Frank Morgan, Franchot Tone, Pat O'Brien, Ivan Lebedeff, Una Merkel, Ted Healy, Isabel Jewell, C. Aubrey Smith, Louise Beavers, Leonard Carey, Mary Forbes

Bon Voyage*
US 1962 133m Technicolor
Walt Disney (Bill Walsh, Ron Miller)

An American family spends a holiday in Paris. Simple-minded, overlong comedy of mishaps, with daddy finally trapped in the sewer. Smoothly done of its kind.

w Bill Walsh, *novel* Marrijane and Joseph Hayes d James Neilson ph William Snyder m Paul Smith

Fred MacMurray, Jane Wyman, Michael Callan, Deborah Walley, Jessie Royce Landis, Tommy Kirk, Ivan Desny

Bond Street

GB 1948 107m bw

ABP / World Screenplays (Anatole de Grunwald)

Four stories, each concerning an item of an expensive wedding trousseau.

Mild and laboured short story compendium.

w Anatole de Grunwald d Gordon Parry ph Otto Heller m Benjamin Frankel

Roland Young, Jean Kent, Paula Valenska, Kathleen Harrison, Derek Farr, *Kenneth Griffith*, Hazel Court, Ronald Howard
'Even a glimpse of actual Bond Street makes little contact with reality.'—*MFB*

Le Bonheur*

France 1965 79m Eastmancolor

Parc / Mag Bodard

A young carpenter is happy with his wife and family, happier still when he finds a mistress, whom he marries when his wife is found drowned.

Slight, good looking, ambivalent little fable which finally expires in a surfeit of style.

wd Agnès Varda ph Jean Rabier, Claude Beausoleil m Mozart

Jean-Claude Drouot, Claire Drouot, Marie-France Boyer

Bonjour Tristesse*

GB 1957 93m Technicolor Cinemascope

(Columbia) Wheel Films (Otto Preminger)

A teenage girl becomes involved with her sophisticated father's amours and causes the death of his would-be mistress.

The novel's rather repellent characters are here played like royal personages against a background of Riviera opulence. The result is very odd but often entertaining, especially when it slips into self-parody.

w Arthur Laurents, *novel* Françoise Sagan d Otto Preminger ph *Georges Périnal* m Georges Auric pd Roger Furse

David Niven, Deborah Kerr, Jean Seberg, Mylene Demongeot, Geoffrey Horne, Juliette Greco, Martita Hunt, Walter Chiari, Jean Kent, Roland Culver
'An elegant, ice-cold charade of emotions.'—*Judith Crist*
'Sagan not so much translated as traduced—opened out, smartened up, the sickness overlaid with Riviera suntan.'—*Alexander Walker*

'Long, untidy, muddled and mushy.'—*Financial Times*
† Shot in monochrome for Paris, colour for the Riviera.

La Bonne Soupe

France / Italy 1963 97m bw

Belstar / Du Siècle / Dear Film (André Hakim)

A high-class prostitute tells her life story.

A saucy frolic complete with three-in-a-bed and rapidly closing doors; quite enjoyable of its kind.

wd Robert Thomas, *play* Félicien Marceau ph Roger Hubert m Raymond le Sénéchal

Annie Girardot, Marie Bell, Gérard Blain, Bernard Blier, Jean-Claude Brialy, Claude Dauphin, Sacha Distel, Daniel Gélin, Blanchette Brunoy, Jane Marken, Raymond Péllégrin. Franchot Tone

Bonnie and Clyde****

US 1967 111m Technicolor

Warner / Seven Arts / Tatira / Hiller (*Warren Beatty*)

In the early thirties, a car thief and the daughter of his intended victim team up to become America's most feared and ruthless bank robbers.

Technically brilliant evocation of sleepy mid-America at the time of the public enemies, using every kind of cinematic trick including fake snapshots, farcical interludes, dreamy soft-focus and a jazzy score. For all kinds of reasons a very influential film which even made extreme violence quite fashionable (and very bloody it is).

w *David Newman, Robert Benton* d *Arthur Penn* ph *Burnett Guffey* m *Charles Strouse*, using 'Foggy Mountain Breakdown' by Flatt and Scruggs

Warren Beatty, Faye Dunaway, Gene Hackman, Estelle Parsons, *Michael J. Pollard*, Dub Taylor, Denver Pyle, Gene Wilder
'They're young . . . they're in love . . . and they kill people!'—*publicity*
'It is a long time since we have seen an American film so perfectly judged.'—*MFB*
'. . . all to the rickety twang of a banjo and a saturation in time and place.'—*Judith Crist*
'The formula is hayseed comedy bursting sporadically into pyrotechnical bloodshed and laced with sentimental pop-Freudianism.'—*John Simon*
'A film from which we shall date reputations and innovations in the American cinema.'—*Alexander Walker*

AA: Burnett Guffey; Estelle Parsons
AAN: best picture; David Newman, Robert
Benton; Arthur Penn; Warren Beatty; Faye
Dunaway; Gene Hackman; Michael J. Pollard

Bonnie Prince Charlie
GB 1948   140m approx (later cut to
    118m)   Technicolor
British Lion / London Films (Edward Black)

The hope of the Stuarts returns from exile but
is eventually forced to flee again.
Good highland photography combines with
appalling studio sets, an initially confused
narrative, a draggy script and uneasy
performances to produce an ill-fated attempt
at a British historical epic. Alexander Korda,
who masterminded it, sulked in public at the
critical roasting, but on this occasion the critics
were right.

w Clemence Dane d Anthony Kimmins
ph Robert Krasker m Ian Whyte

David Niven, Margaret Leighton, Jack
Hawkins, Judy Campbell, Morland Graham,
Finlay Currie, John Laurie

'I have a sense of wonder about this film,
beside which *The Swordsman* seems like a
dazzling work of veracity and art. It is that
London Films, having surveyed the finished
thing, should not have quietly scrapped it.'—
Richard Winnington

'The picture is not lacking in moments of
unconscious levity, what with David Niven
rallying his hardy Highlanders to his standard
in a voice hardly large enough to summon a
waiter.'—*New Yorker*

'Time has made it the film industry's biggest
joke. But the joke turns a little sour when one
reflects how extravagance, recklessness and
sheer bungling administration during the fat
and prosperous years left the British film
industry so poor and vulnerable when the hard
times came along.'—*Gerald Garrett, 1975*

Bonnie Scotland**
US 1935   80m   bw
MGM / Hal Roach

Two Americans journey to Scotland to collect
a non-existent inheritance, then follow their
friend in the army and wind up in India.
Generally disappointing star comedy which
still contains excellent sequences when it is not
vainly trying to preserve interest in a boring
plot. An obvious parody on *Lives of a Bengal
Lancer*, released earlier that year; Scotland
has almost nothing to do with it.

w Frank Butler, Jeff Moffitt d James Horne
ph Art Lloyd, Walter Lundin

Stan Laurel, Oliver Hardy, James Finlayson,
Daphne Pollard, William Janney, June Lang

The Boogie Man Will Get You
US 1944   66m   bw
Columbia

Bodies accumulate when mad doctors get to
work creating supermen in a small village.
Desperately unfunny spoof notable only for
the fact that it was attempted with these
players and at that time.

w Edwin Blum d Lew Landers ph Colbert
Clark md Morris Stoloff

Boris Karloff, Peter Lorre, Maxie
Rosenbloom, Jeff Donnell, Larry Parks,
Maude Eburne, Don Beddoe

Boom!
GB 1968   113m   Technicolor
    Panavision
Universal / World Film Services / Moon
    Lake Productions (John Heyman,
    Norman Priggen)

On the volcanic Mediterranean island which
she owns, a dying millionairess plans to take as
her last lover a wandering poet who is the
angel of death.
Pretentious, boring nonsense, showing that
when talent goes awry it certainly goes boom.

w Tennessee Williams, from his play *The Milk
Train Doesn't Stop Here Any More* d Joseph
Losey ph Douglas Slocombe m John Barry

Elizabeth Taylor, Richard Burton, *Noel
Coward*, Michael Dunn, Joanna Shimkus

Boom Town**
US 1940   120m   bw
MGM (Sam Zimbalist)

Two friendly oil drillers strike it rich.
Enjoyable four-star, big-studio product of its
time: world-wide entertainment of assured
success, with a proven mix of romance, action,
drama and comedy.

w John Lee Mahin, *story* James Edward
Grant d Jack Conway ph Harold Rosson
m Franz Waxman ad Cedric Gibbons

Clark Gable, Spencer Tracy, Claudette
Colbert, Hedy Lamarr, *Frank Morgan*, Lionel
Atwill, Chill Wills

'Western high jinks, a wee child, and
courtroom speeches about individual
enterprise constitute the various come-ons in a
scrambled and inept picture.'—*New York
Herald Tribune*

'More colourful action in the oil fields and
less agitation indoors might have made it a
great picture.'—*Bosley Crowther*

AAN: Harold Rosson

Boomerang***
US 1947 88m bw
TCF (Louis de Rochemont)

In a New England town, a clergyman is shot dead on the street. The DA prevents an innocent man from being convicted, but cannot track down the guilty party.
Incisive real life thriller: based on a true case, it was shot in an innovative documentary style which was much copied, and justice is not seen to be done, though the murderer is known to the audience. A milestone movie of its kind.

w Richard Murphy d Elia Kazan ph Norbert Brodine *m* David Buttolph

Dana Andrews, Jane Wyatt, Lee J. Cobb, Cara Williams, Arthur Kennedy, Sam Levene, Taylor Holmes, Robert Keith, Ed Begley
'A study of integrity, beautifully developed by Dana Andrews against a background of political corruption and chicanery that is doubly shocking because of its documentary understatement.'—*Richard Winnington*
'For the first time in many a moon we are treated to a picture that gives a good example of a typical small American city—the people, their way of living, their mode of government, the petty politics practised, the power of the press.'—*Frank Ward, National Board of Review*
AAN: Richard Murphy

Boots Malone
US 1952 103m bw
Columbia (Milton Holmes)

A would-be jockey tags along with a down-at-heel agent who gets him work and finally persuades him not to throw a crooked race.
Dullish racetrack melodrama bogged down by repetitive and unsympathetic plot twists.

w Milton Holmes d William Dieterle ph Charles Lawton *m* Elmer Bernstein

William Holden, Johnny Stewart, Stanley Clements, Basil Ruysdael, Carl Benton Reid, Ed Begley, Henry Morgan

Border Incident
US 1949 93m bw
MGM (Nicholas Nayfack)

Police stop the illegal immigration of labourers from Mexico.
Routine semi-documentary cops and robbers, well enough made.

w John C. Higgins d Anthony Mann ph John Alton *m* André Previn

Ricardo Montalban, George Murphy, Howard da Silva, James Mitchell, Alfonso Bedoya

Borderline
US 1980 97m colour
ITC (Martin Starger)

A Mexican border patrolman chases illegal immigrants and the big time crooks making money out of them.
Routine, quite effective action programmer.

w Steve Kline, Jerrold Freedman d Jerrold Freedman *ph* Tak Fujimoto *m* Gil Melle

Charles Bronson, Bruno Kirby, Karmin Murcelo, Michael Learner, Ed Harris

Bordertown*
US 1935 90m bw
Warner (Robert Lord)

In a North Mexican town, a shabby lawyer becomes infatuated with the neurotic wife of a businessman.
Satisfying melodrama whose plot climax was later borrowed for *They Drive by Night.*

w Laird Doyle, Wallace Smith, *novel* Carroll Graham *d* Archie Mayo *ph* Tony Gaudio

Paul Muni, Bette Davis, Margaret Lindsay, Eugene Pallette, Robert Barrat, Henry O'Neill, Hobart Cavanaugh
† *Blowing Wild* (qv) was also a partial uncredited remake.

Born Again
US 1978 110m Technicolor
Robert L. Munger / Frank Capra Jnr

Charles Colson, sent to prison after Watergate, becomes a devout Christian.
Part evangelism, part reconstruction through rose-tinted spectacles; not particularly entertaining or instructive as either.

w Walter Block *d* Irving Rapper *ph* Harry Stradling Jnr *m* Les Baxter

Dean Jones, Anne Francis, Jay Robinson, Dana Andrews, Raymond St Jacques, George Brent, Harry Spillman (as Nixon)

Born Free**
GB 1965 95m Technicolor Panavision
Columbia / Open Road (Carl Foreman)

A Kenyan game warden and his wife rear three lion cubs, one of which eventually presents them with a family.
Irresistible animal shots salvage this rather flabbily put together version of a bestselling book. An enormous commercial success, it was followed by the even thinner *Living Free*, by a TV series, and by several semi-professional documentaries.

w Gerald L. C. Copley, *book* Joy Adamson *d* James Hill *ph* Kenneth Talbot *m John Barry*

Virginia McKenna, Bill Travers, Geoffrey Keen

AA: John Barry; title song (*m* John Barry, *ly* Don Black)

Born Losers

US 1967   112m   colour
AIP (Delores Taylor)

California teeny-boppers claim to have been gang-raped by wandering motorcyclists. Teenage shocker, only notable for its credits, and for being the first Billy Jack film.

wd Tom Laughlin   *ph* Gregory Sandor

Tom Laughlin, Jane Russell, Elizabeth James, Jeremy Slate, William Wellman Jnr

Born to be Bad

US 1934   61m   bw
Twentieth Century (William Goetz, Raymond Griffith)

A girl schemes to seduce the man who has adopted her illegitimate son.
Batty mother-love melodrama.

w Ralph Graves   *d* Lowell Sherman
ph Barney McGill   *m* Alfred Newman

Loretta Young, Cary Grant, Jackie Kelk, Henry Travers, Russell Hopton, Andrew Tombes, Harry Green

Born to be Bad

US 1950   94m   bw
RKO (Robert Sparks)

An ambitious girl marries a millionaire but continues her affair with a novelist; finally both men discover her true character.
Tentative bad girl novelette, just about passable.

w Edith Sommer, *novel* All Kneeling by Anne Parrish   *d* Nicholas Ray   *ph* Nicholas Musuraca   *m* Frederick Hollander

Joan Fontaine, Robert Ryan, Zachary Scott, Joan Leslie, Mel Ferrer

Born to Dance*

US 1936   108m   bw
MGM (Jack Cummings)

A sailor meets a girl in New York.
Well remembered musical with good numbers but a rather lame look.

w Jack McGowan, Sid Silvers, B. G. De Sylva   *d* Roy del Ruth   *ph* Ray June   *songs* Cole Porter

Eleanor Powell, James Stewart, Virginia Bruce, Una Merkel, Sid Silvers, Frances Langford, Raymond Walburn, *Reginald Gardiner*, Buddy Ebsen

AAN: song 'I've Got You Under My Skin'

Born to Kill*

US 1947   92m   bw
RKO
GB title: *Lady of Deceit*

A psychotic involves his new wife in his criminal pursuits.
Unusual, heavy-going, well acted melodrama.

w Eve Greene, Richard Macauley   *d* Robert Wise   *ph* Robert de Grasse   *m* Paul Sawtell

Lawrence Tierney, Claire Trevor, Walter Slezak, Philip Terry, Elisha Cook Jnr

Born to Love

US 1931   84m   bw
RKO

During World War I a nurse bears the child of an army pilot who is reported missing; but he turns up after she has married an English milord.
A useful compendium of thirties romantic clichés, quite attractively packaged.

w Ernest Pascal   *d* Paul Stein   *ph* John Mescall

Constance Bennett, Joel McCrea, Paul Cavanagh, Frederick Kerr, Anthony Bushell, Louise Closser Hale, Edmond Breon, Mary Forbes

Born to Win

US 1971   89m   colour

A Times Square junkie with delusions of grandeur runs out of luck. Dim low-life drama unworthy of its talent. George Segal, Paula Prentiss, Karen Black, Hector Elizondo. Written by David Scott Milton; directed by Ivan Passer; for UA.

Born Yesterday**

US 1950   103m   bw
Columbia (S. Sylvan Simon)

The ignorant ex-chorus girl mistress of a scrap iron tycoon takes English lessons, falls for her tutor, and politically outmanoeuvres her bewildered lover.
Pleasant film version of a cast-iron box office play, subtle and intelligent in all departments yet with a regrettable tendency to wave the flag.

w Albert Mannheimer, *play Garson Kanin*
d George Cukor   *ph* Joseph Walker
m Frederick Hollander

Judy Holliday, Broderick Crawford, William Holden, Howard St John

† The original choices for the Judy Holliday role were Rita Hayworth and Jean Parker (who had played it on tour).

AA: Judy Holliday
AAN: best picture; Albert Mannheimer;
George Cukor

Borsalino*

France / Italy 1970   126m   Eastmancolor
Adel-Marianne-Mars (Alain Delon)

In the thirties two Marseilles gangsters become
firm friends and join forces.
Semi-spoof, but with 'real' blood, and period
atmosphere laid on thick. The stars just about
keep it ticking over.

w Jean-Claude Carrière, Claude Sautet,
Jacques Deray, Jean Cau d Jacques Deray
ph Jean-Jacques Tarbès m Claude Bolling

Jean-Paul Belmondo, Alain Delon, Michel
Bouquet, Catherine Rouvel, Corinne
Marchand

'Rather like a Hollywood musical where
someone has forgotten to insert the production
numbers.'—*MFB*

The Boss*

US 1956   89m   bw
UA / Frank N. Seltzer

After World War I, a ne'er-do-well becomes a
corrupt small town political boss.
Low budgeted, complexly plotted,
occasionally quite powerful and efficient crime
melodrama.

w Ben L. Parry d Byron Haskin ph Hal
Mohr

John Payne, William Bishop, Gloria McGhee,
Doe Avedon, Joe Flynn

Boston Blackie

An American second feature series made by
Columbia between 1941 and 1949. There had
been silent films about the character, a
reformed crook and con man who has to solve
crimes because he is suspected by the law.
Cheap but sometimes vigorous productions,
they had a loyal following, and starred Chester
Morris with George E. Stone as his assistant
the Runt.

The titles were:

1941: MEET BOSTON BLACKIE,
CONFESSIONS OF BOSTON BLACKIE
1942: ALIAS BOSTON BLACKIE,
BOSTON BLACKIE GOES TO
HOLLYWOOD
1943: AFTER MIDNIGHT WITH BOSTON
BLACKIE
1944: ONE MYSTERIOUS NIGHT
1945: BOSTON BLACKIE BOOKED ON
SUSPICION, BOSTON BLACKIE'S
RENDEZVOUS

1946: A CLOSE CALL FOR BOSTON
BLACKIE, THE PHANTOM THIEF
1947: BOSTON BLACKIE AND THE LAW
1948: TRAPPED BY BOSTON BLACKIE
1949: BOSTON BLACKIE'S CHINESE
VENTURE
† A television series starring Kent Taylor
followed in 1951.

The Boston Strangler**

US 1968   118m   De Luxe   Panavision
TCF (Robert Fryer)

A semi-factual account of the sex maniac who
terrified Boston in the mid-sixties.
Ambitious *policier* rendered less effective by
pretentious writing and flashy treatment,
including multi-image sequences; the
investigation is more interesting than the
psychoanalysis.

w Edward Anhalt, *book* Gerold Frank
d Richard Fleischer ph Richard Kline
m Lionel Newman

Henry Fonda, *Tony Curtis* (as the murderer),
George Kennedy, Mike Kellin, Hurd Hatfield,
Murray Hamilton, Sally Kellerman, Jeff
Corey, George Voskovec

Botany Bay

US 1952   94m   Technicolor
Paramount (Joseph Sistrom)

On a convict ship in 1787 an American student
unjustly accused of robbery clashes with the
brutal captain for the favours of the only
woman aboard.
Cramped and brutal action melodrama, a
let-down considering the talent involved.

w Jonathan Latimer, *novel* Charles Nordhof
and James Hall d John Farrow ph John
Seitz m Franz Waxman

James Mason, Alan Ladd, Patricia Medina,
Cedric Hardwicke, Murray Matheson,
Jonathan Harris

The Bottom of the Bottle

US 1956   86m   Eastmancolor
   Cinemascope
TCF (Buddy Adler)
GB title: *Beyond the River*

A wealthy attorney is visited by his drunken
brother, on the run from the police and
needing help to escape into Mexico.
Dreary drama in muddy colour, a clearly
misguided enterprise.

w Sydney Boehm, *novel* Georges Simenon
d Henry Hathaway ph Lee Garmes m Leigh
Harline

Joseph Cotten, Van Johnson, Ruth Roman,
Jack Carson

Bottoms Up
US 1934   85m   bw
Fox (B. G. De Sylva)

A slick promoter in Hollywood disguises his pals as British nobility and gets them lucrative jobs.
Mild musical with a rather interesting cast.

w B. G. De Sylva, David Butler, Sid Silvers
d David Butler ph Arthur Miller
md Constantin Bakaleinikoff

Spencer Tracy, Pat Patterson, John Boles, Harry Green, Herbert Mundin, Sid Silvers, Thelma Todd, Robert Emmett O'Connor
'For those who like to laugh and sing when tears get in their eyes!'—*publicity*

Bottoms Up
GB 1960   89m   bw

A seedy schoolmaster passes off his bookie's son as an eastern prince. Rambling film version of a successful TV series, *Whacko!*
Jimmy Edwards, Arthur Howard. Written by Frank Muir and Denis Norden; directed by Mario Zampi; for Transocean / Warner.

Le Boucher**
France / Italy 1969   94m   Eastmancolor
La Boétie / Euro International (André Génovès)
aka: *The Butcher*

Murders in a small French town are traced to the inoffensive-seeming young butcher who is courting the local schoolmistress.
Curious, mainly charming film which can't make up its mind whether to be an eccentric character study or a Hitchcock thriller, but has its moments as each.

wd *Claude Chabrol ph Jean Rabier m* Pierre Jansen

Stéphane Audran, Jean Yanne, Antonio Passalia, Mario Beccaria
'A thriller, but a superlative example of the genre.'—*Times*

Boudu Sauvé des Eaux***
France 1932   87m   bw
Michel Simon / Jean Gehret
aka: *Boudu Saved from Drowning*

A scruffy tramp is not grateful for being rescued from suicide, and plagues the family who invite him to stay.
A minor classic of black comedy, interesting equally for its characterizations, its acting, and its film technique.

wd *Jean Renoir, play* René Fauchois
ph Marcel Lucien m from Raphael and Johann Strauss

Michel Simon, Charles Grandval, Marcelle Hainia, Séverine Lerczinska, Jean Dasté, Jacques Becker
'A beautifully rhythmed film that makes one nostalgic for the period when it was made.'—*New Yorker, 1977*

Bought
US 1931   70m   bw
Warner

An ambitious working girl rebels against her slum existence and seeks a rich man.
Typical star vehicle of its time, with a predictable and unlikely change of heart for a finale.

w Charles Kenyon, Raymond Griffith, *novel* Jackdaw's Strut by Harriet Henry d Archie Mayo ph Ray June

Constance Bennett, Ben Lyon, Richard Bennett, Dorothy Peterson, Ray Milland, Doris Lloyd, Maude Eburne

Bound for Glory*
US 1976   148m   De Luxe   Panavision
UA / Robert F. Blumhofe, Harold Leventhal

In 1936 Woody Guthrie leaves the Texas dust bowl for California, and after various hardships his musical talent is recognized.
Care and occasional beauty in the photography do not obscure memories of *The Grapes of Wrath*, which told much the same story more dramatically and succinctly, and with less earnestness and self-pity.

w Robert Getchell, from Guthrie's autobiography d Hal Ashby ph *Haskell Wexler m* Leonard Rosenman *songs* Woody Guthrie pd Michael Haller

David Carradine, Ronny Cox, Melinda Dillon, Gail Strickland, John Lehne
'The movie spends two-and-a-half hours and seven million dollars gazing wistfully at a little man and a big country, and it ends up prettily embalming them both.'—*Janet Massin, Newsweek*
AA: Haskell Wexler; Leonard Rosenman
AAN: best picture; Robert Getchell

The Bounty Hunter
US 1954   79m   WarnerColor

Three respectable citizens are unmasked as masterminds behind a series of train robberies.
Predictable but enjoyable star action farc.
Randolph Scott, Dolores Dorn, Marie Windsor, Ernest Borgnine. Written by Winston Miller; directed by André de Toth; for Warners.

The Bowery***
US 1933   92m   bw
Twentieth Century (Darryl F. Zanuck)
(Raymond Griffith, William Goetz)

In nineties New York, two boisterous rivals
settle their differences after one has jumped
off the Brooklyn Bridge for a bet.
Roistering saga of cross and double cross on
the seamy side, splendidly vigorous in acting
and treatment.

*w Howard Estabrook, James Gleason d Raoul
Walsh ph Barney McGill m Alfred Newman
ad Richard Day*

Wallace Beery, George Raft, Pert Kelton,
Jackie Cooper, Fay Wray, Herman Bing

The Bowery Boys

A cheap and cheerful series of American
second features, immensely popular between
1946 and 1958, these adventures of a group of
ageing Brooklyn layabouts had their origin in
the 1937 film *Dead End*, from which the Dead
End Kids graduated to other features at
Warner: *Crime School, They Made Me a
Criminal, Angels with Dirty Faces, Angels
Wash their Faces*, etc. A couple of the 'boys'
then defected to Universal and made *Little
Tough Guy* and a series of half a dozen
subsequent pictures; while in 1940 Monogram
took a couple more and built up another group
called the East Side Kids. In 1946 a formal
merger of talent at Monogram consolidated
the remaining members into the Bowery Boys.
The members were Leo Gorcey, Huntz Hall,
Bobby Jordan, Gabriel Dell (all from the
Dead End Kids), Bernard Gorcey, David
Gorcey, Billy Benedict, and Bennie Bartlett.
The films are:

1946: IN FAST COMPANY, BOWERY
BOMBSHELL, LIVE WIRES, SPOOK
BUSTERS, MR HEX
1947: BOWERY BUCKAROOS, HARD
BOILED MAHONEY, NEWS HOUNDS,
ANGELS' ALLEY
1948: JINX MONEY, SMUGGLER'S
COVE, TROUBLE MAKERS
1949: ANGELS IN DISGUISE, FIGHTING
FOOLS, HOLD THAT BABY, MASTER
MINDS
1950: BLONDE DYNAMITE, BLUES
BUSTERS, LUCKY LOSERS, TRIPLE
TROUBLE
1951: BOWERY BATALLION, CRAZY
OVER HORSES, GHOST CHASERS,
LET'S GO NAVY
1952: FEUDIN' FOOLS, HERE COME THE
MARINES, HOLD THAT LINE, NO
HOLDS BARRED

1953: CLIPPED WINGS, JALOPY, LOOSE
IN LONDON, PRIVATE EYES
1954: THE BOWERY BOYS MEET THE
MONSTERS, JUNGLE GENTS, PARIS
PLAYBOYS
1955: BOWERY TO BAGDAD, HIGH
SOCIETY, JAIL BUSTERS, SPY CHASERS
1956: DIG THAT URANIUM, CRASHING
LAS VEGAS, FIGHTING TROUBLE, HOT
SHOTS
1957: SPOOK CHASERS, HOLD THAT
HYPNOTIST, LOOKING FOR DANGER
1958: UP IN SMOKE, IN THE MONEY.

Bowery to Broadway
US 1944   94m   bw
Universal (John Grant)

In the nineties, a Bowery songstress makes it
to the big time.
Simple-minded musical in which the drama has
no drive and the guest stars are given inferior
material.

*w Joseph Lytton, Arthur T. Horman
d Charles Lamont ph Charles Van Enger
md Edward Ward*

Maria Montez, Turhan Bey, Susanna Foster,
Jack Oakie, Donald Cook, Louise Allbritton,
Andy Devine, Rosemary de Camp, Ann
Blyth, Donald O'Connor, Peggy Ryan, Frank
McHugh, Leo Carrillo, Evelyn Ankers,
Mantan Moreland

Boxcar Bertha*
US 1972   88m   De Luxe
AIP (Roger Corman)

In early thirties Arkansas, an unhappy girl
falls in with gangsters and train robbers.
Competent imitation of *Bonnie and Clyde*.

*w Joyce H. and John W. Corrington d Martin
Scorsese ph John Stephens m Gilb Guilbeau,
Thad Maxwell*

Barbara Hershey, David Carradine, Barry
Primus, Bernie Casey, John Carradine

A Boy a Girl and a Bike
GB 1947   92m   bw
Gainsborough (Ralph Keene)

Romantic jealousies arise between members of
a Yorkshire cycling club.
Mild comedy drama with the advantage of
fresh air locations.

w Ted Willis d Ralph Smart ph Ray Elton

John McCallum, Honor Blackman, Patrick
Holt, Diana Dors, Leslie Dwyer, Thora Hird,
Anthony Newley, Megs Jenkins, Maurice
Denham

The Boy and the Bridge
GB 1959 91m bw
Xanadu (Kevin McClory)

A boy who believes he has committed a murder hides in the ramparts of Tower Bridge. This tiny fable adds up to very weak entertainment, despite inventive photography, because it has virtually no plot development.

w Geoffrey Orme, Kevin McClory, Desmond O'Donovan d Kevin McClory ph Ted Scaife m Malcolm Arnold

Ian MacLaine, Liam Redmond, James Hayter, Norman Macowan, Geoffrey Keen, Jack MacGowran, Royal Dano, Rita Webb

Boy, Did I Get a Wrong Number
US 1966 99m De Luxe
UA / Edward Small (George Beck)

Trying to phone his wife, an estate agent gets involved with a runaway actress.
Lifeless and generally resistible star comedy, the first of several hard and unfunny vehicles for an ageing Bob Hope seeming to hark back to the least attractive aspects of burlesque rather than the sympathetic wisecracking which suits him best.

w Burt Styler, Albert E. Lewin, George Kennett d George Marshall ph Lionel Lindon m Richard Lasalle ly By Dunham

Bob Hope, Elke Sommer, Phyllis Diller, Marjorie Lord, Cesare Danova, Benny Baker

The Boy Friend*
GB 1971 125m Metrocolor Panavision
MGM / Russflix (Ken Russell)

On a wet Wednesday afternoon in Portsmouth in the late twenties, a tatty company with backstage problems puts on an empty-headed musical.
Russell the mastermind effectively destroys Sandy Wilson's charming period pastiche, sending up all the numbers (via badly staged dream sequences on the wrong shape screen) in a Busby Berkeley manner which had not yet been invented. Moments do work, but a non-star doesn't help, and the whole thing is an artistic disaster of some significance both to Russell's career and to the cinema of the early seventies.

w Ken Russell, from Sandy Wilson's musical play d Ken Russell ph David Watkin md Ian Whittaker, Peter Greenwell, Peter Maxwell Davies pd Tony Walton

Twiggy, Christopher Gable, Max Adrian, Tommy Tune, Barbara Windsor, Moyra Fraser, Bryan Pringle, Vladek Sheybal, Antonia Ellis, Glenda Jackson

'The glittering, joyless numbers keep coming at you: you never get any relief from Russell's supposed virtuosity.'—New Yorker, 1977

AAN: Ian Whittaker, Peter Greenwell, Peter Maxwell Davies

The Boy from Oklahoma*
US 1953 88m Warnercolor
Warner (David Weisbart)

A genial plainsman studying law becomes sheriff of a small town and uncovers its mayor as a killer.
Modest, pleasing western with the star imitating his father.

w Frank David, Winston Miller d Michael Curtiz ph Robert Burks m Max Steiner

Will Rogers Jnr, Nancy Olson, Lon Chaney Jnr, Anthony Caruso, Wallace Ford, Clem Bevans, Merv Griffin

Boy Meets Girl**
US 1938 86m bw
Warner (George Abbott)

Two crazy Hollywood scenario writers make a star of an infant yet unborn.
Freewheeling film version of a hilarious play: fine crazy comedy and excellent Hollywood satire.

w Bella and Sam Spewack, from their play d Lloyd Bacon ph Sol Polito m Leo Forbstein

James Cagney, Pat O'Brien, Marie Wilson, Ralph Bellamy, Frank McHugh, Dick Foran, Bruce Lester, Ronald Reagan, James Stephenson

Boy on a Dolphin*
US 1957 111m Eastmancolor
Cinemascope
TCF (Samuel G. Engel)

A Greek girl diver discovers a sunken artifact of great value and the news spreads to an American archaeologist and an unscrupulous collector.
Likeable, sunswept Mediterranean adventure romance marred by the miscasting of the male lead.

w Ivan Moffatt, Dwight Taylor, novel David Divine d Jean Negulesco ph Milton Krasner m Hugo Friedhofer md Lionel Newman

Alan Ladd, Sophia Loren, Clifton Webb, Laurence Naismith, Alexis Minotis, Jorge Mistral

AAN: Hugo Friedhofer

The Boy who Cried Werewolf
US 1973   93m   Technicolor

On a camping trip, a boy and his father are attacked by a werewolf, and later on dad starts acting mighty strange . . . Disappointingly straight rewrite of the old hokum. Kerwin Mathews, Elaine Devry, Scott Sealey. Written by Bob Homel; directed by Nathan Juran; for Universal.

The Boy with Green Hair
US 1948   82m   Technicolor
RKO (Dore Schary)

When he hears that his parents were killed in an air raid, a boy's hair turns green; other war orphans encourage him to parade himself publicly as an image of the horror and futility of war.
Muddled, pretentious and unpersuasive fantasy, typical of this producer's do-goodery. One of those oddities which make Hollywood endearing, but not very entertaining apart from Pat O'Brien's garrulous grandpa.

w Ben Barzman, Alfred Lewis Levitt, *story* Betsy Beaton d Joseph Losey ph George Barnes m Leigh Harline
Dean Stockwell, Pat O'Brien, Robert Ryan, Barbara Hale

The Boys
GB 1962   123m   Cinemascope
Gala / Columbia (Sidney J. Furie)

Four boys are on trial for killing a garage attendant.
Elaborate courtroom drama with flashbacks, stars for counsel, a tricksy director, and about forty minutes too much footage.

w Stuart Douglass d Sidney J. Furie ph Gerald Gibbs m The Shadows
Richard Todd, Robert Morley, Felix Aylmer, Dudley Sutton, Ronald Lacey, Tony Garnett, Jess Conrad, Wilfrid Brambell, Allan Cuthbertson, Colin Gordon

The Boys From Brazil**
US / GB 1978   124m   De Luxe
ITC / Producer Circle (Martin Richards, Stanley O'Toole)

A renegade Nazi in hiding has a sinister plot to reconquer the world.
Suspense fantasy firmly based on a gripping book; excellent performances, but a shade too long.

w Heywood Gould, *novel* Ira Levin d Franklin Schaffner ph Henri Decaë m Jerry Goldsmith pd Gil Parrando

Gregory Peck, Laurence Olivier, James Mason, Lilli Palmer, Uta Hagen, Steven Buttenberg, Denholm Elliott, Rosemary Harris, John Dehner, John Rubenstein, Anne Meara, David Hurst, Michael Gough
AAN: Jerry Goldsmith; Laurence Olivier

The Boys from Syracuse*
US 1940   74m   bw
Universal (Jules Levey)

The Comedy of Errors with modern wisecracks, and a few songs.
Predictable well-drilled confusion arises from master and slave having identical twins, but the general tone is a bit flat for an adaptation from a hilarious Broadway success. Still, the songs are lively and the chariot race finale shows spirit.

w Leonard Spiegelgass, Charles Grayson, Paul Gerard Smith, from the play by George Abbott and William Shakespeare d Edward A. Sutherland ph Joseph Valentine m Frank Skinner md Charles Previn songs Rodgers and Hart
Allan Jones, Joe Penner, Charles Butterworth, Rosemary Lane, Irene Hervey, Martha Raye, Alan Mowbray
† The writing credit on screen ends: 'After a play by William Shakespeare . . . long, long after!'

Boys in Brown
GB 1949   84m   bw
Gainsborough (Antony Darnborough)

Life in a Borstal institution.
The stars make elderly boys, but Jack Warner is a cuddly governor. Boring and unpersuasive non-documentary fiction in Britain's most tiresome style.

wd Montgomery Tully, *play* Reginald Beckwith ph Gordon Lang, Cyril Bristow m Doreen Carwithen
Jack Warner, Dirk Bogarde, Michael Medwin, Jimmy Hanley, Richard Attenborough, Alfie Bass, Barbara Murray, Thora Hird
† Made by the Independent Frame method, which blended real backgrounds with studio sets.

The Boys in Company C
Hong Kong 1977   125m   Technicolor
         Panavision
Golden Harvest (Andre Morgan)

Five marines find their lives changed by the Vietnam war.
Crude action melodrama.

w Rick Natkin, Sidney J. Furie d Sidney J. Furie ph Godfrey Godar m Jaime Mendoza-Nava

Stan Shaw, Andrew Stevens, James Canning, Michael Lembeck, Craig Wasson, James Whitmore Jnr
'Laden with barrack room dialogue and played at the enlisted man's level.'—*Variety*
'An exploitation war movie, like dirty TV.'—*New Yorker*

The Boys in the Band*
US 1970   120m   Technicolor
Cinema Center / Leo (Mart Crowley, Kenneth Utt)

Tempers fray and true selves are revealed when a heterosexual is accidentally invited to a homosexual party.
Careful but claustrophobic filming of a Broadway play, which at the screen's closer quarters becomes overpowering well before the end.

w Mart Crowley, from his play d William Friedkin ph Arthur J. Ornitz m none

Leonard Frey, Kenneth Nelson, Cliff Gorman, Frederick Combs, Reuben Greene, Robert La Tourneaux, Laurence Luckinbill, Keith Prentice, Peter White
'They crack jokes while their hearts are breaking.'—*New Yorker*

Boys' Night Out
US 1962   115m   Metrocolor
Cinemascope
MGM / Filmways (Martin Ransohoff)

Three married men and their bachelor friend share a flat and a 'mistress'.
Would-be saucy comedy in which nothing sexy ever happens and the helpless players are as witless as the script.

w Ira Wallach d Michael Gordon ph Arthur E. Arling m Frank de Vol

James Garner, Kim Novak, Tony Randall, Howard Duff, Howard Morris, Oscar Homolka, Janet Blair, Patti Page, Jessie Royce Landis

Boys' Town**
US 1938   93m   bw
MGM (John W. Considine Jnr)

The story of Father Flanagan and his school for juvenile delinquents.
Well-made, highly successful, but sentimental crowd pleaser.

w John Meehan, Dore Schary, *original story* Eleanor Griffin, Dore Schary d Norman Taurog ph Sidney Wagner m Edward Ward

Spencer Tracy, Mickey Rooney, Henry Hull, Gene Reynolds, Sidney Miller, Frankie Thomas, Bobs Watson, Tommy Noonan

'More laughs than Laurel and Hardy! More thrills than *Test Pilot*! More tears than *Captains Courageous*!'—*publicity*
AA: Eleanor Griffin, Dore Schary; Spencer Tracy
AAN: best picture; John Meehan, Dore Schary; Norman Taurog

The Brain
France / US 1969   115m   colour
Paramount (Alain Poiré)

A British colonel leads an international crew in an attempt to rob NATO.
Exhausting and generally misfiring international crook comedy.

w Gerard Oury, Marcel Julian, Daniele Thompson d Gerard Oury ph Vladimir Ivanov, Armand Thirard m Georges Delerue

David Niven, Jean-Paul Belmondo, Bourvil, Eli Wallach, Silvia Monti

Brainstorm
US 1965   110m   bw   Panavision
Warner / Kodima (William Conrad)

A passer-by saves a married woman from suicide, has an affair with her, and conspires to murder her husband. This accomplished, she leaves him and he goes insane.
Overlong thriller which starts off agreeably in the *Double Indemnity* vein; but goes slow and solemn around the half way mark.

w Mann Rubin d William Conrad ph Sam Leavitt m George Duning

Jeffrey Hunter, Anne Francis, Dana Andrews, Viveca Lindfors, Stacy Harris
'A sub-B potboiler for those who find comic books too intellectual.'—*Judith Crist*

The Bramble Bush
US 1960   105m   Technicolor
Warner / United States (Milton Sperling)

A doctor returns to his home town and finds himself involved in old tragedies including the mercy killing of his friend.
Sordid small-town melodrama in the *Peyton Place* vein, with adequate production values but dispiriting treatment.

w Milton Sperling, Philip Yordan, *novel* Charles Mergendahl d Daniel Petrie ph Lucien Ballard m Leonard Rosenman

Richard Burton, Barbara Rush, Jack Carson, Angie Dickinson, James Dunn, Tom Drake, Henry Jones, Frank Conroy, Carl Benton Reid, William Hansen

Branded
US 1950   104m   Technicolor
Paramount (Mel Epstein)

A gunman poses as a rancher's lost heir, but redeems himself by finding the real one. Competent, brisk western.

w Sydney Boehm, Cyril Hume *d* Rudolph Maté *ph* Charles Lang Jnr *m* Roy Webb

Alan Ladd, Charles Bickford, Mona Freeman, Robert Keith, Joseph Calleia, Peter Hansen, Selena Royle, Tom Tully

Brandy for the Parson*
GB 1951 79m bw
Group Three (Alfred O'Shaughnessy)

A couple on a yachting holiday find themselves unwittingly smuggling brandy into Britain.
Pleasant little sub-Ealing comedy with agreeable locations but not much drive.

w John Dighton, Walter Meade, *story* Geoffrey Household *d* John Eldridge *ph* Martin Curtis *m* John Addison

James Donald, Kenneth More, Jean Lodge, Frederick Piper, Charles Hawtrey, Michael Trubshawe, Alfie Bass, Reginald Beckwith

Brannigan*
GB 1975 111m De Luxe Panavision
UA / Wellborn (Jules Levy, Arthur Gardner)

A Chicago policeman is sent to London to pick up a gangster.
Cheerful crime pastiche and tour of London, quite an agreeable entertainment despite its obviously over-age star.

w Christopher Trumbo, Michael Butler, William P. McGivern, William Norton *d* Douglas Hickox *ph* Gerry Fisher *m* Dominic Frontière

John Wayne, Richard Attenborough, Judy Geeson, Mel Ferrer, John Vernon, Daniel Pilon, John Stride, James Booth, Barry Dennen

The Brasher Doubloon*
US 1946 72m bw
TCF
GB title: *The High Window*

Philip Marlowe investigates the theft of a rare coin and finds himself involved in a series of murders.
The poorest of the Chandler adaptations, previously filmed as *Time to Kill*, still contains good moments, though the star is lightweight and the production low-budget.

w Dorothy Bennett, *novel* The High Window by Raymond Chandler *d* John Brahm *ph* Lloyd Ahern *m* David Buttolph

George Montgomery, Nancy Guild, Florence Bates, Conrad Janis, Fritz Kortner

The Brass Bottle
US 1964 89m Eastmancolor
U-I / Scarus (Robert Arthur)

A young architect finds an old brass bottle which contains a troublesome genie.
Simple-minded farce with little invention and poor trickwork.

w Oscar Brodney, *novel* F. Anstey *d* Harry Keller *ph* Clifford Stine *m* Bernard Green *sp* Roswell Hoffman

Tony Randall, Burl Ives, Barbara Eden, Edward Andrews, Ann Doran

The Brass Monkey
GB 1948 84m bw

A radio singer thwarts the theft of a Buddhist idol. Flat thriller based round a radio 'discovery' programme. Carole Landis, Carroll Levis, Herbert Lom, Avril Angers, Ernest Thesiger. Written by Alec Coppel and Thornton Freeland; directed by Thornton Freeland; for Diadem / Alliance / UA. (Aka: *Lucky Mascot.*)

Brass Target
US 1978 111m Metrocolor
MGM (Berle Adams)

The alleged story behind the death of General Patton, who according to these sources was eliminated because he had discovered a bullion robbery attempt.
Good-looking but interminably complex and talkative, with nothing much for its star cast to do.

w Alvin Boretz, *novel* The Algonquin Project by Frederick Nolan *d* John Hough *ph* Tony Imi *m* Laurence Rosenthal

Sophia Loren, George Kennedy, Max Von Sydow, John Cassavetes, Patrick McGoohan, Robert Vaughn, Bruce Davison, Edward Herrmann, Ed Bishop

Brats*
US 1930 20m bw

Stan and Ollie have trouble baby-sitting their own mischievous kids. Fairly ambitious star comedy with trick sets and photography enabling Laurel and Hardy to play their own sons. About half the gags come off. Written by Leo McCarey, H. M. Walker and Hal Roach; directed by James Parrott; for Hal Roach.

The Bravados*
US 1958 98m Eastmancolor
Cinemascope
TCF (Herbert B. Swope)

A widower chases four killers who, he believes, raped and murdered his wife.

Dour western with a downbeat ending; production good, but entertainment uneasy.

w Philip Yordan, *novel* Frank O'Rourke *d* Henry King *ph* Leon Shamroy *m* Lionel Newman

Gregory Peck, Stephen Boyd, Joan Collins, Albert Salmi, Henry Silva, George Voskovec, Barry Coe, Lee Van Cleef

The Brave Bulls
US 1951   108m   bw
Columbia (Robert Rossen)

A Mexican matador regains his courage but loses his girl in a car crash.
Muddled narrative with dollops of bull-fighting mystique; a rather miserable movie despite effort all round.

w John Bright, *novel* Tom Lea *d* Robert Rossen *ph* James Wong Howe, Floyd Crosby

Mel Ferrer, Miroslava, Anthony Quinn, Eugene Iglesias

The Brave Don't Cry°
GB 1952   90m   bw
Group Three (John Baxter)

Over a hundred men are rescued in a Scottish mine disaster.
Semi-documentary based on a real incident: well done on a small budget, but hardly memorable.

w Montagu Slater *d* Philip Leacock *ph* Arthur Grant *m* none

John Gregson, Meg Buchanan, John Rae, Fulton Mackay, Andrew Keir, Russell Waters, Jameson Clark, Jean Anderson, Eric Woodburn

The Brave One°
US 1956   100m   Technicolor
   Cinemascope
King Brothers

A small boy saves the life of his pet bull when it is sent into the ring.
Mildly beguiling minor drama for those who adore small boys and bulls.

w Harry Franklin, Merrill G. White, *original story* Robert Rich *d* Irving Rapper *ph* Jack Cardiff *m* Victor Young

Michel Ray, Rodolfo Hoyos, Elsa Cardenas, Joi Lansing, Carlos Navarro

AA: Robert Rich. (There was much confusion when the mysterious Rich turned out to be Dalton Trumbo, who was blacklisted at the time.)

Brazil
US 1944   91m   bw
Republic (Robert Worth)

A lady novelist goes to Brazil for material; a local composer poses as her guide in order to pay her back for her previous remarks about his country.
Acceptable lower case musical with pleasant tunes and humour.

w Frank Gill Jnr, Laura Kerr *d* Joseph Santley *ph* Jack Marta *songs* Bob Russell and others *m* Walter Scharf

Virginia Bruce, Tito Guizar, Edward Everett Horton, Roy Rogers

AAN: song 'Rio de Janeiro' (*m* Ary Barrosa, *ly* Ned Washington); Walter Scharf

Breach of Promise
GB 1941   79m   bw

A girl chases the man she wants by filing a breach of promise suit against him. Dated but lively comedy with agreeable playing. Clive Brook, Judy Campbell, C. V. France, Margaret Allan, Percy Walsh. Written by Roland Pertwee; directed by Harold Huth and Roland Pertwee; for British Mercury / MGM.

Bread and Chocolate°
Italy 1973   112m   Eastmancolor
Verona Cinematografica (Maurizio Lodo-Fe)

An Italian waiter in Switzerland is accused of murder and indecent exposure.
Amusing and often pathetic account of an inveterate loser, its flavour impossible to define.

w Franco Brusati, Iaia Fiastri, Nino Manfredi *d* Franco Brusati *ph* Luciano Tovoli *md* Daniele Patrucchi

Nino Manfredi, Anna Karina, Johnny Dorelli, Paolo Turco

Bread, Love and Dreams°
Italy 1953   90m   bw
Titanus (Marcello Girosi)

The new sergeant of police in a small rural village comes looking for a wife.
Pleasant rather than exciting rural comedy which spun off a number of vaguely related sequels (*Bread, Love and Jealousy*, etc.).

w Luigi Comencini, *original story* Ettore Margadonna *d* Luigi Comencini *ph* Arturo Gallea *m* Alessandro Cicognini

Vittorio de Sica, Gina Lollobrigida, Marisa Merlini, Roberto Risso

AAN: Ettore Margadonna

Break of Hearts
US 1935   80m   bw
RKO (Pandro S. Berman)

A girl composer falls in love with a distinguished conductor who becomes a dipsomaniac.
Well acted soap opera, not really worthy of its stars.

w Sarah Y. Mason, Victor Heerman, Anthony Veiller d Philip Moeller ph Robert de Grasse m Max Steiner

Katharine Hepburn, Charles Boyer, Jean Hersholt, John Beal, Sam Hardy
'In spite of some capable acting, it lacks a certain compelling warmth. The audience's heart never breaks.'—*Eileen Creelman, New York Sun*

Break the News*
GB 1938   78m   bw
GFD / Jack Buchanan

A dancer arranges his partner's 'death' for publicity reasons but is sent to jail when the partner disappears.
Thin but lively comedy with a remarkable couple of song and dance men. Negative apparently lost.

w Geoffrey Kerr, *novel* La Mort en Fuite by Loid de Gouriadec d René Clair

Jack Buchanan, Maurice Chevalier, June Knight, Marta Labarr, Garry Marsh, Felix Aylmer, Robb Wilton
† Various remakes include *The Art of Love* (qv).

Breaker Morant*
Australia 1980   107m   Eastmancolor
    Panavision
South Australian Film Corporation
    (Matthew Carroll)

During the Boer War three Australian officers are courtmartialled for murdering prisoners.
Careful, moving military drama which gives a more sympathetic view of the facts than history does.

w Jonathan Hardy, Bruce Beresford, David Stevens, *play* Kenneth Ross d Bruce Beresford ph Donald McAlpine md Phil Cuneen

Edward Woodward, Jack Thompson, John Waters, Charles Tingwell, Terence Donovan, Vincent Ball
'It is impossible to suppress a feeling that the spirit of Stanley Kramer is abroad on the veldt.'—*Tim Pulleine, MFB*
AAN: screenplay

Breakfast at Tiffany's*
US 1961   115m   Technicolor
Paramount (Martin Jurow, Richard Shepherd)

A young New York writer has as neighbour the volatile Holly Golightly, a slightly crazy call girl with an exotic social and emotional life.
Impossibly cleaned up and asexual version of a light novel which tried to be the American *I Am a Camera*. Wild parties, amusing scenes and good cameos, but the pace is slow, the atmosphere is unconvincingly clean and luxurious, and the sentimentality kills it.

w George Axelrod, *novel* Truman Capote d Blake Edwards ph Franz Planer m Henry Mancini

Audrey Hepburn, George Peppard, Patricia Neal, Buddy Ebsen, Martin Balsam, *John McGiver* (as the Tiffany salesman), Mickey Rooney
AA: Henry Mancini; *song* 'Moon River' (*m* Henry Mancini, *ly* Johnny Mercer)
AAN: George Axelrod; Audrey Hepburn

Breakfast for Two*
US 1937   65m   bw
RKO (Edward Kaufman)

A Texas heiress turns a playboy into a businessman.
Star crazy comedy with some wildly funny scenes.

w Charles Kaufman, Paul Yawitz, Viola Brothers Shore d Alfred Santell ph J. Roy Hunt

Barbara Stanwyck, Herbert Marshall, Donald Meek, Glenda Farrell, Eric Blore, Etienne Girardot

Breakheart Pass*
US 1975   94m   De Luxe
UA / Elliott Kastner (Jerry Gershwin)

Various mysterious passengers on an 1873 train across the frozen west to Fort Humboldt turn out to have smuggling and murder in mind.
Botched murder mystery on wheels: there are some exciting scenes, but the plot makes little sense and the 'action finale' is muddled.

w Alistair MacLean, from his book d Tom Gries ph Lucien Ballard m Jerry Goldsmith

Charles Bronson, Ben Johnson, Richard Crenna, Jill Ireland, Charles Durning, Archie Moore, Ed Lauter

Breaking Away*
US 1979   101m   De Luxe
TCF (Peter Yates)

An imaginative teenager has trouble adjusting to adult life after high school.
Andy Hardy would have felt at home in this

fragmented comedy of the American hinterland; 1979 audiences found it a welcome relief from the stronger brews to which they had become accustomed.

w *Steve Tesich* d Peter Yates *ph* Matthew F. Leonetti *md* Lionel Newman

Dennis Christopher, Dennis Quaid, Daniel Stern, Jackie Earle Haley, Barbara Barrie, Paul Dooley

'Affection for the middle classes, the landscapes of Indiana, and bicycle racing.'— *New Yorker*

'It is not devoid of pleasures . . . but it fatally lacks a clear purpose and identity.'— *Geoff Brown, MFB*

† An unsuccessful TV series followed in 1980.

Breaking Glass
GB 1980   104m   Technicolor Panavision
GTO / Film and General (Dodi Fayed)

Vicissitudes of a pop band and of its singer who can't stand the pace.
Garish, freakish musical with unattractive characters strung along an oft-told tale. Some commendable vigour in the presentation, but it won't appeal to anybody over 21.

wd Brian Gibson *ph* Stephen Goldblatt *md* Tony Visconti

Hazel O'Connor, Phil Daniels, Jon Finch, Jonathan Pryce

The Breaking Point*
US 1950   97m   bw
Warner (Jerry Wald)

A charterboat owner becomes involved with crooks but turns them in when they have killed his friend.
Adequate if slightly humdrum attempt by Warners to atone for what they had done to a Hemingway novel, the infidelity of *To Have and Have Not* and the unauthorized variation of *Key Largo*. (See also: *The Gun Runners*.)

w Ranald MacDougall, *novel* To Have and Have Not by Ernest Hemingway *d* Michael Curtiz *ph* Ted McCord *m* (uncredited) William Lava, Max Steiner

John Garfield, Patricia Neal, Phyllis Thaxter, Juano Hernandez, Wallace Ford, Edmon Ryan, William Campbell

Breaking Point
Canada 1976   92m   colour   Panavision
TCF / Astral Belle Vue (Harold Greenberg, Harold Pariser)

An innocent witness against the Mafia takes off against them vigilante style when his partner is murdered and his own life threatened.
Comic strip thuggery with performances to match; plenty of excitement for toughies.

w Roger E. Swaybill, Stanley Mann *d* Bob Clark *ph* Marc Champion *m* David McLey

Bo Svenson, Robert Culp, John Colicos, Belinda J. Montgomery, Stephen Young

Breakthrough
US 1950   91m   bw
Warner (Bryan Foy)

Adventures of a US army unit in Normandy after D-Day.
Routine low-budgeter which improves after a slow start.

w Bernard Girard, Ted Sherdeman, Joseph I. Breen Jnr *d* Lewis Seiler *ph* Edwin DuPar *m* William Lava

David Brian, John Agar, Frank Lovejoy, William Campbell, Paul Picerni, Greg McClure, Edward Norris, Matt Willis, Dick Wesson

A Breath of Scandal
US 1960   98m   Technicolor
Paramount / Titanus / Ponti–Girosi (Carlo Ponti, Marcello Girosi)

A spirited Ruritanian princess falls for an American industrialist.
Exceedingly flat-footed and boring international co-production of an old Molnar play; if anyone concerned had bright ideas, they don't show.

w Sidney Howard (presumably in the thirties, for he died in 1939), *play* Olimpia by Ferenc Molnar *d* Michael Curtiz, Mario Russo *ph* Mario Montuori *m* Alessandro Cicognini

Sophia Loren, Maurice Chevalier, John Gavin, Isabel Jeans, Angela Lansbury, Roberto Risso, Frederick Ledebur, Tullio Carminati, Milly Vitale

Breezy
US 1973   107m   Technicolor
Universal / Malpaso (Robert Daley)

A divorced 50-year-old real estate agent is rejuvenated by an affair with a young girl hippy.
An abrasive veneer covers the most stereotyped of January/May love stories. Technically an attractive piece of work.

w Jo Heims *d* Clint Eastwood *ph* Frank Stanley *m* Michel Legrand

William Holden, Kay Lenz, Roger C. Carmel, Marj Dusay, Joan Hotchkis

Brewster McCloud

US 1970   105m   Metrocolor   Panavision
MGM / Adler–Phillips / Lion's Gate (Lou Adler)

A man hides out under the roof of the Houston Astrodrome, prepares to learn to fly with man-made wings, and refuses all offers of help; when he launches himself, he falls to his death.

Anarchic, allegorical fantasy, a delight no doubt for connoisseurs of way-out humour. Everyone else, forget it.

w Doran William Cannon d Robert Altman
ph Lamar Boren, Jordan Cronenweth
m Gene Page

Bud Cort, Sally Kellerman, Michael Murphy, William Windom, Shelley Duvall, René Auberjonois, Stacy Keach, John Shuck, Margaret Hamilton

'Amorphous and rather silly . . . the idea seems to be left over from a Victorian fable, but the style is like a Road Runner cartoon.'— *New Yorker, 1974*

Brewster's Millions*

GB 1935   84m   bw
British and Dominion (Herbert Wilcox)

If he can spend a million pounds within two months, a playboy will inherit many millions more.

Artless but lively version of a famous comedy which provided a good role for its star.

w Arthur Wimperis, Paul Gangelin, Douglas Furber, Clifford Grey, Donovan Pedelty, Wolfgang Wilhelm, *play* George Barr McCutcheon and Winchell Smith, *original novel* George Barr McCutcheon d Thornton Freeland ph Henry Harris, Barney McGill

Jack Buchanan, Lili Damita, Nancy O'Neil, Amy Veness, Sydney Fairbrother, Fred Emney, Sebastian Shaw

Brewster's Millions*

US 1945   79m   bw
Edward Small

Competent American remake of the above.

w Sig Herzig, Charles Rogers d Allan Dwan
ph Charles Lawton Jnr m Hugo Friedhofer

Dennis O'Keefe, Eddie 'Rochester' Anderson, Helen Walker
† Remade as *Three on a Spree* (GB 1961).
AAN: Lou Forbes

The Bribe*

US 1949   98m   bw
MGM (Robert Z. Leonard)

A US agent tracks down a group of criminals in Central America.

Steamy melodrama with pretensions but only moderate entertainment value despite high gloss. The rogues' gallery, however, is impressive.

w Marguerite Roberts d Robert Z. Leonard
ph Joseph Ruttenberg m Miklos Rozsa

Robert Taylor, Ava Gardner, Charles Laughton, Vincent Price, John Hodiak

The Bridal Path*

GB 1959   95m   Technicolor
British Lion / Sidney Gilliat, Frank Launder

A stalwart Hebridean islander journeys to the mainland in search of a wife.

Mild, episodic, very pleasant open-air comedy set amid splendid locations.

w Frank Launder, Geoffrey Willans, *novel* Nigel Tranter d Frank Launder ph Arthur Ibbetson m Cedric Thorpe Davie

Bill Travers, Fiona Clyne, George Cole, Duncan Macrae, Gordon Jackson, Dilys Laye, Bernadette O'Farrell

Bridal Suite

US 1939   70m   bw

A playboy seldom turns up for his own weddings, but his new intended takes him and his mother in hand. Frothy comedy with dependable cast. Robert Young, Annabella, Walter Connolly, Billie Burke, Reginald Owen, Arthur Treacher. Written by Samuel Hoffenstein; directed by William Thiele; for MGM.

Bride by Mistake

US 1944   84m   bw

An heiress tests her suitors by posing as her own secretary. Pleasant little comedy with hard-working cast. Laraine Day, Alan Marshall, Allyn Joslyn, Marsha Hunt. Written by Phoebe and Henry Ephron; directed by Richard Wallace; for RKO.

The Bride Came C.O.D.*

US 1941   92m   bw
Warner (Hal B. Wallis)

A charter pilot agrees to kidnap a temperamental heiress, but is stuck with her when they crashland in the desert.

Feeble comedy with a script totally unworthy of its stars. The mass of talent does however provide a smile or two towards the end.

w Julius J. and Philip G. Epstein d William Keighley ph Ernest Haller m Max Steiner

Bette Davis, James Cagney, Harry Davenport, Stuart Erwin, Eugene Pallette, Jack Carson, George Tobias, William Frawley, Edward Brophy, Chick Chandler

'Neither the funniest comedy ever made, nor the shortest distance between two points, but for the most part a serviceable romp.'— *Theodore Strauss*
'Both of them mug good-naturedly, and it's pleasantly fast.'—*New Yorker, 1977*

The Bride Comes Home*
US 1935   82m   bw
Paramount (Wesley Ruggles)
A penniless socialite helps a wealthy man and his roughneck bodyguard in a magazine venture.
Slight but freshly handled romantic comedy, still worth a look.
w Elizabeth Sanxay Holding, Claude Binyon d Wesley Ruggles ph Leo Tover
Claudette Colbert, Robert Young, Fred MacMurray, William Collier Snr, Donald Meek, Edgar Kennedy, Richard Carle, Jimmy Conlin

Bride for Sale
US 1949   87m   bw
RKO (Jack H. Skirball)
A practical-minded businesswoman has two admirers.
Skittish romantic comedy for ageing stars.
w Bruce Manning, Islin Auster d William D. Russell ph Joseph Valentine m Frederick Hollander
Claudette Colbert, George Brent, Robert Young, Max Baer, Gus Schilling, Charles Arnt, Thurston Hall

The Bride Goes Wild
US 1948   98m   bw
MGM (William H. Wright)
As his lady illustrator finds out, a writer of children's books is not quite the sober uncle she expected, especially when he has to pretend to adopt an unruly orphan.
Scatty comedy with farcical interludes, quite pleasantly played but lacking style.
w Albert Beich d Norman Taurog ph Ray June m Rudolf Kopp
June Allyson, Van Johnson, Jackie 'Butch' Jenkins, Hume Cronyn, Richard Derr

The Bride of Frankenstein****
US 1935   85–90m   bw
Universal (Carl Laemmle Jnr)
Baron Frankenstein is blackmailed by Dr Praetorious into reviving his monster and building a mate for it.
Frankenstein was startlingly good in a primitive way; this sequel is the screen's

sophisticated masterpiece of black comedy, with all the talents working deftly to one end. Every scene has its own delights, and they are woven together into a superb if wilful cinematic narrative which, of its gentle mocking kind, has never been surpassed.
w *John L. Balderston, William Hurlbut* d *James Whale* ph *John Mescall* m *Franz Waxman*
Boris Karloff, Colin Clive, *Ernest Thesiger,* Valerie Hobson, *E. E. Clive,* Dwight Frye, O. P. Heggie, Una O'Connor, *Elsa Lanchester* (as Mary Shelley and the monster's mate), Gavin Gordon (as Byron), Douglas Walton (as Shelley)
'It is perhaps because Whale was by now master of the horror film that this production is the best of them all.'—*John Baxter, 1968*
'An extraordinary film, with sharp humour, macabre extravagance, and a narrative that proceeds at a fast, efficient pace.'—*Gavin Lambert, 1948*
'A great deal of art has gone into it, but it is the kind of art that gives the healthy feeling of men with their sleeves rolled up and working, worrying only about how to put the thing over in the best manner of the medium—no time for nonsense and attitudes and long hair.'— *Otis Ferguson*
'A monster in form but human in his desire for love.'—*publicity*
† The regular release version runs 75m, having dropped part of the Mary Shelley prologue and a sequence in which the monster becomes unsympathetic by murdering the burgomaster.
†† The title was originally to have been *The Return of Frankenstein*.

Bride of Vengeance*
US 1948   91m   bw
Paramount (Richard Maibaum)
The story of the Borgias (whitewashing Lucretia) and the Duke of Ferrara.
Superb looking but appallingly acted and rather stodgily directed piece of historical melodrama. Totally studio-bound, but one of these days it could find a sympathetic audience.
w Cyril Hume, Michael Hogan d Mitchell Leisen ph Daniel L. Fapp m Hugo Friedhofer ad Hans Dreier, Roland Anderson, Albert Nozaki
Paulette Goddard, John Lund, Macdonald Carey, Albert Dekker, Raymond Burr

The Bride Walks Out
US 1936   81m   bw
RKO (Edward Small)

A successful mannequin tries to manage on her engineer husband's lowly salary.

Thin, pleasant marital comedy with no surprises.

w P. J. Wolfson, Philip G. Epstein d Leigh Jason ph J. Roy Hunt m Roy Webb

Barbara Stanwyck, Gene Raymond, Robert Young, Ned Sparks, Helen Broderick, Willie Best, Robert Warwick, Billy Gilbert, Hattie McDaniel, Irving Bacon

The Bride Wore Black*
France / Italy 1967 107m Eastmancolor
Films du Carrosse / Artistes Associés / Dino de Laurentiis (Marcel Bébert)
original title: *La Mariée Était en Noir*

A melancholy lady traces and kills the five men responsible for her fiancé's death.

Uncertain and not very entertaining attempt to turn a Hitchcock situation into a character study.

w François Truffaut, Jean-Louis Richard, *novel* William Irish d François Truffaut ph Raoul Coutard m Bernard Herrmann

Jeanne Moreau, Jean-Claude Brialy, Michel Bouquet, Charles Denner, Claude Rich, Michel Lonsdale

'Truffaut has called the film a love story; others have taken it as a tribute to his master, a Hitchcockian thriller. In fact it is neither; it is a piece of junk.'—*John Simon*

The Bride Wore Boots
US 1946 86m bw
Paramount (Seton I. Miller)

A woman who loves horses is married to a man who does not.

Flimsy, silly, but mainly quite tolerable light comedy sustained by its stars.

w Dwight Mitchell Wiley d Irving Pichel ph Stuart Thompson m Frederick Hollander

Barbara Stanwyck, Robert Cummings, Diana Lynn, Patric Knowles, Peggy Wood, Robert Benchley, Willie Best, Natalie Wood

The Bride Wore Red*
US 1937 103m bw
MGM (Joseph L. Mankiewicz)

A whimsical count arranges for a chorus girl to spend two weeks at an aristocratic Tyrol resort, where she is pursued by two rich men.

Cinderella retold in fancy dress; a typically unreal but quite entertaining star confection of its day.

w Tess Slesinger, Bradbury Foote, *play* The Girl from Trieste by Ferenc Molnar d Dorothy Arzner ph George Folsey m Franz Waxman

Joan Crawford, Robert Young, Franchot Tone, Billie Burke, Reginald Owen, George Zucco, Lynne Carver, Mary Phillips, Paul Porcasi

Brides of Dracula**
GB 1960 85m Technicolor
U-I / Hammer / Hotspur (Anthony Hinds)

Baron Meinster, a disciple of Dracula, is locked up by his mother; but a servant lets him out and he goes on the rampage in a girls' school.

The best of the Hammer *Draculas*, with plenty of inventive action, some classy acting and a good sense of place and period.

w Jimmy Sangster, Peter Bryan, Edward Percy d Terence Fisher ph Jack Asher m Malcolm Williamson

David Peel (as Meinster), *Peter Cushing*, Freda Jackson, *Martita Hunt*, Yvonne Monlaur, Andrée Melly, Mona Washbourne, Henry Oscar, Miles Malleson

The Bridge*
West Germany 1959 106m bw
Fono / Jochen Severin (Hermann Schwerin)

In 1945, only a handful of 16-year-old schoolboys is left to defend the bridge of a small German town.

Painful but memorable war vignette, almost an updating of *All Quiet on the Western Front*.

w Michael Mansfield, Karl-Wilhelm Vivier, *novel* Manfred Gregor d Bernhard Wicki ph Gerd Von Bonen m Hans-Martin Majewski

Vokler Bohnet, Fritz Wepper, Michael Hinz, Frank Glaubrecht, Karl Michael Balzer, Gunther Hoffman

The Bridge at Remagen*
US 1968 116m De Luxe Panavision
UA / Wolper (David L. Wolper)

February 1945: Germans and Americans fight over a Rhine bridge.

Disenchanted, violent war film in which incessant bang-bang, adroitly staged, is all that matters.

w Richard Yates, William Roberts d John Guillermin ph Stanley Cortez m Elmer Bernstein

George Segal, Robert Vaughn, Ben Gazzara, Bradford Dillman, E. G. Marshall, Peter Van Eyck

'Viable viewing if explosions and clichés are your shtick and exciting if you're not sure who won that war.'—*Judith Crist*

The Bridge of San Luis Rey*
US 1944   85m   bw
(UA) Benedict Bogeaus

Five people die when a Peruvian rope bridge
collapses; the film investigates why they were
each on the bridge at the time.

An intriguing novel is turned into tedious film
drama, with actors, director, scenarist and
production designer all making heavy weather.

w Howard Estabrook, *novel* Thornton Wilder
d Rowland V. Lee *ph* John Boyle *m* Dmitri
Tiomkin

Lynn Bari, Francis Lederer, Nazimova, Louis
Calhern, Akim Tamiroff, Blanche Yurka,
Donald Woods

† A silent version, with a few minutes of hasty
talk, was made in 1929 by Charles Brabin for
MGM, from a script by Alice Duer Miller,
Ruth Cummings and Marian Ainslee. The cast
included Lili Damita, Ernest Torrence, Don
Alvarado, Raquel Torres, and Henry B.
Walthall.

AAN: Dmitri Tiomkin

The Bridge on the River Kwai***
GB 1957   161m   Technicolor
   Cinemascope
Columbia / Sam Spiegel

British POWs in Burma are employed by the
Japs to build a bridge; meanwhile British
agents seek to destroy it.

Ironic adventure epic with many fine moments
but too many centres of interest and an
unforgivably confusing climax. It is
distinguished by Guinness' portrait of the
English CO who is heroic in his initial stand
against the Japs but finally cannot bear to see
his bridge blown up: and the physical detail of
the production is beyond criticism.

w Carl Foreman, *novel* Pierre Boulle *d David
Lean ph* Jack Hildyard *m* Malcolm Arnold

Alec Guinness, Jack Hawkins, William
Holden, Sessue Hayakawa, Percy Herbert,
James Donald, Geoffrey Horne, André Morell

'It may rank as the most rousing adventure
film inspired by the last World War.'—*Alton
Cook, New York World Telegram*

AA: best picture; Carl Foreman (credited as
Michael Wilson); David Lean; Jack Hildyard;
Malcolm Arnold; Alec Guinness
AAN: Sessue Hayakawa

Bridge to the Sun*
France / US 1961   112m   bw
MGM / Cité Films (Jacques Bar)

Just before Pearl Harbor, an American girl
marries a Japanese diplomat and goes to live
in Tokyo.

Romantic drama which oddly sides with the
Japanese and shows America in a poor light.
Interesting if not very compelling, with some
unfamiliar views of Japan.

w Charles Kaufman, *autobiography*
Gwendolen Terasaki *d* Etienne Périer
ph Marcel Weiss, Seiichi Kizuka, Bill Kelly
m Georges Auric

Carroll Baker, James Shigeta, James Yagi,
Tetsuro Tamba

'In yet another burst of national flagellation,
Hollywood turns on itself and unthinking
Americans for being so beastly about the
wartime Japanese.'—*MFB*

A Bridge Too Far**
US / GB 1977   175m   Technicolor
   Panavision
UA / Joseph E. Levine (John Palmer)

The story of the Allied defeat at Arnhem in
1944.

Like all large-scale military films, this one fails
to make its tactics clear, and its sober intent
conflicts with its roster of guest stars. For all
that, there are impressive moments of acting
and production.

w William Goldman, *book* Cornelius Ryan
d Richard Attenborough (and Sidney Hayers)
*ph Geoffrey Unsworth, Harry Waxman, Robin
Browne pd* Terence Marsh

Dirk Bogarde, James Caan, Michael Caine,
Sean Connery, Edward Fox, Elliott Gould,
Gene Hackman, Anthony Hopkins, Hardy
Kruger, *Laurence Olivier*, Ryan O'Neal,
Robert Redford, Maximilian Schell, Liv
Ullmann, Arthur Hill, Wolfgang Preiss

'A film too long.'—*Anon.*

'So wearily, expensively predictable that by
the end the viewer will in all likelihood be too
enervated to notice Attenborough's prosaic
moral epilogue.'—*John Pym, MFB*

The Bridges at Toko-Ri*
US 1954   104m   Technicolor
Paramount / Perlberg–Seaton

The comradeship and death of two jet pilots
during the Korean War.

Ambitiously staged action thriller with points
to make about war, death and politics: a
well-worn American formula pitched very
hard.

w Valentine Davies, *novel* James E.
Michener *d* Mark Robson *ph* Loyal Griggs
m Lyn Murray

William Holden, Mickey Rooney, Grace
Kelly, Fredric March, Robert Strauss, Charles
McGraw, Earl Holliman, Willis Bouchey

'A taut, thrilling, top flight documentary
drama of men, war, ships and planes.'—*Cue*

Brief Encounter****
GB 1945   86m   bw
Cineguild (Anthony Havelock-Allan, Ronald
Neame)

A suburban housewife on her weekly shopping
visits develops a love affair with a local doctor;
but he gets a job abroad and they agree not to
see each other again.

An outstanding example of good middle-class
cinema turned by sheer professional craft into
a masterpiece; even those bored by the theme
must be riveted by the treatment, especially
the use of a dismal railway station and its
trains.

w *Noel Coward*, from his one-act play Still
Life *d David Lean ph Robert Krasker*
m Rachmaninov

Celia Johnson, Trevor Howard, Stanley
Holloway, Joyce Carey, Cyril Raymond
'Both a pleasure to watch as a well-
controlled piece of work, and deeply
touching.'—*James Agee*
'Polished as it is this film, its strength does not
lie in movie technique, of which there is
plenty, so much as in the tight realism of its
detail.'—*Richard Winnington*

† A TV film version was made in 1975 by ITC,
starring Richard Burton and Sophia Loren and
directed by Alan Bridges. It was an
unqualified disaster.
AAN: script; David Lean; Celia Johnson

Brigadoon*
US 1954   108m   Anscocolor
Cinemascope
MGM (Arthur Freed)

Two Americans in Scotland find a ghost village
which awakens only once every hundred years.
Likeable but disappointing adaptation of a
Lost Horizonish Broadway musical, marred by
artificial sets and jaded direction.

w Alan Jay Lerner, from his play *d* Vincente
Minnelli *ph* Joseph Ruttenberg *md* Johnny
Green *songs* Frederick Loewe, Alan Jay
Lerner

Gene Kelly, Cyd Charisse, Van Johnson,
Jimmy Thompson, Elaine Stewart, Barry
Jones, Eddie Quillan
'The whimsical dream world it creates holds
no compelling attractions.'—*Penelope
Houston*

The Brigand*
US 1952   93m   Technicolor
Columbia

A Moroccan adventurer looks like the king
and is reprieved from execution if he will
impersonate the latter and root out his
enemies.

Cheeky revamp of *The Prisoner of Zenda*,
quite acceptably done.

w Jesse Lasky Jnr *d* Phil Karlson *ph* W.
Howard Greene *m* Mario Castelnuovo-
Tedesco

Anthony Dexter, Jody Lawrance, Gale
Robbins, Anthony Quinn, Carl Benton Reid,
Ron Randell

The Brigand of Kandahar
GB 1965   81m   Technicolor   'Scope
EMI / Hammer (Anthony Nelson Keys)

A cashiered Bengal Lancer officer throws in
his lot with a troublesome bandit.
Feeble frontier adventure with nothing ringing
true.

wd John Gilling *ph* Reg Wyer *m* Don Banks
pd Bernard Robinson

Oliver Reed, Ronald Lewis, Duncan Lamont,
Yvonne Romain, Catherine Woodville, Glyn
Houston

Brigham Young**
US 1940   112m   bw
TCF (Kenneth MacGowan)

The story of the Mormon trek to Utah.
Ambitious but rather dull interpretation of
history, seen as a western with romantic
fictional trimmings.

w Lamar Trotti, *story* Louis Bromfield
d Henry Hathaway *ph Arthur Miller*
m Alfred Newman

Dean Jagger, Tyrone Power, Linda Darnell,
Brian Donlevy, Jane Darwell, John
Carradine, Mary Astor, Vincent Price, Moroni
Olsen

Bright Eyes*
US 1934   84m   bw
TCF

An orphan finds herself torn between foster-
parents.
The first of Shirley Temple's genuine star
vehicles has a liveliness and cheerfulness hard
to find today. As a production, however, it is
decidedly economical.

w William Conselman *d* David Butler
ph Arthur Miller *m* Samuel Kaylin

Shirley Temple, James Dunn, Lois Wilson,
Jane Withers, Judith Allen

Bright Leaf
US 1950   110m   bw
Warner (Henry Blanke)

A 19th-century tobacco farmer builds a
cigarette empire.

Quite agreeable but disjointed fictional biopic, more about love than tobacco.

w Ranald MacDougall, *novel* Robert Wilder d Michael Curtiz *ph* Karl Freund *m* Victor Young

Gary Cooper, Lauren Bacall, Patricia Neal, Jack Carson, Donald Crisp, Gladys George, Elizabeth Patterson, Jeff Corey, Taylor Holmes

Bright Lights*
US 1935 86m bw

A vaudevillian lets success go to his head. The plot served for a score or more of thirties musicals, but this had Busby Berkeley routines and an unusual star role for Joe E. Brown; with Ann Dvorak, Patricia Ellis, William Gargan. Written by Bert Kalmar and Harry Ruby; directed by Busby Berkeley; for Warner. (GB title: *Funny Face*.) (The same title covered a 1925 MGM silent with Charles Ray as a country boy in love with a Broadway star.)

Bright Road*
US 1953 69m bw
MGM (Sol Baer Fielding)

In an all-black school, a problem child finds himself when he helps to rid the school of a swarm of bees.
Slight but attractive second feature, unostentatiously set in a black community.

w Emmet Lavery d Gerald Mayer *ph* Alfred Gilks *m* David Rose

Dorothy Dandridge, Harry Belafonte, Robert Horton, Philip Hepburn, Barbara Ann Sanders

Bright Victory*
US 1951 97m bw
Universal (Robert Buckner)
GB title: *Lights Out*

A blinded soldier adjusts to civilian life. Well-meaning if rather slow and sticky, this drama is more sentimental than realistic but has good performances.

w Robert Buckner, *novel* Bayard Kendrick d Mark Robson *ph* William Daniels *m* Frank Skinner

Arthur Kennedy, Peggy Dow, Julia Adams, James Edwards, Will Geer, Minor Watson, Jim Backus

AAN: Arthur Kennedy

Brighton Rock***
GB 1947 92m bw
Associated British / The Boultings
US title: *Young Scarface*

The teenage leader of a racetrack gang uses a waitress as alibi to cover a murder, and marries her. He later decides to be rid of her, but fate takes a hand in his murder plot.
A properly 'seedy' version of Graham Greene's 'entertainment', very flashily done for the most part but with a trick ending which allows the heroine to keep her illusions.

w Graham Greene, Terence Rattigan d John Boulting *ph* Harry Waxman *m* Hans May

Richard Attenborough, Hermione Baddeley, *Harcourt Williams*, William Hartnell, Alan Wheatley, Carol Marsh

'The film is slower, much less compelling, and, if you get me, less cinematic than the book, as a child's guide to which I hereby offer it.'—*Richard Winnington*

'It proceeds with the efficiency, the precision and the anxiety to please of a circular saw.'—*Dilys Powell*

The Brighton Strangler
US 1945 67m bw

An actor takes over in real life the part he is playing – of a murderer. This hoary plot had seen better days even in 1945, and was not helped by an establishing shot which put Parliament on the wrong side of the Thames. John Loder, June Duprez. Written by Arnold Philips and Max Nosseck; directed by Max Nosseck; for RKO.

Bring Me the Head of Alfredo Garcia
US 1974 112m De Luxe
UA / Optimus / Churubusco (Martin Baum)

A wealthy Mexican offers a million dollars for the head of a man who seduced his daughter, and claimants find that grave robbing is involved.
Gruesome, sickly action melodrama with revolting detail; the nadir of a director obsessed by violence.

w Gordon Dawson, Sam Peckinpah d Sam Peckinpah *ph* Alex Phillips Jnr *m* Jerry Fielding

Warren Oates, Gig Young, Isela Vega, Robert Webber, Helmut Dantine, Emilio Fernandez, Kris Kristofferson

Bring On the Girls
US 1945 92m Technicolor
Paramount (Fred Kohlmar)

A millionaire joins the navy in the hope that a girl will love him for himself.
A good example of the gaily-coloured but witless drivel which occasionally came out of the big studios towards the end of the war.

w Karl Tunberg, Darrell Ware *d* Sidney
Lanfield *ph* Karl Struss *md* Robert Emmett
Dolan

Veronica Lake, Eddie Bracken, Sonny Tufts,
Marjorie Reynolds, Grant Mitchell, Alan
Mowbray, Porter Hall

Bringing Up Baby***
US 1938   102m   bw
RKO (Howard Hawks)

A zany girl causes a zoology professor to lose
a dinosaur bone and a pet leopard in the same
evening.

Outstanding crazy comedy which barely
pauses for romance and ends up with the
whole splendid cast in jail.

*w Dudley Nichols, Hagar Wilde d Howard
Hawks ph* Russell Metty *m* Roy Webb

*Katharine Hepburn, Cary Grant, May Robson,
Charles Ruggles, Walter Catlett, Fritz Feld,*
Jonathan Hale, Barry Fitzgerald

'I am happy to report that it is funny from
the word go, that it has no other meaning to
recommend it . . . and that I wouldn't swap it
for practically any three things of the current
season.'—*Otis Ferguson*

'It may be the American movies' closest
equivalent to Restoration comedy.'—*Pauline
Kael*

'Crazy comedies continue to become
crazier, and there will soon be few actors and
actresses left who have no straw in their
hair.'—*Basil Wright*

Bringing Up Father
US 1928   approx 70m at 24 fps   bw
     silent

Mild domestic comedy about a henpecked
husband, from the famous comic strip; it
marked the successful comeback of Marie
Dressler (as the maid). J. Farrell MacDonald,
Polly Moran, Gertrude Olmsted, Grant
Withers. Written by Frances Marion; directed
by Jack Conway; for MGM. (Two or three
second features about Jiggs and Maggie,
featuring Renie Riano and Joe Yule, appeared
in the late forties.)

The Brinks Job
US 1978   103m   Technicolor
Universal / Dino de Laurentiis (Ralph
     Serpe)

In 1944, amateur criminals bring off a raid on
the vaults of a Boston security company.
Farcical variation of a much-told true tale.
Despite much mugging by the stars and a
frantic narrative style, it does not come off.

w Walon Green *d* William Friedkin
ph Norman Leigh *m* Richard Rodney
Bennett *pd* Dean Tavoularis

Peter Falk, Warren Oates, Peter Boyle, Allen
Goorwitz, Gena Rowlands, Paul Sorvino,
Sheldon Leonard

Britannia Mews
GB 1948   91m   bw
TCF (William Perlberg)
US title: *The Forbidden Street*

In Victorian times, the widow of a
puppetmaster eventually marries his lookalike
who rebuilds their puppet theatre.

Curious and uncertain comedy drama set
among yesterday's high society, with poorly
played leads but an interesting supporting cast
and technical assurance.

w Ring Lardner Jnr, *novel* Margery Sharp
d Jean Negulesco *ph* Georges Périnal
ad Andrei Andreiev *m* Malcolm Arnold

Dana Andrews, Maureen O'Hara, Sybil
Thorndike, Wilfrid Hyde White, Fay
Compton, A. E. Matthews

British Agent*
US 1934   81m   bw
Warner (Henry Blanke)

In 1910 Russia, a Britisher falls in love with a
lady spy.

Sluggish and dated romantic melodrama,
notable only for Howard's performance and
some directional felicities.

w Laird Doyle, *novel* H. Bruce Lockhart
d Michael Curtiz *ph* Ernest Haller *ad* Anton
Grot

Leslie Howard, Kay Francis, William Gargan,
Irving Pichel, Philip Reed, Walter Byron, J.
Carrol Naish, Halliwell Hobbes

British Intelligence
US 1940   63m   bw
Warner
GB title: *Enemy Agent*

During World War I a German lady spy
becomes a guest in the house of a British war
official, the butler of which is the leader of a
German spy ring.

Second feature remake of *Three Faces East*
(qv); still quite an entertaining melodrama.

w Lee Katz, *play* Anthony Paul Kelly *d* Terry
Morse *ph* Sid Hickox

Boris Karloff, Margaret Lindsay, Maris
Wrixon, Bruce Lester, Leonard Mudie,
Holmes Herbert

Broadway
US 1942 90m bw
Universal (Bruce Manning)

George Raft recalls his days as a hoofer in a
New York speakeasy, and in particular a
murder involving gangsters and chorus girls.
Minor crime melodrama which after
interminable scene-setting paints an effective
picture of the twenties but has too slack a grip
on narrative.

w Felix Jackson, John Bright, *play* Philip
Dunning, George Abbott *d* William A.
Seiter *ph* George Barnes *md* Charles Previn

George Raft, Pat O'Brien, S. Z. Sakall, Janet
Blair, Broderick Crawford, Marjorie
Rambeau

Broadway Bill*
US 1934 104m bw
Columbia (Frank Capra)
GB title: *Strictly Confidential*

A cheerful horse trainer finds he has a winner.
Easygoing romantic comedy with the energetic
Capra style in fairly full bloom.

w Robert Riskin, *story* Mark Hellinger
d Frank Capra *ph* Joseph Walker

Warner Baxter, Myrna Loy, Walter Connolly,
Helen Vinson, Douglass Dumbrille, Raymond
Walburn, Lynne Overman, Clarence Muse,
Margaret Hamilton, Paul Harvey, Claude
Gillingwater, Charles Lane, Ward Bond

'It will be a long day before we see so little
made into so much: it is gay and charming and
will make you happy, and I am sorry to say I
do not know recommendations much
higher.'—*Otis Ferguson*
† Remade as *Riding High* (qv).

Broadway Limited*
US 1941 75m bw
Hal Roach
GB title: *The Baby Vanishes*

On an express train, a Hollywood publicity
stunt backfires.
Wild farce which is not very funny as a whole
but has entertaining comic performances.

w Rian James *d* Gordon Douglas *ph* Henry
Sharp *m* Charles Previn

Victor McLaglen, Patsy Kelly, *Leonid
Kinskey*, Marjorie Woodworth, Dennis
O'Keefe, Zasu Pitts, George E. Stone

Broadway Melody*
US 1929 110m bw (Technicolor scenes)
MGM (Lawrence Weingarten)

Chorus girls try to make it big on Broadway.
The screen's very first musical, exceedingly

primitive by the standards of even a year later,
but rather endearing and with a splendid
score.

w James Gleason, Norman Houston, Edmund
Goulding *d* Harry Beaumont *ph* John
Arnold *songs* Nacio Herb Brown, Arthur
Freed

Charles King, Anita Page, Bessie Love, Jed
Prouty, Kenneth Thomson, Mary Doran,
Eddie Kane

'A basic story with some sense to it, action,
excellent direction, laughs, a tear, a couple of
great performances and plenty of sex.'—
Variety

AA: best picture; Harry Beaumont
AAN: Bessie Love

Broadway Melody of 1936*
US 1935 103m bw
MGM (John W. Considine Jnr)

A Broadway producer is at loggerheads with a
columnist.
Fairly lively musical with lavish numbers.

w Jack McGowan, Sid Silvers, *original
story* Moss Hart *d* Roy del Ruth *ph* Charles
Rosher *songs* Nacio Herb Brown, Arthur
Freed

Jack Benny, Robert Taylor, Una Merkel,
Eleanor Powell, June Knight, Vilma and
Buddy Ebsen, Nick Long Jnr

AAN: best picture; Moss Hart

Broadway Melody of 1938*
US 1937 110m bw
MGM (Jack Cummings)

Backstage problems threaten the opening of a
musical show.
Lavish but fairly forgettable musical with top
talent.

w Jack McGowan, Sid Silvers *d* Roy del
Ruth *ph* William Daniels *songs* Nacio Herb
Brown, Arthur Freed

Eleanor Powell, George Murphy, *Sophie
Tucker*, Judy Garland, Robert Taylor, Buddy
Ebsen, Sid Silvers, Billy Gilbert, Raymond
Walburn

Broadway Melody of 1940*
US 1939 102m bw
MGM (Jack Cummings)

A dance team gets to the top.
Splendidly produced but thinly plotted
extravaganza with good numbers.

w Leon Gordon, George Oppenheimer
d Norman Taurog *ph* Oliver T. Marsh,
Joseph Ruttenberg *songs* Cole Porter

Fred Astaire, Eleanor Powell, George Murphy, Douglas Macphail, Florence Rice, Frank Morgan, Ian Hunter

Broadway Rhythm*
US 1943 113m Technicolor
MGM (Jack Cummings)

Originally intended as *Broadway Melody of 1944*, this putting-on-a-show extravaganza had only the numbers to commend it.

w Dorothy Kingsley, Harry Clark, from the Kern / Hammerstein operetta Very Warm for May *d* Roy del Ruth *ph* Leonard Smith *songs* various

George Murphy, Ginny Simms, Charles Winninger, Gloria de Haven, Lena Horne, Nancy Walker, Hazel Scott, Eddie Anderson, Ben Blue, Tommy Dorsey and his Orchestra
 'It contains perhaps three minutes of good acrobatic dancing and lasts nearly two hours.'—*James Agee*

Broadway Serenade
US 1939 114m bw
MGM (Robert Z. Leonard)
GB title: *Serenade*

Career problems split the marriage of a songwriter and his singing wife.
Lavish but rather dull romantic drama with music.

w Charles Lederer, Lew Lipton, John T. Foote, Hans Kraly *d* Robert Z. Leonard *ph* Oliver T. Marsh *md* Herbert Stothart

Jeanette MacDonald, Lew Ayres, Frank Morgan, Ian Hunter, Rita Johnson, Virginia Grey, William Gargan, Katherine Alexander

Broadway thru a Keyhole*
US 1933 90m bw
UA / William Goetz, Raymond Griffith

A tough New York gangster falls for a singer in his nightclub.
Reputed acid observation of the New York scene distinguishes this low-budget gangster drama.

w Gene Town, *story* Walter Winchell *d* Lowell Sherman *ph* Barney McGill *songs* Mack Gordon, Harry Revel

Constance Cummings, Russ Columbo, Paul Kelly, *Blossom Seeley*, Gregory Ratoff, *Texas Guinan*, Hobart Cavanaugh, C. Henry Gordon

Broadway to Hollywood
US 1933 90m bw

A vaudeville family makes it in movies.
Cliché-strewn rags-to-riches saga with songs;

good moments. Frank Morgan, Alice Brady, Jackie Cooper, Madge Evans, Jimmy Durante, Nelson Eddy, May Robson, Una Merkel, Mickey Rooney. Written and directed by Willard Mack; for MGM. (GB title: *Ring Up the Curtain.*)

Broken Arrow*
US 1950 92m Technicolor
TCF (Julian Blaustein)

A US army scout brings about peace between white man and Apache.
Solemn western which at the time was acclaimed for giving the Indian's point of view (something which had scarcely happened since silent days). As entertainment it was not exciting, but it set Jeff Chandler off on a career playing Cochise with variations, and a TV series of the same name surfaced in 1956.

w Michael Blankfort, *novel* Blood Brother by Elliott Arnold *d* Delmer Daves *ph* Ernest Palmer *m* Hugo Friedhofer *md* Alfred Newman

James Stewart, Jeff Chandler, Debra Paget, Basil Ruysdael, Will Geer, Arthur Hunnicutt, Jay Siverheels
 'It has probably done more to soften racial hostilities than most movies designed to instruct, indict and inspire.'—*Pauline Kael*
AAN: Michael Blankfort; Ernest Palmer; Jeff Chandler

Broken Blossoms**
US 1919 105m (16 fps) bw
UA / D. W. Griffith

In slummy Limehouse, a young Chinaman loves the daughter of a brute, who kills her; the Chinaman then kills him and commits suicide.
Victorian-style melodrama presented by Griffith with all the stops out; sometimes striking, but very dated even on its first appearance.

wd D. W. Griffith, *story* The Chink and the Child in Thomas Burke's Limehouse Nights *ph* G. W. Bitzer

Lillian Gish, Donald Crisp, Richard Barthelmess
 'This is a Limehouse which neither Mr Burke nor anybody else who knows his East End of London will be able to recognize . . . but *Broken Blossoms* is a genuine attempt to bring real tragedy onto the screen as opposed to machine-made drama, and for that Mr Griffith deserves the thanks of all who are convinced of the potentialities of the film.'— *The Times*
 'I know of no other picture in which so much screen beauty is obtained . . .

attributable to the Whistlerian fogs and shadows, with that dock in Limehouse recurring like some pedal point.'—*James Agate, 1928*
† Leslie Henson appeared in a parody, Broken Bottles, in 1920.

Broken Blossoms*
GB 1936 84m bw
Twickenham (Julius Hagen)

A remake originally intended to be directed by Griffith. Quite stylish, and in some ways more interesting than its predecessor.

w Emlyn Williams *d* John Brahm *ph* Curt Courant

Dolly Haas, Arthur Margetson, Emlyn Williams, Donald Calthrop, Ernest Sefton, Kathleen Harrison, Basil Radford

Broken Journey
GB 1948 89m bw
Gainsborough (Sydney Box)

A plane crashes in the Alps, and the survivors take different attitudes to their situation. Unpersuasive and stagey melodrama which wastes some good talent.

w Robert Westerby *d* Ken Annakin *ph* Jack Cox *m* John Greenwood

Phyllis Calvert, James Donald, Margot Grahame, Francis L. Sullivan, Raymond Huntley, Derek Bond, Guy Rolfe, David Tomlinson

Broken Lance*
US 1954 96m De Luxe Cinemascope
TCF (Sol C. Siegel)

An autocratic cattle baron causes dissension among his sons.
Western remake of *House of Strangers*, quite well done.

w Richard Murphy, *original story* Philip Yordan *d* Edward Dmytryk *ph* Joe MacDonald *m* Leigh Harline

Spencer Tracy, Richard Widmark, Robert Wagner, Jean Peters, Katy Jurado, Earl Holliman, Hugh O'Brian, Eduard Franz, E. G. Marshall

AA: Philip Yordan
AAN: Katy Jurado

Broken Lullaby*
US 1932 77m bw
Paramount
GB and original title: *The Man I Killed*

A young Frenchman goes to Germany to seek out the family of the man he killed in the war, and is accepted by them as a friend.

This most untypical Lubitsch film now seems very dated but was deeply felt at the time and has plenty of cinematic grip.

w Ernest Vajda, Samson Raphaelson, *play* L'Homme que J'ai Tué by Maurice Rostand *d* Ernst Lubitsch *ph* Victor Milner *ad* Hans Dreier

Lionel Barrymore, Phillips Holmes, Nancy Carroll, Tom Douglas, Zasu Pitts, Lucien Littlefield, Lois Carver, Emma Dunn

'The best talking picture that has yet been seen and heard.'—*Robert E. Sherwood*

'I cannot remember a film so beautifully made, so completely fine in its execution.'— *John Grierson*

The Broken Wing
US 1932 71m bw
Paramount

A Mexican girl jilts a bandit for an American pilot.
Hokey romantic melodrama.

w Gordon Jones, William Slavens McNutt, *play* Paul Dickey, Charles Goddard *d* Lloyd Corrigan *ph* Henry Sharp

Lupe Velez, Leo Carrillo, Melvyn Douglas, George Barbier, Willard Robertson

Bronco Billy*
US 1980 116m De Luxe
Warner / Second Street (Neal Dubrovsky, Dennis Hackin)

A New Jersey shoe salesman takes over a rundown wild west show.
Enjoyable, sentimental, satirical comedy which unaccountably let down its star's box office record.

w Dennis Hackin *d* Clint Eastwood *ph* David Worth *md* Snuff Garrett, Steve Dorff *ad* Eugene Lourie

Clint Eastwood, Sondra Locke, Geoffrey Lewis, Scatman Crothers, Bill McKinney, Sam Bottoms

'Eastwood seems to have most enjoyed toying with some distinctly old-fashioned materials: a runaway heiress, a murder plot that isn't, some consequent punning on points of identity, and the most mischievously brittle set of greedy Eastern sophisticates since Frank Capra.'—*Richard Combs, MFB*

The Brood
Canada 1979 91m colour

The rage of a mentally disturbed woman produces homicidal 'babies'. Idiotic and repellent shocker. Oliver Reed, Samantha Eggar, Art Hindle, Cindy Hinds. Written and directed by David Cronenberg; for Mutual / Elgin.

Broth of a Boy
Eire 1958   77m   bw
Emmet Dalton (Alec Snowden)

TV covers the village festivities celebrating an old poacher's 110th birthday.
Mildly amusing regional comedy.

w Patrick Kirwan, Blanaid Irvine, *play* The Big Birthday by Hugh Leonard *d* George Pollock *ph* Walter J. Harvey *m* Stanley Black

Barry Fitzgerald, June Thorburn, Tony Wright, Harry Brogan, Eddie Golden, Maire Kean, Godfrey Quigley, Dermot Kelly

Brother Can You Spare a Dime?
GB 1975   109m   bw

A 'documentary' picture of America in the thirties, attempted by an apparently random collage of newsreel and feature film extracts, sometimes difficult to tell one from the other. Sometimes entertaining but mainly unpardonable. Written and directed by Philippe Mora; for VPS / Goodtimes.

Brother John*
US 1970   94m   Eastmancolor
Columbia / E and R (Joel Glickman)

A mysterious black man comes to town for a family funeral and is suspected by the townsfolk of various sinister motives, but when they imprison him he is freed by a sympathizer.
The humans are all mean-minded, the saintly visitor is either Christ or an emissary from another planet. Either way, we have been here before, but although this little fantasy has nothing clear to say it is quite enjoyable on the surface.

w Ernest Kinoy *d* James Goldstone
ph Gerald Perry Finnerman *m* Quincy Jones

Sidney Poitier, Bradford Dillman, Will Geer, Beverly Todd, Ramon Pieri, Warren J. Kemmerling, Paul Winfield, Lincoln Kilpatrick
  'It starts out as an engaging mystery with sociological overtones but ends up as a muddle-headed doomsday parable.'—*Judith Crist, 1977*

Brother Orchid*
US 1940   91m   bw
Warner (Hal B. Wallis)

A gangster, 'taken for a ride' by his former friends, escapes and becomes a monk.
Rather uneasy blend of comedy, drama and religion, with some good scenes.

w Earl Baldwin, *story* Richard Connell
d Lloyd Bacon *ph* Tony Gaudio *m* Heinz Roemheld

Edward G. Robinson, Humphrey Bogart, Donald Crisp, Ann Sothern, Ralph Bellamy, Allen Jenkins, Cecil Kellaway

Brother Rat*
US 1938   89m   bw
Warner (Robert Lord)

Fun and games with the cadets at a military academy.
Brisk but dated farce from a highly successful Broadway original; remade as *About Face*.

w Richard Macaulay, Jerry Wald, *play* Fred Finklehoffe, John Monks *d* William Keighley *ph* Ernest Haller

Wayne Morris, Eddie Albert, Ronald Reagan, Priscilla Lane, Jane Bryan, Jane Wyman, Johnnie Davis, Henry O'Neill

Brother Rat and a Baby
US 1939   87m   bw
Warner (Robert Lord)
GB title: *Baby Be Good*

Scatty follow-up to the above, with the cadets graduating.

w Jerry Wald, Richard Macauley *d* Ray Enright *ph* Charles Rosher

Wayne Morris, Eddie Albert, Ronald Reagan, Priscilla Lane, Jane Wyman, Jane Bryan, Arthur Treacher, Moroni Olsen

Brother Sun, Sister Moon
GB / Italy 1972   122m   Technicolor Panavision
Paramount / Vic Films / Euro International (Luciano Perugia)

The life of Francis of Assisi.
Good-looking but relentlessly boring view of a medieval saint as a kind of early flower person.

w Suso Cecchi d'Amico, Kenneth Ross, Lina Wertmuller, Franco Zeffirelli *d* Franco Zeffirelli *ph* Ennio Guarnieri *m* Donovan

Graham Faulkner, Judi Bowker, Alec Guinness (as Pope Innocent III), Leigh Lawson, Kenneth Cranham, Lee Montague, Valentina Cortese
  'If I were Pope, I would burn it.'—*Stanley Kauffmann*

The Brotherhood*
US 1968   96m   Technicolor
Paramount / Brotherhood Company (Kirk Douglas)

A Mafia executive welcomes his younger brother into the syndicate, but is finally executed by him.

Dour melodrama with tragic pretensions: well made but rather tedious and violent.

w Lewis John Carlino *d* Martin Ritt *ph* Boris Kaufman *m* Lalo Schifrin

Kirk Douglas, Alex Cord, *Luther Adler*, Irene Papas, Susan Strasberg, Murray Hamilton, Eduardo Ciannelli

The Brotherhood of Satan*
US 1970   93m   Techniscope
Columbia / LQJAF / Four Star Excelsior (L. Q. Jones, Alvy Moore)

A village is isolated by an outbreak of diabolism.

Fresh and intriguing minor horror film with imaginative touches.

w William Welch *d Bernard McEveety ph* John Arthur Morril *m* Jaime Mendoza-Nava

Strother Martin, L. Q. Jones, Charles Bateman, Anna Capri, Charles Robinson, Alvy Moore, Geri Reischl

The Brothers**
GB 1947   98m   bw
GFD / Sydney Box

An orphan girl comes to a Skye fishing family at the turn of the century, and causes superstition, sexual jealousy and tragedy.

Wildly melodramatic but good-looking open-air melodrama, a surprising and striking British film of its time.

w Muriel and Sydney Box, *novel* L. A. G. Strong *d David Macdonald ph Stephen Dade*

Patricia Roc, Maxwell Reed, *Duncan Macrae* (a splendidly malevolent performance), Will Fyffe, Andrew Crawford, Finlay Currie

'Heavy breathing, heavier dialect, and any number of quaint folk customs . . . the island and its actual inhabitants are all right; the rest is Mary Webb with hair on her chest.'—*James Agee*

Brothers in Law*
GB 1957   97m   bw
British Lion / the Boultings

A young barrister has comic misdemeanours in and out of court.

The lighter side of the law, from a bestseller by a judge; mechanically amusing and not in the same street as its predecessor *Private's Progress*, though it seemed hilarious at the time.

w Roy Boulting, Frank Harvey, Jeffrey Dell, *novel Henry Cecil d* John Boulting *ph* Max Greene *m* Benjamin Frankel

Ian Carmichael, Terry-Thomas, Richard Attenborough, *Miles Malleson, Eric Barker*, Irene Handl, John Le Mesurier, Olive Sloane, Kynaston Reeves

The Brothers Karamazov*
US 1958   146m   Metrocolor
MGM / Avon (Pandro S. Berman)

In 19th-century Russia, the father of three sons is murdered and the wrong brother is found guilty.

Decent but decidedly unenthralling Hollywood compression of a classic, faithful to the letter but not the spirit of the book, and with few memorable moments or performances.

w Richard Brooks, *novel* Fedor Dostoievsky *d* Richard Brooks *ph* John Alton *m* Bronislau Kaper *ad* William A. Horning, Paul Groesse

Yul Brynner, Maria Schell, Richard Basehart, Claire Bloom, Lee J. Cobb, Albert Salmi, William Shatner, Judith Evelyn

† In 1968 came Ivan Pyryev's massive 220m Russian version, little seen in the west. See also *The Murder of Dmitri Karamazov*.

AAN: Lee J. Cobb

The Brothers Rico
US 1957   91m   bw
Columbia / William Goetz (Lewis J. Rachmil)

An accountant fails to retrieve his brothers from a life of crime.

Moderate gangster fare with good credentials but more talk than action.

w Lewis Meltzer, Ben Perry, *novel* Georges Simenon *d* Phil Karlson *ph* Burnett Guffey *m* George Duning

Richard Conte, James Darren, Dianne Foster, Kathryn Grant, Larry Gates, Lamont Johnson, Harry Bellaver

Brown of Harvard
US 1926   approx 70m at 24 fps   bw silent

Two college students, one academic and one sporty, love the same girl. Best-known version of a 1909 play first filmed in 1917: archetypal campus drama. William Haines; Jack Pickford, Mary Brian. Written by Donald Ogden Stewart and A. P. Younger, from a play by Rida Johnson Young; directed by Jack Conway; for MGM.

Brown on Resolution*
GB 1935 80m bw
Gaumont (Michael Balcon)
Later retitled: *Forever England*; US title:
Born for Glory

In the 1914 war in the Mediterranean, a
seaman holds a German warship at bay with a
rifle.
Uneasy amalgam of adventure heroics and
character study, interesting for its effort.
Remade as *Singlehanded* (qv).

w Michael Hogan, Gerard Fairlie, J. O. C.
Orton, *novel* C. S. Forester *d* Walter Forde
ph Bernard Knowles

John Mills, Betty Balfour, Barry Mackay,
Jimmy Hanley, Howard Marion Crawford, H.
G. Stoker

The Browning Version*
GB 1951 90m bw
GFD / Javelin (Teddy Baird)

Retiring through ill health, a classics master
finds that he is hated by his unfaithful wife, his
headmaster and his pupils. An unexpected act
of kindness gives him courage to face the
future.
A rather thin extension of a one-act play,
capped by a thank-you speech which is wildly
out of character. Dialogue and settings are
smooth, but the actors are not really happy
with their roles.

w Terence Rattigan, from his play *d* Anthony
Asquith *ph* Desmond Dickinson

Michael Redgrave, Jean Kent, Nigel Patrick,
Wilfrid Hyde White, Bill Travers, Ronald
Howard

Brubaker*
US 1980 130m De Luxe
TCF (Ron Silverman)

A new governor fails to make much headway
with his reform plan at Wakefield Prison
Farm.
Fairly brutal but unsurprising prison drama
which takes itself somewhat too seriously.

w W. D. Richter *d* Stuart Rosenberg
ph Bruno Nuytten *m* Lalo Schifrin

Robert Redford, Yaphet Kotto, Jane
Alexander, Murray Hamilton, David Keith,
Morgan Freeman
'It's hard to imagine a broad audience
wanting to share the two hours of agony.'—
Variety

AAN: screenplay

The Brute*
Mexico 1952 83m bw
International Cinematografica
original title: *El Bruto*

Victimized slum tenants call for help to a
slow-witted giant, who kills the landlord and
falls in love with his daughter.
Eccentric melodrama which doesn't quite
seem to make its point.

wd Luis Bunuel *ph* Augustin Jiminez
m Rafael Larista

Pedro Armendariz, *Katy Jurado*, Rosita
Arenas, Andres Soler

Brute Force**
US 1947 96m bw
U-I

Six violent convicts revolt against a sadistic
warden and try to escape.
Vivid and rather repellent prison melodrama
leading up to an explosive climax; its savagery
seemed at the time to break fresh ground.

w Richard Brooks d Jules Dassin ph William
Daniels *m* Miklos Rozsa

Burt Lancaster, Charles Bickford, Hume
Cronyn, Ella Raines, Yvonne de Carlo

The Brute Man
US 1946 60m bw

A disfigured paranoic is helped by a blind
pianist and kills again to help her. Schlock
horror programmer. Rondo Hatton, Tom
Neal, Jane Adams. Written by George Bricker
and M. Coates Webster; directed by Jean
Yarborough; for Universal (who were so
ashamed of it that they farmed it out to PRC).

The Buccaneer*
US 1938 90m bw
Paramount (Cecil B. de Mille)

During the 1812 war, pirate Jean Lafitte helps
president Andrew Jackson to repel the British.
Sprightly adventure romance with generally
good production and acting.

w Jeanie Macpherson, Edwin Justus Mayer,
Harold Lamb, C. Gardner Sullivan *d* Cecil B.
de Mille *ph* Victor Milner *md* Boris Morros
m Georges Antheil

Fredric March, Franciska Gaal, *Akim
Tamiroff*, Margot Grahame, Walter Brennan,
Ian Keith, Spring Byington, Douglass
Dumbrille, Robert Barrat, Hugh Sothern,
Beulah Bondi, Anthony Quinn, Montagu
Love
'From de Mille's skilled craftsmanship have
come other pictures quite as ambitious, none
more adroitly fabricated, skilfully adjusted to
the norm of appeal to the world audience that
such imposing and costly productions must
command.'—*Terry Ramsaye*

AAN: Victor Milner

The Buccaneer
US 1958   121m   Technicolor
Vistavision
Paramount / Cecil B. de Mille (Henry
Wilcoxon)

Slow, slack and stolid remake of the 1938 film,
with practically no excitement or interest and
very obvious studio sets.

w Jesse L. Lasky Jnr, Berenice Mosk, from
the earlier screenplay *d* Anthony Quinn
ph Loyal Griggs *m* Elmer Bernstein

Yul Brynner, Claire Bloom, Charles Boyer,
Inger Stevens, Henry Hull, Charlton Heston,
E. G. Marshall, Douglass Dumbrille, Lorne
Greene, Ted de Corsia, Robert F. Simon

Buccaneer's Girl
US 1949   77m   Technicolor

A New Orleans entertainer helps to free a
pirate who was her friend. Cheerful action
programmer. Yvonne de Carlo, Philip Friend,
Robert Douglas, Elsa Lanchester. Written by
Harold Shumate and Joseph Hoffman;
directed by Frederick de Cordova; for
Universal-International.

Buchanan Rides Alone
US 1958   78m   colour

A wandering Texan helps a young Mexican
accused of murder. Very moderate star
western. Randolph Scott, Craig Stevens, Barry
Kelley, Peter Whitney. Written by Charles
Lang; directed by Budd Boetticher; for
Columbia.

Buck and the Preacher
US 1971   103m   colour
Columbia / E and R / Belafonte (Joel
Glickman)

Nightriders chasing escaped slaves are
outwitted by a wagon train guide and a con
man.
Lively, easygoing western with a largely black
cast, and a message of militancy sugar-coated
by Hollywood hokum.

w Ernest Kinoy *d* Sidney Poitier *ph* Alex
Phillips *m* Benny Carter

Sidney Poitier, Harry Belafonte, Ruby Dee,
Cameron Mitchell, Denny Miller, Nita Talbot,
John Kelly

Buck Privates*
US 1941   84m   bw
Universal (Alex Gottlieb)
GB title: *Rookies*

Two incompetents in the army accidentally
become heroes.

Abbott and Costello's first starring vehicle is a
tired bundle of army jokes and old routines
separated by plot and romance, but it sent the
comedians right to the top, where they stayed
for ten years.

w Arthur T. Horman *d* Arthur Lubin
ph Milton Krasner *md* Charles Previn

Bud Abbott, Lou Costello, Lee Bowman, Alan
Curtis, Jane Frazee, *The Andrews Sisters, Nat
Pendleton*, Samuel S. Hinds, Shemp Howard

AAN: Charles Previn; song 'The Boogie
Woogie Bugle Boy of Company B' (*m* Hugh
Prince, *ly* Don Raye)

Buck Privates Come Home
US 1946   77m   bw
U-I
GB title: *Rookies Come Home*

Incompetent war veterans are demobilized and
find civilian life tough.
Thin star comedy with a good final chase.

w John Grant, Frederic I. Rinaldo, Robert
Lees *d* Charles T. Barton *ph* Charles Van
Enger

Bud Abbott, Lou Costello, Beverly
Simmons,Tom Brown, Nat Pendleton

Buckskin
US 1968   97m   Pathecolor
Paramount / A. C. Lyles

In the frontier town of Gloryhole a gambler is
routed by the new marshal.
Routine old-fashioned western with this
producer's predictable gallery of
weatherbeaten familiar faces.

w Michael Fisher *d* Michael Moore *ph* W.
Wallace Kelley *m* Jimmie Haskell

Barry Sullivan, Joan Caulfield, Lon Chaney
Jnr, John Russell, Richard Arlen, Barbara
Hale, Bill Williams, Barton Maclane

The Buddy Holly Story
US 1978   113m   colour
Columbia / Innavisions / ECA (Fred Bauer)

The life of a fifties rock-and-roller who died
young in an accident.
Solidly carpentered showbiz biopic for the
youth market.

w Robert Gitler *d* Steve Rash *ph* Stevan
Larner *md* Joe Renzetti

Gary Busey, Dan Stroud, Charles Martin
Smith, Bill Jordan, Maria Rochwine
    'A B movie leavened by grade-A talent.'—
Les Keyser, Hollywood in the Seventies

AA: Joe Renzetti
AAN: Gary Busey

Buffalo Bill*
US 1944 89m Technicolor
TCF (Harry Sherman)

A moderately fictitious account of the life of
William Cody, from buffalo hunter to wild
west showman.
Easygoing entertainment which turns from
western excitements to domestic drama.
Generally watchable.

w Aeneas Mackenzie, Clements Ripley, Cecile
Kramer d William Wellman ph Leon
Shamroy m David Buttolph

Joel McCrea, Maureen O'Hara, Linda
Darnell, Thomas Mitchell, Edgar Buchanan,
Anthony Quinn, Moroni Olsen

**Buffalo Bill and the Indians, or Sitting
Bull's History Lesson**
US 1976 118m colour Panavision
UA / Robert Altman

During winter camp for his wild west show,
Buffalo Bill Cody and his friends discuss life
and his own myth.
Anti-action, alienation-effect talk piece which
has some points of interest for sophisticates
but is likely to set western addicts asking for
their money back.

w Alan Rudolph, Robert Altman, play
Indians by Arthur Kopit d Robert Altman
ph Paul Lohmann m Richard Baskin

Paul Newman, Burt Lancaster, Joel Grey,
Kevin McCarthy, Geraldine Chaplin, Harvey
Keitel, John Considine, Denver Pyle

'The western is an enormously resilient
form, but never has that resilience been tested
quite so much as in this movie . . . it isn't
really a movie, it's a happening.'—*Arthur
Knight*

'Whereas Kopit's play offered a
hallucinatory mosaic, Altman's script has the
one-dimensional clarity of a cartoon.'—
Michael Billington, Illustrated London News

'That American history is the creation of
flamboyant lies and showmanship strikes us at
first as an amusing trifle and then quickly
becomes an epigram shaggy-dogging its way
across two hours of eccentric Altmanship.'—
Will Aitken, Take One

Bug
US 1975 101m Movielab
Paramount / William Castle

Large rocklike insects appear after an
earthquake and set fire to themselves and their
victims.
Absurd, overlong and rather nasty horror film
with no visible redeeming features.

w William Castle, Thomas Page, novel The
Hephaestus Plague by Thomas Page
d Jeannot Szwarc ph Michel Hugo, Ken
Middleham m Charles Fox

Bradford Dillman, Joanna Miles, Richard
Gilliland, Jamie Smith Jackson, Alan Fudge,
Patty McCormack

'The finer scientific points are to say the
least elusive.'—*David Robinson*

The Bugle Sounds
US1941 101m bw
MGM (J. Walter Ruben)

An old cavalry sergeant, discharged for
insubordination, rounds up fifth columnists
and is reinstated.
Ho-hum star vehicle on familiar lines but at
undue length.

w Cyril Hume d S. Sylvan Simon ph Clyde
de Vinna m Lennie Hayton

Wallace Beery, Marjorie Main, Lewis Stone,
George Bancroft, William Lundigan, Henry
O'Neill, Donna Reed, Chill Wills, Roman
Bohnen, Jerome Cowan, Tom Dugan, Guinn
Williams, Jonathan Hale.

Bugles in the Afternoon
US 1952 85m Technicolor
William Cagney

In the US army at the time of Custer's last
stand, a young officer is victimized by a
jealous rival.
Modest, adequate western with nice scenery
but no surprises.

w Geoffrey Homes, Harry Brown, novel
Ernest Haycox d Roy Rowland ph Wilfrid
Cline m Dmitri Tiomkin

Ray Milland, Hugh Marlowe, Helena Carter,
Forrest Tucker, Barton Maclane, George
Reeves, James Millican, Gertrude Michael

Bugsy Malone**
GB 1976 93m Eastmancolor
Rank / Bugsy Malone Productions (David
Puttnam, Allan Marshall)

New York 1929: gangster Fat Sam fights it out
with Dandy Dan, and the best man wins the
girl.
Extremely curious musical gangster spoof with
all the parts played by children and the guns
shooting ice cream. Very professionally done,
but one wonders to whom it is supposed to
appeal.

wd Alan Parker ph Michael Seresin, Peter
Biziou m / songs Paul Williams pd Geoffrey
Kirkland

Scott Baio, Jodie Foster, Florrie Digger, John Cassisi

'If for nothing else, you would have to admire it for the sheer doggedness of its eccentricity.'—*David Robinson, Times*

'All the pizazz in the world couldn't lift it above the level of empty camp.'—*Frank Rich, New York Post*

'I only wish the British could make adult movies as intelligent as this one.'—*Michael Billington, Illustrated London News*

AAN: Paul Williams

Bulldog Drummond*
US 1929 90m bw
Samuel Goldwyn

After advertising for adventure, ex-war hero Drummond is approached by an American girl whose uncle is being held prisoner in a fake nursing home by villainous Carl Petersen. This is the closest the screen ever came to the original Drummond character, debonair yet taking personal and unnecessary vengeance on the chief villain. A fairly primitive talkie with little movement, yet consistently interesting.

w Sidney Howard, *play* 'Sapper' (H. C. McNeile) *d* F. Richard Jones *ph* George Barnes, Gregg Toland *ad William Cameron Menzies*

Ronald Colman, Joan Bennett, *Claud Allister* (as Algy), Lilyan Tashman, Montagu Love, Lawrence Grant

AAN: Ronald Colman

Bulldog Drummond Strikes Back*
US 1934 83m bw
Twentieth Century

Drummond gets married, but delays his honeymoon to investigate a mysterious London house with a disappearing body. Slow-starting, then intriguing light mystery which becomes repetitive and silly. Performances and production enjoyable.

w Nunnally Johnson *d* Roy del Ruth *ph* Peverell Marley *m* Alfred Newman

Ronald Colman, Loretta Young, C. Aubrey Smith, *Charles Butterworth* (Algy), Warner Oland, Mischa Auer, Una Merkel
† The full complement of Drummond films is as follows:
BULLDOG DRUMMOND (GB 1922); silent with Carlyle Brackwell.
THE THIRD ROUND (GB 1925); silent with Jack Buchanan.
BULLDOG DRUMMOND (US 1929); see above.
TEMPLE TOWER (US 1930); lost Fox film with Kenneth MacKenna.

THE RETURN OF BULLDOG DRUMMOND (GB 1934); perhaps the most Fascist of the series, with Ralph Richardson.
BULLDOG JACK (GB 1934); amiable spoof with Jack Hulbert (and Richardson as the Moriarty-like villain). Finale in an Underground tunnel.
BULLDOG DRUMMOND STRIKES BACK (US 1934); see above.
BULLDOG DRUMMOND AT BAY (GB 1937); with John Lodge.
BULLDOG DRUMMOND ESCAPES (US 1937); start of minor series with Ray Milland, later replaced by John Howard (and Guy Standing as Colonel Neilson).
BULLDOG DRUMMOND COMES BACK (US 1937); John Howard takes over from Milland, John Barrymore from Standing.
BULLDOG DRUMMOND'S REVENGE (US 1938); Howard and Barrymore.
BULLDOG DRUMMOND'S PERIL (US 1938); ditto.
BULLDOG DRUMMOND IN AFRICA (US 1938); Howard and H. B. Warner.
ARREST BULLDOG DRUMMOND (US 1938); ditto.
BULLDOG DRUMMOND'S SECRET POLICE (US 1939); ditto.
BULLDOG DRUMMOND'S BRIDE (US 1939); ditto.
BULLDOG SEES IT THROUGH (GB 1939); imitation with Jack Buchanan.
BULLDOG DRUMMOND AT BAY (US 1947); second feature with Ron Randell.
BULLDOG DRUMMOND STRIKES BACK (US 1947); ditto.
THE CHALLENGE (US 1948); with Tom Conway.
THIRTEEN LEAD SOLDIERS (US 1948); ditto.
CALLING BULLDOG DRUMMOND (GB 1951); with Walter Pidgeon.
DEADLIER THAN THE MALE (GB 1967); Richard Johnson as a Bond-like Drummond.
SOME GIRLS DO (GB 1970); Johnson again in a feeble sequel.

Bulldog Jack*
GB 1934 72m bw
Gaumont (Michael Balcon)
US title: *Alias Bulldog Drummond*

A playboy poses as Bulldog Drummond when the real man is injured, and manages to foil the thieves and save the girl.
After a slowish start, this comedy thriller works up into a fine frenzy with exciting scenes on the London Underground and in the British Museum.

w H. C. McNeile, Gerard Fairlie, J. O. C. Orton, Sidney Gilliat *d Walter Forde*

Jack Hulbert, Ralph Richardson, Claude
Hulbert, Fay Wray, Athole Fleming, Paul
Graetz

'There is . . . a mad train ride towards the
terminus and destruction, as good as anything
in screen melodrama.'—*Peter John Dyer, 1965*

'A sense of showmanship that is rewarded in
a full quota of thrills and laughs.'—*Kine
Weekly*

Bullet for a Badman
US 1964 80m Technicolor

An ex-Texas Ranger escapes from prison to
prove his innocence of murder. Lively western
programmer. Audie Murphy, Darren
McGavin, Ruta Lee, Skip Homeier, George
Tobias. Written by Mary and Willard
Winningham; directed by R. G. Springsteen;
for Universal-International.

A Bullet for Joey
US 1955 85m bw
UA / Sam Bischoff, David Diamond

A Canadian policeman prevents the murder of
an atomic scientist.
Listless low-budgeter with familiar stars below
par.

w Geoffrey Homes, A. I. Bezzerides d Lewis
Allen ph Harry Neumann m Harry Sukman

Edward G. Robinson, George Raft, Audrey
Totter, George Dolenz, Peter Hanson, Peter
Van Eyck

A Bullet is Waiting
US 1954 82m Technicolor
Columbia / Welsch (Howard Welsch)

A plane accident brings a policeman and his
prisoner to a lonely farm, where a girl and her
father bring a fresh twist to the situation.
Disappointing melodrama full of pretentious
moralizing and fey characterization.

w Thames Williamson, Casey Robinson
d John Farrow ph Franz Planer m Dmitri
Tiomkin

Jean Simmons, Rory Calhoun, Stephen
McNally, Brian Aherne

Bullets or Ballots*
US 1936 81m bw
Warner (Lou Edelman)

A city cop goes undercover to break the mob.
Vivid routine gangster thriller, not quite of the
top flight, but nearly.

w Seton I. Miller d William Keighley ph Hal
Mohr m Heinz Roemheld

Edward G. Robinson, Joan Blondell,
Humphrey Bogart, Barton Maclane, Frank
McHugh, Dick Purcell, George E. Stone

'A good gangster film of the second class
. . . all the old chivalrous situations of *Chums*
and the *Boy's Own Paper* are agreeably
translated into sub-machine gun terms.'—
Graham Greene

The Bullfighter and the Lady
US 1950 87m bw
Republic / John Wayne (Budd Boetticher)

A young American in Mexico is fascinated by
bullfighting but during training accidentally
causes the death of a great matador.
Predictable, rather boring plot given routine
treatment: for aficionados only.

w James Edward Grant d Budd Boetticher
ph Jack Draper m Victor Young

Robert Stack, Gilbert Roland, Joy Page, Katy
Jurado, Virginia Grey, John Hubbard

AAN: original story (Budd Boetticher, Ray
Nazarro)

The Bullfighters*
US 1945 60m bw
TCF (William Girard)

Two detectives in Mexico find that one of
them resembles a famous matador.
Laurel and Hardy's last American feature is
poor enough as a whole, but at least has a few
sequences in their earlier style.

w Scott Darling d Mal St Clair ph Norbert
Brodine m David Buttolph

Stan Laurel, Oliver Hardy, Richard Lane,
Carol Woode

Bullitt**
US 1968 113m Technicolor
Warner / Solar (Philip D'Antoni)

A San Francisco police detective conceals the
death of an underground witness in his charge,
and goes after the killers himself.
Routine cop thriller with undoubted charisma,
distinguished by a splendid car chase which
takes one's mind off the tedious plot.
Technical credits first class.

w Harry Kleiner, Alan R. Trustman, *novel*
Mute Witness by Robert L. Pike d Peter
Yates ph William A. Fraker m Lalo Schifrin

Steve McQueen, Jacqueline Bisset, Robert
Vaughn, Don Gordon, Robert Duvall, Simon
Oakland

'It has energy, drive, impact, and above all,
style.'—*Hollis Alpert*

Bunco Squad
US 1950 67m bw

The police expose a fake medium. Slightly
unusual cop caper. Robert Sterling, Ricardo

Cortez, Joan Dixon. Written by George E. Callahan; directed by Herbert Leeds; for RKO.

Bundle of Joy
US 1956   98m   Technicolor   RKOscope
RKO / Edmund Grainger

A shopgirl finds an abandoned baby and everyone thinks it is hers.
Tame musical remake of *Bachelor Mother*; some laughs, but poor numbers.

w Norman Krasna, Arthur Sheekman, Robert Carson d Norman Taurog ph William Snyder m Josef Myrow

Debbie Reynolds, Eddie Fisher, Adolphe Menjou, Melville Cooper, Tommy Noonan, Nita Talbot, Una Merkel, Robert H. Harris

Bunny Lake is Missing**
GB 1965   107m   bw   Panavision
Columbia / Wheel (Otto Preminger)

The 4-year-old illegitimate daughter of an American girl in London disappears, and no one can be found to admit that she ever existed.
A nightmarish gimmick story, with more gimmicks superimposed along the way to say nothing of a *Psycho*ish ending; some of the decoration works and makes even the unconvincing story compelling, while the cast is alone worth the price of admission.

w John and Penelope Mortimer, *novel* Evelyn Piper d Otto Preminger ph Denys Coop m Paul Glass pd Don Ashton *titles* Saul Bass

Laurence Olivier, Carol Lynley, Keir Dullea, Noel Coward, Martita Hunt, Finlay Currie, Clive Revill, Anna Massey, Lucie Mannheim

'It has the enjoyable hallmarks of really high calibre professionalism.'—*Penelope Houston*

Bunny O'Hare
US 1971   92m   Movielab
AIP (Gerd Oswald, Norman T. Herman)

A middle-aged widow and an ex-con plumber become bank robbers, dressed as hippies and escaping on a motor cycle.
Unappealing, ill-thought-out comedy with pretensions to satire, an unhappy venture for both stars.

w Stanley Z. Cherry, Coslough Johnson d Gerd Oswald ph Loyal Griggs, John Stephens m Billy Strange

Bette Davis, Ernest Borgnine, Jack Cassidy, Joan Delaney, Jay Robinson, John Astin

Buona Sera Mrs Campbell*
US 1968   113m   Technicolor
UA / Connaught (Melvin Frank)

Wartime USAF comrades reassemble twenty years later in an Italian village, and three find that they have been paying paternity money to the same local glamour girl.
Agreeably cast, pleasantly set and photographed, quite funny in parts, this comedy of middle age unfortunately outstays its welcome and lets its invention peter out.

w Melvin Frank, Denis Norden, Sheldon Keller d Melvin Frank ph Gabor Pogany m Riz Ortolani

Gina Lollobrigida, Telly Savalas, Phil Silvers, Peter Lawford, Lee Grant, Marian Moses, Shelley Winters

Bureau of Missing Persons
US 1933   73m   bw

Police chief helps a girl find her husband, who turns out to have been murdered. Fast-moving potboiler typical of its studio. Pat O'Brien, Bette Davis, Lewis Stone, Glenda Farrell, Allen Jenkins, Hugh Herbert. Written by Robert Presnell; directed by Roy del Ruth; for Warner.

The Burglar*
US 1957   80m   bw
Columbia (Louis W. Kellerman)

A burglar is shadowed by a policeman who is also after the loot.
Slightly pretentious but watchable low-budgeter.

w David Goodis from his novel d / ed Paul Wendkos ph Don Malkames m Sol Kaplan

Dan Duryea, Jayne Mansfield, Martha Vickers, Peter Capell

The Burglars
France / Italy 1971   120m   Eastmancolor
                    Panavision
Columbia / Vides (Henri Verneuil)
original title: *La Casse*

A determined policeman chases three burglars and their girl accomplice.
Expensive, camped-up version of *The Burglar*, with plenty going on, most of it borrowed from other films.

w Vahe Katcha, Henri Verneuil, *novel* The Burglar by David Goodis d Henri Verneuil ph Claude Renoir m Ennio Morricone

Omar Sharif, Jean-Paul Belmondo, Dyan Cannon, Robert Hossein, Nicole Calfan, Renato Salvatori

'Electronic equipment, wild action, exotic locales and bland villainy.'—*Tom Milne, MFB*

Burke and Hare

GB 1971   91m   De Luxe
UA / Kenneth Shipman / Armitage (Guido
Coen)

The story of anatomist Dr Knox and his body
snatchers, retold with emphasis on the local
brothel. Depressing in its childish attempts to
be gruesome and perverted.

w Ernie Bradford d Vernon Sewell
ph Desmond Dickinson m Roger Webb

Harry Andrews, Derren Nesbitt, Glynn
Edwards, Yootha Joyce, Dee Sjendery, Alan
Tucker

The Burmese Harp***

Japan 1956   116m   bw
Nikkatsu (Masayuki Takagi)
original title: Biruma no tategoto

A shell-shocked Japanese soldier stays in the
Burmese jungle to bury the unknown dead.
Deeply impressive and horrifying war film with
an epic, folk-tale quality, emphasized by
superbly controlled direction.

w Natto Wada, novel Michio Takeyama
d Kon Ichikawa ph Minoru Yokoyama
m Akira Ifukube

Shoji Yasui, Rentaro Mikuni, Tatsuya Mihashi

The Burning Hills

US 1956   92m   Warnercolor
Cinemascope

A young rancher gets even with a cattle baron
who had his brother killed. Reasonable but
unexciting star vehicle. Natalie Wood, Tab
Hunter, Skip Homeier, Eduard Franz. Earl
Holliman. Written by Irving Wallace, from a
novel by Louis L'Amour; directed by Stuart
Heisler; for Warner.

Burnt Offerings

US 1976   115m   De Luxe
UA / PEA-Dan Curtis (Robert Singer)

An evil house restores itself by feeding on its
tenants.

An agreeably macabre idea for a five-page
story is dragged out to interminable length,
and seizes the attention only by a few shock
moments. The title is mysteriously irrelevant.

w William F. Nolan, Dan Curtis, novel Robert
Marasco d Dan Curtis ph Jacques
Marquette m Robert Colbert pd Eugene
Lourie

Oliver Reed, Karen Black, Bette Davis, Lee
Montgomery, Burgess Meredith, Eileen
Heckart, Dub Taylor

'Before the ludicrous dénouement, the
movie merely piles on one special effect after

another—none of them too special—and stalls
for time.'—Janet Maslin, Newsweek

Bus Riley's Back in Town*

US 1965   93m   Eastmancolor
U-I (Elliott Kastner)

An ex-sailor wants to settle back into small-
town life but finds that his girl friend has
married.
Watchable, middling, routine small-town
drama in the style of Picnic.

w Walter Gage (William Inge) d Harvey
Hart ph Russell Metty m Richard Markowitz

Michael Parks, Ann-Margret, Jocelyn Brando,
Janet Margolin, Kim Darby, Brad Dexter,
Larry Storch, Crahan Denton, Mimsy Farmer,
David Carradine

Bus Stop**

US 1956   96m   Eastmancolor
Cinemascope
TCF (Buddy Adler)
TV title: The Wrong Kind of Girl

In a rodeo town, a simple-thinking cowboy
meets a café singer and asks her to marry him.
Sex comedy-drama, a modest entertainment in
familiar American vein, very well done but
rather over-inflated by its star.

w George Axelrod, play William Inge
d Joshua Logan ph Milton Krasner m Alfred
Newman, Cyril Mockridge

Marilyn Monroe, Don Murray, Betty Field,
Arthur O'Connell, Eileen Heckart, Robert
Bray, Hope Lange, Hans Conried, Casey
Adams

'The film demands of its principal
performers a purely physical display of their
bodies viewed as sexual machinery.'—David
Robinson

AAN: Don Murray

Bush Christmas

GB 1947   77m   bw

Australian children on holiday help catch
horse thieves. Rather stolid family feature
which got a reputation it hardly deserved.
Chips Rafferty, John Fernside. Written and
directed by Ralph Smart; for ABFD.

Busman's Honeymoon*

GB 1940   99m   bw
MGM (Harold Huth)
US title: Haunted Honeymoon

Lord Peter Wimsey finds a murder to be
solved in his honeymoon cottage.
Pleasant, slightly flat film version of a
favourite old-fashioned detective novel.

w Monckton Hoffe, Angus Macphail, Harold Goldman, *novel* Dorothy L. Sayers *d* Arthur Woods *ph* F. A. Young

Robert Montgomery, Constance Cummings, Leslie Banks, Seymour Hicks, Robert Newton, Googie Withers, Frank Pettingell, Joan Kemp-Welch

Buster and Billie
US 1973 99m CFI colour

A sensitive high school senior elects to marry the school's derided 'easy lay', with tragic results. Unattractive reminiscences of rural Georgia with a rather desperate appeal to oversexed teenagers. Jan-Michael Vincent, Pamela Sue Martin, Joan Goodfellow, Clifton James. Written by Ron Turbeville; directed by Daniel Petrie; for Black Creek Billie / Columbia.

The Buster Keaton Story*
US 1957 91m bw Vistavision
Paramount (Sidney Sheldon, Robert Smith)

A biopic of the great silent comedian, with the emphasis on his years of downfall through drink.
An interesting recreation of Hollywood in the twenties and thirties is the main asset of this otherwise dismal tribute to a man whose greatness the star is unable to suggest apart from a few acrobatic moments.

w Robert Smith, Sidney Sheldon *d* Sidney Sheldon *ph* Loyal Griggs *m* Victor Young

Donald O'Connor, Rhonda Fleming, Ann Blyth, Peter Lorre, Larry Keating, Richard Anderson, Dave Willock

Busting
US 1973 92m De Luxe
UA / Chartoff-Winkler (Henry Gellis)

Two Los Angeles vice squad officers fight corruption inside and outside the force. Violent, exhausting, but totally routine police caper of the seventies.

wd Peter Hyams *ph* Earl Rath *m* Billy Goldenberg

Elliott Gould, Robert Blake, Allen Garfield, Antonio Fargas
'The farcical version of *Serpico*.'—*Michael Billington, Illustrated London News*

Busy Bodies**
US 1933 20m bw

Stan and Ollie are involved in various disasters in a sawmill. Though not among their most sympathetic comedies, this is a sustained and brilliantly contrived slapstick sequence. Laurel and Hardy, Tiny Sandford, Charlie Hall. Written by Anon (and Stan Laurel); directed by Lloyd French; for Hal Roach.

The Busy Body
US 1966 102m Techniscope
Paramount / William Castle

A gangster is buried in a suit with a million dollar lining which various people are out to get.
Unfunny black comedy; laboured handling makes it a joke in poor taste.

w Ben Starr, *novel* Donald E. Westlake *d* William Castle *ph* Hal Stine *m* Vic Mizzy

Robert Ryan, Sid Caesar, Arlene Golonka, Anne Baxter, Kay Medford, Charles McGraw

But Not for Me
US 1959 105m bw
Paramount (William Perlberg, George Seaton)

An ageing, washed-up Broadway producer is loved by his young drama student secretary. Rather heavy-going remake of *Accent on Youth*, efficiently performed but lacking the original gaiety.

w John Michael Hayes *d* Walter Lang *ph* Robert Burks *m* Leith Stevens

Clark Gable, Carroll Baker, Lilli Palmer, Lee J. Cobb, Barry Coe, Thomas Gomez

But The Flesh Is Weak
US 1932 82m bw

A widower and his son both decide to marry wealthy widows. Amusing high society comedy from Ivor Novello's *The Truth Game*. Robert Montgomery, C. Aubrey Smith, Heather Thatcher, Edward Everett Horton, Nils Asther. Written by Ivor Novello; directed by Jack Conway; for MGM.

Butch and Sundance: The Early Days*
US 1979 112m De Luxe
TCF (Gabriel Katzka, Stephen Bach)

Early episodes in the careers of the famous outlaws, culminating in a train robbery. 'Prequel' to a more celebrated but not a fresher or more lyrical western.

w Allan Burns *d* Richard Lester *ph* Laszlo Kovacs *m* Patrick Williams *pd* Brian Eatwell

Tom Berenger, William Katt, Jeff Corey, John Schuck, Michael C. Gwynne, Brian Dennehy, Peter Weller

Butch Cassidy and the Sundance Kid***
US 1969 110m De Luxe Panavision
TCF / Campanile (John Foreman)

A hundred years ago, two western train robbers keep one step ahead of the law until finally tracked down to Bolivia.

Humorous, cheerful, poetic, cinematic account of two semi-legendary outlaws, winningly acted and directed. One of the decade's great commercial successes, not least because of the song 'Raindrops Keep Fallin' on My Head'.

w William Goldman d George Roy Hill ph Conrad Hall m Burt Bacharach

Paul Newman, Robert Redford, Katharine Ross, Strother Martin, Henry Jones, Jeff Corey, Cloris Leachman, Ted Cassidy, Kenneth Mars

'A mere exercise in smart-alecky device-mongering, chock-full of out of place and out of period one-upmanship, a battle of wits at a freshman smoker.'—*John Simon*

AA: William Goldman; Conrad Hall; Burt Bacharach; song 'Raindrops Keep Fallin' on My Head' (*m* Burt Bacharach, *ly* Hal David)
AAN: best picture; George Roy Hill

Butley*
US / GB 1973   130m   Eastmancolor
American Express / Ely Landau / Cinevision

Personal problems assail an English lecturer at a university college.

Adequate but not outstanding transcription (for the American Film Theatre) of a successful and percipient play.

w Simon Gray, from his play *d* Harold Pinter
ph Gerry Fisher *m* none

Alan Bates, Jessica Tandy, Richard Callaghan, Susan Engel, Michael Byrne

The Butter and Egg Man
US

This pleasant George S. Kaufman comedy about a cowboy in New York was filmed as a silent in 1928, with Jack Mulhall; in 1932 as *The Tenderfoot* with Joe E. Brown; in 1937 as *Dance Charlie Dance* with Stuart Erwin; and in 1940 as *An Angel from Texas* with Eddie Albert; all for Warner in Hollywood.

The Buttercup Chain*
GB 1970   95m   Technicolor   Panavision
Columbia (Leslie Gilliat, John Whitney, Philip Waddilove)

A hothouse sex quartet changes partners with bewildering rapidity against a background of European splendour.

Chi-chi romance with a fashionably disillusioned and tragic ending. As watchable as the best TV commercials, but totally empty.

w Peter Draper, *novel* Janice Elliott *d* Robert Ellis Miller *ph* Douglas Slocombe *m* Richard Rodney Bennett

Hywel Bennett, Leigh Taylor-Young, Jane Asher, Sven-Bertil Taube, Clive Revill, Roy Dotrice

Butterfield Eight
US 1960   108m   Metrocolor
Cinemascope
MGM / Afton / Linebrook (Pandro S. Berman)

A society call girl has a complex love life.

This coy sex drama seemed mildly daring in 1960, but has since been well outclassed in that field and certainly has nothing else going for it except good production values.

w Charles Schnee, John Michael Hayes, *novel* John O'Hara *d* Daniel Mann *ph* Joseph Ruttenberg, Charles Harten *m* Bronislau Kaper

Elizabeth Taylor, Laurence Harvey, Eddie Fisher, Dina Merrill, Mildred Dunnock, Betty Field, Jeffrey Lynn, Kay Medford, Susan Oliver

'The mixture resolutely refuses to come to the boil.'—*John Gillett*

AA: Elizabeth Taylor
AAN: Joseph Ruttenberg, Charles Harten

Butterflies are Free
US 1972   109m   Eastmancolor
Columbia / M. J. Frankovich

An aspiring actress falls for a blind neighbour but is handicapped by his possessive mother. Three-character comedy-drama from a slight, sentimental but successful Broadway play.

w Leonard Gershe, from his play *d* Milton Katselas *ph* Charles B. Lang *m* Bob Alcivar

Goldie Hawn, Edward Albert, Eileen Heckart

AA: Eileen Heckart
AAN: Charles B. Lang

Buy Me That Town*
US 1941   70m   bw
Paramount (Sol C. Siegel)

Gangsters take over a small town and pull the community out of bankruptcy.

Unusual comedy-drama, quite well done for a second feature.

w Gordon Kahn *d* Eugene Forde
ph Theodor Sparkuhl

Lloyd Nolan, Albert Dekker, Constance Moore, Sheldon Leonard, Vera Vague, Edward Brophy, Horace MacMahon, Warren Hymer

Bwana Devil
US 1952   79m   Anscocolor   3D
(UA) Arch Oboler

At the turn of the century, two man-eating lions threaten an African railroad.
Inept actioner notable only as the first film in 3-D ('Natural Vision'), advertised with the famous slogan 'A lion in your lap'.

wd Arch Oboler ph Joseph Biroc m Gordon Jenkins

Robert Stack, Barbara Britton, Nigel Bruce, Ramsay Hill

By Candlelight*
US 1934   70m   bw
Universal (Carl Laemmle Jnr)

On a transcontinental train a woman meets a butler and takes him for a prince; he does not disillusion her.
Moderately pleasing romantic comedy of the old school.

w Hans Kraly, F. Hugh Herbert, Karen de Wolf, Ruth Cummings, play Siegfried Geyer d James Whale

Elissa Landi, Paul Lukas, Nils Asther
'A dazzling display of romantic confidence trickery which takes on Lubitsch in his own territory.'—Tom Milne, 1978

By Love Possessed*
US 1961   116m   De Luxe   Panavision
UA / Mirat (Walter Mirisch)

A Massachusetts lawyer reflects on the outlandish sexual mores of himself, his family and friends.
Peyton Place moved up in the social scale; a reasonably absorbing melodrama but hardly memorable.

w John Dennis, novel James Gould Cozzens d John Sturges ph Russell Metty m Elmer Bernstein

Lana Turner, Efrem Zimbalist Jnr, Jason Robards Jnr, Barbara Bel Geddes, George Hamilton, Susan Kohner, Thomas Mitchell, Yvonne Craig, Everett Sloane
'A talky succession of soap opera situations.'—Robert Windeler

By the Light of the Silvery Moon*
US 1953   101m   Technicolor
Warner (William Jacobs)

In a small American town in 1918, the Winfield family has several problems arising from the return of daughter Marjorie's soldier boyfriend.
A sequel to On Moonlight Bay (qv), presenting further situations from the Penrod stories retailored for Doris Day. Inoffensive, well-made, old-fashioned entertainment with nostalgic songs and an archetypal family.

w Robert O'Brien, Irving Elinson, from stories by Booth Tarkington d David Butler ph Wilfrid M. Cline m Max Steiner

Doris Day, Gordon Macrae, Leon Ames, Rosemary de Camp, Mary Wickes

Bye Bye Birdie
US 1963   112m   Eastmancolor
     Panavision
Columbia / Fred Kohlmar / George Sidney

Havoc suffuses the last TV show of a pop star before he goes into the army.
Noisy, frenetic musical, hard to follow and even harder to like, with all the satire of the stage original subtracted. For young audiences who enjoy incoherence.

w Irving Brecher, from musical by Michael Stewart d George Sidney ph Joseph Biroc md Johnny Green songs Charles Strouse, Lee Adams

Janet Leigh, Dick Van Dyke, Maureen Stapleton, Ann-Margret, Bobby Rydell, Jesse Pearson, Ed Sullivan, Paul Lynde, Robert Paige

AAN: Johnny Green

Bye Bye Braverman*
US 1968   92m   Technicolor
Warner / Sidney Lumet

New Yorkers get drunk and disillusioned on their way home from the funeral of a friend.
Witty, downbeat Jewish comedy which does not quite come off and would in any case be caviare to the general.

w Herbert Sargent, novel To an Early Grave by Wallace Markfield d Sidney Lumet ph Boris Kaufman m Peter Matz

George Segal, Jack Warden, Joseph Wiseman, Sorrell Booke, Jessica Walter, Phyllis Newman, Zohra Lampert, Alan King, Godfrey Cambridge
'You don't have to be Jewish to love it, but it helps a lot to be a New Yorker.'—Robert Hatch, The Nation

C

Cabaret***
US 1972 123m Technicolor
ABC Pictures / Allied Artists (Cy Feuer)

In the early thirties, Berlin is a hotbed of vice and anti-semitism. In the Kit Kat Klub, singer Sally Bowles shares her English lover with a homosexual German baron, and her Jewish friend Natasha has troubles of her own.
This version of Isherwood's Berlin stories regrettably follows the plot line of the play *I Am a Camera* rather than the Broadway musical on which it is allegedly based, and it lacks the incisive remarks of the MC, but the very smart direction creates a near-masterpiece of its own, and most of the songs are intact.

w Jay Presson Allen, from Goodbye to Berlin by Christopher Isherwood *d / ch Bob Fosse m John Kander ly Fred Ebb ph Geoffrey Unsworth md Ralph Burns pd Rolf Zehetbauer*

Liza Minnelli, Joel Grey, Michael York, Helmut Griem, Fritz Wepper, Marisa Berenson

'A stylish, sophisticated entertainment for grown-up people.'—*John Russell Taylor*
'Film journals will feast for years on shots from this picture; as it rolled along, I saw page after illustrated page from a not-too-distant book called *The Cinema of Bob Fosse*.'—*Stanley Kauffmann*

AA: Bob Fosse (as director); Geoffrey Unsworth; Ralph Burns; Liza Minnelli; Joel Grey
AAN: best picture; Jay Presson Allen

Cabin in the Cotton*
US 1932 79m bw
Warner (Hal B. Wallis)

A sharecropper is almost ruined by a southern belle.
Dated melodrama with interesting style and performances.

w Paul Green, *novel* Harry Harrison Knoll *d* Michael Curtiz *ph* Barney McGill

Richard Barthelmess, Dorothy Jordan, Bette Davis, David Landau, Tully Marshall, Henry B. Walthall, Hardie Albright

Cabin in the Sky**
US 1943 99m bw
MGM (Arthur Freed)

An idle, gambling husband is reformed by a dream of his own death, with God and Satan battling for his soul.
Consistently interesting, often lively, but generally rather stilted all-black musical which must have seemed a whole lot fresher on the stage. Still, a good try.

w Joseph Schrank, *musical play* Lynn Root *d* Vincente Minnelli *ph Sidney Wagner md* George Stoll *new songs: m* Harold Arlen, *ly* E. Y. Harburg *show songs: m* Vernon Duke, *ly* John Latouche, Ted Fetter

Eddie 'Rochester' Anderson, Ethel Waters, Lena Horne, Cab Calloway, Louis Armstrong, John W. Bublett

'Broadway's big, fun-jammed music show is on the screen at last—crowded with stars and songs and spectacle in the famed MGM manner!'—*publicity*

AAN: song 'Happiness Is Just a Thing Called Joe' (*m* Harold Arlen, *ly* E. Y. Harburg)

The Cabinet of Caligari
US 1962 105m bw Cinemascope
TCF / Lippert (Roger Kay)

A young woman whose car breaks down near a country house is held prisoner by the sinister Caligari. Eventually it transpires that the mystery is all in her imagination: he is a psychiatrist and she an old lady whose sexual fantasies he has been curing.
Interminably talkative and frequently (unintentionally) funny trick film with the odd moment of effective suspense. The original ending, which cast some doubt on who was mad and who sane, is no longer available. The actors do not entirely escape absurdity.

w Robert Bloch *d* Roger Kay *ph* John Russell *m* Gerald Fried

Glynis Johns, Dan O'Herlihy, Constance Ford, Dick Davalos, Lawrence Dobkin

'It is impossible to be grateful for the film on any of its levels.'—*MFB*
'The most complete essay in the décor of delirium.'—*New Yorker, 1979*

† The fact that the story is told through the eyes of a mad person is the only link with the 1919 classic.

The Cabinet of Dr Caligari****
Germany 1919   90m approx (16 fps)
bw   silent
Decla-Bioscop (Erich Pommer)

A fairground showman uses a somnambulist for purposes of murder and is finally revealed to be the director of a lunatic asylum; but the whole story is only the dream of a madman. Faded now, but a film of immense influence on the dramatic art of cinema, with its odd angles, stylized sets and hypnotic acting, not to mention the sting in the tail of its story (added by the producer).

w Carl Mayer, Hans Janowitz d Robert Wiene ph Willy Hameister ad Hermann Warm, Walter Röhrig, Walter Reiman

Werner Krauss, Conrad Veidt, Lil Dagover, Friedrich Feher, Hans von Twardowski

Cabiria**
Italy / France 1957   110m   bw
Dino de Laurentiis / Les Films Marceau
original title: *Le Notti di Cabiria*; aka:
Nights of Cabiria

A Roman prostitute has dreams of romance and respectability.
A bitter Cinderella story which was later turned into the Broadway musical *Sweet Charity*. Much of interest, but the leading lady is too Chaplinesque.

w Federico Fellini, Ennio Flaiano, Tullio Pinelli d Federico Fellini ph Aldo Tonti m Nino Rota

Giulietta Masina, François Périer, Amedeo Nazzari, Franca Marzi, Dorian Gray
   'Any nobility in the original conception slowly suffocates in an atmosphere of subjective indulgence bordering dangerously on self-pity.'—*Peter John Dyer*
AA: best foreign film

Caccia Tragica*
Italy 1947   89m   bw
Lux / ANPI
aka: *The Tragic Pursuit*

A bandit is hunted through the Po valley but finally allowed to escape.
Minor peripatetic melodrama, well-handled and exciting but uncertain in mood.

w Giuseppe de Santis, Michelangelo Antonioni, Cesare Zavattini, Carlo Lizzani, Unberto Barbaro d Giuseppe de Santis ph Otello Martelli m Giuseppe Rosati

Massimo Girotti, Andrea Checci, Vivi Gioi

Cactus Flower*
US 1969   103m   Technicolor
Columbia / M. J. Frankovich

To deceive his mistress, a dentist employs his starchy secretary to pose as his wife, and falls for her when she loosens up.
Amusing sophisticated comedy, generally well handled.

w I. A. L. Diamond, *play* Abe Burrows, French original by Pierre Barillet, Jean Pierre Gredy *d* Gene Saks *ph* Charles E. Lang *m* Quincy Jones *pd* Robert Clatworthy

Ingrid Bergman, Walter Matthau, Goldie Hawn, Jack Weston, Rick Lenz, Vito Scotti, Irene Hervey
AA: Goldie Hawn

The Caddy
US 1953   95m   bw
Paramount (Paul Jones)

A music hall comedy act recall how they got together.
Less a feature than a series of short sketches, this ragbag has its choice moments, but they are few.

w Edmund Hartmann, Danny Arnold *d* Norman Taurog *ph* Daniel L. Fapp *m* Joseph L. Lilley

Dean Martin, Jerry Lewis, Donna Reed, Barbara Bates, Joseph Calleia, Fred Clark, Clinton Sundberg, Marshall Thompson
AAN: song 'That's Amore' (*m* Harry Warren, *ly* Jack Brooks)

Caddyshack
US 1980   98m   Technicolor

Misadventures at a golf club. A relentlessly crude and lumbering series of farcical incidents which mainly fail to raise laughs. Chevy Chase, Rodney Dangerfield, Ted Knight, Michael O'Keefe. Written by Brian Doyle-Murray, Harold Ramis and Douglas Kenney; directed by Harold Ramis; for Jon Peters / Orion. 'There are jests about vomiting and nose-picking, while the most elaborate gag sequence involves a chocolate bar falling into a swimming pool and being mistaken for a turd . . . a sustained exercise in tiresomeness.'— *Tim Pulleine, MFB*

Caesar and Cleopatra**
GB 1945   135m   Technicolor
Rank / Gabriel Pascal

An elaborate screen treatment of Bernard Shaw's comedy about Caesar's years in Alexandria.
Britain's most expensive film is an absurd extravaganza for which the producer actually

took sand to Egypt to get the right colour. It has compensations however in the sets, the colour, the performances and the witty lines, though all its virtues are theatrical rather than cinematic and the play is certainly not a major work.

w Bernard Shaw d Gabriel Pascal ph F. A. Young, Robert Krasker, Jack Hildyard, Jack Cardiff m Georges Auric decor, costumes Oliver Messel sets John Bryan

Claude Rains, Vivien Leigh, Cecil Parker, Stewart Granger, Flora Robson, Francis L. Sullivan, Raymond Lovell, Anthony Harvey, Anthony Eustrel, Basil Sydney, Ernest Thesiger, Stanley Holloway, Leo Genn, Jean Simmons, Esmé Percy, Michael Rennie

'It cost over a million and a quarter pounds, took two and a half years to make, and well and truly bored one spectator for two and a quarter hours.'—*Richard Winnington*

'Days of magnificent adventure . . . nights of maddest revelry . . . a temptation in Technicolor!'—*American publicity*

Café Metropole
US 1937 83m bw
TCF (Nunnally Johnson)

An heiress in Paris romances a Russian nobleman who is actually a penniless American.
Lighter-than-air romance which passed the time at the time.

w Jacques Duval d Edward H. Griffith ph Lucien Andriot md Louis Silvers

Loretta Young, Adolphe Menjou, Tyrone Power, Charles Winninger, Gregory Ratoff, Christian Rub, Helen Westley

'Here is a very amusing script, admirable acting . . . all thrown away by inferior direction. The camera is planked down four-square before the characters like a plain, honest, inexpressibly dull guest at a light and loony party.'—*Graham Greene*

Café Society
US 1939 84m bw
Paramount

A publicity-seeking socialite impulsively marries a reporter who has annoyed her, but instead of making a fool of him she falls in love.
Faded light comedy which was never outstanding.

w Virginia Van Upp d Edward H. Griffith ph Ted Tetzlaff

Madeleine Carroll, Fred MacMurray, Shirley Ross, Claude Gillingwater

La Cage aux Folles*
France / Italy 1978 91m Eastmancolor
UA / PAA / Da Ma (Marcello Danon)
aka: *Birds of a Feather*

A homosexual nightclub owner is persuaded by his straight son to behave properly in front of his girl friend's parents, but chaos comes on the night of the party.
Internationally popular near-the-knuckle farce with excellent moments and some *longueurs*.

w Francis Veber, Edouard Molinaro, Marcello Danon, Jean Poiret, play Jean Poiret d Edouard Molinaro ph Armando Nannuzzi m Ennio Morricone

Ugo Tognazzi, Michel Serrault, Michel Galabru, Claire Maurier, Remi Laurent

Cage of Gold*
GB 1950 83m bw
Ealing (Michael Relph)

A girl's philandering ex-husband comes back into her life and is murdered.
Mild mystery melodrama in which the puzzle comes too late.

w Jack Whittingham d Basil Dearden ph Douglas Slocombe m Georges Auric

Jean Simmons, David Farrar, James Donald, Madeleine Lebeau, Maria Mauban, Herbert Lom, Bernard Lee, Gladys Henson, Harcourt Williams, Grégoire Aslan

Caged*
US 1950 96m bw
Warner (Jerry Wald)

After being involved in a robbery a 19-year-old girl is sent to prison, and finds the staff more terrifying than the inmates.
Slick, superficial, hysterically harrowing women-in-prison melodrama; predictably overblown but also effective and powerful.

w Virginia Kellogg, Bernard Schoenfeld d John Cromwell ph Carl Guthrie m Max Steiner

Eleanor Parker, Agnes Moorehead, Ellen Corby, *Hope Emerson*, Betty Garde, Jan Sterling, Lee Patrick, Olive Deering, Jane Darwell, Gertrude Michael, Joan Miller
† Remade in 1962 as *House of Women*, directed by Walter Doniger, with Shirley Knight.

AAN: Virginia Kellogg, Bernard Schoenfeld; Eleanor Parker; Hope Emerson

Cahill, US Marshal
US 1973 103m Technicolor
 Panavision
Warner / Batjac (Michael A. Wayne)

A stalwart western marshal finds that his own young sons are involved in a robbery he is investigating.
Satisfactory but sentimental John Wayne vehicle with the star too often yielding place to the rather boring young folk.

w Harry Julian Fink, Rita M. Fink d Andrew V. McLaglen ph Joseph Biroc m Elmer Bernstein

John Wayne, George Kennedy, Gary Grimes, Neville Brand, Clay O'Brien, Marie Windsor, Royal Dano, Denver Pyle, Jackie Coogan

Cain and Mabel*
US 1936   90m   bw
Warner (Sam Bischoff)
Tribulations of a prizefighter in love with a showgirl.
Generously produced but weakly written comedy drama with rather unexpected musical numbers; not a successful whole, but interesting.

w Laird Doyle, H. C. Witwer d Lloyd Bacon ph George Barnes

Clark Gable, Marion Davies, Allen Jenkins, Roscoe Karns, Walter Catlett, Hobart Cavanaugh, Pert Kelton, Ruth Donelly, E. E. Clive

The Caine Mutiny**
US 1954   125m   Technicolor
Columbia / Stanley Kramer
Jealousies and frustrations among the officers of a peacetime destroyer come to a head when the neurotic captain panics during a typhoon and is relieved of his post. At the resulting trial the officers learn about themselves.
Decent if lamely paced version of a bestseller which also made a successful play; the film skates too lightly over the characterizations and even skimps the courtroom scene, but there are effective scenes and performances.

w Stanley Roberts, novel Herman Wouk d Edward Dmytryk ph Franz Planer m Max Steiner

Humphrey Bogart, Jose Ferrer, Van Johnson, Fred MacMurray, Robert Francis, May Wynn, Tom Tully, E. G. Marshall, Lee Marvin, Arthur Franz

AAN: best picture; Stanley Roberts; Max Steiner; Humphrey Bogart; Tom Tully

Cairo*
US 1941   100m   bw
MGM (Joseph L. Mankiewicz)
An American war reporter in Egypt meets a screen star and thinks she is a spy.

Mildly pleasing light comedy-drama with self-spoofing elements.

w John McClain d W. S. Van Dyke II ph Ray June md Herbert Stothart

Jeanette MacDonald, Robert Young, Ethel Waters, Reginald Owen, Lionel Atwill, Mona Barrie, Eduardo Ciannelli, Dennis Hoey, Dooley Wilson

Cairo
GB 1963   91m   bw
MGM (Ronald Kinnoch)
Crooks plan to steal Tutankhamun's jewels from the Cairo Museum.
Spiritless remake of The Asphalt Jungle (qv).

w Joanne Court d Wolf Rilla ph Desmond Dickinson m Kenneth V. Jones

George Sanders, Richard Johnson, Faten Hamama, John Meillon, Eric Pohlmann, Walter Rilla

Cairo Road
GB 1950   95m   bw
ABP (Aubrey Baring)
An Egyptian police chief lays traps for drug smugglers.
Oddly cast, reasonably lively but routine police adventure in an unfamiliar setting.

w Robert Westerby d David MacDonald ph Oswald Morris m Robert Gill

Eric Portman, Laurence Harvey, Maria Mauban, Karel Stepanek, Harold Lang, Camelia, Grégoire Aslan, Oscar Quitak

Calabuch*
Spain / Italy 1956   93m   bw
Aguila / Constellaxione (Jose Luis Jerez)
An atomic scientist settles delightedly in a peaceful Spanish village, but sacrifices his own privacy when he invents a sky rocket.
Semi-satirical Ealing-type comedy which starts engagingly but runs out of steam.

w Leonardo Martin, Ennio Flaiano, Florentino Soria, Luis Berlanga d Luis Berlanga ph Francisco Sempere m Francesco Lavagnino

Edmund Gwenn, Valentina Cortese, Franco Fabrizi

Calamity Jane**
US 1953   101m   Technicolor
Warner (William Jacobs)
Calamity helps a saloon owner friend find a star attraction, and wins the heart of Wild Bill Hickok.

Agreeable, cleaned-up, studio-set western musical patterned after *Annie Get Your Gun*, but a much friendlier film, helped by an excellent score.

w James O'Hanlon d David Butler ph Wilfrid Cline *songs* Sammy Fain, *Paul Francis Webster* md Ray Heindorf ch Jack Donohue

Doris Day, Howard Keel, Allyn McLerie, Phil Carey, Dick Wesson, Paul Harvey

AA: song 'Secret Love' (*m* Sammy Fain, *ly* Paul Francis Webster)
AAN: Ray Heindorf

Calcutta
US 1946 83m bw
Paramount (Seton I. Miller)

Two fliers seek the murderer of their friend in the hotels and bazaars of Calcutta.
Studio-bound action potboiler, simple-minded but quite good fun.

w Seton I. Miller d John Farrow ph John F. Seitz m Victor Young

Alan Ladd, Gail Russell, William Bendix, June Duprez, Lowell Gilmore

The Calendar
GB 1948 80m bw

A girl trainer helps an owner to prove he didn't nobble his horse. Very average racecourse melodrama from a novel by Edgar Wallace, previously filmed in 1932 with Herbert Marshall and Edna Best. Here with Greta Gynt, John McCallum, Leslie Dwyer, Raymond Lovell, Charles Victor, Barry Jones. Written by Geoffrey Kerr; directed by Arthur Crabtree; for Gainsborough.

California
US 1946 97m Technicolor
Paramount (Seton I. Miller)

An army deserter joins the 1848 California gold rush.
Standard glamorized star western; not bad if you accept the conventions.

w Frank Butler, Theodore Strauss d John Farrow ph Ray Rennahan m Victor Young

Ray Milland, Barbara Stanwyck, Barry Fitzgerald, Albert Dekker, George Coulouris, Anthony Quinn

California Split*
US 1974 109m Metrocolor Panavision
Columbia / Persky–Bright / Reno (Robert Altman, Joseph Walsh)

Two cheerful gamblers get drunk, laid, cheated and happy.

Sporadically entertaining character comedy sunk in a sea of chatter.

w Joseph Walsh d Robert Altman ph Paul Lohmann

Elliott Gould, George Segal, Gwen Welles, Ann Prentiss, Joseph Walsh
'The film seems to be being improvised . . . we catch at events and personalities by the ends of threads.'—*New Yorker*

California Straight Ahead*
US 1937 67m bw
Universal (Trem Carr)

A nationwide race is held between a special train and a convoy of high-powered trucks.
Unusual and quite lively second feature shot on location.

w Herman Boxer d Arthur Lubin ph Harry Neumann m Charles Previn

John Wayne, Louise Latimer, Robert McWade, Tully Marshall

California Suite*
US 1978 103m colour
Columbia / Ray Stark

Misadventures of four groups of guests at the Beverly Hills Hotel.
Two hits, two misses; closer intercutting might have helped. No doubt that Maggie Smith and Michael Caine come off best, with bitcheries about the Academy Awards; Walter Matthau and Elaine May also raise laughs in Jewish farce. But Alan Alda and Jane Fonda in stiff-upper-lip divorce drama are a bore; and the black farce with Richard Pryor and Bill Cosby is scuppered before it starts.

w Neil Simon, from his play d Herbert Ross ph David M. Walsh m Claude Bolling pd Albert Brenner
'By turns silly and thoughtful, tedious and charming, broad and delicate.'—*Frank Rich, Time*

Caligula
Italy / US 1979 150m Eastmancolor
Penthouse Films (Bob Guccione)

The violent life and times of a decadent Roman emperor. What would have been a dull and worthless pseudo-epic has been perked up by violence and hardcore sex. The result is a vile curiosity of interest chiefly to sado-masochists.

w Bob Guccione, after a screenplay by Gore Vidal d Tinto Brass and others ph Silvano Ippoliti m Paul Clemente ph Danilo Donati

Malcolm McDowell, John Gielgud, Peter

O'Toole, Helen Mirren, Teresa Ann Savoy, John Steiner

'An anthology of sexual aberrations in which incest is the only face-saving relationship . . . far more Gore than Vidal.'— *Variety*

Call Her Savage
US 1932 88m bw
Paramount (Sam E. Rork)

Trials and tribulations of a half-breed Indian girl who marries a cad and later takes to the streets.

Rough and ready melodrama for female audiences; the penultimate appearance of a star who did not take to talkies.

w Edwin Burke, *novel* Tiffany Thayer d John Francis Dillon ph Lee Garmes

Clara Bow, Gilbert Roland, Monroe Owsley, Thelma Todd, Estelle Taylor

Call It a Day*
US 1937 89m bw
Warner (Henry Blanke)

An upper-class British family has problems during a single day.

Surprising, and not very effective, Hollywood treatment of a very British comedy.

w Casey Robinson, *play* Dodie Smith d Archie Mayo ph Ernest Haller

Olivia de Havilland, Ian Hunter, Anita Louise, Alice Brady, Roland Young, Frieda Inescort, Bonita Granville, Peggy Wood, Walter Woolf King, Una O'Connor, Beryl Mercer

Call Me Bwana*
GB 1962 93m Eastmancolor
Rank / Eon (Harry Saltzman, Albert R. Broccoli)

A fake African explorer is sent to the jungle to recover a space capsule.

Moderate star farce with occasional bright moments.

w Nate Monaster, Johanna Harwood d Gordon Douglas ph Ted Moore m Monty Norman

Bob Hope, Anita Ekberg, Edie Adams, Lionel Jeffries, Percy Herbert, Paul Carpenter, Orlando Martins

Call Me Madam***
US 1953 114m Technicolor
TCF (Sol C. Siegel)

A Washington hostess is appointed Ambassador to Lichtenberg and marries the foreign minister.

Studio-bound but thoroughly lively transcription of Irving Berlin's last big success, with most of the performers at their peak and some topical gags which may now be mystifying.

w Arthur Sheekman, *play* Howard Lindsay, Russel Crouse m / ly Irving Berlin md Alfred Newman ph Leon Shamroy d Walter Lang ch Robert Alton

Ethel Merman, Donald O'Connor, George Sanders, Vera-Ellen, Billy de Wolfe, Helmut Dantine, Walter Slezak, Steve Geray, Ludwig Stossel

AA: Alfred Newman

Call Me Mister
US 1951 95m Technicolor
TCF (Fred Kohlmar)

A husband-and-wife dance team entertain the troops in Japan and after the war.

Passable musical of a very predictable kind.

w Albert E. Lewin, Burt Styler d Lloyd Bacon ph Arthur E. Arling m Leigh Harline ch Busby Berkeley songs various *original show credits: m* Harold Rome, *book* Arnold Auerbach, Arnold B. Horwitt

Betty Grable, Dan Dailey, Danny Thomas, Dale Robertson, Richard Boone

Call Northside 777**
US 1948 111m bw
TCF (Otto Lang)

A Chicago reporter helps a washerwoman prove her son not guilty of murdering a policeman.

Overlong semi-documentary crime thriller based on a real case. Acting and detail excellent, but the sharp edge of *Boomerang* is missing.

w Jerome Cady, Jay Dratler d Henry Hathaway ph Joe MacDonald m Alfred Newman

James Stewart, Lee J. Cobb, Helen Walker, *Kazia Orzazewski,* Betty Garde, Richard Conte

Call of the Blood
GB 1947 88m bw

A Sicilian fisherman takes revenge on his daughter's seducer. Antediluvian melodrama with stiff-upper-lip English looking on. John Clements, Kay Hammond, John Justin, Lea Padovani, Robert Rietti. Written by John Clements, Akos Tolnay and Basil Mason, from the novel by Robert Hichens; directed by John Clements and Ladislas Vajda; for Pendennis.

Call of the Wild*
US 1935   81m   bw
TCF (Darryl F. Zanuck)

A young widow falls in love with a wild Yukon prospector.
Inaccurate but pleasing adaptation of an adventure novel with dog interest.

w Gene Fowler, Leonard Praskins, *novel* Jack London d William Wellman ph Charles Rosher m Alfred Newman

Clark Gable, Loretta Young, Jack Oakie, Reginald Owen, Frank Conroy

Call of the Wild
GB / Ger / Sp / It / Fr 1972   105m
   Eastmancolor
Massfilms / CCC / Izaro / Oceania / UPF
(Harry Alan Towers)

During the Klondike gold rush, a stolen dog becomes a miner's best friend before joining the wolf-pack.
Closer to the book than the previous version, but curiously scrappy and unsatisfactory.

w Harry Alan Towers, Wyn Wells, Peter Yeldman d Ken Annakin ph John Vabrera, Dudley Lovell m Carlo Rustichelli

Charlton Heston, Michèle Mercier, Raimund Harmstorf, George Eastman

Call Out the Marines*
US 1942   67m   bw

Two adventurers re-enlist in the Marines and foil a spy plot. The last of many action comedies featuring the original Flagg and Quirt from *What Price Glory?* Victor McLaglen, Edmund Lowe, Binnie Barnes, Paul Kelly, Franklin Pangborn. Written and directed by Frank Ryan and William Hamilton; for Universal.

Callan*
GB 1974   106m   Eastmancolor
EMI / Magnum (Derek Horne)

A former secret agent is seconded to a government section devoted to the elimination of undesirables.
Expanded rewrite of the first episode of a long-running TV series, quite fresh and vivid in the circumstances, especially as it comes at the tail end of ten years of similar bouts of blood and thunder.

w James Mitchell, from A Magnum for Schneider d Don Sharp ph Ernest Steward m Wilfred Josephs

Edward Woodward, Eric Porter, Carl Mohner, Catherine Schell, Peter Egan, Russell Hunter, Kenneth Griffith

Callaway Went Thataway*
US 1951   81m   bw
MGM (Melvin Frank, Norman Panama)
GB title: *The Star Said No*

The old movies of a Hollywood cowboy become popular on TV, but the star has become a hopeless drunk and an actor is hired to pose as him for public appearances.
Reasonably engaging comedy using charm rather than acid.

wd Melvin Frank, Norman Panama ph Ray June m Marlin Skiles

Dorothy McGuire, Fred MacMurray, Howard Keel, Jesse White, Natalie Schaefer

Calle Mayor*
Spain / France 1956   95m   bw
Play Art Iberia / Cesareo Gonzales
aka: *Grande Rue*

In a small Spanish town, a young stud pretends for a bet to be in love with a plain spinster.
Interesting but rather unattractive and certainly unconvincing little comedy-drama, rather too obviously styled for its American star after her success in *Marty*.

wd Juan Antonio Bardem ph Michel Kelber m Joseph Kosma

Betsy Blair, Yves Massard, René Blancard, Lila Kedrova

Calling Bulldog Drummond
GB 1951   80m   bw
MGM (Hayes Goetz)

Drummond goes undercover to catch a gang of thieves.
Minor-league quota quickie addition to the exploits of a long-running character (see *Bulldog Drummond*).

w Howard Emmett Rogers, Gerard Fairlie, Arthur Wimperis d Victor Saville ph F. A. Young m Rudolph Kopp

Walter Pidgeon, Margaret Leighton, Robert Beatty, David Tomlinson, Peggy Evans, Charles Victor, Bernard Lee, James Hayter

Calling Doctor Death
US 1943   63m   bw

A doctor's wife is murdered; her lover is arrested; but did the doctor himself do it? Probably not, as the tendency of the tinpot *Inner Sanctum* series, of which this was the first, was to make its star look anguished for six reels and then show him to be as innocent as the film was (mercifully) short. Lon Chaney, Patricia Morison, Fay Helm, David Bruce, Ramsay Ames, J. Carrol Naish.

Written by Edward Dein; directed by
Reginald Le Borg; for Universal.

Camelot**
US 1967   181m   Technicolor
   Panavision 70
Warner (Jack L. Warner)

King Arthur marries Guinevere, loses her to
Lancelot, and is forced into war.
A film version of a long-running Broadway
show with many excellent moments.
Unfortunately the director cannot make up his
mind whether to go for style or realism, and
has chosen actors who cannot sing. The result
is cluttered and overlong, with no real sense of
period or sustained imagination, but the
photography and the music linger in the mind.

w Alan Jay Lerner   m Frederick Loewe
d Joshua Logan   ph Richard H. Kline
pd / costumes John Truscott   ad Edward
Carere   md Ken Darby, Alfred Newman

Richard Harris, Vanessa Redgrave, David
Hemmings, Lionel Jeffries, Laurence
Naismith, Franco Nero

'One wonders whether the fashion for
musicals in which only the chorus can actually
sing may be reaching its final stage.'—MFB
'Three hours of unrelieved glossiness,
meticulous inanity, desperate and charmless
striving for charm.'—John Simon
'The sets and costumes and people seem to
be sitting there on the screen, waiting for the
unifying magic that never happens.'—New
Yorker, 1977

AA: art direction; costumes; music direction
AAN: cinematography

The Camels are Coming
GB 1934   80m   bw

An officer in the camel corps catches Egyptian
drug smugglers. Light, bouncy star vehicle.
Jack Hulbert, Anna Lee, Hartley Power,
Harold Huth, Allan Jeayes. Written by Jack
Hulbert, Guy Bolton and W. P. Lipscomb;
directed by Tim Whelan; for Gainsborough.

The Cameraman***
US 1928   78m approx (24 fps)   bw
   silent
MGM / Buster Keaton Productions

In order to woo a film star, a street
photographer becomes a newsreel cameraman.
Highly regarded chapter of farcical errors,
among the star's top features.

w Clyde Bruckman, Lex Lipton, Richard
Schayer   d Edward Sedgwick   ph Elgin
Lessley, Reggie Manning

Buster Keaton, Marceline Day, Harry
Gribbon, Harold Goodwin
† The film was remade in 1948 for Red
Skelton as Watch the Birdie, with Keaton sadly
supervising the gags but getting no credit.

Camille**
US 1936   108m   bw
MGM (Irving Thalberg, Bernard Hyman)

A dying courtesan falls for an innocent young
man who loves her, and dies in his arms.
This old warhorse is an unsuitable vehicle for
Garbo but magically she carries it off, and the
production is elegant and pleasing.

w Frances Marion, James Hilton, Zoe Akins,
novel Alexandre Dumas   d George Cukor
ph William Daniels   m Herbert Stothart

Greta Garbo, Robert Taylor, Lionel
Barrymore, Henry Daniell, Elizabeth Allan,
Lenore Ulric, Laura Hope Crews, Rex
O'Malley, Jessie Ralph, E. E. Clive

'The slow, solemn production is luxuriant in
its vulgarity: it achieves that glamor which
MGM traditionally mistook for style.'—
Pauline Kael, 1968
'The surprise is to find a story that should by
rights be old hat coming to such insistent life
on the screen.'—Otis Ferguson
'It steadily builds up an impression of being
a spectacle of manners and fashions, a socially
true background for its characters to move
against.'—National Board of Review
'Their lips meet for the first time . . . a
superb thrill seared in your memory
forever!'—publicity
'This is not death as mortals know it. This is
but the conclusion of a romantic ritual.'—
Bosley Crowther
'Luxuriant in its vulgarity, it achieves that
glamour which MGM traditionally mistook for
style.'—New Yorker 1982

AAN: Greta Garbo

Il Cammino della Speranza*
Italy 1950   105m   bw
Lux (Luigi Rovere)
aka: The Road to Hope

Unemployed Sicilian miners travel to France
in search of work.
Episodic location melodrama with a social
conscience, a kind of Italian Grapes of Wrath.
Very watchable, but not moving.

w Federico Fellini, Tullio Pinelli   d Pietro
Germi   ph Leonido Barboni   m Carlo
Rustichelli

Raf Vallone, Elena Varzi, Saro Urzi, Franco
Navarra

The Camp on Blood Island
GB 1958   81m   bw   Megascope
Columbia / Hammer (Anthony Hinds)

The sadistic commandant of a Japanese POW
camp swears to kill all the inmates. Japan
surrenders, and a great effort is made to
prevent the news from reaching him.

Dubious melodrama parading sadism and
brutality as entertainment.

w Jon Manchip White, Val Guest d Val
Guest ph Jack Asher m Gerard Schurmann

André Morell, Carl Mohner, Edward
Underdown, Michael Goodliffe, Ronald
Radd, Walter Fitzgerald, Phil Brown, Barbara
Shelley, Michael Gwynn, Richard
Wordsworth, Marne Maitland, Mary Merrall

Campbell's Kingdom*
GB 1957   102m   Eastmancolor
Rank (Betty E. Box)

A young man who thinks he is dying arrives in
the Canadian Rockies to take over his father's
oil valley, but a scheming contractor opposes
him.

Competent and entertaining romantic thick-
ear.

w Robin Estridge, novel Hammond Innes
d Ralph Thomas ph Ernest Steward
m Clifton Parker

Dirk Bogarde, Stanley Baker, Barbara
Murray, Athene Seyler, Mary Merrall, James
Robertson Justice

Can Can
US 1960   131m   De Luxe   Todd-AO
TCF / Suffolk–Cummings (Jack Cummings)

A Parisian nightclub dancer in the nineties is
sued for performing the Can Can.

Flat film of a dull musical, with just a few
plums in the pudding.

w Dorothy Kingsley, Charles Lederer, play
Abe Burrows songs Cole Porter d Walter
Lang ph William Daniels ch Hermes Pan
md Nelson Riddle

Frank Sinatra, Shirley Maclaine, Maurice
Chevalier, Louis Jourdan, Juliet Prowse,
Marcel Dalio, Leon Belasco

AAN: Nelson Riddle

Can Heironymus Merkin Ever Forget
Mercy Humppe and Find True
Happiness?
GB 1969   117m   Technicolor
Universal / Taralex (Anthony Newley)

A performer on a beach assembles a huge pile
of personal bric-à-brac and reminisces about
his life in the style of a variety show.

Obscure and pointless personal fantasy,
financed at great expense by a major film
company as a rather seedy monument to
Anthony Newley's totally uninteresting sex
life, and to the talent which he obviously
thinks he possesses. The few mildly amusing
moments are not provided by him.

w Herman Raucher, Anthony Newley
d Anthony Newley ph Otto Heller
m Anthony Newley

Anthony Newley, Joan Collins, George Jessel,
Milton Berle, Bruce Forsyth, Stubby Kaye,
Patricia Hayes, Victor Spinetti

'If I'd been Anthony Newley I would have
opened it in Siberia during Christmas week
and called it a day.'—Rex Reed

'The kindest thing for all concerned would
be that every available copy should be quietly
and decently buried.'—Michael Billington,
Illustrated London News

The Candidate**
US 1972   110m   Technicolor
Warner / Redford–Ritchie (Walter Coblenz)

A young Californian lawyer is persuaded to
run for senator; in succeeding, he alienates his
wife and obscures his real opinions.

Put together in a slightly scrappy but finally
persuasive style, this joins a select band of
rousing, doubting American political films.

w Jeremy Larner d Michael Ritchie ph Victor
J. Kemper m John Rubinstein

Robert Redford, Peter Boyle, Don Porter,
Allen Garfield, Karen Carlson, Quinn
Redeker, Morgan Upton, Melvyn Douglas

'Decent entertainment . . . it is never
boring, but it is never enlarging,
informationally or emotionally or
thematically.'—Stanley Kauffmann

AA: Jeremy Larner

Candide
France 1960   90m   bw
CLM / SN Pathé (Clément Duhour)

Ever optimistic, a 20th-century Candide tours
Nazi prison camps, communist countries and
various South American revolutions.

Scrappily-made satire which soon overstays its
welcome.

wd Norbert Carbonneaux, from Voltaire
ph Robert Le Fèbvre m Hubert Rostaing

Jean-Pierre Cassel, Daliah Lavi, Pierre
Brasseur, Nadia Gray, Michel Simon, Louis
de Funès

Candlelight in Algeria
GB 1943   85m   bw

Spies seek whereabouts of Allied rendezvous.
Elementary spy thriller using modest talents.
Carla Lehmann, James Mason, Walter Rilla,
Raymond Lovell, Enid Stamp Taylor. Written
by Katherine Strueby and Brock Williams;
directed by George King; for British Aviation.

Candles at Nine
GB 1944   86m   bw

A young heiress in her benefactor's old
mansion is menaced by his housekeeper.
Elementary *Cat and the Canary* reprise; cast
understandably uneasy. Jessie Matthews, John
Stuart, Beatrix Lehmann, Winifred Shotter,
Reginald Purdell. Written by John Harlow and
Basil Mason, from a novel by Anthony
Gilbert; directed by John Harlow; for British
National.

Candleshoe
GB 1977   101m   Technicolor
Walt Disney Productions (Hugh Attwooll)

An attempt to pass off a fake heiress to an
English stately home is prevented by the
resourceful butler.
Slackly handled comedy adventure full of easy
targets and predictable incidents.

w David Swift, Rosemary Anne Sisson, *novel*
Christmas at Candleshoe by Michael Innes
d Norman Tokar ph Paul Beeson m Ron
Goodwin

David Niven, Helen Hayes, Jodie Foster, Leo
McKern, Veronica Quilligan, Ian Sharrock,
Vivian Pickles

'It might have been conceived by a
computer called upon to produce the definitive
pastiche of a Disney film of the 1970s.'—
Financial Times

Candy
US 1968   124m   Technicolor
Selmur / Dear / Corona (Robert Haggiag)

An innocent girl defends herself from a fate
worse than death in a variety of international
situations.
Witless and charmless perversion of a sex
satire in which the point (if any) was that the
nymphet gladly surrendered herself to all the
gentlemen for their own good. A star cast
flounders helplessly in a morass of bad taste,
bad film-making, and boredom.

w Buck Henry, *novel* Terry Southern
d Christian Marquand ph Giuseppe Rotunno
m Dave Grusin

Ewa Aulin, Richard Burton, Marlon Brando,
James Coburn, Walter Matthau, Charles
Aznavour, John Huston, Elsa Martinelli,
Ringo Starr, John Astin

'Hippy psychedelics are laid on with the
self-destroying effect of an overdose of
garlic.'—*MFB*

'As an emetic, liquor is dandy, but *Candy* is
quicker.'—*John Simon*

Cannon for Cordoba
US 1970   104m   De Luxe   Panavision
UA / Mirisch (Stephen Kandel, Vincent
Fenelly)

In 1912, the Mexican bandit Cordoba is
outgunned and outwitted by a US army
captain.
Fast-moving but rather uninteresting action
adventure.

w Stephen Kandel d Paul Wendkos
ph Antonio Macasoli m Elmer Bernstein

George Peppard, Raf Vallone, Giovanna
Ralli, Pete Duel, Don Gordon, Nico
Minardos, John Russell

Cannonball
US / Hong Kong 1976   93m   Metrocolor
Harbor / Shaw Brothers (Samuel W.
Gelfman)
GB title: *Carquake*

Aggressive drivers compete in the Trans-
American Grand Prix.
The plot is a thin excuse for multiple pile-ups
and other road disasters. Moments amuse, but
the violence quickly palls.

w Paul Bartel, Donald C. Simpson d Paul
Bartel ph Tak Fujimoto m David A.
Axelrod

David Carradine, Bill McKinney, Veronica
Hamel, Gerrit Graham, Judy Canova

'A free-wheeling, stunt-studded, dented and
demented story of a road racer without
rules.'—*publicity*

Canon City*
US 1948   82m   bw
Eagle Lion

Convicts break out of the Colorado State
Prison.
Minor semi-documentary melodrama, quite
effectively presented.

wd Crane Wilbur ph John Alton

Scott Brady, Jeff Corey, Whit Bissell, Stanley
Clements, De Forrest Kelley

Can't Help Singing*
US 1944   90m   Technicolor
Universal (Frank Ross)

A Washington heiress chases her army
lieutenant lover across the wild west to
California.

Lively star musical which could have used a little more wit in its lighthearted script.

w Lewis Foster, Frank Ryan *d* Frank Ryan *ph* Woody Bredell, W. Howard Greene *m* Jerome Kern *ly* E. Y. Harburg *md* Jerome Kern, Hans Salter

Deanna Durbin, David Bruce, Robert Paige, *Akim Tamiroff, Leonid Kinskey*, Ray Collins, Thomas Gomez

'This could have been a beautiful and gay picture, but it is made without much feeling for beauty or gaiety.'—*James Agee*

AAN: Jerome Kern, Hans Salter; song 'More and More' (*m* Jerome Kern, *ly* E. Y. Harburg)

Can't Stop the Music

US 1980   124m   Metrocolor   Panavision
EMI / Allan Carr

A Greenwich Village pop group hits the bigtime.

Curiously old-fashioned youth musical, unwisely touted as something special, which it isn't.

w Bronte Woodward, Allan Carr *d* Nancy Walker
ph Bill Butler *m* Jacques Morali

The Village People, Valerie Perrine, Paul Sand, Bruce Jenner, Tammy Grimes, June Havoc, Barbara Rush, Jack Weston

'The hype disaster of the 80s, a grisly rehash of the let's-start-a-group-of-our-own plot, peopled with butch gay stereotypes of both sexes pretending to be straight. The pervasive tackiness is unrelieved.'—*Time Out*

A Canterbury Tale*

GB 1944   124m   bw
Rank / Archers (Michael Powell, Emeric Pressburger)

A batty magistrate is unmasked by a land girl, an army sergeant and a GI.

Curious would-be propaganda piece with Old England bathed in a roseate wartime glow, but the plot seems to have little to do with Chaucer. Indeed, quite what Powell and Pressburger thought they were up to is hard to fathom, but the detail is interesting.

wd Michael Powell and Emeric Pressburger *ph* Erwin Hillier

Eric Portman, Sheila Sim, John Sweet, Dennis Price, Esmond Knight, Charles Hawtrey, Hay Petrie, George Merritt, Edward Rigby

'To most people the intentions of the film-makers remained highly mysterious; nor did this picture of the British administration of justice commend itself to the authorities, who showed some reluctance to encourage its export to our allies.'—*Basil Wright, 1972*

The Canterbury Tales

Italy / France 1971   109m (English version)   Technicolor
UA / PEA / PAA (Alberto Grimaldi)

Medieval pilgrims amuse each other by telling stories on the way to Canterbury.

A sweaty selection of the tales in their more prurient aspects, with relentless emphasis on excrement and sex perversions.

wd Pier Paolo Pasolini, after Chaucer *ph* Tonino Delli Colli

Pier Paolo Pasolini (as Chaucer), Hugh Griffith, Laura Betti, Tom Baker, Ninetto Davoli, Franco Citti

'Caricature Chaucer, with pilgrims losing the way to Canterbury amid a forest of male genitalia.'—*Sight and Sound*

'The vivid depiction of taboo subjects emerges less as an affirmation of the Chaucerian belief that all human activity lies within the artist's scope, than as a bludgeoning over-emphasis on physical appetite as man's primal motive for action.'—*Nigel Andrews, MFB*

The Canterville Ghost*

US 1943   95m   bw
MGM (Arthur Field)

The young girl heiress of an English castle introduces GIs to the resident ghost.

Leaden comedy a long way after Oscar Wilde, sunk by slow script and direction, but partly salvaged by the respective roguishness and infant charm of its stars.

w Edwin Blum *d* Jules Dassin *ph* Robert Planck *m* George Bassman

Charles Laughton, Margaret O'Brien, Robert Young, William Gargan, Rags Ragland, Peter Lawford, Una O'Connor, Mike Mazurki
† In the mid 1970s, a television version starring David Niven was made by HTV.

Canyon Passage*

US 1946   99m   Technicolor
Universal (Walter Wanger)

In the 1850s along the pioneering tracks the west's first towns were being built . . .

Simple, scrappy but generally pleasing film which gives a vivid picture of pioneering life while minimizing its hardships.

w Ernest Pascal, William Fosche *d* Jacques Tourneur *ph* Edward Cronjager *m* Frank Skinner

Dana Andrews, Patricia Roc, Hoagy
Carmichael, Brian Donlevy, Susan Hayward,
Ward Bond, Andy Devine, Lloyd Bridges
'Miles of beautiful scenery, lavishly
punctuated with rough-and-tumble episodes,
moments of tender romance and a smattering
of folk customs.'—*New York Times*

AAN: song 'Ole Buttermilk Sky' (*m* Hoagy
Carmichael, *ly* Jack Brooks)

Cape Fear
US 1962 106m bw
U-I / Melville–Talbot (Sy Bartlett)

An ex-convict blames a lawyer for his sentence
and threatens to rape the lawyer's wife.
Unpleasant and drawn out suspenser with
characters of cardboard and situations from
stock.

w James R. Webb, *novel* The Executioners by
John D. MacDonald *d* J. Lee-Thompson
ph Sam Leavitt *m* Bernard Herrmann

Gregory Peck, Robert Mitchum, Polly
Bergen, Martin Balsam, Lori Martin, Jack
Kruschen, Telly Savalas

The Caper of the Golden Bulls
US 1966 104m Pathecolor
Embassy (Clarence Greene)
GB title: *Carnival of Thieves*

Ex-air-aces rob banks in order to pay for the
restoration of a French cathedral they had to
bomb; to avoid incrimination they are
blackmailed into doing one last job in
Pamplona.
Ingeniously plotted, flatly executed suspenser
set in Pamplona during the bull run.

w Ed Waters, William Moessinger, *novel*
William P. McGivern *d* Russel Rouse *ph* Hal
Stine *m* Vic Mizzy

Stephen Boyd, Giovanna Ralli, Yvette
Mimieux, Walter Slezak, Vito Scotti

Capetown Affair
US / SA 1967 100m De Luxe
TCF / Killarney (Robert D. Webb)

A pickpocket on a South African bus steals a
purse containing secret microfilm.
Flatulent remake of *Pickup on South Street*
with nothing but the unfamiliar locale to
recommend it.

w Harold Medford, Samuel Fuller *d* Robert
D. Webb *ph* David Millin *m* Bob Adams

James Brolin, Jacqueline Bisset, Claire
Trevor, Bob Courtney, Jon Whiteley

Capone
US 1975 101.m De Luxe
TCF / Santa Fe (Roger Corman)

Exploitation version of the Capone story, with
the emphasis on unpleasant violence.

w Howard Browne *d* Steve Carver *ph* Vilis
Lapenieks *m* David Grisman

Ben Gazzara, Sylvester Stallone, Susan
Blakely, Harry Guardino, John Cassavetes,
John Davis Chandler, Peter Maloney, Royal
Dano

Caprice*
US 1967 98m De Luxe Cinemascope
TCF / Aaron Rosenberg, Marty Melcher

A career girl investigating the death of her
boss discovers that a cosmetics empire is the
front for international drug smuggling.
Incoherent kaleidoscope which switches from
farce to suspense and Bond-style action,
scattering in-jokes along the way. Bits of it
however are funny, and it looks good.

w Jay Jayson, Frank Tashlin *d* Frank Tashlin
ph Leon Shamroy (who also appears)
m Frank de Vol

Doris Day, Richard Harris, Edward Mulhare,
Ray Walston, Jack Kruschen, Lilia Skala,
Irene Tsu, Michael Romanoff, Michael J.
Pollard

Capricious Summer*
Czechoslovakia 1968 75m Eastmancolor
Ceskoslovensky Film (Jan Libora)

The beautiful assistant of a wandering
tightrope walker sets up sexual tensions when
they stop at a sleepy riverside town.
Amusing little period comedy in a period
setting.

wd Jiri Menzel *ph* Jaromir Sofr *m* Jiri Sust

Rudolf Hrusinksy, Vlastimil Brodsky,
Frantisek Rehak, Jana Drchalova, Jiri Menzel

Capricorn One
US 1978 128m CFI colour
Associated General / Lew Grade (Paul N.
   Lazarus III)

A reporter discovers that the first manned
space flight to Mars was a hoax.
Smartly packaged topical adventure thriller
rather marred by its all star cast.

wd Peter Hyams *ph* Bill Butler *m* Jerry
Goldsmith *pd* Albert Brenner

Elliott Gould, James Brolin, Brenda Vaccaro,
Sam Waterston, O. J. Simpson, Hal
Holbrook, Telly Savalas, Karen Black, David
Huddleston
'After weighing in with some Watergate /
Bernstein pretensions, the makers then opt
for boring, Bondish derring-do.'—*Sight and
Sound*

Captain Apache

US / Spain 1971   94m   Technicolor
'Scope
Benmar (Milton Sperling, Philip Yordan,
  Irving Lerner)

An Indian serving with US army intelligence
tracks down a gun runner.
An old formula tarted up with the new
violence.· Very ho-hum.

w Philip Yordan, Milton Sperling, novel S. E.
Whitman d Alexander Singer ph John
Cabrera m Dolores Claman

Lee Van Cleef, Carroll Baker, Stuart
Whitman, Percy Herbert, Tony Vogel

Captain Applejack

US 1931   70m   bw

A timid man turns the tables on crooks who
plan to find treasure beneath his ancestral
home. Early talkie version of a well-worn play
previously filmed in 1923. John Halliday, Kay
Strozzi, Arthur Edmund Carewe, Mary Brian,
Louise Closser Hale. Written by Maude
Fulton, from Ambrose Applejohn's Adventure
by Walter Hackett; directed by Hobart
Henley; for Warner.

Captain Bill

GB 1935   81m   bw

A bargee saves a schoolmistress from trouble
with crooks. By reputation the best of its star's
modest comedies, which have not yet been
rediscovered. Leslie Fuller, Georgie Harris,
Judy Kelly, Hal Gordon, O. B. Clarence.
Written by Val Valentine, Syd Courtenay and
George Harris; directed by Ralph Ceder; for
ABFD.

Captain Black Jack

US / France 1952   90m   bw

A Riviera socialite pretends to be an
undercover agent but is really a smuggler; she
is unmasked by a doctor who is really a
detective. Trashy hodgepodge with a
remarkable cast of ageing stars: George
Sanders, Agnes Moorehead, Herbert
Marshall, Patricia Roc, Marcel Dalio. Written
by Julien Duvivier and Charles Spaak;
directed by Julien Duvivier; for Walter Gould.

Captain Blood**

US 1935   119m   bw
Warner (Harry Joe Brown)

A young British surgeon, wrongly condemned
by Judge Jeffreys for helping rebels, escapes
and becomes a Caribbean pirate.
Modestly produced but quite exhilarating
pirate adventure notable for making a star of
Errol Flynn. Direction makes the most of very
limited production values.

w Casey Robinson, novel Rafael Sabatini
d Michael Curtiz ph Hal Mohr m Erich
Wolfgang Korngold ad Anton Grot

Errol Flynn, Olivia de Havilland, Basil
Rathbone, Lionel Atwill, Guy Kibbee, Ross
Alexander, Henry Stephenson, Forrester
Harvey, Hobart Cavanaugh, Donald Meek

'Here is a fine spirited mix-up with clothes
and wigs which sometimes hark back to the
sixteenth century and sometimes forward to
the period of Wolfe . . . one is quite prepared
for the culminating moment when the Union
Jack breaks proudly, anachronistically forth at
Peter Blood's masthead.'—Graham Greene

AAN: best picture

Captain Boycott*

GB 1947   93m   bw
GFD / Individual (Frank Launder, Sidney
  Gilliat)

In 1880, poor Irish farmers rebel against their
tyrannical English landlords.
Modest historical drama in which a splendid
cast is rather subdued.

w Wolfgang Wilhelm, Frank Launder, Paul
Vincent Carroll, Patrick Campbell,
novel Philip Rooney d Frank Launder
ph Wilkie Cooper m William Alwyn

Stewart Granger, Kathleen Ryan, Alastair
Sim, Robert Donat (a cameo as Parnell), Cecil
Parker, Mervyn Johns, Noel Purcell, Niall
MacGinnis

Captain Carey USA

US 1951   83m   bw
Paramount (Richard Maibaum)
GB title: After Midnight

After the war, a military officer returns to an
Italian village to expose the informer who
betrayed his comrades.
Muddled and rather boring melodrama with a
labyrinthine plot which seems to have stultified
all concerned. It did produce a hit song,
'Mona Lisa'.

w Robert Thoeren, novel Dishonoured by
Martha Albrand d Mitchell Leisen ph John
F. Seitz m Hugo Friedhofer

Alan Ladd, Francis Lederer, Wanda Hendrix,
Joseph Calleia, Celia Lovsky, Angela Clarke,
Jane Nigh, Frank Puglia, Luis Alberni

AA: song 'Mona Lisa' (m / ly Ray Evens, Jay
Livingston)

Captain Caution

US 1940   84m   bw
Hal Roach

In 1812, a girl takes over her dead father's ship and fights the British.
Lively though unconvincing adventure with emphasis on comedy.

w Grover Jones, *novel* Kenneth Roberts
d Richard Wallace ph Norbert Brodine
m Phil Ohman

Victor Mature, Louise Platt, Bruce Cabot, Leo Carrillo, Robert Barrat, Vivienne Osborne, Alan Ladd

Captain China
US 1949 97m bw
Paramount / Pine-Thomas (William H. Pine, William C. Thomas)

A wandering seafarer seeks the mate who betrayed him.
Action melodrama with a second team look; all rather listless.

w Lewis R. Foster, Gwen Bagni d Lewis R. Foster ph John Alton m Lucien Caillet

John Payne, Gail Russell, Jeffrey Lynn, Lon Chaney Jnr, Michael O'Shea, Ellen Corby

Captain Clegg*
GB 1962 82m Technicolor
Universal / Hammer (John Temple-Smith)
US title: *Night Creatures*

The vicar of an 18th-century village in Romney Marsh is really a retired pirate, now doing a little smuggling on the side.
Mild remake of *Dr Syn* with a few moments of violence added; watchable for those who like totally predictable plot development.

w John Elder d Peter Graham Scott
ph Arthur Grant m Don Banks

Peter Cushing, Patrick Allen, Michael Ripper, Oliver Reed, Derek Francis, Milton Reid, Martin Benson, David Lodge

Captain Eddie
US 1945 107m bw
TCF / Eureka

Eddie Rickenbacker, adrift on a life raft after a plane crash in the Pacific, thinks back on his adventurous life in aviation.
Flat and surprisingly poorly made biopic with little to hold the attention.

w John Tucker Battle d Lloyd Bacon ph Joe MacDonald m Cyril Mockridge

Fred MacMurray, Lynn Bari, Thomas Mitchell, Lloyd Nolan, Charles Bickford

Captain from Castile
US 1947 140m Technicolor
TCF (Lamar Trotti)

A young 15th-century Spaniard hopes for fame and fortune in the New World.
Rather empty and boring adventure epic from a bestseller; high production values produce moments of interest.

w Lamar Trotti, *novel* Samuel Shellabarger
d Henry King ph Charles Clarke, Arthur E. Arling m Alfred Newman ad Richard Day, James Basevi

Tyrone Power, Jean Peters, Lee J. Cobb, Cesar Romero, John Sutton, Antonio Moreno, Thomas Gomez, Alan Mowbray, Barbara Lawrence, George Zucco, Roy Roberts, Marc Lawrence
'The first few reels have flow and a kind of boy's-book splendour; the rest is locomotor ataxia.'—*James Agee*

AAN: Alfred Newman

Captain Fury*
US 1939 91m bw
Hal Roach

In 19th-century Australia, an adventurer fights the evil head of a penal colony.
Shades of Zorro and Robin Hood in a brawling, comic actioner typical of this producer.

w Grover Jones, Jack Jevne, William de Mille d Hal Roach ph Norbert Brodine m Marvin Hatley

Brian Aherne, Victor McLaglen, Paul Lukas, June Lang, John Carradine

The Captain Hates the Sea*
US 1934 92m bw
Columbia

Crime and comedy on an ocean voyage.
Zany, rather endearing comedy which gave the star his last role.

w Wallace Smith d Lewis Milestone
ph Joseph August

John Gilbert, Victor McLaglen, Walter Connolly, Alison Skipworth, Wynne Gibson, Helen Vinson, Leon Errol, Walter Catlett, Donald Meek, Arthur Treacher, Akim Tamiroff
'The best neglected picture in two years.'—*Otis Ferguson, 1936*

Captain Horatio Hornblower RN
GB 1951 117m Technicolor
Warner (Raoul Walsh)

Events from the adventure novels about a 19th-century sailor who outwits the Spaniards and the French and marries his admiral's widow.

Sprawling, plotless sea saga with the cast ill at ease in highly unconvincing sets: no air seems to blow across the decks of the *Lydia*.

w Ivan Goff, Ben Roberts, Aeneas Mackenzie, *novels* C. S. Forester *d* Raoul Walsh *ph* Guy Green *m* Robert Farnon *ad* Tom Morahan

Gregory Peck, Virginia Mayo, Robert Beatty, James Robertson Justice, Terence Morgan, Moultrie Kelsall, Richard Hearne, Denis O'Dea

'No point makes a strong enough impression to suggest a main line of criticism.'—*Richard Mallett, Punch*

The Captain Is a Lady*
US 1940   63m   bw

A sea captain is forced by ill-fortune to send his wife to an old ladies' home, but he dresses as a woman to be with her. Absurd-sounding comedy not without a certain lunatic charm.
Charles Coburn, Billie Burke, Beulah Bondi, Dan Dailey, Virginia Grey, Helen Broderick, Helen Westley. Written by Harry Clark, from a play by Rachel Crothers; directed by Robert Sinclair; for MGM.

Captain January*
US 1936   74m   bw
TCF (Darryl F. Zanuck)

A little girl is rescued from a shipwreck by a lighthouse keeper.
Standard Shirley Temple vehicle with pleasing dialogue and numbers.

w Sam Hellman, Gladys Lehman, Harry Tugend, *novel* Laura E. Richards *d* David Butler *ph* John F. Seitz *m* Louis Silvers

Shirley Temple, Guy Kibbee, Buddy Ebsen, Slim Summerville, June Lang, Sara Haden, Jane Darwell

Captain Kidd
US 1945   90m   bw
Benedict Bogeaus

A pirate tricks King William III into giving him royal orders, but enemies he believes dead return to see him hanged.
Rather poorly produced vehicle for a star who however rants and raves to some effect.

w Norman Reilly Raine *d* Rowland V. Lee *ph* Archie Stout *m* Werner Janssen

Charles Laughton, Randolph Scott, Barbara Britton, Reginald Owen, John Carradine, Gilbert Roland, Sheldon Leonard

AAN: Werner Janssen

Captain Lightfoot
US 1955   92m   Technicolor print
      Cinemascope
U-I (Ross Hunter)

Adventures of a 19th-century Irish rebel.
Dullish adventure story with the star ill at ease.

w W. R. Burnett, Oscar Brodney *d* Douglas Sirk *ph* Irving Glassberg *m* Joseph Gershenson

Rock Hudson, Barbara Rush, Jeff Morrow, Kathleen Ryan, Finlay Currie, Denis O'Dea, Geoffrey Toone

Captain Nemo and the Underwater City
GB 1969   106m   Metrocolor Panavision
MGM / Omnia (Steven Pallos, Bertram Ostrer)

Six survivors from an Atlantic shipwreck are picked up by a mysterious submarine and have adventures in a spectacular underwater city. Further adventures of Jules Verne's engaging Victorian character from *Twenty Thousand Leagues under the Sea*. Here however the general production values are stolid rather than solid, and the script makes heavy weather.

w Pip Baker, Jane Baker, R. Wright Campbell *d* James Hill *ph* Alan Hume, Egil Woxholt *m* Walter Stott *ad* Bill Andrews

Robert Ryan, Chuck Connors, Bill Fraser, Kenneth Connor, Nanette Newman, John Turner, Luciana Paluzzi, Allan Cuthbertson

Captain Newman MD*
US 1963   126m   Eastmancolor
Universal–Brentwood–Reynard (Robert Arthur)

At an army air base during World War II, a psychiatrist has varied success with his patients.
A decidedly curious comedy drama on the fringe of bad taste; it should have turned out better than it does, but will entertain those who like hospital heroics drenched in bitter-sweet sentimentality.

w Richard L. Breen, Phoebe and Henry Ephron, *novel* Leo Rosten *d* David Miller *ph* Russell Metty *m* Joseph Gershenson

Gregory Peck, Tony Curtis, Angie Dickinson, Eddie Albert, Bobby Darin, James Gregory, Jane Withers, Bethel Leslie, Robert Duvall, Larry Storch, Robert F. Simon, Dick Sargent

AAN: script; Bobby Darin

Captain Sinbad*
US / Germany 1963   88m
   Eastmancolor   Wonderscope
King Brothers

Sinbad returns to Baristan and by means of
magic deposes a sultan.
Rather splendid adventure fantasy with a
European flavour, good trick effects and full-
blooded performances.

w Samuel B. West, Harry Relis   d Byron
Haskin   ph Gunther Senftleben, Eugen
Shuftan   m Michel Michelet   sp Tom Howard
ad Werner and Isabell Schlicting

Guy Williams, Pedro Armendariz, Heidi
Bruhl, Abraham Sofaer

Captains Courageous**
US 1937   116m   bw
MGM (Louis D. Lighton)

A spoiled rich boy falls off a cruise liner and
lives for a while among fisherfolk who teach
him how to live.
Semi-classic Hollywood family film which is
not all that enjoyable while it's on but is
certainly a good example of the prestige
picture of the thirties. (It also happened to be
good box office.)

w John Lee Mahin, Marc Connelly, Dale Van
Every, novel Rudyard Kipling   d Victor
Fleming   ph Harold Rosson   m Franz
Waxman

Spencer Tracy, Lionel Barrymore, Freddie
Bartholomew, Mickey Rooney, Melvyn
Douglas, Charley Grapewin, Christian Rub,
John Carradine, Walter Kingsford, Leo G.
Carroll, Charles Trowbridge
'Another of those grand jobs of movie-
making we have come to expect from
Hollywood's most profligate studio.'—Frank
S. Nugent, New York Times
† 1977 brought a TV movie remake.

AA: Spencer Tracy
AAN: best picture; script

Captains of the Clouds
US 1942   113m   Technicolor
Warner (Hal. B. Wallis, William Cagney)

A flippant Canadian Air Force pilot proves his
worth under fire.
Recruiting poster heroics, reasonably well
done but lacking the vital spark.

w Arthur T. Horman, Richard Macaulay,
Norman Reilly Raine   d Michael Curtiz
ph Sol Polito, Wilfrid M. Cline   m Max
Steiner

James Cagney, Dennis Morgan, Brenda
Marshall, George Tobias, Alan Hale,

Reginald Gardiner, Reginald Denny, Paul
Cavanagh, Clem Bevans, J. M. Kerrigan
'Pure tribute to the unchanging forcefulness
of James Cagney.'—New York Post

AAN: Sol Polito, Wilfrid M. Cline

The Captain's Paradise*
GB 1953   89m   bw
BL / London (Anthony Kimmins)

The captain of a steamer plying between
Gibraltar and Tangier has a wife in each port,
one to suit each of his personalities.
Over-dry comedy in which the idea is much
funnier than the script. One is left with the
memory of a pleasant star performance.

w Alec Coppel, Nicholas Phipps   d Anthony
Kimmins   ph Ted Scaife   m Malcolm Arnold

Alec Guinness, Celia Johnson, Yvonne de
Carlo, Charles Goldner, Miles Malleson, Bill
Fraser, Nicholas Phipps, Ferdy Mayne,
George Benson

AAN: original story (Alec Coppel)

The Captain's Table*
GB 1958   89m   Eastmancolor
Rank (Joseph Janni)

A cargo skipper is given command of a luxury
liner and has to watch his manners.
Lively adaptation of a frivolous book of
obvious jokes, most of which come up quite
funny amid the luxurious surroundings.

w John Whiting, Bryan Forbes, Nicholas
Phipps, novel Richard Gordon   d Jack Lee
ph Christopher Challis   m Frank Cordell

John Gregson, Peggy Cummins, Donald
Sinden, Reginald Beckwith, Nadia Gray,
Richard Wattis, Maurice Denham, Nicholas
Phipps, Joan Sims, Miles Malleson

The Captive City**
US 1951   91m   bw
UA / Aspen (Theron Warth)

Small-town corruption imposed by the Mafia is
revealed by a crusading editor who defies
threats to his wife and family and tells all to
the Kefauver Commission.
Excellent documentary melodrama made in a
style then original, also notable for use of the
Hoge deep focus lens.

w Karl Lamb, Alvin Josephy Jnr   d Robert
Wise   ph Lee Garmes   m Jerome Moross

John Forsythe, Joan Camden, Harold J.
Kennedy, Marjorie Crossland, Victor
Sutherland, Ray Teal, Martin Milner, Hal K.
Dawson

The Captive Heart**
GB 1946 108m bw
Ealing (Michael Relph)

Stories of life among British officers in a
German POW camp, especially of a Czech
who has stolen the papers of a dead Britisher.
Archetypal POW drama lacing an almost
poetic treatment with humour and melodrama.

w Angus Macphail, Guy Morgan *d Basil
Dearden ph* Lionel Banes, Douglas
Slocombe *m* Alan Rawsthorne

Michael Redgrave, *Jack Warner*, Basil
Radford, Mervyn Johns, Jimmy Hanley,
Gordon Jackson, Ralph Michael, Derek
Bond, Karel Stepanek, Guy Middleton, Jack
Lambert, Gladys Henson, Rachel Kempson,
Meriel Forbes

Captured
US 1933 72m bw

A prisoner-of-war discovers that his best
friend was his wife's lover. Turgid and heavy-
going early variation on a theme which would
become very familiar indeed; the stars couldn't
save it. Leslie Howard, Paul Lukas, Douglas
Fairbanks Jnr, Margaret Lindsay, J. Carrol
Naish, Arthur Hohl. Written by Edward
Chodorov, from a novel by Sir Philip Gibbs;
directed by Roy Del Ruth; for Warner.

The Car
US 1977 98m Technicolor Panavision
Universal (Peter Saphier)

A small southwestern town is terrorized by a
driverless car which may be a creation of the
devil.
Silly suspenser with a draggy midsection.

w Dennis Shyrack, Michael Butler, Lane
Slate *d* Elliot Silverstein *ph* Gerald
Hirschfeld *m* Leonard Rosenman

James Brolin, Kathleen Lloyd, John Marley,
R. G. Armstrong, John Rubenstein

Car 99
US 1935 70m bw

A novice state trooper redeems early failure
by capturing bank robbers. Competent routine
programmer which helped to establish its star.
Fred MacMurray, Ann Sheridan, Sir Guy
Standing. Written by Karl Ditzer and C.
Gardner Sullivan; directed by Charles Barton;
for Paramount.

Caravan
US 1934 101m bw
Fox

A countess marries a gypsy.
Odd romantic drama with music: too
whimsical to succeed.

w Samson Raphaelson *d* Erik Charell
ph Ernest Palmer, Theodor Sparkuhl
songs Werner B. Heymann, Gus Kahn

Loretta Young, Charles Boyer, Jean Parker,
Phillips Holmes, Louise Fazenda, Eugene
Pallette, C. Aubrey Smith, Charley Grapewin,
Noah Beery, Dudley Digges

Caravan
GB 1946 122m bw
Gainsborough (Harold Huth)

A young man on a mission in Spain is left for
dead by emissaries of his rival in love; he is
nursed back to health by a gypsy girl who falls
in love with him.
Artificial, romantic, high-flown period tosh
without the courage of its lack of convictions.
At the time, an exhibitor's dream.

w Roland Pertwee, *novel* Lady Eleanor Smith
d Arthur Crabtree *ph* Stephen Dade

Stewart Granger, Jean Kent, Anne Crawford,
Robert Helpmann, Dennis Price, Gerard
Heinz, Enid Stamp-Taylor, David Horne,
John Salew

Caravan to Vaccares
GB / France 1974 98m Eastmancolor
Panavision
Crowndale (Geoffrey Reeve)

An American drifter on the Riviera is
employed to escort a mysterious Hungarian to
New York.
Lumpy Alistair MacLean action thriller, all a
bit *déjà vu.*

w Paul Wheeler *d* Geoffrey Reeve
ph Frederic Tammes *m* Stanley Myers

David Birney, Charlotte Rampling, Michel
Lonsdale, Marcel Bozzuff, Michael Bryant
'An undernourished plot advanced only by a
series of venerable clichés.'—*MFB*
'The biggest load of schoolboy hokum since
Boy's Own Paper ceased circulation.'—
Michael Billington, Illustrated London News

Caravans
US / Iran 1978 123m Technicolor
Panavision
Ibex / FIDCI (Elmo Williams)

In the Middle East in 1948, a junior diplomat
is sent to bring back the daughter of a US
politician, who has married an arab, left him,
and joined a bedouin caravan.
Curiously halting succession of pretty pictures
and not much plot; what there is tends to take
second place to philosophy and eastern
promise.

w Nancy Voyles Crawford, Thomas A. MacMahon, Lorraine Williams, *novel* James Michener *d* James Fargo *ph* Douglas Slocombe *m* Mike Batt

Anthony Quinn, Michael Sarrazin, Jennifer O'Neill, Christopher Lee, Joseph Cotten, Barry Sullivan, Jeremy Kemp
'A tiresome exercise in anti-climax.'—*Tim Pulleine, MFB*

Carbine Williams
US 1952 93m bw
MGM (Armand Deutsch)
An imprisoned bootlegger perfects a new gun and is pardoned.
Flat fictionalization of a true story, with the star miscast.

w Art Cohn *d* Richard Thorpe *ph* William Mellor *m* Conrad Salinger

James Stewart, Jean Hagen, Wendell Corey, Carl Benton Reid, Paul Stewart, Otto Hulett, James Arness

The Card**
GB 1952 91m bw
Rank / British Film Makers (John Bryan)
US title: *The Promoter*
A bright young clerk from the potteries finds many ingenious ways of improving his bank account and his place in society.
Pleasing period comedy with the star in a made-to-measure role and excellent production values.

w Eric Ambler, *novel* Arnold Bennett *d* Ronald Neame *ph* Oswald Morris *ad* T. Hopwell Ash *m* William Alwyn

Alec Guinness, Glynis Johns, Petula Clark, *Valerie Hobson,* Edward Chapman, Veronica Turleigh, Gibb McLaughlin, Frank Pettingell

Card of Fate see Le Grand Jeu

Cardboard Cavalier*
GB 1949 96m bw
Rank / Two Cities (Walter Forde)
In Cromwellian England, royalists commission a barrow boy to carry a secret letter. Helped by Nell Gwynn, he succeeds after encounters with a castle ghost and custard pies.
A pantomime crossed with an Aldwych farce in a period setting. It failed at the time but now seems a brave try, with nice judgment all round.

w Noel Langley *d* Walter Forde *ph* Jack Hildyard *m* Lambert Williamson

Sid Field, Margaret Lockwood, Mary Clare, Jerry Desmonde, Claude Hulbert, Irene

Handl, Brian Worth, Edmund Willard (as Cromwell)

The Cardinal*
US 1963 175m Technicolor Panavision 70
Gamma / Otto Preminger
A 1917 ordinand becomes a Boston curate, a fighter of the Ku Klux Klan, a Rome diplomat, and finally gets a cardinal's hat.
Heavy-going documentary melodrama with many interesting sequences marred by lack of cohesion, too much grabbing at world problems, and over-sensational personal asides.

w Robert Dozier, *novel* Henry Morton Robinson *d* Otto Preminger *ph* Leon Shamroy *m* Jerome Moross *pd* Lyle Wheeler *titles* Saul Bass

Tom Tryon, *Carol Lynley,* Dorothy Gish, Maggie Macnamara, Cecil Kellaway, John Saxon, *John Huston,* Robert Morse, Burgess Meredith, Jill Haworth, Raf Vallone, Tullio Carminati, Ossie Davis, Chill Wills, Arthur Hunnicutt, Murray Hamilton, Patrick O'Neal, Romy Schneider
'Very probably the last word in glossy dishonesty posturing as serious art.'—*John Simon*
'Mere and sheer wide screen Technicolor movie.'—*Stanley Kauffmann*
AAN: Otto Preminger; Leon Shamroy; John Huston

Cardinal Richelieu*
US 1935 83m bw
Twentieth Century (Darryl F. Zanuck)
Fictionalized biography of the unscrupulous cardinal who was the grey eminence behind Louis XIII.
One of George Arliss' better star vehicles, with not much conviction but excellent production values.

w Maude Howell, Cameron Rogers, W. P. Lipscomb *d* Rowland V. Lee *ph* Peverell Marley *m* Alfred Newman

George Arliss, Maureen O'Sullivan, Edward Arnold, Cesar Romero

Career
US 1939 80m bw
RKO (Robert Sisk)
A respected small-town storekeeper has old scores to settle against the local banker.
Modest, pleasing, rather faded 'B' picture.

w Dalton Trumbo, Bert Granet, *novel* Phil Stong *d* Leigh Jason *ph* Frank Redman

Edward Ellis, Samuel S. Hinds, Anne Shirley, Janet Beecher, Leon Errol, Raymond Hatton, Hobart Cavanaugh

Career*
US 1959   105m   bw
Paramount / Hal B. Wallis (Paul Nathan)

An actor from the midwest finally gets his chance in New York.
A location melodrama with the feel of a documentary, well played but slow and rather indeterminate.

w James Lee, from his play   d Joseph Anthony   ph Joseph La Shelle   m Franz Waxman

Anthony Franciosa, Dean Martin, Shirley Maclaine, Carolyn Jones, Joan Blackman, Robert Middleton, Frank McHugh, Donna Douglas

AAN: Joseph La Shelle

Carefree*
US 1938   85m   bw
RKO (Pandro S. Berman)

A humourless lawyer sends his undecided girl friend to an alienist, with whom she falls in love.
Slight, frothy comedy musical; quite palatable, but it signalled the end of the Astaire–Rogers series.

w Allan Scott, Ernest Pagano   d Mark Sandrich   ph Robert de Grasse   m / ly Irving Berlin   ch Hermes Pan   md Victor Baravelle

Fred Astaire, Ginger Rogers, Ralph Bellamy, Luella Gear, Clarence Kolb, Jack Carson, Franklin Pangborne, Walter Kingsford, Hattie McDaniel

AAN: Victor Baravelle; song 'Change Partners' (m / ly Irving Berlin)

Careful, Soft Shoulder*
US 1942   69m   bw
TCF (Walter Morosco)

A Washington socialite becomes a spy for both sides.
Modest, slightly unusual second feature which over the years has gathered for itself more reputation than it really deserves.

wd Oliver H. P. Garrett   ph Charles Clarke   m Leigh Harline

Virginia Bruce, James Ellison, Aubrey Mather, Sheila Ryan, Ralph Byrd

The Caretaker*
GB 1964   105m   bw
Caretaker Films (Michael Birkett)
US title: The Guest

Two brothers invite a revolting tramp to share their attic.
Rather doleful filming of the fashionable play with its non-plot, irregular conceits and interesting interplay of character. It remains a theatrical experience.

w Harold Pinter   d Clive Donner   ph Nicolas Roeg   m Ron Grainer

Alan Bates, Robert Shaw, Donald Pleasence

The Caretakers*
US 1963   97m   bw
UA / Hall Bartlett
GB title: Borderlines

The interrelationship of several cases in a state mental hospital.
Rather hysterical melodrama, lacking in the stature required for its subject, but sometimes perversely entertaining.

w Henry F. Greenberg, novel Daniel Telfer   d Hall Bartlett   ph Lucien Ballard   m Elmer Bernstein

Polly Bergen, Robert Stack, Joan Crawford, Diane McBain, Janis Paige, Van Williams, Robert Vaughn, Herbert Marshall, Constance Ford

AAN: Lucien Ballard

The Carey Treatment*
US 1972   101m   Metrocolor   Panavision
MGM (William Belasco)

A Boston pathologist investigating the death of an abortion victim becomes the potential murder victim of a father turned killer.
Pretentious thriller with a tendency to make moral points among the bloodshed; vigorously but variably made.

w James P. Bonner, novel A Case of Need by Jeffrey Hudson   d Blake Edwards   ph Frank Stanley   m Roy Budd

James Coburn, Jennifer O'Neill, Skye Aubrey, Pat Hingle, Dan O'Herlihy, Elizabeth Allen, Alex Dreier, Regis Toomey

Caribbean
US 1952   94m   Technicolor
(Paramount) Pine–Thomas (William H. Pine, William C. Thomas)
GB title: Caribbean Gold

An 18th-century pirate captures the nephew of his old enemy.
Adequate but not very exciting swashbuckler with fair production values.

w Frank L. Moss, Edward Ludwig   d Edward Ludwig   ph Lionel Lindon   m Lucien Cailliet

John Payne, Arlene Dahl, Cedric Hardwicke (incredibly cast as the pirate), Francis L. Sullivan, Dennis Hoey

The Caribbean Mystery
US 1945   65m   bw

A Brooklyn detective arrives on a Caribbean island in search of a murderer. Good atmospheric second feature with local colour not getting in the way of the plot. James Dunn, Sheila Ryan, Edward Ryan, Roy Roberts. Written by Jack Andrews and Leonard Praskins; directed by Robert Webb; for TCF.

Carlton-Browne of the FO
GB 1958   88m   bw
British Lion / Charter Films (John Boulting)
US title: *Man in a Cocked Hat*

When valuable mineral deposits are found in a small British colony, the diplomat sent to cement good relations does quite the reverse. Hit-or-miss farcical comedy several rungs below the Ealing style, with all concerned in poor form.

wd Jeffrey Dell, Roy Boulting *ph* Max Greene *m* John Addison

Terry-Thomas, Peter Sellers, Ian Bannen, Thorley Walters, Raymond Huntley, John Le Mesurier, Luciana Paluzzi, Miles Malleson, Kynaston Reeves, Marie Lohr

Carmen Jones*
US 1954   105m   De Luxe   Cinemascope
TCF (Otto Preminger)

A factory girl marries a pilot, and is strangled by him for infidelity.
Black American updating of Bizet's opera, not really satisfactory but given full marks for trying, though the main singing is dubbed and the effect remains doggedly theatrical.

w Harry Kleiner *d* Otto Preminger *ph* Sam Leavitt *ly* Oscar Hammerstein II *titles* Saul Bass *md* Herschel Burke Gilbert

Dorothy Dandridge, Harry Belafonte, *Pearl Bailey*, Olga James, Joe Adams, Roy Glenn, Nick Stewart, Diahann Carroll, Brock Peters

'All one regrets is that the director has been unable to impose a unifying style on this promising material.'—*Gavin Lambert*

AAN: Herschel Burke Gilbert; Dorothy Dandridge

Carnal Knowledge*
US 1971   97m   Technicolor   Panavision
Avco Embassy / Icarus (Mike Nichols)

A college student embarks on an enthusiastic and varied sex life but by middle age is bored and empty.
Hampered by an unsuitable wide screen, this pretentious but fragmented comedy drama is embarrassingly conscious of its own daring in subject and language, and good performances are weighed down by an unsubtle script and tricksy direction.

w Jules Feiffer *d* Mike Nichols *ph* Giuseppe Rotunno *m* various songs *pd* Richard Sylbert

Jack Nicholson, *Arthur Garfunkel*, Candice Bergen, *Ann-Margret*, Rita Moreno

AAN: Ann-Margret

Carnegie Hall
US 1947   134m   bw
Federal Films (Boris Morros, William Le Baron)

The story of New York's music centre, based on a fiction about a cleaner who finally becomes a concert organizer when her son is a famous pianist.
Slim and risible excuse for a classical concert, featuring among others Bruno Walter, Leopold Stokowski, Artur Rubenstein, Jascha Heifitz, Lily Pons, Rise Stevens, Ezio Pinza, Jan Peerce, Harry James, Vaughn Monroe and the New York Philharmonic Symphony Orchestra.

w Karl Lamb *d* Edgar G. Ulmer *ph* William Miller

'The thickest and sourest mess of musical mulligatawny I have yet had to sit down to.'—*James Agee*

Un Carnet de Bal**
France 1936   120m   bw
Lévy / Strauss / Sigma
aka: *Christine*

A rich widow seeks her partners at a ball she remembers from her youth, finding that they are all failures and the ball a village hop.
Considering its fame, this is a lumpy porridge of a picture, good in parts but often slow, pretentious and banal. Its gallery of actors is, however, unique.

w Jean Sarment, Pierre Wolff, Bernard Zimmer, Henri Jeanson, Julien Duvivier *d* Julien Duvivier *ph* Michel Kelber, Philippe Agostini *m* Maurice Jaubert

Marie Bell, Françoise Rosay, *Louis Jouvet, Raimu, Harry Baur, Fernandel, Pierre Blanchar*

† The film's international success took Duvivier to Hollywood, where he half-remade it as *Lydia* and went on to other multi-story films such as *Tales of Manhattan* and *Flesh and Fantasy*.

Carnival
GB 1946   93m   bw
Rank / Two Cities

In the nineties, a ballet dancer marries a dour Cornish farmer, who shoots her when her erstwhile lover comes after her.
Flimsy screen version of a solidly old-fashioned romantic drama.

w Eric Maschwitz, *novel* Compton Mackenzie d Stanley Haynes *ph* Guy Green

Sally Gray, Michael Wilding, Bernard Miles, Cathleen Nesbitt
† The story was previously filmed in 1931, as *Dance Pretty Lady*, with Ann Casson and Carl Harbord. The 1931 film *Carnival*, with Matheson Lang, is based on a story identical to *Men Are Not Gods* and *A Double Life:* an actor becomes obsessed with the part of Othello and strangles his wife.

Carnival in Costa Rica
US 1947 97m Technicolor
TCF (William A. Bacher)

A young Costa Rican, engaged to an American singer, returns home to find that his parents expect him to marry his childhood sweetheart.
Decidedly rundown musical in which incessant carnival largely supplants the wispy plot.

w John Larkin, Samuel Hoffenstein, Elizabeth Reinhardt d Gregory Ratoff *ph* Harry Jackson *ch* Leonide Massine *m / ly* Harry Ruby, Ernesto Lecuona

Dick Haymes, Vera-Ellen, Celeste Holm, J. Carrol Naish, Cesar Romero

Carnival Story
US / Germany 1954 95m Technicolor
The King Brothers

A starving girl becomes a trapezist at a German circus and stirs up jealousy among her partners.
Bleak reworking of *The Three Maxims* (qv), reworked again with more expertise in *Trapeze* (qv); this version is a cheap and unattractive co-production.

w Kurt Neumann, Hans Jacoby d Kurt Neumann *ph* Ernest Haller *m* Willi Schmidt-Genter

Anne Baxter, Steve Cochran, Lyle Bettger, George Nader, Jay C. Flippen

Carny
US 1980 105m Technicolor
Lorimar / Jonathan Taplin (Robbie Robertson)

Three wacky characters join a travelling carnival.
Sordid, sexy melodrama which seems to be doing a *Jules and Jim* with no holds barred.

Not badly made, but full of people one would cross the road to avoid.

w Thomas Baum d Robert Kaylor *ph* Harry Stradling Jnr *m* Alex North

Gary Busey, Jodie Foster, Robbie Robertson, Kenneth McMillan, Meg Foster, Elisha Cook Jnr
'Too dark and turbulent a vision to be palatable to a large public.'—*Variety*

Carolina
US 1934 85m bw
Fox (Darryl F. Zanuck)
GB title: *House of Connelly*

A Yankee farmer's daughter falls in love with a Southern plantation owner.
Mildly pleasing period piece.

w Reginald Berkeley, *play* The House of Connelly by Paul Green d Henry King *ph* Hal Mohr

Janet Gaynor, Lionel Barrymore, Robert Young, Henrietta Crosman, Mona Barrie, Richard Cromwell

Carolina Blues
US 1944 81m bw

A bandleader needs a new singer. Wispy comedy musical towards the end of Kyser's unlikely popularity. Kay Kyser and his band, Ann Miller, Victor Moore. Written by M. M. Musselman, Kenneth Earl, Joseph Hoffman and Al Martin; directed by Leigh Jason; for Columbia.

Caroline Chérie
France 1951 115m approx bw
SNEG / Cinéphonie

Adventures of an attractive and willing young French girl in the days of the revolution.
A cheerful French imitation of *Forever Amber*; witless and not very entertaining despite good period sense and a certain amount of self-mockery.

w Jean Anouilh, *novel* Cécil Saint-Laurent d Richard Poitier *ph* Maurice Barry *m* Georges Auric

Martine Carol, Jacques Dacqmine, Marie Déa, Paul Bernard, Pierre Cressoy
† After several sequels, a colour remake appeared in 1967.

Carousel*
US 1956 128m Eastmancolor
Cinemascope 55
TCF (Henry Ephron)

A ne'er-do-well dies while committing a hold-

up. Fifteen years later he returns from heaven
to set his family's affairs in order.

Based on a fantasy play with an honourable
history, this super-wide-screen version of an
effective stage musical is hollow and boring, a
humourless whimsy in which even the songs
seem an intrusion.

w Phoebe and Henry Ephron, from the
musical based on Ferenc Molnar's play Liliom
d Henry King *ph* Charles G. Clarke
m / ly Rodgers and Hammerstein *ch* Rod
Alexander, Agnes de Mille

Gordon Macrae, Shirley Jones, Cameron
Mitchell,Gene Lockhart, Barbara Ruick,
Robert Rounseville

The Carpetbaggers••
US 1964   150m   Technicolor
  Panavision
Paramount / Embassy (Joseph E. Levine)

A young playboy inherits an aircraft business,
becomes a megalomaniac tycoon, and moves
to Hollywood in his search for power.
Enjoyable pulp fiction clearly suggested by the
career of Howard Hughes. Lashings of old-
fashioned melodrama, quite well pointed by
all concerned.

w John Michael Hayes, *novel* Harold Robbins
d Edward Dmytryk *ph* Joseph MacDonald
m Elmer Bernstein *ad* Hal Pereira, Walter
Tyler

George Peppard, Carroll Baker, *Alan Ladd*
(his last film), *Martin Balsam*, Bob Cummings,
Martha Hyer, Elizabeth Ashley, Lew Ayres,
Ralph Taeger, Archie Moore, Leif Erickson,
Audrey Totter

'One of those elaborate conjuring tricks in
which yards and yards of coloured ribbon are
spread all over the stage merely to prove that
the conjuror has nothing up his sleeve.'—*Tom
Milne*

Carrie••
US 1952   122m   bw
Paramount (William Wyler)

In the early 1900s a country girl comes to
Chicago, loses her innocence and goes on the
stage, meanwhile reducing a wealthy
restaurant manager to penury through love for
her.

A famous satirical novel is softened into an
unwieldy narrative with scarcely enough
dramatic power to sustain interest despite
splendid production values. Heavy pre-release
cuts remain obvious, and the general effect is
depressing; but it is very good to look at.

w Ruth and Augustus Goetz, *novel* Sister
Carrie by Theodore Dreiser *d* William Wyler
ph Victor Milner *m* David Raksin *ad* Hal
Pereira, Roland Anderson

Laurence Olivier, Jennifer Jones, Miriam
Hopkins, Eddie Albert, Basil Ruysdael, Ray
Teal, Barry Kelley, Mary Murphy

'They shot the later episodes for the
strongest dramatic effect only, despite the fact
that the story had stopped following a
melodramatic line and become a sociological
study . . . each additional episode exploits the
audience's hope that things will be brought to
a satisfactory conclusion, but they never
are.'—*Films in Review*

Carrie•
US 1976   98m   MGM-De Luxe
UA / Red Bank (Paul Monash)

A repressed teenager with remarkable mental
powers takes a macabre revenge on classmates
who taunt and persecute her.

Stylish but unattractive shocker which works
its way up to a fine climax of gore and frenzy
and takes care to provide a final frisson just
when the audience thinks it can safely go
home.

w Laurence D. Cohen, *novel* Stephen King
d Brian de Palma *ph* Mario Tosi *m* Pino
Donaggio

Sissy Spacek, *Piper Laurie*, Amy Irving,
William Katt, John Travolta

'Combining Gothic horror, offhand
misogyny and an air of studied triviality,
Carrie is de Palma's most enjoyable movie in a
long while, and also his silliest.'—*Janet
Maslin, Newsweek*

'The horror is effective only once, and the
attempts at humour are never very successful
and come almost when one is inclined to be
moved by somebody's plight, so that the
non-jokes yield authentic bad taste.'—*John
Simon, New York*

AAN: Sissy Spacek; Piper Laurie

Carrington VC•
GB 1954   106m   bw
British Lion / Romulus (Teddy Baird)
US title: *Court Martial*

An army major is courtmartialled for
embezzling mess funds.

Good courtroom drama with a few plot
surprises, convincing characters, and very
serviceable acting and direction.

w John Hunter, *play* Dorothy and Campbell
Christie *d* Anthony Asquith *ph* Desmond
Dickinson

David Niven, Margaret Leighton, Noelle Middleton, Laurence Naismith, Clive Morton, Mark Dignam, Allan Cuthbertson, Victor Maddern, John Glyn-Jones, Raymond Francis, Newton Blick, John Chandos

Carry on Sergeant

GB 1958 83m bw
Anglo Amalgamated / Insignia (Peter Rogers)

An army training sergeant accepts a bet that his last platoon of raw recruits will win the Star Squad award.
Shabby farce with humdrum script and slack direction, saved by energetic performances.

w Norman Hudis, *play* The Bull Boys by R. F. Delderfield *d* Gerald Thomas *ph* Peter Hennessy *m* Bruce Montgomery

Bob Monkhouse, William Hartnell, Kenneth Williams, Charles Hawtrey, Shirley Eaton, Eric Barker, Dora Bryan, Bill Owen, Kenneth Connor
† From this unlikely beginning sprang almost twenty years of *Carry Ons*, their plots gradually disappearing under an accumulation of old jokes which grew steadily bluer. Colour did little to disguise their makeshift construction, and they never raised their sights as high as satire, but they became a British institution like fish and chips, and many of the regulars became stars. Apart from Williams, Hawtrey and Connor, those most regularly featured in the sequels were Sid James, Bernard Bresslaw, Jim Dale, Joan Sims, Hattie Jacques, Peter Butterworth, and Jack Douglas, with occasional guests such as Harry H. Corbett, Juliet Mills and even Phil Silvers. All were produced by Peter Rogers and directed by Gerald Thomas; most were written (or recollected) by Talbot Rothwell. Delivered at the rate of roughly two a year, the sequence of titles was CARRY ON NURSE (a surprising hit in the US), CARRY ON TEACHER, CARRY ON CONSTABLE, CARRY ON REGARDLESS, CARRY ON CRUISING, CARRY ON CABBY, CARRY ON JACK, CARRY ON SPYING, CARRY ON CLEO, CARRY ON COWBOY, CARRY ON SCREAMING, FOLLOW THAT CAMEL (Beau Geste), DON'T LOSE YOUR HEAD (the Scarlet Pimpernel), CARRY ON DOCTOR, CARRY ON UP THE KHYBER, CARRY ON CAMPING, CARRY ON AGAIN DOCTOR, CARRY ON LOVING, CARRY ON UP THE JUNGLE, CARRY ON HENRY (Henry VIII), CARRY ON AT YOUR CONVENIENCE, CARRY ON MATRON, CARRY ON ABROAD, CARRY ON

GIRLS, CARRY ON DICK, CARRY ON BEHIND, CARRY ON ENGLAND, CARRY ON EMMANUELLE.
† CARRY ON ADMIRAL and WHAT A CARRY ON are not part of the series.

Carson City*

US 1952 87m Warnercolor
Warner (David Weisbart)

A stagecoach service suffers from bandit raids, so a local banker finances a railroad.
Agreeably conventional western with plenty of reliable plot and a satisfactory outcome for the goodies.

w Sloan Nibley, Winston Miller *d* André de Toth *ph* John Boyle *m* David Buttolph

Randolph Scott, Raymond Massey, Lucille Norman, Richard Webb, James Millican, Larry Keating, George Cleveland

Cartouche

Italy / US 1954 85m approx bw
Venturini / RKO (John Nasht)

A French prince clears himself of a murder charge and brings the villain to book.
Flat costume drama.

w Louis Stevens, Tullio Pinelli *d* Steve Sekely, Gianni Vernuccio *ph* Massimo Dallamano *m* Bruce Montgomery

Richard Basehart, Patricia Roc, Massimo Serato, Akim Tamiroff

Cartouche**

France / Italy 1961 114m
Eastmancolor Dyaliscope
Ariane / Filmsonor / Vides (Georges Danciger)
aka: *Swords of Blood*

An 18th-century cooper's son becomes a quick-witted and gallant thief.
Slightly bitter fairy tale based on a French legend, vigorously encompassing tragedy, farce, violence and high-flown adventure.

w Daniel Boulanger, Philippe de Broca *d* Philippe de Broca *ph* Christian Matras *m* Georges Delerue

Jean-Paul Belmondo, Claudia Cardinale, Odile Versois, Marcel Dalio, Philippe Lemaire, Jean Rochefort
'A tour de force of virtuosity.'—*Peter John Dyer, MFB*

Carve Her Name with Pride*

GB 1958 119m bw
Rank / Keyboard (Daniel M. Angel)

In 1940, the young British widow of a French officer is enlisted as a spy, and after various

adventures dies before a German firing squad.
Slightly muddled if ultimately moving biopic in
which initial light comedy gives way to
romance, documentary, character study,
blazing war action and finally tragedy.
Generally well made.

w Vernon Harris, Lewis Gilbert, *book* R. J.
Minney *d* Lewis Gilbert *ph* John Wilcox
m William Alwyn

Virginia McKenna (as Violette Szabo), *Paul
Scofield*, Jack Warner, Sidney Tafler, Denise
Grey, Alain Saury, Maurice Ronet, Nicole
Stéphane, Noel Willman, Bill Owen, William
Mervyn, Anne Leon
  'What is missing is the deeply charged
passion which would have gone beyond the
quietly decent statement intermittently
achieved.'—*John Gillett*

Casablanca••••
US 1942   102m   bw
Warner *(Hal B. Wallis)*

Rick's Café in Casablanca is a centre for war
refugees awaiting visas for America. Rick
abandons his cynicism to help an old love
escape the Nazis with her underground leader
husband.
Cinema par excellence: a studio-bound
Hollywood melodrama which after various
chances just fell together impeccably into one
of the outstanding entertainment experiences
of cinema history, with romance, intrigue,
excitement, suspense and humour cunningly
deployed by master technicians and a perfect
cast.

w *Julius J. Epstein, Philip G. Epstein, Howard
Koch*, from an unproduced play, Everybody
Comes to Rick's, by Murray Burnett and Joan
Alison *d* Michael Curtiz *ph* Arthur Edeson
m Max Steiner

*Humphrey Bogart, Ingrid Bergman, Claude
Rains, Paul Henreid, Conrad Veidt, S. Z.
Sakall, Sidney Greenstreet, Peter Lorre,
Dooley Wilson* (singing 'As Time Goes By'),
Marcel Dalio, Leonid Kinskey
  'A picture which makes the spine tingle and
the heart take a leap . . . they have so
combined sentiment, humour and pathos with
taut melodrama and bristling intrigue that the
result is a highly entertaining and even
inspiring film.'—*New York Times*
  'Its humour is what really saves it, being a
mixture of Central European irony of attack
and racy Broadway–Hollywood Boulevard
cynicism.'—*Herman G. Weinberg*
  'The happiest of happy accidents, and the
most decisive exception to the *auteur*
theory.'—*Andrew Sarris, 1968*

  'A film which seems to have been frozen in
time . . . the sum of its many marvellous parts
far exceeds the whole.'—*NFT, 1974*
  'You can tell by the cast it's important!
gripping! big!'—*publicity*
AA: best picture; Julius J. and Philip G.
Epstein, Howard Koch; Michael Curtiz
AAN: Arthur Edeson; Max Steiner;
Humphrey Bogart; Claude Rains

Casanova
Italy 1976   163m (English version)
  Technicolor   Scope
TCF / PEA (Alberto Grimaldi)
aka: *Fellini's Casanova*

Episodes from the life of the eighteenth-
century libertine, in the course of which he
seduces, among others, a nun, a mechanical
doll, and a hunchbacked nymphomaniac.
A curiously rarefied spectacle which seldom
comes to anything like life and despite its vast
expense seems more likely to provoke yawns
than lust.

w Federico Fellini, Barnadino Zapponi
d Federico Fellini *ph* Giuseppe Rotunno
m Nino Rota *pd* Danilo Donati, Federico
Fellini

Donald Sutherland, Tina Aumont, Cicely
Browne, Carmen Scarpitta
  'It may well be the most ponderous
specimen of imaginative vacuity ever
devised.'—*John Simon, New York*

Casanova Brown
US 1944   99m   bw
International / Christie (Nunnally Johnson)

Just as his divorce comes through, a man
discovers that his wife is pregnant.
Very mild star comedy which tiptoes round its
subject.

w Nunnally Johnson, *play* Bachelor Father by
Floyd Dell, Thomas Mitchell *d* Sam Wood
ph John F. Seitz *m* Arthur Lange *ad* Perry
Ferguson

Gary Cooper, Teresa Wright, Frank Morgan,
Anita Louise, Patricia Collinge, Edmond
Breon, Jill Esmond, Isobel Elsom, Mary
Treen, Halliwell Hobbes
  'There is so much clowning with so little
subject that one is exposed to the impression
that anything went for a laugh.'—*Bosley
Crowther, New York Times*
AAN: Arthur Lange; Perry Ferguson

Casanova in Burlesque
US 1944   74m   bw

A professor has a secret summer life as a
burlesque performer. Unusual, amiable

comedy. Joe E. Brown, June Havoc. Written
by Frank Gill; directed by Leslie Goodwins;
for Republic.

Casanova's Big Night
US 1954   86m   Technicolor
Paramount (Paul Jones)

In old Italy, the great lover is fleeing from his
creditors and changes places with a tailor's
apprentice.
The last of Bob Hope's big-budget, big-studio
burlesques is a lumbering vehicle which wastes
its star cast and mistimes its laughs.

w Hal Kanter, Edmund Hartmann *d* Norman
Z. McLeod *ph* Lionel Lindon

Bob Hope, Joan Fontaine (an unhappy
comedy foil), Basil Rathbone, Vincent Price,
Audrey Dalton, Hugh Marlowe, John
Carradine, Primo Carnera, Arnold Moss, Lon
Chaney Jnr

Casbah
US 1948   94m   bw
Universal (Erik Charell)

Remake of *Algiers* (qv) with songs added.
Not too bad in the circumstances, but a wholly
artificial exercise, and another version was
really not needed. The sets seem overlit and
claustrophobic.

w (not credited) *d* John Berry *ph* Irving
Glassberg *m* Harold Arlen

*Tony Martin,*Yvonne de Carlo, Marta Toren,
Peter Lorre, Hugo Haas

AAN: song 'For Every Man There's a
Woman' (*m* Harold Arlen, *ly* Leo Robin)

The Case against Mrs Ames
US 1936   85m   bw
Paramount (Walter Wanger)

The prosecutor in a murder case is convinced
of the defendant's innocence.
Tired rehash of a familiar theme.

w Gene Towne, Graham Baker *d* William A.
Seiter *ph* Lucien Andriot

Madeleine Carroll, George Brent, Arthur
Treacher, Alan Baxter, Beulah Bondi, Alan
Mowbray, Esther Dale, Ed Brophy

The Case of the Black Cat
US 1936   66m   bw

An old man is murdered after changing his
will: Perry Mason investigates. One of the
better tales of the lawyer sleuth. here
impersonated by Ricardo Cortez; with Harry
Davenport, June Travis, Jane Bryan. Written
by F. Hugh Herbert; directed by William
McGann; for Warner.

The Case of the Black Parrot
US 1941   60m   bw

Was it the butler who murdered to steal a case
of diamonds? This sounds like a Perry Mason
but is not; William Lundigan stars as a
reporter who solves the puzzle; with Maris
Wrixon, Eddie Foy Jnr, Paul Cavanagh.
Written by Robert E. Kent, from a play by
Burton Stevenson; directed by Noel Smith; for
Warner.

The Case of the Curious Bride
US 1935   80m   bw

Perry Mason helps a woman who is being
blackmailed by her 'dead' husband. Smoothish
mystery, with Warren William, Margaret
Lindsay, Donald Woods, Claire Dodd, Allen
Jenkins and—briefly—Errol Flynn. Written by
Tom Reed, from an Erle Stanley Gardner
original; directed by Michael Curtiz; for
Warner.

The Case of the Frightened Lady
GB 1940   81m   bw

A dowager knows that her son is mad and tries
to prevent him from strangling his cousin.
Quite a lively suspenser of its time. Marius
Goring, Penelope Dudley Ward, Helen Haye,
Patrick Barr, Felix Aylmer. Written by
Edward Dryhurst, from the novel by Edgar
Wallace; directed by George King; for
Pennant. A previous version was released in
1932 as *The Frightened Lady* (qv).

The Case of the Howling Dog
US 1934   75m   bw

Two men claim the same woman as their wife.
Adequate Perry Mason mystery. Warren
William, Mary Astor, Allen Jenkins, Grant
Mitchell, Helen Trenholme. Written by Ben
Markson, from an Erle Stanley Gardner
original; directed by Alan Crosland; for
Warner.

The Case of the Lucky Legs
US 1935   77m   bw

Perry Mason chases a beauty contest promoter
who skips town with the winnings. Fair light-
hearted mystery, with Warren William as a
somewhat dissipated sleuth; also Genevieve
Tobin, Allen Jenkins, Patricia Ellis, Lyle
Talbot, Barton Maclane. Written by Ben
Markson and Brown Holmes, from an Erle
Stanley Gardner original; directed by Archie
Mayo; for Warner.

The Case of the Stuttering Bishop
US 1937   70m   bw

Perry Mason investigates an heiress who may
be an impostor. Thin mystery with another

different star in the lead: Donald Woods. Also
Ann Dvorak, Anne Nagel, Linda Perry.
Written by Don Ryan and Kenneth Gamet,
from an Erle Stanley Gardner original;
directed by William Clemens; for Warner.

The Case of the Velvet Claws
US 1936   63m   bw

Perry Mason's honeymoon is postponed when
he finds himself on a murder charge. Moderate
light-hearted mystery, but they should have
awarded prizes to anyone who could explain
the title. Warren William, Claire Dodd, Wini
Shaw, Gordon Elliott, Addison Richards.
Written by Tom Reed, from an Erle Stanley
Gardner original; directed by William
Clemens; for Warner.

Casey's Shadow
US 1978   116m   Metrocolor   Panavision
Columbia / Ray Stark (Michael Levee)

A Cajun family in New Mexico breeds a
champion horse which wins the annual race.
Shades of *Maryland*: an old-fashioned movie
of the kind which absolutely nobody should
want to revive, at least not so ineptly or at
such length.

w Carol Sobieski, *story* Ruidoso by John
McPhee d Martin Ritt ph John A. Alonzo
m Patrick Williams

Walter Matthau, Alexis Smith, Robert
Webber, Murray Hamilton, Andrew A.
Rubin, Stephan Burns, Michael Hershewe

Cash McCall
US 1960   102m   Technicolor
Warner (Henry Blanke)

A Napoleon of the stock market gets into
trouble for the first time when love interferes
with business.
Slightly unusual comedy drama, quite sharply
made and played, but not adding up to much.

w Lenore Coffee, Marion Hargrove. *novel*
Cameron Hawley d Joseph Pevney
ph George Folsey m Max Steiner

James Garner, Natalie Wood, Nina Foch,
Dean Jagger, E. G. Marshall, Henry Jones,
Otto Kruger, Roland Winters

Cash on Demand*
GB 1963   86m   bw
Columbia / Woodpecker / Hammer
   (Michael Carreras)

A fussy bank manager outwits a classy robber.
Quietly effective suspenser with an admirable
middle-aged cast and no love interest.

w Lewis Greifer, David T. Chantler, from
Jacques Gillies' TV play d Quentin

Lawrence ph Arthur Grant m Wilfred
Josephs
Peter Cushing, André Morell, Richard Vernon,
Norman Bird, Edith Sharpe

The Casino Murder Case
US 1935   85m   bw

Philo Vance solves a murder in a family of
neurotics. Rather heavy-going detection. Paul
Lukas, Rosalind Russell, Eric Blore, Donald
Cook, Louise Fazenda, Ted Healy, Isabel
Jewell, Leo G. Carroll. Written by Florence
Ryerson and Edgar Allen Woolf, from an S.
S. Van Dine original; directed by Edwin
Marin; for MGM.

Casino Royale
GB 1967   130m   Technicolor
Panavision
Columbia / Famous Artists (Charles K.
   Feldman, Jerry Bresler)

The heads of the allied spy forces call Sir
James Bond out of retirement to fight the
power of *SMERSH*.
Woeful all-star kaleidoscope, a way-out spoof
which generates far fewer laughs than the
original. One of the most shameless wastes of
time and talent in screen history.

w Wolf Mankowitz, John Law, Michael
Sayers, *novel* Ian Fleming d John Huston,
Ken Hughes, Val Guest, Robert Parrish, Joe
McGrath, Richard Talmadge ph Jack
Hildyard m Burt Bacharach pd Michael
Stringer

David Niven, Deborah Kerr, Orson Welles,
Peter Sellers, Ursula Andress, Woody Allen,
William Holden, Charles Boyer, John Huston,
Joanna Pettet, Daliah Lavi, Kurt Kasznar,
Jacqueline Bisset, Derek Nimmo, George
Raft, Ronnie Corbett, Peter O'Toole, Jean-
Paul Belmondo, Geoffrey Bayldon, Duncan
Macrae

'One of those wild wacky extravaganzas in
which the audience is expected to have a great
time because everybody making the film did.
It seldom works out that way, and certainly
doesn't here.'—*John Russell Taylor*
'The dialogue is witless and unhampered by
taste, and the interminable finale is a
collection of clichés in a brawl involving the
cavalry, parachuted Indians, split-second
appearances by George Raft and Jean-Paul
Belmondo, every variety of mayhem, and
Woody Allen burping radiation as a walking
atom bomb.'—*Judith Crist*
'The worst film I ever enjoyed.'—*Donald
Zec*

AAN: song 'The Look of Love' (*m* Burt
Bacharach, *ly* Hal David)

Casque d'Or***
France 1952   96m   bw
Speva / Paris
aka: *Golden Marie*

1898. In the Paris slums, an apache finds
passionate love but is executed for murder.
A tragic romance which on its first release
seemed bathed in a golden glow and is
certainly an impeccable piece of film-making.

w Jacques Becker, Jacques Companeez
d *Jacques Becker* ph *Robert Le Fèbvre*
m Georges Van Parys

Simone Signoret, Serge Reggiani, Claude
Dauphin, Raymond Bussières, Gaston Modot
  'Takes its place alongside *Le Jour Se Lève*
among the masterpieces of the French
cinema.'—*Karel Reisz*
  'A screen alive with sensuousness and
luminous figures.'—*Dilys Powell*

Cass Timberlane*
US 1947   119m   bw
MGM (Arthur Hornblow Jnr)

A judge marries a working class girl, who is
unsettled at first but finally comes to realize
her good fortune.
Solid drama with an understanding star
performance and good production values.

w Donald Ogden Stewart, *novel* Sinclair
Lewis d George Sidney ph Robert Planck
m Roy Webb

Spencer Tracy, Lana Turner, Zachary Scott,
Tom Drake, Mary Astor, Albert Dekker,
Selena Royle, Josephine Hutchinson,
Margaret Lindsay

The Cassandra Crossing
GB / Italy / West Germany 1976   129m
   Technicolor   Panavision
AGF / CCC / International Cine (Lew Grade,
   Carlo Ponti)

A terrorist carrying a deadly plague virus
boards a transcontinental train.
Disaster spectacular with a number of
fashionable interests but no observable film-
making technique.

w Tom Mankiewicz, Robert Katz, George Pan
Cosmatos d George Pan Cosmatos ph Ennio
Guarnieri m Jerry Goldsmith pd Aurelio
Crugnola

Sophia Loren, Richard Harris, Ava Gardner,
Burt Lancaster, Martin Sheen, Ingrid Thulin,
Lee Strasberg, John Phillip Law, Lionel
Stander, Ann Turkel, O. J. Simpson, Alida
Valli

Cast a Dark Shadow*
GB 1955   82m   bw
Frobisher / Daniel M. Angel (Herbert
   Mason)

A wife-murderer marries an ex-barmaid and
tries again.
Unambitious but enjoyable melodrama, well
acted though with directorial opportunities
missed.

w John Cresswell, *play* Murder Mistaken by
Janet Green d Lewis Gilbert ph Jack Asher
m Antony Hopkins

Dirk Bogarde, *Margaret Lockwood*, Kay
Walsh, Kathleen Harrison, Robert Flemyng,
Mona Washbourne, Walter Hudd

Cast a Giant Shadow*
US 1966   141m   De Luxe   Panavision
UA / Mirisch / Llenroc / Batjac (Melville
   Shavelson)

An American military lawyer and ex-colonel
goes to Israel in 1947 to help in the fight
against the Arabs.
Spectacular war biopic with all concerned in
good form but lacking the clarity and narrative
control of a real smash.

w Melville Shavelson, from Ted Berkman's
biography of Col. David Marcus d Melville
Shavelson ph Aldo Tonti m Elmer Bernstein
pd Michael Stringer

Kirk Douglas, Angie Dickinson, Senta Berger,
Luther Adler, Stathis Giallelis, Chaim Topol,
John Wayne, Frank Sinatra, Yul Brynner,
James Donald, Gordon Jackson, Michael
Hordern, Gary Merrill, Allan Cuthbertson,
Jeremy Kemp

Cast a Long Shadow
US 1959   82m   colour

A hard-drinking drifter thinks he may be the
illegitimate son of a dead cattle baron. Would-
be psychological western with not enough
going for it. Audie Murphy, John Dehner,
Terry Moore, James Best, Denver Pyle.
Written by Martin H. Goldsmith and John
McGreevey, from the novel by Wayne D.
Overholser; directed by Thomas Carr; for
Mirisch / UA.

The Castaway Cowboy*
US 1974   91m   Technicolor
Walt Disney (Ron Miller, Winston Hibler)

In 1850, a Shanghaied sailor on Hawaii helps a
lady potato farmer to turn her land into a
cattle ranch.
Unexciting and unexceptional family fare.

w Don Tait d Vincent McEveety ph Andrew
Jackson m Robert F. Brunner

James Garner, Vera Miles, Robert Culp, Eric
Shea, Elizabeth Smith

Castle Keep*
US 1969   107m   Technicolor
  Panavision
Columbia / Filmways (Martin Ransohoff,
John Calley)

During World War II seven battle-weary
American soldiers occupy a 10th-century castle
filled with art treasures, then die defending it.
Or are they dead all the time? The film version
of this fantastic novel never seems quite sure,
and the uncertainty finally deadens it despite
careful work all round.

w Daniel Taradash, David Rayfiel, *novel*
William Eastlake d Sydney Pollack *ph* Henri
Decaë *m* Michel Legrand

Burt Lancaster, Peter Falk, Jean Pierre
Aumont, Patrick O'Neal, Al Freeman Jnr,
Scott Wilson, Tony Bill, Bruce Dern, Astrid
Heeren

Castle on the Hudson*
US 1940   77m   bw
Warner (Sam Bischoff)
GB title: *Years without Days*

A hardened criminal is not helped by his years
in prison.
Adequate, gloomy remake of *Twenty
Thousand Years in Sing Sing.*

w Seton I. Miller, Brown Holmes, Courtney
Terrett d Anatole Litvak *ph* Arthur Edeson
m Adolph Deutsch

John Garfield, Pat O'Brien, Ann Sheridan,
Burgess Meredith, Jerome Cowan, Henry
O'Neill, Guinn Williams, John Litel

The Cat*
France 1973   88m   colour

After twenty-five years of marriage an
embittered trapeze star and her husband
simply don't talk to each other. Absorbing
drama for two characters, brilliantly acted by
Jean Gabin and Simone Signoret, but with a
somewhat unsatisfactory conclusion. Written
by Pascal Jardin; directed by Pierre Granier-
Deferre; for Raymond Danon.

Cat and Mouse*
GB 1958   79m   bw
(Eros) Anvil (Paul Rotha)

The daughter of a man executed for murder is
threatened by criminals seeking hidden loot.
Interesting rather than exciting second feature
thriller directed by a documentary maker.

wd Paul Rotha, *novel* Michael Halliday
ph Wolfgang Suschitzky

Lee Patterson, Ann Sears, Hilton Edwards,
Victor Maddern, George Rose, Roddy
McMillan

The Cat and the Canary***
US 1927   84m (24 fps)   bw   silent
Universal

Greedy relatives assemble in an old house to
hear an eccentric's will, and a young girl's
sanity is threatened.
Archetypal spooky house comedy horror, here
given an immensely stylish production which
influenced Hollywood through the thirties and
was spoofed in *The Old Dark House.*

w Alfred Cohn, Robert F. Hill, *play John
Willard* d Paul Leni *ph Gilbert Warrenton
ad Charles D. Hall*

Creighton Hale, Laura La Plante, Forrest
Stanley, Tully Marshall, Flora Finch, Gertrude
Astor, Arthur Carewe
† Remade for sound by Rupert Julian in 1931
as *The Cat Creeps*, with Raymond Hackett,
Helen Twelvetrees and Jean Hersholt. This
title was also used for a grade Z 1946 second
feature with a different plot.

The Cat and the Canary***
US 1939   72m   bw
Paramount (Arthur Hornblow Jnr)

A superbly staged remake, briskly paced,
perfectly cast and lusciously photographed.
The comedy-thriller par excellence, with Bob
Hope fresh and sympathetic in his first big star
part.

w Walter de Leon, Lynn Starling d Elliott
Nugent ph Charles Lang m Dr Ernst Toch
ad Hans Dreier, Robert Usher

*Bob Hope, Paulette Goddard, Gale
Sondergaard, John Beal, Douglass
Montgomery, Nydia Westman, Elizabeth
Patterson, John Wray, George Zucco*
  'Beautifully shot, intelligently
constructed.'—*Peter John Dyer, 1966*

The Cat and the Fiddle
US 1933   90m   bw

In a taxi in Brussels, a leading lady of
Broadway musicals meets a European
composer. Very lightweight musical comedy.
Jeanette MacDonald, Ramon Novarro,
Charles Butterworth, Frank Morgan, Jean
Hersholt, Vivienne Segal, Henry Armetta.
Written by Sam and Bella Spewack, from the
show by Jerome Kern and Otto Harbach;
directed by William K. Howard; for MGM.

Cat Ballou**
US 1965   96m   Technicolor
Columbia (Harold Hecht)

Young Catherine Ballou hires a drunken
gunfighter to protect her father from a vicious
gunman, but despite her efforts he is shot, so
she turns outlaw.
Sometimes lively, sometimes somnolent

western spoof which considering the talent involved should have been funnier than it is. The linking ballad helps.

w Walter Newman, Frank R. Pierson, *novel* Roy Chanslor d Eliot Silverstein ph Jack Marta m Frank de Vol

Jane Fonda, *Lee Marvin*, Michael Callan, Dwayne Hickman, Nat King Cole, Stubby Kaye, Tom Nardini, John Marley, Reginald Denny

'Uneven, lumpy, coy and obvious.'— *Pauline Kael*

AA: Lee Marvin
AAN: Walter Newman, Frank R. Pierson; Frank de Vol; song 'The Ballad of Cat Ballou' (*m* Jerry Livingston, *ly* Mack David)

The Cat Creeps see The Cat and the Canary (1927)

The Cat from Outer Space
US 1978 103m Technicolor
Walt Disney Productions (Ron Miller)

A superintelligent extraterrestrial cat is forced to land on earth for running repairs. Fairly modest studio offering which pleased its intended market but could have been sharper.

w Ted Key d Norman Tokar ph Charles F. Wheeler m Lalo Schifrin sp Eustace Lycett, Art Cruickshank, Danny Dee

Ken Berry, Roddy McDowall, Sandy Duncan, Harry Morgan, McLean Stevenson, Jesse White, Alan Young, Hans Conried

Cat o'Nine Tails
Italy / France / Germany 1971 112m Techniscope

A blind reporter overhears an industrial espionage plot that turns into murder. Smart surface mechanics camouflage poor storytelling. Karl Malden, James Franciscus, Catherine Spaak. Written and directed by Dario Argento; for Spettacoli / Mondial / Terra / Labrador.

Cat on a Hot Tin Roof**
US 1958 108m Metrocolor
MGM / Avon (Lawrence Weingarten)

A rich plantation owner, dying of cancer, finds his two sons unsatisfactory: one is a conniver, the other a neurotic who refuses to sleep with his wife.
Slightly bowdlerized version of Tennessee Williams' most straightforward melodrama, watchable for the acting but still basically a theatrical experience.

w Richard Brooks, James Poe d Richard Brooks ph William Daniels m uncredited

Paul Newman, Burl Ives, Elizabeth Taylor, Jack Carson, Judith Anderson, Madeleine Sherwood, Larry Gates

AAN: best picture; Richard Brooks, James Poe; Richard Brooks (as director); William Daniels; Paul Newman; Elizabeth Taylor

Cat People**
US 1942 73m bw
RKO (*Val Lewton*)

A beautiful Yugoslavian girl believes she can turn into a panther; before she is found mysteriously dead, several of her acquaintances are attacked by such a beast. The first of Lewton's famous horror series for RKO is a slow starter but has some notable suspense sequences. It was also the first monster film to refrain from showing its monster.

w De Witt Bodeen d Jacques Tourneur ph Nicholas Musuraca m Roy Webb

Simone Simon, Kent Smith, Tom Conway, Jane Randolph, Jack Holt

'(Lewton) revolutionized scare movies with suggestion, imaginative sound effects and camera angles, leaving everything to the fear-filled imagination.'—*Pauline Kael, 1968*
† *Curse of the Cat People* (qv) was a very unrelated sequel.

Catacombs
GB 1964 90m bw

A rich woman is murdered by her husband and her male secretary. Involved melodrama with rather too many twists. Gary Merrill, Neil McCallum, Georgina Cookson, Jane Merrow, Rachel Thomas, Jack Train. Written by Dan Mainwaring; directed by Gordon Hessler; for Parroch / McCallum.

Catch As Catch Can
GB 1937 71m bw

Crooks after a valuable diamond converge on a transatlantic liner. Modest comedy-thriller. James Mason, Viki Dobson, Eddie Pola, Finlay Currie. Written by Richard Llewellyn; directed by Roy Kellino; for Fox British. (Aka: *Atlantic Episode*.)

Catch Me a Spy
GB 1971 94m Technicolor
Rank / Ludgate / Capitol / Films de la Pleiade (Steven Pallos)

A British agent smuggling Russian manuscripts into England falls for the wife of a Russian spy and finally gets his money as well. Complex, patchy comedy thriller with dispirited action scenes in Bucharest and Scotland. Technical credits rather dim.

w Dick Clement, Ian La Frenais, *novel* George Marton, Tibor Meray *d* Dick Clement *ph* Christopher Challis *m* Claude Bolling

Kirk Douglas, Trevor Howard, Tom Courtenay, Marlene Jobert, Patrick Mower, Bernadette Lafont, Bernard Blier

Catch 22*
US 1970 122m Technicolor
Panavision
Paramount / Filmways (John Calley, Martin Ransohoff)

At a US Air Force base in the Mediterranean during World War II, one by one the officers are distressingly killed; a survivor paddles towards neutral Sweden.

Intensely black comedy, more so than *M*A*S*H* and less funny, effectively mordant in places but too grisly and missing several tricks.

w Buck Henry, *novel* Joseph Heller *d* Mike Nichols *ph* David Watkin *m* none
pd Richard Sylbert

Alan Arkin, Martin Balsam, Richard Benjamin, Art Garfunkel, Jack Gilford, Buck Henry, Bob Newhart, Anthony Perkins, Paula Prentiss, Jon Voight, Martin Sheen, Orson Welles

'There are startling effects and good revue touches here and there, but the picture keeps going on and on, as if it were determined to impress us.'—*New Yorker*, 1977

'As hot and heavy as the original was cool and light.'—*Richard Schickel*

Catch Us If You Can
GB 1965 91m bw
Anglo Amalgamated / Bruton (David Deutsch)
US title: *Having a Wild Weekend*

Freelance stuntmen have various adventures in the west of England.

The first film of a pretentious director is a bright but wearisomely high-spirited imitation of *A Hard Day's Night.*

w Peter Nichols *d* John Boorman *ph* Manny Wynn *m* Dave Clark

The Dave Clark Five, Barbara Ferris, David Lodge, Robin Bailey, Yootha Joyce

The Catered Affair*
US 1956 93m bw
MGM (Sam Zimbalist)
GB title: *Wedding Breakfast*

When the daughter of a New York taxi driver gets married, her mother insists on a bigger function than they can afford.

Rather heavy-going comedy with amusing dialogue, from the period when Hollywood was seizing on TV plays like *Marty* and *Twelve Angry Men.*

w Gore Vidal, *TV play* Paddy Chayevsky *d* Richard Brooks *ph* John Alton *m* André Previn

Bette Davis, Ernest Borgnine, Debbie Reynolds, Barry Fitzgerald, Rod Taylor, Robert Simon, Madge Kennedy, Dorothy Stickney

Catherine the Great*
GB 1934 93m bw
Alexander Korda

How Catherine married the mad prince and slowly conquered the Russian court.

Dated but well acted and written account, sober by comparison with *The Scarlet Empress* which came out at the same time.

w Lajos Biro, Arthur Wimperis, Marjorie Deans, *play* The Czarina by Melchior Lengyel, Lajos Biro *d* Paul Czinner *ph* Georges Périnal

Elisabeth Bergner, Douglas Fairbanks Jnr, Flora Robson, Gerald du Maurier, Irene Vanbrugh, Griffith Jones, Joan Gardner, Diana Napier

† The style is typified by a speech given to Grand Duke Peter: 'If she wasn't on the throne she'd be on the street.'

Catlow*
GB 1971 101m Metrocolor
MGM / Euan Lloyd

A likeable outlaw tries to avoid problems while recovering his hidden gold.

Light-hearted, cheerfully cast, fast-moving, Spanish-located western.

w Scot Finch, J. J. Griffith, *novel* Louis L'Amour *d* Sam Wanamaker *ph* Ted Scaife *m* Roy Budd

Yul Brynner, Leonard Nimoy, Richard Crenna, Daliah Lavi, Jo Ann Pflug, Jeff Corey, Bessie Love, David Ladd

The Cat's Paw*
US 1936 90m bw
Harold Lloyd

The son of a Chinese missionary returns home and finds himself in the middle of a Tong war. Very moderate star comedy from the time when he was considering himself a character comedian rather than a slapstick ace.

w Harold Lloyd, Sam Taylor, *story* Clarence Budington Kelland *d* Sam Taylor

Harold Lloyd, George Barbier, Una Merkel, Nat Pendleton, Grant Mitchell, Vince Barnett

Cattle Annie and Little Britches
US 1980   98m   CFI colour
Hemdale / UATC (David Korda)

In 1893, two girls head west in search of
adventure.
Rather winsome family western, with too little
real action and too much romping about.

w Robert Ward, from his novel d Lamont
Johnson ph Larry Pizer m Sanh Berti, Tom
Slocum

Burt Lancaster, John Savage, Rod Steiger,
Diane Lane, Amanda Plummer, Scott Glenn,
Steven Ford

Cattle Empire
US 1958   82m   De Luxe   Cinemascope

A trail boss out of prison gets a new
assignment and signs up helpers who had
previously made life difficult for him. Fair
general western, entirely dependent on its
star. Joel McCrea, Gloria Talbott, Don
Haggerty, Phyllis Coates, Paul Brinegar.
Written by Endre Boehm and Eric Norden;
directed by Charles Marquis Warren; for TCF.

Cattle King
US 1963   90m   Metrocolor
MGM (Nat Holt)
GB title: Guns of Wyoming

A big rancher opposes a cattle trail and starts
a range war.
Moderately expert but very familiar star
western.

w Thomas Thompson d Tay Garnett
ph William E. Snyder

Robert Taylor, Joan Caulfield, Robert
Middleton, Robert Loggia, Larry Gates,
Malcolm Atterbury

Cattle Queen of Montana
US 1954   88m   Technicolor

A tough woman inherits her father's rangeland
and resists cattle rustlers. A western which
runs in predictable grooves, and could have
done with more vigour. Barbara Stanwyck,
Ronald Reagan, Gene Evans, Lance Fuller,
Anthony Caruso, Jack Elam. Written by
Robert Blees and Howard Estabrook; directed
by Allan Dwan; for RKO / Benedict Bogeaus.

Cattle Town
US 1952   71m   bw

After the Civil War, returning ranch owners
find their land appropriated by squatters.
Reach-me-down western programmer. Dennis
Morgan, Amanda Blake, Rita Moreno, Ray

Teal, Philip Carey. Written by Tom
Blackburn; directed by Noel Smith; for
Warner.

Caught*
US 1948   88m   bw
Enterprise (Wolfgang Reinhardt)

The ill-treated wife of a vicious millionaire
leaves him for a doctor, but finds she is to
have the millionaire's baby.
Pretentious film noir, rather typical of its time,
with much talent squandered on a very boring
plot.

w Arthur Laurents, novel Wild Calendar by
Libbie Block d Max Ophuls ph Lee Garmes
m Frederick Hollander

James Mason (the doctor), Robert Ryan (the
millionaire), Barbara Bel Geddes, Natalie
Schaefer, Curt Bois

Caught in the Draft**
US 1941   82m   bw
Paramount (B. G. De Sylva)

A nervous film star cannot avoid being drafted
into the army.
Sprightly comedy from the star's best period,
with gags and supporting cast well up to form.

w Harry Tugend d David Butler ph Karl
Struss m Victor Young

Bob Hope, Lynne Overman, Dorothy
Lamour, Clarence Kolb, Eddie Bracken, Paul
Hurst, Irving Bacon

Caught Short
US 1930   approx 75m   bw

Feuding boarding house landladies play the
stock market—and win. Lumbering comedy
which marked the first big success for the
team of Marie Dressler and Polly Moran;
featuring Charles Morton, Anita Page.
Written by Willard Mack and Robert
Hopkins; directed by Charles Reisner; for
MGM.

Cause for Alarm*
US 1951   74m   bw
MGM (Tom Lewis)

A housewife tries frantically to retrieve a
posted letter containing manufactured
evidence which may put her on a murder
charge.
Minor-league suspenser, watchable but
disappointingly handled.

w Mel Dinelli, Tom Lewis d Tay Garnett
ph Joe Ruttenberg m André Previn

Loretta Young, Barry Sullivan, Bruce
Cowling, Margalo Gillmore, Irving Bacon

Cavalcade**
US 1933   109m   bw
Fox (Winfield Sheehan)

The story of an upper-class English family
between the Boer War and World War I.
Rather static version of the famous stage
spectacular, very similar in setting and style to
TV's later *Upstairs Downstairs*. Good
performances, flat handling.

w Reginald Berkeley, *play Noel Coward*
d Frank Lloyd ph Ernest Palmer *war scenes*
William Cameron Menzies ad William
Darling m Louis de Francesco

Clive Brook, Diana Wynyard, Ursula Jeans,
Herbert Mundin, Una O'Connor, Irene
Browne, Merle Tottenham, Beryl Mercer,
Frank Lawton, Billy Bevan
   'If there is anything that moves the ordinary
American to uncontrollable tears, it is the
plight—the constant plight—of dear old
England . . . a superlative newsreel, forcibly
strengthened by factual scenes, good music,
and wonderful photography.'—*Pare Lorentz*
   'A love that suffered and rose triumphant
above the crushing events of this modern
age.'—*publicity*
   'Greater even than *Birth of a Nation*!'—
Louella Parsons
   'The march of time measured by a human
heart—a mother's heart!'—*more publicity*

AA: best picture; Frank Lloyd
AAN: Diana Wynyard

The Cave Man
US 1926   approx 78m at 24 fps   bw
silent

A bored socialite cuts a high denomination
note in half, throws one half away, and offers
riches to the first man to find it. Typical
twenties comedy which seemed very modern
at the time. Marie Prevost, Matt Moore,
Phyllis Haver, Myrna Loy. Written by Darryl
F. Zanuck; directed by Lewis Milestone; for
Warner.

Cave of Outlaws
US 1951   76m   Technicolor

After surviving a long prison term, a bandit
returns to the caves where his partners hid
their booty. Modest western with scenes shot
in the Carlsbad Caverns. Macdonald Carey,
Alexis Smith, Edgar Buchanan, Victor Jory,
Hugh O'Brian, Houseley Stevenson. Written
by Elizabeth Wilson; directed by William
Castle; for Universal-International.

The Cavern
US / Italy 1966   96m   bw

In the last days of World War II, six soldiers
and a girl are trapped by aerial bombardment
in a cave in the Italian mountains. Enervating
psychological drama, glum to look at and
listen to. John Saxon, Rosanna Schiaffino,
Larry Hagman, Brian Aherne, Nino
Castelnuovo. Written by Michael Pertwee and
Jack Davis; directed and produced by Edgar
G. Ulmer; for Ulmer / TCF.

Ceiling Zero*
US 1935   95m   bw
Warner / Cosmopolitan (Harry Joe Brown)

Amorous and airborne adventures of an
irresponsible but brilliant civil airlines pilot.
Splendid star vehicle which turns maudlin in
the last reel but until then provides crackling
entertainment.

w Frank 'Spig' Wead, from his play
d Howard Hawks ph Arthur Edeson

James Cagney, Pat O'Brien, June Travis,
Stuart Erwin, Henry Wadsworth, Isabel
Jewell, Barton Maclane
   'The best of all airplane pictures.'—*Otis
Ferguson, 1939*
   'Directed at a breakneck pace which
emphasizes its lean fibre and its concentration
on the essentials of its theme.'—*Andrew
Sarris, 1963*
† Remade in 1939 as *International Squadron*.

Cela s'appelle l'Aurore*
France / Italy 1955   108m   bw
Marceau / Laetitia

A Corsican company doctor falls for a young
widow while his wife is on holiday, and events
lead to tragedy.
Efficient melodrama, given an extra dimension
by its *auteur*.

w Luis Bunuel, Jean Ferry, *novel* Emmanuel
Robles d Luis Bunuel ph Robert Le Fèbvre
m Joseph Kosma

Georges Marchal, Lucia Bose, Gianni
Esposito, Julien Bertheau, *Henri Nassiet*

Celine and Julie Go Boating*
France 1974   192m   Eastmancolor
Les Films du Losange (Barbet Schroeder)

Two girls change the outcome of a drama
played daily in a haunted house.
Odd, dreamlike, absurdly long and semi-
improvisational mood piece, with
reverberations from *Alice in Wonderland* and
Orphée. Not an unpleasant experience, but
sometimes a tiresome one.

w Eduardo de Gregorio, Juliet Berto,
Dominique Labourier, Bulle Ogier, Marie-
France Pisier, Jacques Rivette, partly

suggested by two stories by Henry James
ph Jacques Renard *m* Jean-Marie Senia

Juliet Berto, Dominique Labourier, Bulle
Ogier, Marie-France Pisier, Barbet Schroeder
'Rivette uncannily combines slapstick,
suspense and tears in his most watchable
assault on the narrative form.'—*Jan Dawson*
† Shot in 16mm.

Cell 2455 Death Row
US 1955   77m   bw
Columbia (Wallace MacDonald)

A convicted murderer staves off execution
with appeal after appeal.
Cheap run-off of the case of Caryl Chessman,
who was executed ten years after his trial for
rape and murder. Retold in a 1977 TV movie,
Kill Me If You Can.

w Jack de Witt, *book* Caryl Chessman *d* Fred
F. Sears *ph* Fred Jackman Jnr *md* Mischa
Bakaleinikoff

William Campbell, Kathryn Grant, Harvey
Stephens, Marian Carr, Vince Edwards

Centennial Summer**
US 1946   102m   Technicolor
TCF (Otto Preminger)

A Philadelphia family responds to the Great
Exposition of 1876.
Pleasing family comedy with music, the kind
of harmless competence Hollywood used to
throw off with ease but can no longer manage.

w Michael Kanin, *novel* Albert E. Idell
d Otto Preminger *ph* Ernest Palmer
m Alfred Newman *songs* Jerome Kern, Oscar
Hammerstein II, E. Y. Harburg, Leo Robin

Jeanne Crain, Cornel Wilde, Linda Darnell,
William Eythe, Walter Brennan, *Constance
Bennett*, Dorothy Gish

AAN: Alfred Newman; song 'All Through the
Day' (*m* Jerome Kern, *ly* Oscar Hammerstein
II)

Central Airport
US 1933   75m   bw

After the war the only job an ace pilot can get
is as 'chauffeur' to a lady parachutist. Rather
stiff romantic drama with aeronautics thrown
in. Richard Barthelmess, Sally Eilers, Tom
Brown, Glenda Farrell, Harold Huber.
Written by Rian James and James Seymour;
directed by William A. Wellman; for Warner.

The Ceremony
US / Spain 1963   107m   bw
UA / Magla (Laurence Harvey)

In a Tangier jail, a bank robber awaits the

firing squad, but he and his brother have an
escape plan.
Murky and pretentious melodrama with
aspirations to high style and symbolism. A
bore.

w Ben Barzman, *novel* Frederic Grendel
d Laurence Harvey *ph* Oswald Morris
m Gerard Schurmann

Laurence Harvey, Sarah Miles, Robert
Walker, John Ireland, Ross Martin, Lee
Patterson, Jack McGowran, Murray Melvin,
Fernando Rey

A Certain Smile*
US 1958   105m   Eastmancolor
    Cinemascope
TCF (Henry Ephron)

A girl student falls in love with her
philandering uncle.
Another sordid novella by Françoise Sagan
(see *Bonjour Tristesse*), transformed by
Hollywood into a glowing romantic saga of life
among the Riviera rich. On this level, very
competent.

w Frances Goodrich, Albert Hackett *d* Jean
Negulesco *ph* Milton Krasner *m* Alfred
Newman

Christine Carere, Rossano Brazzi, Joan
Fontaine, Bradford Dillman, Eduard Franz,
Kathryn Givney, Steve Geray

AAN: title song (*m* Sammy Fain, *ly* Paul
Francis Webster)

Cervantes
Spain / Italy / France 1968   119m
    Eastmancolor   Supertotalvision
Prisma / Protor / Procinex (Alexander
    Salkind)

Cervantes, an assistant papal envoy, helps
persuade Philip of Spain to join the Holy
League, then turns soldier and has various
adventures.
Rather boring spectacular with conventional
set pieces.

w Enrique Llovet, Enrico Bomba,
novel Bruno Frank *d* Vincent Sherman
ph Edmond Richard *m* Jean Ledrut

Horst Buchholz, Gina Lollobrigida, Louis
Jourdan, Jose Ferrer, Fernando Rey,
Francisco Rabal

César see Marius

César and Rosalie*
France / Italy / West Germany 1972
    105m   Eastmancolor
Fildebroc / UPS / Mega Paramount / Orion
    (Michèle de Broca)

A divorcee living with a rich merchant
becomes attracted to a young artist.
Unexpectedly, the two men become
friends . . .
Wryly amusing comedy for adults.

w Jean-Loup Dabadie, Claude Sautet
d Claude Sautet ph Jean Boffety m Philippe
Sarde
Yves Montand, Romy Schneider, Sami Frey,
Umberto Orsini

Chad Hanna*
US 1940 86m Technicolor
TCF (Darryl F. Zanuck, Nunnally Johnson)

Life in a New York state circus in the 1840s.
Mild romantic drama from a bestseller; local
colour excellent, dramatic interest thin.

w Nunnally Johnson, *novel* Red Wheels
Rolling by Walter D. Edmonds d Henry
King ph Ernest Palmer m David Buttolph

Henry Fonda, Dorothy Lamour, Linda
Darnell, Guy Kibbee, Jane Darwell, John
Carradine, Ted North, Roscoe Ates

Chain Lightning
US 1950 94m bw
Warner (Anthony Veiller)

After World War II a bomber pilot learns how
to control the new jets.
Absolutely routine romance and heroics.

w Liam O'Brien, Vincent Evans d Stuart
Heisler ph Ernest Haller m David Buttolph

Humphrey Bogart, Eleanor Parker, Raymond
Massey, Richard Whorf, James Brown, Roy
Roberts, Morris Ankrum

Chained*
US 1934 77m bw
MGM (Hunt Stromberg)

A devoted wife has a shipboard romance with
another man.
Moderate star romantic drama.

w John Lee Mahin d Clarence Brown
ph George Folsey m Herbert Stothart

Joan Crawford, Clark Gable, Otto Kruger,
Stuart Erwin, Una O'Connor, Akim Tamiroff

The Chalk Garden*
GB 1964 106m Technicolor
U-I / Quota Rentals (Ross Hunter)

The governess in a melancholy household has
an effect on the lives of her aged employer and
the young granddaughter.
Sub-Chekhovian drama in a house by the sea,
flattened by routine handling into something
much less interesting than it was on the stage.

w John Michael Hayes, *novel* Enid Bagnold
d Ronald Neame ph Arthur Ibbetson
m Malcolm Arnold

Edith Evans, Deborah Kerr, Hayley Mills,
John Mills, Felix Aylmer, Elizabeth Sellars,
Lally Bowers, Toke Townley
  'Crashing symbolism, cracker-motto
sententiousness.'—*MFB*

AAN: Edith Evans

A Challenge for Robin Hood*
GB 1967 96m Technicolor
Hammer (Clifford Parkes)

A retelling of the original Robin Hood legend.
Unassuming, lively, predictable adventure
hokum.

w Peter Bryan d C. Pennington-Richards
ph Arthur Grant m Gary Hughes

Barrie Ingham, James Hayter, Leon Greene,
John Arnatt

Chamber of Horrors
US 1966 99m Warnercolor
Warner (Hy Averback)

A maniacal murderer is finally trapped by two
amateur criminologists who run a wax museum
in Baltimore.
Zany horror thriller originally meant for TV; it
turned out a shade too harrowing. Advertised
as 'the picture with the Fear Flasher and the
Horror Horn', shock gimmicks which proved
much more startling than the crude events
they heralded.

w Stephen Kandel d Hy Averback
ph Richard Kline m William Lava

Patrick O'Neal, Cesare Danova, Wilfrid Hyde
White, Laura Devon, Patrice Wymore, Suzy
Parker, Jeanette Nolan, Tony Curtis (guest)

The Champ*
US 1931 87m bw
MGM (Harry Rapf)

A young boy has faith in a washed-up
prizefighter.
Maudlin drama, highly commercial in its day
and a box office tonic for its two stars.
Remade as *The Clown* (qv).

w Leonard Praskins, Frances Marion d King
Vidor ph Gordon Avil

Wallace Beery, Jackie Cooper, Irene Rich,
Roscoe Ates, Edward Brophy
  'The knockout picture of the year!'—
publicity

AA: original story (Frances Marion); Wallace
Beery
AAN: best picture; King Vidor

The Champ*
US 1979 122m Metrocolor
MGM (Dyson Lovell)

A remake of the above, with Florida racetrack asides.
A lush version, so little updated in mood that its tearfulness seems to have strayed from another age.

w Walter Newman d Franco Zeffirelli
ph Fred J. Koenekamp m Dave Grusin
pd Herman A. Blumenthal

Jon Voight, Faye Dunaway, Ricky Schroeder, Jack Warden, Arthur Hill, Strother Martin, Joan Blondell, Elisha Cook

Champagne Charlie*
GB 1944 107m bw
Ealing (John Croydon)

The life of Victorian music hall singer George Leybourne and his rivalry with the Great Vance.
Careful period reconstruction and good songs and acting are somehow nullified by unsympathetic handling and photography.

w Austin Melford, Angus Macphail, John Dighton d Alberto Cavalcanti ph Wilkie Cooper md Ernest Irving

Tommy Trinder, Stanley Holloway, Betty Warren, Austin Trevor, Jean Kent, Guy Middleton, Frederick Piper, Harry Fowler

Champagne for Caesar*
US 1950 99m bw
Cardinal (George Moskov)

A self-confessed genius with a grudge against a soap company determines to win astronomical sums on its weekly radio quiz.
Agreeable, mildly satirical star comedy which tends to peter out halfway.

w Hans Jacoby, Fred Brady d Richard Whorf ph Paul Ivano m Dmitri Tiomkin

Ronald Colman, Vincent Price, Celeste Holm, Barbara Britton, Art Linkletter

The Champagne Murders
France 1967 107m Techniscope
Universal (France) (Jacques Natteau)
original title: Le Scandale

A disturbed champagne millionaire thinks he may be a murderer.
Complex but uninvolving mystery story in which the director's eye seems to be more on satire than on narrative.

w Claude Brûlé, Derek Prouse, Paul Gégauff d Claude Chabrol ph Jean Rabier m Pierre Jansen

Anthony Perkins, Maurice Ronet, Stéphane Audran, Yvonne Furneaux, Suzanne Lloyd

Champagne Waltz
US 1937 90m bw

A press agent takes a swing band to Vienna.
Rather tedious romantic comedy with music.
Fred MacMurray, Gladys Swarthout, Jack Oakie. Written by Don Hartman, Frank Butler from a story by Billy Wilder, H. S. Kraft and Vienna Hall; directed by Edward Sutherland; for Paramount.

Champion**
US 1949 99m bw
Stanley Kramer

An ambitious prizefighter alienates his friends and family, and dies of injuries received in the ring.
Interesting exposé of the fight racket, presented in good cinematic style and acted with great bravura.

w Carl Foreman, story Ring Lardner d Mark Robson ph Franz Planer m Dmitri Tiomkin

Kirk Douglas, Arthur Kennedy, Marilyn Maxwell, Paul Stewart, Ruth Roman, Lola Albright, Luis Van Rooten

AAN: Carl Foreman; Franz Planer; Dmitri Tiomkin; Kirk Douglas; Arthur Kennedy

Chance of a Lifetime*
GB 1950 93m bw
Pilgrim Pictures (Bernard Miles)

The owner of a small engineering works, impatient with the unionism of his men, gives them a chance to run the factory themselves.
Quiet comedy-drama on sub-Ealing lines; always interesting, it never quite catches fire despite a reliable cast.

w Walter Greenwood, Bernard Miles d Bernard Miles ph Eric Cross

Bernard Miles, Basil Radford, Niall MacGinnis, Geoffrey Keen, Julien Mitchell, Josephine Wilson, Kenneth More, Hattie Jacques

Chances*
US 1931 72m bw

In wartime London, two soldiers on leave fall for the same girl. Unexpectedly sensitive and pleasing romance, generally well handled.
Douglas Fairbanks Jnr, Anthony Bushell, Rose Hobart. Written by Waldemar Young, from a novel by Hamilton Gibbs; directed by Allan Dwan; for Warner.

Chandu the Magician*
US 1932 74m bw
Fox

A spiritualist battles against a madman with a death ray which could destroy the world.

Rather dim serial-like thriller, with interesting talent not at its best.

w Philip Klein, Barry Conners *d* Marcel Varnel, William Cameron Menzies *ph* James Wong Howe

Edmund Lowe, Bela Lugosi, Irene Ware, Herbert Mundin, Henry B. Walthall

Chang**
US 1927   71m (24 fps)   bw   silent
Paramount

The life of a rice-grower in Thailand. Influential but now rather boring documentary with animal interest.

wd, ph, ed Merian C. Cooper, Ernest B. Schoedsack

Change of Heart
US 1934   74m   bw
Fox

Four young California students make good in New York.
Minor fairy tale which marked the last of twelve teamings for Gaynor and Farrell.

w Sonya Levien, James Gleason, Samuel Hoffenstein, *novel* Kathleen Norris *d* John G. Blystone *ph* Hal Mohr

Janet Gaynor, Charles Farrell, Ginger Rogers, James Dunn, Beryl Mercer, Gustav Von Seyffertitz, Shirley Temple

Change of Heart
US 1943   87m   bw

A country girl writes songs and a publisher steals them. Slim basis for a so-so musical. Susan Hayward, John Carroll, Eve Arden, Gail Patrick, Walter Catlett, Melville Cooper, Count Basie and his Orchestra. Written by Frank Gill Jnr; directed by Albert S. Rogell; for Republic. (Original title: *Hit Parade of 1943*.)

Change of Mind
US 1969   98m   Eastmancolor
Sagittarius (Seeleg Lester, Richard Wesson)

The life of a liberal white DA can only be 'saved' by transplanting his brain into the body of a dead black man.
Fantasy melodrama with a social conscience, about a half-and-half which is acceptable to neither whites nor blacks. Very obvious and rather boring.

w Seeleg Lester, Richard Wesson *d* Robert Stevens *ph* Arthur J. Ornitz *m* Duke Ellington

Raymond St Jacques, Susan Oliver, Janet McLachlan, Leslie Nielsen

A Change of Seasons
US 1980   102m   De Luxe
TCF / Martin Ransohoff / Film Finance Group Ltd

A college professor takes a mistress and his wife retaliates.
Zestless and unhumorous rehash of *Who's Afraid of Virginia Woolf?* and *Bob and Carol and Ted and Alice*. Not a new thought anywhere.

w Erich Segal, Ronni Kern, Fred Segal *d* Richard Lang *ph* Philip Lathrop *m* Henry Mancini *pd* Bill Kenney

Shirley Maclaine, Anthony Hopkins, Bo Derek, Michael Brandon, Mary Beth Hurt, Ed Winter
'A tired rehash of themes that might have been provocative a decade ago . . . it would take a Lubitsch to do justice to the incredibly tangled relationships.'—*Variety*

The Changeling
Canada 1979   107m   colour   Panavision
Chessman Palk Productions

A widowed academic takes on an old house haunted by the spirit of a murdered child. Tedious and not very brief, this uninspired ghost story comes very late in the horror stakes and contains very little to make one care about its outcome.

w William Gray, Diana Maddox *d* Peter Medak *ph* John Coquillon *m* Rick Wilkins

George C. Scott, Melvyn Douglas, Trish Van Devere, John Colicos, Jean Marsh, Barry Morse
'None of its most eerily untoward occurrences proceed from any spectral intervention, but from the worst abuses of Peter Medak's infuriatingly fidgety camera.'—*Gilbert Adair, MFB*

Channel Crossing*
GB 1933   70m   bw

Various characters converge on a ferry boat to France. Somewhat stilted potboiler with interesting cast: Matheson Lang, Max Miller, Constance Cummings, Edmund Gwenn, Anthony Bushell, Dorothy Dickson, Nigel Bruce. Written by W. P. Lipscomb and Cyril Campion; directed by Milton Rosmer; for Gaumont.

The Chant of Jimmie Blacksmith
Australia 1978   122m   Eastmancolor
Panavision

In 1900, a half-caste mingles with high class whites, goes berserk, and slaughters several of them with an axe. Hard-to-take moral tale for

philosophers with strong stomachs. Tommy
Lewis, Ray Barrett, Jack Thompson, Freddy
Reynolds. Written and directed by Fred
Schepsi, from the novel by Thomas Keneally;
for Film House.

Chapayev*
USSR 1934   94m   bw
Lenfilm

Exploits of a Red Army commander during
the 1919 battles.
Moderately striking propaganda piece.

wd Sergei and Georgy Vasiliev *ph* Alexander
Sigayev *m* Gavril Popov

Boris Babochkin, B. Blinov, Leonid Kmit

The Chapman Report
US 1962   125m   Technicolor
(Warner) Darryl F. Zanuck (Richard D.
   Zanuck)

Dr Chapman conducts a study of female sex
behaviour in an American suburb.
Influenced by the Kinsey report, this
melodramatic compendium takes itself far too
seriously, and the director's smooth style is
barely in evidence.

w Wyatt Cooper, Don M. Mankiewicz, *novel*
Irving Wallace *d* George Cukor *ph* Harold
Lipstein *m* Leonard Rosenman

Shelley Winters, Claire Bloom, *Glynis Johns*,
Efrem Zimbalist Jnr, Jane Fonda, Ray
Danton, Ty Hardin, Andrew Duggan, John
Dehner, Henry Daniell, Corey Allen, Harold
J. Stone
   'We had a preview which went very well,
and then it was sent over to Mr Zanuck, who
did what I thought was a most horrendous job
of cutting it up.'—*George Cukor*

Chapter Two*
US 1979   127m   Metrocolor
Columbia / Rastar (Margaret Booth)

A widowed novelist reluctantly embarks on an
affair with a divorcee.
Simon in sad mood means that the wisecracks
are still there but the pauses between them are
longer. The thin but heavy-going plot finally
militates against enthusiasm.

w Neil Simon *d* Robert Moore *ph* David M.
Walsh, Richard Kratina *m* Marvin Hamlisch
pd Gene Callahan

James Caan, Marsha Mason, Joseph Bologna,
Valerie Harper, Alan Fudge
   'The regular Neil Simon Broadway
takeaway for people who watch movies with
their ears. Over two hours of theatrical smart
talk and unfailing wit-under-pressure as

Simon-surrogate Caan and the real Mrs Simon
swap marital repartee in front of a reverent
camera.'—*Time Out*

Charade**
US 1964   113m   Technicolor
Universal / Stanley Donen

A Parisienne finds her husband murdered.
Four strange men are after her, and she is
helped by a handsome stranger . . . but is he
hero, spy or murderer?
Smoothly satisfying sub-Hitchcock nonsense,
effective both as black romantic comedy and
macabre farce.

w Peter Stone *d* Stanley Donen *ph* Charles
Lang Jnr *m* Henry Mancini

Cary Grant (sixty but concealing the fact by
taking a shower fully clothed), *Audrey
Hepburn, Walter Matthau*, James Coburn,
George Kennedy, Ned Glass, Jacques Marin
   'One hesitates to be uncharitable to a film
like *Charade*, which seeks only to provide a
little innocent merriment and make a pot of
money. . . . Of itself, it is a stylish and
amusing melodrama, but in the context of the
bloodlust that seems unloosed in our land it is
as sinister as the villains who stalk Miss
Hepburn through the cobbled streets of
Paris.'—*Arthur Knight*

AAN: song 'Charade' (*m* Henry Mancini,
ly Johnny Mercer)

The Charge at Feather River*
US 1953   96m   Warnercolor
Warner (David Weisbart)

An army platoon composed of men from the
guardhouse tries to rescue two women
kidnapped by Indians.
Formula western distinguished by 3-D
photography, probably the best to be achieved
in the brief life of the medium. Warnerphonic
sound was less successfully added; the sum
total would be trying for nervous people.

w James R. Webb *d* Gordon Douglas
ph Peverell Marley *m* Max Steiner

Guy Madison, Frank Lovejoy, Vera Miles,
Helen Westcott, Dick Wesson, Onslow
Stevens, Steve Brodie
   'From the start we are involved in a whirl of
frenzied activity: a cavalry charge, knife
throwing, sabre practice, flaming arrows—not
a trick missed.'—*MFB*

The Charge of the Light Brigade***
US 1936   115m   bw
Warner (Hal B. Wallis, Sam Bischoff)

An army officer deliberately starts the

Balaclava charge to even an old score with Surat Khan, who's on the other side.
Though allegedly 'based on the poem by Alfred Lord Tennyson', this is no more than a travesty of history, most of it taking place in India. As pure entertainment however it is a most superior slice of Hollywood hokum and the film which set the seal on Errol Flynn's superstardom.

w Michael Jacoby, Rowland Leigh d Michael Curtiz ph Sol Polito, Fred Jackman m Max Steiner

Errol Flynn, Olivia de Havilland, Patric Knowles, Donald Crisp, C. Aubrey Smith, David Niven, Henry Stephenson, Nigel Bruce, C. Henry Gordon, Spring Byington, E. E. Clive, Lumsden Hare, Robert Barrat, J. Carrol Naish

The Charge of the Light Brigade
GB 1968   141m   De Luxe   Panavision
UA / Woodfall (Neil Hartley)

An historical fantasia with comic, sociological and cartoon embellishments.
This version for the swinging sixties has a few splendid moments but apes *Tom Jones* all too obviously and leaves audiences with an even dimmer view of history than they started with.

w Charles Wood d Tony Richardson ph David Watkin, Peter Suschitsky m John Addison *animation Richard Williams* ad Edward Marshall

Trevor Howard, John Gielgud, David Hemmings, Vanessa Redgrave, Jill Bennett, Harry Andrews, Peter Bowles, Mark Burns

'Considering the lucid book on which it is largely based, it is almost as inexcusably muddled as the British commanders at Balaclava.'—*John Simon*

'The point of the film is to recreate mid-Victorian England in spirit and detail.'—*Stanley Kauffmann*

'Notions for at least three interesting films are on view . . . what seems signally lacking is a guiding hand, an overriding purpose.'—*John Coleman*

Charing Cross Road
GB 1935   72m   bw

Struggling boy and girl singers try to move into high society. Dated and artificial filler. John Mills, June Clyde, Derek Oldham, Jean Colin, Judy Kelly. Written by Con West and Clifford Grey; directed by Albert de Courville; for British Lion.

Charley and the Angel*
US 1974   93m   Technicolor
Walt Disney (Bill Anderson)

A small-town sporting goods storekeeper in the thirties escapes death three times and finds an impatient angel waiting for him.
Mild sentimental whimsy on the lines of *On Borrowed Time*, but with a happy ending and attractive period trappings.

w Roswell Rogers, *novel* The Golden Evenings of Summer by Will Stanton d Vincent McEveety ph Charles F. Wheeler m Buddy Baker

Fred MacMurray, Cloris Leachmann, Harry Morgan, Kurt Russell, Kathleen Cody, Edward Andrews, Barbara Nichols

Charley Moon*
GB 1956   92m   Eastmancolor
Colin Lesslie, Aubrey Baring

A music hall comic becomes swollen-headed but returns to his home village and marries his childhood sweetheart.
Faltering musical lacking the gusto of its background, but providing a generally believable impression of life on the halls.

w / songs Leslie Bricusse, *novel* Reginald Arkell d Guy Hamilton ph Jack Hildyard

Max Bygraves, Dennis Price, Michael Medwin, Florence Desmond, Shirley Eaton, Patricia Driscoll, Reginald Beckwith

Charley Varrick**
US 1973   111m   Technicolor
Universal (Don Siegel)

A bank robber discovers he has stolen Mafia money, and devises a clever scheme to get himself off the hook.
Sharp, smart, well-observed but implausible thriller, astringently handled and agreeably set in Californian backlands. Accomplished, forgettable entertainment.

w Howard Rodman, Dean Reisner, *novel* The Looters by John Reese d Don Siegel ph Michael Butler m Lalo Schifrin

Walter Matthau, Joe Don Baker, Felicia Farr, Andy Robinson, John Vernon, Sheree North, Norman Fell

'It proves there is nothing wrong with an *auteur* director that a good script can't cure.'—*Stanley Kauffmann*

'The narrative line is clean and direct, the characterizations economical and functional, and the triumph of intelligence gloriously satisfying.'—*Andrew Sarris*

Charley's Aunt**
US 1941   81m   bw
TCF (William Perlberg)
GB title: *Charley's American Aunt*

For complicated reasons, an Oxford undergraduate has to impersonate his own rich aunt from Brazil (where the nuts come from). Very adequate version of the Victorian farce, with all concerned in excellent form.

w George Seaton, *play* Brandon Thomas d Archie Mayo *ph* Peverell Marley *m* Alfred Newman *ad* Richard Day, Nathan Juran

Jack Benny, Kay Francis, James Ellison, Anne Baxter, *Laird Cregar*, Edmund Gwenn, Reginald Owen, Richard Haydn, Arleen Whelan, Ernest Cossart

† See also: *Where's Charley?*

Charley's Big-Hearted Aunt
GB 1940   76m   bw
Gainsborough (Edward Black)

Rather disappointing British version of the famous farce, dully assembled and rather unsuitably cast.

w Marriott Edgar, Val Guest d Walter Forde
ph Jack Cox

Arthur Askey, Phyllis Calvert, Moore Marriott, Graham Moffatt, Richard Murdoch, Jeanne de Casalis, J. H. Roberts, Felix Aylmer, Wally Patch

Charlie Bubbles***
GB 1968   91m   Technicolor
Universal / Memorial (Michael Medwin, George Pitcher)

A successful novelist loathes the pointlessness of the good life and tries unsuccessfully to return to his northern working class background.
A little arid and slow in its early stages, and with a rather lame end (our hero escapes by air balloon), this is nevertheless a fascinating, fragmentary character study with a host of wry comedy touches and nimbly sketched characters; in its unassuming way it indicts many of the symbols people lived by in the sixties.

w Shelagh Delaney d Albert Finney ph Peter Suschitzky m Mischa Donat

Albert Finney, Billie Whitelaw, Liza Minnelli, Colin Blakely, Timothy Garland, Diana Coupland, Alan Lake, Yootha Joyce, Joe Gladwin

'A modest thing, but like all good work in minor keys it has a way of haunting the memory.'—*Richard Schickel*

'The supreme deadweight is Liza Minnelli, whose screen debut proves easily the most inauspicious since Turhan Bey's.'—*John Simon*

Charlie Chan
The Oriental detective created by Earl Derr Biggers began his film career as a minor character (played by George Kuwa) in a 1926 serial called HOUSE WITHOUT A KEY. In 1928 Kamiyama Sojin had a bigger role in THE CHINESE PARROT, but in 1929 E. L. Park did almost nothing in BEHIND THAT CURTAIN. In 1931 however began the fully-fledged Chan movies, which entertained a generation. Chan, based on a real-life Chinese detective named Chang Apana, became a citizen of Honolulu and was developed as a polite family man, aided by his impulsive number one or number two son (out of a family of fourteen), in solving murder puzzles. He had a treasury of aphorisms (a whole book of which has been published), and his technique was to gather all the suspects into one room before unmasking one as the murderer. The films built to a peak around 1936–9, but tailed off disastrously in the mid-forties. They were never noted for production values, but many retain interest for their scripts, their puzzles, and their casts of budding stars, as well as the central character. This is a complete list:

For Fox (later Twentieth Century Fox), with *Warner Oland* as Chan:
1931: CHARLIE CHAN CARRIES ON*, THE BLACK CAMEL
1932: CHARLIE CHAN'S CHANCE
1933: CHARLIE CHAN'S GREATEST CASE
1934: CHARLIE CHAN'S COURAGE, CHARLIE CHAN IN LONDON
1935: CHARLIE CHAN IN PARIS*, CHARLIE CHAN IN EGYPT, CHARLIE CHAN IN SHANGHAI
1936: CHARLIE CHAN'S SECRET*, CHARLIE CHAN AT THE CIRCUS*, CHARLIE CHAN AT THE RACE TRACK, CHARLIE CHAN AT THE OPERA**
1937: CHARLIE CHAN AT THE OLYMPICS, CHARLIE CHAN ON BROADWAY*, CHARLIE CHAN AT MONTE CARLO

For Twentieth Century Fox, with *Sidney Toler*:
1938: CHARLIE CHAN IN HONOLULU
1939: CHARLIE CHAN IN RENO, CHARLIE CHAN ON TREASURE ISLAND**, CITY OF DARKNESS
1940: CHARLIE CHAN IN PANAMA, CHARLIE CHAN'S MURDER CRUISE, CHARLIE CHAN AT THE WAX MUSEUM*, MURDER OVER NEW YORK
1941: DEAD MEN TELL, CHARLIE CHAN IN RIO, CASTLE IN THE DESERT*

For Monogram, with Sidney Toler:
1944: CHARLIE CHAN IN THE SECRET
SERVICE, THE CHINESE CAT, BLACK
MAGIC
1945: THE SCARLET CLUE, THE JADE
MASK, SHANGHAI COBRA, RED
DRAGON
1946: SHADOWS OVER CHINATOWN,
DANGEROUS MONEY
1947: THE TRAP

For Monogram, with Roland Winters:
1947: THE CHINESE RING
1948: DOCKS OF NEW ORLEANS,
SHANGHAI CHEST, THE GOLDEN EYE,
THE FEATHERED SERPENT
1949: SKY DRAGON

In the late fifties J. Carrol Naish appeared in a
half-hour TV series as Chan, but the episodes
were dull. In 1971 Universal tried to revive the
character in a 96-minute pilot film *Happiness is
a Warm Clue*, but Ross Martin was woefully
miscast.

Charlotte's Web
US 1972   96m   Technicolor
Hanna-Barbera for Sagittarius

Farmyard animals who sense their fate are
stimulated and encouraged by a resourceful
spider.
Interesting but overlong and rather plodding
version of a stylish book for children; the
animation has no style at all.

w Earl Hanmer Jnr, *novel* E. B. White
d Charles A. Nichols, Iwao Takamoto
m / ly Richard and Robert Sherman

Charming Sinners
US 1929   66m   bw

A society wife schemes to regain the attention
of her wayward husband. Early talkie version
of Somerset Maugham's *The Constant Wife*; of
historical interest only. Ruth Chatterton, Clive
Brook, William Powell, Mary Nolan, Florence
Eldridge. Written by Doris Anderson;
directed by Robert Milton; for Paramount.

Charly*
US 1968   106m   Techniscope
Selmur / Robertson Associates (Ralph
   Nelson)

New methods of surgery cure a mentally
retarded young man, who becomes a genius,
but the effects wear off.
Smooth, unconvincing, rather pointless fantasy
which ultimately leaves a bad taste in the
mouth.

w Sterling Silliphant, *novel* Flowers for
Algernon by Daniel Keyes   *d* Ralph Nelson
ph Arthur J. Ornitz   *m* Ravi Shankar

Cliff Robertson, Claire Bloom, Leon Janney,
Lilia Skala
'The most distressing thing about *Charly* is
not its ticklish subject, nor yet its clumsily
modish surface, but its insistent, persistent
sentimentality.'—*Tom Milne*

AA: Cliff Robertson

Charro
US 1969   98m   Technicolor   Panavision
National General (Charles Marquis Warren)

A reformed outlaw is framed for the theft of a
cannon.
Dismal western with a singing star playing
straight. A bad experience.

wd Charles Marquis Warren   *ph* Ellsworth
Fredericks   *m* Hugo Montenegro

Elvis Presley, Ina Balin, Barbara Werle, Lynn
Kellogg, Victor French, Solomon Sturges

Chartroose Caboose
US 1960   76m   Eastmancolor
   Panavision

A runaway couple take refuge with a retired
train conductor in his converted rolling stock
home. Old-fashioned to the point of seeming
half-witted, this comedy has little to offer but
geniality. Molly Bee, Ben Cooper, Edgar
Buchanan, O. Z. Whitehead, Slim Pickens.
Written by Rod Peterson; directed by William
Reynolds; for Red-Bill / U-I.

The Chase*
US 1947   84m   bw
Nero Pictures (Seymour Nebenzal)

A shell-shocked ex-serviceman foils a criminal
and falls for his wife.
Weird Cuban-set *film noir* with a strange cast
and stranger atmosphere. A genuine bomb,
but worth a look for its pretensions, its cast,
and its trick ending.

w Philip Yordan, *novel* The Black Path of
Fear by Cornell Woolrich   *d* Arthur Ripley
ph Franz Planer   *m* Michel Michelet

Robert Cummings, Michèle Morgan, Peter
Lorre, Steve Cochran, Lloyd Corrigan, Jack
Holt

The Chase*
US 1966   135m   Technicolor
   Panavision
Columbia / Sam Spiegel

When a convict escapes and heads for his
small Texas home town, almost all the
inhabitants are affected in one way or another.
Expensive but shoddy essay in sex and
violence, with Brando as a masochistic sheriff
lording it over Peyton-Place-in-all-but-name.

Literate moments do not atone for the general pretentiousness, and we have all been here once too often.

w Lillian Hellman, *novel* Horton Foote
d Arthur Penn *ph* Joseph La Shelle
pd Richard Day *m* John Barry

Marlon Brando, Jane Fonda, Robert Redford, Angie Dickinson, Janice Rule, James Fox, Robert Duvall, E. G. Marshall, Miriam Hopkins, Henry Hull

'The worst thing that has happened to movies since Lassie played a war veteran with amnesia.'—*Rex Reed*

'Considering all the talent connected with it, it is hard to imagine how *The Chase* went so haywire.'—*Philip T. Hartung*

Chase a Crooked Shadow**
GB 1957   87m   bw
ABP / Associated Dragon Films (Douglas Fairbanks Jnr)

An heiress finds her home invaded by a stranger posing as her dead brother.
Tricksy, lightly controlled suspense melodrama with a perfectly fair surprise ending. Handling equivocal but competent.

w David D. Osborn, Charles Sinclair
d *Michael Anderson* ph Erwin Hillier
m Matyas Seiber

Richard Todd, Anne Baxter, Faith Brook, Herbert Lom, Alexander Knox, Alan Tilvern
† The plot was borrowed from an episode in *The Whistler* TV series, and later reversed for a 1975 TV film, *One of my Wives is Missing*.

Chasing Rainbows
US 1929   80m   bw

True love finds a way while a big musical is rehearsing. Naïve attempt to repeat the success of *Broadway Melody*. Bessie Love, Charles King, Marie Dressler, Polly Moran, Jack Benny. Written by Bess Meredyth; directed by Charles Riesner; for MGM.

The Chastity Belt
Italy 1967   110m   Eastmancolor
Warner / Julia (Francesco Mazzei)
aka: *On My Way to the Crusades I Met a Girl Who . . .*

A 12th-century knight is called to the Crusades just as he is consummating his marriage, and when he locks his wife in a chastity belt she follows him.
Abysmal international romp which looks nice but is killed stone dead by writing, dubbing and direction.

w Luigi Magni, Larry Gelbart *d* Pasquale Festa Campanile *ph* Carlo di Palma *m* Riz Ortolani

Tony Curtis, Virna Lisi, Hugh Griffith, John Richardson, Nino Castelnuovo

Chato's Land
GB 1971   100m   Technicolor
UA / Scimitar (Michael Winner)

An Apache half-breed kills a man in self-defence, subsequently eluding and destroying the sheriff's posse.
Exhaustingly violent western in which the audience is spared no gory detail; efficiently put together for those who like this kind of fracas.

w Gerald Wilson *d* Michael Winner
ph Robert Paynter *m* Jerry Fielding

Charles Bronson, Jack Palance, Richard Basehart, James Whitmore, Simon Oakland, Richard Jordan, Ralph Waite, Victor French, Lee Patterson

Chatterbox
US 1943   77m   bw
Republic (Albert J. Cohen)

A radio cowboy gets a film contract but can't stand horses.
Flat star comedy which borrows some well-worn situations but handles them badly.

w George Carleton Brown, Frank Gill Jnr
d Joseph Santley *ph* Ernest Miller
md Walter Scharf

Joe E. Brown, Judy Canova, Rosemary Lane, John Hubbard, Chester Clute

Che!
US 1969   94m   De Luxe   Panavision
TCF (Sy Bartlett)

Fidel Castro is helped in his subversion of Batista's Cuban regime by an Argentinian doctor named Che Guevara.
Fictionalized biography, and a dull one, of a man who became a myth.

w Michael Wilson, Sy Bartlett *d* Richard Fleischer *ph* Charles Wheeler *m* Lalo Schifrin

Omar Sharif, Jack Palance (as Castro), Cesare Danova, Robert Loggia, Woody Strode, Barbara Luna

The Cheap Detective
US 1978   92m   Metrocolor   Panavision
Columbia / Ray Stark

Forties private eye Lou Peckinpaugh is involved in a complex case with echoes of *Casablanca*, *The Big Sleep*, *The Maltese Falcon* and *Farewell My Lovely*.
Lame spoof which might have seemed funnier on a small screen in black and white; as it is, the strain is evident and desperate.

w Neil Simon *d* Robert Moore *ph* John A. Alonzo *m* Patrick Williams

Peter Falk (Bogart), John Houseman (Greenstreet), Nicol Williamson (Veidt), *Louise Fletcher* (Bergman), Fernando Lamas (Henreid), Madeleine Kahn (Astor), Dom de Luise (Lorre), Paul Williams (Cook), Marsha Mason (Gladys George), Ann-Margret (Claire Trevor), Eileen Brennan (Bacall), Stockard Channing (Lee Patrick), Sid Caesar (Miles Mander), Scatman Crothers (Dooley Wilson); and James Coco, Phil Silvers, Abe Vigoda, Vic Tayback

'Frankly they did this sort of thing just as well, and a lot more quickly, on *The Carol Burnett Show.*'—*Richard Shickel, Time*

'There is about enough talent around for a twenty-minute sketch at the Edinburgh fringe.'—*Derek Malcolm, Guardian*

† The film was a follow-up to the not much more effective but at least more controlled *Murder by Death*.

Cheaper by the Dozen**
US 1950 86m Technicolor
TCF (Lamar Trotti)

Efficiency expert Frank Gilbreth and his wife Lillian have twelve children, a fact which requires mathematical conduct of all their lives.
Amusing family comedy set in the twenties, unconvincing in detail though based on a book by two of the children. A great commercial success and a Hollywood myth-maker. Sequel: *Belles on their Toes* (qv).

w Lamar Trotti, *book* Frank B. Gilbreth Jnr, Ernestine Gilbreth Carey *d* Walter Lang *ph* Leon Shamroy *m* Cyril Mockridge *md* Lionel Newman *ad* Lyle Wheeler, Leland Fuller

Clifton Webb, Myrna Loy, Jeanne Crain, Edgar Buchanan, Barbara Bates, Betty Lynn, Mildred Natwick, Sara Allgood

The Cheat*
US 1915 95m (16 fps) bw silent
Famous Players Lasky / Paramount

A society lady borrows from a rich Japanese, and he brands her when she refuses to become his mistress.
Hoary melodrama which caused a sensation in its day.

w Hector Turnbull *d* Cecil B. de Mille *ph* Alvin Wyckoff

Fanny Ward, Jack Dean, Sessue Hayakawa, James Neill

† Remade in 1923 by George Fitzmaurice, in 1931 by George Abbott, and in 1937 (in France, as *Forfaiture*) by Marcel L'Herbier.

The Cheaters*
US 1945 86m bw
Republic

A selfish and ostentatious family is reformed by the ministrations of a down-and-out actor.
Fairly engaging variation on *The Passing of the Third Floor Back*, with sweetness and light brought into people's lives by a fireside recital of *A Christmas Carol*.

w Francis Hyland *d* Joseph Kane *ph* Reggie Lanning *m* Walter Scharf

Joseph Schildkraut, Billie Burke, Eugene Pallette, Ona Munson, Raymond Walburn

Check and Double Check
US 1932 71m bw
RKO

Comic adventures of a couple of black handymen.
Feeble comedy notable only for the film appearance of radio's immensely popular Amos 'n Andy, played by white actors in blackface.

w Bert Kalmar, Harry Ruby, J. Walter Ruben *d* Melville Brown *ph* William Marshall *m* Max Steiner

Freeman F. Gosden, Charles V. Correll, Sue Carol, Charles Morton, Irene Rich, Ralf Harolde, Duke Ellington and his Orchestra

Checkpoint*
GB 1956 84m Eastmancolor
Rank (Betty Box)

A tycoon sends an industrial spy to Italy in search of new motor racing car designs.
Acceptable hokum, cleanly assembled, with motor race highlights.

w Robin Estridge *d* Ralph Thomas *ph* Ernest Steward *m* Bruce Montgomery

Anthony Steel, Stanley Baker, James Robertson Justice, Odile Versois, Maurice Denham, Michael Medwin, Lee Patterson

Cheer Boys Cheer
GB 1939 84m bw

Brewery owners hate each other but their children fall in love. A highly predictable plot provides some incidental pleasures in this modest precursor of the Ealing comedies. Nova Pilbeam, Edmund Gwenn, Jimmy O'Dea, Moore Marriott, Graham Moffatt, C. V. France, Alexander Knox. Written by Roger MacDougall and Allan MacKinnon; directed by Walter Forde; for ATP.

Cheers for Miss Bishop*
US 1941 94m bw
Paramount (Richard A. Rowland)

The life of a schoolmistress in a small midwestern town.
Acceptable sentimental hokum, quite pleasantly done.

w Adelaide Heinbron, *novel* Bess Streeter Aldrich d Tay Garnett ph Hal Mohr m Edward Ward

Martha Scott, William Gargan, Edmund Gwenn, Sterling Holloway, Sidney Blackmer, Mary Anderson, Dorothy Petersen

AAN: Edward Ward

Cherokee Strip
US 1940 86m bw

A marshal brings law and order to a frontier town. Competent western programmer.
Richard Dix, Florence Rice, William Henry, Victor Jory, Andy Clyde. Written by Herman Houston and Bernard McConville; directed by Lesley Selander; for Harry Sherman / Paramount.

The Chess Players*
India 1977 129m Eastmancolor

In 1856 Lucknow, two noblemen are more interested in playing chess than in their state's imminent annexation by the British. Patchy but frequently charming historical piece with more specifically Indian elements than are usual from its director. Sanjeev Kumar, Saeed Jaffrey, Richard Attenborough, Amjad Khan. Written and directed by Satyajit Ray; for Devki Chitra.

Cheyenne
US 1947 100m bw

A gambler turns lawman, catches a robber and marries his wife. Rather sluggish western which later inspired a long-running TV series.
Dennis Morgan, Bruce Bennett, Jane Wyman, Arthur Kennedy, Janis Paige, Alan Hale. Written by Alan Le May and Thames Williamson; directed by Raoul Walsh; for Warner. (Later retitled: *The Wyoming Kid.*)

Cheyenne Autumn*
US 1964 170m Technicolor
  Panavision 70
Warner / Ford-Smith (Bernard Smith)

In the 1860s, Cheyenne Indians are moved to a new reservation 1500 miles away; wanting aid, they begin a trek back home, and various battles follow.
Dispirited, shapeless John Ford western with little of the master's touch; good to look at, however, with effective cameos, notably an irrelevant and out-of-key comic one featuring James Stewart as Wyatt Earp.

w James R. Webb, *novel* Mari Sandoz d John Ford ph William H. Clothier m Alex North

Richard Widmark, Carroll Baker, Karl Malden, Dolores del Rio, Sal Mineo, Edward G. Robinson, James Stewart, Ricardo Montalban, Gilbert Roland, Arthur Kennedy, Patrick Wayne, Elizabeth Allen, Victor Jory, John Carradine, Mike Mazurki, John Qualen, George O'Brien

'Although one would like to praise the film for its high-minded aims, it is hard to forget how ponderous and disjointed it is.'—*Moira Walsh*

'The acting is bad, the dialogue trite and predictable, the pace funereal, the structure fragmented and the climaxes puny.'—*Stanley Kauffmann*

AAN: William H. Clothier

The Cheyenne Social Club*
US 1970 102m Technicolor
  Panavision
National General (James Lee Barrett, Gene Kelly)

Two itinerant cowboys inherit a high-class brothel.
Disappointing star comedy western with pleasing moments and a lively climactic shoot-out. Perhaps the girls are just a shade too winsome.

w James Lee Barrett d Gene Kelly ph William H. Clothier m Walter Scharf

James Stewart, Henry Fonda, Shirley Jones, Sue Anne Langdon, Robert Middleton, Arch Johnson

'Co-starring Shirley Jones and Rigor Mortis, who enters early and stays through the very last scene.'—*Rex Reed*

Chicago Calling*
US 1951 75m bw
UA / Arrowhead / Joseph Justman (Peter Berneis)

A drunk cannot pay his phone bill and is waiting for a vital call about his daughter's involvement in a car crash.
Moderate, location-shot minor melodrama with a few good ideas.

w John Reinhardt, Peter Berneis d John Reinhardt ph Robert de Grasse

Dan Duryea, Mary Anderson, Gordon Gebert, Ross Elliot

Chicago Confidential
US 1957 74m bw

A gambling syndicate takes over a labour union and frames its incorruptible president for murder. Very routine gangster potboiler.

Brian Keith, Beverly Garland, Dick Foran, Elisha Cook Jnr. Written by Raymond T. Marcus; directed by Sidney Salkow; for Peerless / UA.

Chicago Deadline
US 1949 87m bw
Paramount (Robert Fellows)

A reporter researches the life of a lonely girl who died of tuberculosis.
Flat star vehicle consisting mainly of overplayed cameos.

w Warren Duff, Tiffany Thayer d Lewis Allen ph John F. Seitz m Victor Young

Alan Ladd, Donna Reed, *June Havoc*, Berry Kroeger, Arthur Kennedy, Gavin Muir, Shepperd Strudwick
† Remade for TV as the TV movie *Fame Is the Name of the Game.*

Chicago Syndicate
US 1955 86m bw

A young accountant breaks up an outwardly respectable crime syndicate. Formula racket-busting melodrama. Dennis O'Keefe, Abbe Lane, Paul Stewart, Xavier Cugat, Alison Hayes. Written by Joseph Hoffman; directed by Fred F. Sears; for Clover / Columbia.

Chicken Every Sunday*
US 1949 94m bw
TCF

The Hefferans have run a boarding house for twenty years, but dad's wild schemes run away with any possible profit.
Archetypal, folksy, American small-town chronicle, reasonably well made, for an audience that now watches *The Waltons.*

w George Seaton, Valentine Davies d George Seaton ph Harry Jackson m Alfred Newman

Dan Dailey, Celeste Holm, Colleen Townsend, Alan Young, Natalie Wood

Chickens Come Home*
US 1931 30m bw

Stan helps his boss Ollie to evade the attentions of an old flame. Rather heavy and untypical, but mainly very enjoyable star comedy, a remake of *Love 'Em and Weep* in which all three leading players had appeared four years earlier in different roles. Laurel and Hardy, James Finlayson, Mae Busch, Thelma Todd. Written by H. M. Walker, from a story by Hal Roach; directed by James W. Horne; for Hal Roach.

Chief Crazy Horse
US 1954 86m Technicolor
   Cinemascope
U-I (William Alland)
GB title: *Valley of Fury*

The tribal problems of the Indian chief who defeated Custer at Little Big Horn.
Competent pro-Indian western.

w Franklin Coen, Gerald Drayson Adams d George Sherman ph Harold Lipstein m Frank Skinner

Victor Mature, Suzan Ball, John Lund, Ray Danton, Keith Larsen, Paul Guilfoyle, David Janssen

Un Chien Andalou*
France 1928 17m bw silent
Luis Bunuel

Famous surrealist short which includes dead donkeys on pianos and starts with a woman's eyeball being cut by a razor blade.
It had meaning for its makers, but very few other people saw anything in it but sensationalism.

w *Luis Bunuel, Salvador Dali d, ed Luis Bunuel ph* Albert Dubergen

Simone Mareuil, Pierre Batcheff, Jaime Miravilles, Salvador Dali, Luis Bunuel

La Chienne*
France 1931 85m bw
Braunberger-Richebé

A bank clerk falls for a prostitute and later kills her; her pimp is executed for the crime and the bank clerk becomes a tramp.
Heavy-going, old-fashioned melodrama with some interesting detail.

wd *Jean Renoir, novel* Georges de la Fouchardière ph Theodor Sparkuhl, Roger Hubert

Michel Simon, Janie Marèze, Georges Flament, Jean Gehret
† Remade as Scarlet Street (qv).

Child in the House
GB 1956 88m bw
Eros / Golden Era (Ben Fisz)

When her mother is ill and her father in hiding from the police, a 12-year-old girl goes to stay with her fussy uncle and aunt.
Modest family drama of the novelette type in which adult problems are put right by the wisdom of a child.

wd C. Raker Endfield, *novel* Janet McNeill ph Otto Heller m Mario Nascimbene ad Ken Adam

Eric Portman, Phyllis Calvert, Stanley Baker, Mandy Miller, Dora Bryan, Joan Hickson, Victor Maddern, Percy Herbert

A Child is Born
US 1939 79m bw
Warner (Sam Bischoff)

A slice of life in the maternity ward.
Adequately dramatic sequence of cameos, with mothers-to-be including a gangster's moll: a remake of *Life Begins*.

w Robert Rossen, *play* Mary M. Axelson *d* Lloyd Bacon *ph* Charles Rosher

Geraldine Fitzgerald, Jeffrey Lynn, Gladys George, Gale Page, Spring Byington, Henry O'Neill, John Litel, Gloria Holden, Eve Arden, Nanette Fabares, Hobart Cavanaugh, Johnny Downs, Johnnie Davis

A Child is Waiting**
US 1963 104m bw
UA / Stanley Kramer

A mixed-up spinster joins the staff of a school for mentally handicapped children.
Worthy semi-documentary marred by having a normal boy play the central character (albeit very well). A little over-dramatized but cogent and unsentimental.

w Abby Mann *d* John Cassavetes *ph* Joseph La Shelle *m* Ernest Gold

Burt Lancaster, *Judy Garland, Bruce Ritchey,* Steven Hill, Gena Rowlands, *Paul Stewart,* Lawrence Tierney

The Childhood of Maxim Gorky***
USSR 1938–40 bw
Soyuzdetfilm

Orphan Gorky is raised by his grandparents, and becomes a ship's cook and a painter before going on to university.
This simple and direct story is told in three beautifully detailed if rather overlong films:
'The Childhood of Maxim Gorky': 101m
'Out in the World': 98m
'My Universities': 104m

w Mark Donskoi, I. Grudzev *d Mark Donskoi ph* Pyotr Yermolov *m* Lev Schwartz *ad* I. Stepanov

Alexei Lyarsky, Y. Valbert, M. Troyanovski, Valeria Massalitinova

Children of Hiroshima**
Japan 1952 97m bw
Kendai Eiga Lyokai / Gekidan Mingei

A young teacher returns to Hiroshima seven years after the bomb.
Restrained yet harrowing social documentary

in fiction form, with the most effective use of flashbacks to show the horror of the bomb and its aftermath.

wd Kaneto Shindo, novel Arata Osada *ph Takeo Itoh m* Akira Ifukube

Nobuko Otowa, Chikako Hoshawa, Niwa Saito

The Children of Sanchez
US / Mexico 1978 126m colour
Hall Bartlett

A macho Mexican and one of his daughters have ideas above the semi-slum in which they live.
The star is still looking for another *Zorba the Greek*, but this isn't it. Glum, glum, glum.

w Cesare Zavattini, Hall Bartlett, *novel* Oscar Lewis *d* Hall Bartlett *ph* Gabriel Figueroa *m* Chuck Mangione

Anthony Quinn, Dolores del Rio, Lupita Ferrer, Katy Jurado, Stathis Giallelis

Children of the Damned*
GB 1964 90m bw
MGM (Ben Arbeid)

Six super-intelligent children of various nations are brought to London by UNESCO, and turn out to be invaders from another planet.
Moderate sequel to *Village of the Damned*, well made but with no new twists.

w John Briley *d* Anton M. Leader *ph* David Boulton *m* Ron Goodwin

Ian Hendry, Alan Badel, Barbara Ferris, Alfred Burke, Sheila Allen, Ralph Michael, Martin Miller, Harold Goldblatt

The Children's Hour*
US 1961 108m bw
UA / Mirisch (William Wyler)
GB title: *The Loudest Whisper*

A spoilt schoolgirl spreads a rumour that her schoolmistresses are lesbians.
Frank sixties version of a play originally filmed in a much bowdlerized version as *These Three*. Unfortunately frankness in this case leads to dullness, as nothing is done with the theme once it is stated, and the treatment is heavy-handed.

w Lillian Hellman, from her play *d* William Wyler *ph* Franz Planer *m* Alex North

Audrey Hepburn, Shirley Maclaine, James Garner, Miriam Hopkins, Fay Bainter, Karen Balkin

'All very exquisite, and dead as mutton.'—
Tom Milne

AAN: Franz Planer; Fay Bainter

Child's Play*
US 1972   100m   Movielab
Paramount (David Merrick)

In a Catholic boarding school for boys, an unpopular master is hounded and discredited by another whose motives may be diabolic. Enjoyable overblown melodrama with hints of many nasty goings on, rather spoiled by too much talk and too little local colour.

w Leon Prochnik, play Robert Marasco
d Sidney Lumet ph Gerald Hirschfeld
m Michael Small

James Mason, Robert Preston, Beau Bridges, Ronald Weyand

The Chiltern Hundreds*
GB 1949   84m   bw
Rank / Two Cities (George H. Brown)
US title: The Amazing Mr Beecham

An aged earl is bewildered when his son fails to be elected to parliament as a socialist but his butler gets in as a tory.
Satisfactory filming of an amusing stage comedy, with the aged A. E. Matthews repeating his delightful if irrelevant act as the dotty earl.

w William Douglas Home, Patrick Kirwan, play William Douglas Home d John Paddy Carstairs ph Jack Hildyard m Benjamin Frankel

A. E. Matthews, Cecil Parker, David Tomlinson, Marjorie Fielding, Joyce Carey

Chimes at Midnight*
Spain / Switz 1966   119m   bw
Internacional Films Espanola / Alpine
    (Alessandro Tasca)
aka: Falstaff

Prince Hal becomes King Henry V and rejects his old friend Falstaff.
Clumsy adaptation of Shakespeare with brilliant flashes and the usual Welles vices of hasty production, poor synchronization and recording, etc. One wonders why, if he wanted to make a telescoped version of the plays, he did not spare the time and patience to make it better.

w Orson Welles d Orson Welles ph Edmond Richard m Angelo Francesco Lavagnino

Orson Welles, Keith Baxter, John Gielgud (Henry IV), Margaret Rutherford (Mistress Quickly), Jeanne Moreau (Doll Tearsheet), Norman Rodway, Alan Webb, Marina Vlady, Tony Beckley, Fernando Rey

The Chimp*
US 1932   30m   bw

Stan and Ollie try to get lodgings without revealing that their friend is a chimp, their share of a bankrupt circus. The circus scenes are better than the rather tired farce which follows, especially as it is so similar to Laughing Gravy. Laurel and Hardy, James Finlayson, Billy Gilbert, Tiny Sandford. Written by H. M. Walker; directed by James Parrott; for Hal Roach.

China
US 1943   79m   bw
Paramount (Richard Blumenthal)

An oil salesman joins a Chinese guerrilla force and sacrifices himself.
Solemnly hilarious propaganda piece tailored to its star, showing the immense superiority of one lone American to the entire Japanese army.

w Frank Butler, novel The Fourth Brother by Reginald Forbes d John Farrow ph Leo Tover m Victor Young

Alan Ladd, Loretta Young, William Bendix, Philip Ahn, Iris Wong, Sen Yung, Richard Loo, Tala Birell

China Clipper*
US 1936   89m   bw
Warner (Sam Bischoff)

An aviator neglects his wife while building up a trans-Pacific civil aviation link.
Solid entertainment feature of its day, with adequate production and performance.

w Frank 'Spig' Wead d Ray Enright
ph Arthur Edeson m W. Franke Harling

Pat O'Brien, Beverly Roberts, Ross Alexander, Humphrey Bogart, Marie Wilson, Henry B. Walthall, Joseph Crehan, Addison Richards

China Doll
US 1958   99m   bw
Romina / Batjac (Frank Borzage)

In 1943 an American air force officer accidentally buys the services of a young Chinese housekeeper. He marries her but they are both killed in action; years later their daughter is welcomed to America by members of his old air crew.
Incurably sentimental and icky romantic drama in the style of the director's silent films; something of a curiosity for historians.

w Kitty Buhler d Frank Borzage ph William H. Clothier m Henry Vars

Victor Mature, Li Li Hua, Bob Mathias, Ward Bond, Stuart Whitman

China Gate
US 1957 90m bw Cinemascope
TCF (Samuel Fuller)

A Eurasian girl guides her American husband
to a communist arms dump.
Anti-Red thick ear, slick but undistinguished.

wd Samuel Fuller *ph* Joseph Biroc *m* Victor
Young, Max Steiner

Gene Barry, Angie Dickinson, Nat King Cole,
Paul Dubov, Lee Van Cleef, George Givot

China Girl
US 1943 95m bw
TCF (Ben Hecht)

A newsreel cameraman in China falls in love
with a Eurasian schoolteacher.
Routine adventure romance with splodges of
love and self-sacrifice.

w Ben Hecht *d* Henry Hathaway *ph* Lee
Garmes *m* Hugo Friedhofer

Gene Tierney, George Montgomery, *Lynn
Bari*, Victor McLaglen, Alan Baxter, Sig
Rumann, Myron McCormick, Philip Ahn

China Seas**
US 1935 89m bw
MGM (Albert Lewin)

Luxury cruise passengers find themselves
involved with piracy.
Omnibus shipboard melodrama, tersely
scripted and featuring a splendid cast all
somewhere near their best; slightly dated but
very entertaining.

w Jules Furthman, James Kevin McGuinness,
novel Crosbie Garstin *d* Tay Garnett *ph* Ray
June *m* Herbert Stothart

Clark Gable, Jean Harlow, Wallace Beery,
Rosalind Russell, Lewis Stone, C. Aubrey
Smith, Dudley Digges, Robert Benchley
    'The hell with art this time. I'm going to
produce a picture that will make money.'—
Irving Thalberg

China Sky
US 1945 78m bw
RKO (Maurice Geraghty)

Two American doctors live with Chinese
guerrillas; the jealousy of the wife of one of
them causes problems.
Routine adventure romance with generally
unconvincing production and performance.

w Brenda Weisberg, Joseph Hoffman, *novel*
Pearl Buck *d* Ray Enright *ph* Nicholas
Musuraca *m* Roy Webb

Randolph Scott, Ellen Drew, Ruth Warrick,
Anthony Quinn, Carol Thurston, Richard
Loo, Philip Ahn

The China Syndrome**
US 1979 122m Metrocolor
Columbia / IPC (Bruce Gilbert)

The controller of a nuclear power plant
discovers an operational flaw which could lead
to disaster, but the unscrupulous authorities
want to cover it up.
Topical thriller-with-a-moral, absorbingly
done in the old style but perhaps in the end a
shade too hysterical and self-congratulatory.

w Mike Gray, T. S. Cook, James Bridges
d James Bridges *ph* James Crabe *m* various
pd George Jenkins

Jane Fonda, *Jack Lemmon*, Michael Douglas,
Scott Brady, Peter Donat, James Hampton
    'The performances are so good, and the
screen so bombarded with both action and
informative images . . . that it's only with
considerable hindsight that one recovers
sufficient breath to reproach the script with the
occasional glib symmetry.'—*Jan Dawson,
MFB*

China Venture
US 1953 83m bw

In 1945, American marines are sent into the
Chinese jungle to recover a Japanese admiral
held captive there. Topical thick-ear, played
and presented without conviction. Edmond
O'Brien, Barry Sullivan, Jocelyn Brando,
Richard Loo. Written by George Worthing
Yates and Richard Collins; directed by Don
Siegel; for Anson Bond / Columbia.

Chinatown***
US 1974 131m Technicolor
Panavision
Paramount / Long Road (Robert Evans)

In 1937, a Los Angeles private eye takes on a
simple case and burrows into it until it leads to
murder and a public scandal.
Pretentious melodrama which is basically no
more serious than the Raymond Chandler
mysteries from which it derives; the tragic
ending is merely an irritation, and the title
only allusive. Superficially, however, it is
eminently watchable, with effective individual
scenes and performances and photography
which is lovingly composed though tending to
suggest period by use of an orange filter.

*w Robert Towne d Roman Polanski ph John
A. Alonso m Jerry Goldsmith pd Richard
Sylbert*

Jack Nicholson, Faye Dunaway, John Huston,
Perry Lopez, John Hillerman, Roman
Polanski, Darrell Zwerling, Diane Ladd

AA: Robert Towne
AAN: best picture; Roman Polanski; John A.
Alonso; Jerry Goldsmith; Jack Nicholson;
Faye Dunaway

The Chinese Bungalow
GB 1939   72m   bw
George King
US title: *Chinese Den*

A Chinese merchant plots to kill the lover of
his English wife.
Stolid version of an old melodrama which can
hardly fail; previously filmed in 1926 with
Matheson Lang and Genevieve Townsend
(directed by Sinclair Hill) and in 1930 with
Matheson Lang and Anna Neagle (directed by
J. B. Williams).

w A. R. Rawlinson, George Wellesley, *play*
Matheson Lang, Marian Osmond *d* George
King *ph* Hone Glendinning

Paul Lukas, Jane Baxter, Robert Douglas,
Kay Walsh, Jerry Verno

Chinese Roulette*
West Germany / France 1976   86m
   Eastmancolor
Albatros / Losange (Rainer Werner
   Fassbinder)

Various related people, mainly adulterous,
meet in a country château and play a truth
game which ends in violence.
Interestingly enigmatic character melodrama
reminiscent of Bergman at his prime, but
concerning people who barely seem to matter.

wd Rainer Werner Fassbinder *ph* Michael
Ballhaus *m* Peer Raben

Margit Carstensen, Andrea Schober, Ulli
Lommel, Anna Karina, Macha Meril
   'Locked into their private hell . . . this
vicious octet form their own coherent and
compelling universe.'—*Jan Dawson, MFB*

Chino
US / Italy 1973   98m   colour

A runaway boy helps a half-breed run a ranch
in New Mexico. Undistinguished western.
Charles Bronson, Jill Ireland, Vincent Van
Petten. Written by Clair Huffaker, from a
novel by Lee Hoffman; directed by John
Sturges; for Dino de Laurentiis.

Chisum*
US 1970   110m   Technicolor
   Panavision
Warner / Batjac (Michael Wayne, Andrew J.
   Fenady)

A corrupt businessman plots against the head

of a vast cattle empire, who is saved by the
intervention of numerous friends including Pat
Garrett and Billy the Kid.
Desultory, overlong, friendly western in the
Ford manner. Easy to watch and easier to
forget.

w Andrew J. Fenady *d* Andrew V.
McLaglen *ph* William H. Clothier
m Dominic Frontière

John Wayne, Forrest Tucker, Christopher
George, Ben Johnson, Glenn Corbett, Bruce
Cabot, Andrew Prine, Patric Knowles,
Richard Jaeckel, Linda Day George, John
Agar, Ray Teal, Glenn Langan, Alan Baxter,
Abraham Sofaer
   'A curious mixture of styles and myths.'—
John Gillett

Chitty Chitty Bang Bang
GB 1968   145m   Technicolor   Super
   Panavision 70
UA / Warfield / DFI (Albert R. Broccoli)

An unsuccessful inventor rescues a derelict car
and gives it magical properties, then helps the
children who own it to overthrow the
government of a country which hates children.
A bumpy ride. Sentiment, slapstick, whimsy
and mild scares do not combine but are given
equal shares of the limelight, while poor
trickwork prevents the audience from being
transported.

w Roald Dahl, Ken Hughes *d* Ken Hughes
ph Christopher Challis *m* Irwin Kostal
songs the Sherman Brothers *ad* Ken Adam
decor Rowland Emmett

Dick Van Dyke, Sally Ann Howes (as Truly
Scrumptious), Lionel Jeffries, Robert
Helpmann, Gert Frobe, Benny Hill, James
Robertson Justice

AAN: title song

The Chocolate Soldier*
US 1941   102m   bw
MGM (Victor Saville)

Married opera singers fall out backstage.
Talky musical remake of *The Guardsman*:
nearly comes off but not quite.

w Keith Winter, Leonard Lee *d* Roy del
Ruth *ph* Karl Freund *songs* Oscar Straus
m Herbert Stothart, Bronislau Kaper

Nelson Eddy, Rise Stevens, Nigel Bruce,
Florence Bates, Nydia Westman

AAN: Karl Freund; Herbert Stothart,
Bronislau Kaper

The Choirboys
US 1978   119m   Technicolor
Lorimar / Airone (Lee Rich, Merv Adelson)

Members of a police department are if anything more delinquent, vicious and mentally retarded than their quarries.
A vulgar and repellent anti-establishment display, apparently intended as black comedy. Just the thing to put an end to the art of the movie once and for all.

w Christopher Knopf, *novel* Joseph Wambaugh d Robert Aldrich ph Joseph Biroc m Frank de Vol

Charles Durning, Lou Gossett Jnr, Perry King, Stephen Macht, Tim McIntyre, Clyde Kusatu, Randy Quaid, Don Stroud, Robert Webber, Blair Brown

Chosen Survivors
US 1974 98m colour
Alpine / Metromedia (Charles Fries)

Ten people with special skills are chosen to test human reaction to thermo-nuclear war, but find themselves at the mercy of vampire bats.
Another misfit group united by disaster; more shocks than suspense, and not much characterization, but for adventure / horror addicts it will pass the time.

w H. B. Cross, Joe Red Moffly d Sutton Roley ph Gabriel Torres m Fred Karlin

Jackie Cooper, Alex Cord, Richard Jaeckel, Diana Muldaur, Lincoln Kilpatrick, Bradford Dillman, Pedro Armendariz Jnr, Gwen Mitchell, Barbara Babcock, Christina Moreno

A Christmas Carol*
US 1938 69m bw
MGM (Joseph L. Mankiewicz)

Scrooge the miser is reformed when four ghosts visit him on Christmas Eve.
Standard Dickensian frolic, quite well mounted.

w Hugo Butler d Edwin L. Marin ph Sidney Wagner m Franz Waxman

Reginald Owen, Gene Lockhart, Kathleen Lockhart, Terry Kilburn, Leo G. Carroll, Lynne Carver
† See also *Scrooge*.

Christmas Eve*
US 1947 92m bw
Benedict Bogeaus
aka: *Sinners' Holiday*

An old lady needs the help of her three adopted sons to prevent herself from being swindled.
Basically three short stories sealed by a Christmas Eve reunion, this is old-fashioned sentimental stuff, but it works on its level and the cast is interesting.

w Lawrence Stallings d Edwin L. Marin ph Gordon Avil m Heinz Roemheld

Ann Harding, George Raft, Randolph Scott, George Brent, Joan Blondell, Virginia Field, Reginald Denny

Christmas Holiday
US 1944 93m bw
Universal (Felix Jackson)

A young girl marries a murderer, and later, as a shady songstress in a nightclub, is forced to help him escape.
A weird change of pace for Deanna Durbin, whose forte had been sweetness and light, this relentlessly grim and boring melodrama was also a travesty of the novel on which it was based.

w Herman J. Mankiewicz, *novel* Somerset Maugham d Robert Siodmak ph Elwood Bredell m Hans Salter

Deanna Durbin, Gene Kelly, Dean Harens, Gladys George, Richard Whorf, Gale Sondergaard

AAN: Hans Salter

Christmas in Connecticut*
US 1945 101m bw
Warner (William Jacobs)
GB title: *Indiscretion*

The spinster writer of a successful column about love and marriage has to conjure up a family for herself in the cause of publicity.
Predictable but fairly brisk comedy with excellent talent well deployed.

w Lionel Houser, Adele Commandini d Peter Godfrey ph Carl Guthrie m Frederick Hollander

Barbara Stanwyck, Dennis Morgan, Sydney Greenstreet, Reginald Gardiner, S. Z. Sakall, Robert Shayne, Una O'Connor, Frank Jenks

Christmas in July**
US 1940 67m bw
Paramount

A young clerk and his girl win first prize in a big competition.
Slightly unsatisfactory as a whole, this Preston Sturges comedy has echoes of Clair and a dully predictable plot line, but is kept alive by inventive touches and a gallery of splendid character comedians.

wd Preston Sturges ph Victor Milner m Sigmund Krumgold

Dick Powell, Ellen Drew, Ernest Truex, Al Bridge, Raymond Walburn, William Demarest
'The perfect restorative for battered humors and jangled nerves.'—*Bosley Crowther*

'Agreeable enough, but it lacks the full-fledged Sturges lunacy.'—*New Yorker*, 1977

The Christmas Tree
France / Italy 1969   110m   Eastmancolor
Corona / Jupiter (Robert Dorfmann)

The small son of a millionaire widower is fatally infected by radioactivity.

Painfully sentimental and overdrawn weepie, the most lachrymose film of the sixties.

wd Terence Young, *novel* Michel Bataille
ph Henri Alekan   *m* Georges Auric

William Holden, Virna Lisi, Brook Fuller, Bourvil

'Depending on your taste threshold, there may not be a dry eye—nor a full stomach—in the house.'—*Judith Crist*

Christopher Bean*
US 1933   80m   bw

A dying artist appoints his housekeeper as his executor. Solid family entertainment very typical of its studio. *Marie Dressler* (her last film), Lionel Barrymore, Beulah Bondi, Helen Mack, George Coulouris, H. B. Warner, Jean Hersholt. Written by Laurence Johnson and Sylvia Thalberg, from Sidney Howard's play *The Late Christopher Bean*; directed by Sam Wood; for MGM.

Christopher Columbus
US 1949   104m   Technicolor
Rank / Gainsborough / Sydney Box (Betty E. Box)

Columbus seeks and receives the patronage of the Spanish court for his voyage to the west. An extraordinarily tediously paced historical account of basically undramatic events; interesting without being stimulating.

w Muriel and Sydney Box, Cyril Roberts
d David MacDonald   *ph* Stephen Dade
m Arthur Bliss

Fredric March, Florence Eldridge, Francis L. Sullivan, Linden Travers

'Even ten-year-olds will find it about as thrilling as an afternoon spent looking at Christmas cards.'—*Time*

Christopher Strong*
US 1933   72m   bw
RKO (Pandro S. Berman)

A daring lady aviator has an affair with a married businessman and commits suicide when she finds herself pregnant.

A curious and unsatisfactory yarn for Hepburn's second film; well enough made, it died at the box office.

w Zoe Akins, *novel* Gilbert Frankau
d Dorothy Arzner   *ph* Bert Glennon   *m* Max Steiner

Katharine Hepburn, Colin Clive, Billie Burke, Helen Chandler, Ralph Forbes, Irene Browne, Jack La Rue

'The personal story of a million daughters.' —*publicity*

'She gave herself to the great god Speed, and tried to run away from the fires within her!'—*publicity*

Chronique d'un Eté*
France 1961   90m   bw
Argos

Parisians talk about their lives.

Curious but rather stimulating acted documentary, with two interviewers pontificating; saved by shrewd editing to keep interest at its maximum.

wd Jean Rouch, Edgar Morin ph various

Chu Chin Chow*
GB 1934   102m   bw
Gaumont British / Gainsborough (Michael Balcon)

In old Arabia, a slave girl foils a robber posing as a dead mandarin.

Second screen version (the first was silent) of the old Arabian Nights stage musical. A curiosity.

w Edward Knoblock, L. DuGarde Peach, Sidney Gilliat, *play* Oscar Asche and Frederick Norton   *d* Walter Forde
songs Frederick Norton   *md* Louis Levy
ph Max Greene   *ch* Anton Dolin

George Robey, Fritz Kortner, Anna May Wong, John Garrick, Pearl Argyle, Malcolm MacEachern, Dennis Hoey, Francis L. Sullivan, Sydney Fairbrother

'Gaumont British have broken away for the first time from their careful refinement, and produced something that has guts as well as grace.'—*C. A. Lejeune*

Chubasco
US 1967   100m   Technicolor
           Panavision
Warner Seven Arts (William Conrad)

A wild beach boy takes a job on a tuna fishing boat.

Old-fashioned boy-makes-good melodrama à la Captains Courageous. Excellent action sequences at sea.

wd Allen H. Miner   *ph* Louis Jennings, Paul Ivano   *m* William Lava

Chris Jones, Richard Egan, Susan Strasberg,
Ann Sothern, Simon Oakland, Preston Foster,
Audrey Totter, Peter Whitney

Chuka
US 1967   105m   Technicolor
Paramount / Rod Taylor

A wandering gunfighter defends the
inhabitants of a fort against Indian attack.
Ill-assorted characters under stress is the
theme of this rather pedestrian and slightly
pretentious western.

w Richard Jessup d Gordon Douglas
ph Harold Stine m Leith Stevens

Rod Taylor, Ernest Borgnine, John Mills,
Luciana Paluzzi, James Whitmore, Louis
Hayward, Angela Dorian

A Chump at Oxford**
US 1939   63m   bw
Hal Roach

Two street cleaners foil a bank hold-up and
are presented with an Oxford education.
Patchy but endearing Laurel and Hardy romp,
starting with an irrelevant two reels about
their playing butler and maid, but later
including Stan's burlesque impersonation of
Lord Paddington.

w Charles Rogers, Harry Langdon, Felix
Adler d Alfred Goulding ph Art Lloyd

Stan Laurel, Oliver Hardy, James Finlayson,
Forrester Harvey, Wilfrid Lucas, Peter
Cushing

'Ranks with their best pictures—which, to
one heretic, are more agreeable than
Chaplin's. Their clowning is purer; they aren't
out to better an unbetterable world; they've
never wanted to play Hamlet.'—Graham
Greene

Cimarron*
US 1931   130m   bw
RKO (Louis Sarecky)

The life of an Oklahoma homesteader from
1890 to 1915.
Sprawling western family saga; a big early
talkie, it dates badly.

w Howard Estabrook, novel Edna Ferber
d Wesley Ruggles ph Edward Cronjager
m Max Steiner

Richard Dix, Irene Dunne, Estelle Taylor,
Nance O'Neill, William Collier Jnr, Roscoe
Ates, George E. Stone, Stanley Fields, Edna
May Oliver

AA: best picture; Howard Estabrook
AAN: Wesley Ruggles; Edward Cronjager;
Richard Dix; Irene Dunne

'Earth-shaking in its grandeur! A titanic
canvas sprung to life!'—publicity

Cimarron
US 1961   147m   Metrocolor
Cinemascope
MGM (Edmund Grainger)

Flabby, relentlessly boring remake of the
above.

w Arnold Schulman d Anthony Mann
ph Robert L. Surtees m Franz Waxman

Glenn Ford, Maria Schell, Anne Baxter, Lili
Darvas, Russ Tamblyn, Henry Morgan, David
Opatoshu, Charles McGraw, Aline
MacMahon, Edgar Buchanan, Arthur
O'Connell, Mercedes McCambridge, Vic
Morrow, Robert Keith, Mary Wickes, Royal
Dano, Vladimir Sokoloff

The Cincinnati Kid**
US 1965   113m   Metrocolor
MGM / Filmways (Martin Ransohoff, John
Calley)

In New Orleans in the late thirties, stud poker
experts compete for supremacy.
This is to poker what The Hustler was to pool,
a fascinating suspense study of experts at
work; as before, the romantic asides let down
the effectiveness of the others.

w Ring Lardner Jnr, Terry Southern, novel
Richard Jessup d Norman Jewison ph Philip
Lathrop m Lalo Schifrin

Steve McQueen, Edward G. Robinson, Karl
Malden, Ann-Margret, Tuesday Weld, Joan
Blondell, Rip Torn, Jack Weston, Cab
Calloway, Jeff Corey

Cinderella**
US 1950   75m   Technicolor
Walt Disney

The Perrault fairy tale embroidered with
animal characters.
A feature cartoon rather short on inspiration,
though with all Disney's solid virtues. The
mice are lively and the villainous cat the best
character.

supervisor Ben Sharpsteen d Wilfred Jackson,
Hamilton Luske, Clyde Geronomi m Oliver
Wallace, Paul J. Smith

AAN: Oliver Wallace, Paul J. Smith; song
'Bibbidy Bobbidy Boo' (m / ly Mack David,
Al Hoffman, Jerry Livingston)

Cinderella Jones
US 1946   89m   bw
Warner (Alex Gottlieb)

To collect an inheritance, a girl must marry a brainy man.

Witless comedy for the easily pleased.

w Charles Hoffman, *story* Philip Wylie
d Busby Berkeley *ph* Sol Polito *m* Frederick Hollander

Joan Leslie, Robert Alda, S. Z. Sakall, Edward Everett Horton, Julie Bishop, William Prince, Charles Dingle, Ruth Donnelly, Elisha Cook Jnr, Hobart Cavanaugh, Chester Clute

Cinderella Liberty
US 1974   117m   De Luxe   Panavision
TCF / Sanford (Mark Rydell)

A sailor on shore leave picks up a prostitute and falls in love with her.

Assertively 'modern' yet glutinously sentimental love story in squalid settings. It presumably has an audience.

w Darryl Ponicsan, from his novel d Mark Rydell *ph* Vilmos Zsigmond *m* John Williams

James Caan, Marsha Mason, Eli Wallach, Kirk Calloway, Allyn Ann McLerie

'A sordid, messy affair which wants to jerk tears but just doesn't have the knack.'—*New Yorker*

AA: song 'Nice To Be Around' (*m* John Williams, *ly* Paul Williams)
AAN: John Williams; Marsha Mason

Cinderfella
US 1960   91m   Technicolor
Paramount / Jerry Lewis

Luxury pantomime featuring a male Cinderella.

Annoyingly lavish and empty star vehicle with precious little to laugh at: Lewis' own jokes are strung out to snapping point and no one else gets a look in.

wd Frank Tashlin *ph* Haskell Boggs *m* Walter Scharf

Jerry Lewis, Ed Wynn, Judith Anderson, Anna Maria Alberghetti, Henry Silva, Robert Hutton, Count Basie

'A drought of comic inspiration, followed by a flood of mawkish whimsy, gradually increases one's early misgivings to a degree which finally verges on revulsion.'—*Peter John Dyer*

The Circle
Somerset Maugham's brittle play contrasting noble breeding with vulgar riches was filmed by Frank Borzage as a Hollywood silent, in 1925 for MGM, with Elinor Boardman, Creighton Hale and Alec B. Francis. In 1930

the same studio made it as a talkie under the title *Strictly Unconventional*, with Catherine Dale Owen, Tyrrell Davis and Lewis Stone; directed by David Burton. Neither version really worked.

Circle of Danger*
GB 1951   89m   bw
Coronado / David Rose (Joan Harrison)

An American in England investigates the strange death some years earlier of his brother during a commando raid.

Individual scenes are well milked for suspense and dramatic emphasis, but the plot line has virtually no mystery and absolutely no danger. It all seems mildly reminiscent of several Hitchcock films.

w Philip MacDonald *d Jacques Tourneur*
ph Oswald Morris *m* Robert Farnon

Ray Milland, Patricia Roc, Marius Goring, Hugh Sinclair, Naunton Wayne, Marjorie Fielding, Edward Rigby, Colin Gordon, Dora Bryan

Circle of Deception
GB 1960   100m   bw   Cinemascope
TCF (T. H. Morahan)

An officer is parachuted into Germany with the intention that he should crack under interrogation and reveal false information. Depressing World War II tall tale, with suspense sacrificed by flashback structure.

w Nigel Balchin, Robert Musel, *novel* Alec Waugh d Jack Lee *ph* Gordon Dines *m* Clifton Parker

Bradford Dillman, Harry Andrews, Suzy Parker, Robert Stephens, John Welsh, Paul Rogers, Duncan Lamont, Michael Ripper

Circle of Two
Canada 1980   105m   colour
Film Consortium of Canada (Henk Van der Kolk)

A 60-year-old artist falls for a teenage student. Dreary and uninteresting star drama which never really gets going.

w Thomas Hedley, from A Lesson in Love by Marie Terese Baird *d Jules Dassin ph* Lazlo George *m* Paul Hoffert

Richard Burton, Tatum O'Neal, Nuala Fitzgerald, Kate Reid, Robin Gammell, Patricia Collins

The Circus*
US 1928   72m (24 fps)   bw   silent
(UA) Charles Chaplin

A tramp on the run from the police takes
refuge in a circus and falls for an equestrienne.
Pathos often descends to bathos in this self-
constructed star vehicle which has far too few
laughs.

wd Charles Chaplin *ph* Rollie Totheroh, Jack
Wilson, Mark Marlott

Charles Chaplin, Merna Kennedy, Allan
Garcia, Harry Crocker

AAN: Charles Chaplin (as actor and director)

Circus of Horrors
GB 1960   91m   Eastmancolor
Anglo Amalgamated / Lynx / Independent
  Artists (Norman Priggen)

A plastic surgeon staffs a semi-derelict circus
with criminals whose faces he has altered, and
murders any who try to flee.
Stark horror comic; quite professionally made,
but content-wise a crude concoction of sex and
sadism.

w George Baxt *d* Sidney Hayers *ph* Douglas
Slocombe *m* Franz Reizenstein, Muir
Mathieson

Anton Diffring, Erika Remberg, Yvonne
Monlaur, Donald Pleasance, Jane Hylton,
Kenneth Griffith, Conrad Phillips, Jack
Gwyllim

Circus World
US 1964   138m   Super Technirama
Bronston / Midway (Samuel Bronston)
GB title: *The Magnificent Showman*

An American circus owner tours Europe in
search of his alcoholic ex-wife who left him
when her lover fell to death from the trapeze.
Lethargic big-screen epic which exhausts its
spectacle in the first hour and then settles
down to a dreary will-daughter-guess-who-the-
strange-lady-is plot, without even the plus of
an exciting finale.

w Ben Hecht, Julian Halevy, James Edward
Grant *d* Henry Hathaway *ph* Jack Hildyard
pd John de Cuir *m* Dmitri Tiomkin

John Wayne, *Rita Hayworth*, Claudia
Cardinale, John Smith, Lloyd Nolan, Richard
Conte, Wanda Rotha, Kay Walsh

The Cisco Kid
The Cisco Kid, a ruthless Mexican bandit
originally created by O. Henry in a short
story, was turned by Hollywood into a dashing
wild western Robin Hood in twenty-three
sound features (following a few silent ones)
and a long-running TV series. In most of them
he was accompanied by his fat side-kick
Pancho.

For Fox:
1929: IN OLD ARIZONA (Warner Baxter)
1931: THE CISCO KID (Baxter)

For Twentieth Century Fox:
1939: THE RETURN OF THE CISCO KID
(Baxter), THE CISCO KID AND THE
LADY (Cesar Romero: who played the role in
all the remaining TCF movies).
1940: VIVA CISCO KID, LUCKY CISCO
KID, THE GAY CABALLERO
1941: ROMANCE OF THE RIO GRANDE,
RIDE ON, VAQUERO

For Monogram:
1945: THE CISCO KID RETURNS (Duncan
Renaldo), THE CISCO KID IN OLD NEW
MEXICO (Renaldo), SOUTH OF THE RIO
GRANDE (Renaldo)
1946: THE GAY CAVALIER (Gilbert
Roland), SOUTH OF MONTEREY
(Roland), BEAUTY AND THE BANDIT
(Roland)
1947: RIDING THE CALIFORNIA TRAIL
(Roland), ROBIN HOOD OF MONTEREY
(Roland), KING OF THE BANDITS
(Roland)

For United Artists (all with Renaldo):
1949: THE VALIANT HOMBRE, THE
GAY AMIGO, THE DARING
CABALLERO, SATAN'S CRADLE
1950: THE GIRL FROM SAN LORENZO
† The fifties TV series starred Renaldo with
Leo Carrillo.

Cisco Pike
US 1971   94m   Eastmancolor
Columbia / Acrobat (Gerald Ayres)

A former pop group leader and drug pusher is
blackmailed by a cop into selling heroin.
Low-key, would-be realistic study of a section
of life in seventies LA. Flashy, boring and
almost plotless.

wd Bill L. Norton *ph* Vilis Lapenieks
m various

Kris Kristofferson, Gene Hackman, Karen
Black, Harry Dean Stanton
  'A moody, melancholy little film whose
strength lies in its evocation of the rootless,
aimless, irresponsible life-style of the pop /
drug culture.'—*Brenda Davies*

The Citadel**
GB 1938   113m   bw
MGM (Victor Saville)

A young doctor has a hard time in the mining
villages but is later swayed by the easy rewards
of a Mayfair practice.
Solidly produced adaptation of a bestseller;

the more recent deluge of doctors on television make it appear rather elementary, but many scenes work in a classical way. One of the first fruits of MGM's British studios which were closed by World War II.

w Elizabeth Hill, Ian Dalrymple, Emlyn Williams, Frank Wead, *novel* A. J. Cronin *d* King Vidor *ph* Harry Stradling *m* Louis Levy

Robert Donat, Rosalind Russell, Ralph Richardson, Emlyn Williams, Penelope Dudley Ward, Francis L. Sullivan

'I think any doctor will agree that here is a medical picture with no *Men in White* hokum, no hysterical, incredible melodrama, but with an honest story, honestly told. And that's a rare picture.'—*Pare Lorentz*

'We are grateful that a worthy idea has been handled with intelligence and imagination, that Vidor has shown respect both for his talent and for the sensibilities of the audience.'—*Robert Stebbins*

'Secrets of a doctor as told by a doctor!'— *publicity*

† The parts played by Russell and Richardson were originally intended for Elizabeth Allan and Spencer Tracy

AAN: best picture; script; King Vidor; Robert Donat

Citizen Kane****
US 1941   119m   bw
RKO (Orson Welles)

A newspaper tycoon dies, and a magazine reporter interviews his friends in an effort to discover the meaning of his last words.
A brilliant piece of Hollywood cinema using all the resources of the studio; despite lapses of characterization and gaps in the narrative, almost every shot and every line is utterly absorbing both as entertainment and as craft. See *The Citizen Kane Book* by Pauline Kael, and innumerable other writings.

w Herman J. Mankiewicz, Orson Welles d Orson Welles ph Gregg Toland m Bernard Herrmann ad Van Nest Polglase sp Vernon L. Walker

Orson Welles, Joseph Cotten, Dorothy Comingore, Everett Sloane, Paul Stewart, Ray Collins, Ruth Warrick, Erskine Sanford, Agnes Moorehead, George Coulouris, William Alland, Fortunio Bonanova

'On seeing it for the first time, one got a conviction that if the cinema could do that, it could do anything.'—*Penelope Houston*

'What may distinguish *Citizen Kane* most of all is its extracting the mythic from under the humdrum surface of the American experience.'—*John Simon, 1968*

'Probably the most exciting film that has come out of Hollywood for twenty-five years. I am not sure it isn't the most exciting film that has ever come out of anywhere.'—*C. A. Lejeune*

'At any rate Orson Welles has landed in the movies, with a splash and a loud yell.'—*James Shelley Hamilton*

'More fun than any great movie I can think of.'—*Pauline Kael, 1968*

'It is a fascinating picture, but because of its congestion of technical stunts, it fails to move us.'—*Egon Larsen*

'A quite good film which tries to run the psychological essay in harness with the detective thriller, and doesn't quite succeed.'—*James Agate*

AA: Herman J. Mankiewicz, Orson Welles (script)
AAN: best picture; Orson Welles (as director); Gregg Toland; Bernard Herrmann; Orson Welles (as actor)

La Città Si Difende
Italy 1951   90m   bw
Cines (Carlo Civallero)

A gang is recruited to rob a football stadium. Moderate forerunner of *The Good Die Young*, *The Killing*, and a hundred other caper films.

w Federico Fellini, Tullio Pinelli, Luigi Comencini d Pietro Germi ph Carlo Montuori m Carlo Rustichelli

Fausto Tozzi, Gina Lollobrigida, Patrizia Manca, Enzo Maggio

'As anonymous as the average B picture.'— *Gavin Lambert*

City across the River
US 1949   91m   bw
U-I (Howard Christie)

Brooklyn delinquents get involved in murder. Semi-documentary throwback to the Dead End Kids, with location shooting influenced by *The Naked City*. Dull.

w Maxwell Shane, Dennis Cooper, novel The Amboy Dukes by Irving Shulman *d* Maxwell Shane *ph* Maury Gertsman *m* Walter Scharf

Stephen McNally, Barbara Whiting, Peter Fernandez, Al Ramsen, Joshua Shelley, Anthony Curtis (Tony Curtis in his first film role)

City beneath the Sea
US 1953   87m   Technicolor
U-I (Albert J. Cohen)

Deep sea divers fall out over a sunken treasure.

Adequate double-biller with little to stir the interest.

w Jack Harvey, Ramon Romero *d* Budd Boetticher *ph* Charles P. Boyle

Robert Ryan, Anthony Quinn, Mala Powers, Suzan Ball, George Mathews, Karel Stepanek, Lalo Rios

City beneath the Sea
US 1970   98m   De Luxe   TVM
Warner / Kent / Motion Pictures
   International (Irwin Allen)
GB theatrical release title: *One Hour to Doomsday*

An undersea city is threatened by an errant planetoid.
Futuristic adventure from a familiar stable; it will satisfy followers of *Voyage to the Bottom of the Sea.*

w John Meredyth Lucas *d* Irwin Allen *ph* Kenneth Peach *m* Richard La Salle *ad* Roger E. Maus, Stan Jolley

Stuart Whitman, Robert Wagner, Rosemary Forsyth, Robert Colbert, Burr de Benning, Richard Basehart, Joseph Cotten, James Darren, Sugar Ray Robinson, Paul Stewart

City for Conquest**
US 1940   106m   bw
Warner (Anatole Litvak)

An East Side truck driver becomes a boxer but is blinded in a fight; meanwhile his composer brother gives up pop music for symphonies. Phony but oddly persuasive melodrama set in a studio in New York and heavily influenced by the pretensions of the Group theatre.

w John Wexley, *novel* Aben Kandel *d* Anatole Litvak *ph* Sol Polito, James Wong Howe *m* Max Steiner

James Cagney, Ann Sheridan, Frank Craven, Donald Crisp, *Arthur Kennedy*, Frank McHugh, George Tobias, Anthony Quinn, Jerome Cowan, Lee Patrick, Blanche Yurka, Thurston Hall

'Sometimes we wonder whether it wasn't really the Warner brothers who got New York from the Indians, so diligent and devoted have they been in feeling the great city's pulse, picturing its myriad facets and recording with deep compassion the passing life of its seething population.'—*Bosley Crowther*

City Girl*
US 1930   77m   bw
Fox

A city girl finds rural life has its own drama. Rural drama distinguished by directorial touches.

w Berthold Viertel, Marion Orth, *play* The Mud Turtle by Elliot Lester *d* F. W. *Murnau* *ph* Ernest Palmer *m* Arthur Kay

Charles Farrell, Mary Duncan, David Torrence, Edith Yorke, Dawn O'Day

City Lights***
US 1931   87m   bw   silent (with music and effects)
(UA) Charles Chaplin

A tramp befriends a millionaire and falls in love with a blind girl.
Sentimental comedy with several delightful sequences in Chaplin's best manner.

wd, m Charles Chaplin ph Rollie Totheroh, Mark Marlott, Gordon Pollock

Charles Chaplin, Virginia Cherrill, Harry Myers

City of Bad Men*
US 1953   82m   Technicolor
TCF (Leonard Goldstein)

In Carson City during the Corbett/ Fitzsimmons boxing match, outlaws plan to rob the arena of its receipts.
Slightly unusual western suspenser with generally accomplished handling.

w George W. George, George Slavin *d* Harmon Jones *ph* Charles G. Clarke *md* Lionel Newman

Dale Robertson, Jeanne Crain, Richard Boone, Lloyd Bridges, Carl Betz, Carole Mathews, Whitfield Connor

The City of Beautiful Nonsense
GB 1935   88m   bw

A poor composer wins the girl he loves from a rich man. Thin and dated version of a fashionable novel by E. Temple Thurston. Emlyn Williams, Sophie Stewart, Eve Lister, George Carney. Written by Donovan Pedelty; directed by Adrian Brunel; for Butcher's.

City of Fear*
US 1958   81m   bw
Columbia / Orbit (Leon Chooluck)

A convict escapes with a canister of radioactive cobalt, which he believes to be heroin. After terrifying the city, he finally dies of exposure to it.
Rough-edged but occasionally gripping minor thriller from an independent company.

w Steven Ritch, Robert Dillon *d* Irving Lerner *ph* Lucien Ballard *m* Jerry Goldsmith

Vince Edwards, John Archer, Patricia Blair, Steven Ritch, Lyle Talbot

City of the Dead*
GB 1960 78m bw
Vulcan (Donald Taylor)
US title: *Horror Hotel*

In Massachusetts, a woman burned as a witch
250 years ago is still 'alive', running a local
hotel and luring unwary strangers into
becoming sacrificial victims.
A deadly first half gives way to splendid
cinematic terror when the scene shifts to the
village by night, all dry ice and limpid fog, and
the heroine becomes a human sacrifice. A
superior horror comic.

w George Baxt *d* John Moxey *ph* Desmond
Dickinson *m* Douglas Gamley, Ken Jones

Patricia Jessel, Betta St John, Christopher
Lee, Dennis Lotis, Valentine Dyall, Venetia
Stevenson, Norman Macowan, Fred Johnson

City of Women*
Italy-France 1980 140m Eastmancolor
Opera Film-Gaumont (Renzo Rossellini)
Original title: *La Città delle Donne*

A businessman finds himself trapped and
threatened by women en masse.
Often leaden but sometimes spectacular
fantasy in which the director spews out his
views of the war between men and women.
Fascinating in patches, but generally
indigestible.

w Federico Fellini, Bernardino Zapponi
d Federico Fellini *ph* Giuseppe Rotunno
m Luis Bacalov

Marcello Mastroianni, Anna Prucnal, Bernice
Stegers, Ettore Manni, Donatella Damiani
 'Another visual tour de force in an elaborate
dream framework; narrative thin, overlong,
and finally overweight.'—*Variety*

City on Fire
Canada / US 1979 106m colour

A slum fire threatens an entire city. Shoddy
disaster movie which does its cast no favour.
Barry Newman, Susan Clark, Shelley Winters,
Henry Fonda, Leslie Nielsen, James
Franciscus, Ava Gardner. Written by Jack
Hill, David P. Lewis and Celine La Freniere;
directed by Alvin Rakoff; for Astral-Bellevue-
Pathe / Sandy Howard.

City Streets**
US 1931 86m bw
Paramount (Rouben Mamoulian)

A gangster's daughter is sent to jail for a
murder she did not commit, and on release
narrowly escapes being 'taken for a ride'.
Tense, dated gangland melodrama of primary

interest because of its director's very cinematic
treatment.

w Max Marcin, Oliver H. P. Garrett, Dashiell
Hammett, *story* Ladies of the Mob by Ernest
Booth *d* Rouben Mamoulian *ph* Lee Garmes

Sylvia Sidney, Gary Cooper, Paul Lukas, Guy
Kibbee, William (Stage) Boyd, Stanley Fields,
Wynne Gibson

City That Never Sleeps
US 1953 90m bw
Republic (John H. Auer)

The work of the Chicago police force during
one night.
Adequate minor semi-documentary police
yarn.

w Steve Fisher *d* John H. Auer *ph* John I.
Russell *m* R. Dale Butts

Gig Young, Mala Powers, William Talman,
Edward Arnold, Chill Wills, Paula Raymond,
Marie Windsor

City under the Sea
GB 1965 84m Eastmancolor
    Colorscope
Bruton / AIP (Daniel Haller)
US title: *War Gods of the Deep*

An American heiress in Cornwall meets
Victorian smugglers who have lived a hundred
years under the sea in Lyonesse.
Childlike, unpersuasive nonsense which wastes
some good talent.

w Charles Bennett, Louis M. Heyward
d Jacques Tourneur *ph* Stephen Dade
m Stanley Black

Vincent Price, David Tomlinson, Susan Hart,
Tab Hunter, Henry Oscar, John Le Mesurier

City Without Men
US 1943 75m bw

A boarding house near a prison is filled with
women awaiting the parole of their menfolk.
Stereotyped programmer. Linda Darnell,
Michael Duane, Sara Allgood, Edgar
Buchanan, Glenda Farrell, Leslie Brooks,
Margaret Hamilton, Sheldon Leonard.
Written by W. L. River, George Skier and
Donald Davis; directed by Sidney Salkow; for
Columbia.

Civilization***
US 1916 68m (1931 'sound' version)
    bw silent
Triangle

A mythical country starts war, but one of the
principals has a vision of Christ on the
battlefields and the king is persuaded to sign a
peace treaty.

Surprisingly impressive parable showing this
early director at his best; intended as a pacifist
tract in the middle of World War I.

w C. Gardner Sullivan d Thomas Ince
ph Irwin Willat

Enid Markey, Howard Hickman, J. Barney
Sherry

The Clairvoyant*
GB 1934 80m bw
Gainsborough (Michael Balcon)

A fraudulent mindreader predicts a disaster
which comes true.
Effective minor suspenser on predictable but
enjoyable lines.

w Charles Bennett, Bryan Edgar Wallace,
Robert Edmunds d Maurice Elvey ph Glen
MacWilliams

Claude Rains, Fay Wray, Jane Baxter, Mary
Clare, Athole Stewart, Ben Field, Felix
Aylmer, Donald Calthrop

Clambake
US 1967 98m Techniscope
UA / Rhodes (Laven–Gardner–Levy)

The son of an oil millionaire sets out to see
life.
Painless, forgettable star vehicle.

w Arthur Browne Jnr d Arthur H. Nadel
ph William Margulies m Jeff Alexander

Elvis Presley, Shelley Fabares, Bill Bixby,
James Gregory, Will Hutchins, Gary Merrill

Clarence the Cross-Eyed Lion
US 1965 98m Metrocolor
MGM (Leonard Kaufman)

Adventures of animal farmers in Africa.
Amiable theatrical 'pilot' for the Daktari TV
series.

w Alan Caillou, Marshall Thompson, Art
Arthur d Andrew Marton ph Lamar Boren

Marshall Thompson, Betsy Drake, Richard
Haydn, Cheryl Miller

Clash by Night*
US 1952 105m bw
RKO (Harriet Parsons) (A Wald–Krasna
Production)

In a northern fishing village, jealousy and
near-tragedy are occasioned by the return
home of a hardened girl from the big city.
Absurdly overblown melodrama of the Anna
Christie school, burdened with significance and
doggedly acted by a remarkable cast.

w Alfred Hayes, play Clifford Odets d Fritz
Lang ph Nicholas Musuraca m Roy Webb

Barbara Stanwyck, Paul Douglas, Robert
Ryan, Marilyn Monroe, J. Carrol Naish, Keith
Andes

'When Stanwyck snarls into a pub and belts
down a straight shot, we think we're watching
a remake of Anna Christie; when she is shyly
and ineptly courted by Douglas we think it's a
remake of Min and Bill; a sub-plot involving
Monroe and Andes plays like Gidget Faces an
Identity Crisis.'—Kit Parker catalogue

Class of '44
US 1973 95m Technicolor Panavision
Warner (Paul Bogart)

Sex problems of college students during World
War II.
Thin sequel to Summer of '42, nostalgic to
Americans over forty but not much of a trip
for anyone else.

w Herman Raucher d Paul Bogart
ph Andrew Laszlo m David Shire

Gary Grimes, Jerry Houser, Oliver Conant,
William Atherton, Sam Bottoms, Deborah
Winters

The Class of Miss McMichael
GB 1978 90m colour
Brut / Kettledrum (Judd Bernard)

A dedicated schoolmistress has no chance
against her slum surroundings.
The Blackboard Jungle lives on, very boringly.

w Judd Bernard, novel Sandy Hutson
d Silvio Narizzano ph Alex Thomson
m Stanley Myers

Glenda Jackson, Oliver Reed, John Standing,
Michael Murphy, Rosalind Cash

'Poorly mannered, simple minded, badly
disciplined . . . gives social science a bad
name.'—Variety

Claudelle Inglish
US 1961 99m bw
Warner (Leonard Freeman)
GB title: Young and Eager

A poor farmer's daughter scorns a wealthy
man for a succession of young studs.
Would-be sensational novelette from the
author of Tobacco Road; it does not begin to
be interesting.

w Leonard Freeman, novel Erskine Caldwell
d Gordon Douglas ph Ralph Woolsey
m Howard Jackson

Diane McBain, Arthur Kennedy, Constance
Ford, Chad Everett, Claude Akins, Will
Hutchins, Robert Colbert, Ford Rainey,
James Bell

Claudia•••
US 1943   92m   bw
TCF (William Perlberg)

A middle-class husband helps his child-wife to mature.

Typical of the best of Hollywood's 'woman's pictures' of the period, this is a pleasant domestic comedy-drama featuring recognizably human characters in an agreeable setting.

w Morrie Ryskind, *novel* and *play Rose Franken* d Edmund Goulding *ph* Leon Shamroy *m* Alfred Newman

Dorothy McGuire (her film debut), *Robert Young, Ina Claire*, Reginald Gardiner, Olga Baclanova, Jean Howard, Elsa Janssen

Claudia and David•
US 1946   78m   bw
TCF (William Perlberg)

Claudia and her husband survive assorted crises including their son's illness and David's involvement in a car crash.

Patchwork sequel to *Claudia*, quite pleasant but obviously contrived quickly from scraps.

w Rose Franken, William Brown Meloney d Walter Lang *ph* Joseph La Shelle *m* Cyril Mockridge

Dorothy McGuire, Robert Young, Mary Astor, John Sutton, Gail Patrick, Florence Bates

The Clay Pigeon••
US 1949   63m   bw
RKO (Herman Schlom)

An amnesiac sailor finds himself courtmartialled for treason, but discovers the real culprit.

Tidily efficient second feature thriller; good enjoyable stuff of its kind.

w Carl Foreman d Richard Fleischer ph Robert de Grasse m Paul Sawtell

Bill Williams, Barbara Hale, Richard Quine, Richard Loo, Frank Fenton

Cleo from Five to Seven•
France / Italy 1961   90m   part colour
Rome / Paris (Bruno Drigo)

A girl waiting for the result of a medical examination wanders around Paris thinking she has cancer.

Impressively handled character sketch with gratifying attention to detail.

wd Agnès Varda ph Jean Rabier m Michel Legrand

Corinne Marchand, Antoine Bourseiller, Dorothée Blanck, Michel Legrand

Cleopatra••
US 1934   101m   bw
Paramount / Cecil B. de Mille

After Julius Caesar's death, Cleopatra turns her attention to Mark Antony.

More of the vices than the virtues of its producer are notable in this fustian epic, which is almost but not quite unwatchable because of its stolid pace and miscasting. Some of the action montages and the barge scene, however, are superb cinema.

w Waldemar Young, Vincent Lawrence d Cecil B. de Mille ph Victor Milner m Rudolph Kopp

Claudette Colbert, Henry Wilcoxon (Antony), Warren William (Caesar), Gertrude Michael, Joseph Schildkraut, Ian Keith, C. Aubrey Smith, Leonard Mudie, Irving Pichel, Arthur Hohl

'It is remarkable how Cecil B. de Mille can photograph so much on such a vast scale and still say nothing . . . it reeks of so much pseudo-artistry, vulgarity, philistinism, sadism, that it can only be compared with the lowest form of contemporary culture: Hitlerism. This is the type of "culture" that will be fed to the audience of Fascist America.'—*Irving Lerner, 1968*

'He has certainly made the most sumptuous of Roman circuses out of Roman history . . . a constant succession of banquets, dancers, triumphs, and a fleet set on fire.'—*The Times*

'The love affair that shook the world!'— *publicity*

AA: Victor Milner
AAN: best picture

Cleopatra
US 1963   243m   De Luxe   Todd-AO
TCF (Walter Wanger)

The unsurprising story is told at inordinate length and dullness in this ill-starred epic, one of the most heralded, and mismanaged, in film history. (Its story is best told in the producer's *My Life with Cleopatra*.) The most expensive film ever made, for various reasons which do not appear on the screen.

w Joseph L. Mankiewicz, Ranald MacDougall, Sidney Buchman, and others d Joseph L. Mankiewicz (and others) ph Leon Shamroy m Alex North ad John de Cuir, Jack Martin Smith, and others

Elizabeth Taylor, Richard Burton, Rex Harrison, Pamela Brown, George Cole, Hume Cronyn, Cesare Danova, Kenneth Haigh, Andrew Keir, Martin Landau, Roddy McDowall, Robert Stephens, Francesca Annis, Martin Benson, Herbert Berghof, Grégoire Aslan, Richard O'Sullivan

'Whatever was interesting about it clearly ended up somewhere else: on the cutting room floor, in various hotel rooms, in the newspaper columns . . . it lacks not only the intelligent spectacle of *Lawrence of Arabia* but the spectacular unintelligence of a Cecil B. de Mille product . . .'—*John Simon*
'The small screen does more than justice to this monumental mouse.'—*Judith Crist*
'I only came to see the asp.'—*Charles Addams*

AA: Leon Shamroy
AAN: best picture; Alex North; Rex Harrison

Cleopatra Jones
US 1973 89m Technicolor Panavision

A black female CIA agent eliminates a ring of dope peddlers. Grotesque comic strip fantasy with a high mortality rate. Tamara Dobson, Shelley Winters, Bernie Casey, Brenda Sykes. Written by Max Julien and Sheldon Keller; directed by Jack Starrett; for Warner. 'It hampers the cause of racial entente more effectively than any work since *Uncle Tom's Cabin.*'—*John Baxter, MFB.*

The Climax*
US 1944 86m Technicolor
Universal (George Waggner)

A young opera singer is hypnotized by a mad doctor, who has kept his murdered mistress embalmed for ten years.
Gothic romantic melodrama invented to capitalize on the success—and the sets—of *Phantom of the Opera.* Curiously endearing, with a good eye-rolling part for Karloff.

w Curt Siodmak, Lynn Starling, *play* Edward Cochran d George Waggner ph Hal Mohr, W. Howard Greene m Edward Ward

Boris Karloff, Susanna Foster, Gale Sondergaard, Turhan Bey, Thomas Gomez, Scotty Beckett
'All quite unalarming, which is a bit of a handicap.'—*New Yorker, 1978*

The Clinging Vine*
US 1926 71m (24 fps) bw silent
Cecil B. de Mille

The president's secretary is the real driving force of a paint company, but finds that love is more important than business.
Interesting silent predecessor of many career girl comedies of the thirties and forties.

w Jeannie McPherson d Paul Sloane

Leatrice Joy, Tom Moore, Toby Claude, Robert Edeson

Clive of India*
US 1935 90m bw
TCF (Darryl F. Zanuck, William Goetz, Raymond Griffith)

The life of the 18th-century empire builder, with special emphasis on his marriage.
A very tame and now faded epic, with more romance than adventure. The production relies more on stars than technique, but it works.

w W. P. Lipscomb, R. J. Minney, from their play d Richard Boleslawski ph Peverell Marley m Alfred Newman

Ronald Colman, Loretta Young, Colin Clive, Francis Lister, Montagu Love, Robert Greig, Leo G. Carroll, C. Aubrey Smith, Mischa Auer
'Patriotic pageantry, undistorted by facts.'—*J. R. Parish*

Cloak and Dagger*
US 1946 106m bw
United States Pictures (Milton Sperling)

A physics professor joins the secret service and is parachuted into Germany to interview a kidnapped scientist.
Supposedly authoritative espionage adventure which turned out dull and humourless; plot routine, direction absent-minded.

w Albert Maltz, Ring Lardner Jnr d Fritz Lang ph Sol Polito m Max Steiner

Gary Cooper, Lilli Palmer, Robert Alda, Vladimir Sokoloff, J. Edward Bromberg, Ludwig Stossel, Helene Thimig, Marc Lawrence
'Just a B plot dressed up in A trimmings.'—*Newsweek*
'The moment he fell in love was his moment of greatest danger!'—*ad line*

Clochemerle
France 1948 93m bw
Cinéma Productions (Ralph Baum)

The progressive mayor of a French village erects a gentlemen's convenience in the main street and shocks the local reactionaries.
Most of the book's political satire was ironed out in this cheap and opportunist production which got a few easy laughs but failed to sustain itself.

w Gabriel Chevalier, from his novel d Pierre Chénal ph Robert Le Fèbvre m Henri Sauguet

Brochard, Maximilienne, Simone Michels, Jane Marken, Paul Demange, Felix Oudart, Saturnin Fabre

The Clock**
US 1945 90m bw
MGM (Arthur Freed)
GB title: *Under the Clock*

A girl meets a soldier at New York's Grand
Central Station and marries him during his
24-hour leave.

Everyone now seems far too nice in this
winsome romance full of comedy cameos and
real New York locations, but if you can relive
the wartime mood it still works as a corrective
to the Betty Grable glamour pieces.

w Robert Nathan, Joseph Schrank, *story* Paul
and Pauline Gallico *d Vincente Minnelli*
ph George Folsey *m* George Bassman

Judy Garland, Robert Walker, James
Gleason, Lucile Gleason, Keenan Wynn,
Marshall Thompson, Chester Clute

'Sweetly charming, if maybe too irresistible
. . . fortunately the director fills the edges with
comic characters.'—*New Yorker, 1978*

'The emotion may have been honest, but
the method was too rich for my eyes, and the
writing as used on the screen too weak for my
mind.'—*Stephen Longstreet*

'Strictly a romance . . . safely told,
disappointing and angering in the thought of
the great film it might have been.'—*James
Agee*

A Clockwork Orange*
GB 1971 136m colour
Warner / Polaris (Bernard Williams)

In a future Britain of desolation and violence,
a young gangster guilty of rape and murder
obtains a release from prison after being
experimentally brainwashed: he finds society
more violent than it was in his time.

A repulsive film in which intellectuals have
found acres of social and political meaning;
the average judgement is likely to remain that
it is pretentious and nasty rubbish for sick
minds who do not mind jazzed-up images and
incoherent sound.

wd Stanley Kubrick, *novel* Anthony Burgess
ph John Alcott *m* Walter Carlos *pd* John
Barry

Malcolm McDowell, Michael Bates, Adrienne
Corri, Patrick Magee, Warren Clarke

'Very early there are hints of triteness and
insecurity, and before half an hour is over it
begins to slip into tedium . . . Inexplicably the
script leaves out Burgess' reference to the
title.'—*Stanley Kauffmann*

'It might be the work of a strict and exacting
German professor who set out to make a
porno violent sci-fi comedy.'—*New Yorker,
1980*

AAN: best picture; Stanley Kubrick (as writer
and director)

Close Encounters of the Third Kind*
US 1977 135m Metrocolor Panavision
Columbia / EMI (Julia and Michael Phillips)

A series of UFOs takes Indiana by surprise,
and a workman is led by intuition and
detection to the landing site which has been
concealed from the public.

There's a lot of padding in this slender fantasy,
which has less plot and much less suspense
than *It Came from Outer Space* which was
made on a tiny budget in 1955; but the
technical effects are masterly though their
exposure is over-prolonged, and the
benevolent mysticism filled a current
requirement of popular taste, accounting for
the enormous box-office success of a basically
flawed film. Much of the dialogue is inaudible.

wd Steven Spielberg *ph* Vilmos Zsigmond
m John Williams *sp Douglas Trumbull*
pd Joe Alves

Richard Dreyfuss, Françoise Truffaut, Teri
Garr, Melinda Dillon, Cary Guffey

'It somehow combines Disney and 1950s SF
and junk food into the most persuasive (if
arrested) version of the American dream
yet.'—*Time Out*
† The cost of this film was estimated at
20,000,000 dollars.
†† In 1980 a 'special edition' was released with
some success: this pared down the idiotic
middle section and extended the final scenes of
the space ship, including some new interiors.

AA: Vilmos Zsigmond
AAN: direction; John Williams; Melinda
Dillon

Close to My Heart
US 1951 90m bw
Warner (William Jacobs)

An adopted baby is discovered to have a
murderer for a father; but environment is
proved to be more important than heredity.
Routine sentimental drama.

wd William Keighley, *story* A Baby for Midge
by James R. Webb *ph* Robert Burks *m* Max
Steiner

Ray Milland, Gene Tierney, Fay Bainter,
Howard St John, Mary Beth Hughes

Closely Observed Trains**
Czechoslovakia 1966 92m bw
Ceskoslovensky Film (Zdenek Oves)

During World War II, an apprentice railway
guard at a country station falls in love and
becomes a saboteur.

Warm, amusingly detailed comedy with a disconcerting downbeat ending.

wd Jiri Menzel, novel Bohumil Hrabal *ph* Jaromir Sofr *m* Jiri Pavlik

Vaclav Neckar, Jitka Bendova, Vladimir Valenta, Josef Somr

'Like Forman, Menzel seems incapable of being unkind to anybody.'—*Tom Milne*

AA: best foreign film

Cloud Dancer

US 1977 108m colour

Episodes in the life of a stunt flyer. Technically proficient, loosely assembled amble through the problems of a man with an obsession for danger; not a great crowd-puller. David Carradine, Jennifer O'Neill, Joseph Bottoms, Albert Salmi, Salome Jens, Colleen Camp. Written by William Goodhart; directed by Barry Brown; for Melvin Simon.

Cloudburst

GB 1951 92m bw

A vengeful code expert goes after the criminals who ran down his wife in making a getaway. Watchable potboiler. Robert Preston, Elizabeth Sellars, Colin Tapley, Sheila Burrell, Harold Lang. Written by Leo Marks; directed by Francis Searle; for Hammer.

The Clouded Yellow*

GB 1950 96m bw
Sydney Box (Betty Box)

A sacked secret service agent gets work tending a butterfly collection and finds that this involves him in a murder plot. Implausible but quite engaging thriller in the Hitchcock style, involving a chase across the Lake District.

w Janet Green, Eric Ambler *d* Ralph Thomas *ph* Geoffrey Unsworth

Trevor Howard, Jean Simmons, Barry Jones, Sonia Dresdel, Maxwell Reed, Kenneth More, André Morell

The Clown

US 1952 91m bw
MGM (William H. Wright)

A drunken clown, once a great star, is idolized by his son who believes in a comeback. Maudlin reworking of *The Champ* (qv), with not a surprise in the plot and a star way over the top.

w Martin Rackin *d* Robert Z. Leonard *ph* Paul C. Vogel *m* David Rose

Red Skelton, Jane Greer, Tim Considine, Loring Smith, Philip Ober

Cluny Brown**

US 1946 100m bw
TCF (Ernst Lubitsch)

A plumber's niece goes into service and falls for a Czech refugee guest.
Romantic comedy in a never-never pre-war England; it does no more than poke casual fun at upper-class conventions, but the smooth direction and some excellent character comedy keep it well afloat.

w Samuel Hoffenstein, Elizabeth Reinhardt, *novel* Margery Sharp *d* Ernst Lubitsch *ph* Joseph La Shelle *m* Cyril Mockridge, Emil Newman

Jennifer Jones, Charles Boyer, *Richard Haydn, Una O'Connor*, Peter Lawford, Helen Walker, Reginald Gardiner, Reginald Owen, C. Aubrey Smith, Sara Allgood, Ernest Cossart, Florence Bates, Billy Bevan

Coal Miner's Daughter*

US 1980 124m Technicolor
Universal (Bob Larson)

The wife of a Kentucky hillbilly becomes a pop star.
'With-it' version of the old show business story: gradual success, stardom, nervous breakdown, reconciliation. Based on the life of Loretta Lynn, but mainly notable for its depiction of backwoods Kentucky.

w Tom Rickman *d* Michael Apted *ph* Ralf D. Bode *md* Owen Bradley *pd* John W. Corso

Sissy Spacek, Tommy Lee Jones, Levon Helm, Jennifer Beasley, Phyllis Boyens

AA: Sissy Spacek
AAN: best film; Tom Rickman; Ralf D. Bode; editing (Arthur Schmidt); art direction (John W. Corso, John M. Dwyer)

Cobra Woman

US 1944 71m Technicolor
U-I (George Waggner)

A South Seas girl is abducted by snake worshippers ruled by her evil twin.
A monument of undiluted hokum with some amusing sets and performances but not enough self-mockery in the script.

w Richard Brooks, Gene Lewis *d* Robert Siodmak *ph* George Robinson, W. Howard Greene *m* Edward Ward

Maria Montez, Jon Hall, Sabu, Lon Chaney Jnr, Mary Nash, Edgar Barrier, Lois Collier, Samuel S. Hinds, Moroni Olsen

The Cobweb

US 1955 124m Eastmancolor
Cinemascope
MGM (John Houseman)

Tensions among the staff of a private mental clinic reach a new high over the purchase of curtains.

The patients seem saner than the doctors in this strained and verbose character drama which despite its cast and big studio look never begins to engage the interest.

w John Paxton, *novel* William Gibson
d Vincente Minnelli *ph* George Folsey
m Leonard Rosenman

Richard Widmark, Lauren Bacall, Charles Boyer, *Lillian Gish*, Gloria Grahame, John Kerr, Susan Strasberg, *Oscar Levant*, Tommy Rettig, Paul Stewart, Adèle Jergens
  'An overwrought and elaborately artificial exercise, made scarcely more plausible by reliance on the basic jargon of psychiatry.'— *Penelope Houston*

The Cockeyed Cowboys of Calico County
US 1969   99m   Technicolor

A western blacksmith stops working when his mail order bride doesn't arrive. Styleless American rehash of *La Femme du Boulanger*, with all concerned trying too hard. Dan Blocker, Nanette Fabray, Mickey Rooney. Written by Ranald MacDougall; directed by Tony Leader; for Universal.

The Cockeyed Miracle
US 1946   92m   bw

Family ghosts return to sort out domestic chaos. Moderate 'Topper'-style comedy with amiable cast: Frank Morgan, Cecil Kellaway, Gladys Cooper, Audrey Totter, Marshall Thompson, Leon Ames. Written by Karen de Wolf, from a play by George Seaton; directed by S. Sylvan Simon; for MGM. (GB title: *Mr Griggs Returns*.)

The Cockeyed World*
US 1929   115m   bw
Fox

Further adventures of Sergeants Flagg and Quirt, the boisterous heroes of *What Price Glory*.

Lively early talkie; the adventure comedy remains interesting, though the technique is badly faded.

w William K. Wells, Laurence Stallings, Michael Anderson, Wilson Mizner, Tom Barry d Raoul Walsh ph Arthur Edeson

Victor McLaglen, Edmund Lowe, Lili Damita, Lelia Karnelly, El Brendel, Bobby Burns, Stuart Erwin

Cockfighter
US 1974   83m   Metrocolor
Rio Pinto / New World / Artists
  Entertainment Complex (Roger Corman)
aka: *Born to Kill*

A professional cockfighter ends a run of bad luck but loses his girl.

Not badly made but rather seedy film about appalling people.

w Charles Willeford, from his novel d Monte Hellman ph Nestor Almendros m Michael Franks

Warren Oates, Richard B. Shull, Harry Dean Stanton, Ed Begley Jnr, Laurie Bird, Troy Donahue

Cockleshell Heroes
GB 1955   97m   Technicolor
  Cinemascope
Columbia / Warwick (Phil C. Samuel)

During World War II, ten marines are trained to travel by canoe into Bordeaux harbour and attach limpet mines to German ships.

Absolutely predictable semi-documentary war heroics, with barrack-room humour turning eventually into tragedy. The familiar elements, including a display of stiff upper lips, ensured box office success.

w Bryan Forbes, Richard Maibaum d Jose Ferrer ph John Wilcox, Ted Moore m John Addison

Jose Ferrer, *Trevor Howard*, Dora Bryan, Victor Maddern, Anthony Newley, Peter Arne, David Lodge, Walter Fitzgerald, Beatrice Campbell

The Cocoanuts**
US 1929   96m   bw
Paramount (Walter Wanger, James R.
  Cown)

A chiselling hotel manager tries to get in on the Florida land boom.

Considering its age and the dismal prints which remain, this is a remarkably lively if primitive first film by the Marxes, with some good routines among the excess footage.

w George S. Kaufman, Morrie Ryskind
d Robert Florey ph George Folsey
m / ly Irving Berlin

The Four Marx Brothers, Margaret Dumont, Oscar Shaw, Mary Eaton, Kay Francis, Basil Ruysdael
  'The camerawork showed all the mobility of a concrete fire hydrant caught in a winter freeze.'—*Paul D. Zimmermann*

Coconut Grove
US 1938   85m   bw
Paramount (George Arthur)

A band is fired from an excursion boat but makes it big in a Los Angeles night club.
Vacuous comedy musical with a watchable number or two.

w Sy Bartlett, Olive Cooper d Alfred Santell ph Leo Tover songs various

Fred MacMurray, Harriet Hilliard, The Yacht Club Boys, Ben Blue, Eve Arden, Billy Lee, Rufe Davis

Coiffeur pour Dames
France 1952 87m approx bw
Hoche (Jean Boyer)
GB title: An Artist with Ladies

A Provençal sheep shearer becomes a fashionable ladies' hairdresser with a Champs-Élysées salon, and finds that his clients are all susceptible to his charms.
Obvious star comedy with a fair measure of laughs; more in fact than the much later Shampoo.

w Serge Véber, Jean Boyer, play P. Armont, M. Gerbidon d Jean Boyer ph Charles Suin m Paul Misraki

Fernandel, Blanchette Crunoy, Renée Devillers, Arlette Poirier

Cold Turkey*
US 1970 102m De Luxe
UA / Tandem / DFI (Bud Yorkin, Norman Lear)

A tobacco company offers 25 million dollars to any town which can give up smoking for thirty days.
Rather wild and strained but sporadically amusing satirical comedy, aggressively littered with unpleasant detail.

w Norman Lear, novel I'm Giving Them Up for Good by Margaret and Neil Rau d Norman Lear ph Charles F. Wheeler m Randy Newman

Dick Van Dyke, Pippa Scott, Tom Poston, Edward Everett Horton, Bob Newhart, Vincent Gardenia, Jean Stapleton

'An eager desire to debunk and shock at the same time.'—David McGillivray

A Cold Wind in August*
US 1960 77m bw
UA / Troy Films (Robert L. Ross, Philip Hazleton)

An ageing stripper seduces a 17-year-old janitor but the affair ends when he sees her do her act.
Roughly-made, well-acted sex drama which at the time seemed mildly shocking but can only survive for its central acting performance.

w Burton Wohl, from his novel d Alexander Singer ph Floyd Crosby m Gerald Fried

Lola Albright, Scott Marlowe, Joe de Santis, Herschel Bernardi

The Colditz Story**
GB 1954 97m bw
British Lion / Ivan Foxwell

Adventures of British POWs in the German maximum security prison in Saxony's Colditz Castle during World War II.
Probably the most convincing of the British accounts of POW life, with a careful balance of tragedy and comedy against a background of humdrum, boring daily existence. A TV series followed in 1972.

w Guy Hamilton, Ivan Foxwell, book P. R. Reid d Guy Hamilton ph Gordon Dines m Francis Chagrin

John Mills, Eric Portman, Christopher Rhodes, Lionel Jeffries, Bryan Forbes, Ian Carmichael, Richard Wattis, Frederick Valk, Anton Diffring, Eugene Deckers, Theodore Bikel

The Collector*
US 1965 119m Technicolor
Columbia (Jud Kinberg, John Kohn)

An inhibited young butterfly specialist kidnaps a girl to add to his collection.
Talkative and unrewarding suspenser with pretensions, sluggishly handled and not very interestingly acted.

w Stanley Mann, John Kohn, novel John Fowles d William Wyler ph Robert L. Surtees, Robert Krasker m Maurice Jarre

Terence Stamp, Samantha Eggar, Mona Washbourne

AAN: Stanley Mann, John Kohn; William Wyler; Samantha Eggar

Colleen*
US 1936 89m bw
Warner (Robert Lord)

Boy meets Irish girl in New York.
Typical light musical of the period with standard studio talent.

w Peter Milne, F. Hugh Herbert, Sig Herzig d Alfred E. Green ph Byron Haskin, Sol Polito m / ly Harry Warren, Al Dubin ch Bobby Connolly gowns Orry-Kelly

Dick Powell, Ruby Keeler, Jack Oakie, Joan Blondell, Hugh Herbert, Louise Fazenda, Paul Draper, Marie Wilson, Luis Alberni, Hobart Cavanaugh, Berton Churchill

College Holiday
US 1936 87m bw
Paramount (Harlan Thompson)

Bright young specimens are invited to spend a summer with a lady hotelier interested in eugenics.
Boisterous fun and games which may have seemed funny at the time.

w J. P. McEvoy, Harlan Ware, Jay Gorney, Henry Myers *d* Frank Tuttle *ph* Theodor Sparkuhl *songs* various

Jack Benny, George Burns, Gracie Allen, Mary Boland, Martha Raye, Etienne Girardot, Marsha Hunt, Leif Erickson, Eleanore Whitney, Johnny Downs, Olympe Bradna, Ben Blue, Jed Prouty

College Humor
US 1933 84m bw
Paramount

A freshman discovers that football and necking are at least as important as studies.
Easy-going comedy-musical which helped to establish its star.

w Claude Binyon, Frank Butler, *story* Dean Fales *d* Wesley Ruggles *ph* Leo Tover

Bing Crosby, Jack Oakie, George Burns, Gracie Allen, Richard Arlen, Mary Carlisle

College Swing
US 1938 86m bw
Paramount (Lewis Gensler)
GB title: *Swing, Teacher, Swing*

A dumb girl must graduate if a college is to inherit a fortune.
Mild comedy more notable for its cast than its script.

w Walter de Leon, Francis Martin *d* Raoul Walsh *ph* Victor Milner *songs* various

George Burns, Gracie Allen, Martha Raye, Bob Hope, Edward Everett Horton, Florence George, Ben Blue, Betty Grable, Jackie Coogan, John Payne, Cecil Cunningham, Robert Cummings

Colonel Effingham's Raid
US 1946 70m bw
TCF (Lamar Trotti)
GB title: *Man of the Hour*

A retired southern colonel tries to straighten out a corrupt Georgia town.
Competent, unsurprising programmer.

w Kathryn Scola, *novel* Berry Fleming *d* Irving Pichel *ph* Edward Cronjager *m* Cyril Mockridge

Charles Coburn, Joan Bennett, William Eythe, Allyn Joslyn, Elizabeth Patterson,
Donald Meek, Frank Craven, Thurston Hall, Cora Witherspoon, Emory Parnell, Henry Armetta, Roy Roberts, Charles Trowbridge

Colorado Territory*
US 1949 93m bw
Warner (Anthony Veiller)

An outlaw escapes from prison planning one last robbery but is shot in the attempt.
Moderate western remake of *High Sierra.*

w John Twist, Edmund H. North *d* Raoul Walsh *ph* Sid Hickox *m* David Buttolph

Joel McCrea, Virginia Mayo, Dorothy Malone, Henry Hull, John Archer, James Mitchell, Morris Ankrum, Basil Ruysdael, Frank Puglia

The Colossus of New York
US 1958 70m bw

An international scientist is killed in an accident; his father puts his brain into a robot, which goes on the rampage. Absurd horror comic for kids, with hilariously unexplained detail and poor technical effects. Otto Kruger, Ross Martin, Robert Hutton, John Baragrey, Mala Powers. Written by Thelma Schnee; directed by Eugene Lourie; for William Alland / Paramount.

The Colossus of Rhodes
Italy 1960   129m   Technicolor
SuperTotalScope

In 300 BC, a huge statue doubles as a fortress to prevent the Phoenicians from invading.
Good-looking spectacle with the usual muddled script. Rory Calhoun, Lea Massari, Georges Marchal. Written by Sergio Leone and seven others; directed by Sergio Leone; for Michele Scaglione / MGM.

Colt 45
US 1950   74m   Technicolor

A new kind of gun, intended to bring law and order to the west, gets into the wrong hands.
Routine, watchable western which achieved a surprising popularity. Randolph Scott, Zachary Scott, Ruth Roman, Lloyd Bridges. Written by Thomas Blackburn; directed by Edwin L. Marin; for Warner. (American TV title: *Thundercloud.*)

Coma*
US 1978   113m   Metrocolor
MGM (Martin Erlichman)

A lady doctor suspects that patients are being put deliberately into coma so that their organs can be sold, and finds herself in deadly peril.
Hitchcockian suspense thriller with nobody

but the audience believing the heroine; the fact that there are more dead than living characters makes it slightly too ghoulish at times.

wd Micheal Crichton, *novel* Robin Cook *ph* Victor J. Kemper, Gerald Hirschfeld *m* Jerry Goldsmith *pd* Albert Brenner

Geneviève Bujold, Michael Douglas, Richard Widmark, Elizabeth Ashley, Rip Torn, Lois Chiles, Harry Rhodes

Comanche
US 1955   87m   De Luxe   Cinemascope

In 1875 New Mexico, a renegade Indian prevents peace between white and red man. Cheerful action western, satisfying to the easily pleased. Dana Andrews, Kent Smith, Nestor Paiva, Henry Brandon, John Litel, Lowell Gilmore, Mike Mazurki. Written by Carl Krueger; directed by George Sherman; for Carl Krueger / UA.

Comanche Station
US 1960   74m   Technicolor
Cinemascope

A man seeks his wife, taken prisoner by Indians. Below par star western, indifferently plotted. Randolph Scott, Nancy Gates, Claude Akins, Skip Homeier. Written by Burt Kennedy; directed by Budd Boetticher; for Harry Joe Brown / Columbia.

Comanche Territory
US 1950   76m   Technicolor

Jim Bowie assists the Comanches against treacherous whites. Double bill western, adequate for its purpose. Maureen O'Hara, Macdonald Carey, Will Geer, Charles Drake. Written by Oscar Brodney and Louis Meltzer; directed by George Sherman; for Universal-International.

The Comancheros**
US 1961   107m   De Luxe   Cinemascope
TCF (George Sherman)

A Texas Ranger and his gambler prisoner join forces to clean up renegade gunmen operating from a remote armed compound. Easy-going, cheerfully violent western with lively roughhouse sequences.

w James Edward Grant, Clair Huffaker *d* Michael Curtiz *ph* William H. Clothier *m* Elmer Bernstein

John Wayne, Stuart Whitman, Nehemiah Persoff, Lee Marvin, Ina Balin, Bruce Cabot

Come and Get It*
US 1936   99m   bw
Samuel Goldwyn (Merritt Hulburd)

The life and loves of a lumber tycoon in 19th-century Wisconsin. Disappointingly conventional, mainly studio-bound action drama using top talent of the period.

w Jules Furthman, Jane Murfin, *novel* Edna Ferber *d* Howard Hawks, William Wyler *ph* Gregg Toland, Rudolph Maté *m* Alfred Newman

Edward Arnold, Joel McCrea, Frances Farmer, Walter Brennan, Andrea Leeds

AA: Walter Brennan

Come Back Charleston Blue*
US 1972   101m   Technicolor
Warner / Formosa (Samuel Goldwyn Jnr)

Harlem detectives Coffin Ed Johnson and Gravedigger Jones investigate the case of a long-dead gangster who seems to be still taking vengeance. Occasionally funny but disturbingly violent crime kaleidoscope with a black ambience, more sophisticated and therefore more generally acceptable than its predecessor *Cotton Comes to Harlem* (qv).

w Bontche Schweig, Peggy Elliott, *novel* The Heat's On by Chester Himes *d* Mark Warren *ph* Dick Kratina *m* Donny Hathaway

Godfrey Cambridge, Raymond St Jacques, Peter de Anda, Jonelle Allen, Percy Rodrigues, Minny Gentry

Come Back Little Sheba*
US 1952   99m   bw
Paramount (Hal B. Wallis)

An ex-alcoholic is let down not only by his slovenly wife but by the young girl he idolizes. Stagey but theatrically effective transcription of a popular domestic drama, with one outstanding performance.

w Ketti Frings, *play William Inge* *d* Daniel Mann *ph* James Wong Howe *m* Franz Waxman

Shirley Booth, Burt Lancaster, Terry Moore, Richard Jaeckel

AA: Shirley Booth
AAN: Terry Moore

Come Blow Your Horn*
US 1962   112m   Technicolor
Panavision
Paramount / Lear and Yorkin

A country boy in New York is envious of his older brother's sophisticated life. Amusing characters and funny lines permeate this stolid transcription of an early Neil Simon success; the big screen is not the place for them.

w Norman Lear, *play Neil Simon* d Bud Yorkin *ph* William Daniels *m* Nelson Riddle

Frank Sinatra, Tony Bill, Lee J. Cobb, Molly Picon, Jill St John, Barbara Rush, Dan Blocker

Come Clean**
US 1931 20m bw

Two much-married men go out for ice-cream and bring back a woman of the streets they have saved from suicide. Splendid star comedy with the famous characterizations fully rounded. Laurel and Hardy, Mae Busch, Charlie Hall, Gertrude Astor, Linda Loredo. Written by H. M. Walker; directed by James W. Horne; for Hal Roach. (NB: Remade in 1942 as *Brooklyn Orchid*, with William Bendix and Joe Sawyer.)

Come Fill the Cup*
US 1951 113m bw
Warner (Henry Blanke)

An alcoholic newspaperman cures himself, then his boss's alcoholic son who is involved with gangsters.
Unlikely but solidly entertaining melodrama, powerfully cast.

w Ivan Goff, Ben Roberts, *novel* Harlan Ware d Gordon Douglas *ph Robert Burks* m Ray Heindorf

James Cagney, Gig Young, Raymond Massey, Phyllis Thaxter, James Gleason, Selena Royle, Larry Keating

AAN: Gig Young

Come Fly with Me
US 1962 109m Metrocolor Panavision
MGM / Anatole de Grunwald

The romantic adventures of three air hostesses.
Good-looking girls and airplanes but little else make thin entertainment.

w William Roberts d Henry Levin *ph* Oswald Morris *m* Lyn Murray

Hugh O'Brian, Dolores Hart, Karl Malden, Pamela Tiffin, Lois Nettleton, Karl Boehm

Come Live with Me*
US 1941 86m bw
MGM (Clarence Brown)

In order to stay in America, a girl refugee from Vienna arranges a strictly platonic marriage with a struggling author.
Hypnotically predictable comedy, quite well presented and performed.

w Patterson McNutt, Virginia Van Upp d Clarence Brown *ph* George Folsey m Herbert Stothart

James Stewart, Hedy Lamarr, Ian Hunter, Verree Teasdale, Donald Meek, Barton MacLane, *Adeline de Walt Reynolds*

Come Next Spring*
US 1955 92m Trucolor
Republic

A drunkard returns to his Arkansas farm family and wins the respect of them and the community.
D. W. Griffith-type pastoral melodrama which surprisingly works pretty well and leaves one with the intended warm glow.

w Montgomery Pittman d R. G. Springsteen *ph* Jack Marta m Max Steiner

Ann Sheridan, Steve Cochran, Walter Brennan, Sherry Jackson, Richard Eyer, Edgar Buchanan, Sonny Tufts, Mae Clarke
'An unpretentious film with a good deal of charm.'—*MFB*

The Come On
US 1956 83m bw Superscope
AA (Lindley Parsons)

Husband and wife confidence tricksters get homicidal when she falls in love.
In trade parlance, strictly a lower berth item; but with points of mild interest.

w Warren Douglas, *novel* Whitman Chambers d Russell Birdwell *ph* Ernest Haller m Paul Dunlap

Anne Baxter, Sterling Hayden, John Hoyt, Jesse White, Paul Picerni

Come on George*
GB 1939 88m bw
ATP / Ealing (Jack Kitchin)

A stableboy calms a nervous racehorse and rides him to victory.
Standard comedy vehicle, well mounted, with the star at his box office peak.

w Anthony Kimmins, Leslie Arliss, Val Valentine d Anthony Kimmins *ph* Ronald Neame, Gordon Dines m Ernest Irving

George Formby, Pat Kirkwood, Joss Ambler, Meriel Forbes, Cyril Raymond, George Carney, Ronald Shiner

Come September
US 1961 112m Technicolor
CinemaScope
Universal / 7 Pictures Corporation / Raoul Walsh Enterprises (Robert Arthur)

A wealthy American discovers that his Italian villa is being used as a hotel by his once-a-year mistress, who is about to marry.
Clumsy sex farce with lush trimmings and

generation gap asides; effort more noticeable than achievement.

w Stanley Shapiro, Maurice Richlin d Robert Mulligan ph William Daniels m Hans J. Salter

Rock Hudson, Gina Lollobrigida, Sandra Dee, Bobby Darin, Walter Slezak, Brenda de Banzie, Joel Grey, Rosanna Rory, Ronald Howard

Come to the Stable*
US 1949 94m bw
TCF (Samuel G. Engel)

Two French nuns arrive in New England to build a local hospital, and melt the hearts of the local grumps.
This old-time charmer simply brims with sweetness and light and is produced with high-class studio efficiency.

w Oscar Millard, Sally Benson, story Clare Boothe Luce d Henry Koster ph Joseph La Shelle md Lionel Newman m Cyril Mockridge

Loretta Young, Celeste Holm, Hugh Marlowe, Elsa Lanchester, Thomas Gomez, Dorothy Patrick, Basil Ruysdael, Dooley Wilson, Regis Toomey, Henri Letondal

AAN: Clare Boothe Luce; Joseph La Shelle; Loretta Young; Celeste Holm; Elsa Lanchester; song 'Through a Long and Sleepless Night' (m Alfred Newman, ly Mack Gordon)

The Comedians*
US / Bermuda / France 1967 160m
  Metrocolor Panavision
MGM / Maximilian / Trianon (Peter
  Glenville)

A variety of English-speaking eccentrics are caught up in the violent events of Haiti under Papa Doc Duvalier.
Clumsy and heavy-going compression of a too-topical novel, with most of the plot left in at the expense of character. Neither entertaining nor instructive, but bits of acting please.

w Graham Greene, from his novel d Peter Glenville ph Henri Decaë m Laurence Rosenthal

Richard Burton, Elizabeth Taylor, *Alec Guinness*, Peter Ustinov, Lillian Gish, Paul Ford, Roscoe Lee Browne, James Earl Jones, Raymond St Jacques, Cicely Tyson
  'So thick and fast do the clichés come that one feels the script can only have been salvaged from some *New Statesman* competition.'—*Tom Milne*

'It's pleasant to spend two hours again in Greeneland, still well-stocked with bilious minor crucifixions, furtive fornication, cynical politics, and reluctant hope.'—*Stanley Kauffmann*

The Comedy Man*
GB 1964 92m bw
British Lion–Gray–Consort (Jon
  Pennington)

A middle-aged actor on the skids desperately rounds up his contacts and becomes the star of a TV commercial.
Determinedly depressing satirical melodrama with engaging moments; comedy emphasis would have better suited the talents.

w Peter Yeldham, *novel* Douglas Hayes d Alvin Rakoff ph Ken Hodges m Bill McGuffie

Kenneth More, Cecil Parker, Dennis Price, Billie Whitelaw, Norman Rossington, Angela Douglas, Edmund Purdom, Frank Finlay, Alan Dobie

The Comedy of Terrors*
US 1963 88m Pathecolor Panavision
Alta Vista / AIP (Anthony Carras, Richard
  Matheson)

Two impecunious funeral directors decide to speed up the demise of their prospective clients.
Disappointingly slackly-handled and rather tiresome macabre frolic, notable for a few splendid moments and an imperishable cast.

w Richard Matheson d Jacques Tourneur ph Floyd Crosby m Les Baxter

Vincent Price, Peter Lorre, Boris Karloff, Basil Rathbone, Joe E. Brown, Joyce Jameson

Comes a Horseman
US 1978 118m Technicolor
  Panavision
UA / Chartoff-Winkler (Robert Caan)

In the forties, Montana ranchers have a hard time holding onto their land against the pressures of progress and a villainous cattle baron.
Portentous and wholly unexciting modern western, not helped by a loftily unexplained title and show-off photography.

w Dennis Lynton Clark d Alan J. Pakula ph Gordon Willis m Michael Small pd George Jenkins

Jane Fonda, Jason Robards Jnr, James Caan, George Grizzard, Richard Farnsworth, Jim Davis

The Comic**
US 1969   95m   Technicolor
Columbia (Carl Reiner)

The success, downfall and old age of a silent film comedian in Hollywood.
Remarkably bright and cinematic tragi-comedy obviously based on Buster Keaton, with a *Citizen Kane*-type framework. Not a commercial success, but a must for professionals.

w Carl Reiner, Aaron Rubin d Carl Reiner
ph W. Wallace Kelley m Jack Elliott

Dick Van Dyke, Mickey Rooney (more or less playing Ben Turpin), Cornel Wilde, Carl Reiner, Michele Lee, Pert Kelton
'Offers a variety of delights.'—*Judith Crist*

Coming Home*
US 1978   128m   De Luxe
UA / Jerome Hellman

An embittered Vietnam veteran falls for the wife of a serving soldier.
Self-pitying romantic wallow which must mean more to American audiences than to others. Goodish acting.

w Waldo Salt, Robert C. Jones, *story* Nancy Dowd d Hal Ashby ph Haskell Wexler
pd Mike Haller m various

Jane Fonda, Jon Voight, Bruce Dern, Robert Carradine, Penelope Milford

The Command
US 1954   94m   Warnercolor
  Cinemascope
Warner (David Weisbart)

A cavalry troop escorts a wagon train through Indian country.
Competent but unsurprising 'second team' western.

w Russell Hughes, *novel* James Warner Bellah d David Butler ph Wilfrid M. Cline
m Dmitri Tiomkin

Guy Madison, Joan Weldon, James Whitmore, Carl Benton Reid, Harvey Lembeck, Ray Teal, Bob Nichols

Command Decision*
US 1949   111m   bw
MGM (Sidney Franklin)

War among the back-room boys; a general, his staff and his peers debate the aerial bombardment of Germany.
Plainly reproduced version of a determinedly serious play, with a remarkable cast partly at sea.

w William R. Laidlaw, George Froeschel, *play* William Wister Haines d Sam Wood
ph Harold Rosson m Miklos Rozsa

Clark Gable, Walter Pidgeon, Van Johnson, Brian Donlevy, John Hodiak, Charles Bickford, Edward Arnold, Marshall Thompson, Richard Quine, Cameron Mitchell, Clinton Sundberg, Ray Collins, Warner Anderson, John McIntire, Moroni Olsen
'Heroes, cowards, fighters, braggarts, liars . . . and what goes on in their hearts!'—*publicity*

The Commandos Strike at Dawn*
US 1942   98m   bw
Columbia (Lester Cowan)

Norwegian commandos outwit the Nazis with the help of the British navy.
Standard war adventure shot on Vancouver Island.

w Irwin Shaw, *story* C. S. Forester d John Farrow ph William C. Mellor m Louis Gruenberg

Paul Muni, Anna Lee, Lillian Gish, Cedric Hardwicke, Robert Coote, Ray Collins, Rosemary de Camp, Richard Derr, Alexander Knox, Rod Cameron

AAN: Louis Gruenberg

Common Clay
US 1930   68m   bw
Fox

A speakeasy hostess becomes maid in a wealthy household and falls in love with her betters.
Archetypal soap opera which caused a mild sensation and sent its star into half a dozen imitations.

w Jules Furthman, *novel* Cleves Kincaid
d Victor Fleming ph Glen MacWilliams

Constance Bennett, Lew Ayres, Tully Marshall, Matty Kemp, Purnell Pratt, Beryl Mercer

The Common Touch*
GB 1941   104m   bw
British National (John Baxter)

A rich young man poses as a tramp to save a dosshouse from destruction.
Naive drama with a social conscience, remade from the 1932 talkie *Dosshouse*. A brave try.

w Barbara K. Emery, Geoffrey Orme, *novel* Herbert Ayres d John Baxter

Geoffrey Hibbert, Greta Gynt, Joyce Howard, Harry Welchman, Edward Rigby, George Carney, Bransby Williams, Wally Patch, Eliot Makeham, Bernard Miles, Bill Fraser, John Longden; *guests* Sandy Macpherson, Scott Sanders, Mark Hambourg, Carrol Gibbons

Company Limited*
India 1971 112m bw
Bharat Shumshere Rana
original title: *Seemabadha*

The young export sales manager of a firm of
Delhi electrical appliance manufacturers is
saved from boredom by his wife's younger
sister.
Quietly pleasing but overlong comedy-drama
of modern urban India, very typical of its
director.

wd Satyajit Ray, novel Shankar *ph* Soumendu
Roy

Barun Chanda, Sharmilla Tagore, Parumita
Chowdhary
 'Subtle, witty, intelligent, and beautifully
acted.'—*Michael Billington, Illustrated
London News*

The Company She Keeps
US 1950 83m bw
RKO (John Houseman)

A self-sacrificing parole officer allows a
parolee to steal her fiancé.
Considering the credits, a dismally novelettish
drama of almost no interest.

w Ketti Frings *d* John Cromwell *ph* Nicholas
Musuraca *m* Leigh Harline

Lizabeth Scott, *Jane Greer*, Dennis O'Keefe,
Fay Baker, John Hoyt, James Bell, Don
Beddoe, Bert Freed

The Competition*
US 1980 129m Metrocolor
Columbia / Rastar / William Sackheim

An ageing piano prodigy has one last shot at
fame in a San Francisco piano competition.
Slightly curious, old-fashioned but heavy-
handed romance which aims to do for the
piano what *The Turning Point* did for ballet. It
doesn't sustain its length but at least the milieu
is interesting.

wd Joel Oliansky *ph* Richard H. Kline
m,md Lalo Schifrin *pd* Dale Hennesy

Richard Dreyfuss, Lee Remick, Amy Irving,
Sam Wanamaker, Joseph Cali

AAN: editing (David Blewitt); best song
('People Alone')

Compulsion**
US 1959 103m bw Cinemascope
TCF / Darryl F. Zanuck Productions (Richard
F. Zanuck)

In the twenties, two Chicago students kidnap
and murder a young boy for kicks.
Rather dogged but earnest fictionalization of
the Leopold-Loeb case with solid
performances and production.

w Richard Murphy, *play* Meyer Levin
d Richard Fleischer *ph* William C. Mellor
m Lionel Newman

Dean Stockwell, Bradford Dillman, Orson
Welles (in a cameo court appearance as
Clarence Darrow), Diane Varsi, E. G.
Marshall, Martin Milner, Richard Anderson,
Robert Simon

The Computer Wore Tennis Shoes
US 1970 90m Technicolor

While mending a computer a college student
gets an electric shock and becomes omniscient.
Ho-hum Disney comedy, eager to please but
instantly forgotten. Kurt Russell, Cesar
Romero, Joe Flynn, William Schallert, Alan
Hewitt. Written by Joseph L. McEveety;
directed by Robert Butler; for Disney.

Comrade X*
US 1940 89m bw
MGM (Gottfried Reinhardt)

An American correspondent in Russia is
blackmailed into smuggling a girl out of the
country.
Lame satirical comedy in the wake of
Ninotchka; a few good moments, but generally
heavy-handed.

w Ben Hecht, Charles Lederer, *original story*
Walter Reisch *d* King Vidor *ph* Joseph L.
Ruttenberg *m* Bronislau Kaper

Clark Gable, Hedy Lamarr, Felix Bressart,
Oscar Homolka, Eve Arden, Sig Rumann

AAN: Walter Reisch

The Concorde: Airport '79
US 1979 113m Technicolor
Universal (Jennings Lang)
GB title: *Airport '80: The Concorde*

Various disasters befall the Concorde on its
way from Washington to Paris.
Stultified final (one presumes) effort in the
Airport series; it could hardly be funnier if it
were intended as a comedy, but somehow it
entertains.

w Eric Roth *d* David Lowell Rich *ph* Philip
Lathrop *m* Lalo Schifrin

Alain Delon, Susan Blakely, Robert Wagner,
Sylvia Kristel, George Kennedy, Eddie
Albert, Bibi Andersson, John Davidson,
Martha Raye, Cicely Tyson, Mercedes
McCambridge
 'Larger-than-life characters are thrown
together on a storyboard and must fend for
themselves against attacks, chases and
assorted escapades . . . this would be soporific
even as a transatlantic inflight movie.'—
Martyn Auty, MFB

Condemned*
US 1930 86m bw
Samuel Goldwyn

A bank robber is sent to Devil's Island and
falls in love with the wife of the brutal warden.
Slow-moving but pictorially attractive
melodrama with old-style performances.

w Sidney Howard, *novel* Condemned to
Devil's Island by Blair Niles d Wesley
Ruggles *ph George Barnes, Gregg Toland
sets William Cameron Menzies*

Ronald Colman, Ann Harding, Louis
Wolheim, Dudley Digges, William Elmer
  'A piece of nonsense from which it would
appear that French convicts on Devil's Island
live a life consisting entirely of hot-towel
shaves and flirtations with the governor's
wife.'—*James Agate*

AAN: Ronald Colman

The Condemned of Altona*
Italy / France 1962 113m bw
(TCF) Titanus / SGC (Carlo Ponti)

The head of a German shipping empire
discovers he has only a few months to live and
tries to bring his family to order.
Strident intellectual melodrama whose credits
tell all. Watchable for the acting, but very
glum.

w Abby Mann, Cesare Zavattini, *play* Jean-
Paul Sartre d Vittorio de Sica *ph* Roberto
Gerardi m Dmitri Shostakovich

Fredric March, Sophia Loren, Robert
Wagner, Maximilian Schell, Françoise
Prévost, Alfredo Franchi
  'This film is such a hopeless mess that it is
difficult to know where to begin criticizing
it.'—*Tom Milne*

Condemned to Death*
GB 1932 75m bw
Twickenham (Julius Hagen)

A condemned killer hypnotizes a judge into
murdering those who turned him in.
Irresistible nonsense of the old school, with
spirited direction and a good cast.

w Bernard Merivale, Harry Fowler Mear,
Brock Williams, *play* Jack O'Lantern by
George Goodchild and James Dawson
d Walter Forde ph Sidney Blythe, William
Luff

Arthur Wontner, Gillian Lind, Edmund
Gwenn, Gordon Harker, Jane Welsh, Cyril
Raymond
  'It would be difficult to find a dull
moment.'—*The Bioscope*

Conduct Unbecoming*
GB 1975 107m Technicolor
British Lion / Crown (Michael Deeley, Barry
  Spikings)

In an officers' mess in India in the nineties, a
cadet is accused of assault on a lady but the
real culprit is a paranoic who has taken to
pigsticking in quite the wrong way.
Disappointingly flatly-handled and quite
unatmospheric picturization of an absorbing
West End melodrama. The cast is largely
wasted, but stretches of dialogue maintain
their interest.

w Robert Enders, *play* Barry England
d Michael Anderson *ph* Bob Huke
m Stanley Myers

Michael York, Stacy Keach, Trevor Howard,
Christopher Plummer, Richard Attenborough,
Susannah York, James Faulkner, James
Donald

Cone of Silence*
GB 1960 92m bw
British Lion / Bryanston (Aubrey Baring)
US title: *Trouble in the Sky*

A seasoned pilot is condemned for an error
which caused a crash and later dies in similar
circumstances. A flying examiner discovers
scientific reasons for exonerating him.
Tolerable suspense drama let down by thin
dialogue and confused characterization.

w Robert Westerby, *novel* David Beaty
d Charles Frend *ph* Arthur Grant
m Gerhard Schurmann

Michael Craig, Bernard Lee, Peter Cushing,
George Sanders, Elizabeth Seal, André
Morell, Gordon Jackson, Delphi Lawrence,
Noel Willman, Charles Tingwell

Coney Island**
US 1943 96m Technicolor
TCF (William Perlberg)

Two fairground showmen vie for the affections
of a songstress.
Brassy, simple-minded, entertaining musical.
Very typical of its time; later remade as
Wabash Avenue (qv).

w George Seaton d Walter Lang ph Ernest
Palmer *songs* Leo Robin, Ralph Rainger
m Alfred Newman ch Hermes Pan
ad Richard Day, Joseph C. Wright

Betty Grable, George Montgomery, Cesar
Romero, Charles Winninger, Phil Silvers,
Matt Briggs, Paul Hurst, Frank Orth, Andrew
Tombes, Alec Craig, Hal K. Dawson

AAN: Alfred Newman

Confession
US 1937 90m bw
Warner (Henry Blanke)

An errant mother shoots her former lover to protect her daughter.
Stilted romantic melodrama copied scene for scene from a 1936 German film *Mazurka*.

w Julius J. Epstein, Margaret Le Vino, *original screenplay* Hans Rameau *d* Joe May *ph* Sid Hickox *m* Peter Kreuder *md* Leo F. Forbstein *ad* Anton Grot

Kay Francis, Ian Hunter, Basil Rathbone, Jane Bryan, Donald Crisp, Dorothy Peterson, Laura Hope Crews, Robert Barrat

Confession
GB 1955 90m bw

A murderer stalks the priest who knows his guilt through the confessional but may not reveal it. So-so reworking of the theme that daunted Hitchcock in *I Confess*; some pleasant touches are nullified by slow pacing. Sydney Chaplin, Audrey Dalton, John Welsh, John Bentley, Peter Hammond. Written and directed by Ken Hughes; for Anglo Amalgamated.

The Confession*
France / Italy 1970 160m Eastmancolor
Films Corona / Films Pomereu / Selena
   Cinematografica (Robert Dorfmann)
original title: *L'Aveu*

In Prague in 1951, a minister is secretly imprisoned and interrogated, and finally confesses under duress to anti-communist activities.
Brutally long but frequently impressive anti-Soviet tract, extremely well acted but less exciting than *Z*. Based on a true account.

w Jorge Semprun, *book* Lise and Artur London *d* Costa-Gavras *ph* Raoul Coutard *m* not credited

Yves Montand, Simone Signoret, Gabriele Ferzetti, Michel Vitold

Confessions of a Nazi Spy***
US 1939 102m bw
Warner (Robert Lord)

How G-men ferreted out Nazis in the United States.
Topical exposé with all concerned in top form; a semi-documentary very typical of Warner product throughout the thirties and forties, from *G-Men* to *Mission to Moscow* and *I Was a Communist for the FBI*: well made, punchy, and smartly edited, with a loud moral at the end.

w Milton Krims, John Wexley, from materials gathered by former FBI agent Leon G. Turrou *d* Anatole Litvak *ph* Sol Polito *m* Max Steiner

Edward G. Robinson, Paul Lukas, George Sanders, Francis Lederer, Henry O'Neill, Lya Lys, James Stephenson, Sig Rumann, Dorothy Tree, Joe Sawyer

'The Warner brothers have declared war on Germany with this one . . . with this precedent there is no way any producer could argue against dramatizing any social or political theme on the grounds that he's afraid of domestic or foreign censorship. Everybody duck.'—*Pare Lorentz*

'Has a remarkable resemblance to a full-length *Crime Does Not Pay*.'—*David Wolff*

'One of the most sensational movie jobs on record, workmanlike in every respect and spang across the headlines.'—*Otis Ferguson*

Confessions of an Opium Eater
US 1962 85m bw
Albert Zugsmith
GB title: *Evils of Chinatown*

In San Francisco in the nineties, a seaman falls into the clutches of a tong.
The hero is called De Quincey, but that is the only association with the famous book of the same title. This absurd melodrama is just about bad enough to be funny, but not very.

w Robert Hill *d* Albert Zugsmith *ph* Joseph Biroc *m* Albert Glasser *ad* Eugene Lourié

Vincent Price, Linda Ho, Richard Loo, Philip Ahn, June Kim

'Has to be seen to be believed . . . starved girls captive in cages, secret panels, sliding doors, sewer escape routes, opium dens and nightmares . . .'—*MFB*

Confidential Agent**
US 1945 122m bw
Warner (Robert Buckner)

An emissary of Franco's Spain comes to England in the late thirties to make a munitions deal, and falls in love with the tycoon's daughter.
Heavy-going simplification of Graham Greene's lowering novel, with cast and (especially) set designers all at sea but nevertheless providing striking moments.

w Robert Buckner *d* Herman Shumlin *ph* James Wong Howe *m* Franz Waxman

Charles Boyer, Lauren Bacall, Katina Paxinou, Peter Lorre, Victor Francen, George Coulouris, Wanda Hendrix, George Zucco, Miles Mander

'In some ways an exciting and good picture, the best attempt yet, though still inadequate, to make the best of a Greene novel.'—*James Agee*

Confidential Report*

Spain 1955   99m   bw
Sevilla Studios (Louis Dolivet, Orson Welles)
aka: *Mr Arkadin*

A wealthy and powerful financier employs a young American to seek out figures from his own past, who are soon found dead . . . Silly melodrama which might have been suspenseful if done by Hitchcock, or even by Welles at his peak; as it is, weak writing and sloppy production remove most of the interest and reveal it as a very obvious bag of tricks.

wd Orson Welles   *ph* Jean Bourgoin   *m* Paul Misraki

Orson Welles, Michael Redgrave, Katina Paxinou, Akim Tamiroff, Mischa Auer, Patricia Medina, Jack Watling, Peter Van Eyck, Paola Mori, Robert Arden, Grégoire Aslan, Suzanne Flon
    'Tilted camera angles, heavy atmospheric shots, overlapping dialogue—all the trademarks are here, sometimes over-used to an almost hysterical degree, but they have little significance . . . (the film) springs not from life but from the earlier cinematic world of Welles himself and from the kind of thriller written about thirty years ago by E. Philips Oppenheim.'—*Gavin Lambert*
    'The quality of the soundtrack is quite disastrous, but there is a certain grandeur about the carelessness of the film's construction which makes one forget everything except the immediacy of the moment.'—*Basil Wright, 1972*

Confirm or Deny*

US 1941   78m   bw
TCF (Len Hammond)

An American reporter falls for a wireless operator in wartime London.
Artificial but watchable minor romantic melodrama.

w Jo Swerling, Henry Wales, Samuel Fuller   *d* Archie Mayo   *ph* Leon Shamroy

Don Ameche, Joan Bennett, Roddy McDowall, Arthur Shields, Raymond Walburn, John Loder
† Fritz Lang directed some scenes.

Conflict*

US 1945   86m   bw
Warner (William Jacobs)

A man murders his wife and is apparently haunted by her; but the odd happenings have been arranged by a suspicious psychiatrist.
Leaden and artificial melodrama with both stars miscast; a few effective moments.

w Arthur T. Horman, Dwight Taylor   *d* Curtis Bernhardt   *ph* Merritt Gerstad   *m* Frederick Hollander

Humphrey Bogart, Sydney Greenstreet, Alexis Smith, Rose Hobart, Charles Drake, Grant Mitchell

Conflict of Wings*

GB 1953   84m   Eastmancolor
Group Three (Herbert Mason)
US title: *Fuss over Feathers*

East Anglian villagers fight to save a bird sanctuary from being taken over by the RAF as a rocket range.
Sub-Ealing comedy-drama with a highly predictable outcome; generally pleasant but without much bite.

w Don Sharp, John Pudney   *d* John Eldridge   *ph* Arthur Grant   *m* Philip Green

John Gregson, Muriel Pavlow, Kieron Moore, Niall MacGinnis, Sheila Sweet, Harry Fowler, Barbara Hicks, Charles Lloyd Pack

Congo Crossing

US 1956   85m   Technicolor
U-I (Howard Christie)

Assorted fugitives from justice gather at Congotanga, which has no extradition laws.
The poor man's *Casablanca*, quite good looking but dully written and presented.

w Richard Alan Simmons   *d* Joseph Pevney   *ph* Russell Metty   *m* Joseph Gershenson

George Nader, Virginia Mayo, *Peter Lorre*, Michael Pate, Rex Ingram

Congress Dances*

Germany 1931   92m   bw
UFA (Erich Pommer)
original title: *Der Kongress Tanzt*

At the Congress of Vienna, Metternich attempts to decoy the Tsar with a countess; but the Tsar has a double.
Lubitsch-like treatment of sexual dalliance in high places; no doubt a stunner in its time, but rather faded now.

w Norbert Falk, Robert Liebmann   *d* Erik Charrell   *ph* Carl Hoffmann   *m* Werner Heymann

Conrad Veidt, Henri Garat / Willy Fritsch, Lilian Harvey

A Connecticut Yankee*
US 1931   96m   bw
Fox

A man dreams himself back to the court of
King Arthur, and teaches the Middle Ages a
thing or two about modern living.
First sound version of Mark Twain's classic
fantasy, also filmed in 1921 and 1949. Creaky
now, but amiable.

w William Conselman   d David Butler
ph Ernest Palmer

Will Rogers, Maureen O'Sullivan, Myrna Loy,
Frank Albertson, William Farnum

A Connecticut Yankee in King Arthur's Court*
US 1949   106m   Technicolor
Paramount (Robert Fellows)
GB title: *A Yankee in King Arthur's Court*

Gossamer musical version of the above with
the emphasis on song and knockabout.
Palatable, with the 'Busy Doin' Nothin' '
sequence the most memorable.

w Edmund Beloin   d Tay Garnett   ph Ray
Rennahan   md Victor Young
songs Johnny Burke, Jimmy Van Heusen

Bing Crosby, Rhonda Fleming, William
Bendix, *Cedric Hardwicke*, Murvyn Vye

Connecting Rooms
GB 1969   103m   Technicolor
Telstar / Franklin Gollings (Harry Field)

In a seedy Bayswater boarding house, a
dismissed schoolmaster befriends a failed
cellist whose protégé is a sponging songwriter.
Aggressively dismal melodrama which would
be hilarious if it were not so sadly slow and
naive.

wd Franklin Gollings, *play* The Cellist by
Marion Hart   ph John Wilcox   m Joan
Shakespeare

Bette Davis, Michael Redgrave, Alexis
Kanner, Kay Walsh, Gabrielle Drake, Leo
Genn, Olga Georges-Picot, Richard Wyler,
Brian Wilde

The Connection
US 1961   110m   bw
Shirley Clarke / Lewis Allen

Junkies hang around waiting for a fix and are
filmed by a documentary unit.
Unattractive low-budgeter with occasional
impressive moments.

w Jack Gelber   d Shirley Clarke   ph Arthur J.
Ornitz   m Freddie Redd   ad Richard Sylbert

Warren Finnerty, Jerome Raphael, Jim
Anderson, Carl Lee, Roscoe Browne

The Conqueror
US 1955   112m   Technicolor
Cinemascope
Howard Hughes (Dick Powell)

A romance of the early life of Genghis Khan,
who captures and is enamoured by the
daughter of an enemy.
Solemn pantomime with a measure of
bloodthirsty action and dancing girls, but
featuring too many dull spots between,
especially as the star is the most unlikely of
eastern warriors and the production values
careful but not too steady.

w Oscar Millard   d Dick Powell   ph Joseph La
Shelle, Leo Tover, Harry J. Wild   m Victor
Young

John Wayne, Susan Hayward, Pedro
Armendariz, Agnes Moorehead, Thomas
Gomez, John Hoyt, William Conrad, Ted de
Corsia, Lee Van Cleef

The Conquerors
US 1932   88m   bw
RKO (David O. Selznick)
TV title: *Pioneer Builders*

Nebraska settlers in the 1870s set the seeds of
a banking empire.
Routine family epic with the star playing
himself and his own grandson.

w Robert Lord, *story* Howard Estabrook
d William Wellman   ph Edward Cronjager
m Max Steiner

Richard Dix, Ann Harding, Edna May Oliver,
Guy Kibbee, Donald Cook, Julie Haydon, Jed
Prouty

Conquest**
US 1937   115m   bw
MGM (Bernard Hollyman)
GB title: *Marie Walewska*

The life of Napoleon's most enduring mistress.
Measured, dignified, and often rather dull
historical fiction, lightened by excellent
performances and production.

w Samuel Hoffenstein, Salka Viertel, S. N.
Behrman, from a Polish play dramatized by
Helen Jerome   d Clarence Brown   ph Karl
Freund   m Herbert Stothart

Greta Garbo, *Charles Boyer*, Reginald Owen,
Alan Marshal, Henry Stephenson, Dame May
Whitty, Leif Erickson

AAN: Charles Boyer

Conquest of Cochise
US 1953   78m   Technicolor

An army major is sent to make peace with
Cochise, the Apache. Feeble western cheapie.

Robert Stack, John Hodiak, Joy Page. Written by Arthur Lewis and De Vallon Scott; directed by William Castle; for Sam Katzman / Columbia.

Conquest of the Air
GB 1936   71m   bw

A history of man's discovery of the power of flight. Curious schoolbook documentary, of historical interest. Laurence Olivier (as Lunardi), Franklin Dyall, Henry Victor, Hay Petrie, John Turnbull. Written by Hugh Gray and Peter Bezencenet; directed by Zoltan Korda and others; for Alexander Korda.

Conquest of Space
US 1955   80m   Technicolor
Paramount (George Pal)

In 1980, the Americans have built a space station in the atmosphere, and plan a voyage to the moon but are sent to Mars instead. So history catches up with science fiction. This sober prophecy looks good but very little happens and the result is as dull as it is bright and shiny.

w James O'Hanlon d Byron Haskin
ph Lionel Lindon m Van Cleeve ad Hal Pereira, James McMillan Johnson sp John P. Fulton, Irmin Roberts, Paul Lerpae, Ivyl Burks, Jan Domella

Eric Fleming, Walter Brooke, Mickey Shaughnessy, William Hopper, Ross Martin

Conrack*
US 1974   106m   De Luxe   Panavision
TCF (Martin Ritt, Irving Ravetch)

A young white teacher is assigned to an all-black school in South Carolina, and after some difficulty makes friends with children and parents.
Nostalgically mellow happy-film, lit by bright smiles all round.

w Irving Ravetch, Harriet Frank Jnr, novel The Water Is Wide by Pat Conroy d Martin Ritt ph John Alonzo m John Williams

Jon Voight, Paul Winfield, Hume Cronyn, Madge Sinclair, Tina Andrews

'For all its craftsman-like virtues, it seems a conscious turning aside from the complexities of modern cinema to the simpler alternatives of yesteryear. Indeed, with underprivileged white children instead of black and Greer Garson substituting for Jon Voight, the film might have been made all of thirty years ago.'—John Raisbeck

Consider Your Verdict
GB 1938   40m   bw

A juror proves an accused man not guilty by falsely confessing to the crime himself. Fairly smart little entry into the feature film scene for the Boulting Brothers, from a popular radio play of the time. Marius Goring, Manning Whiley, Olive Sloane, Hay Petrie, George Carney. Written by Francis Miller, from the play by Laurence Housman; directed by Roy Boulting; for Charter.

Conspiracy of Hearts*
GB 1960   113m   bw
Rank (Betty E. Box)

During World War II, Italian nuns smuggle Jewish children across the border from a nearby prison camp.
Highly commercial combination of exploitable sentimental elements: Germans, Jews, nuns, children, war, suspense. Remarkably, it gets by without causing nausea.

w Robert Presnell Jnr d Ralph Thomas
ph Ernest Steward m Angelo Lavagnino

Lilli Palmer, Sylvia Syms, Yvonne Mitchell, Albert Lieven, Ronald Lewis, Peter Arne, Nora Swinburne, Michael Goodliffe. Megs Jenkins, David Kossoff, Jenny Laird, George Coulouris, Phyllis Neilson-Terry

Conspirator
GB 1949   87m   bw
MGM (Arthur Hornblow Jnr)

A guards officer, unknown to his young wife, is a communist spy.
Singularly awful romantic melodrama which never convinces or entertains for a moment.

w Sally Benson, Gerard Fairlie, novel Humphrey Slater d Victor Saville ph E. A. Young m John Wooldridge

Robert Taylor, Elizabeth Taylor, Harold Warrender, Robert Flemyng, Marie Ney

The Conspirators*
US 1944   101m   bw
Warner (Jack Chertok)

A Dutch underground leader escapes to Lisbon and clears up international intrigue. Interestingly cast but often listless wartime melodrama, a doomed attempt to reprise Casablanca without Humphrey Bogart.

w Vladimir Pozner, Leo Rosten, novel City of Shadows by Frederick Prokosch d Jean Negulesco ph Arthur Edeson m Max Steiner

Hedy Lamarr, Paul Henreid, Sydney Greenstreet, Peter Lorre, Victor Francen, Carol Thurston, Vladimir Sokoloff, Joseph Calleia, Edward Ciannelli, Steve Geray, Kurt Katch, George Macready

The Constant Husband*
GB 1954   88m   Technicolor print
British Lion / London Films (Frank Launder,
Sidney Gilliat)

An amnesiac discovers that he is a multiple
bigamist, still wanted by each of his five wives.
Flimsy comedy which never really gets going
despite an attractive cast.

w Sidney Gilliat, Val Valentine d Sidney
Gilliat ph Ted Scaife m Malcolm Arnold

Rex Harrison, Kay Kendall, Margaret
Leighton, Cecil Parker, Nicole Maurey,
George Cole, Raymond Huntley, Michael
Hordern, Eric Pohlmann, Robert Coote

The Constant Nymph*
GB 1933   98m   bw
Gaumont (Michael Balcon)

In the Tyrol, a composer leaves his rich wife
for a schoolgirl suffering from a heart
condition.

Archetypal romantic drama from Margaret
Kennedy's book, first filmed in 1928 by the
same producer (directed by Adrian Brunel,
with Ivor Novello and Mabel Poulton). A
standard production of its time, which seems
to have vanished with the literary copyright.

w Margaret Kennedy, Basil Dean, from their
play based on her novel d Basil Dean
ph Max Greene

Brian Aherne, Victoria Hopper, Leonora
Corbett, Lyn Harding, Mary Clare, Jane
Baxter

  'One can say that it has a beginning, a
middle and an end, but it lacks something
vital.'—E. V. Lucas, Punch

The Constant Nymph*
US 1943   112m   bw
Warner (Henry Blanke)

Artificially well-produced, overlong
Hollywood version of the above.

w Kathryn Scola d Edmund Goulding
ph Tony Gaudio m Erich Wolfgang Korngold

Charles Boyer, Joan Fontaine, Alexis Smith,
Brenda Marshall, Charles Coburn, Dame May
Whitty, Peter Lorre, Joyce Reynolds, Jean
Muir, Edward Ciannelli, Montagu Love,
André Charlot

AAN: Joan Fontaine

Contraband**
GB 1940   92m   bw
British National (John Corfield)
US title: Blackout

A Danish merchant captain and a girl in
wartime London expose a gang of spies using a
cinema as headquarters.

Enjoyable lightweight comedy melodrama on
Hitchcock lines, reuniting the unlikely star
team from The Spy in Black.

w Emeric Pressburger, Michael Powell, Brock
Williams d Michael Powell ph F. A. Young

Conrad Veidt, Valerie Hobson, Esmond
Knight, Hay Petrie, Raymond Lovell, Harold
Warrender, Charles Victor, Manning Whiley

Contraband Spain
GB 1955   82m   Eastmancolor

An American agent in Barcelona investigates
the death there of a compatriot involved in
drug smuggling. Pretty awful formula thick-ear
with bland stars and a boring look. Richard
Greene, Anouk Aimée, Michael Denison,
John Warwick. Written and directed by
Laurence Huntingdon; for Diadem / ABP.

Convention City*
US 1933   78m   bw
Warner (Henry Blanke)

Extra-marital fun and games at a Chicago
convention.

Amusing and rather risqué comedy which
helped to bring down on Hollywood the wrath
of the Legion of Decency.

w Robert Lord d Archie Mayo ph William
Rees

Joan Blondell, Guy Kibbee, Adolphe Menjou,
Dick Powell, Mary Astor, Frank McHugh,
Ruth Donnelly, Hugh Herbert, Hobart
Cavanaugh

The Conversation**
US 1974   113m   Technicolor
Paramount / Francis Ford Coppola

A bugging device expert lives only for his
work, but finally develops a conscience.
Absorbing but extremely difficult to follow in
detail, this personal, timely (in view of
Watergate), Kafkaesque suspense story
centres almost entirely on director and leading
actor, who have a field day.

wd Francis Ford Coppola ph Bill Butler
m David Shire

Gene Hackman, John Cazale, Allen Garfield,
Frederick Forrest

  'A private, hallucinatory study in technical
expertise and lonely guilt.'—Sight and Sound
  'A terrifying depiction of a ransacked
spirit.'—New Yorker, 1977
  'Alert, truthful, unarty and absolutely
essential viewing.'—Michael Billington,
Illustrated London News

AAN: best picture; Francis Ford Coppola (as
writer)

Conversation Piece
Italy / France 1974   121m   Technicolor
    Todd AO 35
Rusconi / Gaumont (Giovanni Bertolucci)
original title: *Gruppo di Famiglia in un
    Interno*

When a reclusive professor is persuaded to let
his top floor to a young couple he is brought
face to face with his latent homosexuality and
his approaching death.
Death in Venice revisited, but with much less
style and even more obscurity.

w Luchino Visconti, Suso Cecchi d'Amico,
Enrico Medioli *d* Luchino Visconti
ph Pasqualino de Santis *m* Franco Mannino

Burt Lancaster, Helmut Berger, Claudia
Marsani, Silvana Mangano

Convict 99**
GB 1938   91m   bw
Gainsborough (Edward Black)

A seedy schoolmaster accidentally becomes a
prison governor and lets the convicts run the
place.
Patchily funny if overlong and in some ways
rather serious Will Hay comedy, not quite
typical of him.

w Marriott Edgar, Val Guest, Ralph Smart,
Jack Davies *d* Marcel Varnel *ph* Arthur
Crabtree *md* Louis Levy

Will Hay, Graham Moffatt, Moore Marriott,
Googie Withers, Garry Marsh, Peter
Gawthorne, Basil Radford, Kathleen Harrison

Convicted*
US 1950   91m   bw
Columbia (Jerry Bresler)

When a prison informer is killed, one convict
knows who did it.
Routine, over-plotted, strongly cast prison
melodrama.

w William Bowers, Fred Niblo Jnr, Seton I.
Miller, *play* Martin Flavin *d* Henry Levin
ph Burnett Guffey *m* George Duning

Glenn Ford, Broderick Crawford, Millard
Mitchell, Dorothy Malone, Frank Faylen, Carl
Benton Reid, Will Geer

Convicts Four*
US 1962   106m   bw
Allied Artists–Lubin–Kaufman (A. Ronald
    Lubin)
original and GB title: *Reprieve*

A convict reprieved from the electric chair
spends eighteen years in prison, becomes a
painter, and is rehabilitated.
Odd and unsatisfactory mixture of

documentary, melodrama, sentimentality and
character study, with stars unexpectedly
popping in for cameo appearances. Something
worthier was obviously intended.

wd Millard Kaufman, from the autobiography
of John Resko *ph* Joseph Biroc *m* Leonard
Rosenman

Ben Gazzara, Vincent Price, Rod Steiger,
Broderick Crawford, Stuart Whitman, Ray
Walston, Jack Kruschen, Sammy Davis Jnr

Convoy*
GB 1941   90m   bw
Ealing (Sergei Nolbandov)

A German pocket battleship menaces a British
convoy, and a merchant ship sacrifices itself to
prevent disaster.
Fluent British war film of the early days, the
only substantial work of a much vaunted
director who was subsequently killed.

w Pen Tennyson, Patrick Kirwan *d* Pen
Tennyson ph Gunther Krampf, Roy Kellino
m Ernest Irving

Clive Brook, John Clements, Edward
Chapman, Judy Campbell, Penelope Dudley
Ward, Edward Rigby, Allan Jeayes, Albert
Lieven

Convoy
US 1978   110m   De Luxe   Panavision
UA / EMI (Robert M. Sherman)

A folk hero truck driver survives several
crashes and his policeman nemesis.
A virtually plotless anthology of wanton
destruction. Too noisy to sleep through.

w B. W.,L. Norton, based on the song by
C. W. McCall *d* Sam Peckinpah *ph* Harry
Stradling Jnr

Kris Kristofferson, Ali MacGraw, Ernest
Borgnine, Burt Young, Madge Sinclair
    'There's a whole lot of nothing going on
here . . . strictly a summer popcorn picture for
the nondiscriminating.'—*Variety*
    'Roughly as much fun as a ride on the New
Jersey turnpike with the window open. It not
only numbs the brain but pollutes the
senses.'—*Richard Schickel, Time*

Coogan's Bluff**
US 1968   94m   Technicolor
Universal (Don Siegel)

An Arizona sheriff takes an escaped killer
back to New York, and when the man escapes
uses western methods to recapture him.
Violent, well-done police story which inspired
the TV series *McCloud*.

w Herman Miller, Dean Riesner, Howard Rodman *d Don Siegel ph* Bud Thackery *m* Lalo Schifrin

Clint Eastwood, Lee J. Cobb, Susan Clark, Don Stroud, Tisha Sterling, Betty Field, Tom Tully

Cool Breeze
US 1972   102m   Metrocolor
MGM / Penelope (Gene Corman)

A miscellaneous gang of crooks is rounded up to commit a robbery, which ultimately fails.
Third, all-black remake of *The Asphalt Jungle* (the others being *The Badlanders* and *Cairo*). Fashionable violence against a Los Angeles backdrop, but not at all memorable.

wd Barry Pollack *ph* Andy Davis *m* Solomon Burke

Thalmus Rasulala, Judy Pace, Jim Watkins, Raymond St Jacques, Lincoln Kilpatrick

Cool Hand Luke**
US 1967   126m   Technicolor
Panavision
Warner / Jalem (Gordon Carroll)

Sentenced to two years' hard labour with the chain gang, a convict becomes a legend of invulnerability but is eventually shot during an escape.
Allegedly a Christ-allegory, this well-made and good-looking film is only partially successful as an entertainment; slow stretches of soul-searching alternate with brutality, and not much acting is possible.

w Donn Pearce, Frank R. Pierson, *novel* Donn Pearce *d* Stuart Rosenberg *ph* Conrad Hall *m* Lalo Schifrin

Paul Newman, George Kennedy, Jo Van Fleet, J. D. Cannon, Lou Antonio, Robert Drivas, Strother Martin, Clifton James

AA: George Kennedy
AAN: Donn Pearce, Frank R. Pierson; Lalo Schifrin; Paul Newman

The Cool Ones
US 1967   96m   Technicolor   Panavision
Warner (William Conrad)

Former pop singer makes a comeback. Zazzy showbiz saga with ear-splitting track, quite professionally assembled.

w Joyce Geller *d* Gene Nelson *ph* Floyd Crosby *m* Ernie Freeman

Roddy McDowall, Debbie Watson, Robert Coote, Phil Harris, Nita Talbot

The Co-Optimists*
GB 1929   83m   bw
New Era (Gordon Craig)

A revue by a popular pierrot troupe of the time.
Famous as Britain's first musical, this is a dated but valuable record of a stage performance of the kind long vanished.

d Edwin Greenwood, Laddie Cliff *ph* Basil Emmott

Davy Burnaby, Stanley Holloway, Laddie Cliff, Phyllis Monkman, Melville Gideon, Gilbert Childs, Betty Chester, Elsa MacFarlane, Peggy Petronella, Harry S. Pepper

Copacabana
US 1947   91m   bw
(UA) Sam Coslow

A quick-thinking agent forms two acts out of one client, which makes things awkward when both are needed at once.
Thinly produced comedy with both stars doing what is expected of them in surroundings less glamorous than those to which they were previously accustomed.

w Laslo Vadnay, Allen Boretz, Howard Harris *d* Alfred E. Green *ph* Bert Glennon *m* Edward Ward

Groucho Marx, Carmen Miranda, Steve Cochran, Gloria Jean, Andy Russell

Copper Canyon
US 1949   84m   Technicolor

After the Civil War, southern veterans trying to rebuild their homes are helped by a gunslinger. Shiny unpersuasive western with stars ill at ease. Ray Milland, Hedy Lamarr, Macdonald Carey, Mona Freeman, Harry Carey Jnr. Written by Jonathan Latimer; directed by John Farrow; for Paramount.

Cops***
US 1922   20m (24 fps)   bw   silent
Associated First National

An innocent disrupts a parade and is pursued by a horde of policemen.
The perfect Keaton short, a careful assembly of perfectly timed gags.

wd Buster Keaton

Buster Keaton, Virginia Fox

Cops and Robbers*
US 1973   89m   De Luxe
UA / EK Corp (Elliott Kastner)

Two New York cops turn crook and pull off a job for the Mafia.
Trendily anti-establishment comedy, quite snappy and smart when you can follow it.

w Donald E. Westlake *d* Aram Avakian *ph* David L. Quaid *m* Michel Legrand

Cliff Gorman, Joe Bologna, Dick Ward, Shepperd Strudwick, Ellen Holly, John P. Ryan

Le Corbeau**
France 1943   92m   bw
L'Atelier Français
US title: *The Raven*
Poison pen letters disturb a small provincial town.
Impressively characterized whodunnit with the usual French qualities of detail and discretion. Remade in Hollywood to less effect as *The Thirteenth Letter* (qv).

w Louis Chavance *d* Henri-Georges Clouzot *ph* Nicholas Hayer *m* none

Pierre Fresnay, Pierre Larquey, Ginette Leclerc, Hélène Manson

'By no means as malign or as brilliant as it's cracked up to be, but a sour, clever, amusing job.'—*James Agee*

Corky
US 1971   88m   colour
An arrogant auto mechanic becomes a stock car racer. Noisy and unattractive movie about an anti-hero. Robert Blake, Patrick O'Neal, Charlotte Rampling, Christopher Connolly, Laurence Luckinbill, Ben Johnson. Written by Eugene Price; directed by Leonard Horn; for Bruce Geller / MGM.

The Corn is Green*
US 1945   118m   bw
Warner (Jack Chertok)
In 1895 Miss Moffat starts a village school for Welsh miners, and after some tribulations sees one of them off to Oxford.
A very theatrical production with unconvincing sets and mannered acting, but the original play has its felicities.

w Casey Robinson, Frank Cavett, *play Emlyn Williams d* Irving Rapper *ph* Sol Polito *m* Max Steiner *ad* Carl Jules Weyl

Bette Davis, John Dall, Nigel Bruce, Joan Lorring, Rhys Williams, Rosalind Ivan, Mildred Dunnock, Arthur Shields

'It's very apparent that Hollywood isn't Wales . . . but the film lingers in the memory anyway.'—*New Yorker, 1978*
† Remade as a TV movie in 1978, with Katharine Hepburn.

AAN: John Dall; Joan Lorring

Cornered*
US 1945   102m   bw
RKO
After demobilization, a French-Canadian pilot tracks down the collaborationist responsible

for the death of his wife. Well-made but humourless revenge thriller.
w John Paxton, *story* John Wexley *d* Edward Dmytryk *ph* Harry J. Wild *m* Roy Webb
Dick Powell, Micheline Cheirel, Walter Slezak, Morris Carnovsky

The Corpse Came COD
US 1947   87m   bw
Columbia (Sam Bischoff)
Rival reporters try to solve the mystery of a wandering body.
Routine crime comedy with too few smart lines.

w George Bricker, Dwight Babcock, *novel* Jimmy Starr *d* Henry Levin *ph* Lucien Andriot *m* George Duning

George Brent, Joan Blondell, Adele Jergens, Jim Bannon, Leslie Brooks, Grant Mitchell, Una O'Connor

Corridor of Mirros
GB 1948   105m   bw
Cartier–Romney–Apollo (Rudolph Cartier)
An eccentric art collector believes that he and his mistress are reincarnations of 400-year-old lovers in a painting; but they are separated by murder.
Pretentious melodrama of no urgent narrative interest, with all concerned sadly at sea.

w Rudolph Cartier, Edana Romney *d* Terence Young *ph* André Thomas *m* Georges Auric

Eric Portman, Edana Romney, Barbara Mullen, Hugh Sinclair

'It has aimed at Art. It is, in fact, Effect. Some members of the cast wander in and out of the scenes as if they are not quite sure what has happened to them. Their confusion is not beyond comprehension.'—*MFB*

Corridors of Blood*
GB 1958   86m   bw
Producers' Associates (John Croydon)
original title: *Doctor from Seven Dials*
Seeking to discover anaesthetics, a Victorian doctor falls a prey to resurrection men. Unpleasant but well-mounted semi-horror backed by strong cast and art direction.

w Jean Scott Rogers *d* Robert Day *ph* Geoffrey Faithfull *m* Buxton Orr *ad* Anthony Masters

Boris Karloff, Christopher Lee, Finlay Currie, Frank Pettingell, Betta St John, Francis Matthews, Adrienne Corri, Marian Spencer
† Not released until 1964.

Corruption
GB 1967   91m   Technicolor
Columbia / Titan (Peter Newbrook)

A surgeon kills for pituitary gland fluid to restore his fiancée's beauty.
Highly derivative shocker with no inspiration of its own except an accumulation of gory detail.

w Donald and Derek Ford d Robert Hartford Davis ph Peter Newbrook m Bill McGuffie

Peter Cushing, Sue Lloyd, Noel Trevarthen, Kate O'Mara, David Lodge

The Corsican Brothers*
US 1942   111m   bw
Edward Small

Siamese twins are separated but remain spiritually tied through various adventures.
Adequately exciting picturization of the Dumas swashbuckler.

w George Bruce, Howard Estabrook d Gregory Ratoff ph Harry Stradling m Dmitri Tiomkin

Douglas Fairbanks Jnr, Akim Tamiroff, Ruth Warrick, J. Carrol Naish, H. B. Warner, Henry Wilcoxon

† In 1953 came an undistinguished sequel, *Bandits of Corsica* (GB: *The Return of the Corsican Brothers*), with Richard Greene, Paul Raymond, Raymond Burr and Dona Drake. Written by Richard Schayer; directed by Ray Nazarro; for Global / UA.

AAN: Dmitri Tiomkin

Corvette K 225*
US 1943   97m   bw
Universal (Howard Hawks)
GB title: *The Nelson Touch*

A Canadian corvette commander encounters submarines and bombers in mid-Atlantic.
Good war film of its period, marred by romantic interest.

w Lt John Sturdy d Richard Rosson ph Tony Gaudio m David Buttolph

Randolph Scott, James Brown, Ella Raines, Barry Fitzgerald, Andy Devine, Richard Lane
AAN: Tony Gaudio

Corvette Summer
US 1979   104m   Metrocolor
MGM / Plotto (Hal Barwood)
GB title: *The Hot One*

A Los Angeles student spends the summer looking for his stolen customized car, and has various adventures around Las Vegas.
There are a few choice moments in this disconnected comedy drama, but the appeal is almost entirely to moonstruck teenagers.

w Hal Barwood, Matthew Robbins d Matthew Robbins ph Frank Stanley m Craig Safan

Mark Hamill, Annie Potts, Eugene Roche, Kim Milford, Richard McKenzie

Cottage on Dartmoor
GB 1929   75m   bw
BIP (Bruce Woolfe)

A farmer's wife shelters her ex-lover when he breaks jail.
Crude early talkie notable only as an immature work of its director.

wd Anthony Asquith ph Stanley Rodwell

Norah Baring, Uno Hemming, Hans Schlettow, Judd Green

Cottage to Let*
GB 1941   90m   bw
Gainsborough (Edward Black)
US title: *Bombsight Stolen*

Evacuated to Scotland, a Cockney helps prevent spies from kidnapping his inventor foster-father.
Stagey but often amusing comedy-thriller which after a shaky start becomes agreeably Hitchcockian.

w Anatole de Grunwald, J. O. C. Orton, *play* Geoffrey Kerr d Anthony Asquith ph Jack Cox

Leslie Banks, *Alastair Sim, John Mills*, Jeanne de Casalis, George Cole, Carla Lehmann, Michael Wilding, Frank Cellier, Wally Patch, Muriel Aked, Muriel George, Catherine Lacey, Hay Petrie

Cotton Comes to Harlem
US 1970   97m   De Luxe

Two black detectives try to beat the police to a bale of cotton containing a fortune in stolen dollars. Rickety vehicle for two amiable black characters presented rather more surely in *Come Back Charleston Blue* (qv). Godfrey Cambridge, Raymond St Jacques, Calvin Lockhart, Judy Pace, Redd Foxx. Written by Arnold Perl and Ossie Davis, from the novel by Chester Himes; directed by Ossie Davis; for Formosa / UA.

The Couch
US 1962   100m   bw

A psychiatrist's patient goes on the rampage with an ice pick. Overstretched suspenser which never really holds the interest. Grant Williams, Shirley Knight, Onslow Stevens. Written by Robert Bloch; directed and produced by Owen Crump; for Warner.

Council of the Gods*
Germany 1950   106m   bw
DEFA (Adolf Fischer)

A research chemist working for a big chemical company denounces them after the war when he finds they have been producing poison gas for the concentration camps.

Self-flagellatory expiation of war crimes encased in an absorbing drama.

w Friedrich Wolff, Philipp Gebb   *d* Kurt Maetzig   *ph* Friedl Behn-Grund   *m* Hanns Eisler, Erwin Lehn

Paul Bildt, Agnes Windeck, Yvonne Merin, Fritz Tillman

Counsellor at Law*
US 1933   78m   bw
Universal (Henry Henigson)

Life in the New York office of a successful Jewish lawyer.

Practised film-making from a Broadway hit.

w Elmer Rice, from his play   *d William Wyler*
ph Norbert Brodine

John Barrymore, Bebe Daniels, Melvyn Douglas, Doris Kenyon, Onslow Stevens, Isabel Jewell, Thelma Todd, Mayo Methot

Counsel's Opinion
GB 1933   76m   bw

A widow wins a barrister by pretending to be a flighty socialite. Semi-sophisticated comedy; this rather thin quickie version was done over four years later and became *The Divorce of Lady X* (qv). Henry Kendall, Binnie Barnes, Cyril Maude, Laurence Grossmith. Written by Dorothy Greenhill and Arthur Wimperis, from a play by Gilbert Wakefield; directed by Allan Dwan; for Alexander Korda.

Count Five and Die*
GB 1957   92m   bw   Cinemascope
TCF / Zonic (Ernest Gartside)

British intelligence seeks to give the Nazis false information about the 1944 invasion, but conviction grows that a double agent is among them.

Terse, downbeat war suspenser, gripping in parts but quite forgettable.

w Jack Seddon, David Pursall   *d* Victor Vicas
ph Arthur Grant   *m* John Wooldridge

Nigel Patrick, Jeffrey Hunter, Anne-Marie Duringer, David Kossoff

The Count of Monte Cristo***
US 1934   114m   bw
Edward Small / Reliance

After spending years in prison, Edmond Dantes escapes and avenges himself on those who framed him.

Classic swashbuckler, extremely well done with due attention to dialogue as well as action; a model of its kind and period.

w Philip Dunne, Dan Totheroh, Rowland V. Lee, *novel* Alexandre Dumas   *d Rowland V. Lee*   *ph* Peverell Marley   *m* Alfred Newman

Robert Donat, Elissa Landi, Louis Calhern, Sidney Blackmer, Raymond Walburn, O. P. Heggie, William Farnum

Count Three and Pray
US 1955   92m   Technicolor
    Cinemascope
Columbia / Copa (Ted Richmond)

After the Civil War a roistering Southerner comes home to rebuild his town and become its parson.

Moderate semi-western, fresh and pleasing but not memorable.

w Herb Meadow   *d* George Sherman
ph Burnett Guffey   *m* George Duning

Van Heflin, Joanne Woodward (debut), Phil Carey, Raymond Burr, Allison Hayes, Myron Healey, Nancy Kulp, James Griffiths

Count Yorga Vampire
US 1970   90m   Moviélab
Erica / AIP (Michael Macready)

Inquisitive Los Angeles teenagers are vampirized by a suave foreign visitor.

A semi-professional film that looks it but amid the longueurs provides one or two nasty frissons.

wd Bob Kelljan   *ph* Arch Archambault
m William Marx

Robert Quarry, Roger Perry, Michael Murphy, Michael Macready, Donna Anders, Judith Lang

† *The Return of Count Yorga* followed a year later.

Count Your Blessings
US 1959   102m   Metrocolor
    Cinemascope
MGM (Karl Tunberg)

An English girl marries an aristocratic Frenchman, but the war and other considerations make them virtual strangers until their son is nine years old, when it becomes clear that daddy is a philanderer.

Slight upper-crust comedy, basically rather tedious but kept buoyant by Chevalier as commentator.

w Karl Tunberg, *novel* The Blessing by Nancy Mitford   *d* Jean Negulesco   *ph* Milton Krasner, George Folsey   *m* Franz Waxman

Deborah Kerr, *Maurice Chevalier*, Rossano
Brazzi, Martin Stephens, Tom Helmore,
Ronald Squire, Patricia Medina, Mona
Washbourne

'Negulesco's aspirations to elegance are now
familiar . . . this is far too absurd an example
of Hollywood's infatuation with Old Europe to
arouse much interest.'—*MFB*

Countdown*
US 1967 101m Technicolor
Panavision
Warner (William Conrad)

Russian and American spaceships race for the
moon.
Earnest, simply-plotted science-fiction in
which technology is the centre of interest.

w Loring Mandel *d* Robert Altman
ph William W. Spencer *m* Leonard
Rosenman *ad* Jack Poplin

James Caan, Robert Duvall, Barbara Baxley,
Joanna Moore, Charles Aidman, Steve Ihnat

Counterattack
US 1945 89m bw
Columbia
GB title: *One against Seven*

Resistance fighters go behind enemy lines for
purposes of sabotage.
Standard World War II actioner, the star
appearing above his surroundings.

w John Howard Lawson, *play* Janet and Philip
Stevenson *d* Zoltan Korda *ph* James Wong
Howe *m* Louis Gruenberg

Paul Muni, Marguerite Chapman, Larry
Parks, George Macready, Roman Bohnen

Counterblast
GB 1948 99m bw

An escaped Nazi poses as a British scientist in
a research laboratory. Overlong espionage
thick ear with some compensations. Robert
Beatty, Mervyn Johns, Nova Pilbeam,
Margaretta Scott, Marie Lohr, Karel
Stepanek, Alan Wheatley. Written by Jack
Whittingham, from a story by Guy Morgan;
directed by Paul Stein; for British National.

The Counterfeit Traitor*
US 1962 140m Technicolor
Paramount / Perlberg–Seaton

An oil importer, a naturalized Swede born in
America, is blackmailed by the Allies into
becoming a spy.
Heavy-going espionage drama which divides
its time between action and moralizing.
Excellent production does not quite make it
exciting.

wd George Seaton, *book* Alexander Klein
ph Jean Bourgoin *m* Alfred Newman

William Holden, Lilli Palmer, Hugh Griffith,
Werner Peters, Eva Dahlbeck

'The picture is too long, it is also incessantly
exciting, occasionally witty . . . and in its
expression of organized sadism comparatively
subtle.'—*Time*

Counterpoint*
US 1967 107m Techniscope
Universal (Dick Berg)

In 1944, an American symphony orchestra is
captured by the Germans and threatened with
execution.
Bizarre war suspenser, quite unconvincing but
with effectively suspenseful moments and an
old-fashioned portrayal of the Nazis as sadistic
music-loving Huns.

w James Lee, Joel Oliansky, *novel* The
General by Alan Sillitoe *d* Ralph Nelson
ph Russell Metty *m* Bronislau Kaper

Charlton Heston, Maximilian Schell, Anton
Diffring, Kathryn Hays, Leslie Nielsen

A Countess from Hong Kong
GB 1967 120m Technicolor
Universal (Jerome Epstein)

An American millionaire diplomat is followed
from Hong Kong by his Russian émigrée girl
friend, and complications mount when his wife
boards the ship at Hawaii.
Flatulent comedy with neither the sparkle of
champagne nor even the fizz of lemonade:
Chaplin's writing, direction and music are
alike soporific, and commiserations are due to
the cast.

wd / m Charles Chaplin *ph* Arthur Ibbetson
pd Don Ashton

Marlon Brando, Sophia Loren, *Patrick
Cargill*, Margaret Rutherford, Charles
Chaplin, Sydney Chaplin, Oliver Johnston,
John Paul

'An unfunny, mindless mess.'—*Robert
Windeler*
'So old-fashioned and dull that one can
hardly believe it was made now.'—*Philip T.
Hartung*

The Countess of Monte Cristo
US 1933 74m bw

A bit player in a musical convinces her friends
she is a countess. Mild comedy remade in 1948
as an even milder vehicle for Sonja Henie. Fay
Wray, Paul Lukas, Patsy Kelly, Reginald
Owen. Written by Karen de Wolf and Gene
Lewis; directed by Karl Freund; for Universal.

Country Dance
GB 1969   112m   Metrocolor
MGM / Keep–Windward (Robert Emmett
    Ginna)
aka: *Brotherly Love*

An eccentric baronet's incestuous love for his
sister finally breaks up her marriage.
Rambling melodrama with O'Toole going mad
in squire's tweeds; tediously fashionable but
too pallid for general success, it was barely
released.

w James Kennaway, from his novel Household
Ghosts *d* J. Lee-Thompson *ph* Ted Moore
m John Addison

Peter O'Toole, Susannah York, Michael
Craig, Harry Andrews, Cyril Cusack, Judy
Cornwell, Brian Blessed

The Country Doctor*
US 1936   94m   bw
TCF (Darryl F. Zanuck)

A rural physician becomes famous when
quintuplets are born to one of his patients.
Fictionalization of the birth of the Dionne
Quintuplets; pleasantly nostalgic even forty
years after its *raison d'être.*

w Sonya Levien *d* Henry King *ph* John F.
Seitz, Daniel B. Clark

Jean Hersholt, the Dionne Quins, Dorothy
Petersen, June Lang, Slim Summerville,
Michael Whalen, Robert Barrat
† Sequels: *Reunion* (1936), *Five of a Kind*
(1938).

The Country Girl*
US 1954   104m   bw
Paramount (William Perlberg)

The wife of an alcoholic singer blossoms when
he is stimulated into a comeback.
Theatrically effective but highly unconvincing,
this rather glum stage success made a cold
film, miscast with an eye on the box office.

w George Seaton, *play* Clifford Odets
d George Seaton *ph* John F. Warren
m Victor Young *songs* Ira Gershwin, Harold
Arlen

Bing Crosby, Grace Kelly, William Holden,
Anthony Ross, Gene Reynolds
    'How far should a woman go to redeem the
man she loves?'—*publicity*
    'The dramatic development is not really
interesting enough to sustain a film of the
intensity for which it strives.'—*Karel Reisz*

AA: George Seaton (as writer); Grace Kelly
AAN: best picture; John F. Warren; Bing
Crosby

County Hospital**
US 1932   20m   bw

Ollie is in hospital; Stan brings him some
hardboiled eggs and some nuts, and nearly
wrecks the place. Archetypal star comedy with
brilliant character and slapstick sequences, let
down by a badly processed car ride home.
Laurel and Hardy, Billy Gilbert. Written by
H. M. Walker; directed by James Parrott; for
Hal Roach.

Courage Fuyons*
France 1979   98m   Eastmancolor
Gaumont / Gueville (Yves Robert)

A middle-aged man embarks on a series of
surprising romantic adventures.
A mainly enjoyable exercise in wish-
fulfilment, sharply written and acted.

w Jean-Loup Dabadie, Yves Robert *d* Yves
Robert *ph* Yves Lafaye *m* Vladimir Cosma

Jean Rochefort, Catherine Deneuve, Robert
Webber, Philippe Leroy-Beaulieu

The Court Jester***
US 1955   101m   Technicolor
    Vistavision
Paramount / Dena (Melvin Frank, Norman
    Panama)

Opposition to a tyrannical king is provided by
the Fox, but it is one of the rebel's meekest
men who, posing as a jester, defeats the
usurper.
One of the star's most delightful vehicles, this
medieval romp has good tunes and lively
action, not to mention an exceptional cast and
the memorable 'chalice from the palace'
routine.

wd Norman Panama, Melvin Frank *ph* Ray
June *songs* Sylvia Fine, Sammy Cahn *ad* Hal
Pereira, Roland Anderson

Danny Kaye, Glynis Johns, *Basil Rathbone*,
Cecil Parker, *Mildred Natwick*, Angela
Lansbury, Edward Ashley, Robert Middleton,
Michael Pate, Alan Napier

The Court Martial of Billy Mitchell*
US 1955   100m   Warnercolor
    Cinemascope
United States Pictures (Milton Sperling)
GB title: *One Man Mutiny*

In the early twenties, an American general of
the Army Air Service is court-martialled for
accusing the war department of criminal
negligence.
Adequate recreation of a historical incident,
with a cast of excellent actors converging for a
courtroom scene of some effectiveness.

w Milton Sperling, Emmet Lavery *d* Otto Preminger *ph* Sam Leavitt *m* Dmitri Tiomkin

Gary Cooper, *Rod Steiger*, Ralph Bellamy, Charles Bickford, Elizabeth Montgomery, Fred Clark, Darren McGavin, James Daly

AAN: Milton Sperling, Emmet Lavery

The Courtneys of Curzon Street*
GB 1947   120m   bw
British Lion / Herbert Wilcox
US title: *The Courtney Affair*

In Victorian times, a baronet's son marries a lady's maid . . . and many years later, their grandson marries a factory worker.
Unbelievable upstairs-downstairs romantic drama spanning three generations; all to be taken with a gigantic pinch of salt, but a huge success when released.

w Nicholas Phipps, *novel* Florence Tranter *d* Herbert Wilcox *ph* Max Greene

Anna Neagle, Michael Wilding, Gladys Young, Coral Browne, Michael Medwin, Daphne Slater, Jack Watling, Helen Cherry, Bernard Lee
    'The dignity of Curzon Street is Hollywoodized, and it is rare in 1945 that people in their sixties look as though they have one foot in the grave.'—*MFB*

The Courtship of Eddie's Father*
US 1962   117m   Metrocolor   Panavision
MGM / Joe Pasternak

The small son of a widower tries to interest Dad in another woman.
Fairly icky American-style sentimental comedy with most of the stops pulled out; way over-length and too self-indulgently solemn in the last part, but with professional touches.

w John Gay, *novel* Muriel Toby *d* Vincente Minnelli *ph* Milton Krasner *m* George Stoll

Glenn Ford, Ronnie Howard, Shirley Jones, Stella Stevens, Dina Merrill
† A TV series starring Bill Bixby followed in 1971.

Cousin, Cousine**
France 1975   95m   Eastmancolor
Pomereu / Gaumont (Bertrand Javal)

Various furtive love affairs centre on a family wedding.
Sprightly satirical comedy full of pleasing touches, mostly jibes at French bourgeois standards.

wd Jean-Charles Tacchella ph Georges Lendi *m* Gerard Anfosso

Marie-France Pisier, Marie-Christine Barrault, Victor Lanoux, Guy Marchand, Ginette Garcin
    'One of those rare delights you want to see again and again just to share the sheer joy of living, zest for love, genuine affection, all-too-human absurdity, and pure happiness of all those delicious people on screen.'—*Judith Crist, Saturday Review*

Les Cousins*
France 1958   110m   bw
AJYM (Claude Chabrol)

A law student stays with his sophisticated cousin in Paris, and his life is altered.
The country cousin fable filled with undramatic detail and given a rather perverse ending without any apparent point.

wd Claude Chabrol ph Henri Decaë *m* Paul Misraki

Jean-Claude Brialy, Gérard Blain, Juliette Mayniel, Claude Cerval

A Covenant with Death
US 1966   97m   Technicolor
Warner (William Conrad)

A half-Mexican judge in a border town convicts a man who accidentally kills the hangman just as the real murderer confesses.
Dreary moral melodrama with accents, nicely photographed but cold, remote and drawn out.

w Larry Marcus, Saul Levitt, *novel* Stephen Becker *d* Lamont Johnson *ph* Robert Burks *m* Leonard Rosenman

George Maharis, Katy Jurado, Earl Holliman, Sidney Blackmer, Laura Devon, Gene Hackman

Cover Girl**
US 1944   107m   Technicolor
Columbia (Arthur Schwartz)

The road to success for magazine cover models.
Wartime glamour musical with a stronger reputation than it really deserves apart from Kelly's solos; it does however manage a certain *joie de vivre* which should not be despised.

w Virginia Van Upp *d* Charles Vidor *ph* Rudolph Maté *md* Morris Stoloff, Carmen Dragon *songs* Jerome Kern, Ira Gershwin

Rita Hayworth, Gene Kelly, Phil Silvers, Lee Bowman, Jinx Falkenberg, Otto Kruger, Eve Arden, Ed Brophy
    'Kelly and Silvers are better than Kelly and Hayworth, though she does look sumptuous, and her big smile could be the emblem of the period.'—*New Yorker, 1977*

'Much of it is not as fresh as it may seem; but its second-handedness and its occasional failures cannot obliterate the pleasure of seeing the work of a production company which obviously knows, cares about and enjoys what it is doing.'—*James Agee*

'Too thrilling for words so they set it to music!'—*publicity*

AA: Morris Stoloff, Carmen Dragon
AAN: Rudolph Maté; song 'Long Ago and Far Away'

Cover Girl Killer
GB 1959   61m   bw

A trap is set for the mad murderer of cover models. Good unpretentious second feature with plenty of suspense. Harry H. Corbett, Felicity Young, Spencer Teakle, Victor Brooks. Written and directed by Terry Bishop; for Parroch / Eros.

Cover Up
US 1948   82m   bw

An insurance investigator finds senior officials conspiring to obscure the facts of a small-town murder. Modest mystery, initially intriguing but finally unsatisfying. Dennis O'Keefe, William Bendix, Barbara Britton, Art Smith. Written by Jerome Odlum and Jonathan Ritz; directed by Alfred E. Green; for Strand / UA.

The Covered Wagon*
US 1923   103m (24 fps)   bw   silent
Paramount / Famous Players-Lasky

Pioneer settlers travel west by wagon train. A classic western which now seems painfully undernourished in terms of plot and character but still retains moments of epic sweep.

w Jack Cunningham, *novel* Emerson Hough
d James Cruze   *ph Karl Brown*

Ernest Torrence, Tully Marshall, J. Warren Kerrigan, Lois Wilson, Alan Hale

'There wasn't a false whisker in the film.'—*James Cruze*

'Forthright, impressive and vigorous, it brought a breath of fresh air into the jazz-ridden film world.'—*Lewis Jacobs*

The Cow and I
France 1959   119m   bw
Cyclope / Omnia (Walter Rupp)
original title: *La Vache et le Prisonnier*

A French soldier escapes from a prison camp and takes a farm cow as cover.
Curiously overlong war adventure which hovers uncertainly between comedy and suspense.

w Henri Verneuil, Henri Jeanson, Jean Manse   d Henri Verneuil   *ph Roger Hubert*   m Paul Durand

Fernandel, René Havard, Albert Remy, Bernard Musson

Cowboy*
US 1957   92m   Technicolor
Columbia / Phoenix

Frank Harris becomes a cattle herder for love of a lady but is quickly disillusioned with the outdoor life.
Fashioned from a lively autobiography, this has interesting moments but is never as fascinating as one would expect.

w Edmund H. North, *book* On the Trail by Frank Harris   d Delmer Daves   *ph* Charles Lawton Jnr   m George Duning

Jack Lemmon, Glenn Ford, Brian Donlevy, Anna Kashfi, Dick York, Richard Jaeckel, King Donovan

The Cowboy and the Lady
US 1938   91m   bw
Samuel Goldwyn

The daughter of a presidential candidate becomes infatuated with a rodeo cowboy. Insubstantial and witless romantic comedy which suffered many sea changes from script to screen.

w Leo McCarey, S. N. Behrman, Sonya Levien   d H. C. Potter   *ph* Gregg Toland   m Alfred Newman

Gary Cooper, Merle Oberon, Patsy Kelly, Walter·Brennan, Fuzzy Knight, Henry Kolker, Harry Davenport

'Just a lot of chestnuts pulled out of other people's dead fires.'—*Otis Ferguson*

AAN: Alfred Newman; title song (*m* Alfred Newman, *ly* Arthur Quenzer)

The Cowboys*
US 1972   128m   Technicolor
Panavision 70
Sanford / Warner (Mark Rydell)

Deserted by his ranch hands, a cattle drover on a long trail enlists the help of eleven schoolboys, who later avenge his death. Ambling, climactically violent, extremely unlikely western with good scenes along the way.

w Irving Ravetch, Harriet Frank Jnr, *novel* William Dale Jennings   d Mark Rydell   *ph Robert Surtees   m* John Williams

John Wayne, Roscoe Lee Browne, Bruce Dern, Colleen Dewhurst, Slim Pickens, Sarah Cunningham

† A TV series followed in 1974 but was shortlived.

Crack in the Mirror
US 1960 97m bw Cinemascope
TCF / Darryl F. Zanuck

A young lawyer and his ageing mentor are at opposite sides of a murder case.
Pointless Paris-set melodrama in which for no obvious reason each of the three stars plays two roles. Relentlessly boring.

w Mark Canfield (Darryl F. Zanuck)
d Richard Fleischer ph William C. Mellor
m Maurice Jarre

Orson Welles, Bradford Dillman, Juliette Greco, William Lucas, Alexander Knox, Catherine Lacey

Crack in the World
US 1965 96m Technicolor
Paramount / Security (Philip Yordan, Bernard Glasser, Lester A. Sansom)

A dying scientist fires a missile into the earth's centre, and nearly blows the planet apart.
Jaded science-fiction melodrama, overburdened with initial chat but waking up when the special effects take over.

w Jon Manchip White, Julian Halevy
d Andrew Marton ph Manuel Berenguer
m John Douglas ad Eugene Lourié sp John Douglas

Dana Andrews, Janette Scott, Kieron Moore, Alexander Knox, Peter Damon, Gary Lasdun

Crack Up
US 1936 65m bw

Espionage agents try to corrupt a test pilot.
Modestly efficient thriller. Peter Lorre, Brian Donlevy, Helen Wood, Ralph Morgan, Thomas Beck. Written by Charles Kenyon and Sam Mintz; directed by Mal St Clair; for TCF.

Crack Up*
US 1946 93m bw
RKO

A museum curator with an eye for forgery is discredited by crooks who make him appear drunk or half-crazed when he recounts a set of strange events which have happened to him . . .
The intriguing mystery of the opening reels, when solved, is replaced by rather dull detection, but this remains a thriller with a difference, generally well presented.

w John Paxton d Irving Reis ph Robert de Grasse m Leigh Harline

Pat O'Brien, Claire Trevor, Herbert Marshall, Ray Collins

Crackerjack*
GB 1938 79m bw

A gentleman thief poses as butler at a stately home. Fairly smart sardonic star vehicle. Tom Walls, Lilli Palmer, Noel Madison, Leon M. Lion, Edmund Breon, Charles Heslop. Written by A. R. Rawlinson, Michael Pertwee and Basil Mason; directed by Albert de Courville; for Gainsborough.

The Cracksman
GB 1963 112m Technicolor Cinemascope

A master locksmith becomes the unwitting dupe of a gang of safecrackers. The most elaborate vehicle devised for this diminutive star; despite bright moments, conventional mounting and over-generous length finally defeat it. Charlie Drake, George Sanders, Dennis Price, Nyree Dawn Porter, Eddie Byrne, Finlay Currie, Percy Herbert. Written by Lew Schwartz and Charlie Drake; directed by Peter Graham Scott; for ABPC.

Craig's Wife*
US 1936 77m bw
Columbia

A middle-class wife lets her house take precedence over her husband.
Capable picturization of a Broadway success, later remade as Harriet Craig (qv).

w Mary McCally Jnr, George Kelly, play George Kelly d Dorothy Arzner ph Lucien Ballard md Morris Stoloff

Rosalind Russell, John Boles, Billie Burke, Jane Darwell, Dorothy Wilson, Alma Kruger, Thomas Mitchell, Elizabeth Risdon, Raymond Walburn

Crainquebille*
France 1922 70m approx (16 fps) bw silent
Trarieux Films

A street trader is unjustly accused and imprisoned, afterwards finding happiness as a tramp.
Somewhere between Chaplin and Kafka, this fable was long admired for its style.

wd Jacques Feyder, story Anatole France
ph Léonce Burel

Maurice de Féraudy, Françoise Rosay, Felix Oudart

† Remade 1933 by Jacques de Baroncelli with Maurice Tramel; 1954 by Ralph Habib with Yves Deniaud.

The Cranes Are Flying**
USSR 1957   94m   bw
Mosfilm
original title: *Letyat Zhuravli*

When her lover goes to war, a girl refuses to
believe later reports of his death even though
she has suffered much, including marriage to a
bully, in the interim.

Sleek, moving love story with most of the
Hollywood production virtues plus an
attention to detail and a realism which are
wholly Russian.

*w Victor Rosov d Mikhail Kalatozov
ph Sergei Urusevski*

Tatiana Samoilova, Alexei Batalov, Vasili
Merkuriev

Crash Dive*
US 1943   105m   Technicolor
TCF (Milton Sperling)

A submarine lieutenant and his commander
love the same girl.

Well-staged war thrills in the final reels are
prefaced by a long romantic comedy build-up,
which probably seemed good propaganda at
the time.

*w Jo Swerling, story W. R. Burnett d Archie
Mayo ph Leon Shamroy m David Buttolph
md Emil Newman sp Fred Sersen*

Tyrone Power, Anne Baxter, Dana Andrews,
James Gleason, Dame May Whitty, Henry
Morgan, Frank Conroy, Minor Watson

'One of those films which have no more
sense of reality about this war than a popular
song.'—*Bosley Crowther*

Crashout
US 1955   83m   bw

Six convicts escape from prison, but most of
them die en route. Watchable melodrama,
fairly savage for its day. William Bendix,
Arthur Kennedy, Luther Adler, William
Talman, Gene Evans, Marshall Thompson,
Beverly Michaels. Written by Hal E. Chester
and Lewis R. Foster; directed by Lewis R.
Foster; for Hal E. Chester / Standard.

Craze
GB 1973   95m   Technicolor
(EMI) Harbour (Herman Cohen)

An African idol accidentally causes a death
which brings money to its owner, who kills
again and again in the hope of more loot.
Crude shocker from the bottom of even this
producer's barrel, notable for the star cast
which was surprisingly roped in.

*w Aben Kandel, Herman Cohen, novel
Infernal Idol by Henry Seymour d Freddie
Francis ph John Wilcox m John Scott*

Jack Palance, Diana Dors, Julie Ege, Edith
Evans, Hugh Griffith, Trevor Howard,
Michael Jayston, Suzy Kendall, Martin Potter,
Percy Herbert, Kathleen Byron

Crazy House
US 1943   80m   bw
Universal (Erle C. Kenton)

Olsen and Johnson go to Hollywood to make a
film.

Lame sequel to *Hellzapoppin;* after an
explosively well edited first reel of panic in the
studio, it degenerates into a slew of below-par
variety turns.

*w Robert Lees, Frederic I. Rinaldo d Edward
Cline ph Charles Van Enger md George
Hale, Milt Rosen*

Ole Olsen, Chic Johnson, Martha O'Driscoll,
Patric Knowles, Percy Kilbride, Cass Daley,
Thomas Gomez, Edgar Kennedy

† Sherlock Holmes fans may or may not wish
to record a two-line comic bit by Basil
Rathbone and Nigel Bruce in character.

Crazy Joe
US / Italy 1973   99m   Technicolor

The rise and fall of a Mafia hood in New York.
Noisy, violent, reasonably proficient gangster
movie which seems to have some pretensions
to play against stereotype. Peter Boyle, Paula
Prentiss, Fred Williamson, Charles Cioffi, Rip
Torn, Luther Adler, Eli Wallach, Henry
Winkler. Written by Lewis John Carlino;
directed by Carlo Lizzani; for Bright-Persky /
De Laurentiis.

The Crazy World of Laurel and Hardy**
US 1964   83m   bw
Hal Roach / Jay Ward

A compilation of Laurel and Hardy extracts
from their classic period.

Although the material is in itself excellent and
some of the build-up sequences well done, the
clips are all too short to achieve maximum
impact, and virtually none is identified.

*w Bill Scott m Jerry Fielding narrator Garry
Moore*

The Creature from the Black Lagoon
US 1954   79m   bw   3-D
U-I (William Alland)

Up the Amazon, scientists encounter a fearful
fanged creature who is half man, half fish.
Unpersuasive and unsuspenseful horror
hokum from the bottom drawer of

imagination: it did, however, coin enough pennies to generate two even worse sequels, *Revenge of the Creature* (1955) and *The Creature Walks Among Us* (1956). And the underwater photography is super.

w Harry Essex, Arthur Ross d Jack Arnold
ph William E. Snyder md Joseph Gershenson

Richard Carlson, Julie Adams, Richard Denning, Antonio Moreno, Nestor Paiva, Ricou Browning (in the rubber suit)

Creatures the World Forgot
GB 1970 95m Technicolor
Columbia / Hammer (Michael Carreras)

Quarrels break out between rival tribes of Stone Age men.
Feeble follow-up to *One Million Years BC* and *When Dinosaurs Ruled the Earth*: someone forgot to order any monsters.

w Michael Carreras d Don Chaffey
ph Vincent Cox m Mario Nascimbene

Julie Ege, Brian O'Shaughnessy, Robert John, Marcia Fox, Rosalie Crutchley

The Creeper
US 1948 63m bw

Scientists disagree over a serum which changes humans into cats. Nonsense horror item with stalwart cast. Ralph Morgan, Eduardo Ciannelli, Onslow Stevens, June Vincent, Richard Lane. Written by Maurice Tombragel; directed by Jean Yarbrough; for TCF.

The Creeping Flesh*
GB 1972 91m Eastmancolor
Tigon / World Film Services (Michael Redbourn)

A Victorian scientist discovers that water causes the recomposing of tissue on the skeleton of a Neanderthal man.
Absurd but persuasive horror film, quite well done in all departments.

w Peter Spenceley, Jonathan Rumbold
d Freddie Francis ph Norman Warwick
m Paul Ferris

Peter Cushing, Christopher Lee, Lorna Heilbron, George Benson, Kenneth J. Warren, Duncan Lamont, Michael Ripper

Crescendo*
GB 1969 95m Technicolor
Warner / Hammer (Michael Carreras)

A girl researcher goes to stay with the widow of a famous composer, and finds herself in mortal danger . . .
Lunatic Hammer horror with the courage of

its shameless borrowings from *Taste of Fear*, *Fanatic*, *Nightmare*, *Maniac* and all the films about mad twin brothers, to which this chaotic brew adds dollops of sex and heroin addiction.

w Jimmy Sangster, Alfred Shaughnessy
d Alan Gibson ph Paul Beeson m Malcolm Williamson

Stefanie Powers, James Olson, Margaretta Scott, Jane Lapotaire, Joss Ackland

Cries and Whispers***
Sweden 1972 91m Eastmancolor
Cinematograph (Ingmar Bergman)
original title: *Viskingar och Rop*

A young woman dying of cancer in her family home is tended by her two sisters.
Quiet, chilling, classical chapter of doom which variously reminds one of Chekhov, Tolstoy and Dostoievsky but is also essential Bergman. Tough but important viewing, it lingers afterwards in the mind like a picture vividly painted in shades of red.

wd Ingmar Bergman ph Sven Nykvist
m Chopin and Bach

Harriet Andersson, Kari Sylwan, Ingrid Thulin, Liv Ullmann

'Harrowing, spare and perceptive, but lacking the humour that helps to put life and death into perspective.'—*Michael Billington, Illustrated London News*

AA: Sven Nykvist
AAN: best picture; Ingmar Bergman (as writer); Ingmar Bergman (as director)

Crime and Punishment*
US 1935 88m bw
Columbia

A student kills a pawnbroker and is tortured by remorse.
Heavy-going rendering of Dostoievsky with some pictorial interest.

w S. K. Lauren, Joseph Anthony d Josef Von Sternberg ph Lucien Ballard m Arthur Honegger md Louis Silvers

Peter Lorre, Edward Arnold, Tala Birell, Marian Marsh, Elizabeth Risdon, Mrs Patrick Campbell

Crime and Punishment USA
US 1958 96m bw
Allied Artists / Sanders Associates (Terry Sanders)

A student murders an old pawnbroker and is driven mad by guilt.
Pointless updating of Dostoievsky by two young film-makers who seemed for years to be on the brink of a masterpiece but never

actually produced it. Some points of interest, but the low budget is cramping.

w Walter Newman d Denis Sanders ph Floyd Crosby m Herschel Burke Gilbert

George Hamilton, Frank Silvera, Mary Murphy, John Harding, Marian Seldes

'There is about it a strange quality of aimlessness which nullifies much of its effect.'—*MFB*

Crime by Night*
US 1944 72m bw
Warner (William Jacobs)

A private detective reluctantly solves a small-town murder, and finds a spy.
Second feature which was thought at the time to have established a new pair of married detectives in the tradition of *The Thin Man*. However, one poor sequel, *Find the Blackmailer*, put paid to the idea.

w Richard Weil, Joel Malone, *novel* Forty Whacks by Geoffrey Homes d William Clemens ph Henry Sharpe

Jerome Cowan, Jane Wyman, Faye Emerson, Charles Lang, Eleanor Parker, Cy Kendall, Creighton Hale

Crime Doctor*
US 1943   66m   bw
Columbia

An amnesiac becomes a successful psychiatrist, then discovers that he was once a wanted gangster.
Time-passing second feature from a popular radio series. Ten *Crime Doctor* films were made between 1943 and 1949, all starring Warner Baxter, all except the first being locked room mysteries which seldom played fair with the audience.

w Graham Baker, Louise Lantz d Michael Gordon m Louis Silvers

Warner Baxter, Margaret Lindsay, John Litel, Ray Collins, Harold Huber, Leon Ames, Don Costello

The sequels:
1943: CRIME DOCTOR'S STRANGEST CASE
1944: SHADOWS IN THE NIGHT, CRIME DOCTOR'S COURAGE
1945: CRIME DOCTOR'S WARNING
1946: CRIME DOCTOR'S MANHUNT, JUST BEFORE DAWN
1947: THE MILLERSON CASE
1948: CRIME DOCTOR'S GAMBLE
1949: CRIME DOCTOR'S DIARY

Crime in the Streets*
US 1956   91m   bw
Allied Artists (Vincent M. Fenelly)

Rival knife gangs bring havoc to tenement dwellers.
Lively semi-documentary low-life melodrama; routine subject, excellent credits.

w *Reginald Rose,* from his TV play d *Don Siegel* ph Sam Leavitt m Franz Waxman

John Cassavetes, James Whitmore, Sal Mineo, Mark Rydell

The Crime of Dr Forbes
US 1936   75m   bw

A gravely injured scientist asks to be put out of his misery, and a colleague is accused of murder. Competently handled minor item, more a mystery story than a consideration of euthanasia. Robert Kent, J. Edward Bromberg, Gloria Stuart, Henry Armetta, Sara Haden, Alan Dinehart. Written by Frances Hyland and Saul Elkins; directed by George Marshall; for TCF.

The Crime of Dr Hallet
US 1938   68m   bw

A doctor working on jungle fever finds it convenient to disappear and take over a dead colleague's identity. Implausible time-passer. Ralph Bellamy, Josephine Hutchinson, William Gargan, Barbara Read. Written by Lester Cole and Brown Holmes; directed by S. Sylvan Simon; for Universal. (Remade in 1946 as *Strange Conquest,* with Lowell Gilmore and Jane Wyatt.)

The Crime of Monsieur Lange**
France 1935   85m   bw
Obéron (André Halley des Fontaines)

When the hated boss of a publishing house is believed killed, the workers turn it into a successful co-operative. When he reappears, they kill him.
The political elements of this fable now seem unimportant, but it still shows its original charm and cinematic skill.

w *Jacques Prévert d Jean Renoir ph* Jean Bachelet m Jean Wiener

René Lefèbvre, Jules Berry, Florelle, Sylvie Bataille, Henri Guisol

Crime of Passion
US 1956   86m   bw
UA / Bob Goldstein (Herman Cohen)

An executive's wife sleeps his way to the top, but when the boss does not come through with promotion she shoots him.
Old-fashioned star melodrama on a low budget.

w Jo Eisinger d Gerd Oswald ph Joseph La Shelle m Paul Dunlap

Barbara Stanwyck, Sterling Hayden, Raymond Burr, Fay Wray, Royal Dano, Virginia Grey

Crime School*
US 1938 86m bw
Warner (Bryan Foy)

Problems of the warden of a reform school. Predictable vehicle for the Dead End Kids; watchable at the time.

w Crane Wilbur, Vincent Sherman *d* Lewis Seiler *ph* Arthur Todd

Humphrey Bogart, Gale Page, Billy Halop, Huntz Hall, Leo Gorcey, Bobby Jordan, Gabriel Dell, Bernard Punsley, Paul Porcasi, Al Bridge

Crime without Passion**
US 1934 82m bw
Paramount (Ben Hecht, Charles MacArthur)

A lawyer is driven to commit murder. Effective melodrama notable for then-new techniques which were blended into the mainstream of movie-making, and for the first appearance in Hollywood of a smart new writer-producer-director team.

wd Ben Hecht, Charles MacArthur, from their story Caballero of the Law *ph Lee Garmes sp* Slavko Vorkapitch

Claude Rains, Margo, Whitney Bourne, Stanley Ridges
'The whole venture seems to take a long stride forward for the movies.'—*Otis Ferguson*
'A flamboyant, undisciplined, but compulsively fascinating film classic.'—*Peter John Dyer, 1966*

Crimes at the Dark House
GB 1939 69m bw
Pennant (George King)

A Victorian landowner kills his wife and conceals the fact by using a lunatic as her double.
Cheeky adaptation of a classic to make one of the star's most lip-smacking barnstormers.

w Edward Dryhurst, Frederick Hayward, H. F. Maltby from The Woman in White by Wilkie Collins *d* George King

Tod Slaughter, Hilary Eaves, Sylvia Marriott, Hay Petrie, David Horne

The Crimes of Stephen Hawke
GB 1936 69m bw

A nineteenth-century moneylender is exposed as the mysterious murderer who had terrorized London. Amusing barnstormer, a vehicle for *Tod Slaughter*; with Eric Portman, Marjorie Taylor, Gerald Barry. Written by H. F.

Maltby; directed by George King; for George King / MGM.

The Criminal*
GB 1960 97m bw
Merton Park (Jack Greenwood)
US title: *The Concrete Jungle*

Sent to jail for a racecourse snatch, a gangster comes out fifteen years later to regain the loot and is followed by other criminals who kill him.
Relentlessly grim saga of prison life, with a few sensational trimmings.

w Alun Owen, Jimmy Sangster *d* Joseph Losey *ph Robert Krasker m* Johnny Dankworth

Stanley Baker, Sam Wanamaker, Margit Saad, *Patrick Magee*, Noel Willman, Grégoire Aslan, Jill Bennett, Kenneth J. Warren, Nigel Green, Patrick Wymark, Murray Melvin
'A savage, almost expressionistic picture of English underworld life.'—*NFT, 1973*

The Criminal Code*
US 1931 97m bw
Columbia (Harry Cohn)

A young man kills in self-defence, is railroaded into jail and becomes involved in another murder.
Impressive melodrama with good performances and sharp handling.

w Seton I. Miller, Fred Niblo Jnr, *play* Martin Flavin *d Howard Hawks ph* James Wong Howe, William O'Connell

Walter Huston, Phillips Holmes, Constance Cummings, Mary Doran, De Witt Jennings, John Sheehan, Boris Karloff
† Remade as *Penitentiary* (1938) with Walter Connolly and *Convicted* (1950) with Broderick Crawford.

AAN: Seton I. Miller, Fred Niblo Jnr

Criminal Court
US 1946 63m bw

A lawyer is blackmailed by a crooked club owner. Stock crime and lawcourt yarn, rather stodgily put together but with interesting moments. Tom Conway, Martha O'Driscoll, Robert Armstrong, Addison Richards. Written by Lawrence Kimble; directed by Robert Wise; for RKO.

The Criminal Life of Archibaldo de la Cruz*
Mexico 1955 91m bw
Alianza Cinematografica (Roberto Figueroa)
original title: *Ensayo de un Crimen*

A fantasist determines to kill all women who cross his path, but fate intervenes.

Cheaply made macabre joke, one of its director's throwaway oddities: not too smooth, but often amusing.

w Luis Bunuel, E. Ugarte d Luis Bunuel ph Augusto Jimenez md Jorge Perez

Ernesto Alonso, Ariadna Welter, Miroslava Stern, Rita Macedo

The Crimson Circle
GB 1936   76m   bw

Scotland Yard rounds up a blackmail gang.
Lively Edgar Wallace adaptation. Hugh Wakefield, Alfred Drayton, Noah Beery, June Duprez, Niall MacGinnis. Written by Howard Irving Young; directed by Reginald Denham; for Wainwright.

The Crimson Curtain*
France 1952   43m   bw
Argos
original title: Le Rideau Cramoisi

An officer billeted with a bourgeois family is visited at night by the beautiful daughter, who finally dies in his arms.

A curious polished fragment with narration replacing spoken dialogue. For those in the mood, it works.

wd Alexandre Astruc, from a story by Barbey d'Aurevilly ph Eugene Schufftan m Jean-Jacques Grunenwald

Jean-Claude Pascal, Anouk Aimée, Madeleine Garcia, Jim Gerald

'In its limited time, with the greatest economy of means, it evokes an authentic sense of the past, as well as telling a story movingly and dramatically.'—Richard Roud

The Crimson Kimono
US 1959   82m   bw
Columbia / Globe (Samuel Fuller)

Detectives seeking the murderer of a stripper in Los Angeles' Little Tokyo both fall in love with a witness.

Self-conscious local colour, though quite freshly observed and well photographed, finally overwhelms an ordinary little murder mystery.

wd Samuel Fuller ph Sam Leavitt m Harry Sukman

Glenn Corbett, James Shigeta, Victoria Shaw, Anna Lee, Paul Dubov

The Crimson Pirate*
GB 1952   104m   Technicolor
Warner / Harold Hecht

An 18th-century pirate and an eccentric inventor lead an island's people in rebellion against a tyrant.

One suspects that this started off as a straight adventure and was turned halfway through production into a spoof; at any rate, the effect is patchy but with spirited highlights, and the star's acrobatic training is put to good use.

w Roland Kibbee d Robert Siodmak ph Otto Heller m William Alwyn

Burt Lancaster, Nick Cravat, Eva Bartok, Torin Thatcher, James Hayter, Margot Grahame, Noel Purcell, Frank Pettingell

Crin Blanc**
France 1953   47m   bw
Albert Lamorisse
aka: Wild Stallion

A small boy befriends and rides a wild horse in the Camargue.

A favourite short film of great beauty, but a shade overlong for its content.

wd Albert Lamorisse ph Edmond Séchan m Maurice Le Roux

Alain Emery, Pascal Lamorisse

Crisis*
US 1950   96m   bw
MGM (Arthur Freed)

A brain surgeon is forced to operate secretly on a South American dictator, and his wife is kidnapped by revolutionaries.

Dour intellectual suspense piece, in key with the genteel enlightenment of the Dore Schary regime at MGM. Well made but cold.

wd Richard Brooks, story George Tabori ph Ray June m Miklos Rozsa

Cary Grant, Jose Ferrer, Signe Hasso, Paula Raymond, Ramon Navarro, Antonio Moreno, Leon Ames, Gilbert Roland

'Original, arresting and considered . . . so far the most striking example of Dore Schary's policy of encouraging the development of new talents.'—Gavin Lambert

Criss Cross*
US 1948   87m   bw
U-I (Michael Draike)

An armoured car guard and his double-crossing ex-wife get mixed up with vicious gangsters.

Sordid film noir with a poor plot but suspenseful sequences.

w Daniel Fuchs d Robert Siodmak ph Franz Planer m Miklos Rozsa

Burt Lancaster, Yvonne de Carlo, Dan
Duryea, Stephen McNally, Richard Long,
Tom Pedi, Alan Napier

'Siodmak's talent for brooding violence and
the sombre urban setting gives the film a
relentlessly mounting tension.'—*Peter John
Dyer*

Critic's Choice
US 1963   100m   Technicolor
Panavision
Warner / Frank P. Rosenberg

A ruthless Broadway critic is forced by his
scruples to write a bad review of his wife's
play.
Unsuitable vehicle for stars who have shorn a
good comedy of wit and strive vainly for
sentiment, wisecracks and pratfalls.

w Jack Sher, *play* Ira Levin *d* Don Weis
ph Charles Lang *m* George Duning

Bob Hope, Lucille Ball, Marilyn Maxwell, Rip
Torn, Jessie Royce Landis, John Dehner, Jim
Backus, Marie Windsor

'For instant stultification.'—*Judith Crist*

Cromwell*
GB 1970   141m   Technicolor
Panavision
Columbia / Irving Allen (Andrew Donally)

An account of the rise of Cromwell to power,
the execution of Charles I, and the Civil War.
Disappointingly dull schoolbook history, with
good production values but glum handling.

wd Ken Hughes *ph* Geoffrey Unsworth
m Frank Cordell *pd* John Stoll

Richard Harris, Alec Guinness, Robert
Morley, Dorothy Tutin, Frank Finlay,
Timothy Dalton, Patrick Wymark, Patrick
Magee, Nigel Stock, Charles Gray, Michael
Jayston, Anna Cropper, Michael Goodliffe

'It tries to combine serious intentions with
the widest kind of popular appeal and falls
unhappily between the two. It will offend the
purists and bore the kiddies.'—*Brenda Davies*

AAN: Frank Cordell

The Crooked Billet
GB 1929   82m   bw

Spies and detectives converge on an old inn
where documents are hidden. Fairly
unwatchable now, this once-entertaining
melodrama was shot as a silent and had sound
clumsily added. Its cast remains notable:
Carlyle Blackwell, Madeleine Carroll, Miles
Mander, Gordon Harker. Written by Angus
Macphail, from the play by Dion Titherage;
directed by Adrian Brunel; for Michael
Balcon / Gainsborough.

The Crooked Road
GB / Yugoslavia 1964   92m   bw

An American journalist plans to expose as a
crook the dictator of a small Balkan state, but
finds himself framed for murder. Lugubrious
and too-talkative melodrama of political
intrigue. Robert Ryan, Stewart Granger,
Marius Goring, Nadia Gray, Catherine
Woodville, George Coulouris. Written by J.
Garrison and Don Chaffey, from the novel
The Big Story by Morris West; directed by
Don Chaffey; for Argo / Triglav.

The Crooked Web
US 1955   77m   bw

A restaurant owner is lured into a scheme to
recover buried Nazi gold from Germany, but
finds it is a means of arresting him on an old
murder charge. Ingenious but somehow
uninteresting puzzle melodrama. Frank
Lovejoy, Richard Denning, Mari Blanchard.
Written by Lou Breslow; directed by Nathan
Juran; for Sam Katzman / Columbia.

Crooks and Coronets
GB 1969   106m   Technicolor
Warner Seven Arts / Herman Cohen
US title: *Sophie's Place*

American gangsters plan to rob a stately home
but are taken over by the dowager in charge.
Overlong and mainly flatulent comedy, with a
good climax involving a vintage plane.

wd Jim O'Connelly *ph* Desmond Dickinson
m Patrick John Scott

Telly Savalas, Edith Evans, Warren Oates,
Nicky Henson, Cesar Romero, Harry H.
Corbett

Crooks Anonymous*
GB 1962   87m   bw
Anglo Amalgamated (Nat Cohen)

A petty thief joins an organization for
reforming criminals, but is tempted again . . .
and so are they.
Amusingly devised and plotted minor comedy
with an exceptional cast.

w Jack Davies, Henry Blyth *d* Ken Annakin
ph Ernest Steward *m* Muir Mathieson, Henry
Martin

Leslie Phillips, Stanley Baxter, Wilfrid Hyde
White, Julie Christie, James Robertson
Justice, Robertson Hare, Charles Lloyd Pack

Crooks in Cloisters
GB 1963   97m   Technicolor   Scope
Forgers pose as monks but are reformed by
the country life. Busy comedy full of familiar
faces; perhaps a small cut above the *Carry*

*On*s. Ronald Fraser, Barbara Windsor, Grégoire Aslan, Bernard Cribbins, Davy Kaye, Wilfred Brambell. Written by Mike Watts; directed by Jeremy Summers; for ABPC.

Crooks' Tour*
GB 1940 84m bw
British National (John Corfield)

English tourists are mistaken for spies by Nazis in Baghdad.
Amusing vehicle for two comic actors who excelled at portraying the English abroad.

w John Watt, Max Kester, from the radio serial by Sidney Gilliat and Frank Launder *d* John Baxter *ph* James Wilson *m* Kennedy Russell

Basil Radford, Naunton Wayne, Greta Gynt, Abraham Sofaer, Gordon McLeod

Cross My Heart*
US 1945 83m bw
Paramount (Harry Tugend)

A romantic girl confesses to murder, is acquitted, and finds the real murderer.
Modest remake of *True Confession* (qv), with frenetic pace but not much style.

w Claude Binyon, Harry Tugend, Charles Schnee *d* John Berry *ph* Charles Lang Jnr *m* Robert Emmett Dolan

Betty Hutton, Sonny Tufts, Michael Chekhov, Rhys Williams, Ruth Donnelly, Al Bridge, Howard Freeman, Iris Adrian

Cross of Iron*
GB / West Germany 1976   133m
    Technicolor
EMI–Rapid Film / Terra Filmkunst (Wolf C. Hartwig)

Militarily and emotionally at the end of its tether, a German battalion is decimated while fighting the Russians in 1943.
Painful to follow, occasionally beautiful to watch, this quite horrid film offers too much opportunity for its director to wallow in unpleasant physical details, and its main plot of bitter rivalry offers no relief.

w Julius J. Epstein, Herbert Asmodi *d* Sam Peckinpah *ph* John Coquillon *m* Ernest Gold

James Coburn, James Mason, Maximilian Schell, David Warner, Klaus Löwitch
   'Morally dubious but technically brilliant.'— *Michael Billington, Illustrated London News*

The Cross of Lorraine*
US 1944   91m   bw
MGM (Edwin Knopf)

In a German camp for French prisoners, an escape leads to a rising by local villagers.
Standard war propaganda piece, made with enthusiasm on unconvincing sets.

w Michael Kanin, Ring Lardner Jnr, Alexander Esway, Robert Andrews *d* Tay Garnett *ph* Sidney Wagner *m* Bronislau Kaper

Gene Kelly, Jean-Pierre Aumont, Cedric Hardwicke, Peter Lorre, Joseph Calleia, Richard Whorf, Hume Cronyn
   'Half a football team worked on the story, yet except for a foolish coda it is one of the most edged, well-characterized, and naturally cinematic scripts of the year.'—*James Agee*

Crossed Swords
Italy / USA 1954   83m   Pathecolor
Viva Films (J. Barrett Mahon, Vittorio Vassarotti)
original title: *Il Maestro di Don Giovanni*

The son of an Italian duke prevents an uprising.
A thin swashbuckler showing the perils of early co-production.

wd Milton Krims *ph* Jack Cardiff

Errol Flynn, Gina Lollobrigida, Cesare Danova, Nadia Gray, Paola Mori

Crossfire****
US 1947   86m   bw
RKO (Adrian Scott)

A Jew is murdered in a New York hotel, and three soldiers are suspected.
Tense, talky thriller shot entirely at night with pretty full expressionist use of camera technique; notable for style, acting, experimentation, and for being the first Hollywood film to hit out at racial bigotry.

w John Paxton, *novel* The Brick Foxhole by Richard Brooks *ph* J. Roy Hunt *d* Edward Dmytryk *m* Roy Webb

Robert Young, Robert Mitchum, *Robert Ryan*, Gloria Grahame, *Paul Kelly*, Sam Levene, Jacqueline White, Steve Brodie

AAN: best picture; John Paxton; Edward Dmytryk; Robert Ryan; Gloria Grahame

The Crossing of the Rhine*
France / Italy / West Germany 1960
    125m   bw
Franco-London-Gibe-Jonia-UFA (Ralph Baum)
original title: *Le Passage du Rhin*

Two French soldiers escape from the Germans in 1940 and after various adventures meet up again in Paris in 1945.
Two crowded plots and not a great deal of point emerge from this watchable war film full of conventional set pieces.

w André Cayatte, Armand Jammot *d* André Cayatte *ph* Roger Fellous *m* Louiguy

Charles Aznavour, Nicole Courcel, Georges Rivière, Cordula Trantow

Crossplot
GB 1969 97m Eastmancolor
UA / Tribune (Robert S. Baker)

An advertising executive gets involved in a spy ring.
Old-fashioned, London-set amalgam of secret codes, disappearing bodies, helicopter attacks, and a finale frustrating the assassination of a statesman in Hyde Park.

w Leigh Vance *d* Alvin Rakoff *ph* Brendan J. Stafford *m* Stanley Black

Roger Moore, Martha Hyer, Alexis Kanner, Francis Matthews, Bernard Lee

Crossroads**
Japan 1928 80m approx bw silent
Shochiku
original title: *Jujiro*

A woman kills her seducer. Her brother thinks he has killed a man and takes refuge with her, only to die of shock when he sees the man alive.
The only widely distributed Japanese silent film, this curious piece is fragmentarily told and will remind many of *Rashomon* with its mixture of flashbacks and dreams.

wd Teinosuke Kinugasa *ph* Kohei Sugiyama

J. Bandoha, A. Tschihaya, Yujiko Ogawa, I. Sohma

Crossroads*
US 1942 84m bw
MGM (Edwin Knopf)

A French diplomat who once lost his memory is blackmailed by crooks who claim he was once a criminal.
Smooth mystery melodrama adapted from the French film *Carrefour*.

w Howard Emmett Rogers, John Kafka *d* Jack Conway *ph* Joseph Ruttenberg *m* Bronislau Kaper

William Powell, Hedy Lamarr, Basil Rathbone, Claire Trevor, Margaret Wycherly, Felix Bressart, Sig Rumann

Crosswinds
US 1951 93m Technicolor

Treasure-hunting boatmen fall out in New Guinea. Adequate outdoor thick-ear; good value for money as the lower half of a double bill. John Payne, Rhonda Fleming, Forrest

Tucker, Robert Lowery, Alan Mowbray, John Abbott. Written and directed by Lewis R. Foster; for Pine / Thomas (Paramount).

The Crowd***
US 1928 98m bw silent
MGM (King Vidor)

Episodes in the life of a city clerk.
A deliberately humdrum story, chosen to show that drama can exist in the lowliest surroundings, retains much of its original power, though some of the director's innovations have become clichés.

w King Vidor, John V. A. Weaver, Harry Behn *d* King Vidor *ph* Henry Sharp *ad* Cedric Gibbons, Arnold Gillespie *ed* Hugh Wynn

James Murray, Eleanor Boardman, Bert Roach, Estelle Clark
'No picture is perfect, but this comes as near to reproducing reality as anything you have ever witnessed.'—*Photoplay*
AAN: King Vidor

The Crowd Roars*
US 1932 85m bw
Warner

A star motor-racing driver tries to prevent his young brother from following in his footsteps. Typical early Cagney vehicle, still spectacularly pacy but dated in its dialogue scenes.

w Kubec Glasmon, John Bright, Niven Busch *d* Howard Hawks *ph* Sid Hickox, John Stumar *md* Leo Forbstein

James Cagney, Joan Blondell, Ann Dvorak, Eric Linden, Guy Kibbee, Frank McHugh, Regis Toomey
'As so often Hawks seems bitter at the world men have created but respects those who have to attempt to live it to the full.'—*NFT, 1963*
'The story is not precisely exciting . . . the closing episode is the best, for it reveals a certain originality in having the injured automobile racers eager to continue the race in ambulances on the way to hospital.'—*Mordaunt Hall, New York Times*
† Remade in 1939 as *Indianapolis Speedway*.

The Crowd Roars*
US 1938 90m bw
MGM (Sam Zimbalist)

A young boxer becomes involved with the underworld.
Standard star vehicle with efficient trimmings.

w Thomas Lennon, George Bruce, George Oppenheimer d Richard Thorpe ph John Seitz m Edward Ward

Robert Taylor, Frank Morgan, Edward Arnold, Maureen O'Sullivan, William Gargan, Frank Craven, Jane Wyman, Lionel Stander, Nat Pendleton

† Remade as *Killer McCoy*.

The Crowded Day
GB 1954   82m   bw

Problems of five assistants in a department store during the Christmas rush. Naïve little portmanteau which suited its purpose. Joan Rice, John Gregson, Freda Jackson, Patricia Marmont, Josephine Griffin, Sonia Holm, Rachel Roberts, Thora Hird, Dora Bryan, Edward Chapman, Sid James, Richard Wattis. Written by Talbot Rothwell; directed by John Guillermin; for Adelphi.

The Crowded Sky
US 1960   104m   Technicolor
Warner (Michael Garrison)

As two planes fly unwittingly towards each other, the passengers muse on their personal problems. An emergency landing averts total disaster.

The format goes back as far as *Friday the Thirteenth*, and forward to *Airport 75*, but this was in fact a cut-rate rehash of *The High and the Mighty*, with dull characters and insufficiently tense handling, not to mention a second team cast.

w Charles Schnee   d Joseph Pevney   ph Harry Stradling   m Leonard Rosenman

Dana Andrews, Rhonda Fleming, Efrem Zimbalist Jnr, John Kerr, Anne Francis, Keenan Wynn, Troy Donahue, Joe Mantell, Patsy Kelly

The Cruel Sea**
GB 1952   126m   bw
Ealing (Leslie Norman)

Life and death on an Atlantic corvette during World War II.

Competent transcription of a bestselling book, cleanly produced and acted; a huge box office success.

w Eric Ambler, *novel* Nicholas Monsarrat
d *Charles Frend* ph Gordon Dines, Jo Jago, Paul Beeson   m Alan Rawsthorne

Jack Hawkins, Donald Sinden, Stanley Baker, John Stratton, Denholm Elliott, John Warner, Bruce Seton, Virginia McKenna, Moira Lister, June Thorburn

'One is grateful nowadays for a film which does not depict war as anything but a tragic and bloody experience, and it is this quality which gives the production its final power to move.'—*John Gillett*

AAN: Eric Ambler

Cruising
US 1980   106m   Technicolor
Lorimar (Jerry Weintraub)

A New York cop becomes degraded in his search among homosexuals for a sadistic killer. Alleged thriller with phoney pretensions and repellent detail.

wd William Friedkin   ph James Contner
m Jack Nitzsche

Al Pacino, Paul Sorvino, Karen Allen, Richard Cox, Don Scardino, Joe Spinell

'Like any approach to the bizarre, it's fascinating for about fifteen minutes. After that, it suffers from the same boring repetition that makes porno so uninteresting generally.'—*Variety*

The Crusades**
US 1935   127m   bw
Paramount / Cecil B. de Mille

Spurred by his wife Berengaria, Richard the Lionheart sets off on his holy wars. Heavily tapestried medieval epic, spectacular sequences being punctuated by wodges of uninspired dialogue. A true de Mille pageant.

w Harold Lamb, Waldemar Young, Dudley Nichols   d *Cecil B. de Mille*   ph Victor Milner
sp Gordon Jennings   m Rudolph Kopp

Henry Wilcoxon, Loretta Young, C. Aubrey Smith, Ian Keith, Katherine de Mille, Joseph Schildkraut, Alan Hale, C. Henry Gordon, George Barbier, Montagu Love, Lumsden Hare, William Farnum, Hobart Bosworth, Pedro de Cordoba, Mischa Auer

'Mr de Mille's evangelical films are the nearest equivalent today to the glossy German colour prints which decorated mid-Victorian bibles. There is the same lack of a period sense, the same stuffy horsehair atmosphere of beards and whiskers, and, their best quality, a childlike eye for detail.'—*Otis Ferguson*

'Cinema addicts by now have some idea what to expect in a de Mille version of the Holy Wars. *The Crusades* should fulfil all expectations. As a picture it is historically worthless, didactically treacherous, artistically absurd. None of these defects impairs its entertainment value. It is a hundred-million-dollar sideshow which has at least three features to distinguish it from the long line of previous de Mille extravaganzas. It is the noisiest; it is the biggest; it contains no baths.'—*Time*

AAN: Victor Milner

Cry for Happy
US 1961   110m   Eastmancolor
Cinemascope
Columbia (William Goetz)

Four navy cameramen in Japan help geishas to found an orphanage.

As bad as it sounds, a repellent mixture of sentiment and knockabout.

w Irving Brecher *d* George Marshall
ph Burnett Guffey *m* George Duning

Glenn Ford, Donald O'Connor, Miiko Taka, James Shigeta, Mikoshi Umeki, Joe Flynn, Howard St John

'Any film which expends most of its energies on a protracted joke about how far you can go with a geisha could hardly fail to be as charmless and witless as this.'—*MFB*

A Cry from the Streets
GB 1958   100m   bw
Film Traders (Ian Dalrymple)

Episodes from the work of child welfare officers.

Mildly pleasing but unconvincing semi-documentary, with children competing with the star at scene-stealing.

w Vernon Harris, *novel* The Friend in Need by Elizabeth Coxhead *d* Lewis Gilbert
ph Harry Gillan *m* Larry Adler

Max Bygraves, Barbara Murray, Colin Petersen, Dana Wilson, Elizabeth Harrison, Eleanor Summerfield, Mona Washbourne

Cry Havoc
US 1943   97m   bw
MGM (Edwin Knopf)

War nurses are caught up in the Bataan retreat.

An all-woman cast adequately handles a stagey melodrama about a tragic situation.

w Paul Osborn, *play* Proof thro' the Night by Allen R. Kenward *d* Richard Thorpe
ph Karl Freund *m* Daniele Amfitheatrof

Margaret Sullavan, Joan Blondell, Ann Sothern, Fay Bainter, Marsha Hunt, Ella Raines, Frances Gifford, Diana Lewis, Heather Angel, Connie Gilchrist

'A sincere fourth-rate film made from a sincere fifth-rate play.'—*James Agee*

'Its popularity will stem less from its probably factual record of nurses starving, sweating and dying in the beleaguered Philippine jungle than from the impressive all-woman cast which MGM has rounded up for the occasion.'—*Newsweek*

A Cry in the Night
US 1956   75m   bw
Warner / Jaguar (George C. Bertholon)

A peeping Tom, caught by a teenage couple, abducts the girl and threatens rape.

Odd little domestic thriller, with parents and police working together. Watchable, but a bit over the top.

w David Dortort *d* Frank Tuttle *ph* John Seitz *m* David Buttolph

Edmond O'Brien, Brian Donlevy, Natalie Wood, Raymond Burr, Richard Anderson, Irene Hervey, Anthony Caruso

Cry of the Banshee
GB 1970   87m   Movielab
AIP (Gordon Hessler)

A 16th-century magistrate is cursed by a witch, who sends a devil in the form of a young man to destroy him.

Modest horror film which fails to do justice to its interesting plot.

w Tim Kelly, Christopher Wicking *d* Gordon Hessler *ph* John Coquillon *m* Les Baxter

Vincent Price, Elisabeth Bergner, Patrick Mower, Essy Persson, Hugh Griffith, Hilary Dwyer, Sally Geeson

Cry of the City**
US 1948   96m   bw
TCF

A ruthless gangster on the run is pursued by a policeman who was once his boyhood friend.

Very well produced but relentlessly miserable New York thriller on the lines of *Manhattan Melodrama* and *Angels with Dirty Faces*.

w Richard Murphy *d* Robert Siodmak
ph Lloyd Aherne *m* Alfred Newman

Victor Mature, Richard Conte, Mimi Agulia, Shelley Winters, Tommy Cook, Fred Clark, Debra Paget

'When the city cries in a movie, it's with the desolate wail of police sirens and with rain-streaked sidewalks; but most of all with poetic justification.'—*Paul Taylor, Time Out, 1980*

Cry Terror**
US 1958   96m   bw
MGM / Andrew Stone

As security against ransom money being delivered, an airline bomber kidnaps a family.

Unabashed suspenser which screws panic situations as far as they will go and farther.

wd Andrew Stone ph Walter Strenge
m Howard Jackson

James Mason, Rod Steiger, Inger Stevens,
Neville Brand, Angie Dickinson, Kenneth
Tobey, Jack Klugman, Jack Kruschen

Cry the Beloved Country*
GB 1951 96m bw
London Films (Alan Paton)
US title: *African Fury*

In South Africa, a white farmer and a black
preacher find friendship through linked family
tragedies.
Well-intentioned, earnest, rather high-flown
racial drama.

w Alan Paton, from his novel *d* Zoltan
Korda *ph* Robert Krasker *m* Raymond
Gallois-Montbrun

Canada Lee, Sidney Poitier, Charles Carson,
Charles McRae, Joyce Carey, Geoffrey Keen,
Michael Goodliffe, Edric Connor

Cry Wolf
US 1947 83m bw
Warner (Henry Blanke)

A widow claims her husband's estate and finds
his mysterious uncle very difficult to deal
with . . .
Rather obvious old dark house mystery with a
not very interesting solution, all relying too
heavily on star performances.

w Catherine Turney, *novel* Marjorie Carleton
d Peter Godfrey *ph* Carl Guthrie *m* Franz
Waxman

Barbara Stanwyck, Errol Flynn (as the
apparent heavy), Geraldine Brooks, Richard
Basehart, Helene Thimig

The Crystal Ball*
US 1943 82m bw
(Richard Blumenthal)

A failed beauty contestant becomes a fortune
teller and is involved in a land swindle.
Pleasant comedy with fanciful moments,
ending with a pie-throwing contest.

w Virginia Van Upp *d* Elliott Nugent *ph* Leo
Tover *m* Victor Young

Paulette Goddard, Ray Milland, Gladys
George, Virginia Field, Cecil Kellaway,
William Bendix, Ernest Truex

Cuba
US 1979 122m Technicolor
UA / Alex Winitsky, Arlene Sellers

Upper-crust characters are caught in Havana
when the Castro revolution starts.
Aimless romantic melodrama which gets

absolutely nowhere and might have been
better played in the *Casablanca* vein.

w Charles Wood *d* Richard Lester *ph* David
Watkin *m* Patrick Williams *pd* Gil Parrando

Sean Connery, Brooke Adams, Jack Weston,
Hector Elizondo, Denholm Elliott, Martin
Balsam, Chris Sarandon

Cuba Si!*
France 1961 58m bw
Films de la Pléïade

A documentary on the Cuban revolution and
Castro's rise to power.
Remarkable and influential at the time for its
use of techniques which are now the
commonplaces of television, this documentary
still has its flashes of interest.

wd, ph Chris Marker m E. G. Mantici, J.
Calzada *ed* Eva Zora
  'An eloquent, personal record of history in
the making.'—*Georges Sadoul*

Cuban Love Song
US 1931 86m bw
MGM

A marine on leave in Cuba falls in love; years
later he returns to retrieve his illegitimate
child, whose mother has died.
Pathetic musical melodrama which did not
advance its singing star's film career.

w John Lynch *d* W. S. Van Dyke *ph* Harold
Rosson *songs* various

Lawrence Tibbett, Lupe Velez, Jimmy
Durante, Ernest Torrence, Karen Morley,
Louise Fazenda

A Cuckoo in the Nest*
GB 1933 85m bw
Gaumont (Ian Dalrymple, Angus MacPhail)

A newlywed husband is forced to spend a
night at an inn with an old flame pretending to
be his wife.
Classic Aldwych farce with the stage company
in excellent form; directorial style on the
stagey side.

w Ben Travers, A. R. Rawlinson, *play Ben
Travers d* Tom Walls

*Ralph Lynn, Tom Walls, Yvonne Arnaud,
Mary Brough*, Veronica Rose, Gordon James,
Cecil Parker, Roger Livesey
  † Remade 1955 as *Fast and Loose.*

Cul de Sac
GB 1966 111m bw
Compton—Tekli (Gene Gutowski)

Two gangsters on the run take refuge in an old
castle on a desolate Northumbrian island, but

find their nemesis in the effeminate owner and his voluptuous wife.

Overlong, eccentric black comedy, more perplexing than entertaining.

w Roman Polanski, Gerard Brach *d* Roman Polanski *ph* Gilbert Taylor *m* Komeda

Lionel Stander, Donald Pleasence, Jack MacGowran, Françoise Dorléac, William Franklyn, Robert Dorning, Renée Houston

The Culpeper Cattle Company*
US 1972 92m De Luxe
TCF (Paul A. Helmick)

A 16-year-old would-be cowboy joins a cattle trail but is shocked at the harsh realities of western life.

Excellent moody photography helps to convince us that the old west was really like this, but the story is more brutal than interesting.

w Eric Bercovici, Gregory Prentiss *d* Dick Richards *ph* *Lawrence Edward Williams, Ralph Woolsey* *m* Tom Scott, Jerry Goldsmith

Gary Grimes, Billy 'Green' Bush, Luke Askew, Bo Hopkins, Geoffrey Lewis, Wayne Sutherlin

Cult of the Cobra
US 1955 79m bw

Six GIs are cursed by the high priest of an Indian cobra cult. Back in New York, a mysterious woman brings about their deaths, and when the survivor kills a cobra, it turns into her. Glossy but wholly unconvincing and unexciting non-horror potboiler. Faith Domergue, Richard Long, Marshall Thompson, Kathleen Hughes, Jack Kelly. Written by Jerry Davis, Cecil Maiden and Richard Collins; directed by Francis D. Lyon; for Universal–International.

A Cup of Kindness
GB 1934 81m bw

Young lovers marry despite parental disapproval on both sides. Farcical updating of *Romeo and Juliet*; it hasn't worn too well, but the stars are at their peak. Tom Walls, Ralph Lynn, Robertson Hare, Claude Hulbert, Dorothy Hyson, Eva Moore. Written by Ben Travers, from his play; directed by Tom Walls; for Michael Balcon / Gaumont.

The Cure••••
US 1917 20m approx bw silent
Mutual

A dipsomaniac sent to a spa gets his booze mixed up with the spa water.

One of the funniest of the Chaplin shorts, with no pathos intervening (nor come to that much plot); it is simply a succession of balletic slapstick scenes of the highest order.

wd Charles Chaplin *ph* William C. Foster, Rollie Totheroh

Charles Chaplin, Edna Purviance, Eric Campbell, Henry Bergman

The Cure for Love
GB 1949 98m bw
London Films (Robert Donat)

An ex-soldier goes home and tries to get married.

Thin Lancashire comedy which seemed an astonishing choice for Robert Donat, whose acting and direction are equally ill at ease.

w Robert Donat, Alexander Shaw, Albert Fennell, *play* Walter Greenwood *d* Robert Donat *ph* Jack Cox *m* William Alwyn

Robert Donat, Renée Asherson, Dora Bryan, Marjorie Rhodes, Charles Victor, Thora Hird, Gladys Henson

'Antediluvian regional farce.'—*MFB*

Curly Top*
US 1935 78m bw
TCF (Darryl F. Zanuck, Winfield Sheehan)

An orphan waif is adopted by a playboy, and not only sets his business right but fixes his romantic interest in her sister.

Archetypal Temple vehicle, a loose remake of *Daddy Longlegs*.

w Patterson McNutt, Arthur Beckhard *d* Irving Cummings *ph* John Seitz *songs* Ray Henderson, Ted Koehler, Edward Heyman, Irving Caesar

Shirley Temple, John Boles, Rochelle Hudson, Jane Darwell, Rafaela Ottiano, Esther Dale, Arthur Treacher, Etienne Girardot

The Curse of Frankenstein••
GB 1957 83m Eastmancolor
Warner / Hammer (Anthony Hinds)

A lurid revamping of the 1931 *Frankenstein*, this time with severed eyeballs and a peculiarly unpleasant and uncharacterized creature, all in gory colour. It set the trend in nasty horrors from which we have all suffered since, and launched Hammer Studios on a long and profitable career of charnelry. But it did have a gruesome sense of style.

w Jimmy Sangster *d* Terence Fisher *ph* Jack Asher *m* James Bernard *ad* Ted Marshall

Peter Cushing, Christopher Lee, Hazel Court, Robert Urquhart, Valerie Gaunt, Noel Hood

The Curse of the Cat People*
US 1944   70m   bw
RKO (*Val Lewton*)

A child is haunted by the spirit of the cat people.
A gentle film ordered by the studio as a sequel to *Cat People* but turned by Lewton into a fantasy of childhood. Slow to start but finally compelling, it's a pleasing and unusual film in a minor key.

w De Witt Bodeen   *d* Robert Wise, Gunther Fritsch   *ph* Nicholas Musuraca   *m* Roy Webb

Kent Smith, Simone Simon, Jane Randolph, Julia Dean, Ann Carter, Elizabeth Russell
   'Full of the poetry and danger of childhood.'—*James Agee*
   'A clumsy coming together of unrealized ideas, gothic effects, and stiff, dull acting.'—*New Yorker, 1979*

Curse of the Crimson Altar
GB 1968   89m   Eastmancolor
Tigon / AIP (Tony Tenser)
aka: *The Crimson Cult*

Witchcraft, diabolism and mystery in an English country house.
A derivative, muddled scribble of a horror film, making no sense and wasting much talent.

w Mervyn Haisman, Henry Lincoln   *d* Vernon Sewell   *ph* John Coquillon   *m* Peter Knight

Boris Karloff (his last appearance), Christopher Lee, Rupert Davies, Mark Eden, Barbara Steele, Michael Gough

Curse of the Undead
US 1959   79m   bw

A black-clad stranger in a western town turns out to be a vampire of Spanish origin.
Abysmal attempt to substitute Wyoming for Transylvania; more skill and sensitivity were required. Michael Pate, Eric Fleming, Kathleen Crowley, John Hoyt. Written and directed by Edward Dein; for Universal-International.

Curse of the Werewolf
GB 1961   92m   Technicolor
U-I / Hammer (Anthony Hinds)

A beggar rapes a servant girl and their offspring grows up to be a werewolf.
Doleful Hammer horror in a Spanish setting, with an absurd but predictable plot and a lack of sympathy for its fancy, hairy hero.

w John Elder (Anthony Hinds)   *d* Terence Fisher   *ph* Arthur Grant   *m* Benjamin Frankel

Oliver Reed, Clifford Evans, Catherine Feller, Yvonne Romain, Anthony Dawson, Richard Wordsworth, Warren Mitchell

The Curse of the Wraydons
GB 1946   94m   bw

The Victorian story of Spring-heeled Jack, here depicted as a mad inventor out for revenge. Too long and stagey to be one of its star's better barnstormers, especially as by this time his girth made the notion of his springing about somewhat hilarious. Tod Slaughter, Bruce Seton, Gabriel Toyne. Written by Michael Barringer; directed by Victor M. Gover; for Bushey.

Curtain Call*
US 1940   63m   bw
RKO

Two Broadway producers buy an awful play in order to get even with a temperamental star, but she likes it.
Amusing second feature, a kind of flashforward to *The Producers*. A reprise the following year, *Footlight Fever*, did not work.

w Dalton Trumbo   *d* Frank Woodruff   *ph* Russell Metty   *m* Roy Webb

Alan Mowbray, Donald MacBride, Helen Vinson, Barbara Read, John Archer

Curtain Call at Cactus Creek*
US 1949   83m   Technicolor
U-I (Robert Arthur)
GB title: *Take the Stage*

A travelling repertory company in the old west exposes a gang of bank robbers.
Cheerful minor comedy with good pace and amusing burlesques of old melodramas.

w Oscar Brodney   *d* Charles Lamont   *ph* Russell Metty   *m* Walter Scharf

Donald O'Connor, Gale Storm, Eve Arden, Vincent Price, Walter Brennan, Chick Chandler

Curtain Up*
GB 1952   85m   bw
Rank / Constellation (Robert Garrett)

A seaside repertory company runs into trouble when the producer is at loggerheads with the author of next week's play.
Fairly amusing farce which has now acquired historical value for the light it throws on the old weekly reps.

w Michael Pertwee, Jack Davies, *play* On Monday Next by Philip King   *d* Ralph Smart   *ph* Stanley Pavey   *m* Malcolm Arnold

Margaret Rutherford, Robert Morley, Olive Sloane, Joan Rice, Charlotte Mitchell, Kay Kendall, Liam Gaffney, Michael Medwin

Custer of the West
US 1968   146m   Super Technirama 70
Cinerama / Security (Louis Dolivet, Philip Yordan, Irving Lerner)

After the Civil War, Custer is offered a cavalry command, becomes disillusioned, and is massacred with his troops at Little Big Horn.
Gloomily inaccurate spectacular with pauses for Cinerama carnival thrills and dour bits of melodrama.

w Bernard Gordon, Julian Halevy *d* Robert Siodmak *ph* Cecilio Paniagua *m* Bernardo Segall

Robert Shaw, Mary Ure, Robert Ryan, Jeffrey Hunter, Ty Hardin, Lawrence Tierney, Kieron Moore

The Cyclops
US 1956   65m   bw
B and H (Bert I. Gordon)

Explorers in Mexico find animals turned by radiation into monsters, plus a one-eyed 25-foot-tall human.
Modest monster movie, quite palatable of its kind.

wd Bert I. Gordon *ph* Ira Morgan *m* Albert Glasser

James Craig, Lon Chaney Jnr, Gloria Talbot, Tom Drake

Cynara**
US 1933   78m   bw
Samuel Goldwyn

A London barrister has an affair with a young girl who commits suicide when he goes back to his wife.
Solidly carpentered, effective star vehicle of the old school, now dated but preserving its dignity.

w Frances Marion, Lynn Starling, *novel* An Imperfect Lover by Robert Gore Brown *d* King Vidor *ph* Ray June *m* Alfred Newman

Ronald Colman, Kay Francis, Phyllis Barry, Henry Stephenson, Paul Porcasi

Cynthia
US 1947   98m   bw
MGM (Edwin H. Knopf)
GB title: *The Rich Full Life*

An over-protected girl finds an outlet in music and her parents finally allow her to lead her own life.
An overlong domestic drama in which thin writing and acting are backed by unsound psychology.

w Harold Buchman, Charles Kaufman, *play* Vina Delmar *d* Robert Z. Leonard *ph* Charles Schoenbaum *m* Bronislau Kaper

Elizabeth Taylor, George Murphy, Mary Astor, S. Z. Sakall, James Lydon, Gene Lockhart, Spring Byington

Cyrano de Bergerac*
US 1950   112m   bw
Stanley Kramer

In the 17th century a long-nosed poet, philosopher and buffoon writes letters enabling a friend to win the lady he loves himself.
The classic romantic verse play does not take kindly to a hole-in-corner black-and-white production, but at the time it was lapped up as a daring cultural breakthrough.

w Brian Hooker, *play* Edmond Rostand *d* Michael Gordon *ph* Franz Planer *m* Dmitri Tiomkin

Jose Ferrer, Mala Powers, William Prince, Morris Carnovsky, Ralph Clanton, Virginia Farmer, Edgar Barrier, Elena Verdugo

AA: Jose Ferrer

D

Daddy Longlegs*
US 1931 73m bw
Fox

An orphan girl grows up to fall in love with
her mysterious benefactor.
Cinderella-like romance, adequately adapted
from a novel which became the classic
American version of the January–May
romance.

w Sonya Levien, *novel* Jean Webster d Alfred
Santell ph Lucien Andriot

Janet Gaynor, Warner Baxter, Una Merkel,
John Arledge, Claude Gillingwater, Louise
Closser Hale
† Other versions were made in 1919 with Mary
Pickford and Mahlon Hamilton, directed by
Marshal Neilan; in 1935 disguised as *Curly
Top* (qv) and in 1955 (see below).

Daddy Longlegs*
US 1955 126m Technicolor
   Cinemascope
TCF (Samuel G. Engel)

Overlong and unsuitably wide-screened
musical version of a popular story (see above).
Generally clumsy and dispirited, but Astaire is
always worth watching and a couple of the
dances are well staged.

w Phoebe and Henry Ephron d Jean
Negulesco ph Leon Shamroy m Alfred
Newman *songs* Johnny Mercer

Fred Astaire, Leslie Caron, *Fred Clark*,
Thelma Ritter, Terry Moore, Charlotte
Austin, Larry Keating

AAN: Alfred Newman; song 'Something's
Gotta Give' (*m / ly* Johnny Mercer)

Daddy's Gone A-Hunting
US 1969 108m Technicolor
Warner / Red Lion (Mark Robson)

A child and its mother are threatened by her
deranged ex-husband.
Unpleasant and protracted suspenser with the
emphasis on sex rather than thrills.

w Larry Cohen, Lorenzo Semple Jnr d Mark
Robson ph Ernest Laszlo m John Williams

Carol White, Paul Burke, Scott Hylands, Mala
Powers, Andrea King

Dad's Army**
GB 1971 95m Technicolor
Columbia / Norcon (John R. Sloan)

Misadventures of a number of elderly gents in
Britain's wartime Home Guard.
Expanded big-screen version of the long-
running TV series, a pleasant souvenir but
rather less effective than was expected because
everything is shown—the town, the Nazis, the
wives—and thus the air of gentle fantasy
disappears, especially in the face of much
coarsened humour.

w Jimmy Perry, David Croft d Norman
Cohen ph Terry Maher m Wilfred Burns

*Arthur Lowe, John Le Mesurier, John Laurie,
James Beck*, Ian Lavender, *Arnold Ridley*, Liz
Fraser, *Clive Dunn*, Bill Pertwee, Frank
Williams, Edward Sinclair

Daisy Kenyon
US 1947 99m bw
TCF (Otto Preminger)

A fashion designer has two men in her life.
Adequate woman's picture which hardly
justifies its cast.

w David Hertz, *novel* Elizabeth Janeway
d Otto Preminger ph Leon Shamroy
m David Raksin

Joan Crawford, Henry Fonda, Dana Andrews,
Ruth Warrick, Martha Stewart, Peggy Ann
Garner

Daisy Miller*
US 1974 92m Technicolor
Paramount / Copa de Oro (Peter
   Bogdanovich)

In the 19th century, an American girl tourist in
Europe falls in love but dies of the Roman
fever.
Curious attempt to film a very mild and
uneventful Henry James story, with careful
production but inadequate leads. The first sign
that Bogdanovich was getting too big for his
boots.

w Frederic Raphael d Peter Bogdanovich
ph Alberto Spagnoli m classical themes
ad Ferdinando Scarfiotti

Cybill Shepherd, Barry Brown, Cloris
Leachman, Mildred Natwick, Eileen Brennan,
James MacMurtry

'A historical film bereft of any feeling for
history, and a literary adaptation which
reveals a fine contempt for literary subtlety.'—
Jan Dawson

'Appallingly crass . . . directed with all the
subtlety of a sledgehammer.'—*Michael
Billington, Illustrated London News*

'Trying to make that little thing he's with
into Daisy Miller was hilarious. God almighty
couldn't do that. She's so coy.'—*Henry
Hathaway*

Dakota
US 1945 82m bw
Republic (Joseph Kane)

The daughter of a railroad tycoon elopes with
a cowboy and becomes involved in a land war.
Adequate star western.

w Lawrence Hazard, *story* Carl Foreman
d Joseph Kane *ph* Jack Marta *m* Walter
Scharf

John Wayne, Vera Hruba Ralston, Walter
Brennan, Ward Bond, Ona Munson, Hugo
Haas, Mike Mazurki, Paul Fix, Grant Withers,
Jack La Rue

Daleks: Invasion Earth 2150 AD see Dr
Who and the Daleks

Dallas*
US 1950 94m Technicolor
Warner (Anthony Veiller)

A renegade ex-Confederate colonel is
pardoned for bringing law and order to Dallas.
Routinely competent top-of-the-bill western.

w John Twist *d* Stuart Heisler *ph* Ernest
Haller *m* Max Steiner

Gary Cooper, Ruth Roman, Raymond
Massey, Steve Cochran, Barbara Payton, Leif
Erickson, Antonio Moreno, Jerome Cowan

The Dam Busters**
GB 1954 125m bw
ABPC (Robert Clark)

In 1943 the Ruhr dams are destroyed by Dr
Barnes Wallis' bouncing bombs.
Understated British war epic with additional
scientific interest and good acting and model
work, not to mention a welcome lack of love
interest.

w R. C. Sheriff, *books* by Guy Gibson and
Paul Brickhill *d* Michael Anderson *ph* Eric
Hillier *m* Leighton Lucas, *Eric Coates
sp* George Blackwell

Michael Redgrave, Richard Todd, Basil
Sydney, Derek Farr, Patrick Barr, Ernest
Clark, Raymond Huntley, Ursula Jeans

Dames**
US 1935 90m bw
Warner (Robert Lord)

A millionaire purity fanatic tries to stop the
opening of a Broadway show.
Typical Warner musical of the period: its real
raison d'être is to be found in the splendidly
imaginative numbers at the finale, but it also
gives very full rein to the roster of comic
actors under contract at the time.

w Delmer Daves *d* Ray Enright *ch* Busby
Berkeley *ph* Sid Hickox, George Barnes
m various

*Joan Blondell, Hugh Herbert, Guy Kibbee,
Zasu Pitts,* Dick Powell, Ruby Keeler

Les Dames du Bois de Boulogne*
France 1946 90m bw
Films Raoul Ploquin

Hélène revenges herself on her bored lover by
arranging for him to marry a prostitute.
Spare, symbolic melodrama which has
occasioned as much irritation as applause.

w Robert Bresson, Jean Cocteau, from
Diderot's Jacques Le Fataliste *d* Robert
Bresson *ph* Philippe Agostini *m* Jean-
Jacques Grunenwald

Maria Casarès, Elina Labourdette, Lucienne
Bogaert, Paul Bernard

'Through abstraction, Bresson has been able
to make a film in which the tragedy is implicit
not only in the plot but also in the form.'—
Richard Roud, MFB, 1966

Damien: Omen Two
US 1978 109m De Luxe Panavision
TCF (Harvey Bernhard)

The antichrist who got rid of the entire cast of
The Omen now, as a teenager, starts in on his
foster parents.
Once was enough.

w Stanley Mann, Michael Hodges *d* Don
Taylor *ph* Bill Butler *m* Jerry Goldsmith

William Holden, Lee Grant, Jonathan Scott-
Taylor, Robert Foxworth, Lucas Donat, Lew
Ayres, Sylvia Sidney, Elizabeth Shepherd

Damn Yankees**
US 1958 110m Technicolor
Warner (George Abbott, Stanley Donen)
GB title: *What Lola Wants*

The devil interferes in the fortunes of a failing
baseball team.

Smartly-styled but very American musical based on *Faust*; brilliant moments but some tedium.

w George Abbott, *novel* Douglas Wallop d George Abbott, Stanley Donen *ph Harold Lipstein m / ly* Richard Adler, Jerry Ross *md* Ray Heindorf

Gwen Verdon, Tab Hunter, Ray Walston, Russ Brown, Shannon Bolin

AAN: Ray Heindorf

Damnation Alley
US 1977   95m   De Luxe
TCF / Hal Landers, Bobby Roberts, Jerome M. Zeitman

Four survivors from World War Three try to reach a colony of fellow-survivors in New York.
Feeble attempt at a low-budget blockbuster.

w Alan Sharp, Lukas Heller, *novel* Roger Zelazny d Jack Smight *ph* Harry Stradling Jnr *m* Jerry Goldsmith *pd* Preston Ames

Jan-Michael Vincent, George Peppard, Dominique Sanda, Paul Winfield

The Damned*
France 1947   105m   bw
Speva Film
original title: *Les Maudits*

In 1945 fanatical Nazis escape in a submarine but make the mistake of stopping to sink a freighter.
Unusual melodrama with a brilliant sense of claustrophobia, good characterization and much suspense.

w Jacques Remy, René Clément, Henri Jeanson *d René Clément ph* Henri Alekan *m* Yves Baudrier

Paul Bernard, Henri Vidal, Marcel Dalio, Michel Auclair, Florence Marly

The Damned*
GB 1961   87m   bw   Hammerscope
Columbia / Hammer–Swallow (Anthony Hinds)
US title: *These Are the Damned*

A scientist keeps radioactive children in a cliff cave, sealed off from the world's corruption.
Absurdly pompous, downcast and confused sci-fi melodrama set in Weymouth, with a secondary plot about motor-cycling thugs.

w Evan Jones, *novel* The Children of Light by H. L. Lawrence *d* Joseph Losey *ph* Arthur Grant *m* James Bernard

Macdonald Carey, Shirley Ann Field, Alexander Knox, Viveca Lindfors, Oliver Reed, Walter Gotell, James Villiers

'A *folie de grandeur.*'—*Tom Milne*
'Out of this wild mishmash some really magnificent images loom.'—*John Coleman*

The Damned**
West Germany / Italy 1969   164m
Eastmancolor
Praesidens / Pegaso
original title: *Götterdämmerung*

A family of German industrialists divides and destroys itself under Nazi influence.
A film which has been called baroque, Wagnerian, and just plain unpleasant; it is also rather a strain to watch, with exaggerated colour and make-up to match the rotting theme.

w Nicola Badalucco, Enrico Medioli, Luchino Visconti *d Luchino Visconti ph* Armando Nannuzzi, Pasquale de Santis *m* Maurice Jarre *ad* Enzo del Prato, Pasquale Romano

Dirk Bogarde, Ingrid Thulin, Helmut Berger, Renaud Verley, Helmut Griem, René Kolldehof, Albrecht Schönhals, Umberto Orsini

'One is left lamenting that such a quondam master of realism as Visconti is making his films look like operas from which the score has been inexplicably removed.'—*MFB*
'The ludicrous flailings of puny puppets in inscrutable wooden frenzies.'—*John Simon*

AAN: script

The Damned Don't Cry
US 1950   103m   bw
Warner (Jerry Wald)

A middle-class housewife leaves her husband for a gambler, and becomes involved with gangsters, but eventually reforms.
Rather dreary stimulation for female audiences who like safe dreams of danger.

w Harold Medford, Jerome Weidman, *novel* Case History by Gertrude Walker *d* Vincent Sherman *ph* Ted McCord *m* Daniele Amfitheatrof

Joan Crawford, Kent Smith, David Brian, Steve Cochran, Hugh Sanders, Selena Royle, Morris Ankrum, Richard Egan

'The private lady of a public enemy!'—*publicity*

A Damsel in Distress*
US 1937   101m   bw
RKO (Pandro S. Berman)

An American dancing star falls for an aristocratic young Englishwoman.
Astaire without Rogers, but the style is the same and there are some very good numbers.

w P. G. Wodehouse, S. K. Lauren, Ernest Pagano *d* George Stevens *ph* Joseph H. August *m* / *ly* George and Ira Gershwin *ch* Hermes Pan

Fred Astaire, George Burns, Gracie Allen, Joan Fontaine, Reginald Gardiner, Constance Collier, Ray Noble, Montagu Love
† Rogers had demanded a break from musicals, so she was replaced by the demure Miss Fontaine, who was generally thought disappointing.

Dance Fools Dance
US 1930 82m bw
MGM

A lady reporter in Chicago proves her worth. Bizarrely-titled gangster thriller based on the Jake Lingle killing. Very moderate of its kind.

w Richard Schayer, Aurania Rouverol *d* Harry Beaumont *ph* Charles Rosher

Joan Crawford, Lester Vail, Cliff Edwards, William Bakewell, William Holden (the other one), Clark Gable, Earle Foxe, Joan Marsh

Dance Girl Dance*
US 1940 88m bw
RKO (Erich Pommer)

Private problems of the members of a nightclub dance troupe.
Competent and sometimes interesting formula drama with a harder edge than usual.

w Tess Slesinger, Frank Davis, *story* Vicki Baum *d* Dorothy Arzner *ph* Russell Metty *m* Edward Ward

Maureen O'Hara, Louis Hayward, Lucille Ball, Maria Ouspenskaya, Ralph Bellamy, Virginia Field, Mary Carlisle, Walter Abel, Edward Brophy, Harold Huber

Dance Hall*
GB 1950 80m bw
Ealing (E. V. H. Emmett)

Four factory girls seek relaxation and various kinds of romance at the local palais.
Untypically flat Ealing slice of life, now watchable only with a smile as musical nostalgia.

w E. V. H. Emmett, Diana Morgan, Alexander Mackendrick *d* Charles Crichton *ph* Douglas Slocombe *md* Ernest Irving

Natasha Parry, Donald Houston, Diana Dors, Bonar Colleano, Jane Hylton, Petula Clark, Gladys Henson, Sydney Tafler; the bands of Geraldo and Ted Heath

Dance Little Lady
GB 1954 87m Eastmancolor

An ambitious man tries to turn his balletomane daughter into a film star. Artless melodrama in poor colour. Terence Morgan, Mai Zetterling, Mandy Miller, Guy Rolfe, Eunice Gayson. Written by Val Guest and Doreen Montgomery; directed by Val Guest; for George Minter / Renown.

Dance Pretty Lady
GB 1932 64m bw

Ballerina loves artist but settles unwisely for respectability. Stilted early talkie from Compton Mackenzie's *Carnival*, qv under its own title. Ann Casson, Carl Harbord, Michael Hogan. Written and directed by Anthony Asquith; for H. Bruce Woolfe / British Instructional.

The Dance of Death*
GB 1968 149m Technicolor
BHE / National Theatre (John Brabourne)

Edgar and Alice live alone on an island, their marriage having become a constant war. Too-literal film transcription of an applauded theatrical production, with the camera anchored firmly in the middle of the stalls.

w August Strindberg (*translation* by C. D. Locock) *d* David Giles *ph* Geoffrey Unsworth

Laurence Olivier, Geraldine McEwan, Robert Lang, Carolyn Jones

Dancers in the Dark
US 1932 76m bw

A taxi dancer with a shady past tries to prove that she's really in love. Banal show business melodrama with authentic-seeming nightclub background. Miriam Hopkins, Jack Oakie, George Raft, William Collier Jnr, Lyda Roberti, Eugene Pallette. Written by Herman J. Mankiewicz; directed by David Burton; for Paramount.

Dancing Co-ed
US 1939 90m bw
MGM (Edgar Selwyn)
GB title: *Every Other Inch a Lady*

A college girl makes it in show business as well as the groves of academe.
Mindless vehicle for a 19-year-old star.

w Albert Mannheimer, *story* Albert Treynor *d* S. Sylvan Simon *ph* Alfred Gilks

Lana Turner, Richard Carlson, Artie Shaw, Leon Errol, Ann Rutherford, Lee Bowman, Monty Woolley, Roscoe Karns, June Preisser, Walter Kingsford

Dancing in the Dark°
US 1949   92m   Technicolor
TCF (George Jessel)

A silent movie idol makes a comeback as a
talent scout, and spots his own daughter.
Thin but unusual Hollywood drama with
music; in the long run too sentimental.

w Mary C. McCall Jnr, *play* The Band Wagon
by George F. Kaufman, Howard Dietz,
Arthur Schwarz d Irving Reis ph Harry
Jackson m Alfred Newman

William Powell, Adolphe Menjou, Mark
Stevens, Betsy Drake, Hope Emerson, Lloyd
Corrigan, Walter Catlett, Jean Hersholt

Dancing Lady°
US 1933   94m   bw
MGM (David O. Selznick)

A successful dancer chooses between a
playboy and her stage manager.
Routine backstage semi-musical with
interesting talent applied rather haphazardly.

w Allen Rivkin, P. J. Wolfson, *novel* James
Warner Bellah d Robert Z. Leonard
ph Oliver T. Marsh m various

Joan Crawford, Clark Gable, *Fred Astaire*,
Franchot Tone, May Robson, Ted Healy and
his Stooges (the Three Stooges), Winnie
Lightner, Robert Benchley, Nelson Eddy

The Dancing Masters
US 1943   63m   bw
TCF (Lee Marcus)

Laurel and Hardy run a ballet school, and get
involved with gangsters and inventors.
Insubstantial star comedy featuring reworkings
of old routines, and a back-projected runaway
bus climax.

w Scott Darling, George Bricker d Mal St
Clair ph Norbert Brodine m Arthur Lange

Stan Laurel, Oliver Hardy, Trudy Marshall,
Bob Bailey, Margaret Dumont, Matt Briggs,
Robert Mitchum

Dancing with Crime
GB 1947   83m   bw

A dance hall is the front for black marketeers,
who are exposed by a resourceful taxi driver.
Tolerable post-war melodrama aping
Hollywood. Richard Attenborough, Barry K.
Barnes, Sheila Sim, Garry Marsh, John
Warwick, Barry Jones. Written by Brock
Williams; directed by John Paddy Carstairs;
for Coronet-Alliance.

The Dancing Years
GB 1949   97m   Technicolor
ABPC (Warwick Ward)

A composer loves a singer who leaves him
after a misunderstanding but later bears his
son . . . all in the Alps pre-1914.
Lamentable transcription of an operetta;
precisely the ingredients which worked so well
on stage seem embarrassing on film, and the
performances and direction do not help.

w Warwick Ward, Jack Whittingham, from
Ivor Novello's operetta d Harold French
ph Stephen Dade m Ivor Novello

Dennis Price, Gisèle Préville, Patricia
Dainton, Anthony Nicholls, Grey Blake,
Muriel George, Olive Gilbert

Dandy Dick
GB 1935   72m   bw

A country vicar becomes innocently involved
with racehorse doping. Flatly-handled farce
which helped to introduce Will Hay to the
screen, though not in his accustomed role;
with Nancy Burne, Esmond Knight, Davy
Burnaby. Written by William Beaudine, Frank
Miller, Clifford Grey and Will Hay, from the
play by Sir Arthur Wing Pinero; directed by
William Beaudine; for Twickenham.

A Dandy in Aspic
GB 1968   107m   Technicolor
   Panavision
Columbia (Anthony Mann)

A double agent in Berlin is given orders to kill
himself.
Muddled, pretentious spy thriller; flat,
nebulous and boring.

w Derek Marlowe, from his novel d Anthony
Mann ph Christopher Challis m Quincy
Jones

Laurence Harvey, Tom Courtenay, Lionel
Stander, Mia Farrow, Harry Andrews, Peter
Cook, Per Oscarsson

† Anthony Mann died during shooting, and
Laurence Harvey completed the direction.

Dandy the All-American Girl
US 1976   90m   Metrocolor   Panavision

A much convicted woman car thief determines
to become the legitimate owner of a Dino
Ferrari. The American dream gone sour again,
this time offering in its wake a curious stream
of moral values. Stockard Channing, Sam
Waterston, Richard Doughty, Franklin Ajaye.
Written by B. J. Perla and Marilyn Goldin;
directed by Jerry Schatzberg; for MGM. (GB
title: *Sweet Revenge*.)

Danger: Diabolik
Italy / France 1967   105m   Technicolor
Dino de Laurentiis / Marianne (Bruno
   Todini)

International police bait a golden trap for a master criminal.
Superior Batman-type adventures with a comic strip hero-villain.

w Dino Maiuri, Adriano Baracco, Mario Bava *d* Mario Bava *ph* Antonio Rinaldi *m* Ennio Morricone

John Phillip Law, Marisa Mell, Michel Piccoli, Adolfo Celi, Terry-Thomas

Danger, Love at Work*
US 1937 84m bw
TCF (Harold Wilson)

A young lawyer needs the signature of a rich crazy family to conclude a land sale.
The title doesn't suggest it, but this is a not inconsiderable comedy in the tradition of *My Man Godfrey* and *You Can't Take It With You*. A highly competent cast does its best.

w James Edward Grant, Ben Markson *d* Otto Preminger *ph* Virgil Miller *md* David Buttolph

Ann Sothern, Jack Haley, Edward Everett Horton, Mary Boland, Walter Catlett, John Carradine, Maurice Cass, Alan Dinehart, E. E. Clive

Danger Route
GB 1967 92m De Luxe
UA / Amicus (Max J. Rosenberg, Milton Subotsky)

An 'eliminator' for the British secret service finds after a series of adventures that he must dispose of his own girl friend.
Dour sub-Bondian thriller with little to commend it.

w Meade Roberts, *novel* The Eliminator by Andrew York *d* Seth Holt *ph* Harry Waxman *m* John Mayer

Richard Johnson, Diana Dors, Sylvia Syms, Carol Lynley, Barbara Bouchet, Gordon Jackson, Sam Wanamaker, Maurice Denham, Harry Andrews

Danger Within**
GB 1958 101m bw
British Lion / Colin Lesslie
US title: *Breakout*

Escape plans of officers in a prisoner-of-war camp are threatened by an informer.
Familiar comedy and melodrama with an added whodunnit element, smartly handled and very entertaining.

w Bryan Forbes, Frank Harvey, *novel* Michael Gilbert *d* Don Chaffey *ph* Arthur Grant *m* Francis Chagrin

Richard Todd, Bernard Lee, Michael Wilding, Richard Attenborough, Dennis Price, Donald Houston, William Franklyn, Vincent Ball, Peter Arne

Dangerous*
US 1935 78m bw
Warner (Harry Joe Brown)

An alcoholic actress is rehabilitated.
Unconvincing and only adequately handled melodrama which won the star her first Oscar, presumably from sympathy at her losing it the previous year for *Of Human Bondage*.

w Laird Doyle *d* Alfred E. Green *ph* Ernest Haller

Bette Davis, Franchot Tone, Margaret Lindsay, Alison Skipworth, John Eldridge, Dick Foran
† Remade 1941 as *Singapore Woman*.
AA: Bette Davis

Dangerous Corner*
US 1934 67m bw
RKO

After dinner conversation reveals what might have been if friends had spoken the truth about a long-ago suicide.
A fascinating trick play makes interesting but scarcely sparkling cinema.

w Anne Morrison Chapin, Madeleine Ruthven, *play* J. B. Priestley *d* Phil Rosen *ph* J. Roy Hunt *m* Max Steiner

Melvyn Douglas, Conrad Nagel, Virginia Bruce, Erin O'Brien Moore, Ian Keith, Betty Furness, Henry Wadsworth

Dangerous Crossing*
US 1953 75m bw
TCF (Robert Bassler)

At the start of an Atlantic sea voyage a woman's husband disappears, and she is assured that he never existed. He does, and is trying to murder her.
Adequately handled twist on the vanishing lady story: grade A production covers lapses of grade B imagination.

w Leo Townsend, *story* John Dickson Carr *d* Joseph M. Newman *ph* Joseph La Shelle *md* Lionel Newman

Jeanne Crain, Michael Rennie, Carl Betz, Casey Adams, Mary Anderson, Willis Bouchey

Dangerous Curves
US 1929 75m bw
Paramount

A bareback rider loves a high wire artist. Obvious circus melodrama, a modest star vehicle.

w Donald David, Florence Ryerson d Lothar Mendes ph Harry Fischbeck

Clara Bow, Richard Arlen, Kay Francis, David Newell, Anders Randolf

Dangerous Exile
GB 1957 90m Eastmancolor
Vistavision
Rank (George H. Brown)

After the French Revolution, the young would-be Louis XVII is brought across the Channel and hidden in Pembrokeshire, where enemies attack him.

Historical romance, ineptly plotted but quite well produced.

w Robin Estridge, novel Vaughan Wilkins d Brian Desmond Hurst ph Geoffrey Unsworth m Georges Auric

Louis Jourdan, Belinda Lee, Keith Michell, Richard O'Sullivan, Martita Hunt, Finlay Currie, Anne Heywood, Jacques Brunius

Dangerous Moonlight*
GB 1941 98m bw
RKO (William Sistrom)
US title: Suicide Squadron

A Polish pianist escapes from the Nazis and loses his memory after flying in the Battle of Britain.

Immensely popular wartime romance which introduced Richard Addinsell's Warsaw Concerto. Production values and script somewhat below par.

w Shaun Terence Young, Brian Desmond Hurst, Rodney Ackland d Brian Desmond Hurst ph Georges Périnal, Ronald Neame

Anton Walbrook, Sally Gray, Derrick de Marney, Cecil Parker, Percy Parsons, Kenneth Kent, Guy Middleton, John Laurie, Frederick Valk

A Dangerous Profession
US 1949 79m bw

An ex-detective tries to help a beautiful woman and becomes involved in murder and the bail bond racket. Undistinguished crime melodrama providing a satisfactory vehicle for its stars: Pat O'Brien, George Raft, Ella Raines, Jim Backus, Bill Williams. Written by Martin Rackin and Warren Duff; directed by Ted Tetzlaff; for RKO.

Dangerous to Know*
US 1938 70m bw
Paramount

A ruthless Chicago gangster comes a cropper when his Chinese mistress discovers he has fallen for a socialite.

Flatly handled but mildly interesting adaptation of a highly successful play, the potential of which seems to have been thrown away.

w William R. Lippmann, Horace McCoy, play On the Spot by Edgar Wallace d Robert Florey ph Theodor Sparkuhl

Akim Tamiroff, Anna May Wong, Gail Patrick, Lloyd Nolan, Harvey Stephens, Anthony Quinn, Porter Hall

Dangerous When Wet**
US 1953 95m Technicolor
MGM (George Wells)

An entire Arkansas family is sponsored to swim the English Channel.

A bright and lively vehicle for an aquatic star, who in one sequence swims with Tom and Jerry. Amusing sequences give opportunities to a strong cast.

w Dorothy Kingsley d Charles Walters ph Harold Rosson songs Johnny Mercer, Arthur Schwarz

Esther Williams, Charlotte Greenwood, William Demarest, Fernando Lamas, Jack Carson, Denise Darcel, Barbara Whiting

Dangerously They Live
US 1941 77m bw
Warner (Ben Stoloff)

American Nazi agents try to get a secret memorized by a British girl agent injured in a car crash.

Watchable, routine spy propaganda fare.

w Marion Parsonnet d Robert Florey ph William O'Connell

John Garfield, Raymond Massey, Nancy Coleman, Moroni Olsen, Lee Patrick, Christian Rub, Frank Reicher

Danny Boy
GB 1941 80m bw

A singer searches for her estranged husband and small son who have become street entertainers. Sentimental drama with music; not for the critical. Ann Todd, Wilfrid Lawson, Grant Tyler, John Warwick, David Farrar. Written by Oswald Mitchell and A. Barr-Carson; directed by Oswald Mitchell; for Butcher's.

Dante's Inferno**
US 1935 89m bw
TCF (Sol M. Wurtzel)

A ruthless carnival owner gets too big for his boots, and has a vision of hell induced by one of his own attractions.

Curiously unpersuasive melodrama with a moral, but the inferno sequence is one of the most unexpected, imaginative and striking pieces of cinema in Hollywood's history.

w Philip Klein, Robert Yost *d Harry Lachman ph Rudolph Maté*

Spencer Tracy, Claire Trevor, Henry B. Walthall, Alan Dinehart, Scotty Beckett, Rita Hayworth (her first appearance, as a dancer)

'We depart gratefully, having seen papier maché photographed in more ways than we had thought possible.'—*Robert Herring*

'One of the most unusual and effectively presented films of the thirties.'—*John Baxter, 1968*

Darby O'Gill and the Little People*
US 1959   90m   Technicolor
Walt Disney

An Irish caretaker falls down a well and is captured by leprechauns, who allow him three wishes to rearrange his life.

Pleasantly barmy Irish fantasy with brilliant trick work but some tedium in between.

w Lawrence Edward Watkin, *stories* H. T. Kavanagh *d* Robert Stevenson *ph* Winton C. Hoch *m* Oliver Wallace *sp Peter Ellenshaw, Eustace Lycett, Joshua Meador*

Albert Sharpe, *Jimmy O'Dea*, Sean Connery, Janet Munro, Kieron Moore, Estelle Winwood, Walter Fitzgerald, Denis O'Dea, J. G. Devlin, Jack MacGowran

'One of the best fantasies ever put on film.'—*Leonard Maltin*

Darby's Rangers
US 1957   121m   bw
Warner (Martin Rackin)
GB title: *The Young Invaders*

A tough American commando unit is trained in Britain before seeing action in Africa and Sicily.

Standard World War II actioner, adequately executed.

w Guy Trosper, *book* Major James Altieri *d* William Wellman *ph* William H. Clothier *m* Max Steiner

James Garner, Etchika Choureau, Jack Warden, Edward Byrnes, Venetia Stevenson, Torin Thatcher, Stuart Whitman, Andrea King, Frieda Inescort, Reginald Owen, Adam Williams

The Daring Game
US 1967   101m   Eastmancolor
Paramount / Tors (Gene Levitt)

A commercial group experiments with airborne and underwater inventions, and rescues a scientist from a police state.

Well photographed but haphazardly assembled adventures, aimed at TV.

w Andy White *d* Laslo Benedek *ph* Edmund Gibson *m* George Bruns

Lloyd Bridges, Nico Minardos, Joan Blackman, Michael Ansara ,

The Dark Angel*
US 1935   105m   bw
Samuel Goldwyn

Tearstained melodrama from another age (see above), neatly packaged for the romantic 1935 public.

w Lillian Hellman, Mordaunt Shairp *d* Sidney Franklin *ph* Gregg Toland *m* Alfred Newman

Merle Oberon, Fredric March, Herbert Marshall, Janet Beecher, John Halliday, Henrietta Crosman, Frieda Inescort, George Breakston, Claud Allister

'It makes a systematic and skilful appeal to those untrustworthy emotions which may suddenly cause the most hardened intellects to dissolve before the most obvious sentimentality.'—*The Times*

AAN: Merle Oberon

The Dark at the Top of the Stairs**
US 1960   124m   Technicolor
Warner (Michael Garrison)

Twenties small town drama about a young boy's awakening to the sexual tensions around him.

Archetypal family drama set in that highly familiar American street. The perfect essence of this playwright's work, with high and low spots, several irrelevancies, but a real feeling for the people and the place.

w Harriet Frank Jnr, Irving Ravetch, *play* William Inge *d* Delbert Mann *ph* Harry Stradling *m* Max Steiner

Robert Preston, Dorothy McGuire, Angela Lansbury, *Eve Arden*, Shirley Knight, Frank Overton, Lee Kinsolving, Robert Eyer

'Every time a woman turns her face away because she's tired or unwilling, there's someone waiting like me . . .'—*publicity*
† The curious title turns out to be a synonym for life, which one should never be afraid of.

AAN: Shirley Knight

The Dark Avenger*
GB 1955   85m   Eastmancolor
  Cinemascope
Allied Artists
US title: *The Warriors*

The Black Prince quells some French rebels.
Good-humoured historical romp with the
ageing star in his last swashbuckling role,
helped by a good cast and brisk pace.

w Daniel B. Ullman *d* Henry Levin *ph* Guy
Green *m* Cedric Thorpe Davie

Errol Flynn, Peter Finch, Joanne Dru,
Yvonne Furneaux, Patrick Holt, Michael
Hordern, Moultrie Kelsall, Robert Urquhart,
Noel Willman

Dark City
US 1950   97m   bw
Paramount / Hal B. Wallis

A bookmaker finds himself on the run from a
revenge-seeking psychopath.
Unattractive and heavily-handled underworld
melodrama, a disappointment from the talents
involved.

w John Meredyth Lucas, Larry Marcus
d William Dieterle *ph* Victor Milner *m* Franz
Waxman

Charlton Heston (his first Hollywood
appearance), Lizabeth Scott, Viveca Lindfors,
Dean Jagger, Don Defore, Jack Webb, Ed
Begley, Henry Morgan, Mike Mazurki
  'A jaded addition to a type of thriller which
has become increasingly tedious and unreal.'—
MFB

Dark Command*
US 1940   92m   bw
Republic (Sol C. Siegel)

In pre-Civil War Kansas, an ambitious ex-
schoolteacher named Cantrill organizes
guerrilla bands to pillage the countryside.
Semi-historical hokum, quite well done with a
good cast.

w Grover Jones, Lionel Houser, F. Hugh
Herbert, *novel* W. R. Burnett *d* Raoul
Walsh *ph* Jack Marta *m* Victor Young

John Wayne, Claire Trevor, Walter Pidgeon,
Roy Rogers, George 'Gabby' Hayes, Porter
Hall, Marjorie Main

AAN: Victor Young

The Dark Corner*
US 1946   98m   bw
TCF (Fred Kohlmar)

A private eye with a criminal record thinks he
is being menaced by an old adversary, but the
latter is found murdered.

Moody, brutish, well-made thriller with a plot
put together from bits and pieces of older,
better movies, notably Clifton Webb's reprise
of his *Laura* performance and William Bendix
ditto *The Glass Key*.

w Jay Dratler, Bernard Schoenfeld, *story* Leo
Rosten *d* Henry Hathaway *ph* Joe
MacDonald *m* Cyril Mockridge

Mark Stevens, Clifton Webb, Lucille Ball,
William Bendix, Kurt Kreuger, Cathy Downs,
Reed Hadley, Constance Collier
  'Not so much a whodunnit as a
whodunnwhat . . . all seem bent on "getting"
each other and their internecine plottings add
up to an alpha thriller.'—*Daily Mail*

Dark Delusion
US 1947   90m   bw

A neurotic girl may have to be committed to
an asylum. Last episode of the Dr Gillespie
series; not a sensation on its own account.
Lionel Barrymore, James Craig, Lucille
Bremer, Edward Arnold, Keye Luke. Written
by Jack Andrews and Harry Ruskin; directed
by Willis Goldbeck; for MGM. (GB title:
Cynthia's Secret.)

Dark Eyes of London*
GB 1939   75m   bw
Pathe / Argyle (John Argyle)
US title: *The Human Monster*

The proprietor of a home for the blind uses a
mute giant to drown insured victims.
Reasonably effective British horror, a rarity at
the time.

w John Argyle, Walter Summers, Patrick
Kirwan, *novel* Edgar Wallace *d* Walter
Summers *ph* Bryan Langley

Bela Lugosi, Hugh Williams, Greta Gynt,
Wilfrid Walter, Edmon Ryan

Dark Hazard
US 1934   72m   bw

A compulsive gambler loses his wife as well as
his money. Modest star drama, remade in 1937
as *Wine, Women and Horses*. Edward G.
Robinson, Glenda Farrell, Robert Barrat,
Hobart Cavanagh. Written by Ralph Block
and Brown Holmes; directed by Alfred E.
Green; for Warner.

The Dark Horse
US 1932   75m   bw

A nitwit runs for governor and nearly makes
it. Mild political satire; closer to farce, really.
Guy Kibbee, Bette Davis, Warren William,

Frank McHugh. Written by Joseph Jackson and Wilson Mizner; directed by Alfred E. Green; for Warner.

Dark Journey*
GB 1937 82m bw
London Films / Victor Saville

In 1915 Stockholm, a French woman spy masquerading as a traitor falls in love with her German spy contact.
Unconvincing but entertaining romantic adventure with good star performances.

w Lajos Biro, Arthur Wimperis, *play* Lajos Biro d Victor Saville ph Georges Périnal, Harry Stradling m Richard Addinsell

Conrad Veidt, Vivien Leigh, Joan Gardner, Anthony Bushell, Ursula Jeans, Eliot Makeham, Austin Trevor, Edmund Willard

The Dark Man
GB 1950 91m bw
Rank / Independent Artists (Julian Wintle)

A mysterious murderer haunts a seaside resort.
Limp, disappointing location police thriller, with too much chat and generally mishandled moments of suspense

wd Jeffrey Dell ph Eric Cross m Hubert Clifford

Maxwell Reed, Edward Underdown, Natasha Parry, Barbara Murray, William Hartnell, Cyril Smith, Geoffrey Sumner
'The contrivances of the script are not helped by stilted dialogue.'—*MFB*

The Dark Mirror**
US 1946 85m bw
International

A police detective works out which of identical twin girls is a murderer.
Unconvincing but highly absorbing thriller with all credits plus; the best brand of Hollywood moonshine.

w Nunnally Johnson, *original story* Vladimir Posner d Robert Siodmak ph Milton Krasner

Olivia de Havilland, Lew Ayres, Thomas Mitchell, Garry Owen
'Smooth and agreeable melodrama . . . the detective work involves inkblot and word association tests and an amusingly sinister tandem of oscillating pens which register concealed emotions as one of the sisters talks.'—*James Agee*

AAN: Vladimir Posner

Dark Passage**
US 1947 106m bw
Warner (Jerry Wald)

A convicted murderer escapes from jail and proves his innocence.
Loosely assembled, totally unconvincing star thriller which succeeds because of its professionalism, some good cameos, and a number of narrative tricks including subjective camera for the first half hour.

w Delmer Daves, *novel* David Goodis d *Delmer Daves* ph Sid Hickox m Franz Waxman

Humphrey Bogart, Lauren Bacall, Agnes Moorehead, Bruce Bennett, *Tom D'Andrea, Houseley Stevenson*
'An almost total drag.'—*New Yorker, 1977*

The Dark Past**
US 1948 75m bw
Columbia (Buddy Adler)

A psychiatrist turns the tables on convicts who break into his home.
Tense, economical remake of *Blind Alley* (qv); a fresh look at a familiar situation (*The Small Voice, The Desperate Hours,* etc) helped by excellent performances.

w Philip Macdonald, Malvin Wald, Oscar Saul d *Rudolph Maté* ph Joseph Walker m George Duning

William Holden, Lee J. Cobb, Nina Foch, Adele Jergens, Stephen Dunne
'A picture so packed with skill and imagination that every minute is absorbing.'—*Richard Mallett, Punch*

Dark Star*
US 1974 83m Metrocolor
Jack H. Harris (John Carpenter)

In the 22nd century, the bored crew of a starship on an intergalactic mission become prey to their own phobias and to the alien mascot they are taking back to earth.
A semi-professional film which turned out to be one of the screen's neatest low-budget entries in the pulp science fiction genre. That doesn't make it wholly entertaining, but its credentials are impeccable.

w John Carpenter, Dan O'Bannon d *John Carpenter* pd, ed Dan O'Bannon ph Douglas Knapp m John Carpenter

Brian Narelle, Dre Pahich, Cal Kuniholm, Dan O'Bannon

The Dark Tower
GB 1943 93m bw
Warner

A circus hypnotist possessively controls a girl trapezist.
Heavy-handed but quite effective melodrama.

w Brock Williams, Reginald Purdell, *play* Alexander Woolcott, George S. Kaufman *d* John Harlow *ph* Otto Heller

Ben Lyon, Anne Crawford, David Farrar, Herbert Lom, William Hartnell, Frederick Burtwell, Josephine Wilson

Dark Victory**
US 1939   106m   bw
Warner (David Lewis)

A good-time society girl discovers she is dying of a brain tumour.
A highly commercial tearjerker of its day, this glutinous star vehicle now works only fitfully.

w Casey Robinson, *play* George Brewer Jnr, Bertram Bloch *d* Edmund Goulding *ph* Ernest Haller *m* Max Steiner

Bette Davis, George Brent, Humphrey Bogart, Ronald Reagan, Geraldine Fitzgerald, Henry Travers, Cora Witherspoon, Dorothy Peterson

'A completely cynical appraisal would dismiss it all as emotional flim-flam . . . but it is impossible to be that cynical about it.'— *Frank S. Nugent*

'A gooey collection of clichés, but Davis slams through them in her nerviest style.'— *New Yorker, 1976*

† Remade 1963 as *Stolen Hours*, with Susan Hayward; 1975 as *Dark Victory* (TV movie) with Elizabeth Montgomery.

AAN: best picture; Bette Davis; Max Steiner

Dark Waters**
US 1944   90m   bw
Benedict Bogeaus

Recovering from being torpedoed, an orphan girl visits her aunt and uncle in Louisiana and has some terrifying experiences.
Competent frightened-lady melodrama helped by its bayou surroundings. Possibly discarded by Hitchcock, but with sequences well in his manner.

w Joan Harrison, Marian Cockrell *d André de Toth ph John Mescall*

Merle Oberon, Franchot Tone, *Thomas Mitchell, Fay Bainter, John Qualen,* Elisha Cook Jnr, Rex Ingram

Darker than Amber
US 1970   96m   Technicolor
Cinema Center / Major Films

A Florida private eye rescues a girl who is subsequently murdered and turns out to be part of a confidence racket.
Routine suspenser from the Travis McGee books; not very stimulating.

w Ed Waters, *novel* John D. MacDonald *d* Robert Clouse *ph* Frank Phillips *m* John Parker

Rod Taylor, Suzy Kendall, Theodore Bikel, James Booth, Jane Russell, Janet McLachlan, William Smith

Darling**
GB 1965   127m   bw
Anglo-Amalgamated / Vic / Appia (Joseph Janni, Victor Lyndon)

An ambitious young woman deserts her journalist mentor for a company director, an effeminate photographer and an Italian prince. Fashionable mid-sixties concoction of smart swinging people and their amoral doings. Influential, put over with high style, and totally tiresome in retrospect.

w Frederic Raphael *d John Schlesinger ph* Ken Higgins *m* John Dankworth

Julie Christie, Dirk Bogarde, Laurence Harvey, Roland Curram, Alex Scott, Basil Henson, Pauline Yates

'As empty of meaning and mind as the empty life it's exposing.'—*Pauline Kael*

AA: Frederic Raphael; Julie Christie
AAN: best picture; John Schlesinger

Darling How Could You
US 1951   96m   bw
Paramount (Harry Tugend)
GB title: *Rendezvous*

Children long separated from their parents have fantasies about them.
Faded-looking Edwardian comedy which does not quite have the style or the cast for success. (Or the title, come to that.)

w Dodie Smith, Lesser Samuels, *play* Alice Sit by the Fire by J. M. Barrie *d* Mitchell Leisen *ph* Daniel L. Fapp *m* Frederick Hollander

Joan Fontaine, John Lund, Mona Freeman, Peter Hanson, David Stollery, Lowell Gilmore, Robert Barrat, Gertrude Michael

Darling Lili*
US 1970   136m   Technicolor
     Panavision
Paramount / Geoffrey (Owen Crump)

During World War I, an American air ace falls for a German lady spy, and waits till the war is over to marry her.
Farce and romance mix oddly with aerial acrobatics in this expensive and dull extravaganza which bore the sub-title *Where Were You the Night I Shot Down Baron Von Richthofen?* (which probably sums up its aims and its failure). A coffee table film, good to look at and with occasional striking moments.

wd Blake Edwards *ph Russell Harlan, Harold
E. Wellman m* Henry Mancini *pd* Fernando
Carrere

Julie Andrews, Rock Hudson, Jeremy Kemp,
Lance Percival, Michael Witney, Jacques
Marin, André Maranne

AAN: Henry Mancini; song 'Whistling Away
the Dark' (*m* Henry Mancini, *ly* Johnny
Mercer)

The Darwin Adventure*
GB 1971   91m   Eastmancolor
(TCF) Palomar (Joseph Strick, Irving
  Lerner)

In 1831, Charles Darwin becomes ship's
naturalist on the *Beagle* and studies wild life in
South America.
Rather naive biopic of Darwin which tries to
cover too much with too slender resources but
makes a pleasant introduction to the subject.

w William Fairchild *d* Jack Couffer
ph Denys Coop, Jack Couffer *m* Marc
Wilkinson

Nicholas Clay, Susan Macready, Ian
Richardson, Christopher Martin, Robert
Flemyng, Aubrey Woods, Hugh Morton
  'The biopic plague, which has ravaged the
screen lives of Pasteur, Juarez, Cole Porter
and countless others, has now struck down the
memory of famed naturalist Charles Darwin.
The filmgoing public's own version of
Darwin's natural selection theory will
immediately weed out this inferior species.'—
Variety

A Date with Judy
US 1948   113m   Technicolor
MGM (Joe Pasternak)

A teenager wrongly suspects her friend of an
illicit affair.
Ambitious but flat comedy musical which
neatly wraps up all kinds of forties people and
institutions: teenagers, small towns, families,
Carmen Miranda and Miss Taylor, not to
mention the producer.

w Dorothy Cooper, Dorothy Kingsley
d Richard Thorpe *ph* Robert Surtees
m / ly various

Wallace Beery, Elizabeth Taylor, Jane Powell,
Carmen Miranda, Xavier Cugat, Robert
Stack, Selena Royle, Scotty Beckett, Leon
Ames

Daughter of Darkness
GB 1947   91m   bw
Kenilworth–Alliance (Victor Hanbury)

A murderous Irish servant girl has a fatal flair
for men.

Absurd melodrama, almost Grand Guignol,
louringly set on the Yorkshire moors but
lethargically handled all round.

w Max Catto, from his play They Walk Alone
d Lance Comfort *ph* Stanley Pavey

Siobhan McKenna, Anne Crawford, Maxwell
Reed, George Thorpe, Barry Morse, Honor
Blackman, Liam Redmond, David Greene

Daughter of Dr Jekyll
US 1957   74m   bw

An evil doctor tells his ward that she is the
daughter of the unfortunate Dr Jekyll and
therefore responsible for a series of werewolf
killings. Bathetic cheapie with risible views of
England and a tendency to mix up several
myths in one package. Arthur Shields, John
Agar, Gloria Talbott, John Dierkes. Written
by Jack Pollexfen; directed by Edgar C.
Ulmer; for Allied Artists.

The Daughter of Rosie O'Grady*
US 1950   104m   Technicolor
Warner (William Jacobs)

A girl determines to follow in her dead
mother's musical comedy footsteps against the
wishes of her still-grieving father.
Absolutely standard period musical, quite
pleasantly handled but with below-par musical
numbers.

w Jack Rose, Mel Shavelson, Peter Milne
d David Butler *ph* Wilfred M. Cline
md David Buttolph

June Haver, Gordon Macrae, *James Barton*,
S. Z. Sakall, Gene Nelson, Debbie Reynolds,
Sean McClory, Jane Darwell

Daughters Courageous*
US 1939   107m   bw
Warner (Hal B. Wallis)

A prodigal father returns to his family and
sorts out their problems.
Following the success of *Four Daughters* (qv)
the cast was reassembled to make this amiable
rehash about a different family.

w Julius and Philip Epstein, *play* Fly Away
Home by Dorothy Bennett, Irving White
d Michael Curtiz *ph James Wong Howe*

Claude Rains, John Garfield, Jeffrey Lynn,
Fay Bainter, Priscilla Lane, Rosemary Lane,
Lola Lane, Gale Page, Donald Crisp, May
Robson, Frank McHugh, Dick Foran, Berton
Churchill
  'For its intelligent use of small town
locations, its skilled acting, fine camerawork
and evenly paced, sympathetic direction, it
surpasses everything of its type.'—*John
Baxter, 1968*

'Attractive people, good dialogue and camerawork, and skilful direction can work wonders.'—*Richard Mallett, Punch*

David and Bathsheba*
US 1952   116m   Technicolor
TCF (Darryl F. Zanuck)

King David loves the wife of one of his captains, and ensures that the latter is killed in battle.
Deliberately sober bible-in-pictures, probably intended as a riposte to Cecil B. de Mille. Somewhat lacking in excitement, but you can't call it gaudy.

w Philip Dunne *d* Henry King *ph* Leon Shamroy *m* Alfred Newman

Gregory Peck, Susan Hayward, James Robertson Justice, Raymond Massey, Kieron Moore, Jayne Meadows, John Sutton, Dennis Hoey, Francis X. Bushman, George Zucco
'Hardly a single unintentional laugh.'— *Richard Mallett, Punch*

AAN: Phillip Dunne; Leon Shamroy; Alfred Newman

David and Lisa*
US 1963   94m   bw
Continental (Paul M. Heller)

Two disturbed adolescents at a special school fall in love.
Case history drama, earnest and well meaning rather than exciting.

w Eleanor Perry, book Theodore Isaac Rubin
d Frank Perry *ph* Leonard Hirschfield
m Mark Lawrence

Keir Dullea, Janet Margolin, Howard da Silva, Neva Patterson, Clifton James, Richard McMurray

AAN: Eleanor Perry; Frank Perry

David Copperfield••••
US 1935   132m   bw
MGM (David O. Selznick)

Disliked by his cruel stepfather and helped by his eccentric aunt, orphan David grows up to become an author and eventually to marry his childhood sweetheart.
Only slightly faded after forty-five years, this small miracle of compression not only conveys the spirit of Dickens better than the screen has normally managed but is a particularly pleasing example of Hollywood's handling of literature and of the deployment of a great studio's resources. It also overflows with memorable character cameos, and it was a box office giant.

w Hugh Walpole, Howard Estabrook, *novel* Charles Dickens *d George Cukor ph* Oliver T. Marsh *m* Herbert Stothart
montages Slavko Vorkapitch *ad* Cedric Gibbons

Freddie Bartholemew (young David), *Frank Lawton* (David as a man), *W. C. Fields* (Micawber), *Roland Young* (Uriah Heep), *Edna May Oliver* (Aunt Betsy), *Lennox Pawle* (Mr Dick), *Basil Rathbone* (Mr Murdstone), Violet Kemble Cooper (Miss Murdstone), Maureen O'Sullivan (Dora), Madge Evans (Agnes), Elizabeth Allan (Mrs Copperfield), *Jessie Ralph* (Peggotty), Lionel Barrymore (Dan Peggotty), Hugh Williams (Steerforth), Lewis Stone (Mr Wickfield), *Herbert Mundin* (Barkis), Elsa Lanchester (Clickett), Jean Cadell (Mrs Micawber), Una O'Connor (Mrs Gummidge), John Buckler (Ham), Hugh Walpole (the Vicar), Arthur Treacher (donkey man)

'Though half the characters are absent, the whole spectacle of the book, Micawber always excepted, is conveyed.'—*James Agee*
'The most profoundly satisfying screen manipulation of a great novel that the camera has ever given us.'—*André Sennwald*
'Perhaps the finest casting of all time.'— *Basil Wright, 1972*

AAN: best picture

David Harum*
US 1934   83m   bw
TCF

A wily old rancher plays matchmaker.
Simple, pleasing small-town comedy-drama, ably fashioned for its star.

w Walter Woods, *play* Edward Westcott
d James Cruze *ph* Hal Mohr *m* Louis de Francesco

Will Rogers, Evelyn Venable, Kent Taylor, Louise Dresser, Stepin Fetchit, Charles Middleton, Noah Beery

Davy*
GB 1957   84m   Technirama
Ealing (Basil Dearden)

A member of a family music hall act auditions at Covent Garden.
Curiously unsuccessful vehicle for a popular singing comic; the script and continuity are simply poor, and swamped by the wide screen.

w William Rose *d* Michael Relph
ph Douglas Slocombe *m* various classics

Harry Secombe, Ron Randell, George Relph, Alexander Knox, Susan Shaw, Bill Owen

Davy Crockett*
US 1955   93m   Technicolor
Walt Disney

Episodes in the career of the famous
Tennessee hunter and Indian scout who died
at the Alamo.

Disjointed and naive but somehow very fresh
and appealing adventures; made for American
television (as 3 × 50m episodes) but elsewhere
an enormous hit in cinemas.

w Tom Blackburn d Norman Foster
ph Charles Boyle m George Bruns

Fess Parker, Buddy Ebsen, Basil Ruysdael,
William Bakewell, Hans Conried, Kenneth
Tobey, Nick Cravat

† 1956 sequel on similar lines: *Davy Crockett
and the River Pirates*.

Dawn at Socorro
US 1954   80m   Technicolor

A gunfighter is trapped into one last duel.
Moderate western programmer. Rory
Calhoun, David Brian, Alex Nicol, Piper
Laurie, Edgar Buchanan. Written by George
Zuckerman; directed by George Sherman; for
Universal-International.

Dawn of the Dead
US 1979   127m   Technicolor

America is filled by legions of carnivorous
zombies. Seemingly endless horror comic with
absurd pretensions to be an allegory of
something or other; occasionally laughable,
otherwise sickening or boring. David Emge,
Ken Foree, Scott H. Reininger, Gaylen Ross.
Written and directed by George A. Romero;
for Laurel Group. (GB title: *Zombies*.)

The Dawn Patrol**
US 1930   82m   bw
Warner

In France during World War I, flying officers
wait their turn to leave on missions which may
mean death.

The second version (see below) is more
watchable today, but this early talkie was
highly effective in its time, and much of its
aerial footage was re-used.

w John Monk Saunders d Howard Hawks
ph Ernest Haller

Richard Barthelmess, Douglas Fairbanks Jnr,
Neil Hamilton, William Hanney, *James
Finlayson*, Clyde Cook, Edmund Breon,
Frank McHugh

· 'Bare, cleancut, uncluttered technique, a
stark story line, terse dialogue . . . and a

pervasive atmosphere of hopelessness
captured with economy and incisiveness.'—
Andrew Sarris, 1963

† TV title is *Flight Commander*, which was the
title of Saunders' original story.

AAN: John Monk Saunders

The Dawn Patrol**
US 1938   103m   bw
Warner (Hal B. Wallis)

A remarkably early but trim and competent
remake of the above, using much of the same
aerial footage.

w Seton I. Miller, Dan Totheroh d Edmund
Goulding ph Tony Gaudio m Max Steiner

Errol Flynn, Basil Rathbone, David Niven,
Melville Cooper, Donald Crisp, Barry
Fitzgerald, Carl Esmond

'A great deal of self-pity and romanticism
have gone into the making of this excellent
ham sandwich.'—*Graham Greene*

A Day at the Races****
US 1937   109m   bw (blue-tinted ballet
sequence)
MGM (Lawrence Weingarten)

The Marxes help a girl who owns a sanatorium
and a racehorse.

Fashions in Marxism change, but this top
quality production, though lacking their
zaniest inspirations, does contain several of
their funniest routines and a spectacularly well
integrated racecourse climax. The musical and
romantic asides are a matter of taste but
delightfully typical of their time.

w *Robert Pirosh, George Seaton, George
Oppenheimer d Sam Wood ph Joseph
Ruttenberg m Franz Waxman

Groucho, Chico, Harpo, Margaret Dumont,
Maureen O'Sullivan, Allan Jones, *Douglass
Dumbrille, Esther Muir, Sig Rumann*

'The money is fairly splashed about; the
capitalists have recognized the Marx Brothers;
ballet sequences, sentimental songs, amber
fountains, young lovers. Easily the best film to
be seen in London, but all the same I feel a
nostalgia for the old cheap rickety sets.'—
Graham Greene

Day for Night***
France / Italy 1973   116m   Eastmancolor
Films du Carrosse / PECF / PIC (Marcel
Bébert)
original title: *La Nuit Américaine*

Frictions and personality clashes beset the
making of a romantic film in Nice.
Immensely enjoyable, richly detailed,

insider's-eye-view of the goings-on in a film studio. A fun film with melodramatic asides.

w François Truffaut, Jean-Louis Richard, Suzanne Schiffman d François Truffaut ph Pierre-William Glenn m Georges Delerue

Jacqueline Bisset, Valentina Cortese, Jean-Pierre Aumont, Jean-Pierre Léaud, Dani, Alexandra Stewart, Jean Champion, François Truffaut, David Markham

'I thought I'd had my last dram of enjoyment out of the Pagliacci theme and studio magic, and Truffaut shows there's life in the old whirl yet.'—Stanley Kauffmann

'Made with such dazzling craftsmanship and confidence that you can never quite believe Truffaut's point that directing a movie is a danger-fraught experience.'—Michael Billington, Illustrated London News

† Graham Greene, as Henry Graham, played an insurance representative.

AA: best foreign film

AAN: script; François Truffaut (as director); Valentina Cortese

A Day in the Death of Joe Egg**
GB 1971   106m   Eastmancolor
Columbia / Domino (David Deutsch)

A teacher and his wife are frustrated by their own inability to cope with the problem of their spastic daughter.
A well-filmed version of a sincerely human play, with humour and fantasy sequences leavening the gloom.

w Peter Nichols, from his play d Peter Medak ph Ken Hodges m Elgar

Alan Bates, Janet Suzman, Peter Bowles, Sheila Gish, Joan Hickson

'It's unsatisfying, and it's not to be missed.'—Stanley Kauffmann

The Day of the Animals
US 1976   98m   De Luxe   Todd AO 35
Film Ventures International (Edward L. Montero)

In the Californian High Sierras, animals of all kinds suddenly turn on human beings, but a day later are all found dead.
Irritatingly pointless horror fable borrowing heavily from The Birds; basically an exploitation shocker, most efficient when most unpleasant.

w William and Eleanor Norton d William Girdler ph Tom McHugh m Lalo Schifrin

Christopher George, Lynda Day George, Leslie Nielsen, Robert Sorrentino, Richard Jaeckel, Michael Ansara, Ruth Roman, Paul Mantee, Gil Lamb

Day of the Badman
US 1957   82m   Eastmancolor
Cinemascope

A circuit judge stands up against threatening outlaws. Uninvolving western which can't fill the wide screen. Fred MacMurray, Joan Weldon, John Ericson, Robert Middleton, Edgar Buchanan. Written by Irving Glassberg; directed by Harry Keller; for Universal-International.

The Day of the Dolphin*
US 1973   104m   Technicolor
Panavision
Avco–Embassy / Icarus (Robert E. Relyea)

A marine biologist researching dolphins off the Florida coast discovers they are being used in a plot to blow up the President's yacht.
A strangely unexpected and unsuccessful offering from the talent involved: thin and repetitive as scientific instruction (the dolphins' language in any case topples it into fantasy), and oddly childlike as spy adventure.

w Buck Henry, novel Robert Merle d Mike Nichols ph William A. Fraker m Georges Delerue pd Richard Sylbert

George C. Scott, Trish Van Devere, Paul Sorvino, Fritz Weaver

'The whole thing seems to have been shoved through the cameras as glibly as possible, so that everyone concerned could grab the money and run.'—Stanley Kauffmann

'An eight and a half million dollar Saturday afternoon special for sheltered nine-year-olds.'—Judith Crist

'Dolphins may live in a state of ecstasy, but the cast of this film seems lost in a state of confusion, wondering whether they are in an enlightened documentary, juvenile fantasy, or lurid soap opera.'—Les Keyser, Hollywood in the Seventies

AAN: Georges Delerue

The Day of the Evil Gun*
US 1968   93m   Metrocolor   Panavision
MGM (Jerry Thorpe)

Returning home after three years, a rancher finds that his wife and child have been carried off by Indians.
Competent standard western which resolves itself into a duel of wits between the hero and his rival.

w Charles Marquis Warren, Eric Bercovici d Jerry Thorpe ph W. Wallace Kelley m Jeff Alexander

Glenn Ford, Arthur Kennedy, Dean Jagger, Paul Fix, John Anderson, Nico Minardos

The Day of the Jackal••
GB / France 1973   142m   Technicolor
Universal / Warwick / Universal France
(John Woolf, David Deutsch)

British and French police combine to prevent
an OAS assassination attempt on de Gaulle by
use of a professional killer.
An incisive, observant and professional piece
of work based on a rather clinical bestseller.
Lack of a channel for sympathy, plus language
confusions, are its main drawbacks.

w Kenneth Ross, *novel* Frederick Forsyth
d Fred Zinnemann ph Jean Tournier
m Georges Delerue

Edward Fox, Michel Lonsdale, Alan Badel,
Eric Porter, Cyril Cusack, Delphine Seyrig,
Donald Sinden, Tony Britton, Timothy West,
Olga Georges-Picot, Barrie Ingham, Maurice
Denham, Anton Rodgers

'Before *Jackal* is five minutes old, you know
it's just going to be told professionally, with no
flavour and no zest.'—*Stanley Kauffmann*
'All plot, with scarcely a character in
sight.'—*Michael Billington, Illustrated London
News*
'A better than average thriller for those who
haven't read the book.'—*Judith Crist*
'A rare lesson in film-making in the good
old grand manner.'—*Basil Wright, 1972*

The Day of the Locust••
US 1975   143m   Technicolor
Paramount / Long Road (Jerome Hellman,
Sheldon Shrager)

In Hollywood in the 1930s, a novice art
director is bewildered by the eccentricities of
life and an innocent man is martyred by the
crowd.
A curious and interesting work from a
savagely satirical novel; full of stimulating
scenes and characters, it barely succeeds as a
whole and was a disaster at the box office.

w Waldo Salt, *novel* Nathanael West   d John
Schlesinger ph Conrad Hall m John Barry
pd Richard MacDonald

Donald Sutherland, William Atherton, Karen
Black, Burgess Meredith, Geraldine Page,
Richard A. Dysart, Bo Hopkins, Lelia
Goldoni

AAN: Conrad Hall; Burgess Meredith

The Day of the Outlaw••
US 1958   96m   bw
UA / Security Pictures (Sidney Harmon)

Two rival cattlemen forget their differences to
fight six outlaws who ride into town.
Bleak and wintry western, well done and
sufficiently unusual to stick in the mind.

w Philip Yordan, *novel* Lee Wells   d André de
Toth ph Russell Harlan m Alexander
Courage

Robert Ryan, Burl Ives, Tina Louise,
Nehemiah Persoff, David Nelson, Venetia
Stevenson, Jack Lambert, Lance Fuller
'In the best William S. Hart tradition.'—
MFB

The Day of the Triffids•
GB 1962   95m   Eastmancolor
   Cinemascope
Philip Yordan (George Pitcher)

Almost everyone in the world is blinded by
meteorites prior to being taken over by
intelligent plants.
Rough and ready adaptation of a famous sci-fi
novel, sometimes blunderingly effective and
with moments of good trick work.

w Philip Yordan, *novel* John Wyndham
d Steve Sekely ph Ted Moore m Ron
Goodwin

Howard Keel, Nicole Maurey, Kieron Moore,
Janette Scott, Alexander Knox

Day of Wrath•••
Denmark 1943   105m   bw
Palladium
original title: *Vredens Dag*

In a 17th-century village an old woman is
burned as a witch and curses the pastor who
judged her. He dies and his mother accuses
her daughter-in-law, in love with another man,
of using witchcraft to kill him.
Harrowing, spellbinding melodrama with a
message, moving in a series of
Rembrandtesque compositions from one
horrifying sequence to another. Depressing,
but marvellous.

w Carl Dreyer, Poul Knudsen, Mogens Skot-
Hansen, *play* Anne Pedersdotter by Hans
Wiers Jenssen d Carl Dreyer ph Carl
Andersson m Poul Schierbeck ad Erik Ases,
Lis Fribert

Thorkild Roose, Lisbeth Movin, Sigrid
Neiiendam, Preben Lerdoff Rye, Anna
Svierkier

The Day the Earth Caught Fire••
GB 1961   99m   bw with filters
   Dyaliscope
British Lion / Pax (Val Guest)

Nuclear tests knock the world off its axis and
send it careering towards the sun.
A smart piece of science fiction told through
the eyes of Fleet Street journalists and
showing a sharp eye for the London scene.

Rather exhaustingly talkative, but genuinely frightening at the time.

w Wolf Mankowitz, *Val Guest d* Val Guest *ph* Harry Waxman *m* Monty Norman

Edward Judd, Janet Munro, Leo McKern, *Arthur Christiansen* (ex-editor of the Daily Express), Michael Goodliffe, Bernard Braden, Reginald Beckwith, Austin Trevor, Renée Asherson, Edward Underdown

The Day the Earth Stood Still**
US 1951 92m bw
TCF (Julian Blaustein)

A flying saucer arrives in Washington and its alien occupant, aided by a robot, demonstrates his intellectual and physical power, warns the world what will happen if wars continue, and departs.
Cold-war wish-fulfilment fantasy, impressive rather than exciting but very capably put over with the minimum of trick work and the maximum of sober conviction.

w Edmund H. North *d* Robert Wise *ph* Leo Tover *m* Bernard Herrmann

Michael Rennie, Patricia Neal, Hugh Marlowe, Sam Jaffe, Billy Gray
  'Quite wry and alarmingly smooth.'—*New Yorker, 1977*

The Day the Fish Came Out
GB / Greece 1967 109m De Luxe
TCF / Michael Cacoyannis

Atomic material contaminates a Mediterranean island.
Addle-pated, would-be satirical mod fantasy with establishment figures cast as world villains.

wd Michael Cacoyannis *ph* Walter Lassally *m* Mikis Theodorakis

Tom Courtenay, Colin Blakely, Sam Wanamaker, Candice Bergen, Ian Ogilvy, Patricia Burke

The Day the Hot Line Got Hot
US 1968 92m Eastmancolor

Russian and American agents are outwitted by their go-between. Feeble espionage comedy teaming two big stars at the end of their careers. Charles Boyer, Robert Taylor, George Chakiris, Marie Dubois. Written by Paul Jarrico, Dominique Fabre and M. Trueblood; directed by Etienne Perier; for Commonwealth United.

The Day They Robbed the Bank of England*
GB 1960 85m bw
MGM / Summit (Jules Buck)

In 1901 Irish patriots plan a coup against the British government . . .
Small-scale, well-detailed period caper story, marred by a slow-starting script and unsympathetic acting.

w Howard Clewes, Richard Maibaum, *novel* John Brophy *d* John Guillermin *ph* Georges Périnal *m* Edwin Astley

Peter O'Toole, Aldo Ray, Elizabeth Sellars, Kieron Moore, Albert Sharpe, Hugh Griffith, John Le Mesurier, Joseph Tomelty, Miles Malleson, Colin Gordon

The Day Will Dawn*
GB 1942 98m bw
Paul Soskin
US title: *The Avengers*

Norwegian freedom fighters destroy a U-boat base and are saved by commandos.
Dated propaganda piece with an interesting cast.

w Terence Rattigan, Anatole de Grunwald, Patrick Kirwan *d* Harold French *ph* Bernard Knowles

Ralph Richardson, Deborah Kerr, Hugh Williams, Griffith Jones, Francis L. Sullivan, Roland Culver, Niall MacGinnis, Finlay Currie, Bernard Miles, Patricia Medina

Daybreak*
US 1931 85m approx bw
MGM

An Austrian guardsman falls in love out of his class.
Elegant romantic fable comparable with *Letter From an Unknown Woman*; equally unpopular and quite forgotten.

w Ruth Cummings, Zelda Sears, Cyril Hume, *play* Arthur Schnitzler *d Jacques Feyder ph* J. Merrit Gerstad

Ramon Novarro, Helen Chandler, C. Aubrey Smith, Karen Morley, Kent Douglass, Jean Hersholt, Glenn Tryon

Daybreak
GB 1946 81m bw
GFD / Triton (Sydney Box)

A barber and part-time hangman marries a destitute girl, loses her to a Swedish seaman, and kills himself in such a way as to implicate the other man.
Dockside melodrama of extraordinary pretentious gloominess; laughable in most respects. A curious follow-up from the *Seventh Veil* team.

w Muriel and Sydney Box, *play* Monckton Hoffe *d* Compton Bennett *ph* Reg Wyer

Ann Todd, Eric Portman, Maxwell Reed,
Edward Rigby, Bill Owen, Jane Hylton,
Maurice Denham

Days of Glory

US 1944   86m   bw
RKO (Casey Robinson)

Russian peasants fight the invading Nazis.
Lower-berth wartime propaganda piece chiefly
notable for introducing Gregory Peck to the
screen.

w Casey Robinson, *story* Melchior Lengyel
d Jacques Tourneur *ph* Tony Gaudio
m Daniele Amfitheatrof

Tamara Toumanova, Gregory Peck, Alan
Reed, Maria Palmer, Lowell Gilmore, Hugo
Haas

Days of Heaven**

US 1978   95m   Metrocolor
Paramount / OP (Bert and Harold
   Schneider)

In the early 20th century, three young
immigrants leave Chicago for the wheatfields.
Visually a superb slice of period life, let down
by obsessively self-important and symbolic
drama; also by imperfect sound recording.

wd Terrence Malick *ph* Nestor Almendros
m Ennio Morricone

Richard Gere, Brooke Adams, Sam Shepard,
Linda Manz

Days of Thrills and Laughter***

US 1961   93m   bw
(TCF) *Robert Youngson*

Appealing if rather miscellaneous silent film
compilation with the accent on action and
thrills as well as comedy. Like the other
Youngson histories, a boon to film archivists
despite a facetious commentary.

m Jack Shaindlin *narrator* Jay Jackson

Stan Laurel, Oliver Hardy, Snub Pollard,
Douglas Fairbanks, Charles Chaplin, Pearl
White, Houdini, Harry Langdon, Ben Turpin,
Charlie Chase, Boris Karloff, Warner Oland,
Fatty Arbuckle, Keystone Kops

Days of Wine and Roses**

US 1962   117m   bw
Warner (Martin Manulis)

A PR man becomes an alcoholic; his wife
gradually reaches the same state, but he
recovers and she does not.
Smart satirical comedy confusingly gives way
to melodrama, then sentimentality; quality is
evident throughout, but all concerned are
happiest with the first hour.

w J. P. Miller d Blake Edwards *ph Philip
Lathrop m Henry Mancini*

*Jack Lemmon, Lee Remick, Charles Bickford,
Jack Klugman*, Alan Hewitt, Debbie
Megowan, Jack Albertson

AA: title song (*m* Henry Mancini, *ly* Johnny
Mercer)
AAN: Jack Lemmon; Lee Remick

A Day's Pleasure*

US 1919   20m   bw   silent
First National

Mishaps of a family picnic.
Very mild Chaplin, reaching for but not
achieving a kind of lyric quality. Amusing bits
rather than scenes.

wd Charles Chaplin *ph* Rollie Totheroh

Charles Chaplin, Edna Purviance, Henry
Bergman, Babe Lincoln

Dayton's Devils

US 1968   103m   Eastmancolor
Madison / Harold Goldman (Robert W.
   Stabler)

A former USAF colonel assembles a group of
misfits and adventurers to steal an army
payroll.
Overlong, routine caper film with a
surprisingly crisp climax (when it comes).

w Fred de Gorter d Jack Shea *ph* Brick
Marquard m Marlin Skiles

Leslie Nielsen, Rory Calhoun, Lainie Kazan,
Hans Gudegast

D-Day the Sixth of June

US 1956   106m   Eastmancolor
   Cinemascope
TCF (Charles Brackett)

On the way to invade France in 1944, a British
colonel and an American captain reminisce
about their love for the same woman.
Turgid war romance with some good action
scenes and the usual hilarious Hollywood view
of London. General effect very wooden.

w Ivan Moffat, Harry Brown, *novel* Lionel
Shapiro d Henry Koster *ph* Lee Garmes
m Lyn Murray

Robert Taylor, Richard Todd, Dana Wynter,
Edmond O'Brien, John Williams, Jerry Paris,
Richard Stapley
   'Reminiscent of *Mrs Miniver* in style and
feeling.'—*MFB*

De Sade*

US / Germany 1969   113m   Movielab
AIP / CCC / Transcontinental (Louis M.
   Heyward, Artur Brauner)

The unbalanced Marquis de Sade is tormented by his wicked uncle with thoughts of his past. Mildly interesting attempt by AIP at European debauchery, with a good theatrical framework for the fantasies but too much flailing about by all concerned, especially in the slow motion orgy sequences, which are relentlessly boring, as is the film.

w Richard Matheson d Cy Endfield ph *Heinz Pehlke ad Jurgen Kiebach m* Billy Strange

Keir Dullea, *John Huston*, Lilli Palmer, Senta Berger, Anna Massey, Uta Levka

Dead End***
US 1937 92m bw
Samuel Goldwyn

A slice of life in New York's east side, where slum kids and gangsters live in a river street next to a luxury apartment block.
Highly theatrical film of a highly theatrical play, more or less preserving the single set and overcoming the limitations of the script and setting by sheer cinematic expertise. It is chiefly remembered, however, for introducing the Dead End Kids to a delighted world.

w Lillian Hellman, *play Sidney Kingsley d William Wyler ph Gregg Toland ad Richard Day m* Alfred Newman

Joel McCrea, Sylvia Sidney, *Humphrey Bogart*, Wendy Barrie, Claire Trevor, Allen Jenkins, *Marjorie Main*, James Burke, Ward Bond, *The Dead End Kids* (Billy Halop, Leo Gorcey, Bernard Punsley, Huntz Hall, Bobby Jordan, Gabriel Dell)

AAN: best picture; Gregg Toland; Claire Trevor

The Dead End Kids
The films in which the original gang of young 'hooligans' (see above) appeared were as follows:

1937: DEAD END
1938: CRIME SCHOOL, ANGELS WITH DIRTY FACES
1939: THEY MADE ME A CRIMINAL, HELL'S KITCHEN, ANGELS WASH THEIR FACES
1940: THE DEAD END KIDS ON DRESS PARADE
Subsequently they broke up into the LITTLE TOUGH GUYS, the EAST SIDE KIDS, and the BOWERY BOYS (all qv)

Dead Heat on a Merry Go Round
US 1968   108m Technicolor
Columbia (Carter de Haven)

An ex-con breaks parole and plans to rob Los Angeles Airport.

Boringly arty caper comedy-melodrama, concentrating less on the robbery than on its hero's sexual prowess. All very superficially flashy, and what the title means is anybody's guess.

wd Bernard Girard ph Lionel Lindon m Stu Phillips

James Coburn, Camilla Sparv, Aldo Ray, Nina Wayne, Robert Webber, Rose Marie, Todd Armstrong, Marian Moses, Severn Darden

'Just fills the space between a frisky title and a tricky TV-comedy ending, but doesn't fill it with any revels that require a viewer's complete attention.'—*Time*

Dead Man's Eyes
US 1944   64m bw

In order to trap a murderer, a blind artist pretends to have recovered his sight. Cheerless lower-case thriller from the disappointing *Inner Sanctum* series. Lon Chaney Jnr, Jean Parker, Paul Kelly. Written by Dwight V. Babcock; directed by Reginald LeBorg; for Universal.

Dead Men Are Dangerous
GB 1938   69m bw

A down-and-out changes clothes with a corpse and is accused of murder. Sprightly thriller of its unassuming type. Robert Newton, Betty Lynne, John Warwick, Peter Gawthorne. Written by Victor Kendall, Harry Hughes and Vernon Clancy; directed by Harold French; for Pathé.

Dead Men Tell No Tales
GB 1938   80m bw

The matron of a school for boys is murdered after winning a lottery. Reasonably intriguing mystery. Emlyn Williams, Hugh Williams, Marius Goring, Lesley Brook, Sara Seegar. Written by Walter Summers and others, from the novel *The Norwich Victims* by Francis Beeding; directed by David MacDonald; for British National.

Dead Men Walk
US 1943   64m bw

A vampire returns from death to destroy his twin brother. Incompetent chiller partly sustained by its star performance. George Zucco, Mary Carlisle. Written by Fred Myton; directed by Sam Newfeld; for PRC.

Dead of Night****
GB 1945   104m bw
Ealing (Michael Balcon)

An architect is caught up in an endless series of recurring dreams, during which he is told other people's supernatural experiences and finally murders the psychiatrist who is trying to help him.

Chillingly successful and influential compendium of the macabre, especially effective in its low-key handling of the linking sequence with its circular ending.

w John Baines, Angus Macphail, based on stories by themselves, H. G. Wells, E. F. Benson *d Cavalcanti, Charles Crichton, Robert Hamer, Basil Dearden ph* Douglas Slocombe, Stan Pavey *m Georges Auric ad Michael Relph*

Mervyn Johns, Roland Culver, Mary Merrall, Judy Kelly, Anthony Baird, *Sally Ann Howes, Frederick Valk, Googie Withers*, Ralph Michael, Esmé Percy, Basil Radford, Naunton Wayne, Miles Malleson, *Michael Redgrave*, Hartley Power, Elizabeth Welch

'In a nightmare within a nightmare are contained five separate ghost stories . . . they have atmosphere and polish, they are eerie, they are well acted.'—*Richard Winnington*

'One of the most successful blends of laughter, terror and outrage that I can remember.'—*James Agee*

'The five ghost stories accumulate in intensity until the trap closes in the surrealist climax.'—*Pauline Kael, 1968*

Dead or Alive

Italy / US 1967   89m   Eastmancolor
Documento / Selmur (Albert Band)
US title: *A Minute to Pray, a Second to Die*

A gunman with a paralysed right arm helps a state governor rid a town of bandits.

Semi-spaghetti western with a strong cast and violent action scenes.

w Ugo Liberatore, Louis Garfinkle *d* Franco Giraldi *ph* Aiace Parolin *m* Carlo Rustichelli

Robert Ryan, Arthur Kennedy, Alex Cord, Nicoletta Machiavelli

Dead Reckoning*

US 1947   100m   bw
Columbia (Sidney Biddell)

Two war veterans are on their way to be decorated in Washington when one disappears.

Dour, complexly plotted thriller, a typical Hollywood *film noir* of the post-war years but a long way behind *Gilda* in likeability. The hero confesses the plot to a priest, and all the way it is more glum than fun.

w Oliver H. P. Garrett, Steve Fisher *d* John Cromwell *ph* Leo Tover *m* Marlin Skiles *md* Morris Stoloff

Humphrey Bogart, Lizabeth Scott, *Morris Carnovsky*, Charles Cane, William Prince, Marvin Miller, Wallace Ford, James Bell

Dead Ringer*

US 1964   116m   bw
Warner (William H. Wright)
GB title: *Dead Image*

A woman shoots her rich twin sister and assumes her identity.

High camp star vehicle, full of memories of long ago but rather drearily assembled and far too long, though Miss Davis as ever is in fighting form.

w Albert Beich, Oscar Millard *d* Paul Henreid *ph* Ernest Haller *m* André Previn

Bette Davis, Karl Malden, Peter Lawford, Philip Carey, Jean Hagen, Estelle Winwood, George Chandler, Cyril Delevanti

Deadfall

GB 1968   120m   De Luxe
TCF / Salamanda (Paul Monash, Jack Rix)

Robbery turns sour when a cat burglar falls in love with the wife of his homosexual partner.

Drearily fashionable romantic melodrama with far too few high spots and generally dull performances.

w Bryan Forbes, *novel* Desmond Cory *d* Bryan Forbes *ph* Gerry Turpin *m* John Barry

Michael Caine, Eric Portman, Giovanna Ralli, Nanette Newman, David Buck

'Exhausted no doubt by their past passions and childhood traumas, the principal protagonists move like so many somnambulists through the turgid labyrinth . . . whatever the intention, *Deadfall* merely falls flat on its somewhat ludicrous face.'—*MFB*

Deadlier Than the Male

GB 1967   101m   Techniscope
Rank / Sydney Box (Betty E. Box)

Bulldog Drummond traces the death of oil company executives to a master criminal using glamorous female assassins.

Just about tolerable recreation of Drummond in the modern world, with too little style, too much violence and sex, and an almost total lack of self-mockery. A sequel *Some Girls Do* (qv), was an unmitigated disaster.

w Jimmy Sangster, David Osborn, Liz Charles-Williams *d* Ralph Thomas *ph* Ernest Steward *m* Malcolm Lockyer *ad* Alex Vetchinsky

Richard Johnson, Nigel Green, Elke Sommer, Sylva Koscina, Suzanna Leigh, Zia Mohyeddin, Steve Carlson

'The original Drummond would have found the whole thing rather distasteful.'—*MFB*

Deadline at Dawn
US 1946 82m bw
RKO

A sailor on leave passes out, finds the girl he was with has been murdered, and is helped by a philosophical taxi driver and a girl.
This could have been another *Crossfire*, but is smothered by pretentious writing and uncertain direction. The credits are interesting, though.

w Clifford Odets *d* Harold Clurman
ph Nicholas Musuraca

Paul Lukas, Bill Williams, Susan Hayward, Osa Massen, Lola Lane

Deadline USA*
US 1952 87m bw
TCF (Sol C. Siegel)
GB title: *Deadline*

Despite threats and the killing of a witness, a crusading newspaper editor goes ahead with a story about the crimes of a powerful gangster. Watchable newspaper melodrama with nothing much to say except that America must wake up to the enemy within. Smooth production, but too much semi-pretentious talk.

wd Richard Brooks *ph* Milton Krasner
m Cyril Mockridge

Humphrey Bogart, Kim Hunter, Ethel Barrymore, Ed Begley, Paul Stewart, Warren Stevens, Martin Gabel, Joe de Santis, Audrey Christie, Jim Backus

The Deadly Affair**
GB 1966 106m Technicolor
Columbia / Sidney Lumet

A Foreign Office man apparently commits suicide; his colleague is unconvinced and finally uncovers a spy ring.
Compulsive if heavy-going thriller from the sour-about-spies era, deliberately glum, photographed against the shabbiest possible London backgrounds in muddy colour. Solidly entertaining for sophisticated grown-ups.

w Paul Dehn, novel Call for the Dead by John Le Carré *d Sidney Lumet ph* Frederick A. Young *m* Quincy Jones

James Mason, Simone Signoret, Harry Andrews, Maximilian Schell, Harriet Andersson, Kenneth Haigh, *Max Adrian*, Robert Flemyng, Roy Kinnear, Lynn Redgrave

The Deadly Bees
GB 1966 83m Technicolor

A pop singer goes on holiday to a remote farm and finds herself menaced by killer bees. Flat little thriller with one very obvious twist and no monster: just those bees. Frank Finlay, Guy Doleman, Suzanna Leigh, Catherine Finn. Written by Robert Bloch and Anthony Marriott; directed by Freddie Francis; for Amicus.

The Deadly Companions*
US 1961 90m Pathecolor Panavision
Warner / Pathe America (Charles B. Fitzsimmons)

An army sergeant, a deserter, a trigger-happy gunman and a saloon hostess join forces to rob a bank.
Disjointed but rather attractive little western let down by corny moments in the script.

w A. S. Fleishman *d Sam Peckinpah*
ph William H. Clothier *m* Martin Skiles, Raoul Kraushaar

Brian Keith, Maureen O'Hara, Chill Wills, Steve Cochran

The Deadly Mantis
US 1957 78m bw

A 'prehistoric' mantis escapes from Arctic ice and travels rapidly towards New York. Absurd and poorly crafted monster movie. Craig Stevens, Alix Talton, William Hopper. Written by Martin Berkeley; directed by Nathan Juran; for Universal-International.

Deadly Strangers
GB 1974 93m Eastmancolor
Rank / Silhouette (Peter Miller)

A girl accepts a lift from a motorist at a time when a mad strangler is on the loose.
Sub-Hitchcock melo-thriller with enough red herrings to sink a ship. Smartly enough done, but the grisliness needed balancing by humour.

w Philip Levene *d* Sidney Hayers
ph Graham Edgar *m* Ron Goodwin

Hayley Mills, Simon Ward, Sterling Hayden, Ken Hutchison, Peter Jeffrey

The Deadly Trackers
US 1973 104m Technicolor
Warner / Cine Film (Ed Rosen, Fouad Said)
A sheriff stalks the bandits who killed his wife and son.
Lurid and ludicrous western started, and abandoned, by Samuel Fuller; the challenge need not have been taken up.

w Lukas Heller *d* Barry Shear *ph* Gabriel
Torres *m* various

Rod Taylor, Richard Harris, Al Lettieri,
Neville Brand, William Smith
'It is no more than the outline of a
shadow.'—*Tony Rayns*
'An incoherent, blood-soaked chase
story.'—*New Yorker, 1977*

The Deadly Trap
France / Italy 1971   100m   Eastmancolor
The children of an American couple in Paris
are kidnapped. Smoothly made thriller which
spends rather too much time being chic. Faye
Dunaway, Frank Langella, Barbara Parkins.
Written by Sidney Buchman and Eleanor
Perry, from the novel *The Children are Gone*
by Arthur Cavanaugh; directed by René
Clément; for Corona / Pomereu / Oceania.

Dear Brigitte
US 1965   100m   De Luxe   Cinemascope
TCF (Henry Koster)
The small son of an American professor writes
a love letter to Brigitte Bardot, and when they
finally go to Paris she is charming to them.
Mild family comedy quaintly set around a
decaying Mississippi riverboat home; despite
assured performances, it all gets a bit icky at
times.

w Hal Kanter, *novel* Erasmus with Freckles by
John Haase *d* Henry Koster *ph* Lucien
Ballard *m* George Duning

James Stewart, Glynis Johns, Fabian, Cindy
Carol, Billy Mumy, John Williams, Jack
Kruschen, Brigitte Bardot, Ed Wynn, Alice
Pearce

Dear Heart*
US 1964   114m   bw
Warner (Martin Manulis)
At a postmasters' convention in New York,
two middle-aged delegates fall in love.
Charming, understated, overlong romantic
drama in the *Marty* tradition; all quite
professional and satisfying.

w Tad Mosel *d* Delbert Mann *ph* Russell
Harlan *m* Henry Mancini

Glenn Ford, Geraldine Page, Angela
Lansbury, Michael Anderson Jnr, Barbara
Nichols, Patricia Barry, Charles Drake, Ruth
McDevitt, Neva Patterson, Alice Pearce,
Richard Deacon

AAN: title song (*m* Henry Mancini, *ly* Jay
Livingston, Ray Evans)

Dear Inspector*
France 1977   105m   Eastmancolor
Ariane / Mondex (Alexander Mnouchkine)
Original title: *Tendre Poulet*
A female detective chases a murderer, helped
by her professor boyfriend.
Very likeable comedy-thriller with neat
performances. Popular in America, it was
translated into a series for television, but
didn't run.

w Michel Audiard, Philippe de Broca,
novel Jean-Paul Rouland and Claude Olivier
d Philippe de Broca *ph* Jean-Paul Schwartz
m Georges Delerue

Annie Girardot, Philippe Noiret, Catherine
Alric, Hubert Deschamps

Dear John*
Sweden 1964   111m   bw
Sandrew (Bo Jonsson)
original title: *Kare John*
An unmarried mother in a seaside village falls
for a seaman.
A slight story effectively tricked out with all
manner of cinematic devices including a
multitude of flashbacks. Very watchable if a
little self-conscious.

wd Lars Magnus Lindgren, *novel* Olle
Lansburg *ph* Rune Ericson *m* Bengt-Arne
Wallin

Jarl Kulle, Christina Schollin, Helena Nilsson,
Morgan Anderson
'It shines with the cool clear light of the
Swedish summer, and despite its glossy surface
manages also to convey strong sensual
pleasure.'—*Brenda Davies*

Dear Mr Prohack
GB 1949   91m   bw
GFD / Wessex (Ian Dalrymple, Dennis Van
Thal)
A treasury official copes admirably with public
money but is helpless when he comes into a
private fortune.
Flat little comedy in which the minor
amusements are incidental to the story.

w Ian Dalrymple, Donald Bull, *novel* Arnold
Bennett *d* Thornton Freeland *ph* H. E.
Fowle *m* Temple Abady

Cecil Parker, Hermione Baddeley, Dirk
Bogarde, Sheila Sim, Glynis Johns, Heather
Thatcher, Henry Edwards, Judith Furse

Dear Murderer
GB 1947   94m   bw
GFD / Gainsborough (Betty E. Box)

Plot and counterplot among an adulterous triangle.
Thoroughly artificial pattern play set among the unreal rich, from one of those unaccountable West End successes, here boringly filmed.

w Muriel and Sydney Box, Peter Rogers, *play* St John L. Clowes *d* Arthur Crabtree *ph* Stephen Dade

Eric Portman, Greta Gynt, Dennis Price, Maxwell Reed, Jack Warner, Hazel Court, Andrew Crawford, Jane Hylton

Dear Octopus**
GB 1943 86m bw
GFD / Gainsborough (Edward Black)
US title: *The Randolph Family*

Members of a well-to-do British family reunite for Golden Wedding celebrations.
Traditional upper-class British comedy drama, and very well done too, with opportunities for excellent character acting.

w R. J. Minney, Patrick Kirwan, *play Dodie Smith* *d* Harold French *ph* Arthur Crabtree

Margaret Lockwood, Michael Wilding, *Helen Haye, Frederick Leister, Celia Johnson, Roland Culver, Athene Seyler*, Basil Radford, Nora Swinburne, Jean Cadell, Kathleen Harrison, Ann Stephens, Muriel George, Antoinette Cellier, Graham Moffatt

Dear Ruth*
US 1947 95m bw
Paramount (Paul Jones)

A schoolgirl causes confusion when she writes love letters to a soldier using her elder sister's photograph.
Smoothly amusing family comedy from a Broadway success.

w Arthur Sheekman, *play* Norman Krasna *d* William D. Russell *ph* Ernest Laszlo *m* Robert Emmett Dolan

Joan Caulfield, William Holden, Mona Freeman, Billy de Wolfe, Edward Arnold, Mary Philips, Virginia Welles
'It is unlikely that 1947 will bring a more satisfying comedy . . . so many surprising and funny twists.'—*John Thompson, New York Mirror*
† Two less amusing sequels were made using virtually the same cast: *Dear Wife* (1949, 88m, *d* Richard Haydn); *Dear Brat* (1951, 82m, *d* William A. Seiter).

Death at Broadcasting House*
GB 1934 71m bw
ABFD / Phoenix (Hugh Perceval)

A radio actor is murdered during a broadcast.
Intriguing little murder mystery with an unusual background.

w Basil Mason, *novel* Val Gielgud *d* Reginald Denham

Ian Hunter, Austin Trevor, Mary Newland, Henry Kendall, Val Gielgud, Peter Haddon, Betty Ann Davies, Jack Hawkins, Donald Wolfit

Death in Venice**
Italy 1971 128m Technicolor
Panavision
Warner / Alfa (Mario Gallo)
original title: *Morte a Venezia*

In a lush Venetian hotel one summer in the early years of the century, a middle-aged German composer on holiday falls for the charms of a silent young boy, and stays in the city too long to escape the approaching plague.
Incredibly extended and rather pointless fable enriched by moments of great beauty and directorial style; these do not quite atone for the slow pace or the muddled storyline.

w Luchino Visconti, Nicola Bandalucco, *novel* Thomas Mann *d* Luchino Visconti *ph* Pasquale de Santis *m* Gustav Mahler *md* Franco Mannino *ad* Ferdinando Scarfiotti

Dirk Bogarde, Bjorn Andresen, Silvana Mangano, Marisa Berenson, Mark Burns
'Maybe a story as elusive as *Death in Venice* simply can't be filmed. Visconti has made a brave attempt, always sensitive to the original; but it's finally not quite the same thing.'— *David Wilson, MFB*

Death of a Cyclist*
Spain / Italy 1955 85m bw
Guion-Suevia / Trionfalcine
original title: *Muerte de un Ciclista*

An accident – a cyclist is knocked down and killed by an adulterous couple – tragically affects the lives of many people.
Rather like a politically conscious version of *An Inspector Calls*, this mannered and unemotional film was most interesting because of its almost Hollywoodian self-assurance.

wd *Juan Antonio Bardem story* Luis de Igoa *ph* Alfredo Fraile *m* Isrido Maiztegui

Lucia Bose, Alberto Closas, Otello Toso, Carlos Casaravilla

Death of a Gunfighter*
US 1969 100m Technicolor
Universal (Richard E. Lyons)

An unpopular marshal refuses to resign, and the situation leads to gunplay.

Downcast character western set in the early years of the century.

w Joseph Calvelli d Robert Totten, Don Siegel ph Andrew Jackson m Oliver Nelson

Richard Widmark, Lena Horne, John Saxon, Carroll O'Connor, Larry Gates, Kent Smith

Death of a Salesman***
US 1951 112m bw
Columbia (Stanley Kramer)

An ageing travelling salesman recognizes the emptiness of his life and commits suicide. A very acceptable screen version of a milestone play which has become an American classic; stage conventions and tricks are cleverly adapted to cinematic use, especially when the hero walks from the present into the past and back again.

w Stanley Roberts, play Arthur Miller d Laslo Benedek ph Franz Planer m Alex North md Morris Stoloff

Fredric March, Kevin McCarthy, Cameron Mitchell, Mildred Dunnock, Howard Smith, Royal Beal, Jesse White

'Its time shifts with light, which were poetic in the theatre, seemed shabby in a medium that can dissolve time and space so easily.'— Stanley Kauffmann

AAN: Franz Planer; Alex North; Fredric March; Kevin McCarthy; Mildred Dunnock

Death of a Scoundrel*
US 1956 119m bw
RKO / Charles Martin

A Czech in New York becomes rich by fraud. Unconvincing but intermittently entertaining melodrama, a vehicle for a male Bette Davis.

wd Charles Martin ph James Wong Howe m Max Steiner

George Sanders, Yvonne de Carlo, Coleen Gray, Victor Jory, Zsa Zsa Gabor, Nancy Gates, John Hoyt, Tom Conway

'Vague moralizing and some attempts at social comment scarcely enliven this protracted study in megalomania.'—MFB

Death on the Nile*
GB 1978 140m Technicolor
EMI (John Brabourne, Richard Goodwin)

Hercule Poirot solves the mystery of who killed the spoilt heiress on a steamer cruising down the Nile. A pleasant thirties atmosphere and the travel poster backgrounds are the chief assets of this rather hesitant whodunnit which plays fair enough with the audience but gives its popular cast too little to do, while its constant

repetitions of the crime become rather ghoulish. On the whole, though, a very passable representation of an old-fashioned genre, and a few points up on Murder on the Orient Express.

w Anthony Shaffer, novel Agatha Christie d John Guillermin ph Jack Cardiff pd Peter Murton m Nino Rota

Peter Ustinov, Bette Davis, Mia Farrow, Angela Lansbury, Jane Birkin, David Niven, George Kennedy, Jack Warden, Simon MacCorkindale, Lois Chiles, Jon Finch, Maggie Smith, Olivia Hussey, Harry Andrews, I. S. Johar

Death Race 2000*
US 1975 79m colour
New World (Roger Corman)

In the year 2000, the world's most popular sport involves motor racers who compete for the highest total of human casualties. Cheaply made macabre satire, quite well enough made to please addicts of the blackest of black comedy.

w Robert Thom, Charles Griffith, Ib Melchior d Paul Bartel ph Tak Fujimoto m Paul Chihara

David Carradine, Simone Griffeth, Sylvester Stallone, Mary Woronov

'The script is hardly Swiftian and therefore treads a thin delicate line between mockery and exploitation.'—Michael Billington, Illustrated London News

Death Ship
Canada 1980 91m CFI color

Survivors of a shipwreck take refuge on a mysterious empty ship which sets about killing them one by one. Yes, that's the synopsis, in the wake of Killdozer and The Car, and this film is stupider than either. George Kennedy, Richard Crenna, Nick Mancuso, Sally Ann Howes, Kate Reid. Written by John Robins; directed by Alvin Rakoff; for Astral Bellevue Pathé / Bloodstar.

Death Takes a Holiday**
US 1934 78m bw
Paramount (E. Lloyd Sheldon)

In the form of a mysterious prince, Death visits an Italian noble family to see why men fear him so. A somewhat pretentious classic from a popular play of the twenties; interesting handling and performances, but a slow pace by modern standards.

w Maxwell Anderson, Gladys Lehman, Walter Ferris based on plays by Maxwell Anderson

and Alberto Casella *d Mitchell Leisen*
ph Charles Lang *ad* Ernst Fegte

Fredric March, Evelyn Venable, Sir Guy
Standing, Katherine Alexander, Gail Patrick,
Helen Westley, Kathleen Howard, Henry
Travers, Kent Taylor

Death Wish*
US 1974 94m Technicolor
Paramount / Dino de Laurentiis (Hal
 Landers, Bobby Roberts, Michael
 Winner)

When his wife dies and his daughter becomes
a vegetable after an assault by muggers, a New
York businessman takes the law into his own
hands.
After a highly unpleasant and sensational
opening, this curious and controversial film
settles down into what amounts to black
comedy, with the audience well on the
vigilante's side. It's not very good, but it keeps
one watching.

w Wendell Mayes, *novel* Brian Garfield
d Michael Winner *ph* Arthur J. Ornitz
m Herbie Hancock

Charles Bronson, Hope Lange, Vincent
Gardenia, Stuart Margolin, Stephen Keats,
William Redfield
 'This urban version of *Walking Tall*
transcends its violence to satisfy every base
instinct that "we liberals" are heir to.'—*Judith
Crist*

Deathsport
US 1978 83m Metrocolor
New World (Roger Corman)

A popular game of the future involves
gladiators willing to lose their lives against
lethal motorcyclists.
Low-budget shocker for teenagers, by
Rollerball out of *Death Race*. Of no possible
interest except as exploitation.

w Henry Suso, Donald Stewart *d* Henry
Suso, Allan Arkush *ph* Gary Graver
m Andrew Stein

David Carradine, Claudia Jennings, Richard
Lynch, William Smithers

Decameron Nights
GB 1952 94m Technicolor
Film Locations (M. J. Frankovich)

Young Boccaccio entertains a glamorous
widow and her three guests with stories.
Feeble costume charade with all the
cuckolding off-screen: insipid and artificial.

w George Oppenheimer *d* Hugo Fregonese
ph Guy Green *m* Antony Hopkins

Louis Jourdan, Joan Fontaine, Binnie Barnes,
Joan Collins, Godfrey Tearle, Eliot Makeham,
Noel Purcell
 'The sort of hybrid international production
of which experience has made one
mistrustful.'—*Gavin Lambert*

Deception**
US 1946 112m bw
Warner (Henry Blanke)

A European cellist returning to America after
the war finds that his former girl friend has a
rich and jealous lover.
Downcast melodrama made when its star was
beginning to slide; today it seems irresistible
bosh with a background of classical music,
done with intermittent style especially by
Claude Rains as the egomaniac lover.

w John Collier, *play* Monsieur Lamberthier by
Louis Verneuil *d* Irving Rapper *ph* Ernest
Haller *m* Erich Wolfgang Korngold

Bette Davis, *Claude Rains*, Paul Henreid,
John Abbott, Benson Fong
 'It's like grand opera, only the people are
thinner . . . I wouldn't have missed it for the
world.'—*Cecelia Ager*
 'Exquisitely foolish: a camp classic.'—*New
Yorker, 1977*
 † Previously filmed in 1929 as *Jealousy*, with
Fredric March and Jeanne Eagels.

Decision before Dawn*
US 1951 119m bw
TCF (Anatole Litvak, Frank McCarthy)

In 1944, anti-Nazi German POWs are
parachuted into Germany to obtain
information.
Meticulous, well made but unexciting spy story
which seldom comes vividly to life.

w Peter Viertel, *novel* Call It Treason by
George Howe *d* Anatole Litvak *ph* Franz
Planer *m* Franz Waxman

Oskar Werner, Richard Basehart, Gary
Merrill, Hildegarde Neff, Dominique
Blanchar, Helene Thimig, O. E. Hasse, Hans
Christian Blech

AAN: best picture

The Decision of Christopher Blake
US 1948 75m bw
Warner (Ranald MacDougall)

A 12-year-old boy reunites his divorcing
parents.
Sentimental slop, surprisingly ill done, but
with a few good lines.

w Ranald MacDougall, *play* Moss Hart
d Peter Godfrey *ph* Karl Freund *m* Max
Steiner

Alexis Smith, Robert Douglas, *Cecil Kellaway*, Ted Donaldson, *Harry Davenport*, John Hoyt, Mary Wickes, Art Baker, Lois Maxwell

The Decks Ran Red
US 1958 84m bw
MGM / Andrew and Virginia Stone

Unscrupulous sailors plan to murder the entire crew of a freighter and claim the salvage money.
Solidly crafted but basically uninteresting melodrama.

w Andrew and Virginia Stone *d* Andrew Stone *ph* Meredith M. Nicholson

James Mason, Broderick Crawford, Dorothy Dandridge, Stuart Whitman

Decline and Fall
GB 1968 113m De Luxe
TCF / Ivan Foxwell
aka: *Decline and Fall of a Birdwatcher*

An innocent, accident-prone Oxford undergraduate is expelled and after various adventures in high and low society is convicted as a white slaver.
Flabby, doomed attempt to film a satirical classic which lives only on the printed page. Odd moments amuse.

w Ivan Foxwell, *novel* Evelyn Waugh *d* John Krish *ph* Desmond Dickinson *m* Ron Goodwin

Robin Phillips, Donald Wolfit, Genevieve Page, Robert Harris, Leo McKern, Colin Blakely, Felix Aylmer, Donald Sinden, Griffith Jones

Dédée d'Anvers°
France 1948 95m bw
Sacha Gordine (André Paulvé)
aka: *Woman of Antwerp; Dédée*

A dockside prostitute falls for a sailor and arouses the jealousy of her protector.
Seamy low life melodrama, presented *con brio*, but rather like a tenth copy of *Quai des Brumes*.

w Yves Allégret, Jacques Sigurd *d* Yves Allégret *ph* Jean Bourgoin *m* Jacques Besse

Simone Signoret, Marcel Pagliero, Bernard Blier, Marcel Dalio, Jane Marken

The Deep
US 1977 124m Metrocolor Panavision
Columbia / EMI / Casablanca (Peter Guber)

Underwater treasure seekers off Bermuda clash with black villains seeking a lost consignment of morphine.

An expensive action picture which is singularly lacking in action and even in plot, but oozes with brutality and overdoes the splendours of submarine life, forty per cent of it taking place under water.

w Peter Benchley, Tracy Keenan Wynn, *novel* Peter Benchley *d* Peter Yates *ph* Christopher Challis, Al Giddings, Stan Waterman *m* John Barry *pd* Tony Masters

Jacqueline Bisset, Robert Shaw, Nick Nolte, Lou Gossett, Eli Wallach

'The ultimate disco experience . . . it dances on the spot for two hours, taking voodoo, buried treasure, morphine, violence and sea monsters in its stride.'—*Time Out*

'Peter Yates has knocked himself out doing masterly underwater action sequences in the service of a woefully crummy book.'—*Russell Davies, Observer*

The Deep Blue Sea°
GB 1955 99m Eastmancolor Cinemascope
TCF / London Films (Anatole Litvak)

A judge's wife attempts suicide when jilted by her ex-RAF lover.
Undistinguished adaptation of a very good play, hampered by wide screen and muddy colour, helped by thoughtful performances.

w Terence Rattigan, from his play *d* Anatole Litvak *ph* Jack Hildyard *m* Malcolm Arnold

Vivien Leigh, Kenneth More, Eric Portman, *Emlyn Williams*, Moira Lister, Arthur Hill, Dandy Nichols, Jimmy Hanley, Miriam Karlin

Deep End°
West Germany / USA 1970 88m Eastmancolor
Maran / Kettledrum / Bavaria Atelier (Judd Bernard)

Sexual problems of two young people on the staff of a London municipal bathhouse.
Interestingly made but rather dreary and vaguely symbolic modern fable.

w Jerzy Skolimowski, Jerzy Gruza, Boleslaw Sulik *d* Jerzy Skolimowski *ph* Charly Steinberger *m* Cat Stevens

Jane Asher, John Moulder-Brown, Diana Dors, Karl Michael Vogler, Christopher Sandford

'A study in the growth of obsession that is both funny and frighteningly exact.'—*Nigel Andrews, MFB*

Deep in My Heart°
US 1954 132m Eastmancolor
MGM (Roger Edens)

Sigmund Romberg, a composer-waiter in New York, is helped by writer Dorothy Donnelly and showman Florenz Ziegfeld to become a famous writer of musicals.

Standard fictionalized biopic with plenty of good turns and a sharper script than usual.

w Leonard Spiegelgass *d* Stanley Donen *ph* George Folsey *m* Sigmund Romberg *ad* Cedric Gibbons, Edward Carfagno *ch* Eugene Loring

Jose Ferrer, Merle Oberon, Paul Henreid (as Ziegfeld), Walter Pidgeon, Helen Traubel, Doe Avedon, Tamara Toumanova, Paul Stewart, Isobel Elsom, David Burns, Jim Backus . . . and Gene Kelly, Fred Kelly, Rosemary Clooney, Jane Powell, Ann Miller, Cyd Charisse, James Mitchell, Howard Keel, Tony Martin, Joan Weldon

The Deep Six
US 1958   110m   Warnercolor
Jaguar (Martin Rackin)

A Quaker is unhappy at being drafted into the submarine service, but after initial unpopularity becomes a hero.

An ageing star contends with many hazards: slipshod production, poor colour, a dull script, and an unplayable part.

w John Twist, Martin Rackin, Harry Brown *d* Rudolph Maté *ph* John Seitz *m* David Buttolph

Alan Ladd, William Bendix, Efrem Zimbalist Jnr, Dianne Foster, Keenan Wynn, James Whitmore, Joey Bishop, Jeanette Nolan

Deep Valley
US 1947   104m   bw
Warner (Henry Blanke)

The daughter of a poor California farmer falls for a convict on a work gang.

Downright peculiar melodrama, a cross between *Tobacco Road* and *Cold Comfort Farm*, with touches of *High Sierra*. For collectors.

w Salka Viertel, Stephen Morehouse Avery, *novel* Dan Totheroh *d* Jean Negulesco *ph* Ted McCord *m* Max Steiner

Ida Lupino, Dane Clark, Wayne Morris, Henry Hull, Fay Bainter, Willard Robertson

Deep Waters
US 1948   85m   bw
TCF

A problem orphan boy is content when adopted by a lobster fisherman.

Forgettable family film, smoothly directed and photographed.

w Richard Murphy *d* Henry King *ph* Joseph La Shelle *m* Cyril Mockridge

Jean Peters, Dana Andrews, Dean Stockwell, Cesar Romero, Anne Revere

The Deer Hunter*
US 1978   182m   Technicolor
Universal / EMI (Barry Spikings, Michael Deeley, Michael Cimino, John Pevera)

Three friends from a small Pennsylvania town go to fight in Vietnam.

The three-hour running time is taken up with crosscutting of a wedding, a deer hunt and a game of Russian roulette. Presumably the audience has to guess the point, if any; meanwhile it may be repelled by this long and savage if frequently engrossing film.

w Deric Washburn, *story* Michael Cimino, Louis Garfinkle, Quinn K. Redeker and Washburn *d Michael Cimino ph* Vilmos Zsigmond *m* Stanley Myers

Robert De Niro, John Cazale, John Savage, Christopher Walken, Meryl Streep

'A hollow spectacle, less about war than its effect on a community, full of specious analogies, incoherent sentimentality and belief in its own self-importance.'—*Time Out*

AA: best picture; direction; Christopher Walken

AAN: Deric Washburn; Vilmos Zsigmond; Robert de Niro; Meryl Streep

The Defector
France / West Germany 1966   101m
Eastmancolor
PECF / Rhein Main (Raoul Lévy)
original title: *L'Espion*

An American physicist in East Germany gets involved in the spy game.

Disenchanted espionage 'realism', not very well styled and hampered by a star at the end of his tether.

w Robert Guenette, Raoul Lévy, *novel* The Spy by Paul Thomas *d* Raoul Lévy *ph* Raoul Coutard *m* Serge Gainsbourg

Montgomery Clift, Hardy Kruger, Macha Meril, Roddy McDowall, David Opatoshu, Christine Delaroche, Jean-Luc Godard

Defiance
US 1980   102m   Movielab

A young seaman staying in New York fights back against the power of an urban gang.

Belated and unnecessary addition to the gang cycle; violent nonsense. Jan Michael Vincent, Theresa Saldana, Danny Lopez. Written by Thomas Michael Donnelly; directed by John Flynn; for AIP.

The Defiant Ones**
US 1958 96m bw
US / Stanley Kramer

A black and a white convict escape from a
chain gang, still linked together but hating
each other.
Schematic melodrama with a moral,
impeccably done and with good performances.

w Nathan E. Douglas, Harold Jacob Smith
d *Stanley Kramer* ph *Sam Leavitt* m Ernest
Gold

Tony Curtis, Sidney Poitier, Theodore Bikel,
Charles McGraw, Lon Chaney Jnr, King
Donovan, Claude Akins, Lawrence Dobkin,
Whit Bissell, Carl 'Alfalfa' Switzer, Cara
Williams

'Probably Kramer's best picture. The
subject matter is relatively simple, though
"powerful"; the action is exciting; the acting is
good. But the singleness of purpose behind it
all is a little offensive.'—*Pauline Kael*

AA: Nathan E. Douglas, Harold Jacob Smith;
Sam Leavitt
AAN: best picture; Stanley Kramer; Tony
Curtis; Sidney Poitier; Theodore Bikel; Cara
Williams

Le Defroqué*
France 1953 111m bw
SFC / SNEG

A defrocked priest performs a gallant action
which persuades an acquaintance to become a
priest himself and try to draw his friend back
into the fold.
Curious but holding moral melodrama
embellished by good acting.

w Leo Joannon, Denys de la Patellière d *Leo
Joannon* ph Nicolas Torporkoff m Jean-
Jacques Grunenwald

Pierre Fresnay, Pierre Trabaud, Nicole
Stéphane, Marcelle Geniat, Guy Decomble,
Leo Joannon, René Blancard

A Delicate Balance*
US 1975 134m colour
American Express / Ely Landau / Cinevision

A quarrelsome Connecticut family is
dominated by an ageing matriarch, and
tensions mount to a climax of fear and threats.
Honourable but slightly boring film version of
an essentially theatrical play: the acting is the
thing.

w Edward Albee, from his play d Tony
Richardson ph David Watkin m none

Katharine Hepburn, Paul Scofield, Joseph
Cotten, Lee Remick, Kate Reid, Betsy Blair

The Delicate Delinquent
US 1956 101m bw Vistavision
Paramount / Jerry Lewis

A New York policeman tries to make friends
with an eccentric youth who mixes with thugs;
the boy decides to train as a policeman.
Jerry Lewis' first film without Dean Martin: a
sobering experience combining zany comedy,
sentiment, pathos and social comment. The
mixture fails to rise.

wd Don McGuire ph Haskell Boggs
m Buddy Bregman

Jerry Lewis, Darren McGavin, Martha Hyer,
Robert Ivers, Horace McMahon

Delicious
US 1931 106m bw
Fox

An Irish girl in New York falls for a rich man.
Early musical, very thin, but an agreeable
museum piece for collectors.

w Guy Bolton, Sonya Levien d David Butler
ph Ernest Palmer songs *George and Ira
Gershwin*

Janet Gaynor, Charles Farrell, El Brendel,
Lawrence O'Sullivan, Virginia Cherrill,
Mischa Auer

Delightfully Dangerous
US 1945 93m bw

A straitlaced girl discovers that her eldest
sister is a burlesque dancer. Mild family
comedy with music. Jane Powell, Constance
Moore, Ralph Bellamy, Arthur Treacher.
Written by Walter De Leon and Arthur
Phillips; directed by Arthur Lubin; for Buddy
Rogers / UA.

Deliverance**
US 1972 109m Technicolor
Panavision
Warner / Elmer Enterprises (John
Boorman)

Four men spend a holiday weekend canoeing
down a dangerous river, but find that the real
danger to their lives comes from themselves
and other humans.
Vigorous, meaningful, almost apocalyptic
vision of man's inhumanity, disguised as a
thrilling adult adventure.

w *James Dickey*, from his novel d John
Boorman ph Vilmos Zsigmond m Eric
Weissberg

Burt Reynolds, Jon Voight, Ned Beatty,
Ronny Cox, James Dickey

'There is fundamentally no view of the material, just a lot of painful grasping and groping.'—*Stanley Kauffmann*

AAN: best picture; John Boorman

Dementia 13*

US / Eire 1963   81m   bw
Filmgroup / AIP (Roger Corman)
GB title: *The Haunted and the Hunted*

An axe murderer attacks members of a noble Irish family at their lonely castle.
Nastily effective macabre piece with interesting credits.

wd Francis Ford Coppola *ph* Charles Hannawalt *m* Ronald Stein

Luana Anders, William Campbell, Bart Patton, Mary Mitchell, Patrick Magee, Eithne Dunn

Demetrius and the Gladiators**

US 1954   101m   Technicolor
Cinemascope
TCF (Frank Ross)

A Greek slave who keeps Christ's robe after the crucifixion is sentenced to be one of Caligula's gladiators and becomes involved in Messalina's wiles.
Lively, efficient sequel to *The Robe*, with emphasis less on religiosity than on the brutality of the arena and our hero's sexual temptations and near-escapes. Good Hollywood hokum.

w Philip Dunne *d* Delmer Daves *ph* Milton Krasner *m* Franz Waxman

Victor Mature, Susan Hayward, Michael Rennie (as Peter), Debra Paget, Anne Bancroft, Jay Robinson, Barry Jones, William Marshall, Richard Egan, Ernest Borgnine

'An energetic attempt to fling the mantle of sanctity over several more millions of the entertainment dollar.'—*The Times*

The Demi-Paradise*

GB 1943   114m   bw
Two Cities (Anatole de Grunwald)
US title: *Adventure for Two*

In 1939, a Russian inventor is sent to observe the British way of life.
Pleasant, aimless little satirical comedy in which this blessed plot seems to be peopled entirely by eccentrics.

w Anatole de Grunwald *d* Anthony Asquith *ph* Bernard Knowles *m* Nicholas Brodszky

Laurence Olivier, Penelope Dudley Ward, *Margaret Rutherford*, Leslie Henson, Marjorie Fielding, Felix Aylmer, Guy Middleton,

Michael Shepley, George Thorpe, Edie Martin, Muriel Aked, Joyce Grenfell

'A backhanded way of showing us poor juvenile-minded cinemagoers that the England of Mr Punch and Mrs Malaprop lives forever.'—*Richard Winnington*

Demon Seed

US 1977   95m   Metrocolor   Panavision
MGM (Herb Jaffe)

A scientist invents too perfect a computer: it locks up his wife, rapes her, and incubates a child . . .
Science fiction at the end of its tether, all very smart and self-conscious, but at this length very tasteless. Hitchcock would have got it into a television half-hour.

w Robert Jaffe, Roger O. Hirson, *novel* Dean R. Koontz *d* Donald Cammell *ph* Bill Butler *m* Jerry Fielding *pd* Edward Carfagno

Julie Christie, Fritz Weaver, Gerrit Graham, Berry Kroeger, Lisa Lu

Denver and Rio Grande

US 1952   89m   Technicolor

Railroad companies compete to lay track through a narrow gorge. Adequate western thick-ear. Edmond O'Brien, Sterling Hayden, Dean Jagger, Laura Elliot, Zasu Pitts, Lyle Bettger, J. Carrol Naish. Written by Frank Gruber; directed by Byron Haskin; for Nat Holt / Paramount.

Derby Day

GB 1952   84m   bw
British Lion / Wilcox-Neagle (Maurice Cowan)
US title: *Four Against Fate*

Intercut comic and melodramatic stories of four people who go to the Derby.
Quietly efficient, class-conscious entertainment on the lines of *Friday the 13th* and *The Bridge of San Luis Rey*. No surprises, but plenty of familiar faces.

w John Baines, Monckton Hoffe, Alan Melville *d* Herbert Wilcox *ph* Max Greene *m* Anthony Collins

Anna Neagle, Michael Wilding, Googie Withers, Gordon Harker, John McCallum, Peter Graves, Suzanne Cloutier, Gladys Henson, Ralph Reader, Alfie Bass, Edwin Styles, Nigel Stock

'Excessive loyalty to a formula has produced far from happy results.'—*Penelope Houston, MFB*

Le Dernier Milliardaire°
France 1934 90m bw
Pathé-Natan

The queen of a small principality invites a
financial wizard to pay court to her daughter.
The girl elopes with a bandleader, the
financier is engaged to the queen, and is then
revealed as a sham.
Rather too determined to be satirical, this
comedy sadly lacks the pace and flair of the
director's best work but there are several
sequences of interest.

wd René Clair ph Rudolph Maté, Louis Née
m Maurice Jaubert

Max Dearly, Renée Saint-Cyr, Marthe Mellot,
Raymond Cordy

Les Dernières Vacances°
France 1947 95m bw
Pathé

During a country house holiday in the
twenties, the last before the house is sold, old
friends conduct amorous intrigues and so do
their teenage progeny.
A moderately charming little fable making a
rather obscure social point.

w R. Breuil, Roger Leenhardt d Roger
Leenhardt ph Philippe Agostini

Berthe Bovy, Renée Devillers, Pierre Dux,
Jean d'Yd, Odile Versois, Michel François

Dersu Uzala°
USSR / Japan 1975 140m colour

A Russian surveyor mapping Siberian wastes
becomes friendly with a wily Mongolian
hunter.
Magnificent vistas punctuate an essentially
plodding propaganda piece which does not
rank with its director's best work. Maxim
Munzuk, Juri Solomine. Written by Yuri
Nagibin and Akira Kurosawa; directed by
Akira Kurosawa; for Mosfilm / Toho.
AA: best foreign film.

The Desert Fox°°
US 1951 88m bw
TCF (Nunnally Johnson)
GB title: *Rommel, Desert Fox*

Rommel returns, disillusioned, to Hitler's
Germany after his North African defeat, and
is involved in the July plot.
Vivid but scrappy account of the last years of a
contemporary hero. At the time it seemed to
show a new immediacy in film-making, and
was probably the first film to use an action
sequence to arrest attention before the credit
titles.

w Nunnally Johnson, book Rommel by
Desmond Young d Henry Hathaway
ph Norbert Brodine m Daniele Amfitheatrof

James Mason, Jessica Tandy, Cedric
Hardwicke, Luther Adler (as Hitler), Everett
Sloane, *Leo G. Carroll, George Macready*,
Richard Boone, Eduard Franz, Desmond
Young

Desert Fury
US 1947 96m Technicolor
Paramount (Hal B. Wallis)

Against advice, a girl is attracted to a neurotic
gambler who may have murdered his first wife.
Muddled melodrama slightly helped by
Arizona colour settings; unconvincing
characters mouth unspeakable lines in an
airless tedium.

w Robert Rossen, novel Desert Town by
Ramona Stewart d Lewis Allen ph Charles
Lang, Edward Cronjager m Miklos Rozsa

Lizabeth Scott, Wendell Corey, Burt
Lancaster, John Hodiak, Mary Astor, Kristine
Miller
  'The only fury I could sense was in my
corner of the balcony.'—*C. A. Lejeune*

The Desert Hawk
US 1950 77m Technicolor

Against an Arabian Nights background, a
cheerful outlaw abducts a princess. Tolerable
cloak-and-sandal action comedy. Richard
Greene, Yvonne de Carlo, Jackie Gleason,
George Macready, Rock Hudson, Carl
Esmond. Written by Aubrey Wisberg, Jack
Pollexfen and Gerald Drayson Adams;
directed by Frederick de Cordova; for
Universal-International.

Desert Legion
US 1953 86m Technicolor
Universal (Ted Richmond)

A Foreign Legion captain rids a lost city of
menacing bandits.
Schoolboy stuff, impudent in its silly story and
its unconvincing Shangri-La, but quite
entertaining for those prepared to let their hair
down.

w Irving Wallace, Lewis Meltzer d Joseph
Pevney ph John Seitz m Frank Skinner

Alan Ladd, Richard Conte, Arlene Dahl,
Akim Tamiroff, Leon Askin

The Desert Rats°
US 1953 88m bw
TCF (Robert L. Jacks)

An English captain commands an Australian
detachment in the siege of Tobruk, and

survives an encounter with Rommel.
Actioner made to cash in on the success of *The Desert Fox* (qv). Stars and battle scenes survive a studio look.

w Richard Murphy *d* Robert Wise *ph* Lucien Ballard *m* Leigh Harline *md* Nathaniel Finston

James Mason (as Rommel), Richard Burton, Robert Newton, Robert Douglas, Torin Thatcher, Chips Rafferty

AAN: Richard Murphy

The Desert Song
US 1929 106m bw
Warner

A romantic and mysterious figure leads North African natives against evil Arabs.
Primitive sound version of the highly successful 1926 operetta.

w Harvey Gates, *play* Otto Harbach, Lawrence Schwab, Frank Mandel *d* Roy del Ruth *ph* Barney McGill *m* Sigmund Romberg *ly* Oscar Hammerstein II

John Boles, Carlotta King, Louise Fazenda, Johnny Arthur, Edward Martindel, Jack Pratt

The Desert Song
US 1943 96m Technicolor
Warner (Robert Florey)

Updated version with Nazis as the real villains.
adaptation Robert Buckner *d* Robert Florey *ph* Bert Glennon *m* Heinz Roemheld

Dennis Morgan, Irene Manning, Bruce Cabot, Lynne Overman, Gene Lockhart, Victor Francen, Faye Emerson, Curt Bois, Jack La Rue, Marcel Dalio, Nestor Paiva, Gerald Mohr

The Desert Song
US 1953 110m Technicolor
Warner (Rudi Fehr)

Well staged straight version of the musical, with full score.
adaptation Roland Kibbee *d* Bruce Humberstone *ph* Robert Burks *m adaptation* Max Steiner

Gordon Macrae, Kathryn Grayson, Steve Cochran, Raymond Massey, Dick Wesson, Allyn McLerie, Ray Collins, Paul Picerni, William Conrad

The Deserter
Italy / Yugoslavia / USA 1970 99m
   Technicolor Panavision
Dino de Laurentiis / Jadran / Heritage
   (Norman Baer, Ralph Serpe)
original title: *La Spina Dorsale del Diavolo*

In the southwest in 1886, a cavalry captain tracks down the Apaches who tortured his wife to death.
Brutal revenge western, as muddled as its international credits would suggest.

w Clair Huffaker *d* Burt Kennedy *ph* Aldo Tonti *m* Piero Piccione *pd* Mario Chiari

Bekim Fehmiu, John Huston, Richard Crenna, Chuck Connors, Ricardo Montalban, Ian Bannen, Brandon de Wilde, Slim Pickens, Albert Salmi, Woody Strode, Patrick Wayne, Fausto Tozzi

Design for Living**
US 1933 88m bw
Paramount (Ernst Lubitsch)

Two friends love and are loved by the same worldly woman, and they set up house together.
Elegant but miscast version of a scintillating play, with all the sex and the sting removed (at the insistence of the Legion of Decency, then coming into power). Ben Hecht claimed to have removed all but one line of Coward's dialogue.

w Ben Hecht, *play* Noel Coward *d* Ernst Lubitsch *ph* Victor Milner *m* Nathaniel Finston *ad* Hans Dreier

Gary Cooper, Fredric March, Miriam Hopkins, Edward Everett Horton, Franklin Pangborn, Isabel Jewell
   'A partial cleansing for the screen of a stage story notorious for its wealth and variety of moral code infractions.'—*Martin Quigley*

Design for Scandal
US 1941 85m bw

A reporter is assigned by his boss to get a lady judge disbarred. Mechanical star comedy.
Rosalind Russell, Walter Pidgeon, Edward Arnold, Guy Kibbee, Lee Bowman. Written by Lionel Houser; directed by Norman Taurog; for MGM.

Designing Woman*
US 1957 118m Metrocolor
   Cinemascope
MGM (Dore Schary)

A sports reporter marries a dress designer and finds that their common interests are few.
Lumbering comedy which aims for sophistication but settles for farce: tolerable for star watchers who have dined well.

w George Wells *d* Vincente Minnelli *ph* John Alton *m* André Previn

Gregory Peck, Lauren Bacall, Dolores Gray, Sam Levene, Tom Helmore, Mickey

Shaughnessey, Jesse White, Chuck Connors, Jack Cole

AAN: George Wells

Desire**
US 1936 89m bw
Paramount (Ernst Lubitsch)

In Spain, an American car designer falls for a glamorous jewel thief.
Romantic comedy which the producer should have worked on longer: it begins brilliantly and keeps its style, but the pace and wit ebb away.

w Edwin Justus Mayer, Waldemar Young, Samuel Hoffenstein, from a German film Die schönen Tage von Aranjuez and a play by Hans Szekely and R. A. Stemmle d Frank Borzage ph Charles Lang, Victor Milner m Frederick Hollander ad Hans Dreier, Robert Usher

Marlene Dietrich, Gary Cooper, John Halliday, William Frawley, Ernest Cossart, Akim Tamiroff, Alan Mowbray, Zeffie Tilbury

'It sparkles and twinkles . . . one of the most engaging pictures of the season.'—Frank S. Nugent, New York Times

'A sure, beautifully written piece about the usual Lubitsch trifles, about crooks and fake countesses breathless before the dawn of romance.'—Alistair Cooke

Desire in the Dust
US 1960 102m bw Cinemascope
TCF / Associated Producers (William F. Claxton)

A wealthy southern aristocrat is involved in a fatal car crash and persuades a young farmhand to take the blame.
Derivative hothouse drama, a little better than its title, with a cast breathing heavily in imitation of refugees from Tennessee Williams or William Faulkner.

w Charles Lang, novel Harry Whittington d William F. Claxton ph Lucien Ballard m Paul Dunlap

Raymond Burr, Martha Hyer, Joan Bennett, Ken Scott, Brett Halsey, Anne Helm, Jack Ging, Edward Binns

Desire Me
US 1947 91m bw
MGM (Arthur Hornblow Jnr)

The wife of a Normandy villager hears that he has died in a concentration camp. She marries the bearer of the news, who turns out to be a psychotic who has left her husband for dead . . . but he is not.

Dreary drama, troubled during production and offering little for the actors to chew on.

w Marguerite Roberts, Zoe Akins, Casey Robinson, novel Leonhard Frank d not credited, but mostly by George Cukor, Melvyn Le Roy, Jack Conway ph Joseph Ruttenberg m Herbert Stothart

Greer Garson, Robert Mitchum, Richard Hart, George Zucco, Morris Ankrum

'The supporting cast includes a number of characters who give the appearance of having come out of a dusty cupboard marked "French Types—Assorted".'—MFB

Desire under the Elms
US 1958 111m bw Vistavision
Paramount (Don Hartman)

A New England farmer brings home a young bride and causes friction with his son.
This bid for culture turns out like a hoary and very slow melodrama, not exactly risible but annoying because it teeters between several styles.

w Irwin Shaw, play Eugene O'Neill d Delbert Mann ph Daniel L. Fapp m Elmer Bernstein

Sophia Loren, Burl Ives, Anthony Perkins, Frank Overton, Pernell Roberts, Anne Seymour

'The film is consistently and unhappily out of its depth.'—Penelope Houston

AAN: Daniel L. Fapp

Desirée
US 1954 110m De Luxe Cinemascope
TCF (Julian Blaustein)

Fictionalized biopic of one of Napoleon's mistresses.
Heavy-going costume piece, with all contributors distinctly uncomfortable.

w Daniel Taradash, novel Annemarie Selinko d Henry Koster ph Milton Krasner m Alex North

Jean Simmons, Marlon Brando, Merle Oberon, Michael Rennie, Cameron Mitchell, Elizabeth Sellars, Cathleen Nesbitt, Isobel Elsom

'Their story is not in the history books. It has never been seen on the screen—until now!'—publicity

The Desk Set**
US 1957 103m Eastmancolor Cinemascope
TCF (Henry Ephron)
GB title: His Other Woman

Ladies in a broadcasting company's reference section are appalled when an electronics

expert is sent to improve their performance.
Thin comedy, altered from a Broadway
success; patchy as a whole, but with several
splendid dialogue scenes for the principals.

w Phoebe and Henry Ephron, *play* William
Marchant d Walter Lang ph Leon Shamroy
m Cyril Mockridge

Spencer Tracy, Katharine Hepburn, Joan
Blondell, Gig Young, Dina Merrill, Neva
Patterson

'They lope through this trifling charade like
a couple of oldtimers who enjoy reminiscing
with simple routines.'—*Bosley Crowther, New
York Times*

Desperadoes
US 1943 85m Technicolor

A gunman rides into town to cause trouble,
but finds romance and renews an old
friendship. Lively star western of its day.
Randolph Scott, Glenn Ford, Evelyn Keyes,
Edgar Buchanan, Claire Trevor, Guinn
Williams. Written by Max Brand, Robert
Carson; directed by Charles Vidor; for Harry
Joe Brown / Columbia.

The Desperados
US 1968 90m Technicolor
Columbia / Meadway (Irving Allen)

After the Civil War, a fanatic 'parson' leads a
tribe of violent outlaws including his three
sons.
Rough-and-tumble western in the modern
savage manner; made in Spain.

w Walter Brough d Henry Levin ph Sam
Leavitt m David Whitaker

Vince Edwards, Jack Palance, George
Maharis, Neville Brand, Sylvia Syms,
Christian Roberts, Kate O'Mara, Kenneth
Cope, John Paul

Desperate Characters*
US 1971 106m colour
ITC (Frank D. Gilroy)

Residents of New York's east side find the
rigours of life hard to take.
Curious but interesting suburban drama, a
kind of deglamorized and updated *City for
Conquest*.

wd Frank D. Gilroy, *novel* Paula Fox ph Urs
Furrer

Shirley Maclaine, Gerald S. O'Loughlin,
Kenneth Mars, Sada Thompson, Jack Somack

'The most blistering indictment of New
York City since *Midnight Cowboy*.'—*Rex
Reed*

'A film of authenticity, of delicately realized
intangibles.'—*Stanley Kauffmann*

The Desperate Hours*
US 1955 112m bw Vistavision
Paramount (William Wyler)

Three escaped convicts take over a suburban
house but are finally outwitted by the family.
Ponderous treatment of an over-familiar
situation with only the acting and an 'A'
picture look to save it.

w Joseph Hayes, from his novel and play
d William Wyler ph Lee Garmes m Gail
Kubik

Fredric March, Humphrey Bogart, Martha
Scott, Arthur Kennedy, Gig Young, Dewey
Martin, Mary Murphy, Robert Middleton,
Richard Eyer

'A solid, deliberate and long-drawn-out
exercise in the mechanics of suspense.'—
Penelope Houston

Desperate Journey**
US 1942 109m bw
Warner (Hal B. Wallis)

Three POWs in Nazi Germany fight their way
back to freedom.
When you pit Errol Flynn against the Nazis,
there's no doubt who wins; and the last line is
'Now for Australia and a crack at those Japs!'
Exhilarating adventure for the totally
uncritical; professional standards high.

w Arthur Horman d Raoul Walsh ph Bert
Glennon m Max Steiner

Errol Flynn, Alan Hale, Ronald Reagan,
Nancy Coleman, Raymond Massey, Arthur
Kennedy, Ronald Sinclair, Albert Basserman,
Sig Rumann, Ilka Gruning, Pat O'Moore

Desperate Moment
GB 1953 88m bw
Rank / George H. Brown

In Poland, a man imprisoned for murder finds
he didn't do it, escapes, and tracks down the
real criminal, his best friend.
Cliché-ridden melodrama climaxing in a car
chase; poor in all departments.

w Patrick Kirwan, George H. Brown,
novel Martha Albrand d Compton Bennett
ph C. Pennington-Richards m Ronald Binge

Dirk Bogarde, Mai Zetterling, Philip Friend,
Albert Lieven, Carl Jaffe, Gerald Heinz

Destination Gobi*
US 1953 90m Technicolor
TCF (Stanley Rubin)

American soldiers get Mongol help against the
Japanese in the Gobi desert.
A curious war adventure, a kind of camel
opera, apparently based on fact; mildly

enjoyable, though the outlandish is gradually replaced by the predictable.

w Everett Freeman d Robert Wise
ph Charles G. Clarke m Sol Kaplan

Richard Widmark, Don Taylor, Casey Adams, Murvyn Vye, Darryl Hickman, Martin Milner, Ross Badgasarian, Rodolfo Acosta

Destination Moon*
US 1950 91m Technicolor
Universal / George Pal

An American inventor gets private backing to build a rocket so that the US can reach the moon before the Russians.
Semi-documentary prophecy with impressive gadgetry encased in a tedious and totally unsurprising script.

w Rip Van Ronkel, Robert Heinlan, James O'Hanlon d Irving Pichel ph Lionel Lindon m Leith Stevens

Warner Anderson, John Archer, Tom Powers, Dick Wesson
'Heavy-handed, unimaginative and very badly acted.'—MFB

Destination Tokyo*
US 1943 135m bw
Warner (Jerry Wald)

A US submarine is sent into Tokyo harbour. Solid, well acted war suspenser, but overlong.

w Delmer Daves, Albert Maltz, original story Steve Fisher d Delmer Daves ph Bert Glennon m Franz Waxman

Cary Grant, John Garfield, Alan Hale, John Ridgely, Dane Clark, Warner Anderson, William Prince, Robert Hutton, Tom Tully, Peter Whitney, Faye Emerson, John Forsythe
'We don't say it is credible; we don't even suggest that it makes sense. But it does make a pippin of a picture from a purely melodramatic point of view.'—Bosley Crowther
'Even moviegoers who have developed a serious allergy for service pictures should find it high among the superior films of the war.'— Newsweek

AAN: Steve Fisher

Destiny*
Germany 1921 100m approx bw silent
Decla-Bioscop
original title: Der Mude Tod

In the 19th-century a young woman tries to save her lover from the presence of Death, who shows her that whatever she does it is inevitable.
A solemn fantasy on the lines of Appointment

in Samarra, the framing story being more effective than the 'illustrations'.

w Thea Von Harbou, Fritz Lang d Fritz Lang ph Fritz Arno Wagner, Erich Nitschmann, Hermann Saalfrank

Lil Dagover, Rudolph Klein-Rogge, Bernhard Götzke, Walter Janssen

Destiny*
US 1944 65m bw
Universal (Roy William Neill)

An escaped convict on the run finds refuge with a blind girl on a lonely farm.
Curious second feature, interesting because it began as a story eliminated from Flesh and Fantasy (qv); extra footage was added to bring it up to the required length. The original footage is mainly the nightmare suffered by the girl.

w Roy Chanslor (F and F Ernest Pascal) d Reginald Le Borg (F and F Julien Duvivier) ph George Robinson (F and F Paul Ivano) m Frank Skinner

Gloria Jean, Alan Curtis (who died in the original but here survives), Frank Craven, Grace McDonald

Destiny of a Man**
USSR 1959 98m bw
Sovexportfilm / Mosfilm (G. Kuznetsov)
original title: Sudba Cheloveka

During World War II a Russian is captured by Nazis but escapes and returns home only to find his family dead.
Strikingly styled sob story whose very glumness prevented it from being hailed as a masterpiece; in technique however it is in the best Russian tradition.

w Y. Lukin, F. Shakhmagonov, story Mikhail Sholokhov d Sergei Bondarchuk ph Vladimir Monakhov m V. Basnov

Sergei Bondarchuk, Zinaida Kirienko, Pavlik Boriskin
'Of all Soviet post-war films, this will be looked on as the greatest and most original work of the period.'—MFB

Destroyer
US 1943 99m bw
Columbia (Louis F. Edelmann)

An old sea dog talks himself into a job on a World War II destroyer but works his men too hard.
Flat propaganda piece, not too well made.

w Frank Wead, Lewis Meltzer, Borden Chase d William A. Seiter ph Franz Planer m Anthony Collins

Edward G. Robinson, Glenn Ford,
Marguerite Chapman, Edgar Buchanan, Leo
Gorcey, Regis Toomey, Ed Brophy

Destry°
US 1954 95m Technicolor
U-I (Stanley Rubin)

Almost scene-for-scene remake of *Destry
Rides Again* (qv). Well enough made and
tolerably acted, but it doesn't have the
sparkle, despite employing the same director.

w Edmund H. North, D. D. Beauchamp
d George Marshall *ph* George Robinson
m Joseph Gershenson

Audie Murphy, Mari Blanchard, Lyle Bettger,
Thomas Mitchell, Edgar Buchanan, Wallace
Ford, Lori Nelson, Alan Hale Jnr, Mary
Wickes

'The impression is of a school revival of the
original production.'—*MFB*

Destry Rides Again°°°°
US 1939 94m bw
Universal (Joe Pasternak)

A mild-mannered sheriff finally gets mad at
local corruption and straps on his guns.
Classic western which manages to encompass
suspense, comedy, romance, tenderness, vivid
characterization, horseplay, songs and
standard western excitements, without moving
for more than a moment from a studio main
street set. It starts with a sign reading
'Welcome to Bottleneck' and an outburst of
gunfire; it ends with tragedy followed by a
running joke. Hollywood expertise at its very
best.

w Felix Jackson, Gertrude Purcell, Henry
Myers, *novel* Max Brand *d* George Marshall
ph Hal Mohr *songs* Frederick Hollander,
Frank Loesser *m* Frank Skinner

*James Stewart, Marlene Dietrich, Brian
Donlevy, Charles Winninger, Samuel S. Hinds,
Mischa Auer*, Irene Hervey, Jack Carson, *Una
Merkel*, Allen Jenkins, Warren Hymer, *Billy
Gilbert*

'I think it was Lord Beaverbrook who said
that Marlene Dietrich standing on a bar in
black net stockings, belting out *See What the
Boys in the Back Room Will Have*, was a
greater work of art than the Venus de Milo.'—
Richard Roud
† An early sound version in 1932 starred Tom
Mix; *Frenchie* (1950) was a slight variation.
See also *Destry*.

The Detective°°
US 1968 114m De Luxe Panavision
TCF / Arcola / Millfield (Aaron Rosenberg)

A New York police detective fights crime and
corruption.
Determinedly sleazy and 'frank' cop stuff,
quite arrestingly narrated and with something
to say about police methods. Good violent
entertainment, with just a shade too many
homosexuals and nymphomaniacs for balance.

w Abby Mann, *novel* Roderick Thorp
d Gordon Douglas *ph* Joseph Biroc *m* Jerry
Goldsmith

Frank Sinatra, Lee Remick, Jacqueline Bisset,
Ralph Meeker, Jack Klugman, Horace
MacMahon, Lloyd Bochner, William
Windom, Tony Musante, Al Freeman Jnr,
Robert Duvall

'It vacillates uncertainly between murder
mystery, political allegory, and a psychological
study of the hero.'—*Jan Dawson*

Detective Story°°°
US 1951 103m bw
Paramount (William Wyler)

A day in a New York precinct police station,
during which a detective of almost
pathological righteousness discovers a stain on
his family and himself becomes a victim of
violence.
Clever, fluent transcription of a Broadway
play with some of the pretensions of Greek
tragedy; it could have been the negation of
cinema, but professional handling makes it the
essence of it.

w Philip Yordan, Robert Wyler, *play* Sidney
Kingsley *d* William Wyler *ph* Lee Garmes

Kirk Douglas, Eleanor Parker, William
Bendix, Cathy O'Donnell, George Macready,
Horace MacMahon, Gladys George, *Joseph
Wiseman*, Lee Grant, Gerald Mohr, Frank
Faylen, Luis Van Rooten

'The admirably directed interaction of
movement and talk all over the big room is
what gives the thing its satisfying texture.'—
Richard Mallett, Punch

AAN: Philip Yordan, Robert Wyler; William
Wyler; Eleanor Parker; Lee Grant

Devi°
India 1960 93m bw
Satyajit Ray Productions
aka: *The Goddess*

While his son is away at university, a farmer
persuades his daughter-in-law that she is a
goddess, and the events which follow,
including the death of her son, are too much
for her reason.
A curious, 'foreign' story which does not have
the usual Ray tempo or feeling for character,
but wins one's attention by its very
strangeness.

wd Satyajit Ray, *story* Prabhat Kumar Mukherjee *ph* Subrata Mitra *m* Ali Akbar Khan

Chhabi Biswas, Sharmila Tagore, Soumitra Chatterjee, Karuna Bannerjee

The Devil and Miss Jones**
US 1941 97m bw
RKO / Frank Ross, Norman Krasna

A millionaire masquerades as a clerk in his own department store to investigate worker complaints.
Attractive comedy with elements of the crazy thirties and the more socially conscious forties.

w Norman Krasna d Sam Wood *ph* Harry Stradling

Jean Arthur, *Charles Coburn*, Robert Cummings, Spring Byington, S. Z. Sakall, William Demarest

AAN: Norman Krasna; Charles Coburn

Devil and the Deep*
US 1932 73m bw
Paramount (Emmanuel Cohen)

A submarine commander goes mad with jealousy of his faithless wife.
A turgid melodrama notable for its stars.

w Benn Levy *d* Marion Gering *ph* Charles Lang

Tallulah Bankhead, Charles Laughton, Gary Cooper, Cary Grant, Paul Porcasi

The Devil and the Nun*
Poland 1960 108m bw
Kadr
original title: *Matka Joanna od Aniolow;*
aka: *Mother Joan of the Angels*

In a 17th-century convent nuns are possessed by devils. A priest who tries to help is burned at the stake; another becomes possessed himself.
Reasonably dispassionate and fairly stylized version of the same facts that were treated so hysterically by Ken Russell in *The Devils.*

w Tadeusz Konwicki, Jerzy Kawalerowicz, *novel* Jaroslav Iwaszkiewicz *d* Jerzy Kawalerowicz *ph* Jerzy Wojcik *m* Adam Walacinski

Lucyna Winnicka, Mieczyslaw Voit, Anna Ciepielewska

The Devil at Four o'Clock
US 1961 126m Eastmancolor
Columbia / Leroy / Kohlmar (Fred Kohlmar)

A drunken missionary and three convicts save a colony of leper children from a South Seas volcano.

Muddled adventure melodrama with a downbeat ending long delayed.

w Liam O'Brien, *novel* Max Catto *d* Mervyn Le Roy *ph* Joseph Biroc *m* George Duning

Spencer Tracy, Frank Sinatra, Kerwin Mathews, Jean-Pierre Aumont, Grégoire Aslan, Alexander Scourby, Barbara Luna

The Devil Bat
US 1942 70m bw

A crazed scientist trains bats to kill at the scent of a certain perfume. Horror comic hokum from the bottom of the barrel. Bela Lugosi, Suzanne Kaaren, Dave O'Brien. Written by John Neville; directed by Jean Yarbrough; for PRC. *Devil Bat's Daughter* (1946), with Rosemary La Planche, was an even tamer sequel.

The Devil Commands*
US 1941 65m bw
Columbia (Wallace MacDonald)

An electrical scientist tries to communicate with his dead wife through a medium.
Modestly effective horror thriller, though rather too deliberately paced.

w Robert D. Andrews, Milton Gunzberg, *story* The Edge of Running Water by William Sloane *d* Edward Dmytryk *ph* Allan G. Siegler *md* Morris Stoloff

Boris Karloff, Richard Fiske, Amanda Duff, Anne Revere, Ralph Penney

Devil Dogs of the Air**
US 1935 86m bw
Warner (Lou Edelman)

Rivalry and romance in the Marine Flying Corps.
Standard, lively vehicle for Cagney and O'Brien, with excellent stunt flying sequences.

w Malcolm Stuart Boylan, Earl Baldwin, *novel* John Monk Saunders *d* Lloyd Bacon *ph* Arthur Edeson *md* Leo F. Forbstein

James Cagney, Pat O'Brien, Margaret Lindsay, Frank McHugh, Helen Lowell, John Arledge, Robert Barrat, Russell Hicks, Ward Bond

'A loud and roughneck screen comedy, both amusing and exciting.'—*André Sennwald*

The Devil Doll**
US 1936 79m bw
MGM (E.J.Mannix)

A refugee from Devil's Island disguises himself as an old lady who sells human dolls which murder those responsible for his imprisonment.

Interesting rather than exciting tall tale with a Paris backdrop; despite impressive moments it does not quite have the right *frisson*.

w Tod Browning, Garrett Fort, Erich Von Stroheim, Guy Endore, *novel* Burn Witch Burn by A. A. Merritt d *Tod Browning* ph Leonard Smith m Franz Waxman ad Cedric Gibbons

Lionel Barrymore, Maureen O'Sullivan, Frank Lawton, Henry B. Walthall, Rafacla Ottiano, Grace Ford, Arthur Hohl
'Grotesque, slightly horrible and consistently interesting.'—*Frank Nugent, New York Times*

The Devil Is a Sissy
US 1936   92m   bw
MGM (Frank Davis)
aka: *The Devil Takes the Count*

The young son of divorcing parents gets into bad company.
Adequate juvenile melodrama

w John Lee Mahin, Richard Schayer, Roland Brown d W. S. Van Dyke ph Harold Rosson, George Schneidermann m Herbert Stothart
Freddie Bartholemew, Jackie Cooper, Mickey Rooney, Ian Hunter, Peggy Conklin, Katherine Alexander, Gene Lockhart, Dorothy Peterson

The Devil Is a Woman*
US 1935   82m   bw
Paramount

In Seville in the 1890s a *femme fatale* has several admirers.
The last Dietrich vehicle to be directed by Von Sternberg, and rather splendid in its highly decorative and uncommercial way; a treat for addicts.

w John Dos Passos, S. K. Winston, *novel* La Femme et le Pantin by Pierre Louÿs d *Josef Von Sternberg* ph Josef Von Sternberg, Lucien Ballard ad Hans Dreier

Marlene Dietrich, Lionel Atwill, Cesar Romero, Edward Everett Horton, Alison Skipworth, Don Alvarado, Morgan Wallace, Tempe Pigott
'One of the most sophisticated films ever produced in America.'—*André Sennwald, New York Times*
'Light and shadow are splashed liberally around over the white-painted sets; cafés, tobacco factories, stairs and balconies are decorated with every conceivable device and camera-level.'—*Peter John Dyer, 1964*
'A clever, perversely dehumanized picture said to be one of Von Sternberg's favourites.'—*New Yorker, 1977*

The Devil Makes Three
US 1952   90m   bw
MGM (Richard Goldstone)

An American intelligence officer in post-war Germany becomes involved with neo-Nazis. A curious break from dancing for Gene Kelly, this obscurely titled thriller has little to commend it but authentic locations.

w Jerry Davis, *story* Lawrence Bachmann d Andrew Marton ph Vaclav Vich m Rudolph G. Kopp
Gene Kelly, Pier Angeli, Richard Rober, Richard Egan, Claus Clausen

The Devil Rides Out*
GB 1967   95m   Technicolor
Hammer (Anthony Nelson Keys)
US title: *The Devil's Bride*

The Duc de Richleau rescues a friend from a group of Satanists.
Rather stodgy adaptation of a frightening novel; moments of suspense.

w Richard Matheson, *novel* Dennis Wheatley d Terence Fisher ph Arthur Grant m James Bernard
Christopher Lee, *Charles Gray*, Leon Greene, Patrick Mower, Gwen Ffrangcon Davies

The Devil to Pay*
US 1931   65m   bw
Samuel Goldwyn

The prodigal son of a snooty English family returns to cheer them all up.
Agreeably lighthearted star comedy in the drawing-room tradition.

w Frederick Lonsdale d George Fitzmaurice ph Gregg Toland, George Barnes m Alfred Newman
Ronald Colman, Loretta Young, Myrna Loy, Frederick Kerr
'Six reels of Mr Colman being charming . . . a polished, tasteful and entirely likeable screen comedy.'—*New York Herald Tribune*

A Devil with Women
US 1930   76m   bw
Fox (George Middleton)

Soldiers of fortune in a banana republic end the regime of a notorious bandit and compete for a fair señorita.
Primitive Flagg-and-Quirt style knockabout.

w Dudley Nichols, Henry M. Johnson, *novel* Dust and Sun by Clements Ripley d Irving Cummings ph Arthur Todd m Peter Brunelli
Victor McLaglen, Humphrey Bogart, Mona Maris, Michael Vavitch

The Devils*
GB 1970 111m Technicolor
Panavision
Warner / Russo (Robert H. Solo, Ken
Russell)

An account of the apparent demoniacal possession of the 17th-century nuns of Loudun, climaxing in the burning of their priest as a sorcerer.
Despite undeniable technical proficiency this is its writer-director's most outrageously sick film to date, campy, idiosyncratic and in howling bad taste from beginning to end, full of worm-eaten skulls, masturbating nuns, gibbering courtiers, plague sores, rats and a burning to death before our very eyes . . . plus a sacrilegious dream of Jesus. A pointless pantomime for misogynists.

wd Ken Russell, *play* John Whiting, *book* The Devils of Loudun by Aldous Huxley
ph David Watkin *m* Peter Maxwell Davies
ad Robert Cartwright

Vanessa Redgrave, Oliver Reed, Dudley Sutton, Max Adrian, Gemma Jones, Murray Melvin, Michael Gothard, Graham Armitage
'Ken Russell doesn't report hysteria, he markets it.'—*New Yorker, 1976*
'Russell's swirling multi-colored puddle . . . made me glad that both Huxley and Whiting are dead, so that they are spared this farrago of witless exhibitionism.'—*Stanley Kauffmann*
'A garish glossary of sado-masochism . . . a taste for visual sensation that makes scene after scene look like the masturbatory fantasies of a Roman Catholic boyhood.'—*Alexander Walker*

The Devil's Advocate
West Germany 1977 109m colour
Geria (Lutz Hengst)

A dying priest is summoned to Rome to investigate the cult of a dead partisan nominated for sainthood.
Well-meaning but rather tepid and inconclusive adaptation of a bestseller which presumably made its points more firmly.

w Morris West, from his novel *d* Guy Green *ph* Billy Williams *m* Bert Grund

John Mills, Stéphane Audran, Jason Miller, Timothy West, Patrick Mower, Paola Pitagora, Daniel Massey, Leigh Lawson, Raf Vallone, Jack Hedley

The Devil's Brigade
US 1968 132m De Luxe Panavision
UA / David L. Wolper

For combat in Norway and Italy during World War II a US officer assembles a platoon of thugs and misfits to work with crack Canadian commandos.
Flagrant but routine imitation of *The Dirty Dozen*, quite undistinguished.

w William Roberts *d* Andrew V. McLaglen *ph* William Clothier *m* Alex North

William Holden, Cliff Robertson, Vince Edwards, Andrew Prine, Claude Akins, Carroll O'Connor, Richard Jaeckel
'After nearly three decades of World War II films, it is hardly surprising that Hollywood is beginning to suffer from combat fatigue.'—*Time*

Devil's Canyon
US 1953 92m Technicolor 3-D
RKO / Edmund Grainger

Life in a notorious Arizona prison in the 1880s; a marshal is unjustly convicted but wins his pardon.
Fairly brutal western, quite unmemorable.

w Frederick Hazlitt Brennan *d* Alfred Werker *ph* Nicholas Musuraca *m* Daniele Amfitheatrof

Dale Robertson, Virginia Mayo, Stephen McNally, Arthur Hunnicutt, Robert Keith, Jay C. Flippen, Whit Bissell

The Devil's Disciple*
GB 1959 82m bw
UA / Hecht–Hill–Lancaster / Brynaprod
(Harold Hecht)

In 1777 an American ne'er-do-well almost allows himself to be hanged by the British in mistake for a rebel pastor.
Star-studded but indifferently staged adaptation of a minor Shavian frolic. Patchy, with good moments.

w John Dighton, Roland Kibbee, *play* Bernard Shaw *d* Guy Hamilton *ph* Jack Hildyard *m* Richard Rodney Bennett *ad* Terence Verity, Edward Carere

Burt Lancaster, Kirk Douglas, *Laurence Olivier* (as General Burgoyne), Eva Le Gallienne, Janette Scott, Harry Andrews, Basil Sidney, George Rose, Neil McCallum, David Horne, Mervyn Johns

Devil's Doorway
US 1950 84m bw
MGM (Nicholas Nayfack)

A Shoshone Indian fights valiantly in the Civil War but on his return to Wyoming finds himself hated and threatened by his former colleagues.
Dull pro-Indian western with a most unsuitable star.

w Guy Trosper *d* Anthony Mann *ph* John Alton *m* Daniele Amfitheatrof

Robert Taylor, Louis Calhern, Paula Raymond, Marshall Thompson, James Mitchell, Edgar Buchanan, Rhys Williams, Spring Byington

The Devil's Eye°
Sweden 1960 90m bw
Svensk Filmindustri

An old proverb says that a woman's chastity is a stye in the devil's eye. So when Satan has a sore eye he comes down to earth to put things right.
Surprisingly shoddily-made comedy with just a few of the sharpnesses of technique and mystifications of plot which one had come to expect from this maestro.

wd Ingmar Bergman *ph* Gunnar Fischer *m* Domenico Scarlatti

Jarl Kulle, Bibi Andersson, Nils Poppe, Stig Järrel, Gunnar Björnstrand

The Devil's General
West Germany 1955 121m bw
Ryal (Gyula Trebitsch)

In 1941 a German air ace becomes estranged from the high command and is tortured by the Gestapo. On release he helps a Jewish couple . . .
Heavy-going melodrama which nevertheless paints a convincing picture of Berlin during the war.

w George Hurdalek, Helmut Kautner, *play* Carl Zuckmayer *d* Helmut Kautner *ph* Albert Benitz

Curt Jurgens, Victor de Kowa, Karl John, Eva-Ingeborg Scholz

The Devil's Hairpin
US 1957 83m Technicolor Vistavision
Paramount / Cornel Wilde

A former motor racing champion makes a comeback, and redeems his past boorish behaviour.
Efficient routine melodramatics with good action sequences.

w James Edmiston, Cornel Wilde *d* Cornel Wilde *ph* Daniel Fapp *m* Van Cleave

Cornel Wilde, Jean Wallace, Arthur Franz, *Mary Astor*, Paul Fix

Devil's Island°
US 1939 63m bw
Warner (Bryan Foy)

A surgeon is sent to Devil's Island for aiding an escaped convict.

Sharply-made exposé of the notorious French penal colony; commendable pace and vigour all round.

w Kenneth Gamet, Don Ryan *d* William Clemens

Boris Karloff, James Stephenson, Nedda Harrigan, Adia Kuznetzoff, Robert Warwick, Pedro de Cordoba

The Devil's Mask
US 1946 66m bw

An unclaimed parcel containing a shrunken head is found after a plane crash; murder follows. Involved but amusing entry in the *I Love a Mystery* series. Jim Bannon, Anita Louise, Michael Duane, Mona Barrie, Byron Foulger. Written by Charles O'Neal; directed by Henry Levin; for Columbia.

The Devil's Playground°
Australia 1976 107m Eastmancolor
The Feature Film House (Fred Schepsi)

Tensions between masters and boys in a Catholic seminary in the fifties.
Well made but rather dislikeable intrusion into *Mr Perrin and Mr Traill* country with the addition of modern frankness.

wd Fred Schepsi *ph* Ian Baker *m* Bruce Smeaton

Arthur Dignam, Nick Tate, Simon Burke, Charles McCallum, John Frawley

The Devil's Rain
US 1975 86m colour Todd-AO 35
Sandy Howard

Witchcraft in the modern west causes victims to melt; the son of one of them takes arms against the leading Satanist.
Interestingly cast example of the low-budget seventies exploitation picture, with more nastiness than logic.

w Gabe Essoe, James Ashton, Gerald Hopman *d* Robert Fuest *ph* Alex Phillips Jnr *m* Al de Lory

Ernest Borgnine, Ida Lupino, Eddie Albert, William Shatner, Keenan Wynn, Tom Skerritt

Devils of Darkness
GB 1964 90m Eastmancolor

A vampire disguises himself as a French count and preys on young girls. Mainly tatty shocker with a few lively scenes. William Sylvester, Hubert Noel, Tracy Reed, Diana Decker, Rona Anderson. Written by Lyn Fairhurst; directed by Lance Comfort; for Tom Blakeley / Planet.

The Devil's Wanton*
Sweden 1949   80m   bw
Terrafilm
original title: *Fängelse*
aka: *Prison*

Film-makers discuss some rather unpleasant
projects but put them aside as unsatisfactory.
A bit of a Scandinavian wallow, with heavy
expressionism and low-life themes.

wd Ingmar Bergman *ph* Göran Strindberg
m Erland von Koch

Doris Svedlund, Birger Malmsten, Eva
Henning, Hasse Ekman

'It employs all the paraphernalia associated
with Scandinavian angst.'—*John Gillett, MFB*

Devotion
US 1931   84m   bw

A woman falls in love with a barrister and
takes a job as governess to his son. Rather
winsome tear-jerker entirely dependent on its
stars. Ann Harding, Leslie Howard, Robert
Williams, O. P. Heggie, Louise Closser Hale,
Dudley Digges. Written by Graham John and
Horace Jackson, from the novel *A Little Flat
in the Temple* by Pamela Wynne; directed by
Robert Milton; for RKO-Pathé.

Devotion**
US 1944   107m   bw
Warner (Robert Buckner)

A highly romanticized account of the lives of
the Brontë sisters and their brother Branwell.
An enjoyably bad example of a big-budget
Hollywood production which tampers with
things it cannot understand, in this case life in
a Yorkshire parsonage in Victorian times. An
excuse is found to give the curate an Austrian
accent to fit the available actor, but this and
other *faux pas* are atoned for by the vividness
of Emily's recurrent dream of death as a
silhouetted man on horseback. In general, an
interesting period piece in more senses than
one.

w Keith Winter *d* Curtis Bernhardt *ph* Ernest
Haller *m* Erich Wolfgang Korngold

Ida Lupino (Emily), Olivia de Havilland
(Charlotte), Nancy Coleman (Anne), Arthur
Kennedy (Branwell), Montagu Love (Revd
Brontë), Paul Henreid (Revd Nicholls), Ethel
Griffies (Aunt Branwell), Sidney Greenstreet
(Thackeray), Eily Malyon, Forrester Harvey,
Victor Francen

'I found it painless. It never got nearer to
the subject than names and consequently

didn't hurt. But I would like to know who was
devoted to whom and why.'—*Richard
Winnington*
    'It tells *all* about those Brontë sisters . . .'—
publicity

The DI
US 1957   106m   bw
Warner / Mark VII (Jack Webb)

A tough marine drill instructor takes a special
interest in a backward member of his platoon.
Noisy recruiting poster heroics in which the
producer gives himself a loud but boring part.
The drill sequences are well done, but the film
is overlong and repetitive.

w James Lee Barrett *d* Jack Webb
ph Edward Colman *m* David Buttolph

Jack Webb, Don Dubbins, Jackie Loughery,
Lin McCarthy, Monica Lewis

Le Diable au Corps*
France 1947   110m   bw
Transcontinental
US title: *Devil in the Flesh*

When her husband is away at war, a young
married woman falls for a college student and
dies bearing his child.
A love story of World War I; a great
commercial success, but tending to be slow
and dreary.

w Jean Aurenche, Pierre Bost,
novel Raymond Radiguet *d* Claude Autant-
Lara *ph* Michel Kelber *m* René Cloërc

Micheline Presle, Gérard Philipe, Jean
Debucourt, Denise Grey, Jacques Tati

Les Diaboliques***
France 1954   114m   bw
Filmsonor (Henri-Georges Clouzot)
aka: *Diabolique; The Fiends*

A sadistic headmaster's wife and mistress
conspire to murder him; but his body
disappears and evidence of his presence haunts
them.
Highly influential, suspenseful and scary
thriller with a much-copied twist typical of its
authors. Slow to start and shabby-looking as
befits its grubby school setting, it gathers
momentum with the murder and turns the
screw with fine professionalism.

w Henri-Georges Clouzot, G. Geronimi,
novel The Woman Who Was by Pierre
Boileau and Thomas Narcejac *d* Henri-
Georges Clouzot *ph* Armand Thirard
m Georges Van Parys

Simone Signoret, Vera Clouzot, Charles
Vanel, Paul Meurisse

'Scary, but so calculatedly sensational that it's rather revolting.'—*New Yorker, 1978*

'It depends very much on the intimate details of the seedy fourth-rate school, with its inadequate education and uneatable food, its general smell of unwashed children, hatred and petty perversions.'—*Basil Wright, 1972*

† Remade in 1976 as a TV movie, *Reflections of Murder.*

Diagnosis: Murder

GB 1974   90m   Eastmancolor
Silhouette (Patrick Dromgoole, Peter Miller)

A psychiatrist's wife disappears, and the police suspect her husband.

Well-upholstered but sadly old-fashioned domestic crime thriller; one is vaguely surprised to see it in colour, having seen it so often in black-and-white.

w Philip Levene *d* Sidney Hayers *ph* Bob Edwards *m* Laurie Johnson

Jon Finch, Judy Geeson, Christopher Lee, Tony Beckley, Dilys Hamlett, Jane Merrow, Colin Jeavons

Dial M For Murder**

US 1954   105m   Warnercolor   3-D
Warner (Alfred Hitchcock)

An ageing tennis champion tries to arrange the death of his wife so that he will inherit, but his complex plan goes wrong.

Hitchcock did not try very hard to adapt this highly commercial play for the cinema, nor did he exploit the possibilities of 3-D. But for a one-room film with a not very exciting cast the film holds its grip pretty well.

w Frederick Knott, from his play *d Alfred Hitchcock ph* Robert Burks *m* Dmitri Tiomkin

Ray Milland, John Williams, Grace Kelly, Robert Cummings, Anthony Dawson

'All this is related with Hitchcock's ghoulish chic but everyone in it seems to be walking around with tired blood.'—*Pauline Kael, 1968*

Dial 1119*

US 1950   75m   bw
MGM (Richard Goldstone)
GB title: *The Violent Hour*

An assortment of people are held up in a bar by a maniac.

Suspenseful thriller when it sticks to its central theme; dullish when it tries characterization. A good second feature.

w John Monks Jnr *d* Gerald Mayer *ph* Paul Vogel *m* André Previn

Marshall Thompson, Virginia Field, Andrea King, Leon Ames, Keefe Brasselle, Richard Rober, James Bell, William Conrad

Diamond City

GB 1949   90m   bw
GFD / Gainsborough (A. Frank Bundy)

Law and order is maintained during the working of a South African diamond field.

British imitation of a Wyatt Earp western; very milk-and-water.

w Roger Bray, Roland Pertwee *d* David MacDonald *ph* Reginald Wyer *m* Clifton Parker

David Farrar, Honor Blackman, Diana Dors, Niall MacGinnis, Andrew Crawford, Mervyn Johns, Bill Owen, Phyllis Monkman

Diamond Frontier

US 1940   72m   bw

An honest diamond dealer is framed and sent to prison. Co-feature action stuff, with South Africa standing in for the west. Victor McLaglen, Anne Nagel, John Loder, Philip Dorn, Cecil Kellaway. Written by Edmund L. Hartmann and Stanley Rubin; directed by Harold Schuster; for Universal.

Diamond Head

US 1962   107m   Eastmancolor
      Panavision
Columbia (Jerry Bresler)

A domineering Hawaiian landowner almost ruins the lives of his family.

Predictable, heavy-going transcription of a bestseller.

w Marguerite Roberts, *novel* Peter Gilman *d* Guy Green *ph* Sam Leavitt *m* Johnny Williams

Charlton Heston, Yvette Mimieux, George Chakiris, France Nuyen, James Darren, Aline MacMahon, Elizabeth Allen, Richard Loo

Diamond Horseshoe

US 1945   104m   Technicolor
TCF (William Perlberg)
aka: *Billy Rose's Diamond Horseshoe*

A nightclub singer gives up her career for a medical student.

Lavish but humourless star vehicle with standard numbers.

wd George Seaton, *play* The Barker by Kenyon Nicholson *ph* Ernest Palmer *songs* Mack Gordon, Harry Warren

Betty Grable, Dick Haymes, *William Gaxton*, Phil Silvers, Beatrice Kay, Carmen Cavallero, Margaret Dumont

Diamond Jim*
US 1935   93m   bw
Universal (Edmund Grainger)

A fantasia on the life of the nineties
millionaire who sailed pretty close to the wind
in business, adored Lillian Russell, and
developed a gargantuan appetite.
Cheerful period comedy drama with plenty of
gusto.

w Preston Sturges d A. Edward Sutherland
ph George Robinson m Ferde Grofe, Franz
Waxman

Edward Arnold, Jean Arthur, Binnie Barnes,
Cesar Romero, Eric Blore

Diamonds
US 1975   108m   Eastmancolor
Avco Embassy / AmeriEuro (Menahem
Golan)

A London diamond merchant sets himself up
to be robbed so that he can blackmail the
culprits into a raid on the Tel Aviv diamond
repository.
Cheerful but unremarkable caper movie with
an upbeat ending.

w David Paulsen, Menahem Golan
d Menahem Golan ph Adam Greenberg
m Roy Budd

Robert Shaw, Richard Roundtree, Barbara
Seagull, Shelley Winters

Diamonds Are Forever*
GB 1971   120m   Technicolor
Panavision
UA / Eon / Danjaq (Harry Saltzman, Albert
R. Broccoli)

Seeking a diamond smuggler, James Bond has
adventures in Amsterdam, a Los Angeles
crematorium, various Las Vegas gambling
parlours, and a secret installation in the
desert.
Campy, rather vicious addition to a well-worn
cycle, with an element of nastiness which
big-budget stunts cannot conceal. Panavision
does not help, and Connery's return to the
role for a final throw is disappointing.

w Richard Maibaum, Tom Mankiewicz, novel
Ian Fleming d Guy Hamilton ph Ted Moore
m John Barry pd Ken Adam

Sean Connery, Jill St John, Charles Gray,
Lana Wood, Jimmy Dean, Bruce Cabot,
Bernard Lee, Lois Maxwell

Diamonds for Breakfast
GB 1968   102m   Eastmancolor
Paramount / Bridge Films (Carlo Ponti,
Pierre Rouve)

An impoverished Russian aristocrat decides to
retrieve from a museum the crown jewels of
his ancestors, and seduces seven female
accomplices.
Yawning caper yarn embellished with sex and
slapstick.

w N. F. Simpson, Pierre Rouve, Ronald
Harwood d Christopher Morahan ph Gerry
Turpin m Norman Kay

Marcello Mastroianni, Rita Tushingham,
Elaine Taylor, Warren Mitchell, Nora
Nicholson, Bill Fraser, Leonard Rossiter

Diane
US 1956   110m   Eastmancolor
Cinemascope
MGM (Edwin H. Knopf)

Diane de Poitier becomes a consultant to the
king and falls in love with his son.
Solidly boring slice of Hollywood history, with
all concerned out of their depth.

w Christopher Isherwood d David Miller
ph Robert Planck m Miklos Rozsa

Lana Turner, Roger Moore, Cedric
Hardwicke, Pedro Armendariz, Marisa Pavan

The Diary of a Chambermaid*
US 1946   86m   bw
Benedict Bogeaus (Burgess Meredith,
Paulette Goddard)

A 19th-century serving girl causes sexual
frustration and other troubles in two
households.
Hollywood notables were all at sea in this
wholly artificial and unpersuasive adaptation
of a minor classic.

w Burgess Meredith, novel Octave Mirbeau
d Jean Renoir ph Lucien Andriot pd Eugene
Lourié

Paulette Goddard, Burgess Meredith, Hurd
Hatfield, Francis Lederer, Judith Anderson,
Florence Bates, Irene Ryan, Reginald Owen,
Almira Sessions

The Diary of a Chambermaid*
France / Italy 1964   98m   bw   Franscope
Speva / Ciné Alliance / Filmsonor / Dear
(Serge Silberman, Michel Sabra)
original title: Le Journal d'une Femme de
Chambre

Interesting but not especially successful
Bunuel version: the subject is certainly up his
street, but the novel seems to restrict him and
the visual quality is unattractive.

w Luis Bunuel, Jean-Claude Carrière d Luis
Bunuel ph Roger Fellous m none

Jeanne Moreau, Georges Géret, Michel Piccoli, Françoise Lugagne

The Diary of a Country Priest•••
France 1950   120m   bw
Union Générale Cinématographique (Léon Carré)
original title: *Journal d'un Curé de Campagne*
A lonely young priest fails to make much impression in his first parish; and, falling ill, he dies alone.
Striking, depressing, slow and austere, with little dialogue but considerable visual beauty; a very typical work of its director.
wd Robert Bresson, novel Georges Bernanos *ph* L. Burel *m* Jean-Jacques Grunenwald
Claude Laydu, Jean Riveyre, Armand Guibert, Nicole Ladmiral

Diary of a Lost Girl••
Germany 1929   110m approx   bw   silent
G. W. Pabst Film
original title: *Tagebuch einer Verlorenen*
A rich man's daughter is seduced, has an illegitimate child, is placed in a house of correction and finds herself later in a brothel.
Heavily Germanic Road to Ruin, superbly mounted in best cinematic style, with several memorable sequences. Heavily mutilated by censors; according to the screenwriter the film ends just after the middle of his script.
w Rudolf Leonhardt, *novel* Margaret Böhme *d G. W. Pabst ph* Sepp Allgeier
Louise Brooks, Fritz Rasp, Josef Ravensky
† A previous version had been made in 1918, written and directed by Richard Oswald.

Diary of a Mad Housewife••
US 1970   95m   Technicolor
Universal / Frank Perry
The bored and repressed wife of a lawyer tries an affair, walks out on her husband, and opts for group therapy.
An agreeably mordant view of the contemporary American scene, with good dialogue and performances, but the little bits of satire do not really add up to a satisfactory film.
w Eleanor Perry, novel Sue Kaufman *d Frank Perry ph* Gerald Hirschfeld
Carrie Snodgress, Richard Benjamin, Frank Langella, Lorraine Cullen, Frannie Michel
'A prototypical contemporary American artifact . . . all its assorted talents and

technological smartness are turned to the varnishing of mediocrity.'—*Stanley Kauffmann*
AAN: Carrie Snodgress

The Diary of a Madman
US 1962   96m   Technicolor
UA / Admiral (Robert E. Kent)
A murderer explains to a magistrate that he was possessed by an evil spirit.
Ponderous transcription of a Maupassant story with a few moments of horror.
w Robert E. Kent *d* Reginald Le Borg *ph* Ellis W. Carter *m* Richard La Salle
Vincent Price, Nancy Kovack, Chris Warfield, Stephen Roberts

The Diary of a Married Woman
Germany 1953   83m   bw
Magna
original title: *Tagebuch einer Verliebten*
A wife divorces her adulterous husband, but their small son brings them together again.
One long Hollywood cliché, assembled with some spirit; notable only as one of the rare post-war German films to get distribution in English-speaking countries.
w Emil Burri, Johann Mario Simmel *d* Josef Von Baky *ph* Oskar Snirch *m* Alois Melichar
Maria Schell, O. W. Fischer, Franco Andrei

The Diary of Anne Frank••
US 1959   170m   bw   Cinemascope
TCF / George Stevens
In 1942, a family of Dutch Jews hides in an attic from the Nazis; just before the war ends they are found and sent to concentration camps.
Based on the famous diaries of a girl who died at Auschwitz, this solemn adaptation is elephantine in its length, its ponderousness and its use of Cinemascope when the atmosphere is supposed to be claustrophobic.
w Frances Goodrich, Albert Hackett, from their play based on Anne Frank's diaries
d George Stevens *ph William C. Mellor m* Alfred Newman
Millie Perkins, *Joseph Schildkraut, Shelley Winters*, Ed Wynn, Richard Beymer, Gusti Huber, Lou Jacobi, Diane Baker
AA: William C. Mellor; Shelley Winters
AAN: best picture; George Stevens; Alfred Newman; Ed Wynn

The Diary of Major Thompson

France 1955 83m bw
SNE Gaumont / Paul Wagner
original title: *Les Carnets de Major
  Thompson;* US title: *The French They
  Are a Funny Race*

An Englishman married to a Frenchwoman
keeps notes on the French way of life.
Tatty filming of a mildly amusing book; it falls
away into a number of badly-timed and
presented gags, and one can't believe that its
creator was once the top comedy genius of
Hollywood.

wd Preston Sturges *ph* Maurice Barry,
Christian Matras *m* Georges Van Parys

Jack Buchanan, Martine Carol, Noel-Noel,
Genevieve Brunet

'Even allowing for the appalling editing and
the frequently incomprehensible dubbed
soundtrack, there is little evidence to suggest
that this film could ever have been anything
but a shambles.'—*Peter John Dyer, MFB*

Dick Tracy

US 1945 61m bw
RKO (Herman Schlom)
GB title: *Splitface*

The jut-jawed detective routs a disfigured
criminal named Splitface.
Vigorous second feature from the comic strip.

w Eric Taylor, *strip* Chester Gould *d* William
Berke *ph* Frank Redman *m* Roy Webb

Morgan Conway, Jane Greer, Mike Mazurki,
Anne Jeffreys, Lyle Latell, Joseph Crehan,
Trevor Bardette

† Sequels: *Dick Tracy vs Cueball* (1946) with
Morgan Conway, *d* John Rawlins; *Dick Tracy
Meets Gruesome* (1947) with Ralph Byrd,
Boris Karloff, *d* John Rawlins; *Dick Tracy's
Dilemma* (1947), with Ralph Byrd, *d* John
Rawlins. There had been several Republic
serials featuring Tracy, and in the fifties a
cartoon series appeared.

Dick Turpin

GB 1933 79m bw
Stoll-Stafford (Clyde Cook)

In this version the highwayman's ride to York
is to prevent an enforced marriage.
Mild British costume piece which sent its star
to Hollywood.

w Victor Kendall, *novel* Rookwood by
Harrison Ainsworth *d* Victor Hanbury, John
Stafford *ph* Desmond Dickinson

Victor McLaglen, Jane Carr, Frank Vosper,
James Finlayson, Gillian Lind

The Dictator*

GB 1936 86m bw
Toeplitz
aka: *For Love of a Queen; The Loves of a
Dictator*

In 18th-century Denmark, a country doctor
falls in love with his queen and overthrows the
mad king.
Stiff-backed middle-class romance, an
interesting example of English-German co-
production at the time.

w Benn Levy, Hans Wilhelm, H. G. Lustig,
Michael Hogan *d* Victor Saville, Alfred
Santell *ph* Franz Planer

Clive Brook, Madeleine Carroll, Helen Haye,
Emlyn Williams, Isabel Jeans, Alfred
Drayton, Frank Cellier

Did You Hear the One about the Travelling Saleslady?

US 1967 96m Techniscope
Universal (Si Rose)

In a Kansas town in 1910 an eccentric
saleslady offers pianolas which tend to go
berserk.
Cornbelt comedy vehicle for an unappealing
star.

w John Fenton Murray *d* Don Weis *ph* Bud
Thackery *m* Vic Mizzy

Phyllis Diller, Bob Denver, Joe Flynn,
Jeanette Nolan

Die Laughing

US 1980 108m Technicolor

After the murder of a nuclear scientist, a
young musician who knows too much is chased
by the murderers and the FBI. Witless black
comedy rehash of *The 39 Steps.* Robby
Benson, Linda Grovenor, Charles Durning,
Elsa Lanchester, Bud Cort. Written by Jerry
Segal, Robby Benson and Scott Parker;
directed by Jeff Werner; for Jon Peters /
Orion / Warner.

Dieu A Besoin des Hommes*

France 1950 100m bw
Transcontinental (Paul Graetz)
aka: *Isle of Sinners; God Needs Men*

The priest of a Breton island leaves in horror
at the sinfulness of his flock, and the fisherfolk
appoint one of their number as priest.
Cold, gloomy, rather pointless fable, often a
pleasure to look at.

w Jean Aurenche, Pierre Bost, *novel* Un
Recteur de l'Ile de Sein by H. Quefflec
d Jean Delannoy *ph* Robert Le Fèbvre
m René Cloërc

Pierre Fresnay, Madeleine Robinson, Daniel Gélin, Andrée Clément, Sylvie, Jean Brochard

A Different Story
US 1978   106m   CFI color
Avco / Alan Belkin

A homosexual falls in love with a lesbian. One supposes it had to come, but one doesn't really have to watch it.

w Henry Olek d Paul Aaron ph Philip Lathrop m David Frank

Perry King, Meg Foster, Valerie Curtin, Peter Donat

'There's something in *A Different Story* to turn off audiences of every sexual persuasion—and movie lovers most of all.'—*Richard Schickel, Time*

Dillinger*
US 1945   70m   bw
Monogram

The life of American public enemy number one who was shot by the police in 1934. Slick, speedy gangster thriller, possibly the most tolerable movie to come from this low-budget studio.

w Philip Yordan d Max Nosseck ph Jackson Rose m Dmitri Tiomkin

Lawrence Tierney, Edmund Lowe, Anne Jeffreys

AAN: Philip Yordan

Dillinger*
US 1973   107m   Movielab
AIP (Buzz Feitshans)

Violence-soaked version, with black comedy touches, of the last year of Dillinger's life. Not badly done, with a style reminiscent of *Bonnie and Clyde.*

wd John Milius ph Jules Brenner m Barry Devorzon

Warren Oates, Ben Johnson (as Melvin Purvis), Michelle Philips, Cloris Leachman, Harry Dean Stanton, Richard Dreyfuss

Dimples**
US 1936   82m   bw
TCF (Darryl F. Zanuck, Nunnally Johnson)

In the New York Bowery in pre-Civil War days, a child and her reprobate grandfather win the hearts of high society.
Excellent Temple vehicle with good period flavour.

w Arthur Sheekman, Nat Perrin d William A. Seiter ph Bert Glennon m Louis Silvers
songs Jimmy McHugh, Ted Koehler

Shirley Temple, Frank Morgan, Helen Westley, Berton Churchill, Robert Kent, Delma Byron, Astrid Allwyn

Dinner at Eight***
US 1933   113m   bw
MGM (David O. Selznick)

Guests at a society dinner party all find themselves in dramatic circumstances.
Artificial but compelling pattern play from a Broadway success.

w Frances Marion, Herman J. Mankiewicz, *play* George S. Kaufman, Edna Ferber
d George Cukor ph William Daniels
m William Axt

Marie Dressler, John Barrymore, Lionel Barrymore, Billie Burke, Wallace Beery, *Jean Harlow,* Lee Tracy, Edmund Lowe, Madge Evans, Jean Hersholt, Karen Morley, Louise Closser Hale, Phillips Holmes, May Robson, Grant Mitchell, Elizabeth Patterson

Dinner at the Ritz
GB 1937   77m   bw
New World (Robert T. Kane)

A French girl exposes swindlers who faked her father's suicide.
Once-diverting comedy melodrama with an international cast.

w Roland Pertwee, Romney Brent d Harold Schuster ph Philip Tannura

Annabella, Paul Lukas, David Niven, Romney Brent, Stewart Rome, Francis L. Sullivan, Nora Swinburne, Frederick Leister
'It moves with old world decorum and occasional touches of gout.'—*New York Times*

Diplomatic Courier*
US 1952   98m   bw
TCF (Casey Robinson)

American and Russian agents clash on a train between Salzburg and Trieste; an unexpected master spy is revealed after several chases.
Lively cold war intrigue, well produced and played with relish.

w Casey Robinson, Liam O'Brien, *novel* Sinister Errand by Peter Cheyney d Henry Hathaway ph Lucien Ballard md Lionel Newman m Sol Kaplan

Tyrone Power, Patricia Neal, Stephen McNally, Hildegarde Neff, Karl Malden, James Millican, Herbert Berghof
'A reversion to the oldest tradition of spy fiction.'—*Penelope Houston*

Dirigible*
US 1931   102m   bw
Columbia

The story of an airship disaster.
Economical epic with a few Capra touches.

w Jo Swerling, Dorothy Howell, *story* 'Spig'
Wead *d* Frank Capra *ph* Joe Wilbur, Elmer
Dyer, Joseph Walker

Jack Holt, Fay Wray, Ralph Graves, Hobart
Bosworth, Roscoe Karns

Dirty Dingus Magee
US 1970 91m Metrocolor Panavision
MGM (Burt Kennedy)

A likeable western outlaw crosses swords with
an old enemy.
Fair burlesque western often stooping to
vulgarity.

w Tom Waldman, Frank Waldman, Joseph
Heller, *novel* David Markson *d* Burt
Kennedy *ph* Harry Stradling *m* Jeff
Alexander

Frank Sinatra, George Kennedy, Anne
Jackson, Lois Nettleton, Jack Elam, John
Dehner, Henry Jones, Harry Carey Jnr, Paul
Fix

'Skittish burlesque, scripted in the brash and
undisciplined style of a TV show . . . heavily
reliant on the *Carry On* brand of humour.'—
David McGillivray

The Dirty Dozen**
US / Spain 1967 150m Metrocolor
70mm
MGM / Kenneth Hyman (Raymond Anzarut)

In 1944, twelve convicts serving life sentences
are recruited for a commando suicide mission.
Professional, commercial but unlikeable slice
of wartime thick ear; pretensions about capital
punishment are jettisoned early on in favour
of frequent and violent bloodshed. Much
imitated, e.g. by *The Devil's Brigade, A
Reason to Live, a Reason to Die*, etc.

w Nunnally Johnson, Lukas Heller *d* Robert
Aldrich *ph* Edward Scaife *m* Frank de Vol

Lee Marvin, Ernest Borgnine, Robert Ryan,
Charles Bronson, Jim Brown, John
Cassavetes, George Kennedy, Richard
Jaeckel, Trini Lopez, Telly Savalas, Ralph
Meeker, Clint Walker, Robert Webber,
Donald Sutherland

AAN: John Cassavetes

Dirty Harry**
US 1971 103m Technicolor
Panavision
Warner / Malpaso (Don Siegel)

A violently inclined San Francisco police
inspector is the only cop who can bring to

book a mad sniper. When the man is released
through lack of evidence, he takes private
revenge.
A savage cop show which became a cult and
led to a spate of dirty cop movies, including
two sequels, *Magnum Force* (qv) and *The
Enforcer*. Well done for those who can take it.

w Harry Julian Fink, Rita M. Fink, Dean
Riesner *d Don Siegel* *ph* Bruce Surtees
m Lalo Schifrin

Clint Eastwood, Harry Guardino, Reni
Santoni, John Vernon, Andy Robinson, John
Larch, John Mitchum

Dirty Little Billy
US 1972 92m Eastmancolor
Columbia / WRG / Dragoti (Jack L. Warner)

The violent young life of Billy the Kid.
Squalid little western with few attractive
aspects except that it presents its hero as the
mentally retarded delinquent which history
says he was.

w Charles Moss, Stan Dragoti *d* Stan
Dragoti *ph* Ralph Woolsey *m* Sascha
Burland

Michael J. Pollard, Lee Purcell, Richard
Evans, Charles Aidman

'The gap between its ostensible aims and its
manner of realizing them continually leaves
the film bogged down in its own scrupulously
realistic mud.'—*Tony Rayns*

Dirty Mary, Crazy Larry
US 1974 92m De Luxe
Academy Pictures Corporation (Norman T.
Herman)

Two racing drivers and a kooky groupie rob a
supermarket and almost elude their police
pursuers.
Elaborately stunted chase film, agreeable
enough to watch if the characters were not so
disagreeable.

w Leigh Chapman, Antonio Santean, *novel*
The Chase by Richard Unekis *d* John Hough
ph Mike Margulies *m* Jimmie Haskell

Peter Fonda, Susan George, Adam Roarke,
Vic Morrow, Kenneth Tobey, Roddy
McDowall, Eugene Daniels

'The film's general delight in destruction and
despoliation makes one wonder if it is the
cinema that reflects the ugliness of modern
society or the ugliness of modern society that
reflects trends in the cinema.'—*Michael
Billington, Illustrated London News*

Dirty Work***
US 1933   20m   bw

Chimney sweeps cause havoc in the house of an eccentric scientist. Hilarious star comedy with splendid timing and comedy touches. Laurel and Hardy, Lucien Littlefield, Sam Adams. Written by H. M. Walker; directed by Lloyd French; for Hal Roach.

Dirty Work
GB 1934   78m   bw
Gaumont (Michael Balcon)

Shop assistants pose as crooks in order to catch thieves.
Rather thin Ben Travers farce with some authentic moments.

w Ben Travers, from his play d Tom Walls

Ralph Lynn, Gordon Harker, Robertson Hare, Lillian Bond, Basil Sydney, Cecil Parker, Margaretta Scott, Gordon James, Peter Gawthorne

The Discreet Charm of the Bourgeoisie***
France / Spain / Italy 1972   105m
    Eastmancolor
Greenwich (Serge Silberman)
original title: *Le Charme Discret de la Bourgeoisie*

The efforts of a group of friends to dine together are continually frustrated.
A frequently hilarious, sometimes savage surrealist fable which makes all its points beautifully and then goes on twenty minutes too long. The performances are a joy.

w *Luis Bunuel, Jean-Claude Carrière d Luis Bunuel ph* Edmond Richard

Fernando Rey, Delphine Seyrig, Stéphane Audran, Bulle Ogier, Jean-Pierre Cassel, Paul Frankeur, Julien Bertheau
    'A perfect synthesis of surreal wit and blistering social assault.'—*Jan Dawson, MFB*

AA: best foreign film
AAN: Luis Bunuel, Jean-Claude Carrière (script)

Dishonored**
US 1931   91m   bw
Paramount

An officer's widow turned streetwalker is hired by the German government as a spy.
Rather gloomy melodrama which helped to establish its star as a top American attraction; but the heavy hand of her Svengali, Von Sternberg, was already evident.

w Daniel H. Rubin d *Josef Von Sternberg
ph Lee Garmes m* Karl Hajos

Marlene Dietrich, Victor McLaglen, Lew Cody, Gustav Von Seyffertitz, Warner Oland, Barry Norton, Wilfred Lucas
    'The most exciting movie I have seen in several months . . . yet I hope I may die young if I ever again have to listen to a manuscript so full of recusant, stilted, outmoded theatrical mouthings.'—*Pare Lorentz*
    'The whole film has a kind of magnificent grandeur embellished, of course, by its shining central performance.'—*John Gillett, 1964*

Dishonored Lady
US 1947   85m   bw
Mars Film (Hedy Lamarr)

A girl with a past is cleared of a murder charge by her psychiatrist.
Melodramatic showpiece designed for herself by a glamorous star; OK for the silly season.

w Edmund H. North, *play* Edward Sheldon, Margaret Ayer Barnes d Robert Stevenson
ph Lucien Andriot m Carmen Dragon

Hedy Lamarr, John Loder, Dennis O'Keefe, Paul Cavanagh, William Lundigan, Natalie Schaefer, Morris Carnovsky
    'She insulted her soul!'—*publicity*

Dishonour Bright*
GB 1936   82m   bw
GFD / Cecil (Herman Fellner, Max Schach)

An ageing playboy is blackmailed about a past affair.
Interesting semi-smart comedy of the period, tailored for its star.

w Ben Travers d Tom Walls

Tom Walls, Eugene Pallette, Betty Stockfield, Diana Churchill, Arthur Wontner, Cecil Parker, George Sanders, Henry Oscar, Basil Radford

A Dispatch from Reuters**
US 1940   90m   bw
Warner (Hal B. Wallis)
GB title: *This Man Reuter*

The story of the man who provided Europe's first news service.
Acceptable if slightly dull addition to Warner's prestige biopics; well made and acted.

w Milton Krims d *William Dieterle ph James Wong Howe m* Max Steiner

Edward G. Robinson, Edna Best, Eddie Albert, Albert Basserman, Gene Lockhart, Otto Kruger, Montagu Love, Nigel Bruce, James Stephenson

Disputed Passage*
US 1939 90m bw
Paramount (Harlan Thompson)

A young scientist who wants to marry meets
resistance from his mentor.
Adequate screen version of a bestseller.

w Anthony Veiller, Sheridan Gibney, *novel*
Lloyd C. Douglas d Frank Borzage
ph William C. Mellor *m* Frederick Hollander,
James Leopold

Dorothy Lamour, John Howard, Akim
Tamiroff, Judith Barrett, William Collier Snr,
Victor Varconi, Keye Luke, Elizabeth Risdon

'I should describe the flavour as a rather
nauseating blend of iodine and glucose.'—
Graham Greene

Disraeli*
US 1929 89m bw
Warner

Fictionalized episodes in the life of the
Victorian statesman, including his activities as
a matchmaker.
Very early star talkie, of primarily archival
interest; Arliss had appeared in a silent
version in 1921.

w Julian Josephson, *play* Louis N. Parker
d Alfred E. Green *ph* Lee Garmes

George Arliss, Joan Bennett, Florence Arliss,
Anthony Bushell, David Torrence, Ivan
Simpson, Doris Lloyd

AA: George Arliss
AAN: best picture; Julian Josephson

Distant Drums
US 1951 101m Technicolor
United States Pictures (Milton Sperling)

In 1840 Florida, an army officer rescues
prisoners from an Indian fort and decimates
the Seminoles who threaten their return
journey.
Overlong action saga, with dull stretches
compensated by a dominating star and some
lively incident.

w Niven Busch, Martin Rackin d Raoul
Walsh *ph* Sid Hickox *m* Max Steiner

Gary Cooper, Mari Aldon, Richard Webb,
Ray Teal, Arthur Hunnicutt, Robert Barrat

'Don't look for surprises. Mr Cooper is kept
steady and laconic throughout, the action is
serio-comic, and the pace is conventionally
maintained.'—*Bosley Crowther, New York
Times*

A Distant Trumpet
US 1964 116m Technicolor
 Panavision
Warner (William H. Wright)

The new commander of a cavalry outpost
tightens up discipline, which serves him well
when Indian trouble erupts.
Moderate western, quite well staged but with a
second team cast.

w John Twist, *novel* Paul Horgan d Raoul
Walsh *ph* William Clothier *m* Max Steiner

Troy Donahue, Suzanne Pleshette, James
Gregory, Diane McBain, William Reynolds,
Claude Akins, Kent Smith, Judson Pratt

Ditte, Child of Man*
Denmark 1946 106m bw
Nordisk
original title: *Ditte Menneskebarn*

An unmarried mother abandons her daughter,
who grows up to be a servant and to be
seduced in her turn.
Impressive, doom-laden Scandinavian saga,
highly thought of on its release.

wd Astrid and Bjarne Henning-Jensen,
novel Martin Andersen *ph* Werner Jenssen
m Herman Koppel

Tove Maes, Rasmus Ottesen, Karen Poulsen

Dive Bomber*
US 1941 133m Technicolor
Warner (Hal B. Wallis)

Aviation scientists work to eliminate pilot
blackout.
Somewhat rarefied propaganda piece with too
many reels of romantic banter but tense
climactic scenes and good star performances.

w Frank 'Spig' Wead, Robert Buckner
d Michael Curtiz *ph* Bert Glennon, Winton
C. Hoch *m* Max Steiner *md* Leo F. Forbstein

Errol Flynn, Fred MacMurray, Ralph
Bellamy, Alexis Smith, Regis Toomey, Robert
Armstrong, Allen Jenkins, Craig Stevens,
Moroni Olsen, Gig Young, William Hopper,
Charles Drake, Russell Hicks, Addison
Richards, Ann Doran, Herbert Anderson

AAN: Bert Glennon, Winton C. Hoch

The Divided Heart**
GB 1954 89m bw
Ealing (Michael Truman)

A boy believed to be a war orphan is lovingly
brought up by foster parents; then his real
mother turns up and wants him back.
Effective 'woman's picture' set in Europe and
giving a genuine sense of post-war feelings and
problems.

w Jack Whittingham d Charles Crichton
ph Otto Heller *m* Georges Auric

Cornell Borchers, Yvonne Mitchell, Armin
Dahlen, Alexander Knox, Geoffrey Keen,
Michel Ray, Liam Redmond, Eddie Byrne

The Divine Lady*
US 1929   100m   bw
Warner

The adventures of Emma, Lady Hamilton.
Historical charade which titillated at the time.

w Agnes Christine Johnson, Forrest Halsey
d Frank Lloyd *ph* John Seitz

Corinne Griffith, Victor Varconi, H. B.
Warner, Montagu Love, Marie Dressler

AA: Frank Lloyd
AAN: John Seitz

The Divine Woman*
US 1927   95m approx (24 fps)   bw
silent
MGM

The loves of Sarah Bernhardt.
Garbo's first star role; a typical Hollywood
melodramatization of facts.

w Dorothy Farnum, *play* Starlight by Gladys
Unger *d* Victor Sjostrom

Greta Garbo, Lars Hanson, Lowell Sherman,
John Mack Brown, Polly Moran

Divorce American Style**
US 1967   109m   Technicolor
Columbia / Tandem (Norman Lear)

Well-heeled Los Angeles suburbanites toy
with divorce but eventually resume their
domestic bickering.
Rather arid and patchy but often sharply
sardonic comedy about a society in which
people can't afford to divorce.

w Norman Lear d Bud Yorkin *ph* Conrad
Hall *m* David Grusin *pd* Edward Stephenson

*Dick Van Dyke, Debbie Reynolds, Jean
Simmons,* Jason Robards Jnr, Van Johnson,
Joe Flynn, Shelley Berman, Martin Gabel,
Lee Grant, Tom Bosley, Dick Gautier

AAN: Norman Lear

Divorce Italian Style**
Italy 1961   108m   bw
Lux / Vides / Galatea (Franco Cristaldi)
original title: *Divorzio all'Italiana*

A Sicilian nobleman explains how, wishing to
be rid of his wife, he arranged for her to be
seduced and later shot by a jealous lover.
Sardonic, stylized comedy which, rather in the
manner of *Kind Hearts and Coronets,* manages
while retailing a black comedy plot to satirize
Italian manners and institutions.

w Ennio de Concini, Pietro Germi, *Alfredo
Gianetti d Pietro Germi ph* Leonida Barboni
m Carlo Rustichelli

Marcello Mastroianni, Daniela Rocca, Stefania
Sandrelli, Leopoldo Trieste

AA: script
AAN: Pietro Germi; Marcello Mastroianni

The Divorce of Lady X**
GB 1937   92m   Technicolor
London Films (Alexander Korda)

A nobleman's daughter wins a barrister by
posing as a divorce client.
Pleasing comedy with high production
standards of its time, deftly performed by a
distinguished cast.

w Lajos Biro, Arthur Wimperis, Ian
Dalrymple, *play* Counsel's Opinion by Gilbert
Wakefield *d Tim Whelan ph* Harry Stradling
m Miklos Rozsa

Laurence Olivier, Merle Oberon, Binnie
Barnes, Ralph Richardson, Morton Selten, J.
H. Roberts

The Divorcee*
US 1930   83m   bw
MGM

Would-be liberal young marrieds divorce when
she puts up with his affairs but he can't
tolerate hers. She falls in love with another
married man but sends him back to his wife.
Rather wan illustration of the double standard
which was being much discussed in society at
the time.

w John Meehan, Nick Grinde, Zelda Sears,
novel Ex-Wife by Ursula Parrott *d* Robert Z.
Leonard *ph* Norbert Brodine *ad* Cedric
Gibbons

Norma Shearer, Chester Morris, Conrad
Nagel, Robert Montgomery, Florence
Eldridge

AA: Norma Shearer
AAN: best picture; Robert Z. Leonard; John
Meehan, Nick Grinde, Zelda Sears

Dixie*
US 1943   90m   Technicolor
Paramount (Paul Jones)

The life of old-time minstrel man Dan
Emmett.
Lighter-than-air fictionalized biography with
pleasing mid-19th-century settings.

w Karl Tunberg, Darrell Ware *d* A. Edward
Sutherland *ph* William C. Mellor *m* Robert
Emmet Delan *songs* Johnny Burke, Jimmy
Van Heusen

Bing Crosby, Dorothy Lamour, Marjorie
Reynolds, *Lynne Overman, Eddie Foy Jnr,
Billy de Wolfe, Raymond Walburn*, Grant
Mitchell

DOA**
US 1949 81m bw
Cardinal Pictures (Leo C. Popkin)

A businessman discovers that he has
effectively been murdered by a slow-acting
poison. In the few hours left to him he tracks
down and kills his murderer, and confesses to
the police.
Unusual and effective thriller, well
photographed on location in San Francisco
and Los Angeles.

*w Russell Rouse, Clarence Greene d Rudolph
Maté ph Ernest Laszlo m* Dmitri Tiomkin

Edmond O'Brien, Luther Adler, Pamela
Britton, William Ching

† Remade 1970 as *Colour Me Dead*, with Tom
Tryon.

Do Not Disturb
US 1965 102m De Luxe Cinemascope
TCF / Melcher / Arcola (Aaron Rosenberg,
Martin Melcher)

An American wool executive is posted to
London; his dizzy wife makes him jealous by
flirting with a French antique dealer.
Silly farce which paints a lunatic picture of
English and French life but occasionally raises
a wild laugh or two. Thin script and
production.

w Milt Rosen, Richard Breen, *play* William
Fairchild *d* Ralph Levy *ph* Leon Shamroy
m Lionel Newman

Doris Day, Rod Taylor, *Sergio Fantoni*,
Reginald Gardiner, Hermione Baddeley, Leon
Askin

Do You Like Women?
France / Italy 1964 100m bw
Francoriz / Number One / Federiz (Pierre
Kalfon)
original title: *Aimez-Vous Les Femmes?*

Secret rival sects of woman-eaters cause an
outbreak of murders in Paris.
Bizarre black comedy that doesn't quite work
but provides ghoulish fun along the way.

w Roman Polanski, Gérard Brach,
novel Georges Bardawil *d* Jean Léon
ph Sacha Vierny *m* Ward Swingle

Sophie Daumier, Guy Bédos, Edwige
Feuillère, Grégoire Aslan, Roger Blin

'It has the provoking quality of a carefully-
prepared firework display which, due to faulty
timing or bad connections, is never actually
ignited.'—*MFB*

Do You Love Me?
US 1946 91m Technicolor
TCF (George Jessel)

The lady dean of a music school gets herself
glamorized.
Thin, mildly agreeable but forgettable musical.

w Robert Ellis, Helen Logan *d* Gregory
Ratoff *ph* Edward Cronjager *songs* various

Maureen O'Hara, Dick Haymes, Harry James
and his Orchestra, Reginald Gardiner,
Richard Gaines, Stanley Prager

Doc*
US 1971 96m De Luxe
UA / Frank Perry

Doc Holliday goes to Tombstone to die of TB,
but is drawn into the feud between the
Clantons and his friend Wyatt Earp, whose
motives are not of the highest.
A somewhat glum debunking of the west's
most heroic myth, backing dour character
study with grubby pictures. The result lacks
excitement but maintains interest.

w Pete Hamill *d* Frank Perry *ph* Gerald
Hirschfeld *m* Jimmy Webb

Stacy Keach (Doc), Harris Yulin (Earp), Faye
Dunaway (Kate Elder), Mike Witney, Denver
John Collins, Dan Greenberg

'The physical realism that *Doc* is at pains to
establish becomes simply a convention of its
own.'—*Richard Combs*

Doc Savage, Man of Bronze
US 1975 100m Technicolor
Warner (George Pal)

A thirties superman and his assistants the
Amazing Five fly to South America to avenge
the death of Doc's father.
Stolid, humourless adaptation from a comic
strip, totally lacking in the necessary panache.

w George Pal, Joe Morhaim, *stories* Kenneth
Robeson *d* Michael Anderson *ph* Fred
Koenekamp *m* John Philip Sousa

Ron Ely, Paul Gleason, Bill Lucking, Michael
Miller, Eldon Quick

'A slick, ultra-self-conscious camp that
denies the material its self-respect.'—*Colin
Pahlow*

'Nothing in this unfortunate enterprise is
likely to please anyone: former Savage fans
will be enraged, newcomers bored, and
children will probably feel superior to the
whole mess . . .'—*New Yorker*

The Dock Brief
GB 1962 88m bw
(MGM) Dimitri de Grunwald
US title: *Trial and Error*

An incompetent barrister defends his client on a murder charge. The client is found guilty but the sentence is quashed on the grounds of inadequate defence.

Flat filming of a TV play which was a minor milestone; the film is twice the length and half as funny, and both stars quickly become tiresome.

w John Mortimer, Pierre Rouve, *play* John Mortimer *d* James Hill *ph* Ted Scaife *m* Ron Grainer

Peter Sellers, Richard Attenborough

Docks of New York**
US 1928 80m (24 fps) bw silent
Paramount

A stoker marries a girl he has saved from suicide. Further unfortunate incidents result in his going to prison, but she waits for him.

Glum melodrama chiefly remarkable for its sets and lighting, reminiscent of the later *Quai des Brumes*.

w Jules Furthman, *story* The Dock Walloper by John Monk Saunders *d Josef Von Sternberg ph Harold Rosson ad Hans Dreier*

George Bancroft, Betty Compson, Olga Baclanova, Clyde Cooke, Gustav Von Seyffertitz

'One comes away with the memory of a film impregnated with a life whose essential is in its energy and force.'—*Louis Chavance*

Dr Christian
Following the success of THE COUNTRY DOCTOR (qv), a rival studio (RKO) made a series of second features about a fictional country doctor, the rights to Dr Dafoe's life story being unavailable. Jean Hersholt again played the leading role and the films were immensely popular in small towns. A TV series followed in the fifties, starring Macdonald Carey.

1939: MEET DR CHRISTIAN
1940: THE COURAGEOUS DR CHRISTIAN, DR CHRISTIAN MEETS THE WOMEN, REMEDY FOR RICHES
1941: MELODY FOR THREE, THEY MEET AGAIN

Dr Crippen*
GB 1962 98m bw
ABP / John Clein

A quiet doctor murders his wife and elopes with a typist.

Straightforward account of a famous and rather unsurprising Edwardian murder case; well enough made but with no special *raison d'être*.

w Leigh Vance *d* Robert Lynn *ph* Nicolas Roeg

Donald Pleasence, Coral Browne, Samantha Eggar, Donald Wolfit

Dr Cyclops*
US 1940 76m Technicolor
Paramount (Merian C. Cooper)

Jungle travellers are captured and miniaturized by a mad scientist.

Splendid special effects and an appropriately sombre atmosphere are hampered by a slow-paced narrative in this minor horror classic.

w Tom Kilpatrick *d* Ernest Schoedsack *ph Henry Sharp, Winton Hoch m* Ernst Toch, Gerard Carbonera, Albert Hay Malotte

Albert Dekker, Janice Logan, Victor Kilian, Thomas Coley, Charles Halton

'The picture made behind locked doors!'— *publicity*

Dr Dolittle
US 1967 152m De Luxe Todd-AO
TCF / APJAC (Arthur P. Jacobs)

In a Victorian English village, Dr Dolittle is a veterinary surgeon who talks to his patients; escaping from a lunatic asylum, he travels with friends to the South Seas in search of the Great Pink Sea Snail.

Lumpish family spectacular with no imagination whatever, further handicapped by charmless performances and unsingable songs.

w / songs Leslie Bricusse, *novels* Hugh Lofting *d* Richard Fleischer *ph* Robert Surtees *pd* Mario Chiari *md* Lionel Newman, Alex Courage

Rex Harrison, Anthony Newley, Samantha Eggar, *Richard Attenborough*, William Dix, Peter Bull

AA: song 'Talk to the Animals'
AAN: best picture; Robert Surtees; Lionel Newman, Alex Courage; Leslie Bricusse (*m*)

Dr Ehrlich's Magic Bullet***
US 1940 103m bw
Warner (Wolfgang Reinhardt)
aka: *The Story of Dr Ehrlich's Magic Bullet*

A German scientist develops a cure for venereal disease.

Excellent period biopic: absorbing, convincing and extremely well put together.

w John Huston, Heinz Herald, Norman Burnside *d William Dieterle ph James Wong Howe m* Max Steiner

Edward G. Robinson, Ruth Gordon, Otto Kruger, Donald Crisp, Maria Ouspenskaya, Montagu Love, Sig Rumann, Donald Meek, Henry O'Neill, Albert Basserman, Edward

Norris, Harry Davenport, Louis Calhern,
Louis Jean Heydt
    'A superb motion picture.'—*Pare Lorentz*
AAN: John Huston, Heinz Herald, Norman
Burnside

Dr Faustus
GB 1967 93m Technicolor
Columbia / Oxford University Screen
    Productions / Nassau Films / Venfilms
    (Richard Burton, Richard McWhorter)
A medieval scholar conjures up
Mephistopheles and offers his soul in exchange
for a life of voluptuousness.
Marlowe's play has been adapted and
'improved', and there is some good handling
of the poetry, but the production is flat, dingy
and uninspired, as well as ludicrous when Miss
Taylor makes her silent appearances.

w Nevill Coghill, *play* Christopher Marlowe
d Richard Burton, Nevill Coghill *ph* Gabor
Pogany *m* Mario Nascimbene *pd* John de
Cuir

Richard Burton, Andreas Teuber, Ian Marter,
Elizabeth Donovan, Elizabeth Taylor (as
Helen of Troy)
    'It is of an awfulness that bends the mind.
The whole enterprise has the immense
vulgarity of a collaboration in which academe
would sell its soul for a taste of the glamour of
Hollywood, and the stars are only too happy
to appear a while in academe.'—*John Simon*
    'It turns out to be the story of a man who
sold his soul for Elizabeth Taylor.'—*Judith
Crist*

Dr Gillespie's Criminal Case
US 1943 89m bw

The elderly doctor solves a murder for which
an innocent man is in prison. Skilled
programme filler with beloved characters.
Lionel Barrymore, Margaret O'Brien, Donna
Reed, Van Johnson, Keye Luke, Marilyn
Maxwell. Written by Martin Berkeley, Harry
Ruskin and Lawrence Bachmann; directed by
Willis Goldbeck; for MGM. (GB title: *Crazy
to Kill*.) See also *Dr Kildare*.

Dr Gillespie's New Assistant
US 1942 88m bw

Shorn of young Dr Kildare, Gillespie chooses
a new support from three interns, and
meanwhile concentrates on an amnesia case.
Slick series entry which played widely as top of
the bill. Lionel Barrymore, Van Johnson,
Keye Luke, Richard Quine, Susan Peters.
Written by Willis Goldbeck, Harry Ruskin and
Lawrence Bachmann; directed by Willis
Goldbeck; for MGM. See also *Dr Kildare*.

Dr Goldfoot and the Bikini Machine
US 1965 90m Pathecolor Panavision
AIP (Anthony Carras)

Dr G. makes girl robots programmed to lure
wealthy men into their clutches.
Way-out farce for the jaded end of the teenage
market; a few lively touches and a climactic
chase partly atone for the general
tastelessness.

w Elwood Ullman, Robert Kaufman
d Norman Taurog *ph* Sam Leavitt *m* Les
Baxter *ad* Daniel Haller

Vincent Price, Fred Clark, Frankie Avalon,
Dwayne Hickman, Susan Hart, Jack Mullaney

Dr Heckyl and Mr Hype
US 1980 99m Metrocolor

An ugly scientist is transformed into a
handsome young sadist. Would-be comic
variation on a well-worn theme; the level of
comedy is indicated by the title. Oliver Reed,
Sunny Johnson, Mel Wells, Maia Danziger.
Written and directed by Charles B. Griffith;
for Golan-Globus

Doctor in the House**
GB 1954 91m Eastmancolor
Rank (Betty Box)

Amorous and other misadventures of medical
students at St Swithin's Hospital.
A comedy with much to answer for: several
sequels and an apparently endless TV series.
The original is not bad, as the students,
though plainly over age, constitute a
formidable mass of British talent at its peak.

w Nicholas Phipps, *book* Richard Gordon
d Ralph Thomas *ph* Ernest Steward *m* Bruce
Montgomery

Dirk Bogarde, Kenneth More, Donald Sinden,
Donald Houston, Kay Kendall, Muriel
Pavlow, *James Robertson Justice*, Geoffrey
Keen
    'Works its way with determined high spirits
through the repertoire of medical student
jokes.'—*MFB*
† Sequels, of increasing inanity and decreasing
connection with the original characters, were:
*Doctor at Sea, Doctor at Large, Doctor in
Love, Doctor in Distress, Doctor in Clover* and
Doctor in Trouble. Carry on Doctor and *Carry
on Again Doctor* were horses of a different
colour.

Doctor in the Village*
Holland 1958 92m bw
Nationale Filmproductie Maatschappij
    (Bobby Roosenboom)
original title: *Dorp aan de Rivier*

Stories are recalled of an eccentric but respected country doctor at the turn of the century.
Tragi-comic incidents in the vein of Pagnol, a little too rich in farce and melodrama to be convincingly human.

w Hugo Claus, *novel* Antoon Coolen d Fons Rademakers *ph* Eduard J. R. van der Enden *m* Jurriaan Andriessen

Max Croiset, Mary Dresselhuys, Bernhard Droog, Jan Teulings
'Scenes which should have had disturbing power crowd one upon another with an almost repellent relish which falls over into parody.'—*Peter John Dyer, MFB*

Doctor Jack*
US 1922   72m approx (24 fps)   bw
  silent
Pathé / Rolin

A quack country doctor does more good than the licensed medicos.
Pleasing but not hilariously funny star vehicle.

w Sam Taylor, Jean Havez d Fred Newmeyer
Harold Lloyd, Mildred Davis, John Prince, Eric Mayne

Doctor Jekyll and Mr Hyde****
US 1931   90m   bw
Paramount (Rouben Mamoulian)

A Victorian research chemist finds a formula which separates the good and evil in his soul; when the latter predominates, he becomes a rampaging monster.
The most exciting and cinematic version by far of the famous horror story; the make-up is slightly over the top, but the gas-lit London settings, the pace, the performances and clever camera and sound tricks make it a film to enjoy over and over again. Subjective camera is used at the beginning, and for the first transformation the actor wore various layers of make up which were sensitive to different colour filters and thus produced instant change.

w *Samuel Hoffenstein, Percy Heath, novel Robert Louis Stevenson d Rouben Mamoulian ph Karl Struss ad Hans Dreier*

Fredric March, Miriam Hopkins, Rose Hobart, Holmes Herbert, Halliwell Hobbes, Edgar Norton
'As a work of cinematic imagination this film is difficult to fault.'—*John Baxter, 1968*
'Strange desires! Loves and hates and secret yearnings . . . hidden in the shadows of a man's mind.'—*publicity*

† The screenplay with 1,400 frame blow-ups was published in 1976 in the Film Classics Library (editor Richard J. Anobile).

AA: Fredric March
AAN: Samuel Hoffenstein, Percy Heath; Karl Struss

Dr Jekyll and Mr Hyde**
US 1941   122m   bw
MGM (Victor Saville, Victor Fleming)

Curiously misconceived, stately, badly cast version with elaborate production including Freudian dream sequences. Always worth watching, but not a success.

w John Lee Mahin d Victor Fleming ph Joseph Ruttenberg m Franz Waxman

Spencer Tracy, Ingrid Bergman, Lana Turner, Ian Hunter, C. Aubrey Smith, Donald Crisp, Sara Allgood
'Not so much evil incarnate as ham rampant . . . more ludicrous than dreadful.'—*New York Times*
'A romantic gentleman by day—a love-mad beast at night!'—*publicity*
† Other versions: *The Two Faces of Dr Jekyll* (1960), *I Monster* (1970). Variations: *Daughter of Dr Jekyll* (1957), *Abbott and Costello Meet Dr Jekyll and Mr Hyde* (1954), *Son of Dr Jekyll* (1951), *The Ugly Duckling* (1960), *House of Dracula* (1945), *The Nutty Professor* (1963), *Dr Jekyll and Sister Hyde* (1971).

AAN: Joseph Ruttenberg; Franz Waxman

Dr Jekyll and Sister Hyde*
GB 1971   97m   Technicolor
Hammer

A twist: Jekyll now turns into a young and beautiful woman, and kills prostitutes so that he can continue his research.
Half-successful attempt to link the legend with Jack the Ripper, killed by gore and overlength.

w Brian Clemens d Roy Ward Baker ph Norman Warwick m David Whitaker

Ralph Bates, Martine Beswick, Gerald Sim, Lewis Fiander, Dorothy Alison

Dr Kildare
This long-running screen hero was a young intern at Blair Hospital, under the cranky tutelage of old Dr Gillespie. Created by Max Brand in a series of novels, he first appeared on the screen in a 1937 Paramount double-biller called INTERNS CAN'T TAKE MONEY, played by Joel McCrea with Barbara Stanwyck, no less, providing the love interest. Kildare came up against gangsters;

Gillespie did not appear. MGM then took over the property and went to town with it, making fifteen films in ten years. They were as follows:

1938: YOUNG DR KILDARE
1939: CALLING DR KILDARE, THE SECRET OF DR KILDARE
1940: DR KILDARE'S STRANGE CASE (qv), DR KILDARE GOES HOME (qv), DR KILDARE'S CRISIS (qv)
1941: THE PEOPLE vs DR KILDARE
1942: DR KILDARE'S WEDDING DAY (qv)
1942: DR KILDARE'S VICTORY (qv), CALLING DR GILLESPIE, DR GILLESPIE'S NEW ASSISTANT (qv)
1943: DR GILLESPIE'S CRIMINAL CASE (qv)
1944: THREE MEN IN WHITE, BETWEEN TWO WOMEN
1947: DARK DELUSION

Lew Ayres played Kildare, but in 1942 declared himself a conscientious objector and was dropped. The emphasis shifted to Gillespie, played by Lionel Barrymore from a wheelchair, and he proceeded to deal with a whole series of interns. The films were well enough made on medium budgets; nine were directed by Harold S. Bucquet and the last five by Willis Goldbeck, one by W. S. Van Dyke. In 1961 a TV series began with Richard Chamberlain and Raymond Massey, and ran for seven years.

Dr Kildare Goes Home
US 1940   79m   bw

Young Dr Kildare temporarily deserts Blair Hospital to help his father establish a small-town clinic. Rather below par episode with obvious outcome. Lew Ayres, Lionel Barrymore, Laraine Day, Samuel S. Hinds, Gene Lockhart. Written by Willis Goldbeck and Harry Ruskin; directed by Harold S. Bucquet; for MGM.

Dr Kildare's Strange Case
US 1940   77m   bw

The young doctor cures a mental patient by the newest methods. Crisp series episode. Lew Ayres, Lionel Barrymore, Laraine Day, Shepperd Strudwick, Samuel S. Hinds. Written by Willis Goldbeck and Harry Ruskin; directed by Harold S. Bucquet; for MGM.

Dr Kildare's Crisis
US 1940   75m   bw

Dr Kildare's fiancée may have epilepsy in the family. The series at its peak. Lew Ayres,

Lionel Barrymore, Robert Young, Laraine Day, Nat Pendleton, Marie Blake. Written by Willis Goldbeck and Harry Ruskin; directed by Harold S. Bucquet; for MGM.

Dr Kildare's Victory
US 1942   92m   bw

Back at Blair, Dr Kildare fights ambulance zoning regulations. Rather heavy-going episode, its star's last before becoming a conscientious objector and leaving Hollywood for the duration. Lew Ayres, Lionel Barrymore, Ann Ayars, Robert Sterling. Written by Harry Ruskin and Willis Goldbeck; directed by W. S. Van Dyke; for MGM.

Dr Kildare's Wedding Day
US 1942   83m   bw

Dr Kildare's fiancée is killed in a road accident. Rather deliberately downbeat episode, well enough assembled. Lew Ayres, Lionel Barrymore, Laraine Day, Red Skelton, Nils Asther. Written by Lawrence Bachmann and Ormond Ruthven; directed by Harold S. Bucquet; for MGM. (GB title: *Mary Names the Day*.)

Doctor Mabuse***
Germany 1922   101m (24 fps)   bw
silent
UFA
original title: *Doktor Mabuse, der Spieler*

A criminal mastermind uses hypnotism and blackmail in his efforts to obtain world domination, but when finally cornered is discovered to be a raving maniac.
A real wallow in German post-war depression and melodrama, in the form of a Fu Manchu / Moriarty type thriller. Fascinating scene by scene, but by now a slightly tiresome whole.

w Thea Von Harbou, Fritz Lang,
novel Norbert Jacques   d Fritz Lang   ph Carl Hoffman   ad Otto Hunte, Stahl-Urach, Erich Kettelhut, Karl Vollbrecht

Rudolph Klein-Rogge, Alfred Abel, Gertrude Welcker, Lil Dagover, Paul Richter
† Originally issued in Germany in two parts, *Der Grosse Spieler* and *Inferno*, adding up to a much longer running time.
†† See sequels, *The Testament of Dr Mabuse* and *The Thousand Eyes of Dr Mabuse*.

Doctor No***
GB 1962   111m   Technicolor
UA / Eon (Harry Saltzman, Albert R. Broccoli)

A British secret service agent foils a master criminal operating in the West Indies.

First of the phenomenally successful James
Bond movies, mixing sex, violence and campy
humour against expensive sets and exotic
locales. Toned down from the original novels,
they expressed a number of sixties attitudes,
and proved unstoppable box office attractions
for nearly fifteen years. The first was, if not
quite the best, reasonably representative of
the series.

w *Richard Maibaum*, Johanna Harwood,
Berkely Mather, *novel* Ian Fleming *d* Terence
Young *ph* Ted Moore *m* Monty Norman

Sean Connery, Ursula Andress, Jack Lord,
Joseph Wiseman, John Kitzmiller, Bernard
Lee, Lois Maxwell, Zena Marshall, Eunice
Gayson, Anthony Dawson
† The subsequent titles, all qv, were *From
Russia with Love* (1963), *Goldfinger* (1964),
Thunderball (1965), *You Only Live Twice*
(1967), *On Her Majesty's Secret Service* (1969),
Diamonds Are Forever (1971), *Live and Let
Die* (1973), *The Man with the Golden Gun*
(1974), *The Spy Who Loved Me* (1977),
Moonraker (1979), *For Your Eyes Only*
(1981), *Octopussy* (1983).
Casino Royale (1967) was a Bond spoof made
by other hands.

Dr Phibes Rises Again*
GB 1972 89m De Luxe
AIP (Richard Dalton)

The immortal Phibes and his wife rise from the
dead to seek an Egyptian elixir of life, and
cross swords with a satanic Egyptologist.
Uncertainly paced but generally zippy comic
strip for adults, with all concerned entering
gleefully into the evil spirit of the thing. See
prequel, *The Abominable Dr Phibes*.

w Robert Fuest, Robert Blees *d* Robert
Fuest *ph* Alex Thomson *m* John Gale
ad Brian Eatwell

Vincent Price, Robert Quarry, Valli Kemp,
Fiona Lewis, Peter Cushing, Beryl Reid,
Terry-Thomas, Hugh Griffith, *Peter Jeffrey*,
Gerald Sim, John Thaw, John Cater, Lewis
Fiander
   'It's refreshing to find a sequel which is
better than its prototype.'—*Philip Strick, MFB*

Dr Renault's Secret
US 1942 58m bw

A scientist turns an ape into a semi-human,
which runs amok. Fairly well done horror
support. George Zucco, J. Carrol Naish, John
Shepperd, Lynne Roberts. Written by William
Bruckner and Robert F. Metzler; directed by
Harry Lachman; for TCF.

Dr Rhythm*
US 1938 80m bw

A veterinary surgeon goes into show business.
Easy-going star musical with pleasant songs.
Bing Crosby, Beatrice Lillie, Mary Carlisle,
Andy Devine, Laura Hope Crews, Rufe
Davis. Written by Jo Swerling, Richard
Connell, from a story by O. Henry; directed
by Frank Tuttle; for Paramount.

Dr Socrates**
US 1935 70m bw
Warner (Robert Lord)

A small-town doctor is forced to help
wounded gangsters, and becomes involved.
Good star melodrama.

w Robert Lord, *novel* W. R. Burnett
d William Dieterle *ph* Tony Gaudio *md* Leo
F. Forbstein

Paul Muni, Ann Dvorak, Barton Maclane,
Robert Barrat, John Eldridge, Hobart
Cavanaugh, Mayo Methot, Samuel S. Hinds,
Henry O'Neill
† Remade as *King of the Underworld* and
Bullet Scars.

Dr Strangelove; or, How I Learned to
Stop Worrying and Love the Bomb***
GB 1963 93m bw
Columbia / Stanley Kubrick (Victor Lyndon)

A mad USAF general launches a nuclear
attack on Russia, and when recall attempts
fail, and retaliation is inevitable, all concerned
sit back to await the destruction of the world.
Black comedy resolving itself into a series of
sketches, with the star playing three parts (for
no good reason): the US president, an RAF
captain, and a mad German-American
scientist. Historically an important film in its
timing, its nightmares being those of the early
sixties, artistically it clogs its imperishable
moments by untidy narrative and
unattractively contrasty photography.

w Stanley Kubrick, Terry Southern, Peter
George, *novel* Red Alert by Peter George
d Stanley Kubrick *ph* Gilbert Taylor
m Laurie Johnson *ad* Ken Adam

Peter Sellers, George C. Scott, Peter Bull,
Sterling Hayden, Keenan Wynn, Slim Pickens,
James Earl Jones, Tracy Reed
   'Scarcely a picture of relentless originality;
seldom have we seen so much made over so
little.'—*Joan Didion*
† *Fail Safe* (qv), which took the same theme
more seriously, was released almost
simultaneously.

AAN: best picture; script; Stanley Kubrick (as
director); Peter Sellers

Dr Syn°
GB 1937 80m bw
Gaumont

The vicar of Dymchurch in 1780 is really a
pirate believed dead.
This now obscure, lively pirate yarn was its
star's last film.

w Michael Hogan, Roger Burford, *novel*
Russell Thorndike d *Roy William Neill*
ph Jack Cox md Louis Levy

George Arliss, Margaret Lockwood, John
Loder, Roy Emerton, Graham Moffatt,
Frederick Burtwell, Meinhart Maur, George
Merritt

Dr Syn Alias the Scarecrow
GB 1962 98m Technicolor
Walt Disney (Bill Anderson)

The vicar of Dymchurch is really a smuggler
who manages to outwit a rascally general and
save a prisoner from Dover Castle.
Oddly released the same year as another
version of the story, *Captain Clegg*, this rather
set-bound adventure yarn turns its hero into a
Robin Hood figure. It was originally made to
be shown in three parts on American TV.

w Robert Westerby, *novel* Christopher Syn by
Russell Thorndike, William Buchanan
d James Neilson ph Paul Beeson m Gerard
Schurmann

Patrick McGoohan, George Cole, Tony
Britton, Geoffrey Keen, Kay Walsh, Patrick
Wymark, Alan Dobie, Eric Pohlmann

The Doctor Takes a Wife°
US 1940 89m bw
Columbia (William Perlberg)

A young doctor has to pretend to be the
husband of a socialite.
Typical high life comedy of its period, quite
brisk and diverting.

w George Seaton, Ken Englund d Alexander
Hall ph Sid Hickox m Frederick Hollander
md Morris Stoloff

Loretta Young, Ray Milland, Edmund
Gwenn, Reginald Gardiner, Gail Patrick,
Frank Sully, George Metaxa, Charles Halton,
Chester Clute

Dr Terror's House of Horrors
GB 1965 98m Techniscope
Amicus (Milton Subotsky)

An eccentric, who turns out to be Death
himself, tells the fortunes of five men in a
railway carriage.
One of the first Amicus horror compendiums
and a weak one, not helped by wide screen, a
couple of naïve scripts and ho-hum acting. The
book-ends are quite pleasant, though.

w Milton Subotsky d Freddie Francis
ph Alan Hume m Elisabeth Lutyens

Peter Cushing, Ursula Howells, Max Adrian,
Roy Castle, Alan Freeman, Bernard Lee,
Jeremy Kemp, Kenny Lynch, Christopher
Lee, Michael Gough, Donald Sutherland
† Later collections from the same stable
include *Torture Garden, Tales from the Crypt,
Vault of Horror* and *Asylum*.

Dr Who and the Daleks
GB 1965 83m Techniscope
British Lion / Regal / Aaru (Milton
  Subotsky, Max J. Rosenberg)

Three children and their grandfather
accidentally start his time machine and are
whisked away to a planet where villainous
robots rule.
Junior science fiction from the BBC series.
Limply put together, and only for indulgent
children.

w Milton Subotsky d Gordon Flemyng
ph John Wilcox m Malcolm Lockyer

Peter Cushing, Roy Castle, Jennie Linden,
Roberta Tovey, Barrie Ingham
† A sequel, no better, emerged in 1966:
Daleks: Invasion Earth 2150 AD, with similar
credits except that Bernard Cribbins instead of
Roy Castle provided comic relief.

Dr X°°
US 1932 82m Technicolor
Warner (Hal Wallis)

A reporter investigates a series of moon
murders and narrows his search to one of
several doctors at a medical college.
Fascinating, German-inspired, overblown and
generally enjoyable horror mystery whose
armless villain commits murders by growing
limbs from 'synthetic flesh'.

w Earl Baldwin, Robert Tasker, *play* Howard
W. Comstock, Allen C. Miller d *Michael
Curtiz ph Richard Tower, Ray Rennahan*
md Leo Forbstein

Lee Tracy, Lionel Atwill, Preston Foster, Fay
Wray, George Rosener, Mae Busch, Arthur
Edmund Carewe, John Wray
  'The settings, lighting and final battle with
the man-monster are quite stunning.'—*NFT,
1974*

Doctor You've Got to be Kidding
US 1967 93m Metrocolor Panavision
MGM / Trident (Douglas Laurence)

A girl arrives at a maternity hospital chased by
three prospective husbands.

Wild and wacky farce which leaves little impression.

w Phillip Shuken, *novel* Patte Wheat Mahan
d Peter Tewkesbury *ph* Fred Koenekamp
m Kenyon Hopkins

Sandra Dee, George Hamilton, Celeste Holm, Bill Bixby, *Dwayne Hickman*, Dick Kallman, Mort Sahl, Allen Jenkins

Doctor Zhivago•••
US 1965   192m   Technicolor
  Panavision 70
MGM / Carlo Ponti

A Moscow doctor is caught up in World War I, exiled for writing poetry, forced into partisan service and separated from his only love.
Beautifully photographed and meticulously directed, this complex epic has been so reduced from the original novel that many parts of the script simply do not make any kind of sense. What remains is a collection of expensive set pieces, great for looking if not listening.

w Robert Bolt, *novel* Boris Pasternak
d *David Lean ph Frederick A. Young*
m Maurice Jarre

Omar Sharif, Julie Christie, Rod Steiger, Alec Guinness, Rita Tushingham, Ralph Richardson, Tom Courtenay, Geraldine Chaplin, Siobhan McKenna, Noel Willman, Geoffrey Keen, Adrienne Corri
'A long haul along the road of synthetic lyricism.'—*MFB*
'David Lean's *Doctor Zhivago* does for snow what his *Lawrence of Arabia* did for sand.'—*John Simon*
'It isn't shoddy (except for the music); it isn't soap opera; it's stately, respectable, and dead.'—*Pauline Kael*

AA: Robert Bolt; Frederick A. Young; Maurice Jarre
AAN: best picture; David Lean; Tom Courtenay

The Doctor's Dilemma•
GB 1958   99m   Metrocolor
MGM / Anatole de Grunwald

Eminent Harley Street surgeons debate the case of a devoted wife and her tubercular artist husband.
Well acted but curiously muffled filming of Shaw's Edwardian play about ethics and human values.

w Anatole de Grunwald, *play* Bernard Shaw
d Anthony Asquith *ph* Robert Krasker
m Joseph Kosma *ad* Paul Sheriff

Leslie Caron, Dirk Bogarde, *John Robinson*, Alastair Sim, Felix Aylmer, Robert Morley, Michael Gwynn, Maureen Delany, Alec McCowen

Doctors' Wives
US 1970   102m   Eastmancolor
Columbia / M. J. Frankovich

When Dr Dellman shoots his unfaithful wife, his colleagues reconsider their sex lives.
Adult soap opera from talents who at other times have found better things to do. In the sensational circumstances, two sanguinary operation sequences are tastelessly irrelevant.

w Daniel Taradash, *novel* Frank G. Slaughter
d George Schaefer *ph* Charles B. Lang
m Elmer Bernstein

Richard Crenna, Janice Rule, Gene Hackman, John Colicos, Dyan Cannon, Diana Sands, Rachel Roberts, Carroll O'Connor, Cara Williams, Ralph Bellamy, Richard Anderson
'Crisis follows hard on crisis to breathlessly ludicrous effect.'—*Tom Milne*

Dodge City•••
US 1939   104m   Technicolor
Warner (Robert Lord)

An ex-soldier and trail boss helps clean up the west's great railroad terminus.
Standard, satisfying big-scale western with all clichés intact and very enjoyable, as is the soft, rich early colour. The story is plainly inspired by the exploits of Wyatt Earp.

w Robert Buckner *d Michael Curtiz ph Sol Polito, Ray Rennahan m* Max Steiner

Errol Flynn, Olivia de Havilland, Ann Sheridan, Bruce Cabot, Alan Hale, Frank McHugh, John Litel, Victor Jory, William Lundigan, Henry Travers, Henry O'Neill, Guinn Williams, Gloria Holden
'It looks programmed and underpopulated, though in an elegantly stylized way.'—*New Yorker, 1980*

Dodsworth•••
US 1936   101m   bw
Samuel Goldwyn

An American businessman takes his wife on a tour of Europe, and their lives are changed.
Satisfying, well-acted drama from a bestselling novel; production values high.

w *Sidney Howard, novel Sinclair Lewis*
d *William Wyler ph* Rudolph Maté *m* Alfred Newman

Walter Huston, Mary Astor, Ruth Chatterton, David Niven, Paul Lukas, Gregory Gaye, *Maria Ouspenskaya*, Odette Myrtil, Spring Byington, John Payne

'No one, I think, will fail to enjoy it, in spite of its too limited and personal plot, the sense it leaves behind of a very expensive, very contemporary, Bond Street vacuum flask.'—*Graham Greene*

'William Wyler has had the skill to execute it in cinematic terms, and a gifted cast has been able to bring the whole alive to our complete satisfaction.'—*New York Times*

AAN: best picture; Sidney Howard; William Wyler; Walter Huston; Maria Ouspenskaya

Dog Day Afternoon**
US 1975   130m   Technicolor
Warner / AEC (Martin Bregman, Martin Elfland)

Two incompetent robbers are cornered in a Brooklyn bank.
Recreation of a tragi-comic episode from the newspaper headlines; for half its length a fascinating and acutely observed film which then bogs itself down in a surplus of talk and excessive sentiment about homosexuality.

w Frank Pierson, *book* Patrick Mann
d Sidney Lumet *ph* Victor J. Kemper *m* none

Al Pacino, John Cazale, *Charles Durning*, Sully Boyar, James Broderick, *Chris Sarandon*
'There is plenty of Lumet's vital best here in a film that at least glancingly captures the increasingly garish pathology of our urban life.'—*Jack Kroll*
'Scattered moments of wry humour, sudden pathos and correct observation.'—*John Simon*
'The mask of frenetic cliché doesn't spoil moments of pure reporting on people in extremity.'—*New Yorker*
'A long and wearying case history of the beaten, sobbing, despairing and ultimately powerless anti-hero.'—*Karyn Kay, Jump Cut*
'Full of galvanic mirth rooted in human desperation.'—*Michael Billington, Illustrated London News*

AA: Frank Pierson
AAN: best picture; Sidney Lumet; Al Pacino; Chris Sarandon

A Dog of Flanders
US 1959   97m   De Luxe   Cinemascope
TCF / Associated Producers (Robert B. Radnitz)

A small boy wants to be an artist; when he runs away in frustration, his shaggy dog, formerly a stray, leads his family to him.
Old-fashioned tear-jerker for well-brought-up children, previously filmed as a silent; quite accomplished in presentation.

w Ted Sherdeman, *novel* Ouida *d* James B. Clark *ph* Otto Heller *m* Paul Sawtell, Bert Shefter

David Ladd, Donald Crisp, Theodore Bikel, Max Croiset, Monique Ahrens

A Dog's Life*
US 1918   30m approx   bw   silent
First National

A tramp and a stray mongrel help each other towards a happy ending.
Threatening sentiment is kept at bay by amusing sight gags in this pleasing star featurette.

wd Charles Chaplin ph Rollie Totheroh

Charles Chaplin, Edna Purviance, Chuck Riesner, Henry Bergman, Albert Austin, Scraps

The Dogs of War
GB 1980   118m   Technicolor
UA / Silverwold (Norman Jewison, Patrick Palmer)

A disenchanted mercenary becomes involved in a plot to take over an impoverished West African state.
Tough but seemingly dated modern irony, somewhat lacking in action and surprise.

w Gary DeVore, George Malko
novel Frederick Forsyth *d* John Irvin *ph* Jack Cardiff *m* Geoffrey Burgon

Christopher Walken, Tom Berenger, Colin Blakely, Hugh Millais, Paul Freeman, Robert Urquhart

La Dolce Vita**
Italy / France 1960   173m   bw   Totalscope
Riama / Pathé Consortium (Giuseppe Amato)
aka: *The Sweet Life*

A journalist mixes in modern Roman high society and is alternately bewitched and sickened by what he sees.
Episodic satirical melodrama, a marathon self-indulgent wallow with a wagging finger never far away. Not a successful whole, but full of choice moments such as a statue of Christ being flown by helicopter over the city.

w Federico Fellini, Tullio Pinelli, Ennio Flaiano, Brunello Rondi *d Federico Fellini
ph* Otello Martelli *m* Nino Rota *ad* Piero Gherardi

Marcello Mastroianni, Anita Ekberg, Anouk Aimée, Alain Cuny, Yvonne Furneaux, Magali Noel, Nadia Gray, Lex Barker
'Its personification of various familiar symbols—love, death, purity, sin, reason and so on—never succeeds in reflecting human values or creating intellectual excitement . . .

Its actual significance rests in the way its
(albeit specious) social attack has stirred the
imagination of other Italian film-makers, as
well as public interest in their work.'—*Robert
Vas, MFB*

AAN: script; Federico Fellini

Doll Face
US 1945   80m   bw
TCF (Bryan Foy)
GB title: *Come Back to Me*

A burlesque queen goes to Broadway.
Lower case musical of minimal interest.

w Leonard Praskins *d* Lewis Seiler
ph Joseph La Shelle *songs* Harold Adamson,
Jimmy McHugh

Vivian Blaine, Dennis O'Keefe, Carmen
Miranda, Perry Como, Martha Stewart,
Michael Dunne, Reed Hadley, George E.
Stone, Donald McBride, Edgar Norton

Dollars°
US 1971   120m   Technicolor
Columbia / M. J. Frankovich
GB title: *The Heist*

An American security expert installs an
electronic system in a Hamburg bank which he
plans to rob himself.
Overlong caper comedy-drama which is quite
good to watch when it starts moving, though
the quick cutting, short takes and deliberately
obscure narrative leave one breathless.

wd Richard Brooks *ph* Petrus Schloemp
m Quincy Jones

Warren Beatty, Goldie Hawn, Gert Frobe,
Robert Webber, Scott Brady, Arthur Brauss

'An essay in virtuoso film construction . . .
rather as if one were watching a perfect
machine in full throttle but with nowhere to
go.'—*John Gillet*

A Doll's House°
GB 1973   95m   Eastmancolor
Elkins / Freeward (Hillard Elkins)

A wife begins to resist her husband's will.
Ibsen's feminist play was always good value;
set in Norway in the nineties, it was taken up
eighty years later as a precursor of women's
lib, which accounts for two film versions in one
year. This one is simply staged and well
performed, but suffers from a bad translation.

w Christopher Hampton, *play* Henrik Ibsen
d Patrick Garland *ph* Arthur Ibbetson
m John Barry

Claire Bloom, Anthony Hopkins, Ralph
Richardson, Denholm Elliott, Anna Massey,
Edith Evans

A Doll's House
GB / France 1973   106m   Eastmancolor
World Film Services / Les Films de la
   Boétie (Joseph Losey)

Opened out but less effective version of the
above, with too much solemnity and the
central part miscast.

w David Mercer, *play* Henrik Ibsen *d* Joseph
Losey *ph* Gerry Fisher *m* Michel Legrand

Jane Fonda, David Warner, Trevor Howard,
Edward Fox, Delphine Seyrig, Anna Wing

The Dolly Sisters°°
US 1945   114m   Technicolor
TCF (George Jessel)

The lives of a Hungarian sister act in
American vaudeville.
Fictionalized biographical musical, only fair in
the script department but glittering to look at
in superb colour, and enriched by splendid
production values. Undoubtedly among the
best of its kind.

w John Larkin, Marian Spitzer *d* Irving
Cummings *ph* Ernest Palmer *md* Alfred
Newman, Charles Henderson *songs* various
ch Seymour Felix *ad* Lyle Wheeler, Leland
Fuller

Betty Grable, June Haver, John Payne, S. Z.
Sakall, Reginald Gardiner, Frank Latimore,
Gene Sheldon, Sig Rumann, Trudy Marshall

AAN: song 'I Can't Begin to Tell You'
(*m* Johnny Monaco, *ly* Mack Gordon)

w Alfred Machard, Leonide Moguy
d Leonide Moguy *ph* Mario Craveri, Renato
del Frate *m* Alessandro Cicognini

Vittorio de Sica, Lois Maxwell, Gabrielle
Dorziat, Anna Maria Pierangeli, Gino Leurini

Dominique
GB 1978   100m   colour
Grand Prize / Melvin Simon (Milton
   Subotsky, Andrew Donally)

A woman who was convinced that her
husband was deliberately driving her mad is
found dead, and buried, but seemingly
returns . . .
The old *Diabolique* syndrome revamped in a
very parsimonious production with little to
hold the interest.

w Edward and Valerie Abraham, *novel* What
Beckoning Ghost by Harold Lawlor
d Michael Anderson *ph* Ted Moore *m* David
Whitaker

Cliff Robertson, Jean Simmons, Jenny
Agutter, Simon Ward, Ron Moody, Judy
Geeson, Michael Jayston, Flora Robson,
David Tomlinson, Jack Warner.

The Domino Principle
US 1977   100m   CFI color
Associated General Films (Lew Grade,
   Martin Starger) / Stanley Kramer
GB title: *The Domino Killings*
A murderer is offered his freedom if he will
assassinate a national figure.
Fashionable, complex and rather boring
political thriller.

w Adam Kennedy, from his novel *d* Stanley
Kramer *ph* Fred Koenekamp, Ernest Laszlo
m Billy Goldenberg

Gene Hackman, Richard Widmark, Candice
Bergen, Mickey Rooney, Edward Albert, Eli
Wallach, Ken Swofford, Neva Patterson
   'Terrible movies tend to start with a
preposterous premise and then laboriously
work their way to an impossible conclusion.
This one however starts with an arrant
impossibility and works its way to whatever
lies beyond and below that.'—*John Simon*

Don Camillo's Last Round*
Italy 1955   98m   bw
Rizzoli
original title: *Don Camillo e l'Onorevole
   Peppone*
The village Catholic priest tries to stop the
re-election of the communist mayor.
Pleasant third collection of encounters with
familiar characters.

w Giovanni Guareschi and others, from his
books *d* Carmine Gallone *ph* Anchise Brizzi
m Alessandro Cicognini

Fernandel, Gino Cervi, Claude Silvain, Leda
Gloria
   'The episodic narrative is full of mildly
amusing incident.'—*MFB*

Don Giovanni
France-Italy-Germany 1979   184m   colour
Gaumont-Opera-Camera One (Michel
   Seydoux)
Grandiose but artistically somewhat hesitant
version of Mozart's opera; little here for film
buffs.
cinematic conception Rolf Lieberman
d Joseph Losey *ph* Gerry Fisher
ad Alexander Trauner

Ruggero Raimondi, John Macurdy, Edda
Moser, Kiri Te Kanawa

The Don is Dead
US 1973   117m   Technicolor
Universal / Hal B. Wallis (Paul Nathan)
Cross and double cross among Mafia families.
A failed attempt to cash in on *The Godfather*,

this endless melodrama is boringly violent and
totally predictable.
w Marvin H. Albert, from his novel
d Richard Fleischer *ph* Richard H. Kline
m Jerry Goldsmith

Anthony Quinn, Frederic Forrest, Robert
Forster, Al Lettieri, Angel Tompkins, Charles
Cioffi

Don Juan**
US 1926   126m (synchronized)   bw
Warner
Exploits of the famous lover and adventurer at
Lucretia Borgia's court.
Lithe swashbuckler in the best silent tradition,
but with a synchronized score (by William
Axt) which made it a sensation and led directly
to the talkie revolution.
w Bess Meredyth *d* Alan Crosland *ph* Byron
Haskin

John Barrymore, Mary Astor, Warner Oland,
Estelle Taylor, Myrna Loy, Phyllis Haver,
Willard Louis, Montagu Love

Don Juan Quilligan
US 1945   76m   bw
A would-be romantic bargee becomes engaged
to two girls simultaneously, one on each side
of the Hudson. Thin comedy of bigamy,
similar to *The Captain's Paradise*, which came
later. William Bendix, Phil Silvers, Joan
Blondell, Mary Treen, Anne Revere, George
Macready. Written by Arthur Kober and
Frank Gabrielson; directed by Frank Tuttle;
for TCF.

Don Q Son of Zorro*
US 1925   170m (16 fps)   bw   silent
United Artists
Further adventures in the manner of the star's
1920 hit (see *The Mark of Zorro*).
w K. and H. Pritchard *d* Donald Crisp
Douglas Fairbanks, Mary Astor, Donald
Crisp, Jack McDonald, Jean Hersholt

Don Quixote*
France 1933   82m   bw
Vandor / Nelson / Wester
An adequate potted version starring Fedor
Chaliapin and in the English version George
Robey (French version: Dorville).
w Paul Morand, Alexandre Arnoux, from
Cervantes *d* G. W. Pabst *ph* Nikolas Farkas,
Paul Portier *ad* André Andreiev *m* Jacques
Ibert

Don Quixote••
USSR 1957 105m Agfacolor Sovscope
Lenfilm

An extremely handsome version with a
commanding star performance.

w E. Schwarz *d* Grigori Kozintsev *ph* Andrei
Moskvin, Apollinari Dudko *ad* Yevgeny
Yenei *m* Kara-Karayev

Nikolai Cherkassov, Yuri Tolubeyev
† Other versions came from France in 1902
and 1908, Italy in 1910, France in 1911, USA
in 1915, Britain in 1923, Denmark in 1926,
Spain in 1927, Britain in 1972, and Britain
(ballet version with Nureyev) in 1975.

Dona Flor and Her Two Husbands
Brazil 1976 110m Eastmancolor
Carnaval (Luis Carlos Barreto)

A young widow remarries, and has to share
her bed with her late husband's ghost.
Semi-pornographic comedy which achieved
some fashionable success.

wd Bruno Barreto *ph* Maurito Salles
m Chico Buarque de Holanda

Sonia Braga, Jose Wilker, Mauro Mendonca

Dondi
US 1960 80m bw

GIs in Italy adopt an orphan boy, who stows
away to be with them in America. Glutinous,
sentimental comedy-drama. David Janssen,
Patti Page, Walter Winchell, Mickey
Shaughnessy, Robert Strauss, Arnold Stang,
Gale Gordon. Written by Albert Zugsmith
and Gus Edson, from a comic strip; directed
by Albert Zugsmith; for Allied Artists.

Donovan's Brain•
US 1953 81m bw
UA / Dowling (Tom Gries)

An unscrupulous tycoon is fatally injured, but
his brain is kept alive by a surgeon who finds
himself dominated by it.
Modest competence marks this version of a
much filmed novel, with quiet suspense and a
firm central performance.

w Felix Feist, *novel* Curt Siodmak *d* Felix
Feist *ph* Joseph Biroc *m* Eddie Dunstedter

Lew Ayres, Gene Evans, Nancy Davis, Steve
Brodie, Lisa K. Howard

Donovan's Reef
US 1963 108m Technicolor
Paramount (John Ford)

War veterans settle down on a South Sea
island; when the daughter of one of them
comes to visit, his reputation must be
protected.
Good-humoured but finally enervating mixture
of rough-house and slapstick, with the
appearance of an old friends' benefit and the
director in familiar sub-standard form.

w Frank Nugent, James Edward Grant
d John Ford *ph* William H. Clothier *m* Cyril
Mockridge

John Wayne, Lee Marvin, Jack Warden,
Elizabeth Allen, Dorothy Lamour, Cesar
Romero, Mike Mazurki

Don's Party•
Australia 1976 90m Eastmancolor

In suburban Sydney, a political celebration
party turns into a pretence of wife-swapping.
Fairly acute observation of middle-class
antipodean mores, interrupted with
predictable bouts of antipodean crudeness.
Ray Barrett, Clare Binney, Pat Bishop,
Graeme Blundell, John Hargreaves. Written
by David Williamson, from his own play;
directed by Bruce Beresford; for Double
Head / AFC.

Don't Bother to Knock•
US 1952 76m bw
TCF (Julian Blaustein)

A deranged girl gets a baby-sitting job in a
hotel and terrifies all concerned by threatening
to kill her charge.
Curious vehicle for the emergent Monroe,
who is not up to it, as who would be?
Technical credits par, but entertainment value
small.

w Daniel Taradash, *novel* Charlotte
Armstrong *d* Roy Baker *ph* Lucien Ballard
m Lionel Newman

Marilyn Monroe, Richard Widmark, Anne
Bancroft, Donna Corcoran, Jeanne Cagney,
Lurene Tuttle, Jim Backus, Elisha Cook Jnr

Don't Bother to Knock
GB 1961 89m Technicolor
      Cinemascope
ABP / Haileywood (Frank Godwin)
US title: *Why Bother to Knock*

A Casanova travel agent gives each of his girl
friends a key to his Edinburgh flat.
Poorly developed and self-conscious sex farce.

w Dennis Cannan, Frederick Gotfurt, Frederic
Raphael, *novel* Clifford Hanley *d* Cyril
Frankel *ph* Geoffrey Unsworth *m* Elisabeth
Lutyens

Richard Todd, *Judith Anderson*, Elke
Sommer, June Thorburn, Nicole Maurey, Rik
Battaglia, Eleanor Summerfield, John Le
Mesurier

Don't Ever Leave Me
GB 1949 85m bw

A kidnapped teenager falls for her abductor.
No Orchids for Miss Blandish played as a
family comedy; quite unmemorable. Jimmy
Hanley, Petula Clark, Edward Rigby, Hugh
Sinclair, Linden Travers, Anthony Newley.
Written by Robert Westerby, from Anthony
Armstrong's novel *The Wide Guy*; directed by
Arthur Crabtree; for Triton / Rank.

Don't Go Near the Water°
US 1957 107m Metrocolor
Cinemascope
MGM / Avon (Lawrence Weingarten)

The US Navy sets up a public relations unit on
a South Pacific island.
Loosely cemented service farce full of
fumbling lieutenants and bumbling
commanders, a more light-hearted *M*A*S*H*.
Boring romantic interludes separate some very
funny farcical sequences.
w Dorothy Kingsley, George Wells, *novel*
William Brinkley *d* Charles Walters
ph Robert Bronner *m* Bronislau Kaper
Glenn Ford, Fred Clark, Gia Scala, Romney
Brent, Mickey Shaughnessey, Earl Holliman,
Anne Francis, Keenan Wynn, Eva Gabor,
Russ Tamblyn, Jeff Richards, Mary Wickes

Don't Just Stand There
US 1967 99m Techniscope
Universal (Stan Margulies)

A mild-mannered watch smuggler gets himself
involved with kidnapping, murder, and
finishing a sex novel.
Frantic but ineffective farce which keeps on
the move but does not arrive anywhere.
w Charles Williams, from his novel The
Wrong Venus *d* Ron Winston *ph* Milton
Krasner *m* Nick Perito
Mary Tyler Moore, Robert Wagner, *Barbara
Rhoades*, Glynis Johns, Harvey Korman
'Paris locations might have helped, but
we're stuck with the San Fernando Valley.'—
Robert Windeler

Don't Look Now°°°
GB 1973 110m Technicolor
BL / Casey / Eldorado (Peter Katz)

After the death of their small daughter, the
Baxters meet in Venice two old sisters who
claim mediumistic connection with the dead
girl. The husband scorns the idea, but
repeatedly sees a little red-coated figure in
shadowy passages by the canals. When he
confronts it, it proves to be a maniac dwarf
who stabs him to death.
A macabre short story has become a
pretentious and puzzling piece of high cinema
art full of vague suggestions and unexplored
avenues. Whatever its overall deficiencies, it is
too brilliant in surface detail to be dismissed.
Depressingly but fascinatingly set in wintry
Venice, it has to be seen to be appreciated.
w Allan Scott, Chris Bryant, *story* Daphne du
Maurier *d* Nicolas Roeg *ph* Anthony
Richmond *m* Pino D'Onnagio *ad* Giovanni
Soccol
Donald Sutherland, Julie Christie, Hilary
Mason, Clelia Matania, Massimo Serrato
'The fanciest, most carefully assembled
enigma yet seen on the screen.'—*New Yorker*
'A powerful and dazzling visual texture.'—
Penelope Houston

Don't Look Now . . . We're Being Shot At!°
France 1966 130m Eastmancolor
Panavision
Les Films Corona (Robert Dorfmann)
original title: *La Grande Vadrouille*

During World War II three members of a
British bomber crew bale out over Paris and
make a frantic escape to the free zone by
means of various wild disguises.
Freewheeling star farce, a shade lacking in
control, but with some funny sequences.
wd Gérard Oury *ph* Claude Renoir
m Georges Auric
Terry-Thomas, Bourvil, Louis de Funès,
Claudio Brook, Mike Marshall
'Both the sight gags and the characters
evoke pale echoes of Laurel and Hardy, but it
is not familiarity that breeds contempt here so
much as the debasement of the familiar.'—
MFB

Don't Make Waves
US 1967 97m Metrocolor Panavision
MGM / Filmways (Julian Bercovici)

A swimming-pool salesman attempts to get his
own back on an impulsive young woman who
has wrecked his car.
Malibu beach farce for immature adults, made
by professionals helpless in the face of a weak
script, but boasting a funny climax with a
house teetering on the edge of a cliff.

w Ira Wallach, George Kirgo, *novel* Muscle
Beach by Ira Wallach *d* Alexander
Mackendrick *ph* Philip Lathrop *m* Vic Mizzy

Tony Curtis, Claudia Cardinale, Robert
Webber, Joanna Barnes, Sharon Tate, Jim
Backus, Mort Sahl

Don't Raise the Bridge, Lower the River
GB 1967 100m Technicolor
Columbia / Walter Shenson

An American turns his English wife's home
into a discotheque.
Dreary comedy apparently intent on proving
that its star can be just as unfunny abroad as
at home.

w Max Wilk *d* Jerry Paris *ph* Otto Heller
m David Whitaker

Jerry Lewis, Terry-Thomas, Jacqueline
Pearce, Bernard Cribbins, Patricia Routledge,
Nicholas Parsons, Michael Bates

Don't Take it to Heart*
GB 1944 90m bw
GFD / Two Cities (Sydney Box)

A genial castle ghost is unleashed by a bomb
and affects the love affair of a researcher with
the daughter of the house.
Amiably lunatic British-upper-class
extravaganza with eccentric characters and
some felicitous moments.

wd Jeffrey Dell *ph* Eric Cross

Richard Greene, *Edward Rigby*, Patricia
Medina, Alfred Drayton, Richard Bird, Wylie
Watson, Moore Marriott, Brefni O'Rourke,
Amy Veness, Claude Dampier, Joan Hickson,
Joyce Barbour, Ronald Squire, Ernest
Thesiger
  'A cheerful and rewarding entertainment.'—
Richard Mallett, Punch

The Doolins of Oklahoma
US 1949 90m bw

When his old gang claims his return to
lawlessness, Bill Doolin walks into the sheriff's
guns rather than cause his wife unhappiness.
Moderate western with an unusually less-than-
sympathetic role for its star. Randolph Scott,
George Macready, Louise Allbritton, John
Ireland, Noah Beery Jnr, Dona Drake.
Written by Kenneth Gamet; directed by
Gordon Douglas; for Harry Joe Brown /
  Columbia. (GB title: *The Great Manhunt*.)

Doomwatch
GB 1972 92m colour
Tigon (Tony Tenser)

An investigator of coastal pollution discovers a
village in which dumped chemicals have given
all the inhabitants a distorting disease called
acromegaly.
An unsatisfactory horror film is drawn from a
moderately serious TV series about ecology.

w Clive Exton *d* Peter Sasdy *ph* Kenneth
Talbot *m* John Scott

Ian Bannen, Judy Geeson, John Paul, Simon
Oates, George Sanders, Percy Herbert,
Geoffrey Keen, Joseph O'Conor

The Door in the Wall*
GB 1956 29m Technicolor Vistavision
AB Pathé / BFI / Lawrie (Howard Thomas)

A man is obsessed by a childhood dream of a
green door which leads into a beautiful
garden.
The story is chosen to experiment with
Dynamic Frame, a system in which the picture
changes shape and size according to the
subject matter. In this case the results are
entertaining enough.

wd Glenn H. Alvey Jnr *ph* Jo Jago *m* James
Bernard

Stephen Murray, Ian Hunter

The Door with Seven Locks
GB 1940 89m bw
Rialto (John Argyle)
US title: *Chamber of Horrors*

A mad doctor abducts an heiress in the hope
of gaining her wealth.
Old-fashioned barnstormer, ineptly made.

w Norman Lee, John Argyle, Gilbert Gunn,
novel Edgar Wallace *d* Norman Lee

Leslie Banks, Lilli Palmer, Romilly Lunge,
Gina Malo, Richard Bird, David Horne,
Cathleen Nesbitt

Dosshouse*
GB 1933 53m bw
Sound City (John Baxter)

An escaped convict is captured by a reporter
and detective posing as tramps.
Low-budget featurette which deserves a
footnote in film history for its social
consciousness, rare at the time, especially in
the dosshouse scenes.

w Herbert Ayres *d* John Baxter

Frank Cellier, Arnold Bell, Herbert Franklyn,
J. Hubert Leslie

Double Confession
GB 1950 85m bw
ABP / Harry Reynolds

At a seaside resort, a man finds his wife dead and tries to frame her lover, but becomes confused with two real murderers with a different purpose.

Confused and unlikely melodrama which signally lacks the ancient mariner's eye.

w William Templeton, *novel* All on a Summer's Day by John Garden *d* Ken Annakin *ph* Geoffrey Unsworth *m* Benjamin Franklin

Derek Farr, Peter Lorre, William Hartnell, Joan Hopkins, Naunton Wayne, Ronald Howard, Kathleen Harrison, Leslie Dwyer, Edward Rigby

Double Crossbones
US 1950 75m Technicolor

Circumstances force our hero to assume the identity of a pirate, in which disguise he rescues a fair lady. Lamebrained burlesque unworthy of its star. Donald O'Connor, Helena Carter, Will Geer, John Emery, Hope Emerson, Charles McGraw, Alan Napier. Written by Oscar Brodney; directed by Charles R. Barton; for Universal-International.

Double Dynamite
US 1951 (produced 1948) 80m bw
RKO (Irving Cummings)
aka: *It's Only Money*

A bank teller wins a fortune at the race track but is afraid his winnings will be thought the proceeds of a bank robbery.

Insultingly mild comedy, nearly saved by a few quips from Groucho.

w Melville Shavelson, Harry Crane, Leo Rosten *d* Irving Cummings *ph* Robert de Grasse *m* Leigh Harline

Frank Sinatra, Jane Russell, Groucho Marx, Don McGuire, Howard Freeman

Double Indemnity: see River's End

Double Indemnity****
US 1944 107m bw
Paramount (Joseph Sistrom)

An insurance agent connives with the glamorous wife of a client to kill her husband and collect.

Archetypal *film noir* of the forties, brilliantly filmed and incisively written, perfectly capturing the decayed Los Angeles atmosphere of a Chandler novel but using a simpler story and more substantial characters. The hero / villain was almost a new concept.

w Billy Wilder, Raymond Chandler, *novel James M. Cain d Billy Wilder ph John Seitz m Miklos Rozsa*

Fred MacMurray, Barbara Stanwyck, Edward G. Robinson, Tom Powers, Porter Hall, Jean Heather, Byron Barr, Richard Gaines

'The sort of film which revives a critic from the depressive effects of bright epics about the big soul of America or the suffering soul of Europe and gives him a new lease of faith.'— *Richard Winnington*

'Masturbation fantasy triple distilled.'— *James Agee*

'The most pared-down and purposeful film ever made by Billy Wilder.'—*John Coleman, 1966*

'Profoundly, intensely entertaining,'— *Richard Mallett, Punch*

'One of the highest summits of *film noir . . .* without a single trace of pity or love.'— *Charles Higham, 1971*

AAN: best picture; script; direction; John Seitz; Miklos Rozsa; Barbara Stanwyck

A Double Life**
US 1947 103m bw
Kanin Productions

An actor playing Othello is obsessed by the role and murders a woman he imagines to be Desdemona.

An old theatrical chestnut (cf *Men Are Not Gods*) is decked out with smartish backstage dialogue but despite a pleasant star performance remains unrewarding if taxing, and the entertainment value of the piece is on the thin side considering the mighty talents involved

w Ruth Gordon, Garson Kanin *d* George Cukor *ph* Milton Krasner *m* Miklos Rozsa

Ronald Colman, Shelley Winters, Signe Hasso, Edmond O'Brien, Millard Mitchell

AA: Miklos Rozsa; Ronald Colman
AAN: Ruth Gordon, Garson Kanin; George Cukor

The Double Man*
GB 1968 105m Technicolor
Warner / Hal E. Chester

A CIA agent investigates the death of his son on a Swiss skiing holiday and finds the murder was a lure to get him there so that an enemy lookalike can substitute for him.

Rather ruthless but good-looking and generally watchable spy melodrama.

w Frank Tarloff, Alfred Hayes, *novel* Henry S. Maxfield *d* Franklin Schaffner *ph* Denys Coop

Yul Brynner, Clive Revill, Anton Diffring, Britt Ekland, Moira Lister

Double Negative
Canada 1980 96m colour

A photo journalist tries to find the murderer of his wife, and discovers he's an amnesiac and did it himself. Ho-hum mystery thriller centring on an ancient wheeze; treatment resolutely plodding. Michael Sarrazin, Susan Clark, Anthony Perkins, Howard Duff, Kate Reid. Written by Thomas Hedley Jnr, Janis Allen and Charles Dennis, from *The Three Roads* by Ross Macdonald; directed by George Bloomfield; for Quadrant.

Double Wedding
US 1937 87m bw
MGM (Joseph L. Mankiewicz)

A bohemian artist makes a play for the lady of his choice by romancing her sister.
Zany star comedy which doesn't quite come off.

w Jo Swerling, *play* Great Love by Ferenc Molnar *d* Richard Thorpe *ph* William Daniels *m* Edward Ward

William Powell, Myrna Loy, John Beal, Florence Rice, Jessie Ralph, Edgar Kennedy, Sidney Toler, Barnett Parker, Katherine Alexander, Donald Meek

Double Whoopee**
US 1928 20m bw silent

Incompetent doormen at a swank hotel cause havoc. Simple-minded but pleasing star farce. Laurel and Hardy, Jean Harlow, Charlie Hall. Written by Leo McCarey and H. M. Walker; directed by Lewis R. Foster; for Hal Roach.

Douce*
France 1943 106m bw
Société Parisienne de l'Industrie Cinématographique

In 1887 Paris a sheltered young rich girl falls for a steward and encounters family opposition.
A charming old-fashioned story which provides a well-taken opportunity for a portrait of the old bourgeoisie.

w Jean Aurenche, Pierre Bost *d* Claude Autant-Lara *ph* Gaston Thonnart *m* René Cloërc

Odette Joyeux, Jean Debucourt, Marguerite Moreno, Roger Pigaut, Madeleine Robinson
'Direction and camerawork constantly reveal touches of felicity.'—*MFB*

Doughboys*
US 1930 80m approx bw
MGM / Buster Keaton (Lawrence Weingarten)
GB title: *Forward March*

A young eccentric joins the army.
Simple-minded farce with a few good routines for the star.

w Richard Schayer *d* Edward Sedgwick *ph* Leonard Smith

Buster Keaton, Sally Eilers, Cliff Edwards, Edward Brophy

The Doughgirls*
US 1944 102m bw
Warner (Mark Hellinger)

In a crowded wartime Washington hotel, a honeymoon is frustrated by constant interruption, not to mention the discovery that the wedding was not legal.
Frantic farce, generally well adapted, and certainly played with gusto.

w James V. Kern, Sam Hellman, *play* Joseph Fields *d* James V. Kern *ph* Ernest Haller *m* Adolph Deutsch

Alexis Smith, Jane Wyman, Jack Carson, Ann Sheridan, Irene Manning, *Eve Arden*, Charlie Ruggles, John Alexander, John Ridgely, Craig Stevens, Alan Mowbray, Donald MacBride
'There's nothing so good in it that you must attend, just as there is nothing bad enough to keep you away.'—*Archer Winsten*

The Dove*
US 1974 104m Technicolor Panavision
St George Productions (Gregory Peck)

Yachtsman Robin Lee Graham makes a five-year voyage around the world.
Bland, rather stolid adventure story for boatniks, based on real incidents; good to look at.

w Peter Beagle, Adam Kennedy *d* Charles Jarrott *ph* Sven Nykvist *m* John Barry

Joseph Bottoms, Deborah Raffin, John McLiam, Dabney Coleman
'Postcard views flick by to the strains of a saccharine score.'—*David McGillivray*

Down Argentine Way*
US 1940 94m Technicolor
TCF (Harry Joe Brown)

A wealthy American girl falls in love with an Argentinian horse-breeder.
A very moderate musical which happened to bring both Grable and Miranda to star stature and set Fox off on their successful run of forties extravaganzas, reasonably pleasant to look at but empty-headed.

w Karl Tunberg, Darrell Ware *d* Irving Cummings *ph* Ray Rennahan, Leon Shamroy *songs* Harry Warren, Mack Gordon

Betty Grable, Carmen Miranda, Don Ameche, Charlotte Greenwood, J. Carrol Naish, Henry Stephenson, Leonid Kinskey, The Nicholas Brothers

'I dislike Technicolor in which all pinks resemble raspberry sauce, reds turn to sealing wax, blues shriek of the washtub, and yellows become suet pudding.'—*James Agate*

'So outrageous—that it's hard to believe it isn't at least partly intentional—but why would anybody make this picture on purpose.'—*New Yorker, 1976*

AAN: Ray Rennahan, Leon Shamroy; title song (*m* Harry Warren, *ly* Mack Gordon)

Down Three Dark Streets*
US 1954   85m   bw
UA / Edward Small (Arthur Gardner, Jules V. Levy)

An FBI agent is shot on duty, and his friend avenges him in the course of clearing up three cases in which he was involved.
Competent, enjoyable police film with three cases for the price of one.

w The Gordons, Bernard C. Schoenfeld, *book* Case File FBI by the Gordons *d* Arnold Laven *ph* Joseph Biroc *m* Paul Sawtell

Broderick Crawford, Ruth Roman, Martha Hyer, Marisa Pavan, Casey Adams, Kenneth Tobey
† One of the first collaborations of the prolific production company Laven-Gardner-Levy.

Down to Earth*
US 1947   101m   Technicolor
Columbia (Don Hartman)

The muse Terpsichore comes down to help a Broadway producer fix a new show in which she is featured.
Pleasant but undistinguished musical fantasy, a sequel to *Here Comes Mr Jordan*. The heavenly sequences promise more amusement than they produce.

w Edwin Blum, Don Hartman *d* Alexander Hall *ph* Rudolph Maté *m* Heinz Roemheld

Rita Hayworth, Larry Parks, Roland Culver (as Mr Jordan), *Edward Everett Horton* (repeating as Messenger 7013), Marc Platt, James Gleason

'Just the film to make the spectator forget the troubles of life.'—*MFB*

'Celestial whimsy musical, with arch acting and a dull score.'—*New Yorker, 1977*

Down to the Sea in Ships*
US 1948   120m   bw
TCF

An old whaling skipper wants his grandson to follow in his footsteps.

Seagoing spectacle with strong characters; all concerned show Hollywood in its most professional form, but the film somehow fails to catch the imagination or live in the memory.

w John Lee Mahin, Sy Bartlett *d* Henry Hathaway *ph* Joe MacDonald *m* Alfred Newman

Lionel Barrymore, Dean Stockwell, Richard Widmark, Cecil Kellaway, Gene Lockhart

Downhill
GB 1927   80m approx (24 fps)   bw silent
Gainsborough (Michael Balcon)
US title: *When Boys Leave Home*

A sixth-form schoolboy, accused of theft, is expelled and goes to the bad in Marseilles before being found innocent.
Absurd novelette with only marginal glimpses of the director's emerging talent.

w Eliot Stannard, *play* Ivor Novello and Constance Collier *d* Alfred Hitchcock *ph* Claude McDonnell *ed* Ivor Montagu

Ivor Novello, Ben Webster, Robin Irvine, Sybil Rhoda, Lillian Braithwaite, Isabel Jeans, Ian Hunter

Downhill Racer*
US 1969   101m   Technicolor
Paramount / Wildwood (Richard Gregson)

An ambitious American skier gains a place on the team competing in Europe.
Virtually plotless, casually assembled study of a man and a sport, good to look at, often exciting, but just as frequently irritating in its throwaway style.

w James Salter, *novel* Oakley Hall *d* Michael Ritchie *ph* Brian Probyn *m* Kenyon Hopkins

Robert Redford, Gene Hackman, Camilla Sparv, Joe Jay Jalbert, Timothy Kirk, Dabney Coleman

Downstairs*
US 1932   84m   bw

Life below stairs: a butler clashes with a chauffeur over the love of a maid. Surprisingly sharp little drama from a story by the star.
John Gilbert, Paul Lukas, Virginia Bruce, Hedda Hopper, Reginald Owen. Written by Lenore Coffee and Melville Baker; directed by Monta Bell; for MGM.

Dracula***
US 1931   84m   bw
Universal (Carl Laemmle Jnr)

A Transylvanian vampire count gets his come-uppance in Yorkshire.

A film which has much to answer for. It started its star and its studio off on horror careers, and it launched innumerable sequels (see below). In itself, after two eerie reels, it becomes a pedantic and slow transcription of a stage adaptation, and its climax takes place offscreen; but for all kinds of reasons it remains full of interest.

w Garrett Fort, *play* Hamilton Deane, John Balderston, *novel Bram Stoker d* Tod Browning *ph* Karl Freund *m* Tchaikovsky

Bela Lugosi, Helen Chandler, David Manners, Dwight Frye, Edward Van Sloan

'A too literal adaptation of the play (*not* the book) results in a plodding, talkative development, with much of the vital action taking place off-screen.'—*William K. Everson*

'The mistiest parts are the best; when the lights go up the interest goes down.'—*Ivan Butler*

'The strangest love a man has ever known!'— *publicity*

† Sequels include *Dracula's Daughter* (qv), *Son of Dracula* (qv); the later Hammer sequence consists of *Dracula* (see below), *Brides of Dracula* (qv), *Dracula Prince of Darkness* (qv), *Dracula Has Risen From the Grave* (qv), *Taste the Blood of Dracula* (qv), *Scars of Dracula* (qv), *Dracula AD 1972* (qv), *The Satanic Rites of Dracula* (qv). Other associated films in which the Count or a disciple appears include (all qv) *Return of the Vampire* (1944), *House of Frankenstein* (1945), *House of Dracula* (1945), *Abbott and Costello Meet Frankenstein* (1948), *The Return of Dracula* (1958), *Kiss of the Vampire* (1963), *The Fearless Vampire Killers* (1967), *Count Yorga Vampire* (1969), *Countess Dracula* (1970), *Vampire Circus* (1970), *The House of Dark Shadows* (1970), *Vampire Lovers* (1971), *Blacula* (1972). Minor potboilers are legion.

Dracula***
GB 1958   82m   Technicolor
Hammer (Anthony Hinds)
US title: *Horror of Dracula*

A remake of the 1930 film. Commendably brief in comparison with the later Hammer films, this was perhaps the best horror piece they turned out as well as the most faithful to its original. Decor and colour were well used, and the leading performances are striking.

w Jimmy Sangster d Terence Fisher ph Jack Asher m James Bernard ad Bernard Robinson

Peter Cushing (as Van Helsing), *Christopher Lee* (as Dracula), Melissa Stribling, Carol

Marsh, Michael Gough, John Van Eyssen, Valerie Gaunt, Miles Malleson

Dracula*
GB 1979   112m   Technicolor
Panavision
Universal / Mirisch (Marvin Mirisch / Tom Pevsner)

A lush, expensive and romantic version which presents the count as a matinée idol and spends too much time on the romantic scenes to distract attention from an old old story.

w W. D. Richter d John Badham ph Gilbert Taylor pd Peter Murton m John Williams

Frank Langella, Laurence Olivier, Donald Pleasence, Kate Nelligan, Trevor Eve

'A triumphantly lurid creation that seems bound to be either under-valued for its circus effects or over-valued for the stylishness with which it steers between the reefs of camp and theatrical indulgence.'—*Richard Combs, MFB*

Dracula AD 1972
GB 1972   95m   Eastmancolor
Warner / Hammer (Josephine Douglas)

Dracula reappears among Chelsea teenagers practising black magic.

Depressed attempt to update a myth; the link with modern sin makes it seem not only tarnished but tasteless, and the film itself is lamentably short on excitement.

w Don Houghton d Alan Gibson ph Richard Bush m Michael Vickers

Peter Cushing, Christopher Lee, Stephanie Beacham, Michael Coles, Christopher Neame, William Ellis

Dracula Has Risen from the Grave
GB 1968   92m   Technicolor
Hammer (Aida Young)

Dracula again terrorizes the village in the shadow of his castle, and is routed by a bishop.

Tedious, confined and repetitive shocker with little conventional action and an unusual emphasis on sex.

w John Elder (Anthony Hinds) d Freddie Francis ph Arthur Grant m James Bernard

Christopher Lee, Rupert Davies, Veronica Carlson, Barbara Ewing, Barry Andrews, Ewan Hooper

'A bloody bore.'—*Judith Crist*

Dracula Prince of Darkness
GB 1965   90m   Techniscope
Warner / Hammer (Anthony Nelson Keys)

Stranded travellers are made welcome at the late count's castle by his sinister butler, who proceeds to use the blood of one of them to revivify his master.
Ingenious rehash of incidents from the original story, largely dissipated by poor colour and unsuitable wide screen.

w John Sansom *d* Terence Fisher *ph* Michael Reed *m* James Bernard

Christopher Lee, *Philip Latham*, Barbara Shelley, Thorley Walters, Andrew Keir, Francis Matthews, Suzan Farmer, Charles Tingwell
'Run-of-the-coffin stuff . . . only for ardent fang-and-cross fans.'—*Judith Crist*

Dracula's Daughter**
US 1936 70m bw
Universal

The daughter of the old count follows his remains to London.
Lively sequel which develops in the manner of a Sherlock Holmes story.

w Garrett Fort *d* Lambert Hillyer *ph* George Robinson *m* Heinz Roemheld

Otto Kruger, Marguerite Churchill, Edward Van Sloan, Gloria Holden, Irving Pichel, Nan Grey, Hedda Hopper, Gilbert Emery, Claud Allister, E. E. Clive, Halliwell Hobbes, Billy Bevan
'More sensational than her unforgettable father!'—*publicity*

Dracula's Dog
US 1977 88m De Luxe
Vic (Albert Band, Frank Ray Perelli)
GB title: *Zoltan, Hound of Dracula*

The resurrected servant of Dracula tries to use his vampire dog to create a new master.
Ingenious but unattractive addition to the saga, with dogs as chief villains; the style varies between spoof and rather nasty horror.

w Frank Ray Perelli *d* Albert Band *ph* Bruce Logan *m* Andrew Belling

Jose Ferrer, Reggie Malder, Michael Pataki, Jan Shutan

Dragnet*
US 1954 93m Warnercolor
Mark VII (Jack Webb)

Sgt Joe Friday solves the murder of an ex-convict.
Moderately interesting but overlong attempt to transfer television techniques to the big screen; laconic dialogue, question and answer, cheap sets, close-ups and convenient Los Angeles locations.

w Richard Breen *d Jack Webb ph* Edward Colman

Jack Webb, Ben Alexander, Richard Boone, Stacy Harris, Ann Robinson, Virginia Gregg

Dragon Seed*
US 1944 144m bw
MGM (Pandro S. Berman)

Chinese peasants fight the Japs.
Ill-advised attempt to follow the success of *The Good Earth*; badly cast actors mouth propaganda lines in a mechanical script which provokes more boredom and unintentional laughter than sympathy.

w Marguerite Roberts, Jane Murfin, *novel* Pearl S. Buck *d* Jack Conway, Harold S. Bucquet *ph* Sidney Wagner *m* Herbert Stothart

Katharine Hepburn, Walter Huston, Turhan Bey, Aline MacMahon, Akim Tamiroff, Hurd Hatfield, Frances Rafferty, Agnes Moorehead, Henry Travers, J. Carrol Naish
'A kind of slant-eyed *North Star*. Often awkward and pretentious, it nevertheless has moments of moral and dramatic grandeur.'—*Time*

AAN: Sidney Wagner; Aline MacMahon

Dragonwyck*
US 1946 103m bw
TCF (Darryl F. Zanuck)

In the 1840s a farmer's daughter marries her rich cousin, not knowing that he has poisoned his first wife.
Good-looking but rather tedious romance of the Jane Eyre / Rebecca school: tyrannical recluse, mystery upstairs, spooky house, etc. Heavy going.

w Joseph L. Mankiewicz, *novel* Anya Seton *d* Joseph L. Mankiewicz *ph Arthur Miller m* Alfred Newman

Gene Tierney, Vincent Price, Glenn Langan, Walter Huston, Anne Revere, Spring Byington, Henry Morgan, Jessica Tandy

Drake of England
GB 1935 104m bw
Wardour (Walter C. Mycroft)
US titles: *Drake the Pirate; Elizabeth of England*

Sir Francis Drake is knighted by Queen Elizabeth for his seafaring exploits, and defeats the Spanish Armada.
Stiffly moving historical pageant; you can smell the mothballs.

w Clifford Grey, Akos Tolney, Marjorie Deans, Norman Watson *d* Arthur Woods *ph* Claude Friese-Greene

Matheson Lang, Athene Seyler, Jane Baxter, Donald Wolfit, Henry Mollison, George Merritt, Amy Veness, Sam Livesey, Ben Webster

Dramatic School*
US 1938 80m bw
MGM (Mervyn Le Roy)

Young actresses compete for success.
Another, less lively, *Stage Door*; tolerable but not exciting.

w Ernst Vajda, Mary McCall Jnr, *play* School of Drama by Hans Szekely, Zoltan Egyed d Robert B. Sinclair Jnr ph William Daniels m Franz Waxman

Luise Rainer, Paulette Goddard, Alan Marshal, Lana Turner, Anthony Allan (later John Hubbard), Henry Stephenson, Genevieve Tobin, Gale Sondergaard, Melville Cooper, Erik Rhodes, Ann Rutherford, Margaret Dumont, Virginia Grey, Hans Conried

Drango
US 1957 92m bw
UA / Hall Bartlett

After the Civil War, a Union Army officer is assigned to bring law and order to a Georgia community.
Eccentric, downbeat semi-western with aspirations to be some kind of *film noir*; does not come off.

wd Hall Bartlett ph *James Wong Howe* m Elmer Bernstein

Jeff Chandler, Ronald Howard, Joanne Dru, Julie London, Donald Crisp, John Lupton, Morris Ankrum

Dream Girl
US 1947 86m bw
Paramount (P. J. Wolfson)

A girl revels in her own romantic dreams, one of which nearly comes true.
Potentially pleasant comedy about a female Walter Mitty does not work because the director has run out of ideas, the star is miscast and Hollywood has insisted on making the girl rich to begin with, which robs the dreams of any point.

w Arthur Sheekman, *play* Elmer Rice d Mitchell Leisen ph Daniel L. Fapp m Victor Young

Betty Hutton, Macdonald Carey, Walter Abel, Patric Knowles, Virginia Field, Peggy Wood, Lowell Gilmore

A Dream of Kings
US 1969 110m Technicolor
National General (Jules Schermer)

Episodes in the life of an improvident, lusty, poetical Chicago Greek with a dying son.
The part screamed for Anthony Quinn and got him, with the result that it has all been seen before, too frequently. Well made, with strong appeal to Chicago Greeks.

w Harry Mark Patrakis, Ian Hunter, *novel* Harry Mark Patrakis d Daniel Mann ph Richard H. Kline m Alex North

Anthony Quinn, Irene Papas, Inger Stevens, Sam Levene, Val Avery, Tamara Daykarhanova

A Dream of Passion
Greece 1978 110m Eastmancolor
Branfilm / Melinafilm (Jules Dassin)

A woman who, Medea-like, has killed her children is drawn into an eccentric relationship with an actress playing Medea on the stage.
Weird and ineffective character drama which badly needs discipline.

wd Jules Dassin ph George Arvanitis m Ionnis Markopoulos

Melina Mercouri, Ellen Burstyn, Andreas Voutsinas, Despo Diamantidou

Dream Street*
US 1921 89m (at 24 fps) bw silent
D. W. Griffith Inc

Three Limehouse folk, torn between good and evil, act out their dreams.
Trilogy of moral tales, fancifully and often charmingly assembled by the master director who often reminds one of a Victorian lace maker.

wd D. W. Griffith, from stories by Thomas Burke ph Henrik Sartov

Carol Dempster, Ralph Graves, Charles Emmett Mack, Edwart Peil, Tyrone Power Snr, W. J. Ferguson

Dream Wife
US 1953 99m bw
MGM (Dore Schary)

An executive leaves his ambitious wife for a sheik's daughter schooled in the art of pleasing men, but naturally finds drawbacks.
Very moderate comedy with strained situations and few laughs. The stars work hard.

w Sidney Sheldon, Herbert Baker, Alfred L. Levitt d Sidney Sheldon ph Milton Krasner m Conrad Salinger

Cary Grant, Deborah Kerr, Walter Pidgeon, Betta St John, Eduard Franz, Buddy Baer, Les Temayne

Dreamboat*
US 1952 83m bw
TCF (Sol C. Siegel)

A romantic star of the silent film era is embarrassed when his old movies turn up on television.

Hollywood rather blunderingly makes fun of its arch enemy in this sometimes sprightly but often disappointing comedy which should have been a bulls-eye.

wd Claude Binyon *ph* Milton Krasner *m* Cyril Mockridge

Clifton Webb, Ginger Rogers, Anne Francis, Jeffrey Hunter, Elsa Lanchester, Fred Clark, Ray Collins, Paul Harvey

Dreaming Lips*
GB 1937 94m bw
Trafalgar (Paul Czinner)

The wife of an invalid musician has an affair with another man and commits suicide.
Standard star fare, possibly Miss Bergner's most notable film, also available in a German version.

w Margaret Kennedy, Lady Cynthia Asquith, Carl Mayer, *play* Henry Bernstein *d* Paul Czinner, Lee Garmes *ph* Lee Garmes *m* William Walton

Elisabeth Bergner, Romney Brent, Raymond Massey, Joyce Bland, Sydney Fairbrother, Felix Aylmer, Donald Calthrop

Dreams That Money Can Buy*
US 1946 81m Technicolor
Art of the Century (Hans Richter, Peggy Guggenheim, Kenneth MacPherson)

A young itinerant sells dreams to people who need them.
Semi-underground surrealist film, momentarily of interest, but disjointed and with no real apparent purpose.

wd Hans Richter ph Arnold Eagle *md* Louis Applebaum

† The individual dreams are directed by Max Ernst, Man Ray, Fernand Leger, Marcel Duchamp and Alexander Calder as well as Richter.
'Arch, snobbish and sycophantic, about as genuinely experimental as a Chemcraft set.'— *James Agee*

Dreaming
GB 1944 78m bw

A soldier on leave gets a bump on the head, and dreams . . . Rather elementary series of sketches with a few good laughs and interesting guest appearances. Flanagan and Allen, Hazel Court, Dick Francis, Philip Wade, Teddy Brown, Reginald Foort, Gordon Richards, Alfredo Campoli. Written by Bud Flanagan and Reginald Purdell; directed by John Baxter; for Ealing.

Drei von der Tankstelle*
Germany 1930 80m bw
UFA

Three penniless young men find happiness as petrol station attendants.
Light-hearted operetta of the Depression era, well received at the time.

w Franz Schultz, Paul Frank *d William Thiele ph* Franz Planer *m* Werner Heymann

Willy Fritsch, Lilian Harvey, Oskar Karlweis, Heinz Ruhmann, Olga Tchekhova
† Remade 1955 by Hans Wolff, with a cast still led by Willy Fritsch.

Die Dreigroschenoper**
Germany 1931 114m bw
Warner / Tobis / Nero
US title: *The Threepenny Opera*

In turn-of-the-century London, Mack the Knife marries the daughter of the beggar king and runs into trouble.
Heavy-footed but interesting updating of *The Beggar's Opera*, with splendid sets.

w Bela Balazs, Leo Lania, Ladislas Vajda, from Bertolt Brecht's version *d G. W. Pabst ph* Fritz Arno Wagner *m* Kurt Weill *ad Andrei Andreiev*

Lotte Lenya, Rudolf Forster, Fritz Rasp, Caroline Neher, Reinhold Schunzel, Valeska Gert, Vladimir Sokoloff
† Brecht disliked the film and sued the makers, but lost.
†† A French version was also released under the title *L'Opéra de Quat'sous*, with Albert Préjean.

Dressed to Kill**
US 1980 105m Technicolor
Filmways / Samuel Z. Arkoff / Cinema 77 (George Litto)

A sexually disturbed matron under analysis is murdered by a transvestite slasher, who then goes after a witness.
Occasionally brilliant, generally nasty suspenser clearly derived from many viewings of *Psycho*. Certainly not for the squeamish.

wd Brian de Palma ph Ralf Bode *m* Pino Donaggio *pd* Gary Weist

Michael Caine, Angie Dickinson, Nancy Allen, Keith Gordon, Dennis Franz

'De Palma goes right for the audience jugular . . . it fully milks the boundaries of its "R" rating.'—*Variety*

Dreyfus°
GB 1931   90m   bw
Wardour (F. W. Kraemer)

In 1894 France, a Jewish officer is accused of spying.
Primitive version of a much-filmed story (cf *The Life of Emile Zola, I Accuse*).

w Rehfisch Herzog, Reginald Berkeley, Walter C. Mycroft   *d* F. W. Kraemer, Milton Rosmer   *ph* Willy Minterstein

Cedric Hardwicke, George Merritt (as Zola), Charles Carson, Sam Livesey, Garry Marsh (as Esterhazy), Randle Ayrton, George Zucco

Drifters°
GB 1929   40m approx   bw
Empire Marketing Board

A documentary of the North Sea fishing fleet.
A highly influential documentary, made at a time when British films were totally unrealistic and studio-bound. Unfortunately it now seems extremely dull.

wd, ed John Grierson   *ph* Basil Emmott

Driftwood
US 1947   90m   bw

An orphan is adopted by a kindly doctor.
Lavender-scented family yarn with pleasant backgrounds and expert performances. Natalie Wood, Ruth Warrick, Walter Brennan, Dean Jagger, Charlotte Greenwood. Written by Mary Loos and Richard Sale; directed by Allan Dwan; for Republic.

Drive a Crooked Road
US 1954   82m   bw
Columbia (Jonie Taps)

A garage mechanic falls in with bank robbers.
Terse crime melodrama, quite watchable.

w Blake Edwards   *d* Richard Quine
ph Charles Lawton Jnr   *md* Ross di Maggio

Mickey Rooney, Kevin McCarthy, Dianne Foster

Drive He Said
US 1970   90m   colour
Columbia / Drive Productions / BBS (Steve Blauner)

An easygoing college basketball star is helped by an eccentric rebel to ensure his own

unfitness for military service. Both run into trouble.
Flabby celebration of against-the-government attitudes, expressed partly through sex and bad language. Defiantly hard to like.

w Jeremy Larner, Jack Nicholson   *d* Jack Nicholson   *ph* Bill Butler   *m* David Shire

Michael Margotta, William Tepper, Bruce Dern, Karen Black, Robert Towne, Henry Jaglom

The Driver°
US 1978   91m   De Luxe
TCF / EMI / Lawrence Gordon

A detective determines to catch an old enemy, a getaway driver.
Noisy melodrama, very proficient in the screeching tyre department but extremely empty as a character.

wd Walter Hill   *ph* Philip Lathrop   *m* Michael Small

Ryan O'Neal, Bruce Dern, Isabelle Adjani, Ronee Blakeley

Drôle de Drame°
France 1936   100m approx   bw

A complicated chain of bizarre events is set in motion when a botanist pretends not to be a detective story writer, a bishop tries to be a detective, and a murderer seeks revenge for libel.
A curious satirical comedy which is never quite as funny as it seems about to be, but should be seen for its downright peculiar London sets and its array of actors in top form.

w Jacques Prévert, *novel* The Lunatic at Large by J. Storer Clouston   *d* Marcel Carné

Françoise Rosay, Michel Simon, Louis Jouvet, Jean-Louis Barrault, Jean-Pierre Aumont

'No one with any taste for nonsense should miss it.'—*Richard Mallett, Punch*

Drop Dead Darling
GB 1966   100m   Technicolor Panavision
Seven Arts (Ken Hughes)
US title: *Arrivederci Baby*

A con man who marries and murders rich women meets a con lady with similar intentions.
Loud, restless black comedy which squanders its moments of genuine inventiveness among scenes of shouting, confusion and action for action's sake.

wd Ken Hughes, *story* The Careful Man by Richard Deeming   *ph* Denys Coop   *m* Dennis Farnon

Tony Curtis, Rosanna Schiaffino, Lionel Jeffries, Zsa Zsa Gabor, Nancy Kwan, Fenella Fielding, Anna Quayle, Warren Mitchell, Mischa Auer

The Drowning Pool
US 1975 108m Technicolor Panavision
Warner / Coleytown (Lawrence Turman, David Foster)

Private eye Lew Harper goes to New Orleans to investigate an anonymous letter which ends in murder.
Dreary sequel to *Harper* (qv), full of boring characters uninventively deployed.

w Tracy Keenan Wynn, Lorenzo Semple Jnr, Walter Hill, *novel* John Ross MacDonald *d* Stuart Rosenberg *ph* Gordon Willis *m* Michael Small

Paul Newman, Joanne Woodward, Coral Browne, Tony Franciosa, Murray Hamilton, Gail Strickland, Linda Hayes, Richard Jaeckel

'The impenetrable mystery is not particularly gripping; and the general air of pointlessness is only intensified by the sudden rush of clarifications at the end.'—*Tom Milne*
'It recycles every private eye cliché known to civilized man as it crawls through Louisiana talking all the way.'—*Paul D. Zimmermann*
'All the clichés of cheapjack TV private eye capers have been added to MacDonald's book; whatever separates him from the paperback hacks has been deleted.'—*Judith Crist*

The Drum°
GB 1938 96m Technicolor
London Films (Alexander Korda)
US title: *Drums*

The British army helps an Indian prince to resist his usurping uncle.
Reasonably entertaining story of the Raj, with adequate excitement after a meandering start.

w Lajos Biro, Arthur Wimperis, Patrick Kirwan, Hugh Gray, *novel* A. E. W. Mason *d* Zoltan Korda *ph* Georges Périnal *m* John Greenwood, Miklos Rozsa

Sabu, Roger Livesey, Raymond Massey, Valerie Hobson, Desmond Tester, David Tree, Francis L. Sullivan, Roy Emerton, Edward Lexy

Drum
US 1976 100m Metrocolor Panavision
Dino de Laurentiis (Ralph Serpe)

In 1860 New Orleans, a bordello house slave faces all manner of sexual predators.
Tediously single-minded sequel to the appalling *Mandingo*.

w Norman Wexler, *novel* Kyle Onstott *d* Steve Carver *ph* Lucien Ballard *m* Charles Smalls

Warren Oates, Ken Norton, Isela Vega, Yaphet Kotto, John Colicos

'Shamelessly it exploits the factors which explain the success of the prototype: a feeble pretence at outraged historical exposé of the abuses of the slave trade provides the excuse for an orgy of wish dreams, of sadism, flagellation, domination, sexuality of all tastes, popular fantasies of negro potency.'—*David Robinson, The Times*

Drumbeat
US 1954 111m Warnercolor
Jaguar (no producer credited)

An Indian fighter sets out to make peace with a renegade.
Long, dull western, stolid all round.

wd Delmer Daves *ph* J. Peverell Marley *m* Victor Young

Alan Ladd, Audrey Dalton, Marisa Pavan, Robert Keith, Rodolpho Acosta, Charles Bronson, Warner Anderson, Elisha Cook Jnr, Anthony Caruso

Drums along the Mohawk°°°
US 1939 103m Technicolor
TCF (Raymond Griffith)

Colonists survive Indian attacks in upstate New York during the Revolutionary War.
Patchy, likeable period adventure story with domestic and farming interludes; in its way a key film in the director's canon.

w Lamar Trotti, Sonya Levien, *novel* Walter Edmonds *d* John Ford *ph* Bert Glennon, Ray Rennahan *m* Alfred Newman

Claudette Colbert, Henry Fonda, Edna May Oliver, Eddie Collins, John Carradine, Dorris Bowdon, Jessie Ralph, Arthur Shields, Robert Lowery, Roger Imhof, Ward Bond

AAN: Edna May Oliver

Drums in the Deep South
GB 1951 87m Supercinecolor

A Confederate officer finds himself fighting a lonely battle with his best friend from West Point. Barely stimulating semi-western in appalling colour. James Craig, Barbara Payton, Guy Madison, Barton Maclane, Craig Stevens, Tom Fadden, Taylor Holmes. Written by Philip Yordan and Sidney Harmon; directed by William Cameron Menzies (also production designer); for King Brothers / RKO.

Dry Rot
GB 1956   87m   bw
Romulus (Jack Clayton)

Three bookmakers plot to make a fortune by
substituting a doped horse for the favourite.
Flat filming of a long-running theatrical farce.

w John Chapman, from his play d Maurice
Elvey ph Arthur Grant m Peter Akister

Ronald Shiner, Brian Rix, Sid James, Michael
Shepley, Joan Haythorne, Joan Sims, Heather
Sears, Lee Patterson, Peggy Mount.

Dual Alibi
GB 1947   81m   bw
British National (Louis H. Jackson)

Twin trapezists fall out over a lottery ticket
and a worthless woman, but later extract a
unique revenge.
Sprightly circus melodrama, shot on a
shoestring.

w Alfred Travers, Stephen Clarkson d Alfred
Travers ph James Wilson

Herbert Lom, Phyllis Dixey, Ronald Frankau,
Terence de Marney, Abraham Sofaer, Eugene
Deckers

Dubarry Was a Lady
US 1943   101m   Technicolor
MGM (Arthur Freed)

A New Yorker imagines himself back at the
court of Louis XIV.
Dull, stiff adaptation of a Broadway musical
comedy, with changed songs.

w Irving Brecher, book B. G. De Sylva,
Herbert Fields d Roy del Ruth ph Karl
Freund md George Stoll songs Cole Porter

Gene Kelly, Lucille Ball, Red Skelton,
Virginia O'Brien, Zero Mostel, Rags Ragland,
Tommy Dorsey and his Orchestra

The Duchess and the Dirtwater Fox
US 1976   104m   De Luxe   Panavision
TCF (Melvin Frank)

A Barbary Coast con man and a saloon singer
have various hectic adventures.
Wild and woolly spoof western which fires off
aimlessly in a variety of styles and becomes
merely tiresome despite good scenes.

w Melvin Frank, Barry Sandler d Melvin
Frank ph Joseph Biroc m Charles Fox

George Segal, Goldie Hawn, Conrad Janis,
Thayer David, Roy Jenson, Bob Hoy, Bennie
Dobbins

'The classic western has now been shot to
death by Sam Peckinpah, laughed to death by
Mel Brooks and pondered to death by Arthur
Penn, and Frank is like a scavenger picking up
stray relics from its body.'—*Newsweek*

'The relentless vulgarity of the enterprise
suggests that Mr Frank, having been so long
constrained by the Hollywood Production
Code when churning out vehicles for Bob
Hope and Danny Kaye, is still making up for
lost time.'—*Philip French, The Times*

The Duchess of Idaho
US 1950   98m   Technicolor
MGM (Joe Pasternak)

Romantic misunderstandings among
candidates for Miss Idaho Potato.
Lightweight musical, quite pleasant if routine,
with guest spots.

w Dorothy Cooper, Jerry Davis d Robert Z.
Leonard ph Charles Schoenbaum
md Georgie Stoll

Esther Williams, Van Johnson, John Lund,
Paula Raymond, Clinton Sundberg; guests
Red Skelton, Eleanor Powell, Lena Horne

Duck Soup••••
US 1933   68m   bw
Paramount

An incompetent becomes President of
Fredonia and wages war on its scheming
neighbour.
The satirical aspects of this film are fascinating
but appear to have been unintentional. Never
mind, it's also the most satisfying and
undiluted Marx Brothers romp, albeit the one
without instrumental interludes. It does
include the lemonade stall, the mirror
sequence, and an endless array of one-liners
and comedy choruses.

w Bert Kalmar, Harry Ruby, Arthur
Sheekman, Nat Perrin d Leo McCarey
ph Henry Sharp m / ly Bert Kalmar, Harry
Ruby ad Hans Dreier, Wiard Ihnen

The Four Marx Brothers, Margaret Dumont,
Louis Calhern, Edgar Kennedy, Raquel
Torres

'So much preliminary dialogue is necessary
that it seems years before Groucho comes on
at all; and waiting for Groucho is agony.'
—*E. V. Lucas, Punch*

Due Soldi di Speranza•
Italy 1952   98m   bw
Universalcine (Sandro Ghenzi)
GB title: *Two Pennyworth of Hope*

Demobilized after World War II, Antonio
finds life in his native village hard to take.
Neo-realist comedy-melodrama full of
gesticulating rustics; good for those who like
this sort of thing.

w Renato Castellani, Titina de Filippo
d Renato Castellani *ph* Arturo Gallea
m Alessandro Cicognini

Vincenzo Musolino, Maria Fiore, Filumena
Russo, Luigi Astarita

Duel at Diablo°

US 1965 103m De Luxe
UA / Nelson / Engel / Cherokee / Rainbow /
Brien

White and black man fight together as apaches
attack.
Well-paced, old-fashioned, shoot-em-up star
western.

w Marvin H. Albert, Michel M. Grilikhes
d Ralph Nelson *ph* Charles F. Wheeler
m Neal Hefti

Sidney Poitier, James Garner, Bibi
Andersson, Bill Travers, William Redfield,
John Hoyt, John Hubbard

Duel at Silver Creek

US 1952 77m Technicolor
U-I (Leonard Goldstein)

An honest man is murdered by claim jumpers,
and the Silver Kid is suspected.
Modest, efficient western.

w Gerald Drayson Adams, Joseph Hoffman
d Don Siegel *ph* Irving Glassberg *m* Hans
Salter

Audie Murphy, Stephen McNally, Faith
Domergue, Susan Cabot, Gerald Mohr,
Eugene Iglesias, Lee Marvin, Walter Sande

Duel in the Jungle

GB 1954 101m Technicolor
ABP / Marcel Hellman

An African explorer intends to defraud an
insurance company and sets traps for the
investigator who pursues him.
Lackadaisical romp in the studio jungle, none
of it with much style or film sense.

w Sam Marx, T. J. Morrison *d* George
Marshall *ph* Erwin Hillier *m* Mischa
Spoliansky

Dana Andrews, Jeanne Crain, David Farrar,
Patrick Barr

Duel in the Sun°°°

US 1946 135 or 138m Technicolor
David O. Selznick

A half-breed girl causes trouble between two
brothers.
Massive western, dominated and fragmented
by its producer, who bought the best talent
and proceeded to interfere with it, so that
while individual scenes are marvellous, the

narrative has little flow. The final gory shoot-
up between two lovers was much discussed at
the time.

w David O. Selznick, Oliver H. P. Garrett,
novel Niven Busch *d King Vidor* (and others)
*second unit B. Reeves Eason, Otto Brower
ph Lee Garmes, Harold Rosson, Ray
Rennahan m Dmitri Tiomkin ad James
Basevi pd J. McMillan Johnson*

Jennifer Jones, Joseph Cotten, Gregory Peck,
Lionel Barrymore, Lillian Gish, Walter
Huston, Herbert Marshall, Charles Bickford,
Tilly Losch, Joan Tetzel, Harry Carey, Otto
Kruger, Sidney Blackmer

'A razzmatazz of thunderous naïvety
simmering into a kind of majestic dottiness.'—
Basil Wright, 1972

AAN: Jennifer Jones; Lillian Gish

The Duellists°

GB 1977 101m colour
Scott Free / NFFC / David Puttnam

In the early 1800s, two Hussar Officers
challenge each other to a series of duels; after
sixteen years an ironic truce is called. A
singularly pointless anecdote; its main virtue is
that it is coldly attractive to look at.

w Gerald Vaughan-Hughes, *story* The Point of
Honour by Joseph Conrad *d* Ridley Scott
ph Frank Tidy *m* Howard Blake *pd* Peter J.
Hampton

Keith Carradine, Harvey Keitel, Albert
Finney, Edward Fox, Cristina Raines, Tom
Conti, Robert Stephens, John McEnery

Duffy

GB 1968 101m Technicolor
Columbia / Martin Manulis

Two half-brothers plan to rob their millionaire
father.
Would-be with-it caper film, all flashy
fragments and pop art, like sitting through a
feature-length commercial. Exasperating.

w Donald Cammell, Harry Joe Brown Jnr
d Robert Parrish *ph* Otto Heller *m* Ernie
Freeman

James Coburn, James Mason, James Fox,
Susannah York, John Alderton, Guy Deghy,
Tutte Lemkow, Carl Duering, Marne
Maitland

Duffy's Tavern

US 1945 97m bw
Paramount (Danny Dare)

The owner of a bar is helped by Hollywood
stars.
Flat comedy based on a radio show and not
helped by dismal guest star appearances.

w Melvin Frank, Norman Panama *d* Hal
Walker *ph* Lionel Lindon *m* Robert Emmet
Dolan

Ed Gardner, Victor Moore, Marjorie
Reynolds, Barry Sullivan and guests including
Bing Crosby, Bob Hope, Betty Hutton, Alan
Ladd, Dorothy Lamour, Veronica Lake,
William Bendix, Joan Caulfield

The Duke of West Point*
US 1938   112m   bw
Edward Small

An extrovert army cadet finds the going tough.
Dated romantic flagwaver which pleased at the
time.

w George Bruce *d* Alfred E. Green
ph Robert Planck

Louis Hayward, Joan Fontaine, Tom Brown,
Richard Carlson, Alan Curtis, Donald Barry,
Gaylord Pendleton, Jed Prouty, Marjorie
Gateson

Dulcima
GB 1971   98m   Technicolor
EMI (Basil Rayburn)

A farmer's daughter reluctantly moves in with
a persistent, lecherous old miser.
Weird sex melodrama from *Cold Comfort
Farm* country, more risible than interesting.

wd Frank Nesbitt, *story* H. E. Bates *ph* Tony
Imi *m* Johnny Douglas

John Mills, Carol White, Stuart Wilson,
Bernard Lee, Dudley Foster

Dumbo***
US 1941   64m   Technicolor
Walt Disney

A baby circus elephant finds that his big ears
have a use after all.
Delightful cartoon feature notable for set
pieces such as the drunken nightmare and the
crows' song.

w various *d* Ben Sharpsteen *m* Frank
Churchill, Oliver Wallace

AA: music
AAN: song, 'Baby Mine' (*m* Frank Churchill,
ly Ned Washington)

The Dummy Talks
GB 1943   85m   bw

A ventriloquist turns to blackmail and is
murdered backstage. Curious, oddly cast
murder mystery, not unentertaining at the
time. Jack Warner, Claude Hulbert, Beryl
Orde, G. H. Mulcaster, Ivy Benson, Manning
Whiley. Written by Michael Barringer;
directed by Oswald Mitchell; for British
National.

Dunkirk**
GB 1958   135m   bw
MGM / Ealing (Michael Balcon)

In 1940 on the Normandy beaches, a small
group gets detached from the main force.
Sober, small-scale approach to an epic subject;
interesting but not inspiring, with
performances to match.

w W. P. Lipscomb, David Divine *d* Leslie
Norman *ph* Paul Beeson *m* Malcolm Arnold

John Mills, Richard Attenborough, Bernard
Lee, Robert Urquhart, Ray Jackson

The Dunwich Horror*
US 1970   90m   Movielab
AIP (Roger Corman, Jack Bohrer)

A young warlock plans to use his girl friend in
a fertility rite.
Bookish horror story, quite well done against
a village background.

w Curtis Lee Hanson, Henry Rosenbaum,
Ronald Silkosky, *story* H. P. Lovecraft
d Daniel Haller *ph* Richard C. Glouner
m Les Baxter

Dean Stockwell, Sandra Dee, Ed Begley, Sam
Jaffe, Lloyd Bochner

Duped Till Doomsday*
East Germany 1957   97m   bw
DEFA (Adolf Fischer)
original title: *Betrogen bis zum Jungsten
Tag*

Three Nazi NCOs go to the bad.
Propagandist anti-Nazi war melodrama, very
well made in parts.

w Kurt Bortfeldt, *novel* Kameraden by Franz
Fuhmann *d* Kurt Jung-Alsen *ph* Walter
Fehdmer

Wolfgang Kieling, Rudolph Ulrich, Hans-
Joachim Martens

Dust Be My Destiny*
US 1939   88m   bw
Warner (Lou Edelman)

A young misfit tries to find himself in the
country.
Dated but well made social melodrama.

w Robert Rossen, *story* Jerome Odlum
d Lewis Seiler *ph* James Wong Howe *m* Max
Steiner

John Garfield, Priscilla Lane, Alan Hale,
Frank McHugh, John Litel, Charles
Grapewin, Billy Halop, Bobby Jordan,
Stanley Ridges
   'You can tell from the title that John
Garfield has his usual part—the angry, bitter,

tough, poor young man with slight persecution
mania.'—*Richard Mallett, Punch*
† Remade 1942 as *I Was Framed*, with
Michael Ames.

Dutchman*
GB 1966 56m bw
Gene Persson

On a New York subway train a woman
humiliates a black man and finally knifes him.
An allegory for addicts who can ferret out the
meaning; on the surface, vaguely Pinterish and
mainly boring.

w LeRoi Jones, from his play *d* Anthony
Harvey *ph* Gerry Turpin *m* John Barry

Shirley Knight, Al Freeman Jnr

Dynamite**
US 1929 129m bw
MGM (Cecil B. de Mille)

In order to gain an inheritance, a socialite
marries a man about to be executed . . . but
he is reprieved.
Dated but still dynamic social melodrama of
the early talkie period.

w Jeanie Macpherson *d* Cecil B. de Mille
ph Peverell Marley *m* Herbert Stothart

Kay Johnson, Charles Bickford, Conrad
Nagel, Julia Faye, Joel McCrea
'Exuberant, wonderfully vigorous, the film
skilfully evokes the look and character of the
Jazz Age.'—*Charles Higham*
'An astonishing mixture, with artificiality
vying with realism and comedy hanging on the
heels of grim melodrama.'—*Mordaunt Hall,
New York Times*

E

Each Dawn I Die*
US 1939 84m bw
Warner (David Lewis)

A crusading reporter is framed for
manslaughter and becomes a hardened
prisoner.
Efficient, vigorous yet slightly disappointing
star vehicle; the talents are in the right
background, but the script is wobbly.

w Norman Reilly Raine, Warren Duff,
Charles Perry, *novel* Jerome Odlum
d William Keighley *ph* Arthur Edeson
m Max Steiner

James Cagney, George Raft, Jane Bryan,
George Bancroft, Maxie Rosenbloom, Stanley
Ridges, Alan Baxter, Victor Jory

The Eagle and the Hawk**
US 1933 72m bw
Paramount

In 1918 France, two American army fliers
dislike each other but come together before
the death of one of them.
Dawn Patrol melodrama, well done with
unusually vivid dialogue and acting.

w Bogart Rogers, Seton I. Miller, *story* John
Monk Saunders d Stuart Walker *ph* Harry
Fischbeck

Fredric March, Cary Grant, Carole Lombard,
Sir Guy Standing, Jack Oakie, Forrester
Harvey

The Eagle and the Hawk
US 1949 86m bw
(Paramount) Pine-Thomas

During the Mexican wars, a US government
agent tracks down a traitor who is supplying
arms to the rebel Juarez.
Stolid adventure yarn, energetically played.

w Geoffrey Homes, Lewis R. Foster d Lewis
R. Foster *ph* James Wong Howe *m* David
Chudnow

John Payne, Dennis O'Keefe, Rhonda
Fleming, Thomas Gomez, Fred Clark, Frank
Faylen, Eduardo Noriega

The Eagle Has Landed*
GB 1976 135m Eastmancolor
Panavision
ITC / Associated General (Jack Wiener,
David Niven Jnr)

During World War II, enemy aliens infiltrate
an English village in the hope of killing
Churchill.
Elaborately plotted but uninvolving spy
melodrama, lethargically directed, muddily
coloured and too concerned to create some
good Germans.

w Tom Mankiewicz, *novel* Jack Higgins
d John Sturges *ph* Anthony Richmond
m Lalo Schifrin

Michael Caine, Donald Sutherland, Robert
Duvall, Jenny Agutter, Donald Pleasence,
Anthony Quayle, Jean Marsh, Sven-Bertil
Taube, John Standing, Judy Geeson, Larry
Hagman, Maurice Roeves

Eagle in a Cage*
GB 1970 103m Eastmancolor
Group W / Ramona (Millard Lampell, Albert
Schwarz)

In 1815, a professional soldier becomes
governor of St Helena and jailer to Napoleon.
Talkative, anecdotal, heavily serious historical
reconstruction with good acting but little
control.

w Millard Lampell d Fielder Cook *ph* Frano
Vodopivec *m* Marc Wilkinson

John Gielgud, Ralph Richardson, Kenneth
Haigh, Billie Whitelaw, Moses Gunn, Ferdy
Mayne, Lee Montague

Eagle Squadron
US 1942 102m bw
Universal (Walter Wanger)

During World War II, American fliers join the
RAF.
Studio-bound air epic, leavened with
conventional romance but little humour or
sympathy.

w Norman Reilly Raine, *story* C. S. Forester
d Arthur Lubin *ph* Stanley Cortez *m* Frank
Skinner

Robert Stack, Diana Barrymore, John Loder, Eddie Albert, Nigel Bruce, Leif Erickson, Edgar Barrier, Jon Hall, Evelyn Ankers, Isobel Elsom, Alan Hale Jnr, Don Porter, Frederick Worlock, Gladys Cooper

Eagle's Wing
GB 1979 111m Eastmancolor
Panavision
Rank / Peter Shaw (Ben Arbeid)

A Comanche chief pursues a white man who has stolen a prize Indian horse.
Would-be poetic western which emerges as very pretty but stultifyingly dull; an odd thing indeed to come from a moribund British studio.

w John Briley d Anthony Harvey ph Billy Williams m Marc Wilkinson pd Herbert Westbrook

Martin Sheen, Sam Waterston, Harvey Keitel, Stephane Audran, John Castle

Earl Carroll Vanities
US 1945 91m bw
Republic (Albert J. Cohen)

A Ruritanian princess in need of a loan becomes the singing star of a New York night club.
Nit-witted musical with no style but an engaging cast.

w Frank Gill Jnr d Joseph Santley ph Jack Marta md Walter Scharf songs Walter Kent, Kim Gannon

Constance Moore, Dennis O'Keefe, Alan Mowbray, Eve Arden, Otto Kruger (as Earl Carroll), Pinky Lee, Mary Forbes, Stephanie Bachelor, Parkyakarkus, Leon Belasco, Robert Greig

AAN: song 'Endlessly' (ly Kim Gannon, m Walter Kent)

The Earl of Chicago*
US 1940 87m bw
MGM (Victor Saville)

An American gangster accedes to an English earldom but is tried for murder.
Unusual but unsatisfactory comedy-drama which rambles to a dismal conclusion but has entertaining passages.

w Lesser Samuels, novel Brock Williams d Richard Thorpe ph Ray June m Werner Heymann

Robert Montgomery, Edward Arnold, Reginald Owen, Edmund Gwenn

The Early Bird
GB 1965 98m Eastmancolor
Rank / Hugh Stewart

A milkman gets involved in an inter-company war.
Star farcical comedy; not the worst of Wisdom, but overlong and mainly uninventive.

w Jack Davies, Norman Wisdom, Eddie Leslie, Henry Blyth d Robert Asher ph Jack Asher m Ron Goodwin

Norman Wisdom, Edward Chapman, Jerry Desmonde, Paddie O'Neil, Bryan Pringle, Richard Vernon, John Le Mesurier, Peter Jeffrey

Early to Bed
US 1928 20m bw silent

Stan becomes Ollie's butler but rebels when his friend's fortune goes to his head. One of the most untypical and seldom seen Laurel and Hardy comedies, with both stars prankishly out of characters. On its own account however it is mainly very funny.
Written by H. M. Walker; directed by Emmett Flynn; for Hal Roach.

Earth***
USSR 1930 63m approx (24 fps) bw silent
VUFKU
original title: Zemlya

Trouble results in a Ukrainian village when a landowner refuses to hand over his land for a collective farm.
The melodramatic little plot takes second place to lyrical sequences of rustic beauty, illustrating life, love and death in the countryside.

wd, ed Alexander Dovzhenko ph Danylo Demutsky

Semyon Svashenko, Stephan Shkurat, Mikola Nademsky, Yelena Maximova

'Stories in themselves do not interest me. I choose them in order to get the greatest expression of essential social forms.'—Dovzhenko
'A picture for filmgoers who are prepared to take their cinema as seriously as Tolstoy took the novel.'—James Agate

Earthquake*
US 1974 123m Technicolor
Panavision
Universal / Jennings Lang / Mark Robson

Various personal stories intertwine in a Los Angeles earthquake.
Dreary drama with very variable special effects, gimmicked up by Sensurround. A box office bonanza.

w George Fox, Mario Puzo d Mark Robson
ph Philip Lathrop m John Williams
pd Alexander Golitzen sp Albert Whitlock

Charlton Heston, Ava Gardner, Lorne
Greene, Marjoe Gortner, Barry Sullivan,
George Kennedy, Richard Roundtree,
Geneviève Bujold, Walter Matthau (under the
alias of his real name)

AAN: Philip Lathrop

Earthworm Tractors
US 1936 69m bw

A salesman whose fiancée wants him to think
big turns to tractors. One of the star's livelier
comedies. *Joe E. Brown*, June Travis, Guy
Kibbee, Dick Foran. Written by Richard
Macauley, Joe Traub and Hugh Cummings;
directed by Ray Enright; for Warner.(GB
title: *A Natural Born Salesman*.)

East Lynne
US 1931 102m bw
Fox

A Victorian lady is unjustly divorced by her
husband, and later loses both her lover and
her sight.
Much caricatured melodrama, here presented
in stolidly acceptable form.

w Bradley King, Tom Barry, *novel* Mrs Henry
Wood d Frank Lloyd ph John Seitz
m Richard Fall

Ann Harding, Clive Brook, O. P. Heggie,
Conrad Nagel, Cecilia Loftus, Beryl Mercer,
Flora Sheffield

† Previous versions had been made by Fox, in
1916 with Theda Bara and in 1925 with Alma
Rubens.

AAN: best picture

East Meets West
GB 1936 74m bw

A proud sultan learns that his son is having an
affair with the wife of a crook. Derivative star
vehicle, very stagey even then. George Arliss,
Godfrey Tearle, Lucie Mannheim, Romney
Brent, Ballard Berkeley, John Laurie. Written
by Maude Howell, from Edwin Greenwood's
play *The Lake of Life*; directed by Herbert
Mason; for Gaumont.

East of Eden**
US 1954 115m Warnercolor
  Cinemascope
Warner (Elia Kazan)

In a California farming valley in 1913 a wild
adolescent rebels against his stern father and
discovers that his mother, believed dead, runs
a nearby brothel.

Turgid elaboration of Genesis with strong
character but nowhere to go. Heavily overdirected and rousingly acted.

w Paul Osborn, *novel* John Steinbeck d Elia
Kazan ph Ted McCord m Leonard
Rosenman ad James Basevi, Malcolm Bert

Raymond Massey, James Dean (his first star
role), Julie Harris, Dick Davalos, *Jo Van
Fleet*, Burl Ives, Albert Dekker
  'Of what a boy did . . . of what a girl did
. . . of ecstasy and revenge!'—*publicity*
  'The first distinguished production in
Cinemascope.'—*Eugene Archer*

AA: Jo Van Fleet
AAN: Paul Osborn; Elia Kazan; James Dean

East of Elephant Rock
GB 1976 92m colour
Boyd's Company / Kendon (Don Boyd)

In 1948 Malaya a womanizing civil servant is
shot by his jealous mistress.
Style-less and quite uncredited re-hash of *The
Letter*, striving vainly to recreate the spirit of
Somerset Maugham.

wd Don Boyd ph Keith Goddard m Peter
Skellern

Judi Bowker, Jeremy Kemp, John Hurt,
Christopher Cazenove, Anton Rodgers,
Vajira, Tariq Yunus
  'Punishingly inept in every department.'—
David Badder, MFB

East of Piccadilly
GB 1940 79m bw
ABPC (Walter C. Mycroft)
US title: *The Strangler*

A novelist and a girl reporter catch a silk
stocking murderer.
Adequate lower case mystery with good
atmosphere.

w Lesley Storm, J. Lee-Thomson,
novel Gordon Beckles d Harold Huth

Sebastian Shaw, Judy Campbell, Henry
Edwards, Niall MacGinnis, George Pughe,
Martita Hunt, George Hayes, Cameron Hall,
Edana Romney

East of Sudan
GB 1964 94m Techniscope
Columbia / Ameran (Charles H. Schneer)

A trooper, a governess and others escape
downriver from one of General Gordon's
outposts.
Shameless borrowing of plot from *The African
Queen* and footage from *The Four Feathers*.
The purest hokum.

w Jud Kinberg *d* Nathan Juran *ph* Wilkie Cooper *m* Laurie Johnson

Anthony Quayle, Sylvia Syms, Jenny Agutter.

'Nathan Juran could direct this kind of thing blindfold, and for once would appear to have done so.'—*MFB*

East of Sumatra*
US 1953 82m Technicolor
U-I (Albert J. Cohen)

A mining engineer has trouble with the ruthless chief of a Pacific island.
A good example of routine Hollywood hokum, efficiently staged and acted.

w Frank Gill Jnr *d* Budd Boetticher
ph Clifford Stine

Jeff Chandler, Anthony Quinn, Marilyn Maxwell, John Sutton

East of the River
US 1940 73m bw

A young gangster and his respectable brother both love the same girl. Tedious formula melodrama in a studio New York. John Garfield, William Lundigan, Brenda Marshall, Marjorie Rambeau, George Tobias. Written by Fred Niblo Jnr; directed by Alfred E. Green; for Warner.

East Side of Heaven
US 1939 90m bw

A singing taxi driver looks after an abandoned baby. Modestly pleasing comedy with music and sentiment; Baby Sandy subsequently starred in her own series. Bing Crosby, Joan Blondell, Mischa Auer, C. Aubrey Smith, Irene Hervey. Written by William Consetman; directed by David Butler; for Universal.

East Side West Side*
US 1949 108m bw
MGM (Voldemar Veltuguin)

A New York businessman is torn between his wife and another woman.
High class soap opera with all the production stops pulled out; generally well acted and reasonably entertaining.

w Isobel Lennart, *novel* Marcia Davenport
d Mervyn Le Roy *ph* Charles Rosher
m Miklos Rozsa

James Mason, Barbara Stanwyck, Van Heflin, Ava Gardner, *Gale Sondergaard,* Cyd Charisse, Nancy Davis, William Conrad

'No company is quite so adept as MGM at presenting basically uninteresting material with such style, and such a strong cast, that it cannot fail to entertain.'—*Penelope Houston*

Easter Parade**
US 1948 109m Technicolor
MGM (Arthur Freed)

A song and dance man quarrels with one partner but finds another.
A musical which exists only in its numbers, which are many but variable. All in all, an agreeable lightweight entertainment without the style to put it in the top class.

w Sidney Sheldon, Frances Goodrich, Albert Hackett *d* Charles Walters *ph* Harry Stradling *m / ly Irving Berlin md* Roger Edens, Johnny Green

Fred Astaire, Judy Garland, Ann Miller, Peter Lawford, Clinton Sundberg, Jules Munshin

'The important thing is that Fred Astaire is back, with Irving Berlin calling the tunes.'—*Newsweek*

† Fred Astaire was actually second choice, replacing Gene Kelly who damaged an ankle.

AA: Roger Edens, Johnny Green

Easy Living***
US 1937 91m bw
Paramount (Arthur Hornblow Jnr)

A fur coat is thrown out of a window and lands on a typist . . .
Amusing romantic comedy with farcical trimmings; it now stands among the classic crazy comedies of the thirties.

w Preston Sturges *d* Mitchell Leisen *ph* Ted Tetzlaff *md* Boris Morros

Jean Arthur, Ray Milland, *Edward Arnold*, Luis Alberni, Mary Nash, Franklin Pangborn, William Demarest, Andrew Tombes

'Secretaries, millionaires, jokes, sight gags, furies, attacks of cool sense—there are always three things going on at once.'—*New Yorker, 1977*

Easy Living
US 1949 77m bw
RKO (Robert Sparks)

An ageing football star wants to retire but has to satisfy the living standards of his ambitious wife.
Dim drama.

w Charles Schnee, *story* Irwin Shaw
d Jacques Tourneur *ph* Harry J. Wild *m* Roy Webb

Victor Mature, Lucille Ball, Lizabeth Scott, Sonny Tufts, Lloyd Nolan, Paul Stewart, Jack Paar, Jeff Donnell

Easy Money
GB 1948 93m bw
GFD / Gainsborough (A. Frank Bundy)

Four people win big prizes on the football
pools.
Short story compendium; very average.

w Muriel and Sydney Box, *play* Arnold
Ridley *d* Bernard Knowles

Edward Rigby, Greta Gynt, Dennis Price,
Jack Warner, Mervyn Johns, Petula Clark,
Marjorie Fielding, Bill Owen, Raymond
Lovell

Easy Rider*
US 1969   94m   Technicolor
Columbia / Pando / Raybert (Peter Fonda)

Two drop-outs ride across America on
motorcycles.
Happening to please hippies and motor-cycle
enthusiasts as well as amateur politicians, this
oddball melodrama drew freakishly large
audiences throughout the world and was much
imitated though never equalled in its casual
effectiveness, nor did promising careers ensue
for the actors mainly concerned.

w Peter Fonda, Dennis Hopper, Terry
Southern *d* Dennis Hopper *ph* Laszlo
Kovacs *m* various recordings

Peter Fonda, Dennis Hopper, *Jack Nicholson*

'*Cinéma-vérité* in allegory terms.'—*Peter
Fonda*

'Ninety-four minutes of what it is like to
swing, to watch, to be fond, to hold opinions
and to get killed in America at this
moment.'—*Penelope Gilliatt*

AAN: script; Jack Nicholson

Easy Street**
US 1916   22m approx   bw   silent
Mutual

In a slum street, a tramp is reformed by a
dewy-eyed missionary, becomes a policeman,
and tames the local bully.
Quintessential Chaplin, combining
sentimentality and social comment with
hilarious slapstick.

wd Charles Chaplin *ph* William C. Foster,
Rollie Totheroh

Charles Chaplin, Edna Purviance, Albert
Austin, Eric Campbell

Easy to Love
US 1953   96m   Technicolor
MGM (Joe Pasternak)

The romances of an aqua-queen in Florida's
Cypress Gardens.
Thin, humourless and forgettable musical
vehicle sustained by spectacular water ballets.

w Laslo Vadnay, William Roberts *d* Charles

Walters *ph* Ray June *md* Lennie Hayton,
George Stoll; numbers staged by *Busby
Berkeley*

Esther Williams, Tony Martin, Van Johnson

Easy to Wed*
US 1946   110m   Technicolor
MGM (Jack Cummings)

A socialite threatens a newspaper editor with
libel; he postpones his own wedding and sets a
friend to compromise her.
Bright but tasteless remake of *Libelled Lady*,
with a second team cast trying hard.

w Dorothy Kingsley, Maurine Watkins,
Howard Emmett Rogers, George
Oppenheimer *d* Edward Buzzell *ph* Harry
Stradling *m* Johnny Green

Van Johnson, Esther Williams, *Lucille Ball*,
Keenan Wynn, Cecil Kellaway, Carlos
Ramirez, Ben Blue, Ethel Smith

Easy Virtue
GB 1927   73m (24 fps)   bw   silent
Gainsborough (Michael Balcon)

A drunkard's wife falls for a young man who
kills himself. Her past then prevents her
attempts to lead a respectable life.
Vapid social melodrama with minimal points
of interest despite its credits.

w Eliot Stannard, *play* Noël Coward *d* Alfred
Hitchcock *ph* Claude McDonnell *ed* Ivor
Montagu

Isabel Jeans, Franklyn Dyall, Eric Bransby
Williams, Ian Hunter, Violet Farebrother,
Robin Irvine

Ebb Tide**
US 1937   92m   Technicolor
Paramount (Lucien Hubbard)

Sailors are stranded with a dangerous fanatic
on a South Sea island.
Interesting adaptation of Stevenson, notable
both for its early colour and its genuinely sour,
anti-romantic mood, almost unique for
Hollywood in this period.

w Bertram Millhauser, *novel* R. L. Stevenson
and Lloyd Osbourne *d* James Hogan *ph* Leo
Tover *m* Victor Young

Ray Milland, Frances Farmer, Oscar
Homolka, Barry Fitzgerald, Lloyd Nolan
† Remade 1946 as *Adventure Island*.

Echoes of a Summer
US / Canada 1975   98m   Eastmancolor
Beata / Castle / Astral / Bryanston (Robert L.
Joseph)

An 11-year-old girl dying of heart disease spends her last summer with her parents on holiday in a Nova Scotian village. Excruciating.

w Robert L. Joseph d Don Taylor ph John Coquillon m Terry James

Jodie Foster, Richard Harris, Lois Nettleton, Geraldine Fitzgerald, William Windom, Brad Savage

'The only honest thing about this movie is its desire to make a buck.'—*Frank Rich, New York Post*

The Eclipse°
Italy / France 1962 125m bw
Interopa-Cineriz / Paris Film (Robert and Raymond Hakim)
original title: *L'Eclisse*

A young Roman woman breaks off one affair and begins another.
A portrait in depth, rather tiresomely long and with at least one totally irrelevant stock-market sequence; but superbly done for connoisseurs.

wd *Michelangelo Antonioni,* Tonino Guerra, Elio Bartolini, Ottiero Ottieri ph Gianni di Venanzo m Giovanni Fusco

Monica Vitti, Alain Delon, Francisco Rabal

L'Ecole Buissonière°
France 1948 89m bw
UGC / CGCF
US title: *I Have a New Master*

At a provincial village school, a new teacher introduces new methods and takes a while to win over the locals.
Rustic comedy-drama of a kind the French do well.

w Jean-Paul Le Chanois, Elise Freinet d Jean-Paul Le Chanois ph Marc Fossard, Maurice Pecqueux, André Dumaitre m Joseph Kosma

Bernard Blier, Juliette Fabre, Edouard Delmont

The Eddie Cantor Story
US 1953 116m Technicolor
Cinemascope
Warner (Sidney Skolsky)

After a tough childhood on New York's east side, Israel Iskowitz becomes a famous entertainer.
Deliberately patterned after the success of *The Jolson Story,* this is an unhappy example of how close are success and failure; the elements are the same, but this film suffers from unsure timing, lack of humour, rather apologetic numbers, a really dismal script and a caricature performance in the lead.

w Jerome Weidman, Ted Sherdeman, Sidney Skolsky d Alfred E. Green ph Edwin DuPar md Ray Heindorf *songs* various ch Le Roy Prinz

Keefe Brasselle, Marilyn Erskine, Aline MacMahon, Arthur Franz, Alex Gerry, Gerald Mohr, William Forrest (as Ziegfeld), Will Rogers Jnr (as Will Rogers), and Eddie Cantor (who also sings the songs off screen)

The Eddy Duchin Story
US 1955 123m Technicolor
Cinemascope
Columbia (Jonie Taps, Jerry Wald)

The success story of a pianist who died of leukemia.
Predictable, glossy, sentimental musical biopic.

w Samuel Taylor, *original story* Leo Katcher d George Sidney ph Harry Stradling md George Duning *piano* Carmen Cavallero

Tyrone Power, Kim Novak, *Victoria Shaw,* James Whitmore, Shepperd Strudwick, Frieda Inescort, Gloria Holden, Larry Keating

AAN: Leo Katcher; Harry Stradling; George Duning

Edgar Wallace
Between 1960 and 1963 no fewer than 47 second features emerged from Jack Greenwood's production unit at the London suburban studios of Merton Park, under the Edgar Wallace banner and prefaced by a sinister revolving bust of the author (though few had very much to do with his original stories). All maintained a better standard than any other crime second features of the period, and a few were seized on with delight by the critics. They were subsequently popular on television, though the Independent Broadcasting Authority banned repeats on the grounds that they were without merit. In this complete list, details are given for the more interesting items:

THE CLUE OF THE TWISTED CANDLE
A MARRIAGE OF CONVENIENCE
THE MALPAS MYSTERY
THE MAN WHO WAS NOBODY
THE CLUE OF THE NEW PIN*
(w Philip Mackie, d Allan Davis, with Paul Daneman, Bernard Archard)
PARTNERS IN CRIME
THE FOURTH SQUARE
THE MAN AT THE CARLTON TOWER
THE CLUE OF THE SILVER KEY
ATTEMPT TO KILL
THE SINISTER MAN*
(w Philip Mackie, d Clive Donner, with Patrick Allen, John Bentley)

NEVER BACK LOSERS
MAN DETAINED
RICOCHET
THE DOUBLE
THE RIVALS
TO HAVE AND TO HOLD
THE PARTNER
FIVE TO ONE
ACCIDENTAL DEATH
WE SHALL SEE
DOWNFALL
THE VERDICT
WHO WAS MADDOX?*
(w Roger Marshall, d Geoffrey Nethercott,
with Bernard Lee, Finlay Currie)
ACT OF MURDER*
(w Lewis Davidson, d Alan Bridges, with
John Carson, Anthony Bate)
FACE OF A STRANGER
NEVER MENTION MURDER*
(w Robert Banks Stewart, d John Nelson
Burton, with Maxine Audley, Dudley Foster)
THE MAIN CHANCE
GAME FOR THREE LOSERS
DEAD MAN'S CHEST
CHANGE PARTNERS
STRANGLER'S WEB*
(w George Baxt, d John Moxey, with Griffith
Jones, Gerald Harper)
BACKFIRE
CANDIDATE FOR MURDER*
(w Lukas Heller, d David Villers, with
Michael Gough, John Justin)
FLAT TWO
THE SHARE-OUT
NUMBER SIX
TIME TO REMEMBER
PLAYBACK*
(w Robert Banks Stewart, d John Nelson
Burton, with Maxine Audley, Dudley Foster)
SOLO FOR SPARROW
LOCKER 69
DEATH TRAP
THE SET-UP
ON THE RUN
THE £20,000 KISS
INCIDENT AT MIDNIGHT
RETURN TO SENDER

Edge of Darkness*
US 1943   124m   bw
Warner (Henry Blanke)

Norwegian village patriots resist the Nazis.
High-intentioned, ambitiously cast but
ultimately bathetic resistance melodrama, high
principled down to its tragic finale but
compromised by backlot shooting and the
presence of Errol Flynn.

w Robert Rossen   d Lewis Milestone   ph Sid
Hickox   m Franz Waxman

Errol Flynn, Ann Sheridan, Walker Huston,
Judith Anderson, Ruth Gordon, Nancy
Coleman, Helmut Dantine, Morris Carnovsky,
Charles Dingle, John Beal, Richard Fraser,
Helene Thimig

Edge of Doom
US 1950   97m   bw
Samuel Goldwyn
GB title: Stronger than Fear

A desperate youth kills a priest and struggles
with his conscience.
A sanctimonious weirdie, extremely odd
coming from this producer, and unhappily
re-edited before release. Someone was
interested enough to want to make it, but it
seems to have been killed by the cast and the
front office.

w Philip Yordan, novel Leo Brady   d Mark
Robson   ph Harry Stradling   m Hugo
Friedhofer

Dana Andrews, Farley Granger, Joan Evans,
Robert Keith, Paul Stewart, Mala Powers,
Adele Jergens, Harold Vermilyea, Mabel
Paige

Edge of Eternity*
US 1959   80m   Technicolor
   Cinemascope
Columbia / Thunderbird (Kendrick Sweet)

A Grand Canyon sheriff traces three murders
to an ownership struggle over a disused mine.
Routine but suspenseful thriller with splendid
locations.

w Knut Swenson, Richard Collins   d Don
Siegel   ph Burnett Guffey   m Daniele
Amfitheatrof

Cornel Wilde, Victoria Shaw, Edgar
Buchanan, Mickey Shaughnessy, Jack Elam

Edge of the City**
US 1957   85m   bw
MGM / Jonathan (David Susskind, Jim di
   Ganci)
GB title: A Man is Ten Feet Tall

Racial tensions lead to tragedy in the railroad
yards of New York's waterfront.
Tense, brutal melodrama, which has historical
interest as an effective opening-up in cinematic
terms of a TV play, in its imitation of On the
Waterfront, and in its rebel hero and relaxed
black friend.

w Robert Alan Arthur, from his play   d Martin
Ritt   ph Joseph Brun   m Leonard Rosenman
Sidney Poitier, John Cassavetes, Jack Warden,
Kathleen Maguire, Ruby Dee, Robert Simon,
Ruth White

Edge of the World ••
GB 1937   80m   bw
GFD / Rock (Joe Rock)

Life, love and death on Foula, a remote
Shetland island.
Rare for its time, a vigorous location drama in
the Flaherty tradition; sometimes naïve,
usually exhilarating.

wd Michael Powell ph Ernest Palmer and
others

Niall MacGinnis, Belle Chrystal, John Laurie,
Finlay Currie, Eric Berry

Edison the Man ••
US 1940   107m   bw
MGM (John W. Considine Jnr)

Edison struggles for years in poverty before
becoming famous as the inventor of the
electric light bulb.
Standard, well-made biopic following on from
Young Tom Edison; reasonably absorbing, but
slightly suspect in its facts.

w Dore Schary, Talbot Jennings, Bradbury
Foote, Hugo Butler *d Clarence Brown*
ph Harold Rosson *m* Herbert Stothart

Spencer Tracy, Rita Johnson, Lynne
Overman, Charles Coburn, Gene Lockhart,
Henry Travers, Felix Bressart
'The love of a woman . . . the courage of a
fighting America . . . lifted him from obscurity
to thrilling fame!'—*publicity*

AAN: Dore Schary, Hugo Butler (original
story)

Edouard et Caroline ••
France 1951   99m   bw
UGC / CICC

A young pianist and his wife quarrel while
preparing for an important recital.
Gay, slight, charming comedy, a two-hander
taking place within the course of a few hours.

w Annette Wademant, Jacques Becker
d Jacques Becker ph Robert Le Fèbvre
m Jean-Jacques Grunenwald

Daniel Gélin, Anne Vernon, Jacques François,
William Tubbs, Jean Galland, Elina
Labourdette, Betty Stockfield
'It lifts its weighty trivialities into a world of
enchantment.'—*Sunday Times*

Educated Evans
GB 1936   86m   bw

A racetrack bookie becomes a trainer. Rather
unyielding vehicle for a fast-talking star. Max
Miller, Nancy O'Neil, Clarice Mayne, Albert
Whelan, Hal Walters. Written by Frank

Launder and Robert Edmunds, from an Edgar
Wallace character; directed by William
Beaudine; for Warner.

Edward My Son
GB 1949   112m   bw
MGM (Edwin H. Knopf)

A rich, unscrupulous man remembers the
people he has made unhappy, and the son to
whom he never behaved as a father should.
Unsatisfactory, rather ugly-looking adaptation
of a gripping piece of theatre, with casting and
direction remarkably uncertain from such
professionals.

w Donald Ogden Stewart, *play* Robert
Morley *d* George Cukor *ph* F. A. Young
m John Woolbridge, Malcolm Sargent

Spencer Tracy, Deborah Kerr, Ian Hunter,
James Donald, Leueen McGrath, Mervyn
Johns

AAN: Deborah Kerr

**The Effect of Gamma Rays on
Man-in-the-Moon Marigolds**
US 1972   101m   De Luxe
Newman–Foreman

A slatternly middle-aged woman dreams of
better times for herself and her children.
Well-written but essentially banal and
pretentious domestic drama, the kind of film
that only gets made when powerful stars see in
it a juicy role.

w Alvin Sargent, *play* Paul Zendel *d* Paul
Newman *ph* Adam Holender *m* Maurice
Jarre

Joanne Woodward, Nell Potts, Roberta
Wallach, Judith Lowry

The Egg and I •
US 1947   104m   bw
U-I (Chester Erskine)

A city couple try to become gentleman
farmers.
Mild, pleasant comedy notable chiefly for
introducing a hillbilly couple, Ma and Pa
Kettle, who went on, in the personae of Main
and Kilbride, to make several later features.
(See under Kettles.)

w Chester Erskine, Fred Finkelhoffe,
novel Betty Macdonald *d* Chester Erskine
ph Milton Krasner *m* Frank Skinner

Claudette Colbert, Fred MacMurray, *Marjorie
Main, Percy Kilbride*, Louise Allbritton,
Richard Long, Billy House, Ida Moore,
Donald MacBride

'Marjorie Main, in an occasional fit of fine, wild comedy, picks the show up and brandishes it as if she were wringing its neck. I wish to God she had.'—*James Agee*

AAN: Marjorie Main

The Egyptian*
US 1954   140m   De Luxe   Cinemascope
TCF (Darryl F. Zanuck)

In ancient Egypt an abandoned baby grows up to be physician to the pharaoh.
More risible than reasonable, sounding more like a parody than the real thing, this pretentious epic from a bestseller flounders helplessly between its highlights but has moments of good humour and makes an excellent example of the pictures they don't make 'em like any more.

w Philip Dunne, Casey Robinson, *novel* Mika Waltari d Michael Curtiz ph Leon Shamroy m Bernard Herrmann, Alfred Newman ad Lyle Wheeler, George W. Davis

Edmund Purdom, Victor Mature, *Peter Ustinov*, Bella Darvi, Gene Tierney, Michael Wilding, Jean Simmons, Judith Evelyn, Henry Daniell, John Carradine, Carl Benton Reid

'The novel . . . supplied the reader with enough occurrences and customs of Akhnaton's time . . . to hide some of the more obvious contrivances of the story. The film does not do this.'—*Carolyn Harrow, Films in Review*

AAN: Leon Shamroy

The Eiger Sanction*
US 1975   125m   Technicolor
Panavision
Universal / Malpaso (Jennings Lang)

An art teacher returns to the CIA as an exterminator, and finds himself in a party climbing the Eiger.
Silly spy melodrama with some breathtaking mountain sequences.

w Warren B. Murphy, Hal Dresner, Rod Whitaker, *novel* Trevanian d Clint Eastwood ph Frank Stanley, John Cleare, Jeff Schoolfield, Peter Pilafian, Pete White m John Williams

Clint Eastwood, George Kennedy, Vonetta McGee, Jack Cassidy, Heidi Bruhl, Thayer David

'All the villains have been constructed from prefabricated Bond models.'—*Richard Combs*

Eight and a Half**
Italy 1963   138m   bw
Cineriz (Angelo Rizzoli)
original title: *Otto e Mezzo*

A successful film director on the verge of a nervous breakdown has conflicting fantasies about his life.
A Fellini self-portrait in which anything goes. Some of it is fascinating, some not worth the trouble of sorting out.

w Federico Fellini, Ennio Flaiano, Tullio Pinelli, Brunello Rondi d Federico Fellini ph Gianni di Venanzo m Nino Rota ad Piero Gherardi

Marcello Mastroianni, Claudia Cardinale, Anouk Aimée, Sandra Milo, Rossella Falk, Barbara Steele, Madeleine Lebeau

'The whole may add up to a magnificent folly, but it is too singular, too candid, too vividly and insistently alive to be judged as being in any way diminishing.'—*Peter John Dyer, MFB*

'Fellini's intellectualizing is not even like dogs dancing; it is not done well, nor does it surprise us that it is done at all. It merely palls on us, and finally appals us.'—*John Simon*

AAN: best foreign film; script; direction

Eight Iron Men
US 1952   80m   bw
Columbia / Stanley Kramer

In the ruins of an Italian village, eight American infantrymen wait for relief.
Quickie war film in which everyone talks a lot and they all survive; from the time when Kramer was discovering how fast he could turn 'em out.

w Harry Brown, from his play A Sound of Hunting d Edward Dmytryk ph Roy Hunt m Leith Stevens pd Rudolph Sternad

Bonar Colleano, Lee Marvin, Arthur Franz, Richard Kiley, Nick Dennis, James Griffith, Dick Moore, George Cooper

Eight O'Clock Walk
GB 1953   87m   bw
British Lion / George King

A young barrister proves a taxi driver innocent of murder.
Minor-league courtroom stuff, an adequate time-passer.

w Katherine Strueby, Guy Morgan, *story* Jack Roffey, Gordon Harbord d Lance Comfort ph Brendan Stafford m George Melachrino

Richard Attenborough, Derek Farr, Cathy O'Donnell, Ian Hunter, Maurice Denham, Bruce Seton, Harry Welchman

Eighty Thousand Suspects*
GB 1963   113m   bw   Cinemascope
Rank / Val Guest

A smallpox epidemic terrorizes the city of Bath.
Predictable melodrama which adequately passes the time.

w Val Guest, *novel* Pillars of Midnight by Elleston Trevor *d* Val Guest *ph* Arthur Grant *m* Stanley Black

Claire Bloom, Richard Johnson, Yolande Donlan, Cyril Cusack, Michael Goodliffe, Mervyn Johns, Kay Walsh, Basil Dignam, Ray Barrett

El**
Mexico 1952 91m bw
Nacional Film (Oscar Dancigers)
aka: *This Strange Passion; Torments*

A middle-aged aristocrat marries a beautiful young girl and falls victim to insane jealousy.
A tragi-comic case history with chilling and memorable details; not one of its director's great works, but an engaging minor one.

w Luis Bunuel, Luis Alcoriza, *novel* Pensamientos by Mercedes Pinto *d* Luis Bunuel *ph* Gabriel Figueroa *m* Luis Hernandez Breton

Arturo de Cordova, Delia Garces, Luis Beristain, Aurora Walker

El Cid*
US / Spain 1961 184m Super Technirama
Samuel Bronston

A legendary 11th-century hero drives the Moors from Spain.
Endless glum epic with splendid action sequences as befits the high budget.

w Frederic M. Frank, Philip Yordan *d* Anthony Mann *ph* Robert Krasker *m* Miklos Rozsa

Charlton Heston, Sophia Loren, Raf Vallone, Geraldine Page, John Fraser, Gary Raymond, Herbert Lom, Hurd Hatfield, Massimo Serato, Andrew Cruickshank, Michael Hordern, Douglas Wilmer, Frank Thring

AAN: Miklos Rozsa; song 'The Falcon and the Dove' (*m* Miklos Rozsa, *ly* Paul Francis Webster)

El Condor
US 1970 102m Technicolor
National General / Carthay Continental (André de Toth)

An escaped convict and a con man seek a fortune in gold believed to be hidden in a fortress in the Mexican desert.
Blood and guts western with few moments of interest.

w Larry Cohen, Steven Carabatsos *d* John Guillermin *ph* Henri Persin *m* Maurice Jarre

Jim Brown, Lee Van Cleef, Patrick O'Neal, Marianna Hill, Iron Eyes Cody, Elisha Cook Jnr

'The kind of fun you can find at your friendly neighbourhood abattoir.'—*Judith Crist, 1977*

El Dorado*
US 1966 126m Technicolor
Paramount / Laurel (Howard Hawks)

A gunfighter and a drunken sheriff tackle a villainous cattle baron.
Easy-going, semi-somnolent, generally likeable but disappointing western . . . an old man's movie all round.

w Leigh Brackett, *novel* The Stars in their Courses by Harry Joe Brown *d* Howard Hawks *ph* Harold Rosson *m* Nelson Riddle

John Wayne, Robert Mitchum, James Caan, Charlene Holt, Michele Carey, Ed Asner, Arthur Hunnicutt, R. G. Armstrong, Paul Fix, Christopher George

'A rumbustious lament for the good days of the bad old west.'—*Tom Milne*

'A claustrophobic, careless and cliché-ridden thing, wavering constantly between campy self-deprecation and pretentious pomposity.'—*Richard Schickel*

El Greco
Italy / France 1964 94m Eastmancolor Cinemascope
(TCF) Artistiche Internazionale / Arco-Films du Siècle (Alfredo Bini, Mel Ferrer)

In the 16th century, a Greek-Italian painter finds favour in Spain and falls in love with an aristocratic girl.
Heavily embellished history with a few good scenes.

w Guy Elmes, Massimo Franciosa, Luigi Magni, Luciano Salce *d* Luciano Salce *ph* Leonida Barboni *m* Ennio Morricone

Mel Ferrer, Rosanna Schiaffino, Adolfo Celi, Angel Aranda

El Topo*
Mexico 1971 124m Eastmancolor
Producciones Panic

An evil gunfighter rides through the old west and has various encounters, after which he sets himself on fire.
Curious, perverse, powerful surrealist allegory which takes in the life of Christ and the fate of man among some exceedingly unpleasant violence. A treat for connoisseurs of the unpleasantly absurd.

w, d, m, ad Alexandro Jodorowsky
ph Raphael Corkidi
Alexandro Jodorowsky, Brontis Jodorowsky,
Mara Lorenzio, David Silva

Electra Glide in Blue*
US 1973   113m   De Luxe   Panavision
UA / James William Guercio / Rupert Hitzig

A small-town motor-cycle cop becomes
disillusioned.
Agreeable desert melodrama in the wake of
Easy Rider, freshly observed with mordant
humour, marred by a fashionable downbeat
ending.

w Robert Boris *d / m* James William Guercio
ph Conrad Hall

Robert Blake, Billy Green Bush, Mitch Ryan,
Jeannine Riley, Elisha Cook Jnr, Royal Dana

The Electric Horseman*
US 1979   120m   Technicolor
Panavision
Columbia / Universal (Ray Stark /
  Wildwood)

A horseman advertising breakfast cereal in
Las Vegas suddenly tires of it all and heads for
the wilderness.
Pretty but slightly sheepish moral saga with
too much technique for its own good.

w Robert Garland *d* Sydney Pollack
ph Owen Roizman *m* Dave Grusin
pd Stephen Grimes

Robert Redford, Jane Fonda, Valerie Perrine,
Willie Nelson, John Saxon, Nicholas Coster
'Overlong, talky and diffused.'—*Variety*

Elephant Boy**
GB 1937   80m   bw
Alexander Korda

In India, a boy elephant keeper helps
government conservationists.
Documentary drama which seemed fresh and
extraordinary at the time, has dated badly
since, but did make an international star of
Sabu.

w John Collier, Akos Tolnay, Marcia de
Sylva *d* Robert Flaherty, Zoltan Korda
ph Osmond Borradaile *m* John Greenwood

Sabu, Walter Hudd, Allan Jeayes, W. E.
Holloway, Wilfrid Hyde White
'This is a fractured film, its skeleton is awry,
its bones stick out through the skin.'—*Richard
Griffith, 1941*
'It has gone the way of *Man of Aran*:
enormous advance publicity, director out of

touch with the press for months, rumours of
great epics sealed in tins, and then the
disappointing diminutive achievement.'—
Graham Greene

The Elephant Man**
US 1980   124m   bw   Panavision
EMI / Brooksfilms (Stuart Cornfield)

In 1884 London, a penniless man deformed by
a rare illness is rescued by a doctor from a
fairground freak show, and becomes a
member of fashionable society.
A curious story which happens to be true; the
film sets its scene superbly, has splendid
performances and a fascinating make-up. Yet
it fails to move quite as it should, perhaps
because the central figure is treated as a
horrific come-on, like the hunchback of Notre
Dame.

w Christopher de Core, Eric Bergren, David
Lynch, from various memoirs *d* David Lynch
ph Freddie Francis *m* John Morris *pd* Stuart
Craig

Anthony Hopkins, *John Hurt*, John Gielgud,
Anne Bancroft, Freddie Jones, Wendy Hiller,
Michael Elphick, Hannah Gordon
'If there's a wrong note in this unique
movie—in performance, production design,
cinematography or anywhere else—I must
have missed it.'—*Paul Taylor, Time Out*
AAN: best film; screenplay; David Lynch;
editing (Anne V. Coates); art direction (Stuart
Craig, Bob Cartwright, Hugh Scaife); John
Morris; costume design (Patricia Norris); John
Hurt
BFA: best film; production design; John Hurt

Elephant Walk*
US 1954   103m   Technicolor
Paramount (Irving Asher)

The owner of a Ceylon tea plantation takes
back an English wife who finds the atmosphere
strange and turns to a friendly overseer for
comfort.
Echoes of *Jane Eyre* and *Rebecca*, with
stampeding elephants instead of a mad or dead
wife. Grade A fiction for ladies.

w John Lee Mahin, *novel* Robert Standish
d William Dieterle *ph* Loyal Griggs *m* Franz
Waxman

Elizabeth Taylor, Peter Finch, Dana Andrews,
Abraham Sofaer
'The climactic elephant stampede's a
rouser—if you're still awake.'—*Judith Crist*

Eleven Harrowhouse*
GB 1974   108m   De Luxe   Panavision
TCF / Harrowhouse (Elliott Kastner)

An American diamond merchant is robbed of a valuable jewel, and finds himself in the middle of an ingenious plot.
Amusing caper story marred by sudden changes of mood.

w Jeffrey Bloom, *novel* Gerald A. Browne d Aram Avakian *ph* Arthur Ibbetson *m* Michael J. Lewis

Charles Grodin, *James Mason*, Trevor Howard, John Gielgud, Candice Bergen, Peter Vaughan, Helen Cherry, Jack Watson, Jack Watling

Elizabeth of Ladymead

GB 1948 97m Technicolor
BL / Imperadio (Herbert Wilcox)

Four husbands of different generations come home from war (1854, 1903, 1919, 1946) to find their wives altered.
Thin star vehicle turns into an amateur-night compendium with a few funny moments.

w Frank Harvey, from his play *d* Herbert Wilcox *ph* Max Greene

Anna Neagle, Hugh Williams, Bernard Lee, Michael Laurence, Nicholas Phipps, Isobel Jeans, Michael Shepley, Jack Allen

Ellery Queen

The debonair detective created by Manfred B. Lee and Frederic Dannay was seen in several unremarkable second features, usually with his secretary Nikki and his police inspector father. The first two were made for Republic, the rest for Columbia.

1935: THE SPANISH CAPE MYSTERY with Donald Cook
1936: THE MANDARIN MYSTERY (Eddie Quillan)
1940: ELLERY QUEEN MASTER DETECTIVE (Ralph Bellamy)
1941: ELLERY QUEEN'S PENTHOUSE MYSTERY, ELLERY QUEEN AND THE PERFECT CRIME, ELLERY QUEEN AND THE MURDER RING (all Bellamy)
1942: A CLOSE CALL FOR ELLERY QUEEN, A DESPERATE CHANCE FOR ELLERY QUEEN, ENEMY AGENTS MEET ELLERY QUEEN (all William Gargan)
In 1971 Peter Lawford starred in a TV pilot, *Don't Look behind You*, and in 1975 a one-season series starred Jim Hutton. The books, pseudonymously authored by Ellery Queen, were far more popular than any of the movies.

Elmer Gantry**

US 1960 146m Eastmancolor
UA / Bernard Smith

The exploits of an American evangelist in the twenties.
Mainly gripping but overlong exposé of commercialized small-town religion

wd Richard Brooks, *novel* Sinclair Lewis *ph* John Alton *m* André Previn *ad* Edward Carrere

Burt Lancaster, Jean Simmons, Arthur Kennedy, *Shirley Jones*, Dean Jagger, Edward Andrews, Patti Page, John McIntire

AA: Richard Brooks (as writer); Burt Lancaster; Shirley Jones
AAN: best picture; André Previn

Elopement

US 1952 82m bw
TCF (Fred Kohlmar)

A girl student eloping with her professor is chased by her father.
Unconvincing domestic comedy with some lively chase sequences.

w Bess Taffell *d* Henry Koster *ph* Joseph La Shelle *m* Cyril Mockridge

Clifton Webb, Charles Bickford, Anne Francis, William Lundigan, Margalo Gillmore, Evelyn Varden, Reginald Gardiner
'A picture that goes beyond what men think about . . . because no man ever thought about it in quite this way!'—*publicity*

Elstree Calling**

GB 1930 86m bw and colour
BIP / Wardour

A film studio mounts a television show.
Slender excuse for an all-star revue which luckily preserves much light entertainment talent of the time.

w Adrian Brunel, Walter C. Mycroft, Val Valentine *d* Adrian Brunel, Alfred Hitchcock, Jack Hulbert, André Charlot, Paul Murray *ph* Claude Friese-Greene

Tommy Handley, Jack Hulbert, Cicely Courtneidge, Will Fyffe, Lily Morris, Teddy Brown, Anna May Wong, Gordon Harker, Donald Calthrop, John Longden, Jameson Thomas, Bobbie Comber

The Elusive Pimpernel*

GB 1950 109m Technicolor
BL / London Films (Michael Powell, Emeric Pressburger)

A foppish 18th-century London dandy is actually the hero who rescues French aristocrats from the guillotine.
Expensive remake of *The Scarlet Pimpernel* which fails to please, apparently because the talents were not congenial to the subject. Interesting detail, though.

wd Michael Powell, Emeric Pressburger,
novel Baroness Orczy *ph* Christopher Challis
m Brian Easdale *ph* Hein Heckroth

David Niven, Margaret Leighton, Cyril
Cusack, Jack Hawkins, David Hutcheson,
Robert Coote
'The quality of excitement which should
carry the film is quite lost. *The Elusive
Pimpernel* is highly—often too highly—
coloured, and has an artificiality quite
different in character from that of the
original.'—*Penelope Houston*
'I never thought I should feel inclined to
leave a Powell and Pressburger film before the
end; but I did here.'—*Richard Mallett, Punch*
'Niven plays the Scarlet Pimpernel with the
sheepish lack of enthusiasm of a tone deaf
man called upon to sing solo in church. His
companions lumber through their parts like
schoolboys about to go down with mumps.'—
Daily Express

Elvira Madigan°
Sweden 1967   95m   Eastmancolor
Europa Film (Waldemar Bergendahl)

A married army officer runs off with a
tightrope dancer; when they run out of money
they live in the woods and finally commit
suicide rather than part.
A simple Victorian romantic idyll, based on a
true incident; a director's and photographer's
piece which entrances the eyes and ears while
starving the mind.

wd Bo Widerberg *ph* Jorgen Persson
m Mozart

Thommy Berggren, Pia Degermark

Embassy°
US 1972   90m   colour
Hemdale / Triad / Weaver (Mel Ferrer)

At the US Embassy in Beirut, a Soviet official
seeking asylum is in danger from a KGB
killer.
Goodish suspenser with reasonably literate
dialogue and several Hitchcockian sequences.

w William Fairchild *d* Gordon Hessler
ph Raoul Coutard *m* Jonathan Hodge

Richard Roundtree, Chuck Connors, Max
Von Sydow, Broderick Crawford, Ray Milland

Embraceable You
US 1948   80m   bw

A gangster on the run fatally injures a young
girl, and stays to nurse her during her last
weeks. Incredible heavy-handed romantic
melodrama. Dane Clark, Geraldine Brooks,
Wallace Ford, S. Z. Sakall, Richard Rober.

Written by Edna Anhalt; directed by Felix
Jacoves; for Warner.

Embryo
US 1976   104m   colour
Cine Artists

A researcher experiments on foetuses with
growth hormones, and lives to regret it.
Rather unpleasant mixture of science fiction
and old-fashioned horror; slickness can't
conceal a total lack of taste.

w Anita Doohan, Jack W. Thomas *d* Ralph
Nelson *ph* Fred Koenekamp *m* Gil Melle

Rock Hudson, Diane Ladd, Barbara Carrera,
Roddy McDowall

The Emigrants°
Sweden 1970   191m   Technicolor
Svensk Filmindustri (Bengt Forslund)
original title: *Utvandrarna*

A family of farmers leaves famine-stricken
19th-century Sweden for America, and builds
a homestead in Minnesota.
Solemn, forceful, overlong epic which while
full of trial and tribulation is sufficiently well
made to cast a hypnotic spell and was a major
hit among Swedish-Americans.

w Jan Troell, Bengt Forslund, from four
novels by Vilhelm Moberg *d, ph, ed* Jan
Troell *m* Erik Nordgren

Max Von Sydow, Liv Ullmann, Eddie Axberg,
Svenolof Bern
'A Fordian canvas without the Fordian
warmth.'—*Sight and Sound*
† A sequel, *The New Land*, shortly appeared,
and this was also the title of a short-lived TV
series on the subject.

AAN: best picture; Jan Troell (direction and
script); Liv Ullmann

Emil and the Detectives°
Germany 1931   80m   bw
UFA

City children discover and chase a crook, who
is finally arrested.
A pleasing fable for children which has
survived several subsequent versions; the
original is probably the best.

w Billy Wilder, *novel* Erich Kästner
d Gerhard Lamprecht *ph* Werner Brandes
m Allan Grey

Fritz Rasp, Kathe Haack
† Other versions: Britain 1934, directed by
Milton Rosmer, with George Hayes; West
Germany 1954, directed by R. A. Stemmle,
with Kurt Meisel; US 1964 (Walt Disney),
directed by Peter Tewkesbury, with Walter
Slezak.

Emma*
US 1932 73m bw
MGM

A servant marries into the family.
Predictably cosy family drama tailored for its
star.

w Frances Marion, Leonard Praskins, Zelda
Sears d Clarence Brown ph Oliver T. Marsh

Marie Dressler, Richard Cromwell, Jean
Hersholt, Myrna Loy, John Miljan, Purnell E.
Pratt

AAN: Marie Dressler

Emmanuelle*
France 1974 94m Eastmancolor
Trinacra / Orphée (Yves Rousset-Rouard)

The bored bride of a French Embassy official
in Siam is initiated by well-meaning friends
into various forms of sexual activity.
Not much sexier than a Sunday colour
supplement, this fashionable piece of sub-
eroticism took off like a bomb and spawned
half-a-dozen so-called sequels. Future students
may well wonder why.

w Jean-Louis Richard, *novel* Emmanuelle
Arsan d Just Jaeckin ph Richard Suzuki,
Marie Saunier m Pierre Bachelet

Sylvia Kristel, Marika Green, Daniel Sarky,
Alain Cuny
  'Much hazy, soft-focus coupling in
downtown Bangkok.'—*Michael Billington,
Illustrated London News*

The Emperor Jones*
US 1933 72m bw

A train porter becomes king of the Haitian
jungle. Stagey transcript of a stagey play, with
acting of some interest at the time. *Paul
Robeson*, *Dudley Digges*, Frank Wilson. From
the play by Eugene O'Neill; directed by
Dudley Murphy; for UA.

Emperor of the North Pole*
US 1973 119m De Luxe
TCF / Inter Hemisphere (Robert Aldrich)
GB title: *Emperor of the North*

In 1933 Oregon, freeloading hobos are
brutally attacked by a sadistic train guard.
Unlikely melodrama with vicious but
exhilarating high spots separating acres of
verbiage.

w Christopher Knopf d Robert Aldrich
ph Joseph Biroc m Frank de Vol

Lee Marvin, Ernest Borgnine, Keith
Carradine, Charles Tyner, Malcolm
Atterbury, Elisha Cook Jnr

  'It's hard, contrived, pointless in its thesis,
repulsive in its people, and it's singularly
joyless and contemptible in its glorification of
the bum and freeloader.'—*Judith Crist*

The Emperor Waltz
US 1948 106m Technicolor
Paramount (Charles Brackett)

In 1901 Austria, a countess falls for an
American phonograph salesman.
Thin to the point of emaciation, this witless
comedy with music, dully set-bound, proved
its director's strangest and most unsatisfactory
choice.

w Charles Brackett, Billy Wilder d Billy
Wilder ph George Barnes m Victor Young
songs Johnny Burke, Jimmy Van Heusen
ad Hans Dreier, Franz Bachelin

Bing Crosby, Joan Fontaine, Roland Culver,
Lucile Watson, Richard Haydn, Harold
Vermilyea, Sig Rumann, Julie Dean

AAN: Victor Young

The Emperor's Candlesticks*
US 1937 89m bw
MGM (John Considine Jnr)

In old Russia, spies on opposite sides fall in
love.
Lavish romantic comedy drama, generally well
handled; superior Hollywood moonshine.

w Monckton Hoffe, Herman J. Mankiewicz,
Harold Goldman, *novel* Baroness Orczy
d George Fitzmaurice ph Harold Rosson
m Franz Waxman

William Powell, Luise Rainer, Maureen
O'Sullivan, Robert Young, Frank Morgan,
Douglass Dumbrille

Empire of the Ants
US 1977 89m Movielab
AIP / Cinema 77 (Bert I. Gordon)

Giant ants menace a stretch of the Florida
coast.
A long way behind *Them*, but as exploitation
it could be worse.

w Jack Turley, *story* H. G. Wells d Bert I.
Gordon ph Reginald Morris m Dana Kaproff

Joan Collins, Robert Lansing, John David
Carson, Albert Salmi, Jaqueline Scott

The Empire Strikes Back**
US 1980 124m Eastmancolor
  Panavision
TCF / Lucasfilm (Gary Kurtz)

The Rebel Alliance takes refuge from Darth
Vader on a frozen planet.

More exhilarating interplanetary adventures,
as mindless as *Star Wars* but just as enjoyable
for aficionados.

w Leigh Brackett, Lawrence Kasdan, *story*
George Lucas *d* Irvin Kershner *ph* Peter
Suschitzky *m* John Williams *pd* Norman
Reynolds

Mark Hamill, Harrison Ford, Carrie Fisher,
Billy Dee Williams

   'Slightly encumbered by some mythic and
neo-Sophoclean overtones, but its
inventiveness, humour and special effects are
scarcely less inspired than those of its
phenomenally successful predecessor.'—*New
Yorker*

AAN: art direction
BFA: music

Employees' Entrance*
US 1933 75m bw

A ruthless department store manager gets his
comeuppance. Smart comedy-melodrama with
solidly familiar cast. *Warren William*, Loretta
Young, Alice White, Wallace Ford, Allen
Jenkins, Marjorie Gateson. Written by Robert
Presnell, from a play by David Boehm;
directed by Roy del Ruth; for Warner.

The Empty Canvas
Italy / France 1964   118m   bw
CC Champion / Concordia (Joseph E.
  Levine, Carlo Ponti)
original title: *La Noia*

A young painter, obsessed by his own spiritual
emptiness, becomes paranoically jealous of his
promiscuous young mistress.
An extraordinarily boring film version of a
novel which needed Bunuel, if anybody, to
handle it.

w Tonino Guerra, Ugo Liberatore, Damiano
Damiani, *novel* Alberto Moravia *d* Damiano
Damiani *ph* Roberto Gerardi *m* Luis
Enriquez Bacalov

Horst Buchholz, Catherine Spaak, Bette
Davis, Isa Miranda, Lea Padovani

En Cas de Malheur*
France / Italy 1958   120m   bw
Iena / UCIL / Incom
aka: *Love Is My Profession*

A wealthy, middle-aged lawyer leaves his wife
for a worthless young wanton whom he is
defending on a robbery charge.
Good solid melodrama with excellent credits:
it caught all concerned on top form and had
international success, but the theme is not in
itself very interesting.

w Jean Aurenche, Pierre Bost, *novel* Georges
Simenon *d Claude Autant-Lara ph* Jacques
Natteau *m* René Cloërc

Jean Gabin, Edwige Feuillère, Brigitte Bardot,
Franco Interlenghi

En Rade*
France 1927   60m approx   bw   silent
Neofilm

A Marseilles docker dreams of escaping his
pent-in existence and fleeing with his mistress
to the South Seas.
More realistic than Pagnol's *Marius* trilogy,
which used the same setting, this remains an
interesting slice of romantic realism, with good
attention to detail.

w Alberto Cavalcanti, Claude Heymann
d Alberto Cavalcanti *ph* Jimmy Rogers, A.
Fairli, P. Enberg

Catherine Hessling, Philippe Heriat, Georges
Charlia

The Enchanted Cottage*
US 1945   92m   bw
RKO

A plain girl and a disfigured man are beautiful
to each other.
Wartime updating of a sentimental old play;
insufficiently well considered to be more than
tolerable.

w De Witt Bodeen, Herman J. Mankiewicz,
play Sir Arthur Wing Pinero *d* John
Cromwell *ph* Ted Tetzlaff *m* Roy Webb

Dorothy McGuire, Robert Young, Herbert
Marshall, Mildred Natwick

AAN: Roy Webb

The Enchanted Forest*
US 1945   77m   Cinecolor
PRC

Old John the Hermit talks to trees and
animals, and rescues a lost child.
Surprising piece of Victorian whimsy,
remarkably effective in its unambitious way,
especially as a product of this studio. The best
known example of Cinecolor.

w Robert Lee Johnson, John Le Bar, Lou
Brock *d* Lew Landers *ph* Marcel Le Picard
m Alfred Hay Malotte

Harry Davenport, Edmund Lowe, Brenda
Joyce, Billy Severn

Enchanted Island
US 1958   94m   Technicolor
Waverly (Benedict Bogeaus)

In the 1840s two sailors jump ship and settle

on what they later discover to be a cannibal island.
Tame adaptation of a minor classic, with the actors all at sea.

w James Leicester, Harold Jacob Smith, *novel* Typee by Herman Melville *d* Allan Dwan *ph* George Stahl *m* Raul Lavista

Jane Powell (an unconvincing Polynesian), Dana Andrews, Don Dubbins, Arthur Shields, Ted de Corsia, Friedrich Ledebur

Enchantment**

US 1948 101m bw
Samuel Goldwyn

A London house tells the story of three generations.
Yes, a house tells the story, and the leading characters are called Rollo and Lark, but this is a very appealing piece of period romantic nonsense, with the highest possible gloss upon it.

w John Patrick, novel A Fugue in Time by Rumer Godden *d Irving Reis ph Gregg Toland m* Hugo Friedhofer

David Niven, Teresa Wright, Evelyn Keyes, Farley Granger, Jayne Meadows, Leo G. Carroll

Encore*

GB 1951 88m bw
GFD / Two Cities (Antony Darn' orough)

Three more Somerset Maugham short stories introduced by the author.
The final follow-up to the success of *Quartet* and *Trio*; television playlets quickly made this kind of short story seem old-fashioned, but the standard here was high.

w T. E. B. Clarke, Arthur Macrae, Eric Ambler, *stories* The Ant and the Grasshopper, Winter Cruise, Gigolo and Gigolette *d* Pat Jackson, Anthony Pelissier, Harold French *ph* Desmond Dickinson *m* Richard Addinsell

Nigel Patrick, Roland Culver, *Kay Walsh*, Noel Purcell, Ronald Squire, John Laurie, Glynis Johns, Terence Morgan, David Hutcheson

The End

US 1978 100m De Luxe
UA / Lawrence Gordon (Hank Moonjean)

A selfish man finds he is dying and unsuccessfully tries to change what remains of his life.
Presumably intended as an ironic black comedy, this comes over as tasteless ham; nobody involved, least of all the director-star, has any idea how to handle it.

w Jerry Belson *d* Burt Reynolds *ph* Bobby Byrne *m* Paul Williams *pd* Jan Scott

Burt Reynolds, Dom de Luise, Sally Field, Strother Martin, David Steinberg, Joanne Woodward, Norman Fell, Myrna Loy, Pat O'Brien, Robby Benson, Carl Reiner

The End of St Petersburg**

USSR 1927 110m approx bw silent
Mezhrabpom-Russ
original title: *Konyets Sankt-Peterburga*

A peasant comes to live in St Petersburg in 1914, understands the workers' problems, and joins in the revolution.
Exhilarating propaganda, reprehensible but superbly conceived, with an especially rousing climax.

w Nathan Zarkhi *d V. I. Pudovkin*
ph Anatoli Golovnya, K. Vents
ad S. Kozlovsky

Ivan Chuvelov, Vera Baranovskaya, A. P. Christiakov

† The film was officially commissioned as part of the 10th anniversary celebrations.

The End of the Affair

GB 1954 106m bw
Columbia / Coronado (David Lewis)

In wartime London, a repressed wife has an affair with a writer but develops religious guilt which leads indirectly to her death.
Glum sinning in Greeneland; over-ambitious, miscast, and poor-looking.

w Lenore Coffee, *novel* Graham Greene
d Edward Dmytryk *ph* Wilkie Cooper
m Benjamin Frankel

Deborah Kerr, Van Johnson, Peter Cushing, John Mills, Stephen Murray, Nora Swinburne, Charles Goldner

End of the Game*

US / West Germany 1976 104m colour
TCF / Maximilian Schell

A retiring police inspector intensifies his vendetta against the crooked industrialist who thirty years earlier killed the woman they both loved.
Chess-like revenge melodrama very typical of its author, with no light relief and a few existentialist touches added for general confusion. Well made and sometimes fascinating, but finally annoying.

w Maximilian Schell and Friedrich Durrenmatt, from Durrenmatt's novel *The Judge and his Hangman d* Maximilian Schell *ph* Ennio Guarnieri, Klaus Koenig, Roberto Gerardi

Jon Voight, Robert Shaw, Martin Ritt, Jacqueline Bisset

'A more addled, overreaching, misjudged, ill-made, wasteful, posturizing, uninteresting and tedious little epic has not toddled into town in years.'—*Charles Champlin, Los Angeles Times*

The End of the River*
GB 1947 83m bw
GFD / The Archers (Michael Powell, Emeric Pressburger)

A South American Indian boy flees to the outside world and finds life in the city as dangerous as in the jungle.
Strange but oddly impressive departure for British film-makers at this time. A commercial and critical disaster.

w Wolfgang Wilhelm *d* Derek Twist *ph* Christopher Challis *m* Lambert Williamson

Sabu, Esmond Knight, Bibi Ferreira, Robert Douglas, Antoinette Cellier, Raymond Lovell, Torin Thatcher

The End of the Road
GB 1936 71m bw

A travelling singer loses heart when he hears of the death of his daughter. Stilted star vehicle of archival interest. Harry Lauder, Ruth Haven, Ethel Glendinning, Bruce Seton. Written by Edward Dryhurst; directed by Alan Bryce; for Fox British.

The End of the Road*
GB 1954 77m bw
Group Three (Alfred Shaughnessy)

A retired engineer becomes frustrated by idleness, and his family contemplate sending him to an old people's home.
Reasonably absorbing study of old age, suffering from a contrived end.

w James Forsyth, Geoffrey Orme *d* Wolf Rilla *ph* Arthur Grant *m* John Addison

Finlay Currie, Duncan Lamont, Naomi Chance, David Hannaford

Endless Night*
GB 1971 99m Eastmancolor
BL / EMI (Leslie Gilliat)

An American girl buys an English stately home and marries a chauffeur, but is later frightened to death.
Bumpy British thriller, structurally weak and peopled by the dullest conceivable characters, but with watchably scary sequences.

wd Sidney Gilliat, *novel* Agatha Christie *ph* Harry Waxman *m* Bernard Herrmann

Hayley Mills, Hywel Bennett, George Sanders, Britt Ekland, Per Oscarsson, Lois Maxwell

The Endless Summer
US 1966 95m Technicolor

A study of surfing round the world. A documentary which became a cult for those influenced by this Californian obsession; smashing photography hardly atones for an approach so naïve as to become fatuous.
Written, directed, photographed and edited by *Bruce Brown,* for Bruce Brown Films / Columbia.

The Enemy Below*
US 1957 98m Technicolor Cinemascope
TCF (Dick Powell)

During World War II an American destroyer in the South Atlantic is involved in a cat-and-mouse operation with a U-boat.
Well-staged, unsurprising naval thriller with good pace and a pat let's-not-be-nasty-to-each-other ending.

w Wendell Mayes, *novel* Commander D. A. Rayner *d Dick Powell ph* Harold Rosson *m* Leigh Harline

Robert Mitchum, Curt Jurgens, Theodore Bikel, David Hedison

The Enemy General
US 1960 74m bw
Columbia (Sam Katzman)

An American officer takes revenge on the German general who executed his fiancée. Routine World War II heroics with a plot deserving a rather better production.

w Dan Pepper, Burt Picard *d* George Sherman *ph* Basil Emmott *md* Mischa Bakaleinikoff

Van Johnson, Jean-Pierre Aumont, John Van Dreelen, Dany Carrel, Françoise Prévost

An Enemy of the People*
US 1977 103m Metrocolor
First Artists (George Schaefer)

A small-town doctor discovers that for commercial reasons his colleagues propose to conceal the fact that the local spa is contaminated by tannery waste.
Ibsen's plot is well intentioned but well worn – it more or less served as the starting point for *Jaws* – so in any modern version the acting is all. Here it isn't enough, though the star so

badly wanted to do it that arguments and sulks kept him off the screen for three years.

w Alexander Jacobs, from Arthur Miller's version of the play by Henrik Ibsen d George Schaefer ph Paul Lohmann

Steve McQueen, Charles Durning, Bibi Andersson, Eric Christmas, Richard Bradford, Richard A. Dysart

L'Enfant Sauvage*
France 1969 84m bw
UA / Films du Carrosse (Marcel Berbert)
US title: *The Wild Child*

In 1797, a scientist tames and studies a young boy who has mysteriously been living wild in the forest.
Slightly flat but generally interesting reconstruction of a true event, the same one which subsequently inspired TV projects such as *Stalk the Wild Child* and *Lucan*.

w François Truffaut, Jean Gruault d François Truffaut ph Nestor Almendros m Vivaldi

Jean-Pierre Cargol, François Truffaut, Jean Dasté, Françoise Seigner

Les Enfants du Paradis****
France 1945 195m bw
Pathé
US title: *Children of Paradise*

In the 'theatre street' of Paris in the 1840s, a mime falls in love with the elusive Garance, but her problems with other men keep them apart.
A magnificent evocation of a place and a period, this thoroughly enjoyable epic melodrama is flawed only by its lack of human warmth and of a real theme. It remains nevertheless one of the cinema's most memorable films.

w Jacques Prévert d Marcel Carné ph Roger Hubert m Maurice Thiriet, Joseph Kosma, G. Mouque ad Alexandre Trauner, Léon Barsacq, Raymond Gabutti

Arletty, Jean-Louis Barrault, Pierre Brasseur, Marcel Herrand, Maria Casarès, Louis Salou, Pierre Renoir, Gaston Modot, Jane Marken
'A magnificent scenario . . . Prévert is as adept with wit as with poignancy . . . I don't believe a finer group of actors was ever assembled on film'—*John Simon*

AAN: Jacques Prévert

Les Enfants Terribles*
France 1950 100m bw
Jean-Pierre Melville
aka: *The Strange Ones*

The hothouse relationship of an adolescent brother and sister leads to tragedy.
Rough-edged, stage-bound but occasionally quite powerful exploration into familiar Cocteau territory.

wd Jean-Pierre Melville, novel Jean Cocteau ph Henri Decaë m Bach, Vivaldi

Nicole Stéphane, Edouard Dermithe, Renée Cosima, Jacques Bernard

The Enforcer***
US 1950 87m bw
United States Pictures (Milton Sperling)
GB title: *Murder, Inc*

A crusading District Attorney tracks down the leader of a gang which murders for profit.
Extremely suspenseful and well-characterized police yarn based on fact. One of the very best of its kind.

w Martin Rackin d Bretaigne Windust ph Robert Burks m David Buttolph

Humphrey Bogart, Everett Sloane, Zero Mostel, Ted de Corsia, Roy Roberts, King Donovan
'A tough, very slickly-made thriller with a host of fine character parts.'—*NFT, 1969*
'Absorbing and exciting, with little of the violence that so often disfigures films of this kind.'—*Richard Mallett, Punch*

The Enforcer
US 1976 96m De Luxe Panavision
Warner / Malpaso (Robert Daley)

Brutal Inspector Callahan of the San Francisco police redeems himself by rounding up a group of psychopathic hoodlums.
Dirty Harry, phase three: for hardened veterans only.

w Stirling Silliphant, Dean Riesner d James Fargo ph Richard Glouner m Jerry Fielding

Clint Eastwood, Tyne Daly, Harry Guardino, Bradford Dillman, John Mitchum, DeVeren Brookwalter, John Crawford
'A new low in mindless violence is reached in this film, which is so bad it would be funny if it were not for the gut-thumping killings from beginning to end.'—*William F. Fore, Film Information*

England Made Me**
GB 1972 100m Eastmancolor
Hemdale / Atlantic (Jack Levin)

In 1935 a sponging Englishman becomes involved through his sister with a German financier.
Somewhat altered from the novel, this unusual film remains a lively, intelligent character melodrama.

w Desmond Cory, Peter Duffell, *novel*
Graham Greene *d Peter Duffell ph* Ray
Parslow *m* John Scott

Peter Finch, Michael York, Hildegarde Neil,
Michael Hordern, Joss Ackland

English without Tears°
GB 1944   89m   bw
GFD / Two Cities (Anatole de Grunwald,
Sydney Box)
US title: *Her Man Gilbey*

World War II a rich ATS girl falls for her
butler who has become a lieutenant.
Wispy satirical comedy with amusing
moments, chiefly interesting for the pre-war
League of Nations sequences.

w Terence Rattigan, Anatole de Grunwald
d Harold French

Lilli Palmer, Michael Wilding, *Margaret
Rutherford*, Penelope Dudley Ward, Albert
Lieven, Roland Culver, Peggy Cummins

An Englishman's Home
GB 1939   79m   bw

An English family plays unwitting host to a
foreign spy. Hilarious clinker, far too
unintentionally funny to make the effective
propaganda intended. Edmund Gwenn, Mary
Maguire, Paul Von Hernreid, Geoffrey
Toone, Richard Ainley, Desmond Tester.
Written by (catch them all) Dennis Wheatley,
Edward Knoblock, Ian Hay, Robert
Edmunds, Dora Nirva, Clifford Grey, Richard
Llewellyn and Rodney Ackland; directed by
Albert de Courville; for Aldwych. 'There is
nothing to be said for this film—though it
might prove useful propaganda in enemy
countries, purporting to illustrate the
decadence of English architecture and
taste.'—*Graham Greene.*

Ensign Pulver
US 1964   104m   Technicolor
Panavision
Warner (Joshua Logan)

Further naval misadventures of the character
from *Mr Roberts.*
Threadbare naval comedy with every expected
cliché.

w Joshua Logan, Peter S. Feibleman, *play*
Joshua Logan, Thomas Heggen *d* Joshua
Logan *ph* Charles Lawton *m* George Duning

Robert Walker, Burl Ives, Walter Matthau,
Tommy Sands, Millie Perkins, Kay Medford,
Larry Hagman, James Farentino, James Coco,
Al Freeman Jnr

Enter Laughing°
US 1967   111m   Technicolor
Columbia / Acre / Sajo (Carl Reiner, Joseph
Stein)

In New York in the thirties, a young man
about to train as a pharmacist decides to
become an actor instead.
Strident Jewish comedy based on the writer-
director's own youthful experiences, which
might have been more effectively strained by
another hand. The talent is there, though.

w Joseph Stein, Carl Reiner, *play* Carl Reiner
d Carl Reiner *ph* Joseph Biroc *m* Quincy
Jones

Reni Santoni, Jose Ferrer, Shelley Winters,
Elaine May, Jack Gilford, Janet Margolin,
David Opatoshu, Michael J. Pollard

Enter Madame
US 1935   83m   bw

A millionaire is humbled when he marries a
glamorous opera singer. Modest comedy
operetta, with the star's voice dubbed by Nina
Koshetz. Elissa Landi, Cary Grant, Lynne
Overman, Sharon Lynne, Paul Porcasi.
Written by Charles Brackett and Gladys
Lehmann, from the play by Gilda Varesi
Archibald and Dorothea Donn-Byrne;
directed by Elliott Nugent; for Paramount.

Enter the Dragon°°
US / Hong Kong 1973   99m
Technicolor   Panavision
Warner / Concord (Fred Weintraub, Paul
Heller)

A master of martial arts is enlisted by British
intelligence to stop opium smuggling.
The first Hollywood-based Kung Fu actioner;
not bad, on the lines of a more violent James
Bond.

w Michael Allin *d* Robert Clouse *ph* Gilbert
Hubbs *m* Lalo Schifrin

Bruce Lee, John Saxon, Shih Kien, Jim Kelly,
Bob Wall

The Entertainer°
GB 1960   96m   bw
BL / Bryanston / Woodfall / Holly (John
Croydon)

A faded seaside comedian reflects on his
failure as an entertainer and as a man.
Even with Olivier repeating his stage triumph,
or perhaps because of it, this tragi-comedy
remains defiantly theatrical and does not take
wing on film.

w John Osborne, Nigel Kneale, *play* John
Osborne *d* Tony Richardson *ph* Oswald
Morris *m* John Addison

Laurence Olivier, Joan Plowright, Brenda de Banzie, *Roger Livesey*, Alan Bates, Shirley Anne Field, Albert Finney, Thora Hird, Daniel Massey

'No amount of deafening sound effects and speciously busy cutting can remove one's feeling that behind this distracting façade of heightened realism lurks a basic lack of confidence.'—*Peter John Dyer*

AAN: Laurence Olivier

† For the television version starring Jack Lemmon and Ray Bolger, see *Television Companion*.

Entertaining Mr Sloane*
GB 1969 94m Technicolor
Pathe / Canterbury (Douglas Kentish)

A lodger attracts the amorous attention of both the middle-aged daughter and older son of the house.

A Gothic *tour de force* of bad taste which worked better on the stage but has its moments.

w Clive Exton, *play* Joe Orton *d* Douglas Hickox *ph* Wolfgang Suschitzky *m* Georgie Fame

Beryl Reid, Harry Andrews, Peter McEnery, Alan Webb

Entr'acte**
France 1924 20m approx bw silent
Ballets Suédois

Various eccentric characters become involved in a crazy chase.

Hilarious nonsense short, devised originally to be shown between the acts of a Dadaist ballet. Very clearly the start of a famous directorial career.

w Francis Picabia *d, ed* René Clair
ph J. Berliet

Jean Borlin, Inge Fries, Francis Picabia, Man Ray, Georges Auric, Marcel Achard, Marcel Duchamps

Entre Onze Heures et Minuit*
France 1948 103m bw
Francinex (Jacques Roitfeld)

A police detective solves his case by impersonating one of the victims.

Twisty, elaborate murder mystery, very competently performed but a little overlong.

w Henri Decoin, Marcel Rivet, *novel* Le Sosie de la Morgue by Claude Luxel *d* Henri Decoin *ph* Nicolas Hayer *m* Henri Saguet

Louis Jouvet, Madeleine Robinson, Robert Arnoux, Gisèle Casadeus

Equus*
GB 1977 137m colour
UA / Winkast (Denis Holt)

A middle-aged psychiatrist tries to find out why a 17-year-old boy blinded six horses.

Overlong film version of a play which was a *succès d'estime*; it makes the fatal mistake of showing the tragic events realistically instead of stylistically as was done on the stage, and as a study in abnormal psychology it is scarcely gripping or revealing.

w Peter Shaffer, from his play *d* Sidney Lumet *ph* Oswald Morris *m* Richard Rodney Bennett *pd* Tony Walton

Richard Burton, Peter Firth, Colin Blakely, Joan Plowright, Harry Andrews, Eileen Atkins, Jenny Agutter, Kate Reid

AAN: Peter Shaffer; Richard Burton; Peter Firth

Eroica*
Poland 1957 83m bw
Kadr
aka: *Heroism*

Two ironic episodes of war; in the 1944 Warsaw uprising and in a POW camp.

Nicely-judged little stories with a sting.

w Jerzy Stefan Stawinski, from his novels *d* Andrzej Munk *ph* Jerzy Wojcik *m* Jan Krenz

Barbara Polomska, L. Niemszyk, Edward Dziewonski, K. Rudzki, Roman Klosowski, Josef Nowak

Erotikon*
Sweden 1920 85m approx bw silent
Svensk Filmindustri

When a professor discovers that his wife is unfaithful, he consoles himself with his young niece.

Sophisticated comedy drama filled with material which might later have appealed to Lubitsch; a little faded now, but it still has charm.

w Gustav Molander, Mauritz Stiller, *play* Franz Herzeg *d* Mauritz Stiller *ph* Henrik Jaenzon

Lars Hanson, Karin Molander, Tora Teje, Anders de Wahl

Erotikon*
Czechoslovakia 1929 85m approx bw silent
Gem Film

A stationmaster's daughter takes a rich lover. Atmospheric little sex drama which sufficiently justified its title to be a big international success.

wd *Gustav Machaty* ph Vaclav Vich

Ita Rina, Karel Schleichert, Olaf Fjord, Theo Pistek

The Errand Boy
US 1961   92m   bw
Paramount / Jerry Lewis (Ernest D. Glucksman)

A dimwit paperhanger causes havoc in a Hollywood studio but is eventually signed up as a comic to rival Jerry Lewis.
Feeble comedy with the star at his self-satisfied worst.

wd Jerry Lewis   ph W. Wallace Kelley
m Walter Scharf

Jerry Lewis, Brian Donlevy, Sig Rumann, Fritz Feld, Isobel Elsom, Iris Adrian

Escapade
US 1935   87m   bw
MGM (Bernard Hyman)

Affairs of a Viennese artist.
Turgid romantic drama copied from the more successful German film *Maskerade*.

w Herman J. Mankiewicz, *original* Walter Reisch   d Robert Z. Leonard   ph Ernest Haller   m Bronislau Kaper, Walter Jurmann

William Powell, Luise Rainer, Virginia Bruce, Mady Christians, Reginald Owen, Frank Morgan, Laura Hope Crews, Henry Travers

Escapade*
GB 1955   87m   bw
Pinnacle (Daniel Angel)

Parents row with a headmaster when their three sons steal an aeroplane, but all is well when it turns out that they are on a peace mission.
Whimsical comedy-drama with a rather foolish point; the cast however can hardly fail to provide entertaining moments.

w Gilbert Holland (Donald Ogden Stewart), *play* Roger MacDougall   d Philip Leacock   ph Eric Cross   m Bruce Montgomery

John Mills, Alastair Sim, Yvonne Mitchell, Colin Gordon, Marie Lohr

Escapade in Florence
US 1962   80m   Technicolor
Walt Disney (Bill Anderson)

Two American students in Florence uncover art thefts.
Cheerful adventure for children, well enough produced on location, but quite unmemorable.

w Maurice Tombragel   d Steve Previn
ph Kurt Grigoleit   m Buddy Baker

Ivan Desny, Tommy Kirk, Annette Alliotto, Nino Castelnuovo

Escapade in Japan
US 1957   93m   Technirama
RKO (Arthur Lubin)

An American boy survives a plane crash in Tokyo and the crisis reunites his parents.
Nicely photographed travelogue with a thread of plot; pleasant but hardly sustaining.

w Winston Miller   d Arthur Lubin
ph William Snyder   m Max Steiner

Cameron Mitchell, Teresa Wright, Jon Prevost, Philip Ober

Escape
GB 1930   69m   bw
ATP

An escaped convict on Dartmoor is helped and hindered by various chance encounters.
Episodic, unsatisfactory drama from a stilted play.

wd Basil Dean, *play* John Galsworthy
ph Jack Mackenzie

Gerald du Maurier, Edna Best, Madeleine Carroll, Gordon Harker, Horace Hodges, Mabel Poulton, Lewis Casson, Ian Hunter, Felix Aylmer

Escape**
US 1940   104m   bw
MGM (Lawrence Weingarten)
reissue title: *When the Door Opened*

An American gets his mother out of a Nazi concentration camp before World War II.
Ingenious but somewhat slow-moving melodrama with an exciting climax and good production values.

w Arch Oboler, Marguerite Roberts, *novel* Ethel Vance   d Mervyn Le Roy   ph Robert Planck   m Franz Waxman

Norma Shearer, Robert Taylor, *Conrad Veidt, Nazimova,* Felix Bressart, Albert Basserman, Philip Dorn, Bonita Granville

'It takes an hour to get started and makes just another feeble fable from headlines.'— *Otis Ferguson*
'Far and away the most dramatic and hair-raising picture yet made on the sinister subject of persecution in a totalitarian land.'—*Bosley Crowther, New York Times*

Escape
GB 1948   79m   bw
TCF (William Perlberg)

Wholly artificial, predictable and uninteresting remake of the 1930 film.

w Philip Dunne *d* Joseph L. Mankiewicz *ph* Frederick A. Young *m* William Alwyn

Rex Harrison, Peggy Cummins, William Hartnell, Norman Wooland, Jill Esmond

Escape from Alcatraz*

US 1979 112m De Luxe
Paramount / Malpaso (Don Siegel)

The allegedly true story of a 1960 escape from the prison on a rock in San Francisco Bay.
A dour, terse, depressing prison movie which makes an uncomfortable star vehicle and not very much of an entertainment, but does preserve a certain integrity right to its ambiguous ending.

w Richard Tuggle, *book* J. Campbell Bruce *d* Don Siegel *ph* Bruce Surtees *m* Jerry Fielding *pd* Allen Smith

Clint Eastwood, Patrick McGoohan, Roberts Blossom, Jack Thibeau, Larry Hankin
'An almost entirely interior film masquerading as an exterior one.'—*Tom Milne, MFB*

Escape from East Berlin

Germany / US 1962 94m bw
MGM / Walter Wood / Hans Albin
aka: *Tunnel 28*

An East German chauffeur is persuaded to help an escape attempt by digging and tunnelling under the Berlin Wall.
Cheerless escape melodrama, thinly based on fact but without much suspense.

w Gabrielle Upton, Peter Berneis, Millard Lampell *d* Robert Siodmak *ph* Georg Krause *m* Hans-Martin Majewski

Don Murray, Christine Kaufmann, Werner Klemperer, Ingrid van Bergen

Escape from Fort Bravo*

US 1953 98m Anscocolor
MGM (Nicholas Nayfack)

A girl helps her Confederate lover to escape from a Yankee fort in Arizona; the commander then tries to save them from Indians.
Grade A western, effectively shot in Death Valley.

w Frank Fenton *d* John Sturges *ph* Robert Surtees *m* Jeff Alexander

William Holden, Eleanor Parker, John Forsythe, William Demarest

Escape from the Dark

GB 1976 104m Technicolor
Walt Disney (Ron Miller)

In 1909 Yorkshire, two boys save pit ponies from the slaughterhouse.
Efficient family fare with plenty of suspense and good character cameos.

w Rosemary Anne Sisson *d* Charles Jarrott *ph* Paul Beeson *m* Ron Goodwin

Alastair Sim, Peter Barkworth, Maurice Colbourne, Susan Tebbs, Geraldine McEwan, Prunella Scales, Leslie Sands, Joe Gladwin

Escape from Zahrain

US 1961 93m Technicolor Panavision
Paramount (Ronald Neame)

Prisoners escape across the desert from an oil sheikdom.
Slow, boring adventure film; good to look at, with James Mason unbilled in a tiny part.

w Robin Estridge *d* Ronald Neame *ph* Ellsworth Fredericks *m* Lyn Murray

Yul Brynner, Sal Mineo, Madlyn Rhue, Jack Warden, Jay Novello

Escape in the Desert

US 1945 81m bw
Warner (Alex Gottlieb)

An American flier outwits renegade Nazis.
Oddball remake of *The Petrified Forest*, with Nazis sitting in for gangsters. Of no interest in itself.

w Thomas Job, *play* Robert E. Sherwood *d* Edward A. Blatt *ph* Robert Burks *m* Adolph Deutsch

Philip Dorn, Helmut Dantine, Alan Hale, Jean Sullivan, Irene Manning, Samuel S. Hinds

Escape in the Fog

US 1945 65m bw

A nurse sees a man attacked in a dream, and helps to save him when the events recur in real life. Muddy little spy story with premonition used as a book-end. Nina Foch, Otto Kruger, William Wright. Written by Aubrey Wisberg; directed by Budd Boetticher; for Columbia.

Escape Me Never*

GB 1935 95m bw
B and D (Herbert Wilcox)

The mother of an illegitimate baby marries a composer who loves someone else.
Archetypal romantic weepie which has probably the star's most memorable and likeable performance.

w Carl Zuckerman, Robert Cullen, *play*

Margaret Kennedy *d* Paul Czinner
ph Georges Périnal

Elisabeth Bergner, Hugh Sinclair, Griffith
Jones, Penelope Dudley Ward, Irene
Vanbrugh, Leon Quartermaine, Lyn Harding
   'That it is a thoroughly British film is proved
by the fact that among the staff one can see
names like Andrejiev, Allgeier and Strassner,
that the principal actress is German, and the
producer is German too.'—*James Agate*

AAN: Elisabeth Bergner

Escape Me Never

US 1947   104m   bw
Warner (Henry Blanke)

Muddled remake of the above with shifted
emphasis. So ill-conceived it's like watching
through frosted glass.

w Thomas Williamson *d* Peter Godfrey
ph Sol Polito *m* Erich Wolfgang Korngold

Errol Flynn, Ida Lupino, Eleanor Parker, Gig
Young, Reginald Denny, Isobel Elsom, Albert
Basserman, Ludwig Stossel, Helene Thimig

Escape Route

GB 1952   79m   bw

Man on the run turns out to be FBI agent on
the spy trail. A moderate co-feature, as
unremarkable as its plot. George Raft, Sally
Gray, Clifford Evans, Reginald Tate. Written
by John Baines and Nicholas Phipps; directed
by Seymour Friedman and Peter Graham
Scott; for Banner / Eros.

Escape to Athena

GB 1979   117m   Eastmancolor
   Panavision
ITC / Pimlico (David Niven Jnr, Jack
   Wiener)

Prisoners-of-war on a Greek island during
World War II recruit the aid of their
sympathetic camp commandant in harassing
the SS.
Expensive but not very involving thick-ear,
hampered by tediously typecast actors and an
uninventive script.

w Edward Anhalt, Richard S. Lochte
d George Pan Cosmatos *ph* Gil Taylor
m Lalo Schifrin

Roger Moore, David Niven, Elliott Gould,
Sonny Bono, Telly Savalas, Claudia
Cardinale, Stefanie Powers, Richard
Roundtree, Anthony Valentine
   'Performing as though they had met up by
chance on holiday . . . the clutch of box office
stars do what they can in a situation where

they are the stand-ins and the stuntmen
(especially the motorcyclists) dominate the
screen.'—*Martyn Auty, MFB*

Escape to Burma

US 1955   88m   Technicolor   Superscope
Benedict Bogeaus

An adventurer suspected of murder hides out
on the tea plantation of an indomitable
American woman.
Far Eastern hokum in which the heroine has a
way with elephants.

w Talbot Jennings, Herbert Donovan *d* Allan
Dwan *ph* John Alton *m* Louis Forbes

Barbara Stanwyck, Robert Ryan, David
Farrar, Murvyn Vye, Reginald Denny

Escape to Danger

GB 1943   92m   bw
RKO (William Sistrom)

A British schoolmistress becomes a spy.
Adequate propaganda hokum.

w Wolfgang Wilhelm, Jack Whittingham
d Lance Comfort *ph* Max Greene *m* William
Alwyn

Eric Portman, Ann Dvorak, Karel Stepanek,
Ronald Ward, Ronald Adam, Lily Kann,
David Peel, Felix Aylmer, A. E. Matthews

Escape to Glory

US 1940   74m   bw
Columbia (Sam Bischoff)
aka: *Submarine Zone*

A merchant ship with a variety of passengers
is stalked by a Nazi submarine.
Minor *Grand Hotel* afloat: quite brisk and
watchable.

w P. J. Wolfson *d* John Brahm *ph* Franz
Planer

Pat O'Brien, Constance Bennett, John
Halliday, Alan Baxter, Melville Cooper,
Edgar Buchanan, Marjorie Gateson

Escape to Witch Mountain°

US 1974   97m   Technicolor
Walt Disney (Jerome Courtland)

Two mysterious orphan children have
extraordinary powers, are chased by a
scheming millionaire, and prove to come from
another planet.
Mildly ingenious story frittered away by poor
scripting and special effects. A stimulating
change in children's films, however.

w Robert Malcolm Young, *novel* Alexander Key *d* John Hough *ph* Frank Phillips *m* Johnny Mandel *sp* Art Cruickshank, Danny Lee

Ray Milland, Donald Pleasence, Eddie Albert, Kim Richards, Ike Eisenmann, Walter Barnes, Reta Shaw, Denver Pyle

Escort West

US 1959 75m bw Cinemascope

An ex-Confederate soldier helps the survivors of a Union wagon train attack. Watchable lower-berth western. Victor Mature, Elaine Stewart, Faith Domergue, Noah Beery Jnr, Rex Ingram, John Hubbard. Written by Leo Gordon and Fred Hartsook; directed by Francis D. Lyon; for Batjac / Romina / UA.

Espionage*

US 1937 67m bw
MGM (Harry Rapf)

Spies and counter spies mingle on the Orient Express.
Lively second feature on familiar lines.

w Manuel Seff, Leonard Lee, Ainsworth Morgan, *play* Walter Hackett *d* Kurt Neumann *ph* Ray June

Edmund Lowe, Madge Evans, Paul Lukas, Ketti Gallian, Skeets Gallagher, Leonid Kinskey, Barnett Parker, Frank Reicher

Espionage Agent

US 1939 83m bw
Warner (Louis F. Edelmann)

An American diplomat falls in love with a spy. Anti-isolationist, semi-documentary exposé, a rather sketchy cross between *Foreign Correspondent* and *Confessions of a Nazi Spy*.

w Warren Duff, Michael Fessier, Frank Donaghue, Robert Buckner *d* Lloyd Bacon *ph* Charles Rosher

Joel McCrea, Brenda Marshall, Jeffrey Lynn, George Bancroft, Stanley Ridges, James Stephenson, Nana Bryant

Espoir*

France / Spain 1938–45 73m bw
Cornignion / Moligniec
aka: *Days of Hope; Man's Hope*

Events of the Spanish Civil War, recreated by surviving combatants.
Anti-fascist propaganda which seems a good deal less inspiring than on its first release, but has some vivid cinematic ideas.

wd André Malraux ph Louis Page *m* Darius Milhaud

Mejuto, Nicolas Rodriguez, Jose Lado

Esther and the King

US 1960 109m Technicolor
Cinemascope
TCF / Galatea (Raoul Walsh)

A Persian king selects a new bride who helps defend him from his enemies.
Tedious biblical hokum with a muddled script and the usual co-production deficiencies.

w Raoul Walsh, Michael Elkins *d* Raoul Walsh *ph* Mario Bava *m* Francesco Lavagnino, Roberto Nicolosi

Richard Egan, Joan Collins, Dennis O'Dea, Sergei Fantoni, Rik Battaglia

Esther Waters

GB 1947 108m bw
GFD / Wessex (Ian Dalrymple)

In the 1870s, a maid is seduced by a squire but insists on bringing up her child without help. Faded costumer with tentative performances and little else to recommend it.

w Michael Gordon, William Rose, Gerard Tyrrell, *novel* George Moore *d* Ian Dalrymple, Peter Proud
ph C. Pennington-Richards, H. E. Fowle *m* Gordon Jacob

Kathleen Ryan, Dirk Bogarde, Cyril Cusack, Ivor Barnard, Fay Compton, Mary Clare, Morland Graham

The Eternal Sea

US 1955 96m bw
Republic (John H. Auer)

The career of an aircraft carrier captain in World War II and Korea.
Solemn biopic of John Hoskins: competent but quite uninspired.

w Allen Rivkin *d* John H. Auer *ph* John L. Russell Jnr *m* Elmer Bernstein

Sterling Hayden, Alexis Smith, Dean Jagger, Virginia Grey

Eternally Yours*

US 1939 95m bw
Walter Wanger

A magician's wife thinks he is too interested in his tricks.
Slightly scatty romantic comedy, amiable if not quite good enough to stand the test of time, but with a great cast.

w Gene Towne, Graham Baker *d* Tay Garnett *ph* Merritt Gerstad *m* Werner Janssen

Loretta Young, David Niven, Broderick Crawford, Hugh Herbert, Billie Burke, C. Aubrey Smith, Raymond Walburn, Zasu Pitts,

Virginia Field, Eve Arden, Herman the
Rabbit
'An amusing and irresponsible picture,
though on the whole more irresponsible than
amusing.'—*New York Times*
AAN: Werner Janssen

Eureka Stockade
GB ,1948   103m   bw
Ealing (Leslie Norman)
US title: *Massacre Hill*
In 1854, Australian gold miners revolt against
a harsh governor.
Unconvincingly made historical actioner from
Ealing's antipodean period.
w Harry Watt, Walter Greenwood, Ralph
Smart *d* Harry Watt *ph* Gerald Heath
m John Greenwood
Chips Rafferty, Jane Barrett, Gordon
Jackson, Jack Lambert, Peter Illing, Ralph
Truman, Peter Finch

Europa 51*
Italy 1952   110m   bw
Ponti / de Laurentiis
An American society woman living in Rome
seeks vainly for truth in the chaotic post-war
world and is committed to an asylum by her
husband.
A despairing, ironic comment on a period
which unfortunately does not convince on the
personal level.
w Roberto Rossellini and others *d* Roberto
Rossellini *ph* Aldo Tonti *m* Renzo Rossellini
Ingrid Bergman, Alexander Knox, Ettore
Giannini, Giulietta Masina

The Europeans*
GB 1979   83m   colour
Merchant Ivory (Ismail Merchant)
In 1850, a European baroness arrives in
Boston in search of a husband.
Charming if rather tentative period mood
piece, probably the most professional and
judicious of all the overpraised Merchant
Ivory offerings.
w Ruth Prawer Jhabvala, *novel* Henry James
d James Ivory *ph* Larry Pizer *m* Richard
Robbins *ad* Jeremiah Rusconi
Lee Remick, Robin Ellis, Tim Woodward,
Wesley Addy, Lisa Eichhorn
'A film of astonishing delicacy and richness
in which the tiniest gesture or intonation
reverberates with a world of meanings.'—*Tom
Milne, MFB*

Eva
France / Italy 1962   135m   bw
Paris / Interopa (Robert and Raymond
Hakim)
A raw Welsh novelist in Venice is humiliated
by a money-loving Frenchwoman who
erotically ensnares him.
Foolish story of a *femme fatale*; elegantly
Freudian at moments, it long outstays its
welcome.
w Hugo Butler, Evan Jones, *novel* James
Hadley Chase *d* Joseph Losey *ph* Gianni di
Venanzo *m* Michel Legrand
Stanley Baker, Jeanne Moreau, Virna Lisi,
James Villiers

The Eve of St Mark
US 1944   95m   bw
TCF (William Perlberg)
A small-town boy goes to war and his
sweetheart waits for him.
Poetic propaganda based on a sticky play
which however had a tragic ending which the
film eschews. Smartly made is all one can say.
w George Seaton, *play* Maxwell Anderson
d John M. Stahl *ph* Joseph La Shelle *m* Cyril
Mockridge
William Eythe, Anne Baxter, Michael O'Shea,
Vincent Price, Ruth Nelson, Ray Collins,
Stanley Prager, Henry Morgan

Eve Wants to Sleep*
Poland 1957   98m   bw
Film Polski (Wislaw Mincer)
An innocent country girl arrives in a city
overrun by subversives.
Curious yet sympathetic black farce, like a
cross between *Hellzapoppin* and *M*. One on its
own.
wd Tadeusz Chmielewski *ph* Stefan
Matyjaskiewicz *m* Henryk Czyz
Barbara Kwiatkowska, Stanislaw Mikulski,
Ludwik Benoit

Evel Knievel
US 1971   90m   Metrocolor
(MGM) Fanfare (George Hamilton)
Episodes from the life of a motor-cycle
stuntman.
Mildly entertaining ragbag of action sequences
and fragments of philosophy which might have
been more tolerable had EK played himself.
w Alan Caillou, John Milius *d* Marvin
Chomsky *ph* David Walsh *m* Pat Williams

George Hamilton, Sue Lyon, Bert Freed, Rod Cameron

Evelyn Prentice
US 1934   80m   bw
MGM (John W. Considine Jnr)

The wife of a criminal lawyer has an affair with a man who blackmails her.
Moderate domestic-cum-courtroom melodrama, heavily reliant on its popular stars.

w Lenore Coffee, *novel* W. E. Woodward
d William K. Howard ph Charles G. Clarke
md Oscar Radin

Myrna Loy, William Powell, Una Merkel, Harvey Stephens, Isabel Jewell, Rosalind Russell, Henry Wadsworth, Edward Brophy

Evenings for Sale
US 1932   68m   bw

An impoverished count becomes a dancing master. Scented Viennese romance intended to extend the star's success in *Trouble in Paradise*. Herbert Marshall, Sari Maritza, Mary Boland, Charles Ruggles. Written by S. K. Lauren, Agnes Brand Leahy from a novel by I. A. R Wylie; directed by Stuart Walker; for Paramount.

Evensong°
GB 1934   84m   bw
Gaumont (Michael Balcon)

At the turn of the century, an Austrian prima donna gives up her career for love.
Well-made romantic drama of its type, notable as the best of its star's few films.

w Edward Knoblock, Dorothy Farnum, *play* Beverly Nichols d Victor Saville ph Max Greene

Evelyn Laye, Fritz Kortner, Carl Esmond, Alice Delysia, Emlyn Williams, Muriel Aked

Ever Since Eve
US 1937   80m   bw
Warner (Earl Baldwin)

A publisher falls for a pretty girl, not realizing that she is his own plain secretary in disguise.
Silly romantic comedy which sadly lacks wit, style and believability.

w Lawrence Riley, Earl Baldwin, Lillie Hayward d Lloyd Bacon ph George Barnes
m Heinz Roemheld

Marion Davies (her last film), Robert Montgomery, Frank McHugh, Patsy Kelly, Louise Fazenda, Barton MacLane, Mary Treen

Evergreen°°
GB 1934   90m   bw
Gaumont (Michael Balcon)

A star's daughter takes her mother's place, with romantic complications.
Pleasant musical with more wit and style than might be expected.

w Emlyn Williams, Marjorie Gaffney, *play* Benn W. Levy d Victor Saville ph Glen MacWilliams *songs* Rodgers and Hart

Jessie Matthews, Sonnie Hale, Betty Balfour, Barry Mackay, Ivor McLaren, Hartley Power

Every Day's a Holiday°
US 1937   79m   bw
Paramount (Emmanuel Cohen)

A confidence girl in the old Bowery sells Brooklyn Bridge to suckers.
The most satisfactory example of post-Legion of Decency Mae West, the smut being replaced by a lively cast of comedians.

w *Mae West* d A. Edward Sutherland
ph Karl Struss *songs* various

Mae West, Edmund Lowe, Charles Butterworth, Charles Winninger, Walter Catlett, Lloyd Nolan, Herman Bing, Roger Imhof, Chester Conklin

Every Girl Should be Married
US 1948   84m   bw
RKO (Don Hartman, Dore Schary)

A determined girl sets her cap at a bachelor pediatrician.
Woefully thin star comedy with few laughs.

w Stephen Morehouse Avery, Don Hartman
d Don Hartman ph George E. Diskant
m Leigh Harline

Cary Grant, Betsy Drake, Franchot Tone, Diana Lynn, Alan Mowbray, Elizabeth Risdon, Richard Gaines

'In the past, Cary Grant has shown a talent for quietly underplaying comedy. In this picture, he has trouble finding comedy to play.'—*Time*

Every Home Should Have One
GB 1970   94m   Eastmancolor
British Lion / Example (Ned Sherrin)

An advertising man goes berserk when he tries to think up an erotic way of selling porridge.
Tiresomely frenetic star comedy with the emphasis on smut.

w Marty Feldman, Barry Took, Denis Norden d James Clark ph Ken Hodges
m John Cameron

Marty Feldman, Shelley Berman, Judy
Cornwell, Julie Ege, Patrick Cargill, Jack
Watson, Patience Collier, Penelope Keith,
Dinsdale Landen

Every Little Crook and Nanny
US 1972 92m Metrocolor
MGM (Leonard J. Ackerman)

A Mafia chief finds his child's new nanny has a
grudge against him.
Sporadically amusing farce.

w Cy Howard, Jonathan Axelrod, Robert
Klane d Cy Howard ph Philip Lathrop
m Fred Karlin

Victor Mature, Lynn Redgrave, Paul Sand,
Maggie Blye, Austin Pendleton, John Astin,
Dom De Luise

Every Night at Eight
US 1935 80m bw
Paramount (Walter Wanger)

Three sisters become a successful radio singing
team.
Forgettable comedy musical with a mildly
interesting cast.

w Gene Towne, Graham Baker d Raoul
Walsh ph James Van Trees songs Dorothy
Fields, Jimmy McHugh

George Raft, Alice Faye, Frances Langford,
Patsy Kelly, The Radio Rogues, Walter
Catlett, Herman Bing

Every Which Way But Loose
US 1978 114m De Luxe
Warner / Malpaso

A Los Angeles trucker wins an orang-utan in a
prize fight and becomes involved in sundry
brawls and chases.
Easy-going, shambling star vehicle which was
liked by nobody but the public.

w Jeremy Joe Kronsberg d James Fargo
ph Rexford Metz md Steve Dorff

Clint Eastwood, Sondra Locke, Ruth Gordon,
Geoffrey Lewis, Walter Barnes
† The 1980 sequel, almost indistinguishable,
was *Any Which Way You Can*.

Everybody Dance
GB 1936 74m bw

A nightclub singer is forced to pose as a rural
do-gooder. Thin comedy vehicle. Cicely
Courtneidge, Ernest Truex, Charles Riesner
Jnr, Billie de la Volta, Percy Parsons. Written
by Stafford Dickens, Ralph Spence and Leslie
Arliss; directed by Charles Riesner; for
Gaumont.

Everybody Does It
US 1949 98m bw
TCF (Nunnally Johnson)

A stage-struck wife is chagrined to see her dull
husband accidentally become an opera singer.
Very mild remake of *Wife, Husband and
Friend*; everyone tries to be zany, but the
result is often just silly.

w Nunnally Johnson d Edmund Goulding
ph Joseph La Shelle m Alfred Newman

Paul Douglas, Celeste Holm, Linda Darnell,
Charles Coburn, Millard Mitchell, Lucile
Watson, John Hoyt, George Tobias, Leon
Belasco

'For sheer momentary enjoyment it would
be hard to beat.'—*Richard Mallett, Punch*

Everybody Sing*
US 1937 80m bw
MGM (Harry Rapf)

An eccentric theatrical family is upstaged by
its servants, who put on a Broadway show.
Agreeably zany comedy with music.

w Florence Ryerson, Edgar Allan Woolf
d Edwin L. Marin ph Joseph L. Ruttenberg
m William Axt

Allan Jones, *Fanny Brice, Judy Garland*,
Reginald Owen, Billie Burke, Lynne Carver,
Monty Woolley, Reginald Gardiner, Henry
Armetta

Everything But the Truth
US 1956 83m Technicolor
U-I (Howard Christie)

A small boy embarrasses his family by telling
the truth at all times.
Dum-dum formula comedy made with jaded
professionalism.

w Herb Meadow d Jerry Hopper ph Maury
Gertsman m Milton Rosen

Maureen O'Hara, John Forsythe, Tim Hovey,
Frank Faylen, Barry Atwater

Everything Happens at Night
US 1939 77m bw
TCF (Harry Joe Brown)

Two reporters fall for the daughter of a Nobel
Peace Prize winner on the run from the
Gestapo.
The star's sixth American film plays down the
music and skating in favour of rather jaded spy
comedy. Modest entertainment.

w Art Arthur, Robert Harari d Irving
Cummings ph Edward Cronjager m various

Sonja Henie, Ray Milland, Robert Cummings, Maurice Moscovitch, Leonid Kinskey, Alan Dinehart, Fritz Feld, Victor Varconi

Everything I Have Is Yours
US 1952 92m Technicolor
MGM (George Wells)

A song and dance team is disrupted when the wife decides to become a mother.
Uninventive but lively musical vehicle for the Champions.

w George Wells d Robert Z. Leonard
ph William V. Skall md David Rose ch Nick Castle, Gower Champion

Marge and Gower Champion, Dennis O'Keefe, Eduard Franz

Everything Is Rhythm
GB 1936 73m bw

A dance band leader wins a European princess. Modest programme filler remarkable only for its record of a top band of its time.
Harry Roy and his Band, Princess Pearl, Ivor Moreton, Dave Kaye. Written by Syd Courtenay, Jack Byrd and Stanley Haynes; directed by Alfred Goulding; for Joe Rock.

Everything Is Thunder*
GB 1936 76m bw
Gaumont-British

A German girl helps a British prisoner of war to escape.
Tolerable let's-not-be-beastly melodrama, quite unusual in its time.

w Marion Dix, John Orton, novel J. B. Hardy d Milton Rosmer ph Gunther Krampf

Constance Bennett, Douglass Montgomery, Oscar Homolka, Roy Emerton, Frederick Lloyd, George Merritt

Everything You Always Wanted to Know About Sex*
US 1972 87m De Luxe
US / Jack Rollins / Charles H. Joffe / Brodsky / Gould

Seven sketches on sexual themes.
Dishevelled revue with a reasonable number of laughs for broadminded audiences.

wd Woody Allen, book Dr David Reuben
ph David M. Walsh m Mundell Lowe
pd Dale Hennesy

Woody Allen, Lynn Redgrave, Anthony Quayle, John Carradine, Lou Jacobi, Louise Lasser, Tony Randall, Burt Reynolds, Gene Wilder

Everything's Ducky
US 1961 81m bw

Two naval ratings adopt a talking duck.
Anything-goes service farce, with material below the standard of the talent available.
Mickey Rooney, Buddy Hackett, Jackie Cooper, Joanie Summers, Roland Winters. Written by John Fenton Murray and Benedict Freedman; directed by Don Taylor; for Barboo / Columbia.

The Evictors
US 1979 92m Movielab

Axe murders abound when a young couple move into an old house with a history. Old-hat horror, out of Psycho and The Amityville Horror: strictly for drive-ins. Michael Parks, Jessica Harper, Vic Morrow, Sue Ane Langdon. Written by Charles B. Pierce, Gary Rusoff and Paul Fisk; directed by Charles B. Pierce; for AIP.

The Evil
US 1978 89m Movielab
New World / Rangoon (Ed Carlin)

A psychologist takes a team to investigate a haunted house, and is soon sorry he meddled. Another variation on the theme of The Haunting and The Legend of Hell House; more this time on the horror comic level, but reasonably effective.

w Donald G. Thompson d Gus Trikonis
ph Mario Di Leo m Johnny Harris

Richard Crenna, Joanna Pettet, Andrew Prine, Cassie Yates, Victor Buono, Lynne Maddy

The Evil of Frankenstein
GB 1964 94m Technicolor
U-I / Hammer (Anthony Hinds)

Frankenstein returns to his derelict castle and finds the Monster preserved in a glacier. For their third Frankenstein film Hammer made a distribution deal with Universal and thus for the first time were able to use fragments of the old plots as well as something approximating to the Karloff make-up. Production and writing, however, are sadly dispirited except when relying on sadism.

w John Elder (Anthony Hinds) d Freddie Francis ph John Wilcox m Don Banks

Peter Cushing, Peter Woodthorpe, Sandor Eles, Kiwi Kingston (as the monster), Duncan Lamont, Katy Wild, David Hutcheson

Ex-Lady*
US 1933 70m bw

A lady artist has ultra-modern views on sex and marriage, but turns conventional when she falls in love. Mildly shocking in its day, this romantic drama was one of the contributing factors to the onslaught of the Legion of Decency which transformed Hollywood output in the following year. Bette Davis (her first starring role), Gene Raymond, Frank McHugh, Monroe Owsley, Clare Dodd. Written by David Boehm from a story by Edith Fitzgerald and Robert Riskin (previously filmed in 1931 as *Illicit*); directed by Robert Florey; for Warner.

The Ex-Mrs Bradford*
US 1936 87m bw
MGM (Edward Kaufman)

A doctor's scatty ex-wife involves him in solving a murder plot.
Amusing crime comedy, just a little way behind *The Thin Man*.

w Anthony Veiller, James Edward Grant
d Stephen Roberts ph J. Roy Hunt m Roy Webb

William Powell, Jean Arthur, James Gleason, Eric Blore, Robert Armstrong, Lila Lee, Grant Mitchell, Ralph Morgan

Exclusive
US 1937 76m bw

Journalist sacrifices himself for daughter whose views he despises. Solid newspaper drama jinxed by the excellent tragic performance of a star too long regarded as a comedian. *Charles Ruggles*, Fred MacMurray, Frances Farmer, Lloyd Nolan. Written by John C. Moffitt, Sidney Salkow, Rian James; directed by Alexander Hall; for Paramount.
'In the tough race it falls behind—it can't make the 1937 speed in murder, and the result, like lavender, is not unagreeable.'—*Graham Greene*.

Exclusive Story
US 1934 75m bw

A newspaperman has a go at the numbers racket. Tolerable anti-gangster crusade.
Franchot Tone, Madge Evans, *Joseph Calleia*, Stuart Erwin, J. Carrol Naish. Written by Michael Fessier and Martin Mooney; directed by George B. Seitz; for MGM.

Excuse My Dust*
US 1951 82m Technicolor
MGM (Jack Cummings)

The inventor of a horseless carriage loves the daughter of a livery stable owner.
Innocuous small-town nineties comedy with a race climax. Quite pleasant.

w George Wells d Roy Rowland ph Alfred Gilks m Arthur Schwarz

Red Skelton, Sally Forrest, Macdonald Carey, William Demarest

The Executioner*
GB 1970 107m Technicolor
Panavision
Columbia / Ameran (Charles H. Schneer)

A British spy suspects a colleague of being a double agent.
Dour espionage thriller with a reasonably holding narrative and predictable performances.

w Jack Pulman d Sam Wanamaker ph Denys Coop m Ron Goodwin

George Peppard, Nigel Patrick, Joan Collins, Judy Geeson, Oscar Homolka, Charles Gray, Keith Michell, George Baker, Alexander Scourby, Peter Bull, Ernest Clark, Peter Dyneley
'Does not escape from the well-worn shallow groove in which the contemporary spy film is in danger of becoming stuck.'—*Russell Campbell*

Executive Action**
US 1973 91m colour
EA Enterprises / Wakefield Orloff (Edward Lewis)

An imaginative version of the facts behind the 1963 assassination of President Kennedy. Interesting but rather messy mixture of fact and fiction; makes one sit up while it's unreeling.

w Dalton Trumbo, *story* Mark Lane, Donald Freed d David Miller ph Robert Steadman m Randy Edelman

Burt Lancaster, Robert Ryan, Will Geer, Gilbert Green, John Anderson

Executive Suite***
US 1954 104m bw
MGM (John Houseman)

When the president of a big company dies, the boardroom sees a battle for control.
First of the boardroom films of the fifties, a calculatedly commercial mixture of business ethics and domestic asides, with an all-star cast working up effective tensions.

w *Ernest Lehman, novel* Cameron Hawley
d *Robert Wise ph* George Folsey

Fredric March, William Holden, June Allyson, *Barbara Stanwyck,* Walter Pidgeon, Shelley Winters, Paul Douglas, *Louis Calhern,* Dean Jagger, *Nina Foch,* Tim Considine

'Not a classic, not a milestone in movie making, but it does suggest a standard of product that could bring back to the box office those vast audiences long alienated by trivia.'—*Arthur Knight*

'The only trouble with all these people is that they are strictly two-dimensional. They give no substantial illusion of significance, emotion or warmth.'—*Bosley Crowther, New York Times*

† A TV series followed in 1976.

AAN: George Folsey; Nina Foch

The Exile*
US 1948 90m bw
U-I (Douglas Fairbanks Jnr)

The man who is to return to the English throne as Charles II hides in Holland, receives his friends and despatches his enemies.
Curious, talkative swashbuckler with only a few moments of action; the available talents are simply not used, though the director imposes a nice pictorial style.

w Douglas Fairbanks Jnr, *novel* His Majesty the King by Cosmo Hamilton *d Max Ophuls ph Franz Planer m* Frank Skinner

Douglas Fairbanks Jnr, Maria Montez, Paula Corday, Henry Daniell, Nigel Bruce, Robert Coote

† Originally released in sepia.

Exit Smiling**
US 1926 71m (24 fps) bw silent
MGM (Sam Taylor)

The worst actress in a stock company saves the show.
Amusing comedy for a star who never quite made it in films: this is the best of her vehicles.

w Sam Taylor, Tim Whelan, *play* Marc Connelly *d* Sam Taylor *ph* Andre Barlatier

Beatrice Lillie, Jack Pickford, Harry Myers, Doris Lloyd, DeWitt Jennings, Louise Lorraine, Franklin Pangborn

Exodus*
US 1960 220m Technicolor Super Panavision 70
UA / Carlyle / Alpha (Otto Preminger)

The early years of the state of Israel, seen through various eyes.
Heavy-going modern epic, toned down from a passionate novel.

w Dalton Trumbo, *novel* Leon Uris *d* Otto Preminger *ph* Sam Leavitt *m* Ernest Gold

Paul Newman, Eva Marie Saint, Ralph Richardson, Peter Lawford, Lee J. Cobb, Sal Mineo, John Derek, Hugh Griffith, Gregory Ratoff, Felix Aylmer, David Opatoshu, Jill Haworth, Alexandra Stewart, Martin Benson, Martin Miller

'Professionalism is not enough—after three and a half hours the approach seems more exhausting than exhaustive.'—*Penelope Houston*

† Jewish comedian Mort Sahl, invited by the director to a preview, is said to have stood up after three hours and said: 'Otto—let my people go!'

AA: Ernest Gold
AAN: Sam Leavitt; Sal Mineo

The Exorcist*
US 1973 122m Metrocolor
Warner / Hoya (William Peter Blatty)

A small girl is unaccountably possessed by the devil and turned into a repellent monster who causes several violent deaths before she is cured.
Spectacularly ludicrous mishmash with uncomfortable attention to physical detail and no talent for narrative or verisimilitude. Its sensational aspects, together with a sudden worldwide need for the supernatural, assured its enormous commercial success.

w William Peter Blatty, from his novel *d* William Friedkin *ph* Owen Roizman *m* George Crumb and others *pd* Bill Malloy

Ellen Burstyn, Max Von Sydow, Jason Miller, Linda Blair, Lee J. Cobb, Kitty Winn, Jack McGowran

'No more nor less than a blood and thunder horror movie, foundering heavily on the rocks of pretension.'—*Tom Milne*

'*The Exorcist* makes no sense, [but] if you want to be shaken, it will scare the hell out of you.'—*Stanley Kauffmann*

'It exploits the subject of diabolic possession without telling you anything about it . . . just a stylistic exercise.'—*Michael Billington, Illustrated London News*

'There is a little exposition, some philosophy and theology, a quiet interlude, and then pandemonium reigns: rooms shake, heads turn full circle on bodies, wounds fester, vomit spews forth in bilious clouds besmirching a saintly priest, a possessed adolescent girl masturbates bloodily on a crucifix as she barks blasphemies and obscenities, and hoary demons freeze the soul.'—*Les Keyser, Hollywood in the Seventies*

'I know how to do it. I just throw everything at the audience and give them a real thrill. That's what they want. They don't want to go into a theater and treat it like a book. They don't even read books!'—*William Peter Blatty*
† Published 1974: *The Story Behind the Exorcist* by Peter Travers and Stephanie Reiff.

AA: William Peter Blatty
AAN: best picture; William Friedkin; Owen Roizman; Ellen Burstyn; Jason Miller; Linda Blair

Exorcist II: The Heretic
US 1977   117m   Technicolor
Warner (Richard Lederer, John Boorman)

Father Lamont, investigating the case related in *The Exorcist*, finds that the evil in Regan, apparently exorcized, is only dormant.
Highly unsatisfactory psychic melodrama which, far from the commercial route of the shocker followed by its predecessor, falls flat on its face along some wayward path of metaphysical and religious fancy. A commercial disaster, it was released in two versions and is unintelligible in either.

w William Goodhart *d* John Boorman *ph* William A. Fraker *m* Ennio Morricone *pd* Richard MacDonald

Richard Burton, Linda Blair, Louise Fletcher, Kitty Winn, Max Von Sydow, Paul Henreid, James Earl Jones, Ned Beatty

Experiment in Terror°°
US 1962   123m   bw
Columbia / Geoffrey-Kate Productions (Blake Edwards)
GB title: *The Grip of Fear*

An asthmatic stranger threatens the life of a bank teller and her sister if she does not help him commit a robbery.
Detailed, meticulous police thriller with San Francisco locations. Good stuff, a bit long.

w The Gordons, from their novel Operation Terror *d* Blake Edwards *ph* Philip Lathrop *m* Henry Mancini

Glenn Ford, Lee Remick, Ross Martin

Experiment Perilous°
US 1944   91m   bw
RKO (Warren Duff)

A woman's wealthy husband is killed in mysterious circumstances, and she is suspected.
Enjoyable mystery melodrama which takes itself with a pinch of salt.

w Warren Duff, *novel* Margaret Carpenter *d Jacques Tourneur ph* Tony Gaudio *m* Roy Webb

Hedy Lamarr, Paul Lukas, George Brent, Albert Dekker, Margaret Wycherly

The Exploits of Elaine°
US 1914   14 episodes, each 20m approx
    bw   silent
Pathé / Wharton

Detective Craig Kennedy helps his girl friend avenge her father's murder.
Archetypal cliffhanger serial following on the success of *The Perils of Pauline*. It was itself followed within a year by *The New Exploits of Elaine* and *The Romance of Elaine*. Chapter headings included such now familiar clichés as 'The Clutching Hand', 'The Vanishing Jewels', 'The Poisoned Room', 'The Death Ray' and 'The Devil Worshippers'. The films were much praised by critics for their pace and inventiveness.

w Charles W. Goddard, George B. Seitz, from stories by Arthur B. Reeve *d* Louis Gasnier, George B. Seitz

Pearl White, Creighton Hale, Sheldon Lewis, Arnold Daly

Expresso Bongo°
GB 1959   111m   bw   Dyaliscope
BL / Britannia / Conquest (Val Guest)

A Soho agent turns a nondescript teenage singer into an international star.
Heavily vulgarized version of a stage skit on the Tommy Steele rock phenomenon, divested of most of its satirical barbs and only intermittently amusing.

w Wolf Mankowitz, from his play *d* Val Guest *ph* John Wilcox *songs* David Heneker, Monty Norman

Laurence Harvey, Sylvia Syms, Yolande Donlan, Cliff Richard, *Meier Tzelniker*, Gilbert Harding, Ambrosine Philpotts, Eric Pohlmann, Wilfrid Lawson, Hermione Baddeley, Reginald Beckwith, Martin Miller

The Exquisite Sinner
US 1926   80m approx at 24 fps   bw
    silent

A young French industrialist becomes bored with his society and takes off with a band of gypsies. Curious and unsatisfactory farrago originally directed by Josef von Sternberg, but with extensive retakes by Phil Rosen (who also took credit the following year for an almost exactly similar film with a different title, *Heaven on Earth,* but featuring the same stars: Conrad Nagel and Renee Adoree). Written by Josef von Sternberg and Alice Duer Miller; for MGM.

Extase°

Czechoslovakia 1932   90m   bw
Universal Elektra Film
aka: *Ecstasy*

A country girl takes a lover.
Simple love story with Freudian sequences,
quite successfully and cinematically done. It
caused a sensation at the time and was issued
in various censored versions; the star's
husband later tried to destroy all the copies.

w Gustav Machaty, story Viteslav Nezval
d Gustav Machaty   *ph* Jan Stallich
m Giuseppe Becce

Hedy Kiesler (later Hedy Lamarr), Aribert
Mog

The Exterminating Angel°°°

Mexico 1962   95m   bw
Uninci-Films 59
original title: *El Angel Exterminador*

High society dinner guests find themselves
unable to leave the room, stay there for days,
and go totally to the bad before the strange
spell is broken; when they go to church to give
thanks, they find themselves unable to leave.
Fascinating surrealist fantasia on themes
elaborated with even more panache in *The
Discreet Charm of the Bourgeoisie*.
Nevertheless, one of its director's key films.

wd Luis Bunuel (story assistance from Luis
Alcoriza)   *ph* Gabriel Figueroa   *ad* Jesus
Bracho

Silvia Pinal, Enrique Rambal, Jacqueline
Andere, Jose Baviera
    'An unsound and unsightly mixture of
spurious allegory and genuine craziness.'—
John Simon

The Extra Girl°

US 1923   69m   bw   silent
Mack Sennett

A small town girl wins a beauty contest and
goes to Hollywood.
A comparatively restrained comedy with
slapstick interludes, this charming film shows
its star at her best and admirably illustrates
Hollywood in the early twenties.

d Mack Sennett   *m* Jack Ward

Mabel Normand, Max Davidson, Ralph
Graves, George Nicholls

The Extraordinary Seaman

US 1968   80m   Metrocolor   Panavision
MGM / John Frankenheimer / Edward
    Lewis (John H. Cushingham, Hal
    Dresner)

Four stranded sailors come upon the ghostly
Royal Navy captain of a ghostly World War II
ship.
Curious sixties attempt at forties fantasy;
obviously, from its short running time and
fragmented style, something went sadly adrift
during its making, and the wide screen does
not help, but there are scattered funny
moments.

w Philip Rock, Hal Dresner   *d* John
Frankenheimer   *ph* Lionel Lindon   *m* Maurice
Jarre

David Niven, Faye Dunaway, Alan Alda,
Mickey Rooney, Jack Carter, Juano
Hernandez, Barry Kelley
    'A cleverly made curiosity, not so much
produced as manufactured.'—*Marjorie Bilbow*

An Eye for an Eye

France / Italy 1956   93m   Technicolor
    VistaVision
UGC / Jolly (Andre Cayatte)

A doctor finds himself trekking across the
desert with a demented man whose wife has
died in his care.
Initially striking melodrama which becomes
increasingly unconvincing and has a tendency
to harp on unpleasant detail.

wd Andre Cayatte, *novel* Vahe Katcha
ph Christian Matras   *m* Louiguy

Curt Jurgens, Folco Lulli, Lea Padovani

Eye of the Cat°

US 1969   102m   Technicolor
Universal / Joseph M. Schenck (Bernard
    Schwarz, Philip Hazelton)

A young man who hates cats goes to stay with
his crippled aunt who keeps a house full of
them.
Odd, *Psycho*-like thriller (from the same
screen writer) with plenty of scary sequences
but an inadequate resolution.

w Joseph Stefano   *d* David Lowell Rich
ph Russell Metty, Ellsworth Fredericks   *m* Lalo
Schifrin   *cat trainer* Ray Berwick

Eleanor Parker, Michael Sarrazin, Gayle
Hunnicutt, Tim Henry, Laurence Naismith
    'Not so much a good film as an
extravagantly enjoyable one.'—*MFB*

Eye of the Devil°

GB 1967   92m   bw
MGM / Filmways (John Calley, Ben Kadish)

A French nobleman is obsessed by a family
tradition of pagan self-sacrifice.
Diabolical goings-on in a spooky castle, not
really helped by a glittering supporting cast

any more than by miscast stars, sluggish direction or a general atmosphere of gloom rather than suspense.

w Robin Estridge, Dennis Murphy, *novel* Day of the Arrow by Philip Loraine *d* J. Lee-Thompson *ph* Erwin Hillier *m* Gary McFarland

David Niven, Deborah Kerr, Emlyn Williams, Flora Robson, Donald Pleasence, Edward Mulhare, David Hemmings, Sharon Tate, John Le Mesurier, Donald Bisset

'It is hard to say why the total effect is so constantly hilarious.'—*MFB*

† The film had a chequered career. The first attempt to make it was abandoned because of Kim Novak's inadequacy; it then went through three titles and a lot of trouble with the censor.

Eye Witness
GB 1956 82m bw
Rank / Sydney Box

A maniacal burglar pursues a witness of his crime into the emergency ward of a local hospital.
Naïve but adequate suspenser with too many character cameos getting in the way of the plot.

w Janet Green *d* Muriel Box *ph* Reg Wyer *m* Bruce Montgomery

Donald Sinden, Muriel Pavlow, Belinda Lee, Michael Craig, Nigel Stock, Susan Beaumont, David Knight, *Ada Reeve*

Eyes in the Night*
US 1942 80m bw
MGM (Jack Chertok)

A blind detective sets out to discover whether a mysterious man engaged to an heiress is really a Nazi spy.
Tolerable wartime puzzler.

w Guy Trosper, Howard Emmett Rogers, *novel* Odor of Violets by Bayard Kendrick *d* Fred Zinnemann *ph* Robert Planck, Charles Lawton *m* Lennie Hayton

Edward Arnold, Ann Harding, Donna Reed, Allen Jenkins, John Emery, Stephen McNally, Reginald Denny, Rosemary de Camp, Stanley Ridges

† Edward Arnold appeared once more as Duncan Maclain, in *The Hidden Eye* (1944).

Eyes of Laura Mars
US 1978 104m Metrocolor
Columbia / Jon Peters (Jack H. Harris)

A fashion photographer has violent premonitions about a series of murders.
Silly and often unpleasant suspenser which despite its chic appearance never bothers to explain itself.

w John Carpenter, David Zelag Goodman *d* Irvin Kershner *ph* Victor J. Kemper *m* Artie Kane

Faye Dunaway, Tommy Lee Jones, Brad Dourif, René Auberjonois, Raul Julia, Frank Adonis

'Long on trendy settings, high-priced actors and vicious murders, but devoid of narrative thrills.'—*Richard Schickel, Time*

'Perhaps the most austerely elegant horror film ever made.'—*New Yorker*

Eyes without a Face*
France / Italy 1959 90m bw
Champs Elysées / Lux (Jules Borkon)
original title: *Les Yeux sans Visage*

When his daughter is mutilated in a car accident, a mad professor murders young girls in the process of grafting their faces onto hers.
Unpleasant horror film which its director seems to have made as a joke; the years have made it a cult.

w Jean Redon, from his novel *d Georges Franju* *ph* Eugen Schufftan *m* Maurice Jarre

Pierre Brasseur, Alida Valli, Edith Scob, François Guérin

Eyewitness*
GB 1970 91m Technicolor
ITC / ABP (Paul Maslansky)

A boy is the sole witness to an assassination, but no one believes him except the assassins.
The Window all over again, the standard clichés being tricked out with fancy photography, sub-Hitchcock set-ups and Mediterranean locations, which make it all very tolerable.

w Ronald Harwood, *novel* Mark Hebden *d* John Hough *ph* David Holmes *m* Fairfield Parlour, David Whitaker

Mark Lester, Lionel Jeffries, Susan George, Tony Bonner, Jeremy Kemp, Peter Vaughan, Peter Bowles, Betty Marsden

F

F for Fake*
France / Iran / West Germany 1973   85m
colour
Astrophore / Saco / Janus (Dominique
Antoine, François Reichenbach)
French title: *Vérités et Mensonges*

Orson Welles, at a railway station, lectures the
audience in truth and falsehood, in art, in films
and in life.
A ragbag of an entertainment, cannibalizing as
it does more than one unsold documentary,
shredded at the editing table to match the
narrator's illusionist style. Despite the raptures
of some critics, this is an irritating effusion,
and Welles now looks more like a clever
charlatan than a master film-maker.

w Orson Welles, Oja Palinkas *d* Orson
Welles *ph* Gary Graver, Christian Odasso
m Michel Legrand
'Welles stretches his material and his legend
just about as thin as possible in this tedious
treatise on truth and illusion.'—*Kevin
Thomas, Los Angeles Times*

F.P.1*
GB / Germany 1933   93m   bw
Gaumont / UFA (Erich Pommer)

Financiers try to destroy the first floating
aerodrome.
'Futuristic' melodrama about an aircraft
carrier. Very well done, and shot in two
languages, but now dated in most respects.

w Curt Siodmak, Walter Reisch, Robert
Stevenson, Peter Macfarlane *d* Karl Hartl
ph Gunther Rittau, Konstantin Tochet

Conrad Veidt, Leslie Fenton, Jill Esmond,
George Merritt, Donald Calthrop, Nicholas
Hannen, Francis L. Sullivan

The Fabulous Adventures of Marco Polo
France / Italy / Yugoslavia / Egypt /
Afghanistan 1964   115m
Eastmancolor   Franscope
Ittac / Prodi / Avala / Mounir Rafla / Italaf
Kaboul (Raoul Lévy)
aka: *Marco the Magnificent*

In 1271 Marco Polo carries a message of peace
to Kubla Khan.

Curious mixture of melodrama and
pantomime, with a star cast half playing for
laughs.

w Raoul Lévy, Denys de la Patellière
d Denys de la Patellière, Noel Howard
ph Armand Thirard *m* George Garvarentz

Horst Buchholz, Anthony Quinn, Orson
Welles, Akim Tamiroff, Robert Hossein,
Omar Sharif, Elsa Martinelli, Grégoire Aslan,
Massimo Girotti, Folco Lulli

The Fabulous Dorseys
US 1947   91m   bw
UA (Charles R. Rogers)

Two quarrelling bandleader brothers are
reunited on the death of their father.
Slight, comedic biopic with the Dorseys
playing well and trying hard.

w Richard English, Art Arthur, Curtis
Kenyon *d* Alfred E. Green *ph* James Van
Trees *m* Leo Shuken

Tommy Dorsey, Jimmy Dorsey (and their
bands), Janet Blair, Paul Whiteman, William
Lundigan

The Face***
Sweden 1958   103m   bw
Svensk Filmindustri
original title: *Ansiktet;* US title: *The
Magician*

In 19th-century Sweden, a mesmerist and his
troupe are halted at a country post to be
examined by three officials. Partly exposed as
a fraud, he takes a frightening revenge.
A virtually indecipherable parable which may
be about the survival of Christianity (and may
not), this wholly personal Bergman fancy has
to be enjoyed chiefly for its surface frissons,
for its acting and its look, which are almost
sufficient compensation.

wd Ingmar Bergman *ph* Gunnar Fischer
m Erik Nordgren

Max Von Sydow, Ingrid Thulin, *Gunnar
Bjornstrand*, Naima Wifstrand, Ake Fridell,
Lars Ekborg, Bengt Ekerot

The Face at the Window*
GB 1939   65m   bw
Pennant / Ambassador (George King)

In 1880 Paris, a murderer uses his moronic half-brother to distract his victims but is foiled when a dead man apparently incriminates him. Roistering melodrama which provided Tod Slaughter with one of his juiciest roles and is here effectively presented, which is more than can be said for the screen treatments of most of his other vehicles.

w A. R. Rawlinson, Randall Faye, play F. Brooke Warren d George King

Tod Slaughter, Marjorie Taylor, John Warwick, Leonard Henry, Aubrey Mallalieu

'One of the best English pictures I have seen . . . leaves the American horror films far behind.'—Graham Greene

The Face behind the Mask*
US 1941   69m   bw
Columbia (Wallace MacDonald)

When his face is disfigured in a fire, an immigrant turns to a life of crime. Effective second feature melodrama with a good star performance.

w Allen Vincent, Paul Jarrico, play Thomas O'Connell d Robert Florey ph Franz Planer md Sidney Cutner

Peter Lorre, Evelyn Keyes, Don Beddoe, George E. Stone

A Face in the Crowd***
US 1957   126m   bw
(Warner) Newton (Elia Kazan)

A small-town hick becomes a megalomaniac when television turns him into a cracker-barrel philosopher. Brilliantly cinematic melodrama of its time which only flags in the last lap and paints a luridly entertaining picture of modern show business.

w Budd Schulberg, from his story Your Arkansas Traveller d Elia Kazan ph Harry Stradling, Gayne Rescher m Tom Glazer

Andy Griffith, Lee Remick, Walter Matthau, Patricia Neal, Anthony Franciosa, Percy Waram, Marshall Neilan

'Savagery, bitterness, cutting humour.'— Penelope Houston

'If Kazan and Schulberg had been content to make their case by implication, it might have been a completely sophisticated piece of movie-making. Instead, everything is elaborately spelled out, and the film degenerates into preposterous liberal propaganda.'—Andrew Sarris

A Face in the Rain*
US 1963   80m   bw
Filmways / Calvic (John Calley)

During World War II an American spy in Italy bungles his mission, and hides in the apartment of a professor's wife. Offbeat, talkative melodrama with a few neat touches.

w Hugo Butler, Jean Rouverol d Irvin Kershner ph Haskell Wexler m Richard Markowitz

Rory Calhoun, Marina Berti, Niall MacGinnis

Face of a Fugitive*
US 1959   81m   Eastmancolor
Columbia / Morningside

A man falsely accused of murder makes a new life in a frontier town. Lively western melodrama with good atmosphere.

w David T. Chantler d Paul Wendkos ph Wilfrid M. Cline m Jerry Goldsmith

Fred MacMurray, Lin McCarthy, Alan Baxter, James Coburn

The Face of Fu Manchu**
GB 1965   96m   Techniscope
Anglo–EMI / Hallam (Harry Alan Towers)

In the twenties, Nayland Smith of Scotland Yard links an oriental crime wave with evil mastermind Fu Manchu. A splendidly light touch and attention to detail make this entertaining spoof like a tuppenny blood come to life.

w Peter Welbeck (Harry Alan Towers) d Don Sharp ph Ernest Steward m Chris Whelan ad Frank White

Nigel Green, Christopher Lee, Tsai Chin, Howard Marion Crawford

Faces*
US 1968   130m   bw
Maurice McEndree

A discontented Los Angeles executive tries but fails to go through with a divorce. A personal, probing study of middle-aged loneliness, made with the director's usual long-winded relentlessness but quite frequently compelling.

wd John Cassavetes ph Al Ruban m Jack Ackerman

John Marley, Gena Rowlands, Lynn Carlin, Fred Draper, Seymour Cassell

'The cast are all painfully and overpoweringly real.'—Jan Dawson

AAN: John Cassavetes (as writer); Lynn Carlin; Seymour Cassell

Faces in the Dark*
GB 1960 85m bw
Rank / Welbeck / Penington Eady (Jon
  Penington)

A blind man survives a plot against his life.
Unlikely but watchable puzzler, betrayed by
lifeless handling. Hitchcock could have
worked wonders with such a plot.

w Ephraim Kogan, John Tulley, *novel* Pierre
Boileau, Thomas Narcejac *d* David Eady
ph Ken Hodges *m* Edwin Astley

John Gregson, Mai Zetterling, Michael
Denison, John Ireland, Tony Wright, Nanette
Newman

The Facts of Life*
US 1960 103m bw
(UA) HLP (Norman Panama)

Two middle-aged married suburbanites have
an abortive affair.
Star comedy with muted slapstick and earnest
acting, a good try, but less effective than their
normal pratfalls.

w Norman Panama, Melvin Frank *d* Melvin
Frank *ph* Charles Lang Jnr *m* Leigh Harline

Bob Hope, Lucille Ball, Ruth Hussey, Don
Defore, Louis Nye, Philip Ober
  'Random shots of mockery aimed effectively
at the American middle-class way of life.'—
Peter John Dyer

AAN: Norman Panama, Melvin Frank
(script); Charles Lang Jnr; title song (*m /
ly* Johnny Mercer)

Fahrenheit 451*
GB 1966 112m Technicolor
Rank / Anglo Enterprise / Vineyard (Lewis
  M. Allen)

In a fascist future state, a fireman's job is to
burn books.
1984 stuff, a litt̩ ɔ lacking in plot and rather
tentatively directed, but with charming
moments.

w François Truffaut, Jean-Louis Richard,
novel Ray Bradbury *d* François Truffaut
ph Nicolas Roeg *m* Bernard Herrmann
design consultant Tony Walton

Oskar Werner, Julie Christie, Cyril Cusack,
Anton Diffring, Jeremy Spenser

Fail Safe*
US 1964 111m bw
Columbia / Max E. Youngstein / Sidney
  Lumet

An American atomic bomber is accidentally
set to destroy Moscow, and the president has
to destroy New York in retaliation.

Despite a confusing opening, this deadly
earnest melodrama gets across the horror of its
situation better than the contemporaneous *Dr
Strangelove* which treated the same plot as
black comedy. Here the details are both
terrifying and convincing.

w Walter Bernstein, *novel* Eugene Burdick,
Harvey Wheeler *d* Sidney Lumet *ph* Gerald
Hirschfeld *m* none

Henry Fonda, Walter Matthau, Dan
O'Herlihy, Frank Overton, Fritz Weaver,
Edward Binns, Larry Hagman, Russell Collins
  'It will have you sitting on the brink of
eternity.'—*publicity*

Fair Wind to Java
US 1952 92m Trucolor
Republic (Joseph Kane)

A sailor with a mutinous crew seeks a South
Sea treasure.
Routine adventure culminating in a volcanic
explosion.

w Richard Tregaskis, *novel* Garland Roark
d Joseph Kane *ph* Jack Marta *m* Victor
Young

Fred MacMurray, Vera Hruba Ralston,
Robert Douglas, Victor McLaglen

Faithful in My Fashion
US 1946 81m bw

A soldier on leave causes havoc in a
department store where his girl friend is
manager. Sentimental comedy, forgettable for
itself but containing endearing performances
by a number of favourite character actors.
Tom Drake, Donna Reed, Edward Everett
Horton, Spring Byington, Harry Davenport,
Sig Rumann, Margaret Hamilton, Hobart
Cavanaugh. Written by Lionel Houser;
directed by Sidney Salkow; for MGM.

Faithless
US 1932 76m bw
MGM

A spoiled rich girl and her beau both descend
to working-class level and almost further.
Would-be sensational drama ruined by
censorship and miscasting.

w Carey Wilson, *novel* Tinfoil by Mildred
Cram *d* Harry Beaumont *ph* Oliver T. Marsh

Tallulah Bankhead, Robert Montgomery,
Hugh Herbert, Maurice Murphy, Louise
Closser Hale, Lawrence Grant, Henry Kolker

The Falcon
A debonair solver of crime puzzles allegedly
created by Michael Arlen but owing much to

The Saint and resulting from a need by RKO for more of the same. Helped by a tough / comic manservant, he flourished during the forties in sixteen second features (the last three for Film Classics). After three episodes George Sanders tired of the role and was written out by being 'shot' and having his real-life brother Tom Conway take over as his fictional one. The performances of these two actors are pleasant, though the films are now fairly unwatchable, but John Calvert who took over for the last three was not a success.

1941: THE GAY FALCON, A DATE WITH THE FALCON
1942: THE FALCON TAKES OVER (the plot was borrowed from Raymond Chandler's FAREWELL MY LOVELY), THE FALCON'S BROTHER
1943: THE FALCON STRIKES BACK, THE FALCON AND THE CO-EDS, THE FALCON IN DANGER
1944: THE FALCON IN HOLLYWOOD, THE FALCON IN MEXICO, THE FALCON OUT WEST
1945: THE FALCON IN SAN FRANCISCO
1946: THE FALCON'S ALIBI, THE FALCON'S ADVENTURE
1948: THE DEVIL'S CARGO, APPOINTMENT WITH MURDER, SEARCH FOR DANGER

The Fall°
Argentina 1958   86m   bw
Argentine Sono (Leopoldo Torre Nilsson)
original title: *La Caida*

A strictly brought-up college girl lodges with an eccentric family whose strange world comes to mean more to her than the love of a young lawyer.
Odd, claustrophobic melodrama from a very personal film-maker.

w Beatriz Guido, Leopoldo Torre Nilsson, *novel* Beatriz Guido *d Leopoldo Torre Nilsson ph* Alberto Etchebehere *m* Juan Carlos Paz

Elsa Daniel, Duilio Marzia, Lydia Lamaison, Carlos Lopez Monet

The Fall of Berlin°
USSR 1949   160m   Agfacolor
Mosfilm

A steel worker turns soldier, sees all the major Russian battles of World War II, and has his hand shaken by Stalin.
Out-and-out propaganda, with caricatures of famous people and magnificently staged battles.

w M. Chiaureli, P. A. Pavlenko
d M. Chiaureli *ph* L. V. Kosmatov *m* Dmitri Shostakovich

B. Andreyev, M. Gelovani (as Stalin), V. Stanitsine (as Churchill), M. Kovaleva

The Fall of the Roman Empire°°
US / Spain 1964   187m   Technicolor
Ultra Panavision 70
Samuel Bronston

After poisoning the Emperor Marcus Aurelius his mad son Commodus succumbs to dissipation and allows Rome to be ravaged by pestilence and the Barbarians.
Would-be distinguished epic with an intellectual first hour; unfortunately the hero is a priggish bore, the villain a crashing bore, the heroine a saintly bore, and the only interesting character is killed off early. A chariot race, a javelin duel, some military clashes and a mass burning at the stake keep one watching, and the production values are high indeed.

w Ben Barzman, Philip Yordan *d Anthony Mann ph* Robert Krasker, John Moore *m* Dmitri Tiomkin *pd* Venerio Colasanti

Alec Guinness, Christopher Plummer, Stephen Boyd, James Mason, Sophia Loren, John Ireland, Eric Porter, Anthony Quayle, Mel Ferrer, Omar Sharif
'The film works from a restricted palette, and the result is weirdly restraining and severe, a dignified curb on absurdities.'—*John Coleman*

AAN: Dmitri Tiomkin

Fallen Angel°
US 1945   97m   bw
TCF (Otto Preminger)

A man plans to get rid of his wife and marry another woman, but it is the latter who is murdered.
Oddly sleazy melodrama, not more successful then because it was unexpected than now because it is miscast. Some good sequences, though.

w Harry Kleiner, *novel* Marty Holland *d Otto Preminger ph Joseph La Shelle m* David Raksin

Dana Andrews, Alice Faye, Linda Darnell, Charles Bickford, Anne Revere, Bruce Cabot, John Carradine, Percy Kilbride
'It holds you by its undertones of small-town life and frustration.'—*Richard Winnington*

The Fallen Idol°°°
GB 1948   94m   bw
British Lion / London Films
US title: *The Lost Illusion*

An ambassador's small son nearly incriminates his friend the butler in the accidental death of his shrewish wife.

A near-perfect piece of small-scale cinema, built up from clever nuances of acting and cinematic technique.

w Graham Greene, from his story The Basement Room *d Carol Reed ph Georges Périnal m* William Alwyn

Ralph Richardson, Michèle Morgan, *Bobby Henrey,* Sonia Dresdel, Jack Hawkins

'A short story has become a film which is compact without loss of variety in pace and shape.'—*Dilys Powell*

AAN: Graham Greene; Carol Reed

The Fallen Sparrow°
US 1943 93m bw
RKO (Robert Fellows)

An American veteran of the Spanish Civil War finds himself hounded in New York by Nazis seeking the Spanish flag of freedom.

Obscure melodrama, very good to look at but hardly worth unravelling; a precursor to Hollywood's post-war *films noirs.*

w Warren Duff, *novel* Dorothy B. Hughes *d* Richard Wallace *ph Nicholas Musuraca md* Roy Webb, Constantin Bakaleinikoff

John Garfield, Maureen O'Hara, Walter Slezak, Martha O'Driscoll, Patricia Morison, Bruce Edwards, John Banner, John Miljan

AAN: Roy Webb, Constantin Bakaleinikoff

Falling in Love Again°
US 1980 103m colour
International Picture Show of Atlanta (Steven Paul)

A middle-aged New Yorker remembers his young romances and his dreams of success.

Warm little independent production harking back to the days of *H. M. Pulham Esquire* and none the worse for that.

w Steven Paul, Ted Allan, Susannah York *d* Steven Paul *ph* Michael Mileham, Dick Bush, Wolfgang Suschitzky *m* Michel Legrand

Elliott Gould, Susannah York, Stuart Paul, Kaye Ballard

Falling for You°
GB 1933 88m bw
Gainsborough (Michael Balcon)

Fleet Street journalists in Switzerland try to outsmart each other.

Dated comedy very typical of the stars' extremely casual style, with immaculate set pieces.

w Jack Hulbert, Douglas Furber, Robert Stevenson, *story* Sidney Gilliat *d* Jack Hulbert, Robert Stevenson *ph* Bernard Knowles *songs* Vivian Ellis, Douglas Furber

Jack Hulbert, Cicely Courtneidge, Tamara Desni, Garry Marsh, Alfred Drayton, O. B. Clarence, Morton Selten

Fame°
US 1980 133m Metrocolor
MGM (David de Silva, Alan Marshall)

Assorted teenagers attend Manhattan's High School for the Performing Arts.

Cleverly shot and edited slice of life which unfortunately features people whose language and personalities are fairly repellent. The result is like *A Chorus Line* without the music.

w Christopher Gore *d Alan Parker ph* Michael Seresin *m* Michael Gore and others *pd* Geoffrey Kirkland

Irene Cara, Lee Curreri, Laura Dean, Paul McCrane, Barry Miller, Gene Anthony Ray

'Our film, I hope, will be a microcosm of New York . . . a dozen races pitching in and having their own crack at the American dream.'—*Alan Parker*

'Its soft-centred view of human relationships is periodically undercut by what can only be described as the grotesque.'—*John Pym*

AA: screenplay; best original song (Michael Gore, Dean Pitchford); editing (Gerry Hambling)

Fame Is the Spur°
GB 1947 116m bw
GFD / Two Cities / Charter Films (John Boulting)

The rise to political eminence of a working-class socialist.

Disappointingly flat historical drama from a novel allegedly based on the career of Ramsay MacDonald. Interesting moments.

w Nigel Balchin, *novel* Howard Spring *d* Roy Boulting *ph* Gunther Krampf, Harry Waxman

Michael Redgrave, Rosamund John, Bernard Miles, Carla Lehmann, Hugh Burden, Marjorie Fielding, Seymour Hicks

A Family Affair°
US 1937 69m bw
MGM (Lucien Hubbard)

A small-town judge faces a few family problems.

The second feature that started the highly successful Hardy family series (qv under *Hardy*). In this case the judge and his wife were played by actors who did not persevere into the series, but the stage was otherwise set for a long run, and the town of Carvel came to mean home to many Americans abroad.

w Kay Van Riper, *play* Skidding by Aurania Rouverol *d* George B. Seitz *ph* Lester White

Lionel Barrymore, Spring Byington, *Mickey Rooney*, Eric Linden, Cecilia Parker, Sara Haden, Charles Grapewin, Julie Haydon

Family Honeymoon
US 1948   90m   bw
U-I (John Beck, Z. Wayne Griffin)

A college professor marries a widow whose three children join them on their Grand Canyon honeymoon.
Very ordinary and predictable star comedy.

w Dane Lussier, Homer Croy *d* Claude Binyon *ph* William Daniels *m* Frank Skinner

Claudette Colbert, Fred MacMurray, Rita Johnson, Gigi Perreau, Peter Miles, Jimmy Hunt, Hattie McDaniel, Chill Wills

The Family Jewels
US 1965   100m   Technicolor
Paramount / York / Jerry Lewis

A child heiress chooses a new father from among her five uncles.
Unfunny star farce with multiple impersonations.

w Jerry Lewis, Bill Richmond *d* Jerry Lewis *ph* W. Wallace Kelley *m* Pete King

Jerry Lewis, Donna Butterworth, Sebastian Cabot, Robert Strauss

Family Life**
GB 1971   108m   Technicolor
EMI / Kestrel (Tony Garnett)

A 19-year-old girl is driven into a mental collapse by emotional and family problems.
A slice of suburban life and an indictment of it, put together with unknown actors and probing TV techniques. Somewhat too harrowing for fiction, but extraordinarily vivid.

w David Mercer, from his play In Two Minds *d* Ken Loach *ph* Charles Stewart *m* Marc Wilkinson

Sandy Ratcliff, Bill Dean, Grace Cave

Family Plot**
US 1976   126m   Technicolor
Universal (Alfred Hitchcock)

A fake medium tries for easy money by producing a lost heir.
Talkative, complex, patchy, low-key but always interesting Hitchcock suspenser in an unusually friendly vein.

w Ernest Lehman, *novel* The Rainbird Pattern by Victor Canning *d* Alfred Hitchcock *ph* Leonard J. South *m* John Williams *pd* Henry Bumstead

Karen Black, Bruce Dern, Barbara Harris, William Devane, Ed Lauter, Cathleen Nesbitt
'Full of benign mischief, beautiful craftsmanship and that elusive sense of cinematic rhythm that has always been Hitchcock's trump card.'—*Michael Billington, Illustrated London News*
'The picture bogs down in one talky, undramatic sequence after another, and the plot, with all its exposition and loose ends, is involved beyond belief.'—*De Witt Bodeen, Films in Review*

The Family Secret
US 1951   85m   bw
Columbia / Santana (Robert Lord, Henry S. Kesler)

The son of a suburban family kills his best friend in a brawl, and his mother insists he conceal the truth even when another man is charged.
Television-style pattern play, not even very interesting at the time.

w Francis Cockrell, Andrew Solt *d* Henry Levin *ph* Burnett Guffey *m* George Duning

John Derek, Lee J. Cobb, Erin O'Brien Moore, Jody Lawrance, Henry O'Neill, Carl Benton Reid
'The general atmosphere is one of outward torment unbacked by inner emotion.'—*MFB*

The Family Way*
GB 1966   115m   Eastmancolor
BL / Jambox (John Boulting)

There is consternation in a Lancashire family when the son cannot consummate his marriage.
Overstretched domestic farce-drama. Good scenes and performances, but it was all much sharper as a one-hour TV play.

w Bill Naughton, from his play Honeymoon Deferred *d* Roy Boulting *ph* Harry Waxman *m* Paul McCartney

John Mills, *Marjorie Rhodes*, Hywel Bennett, Hayley Mills, *Avril Angers*, Murray Head, Wilfred Pickles, Barry Foster, Liz Fraser

The Fan*
US 1949   79m   bw
TCF (Otto Preminger)
GB title: *Lady Windermere's Fan*

Scandal almost results when Lady Windermere loses her fan.

Reasonably polished, rather dull version of an
old play, not really helped by modern
bookends.

w Walter Reisch, Dorothy Parker, Ross
Evans, *play* Lady Windermere's Fan by Oscar
Wilde *d* Otto Preminger *ph* Joseph La
Shelle *m* Daniele Amfitheatrof

George Sanders, Madeleine Carroll, Jeanne
Crain, Richard Greene, Martita Hunt, John
Sutton, Hugh Dempster, Richard Ney

Fanatic°
GB 1965 96m Technicolor
Hammer / Seven Arts (Anthony Hinds)
US title: *Die! Die! My Darling*

An American girl in England visits the mother
of her dead fiancé and finds herself the
prisoner of a religious maniac.
Boringly overlong Grand Guignol which even
defeats its gallantly unmade-up and deathly-
looking star; mildly notable however as a
record of one of her last performances.

w Richard Matheson, *novel* Nightmare by
Anne Blaisdell *d* Silvio Narizzano *ph* Arthur
Ibbetson *m* Wilfrid Josephs *pd* Peter Proud

Tallulah Bankhead, Stefanie Powers, Peter
Vaughan, Yootha Joyce, Donald Sutherland

The Fanatics°
France 1957 92m bw
Cinégraphe-Regent (Pierre Lévy)

Patriots quarrel over the assassination by
bomb of a South American dictator when he
travels by public plane.
Suspense melodrama with many artificial
twists, but slick and well acted.

w Alex Joffé, Jean Levitte *d* Alex Joffé
ph L. H. Burel *m* Paul Misraki

Pierre Fresnay, Michel Auclair, Grégoire
Aslan, Betty Schneider

Fancy Pants°°
US 1950 92m Technicolor
Paramount (Robert Welch)

A British actor stranded in the far west poses
as a butler.
Lively western comedy remake of *Ruggles of
Red Gap* (qv), one of the star's better vehicles.

w Edmund Hartman, Robert O'Brien
d George Marshall *ph* Charles Lang Jnr
m Van Cleave

Bob Hope, Lucille Ball, Bruce Cabot, Jack
Kirkwood, Lea Penman, Eric Blore, John
Alexander, Norma Varden

Fanfan la Tulipe°
France 1951 98m bw
Filmsonor-Ariane-Amato

Recruited into the army of Louis XV by a
prophecy that he will marry the king's
daughter, a young braggart does everything he
can to live up to it.
Rather like a spoof Errol Flynn effort, this
likeable swashbuckler can't quite summon up
enough buckle or swash to be the minor classic
it clearly intends.

w René Wheeler, Jean Fallet *d* Christian-
Jaque *ph* Christian Matras *m* Georges Van
Parys, Maurice Thiriet

Gérard Philipe, Gina Lollobrigida, Noel
Roquevert, Marcel Herrand
  'A daring and delightful piece of work.'—
Times

Fanny (Pagnol) see Marius

Fanny°
US 1960 133m Technicolor
Warner / Mansfield (Joshua Logan)

Life on the Marseilles waterfront, and in
particular the story of two old men and two
lovers.
Lumbering adaptation of three Pagnol films of
the thirties (*Marius, Fanny, César*—see
Marius) previously seen as a 1938 Hollywood
film (*Port of Seven Seas*) and later as a
Broadway musical. This is the dullest version
despite fine photography and a couple of good
performances.

w Julius J. Epstein, *play* S. N. Behrman,
Joshua Logan, *films* Marcel Pagnol *d* Joshua
Logan *ph* Jack Cardiff *m* Harold Rome
md Morris Stoloff, Harry Sukman

Charles Boyer, Maurice Chevalier, Leslie
Caron, Horst Buchholz, Georgette Anys,
Salvatore Baccaloni, Lionel Jeffries, Raymond
Bussières, Victor Francen
† The film was proudly advertised as 'Joshua
Logan's *Fanny*' until the press pointed out the
double meaning.

AAN: best picture; Jack Cardiff; Morris
Stoloff, Harry Sukman; Charles Boyer

Fanny by Gaslight°°
GB 1944 108m bw
GFD / Gainsborough (Edward Black)
US title: *Man of Evil*

The illegitimate daughter of a cabinet minister
is saved from a lustful Lord.
Highly-coloured Victorian romantic
melodrama, enjoyably put over with no holds
barred and a pretty high budget for the time.

w Doreen Montgomery, Aimée Stuart, *novel*
Michael Sadleir *d* Anthony Asquith
ph Arthur Crabtree *m* Cedric Mallabey

James Mason, Phyllis Calvert, Stewart
Granger, Wilfrid Lawson, John Laurie,
Margaretta Scott, Stuart Lindsell, Jean Kent
   'Seldom have I seen a film more agreeable
to watch, from start to finish.'—*William
Whitebait*
   'Mr Asquith does not seem to have made
much effort to freshen it by interesting
treatment, so that the rare unusual device
seems quite out of key among so much that is
simple, obvious, hackneyed.'—*Richard
Mallett, Punch*
† One of several costume melodramas
patterned after the success of *The Man in Grey*
(qv).

Fantasia****
US 1940   135m   Technicolor
Walt Disney

A concert of classical music is given cartoon
interpretations. The pieces are:
   Bach: Toccata and Fugue in D Minor
   Tchaikovsky: The Nutcracker Suite
   Dukas: The Sorcerer's Apprentice
   Stravinsky: The Rite of Spring
   Beethoven: The Pastoral Symphony
   Ponchielli: Dance of the Hours
   Moussorgsky: Night on a Bare Mountain
   Schubert: Ave Maria
Brilliantly inventive for the most part, the
cartoons having become classics in themselves.
The least part (the Pastoral Symphony) can be
forgiven.
supervisor Ben Sharpsteen   *md* Edward H.
Plumb

Leopold Stokowski, the Philadelphia
Orchestra, Deems Taylor
   'Dull as it is towards the end, ridiculous as it
is in the bend of the knee before Art, it is one
of the strange and beautiful things that have
happened in the world.'—*Otis Ferguson*
   'It is ambitious, and finely so, and one feels
that its vulgarities are at least unintentional.'—
James Agate
† Multiplane cameras, showing degrees of
depth in animation, were used for the first
time.

Fantastic Voyage*
US 1966   100m   De Luxe   Cinemascope
TCF (Saul David)

When a top scientist is shot and suffers brain
damage, a team of doctors and a boat are
miniaturized and injected into his blood
stream . . . but one is a traitor.
Engagingly absurd science fiction which keeps
its momentum but is somewhat let down by its
decor.

w Harry Kleiner   *d Richard Fleischer
ph* Ernest Laszlo   *m* Leonard Rosenman
ad Dale Hennesy, Jack Martin Smith   *sp* L. B.
Abbott, Art Cruickshank, Emil Kosa Jnr

Stephen Boyd, Raquel Welch, Edmond
O'Brien, Donald Pleasence, Arthur Kennedy,
Arthur O'Connell, William Redfield
   'The process shots are so clumsily matted
. . . that the actors look as if a child has cut
them out with blunt scissors.'—*Pauline Kael*

AA: art direction
AAN: Ernest Laszlo

The Far Country*
US 1955   97m   Technicolor
U-I (Aaron Rosenberg)

Two cowboys on their way to the Alaska
goldfields are beset by swindlers.
Sturdy star western with good production
values.

w Borden Chase   *d* Anthony Mann
ph William Daniels   *m* Joseph Gershenson

James Stewart, Walter Brennan, Ruth Roman,
Corinne Calvet, John McIntire

Far from the Madding Crowd*
GB 1967   175m   Technicolor
   Panavision 70
EMI / Vic / Appia (Joseph Janni)

In Victorian Wessex a headstrong girl causes
unhappiness and tragedy.
Good-looking but slackly handled version of a
melodramatic and depressing novel.

w Frederic Raphael, *novel* Thomas Hardy
d John Schlesinger   *ph* Nicolas Roeg
m Richard Rodney Bennett   *pd* Richard
Macdonald

Julie Christie, Peter Finch, Alan Bates,
Terence Stamp, Prunella Ransome
   'In this rather plodding film the insufficiency
of the foreground is partly offset by the
winsomeness of the backgrounds. The very
sheep are so engaging as to entice our gaze
into some extremely amiable
woolgathering.'—*John Simon*

AAN: Richard Rodney Bennett

The Far Horizons
US 1955   108m   Technicolor
   Vistavision
(Paramount) Pine–Thomas

The story of Lewis and Clark's 1803
expedition west through the Louisiana
Purchase territory.
Flabbily-handled historical hokum; potential
interest quickly dissipated.

w Winston Miller, Edmund H. North
d Rudolph Maté *ph* Daniel L. Fapp *m* Hans
Salter

Fred MacMurray, Charlton Heston, Donna
Reed, Barbara Hale, William Demarest

Farewell Again**
GB 1937 85m bw
Pendennis / London Films (Erich Pommer)
US title: *Troopship*

Soldiers returning from India have six hours'
shore leave to sort out their problems.
Dated but sharply made compendium drama,
a solid success of its time.

w Clemence Dane, Patrick Kirwan *d* Tim
Whelan *ph* James Wong Howe, Hans
Schneeberger

Flora Robson, Leslie Banks, Robert Newton,
René Ray, Patricia Hilliard, Sebastian Shaw,
Leonora Corbett, Anthony Bushell, Edward
Lexy, Wally Patch, Edmund Willard, Martita
Hunt, John Laurie

Farewell My Lovely***
US 1944 95m bw
RKO (Adrian Scott)
aka: *Murder My Sweet*

A private eye searches for an ex-convict's
missing girl friend.
A revolutionary crime film in that it was the
first to depict the genuinely seedy milieu
suggested by its author. One of the first *films
noirs* of the mid-forties, a minor masterpiece
of expressionist film making, and a total
change of direction for a crooner who
suddenly became a tough guy.

w John Paxton, novel Raymond Chandler
d Edward Dmytryk *ph* Harry J. Wild *m* Roy
Webb

Dick Powell, Claire Trevor, Anne Shirley,
Mike Mazurki, Otto Kruger, Miles Mander,
Douglas Walton, Ralf Harolde, Don Douglas,
Esther Howard
'A nasty, draggled bit of dirty work,
accurately observed.'—*C. A. Lejeune*

Farewell My Lovely**
US 1975 95m Technicolor
Avco Embassy / Elliott Kastner / ITC
  (George Pappas, Jerry Bruckheimer)

A pretty sharp remake of the above, with the
plot slightly rewritten but tightened, and an
excellent performance from a rather over-age
star.

w David Zelag Goodman *d* Dick Richards
ph John A. Alonzo *m* David Shire *pd* Dean
Tavouraris

Robert Mitchum, Charlotte Rampling, John
Ireland, Sylvia Miles, Anthony Zerbe, Jack
O'Halloran, Kate Murtagh
'A moody, bluesy, boozy recreation of
Marlowe's tacky, neon-flashed Los Angeles of
the early forties.'—*Judith Crist*
'A delicious remake with a nice, smoky
1940s atmosphere.'—*Michael Billington,
Illustrated London News*
AAN: Sylvia Miles

A Farewell to Arms**
US 1932 78m bw
Paramount

In World War I, a wounded American
ambulance driver falls in love with his nurse.
Now very dated but important in its time, this
romantic drama was one of the more
successful Hemingway adaptations to be
filmed.

w Benjamin Glazer, Oliver H. P. Garrett,
*novel Ernest Hemingway d Frank Borzage
ph* Charles Lang *m* W. Franke Harling

Gary Cooper, *Helen Hayes*, Adolphe Menjou,
Mary Philips, Jack La Rue, Blanche Frederici,
Henry Armetta
'Too much sentiment and not enough
strength.'—*Mordaunt Hall, New York Times*
'Borzage has invested the war scenes with a
strange, brooding expressionist quality . . .
indeed, the overall visual style is most
impressive.'—*NFT, 1974*
† Remade as *Force of Arms* (qv) and see
below.

AA: Charles Lang
AAN: best picture

A Farewell to Arms
US 1957 150m De Luxe Cinemascope
TCF / David O. Selznick

Elaborate ill-fated remake which tried to make
an adventure epic out of a low-key war drama.
Its failure caused David O. Selznick to
produce no more films.

w Ben Hecht *d* Charles Vidor *pd* Alfred
Junge *ph* Piero Portalupi, Oswald Morris
m Mario Nascimbene

Rock Hudson, Jennifer Jones, Vittorio de
Sica, Alberto Sordi, Kurt Kasznar, Mercedes
McCambridge, Oscar Homolka, Elaine
Stritch, Victor Francen
AAN: Vittorio de Sica

The Farmer Takes a Wife*
US 1935 91m bw
TCF (Winfield Sheehan)

By the Erie Canal in the 1820s, a wandering
girl finds security with a farmer.
Pleasantly 'different' romantic drama, quite
ably executed and introducing Henry Fonda to
the screen.

w Edwin Burke, *play* Frank B. Elser and Marc
Connelly, *novel* Rome Haul by Walter D.
Edmonds *d* Victor Fleming *ph* John Seitz
m Arthur Lange

Janet Gaynor, Henry Fonda, Charles
Bickford, Slim Summerville, Andy Devine,
Roger Imhof, Jane Withers, Margaret
Hamilton, Sig Rumann, John Qualen

The Farmer Takes a Wife*
US 1953   81m   Technicolor
TCF (Frank P. Rosenberg)

Musical remake with an agreeably stylized
look, hampered by a slowish script and dull
cast.

w Walter Bulloch, Sally Benson, Joseph
Fields *d* Henry Levin *ph* Arthur E. Arling
m Cyril Mockridge *ad Lyle Wheeler, Addison
Hehr*

Betty Grable, Dale Robertson, Thelma Ritter,
Eddie Foy Jnr, John Carroll

The Farmer's Daughter
US 1940   60m   bw
Paramount (William C. Thomas)

A stage struck country girl tries to horn in on a
Broadway musical rehearsing nearby.
Feeble comedy for the sticks.

w Lewis R. Foster, Delmer Daves *d* James
Hogan *ph* Leo Tover

Martha Raye, Charles Ruggles, Richard
Denning, Gertrude Michael, William Frawley,
William Demarest, Jack Norton

The Farmer's Daughter**
US 1947   97m   bw
David O. Selznick (Dore Schary)

The Swedish maid of a congressman becomes
a political force.
Well-made Cinderella story with a touch of
asperity and top notch production values and
cast.

*w Allen Rivkin, Laura Kerr d H. C. Potter
ph Milton Krasner m* Leigh Harline

*Loretta Young, Joseph Cotten, Ethel
Barrymore, Charles Bickford*, Rose Hobart,
Rhys Williams, Harry Davenport, Tom
Powers

  'Patricians, politicians, even peasants are
portrayed with unusual perception and wit.'—
James Agee

AA: Loretta Young
AAN: Charles Bickford

The Farmer's Wife
GB 1928   67m approx   bw   silent
BIP (John Maxwell)

A farmer seeks a wife and after three
disappointments settles for his housekeeper.
A simple and not very interesting silent screen
version of a stage success which depended
largely on dialogue.

wd Alfred Hitchcock, *play* Eden Phillpotts
ph Jack Cox

James Thomas, Gordon Harker, Lillian Hall-
Davis

The Farmer's Wife
GB 1940   82m   bw

Talkie remake of the above, a perfectly
adequate photographed play. Basil Sydney,
Wilfrid Lawson, Nora Swinburne, Patricia
Roc, Michael Wilding. Written by Norman
Lee, Leslie Arliss and J. E. Hunter; directed
by Norman Lee and Leslie Arliss; for Pathé.

Farrebique**
France 1947   85m   bw
L'Ecran Français / Les Films Etienne Lallier

Problems of a peasant family in central
France.
Superbly-filmed semi-documentary, acted by a
real family.

*wd Georges Rouquier ph André Dantan
m* Henri Sauguet

  'Definitely a film for posterity.'—*MFB*

Fashions of 1934*
US 1934   78m   bw
Warner (Henry Blanke)

A confidence trickster conquers the French
fashion world.
Slight musical comedy with a couple of
splendid Berkeley numbers.

w F. Hugh Herbert, Carl Brickson *d* William
Dieterle *ch Busby Berkeley ph* William
Rees *m / ly* Sammy Fain, Irving Kahal
ad Jack Okey

William Powell, Bette Davis, Verree
Teasdale, Frank McHugh, Reginald Owen,
Hugh Herbert, Henry O'Neill

Fast and Loose
US 1930   70m   bw
Paramount

A spoiled rich girl falls in love with a car
mechanic.
Tiresome melodrama, dully scripted.

w Doris Anderson, Jack Kirkland, Preston
Sturges, *play* The Best People by Avery
Hopwood, David Gray *d* Fred Newmeyer
ph William Steiner

Miriam Hopkins, Carole Lombard, Frank
Morgan, Charles Starrett, Henry Wadsworth,
David Hutcheson, Ilka Chase

Fast and Loose*
US 1939 80m bw
MGM (Frederick Stephani)

Married detectives and rare book experts solve
the mystery of a missing Shakespeare
manuscript.
Pleasing comedy mystery in the wake of *The
Thin Man*.

w Harry Kurnitz *d* Edwin L. Marin
ph George Folsey

Robert Montgomery, Rosalind Russell, Ralph
Morgan, Reginald Owen, Etienne Girardot,
Alan Dinehart, Joan Marsh, Sidney Blackmer

Fast and Loose
GB 1954 75m bw

By a series of accidents, a married man has to
spend a night at an inn with an old flame.
Spiritless and miscast remake of *A Cuckoo in
the Nest*; all talents below form. Brian Reece,
Stanley Holloway, Kay Kendall, Reginald
Beckwith, Charles Victor, June Thorburn.
Written by A. R. Rawlinson and Ben Travers,
from the latter's play; directed by Gordon
Parry; for Group Films / Rank.

Fast Company*
US 1938 75m bw

A couple in the rare book business are
implicated in the murder of a rival. First of
three whodunnits featuring Joel and Garda
Page, whose style was not at all dissimilar
from that of Nick and Nora Charles in the
Thin Man series. A polished time-passer.
Melvyn Douglas, Florence Rice, Clare Dodd,
Louis Calhern, George Zucco. Written by
Marco Page (Harry Kurnitz); directed by
Edward Buzzell; for MGM. (NB: The follow-
ups had different stars as the pair of sleuths.
Fast and Loose (qv) featured Robert
Montgomery and Rosalind Russell; Sidney
Blackmer, Ralph Morgan and Reginald Owen
supported. *Fast and Furious*, also released in
1939, starred Franchot Tone and Ann
Sothern, with Ruth Hussey, Lee Bowman and
Allyn Joslyn.)

The Fast Lady**
GB 1962 95m Eastmancolor
Rank / Group Films (Teddy Baird)

A bashful suitor buys an old Bentley, becomes
a roadhog, passes his test, captures some
crooks and gets the girl.
Spirited if aimless farcical comedy which crams
in all the jokes about cars anyone can think of.

w Jack Davies, Henry Blyth *d* Ken Annakin
ph Reg Wyer *m* Norrie Paramor

Stanley Baxter, James Robertson Justice,
Leslie Phillips, Julie Christie, Dick Emery

Fast Workers
US 1933 68m bw

Rivalries erupt among skyscraper workers.
Standard action programmer with which
MGM terminated John Gilbert's contract after
an illustrious rise and dramatic fall. Also cast:
Mae Clarke, Willard Mack, Robert
Armstrong. Written by Laurence Stallings;
directed by Tod Browning; for MGM.

The Fastest Gun Alive*
US 1956 89m bw
MGM (Clarence Greene)

A mild-mannered western storekeeper proves
to be the son of a famous gunfighter, and is
put to the test.
Flimsily contrived mini-western helped by
good performances.

w Frank D. Gilroy, Russel Rouse *d* Russel
Rouse *ph* George Folsey *m* André Previn

Glenn Ford, Broderick Crawford, Jeanne
Crain, Russ Tamblyn, Allyn Joslyn, Leif
Erickson, John Dehner

Fat City*
US 1972 96m Eastmancolor
Columbia / Rastar (Ray Stark)

In a small Californian town, a has-been boxer
tries to get back to the top, but loses his self
respect and becomes a hobo.
Vivid but over-casual exploration of failure,
with more interest in the characters than the
sport.

w Leonard Gardner, from his novel *d* John
Huston *ph* Conrad Hall *md* Marvin
Hamlisch *pd* Richard Sylbert

Stacy Keach, Jeff Bridges, Susan Tyrell

AAN: Susan Tyrell

The Fat Man
US 1950 77m bw
U-I (Aubrey Schenck)

The murder of a dentist leads to the circus.
Dense murder mystery featuring a gourmet
17-stone detective; understandably, no series
resulted.

---

w Harry Essex, Leonard Lee d William Castle ph Irving Glassberg m Bernard Green

J. Scott Smart, Rock Hudson, Julie London, Clinton Sundberg, Jerome Cowan, Jayne Meadows

The Fatal Night*
GB 1948 49m bw
(Columbia) Mario Zampi

A joke haunting has unfortunate consequences.
A small, cheaply-made film which really thrilled.

w Gerald Butler, *story* The Gentleman from America by Michael Arlen d Mario Zampi ph Cedric Williams m Stanley Black

Lester Ferguson, Jean Short, Leslie Armstrong, Brenda Hogan, Patrick MacNee

Fate Is the Hunter
US 1964 106m bw Cinemascope
TCF / Arcola (Aaron Rosenberg)

An airline executive investigates the cause of a fatal crash in which his friend the pilot was a victim.
Watchable how-did-it happen melodrama marred by pretentious dialogue.

w Harold Medford, *novel* Ernest K. Gann d Ralph Nelson ph Milton Krasner m Jerry Goldsmith

Glenn Ford, Rod Taylor, Nehemiah Persoff, Nancy Kwan, Suzanne Pleshette, Jane Russell

AAN: Milton Krasner

Father Brown***
GB 1954 91m bw
(Columbia) Facet (Vivian A. Cox)
US title: *The Detective*

A Catholic clergyman retrieves a priceless church cross from master thief Flambeau.
Delightfully eccentric comedy based closely on the famous character, with a sympathetic if rather wandering script, pointed direction and some delicious characterizations. A thoroughly civilized entertainment.

w Thelma Schnee, *story* The Blue Cross by G. K. Chesterton d Robert Hamer ph Harry Waxman m Georges Auric

Alec Guinness, Joan Greenwood, Peter Finch, Sidney James, Cecil Parker, Bernard Lee, Ernest Thesiger, Marne Maitland

Father Came Too*
GB 1963 93m Eastmancolor
Rank / Independent Artists

Honeymooners agree to live with her overbearing actor manager father.

Less funny sequel to *The Fast Lady*, with comic household disasters striking every couple of minutes. Easy-going, and predictably amusing in spots.

w Jack Davies, Henry Blyth d Peter Graham Scott ph Reg Wyer m Norrie Paramor

Stanley Baxter, James Robertson Justice, Sally Smith, Ronnie Barker, Timothy Bateson, Philip Locke

Father Goose*
US 1964 116m Technicolor
U-I / Granox (Robert Arthur)

During World War II a South Seas wanderer is compelled by the Australian navy to act as sky observer on a small island, where he finds himself in charge of six refugee schoolchildren and their schoolmistress.
Eager-to-please but unsatisfactory film which wanders between farce, adventure and sex comedy, taking too long about all of them.

w Peter Stone, Frank Tarloff d Ralph Nelson ph Charles Lang Jnr m Cy Coleman

Cary Grant, Leslie Caron, Trevor Howard
'Reasoning would indicate a made-to-order Christmas package for the family trade. However, the more sophisticated may be bored and exasperated after some of the initial brightness wears off.'—*Cue*
'Cary Grant wrings what there is to be wrung from the role, but never quite enough to conceal the fact that *Father Goose* is a waste of his talent and the audience's time.'—*Arthur Knight*

AA: Peter Stone, Frank Tarloff

Father Is a Bachelor
US 1950 85m bw
Columbia (S. Sylvan Simon)

A young tramp cares for a family of orphaned children.
Boringly sentimental semi-western.

w Aleen Leslie, James Edward Grant d Norman Foster, Abby Berlin ph Burnett Guffey m Arthur Morton

William Holden, Coleen Gray, Charles Winninger, Stuart Erwin, Sig Rumann
'Saccharine, paper thin. At least one spectator at the Palace yesterday couldn't take it—a tot of about four, wearing a cowboy suit, who aimed a toy pistol at the screen and popped off the cast one by one.'—*New York Times*

Father Is a Prince: see Big Hearted Herbert

Father of the Bride**
US 1950 93m bw
MGM (Pandro S. Berman)

A dismayed but happy father surveys the cost
and chaos of his daughter's marriage.
Fragmentary but mainly delightful suburban
comedy which finds Hollywood in its best light
vein and benefits from a strong central
performance.

w Frances Goodrich, Albert Hackett, novel
Edward Streeter d Vincente Minnelli ph John
Alton m Adolph Deutsch

Spencer Tracy, Joan Bennett, Elizabeth
Taylor, Don Taylor, Billie Burke, Moroni
Olsen, Leo G. Carroll, Taylor Holmes,
Melville Cooper

'The idealization of a safe sheltered
existence, the good life according to MGM: 24
carat complacency.'—New Yorker, 1980
'The bride gets the thrills! Father gets the
bills!'—publicity
† Jack Benny badly wanted the role but was
thought unsuitable.

AAN: best picture; Frances Goodrich, Albert
Hackett; Spencer Tracy

Father Takes a Wife*
US 1941 80m bw
RKO (Lee S. Marcus)

A famous actress marries a shipping magnate
and runs into resentment from her children.
Disappointing comedy with a script too flat for
the stars to make interesting.

w Dorothy and Herbert Fields d Jack Hively
ph Robert de Grasse m Roy Webb

Gloria Swanson, Adolphe Menjou, Desi
Arnaz, John Howard, Helen Broderick,
Florence Rice, Neil Hamilton

Father Was a Fullback
US 1949 84m bw
TCF (Fred Kohlmar)

The coach of a college football team has
domestic problems.
Thin star comedy, strictly double bill.

w Aleen Leslie, Casey Robinson, Richard
Sale, Mary Loos, play Clifford Goldsmith
d John M. Stahl ph Lloyd Ahern m Cyril
Mockridge

Fred MacMurray, Maureen O'Hara, Betty
Lynn, Natalie Wood, Rudy Vallee, Jim
Backus

Father's Doing Fine
GB 1952 83m Technicolor

An impoverished lady has trouble with her
daughters, one of whom is pregnant.

Agreeable madcap farce from a long-running
stage success (so why did they change the
title?). Heather Thatcher, Richard
Attenborough, Susan Stephen, Noel Purcell,
George Thorpe. Written by Anne Burnaby,
from the play Little Lambs Eat Ivy by Noel
Langley; directed by Henry Cass; for Marble
Arch / ABP.

Father's Little Dividend
US 1951 81m bw
MGM (Pandro S. Berman)

Sequel to Father of the Bride, in which the
newlyweds have a baby.
A very flat follow-up, palatable enough at the
time but quite unmemorable.

w Frances Goodrich, Albert Hackett
d Vincente Minnelli ph John Alton m Albert
Sandrey

Spencer Tracy, Joan Bennett, Elizabeth
Taylor, Don Taylor, Billie Burke, Moroni
Olsen, Frank Faylen, Marietta Canty, Russ
Tamblyn

Fathom
GB 1967 99m De Luxe Franscope
TCF (John Kohn)

Adventures of a glamorous sky-diving spy.
Watchable romp with nothing memorable
about it.

w Lorenzo Semple Jnr, novel Larry Forrester
d Leslie Martinson ph Douglas Slocombe,
Ken Vos m Johnny Dankworth

Raquel Welch, Tony Franciosa, Clive Revill,
Ronald Fraser, Greta Chi, Richard Briers,
Tom Adams

'Belongs not in the category of High Camp
but in that of Good Wholesome Fun.'—MFB
'The world's most uncovered undercover
agent!'—publicity

Fatso
US 1980 93m De Luxe

A fat man fails to make much headway at
slimming, and gives up. Unappealing mixture
of sentiment, satire, shouting and crude
humour. Dom DeLuise, Anne Bancroft, Ron
Carey, Candice Azzara. Written and directed
by Anne Bancroft; for Brooksfilms / TCF. 'As
bumbling and sluggish as its title might
suggest, a lamentable affair which ricochets
uncontrollably between attempts at hilarity
and pathos.'—Variety.

Faust**
Germany 1926 100m approx bw silent
UFA

A superbly stylish version of the legend about

a man who sells his soul to the devil. The best of many silent versions; see also *All That Money Can Buy*.

w Hans Kyser *d* F. W. *Murnau* *ph* Carl Hoffman

Emil Jannings, Gosta Ekman, Camilla Horn, Yvette Guilbert, William Dieterle

The FBI Story*
US 1959 149m Technicolor
Warner (Mervyn Le Roy)

An FBI agent thinks back on his career with the bureau.

Predictable mix of domestic sentimentality (very trying) and competent crime capsules: mad bomber, Ku Klux Klan, thirties hoodlums, Nazi spy rings and the cold war.

w Richard L. Breen, John Twist *d* Mervyn Le Roy *ph* Joseph Biroc *m* Max Steiner
ad John Beckman

James Stewart, Vera Miles, Larry Pennell, Nick Adams, Murray Hamilton
'Insufferably cosy.'—*MFB*

Fear
US 1946 68m bw
Monogram

A student kills his professor, and a detective taunts him to the point of confession.

Cheeky second feature version of *Crime and Punishment*, with a twist ending. Not too bad in its way.

w Alfred Zeisler, Dennis Cooper *d* Alfred Zeisler *ph* Jackson Rose

Warren William, Peter Cookson, Anne Gwynne, Nestor Paiva

Fear Eats the Soul*
West Germany 1973 92m colour
Tango Film (Christian Hohoff)

A Moroccan immigrant in Munich comes up against social and racial prejudice when he marries a sixty-year-old charwoman.

Unexceptionable moral tale which can hardly have been necessary in view of the infrequency of such cases.

wd Rainer Werner Fassbinder *ph* Jürgen Jürges

Brigitti Mira, El Hedi Ben Salem, Barbara Valentin, Irm Hermann, Rainer Werner Fassbinder

Fear in the Night**
US 1947 72m bw
Maxwell Shane

A man suffering from a strange nightmare

discovers he has been hypnotized into committing a murder.

Intriguing small-scale puzzler later remade to less effect as *Nightmare* (qv). Adequate performances and handling, but the plot's the thing.

wd Maxwell Shane *ph* Jack Grennhalgh
m Rudy Schraeger

Paul Kelly, De Forrest Kelley, Ann Doran, Kay Scott

Fear in the Night*
GB 1972 85m Technicolor
Hammer (Jimmy Sangster)

A girl recovering from a nervous breakdown is deluded into committing a murder.

Yet another variant on *Les Diaboliques*, ingeniously worked out with good touches of detail to produce an air of general competence.

w Jimmy Sangster, Michael Syson *d* Jimmy Sangster *ph* Arthur Grant *m* John McCabe

Peter Cushing, Judy Geeson, Joan Collins, Ralph Bates

Fear Is the Key*
GB 1972 108m Technicolor
Panavision
EMI / KLK (Alan Ladd Jnr, Elliott Kastner)

A man conceives an elaborate plot to track down those responsible for killing his wife and family in a plane crash.

Reasonably absorbing, surprise-plotted thriller.

w Robert Carrington, *novel* Alistair MacLean
d Michael Tuchner *ph* Alex Thomson *m* Roy Budd

Suzy Kendall, Barry Newman, John Vernon, Dolph Sweet, Ben Kingsley, Ray McAnally

Fear Strikes Out
US 1957 100m bw Vistavision
Paramount / Alan Pakula

A father wants his son to become a professional baseball player, and the son in consequence suffers a nervous breakdown.

Rather flat biopic of Jim Piersall; well-intentioned and careful in its psychological insights, but too often just plain dull.

w Ted Berkman, Raphael Blau *d* Robert Mulligan *ph* Haskell Boggs *m* Elmer Bernstein

Anthony Perkins, Karl Malden, Norma Moore, Perry Wilson

The Fearless Vampire Killers, or Pardon Me, Your Teeth Are in My Neck*
US 1967 124m Metrocolor Panavision
MGM / Cadre Films / Filmways (Gene Gutowski)
aka: *Dance of the Vampires*

A professor and his assistant stake a Transylvanian vampire.

Heavy, slow spoof of *Dracula*, most of which shows that sense of humour is very personal; a few effective moments hardly compensate for the prevailing stodge.

w Gerard Brach, Roman Polanski d Roman Polanski ph Douglas Slocombe m Krzystof Komeda pd Wilfrid Shingleton

Jack McGowran, Roman Polanski, Alfie Bass, Sharon Tate, *Ferdy Mayne*, Iain Quarrier, Terry Downes

 'An engaging oddity . . . long stretches might have been lifted intact from any Hammer horror.'—*Tom Milne*

The Fearmakers
US 1958 85m bw
Pacemaker (Martin H. Lancer)

A brainwashed Korean War veteran returns to Washington and finds that his PR firm has been taken over by communist racketeers. Unusual but cheaply made anti-Red propaganda, too talkative to be very entertaining.

w Elliot West, Chris Appley, *novel* Darwin Teilhet d Jacques Tourneur ph Sam Leavitt m Irving Gertz

Dana Andrews, Dick Foran, Mel Tormé

A Feather in Her Hat
US 1935 72m bw
Columbia

A London widow with delusions of grandeur tells her son that his real mother was a famous actress.
Outmoded mother-love drama, interestingly cast.

w Lawrence Hazard, *story* I. A. R. Wylie d Alfred Santell ph Joseph Walker

Pauline Lord, Basil Rathbone, Louis Hayward, Billie Burke, Wendy Barrie, J. M. Kerrigan, Victor Varconi, Nydia Westman, Thurston Hall

Feather Your Nest*
GB 1937 86m bw
ATP (Basil Dean)

A gramophone record technician substitutes his own voice for a star and becomes world famous.

The star in less farcical vein than usual; this is the one in which he sings 'Leaning on a Lamp-post'.

w Austin Melford, Robert Edmunds, Anthony Kimmins d William Beaudine

George Formby, Polly Ward, Enid Stamp Taylor, Val Rosing, Davy Burnaby

Fedora*
West Germany / France 1978 110m Eastmancolor
Geria / SFP (Billy Wilder)

An ageing star who seems miraculously to have kept her beauty comes out of retirement. *Sunset Boulevard* revisited, with a less bitter approach and less effectiveness; but any civilized film is welcome in the late seventies.

w I. A. L. Diamond, Billy Wilder, from a story in Crowned Heads by Tom Tryon d Billy Wilder ph Gerry Fisher m Miklos Rozsa

William Holden, Marthe Keller, Hildgarde Knef, Jose Ferrer, Mario Adorf, Henry Fonda, Michael York

 'Rife with Wilderean gallows humour and a sumptuous sense of decay in never-never land.'—*Sight and Sound*

Feet First**
US 1930 88m bw
Harold Lloyd

A shoe salesman gets entangled with crooks and has a narrow escape when hanging from the side of a building.
Very funny early talkie comedy, probably the comedian's last wholly satisfactory film.

w Lex Neal, Felix Adler, Paul Gerard Smith d Clyde Bruckman ph Walter Ludin, Henry Kohler

Harold Lloyd, Robert McWade, Barbara Kent

Female*
US 1933 60m bw

A high-powered lady president of a motor car company has a secret night life. Slick star vehicle reminiscent of *Peg's Paper* but absorbing while on screen. Ruth Chatterton, George Brent, Johnny Mack Brown, Ruth Donnelly, Douglass Dumbrille, Lois Wilson. Written by Gene Markey and Kathryn Scola, from a story by Donald Henderson Clarke; directed by Michael Curtiz and William Dieterle; for Warner.

The Female Animal
US 1957 82m bw Cinemascope
U-I (Albert Zugsmith)

A beach bum becomes the lover of a film star,
then falls in love with her daughter.
Dreary and humourless melodrama notable
only for the comeback appearance of one of
the screen's legendary glamour queens.

w Robert Hill d Harry Keller ph Russell
Metty m Hans Salter

Hedy Lamarr, Jan Sterling, Jane Powell,
George Nader, James Gleason

The Female on the Beach
US 1955 97m bw
U-I (Albert Zugsmith)

A wealthy widow visits her late husband's
beach house and falls for the gigolo next door,
who later seems intent on murdering her.
Absurd and jaded melodrama, a rehash of
Love from a Stranger, enlivened by some
hilarious love-hate dialogue.

w Robert Hill, Richard Alan Simmons
d Joseph Pevney ph Charles Lang m Joseph
Gershenson

Joan Crawford, Jeff Chandler, Jan Sterling,
Cecil Kellaway, Natalie Schaefer

La Femme de Nulle Part*
France 1922 70m approx bw   silent
aka: *The Woman from Nowhere*

A woman who feels that her life has been
ruined through love returns home and
persuades a young girl not to do the same.
A minor atmospheric piece of some power,
comparable with *Partie de Campagne* and
cinematically very interesting.

wd *Louis Delluc* ph Lucas Gibory
ad F. Jourdain

Eve Francis, Roger Karl, Gine Avril

La Femme du Boulanger**
France 1938 110m bw
Marcel Pagnol
aka: *The Baker's Wife*

Villagers put a stop to the infidelity of the
baker's wife because her husband no longer
has the heart to make good bread.
Best-known of Pagnol's rustic fables, this
rather obvious and long-drawn-out joke is
important because international critics hailed
it as a work of art (which it isn't) and because
it fixed an image of the naughty bucolic
French.

wd *Marcel Pagnol, novel* Jean Le Bleu by
Jean Giono ph G. Benoit, R. Lendruz, N.
Daries m Vincent Scotto

Raimu, Ginette Leclerc, Charles Moulin,
Charpin, Maximilienne

'It is a long film with a small subject, but the
treatment is so authentic that it seems over far
too soon, and the acting is superb.'—*Graham
Greene*

La Femme Infidèle**
France / Italy 1968 98m Eastmancolor
La Boétie / Cinégai (André Génovès)
aka: *The Unfaithful Wife*

A middle-aged insurance broker, set in his
ways, murders his wife's lover; when she
suspects the truth, they are drawn closer
together.
Almost a Bunuel-like black comedy, spare and
quiet, with immaculate performances.

wd *Claude Chabrol* ph Jean Rabier m Pierre
Jansen

Stéphane Audran, Michel Bouquet, Maurice
Ronet

'On any level, this bizarre murder framed by
whiskies emerges as Chabrol's most flawless
work to date.'—*Jan Dawson, MFB*

Femmes de Paris*
France 1954 85m approx Agfacolor
Optimax-Lux (Edgar Bacquet)
aka: *Ah! Les Belles Bacchantes*

A touring revue is almost run out of town for
indecency.
A rather crude but quite valuable record of
Dhéry's stage revue, which convulsed London
in the fifties.

w Robert Dhéry d Jean Loubignac ph René
Colas m Gérard Calvi

Robert Dhéry, Colette Brosset, Louis de
Funès, Raymond Bussières, the Bluebell Girls

La Ferme du Pendu*
France 1946 90m bw
Corona
aka: *Hanged Man's Farm*

The lecherous son of a farming family brings
tragedy to the lives of himself and his brothers
and sister.
Cold Comfort Farm with a vengeance,
appropriately played: arrant melodrama, but
watchable.

w André-Paul Antoine d Jean Dréville
ph André Thomas

Alfred Adam, Charles Vanel, Arlette Merry

Ferry to Hong Kong
GB 1958 113m Eastmancolor
   Cinemascope
Rank (George Maynard)

An Austrian layabout can land at neither of
the Hong Kong ferry's ports of call, but shows

his true worth when a typhoon strikes.
Silly storyline and rampant bad acting ruin the
Rank Organization's first attempt at an
international epic.

w Vernon Harris, Lewis Gilbert *d* Lewis
Gilbert *ph* Otto Heller *m* Kenneth V. Jones

Curt Jurgens, Sylvia Syms, Orson Welles,
Jeremy Spenser, Noel Purcell

La Fête à Henriette*
France 1952   113m   bw
Regina-Filmsonor
aka: *Holiday for Henrietta*

Two screenwriters disagree whether or not to
give their hero and heroine a happy ending.
A rather heavy-handed romantic joke which
does have its moments and was later—
fatally—Americanized as *Paris When It
Sizzles.*

w Julien Duvivier, Henri Jeanson *d Julien
Duvivier ph* Roger Hubert *m* Georges Auric

Dany Robin, Michel Auclair, Hildegarde
Neff, Michel Roux, Saturnin Fabre, Julien
Carette

Feudin', Fussin' and A-fightin'
US 1948   78m   bw

A fast-running travelling salesman is
kidnapped by a hillbilly town which needs him
in its annual sports. Unpretentious lower-berth
comedy for middle America. Donald
O'Connor, Marjorie Main, Percy Kilbride,
Penny Edwards, Joe Besser. Written by D. D.
Beauchamp; directed by George Sherman; for
Universal-International.

Le Feu Follet*
France / Italy 1963   110m   bw
Nouvelles Editions / Arco
aka: *Will o' the Wisp; A Time to Live and a
Time to Die*

The last 24 hours, before his suicide, in the life
of an ex-alcoholic playboy.
Not quite as weary as it sounds, and full of
admirable touches, this is nevertheless a fairly
downbeat film and a pointless one.

wd Louis Malle, novel Pierre Drieu la
Rochelle *ph* Ghislain Cloquet *m* Erik Satie

Maurice Ronet, Léna Skerla, Yvonne Clech,
Hubert Deschamps, Jeanne Moreau

A Fever in the Blood
US 1960   117m   bw
Warner (Roy Huggins)

Candidates for governor sharpen their
campaigns on a murder trial.
Interestingly-cast, flabbily-written melodrama.

w Roy Huggins, Harry Kleiner, *novel* William
Pearson *d* Vincent Sherman *ph* J. Peverell
Marley *m* Ernest Gold

Efrem Zimbalist Jnr, Angie Dickinson, Don
Ameche, Herbert Marshall, Jack Kelly, Ray
Danton, Jesse White, Rhodes Reason, Robert
Colbert

Fiddler on the Roof**
US 1971   180m   Technicolor
Panavision 70
UA / Mirisch (Norman Jewison)

In a pre-revolutionary Russian village, Tevye
the Jewish milkman survives family and
political problems and when the pogroms
begin cheerfully emigrates to America.
Self-conscious, grittily realistic adaptation of
the stage musical, with slow and heavy patches
in its grossly overlong celebration of a
vanished way of life. The big moments still
come off well though the songs tend to be
thrown away and the photography is
unnecessarily murky.

w Joseph Stein, from his play and Sholom
Aleichem's story Tevye and his Daughters
d Norman Jewison *ph* Oswald Morris
m Jerry Bock md John Williams *pd* Robert
Boyle *ly* Sheldon Harnick

Topol, Norma Crane, Leonard Frey, Molly
Picon

'Jewison hasn't so much directed a film as
prepared a product for world consumption.'—
Stanley Kauffmann

AA: Oswald Morris; John Williams
AAN: best picture; Norman Jewison (as
director); Topol; Leonard Frey

Fiddlers Three*
GB 1944   87m   bw
Ealing (Robert Hamer)

Sailors struck by lightning on Salisbury Plain
are transported back to ancient Rome.
Sequel to *Sailors Three*; despite a harsh and
unattractive look, every conceivable joke
about old Romans is deftly mined and the
good humour flows free.

w Diana Morgan, Angus Macphail d Harry
Watt *ph* Wilkie Cooper *m* Spike Hughes

*Tommy Trinder, Sonnie Hale, Frances Day,
Francis L. Sullivan*, Ernest Milton, Diana
Decker, Elizabeth Welch, Mary Clare

The Fiend Who Walked the West
US 1958   101m   bw   Cinemascope
TCF (Herbert B. Swope Jnr)

A sadistic killer released from prison tracks
down the associates of a cellmate and
terrorizes the district.

Western remake of *Kiss of Death*, with
babyface Robert Evans in the Widmark role.
Violent and dull.

w Harry Brown, Philip Yordan *d* Gordon
Douglas *ph* Joe MacDonald *m* Leon
Klatzkin

Hugh O'Brian, Dolores Michaels, Robert
Evans, Linda Cristal, Stephen McNally,
Edward Andrews

The Fiend without a Face
GB 1957   75m   bw
Producers' Associates (John Croydon)

A scientist working on materialized thought
produces monsters from his own id.
Tepid shocker with well-organized mobile
brains.

w H. J. Leder *d* Arthur Crabtree *ph* Lionel
Banes *m* Buxton Orr *sp* Ruppel and
Nordhoff

Kynaston Reeves, Terry Kilburn, Marshall
Thompson

The Fiendish Plot of Dr Fu Manchu
US 1980   108m   Technicolor
Warner / Orion / Playboy (Hugh Hefner)

The 'yellow peril' returns to the western world
to mastermind diamond thefts.
Feeble spoof with a history of production
troubles; clearly the only thing in anybody's
mind was to get it over with.

w Jim Moloney, Rudy Dochtermann *d* Piers
Haggard *ph* Jean Tournier *m* Marc
Wilkinson *pd* Alexander Trauner

Peter Sellers, Helen Mirren, David
Tomlinson, Sid Caesar, Simon Williams, Steve
Franken, Stratford Johns, John Le Mesurier,
Clive Dunn

The Fiercest Heart
US 1961   90m   De Luxe   Cinemascope
TCF (George Sherman)

A British army deserter joins a Boer trek into
South Africa.
Pioneer 'western', poorly done but with
novelty value.

w Edmund H. North, *novel* Stuart Cloete
d George Sherman *ph* Ellis Carter *m* Irving
Gertz

Stuart Whitman, Juliet Prowse, Raymond
Massey, Ken Scott, Geraldine Fitzgerald,
Rafer Johnson

Fièvre*
France 1921   50m approx   bw   silent
Alhambre

A brawl in a Marseilles bar ends in murder.
A dramatic sketch, filmed with remarkable
detail and artistry.

wd Louis Delluc ph A. Gibory *ad* Bécan

Eve Francis, Edmond Van Daele, Gaston
Modot

Fifi la Plume
France 1964   80m   bw
Les Films Montsouris (Albert Lamorisse)

A burglar becomes a circus bird-man, learns to
fly, and is everywhere mistaken for an angel.
A likeable fantasy idea which doesn't quite
come off, alternating uneasily between
slapstick and sentiment.

wd Albert Lamorisse *ph* Pierre Petit *m* Jean-
Michel Defaye

Philippe Avron, Mireille Nègre, Henri
Lambert, Raoul Delfosse

Fifth Avenue Girl*
US 1939   83m   bw
RKO (Gregory La Cava)

An unemployed girl is persuaded by a
millionaire to pose as a gold digger and annoy
his avaricious family.
Brightish comedy of the Cinderella kind.

w Allan Scott *d* Gregory La Cava *ph* Robert
de Grasse

Ginger Rogers, Walter Connolly, Verree
Teasdale, Tim Holt, James Ellison, Franklin
Pangborn, Kathryn Adams, Louis Calhern

The Fifth Musketeer
Austria 1978   106m   Eastmancolor
Sascha-Wien Film / Ted Richmond

Louis XIII and his twin brother Philippe vie
for the crown of France.
Virtually a remake of *The Man in the Iron
Mask*, with patchy style and a few excisable
sex scenes added. The 1939 version was better.

w David Ambrose *d* Ken Annakin *ph* Jack
Cardiff *m* Riz Ortolani

Beau Bridges, Sylvia Kristel, Ursula Andress,
Cornel Wilde (as D'Artagnan), Lloyd Bridges,
Alan Hale Jnr, Jose Ferrer (the ageing
musketeers), Rex Harrison (Colbert), Olivia
de Havilland (Queen Anne), Ian McShane,
Helmut Dantine

55 Days at Peking*
US / Spain 1962   154m   Super
      Technirama 70
Samuel Bronston

In 1900 Peking, Boxer fanatics are encouraged
by the Empress to take over the city and

besiege the international diplomatic quarter;
an American major leads the defence.
Spasmodically lively action spectacular
weighed down by romantic stretches.

w Philip Yordan, Bernard Gordon d Nicholas
Ray, Andrew Marton ph Jack Hildyard,
Manuel Berenguer m Dmitri Tiomkin
ad Venerio Colasanti, John Moore

Charlton Heston, David Niven, Ava Gardner,
Flora Robson, Robert Helpmann, Leo Genn,
Paul Lukas, John Ireland, Harry Andrews,
Elizabeth Sellars, Massimo Serrato, Jacques
Sernas, Geoffrey Bayldon
   'An open-air western in Chinese.'—*David
Niven*
   'Pictorially this is a beautiful film, but the
characters are conventional siege figures.'—
Sunday Times

AAN: Dmitri Tiomkin; song 'So Little Time'
(*m* Dmitri Tiomkin, *ly* Paul Francis Webster)

Fifty Roads to Town
US 1937 80m bw

Mistaken identities abound in a snowbound
cabin. Fairly funny minor comedy. Don
Ameche, Ann Sothern, Slim Summerville,
Jane Darwell, John Qualen, Douglas Fowley,
Stepin Fetchit. Written by George Marion Jnr
and William Conselman; directed by Norman
Taurog; for TCF.

52nd Street
US 1937 83m bw

A strictly-brought-up young woman shocks her
family by falling for a singer. Tame romantic
comedy with musical items. Kenny Baker, Ella
Logan, Ian Hunter, Zasu Pitts, Leo Carrillo.
Written by Grover Jones; directed by Harold
Young; for Walter Wanger.

The Fighter
US 1952 78m bw
GH (Alex Gottlieb)

A Mexican fisherman whose family is
murdered by government troops becomes a
prizefighter to earn money for the rebels.
A rather glum attempt to turn a few ringside
clichés.

w Aben Kandel, Herbert Kline, *story* The
Mexican by Jack London d Herbert Kline
ph James Wong Howe m Vincente Gomez

Richard Conte, Vanessa Brown, Lee J. Cobb,
Frank Silvera

Fighter Squadron
US 1948 96m Technicolor
Warner (Seton I. Miller)

In World War II, a dedicated flier risks his
friends' lives.
Routine aerial actioner.

w Seton I. Miller d Raoul Walsh ph Sid
Hickox, Wilfrid M. Cline m Max Steiner

Edmond O'Brien, Robert Stack, John
Rodney, Tom D'Andrea, Henry Hull, Walter
Reed, Shepperd Strudwick, Rock Hudson

Fighting Father Dunne
US 1948 93m bw
RKO

A clergyman looks after unfortunate boys.
A slum melodrama which all concerned could
have made with their eyes closed, and
probably did.

w Martin Rackin, Frank Davis d Ted
Tetzlaff ph George E. Diskant m Roy Webb

Pat O'Brien, Darryl Hickman, Charles
Kemper, Una O'Connor

The Fighting Guardsman
US 1945 84m bw

Under the tyrannical reign of Louis XVI a
young nobleman leads a peasants' revolt. Stiff
swashbuckler in which the actors appear to
have been only recently introduced to their
clothes. Willard Parker, Anita Louise, George
Macready, John Loder. Written by Franz
Spencer and Edward Dein; directed by Henry
Levin; for Columbia.

The Fighting Kentuckian
US 1949 100m bw
Republic (John Wayne)

In 1810 a farmer combats land-grabbing
criminals.
Standard star western for the family.

wd George Waggner ph Lee Garmes
m George Antheil

John Wayne, Vera Ralston, Oliver Hardy,
Philip Dorn, Marie Windsor, Mae Marsh

Fighting Mad
US 1976 90m De Luxe
TCF / Santa Fe (Roger Corman)

A rancher and his son are murdered by a local
industrialist who wants their land, and the
rancher's city-bred son takes revenge.
Another vigilante western in modern dress,
very laborious and violent without being very
exciting.

wd Jonathan Demme ph Bill Birch m Bruce
Langhorne

Peter Fonda, Lynn Lowry, John Doucette,
Philip Carey, Scott Glen

'Demme has allowed violence to outweigh
ideas to such a degree that the picture
becomes a turnoff, little more than a blatantly
obvious play to the yahoo mentality.'—*Kevin
Thomas, Los Angeles Times*

The Fighting O'Flynn
US 1949   94m   bw
U-I (Douglas Fairbanks Jnr)

In 18th-century Ireland, a penniless young
adventurer aborts Napoleon's plan for
invasion.
Lively minor-league adventure.

w Douglas Fairbanks Jnr, Robert Thoeren,
novel Justin Huntly McCarthy *d* Arthur
Pierson *ph* Arthur Edeson *m* Frank Skinner

Douglas Fairbanks Jnr, Helena Carter,
Richard Greene, Patricia Medina, Arthur
Shields, J. M. Kerrigan

'Fairbanks plays the irrepressible O'Flynn
with unflagging energy and tongue in cheek
good humour; the rest of the cast stolidly
refuses to see the joke.'—*MFB*

The Fighting Prince of Donegal
GB 1966   104m   Technicolor
Walt Disney (Bill Anderson)

Adventures of an Irish rebel in the reign of
Elizabeth I.
Adequate Boys' Own Paper romp.

w Robert Westerby, *novel* Red Hugh, Prince
of Donegal by Robert T. Reilly *d* Michael
O'Herlihy *ph* Arthur Ibbetson *m* George
Bruns

Peter McEnery, Susan Hampshire, Tom
Adams, Gordon Jackson, Andrew Keir,
Norman Woolland, Richard Leech

The Fighting Seabees
US 1944   100m   bw
Republic (Albert J. Cohen)

During World War II in the Pacific,
construction workers attack the Japanese.
Routine, studio-staged war melodrama,
heavily fleshed out with love interest.

w Borden Chase, Aeneas Mackenzie
d Edward Ludwig *ph* William Bradford
m Walter Scharf, Roy Webb

John Wayne, Susan Hayward, Dennis
O'Keefe, William Frawley, Duncan Renaldo,
Addison Richards, Leonid Kinskey, Paul Fix

AAN: Walter Scharf, Roy Webb

The Fighting 69th*
US 1940   89m   bw
Warner (Hal B. Wallis)

During World War I in the trenches, a cocky
recruit becomes a hero and loses his life in the
process.
Recruiting poster stuff, all well enough done
but bewildering in its changes of mood.

w Norman Reilly Raine, Fred Niblo Jnr, Dean
Franklin *d* William Keighley *ph* Tony
Gaudio *m* Adolph Deutsch

James Cagney, Pat O'Brien, George Brent,
Jeffrey Lynn, Alan Hale, Frank McHugh,
Dennis Morgan, Dick Foran, William
Lundigan, Guinn Williams, John Litel, Henry
O'Neill

'The picture is better if you can manage to
forget the plot and think of it instead as the
human, amusing and frequently gripping
record of a regiment marching off to war.'—
Frank Nugent, New York Times

Fighting Stock
GB 1935   68m   bw

The family gets together to save a girl from a
blackmailer. Fair example of the Aldwych
farces, with the trio in good form. Tom Walls,
Ralph Lynn, Robertson Hare, Marie Lohr,
Lesley Waring. Written by Ben Travers;
directed by Tom Walls; for Gaumont.

Figures in a Landscape
GB 1970   110m   Technicolor
Panavision
Cinecrest (John Kohn)

Two men on the run are pursued by soldiers
and helicopters; only one crosses the frontier.
Portentous Pinterish parable, very long-
winded and relentlessly boring though good to
look at. Everything is symbolic, nothing is
specific, not even the country.

w Robert Shaw, *novel* Barry England
d Joseph Losey *ph* Henri Alekan *m* Richard
Rodney Bennett

Robert Shaw, Malcolm McDowell

The File of the Golden Goose
GB 1969   109m   De Luxe
UA / Theme / Caralan / Dador (David E.
Rose)

An American agent works with Scotland Yard
to track down counterfeiters.
Incredibly predictable spy thriller which
almost makes an eccentricity out of collecting
so many clichés and so many tourist views of
London. Like ten TV episodes cut together.

w John C. Higgins, James B. Gordon *d* Sam
Wanamaker *ph* Ken Hodges *m* Harry
Robinson

Yul Brynner, Edward Woodward, Charles Gray, John Barrie, Bernard Archard, Ivor Dean, Adrienne Corri, Graham Crowden, Karel Stepanek

'The film plods wearily homewards through an exceptionally uninteresting batch of fights, intrigues and sinister encounters.'—*MFB*

The File on Thelma Jordon*
US 1949 100m bw
Paramount (Hal B. Wallis)
aka: *Thelma Jordon*

A district attorney falls for a murder suspect and has her acquitted by losing the case. Stylishly made, murkily plotted melodrama and a superior star vehicle of its time.

w Ketti Frings *d* Robert Siodmak *ph* George Barnes *m* Victor Young

Barbara Stanwyck, Wendell Corey, Paul Kelly, Joan Tetzel, Stanley Ridges, Richard Rober, Minor Watson, Barry Kelley

La Fille du Puisatier*
France 1946 131m bw
Marcel Pagnol
aka: *The Well-Digger's Daughter*

A stern old well-digger feels bound to send his daughter away when she becomes pregnant. More country matters from Pagnol, this time with an East Lynne type plot getting in the way of some fine acting. Not much comedy.

wd Marcel Pagnol

Raimu, Fernandel, Charpin, Josette Day

'There is a feeling in France that such films are made for the foreigner and exploit the eccentricities of French rural life rather than the realities.'—*MFB*

Film ohne Titel*
West Germany 1947 100m bw
Camera Film (Erwin Gitt)
aka: *Film without Title*

Scriptwriters discuss how it is possible to make a comedy film in post-war Germany, and evolve a story with alternative endings. Elegantly conceived but rather humourlessly executed, this interesting film was one of the first post-war German exports, but failed to start a trend. It has similarities to *La Fête à Henriette* and *Rashomon*.

w Helmut Kautner, Ellen Fechner, Rudolf Jugert *d* Rudolf Jugert *ph* Igor Oberberg *m* Bernard Eichhorn

Hans Söhnker, Hildegarde Knef, *Irene Von Meyendorff*, Willy Fritsch

The Final Countdown*
US 1980 105m TVC colour
UA / Bryna (Peter Vincent Douglas)

An aircraft carrier on manoeuvres near Hawaii passes through a strange storm and finds itself back at Pearl Harbor.

Quite an enjoyable bit of schoolboy science fiction, but containing no more body than an episode of *Twilight Zone*. The ending, as so often, is impenetrable.

w David Ambrose, Gerry Davis, Thomas Hunter, Peter Powell *d* Don Taylor *ph* Victor J. Kemper *m* John Scott *pd* Fernando Carrere

Kirk Douglas, Martin Sheen, Katherine Ross, James Farentino, Ron O'Neal, Charles Durning

The Final Programme
GB 1973 89m Technicolor
Goodtimes / Gladiole (John Goldstone, Sanford Lieberson)
US title: *The Last Days of Man on Earth*

In the future, when the world is torn by famine and war, a scientist awaits a new messiah.

Intellectualized sci-fi, hard to take as entertainment but very glossy.

wd Robert Fuest, *novel* Michael Moorcock *ph* Norman Warwick *m* Paul Beaver, Bernard Krause

Jon Finch, Jenny Runacre, Sterling Hayden, Hugh Griffith

'Clumsy and almost incomprehensible.'— *Sight and Sound*

The Final Test
GB 1953 90m bw
Rank / ACT (R. J. Minney)

A cricketer looks forward to his last game but is out for a duck; he is however cheered by the crowd and comforted by his son.

Flat character study some way below the author's best style, cluttered up with real cricketers and stymied by lack of action.

w Terence Rattigan *d* Anthony Asquith *ph* Bill McLeod *m* Benjamin Franklin

Jack Warner, Robert Morley, George Relph

Finders Keepers
GB 1966 94m Eastmancolor
UA / Interstate (George H. Brown)

The Americans lose an atomic bomb off the Spanish coast, and it's found by a pop group. Harmless youth musical without much style. Tunes poor, comedy rather too easy-going.

w Michael Pertwee d Sidney Hayers ph Alan Hume m The Shadows, Norrie Paramor

Cliff Richard, The Shadows, Robert Morley, Peggy Mount, Viviane Ventura, Graham Stark, John Le Mesurier, Robert Hutton

A Fine Madness*
US 1966   104m   Technicolor
Warner Seven Arts (Jerome Hellman)

A frustrated New York poet has outbursts of violence.
Patchy, interesting, with-it comedy which suffers from too many changes of mood.

w Elliot Baker, from his novel d Irvin Kershner ph Ted McCord m John Addison

Sean Connery, Jean Seberg, Joanne Woodward, Patrick O'Neal, Colleen Dewhurst, Clive Revill

'Straddling a no man's land somewhere between the nouvelle vague and the crazy comedies of Old Hollywood.'—Tom Milne

The Finger Points
US 1931   88m   bw

A crime reporter succumbs to pressures from the underworld. Humourless and low-geared exposé-style melodrama. Richard Barthelmess, Clark Gable, Fay Wray, Regis Toomey. Written by John Monk Saunders, W. R. Burnett and Robert Lord; directed by John Francis Dillon; for Warner.

Fingers*
US 1977   90m   Technicolor

A would-be concert pianist gets involved with his father's gangster friends, and violence results. Lively and interesting skirmish with an overworked and essentially downbeat subject. Harvey Keitel, Tisa Farrow, Jim Brown, Marion Seldes. Written and directed by James Toback; for Brut.

Fingers at the Window
US 1942   90m   bw
MGM (Irving Starr)

A stage magician hypnotizes lunatics into murdering all those who stand between him and an inheritance.
Slow-starting thriller which never achieves top gear.

w Rose Caylor, Lawrence P. Bachmann d Charles Lederer ph Harry Stradling, Charles Lawton m Bronislau Kaper

Basil Rathbone, Lew Ayres, Laraine Day, Walter Kingsford, Miles Mander, Russell Gleason

'The kind of picture actors do when they need work.'—Lew Ayres

Finian's Rainbow*
US 1968   140m   Technicolor
Panavision 70
Warner Seven Arts (Joseph Landon)

A leprechaun tries to retrieve a crock of gold from an old wanderer who has taken it to America.
Musical whimsy-whamsy, a long way after a 1947 Broadway success; in this overlong and overblown screen version the elements and the style do not jell and there is too much sentimental chat, but moments of magic shine through.

w E. Y. Harburg, Fred Saidy, from their play d Francis Ford Coppola ph Philip Lathrop m Burton Lane ly E. Y. Harburg pd Hilyard M. Brown md Ray Heindorf

Fred Astaire, Petula Clark, Tommy Steele, Don Francks, Keenan Wynn, Barbara Hancock, Al Freeman Jnr

AAN: Ray Heindorf

Finis Terrae*
France 1929   90m approx   bw   silent
Société Générale des Films

A re-enacted account of the lives of fishermen on remote Brittany islands.
A feature documentary which was impressive at the time; very similar to Flaherty's Man of Aran.

wd Jean Epstein ph Joseph Barth, Joseph Kottula

Finishing School
US 1934   73m   bw
RKO (Kenneth MacGowan)

A girl at an exclusive school falls for an intern. Modest pap for the teenage audience.

w Wanda Tuchock, Laird Doyle d George Nicholls Jnr ph J. Roy Hunt m Max Steiner

Frances Dee, Ginger Rogers, Billie Burke, Bruce Cabot, John Halliday, Beulah Bondi, Sara Haden

The Finishing Touch*
US 1928   20m   bw; silent

Stan and Ollie accidentally destroy the house they are building. Excellent early star slapstick with predictable but enjoyable gags. Laurel and Hardy, Edgar Kennedy, Dorothy Coburn. Written by H. M Walker; directed by Clyde Bruckman; for Hal Roach.

Fire Down Below
GB 1957   116m   Technicolor
Cinemascope
Columbia / Warwick (Irving Allen, Albert
Broccoli)

Partners in a Caribbean fishing and smuggling
business fall out over a woman.
Overheated melodrama with thin characters,
predictable incident and ill-advised casting.

w Irwin Shaw, *novel* Max Catto d Robert
Parrish ph Desmond Dickinson m Arthur
Benjamin

Rita Hayworth, Robert Mitchum, Jack
Lemmon, Herbert Lom, Bonar Colleano,
Bernard Lee, Edric Connor, Peter Illing

A Fire Has Been Arranged
GB 1935   70m   bw
Twickenham (Julius Hagen)

Ex-convicts find a building in the field where
they buried the loot.
Modest star comedy. Was this the first use of
this well-worn plot?

w H. Fowler Mear, Michael Barringer
d Leslie Hiscott

Bud Flanagan, Chesney Allen, Alastair Sim,
Robb Wilton, Mary Lawson, Harold French,
C. Denier Warren

Fire Over England**
GB 1936   92m   bw
Pendennis (Erich Pommer)

Elizabeth I and her navy overcome the
Spanish Armada.
Though the film has a faded air and the action
climax was always a bath-tub affair, the
splendid cast keeps this pageant afloat and
interesting.

w Clemence Dane, Sergei Nolbandov, *novel*
A. E. W. Mason d William K. Howard
ph James Wong Howe m Richard Addinsell

Flora Robson, Laurence Olivier, Leslie
Banks, Vivien Leigh, Raymond Massey,
Tamara Desni, Morton Selten, Lyn Harding,
James Mason

'Pommer and Howard have done one
remarkable thing: they have caught the very
spirit of an English public schoolmistress's
vision of history.'—*Graham Greene*

Fire Sale*
US 1977   88m   De Luxe
TCF (Marvin Worth)

Misadventures of a frantic, eccentric New
York-Jewish family who own a department
store.
Frenzied black farce for ethnic audiences.

w Robert Klane, from his novel d Alan
Arkin ph Ralph Woolsey m Dave Grusin

Alan Arkin, Rob Reiner, Vincent Gardenia,
Anjanette Comer, Kay Medford, Sid Caesar,
Alex Rocco

'It moves fast enough to carry the occasional
lapses from its own high standards of
tastelessness.'—*Jan Dawson, MFB*

Firecreek
US 1968   104m   Technicolor
Panavision
Warner Seven Arts (Philip Leacock)

The people of Firecreek protect themselves
from wandering gunmen.
Dour, predictable little western which does
not show its stars at their best.

w Calvin Clements d Vincent McEveety
ph William Clothier m Alfred Newman

James Stewart, Henry Fonda, Inger Stevens,
Gary Lockwood, Dean Jagger, Ed Begley, Jay
C. Flippen, Jack Elam, James Best, Barbara
Luna

'This cramped and clumsy western grinds to
a standstill in its attempts to give Firecreek
symbolic status . . . while the gunmen roister
like mad and the townsfolk rhubarb glumly in
the background.'—*MFB*

The Firefly*
US 1937   131m   bw
MGM (Hunt Stromberg)

Adventures of a Spanish lady spy during the
Napoleonic war.
Solid production of a romantic operetta;
splendid stuff for connoisseurs.

w Frances Goodrich, Albert Hackett, Ogden
Nash d Robert Z. Leonard ph Oliver Marsh
original book / *ly* Otto Harbach m Rudolf
Friml md Herbert Stothart

Jeanette MacDonald, *Allan Jones* (who sings
the Donkey Serenade), Warren William, Billy
Gilbert, Henry Daniell, George Zucco,
Douglass Dumbrille

'A lavish musical monstrosity.'—*New
Yorker, 1978*

'It will make 1937 remembered always as
the year of the first romantic dramatic musical
film!'—*publicity*

Fireman Save My Child
US 1954   80m   bw
U-I (Howard Christie)

In 1910 San Francisco, incompetent firemen
accidentally catch a gang of crooks.
Slapstick farce intended for Abbott and
Costello, taken over by a new team which did

not catch on, played like the Keystone Kops. Mildly funny during the chases.

w Lee Loeb, John Grant d Leslie Goodwins ph Clifford Stine m Joseph Gershenson

Buddy Hackett, Spike Jones and the City Slickers, Hugh O'Brian, Adèle Jergens

The Firemen's Ball*
Czechoslovakia / Italy   1967   73m Eastmancolor
Barrandov / Carlo Ponti
original title: Hori, Ma Panenko

In a small provincial town, arrangements for the firemen's annual ball go wrong at every turn.
Vaguely amusing Tati-esque comedy with not quite enough funny moments and a prevailing atmosphere of pessimism.

w Milos Forman, Ivan Passer, Jaroslav Papousek d Milos Forman ph Miroslav Ondricek m Karel Mares

Jan Vostrcil, Josef Kolb, Josef Svet, Frantisek Debelka

'A compendium of superb items.'—Philip Strick

AAN: best foreign film

Firepower
GB 1979   104m   Technicolor
ITC / Michael Winner

A chemist about to expose contaminated drugs is murdered; his widow persuades the US Justice Department to hire her ex-lover, a gangster, to track down his killers.
Globe-trotting kaleidoscope of the familiar patterns of violence; tolerable for those who haven't been here a hundred times before.

w Gerald Wilson d Michael Winner ph Robert Paynter, Dick Kratina md Jay Cattaway

Sophia Loren, James Coburn, Anthony Franciosa, O. J. Simpson, Eli Wallach, George Grizzard, Vincent Gardenia, Victor Mature

'The nearest thing yet to film-making by numbers, with identikit characters jet-setting across a travel brochure landscape to an orchestration of gunfire, car smashes and colourful explosions.'—Clyde Jeavons, MFB

Fires on the Plain**
Japan 1959   108m   bw
Daiei (Masaichi Nagata)
original title: Nobi

In the Philippines during World War II, a half-demented Japanese private takes to the hills, becomes a cannibal, and is shot by the Americans when he tries to surrender.
Stomach-turning anti-war epic with fine scenes and performances but dubious intent.

w Natto Wada, novel Shohei O-oka d Kon Ichikawa ph Setsuo Kobayashi m Yasushi Akatagawa

Eiji Funakoshi, Osamu Takizawa, Micky Curtis

Fires Were Started**
GB 1942   63m   bw
Crown Film Unit (Ian Dalrymple)
aka: I Was a Fireman

One day and night in the life of a National Fire Service unit during the London blitz.
Thoughtful, slow-moving, poetic documentary originally intended as a training film but generally released to boost morale. Not its director's finest work, but perhaps his most ambitious.

wd Humphrey Jennings ph C. Pennington-Richards m William Alwyn

'An astonishingly intimate portrait of an isolated and besieged Britain . . . an unforgettable piece of human observation, affectionate, touching, and yet ironic.'—Georges Sadoul

† The firemen were real firemen, but the scenes were re-enacted.

First a Girl
GB 1935   94m   bw

A messenger girl attracts attention by posing as a boy, and becomes a star. Moderate light star vehicle. Jessie Matthews, Sonnie Hale, Griffith Jones, Anna Lee, Alfred Drayton, Martita Hunt, Eddie Gray. Written by Marjorie Gaffney, from the play Viktor und Viktoria by Reinhold Schunzel; directed by Victor Saville; for Gaumont.

First Comes Courage
US 1943   88m   bw
Columbia (Harry Joe Brown)

During World War II, a Norwegian girl appears to be a Quisling but is really a spy getting information from the Nazis by fraternizing with them.
Doleful war drama with little to commend it except propaganda.

w Lewis Meltzer, Melvin Levy, novel The Commandos by Elliott Arnold d Dorothy Arzner ph Joseph Walker m Ernst Toch

Merle Oberon, Brian Aherne, Carl Esmond, Fritz Leiber, Erik Rolf, Reinhold Schunzel, Isobel Elsom

The First Gentleman*
GB 1948 111m bw
Columbia (Joseph Friedman)
US title: *Affairs of a Rogue*

The affairs and foibles of the Prince Regent.
Dullish adaptation of a successful West End
play about 18th-century court life; script and
performances still entertain.

w Nicholas Phipps, Reginald Long, *play
Norman Ginsbury d* Cavalcanti *ph* Jack
Hildyard

Cecil Parker, Jean-Pierre Aumont, Joan
Hopkins, Margaretta Scott, Jack Livesey,
Ronald Squire, Athene Seyler, Hugh Griffith

The First Great Train Robbery*
GB 1978 108m Technicolor
UA / Starling (John Foreman)

In 1855, an elegant but ruthless crook picks
out a gang to help him rob the Folkestone
express of gold bullion.
Patchy but generally very likeable period
crime story, with just a few lapses of pace and
taste.

wd Michael Crichton, from his novel
ph Geoffrey Unsworth *m* Jerry Goldsmith
ph Maurice Carter

Sean Connery, Donald Sutherland, Lesley-
Anne Down, Alan Webb, Robert Lang,
Malcolm Terris

'My dream was that the historical world was
going to be lovingly recreated, and then I was
going to shoot *The French Connection* inside
it.'—*Michael Crichton*

First Lady*
US 1937 82m bw
Warner (Hal B. Wallis)

The President's wife is a power behind the
scenes.
Solidly entertaining Washington comedy.

w Rowland Leigh, *play* George S. Kaufman,
Katherine Dayton *d* Stanley Logan *ph* Sid
Hickox

Kay Francis, Preston Foster, Anita Louise,
Walter Connolly, Verree Teasdale, Victor
Jory, Marjorie Rambeau, Louise Fazenda

The First Legion*
US 1951 86m bw
Sedif (Douglas Sirk)

Priests are bewildered when one of their
number is the victim of an apparent miracle.
Talkative religious drama of a peculiarly
American kind which likes to have its cake
and eat it; watchable for the performances.

w Emmet Lavery, from his play *d* Douglas
Sirk *ph* Robert de Grasse *m* Hans Sommer

Charles Boyer, William Demarest, Lyle
Bettger, Barbara Rush, Leo G. Carroll,
Walter Hampden, George Zucco, Taylor
Holmes

First Love*
US 1939 84m bw
Universal (Joe Pasternak)

An orphaned teenager goes to live with her
uncle and his snobbish family, and falls for a
local bigwig's son.
A vehicle carefully conceived to introduce its
star to grown-up romance. The compromises
show, but it's palatable enough.

w Bruce Manning, Lionel Houser *d* Henry
Koster *ph* Joseph Valentine *m* Frank
Skinner *md* Charles Previn

Deanna Durbin, Robert Stack, Eugene
Pallette, Helen Parrish, Lewis Howard,
Leatrice Joy

'The most obvious Cinderella story I ever
met with, apart from *Cinderella*.'—*Richard
Mallett, Punch*

'There is nothing at all to resent in the
picture: it is admirably directed, amusingly
written, and acted with immense virtuosity by
a fine cast.'—*Graham Greene*

AAN: Charles Previn

First Man into Space
GB 1958 78m bw
Producers' Associates (John Croydon)

An astronaut runs into a cloud of meteor dust
and returns to earth a vampirish killer.
Quatermass-like shocker with modest budget
but firm control.

w John C. Cooper, Lance Z. Hargreaves
d Robert Day *ph* Geoffrey Faithfull
m Buxton Orr

Marshall Thompson, Marla Landi, Bill
Edwards

First Men in the Moon*
GB 1964 103m Technicolor
  Panavision
Columbia / Ameran (Charles H. Schneer)

A Victorian eccentric makes a voyage to the
moon and is forced to stay there.
Rather slack in plot development, but an
enjoyable schoolboy romp with a good eye for
detail and tongue firmly in cheek.

w Nigel Kneale, Jan Read, *novel* H. G. Wells
d Nathan Juran *ph* Wilkie Cooper *m* Laurie
Johnson *sp* Ray Harryhausen

Lionel Jeffries, Edward Judd, Martha Hyer
† Uncredited, Peter Finch played the bit part
of a process server.

The First of the Few**
GB 1942   117m   bw
Melbourne / British Aviation (Leslie
  Howard, George King, Adrian Brunel,
  John Stafford)
US title: *Spitfire*

The story of R. J. Mitchell who saw World
War II coming and devised the Spitfire.
Low-key but impressive biopic with firm acting
and good dialogue scenes. Production values
slightly shaky.

w Anatole de Grunwald, Miles Malleson,
Henry C. James, Katherine Strueby *d* Leslie
Howard *ph* Georges Perinal *m* William
Walton

Leslie Howard, David Niven, Rosamund
John, Roland Culver, David Horne

The First Texan
US 1956   82m   Technicolor
  Cinemascope
Allied Artists (Walter Mirisch)

The Governor of Tennessee helps Texas win
its independence.
Generally well done biopic of Sam Houston,
with the usual western excitements.

w Daniel B. Ullman *d* Byron Haskin
ph Wilfrid Cline *m* Roy Webb

Joel McCrea, Felicia Farr, Jeff Morrow,
Wallace Ford, Abraham Sofaer

The First Time
US 1968   90m   De Luxe
UA / Mirisch / Rogallan (Roger Smith, Allan
  Carr)
GB title: *You Don't Need Pajamas at
  Rosie's*

Three teenage boys who fantasize about sex
help a stranded girl under the impression that
she is a prostitute.
Embarrassingly sentimental teenage sex
comedy, all the more irritating by its restraint.
Not a patch on *Summer of '42*.

w Jo Heims, Roger Smith *d* James Nielson
ph Ernest Laszlo *m* Kenyon Hopkins

Jacqueline Bisset, Wes Stern, Rick Kelman,
Wink Roberts, Sharon Acker

First to Fight
US 1967   97m   Technicolor   Panavision
Warner (William Conrad)

A World War II hero is taken home and fêted,
but on returning to the front he loses his
nerve.

War film in the guise of a psychological study;
competently done but very American in its
sentiments and a bit shaky on period detail.

w Gene L. Coon *d* Christian Nyby
ph Harold Wellman *m* Fred Steiner

Chad Everett, Gene Hackman, Dean Jagger,
Marilyn Devon, Claude Akins

The First Travelling Saleslady
US 1956   92m   Technicolor
RKO (Arthur Lubin)

Two women set out to sell barbed wire in the
old west.
Strained comedy with very few effective
moments.

w Devery Freeman, Stephen Longstreet
d Arthur Lubin *ph* William Snyder *m* Irving
Gertz

Ginger Rogers, Carol Channing, Barry
Nelson, James Arness, David Brian, Clint
Eastwood

F.I.S.T.*
US 1978   145m   Technicolor
UA / Norman Jewison (Gene Corman)

The rise and fall of a union boss.
Reminiscent of *All the King's Men* and *On the
Waterfront*, this much overlong melodrama has
compelling passages, but the star is not quite
equal to it and parts are both repetitive and
obscure.

w Joe Eszterhas, Sylvester Stallone *d* Norman
Jewison *ph* Laszlo Kovacs *m* Bill Conti
pd Richard MacDonald

Sylvester Stallone, Rod Steiger, Peter Boyle,
Melinda Dillon, David Huffman, Tony L.
Bianco, Cassie Yates, Peter Donat, Henry
Wilcoxon

A Fistful of Dollars*
Italy / Germany / Spain 1964   100m
  Techniscope
UA / Jolly / Constantin / Ocean (Arrigo
  Colombo, Georgio Papi)

An avenging stranger, violent and mysterious,
cleans up a Mexican border town.
A film with much to answer for: it began the
craze for 'spaghetti westerns', took its director
to Hollywood, and made a TV cowboy into a
world star. In itself it is simple, noisy, brutish
and actionful.

w Sergio Leone, Duccio Tessari *d* Sergio
Leone *ph* Massimo Dallamano *m* Ennio
Morricone

Clint Eastwood, Gian Maria Volonte,
Marianne Koch

† Direct sequels by Leone, apart from numerous imitations, are *For a Few Dollars More* and *The Good, the Bad and the Ugly*.

A Fistful of Dynamite
Italy 1971 150m Techniscope
UA / Rafran / San Marco / Miura (Fulvio Morsella)
aka: *Duck, You Sucker*

In 1913 a Mexican bandit and an ex-IRA explosives expert join forces to rob a bank.
Overblown action spectacular, far too long to be sustained by its flashes of humour and excitement. A good instance of what happens to a small talent when success goes to its head.
wd Sergio Leone ph Giuseppe Ruzzolini *m* Ennio Morricone

Rod Steiger, James Coburn

Fists in the Pocket*
Italy 1965 113m bw
Doria (Ezio Passadore)
original title: *I Pugni in Tasca*

One of a family of epileptics murders most of the others in order to help his normal eldest brother.
Complex black melodrama which makes its points, if it has any, with great style.
wd Marco Bellocchio ph Alberto Marrama *m* Ennio Morricone

Lou Castel, Paola Pitagora, Liliona Gerace
'There have been few debuts as exciting as this in recent years.'—*Tom Milne, MFB*

Fitzwilly*
US 1967 102m De Luxe Panavision
UA / Dramatic Features Inc / Walter Mirisch
GB title: *Fitzwilly Strikes Back*

A New York butler, in order to keep his lady in style, has to organize the staff into a crime syndicate.
Moderately inventive, good-looking comedy with rather too much plot and not enough funny lines.
w Isobel Lennart, *novel* A Garden of Cucumbers by Poyntz Tyler *d* Delbert Mann *ph* Joseph Biroc *m* Johnny Williams

Dick Van Dyke, Edith Evans, Barbara Feldon, John McGiver, Harry Townes, John Fiedler, Norman Fell, Cecil Kellaway, Anne Seymour, Sam Waterston, Billy Halop

Five
US 1951 89m bw
Columbia (Arch Oboler)

There are only five survivors of an atomic holocaust, and their political and racial tensions soon reduce the number to two.
Gutless talkfest which becomes interesting only when the camera moves out of doors; otherwise, too pretentious and dull by half.
wd Arch Oboler *ph* Lou Stoumen, Ed Spiegel, Sid Lubow *m* Henry Russell

William Phipps, Susan Douglas, James Anderson, Charles Lampkin, Earl Lee
'The talk leaves one with a strong impression that in this case the fittest did not survive.'—*Penelope Houston*

Five Against the House
US 1955 84m bw
Columbia (Sterling Silliphant, John Barnwell)

College students try to rob a casino.
Meandering caper melodrama with too much flabby dialogue.
w Sterling Silliphant, John Barnwell, *novel* Jack Finney *d* Phil Karlson *ph* Leslie White *m* George Duning

Guy Madison, Kim Novak, Brian Keith, Kerwin Mathews, William Conrad

Five and Ten
US 1931 88m bw

A chain store heiress elopes with a married man, but is tamed by family misfortune. Solid star drama which maintains points of interest.
Marion Davies, Leslie Howard, Richard Bennett, Irene Rich, Kent Douglass, Halliwell Hobbes. Written by A. P. Younger and Edith Fitzgerald, from the novel by Fannie Hurst; directed by Robert Z. Leonard; for MGM.
(GB title: *Daughter of Luxury*.)

Five Boys from Barska Street*
Poland 1953 115m Agfacolor
Film Polski
original title: *Piatka z Ulicy Barskiej*

Five city boys are placed on probation and gradually change their attitudes towards life and society.
Rather dated propaganda piece with a plot which surprisingly follows western models.
wd Aleksander Ford, *novel* Kazimierz Kozniewski *ph* Jaroslav Tuzar *m* Kazimierz Serocki

Tadeusz Janczar, Aleksandra Slaska, Andrzej Kozak

Five Branded Women
Italy / US 1960 100m bw
Paramount / Dino de Laurentiis

Five Yugoslav girls have their heads shaved for associating with German soldiers, and after various adventures join the partisans. Rough, tough war adventure which makes a few boring points about love and war.

w Ivo Perelli, *novel* Ugo Pirro d Martin Ritt ph Giuseppe Rotunno m Francesco Lavagnino

Silvana Mangano, Van Heflin, Vera Miles, Barbara Bel Geddes, Jeanne Moreau, Richard Basehart, Harry Guardino, Steve Forrest, Alex Nicol

'For the most part the film is devoted to unexciting guerrilla action and uninviting partisan life . . . obstinately unreal despite lashings of blood, mutilation, childbirth and death.'—*MFB*

Five Came Back**
US 1939 75m bw
RKO (Robert Sisk)

A passenger plane crashlands in the jungle. It can carry back only five survivors, and headhunters are coming closer . . .
A minor film which gradually achieved cult status and was remade as *Back to Eternity* as well as being the starting point for many variations. Still gripping in its dated way.

w Jerry Cady, Dalton Trumbo, Nathanael West d *John Farrow* ph Nicholas Musuraca m Roy Webb

Chester Morris, Lucille Ball, C. Aubrey Smith, Elizabeth Risdon, Wendy Barrie, John Carradine, Joseph Calleia, Allen Jenkins, Kent Taylor, Patric Knowles

Five Card Stud
US 1968 103m Technicolor
Paramount / Hal. B. Wallis

Members of a lynching party are murdered one by one.
Would-be nonchalant murder mystery western: the stars just about hold it together, but it's an uphill fight.

w Marguerite Roberts, *novel* Ray Gaulden d Henry Hathaway ph Daniel L. Fapp m Maurice Jarre

Dean Martin, Robert Mitchum, Inger Stevens, Roddy McDowall, Katherine Justice, John Anderson, Yaphet Kotto

'Marginally watchable . . . but destined to sink without trace minutes after one leaves the cinema.'—*Gavin Millar*
'So mediocre you can't get mad at it.'—*Judith Crist*

Five Easy Pieces**
US 1970 98m Technicolor
Columbia / Bert Schneider (Bob Rafelson, Richard Wechsler)

A middle-class drifter jilts his pregnant mistress for his brother's fiancée, but finally leaves both and hitches a ride to nowhere in particular.
Echoes of *Easy Rider, The Graduate* and *Charlie Bubbles* abound in this generally likeable but insubstantial modern anti-drama which at least takes place in pleasant surroundings and is firmly directed.

w Adrien Joyce d Bob Rafelson ph Laszlo Kovacs m various

Jack Nicholson, Karen Black, Susan Anspach, Lois Smith, Billy 'Green' Bush, Fannie Flagg

AAN: best picture; Adrien Joyce; Jack Nicholson; Karen Black

Five Finger Exercise
US 1962 109m bw
Columbia / Sonnis (Frederick Brisson)

A snobbish wife falls in love with a young house guest, with dire effect on her husband and son.
This West End study of a neurotic family is probably not good film material, certainly not adaptable to California, and above all not suitable to this star's whizzbang dramatics. Numbing hysteria arrives early and stays till the end.

w Frances Goodrich, Albert Hackett, *play* Peter Shaffer d Daniel Mann ph Harry Stradling m Jerome Moross

Rosalind Russell, Jack Hawkins, Maximilian Schell, Richard Beymer

'There are many kinds of love, but are there any without guilt?'—*publicity*

Five Fingers***
US 1952 108m bw
TCF (Otto Lang)

The valet of the British ambassador in Ankara sells military secrets to the Germans, who pay him but never use the information.
Absorbing, lightweight film adaptation of a true story of World War II; civilized suspense entertainment with all talents contributing nicely.

w *Michael Wilson, book* Operation Cicero by L. C. Moyzich d *Joseph L. Mankiewicz* ph Norbert Brodine m Bernard Herrmann ad Lyle Wheeler, George W. Davis

James Mason, Danielle Darrieux, Michael Rennie, Walter Hampden, Oscar Karlweis, Herbert Berghof, John Wengraf, Michael Pate

'One of the highest, fastest and most absorbing spy melodramas since Hitchcock crossed the Atlantic.'—*Arthur Knight*

AAN: Michael Wilson; Joseph L. Mankiewicz

Five Golden Dragons
GB 1965   92m   Techniscope

An American playboy in Hong Kong becomes involved in the affairs of five master criminals preparing to sell out to the Mafia. Anything-goes comedy-thriller, patchy at best, unintelligible at worst, and filled with ageing stars. Robert Cummings, Rupert Davies, Margaret Lee, Maria Perschy, Klaus Kinski, Dan Duryea, Brian Donlevy, Christopher Lee, George Raft. Written by Harry Alan Towers; directed by Jeremy Summers; for Harry Alan Towers.

Five Golden Hours
GB / Italy 1960   90m   bw
(Columbia) Anglofilm / Fabio Jegher (Mario Zampi)

A con man tries to murder three widows who have invested money in one of his schemes. Ill-judged black comedy, sadly lacking style.

w Hans Wilhelm   d Mario Zampi
ph Christopher Challis   m Stanley Black

Ernie Kovacs, Cyd Charisse, Kay Hammond, George Sanders, Dennis Price, Reginald Beckwith, Martin Benson, Ron Moody, Finlay Currie, Avis Landone, Sidney Tafler, John Le Mesurier, Clelia Matania

Five Graves to Cairo***
US 1943   96m   bw
Paramount (Charles Brackett)

During the North Africa campaign, British spies try to destroy Rommel's secret supply dumps.
Intriguing spy melodrama set in a desert hotel, a notable example of Hollywood's ability to snatch polished drama from the headlines.

w Charles Brackett, Billy Wilder, play Lajos Biro   d Billy Wilder   m Miklos Rozsa   ph John Seitz

Franchot Tone, Anne Baxter, Erich Von Stroheim (as Rommel), Akim Tamiroff, Peter Van Eyck, Miles Mander
'Billy Wilder must have had something a little grander in mind: the cleverness lacks lustre.'—New Yorker, 1978
'A fabulous film fable, but it has been executed with enough finesse to make it a rather exciting pipe dream.'—Howard Barnes, New York Herald Tribune

AAN: John Seitz

Five Miles to Midnight*
France / Italy 1962   110m   bw
UA / Filmsonor / Dear Film (Anatole Litvak)

A neurotic believed dead forces his terrified wife to collect his life insurance.

Hysterical melodrama, smoothly made with all the familiar expressionist devices, but far too long for its content.

w Peter Viertel, Hugh Wheeler   d Anatole Litvak   ph Henri Alekan   m Mikis Theodorakis

Sophia Loren, Anthony Perkins, Gig Young, Jean-Pierre Aumont, Yolande Turner, Tommy Norden
'From the polished immediacy of the cars, streets, shop windows and café tables to the off-focus vertigo shots of panic, from the overhead view of neighbours on stairs . . . to the close-ups of hands in filing trays touching off the details of fear and guilt, there is a thread of colour to keep you watching.'—MFB
'One of those movies without a country that are becoming as fixed a part of the international scene as the Duke and Duchess of Windsor.'—Arthur Schlesinger Jnr, Show

The Five Pennies*
US 1959   117m   Technicolor Vistavision
Paramount / Dena (Jack Rose)

The rags-to-riches success story of cornet player Red Nichols.
The only touch of originality in this biopic is that the subject is given touches of irascibility. Production values reach a good standard.

w Jack Rose, Melville Shavelson   d Melville Shavelson   ph Daniel L. Fapp   md Leith Stevens   ad Hal Pereira, Tambi Larsen   songs Sylvia Fine   trumpet solos Red Nichols

Danny Kaye, Barbara Bel Geddes, Louis Armstrong, Bob Crosby, Harry Guardino, Tuesday Weld, Ray Anthony

AAN: Daniel L. Fapp; Leith Stevens; title song (m / ly Sylvia Fine)

Five Star Final**
US 1931   89m   bw
Warner

A sensation-seeking newspaper editor causes tragedy.
Dated but still powerful melodrama which set the pattern for all the newspaper films of the thirties.

w Robert Lord, Byron Morgan, play Louis Weitzenkorn   d Mervyn Le Roy   ph Sol Polito   md Leo F. Forbstein

Edward G. Robinson, H. B. Warner, Marian Marsh, Anthony Bushell, George E. Stone, Ona Munson, Aline MacMahon, Boris Karloff
'All the elements to make a hit attraction.'—Variety

† Remade in 1936 with Humphrey Bogart, as
Two Against the World.

AAN: best picture

Five Steps to Danger
US 1956   80m   bw
UA / HSK

A girl possessing secret information from her
dead scientist brother has a mental
breakdown, and is pursued by spies.
Lively if cliché-ridden espionage melodrama,
like an old-time serial.

wd Henry S. Kesler, *novel* Donald Hamilton
ph Kenneth Peach   *m* Paul Sawtell, Bert
Shefter

Sterling Hayden, Ruth Roman, Werner
Klemperer, Richard Gaines

The Five Thousand Fingers of Doctor T**
US 1953   88m   Technicolor
Columbia / *Stanley Kramer*

A boy who hates piano lessons dreams of his
teacher as an evil genius who keeps five
hundred boys imprisoned in a castle of musical
instruments.
Badly scripted fantasy with gleaming
sophisticated dream sequences which deserve
a better frame. A real oddity to come from
Hollywood at this time, even though Dr Seuss'
books were and are bestsellers.

w Dr Seuss (Theodore Geisel), Alan Scott
d Roy Rowland   *ph Franz Planer*
m Frederick Hollander   *ly* Dr Seuss
pd Rudolph Sternad   ch Eugene Loring

Hans Conried, Tommy Rettig, Peter Lind
Hayes, Mary Healy

AAN: Frederick Hollander

Five Weeks in a Balloon
US 1962   101m   De Luxe   Cinemascope
TCF (Irving Allen)

In 1862 a professor is financed on a balloon
trip into central Africa.
Would-be humorous semi-fantasy which
strives to equal *Journey to the Center of the
Earth* but unfortunately falls flat on its face
despite the interesting talent available. Limp
comedy situations, poor production values.

w Charles Bennett, Irving Allen, Albert Gail,
novel Jules Verne   *d* Irving Allen   *ph* Winton
Hoch   *m* Paul Sawtell   *ad* Jack Martin Smith,
Alfred Ybarra

Cedric Hardwicke, Peter Lorre, Red Buttons,
Fabian, Richard Haydn, Billy Gilbert, Herbert
Marshall, Reginald Owen, Henry Daniell

Fixed Bayonets
US 1951   93m   bw
TCF (Jules Buck)

An American division in Korea fights a
rearguard action.
Downbeat war melodrama of a familiar kind,
with more characterization than action.

wd Samuel Fuller   *ph* Lucien Ballard   *m* Roy
Webb

Richard Basehart, Gene Evans, Michael
O'Shea, Richard Hylton, Craig Hill

The Fixer
US 1968   130m   Metrocolor
MGM / Edward Lewis, John Frankenheimer

A Jew in Tsarist Russia denies his race but
becomes a scapegoat for various crimes and is
imprisoned without trial until he becomes a
cause célèbre.
Worthy but extremely dreary realist
melodrama.

w Dalton Trumbo, *novel* Bernard Malamud
d John Frankenheimer   *ph* Marcel Grignon
m Maurice Jarre

Alan Bates, Dirk Bogarde, Georgia Brown,
Jack Gilford, Hugh Griffith, Elizabeth
Hartman, Ian Holm, David Warner, Carol
White, Murray Melvin, Peter Jeffrey, Michael
Goodliffe
'The kind of film in which one has to admire
much of the acting simply because it is all
there is to admire.'—*David Pirie*
'A totally false film, devoid of a breath of
human life or truth.'—*Arthur Schlesinger Jnr*
'Alan Bates's bare posterior, known to us
from *Georgy Girl* and *King of Hearts*, makes
another timely appearance here, thus
becoming one of the most exposed arses in
cinematic annals.'—*John Simon*

AAN: Alan Bates

The Fixer Uppers
US 1935   20m   bw

Christmas card salesmen try to help a bored
wife, but her jealous husband challenges Ollie
to a duel. Rather flat comedy marking a
tailing-off from the stars' best period. Laurel
and Hardy, Mae Busch, Charles Middleton,
Arthur Housman. Writer uncredited; directed
by Charles Rogers; for Hal Roach. (NB: A
remake of an early silent, *Slipping Wives*.)

The Flag Lieutenant
GB 1933   85m   bw
British and Dominions (Herbert Wilcox)

A naval lieutenant, thought to be a coward,
shows his true courage when a fort is
beleaguered.

Boy's Own Paper stuff from a popular play previously filmed in 1919 (with George Wynn) and 1926 (with Henry Edwards).

w W. P. Drury, Leo Tover, from their play d Henry Edwards

Henry Edwards, Anna Neagle, Joyce Bland, Peter Gawthorne, Sam Livesey, O. B. Clarence, Abraham Sofaer

The Flame
US 1947 97m bw
Republic (John H. Auer)

A nurse marries for money, but her ailing spouse recovers and she falls in love with him. Turgid melodrama, ineptly presented.

w Lawrence Kimble d John H. Auer ph Reggie Lanning m Heinz Roemheld

Vera Hruba Ralston, John Carroll, Robert Paige, Broderick Crawford, Henry Travers, Blanche Yurka, Constance Dowling, Hattie McDaniel, Sen Yung
'A good picture to stay away from, with or without a good book.'—*Cue*

The Flame and the Arrow*
US 1950 88m Technicolor
(Warner) Harold Hecht, Frank Ross

In medieval Italy, a rebel leader seeks victory over a tyrant.
Good-humoured Robin Hood stuff with the star at his most acrobatic.

w Waldo Salt d Jacques Tourneur ph Ernest Haller m Max Steiner ad Edward Carrere

Burt Lancaster, Virginia Mayo, Robert Douglas, Aline MacMahon, Frank Allenby, Nick Cravat
'I never found a Technicolor costume picture so entertaining.'—*Richard Mallett, Punch*

AAN: Ernest Haller; Max Steiner

The Flame and the Flesh
US 1954 104m Technicolor
MGM (Joe Pasternak)

An unscrupulous American woman in Naples has a fatal fascination for the local menfolk.
Dreary remake of *Naples au Baiser du Feu* (France 1937), with the dullest possible handling all round.

w Helen Deutsch, *novel* Auguste Bailly d Richard Brooks ph Christopher Challis m Nicholas Brodszky

Lana Turner, Carlos Thompson, Bonar Colleano, Pier Angeli, Charles Goldner, Peter Illing

Flame in the Streets
GB 1961 93m colour Cinemascope
Rank / Somerset (Roy Baker)

A liberal-minded union man erupts when his daughter proposes to marry a black man.
Predictable East End problem picture, unconvincingly set and acted and boring into the bargain.

w Ted Willis, from his TV play Hot Summer Night d Roy Baker ph Christopher Challis m Phil Green

John Mills, Brenda de Banzie, Sylvia Syms, Earl Cameron, Johnny Sekka, Ann Lynn, Wilfred Brambell
'Its methods belong more to the writer's study than to life.'—*John Gillett*

The Flame of New Orleans*
US 1941 79m bw
Universal (Joe Pasternak)

A European adventuress settles in America.
Fluffy comedy romance with the exiled director scarcely in top form.

w Norman Krasna d René Clair ph Rudolph Maté m Frank Skinner

Marlene Dietrich, Roland Young, Bruce Cabot, Mischa Auer, Andy Devine, Frank Jenks, Eddie Quillan, Laura Hope Crews, Franklin Pangborn
† Remade as *Scarlet Angel*.

Flame of the Barbary Coast
US 1945 97m bw
Republic (Joseph Kane)

In old San Francisco, a cowboy becomes involved with a night club queen, and their fortunes are resolved by the earthquake.
Tolerable period melodrama, and the one in which Wayne played a character named Duke: the nickname stuck.

w Borden Chase d Joseph Kane ph Robert de Grasse m Dale Butts sp Howard and Theodore Lydecker

John Wayne, Ann Dvorak, Joseph Schildkraut, William Frawley, Virginia Grey, Russell Hicks, Jack Norton, Paul Fix, Marc Lawrence

AAN: Dale Butts

Flame of the Islands
US 1955 90m Trucolor
Republic (Edward Ludwig)

A girl invests a bequest in a Bahamas night club, and there becomes involved with four men.
Barely competent time-filler.

w Bruce Manning *d* Edward Ludwig *ph* Bud Thackery *m* Nelson Riddle

Yvonne de Carlo, Howard Duff, Zachary Scott, Kurt Kasznar, Barbara O'Neil, James Arness, Frieda Inescort

The Flame Within
US 1935   73m   bw

A lady psychiatrist falls for the husband of one of her patients. Decent star melodrama. Ann Harding, Maureen O'Sullivan, Louis Hayward, Henry Stephenson, Herbert Marshall. Written, directed (and produced) by *Edmund Goulding*; for MGM.

Flaming Star*
US 1960   92m   De Luxe   Cinemascope
TCF (David Weisbart)

A half-breed family is torn between two loyalties.
Solemn, unusual Civil War western with a downbeat ending.

w Clair Huffaker, Nunnally Johnson *d* Don Siegel *ph* Charles G. Clarke *m* Cyril Mockridge

Elvis Presley, Dolores del Rio, Steve Forrest, Barbara Eden, John McIntire, Rodolpho Acosta

'Despite familiar absurdities, it has more than its share of good moments.'—*MFB*

Flamingo Road*
US 1949   94m   bw
Warner (Jerry Wald)

A tough carnival dancer is stranded in a small town and soon affects the lives of the local politicians.
Standard melodrama from a bestseller, absurd but well performed.

w Robert Wilder, from his novel *d* Michael Curtiz *ph* Ted McCord *m* Max Steiner

Joan Crawford, David Brian, Sidney Greenstreet, Zachary Scott, Gladys George, Virginia Huston, Fred Clark

Flap
US 1970   106m   Technicolor
  Panavision
Warner (Jerry Adler)
GB title: *The Last Warrior*

A drunken Indian on a dilapidated modern reservation starts a public relations war and leads a march on the city.
Unendearing comedy with a tragic end tacked on, not very entertaining as whimsy, farce or social conscience.

w Clair Huffaker, from his novel Nobody Loves a Drunken Indian *d* Carol Reed *ph* Fred Koenekamp *m* Marvin Hamlisch

Anthony Quinn, Claude Atkins, Tony Bill, Victor Jory, Shelley Winters

Flare Up
US 1969   98m   Metrocolor
MGM / GMF (Leon Fromkes)

A man kills his wife and threatens her friends who he feels are responsible for the break-up of his marriage.
Sensationally violent melodrama with a plot that goes back to *Sudden Fear* and further. Adequately made.

w Mark Rodgers *d* James Neilson *ph* Andrew J. McIntyre *m* Les Baxter

Raquel Welch, James Stacy, Luke Askew, Don Chastain, Ron Rifkin

Flash Gordon
The hero of the 25th century was created in comic strip form by Alex Raymond and his chief claims to film fame are three wild and woolly serials made by Universal: *Flash Gordon* (1936), *Flash Gordon's Trip to Mars* (1938), and *Flash Gordon Conquers the Universe* (1940), all starring Buster Crabbe with Charles Middleton as the wily Emperor Ming. Their cheap and cheerful futuristic sets and their non-stop action have kept them popular with film buffs through the years. In 1974 a semi-porno spoof, *Flesh Gordon*, appeared.

Flash Gordon*
GB 1980   115m   Technicolor   Todd-AO
EMI / Famous / Starling (Dino de Laurentiis)

A football hero, his girl friend, and Dr Zarkov have adventures on the planet Mongo.
Lively comic strip addition to the increasing numbers of such things being restaged at enormous expense fifty years after their prime.

w Lorenzo Semple Jnr, from characters created by Alex Raymond *d* Michael Hodges *ph* Gil Taylor *m* Queen *pd* Danilo Donati

Sam J. Jones, Melody Anderson, Topol, Max Von Sydow, Timothy Dalton, Brian Blessed, Peter Wyngarde

'An expensively irrelevant gloss on its sources.'—*Richard Combs, MFB*

Flaxy Martin
US 1948   86m   bw
Warner

A lawyer falls for a racketeer's girl friend and finds himself framed for murder.

Flatly-handled melodrama with unsympathetic characters.

w David Lang d Richard Bare ph Carl Guthrie

Zachary Scott, Virginia Mayo, Dorothy Malone, Tom d'Andrea, Elisha Cook Jnr

A Flea in Her Ear*
US / France 1968 94m De Luxe Panavision
TCF (Fred Kohlmar)

Various suspicious wives and husbands converge on the notorious Hotel Coq d'Or. Disappointing filming of a Feydeau farce, which needs to be much more cleverly handled to come over with its full theatrical force.

w John Mortimer, play La Puce à l'Oreille by Georges Feydeau d Jacques Charon ph Charles Lang m Bronislau Kaper pd Alexander Trauner

Rex Harrison, Rachel Roberts, Rosemary Harris, Louis Jourdan, John Williams, Grégoire Aslan, Edward Hardwicke, Frank Thornton, Victor Sen Yung
'The plunge into madness never comes, and one is left with the sight of a group of talented players struggling with alien material.'— Michael Billington, Illustrated London News

The Fleet's In*
US 1942 93m bw
Paramount (Paul Jones)

A sailor on leave in San Francisco takes a bet that he can kiss the glamorous owner of a swank nightclub.
Mindless wartime musical which happened to set the seal of success on a number of young talents. Previously a Clara Bow vehicle.

w Walter de Leon, Sid Silvers d Victor Schertzinger ph William Mellor m / ly Victor Schertzinger, Johnny Mercer

Dorothy Lamour, William Holden, Eddie Bracken, Betty Hutton, Cass Daley, Gil Lamb, Leif Erickson, Betty Jane Rhodes
'A slim and obvious comedy with some good tunes. Much of the film is a roughhouse; several reels towards the end are turned over to straight vaudeville.'—Eileen Creelman, New York Sun

The Flemish Farm
GB 1943 82m bw
Two Cities (Sydney Box)

An attempt is made to retrieve a buried flag from occupied Belgium.
Tolerable wartime flagwaver.

w Jeffrey Dell, Jill Craigie d Jeffrey Dell

Clive Brook, Clifford Evans, Jane Baxter, Philip Friend, Brefni O'Rourke

Flesh*
US 1932 95m bw
MGM

A German wrestler in the US falls for a street waif.
Unusual, rather unattractive, but vivid melodrama.

w Edmund Goulding, Moss Hart d John Ford ph Arthur Edeson

Wallace Beery, Ricardo Cortez, Karen Morley, John Miljan, Jean Hersholt, Herman Bing, Edward Brophy

Flesh and Blood
GB 1951 102m bw
BL / Harefield (Anatole de Grunwald)

Three generations of a family suffer from the effects of heredity.
Fragmented Scottish period piece which never settles down long enough to make an impact with any group of characters.

w Anatole de Grunwald, play A Sleeping Clergyman by James Bridie d Anthony Kimmins ph Otto Heller m Charles Williams

Richard Todd, Glynis Johns, Joan Greenwood, André Morell, Ursula Howells, Freda Jackson, George Cole, James Hayter, Ronald Howard, Muriel Aked

Flesh and Fantasy*
US 1943 94m bw
Universal (Charles Boyer, Julien Duvivier)

A club bore tells three strange stories.
A portmanteau with ingredients of varying interest, attempting to emulate the success of Tales of Manhattan. The fourth episode planned was deleted and turned up as Destiny (qv). All quite stylish, the best section being Lord Arthur Savile's Crime.

w Ernest Pascal, Samuel Hoffenstein, Ellis St Joseph, stories Ellis St Joseph, Oscar Wilde, Laslo Vadnay d Julien Duvivier ph Paul Ivano, Stanley Cortez m Alexandre Tansman

Robert Benchley, Edward G. Robinson, Barbara Stanwyck, Charles Boyer, Betty Field, Robert Cummings, Thomas Mitchell, C. Aubrey Smith, Dame May Whitty, Edgar Barrier, David Hoffman

Flesh and the Devil*
US 1926 109m bw silent
MGM

A temptress toys with three men.
Hokey but good-looking star melodrama,

climaxing with death on an ice floe. A huge commercial success because of the off-screen Garbo-Gilbert romance.

w Benjamin Glazer, *novel* The Undying Past by Hermann Sudermann d *Clarence Brown*

Greta Garbo, John Gilbert, Lars Hanson, Marc McDermott, Barbara Kent

'A film of more than passing cleverness . . . the theme is sheer undiluted sex, and Brown uses a series of close-ups to get this across with considerable effect.'—*Paul Rotha, The Film Till Now*

The Flesh and the Fiends

GB 1959   97m   bw   Dyaliscope
Regal / Triad (Robert Baker, Monty Berman)

In 1820 Edinburgh, 'resurrection men' commit murders to keep anatomists supplied.
Dr Robert Knox rides again, in a version more bloody but less entertaining than *The Body Snatcher.*

w John Gilling, Leon Griffiths d John Gilling ph Monty Berman m Stanley Black

Peter Cushing, June Laverick, George Rose, Donald Pleasence, Renée Houston, Billie Whitelaw, Dermot Walsh

Flight Command

US 1940   116m   bw
MGM (J. Walter Ruben)

A cocky recruit makes good in the naval air arm.
Routine flagwaver.

w Wells Root, Cmdr Harvey Haislip d Frank Borzage ph Harold Rosson m Franz Waxman

Robert Taylor, Ruth Hussey, Walter Pidgeon, Paul Kelly, Nat Pendleton, Red Skelton, Shepperd Strudwick, Dick Purcell

Flight for Freedom

US 1943   101m   bw
RKO (David Hempstead)

Biography of an intrepid aviatrix and her husband.
Patchy job based on the life of Amelia Earhart, suggesting that her final disappearance was on a government mission. Dull production.

w Oliver H. P. Garrett, S. K. Lauren d Lothar Mendes ph Lee Garmes m Roy Webb

Rosalind Russell, Fred MacMurray, Herbert Marshall, Eduardo Ciannelli, Walter Kingsford

Flight from Ashiya*

US / Japan 1963   102m   Eastmancolor
Panavision
UA / Harold Hecht / Daiei

When a cargo vessel sinks off the coast of Japan during a typhoon, the helicopter rescue service springs into action.
Conventional Grade A action thriller with flashbacks to earlier disasters in the lives of its heroes.

w Elliot Arnold, Waldo Salt d Michael Anderson ph Joe MacDonald, Burnett Guffey m Frank Cordell pd Eugène Lourié

Yul Brynner, Richard Widmark, George Chakiris, Shirley Knight, Daniele Gaubert, Suzy Parker

Flight from Destiny

US 1941   74m   bw

An elderly professor with six months to live determines on one good deed . . . which includes murder. Likeable minor melodrama, well put together. Thomas Mitchell, Geraldine Fitzgerald, Jeffrey Lynn, Mona Maris. Written by Barry Trivers, from a play by Anthony Berkeley; directed by Vincent Sherman; for Warner.

Flight from Folly

GB 1944   93m   bw

A chorus girl cures a playwright's amnesia. Leadenly-titled and played variation on *Random Harvest,* with dreary musical numbers. Pat Kirkwood, Hugh Sinclair, Sydney Howard, Marian Spencer, Tamara Desni, Jean Gillie, A. E. Matthews. Written by Basil Woon, Lesley Storm and Katherine Strueby; directed by Herbert Mason; for Warner.

Flight of the Doves*

US 1971   101m   colour
Columbia / Rainbow (Ralph Nelson)

Two children run away from their bullying stepfather to join their Irish grandmother, but are chased by a wicked uncle who knows they are heirs to a fortune.
Pantomimish whimsy which works in fits and starts, but has little real humour or charm.

wd Ralph Nelson, *novel* Walter Macken ph Harry Waxman m Roy Budd

Ron Moody, Dorothy McGuire, Helen Raye, Dana, Jack Wild, Stanley Holloway, William Rushton

The Flight of the Phoenix*

US 1965   149m   De Luxe
TCF / Associates and Aldrich

A cargo passenger plane crashes in the desert, and the survivors try to avert disaster.
Achingly slow character adventure; an all-star cast works desperately hard but the final flight of the rebuilt plane seems almost an anti-climax after the surfeit of personal melodramatics.

w Lukas Heller, *novel* Elleston Trevor
d Robert Aldrich *ph* Joseph Biroc *m* Frank de Vol

James Stewart, Richard Attenborough, Hardy Kruger, Peter Finch, Dan Duryea, Ernest Borgnine, Ian Bannen, Ronald Fraser, Christian Marquand, George Kennedy

AAN: Ian Bannen

The Flight that Disappeared
US 1961 73m bw
UA / Harvard (Robert E. Kent)

Atomic scientists on an airliner find themselves in 'heaven' being tried by people of the future.
Eccentric anti-bomb curiosity, a second feature *Outward Bound*.

w Ralph Hart, Judith Hart, Owen Harris
d Reginald Le Borg *ph* Gilbert Warrenton *m* Richard La Salle

Gregory Morton, Addison Richards, Craig Hill, Paula Raymond, Dayton Lummis

Flight to Mars
US 1951 75m Cinecolor

After a rocket flight, four scientists discover that the inhabitants of Mars speak perfect American, learned by radio. Pioneering science-fiction entry with nothing going for it but being first: writing, production and acting are alike abysmal. Cameron Mitchell, Marguerite Chapman, Arthur Franz, Virginia Huston, John Litel. Written by Arthur Strawn; directed by Lesley Selander; for Monogram.

Flight to Tangier
US 1953 90m Technicolor 3-D
Paramount (Nat Holt)

A female FBI agent chases a three million dollar letter of credit.
Forced and boring action romance without much of either element.

wd Charles Marquis Warren *ph* Ray Rennahan *m* Paul Sawtell

Joan Fontaine, Jack Palance, Corinne Calvet, Robert Douglas, Marcel Dalio, Jeff Morrow, Murray Matheson, John Doucette

The Flim Flam Man*
US 1967 104m De Luxe Panavision
TCF / Lawrence Turman
GB title: *One Born Every Minute*

An army deserter joins forces with an elderly con man.
Folksy comedy in a small-town setting; none of it really comes to the boil after a couple of early chase sequences.

w William Rose, *novel* Guy Owen *d* Irvin Kershner, *Yakima Canutt ph* Charles Lang *m* Jerry Goldsmith

George C. Scott, Michael Sarrazin, Sue Lyon, Harry Morgan, Jack Albertson, Alice Ghostley, Albert Salmi

Flipper
US 1963 87m Metrocolor
(MGM) Ivan Tors

A fisherman's son on the Florida Keys befriends a dolphin.
Harmless boy-and-animal adventure which spawned two sequels and a TV series.

w Arthur Weiss *d* James B. Clark *ph* Lamar Boren, Joseph Brun *m* Henry Vars

Chuck Connors, Luke Halpin, Kathleen Maguire, Connie Scott

Flirtation Walk*
US 1934 97m bw
Warner (Frank Borzage)

Love affairs of West Point cadets.
Light musical very typical of its period, with a few agreeable numbers.

w Delmer Daves *d* Frank Borzage *ch* Bobby Connelly *ph* Sol Polito, George Barnes *m / ly* Allie Wrubel, Mort Dixon

Dick Powell, Ruby Keeler, Pat O'Brien, Ross Alexander, John Arledge, Henry O'Neill, Guinn Williams

'A rousing recruiting poster . . . and a splendid laboratory specimen of the adolescent cinema.'—*André Sennwald, New York Times*

AAN: best picture

Floods of Fear*
GB 1958 84m bw
Rank / Sydney Box

Two escaped convicts, a warder, and a pretty girl are trapped by floods in a lonely house.
Adequate melodrama with impressively gloomy production and performances but not many surprises.

wd Charles Crichton, *novel* Joan and Ward Hawkins *ph* Christopher Challis *m* Alan Rawsthorne

Howard Keel, Anne Heywood, Harry H.
Corbett, Cyril Cusack

Floodtide
GB 1949   90m   bw

A Clydebank apprentice becomes a ship
designer. Boring inspirational drama hindered
by the Independent Frame method. Gordon
Jackson, Rona Anderson, John Laurie, Jack
Lambert, Elizabeth Sellars. Written by
Donald B. Wilson and George Blake; directed
by Frederick Wilson; for Aquila / Rank.

The Florentine Dagger
US 1935   69m   bw

A mysterious Borgia influence is brought to
bear on the murder of an art dealer. Vaguely
unsatisfactory whodunnit with some intriguing
and some pretentious elements. Margaret
Lindsay, Donald Woods, C. Aubrey Smith,
Robert Barrat, Henry O'Neill. Written by
Brown Holmes and Tom Reed, from the novel
by Ben Hecht; directed by Robert Florey; for
Warner.

Florian
US 1940   91m   bw
MGM (Winfield Sheehan)

In 1910 Austria, a poor boy and a rich girl are
united by their love of a Lippizaner stallion.
Not kinky, but strangely dull.

w Noel Langley, Geza Herczeg, James K.
McGuinness d Edwin L. Marin ph Karl
Freund, Richard Rosson m Franz Waxman

Robert Young, Helen Gilbert, Charles
Coburn, Lee Bowman, Reginald Owen, S. Z.
Sakall, Lucile Watson, Irina Baronova

Flower Drum Song*
US 1961   133m   Technicolor
   Panavision
U-I / Rodgers and Hammerstein / Joseph
   Fields

Romantic problems among the immigrants in
San Francisco's Chinatown.
A Broadway musical which on the screen
seems old-fashioned, remorselessly cute, and
even insulting to the Chinese characters.
Within its limits, however, it is well enough
staged and performed.

w Joseph Fields d Henry Koster m / ly
Richard Rodgers, Oscar Hammerstein II
md Alfred Newman, Ken Darby ph Russell
Metty ad Alexander Golitzen, Joseph Weight
costumes Irene Sharaff ch Hermes Pan

Nancy Kwan, James Shigeta, Juanita Hall,
Myoshi Umeki, James Soo, Sen Yung

AAN: Alfred Newman, Ken Darby; Russell
Metty

Flowing Gold
US 1940   82m   bw

A fugitive from justice finds himself in a
western oilfield. Routine melodrama with
climactic heroics and nothing to remember
next day. John Garfield, Pat O'Brien, Frances
Farmer, Raymond Walburn, Cliff Edwards.
Written by Kenneth Gamet; directed by
Alfred E. Green; for Warner.

Fluffy
US 1964   92m   Eastmancolor
U-I / Scarus (Gordon Kay)

A biologist manages to tame a lion.
Mindless, cheerful animal comedy.

w Samuel Rocca d Earl Bellamy ph Clifford
Stine m Irving Gertz

Tony Randall, Shirley Jones, Edward
Andrews, Ernest Truex, Howard Morris, Jim
Backus, Frank Faylen

The Flute and the Arrow*
Sweden 1957   75m   Technicolor
   Agascope
Sandrews (Arne Sucksdorff)
original title: En Djungelsaga

The story of a remote Indian tribe and a
prowling leopard thought to be possessed by a
demon.
Superbly photographed but rather dull:
Sucksdorff failed to provide enough story for a
feature.

wd, ph Arne Sucksdorff m Ravi Shankar

The Fly
US 1958   94m   Eastmancolor
   Cinemascope
TCF (Kurt Neumann)

A scientist invents a method of transmitting
and reassembling atoms. He transmits himself
and does not notice a fly in the
compartment . . .
Unpleasant horror film which becomes
ludicrous but not funny.

w James Clavell d Kurt Neumann ph Karl
Struss m Paul Sawtell

David Hedison, Patricia Owens, Herbert
Marshall, Vincent Price

  'The monster created by atoms gone
wild!'—publicity
† Sequels were Return of the Fly (1960) and
Curse of the Fly (1965), neither worth noting
in detail.

Fly By Night
US 1942   74m   bw

A doctor, accused of murdering a scientist,
goes on the run and uncovers a Nazi spy ring.

Hoary *39 Steps* imitation, commendably done on a low budget to furnish wartime propaganda. Richard Carlson, Nancy Kelly, Albert Basserman, Walter Kingsford, Martin Kosleek, Miles Mander. Written by Jay Dratler and F. Hugh Herbert; directed by Robert Siodmak; for Paramount. (GB title: *Secrets of G32.*)

The Flying Deuces*
US 1939 67m bw
Boris Morros

Laurel and Hardy join the Foreign Legion. Patchy comedy from the end of the comedians' period of glory, and showing signs of decline.

w Ralph Spence, Harry Langdon, Charles Rogers, Alfred Schiller *d* Edward Sutherland *ph* Art Lloyd, Elmer Dyer

Stan Laurel, Oliver Hardy, Jean Parker, James Finlayson, Reginald Gardiner, Charles Middleton

'Mechanical stuff . . . seemed like *Beau Hunks* and *Bonnie Scotland* all over again.'— *William K. Everson*

Flying Down to Rio**
US 1933 89m bw
RKO (Merian C. Cooper, Lou Brock)

A dance band is a big success in Rio de Janeiro.
A thin musical electrified by the finale in which girls dance on the wings of moving airplanes, and by the teaming of Astaire and Rogers for the first time. Now an irresistible period piece.

w Cyril Hume, H. W. Hannemann, Erwin Gelsey, *play* Anne Caldwell *d* Thornton Freeland *ph* J. Roy Hunt *m* Vincent Youmans *ly* Edward Eliscu, Gus Kahn *ch* Dave Gould

Dolores del Rio, Gene Raymond, Raul Roulien, *Ginger Rogers, Fred Astaire*, Blanche Frederici, Walter Walker, Franklin Pangborn, Eric Blore

AAN: song 'The Carioca'

Flying Elephants
US 1927 20m bw silent

A caveman has the toothache. Fragmentary and generally unsatisfactory comedy starring Laurel and Hardy before they properly teamed, but released after their joint success. Written by Hal Roach and H. M. Walker; directed by Fred Butler and Hal Roach; for Hal Roach.

Flying Fortress
GB 1942 104m bw
Warner

A Canadian becomes a hero of bombing missions over Berlin.
Cardboard propaganda with silly love interest and a hilarious climax in which the hero does his stuff on the wing of a flying plane.

w Brock Williams, Gordon Wellesley, Edward Dryhurst *d* Walter Forde *ph* Gus Drisse, Basil Emmott

Richard Greene, Carla Lehmann, Betty Stockfield, Donald Stewart, Charles Heslop, Sidney King, Basil Radford, John Stuart

Flying High
US 1931 80m bw

A zany inventor breaks a long-distance flight record because he doesn't know how to land. Primitive comedy musical with inept dialogue and a static camera, partially salvaged by two early Busby Berkeley routines. Bert Lahr, Charlotte Greenwood, Pat O'Brien, Charles Winninger, Guy Kibbee, Hedda Hopper. Written by Robert Hopkins, A. P. Younger and Charles Riesner; directed by Charles Riesner; for MGM. (GB title: *Happy Landing.*)

Flying Leathernecks
US 1951 102m Technicolor
RKO (Edmund Grainger)

Two marine officers fight the Japs and each other on Guadalcanal.
Empty, violent war actioner full of phoney heroics.

w James Edward Grant *d* Nicholas Ray *ph* William E. Snyder *m* Roy Webb

John Wayne, Robert Ryan, Janis Carter, Don Taylor, Jay C. Flippen, William Harrigan, James Bell

'Ray's treatment is depressingly second rate and does nothing to alleviate the unpleasant impression of this disturbingly violent production.'—*Penelope Houston*

The Flying Missile
US 1950 92m bw
Columbia (Jerry Bresler)

A submarine commander defies authority to prove that rockets can be launched from the deck of a submarine.
Dated semi-documentary melodrama which was pretty flat on first viewing.

w Richard English, James Gunn *d* Henry Levin *ph* William Snyder *m* George Duning

Glenn Ford, Viveca Lindfors, Henry O'Neill, Carl Benton Reid, Joe Sawyer, John Qualen

The Flying Scotsman
GB 1929 63m bw

An ex-employee tries to wreck a crack train. Fairly presentable example of an early talkie film originally shot silent; one or two climactic thrills. Moore Marriott, Pauline Jameson, Ray Milland, Dino Galvani. Written by Victor Kendal and Garnett Weston; directed by Castleton Knight; for BIP.

Flying Tigers
US 1942 100m bw
Republic (Edmund Grainger)

American airmen fight the Japs over World War II China.
More mock heroics with noisy but unconvincing action sequences.

w Kenneth Gamet, Barry Trivers d David Miller ph Jack Marta m Victor Young

John Wayne, John Carroll, Anna Lee, Paul Kelly, Mae Clarke

AAN: Victor Young

FM (aka Citizens' Band)
US 1978 104m Technicolor

Problems of a commercial radio station whose disc jockeys seek integrity above commerce.
Footling cause-pleading is all this 'with-it' movie has to offier apart from its picture of commercial radio in the late seventies, which should be of interest to social historians.
Michael Brandon, Eileen Brennan, Alex Karras, Cleavon Little, Martin Mull. Written by Ezra Sacks; directed by John A. Alonzo; for Universal.

The Fog°
US 1979 91m Metrocolor Panavision
Avco / Debra Hill

A small Californian town is invaded by the leprous ghosts of mariners wrecked on the coast a hundred years before.
Silly but beguiling horror film with shock effects typical of its director.

w John Carpenter, Debra Hill d John Carpenter ph Dean Cundey m John Carpenter pd Tommy Lee Wallace

Adrienne Barbeau, Hal Holbrook, John Houseman, Janet Leigh, Jamie Lee Curtis, Tom Atkins

'An uneasy venture down a blind alley.'—
Tom Milne, MFB

Fog over Frisco°°°
US 1934 68m bw
Warner (Henry Blanke)

A San Francisco heiress gets herself murdered.
Silly whodunnit highly notable for its cinematic style, all dissolves, wipes and quick takes. Probably the fastest moving film ever made, and very entertaining despite its plot inadequacy.

w Robert N. Lee, novel George Dyer d William Dieterle ph Tony Gaudio md Leo F. Forbstein ed Harold McLernon

Bette Davis, Donald Woods, Margaret Lindsay, Lyle Talbot, Hugh Herbert, Arthur Byron, Robert Barrat, Douglass Dumbrille, Henry O'Neill, Irving Pichel, Alan Hale

'It reveals those qualities of pace and velocity and sharpness which make the Hollywood product acceptable even when the shallow content of ideas makes you want to scream.'—Robert Forsythe

'Its speed is artificially created by pacing, wipes, opticals, overlapping sound, camera movement and placing of characters, and by its habit of never having time really to begin or end scenes.'—William K. Everson
† Remade 1942 as Spy Ship, a second feature.

Folies Bergère°°°
US 1935 84m bw
Twentieth Century (William Goetz, Raymond Griffith)
GB title: The Man from the Folies Bergère

A Parisian banker persuades a music hall artist to impersonate him, but the wife and girl friend become involved in the confusion.
Amusing star vehicle with inventive Berkeleyish numbers and some remarkably sexy dialogue.

w Bess Meredyth, Hal Long, play The Red Cat by Rudolph Lothar, Hans Adler d Roy del Ruth ph Barney McGill, Peverell Marley md Alfred Newman ch Dave Gould

Maurice Chevalier, Merle Oberon, Ann Sothern, Eric Blore
† Remade as That Night in Rio, with Don Ameche, and On the Riviera, with Danny Kaye (both qv).

Follow a Star
GB 1959 104m bw
Rank (Hugh Stewart)

A shy amateur singer allows a fading star to mime to his voice.
Star comedy with an antique plot and a superfluity of pathos.

w Jack Davies, Henry Blyth, Norman Wisdom d Robert Asher ph Jack Asher m Philip Green

Norman Wisdom, Jerry Desmonde, June Laverick, Hattie Jacques, Richard Wattis, John Le Mesurier, Fenella Fielding, Ron Moody

'Such comedy as there is is mostly muffed by the lack of any sense of comic timing.'—*MFB*

Follow Me

GB 1971 93m Technicolor Panavision
Universal / Hal B. Wallis (Paul Nathan)
US title: *The Public Eye*

An eccentric private eye is hired to follow an accountant's wife, and she finds him fascinating.
Dullish, whimsical rendering of a dullish, whimsical one-act play; it never springs to life or interest.

w Peter Shaffer, from his play d Carol Reed
ph Christopher Challis m John Barry

Topol, Michael Jayston, Mia Farrow
'An uneasy mixture of broad comedy and high romance.'—*Sight and Sound*

Follow Me Boys

US 1966 132m Technicolor
Walt Disney (Winston Hibler)

The domestic trials and tribulations of a small-town schoolmaster.
Sentimental family saga full of patriotic fervour.

w Louis Pelletier, *novel* God and My Country by Mackinlay Kantor d Norman Tokar
ph Clifford Stine m George Bruns

Fred MacMurray, Vera Miles, Lillian Gish, Charlie Ruggles, Elliott Reid, Kurt Russell, Luana Patten, Ken Murray
'Demands an extremely strong stomach.'—*MFB*

Follow That Dream

US 1962 110m De Luxe Panavision
UA / Mirisch (David Weisbart)

A wandering family sets up house on a Florida beach.
Tiresomely cute comedy vehicle for a resistible star.

w Charles Lederer, *novel* Pioneer Go Home by Richard Powell d Gordon Douglas
ph Leo Tover m Hans Salter

Elvis Presley, Arthur O'Connell, Joanna Moore, Anne Helm, Jack Kruschen

Follow the Boys*

US 1944 109m bw
Universal (Charles K. Feldman)

A song and dance man organizes entertainment for the US troops during World War II.
Scrappy, unattractive propaganda tribute by the stars to the stars, enlivened only by a few guest spots.

w Lou Breslow, Gertrude Purcell
d A. Edward Sutherland ph David Abel
m Leigh Harline and others

George Raft, Vera Zorina, Charley Grapewin, Grace MacDonald, Charles Butterworth, George Macready, Elizabeth Patterson; and Orson Welles, Marlene Dietrich, Jeanette MacDonald, Dinah Shore, Donald O'Connor, Peggy Ryan, W. C. Fields, the Andrews Sisters, Artur Rubenstein, Sophie Tucker, Ted Lewis and his band, etc

AAN: song 'I'll Walk Alone' (m Jule Styne, ly Sammy Cahn)

Follow the Boys

US 1963 95m Metrocolor Panavision
MGM / Franmet (Laurence P. Bachmann)

An American warship is diverted from Cannes to Santa Margarita, and the waiting wives have to follow by road.
Harmless star comedy musical.

w David T. Chantler, David Osborn
d Richard Thorpe ph Ted Scaife

Connie Francis, Paula Prentiss, Dany Robin, Russ Tamblyn, Richard Long

Follow the Fleet**

US 1936 110m bw
RKO (Pandro S. Berman)

Sailors on shore leave romance a couple of girl singers.
Amiable star musical which makes heavy weather of a listless and overlong script, but has good numbers for those who can wait.

w Dwight Taylor, *play* Shore Leave by Hubert Osborne, Allan Scott d Mark Sandrich
ph David Abel m / ly Irving Berlin

Fred Astaire, Ginger Rogers, Randolph Scott, Harriet Hilliard, Astrid Allwyn, Harry Beresford, Lucille Ball, Betty Grable, Tony Martin

Follow the Sun

US 1951 93m bw
TCF (Samuel G. Engel)

Ben Hogan, a professional golfer, recovers slowly and painfully from a car crash and for the first time gains the affection of the crowd.
Modest sporting biopic, generally watchable but rising to no great heights.

w Frederick Hazlitt Brennan d Sidney Lanfield ph Leo Tover m Cyril Mockridge

Glenn Ford, Anne Baxter, Dennis O'Keefe, June Havoc, Larry Keating, Nana Bryant, Roland Winters

Folly to be Wise*
GB 1952   91m   bw
London Films / Launder and Gilliat

A brains trust at an army unit starts off a
battle of the sexes.
Typical James Bridie comedy which starts
brightly and whimsically, then peters out and
is saved by the acting.

w Frank Launder, John Dighton, *play* It
Depends What You Mean by James Bridie
d Frank Launder *ph* Jack Hildyard
m Temple Abady

Alastair Sim, Roland Culver, Elizabeth Allen,
Martita Hunt, Colin Gordon

The Food of the Gods
US 1976   88m   Movielab
AIP (Bert I. Gordon)

A curious substance which oozes out of the
ground turns common beasts into monsters.
Rather crude horror movie which has little
affinity with its literary original.

wd Bert I. Gordon, *story* H. G. Wells
ph Reginald Morris *m* Elliot Kaplan

Marjoe Gortner, Pamela Franklin, Ida
Lupino, Ralph Meeker, John McLiam
    'Not only sick, but sickening.'—*Arthur
Knight*
    'I wish I hadn't seen the movie, so I could
avoid it like the plague.'—*John Simon*
    'More plot holes than any movie in recent
memory, and enough dopey lines to make a
Saturday night audience howl in all the wrong
places.'—*David Sterritt, Christian Science
Monitor*

A Fool There Was*
US 1914   67m (24 fps)   bw   silent
William Fox

A financier in Europe forsakes all for a *femme
fatale*, and dies in her arms.
Antediluvian moral melodrama which made a
star of Bara and added the word 'vamp' to the
language.

wd Frank Powell, play Porter Emerson
Browne suggested by Rudyard Kipling's poem
The Vampire

Theda Bara, Edward Jose, Mabel Frenyer,
May Allison

Foolin' Around
US 1979   101m   De Luxe
Columbia / Arnold Kopelson

A country bumpkin wins a runaway heiress.
Uneasy harkback to the innocence of *It
Happened One Night*, with willing performers
in search of a script and setting.

w Mike Kane, David Swift *d* Richard T.
Heffron *ph* Philip Lathrop *m* Charles
Bernstein

Gary Busey, Annette O'Toole, John Calvin,
Eddie Albert, Cloris Leachman, Tony Randall

Foolish Wives**
US 1921   85m approx (24 fps); originally
    much longer   bw   silent
Universal

In Monte Carlo, a fake count seduces and
blackmails rich women.
Weird melodrama with memorable moments
and a vast set; Stroheim's most vivid star
performance and one of his most lavish
productions.

wd Erich Von Stroheim ph Ben Reynolds,
William Daniels *ad Erich Von Stroheim,
Richard Day*

Erich Von Stroheim, Mae Busch, Maud
George, Cesare Gravina
    'A very superior piece of photoplay
craftsmanship, original in ideas and treatment
and deserving of higher rating than *Orphans of
the Storm, Loves of Pharaoh, The Storm* and
other second-class material which however
brought forth applause and bravos from screen
public and scribes.'—*Tamar Lane, What's
Wrong with the Movies*

Fools
US 1970   93m   Eastmancolor

An unsuccessful actor has an idyllic love affair
with a girl he meets in a park; but her jealous
millionaire husband shoots her dead. Foolish
is the word for those who concocted this
tedious parable about the innocence of love
and the sickness of society. Jason Robards Jnr,
Katharine Ross, Scott Hylands. Written by
Robert Rudelson; directed by Tom Gries; for
Translor.

Fools for Scandal*
US 1938   81m   bw
Warner (Mervyn Le Roy)

A Hollywood movie star falls in love with a
French nobleman.
Disappointingly leaden romantic comedy.

w Herbert and Joseph Fields, *play* Return
Engagement by Nancy Hamilton, Rosemary
Casey, James Shute *d* Mervyn Le Roy
ph Ted Tetzlaff *m* Richard Rodgers, Lorenz
Hart

Carole Lombard, Fernand Gravet, Ralph
Bellamy, Allen Jenkins, Isabel Jeans, Marie
Wilson, Ottola Nesmith

Fools Parade**
US 1971   98m   Eastmancolor
Columbia / Stanmore / Penbar (Andrew V.
  McLaglen)
GB title: *Dynamite Man from Glory Jail*

An ex-con has trouble cashing a cheque for his
prison savings, especially as outlaws are after
it.
Curious admixture of comedy, adventure and
violence with a thirties setting, from the
author of *Night of the Hunter*; generally
gripping entertainment.

*w James Lee Barrett, novel Davis Grubb
d* Andrew V. McLaglen *ph* Harry Stradling
Jnr *m* Henry Vars

James Stewart, George Kennedy, Strother
Martin, Anne Baxter, Kurt Russell, William
Windom, Mike Kellin
  'A quintessentially American tribute to the
quiet heroism of the self-made man.'—*Nigel
Andrews*

Fools Rush In
GB 1949   82m   bw

A girl changes her mind on her wedding day,
and causes repercussions through the family.
Thin, flat film version of a successful play.
Sally Ann Howes, Guy Rolfe, Nora
Swinburne, Nigel Buchanan, Raymond Lovell,
Thora Hird. Written by Geoffrey Kerr, from
the play by Kenneth Horne; directed by John
Paddy Carstairs; for Rank.

Footlight Parade***
US 1933   104m   bw
Warner (Robert Lord)

A determined producer of cine-variety
numbers gets the show going despite great
difficulty.
Classic putting-on-a-show musical
distinguished by rapid-fire dialogue, New York
setting, star performances and some of the
best Busby Berkeley numbers.

w Manuel Seff, James Seymour *d Lloyd
Bacon ch Busby Berkeley ph* George Barnes
ad Anton Grot, Jack Okey m / ly Harry
Warren, Al Dubin, Sammy Fain, Irving Fahal
James Cagney, Joan Blondell, Ruby Keeler,
Dick Powell, Frank McHugh, Guy Kibbee,
Ruth Donnelly, Hugh Herbert, Claire Dodd,
Herman Bing
  '1,000 surprises! 300 beauties! 20 big
stars!'—*publicity*
  'Bevies of beauty and mere males disport
themselves in a Honeymoon Hotel, by (and
in) a Waterfall, and over several acres of
Shanghai.'—*C. A. Lejeune*

Footlight Serenade
US 1942   80m   bw
TCF (William LeBaron)

A boxer romances a showgirl.
Indifferent star musical.

w Robert Ellis, Helen Logan, Lynn Starling
d Gregory Ratoff *ph* Lee Garmes
md Charles Henderson *songs* Ralph Rainger,
Leo Robin

Betty Grable, John Payne, Victor Mature,
James Gleason, Phil Silvers, Jane Wyman,
Cobina Wright Jnr, June Lang, Mantan
Moreland

Footsteps in the Dark
US 1941   96m   bw
Warner (Robert Ford)

A would-be detective novelist on the lookout
for story material finds himself solving a
murder.
Lethargic modern vehicle for Flynn between
his swashbucklers, a poor imitation of the *Thin
Man* style.

w Lester Cole, John Wexley, *play* Blondie
White by Ladislas Fodor *d* Lloyd Bacon
ph Ernest Haller *m* Frederick Hollander

Errol Flynn, Brenda Marshall, Ralph Bellamy,
Alan Hale, Lucile Watson, Allen Jenkins, Lee
Patrick, William Frawley, Roscoe Karns,
Grant Mitchell
  'The footsteps were those of restless patrons
on their way out to buy popcorn.'—*Clive
Hirschhorn*

Footsteps in the Fog*
GB 1955   90m   Technicolor
Columbia / Mike Frankovich (Maxwell
  Setton)

A Victorian murderer plans to eliminate a
blackmailing maid.
This variation on *Gaslight* turns into a black
comedy without laughs, but it has effective
moments and is efficiently if charmlessly
made.

w Dorothy Reid, Lenore Coffee, *story* The
Interruption by W. W. Jacobs *d* Arthur
Lubin *ph* Christopher Challis *m* Benjamin
Frankel *ad* Wilfrid Shingleton

Stewart Granger, Jean Simmons, Bill Travers,
Ronald Squire, Finlay Currie, Peter Bull

For a Few Dollars More
Italy / Spain / West Germany 1965   130m
  Techniscope
PEA / Gonzales / Constantin (Alberto
  Grimaldi)

Bounty hunters in El Paso agree to work
together.

Vague, inflated, sometimes good-looking sequel to *A Fistful of Dollars*, with customary violence and predictably mean performances.

wd Sergio Leone *ph* Massimo Dallamano *m* Ennio Morricone

Clint Eastwood, Lee Van Cleef, Gian Maria Volonte, Klaus Kinski

For Freedom
GB 1940 88m bw
GFD / Gainsborough (Edward Black, Castleton Knight)

Events surrounding the Battle of the River Plate and the sinking of the Graf Spee. Economical wartime potboiler with much use of newsreel.

w Miles Malleson, Leslie Arliss *d* Maurice Elvey

Will Fyffe, Anthony Hulme, E. V. H. Emmett, Guy Middleton, Albert Lieven

For Heaven's Sake
US 1950 92m bw
TCF (William Perlberg)

Two angels are sent to earth to mend a Broadway producer's marriage.
Silly, flat whimsy of the *Here Comes Mr Jordan* school, and originating from the same author. Stale beer, but historically interesting.

w George Seaton, *play* Harry Segall *d* George Seaton *ph* Lloyd Ahern *m* Alfred Newman

Clifton Webb, Edmund Gwenn, Robert Cummings, Joan Bennett, Joan Blondell, Gigi Perreau, Jack La Rue

For Love of Ivy
US 1968 100m Perfectcolor
Cinerama / Palomar (Edgar J. Scherick, Jay Weston)

An invaluable coloured maid gives notice, and the family blackmails a likeable black ne'er-do-well to make love to her so that she will stay.
Unhappy whimsy with an extremely laboured script and no jokes, notable only as Hollywood's first bow towards a black love affair.

w Robert Alan Aurthur, *story* Sidney Poitier *d* Daniel Mann *ph* Joseph Coffey *m* Quincy Jones

Sidney Poitier, Abby Lincoln, Beau Bridges, Carroll O'Connor, Nan Martin, Lauri Peters

AAN: title song (*m* Quincy Jones, *ly* Bob Russell)

For Love or Money
US 1963 108m Technicolor
U-I (Robert Arthur)

A rich widow hires a lawyer to look after the affairs of her three wayward daughters; he picks the eldest for himself.
Slow, thin, overlong comedy with a surfeit of witless chat.

w Larry Marks, Michael Morris *d* Michael Gordon *ph* Clifford Stine *m* Frank de Vol

Kirk Douglas, Mitzi Gaynor, Thelma Ritter, William Bendix, Gig Young

For Me and My Gal***
US 1942 104m bw
MGM (Arthur Freed)

Just before World War I, a girl vaudevillian chooses between two partners.
A routine musical romance at the time of its production, this film now stands out because of its professional execution, its star value, and the fact that they don't make 'em like that any more.

w Richard Sherman, Sid Silvers, Fred Finkelhoffe *d* Busby Berkeley *ph* William Daniels *md* Georgie Stoll, Roger Edens

Judy Garland, Gene Kelly, George Murphy, Marta Eggerth, Ben Blue, Richard Quine, Stephen McNally

'A touch of imagination and a deal more than a touch of energy.'—*The Times*

AAN: Georgie Stoll, Roger Edens

For Pete's Sake*
US 1974 90m Eastmancolor
Columbia / Rastar / Persky–Bright–Barclay (Martin Erlichmann, Stanley Shapiro)

A New York taxi driver's wife borrows money and finds herself heavily committed to work off the debt.
Involved farcical comedy with amusing passages.

w Stanley Shapiro, Martin Richlin *d* Peter Yates *ph* Laszlo Kovacs *m* Artie Butler

Barbra Streisand, Michael Sarrazin, Estelle Parsons, William Redfield, Molly Picon

'Revives memories of how much more inventively they used to do it thirty years ago.'—*Sight and Sound*

For the First Time
US 1959 97m Technirama
MGM / Corona / Orion (Alexander Gruter)

A famous tenor slips off incognito to Capri and falls in love with a deaf girl.
Slipshod co-production (with West Germany)

with a hoary sentimental plot, a fat star, and some agreeable picture postcard views.

w Andrew Solt *d* Rudolph Maté *ph* Aldo Tonti *md* Georgie Stoll

Mario Lanza, Johanna von Koczian, Kurt Kasznar, Zsa Zsa Gabor, Hans Sohnker

For the Love of Mike*

US 1960 84m De Luxe Cinemascope
TCF / Shergari (George Sherman)
GB title: *None But the Brave*

An Indian boy in New Mexico is helped by a priest to care for sick animals.
Sentimental outdoor film for young people with a pleasantly light touch.

w D. D. Beauchamp *d* George Sherman *ph* Alex Phillips *m* Raul La Vista

Richard Basehart, Stuart Erwin, Arthur Shields, Armando Silvestre

For Them That Trespass

GB 1948 93m bw
ABP (Victor Skutezky)

A man proves himself innocent of the crime for which he has served fifteen years in prison.
Tedious melodrama which served to introduce Richard Todd to the screen.

w J. Lee-Thompson *d* Alberto Cavalcanti *ph* Derick Williams *m* Philip Green

Richard Todd, Stephen Murray, Joan Dowling, Patricia Plunkett, Michael Laurence, Rosalyn Boulter

For Those in Peril

GB 1943 67m bw

Exploits of the air / sea rescue service.
Standard semi-documentary morale-raiser.
David Farrar, Ralph Michael, Robert Wyndham, John Slater. Written by Harry Watt, J. O. C. Orton and T. E. B. Clarke; directed by Charles Crichton; for Ealing.

For Those Who Think Young

US 1964 96m Techniscope
UA / Aubrey Schenck-Howard W. Koch
(Hugh Benson)

College students save their favourite club from closure.
Tedious beach party frolic, very typical of its day, with some odd cameo appearances.

w James and George O'Hanlon, Dan Beaumont *d* Leslie H. Martinson *ph* Harold E. Stine *m* Jerry Fielding

James Darren, Pamela Tiffin, Woody Woodbury, Nancy Sinatra, Tina Louise, Paul Lynde, Bob Denver, Jack La Rue, George Raft, Allen Jenkins, Robert Armstrong, Roger Smith

For Valour*

GB 1937 95m bw
GFD / Capitol (Max Schach)

Adventures in two wars of a major, his shady friend, and their sons.
Agreeable adult farce with the stars each playing father and son.

w Ben Travers *d* Tom Walls

Tom Walls, Ralph Lynn, Veronica Rose, Joan Marion, Hubert Harben

'A very pleasant antidote to the Coronation, though a little marred by its inability to remain wholly flippant.'—*Graham Greene*

For Whom the Bell Tolls**

US 1943 168m Technicolor
Paramount (Sam Wood)

An American joins partisan fighters in the Spanish Civil War and falls in love with a refugee girl before going on a suicide mission.
Portentous, solemn adventure story based on a modern classic but without much cinematic impetus despite careful handling and useful performances. It looks expensive, though.

w Dudley Nichols, *novel* Ernest Hemingway *d* Sam Wood *ph* Ray Rennahan *m* Victor Young *pd* William Cameron Menzies

Gary Cooper, Ingrid Bergman, Akim Tamiroff, Arturo de Cordova, *Katina Paxinou*, Vladimir Sokoloff, Mikhail Rasumny, Victor Varconi, Joseph Calleia, Alexander Granach

'168 minutes of breathless thrills and romance!'—*publicity*

'The rhythm of this film is the most defective I have ever seen in a super-production . . . colour is very nice for costume pieces and musical comedies, and has a great aesthetic future in films, but it still gets fatally in the way of any serious imitation of reality.'—*James Agee*

AA: Katina Paxinou
AAN: best picture; Ray Rennahan; Victor Young; Gary Cooper; Ingrid Bergman; Akim Tamiroff

For You Alone

GB 1944 98m bw

Romance of a naval officer and a vicar's daughter. Sentimental drama with music; you can smell the lavender a mile off, but it was probably the most ambitious production of this indefatigable Poverty Row production company. Lesley Brook, Jimmy Hanley, Dinah Sheridan, G. H. Mulcaster, Manning Whiley. Written by Montgomery Tully; directed by Geoffrey Faithfull; for Butcher's.

Forbidden
US 1932   83m   bw

Our heroine loves the DA, but to save his
marriage she marries someone else. Turgid
renunciation drama with some interest added
by stars and director. Barbara Stanwyck,
Adolphe Menjou, Ralph Bellamy. Written by
Frank Capra and Jo Swerling; directed by
Frank Capra; for Columbia.

Forbidden
GB 1949   87m   bw

A man in love with another woman tries to
poison his extravagant wife. Turgid
melodrama with funfair background. Douglass
Montgomery, Hazel Court, Patricia Burke,
Garry Marsh, Ronald Shiner, Kenneth
Griffith. Written by Katherine Strueby;
directed by George King; for Pennant / British
Lion.

Forbidden
US 1953   85m   bw

A detective falls in love with the woman a
mobster has hired him to find. Would-be
intense *film noir*; talent does not enable it to
register. Tony Curtis, Joanne Dru, Lyle
Bettger, Marvin Miller, Sen Yung. Written by
William Sackheim and Gil Doud; directed by
Rudolph Maté; for Universal-International.

Forbidden Cargo
GB 1954   85m   bw
Rank / London Independent Productions
(Sydney Box)

A customs investigator prevents a large
consignment of drugs from reaching its English
outlets.
Routine British thick ear.

w Sydney Box d Harold French ph C.
Pennington-Richards m Lambert Williamson

Nigel Patrick, Elizabeth Sellars, Terence
Morgan, Jack Warner

Forbidden Fruit*
France 1952   103m   bw
Gray Film
original title: *Le Fruit Défendu*

A widowered doctor marries again, then falls
for a prostitute.
One of the rather solemn romantic
melodramas in which the star insisted from
time to time in becoming involved.

w Jacques Companeez, Henri Verneuil, Jean
Manse, *novel* Lettre à Mon Juge by Georges
Simenon d Henri Verneuil ph Henri Alekan
m Paul Durand

Fernandel, Claude Nollier, Françoise Arnoul,
Sylvie

Forbidden Planet**
US 1956   98m   Eastmancolor
  Cinemascope
MGM (Nicholas Nayfack)

In AD 2200 a space cruiser visits the planet
Altair Four to discover the fate of a previous
mission.
Intriguing sci-fi with a plot derived from *The
Tempest* and a Prospero who unwittingly
creates monsters from his own id. High spirits
and suspense sequences partially cancelled out
by wooden playing from the younger actors
and some leaden dialogue.

w Cyril Hume d Fred M. Wilcox ph George
Folsey m Louis and Bebe Barron ad Cedric
Gibbons, Arthur Lonergan

Walter Pidgeon, Anne Francis, Leslie Nielsen,
Warren Stevens, Jack Kelly, Richard
Anderson, Earl Holliman
  'It's a pity they didn't lift some of
Shakespeare's language.'—*New Yorker, 1977*

The Forbin Project**
US 1969   100m   Technicolor
  Panavision
Universal (Stanley Chase)
GB title: *Colossus, The Forbin Project*

An enormous computer takes over the defence
of the western world; but it goes into
collaboration with the Russian one.
Good-looking sci-fi for intellectual addicts.

w James Bridges, *novel* Colossus by D. F.
Jones d Joseph Sargent ph Gene Polito
m Michel Columbier

Eric Braeden, Gordon Pinsent, Susan Clark,
William Schallert

Force of Arms*
US 1951   100m   bw
Warner (Anthony Veiller)

A soldier in the Italian campaign falls in love
with his nurse.
Routine variation on *A Farewell to Arms*,
adequately but unexcitingly mounted.

w Orin Jannings, *story* Richard Tregaskis
d Michael Curtiz ph Ted McCord m Max
Steiner

William Holden, Nancy Olson, Frank
Lovejoy, Gene Evans, Dick Wesson, Paul
Picerni
  'The romance rings true and the battle
scenes are dangerously alive.'—*Variety*

Force of Evil***
US 1948 78m bw
MGM / Enterprise (Bob Roberts)

A racketeer's lawyer finds that his boss has killed the lawyer's brother.
Involved, atmospheric melodrama about the numbers racket, moodily and brilliantly photographed in New York streets, gloweringly well acted and generally almost as hypnotic as *Citizen Kane*.

w Abraham Polonsky, Ira Wolfert, *novel* Tucker's People by Ira Wolfert *d Abraham Polonsky ph* George Barnes *m* David Raksin

John Garfield, *Thomas Gomez*, Beatrice Pearson, Marie Windsor
'It credits an audience with intelligence in its ears as well as its eyes.'—*Dilys Powell*

Force Ten from Navarone
GB 1978 118m Technicolor Panavision
Columbia / AIP / Guy Hamilton (Oliver A. Unger)

During World War II, commandos are detailed to blow up a vital bridge separating the Germans and partisans in Yugoslavia.
Routine war hokum with plenty of explosions and sudden death, but not much sense. Nothing, really, to do with *The Guns of Navarone*.

w Robin Chapman, *novel* Alistair MacLean *d* Guy Hamilton *ph* Chris Challis *m* Ron Goodwin *pd* Geoffrey Drake

Robert Shaw, Edward Fox, Franco Nero, Harrison Ford, Barbara Bach, Richard Kiel

A Foreign Affair**
US 1948 116m bw
Paramount (Charles Brackett)

A deputation of American politicians goes to visit post-war Berlin and a congresswoman finds herself in an emotional triangle with a captain and his German mistress.
Bleakly sophisticated comedy from this team's headline-grabbing period; full of interest and amusement, it never quite sparkles enough to remove the doubtful taste.

w Charles Brackett, Billy Wilder, Richard Breen *d* Billy Wilder *ph* Charles Lang Jnr *m* Frederick Hollander

Jean Arthur, Marlene Dietrich, John Lund, Millard Mitchell, Peter Von Zerneck, Stanley Prager
'This deliberately cynical political farce . . . often seems on the verge of being funny, but the humour is too clumsily forced.'—*New Yorker, 1980*

AAN: script; Charles Lang Jnr

Foreign Affaires
GB 1935 71m bw
Gainsborough (Michael Balcon)

A gambler and a car salesman get mixed up with a phoney casino.
Mild star farce.

w Ben Travers *d* Tom Walls

Tom Walls, Ralph Lynn, Robertson Hare, Norma Varden, Marie Lohr, Diana Churchill, Cecil Parker

Foreign Correspondent****
US 1940 120m bw
Walter Wanger

An American journalist is sent to Europe in 1938 and becomes involved with spies.
Thoroughly typical and enjoyable Hitchcock adventure with a rambling script which builds up into brilliantly managed suspense sequences: an assassination, a windmill, an attempted murder in Westminster Cathedral, a plane crash at sea. The final speech was an attempt to encourage America into the war.

w *Charles Bennett, Joan Harrison, James Hilton, Robert Benchley*, from Personal History by Vincent Sheean *d Alfred Hitchcock ph Rudolph Maté m* Alfred Newman *sp* Lee Zavitz *ad* Alexander Golitzen

Joel McCrea, Laraine Day, *Herbert Marshall, Albert Basserman, Edmund Gwenn, George Sanders, Eduardo Cianelli, Robert Benchley, Harry Davenport*, Martin Kosleck
'If you have any interest in the true motion and sweep of pictures, watching that man work is like listening to music . . . If you would like a seminar in how to make a movie travel the lightest and fastest way, in a kind of beauty that is peculiar to movies alone, you can see this once, and then again to see what you missed, and then study it twice.'—*Otis Ferguson*
'The most excitingly shot and edited picture of the year.'—*Basil Wright*
'A masterpiece of propaganda, a first class production which no doubt will make a certain impression upon the broad masses of the people in enemy countries.'—*Joseph Goebbels*
'This juxtaposition of outright melodramatics with deadly serious propaganda is eminently satisfactory . . . Hitchcock uses camera tricks, cinematic rhythm and crescendo to make his points.'—*Howard Barnes, New York Herald Tribune*
'Easily one of the year's finest pictures.'—*Time*

AAN: best picture; script; Rudolph Maté; Albert Basserman

Foreign Intrigue*
US 1956 100m Eastmancolor
UA / Sheldon Reynolds

A press agent investigates the death of a man who had been blackmailing potential traitors.
Location espionage melodrama of the cold war fifties, quite well done in a rather dismal vein, but a long way from *Foreign Correspondent*.

wd Sheldon Reynolds *ph* Bertil Palmgrem *m* Paul Durand

Robert Mitchum, Genevieve Page, Ingrid Thulin, Eugene Deckers

The Foreman Went to France**
GB 1941 87m bw
Ealing (Alberto Cavalcanti)
US title: *Somewhere in France*

Before Dunkirk, a Welsh foreman is sent on a mission to salvage secret French machinery.
Fresh, appealing comedy drama based on a true incident of World War II.

w John Dighton, Angus Macphail, Leslie Arliss, Roger Macdougall, Diana Morgan, *story* J. B. Priestley *d* Charles Frend *ph* Wilkie Cooper *m* William Walton

Tommy Trinder, Constance Cummings, Clifford Evans, Robert Morley, Gordon Jackson, Ernest Milton

The Forest Rangers*
US 1942 85m Technicolor
Paramount (Robert Sisk)

A socialite marries a district ranger and rescues her disgruntled rival during a forest blaze.
Routine, competent, box office actioner of its time, with popular stars, adequate plot, but precious little inventiveness.

w Harold Shumate *d* George Marshall *ph* Charles Lang *m* Victor Young

Fred MacMurray, Paulette Goddard, Susan Hayward, Lynne Overman, Albert Dekker, Eugene Pallette, Regis Toomey, Rod Cameron

  'Another tale of the tall timbers, complete with conflagrations, he-men, and women like cats.'—*New York Times*

Forever Amber*
US 1947 137m Technicolor
TCF (William Perlberg)

Adventures of a desirable young lady during the reign of Charles II.
Much-bowdlerized version of a sensational novel of the forties; pretty but rather thin, with a colourless cast, saved by lively action sequences.

w Philip Dunne, Ring Lardner Jnr, *novel* Kathleen Winsor *d* Otto Preminger *ph* Leon Shamroy *m* David Raksin *ad* Lyle Wheeler

Linda Darnell, Cornel Wilde, *George Sanders* (as Charles II), Richard Greene, Glenn Langan, Richard Haydn, Jessica Tandy, Anne Revere, Robert Coote, John Russell, Leo G. Carroll

AAN: David Raksin

Forever and a Day**
US 1943 104m bw
RKO (Herbert Wilcox, Victor Saville)

The history of a London house from 1804 to the blitz of World War II.
Made for war charities by a combination of the European talents in Hollywood, this series of sketches was unavoidably patchy but gave good opportunities to several familiar performers and stands as a likeable quick reference to their work at this period.

w Charles Bennett, C. S. Forester, Lawrence Hazard, Michael Hogan, W. P. Lipscomb, Alice Duer Miller, John Van Druten, Alan Campbell, Peter Godfrey, S. M. Herzig, Christopher Isherwood, Gene Lockhart, R. C. Sherriff, Claudine West, Norman Corwin, Jack Hartfield, James Hilton, Emmet Lavery, Frederick Lonsdale, Donald Ogden Stewart, Keith Winter *ph* Robert de Grasse, Lee Garmes, Russell Metty, Nicholas Musuraca *m* Anthony Collins *d* René Clair, Edmund Goulding, Cedric Hardwicke, Frank Lloyd, Victor Saville, Robert Stevenson, Herbert Wilcox *ad* Albert D'Agostino, Lawrence Williams, Al Herman

Anna Neagle, Ray Milland, *Claude Rains*, *C. Aubrey Smith*, Dame May Whitty, Gene Lockhart, Ray Bolger, Edmund Gwenn, Charles Coburn, Ian Hunter, *Jessie Matthews*, *Charles Laughton*, Montagu Love, *Cedric Hardwicke*, Reginald Owen, *Buster Keaton*, Wendy Barrie, Ida Lupino, *Brian Aherne*, Edward Everett Horton, June Duprez, Eric Blore, Merle Oberon, Una O'Connor, Nigel Bruce, *Roland Young, Gladys Cooper*, Robert Cummings, Richard Haydn, Elsa Lanchester, Sara Allgood, Robert Coote, Donald Crisp, Ruth Warrick, Kent Smith, Herbert Marshall, Victor McLaglen, many others in bit parts

  'One of the most brilliant casts of modern times has been assembled to bolster up one of the poorest pictures.'—*James Agate*

Forever Darling
US 1956 91m Eastmancolor
MGM / Zanra (Desi Arnaz)

A couple's matrimonial difficulties are solved by her guardian angel.

Cutesy-pie comedy with all concerned
embarrassed by their material.

w Helen Deutsch *d* Alexander Hall
ph Harold Lipstein *m* Bronislau Kaper

Lucille Ball, Desi Arnaz, James Mason (as the
angel), John Emery, Louis Calhern, John
Hoyt, Natalie Schaefer

Forever England see Brown on
Resolution

Forever Female
US 1953 93m bw
Paramount (Pat Duggan)

A young writer sells his play to a Broadway
producer who wants to transform it into a
vehicle for his ex-wife; she falls for the writer
but eventually discourages him.
Talky romantic comedy without much style or
sense of Broadway; a long way from *All About
Eve.*

w Julius J. Epstein, Philip G. Epstein, *play*
Rosalind by J. M. Barrie *d* Irving Rapper
ph Harry Stradling *m* Victor Young

Ginger Rogers, William Holden, Paul
Douglas, James Gleason, Pat Crowley

Forfaiture see The Cheat

Forget Me Not
GB 1934 72m bw
London Films (Alexander Korda)
US title: *Forever Yours*

On board ship, a young girl falls for a
widowed tenor.
Bland romance, notable only for the star's
singing.

w Hugh Gray, Arthur Wimperis *d* Zoltan
Korda, Stanley Irving *ph* Hans Schneeberger

Beniamino Gigli, Joan Gardner, Ivan Brandt,
Hugh Wakefield

Forsaking All Others*
US 1934 84m bw
MGM (Bernard H. Hyman)

A wife nearly breaks up her rather dull
marriage, but thinks better of it.
Star power carries this thin comedy drama.

w Joseph L. Mankiewicz, *play* Edward Barry
Roberts, Frank Morgan Cavett *d* W. S. Van
Dyke *ph* Gregg Toland, George Folsey
m William Axt

Clark Gable, Joan Crawford, Robert
Montgomery, *Charles Butterworth*, Billie
Burke, Frances Drake, Rosalind Russell,
Arthur Treacher

Fort Algiers
US 1952 85m bw

A female French agent loves a fellow spy who
turns up as a Foreign Legionnaire, working
against an evil Emir. Quite lively old-
fashioned hokum, satisfactory on its level.
Yvonne de Carlo, Carlos Thompson,
Raymond Burr, Leif Erickson, Anthony
Caruso. Written by Theodore St John;
directed by Lesley Selander; for Erco / UA.

Fort Apache**
US 1948 127m bw
RKO (John Ford, Merian C. Cooper)

In the old west, a military martinet has trouble
with his family as well as the Indians.
Rather stiff and unsatisfactory epic western
which yet contains sequences in its director's
best manner.

w Frank S. Nugent, *story* Massacre by James
Warner Bellah *d John Ford* *ph* Archie Stout
m Richard Hageman

Henry Fonda, John Wayne, Shirley Temple,
Pedro Armendariz, Ward Bond, Irene Rich,
George O'Brien, John Agar, Victor
McLaglen, Anna Lee, Dick Foran, Guy
Kibbee
'A visually absorbing celebration of violent
deeds.'—*Howard Barnes*
'The whole picture is bathed in a special
form of patriotic sentimentality: scenes are
held so that we cannot fail to appreciate the
beauty of the American past.'—*New Yorker,
1976*
'Shirley Temple and her husband handle the
love interest as though they were sharing a
soda fountain special, and there is enough
Irish comedy to make me wish Cromwell had
done a more thorough job.'—*James Agee*

Fort Dobbs
US 1957 90m bw

Man on the run rescues widow from
Comanches and clears his name. Very routine
medium-scale western showcasing a TV star.
Clint Walker, Virginia Mayo, Brian Keith,
Richard Eyer. Written by George W. George
and Burt Kennedy; directed by Gordon
Douglas; for Warner.

Fort Massacre
US 1958 80m De Luxe Cinemascope

A cavalry sergeant becomes reckless when he
has to lead to safety the survivors of an Indian
attack. Psychological western without the skill
necessary to realize its pretensions. Joel
McCrea, Forrest Tucker, Susan Cabot, John

Russell. Written by Martin N. Goldsmith; directed by Joseph Newman; for Mirisch / UA.

Fort Ti
US 1953   73m   Technicolor   3-D
Columbia (Sam Katzman)

In 1759 a platoon of Rogers' Rangers marches north to defend their territory against Indians. Cheap and feeble western memorable only for the amount of miscellaneous objects thrown at the audience via 3-D photography.

w Robert E. Kent d William Castle
ph Lester E. White, Lathrop B. Worth
md Ross di Maggio

George Montgomery, Joan Vohs, Irving Bacon, James Seay

'The lack of restraint is remarkable. To the injury of tomahawks, rifle shots, cannon balls, flaming arrows, broken bottles and blazing torches is added the insult of grubby redskins hurled judo style into one's lap.'—*David Robinson*

Fort Worth
US 1951   80m   Technicolor

A newspaper editor combats a would-be dictator. Satisfying star western. Randolph Scott, Phyllis Thaxter, David Brian, Dick Jones, Paul Picerni. Written by John Twist; directed by Edwin L. Marin; for Warner.

The Fortune
US 1975   88m   Technicolor   Panavision
Columbia (Hank Moonjean)

A twenties heiress elopes with her lover and his dim-witted friend but discovers that they mean to murder her for her money.
Bungled black comedy with top talent overconfident of carrying it.

w Adrien Joyce (Carole Eastman) d Mike Nichols ph John A. Alonzo m various songs
pd Richard Sylbert

Jack Nicholson, Warren Beatty, Stockard Channing, Florence Stanley, Richard B. Shull, John Fiedler

'Like the ill-assorted styles of the film generally, the stars themselves frequently seem to belong in different movies.'—*Richard Combs*

'A silly, shallow, occasionally enjoyable comedy trifle . . . classy 20's production values often merit more attention than the plot.'—*Variety*

Fortune and Men's Eyes
Canada / US 1971   102m   Metrocolor
MGM / Cinemex / CFD (Lester Persky, Lewis M. Allen)

Life among homosexuals in a Canadian jail. A welter of sensational incident outweighs any point the author may have had; this prison seems to be beyond reform.

w John Herbert, from his play d Harvey Hart ph Georges Dufaux m Galt McDermot

Wendell Burton, Michael Greer

The Fortune Cookie*
US 1966   125m   bw   Panavision
UA / Mirisch / Phalanx / Jalem (Billy Wilder)
GB title: *Meet Whiplash Willie*

A crooked lawyer forces his slightly injured client to sue for a million dollars.
Flat, stretched-out, only occasionally effective comedy which relies too much on mordant attitudes and a single star performance.

w Billy Wilder, I. A. L. Diamond d Billy Wilder ph Joseph La Shelle m André Previn

Walter Matthau, Jack Lemmon, Ron Rich, Cliff Osmond, Lurene Tuttle

'A jackhammer of a film savagely applied to those concrete areas of human spirit where cupidity and stupidity have been so long entrenched.'—*Richard Schickel*

AA: Walter Matthau
AAN: Billy Wilder, I. A. L. Diamond (script); Joseph La Shelle

Fortune Is a Woman*
GB 1956   95m   bw
Columbia / Frank Launder, Sidney Gilliat
US title: *She Played with Fire*

An insurance assessor investigates a fire, finds a murder, marries the victim's widow, and is blackmailed . . .
Slackly-handled mystery thriller, a disappointment from the talents involved.

w Frank Launder, Sidney Gilliat, *novel* Winston Graham d Sidney Gilliat ph Gerald Gibbs m William Alwyn

Jack Hawkins, Arlene Dahl, Dennis Price, Geoffrey Keen, Violet Farebrother, John Robinson, Bernard Miles, Greta Gynt

Forty Carats*
US 1973   109m   Metrocolor
Columbia / M. J. Frankovich

A 40-year-old divorcee on holiday in Greece has a brief affair with a 22-year-old man. Curiously miscast and mishandled comedy for the smart set; scores a laugh or two but never really takes off.

w Leonard Gershe, *play* Pierre Barillet, Jean-Pierre Gredy *d* Milton Katselas *ph* Charles Lang Jnr *m* Michel Legrand

Liv Ullmann, Edward Albert, Gene Kelly, Billy 'Green' Bush, Binnie Barnes, Nancy Walker, Deborah Raffin, Don Porter, Natalie Schaefer, Rosemary Murphy

The Forty First*
USSR 1927   80m approx   bw   silent
Mezhrabpom
original title: *Sorok Pervyi*

During the Civil War in Turkestan, a girl sniper for the Reds becomes the companion in adventure of a White lieutenant. But in the end he becomes her 41st victim.
Strong action melodrama which found an international audience.

w Boris Lavryenov, from his novel *d* Yakov Protazanov *ph* Pyotr Yermolov

Ada Voitsik, Ivan Kovan-Samborsky
† Remade in 1956 by Grigori Chukrai, in colour.

Forty Guns
US 1957   80m   bw   Cinemascope
TCF / Globe (Samuel Fuller)

A powerful ranchwoman protects her hoodlum brother.
Heavily melodramatic and slow-moving western with a few effective moments.

wd Samuel Fuller *ph* Joseph Biroc *m* Harry Sukman

Barbara Stanwyck, Barry Sullivan, Dean Jagger, Gene Barry, John Ericson

Forty Guns to Apache Pass
US 1967   95m   Technicolor

A cavalry captain protects homesteaders when Cochise attacks. Flat and overlong star western compounded of excessively familiar elements. Audie Murphy, Michael Burns, Kenneth Tobey, Laraine Stephens. Written by Willard and Mary Willingham; directed by William Witney; for Admiral / Columbia.

Forty Little Mothers
US 1940   90m   bw
MGM (Harry Rapf)

A teacher in a girls' school finds himself in charge of a baby.
Ill-advised star vehicle composed largely of whimsy . . . and no musical numbers.

w Dorothy Yost, Ernest Pagano *d* Busby Berkeley *ph* Charles A. Lawton Jnr

Eddie Cantor, Judith Anderson, Bonita Granville, Rita Johnson, Diana Lewis, Nydia Westman, Martha O'Driscoll

Forty Ninth Parallel***
GB 1941   123m   bw
GFD / Ortus (John Sutro, Michael Powell)
US title: *The Invaders*

In Canada, five stranded U-boat men try to escape into the US.
Episodic, effective propaganda piece which develops some nice Hitchcockian touches and allows a range of star actors to make impact.

w Emeric Pressburger, Rodney Ackland *d* Michael Powell *ph* F. A. Young *m* Ralph Vaughan Williams

Eric Portman, Laurence Olivier, *Anton Walbrook, Leslie Howard, Raymond Massey*, Glynis Johns, Niall MacGinnis, Finlay Currie, Raymond Lovell, John Chandos
'Some of the plotting and characterization look rather rusty at this remove, but the sense of landscape and figures passing through it remains authoritatively dynamic.'—*Tony Rayns, Time Out, 1979*

AA: original story (Emeric Pressburger)
AAN: best picture; script

Forty Pounds of Trouble*
US 1963   105m   Eastmancolor
   Panavision
U-I / Curtis Enterprises (Stan Margulies)

A casino manager is chased by his ex-wife's detective for alimony payments, and also has to look after an abandoned six-year-old girl.
Standard sentimental comedy with some verve and a lively climactic chase through Disneyland.

w Marion Hargrove *d* Norman Jewison *ph* Joe MacDonald *m* Mort Lindsey

Tony Curtis, Phil Silvers, Suzanne Pleshette, Edward Andrews

Forty-Second Street****
US 1933   89m   bw
Warner (Hal B. Wallis)

A Broadway musical producer has troubles during rehearsal but reaches a successful opening night.
Archetypal Hollywood putting-on-a-show musical in which the leading lady is indisposed and a chorus girl is told to get out there and come back a star. The clichés are written and performed with great zest, the atmosphere is convincing, and the numbers when they come are dazzlers.

w James Seymour, Rian James, novel Bradford Ropes *d* Lloyd Bacon *ch* Busby Berkeley *ph* Sol Polito *m / ly* Al Dubin, Harry Warren

Warner Baxter, Ruby Keeler, Bebe Daniels, George Brent, Una Merkel, Guy Kibbee, Dick Powell, *Ginger Rogers* (as Anytime Annie), *Ned Sparks*, George E. Stone, Allen Jenkins

'The story has been copied a hundred times since, but never has the backstage atmosphere been so honestly and felicitously caught.'— *John Huntley, 1966*

'It gave new life to the clichés that have kept parodists happy.'—*New Yorker, 1977*

AAN: best picture

Foul Play*
US 1978   116m   Movielab
Paramount / Thomas L. Miller, Edward K. Milkis

Two innocents in San Francisco get involved in a plot to assassinate the visiting pope. Sometimes sprightly, sometimes tired rehash of Hitchcock elements, rather on the level of the similar *Silver Streak*.

wd Colin Higgins *ph* David M. Walsh *m* Charles Fox

Goldie Hawn, Chevy Chase, Burges Meredith, Rachel Roberts, Eugene Roche, Dudley Moore, Billy Barty

AAN: song, 'Ready to Take a Chance Again'

The Fountain
US 1934   84m   bw
RKO (Pandro S. Berman)

During World War I a British woman is tempted to forsake her mangled German air ace husband for her childhood sweetheart. A slice of impenetrable gloom from an intractable novel.

w Jane Murfin, Samuel Hoffenstein, *novel* Charles Morgan *d* John Cromwell *ph* Henry W. Gerrard *m* Max Steiner

Ann Harding, Brian Aherne, Paul Lukas, Jean Hersholt, Ralph Forbes, Violet Kemble-Cooper, Sara Haden

'One of the talkiest talkies yet.'—*Variety*
'Long and solemn and wonderfully empty.'—*Otis Ferguson*

The Fountainhead**
US 1949   114m   bw
Warner (Henry Blanke)

An idealistic architect clashes with big business.
Overripe adaptation of a rather silly novel, full of Freudian symbols and expressionist

techniques with which the star really can't cope; but an enjoyable field day for the director and the rest of the cast.

w Ayn Rand, from her novel *d King Vidor ph* Robert Burks *m* Max Steiner

Gary Cooper, *Patricia Neal, Raymond Massey*, Kent Smith, Robert Douglas, Henry Hull, Ray Collins, Moroni Olson, Jerome Cowan

'If you like deep thinking, hidden meanings, plus pure modern architecture, then this is something for which you have been waiting a long time.'—*Screenland*
'The most bizarre movie in both Vidor's and Cooper's filmographies, this adaptation mutes Ms Rand's neo-Nietzschian philosophy of "objectivism" but lays on the expressionist symbolism with a "free enterprise" trowel.'— *Time Out, 1980*

Four Daughters***
US 1938   90m   bw
Warner (Henry Blanke)

Domestic and romantic adventures of a small-town family.
Standard small-town hearth-fire hokum, impeccably done and really quite irresistible.

w Julius Epstein, Lenore Coffee, *novel* Sister Act by Fannie Hurst *d* Michael Curtiz *ph* Ernest Haller *m* Max Steiner

Claude Rains, John Garfield (a sensation in his first role), Priscilla Lane, Rosemary Lane, Lola Lane, Gale Page, Jeffrey Lynn, Frank McHugh, *May Robson*, Dick Foran

'It may be sentimental, but it's grand cinema.'—*New York Times*
† An immediate sequel was required, but the Garfield character had been killed off, so to accommodate him a variation was written under the title *Daughters Courageous*; then came two proper sequels without him, *Four Wives* and *Four Mothers*. In 1955 the original was remade as *Young at Heart* (qv).

AAN: best picture; script; Michael Curtiz; John Garfield

The Four Days of Naples*
Italy 1962   119m   bw
Titanus-Metro (Goffredo Lombardo)

A reconstruction of the 1943 city battle in which the Nazis were driven out by civilian fury.
A kind of update of *Open City*: much admired, but a little ill-timed.

w Nanni Loy and others *d* Nanni Loy *ph* Marcello Gatti *m* Carlo Rustichelli

Lea Massari, Frank Wolff, Domenico Formato, Raffaele Barbato

AAN: script

The Four Feathers**
US 1929 83m bw
Paramount (David O. Selznick)

During the Sudan campaign of the nineties, a stay-at-home receives four white feathers as a symbol of cowardice; but he goes undercover, becomes a hero, and rescues his best friend.
Ambitious early talkie based on a famous adventure novel, partly filmed in Africa; interesting but now very stilted.

w Howard Estabrook, novel A. E. W. Mason d Lothar Mendes, Merian C. Cooper, Ernest Schoedsack ph Robert Kurlle, Merian C. Cooper, Ernest Schoedsack m William F. Peters

Richard Arlen, Fay Wray, Clive Brook, William Powell, George Fawcett, Theodore Von Eltz, Noah Beery

The Four Feathers****
GB 1939 130m Technicolor
London (Alexander Korda, Irving Asher)

The standard version of the above, perfectly cast and presented, with battle scenes which have since turned up in a score of other films from Zarak to Master of the World; also a triumph of early colour.

w R. C. Sheriff, Lajos Biro, Arthur Wimperis d Zoltan Korda ph Georges Périnal, Osmond Borradaile, Jack Cardiff m Miklos Rozsa

John Clements, Ralph Richardson, C. Aubrey Smith, June Duprez, Allan Jeayes, Jack Allen, Donald Gray, Henry Oscar, John Laurie

'It cannot fail to be one of the best films of the year . . . even the richest of the ham goes smoothly down, savoured with humour and satire.'—Graham Greene

† Remade 1956 as Storm over the Nile (qv).

Four for Texas
US 1963 124m Technicolor
Warner / Sam Company (Robert Aldrich)

Two survivors of a stagecoach raid doublecross each other for the loot and become rival saloon owners.
Flabby western comedy, tediously directed and casually performed.

w Teddi Sherman, Robert Aldrich d Robert Aldrich ph Ernest Laszlo m Nelson Riddle

Dean Martin, Frank Sinatra, Anita Ekberg, Ursula Andress, Charles Bronson, Victor Buono, the Three Stooges

'The major laughs come from the Three Stooges doing an ancient routine and an old lady falling out of her wheelchair. Zowie.'—Judith Crist

'One suspects that the most amusing antics were those that went on off-screen.'—Films and Filming

Four Frightened People*
US 1934 78m bw
Paramount / Cecil B. de Mille

A bubonic plague outbreak on board ship causes four survivors to escape via a lifeboat and trek through dangerous jungle.
Studio-bound but interesting action melodrama, of a type unusual from this director.

w Bartlett Cormack, Lenore Coffee, novel E. Arnot Robertson d Cecil B. de Mille ph Karl Struss m Karl Hajos and others

Claudette Colbert, Herbert Marshall, William Gargan, Mary Boland, Leo Carrillo, Nella Walker, Tetsu Komai, Ethel Griffies

'A cumbersome sort of melodrama . . . despite some mildly entertaining jungle scenes.'—Literary Digest

Four Girls in Town
US 1956 85m Technicolor
Cinemascope
U-I (Aaron Rosenberg)

Girls from various countries are chosen for Hollywood screen tests.
Formula romantic comedy adequately exposing young talent.

wd Jack Sher ph Irving Glassberg m Alex North

George Nader, Julie Adams, Marianne Cook, Elsa Martinelli, Gia Scala, Sidney Chaplin, Grant Williams, John Gavin

Four Guns to the Border
US 1954 83m Technicolor

Things go wrong for four bank robbers after a raid. Rather downbeat western with insufficient excitement. Rory Calhoun, Walter Brennan, Coleen Miller, George Nader, Nina Foch, John McIntire, Charles Drake. Written by George Van Marter and Franklin Coen; directed by Richard Carlson; for Universal-International.

The Four Horsemen of the Apocalypse**
US 1921 150m approx bw silent
Metro

A young Argentinian fights for his father's country, France, in World War I.

Highly derivative dramatic spectacle, almost a pageant, from a fairly unreadable novel. Despite its variable if exotic style, it made a star of Rudolph Valentino.

w June Mathis, *novel* Vicente Blasco-Ibanez d Rex Ingram ph John F. Seitz

Rudolph Valentino, Alice Terry, Nigel de Brulier, Alan Hale, Jean Hersholt, Wallace Beery

'A blend of exotic settings, striking composition, dramatic lighting, and colourful if sordid atmosphere.'—*Lewis Jacobs*

'Not only was it marvellously effective in its appeal to the eye, but the logical and dramatic unfolding of the basic story was a striking revelation of the valuable service that an expert scenario-writer may render to the professional writer of novels.'—*Edward S. Van Zile, That Marvel the Movie*

The Four Horsemen of the Apocalypse*
US 1961   153m   Metrocolor
    Cinemascope
MGM (Julian Blaustein)

In this ill-fated modernization, the idle grandson of an Argentinian beef tycoon finds his manhood at last as a member of the French resistance during World War II. The visionary skyriding figures of death and pestilence simply do not fit in with bombs and concentration camps. Glum acting by a too elderly company, ugly colour and the usual hindrances of Cinemascope.

w Robert Ardrey, John Gay d Vincente Minnelli ph Milton Krasner m André Previn

Glenn Ford, Ingrid Thulin, Charles Boyer, Paul Henreid, Lee J. Cobb, Paul Lukas, Karl Boehm, Yvette Mimieux

'An elephantine helping of hysteria and hokum.'—*Judith Crist, 1973*

Four Hours to Kill**
US 1935   74m   bw
Paramount (Arthur Hornblow Jnr)

A psychopathic gangster gets loose during an evening at the theatre.
Tense, well-handled melodrama making full use of its setting.

w Norman Krasna, from his play Small Miracle d Mitchell Leisen ph Theodor Sparkuhl

Richard Barthelmess, Ray Milland, Gertrude Michael, Joe Morrison, Helen Mack, Dorothy Tree, Roscoe Karns, Henry Travers

The Four Hundred Blows**
France 1958   94m   bw   Dyaliscope
Films du Carrosse / SEDIF
original title: *Les Quatre Cents Coups*

A 12-year-old boy, unhappy at home, finds himself in a detention centre but finally escapes and keeps running.
Little more in plot terms than a piece of character observation, this engaging film is so controlled and lyrical as to be totally refreshing, and it gives a very vivid picture of the Paris streets.

wd François Truffaut ph Henri Decaë m Jean Constantin

Jean-Pierre Léaud, Claire Maurier, Albert Rémy

† The film is said to be based on Truffaut's own childhood.

AAN: script

Four in a Jeep*
Switzerland 1951   96m   bw
Praesensfilm (Lazar Wechsler)

In the post-war international zone of Vienna, the four nationals of a police patrol come to blows over the cases they encounter.
Historically interesting but rather bland illustration of an untenable and even tragic political situation which was treated more melodramatically in *The Third Man*.

w Richard Schweizer d Leopold Lindtberg ph Emil Barna m Robert Blum

Viveca Lindfors, Ralph Meeker, Yoseph Yadin, Michael Medwin

Four Jills in a Jeep
US 1944   89m   bw
TCF (Irving Starr)

Four Hollywood glamour girls entertain the troops.
Condescending, dispirited 'semi-documentary' war musical.

w Robert Ellis, Helen Logan, Snag Werris d William A. Seiter ph Peverell Marley md Emil Newman

Kay Francis, Martha Raye, Carole Landis, Mitzi Mayfair, Jimmy Dorsey and his band, John Harvey, Phil Silvers, Dick Haymes; guest stars Alice Faye, Betty Grable, Carmen Miranda, George Jessel

'It gives the painful impression of having been tossed together in a couple of hours.'—*Bosley Crowther*

The Four Just Men*
GB 1939   85m   bw
Ealing—Capad (S. C. Balcon)
US title: *The Secret Four*

To save the Empire, four stalwart Britishers agree to murder a villainous MP.
Bright, unusual but dated thriller from a popular novel.

w Roland Pertwee, Angus Macphail, Sergei Nolbandov, *novel* Edgar Wallace *d* Walter Forde *ph* Ronald Neame

Hugh Sinclair, Francis L. Sullivan, Frank Lawton, Griffith Jones, Anna Lee, Basil Sidney, Alan Napier, Athole Stewart, Edward Chapman, Garry Marsh, Ellaline Terriss, Lydia Sherwood, George Merritt

† The TV series of the late fifties restrained its heroes from criminal acts; the men were Jack Hawkins, Richard Conte, Dan Dailey, Vittorio de Sica.

Four Men and a Prayer**
US 1938 97m bw
TCF (Kenneth MacGowan)

Four young Englishmen set out to clear the name of their dishonoured father.
Pleasantly performed mystery which improves after a slowish start.

w Richard Sherman, Sonya Levien, Walter Ferris, *novel* David Garth *d John Ford ph* Ernest Palmer *md* Louis Silvers

Loretta Young, Richard Greene, George Sanders, David Niven, William Henry, C. Aubrey Smith, J. Edward Bromberg, John Carradine, Alan Hale, Reginald Denny, Barry Fitzgerald, Berton Churchill, John Sutton
   'Energetically told, compactly presented.'— *New York Times*

The Four Musketeers (The Revenge of Milady)*
Panama 1974 103m Technicolor
TCF / Film Trust / Este (Alexander Salkind, Michael Salkind)

Athos, Porthos, Aramis and D'Artagnan have a final battle with Rochefort.
Perfunctory sequel to the same team's *The Three Musketeers*; allegedly the two films were intended as one, but if so the first ten reels were by far the best, though this section has its regulation quota of high spirits and lusty action.

w George MacDonald Fraser *d* Richard Lester *ph* David Watkin *m* Lalo Schifrin *pd* Brian Eatwell

Michael York, Oliver Reed, Frank Finlay, Richard Chamberlain, Raquel Welch, Faye Dunaway, Charlton Heston, Christopher Lee, Simon Ward, Geraldine Chaplin, Jean-Pierre Cassel, Roy Kinnear
   'The whole sleek formula has rolled over to reveal a very soft, very flabby underside.'— *Tony Rayns*

The Four-Poster
US 1952 103m bw
Columbia / Stanley Kramer

The history of a marriage told in a series of bedroom scenes.
Hastily shot and rather tatty looking version of a stage play; unfortunately film can't contrast the comedy of the opening and the tragedy of the close within one small set, and the UPA cartoon bridges, though smart in themselves, are merely an irritation.

w Allan Scott, *play* Jan de Hartog *d* Irving Reis *ph* Hal Mohr *m* Dmitri Tiomkin

Rex Harrison, Lilli Palmer

AAN: Hal Mohr

The Four Skulls of Jonathan Drake
US 1959 70m bw
UA / Vogue (Robert E. Kent)

A family is cursed by a head-hunting Equadorian medicine man.
Cheaply made but full-blooded occult horror, rather effectively done by a cast that knows how.

w Orville H. Hampton *d* Edward L. Cahn *ph* Maury Gertsman *m* Paul Dunlap

Henry Daniell, Eduard Franz, Valerie French, Grant Richards, Paul Cavanagh
   'Amazonian Indians may find the plot a shade far-fetched.'—*MFB*

Four Sons*
US 1940 89m bw
TCF

A Czech family is divided when the Nazis take over.
Predictable po-faced anti-Hitler melodrama released to an indifferent public well before America entered the war. A remake of a silent film set during World War I.

w John Howard Lawson *d* Archie Mayo *ph* Leon Shamroy *m* David Buttolph

Don Ameche, Eugenie Leontovich, Mary Beth Hughes, Alan Curtis, George Ernest, Robert Lowery, Sig Rumann, Lionel Royce, Ludwig Stossel
   'It partakes more of sentimental melodrama than of tragedy. . . . Neither in its performance nor its writing does the film ever rise to any passion.'—*New York Times*

Four Steps in the Clouds*
Italy 1942 90m bw
Cines Amato
original title: *Quattro Passi fra le Nuvole*

A travelling salesman on a bus gets involved with the problems of a pregnant girl, but

misunderstandings are finally cleared up to general satisfaction.
A comedy on the American model which was a great success in wartorn Italy. Not particularly remarkable in itself, it was remade in 1957, as *The Virtuous Bigamist*, with Fernandel. It does show the lighter side of Italian neo-realism.

w Cesare Zavattini, Giuseppe Amato, Piero Tellini, Aldo de Benedetti *d* Alessandro Blasetti *ph* Vaclav Vich *m* Alessandro Cicognini

Gino Cervi, Adriana Benetti, Giuditta Rissone

Four's a Crowd
US 1938   91m   bw
Warner (Hal B. Wallis / David Lewis)

A public relations man has the job of promoting a mean-spirited millionaire, and falls in love with his daughter.
Floppy comedy, neither very witty nor as crazy as might have been expected. However, it ambles along quite engagingly.

w Casey Robinson, Sig Herzig *d* Michael Curtiz *ph* Ernest Haller *m* Heinz Roemheld, Ray Heindorf

Errol Flynn, Rosalind Russell, Olivia de Havilland, Patric Knowles, Walter Connolly, Hugh Herbert, Melville Cooper, Franklin Pangborn, Herman Bing, Margaret Hamilton

Fourteen Hours***
US 1951   92m   bw
TCF (Sol C. Siegel)

A man stands on the ledge of a tall building and threatens to jump.
Well-made documentary drama based on a true occurrence but given a happy ending. First class detail gives an impression of realism.

w John Paxton, article Joel Sayre *d* Henry Hathaway *ph* Joe MacDonald *m* Alfred Newman

Richard Basehart, Paul Douglas, Barbara Bel Geddes, Grace Kelly, Debra Paget, Agnes Moorehead, Robert Keith, Howard da Silva, Jeffrey Hunter, Martin Gabel, Jeff Corey
'A model of craftsmanship in all departments.'—*Penelope Houston*
'A highly enjoyable small scale picture, with a strength immensely greater than its size would suggest.'—*Richard Mallett, Punch*

The Fox*
US / Canada 1967   110m   De Luxe
Warner / Raymond Stross / Motion Pictures International (Howard Koch)

On an isolated farm, two lesbians are disturbed by the arrival of a wandering seaman.
Rather obvious sexual high jinks full of symbolism and heavy breathing.

w Lewis John Carlino, Howard Koch, *novel* D. H. Lawrence *d* Mark Rydell *ph* Bill Fraker *m* Lalo Schifrin

Anne Heywood, Sandy Dennis, Keir Dullea

AAN: Lalo Schifrin

Fox Follies of 1929
US 1929   82m   bw (sequence in colour)
Fox
GB title: *Movietone Follies of 1929*

An all-star review.
Every studio had its early talkie musical using up its contract stars; this was perhaps the least interesting.

wd David Butler, William K. Wells
ph Charles Van Enger

Sue Carol, Lola Lane, Dixie Lee, Sharon Lynn, Stepin Fetchit

Foxes
US 1980   106m   Technicolor

Four teenage girls battle with sex, drugs and life in general. Well-meaning but entirely resistible melodrama from behind the headlines. Jodie Foster, Scott Baio, Sally Kellerman, Randy Quaid, Adam Faith. Written by Gerald Ayres; directed by Adrian Lyne; for Casablanca / UA. 'Almost nil adult appeal.'—*Variety*.

The Foxes of Harrow
US 1947   117m   bw
TCF (William A. Bacher)

In 1820 New Orleans, a philanderer seeks advancement by breaking up his marriage.
Tolerable but rather flat adaptation of a bestseller, stultified by central miscasting.

w Wanda Tuchock, *novel* Frank Yerby *d* John M. Stahl *ph* Joseph La Shelle *m* Alfred Newman

Rex Harrison, Maureen O'Hara, Richard Haydn, Victor McLaglen, Vanessa Brown, Patricia Medina, Gene Lockhart, Hugo Haas

Foxfire
US 1955   92m   Technicolor
U-I (Aaron Rosenberg)

A rich New York girl on holiday in Arizona is attracted to a half-Apache miner.
Romantic melodrama with action asides; watchable for women who like that sort of thing.

w Ketti Frings, *novel* Anya Seton *d* Joseph
Pevney *ph* William Daniels *m* Frank Skinner

Jane Russell, Jeff Chandler, Frieda Inescort,
Dan Duryea

Foxhole in Cairo
GB 1960 80m bw
Omnia (Steven Pallos, Donald Taylor)

A German agent in Libya is allowed to get
back to Rommel with false information.
Interesting true spy story deflated by muddled
handling.

w Leonard Mosley, from his book The Cat
and the Mice *d* John Moxey *ph* Desmond
Dickinson *m* Wolfram Rohrig, Douglas
Gamley, Ken Jones

James Robertson Justice, Adrian Hoven,
Albert Lieven (as Rommel), Niall MacGinnis,
Peter Van Eyck, Robert Urquhart, Fenella
Fielding

Fra Diavolo**
US 1933 90m bw
MGM / Hal Roach
aka: *The Devil's Brother*

Two incompetent bandits are hired as
manservants by a real bandit.
Auber's 1830 operetta becomes a vehicle for
Laurel and Hardy, setting a pattern they
followed with *Babes in Toyland* and *The
Bohemian Girl*. They have excellent
sequences, but overall the film lacks pace.

w Jeanie McPherson *d* Hal Roach, Charles
Rogers *ph* Art Lloyd, Hap Depew *md* Le
Roy Shield

Stan Laurel, Oliver Hardy, Dennis King,
James Finlayson, Thelma Todd

Fragment of an Empire*
USSR 1929 100m approx bw silent
Sovkino

A young man who lost his memory in World
War I regains it in 1928 and surveys the
changed social order.
Mildly satirical propaganda piece with a vivid
impression of Leningrad at the time.

w Friedrich Ermier, Katerina Vinogradskaya
d Friedrich Ermler *ph* Yevgeni Schneider

Fyoder Nikitin, Yakov Gudkin, Ludmila
Semyonova

Fragment of Fear*
GB 1970 95m Technicolor
Columbia (John R. Sloan)

A young writer investigates the murder of his
aunt, but finds that he may himself be mad.
What appears to be a whodunnit turns into a

flashy, fashionable, sub-Antonioni puzzle with
no ending, but despite the considerable
irritation this causes, the details and character
cameos are excellent.

w Paul Dehn, *novel* John Bingham *d* Richard
C. Sarafian *ph* Oswald Morris *m* Johnny
Harris

David Hemmings, Gayle Hunnicutt, Roland
Culver, Daniel Massey, Flora Robson, Wilfrid
Hyde White, Adolfo Celi, Mona Washbourne

Framed
US 1947 82m bw

A drunken out-of-work engineer is used as fall
guy by two thieves planning an elaborate
coup. Lugubrious mixture of puzzle, character
drama and gloomy philosophizing, complete
with femme fatale who is handed over to the
cops at the end. Glenn Ford, Janis Carter,
Barry Sullivan. Written by Ben Maddow;
directed by Richard Wallace; for Columbia.
(GB title: *Paula*.)

Framed
US 1974 106m Metrocolor

A Tennessee gambler inadvertently kills a
sheriff, is sent to prison, gets out on parole
and wreaks revenge on those who framed him.
Violent thick-ear update of *The Count of
Monte Cristo*, of interest only to connoisseurs
of gratuitous nastiness. Joe Don Baker, Conny
Van Dyke, Gabriel Dell, Brock Peters, John
Marley, John Larch. Written by Mort Briskin;
directed by Phil Karlson; for Paramount.

The Franchise Affair*
GB 1950 88m bw
ABP (Robert Hall)

A young girl accuses two gentlewomen of
kidnapping and ill-treating her.
Unusual and absorbing mystery based on a
true 18th-century case; the treatment however
is rather too mild.

w Robert Hall, Lawrence Huntington, *novel*
Josephine Tey *d* Lawrence Huntington
ph Gunther Krampf *m* Philip Green

Michael Denison, Dulcie Gray, Anthony
Nicholls, Marjorie Fielding, Athene Seyler,
Ann Stephens, Hy Hazell, John Bailey,
Kenneth More

Francis*
US 1950 90m bw
U-I (Robert Arthur)

An army private makes friends with a talking
mule who causes him some embarrassment.
Simple-minded, quite agreeable if rather slow-
moving fantasy farce which was popular

enough to spawn several sequels and later a TV series called *Mister Ed.*

w David Stern, from his novel *d* Arthur Lubin *ph* Irving Glassberg *m* Frank Skinner

Donald O'Connor, Patricia Medina, Zasu Pitts, Ray Collins, John McIntyre, Eduard Franz, Robert Warwick, and Chill Wills as Francis' voice.

Sequels (the first six with Donald O'Connor):
1951: FRANCIS GOES TO THE RACES
1952: FRANCIS GOES TO WEST POINT
1953: FRANCIS COVERS BIG TOWN
1954: FRANCIS JOINS THE WACS
1955: FRANCIS IN THE NAVY
1956: FRANCIS IN THE HAUNTED HOUSE (with Mickey Rooney)

Francis of Assisi
US 1961   107m   De Luxe   Cinemascope
TCF / Perseus (Plato A. Skouras)

The son of a medieval cloth merchant takes a vow of poverty, cares for animals and dies a hermit.
Tedious biopic.

w Eugene Vale, Jack Thomas, James Forsyth *d* Michael Curtiz *ph* Piero Portalupi *m* Mario Nascimbene

Bradford Dillman, Dolores Hart, Stuart Whitman, Eduard Franz, Pedro Armendariz, Cecil Kellaway, Finlay Currie, Mervyn Johns, Athene Seyler

Frankenstein****
US 1931   71m   bw
Universal (Carl Laemmle Jnr)

A research scientist creates a living monster from corpses, but it runs amok.
Whole books have been written about this film and its sequels. Apart from being a fascinating if primitive cinematic work in its own right, it set its director and star on interesting paths and established a Hollywood attitude towards horror (mostly borrowed from German silents such as *The Golem*). A seminal film indeed, which at each repeated viewing belies its age.

w Garrett Fort, Francis Edward Faragoh, John L. Balderston, from the play by Peggy Webling and the novel by Mary Wollstonecraft Shelley *d* James Whale, *ph* Arthur Edeson *m* David Broekman *ad* Charles D. Hall

Boris Karloff, Colin Clive, Mae Clarke, John Boles, *Edward Van Sloan, Frederick Kerr, Dwight Frye*

'Still the most famous of all horror films, and deservedly so.'—*John Baxter, 1968*
'The horror is cold, chilling the marrow but never arousing malaise.'—*Carlos Clarens*

† Direct sequels by the same studio (all qv) include *The Bride of Frankenstein, Son of Frankenstein, Ghost of Frankenstein, Frankenstein Meets the Wolf Man, House of Frankenstein, House of Dracula, Abbott and Costello Meet Frankenstein.* The later Hammer series, which told the story all over again in gorier vein, includes (all qv) *The Curse of Frankenstein, The Revenge of Frankenstein, The Evil of Frankenstein, Frankenstein Created Woman, Frankenstein Must be Destroyed, Horror of Frankenstein, Frankenstein and the Monster from Hell.* Other Frankenstein films date from as early as 1908, and scores have been made in various languages. *Young Frankenstein* (qv) is a partly effective spoof on the Hollywood series; *The Munsters* was a sixties comedy series for TV which used the monster as its leading character in a domestic setting.
†† Robert Florey is said to have contributed to the script, having been the first choice for director.

Frankenstein and the Monster from Hell
GB 1973   99m   Technicolor

The Baron turns an injured lunatic into a hairy ape man. Cheaply made and very ghoulish horror comic in the unattractive setting of an asylum; very little entertainment is provided.
Peter Cushing, Shane Briant, Madeleine Smith, John Stratton, Bernard Lee, Dave Prowse. Written by John Elder (Anthony Hinds); directed by Terence Fisher; for Hammer / Avco.

Frankenstein Created Woman
GB 1966   86m   Technicolor

The Baron invests the body of a dead girl with the soul of her dead lover, and a murder spree results. Crude and gory farrago, with the central laboratory sequence apparently excised at the last moment. Peter Cushing, Thorley Walters, Susan Denberg, Robert Morris, Duncan Lamont. Written by John Elder (Anthony Hinds); directed by Terence Fisher; for Hammer / Warner.

Frankenstein Meets the Wolf Man**
US 1943   73m   bw
Universal (George Waggner)

Lawrence Talbot, the wolf man, travels to Vasaria in the hope of a cure, and finds the Frankenstein monster being reactivated. Once one recovered from the bargain basement combination of two monsters in one picture, this was a horror comic with stylish sequences, weakened by cuts in the script and a miscast Bela Lugosi.

w Curt Siodmak *d Roy William Neill*
ph George Robinson *m* Hans Salter

Lon Chaney Jnr, Ilona Massey, Bela Lugosi
(as the monster), Patric Knowles, *Maria
Ouspenskaya*

Frankenstein Must Be Destroyed
GB 1969 96m Technicolor

The Baron transplants the brain of one
colleague into the body of another. Spirited
but decidedly unpleasant addition to the cycle,
made more so by a genuine note of pathos.

Peter Cushing, Freddie Jones, Veronica
Carlson, Simon Ward, Thorley Walters,
Maxine Audley. Written by Bert Batt;
directed by Terence Fisher; for Hammer /
Warner-Pathé.

Frankenstein '70
US 1958 83m bw Cinemascope
Allied Artists (Aubrey Schenck)

Television film-makers descend on Castle
Frankenstein; the current Count needs the
money to finance some monster making of his
own.
Boringly talkative and very silly 'futuristic'
blot on an honourable name, apart from a
rather frightening pre-credits sequence.

w Richard Landau, G. Worthing Yates
d Howard W. Koch *ph* Carl Guthrie *m* Paul
Dunlap

Boris Karloff, Tom Duggan, Jana Lund

Frankie and Johnny*
US 1966 87m Technicolor
UA / F and J (Edward Small)

On a Mississippi riverboat, a gambling singer
is the despair of his lady partner.
Mildly amusing pastiche both of the old song
and of the various riverboat dramas.

w Alex Gottlieb *d* Frederick de Cordova
ph John Marquette *m* Fred Karger

Elvis Presley, Donna Douglas, Sue Ane
Langdon, Harry Morgan, Nancy Kovack,
Audrey Christie, Jerome Cowan

Fräulein
US 1958 100m Eastmancolor
Cinemascope
TCF (Walter Reisch)

During World War II an American prisoner of
war escapes and is helped by the daughter of a
German professor.
Studio-bound war heroics with little conviction
achieved or aimed at.

w Lee Townsend, *novel* James McGowan
d Henry Koster *ph* Leo Tover *m* Daniele
Amfitheatrof

Dana Wynter, Mel Ferrer, Margaret Hayes,
Dolores Michaels, Theodore Bikel, Helmut
Dantine

Fräulein Doktor
Italy / Yugoslavia 1968 104m
Technicolor
(Paramount) Dino de Laurentiis / Avala

In World War I, a German lady spy outwits
British intelligence.
Rather glum international action melodrama.

w Diulio Coletti, H. A. L. Craig, Stanley
Mann, Vittoriano Petrilli, Alberto Lattuada
d Alberto Lattuada *ph* Luigi Kuveiller
m Ennio Morricone

Suzy Kendall, Kenneth More, James Booth,
Capucine, Alexander Knox, Nigel Green,
Roberto Bisacco
† A similar story was filmed in 1936 as
Mademoiselle Docteur.

Freaks**
US 1932 64m bw
MGM (Tod Browning)

A lady trapeze artist marries a midget, then
poisons him for his money; his abnormal
friends take revenge by turning her into a
freak.
Made but disowned by MGM after accusations
of tastelessness, this strident and silly
melodrama has dated badly but has sequences
of great power, especially the final massing of
the freaks, slithering to their revenge in a
rainstorm. It would have been better as a
silent; the dialogue kills it.

w Willis Goldbeck, Leon Gordon, *novel* Spurs
by Tod Robbins *d Tod Browning ph* Merrit
B. Gerstad

Wallace Ford, Olga Baclanova, Leila Hyams,
Roscoe Ates
'It is a skilfully presented production but of
a character which in consideration of the
susceptibilities of mass audiences should be
avoided.'—*Martin Quigley*
'For pure sensationalism it tops any picture
yet produced.'—*Louella Parsons*

Freaky Friday
US 1976 100m Technicolor
Walt Disney (Ron Miller)

A 13-year-old and her mother, each
discontented with their lot, express a wish to
change places—and do.
A trendy update of *Vice Versa*, padded out
with Disney irrelevancies and long outstaying
its welcome.

w Mary Rodgers, from her novel *d* Gary
Nelson *ph* Charles F. Wheeler *m* Johnny
Mandel

Jodie Foster, Barbara Harris, John Astin.
Patsy Kelly, Dick Van Patten, Sorrell Booke,
Marie Windsor

Free and Easy
US 1930 75m bw
MGM

A beauty contest winner is taken to
Hollywood by her accident-prone manager.
Primitive talkie showing a great silent
comedian all at sea with the new techniques,
and the MGM studio offering entertainment
on the level of a very bad school concert.

w Al Boasberg, Richard Schayer d Edward
Sedgwick ph Leonard Smith

Buster Keaton, Anita Page, Robert
Montgomery, Trixie Freganza

Free for All
US 1949 83m bw
U-I (Robert Buckner)

A young inventor finds a way of turning water
into petrol.
Scatty comedy with mildly amusing moments.

w Robert Buckner d Charles T. Barton
ph George Robinson m Frank Skinner

Robert Cummings, Ann Blyth, Percy Kilbride,
Ray Collins, Donald Woods, Mikhail
Rasumny

A Free Soul*
US 1931 91m bw
MGM

An unconventional lawyer regrets allowing his
daughter to consort with a gangster.
Heavy melodrama with outdated attitudes, but
an impressive example of the studio's style in
the early thirties.

w John Meehan, novel Adela Rogers St John
d Clarence Brown ph William Daniels
m William Axt

Lionel Barrymore, Norma Shearer, Leslie
Howard, Clark Gable, Lucy Beaumont, James
Gleason
† Remade 1953 as *The Girl Who Had
Everything*.
AA: Lionel Barrymore
AAN: Clarence Brown; Norma Shearer

Freebie and the Bean*
US 1974 113m Technicolor
Panavision
Warner (Richard Rush)

Two vaguely incompetent cops try to link a
mobster with the numbers racket.
Violent comedy melodrama with a high
mortality rate, amoral outlook, and the usual
seventies reliance on incoherent plot, bumbled
dialogue and excessive background noise.
Occasionally funny all the same.

w Richard Kaufman d Richard Rush
ph Laszlo Kovacs m Dominic Frontière

Alan Arkin, James Caan, Loretta Swit, Jack
Kruschen, Mike Kellin

'It summarizes Hollywood's favourite
thematic elements of the early seventies:
platonic male love affair, police corruption,
comic violence, cynicism in high places, San
Francisco, gay villains, the car chase. A return
to the Keystone Kops, with character
trimmings and lashings of sado-masochistic
mayhem.'—*Clyde Jeavons*

'A tasteless film from a spitball script.'—
Variety

'There is a beating or a killing, or at least a
yelling scene, every couple of minutes.'—*New
Yorker, 1980*

Freedom Radio
GB 1941 95m bw
Columbia / Two Cities (Mario Zampi)
US title: *A Voice in the Night*

In Vienna during World War II, the husband
of a Nazi actress runs a secret radio
transmitter for Allied propaganda.
Moderate wartime flagwaver.

w Basil Wood, Gordon Wellesley, Louis
Golding, Anatole de Grunwald, Jeffrey Dell,
Bridget Boland, Roland Pertwee d Anthony
Asquith ph Bernard Knowles

Diana Wynyard, Clive Brook, Raymond
Huntley, Joyce Howard, Derek Farr, Howard
Marion Crawford, Morland Graham

French Can-Can**
France / Italy 1955 105m Technicolor
Franco-London / Jolly

How the can-can was launched in Paris night
clubs.
A dramatically thin vehicle splendidly evoking
a vision of vanished Paris: a feast for the eyes.

w André-Paul Antoine d Jean Renoir
ph Michel Kelber m Georges Van Parys

Jean Gabin, Françoise Arnoul, Maria Félix,
Jean-Roger Caussimon, Edith Piaf, Patachou

The French Connection***
US 1971 104m De Luxe
TCF / Philip D'Antoni

New York police track down a consignment of
drugs entering the country in a car.
Lively semi-documentary based on the true
exploits of a tough cop named Eddie Egan

who liked to break a few rules. Most memorable for a car chase scene involving an elevated railway, for showing the seamy side of New York more or less as it is, and for the most mumbled dialogue and the poorest sound track in years.

w Ernest Tidyman, *book* Robin Moore *d William Friedkin ph* Owen Roizman *m* Don Ellis

Gene Hackman, Roy Scheider, *Fernando Rey*, Tony Lo Bianco

AA: best picture; Ernest Tidyman; William Friedkin; Gene Hackman

AAN: Owen Roizman; Roy Scheider

French Connection II
US 1975   119m   De Luxe
TCF (Robert L. Rosen)

The New York cop who in *The French Connection* smashed most of a drug ring arrives in Marseilles to track down its elusive leader.
Sleazy, virtually plotless and unattractive sequel which rises to a few good action moments but is bogged down by bad language, unconvincing characterization and an interminable and irrelevant 'cold turkey' sequence.

w Robert Dillon, Laurie Dillon, Alexander Jacobs *d* John Frankenheimer *ph* Claude Renoir *m* Don Ellis

Gene Hackman, Fernando Rey, Bernard Fresson, Jean-Pierre Castaldi

'Visually as well as morally the film makes you uncertain where its feet are.'—*New Yorker*

French Dressing
GB 1963   86m   bw
ABP / Kenwood (Kenneth Harper)

A deckchair attendant and a local reporter believe that what Bardot can do for St Tropez they can do for Gormleigh-on-Sea.
Cinema's *enfant terrible* directs this his first theatrical film at breakneck speed with echoes of Tati, Keaton and the Keystone Kops. Alas, lack of star comedians and firm control make its exuberance merely irritating.

w Peter Myers, Ronald Cass, Peter Britt *d Ken Russell ph* Ken Higgins *m* Georges Delerue

James Booth, Roy Kinnear, Marisa Mell, Bryan Pringle

The French Line
US 1953   102m   Technicolor   3-D
RKO (Edmund Grainger)

A cheery Texas oil heiress finds a husband while travelling to France.
Very thinly plotted but quite attractive light musical with a good-humoured star wearing costumes once thought censorable.

w Mary Loos, Richard Sale *d* Lloyd Bacon *ph* Harry J. Wild *m* Walter Scharf *md* Lionel Newman *ch* Jack Cole

Jane Russell, Gilbert Roland, Arthur Hunnicutt, Mary McCarty

'A slouching Amazon, her clothes appear to stay put just as long as she agrees not to burst out of them; essentially a good sort, she has an ever-annihilating sneer for the false, the pretentious and the fresh.'—*MFB*

A French Mistress
GB 1960   98m   bw
British Lion / Charter (John Boulting)

An attractive new mistress causes havoc at a boys' school.
Sloppy, predictable comedy with practised performers getting a few easy laughs. The producers tried to excuse its imperfections by promoting it as 'a romp'.

w Roy Boulting, Jeffrey Dell, *play* Robert Monro (Sonnie Hale) *d* Roy Boulting *ph* Max Greene *m* John Addison

James Robertson Justice, Cecil Parker, Raymond Huntley, Ian Bannen, Agnes Laurent, Thorley Walters, Edith Sharpe, Athene Seyler, Kenneth Griffith

French without Tears*
GB 1939   85m   bw
Paramount / Two Cities (David E. Rose)

Young Britons at a French crammers fall for the young sister of one of their number.
Pleasant light comedy from a successful West End play.

w Terence Rattigan, Anatole de Grunwald, Ian Dalrymple, *play* Terence Rattigan *d* Anthony Asquith *ph* Bernard Knowles

Ray Milland, Ellen Drew, *Guy Middleton, Ronald Culver*, David Tree, Jim Gerald, Janine Darcy, Kenneth Morgan

'There is always something a little shocking about English levity. The greedy exhilaration of these blithe young men when they learn that another fellow's girl is to join them at the establishment where they are learning French, the scramble over her luggage, the light-hearted badinage, the watery and libidinous eye—that national mixture of prudery and excitement—would be unbearable if it were not for Mr Asquith's civilized direction.'—*Graham Greene*

Frenchie
US 1950   80m   Technicolor
U-I (Michael Kraike)

A saloon queen sets up shop in Bottleneck,
her real aim being to track down her father's
murderers.
Modest western of the *Destry Rides Again*
school.

w Oscar Brodney *d* Louis King *ph* Maury
Gertsman *m* Hans Salter

Shelley Winters, Joel McCrea, Paul Kelly,
Elsa Lanchester, Marie Windsor, John Emery,
George Cleveland, John Russell

Frenchman's Creek**
US 1944   112m   Technicolor
Paramount (B. G. De Sylva)

In Restoration England, a lady flees from a
lascivious nobleman to her family home in
Cornwall, where she falls in love with a French
pirate.
Enjoyable Girls' Own Paper romance, dressed
to kill and entertaining despite its many
palpable absurdities.

w Talbot Jennings, *novel* Daphne du Maurier
d Mitchell Leisen ph George Barnes m Victor
Young *ad Hans Dreier, Ernest Fegte*

Joan Fontaine, Arturo de Cordova, Basil
Rathbone, Nigel Bruce, *Cecil Kellaway*, Ralph
Forbes, Moyna McGill

Frenzy*
Sweden 1944   101m   bw
Svensk Filmindustri
original title: *Hets;* aka: *Torment*

A sadistic Latin teacher and his sensitive pupil
find themselves competing for the same girl.
Hothouse melodrama of the *Blue Angel*
school: it seemed pretty powerful at the time.

w Ingmar Bergman *d Alf Sjöberg ph* Martin
Bodin *m* Hilding Rosenberg

Stig Jarrel, Alf Kjellin, Mai Zetterling

Frenzy*
GB 1972   116m   Technicolor
Universal / Alfred Hitchcock

A disillusioned and aggressive ex-RAF officer
is suspected through circumstantial evidence of
being London's 'necktie murderer'.
Has-been, unconvincing, cliché-ridden thriller,
an old man's sex suspenser, which would have
been derided if anyone but Hitchcock had
made it. As it is, a few comic and suspenseful
touches partly atone for the implausibilities
and lapses of taste.

w Anthony Shaffer, *novel* Goodbye Piccadilly,
Farewell Leicester Square by Arthur La Bern

d Alfred Hitchcock *ph* Gilbert Taylor *m* Ron
Goodwin

Jon Finch, *Alec McCowen, Barry Foster,*
Vivien Merchant, Anna Massey

'Hitchcock's most stodgy piece since *Dial M
for Murder* and possibly his least interesting
film from any period.'—*William S. Pechter*

The Freshman**
US 1925   75m (24 fps)   bw   silent
Harold Lloyd

An awkward college student accidentally
becomes a star football player.
A rather slow but striking star vehicle with
assured set-pieces. The football game climax
was later used as the first reel of *Mad
Wednesday.*

w Sam Taylor, Ted Wilde, Time Whelan,
John Grey *d* Fred Newmeyer, Sam Taylor
ph Walter Lundin, Henry Kohler

Harold Lloyd, Jobyna Ralston, Brooks
Benedict

Freud**
US 1963   140m   bw
U-I (Wolfgang Reinhardt)

Vienna 1865; Dr Sigmund Freud, a
neurologist, uses hypnotism to treat hysteria,
and finds new interest in the case of a boy
whose hatred of his father springs from
incestuous love of his mother, a failing which
Freud finds in himself.
Earnest and competent biopic harking back to
Warners' similar films of the thirties, with the
addition of franker language. Generally
absorbing, but undeniably hard tack.

w Charles Kaufman, Wolfgang Reinhardt
d John Huston ph Douglas Slocombe
m Jerry Goldsmith

Montgomery Clift, Larry Parks, Susannah
York, Eileen Herlie, Susan Kohner, David
McCallum

'The dream sequences, photographed
mostly in negative or overexposure, belong
not on the couch of Dr Freud but in the
Cabinet of Dr Caligari.'—*John Simon*

'It is impossible, I would think, for any
educated person to sit through *Freud* without
bursting into laughter at least once.'—*Ernest
Callenbach, Film Quarterly*

AAN: script; Jerry Goldsmith

Friday the Thirteenth***
GB 1933   84m   bw
Gainsborough (Michael Balcon)

Several people are involved in a bus crash, and
we turn back the clock to see how they came
to be there.

Highly competent compendium of comedies and dramas looking back to *The Bridge of San Luis Rey* and forward to the innumerable all-star films of the forties.

w G. H. Moresby-White, Sidney Gilliat, Emlyn Williams *d* Victor Saville *ph* Charles Van Enger

Sonnie Hale, Cyril Smith, *Eliot Makeham*, Ursula Jeans, *Emlyn Williams*, Frank Lawton, Belle Chrystal, *Max Miller*, Alfred Drayton, Edmund Gwenn, Mary Jerrold, Gordon Harker, *Robertson Hare*, Martita Hunt, Leonora Corbett, Jessie Matthews, Ralph Richardson

Friday the Thirteenth
US 1980 95m colour
Georgetown (Sean S. Cunningham)

When a summer camp is reopened after many years, the grisly murders which closed it down begin again.
Horror suspense story with no *raison d'être* but a series of inventively gory shock moments, which were enough however for it to ring the box office bell.

w Victor Miller *d* Sean S. Cunningham *ph* Barry Abrams

Betsy Palmer, Adrienne King, Jeannine Taylor, Robbi Morgan
'An oversexed couple makes love in the bottom bunk, there's a dead body in the top bunk and the rest of the bunk is in the television commercials.'—*Variety*

Frieda*
GB 1947 97m bw
Ealing (Michael Relph)

An RAF officer marries and takes home a girl who helped him escape from a POW camp. Stuffy and dated drama about how one English family learned to love one particular German. Timely when it appeared, however, and well made within its conventions.

w Angus Macphail, Ronald Millar, *play* Ronald Millar *d* Basil Dearden *ph* Gordon Dines *m* John Greenwood

Mai Zetterling, David Farrar, Glynis Johns, Flora Robson, Albert Lieven

Friendly Persuasion**
US 1956 139m De Luxe
AA (William Wyler)

At the outbreak of the Civil War, a family of Quakers has to consider its position.
Sentimental, homespun western fare, well done without being especially engrossing.

w Michael Wilson, *novel* Jessamyn West *d* William Wyler *ph* Ellsworth Fredericks *m* Dmitri Tiomkin

Gary Cooper, Dorothy McGuire, Anthony Perkins, Marjorie Main, Richard Eyer, Robert Middleton, Walter Catlett
'The material is a little tenuous . . . but Wyler's sure-handed direction constantly illuminates it with a humour, a gentle charm and a feeling for fundamental values that are rare indeed.'—*Moira Walsh, America*
† For TV movie remake, see *Television Companion*.

AAN: best picture; Michael Wilson; William Wyler; Anthony Perkins; song 'Thee I Love' (*m* Dmitri Tiomkin, *ly* Paul Francis Webster)

Friends
GB 1971 102m Technicolor
Paramount (Lewis Gilbert)

Teenage lovers run away to a country cottage and have a child.
Peculiar idyll given corny 'poetic' treatment: a real non-starter.

w Jack Russell, Vernon Harris *d* Lewis Gilbert *ph* Andrew Winding *m* Elton John

Sean Bury, Anicee Alvina, Toby Robbins, Ronald Lewis

The Friends of Eddie Coyle*
US 1973 102m Technicolor
Paramount (Paul Monash)

An ageing hoodlum agrees to become a police informer and is hunted down by his former associates.
Dour gangster melodrama held together by its central performance.

w Paul Monash, *novel* George V. Higgins *d* Peter Yates *ph* Vernon J. Kemper *m* Dave Grusin

Robert Mitchum, Peter Boyle, Richard Jordan, Steven Keats, Mitch Ryan, Alex Rocco

Friends of Mr Sweeney*
US 1934 68m bw

A brow-beaten reporter gets drunk, faces life, and changes his personality. Amusing minor comedy of a kind no longer made. *Charles Ruggles*, Eugene Pallette, Berton Churchill, Robert Barrat, Ann Dvorak. Written by Warren Duff and Sidney Sutherland, from the novel by Elmer Davis; directed by Edward Ludwig; for Warner.

The Frightened Lady
GB 1932 87m bw

A mad young lord is protected by his mother. Modest chiller remade later as *The Case of the Frightened Lady* (qv). Norman McKinnel, Cathleen Nesbitt, Emlyn Williams, Gordon Harker, Belle Chrystall, Finlay Currie. Written by Angus McPhail and Bryan Edgar Wallace, from the play by Edgar Wallace; directed by T. Hayes Hunter; for Gainsborough.

Frisco Jenny
US 1933   73m   bw

A Barbary Coast lady is prosecuted for murder by her own son. Antediluvian melodramatic plot, borrowed from *Madame X*, provides an adequate star vehicle. Ruth Chatterton, Donald Cook, Louis Calhern, J. Carrol Naish, James Murray. Written by Wilson Mizner and Robert Lord; directed by William A. Wellman; for Warner.

The Frisco Kid*
US 1935   77m   bw
Warner (Samuel Bischoff)

A Shanghaied sailor rises to power among the riff raff of the Barbary Coast in the 1860s. Fair melodrama with the star in action and (less interestingly) in love.

w Warren Duff, Seton I. Miller *d* Lloyd Bacon *ph* Sol Polito *md* Leo F. Forbstein

James Cagney, Margaret Lindsay, Ricardo Cortez, Lili Damita, Donald Woods, Barton MacLane, George E. Stone, Addison Richards

The Frisco Kid
US 1979   108m   Technicolor
Warner (Howard W. Koch Jnr)

In the old west, a rabbi heading for San Francisco makes friends with an outlaw. Unsuccessful episodic comedy, unreasonably alternating farce with sentimentality.

w Michael Elias, Frank Shaw *d* Robert Aldrich *ph* Robert B. Hauser *m* Frank De Vol

Gene Wilder, Harrison Ford, Ramon Bieri, Leo Fuchs, Penny Peyser

'A very forced comedy, made all the worse by the fact that Aldrich seems to time and edit comedy as though it were a melodrama only played a little slower.'—*Richard Combs, MFB*

Frisco Lil
US 1942   62m   bw

A girl law student traps a killer and clears her dad. Formula second feature, quite adequate in its way. Irene Hervey, Kent Taylor, Minor

Watson, Jerome Cowan. Written by George Bricker and Michael Jacoby; directed by Erle C. Kenton; for Universal.

Frisco Sal
US 1945   63m   bw

A New England girl goes to California to avenge her brother's murder. Minor musical vehicle for a star being groomed as a rival to Deanna Durbin. Susanna Foster, Turhan Bey, Alan Curtis, Andy Devine, Thomas Gomez, Samuel S. Hinds. Written by Curt Siodmak and Gerald Geraghty; directed by George Waggner; for Universal.

Fritz the Cat**
US 1971   78m   De Luxe
Fritz Productions / Aurica (Steve Krantz)

An alleycat student in New York seeks new and varied experience.
Cartoon feature which applies the old anthropomorphism to the contemporary scene, and whips up more obscenity and violence than Disney ever dreamed of. A fast-moving orgy of outrage which could never have got by in live form.

wd / animator Ralph Bakshi, comic strip R. H. Crumb

'A bitter and snarling satire that refuses to curl up in anyone's lap.'—*Bruce Williamson*

The Frog*
GB 1937   75m   bw
Herbert Wilcox

The mysterious leader of a criminal organization is unmasked.
Lively old-fashioned mystery melodrama.

w Ian Hay, Gerald Elliott, *novel* The Fellowship of the Frog by Edgar Wallace *d* Jack Raymond

Gordon Harker, Carol Goodner, Noah Beery, Jack Hawkins, Richard Ainley, Esmé Percy, Felix Aylmer

'Badly directed, badly acted, it is like one of those plays produced in country towns by stranded actors. It has an old-world charm: Scotland Yard is laid up in lavender.'— *Graham Greene*
† Sequel 1938: *The Return of the Frog.*

The Frogmen
US 1951   96m   bw
TCF (Samuel G. Engel)

Underwater demolition experts pave the way for the invasion of a Japanese-held island. Standard, efficient war fare.

w John Tucker Battle *d* Lloyd Bacon
ph Norbert Brodine *m* Cyril Mockridge

Richard Widmark, Dana Andrews, Gary
Merrill, Jeffrey Hunter, Warren Stevens,
Robert Wagner, Harvey Lembeck
'Competent, unpretentious and free from
jingoism.'—*MFB*
AAN: original story (Oscar Millard); Norbert
Brodine

Frogs*
US 1972 91m Movielab
AIP (George Edwards, Peter Thomas)

A remote, inhabited island in the southern
States is overtaken by reptiles.
As Hitchcock might have said, the frogs is
coming; instead of monsters, ordinary creepy-
crawlies in their thousands devour most of the
cast. Well enough done for those with strong
stomachs.

w Robert Hutchison, Robert Blees d George
McCowan ph Mario Tosi m Les Baxter
Ray Milland, Joan Van Ark, Sam Elliott,
Adam Roarke, Judy Pace
'One of the most remarkable and impressive
onslaughts since *King Kong*.'—*David Pirie*

From Beyond the Grave*
GB 1973 98m Technicolor
Warner / Amicus (Milton Subotsky)

The proprietor of an East End antique shop
involves his customers in horrific situations.
Reasonably lively portmanteau of tall tales
from a familiar stable.

w Robin Clarke, Raymond Christodoulou
d Kevin Connor ph Alan Hume m David
Gamley pd Maurice Carter
David Warner, Donald Pleasence, Ian
Bannen, Diana Dors, Margaret Leighton, Ian
Carmichael, Nyree Dawn Porter, Ian Ogilvy

From Headquarters
US 1933 63m bw
Warner

The police solve a murder by scientific
methods.
Efficient, rather boring programmer.

w Robert N. Lee, Peter Milne d William
Dieterle ph William Reese
George Brent, Margaret Lindsay, Eugene
Pallette, Hugh Herbert, Hobart Cavanaugh,
Robert Barrat, Henry O'Neill, Edward Ellis

From Hell to Texas
US 1958 100m Eastmancolor
Cinemascope
TCF (Robert Buckner)
GB title: *Manhunt*

After accidentally killing a man, a cowboy is
vengefully pursued by the victim's father.
Competent chase western with a stand against
violence.

w Robert Buckner, Wendell Mayes d Henry
Hathaway ph Wilfrid Cline m Daniele
Amfitheatrof
Don Murray, Diane Varsi, Chill Wills, Dennis
Hopper, R. G. Armstrong, Margo, Jay C.
Flippen

From Here to Eternity***
US 1953 118m bw
Columbia (Buddy Adler)

Life in a Honolulu barracks at the time of
Pearl Harbor.
Cleaned up and streamlined version of a
bestseller in which the mainly sexual
frustrations of a number of unattractive
characters are laid bare. As a production, it is
Hollywood in good form, and certainly took
the public fancy as well as establishing Sinatra
as an acting force.

w Daniel Taradash, *novel* James Jones d Fred
Zinnemann ph Burnett Guffey m George
Duning
Burt Lancaster, Deborah Kerr, *Frank Sinatra*,
Donna Reed, Ernest Borgnine, Montgomery
Clift, Philip Ober, Mickey Shaughnessy
'This is not a theme which one would expect
Zinnemann to approach in the hopeful,
sympathetic mood of his earlier films; but
neither could one expect the negative shrug of
indifference with which he seems to have
surrendered to its hysteria.'—*Karel Reisz,
Sight and Sound*
† The story was remade for TV in 1979 as a
six-hour mini-series.
AA: best picture; Daniel Taradash; Fred
Zinnemann; Burnett Guffey; Frank Sinatra;
Donna Reed
AAN: George Duning; Burt Lancaster;
Deborah Kerr; Montgomery Clift

From Noon Till Three
US 1976 99m De Luxe
UA / Frankovich-Self

A bank robber becomes a local legend when
he interrupts a raid to dally with an attractive
widow. Later, when someone else is shot in
mistake for him, he is reduced to penury,
unable to prove his identity or live up to his
own legend.
Curious, shapeless, lumpy western satire,
difficult to synopsize or analyse. Despite effort
all round, it's just plain unsatisfactory.

wd Frank D. Gilroy, from his novel
ph Lucien Ballard m Elmer Bernstein

Charles Bronson, Jill Ireland, Douglas Fowley, Stan Haze, Damon Douglas

'It squanders its early sparkle for a pot of message.'—*Michael Billington, Illustrated London News*

'The main thing—hell, the only thing—worth noting about *From Noon Till Three* is that it is profoundly weird, which is not quite the same thing as being good.'—*Frank Rich, New York Post*

From Russia with Love***
GB 1963 118m Technicolor
UA / Eon (Harry Saltzman, Albert Broccoli)

A Russian spy joins an international crime organization and develops a plan to kill James Bond and steal a coding machine.

The second Bond adventure and possibly the best, with Istanbul and Venice for backdrops and climaxes involving a speeding train and a helicopter. Arrant nonsense with tongue in cheek, on a big budget.

w Richard Maibaum, Johanna Harwood, novel Ian Fleming *d* Terence Young *ph Ted Moore m* John Barry *titles Robert Brownjohn*

Sean Connery, Robert Shaw, Pedro Armendariz, Daniela Bianchi, *Lotte Lenya,* Bernard Lee, Eunice Gayson, Lois Maxwell

From Soup to Nuts*
US 1928 20m bw silent

Two temporary waiters wreck a dinner party.

Very funny slapstick which the stars subsequently reworked into *A Chump at Oxford.* Laurel and Hardy, Anita Garvin, Tiny Sandford. Written by H. M. Walker; directed by Edgar Kennedy; for Hal Roach.

From the Earth to the Moon
US 1958 100m Technicolor
Waverley (Benedict Bogeaus)

In the 1880s an armaments millionaire finances a trip to the moon in a projectile fired by his own invention.

Cardboard science fiction, with an imposing cast at sea in an unspeakable script and an unseaworthy production.

w Robert Blees, James Leicester, novel Jules Verne *d* Byron Haskin *ph* Edwin DuPar *m* Louis Forbes *ad* Hal Wilson Cox

Joseph Cotten, George Sanders, Henry Daniell, Carl Esmond, Melville Cooper, Don Dubbins, Debra Paget, Patric Knowles

From the Life of the Marionettes*
West Germany 1980 104m colour / bw
ITC / Martin Starger

An inquiry into the killing of a prostitute by a rich businessman.

A film somehow very typical of its director, but far from his most interesting work.

wd Ingmar Bergman *ph* Sven Nykvist *m* Rols Wilhelm *pd* Rolf Zechetbauer

Robert Atzorn, Christine Buchegger, Martin Benrath

From the Terrace
US 1960 144m De Luxe Cinemascope
TCF / Linebrook (Mark Robson)

Life among Pennsylvania's idle rich.

Heavy-going family melodrama from a bestseller peopled with boorish characters.

w Ernest Lehman, *novel* John O'Hara *d* Mark Robson *ph* Leo Tover *m* Elmer Bernstein

Paul Newman, Joanne Woodward, Myrna Loy, Ina Balin, Leon Ames, Felix Aylmer, George Grizzard, Patrick O'Neal, Elizabeth Allen

From This Day Forward***
US 1946 95m bw
RKO (William L. Pereira)

After World War II, a New York couple think back to their early years in the poverty-stricken thirties.

Effective sentimental realism coupled with Hollywood professionalism made this film more memorable than it may sound.

w Hugo Butler, Garson Kanin, *novel* All Brides Are Beautiful by Thomas Bell *d John Berry ph George Barnes m* Leigh Harline

Joan Fontaine, Mark Stevens, Rosemary de Camp, Henry Morgan, Wally Brown, Arline Judge, Bobby Driscoll, Mary Treen

'Distinguished from the usual film about Young Love and Young Marriage by irony, poetry and realism.'—*Richard Winnington*

The Front*
US 1976 95m Metrocolor Panavision
Columbia / Persky-Bright, Devon (Martin Ritt, Charles H. Joffe)

For a small commission, a bookmaker puts his name to scripts by blacklisted writers.

Rather bland satire on the communist witch hunts of the fifties; interesting, but neither funny nor incisive enough.

w Walter Bernstein *d* Martin Ritt *ph* Michael Chapman *m* Dave Grusin

Woody Allen, Zero Mostel, Herschel Bernardi, Michael Murphy, Andrea Marcovicci, Lloyd Gough

'The pacing is off, the sequences don't flow, and the film seems sterile, unpopulated and flat.'—*New Yorker*

'A light comedy forged out of dark and authentic pain.'—*Frank Rich, New York Post*

AAN: Walter Bernstein

The Front Page***
US 1931 101m bw
Howard Hughes

A Chicago reporter wants to retire and marry, but is tricked by his scheming editor into covering one last case.

Brilliant early talkie perfectly transferring into screen terms a stage classic of the twenties. Superficially a shade primitive now, its essential power remains.

w Bartlett Cormack, Charles Lederer, *play Charles MacArthur, Ben Hecht d Lewis Milestone ph* Glen MacWilliams

Adolphe Menjou, Pat O'Brien, Mary Brian, Edward Everett Horton, Walter Catlett, George E. Stone, Mae Clarke, Slim Summerville, Frank McHugh

'The most riproaring movie that ever came out of Hollywood.'—*Pare Lorentz*

'It excelled most of the films of its day by sheer treatment. The speedy delivery of lines and business and the re-emphasis upon cutting as a prime structural element made the film a model of mobility for confused directors who did not know yet how to handle sound.'— *Lewis Jacobs, The Rise of the American Film* † Remade 1940 as *His Girl Friday* (qv).

AAN: best picture; Lewis Milestone; Adolphe Menjou

The Front Page**
US 1974 105m Technicolor
Panavision
U-I (Paul Monash)

Disappointing Billy Wilder remake, relying overmuch on bad language and farcical intrusions, while tending to jettison the plot in the latter half. Some laughs nevertheless.

w Billy Wilder, I. A. L. Diamond *d* Billy Wilder *ph* Jordan S. Cronenweth *m* Billy May

Walter Matthau, Jack Lemmon, Susan Sarandon, *David Wayne*, Carol Burnett, Vincent Gardenia, Allen Garfield, Herb Edelmann, Charles Durning, *Austin Pendleton*

'The signs of coarsening in Wilder's comedy technique are unmistakable.'—*MFB*

'I can't think of a better tonic for the winter glooms.'—*Michael Billington, Illustrated London News*

Front Page Story*
GB 1953 99m bw
British Lion / Jay Lewis

A day in the life of a Fleet Street newspaper, when the editor is torn between several big stories and nearly loses his wife.

Dogged 'slice of life' drama with few excitements but some incidental entertainment and a production of routine competence.

w Jay Lewis, Jack Howells *d* Gordon Parry *ph* Gilbert Taylor *m* Jackie Brown

Jack Hawkins, Elizabeth Allan, Derek Farr, Michael Goodliffe, Martin Miller

Front Page Woman**
US 1935 82m bw
Warner (Samuel Bischoff)

Rival reporters try to outshine each other. Lively comedy-melodrama very typical of its style and time.

w Laird Doyle, Lillie Hayward, Roy Chanslor *d* Michael Curtiz *ph* Tony Gaudio *m* Heinz Roemheld *md* Leo Forbstein

Bette Davis, George Brent, Roscoe Karns, Wini Shaw, J. Carroll Naish, Walter Walker

Frontier Gal
US 1945 84m Technicolor
Universal (Michael Fessier, Ernest Pagano)
GB title: *The Bride Wasn't Willing*

An outlaw weds a saloon girl at pistol point; emerging five years later from prison, he finds he has a daughter.

Rambling western with some pretensions to humour and sentiment; not a success, but it established de Carlo as a star.

w Michael Fessier, Ernest Pagano *d* Charles Lamont *ph* George Robinson, Charles Boyle *m* Frank Skinner

Yvonne de Carlo, Rod Cameron, Sheldon Leonard, Andy Devine, Fuzzy Knight, Andrew Tombes, Clara Blandick

Frontier Marshal*
US 1939 70m bw
TCF (Sol M. Wurtzel)

Wyatt Earp cleans up Tombstone. Simple-minded, pleasing western, later worked over by Ford as *My Darling Clementine*.

w Sam Hellman *book* Stuart N. Lake *d* Allan Dwan *ph* Charles Clarke *m* Samuel Kaylin

Randolph Scott, Nancy Kelly, Cesar Romero (as Doc Holliday), Binnie Barnes, John Carradine, Joe Sawyer, Lon Chaney Jnr, Ward Bond, Edward Norris, Eddie Foy Jnr

The Frozen Ghost
US 1945   61m   bw

When a drunk dies while under his influence, a hypnotist fears he has the will and power to kill. Absurdly titled and insufficiently vigorous entry in the *Inner Sanctum* series. Lon Chaney Jnr, Evelyn Ankers, Martin Kosleck, Milburn Stone, Tala Birell, Douglass Dumbrille. Written by Bernard Schubert and Luci Ward; directed by Harold Young; for Universal.

The Frozen Limits*
GB 1939   84m   bw
Gainsborough (Edward Black)

Six impecunious comedians hear of the Yukon gold rush, and join it . . . forty years too late. The Crazy Gang not quite at its best, but working hard, with a few hilarious moments and a special assist from Moore Marriott.

w Marriott Edgar, Val Guest, J. O. C. Orton d Marcel Varnel ph Arthur Crabtree

Flanagan and Allen, Nervo and Knox, Naughton and Gold, *Moore Marriott*, Eileen Bell, Anthony Hulme, Bernard Lee, Eric Clavering

'The funniest English picture yet produced . . . it can bear comparison with *Safety Last* and *The General*.'—*Graham Greene*

Fu Manchu
The Yellow Peril, or evil Oriental master criminal, was created by Sax Rohmer in a 1911 novel, which led to 13 more plus some short stories. A long series of British two-reelers was made in the twenties, and talking films are as follows:

1929: THE MYSTERIOUS DR FU MANCHU, with Warner Oland (Paramount)
1930: THE RETURN OF DR FU MANCHU (ditto)
1931: DAUGHTER OF THE DRAGON (ditto)
1932: THE MASK OF FU MANCHU (qv) with Boris Karloff (MGM)
1939: DRUMS OF FU MANCHU, with Henry Brandon (Republic serial).

The remainder are British productions by Harry Alan Towers, with Christopher Lee:
1965: THE FACE OF FU MANCHU (qv)
1966: BRIDES OF FU MANCHU
1968: THE VENGEANCE OF FU MANCHU
1969: THE BLOOD OF FU MANCHU
1970: THE CASTLE OF FU MANCHU

The Fugitive*
US 1947   104m   bw
Argosy (Merian C. Cooper, John Ford)

In an anti-clerical country, a priest is on the run.
Ford's attempt to do a Mexican *Informer* is slow and rather boring, but the pictures are nice to look at even though the original novel has been totally emasculated.

w Dudley Nichols, novel The Power and the Glory by Graham Greene *d John Ford ph Gabriel Figueroa m* Richard Hageman

Henry Fonda, Dolores del Rio, Pedro Armendariz, J. Carrol Naish, Leo Carrillo, Ward Bond, Robert Armstrong, John Qualen

'A symphony of light and shade, of deafening din and silence, of sweeping movement and repose.'—*Bosley Crowther*
'The most pretentious travesty of a literary work since *For Whom the Bell Tolls*.'—*Richard Winnington*

The Fugitive Kind
US 1960   121m   bw
UA / Martin Jurow / Richard A. Shepherd / Pennebaker

A Mississippi drifter in a small strange town runs into trouble with women.
Doom-laden melodrama, almost a parody of the author's works, full of cancer patients, nympho-dipsos, and cemetery seductions; we are however spared the final castration.

w Tennessee Williams, Meade Roberts, play Orpheus Descending by Tennessee Williams *d* Sidney Lumet *ph* Boris Kaufman *m* Kenyon Hopkins *pd* Richard Sylbert

Marlon Brando, Anna Magnani, Joanne Woodward, Victor Jory, Maureen Stapleton, R. G. Armstrong

'A series of mythological engravings, determined by a literary text and a lurid concept of hell on earth.'—*Peter John Dyer*
'Sidney Lumet is usually clever at least part of the time—an acquisitive magpie who has picked up, along with the selly trash, a few small gems. This time he brings us nothing but bits of coloured glass.'—*Stanley Kauffmann*

Full Circle
GB / Canada 1976   97m   Eastmancolor
Paramount / Fetter-Classic (Peter Fetterman, Alfred Parisier)

After the death of her small daughter, a woman leaves home to live in an old house which is haunted by the malevolent spirit of another dead child.
Unpleasant and incompetent supernatural nonsense, seeking a niche somewhere between *Don't Look Now* and *The Exorcist*.

w Dave Humphries, *novel* Julia by Peter
Straub *d* Richard Loncraine *ph* Peter
Hannan *m* Colin Towns

Mia Farrow, Keir Dullea, Tom Conti, Jill
Bennett, Robin Gammell, Cathleen Nesbitt,
Mary Morris, Edward Hardwicke

Full Confession
US 1939 73m bw

A priest bound by the sanctity of confession
urges a murderer to give himself up. Neat little
melodrama with a plot much copied
subsequently. Victor McLaglen, Barry
Fitzgerald, Sally Eilers. Written and directed
by John Farrow; for RKO.

Full of Life*
US 1956 91m bw
Columbia (Fred Kohlmar)

A poor New York / Italian couple expect a
baby.
Domestic comedy drama with good scenes but
fatally uncertain mood.

w John Fante, from his novel *d* Richard
Quine *ph* Charles Lawton Jnr *m* George
Duning

Judy Holliday, Richard Conte, Esther
Minciotti, Salvatore Baccaloni

The Full Treatment
GB 1960 109m bw Megascope
Columbia / Hilary / Falcon (Val Guest)
US title: *Stop Me Before I Kill*

A racing driver crashes and subsequently tries
to murder his wife; psychiatric help leads to
further gruesome goings-on.
Variation on *Les Diaboliques*, with very little
mystery and too much talk from boring
characters.

w Val Guest, Ronald Scott Thorn, *novel*
Ronald Scott Thorn *d* Val Guest *ph* Gilbert
Taylor *m* Stanley Black

Ronald Lewis, Diane Cilento, Claude
Dauphin, Françoise Rosay, Bernard Braden

The Fuller Brush Girl*
US 1950 85m bw
Columbia (S. Sylvan Simon)
GB title: *Affairs of Sally*

A cosmetics saleslady gets involved in murder.
Fairly amusing slapstick mystery with the star
in good form.

w Frank Tashlin *d* Lloyd Bacon *ph* Charles
Lawton *m* Heinz Roemheld

Lucille Ball, Eddie Albert, Carl Benton Reid,
Gale Robbins, Jeff Connell, John Litel,
Jerome Cowan, Lee Patrick

The Fuller Brush Man*
US 1948 93m bw
Columbia (S. Sylvan Simon)
GB title: *That Mad Mr Jones*

A door-to-door salesman gets involved in
homicide.
Bright star comedy with slow patches.

w Frank Tashlin, Devery Freeman
d S. Sylvan Simon *ph* Leslie White
m Heinz Roemheld

Red Skelton, Janet Blair, Don McGuire,
Adele Jergens

Fun and Fancy Free*
US 1947 73m Technicolor
Walt Disney (Ben Sharpsteen)

Cartoon stories told by and to Jiminy Cricket
and Edgar Bergen.
Variable Disney ragbag including *Bongo* the
Bear, and a lengthy version of *Jack and the
Beanstalk*.

w various *d* various

Fun in Acapulco
US 1963 97m Technicolor
Paramount / Hal B. Wallis

A trapeze artist becomes a lifeguard and is
pursued by a lady bullfighter.
Dim comedy musical.

w Allan Weiss *d* Richard Thorpe *ph* Daniel
Fapp *m* Joseph J. Lilley

Elvis Presley, Ursula Andress, Paul Lukas

Fun with Dick and Jane
US 1976 100m Metrocolor
Columbia / Peter Bart, Max Pelevsky

When an aerospace executive is fired, in order
to keep up with the Joneses he and his wife
embark on a life of crime.
This being a 1970s satire, they actually get
away with it, providing some, but not enough,
fun on the way.

w David Giler, Jerry Belson, Mordecai
Richler, *story* Gerald Gaiser *d* Ted Kotcheff
ph Fred J. Koenekamp *m* Ernest Gold

George Segal, Jane Fonda, Ed McMahon,
Dick Gautier, Alan Miller
  'A nitwit mixture of counterculture politics,
madcap comedy and toilet humour.'—*New
Yorker*
† The sequence in which the heroine discusses
the family predicament while sitting on a toilet
was later deleted, reducing the running time
by two minutes.

Funeral in Berlin*
GB 1967   102m   Technicolor
Paramount / Harry Saltzman (Charles Kasher)

Harry Palmer is sent to Berlin to check a story that a Russian colonel wants to defect.
Initially intriguing, finally confusing, always depressing spy yarn in the sixties manner, i.e. with every character devious and no one a hero. Good production.

w Evan Jones, *novel* The Berlin Memorandum by Len Deighton d Guy Hamilton ph Otto Heller m Konrad Elfers pd Ken Adam

Michael Caine, *Oscar Homolka*, Eva Renzi, Paul Hubschmid, *Hugh Burden*, Guy Doleman, Rachel Gurney

'So many twists that even Sherlock Holmes might have been baffled . . . before long it becomes difficult to remember who is watching whom and why, or indeed whether anybody *was* watching anybody at any given moment.'—*Tom Milne*

† Second in the Harry Palmer series, of which the first was *The Ipcress File* and the third *Billion Dollar Brain* (both qv).

Funny Face**
US 1956   103m   Technicolor
Vistavision
Paramount (Roger Edens)

A fashion editor and photographer choose a shy bookstore attendant as their 'quality woman'.
Stylish, wistful musical with good numbers but drawn-out dialogue; finally a shade too sophisticated and a whole lot too fey.

w Leonard Gershe d Stanley Donen ph Ray June m / ly George and Ira Gershwin

Fred Astaire, Audrey Hepburn, Kay Thompson, Michel Auclair, Robert Flemyng

AAN: Leonard Gershe; Ray June

Funny Girl**
US 1968   169m   Technicolor
Panavision 70
Columbia / Rastar (Ray Stark)

Fanny Brice, an ugly Jewish girl from New York's east side, becomes a big Broadway star but loses her husband in the process.
Interminable cliché-ridden musical drama relieved by a few good numbers, high production gloss and the unveiling of a new powerhouse star.

w Isobel Lennart, from her play d William Wyler ph Harry Stradling md Walter Scharf m Jule Styne ly Bob Merrill pd Gene Callahan

Barbra Streisand, Omar Sharif, Walter Pidgeon, Kay Medford, Anne Francis, Lee Allen, Gerald Mohr, Frank Faylen

AA: Barbra Streisand
AAN: best picture; Harry Stradling; Walter Scharf; Kay Medford; title song

Funny Lady*
US 1975   138m   Eastmancolor
Columbia / Rastar / Persky–Bright / Vista (Ray Stark)

Fanny Brice marries Billy Rose.
Unnecessary sequel to the above, entirely predictable and far from the truth, but with the occasional pleasures that a high budget brings.

w Jay Presson Allen, Arnold Schulman d Herbert Ross ph James Wong Howe m / ly various md Peter Matz pd George Jenkins

Barbra Streisand, James Caan, *Ben Vereen*, Omar Sharif, Roddy McDowall, Larry Gates

'The plot line is as slackly handled as the milieu.'—*Geoff Brown*

'As Fanny Brice, Streisand is no longer human; she's like a bitchy female impersonator imitating Barbra Streisand.'—*New Yorker*

AAN: James Wong Howe; Peter Matz; song 'How Lucky Can You Get' (m / ly Fred Ebb, John Kander)

A Funny Thing Happened on the Way to the Forum**
GB 1966   99m   De Luxe
UA / Quadrangle (Melvin Frank)

In ancient Rome, a conniving slave schemes to win his freedom.
Bawdy farce from a Broadway musical inspired by Plautus but with a New York Jewish atmosphere. The film pays scant attention to the comic numbers that made the show a hit, but adds some style of its own, including a free-for-all slapstick climax.

w Melvin Frank, Michael Pertwee, *musical comedy* Burt Shevelove, Larry Gelbart m / ly Stephen Sondheim md Ken Thorne d Richard Lester ph Nicolas Roeg pd Tony Walton titles Richard Williams

Zero Mostel, Phil Silvers, Michael Crawford, Jack Gilford, *Michael Hordern*, Buster Keaton, Patricia Jessel, Leon Greene, Beatrix Lehmann

'Actors have to be very fast and very sly to make themselves felt amid the flash and glitter of a characteristic piece of Lester film-mosaic.'—*John Russell Taylor*

'He proceeds by fits and starts and leaves jokes suspended in mid-air . . . like coitus interruptus going on forever.'—*Pauline Kael*

AA: Ken Thorne

Funnyman
US 1967 100m bw and colour
Korty Films (Hugh McGraw, Stephen Schmidt)

A satirical comedian seeks some better occupation in life, but finally agrees he's best as a comic.

One suspects Korty has seen *Sullivan's Travels* several times; but even though his film tries hard, it finally provides more yawns than appreciative chuckles.

w John Korty, Peter Bonerz *d* John Korty *ph* John Korty *m* Peter Schickele

Peter Bonerz, Sandra Archer, Carol Androsky, Gerald Hiken

'It has its dull patches, but it made me laugh louder and more often than any other film this year.'—*Michael Billington, Illustrated London News*

The Furies*
US 1950 109m bw
Paramount / Hal B. Wallis

A cattle baron feuds with his tempestuous daughter.

Interesting but heavy-going western, more solemn than stimulating despite its Freudian excesses.

w Charles Schnee, *novel* Niven Busch *d* Anthony Mann *ph* Victor Milner *m* Franz Waxman

Barbara Stanwyck, *Walter Huston*, Wendell Corey, Judith Anderson, Gilbert Roland, Thomas Gomez, Beulah Bondi, Wallace Ford, Albert Dekker, Blanche Yurka

'An immoral saga, capably mounted, with some pretentious psychological trimmings.'—*MFB*

AAN: Victor Milner

The Further Perils of Laurel and Hardy***
US 1967 99m bw
TCF / *Robert Youngson*

A compilation of longish extracts from the stars' silent comedies, including *Early to Bed, The Second Hundred Years, Should Married Men Go Home, You're Darn Tootin', Habeas Corpus, That's My Wife,* and *Leave 'Em Laughing.* The producer is to be congratulated on refurbishing so many deteriorating negatives, though the commentary leaves much to be desired.

w, ed Robert Youngson *m* John Parker

Fury***
US 1936 94m bw
MGM (Joseph L. Mankiewicz)

A traveller in a small town is mistaken for a murderer and apparently lynched; he escapes in a fire but determines to have his persecutors hanged for his murder.

Powerful drama which becomes artificial in its latter stages but remains its director's best American film.

w Bartlett Cormack, Fritz Lang, *story* Norman Krasna *d* Fritz Lang *ph* Joseph Ruttenberg *m* Franz Waxman

Spencer Tracy, Sylvia Sidney, Bruce Cabot, Walter Abel, Edward Ellis, Walter Brennan, Frank Albertson

'The surface of American life has been rubbed away: *Fury* gets down to the bones of the thing and shows them for what they are.'—*C. A. Lejeune*

'Since the screen began to talk, no other serious film except *The Front Page* has so clearly shown that here is a new art and what this new art can do.'—*John Marks*

'Everyday events and people suddenly took on tremendous and horrifying proportion; even the most insignificant details had a pointed meaning.'—*Lewis Jacobs*

'For half its length a powerful and documented piece of fiction about a lynching, and for the remaining half a desperate attempt to make love, lynching and the Hays Office come out even.'—*Otis Ferguson*

'Astonishing, the only film I know to which I have wanted to attach the epithet of *great*.'—*Graham Greene*

AAN: Norman Krasna

The Fury*
US 1978 117m De Luxe
TCF / Frank Yablans (Ron Preissman)

The head of a government institute for psychic research finds that his own son is wanted by terrorists who wish to use his lethal psychic powers.

Flashy, kaleidoscopic nonsense which never even begins to make sense but is used as the basis for the director's showing-off, which is occasionally worth a glance for those with hardened stomachs.

w John Farris, from his novel *d* Brian de Palma *ph* Richard H. Kline *m* John Williams

Kirk Douglas, John Cassavetes, Carrie Snodgress, Charles Durning, Andrew Stevens, Amy Irving, Fiona Lewis

'A conception of cinema that is closer to Ken Russell than Alfred Hitchcock.'—*Richard Combs, MFB*

Fury at Furnace Creek*
US 1948   88m   bw
TCF

A westerner clears the name of his father, a general accused of diverting a wagon train into hostile Indian territory.
Adequate old-fashioned western with a good story line and standard excitements.

w Charles G. Booth   *d* H. Bruce Humberstone   *ph* Harry Jackson   *m* David Raksin   *md* Alfred Newman

Victor Mature, Coleen Gray, Glenn Langan, Reginald Gardiner

Fury at Smugglers' Bay
GB 1960   96m   Eastmancolor
  Panascope
(Regal) Mijo (Michael Green, Joe Vegoda)

The squire of a Cornish village is being blackmailed by the vicious leader of a gang of wreckers.
Watchable, then forgettable variation on *Jamaica Inn*.

wd John Gilling   *ph* Harry Waxman
m Harold Geller

Peter Cushing, John Fraser, Bernard Lee, William Franklyn, June Thorburn, Miles Malleson, Michele Mercier, George Coulouris

Futureworld*
US 1976   107m   Metrocolor
AIP (James T. Aubrey Jnr, Paul Lazarus III)

The robot factory seen in *Westworld* (qv) now aims at world domination by duplicating influential figures.

Amusing and fairly suspenseful fantasy with a bigger budget than its predecessor.

w Mayo Simon, George Schenck   *d* Richard T. Heffron   *ph* Howard Schwarz, Gene Polito   *m* Fred Karlin

Peter Fonda, Blythe Danner, Arthur Hill, Yul Brynner, John Ryan, Stuart Margolin, Jim Antonio

Fuzz*
US 1972   93m   De Luxe
UA / Filmways / Javelin (Jack Farren)

Detectives of Boston's 87th precinct try to catch a rapist.
A black farce devoted to police incompetence, though taken from a straight 'Ed McBain' story. Brisk and sometimes funny.

w *Evan Hunter* ('Ed McBain')   *d* Richard A. Colla   *ph* Jacques Marquette   *m* Dave Grusin

Burt Reynolds, Raquel Welch, Jack Weston, Yul Brynner, Tom Skerritt, James McEachin

The Fuzzy Pink Nightgown
US 1957   88m   bw
UA / Russ–Field (Robert Waterfield)

A glamorous film star falls in love with her kidnapper.
Unendurable cheap romantic farce.

w Richard Alan Simmons, *novel* Sylvia Tate   *d* Norman Taurog   *ph* Joseph La Shelle   *m* Billy May

Jane Russell, Ralph Meeker, Keenan Wynn, Fred Clark

G

Gi Blues
US 1960   104m   Technicolor
Paramount / Hal B. Wallis (Paul Nathan)

A guitar-playing gunner with the American army in West Germany falls for a cabaret dancer.
Routine star vehicle marking Presley's return from military service.

w Edmund Beloin, Henry Garson d Norman Taurog ph Loyal Griggs m Joseph J. Lilley

Elvis Presley, Juliet Prowse, Robert Ivers, Leticia Roman, Arch Johnson

G Men***
US 1935   85m   bw
Warner (Lou Edelman)

A young lawyer becomes a G-man to avenge the murder of his best friend, and finds himself tracking down another old friend who is a gangster.
In the face of mounting criticism of their melodramas making heroes of gangsters, Warners pulled a clever switch by showing the same crimes from a different angle, that of the law enforcer. As an action show it became pretty good after a slow start.

w Seton I. Miller d William Keighley ph Sol Polito md Leo F. Forbstein

James Cagney, Ann Dvorak, Margaret Lindsay, Robert Armstrong, Barton MacLane, Lloyd Nolan, William Harrigan

'The gangster is back, racing madly through one of the fastest melodramas ever made.'— New York Sun
'The headiest dose of gunplay that Hollywood has unleashed in recent months.'— André Sennwald, New York Times

Gable and Lombard
US 1976   131m   Technicolor
Universal (Harry Korshak)

After Carole Lombard's death in a 1942 air crash, Clark Gable recalls their years together.
Vulgar and inaccurate representation of two Hollywood stars of the thirties; it fails even as titillation.

w Barry Sandler d Sidney J. Furie ph Jordan S. Cronenweth m Michel Legrand pd Edward Carfagno

James Brolin, Jill Clayburgh, Allen Garfield (as Louis B. Mayer), Red Buttons, Joanne Linville

'A limply raunchy, meaningless movie with nothing to say about the movies, about love, or about stardom.'—New Yorker
'An uneven combination of smut and sentimentality.'—Les Keyser, Hollywood in the Seventies

Gabriel over the White House*
US 1933   87m   bw
MGM / Walter Wanger

A crook becomes president and mysteriously reforms.
Pleasing, dated New Deal fantasy.

w Carey Wilson, Bertram Bloch, novel Rinehard by T. F. Tweed d Gregory La Cava ph Bert Glennon m William Axt

Walter Huston, Karen Morley, Franchot Tone, C. Henry Gordon, Samuel S. Hinds, Jean Parker, Dickie Moore

'The picture that will make 1933 famous!'— publicity

Gaby
US 1956   97m   Eastmancolor Cinemascope
MGM (Edwin H. Knopf)

Flabby remake of Waterloo Bridge (qv); saccharine, fussy and outmoded, despite updated settings and a happy ending.

w Albert Hackett, Frances Goodrich, Charles Lederer d Curtis Bernhardt ph Robert Planck m Conrad Salinger

Leslie Caron, John Kerr, Cedric Hardwicke, Taina Elg, Margalo Gillmore

Gaiety George
GB 1946   98m   bw
Embassy (George King)
US title: Showtime

The career in the London theatre of Irish impresario George Howard in the early part of the century.
Tepid musical biopic.

w Katherine Strueby d George King ph Otto Heller

Richard Greene, Ann Todd, Peter Graves, Hazel Court, Leni Lynn, Ursula Jeans, Morland Graham, Frank Pettingell

Gaily, Gaily**
US 1969   117m   De Luxe
UA / Mirisch / Cartier
GB title: *Chicago, Chicago*

The early life on a Chicago newspaper of Ben Hecht.
Busy, farcical, melodramatic, always interesting biopic of the formative years of a celebrated literary figure.

w Abram S. Ginnes, book Ben Hecht d Norman Jewison ph Richard Kline *m* Henry Mancini *pd* Robert Boyle

Beau Bridges, Melina Mercouri, *Brian Keith*, George Kennedy, Hume Cronyn, Margot Kidder, Wilfrid Hyde White, Melodie Johnson, John Randolph

The Gal Who Took the West
US 1949   84m   Technicolor

In 1890, an opera singer travels west and is the object of romantic rivalry. Lame attempt to equal the splendid idiocy of *Salome Where She Danced*. Yvonne de Carlo, Charles Coburn, Scott Brady, John Russell, James Millican. Written by William Bowers and Oscar Brodney; directed by Frederick de Cordova; for Universal-International.

Galileo*
GB 1975   145m   Eastmancolor
Ely Landau / Cinevision

In the 17th century, a poor Italian mathematics teacher has trouble establishing his 'heretical' astronomical theories.
Overlong play-on-celluloid for the American Film Theatre: very decently made and acted, it lacks inspiration.

w Barbara Bray, Joseph Losey, *play* Bertolt Brecht *d* Joseph Losey *ph* Michael Reed *m* Hanns Eisler

Topol, Edward Fox, Michel Lonsdale, Richard O'Callaghan, Tom Conti, Judy Parfitt, Patrick Magee, Michael Gough, John Gielgud, Colin Blakely, Margaret Leighton, Clive Revill

Gallant Bess
US 1946   99m   Cinecolor

A soldier's horse saves his life and becomes his peacetime friend. Boy-and-horse story with a wartime setting; good for small towns.
Marshall Thompson, George Tobias, Clem Bevans, Donald Curtis. Written by Jeanne Bartlett; directed by Andrew Marton; for MGM.

The Gallant Blade
US 1948   81m   Cinecolor

In France in 1648, a dashing young lieutenant rescues his general from the plot of a would-be revolutionary. Pinchpenny swashbuckler which maintains a commendable verve. Larry Parks, Marguerite Chapman, Victor Jory, George Macready. Written by Walter Ferris and Morton Grant; directed by Henry Levin; for Columbia.

The Gallant Hours*
US 1959   115m   bw
UA / James Cagney / Robert Montgomery

Episodes in the career of Admiral William F. Halsey.
Adulatory but physically restrained biopic which covers World War II with barely a scene outside control room sets: interesting but finally too talky.

w Beirne Lay Jnr, Frank D. Gilroy *d* Robert Montgomery *ph* Joe MacDonald *m* Roger Wagner

James Cagney, Dennis Weaver, Richard Jaeckel, Ward Costello, Carl Benton Reid
'Imaginatively conceived but erroneously realized.'—*Robert Vas*

Gallant Journey
US 1946   86m   bw
Columbia

The life of an early American aviation pioneer.
Curious biopic, very tentatively done, about an inventor so obscure as to be virtually fictitious. Sentimental, artificial, but harmless.

w Byron Morgan, William A. Wellman *d* William A. Wellman *ph* Burnett Guffey *m* Marlin Skiles

Glenn Ford, Janet Blair, Charles Ruggles, Henry Travers, Arthur Shields

Gallant Lady
US 1933   84m   bw
Darryl F. Zanuck

A woman allows her illegitimate son to be adopted, but years later marries his stepfather. A tearjerker very typical of its time, moderately well assembled; later remade as *Always Goodbye* (qv).

w Sam Mintz, *story* Gilbert Emery, Doug Doty *d* Gregory La Cava *ph* Peverell Marley *m* Alfred Newman

Ann Harding, Clive Brook, Otto Kruger, Tullio Carminati, Dickie Moore, Janet Beecher

The Galloping Major*
GB 1951   82m   bw
British Lion / Romulus (Monja Danischewsky)

A group of suburbanites form a syndicate to buy a racehorse.
Rather contrived and imitative sub-Ealing comedy which fails to generate much steam.

w Monja Danischewsky, Henry Cornelius
d Henry Cornelius ph Stan Pavey m Georges Auric

Basil Radford, Janette Scott, Hugh Griffith, Jimmy Hanley, René Ray, Joyce Grenfell, Sidney Tafler, Charles Victor, A. E. Matthews

Gambit**
US 1966   109m   Techniscope
Universal (Leo L. Fuchs)

A cockney thief conspires with a Eurasian girl to rob a multi-millionaire of a prize statue.
An enjoyably light pattern of cross and double cross is well sustained to the end.

w Jack Davies, Alvin Sargent d Ronald Neame ph Clifford Stine m Maurice Jarre

Michael Caine, Shirley Maclaine, Herbert Lom, John Abbott, Roger C. Carmel, Arnold Moss

The Gambler**
US 1975   111m   Eastmancolor
Paramount (Irwin Winkler, Robert Chartoff)

A compulsive gambler has a will to lose.
Flashily made but basically uninteresting sub-Freudian study, vaguely based on Dostoievsky.

w James Tomack d Karel Reisz ph Victor J. Kemper m Mahler md Jerry Fielding

James Caan, Paul Sorvino, Lauren Hutton, Morris Carnovsky, Jacqueline Brookes, Burt Young

Gambler from Natchez
US 1954   88m   Technicolor
TCF / Panoramic

A professional gambler returns to New Orleans to avenge his father's murder, and disposes of his enemies one by one.
Mildly watchable semi-western with a plot borrowed from The Count of Monte Cristo.

w Gerald Drayson Adams, Irving Wallace
d Henry Levin ph Lloyd Ahern md Lionel Newman

Dale Robertson, Debra Paget, Thomas Gomez, Kevin McCarthy

Gambling House
US 1950   80m   bw

An immigrant gambler is threatened with deportation when involved in a murder. Heavy melodrama with assumed social conscience.
Victor Mature, Terry Moore, William Bendix, Basil Ruysdael. Written by Marvin Borowsky and Allen Rivkin; directed by Ted Tetzlaff; for RKO.

Gambling Lady*
US 1934   66m   bw
Warner

The daughter of a gambling suicide follows in father's footsteps and becomes involved in murder.
Fast-paced melodrama with a happy ending: smart entertainment of its time.

w Ralph Block, Doris Malloy d Archie Mayo ph George Barnes

Barbara Stanwyck, Joel McCrea, Pat O'Brien, Claire Dodd, C. Aubrey Smith, Robert Barrat, Philip Reed

A Game for Vultures
GB 1979   106m   colour

In Rhodesia, a sanctions-buster comes to understand a black freedom fighter. After a lot of violence and attitudinizing, that is, in this unattractively pretentious piece of bloodthirsty hokum. Richard Harris, Richard Roundtree, Ray Milland, Joan Collins, Sven Bertil Taube, Denholm Elliott. Written by Phillip Baird, from a novel by Michael Hartmann; directed by James Fargo; for Columbia.

A Game of Death
US 1945   72m   bw
RKO

Cheap remake of The Most Dangerous Game (qv); excitement dissipated by poor handling.

w Norman Houston d Robert Wise
ph J. Roy Hunt m Paul Sawtell

John Loder, Audrey Long, Edgar Barrier, Russell Wade, Russell Hicks

Games*
US 1967   100m   Techniscope
Universal (George Edwards)

A sophisticated New York couple play complex games, one of which turns out to have a deadly effect.
Tedious variation on Les Diaboliques, with interesting moments.

w Gene Kearney d Curtis Harrington
ph William A. Fraker m Samuel Matlovsky

Simone Signoret, James Caan, Katharine Ross, Don Stroud, Kent Smith, Estelle Winwood, Marjorie Bennett

The Games*
GB 1970   97m   De Luxe   Panavision
TCF (Lester Linsk)

Four men in various parts of the world prepare to take part in the marathon at the Rome Olympics.
Tepid multi-drama with good locations and a well-shot and exciting climactic race.

w Erich Segal, *novel* Hugh Atkinson
d Michael Winner   *ph Robert Paynter*
m Francis Lai

Stanley Baker, Michael Crawford, Ryan O'Neal, Charles Aznavour, Jeremy Kemp, Elaine Taylor, Kent Smith, Mona Washbourne

The Gamma People
GB 1955   79m   bw

Journalists in a Balkan state uncover a plot by a mad scientist to control the minds of children by gamma rays. Artless serial-like thriller with little suspense. Paul Douglas, Leslie Phillips, Eva Bartok, Walter Rilla, Philip Leaver. Written by John Gilling and John Gossage; directed by John Gilling; for Warwick / Columbia.

The Gang That Couldn't Shoot Straight
US 1971   96m   Metrocolor
MGM (Robert Chartoff, Irwin Winkler)

Members of the New York Mafia organize a cycle race and start antagonisms that end in mass murder.
Unfunny black comedy with all concerned gesticulating wildly.

w Waldo Salt, *novel* Jimmy Breslin d James Goldstone *ph* Owen Roizman *m* Dave Grusin

Jerry Orbach, Leigh Taylor-Young, Jo Van Fleet, Lionel Stander, Robert de Niro, Herve Villechaize, Joe Santos

The Gang's All Here*
GB 1939   77m   bw
ABP (Walter C. Mycroft, Jack Buchanan)
US title: *The Amazing Mr Forrest*

An insurance investigator goes undercover among gangsters.
Lively comedy-melodrama.

w Ralph Spence d Thornton Freeland

Jack Buchanan, Googie Withers, Edward Everett Horton, Syd Walker, Otto Kruger, Jack La Rue, Walter Rilla

The Gang's All Here**
US 1943   103m   Technicolor
TCF (William Le Baron)
GB title: *The Girls He Left Behind*

A serviceman is caught between a fiery entertainer and a Park Avenue socialite.
Frenetic wartime musical with some of Busby Berkeley's most outré choreography (e.g. The Lady in the Tutti Frutti Hat) and gleamingly effective Technicolor.

w Walter Bullock *d / ch Busby Berkeley*
ph Edward Cronjager md Alfred Newman
songs Leo Robin, Harry Warren

Alice Faye, Carmen Miranda, James Ellison, Phil Baker, Benny Goodman, Charlotte Greenwood, Eugene Pallette, Edward Everett Horton

'Those who consider Berkeley a master consider this film his masterpiece.'—*New Yorker, 1976*

'Mainly made up of Busby Berkeley's paroxysmic production numbers, which amuse me a good deal.'—*James Agee*

The Gangster
US 1947   84m   bw

Rival gangs rub each other out. Shoddy-looking Poverty Row melodrama with little rhyme, reason or interest. Barry Sullivan, Akim Tamiroff, Belita, John Ireland. Written by Daniel Fuchs; directed by Gordon Wiles; for Monogram / King Bros.

Gangway*
GB 1937   89m   bw
GFD / Gaumont

A girl reporter poses as a star's maid and is accused of theft.
Mildly pleasing star vehicle.

w Lesser Samuels, Sonnie Hale d Sonnie Hale *ph* Glen MacWilliams

Jessie Metthews, Barry Mackay, Pat Pendleton, Noel Madison, Alastair Sim

Gangway for Tomorrow
US 1943   69m   bw

Five defence workers with problematical pasts unite in the cause of war. Naïve but oddly stirring little propaganda piece. Robert Ryan, Margo, John Carradine. Written by Arch Oboler; directed by John H. Auer; for RKO.

The Garden of Allah**
US 1936   80m   Technicolor
David O. Selznick

A disenchanted socialite falls in love with a renegade monk in the Algerian desert.

Arty old-fashioned romantic star vehicle; great
to look at, and marking a genuine advance in
colour photography, but dramatically a bit of a
drag.

w W. P. Lipscomb, Lynn Riggs, *novel* Robert
Hichens *d* Richard Boleslawski
ph W. *Howard Greene, Harold Rosson m Max
Steiner ad* Sturges Carne, Lyle Wheeler,
Edward Boyle

Marlene Dietrich, Charles Boyer, Basil
Rathbone, Tilly Losch

'Hopelessly dated folderol.'—*J. R. Parish*
'The juiciest tale of woe ever, produced in
poshly lurid colour, with a Max Steiner score
poured on top.'—*Judith Crist*

'Alas! my poor church, so picturesque, so
noble, so superhumanly pious, so intensely
dramatic. I really prefer the *New Statesman*
view, shabby priests counting pesetas on their
dingy fingers before blessing tanks.'—*Graham
Greene*

† Previous, silent, versions had been made in
1917, with Tom Santochi and Helen Ware,
and in 1927 with Ivan Petrovich and Alice
Terry.

AA: photography
AAN: Max Steiner

Garden of Evil*
US 1954   100m   Technicolor
  Cinemascope
TCF (Charles Brackett)

En route to the Californian goldfields an
ex-sheriff and a gambler help a woman to
rescue her husband from a mine, but are
trapped by Indians.
High-flying western melodrama with the
principals glowering at each other. Stock
situations quite skilfully compiled.

w Frank Fenton *d* Henry Hathaway
ph Milton Krasner *m Bernard Herrmann*

Susan Hayward, Gary Cooper, Richard
Widmark, Hugh Marlowe, Cameron Mitchell

The Garden of the Finzi-Continis**
Italy / West Germany 1970   95m
  Eastmancolor
Documento Film / CCC Filmkunst (Gianni
  Hecht Lucari, Arthur Cohn)

In 1938, a family of wealthy Italian Jews sees
its world collapse, with a concentration camp
as the next destination.
A dreamlike, poignant, and very beautiful
film.

w Tullio Pinelli, Valerio Zurlini, Franco
Brusati, Ugo Pirro, Vittorio Bonicelli, Alain
Katz, *novel* Giorgio Bassani *d Vittorio de*

Sica ph Ennio Guarnieri m Manuel de Sica
Dominique Sanda, Lino Capolicchio, Helmut
Berger, Romolo Valli, Fabio Testi

AAN: script

The Garment Jungle*
US 1957   88m   bw
Columbia (Harry Kleiner)

Union and gangster problems abound for a
family in the New York clothing business.
Reasonably powerful melodrama fashioned
from familiar material in the wake of *On the
Waterfront.*

w Harry Kleiner *d* Robert Aldrich, Vincent
Sherman *ph* Joseph Biroc *m* Leith Stevens

Lee J. Cobb, Kerwin Mathews, Gia Scala,
Richard Boone, Valerie French, Robert
Loggia, Joseph Wiseman

Gas! or It Became Necessary to Destroy the World in Order to Save It
US 1970   79m   Movielab
AIP / San Jacinto (Roger Corman)

A gas which speeds up the ageing process is
accidentally released and kills everyone over
twenty-five.
Psychedelic sci-fi for the Easy Rider set. Very
mildly diverting.

w Graham Armitage *d* Roger Corman
ph Ron Dexter *m* Country Joe and the Fish

Robert Corff, Elaine Giftos, Pat Patterson,
Graham Armitage, Alex Wilson, Ben Vereen,
Bud Cort

Gasbags*
GB 1940   77m   bw
Gainsborough (Edward Black)

Airmen stranded in Germany by a barrage
balloon return in a captured secret weapon.
Fast-moving knockabout from the Crazy
Gang; often inventive despite reach-me-down
script and production.

w Val Guest, Marriott Edgar *d* Marcel
Varnel

Flanagan and Allen, Nervo and Knox,
Naughton and Gold, Moore Marriott, Wally
Patch, Peter Gawthorne, Frederick Valf

Gaslight****
GB 1939   88m   bw
British National (John Corfield)
US title: *Angel Street*

A Victorian schizophrenic drives his wife
insane when she seems likely to stumble on his
guilty secret of an old murder and hidden
rubies.

Modest but absolutely effective film version of a superb piece of suspense theatre.

w A. R. Rawlinson, Bridget Boland, play Patrick Hamilton d Thorold Dickinson ph Bernard Knowles m Richard Addinsell

Anton Walbrook, Diana Wynyard, Frank Pettingell, Cathleen Cordell, Robert Newton, Jimmy Hanley

'The electric sense of tension and mid-Victorian atmosphere are entirely cinematic.'—Sequence, 1950

Gaslight°°
US 1944 114m bw
MGM (Arthur Hornblow Jnr)
GB title: The Murder in Thornton Square

Grossly overblown and less effective version of the above, but with moments of power, effective performances and superior production.

w John Van Druten, Walter Reisch, John L. Balderston d George Cukor ph Joseph Ruttenberg m Bronislau Kaper ad Cedric Gibbons

Charles Boyer, Ingrid Bergman, Joseph Cotten, Dame May Whitty, Barbara Everest, Angela Lansbury, Edmund Breon, Halliwell Hobbes

'This is love . . . clouded by evil . . . darkened by a secret no one dared to guess! The strange drama of a captive sweetheart!'—publicity

AA: Ingrid Bergman
AAN: best picture; script; Joseph Ruttenberg; Charles Boyer; Angela Lansbury

Gate of Hell°
Japan 1953 90m Eastmancolor
original title: Jigokumon

After a 12th-century war, a soldier demands as his prize a woman who has helped him; but she is married.
Curious traditional Japanese saga, its emphases strange to western eyes and ears. Its colour, however, is devastatingly beautiful.

wd Teinosuke Kinugasa, novel Kan Kikuchi ph Kohei Sugiyama m Yasushi Akutagawa

Machiko Kyo, Kazuo Hasegawa, Isao Yamagata

AA: best foreign film

Gateway°
US 1938 75m bw
TCF (Darryl F. Zanuck)

An Irish girl emigrating to the US is helped on board ship by a war correspondent.
Brisk romantic drama which provides an interesting recreation of the Ellis Ireland procedures still effective in the thirties.

w Lamar Trotti d Alfred Werker ph Edward Cronjager

Don Ameche, Arleen Whelan, Gregory Ratoff, Raymond Walburn, Binnie Barnes, Gilbert Roland, John Carradine, Harry Carey

A Gathering of Eagles
US 1962 115m Eastmancolor
U-I (Sy Bartlett)

A colonel becomes unpopular when he strives to improve the efficiency of a Strategic Air Command base.
Tame revamp of Twelve O'clock High without the justification of war; all strictly routine and perfectly dull.

w Robert Pirosh d Delbert Mann ph Russell Harlan m Jerry Goldsmith

Rock Hudson, Mary Peach, Rod Taylor, Barry Sullivan, Kevin McCarthy

Gator
US 1976 116m De Luxe Todd AO 35
UA / Levy-Gardner-Laven

A convicted moonshiner is blackmailed into becoming a government undercover man in the organization of a hoodlum.
Shambling mixture of action, violence, and raw humour.

w William Norton d Burt Reynolds ph William A. Fraker m Charles Bernstein

Burt Reynolds, Jack Weston, Lauren Hutton, Jerry Reed, Alice Ghostley, Dub Taylor, Mike Douglas

'The relentless violence, the sentimentality, the raucous stag party humour, the inability to cut off a scene once it has made its point, attest to the influence of Robert Aldrich.'—Philip French, The Times

The Gaunt Stranger°
GB 1938 73m bw
Northwood / Capad (Ealing) (S. C. Balcon)
US title: The Phantom Strikes

A criminal master of disguise threatens to kill a much more despicable criminal at an appointed hour . . . and does so despite police protection.
A highly reliable suspenser of which this is perhaps the best film version.

w Sidney Gilliat, novel and play The Ringer by Edgar Wallace d Walter Forde ph Ronald Neame

Sonnie Hale, Wilfrid Lawson, Alexander Knox, Louise Henry, Patricia Roc, Patrick Barr, John Longden, George Merritt

† Other versions, as *The Ringer*, appeared in 1931 and 1953.

The Gauntlet*
US 1977   109m   De Luxe   Panavision
Warner / Malpaso (Robert Daly)

A disreputable cop is assigned to escort a foul-mouthed prostitute to a courtroom across country, through the gauntlet of baddies who want them both dead.

The epitome of seventies violence, with no excuse except to stage one detailed shoot-up or explosion after another. Well done for those who like this sort of thing.

w Michael Butler, Dennis Shryack *d* Clint Eastwood *ph* Rexford Metz *m* Jerry Fielding

Clint Eastwood, Sondra Locke, Pat Hingle, William Prince

Gawain and the Green Knight*
GB 1973   93m   Technicolor   Panavision
UA / Sancrest (Philip Breen)

The medieval legend of a supernatural knight who challenges the king's men to kill him.
Enterprising if unsuccessful low-budget attempt to create a medieval world; too long by half.

w Philip Green, Stephen Weeks *d* Stephen Weeks *ph* Ian Wilson *m* Ron Goodwin
ad Anthony Woollard

Murray Head, Ciaran Madden, Nigel Green, Anthony Sharp, Robert Hardy, Murray Melvin

The Gay Bride
US 1934   80m   bw
MGM

A gold-digging chorus girl marries a racketeer but soon becomes a widow.
Misfiring satirical melodrama which quickly becomes tedious.

w Bella and Samuel Spewack, *story* Repeal by Charles Francis Coe *d* Jack Conway *ph* Ray June

Carole Lombard, Chester Morris, Zasu Pitts, Nat Pendleton, Leo Carrillo

The Gay Deception*
US 1935   79m   bw
TCF (Jesse L. Lasky)

A Ruritanian prince becomes a doorman at a swank New York hotel, and marries a secretary.
Lightly-handled Cinderella story showing most of its director's accomplishment.

w Stephen Morehouse Avery, Don Hartman
d William Wyler *ph* Joseph Valentine
m Louis de Francesco

Francis Lederer, Frances Dee, Benita Hume, Alan Mowbray, Akim Tamiroff, Lennox Pawle, Richard Carle, Lionel Stander

AAN: script

The Gay Desperado**
US 1936   85m   bw
Mary Pickford

An heiress is held for ransom by a romantic bandit.
Very light, quite amusing, sometimes irritatingly skittish musical spoof sparked by the director's ideas.

w Wallace Smith, *story* Leo Birinski
d Rouben Mamoulian *m* Alfred Newman
ph Lucien Andriot

Ida Lupino, Nino Martini, Leo Carrillo, Harold Huber, Mischa Auer

'One of the best light comedies of the year . . . Mr Mamoulian's camera is very persuasive.'—*Graham Greene*

'While some of the show is fetching, the ideas mostly misfire and the spell is fitful and unsure.'—*Otis Ferguson*

'It has the lightness of touch which goes into the making of the perfect meringue.'—*Basil Wright*

The Gay Divorcee****
US 1934   107m   bw
RKO (Pandro S. Berman)
GB title: *The Gay Divorce*

A would-be divorcee in a Brighton hotel mistakes an author who loves her for a professional co-respondent.
Wildly and hilariously dated comedy musical with splendidly archaic comedy routines supporting Hollywood's great new dance team in their first big success. Not much dancing, but 'The Continental' is a show-stopper.

w George Marion Jnr, Dorothy Yost, Edward Kaufman, *musical comedy* Dwight Taylor
d Mark Sandrich *ph* David Abel *md* Max Steiner *songs* various *sp* Vernon Walker
ad Van Nest Polglase, Carroll Clark

Fred Astaire, Ginger Rogers, Edward Everett Horton, Alice Brady, Erik Rhodes, Eric Blore, Lillian Miles, Betty Grable

'The gayest of mad musicals!'—*publicity*

'The plot is trivial French farce, but the dances are among the wittiest and most lyrical expressions of American romanticism on the screen.'—*New Yorker, 1977*

AA: song 'The Continental' (*m* Con Conrad, *ly* Herb Magidson)
AAN: best picture; musical adaptation (Ken Webb, Samuel Hoffenstein)

The Gay Intruders

US 1948 68m bw

Quarrelling stage marrieds consult psychiatrists, who end up more confused than the patients. Unusual second feature comedy with a few good laughs; allegedly based on Tallulah Bankhead. Tamara Geva, John Emery, Leif Erickson, Virginia Gregg. Written by Francis Swann; directed by Ray McCarey; for TCF.

Gay Purree*

US 1962 85m Technicolor
UPA

A country cat goes to Paris and is Shanghaied.
Feature cartoon similar to Disney's later *The Aristocats* and about as good, i.e. not quite up to the best standards.

w Dorothy and Chuck Jones *d* Abe Levitow *md* Mort Lindsey

voices Judy Garland, Robert Goulet, Hermione Gingold

The Gay Sisters*

US 1942 110m bw
Warner (Henry Blanke)

Three sisters refuse to sell their aristocratic New York mansion to make way for development.
Slowish but quite interesting family drama with Chekhovian touches.

w Lenore Coffee, *novel* Stephen Longstreet *d* Irving Rapper *ph* Sol Polito *m* Max Steiner

Barbara Stanwyck, George Brent, Geraldine Fitzgerald, Donald Crisp, Gig Young (so named after his part in this film; formerly Byron Barr), Nancy Coleman, Gene Lockhart, Larry Simms, Donald Woods, Grant Mitchell

The Gazebo*

US 1959 102m bw
MGM / Avon (Lawrence Weingarten)

A TV writer kills a blackmailer (he thinks) and hides his body in the garden.
Frenetic black comedy which must have worked better on the stage but produces a few laughs.

w George Wells, *play* Alec Coppel *d* George Marshall *ph* Paul C. Vogel *m* Jeff Alexander

Glenn Ford, Debbie Reynolds, Carl Reiner, John McGiver, Mabel Albertson, Doro Merande, Zasu Pitts, Martin Landau

The Geisha Boy

US 1958 98m Technicolor Vistavision
Paramount (Jerry Lewis)

A third-rate magician joins a USO entertainment tour in Japan.
Disconnected farce which amuses only fitfully, and actively displeases when it becomes sentimental with the star drooling over a baby.

wd Frank Tashlin *ph* Haskell Boggs *m* Walter Scharf

Jerry Lewis, Marie MacDonald, Barton MacLane, Sessue Hayakawa, Suzanne Pleshette

The Gene Krupa Story

US 1959 101m bw
Columbia (Philip A. Waxman)
GB title: *Drum Crazy*

A successful jazz drummer is convicted on a drugs charge and falls from grace.
Dreary biopic with the expected music track.

w Orin Jannings *d* Don Weis *ph* Charles Lawton Jnr *m* Leith Stevens

Sal Mineo, Susan Kohner, James Darren, Susan Oliver, Yvonne Craig, Lawrence Dobkin, Celia Lovsky; and Red Nichols, Shelly Manne, Buddy Lester

The General****

US 1926 80m approx (24 fps) bw
silent
UA / Buster Keaton (Joseph M. Schenck)

A confederate train driver gets his train and his girl back when they are stolen by Union soldiers.
Slow-starting, then hilarious action comedy, often voted one of the best ever made. Its sequence of sight gags, each topping the one before, is an incredible joy to behold.

w Al Boasberg, Charles Smith d Buster Keaton, Clyde Bruckman ph J. Devereux Jennings, Bert Haines

Buster Keaton, Marion Mack, Glen Cavander

'It has all the sweet earnestness in the world. It is about trains, frontier America, flower-faced girls.'—*New Yorker, 1977*

'The production itself is singularly well mounted, but the fun is not exactly plentiful . . . here he is more the acrobat than the clown, and his vehicle might be described as a mixture of cast iron and jelly.'—*Mordaunt Hall, New York Times*

† The story is based on an actual incident of the Civil War, treated more seriously in *The Great Locomotive Chase*.

†† The screenplay with 1,400 freeze frames was issued in 1976 in the Film Classics Library (editor, Richard Anobile).

General Crack

US 1930 100m approx bw

Exploits of an eighteenth-century brigand prince. Elaborate swashbuckler which provided the star with his first talkie but boringly demonstrates the technical problems of films of this period, however highly budgeted. John Barrymore, Marian Nixon, Hobart Bosworth, Armida, Lowell Sherman. Written by J. Grubb Alexander and others; directed by Alan Crosland; for Warner.

The General Died at Dawn**
US 1936 93m bw
Paramount (William le Baron)

A mercenary in China overcomes an evil warlord and falls in love with a spy.
Heavy-going but very decorative studio-bound intrigue which seems to take place on the old *Shanghai Express* sets with an extra infusion of dry ice. An intellectual's picture of its day.

w Clifford Odets, *novel* Charles Booth
d Lewis Milestone ph Victor Milner
m Werner Janssen, Gerard Carbonara

Gary Cooper, Madeleine Carroll, *Akim Tamiroff, Dudley Digges,* Porter Hall, *William Frawley*

'If it were not for a rather ludicrous ending, this would be one of the best thrillers for some years.'—*Graham Greene*
'In terms of cinematic invention, a fascinating technical exercise.'—*John Baxter, 1968*
'A curious study in exoticism.'—*NFT, 1974*
'In direction and photography it has undeniable class . . . but like most movies, it is empty of any ideas or characters that stay with you longer than it takes to reach the nearest subway entrance.'—*Brooklyn Daily Eagle*
AAN: Victor Milner; Werner Janssen; Akim Tamiroff

The General Line**
USSR 1929 90m (24 fps) bw silent
Sovkino
original title: *Staroye i Novoye;* aka: *Old and New*

A country woman helps to start a village co-operative.
A slight piece of propaganda, put together with all of Eisenstein's magnificent cinematic resources: the cream separator demonstration is one of the most famous montage sequences in cinema history.

wd Sergei Eisenstein co-d Grigori Alexandrov ph Edouard Tissé.

Marta Lapkina and a cast of non-professionals

General Spanky
US 1936 75m approx bw

A small boy is instrumental in a famous Civil War victory. Uneasy sentimental melodrama vehicle for one of the moppet stars of 'Our Gang'. Spanky McFarland, Phillips Holmes, Hobart Bosworth, Ralph Morgan, Irving Pichel. Written by Richard Flournoy, Hal Yates and John Guedal; directed by Gordon Douglas and Fred Newmeyer; for Hal Roach / MGM.

Il Generale della Rovere
Italy / France 1959 137m bw
Zebra / Gaumont (Morris Ergas)

During World War II, a con man is persuaded to impersonate a dead general, and becomes so imbued with the latter's code of honour that he goes before a firing squad rather than expose a partisan.
An unlikely piece of tragic whimsy with some good acting, but imperfectly assembled and at too great length.

w Sergio Amidei, Diego Fabbri, Indro Montanelli, Roberto Rossellini d Roberto Rossellini ph Carlo Carlini m Renzo Rossellini

Vittorio de Sica, Hannes Messemer, Sandra Milo, Giovanna Ralli, Anne Vernon

AAN: script

Generation*
Poland 1954 90m bw
Film Polski
original title: *Pokolenie*

In occupied Warsaw in 1942 a teenager becomes hardened by life and joins the resistance.
Heavy-going but quite striking propaganda piece, amply demonstrating its director's talents.

w Bohdan Czeszko, from his novel d Andrzej Wajda ph Jerzy Lipman m Andrzej Markowski

Tadeusz Lomnicki, Urszula Modrzynska, Roman Polanski, Zbigniew Cybulski

Genevieve****
GB 1954 86m Technicolor
GFD / Sirius (Henry Cornelius)

Two friendly rivals engage in a race on the way back from the Brighton veteran car rally. One of those happy films in which for no very good or expected reason a number of modest elements merge smoothly to create an aura of high style and memorable moments. A charmingly witty script, carefully pointed direction, attractive actors and locations, an atmosphere of light-hearted British sex and a lively harmonica theme turned it, after a slowish start, into one of Britain's biggest commercial hits and most fondly remembered comedies.

w *William Rose* d *Henry Cornelius*
ph Christopher Challis *m Larry Adler* (who also played it) *md* Muir Mathieson
ad Michael Stringer

Dinah Sheridan, John Gregson, Kay Kendall, Kenneth More, Geoffrey Keen, Joyce Grenfell, Reginald Beckwith, Arthur Wontner

'One of the best things to have happened to British films over the last five years.'—*Gavin Lambert*

AAN: William Rose; Muir Mathieson

Genghis Khan*
US 1964   126m   Technicolor
Panavision
Columbia / Irving Allen / CCC / Avala

Temujin raises a Mongol army and revenges himself on his old enemy Jamuga.
Meandering epic in which brutality alternates with pantomimish comedy and bouts of sex.
Necessarily patchy but reasonably watchable.

w Clarke Reynolds, Beverly Cross d Henry Levin ph Geoffrey Unsworth m Ducan Radic

Omar Sharif, Stephen Boyd, Françoise Dorléac, *James Mason*, Robert Morley, Telly Savalas, Woody Strode, Eli Wallach, Yvonne Mitchell

The Gentle Giant
US 1967   93m   Eastmancolor

A small boy in Florida befriends a bear, which later saves his disapproving father's life.
Lumbering family movie which provided the impetus for a TV series. Dennis Weaver, Clint Howard, Vera Miles, Ralph Meeker, Huntz Hall. Written by Edward J. Lakso and Andy White, from the novel *Gentle Ben* by Walt Morey; directed by James Neilson; for Ivan Tors / Paramount.

The Gentle Sex**
GB 1943   93m   bw
Rank / Two Cities / Concanen (Leslie Howard, Derrick de Marney)

Seven girls from different backgrounds are conscripted into the ATS.
Unassuming war propaganda, quite pleasantly done and historically very interesting.

w Moie Charles, Aimée Stuart, Phyllis Rose, Roland Pertwee d Leslie Howard, Maurice Elvey

Rosamund John, Joan Greenwood, Joan Gates, Jean Gillie, Lilli Palmer, Joyce Howard, Barbara Waring, John Justin, Frederick Leister, Mary Jerrold, Everley Gregg

A Gentleman after Dark
US 1942   74m   bw
Edward Small

A jewel thief comes out of prison to pay back his vindictive wife for shopping him.
Efficient melodrama of a dated kind.

w Patterson McNutt, George Bruce, *story* A Whiff of Heliotrope by Richard Washburn Child d Edwin L. Marin ph Milton Krasner m Dmitri Tiomkin

Brian Donlevy, Miriam Hopkins, Preston Foster, Harold Huber, Philip Reed, Gloria Holden, Douglass Dumbrille, Ralph Morgan
† Previously filmed in 1920 as *Heliotrope* with Fred Burton; in 1928 as *Forgotten Faces* with Clive Brook; and in 1936 as *Forgotten Faces* with Herbert Marshall.

Gentleman Jim**
US 1942   104m   bw
Warner (Robert Buckner)

The rise to fame of boxer Jim Corbett.
Cheerful biopic of a nineties show-off, mostly played for comedy.

w Vincent Lawrence, Horace McCoy, *book* The Roar of the Crowd by James J. Corbett d Raoul Walsh ph Sid Hickox m Heinz Roemheld

Errol Flynn, Alan Hale, Alexis Smith, John Loder, Jack Carson, *Ward Bond*, William Frawley, Rhys Williams, Arthur Shields
'Good-natured enough, but it lacks flavour.'—*New Yorker, 1976*

Gentleman's Agreement**
US 1947   118m   bw
TCF (Darryl F. Zanuck)

A journalist poses as a Jew in order to write about anti-semitism.
Worthy melodrama which caused a sensation at the time but as a film is alas rather dull and self-satisfied.

w Moss Hart, *novel* Laura Z. Hobson d Elia Kazan ph Arthur Miller m Alfred Newman

Gregory Peck, Dorothy McGuire, *John Garfield*, Celeste Holm, *Anne Revere*, June Havoc, Albert Dekker, Jane Wyatt, Dean Stockwell

AA: best picture; Elia Kazan; Celeste Holm
AAN: Moss Hart; Gregory Peck; Dorothy McGuire; Anne Revere

A Gentleman's Gentleman
GB 1939   70m   bw

A valet thinks his master is a murderer, and
tries a little blackmail. Uneasy serio-comic
vehicle for a London stage character who had
made his name in Hollywood. Eric Blore,
Peter Coke, Marie Lohr, David Hutcheson.
Written by Austin Melford and Elizabeth
Meehan, from the play by Philip MacDonald;
directed by Roy William Neill; for Warner.

Gentlemen Are Born
US 1934   74m   bw

College graduates find it hard to get jobs.
Tedious and uninventive quartet of linked
stories. Franchot Tone, Ross Alexander, Dick
Foran, Robert Light, Jean Muir, Margaret
Lindsay, Ann Dvorak, Charles Starrett.
Written by Eugene Solow and Robert Lee
Johnson; directed by Alfred E. Green; for
Warner.

Gentlemen Marry Brunettes
US 1955   95m   Technicolor
Cinemascope
UA / Russ–Field (Richard Sale, Robert
Waterfield)

Two American shopgirls seek rich husbands in
Paris, and find that their aunts were notorious
there.
Jaded sequel to *Gentlemen Prefer Blondes*; it
barely raises a smile and the numbers are
dismal.

w Mary Loos, Richard Sale d Richard Sale
ph Desmond Dickinson m Robert Farnon
ad Paul Sheriff ch Jack Cole

Jane Russell, Jeanne Crain, Alan Young,
Scott Brady, Rudy Vallee

Gentlemen Prefer Blondes°
US 1953   91m   Technicolor
TCF (Sol. C. Siegel)

A dumb blonde and a showgirl go to Paris in
search of rich husbands.
Musicalized and updated version of the
twenties satire; no real vigour, but not too
bad.

w Charles Lederer, *novel* Anita Loos
d Howard Hawks ph Harry J. Wild
md Lionel Newman songs Jule Styne, Leo
Robin ch Jack Cole

*Jane Russell, Marilyn Monroe, Charles
Coburn*, Tommy Noonan, Norma Varden,
Elliott Reid, George Winslow

Geordie°
GB 1955   99m   Technicolor
British Lion / Argonaut (Sidney Gilliat,
Frank Launder)
US title: *Wee Geordie*

A weakly Scottish boy takes a physical culture
course and becomes an Olympic hammer-
thrower.
Slight comic fable, good to look at but without
the necessary style to follow it through.

w Sidney Gilliat, Frank Launder, *novel* David
Walker d Frank Launder ph Wilkie Cooper
m William Alwyn

Bill Travers, Alastair Sim

George and Margaret
GB 1940   77m   bw

The frictions of a suburban family come to
boiling point. Fairly spruce film version of a
stage comedy in which the title pair were much
talked of but never seen. Judy Kelly, Marie
Lohr, Oliver Wakefield, Noel Howlett, Ann
Casson, Arthur Macrae. Written by Brock
Williams and Rodney Ackland, from the play
by Gerald Savory; directed by George King;
for Warner.

George and Mildred
GB 1980   93m   colour

A suburban husband on a weekend package
holiday is mistaken for a hired killer. Abysmal
TV spinoff, seeming even more lugubrious
since it was released after the death of the
female star. Yootha Joyce, Brian Murphy,
Stratford Johns, Norman Eshley, Sheila
Fearn, Kenneth Cope. Written by Dick
Sharples; directed by Peter Frazer Jones; for
Chips / ITC. 'Flaccid entertainment even by
routine sit-com standards.'—*Martyn Auty,
MFB.*

George in Civvy Street
GB 1946   79m   bw
Columbia (Marcel Varnel, Ben Henry)

A soldier returns to his country pub and finds
himself in the middle of a beer war.
The star's last film was oddly lacklustre and
compared very badly with his earlier successes.

w Peter Fraser, Ted Kavanaugh, Max Kester,
Gale Pedrick d Marcel Varnel ph Phil
Grindrod

George Formby, Rosalyn Boulter, Ronald
Shiner, Ian Fleming, Wally Patch

The George Raft Story
US 1961   105m   bw
Allied Artists (Ben Schwab)
GB title: *Spin of a Coin*

In twenties New York, a dancer falls in with gangsters, but eludes them when he goes to Hollywood, where his acting career is harmed by temperament.

Tepid, unconvincing biopic, rather shoddily made but with flashes of interest.

w Crane Wilbur d Joseph M. Newman
ph Carl Guthrie m Jeff Alexander

Ray Danton, Julie London, Jayne Mansfield, Frank Gorshin, Neville Brand (as Al Capone)

George Washington Slept Here
US 1942 93m bw
Warner (Jerry Wald)

A New York couple move to a dilapidated country house.

Disappointingly stiff and ill-timed version of a play that should have been a natural.

w Everett Freeman, *play* George Kaufman, Moss Hart d William Keighley ph Ernest Haller m Adolph Deutsch

Jack Benny, Ann Sheridan, Percy Kilbride, Charles Coburn, Hattie McDaniel, William Tracy, Lee Patrick, John Emery, Charles Dingle

George White's Scandals*
US 1934 79m bw
Fox (Winfield Sheehan)

Romance blossoms backstage during the production of a big musical.

Revue with minimum plot and some impressive numbers.

w Jack Yellen, from the Broadway show directed by George White d Thornton Freeland, Harry Lachman, George White ph Lee Garmes, George Schneiderman *songs* various

George White, Rudy Vallee, Alice Faye, Jimmy Durante, Dixie Dunbar, Adrienne Ames, Cliff Edwards, Gertrude Michael, Gregory Ratoff

George White's 1935 Scandals*
US 1935 83m bw
Fox (Winfield Sheehan)

A small-town star is discovered by a Broadway producer.

Again, basic plot serves to introduce some pretty good acts.

w Jack Yellen, Patterson McNutt d George White ph George Schneiderman *songs* various

George White, Alice Faye, James Dunn, Eleanor Powell, Ned Sparks, Lyda Roberti, Cliff Edwards, Arline Judge

George White's Scandals*
US 1945 95m bw
RKO (Jack J. Gross, Nat Holt, George White)

Ex-Scandals girls get together, and one disappears.

Lively comedy-musical with vaudeville orientations.

w Hugh Wedlock, Parker Levy, Howard Green d Felix E. Feist m Leigh Harline ph Robert de Grasse *songs* various

Joan Davis, Jack Haley, Philip Terry, Martha Holliday, Ethel Smith, Margaret Hamilton, Glenn Tryon, Jane Greer, Fritz Feld, Rufe Davis

Georgy Girl*
GB 1966 100m bw
Columbia / Everglades (Otto Plaschkes, Robert A. Goldston)

An unattractive girl is fancied by her middle-aged employer but escapes to look after the illegitimate baby of her ungrateful friend.

Frantic black farce which seems determined to shock, but has a few good scenes once you get attuned to the mood. A censorship milestone.

w Margaret Forster, Peter Nichols, *novel* Margaret Forster d Silvio Narizzano ph Ken Higgins m Alexander Faris

James Mason, Lynn Redgrave, Charlotte Rampling, Alan Bates, Bill Owen, Clare Kelly, Rachel Kempson

'Another swinging London story filled with people running through London late at night, dancing madly in the rain, and visiting deserted children's playgrounds to ride on the roundabouts.'—*MFB*

'So glib, so clever, so determinedly kinky that everything seems to be devalued.'—*Pauline Kael*

'Its barrage of fashionable tricks proves exhausting.'—*Sight and Sound*

AAN: Ken Higgins; James Mason; Lynn Redgrave; title song (*m* Tom Springfield, *ly* Jim Dale)

Germany Year Zero*
France / Italy 1947 78m bw
Union Générale Cinématographique / DEFA

Life in post-war Germany is so appalling that a boy kills his father and then himself.

Both realistic and pessimistic, this depressing film has a savage power of its own but totally fails to be constructive.

wd Roberto Rossellini ph Robert Juillard m Renzo Rossellini

Franz Gruger and a cast of non-professionals

Geronimo!
US 1939 89m bw
Paramount

The seventh cavalry gives the Indians a run for their money.

Muddled western of no discernible merit.

wd Paul H. Sloane ph Henry Sharp
m Gerald Carbonara

Ellen Drew, Preston Foster, Andy Devine, Gene Lockhart, Ralph Morgan, William Henry

Geronimo
US 1962 101m Technicolor
Panavision
UA / Laven–Gardner–Levy

In 1883 Geronimo and his remaining Apaches seek peace but are betrayed.

Moderate western held back by script and performances.

w Pat Fielder d Arnold Laven ph Alex Phillips m Hugo Friedhofer

Chuck Connors, Ross Martin, Kamala Devi

Gervaise*
France 1956 116m bw
Agnès Delahaye–Silver Films–CLCC

In 19th-century Paris, a laundrymaid is deserted by her lover, settles with another man and is able to open her own laundry, but they both take to drink.

The French equivalent of David Lean's Dickens films, superbly detailed and wonderful to look at, but with a plot which finally seems worthless and depressing.

w Jean Aurenche, Pierre Bost,
novel L'Assommoir by Emile Zola d René Clément ph René Juillard m Georges Auric decor Paul Bertrand

Maria Schell, François Périer, Suzy Delair, Mathilde Casadeus

'A tremendous tour de force of literal realism . . . a piece for the admiration of technicians, or for those whose consciences are purged and hands kept clean by the vicarious contemplation of how the other half lived—once upon a time.'—David Robinson, MFB
† Other French versions were made in 1902, 1909, 1911 and 1933.

Get Carter*
GB 1971 112m Metrocolor
MGM / Mike Klinger

A racketeer goes to Newcastle to avenge his brother's death at the hands of gangsters. He kills those responsible but is himself shot by a sniper.

Brutal British crime melodrama with faint echoes of Raymond Chandler. Sex and thuggery unlimited, narrative disjointed, rewards few.

wd Mike Hodges, novel Jack's Return Home by Ted Lewis ph Wolfgang Suschitzky m Roy Budd

Michael Caine, John Osborne, Ian Hendry, Britt Ekland

'TV on the big screen—more sex, more violence, but no more attention to motivation or plot logic.'—Arthur Knight

Get Cracking*
GB 1942 96m bw
Columbia (Ben Henry)

George joins the home guard.

Adequate star comedy.

w L. DuGarde Peach d Marcel Varnel

George Formby, Edward Rigby, Frank Pettingell, Dinah Sheridan, Ronald Shiner, Wally Patch, Irene Handl

Get Off My Foot
GB 1935 83m bw
Warner (Irving Asher)

A Smithfield porter becomes a butler, and later finds himself heir to a fortune.

The nearest Max Miller came to being a genuine film star was in this first of eight Warner comedies, but the screen simply couldn't contain him.

w Frank Launder, Robert Edmunds,
play Money By Wire by Edward Paulton
d William Beaudine ph Basil Emmott

Max Miller, Chili Bouchier, Morland Graham, Jane Carr, Norma Varden, Reginald Purdell, Wally Patch

The Getaway**
US 1972 122m Technicolor Todd-AO 35
Solar / First Artists (David Foster, Mitchell Brower)

A convict leaves jail and promptly joins his wife in a bank robbery.

Violent, amoral, terse and fast-moving action melodrama which generally holds the interest despite its excesses.

w Walter Hill, novel Jim Thompson d Sam Peckinpah ph Lucien Ballard m Quincy Jones

Steve McQueen, Ali MacGraw, Ben Johnson, Sally Struthers, Al Lettieri, Slim Pickens

'This pair have no mission or "meaning". As in all romances, The Getaway simply extracts one element of reality and dwells on it. Nor is the violence "American". Pictures like this don't fail overseas.'—*Stanley Kauffmann*

Getting Straight*
US 1970   125m   Eastmancolor
Columbia / The Organization (Richard Rush)

A political activist returns to college in order to teach and discovers the foolishness of most contemporary attitudes.
Modish comedy, too long, far too pleased with itself, and now irrevocably dated.

w Robert Kaufman *novel* Ken Kolb
d Richard Rush *ph* Laszlo Kovacs *m* Ronald Stein

Elliott Gould, Candice Bergen, Robert F. Lyons, Jeff Corey, Max Julien, Cecil Kellaway

The Ghost and Mr Chicken
US 1965   90m   Techniscope
Universal (Edward J. Montagne)

An incompetent small-town reporter finds ghosts in a local murder mansion.
Old-fashioned scare comedy starring a highly resistible comic. A big hit in American small towns.

w James Fritzell, Everett Greenbaum *d* Alan Rafkin *ph* William Margulies *m* Vic Mizzy

Don Knotts, Skip Homeier, Joan Staley, Liam Redmond, Dick Sargent, Reta Shaw

The Ghost and Mrs Muir**
US 1947   104m   bw
TCF (Fred Kohlmar)

A widow refuses to be frightened away from her seaside home by the ghost of a sea captain, with whom she falls in love.
Charming sentimental fable in Hollywood's best style.

w Philip Dunne, *novel* R. A. Dick *d* Joseph L. Mankiewicz *ph Charles Lang m Bernard Herrmann ad Richard Day*

Gene Tierney, Rex Harrison, George Sanders, Edna Best, Vanessa Brown, Anna Lee, Robert Coote, Natalie Wood, Isobel Elsom

AAN: Charles Lang

The Ghost Breakers***
US 1940   85m   bw
Paramount (Arthur Hornblow Jnr)

A girl inherits a West Indian castle and finds herself up to her neck in ghosts, zombies and buried treasure.
Archetypal comedy horror, very well done; a follow-up to the success of *The Cat and the Canary*, and just about as entertaining.

w Paul Dickey, Walter de Leon, *play* Paul Dickey, Charles W. Goddard *d* George Marshall *ph* Charles Lang *m* Ernst Toch *ad* Hans Dreier

Bob Hope, Paulette Goddard, Paul Lukas, *Willie Best*, Richard Carlson, *Lloyd Corrigan*, Anthony Quinn, Noble Johnson, Pedro de Cordova

† Previously filmed in 1914 with H. B. Warner; in 1922 with Wallace Reid; and remade in 1953 as *Scared Stiff*.

The Ghost Goes West***
GB 1936   85m   bw
London Films (Alexander Korda)

When a millionaire buys a Scottish castle and transports it stone by stone to America, the castle ghost goes too.
Amusing whimsy which is always pleasant but never quite realizes its full potential; fondly remembered for its star performance.

w Robert E. Sherwood, Geoffrey Kerr, *story* Eric Keown *d René Clair ph* Harold Rosson

Robert Donat, Jean Parker, Eugene Pallette, Elsa Lanchester, Ralph Bunker, Patricia Hilliard, Morton Selten

'Although the film is not cast in the fluid, rapidly paced style of Clair's typical work, it has a sly wit and an adroitness of manner that make it delightful.'—*André Sennwald, New York Times*

'It is typical of the British film industry that M. René Clair should be brought to this country to direct a Scottish film full of what must to him be rather incomprehensible jokes about whisky and bagpipes, humorous fantasy without any social significance, realistic observation, or genuine satire.'—*Graham Greene*

The Ghost of Frankenstein
US 1942   67m   bw
Universal (George Waggner)

Frankenstein's second son implants evil shepherd Igor's brain into the monster.
The rot set in with this flatly-handled potboiler, which had none of the literary mood or cinematic interest of *Bride* or *Son* which preceded it, and suffered from a particularly idiotic script.

w W. Scott Darling, *story* Eric Taylor *d* Erle C. Kenton *ph* Milton Krasner, Woody Bredell *m* Charles Previn *ad* Jack Otterson

Cedric Hardwicke, Lon Chaney Jnr (as the monster), Bela Lugosi, Lionel Atwill, Evelyn Ankers, Ralph Bellamy

'You can't keep a good monster down!'—*publicity*

† See *Frankenstein* for other episodes in series

The Ghost of St Michael's**
GB 1941 82m bw
Ealing (Basil Dearden)

A school is evacuated to the Isle of Skye, and
the local ghost turns out to be an enemy agent.
The star's schoolmaster character is here at its
seedy best, and he is well supported in a
comedy-thriller plot.

w Angus Macphail, John Dighton d Marcel
Varnel ph Derek Williams

Will Hay, Claude Hulbert, Felix Aylmer,
Raymond Huntley, Elliot Mason, Charles
Hawtrey, John Laurie, Hay Petrie, Roddy
Hughes, Manning Whiley

Ghost Story*
GB 1974 89m Fujicolor
Stephen Weeks

Former college acquaintances spend a
weekend at a country house, and one of them
is drawn into tragic events of forty years
before.
Overlong chiller, ingeniously shot in India but
very variably acted; aims for the M. R. James
style and sometimes achieves it, but badly
needs cutting.

w Rosemary Sutcliff, Stephen Weeks
d Stephen Weeks ph Peter Hurst m Ron
Geesin

Murray Melvin, Larry Dann, Vivian
Mackerall, Marianne Faithfull, Anthony Bate,
Leigh Lawson, Barbara Shelley

The Ghost That Walks Alone
US 1943 63m bw

Honeymooners find a dead radio producer in
their suite. Ho-hum second feature mystery.
Arthur Lake, Janis Carter, Frank Sully, Lynne
Roberts. Written by Doris Shattuck and
Clarence Upson Young; directed by Lew
Landers; for Columbia.

The Ghost Train***
GB 1931 72m bw
Gainsborough (Michael Balcon)

Passengers stranded at a haunted station in
Cornwall include a detective posing as a silly
ass in order to trap smugglers.
Excellent early sound version of a comedy-
thriller play which has not only been among
the most commercially successful ever written
but also provided the basic plot for many
another comedy: Oh Mr Porter, The Ghost of
St Michael's, Back Room Boy, Hold That
Ghost, etc. Previously filmed as a silent in
1927, with Guy Newall.

w Angus Macphail, Lajos Biro, play Arnold
Ridley d Walter Forde

Jack Hulbert, Cicely Courtneidge, Donald
Calthrop, Ann Todd, Cyril Raymond, Angela
Baddeley, Allan Jeayes

The Ghost Train**
GB 1941 85m bw
Gainsborough (Edward Black)

Adequate remake with the lead split into two
characters, which doesn't work quite so well.

w Marriott Edgar, Val Guest, J. O. C. Orton
d Walter Forde ph Jack Cox

Arthur Askey, Richard Murdoch, Kathleen
Harrison, Morland Graham, Linden Travers,
Peter Murray Hill, Herbert Lomas

The Ghost Walks
US 1934 70m bw

A hired 'ghost' engaged for a party is scared
off by a real one. Cheeseparing spooky house
comedy-thriller. John Miljan, June Collyer,
Richard Carle. Written by Edward T. Lowe;
directed by Frank Strayer; for Chesterfield.

The Ghosts of Berkeley Square*
GB 1947 89m bw
British National (Louis H. Jackson)

Two 18th-century ghosts are doomed to haunt
a London house until royalty visits.
Thin, skittish whimsy with pleasant moments.

w James Seymour, novel No Nightingales by
S. J. Simon, Caryl Brahms d Vernon Sewell

Robert Morley, Claude Hulbert, Felix
Aylmer, Yvonne Arnaud, Abraham Sofaer,
Ernest Thesiger, Marie Lohr, Martita Hunt,
A. E. Matthews, John Longden, Ronald
Frankau, Wilfrid Hyde White, Esmé Percy,
Mary Jerrold, Wally Patch, Martin Miller

The Ghoul**
GB 1933 79m bw
Gaumont (Michael Balcon)

An Egyptologist returns from the tomb to
uncover stolen jewels and a murderer.
Fascinating minor horror piece reminiscent of
The Old Dark House, with many effective
moments and a ripe cast.

w Frank King, Leonard Hines, L. DuGarde
Peach, Roland Pertwee, John Hastings
Turner, Rupert Downing, novel Frank King
d T. Hayes Hunter ph Gunther Krampf
make-up Heinrich Heitfeld

Boris Karloff, Cedric Hardwicke, Ralph
Richardson, Kathleen Harrison, Ernest
Thesiger, Dorothy Hyson, Anthony Bushell,
D. A. Clarke-Smith

† Remade after a fashion as *What A Carve Up* (1962).

The Ghoul
GB 1975 87m Eastmancolor
Tyburn (Kevin Francis)

In the twenties, a group of stranded travellers is reduced in number when they take shelter in the house of a former clergyman.

The build-up is too slow, the revelation too nasty, and the whole thing is a shameless rip-off of the structure of *Psycho*.

w John Elder *d* Freddie Francis *ph* John Wilcox *m* Harry Robinson

Peter Cushing, Alexandra Bastedo, John Hurt, Gwen Watford, Veronica Carlson, Don Henderson

'Peter Cushing brings out his violin for a soothing spot of the classics, the local copper mutters veiled warnings before trundling off on his bike, and thick fog swirls round the exterior sets at the drop of a canister.'—*Geoff Brown*

Giant**
US 1956 197m Warnercolor
Warner (George Stevens, Henry Ginsburg)

The life of a Texas cattle rancher through two generations.

Sprawling, overlong family saga with unconvincing acting but good visual style.

w Fred Guiol, Ivan Moffat, *novel* Edna Ferber *d George Stevens ph* William C. Mellor, Edwin DuPar *m Dmitri Tiomkin*

Rock Hudson, Elizabeth Taylor, James Dean, Mercedes McCambridge, Carroll Baker, Chill Wills, Jane Withers, Dennis Hooper, Sal Mineo, Rod Taylor, Judith Evelyn, Earl Holliman, Alexander Scourby, Paul Fix

AA: George Stevens
AAN: best picture; script; Dmitri Tiomkin; Rock Hudson; James Dean; Mercedes McCambridge

Gideon's Day*
GB 1958 91m Technicolor
Columbia / John Ford (Michael Killanin)
US title: *Gideon of Scotland Yard*

A Scotland Yard Inspector has an eventful but frustrating day.

Pleasant, ordinary little TV style police yarn showing no evidence of its director's particular talents.

w T. E. B. Clarke, *novel* John Creasey *d* John Ford *ph* Frederick A. Young *m* Douglas Gamley *ad* Ken Adam

Jack Hawkins, Dianne Foster, Anna Lee, Andrew Ray, Anna Massey, Frank Lawton, John Loder, Cyril Cusack

Gidget
US 1959 95m Eastmancolor
  Cinemascope
Columbia (Lewis J. Rachmil)

A 16-year-old girl falls for a surfer; her parents disapprove until he turns out to be the son of their best friend.

Commercial mixture of domestic comedy and beach athletics, for nice teenagers and their moms and pops.

w Gabrielle Upton, *novel* Frederick Kohner *d* Paul Wendkos *ph* Burnett Guffey *m* George Duning *md* Morris Stoloff

Sandra Dee, Cliff Robertson, James Darren, Arthur O'Connell

† Sequels include *Gidget Goes Hawaiian* (1961) with Deborah Walley; *Gidget Goes to Rome* (1962) with Cindy Carol; and two TV movies.

The Gift Horse*
GB 1952 100m bw
British Lion / Molton (George Pitcher)
US title: *Glory at Sea*

In 1940 an old US destroyer is given to Britain, and an officer reluctantly takes charge of it.

Conventional, popular seafaring war adventure.

w William Fairchild, Hugh Hastings, William Rose *d* Compton Bennett *ph* Harry Waxman *m* Clifton Parker

Trevor Howard, Richard Attenborough, Sonny Tufts, James Donald, Joan Rice, Bernard Lee, Dora Bryan, Hugh Williams, Robin Bailey

The Gift of Gab
US 1934 71m bw
Universal

A conceited radio announcer gets his comeuppance.

Odd little comedy drama notable only for its long list of stars making cameo appearances.

w Rian James, Lou Breslow *d* Karl Freund *m* Albert Von Tilzer, Con Conrad, Charles Tobias

Edmund Lowe, Gloria Stuart, Ruth Etting, Phil Baker, Alexander Woollcott, Ethel Waters, Victor Moore, Boris Karloff, Bela Lugosi, Paul Lukas, Chester Morris, Binnie Barnes, Douglass Montgomery, Wini Shaw

The Gift of Love
US 1958 105m Eastmancolor
Cinemascope
TCF (Charles Brackett)

A dying wife adopts an orphan girl so that her husband will not be lonely.
Incredibly cloying and miscast remake of *Sentimental Journey* (qv).

w Luther Davis *d* Jean Negulesco *ph* Milton Krasner *m* Cyril Mockridge

Lauren Bacall, Robert Stack, Evelyn Rudie, Lorne Greene

Gigi*
France 1948 109m bw
Codo Cinema (Claude Dolbert)

In Paris in the nineties, a young girl is trained by her aunt to be a cocotte, but when married off to a rake she reforms him.
Charming, overlong, non-musical version of a famous story, chiefly memorable for its local colour.

w Pierre Laroche, *novel* Colette *d* Jacqueline Audry *ph* Gérard Perrin *m* Marcel Landowski

Daniele Delorme, *Gaby Morlay, Yvonne de Bray*, Frank Villard, Jean Tissier, Madeleine Rousset

Gigi***
US 1958 119m Metrocolor
Cinemascope
MGM (Arthur Freed)

Laundered and musicalized version; delightfully set, costumed and performed, but oddly lacking dance numbers.

w / ly Alan Jay Lerner *m* Frederick Loewe *d* Vincente Minnelli *ph* Joseph Ruttenberg *md* André Previn *pd / cost* Cecil Beaton

Leslie Caron, Louis Jourdan, Maurice Chevalier, Hermione Gingold, Isabel Jeans, Jacques Bergerac, Eva Gabor, John Abbott

'It has the sureness expected when a group of the most sophisticated talents are able to work together on material entirely suited to them.'—*Penelope Houston*

AA: best picture; Alan Jay Lerner; Vincente Minnelli; Joseph Ruttenberg; André Previn; Cecil Beaton; Adrienne Fazan (editing); Preston Ames and Keogh Gleason (art directors); title song (*m* Frederick Loewe, *ly* Alan Jay Lerner); Maurice Chevalier (special award)

Gigot
US 1962 104m De Luxe
TCF / Seven Arts (Kenneth Hyman)

The mute caretaker of a Montmartre boarding house looks after an ailing prostitute and her child.
From Paris, Hollywood, comes a grotesque piece of self-indulgence, the arch example of the clown who wanted to play Hamlet.
Plotless, mawkish and wholly unfunny.

w John Patrick, Jackie Gleason *d* Gene Kelly *ph* Jean Bourgoin *m* Jackie Gleason *md* Michael Magne *ad* Auguste Capelier

Jackie Gleason, Katherine Kath, Gabrielle Dorziat, Jean Lefebvre, Jacques Marin

'Chaplinesque pretensions have proved fatal before to artists who will not accept their own limitations.'—*Gavin Lambert*

AAN: Michael Magne

Gilda****
US 1946 110m bw
Columbia (Virginia Van Upp)

A gambler in a South American city resumes a love-hate relationship with an old flame . . . but she is now married to his dangerous new boss.
Archetypal Hollywood *film noir*, wholly studio-bound and the better for it, with dialogue that would seem risible if it did not happen to be dealt with in this style and with these actors, who keep the mood balanced between suspense and absurdity.

w Marion Parsonnet, *story* E. A. Ellington *d* Charles Vidor *ph* Rudolph Maté *md* Morris Stoloff, Marlin Skiles

Rita Hayworth, Glenn Ford, George Macready, Steve Geray, Joseph Calleia, Joe Sawyer, Gerald Mohr, Ludwig Donath

'There never was a woman like Gilda!'—*publicity*

'From a quietly promising opening the film settles into an intractable obscurity of narrative through which as in a fog three characters bite off at each other words of hate.'—*Richard Winnington*

The Gilded Lily*
US 1935 80m bw
Paramount (Albert Lewis)

A poor stenographer who meets her reporter boy friend on a park bench is wooed by a British peer.
Good depression era romantic comedy with the heroine inevitably choosing poverty.

w Claude Binyon *d* Wesley Ruggles *ph* Victor Milner

Claudette Colbert, Fred MacMurray, Ray Milland, C. Aubrey Smith, Luis Alberni, Donald Meek

A Girl, a Guy and a Gob
US 1941   91m   bw
Harold Lloyd
GB title: *The Navy Steps Out*

A secretary and her sailor boy friend teach her
stuffy boss how to enjoy life.
Did producer Lloyd intend himself for the role
played by O'Brien? If so, he would have
needed a stronger script to prevent this
Capraesque comedy from falling flat.

w Frank Ryan, Bert Granet d Richard
Wallace ph Russell Metty m Roy Webb

Lucille Ball, Edmond O'Brien, George
Murphy, George Cleveland, Henry Travers,
Franklin Pangborn, Marguerite Churchill,
Lloyd Corrigan

The Girl and the General
Italy / France 1967   113m   Technicolor
MGM / Champion / Corcordia (Carlo Ponti)

During World War I, a captured Austrian
general escapes with a girl partisan.
Turgid war epic veering from melodrama to
comedy.

w Luigi Malerba, Pasquale Festa Campanile
d Pasquale Festa Campanile ph Ennio
Guarnieri m Ennio Morricone

Rod Steiger, Virna Lisi, Umberto Orsini

The Girl Can't Help It°
US 1956   97m   Eastmancolor
  Cinemascope
TCF (Frank Tashlin)

A theatrical agent grooms a gangster's dumb
girl friend for stardom.
Scatty, garish pop scene spoof with a plot
borrowed from *Born Yesterday* and a lot of
jokes about its new star's superstructure.
Some scenes are funny, and it puts the first
rock and roll stars in pickle for all time.

w Frank Tashlin, Herbert Baker, *story* Do Re
Mi by Garson Kanin d Frank Tashlin
ph Leon Shamroy md Lionel Newman

*Jayne Mansfield, Tom Ewell, Edmond
O'Brien*, Henry Jones, John Emery; and Julie
London, Ray Anthony, Fats Domino, Little
Richard, the Platters

Girl Crazy°
US 1943   99m   bw
MGM (Arthur Freed)
aka: *When the Girls Meet the Boys*

Romance at a desert college.
Predictable star musical with good tunes.

w Fred F. Finklehoffe, *play* Guy Bolton, Jack
McGowan d Norman Taurog ph William
Daniels, Robert Planck md Georgie Stoll
songs George and Ira Gershwin

Judy Garland, Mickey Rooney, Guy Kibbee,
Gil Stratton, Robert E. Strickland, Rags
Ragland, June Allyson, Nancy Walker,
Tommy Dorsey and his band
† Remade 1965 as *When the Girls Meet the
Boys*.

The Girl Downstairs
US 1938   77m   bw

A rich bachelor in Europe chooses the maid
instead of the mistress. Feeble rewrite of
Cinderella. Franchot Tone, Franciska Gaal,
Walter Connolly, Rita Johnson, Reginald
Owen, Reginald Gardiner, Franklin
Pangborn, Robert Coote. Written by Harold
Goldman, Felix Jackson and Karl Noti;
directed by Norman Taurog; for MGM.

The Girl from Jones Beach
US 1949   78m   bw

A commercial artist meets a schoolteacher
who is the real-life counterpart of his 'perfect
girl'. Predictable comedy with only the
dimmest professional sparkle. Ronald Reagan,
Virginia Mayo, Eddie Bracken, Dona Drake,
Henry Travers, Florence Bates. Written by
I. A. L. Diamond; directed by Peter Godfrey;
for Warner.

The Girl from Manhattan
US 1948   81m   bw
UA / Benedict Bogeaus

A model returns home to help her uncle with
his mortgaged boarding house.
Mouldy comedy-drama full of kind thoughts,
charming failures and worldly priests.
Interesting for cast.

w Howard Estabrook d Alfred E. Green
ph Ernest Laszlo md David Chudnow
m Heinz Roemheld

Dorothy Lamour, Charles Laughton, George
Montgomery, Ernest Truex, Hugh Herbert,
Constance Collier, Sara Allgood, Frank Orth,
Howard Freeman, Adeline de Walt Reynolds,
George Chandler, Maurice Cass

The Girl from Maxim's
GB 1933   79m   bw

Circumstances force a doctor to pass off a
singer as his wife. Tolerable period farce from
a Feydeau original. Leslie Henson, Francis
Day, George Grossmith, Lady Tree, Stanley
Holloway. Written by Arthur Wimperis and
Harry Graham; directed by Alexander Korda;
for London Films.

The Girl from Mexico see Mexican
Spitfire

The Girl from Missouri*
US 1934   75m   bw
MGM (Bernard H. Hyman)
aka: *100% Pure*

A chorus girl determines to remain virtuous
until the right millionaire comes along.
Smart, amusing comedy very typical of its
period.

w Anita Loos, John Emerson d Jack Conway
ph Ray Junc *m* William Axt

Jean Harlow, Franchot Tone, Lionel
Barrymore, Lewis Stone, Patsy Kelly, Alan
Mowbray, Clara Blandick, Henry Kolker
'Noisily defiant, rip-roaring and raucous in
spots . . . fast and furious adult fare.'—
Photoplay

The Girl from Petrovka
US 1974   103m   Technicolor
Universal / Richard Zanuck, David Brown

An American correspondent in Moscow falls
for a Russian girl.
Lugubrious and lethargic romantic comedy-
drama.

w Allan Scott, Chris Bryant *d* Robert Ellis
Miller *m* Henry Mancini

Goldie Hawn, Hal Holbrook. Anthony
Hopkins, Grégoire Aslan, Anton Dolin

The Girl from Tenth Avenue
US 1935   69m   bw
Warner (Robert Lord)
GB title: *Men on Her Mind*

A jilted attorney drowns his sorrows and
marries on the rebound.
Watchable 'woman's picture'.

w Charles Kenyon, *play* Hubert Henry
Davies *d* Alfred E. Green *ph* James Van
Trees

Bette Davis, Ian Hunter, Colin Clive, Alison
Skipworth, Katherine Alexander, John
Eldredge, Philip Reed

Girl Happy
US 1965   96m   Metrocolor   Panavision
MGM / Euterpe (Joe Pasternak)

A pop singer in Florida is forced to chaperone
a group of college girls including a gangster's
daughter.
Standard star vehicle, quite professionally
made and totally forgettable.

w Harvey Bullock, R. S. Allen *d* Boris Sagal
ph Philip Lathrop *m* George Stoll

Elvis Presley, Harold J. Stone, Shelley
Fabares, Gary Crosby, Nita Talbot

The Girl He Left Behind
US 1956   103m   bw
Warner (Frank P. Rosenberg)

The army makes a man of a spoiled youth.
Platitudinous recruiting comedy for dim
American teenagers.

w Guy Trosper, *book* Marion Hargrove
d David Butler *ph* Ted McCord *m* Ray
Heindorf

Tab Hunter, Natalie Wood, Jessie Royce
Landis, Jim Backus, Henry Jones, Murray
Hamilton, Alan King, James Garner, David
Janssen

The Girl Hunters
GB 1963   100m   bw   Panavision
Present Day (Robert Fellows)

Private eye Mike Hammer solves a few
murders plus the disappearance of his own
ex-secretary.
Comic strip thuggery with the author playing
his own slouchy hero; the general
incompetence gives this cheap production an
air of Kafkaesque menace.

w Mickey Spillane, Roy Rowland, Robert
Fellows *d* Roy Rowland *ph* Ken Talbot
m Phil Green

Mickey Spillane, Shirley Eaton, Lloyd Nolan

A Girl in a Million
GB 1946   90m   bw

Having divorced a nagging wife, a chemist
marries a dumb girl, but when he cures her
. . . Thin comedy which must have seemed
funnier on the page than it does on the screen.
Joan Greenwood, Hugh Williams, Basil
Radford, Naunton Wayne, Wylie Watson,
Yvonne Owen. Written by Muriel and Sydney
Box; directed by Francis Searle; for Boca /
British Lion.

The Girl in Black
Greece 1955   93m   bw
Hermes
original title: *To Koritsi me ta Mavra*

A writer holidaying on a remote fishing island
causes tension and tragedy when he falls for a
local maiden.
Watchable mood piece benefiting from its star
female performance.

wd Michael Cacoyannis *ph* Walter Lassally
m Argyris Kounadis, Manos Hadjidakis

Elle Lambetti, George Foundas, Dimitri
Horna

A Girl in Every Port*
US 1928   62m (24 fps)   bw   silent
Fox

Two sailors brawl over women.
Adventure comedy with themes typical of its
director.

w Seton Miller, James K. McGuinness
d Howard Hawks ph R. J. Bergquist, L. W.
O'Connel m William Perry

Victor McLaglen, Natalie Joyce, Dorothy
Matthews, Maria Casajuana, Louise Brooks,
Francis McDonald
    'Brief and essentially anecdotal, it now
looks more than anything else like a
preliminary sketch for concerns which Hawks
would later elaborate.'—*Tim Pulleine, MFB*

A Girl in Every Port
US 1951   87m   bw
RKO (Irwin Allen, Irving Cummings Jnr)

Two accident-prone sailors have trouble with a
racehorse.
Dismally mechanical farce.

wd Chester Erskine ph Nicholas Musuraca
m Roy Webb

Groucho Marx, William Bendix, Marie
Wilson, Don Defore, Gene Lockhart

The Girl in the Headlines*
GB 1963   93m   bw
Bryanston / Viewfinder (John Davis)
US title: *The Model Murder Case*

Scotland Yard investigates the murder of a
model.
Standard police mystery, well enough done.

w Vivienne Knight, Patrick Campbell, *novel*
The Nose on My Face by Laurence Payne
d Michael Truman ph Stan Pavey m John
Addison

Ian Hendry, Ronald Fraser, Margaret
Johnston, Natasha Parry

The Girl in the News*
GB 1940   78m   bw
TCF (Edward Black)

A nurse is framed for the death of her
employer.
Easy-going British mystery of the Agatha
Christie school.

w Sidney Gilliat, *novel* Roy Vickers d Carol
Reed ph Otto Kanturek md Louis Levy

Margaret Lockwood, Barry K. Barnes, Emlyn
Williams, Margaretta Scott, Roger Livesey,
Basil Radford, Wyndham Goldie, Irene
Handl, Mervyn Johns, Kathleen Harrison,
Richard Bird, Michael Hordern, Roland
Culver, Edward Rigby

The Girl in the Red Velvet Swing*
US 1955   109m   De Luxe   Cinemascope
TCF (Charles Brackett)

In New York at the turn of the century, a rich
unstable man shoots his mistress's former
lover.
Plushy but not very interesting recounting of a
celebrated murder case in which the victim
was a famous architect, Stanford White.

w Walter Reisch, Charles Brackett d Richard
Fleischer ph Milton Krasner m Leigh
Harline ad Lyle R. Wheeler, Maurice
Ransford

Ray Milland, Farley Granger, Joan Collins,
Glenda Farrell, Luther Adler, Cornelia Otis
Skinner, Philip Reed, John Hoyt
    'A needlessly long-winded piece of lush
sensationalism.'—*Penelope Houston*

The Girl in the Taxi
GB 1937   72m   bw

The head of the purity league is drawn into an
adulterous flirtation. Moderately piquant
comedy shot in English and French versions.
Frances Day, Henri Garat, Lawrence
Grossmith, Jean Gillie, Mackenzie Ward,
Helen Haye, Albert Whelan. Written by
Austin Melford, Val Valentine and Fritz
Gottfurcht, from the play by George
Okonowski; directed by André Berthomieu;
for British Unity.

The Girl in White*
US 1952   93m   bw
MGM (Armand Deutsch)
GB title: *So Bright the Flame*

The story of Dr Emily Dunning, the first
woman to become an intern in one of New
York's hospitals.
Bland biopic, modestly produced, with
predictable plot crises.

w Irmgard Von Cube, Allen Vincent, *book*
Bowery to Bellevue by Emily Dunning
Barringer d John Sturges ph Paul C. Vogel
m David Raksin

June Allyson, Arthur Kennedy, Gary Merrill,
Mildred Dunnock, Jesse White, Marilyn
Erskine

The Girl Most Likely
US 1956   98m   Technicolor   RKOscope
RKO (Stanley Rubin)

A girl finds herself engaged to three men at
the same time, and envisions marriage with
each.
Dully cast, quite brightly handled remake of
Tom, Dick and Harry, with modest songs and
dances.

w Devery Freeman d Mitchell Leisen
ph Robert Planck m Nelson Riddle
songs Ralph Blane, Hugh Martin

Jane Powell, Cliff Robertson, Keith Andes, Tommy Noonan, Kaye Ballard, Una Merkel
† For Mitchell Leisen and RKO studios, their last film.

A Girl Must Live**
GB 1939   92m   bw
Gainsborough (Edward Black)

A runaway schoolgirl falls among chorus girls planning to marry into the nobility.
Light, peppery comedy with a strong cast.

w Frank Launder, Michael Pertwee, *novel* Emery Bonnet d Carol Reed ph Jack Cox md Louis Levy

Margaret Lockwood, Renée Houston, Lilli Palmer, George Robey, Hugh Sinclair, Naunton Wayne, Moore Marriott, Mary Clare, David Burns, Kathleen Harrison, Martita Hunt, Helen Haye

'An unabashed display of undressed femininity, double-meaning dialogue alternating between piquancy and vulgarity, and hearty knockabout involving scantily attired young viragos who fight furiously in a whirligig of legs and lingerie.'—*Kine Weekly*

A Girl Named Tamiko
US 1962   119m   Technicolor
Panavision
Paramount / Hal B. Wallis (Paul Nathan)

A Eurasian photographer uses his women in an attempt to get American nationality.
Humdrum romantic melodrama with dim performances.

w Edward Anhalt, *novel* Ronald Kirkbride d John Sturges ph Charles Lang Jnr m Elmer Bernstein

Laurence Harvey, France Nuyen, Martha Hyer, Michael Wilding, Miyoshi Umeki

The Girl Next Door
US 1953   92m   Technicolor
TCF (Robert Bassler)

A Broadway musical star falls for her suburban neighbour.
Mild musical linked by UPA cartoon sequences.

w Isobel Lennart d Richard Sale ph Leon Shamroy md Lionel Newman songs Josef Myrow, Mack Gordon ch Richard Barstow

Dan Dailey, June Haver, Natalie Schaefer, Dennis Day, Cara Williams

The Girl of the Golden West
US 1930   81m   bw
Warner (Robert North)

A gun-toting, saloon-owning girl marries an outlaw and saves him from the sheriff.

Straight version of a dusty old Broadway success, later musicalized under the same title (see below).

w Waldemar Young, *play* David Belasco d John Francis Dillon ph Sol Polito

Ann Harding, James Rennie, Harry Bannister, Ben Hendricks Jnr, J. Farrell MacDonald

† A silent version was made in 1923 by First National, with Sylvia Breamer and J. Warren Kerrigan, directed by Edwin Carewe.

The Girl of the Golden West
US 1938   121m   bw (sepia release)
MGM (William Anthony McGuire)

In backwoods Canada, a girl loves a bandit who is being chased by the Mounties.
Solemn musical melodrama in which the stars seem miscast and a bit of pep is badly needed. Taken from a hoary David Belasco spectacular, and looks it.

w Isobel Dawn, Boyce DeGaw d Robert Z. Leonard ph Oliver Marsh songs Sigmund Romberg, Gus Kahn

Jeanette MacDonald, Nelson Eddy, Walter Pidgeon, Leo Carrillo, Buddy Ebsen, Olin Howland

Girl on a Motorcycle
GB / France 1968   91m   Technicolor
Mid Atlantic / Ares (William Sassoon)
US title: *Naked under Leather;* French title: *La Motocyclette*

A married woman leaves her husband, zooms off on her motorcycle to see her lover, and crashes to her death while indulging in sexual reverie.
An incredibly plotless and ill-conceived piece of sub-porn claptrap, existing only as a long series of colour supplement photographs.

w Ronald Duncan, *novel* La Motocyclette by André Pieyre de Mandiargues d Jack Cardiff ph Jack Cardiff, René Guissart m Les Reed

Marianne Faithfull, Alain Delon, Roger Mutton

The Girl on the Boat
GB 1962   91m   bw
UA / Knightsbridge (John Bryan)

On a transatlantic liner in the twenties, two Englishmen fall in love.
Curious attempt to do something different with a star comic, who is clearly outclassed by the lighter talents at hand.

w Reuben Ship, *story* P. G. Wodehouse d Henry Kaplan ph Denys Coop m Kenneth V. Jones

Norman Wisdom, *Richard Briers*, Millicent Martin, Athene Seyler, Sheila Hancock, Philip Locke

The Girl on the Front Page
US 1936   74m   bw

The lady owner of a newspaper gets a job on it under an assumed name, and helps the editor solve a mystery. Fairly pleasing programmer.

Edmund Lowe, Gloria Stuart, Spring Byington, Reginald Owen. Written by Austin Parker, Albert R. Perkins and Alice Duer Miller; directed by Harry Beaumont; for Universal.

The Girl Rosemarie
West Germany 1958   100m   bw
Roxy
original title: *Das Mädchen Rosemarie*

Corrupt industrialists and investigators alike are relieved when a girl who had been the mistress of all of them is murdered .
Slick melodrama based on an actual case; almost a documentary exposé.

w Erich Kuby, Rolf Thiele, Joe Herbst, Rolf Urich *d* Rolf Thiele *ph* Klaus von Rautenfeld *m* Norbert Schultze

Nadja Tiller, Peter Van Eyck, Carl Raddatz, Gert Frobe, Mario Adorf, Horst Frank

The Girl Rush
US 1955   85m   Technicolor   Vistavision
Paramount (Frederick Brisson, Robert Alton)

A gambler's daughter inherits a half share in a Las Vegas hotel.
Dull charmless semi-musical vehicle for a star who can't quite carry it.

w Phoebe and Henry Ephron *d* Robert Pirosh *ph* William Daniels *m* Herbert Spencer, Earle Hagen *ch* Robert Alton

Rosalind Russell, Eddie Albert, Fernando Lamas, James Gleason, Gloria de Haven, *Marion Lorne*

Girl Stroke Boy
GB 1971   88m   Eastmancolor
Hemdale / Virgin (Ned Sherrin, Terry Glinwood)

A well-to-do couple try to find out whether their son's house guest is male or female. Initially funny but appallingly extended one-joke comedy which many will find merely embarrassing.

w Caryl Brahms, Ned Sherrin, *play* Girlfriend by David Percival *d* Bob Kellett *ph* Ian Wilson *m* John Scott

Joan Greenwood, Michael Hordern, Clive Francis, Patricia Routledge, Peter Bull, Rudolph Walker, Elizabeth Welch

The Girl Who Couldn't Say No
Italy 1968   104m   Techniscope

A medical assistant has an on-off relationship with an eccentric girl. Downright peculiar romantic comedy with an American star all at sea in the Mediterranean. George Segal, Virna Lisi, Lila Kedrova. Written by Franco Brusati and Ennio de Concini; directed by Franco Brusati; for INC / PC / Fulcro. (Original title: *Il Suo Modo di Fari.*)

The Girl Who Had Everything
US 1953   69m   bw
MGM (Adolph Deutsch)

The daughter of a wealthy criminal lawyer falls in love with one of her father's crooked clients.
Glossy melodrama of purely superficial interest.

w Art Cohn, *novel* Adela Rogers St John *d* Richard Thorpe *ph* Paul Vogel *m* André Previn

Elizabeth Taylor, William Powell, Fernando Lamas, Gig Young
† Remake of *A Free Soul.*

Girl with Green Eyes**
GB 1963   91m   bw
UA / Woodfall (Oscar Lewenstein)

An artless young Dublin girl falls for a middle-aged writer.
Lyrical romance which just about preserves its charm by good location sense.

w Edna O'Brien, from her novel The Lonely Girl *d* Desmond Davis *ph* Manny Wynn *m* John Addison

Peter Finch, Rita Tushingham, Lynn Redgrave

Girlfriends*
US 1978   86m   Du Art
Cyclops (Claudia Weill, Jan Saunders)

A Jewish girl photographer in New York is ditched by her girl friend and considers men. Mild, amusing, well-observed little comedy-drama which goes nowhere in particular and slightly outstays its welcome.

w Vicki Polon *d* Claudia Weill *ph* Fred Murphy *m* Michael Small

Melanie Mayron, Eli Wallach, Anita Skinner, Bob Balaban

Les Girls*

US 1957 114m Metrocolor
Cinemascope
MGM (Sol. C. Siegel)

Two members of a girl dancing troupe sue
over a memoir written by the third.
Disappointing, talent-laden comedy-musical
with a *Rashomon*-like flashback plot and a
curious absence of the expected wit and style.

w John Patrick, *novel* Vera Caspary d George
Cukor ph Robert Surtees m / ly Cole Porter
ch Jack Cole

Gene Kelly, *Kay Kendall*, Mitzi Gaynor,
Taina Elg, Jacques Bergerac, Leslie Phillips,
Henry Daniell, Patrick MacNee

Girls' Dormitory*

US 1936 66m bw
TCF

A college girl falls for her headmaster.
Old-fashioned romance for nice young people,
smoothly produced in the Fox mid-thirties
manner.

w Gene Markey, *story* Ladislaus Fodor
d Irving Cummings m Arthur Lange ph J.
Merrit Gerstad

Herbert Marshall, *Simone Simon*, Ruth
Chatterton, Constance Collier, J. Edward
Bromberg, Dixie Dunbar, Tyrone Power

Girls, Girls, Girls

US 1962 106m Technicolor
Wallis–Hazen (Hal B. Wallis)

A nightclub singer runs a fishing boat as a
hobby.
Empty-headed, lighter than air vehicle for star
fans.

w Edward Anhalt, Allan Weiss d Norman
Taurog ph Loyal Griggs m Joseph J. Lilley

Elvis Presley, Stella Stevens, Laurel Goodwin,
Jeremy Slate

The Girls of Pleasure Island

US 1953 96m Technicolor
Paramount (Paul Jones)

In 1945 the Marines land on a tiny Pacific
island, disturbing the life of an English
gentleman and his three inexperienced but
beautiful daughters.
Tedious and wholly artificial comedy with a
leaden touch, devised as a try-out for young
talent.

w F. Hugh Herbert d F. Hugh Herbert, Alvin
Ganzer ph Daniel Fapp m Lyn Murray

Leo Genn, Gene Barry, Don Taylor, Elsa
Lanchester, Dorothy Bromiley, Audrey
Dalton, Joan Elan

Give a Girl a Break*

US 1953 84m Technicolor
MGM (Jack Cummings)

A Broadway star walks out on a show and
three girls audition as replacements.
Minor musical vehicle for the Champions; an
agreeable time-passer.

w Frances Goodrich, Albert Hackett
d Stanley Donen ph William Mellor
md André Previn songs Ira Gershwin, Burton
Lane ch Stanley Donen, Gower Champion

Marge and Gower Champion, Debbie
Reynolds, Bob Fosse, Kurt Kasznar

Give Her a Ring

GB 1934 79m bw

A telephonist falls for her employer. Curious
romantic comedy attempting to woo
continental audiences. Clifford Mollison,
Wendy Barrie, Zelma O'Neal, Erik Rhodes,
Bertha Belmore, Stewart Granger (in a bit).
Written by Clifford Grey, Ernst Wolff,
Marjorie Deans and Wolfgang Wilhelm, from
a play by H. Rosenfeld; directed by Arthur
Woods; for BIP. 'Delightful and
unassuming'—*National Film Theatre, 1970*.

Give Me a Sailor

US 1938 80m bw
Paramount (Jeff Lazarus)

An ugly girl envies her sister her beaux, but
ends up winning a competition for beautiful
legs.
One of the double bill comedies which got
Bob Hope's career off to a shaky start.

w Doris Anderson, Frank Butler, *play* Anne
Nichols d Elliott Nugent ph Victor Milner
md Boris Morros

Martha Raye, Bob Hope, Betty Grable, Jack
Whiting, Clarence Kolb

Give Me Your Heart

US 1936 88m bw

A socialite has a child by a married man.
Dated tearjerker. Kay Francis, George Brent,
Patric Knowles, Roland Young, Henry
Stephenson, Frieda Inescort. Written by Casey
Robinson, from the play *Sweet Aloes* by Joyce
Carey; for Warner. (GB title: *Sweet Aloes*.)

Give My Regards to Broadway*

US 1948 89m Technicolor
TCF (Walter Morosco)

An old-time vaudevillian yearns to get back
into show business.
Pleasantly performed, sentimental family
musical with familiar tunes.

w Samuel Hoffenstein, Elizabeth Reinhardt
d Lloyd Bacon *ph* Harry Jackson

Dan Dailey, *Charles Winninger*, Fay Bainter,
Charles Ruggles, Nancy Guild

'Vaudeville is dead. I wish to God someone
would bury it.'—*James Agee*

Give Us the Moon
GB 1944   95m   bw
GFD / Gainsborough (Edward Black)

In post-war London a club is opened for idle
members only.
Whimsical comedy which fell with a dull thud.

wd Val Guest, *novel* The Elephant is White by
Caryl Brahms, S. J. Simon

Margaret Lockwood, Vic Oliver, Peter
Graves, Max Bacon, Roland Culver, Frank
Cellier, Jean Simmons

Give Us This Day
GB 1949   120m   bw
Plantagenet (Rod E. Geiger, N. A. Bronsten)
US title: *Salt to the Devil*

Depression struggles of an Italian immigrant
family in New York.
An unconvincing, self-pitying wallow, a very
curious enterprise for a British studio.

w Ben Barzman, *story* Christ in Concrete by
Pietro di Donato *d* Edward Dmytryk
ph C. Pennington Richards *m* Benjamin
Frankel

Sam Wanamaker, Lea Padovani, Kathleen
Ryan, Charles Goldner, Bonar Colleano,
William Sylvester, Karel Stepanek, Sidney
James

'Dmytryk insisted on cutting the film himself
and he has left in at least three spare reels.'—
Richard Winnington

'Worth making and worth seeing, but
cramped by its symbolism and its language.'—
Richard Mallett, Punch

Glamorous Night
GB 1937   81m   bw
ABP (Walter C. Mycroft)

An opera singer and her gypsy friends save a
Ruritanian king from his scheming prime
minister.
Modest transcription of a popular stage
musical.

w Dudley Leslie, Hugh Brooke, William
Freshman, *play* Ivor Novello *d* Brian
Desmond Hurst *m* Ivor Novello

Mary Ellis, Otto Kruger, Victor Jory, Barry
Mackay, Trefor Jones

Glamour
US 1934   74m   bw
Universal

A day in the life of a Broadway star.
Competent minor entertainment.

w Doris Anderson, *story* Edna Ferber
d William Wyler *ph* George Robinson

Constance Cummings, Paul Lukas, Philip
Reed, Joseph Cawthorne, Doris Lloyd, Olaf
Hytten

The Glass Bottom Boat
US 1966   110m   Metrocolor   Panavision
MGM / Arwin—Reame (Martin Melcher)

A young widow gets involved with spies.
Frantic spy spoof, pleasantly set on the
Californian coast, but overflowing with
pratfalls, messy slapstick and pointless guest
appearances.

w Everett Freeman *d* Frank Tashlin *ph* Leon
Shamroy *m* Frank de Vol

Doris Day, Rod Taylor, Arthur Godfrey, Paul
Lynde, John McGiver, Edward Andrews, Eric
Fleming, Dom De Luise

The Glass Key**
US 1935   87m   bw
Paramount (E. Lloyd Sheldon)

A slightly corrupt but good-natured politician
is saved by his henchman from being
implicated in a murder.
Lively transcription of a zesty crime novel.

w Kathryn Scola, Kubec Glasmon, Harry
Ruskin, *novel Dashiell Hammett d* Frank
Tuttle *ph* Henry Sharp

Edward Arnold, George Raft, Claire Dodd,
Rosalind Keith, Guinn Williams, Ray Milland

The Glass Key**
US 1942   85m   bw
Paramount (Fred Kohlmar)

Nifty remake of the above which finds some
limited talents in their best form, helped by a
plot which keeps one watching.

w Jonathan Latimer *d* Stuart Heisler
ph Theodor Sparkuhl m Victor Young

Brian Donlevy, Alan Ladd, Veronica Lake,
Bonita Granville, *William Bendix*, Richard
Denning, Joseph Calleia, Moroni Olsen

The Glass Menagerie**
US 1950   107m   bw
Warner (Jerry Wald, Charles K. Feldman)

A shy crippled girl seeks escape from the
shabby reality of life in St Louis and from her
mother's fantasies.

Pleasantly moody version of one of its author's lighter and more optimistic plays; fluent and good-looking production, memorable performances.

w *Tennessee Williams* (with Peter Berneis) from his play d *Irving Rapper* ph *Robert Burks* m Max Steiner

Gertrude Lawrence, Jane Wyman, Kirk Douglas, Arthur Kennedy
† For the TV movie starring Katharine Hepburn, see *Television Companion*.

The Glass Mountain
GB 1949 98m bw
Victoria (John Sutro, Joseph Janni, Fred Zelnik)

In the Dolomites, a married composer loves an Italian girl who saved his life during the war.
Tedious sudser, ineptly produced; an enormous British box office success because of its theme music.

w Joseph Janni, John Hunter, Emery Bonnet, Henry Cass, John Cousins d Henry Cass ph Otello Martelli, William McLeod m Nino Rota

Michael Denison, Dulcie Gray, Valentina Cortese, Tito Gobbi, Sebastian Shaw

The Glass Slipper
US 1954 94m Eastmancolor
MGM (Edwin H. Knopf)

The story of Cinderella.
To those used to the pantomime version this is dull, dreary, high-flown stuff: limbo sets, ballets, psychological rationalization and virtually no comedy.

w / ly Helen Deutsch d Charles Walters ph Arthur E. Arling m Bronislau Kaper ch Roland Petit

Leslie Caron, Michael Wilding, Elsa Lanchester, Barry Jones, *Estelle Winwood* (as Fairy Godmother)

The Glass Sphinx
Spain / Italy 1968 98m colour

An archaeologist is in danger because of his discoveries. Multi-national mish-mash only notable as one of the last films of its star.
Robert Taylor, Anita Ekberg, Gianna Sera, Jack Stuart. Written by Adriano Bolzoni and Louis M. Heyward; directed by Fulvio Lucisano; for AIP.

The Glass Web
US 1954 81m bw 3-D
U-I (A. J. Cohen)

A TV executive kills a blackmailing actress and allows a young scriptwriter to be accused. Boring thriller set in a TV studio.

w Robert Blees, Leonard Lee d Jack Arnold ph Maury Gertsman m Joseph Gershenson

Edward G. Robinson, John Forsythe, Marcia Henderson, Richard Denning

The Glenn Miller Story**
US 1954 116m Technicolor
U-I (Aaron Rosenberg)

The life of the unassuming trombonist and bandleader whose plane disappeared during World War II.
Competent musical heartwarmer with a well-cast star and successful reproduction of the Miller sound. A big box office hit.

w Valentine Davies, Oscar Brodney d Anthony Mann ph William Daniels md Henry Mancini, Joseph Gershenson

James Stewart, June Allyson, Harry Morgan, Charles Drake, Frances Langford, Louis Armstrong, Gene Krupa

AAN: script; music direction

A Global Affair
US 1963 84m bw
Seven Arts / Hall Bartlett

A United Nations official has to look after an abandoned baby.
Flat sentimental farce which embarrassingly tries to say something about the UN.

w Arthur Marx, Bob Fisher, Charles Lederer d Jack Arnold ph Joseph Ruttenberg m Dominic Frontière

Bob Hope, Lilo Pulver, Michèle Mercier, Yvonne de Carlo
  'Squaresville incarnate, with a side trip into Leersville.'—*Judith Crist, 1973*

Glorifying the American Girl*
US 1929 87m bw, colour sequence
Paramount (Florenz Ziegfeld)

A chorus girl rejects her boy friend for the sake of stardom.
Archetypal show-must-go-on musical.

w J. P. McEvoy, Millard Webb d Millard Webb, John Harkrider ph George Folsey md Frank Tours

Mary Eaton, Edward Crandall; and as guests Eddie Cantor, Helen Morgan, Rudy Vallee, Florenz Ziegfeld, Adolph Zukor, Otto Kahn, Texas Guinan, Mayor Jimmy Walker, Ring Lardner, Noah Beery, Johnny Weissmuller

The Glorious Adventure*
GB 1921 100m (approx) Prizmacolor silent
Stoll / J. Stuart Blackton

Various lives are affected by the Great Fire of London in 1666.
Stagey costume drama, notable only as the first British film in colour.

w Felix Orman d J. Stuart Blackton
ph William T. Crespinal

Lady Diana Manners, Victor McLaglen, Gerald Lawrence, Cecil Humphreys, Alex Crawford, Lennox Pawle (as Pepys)

Glorious Betsy
US 1928   90m approx   bw   silent

Napoleon's younger brother loves an American girl. Popular period romance of its day. Conrad Nagel, Dolores Costello, John Miljan, Betty Blythe. Written by Anthony Coldeway, from the play by Rida Johnson Young; directed by Alan Crosland; for Warner. (NB: Remade as *Hearts Divided*.)

Glory
US 1955   100m   Technicolor
   Superscope
RKO (David Butler)

Girl loves horse more than boy.
Conventional young love / Kentucky Derby marshmallow.

w Peter Milne d David Butler ph Wilfrid Cline m Frank Perkins

Margaret O'Brien, Walter Brennan, Charlotte Greenwood, John Lupton

Glory Alley
US 1952   79m   bw
MGM (Nicholas Nayfack)

A sullen young boxer has trouble with his girl, her father and the demon rum.
Flat, boring second feature with musical interludes.

w Art Cohn d Raoul Walsh ph William Daniels md Georgie Stoll

Leslie Caron, Ralph Meeker, Kurt Kasznar, Gilbert Roland, John McIntire, Louis Armstrong, Jack Teagarden
'This is the kind of film that contains bits of everything. New Orleans night life and an episode of the Korean war; an arty French ballet sequence and jazz from Louis Armstrong; a boxer who acquired a neurosis in childhood when his father hit him over the head and a blind old father with a French accent, who knows all about everything.'— *MFB*

The Glory Brigade
US 1953   82m   bw
TCF (William Bloom)

Greek soldiers fight in Korea alongside the Americans.
Modest war adventure with predictable racial tensions.

w Franklin Coen d Robert D. Webb
ph Lucien Andriot md Lionel Newman

Victor Mature, Alexander Scourby, Lee Marvin, Richard Egan

The Glory Guys*
US 1965   112m   De Luxe   Panavision
UA / Levy–Gardner–Laven

Officers of the US cavalry disagree about dealing with the Indians.
Standard big-budget western.

w Sam Peckinpah, *novel* The Dice of God by Hoffman Birney d Arnold Laven ph James Wong Howe m Riz Ortolani

Tom Tryon, Harve Presnell, Senta Berger, Andrew Duggan, James Caan, Slim Pickens, Michael Anderson Jnr

The Gnome-Mobile*
US 1967   90m   Technicolor
Walt Disney (James Algar)

A millionaire and his family go for a forest picnic and help a colony of gnomes.
Cheerful adventures for small children, with good trick work.

w Ellis Kadison, *novel* Upton Sinclair
d Robert Stevenson ph Edward Colman
m Buddy Baker

Walter Brennan, Matthew Garber, Karen Dotrice, Richard Deacon, Sean McClory, Ed Wynn, Jerome Cowan, Charles Lane

The Go-Between**
GB 1970   116m   Technicolor
EMI / World Film Services (John Heyman, Norman Priggen)

Staying at a stately home around the turn of the century, 12-year-old Leo carries love letters from a farmer to his friend's sister.
A rather tiresome plot sustains a rich picture of the Edwardian gentry, a milieu with which however the director is not at home and treats far too slowly and trickily.

w Harold Pinter, *novel* L. P. Hartley
d Joseph Losey ph Geoffrey Fisher m Michel Legrand ad Carmen Dillon

Alan Bates, Julie Christie, Michael Redgrave, Dominic Guard, Michael Gough, Margaret Leighton, Edward Fox
'It's an almost palpable recreation of a past environment, and that environment is the film's real achievement, not the drama enacted within it.'—*Stanley Kauffmann*

AAN: Margaret Leighton

The Go-Getter
US 1937 90m bw
Warner (Sam Bischoff)

A one-legged navy veteran is determined that his injury will not prevent him from becoming a success.
Moderate comedy-drama, agreeably played.

w Delmer Daves, Peter B. Kyne d Busby Berkeley ph Arthur Edeson md Leo F. Forbstein

George Brent, Charles Winninger, Anita Louise, John Eldredge, Henry O'Neill, Willard Robertson, Eddie Acuff

Go for a Take
GB 1972 90m colour ·
Rank / Century Films (Roy Simpson)

Two waiters in debt to a gangster take refuge in a film studio.
Painful British farce.

w Alan Hackney d Harry Booth ph Mark McDonald m Glen Mason

Reg Varney, Norman Rossington, Sue Lloyd, Dennis Price, Julie Ege, Patrick Newell, David Lodge

Go for Broke
US 1951 93m bw
MGM (Dore Schary)

World War II exploits of Japanese-American soldiers.
Absolutely unsurprising war film with all the anti-Japs converted by the end. Production quite good.

wd Robert Pirosh ph Paul C. Vogel m Alberto Columbo

Van Johnson, Lane Nakano, George Miki, Akira Fukunaga, Warner Anderson, Don Haggerty

AAN: Robert Pirosh (as writer)

Go into Your Dance**
US 1935 89m bw
Warner (Sam Bischoff)
GB title: Casino de Paree

A big-headed star gets his come-uppance and finds happiness.
Moderate backstage musical notable for the only teaming of Jolson and Keeler, who were then married.

w Earl Baldwin d Archie Mayo ph Tony Gaudio. Sol Polito songs Harry Warren, Al Dubin

Al Jolson, Ruby Keeler, Glenda Farrell, Benny Rubin, Phil Regan, Barton MacLane, Sharon Lynne, Akim Tamiroff, Helen Morgan, Patsy Kelly

Go Man Go
US 1954 82m bw
Alfred Palca (Anton M. Leader)

How Abe Saperstein moulded and trained the Harlem Globetrotters basketball team.
Not so much a film as an athletic demonstration with some actors round the edges.

w Arnold Becker d James Wong Howe ph Bill Steiner m Alex North

Dane Clark, Sidney Poitier, Pat Breslin, Edmond Ryan

Go Naked in the World
US 1960 103m Metrocolor Cinemascope
MGM / Arcola (Aaron Rosenberg)

A prostitute causes a rift between son and millionaire father.
Antediluvian melodrama with overblown performances.

wd Ranald MacDougall, novel Tom Chanales ph Milton Krasner m Adolph Deutsch

Gina Lollobrigida, Tony Franciosa, Ernest Borgnine, Luana Patten, Will Kuluva, Philip Ober

'A good example of how the increased liberation of Hollywood can be misused.'— MFB

Go Tell the Spartans
US 1978 114m CFI color
Spartan Company (Allan F. Badah, Mitchell Cannold)

In Vietnam, a seasoned commander tries to get a platoon of raw soldiers out of a Vietcong ambush.
We have been here before, in other wars, and since there is little heroism to be had from Vietnam it is difficult to see why we are invited again.

w Wendell Mayes, story Daniel Ford d Ted Post ph Harry Stradling Jnr m Dick Halligan

Burt Lancaster, Craig Wasson, Jonathan Goldsmith, Marc Singer

Go to Blazes
GB 1961 84m Technicolor Cinemascope
ABP (Kenneth Harper)

Ex-convicts become firemen, intending to use the engine for smash and grab raids.
Mild comedy ruined by wide screen.

w Patrick Campbell, Vivienne Knight d Michael Truman ph Erwin Hillier m John Addison

Dave King, Daniel Massey, Norman Rossington, Wilfrid Lawson, Maggie Smith, Robert Morley, Coral Browne

Go West*
US 1925   70m (24 fps)   bw   silent
Metro-Goldwyn / Buster Keaton (Joseph M. Schenck)

A tenderfoot makes friends with a cow and takes it everywhere.
Disappointingly slow star comedy with splendid moments.

w Raymond Cannon d Buster Keaton
ph Bert Haines, E. Lessley

Buster Keaton, Howard Truesdall, Kathleen Myers

Go West**
US 1940   82m   bw
MGM (Jack Cummings)

Three zanies tackle a western villain.
Minor Marx comedy with a good start (the ticket office sketch) and a rousing finale as they take a moving train to bits, but some pretty soggy stuff in between.

w Irving Brecher d Edward Buzzell
ph Leonard Smith m Bronislau Kaper
md Georgie Stoll

Groucho, Harpo, Chico, John Carroll, Diana Lewis, Robert Barrat

Go West Young Lady
US 1940   70m   bw

A lawless western town expects a sheriff who turns out to be a girl. Mildly pleasing variation on *Destry Rides Again*. Glenn Ford, Penny Singleton, Charles Ruggles. Written by Karen de Wolf and Richard Flournoy; directed by Frank Strayer; for Columbia.

Go West Young Man
US 1936   80m   bw
Paramount (Emmanuel R. Cohen)

A movie star has a car breakdown in Pennsylvania and falls for a local lad.
Cleaned-up Mae West vehicle, all rather boring.

w Mae West, *play* Personal Appearance by Lawrence Riley d Henry Hathaway ph Karl Struss m George Stoll

Mae West, Randolph Scott, Warren William, Lyle Talbot, Alice Brady, Isabel Jewell, Elizabeth Patterson

'Quite incredibly tedious, as slow and wobbling in its pace as Miss West's famous walk. The wisecracks lack the old impudence, and seldom have so many feet of film been expended on a mere dirty look.'—*Graham Greene*

God Is My Co-Pilot
US 1945   89m   bw
Warner (Robert Buckner)

Pacific air adventures during World War II.
Adequate flagwaver.

w Peter Milne, Abem Finkel, *book* Col.
Robert Lee Scott Jnr d Robert Florey ph Sid Hickox m Franz Waxman

Dennis Morgan, Dane Clark, Raymond Massey, Alan Hale, Andrea King, John Ridgely, Stanley Ridges, Craig Stevens
  'A slapped-together attraction . . . all the flashbacks, supposedly emotional scenes, and fragments of philosophy which punctuate the aerial action vitiate a tale which might have been a notable addition to the screen's extensive considerations of the far-flung theatres of the war.'—*Howard Barnes, New York Herald Tribune*

The Goddess°
US 1958   105m   bw
Columbia (Milton Perlman)

A small-town girl becomes a Hollywood sex symbol and lives to regret it.
Savage attack on the Marilyn Monroe cult, a bit lachrymose and compromised by miscasting, but with interesting detail.

w *Paddy Chayevsky* d John Cromwell
ph Arthur J. Ornitz m Virgil Thompson

Kim Stanley, Lloyd Bridges, Steven Hill, Betty Lou Holland

AAN: Paddy Chayevsky

The Godfather°°°
US 1971   175m   Technicolor
Paramount / Alfran (Albert S. Ruddy)

When, after ruling for two generations, the Mafia's New York head dies of old age, his son takes over reluctantly but later learns how to kill.
A brilliantly-made film with all the fascination of a snake pit: a warm-hearted family saga except that the members are thieves and murderers. Cutting would help, but the duller conversational sections do heighten the cunningly judged moments of suspense and violence.

w Francis Ford Coppola, Mario Puzo, *novel* Mario Puzo d *Francis Ford Coppola*
ph Gordon Willis m Nino Rota pd Dean Tavoularis

Marlon Brando (unintentionally comic in an absurd make-up), *Al Pacino*, Robert Duvall, James Caan, Richard Castellano, Diane Keaton, Talia Shire, Richard Conte, John Marley

'The immorality lies in his presentation of murderers as delightful family men—the criminal is the salt of the earth—and to our shame we rub it into the wounds of our Watergate-world morality and even ask for more.'—*Judith Crist, 1974*

'They have put pudding in Brando's cheeks and dirtied his teeth, he speaks hoarsely and moves stiffly, and these combined mechanics are hailed as great acting . . . Like star, like film, the keynote is inflation. *The Godfather* was made from a big bestseller, a lot of money was spent on it, and it runs over three hours. Therefore it's important.'—*Stanley Kauffmann*

AA: best picture; script; Marlon Brando
AAN: Francis Ford Coppola (as director); Al Pacino; Robert Duvall; James Caan

The Godfather, Part Two***
US 1974   200m   Technicolor
Paramount / the Coppola Company
  (Francis Ford Coppola)

In 1958, Michael Corleone reflects on the problems of himself and his father before him. Curious rehash of part of the original with new scenes, a shade difficult to follow but full of good scenes and performances.

w Francis Ford Coppola, Mario Puzo
d Francis Ford Coppola ph Gordon Willis
m Nino Rota pd Dean Tavoularis

Al Pacino, *Robert de Niro*, Diane Keaton, Robert Duvall, John Cazale, Lee Strasberg, Michael V. Gazzo, Talia Shire, Troy Donahue
'The complete work is an epic vision of the corruption of America.'—*New Yorker*
† The two films were eventually combined and extended for television into a ten-hour serial, *The Godfather Saga.*

AA: best picture; script; Francis Ford Coppola (as director); Nino Rota; Robert de Niro
AAN: Al Pacino; Lee Strasberg; Michael V. Gazzo; Talia Shire

God's Country and the Woman
US 1936   80m   Technicolor
Warner (Lou Edelman)

The junior partner of a lumber company goes to work undercover in an opponent's camp, causes trouble, and falls in love.
Adequate outdoor melodrama in early colour.

w Norman Reilly Raine, *novel* James Oliver Curwood d William Keighley ph Tony Gaudio m Max Steiner

George Brent, Beverly Roberts, Barton MacLane, Robert Barrat, Alan Hale, Addison Richards, El Brendel, Roscoe Ates, Billy Bevan

God's Little Acre*
US 1958   110m   bw
Security (Sidney Harmon)

A poor white farmer in Georgia neglects his land in a fruitless search for gold.
Tobacco Road under another name, and not so lively: bowdlerized and eventually tedious despite a welter of sensational incident and depraved characters.

w Philip Yordan, *novel* Erskine Caldwell
d Anthony Mann ph Ernest Haller m Elmer Bernstein

Robert Ryan, Aldo Ray, Tina Louise, Buddy Hackett, Jack Lord, Vic Morrow, Rex Ingram

Godspell*
US 1973   102m   TVC color
Columbia / Lansbury / Duncan / Beruh
  (Edgar Lansbury)

The Gospel according to St Matthew played out musically by hippies in the streets of New York.
Wild and woolly film version of the successful theatrical fantasy, surviving chiefly by virtue of its gleaming photography.

w David Greene, John Michael Tebelak, *play* John Michael Tebelak d David Greene ph Richard G. Heimann m / ly Stephen Schwarz

Victor Garber, David Haskell, Jerry Sroka, Lynne Thigpen, Robin Lamont
'A patch of terra incognita somewhere between *Sesame Street* and the gospel according to *Laugh-In*.'—*Bruce Williamson*

Gog*
US 1954   85m   Color Corporation   3D
Ivan Tors

In an underground laboratory in New Mexico, a giant computer controls two robots, and a spy programmes it to kill.
Brisk, imaginative low-budget sci-fi in gleaming colour, well staged and developed.

w Tom Taggart d Herbert B. Strock
ph Lothrop B. Worth m Harry Sukman

Richard Egan, Constance Dowling, Herbert Marshall

Goha
France / Tunisia 1957   90m   Agfacolor
Films Franco-Africains

A young Arab helps a blind musician and falls in love with a wise man's young bride.
Curiously winning, good-looking little romance which, apart from an unexpected sad ending, plays like an update of the Arabian Nights.

w Georges Schéhadé, *novel* Le Livre de Goha le Simple by A. Ades, A. Jospiovici *d* Jacques Baratier *ph* Jean Bourgoin *m* Maurice Ohana

Omar Chérif (later Sharif), Zina Bouzaiane, Lauro Gazzolo

Going Bye Bye**
US 1934 20m bw

A violent convict escapes to take vengeance on the two innocents whose evidence sent him up. Splendid star comedy displaying most of the team's most endearing aspects. Laurel and Hardy, Walter Long, Mae Busch. Written by Anon; directed by Charles Rogers; for Hal Roach.

Going Hollywood*
US 1933 80m bw

A crooner is pursued by a girl who poses as a French maid. Lively comedy with a studio setting; anything goes. Bing Crosby, Marion Davies, Patsy Kelly, Stuart Erwin. Written by Donald Ogden Stewart; directed by Raoul Walsh; for MGM.

Going Home
US 1971 98m colour

An ex-convict who killed his wife while drunk assumes an ambivalent relationship with his son. Thoroughly uninteresting melodrama which was barely released. Robert Mitchum, Jan-Michael Vincent, Brenda Vaccaro. Written by Lawrence Marcus; directed by Herbert B. Leonard; for MGM.

Going in Style
US 1979 97m Technicolor
Warner / Tony Bill

Three bored elderly men decide to plan a bank robbery.
Curiously aimless sentimental comedy-drama which is simply neither funny enough, thrilling enough or moving enough to hold the interest.
wd Martin Brest *ph* Billy Williams *m* Michael Small

George Burns, Art Carney, Lee Strasberg

Going My Way**
US 1944 126m bw
Paramount (Leo McCarey)

A young priest comes to a New York slum parish and after initial friction charms the old pastor he is to succeed.
Sentimental comedy which got away with it wonderfully at the time, largely through careful casting, though it seems thin and obvious now.

w Frank Butler, Frank Cavett, Leo McCarey *d* Leo McCarey *ph* Lionel Lindon *m* Robert Emmett Dolan *songs* Johnny Burke, James Van Heusen, J. R. Shannon

Bing Crosby, Barry Fitzgerald, Rise Stevens, Frank McHugh, James Brown, Gene Lockhart, Jean Heather, Porter Hall
'I should not feel safe in recommending it to anyone but a simple-hearted sentimentalist with a taste for light music.'—*Richard Mallett, Punch*
'The lessons, if I read them right, are that leisureliness can be excellent, that if you take a genuine delight in character the universe is opened to you, and perhaps above all that a movie, like any other genuine work of art, must be made for love. But I am willing to bet that the chief discernible result of *Going My Way* will be an anxiety-ridden set of vaudeville sketches about Pat and Mike in cassocks.'— *James Agee*
† Father O'Malley reappeared in *The Bells of St Mary's* and *Say One for Me* (both qv).
AA: best picture; script; original story (Leo McCarey); Leo McCarey (direction); Bing Crosby; Barry Fitzgerald, song, 'Swinging on a Star' (*m* James Van Heusen, *ly* Johnny Burke)
AAN: Lionel Lindon

Going Places
US 1939 84m bw

A sporting goods salesman poses as a jockey and has to ride a horse to victory. Thin musical spurred by the hit song 'Jeepers Creepers'. Dick Powell, Anita Louise, Ronald Reagan, Louis Armstrong, Allen Jenkins, Walter Catlett. Written by Jerry Wald, Sig Herzig and Maurice Leo, from the play *The Hottentot* (filmed thrice previously) by Victor Mapes and William Collier; directed by Ray Enright; for Warner.

Goin' South
US 1978 101m Metrocolor
Paramount (Henry Gittes, Harold Schneider)

An unwashed outlaw is saved from the rope when a young girl promises to marry and reform him . . .
. . . for no very good reason. Curious semi-comic western which might have made a good two-reeler.

w John Herman Shaner, Al Ramrus, Charles Shyer, Alan Mandel *d* Jack Nicholson *ph* Nestor Almendros *m* Van Dyke Parks, Perry Botkin Jnr

Jack Nicholson, Mary Steenburgen, Christopher Lloyd, John Belushi, Veronica Cartwright, Richard Bradford

Going to Town*
US 1935 74m bw
Paramount (William Le Baron)

A western oil heiress moves into society.
Reasonably satisfactory Mae West vehicle, the
last in fact before the censor killed her style.

w Mae West d Alexander Hall ph Karl
Struss songs Sammy Fain, Irving Kahal

Mae West, Paul Cavanagh, Ivan Lebedeff,
Tito Coral, Marjorie Gateson, Fred Kohler
Snr, Monroe Owsley

Gold**
GB 1974 124m Technicolor
  Panavision
Hemdale / Avton (Michael Klinger)

A South African mining engineer falls for the
boss's granddaughter and exposes a
conspiracy.
Old-fashioned thick ear with spectacular
underground sequences and a rousing finale.

w Wilbur Smith, Stanley Price d Peter Hunt
ph Ousama Rawi m Elmer Bernstein

Roger Moore, Susannah York, Ray Milland,
Bradford Dillman, John Gielgud, Tony
Beckley

AAN: song 'Wherever Love Takes Me'
(m Elmer Bernstein, ly Don Black)

Gold Diggers of Broadway*
US 1929 98m Technicolor
Warner

Three Broadway chorus girls seek rich
husbands.
Fascinating primitive musical.

w Robert Lord, play The Gold Diggers by
Avery Hopwood d Roy del Ruth ph Barney
McGill, Ray Rennahan songs Al Dubin, Joe
Burke

Nancy Welford, Conway Tearle, Winnie
Lightner, Ann Pennington, Lilyan Tashman,
William Bakewell, Nick Lucas

'Exceeds in pretentiousness and beauty
anything which has yet appeared on the
screen!'—publicity

† Other versions of the play include The Gold
Diggers (1923), Gold Diggers of 1933 (qv),
Painting the Clouds with Sunshine (qv).

Gold Diggers of 1933*
US 1933 96m bw
Warner (Robert Lord)

Cheerful, competent, well-cast remake of the
above; numbers include 'My Forgotten Man',
'We're in the Money' and 'Pettin' in the Park'.

w Erwin Gelsey, James Seymour, David
Boehm, Ben Markson d Mervyn Le Roy
ch Busby Berkeley songs Harry Warren, Al
Dubin ph Sol Polito

Warren William, Joan Blondell, Aline
MacMahon, Ruby Keeler, Dick Powell, Guy
Kibbee, Ned Sparks, Ginger Rogers, Clarence
Nordstrom

'It sums up what is meant by the phrase
"pure thirties": electrically wired chorus girls
singing "In the Shadows Let Me Come and
Sing to You" merge to form a big illuminated
violin.'—New Yorker, 1979

'It is memorable chiefly because Busby
Berkeley created a mad geometry of patterned
chorines. . . . The innocent vulgarity of the
big numbers is charming and uproarious, and
aesthetically preferable to the pretentious
ballet finales of fifties musicals like An
American in Paris. Even those of us who were
children at the time did not mistake Gold
Diggers for art—and certainly no one took it
for life.'—Pauline Kael, 1968

'Your dream of perfect beauty come
true!'—publicity

Gold Diggers of 1935**
US 1935 95m bw
Warner (Robert Lord)

A socialite puts on a Broadway show at her
country home, and is taken in by a swindler.
Heavy-handed but laugh-provoking comedy
with familiar faces of the day, climaxed by big
numbers including 'Lullaby of Broadway'.

w Manuel Seff, Peter Milne, Robert Lord
d / ch Busby Berkeley ph George Barnes
songs Al Dubin, Harry Warren

Dick Powell, Adolphe Menjou, Gloria Stuart,
Alice Brady, Hugh Herbert, Glenda Farrell,
Frank McHugh, Grant Mitchell, Wini Shaw

'Busby Berkeley, the master of scenic
prestidigitation, continues to dazzle the eye
and stun the imagination.'—André Sennwald,
New York Times

'A decidedly heady mixture.'—Pare Lorentz

AA: song 'Lullaby of Broadway'

Gold Diggers of 1937*
US 1937 100m bw
Warner (Hal B. Wallis)

A group of insurance salesmen back a show.
Mild tailing-off of the Gold Diggers series,
though with the accustomed production
polish.

w Warren Duff, play Richard Maibaum,
Michael Wallach, George Haight d Lloyd
Bacon ch Busby Berkeley ph Arthur Edeson
songs Harry Warren, Al Dubin, E. Y. Harburg,
Harold Arlen

Dick Powell, Joan Blondell, Glenda Farrell, Victor Moore, Lee Dixon, Osgood Perkins, Charles D. Brown

Gold Diggers in Paris*
US 1938   95m   bw
Warner (Sam Bischoff)
GB title: *The Gay Imposters*

Three girls chase rich husbands abroad.
A thin end to the series, saved by an agreeable cast.

w Earl Baldwin, Warren Duff   *d* Ray Enright *ph* Sol Polito, George Barnes   *ch* Busby Berkeley   *songs* Harry Warren, Al Dubin, Johnny Mercer

Rudy Vallee, Rosemary Lane, Hugh Herbert, Allen Jenkins, Gloria Dickson, Melville Cooper, Fritz Feld, Ed Brophy, Curt Bois

Gold Is Where You Find It*
US 1938   90m   Technicolor
Warner (Sam Bischoff)

Gold rush miners settle as California farmers.
Agreeable western in excellent early colour.

w Warren Duff, Clements Ripley, Robert Buckner   *d* Michael Curtiz   *ph* Sol Polito *m* Max Steiner

George Brent, Olivia de Havilland, Claude Rains, Margaret Lindsay, John Litel, Marcia Ralston, Barton MacLane, Tim Holt, Sidney Toler

Gold of Naples
Italy 1955   135m   bw
Ponti-de Laurentiis
original title: *L'Oro di Napoli*

Six sketches, comic and tragic, give an impression of Naples today.
A variable collection, mainly shown around the world in abridged versions.

w Cesare Zavattini, Vittorio de Sica, Giuseppe Marotta   *d* Vittorio de Sica *ph* Otello Martelli   *m* Alessandro Cicognini

Vittorio de Sica, Eduardo de Filippo, Toto, Sophia Loren, Paolo Stoppa, Silvana Mangano

Gold of the Seven Saints
US 1961   89m   bw   Warnerscope
Warner (Leonard Freeman)

Cowboys compete in a search for lost gold.
Adequate minor western using TV stars.

w Leigh Brackett, Leonard Freeman *d* Gordon Douglas   *ph* Joseph Biroc *m* Howard Jackson

Clint Walker, Roger Moore, Leticia Roman, Robert Middleton, Chill Wills, Gene Evans

The Golden Age of Buster Keaton**
US 1975   97m   bw
Jay Ward (Raymond Rohauer)

A useful introductory package to the shorts and features of Buster Keaton, with most of the great silent scenes present.
commentary Bill Scott

The Golden Age of Comedy****
US 1957   78m   bw
Robert Youngson Productions

First of the scholarly compilations of silent comedy which saved many negatives from destruction, this is a fast-paced general survey which despite a facetious sound track does provide a laugh a minute. It particularly brought Laurel and Hardy back into public notice, and includes sections from *Two Tars* and *The Battle of the Century*.

wd Robert Youngson   *narrators* Dweight Weist, Ward Wilson   *m* George Steiner

Stan Laurel, Oliver Hardy, Harry Langdon, Ben Turpin, Will Rogers, Billy Bevan, Charlie Chase, Andy Clyde

Golden Arrow
US 1936   68m   bw

An heiress tricks a newspaper reporter into a marriage of convenience. Dull, schematic romantic comedy. Bette Davis, George Brent, Eugene Pallette, Dick Foran. Written by Charles Kenyon, from the play by Michael Arlen; directed by Alfred E. Green; for Warner.

Golden Arrow
GB 1949   82m   bw

On a transcontinental train, three men have different daydreams about the same girl. Transparent portmanteau comedy which didn't click. Jean Pierre Aumont, Paula Valenska, Richard Murdoch, Kathleen Harrison, Karel Stepanek, Edward Lexy. Written by Paul Darcy and Sid Colin; directed by Gordon Parry; for Anatole de Grunwald. (Alternative title: *Three Men and a Girl*.)

The Golden Blade
US 1953   80m   Technicolor
U-I (Richard Wilson)

With the help of a magic sword, Harun saves a princess and captures a rebel.
Standard cut-rate Arabian Nights adventure, very typical of its studio during the fifties.

w John Rich   *d* Nathan Juran   *ph* Maury Gertsman   *m* Joseph Gershenson

Rock Hudson, Piper Laurie, George Macready, Gene Evans, Kathleen Hughes

Golden Boy*
US 1939 101m bw
Columbia (William Perlberg)

A poor boy is torn between two absorbing interests: prizefighting and the violin. Personalized version of a socially conscious play; moderately effective with smooth production and good cast.

w Lewis Meltzer, Daniel Taradash, Sarah Y. Mason, Victor Heerman, *play* Clifford Odets *d* Rouben Mamoulian *ph* Nicholas Musuraca, Karl Freund *m* Victor Young *md* Morris Stoloff

Barbara Stanwyck, *William Holden*, Adolphe Menjou, Joseph Calleia, *Lee J. Cobb*, Sam Levene, Edward Brophy, Don Beddoe
'A slick, swift, exciting but insensitive movie.'—*Gordon Sager*
'Interesting, entertaining, dramatic, but scarcely first-rate.'—*Frank Nugent, New York Times*

AAN: Victor Young

The Golden Coach
Italy / France 1952 100m Technicolor
Hoche / Panaria (Francesco Alliata)
original title: *Le Carrosse d'Or*

In Spanish South America in the 18th century, the leading lady of a band of strolling players turns all heads including that of the viceroy, who scandalizes all by making her a present of his official golden coach.
The director seems to have been chiefly interested in the colour and the backgrounds: the story is a bore and the leading lady ill-chosen.

w Jean Renoir, Jack Kirkland, Renzo Avanzo, Giulio Macchi *d* Jean Renoir *ph Claude Renoir m* Vivaldi

Anna Magnani, Duncan Lamont, Paul Campbell, Ricardo Rioli, William Tubbs

Golden Earrings*
US 1947 95m bw
Paramount (Harry Tugend)

A British Intelligence officer is helped by a gypsy to sneak a poison gas formula out of Nazi Germany.
One of the silliest stories of all time, despite the presence of Quentin Reynolds asserting that he believed it; also lacking in the humour which might have saved it, but produced with polish and interesting for the two stars at this stage in their careers.

w Abraham Polonsky, Frank Butler, Helen Deutsch, *novel* Yolanda Foldes *d* Mitchell Leisen *ph* Daniel L. Fapp *m* Victor Young

Ray Milland, Marlene Dietrich, Murvyn Vye, Bruce Lester, Dennis Hoey, Reinhold Schuntzel, Ivan Triesault
'A good deal of torso work goes on which I can't help feeling they're a bit old for.'—*Richard Winnington*

Golden Girl*
US 1951 108m Technicolor
TCF (George Jessel)

The story of Lotta Crabtree, who after the Civil War determined to become a great musical star.
Harmless semi-western biopic with good tunes.

w Walter Bullock, Charles O'Neal, Gladys Lehman *d* Lloyd Bacon *ph* Charles G. Clarke *md* Lionel Newman *ch* Seymour Felix

Mitzi Gaynor, Dale Robertson, Dennis Day, James Barton, Una Merkel, Raymond Walburn, Gene Sheldon

AAN: song 'Never' (*m* Lionel Newman, *ly* Eliot Daniel)

Golden Gloves
US 1940 69m bw

A sports reporter cleans up a boxing racket. Competent second feature. Richard Denning, Jeanne Cagney, William Frawley, Robert Ryan. Written by Maxwell Shane and Lewis R. Foster; directed by Edward Dmytryk; for Paramount.

The Golden Hawk
US 1952 83m Technicolor

A pirate determines to avenge his mother's death at the hands of the governor of Cartagena. Clean-cut period romp for boys who don't demand realism. Sterling Hayden, Rhonda Fleming, John Sutton, Helena Carter, Paul Cavanagh. Written by Robert E. Kent, from the novel by Frank Yerby; directed by Sidney Salkow; for Columbia.

The Golden Head
US / Hungary 1964 115m
   Technirama 70
Cinerama / Hungarofilm

Passengers on a Danube pleasure boat become involved in the theft of the golden head of St Laszlo.
Travelogue with a thin plot, somewhat slow moving but suitable for children.

w Stanley Boulder, Ivan Boldizsar *d* Richard Thorpe *ph* Istvan Hildebrand *m* Peter Fenyes

George Sanders, Buddy Hackett, Douglas Wilmer, Jess Conrad, Robert Coote

The Golden Horde
US 1951　76m　Technicolor
U-I (Howard Christie)
aka: *The Golden Horde of Genghis Khan*

Crusaders meet Mongols in Samarkand, and
Sir Guy wins a princess.
Rather priceless idiocies are perpetrated in
this variation on the studio's favourite Arabian
Nights theme, but somehow they fail to make
one laugh, which should be the only possible
response to such a farrago.

w Gerald Drayson Adams *d* George
Sherman *ph* Russell Metty *m* Hans Salter

David Farrar, Ann Blyth, George Macready,
Henry Brandon, Richard Egan, Marvin Miller

The Golden Madonna
GB 1949　88m　bw
IFP / Pendennis (John Stafford)

Two young people search Italy for a religious
painting stolen by thieves.
Stilted but eager to please, this romantic
comedy-drama seemed a bit lacking in drive.

w Akos Tolnay *d* Ladislas Vajda *ph* Anchise
Brizzi

Phyllis Calvert, Michael Rennie, Tullio
Carminati, David Greene, Aldo Silvani

The Golden Mistress*
US 1954　80m　Technicolor
UA / RK (Richard Kay, Harry Rybnick)

An American and his girl friend search the sea
bed for the forbidden treasure of a Haitian
tribe.
Curious independent production, an adventure
in the style of silent serials; amateur in many
ways, yet with a freshness of photography and
location plus some powerful voodoo scenes.

wd Fred Judge *ph* William C. Thompson
m Raoul Kraushaar

John Agar, Rosemarie Bowe, Abner
Biberman

Golden Needles
US 1974　92m　Movielab　Panavision
AIP / Sequoia (Fred Weintraub, Paul Heller)

Various factions seek a Hong Kong statue
showing seven miraculous acupuncture points.
Youth / sex / Kung Fu / James Bond action
amalgam.

w S. Lee Pogostin, Sylvia Schneble *d* Robert
Clouse *ph* Gilbert Hubbs *m* Lalo Schifrin

Joe Don Baker, Elizabeth Ashley, Jim Kelly,
Burgess Meredith, Ann Sothern

Golden Rendezvous
US 1977　109m　colour
Film Trust / Milton Okun (Andre Pieterse)

Murderous mercenaries take over a freighter,
but reckon without the courageous first officer.
Blood-and-thunder hokum with many
casualties but not much sense.

w Stanley Price, *novel* Alistair MacLean
d Ashley Lazarus *ph* Ken Higgins *m* Jeff
Wayne

Richard Harris, Ann Turkel, David Janssen,
Burgess Meredith, John Vernon, Gordon
Jackson, Keith Baxter, Dorothy Malone, John
Carradine, Robert Flemyng, Leigh Lawson,
Robert Beatty

The Golden Salamander
GB 1949　87m　bw
GFD / Pinewood (Ronald Neame,
　Alexander Galperson)

An Englishman in Tunis defeats gun runners.
Boring and unconvincing action hokum.

w Lesley Storm, Victor Canning, Ronald
Neame, *novel* Victor Canning *d* Ronald
Neame *ph* Oswald Morris *m* William Alwyn

Trevor Howard, Anouk Aimée, Herbert Lom,
Miles Malleson, Walter Rilla, Jacques Sernas,
Wilfrid Hyde-White, Peter Copley

The Golden Voyage of Sinbad*
GB 1973　105m　Eastmancolor
Columbia / Morningside (Charles H.
　Schneer)

Sinbad finds a strange map and crosses swords
with a great magician.
Routine, rather uninspired fantasy enlivened
by grotesque trick effects.

w Brian Clemens, Ray Harryhausen
d Gordon Hessler *ph* Ted Moore *m* Miklos
Rozsa *sp* Ray Harryhausen *pd* John Stoll

John Philip Law, Caroline Munro, Tom
Baker, Douglas Wilmer, Grégoire Aslan

Goldfinger**
GB 1964　112m　Technicolor
UA / Eon (Harry Saltzman, Albert R.
　Broccoli)

James Bond prevents an international gold
smuggler from robbing Fort Knox.
Probably the liveliest and most amusing of the
Bond spy spoofs, with a fairly taut plot
between the numerous highlights. The big
budget is well used.

w Richard Maibaum, Paul Dehn, *novel* Ian
Fleming *d* Guy Hamilton *ph* Ted Moore
m John Barry *pd* Ken Adam　titles Robert
Brownjohn

Sean Connery, Honor Blackman, Gert Frobe,
Harold Sakata, Shirley Eaton, Bernard Lee,
Lois Maxwell, Desmond Llewellyn

'A dazzling object lesson in the principle
that nothing succeeds like excess.'—*Penelope*
Gilliatt

'A diverting comic strip for grown-ups.'—
Judith Crist

The Goldwyn Follies**
US 1938   115m   Technicolor
Samuel Goldwyn

A Hollywood producer seeks the average girl
to test his scripts.
Goldwyn's failure to become Ziegfeld, chiefly
due to a lack of humour in the script, still has
a soupçon of effective Hollywood satire and
some excellent numbers.

w Ben Hecht *d* George Marshall *ph* Gregg
Toland *m* Alfred Newman *ch* George
Balanchine *ad* Richard Day

Kenny Baker, Vera Zorina, *the Ritz Brothers,*
Adolphe Menjou, Edgar Bergen and Charlie
McCarthy, Helen Jepson, Phil Baker, Ella
Logan, Bobby Clark, Jerome Cowan, Nydia
Westman, Andrea Leeds

AAN: Alfred Newman

The Golem***
Germany 1920   75m approx   bw   silent
UFA

In 16th-century Prague a Jewish Rabbi
constructs a man of clay to defend his people
against a pogrom.
There were several versions of this story
(Germany 1913, sequel 1917; Czechoslovakia
1935 and 1951), but this is almost certainly the
best, its splendid sets, performances and
certain scenes all being clearly influential on
later Hollywood films, especially *Frankenstein.*

w Paul Wegener, Henrik Galeen *d* Paul
Wegener, Carl Boese *ph* Karl Freund, Guido
Seeber *ad* Hans Poelzig
Paul Wegener, Albert Steinruck, Ernst
Deutsch

Gone to Earth
GB 1948   110m   Technicolor
London Films / David O. Selznick
US title: *The Wild Heart*

In the 1890s, a wild Shropshire girl is desired
by the local squire.
Unintentionally funny film version of an
intractable novel.

w / p / d Michael Powell and Emeric
Pressburger, *novel* Mary Webb
ph Christopher Challis *m* Brian Easdale
pd Hein Heckroth

Jennifer Jones, David Farrar, Cyril Cusack,
Esmond Knight, Sybil Thorndike, Edward
Chapman, George Cole, Hugh Griffith,
Beatrice Varley

'It tries hard to be a powerful work of art,
but it is intrinsically artificial and
pretentious.'—*Richard Mallett, Punch*

Gone with the Wind****
US 1939   220m   Technicolor
MGM / *David O. Selznick*

An egotistic Southern girl survives the Civil
War but finally loses the only man she cares
for.
The only film in history which could be
profitably revived for forty years: 'still pure
gold', said the *Daily Mirror* in 1975. Whole
books have been written about it; its essential
appeal is that of a romantic story with strong
characters and an impeccable production. The
widescreen version produced in the late sixties
ruined its composition and colour, but it is to
be hoped that the original negative still
survives.

w Sidney Howard (and others), *novel*
Margaret Mitchell d Victor Fleming (and
George Cukor, Sam Wood) *ph Ernest Haller,*
Ray Rennahan m Max Steiner pd William
Cameron Menzies ad Lyle Wheeler

Clark Gable, Vivien Leigh, Olivia de
Havilland, Leslie Howard, Thomas Mitchell,
Barbara O'Neil, *Hattie McDaniel, Butterfly*
McQueen, Victor Jory, Evelyn Keyes, Ann
Rutherford, Laura Hope Crews, Harry
Davenport, Jane Darwell, Ona Munson, Ward
Bond

'A major event in the history of the industry
but only a minor event in motion picture art.
There are moments when the two categories
meet on good terms, but the long stretches
between are filled with mere spectacular
efficiency.'—*Franz Hoellering, The Nation*

'Shakespeare's *The Taming of the Shrew*
seems to have got mixed up with one of the
novels of Ethel M. Dell.'—*James Agate*

'Perhaps the key plantation movie.'—*Time*
Out, 1980

'Forget it, Louis, no Civil War picture ever
made a nickel.'—*Irving Thalberg to Louis B.*
Mayer, 1936

† The best account of the film's making is in
Gavin Lambert's 1975 book, *GWTW.*
†† In the early seventies a stage musical
version toured the world; music by Harold
Rome.

AA: best picture; Sidney Howard; Victor
Fleming; Ernest Haller, Ray Rennahan; Lyle
Wheeler; Vivien Leigh; Hattie McDaniel; Hal
C. Kern and James E. Newcom (editors)
AAN: Max Steiner; Clark Gable; Olivia de
Havilland

The Good Companions***
GB 1932 113m bw
Gaumont / Welsh–Pearson (T. A. Welsh,
George Pearson)

Three ill-assorted people take to the road and
in various capacities join the Dinky Doos
pierrot troupe.
Gallant, mini-budgeted version of Priestley's
popular picaresque novel. A little faded now,
it retains some of its vigour, and the
performances please.

w W. P. Lipscomb, Angus Macphail, Ian
Dalrymple *novel J. B. Priestley d* Victor
Saville *ph* Bernard Knowles

Edmund Gwenn, Mary Glynne, John Gielgud,
Jessie Matthews, Percy Parsons, A. W.
Baskomb, Dennis Hoey, Richard Dolman,
Frank Pettingell, Finlay Currie, *Max Miller*,
Jack Hawkins, George Zucco

The Good Companions*
GB 1956 104m Technicolor
   Cinemascope
ABP (Hamilton Inglis, J. Lee-Thompson)

Faint-hearted remake of the above, unwisely
Cinemascoped and leaving no impression.

w T. J. Morrison *d* J. Lee-Thompson
ph Gilbert Taylor *m* Laurie Johnson

Eric Portman, Celia Johnson, John Fraser,
Janette Scott, Hugh Griffith, Bobby Howes,
Rachel Roberts, John Salew, Thora Hird

† A stage musical version (music by André
Previn) had moderate success in London in
1974.

Good Dame
US 1934 77m bw

A penniless chorus girl falls for a cardsharp.
Unsurprising pattern play for two miscast
stars. Sylvia Sidney, Fredric March, Jack La
Rue, Noel Francis, Russell Hopton. Written
by William K. Lipman, Vincent Lawrence,
Frank Partos and Sam Hellman; directed by
Marion Gering; for Paramount. (GB title:
Good Girl.)

Good Day for a Hanging
US 1959 85m Columbia Color

A young outlaw is arrested and seems destined
to be lynched; the marshal tries to see fair
play. Moody western in which the protected
hero turns out to be very guilty after all. Fred
MacMurray, Robert Vaughn, Maggie Hayes,
Joan Blackman, James Drury. Written by
Daniel B. Ullman and Maurice Zimm;
directed by Nathan Juran; for Columbia.

The Good Die Young*
GB 1954 98m bw
Remus (Jack Clayton)

Four crooks, all with private problems, set out
to rob a mail van.
Glum all-star melodrama which set a pattern
for such things; worth waiting for is the
climactic chase through underground stations.

w Vernon Harris, Lewis Gilbert *d* Lewis
Gilbert *ph* Jack Asher *m* Georges Auric

Laurence Harvey, Margaret Leighton, Gloria
Grahame, Richard Basehart, Joan Collins,
John Ireland, René Ray, Stanley Baker,
Robert Morley

The Good Earth***
US 1937 138m bw
MGM (*Irving Thalberg*)

A Chinese peasant grows rich but loses his
beloved wife.
A massive, well-meaning and fondly
remembered production which is nevertheless
artificial, unconvincing and pretty undramatic
in the second half. The star performances
impress to begin with, then wear thin, but the
final locust attack is as well done as it
originally seemed. Historically valuable as a
Hollywood prestige production of the thirties.

w Talbot Jennings, Tess Schlesinger, Claudine
West, *play* Owen and Donald Davis, *novel*
Pearl S. Buck *d Sidney Franklin ph* Karl
Freund *m* Herbert Stothart *montage* Slavko
Vorkapitch *ad* Cedric Gibbons

Paul Muni, Luise Rainer, Walter Connolly,
Tilly Losch, Jessie Ralph, Charley Grapewin,
Keye Luke, Harold Huber

'One of the superb visual adventures of the
period.'—*John Baxter, 1968*

'Prestigious boredom, and it goes on for a
very long time.'—*New Yorker, 1977*

AA: Karl Freund; Luise Rainer
AAN: best picture; Sidney Franklin

The Good Fairy*
US 1935 90m bw
Universal (Henry Henigson)

A beautiful but naïve cinema usherette
ensnares three rich men.
Unusual, rather lumpy romantic comedy using
top talent.

w *Preston Sturges, play* Ferenc Molnar
d William Wyler ph Norbert Brodine

Margaret Sullavan, Herbert Marshall, Frank
Morgan, Reginald Owen, Alan Hale, Beulah
Bondi, Cesar Romero, Eric Blore, Al Bridge

† Remade as *Because of Him* (qv).

The Good Fellows
US 1943 70m bw

A family man spends too much time with his fraternal order. Mild, pleasant family comedy.
Cecil Kellaway, Helen Walker, James Brown, Mabel Paige. Written by Hugh Wedlock Jnr and Howard Snyder, from a play by George S. Kaufman and Herman Mankiewicz; directed by Jo Graham; for Paramount.

Good Girls Go To Paris*
US 1939 75m bw
Columbia (William Perlberg)

After several zany adventures, a Greek professor marries a gold digger.
Amusingly crazy comedy, one of the last of its type.

w Gladys Lehman, Ken Englund d Alexander Hall ph Henry Freulich md Morris Stoloff

Melvyn Douglas, Joan Blondell, Walter Connolly, Alan Curtis, Joan Perry, Isabel Jeans, Alexander D'Arcy, Clarence Kolb

The Good Guys and the Bad Guys*
US 1969 90m Technicolor Panavision
Warner (Robert M. Goldstein)

An ageing sheriff and a train robber have one last showdown.
Good-humoured, black-flavoured western set in the early days of automobiles.

w Ronald M. Cohen, Dennis Shyrack d Burt Kennedy ph Harry Stradling Jnr m William Lava

Robert Mitchum, George Kennedy, David Carradine, Tina Louise, Douglas Fowley, Martin Balsam, Lois Nettleton, John Davis Chandler, John Carradine, Marie Windsor

Good Morning Boys**
GB 1937 79m bw
GFD / Gainsborough (Edward Black)

A schoolmaster takes his troublesome pupils to Paris and becomes involved with an art theft.
Sprightly vehicle for the star's seedy schoolmaster persona: it established him as a major draw in British films.

w Marriott Edgar, Val Guest, Anthony Kimmins d Marcel Varnel

Will Hay, Graham Moffatt, Lilli Palmer, Mark Daly, Peter Gawthorne, Martita Hunt, Charles Hawtrey, Will Hay Jnr
† Remade with Ronald Shiner as *Top of the Form.*

Good Morning Miss Dove
US 1955 107m Eastmancolor
Cinemascope
TCF (Samuel G. Engel)

While recovering from an operation, a small-town schoolmistress looks back on her career.
A fairly spirited weepie with a happy ending and a strong sense of cynicism behind the scenes.

w Eleanore Griffin, *novel* Frances Gray Patton d Henry Koster ph Leon Shamroy m Leigh Harline

Jennifer Jones, Robert Stack, Robert Douglas, Kipp Hamilton, Peggy Knudsen, Marshall Thompson, Chuck Connors, Mary Wickes
  'Mr Chips has changed sex and habitat while preserving intact his ability to provoke epidemics of sentimentality.'—*MFB*

Good Neighbour Sam
US 1964 130m Eastmancolor
Columbia / David Swift

A prissy suburban advertising man becomes innocently involved in a pretence to be the husband of the divorcee next door.
A promising comic idea is here ruined by lengthiness, lack of funny lines, and no apparent idea of how to film a farce. The actors are driven to repeating every trick a dozen times.

w James Fritzell, Everett Greenbaum, David Swift, *novel* Jack Finney d David Swift ph Burnett Guffey m Frank de Vol

Jack Lemmon, Romy Schneider, Dorothy Provine, Senta Berger, Edward G. Robinson, Mike Connors, Edward Andrews, Louis Nye

Good News
US 1930 85m approx bw
MGM

Fraternity tensions are sorted out in time for the big football game.
Spirited early talkie musical.

w Frances Marion, Joe Farnham d Nick Grinde, Edgar McGregor ph Percy Hilburn *songs* De Sylva, Brown and Henderson

Bessie Love, Stanley Smith, Gus Shy, Mary Lawlor, Lola Lane, Dorothy McNulty, Cliff Edwards

Good News*
US 1947 83m Technicolor
MGM (Arthur Freed)

Bright, good-humoured remake of the above.

w Betty Comden, Adolph Green d Charles Walters ph Charles Schoenbaum md Lennie Hayton

June Allyson, Peter Lawford, Patricia Marshall, *Joan McCracken*, Mel Tormé

AAN: song 'Pass that Peace Pipe' (*m / ly* Ralph Blane, Hugh Martin, Roger Edens)

The Good Old Days
GB 1939   79m   bw
Warner

A noble child is kidnapped by a chimney
sweep and saved by strolling players.
Curious Victorian vehicle for a snappy 20th-
century star.

w Austin Melford, John Dighton d Roy
William Neill

Max Miller, Hal Walters, Kathleen Gibson,
H. F. Maltby, Martita Hunt, Allan Jeayes,
Roy Emerton

Good Sam
US 1948   114m   bw
Rainbow (Leo McCarey)

A small-town business man is so charitable
that he finds himself bankrupt.
Poor, disjointed, overlong and obvious
comedy in the Capra style.

w Ken Englund d Leo McCarey ph George
Barnes m Robert Emmett Dolan

Gary Cooper, Ann Sheridan, Ray Collins,
Edmund Lowe, Joan Lorring, Ruth Roman,
Clinton Sundberg

'A bit too long, but in its incidentals often
very enjoyable.'—*Richard Mallett, Punch*

Good Time Girl
GB 1948   93m   bw

A girl escapes from a remand home and starts
on the road to ruin.
 Risible vehicle for a rising star; at the time it
set the box offices clicking. Jean Kent, Dennis
Price, Flora Robson, Griffith Jones, Herbert
Lom, Bonar Colleano. Written by Muriel and
Sidney Box and Ted Willis, from the novel
Night Darkens the Street by Arthur La Bern;
directed by David MacDonald; for Triton /
Rank.

The Good, the Bad and the Ugly
Italy 1966   180m   Techniscope
PEA (Alberto Grimaldi)
original title: *Il Buono, il Bruto, il Cattivo*

During the American Civil War, three men
seek hidden loot.
Intermittently lively, very violent, and
interminably drawn out western with a number
of rather hilarious stylistic touches.

w Age Scarpelli, Luciano Vincenzoni, Sergio
Leone d Sergio Leone ph Tonino delli Colli
m Ennio Morricone

Clint Eastwood, Eli Wallach, Lee Van Cleef

Goodbye Again
US 1933   66m   bw

An author's secretary is jealous of his
rekindled interest in an old flame. Unassuming
star comedy which entertained at the time.
Warren William, Joan Blondell, Genevieve
Tobin, Hugh Herbert, Helen Chandler, Ruth
Donnelly. Written by Ben Markson, from the
play by George Haight and Allan Scott;
directed by Michael Curtiz; for Warner. (NB:
Honeymoon for Three in 1941 [qv] was a
leaden remake.)

Goodbye Again*
US 1961   120m   bw
UA / Mercury / Argus / Anatole Litvak

A woman of forty swaps her rich lover for a
young law student.
Melancholy romantic drama, well produced
and staged on Paris locations.

w Samuel Taylor, *novel* Aimez-vous Brahms
by Françoise Sagan d Anatole Litvak
ph Armand Thirard m Georges Auric

Ingrid Bergman, Anthony Perkins, Yves
Montand, Jessie Royce Landis, Jackie Lane
  'A grey-toned Sagan novella, spread wide
and lush over two hours of screen time.'—
MFB

'The kind of "woman's picture" that gives
women a bad name.'—*Judith Crist, 1973*

Goodbye Charlie*
US 1964   116m   De Luxe   Cinemascope
TCF / Venice (David Weisbart)

A philandering gangster, shot dead by an irate
husband, is reincarnated in his friend's house
as a dishy blonde.
Overlong but amusing Broadway comedy for
wisecrackers, uninventively adapted.

w Harry Kurnitz, *play* George Axelrod
d Vincente Minnelli ph Milton Krasner
m André Previn

Debbie Reynolds, Pat Boone, Walter Matthau,
Tony Curtis

Goodbye Columbus**
US 1969   105m   Technicolor
Paramount / Willow Tree (Stanley Jaffe)

A young Jewish librarian has an affair with the
wilful daughter of a *nouveau riche* family.
An amusing and well-observed delineation of
two kinds of Jewish life in New York; the
story, despite its frank talk of penises and
diaphragms, leaves much to be desired, and
the style is post-*Graduate*.

w Arnold Schulman, *novel* Philip Roth
d Larry Peerce ph Gerald Hirschfeld
m Charles Fox

Richard Benjamin, Ali MacGraw, Jack
Klugman, Nan Martin, Michael Meyers, Lori
Shelle

'Every father's daughter is a virgin!'—
publicity

AAN: Arnold Schulman

The Goodbye Girl*
US 1977   110m   Metrocolor
Warner / Rastar (Ray Stark)

A misunderstanding about the lease of an apartment results in a girl dancer agreeing to share it with a would-be actor.

A very moderate script assisted by excellent acting and the usual array of Neil Simon one-liners. Nothing at all new, but enjoyable.

w Neil Simon *d* Herbert Ross *ph* David M. Walsh *m* Dave Grusin

Richard Dreyfuss, Marsha Mason, Quinn Cummings, Paul Benedict, Barbara Rhoades

AA: Richard Dreyfuss
AAN: best picture; Neil Simon; Marsha Mason; Quinn Cummings

Goodbye Mr Chips***
GB 1939   114m   bw
MGM (Victor Saville)

The life of a shy schoolmaster from his first job to his death.

Sentimental romance in MGM's best style, a long-standing favourite for its performances and humour; but the production seems slightly unsatisfactory these days.

w R. C. Sherriff, Claudine West, Eric Maschwitz, *novel* James Hilton *d* Sam Wood *ph* Frederick A. Young *m* Richard Addinsell

Robert Donat, Greer Garson, Paul Henreid, Lyn Harding, Austin Trevor, Terry Kilburn, John Mills, Milton Rosmer, Judith Furse

'The whole picture has an assurance, bears a glow of popularity like the face of a successful candidate on election day. And it is wrong to despise popularity in the cinema.'—*Graham Greene*

'The picture has no difficulty in using two hours to retell a story that was scarcely above short story length. *Mr Chips* is worth its time.'—*New York Times*

AA: Robert Donat
AAN: best picture; script; Sam Wood; Greer Garson

Goodbye Mr Chips*
GB 1969   147m   Metrocolor
   Panavision 70
MGM / APJAC (Arthur P. Jacobs)

Elaborate musical remake of the above. Slow and slushy, with no improvement visible whatever; but a few of the trimmings please.

w Terence Rattigan *d* Herbert Ross
ph Oswald Morris *m* Leslie Bricusse *pd* Ken Adam *ad* John Williams

Peter O'Toole, Petula Clark, Michael Bryant, Michael Redgrave, George Baker, Jack Hedley, Sian Phillips, Alison Leggatt

'The sum total is considerably less than the parts.'—*Variety*

'He is a shy schoolmaster. She is a music hall star. They marry and immediately have 283 children—all boys!'—*publicity*

† Originally sought for the title role, in order of preference, were Richard Burton and Rex Harrison; for the female lead, Samantha Eggar and Lee Remick.

AAN: Leslie Bricusse; John Williams; Peter O'Toole

Goodbye My Fancy
US 1951   107m   bw
Warner (Henry Blanke)

A congresswoman returns to her old college for an honorary degree, and falls in love. Tolerable romantic flim-flam.

w Ivan Goff, Ben Roberts, *play* Fay Kanin *d* Vincent Sherman *ph* Ted McCord *m* Daniele Amfitheatrof

Joan Crawford, Robert Young, Frank Lovejoy, Eve Arden, Janice Rule

Goodbye My Lady*
US 1956   95m   bw
Batjac

A Mississippi swamp boy finds a valuable dog but eventually returns it to its owner. Reliable, slightly unusual family film.

w Sid Fleischman, *novel* James Street *d* William Wellman *ph* William H. Clothier, Archie Stout *m* Laurindo Almeida, George Field

Brandon de Wilde, Walter Brennan, Phil Harris, Sidney Poitier, William Hopper, Louise Beavers

Goodnight Vienna
GB 1933   76m   bw
British and Dominions (Herbert Wilcox)
US title: *Magic Night*

In 1913 Vienna, a general's son falls for a shopgirl.

Already dated when it was made, this thin musical romance nevertheless made a star of Anna Neagle and re-established Jack Buchanan on the screen.

w Holt Marvel, George Posford, from their radio play *d* Herbert Wilcox *ph* F. A. Young

Jack Buchanan, Anna Neagle, Gina Malo, Clive Currie, William Kendall

The Goose Steps Out*
GB 1942   79m   bw
Ealing (S. C. Balcon)

To steal a secret weapon, an incompetent
teacher is sent into Germany in place of his
Nazi double.
Quite amusing star vehicle, not up to his best
standards.

w Angus Macphail, John Dighton d Will
Hay, Basil Dearden ph Ernest Palmer
m Bretton Byrd

Will Hay, Charles Hawtrey, Frank Pettingell,
Julien Mitchell, Peter Croft, Jeremy Hawk,
Peter Ustinov, Raymond Lovell, Barry Morse

The Goose Woman
US 1925   90m approx   bw   silent
Universal

A young actress falls for the son of an
embittered old one.
Interesting character melodrama of which
prints have survived.

w Melville Brown, *story* Rex Beach
d Clarence Brown ph Milton Moore

Louise Dresser, Jack Pickford, Constance
Bennett, James Barrows

Gordon's War
US 1973   90m   TVC color
TCF / Palomar (Robert L. Schaffel)

A black Vietnam veteran returns to Harlem
and avenges the death of his wife.
Violent vigilante melodrama with vivid
locations.

w Howard Friedlander, Ed Spielman d Ossie
Davis ph Victor J. Kemper m Andy Bodale,
Al Ellis

Paul Winfield, Carl Lee, David Downing

The Gorgeous Hussy*
US 1936   105m   bw
MGM (Joseph L. Mankiewicz)

The love life of Peggy O'Neal, protégée of
President Andrew Jackson.
Bowdlerized all-star historical drama; the
production values are better than the script.

w Ainsworth Morgan, Stephen Morehouse
Avery, *novel* Samuel Hopkins Adams
d Clarence Brown ph George Folsey
m Herbert Stothart

Joan Crawford, Lionel Barrymore, Franchot
Tone, Melvyn Douglas, Robert Taylor, James
Stewart, Alison Skipworth, Louis Calhern,
Beulah Bondi, Melville Cooper, Sidney Toler,
Gene Lockhart

AAN: George Folsey; Beulah Bondi

Gorgo
GB 1960   78m   Technicolor
King Brothers (Wilfrid Eades)

A prehistoric monster is caught in Irish waters
and brought to London, but rescued by its
mother.
Amiable monster hokum with a happy ending
but not much technical resource.

w John Loring, Daniel Hyatt d Eugene
Lourié ph Frederick A. Young m Angelo
Lavagnino sp Tom Howard

Bill Travers, William Sylvester, Vincent
Winter, Christopher Rhodes, Joseph
O'Conor, Bruce Seton, Martin Benson

The Gorgon*
GB 1964   83m   Technicolor
Hammer (Anthony Nelson Keys)

A castle ruin near a German village is infested
by Megaera, the gorgon of ancient myth,
whose gaze turns people to stone and who can
take over the form of an unknowing villager.
Writhing snakes in the hair-do being too great
a challenge to the make-up man, the monster
is barely glimpsed and the film becomes a
who-is-it, all quite suspenseful despite the
central idea being too silly for words.

w John Gilling d Terence Fisher ph Michael
Reed m James Bernard

Peter Cushing, Christopher Lee, Barbara
Shelley, Richard Pasco, Patrick Troughton

The Gorilla*
US 1939   66m   bw
TCF

A murderer blames an escaped gorilla for his
crimes.
Spooky house mystery comedy revamped as a
Ritz Brothers vehicle; not much suspense, but
it all looks good and the cast is highly
satisfactory.

w Rian James, Sid Silvers, *play* Ralph Spence
d Allan Dwan ph Edward Cronjager
m David Buttolph

The Ritz Brothers, Bela Lugosi, Lionel Atwill,
Patsy Kelly, Joseph Calleia, Anita Louise,
Edward Norris, Wally Vernon
† There were two previous versions, in 1927
with Charlie Murray and 1931 with Joe Frisco.

Gorilla at Large
US 1954   93m   Technicolor   3-D
TCF / Panoramic (Robert L. Jacks)

A circus gorilla is used as a cover for murder.
Silly thriller with the gorilla as unconvincing as
the story.

w Leonard Praskins, Barney Slater d Harmon
Jones ph Lloyd Aherne m Lionel Newman

Anne Bancroft, Lee J. Cobb, Cameron
Mitchell, Lee Marvin, Raymond Burr,
Charlotte Austin, Peter Whitney, Warren
Stevens

The Gorilla Man
US 1942 63m bw

A wounded commando discovers that his
hospital is run by Nazis, who then try to prove
him insane so that he won't be believed. There
must have been less laborious ways, one
assumes, but at least this farrago is good for a
few unintentional laughs. John Loder, Ruth
Ford, Richard Fraser, Paul Cavanagh, John
Abbott. Written by Anthony Coldeway;
directed by D. Ross Lederman; for Warner.

The Gospel According to St Matthew*
Italy / France 1964 142m bw
Arco / Lux (Alfredo Bini)
original title: *Il Vangelo Secondo Matteo*

The life of Christ seen almost as a ciné-vérité
documentary: the tone is realist but not
notably iconoclastic.

wd Pier Paolo Pasolini *ph* Tonino delli Colli
m Bach, Mozart, Prokofiev *md* Luis Enrique
Bacalov

Enrique Irazoqui, Susanna Pasolini, Mario
Socrate

AAN: Luis Enrique Bacalov

Goupi Mains Rouges*
France 1943 95m bw
Minerva
US title: *It Happened at the Inn*

A French village is largely populated by
members of the same family, and one of them
murders another.
An odd little black comedy which
strengthened its director's reputation.

w Pierre Véry, Jacques Becker, *novel* Pierre
Véry *d* Jacques Becker *ph* Pierre Montazel,
Jean Bourgoin *m* Jean Alfaro

Fernand Ledoux, Georges Rollin, Blanchette
Brunoy, Robert Le Vigan

Government Girl
US 1943 94m bw

War Department secretaries find their love
lives confused in wartime Washington, where
rooms have to be shared. Thin variation on a
theme curiously dear to Hollywood at the
time. Olivia de Havilland, Sonny Tufts, Anne
Shirley, James Dunn, Paul Stewart, Agnes
Moorehead, Harry Davenport, Una
O'Connor, Sig Rumann, Jane Darwell.
Written and directed by Dudley Nichols; from
an adaptation by Budd Schulberg of a story by
Adela Rogers St John; for RKO.

The Gracie Allen Murder Case see Philo
Vance

The Graduate***
US 1967 105m Technicolor
Panavision
UA / Embassy (Lawrence Turman)

A rich Californian ex-student is led into an
affair with the wife of his father's friend, then
falls in love with her daughter.
Richly reflecting the anything-goes mood of
the late sixties, this lushly-filmed sex comedy
opened a few new doors, looked ravishing,
was well acted and had a popular music score,
so that few people noticed that only the first
half was any good.

w Calder Willingham, Buck Henry, *novel*
Charles Webb d Mike Nichols ph Robert
Surtees songs Paul Simon singers Simon and
Garfunkel m Dave Grusin pd Richard
Sylbert

Dustin Hoffman, Anne Bancroft, Katharine
Ross, Murray Hamilton, William Daniels,
Elizabeth Wilson

'Seeing *The Graduate* is a bit like having
one's most brilliant friend to dinner, watching
him become more witty and animated with
every moment, and then becoming aware that
what one may really be witnessing is the onset
of a nervous breakdown.'—*Renata Adler*

'Yes, there are weaknesses . . . But in
cinematic skill, in intent, in sheer connection
with us, *The Graduate* is a milestone in
American film history.'—*Stanley Kauffmann*

AA: Mike Nichols
AAN: best picture; script; Robert Surtees;
Dustin Hoffman; Anne Bancroft; Katharine
Ross

Grand Central Murder
US 1942 72m bw
MGM (B. F. Zeidman)

A murder is solved in New York's giant
railway station.
Very moderate time-filler with a rather
lethargic script.

w Peter Ruric, *novel* Sue McVeigh *d* S.
Sylvan Simon *ph* George F. Folsey *m* David
Snell

Van Heflin, Cecilia Parker, Sam Levene,
Connie Gilchrist, Millard Mitchell, Tom
Conway, Virginia Grey, Samuel S. Hinds

Grand Hotel***
US 1932 115m bw
MGM (Irving Thalberg)

The lives of various hotel guests become
intertwined and reach their climaxes.

It's a little faded now, but much of the magic still works in this first of the portmanteau movies; the production is opulent yet somehow stiff, and the performances have survived with varying success.

w William A. Drake, *novel* Vicki Baum *d* Edmund Goulding *ph* William Daniels *ad* Cedric Gibbons

Greta Garbo, *John Barrymore*, Lionel Barrymore, Joan Crawford, Wallace Beery, Jean Hersholt, Lewis Stone
† Remade as *Weekend at the Waldorf* (qv).

AA: best picture

Le Grand Jeu*
France 1934   115m   bw

A young man joins the Foreign Legion to forget a woman, meets another who reminds him of her, and is condemned to death for murdering the second woman's lover.
Hokey melodrama whose great interest lay in its picture of life in the Legion.

w Charles Spaak, Jacques Feyder *d* Jacques Feyder *ph* Harry Stradling, Maurice Forster *m* Hanns Eisler

Pierre-Richard Wilm, Marie Bell (in a dual role), Françoise Rosay, Charles Vanel
† A remake appeared in 1953, directed by Robert Siodmak and starring Jean-Claude Pascal, Gina Lollobrigida and Arletty.
Sometimes known as *Card of Fate*, it is of little interest.

Grand National Night
GB 1953   80m   bw
Talisman (George Minter)
US title: *The Wicked Wife*

A stable owner accidentally kills his drunken wife, but fate and a complex series of events clear him.
Slightly dubious morally, but otherwise an adequate detective story with the outcome hinging on train timetables and the like.

w Dorothy and Campbell Christie, from their play *d* Bob McNaught *ph* Jack Asher *m* John Greenwood

Nigel Patrick, Moira Lister, Beatrice Campbell, Betty Ann Davies, Michael Hordern, Noel Purcell, Leslie Mitchell, Barry Mackay, Colin Gordon

Grand Prix*
US 1966   179m   Metrocolor
Super Panavision
MGM (Edward Lewis)

Motor racers converge on Monte Carlo and other European centres.

Seemingly endless montage, mostly in multi-split screens, of motor races, with some very jaded personal footage between. It looks a dream but quickly becomes a bore.

w Robert Alan Aurthur *d* John Frankenheimer *ph* Lionel Lindon *m* Maurice Jarre *pd* Richard Sylbert

James Garner, Eva Marie Saint, Brian Bedford, Yves Montand, Toshiro Mifune, Jessica Walter, Françoise Hardy, Adolfo Celi, Claude Dauphin, Genevieve Page
'The same old story with the same types we've seen flying planes and riding horses in dozens of fast, cheap, hour-and-a-quarter movies.'—*Pauline Kael*
'Nothing more nor less than a paean to the racing car . . . off the track, though, the film is firmly stuck in bottom gear.'—*MFB*

Grand Slam
Italy / Spain / West Germany 1967   120m
Techniscope
(Paramount) Jolly-Coral-Constantin (Harry Columbo, George Papi)
original title: *Ad Ogni Costo*

A retired professor has a plan for a diamond robbery, but recruits his aides unwisely.
Long-drawn-out caper melodrama with good sequences but nothing at all new; a very poor man's *Rififi*.

w Mino Roli, Caminito, Marcello Fondato, Antonio de la Loma *d* Giuliano Montaldo *ph* Antonio Macasoli *m* Ennio Morricone

Janet Leigh, Edward G. Robinson, Klaus Kinski, Robert Hoffman, Georges Rigaud, Adolfo Celi

La Grande Illusion***
France 1937   117m   bw
RAC

During World War I, three captured French pilots have an uneasy relationship with their German commandant.
Celebrated mood piece with much to say about war and mankind; more precisely, it is impeccably acted and directed and has real tragic force.

w Jean Renoir, Charles Spaak *d* Jean Renoir *ph* Christian Matras, Claude Renoir, Bourgoin, Bourreaud *m* Joseph Kosma

Pierre Fresnay, Erich Von Stroheim, Jean Gabin, Julien Carette, Marcel Dalio, Gaston Modot, Jean Dasté, Dita Parlo
'The story is true. It was told to me by my friends in the war . . . notably by Pinsard who flew fighter planes. I was in the reconnaissance squadron. He saved my life many times when the German fighters became too persistent. He

himself was shot down seven times. His escapes are the basis for the story.'—*Jean Renoir*

AAN: best picture

Les Grandes Manoeuvres*
France / Italy 1955   106m   Eastmancolor
Filmsonor / Rizzoli
aka: *Summer Manoeuvres*

In 1913, an army lieutenant takes a bet that he can win any woman in the town in which his regiment is quartered during manoeuvres.
An elegant, but surprisingly unwitty film from this director, saddled with a well-worn and very predictable plot.

wd René Clair *ph* Robert Le Fèbvre, Robert Juillard *m* Georges Van Parys

Gérard Philipe, Michèle Morgan, Brigitte Bardot, Yves Robert, Jean Desailly, Pierre Dux

Granny Get Your Gun
US 1939   56m   bw

An indomitable old lady turns sheriff to get her granddaughter off the hook for murder.
Energetic second feature comedy mystery from a Perry Mason story; pleasant performances. May Robson, Harry Davenport, Margot Stevenson, Hardie Albright. Written by Kenneth Gamet; directed by George Amy; for Warner.

The Grapes of Wrath••••
US 1940   128m   bw
TCF (Nunnally Johnson)

After the dust-bowl disaster of the thirties, Oklahoma farmers trek to California in the hope of a better life.
A superb film which could scarcely be improved upon. Though the ending is softened from the book, there was too much here for filmgoers to chew on. Acting, photography, direction combine to make this an unforgettable experience, a poem of a film.

w Nunnally Johnson, novel John Steinbeck *d John Ford ph* Gregg Toland *m* Alfred Newman

Henry Fonda, Jane Darwell, John Carradine, Charley Grapewin, Dorris Bowdon, Russell Simpson, Zeffie Tilbury, O. Z. Whitehead, John Qualen, Eddie Quillan, Grant Mitchell
'A genuinely great motion picture which makes one proud to have even a small share in the affairs of the cinema.'—*Howard Barnes*
'The most mature motion picture that has ever been made, in feeling, in purpose, and in the use of the medium.'—*Otis Ferguson*

'A sincere and searing indictment of man's cruel indifference to his fellows.'—*Basil Wright*
'The thousands who have read the book will know why WE WILL NOT SELL ANY CHILDREN TICKETS to see this picture!'—*publicity*

AA: John Ford; Jane Darwell
AAN: best picture; Nunnally Johnson; Henry Fonda

Grass*
US 1925   50m approx   bw   silent
Famous Players-Lasky

Nomadic Iranian tribes make an annual migration in search of fresh pasture.
Striking early documentary marred by facetious sub-titles.

w, d, ph Merian C. Cooper, Ernest Schoedsack *titles* Terry Ramsaye

The Grass Is Greener*
GB 1960   104m   Technirama
Grandon (Stanley Donen)

The wife of an English earl falls for an American millionaire tourist.
Heavy-going and unsuitably widescreened version of an agreeable piece of West End fluff. Performances just about save it.

w Hugh and Margaret Williams, from their play *d* Stanley Donen *ph* Christopher Challis *m / ly* Noel Coward *md* Muir Mathieson

Cary Grant, Deborah Kerr, Robert Mitchum, *Jean Simmons, Moray Watson*
'It's too bad Coward couldn't have written the wisecracks too.'—*Philip T. Hartung*
'The stars do not glitter or even glow. Instead of being liberated and propelled by the screenplay, they are chained and sunk. It is one of the year's most disappointing films.'—*James Powers, Hollywood Reporter*

The Grasshopper
US 1969   98m   Technicolor
NGP (Jerry Belson, Barry Marshall)

A small-town girl goes from man to man in Los Angeles and Las Vegas, finally becoming a call girl.
The road to ruin in modern dress; nicely made and quite entertaining in its gaudy way.

w Jerry Belson, *novel* The Passing of Evil by Mark MacShane *d* Jerry Paris *ph* Sam Leavitt *m* Billy Goldenberg

Jacqueline Bisset, Jim Brown, Joseph Cotten, Corbett Monica

The Gravy Train
US 1974   96m   Eastmancolor
Tomorrow (Jonathan T. Taplin)
aka: *The Dion Brothers*

A canning factory worker throws up his job to
hijack a treasury van and open a seafood
restaurant.
Old-hat caper story.

w David Whitney, Bill Kirby *d* Jack Starrett
ph Jerry Hirschfeld *m* Fred Karlin

Stacy Keach, Frederic Forrest, Margot
Kidder, Barry Primus

Gray Lady Down
US 1978   111m   Technicolor
Panavision
Universal / Mirisch (Walter Mirisch)

After a collision, an American submarine
lodges in the neck of an underwater canyon.
A rather boring update of *Morning Departure*
with added technology.

w James Whittaker, Howard Sackler, *novel*
Event 1000 by David Levallee *d* David
Greene *ph* Stevan Larner *m* Jerry Fielding

Charlton Heston, David Carradine, Stacy
Keach, Ned Beatty, Stephen McHattie, Ronny
Cox, Dorian Harewood, Rosemary Forsyth

'The crew eventually reach the surface, but
the film deserves to sink without trace.'—
Nicholas Wapshott, The Times

Grease••
US 1978   110m   Metrocolor   Panavision
Paramount / Robert Stigwood, Allan Carr

The path of true love in a fifties high school
does not run smoothly.
Amiable 'period' musical for teenagers: a
highly fashionable exploitation of the new star
John Travolta, its commercialism was
undeniable, and it carefully built in appeal to
older age groups.

w Bronte Woodard, *stage musical play* Jim
Jacobs, Warren Casey *d* Randal Kleiser
ph Bill Butler *pd* Phil Jefries *titles* John
Wilson

John Travolta, Olivia Newton-John, Stockard
Channing, Eve Arden, Frankie Avalon, Joan
Blondell, Edd Byrnes, Sid Caesar, Alice
Ghostley, Sha Na Na, Jeff Conaway, Barry
Pearl, Michael Tucci

'A bogus, clumsily jointed pastiche of late
fifties high school musicals, studded with
leftovers from *West Side Story* and *Rebel
Without A Cause.*'—*New Yorker*

AAN: song, 'Hopelessly Devoted to You'

Greased Lightning
US 1977   96m   Movielab
Third World (Hannah Weinstein)

A black Virginian moonshiner becomes a
famous stock car racer.
Fashionable action hokum based on a real
character.

w Kenneth Vose, Lawrence DuKore, Melvin
Van Peebles, Leon Capetanos *d* Michel
Schultz *ph* George Bouillet *m* Fred Karlin

Richard Pryor, Beau Bridges, Pam Grier,
Cleavon Little, Vincent Gardenia

The Great Adventure••
Sweden 1953   73m   bw
Arne Sucksdorff

Two boys on a farm rescue an otter and keep
it as a pet.
Superbly photographed wild life film featuring
a variety of small animals.

w, d, ph, ed Arne Sucksdorff

Anders Norberg, Kjell Sucksdorff, Arne
Sucksdorff

The Great American Broadcast•
US 1941   90m   bw
TCF (Kenneth MacGowan)

A romantic triangle set against the burgeoning
years of the radio industry.
Pleasant musical, amusing if historically
inaccurate.

w Don Ettlinger, Edwin Blum, Robert Ellis,
Helen Logan *d* Archie Mayo *ph* Leon
Shamroy, Peverell Marley *songs* Mack
Gordon, Harry Warren

Alice Faye, John Payne, Jack Oakie, Cesar
Romero, The Ink Spots, The Nicholas
Brothers, The Wiere Brothers

The Great American Pastime
US 1956   89m   bw
MGM (Henry Berman)

A mild lawyer takes over a junior baseball
team but incurs parental jealousy.
Thin lower-bracket comedy.

w Nathaniel Benchley *d* Herman Hoffman
ph Arthur E. Arling *m* Jeff Alexander

Tom Ewell, Anne Francis, Ann Miller, Dean
Jones, Raymond Bailey

The Great Bank Robbery•
US 1969   98m   colour   Panavision
Warner (Malcolm Stuart)

Would-be bank robbers turn up in a western
town disguised as priests.
Western spoof without the courage of its
convictions, but easy enough to watch.

w William Peter Blatty, novel Frank O'Rourke *d* Hy Averback *ph* Fred J. Koenekamp *m* Nelson Riddle

Kim Novak, Zero Mostel, Clint Walker, Claude Akins, Akim Tamiroff, Larry Storch, John Anderson, Sam Jaffe, Ruth Warrick, Elisha Cook Jnr

The Great Caruso**
US 1950 109m Technicolor
MGM (Joe Pasternak)

Semi-fictional biography of the Italian tenor. Dramatically flat but opulently staged biopic, turned into a star vehicle and a huge commercial success.

w Sonya Levien, William Ludwig *d* Richard Thorpe *ph* Joseph Ruttenberg *md* Johnny Green, Peter Herman Adler

Mario Lanza, Ann Blyth, Dorothy Kirsten, Jarmila Novotna, Carl Benton Reid, Eduard Franz, Richard Hageman, Ludwig Donath, Alan Napier

AAN: Johnny Green, Peter Herman Adler

Great Catherine
GB 1968 98m Technicolor
Warner / Keep Films (Jules Buck)

An English captain visits the court of Catherine the Great.
Chaos results from the attempt to inflate an ill-considered Shavian whimsy into a feature film: the material is simply insufficient and the performances flounder in irrelevant production values.

w Hugh Leonard, *play* Bernard Shaw *d* Gordon Flemyng *ph* Oswald Morris *m* Dmitri Tiomkin *pd* John Bryan

Jeanne Moreau, Peter O'Toole, Zero Mostel, Jack Hawkins, Marie Lohr, Akim Tamiroff, Marie Kean, Kenneth Griffith

'All Shaw's jokes work very well, but the film has been padded out with Cossack dances, frantic chases, and unfunny slapstick.'— *Michael Billington, Illustrated London News*

The Great Chase
US 1963 82m bw

A compendium of chase sequences from silent films, including William S. Hart, Douglas Fairbanks Snr, and Buster Keaton (in *The General*). Written by Harvey Kort, Paul Killiam and Saul Turrell; for Continental.

Great Day
GB 1945 79m bw
RKO British (Victor Hanbury)

A village Women's Institute prepares for a visit by Mrs Roosevelt.
Modestly pleasing little drama from a successful play.

w Wolfgang Wilhelm, John Davenport, *play* Lesley Storm *d* Lance Comfort *ph* Erwin Hillier

Eric Portman, Flora Robson, Sheila Sim, Isabel Jeans, Walter Fitzgerald, Philip Friend, Marjorie Rhodes, Maire O'Neill, Beatrice Varley

Great Day in the Morning
US 1955 92m Technicolor Superscope
RKO (Edmund Grainger)

At the outbreak of the Civil War, Denver has divided loyalties.
Solemn semi-western without much excitement.

w Lesser Samuels, *novel* Robert Hardy Andrews *d* Jacques Tourneur *ph* William Snyder *m* Leith Stevens

Robert Stack, Virginia Mayo, Ruth Roman, Alex Nicol, Raymond Burr, Regis Toomey

The Great Diamond Robbery
US 1954 69m bw

Crooks convince a dumb jewellery apprentice to help them. Tedious second feature comedy, the star's last for the studio. Red Skelton, Cara Williams, James Whitmore, Kurt Kasznar, Reginald Owen. Written by Laslo Vadnay; directed by Robert Z. Leonard; for MGM.

The Great Dictator**
US 1940 129m bw
Charles Chaplin

A Jewish barber is mistaken for dictator Adenoid Hynkel.
Chaplin's satire on Hitler has a few funny moments, but the rest is heavy going, the production is cheeseparing, and the final speech to the world is a grave mistake.

wd Charles Chaplin *ph* Karl Struss, Rollie Totheroh *md* Meredith Willson *ad* J. Russell Spencer

Charles Chaplin, Paulette Goddard, *Jack Oakie* (as Napaloni), Reginald Gardiner, Henry Daniell, Billy Gilbert, Maurice Moscovitch

'For this film he takes on more than a mimed representation of common humanity; he states, and accepts, the responsibility of being one of humanity's best and most widely-known representatives.'—*Basil Wright*

'The last impassioned speech about peace and serenity still wrecks everything that has gone before: Chaplin mawkish can always overrule Chaplin the innocent mime.'—*New Yorker, 1978*

'You must go back to *Intolerance* for another motion picture that is so completely one man's personal expression of his attitude on something about which he feels deeply and passionately.'—*James Shelley Hamilton, National Board of Review*

'No time for comedy? Yes, I say, time for comedy. Time for Chaplin comedy. No time ever for Chaplin to preach as he does in those last six minutes, no matter how deeply he may feel what he wrote and says. He is not a good preacher. Indeed, he is frighteningly bad.'— *John O'Hara*

AAN: best picture; Charles Chaplin (as writer and actor); Meredith Willson; Jack Oakie

The Great Escape**
US 1963   173m   De Luxe   Panavision
UA / Mirisch / Alpha (John Sturges)

Allied prisoners plan to escape from a German prison camp.
Pretty good but overlong POW adventure with a tragic ending.

w James Clavell, W. R. Burnett, *book* Paul Brickhill d John Sturges ph Daniel Fapp m Elmer Bernstein

James Garner, *Steve McQueen*, Richard Attenborough, James Donald, Charles Bronson, Donald Pleasence, James Coburn, David McCallum, Gordon Jackson, John Leyton, Nigel Stock

Great Expectations
US 1934   100m   bw
Universal

A poor boy becomes unexpectedly rich and mistakes the source of his good fortune.
Solidly carpentered but never inspired version of a sprawling novel later tackled with much more style by David Lean. See below.

w Gladys Unger *novel* Charles Dickens
d Stuart Walker

Phillips Holmes (Pip), Jane Wyatt (Estella), Henry Hull (Magwitch), Florence Reed (Miss Havisham), Alan Hale (Joe Gargery), Rafaela Ottiano (Mrs Joe), Francis L. Sullivan (Jaggers)

Great Expectations****
GB 1946   118m   bw
Rank / Cineguild (Anthony Havelock-Allan)

A boy meets an escaped convict on the Romney Marshes, with strange consequences for both of them.

Despite the inevitable simplifications, this is a superbly pictorial rendering of a much-loved novel, with all the famous characters in safe hands and masterly judgement in every department.

w Ronald Neame, David Lean, Kay Walsh, Cecil McGivern, Anthony Havelock-Allan d David Lean ph Guy Green ad John Bryan

John Mills, Bernard Miles, *Finlay Currie, Martita Hunt*, Valerie Hobson, *Jean Simmons*. Alec Guinness, Francis L. Sullivan, Anthony Wager, Ivor Barnard, Freda Jackson, Hay Petrie, O. B. Clarence, George Hayes, Torin Thatcher, Eileen Erskine

'The first big British film to have been made, a film that sweeps our cloistered virtues out into the open.'—*Richard Winnington*

'The best Dickens adaptation, and arguably David Lean's finest film.'—*NFT, 1969*

'It does for Dickens what *Henry V* did for Shakespeare. That is, it indicates a sound method for translating him from print to film . . . almost never less than graceful, tasteful and intelligent, and some of it better than that.'—*James Agee*

† See *Television Companion* for the later TV version with Michael York.

AA: Guy Green; John Bryan
AAN: best picture; script; David Lean (as director)

The Great Flamarion
US 1945   78m   bw

A jealous vaudeville sharpshooter hunts down and kills the woman he loves because she prefers another. Heavy-handed melodrama reminiscent of German silents but without their flair. Erich Von Stroheim, Dan Duryea, Mary Beth Hughes. Written by Heinz Harald, Ann Widton and Richard Weil; directed by Anthony Mann; for Republic.

The Great Gabbo
US 1929   88m   bw

A ventriloquist's personality is taken over by that of his dummy. Yes, that old chestnut, here in tedious and primitive early talkie form. Erich Von Stroheim, Betty Compson, Margie Kane. Written by F. Hugh Herbert from a story by Ben Hecht; directed by James Cruze; for Sono Art.

The Great Garrick**
US 1937   91m   bw
Warner (Mervyn Le Roy)

When Garrick goes to act in Paris, members of the Comédie Française take over a wayside inn and try to teach him a lesson, but the plan goes awry.

A pleasant unhistorical conceit makes a rather literary film to have come from Hollywood, but it is all very winning and cast and director keep the fun simmering happily.

w *Ernest Vajda* d *James Whale* ph *Ernest Haller* m *Adolph Deutsch*

Brian Aherne, Edward Everett Horton, Olivia de Havilland, Lionel Atwill, *Melville Cooper, Luis Alberni, Étienne Girardot*, Marie Wilson, Lana Turner, Albert Dekker, Fritz Leiber, Dorothy Tree, Chester Clute

'As elegantly witty as anything Whale ever did.'—*Tom Milne*

'A jestful and romantic piece.'—*Frank S. Nugent, New York Times*

The Great Gatsby*
US 1949 90m bw
Paramount

Events leading to the death of a retired gangster and mysterious Long Island plutocrat.
Rather bland and uninteresting attempt to accommodate a unique author to a formula star.

w Richard Maibaum, *novel* F. Scott Fitzgerald d Elliott Nugent ph John Seitz m Robert Emmett Dolan

Alan Ladd, Macdonald Carey, Betty Field, Barry Sullivan, Howard da Silva

The Great Gatsby**
US 1974 146m Eastmancolor
Paramount / Newdon (David Merrick)

Plush version with lavish production values and pleasing period sense but not much grip on the story or characters. Overlong footage is not made to seem shorter by snail's pace and dull performances.

w Francis Ford Coppola d Jack Clayton ph *Douglas Slocombe* m Nelson Riddle pd John Box

Robert Redford, Mia Farrow, Karen Black, Scott Wilson, *Sam Waterston*, Lois Chiles

'Pays its creator the regrettable tribute of erecting a mausoleum over his work.'—*Richard Combs*

'Leaves us more involved with six-and-a-half-million dollars' worth of trappings than with human tragedy.'—*Judith Crist*

'A total failure of every requisite sensibility.'—*Stanley Kauffmann*

'Profoundly unfilmable: a poetic and ultimately pessimistic comment on the American dream is transformed by cinematic realism into pure prose.'—*Michael Billington, Illustrated London News*

AA: Nelson Riddle

Great Guns*
US 1941 74m bw
TCF (Sol M. Wurtzel)

A young millionaire's retainers join the army with him.
Disappointing Laurel and Hardy comedy, their first for Fox and the beginning of their decline. A few good jokes, but no overall control or inventiveness.

w Lou Breslow d Monty Banks ph Glen MacWilliams m Emil Newman

Stan Laurel, Oliver Hardy, Sheila Ryan, Dick Nelson, Edmund Macdonald, Charles Trowbridge, Ludwig Stossel, Mae Marsh

Great Guy*
US 1936 73m bw
Grand National (Douglas Maclean)
GB title: *Pluck of the Irish*

An ex-prizefighter joins the bureau of weights and measures and fights corruption.
Rather tame racket film, Cagney's first independent venture away from Warners. He atones for rather thin production values.

w Henry McCarthy, Henry Johnson, James Edward Grant, Harry Ruskin d John G. Blystone ph Jack McKenzie m Marlin Skiles

James Cagney, Mae Clarke, James Burke, Edward Brophy, Henry Kolker

'It's all typical Cagney stuff, and that's the trouble with it.'—*Variety*

The Great Hospital Mystery
US 1937 59m bw

The lady superintendent of a hospital has a busy night including impersonation and murder. Confused but watchable second feature. Jane Darwell, Joan Davis, Sig Rumann, Sally Blane, Thomas Beck, William Demarest. Written by Bess Meredyth, William Conselman and Jerry Cady, from a novel by Mignon G. Eberhardt; directed by James Tinling; for TCF.

The Great Hotel Murder
US 1934 70m bw

Rival sleuths find the truth about a murder less important than being first to find it out. Lively programme filler of its day, with the stars still doing their Flagg and Quirt act. Edmund Lowe, Victor McLaglen, Rosemary Ames, Mary Carlisle. Written by Arthur Kober from a story by Vincent Starrett; directed by Eugene Forde; for TCF.

The Great Impersonation*
US 1935 81m bw
Universal (Edmund Grainger)

During World War I, a German murders an English nobleman and, being his double, takes over.
Reliable espionage melodrama with atmospheric country house asides, from a sturdily compelling novel, previously filmed in 1921 with James Kirkwood.

w Frank Wead, Eve Greene, *novel* E. Phillips Oppenheim *d* Alan Crosland *ph* Milton Krasner *m* Franz Waxman

Edmund Lowe, Valerie Hobson, Vera Engels, Henry Mollison, Lumsden Hare, Spring Byington, Charles Waldron, Dwight Frye

The Great Impersonation*
US 1942 71m bw
Universal (Paul Malvern)

Okay quickie updating of the above, serviceable rather than inventive.

w W. Scott Darling *d* John Rawlins *ph* George Robinson *m* Hans Salter

Ralph Bellamy, Evelyn Ankers, Aubrey Mather, Edward Norris, Karen Verne, Henry Daniell, Ludwig Stossel

The Great Imposter*
US 1961 112m bw
U-I (Robert Arthur)

The career of Ferdinand Waldo Demara, a marine and Trappist monk who also impersonated a Harvard research fellow, a prison warden, a naval doctor and a schoolteacher.
Uncertain mood hampers this biopic of a likeable fantasist.

w Liam O'Brien, *book* Robert Crichton *d* Robert Mulligan *ph* Robert Burks *m* Henry Mancini

Tony Curtis, Raymond Massey, Karl Malden, Edmond O'Brien, Arthur O'Connell, Gary Merrill, Frank Gorshin, Joan Blackman, Robert Middleton

The Great Jewel Robber
US 1950 91m bw

The exploits of real-life society thief Gerald Graham Dennis. Surprisingly acceptable and entertaining reconstruction. David Brian, Marjorie Reynolds, John Archer, Jacqueline de Wit. Written by Borden Chase; directed by Peter Godfrey; for Warner.

The Great John L.
US 1945 96m bw
UA (Frank Mastroly, James Edward Grant)
GB title: *A Man Called Sullivan*

Women in the life of prizefighter John L. Sullivan.

Very mild period biopic without the zest of *Gentleman Jim*.

w James Edward Grant *d* Frank Tuttle *ph* James Van Trees *m* Victor Young

Greg McClure, Linda Darnell, Barbara Britton, Lee Sullivan, Otto Kruger, Wallace Ford, Robert Barrat

The Great Lie***
US 1941 107m bw
Warner (Hal B. Wallis, Henry Blanke)

A determined girl loses the man she loves, believes him dead in a plane crash, and takes over the baby which his selfish wife does not want.
Absurd melodrama becomes top-flight entertainment with all concerned in cracking form and special attention on the two bitchy female leads, splendidly played. Classical music trimmings, too.

w Lenore Coffee, novel Polan Banks *d* Edmund Goulding *ph* Tony Gaudio *m* Max Steiner

Bette Davis, Mary Astor, George Brent, Lucile Watson, Hattie McDaniel, Grant Mitchell, Jerome Cowan

AA: Mary Astor

The Great Locomotive Chase*
US 1956 76m Technicolor
    Cinemascope
Walt Disney (Lawrence Edward Watkin)

During the Civil War, Union spies steal a train and destroy track and bridges behind them.
A serious version of Buster Keaton's *The General*, based on a true incident; good sequences but no overall pace.

w Lawrence Edward Watkin *d* Francis D. Lyon *ph* Charles Boyle *m* Paul Smith

Fess Parker, Jeffrey Hunter, Jeff York, John Lupton, Kenneth Tobey

The Great Lover
US 1931 77m bw

Capers of a philandering opera star.
Satisfactory drama-comedy vehicle for a durable star. Adolphe Menjou, Irene Dunne, Neil Hamilton, Olga Baclanova. Written by Gene Markey; directed by Harry Beaumont; for MGM.

The Great Lover*
US 1949 80m bw
(Paramount) Hope Enterprises (Edmund Beloin)

On a transatlantic liner, a timid scoutmaster catches a strangler.

Amusing suspense comedy, a good star vehicle.

w Edmund Beloin, Melville Shavelson, Jack Rose d Alexander Hall ph Charles Lang m Joseph J. Lilley

Bob Hope, Rhonda Fleming, *Roland Young*, Jim Backus, Roland Culver, George Reeves

The Great McGinty**
US 1940 83m bw
Paramount
GB title: *Down Went McGinty*

A hobo and a crook have a hectic political career.
Lively comedy-drama which signalled the arrival as director of a new and stimulating Hollywood talent.

wd Preston Sturges ph William C. Mellor *m* Frederick Hollander

Brian Donlevy, Akim Tamiroff, Muriel Angelus, Louis Jean Heydt, Arthur Hoyt

'This is his first directing job and where has he been all our lives? He has that sense of the incongruous which makes some of the best gaiety.'—*Otis Ferguson*

'The tough dialogue is matched by short, snappy scenes; the picture seems to have wasted no time, no money.'—*Gilbert Seldes*

'A director as adroit and inventive as any in the business . . . it starts like a five-alarm fire and never slackens pace for one moment until its unexpected conclusion.'—*Pare Lorentz*

'Sturges takes the success ethic and throws it in the face of the audience.'—*James Orsini*

'Capra with the gloves off.'—*Raymond Durgnat*

AA: script

The Great Man**
US 1956 92m bw
U-I (Aaron Rosenberg)

A memorial programme to a much-loved TV personality turns into an exposé.
Patchy melodrama with a *Citizen Kane* framework; the best bits are very effective.

w Jose Ferrer, Al Morgan, novel Al Morgan *d* Jose Ferrer *ph* Harold Lipstein *m* Herman Stein

Jose Ferrer, Dean Jagger, Keenan Wynn, *Julie London*, Joanne Gilbert, *Ed Wynn*, Jim Backus

'Its distinction is in its unwavering tone— one of blunt and frequently savage irony and cynicism.'—*MFB*

'The movie is almost over before one realizes what a slick, fast sell it is (resembling nothing so much as what it is attacking).'— *Pauline Kael, 1968*

The Great Man Votes*
US 1939 72m bw
RKO

A drunken professor turns out to have the casting vote in a local election.
Slow-starting but progressively funny political comedy with some favourite talents in good form.

w John Twist, *story* Gordon Malherbe Hillman *d Garson Kanin ph* Russell Metty *m* Roy Webb

John Barrymore, Virginia Weidler, Peter Holden, *William Demarest, Donald MacBride*

The Great Man's Lady*
US 1942 90m bw
Paramount (William A. Wellman)

A western pioneer is inspired and encouraged by his wife.
Adequate but unsurprising flashback family drama starting with its star as a lady of 109.

w W. L. Rivers, *story* Vina Delmar *d* William L. Wellman *ph* William C. Mellor *m* Victor Young

Barbara Stanwyck, Joel McCrea, Brian Donlevy, Katharine Stevens, Thurston Hall, Lloyd Corrigan

The Great Mr Handel*
GB 1942 103m Technicolor
Rank / GHW (James B. Sloan)

How the 18th-century composer came to write the Messiah.
Earnest, unlikely biopic, naïve but rather commendable.

w Gerald Elliott, Victor MacClure, *play* L. DuGarde Peach *d* Norman Walker *ph* Claude Friese-Greene

Wilfrid Lawson, Elizabeth Allan, Malcolm Keen, Michael Shepley, Hay Petrie, A. E. Matthews

The Great Moment**
US 1944 83m bw
Paramount

How anaesthetics may have been invented.
Curious biopic of Dr W. T. G. Morgan, poised somewhere between utter seriousness and pratfall farce. The beginning of its director's decline, but always interesting in itself.

wd Preston Sturges, book Triumph over Pain by René Fulop-Miller *ph* Victor Milner *m* Victor Young

Joel McCrea, Betty Field, William Demarest, Harry Carey, Franklin Pangborn, Porter Hall, Grady Sutton

The Great Northfield Minnesota Raid*
US 1971   91m   Technicolor
Universal / Robertson and Associates /
    Jennings Lang

In 1876 a gang of bandits, technically
pardoned, plan a bank robbery.
'Realistic' western in which the settings and
photography have an impressively rough look
but the script leaves much to be desired.

wd Philip Kaufman *ph Bruce Surtees m* Dave
Grusin

Cliff Robertson, Robert Duvall, Luke Askew,
Elisha Cook Jnr

The Great Profile*
US 1940   82m   bw
TCF (Raymond Griffith)

A dissipated actor disgraces his family and
becomes an acrobat.
Shapeless farce in which a great talent on his
last legs parodies himself.

w Milton Sperling, Hilary Lynn *d* Walter
Lang *ph* Ernest Palmer *m* Cyril Mockridge
John Barrymore, Mary Beth Hughes, Gregory
Ratoff, Anne Baxter, John Payne, Lionel
Atwill, Edward Brophy, Willie Fung

The Great Race***
US 1965   163m   Technicolor
    Super Panavision
Warner / Patricia / Jalem / Reynard (Martin
    Jurow)

In 1908, the Great Leslie and Professor Fate
are leading contenders in the first New York
to Paris car race.
Elaborate comedy spectacular with many good
moments, notably the early disasters, a
western saloon brawl, and a custard pie fight.
Elsewhere, there is more evidence of an
oversize budget than of wit or finesse, and the
entire Prisoner of Zenda spoof could have
been omitted. Excellent production detail and
general good humour.

w Arthur Ross *d* Blake Edwards *ph Russell
Harlan m Henry Mancini pd Fernando
Carrere*

*Jack Lemmon, Tony Curtis, Peter Falk,
Natalie Wood*, George Macready, Ross
Martin, Vivian Vance, Dorothy Provine

AAN: Russell Harlan; song 'The Sweetheart
Tree' (*m* Henry Mancini, *ly* Johnny Mercer)

The Great Rupert
US 1950   87m   bw

A family of impoverished acrobats are assisted
by a pet squirrel which proves lucky in more
ways than one. Modest whimsical comedy
which outstays its welcome. Jimmy Durante,

Terry Moore, Tom Drake, Sara Haden,
Frank Orth. Written by Laslo Vadnay;
directed by Irving Pichel; for George Pal /
    Eagle Lion. (NB: The squirrel was part
puppet.)

The Great Santini*
US 1979   115m   Technicolor
Warner / Orion / Bing Crosby Productions

A crack fighter pilot has difficulty adjusting to
peacetime domestic life.
Overlong but generally absorbing star
character drama.

wd Lewis John Carlino, *novel* Pat Conway
ph Ralph Woolsey *m* Elmer Bernstein
pd Jack Poplin

Robert Duvall, Blythe Danner, Michael
O'Keefe, Lisa Jane Perskey, Julie Anne
Haddock
    AAN: Robert Duvall; Michael O'Keefe
(supporting actor)

**The Great Scout and Cathouse
Thursday**
US 1976   102m   Technicolor
AIP (Jules Buck and David Korda)
reissue title: *Wildcat*

While trying to revenge himself on an
absconding partner, an old cowboy falls for a
young prostitute.
Downright peculiar comedy western which
never seems to make up its mind what it's
trying to be, and too often is merely
embarrassing.

w Richard Shapiro *d* Don Taylor *ph* Alex
Phillips Jnr *m* John Cameron *pd* Jack Martin
Smith

Lee Marvin, Oliver Reed, Kay Lenz, Robert
Culp, Elizabeth Ashley, Strother Martin,
Sylvia Miles
    'It takes more than a dollop or two of
sentiment and acres of dirty talk to make a
movie.'—*Michael Billington, Illustrated
London News*
    'It sounds like the latest in the cute twosome
series launched by *Butch Cassidy and the
Sundance Kid.* In fact it features not two but
seven wacky westerners who all seem addicted
to stealing, hee-hawing, falling into puddles
and punching each other in the privates.'—
Janet Maslin, Newsweek

The Great Sinner*
US 1949   110m   bw
MGM (Gottfried Reinhardt)

A serious young writer becomes a compulsive
gambler.
Rather pointless and heavy-handed but
extremely good-looking and splendidly cast

period drama vaguely based on Dostoievsky.

w Ladislas Fodor, Christopher Isherwood
d Robert Siodmak *ph George Folsey*
m Bronislau Kaper *ad Cedric Gibbons, Hans
Peck*

Gregory Peck, *Walter Huston*, Ava Gardner,
Agnes Moorehead, Ethel Barrymore, Melvyn
Douglas, Frank Morgan

The Great Sioux Massacre

US 1965 93m Eastmancolor
Cinemascope
Columbia / FF (Leon Fromkess)

Two officers are court-martialled after Custer's
last stand.
Fragmentary flashback western let down by
production and performances.

w Fred C. Dobbs *d* Sidney Salkow *ph* Irving
Lippman *m* Emil Newman, Edward B.
Powell

Joseph Cotten, Darren McGavin, Phil Carey,
Nancy Kovack, Julie Sommars, Michael Pate

The Great Sioux Uprising

US 1953 80m Technicolor
U-I (Albert J. Cohen)

Indians rebel when their horses are stolen for
sale to the commander of Fort Laramie.
Moderate western programmer.

w Richard Breen, Gladys Atwater *d* Lloyd
Bacon *ph* Maury Gertsman *m* Joseph
Gershenson

Jeff Chandler, Faith Domergue, Lyle Bettger

The Great Train Robbery***

US 1903 10m approx bw silent
Edison

Bandits tie up a telegraph operator and rob a
train, but are arrested.
In its day this was a real pioneer. It was among
the longest films then made, it had the most
complicated story line, it was the first western
and it used new technical tricks such as the
pan and the close-up. Needless to say, it must
now be viewed with sympathy.

wd Edwin S. Porter

Marie Murray, Broncho Billy Anderson,
George Barnes

The Great Victor Herbert*

US 1939 91m bw
Paramount (Andrew L. Stone)

At the turn of the century a famous composer
plays cupid to two young singers.
Pleasant minor musical with excellent songs
and an infectious cheerfulness.

w Russel Crouse, Robert Lively *d Andrew L.
Stone ph* Victor Milner *md* Phil Boutelje,
Arthur Lange

Walter Connolly, Allan Jones, Mary Martin,
Susanna Foster, Lee Bowman

AAN: Phil Boutelje, Arthur Lange

The Great Waldo Pepper**

US 1975 108m Technicolor Todd-
AO 35
Universal (George Roy Hill)

In the twenties, a World War I flier becomes
an aerial stuntman.
Whimsical spectacular which concentrates less
on the mystique of flying than on a series of
splendid stunts.

w William Goldman *d George Roy Hill
ph Robert Surtees m* Henry Mancini

Robert Redford, Bo Svenson, Bo Brundin,
Susan Sarandon, Geoffrey Lewis
'Charged with enthralling balletic
precision.'—*Tom Milne*
'One hundred per cent pure plastic
adolescent male fantasy.'—*New Yorker*

The Great Waltz***

US 1938 103m bw
MGM (Bernard Hyman)

Young Johann Strauss becomes Vienna's waltz
king.
Exhilarating old-fashioned studio-set musical
located in Hollywood's endearing vision of
Old Vienna, assisted by streamlined
production and excellent cast. Musical
schmaltz.

w Walter Reisch, Samuel Hoffenstein, *story*
Gottfried Reinhardt *d Julien Duvivier
ph* Joseph Ruttenberg *m* Dmitri Tiomkin

Fernand Gravet, Luise Rainer, Miliza Korjus,
Lionel Atwill, Hugh Herbert, Herman Bing,
Curt Bois
'Miliza Korjus—rhymes with gorgeous!'—
publicity

AA: Joseph Ruttenberg
AAN: Miliza Korjus

The Great Waltz*

US 1972 134m Metrocolor
Panavision 70
MGM (Andrew L. Stone)

Heavy-going remake set on real locations and
hampered by them, styled in the manner of
the same director's *Song of Norway*, i.e. with
no real style at all. The music survives.

wd Andrew L. Stone *ph* David Boulton
ad William Albert Havenmeyer *ch* Onna
White

Horst Buchholz, Nigel Patrick, Mary Costa,
Rossano Brazzi, Yvonne Mitchell
'Take a box of chocolates—soft-centred, of
course.'—*Michael Billington, Illustrated
London News*

The Great White Hope**

US 1970   103m   De Luxe   Panavision
TCF (Lawrence Turman)

In 1910, a black boxer becomes world
heavyweight champ but has trouble through
his affair with a white girl.

Vivid, slightly whitewashed biopic of Jack
Johnson (called Jefferson). Dramatic
deficiencies outweighed by excellent period
detail and a spellbinding central performance.

w Howard Sackler, from his play d Martin
Ritt ph Burnett Guffey m negro traditionals
pd John de Cuir

James Earl Jones, Jane Alexander, Lou
Gilbert, Joel Fluellen, Chester Morris, Robert
Webber, Hal Holbrook

AAN: James Earl Jones; Jane Alexander

The Great Ziegfeld**

US 1936   179m   bw
MGM (Hunt Stromberg)

The growth and Broadway fame of impresario
Florenz Ziegfeld.

Mammoth biopic which despite a few show-
stopping numbers never takes off dramatically
and becomes something of an endurance test;
interesting, however, as a spectacular of its
time.

w William Anthony McGuire d Robert Z.
Leonard ph Oliver T. Marsh, Ray June,
George Folsey md Arthur Lange ad Cedric
Gibbons

William Powell, Luise Rainer (as Anna Held),
Myrna Loy (as Billie Burke), Frank Morgan,
Reginald Owen, Nat Pendleton, Virginia
Bruce, Ray Bolger, Harriett Hoctor, Ernest
Cossart, Fanny Brice, Robert Greig, Gilda
Gray, Leon Errol, Stanley Morner (Dennis
Morgan)

'This huge inflated gas-blown object bobs
into the critical view as irrelevantly as an
airship advertising somebody's toothpaste at a
south coast resort. It lasts three hours. That is
its only claim to special attention.'—Graham
Greene

'Everything should have been tightened—
not in the team job of cutting those miles of
negative, but in boiling down the script, saving
a line here, combining two scenes into one.'—
Otis Ferguson

AA: best picture; Luise Rainer
AAN: William Anthony McGuire; Robert Z.
Leonard

The Greatest

US / GB 1977   101m   Metrocolor
Columbia / EMI (John Marshall)

The life and times of Muhammed Ali.
Bland confection of rags to riches in the
boxing ring, its only plus being that Ali plays
himself and offers a predictable array of
enjoyable one-liners.

w Ring Lardner Jnr, from Ali's autobiography
The Greatest d Tom Gries ph Harry
Stradling m Michael Masser

Muhammed Ali, Ernest Borgnine, Roger E.
Mosley, Lloyd Haynes, Malachi Throne, John
Marley, Robert Duvall, David Huddleston,
Ben Johnson, James Earl Jones, Dina Merrill,
Paul Winfield

The Greatest Show on Earth*

US 1952   153m   Technicolor
Paramount / Cecil B. de Mille (Henry
   Wilcoxon)

Various dramas come to a head under the big
top.
Moribund circus drama with bad acting, stilted
production, an irrelevant train crash climax
and a few genuinely spectacular and enjoyable
moments.

w Fredric M. Frank, Theodore St John, Frank
Cavett, Barre Lyndon d Cecil B. de Mille
ph George Barnes, Peverell Marley, Wallace
Kelley m Victor Young ad Hal Pereira,
Walter Tyler

Betty Hutton, Cornel Wilde, James Stewart,
Charlton Heston, Dorothy Lamour, Gloria
Grahame, Lyle Bettger, Henry Wilcoxon,
Emmett Kelly, Lawrence Tierney, John
Kellogg, John Ringling North

AA: best picture
AAN: original story (Fredric M. Frank,
Theodore St John, Frank Cavett); Cecil B. de
Mille (as director)

The Greatest Story Ever Told**

US 1965   225m   Technicolor   Ultra
   Panavision 70
UA / George Stevens

Solemn spectacular with an elephantine pace,
shot in Utah because allegedly it looked more
like Palestine than Palestine did. All frightfully
elegant and reverent, but totally unmoving,
partly because of the fatal casting of stars in
bit parts. (John Wayne looks in merely to say
'Truly this man was the son of God.')

w James Lee Barrett, George Stevens, from
various sources d George Stevens ph William
C. Mellor, Loyal Griggs m Alfred Newman
ad Richard Day, William Creber

Max Von Sydow, Dorothy McGuire, Claude
Rains, Jose Ferrer, David McCallum,
Charlton Heston, Sidney Poitier, Donald

Pleasence, Roddy McDowall, Gary Raymond, Carroll Baker, Pat Boone, Van Heflin, Sal Mineo, Shelley Winters, Ed Wynn, John Wayne, Telly Savalas, Angela Lansbury, Joseph Schildkraut, Victor Buono, Nehemiah Persoff

'George Stevens was once described as a water buffalo of film art. What this film more precisely suggests is a dinosaur.'—*MFB*

'God is unlucky in *The Greatest Story Ever Told*. His only begotten son turns out to be a bore . . . the photography is inspired mainly by Hallmark Cards . . . as the Hallelujah Chorus explodes around us stereophonically and stereotypically it becomes clear that Lazarus was not so much raised from the tomb as blasted out of it. As for pacing, the picture does not let you forget a single second of its four hours.'—*John Simon*

'No more than three minutes have elapsed before we suspect that Stevens' name and fame have been purchased by the Hallmark Greeting Card Company, and that what we are looking at is really a lengthy catalogue of greeting cards for 1965—for Those Who Care Enough to Send the Very Best.'—*Stanley Kauffmann*

AAN: William C. Mellor, Loyal Griggs; Alfred Newman

Greed•••
US 1923 110m (24 fps) bw silent
Metro-Goldwyn (Erich Von Stroheim, Irving Thalberg)

An ex-miner dentist kills his avaricious wife. Later in Death Valley he also kills her lover, but is bound to him by handcuffs.
This much-discussed film is often cited as its director's greatest folly: the original version ran eight hours. Re-edited by June Mathis, it retains considerable power sequence by sequence, but is necessarily disjointed in development. However, it must be seen to be appreciated.

wd Erich Von Stroheim, *novel* McTeague by Frank Norris *ph* Ben Reynolds, William Daniels, Ernest B. Schoedsack *ad* Richard Day, Cedric Gibbons, Erich Von Stroheim

Gibson Gowland, Zasu Pitts, *Jean Hersholt*, Chester Conklin, Dale Fuller

'The end leaves one with an appalling sense of human waste, of futility, of the drabness and cruelty of lives stifled by genteel poverty. Every character in the film is overwhelmed by it.'—*Gavin Lambert*

'Von Stroheim is a genius—*Greed* established that beyond all doubt—but he is badly in need of a stopwatch.'—*Robert E. Sherwood*

† In 1972 Herman G. Weinberg published a complete screenplay with 400 stills.

The Greed of William Hart
GB 1948 78m bw
Bushey (Gilbert Church)

In old Edinburgh, grave robbers procure corpses for an anatomist.
Cheapie version of a much filmed subject. This scenario was refurbished eleven years later by the same writer as *The Flesh and the Fiends*; see also *The Body Snatcher, Burke and Hare*.

w John Gilling *d* Oswald Mitchell *ph* S. D. Onions

Tod Slaughter, Henry Oscar, Aubrey Woods, Arnold Bell

The Greek Tycoon
US 1978 106m Technicolor Panavision
Universal / ABKCO (Allan Klein, Ely Landau)

A billionaire shipping tycoon marries the widow of an American president.
Rather messy 'faction' based on Onassis and Jacqueline Kennedy; entirely uninteresting save for glossy backgrounds and the relentlessness with which the characters swear at each other.

w Mort Fine *d* J. Lee Thompson *ph* Tony Richmond *m* Stanley Myers *pd* Michael Stringer

Anthony Quinn, Jacqueline Bisset, Raf Vallone, Edward Albert, James Franciscus, Camilla Sparv

The Greeks Had a Word for Them•
US 1932 77m bw
UA

Adventures of three New York gold diggers.
Smart early talkie which helped launch the *Gold Diggers* series and TCF's parallel *Three Little Mice / Moon over Miami / How to Marry a Millionaire* series.

w Sidney Howard, *play* Zoe Akins *d* Lowell Sherman *ph* George Barnes *m* Alfred Newman

Joan Blondell, Madge Evans, Ina Claire, David Manners, Lowell Sherman, Phillips Smalley, Betty Grable

The Green Berets
US 1968 141m Technicolor Panavision
Warner / Batjac (Michael Wayne)

After extensive training, two tough army detachments see service in Vietnam.

Overlong actioner criticized for unquestioningly accepting the Vietnam cause; in itself, violent, exhausting and dull.

w James Lee Barrett, *novel* Robin Moore d John Wayne, Ray Kellogg *ph* Winton C. Hoch *m* Miklos Rozsa

John Wayne, David Janssen, Jim Hutton, Aldo Ray, Raymond St Jacques, Jack Soo, Bruce Cabot, Patrick Wayne, Irene Tsu, Jason Evers, Luke Askew

'Propaganda as crude as this can only do damage to its cause.'—*David Wilson*

'A film best handled from a distance and with a pair of tongs.'—*Penelope Gilliatt*

The Green Cockatoo
GB 1937   65m   bw
TCF / New World (Robert T. Kane)
aka: *Four Dark Hours; Race Gang*

A man seeks revenge on the gangsters who killed his brother.
Sleazy little Soho-set thriller, mainly remarkable for cast and credits.

w Edward O. Berkman, Arthur Wimperis, *story* Graham Greene d William Cameron Menzies

John Mills, Robert Newton, Rene Ray, Bruce Seton, Charles Oliver

Green Dolphin Street
US 1947   141m   bw
MGM (Carey Wilson)

A Channel Islander emigrates to New Zealand and sends home for the wrong bride.
Silly 19th-century romance climaxed by rather a good earthquake. Expensively but falsely produced.

w Samson Raphaelson, *novel* Elizabeth Goudge d Victor Saville *ph* George Folsey *m* Bronislau Kaper

Lana Turner, Richard Hart, Edmund Gwenn, Van Heflin, Donna Reed

AAN: George Folsey

Green Fingers
GB 1946   83m   bw

An unqualified osteopath tries to achieve respectability. Unsurprising and flatly made drama of eventual success against all odds. Robert Beatty, Carol Raye, Nova Pilbeam, Felix Aylmer, Moore Marriott, Edward Rigby. Written by Jack Whittingham, from the novel *Persistent Warrior* by Edith Arundel; directed by John Harlow; for British National.

Green Fire
US 1954   100m   Eastmancolor
  Cinemascope
MGM (Armand Deutsch)

Two engineers disagree over their mining of Colombia emeralds.
Routine adventure story with good action highlights including landslide, flood and storm, all deadened by dull dialogue and romantic complications.

w Ivan Goff, Ben Roberts d Andrew Marton *ph* Paul Vogel *m* Miklos Rozsa

Stewart Granger, Paul Douglas, Grace Kelly

Green for Danger****
GB 1946   93m   bw
Rank / Individual (Frank Launder, Sidney Gilliat)

A mysterious murderer strikes on the operating table at a wartime emergency hospital.
Classic comedy-thriller, with serious detection balanced by excellent jokes and performances, also by moments of fright.

w *Sidney Gilliat, Claud Gurney, novel* Christianna Brand d *Sidney Gilliat ph Wilkie Cooper m* William Alwyn

Alastair Sim, Sally Gray, Rosamund John, Trevor Howard, Leo Genn, Megs Jenkins, Judy Campbell, Ronald Ward, Moore Marriott

The Green Glove
US / France 1952   89m   bw
UA / Benagoss (George Maurer)

A paratrooper against all odds returns a jewelled relic to its proper place in a French church.
An unsatisfactory concoction by people who have clearly seen *The Maltese Falcon* as well as lots of Hitchcock films, this interestingly cast and credited independent production never really takes off.

w Charles Bennett d Rudolph Maté *ph* Claude Renoir *m* Joseph Kosma

Glenn Ford, Cedric Hardwicke, Geraldine Brooks, George Macready, Gaby André, Roger Treville

The Green Goddess*
US 1930   74m   bw
Warner

An Indian potentate holds Britishers prisoner.
Early talkie star vehicle which was also successful on the stage and as a silent but has little appeal now.

w Julian Josephson, *play* William Archer
d Alfred E. Green *ph* James Van Trees

George Arliss, Alice Joyce, H. B. Warner,
Ralph Forbes, David Tearle
† Remade 1942 as *Adventure in Iraq*.

AAN: George Arliss

Green Grass of Wyoming

US 1948 88m Technicolor
TCF

A rancher captures his runaway white stallion
and wins the local trotting races.
Predictable, good-looking family film shot on
location; a second sequel to *My Friend Flicka*.

w Martin Berkeley, *novel* Mary O'Hara
d Louis King *ph* Charles G. Clarke *m* Cyril
Mockridge

Peggy Cummins, Charles Coburn, Robert
Arthur, Lloyd Nolan

AAN: Charles G. Clarke

Green Grow the Rushes

GB 1951 77m bw
ACT Films

Civil servants discover that a Kentish village is
devoted to smuggling.
Amiable but disappointingly feeble imitation
of Ealing comedy by a company formed from
the technicians' union; it simply hasn't got the
right snap in any department.

w Derek Twist, Howard Clewes,
novel Howard Clewes *d* Derek Twist
ph Harry Waxman *m* Lambert Williamson

Roger Livesey, Richard Burton, Honor
Blackman, Frederick Leister, John Salew,
Colin Gordon, Geoffrey Keen, Harcourt
Williams, Vida Hope

Green Hell*

US 1940 87m bw
Universal (Harry Edgington)

Explorers seek Inca treasure in the South
American Jungle.
Studio-bound potboiler unworthy of its
director but mainly enjoyable as a romp.

w Frances Marion *d* James Whale *ph* Karl
Freund

Douglas Fairbanks Jnr, Joan Bennett, George
Sanders, Vincent Price, Alan Hale, Gene
Garrick, George Bancroft, John Howard
† The temple set was re-used the same year in
The Mummy's Hand.

The Green Light*

US 1937 85m bw
Warner (Henry Blanke)

A dedicated doctor gives up his practice when
a patient dies.
Adequate star melodrama.

w Milton Krims, *novel* Lloyd C. Douglas
d Frank Borzage *ph* Byron Haskin *m* Max
Steiner

Errol Flynn, Anita Louise, Margaret Lindsay,
Cedric Hardwicke, Henry O'Neill, Spring
Byington

The Green Man*

GB 1956 80m bw
BL / Grenadier (Frank Launder, Sidney
Gilliat)

A professional assassin stalks a pompous
politician.
Cheerful but not very subtle black comedy,
suffering from the attempt to make a star part
out of a very minor character.

w Sidney Gilliat, Frank Launder, from their
play Meet a Body *d* Robert Day *ph* Gerald
Gibbs *m* Cedric Thorpe Davie

Alastair Sim, George Cole, Jill Adams, Terry-
Thomas, Avril Angers, John Chandos, Dora
Bryan, Colin Gordon, Raymond Huntley

Green Mansions

US 1959 104m Metrocolor
Cinemascope
MGM / Avon (Edmund Grainger)

In a remote Amazon forest an adventurer
encounters Rima, a child of nature who takes
him on a quest for truth.
Absurd studio-bound Shangri-La story based
on an Edwardian fantasy that may well have
suited the printed page, but not the wide
screen. Dismally photographed in shades of
green, with all concerned looking acutely
uncomfortable.

w Dorothy Kingsley, *novel* W. H. Hudson
d Mel Ferrer *ph* Joseph Ruttenberg
m Bronislau Kaper, Hector Villa-Lobos

Anthony Perkins, Audrey Hepburn, Lee J.
Cobb, Henry Silva

The Green Pastures****

US 1936 93m bw
Warner (Henry Blanke)

Old Testament stories as seen through simple-
minded negro eyes.
Though recently attacked as setting back the
cause of black emancipation, this is a
brilliantly sympathetic and humorous film,
very cunningly adapted for the screen in a
series of dramatic scenes which make the
material work even better than it did on the
stage.

w Marc Connelly, from his play and stories by Roark Bradford *d William Keighley, Marc Connelly ph Hal Mohr m Erich Wolfgang Korngold*

Rex Ingram, Oscar Polk, Eddie Anderson, Frank Wilson, George Reed

'I imagine God has a sense of humour, and I imagine that He is delighted with *The Green Pastures.*'—*Don Herold*

'That disturbance around the Music Hall yesterday was the noise of shuffling queues in Sixth Avenue and the sound of motion picture critics dancing in the street.'—*Bosley Crowther, New York Times*

'This is as good a religious play as one is likely to get in this age from a practised New York writer.'—*Graham Greene*

The Green Scarf
GB 1954   96m   bw
B and A (Bertram Ostrer, Albert Fennell)

An elderly French lawyer takes on the defence of a blind, deaf and dumb murder suspect.
Plodding courtroom drama with familiar faces in unconvincing French guise.

w Gordon Wellesley, novel The Brute by Guy des Cars *d George More O'Ferrall ph Jack Hildyard m Brian Easdale*

Michael Redgrave, Ann Todd, Leo Genn, Kieron Moore

The Green Years*
US 1946   127m   bw
MGM (Leon Gordon)

A young boy brought up strictly in Ireland makes friends with his mischievous grandfather.
Period family film in familiar style, sparked only by its scene-stealing star performance.

w Robert Ardrey, Sonya Levien, novel A. J. Cronin *d Victor Saville ph George Folsey m Herbert Stothart ad Cedric Gibbons, Hans Peters*

Charles Coburn, Dean Stockwell, Tom Drake, Beverly Tyler, Hume Cronyn, Gladys Cooper, Selena Royle, Jessica Tandy, Richard Haydn, Andy Clyde

'It has been described in the ads as "wonderful" by everyone within Louis B. Mayer's purchasing power except his horses, so I hesitate to ask you to take my word for it: the picture is awful.'—*James Agee*

AAN: George Folsey; Charles Coburn

The Greengage Summer*
GB 1961   99m   Technicolor
Columbia / PKL (Victor Saville, Edward Small)
US title: *Loss of Innocence*

A young girl staying at a hotel falls in love with a jewel thief but is accidentally responsible for his capture.
Old-fashioned and not very interesting story with an appeal, one supposes, to well-brought-up young women. Decently made.

w Howard Koch, novel Rumer Godden *d Lewis Gilbert ph Frederick A. Young m Richard Addinsell*

Kenneth More, Danielle Darrieux, Susannah York, Claude Nollier, Jane Asher, Elizabeth Dear, Maurice Denham

Greenwich Village*
US 1944   82m   Technicolor
TCF (William Le Baron)

In the twenties, a hick composer in New York allows his concerto to be used in a jazz musical.
Lightweight musical romp.

w Michael Fessier, Ernest Pagano d Walter Lang ph Leon Shamroy, Harry Jackson songs Leo Robin, Nacio Herb Brown

Carmen Miranda, Don Ameche, William Bendix, Vivian Blaine, Felix Bressart, Tony and Sally De Marco, Adolph Green, Betty Comden, Alvin Hammer, Judy Holliday

Greetings*
US 1968   88m   Eastmancolor

A draftee tries every which way to be exempted, then subjects himself to a whirl of physical experience. Kaleidoscopic stringing together of fleeting satirical bits; talent undeniable but equally uncontrolled. Jonathan Warden, Robert de Niro, Gerrit Graham, Megan McCormick. Written by Charles Hirsch and Brian de Palma; directed and edited by Brian de Palma; for West End Films.

Greyfriars Bobby*
GB 1960   91m   Technicolor
Walt Disney (Hugh Attwooll)

A Skye terrier keeps persistent vigil over his master's grave and is made a freeman of the city of Edinburgh.
Adequately produced film of a charming old Victorian story.

w Robert Westerby d Don Chaffey ph Paul Beeson m Francis Chagrin

Donald Crisp, Laurence Naismith, Alexander Mackenzie, Kay Walsh, Andrew Cruickshank, Vincent Winter, Moultrie Kelsall, Duncan Macrae

'The better Disney qualities of exact period detail and childlike directness are apparent.'—*MFB*

† The story was previously filmed as *Challenge to Lassie*.

Il Grido*
Italy 1957 102m bw
SPA Cinematografica / Robert Alexander
aka: *The Cry*

A man whose wife has left him travels across
the Po Valley with his daughter in search of
new happiness, but fails to find it and commits
suicide.
Watchable but rather aimlessly depressing
character drama.

w Michelangelo Antonioni, Elio Bartolini,
Ennio de Concini *d* Michelangelo Antonioni
ph Gianni di Venanzo *m* Giovanni Fusco

Steve Cochran, Alida Valli, Dorian Gray,
Betsy Blair, Lynn Shaw

Grip of the Strangler*
GB 1958 78m bw
Producers' Associates (John Croydon)
US title: *The Haunted Strangler*

A novelist investigating an old murder case
finds that he was himself the murderer.
Moderate thriller with a predictable but
efficient plot.

w Jan Read *d* Robert Day *ph* Lionel Banes
m Buxton Orr

Boris Karloff, Elizabeth Allan, Jean Kent,
Vera Day, Anthony Dawson

The Grissom Gang
US 1971 128m Metrocolor
Associates and Aldrich / ABC

In 1931, a New York heiress is kidnapped by
gangsters and comes to like it.
Unpleasant remake of *No Orchids for Miss
Blandish* (previously filmed under that title,
incredibly badly, in GB in 1948), with too
much footage of lush blonde being slobbered
over by psychotic thug, and an inevitable
emphasis on violence.

w Leon Griffiths, *novel* James Hadley Chase
d Robert Aldrich *ph* Joseph Biroc *m* Gerald
Fried *ad* James Dowell Vance

Scott Wilson, Kim Darby, Tony Musante,
Robert Lansing, Irene Dailey, Connie
Stevens, Wesley Addy
    'Offensive, immoral and perhaps even
lascivious.'—*Vincent Canby*

Grizzly
US 1976 91m Movielab Todd AO 35
Film Ventures International (David
    Sheldon, Harvey Flaxman)
aka: *Killer Grizzly*

A mammoth bear preys upon campers in a
national park.
Inept and boring shocker in the wake of *Jaws*.

w Harvey Flaxman, David Sheldon *d* William
Girdler *ph* William Asman *m* Robert O.
Ragland

Christopher George, Andrew Prine, Richard
Jaeckel, Joan McCall

Grounds for Marriage
US 1950 90m bw

A divorced couple meet again and find they
have strange effects on each other. Stolid
romantic comedy with second team talent.
Van Johnson, Kathryn Grayson, Paula
Raymond, Lewis Stone, Reginald Owen,
Barry Sullivan. Written by Allen Rivkin and
Laura Kerr; directed by Robert Z. Leonard;
for MGM.

The Groundstar Conspiracy*
US 1972 96m Technicolor Panavision
Universal / Hal Roach International (Trevor
    Wallace)

An explosion rips apart a top secret space
project, and the surviving scientist loses his
memory.
Gimmicky but generally compulsive sci-fi
mystery yarn, with an effective though
predictable climax.

w Matthew Howard, *novel* The Alien by L. P.
Davies *d* Lamont Johnson *ph* Michael Reed
m Paul Hoffert

George Peppard, Michael Sarrazin, James
Olson, Christine Belford, Tim O'Connor,
James McEachin

The Group***
US 1966 152m De Luxe
UA / Famous Artists (Sidney Buchman)

The subsequent love lives of a group of girls
who graduate from Vassar in 1933.
Patchy but generally fascinating series of
interwoven sketches and character studies,
with mainly tragic overtones; good attention to
period detail, and dazzling array of new talent.

*w Sidney Buchman, novel Mary McCarthy
d Sidney Lumet ph Boris Kaufman
m* Charles Gross *pd Gene Callahan*

Joanna Pettet, Candice Bergen, *Jessica Walter,
Joan Hackett*, Elizabeth Hartman, Mary
Robin-Redd, *Kathleen Widdoes*, Shirley
Knight, Larry Hagman, *Hal Holbrook, Robert
Emhardt*, Robert Mulligan, James Congdon,
James Broderick
    'Although it is a strange, inclusive, no-
holds-barred movie that runs the gamut from
scenes that are almost soap-operaish, to
amusing scenes that are almost satire, to
outrageously frank scenes that are almost

voyeuristic, it is still greatly exhilarating while it provokes thought and pushes the viewer into examining his own conscience.'—*Philip T. Hartung, Commonweal*

Guadalcanal Diary*
US 1943   93m   bw
TCF (Bryan Foy)

Marines fight for a vital Pacific base.
Standard war propaganda, with good action scenes.

w Lamar Trotti, *book* Richard Tregaskis *d* Lewis Seiler *ph* Charles G. Clarke *m* David Buttolph

Preston Foster, Lloyd Nolan, William Bendix, Richard Conte, Anthony Quinn, Richard Jaeckel, Roy Roberts, Minor Watson, Ralph Byrd, Lionel Stander, Miles Mander, Reed Hadley

The Guardsman*
US 1931   83m   bw
MGM (Albert Lewin)

A jealous actor tests his wife's fidelity.
Theatrically effective comedy filmed for the sake of its stars; later remade as a musical, *The Chocolate Soldier* (qv).

w Ernest Vajda, Claudine West, *play* Ferenc Molnar *d* Sidney Franklin *ph* Norbert Brodine

Alfred Lunt, Lynn Fontanne, Roland Young, Zasu Pitts, Maude Eburne, Herman Bing, Ann Dvorak

AAN: Alfred Lunt; Lynn Fontanne

La Guerre Est Finie
France / Sweden 1966   122m   bw
Sofracima / Europa Film
aka: *The War Is Over*

A Spanish revolutionary maintains his ideals even though he is warned that he will be sold out.
Dreary drama with romantic interludes and a fussy technique involving what appears to be the first use of flashforwards.

w Jorge Semprun *d* Alain Resnais *ph* Sacha Vierny *m* Giovanni Fusco

Yves Montand, Ingrid Thulin, Geneviève Bujold, Michel Piccoli

AAN: Jorge Semprun

Guess Who's Coming to Dinner**
US 1967   112m   Technicolor
Columbia / Stanley Kramer

A well-to-do San Francisco girl announces that she is going to marry a black man, and her parents find they are less broad-minded than they thought.
The problem picture that isn't really, since everyone is so nice and the prospective bridegroom is so eligible. It looks like a photographed play, but isn't based on one; the set is unconvincing; but the acting is a dream.

w William Rose *d* Stanley Kramer *ph* Sam Leavitt *md* Frank de Vol *pd* Robert Clatworthy

Spencer Tracy, Katharine Hepburn, Katharine Houghton (Hepburn's niece), *Sidney Poitier*, Cecil Kellaway, Roy E. Glenn Snr, Beah Richards, Isabell Sanford, Virginia Christine

'Suddenly everybody's caught up in a kind of integrated drawing-room comedy, and unable to decide whether there's anything funny in it or not.'—*Ann Birstein, Vogue*

'A load of embarrassing rubbish. In the circumstances there is little that director Stanley Kramer can do but see that his camera plod from room to room and make the most of people sitting down and getting up again.'—*Penelope Mortimer*

'What Rose and Kramer have done is to create a number of elaborate Aunt Sallies, arrange them in attractive patterns, and dispose of them with the flick of a feather.'—*Basil Wright, 1972*

'Mendacious and sanctimonious drivel.'—*John Simon*

AA: William Rose; Katharine Hepburn
AAN: best picture; Stanley Kramer; Frank de Vol; Spencer Tracy; Cecil Kellaway; Beah Richards

Guest in the House*
US 1944   121m   bw
Hunt Stromberg

A seemingly pleasant young woman is invited to stay with a family and brings tragedy and hatred to them.
Theatrical and rather unconvincing melodrama.

w Ketti Frings, *play* Dear Evelyn by Dale Eunson, Hagar Wilde *d* John Brahm *ph* Lee Garmes *m* Werner Janssen *pd* Nicolai Remisoff

Anne Baxter, Ralph Bellamy, Aline MacMahon, Ruth Warrick, Scott McKay, Jerome Cowan, Marie McDonald, Percy Kilbride, Margaret Hamilton

AAN: Werner Janssen

Guest Wife
US 1945   90m   bw
(UA) Jack H. Skirball

For business purposes a man allows his wife to pretend to be the wife of another.
Stereotyped star farce which seemed tolerable at the time.

w Bruce Manning, John Klorer *d* Sam Wood *ph* Joseph Valentine *md* Daniele Amfitheatrof

Claudette Colbert, Don Ameche, Dick Foran, Charles Dingle, Grant Mitchell

'Mr Wood is a big gun to be trained on so trivial a target, but the result justifies the choice.'—*Richard Mallett, Punch*

AAN: Daniele Amfitheatrof

A Guide for the Married Man**
US 1967   91m   De Luxe   Panavision
TCF (Frank McCarthy)

A practised wolf explains to a perfect husband how to be unfaithful.
Generally funny revue with as many hilarious moments as flat spots.

w Frank Tarloff *d* Gene Kelly *ph* Joe Macdonald *m* Johnny Williams

Walter Matthau, Inger Stevens, *Robert Morse*, Sue Anne Langdon, Lucille Ball, Art Carney, Jack Benny, Polly Bergen, Joey Bishop, Sid Caesar, Wally Cox, Jayne Mansfield, Carl Reiner, Phil Silvers, Jeffrey Hunter, Terry-Thomas, Ben Blue

'One of the funniest films of the last several seasons . . . it has sense enough to sit down when it's through.'—*Robert Windeler*

Guilt Is My Shadow
GB 1950   86m   bw

A girl kills her villainous husband and is helped by a farmer. Tedious melodrama, stiffly told and not helped by rural surroundings. Patrick Holt, Elizabeth Sellars, Peter Reynolds, Lana Morris, Avice Landone. Written by Ivan Foxwell, Roy Kellino and John Gilling, from the novel *You're Best Alone* by Peter Curtis; directed by Roy Kellino; for Ivan Foxwell.

The Guilt of Janet Ames
US 1948   83m   bw
Columbia

A paralysed war widow seeks to discover whether her husband's sacrifice was worthwhile.
Embarrassing attempt by a comedienne to play Hamlet.

w Louella Macfarlane, Allen Rivkin, Devery Freeman, *story* Lenore Coffee *d* Henry Levin *ph* Joseph Walker *m* Morris Stoloff

Rosalind Russell, Melvyn Douglas, Sid Caesar, Betsy Blair, Nina Foch, Harry Von Zell, Arthur Space

Guilty?
GB 1956   93m   bw
Grand National / Gibraltar (Charles A. Leeds)

An ex-resistance heroine is on trial for murder at the Old Bailey; her young solicitor goes to Avignon to prove her innocence.
Solidly cast old-fashioned mystery with a courtroom climax.

w Maurice J. Wilson, *novel* Death Has Deep Roots by Michael Gilbert *d* Edmond Greville *ph* Stan Pavey *m* Bruce Montgomery

John Justin, Barbara Laage, Donald Wolfit, Stephen Murray, Norman Wooland, Frank Villard, Sydney Tafler, Betty Stockfield

Guilty of Treason
US 1950   86m   bw

An account of the trial by the Russians of the Hungarian primate Cardinal Mindzenty.
Gutter press version of real events, with cheap production and fictional frills. Charles Bickford, Paul Kelly, Bonita Granville, Richard Derr, Barry Kroeger, Elisabeth Risdon. Written by Emmet Lavery; directed by Felix Feist; for Eagle Lion. (GB title: *Treason*.)

The Guinea Pig**
GB 1949   97m   bw
Pilgrim (The Boultings)
US title: *The Outsider*

The first poor boy to win a scholarship to a famous public school has a hard time.
Enjoyable though unrealistic school drama with chief interest centring on the staff. A rude word ('kick up the arse') ensured its popularity.

w Bernard Miles, Warren Chetham Strode, from the latter's play *d* Roy Boulting *ph* Gilbert Taylor *m* John Wooldridge

Richard Attenborough, *Robert Flemyng, Cecil Trouncer*, Sheila Sim, Bernard Miles, Joan Hickson

Gulliver's Travels***
US 1939   74m   Technicolor
(Paramount) Max Fleischer

Animated cartoon version which invents a Romeo-Juliet romance between Lilliput and Blefuscu and has the usual trouble with romantic humans. At the time it represented a genuine challenge to Disney, but has not worn well in terms of pace or inventiveness. Fleischer made one more feature cartoon, *Mr Bug Goes to Town.*

d Dave Fleischer *m* Victor Young
songs Ralph Rainger, Leo Robin

AAN: song 'Faithful Forever'; Victor Young

Gulliver's Travels
GB 1976 81m Eastmancolor
EMI / Valeness-Belvision (Josef Shaftel)

An ineffective treatment, again aimed at children, in which Gulliver is the only human element and all the Lilliputians are cartooned.

w Don Black *d* Peter Hunt *ph* Alan Hume
pd Michael Stringer *m* Michel Legrand

Richard Harris, Catherine Schell, Norman Shelley
    'Bonelessly inoffensive.'—*Sight and Sound*

The Gumball Rally
US 1976 107m Technicolor
Warner / First Artists (Chuck Bail)

A variety of vehicles take part in a crazy race from New York to Long Beach.
The stuntmen are the real stars of this good-looking but dramatically deficient chase and destruction extravaganza.

w Leon Capetanos *d* Chuck Bail *ph Richard Glouner m* Dominic Frontière *stunt co-ordinator* Eddie Donno

Michael Sarrazin, Normann Burton, Gary Busey, John Durren, Susan Flannery

Gumshoe**
GB 1971 85m Eastmancolor
Columbia / Memorial (David Barber)

A Liverpool bingo caller dreams of becoming a Bogart-like private eye and finds himself in the middle of a murder case.
A likeable spoof which is never quite as funny as it means to be. Billy Liar did it better, but there's plenty of amusing detail.

w Neville Smith *d* Stephen Frears *ph* Chris Menges *m* Andrew Lloyd Webber

Albert Finney, Billie Whitelaw, Fulton Mackay, Frank Finlay, Janice Rule

Gun Crazy*
US 1950 87m bw
King Brothers
reissue title: *Deadly is the Female*

A boy and girl set off on a trail of armed robbery and murder.
Modernized Bonnie and Clyde story which has become a minor cult film.

w Mackinlay Kantor, Millard Kaufman
d Joseph H. Lewis ph Russell Harlan
m Victor Young

John Dall, Peggy Cummins, Morris Carnovsky, Barry Kroger, Annabel Shaw, Harry Lewis

Gun Fury
US 1953 80m Technicolor 3-D
Columbia (Lewis J. Rachmil)

Outlaws rob a stagecoach and abduct a girl; her fiancé follows and takes revenge.
Adequate western programmer.

w Irving Wallace, Roy Huggins *d* Raoul Walsh *ph* Lester H. White *md* Mischa Bakaleinikoff

Rock Hudson, Donna Reed, Phil Carey, Lee Marvin, Neville Brand

Gun Glory
US 1957 89m Metrocolor
    Cinemascope
MGM (Nicholas Nayfack)

A gunfighter returns home to settle down, but finds his wife dead and his son resentful.
Dull, unexciting star western.

w William Ludwig, *novel* Man of the West by Philip Yordan *d* Roy Rowland *ph* Harold J. Marzorati *m* Jeff Alexander

Stewart Granger, Rhonda Fleming, Chill Wills, Steve Rowland, James Gregory

The Gun Runners*
US 1958 82m bw
UA / Seven Arts (Clarence Greene)

The owner of a Florida motor cruiser innocently rents it to a gun merchant.
Modestly effective action melodrama, the third version of *To Have and Have Not* (qv).

w Daniel Mainwaring, Paul Monash *d Don Siegel ph* Hal Mohr *m* Leith Stevens

Audie Murphy, Eddie Albert, Patricia Owens, Everett Sloane

A Gunfight*
US 1970 94m Technicolor
Harvest / Thoroughbred / Bryna (Ronnie Lubin, Harold Jack Bloom)

Two famous gunfighters on their uppers stage a duel for money.
Austere and anti-climactic western supposedly against popular blood lust.

w Harold Jack Bloom *d* Lamont Johnson
ph David M. Walsh *m* Laurence Rosenthal

Kirk Douglas, Johnny Cash, Karen Black, Raf Vallone, Jane Alexander

Gunfight at Comanche Creek
US 1963 90m De Luxe Panavision

In 1875 a detective goes undercover to unmask the brains behind a robber gang with complex methods. Ingenious but over-emphatic western programmer. Audie Murphy, Ben Cooper, Coleen Miller, John Hubbard, DeForrest Kelley. Written by Edward Bernds; directed by Frank McDonald; for Allied Artists.

Gunfight at Dodge City
US 1958 81m De Luxe Cinemascope
UA / Mirisch

After various problems, Bat Masterson is elected sheriff of Dodge City.
Fair standard western with emphasis on plot and character.

w Daniel B. Ullman, Martin M. Goldsmith *d* Joseph M. Newman *ph* Carl Guthrie *m* Hans Salter

Joel McCrea, Julie Adams, John McIntire, Richard Anderson, Nancy Gates

Gunfight at the OK Corral**
US 1957 122m Technicolor
Vistavision
Paramount / Hal Wallis

Wyatt Earp and Doc Holliday defeat the Clanton Gang.
Watchable, ambitious, but vaguely disappointing super-western.

w Leon Uris *d* John Sturges *ph* Charles B. Lang *m* Dmitri Tiomkin

Burt Lancaster, Kirk Douglas, Jo Van Fleet, Rhonda Fleming, John Ireland, Frank Faylen, Kenneth Tobey, Earl Holliman
'Carefully and lavishly mounted, but overlong and overwrought.'—*John Cutts*

Gunfight in Abilene
US 1967 86m Technicolor

After the Civil War, an officer goes home to find strife between farmers and cattlemen.
Fairly sensible and pleasing lower-berth western. Bobby Darin, Emily Banks, Leslie Nielsen, Donnelly Rhodes, Don Galloway, Michael Sarrazin. Written by Berne Giler and John D. F. Black; directed by Joseph Kenny; for Universal.

The Gunfighter**
US 1950 84m bw
TCF (Nunnally Johnson)

A gunfighter fails to shake off his past. Downbeat, small-scale but very careful adult western set in a believable community.

w William Bowers, William Sellers *d* Henry King *ph* Arthur Miller *m* Alfred Newman

Gregory Peck, Helen Westcott, Millard Mitchell, Jean Parker, Karl Malden, Skip Homeier, Mae Marsh
'Preserves throughout a respectable level of intelligence and invention.'—*Lindsay Anderson*
'Not merely a good western, a good film.'—*Richard Mallett, Punch*
'The movie is done in cold, quiet tones of gray, and every object in it—faces, clothing, a table, the hero's heavy moustache—is given an air of uncompromising authenticity, suggesting those dim photographs of the nineteenth-century west. . .'—*Robert Warshow, The Immediate Experience*

AAN: original story (William Bowers)

Gunfighters
US 1947 87m Cinecolor

A retired gunfighter is suspected of the murder of his best friend. Presentable star western. Randolph Scott, Barbara Britton, Dorothy Hart, Bruce Cabot, Forrest Tucker. Written by Alan Le May, from the novel *Twin Sombreros* by Zane Grey; directed by George Waggner; for Columbia. (GB title: *The Assassin.*)

Gung Ho!
US 1943 88m bw
Universal / Walter Wanger

Adventures of the Marines in the Pacific War. Trite flagwaver, popular at the time.

w Lucien Hubbard, based on the experiences of Captain W. S. LeFrancois USMC *d* Ray Enright *ph* Milton H. Krasner *m* Frank Skinner, Hans Salter

Randolph Scott, Grace MacDonald, Alan Curtis, Noah Beery Jnr, J. Carrol Naish, David Bruce, Peter Coe, Robert Mitchum

Gunga Din***
US 1939 117m bw
RKO (George Stevens)

Three cheerful army veterans meet adventure on the North-West Frontier.
Rousing period actioner with comedy asides, one of the most entertaining of its kind ever made.

w Joel Sayre, Fred Guiol, Ben Hecht, Charles MacArthur, *poem* Rudyard Kipling *d* George Stevens *ph* Joseph H. August *m* Alfred Newman *ad* Van Nest Polglase

Cary Grant, Victor McLaglen, Douglas Fairbanks Jnr, Sam Jaffe, Eduardo Ciannelli, Joan Fontaine, Montagu Love, Robert Coote, Cecil Kellaway, Abner Biberman, Lumsden Hare

'One of the most enjoyable nonsense-adventure movies of all time.'—*Pauline Kael, 1968*

'Bravura is the exact word for the performances, and Stevens' composition and cutting of the fight sequences is particularly stunning.'—*NFT, 1973*

'Romance aflame through dangerous days and nights of terror! In a land where anything can happen—most of all to a beautiful girl alone!'—*publicity*

Gunman's Walk*
US 1958   97m   Technicolor
   Cinemascope
Columbia (Fred Kohlmar)

A tough westerner has two sons, one of whom follows too literally in his footsteps.
Competent action melodrama with good characterization.

w Frank Nugent *d* Phil Karlson *ph* Charles Lawton *m* George Duning

Van Heflin, Tab Hunter, James Darren, Kathryn Grant

Gunn*
US 1967   95m   Technicolor
Paramount / Geoffrey (Owen Crump)

A private eye is hired to find a gangster's killer.
Tongue-in-cheek violence from the television series, with Craig Stevens doing a Cary Grant imitation.

w Blake Edwards, William Peter Blatty *d* Blake Edwards *ph* Philip Lathrop *m* Henry Mancini

Craig Stevens, Laura Devon, Ed Asner, Sherry Jackson, Helen Traubel, J. Pat O'Malley, Regis Toomey

'Falters between parody and straight action.'—*MFB*

Gunpoint
US 1966   86m   Technicolor

A Colorado sheriff goes after train robbers.
Simple-minded but quite professional and good-looking western programmer. Audie Murphy, Joan Staley, Warren Stevens, Edgar Buchanan, Denver Pyle. Written by Mary and Willard Willingham; directed by Earl Bellamy; for Universal.

Guns at Batasi*
GB 1964   103m   bw   Cinemascope
TCF / George H. Brown

The headquarters of an Anglo-African regiment is threatened by rebels.
Basically the old chestnut about a group of disparate types trapped in a dangerous situation, this is given shape and stature by the star's lively performance as the martinet of an RSM.

w Robert Hollis, from his novel The Siege of Battersea *d* John Guillermin *ph* Douglas Slocombe *m* John Addison

Richard Attenborough, Flora Robson, Mia Farrow, Jack Hawkins, Cecil Parker, Percy Herbert, Errol John, John Leyton, Earl Cameron

Guns for San Sebastian
France / Mexico / Italy 1967   111m
   Eastmancolor   Franscope
MGM / Cipra / Filmes / Ernesto Enriques
   (Jacques Bar)

In Mexico in 1746, a rebel on the run stays to defend a besieged village.
Multi-national actioner, violent but quite undistinguished.

w Serge Ganz, Miguel Morayta, Ennio de Concini *d* Henri Verneuil *ph* Armand Thirard *m* Ennio Morricone

Anthony Quinn, Charles Bronson, Sam Jaffe, Anjanette Comer, Silvia Pinal

Guns of Darkness
GB 1962   102m   bw
ABP / Cavalcade (Thomas Clyde)

A British plantation boss in Latin America escapes with his wife when rebels strike.
Chase / escape film with a few tiny comments about violence.

w John Mortimer, *novel* Act of Mercy by Francis Clifford *d* Anthony Asquith *ph* Robert Krasker *m* Benjamin Frankel

David Niven, Leslie Caron, James Robertson Justice, David Opatoshu

The Guns of Fort Petticoat
US 1957   79m   Technicolor
Columbia / Brown-Murphy (Harry Joe Brown)

During the Civil War, a wandering Texan trains townswomen into a fighting force.
Unlikely western which passes the time.

w Walter Doniger *d* George Marshall *ph* Ray Rennahan *m* Mischa Bakaleinikoff

Audie Murphy, Kathryn Grant, Hope Emerson, Jeff Donnell, Isobel Elsom

The Guns of Loos*
GB 1927   89m (24 fps)   bw   silent
Stoll / New Era

A blinded hero of the war returns home to run an industrial empire and is confronted by a strike.
One of the better British silents, with a strong plot and an interesting cast.

w L. H. Gordon, Reginald Fogwell, Sinclair Hill d Sinclair Hill ph Desmond Dickinson

Henry Victor, Madeleine Carroll, Bobby Howes, Hermione Baddeley

The Guns of Navarone**
GB 1961   157m   Technicolor
   Cinemascope
Columbia / Carl Foreman (Cecil F. Ford)

In 1943 a sabotage team is sent to destroy two giant guns on a Turkish island.
Ambitiously produced Boy's Own Paper heroics, with lots of noise and self-sacrifice; intermittently exciting but bogged down by philosophical chat.

w Carl Foreman, *novel* Alistair Maclean d J. Lee-Thomson ph Oswald Morris m Dmitri Tiomkin ad Geoffrey Drake

Gregory Peck, David Niven, Stanley Baker, Anthony Quinn, Anthony Quayle, James Darren, Gia Scala, James Robertson Justice, Richard Harris, Irene Papas, Bryan Forbes
   'A desperate imbalance: the moral arguments cut into the action without extending it.'—*Penelope Houston*

AAN: best picture; Carl Foreman; J. Lee-Thompson; Dmitri Tiomkin

Guns of the Timberland
US 1960   91m   Technicolor
Jaguar (Aaron Spelling)

Loggers are opposed by cattle interests.
Routine star western with tolerable production values.

w Joseph Petracca, Aaron Spelling d Robert D. Webb ph John Seitz m David Buttolph

Alan Ladd, Jeanne Crain, Gilbert Roland, Frankie Avalon, Lyle Bettger, Noah Beery Jnr

Gunsmoke
US 1953   79m   Technicolor

A cowboy befriends the rancher he has been hired to kill. Moderate western with too many pauses for sentiment. Audie Murphy, Paul Kelly, Susan Cabot, Mary Castle, Charles Drake. Written by D. D. Beauchamp; directed by Nathan Juran; for Universal.

The Guru
US / India 1969   112m   De Luxe
TCF / Arcadia (Ismail Merchant)

In India, an English pop singer succumbs to the local atmosphere.
Pleasant, affectionate but forgettable anecdote of modern India.

w Ruth Prawer Jhabvala, James Ivory d James Ivory ph Subrata Mitra m Ustad Vilayat Khan

Michael York, Rita Tushingham, Utpal Dutt, Aparna Sen, Barry Foster

Gus
US 1976   96m   Technicolor
Walt Disney (Ron Miller)

A football team co-opts a mule which can kick a hundred yard ball.
Predictable Disney fantasy comedy with a direct line back to *The Absent Minded Professor*.

w Arthur Alsberg, Don Nelson d Vincent McEveety ph Frank Phillips m Robert F. Brunner

Ed Asner, Don Knotts, Gary Grimes, Tim Conway, Liberty Williams, Bob Crane, Harold Gould, Tom Bosley, Dick Van Patten
   'In the current comedy climate, when humour so often hinges on a four-letter word or its lengthier variant, a light-hearted football game spoof is a breath of fresh air.'—*Tatiana Balkoff Lipscomb, Films in Review*

The Guvnor
GB 1935   88m   bw
Gaumont (Michael Balcon)
US title: *Mr Hobo*

By chance a tramp becomes a bank director.
Predictable star vehicle with Arliss a most unlikely tramp.

w Maude Howell, Guy Bolton d Milton Rosmer ph Max Greene

George Arliss, Gene Gerrard, Viola Keats, Patric Knowles, Frank Cellier, Mary Clare, George Hayes
   'His admirers need not fear that he has lost any of his usual refinement or sentiment, his cultured English accent, his Universal certificate.'—*Graham Greene*

A Guy Named Joe
US 1944   120m   bw
MGM (Everett Riskin)

A flier is killed but comes back as a ghost to supervise his ex-girl's new romance.
Icky romantic comedy-drama with strong propaganda intent; the stars make it tolerable.

w Dalton Trumbo *d* Victor Fleming
ph George Folsey, Karl Freund *m* Herbert
Stothart

Spencer Tracy, Irene Dunne, Ward Bond,
Van Johnson, James Gleason, Lionel
Barrymore, Barry Nelson, Don Defore, Henry
O'Neill

'As far as I could judge, the audience loved
it: melodrama, farce, fake philosophy,
swimming eyes and all.'—*Richard Mallett,
Punch*

'It neatly obtunds death's sting as ordinary
people suffer it by not only assuming but
photographing a good, busy, hearty
hereafter.'—*James Agee*
† The title was explained by one of the
characters who observed that 'in the Army Air
Corps, any fellow who is a right fellow is
called Joe'.

AAN: original story (David Buchan, Chandler
Sprague)

The Guy Who Came Back
US 1951   92m   bw

A pro football player hates the thought of
retiring. Sentimental sporting drama without
much life in it. Paul Douglas, Joan Bennett,
Linda Darnell, Don Defore, Zero Mostel.
Written by Allan Scott; directed by Joseph
Newman; for TCF.

Guys and Dolls*
US 1955   149m   Eastmancolor
   Cinemascope
Samuel Goldwyn

A New York gangster takes a bet that he can
romance a Salvation Army lady.
The artifices of Runyonland are made more so
by a defiantly studio-bound production and
thoroughly flat handling; but the songs and
sometimes the performances survive.

wd Joseph L. Mankiewicz, *musical* Jo
Swerling and Abe Burrows *ph* Harry
Stradling, *songs Frank Loesser md* Cyril
Mockridge, Jay Blackton *ch* Michael Kidd
ad Joseph Wright *pd* Oliver Smith

Frank Sinatra, Marlon Brando, Jean
Simmons, *Vivian Blaine, Stubby Kaye*, B. S.
Pully, Robert Keith, Sheldon Leonard,
George E. Stone
'Quantity has been achieved only at the cost
of quality.'—*Penelope Houston*

AAN: Harry Stradling; Cyril Mockridge, Jay
Blackton

Gypsy
GB 1936   78m   bw

An ageing playboy marries a gypsy but gives

her back to her true love. Hard-to-swallow
drama with insufficient comedy relief for its
star. Roland Young, Chili Bouchier, Hugh
Williams, Frederick Burtwell. Written by
Brock Williams and Terence Rattigan, from
the novel *Tsigane* by Lady Eleanor Smith;
directed by Roy William Neill; for Warner.

Gypsy*
US 1962   149m   Technirama
Warner (Mervyn Le Roy)

The early days of stripteaser Gypsy Rose Lee,
and the exploits of her ambitious mother.
A vaudeville musical that is nowhere near
raucous enough, or brisk enough, for its
subject, and is miscast into the bargain. The
songs are great, but not here: Miss Russell is
as boring as an electric drill in a role that
should have been reserved for Ethel Merman.

w Leonard Spiegelgass, *book* Arthur
Laurents *d* Mervyn Le Roy *m Jule Styne
ly Stephen Sondheim ph* Harry Stradling
md Frank Perkins *ad* John Beckman

Rosalind Russell, Natalie Wood, *Karl Malden*,
James Milhollin

AAN: Harry Stradling; Frank Perkins

Gypsy Colt
US 1954   72m   Ansco Color

A cherished colt has to be sold, but makes its
way back home. Disguised second feature
remake of *Lassie Come Home*; good for
children. Donna Corcoran, Ward Bond,
Frances Dee, Larry Keating, Lee Van Cleef.
Written by Martin Berkeley; directed by
Andrew Marton; for MGM.

The Gypsy and the Gentleman
GB 1957   107m   Eastmancolor
Rank (Maurice Cowan)

A penniless Regency rake marries a
tempestuous gypsy, with melodramatic and
tragic results.
Expensive and typically mistimed Rank
attempt to re-do *The Man in Grey*; a
barnstormer notable only for waste of talent.

w Janet Greene, *novel* Darkness I Leave You
by Nina Warner Hooke *d* Joseph Losey
ph Jack Hildyard *m* Hans May *ad* Ralph
Brinton

Melina Mercouri, Keith Michell, Patrick
McGoohan, June Laverick, Flora Robson,
Helen Haye

The Gypsy Moths*
US 1969   110m   Metrocolor
MGM (Hal Landers, Bobby Roberts)

Sky-diving stuntmen find love and death on a small-town tour.

Brilliantly breathtaking actioner which too frequently gets grounded, and does not find a reason for being so glum.

w William Hanley, *novel* James Drought *d* John Frankenheimer *ph* Philip Lathrop *aerial ph* Carl Boenisch *m* Elmer Bernstein

Burt Lancaster, Deborah Kerr, Gene Hackman, Scott Wilson, William Windom, Bonnie Bedelia, Sheree North

'A Bergmanesque world of inner emotions and ambiguous means. . . . As in many of Frankenheimer's films it rains, and the wind in the trees in the park and the sound of traffic all contribute to the realism that makes his work so satisfying.'—*Gerald Pratley*

Gypsy Wildcat
US 1944   77m   Technicolor
Universal (George Waggner)

A Transylvanian gypsy girl is really a long lost countess.

Universal's Frankenstein sets are put to lighter use in a quite incredible piece of downright hokum.

w James Hogan, Gene Lewis, James M. Cain *d* Roy William Neill *ph* George Robinson, W. Howard Greene *m* Edward Ward

Maria Montez, Jon Hall, Leo Carrillo, Gale Sondergaard, Douglass Dumbrille, Nigel Bruce, Peter Coe, Curt Bois

'The picture's so bad, it's bound to make money.'—*Cue*

H

H. M. Pulham Esquire**
US 1940 120m bw
MGM (King Vidor)

A moderately successful Bostonian
businessman looks back over his rather stuffy
life and has a fling.
Solidly upholstered drama which does not
quite do justice to the book on which it is
based.

w King Vidor, Elizabeth Hill, *novel* John P.
Marquand *d* King Vidor *ph* Ray June
*Robert Young, Ruth Hussey, Hedy Lamarr,
Charles Coburn, Van Heflin, Fay Holden,
Bonita Granville*

Habeas Corpus*
US 1928 20m bw silent

A mad professor sends two vagabonds out to
look for a body. Unusual star comedy, more
grotesque and pantomimish than any of the
others. Laurel and Hardy, Richard Carle.
Written by H. M. Walker; directed by James
Parrott; for Hal Roach.

Hail the Conquering Hero***
US 1944 101m bw
Paramount (Preston Sturges)

An army reject is accidentally thought a hero
when he returns to his small-town home.
Skilfully orchestrated Preston Sturges romp,
slightly marred by an overdose of sentiment
but featuring his repertory of comic actors at
full pitch.

wd Preston Sturges *ph* John Seitz *m* Werner
Heymann

Eddie Bracken, William Demarest, Ella
Raines, *Franklin Pangborn*, Elizabeth
Patterson, *Raymond Walburn, Alan Bridge*,
Georgia Caine, Freddie Steele, Jimmy Conlin,
Torben Meyer

'Mob scenes, rough-houses and sharply
serious passages are played for all the
pantomime they are worth . . . one of the
happiest, heartiest comedies in a
twelvemonth.'—*Otis L. Guernsey Jnr*
'First rate entertainment, a pattern of film
making, not to be missed.'—*Richard Mallett,
Punch*

'The energy, the verbal density, the rush of
Americana and the congestion seen
periodically in *The Miracle of Morgan's Creek*
stagger the senses in this newest film.'—*James
Ursini*
'He uses verbal as well as visual slapstick,
and his comic timing is so quirkily effective
that the dialogue keeps popping off like a
string of firecrackers.'—*New Yorker, 1977*

AAN: Preston Sturges (as writer)

Hair*
US 1979 121m Technicolor
UA / CIP (Lester Persky, Michael Butler)

An Oklahoman on his way to enlist for
Vietnam service stops off in New York and
becomes embroiled with the flower people.
Slick, vigorous but eventually unsatisfying
version of a quickly dated musical frolic with
some obvious points to make.

w Michael Weller, *musical play* Galt
MacDermot (music) and Gerome Ragni /
 James Rado (book) *d* Milos Forman
ph Miroslav Ondricek, Richard Kratina, Jean
Talvin

John Savage, Treat Williams, Beverly
D'Angelo, Annie Golden, Dorsey Wright

The Hairy Ape
US 1944 91m bw
Jules Levy

A ship's stoker aims to kill a socialite who has
insulted him.
Patchy treatment of an intractable and dated
play.

w Jules Levy, *play* Eugene O'Neill *d* Alfred
Santell *ph* Lucien Andriot *m* Michel
Michelet, Edward Paul

William Bendix, Susan Hayward, John Loder,
Dorothy Comingore, Roman Bohnen, Alan
Napier

AAN: Michel Michelet, Edward Paul

Half a Hero
US 1953 71m bw

A timid journalist has problems with wife,
baby, boss and new house. Aimless comedy

quite unsuited to its star. Red Skelton, Jean
Hagen, Charles Dingle, Mary Wickes, Polly
Bergen. Written by Max Shulman; directed by
Don Weis; for MGM.

Half a Sixpence*
GB 1967   148m   Technicolor
Panavision
Paramount / Ameran (Charles H. Schneer,
George Sidney)

A draper's assistant inherits a fortune and
moves into society.
Mildly likeable but limp and overlong musical
which would have benefited from more
intimate, sharper treatment than the wide
screen can give. The period decor and lively
numbers seem insufficient compensation for
the longueurs.

w Beverly Cross, from his play based on Kipps
by H. G. Wells d George Sidney
ph Geoffrey Unsworth m / ly David
Heneker pd Ted Haworth ch Gillian Lynne

Tommy Steele, Julia Foster, Cyril Ritchard,
Penelope Horner, Elaine Taylor, Hilton
Edwards, Pamela Brown, James Villiers

Half Angel
US 1951   80m   Technicolor

A prim and proper nurse has a more forthright
personality when she sleepwalks. Silly
romantic comedy with amusing moments.
Loretta Young, Joseph Cotten, Cecil
Kellaway, Basil Ruysdael, Jim Backus, Irene
Ryan. Written by Robert Riskin; directed by
Richard Sale; for TCF.

The Half Naked Truth*
US 1932   67m   bw
RKO (David O. Selznick)

A publicity agent has trouble with a
temperamental actress whose schemes are
always over the top.
Amusing wisecracking comedy.

w Bartlett Cormack, Corey Ford d Gregory
La Cava ph Bert Glennon m Max Steiner

Lee Tracy, Lupe Velez, Eugene Pallette,
Frank Morgan, Bob McKenzie

The Halfway House*
GB 1944   99m   bw
Ealing (Cavalcanti)

Overnight guests at an inn find it was bombed
a year before and they have all been given a
supernatural chance to reconsider their lives.
Interesting pattern play which would have
benefited from lighter handling.

w Angus Macphail, Diana Morgan, play Denis
Ogden d Basil Dearden ph Wilkie Cooper
m Lord Berners

Françoise Rosay, Tom Walls, Alfred Drayton,
Sally Ann Howes, Mervyn Johns, Glynis
Johns, Esmond Knight, Richard Bird, Guy
Middleton

Hallelujah!**
US 1929   106m   bw
MGM (King Vidor)

A black cotton worker accidentally kills a man
and decides to become a preacher.
Hollywood's unique black melodrama now
seems stilted because of its early talkie
technique, but at the time its picture of negro
life had a freshness and truth which was not
reached again for thirty years.

w Wanda Tuchock, King Vidor d King Vidor
ph Gordon Avil md Eva Jessye

Daniel Haynes, Nina Mae McKinney, William
Fountaine, Fannie Belle De Knight, Harry
Gray

'The central theme became swamped by the
forty or so singing sequences of folk songs,
spirituals, baptism wails, love songs and
blues.'—Peter Noble, The Negro in Films

AAN: King Vidor

Hallelujah, I'm a Bum**
US 1933   80m   bw
Lewis Milestone
GB titles: Hallelujah I'm a Tramp; Lazy
Bones

The leader of a group of Central Park tramps
smartens himself up for love of a lady who lost
her memory. When she recovers it, he
becomes a tramp again.
Curious whimsy expressed mainly in recitative,
with embarrassing stretches relieved by
moments of visual and verbal inspiration.
Very typical of the Depression, with the
tramps knowing best how life should be lived.

w S. N. Behrman, Ben Hecht d Lewis
Milestone ph Lucien Andriot ad Richard
Day rhymes / m / ly Richard Rodgers, Lorenz
Hart

Al Jolson, Harry Langdon, Madge Evans,
Frank Morgan, Chester Conklin

The Hallelujah Trail
US 1965   167m   Technicolor
Ultra Panavision 70
UA / Mirisch / Kappa (John Sturges)

In 1867 a wagonload of whisky bound for
Denver is waylaid by Indians, temperance
crusaders and the civilian militia.

Absurdly inflated, prolonged, uninventive comedy western with poor narrative grip; all dressed up and nowhere to go.

w John Gay, *novel* Bill Gulick *d* John Sturges *ph* Robert Surtees *m* Elmer Bernstein

Burt Lancaster, Lee Remick, Brian Keith, Jim Hutton, Donald Pleasence, Martin Landau

Halloween*
US 1978 91m Metrocolor Panavision
Falcon International (Irwin Yablans)

In a small Illinois town, a mad killer escapes from the asylum.
Single-minded shocker with virtually no plot, just a succession of bloody attacks in semi-darkness. Very well done if you like that kind of thing, though the final suggestion of the supernatural is rather baffling.

w John Carpenter, Debra Hill *d John Carpenter ph* Dean Cundy *m* John Carpenter *pd* Tommy Wallace

Donald Pleasence, Jamie Lee Curtis, Nancy Loomis, P. J. Soles
'One of the cinema's most perfectly engineered devices for saying Boo!'—*Richard Combs, MFB*

The Halliday Brand*
US 1956 78m bw
UA / Collier Young

A tough farmer / sheriff conflicts with his son over his attitude to Indians.
Dour, reliable western melodrama with a good cast.

w George W. George, George S. Slavin *d* Joseph H. Lewis *ph* Ray Rennahan *m* Stanley Wilson

Joseph Cotten, Viveca Lindfors, Ward Bond, Betsy Blair, Bill Williams, Jay C. Flippen

Halls of Anger
US 1969 99m De Luxe
UA / Mirisch (Herbert Hirschman)

A black basketball star goes to teach in his home town and faces segregation problems.
Schematic melodrama, as well meaning as it is boring.

w John Shaner, Al Ramrus *d* Paul Bogart *ph* Burnett Guffey *m* Dave Grusin

Calvin Lockhart, Janet McLachlan, Jeff Bridges

Halls of Montezuma*
US 1950 113m Technicolor
TCF (Robert Bassler)

Marines fight World War II in the Pacific.
Well-mounted, simple-minded actioner.

w Michael Blankfort *d* Lewis Milestone *ph* Winton C. Hoch, Harry Jackson *m* Sol Kaplan *md* Lionel Newman

Richard Widmark, Jack Palance, Reginald Gardiner, Robert Wagner, Karl Malden, Richard Hylton, Richard Boone, Skip Homeier, Jack Webb, Bert Freed, Neville Brand, Don Hicks, Martin Milner
'By far the noisiest war film I ever encountered.'—*Richard Mallett, Punch*

Ham and Eggs at the Front
US 1927 70m approx at 24 fps bw
silent

Two black soldiers have adventures in the trenches. Irresistibly-titled war farce with our heroes played by whites in blackface. Tom Wilson, Charlie Conklin, Myrna Loy. Written by Darryl F. Zanuck; directed by Roy Del Ruth; for Warner.

Hamlet**
GB 1948 142m bw
Rank / Two Cities (Laurence Olivier)

Prince Hamlet takes too long making up his mind to revenge his father's death.
The play is sharply cut, then time is wasted having the camera prowl pointlessly along gloomy corridors . . . but much of the acting is fine, some scenes compel, and the production has a splendid brooding power.

w William Shakespeare *d* Laurence Olivier *ph* Desmond Dickinson pd Roger Furse *m* William Walton *ad* Carmen Dillon

Laurence Olivier, Eileen Herlie, Basil Sydney, Jean Simmons, Felix Aylmer, Norman Wooland, Terence Morgan, *Stanley Holloway,* Peter Cushing, Esmond Knight, Anthony Quayle, Harcourt Williams, John Laurie, Niall MacGinnis, Patrick Troughton

AA: best picture; Laurence Olivier (as actor)
AAN: Laurence Olivier (as director); William Walton; Jean Simmons

Hamlet*
USSR 1964 150m bw Sovscope
Lenfilm

A Russian version of the play, with lowering sets, brooding photography and strong acting.

translation Boris Pasternak *d* Grigori Kozintsev *ph* I. Gritzys *m* Dmitri Shostakovich

Innokenti Smoktunovsky, Mikhail Nazvanov, Elsa Radzin, Anastasia Vertinskaya
'An opportunity almost deliberately missed.'—*Basil Wright, 1972*

Hammerhead

GB 1968   99m   Technicolor
Columbia / Irving Allen

An American secret agent captures a master
criminal.
Jaded James Bond imitation, full of would-be
fashionable detail.

w William Bast, Herbert Baker, *novel* James
Mayo d David Miller ph Kenneth Talbot,
Wilkie Cooper m David Whitaker

Vince Edwards, Peter Vaughan, Judy Geeson,
Diana Dors, Michael Bates, Beverly Adams,
Patrick Cargill, Patrick Holt

Hammersmith Is Out*

US 1972   114m   Du Art Color
Cinerama / J. Cornelius Cream (Alex Lucas)

With the help of a male nurse, a homicidal
mental inmate escapes and becomes the most
influential man in the country.
Pretentious updating of Faust into a kind of
black farce that seldom amuses but is
interesting in fits and starts.

w Stanford Whitmore d Peter Ustinov
ph Richard Kline m Dominic Frontière

Richard Burton, Elizabeth Taylor, Peter
Ustinov, Beau Bridges, Leon Ames, John
Schuck, George Raft

Hand in Hand*

GB 1960   80m   bw
ABP / Helen Winston

The friendship of two 7-year-olds is affected
by racial prejudice because one is Catholic and
the other Jewish; but after misunderstandings
their friendship is confirmed by priest and
rabbi.
Pleasant, well-meaning drama apparently
intended for older children.

w Diana Morgan d Philip Leacock
ph Frederick A. Young m Stanley Black

Lorette Parry, Phillip Needs, Sybil Thorndike,
John Gregson, Finlay Currie

Handle with Care*

US 1958   82m   bw
MGM (Morton Fine)

Small-town college students stage a mock trial
and come up with some embarrassing answers.
Interesting melodrama with a disappointing
ending; a well done second feature.

w Morton Fine, David Friedkin d David
Friedkin ph Harold J. Marzorati
m Alexander Courage

Dean Jones, Joan O'Brien, Thomas Mitchell,
Walter Abel, John Smith

Hands across the Table**

US 1935   81m   bw
Paramount (E. Lloyd Sheldon)

A manicurist determines to marry a rich man.
Lively romantic comedy, smoothly made and
typical of its time.

w Norman Krasna, Vincent Lawrence,
Herbert Fields d Mitchell Leisen ph Ted
Tetzlaff m Sam Coslow, Frederick Hollander

Carole Lombard, Fred MacMurray, Ralph
Bellamy, Astrid Allwyn, Ruth Donnelly,
Marie Prévost, William Demarest, Ed Gargan

'A happy mixture of brainwork and
horseplay and a reminder that when
intelligence goes for a walk among even the
oldest props, the props may come to life.'—
Otis Ferguson

The Hands of Orlac

GB / France 1960   105m   bw
Riviera / Pendennis (Steven Pallos, Don
Taylor)

A concert pianist's hands are crushed in an
accident, and a mad surgeon grafts on those of
an executed murderer.
Flatulent remake of the 1926 German silent
and the 1935 American *Mad Love*. Stilted,
hammy, threadbare and overlong.

w John Baines, Edmond T. Gréville, *novel*
Maurice Renard d Edmond T. Gréville
ph Desmond Dickinson m Claude Bolling

Mel Ferrer, Donald Wolfit, Christopher Lee

Hands of the Ripper

GB 1971   85m   Technicolor
Hammer (Aida Young)

Jack the Ripper stabs his wife to death in view
of his small daughter, who grows up a sexually
repressed murderess.
Gory Hammer horror with well done scenes.

w L. W. Davidson d Peter Sasdy ph Kenneth
Talbot m Christopher Gunning ad Roy
Stannard

Angharad Rees, Eric Porter, Dora Bryan,
Jane Merrow, Derek Godfrey

Hands over the City

Italy 1963   105m   bw
Galatea
original title: *Le Mani sulla Città*

A property tycoon wangles local politicians so
that he gets development on the property he
controls.
An angry political film which is too strident to
have much entertainment value.

w Enzo Provencale, Enzo Forcella, Raffaele
La Capria, Francesco Rosi d Francesco Rosi

m Piero Piccioni *ph* Gianni di Venanzo
Rod Steiger, Salvo Randone, and non-
professionals

Handy Andy
US 1934   82m   bw
Fox

A midwestern druggist is married to a snob.
Competent star vehicle overflowing with
crackerbarrel philosophy.

w William Counselman, Henry Johnson, *play*
Merry Andrew by Lewis Beach *d* David
Butler *ph* Arthur Miller

Will Rogers, Peggy Wood, Conchita
Montenegro, Mary Carlisle, Roger Imhof,
Robert Taylor (his first film), Paul Harvey

Hangar 18
US 1980   97m   Technicolor

A UFO crashlands and is cared for in secret by
the American government. A cinematic
equivalent to the yellow press, supposing
villainous behaviour by all concerned but
eager only to provide low grade thriller
entertainment. Darren McGavin, Robert
Vaughn, Gary Collins, Philip Abbott. Written
by Steven Thornley; directed by James L.
Conway; for Sunn Classic.

Hang 'em High
US 1967   114m   De Luxe
UA / Malpaso / Leonard Freeman

A cowboy is rescued from lynching and takes
revenge on his persecutors.
Hollywood's first attempt to imitate the gore
and brutality of spaghetti westerns and to take
back its own errant star. Emetic and
interminable.

w Leonard Freeman, Mel Goldberg *d* Ted
Post *ph* Leonard South, Richard Kline
m Dominic Frontière

Clint Eastwood, Inger Stevens, Ed Begley, Pat
Hingle, James MacArthur, Arlene Golonka,
Charles McGraw, Ben Johnson, L. Q. Jones

The Hanging Tree*
US 1958   106m   Technicolor
Warner / Baroda (Martin Jurow, Richard
   Shepherd)

Life is tough in a Montana gold-mining camp,
especially for a doctor who has killed his
unfaithful wife.
Lowering western with a feeling for place and
period, plus a welter of melodramatic incident.

w Wendell Mayes, Halstead Welles, *novel*
Dorothy M. Johnson *d* Delmer Daves
ph Ted McCord *m* Max Steiner

Gary Cooper, Maria Schell, Karl Malden, Ben
Piazza, George C. Scott
AAN: title song (*m* Jay Livingston, *ly* Ray
Evans)

The Hangman
US 1959   86m   bw
Paramount (Frank Freeman Jnr)

A marshal with a reputation for getting his
man deliberately allows one to escape.
Dour, low-key western, competent but rather
flat and uninteresting.

w Dudley Nichols *d* Michael Curtiz *ph* Loyal
Griggs *m* Harry Sukman

Robert Taylor, Jack Lord, Fess Parker, Tina
Louise, Mickey Shaughnessy

Hangman's House
US 1928   72m (24 fps)   bw   silent
Fox

To please her dying father, an Irish girl
marries a wastrel instead of the man she loves,
but her husband is killed in a duel.
Blarney-filled melodrama, like a sober *Quiet
Man*. John Wayne can be glimpsed as an
extra.

w Marion Orth, *story* Don Byrne *d* John
Ford *ph* George Schneiderman

June Collyer, Larry Kent, Earle Foxe, Victor
McLaglen, Hobart Bosworth

Hangman's Knot
US 1952   81m   Technicolor

Confederate soldiers returning home with
Union booty are waylaid at a way station by
renegades. Adequate suspense western.
Randolph Scott, Donna Reed, Claude Jarman
Jnr, Frank Faylen, Glenn Langan, Richard
Denning, Lee Marvin, Jeanette Nolan.
Written and directed by Roy Huggins; for
Harry Joe Brown / Columbia.

Hangmen Also Die*
US 1943   131m   bw
Arnold Pressburger / Fritz Lang (T. W.
   Baumfield)
Reissue title: *Lest We Forget*

The Nazis take revenge for the killing of
Heydrich.
Disappointingly heavy-handed, though deeply
felt war propaganda set in Hollywood's idea of
Czechoslovakia. Only moments of interest
remain.

w John Wexley, *story* Fritz Lang, Bertolt
Brecht *d* Fritz Lang *ph* James Wong Howe
m Hanns Eisler

Brian Donlevy, Anna Lee, Walter Brennan, Gene Lockhart, Dennis O'Keefe, Alexander Granach, Margaret Wycherly, Nana Bryant, Hans von Twardowski (as Heydrich), Jonathan Hale, Lionel Stander

'Lang, working with American actors on an American theme, has produced *Fury*. Lang trying to recreate his own Central Europe on a Hollywood set is completely at sea.'—*Paul Rotha, 1949*

'Directed with a skill which excites and delights . . . brilliant use of the tiny, shocking detail.'—*Dilys Powell*

'They have chosen to use brutality, American gangster idiom, and middle high German cinematic style to get it across, and it is rich with clever melodrama, over-*maestoso* directional touches, and the sort of Querschnitt sophistication for detail which Lang always has.'—*James Agee*

AAN: Hanns Eisler

Hangover Square*
US 1944 77m bw
TCF (Robert Bassler)

In 1903 London, a psychopathic composer murders pretty women.
This rather empty melodrama has almost nothing to do with the book from which it is allegedly taken, but the Hollywoodian evocation of gaslit London is richly entertaining and good to look at.

w Barre Lyndon, *novel* Patrick Hamilton *d* John Brahm *ph* Joseph La Shelle *m* Bernard Herrmann *ad* Lyle Wheeler, Maurice Ransford

Laird Cregar, Linda Darnell, George Sanders, Glenn Langan, Faye Marlowe, Alan Napier, Frederick Worlock

'Cregar lumbers around with a Karloffian glare in the spacious mists which happily blur the architectural decor.'—*Richard Winnington*

'Distinguished photography gets the last glint of fancy fright out of the pomps and vanities of the turn of the century.'—*Time*

'A half-chewed collection of reminiscences of *Dr Jekyll and Mr Hyde* and *The Lodger*.'—*Richard Mallett, Punch*

'The worst betrayal of a first class novel that I can remember.'—*James Agate*

'A better than average horror picture up to, but not including, its wildly overloaded climax.'—*James Agee*

† Tragically, Laird Cregar died after slimming for this role, to which he was in any case unsuited.

Hannibal
Italy 1959 103m Technicolor Supercinescope
Liber Film (Ottavio Poggi)

Hannibal crosses the Alps and falls for the daughter of a Roman senator.
Unhistorical farrago which totally fails to entertain on any level.

w Mortimer Braus *d* Carlo Ludovico Bragaglia, Edgar G. Ulmer *ph* Raffaele Masciocchi *m* Carlo Rustichelli

Victor Mature, Rita Gam, Gabriele Ferzetti, Milly Vitale, Rik Battaglia

'Not even the elephants emerge with dignity.'—*MFB*

Hannibal Brooks
GB 1968 102m De Luxe
UA / Scimitar (Michael Winner)

A British POW in Germany escapes over the Alps with an elephant.
Curious action adventure which seems undecided whether to take itself seriously. Some passable sequences.

w Dick Clement, Ian La Frenais *d* Michael Winner *ph* Robert Paynter *m* Francis Lai

Oliver Reed, Michael J. Pollard, Wolfgang Preiss, Karen Baal

Hannie Caulder
GB 1971 85m colour Panavision
Tigon / Curtwel (Tony Tenser)

Raped by three outlaws who murdered her husband, a western woman takes revenge.
Unintentionally comical action melodrama with the star defeating all comers.

w Z. X. Jones (Burt Kennedy, David Haft) *d* Burt Kennedy *ph* Ted Scaife *m* Ken Thorne

Raquel Welch, Robert Culp, Ernest Borgnine, Strother Martin, Jack Elam, Christopher Lee, Diana Dors

Hanover Street
GB 1979 108m Technicolor
Columbia (Paul N. Lazarus III)

In 1943, an American bomber pilot meets a Red Cross nurse in a bus queue.
Wartime romance of a rather sticky sort, which turns with little warning into escape adventure, with our hero rescuing his loved one's husband from certain death.

wd Peter Hyams *ph* David Watkin *m* John Barry *pd* Philip Harrison

Harrison Ford, Lesley-Anne Down, Christopher Plummer, Alec McCowen, Richard Masure, Michael Sacks, Max Wall

Hans Christian Andersen*
US 1952   112m   Technicolor
Samuel Goldwyn

A storytelling cobbler leaves his village to make shoes for the prima ballerina in Copenhagen.
Artificial, sugary confection with little humour and far too little magic of any kind; the star carries it nicely, but he is on his own apart from the songs.

w Moss Hart d Charles Vidor ph Harry Stradling md Walter Scharf songs Frank Loesser ad Richard Day ch Roland Petit

Danny Kaye, Zizi Jeanmaire, Farley Granger, John Qualen, Joey Walsh

AAN: Harry Stradling; Walter Scharf; song 'Thumbelina' (m / ly Frank Loesser)

The Happening
US 1967   101m   Technicolor
Columbia / Horizon / Dover (Jud Kinberg)

Four young hippies kidnap a wealthy businessman and don't know what to do with him; he turns the tables.
Freewheeling irresponsible comedy which even at the time of swinging cities seemed very irritating.

w Frank R. Pierson, James D. Buchanan, Ronald Austin d Eliot Silverstein ph Philip Lathrop m Frank de Vol pd Richard Day

Anthony Quinn, George Maharis, Michael Parks, Faye Dunaway, Robert Walker, Oscar Homolka, Martha Hyer, Milton Berle, Jack Kruschen

'A wacky comedy à la mode, oddly mixed and only spasmodically effective.'—Variety

The Happiest Days of Your Life***
GB 1950   81m   bw
British Lion / Individual (Frank Launder)

A ministry mistake billets a girls' school on a boys' school.
Briskly handled version of a semi-classic post-war farce, with many familiar talents in excellent form.

w Frank Launder, John Dighton, play John Dighton d Frank Launder ph Stan Pavey m Mischa Spoliansky

Alastair Sim, Margaret Rutherford, Joyce Grenfell, Richard Wattis, Edward Rigby, Guy Middleton, Muriel Aked, John Bentley, Bernadette O'Farrell

'Absolutely first rate fun.'—Richard Mallett, Punch

The Happiest Millionaire
US 1967   159m   Technicolor
Walt Disney (Bill Anderson)

In 1916, a sporting millionaire has several surprising interests but finds time to sort out family problems.
Drearily inept family entertainment with a couple of good songs and an amusing alligator sequence but acres of yawning boredom in between.

w A. J. Carothers, play Kyle Crichton, book My Philadelphia Father by Cornelia Drexel Biddle d Norman Tokar ph Edward Colman m / ly Richard M. and Robert B. Sherman

Fred MacMurray, Tommy Steele, Greer Garson, John Davidson, Gladys Cooper, Lesley Anne Warren, Geraldine Page, Hermione Baddeley

Happy Anniversary
US 1959   83m   bw
UA / Ralph Fields

A television set causes family trouble.
Marital farce designed to take a few sideswipes at TV.

w Joseph Fields, Jerome Chodorov, from their play Anniversary Waltz d David Miller ph Lee Garmes m Sol Kaplan, Robert Allan

David Niven, Mitzi Gaynor, Carl Reiner, Loring Smith, Patty Duke, Phyllis Povah

Happy Birthday Wanda June*
US 1971   105m   Technicolor
Columbia

An adventurer believed dead returns just as his wife is about to choose one of two suitors.
A farcical situation becomes in this writer's hands an investigation of the hero cult, with many zany jokes, episodes in heaven, and bad language. Interesting in spots, but it would have worked better with a more fluent cinematic technique.

w Kurt Vonnegut Jnr, from his play d Mark Robson ph Fred J. Koenekamp

Rod Steiger, Susannah York, George Grizzard, Don Murray

'We can only assume that Mr Robson deserted the filmic instincts that brought him commercial success because here he was, finally, in the presence of Art.'—Hollis Alpert

'Nothing more than a miscast film record of the dialogue and plot outline of the stage work.'—Judith Crist

The Happy Ending*
US 1969   112m   Technicolor
   Panavision
UA / Pax Films (Richard Brooks)

A middle-aged woman reflects over sixteen years of unhappy marriage.
Sometimes glib, sometimes trenchant

sophisticated drama with enough interesting
scenes to make it more than merely a
'woman's picture'.

wd Richard Brooks *ph* Conrad Hall
m Michel Legrand

Jean Simmons, John Forsythe, Shirley Jones,
Lloyd Bridges, Teresa Wright, Dick Shawn,
Nanette Fabray, Bobby Darin, Tina Louise
'Packed with punchy little epigrams floating
in a vacuum of glossy superficiality.'—*David
Wilson*
'The truth about the process of ageing is
what binds this film together like cement.'—
Alexander Walker
'We don't love. We just make love. And
damn little of that!'—*publicity*
AAN: Jean Simmons; song 'What Are You
Doing the Rest of Your Life' (*m* Michel
Legrand, *ly* Alan and Marilyn Bergman)

Happy Ever After

GB / Germany 1932   86m   bw
UFA (Erich Pommer)

Window-cleaners put a young actress on the
way to stardom.
Cheerful comedy, set and made in Germany
by mainly British talent.

w Jack Hulbert, Douglas Furber, from a story
by Walter Reisch and Billy Wilder *d* Paul
Martin, Robert Stevenson

Lilian Harvey, Jack Hulbert, Cicely
Courtneidge, Sonnie Hale, Edward Chapman

Happy Ever After*

GB 1954   87m   Technicolor
ABP / Mario Zampi
US title: *Tonight's the Night*

Irish villagers draw lots for the privilege of
murdering their rascally squire.
Fairly hilarious black comedy with a good cast
entering into the spirit of the thing.

w Jack Davies, Michael Pertwee, L. A. G.
Strong *d* Mario Zampi *ph* Stan Pavey
m Stanley Black

David Niven, Yvonne de Carlo, A. E.
Matthews, Michael Shepley, George Cole,
Barry Fitzgerald

The Happy Family

GB 1952   86m   bw

A shopkeeper refuses to move and provide a
site for the Festival of Britain. Pale Ealing
imitation with amiable cast. Stanley Holloway,
Kathleen Harrison, Naunton Wayne, George
Cole, Dandy Nichols, Miles Malleson. Written
by Muriel and Sydney Box, from a play by
Michael Clayton Hutton; directed by Muriel
Box; for London Independent. (US title: *Mr
Lord Says No.*)

Happy Go Lovely

GB 1950   97m   Technicolor
ABP (Marcel Hellman)

A chorus girl meets a millionaire during the
Edinburgh Festival.
For a semi-official contribution to the Festival
of Britain this is a lamentably unspontaneous
musical with no use of cinema techniques or
natural locales. Even allowing for the flat
handling, it is tedious.

w Val Guest *d* Bruce Humberstone
ph Erwin Hillier *m* Mischa Spoliansky

David Niven, Vera-Ellen, Cesar Romero,
Bobby Howes, Diane Hart, Gordon Jackson,
Barbara Couper, Gladys Henson, Joyce Carey

Happy Go Lucky

US 1943   81m   Technicolor
Paramount (Harold Wilson)

A cigarette girl chases a millionaire to a
Caribbean island.
Flimsy musical for those who like the stars.

w Walter de Leon, Melvin Frank, Norman
Panama *d* Curtis Bernhardt *ph* Karl Struss,
Wilfrid Cline *songs* Frank Loesser, Jimmy
McHugh

Mary Martin, Dick Powell, Betty Hutton
(singing 'Murder He Says'), Rudy Vallee,
Eddie Bracken, Mabel Paige, Eric Blore,
Clem Bevans

Happy Gypsies*

Yugoslavia 1967   90m   Eastmancolor
Avala
aka: *I Even Knew Happy Gypsies*

A handsome, cruel-natured gypsy and his wife
have violent adventures and find themselves
on the run from the police.
The first film in the gypsy language does not
make one too sympathetic to their cause, but
some scenes are well managed and the colour
is fine.

wd Alexander Petrovic *ph* Tomislav Pinter
m gypsy melodies

Bekim Fehmiu, Olivera Vuco, Bata
Zivojinovic

The Happy Hooker

US 1975   98m   Movielab
Double H / Cannon-Happy (Fred Caruso)

A Dutch girl in New York starts a career as a
prostitute and finds she enjoys it.
Glum sex comedy based on the supposed
exploits of a real madam; crude and not very
funny. If this is emancipation, Shirley Temple
seems more attractive by the minute.

w William Richert, *book* Xaviera Hollander
d Nicholas Sgarro *ph* Dick Kratina *m* Don
Elliott

Lynn Redgrave (hilariously miscast), Jean-
Pierre Aumont, Lovelady Powell, Nicholas
Pryor, Elizabeth Wilson, Tom Poston, Conrad
Janis, Richard Lynch

Happy Is the Bride*
GB 1957   84m   bw
British Lion / Paul Soskin

A couple planning a quiet summer wedding
reckon without the intervention of her
parents.
Tame remake of *Quiet Wedding*; the right
spirit but not much sparkle.

w Jeffrey Dell, Roy Boulting, *play* Dodie
Smith *d* Roy Boulting *ph* Ted Scaife
m Benjamin Frankel

Ian Carmichael, Janette Scott, Cecil Parker,
Joyce Grenfell, Terry-Thomas, John Le
Mesurier, Eric Barker, Edith Sharpe, Athene
Seyler

Happy Land*
US 1943   75m   bw
TCF (Kenneth MacGowan)

Grandfather's ghost comes back to comfort a
family which has lost its son at war.
Sentimental flagwaver very typical of its time;
well made, it ensured not a dry eye in the
house.

w Kathryn Scola, Julien Josephson,
novel Mackinlay Kantor *d* Irving Pichel
ph Joseph La Shelle *m* Cyril Mockridge

Don Ameche, Frances Dee, Harry Carey,
Ann Rutherford, Cara Williams, Henry
Morgan, Richard Crane, Dickie Moore

Happy Landing*
US 1938   102m   bw
TCF (David Hempstead)

A Norwegian girl falls for an American flier
who crashes near her home.
Lightweight skating musical, well put together.

w Milton Sperling, Boris Ingster *d* Roy del
Ruth *ph* John Mescall *md* Louis Silvers

Sonja Henie, Don Ameche, Cesar Romero,
Ethel Merman, Jean Hersholt, Billy Gilbert,
Wally Vernon, El Brendel

The Happy Road*
US / France 1956   100m   bw
MGM / Thor (Gene Kelly)

Two children run away from a Swiss school
and are pursued by the American father of
one of them.

Whimsical peripatetic comedy which fails to
come off despite charming passages.

w Arthur Julian, Joseph Morhain, Harry
Kurnitz *d* Gene Kelly *ph* Robert Juillard
m Georges Van Parys

Gene Kelly, Barbara Laage, Michael
Redgrave, Bobby Clark, Brigitte Fossey

The Happy Thieves
US 1962   88m   bw
UA / Hillworth (James Hill, Rita Hayworth)

A gentleman thief and his accomplice become
unwittingly involved in murder.
Dreary comedy which turns into equally
dreary drama and makes its European
backgrounds look ugly.

w John Gay, *novel* The Oldest Confession by
Richard Condon *d* George Marshall *ph* Paul
Beeson *m* Mario Nascimbene

Rex Harrison, Rita Hayworth, Grégoire
Aslan, Joseph Wiseman, Alida Valli

The Happy Time***
US 1952   94m   bw
Columbia / Stanley Kramer (Earl Felton)

Domestic misadventures of a family of French
Canadians during the twenties.
Basically concerned with adolescent sexual
stirrings, this very agreeable film has a light
touch and is most deftly directed and acted.

w Earl Felton, play Samuel A. Taylor
*d Richard Fleischer ph Charles Lawton Jnr
m* Dmitri Tiomkin *pd* Rudolph Sternad

*Charles Boyer, Louis Jourdan, Bobby
Driscoll*, Marsha Hunt, Marcel Dalio, Kurt
Kasznar, Linda Christian, Jeanette Nolan,
Jack Raine, Richard Erdman

Hara Kiri*
Japan 1962   135m   bw   Grandscope
Shochiku
original title: *Seppuku*

17th-century samurai often pretend to commit
hara kiri so that a grand lord will have
sympathy and take them on. One of them is
forced to go through with it.
Strange, traditional, slow and explicitly brutal
costume piece, for specialized western eyes
only.

w Shinodu Hashimoto *d* Masaki Kobayashi
ph Yoshio Miyajima *m* Toru Takemitsu
ad Junichi Ozumi

Tatsuya Nakadai, Shimai Iwashita, Akira
Isahama

Hard Contract
US 1969 106m De Luxe Panavision
TCF (Marvin Schwarz)

A professional killer has sexual hang-ups.
Heavy-going modern thriller with lively scenes
separated by too much self-analytical chat, not
to mention a tour of Europe.

wd S. Lee Pogostin *ph* Jack Hildyard *m* Alex
North

James Coburn, Lilli Palmer, Lee Remick,
Burgess Meredith, Patrick Magee, Sterling
Hayden, Helen Cherry, Karen Black, Claude
Dauphin

'Behind it one glimpses a much better film
than its surface suggests.'—*MFB*

'Like a flat-footed James Bond story that
soaked its feet in a hot bath of
existentialism.'—*John Simon*

A Hard Day's Night****
GB 1964 85m bw
UA / Proscenium (Walter Shenson)

Harassed by their manager and Paul's
grandpa, the Beatles embark from Liverpool
by train for a London TV show.
Comic fantasia with music; an enormous
commercial success with the director trying
every cinematic gag in the book, it led directly
to all the kaleidoscopic swinging London spy
thrillers and comedies of the later sixties, and
so has a lot to answer for; but at the time it
was a sweet breath of fresh air, and the
Beatles even seemed willing and likeable.

*w Alun Owen d Richard Lester ph Gilbert
Taylor songs The Beatles md George Martin*

The Beatles, Wilfrid Brambell, Norman
Rossington, *Victor Spinetti*

'A fine conglomeration of madcap clowning
. . . with such a dazzling use of camera that it
tickles the intellect and electrifies the
nerves.'—*Bosley Crowther*

'All technology was enlisted in the service of
the gag, and a kind of nuclear gagmanship
exploded.'—*John Simon*

AAN: Alun Owen; George Martin

Hard, Fast and Beautiful
US 1951 76m bw
RKO / The Filmmakers (Collier Young)

A girl tennis player is influenced by her
ambitious mother.
Unusual but not very effective melodrama.

w Martha Wilkerson, *novel* John R. Tunis
d Ida Lupino *ph* Archie Stout *m* Roy Webb

Claire Trevor, Sally Forrest, Carleton Young,
Robert Clarke, Kenneth Patterson, Joseph
Kearns

Hard Steel
GB 1942 86m bw
GFD / GHW (James B. Sloan)
reissue title: *What Shall It Profit*

A steel worker is promoted and loses his
humanity, but comes to his senses when his
wife leaves him.
Modest moral drama from the uplift side of
the Rank empire.

w Lydia Hayward, *novel* Steel Saraband by
Roger Dataller *d* Norman Walker

Wilfrid Lawson, Betty Stockfield, John Stuart,
George Carney, Joan Kemp-Welch, Hay
Petrie

Hard Times*
US 1975 93m Metrocolor Panavision
Columbia (Lawrence Gordon)
GB title: *The Streetfighter*

In New Orleans in the Depression-hit thirties,
a prizefighter and a promoter help each other.
Interesting, atmospheric melodrama on the
lone stranger theme.

w Walter Hill, Bryan Gindorff, Bruce
Henstell *d* Walter Hill *ph* Philip Lathrop
m Barry DeVorzon

Charles Bronson, James Coburn, Jill Ireland,
Strother Martin, Maggie Blye

Hard to Get
US 1938 80m bw

An architect is reduced to working at a gas
station; here he meets and falls in love with a
millionairess. Arch romantic comedy which
failed to enhance its stars. Dick Powell, Olivia
de Havilland, Charles Winninger, Thurston
Hall, Isabel Jeans, Penny Singleton, Allen
Jenkins. Written by Jerry Wald, Maurice Leo
and Richard Macauley; directed by Ray
Enright; for Warner.

Hard to Handle**
US 1933 75m bw
Warner (Robert Lord)

The success story of a cheerful public relations
man.
Punchy star comedy with interesting sidelights
on the social fads of the early thirties including
marathon dancing, get-rich-quick schemes and
grapefruit diets.

w Wilson Mizner, Robert Lord *d* Mervyn Le
Roy *ph* Barney McGill

James Cagney, Ruth Donnelly, Mary Brian,
Allen Jenkins, Claire Dodd

'A violent, slangy, down-to-the-pavement
affair which has many a mirthful moment.'—
Mordaunt Hall

The Hard Way*
US 1942   109m   bw
Warner (Jerry Wald)

A strong-willed girl pushes her reluctant sister
to the heights of show business.
Unconvincing but well-mounted drama.

w Daniel Fuchs, Peter Viertel   d Vincent
Sherman   ph James Wong Howe   m Heinz
Roemheld   md Leo F. Forbstein

Ida Lupino, Joan Leslie, Dennis Morgan, Jack
Carson, Gladys George, Faye Emerson, Paul
Cavanagh, Roman Bohnen

Hardcore*
US 1978   108m   Metrocolor
Columbia / A-Team (John Milius)
GB title: *The Hardcore Life*

A religious man from Michigan journeys to
Los Angeles in search of his daughter, who
has taken to acting in porno films.
Intense and solemn treatment of a situation
that could have gone over the top, and very
nearly does; the acting saves it.

wd Paul Schraeder   ph Michael Chapman
m Jack Nitzsche

George C. Scott, Peter Boyle, Season Hubley,
Dick Sargent, Leonard Gaines

The Harder They Fall*
US 1956   109m   bw
Columbia (Philip Yordan)

A press agent exposes the crooked fight game.
Wearily efficient sporting melodrama.

w Philip Yordan, *novel* Budd Schulberg
d Mark Robson   ph Burnett Guffey   m Hugo
Friedhofer

Humphrey Bogart (his last performance), Rod
Steiger, Jan Sterling, Mike Lane, Max Baer,
Edward Andrews, Harold J. Stone

AAN: Burnett Guffey

The Hardy Family
America's favourite fictional characters just
before and during World War II were the
family of a small-town judge, who seemed to
personify all that everyone was fighting for,
especially as the young son was always getting
into amusing scrapes. Designed by a delighted
MGM as low-budgeters, they paid for many an
expensive failure, and introduced, as young
Andy's girl friends, a series of starlets who
went on to much bigger things. The basic
family was Lewis Stone, Fay Holden, Mickey
Rooney, Cecilia Parker and Sara Haden (as
the spinster aunt); but in the very first episode
Lionel Barrymore and Spring Byington played
the judge and his wife.

A FAMILY AFFAIR (1936); 69m; *d* George
B. Seitz; *w* Kay Van Riper, *play* Aurania
Rouverol
YOU'RE ONLY YOUNG ONCE (1938);
78m; *d* George B. Seitz; *w* Kay Van Riper;
introducing Ann Rutherford (who became a
regular)
JUDGE HARDY'S CHILDREN (1938);
78m; *d* George B. Seitz; *w* Kay Van Riper;
with Ruth Hussey
LOVE FINDS ANDY HARDY (1938); 90m;
d George B. Seitz; *w* William Ludwig; *with*
Judy Garland, Lana Turner
OUT WEST WITH THE HARDYS (1938);
90m; *d* George B. Seitz; *w* Kay Van Riper,
Agnes Christine Johnson, William Ludwig
THE HARDYS RIDE HIGH (1939); 81m;
d George B. Seitz; *w* as above
ANDY HARDY GETS SPRING FEVER
(1939); 85m; *d* W. S. Van Dyke II; *w* Kay
Van Riper
JUDGE HARDY AND SON (1939); 90m;
d George B. Seitz; *w* Carey Wilson; *with* June
Preisser, Maria Ouspenskaya
ANDY HARDY MEETS A DEBUTANTE
(1940); 89m; *d* George B. Seitz; *w* Annalee
Whitmore, Thomas Seller; *with* Judy Garland
ANDY HARDY'S PRIVATE SECRETARY
(1941); 101m; *d* George B. Seitz; *w* Jane
Murfin, Harry Ruskin; *with* Kathryn Grayson,
Ian Hunter
LIFE BEGINS FOR ANDY HARDY (1941);
100m; *d* George B. Seitz; *w* Agnes Christine
Johnson; *with* Judy Garland
THE COURTSHIP OF ANDY HARDY
(1942); 93m; *d* George B. Seitz; *w* Agnes
Christine Johnson; *with* Donna Reed
ANDY HARDY'S DOUBLE LIFE (1942);
92m; *d* George B. Seitz; *w* Agnes Christine
Johnson; *with* Esther Williams, Susan Peters
ANDY HARDY'S BLONDE TROUBLE
(1944); 107m; *d* George B. Seitz; *w* Harry
Ruskin, William Ludwig, Agnes Christine
Johnson; *with* Bonita Granville, Jean Porter,
Herbert Marshall, the Wilde twins
LOVE LAUGHS AT ANDY HARDY
(1946); 94m; *d* Willis Goldbeck; *w* Harry
Ruskin, William Ludwig; *with* Bonita
Granville
ANDY HARDY COMES HOME (1958);
80m; *d* Howard Koch; *w* Edward Everett
Hutshing, Robert Morris Donley; *without*
Lewis Stone

Harlequin
Australia 1980   93m   Eastmancolor
   Panavision

A faith healer cures a politician's son, seduces
his wife, and proves to be of supernatural

origin. Muddled and unsatisfactory fantasy in the manner of *The Passing of the Third Floor Back*; in this case far too much is left unexplained, and the film is scarcely entertaining despite effort all round. Robert Powell, David Hemmings, Carmen Duncan, Broderick Crawford. Written by Everett de Roche; directed by Simon Wincer; for FG Films.

Harlow
US 1965 125m Technicolor
Panavision
Paramount / Embassy / Prometheus
(Joseph E. Levine)

In 1929, starlet Jean Harlow is shot to fame by her agent Arthur Landau.
Absurdly whitewashed and excruciatingly boring rags-to-riches yarn with most of the characters fictitious and little to do with the real Jean Harlow. Only the studio scenes are mildly interesting.

w John Michael Hayes *d* Gordon Douglas *ph* Joseph Ruttenberg *m* Neal Hefti *ad* Hal Pereira, Roland Anderson *costumes* Edith Head

Carroll Baker, Peter Lawford, Mike Connors, Red Buttons, Raf Vallone, Angela Lansbury, *Martin Balsam*

'Hollywood once again succeeds in reducing one of its few fascinating realities to the sleazy turgid level of its more sordid fictions.'— *Judith Crist*

† A rather better television tape drama of the same title, starring Carol Lynley and Ginger Rogers, was made almost simultaneously. It was converted to film ('Electronovision') but had few bookings.

Harmony Heaven*
GB 1930 61m colour
BIP

A composer becomes famous with the help of his girl friend.
Unbelievably naïve musical, notable only as British and in colour. Not tolerable today as entertainment.

w Arthur Wimperis, Randall Faye *d* Thomas Bentley *ph* Theodor Sparkuhl *songs* Edward Brandt, Eddie Pola

Polly Ward, Stuart Hall, Trilby Clark, Jack Raine

Harold and Maude*
US 1971 92m Technicolor
Paramount / Mildred Lewis / Colin Higgins

A repressed young man, fixated on death and funerals, has an affair with an 80-year-old woman.
Often hilarious black comedy for those who can stand it; the epitome of bad taste, splashed around with wit and vigour, it became a minor cult.

w Colin Higgins *d* Hal Ashby *ph* John A. Alonzo *m* Cat Stevens

Bud Cort, Ruth Gordon, Vivian Pickles, Cyril Cusack

Harold Lloyd's Funny Side of Life***
US 1963 99m bw
Harold Lloyd (Duncan Mansfield)

Excerpts from twenties comedies plus a shortened version of *The Freshman* (1925). Excellent compilation, though the mini-feature makes it a little unbalanced.

w Arthur Ross *m* Walter Scharf
Harold Lloyd

Harold Lloyd's World of Comedy****
US 1962 97m bw
Harold Lloyd

Generous clips from the comic climaxes of Lloyd's best silent and sound comedies including *Safety Last, The Freshman, Hot Water, Why Worry, Girl Shy, Professor Beware, Movie Crazy* and *Feet First*.
As Lloyd's work lends itself well to extract, this can hardly fail to be a superb anthology capsuling the appeal of one of America's greatest silent comedians. The timing is just perfect.

m Walter Scharf *commentary* Art Ross

Harold Teen
US 1934 66m bw

A young reporter saves a small-town bank from collapse. Teenage romantic comedy previously filmed in 1928 (with Arthur Lake and Mary Brian, directed by Mervyn Le Roy) and here reduced to second feature status. Hal Le Roy, Rochelle Hudson, Patricia Ellis, Guy Kibbee, Hobart Cavanagh. Written by Paul Gerard Smith and Al Cohn, from the comic strip by Carl Ed; directed by Murray Roth; for Warner. (GB title: *Dancing Fool*.)

Harper*
US 1966 121m Technicolor
Panavision
Warner / Gershwin–Kastner
GB title: *The Moving Target*

A Los Angeles private eye is hired by a rich woman to find her missing husband.

Formula Californian detection distinguished by its cast rather than by any special talent in the writing or presentation. It seemed likely to produce a new Chandleresque school, but imitations proved very sporadic; the star repeated the role less successfully in *The Drowning Pool* (qv).

w William Goldman, *novel* The Moving Target by John Ross Macdonald d Jack Smight *ph* Conrad Hall *m* Johnny Mandel

Paul Newman, Lauren Bacall, Shelley Winters, Arthur Hill, Julie Harris, Janet Leigh, Pamela Tiffin, Robert Wagner, Robert Webber, Strother Martin

'It isn't a bad try, but it never really slips into overdrive.'—*Penelope Houston*

'Nothing needs justification less than entertainment; but when something planned only to entertain fails, it has no justification. A private-eye movie without sophistication and style is ignominious.'—*Pauline Kael, 1968*

The Harrad Experiment
US 1973 97m Eastmancolor
Cinerama / Cinema Arts (Dennis F. Stevens)

A college professor conducts a series of tests on sexual relationships.
Low-keyed Kinsey Report for the seventies, pleasantly made but not very stimulating.

w Michael Werner, Ted Cassidy, *novel* Robert H. Rimmer d Ted Post *ph* Richard Kline *m* Artie Butler

James Whitmore, Tippi Hedren, Don Johnson, Laurie Walters, Robert Middleton

'Ludicrously sober-sided amalgam of nude yoga and extra-curricular groping, which should set sex educational theory back ten years.'—*Sight and Sound*

Harriet Craig
US 1950 94m bw
Columbia (William Dozier)

A wife's only real love is her meticulously kept and richly appointed house.
Ho-hum remake of a sturdy thirties film *Craig's Wife* (qv).

w Anne Froelick, James Gunn, *play* Craig's Wife by George Kelly d Vincent Sherman *ph* Joseph Walker *m* George Duning *md* Morris Stoloff

Joan Crawford, Wendell Corey, Allyn Joslyn, Lucile Watson, William Bishop, K. T. Stevens, Raymond Greenleaf

Harry and Tonto*
US 1974 115m De Luxe
TCF (Paul Mazursky)

An elderly New York widower and his cat are evicted and trek to Chicago.
Amiable character study, very watchable but rather pointless.

w Paul Mazursky, Josh Greenfield d Paul Mazursky *ph* Michael Butler *m* Bill Conti

Art Carney, Ellen Burstyn, Chief Dan George, Geraldine Fitzgerald, Larry Hagman, Arthur Hunnicutt, Herbert Berghof

'A vivacious and affectionate folk tale.'—*New Yorker*

'It has a life-affirming quality as welcome contrast to the destructive delirium of most modern movies.'—*Michael Billington, Illustrated London News*

AA: Art Carney
AAN: Paul Mazursky (as writer)

Harry and Walter go to New York.
US 1976 120m Metrocolor Panavision
Columbia (Don Devlin, Harry Gittes)

In oldtime New York, two carnival entertainers get involved with suffragettes and a safecracker.
Extended period romp in which the high humour soon palls and a general lack of talent makes itself felt.

w John Byrum, Robert Kaufman d Mark Rydell *ph* Laszlo Kovacs *m* David Shire *pd* Harry Horner

James Caan, Elliott Gould, Michael Caine, Diane Keaton, Charles Durning, Lesley Ann Warren, Jack Gilford

'A charmless mishmash.'—*Sight and Sound*

'This film fails to work as a light comedy, as a period piece, as a jigsaw puzzle . . . mainly, it just sits there and dies.'—*Frank Rich, New York Post*

'Strictly for those who'll laugh at anything.'—*Kevin Thomas, Los Angeles Times*

Harry Black and the Tiger
GB 1958 117m Technicolor Cinemascope
TCF (John Brabourne)
US title: *Harry Black*

A famous tiger hunter allows his best friend to prove himself a hero, and falls in love with the friend's wife.
Lethargic melodrama with good Indian backgrounds.

w Sydney Boehm, *novel* David Walker d Hugo Fregonese *ph* John Wilcox *m* Clifton Parker

Stewart Granger, Anthony Steel, Barbara Rush, *I. S. Johar*

Harry in Your Pocket
US 1973 103m De Luxe Panavision
UA / Cinema Video (Bruce Geller)

Adventures of a young, a middle-aged and an old pickpocket.
Partly pleasant but rather aimless comedy drama, agreeably set in Seattle and Salt Lake City.

w Ron Austin, James Buchanan d Bruce Geller ph Fred Koenekamp m Lalo Schifrin

James Coburn, *Walter Pidgeon*, Michael Sarrazin, Trish Van Devere

Harvest
France 1937 122m bw Marcel Pagnol
original title: *Regain*

A poacher and an itinerant girl set up house in a deserted village and bring it back to life.
Somewhat charming but interminably slow rustic parable.

wd Marcel Pagnol, *novel* Jean Giono
ph Willy m Arthur Honegger

Gabriel Gabrio, Fernandel, Orane Demazis, E. Delmont

Harvey***
US 1950 104m bw
U-I (John Beck)

A middle-aged drunk has an imaginary white rabbit as his friend, and his sister tries to have him certified.
An amiably batty play with splendid lines is here transferred virtually intact to the screen and survives superbly thanks to understanding by all concerned, though the star is as yet too young for a role which he later made his own.

w *Mary Chase* (with Oscar Brodney) from her play d Henry Koster ph William Daniels m Frank Skinner

James Stewart, Josephine Hull, Victoria Horne, Peggy Dow, *Cecil Kellaway*, Charles Drake, *Jesse White*, Nana Bryant, Wallace Ford

AA: Josephine Hull
AAN: James Stewart

The Harvey Girls**
US 1946 101m Technicolor
MGM (Arthur Freed)

A chain of 19th-century restaurants hires young ladies to go out west as waitresses.
Sprightly if overlong musical based on fact; a good example of an MGM middle-budget extravaganza.

w Edmund Beloin, Nathaniel Curtis
d George Sidney ph George Folsey
md Lennie Hayton *songs* Johnny Mercer, Harry Warren

Judy Garland, Ray Bolger, John Hodiak, Preston Foster, Virginia O'Brien, Angela Lansbury, Marjorie Main, Chill Wills, Kenny Baker, Selena Royle

'Anybody who did anything at all in America up to 1900 is liable to be made into a film by MGM.'—*Richard Winnington*

AA: song 'On the Atcheson, Topeka and the Santa Fe'
AAN: Lennie Hayton

Harvey Middleman Fireman*
US 1965 76m Eastmancolor
Columbia (Robert L. Lawrence)

A frustrated middle-aged fireman begins an affair; the resulting guilt complex drives him to a psychiatrist.
Grotesque satirical comedy from one of the sixties' most fashionable cartoonists. Mild, quite pleasing, occasionally crude.

wd / m Ernest Pintoff ph Karl Malkames

Gene Troobnick, Hermione Gingold, Pat Harty

Has Anybody Seen My Gal?**
US 1952 89m Technicolor
U-I (Ted Richmond)

A multi-millionaire pretends to be poor and moves in with distant relatives to test their worthiness.
Very agreeable comedy set in the twenties and centring on a satisfying star performance.

w Joseph Hoffman d Douglas Sirk
ph Clifford Stine m Joseph Gershenson
ad Bernard Herzbrun, Hilyard Brown

Charles Coburn, Piper Laurie, Rock Hudson, Gigi Perreau, Lynn Bari, Larry Gates, William Reynolds, Skip Homeier, James Dean

The Hasty Heart*
GB 1949 104m bw
ABP (Vincent Sherman)

At an army hospital in Burma, attitudes to an arrogant young Scot change when it is learned that he has only a few weeks to live.
Flat, adequate filming of a successful sentimental stage play.

w Ranald MacDougall, *play* John Patrick
d Vincent Sherman ph Wilkie Cooper
m Jack Beaver

Richard Todd, Patricia Neal, Ronald Reagan, Orlando Martins, Howard Marion-Crawford

AAN: Richard Todd

Hatari!*
US 1962 158m Technicolor
Paramount / Malabar (Howard Hawks)

International hunters in Tanganyika catch game to send to zoos.
Plotless adventure film with good animal sequences but no shape or suspense; a typical folly of its director, whose chief interest is seeing smart men and women in tough action. The elephants steal this overlong show.

w Leigh Brackett d Howard Hawks
ph Russell Harlan m Henry Mancini

John Wayne, Elsa Martinelli, Red Buttons, Hardy Kruger
  'Hawks was taking his friends and cast and crew on a trip he wanted to make personally, and the film is both the incidental excuse for and the record of that experience.'—*Joseph Gelmis, 1970*

AAN: Russell Harlan

The Hatchet Man
US 1932   74m   bw
Warner
GB title: *The Honourable Mr Wong*

The executioner of a San Francisco tong dutifully kills his best friend but promises to care for his daughter.
Unconvincing Chinese-American melodrama.

w J. Grubb Alexander, *play* Achmed Abdullah, David Belasco d William A. Wellman *ph* Sid Hickox

Edward G. Robinson, Loretta Young, Dudley Digges, Leslie Fenton, Edmund Breese, Tully Marshall, J. Carrol Naish, Noel Madison, Blanche Frederici

A Hatful of Rain*
US 1957   108m   bw   Cinemascope
TCF / (Buddy Adler)

A war veteran becomes a drug addict and upsets his wife and family.
One of the first drug dramas: straightforward, well acted, and quite powerful.

w Michael V. Gazzo (with Alfred Hayes), from his play d Fred Zinnemann ph Joe Macdonald m Bernard Herrmann

Eva Marie Saint, Don Murray, Anthony Franciosa, Lloyd Nolan, Henry Silva

AAN: Anthony Franciosa

Hatter's Castle**
GB 1941   102m   bw
Paramount British (Isadore Goldsmith)

In the nineties, a megalomaniac Scottish hatter ruins the lives of his wife and daughter.
Enjoyable period melodrama with a rampant star performance and pretty good detail.

w Rodney Ackland, *novel* A. J. Cronin
d Lance Comfort ph Max Greene m Horace Shepherd

Robert Newton, Deborah Kerr, James Mason, Beatrice Varley, Emlyn Williams, Henry Oscar, Enid Stamp-Taylor, Brefni O'Rourke

The Haunted Palace
US 1963   85m   Pathecolor   Panavision
AIP / Alta Vista (Roger Corman)

In 1875 a New Englander claims an old mansion as his inheritance and is haunted by his vicious ancestor.
Plodding horror comic, too slow to give opportunities to its stalwart cast.

w Charles Beaumont, from material by H. P. Lovecraft and Edgar Allan Poe d Roger Corman ph Floyd Crosby m Ronald Stein

Vincent Price, Lon Chaney Jnr, Debra Paget, Frank Maxwell, Leo Gordon, Elisha Cook Jnr, John Dierkes
  'For those of ghoulish bent, or lovers of the perfectly awful.'—*Judith Crist*

The Haunting*
GB 1963   112m   bw   Panavision
MGM / Argyle (Robert Wise)

An anthropologist, a sceptic and two mediums spend the weekend in a haunted Boston mansion.
Quite frightening but exhausting and humourless melodrama with a lot of suspense, no visible spooks, and not enough plot for its length. The wide screen is a disadvantage.

w Nelson Gidding, *novel* The Haunting of Hill House by Shirley Jackson d Robert Wise
ph David Boulton m Humphrey Searle
pd Elliot Scott

Richard Johnson, Claire Bloom, Russ Tamblyn, Julie Harris, Lois Maxwell, Valentine Dyall
  'You may not believe in ghosts, but you cannot deny terror!'—*publicity*

Having a Wonderful Crime
US 1945   70m   bw

Three amateur detectives solve the mystery of a disappearing magician. Easy-going comedy thriller. Pat O'Brien, Carole Landis, George Murphy. Written by Howard J. Green, Stewart Sterling and Parke Levy; directed by Eddie Sutherland; for RKO.

Having Wonderful Time
US 1938   70m   bw
RKO (Pandro S. Berman)

A New York girl falls in love at a summer camp.
Mild comedy which, robbed of its original Jewish milieu, falls resoundingly flat.

w Arthur Kober, from his play d Alfred Santell ph Robert de Grasse m Roy Webb

Ginger Rogers, Douglas Fairbanks Jnr, Peggy Conklin, Lucille Ball, Lee Bowman, Eve Arden, Red Skelton, Donald Meek, Jack Carson

Hawaii*
US 1966 186m De Luxe Panavision
UA / Mirisch (Lewis J. Rachmil)

In 1820 a pious Yale divinity student becomes a missionary to the Hawaiian islands.
Ambitious attempt to contrast naïve dogma with native innocence, ruined by badly handled sub-plots, storms, a childbirth sequence and other distractions, all fragments of an immense novel. Heavy going.

w Daniel Taradash, Dalton Trumbo, *novel* James A. Michener d George Roy Hill ph Russell Harlan m Elmer Bernstein *2nd unit Richard Talmadge pd Cary Odell*

Max Von Sydow, Julie Andrews, Richard Harris, *Jocelyn la Garde*, Carroll O'Connor, Torin Thatcher, Gene Hackman
    'Consistently intelligent humanism gives it a certain stature among the wide screen spectacles.'—*Brenda Davies*

AAN: cinematography; Jocelyn La Garde

The Hawaiians
US 1970 132m De Luxe Panavision
UA / Mirisch (Walter Mirisch)
GB title: *Master of the Islands*

A young scion of a shipping business leaves after an argument and strikes oil in terrain supposedly barren.
More fragments from Michener, covering 1870 to 1900 and comprising an absolutely uninteresting family chronicle with moments of spectacle.

w James R. Webb d Tom Gries ph Philip Lathrop m Henry Mancini pd Cary Odell

Charlton Heston, Tina Chen, Geraldine Chaplin, John Philip Law, Alec McCowen, Mako, Ann Knight, Lyle Bettger, Keye Luke
    'A quickfire succession of corruption, revolution, plague, fire and questions of moral responsibility.'—*MFB*
    'Total relaxation—preferably of the brain—is recommended.'—*Judith Crist*

Hawk the Slayer
GB 1980 93m colour
ITC / Chips (Harry Robertson)

Good and evil brothers compete for possession of a magical flying sword.
Curiously unexciting and rather gloomy sword-and-sorcery epic.

w Terry Marcel, Harry Robertson d Terry Marcel ph Paul Beeson m Harry Robertson

Jack Palance, John Terry, Bernard Bresslaw, Ray Charleson, Annette Crosbie, Cheryl Campbell, Peter O'Farrell

Hawmps
US 1976 127m colour

The Texas cavalry experiments with the use of camels in the southwestern desert. Incredibly overstretched and tedious period comedy with some bright patches. James Hampton, Christopher Connelly, Slim Pickens, Denver Pyle, Jennifer Hawkins, Jack Elam. Written by William Bickley and Michael Warren; directed by Joe Camp; for Mulberry Square.

Hazard
US 1948 95m bw
Paramount (Mel Epstein)

A compulsive lady gambler agrees to marry the winner of a dice game, but runs away and is chased by a private detective.
Silly, unamusing romantic comedy-drama.

w Arthur Sheekman, Roy Chanslor d George Marshall ph Daniel L. Fapp m Frank Skinner

Paulette Goddard, Macdonald Carey, Fred Clark, Stanley Clemens, Maxie Rosenbloom, Charles McGraw
    'A good bit this side of inspired.'—*New York Times*

He Knows You're Alone
US 1980 92m Metrocolor

A sex-starved maniac attacks teenage girls. Cheapjack horror comic full of fashionable slashing and screaming; of no cinematic interest whatever. Don Scardino, Elizabeth Kemp. Written by Scott Parker; directed by Armand Mastroianni; for Lansbury-Beruh / MGM. 'At this point in the killer-with-a-knife sweepstakes, every company in Hollywood is getting into the act . . . more ingenuity is going into the titles and campaigns than into the films.'—*Variety*.

He Laughed Last*
US 1956 77m Technicolor
Columbia (Jonie Taps)

In the twenties, New York gangsters battle for control of a night club.
Small-scale gangster burlesque which comes off rather better than its credits suggest.

wd Blake Edwards *ph* Henry Freulich
m Arthur Morton

Frankie Laine, Lucy Marlow, Anthony
Dexter, *Jesse White*

He Ran All the Way*
US 1951   78m   bw
UA / Bob Roberts

. A hoodlum on the run from the police
virtually picks up a girl and hides in her
family's apartment.
Uninteresting situation melodrama helped by
intelligent acting and handling.

w Guy Endore, Hugo Butler, *novel* Sam Ross
d John Berry *ph* James Wong Howe *m* Franz
Waxman

John Garfield, Shelley Winters, Wallace Ford,
Selena Royle, Gladys George, Norman Lloyd,
Bobby Hyatt

He Snoops to Conquer
GB 1944   103m   bw
Columbia (Ben Henry, Marcel Varnel)

A local handyman exposes a corrupt council.
Spotty star comedy with insufficient zest for its
great length.

w Stephen Black, Howard Irving Young,
Norman Lee, Michael Vaughan, Langford
Reed *d* Marcel Varnel *ph* Roy Fogwell

George Formby, Robertson Hare, Elizabeth
Allen, Aubrey Mallalieu

He Stayed for Breakfast
US 1940   89m   bw
Columbia (B. P. Schulberg)

A Parisian communist waiter hides out in the
apartment of American capitalists, and learns
from them.
Post-*Ninotchka* comedy, not bad but somehow
rather uninteresting and mechanical.

w P. J. Wolfson, Michael Fessier, Ernest
Vajda, *play* Liberté Provisoire by Michel
Duran *d* Alexander Hall *ph* Joseph Walker
m Werner Heymann

Melvyn Douglas, Loretta Young, Alan
Marshal, Eugene Pallette, Una O'Connor,
Curt Bois, Leonid Kinskey

He Walked by Night*
US 1948   80m   bw
Eagle–Lion / Bryan Foy

A burglar becomes a cop-killer and is hunted
down by the police.
Interesting if rather flatly handled
documentary melodrama in clear imitation of
Naked City.

w John C. Higgins, Crane Wilbur *d* Alfred
Werker *ph* John Alton *m* Leonid Raab

Richard Basehart, Scott Brady, Roy Roberts,
Whit Bissell

He Was Her Man
US 1934   70m   bw

A safecracker goes straight in order to get
even with old rivals. Sassy comedy-drama, not
quite smart enough to match its star. James
Cagney, Joan Blondell, Victor Jory, Frank
Craven, Harold Huber. Written by Niven
Busch and Tom Buckingham; directed by
Lloyd Bacon; for Warner.

He Who Gets Slapped*
US 1924   80m approx (24 fps)   bw
    silent
MGM

A scientist starts a new life as a circus clown.
Odd poetic tragedy, Metro-Goldwyn-Mayer's
very first production; the public took to it
surprisingly well.

w Victor Sjostrom, Carey Wilson, *play* Leonid
Andreyev *d* Victor Sjostrom

Lon Chaney, Norma Shearer, John Gilbert,
Tully Marshall, Ford Sterling
    'For dramatic value and a faultless
adaptation of a play, this is the finest
production we have yet seen.'—*New York
Times*

He Who Must Die*
France / Italy 1957   126m   bw
    Cinemascope
original title: *Celui Qui Doit Mourir*

In a Greek village in 1921, preparations for a
passion play are interrupted by the arrival of
refugees from the mountains.
Occasionally striking, but mainly arty and
pretentious parable; however well meant, a
bore to watch.

w Ben Barzman, Jules Dassin, *novel* Nikos
Kazantzakis *d* Jules Dassin *ph* Jacques
Natteau *m* Georges Auric

Jean Servais, Carl Mohner, Pierre Vaneck,
Melina Mercouri, Fernand Ledoux

He Who Rides a Tiger
GB 1965   103m   bw
British Lion / David Newman

A feckless burglar comes out of prison and
returns to the old life.
Cliché crime yarn which tries rather
desperately after fresh detail but bogs down in
romantic asides.

w Trevor Peacock *d* Charles Crichton
ph John Von Kotze *m* Alexander Faris

Tom Bell, Judi Dench, Paul Rogers, Kay Walsh, Ray McAnally, Jeremy Spenser

Head°
US 1968 85m Technicolor
Columbia (Bert Schneider)

Fantasia on the life of a sixties pop group.
A psychedelic trip of a movie which does for the Monkees what *A Hard Day's Night* and *Yellow Submarine* did for the Beatles, and what *Monty Python* did for us all. Sometimes funny, slick and clever; often just plain silly.

w Jack Nicholson, Bob Rafaelson *d* Bob Rafaelson *ph* Michael Hugo *m* Ken Thorne *sp* Chuck Gaspar

The Monkees, Victor Mature, Annette Funicello, Timothy Carey

'Random particles tossed around in some demented jester's wind machine.'—*Richard Combs, MFB, 1978*

Head Over Heels°
GB 1937 81m bw
Gaumont (S. C. Balcon)
US title: *Head Over Heels in Love*

A singing star can't make up her mind between two men.
Interestingly dated light star vehicle.

w Dwight Taylor, Fred Thompson, Marjorie Gaffney, *play* Francois de Croisset *d* Sonnie Hale *ph* Glen McWilliams

Jessie Matthews, Robert Flemyng, Louis Borell, Romney Brent, Helen Whitney Bourne, Eliot Makeham

Head Over Heels
US 1980 97m Technicolor

A government office worker thinks back on his on-again off-again relationship with the woman he loves. Quirky comedy drama without the zest of *Annie Hall*, which it much resembles; too much like a television play for box office success. John Heard, Mary Beth Hurt, Peter Riegert, Kenneth McMillan, Gloria Grahame. Written and directed by Joan Macklin Silver, from the novel *Chilly Scenes of Winter* by Ann Beattie; for Triple Play / UA.

Health°
US 1979 102m De Luxe
TCF / Robert Altman

Complications result when a health foods convention is staged in a Florida hotel.
Zany satirical all-star romp on the lines of *A Wedding* but by no means as likeable or laughable, considering its cast, as it should be.

w Robert Altman, Paul Dooley, Frank Barhydt *d* Robert Altman *ph* Edmond L. Koons *m* Joseph Byrd

Lauren Bacall, Glenda Jackson, James Garner, Dick Cavett, Carol Burnett, Paul Dooley, Henry Gibson, Donald Moffat

Hear Me Good
US 1957 82m bw VistaVision

Adventures of a confidence trickster in the beauty contest racket. Sub-Damon Runyon goings on, featuring a brash new comedian who was subsequently little heard from. Hal March, Jean Willes, Joe E. Ross, Merry Anders, Milton Frome. Written and directed by Don McGuire; for Paramount.

Heart Beat
US 1979 109m Technicolor

The literary career of Jack Kerouac is paralleled with his curious sex life. Hesitant and generally unsatisfactory analysis of the so-called beat generation. John Heard, Nick Nolte, Sissy Spacek, Ray Sharkey, Tony Bill. Written and directed by John Byrun; for Orion / Warner.

The Heart is a Lonely Hunter°
US 1968 123m Technicolor
Warner Seven Arts (Joel Freeman)

Incidents in the life of a gentle deaf mute in a small southern town.
Wispy film of a wistful novel; quite well done but overlong and hard to cheer at.

w Thomas C. Ryan, *novel* Carson McCullers *d* Robert Ellis Miller *ph James Wong Howe* *m* Dave Grusin

Alan Arkin, Sondra Locke, Stacy Keach, Laurinda Barrett, Chuck McCann, Biff McGuire, Percy Rodriguez, Cicely Tyson

AAN: Alan Arkin; Sondra Locke

Heart of Glass°
West Germany 1976 94m Eastmancolor
Werner Herzog

A wandering herdsman with special powers supplies a factory owner with the secret of making a very precious glass.
Apocalyptic visionary parable which may mean everything, or nothing, but amuses fitfully while it's on the screen.

wd Werner Herzog, *text* Herbert Achternbusch *ph* Jorg Schmidt-Reitwin *m* Popol Vuh

Josef Bierbichler, Stefan Guttler, Clemens Scheitz, Sepp Müller

Heart of New York*
US 1932   74m   bw

A plumber invents a washing machine and
becomes a millionaire. Ethnic farce set in New
York's Jewish quarter; of considerable
curiosity value. Smith and Dale, George
Sidney, Anna Apfel, Aline MacMahon,
Donald Cook. Written and directed by
Mervyn Le Roy; for Warner.

The Heart of the Matter*
GB 1953   105m   bw
British Lion / London Films (Ian Dalrymple)

In 1942 in an African colony a police officer
has an affair while his wife is away, is
blackmailed, and plans suicide despite his
staunch Catholic belief.
Rather stodgy attempt to film Graham
Greene; perhaps everyone tries a little too
hard, and in any case the ending is
compromised.

w Ian Dalrymple, Lesley Storm, *novel*
Graham Greene d George More O'Ferrall
ph Jack Hildyard *m* Brian Easdale

Trevor Howard, Maria Schell, Elizabeth
Allan, Denholm Elliott, Peter Finch, Gérard
Oury, George Coulouris, Earl Cameron,
Michael Hordern, Colin Gordon, Cyril
Raymond, Orlando Martins
  'A curious choice for commercial filming.'—
Lindsay Anderson

Heartbeat
US 1946   102m   bw
RKO / Robert and Raymond Hakim

A French gamin released from reform school
becomes a professional pickpocket.
Unamusing remake of *Battement de Coeur*,
with script and most performances very
strained.

w Hans Wilhelm, Max Kolpe, Michel Druan,
Morrie Ryskind d Sam Wood *ph* Joe
Valentine *m* Paul Misraki

Ginger Rogers, Jean-Pierre Aumont, Adolphe
Menjou, *Basil Rathbone*, Mikhail Rasumny,
Melville Cooper, Mona Maris, Henry
Stephenson
  'The heartbeat is irregular and sadly
ailing.'—*Photoplay*

The Heartbreak Kid*
US 1972   106m   De Luxe
(TCF) Palomar (Edgar J. Scherick)

Disappointed with his honeymoon, a sporting
goods salesman promptly sets his cap at a
richer, prettier prospective spouse.
Heartless modern comedy reminiscent of *The*

Graduate; quite well done but unsympathetic
and somehow too American to export
satisfactorily.

w Neil Simon, *story* A Change of Plan by
Bruce Jay Friedman d Elaine May *ph* Owen
Roizman *m* Garry Sherman

Charles Grodin, Cybill Shepherd, Jeannie
Berlin, Eddie Albert, Audra Lindley, William
Prince, Art Metrano
  'The latest in a relatively new kind of
American film—glittery trash.'—*Stanley
Kauffmann*

AAN: Jeannie Berlin; Eddie Albert

Heart's Desire
GB 1935   82m   bw

In old Vienna, a tenor finds that a glamorous
socialite wants him for his voice rather than
himself. Dated operetta, but the star still
reigns supreme. *Richard Tauber*, Leonora
Corbett, Diana Napier, Frank Vosper.
Written by Clifford Grey, L. DuGarde Peach,
Jack Davies, Roger Burford and Bruno Frank;
directed by Paul Stein; for BIP.

Hearts Divided
US 1936   76m   bw

Napoleon's brother weds a Baltimore beauty.
Uneasy remake of *Glorious Betsy* (qv) with a
couple of musical numbers added; a splendid
cast retires defeated. Marion Davies, Dick
Powell, Edward Everett Horton, Claude
Rains, Charles Ruggles, Arthur Treacher,
Henry Stephenson. Written by Laird Doyle
and Casey Robinson; directed by Frank
Borzage; for Warner.

Hearts of the West*
US 1975   103m   Metrocolor
MGM / Bill–Zieff (Tony Bill)
GB title: *Hollywood Cowboy*

In the early thirties a naïve mid-westerner
almost accidentally becomes a Hollywood star.
Overstretched comedy poking gentle fun at
old Hollywood: likeable but finally
disappointing, as it obviously needed a Buster
Keaton.

w Rob Thompson d Howard Zieff *ph* Mario
Tosi *m* Ken Lauber

Jeff Bridges, Alan Arkin, Andy Griffith,
Blythe Danner, Donald Pleasence, Richard B.
Shull, Herb Edelman

Heat Lightning
US 1934   63m   bw

A lady gas station attendant in the hot
southwest becomes involved with two

murderers on the run. Cautionary tale which does not quite jell despite effort all round. Aline MacMahon, Ann Dvorak, Preston Foster, Lyle Talbot, Glenda Farrell, Frank McHugh, Ruth Donnelly. Written by Brown Holmes and Warren Duff, from the play by George Abbott and Leon Abrams; directed by Mervyn Le Roy; for Warner. (NB: remade in 1941 as *Highway West*.)

The Heat's On
US 1943 79m bw
Columbia (Milton Carter)
GB title: *Tropicana*

A star seeks financial backing from an elderly angel whose sister runs the Legion of Purity. Dim musical vehicle for a fading star; her last film for twenty-seven years.

w Fitzroy Davis, George S. George, Fred Schiller *d* Gregory Ratoff *ph* Franz Planer *md* Yasha Bunchuk

Mae West, Victor Moore, William Gaxton, Almira Sessions, Lester Allan, Mary Roche, Hazel Scott, Alan Dinehart, Lloyd Bridges, Xavier Cugat and his Orchestra
   'A stale-ale musical in which a lot of good people apathetically support the almost equally apathetic Mae West.'—*James Agee*

Heaven Can Wait***
US 1943 112m Technicolor
TCF (Ernst Lubitsch)

On arrival in Hades, an elderly playboy reports his peccadilloes to Satan, who sends him Upstairs.
Charming period piece with fantasy bookends; the essence of the piece is its evocation of American society in the nineties, and in its director's waspish way with a funny scene.

w Samson Raphaelson, *play* Birthday by Lazlo Bus-Fekete *d* Ernst Lubitsch *ph* Edward Cronjager *m* Alfred Newman *ad* James Basevi, Leland Fuller

Don Ameche, Gene Tierney, *Laird Cregar*, *Charles Coburn*, *Marjorie Main*, Eugene Pallette, *Allyn Joslyn*, Spring Byington, Signe Hasso, Louis Calhern
   'It was so good I half believed Lubitsch could still do as well as he ever did, given half a chance.'—*James Agee*

AAN: best picture; Ernst Lubitsch; Edward Cronjager

Heaven Can Wait*
US 1978 100m Movielab
Paramount / Warren Beatty (Howard W. Koch Jnr, Charles H. McGuire)

A football star finds himself accidentally in heaven after a car accident; when he is allowed to return, his body has been cremated, so he has to find another. Unexpectedly commercially successful (the late seventies clearly need religion) remake of 1941's *Here Comes Mr Jordan*. It lacks the sharpness and style of its predecessor, and despite amusing moments is often merely tacky.

w Warren Beatty, Elaine May, *play* Harry Segall *d* Warren Beatty, Buck Henry *ph* William A. Fraker *m* Dave Grusin *pd* Paul Sylbert

Warren Beatty, Julie Christie, James Mason (as Mr Jordan), Jack Warden, Charles Grodin, *Dyan Cannon*, Buck Henry, Vincent Gardenia, Joseph Maher

AAN: best picture; script; direction; photography; music; Warren Beatty (as actor); Jack Warden; Dyan Cannon

Heaven Fell That Night
France / Italy 1958 90m Eastmancolor Cinemascope
IENA / CEIAP (Raoul Levy)
original title: *Les Bijoutiers du Clair de Lune*

A young girl becomes involved in a revenge plot and finds herself on the run with a killer Heavy going sex-and-violence hokum.

w Roger Vadim, Peter Viertel, *novel* Albert Vidalie *d* Roger Vadim *ph* Armand Thirard *m* Georges Auric

Brigitte Bardot, Alida Valli, Stephen Boyd, Pepe Nieto

Heaven Is Round the Corner
GB 1943 94m bw

A war veteran is helped to find his long-lost love. Sentimental tosh with music, a second team effort which went down well enough in wartime. Will Fyffe, Leni Lynn, Austin Trevor, Magda Kun, Peter Glenville. Written by Austin Melford; directed by Fred Zelnick; for British National.

Heaven Knows Mr Allison*
US 1957 105m Technicolor Cinemascope
TCF (Buddy Adler, Eugene Franks)

Marooned on a small Pacific island during World War II, a marine and a nun, antagonistic to each other, combine to outwit the Japs.
Silly adventure story with predictably well-handled action sequences separated by even more predictable dialogue, lots of it.

w John Lee Mahin, John Huston, *novel*
Charles Shaw *d* John Huston *ph* Oswald
Morris *m* Georges Auric

Robert Mitchum, Deborah Kerr

AAN: script; Deborah Kerr

Heaven on Earth: see The Exquisite
Sinner

Heaven Only Knows
US 1947 98m bw
(UA) Seymour Nebenzal

An angel is sent to the old west to reform a
bad man.
Whimsical comedy-drama which doesn't work
at all, even as a distant cousin of *Here Comes
Mr Jordan*.

w Art Arthur, Rowland Leigh *d* Albert S.
Rogell *ph* Karl Struss *m* Heinz Roemheld

Robert Cummings, Brian Donlevy, Marjorie
Reynolds, Bill Goodwin, John Litel, Stuart
Erwin

Heaven with a Barbed Wire Fence
US 1939 61m bw

A New York clerk hitch-hikes his way to
Arizona, where he has bought a piece of land.
Subdued flagwaver with everybody behaving
just swell in God's own country. Glenn Ford
(his first film), Jean Rogers, Richard Conte,
Marjorie Rambeau, Raymond Walburn,
Eddie Collins, Ward Bond. Written by Dalton
Trumbo, Leonard Hoffman and Ben Grauman
Kohn; directed by Ricardo Cortez; for TCF.

Heaven with a Gun
US 1969 101m Metrocolor Panavision

The determined new preacher of a small
western town is an ex-gunfighter. Solidly
carpentered half-a-bill western. Glenn Ford,
Carolyn Jones, David Carradine, J. D.
Cannon, Barbara Hershey, Noah Beery Jnr.
Written by Richard Carr; directed by Lee
Katzin; for King Brothers / MGM.

The Heavenly Body
US 1943 93m bw
MGM (Arthur Hornblow Jnr)

An astronomer is too busy to notice his wife,
so she takes up astrology and meets a dark
handsome stranger as predicted.
Thin romantic comedy which despite crazy
touches never actually makes one laugh.

w Michael Arlen, Walter Reisch *d* Alexander
Hall *ph* Robert Planck *m* Bronislau Kaper

William Powell, Hedy Lamarr, James Craig,
Fay Bainter, Henry O'Neill, Spring Byington,
Morris Ankrum, Connie Gilchrist

Heavens Above*
GB 1963 118m bw
British Lion / Charter (Roy Boulting)

A northern parson with proletarian sympathies
is accidentally appointed to a snobby village
where he converts the dowager aristocrat to
works of absurd charity. Eventually he has the
whole country in an uproar and takes the place
of an astronaut.
Patchy satirical comedy which takes unsteady
aim at too many targets but scores some
predictable laughs.

w Frank Harvey, John Boulting *d* John
Boulting *ph* Max Greene *m* Richard Rodney
Bennett

Peter Sellers, Isabel Jeans, Cecil Parker,
Brock Peters, Ian Carmichael, Irene Handl,
Eric Sykes, Bernard Miles

Heaven's Gate
US 1980 219m Technicolor
UA / Michael Cimino

1890 Wyoming: established cattlemen fight
immigrants.
Totally incoherent, showy western which was
lambasted by the critics and quickly
withdrawn. A vital turning point in Hollywood
policy, hopefully marking the last time a whiz
kid with one success behind him is given a
blank cheque to indulge in self-abuse.

wd Michael Cimino *ph* Vilmos Zsigmond
m David Mansfield

Kris Kristofferson, Christopher Walken, John
Hurt, Sam Waterston, Brad Dourif, Isabelle
Huppert, Joseph Cotten, Jeff Bridges
    'The trade must marvel that directors now
have such power that no one, in the endless
months since work on the picture began, was
able to impose some structure and sense.'—
Variety

Hedda*
GB 1975 102m Technicolor
Brut (Robert Enders)

A selfish pregnant woman is bored by her
husband and revolted at the idea of carrying
his child. She takes an opportunity to revenge
herself on an old lover, but the scheme
rebounds on herself.
Rather flat rendering of a play which has
received more than its due share of attention.

wd Trevor Nunn, *play* Henrik Ibsen
ph Douglas Slocombe *m* Laurie Johnson

Glenda Jackson, Peter Eyre, Timothy West,
Jennie Linden, Patrick Stewart

AAN: Glenda Jackson

Heidi*
US 1937 88m bw
TCF (Raymond Griffith)

An orphan is sent to stay with her crusty
grandfather in a mountain village.
Star-tailored version of a favourite children's
story; just what the box office ordered at the
time.

w Walter Ferris, Julian Josephson, *novel*
Johanna Spyri d Allan Dwan *ph* Arthur
Miller *md* Louis Silvers

Shirley Temple, Jean Hersholt, Arthur
Treacher, Helen Westley, Pauline Moore,
Mary Nash, Thomas Beck, Sidney Blackmer,
Mady Christians, Sig Rumann, Marcia Mae
Jones, Christian Rub

The Heiress**
US 1949 115m bw
Paramount (William Wyler)

A plain but rich young woman takes revenge
on her fortune-seeking lover.
Richly-decorated and generally pleasing
version of a stage success based on a Henry
James story set in the nineties.

w Ruth and Augustus Goetz, from their play
and Henry James's Washington Square
d William Wyler ph Leo Tover *m* Aaron
Copland *ad John Meehan*

Olivia de Havilland, Ralph Richardson,
Montgomery Clift, Miriam Hopkins, Vanessa
Brown, Mona Freeman, Ray Collins
   'Wyler is that rarest of craftsmen who can
take such a drama, already completely fulfilled
in theatre terms, and convert it to film without
ever permitting the play-form to dominate the
screen.'—*Hermione Isaacs, Films in Review*

AA: Aaron Copland; Olivia de Havilland
AAN: best picture; William Wyler; Leo
Tover; Ralph Richardson

The Helen Morgan Story
US 1957 118m bw Cinemascope
Warner (Martin Rackin)
GB title: *Both Ends of the Candle*

A young singer rises from vaudeville to
Broadway but becomes an alcoholic.
Moderately truthful biopic with effective
twenties trimmings.

w Oscar Saul, Dean Riesner, Stephen
Longstreet, Nelson Gidding *d* Michael Curtiz
ph Ted McCord *m* various *ad* John Beckman

Ann Blyth, Paul Newman, Richard Carlson,
Gene Evans, Alan King, Cara Williams,
Walter Woolf King (as Ziegfeld)

Helen of Troy
US / Italy 1955 118m Warnercolor
   Cinemascope
Warner (Robert Wise)

Helen is kidnapped by Paris and regained by
use of the Trojan Horse.
Dingy historical spectacular, stultifyingly
boring until the final spectacle, with the actors
obviously wishing themselves doing anything
but mouthing the doggerel dialogue.

w John Twist, Hugh Gray *d* Robert Wise
ph Harry Stradling *m* Max Steiner

Rosanna Podesta, Jacques Sernas, Cedric
Hardwicke, Niall MacGinnis, Stanley Baker,
Nora Swinburne, Robert Douglas, Torin
Thatcher, Harry Andrews, Janette Scott,
Ronald Lewis, Brigitte Bardot

Hell and High Water
US 1954 103m Technicolor
   Cinemascope
TCF (Raymond A. Klune)

A privately-financed anti-Red scientific
expedition sets off for Alaska to prevent a
Chinese anti-American plot.
Early scoper which mixes deviously plotted
schoolboy fiction with submarine spectacle and
cold war heroics.

wd Samuel Fuller *ph* Joe MacDonald
m Alfred Newman

Richard Widmark, Bella Darvi, Victor
Francen, David Wayne, Cameron Mitchell,
Gene Evans

Hell Below
US 1933 105m bw
MGM

Tensions mount at a Mediterranean submarine
base during World War I.
Adequate war actioner with appropriate
trimmings of heroism, tragedy, comedy and
romance.

w John Lee Mahin, John Meehan, Laird
Doyle, Raymond Schrock, *novel* Pigboats by
Commander Edward Ellsberg *d* Jack
Conway *ph* Harold Rosson

Robert Montgomery, Walter Huston, Madge
Evans, Jimmy Durante, Eugene Pallette,
Robert Young, Edwin Styles, John Lee
Mahin, Sterling Holloway

Hell below Zero
GB 1954 91m Technicolor
Columbia / Warwick (Irving Allen, Albert
   Broccoli)

An American adventurer accompanies the
daughter of a whaling captain to the Antarctic
to discover who killed her father.

Adequate outdoor thick ear with an unusual setting and lively cast.

w Alec Coppel, Max Trell, *novel* The White South by Hammond Innes *d* Mark Robson *ph* John Wilcox *m* Clifton Parker

Alan Ladd, Joan Tetzel, Basil Sydney, Stanley Baker, Jill Bennett, Niall MacGinnis

Hell Divers*
US 1931   113m   bw
MGM

Friendly rivalry exists between two officers in the Naval Air Force.
Routine romantic melodrama with action highlights; a crowdpuller of its day.

w Harvey Gates, Malcolm Stuart Boylan, *story* Spig Wead *d* George Hill *ph* Harold Wenstrom

Wallace Beery, Clark Gable, Conrad Nagel, Dorothy Jordan, Marjorie Rambeau, Marie Prévost, Cliff Edwards

'It's a matter of squadron after squadron of planes, the mechanics attached thereto, the cutting in and around newsreel material, which Metro does so well, and Beery's excellent personal performance.'—*Hollywood Reporter*

Hell Drivers*
GB 1957   108m   bw   Vistavision
Rank / Aqua (Ben Fisz)

Fast driving on death-trap roads is required of rival lorry drivers for a cheapjack haulage firm.
Absurd, violent, hilarious and constantly surprising melodrama with the silliest of premises backed by a good cast and well handled thrill sequences.

w John Kruse, C. Raker Endfield *d* C. Raker Endfield *ph* Geoffrey Unsworth *m* Hubert Clifford

Stanley Baker, Patrick McGoohan, Herbert Lom, Peggy Cummins, William Hartnell, Wilfrid Lawson, Sidney James, Jill Ireland, Alfie Bass, Gordon Jackson

'This extraordinary film may interest future historians for its description of road haulage and masculine social behaviour in the mid-20th century . . . though produced with efficiency and assurance it is disagreeable and occasionally vicious.'—*MFB*

Hell in the Pacific*
US 1969   104m   Technicolor
Panavision
Cinerama / Selmur (Reuben Bercovitch)

During World War II, an American pilot and a Japanese naval officer who are stranded on the same tiny Pacific island almost become friends.
Highly artificial and pretentious allegorical two-parter which is occasionally well acted and good to look at.

w Alexander Jacobs, Eric Bercovici *d* John Boorman *ph* Conrad Hall *m* Lalo Schifrin

Lee Marvin, Toshiro Mifune

'No real reverberation and no real excitement, intellectual or physical.'—*Tom Milne*

Hell Is a City*
GB 1959   93m   bw   Hammerscope
ABP / Hammer (Michael Carreras)

A jewel thief breaks jail and is hunted by the Manchester police.
Lively semi-documentary, cameo-filled cop thriller filmed on location.

wd Val Guest, *novel* Maurice Proctor *ph* Arthur Grant *m* Stanley Black

Stanley Baker, John Crawford, Donald Pleasence, Maxine Audley, Billie Whitelaw, Joseph Tomelty, George A. Cooper, Vanda Godsell

'A hectic pace, with frequent scene changes, mobility of camera and performers, and much rapid, loud, intense dialogue.'—*MFB*

Hell Is for Heroes*
US 1962   90m   bw
Paramount (Henry Blanke)

In 1944, embittered GIs fight and die while taking a German pillbox near the Siegfried line.
Fairly routine anti-war film with a strong cast and effectively-directed moments battling a generally artificial look.

w Robert Pirosh, Richard Carr *d* Don Siegel *ph* Harold Lipstein *m* Leonard Rosenman

Steve McQueen, Bobby Darin, Fess Parker, James Coburn, Bob Newhart, Harry Guardino

Hell Is Sold Out
GB 1951   84m   bw

A novelist returns from the supposed dead to find that a glamorous woman is posing as his widow and issuing best-sellers under his name. Downright peculiar comedy-drama which never jells for long enough to be enjoyable. ('Hell Is Sold Out' is the title of a book in the story.) Herbert Lom, Mai Zetterling, Richard Attenborough. Written by Guy Morgan and Moie Charles; directed by Michael Anderson; for Raymond Stross / Eros.

Hell on Frisco Bay
US 1955 98m Warnercolor
Cinemascope
Jaguar (George Berthelon)

An ex-cop sets out to find the man who
framed him for manslaughter.
Tedious actioner enlivened by the character
parts and a violent climax.

w Sidney Boehm, Martin Rackin, *novel*
William P. McGivern d Frank Tuttle
ph John Seitz m Max Steiner

Alan Ladd, Edward G. Robinson, Joanne
Dru, *Paul Stewart*, William Demarest, Fay
Wray

Hell to Eternity
US 1960 132m bw
Allied Artists / Atlantic (Irving H. Levin)

Marine Guy Gabaldon, brought up by
Japanese foster parents, has divided loyalties
after Pearl Harbor.
Battle-strewn biopic which after two hours
seems to lose its point, if it ever had one, but
is efficiently made.

w Ted Sherdeman, Walter Roeber Schmidt
d Phil Karlson ph Burnett Guffey m Leith
Stevens

Jeffrey Hunter, David Janssen, Vic Damone,
Patricia Owens, Richard Eyer, Sessue
Hayakawa

The Hell with Heroes
US 1968 102m Techniscope
Universal (Stanley Chase)

Air cargo experts find themselves unwittingly
smuggling cigarettes into France, and
American counter-intelligence steps in.
Unremarkable, totally predictable action
melodrama.

w Halsted Welles, Harold Livingston
d Joseph Sargent ph Bud Thackery
m Quincy Jones

Rod Taylor, Claudia Cardinale, Harry
Guardino, Kevin McCarthy, Pete Deuel,
William Marshall

Hellcats of the Navy
US 1957 82m bw

Exploits of a daring submarine commander in
the war against Japan. Flimsy jingoistic
potboiler. Ronald Reagan, Nancy Davis,
Arthur Franz, Robert Arthur. Written by
David Lang; directed by Nathan Juran; for
Charles H. Schneer / Columbia.

Heller in Pink Tights*
US 1960 100m Technicolor
Vistavision
Paramount / Ponti–Girosi

Adventures of a dramatic company touring the
west in the 1880s.
Genteel spoof western which does not quite
come off.

w Dudley Nichols, Walter Bernstein, *novel*
Louis L'Amour d George Cukor ph Harold
Lipstein m Daniele Amfitheatrof ad Hal
Pereira, Eugene Allen

Sophia Loren, Anthony Quinn, Steve Forrest,
Eileen Heckart, Edmund Lowe, Margaret
O'Brien, Ramon Novarro
'It has a welcome individuality which is
never quite smothered by its lapses into
convention.'—*Penelope Houston*

Hellfighters
US 1969 120m Technicolor
Panavision
Universal (Robert Arthur)

Oil well fire-fighting specialists have problems
among themselves and with their womenfolk.
Ham-fisted story line and performances are
slightly, but only slightly, compensated by
excellent special effects.

w Clair Huffaker d Andrew V. McLaglen
ph William H. Clothier m Leonard
Rosenman

John Wayne, Jim Hutton, Katharine Ross,
Vera Miles, Jay C. Flippen, Bruce Cabot,
Barbara Stuart
'The overall effect is unpardonably
tedious.'—*MFB*

The Hellfire Club*
GB 1960 93m Eastmancolor
Dyaliscope
Regal / New World (Robert S. Baker, Monty
Berman)

In the 18th century, a nobleman's child
escapes from his degenerate father, joins a
travelling circus, and later returns to claim his
inheritance.
Sprightly historical romantic melodrama
lightly based on the nefarious activities of the
real Hellfire Club; energetic and entertaining
if slightly too jokey.

w Leon Griffiths, Jimmy Sangster
d / ph Robert S. Baker, Monty Berman
m Clifton Parker

Keith Michell, Peter Arne, Adrienne Corri,
Kai Fischer, Bill Owen, Peter Cushing, David
Lodge, Francis Matthews

Hellgate
US 1952 87m bw

In the 1860s a veterinary surgeon is wrongly convicted and sent to a savage prison.
Competent exploitation melodrama, not apparently based on truth. Sterling Hayden, Ward Bond, Joan Leslie, Jim Arness, Peter Coe. Written and directed by Charles Marquis Warren; for Commander Films / Lippert.

The Hellions
GB 1961 80m Technirama
Columbia / Irving Allen, Jamie Uys (Harold Huth)

In the 1860s, a family of South African outlaws starts a reign of terror in a small village.
A British attempt to restage the OK Corral; it goes sadly awry.
w Harold Swanton, Patrick Kirwan, Harold Huth d Ken Annakin ph Ted Moore m Larry Adler

Richard Todd, Lionel Jeffries, James Booth, Jamie Uys, Ronald Fraser, Anne Aubrey, Zena Walker, Marty Wilde, Colin Blakely
'Unconvincingly staged and plotted, tediously violent, uncertainly directed and very badly acted.'—MFB

Hello Dolly**
US 1969 129m De Luxe Todd-AO
TCF / Chenault (Ernest Lehman)

In 1890 New York, a widowed matchmaker has designs on a wealthy grain merchant.
Generally agreeable but overblown musical based on a slight but much worked-over farce, fatally compromised by the miscasting of a too-young star. Some exhilarating moments.
w Ernest Lehman, musical Jerry Herman (m / ly) and Michael Stewart (book), from Thornton Wilder's play The Matchmaker d Gene Kelly ph Harry Stradling md Lennie Hayton, Lionel Newman pd John de Cuir ch Michael Kidd

Barbra Streisand, Walter Matthau, Michael Crawford, Marianne McAndrew, E. J. Peaker, Tommy Tune, David Hurst
'The film leaves an oddly negative impression; a good deal of synthetic effervescence . . . but very little real vitality.'—David Wilson
AA: music direction; art direction; set decoration
AAN: best picture; photography

Hello Down There
US 1969 98m Eastmancolor

The designer of an underwater house volunteers to live in it for a month. Curious comedy with predictable obstacles to the happy ending. Tony Randall, Janet Leigh, Jim Backus, Roddy McDowall, Merv Griffin, Ken Berry, Richard Dreyfuss. Written by Frank Telford and John McGreevey; directed by Jack Arnold; for Ivan Tors / MGM.

Hello Frisco Hello*
US 1943 98m Technicolor
TCF (Milton Sperling)

On the Barbary Coast, a girl singer becomes a star.
Moderately pleasing period musical with plenty going on but nothing very striking.
w Robert Ellis, Helen Logan, Richard Macauley d Bruce Humberstone ph Charles Clarke, Allen Davey songs various ad James Basevi, Boris Leven

Alice Faye, John Payne, Jack Oakie, Lynn Bari, Laird Cregar, June Havoc, Ward Bond, Aubrey Mather, George Barbier, Frank Orth
AA: song 'You'll Never Know' (m Harry Warren, ly Mack Gordon)
AAN: Charles Clarke, Allen Davey

Hello Goodbye
US 1970 101m De Luxe
TCF (André Hakim)

A cheerful young Englishman falls for a mysterious Frenchwoman who turns out to be the wife of a Baron.
Modest, aimless, forgettable romantic comedy, full of old-fashioned clichés imperfectly remembered.
w Roger Marshall d Jean Negulesco ph Henri Decaë m Francis Lai pd John Howell ad Auguste Capelier

Michael Crawford, Geneviève Gilles, Curt Jurgens, Ira Furstenberg

Hello Sister*
US 1933 62m bw
Fox (Winfield Sheehan)
aka: Walking down Broadway

Boy meets girl in New York.
A mild little romance, only notable because it was edited down from an original by Erich Von Stroheim, and touches of his work remain.
w Erich Von Stroheim, Leonard Spiegelgass, novel Dawn Powell d Erich Von Stroheim, Alfred Werker ph James Wong Howe

James Dunn, Boots Mallory, Zasu Pitts, Minna Gombell

Hell's Angels****
US 1930   135m   bw (some scenes in colour)
Howard Hughes

Two Americans become fliers in World War I. Celebrated early talkie spectacular, with zeppelin and flying sequences that still thrill. The dialogue is another matter, but all told this expensive production, first planned as a silent, is a milestone of cinema history.

w Howard Estabrook, Harry Behn d Howard Hughes ph Tony Gaudio, Harry Perry, E. Burton Steene m Hugo Reisenfeld

Ben Lyon, James Hall, Jean Harlow, John Darrow, Lucien Prival

'It is not great, but it is as lavish as an eight-ring circus, and when you leave the theatre you will know you have seen a movie and not a tinny reproduction of a stage show.'—Pare Lorentz

AAN: Tony Gaudio, Harry Perry, E. Burton Steene

Hell's Five Hours
US 1958   75m   bw

A psychopath takes hostages and threatens to blow up a rocket fuel plant. Standard suspense programmer, tolerable but entirely forgettable. Stephen McNally, Vic Morrow, Coleen Gray. Written and directed by Jack L. Copeland; for Allied Artists.

Hell's Half Acre
US 1953   91m   bw

A soldier missing after Pearl Harbor turns up years later in Hawaii under a different identity. Complex melodrama ending in self-sacrifice; amusing bits don't make it hang together. Wendell Corey, Evelyn Keyes, Elsa Lanchester, Nancy Gates, Philip Ahn, Keye Luke. Written by Steve Fisher; directed by John H. Auer; for Republic.

Hell's Heroes
US 1930   65m   bw
Universal

Three cowboys find an abandoned baby. Yet another version of Three Godfathers; maybe not the best but the shortest.

w Tom Reed, novel Peter Kyne d William Wyler ph George Robinson

Charles Bickford, Raymond Hatton, Fred Kohler, Fritzi Ridgeway

Hell's House
US 1932   72m   bw

A boy is wrongly sentenced to a corrupt reform school. Primitive cheapie notable only for the early appearance of Bette Davis; with Pat O'Brien, Junior Durkin, Junior Coghlan, Emma Dunn, Charley Grapewin. Written by Paul Gangelin and B. Harrison Orkow; directed by Howard Higgins; for Capital Films.

Hell's Island*
US 1955   84m   Technicolor Vistavision
Paramount / Pine–Thomas

Crooks congregate on a Caribbean island in search of a famous ruby. Cheeky rehash of The Maltese Falcon, not bad in its own routine way.

w Maxwell Shane d Phil Karlson ph Lionel Lindon md Irvin Talbot

John Payne, Mary Murphy, Francis L. Sullivan, Arnold Moss

The Hellstrom Chronicle
US 1971   90m   CFI colour

A scientist explains the range and variety of insect life. Odd documentary in fictional bookends; smart and quite sensational for those with strong stomachs. Laurence Pressman as Nils Hellstrom. Written by David Seltzer; directed by Walon Green; for David Wolper.

Hellzapoppin***
US 1942   84m   bw
Universal / Mayfair (Glenn Tryon, Alex Gottlieb)

Two incompetent comics make a picture. Zany modification of a smash burlesque revue; the crazy jokes are toned down and a romantic interest is added (and tentatively sent up). The result is patchy but often hilarious, and the whole is a handy consensus of forties humour and pop music.

w Nat Perrin, Warren Wilson d H. C. Potter ph Woody Bredell md Charles Previn

Ole Olsen, Chic Johnson, Hugh Herbert, Martha Raye, Mischa Auer, Robert Paige, Jane Frazee, Shemp Howard, Elisha Cook Jnr, Richard Lane

Help!*
GB 1965   92m   Eastmancolor
UA / Walter Shenson / Suba Films

An oriental high priest chases the Beatles around the world because one of them has a sacred ring. Exhausting attempt to outdo A Hard Day's Night in lunatic frenzy, which goes to prove that some talents work better on low budgets. The humour is a frantic cross between Hellzapoppin, the Goons, Bugs Bunny and the shade of Monty Python to come. It looks good but becomes too tiresome to entertain.

w Charles Wood, Marc Behm *d* Dick Lester *ph David Watkin m The Beatles ad Ray Simm*

The Beatles, Leo McKern, Eleanor Bron, Victor Spinetti

Helpmates***
US 1932 20m bw

Stan helps Ollie clean up after a wild party while the wife was away. A brilliant succession of catastrophe gags in the stars' best tradition. Laurel and Hardy. Written by H. M. Walker; directed by James Parrott; for Hal Roach.

Helter Skelter
GB 1949 75m bw
GFD / Gainsborough

An heiress with hiccups is helped by the staff of the BBC.
Scatty comedy which tries everything, from custard pies and guest stars to a clip from a silent Walter Forde comedy. It isn't the British *Hellzapoppin* it sets out to be, but hardened buffs will find it worth a look.

w Patrick Campbell *d* Ralph Thomas *ph* Jack Asher *m* Francis Chagrin

Carol Marsh, David Tomlinson, Mervyn Johns, Peter Hammond, Jimmy Edwards, Richard Hearne, Jon Pertwee, Terry-Thomas

Hemingway's Adventures of a Young Man*
US 1962 145m De Luxe Cinemascope
TCF (Jerry Wald)
aka: *Adventures of a Young Man*

The son of a weak doctor and a religious mother breaks away from his family circle on a voyage of discovery.
Curious mélange of ill-assimilated Hemingway stories based on his Nick Adams character. The film has good intentions but no shape or style, and the guest stars don't help.

w A. E. Hotchner, *stories* Ernest Hemingway *d* Martin Ritt *ph* Lee Garmes *m* Franz Waxman

Richard Beymer, Diane Baker, Corinne Calvet, Fred Clark, Dan Dailey, James Dunn, Juano Hernandez, Arthur Kennedy, Ricardo Montalban, Susan Strasberg, Paul Newman, Jessica Tandy, Eli Wallach

Hennessy
GB 1975 104m colour
AIP / Marseilles (Peter Snell)

Angered at the death of his family in the Belfast troubles, an Irish revolutionary hurries to London to blow up the Houses of Parliament.
Unattractive, uninventive thriller with a silly script and not an ounce of real suspense.

w John Gay, *story* Richard Johnson *d* Don Sharp *ph* Ernest Steward *m* John Scott *pd* Ray Simm

Rod Steiger, Richard Johnson, Lee Remick, Trevor Howard, Eric Porter, Peter Egan, David Collings

Henry Aldrich
Henry was originally a radio character created by Ezra Stone, an awkward small-town youth who like Andy Hardy was always getting into scrapes. Clifford Goldsmith wrote the original play which hit Broadway as well as the radio waves before starting a Hollywood series of amiable Paramount second features, most of them starring Jimmy Lydon with Charles Smith as his friend Dizzy.

1939: WHAT A LIFE (with Jackie Cooper)
1941: LIFE WITH HENRY (with Jackie Cooper), HENRY ALDRICH FOR PRESIDENT
1942: HENRY AND DIZZY, HENRY ALDRICH EDITOR
1943: HENRY ALDRICH GETS GLAMOUR, HENRY ALDRICH SWINGS IT, HENRY ALDRICH HAUNTS A HOUSE
1944: HENRY ALDRICH BOY SCOUT, HENRY ALDRICH PLAYS CUPID, HENRY ALDRICH'S LITTLE SECRET

Henry V****
GB 1944 137m Technicolor
Rank / Two Cities (Laurence Olivier)

Shakespeare's historical play is seen in performance at the Globe Theatre in 1603; as it develops, the scenery becomes more realistic.
Immensely stirring, experimental and almost wholly successful production of Shakespeare on film, sturdy both in its stylization and its command of more conventional cinematic resources for the battle.

w Laurence Olivier, Alan Dent, *play* William Shakespeare *d Laurence Olivier ph Robert Krasker m William Walton ad Paul Sheriff*

Laurence Olivier, *Robert Newton, Leslie Banks, Esmond Knight*, Renée Asherson, George Robey, *Leo Genn*, Ernest Thesiger, Ivy St Helier, Ralph Truman, Harcourt Williams, Max Adrian, Valentine Dyall, Felix Aylmer, John Laurie, Roy Emerton

AAN: best picture; William Walton; Laurence Olivier (as actor)

Henry VIII and His Six Wives*
GB 1972   125m   Technicolor
EMI (Roy Baird)

Dullish historical account of the king's reign,
staged as recollections from his deathbed but
lacking any of the sparkle of *The Private Life
of Henry VIII* made forty years previously.
Accurate sets and costumes fail to compensate
for lack of film flair.

w Ian Thorne *d* Waris Hussein *ph* Peter
Suschitsky *m* David Munro

Keith Michell, Frances Cuka (Aragon),
Charlotte Rampling (Boleyn), Jane Asher
(Seymour), Jenny Bos (Cleves), Lynne
Frederick (Howard), Barbara Leigh-Hunt
(Parr), Donald Pleasence (Thomas Cromwell)
† The production was stimulated by a highly
successful BBC TV series, *The Six Wives of
Henry VIII*

Her Cardboard Lover*
US 1942   93m   bw
MGM (J. Walter Ruben)

A flirtatious lady hires a lover to make her
fiancé jealous.
Paper-thin comedy previously filmed in silent
days as *The Passionate Plumber* (with Buster
Keaton). It did nobody any good, but
preserves some style despite a witless script.

w Jacques Deval, John Collier, Anthony
Veiller, William H. Wright, *play* Jacques
Deval *d* George Cukor *ph* Harry Stradling,
Robert Planck *m* Franz Waxman

Norma Shearer, Robert Taylor, George
Sanders, Frank McHugh, Elizabeth Patterson,
Chill Wills

Her Favourite Husband
GB 1950   79m   bw

A wife finds that her husband has been
replaced by a gangster who aims to rob a
bank. Rather tiresome Italian-set comedy with
funny moments. Jean Kent, Robert Beatty,
Gordon Harker, Margaret Rutherford, Rona
Anderson, Max Adrian. Written by Noel
Langley and W. F. Templeton, from a play by
Pepine de Felipe; directed by Mario Soldati;
for Orlux / Renown.

Her Highness and the Bellboy
US 1945   112m   bw
MGM (Joe Pasternak)

A hotel bellboy forsakes his crippled
sweetheart to woo a visiting princess.
Glutinous sentimental mishmash; one waits for
musical numbers which never happen.

w Richard Connell, Gladys Lehmann
d Richard Thorpe *ph* Harry Stradling
m Georgie Stoll

Hedy Lamarr, Robert Walker, June Allyson,
Rags Ragland, Agnes Moorehead, Carl
Esmond, Warner Anderson, Ludwig Stossel

Her Husband's Affairs*
US 1947   83m   bw
Columbia (Raphael Hakim)

A husband and wife team of advertising agents
promote a depilatory which turns out to grow
hair instead.
Mildly amiable crazy comedy.

w Ben Hecht *d* S. Sylvan Simon *ph* Charles
Lawton Jnr *m* George Duning

Lucille Ball, Franchot Tone, Edward Everett
Horton, Mikhail Rasumny, Gene Lockhart,
Nana Bryant, Jonathan Hale, Mabel Paige

Her Jungle Love*
US 1938   81m   Technicolor
Paramount (George M. Arthur)

An aviator crashlands in the jungle, where he
is comforted by a lovely lady, a chimp and a
lion but distressed by an earthquake, a
volcano and assorted villains.
Second of Dorothy Lamour's jungle hokum
shows, and the first in colour; despite its fair
technical proficiency, the fact that it once
packed 'em in is tribute to the changing tastes
of mankind.

w Joseph M. March, Lillie Hayward, Eddie
Welch *d* George Archainbaud *ph* Ray
Rennahan *m* Gregory Stone

Dorothy Lamour, Ray Milland, Lynne
Overman, J. Carrol Naish, Dorothy Howe

Her Kind of Man
US 1946   78m   bw

A singer finds a gangster irresistible but
eventually settles for a newspaper columnist.
Shiny, nondescript forties copy of a thirties
style; more yawns than thrills. Dane Clark,
Zachary Scott, Janis Paige, Faye Emerson,
George Tobias, Sheldon Leonard. Written by
Gordon Kahn and Leopold Atlas; directed by
Frederick de Cordova; for Warner.

Her Majesty Love
US 1931   76m   bw

A well-born Berliner finds it easier to court
the barmaid he loves after she has married a
baron. Heavy-handed musical comedy worth
excavating for the odd talents involved.
Marilyn Miller, Ben Lyon, W. C. Fields, Leon

Errol, Chester Conklin, Ford Sterling. Written
by Robert Lord and Arthur Caesar; directed
by William Dieterle; for Warner.

Her Twelve Men
US 1954 91m Anscocolor
MGM (John Houseman)

A woman teacher in a boys' school reforms a
difficult class.
Predictable, sugary and artificial school story
with the star exuding sweetness and light.

w William Roberts, Laura Z. Hobson
d Robert Z. Leonard ph Joseph Ruttenberg
m Bronislau Kaper

Greer Garson, Robert Ryan, Richard Haydn,
Barry Sullivan

Herbie Goes Bananas
US 1980 100m Technicolor

Two Americans take their magical
Volkswagen on a South American holiday.
Listless addition to a series which has already
gone on too long. Charles Martin Smith,
Stephan W. Burns, Cloris Leachman, John
Vernon. Don Tait; directed by Vincent
McEveety; for Walt Disney.

Herbie Goes to Monte Carlo
US 1977 105m Technicolor
Walt Disney (Ron Miller)

The Volkswagen with a mind of its own enters
the Monte Carlo rally and routs a gang of
thieves.
Utterly predictable, patchily made family
comedy.

w Arthur Alsberg, Don Nelson d Vincent
McEveety ph Leonard J. South m Frank de
Vol

Dean Jones, Don Knotts, Julie Sommars,
Jacques Marin, Roy Kinnear, Bernard Fox
† Second sequel to The Love Bug.

Hercules
Italy 1957 105m Eastmancolor
    Dyaliscope
Oscar / Galatea
original title: Le Fatiche di Ercole

Hercules helps Jason find the golden fleece.
The strong man epic which started a genre; of
little interest in itself.

w Pietro Francisci, Ennio de Concini, Gaio
Frattini d Pietro Francisci ph Mario Bava
m Enzo Masetti

Steve Reeves, Sylva Koscina, Gianna Maria
Canale, Fabrizio Mione

Hercules Unchained
Italy / France 1959 105m
    Eastmancolor Dyaliscope
Lux / Galatea
original title: Ercole e la Regina di Lidia

Hercules has problems with the king of Thebes
and the queen of Lidia.
More comic-strip versions of old legends. This
item had more spent on it in publicity than in
production cost, and consequently was seen by
vast audiences around the world. It isn't very
good.

w Pietro Francisci, Ennio di Concini d Pietro
Francisci ph Mario Bava m Enzo Masetti

Steve Reeves, Sylva Koscina, Sylvia Lopez,
Primo Carnera
† Many sequels followed, the hero sometimes
being known as Ursus or Goliath.

Here Come the Coeds
US 1945 88m bw
Universal (John Grant)

Janitors help to forestall a mortgage
foreclosure on a college for women.
Routine star vehicle with few highlights.

w Arthur T. Horman, John Grant d Jean
Yarbrough ph George Robinson songs Jack
Brooks, Edgar Fairchild

Bud Abbott, Lou Costello, Lon Chaney Jnr,
Peggy Ryan, Martha O'Driscoll, Donald
Cook, June Vincent, Charles Dingle

Here Come the Girls°
US 1953 78m Technicolor
Paramount (Paul Jones)

In the nineties an ageing chorus boy traps a
mysterious murderer.
Spotty, ineptly titled star comedy with music;
in fact among the last of his passable vehicles,
with excellent production backing.

w Edmund Hartmann, Hal Kanter d Claude
Binyon ph Lionel Lindon md Lyn Murray
ad Hal Pereira, Roland Anderson

Bob Hope, Rosemary Clooney, Tony Martin,
Arlene Dahl, Millard Mitchell, Fred Clark,
William Demarest, Robert Strauss

Here Come the Huggetts°
GB 1948 93m bw
Rank / Gainsborough (Betty Box)

A suburban family has its ups and downs.
Cosy domestic comedy drama, a presage of
TV soap operas to come, or Britain's answer
to the Hardys, depending how you look at it.
Tolerable at the time.

w Mabel and Denis Constanduros, Muriel and Sydney Box, Peter Rogers *d* Ken Annakin *ph* Reg Wyer

Jack Warner, Kathleen Harrison, Jane Hylton, Susan Shaw, Petula Clark, Jimmy Hanley, David Tomlinson, Diana Dors, Peter Hammond, John Blythe

† The Huggetts had actually originated in *Holiday Camp* the previous year, and appeared again in *Vote for Huggett* and *The Huggetts Abroad*; Warner and Harrison became an inseparable duo for many years.

Here Come the Waves
US 1944 98m bw
Paramount (Mark Sandrich)

A sailor falls in love with identical twin Waves.
Empty-headed, professionally executed musical recruiting poster.

w Allen Scott, Ken Englund, Zion Myers *d* Mark Sandrich *ph* Charles Lang *md* Robert Emmett Dolan *songs* Harold Arlen, Johnny Mercer

Bing Crosby, Betty Hutton, Sonny Tufts, Ann Doran, Gwen Crawford
'An almost totally negligible musical.'— *James Agee*

AAN: song 'Accentuate the Positive' (*m* Harold Arlen, *ly* Johnny Mercer)

Here Comes Mr Jordan•••
US 1941 93m bw
Columbia (Everett Riskin)

A prizefighter who is also an amateur saxophonist crashes in his private plane and goes to heaven by mistake: he was supposed to survive and live another forty years.
Unfortunately when he goes back for his body it has been cremated, so he has to find another one, recently deceased . . .
Weird heavenly fantasy which succeeded because of its novelty and because heaven in wartime was a comforting vision. As a movie taken on its own merits, it suffers from illogicalities, a miscast star and a wandering plot, but scene for scene there is enough firmness and control to make it memorable. It certainly had many imitations, including *Angel on My Shoulder*, *Down to Earth*, *A Guy Named Joe*, *Heaven Only Knows*, *The Horn Blows at Midnight* and *That's the Spirit*.

w Seton I. Miller, Sidney Buchman, *play* Halfway to Heaven by Harry Segall *d* Alexander Hall *ph* Joseph Walker *m* Frederick Hollander *md* Morris Stoloff

Robert Montgomery, Evelyn Keyes, Rita

Johnson, *Claude Rains, James Gleason, Edward Everett Horton*, John Emery, *Donald MacBride*, Halliwell Hobbes, Don Costello
'There is something about this original so sweet-spirited and earnest that it transcends its plot devices and shines through its comedic asides to beome a true morality play without once becoming either preachy or mawkish.'— *Kit Parker catalogue, 1980*

† Remade 1978 as *Heaven Can Wait*.

AA: original story (Harry Segall); script
AAN: best picture; Seton I. Miller, Sidney Buchman; Alexander Hall; Joseph Walker; Robert Montgomery; James Gleason

Here Comes the Groom•
US 1951 114m bw
Paramount (Frank Capra)

A journalist adopts war orphans and reforms his selfish fiancée.
Tired attempt by Capra to recapture his pre-war mood; despite intermittent pleasures it has neither the right style nor the topical substance.

w Virginia Van Upp, Myles Connelly, Liam O'Brien, *story* Robert Riskin *d* Frank Capra *ph* George Barnes *md* Joseph Lilley *songs* Jay Livingston, Ray Evans

Bing Crosby, Jane Wyman, Franchot Tone, Alexis Smith, James Barton, Connie Gilchrist, Robert Keith, Anna Maria Alberghetti
'The general impression is of a loud, strident, rather vulgar comedy in which technique is used to disappointingly mechanical ends, and which a few bright lines of dialogue cannot rescue from tedium.'— *Penelope Houston*

AA: song 'In the Cool Cool Cool of the Evening' (*m* Hoagy Carmichael, *ly* Johnny Mercer)
AAN: Robert Riskin

Here Comes the Navy•
US 1934 86m bw
Warner

An aggressive young naval rating fights with his former friend, now Petty Officer.
Breezy comedy melodrama teaming Cagney and O'Brien for the first time and offering star heroics as a sop to the Legion of Decency.

w Ben Markson, Earl Baldwin *d* Lloyd Bacon *ph* Arthur Edeson *m* Leo F. Forbstein

James Cagney, Pat O'Brien, Dorothy Tree, Gloria Stuart, Frank McHugh, Robert Barrat
'Rapid and reasonably authentic, a satisfactory addition to a series of cinema

cartoons which, because their colour and mood are indigenous and timely, may be more interesting twenty years from now.'—*Time*

AAN: best picture

Here I Am a Stranger
US 1939   82m   bw

A young man meets the ex-alcoholic father he has never seen. Competent formula drama.
Richard Greene, Richard Dix, Gladys George, Brenda Joyce, Roland Young.
Written by Milton Sperling and Sam Hellman; directed by Roy Del Ruth; for TCF.

Here We Go round the Mulberry Bush*
GB 1967   96m   Technicolor
UA / Giant (Larry Kramer, Clive Donner)

A school-leaver is obsessed by sex and determines to lose his virginity.
Repetitive comedy which certainly opened new avenues in British humour and seemed pretty permissive at the time (pre-*Graduate*). In itself, however, more modish than sympathetic.

w Hunter Davies (with Larry Kramer), from his novel d Clive Donner ph Alex Thomson m various groups

Barry Evans, Judy Geeson, Angela Scoular, Adrienne Posta, Sheila White, Vanessa Howard, Denholm Elliott, Maxine Audley, Moyra Fraser, Michael Bates
'The only incongruity is that it should have been made by adults, so completely does it enter into the teenager's view of himself.'—*MFB*

A Hero Ain't Nothing but a Sandwich
US 1977   107m   CFI color
New World / Radnitz-Mattel (Robert B. Radnitz)

Problems for an urban family in the black ghetto.
Well-intentioned but ultimately wearisome and cliché-strewn melodrama.

w Alice Childress, from her novel d Ralph Nelson ph Frank Stanley m Tom McIntosh

Cicely Tyson, Paul Winfield, Larry B. Scott, Helen Martin, Glynn Turman
'The sort of dreaded wholesome film that cultural and societal groups heavily endorse but nobody pays money to go see.'—*Variety*

Hero at Large
US 1980   98m   Metrocolor

An actor playing Captain Avenger accidentally becomes a real-life hero, but his fans turn against him when they find he's just an ordinary guy. Muddled satirical comedy-melodrama with too many pauses for love interest. John Ritter, Anne Archer, Bert Convy, Kevin McCarthy, Harry Bellaver. Written by A. J. Carothers; directed by Martin Davidson; for Stephen Freedman / MGM.

Heroes
US 1977   113m   Technicolor
Universal (David Foster, Lawrence Turman)

A Vietnam veteran, made slightly kooky by his experiences, settles down after several adventures when he falls in love.
Just plain awful: a would-be star vehicle that doesn't work.

w James Carabatsos (and, uncredited, David Freeman) d Jeremy Paul Kagan ph Frank Stanley m Jack Nitzche, Richard Hazard

Henry Winkler, Sally Field, Harrison Ford, Val Avery

The Heroes Are Tired
France 1955   101m   bw
Cila-Terra
original title: *Les Héros Sont Fatigués*

Two ex-wartime pilots, one Free French and the other German, set up an air charter service in Liberia but come to grief over stolen diamonds.
Gloomy post-war *film noir* set in a peculiarly depressing atmosphere, and not really sharp enough to overcome its squalid plot.

w Yves Ciampi, Jacques-Laurent Bost, *novel* Christine Garnier d Yves Ciampi ph Henri Alekan m Louiguy

Yves Montand, Maria Félix, Jean Servais, Curt Jurgens, Gérard Oury

Heroes for Sale
US 1933   73m   bw

A war veteran becomes in turn a drug addict, a millionaire and the central figure in a labour dispute. Minor social-conscience melodrama with watchable elements. Richard Barthelmess, Aline MacMahon, Loretta Young, Berton Churchill, Robert Barrat. Written by Robert Lord and Wilson Mizner; directed by William A. Wellman; for Warner.

The Heroes of Telemark*
GB 1965   131m   Technicolor
    Panavision
Rank / Benton (Ben Fisz)

Norwegian resistance workers in World War II help the Allies to smash a heavy water plant. Ambling narrative with big action sequences which often seem irrelevant, so that the story as a whole fails to excite.

w Ivan Moffat, Ben Barzman *d* Anthony Mann *ph Robert Krasker m* Malcolm Arnold

Kirk Douglas, Richard Harris, Ulla Jacobsson, Roy Dotrice, Anton Diffring, Michael Redgrave

Hero's Island*
US 1962 94m Technicolor Panavision
UA / Daystar / Portland (James Mason, Leslie Stevens)

In 1718 bondslaves settle on a Carolina island, are attacked by fishermen and protected by Blackbeard the Pirate.
An oddly personal, patchy, rather mysterious film with a rhetorical script and rather good action sequences.

wd Leslie Stevens *ph* Ted McCord *m* Dominic Frontière

James Mason, Kate Manx, Neville Brand, Rip Torn

Herr Puntila and his Servant Matti*
Austria 1955 95m Agfacolor
Bauerfilm

A rich landowner, usually drunk, is rescued from scrapes by his patient valet.
A cogent comedy which its author is said to have approved in this version.

w Alberto Cavalcanti, Vladimir Pozner, Ruth Wieden, *play* Bertolt Brecht *d* Alberto Cavalcanti *ph* André Bac, Arthur Hämmerer *m* Hanns Eisler

Curt Bois, Hans Engelmann, Maria Emo, Edith Prager

Hers to Hold
US 1943 94m bw
Universal (Felix Jackson)

A girl decides whether or not to marry a serviceman.
Limp star vehicle, a sequel to *Three Smart Girls* (qv).

w Lewis R. Foster *d* Frank Ryan *ph* Elwood Bredell *md* Charles Previn *m* Frank Skinner

Deanna Durbin, Joseph Cotten, Charles Winninger, Nella Walker, Gus Schilling, Ludwig Stossel

AAN: song 'Say a Prayer for the Boys Over There' (*m* Jimmy McHugh, *ly* Herb Magidson)

He's a Cockeyed Wonder
US 1950 77m bw

An orange sorter goes into the magic business.
Energetic low-budget comedy vehicle for unsophisticated audiences. Mickey Rooney, Terry Moore, William Demarest, Charles Arnt, Mike Mazurki. Written by Jack Henley; directed by Peter Godfrey; for Columbia.

Hester Street*
US 1974 89m bw
Midwest Films (Raphael D. Silver)

How Jewish immigrants settled in East Side New York in the nineties.
Modest, humorous, but not always smooth or dramatically emphatic chronicle of a familiar background; the detail however is excellent.

wd Joan Macklin Silver, *story* Yeki by Abraham Cahan *ph* Kenneth Van Sickle *m* William Bolcom

Steven Keats, Carol Kane, Mel Howard, Dorrie Kavanaugh, Doris Roberts

'A small, beautifully detailed, slightly shaggy independent film of charm and substance.'—*Judith Crist*
'For old diehards who still go to the cinema seeking humanity, tenderness and insight.'—*Michael Billington, Illustrated London News*

AAN: Joan Macklin Silver (as writer); Carol Kane

Hey! Hey! USA
GB 1938 92m bw

An education expert sails to America, falls in with gangsters, and saves a boy from being kidnapped by them. Misconceived star vehicle which provides some laughs, but not of the expected kind. Will Hay, Edgar Kennedy, David Burns, Fred Duprez. Written by J. O. C. Orton; directed by Marcel Varnel; for Gainsborough.

Hi Diddle Diddle*
US 1943 72m bw
UA / Andrew Stone
aka: *Try and Find It*

Young lovers are hampered by con artist parents.
Scatty comedy with amusing patches and some zest in the telling.

w Edmund L. Hartmann *d* Andrew L. Stone *ph* Charles Van Enger *m* Phil Boutelje

Adolphe Menjou, Pola Negri, Dennis O'Keefe, Billie Burke, Martha Scott, June Havoc

AAN: Phil Boutelje

Hi Gang
GB 1941 100m bw
Rank / Gainsborough (Edward Black)

American expatriates in London get involved in a case of mistaken identity.

Icky farce based faintly on a wartime radio variety series, notable only for preserving the three stars involved.

w Val Guest, Marriott Edgar, J. O. C. Orton, Howard Irving Young *d* Marcel Varnel *ph* Jack Cox

Bebe Daniels, Ben Lyon, Vic Oliver, Graham Moffatt, Moore Marriott, Felix Aylmer, Sam Browne

Hi, Mom!*
US 1969   86m   Movielab

Adventures of a young porno film maker and of the eccentrics who live in the same building. Busy comedy of the drop-out life, full of random satirical jabs and *hommages* to other film makers. Robert de Niro, Allen Garfield, Gerrit Graham, Jennifer Salt. Written and directed by *Brian de Palma;* for West End films.

Hi Nellie*
US 1934   79m   bw
Warner (Robert Presnell)

An ex-editor is demoted to advice to the lovelorn and gets involved in city rackets. Minor, effective star comedy-melodrama.

w Abem Finkel, Sidney Sutherland *d* Mervyn Le Roy *ph* Sol Polito

Paul Muni, Glenda Farrell, Ned Sparks, Robert Barrat, Hobart Cavanaugh, Berton Churchill, Donald Meek, Douglass Dumbrille, Edward Ellis

† Remade in 1935 as *Front Page Woman*; 1937 as *Love Is on the Air*; 1942 as *You Can't Escape Forever*; 1949 as *The House across the Street*.

Hickey and Boggs
US 1972   111m   De Luxe
UA / Film Guarantors Ltd (Fouad Said)

Two down and out private eyes, hired to find a girl, keep falling over dead bodies. Extraordinarily confused thriller with moments of humour and well staged action sequences.

w Walter Hill *d* Robert Culp *ph* Wilmer Butler *m* Ted Ashford

Robert Culp, Bill Cosby, Rosalind Cash

The Hidden Eye
US 1945   69m   bw

A blind detective gets on the trail of a murderer who deliberately leaves confusing clues. Thin successor to *Eyes in the Night*: no style at all. Edward Arnold, Frances Rafferty, William Phillips, Ray Collins, Thomas

Jackson. Written by George Harmon Coxe and Harry Ruskin; directed by Richard Whorf; for MGM.

Hidden Fear
US 1957   83m   bw

An American cop in Copenhagen clears his sister of a murder charge. Patchy, tough thriller with some pretensions to style sabotaged by a muddled script. John Payne, Anne Neyland, Alexander Knox, Conrad Nagel, Elsy Albiin. Written by André de Toth and John Ward Hawkins; directed by André de Toth; for St Aubrey-Kohn / UA.

The Hidden Fortress*
Japan 1958   123m   bw   Tohoscope
Toho (Masumi Fujimoto)
original title: *Kakushi Toride No San-Akunin*

In medieval Japan, the heiress of a feudal lord is saved from a bandit by a samurai. Roistering eastern western.

w Ryuzo Kikushima, Hideo Oguni, Shinobu Hashimoto, Akira Kurosawa *d* Akira Kurosawa *ph* Ichio Yamazaki *m* Masaru Sato

Toshiro Mifune, Misa Uehara, Minoru Chiaki

The Hidden Hand
US 1942   67m   bw

Murders proliferate in the house of a wealthy old spinster. Heavy-going spoof of the thunderstorm mystery; sometimes amusing for connoisseurs of the genre. Craig Stevens, Elizabeth Fraser, Julie Bishop, Willie Best, Milton Parsons. Written by Anthony Coldeway; directed by Ben Stoloff; for Warner.

Hide in Plain Sight
US 1980   92m   Metrocolor
MGM (Robert Christiansen, Rick Rosenberg)

A factory worker searches for his children when his former wife is hidden by the government to protect her husband, an informer.
Unpersuasive melodrama with little more than its unusual plot to commend it.

w Spencer Eastman *book* Leslie Waller *d* James Caan *ph* Paul Lohmann *m* Leonard Rosenman

James Caan, Jill Eikenberry, Robert Viharo

Hideout
US 1934 83m bw

An injured racketeer takes refuge with a farm family and is reformed by the simple life and true love. Schematic eat-your-cake-and-have-it melodrama which pleased audiences at the time. Robert Montgomery, Maureen O'Sullivan, Mickey Rooney, Edward Arnold, C. Henry Gordon, Elizabeth Patterson, Edward Brophy, Herman Bing. Written by Frances Goodrich and Albert Hackett; directed by W. S. Van Dyke; for MGM.

High and Low*
Japan 1963 142m bw Tohoscope
Toho (Tomoyuki Tanaka)

A wealthy shoe manufacturer's chauffeur's son is kidnapped in mistake for his own, and he faces a moral dilemma.
Interesting, rather gloomy Japanese version of a light American thriller with all the style expected of the director.

w Hideo Oguni, Ryuzo Kikushima, Eijiro Hisaito, Akira Kurosawa, *novel* The King's Ransom by Ed McBain *d* Akira Kurosawa *ph* Asakazu Makai, Takao Saito *m* Masaru Sato

Toshiro Mifune, Kyoko Kagawa, Tatsuya Nakadai

The High and the Mighty*
US 1954 147m Warnercolor
Cinemascope
Wayne–Fellows

A big passenger plane is in trouble over the Pacific, and its occupants react in various ways to the prospect of a crash landing.
Compendium fiction with even the pilot having a personal problem which could cloud his judgment. Tolerable, well made hokum.

w Ernest K. Gann, from his novel *d* William Wellman *ph* William Clothier *m* Dmitri Tiomkin

John Wayne, Robert Newton, Robert Stack, Doe Avedon, Claire Trevor, Laraine Day, Jan Sterling, Phil Harris, Sidney Blackmer, John Howard

AA: Dmitri Tiomkin
AAN: William Wellman; Claire Trevor; Jan Sterling; title song (*m* Dmitri Tiomkin, *ly* Ned Washington)

High Anxiety*
US 1977 94m De Luxe
TCF / Crossbow (Mel Brooks)

A psychologist taking up a new appointment suspects that his predecessor may have been murdered.

Elementary but somewhat entertaining spoof of various Hitchcock movies (*Spellbound, North by Northwest, The Birds*), with the level of humour as unsubtle and lavatorial as one has come to expect.

w Mel Brooks, Ron Clark, Rudy DeLuca, Barry Levinson *d* Mel Brooks *ph* Paul Lohmann *m* John Morris

Mel Brooks, Madeline Kahn, Cloris Leachman, Harvey Korman, Ron Carey, Howard Morris, Dick Van Patten

'It basically just shambles along, in search of the next big set-piece to send up.'—*Richard Combs, MFB*
'Brooks has no idea of how to build a sequence, how to tell a story, when to leave well enough (or ill enough) alone.'—*Philip French, Observer*
'A child's idea of satire—imitations, with a comic hat and a leer.'—*New Yorker*

High-Ballin'
US 1978 100m Movielab
AIP / Stanley Chase / Pando (Jan Slan)

An independent trucker battles hijackers as well as pressures from a giant trucking firm.
Routine action hokum, a long way behind 1948's *Thieves' Highway* and even less entertaining than TV's *Movin' On*.

w Paul Edwards *d* Peter Carter *ph* René Verzier *m* Paul Hoffert

Peter Fonda, Jerry Reed, Helen Shaver, Chris Wiggins

High Barbaree
US 1947 91m bw
MGM (Everett Riskin)

A pilot crashlands in the Pacific and finds himself drifting towards a Utopian island fancifully described by his favourite uncle.
Thin Hollywood mysticism on Shangri-La lines but without the solid virtues of plot, dialogue and imagination.

w Anne Morrison Chapin, Whitfield Cook, Cyril Hume *d* Jack Conway *ph* Sidney Wagner *m* Herbert Stothart

Van Johnson, June Allyson, Thomas Mitchell, Marilyn Maxwell

The High Bright Sun
GB 1965 114m Technicolor
Rank (Betty Box)
US title: *McGuire Go Home*

In 1957 Cyprus the British army is beleaguered by partisans, and an officer tries to contact a leading rebel.

Confused and boring attempt to make romantic drama out of an intractably sad situation.

w Ian Stuart Black, from his novel *d* Ralph Thomas *ph* Ernest Steward *m* Angelo Lavagnino

Dirk Bogarde, Susan Strasberg, George Chakiris, Denholm Elliott

The High Command*
GB 1936 88m bw
ABFD / Fanfare / Wellesley (Gordon Wellesley)

The general of a West African garrison has a guilty secret known to his young medical officer.
Dated melodrama, rather interestingly performed and directed.

w Katherine Strueby, *novel* The General Goes Too Far by Lewis Robinson *d* Thorold Dickinson *ph* Otto Heller *m* Ernest Irving

James Mason, Lionel Atwill, Lucie Mannheim, Steve Geray, Leslie Perrins

The High Cost of Loving*
US 1958 87m bw Cinemascope
MGM (Milo O. Frank Jnr)

A happily married middle class couple have doubts about their future.
Pleasant, mildly satirical romantic comedy which doesn't really get anywhere.

w Rip Van Ronkel *d* Jose Ferrer *ph* George J. Folsey *m* Jeff Alexander

Jose Ferrer, Gena Rowlands, Joanne Gilbert, Jim Backus, Bobby Troup, Philip Ober, Edward Platt, Werner Klemperer

High Flight
GB 1957 102m Technicolor
Cinemascope
Columbia / Warwick (Phil C. Samuel)

Cadets train at the Royal Air Force College.
Simple-minded peacetime flagwaver.

w Joseph Landon, Ken Hughes *d* John Gilling *ph* Ted Moore *md* Muir Mathieson *m* Kenneth V. Jones, Douglas Gamley *title march* Eric Coates

Ray Milland, Bernard Lee, Kenneth Haigh, Anthony Newley, Kenneth Fortescue, Sean Kelly, Helen Cherry

High Flyers
US 1937 70m bw
RKO (Lee Marcus)

Two incompetents are duped into smuggling contraband gems.
Feeble finale to the career of two comedians.

w Benny Rubin, Bert Granet, *play* Victor Mapes *d* Edward Cline *ph* Jack Mackenzie *songs* Herman Ruby, Dave Dreyer

Bert Wheeler, Robert Woolsey, Lupe Velez, Marjorie Lord, Margaret Dumont, Jack Carson, Paul Harvey

High Lonesome
US 1950 80m Technicolor

A young man believed to be crazed and homicidal flees into the desert and returns to establish his innocence. Thinly-stretched western not helped by an exhibitionist star performance. John Barrymore Jnr, Chill Wills, Kristine Miller, Lois Butler. Written and directed by Alan Le May; for Eagle Lion.

High Noon****
US 1952 85m bw
Stanley Kramer

A marshal gets no help when he determines to defend his town against revengeful badmen.
A minor western with a soft-pedalled message for the world, this turned out to be a classic simply because it was well done, with every scene and performance clearly worked out. Cinematically it was pared to the bone, and the theme tune helped.

w Carl Foreman, *story* The Tin Star by John W. Cunningham *d* Fred Zinnemann *ph* Floyd Crosby *m* Dmitri Tiomkin *singer* Tex Ritter

Gary Cooper, Grace Kelly, Thomas Mitchell, Lloyd Bridges, Katy Jurado, Otto Kruger, Lon Chaney, Henry Morgan

'When the hands point up . . . the excitement starts!'—*publicity*

'Like nearly all the Kramer productions, this is a neat, well-finished and literate piece of work, though its limitations are more conventional than most.'—*Gavin Lambert*

'A western to challenge *Stagecoach* for the all-time championship.'—*Bosley Crowther*

'A series of crisp and purposeful scenes that interpret each other like the pins on a strategist's war map.'—*Robert L. Hatch*

'It is astonishing how much of the simple western story is told visually by rapid cross-cutting.'—*Films in Review*

'Few recent westerns have gotten so much tension and excitement into the classic struggle between good and evil.'—*Life*

AA: Dmitri Tiomkin; Gary Cooper; title song (*m* Dmitri Tiomkin, *ly* Ned Washington)
AAN: best picture; Carl Foreman; Fred Zinnemann

High Plains Drifter*
US 1972 105m Technicolor
Panavision
Universal / Malpaso (Robert Daley)

A mysterious stranger rides into town and
terrifies the inhabitants.
Semi-supernatural, mystical revenge western
with an overplus of violence. Very watchable,
but irritating.

w Ernest Tidyman d Clint Eastwood
ph Bruce Surtees m Dee Barton ad Henry
Bumstead

Clint Eastwood, Verna Bloom, Marianna Hill,
Mitch Ryan, Jack Ging
'Ritualized violence and plodding symbolism
make for heavy going.'—Sight and Sound
'A nervously humorous, self-conscious near-
satire on the prototype Eastwood formula.'—
Variety

High Pressure*
US 1932 74m bw

A would-be tycoon believes there's a fortune
to be made in artificial rubber. Amusing con
man comedy with good work all round.
William Powell, Evelyn Brent, George Sidney,
Guy Kibbee, Frank McHugh. Written by
Joseph Jackson, from Abem Kandel's play Hot
Money; directed by Mervyn Le Roy; for
Warner.

High Sierra*
US 1941 96m bw
Warner (Hal. B. Wallis, Mark Hellinger)

An ex-con gangster plans one last heist in the
Californian mountains, but is mortally
wounded through his involvement with two
women.
Rather dreary action melodrama which gave
Bogart his first real star part (after George
Raft turned it down). Remade 1955 as I Died
a Thousand Times (qv); also in 1949 as a
western, Colorado Territory.

w John Huston, W. R. Burnett, novel W. R.
Burnett d Raoul Walsh ph Tony Gaudio
m Adolph Deutsch

Humphrey Bogart, Ida Lupino, Joan Leslie,
Alan Curtis, Arthur Kennedy, Henry Hull,
Henry Travers, Jerome Cowan
'The last swallow, perhaps, of the gangsters'
summer.'—William Whitebait
'Like it or not, I'll be damned if you leave
before the end, or go to sleep.'—Otis
Furguson
'As gangster pictures go, this one has
everything—speed, excitement, suspense, and
that ennobling suggestion of futility which
makes for irony and poetry.'—New York
Times

High Society
US 1956 107m Technicolor
Vistavision
MGM (Sol C. Siegel)

A haughty rich girl chooses between several
suitors.
Cold, flat, dull musical reworking of The
Philadelphia Story (qv), with ill-cast
performers and just a few bright moments.

w John Patrick d Charles Walters ph Paul C.
Vogel m / ly Cole Porter md Johnny Green,
Saul Chaplin ad Cedric Gibbons, Hans Peters

Bing Crosby, Grace Kelly, Frank Sinatra,
Celeste Holm, Louis Armstrong, Sidney
Blackmer, Margalo Gillmore, Louis Calhern,
Lydia Reed, John Lund

AAN: Johnny Green, Saul Chaplin; song
'True Love'

High Society Blues
US 1930 102m bw
Fox

A girl ditches a French count in favour of an
all-American hero.
Frothy musical romance which did nothing for
its stars and is now unwatchable.

w Howard J. Green d David Butler
ph Charles Van Enger songs Joe McCarthy,
James Hanley

Janet Gaynor, Charles Farrell, William Collier
Snr, Hedda Hopper, Louise Fazenda, Lucien
Littlefield, Joyce Compton

High Tension
US 1936 63m bw

Exploits of a cable layer in Hawaii. Routine
brawling comedy. Brian Donlevy, Norman
Foster, Glenda Farrell, Helen Wood, Robert
McWade. Written by Lou Breslow, Edward
Eliscu and John Patrick; directed by Allan
Dwan; for TCF.

The High Terrace
GB 1956 82m bw

A theatrical producer is murdered, and
members of the cast protect their leading lady;
but she is guilty. Rather solemn, enclosed little
mystery which evokes no compulsion to go on
watching. Lois Maxwell, Dale Robertson,
Derek Bond, Eric Pohlmann, Mary Laura
Wood, Lionel Jeffries. Written by Alfred
Shaughnessy and Norman Hudis; directed by
Henry Cass; for CIPA / Robert S. Baker.

High Tide at Noon
GB 1957 111m bw
Rank (Julian Wintle)

Passions run high among lobster fishermen in Nova Scotia.

Neat, clean romantic melodrama in agreeable surroundings.

w Neil Paterson *d* Philip Leacock *ph* Eric Cross *m* John Veale

Betta St John, Michael Craig, Patrick McGoohan, William Sylvester, Flora Robson, Alexander Knox, Peter Arne, Patrick Allen, Susan Beaumont

High Time
US 1960   103m   De Luxe   Cinemascope
TCF / Bing Crosby (Charles Brackett)

A middle-aged widower goes back to college.

Flaccid comedy-musical with some undergraduatish jokes.

w Tom and Frank Waldman *d* Blake Edwards *ph* Ellsworth Fredericks *m* Henry Mancini *songs* Sammy Cahn, Jimmy Van Heusen

Bing Crosby, Tuesday Weld, Fabian, Richard Beymer, Nicole Maurey

AAN: song 'The Second Time Around' (*m* Jimmy Van Heusen, *ly* Sammy Cahn)

High Treason
GB 1929   90m   bw

In 1940, women unite to prevent a second world war. Tired little prophetic fable with primitive techniques. Jameson Thomas, Benita Hume, Basil Gill, Humberston Wright. Written by L'Estrange Fawcett, from the play by Noel Pemberton-Billing; directed by Maurice Elvey; for Gaumont.

High Treason*
GB 1951   93m   bw
GFD / Conqueror (Paul Soskin)

Saboteurs are routed by the London police. Unconvincing documentary melodrama which moves fast enough to be entertaining.

w Frank Harvey, Roy Boulting *d* Roy Boulting *ph* Gilbert Taylor *m* John Addison

Liam Redmond, André Morell, Anthony Bushell, Kenneth Griffith, Patric Doonan, Joan Hickson, Anthony Nicholls, Mary Morris, Geoffrey Keen, Dora Bryan

High Wall
US 1947   99m   bw
MGM (Robert Lord)

A war veteran is put in an asylum after confessing to killing his wife, but later events prove that he was drugged into saying so. Adequately entertaining, supremely unconvincing mystery melodrama.

w Sydney Boehm *d* Curtis Bernhardt *ph* Paul C. Vogel *m* Bronislau Kaper

Robert Taylor, Herbert Marshall, Audrey Totter, Dorothy Patrick, H. B. Warner, Warner Anderson

High, Wide and Handsome*
US 1937   110m   bw
Paramount (Arthur Hornblow Jnr)

Pennsylvania 1859: a travelling showgirl falls in love with a farmer.

Disappointingly stilted period musical with most of the talent ill at ease until the final reel.

w Oscar Hammerstein II *d* Rouben Mamoulian *ph* Victor Milner, Theodore Sparkuhl *ch* LeRoy Prinz *songs* Jerome Kern, Oscar Hammerstein II *md* Boris Morros *ad* Hans Dreier, John Goodman

Irene Dunne, Randolph Scott, Dorothy Lamour, Raymond Walburn, Alan Hale, Elizabeth Patterson, Charles Bickford, William Frawley, Akim Tamiroff, Ben Blue, Irving Pichel, Lucien Littlefield

'There are two hours of this long, dumb and dreary picture . . . one is left with a few dim distressing memories.'—*Graham Greene*

A High Wind in Jamaica*
GB 1965   104m   De Luxe   Cinemascope
TCF (John Croydon)

In Victorian days, English children en route home from Jamaica are captured by pirates and influence their lives.

Semi-serious adventure story with a highly unlikely ending in which the chief pirate allows himself to be executed for a murder committed by a child. There are however pleasures along the way.

w Stanley Mann, Ronald Harwood, Denis Cannan, *novel* Richard Hughes *d* Alexander Mackendrick *ph* Douglas Slocombe *m* Larry Adler

Deborah Baxter, Anthony Quinn, James Coburn, Isabel Dean, Nigel Davenport, Gert Frobe, Lila Kedrova

Higher and Higher*
US 1943   90m   bw
RKO (Tim Whelan)

Servants have an elaborate plan to restore the family fortune.

Unamusing musical which undernourishes several talents.

w Jay Dratler, Ralph Spence, *play* Gladys Hurlbut, Joshua Logan *d* Tim Whelan *ph* Robert de Grasse *md* Constantin Bakaleinikoff *songs* Jimmy McHugh, Harold Adamson

Michele Morgan, Jack Haley, *Frank Sinatra*,
Leon Errol, Marcy McGuire, *Victor Borge*,
Mary Wickes, Barbara Hale, Elizabeth Risdon

AAN: Constantin Bakaleinikoff; song 'I
Couldn't Sleep a Wink Last Night (*m* Jimmy
McHugh, *ly* Harold Adamson)

The Highwayman
US 1951   82m   Cinecolor
Allied Artists / Jack Dietz (Hal. E. Chester)

A 17th-century nobleman disguises himself as
a Quaker and becomes a highwayman to right
wrongs.

Curious Poverty Row period actioner with
ideas generally above its station, not to
mention an unexpected tragic ending.

w Jan Jeffries, *poem* Alfred Noyes *d* Lesley
Selander *ph* Harry Neumann *m* Herschel
Burke Gilbert

Philip Friend, Charles Coburn, Victor Jory,
Wanda Hendrix, Cecil Kellaway, Scott
Forbes, Virginia Huston, Dan O'Herlihy

Hilda Crane
US 1956   87m   Technicolor
  Cinemascope
TCF (Herbert B. Swope Jnr)

An unhappy woman marries for the third time
and convinces herself it won't work.

Emotional melodrama of the old school: very
moderate in all departments.

wd Philip Dunne, *play* Samson Raphaelson
ph Joe MacDonald *m* David Raksin

Jean Simmons, Guy Madison, Jean-Pierre
Aumont, *Evelyn Varden*, Judith Evelyn,
Peggy Knudsen

The Hill**
GB 1965   122m   bw
MGM / Seven Arts (Kenneth Hyman)

Prisoners rebel against the harsh discipline of a
British military detention centre in North
Africa during World War II.

Lurid melodrama which descends fairly
quickly into black farce with a number of
sweaty actors outshouting each other.
Enjoyable on this level when you can hear the
dialogue through the poor sound recording.

w Ray Rigby, from his TV play *d* Sidney
Lumet *ph* Oswald Morris *m* none

Sean Connery, Harry Andrews, Michael
Redgrave, Ian Bannen, Alfred Lynch, *Ossie
Davis*, Roy Kinnear, Jack Watson, Ian
Hendry

A Hill in Korea
GB 1956   81m   bw
British Lion / Wessex (Anthony Squire)
US title: *Hell in Korea*

During the Korean war, a small patrol guards
a hill.

Minor war talk-piece, shot in Surrey and
looking it.

w Ian Dalrymple, Anthony Squire, Ronald
Spencer, *novel* Max Catto *d* Julian Amyes
ph Freddie Francis *m* Malcolm Arnold

George Baker, Harry Andrews, Stanley
Baker, Michael Medwin, Ronald Lewis,
Stephen Boyd, Victor Maddern, Harry Landis
  'Character is adequately sketched into a
suitably laconic script.'—*MFB*

Hill 24 Doesn't Answer
Israel 1954   101m   bw
Sikor (Thorold Dickinson, Peter Frye)

Four friends defend Hill 24 against the Arabs
on the eve of the cease-fire, and are all killed.
Israel's first feature film, a curious amalgam of
the slick and the amateur, with long flashbacks
which make it resemble *The Bridge of San
Luis Rey*.

w Zvi Kolitz, Peter Frye, Joanna and Thorold
Dickinson *d* Thorold Dickinson *ph* Gerald
Gibbs *m* Paul Ben-Haim

Michael Wager, Edward Mulhare, Haya
Hararit, Arie Lavi, Michael Shilo

The Hills Have Eyes
US 1977   90m   Movielab

Holidaymakers are waylaid and killed by a
family of desert cannibals. Low-grade shocker
which mysteriously achieved some cult status.
John Steadman, Janus Blythe, Arthur King,
Russ Grieve. Written and directed by Wes
Craven; for Blood Relations. 'Simultaneously
risible and nauseating.'—*Tim Pulleine, MFB*.

The Hills of Home
US 1948   95m   Technicolor

A doctor returns to his Scottish village to
practise medicine, and brings his faithful
collie. Adequate addition to the Lassie saga,
with competent work all round. Edmund
Gwenn, Tom Drake, Donald Crisp, Rhys
Williams, Reginald Owen. Written by William
Ludwig; directed by Fred Wilcox; for MGM.
(GB title: *Master of Lassie*.)

The Hindenburg*
US 1975   125m   Technicolor
  Panavision
Universal / Filmmakers (Robert Wise)

In 1937, sabotage causes the airship
Hindenburg to crash on arrival at New York.
An extremely uninteresting guess at the cause
of this famous disaster. The plot and dialogue
are leaden, and such actors as have more than
a couple of lines look extremely glum. The
special effects, however, are fine despite
curious blue-rinse photographic processing.

w Nelson Gidding, *novel* Michael M. Mooney
d Robert Wise *ph* Robert Surtees
pd Edward Carfagno *sp Albert Whitlock*
m David Shire

George C. Scott, Anne Bancroft, Burgess
Meredith, William Atherton, Roy Thinnes,
Gig Young, Charles Durning, Robert Clary,
René Auberjonois

'The tackiest disaster movie yet—a cheap
and chaotic collage of painted drops, wooden
actors and not-so-special effects that manages
to make one of this century's most sensational
real-life catastrophes seem roughly as
terrifying as a badly stubbed toe.'—*Frank Rich*

AAN: Robert Surtees

Hindle Wakes
GB 1952 82m bw

A Lancashire millgirl spends a week at
Blackpool with the master's son but causes a
scandal when she refuses to marry him.
Modestly competent version of a semi-classic
play about class distinctions. Lisa Daniely,
Leslie Dwyer, Brian Worth, Sandra Dorne,
Ronald Adam. Written by John Baines, from
the play by Stanley Houghton; directed by
Arthur Crabtree; for Monarch. (NB: A
probably better, but unavailable version was
made in 1931 by Victor Saville for Gaumont,
with Belle Chrystall, Edmund Gwenn, John
Stuart, Ruth Peterson, Norman McKinnel and
Sybil Thorndike.)

The Hired Hand
US 1971 93m Technicolor
Universal / Pando (William Hayward)

Two western drifters avenge the killing of their
friend and settle down to work on a farm; but
violence follows them.
A potentially enjoyable small-scale western is
spoiled by pretentious direction and effects
which bore the spectator to death.

w Alan Sharp d Peter Fonda *ph* Vilmos
Zsigmond *m* Bruce Langhorne

Peter Fonda, Warren Oates, Verna Bloom,
Severn Darden

'The first slow-motion western, with endless
artsy photography not quite succeeding in
obscuring the rambling plot.'—*Judith Crist,
1973*

'When a film begins with a "lyrical" shot,
your heart has a right to sink.'—*Stanley
Kauffmann*

The Hireling*
GB 1973 108m colour
Columbia / World Film Services (Ben
Arbeid)

In the twenties, a lady's chauffeur falls in love
with her.
Talkative drama, elegant but not much fun.

w Wolf Mankowitz, *novel* L. P. Hartley
d Alan Bridges ph Michael Reed *m* Marc
Wilkinson *pd Natasha Kroll*

Sarah Miles, Robert Shaw, Peter Egan,
Elizabeth Sellars, Caroline Mortimer

Hiroshima Mon Amour*
France / Japan 1959 91m bw
Argos / Comei / Pathé / Daiei

A French actress working in Hiroshima falls
for a Japanese architect and remembers her
tragic love for a German soldier during the
occupation.
Jumbled mixture of flashbacks and
flashforwards which can now be recognized as
typical of this director and on its first
appearance was hailed as a work of art in an
innovative new style.

w Marguerite Duras *d Alain Resnais*
ph Sacha Vierny, Takahashi Michio
m Giovanni Fusco, Georges Delerue

Emmanuele Riva, Eiji Okada

AAN: Marguerite Duras

His Brother's Wife*
US 1936 91m bw
MGM (Lawrence Weingarten)

A young scientist is helped out of trouble by
his brother, on condition he disappears; the
brother then weds the scientist's girl friend.
Heavy romantic melodrama containing
everything including jungle fever, flung
together to take advantage of the stars' real-
life romance.

w Leon Gordon, John Meehan, *story* George
Auerbach *d* W. S. Van Dyke II *ph* Oliver T.
Marsh *m* Franz Waxman

Robert Taylor, Barbara Stanwyck, Joseph
Calleia, John Eldredge, Jean Hersholt,
Samuel S. Hinds, Leonard Mudie, Jed Prouty

His Butler's Sister*
US 1943 94m bw
Universal (Felix Jackson)

A temporary maid falls for her sophisticated boss.

Pleasant comedy musical: no great shakes, but the principals give the air of enjoying themselves.

w Samuel Hoffenstein, Betty Reinhardt d Frank Borzage ph Elwood Bredell m Hans Salter

Deanna Durbin, Franchot Tone, Pat O'Brien, Evelyn Ankers, Walter Catlett, Alan Mowbray, Akim Tamiroff, Else Janssen, Iris Adrian

His Excellency
GB 1951 84m bw
Ealing (Michael Truman)

The Labour government sends a trade union official to govern a Mediterranean colony. Disappointingly tacky-looking and stagebound version of an unpersuasive West End comedy.

w Robert Hamer, W. P. Lipscomb, play Dorothy and Campbell Christie d Robert Hamer ph Douglas Slocombe m selections from Handel

Eric Portman, Cecil Parker, Helen Cherry, Susan Stephen, Edward Chapman, Clive Morton, Robin Bailey, Geoffrey Keen

His Girl Friday****
US 1940 92m bw
Columbia (Howard Hawks)

A remake of *The Front Page* (qv), with Hildy Johnson turned into a woman.
Frantic, hilarious black farce with all participants at their best; possibly the fastest comedy ever filmed, and one of the funniest.

w Charles Lederer, play The Front Page by Charles MacArthur, Ben Hecht d Howard Hawks ph Joseph Walker m Sydney Cutner md Morris Stoloff

Rosalind Russell, Cary Grant, Ralph Bellamy, Gene Lockhart, Porter Hall, Ernest Truex, Cliff Edwards, Clarence Kolb, Roscoe Karns, Frank Jenks, Abner Biberman, Frank Orth, John Qualen, Helen Mack, Billy Gilbert, Alma Kruger

'The kind of terrific verbal slam-bang that has vanished from current film-making.'—*New Yorker, 1975*

'One of the fastest of all movies, from line to line and from gag to gag.'—*Manny Farber, 1971*

'Overlapping dialogue carries the movie along at breakneck speed; word gags take the place of the sight gags of silent comedy, as this vanished race of brittle, cynical, childish people rush around on corrupt errands.'—*Pauline Kael, 1968*

'The main trouble is that when they made *The Front Page* the first time, it stayed made.'—*Otis Ferguson*

His Glorious Night
US 1929 85m bw
MGM
GB title: *Breath of Scandal*

A princess falls in love with a commoner. Soporific early talkie, remade in 1960 as *A Breath of Scandal*. The movie which first exposed its star's high-pitched voice, it is credited with killing his career.

w Willard Mack, play Olimpia by Ferenc Molnar d Lionel Barrymore ph Percy Hilburn

John Gilbert, Catherine Dale Owen, Hedda Hopper, Gustav von Seyffertitz, Nance O'Neil

His Kind of Woman*
US 1951 120m bw
RKO (Howard Hughes, Robert Sparks)

At a remote Mexican ranch resort, a gangster on the run holds up residents including a fortune-hunting girl and a fading matinee idol. Agreeable tongue-in-cheek melodrama which slightly outstays its welcome but is generally good fun.

w Frank Fenton, d John Farrow ph Harry J. Wild m Leigh Harline md Constantin Bakaleinikoff

Robert Mitchum, Jane Russell, Vincent Price, Raymond Burr, Tim Holt, Charles McGraw, Marjorie Reynolds, Jim Backus

His Lordship*
GB 1936 71m bw
Gaumont (S. C. Balcon)
US title: *Man of Affairs*

A politician's twin takes his place to expose an old murder.
Comfortable star comedy-drama.

w Maude Howell, Edwin Greenwood, L. DuGarde Peach, play The Nelson Touch by Neil Grant d Herbert Mason

George Arliss, Rene Ray, Romilly Lunge, Jessie Winter, Allan Jeayes

His Majesty O'Keefe
GB 1954 90m Technicolor
Warner / Harold Hecht

Native islanders are taught by an easygoing mariner how to exploit their natural resources and defend themselves against pirates.
Thin adventure romance with too little for its star to do.

w Borden Chase, James Hill d Byron Haskin ph Otto Heller m Robert Farnon

Burt Lancaster, Joan Rice, André Morell,
Abraham Sofaer, Benson Fong, Archie
Savage

His Woman
US 1931   80m   bw
Paramount

The captain of a tramp freighter finds himself
in charge of an abandoned baby and a
runaway girl.
Slow, indifferent comedy drama, previously
filmed in 1929 as *Sal of Singapore*.

w Adelaide Heilbron, Melville Baker,
novel The Sentimentalist by Dale Collins
d Edward Sloman ph William Steiner, Arthur
Ellis
Gary Cooper, Claudette Colbert, Averill
Harris, Richard Spiro, Douglass Dumbrille,
Joseph Calleia, Harry Davenport

Une Histoire D'Amour*
France 1951   95m   bw
Jacques Roitfeld / Cité Films
GB title: *Love Story* ·

A police inspector discovers that a young
couple killed themselves because of parental
opposition.
A rather soggy little drama made watchable by
its careful detail and immaculate leading
performance.

w Michel Audiard d Robert Clavel ph Louis
Page m Paul Misraki

Louis Jouvet, Daniel Gélin, Dany Robin

History Is Made at Night*
US 1937   97m   bw
Walter Wanger

A divorcee and her new love have trouble
from her ex-husband.
Atmospheric, artificial, generally entertaining
romantic comedy-drama of a kind which went
out of fashion long ago.

w Gene Towne, Graham Baker d Frank
Borzage ph Gregg Toland m Alfred
Newman

Charles Boyer, Jean Arthur, Leo Carrillo,
Colin Clive
'So souped up with demonic passions and
tender glances and elegant photography that
it's rather fun.'—*New Yorker, 1978*
'Frank Borzage, who could turn
Frankenstein Meets the Wolf Man into a
romantic reverie, is quite undeterred by the
venality rampant in the script and interjects his
vision of what Andrew Sarris called love over
probability. Oh, there's an iceberg disaster
too.'—*Kit Parker catalogue*

The History of Mr Polly*
GB 1949   94m   bw
GFD / Two Cities (John Mills)

A draper's assistant buys a small shop but tires
of his nagging wife and decides the time has
come for a change.
Patchy but generally amusing version of a
popular comic novel, very English and rather
appealingly done.

w Anthony Pelissier, *novel* H. G. Wells
d Anthony Pelissier ph Desmond Dickinson
m William Alwyn

John Mills, Sally Ann Howes, Megs Jenkins,
Finlay Currie, Betty Ann Davies, Edward
Chapman

Hit!
US 1973   134m   Technicolor
    Panavision
Paramount (Harry Korshak)

A federal agent takes personal action against a
drug ring which caused his daughter's death.
Black vigilante melodrama, very violent and
interminably padded out with irrelevancies.

w Alan Trustman, David M. Wolf d Sidney J.
Furie ph John A. Alonzo m Lalo Schifrin

Billy Dee Williams, Richard Pryor, Paul
Hampton, Gwen Welles
'No more under-the-armpit shots, but
obscurity is still the keynote of this Sidney
Furie effort in the urban vigilante genre.'—
Sight and Sound

Hit the Deck
US 1954   112m   Eastmancolor
    Cinemascope
MGM (Joe Pasternak)

Romantic adventures of three sailors on shore
leave in San Francisco.
Boring situations and performances reduce the
temperature of this youth musical which is not
another *On the Town*.

w Sonya Levien, William Ludwig, *musical
play* Herbert Fields, *novel* Shore Leave by
Hubert Osborn ph George Folsey m Vincent
Youmans ly Leo Robin ch Hermes Pan

Tony Martin, Jane Powell, Ann Miller,
Debbie Reynolds, Walter Pidgeon, Vic
Damone, Gene Raymond

Hitler
US 1961   107m   bw
Three Crown / E. Charles Straus

A sex-oriented, semi-fictional biopic of the
German dictator, from the murder of his niece
to his final madness and suicide.
Enterprising sensationalism which deserves a
nod for sheer audacity.

w Sam Neuman *d* Stuart Heisler *ph* Joseph Biroc *m* Hans Salter

Richard Basehart, Maria Emo, Martin Kosleck, John Banner

The Hitler Gang**
US 1944 101m bw
Paramount (B. G. De Sylva)

The rise to power of Hitler and his henchmen. Though at the time it seemed rather like a serious cabaret turn, this fictionalization of historical fact has some good impersonations and dramatically effective scenes.

w Frances Goodrich, Albert Hackett *d* John Farrow *ph* Ernest Laszlo *m* David Buttolph

Robert Watson, Martin Kosleck (Goebbels), Victor Varconi (Hess), Luis Van Rooten (Himmler), Alexander Pope (Goering), Roman Bohnen, Ivan Triesault, Helene Thimig, Reinhold Schunzel, Sig Rumann, Alexander Granach

Hitler—The Last Ten Days
GB / Italy 1973 104m Technicolor
MGM / Wolfgang Reinhardt / Westfilm

With Adolf and Eva in the bunker. Claustrophobic historical reconstruction with an uncomfortable star.

w Ennio de Concini, Maria Pia Fusco, Wolfgang Reinhardt, Ivan Moffat *d* Ennio de Concini *ph* Ennio Guarnieri *m* Mischa Spoliansky

Alec Guinness, Simon Ward, Doris Kunstmann, Adolfo Celi, Diane Cilento, Eric Porter, Joss Ackland

Hitler's Children*
US 1943 83m bw
RKO (Edward A. Golden)

A family reacts to Hitler and the Hitler Youth. Artificial melodrama set in an unlikely Germany but successful at the time because of its topicality and its refusal to play the Nazis as idiots, which was the usual Hollywood line.

w Emmet Lavery, *book* Education for Death by Gregor Ziemer *d* Edward Dmytryk *ph* Russell Metty *m* Roy Webb

Tim Holt, Bonita Granville, Otto Kruger, Kent Smith, H. B. Warner, Lloyd Corrigan, Erford Gage, Gavin Muir, Hans Conried

'A curiously compromised production . . . strong anti-Nazi propaganda, it has not been woven into a defined and moving show.'—*Howard Barnes, New York Herald Tribune*

'The truth about the Nazis from the cradle to the battlefront!'—*publicity*

Hitler's Madman*
US 1943 84m bw
(MGM) PRC / Seymour Nebenzal
aka: *Hitler's Hangman*

Heydrich is assassinated in Czechoslovakia and the Nazis take revenge on the village of Lidice.
Cheapjack sensationalism based on a horrifying incident of World War II; despite its imperfections it generates a certain raw power.

w Peretz Hirshbein, Melvin Levy, Doris Malloy *d* Douglas Sirk *m* Karl Hajos

Patricia Morison, *John Carradine,* Alan Curtis, Ralph Morgan, Ludwig Stossel, Edgar Kennedy, Al Shean, Jimmy Conlin, Blanche Yurka, Victor Kilian

'Newspaper accounts of the bombing of German cities will be pleasant antidotes for the unhappy feeling brought on by the final grim scenes of *Hitler's Madman.'—New York Herald Tribune*

'Even in its poorly depicted scenes of brutality, it inflames a common anger.'—*Theodore Strauss, New York Times*

HMS Defiant*
GB 1962 101m Technicolor
Cinemascope
Columbia / GW (John Brabourne)
US title: *Damn the Defiant*

Mutiny erupts on an 18th-century British sailing ship.
Rather unpleasant and unenterprising sea fare reminiscent of the goings-on aboard the *Bounty.* Well enough staged and acted but not very remarkable or memorable.

w Nigel Kneale, Edmund H. North, *novel* Mutiny by Frank Tilsley *d* Lewis Gilbert *ph* Christopher Challis *m* Clifton Parker

Alec Guinness, Dirk Bogarde, Anthony Quayle, Tom Bell, Nigel Stock, Murray Melvin, Victor Maddern, Maurice Denham, Walter Fitzgerald

'It authentically if superficially recreates the days of press gangs, maggots and the cat.'—*Peter John Dyer*

Hobson's Choice***
GB 1953 107m bw
British Lion / London (Norman Spencer)

In the 1890s a tyrannical Lancashire bootmaker is brought to heel by his plain-speaking daughter and her simple-minded husband.
Brilliantly played version of a famous working-class comedy, memorably set and photographed; one regrets only the slight decline of the predictable third act.

w Norman Spencer, Wynard Browne, *play* Harold Brighouse *d David Lean ph Jack Hildyard m Malcolm Arnold ad Wilfrid Shingleton*

Charles Laughton, Brenda de Banzie, John Mills, Richard Wattis, Helen Haye, Daphne Anderson, Prunella Scales
† Previously filmed in 1931 by Thomas Bentley for BIP from a screenplay by Frank Launder, with James Harcourt, Viola Lyel and Frank Pettingell.

Hoffman
GB 1970   113m   Technicolor
ABP / Longstone (Ben Arbeid)

A middle-aged misfit blackmails a typist into spending a week with him.
Interminable sex comedy padded out from a short TV play; it quickly becomes claustrophobic, tasteless, and boring.

w Ernest Gebler, from his novel and play *d* Alvin Rakoff *ph* Gerry Turpin *m* Ron Grainer

Peter Sellers, Sinead Cusack, Jeremy Bulloch, Ruth Dunning
'Hope never dies for a man with a good dirty mind.'—*publicity*

Hog Wild***
US 1930   20m   bw

Stan helps Ollie to put a radio aerial on the roof of his house. Brilliantly sustained slapstick makes this one of the best star comedies of Laurel and Hardy. Written by H. M. Walker and Leo McCarey; directed by James Parrott; for Hal Roach.

Hold Back the Dawn*
US 1941   115m   bw
Paramount (Arthur Hornblow Jnr)

A would-be immigrant into the US via Mexico marries a schoolteacher he does not love. Surprisingly effective romantic melodrama with a nice style and some mordant lines in the script.

w Charles Brackett, Billy Wilder d Mitchell Leisen ph Leo Tover m Victor Young

Charles Boyer, Olivia de Havilland, Paulette Goddard, Victor Francen, Walter Abel, Curt Bois, Rosemary de Camp, Nestor Paiva, Mitchell Leisen
'All those years with all the others I closed my eyes and thought of you.'—*sample dialogue spoken by Paulette Goddard*

AAN: best picture; Charles Brackett, Billy Wilder; Leo Tover; Victor Young; Olivia de Havilland

Hold Back the Night
US 1956   80m   bw

From World War II to Korea, a marine commander carries with him a lucky whisky bottle. Pointlessly titled war heroics, competently mounted. John Payne, Mona Freeman, Peter Graves, Chuck Connors, Audrey Dalton. Written by John C. Higgins and Walter Doniger, from the novel by Pat Frank; directed by Allan Dwan; for Allied Artists.

Hold Back Tomorrow
US 1956   75m   bw

A convicted killer's last request is for a woman to spend his last night with him. They fall in love before he is executed. A ripe example of the higher tosh, indifferently made and acted. Cleo Moore, John Agar, Frank de Kova, Dallas Boyd. Written, directed and produced by Hugo Haas; for Universal-International.

Hold That Blonde
US 1945   75m   bw
Paramount (Paul Jones)

A psychiatrist suggests that romance may cure a kleptomaniac, but the patient unfortunately chooses a jewel thief.
Thin comedy which erupts into frantic farce, with some energetic slapstick and a Harold Lloyd style finale.

w Walter de Leon, Earl Baldwin, E. Edwin Moran *d* George Marshall *ph* Daniel L. Fapp *m* Werner Heymann

Eddie Bracken, Veronica Lake, Albert Dekker, Frank Fenton, George Zucco, Donald MacBride, Norma Varden, Willie Best

Hold That Co-Ed*
US 1938   80m   bw
TCF (David Hempstead)
GB title: *Hold That Girl*

A girl dressed as a boy wins a university football match and thereby helps a governor get re-elected.
Intriguingly-cast crazy comedy which works up into a fine frenzy.

w Karl Tunberg, Don Ettinger, Jack Yellen *d* George Marshall *ph* Robert Planck *md* Arthur Lange

John Barrymore, Joan Davis, George Murphy, Marjorie Weaver, Jack Haley, George Barbier, Donald Meek, Johnny Downs, Guinn Williams

Hold That Ghost*
US 1941   86m   bw
Universal (Burt Kelly, Glenn Tryon)

A group of strangers are stranded in an apparently haunted house.
Long thought of as Abbott and Costello's best comedy, this now seems pretty strained and slow to start, but it has its classic moments.

w Robert Lees, Fred Rinaldo, John Grant
d Arthur Lubin ph Elwood Bredell, Joe Valentine m Hans Salter

Bud Abbott, Lou Costello, Joan Davis, the Andrews Sisters, Richard Carlson, *Ted Lewis* and his band, Evelyn Ankers, Marc Lawrence, Mischa Auer

Hold Your Man*
US 1933 89m bw
MGM (Sam Wood)

A hard-boiled young woman falls for a confidence man, has his baby, and waits for him to emerge from prison.
Briskly-fashioned star comedy-drama with entertaining moments.

w Anita Loos, Howard Emmett Rogers
d Sam Wood ph Harold Rosson

Jean Harlow, Clark Gable, Stuart Erwin, Dorothy Burgess, Muriel Kirkland, Paul Hurst
'The sudden transition from wise-cracking romance to sentimental penitence provides a jolt.'—*Frank S. Nugent*

The Hole*
France / Italy 1959 123m bw
Play-Art / Filmsonor / Titanus (Serge Silberman)
original title: *Le Trou*

Four convicts in a Paris prison dig a tunnel to freedom and almost make it.
Meticulous escape drama nicely shot in very limited sets: hypnotic for those with the patience to adjust to its pace.

w Jacques Becker, José Giovanni, Jean Aurel, *novel* José Giovanni d Jacques Becker
ph Ghislain Cloquet

Philippe Leroy, Mark Michel, Jean Kéraudy, Michel Constantine

A Hole in the Head*
US 1959 120m De Luxe Cinemascope
UA / Sincap (Frank Sinatra)

A Miami hotelier is threatened with foreclosure and tries to raise the money from his provident elder brother.
Easy-going comedy without much point, but various amusing facets artfully deployed.

w Arnold Shulman, from his TV and stage play d Frank Capra ph William H. Daniels
m Nelson Riddle

Frank Sinatra, Edward G. Robinson, Eleanor Parker, Eddie Hodges, Carolyn Jones, Thelma Ritter, Keenan Wynn, Joi Lansing

AA: song 'High Hopes' (*m* Jimmy Van Heusen, *ly* Sammy Cahn)

The Hole in the Wall
US 1929 73m bw
Paramount

A gangster falls for a phony fortune teller on a revenge scheme.
Involved melodrama, a primitive talkie notable chiefly for its stars.

w Pierre Collings, *play* Fred Jackson
d Robert Florey ph George Folsey

Edward G. Robinson, Claudette Colbert, David Newell, Nelly Savage, Donald Meek, Louise Closser Hale

Holiday*
US 1930 99m bw
Pathe (E. B. Derr)

A bright-minded rich girl steals her sister's fiancé, a struggling young lawyer.
Competent early talkie version of a hit play.

w Horace Jackson, *play* Philip Barry
d Edward H. Griffith ph Norbert Brodine
m Josiah Zuro

Ann Harding, Robert Ames, Mary Astor, Edward Everett Horton, Hedda Hopper, Monroe Owsley, William Holden

AAN: Horace Jackson; Ann Harding

Holiday***
US 1938 93m bw
Columbia (Everett Riskin)
GB titles: *Free to Live; Unconventional Linda*

Elegant, highly successful remake of the above; still a stage play on film, but subtly devised to make the very most of the lines and performances.

w Donald Ogden Stewart d George Cukor
ph Franz Planer m Sidney Cutner

Katharine Hepburn, Cary Grant, Doris Nolan, *Edward Everett Horton* (same role), *Ruth Donnelly, Lew Ayres,* Henry Kolker, Binnie Barnes
'The comedy is full of the best of humour, edged with pathos never allowed to drop into sentimentality. It is played with the greatest cheerfulness and a winning skill.'—*Arthur Pollock, Brooklyn Daily Eagle*
'I suppose actually it is a neat and sometimes elegant job, but under its surface of too much brightness and too many words it

seems so deadly bored and weary. Hell, save your money and yawn at home.'—*Otis Ferguson*

Holiday Affair
US 1949 87m bw
RKO (Don Hartman)

A young widow falls for an easy-going boat builder.
Flimsy star-shaped romantic comedy with nice touches.

w Isobel Lennart *d* Don Hartman *ph* Milton Krasner *m* Roy Webb

Robert Mitchum, Janet Leigh, Wendell Corey, Griff Barnett, Esther Dale, Gordon Gebert, Henry O'Neill, Harry Morgan

Holiday Camp*
GB 1947 97m bw
GFD / Gainsborough (Sydney Box)

At a summer holiday camp, a murderer on the prowl affects people's enjoyment in various ways.
Seminal compendium comedy drama, a bore in itself but establishing several post-war norms of the British cinema, including the Huggetts.

w Muriel and Sidney Box, Ted Willis, Peter Rogers, Mabel and Denis Constanduros
d Ken Annakin

Jack Warner, Kathleen Harrison, Flora Robson, Dennis Price, Hazel Court, Emrys Jones, Yvonne Owen, Esmond Knight, Jimmy Hanley, Peter Hammond, Esma Cannon, John Blythe, Susan Shaw

Holiday for Lovers
US 1959 103m De Luxe Cinemascope
TCF (David Weisbart)

To distract his teenage daughter from boys, a Boston psychiatrist organizes a family holiday in South America.
Frail old-fashioned family comedy with entirely predictable situations culminating in a drunk scene for stuffy father.

w Luther Davis *d* Henry Levin *ph* Charles G. Clarke *m* Leigh Harline

Clifton Webb, Jane Wyman, Paul Henreid, Carol Lynley, Jill St John, Gary Crosby, José Greco

Holiday for Sinners
US 1952 72m bw
MGM (John Houseman)

In New Orleans during the Mardi Gras three old friends meet crises in their lives.

Slightly curious but not very interesting portmanteau drama.

w A. I. Bezzerides, *novel* Hamilton Basso
d Gerald Mayer *ph* Paul Vogel *md* Alberto Columbo

Gig Young, Keenan Wynn, Janice Rule, Richard Anderson, William Campbell, Michael Chekhov, Sandro Giglio, Edith Barrett, Porter Hall

'It gives an impression of blurred, rather heavy-going sincerity.'—*MFB*

Holiday in Mexico
US 1946 127m Technicolor
MGM (Joe Pasternak)

The daughter of the American Ambassador to Mexico falls for Jose Iturbi.
Travel brochure musical in which the occasional plums do not redeem the sogginess of the pudding.

w Isobel Lennart *d* George Sidney *ph* Harry Stradling

Walter Pidgeon, Ilona Massey, Jane Powell, Jose Iturbi, Roddy McDowall

Holiday Inn**
US 1942 101m bw
Paramount (Mark Sandrich)

The joint proprietors of a roadhouse hotel love the same girl.
Plain, simple-minded musical which provided a peg for pleasant performances and good numbers. It hit the box office spot, especially as it introduced 'White Christmas'.

w Claude Binyon, Elmer Rice *d* Mark Sandrich *ph* David Abel *m / ly* Irving Berlin *md* Robert Emmett Dolan

Bing Crosby, Fred Astaire, Walter Abel, Marjorie Reynolds, Virginia Dale, Louise Beavers, Irving Bacon, James Bell

AA: song 'White Christmas'
AAN: original story (Irving Berlin); Robert Emmett Dolan

The Holly and the Ivy*
GB 1952 83m bw
British Lion / London (Anatole de Grunwald)

Christmas brings family revelations in a remote Norfolk rectory.
A badly-filmed stage success which succeeds because of its performances.

w Anatole de Grunwald, *play* Wynard Browne *d* George More O'Ferrall *ph* Ted Scaife *m* Malcolm Arnold

Ralph Richardson, Celia Johnson, Margaret Leighton, Denholm Elliott, John Gregson,

Hugh Williams, Margaret Halstan, Maureen Delany, William Hartnell, Robert Flemyng, Roland Culver

'This type of direct translation to the screen, using none of the cinema's resources, can only do harm to the play itself.'—*Penelope Houston*

Hollywood Boulevard*
US 1936 75m bw
Paramount (A. M. Botsford)

A washed-up Hollywood actor writes a sensational memoir for publication, but lives to regret it.
Entertaining melodrama with famous names in bit parts.

w Marguerite Roberts *d* Robert Florey
ph Karl Struss *m* Gregory Stone

John Halliday, Marsha Hunt, Robert Cummings, C. Henry Gordon, Frieda Inescort, Esther Dale; and Gary Cooper, Francis X. Bushman, Maurice Costello, Mae Marsh, Charles Ray, Jane Novak, Bryant Washburn, Jack Mulhall, Creighton Hale, Bert Roach

'A pretty hoary melodrama and a slight enough excuse for a whole series of homilies upon the uncertainty of fame and fortune in the glamour city.'—*New York Times*

Hollywood Canteen*
US 1944 123m bw
Warner (Alex Gottlieb)

The stars give their evenings to entertaining soldiers.
Shoddily made but sociologically fascinating record of Hollywood doing its bit in World War II.

wd Delmer Daves *ph* Bert Glennon *m* Ray Heindorf *md* Leo F. Forbstein

Joan Leslie, Robert Hutton, Dane Clark, Janis Paige; and The Andrews Sisters, Jack Benny, Joe E. Brown, Eddie Cantor, Joan Crawford, Bette Davis, John Garfield, Sidney Greenstreet, Paul Henreid, Peter Lorre, Ida Lupino, Dennis Morgan, Roy Rogers, S. Z. Sakall, Alexis Smith, Barbara Stanwyck, Jane Wyman, etc etc

'The corporal steps slowly backwards, in his eyes that look of glazed ecstasy which Jennifer Jones wore all through *The Song of Bernadette*. He has just been kissed by Joan Leslie.'—*Richard Winnington*

AAN: Ray Heindorf; song 'Sweet Dreams, Sweetheart' (*m* M. K. Jerome, *ly* Ted Koehler)

Hollywood Cavalcade**
US 1939 96m Technicolor
TCF (Harry Joe Brown)

The career of an old-time Hollywood producer.
A lively first half with amusing re-staging of early slapstick comedies gives way depressingly to personal melodrama, but there is enough historical interest to preserve the balance.

w Ernest Pascal *d* Irving Cummings *ph* Allen M. Davey, Ernest Palmer *ad* Richard Day, Wiard B. Ihnen *md* Louis Silvers

Don Ameche, Alice Faye, *J. Edward Bromberg*, Alan Curtis, Stuart Erwin, Jed Prouty, Buster Keaton, Donald Meek, and the original Keystone Kops

Hollywood Hotel
US 1937 109m bw
Warner (Sam Bischoff)

A Hollywood radio show has its problems.
Half-hearted, overlong Warner musical with little of the expected zip.

w Jerry Wald, Maurice Leo, Richard Macauley *d* Busby Berkeley *ph* Charles Rosher, George Barnes *m / ly* Johnny Mercer, Richard Whiting

Dick Powell, Rosemary Lane, Lola Lane, Hugh Herbert, Ted Healy, Glenda Farrell, Louella Parsons, Alan Mowbray, Frances Langford, Allyn Joslyn, Benny Goodman, Edgar Kennedy

Hollywood or Bust
US 1956 95m Technicolor Vistavision
(Paramount) Hal Wallis

Two halfwits win a car and drive across country to Hollywood.
Dopey comedy with more misses than hits; the last film of Martin and Lewis as a team.

w Erna Lazarus *d* Frank Tashlin *ph* Daniel Fapp *m* Walter Scharf

Dean Martin, Jerry Lewis, Pat Crowley, Maxie Rosenbloom, Anita Ekberg

Hollywood Party
US 1934 68m bw (Technicolor sequence)
MGM (Harry Rapf)

A mad Russian throws a party which ends in disaster.
Dismal 'all-star' comedy relieved by guest appearances.

w Howard Dietz, Arthur Kober
d (uncredited) Richard Boleslawski, Allan Dwan, Roy Rowland *ph* James Wong Howe

Laurel and Hardy, Jimmy Durante, Lupe Velez, Charles Butterworth, Eddie Quillan, Ted Healy and the Stooges, Polly Moran

The Hollywood Revue of 1929**
US 1929   116m   part-Technicolor
MGM (Harry Rapf)

A variety show featuring most of MGM's talent in slightly surprising acts, this is something of a bore to sit through but an archival must; and just occasionally it boasts surprising vitality.

w Al Boasberg, Robert E. Hopkins *d* Charles F. Reisner *ph* John Arnold, Irving Ries, Maximillian Fabian *ch* Sammy Lee *m / ly* various

Jack Benny, Buster Keaton, Joan Crawford, John Gilbert, Norma Shearer, Laurel and Hardy, Marion Davies, Marie Dressler, William Haines, Lionel Barrymore, Conrad Nagel, Bessie Love, Cliff Edwards, Nils Asther

AAN: best picture

Hollywood Story*
US 1951   76m   bw
U-I (Leonard Goldstein)

A young producer solves a 20-year-old studio murder mystery.
Adequate potboiler with a reasonably absorbing plot and glimpses of silent stars.

w Frederick Kohner, Fred Brady *d* William Castle *ph* Carl Guthrie *m* Joseph Gershenson

Richard Conte, Julia Adams, Richard Egan, Henry Hull, Fred Clark, Jim Backus, Paul Cavanagh; and Francis X. Bushman, William Farnum, Betty Blythe, Helen Gibson, Joel McCrea

Holocaust 2000
GB / Italy 1977   102m   Technicolor
    Technovision
(Rank) Aston / Embassy (Edmondo Amati)
aka: *The Chosen*

The executive in charge of a thermonuclear plant in the Middle East is drawn into a legend about the rebirth of the anti-Christ, and discovers that the evil one is his own son.
Extraordinary mishmash of horror, religiosity and social conscience which scarcely works on any level.

w Sergio Donati, Alberto de Martino, Michael Robson *d* Alberto de Martino *ph* Erico Menczer *m* Ennio Morricone

Kirk Douglas, Simon Ward, Agostina Belli, Anthony Quayle, Virginia McKenna, Spiros Focas, Alexander Knox, Adolfo Celi

'The wildest farrago yet to have come out of the demonology genre.'—*Richard Combs, MFB*

Holy Matrimony*
US 1943   87m   bw
TCF (Nunnally Johnson)

A famous painter comes back from exile for a knighthood; but when his valet dies of pneumonia, has him buried as himself in Westminster Abbey.
Slightly stilted but generally warmly amusing version of a favourite novel, with excellent star performances.

w Nunnally Johnson, *novel* Arnold Bennett *d* John Stahl *ph* Lucien Ballard *m* Cyril Mockridge

Monty Woolley, Gracie Fields, Laird Cregar, Eric Blore, Una O'Connor

'A pleasant hour and a half, very well produced and acted.'—*James Agate*

AAN: Nunnally Johnson

Hombre**
US 1967   111m   De Luxe   Panavision
TCF / Hombre Productions (Martin Ritt, Irving Ravetch)

Stagecoach passengers at the mercy of a robber are helped by a despised half-caste.
Slow but suspenseful western melodrama which works up to a couple of good climaxes but falls away in an unnecessary tragic ending.

w Irving Ravetch, Harriet Frank, *novel* Elmore Leonard *d Martin Ritt ph* James Wong Howe *m* David Rose

Paul Newman, *Diane Cilento, Fredric March*, Richard Boone, Martin Balsam, Barbara Rush, Cameron Mitchell

'A fine array of quirkish characters . . . and some unusually literate dialogue.'—*Tom Milne*

Home at Seven
GB 1952   85m   bw
British Lion / London (Maurice Cowan)
US title: *Murder on Monday*

A clerk suffers a 24-hour loss of memory and may have been involved in a murder.
Intriguing suburban mystery, well acted but all too flatly transferred from the stage.

w Anatole de Grunwald, *play* R. C. Sherriff *d* Ralph Richardson *ph* Jack Hildyard, Edward Scaife

Ralph Richardson, Margaret Leighton, Jack Hawkins, Campbell Singer, Michael Shepley, Margaret Withers, Meriel Forbes, Frederick Piper

'A film with a notable absence of imagination in conception, direction and acting is not vindicated because it was made very cheaply in fifteen days . . . it seems ominous that the technique closely resembles that of television.'—*MFB*

Home before Dark
US 1958   137m   bw
Warner (Mervyn Le Roy)

A college professor brings his wife home after a year in a mental hospital, but trouble starts again as the circumstances are unchanged.
Overlong, heavygoing, well-made soap opera, quite unconvincing despite firm performances and a suitably gloomy *mise-en-scène*.

w Eileen and Robert Bassing *d* Mervyn Le Roy *ph* Joseph Biroc *m* Franz Waxman *md* Ray Heindorf

Jean Simmons, Efrem Zimbalist Jnr, Dan O'Herlihy, Rhonda Fleming, Mabel Albertson

Home from the Hill
US 1959   150m   Metrocolor
   Cinemascope
MGM / Sol C. Siegel (Edmund Grainger)

A southern landowner with a voracious sexual appetite has trouble with his two sons, legitimate and illegitimate.
Shades of *Cold Comfort Farm* and *Tobacco Road* . . . and this solemn family saga does go on a bit.

w Irving Ravetch, Harriet Frank, *novel* William Humphrey *d* Vincente Minnelli *ph* Milton Krasner *m* Bronislau Kaper

Robert Mitchum, George Hamilton, George Peppard, Eleanor Parker, Luana Patten, Everett Sloane, Constance Ford, Ray Teal

Home in Indiana
US 1944   103m   Technicolor
TCF (André Daven)

Farmers compete in trotting races and their progeny fall in love.
Archetypal homespun Americana, well enough made according to its lights, but now like something from another world . . . an innocent one.

w Winston Miller, *novel* The Phantom Filly by George Agnew Chamberlain *d* Henry Hathaway *ph* Edward Cronjager *m* Hugo Friedhofer *md* Emil Newman

Jeanne Crain, June Haver, Lon McCallister, Walter Brennan, Charlotte Greenwood, Ward Bond, Charles Dingle, Willie Best
† Remade as *April Love*.
AAN: Edward Cronjager

Home of the Brave*
US 1949   86m   bw
Stanley Kramer

During World War II, a black man finds himself the butt of racist behaviour from the rest of his platoon.
One of the first films to touch the subject of anti-black bias, this now seems pretty tame and dated, and in fact never was much more than a filmed play (in which the butt was originally a Jew).

w Carl Foreman, *play* Arthur Laurents *d* Mark Robson *ph* Robert de Grasse *m* Dmitri Tiomkin

Frank Lovejoy, Lloyd Bridges, Douglas Dick, James Edwards, Steve Brodie, Jeff Corey, Cliff Clark

Home Sweet Homicide
US 1946   90m   bw
TCF

Children solve a murder mystery with the help of their mother, a detective novelist.
Mild family fare.

w F. Hugh Herbert, *novel* Craig Rice *d* Lloyd Bacon *ph* John Seitz *m* David Buttolph

Lynn Bari, Randolph Scott, Peggy Ann Garner, Connie Marshall, Dean Stockwell, Barbara Whiting

The Home Towners
US 1928   84m   bw

A wealthy man falls for a girl half his age and is warned by a hometown friend that she may be a gold digger. Fairly fluent early talkie which pleased at the time. Richard Bennett, Robert Mc'Vade, Doris Kenyon, Stanley Taylor. Written by Addison Burkhart, from the play by George M. Cohan; directed by Bryan Foy; for Warner. (Remakes include *Times Square Playboy* [1936] with Warren William, Gene Lockhart and June Travis, directed by William McGann; and *Ladies Must Live* [1940] with Wayne Morris, Priscilla Lane and Roscoe Karns; both for Warner.)

Homecoming
US 1948   113m   bw
MGM (Sidney Franklin)

A ruthless society doctor is called up in World War II and has his life changed by a brief affair with a nurse who is killed in action.
Ho-hum romantic melodrama which stumbles most badly when it aims to be serious.

w Paul Osborn *d* Mervyn Le Roy *ph* Harold Rosson *md* Charles Previn *m* Bronislau Kaper

Clark Gable. Lana Turner. Anne Baxter. John
Hodiak. Ray Collins. Gladys Cooper.
Cameron Mitchell. Marshall Thompson
  'Its basic substance. like the base of a
perfume. has a terrible smell; but to many
moviegoers the end-product will seem quite
pleasant.'—*Time*

The Homecoming*
GB 1973   114m   colour
American Express / Ely Landau

Tensions mount and sexual revelations abound
in the house of a retired London butcher.
Plain treatment of an anything-but-plain Pinter
play. The result is a record of a performance
rather than a film.

w Harold Pinter. from his play *d* Peter Hall
ph David Watkin *m* Thelonious Monk
pd John Bury

Paul Rogers. Cyril Cusack. Michael Jayston.
Ian Holm. Vivien Merchant. Terence Rigby
  'Shocking in its own lucidity. and fascinating
as an arrangement of mutually reflecting
prisms . . . the remarkable control of Pinter's
language guarantees that the dramatic
situations are revealed to be even *more*
abstract and diagrammatic as they steadily
accumulate psychological density.'—*Jonathan
Rosenbaum*

Homicidal
US 1961   87m   bw
Columbia / William Castle

A murderous blonde and a very strange young
man both live in the house of a paralysed old
lady.
Transvestite horror comic allegedly based on a
true case; made on a low budget and played
for cheap shocks.

w Robb White *d* William Castle *ph* Burnett
Guffey *m* Hugo Friedhofer

Jean Arless. Glenn Corbett. Patricia Breslin.
Eugenie Leontovitch. Alan Bunce. Richard
Rust
† The film was played with a 'fright break'
during which faint-hearted members of the
audience might leave before the final
onslaught.

L'Homme au Chapeau Rond*
France 1946   91m   bw
Alcina

When his wife dies. a man becomes obsessed
with causing the downfall of her two lovers.
Heavy-going melodrama without much in the
way of light relief; chiefly memorable for its
central performance.

w Charles Spaak. Jean Loubignic. *novel* The
Eternal Husband by Dostoevsky *d* Pierre
Billon *ph* Nicolas Torporkoff *m* Maurice
Thiriet

Raimu. Aimé Clariond. Lucy Valnor

Hondo*
US 1954   93m   Warnercolor   3-D
Wayne–Fellows

In 1874 New Mexico a cavalry despatch rider
stops to defend a lonely widow and her son
against Indians.
Overwritten but pleasant-looking western.
clearly patterned after *Shane*.

w James Edward Grant *d* John Farrow
ph Robert Burks. Archie Stout *m* Emil
Newman. Hugo Friedhofer

John Wayne. Geraldine Page. Ward Bond.
Michael Pate

AAN: Geraldine Page

The Honey Pot*
US 1966   150m   Technicolor
UA / Famous Artists (Charles K. Feldman)
  (Joseph L. Mankiewicz)

A millionaire pretends to be dying in order to
trick three former mistresses; but one of them
is murdered.
Uneasy variation. via two other variations. on
Ben Jonson's *Volpone*; despite bright
moments. the mood is fatally inconsistent. and
a cloud of pseudo-sophisticated dialogue hangs
over the whole thing like a pall.

wd Joseph L. Mankiewicz. *play* Mr Fox of
Venice by Frederick Knott. *novel* The Evil of
the Day by Thomas Sterling *ph* Gianni di
Venanzo *m* John Addison *pd* John De Cuir

Rex Harrison. Susan Hayward. *Maggie Smith*.
Cliff Robertson. Capucine. Edie Adams.
Adolfo Celi. Herschel Bernardi
  'One of the talkiest pictures ever made.'—
Stephen Farber

Honeymoon
US 1947   74m   bw
RKO (Warren Duff)
GB title: *Two Men and a Girl*

An 18-year-old elopes to Mexico City with an
army corporal but meets a sophisticated older
man.
Emaciated comedy. one of the reasons for
Shirley Temple's early retirement.

w Michael Kanin. *story* Vicki Baum
d William Keighley *ph* Edward Cronjager
m Leigh Harline

Shirley Temple, Franchot Tone, Guy
Madison, Lina Romay, Gene Lockhart, Grant
Mitchell

Honeymoon

Spain / GB 1959   109m   Technicolor
 Technirama / Dimension 180
Suevia / Everdene (Cesario Gonzalez,
 Michael Powell)
Spanish title: *Luna de Miel*

An ex-ballerina in Spain with her new husband
is tempted to return to the boards.
Incredibly shapeless travel poster with some
dancing and two interpolated ballets to
provide moments of musical interest. An
unbelievable disaster from the co-creator of
The Red Shoes.

w Michael Powell, Luis Escobar *d* Michael
Powell *ph* Georges Périnal, Gerry Turpin
m Mikis Theodorakis

Anthony Steel, Ludmilla Tcherina, Antonio,
Leonide Massine

Honeymoon Deferred

US 1940   84m   bw

An insurance investigator is called away from
honeymoon when his boss is murdered.
Unremarkable star programmer. Edmund
Lowe, Margaret Lindsay, Elizabeth Risdon,
Joyce Compton, Chick Chandler. Written by
Roy Chanslor and Eliot Gibbons; directed by
Lew Landers; for Universal.

Honeymoon Deferred

GB 1951   79m   bw

A war veteran returns for his honeymoon to
the Italian village he helped to liberate, but
finds himself accused of ruining the crops.
Curious hybrid comedy which fails to jell on
all levels. Griffith Jones, Sally Ann Howes,
Kieron Moore, Lea Padovani. Written by Suso
d'Amico and A. Pietrangeli; directed by Mario
Camerini; for Vic Films.

Honeymoon for Three

US 1941   77m   bw

An author is protected from adoring females
by his secretary. Fairly flaccid romantic
comedy, a remake of *Goodbye Again* (1933).
George Brent, Ann Sheridan, Osa Massen,
Charles Ruggles, Jane Wyman, Lee Patrick.
Written by Julius J. Epstein, Philip G. Epstein
and Earl Baldwin; directed by Lloyd Bacon;
for Warner.

Honeymoon Hotel

US 1964   98m   Metrocolor
 Cinemascope
MGM / Avon (Lawrence Weingarten)

A jilted swain goes off with a philandering
friend on what was to have been his
honeymoon trip . . . only to be followed by his
repentant fiancée.
Rather unattractive farce with insufficient
funny moments.

w R. S. Allen, Harvey Bulloch *d* Henry
Levin *ph* Harold Lipstein *m* Walter Scharf

Nancy Kwan, Robert Goulet, Robert Morse,
Jill St John, Elsa Lanchester, Keenan Wynn

The Honeymoon Machine

US 1961   91m   Metrocolor
 Cinemascope
MGM / Avon (Lawrence Weingarten)

A naval lieutenant uses the ship's computer to
break the bank at the Venice casino.
Stolid, expensive-looking comedy which barely
raises a laugh.

w George Wells, *play* The Golden Fleecing by
Lorenzo Semple Jnr *d* Richard Thorpe
ph Joseph La Shelle *m* Leigh Harline

Steve McQueen, Brigid Bazlen, Jim Hutton,
Paula Prentiss, Dean Jagger, Jack Weston,
Jack Mullaney

Honeysuckle Rose

US 1980   119m   Technicolor

A happily married country and western star
takes to the bottle whenever he goes on the
road. Glum modern drama with music, a
semi-autobiographical star vehicle; for fans
only. Willie Nelson, Dyan Cannon, Amy
Irving, Slim Pickens. Written by Carol
Sobieski, William D. Wittliff and John Binder;
directed by Jerry Schatzberg; for Sydney
Pollack / Warner.

The Honkers*

US 1971   102m   De Luxe
UA / Levy–Gardner–Laven

An ageing rodeo rider has trouble with his
wife.
Quiet, carefully accomplished study of a man
and his milieu.

w Steve Ihnat, Stephen Lodge *d* Steve Ihnat
ph John Crabe *m* Jimmie Haskell

James Coburn, Lois Nettleton, Slim Pickens,
Richard Anderson

Honky Tonk

US 1929   80m   bw

A nightclub entertainer sacrifices everything
for her daughter's education. Primitive cross
between *Applause* and *Imitation of Life*, with
spirited moments from Sophie Tucker the only
plus; also Lila Lee, Audrey Ferris, George

Duryea, Mahlon Hamilton. Written by C. Graham Baker and Jack Yellen; directed by Lloyd Bacon; for Warner.

Honky Tonk*
US 1941   104m   bw
MGM (Pandro S. Berman)

A western con man meets his match in the daughter of a fake judge.
Generally amusing comedy melodrama that ambles along between two styles but leaves a pleasant after-effect.

w Marguerite Roberts, John Sandford *d* Jack Conway *ph* Harold Rosson *m* Franz Waxman

Clark Gable, Lana Turner, Frank Morgan, Claire Trevor, Marjorie Main, Albert Dekker, Henry O'Neill, Chill Wills, Betty Blythe
'A lively, lusty western that makes you wish you had been there.'—*Variety*

Honolulu
US 1938   83m   bw
MGM (Jack Cummings)

A movie star is mistaken for his double.
Sloppy comedy with a few musical numbers.

w Herbert Fields, Frank Partos *d* Edward Buzzell *ph* Ray June *m* Franz Waxman

Robert Young, Eleanor Powell, George Burns, Gracie Allen, Rita Johnson, Ruth Hussey, Clarence Kolb, Sig Rumann, Eddie Anderson
'The whole thing seems to have been thrown together so that Eleanor Powell can do a frenetic hula.'—*New Yorker, 1977*

An Honourable Murder*
GB 1959   70m   bw
Danziger

Boardroom executives scheme to be rid of their chairman.
Oddball, interesting attempt to play *Julius Caesar* in modern dress. Not entirely successful, but full marks for trying.

w Brian Clemens, Eldon Howard *d* Godfrey Grayson

Norman Wooland, Margaretta Scott, Lisa Daniely, Douglas Wilmer, Philip Saville, John Longden

Hoodlum Empire
US 1952   98m   bw
Republic (Joseph Kane)

A Congressional committee investigates a racketeer.
Moderate semi-documentary potboiler inspired by the Kefauver investigations.

w Bruce Manning, Bob Considine *d* Joseph Kane *ph* Reggie Lanning *m* Nathan Scott

Brian Donlevy, Forrest Tucker, Claire Trevor, Vera Ralston, Luther Adler, John Russell, Gene Lockhart, Grant Withers, Taylor Holmes
'Familiar gangster melodramatics and repentances, played out in a rigmarole of flashbacks.'—*MFB*

The Hoodlum Priest*
US 1961   100m   bw
UA / Don Murray–Walter Wood

A Jesuit teacher tries to help young criminals, especially a condemned murderer.
Moderately well done, very depressing and downbeat chunk of social conscience based on the life of Charles Dismas Clark.

w Don Mankiewicz, Joseph Landon *d* Irvin Kershner *ph* Haskell Wexler *m* Richard Markowitz

Don Murray, Keir Dullea, Larry Gates, Cindi Wood, Logan Ramsey

The Hoodlum Saint
US 1946   93m   bw
MGM (Cliff Reid)

A cynical newspaperman turns to religion and succours thieves.
Hard-boiled sentimentality, a downright peculiar and doleful comedy drama in deflated post-war mood.

w Frank Wead, James Hill *d* Norman Taurog *ph* Ray June *m* Nathaniel Shilkret

William Powell, Esther Williams, Angela Lansbury, James Gleason, Lewis Stone, Rags Ragland, Frank McHugh, Slim Summerville, Roman Bohnen, Louis Jean Heydt, Charles Arnt, Charles Trowbridge, Henry O'Neill

The Hook
US 1962   98m   bw   Panavision
MGM / Perlberg–Seaton

Three GIs escaping from Korea are ordered to execute a prisoner but cannot bring themselves to do it.
Predictable, claustrophobic drama which becomes a slick exercise in morality.

w Henry Denker, from his novel Vahe Katcha *d* George Seaton *ph* Joe Ruttenberg

Kirk Douglas, Robert Walker, Nick Adams, Nehemiah Persoff

Hook, Line and Sinker
US 1968   92m   Technicolor
Columbia / Jerry Lewis

A salesman who thinks he is dying goes on a spending spree; when he learns the truth, he has to disappear because of his huge debts. Miserable comedy with frantic slapstick interludes. The plot might have served Preston Sturges.

w Rod Amateau d George Marshall
ph W. Wallace Kelley m Dick Stabile

Jerry Lewis, Peter Lawford, Anne Francis, Pedro Gonzales Gonzales

Hooper*
US 1978 99m Metrocolor
Warner / Burt Reynolds, Lawrence Gordon (Hank Moonjean)

An ageing stunt man decides on one last sensational stunt before retiring.
There are some agreeably striking moments, but you can't make a movie out of stunts and loud camaraderie. This one palls half way through.

w Thomas Rickman, Bill Kerby d Hal Needham ph Bobby Byrne m Bill Justis

Burt Reynolds, Sally Field, Brian Keith, Jan-Michael Vincent, John Marley, Robert Klein, James Best, Adam West

'Burt Reynolds's annual Kleenex of a movie: something to use and throw away without any thought beyond a certain gratitude for the convenience of the thing.'— Richard Schickel, Time

The Hoosegow**
US 1929 20m bw

Stan and Ollie, in prison, contrive to fell a tree on the cook's tent and to smother the governor in boiled rice. Splendid slapstick leading up to one of their best tit-for-tat routines. Laurel and Hardy, James Finlayson, Tiny Sandford. Written by Leo McCarey and H. M. Walker; directed by James Parrott; for Hal Roach.

Hoots Mon*
GB 1939 77m bw

A cockney comedian starts a popularity contest with a female impressionist. Tolerable comedy whose value is that it preserves, albeit in cleaned-up form, portions of Max Miller's variety act. Florence Desmond isn't bad either. With Hal Walters, Davina Craig, Garry Marsh. Written by Roy William Neill, Jack Henley and John Dighton; directed by Roy William Neill; for Warner.

Hopalong Cassidy
Cassidy, a creation of Clarence E. Mulford, was a fictitious gentleman cowboy who oddly enough wore black; 26 books about him were published between 1912 and 1956 when Mulford died. 66 films were made starring William Boyd as Hoppy, with either George Gabby Hayes or Andy Clyde as comic sidekick: Harry Sherman produced them, first for Paramount and then for UA, and they were later edited down for TV, in which medium Boyd became a folk hero and eventually made a further series. The films were easy-going, slow-moving second features which always pointed an admirable moral for children; their main directors were Howard Bretherton, Nate Watt, Lesley Selander and George Archainbaud.

1935: HOPALONG CASSIDY, THE EAGLE'S BROOD, BAR 20 RIDES AGAIN
1936: CALL OF THE PRAIRIE, THREE ON THE TRAIL, HEART OF THE WEST, HOPALONG CASSIDY RETURNS, TRAIL DUST
1937: BORDERLAND, HILLS OF OLD WYOMING, NORTH OF THE RIO GRANDE, RUSTLERS' VALLEY, HOPALONG RIDES AGAIN, TEXAS TRAIL
1938: HEART OF ARIZONA, BAR 20 JUSTICE, PRIDE OF THE WEST, IN OLD MEXICO, SUNSET TRAIL, THE FRONTIERSMAN, PARTNERS OF THE PLAINS, CASSIDY OF BAR 20
1939: RANGE WAR, LAW OF THE PAMPAS, SILVER ON THE SAGE, RENEGADE TRAIL
1940: SANTA FE MARSHAL, THE SHOWDOWN, HIDDEN GOLD, STAGECOACH WAR, THREE MEN FROM TEXAS
1941: DOOMED CARAVAN, IN OLD COLORADO, BORDER VIGILANTES, PIRATES ON HORSEBACK, WIDE OPEN TOWN, OUTLAWS OF THE DESERT, RIDERS OF THE TIMBERLINE, SECRETS OF THE WASTELAND, ST'CK TO YOUR GUNS, TWILIGHT ON THE TRAIL
1942: UNDERCOVER MAN
1943: COLT COMRADES, BAR 20, LOST CANYON, HOPPY SERVES A WRIT, BORDER PATROL, THE LEATHER BURNERS, FALSE COLOURS, RIDERS OF THE DEADLINE
1944: MYSTERY MAN, FORTY THIEVES, TEXAS MASQUERADE, LUMBERJACK
1946: THE DEVIL'S PLAYGROUND
1947: FOOL'S GOLD, HOPPY'S HOLIDAY, MARAUDERS, UNEXPECTED GUEST, DANGEROUS VENTURE

1948: SINISTER JOURNEY, SILENT
CONFLICT, STRANGE GAMBLE,
BORROWED TROUBLE, THE DEAD
DON'T DREAM, FALSE PARADISE

Hopscotch*
US 1980   104m   Movielab
Avco / Edie and Ely Landau (Otto
 Plaschkes)

An ex-CIA man writes a revealing book and
foils the consequent attempts on his life.
Genial but patchy spy comedy caper; a filler
for all concerned.

w Brian Garfield, Bryan Forbes, from
Garfield's novel d Ronald Neame ph Arthur
Ibbetson m Ian Fraser

Walter Matthau, Glenda Jackson, Ned Beatty,
Sam Waterston, Herbert Lom, George Baker

Horizons West
US 1952   81m   Technicolor
U-I (Albert J. Cohen)

After the Civil War, a rancher builds an
empire on greed and ruthlessness, and his
brother has to bring him to trial.
Rather lugubrious western with the usual
quota of effective action scenes.

w Louis Stevens d Budd Boetticher
ph Charles P. Boyle md Joseph Gershenson

Rock Hudson, Robert Ryan, Julia Adams,
John McIntire, Raymond Burr, Dennis
Weaver, Judith Braun

The Horizontal Lieutenant
US 1962   90m   Metrocolor
 Cinemascope
MGM / Euterpe (Joe Pasternak)

World War II Hawaii; an amorous intelligence
officer accidentally captures a Japanese
guerrilla.
Very moderate army farce of no great skill or
memorability.

w George Wells d Richard Thorpe
ph Robert Bronner m George Stoll

Jim Hutton, Paula Prentiss, Jim Backus,
Miyoshi Umeki, Jack Carter

The Horn Blows at Midnight*
US 1945   80m   bw
Warner (Mark Hellinger)

An angel is sent to earth to destroy the planet
with Gabriel's horn.
Wacky comedy inspired by *Here Comes Mr
Jordan*, but on a broader slapstick level; much
better than its star always pretended.

w Sam Hellman, James V. Kern d Raoul
Walsh ph Sid Hickox m Franz Waxman

Jack Benny, Alexis Smith, Dolores Moran,
Allyn Joslyn, Guy Kibbee, Reginald Gardiner,
Franklin Pangborn, John Alexander, Margaret
Dumont

Hornet's Nest
US 1969   109m   De Luxe
UA / Triangle (Stanley S. Kanter)

In World War II Italy, a wounded US army
demolitions expert is nursed back to health by
child partisans, who help him destroy a
German-held dam.
Overlong war exploits with the children used
as a tiresome gimmick.

w S. S.Schweitzer d Phil Karlson ph Gabor
Pogani m Ennio Morricone

Rock Hudson, Sergio Fantoni, Sylva Koscina,
Jacques Sernas

Horror Island
US 1941   60m   bw

Various people travel to an island where
buried treasure might be hidden. Feeble little
mystery with very little interest in who done
what to whom. Dick Foran, Leo Carrillo,
Peggy Moran, Fuzzy Knight, John Eldredge,
Walter Catlett, Hobart Cavanaugh. Written by
Maurice Tombragel and Victor McLeod;
directed by George Waggner; for Universal.

The Horror of Frankenstein
GB 1970   95m   Technicolor

Victor Frankenstein is not above murdering
his acquaintances for the sake of his
experiments in bringing the dead back to life.
Ill-advised attempt to remake the original
story as a black comedy, with Frankenstein
frankly villainous from the start. The last in
the Hammer series. Ralph Bates, Kate
O'Mara, Graham James, Veronica Carlson,
Bernard Archard, Dennis Price, Joan Rice,
Dave Prowse. Written and directed by Jimmy
Sangster; for Hammer / EMI.

Horse Feathers****
US 1932   69m   bw
Paramount (Herman J. Mankiewicz)

A college needs to win at football, and its
corrupt new president knows just how to do it.
Possibly the Marxes' wildest yet most
streamlined kaleidoscope of high jinks and
irreverence, with at least one bright gag or line
to the minute and lively musical interludes to
boot. A classic of zany comedy.

w Bert Kalmar, Harry Ruby, S. J. Perelman,
Will B. Johnstone d Norman Z. McLeod
ph Ray June m / ly Bert Kalmar, Harry Ruby

Groucho, Chico, Harpo, Zeppo, *Thelma Todd,* Robert Greig

'The current Marx comedy is the funniest talkie since the last Marx comedy, and the record it establishes is not likely to be disturbed until the next Marx comedy comes along. As for comparisons, I was too busy having a good time to make any.'—*Philip K. Scheuer*

The Horse in the Grey Flannel Suit
US 1969   112m   Technicolor

A teenager's horse beomes the central figure in an advertising campaign for a stomach pill. Interminable kiddie movie which in its virtual absence of plot or excitement is likely to bore kiddies to death. Dean Jones, Fred Clark, Diane Baker, Lloyd Bochner, Morey Amsterdam. Written by Louis Pelletier, from the novel *The Year of the Horse* by Eric Hatch; directed by Norman Tokar; for Walt Disney.

The Horse Soldiers*
US 1959   119m   De Luxe
UA / Mirisch (John Lee Mahin, Martin Rackin)

In 1863 a Union cavalry officer is sent three hundred miles into Confederate territory to demolish a railroad junction.
Typically sprawling John Ford cavalry western with not too many high spots and more sombre ingredients than usual.
w John Lee Mahin, Martin Rackin   *d* John Ford   *ph* William Clothier   *m* David Buttolph
John Wayne, William Holden, Constance Towers, Hoot Gibson

The Horse without a Head**
GB 1963   89m   Technicolor
Walt Disney (Hugh Attwooll)

Stolen money is hidden in an old toy horse, and crooks trying to get it back clash with police and children.
Excellent children's adventure with scenes on trains and in a toy factory.
w T. E. B. Clarke   d Don Chaffey   *ph* Paul Beeson   *m* Eric Rogers
Leo McKern, Jean-Pierre Aumont, Herbert Lom, Pamela Franklin, Vincent Winter

The Horsemen
US 1970   109m   colour
   Super Panavision
Columbia / John Frankenheimer–Edward Lewis

An Afghan tribesman is determined to rival his father at horsemanship.

Rather tedious variant on *Taras Bulba*; plenty of action but not much characterization, or taste, or interest.
w Dalton Trumbo, *novel* Joseph Kessel
d John Frankenheimer   *ph* Claude Renoir
m Georges Delerue
Omar Sharif, Jack Palance, Leigh Taylor-Young, Peter Jeffrey, Eric Pohlmann, Despo, David De Keyser

The Horse's Mouth*
GB 1958   93m   Technicolor
UA / Knightsbridge (John Bryan)

An obsessive painter is a liability to his friends.
Thin but fitfully amusing light study of a social outcast, with a background of London river and streets. Too slight for real success.
w Alec Guinness, *novel* Joyce Cary   *d* Ronald Neame   *ph Arthur Ibbetson   m* K. V. Jones from Prokofiev   *paintings* John Bratby
Alec Guinness, Kay Walsh, Renée Houston, Robert Coote, Arthur Macrae, Michael Gough, Ernest Thesiger
AAN: Alec Guinness (as writer)

The Hospital**
US 1971   101m   De Luxe   Panavision
UA / Simcha (Howard Gottfried)

A city hospital is beset by weird mishaps, and it transpires that a killer is on the loose.
Black comedy with the emphasis on sex and medical ethics; in the same genre as *M*A*S*H*, and very funny if you can take it.
w Paddy Chayevsky   d Arthur Hiller
ph Victor Kemper   *m* Morris Surdin
George C. Scott, Diana Rigg, Barnard Hughes, Nancy Marchand, Richard Dysart
AA: Paddy Chayevsky
AAN: George C. Scott

Hostages
US 1943   88m   bw
Paramount (Sol C. Siegel)

In occupied Prague, the Nazis seize a variety of hostages and threaten them with death as a reprisal for underground activities.
Modest morale-builder, unfortunately padded out with melodramatics and overacting.
w Lester Cole, Frank Butler, *novel* Stefan Heym   *d* Frank Tuttle   *ph* Victor Milner
m Victor Young
Luise Rainer, Paul Lukas, William Bendix, Oscar Homolka, Arturo de Cordova, Katina Paxinou, Roland Varno

Hostile Witness
GB 1968   101m   De Luxe
UA / Caralan / Dador (David E. Rose)

A barrister suffers a nervous breakdown after
the death of his daughter and finds himself
accused of murder.

Complex courtroom thriller, filmed in a flatly
boring way with stagey sets and performances.
The plot is the only interest.

w Jack Roffey, from his play d Ray Milland
ph Gerry Gibbs

Ray Milland, Sylvia Sims, Felix Aylmer,
Raymond Huntley, Geoffrey Lumsden,
Norman Barrs, Percy Marmont, Ewan
Roberts

Hostile Guns
US 1967   91m   Techniscope

A marshal has to deliver four dangerous
convicts to the penitentiary. Rather crude
addition to the A. C. Lyles series distinguished
only by nostalgic casting. George
Montgomery, Tab Hunter, Yvonne de Carlo,
Brian Donlevy, Fuzzy Knight, John Russell,
Leo Gordon, Robert Emhardt, Richard
Arlen. Written by Steve Fisher and Sloan
Nibley; directed by R. G. Springsteen; for
A. C. Lyles / Paramount.

Hot Blood
US 1955   85m   Technicolor
    Cinemascope
Columbia (Howard Welsch)

A dying gypsy king wants his young brother to
get married and succeed him.

What promises to be a boring musical proves
to be a boring melodrama. Artificial Romany
hokum.

w Jesse Lasky Jnr d Nicholas Ray ph Ray
June m Les Baxter

Cornel Wilde, Jane Russell, Joseph Calleia,
Helen Westcott, Mikhail Rasumny

'Be there when Jane Russell shakes her
tambourines!'—publicity

Hot Enough for June
GB 1963   98m   Eastmancolor
Rank (Betty E. Box)
US title: Agent 8¾

A penniless writer is sent to Czechoslovakia
on a goodwill mission and finds himself being
used as a spy.

Very moderate spoof, neither very funny nor
very thrilling.

w Lukas Heller, novel The Night before
Wenceslas by Lionel Davidson d Ralph
Thomas ph Ernest Steward m Angelo
Lavagnino

Dirk Bogarde, Sylva Koscina, Robert Morley,
Leo McKern, John Le Mesurier

Hot Millions*
US 1968   106m   colour
MGM / Mildred Freed Alberg

A confidence trickster makes a fortune out of
fictitious companies.

Elaborate, talky, overlong comedy with
irresistible star performances.

w Ira Wallach, Peter Ustinov d Eric Till

Peter Ustinov, Maggie Smith, Bob Newhart,
Karl Malden, Robert Morley, Cesar Romero

AAN: Ira Wallach, Peter Ustinov (script)

Hot Pepper
US 1933   76m   bw
Fox

Ex-Marines Flagg and Quirt become
bootleggers and quarrel over a fiery South
American entertainer.

Fourth and last in the comedy-melodrama
series stemming from What Price Glory? Mild,
stereotyped entertainment.

w Barry Connors, Philip Klein, Dudley
Nichols d John G. Blystone ph Charles G.
Clarke

Edmund Lowe, Victor McLaglen, Lupe Velez,
El Brendel, Lillian Bond

The Hot Rock***
US 1972   105m   De Luxe   Panavision
TCF (Hal Landers, Bobby Roberts)
GB title: How to Steal a Diamond in Four
    Uneasy Lessons

Four crooks plan to rob the Brooklyn Museum
of a priceless diamond.

Enjoyable variation on the caper theme, with
relaxed comic performances and highly skilled
technical back-up. It's refreshing to come
across a film which hits its targets so precisely.

w William Goldman, novel Donald E.
Westlake d Peter Yates ph Ed Brown
m Quincy Jones

Robert Redford, George Segal, Zero Mostel,
Paul Sand, Ron Leibman, Moses Gunn,
William Redfield

'A funny, fast-paced, inventive and infinitely
clever crime comedy, almost as if The French
Connection had been remade as a piece of
urban humour.'—Michael Korda

Hot Saturday
US 1932   73m   bw

Malicious gossip in a small town causes a girl
to lose her job. Small town, small potatoes;
interesting chiefly for its two budding male

stars. Nancy Carroll, Cary Grant, Randolph
Scott, Edward Woods, Lillian Bond, Jane
Darwell, William Collier Snr. Written by
Seton I. Miller from the novel by Harvey
Ferguson; directed by William A. Seiter; for
Paramount.

Hot Spell*
US 1958 86m bw Vistavision
Paramount / Hal Wallis

In a small southern town, a husband seeks to
leave his wife and family for a 20-year-old girl.
Overwrought domestic drama slipping
perilously close to farce at times, but a good
theatrical vehicle for its stars.

w James Poe, *play* Next of Kin by Lonnie
Coleman d Daniel Mann ph Loyal Griggs
m Alex North

Anthony Quinn, Shirley Booth, Shirley
Maclaine, Earl Holliman, Eileen Heckart

Hot Stuff
US 1979 91m Metrocolor
Columbia / Rastar / Mort Engleberg

Members of a Burglary Task Force need
convictions, so they set up fences in order to
lure criminals, and are embarrassed by the
results.
Slightly unusual but rather frantically
assembled comedy which wears out its
welcome long before the end.

w Michael Kane, Donald E. Westlake d Dom
DeLuise ph James Pergola m Patrick
Williams

Dom DeLuise, Suzanne Pleshette, Ossie
Davis, Jerry Reed, Luis Avalos, Marc
Lawrence

'Heavy farce in which a bright comedy is
struggling to escape.'—*Tom Milne, MFB*

Hot Summer Night*
US 1957 85m bw
MGM (Morton S. Fine)

A foolhardy reporter determines on an
interview with a notorious outlaw, and has to
be rescued.
Interesting but disappointing low-budget
experiment.

w Morton S. Fine, David Friedkin d David
Friedkin ph Harold S. Marcorati m André
Previn

Leslie Nielsen, Colleen Miller, Edward
Andrews, Jay C. Flippen, James Best, Paul
Richards, Robert Wilke, Claude Akins

Hotel*
US 1967 124m Technicolor
Warner (Wendell Mayes)

Guests at a luxurious New Orleans hotel have
various problems.
Old-fashioned omnibus drama from a
bestseller, quite brightly done.

w Wendell Mayes, *novel* Arthur Hailey
d Richard Quine ph Charles Lang m Johnny
Keating

Rod Taylor, Catherine Spaak, Karl Malden,
Melvyn Douglas, Merle Oberon, Richard
Conte, Michael Rennie, Kevin McCarthy,
Alfred Ryder

Hotel Berlin*
US 1945 98m bw
Warner (Louis F. Edelman)

Various lives intertwine in a Berlin hotel
towards the end of the war.
After five years of total war this view of life on
the other side can hardly fail to be
unconvincing, but the actors gleefully seize on
moments of melodrama.

w Thomas Job, *novel* Vicki Baum d Peter
Godfrey ph Carl Guthrie m Franz Waxman

Raymond Massey, Peter Lorre, Faye
Emerson, Helmut Dantine, Andrea King,
Alan Hale, George Coulouris, Henry Daniell,
Helene Thimig, Kurt Kreuger, Steve Geray,
Frank Reicher

'The most heavily routine of Warners'
political melodramas, stuffed with sympathetic
veterans.'—*James Agee*

Hotel for Women
US 1939 83m bw
TCF (Raymond Griffith)

Young city gold diggers are encouraged by a
matron.
Slight comedy drama notable for the acting
debut of hostess Elsa Maxwell.

w Katherine Scola, Darrell Ware d Gregory
Ratoff ph Peverell Marley m David Buttolph
Elsa Maxwell, Linda Darnell, Ann Sothern,
James Ellison, John Halliday, Lynn Bari, Alan
Dinehart

Hotel Haywire
US 1937 66m bw
Paramount (Harold Hurley)

An astrologer makes eyes at a dentist's wife,
and causes much confusion in a hotel.
Frantic farce which might have been funnier if
it had stuck to the original script and cast (it
was intended for Burns and Allen).

w Preston Sturges (before studio revision)
d George Archainbaud ph Henry Sharp

Leo Carrillo, Lynne Overman, Mary Carlisle,
Benny Baker, Spring Byington, George

Barbier, Porter Hall, Lucien Littlefield, John Patterson

Hotel Imperial
US 1939   67m   bw
Paramount

Balkans, 1916: a Polish dancer suspects a Hungarian officer of being responsible for her sister's death.
Dim romantic melodrama with espionage trimmings.

w Gilbert Gabriel, Robert Thoeren, *play* Lajos Biro *d* Robert Florey *ph* William Mellor *md* Boris Morros

Ray Milland, Isa Miranda, Reginald Owen, Gene Lockhart, J. Carrol Naish, Curt Bois, Henry Victor, Albert Dekker
'A very competent rehash . . . for the unexacting the picture has its moments.'— *Graham Greene*
† Previously made in 1926 by Erich Pommer, with Pola Negri.

Hotel Paradiso*
US 1966   99m   Metrocolor   Panavision
MGM (Peter Glenville)

Various romantic affairs come to a head one evening at a seedy hotel.
A famous boulevard farce seems jellied in aspic in this good-looking but very flatly handled film version, in which famous artists are left to caper about on an unsuitable wide screen with no help from the director.

w Peter Glenville, Jean-Claude Carrière, *play* Georges Feydeau *d* Peter Glenville *ph* Henri Decaë *m* Laurence Rosenthal *pd* François de Lamothe

Alec Guinness, Gina Lollobrigida, Robert Morley, Peggy Mount, Douglas Byng, Akim Tamiroff, Robertson Hare

Hotel Reserve
GB 1944   89m   bw
RKO (Victor Hanbury)

An Austrian refugee in the south of France is asked by the police to track down a spy among his fellow hotel guests.
Slow, obvious and poorly made suspenser from a good novel.

w John Davenport, *novel* Epitaph for a Spy by Eric Ambler *d* Victor Hanbury, Lance Comfort, Max Greene *ph* Max Greene

James Mason, Lucie Mannheim, Raymond Lovell, Julien Mitchell, Martin Miller, Herbert Lom, Frederick Valk, Valentine Dyall

Hotel Sahara*
GB 1951   96m   bw
GFD / Tower (George H. Brown)

In North Africa during World War II, a small hotel changes its loyalties to suit its occupiers.
Overstretched, studio-bound, fitfully amusing comedy.

w George H. Brown, Patrick Kirwan *d* Ken Annakin *ph* David Harcourt *m* Benjamin Franklin

Peter Ustinov, Yvonne de Carlo, David Tomlinson, Roland Culver, Albert Lieven, Bill Owen, Sidney Tafler, Ferdy Mayne
'Cheerful, uncomplicated empty stuff . . . no more subtle than a music hall sketch.'— *Richard Mallett, Punch*

The Hottentot
US 1929   77m   bw

A horse lover is forced to masquerade as a champion jockey. Early talkie version of a well-worn theme which had previously appeared as a silent in 1923 with Douglas MacLean; it later turned up as a Joe E. Brown vehicle and in 1938 became *Going Places*, a Dick Powell musical. The 1929 version also starred Patsy Ruth Miller and Douglas Gerrard; written by Harvey Thew, from the play by Victor Mapes and Willie Collier; directed by Roy del Ruth; for Warner.

Houdini*
US 1953   106m   Technicolor
Paramount (George Pal)

In the 1890s a fairground magician shows a passionate talent for escapology and finally kills himself by undertaking increasingly impossible tricks.
Superficial biopic with more attention to romance than to interesting detail. Some zest in the playing is killed by claustrophobic studio sets.

w Philip Yordan *d* George Marshall *ph* Ernest Laszlo *m* Roy Webb

Tony Curtis, Janet Leigh, Torin Thatcher, Sig Rumann, Angela Clarke

The Hound Dog Man
US 1959   87m   colour   Cinemascope
TCF / Company of Artists (Jerry Wald)

An irresponsible country boy gets his come-uppance.
Mild, competent backwoods comedy drama introducing a teenage rave.

w Fred Gipson, Winston Miller *d* Don Siegel *ph* Charles G. Clarke *m* Cyril Mockridge

Fabian, Stuart Whitman, Carol Lynley, Arthur O'Connell, Betty Field, Royal Dano, Jane Darwell, Edgar Buchanan, Claude Akins

The Hound of the Baskervilles**
US 1939 80m bw
(TCF) Gene Markey

Sherlock Holmes solves the mystery of a supernatural hound threatening the life of a Dartmoor baronet.

Basil Rathbone's first appearance as Sherlock Holmes is in a painstaking studio production which achieves good atmosphere and preserves the flavour if not the letter of the book but is let down by a curious lack of pace.

w Ernest Pascal, *novel* Arthur Conan Doyle
d Sidney Lanfield ph Peverell Marley
m Cyril Mockridge ad Thomas Little

Basil Rathbone, Nigel Bruce, Richard Greene, Wendy Barrie, Lionel Atwill, Morton Lowry, John Carradine, Barlowe Borland, Beryl Mercer, Ralph Forbes, E. E. Clive, Eily Malyon, Mary Gordon
   'Lush dialogue, stagey sets and vintage supporting cast make it a delectable Hollywood period piece.'—*Judith Crist, 1980*
† For Rathbone's other appearances as Holmes see under *Sherlock Holmes.*

The Hound of the Baskervilles*
GB 1959 86m Technicolor
UA / Hammer (Anthony Hinds)

Spirited remake let down by dogged Hammer insistence on promises of horror and sex; good atmosphere also let down by poor colour.

w Peter Bryan d Terence Fisher ph Jack Asher m James Bernard

Peter Cushing, André Morell, Christopher Lee, Marla Landi, Ewen Solon, Francis de Wolff

The Hound of the Baskervilles
GB 1977 85m Technicolor
Hemdale / Michael White Ltd (John Goldstone)

A pointless, pitiful and vulgar spoof of an enjoyable original.

w Dudley Moore, Peter Cook, Paul Morrissey
d Paul Morrissey ph Dick Bush, John Wilcox
m Dudley Moore

Peter Cook (Sherlock Holmes), Dudley Moore (Watson), Denholm Elliot (Stapleton), Terry-Thomas (Mortimer), Joan Greenwood, Max Wall, Irene Handl, Kenneth Williams, Hugh Griffith, Roy Kinnear, Penelope Keith, Dana Gillespie, Prunella Scales, Jessie Matthews, Spike Milligan

The Hour before the Dawn
US 1944 75m bw
Paramount (William Dozier)

When a pacifist English nobleman discovers during World War II that he has married a Nazi spy, he strangles her and joins the forces. Stultifyingly absurd, badly made and acted melodrama which its author clearly wished he had never written, as it was later withdrawn from his canon.

w Michael Hogan, Lester Samuels, *novel* W. Somerset Maugham d Frank Tuttle ph John F. Seitz m Miklos Rozsa

Franchot Tone, Veronica Lake, John Sutton, Binnie Barnes, Henry Stephenson, Philip Merivale, Nils Asther, Edmund Breon

Hour of the Gun**
US 1967 101m De Luxe Panavision
UA / Mirisch / Kappa (John Sturges)

After the gunfight at the OK corral, Wyatt Earp tracks down the rest of the Clanton gang. Vividly set, slowly developed western which makes an ambiguous but forceful figure of Earp. Generally confident and interesting.

w *Edward Anhalt d John Sturges ph Lucien Ballard m* Jerry Goldsmith

James Garner, Jason Robards Jnr, Robert Ryan, Steve Ihnat, Michael Tolan, Frank Converse, Sam Melville, Monte Markham, Albert Salmi, Jon Voight, William Windom, Charles Aidman

The Hour of the Wolf*
Sweden 1967 89m bw
Svensk Filmindustri (Lars-Owe Carlberg)
original title: *Vargtimmen*

A painter, at his summer island home with his wife, is terrorized by monstrous nightmares and by memories of his own adulterous past. Rather like the gloomy side of *Smiles of a Summer Night*, this very typical Bergman melodrama doesn't quite flow as intended, and whatever its meaning may be, its surface is less entertaining than usual.

wd Ingmar Bergman ph Sven Nykvist m Mars Johan Werle

Max Von Sydow, Liv Ullmann, Ingrid Thulin, Erland Josephson

The Hour of Thirteen
GB 1952 78m bw
MGM (Hayes Goetz)

Edwardian London is shocked when policemen are stabbed one by one. Jaded Hollywood-English thriller, a remake of *The Mystery of Mr X* (qv).

w Leon Gordon, Howard Emmett Rogers,
novel X vs Rex by Philip MacDonald
d Harold French *ph* Guy Green *m* John
Addison

Peter Lawford, Dawn Addams, Roland
Culver, Derek Bond, Leslie Dwyer, Michael
Hordern, Colin Gordon, Heather Thatcher

The House across the Bay
US 1940   88m   bw
(UA) Walter Wanger

To protect her racketeer husband from his
enemies, his wife has him convicted of income
tax evasion.
Unpersuasive melodrama, a star potboiler.

w Kathryn Scola *d* Archie Mayo *ph* Merritt
Gerstad *m* Werner Janssen

Joan Bennett, George Raft, Lloyd Nolan,
Walter Pidgeon, Gladys George, June Knight

House Calls*
US 1978   98m   Technicolor
Universal (Alex Winitsky, Arlene Sellers)

A middle-aged doctor finds himself widowed
and seeks a new mate.

Spotty comedy which tries to combine
conventional romantic spats with medical
satire, and comes off only in fits and starts.

w Max Shulman, Julius J. Epstein, Alan
Mandel, Charles Shyer *d* Howard Zieff
ph David M. Walsh *m* Henry Mancini

Walter Matthau, Glenda Jackson, Art Carney,
Richard Benjamin, Candice Azzara, Thayer
David, Dick O'Neill

A House Divided*
US 1931   70m   bw
Universal (Paul Kohner)

A tough widowed fisherman seeks a new wife,
but she falls in love with his son.
Glum variation on *Desire under the Elms*,
interesting for early Wyler touches.

w John P. Clymer, Dale Van Every, John
Huston, *story* Heart and Hand by Olive
Edens *d William Wyler ph* Charles Stumar

Walter Huston, Kent Douglass, Helen
Chandler, Vivian Oakland, Frank Hagney,
Mary Foy

The House in Nightmare Park*
GB 1973   95m   Technicolor
EMI / Associated London Films

In 1907, a ham actor is asked to perform at an
old dark house in the country where an axe
murderer prowls during the night.
Standard creepy house comedy thriller, well

enough done though it would have been better
with Bob Hope.

w Clive Exton, Terry Nation *d* Peter Sykes
ph Ian Wilson *m* Harry Robinson

Frankie Howerd, Ray Milland, Hugh Burden,
Kenneth Griffith, John Bennett, Rosalie
Crutchley, Ruth Dunning

The House in the Square*
GB 1951   91m   Technicolor
   (b / w endpieces)
TCF (Sol C. Siegel)
US title: *I'll Never Forget You*

An American atomic chemist living in London
becomes his own ancestor of two hundred
years ago, and falls in love.
Slow-starting but thereafter quite acceptable
remake of *Berkeley Square* (qv), with some
interesting dialogue and a genuinely affecting
fade-out.

w Ranald MacDougall, *play* John L.
Balderston *d* Roy Baker *ph* Georges Périnal
m William Alwyn *ad* C. P. Norman

Tyrone Power, Ann Blyth, Michael Rennie,
Beatrice Campbell, Dennis Price, Raymond
Huntley, Irene Browne, Robert Atkins (as Dr
Johnson)

A House Is Not a Home
US 1964   98m   bw
(Paramount) Embassy (Clarence Greene)

The life story of New York's most famous
madam, Polly Adler.
Dismal, unappealing, laundered biopic,
cheaply made in an unconvincing period
setting.

w Russel Rouse, Clarence Greene *d* Russel
Rouse *ph* Harold Stine *m* Joseph Weiss

Shelley Winters, Robert Taylor, Cesar
Romero, Ralph Taeger, Broderick Crawford

The House of a Thousand Candles
US 1936   54m   bw

A young man must live in an unfinished
mansion to inherit under the terms of his
grandfather's will. Odd but basically
unremarkable little mystery; the title is more
interesting than the movie. Phillips Holmes,
Mae Clarke, Irving Pichel, Rosita Moreno.
Written by H. W. Hanemann and Endre
Boehm from the novel by Meredith Nicholson;
directed by Arthur Lubin; for Republic.

House of Bamboo
US 1955   102m   De Luxe   Cinemascope
TCF (Buddy Adler)

Japanese and American authorities move into undercover action against Tokyo gangsters.
Routine big-budget crime drama with only the location in its favour; a time passer, vaguely adapted from *The Street with No Name* (qv).

w Harry Kleiner *d* Samuel Fuller *ph* Joe MacDonald *m* Leigh Harline

Robert Stack, Robert Ryan, Shirley Yagamuchi, Cameron Mitchell, Sessue Hayakawa

House of Cards
US 1968 100m Techniscope
Universal / Westward (Dick Berg)

An American becomes tutor in the Paris household of a French general's widow, and finds himself a pawn in a high-powered game of international intrigue.
Good-looking location thriller which after an intricate opening settles into a *39 Steps*-style chase, but makes little of it.

w James P. Bonner, *novel* Stanley Ellin *d* John Guillermin *ph* Piero Portalupi *m* Francis Lai

George Peppard, Inger Stevens, Orson Welles, Keith Michell, William Job, Maxine Audley, Peter Bayliss

House of Dracula°
US 1945 67m bw
U–I (Paul Malvern)

As a result of being visited in one evening by Count Dracula, the Wolf Man and the Frankenstein monster, a sympathetic doctor goes on the rampage.
Mind-boggling finale to the first Universal monster cycle, with a happy ending for the Wolf Man. Cheaply made and not really inventive, but has to be seen to be believed.

w Edward T. Lowe *d* Erle C. Kenton *ph* George Robinson *m* Edgar Fairchild

Onslow Stevens, John Carradine, Lon Chaney Jnr, Glenn Strange, Lionel Atwill, Martha O'Driscoll, Jane Adams

The House of Fear see The Last Warning (1929)

House of Frankenstein°
US 1944 71m bw
U–I (Paul Malvern)

A mad doctor thaws out the monster and the Wolf Man (frozen at the end of *Frankenstein Meets the Wolf Man*) but comes to a sticky end.
Originally called *Chamber of Horrors*, this was the studio's first attempt to package its

monsters (the first two reels are about Dracula). It could have been pacier in view of the possibilities, but it has its interest.

w Edward T. Lowe, Curt Siodmak *d* Erle C. Kenton *ph* George Robinson *m* Hans Salter

Boris Karloff, John Carradine, Lon Chaney Jnr, George Zucco, J. Carrol Naish, Anne Gwynne, Elena Verdugo, Lionel Atwill, Sig Rumann, Glenn Strange

House of Numbers
US 1957 92m bw Cinemascope
MGM (Charles Schnee)

A man helps his thuggish twin brother escape from prison.
An original melodramatic idea is frittered away through slow pacing.

w Russel Rouse, Don M. Mankiewicz, *novel* Jack Finney *d* Russel Rouse *ph* George J. Folsey *m* André Previn

Jack Palance, Barbara Lang, Harold J. Stone, Edward Platt

The House of Rothschild°
US 1934 87m bw (Technicolor sequence)
Twentieth Century (William Goetz, Raymond Griffith)

The chronicles of the famous banking family at the time of the Napoleonic Wars.
Lavish historical pageant with interesting scenes and performances.

w Nunnally Johnson, *play* George Hembert Westley *d* Alfred Werker *ph* Peverell Marley *m* Alfred Newman

George Arliss, Loretta Young, Boris Karloff, Robert Young, C. Aubrey Smith, Arthur Byron, Helen Westley, Reginald Owen, Florence Arliss, Alan Mowbray, Holmes Herbert
'A good dramatic photoplay, finely presented, packed with ripe incident and quite beautiful photography.'—*C. A. Lejeune*

AAN: best picture

House of Secrets
GB 1956 97m Technicolor Vistavision Rank / Julian Wintle (Vivian A. Cox)

A naval officer is asked to impersonate a lookalike counterfeiter and work undercover to expose the gang.
Old-hat Boys' Own Paper adventure story, mindlessly watchable.

w Robert Buckner, Bryan Forbes *d* Guy Green *ph* Harry Waxman *m* Hubert Clifford

Michael Craig, Julia Arnall, Brenda de Banzie, David Kossoff, Barbara Bates, Gerard Oury, Geoffrey Keen, Anton Diffring

The House of Seven Gables
US 1940   89m   bw
Universal

In 17th-century New England, a jealous
brother sends his sister's fiancé to prison.
Flat adaptation of a grim, brooding novel; it
never grips.

w Lester Cole, *novel* Nathaniel Hawthorne
d Joe May *ph* Milton Krasner *m* Frank
Skinner

George Sanders, Margaret Lindsay, Vincent
Price, Alan Napier, Nan Grey, Cecil
Kellaway, Dick Foran, Miles Mander

AAN: Frank Skinner

House of Strangers**
US 1949   101m   bw
TCF (Sol C. Siegel)

An Italian-American banker who rigidly
controls his three sons is arrested for illegal
practices, and the family ties slacken.
Interesting ethnic melodrama with good script
and performances; much remade, e.g. as
Broken Lance.

w *Philip Yordan, novel* Jerome Weidman
d Joseph L. Mankiewicz *ph* Milton Krasner
m Daniele Amfitheatrof

Edward G. Robinson, Richard Conte, Susan
Hayward, *Luther Adler*, Paul Valentine,
Efrem Zimbalist Jnr, Debra Paget, Hope
Emerson, Esther Minciotti, Diana Douglas

The House of the Angel**
Argentina 1957   73m   bw
Argentina Sono Film (Leopoldo Torre
  Nilsson)
original title: *La Casa del Angel*

A repressed girl is obsessed for life by the
shame of her first love affair.
Fascinating minor classic in a heavily
Wellesian style.

w Beatriz Guido, Leopoldo Torre Nilsson,
Martin Rodriguez Mentasti, *novel* Beatriz
Guido *d Leopoldo Torre Nilsson ph* Anibal
Gonzalez Paz *m* Juan Carlos Paz

Elsa Daniel, Lautaro Murua, Guillermo
Battaglia

'The first major work of a director of
individual vision and strongly national style.'—
Robert Vas, MFB

The House of the Arrow
GB 1940   66m   bw

A wealthy Frenchwoman is murdered and her
English companion is under suspicion. A case
for Inspector Hanaud; very tolerable
whodunnit. Keneth Kent, Diana Churchill,

Belle Chrystall, Peter Murray Hill, Clifford
Evans, Catherine Lacey. Written by Doreen
Montgomery, from the novel by A. E. W.
Mason; directed by Harold French; for ABPC.
(A previous version in 1930 starred Dennis
Neilson Terry and was directed by Leslie
Hiscott.)

House of the Damned*
US 1963   63m   bw
TCF / Associated Producers (Maury Dexter)

An architect is asked to make a survey of an
old empty castle, but he and his wife find that
someone or something is in hiding there.
Corny but mildly effective second feature with
a few neat touches.

w Harry Spalding *d Maury Dexter ph* John
Nickolaus Jnr *m* Henry Vars

Ronald Foster, Merry Anders

House of the Seven Hawks
GB 1959   92m   bw
MGM / David E. Rose

An American adventurer becomes involved in
a search by criminals for buried Nazi loot.
Cliché-ridden thick ear, adequately produced
but of no interest.

w Jo Eisinger, *novel* The House of Seven Flies
by Victor Canning *d* Richard Thorpe *ph* Ted
Scaife *m* Clifton Parker

Robert Taylor, Nicole Maurey, Linda
Christian, Donald Wolfit, David Kossoff, Eric
Pohlmann, Gerard Heinz

House of Usher*
US 1960   85m   Eastmancolor
  Cinemascope
AIP / Alta Vista (Roger Corman)
GB title: *The Fall of the House of Usher*

The last of the Usher line, prone to catalepsy,
is buried alive by her brother and returns to
wreak vengeance.
Stylish but grottily-coloured low-budget horror
which started the Poe cycle of the sixties. A bit
slow, it would have worked better in the
standard screen ratio, but there is a tense and
spectacular finale.

w Richard Matheson, *story* Edgar Allan Poe
d Roger Corman *ph* Floyd Crosby *m* Les
Baxter *ad* Daniel Haller

Vincent Price, Myrna Fahey, Mark Damon,
Harry Ellerbe

House of Wax**
US 1953   88m   Warnercolor   3-D
Warner (Bryan Foy)

Mutilated in a fire at his wax museum, a
demented sculptor arranges a supply of dead

bodies to be covered in wax for exhibition at his new showplace.

Spirited remake of *The Mystery of the Wax Museum* (qv); as a piece of screen narrative it leaves much to be desired, but the sudden shocks are well managed, perhaps because this is the first Grade-A 3-D film, packed with gimmicks irrelevant to the story and originally shown with stereophonic sound.

w Crane Wilbur *d* André de Toth *ph* Bert Glennon *m* David Buttolph

Vincent Price (whose horror career began here), Carolyn Jones, Paul Picerni, Phyllis Kirk, Frank Lovejoy

† The director could not see the 3-D effect, being blind in one eye.

House of Women
US 1962 85m bw

A pregnant woman is sent to prison for a robbery she didn't commit. Loose remake of *Caged*, with very little sense or vigour. Shirley Knight, Andrew Duggan, Constance Ford, Barbara Nichols, Margaret Hayes. Written by Crane Wilbur; directed by Walter Doniger; for Warner.

House on Haunted Hill
US 1958 75m bw
Allied Artists / William Castle

An old house which has seen several murders is the setting for a millionaire's party.
Gimmick ghost story with some (unexplained) gruesome moments; the most outlandish of its producer's cheapjack trick films (*Thirteen Ghosts*, *The Tingler*, *Macabre*, etc), it was originally billed as being in Emergo, which meant that at an appropriately horrific moment an illuminated skeleton on wires was suddenly trundled over the heads of the audience.

w Robb White *d* William Castle *ph* Carl Guthrie *m* Von Dexter

Vincent Price, Richard Long, Carol Ohmart, Alan Marshal, Elisha Cook Jnr

The House on 92nd Street****
US 1945 88m bw
TCF (*Louis de Rochemont*)

During World War II in New York, the FBI routs Nazi spies after the atomic bomb formula.
Highly influential documentary-style 'now it can be told' spy drama, which borrowed the feel of its producer's *March of Time* series and applied them to a fairly true story set on genuine locations though with a modicum of fictional mystery and suspense.

Highly effective in its own right, it looked forward to *The Naked City* three years later; the later film unaccountably got most of the credit for taking Hollywood out into the open air.

w Barre Lyndon, Charles G. Booth, John Monks Jnr *d* Henry Hathaway *ph* Norbert Brodine *m* David Buttolph

William Eythe, Lloyd Nolan, Signe Hasso, *Leo G. Carroll*, Gene Lockhart, Lydia St Clair, Harry Bellaver

'Recommended entertainment for those who believe that naïve Americans are no match for wily Europeans in the spy trade, and for those who just like their movies to move.'—*Time*

'Imagine an issue of *The March of Time*. The hard agglomeration of fact; the road drill style; the voice. Prolong it to four times its usual length, throw in a fictional climax, and there you have *The House on 92nd Street*.'—*William Whitebait, New Statesman*

AA: original story (Charles G. Booth)

The House on Telegraph Hill
US 1951 93m bw
TCF (Robert Bassler)

A woman in a concentration camp assumes her dead friend's identity so that on release she can be sent to America; but murder threatens there.
Modernized amalgam of *Gaslight* and *Suspicion*, not as good as either, but the complexities of the story hold adequate interest.

w Elick Moll, Frank Partos, *novel* Dana Lyon *d* Robert Wise *ph* Lucien Ballard *m* Sol Kaplan

Richard Basehart, Valentina Cortesa, William Lundigan, Fay Baker, Gordon Gebert, Steve Geray

The House that Dripped Blood*
GB 1970 102m Eastmancolor
Amicus (Milton Subotsky)

A Scotland Yard man investigating a disappearance is led to a house with a murderous history.
Quartet of stories in *Dead of Night* style, neatly made and generally pleasing despite a low level of originality in the writing.

w Robert Bloch *d* Peter John Duffell *ph* Robert Parslow *m* Michael Dress

John Bennett, Christopher Lee, Peter Cushing, Denholm Elliott, Joanna Dunham, Nyree Dawn Porter, Jon Pertwee, Ingrid Pitt

Houseboat
US 1958   110m   Technicolor
Vistavision
Paramount / Scribe (Jack Rose)

A widower with three children engages a maid who is really a socialite, and they all set up house on a boat.

Artificial sentimental comedy with A-1 credits but little style or bite.

w Melville Shavelson, Jack Rose d Melville Shavelson ph Ray June m George Duning

Cary Grant, Sophia Loren, Martha Hyer, Eduardo Ciannelli, Harry Guardino

'The kind of picture to which you can take your stuffy maiden aunt, your wicked sophisticated uncle and your ten-year-old child, and they will all have a wonderful time.'—*Ruth Waterbury, Los Angeles Examiner*

AAN: script; song 'Almost In Your Arms' (*m / ly* Jay Livingston, Ray Evans)

The Housekeeper's Daughter*
US 1939   71m   bw
Hal Roach

A gangster's moll returns to mama for a visit and falls in love with the stuffy son of the household.

Zany crime farce which too often lets its zip fade, but atones in a crazy firework finale.

w Rian James, Gordon Douglas, *novel* Donald Henderson Clarke d Hal Roach ph Norbert Brodine m Amedeo de Filippi

Joan Bennett, John Hubbard, Adolphe Menjou, William Gargan, George E. Stone, Peggy Wood, Donald Meek, Marc Lawrence, Lilian Bond, Victor Mature, Luis Alberni

Housemaster*
GB 1938   95m   bw
ABPC (Walter C. Mycroft)

A schoolmaster sides with his boys against the new headmaster's dictatorial methods.

Pleasing photographed play with all concerned in good form.

w Dudley Leslie, Elizabeth Meehan, *play* Bachelor Born by Ian Hay d Herbert Brenon

Otto Kruger, Diana Churchill, Phillips Holmes, Joyce Barbour, Kynaston Reeves, Rene Ray, Walter Hudd, John Wood, Cecil Parker, Michael Shepley, Jimmy Hanley

Housewife
US 1934   69m   bw
Warner

For an advertising copywriter, success almost brings divorce.

Modestly efficient romantic programmer of its day.

w Manuel Seff, Lillie Hayward d Alfred E. Green ph William Rees m Leo F. Forbstein

Bette Davis, George Brent, Ann Dvorak, John Halliday, Ruth Donnelly, Hobart Cavanaugh, Robert Barrat, Phil Regan

'The dramatic punches are not merely telegraphed, but radioed.'—*Frank S. Nugent*

How Do I Love Thee
US 1970   109m   Metrocolor
ABC (Robert Enders, Everett Freeman)

A philosophy professor recalls the odd career of his atheist father.

Curious comedy about an eccentric and his family relationships, a kind of *Cheaper by the Dozen* with religion added. Not on in 1970.

w Everett Freeman, *novel* Let Me Count the Ways by Peter De Vries d Michael Gordon ph Russell Metty m Randy Sparks

Jackie Gleason, Maureen O'Hara, Shelley Winters, Rick Lenz, Rosemary Forsyth

'Nauseated embarrassment for participants and onlookers alike.'—*Judith Crist*

How Green Was My Valley***
US 1941   118m   bw
TCF (Darryl F. Zanuck)

Memories of childhood in a Welsh mining village.

Prettified and unconvincing but dramatically very effective tearjerker in the style which lasted from Cukor's *David Copperfield* to *The Green Years*. High production values here add a touch of extra class, turning the result into a Hollywood milestone despite its intrinsic inadequacies.

w Philip Dunne, *novel* Richard Llewellyn d *John Ford* ph *Arthur Miller* m Alfred Newman

Walter Pidgeon, Maureen O'Hara, Roddy McDowall, Donald Crisp, Sara Allgood, Anna Lee, John Loder, Barry Fitzgerald, Patric Knowles, Morton Lowry, Arthur Shields, Frederic Worlock

'Perfection of cinematic narrative . . . pure visual action, pictures powerfully composed, dramatically photographed, smoothly and eloquently put together.'—*James Shelley Hamilton*

AA: best picture; John Ford; Arthur Miller; Donald Crisp
AAN: Philip Dunne; Alfred Newman; Sara Allgood

How I Won the War

GB 1967 110m Eastmancolor
UA / Petersham (Richard Lester)

During World War II an earnest young man becomes an officer and survives many tribulations including the death of his comrades.

Appalling kaleidoscope of black comedy and the director's own brand of uncontrolled cinematic zaniness, with echoes of *Candide* and *Oh What a Lovely War!* Just the way to alienate a paying audience.

w Charles Wood, *novel* Patrick Ryan *d* Richard Lester *ph* David Watkin *m* Ken Thorne

Michael Crawford, John Lennon, Roy Kinnear, Lee Montague, Jack McGowran, Michael Hordern, Jack Hedley, Karl Michael Vogler, Ronald Lacey, James Cossins, Alexander Knox

'Pretentious tomfoolery.'—*John Simon*
'One feels that Lester has bitten off more than he can chew . . . the ideas misfire, lost somewhere between the paper on which they were conceived and the celluloid on which they finally appear.'—*MFB*

How Sweet It Is*

US 1968 98m Technicolor Panavision
Warner / Cherokee / National General
(Garry Marshall, Jerry Belson)

Suspicious of their son's intentions towards his girl friend on a European holiday, a middle-aged American couple decide to follow.

Good-looking, rather silly comedy, plain spoken in the modern manner but without much entertainment value except when farce gets the upper hand.

w Garry Marshall, Jerry Belson, *novel* The Girl in the Turquoise Bikini by Muriel Resnik *d* Jerry Paris *ph* Lucien Ballard *m* Pat Williams

James Garner, Debbie Reynolds, Maurice Ronet, Paul Lynde, Marcel Dalio, Terry-Thomas, Donald Losby, Hilarie Thompson

'One of those slender marital farces in which the behaviour of the adults is consistently more juvenile than that of the teenagers.'—*MFB*

How the West Was Won*

US 1962 162m Technicolor Cinerama
MGM / Cinerama (Bernard Smith)

Panoramic western following the daughter of a pioneering family from youth (1830) to old age, with several half-relevant stories along the way.

Muddled spectacular with splendid set-pieces but abysmal dullness in between, especially if not seen in three-strip Cinerama (the Cinemascope prints are muddy and still show the dividing lines). An all-star fairground show of its time.

w James R. Webb *d* Henry Hathaway (first half), John Ford (Civil War), George Marshall (train) *ph* William Daniels, Milton Krasner, Charles Lang Jnr, Joseph La Shelle *m* Alfred Newman *ad* George W. Davis, William Ferrari, Addison Hehr

Debbie Reynolds, Carroll Baker, Lee J. Cobb, Henry Fonda, Carolyn Jones, Karl Malden, Gregory Peck, George Peppard, Robert Preston, James Stewart, Eli Wallach, John Wayne, Richard Widmark, Brigid Bazlen, Walter Brennan, David Brian, Andy Devine, Raymond Massey, Agnes Moorehead, Henry Morgan, Thelma Ritter, Russ Tamblyn, Spencer Tracy (narrator)

'That goddamned Cinerama . . . do you know a waist shot is as close as you could get with that thing?'—*Henry Hathaway*

AA: James R. Webb
AAN: best picture; photography; music

How to Be Very Very Popular

US 1955 89m De Luxe Cinemascope
TCF (Nunnally Johnson)

Two belly dancers on the run from gangsters hide out in a co-ed college.

Wacky remake of *She Loves Me Not* (qv); tries hard for a vein of freewheeling lunacy but only occasionally achieves it. A few numbers might have helped.

wd Nunnally Johnson *ph* Milton Krasner *m* Cyril Mockridge

Betty Grable, Sheree North, *Charles Coburn*, Robert Cummings, Orson Bean, Fred Clark, Tommy Noonan

How to Beat the High Cost of Living

US 1980 110m Movielab

Three middle-class women take to robbery when they can't make the housekeeping balance. Undercast, reprehensible and almost totally unfunny alleged comedy. Susan Saint James, Jane Curtin, Jessica Lange, Richard Benjamin, Fred Willard, Eddie Albert. Written by Robert Kaufman; directed by Robert Scheerer; for Filmways.

How to Commit Marriage

US 1969 98m Technicolor
Cinerama / Naho (Bill Larence)

A couple decide to divorce, with repercussions on their family and in-laws.
Tiresome generation-gap comedy.

w Ben Starr, Michael Kanin *d* Norman Panama *ph* Charles Lang *m* Joseph J. Lilley

Bob Hope, Jackie Gleason, Jane Wyman, Leslie Nielsen, Maureen Arthur, Paul Stewart, Tina Louise

How to Marry a Millionaire**
US 1953   96m   Technicolor
   Cinemascope
TCF (Nunnally Johnson)

Three girls rent an expensive New York apartment and set out to trap millionaires.
Cinemascope's first attempt at modern comedy was not quite as disastrous as might have been expected, largely because of the expensiveness of everything and the several stars still brightly twinkling, but the handling of this variation on the old *Golddiggers* theme, while entirely amiable, is dramatically very slack.

w Nunnally Johnson *d* Jean Negulesco
ph Joe MacDonald *md* Alfred Newman
m Cyril Mockridge

Lauren Bacall, Marilyn Monroe, Betty Grable, *William Powell*, Cameron Mitchell, David Wayne, Rory Calhoun, Alex D'Arcy, Fred Clark

How to Murder a Rich Uncle
GB 1957   80m   bw   Cinemascope
Columbia / Warwick (Ronald Kinnoch)

An impoverished nobleman decides to murder his rich old uncle.
Feebly-handled black comedy which does not come off at all despite a highly talented cast.

w John Paxton, *play* Il faut tuer Julie by Dider Daix *d* Nigel Patrick *ph* Ted Moore

Nigel Patrick, Charles Coburn, *Katie Johnson*, Wendy Hiller, Anthony Newley, Athene Seyler, Michael Caine, Noel Hood, Kenneth Fortescue

How to Murder Your Wife*
US 1964   118m   Technicolor
UA / Murder Inc (George Axelrod)

A strip cartoonist tests out his violent scenes in real life; when his wife disappears he finds himself accused of murder.
Amusing preliminaries give way to dreary plot complications and an overlong courtroom scene. Leave after the first hour.

w George Axelrod *d* Richard Quine
ph Harry Stradling *m* Neal Hefti *pd Richard Sylbert*

Jack Lemmon, Virna Lisi, *Terry-Thomas, Eddie Mayehoff*, Sidney Blackmer, Claire Trevor

How to Save a Marriage and Ruin Your Life
US 1968   102m   Technicolor
   Panavision
Columbia / Nob Hill (Stanley Shapiro)

An attorney takes it upon himself to convince his friend of the infidelity of the friend's mistress . . .
Tedious sex antics without any sex; a few smiles are not enough to endear it.

w Stanley Shapiro, Nate Monaster *d* Fielder Cook *ph* Lee Garmes *m* Michel Legrand

Dean Martin, Eli Wallach, Stella Stevens, Anne Jackson, Betty Field, Jack Albertson, Katharine Bard
'Another variation on Hollywood's patent version of the Restoration comedy, which as usual abandons the lustiness of its 17th-century prototype in favour of guilt-ridden lechery and a fundamental respect for the married state.'—*MFB*

How to Steal a Million*
US 1966   127m   De Luxe   Panavision
TCF / World Wide (Fred Kohlmar)

The daughter of an art forger mistakenly involves a private detective in a robbery.
High-class but rather boring romantic comedy; the credits promise much but interest wanes quickly owing to uncertain handling.

w Harry Kurnitz *d* William Wyler *ph* Charles Lang *m* Johnny Williams

Audrey Hepburn, Peter O'Toole, Charles Boyer, Hugh Griffith, Eli Wallach, Fernand Gravet, Marcel Dalio
'Terribly wordy and slow . . . Wyler hasn't got the touch nowadays.'—*Sight and Sound*

How to Succeed in Business without Really Trying**
US 1967   121m   De Luxe   Panavision
UA / Mirisch (David Swift)

A window cleaner cajoles his way to the top of a New York company.
Cinematically uninventive but otherwise brisk and glowing adaptation of a sharp, slick Broadway musical.

w David Swift, *musical book* Abe Burrows, Jack Weinstock, Willie Gilbert, *book* Shepherd Mead *d* David Swift *ph* Burnett Guffey *m / ly Frank Loesser *ch* Dale Moreda after Bob Fosse

Robert Morse, Rudy Vallee, Michele Lee, Anthony Teague, Maureen Arthur, Murray Matheson
'Shows how taste and talent can succeed in bringing a stage musical to the screen with its virtues intact.'—*John Cutts*

The Howards of Virginia
US 1940 117m bw
Columbia (Frank Lloyd)
GB title: *The Tree of Liberty*

A Virginian surveyor finds himself involved in the Revolutionary War.

Historical cavalcade in which central miscasting seems to cast a shadow of artifice over the whole. Interesting but seldom stimulating.

w Sidney Buchman, *novel* The Tree of Liberty by Elizabeth Page d Frank Lloyd ph Bert Glennon m Richard Hageman

Cary Grant, Martha Scott, Cedric Hardwicke, Alan Marshal, Richard Carlson, Paul Kelly, Irving Bacon, Elizabeth Risdon

AAN: Richard Hageman

Huckleberry Finn
US 1931 71m bw
Paramount

The river adventures of Mark Twain's scapegrace hero.

Adequate early talkie family film.

w Grover Jones, William Slavens McNutt d Norman Taurog ph David Abel

Jackie Coogan, Junior Durkin, Mitzi Green, Jackie Searl, Eugene Pallette

Huckleberry Finn**
US 1939 90m bw
MGM (Joseph L. Mankiewicz)

Solidly competent remake with excellent production values and several entertaining sequences.

w Hugo Butler d Richard Thorpe ph John Seitz m Franz Waxman

Mickey Rooney, Walter Connolly, William Frawley, Rex Ingram

Huckleberry Finn*
US 1960 107m Metrocolor
MGM (Samuel Goldwyn Jnr)
aka: *The Adventures of Huckleberry Finn*

Another patchy remake.

w James Lee d Michael Curtiz ph Ted McCord m Jerome Moross

Eddie Hodges, Tony Randall, Archie Moore, Neville Brand, Judy Canova, Buster Keaton, Andy Devine

Huckleberry Finn
US 1974 118m De Luxe Panavision
UA / Apjac / Readers Digest (Robert Greenhut)

Ambitious but lustreless version of the famous story, with songs.

w / ly / m Richard M. Sherman, Robert B. Sherman d J. Lee-Thompson ph Laszlo Kovacs pd Philip Jeffries

Jeff East, Paul Winfield, David Wayne, Harvey Korman, Arthur O'Connell, Gary Merrill, Natalie Trundy

'It expires in a morass of treacle.'—*Tom Milne*

'It transforms a great work of fiction into something bland, boring and tasteless.'— *Michael Billington, Illustrated London News*

The Hucksters**
US 1947 115m bw
MGM (Arthur Hornblow Jnr)

Back from the war, an advertising executive finds it difficult to put up with his clients' tantrums.

Good topical entertainment which still entertains and gives a good impression of its period.

w Luther Davis, *novel* Frederic Wakeman d Jack Conway ph Harold Rosson m Lennie Hayton

Clark Gable, Deborah Kerr, Ava Gardner, *Sidney Greenstreet*, Adolphe Menjou, Keenan Wynn, Edward Arnold, Aubrey Mather

'A good picture, quick and to the point.'— *Photoplay*

Hud***
US 1963 112m bw Panavision
Paramount / Salem / Dover (Martin Ritt, Irving Ravetch)

Life is hard on a Texas ranch, and the veteran owner is not helped by his sexually arrogant ne'er-do-well son, who is a bad influence on the household.

Superbly set in an arid landscape, this incisive character drama is extremely well directed and acted but somehow lacks the touch of greatness.

w Irving Ravetch, Harriet Frank, *novel* Horseman Pass By by Larry McMurty d Martin Ritt ph James Wong Howe m Elmer Bernstein

Paul Newman, Patricia Neal, Melvyn Douglas, Brandon de Wilde

AA: James Wong Howe; Patricia Neal; Melvyn Douglas
AAN: script; Martin Ritt; Paul Newman

Huddle
US 1932 104m bw

A steel worker's son makes good at Harvard, and wants to marry out of his class. Would-be serious class drama which fell over its own feet. Ramon Novarro, Madge Evans, Una

Merkel, Conrad Nagel, Arthur Byron, Cliff Edwards. Written by Robert Johnson, C. Gardner Sullivan, Arthur Hyman and Walton Smith; directed by Sam Wood; for MGM. (GB title: *The Impossible Lover*.)

Hudson's Bay**
US 1940 95m bw
TCF (Kenneth MacGowan)

Pierre Radisson, a French Canadian trapper, opens up millions of acres of northern wilderness for England.
Well-made historical saga with good production and performances.

w Lamar Trotti d Irving Pichel ph Peverell Marley, George Barnes *m* Alfred Newman *ad* Richard Day, Wiard B. Ihnen

Paul Muni, Laird Cregar, Gene Tierney, John Sutton, Virginia Field, Vincent Price (as King Charles II), Nigel Bruce, Morton Lowry, Robert Greig, Frederic Worlock, Montagu Love

Hue and Cry***
GB 1946 82m bw
Ealing (Henry Cornelius)

East End boys discover that their favourite boys' paper is being used by crooks to pass information.
The first 'Ealing comedy' uses vivid London locations as background for a sturdy comic plot with a climax in which the criminals are rounded up by thousands of boys swarming over dockland.

w T. E. B. Clarke d Charles Crichton ph Douglas Slocombe, John Seaholme *m* Georges Auric

Alastair Sim, Jack Warner, Harry Fowler, Valerie White, Frederick Piper
   'Refreshing, bloodtingling and disarming.'—*Richard Winnington*

Hugo the Hippo
US 1975 78m colour
Brut (Robert Halmi)

An independently-minded hippo combats a Zanzibar magician.
Uninventive cartoon feature, endearing neither in characterization nor in draughtsmanship.

w Thomas Baum *d* William Feigenbaum *md* Bert Keyes

Hugs and Kisses*
Sweden 1966 96m bw
Sandrews (Göran Lindgren)
original title: *Puss och Kram*

A destitute bohemian takes over the house and the wife of the old executive friend who shelters him out of pity.
Rather like a comedy version of the Dirk Stroeve section of *The Moon and Sixpence*, this sophisticated film came under censorship fire for depicting the first full frontal female.

wd Jonas Cornell *ph* Lars Swanberg *m* Bengt Ernryd

Sven-Bertil Taube, Agneta Ekmanner, Hakan Serner
   'The brilliance of the film lies in the way humour and sadness are kept in perfect equilibrium.'—*MFB*

Huis Clos*
France 1954 99m bw
Films Marceau

Two women and a man die, go to hell, and are locked up for ever in an elegant room.
Rather flat intellectual fantasy from a play which made great waves when first performed.

w Pierre Laroche, *play* Jean-Paul Sartre *d* Jacqueline Audry *ph* Robert Juillard *m* Joseph Kosma

Arletty, Frank Villard, Gaby Sylvia
   'Without the ecstasy, terror and poetic imagination of a Cocteau, the subject becomes a fatally stationary one.'—*Peter John Dyer, MFB*

The Human Comedy*
US 1943 117m bw
MGM (Clarence Brown)

In a small town during the war, a telegram boy brings tragedy to others and is touched by it himself.
Gooey, sentimental morale booster in the best MGM tradition, a variant on the Hardy family series but with all the pretensions of its author.

w Howard Estabrook, *novel* William Saroyan *d Clarence Brown ph* Harry Stradling *m* Herbert Stothart

Mickey Rooney, Frank Morgan, James Craig, Marsha Hunt, Jackie Jenkins, Fay Bainter, Ray Collins, Van Johnson, Donna Reed
   'The dignity and simplicity of the ideas shade off into cheap pretentiousness.'—*Bosley Crowther*
   'The best one can say of it . . . is that it tries on the whole to be "faithful" to Saroyan; not invariably a good idea.'—*James Agee*
   'The Saroyan touch leaves nothing ordinary: the film is electric with the joy of life.'—*Time*

AA: original story
AAN: best picture; Clarence Brown; Harry Stradling; Mickey Rooney

Human Desire

US 1954 90m bw
Columbia (Lewis J. Rachmil)

A jealous railway official forces his wife to
help him murder her suspected lover.
Drab and unattractive remake of *La Bête
Humaine*.

w Alfred Hayes *d* Fritz Lang *ph* Burnett
Guffey *m* Daniele Amfitheatrof

Gloria Grahame, Glenn Ford, Broderick
Crawford, Edgar Buchanan

The Human Factor

GB 1979 114m Technicolor
Panavision
(Rank) Wheel / Sigma / Otto Preminger

An innocent man is suspected of being the
'mole' in the Foreign Office.
Quietly sardonic scenes of diplomatic chess are
played far too broadly and literally in this
ill-advised and poorly executed foray into the
serious spy scene, which despite its stars
becomes merely risible before the end.

w Tom Stoppard, *novel* Graham Greene
d Otto Preminger *ph* Mike Malloy
m Richard and Gary Logan

Nicol Williamson, Richard Attenborough,
Derek Jacobi, Robert Morley, John Gielgud,
Ann Todd, Richard Vernon, Joop Doderer,
Iman

'Unfortunately, Preminger stages it all as if
he was just trying to get all the actors through
their line readings in under two hours,
allowing no breathing room or time for
character nuance in a tale which resolutely
calls for quiet moments.'—*Variety*

Humanoids of the Deep

US 1980 81m Metrocolor
New World (Martin B. Cohen)
GB title: *Monster*

Gruesome amphibious creatures rise from the
ocean to stalk and destroy the most nubile
women in sight.
Lurid, nonsensical but very violent horror
flick, with much rape and nudity; like a
Corman quickie of the fifties but with added
gore.

w Frederick James *d* Barbara Peeters (*sic*)
ph Daniele Lacambre *m* James Horner
costumes Rob Bottin

Vic Morrow, Doug McClure, Ann Turkel

Humoresque**

US 1947 125m bw
Warner (Jerry Wald)

An ambitious violinist gets emotionally
involved with his wealthy patroness.
Lush soaper about suffering in high society,
complete with tragic end and lashings of
classical music (Isaac Stern on the sound
track).

w Clifford Odets, Zachary Gold, *novel* Fannie
Hurst *d Jean Negulesco ph Ernest Haller*
md Franz Waxman

Joan Crawford, John Garfield, Oscar Levant,
J. Carrol Naish, Joan Chandler, Tom
D'Andrea, Craig Stevens, Ruth Nelson

AAN: Franz Waxman

The Hunchback of Notre Dame**

US 1923 120m approx (24 fps) bw
silent
Universal

The deformed Notre Dame bellringer rescues
a gypsy girl from the evil intentions of her
guardian.
Victorian gothic version with a riveting star
performance.

w Percy Poore Sheehan, Edward T. Lowe Jnr,
novel Notre Dame de Paris by Victor Hugo
d Wallace Worsley *ph* Robert S. Newhard,
Tony Kornman

Lon Chaney, Patsy Ruth Miller, Norman
Kerry, Ernest Torrence, Gladys Brockwell,
Kate Lester, Brandon Hurst, Tully Marshall

The Hunchback of Notre Dame****

US 1939 117m bw
RKO (Pandro S. Berman)

This superb remake is one of the best
examples of Hollywood expertise at work: art
direction, set construction, costumes, camera,
lighting and above all direction brilliantly
support an irresistible story and bravura
acting.

w Sonya Levien, Bruno Frank *d* William
Dieterle *ph Joseph H. August m Alfred
Newman ad Van Nest Polglase*

*Charles Laughton, Cedric Hardwicke,
Maureen O'Hara, Edmond O'Brien, Thomas
Mitchell, Harry Davenport*, Walter Hampden,
Alan Marshal, George Zucco, Katherine
Alexander, Fritz Leiber, Rod la Rocque

'Has seldom been bettered as an evocation
of medieval life.'—*John Baxter, 1968*
'It exceeds in sheer magnificence any similar
film in history. Sets are vast and rich in detail,
crowds are immense, and camera uses of both
are versatile, varied and veracious.'—*Motion
Picture Herald*

† Other versions: *Esmeralda* (1906, French);
Notre Dame de Paris (1911, French); *The
Darling of Paris* (1917, US, with Theda Bara);
and see above and below.

AAN: Alfred Newman

The Hunchback of Notre Dame
France / Italy 1956 107m
    Eastmancolor Cinemascope
Paris Films / Panitalia (Robert and
    Raymond Hakim)

Crude international rehash with nothing to
commend it, though the script before dubbing
may have been interesting.

w Jacques Prévert, Jean Aurenche *d* Jean
Delannoy *ph* Michel Kelber *m* Georges
Auric

Anthony Quinn, Gina Lollobrigida, Jean
Danet, Alain Cuny, Robert Hirsch

The Hundred Pound Window
GB 1943 84m bw
Warner

A racecourse clerk becomes involved with
gamblers who bribe him to rig the totalizator,
but he finally exposes them.
Routine programmer notable only for giving a
leading role to an old character actor.

w Abem Finkel, Brock Williams, Rodney
Ackland *d* Brian Desmond Hurst *ph* Otto
Heller

Frederick Leister, Mary Clare, Anne
Crawford, Richard Attenborough, David
Farrar, Niall MacGinnis, David Hutcheson

Hungry Hill
GB 1946 92m bw
GFD / Two Cities (William Sistrom)

An Irish family feud spans three generations.
Rather uninteresting costume melodrama.

w Daphne du Maurier, Terence Young,
Francis Crowdy *d* Brian Desmond Hurst
ph Desmond Dickinson

Margaret Lockwood, Dennis Price, Cecil
Parker, Michael Denison, F. J. McCormick,
Dermot Walsh, Jean Simmons, Eileen Herlie,
Siobhan McKenna, Eileen Crowe, Dan
O'Herlihy

Hunted*
GB 1952 84m bw
GFD / Independent Artists (Julian Wintle)
US title: *The Stranger in Between*

A runaway boy joins forces with a runaway
murderer, and the latter sacrifices himself for
the boy's safety.

Predictable pattern melodrama, nicely made
and acted.

w Jack Whittingham *d* Charles Crichton
ph Eric Cross *m* Hubert Clifford

Dirk Bogarde, Jon Whiteley, Kay Walsh,
Elizabeth Sellars, Frederick Piper, Geoffrey
Keen, Julian Somers

Hunted Men*
US 1938 67m bw
Paramount

A killer on the run moves into a private home
and is outwitted by the head of the house.
Competent second feature which sticks in the
memory.

w Horace McCoy, William R. Lipman
d Louis King *ph* Victor Milner

Lloyd Nolan, Lynne Overman, Mary Carlisle,
J. Carrol Naish, Anthony Quinn, Dorothy
Peterson

The Hunter
US 1980 117m Metrocolor
Paramount / Rastar / Mort Engelberg

Episodes in the violent career of an urban
bounty hunter.
The action scenes salvage a mysteriously banal
screenplay full of continuity lapses and
unexplained characters.

w Ted Leighton, Peter Hyams
book Christopher Keane, and the life of Ralph
Thorson *d* Buzz Kulik *ph* Fred J.
Koenekamp *m* Michel Legrand

Steve McQueen (his last film), Eli Wallach,
Kathryn Harrold, LeVar Burton, Ben Johnson

The Hunters
US 1958 108m De Luxe Cinemascope
TCF (Dick Powell)

A fearless American pilot is sent to Korea on
a special mission.
Standard war thriller, good to look at when
airborne but pretty boring on the ground;
propaganda element very strong.

w Wendell Mayes *d* Dick Powell *ph* Charles
G. Clarke *m* Paul Sawtell

Robert Mitchum, Robert Wagner, Richard
Egan, Mai Britt

The Hunting Party
US 1971 108m De Luxe
UA / Brighton / Levy–Gardner–Levy

A sadistic Texas baron sets out to shoot one
by one the outlaws who have kidnapped his
wife.

Crude, brutish and repellent melodrama: the epitome of permissiveness, replete with gore, rape and sadism.

w William Norton, Gilbert Alexander, Lou Morheim *d* Don Medford *ph* Cecilio Paniagua *m* Riz Ortolani

Gene Hackman, Candice Bergen, Oliver Reed

The Hurricane**
US 1937 110m bw
Samuel Goldwyn (Merritt Hulburd)

The simple life on a South Pacific island is disrupted, not only by a vindictive governor but by a typhoon.
Tolerable island melodrama with a spectacular climax and a generally good cast.

w Dudley Nichols, Oliver H. P. Garrett, *novel* Charles Nordhof, James Norman Hall *d John Ford, Stuart Heisler ph Bert Glennon m* Alfred Newman

Dorothy Lamour, Jon Hall, *C. Aubrey Smith, Mary Astor, Raymond Massey, Thomas Mitchell*, John Carradine, Jerome Cowan
† Remade in 1979.

AAN: Alfred Newman; Thomas Mitchell

Hurricane
US 1979 120m Technicolor Todd AO 70
Dino de Laurentiis / Famous Films (Lorenzo Semple Jnr)

A remake of the 1937 film, lacking the style, the innocence, and even the technical splendour.

w Lorenzo Semple Jnr *d* Jan Troell *ph* Sven Nykvist *m* Nino Rota *pd* Danilo Donati

Jason Robards, Mia Farrow, Trevor Howard, Max Von Sydow, Dayton Ka'ne, Timothy Bottoms, James Keach

Hurricane Smith
US 1952 90m Technicolor
Paramount / Nat Holt

An adventurer charters a boat to find a South Sea treasure but the boat owner turns the tables on him.
Standard thick ear with plenty of action.

w Frank Gruber *d* Jerry Hopper *ph* Ray Rennahan *m* Paul Sawtell

John Ireland, Yvonne de Carlo, James Craig, Forrest Tucker

Hurry Sundown
US 1967 146m Technicolor Panavision
Paramount / Sigma (Otto Preminger)

Post-war racial problems in Georgia farmland, with degenerate whites and noble blacks.
Incredibly cliché-ridden epic melodrama with action and sex asides, from a rock bottom bestseller. It long outstays its welcome even for unintentional hilarity.

w Thomas C. Ryan, Horton Foote, *novel* K. B. Gilden *d* Otto Preminger *ph* Loyal Griggs, Milton Krasner *m* Hugo Montenegro

Jane Fonda, Michael Caine, Rex Ingram, Diahann Carroll, Burgess Meredith, John Philip Law, Robert Hooks, Faye Dunaway, Beah Richards, George Kennedy, Madeleine Sherwood

'Critic Wilfrid Sheed wrote recently that no film is ever so bad that you can't find some virtue in it. He must not have seen *Hurry Sundown.*'—*Rex Reed*
'To criticize it would be like tripping a dwarf.'—*Wilfrid Sheed*
'A pantomime version of Greek tragedy.'—*MFB*

Husbands*
US 1970 154m De Luxe
Columbia / Faces Music Inc (Al Ruban)

Three married men, shocked by the death of their friend, impulsively get drunk, fly to London and set out on a weekend of dissipation.
Irritatingly rough hewn and insanely overlong, this half-improvised tragi-comedy forces three good actors to overplay embarrassingly; but its best moments are memorable.

wd John Cassavetes ph Victor Kemper *m* none

Peter Falk, John Cassavetes, Ben Gazzara

Hush Hush Sweet Charlotte**
US 1964 133m bw
TCF / Associates and Aldrich

A southern belle lives thirty-seven years in a lonely mansion tormented by nightmarish memories of her fiancé's murder. Suddenly, after a series of apparent hauntings and other strange events, she finds she didn't do it.
Padded but generally enjoyable replay of elements from *Whatever Happened to Baby Jane*, with a large helping of *Les Diaboliques*. The stars help more than the director.

w Henry Farrell, Lukas Heller *d* Robert Aldrich *ph Joseph Biroc m* Frank de Vol *ad* William Glasgow

Bette Davis, Olivia de Havilland, Joseph Cotten, Cecil Kellaway, Victor Buono, William Marshall, Mary Astor, Agnes Moorehead

'The blood is on the cleaver, the madwoman is on the loose, the headless corpse is on the prowl and the Guignol is about as grand as it can get.'—*Judith Crist*

AAN: Joseph Biroc; Frank de Vol; Agnes Moorehead; title song (*m* Frank de Vol, *ly* Mack David)

Hussy

GB 1979 94m Eastmancolor

A high-class prostitute becomes involved with gangsters but eventually finds a new life for herself and her offspring. Tedious exploitation melodrama, shot like a ninety-minute commercial. Helen Mirren, John Shea, Daniel Chasin, Jenny Runacre. Written and directed by Matthew Chapman; for Boyd's Company.

Hustle

US 1975 118m Eastmancolor
Paramount / RoBurt (Robert Aldrich)

A police lieutenant lives with a call girl and is drawn into her corrupt life.
Doleful crime melodrama with both eyes in the gutter.

w Steve Shagan *d* Robert Aldrich *ph* Joseph Biroc *m* Frank de Vol

Burt Reynolds, Catherine Deneuve, Ben Johnson, Paul Winfield, Eileen Brennan, Eddie Albert, Ernest Borgnine, Catherine Bach, Jack Carter

'A fine companion piece to *Kiss Me Deadly* in its vision of a journey to the end of the night in quest of a myth.'—*Tim Milne*

'Even with such a meandering script as this, one expects more than the paltry fare Aldrich offers.'—*Paul Coleman*

The Hustler**

US 1961 135m bw Cinemascope
TCF / Robert Rossen

A pool room con man comes to grief when he falls in love.

Downbeat melodrama with brilliantly handled and atmospheric pool table scenes; the love interest is redundant.

w Robert Rossen, Sidney Carroll, *novel* Walter Tevis *d* Robert Rossen *ph* Eugen Schufftan *m* Kenyon Hopkins

Paul Newman, Jackie Gleason, George C. Scott, Piper Laurie, Myron McCormick, Murray Hamilton, Michael Constantine

'There is an overall impression of intense violence, and the air of spiritual decadence has rarely been conveyed so vividly.'—*David Robinson*

AA: Eugen Schufftan
AAN: best picture; script; Robert Rossen (as director); Paul Newman; Jackie Gleason; George C. Scott; Piper Laurie

Hyde Park Corner

GB 1935 84m bw

Events of 1780 at Hyde Park Corner seem to happen again in modern times. Half-hearted reincarnation romance with good moments. Gordon Harker, Binnie Hale, Gibb McLaughlin, Harry Tate, Eric Portman, Donald Wolfit. Written by D. B. Wyndham-Lewis, from the play by Walter Hackett; directed by Sinclair Hill; for Grosvenor.

Hysteria

GB 1964 85m bw
MGM / Hammer (Jimmy Sangster)

An American suffering from amnesia is discharged from a London clinic and walks into a murder plot.
Complicated and rather unsympathetic Hammer twister.

w Jimmy Sangster *d* Freddie Francis *ph* John Wilcox *m* Don Banks

Robert Webber, Lelia Goldoni, Anthony Newlands, Jennifer Jayne, *Maurice Denham,* Peter Woodthorpe

I

I Accuse*
GB 1958 99m bw Cinemascope
MGM (Sam Zimbalist)

In 1894 Paris, Alfred Dreyfus is tried for treason and later defended by Emile Zola.
A well tried historical incident is stolidly retold and unsuitably wide-screened; the star cast tends to flounder for lack of assistance.

w Gore Vidal d Jose Ferrer ph Frederick A. Young m William Alwyn

Jose Ferrer (Dreyfus), *Anton Walbrook* (Esterhazy), Emlyn Williams (Zola), Viveca Lindfors, David Farrar, Leo Genn, Herbert Lom, Harry Andrews, Felix Aylmer, George Coulouris, Donald Wolfit

I Aim at the Stars
US 1960 107m bw
Columbia / Morningside / Fama (Charles H. Schneer)

The story of German rocket expert Wernher Von Braun and his later work on American space vehicles.
Shaky biopic of a controversial scientist who changed sides.

w Jay Dratler d J. Lee-Thompson ph Wilkie Cooper m Laurie Johnson

Curt Jurgens, Herbert Lom, James Daly, Gia Scala, Victoria Shaw, Adrian Hoven, Karel Stepanek

'Mannered panning shots and crafty cutting abound, leading to a stylistic St Vitus' Dance.'—*John Gillett*

I Am a Camera
GB 1955 99m bw
Romulus (Jack Clayton)

A young English writer observes life in Berlin in the early thirties, and has a platonic relationship with an amoral and reckless young English girl.
A rather flat and flabby treatment of the stories by Christopher Isherwood and the play by John Van Druten, all better known these days in the form of *Cabaret*. Disappointingly unstylish.

w John Collier d Henry Cornelius ph Guy Green m Malcolm Arnold

Julie Harris, Laurence Harvey, Shelley Winters, Ron Randell, Anton Diffring

I Am a Fugitive from a Chain Gang****
US 1932 90m bw
Warner (Hal B. Wallis)

An innocent man is convicted and after brutal treatment with the chain gang becomes a vicious criminal on the run.
Horrifying story in the semi-documentary manner; a milestone in Hollywood history and still a fairly compelling piece of shock entertainment.

w *Sheridan Gibney, Brown Holmes, Robert E. Burns d Mervyn Le Roy ph Sol Polito*

Paul Muni, Glenda Farrell, Helen Vinson, Preston Foster, Allen Jenkins, Edward J. Macnamara, Berton Churchill, Edward Ellis

'To be enthusiastically commended for its courage, artistic sincerity, dramatic vigour, high entertainment concept and social message.'—*Wilton A. Barrett*

'I quarrel with the production not because it is savage and horrible, but because each step in an inevitable tragedy is taken clumsily, and because each character responsible for the hero's doom is shown more as a caricature than as a person.'—*Pare Lorentz*

'Six sticks of dynamite that blasted his way to freedom . . . and awoke America's conscience!'—*publicity*

AAN: best picture; Paul Muni

I Am the Law*
US 1938 83m bw
Columbia (Everett Riskin)

A law professor is asked by a civic leader to become a special prosecutor cleaning up rackets..
Adequate star potboiler, quite enjoyable.

w Jo Swerling d Alexander Hall ph Henry Freulich md Morris Stoloff

Edward G. Robinson, Otto Kruger, John Beal, Barbara O'Neil, Wendy Barrie, Arthur Loft, Marc Lawrence

I Believe in You*
GB 1952 95m bw
Ealing (Michael Relph)

Interwoven stories of probation officers; watchable and reasonable but not very compelling.

w Michael Relph, Basil Dearden, Jack Whittingham, Nicholas Phipps d Basil Dearden ph Gordon Dines m Ernest Irving

Celia Johnson, Cecil Parker, Godfrey Tearle, Harry Fowler, George Relph, Joan Collins, Laurence Harvey, Ernest Jay, Ursula Howells, Sidney James, Katie Johnson, Ada Reeve, Brenda de Banzie

I Bury the Living
US 1957 77m bw

The honorary chairman of a cemetery seems to have the power to mark people for death. Unusual enough to be encouraging, sloppy enough to disappoint even mystery lovers. Richard Boone, Theodore Bikel, Herbert Anderson, Peggy Maurer. Written by Louis Garfinkle; directed by Albert Band; for Maxim / UA.

I Can Get It for You Wholesale*
US 1951 89m bw
TCF (Sol C. Siegel)
GB title: This Is My Affair
American TV title: Only the Best

An ambitious young mannequin starts her own dressmaking firm and sets her sights high. Watchable comedy-drama which quickly sheds the edge of satire which might have made it the dressmaker's All About Eve.

w Abraham Polonsky, novel Jerome Weidman d Michael Gordon ph Milton Krasner m Sol Kaplan md Lionel Newman

Susan Hayward, Dan Dailey, George Sanders, Sam Jaffe, Randy Stuart, Marvin Kaplan, Harry Von Zell

I Confess**
US 1953 94m bw
Warner / Alfred Hitchcock

A priest hears the confession of a murderer and cannot divulge it to the police even though he is himself suspected.
Hitchcock is always worth watching, and although this old chestnut gives him very restricted scope he imbues the story with a strong feeling for its setting (Quebec) and an overpowering sense of doom.

w George Tabori, William Archibald, play Paul Anthelme d Alfred Hitchcock ph Robert Burks m Dmitri Tiomkin

Montgomery Clift, Anne Baxter, Brian Aherne, Karl Malden, Dolly Haas, O. E. Hasse

'Whatever its shortcomings, it has the professional concentration of effect, the narrative control, of a story teller who can still make most of his rivals look like amateurs.'— MFB

I Could Go on Singing*
GB 1963 99m Eastmancolor
  Panavision
UA / Barbican (Lawrence Turman)

An American singing star in Britain looks up an old lover and tries to take over their illegitimate son, but the call of the footlights proves stronger.
The star enjoys her last specially-tailored role; a banal, old-fashioned agreeable one-woman show.

w Mayo Simon d Ronald Neame ph Arthur Ibbetson m Mort Lindsey

Judy Garland, Dirk Bogarde, Aline MacMahon, Jack Klugman
'Merely standard fare in an age without standards.'—John Simon

I Cover the Waterfront*
US 1933 75m bw
(UA) Twentieth Century (Edward Small)

A reporter uses a girl's friendship to expose her father's smuggling activities.
In its time a tough, even daring melodrama, this plot has now become the stuff of every other TV series episode.

w Wells Root, Jack Jevne, Max Miller d James Cruze ph Ray June m Alfred Newman

Claudette Colbert, Ben Lyon, Ernest Torrence, Hobart Cavanaugh
'A bit raw and a bit sentimental and a bit routine, the film does let life in through the cracks.'—Graham Greene
† Credited with being the origin of the phrase, 'Not tonight, Josephine!'

I Didn't Do It
GB 1945 97m bw
Columbia (Ben Henry, Marcel Varnel)

Murder in a theatrical boarding house, with suspicion pointing at Our George.
One of the star's last vehicles: not too bad at all, but without the sweet smell of success.

w Howard Irving Young, Stephen Black, Norman Lee, Peter Fraser, Michael Vaughan d Marcel Varnel ph Roy Fogwell

George Formby, Billy Caryll, Hilda Mundy, Gaston Palmer, Jack Daly, Carl Jaffe, Marjorie Browne, Wally Patch

I Died a Thousand Times
US 1955   109m   Warnercolor
Cinemascope
Warner (Willis Goldbeck)

An ex-convict plans a big hotel robbery, but
things go wrong within his gang.
Overlong, heavygoing, tedious gangster
melodrama with too much talk.

w W. R. Burnett d Stuart Heisler ph Ted
McCord m David Buttolph

Jack Palance, Shelley Winters, Lori Nelson,
Lon Chaney Jnr, Lee Marvin, Gonzales
Gonzales, Earl Holliman, Perry Lopez

'This remake of *High Sierra* is scarcely more
inspired than its title.'—*MFB*

'It is an insult to the intelligence to pull this
old mythological hero out of the archives and
set him on a mountaintop again.'—*New York
Times*

The I Don't Care Girl*
US 1953   78m   Technicolor
TCF (George Jessel)

The life of musical entertainer Eva Tanguay,
at her height during World War I, as told by
three men in her life.
Breezy, conventional backstage musical
biopic.

w Walter Bullock d Lloyd Bacon ph Arthur
Arling md Lionel Newman ch Jack Cole,
Seymour Felix

Mitzi Gaynor, David Wayne, Oscar Levant,
George Jessel, Warren Stevens

I Don't Want to be Born
GB 1975   94m   Eastmancolor
(Rank) Unicapital (Norma Corney)
US title: *The Devil within Her*

An ex-stripper gives birth to a monstrous baby
which goes on a murderous rampage.
Sick horror stuff with a high death rate and no
notable credits.

w Stanley Price d Peter Sasdy ph Ken
Talbot m Ron Grainer

Joan Collins, Ralph Bates, Donald Pleasence,
Eileen Atkins, George Claydon

I Dood It!
US 1943   102m   bw
MGM (Jack Cummings)
GB title: *By Hook or by Crook*

A tailor falls for a Hollywood star.
Boring star comedy with interpolated musical
numbers.

w Sig Herzig, Fred Saidy d Vincente
Minnelli ph Ray June md Georgie Stoll

Red Skelton, Eleanor Powell, John Hodiak,
Lena Horne, Jimmy Dorsey and his
Orchestra, Hazel Scott, Richard Ainley

I Dream Too Much
US 1935   95m   bw
RKO (Pandro S. Berman)

A French girl singer marries an American
composer.
Forgettable vehicle for an operatic star.

w Edmund North, James Gow d John
Cromwell ph David Abel songs Jerome
Kern, Dorothy Fields

Lily Pons, Henry Fonda, Eric Blore, Osgood
Perkins, Lucien Littlefield, Lucille Ball,
Esther Dale, Mischa Auer, Paul Porcasi

I Escaped from Devil's Island
US 1973   81m   De Luxe
UA Roger Corman, Gene Corman

In 1918, a black convict makes his plans for
escape.
Rough, brutish melodrama which plainly
aimed to beat *Papillon* to the box office.

w Richard L. Adams d William Witney
ph Rosalio Solano m Les Baxter

Jim Brown, Christopher George, Rick Ely,
James Luisi, Richard Rust

'Exploitation's own *Papillon*, mercifully free
from big brother's pretentiousness.'—*Sight
and Sound*

I Found Stella Parish
US 1935   85m   bw

An actress tries to keep her naughty past from
her child, but a blackmailer strikes. One for
the ladies, who flocked to it in its day. Kay
Francis, Paul Lukas, Ian Hunter, Sybil Jason,
Jessie Ralph, Barton Maclane. Written by
Casey Robinson; directed by Mervyn Le Roy;
for Warner.

I Killed Rasputin
France / Italy 1967   100m
   Eastmancolor   Franscope
Copernic / CGC (Raymond Danon)

The evil monk of the Russian court is killed by
Prince Yusopov.
Dull version of a much told story. One of the
big international films that never seems to get
shown anywhere.

w Alain Decaux, Claude Desailly, Robert
Hossein d Robert Hossein ph Henri Persin
m André Hossein

Gert Frobe, Peter McEnery, Robert Hossein,
Geraldine Chaplin, Ira Furstenberg, Patrick
Balkany

'A tedious illustrated history lesson which actually manages to obscure the motivation behind the murder.'—*MFB*
† The script was authorized by Prince Yusopov

I Killed the Count
GB 1939 . 89m bw
Grafton (Isadore Goldschmidt)

Four people confess to the murder of a philanderer.
Inept version of a West End success.

w Alec Coppel, Lawrence Huntington, *play* Alec Coppel *d* Fred Zelnik

Syd Walker, Ben Lyon, Terence de Marney, Barbara Blair, Antoinette Cellier, Kathleen Harrison, Athole Stewart, Leslie Perrins, Ronald Shiner

I Know Where I'm Going**
GB 1945 91m bw
GFD / The Archers (Michael Powell, Emeric Pressburger)

A determined girl travels to the Hebrides to marry a wealthy old man, but is stranded on Mull and marries a young naval officer instead.
A strange assembling of attractive but disparate elements: romance, comedy, bleak scenery, a trained hawk and a dangerous whirlpool. At the time it seemed to represent the Elizabethan age of the British cinema, and remains entertaining for its parts though a bit of a puzzle as a whole.

wd Michael Powell, Emeric Pressburger
ph Erwin Hillier

Wendy Hiller, Roger Livesey, Pamela Brown, Nancy Price, Finlay Currie, John Laurie, George Carney, Walter Hudd

'Continuously fresh and interesting, intelligently written and played, and full of beautiful photography.'—*Richard Mallett, Punch*

'The sensitive photography and the intelligent if not very imaginative use of sound do more than enough to make eloquent the influence of place on people; and the whole thing is undertaken with taste and modesty.'—*James Agee*

I Live for Love
US 1935 83m bw
Warner (Bryan Foy)
GB title: *I Live For You*

A socialite has show business leanings.
Minor musical.

w Jerry Wald, Julius Epstein, Robert Andrews *d / ch* Busby Berkeley *ph* George Barnes *md* Leo F. Forbstein

Dolores del Rio, Everett Marshall, Allen Jenkins, Eddie Conrad, Guy Kibbee, Berton Churchill

I Live in Grosvenor Square
GB 1945 113m bw
ABP (Herbert Wilcox)
US title: *A Yank in London*

A duke's daughter falls in love with an American air force sergeant.
Sloppily-made topical romance which was hot box office at the time and started the producer's 'London' romances: *Piccadilly Incident, Spring in Park Lane, Maytime in Mayfair*, etc.

w Nicholas Phipps, William D. Bayles, Maurice Cowan *d* Herbert Wilcox *ph* Max Greene

Anna Neagle, *Dean Jagger*, Rex Harrison, Robert Morley, Jane Darwell, Nancy Price, Irene Vanbrugh, Edward Rigby, Walter Hudd

I Live My Life
US 1935 85m bw
MGM (Bernard H. Hyman)

A bored society girl falls for a working class archaeologist.
Standard star romance.

w Joseph L. Mankiewicz, *story* Claustrophobia by A. Carter Goodloe *d* W. S. Van Dyke II *ph* George Folsey *m* Dmitri Tiomkin

Joan Crawford, Brian Aherne, Frank Morgan, Aline MacMahon, Eric Blore, Jessie Ralph, Arthur Treacher, Hedda Hopper, Etienne Girardot, Ed Brophy

I Lived with You
GB 1933 100m bw

A cockney family find that their lodger is an exiled Russian prince. Overlong whimsy from a successful West End play. Ivor Novello, Ursula Jeans, Ida Lupino, Minnie Rayner, Eliot Makeham, Jack Hawkins. Written by H. Fowler Mear, from the play by Ivor Novello; directed by Maurice Elvey; for Twickenham.

I Love a Mystery*
US 1945 68m bw
Columbia

An eastern secret society offers a businessman a large sum for his head when he dies, as he resembles their founder whose embalmed head is deteriorating.

Start of a short series of mysteries from a radio series; the production was never up to the ingenious plots.

w Charles O'Neal *d* Henry Levin *ph* Burnett Guffey

George Macready, Jim Bannon, Nina Foch

I Love a Soldier
US 1944 106m bw
Paramount (Mark Sandrich)

A San Francisco girl thinks hard before embarking on a wartime marriage.
Glossy, insubstantial sudser chiefly memorable for casting its leading lady as a welder.

w Allan Scott *d* Mark Sandrich *ph* Charles Lang *m* Robert Emmett Dolan

Paulette Goddard, Sonny Tufts, Beulah Bondi, Walter Sande, Mary Treen, Ann Doran, Barry Fitzgerald

I Love Melvin*
US 1953 77m Technicolor
MGM (George Wells)

A photographer's assistant falls for a high-born chorus girl.
Zippy little musical with all concerned working hard with thin material.

w George Wells *d* Don Weis *ph* Harold Rosson *m / ly* Josef Myrow, Mack Gordon *md* George Stoll *ch* Robert Alton

Donald O'Connor, Debbie Reynolds, Una Merkel, Allyn Joslyn

I Love My Wife
US 1970 95m Technicolor
Universal (Robert Kaufman)

The affairs of a successful doctor with a guilt complex about sex.
Frantic, fashionable comedy drama with wildly erratic treatment and performances.

w Robert Kaufman *d* Mel Stuart *ph* Vilis Lapenieks *m* Lalo Schifrin

Elliott Gould, Brenda Vaccaro, Angel Tompkins
  'A leer-laden, anti-feminist tract disguised as a comedy.'—*Judith Crist*

I Love You Again*
US 1940 99m bw
MGM (Lawrence Weingarten)

A much married man gets amnesia and turns into a gay Lothario.
Sprightly romantic comedy with all concerned letting rip until the pace slows.

w Charles Lederer, George Oppenheimer, Harry Kurnitz *d* W. S. Van Dyke II *ph* Oliver T. Marsh *m* Franz Waxman

William Powell, Myrna Loy, Frank McHugh, Edmund Lowe, Donald Douglas, Nella Walker, Pierre Watkin

I Love You, Alice B. Toklas*
US 1968 93m Technicolor
Warner Seven Arts / Paul Mazursky, Larry Tucker

An asthmatic Los Angeles lawyer escapes his bullying fiancée by joining the flower people.
Quite amusing satirical farce about the dangers of marijuana, Gertrude Stein and Jewish mothers, thrown together with no great sense of style but achieving hilarious moments among the longueurs.

w Paul Mazursky, Larry Tucker *d* Hy Averback *ph* Philip Lathrop *m* Elmer Bernstein *pd* Pato Guzman

Peter Sellers, Jo Van Fleet, Joyce Van Patten, Leigh Taylor-Young, David Arkin, Herb Edelman

I Loved a Woman*
US 1933 90m bw
Warner (Henry Blanke)

The career of a Chicago meat packer is hampered by his social-climbing wife.
Potboiling star melodrama which still holds some interest.

w Charles Kenyon, Sidney Sutherland *d* Alfred E. Green *ph* James Van Trees

Edward G. Robinson, Kay Francis, Genevieve Tobin, J. Farrell MacDonald, Henry Kolker, Robert Barrat

I Married a Doctor
US 1936 87m bw

An idealistic city girl marries a small-town doctor. Solidly carpentered version of Sinclair Lewis's *Main Street* (filmed under its own title in 1923, with Florence Vidor, directed by Harry Beaumont). Josephine Hutchinson, Pat O'Brien, Ross Alexander, Guy Kibbee, Louise Fazenda. Written by Casey Robinson, Harriet Ford and Harvey O'Higgin; directed by Archie Mayo; for Warner.

I Married a Monster from Outer Space*
US 1958 78m bw
Paramount / Gene Fowler Jnr

A young man is taken over by alien invaders but his wife helps to destroy them and bring him back to normal.
Decent, plodding, reasonably effective low-budget science fiction on a well-trampled theme; its minor virtues have been effaced by its silly title.

w Louis Vittes *d* Gene Fowler Jnr
ph Haskell Boggs *sp* John P. Fulton

Tom Tryon, Gloria Talbott, Robert Ivers

I Married a Witch••••
US 1942   82m   bw
(UA) Cinema Guild / René Clair

A Salem witch and her sorcerer father come
back to haunt the descendant of the Puritan
who had them burned.
Delightful romantic comedy fantasy which
shows all concerned at the top of their form.
Hollywood moonshine, impeccably distilled.

w Robert Pirosh, Marc Connelly, novel The
Passionate Witch by Thorne Smith *d René
Clair ph* Ted Tetzlaff *m* Roy Webb

*Fredric March, Veronica Lake, Cecil
Kellaway, Robert Benchley*, Susan Hayward,
Elizabeth Patterson, Robert Warwick
   'She knows all about love potions . . . and
lovely motions!'—*publicity*

AAN: Roy Webb

I Married a Woman
US 1956   85m   bw (colour sequence)
   RKOscope
RKO

A nervous young advertising executive
neglects his wife, who determines to make him
jealous.
Simple-minded comedy tailored to
unsympathetic stars.

w Goodman Ace *d* Hal Kanter *ph* Lucien
Ballard *m* Cyril Mockridge

George Gobel, Diana Dors, Adolphe Menjou,
Jessie Royce Landis, Nita Talbot

I Married an Angel
US 1942   84m   bw
MGM (Hunt Stromberg)

An attractive angel lures a playboy from his
earthly girl friends.
Silly musical fantasy which spelled the end of a
great musical star partnership.

w Anita Loos, *play* Vilismary Janos *d* W. S.
Van Dyke *ph* Ray June *m / ly* Richard
Rodgers, Lorenz Hart

Jeanette MacDonald, Nelson Eddy, Edward
Everett Horton, Binnie Barnes, Reginald
Owen, Douglass Dumbrille
   'As bland as operetta but without its
energy.'—*New Yorker, 1978*

I Met a Murderer•
GB 1939   78m   bw
Grand National / Gamma (Roy Kellino,
   Pamela Kellino, James Mason)

A murderer on the run meets a girl novelist
who is touring in her motor caravan.
Semi-professional location melodrama which
won commendation at the time but now seems
very faded.

w Pamela Kellino, James Mason *d* Roy
Kellino *ph* Roy Kellino *m* Eric Ansell

James Mason, Pamela Kellino, Sylvia
Coleridge, William Devlin, Peter Coke
   'Graceful, gallant, resourceful . . . better
and more enjoyable than most studio
pictures.'—*James Agee*
   'That it has a number of defects does not
mean that it is not worthy of serious
consideration.'—*Basil Wright*

I Met Him in Paris•
US 1937   86m   bw
Paramount (Wesley Ruggles)

A fashion designer spends five years' savings
on a fling in Paris and finds herself pursued to
Switzerland by two philanderers.
Not very witty but likeable romantic comedy
with polished performers near their best.

w Claude Binyon *d* Wesley Ruggles *ph* Leo
Tover *m* John Leopold *md* Boris Morros

*Claudette Colbert, Melvyn Douglas, Robert
Young*, Lee Bowman, Mona Barrie
   'At least half the footage is a perfect
scream, and if you miss it you are an old
sobersides, and who cares.'—*Otis Ferguson*

I Met My Love Again
US 1937   77m   bw
Walter Wanger

A small-town girl marries a drunken writer,
but on his death returns to her first love, a
biology professor.
Mildly pleasing, rather dated romantic drama
with good local colour.

w David Hertz, *novel* Summer Lightning by
Aileen Corliss *d* Joshua Logan, Arthur
Ripley *ph* Hal Mohr

Henry Fonda, Joan Bennett, Alan Marshal,
Dorothy Stickney, Dame May Whitty, Alan
Baxter, Louise Platt, Tim Holt, Florence Lake

I, Mobster
US 1958   80m   bw   Cinemascope
Edward L. Alperson

A slum teenager becomes a top gangster.
Routine gangland thriller.

w Steve Fisher, *novel* Joseph Hilton Smith
d Roger Corman *ph* Floyd Crosby *m* Gerald
Fried

Steve Cochran, Lita Milan, Robert Strauss,
Celia Lovsky, Grant Withers

I, Monster*

GB 1970 75m Eastmancolor
Amicus (Milton Subotsky)

A straight remake of *Dr Jekyll and Mr Hyde*,
holding closely to the original novel but
mysteriously using different names.
Interesting minor work.

w Milton Subotsky d Stephen Weeks
ph Moray Grant m Carl Davis ad Tony
Curtis

Christopher Lee, Peter Cushing, Richard
Hurndall, George Merritt

I Never Promised You a Rose Garden

US 1977 96m colour
New World / Imorh / Fadsin (Roger
Corman)

A suicidal teenage girl is treated in a
psychiatric hospital.
Careful, thoughtful case history which can't
help, after so many TV movies of the kind,
seeming rather too simple for a theatrical
feature, as well as too heavy-going despite the
upbeat ending.

w Gavin Lambert, Lewis John Carlino,
novel Hannah Green d Anthony Page
ph Bruce Logan m Paul Chihara pd Toby
Rafelson

Kathleen Quinlan, Bibi Andersson, Sylvia
Sidney, Ben Piazza, Lorraine Gary, Reni
Santoni, Signe Hasso

I Never Sang for My Father*

US 1969 92m Technicolor
Columbia / Jamel (Gilbert Cates)

When his mother dies, a middle-aged widower
is saddled with his cantankerous father, who
tries to prevent him from remarrying.
Literal transcription of a Eugene O'Neillish
play, a fascinating if depressing character
study.

w *Robert Anderson*, from his play d *Gilbert
Cates* ph Morris Hartzband, George Stoetzel
m Al Gorgoni, Barry Mann

*Melvyn Douglas, Gene Hackman, Dorothy
Stickney*, Estelle Parsons

AAN: Robert Anderson; Melvyn Douglas;
Gene Hackman

I Passed for White

US 1960 92m bw
Allied Artists (Fred M. Wilcox)

A light-skinned negress comes to New York
but fails to achieve happiness by pretending to
be white.
Earnest, rather dreary social drama which
doesn't get anywhere.

d Fred M. Wilcox ph George J. Folsey
m Johnny Williams

Sonya Wilde, James Franciscus, Pat Michon,
Elizabeth Council

I Remember Mama**

US 1948 134m bw
RKO (George Stevens)

A novelist remembers some of the adventures
of growing up with her Norwegian–American
family.
Overlong, but well-upholstered nostalgia:
warm-hearted, sentimental, nicely detailed,
richly acted but just a little boring in spots.

w De Witt Bodeen, *play* John Van Druten,
book Mama's Bank Account by Kathryn
Forbes d George Stevens ph Nicholas
Musuraca m Roy Webb

*Irene Dunne, Barbara Bel Geddes, Oscar
Homolka, Edgar Bergen, Philip Dorn, Ellen
Corby*, Florence Bates, Cedric Hardwicke,
Barbara O'Neil, Rudy Vallee

AAN: Nicholas Musuraca; Irene Dunne;
Barbara Bel Geddes; Oscar Homolka; Ellen
Corby

I Saw What You Did

US 1965 82m bw
Universal / William Castle

A murderer thinks that two playful teenagers
have witnessed his deed, and sets out to kill
them too.
Predictable and long-winded suspenser, very
short of inventive detail.

w William McGivern, *novel* Ursula Curtiss
d William Castle ph Joseph Biroc m Van
Alexander

John Ireland, Joan Crawford, Leif Erickson

I See a Dark Stranger**

GB 1945 112m bw
GFD / Individual
US title: *The Adventuress*

An Irish colleen who hates the English comes
to England to spy for the Germans but falls in
love with a young English officer.
Slipshod plotting does not quite destroy the
jolly atmosphere of this comedy-thriller which
has the cheek to take an IRA member as its
heroine. Good fun, very well staged.

w *Frank Launder, Sidney Gilliat, Wolfgang
Wilhelm d Frank Launder* ph Wilkie Cooper
m William Alwyn

Deborah Kerr, Trevor Howard, Raymond
Huntley, Norman Shelley, Michael Howard,
Brenda Bruce, Liam Redmond, Brefni
O'Rourke

'It is the cinematic equivalent of Irish blarney which inspires most of this picture.'— *MFB*

'There is some intelligence, grace and fun here, but essentially this seems to me a supercilious drama, as if it had been made by bright young men who had decided to package and toss a bone to the groundlings.'—*James Agee*

I See Ice
GB 1938 81m bw

The property man in an ice ballet company is a keen amateur photographer who accidentally snaps crooks at work. Fair star comedy with good production. George Formby, Kay Walsh, Betty Stockfield, Cyril Ritchard, Garry Marsh. Written by Anthony Kimmins and Austin Melford; directed by Anthony Kimmins; for ATP.

I Start Counting
GB 1969 105m De Luxe
UA / Triumvirate (David Greene)

A young girl thinks her foster-brother may be the sex murderer known to be rampant in the locality. But after a great many red herrings, of course, he is not. Strained psychological suspenser with good moments between the *longueurs*.

w Richard Harris, *novel* Audrey Erskine Lindop *d* David Greene *ph* Alex Thomson *m* Basil Kirchin *pd* Brian Eatwell

Jenny Agutter, Bryan Marshall, Clare Sutcliffe, Simon Ward, Lana Morris, Billy Russell, Fay Compton, Lally Bowers

I Stole a Million
US 1939 89m bw
Universal (Burt Kelly)

A cab driver cheated by a finance company becomes a criminal to support his family. Ho-hum star melodrama.

w Nathanael West, *story* Lester Cole *d* Frank Tuttle *ph* Milton Krasner

George Raft, Claire Trevor, Dick Foran, Henry Armetta, Victor Jory, Joe Sawyer, Stanley Ridges

I Take This Woman
US 1931 74m bw
Paramount

A reckless society girl falls for a cowhand and agrees to live in his ramshackle house. Patchy romantic comedy–drama of little remaining interest.

w Vincent Lawrence, *novel* Lost Ecstasy by Mary Roberts Rinehart *d* Marion Gering, Slavko Vorkapitch *ph* Victor Milner

Gary Cooper, Carole Lombard, Helen Ware, Lester Vail, Charles Trowbridge, Clara Blandick

I Take This Woman
US 1939 97m bw
MGM (Louis B. Mayer)

A doctor marries a beautiful European and decides too late that he does not love her. Thin comedy–drama which Louis B. Mayer unaccountably took it into his head to produce personally. The results had to be re-shot so much and so often that Hollywood dubbed the film *I Re-Take This Woman*. It offers little in the way of entertainment.

w James Kevin McGuinness, *story* Charles MacArthur *d* W. S. Van Dyke *ph* Harold Rosson *m* Bronislau Kaper

Spencer Tracy, Hedy Lamarr, Verree Teasdale, Kent Taylor, Laraine Day, Mona Barrie, Jack Carson, Paul Cavanagh, Marjorie Main

I Thank a Fool
GB 1962 100m Metrocolor
   Cinemascope
MGM (Anatole de Grunwald)

A woman found guilty of the murder of her lover is offered a fresh start in the home of the prosecutor's family . . . but another nightmare situation builds up.
Jane Eyre melodrama of the loonier type, with good actors struggling through a wild but unrewarding script.

w Karl Tunberg, *novel* Audrey Erskine Lindop *d* Robert Stevens *ph* Harry Waxman *m* Ron Goodwin

Peter Finch, Susan Hayward, Diane Cilento, Cyril Cusack, Kieron Moore, Athene Seyler

I Thank You
GB 1941 81m bw

Actors seeking a backer become servants to a titled ex-star. Acceptable comedy vehicle. Arthur Askey, Richard Murdoch, Lily Morris, Moore Marriott, Graham Moffatt, Kathleen Harrison. Written by Howard Irving Young, Val Guest and Marriott Edgar; directed by Marcel Varnel; for Gainsborough.

I the Jury
US 1953 87m bw 3-D
Parklane (Victor Saville)

Private eye Mike Hammer avenges the murder of his friend.

Charmless toughie, roughly made and devoid of plot or character interest.

wd Harry Essex *ph* John Alton *m* Franz Waxman

Biff Elliott, Peggie Castle, Preston Foster, Elisha Cook Jnr, John Qualen

I Wake Up Screaming**
US 1941 79m bw
TCF (Milton Sperling)
GB and alternative title: *Hot Spot*

A model is murdered and her sister joins forces with the chief suspect to find the real killer.
Moody thriller with plenty going for it including one memorable performance.

w Dwight Taylor, *novel* Steve Fisher *d* H. Bruce Humberstone *ph* Edward Cronjager *m* Cyril Mockridge

Betty Grable, Victor Mature, Carole Landis, *Laird Cregar*, William Gargan, Alan Mowbray, Allyn Joslyn, Elisha Cook Jnr

† Remade as *Vicki* (qv).

I Walk Alone*
US 1948 98m bw
Paramount (Hal B. Wallis)

An ex-smuggler comes out seeking vengeance after fourteen years in prison.
Dreary gangster drama unworthy of its stars.

w Charles Schnee, *play* Beggars Are Coming to Town by Theodore Reeves *d* Byron Haskin *ph* Leo Tover *m* Victor Young

Burt Lancaster, Kirk Douglas, Lizabeth Scott, Wendell Corey, Kristine Miller, George Rigaud, Marc Lawrence, Mike Mazurki

'The picture deserves, like four out of five other movies, to walk alone, tinkle a little bell, and cry Unclean, unclean.'—*James Agee*

I Walk the Line*
US 1970 97m Eastmancolor
Panavision
Columbia / Frankenheimer / Lewis / Halcyon / Atticus (Harold D. Cohen)

A Tennessee sheriff protects moonshiners for the favours of their daughter; when an investigator arrives, bloodshed results.
Competent but uninteresting hothouse melodrama in which only the plot twists compel attention.

w Alvin Sargent, *novel* An Exile by Madison Jones *d* John Frankenheimer *ph* David M. Walsh *md* Robert Johnson

Gregory Peck, Tuesday Weld, Estelle Parsons, Ralph Meeker

I Walked with a Zombie*
US 1943 68m bw
RKO (*Val Lewton*)

A nurse is retained by a Caribbean planter to care for his voodoo-sick wife.
Mild horror from the famous Lewton package; some style, but generally thin stuff, the plot having been mirthfully borrowed from *Jane Eyre*.

w Curt Siodmak, Ardel Wray *d* Jacques Tourneur *ph* J. Roy Hunt *m* Roy Webb

Frances Dee, James Ellison, Tom Conway, Christine Gordon, Edith Barrett, James Bell, Sir Lancelot

I Wanna Hold Your Hand
US 1978 104m Technicolor
Universal / Steven Spielberg (Tamara Asseyev, Alex Rose)

A day in 1964 finds assorted New Jersey teenagers eagerly awaiting the Beatles' appearance on the Ed Sullivan Show. Modest period comedy utilizing fresh young talent.

w Robert Zemeckis, Bob Gale *d* Robert Zemeckis *ph* Donald M. Morgan *m* Meredith Wilson

Nancy Allen, Bobby diCicco, Marc McClure, Susan Kendall Newman

I Want a Divorce
US 1940 74m bw
Paramount

A young law student marries rashly, but is prevented from doing anything about it by examples of the unhappiness brought by divorce.
Peculiar comedy-drama which never seems to make up its mind to any particular course.

w Frank Butler, *story* Adela Rogers St John *d* Ralph Murphy *ph* Ted Tetzlaff *m* Victor Young

Dick Powell, Joan Blondell, Frank Fay, Gloria Dickson, Jessie Ralph, Conrad Nagel, Harry Davenport, Sidney Blackmer, Louise Beavers

I Want to Live*
US 1958 120m bw
(UA) Walter Wanger

A vagrant prostitute is executed in the gas chamber despite growing doubt as to her guilt.
Sober, harrowing treatment of the Barbara Graham case, uneasily adapted to provide a star role amid the tirade against capital punishment.

w Nelson Gidding, Don Mankiewicz *d* Robert Wise *ph* Lionel Lindon *m* John Mandel

Susan Hayward, Simon Oakland, Virginia
Vincent, Theodore Bikel, Wesley Lau, Philip
Coolidge
   'An inconclusive amalgam of variously
unexplored themes.'—*Peter John Dyer*
AA: Susan Hayward
AAN: Nelson Gidding, Don Mankiewicz;
Robert Wise; Lionel Lindon

I Want What I Want
GB 1971   105m   Eastmancolor
Marayan (Raymond Stross)

Roy has a sex change operation and becomes
Wendy.
Although based on an actual trans-sexual
experience, this film confuses more than it
informs, and provokes unintentional mirth
when its glamorous star is playing a boy.

w Gillian Freeman, *novel* Geoff Brown
d John Dexter *ph* Gerry Turpin *m* Johnny
Harris

Anne Heywood, Paul Rogers, Harry
Andrews, Jill Bennett

I Want You
US 1951   101m   bw
Samuel Goldwyn

A family reacts to the Korean war.
Glossy small-town flagwaver; no *Best Years of
Our Lives*.

w Irwin Shaw *d* Mark Robson *ph* Harry
Stradling *m* Leigh Harline *ad* Richard Day

Dorothy McGuire, Dana Andrews, Farley
Granger, Peggy Dow, Robert Keith, Ray
Collins, Mildred Dunnock, Martin Milner, Jim
Backus
   'A recruiting picture which seems to accept
a third world war almost as a present
reality.'—*Penelope Houston*
   'Below the entertaining surface it has very
little of value to offer.'—*Richard Mallett,
Punch*

I Wanted Wings*
US 1941   131m   bw
Paramount (Arthur Hornblow Jnr)

The fortunes of three recruits to the American
Air Force.
Cheerful, overlong recruiting poster with
concessions to melodrama.

w Richard Maibaum, Beirne Lay Jnr, Sig
Herzig *d* Mitchell Leisen *ph* Leo Tover,
Elmer Dyer *m* Victor Young

Ray Milland, William Holden, Brian Donlevy,
Wayne Morris, Veronica Lake, Constance
Moore, Harry Davenport, Phil Brown
   'Far more a poster than a drama.'—*Howard
Barnes, New York Herald Tribune*

I Was a Communist for the FBI
US 1951   83m   bw
Warner (Bryan Foy)

Matt Cvetic, a Pittsburgh steel worker, is
actually an FBI agent working undercover to
trap communists.
Crude and shoddy Red-baiting melodrama, a
kind of updating of *Confessions of a Nazi Spy*
but using a sadly deteriorated technique.

w Crane Wilbur, Matt Cvetic *d* Gordon
Douglas *ph* Edwin DuPar *m* Max Steiner

Frank Lovejoy, Dorothy Hart, Phil Carey,
James Millican, Richard Webb, Paul Picerni,
Konstantin Shayne
   'It seems that this is a subject which
Hollywood is incapable of tackling even at its
customary level of journalistic efficiency.'—
Penelope Houston

I Was a Male War Bride**
US 1949   105m   bw
TCF (Sol C. Siegel)
GB title: *You Can't Sleep Here*

A WAC in Europe marries a French officer
and can't get him home.
High-spirited farce against realistic
backgrounds of war-torn Europe, which
scarcely accord with Cary Grant's pretending
to be a Frenchman (and later a
Frenchwoman). Funny, though.

w Charles Lederer, Hagar Wilde, Leonard
Spiegelgass *d* Howard Hawks *ph* Norbert
Brodine, Osmond Borradaile *m* Cyril
Mockridge *md* Lionel Newman

Cary Grant, *Ann Sheridan*, Marion Marshall,
Randy Stuart

I Was a Spy**
GB 1933   89m   bw
Gaumont (Michael Balcon)

In Belgium 1914, a nurse is trained as a spy.
Good standard war espionage melodrama.

w W. P. Lipscomb, Ian Hay, *book* Marthe
McKenna *d* Victor Saville *ph* Charles Van
Enger

Madeleine Carroll, Conrad Veidt, Herbert
Marshall, Gerald du Maurier, Edmund
Gwenn, Donald Calthrop, Nigel Bruce,
Anthony Bushell, Martita Hunt

I Was a Teenage Frankenstein
US 1957   72m   bw
American International (Herman Cohen)
GB title: *Teenage Frankenstein*

Professor Frankenstein fashions a creature
from selected morsels of old corpses, and kills
a teenager to give it a more handsome head.

It seemed gruesome enough at the time, but by 1980 standards this is tame, cheap stuff, only notable for its occasional bravura.

w Kenneth Langtry d Herbert J. Strock ph Lothrop Worth m Paul Dunlap

Whit Bissell, Phyllis Coates, Gary Conway, Robert Burton

† In-joke: when the professor crates up the monster to send it to London, the address is 113 Wardour Street, which is Hammer House . . .

I Was a Teenage Werewolf
US 1957 76m bw
AIP / Sunset (Herman Cohen)

A scientist experiments on an aggressive student and turns him into a werewolf.
Hilarious farrago with a title which achieved a splendour of its own.

w Ralph Thornton d Gene Fowler Jnr ph Joseph La Shelle m Paul Dunlap

Michael Landon, Whit Bissell, Yvonne Lime

I Was An Adventuress*
US 1940 81m bw
TCF (Darryl F. Zanuck)

A ballerina works as decoy for a pair of confidence tricksters.
Pleasing comedy drama with striking cast.

w Karl Tunberg, Don Ettlinger, John O'Hare d Gregory Ratoff ph Leon Shamroy, Edward Cronjager md David Buttolph

Vera Zorina, Erich Von Stroheim, Peter Lorre, Richard Greene, Sig Rumann, Fritz Feld, Cora Witherspoon

I Was Happy Here*
GB 1965 91m bw
Partisan (Roy Millichip)
US title: Time Lost and Time Remembered

A girl leaves her husband in London and returns to the little Irish port of her childhood.
Nicely made, over-mannered study in nostalgia and lost illusions.

w Edna O'Brien, Desmond Davis d Desmond Davis ph Manny Wynn m John Addison

Sarah Miles, Cyril Cusack, Julian Glover, Sean Caffrey, Marie Kean

I Was Monty's Double**
GB 1958 100m bw
ABP / Maxwell Setton
US title: Hell, Heaven and Hoboken

To distract the Nazis in Africa, an actor is hired to pose as General Montgomery.
An amusing and intriguing first hour gives way to spy chases, but the overall provides solid entertainment.

w Bryan Forbes, book M. E. Clifton-James d John Guillermin ph Basil Emmott m John Addison

John Mills, Cecil Parker, M. E. Clifton-James, Patrick Allen, Leslie Phillips, Michael Hordern, Marius Goring

I Wonder Who's Kissing Her Now*
US 1947 104m Technicolor
TCF (George Jessel)

The career of nineties songwriter Joseph E. Howard.
Routine biopic, quite pleasantly handled.

w Lewis R. Foster d Lloyd Bacon ph Ernest Palmer md Alfred Newman ad Richard Day, Boris Leven ch Hermes Pan

Mark Stevens, June Haver, Martha Stewart, Reginald Gardiner, Lenore Aubert, William Frawley, Gene Nelson

Ice Castles
US 1978 109m Metrocolor
Columbia / International Cinemedia Center (John Kemeny)

Nick and Lexie meet and fall in love at the ice rink. He goes into professional ice hockey; she becomes an Olympic champion but an accident leaves her blind.
Slick, empty, three-handkerchief wallow in the modern manner; well made but instantly forgettable.

w Donald Wrye, Gary L. Baim d Donald Wrye ph Bill Butler m Marvin Hamlisch pd Joel Schiller

Robby Benson, Lynn-Holly Johnson, Colleen Dewhurst, Tom Skerritt, Jennifer Warren, David Huffman

Ice Cold in Alex**
GB 1958 132m bw
ABP (W. A. Whittaker)
US title: Desert Attack

In 1942 Libya, the commander of a motor ambulance gets his vehicle and passengers to safety despite the hazards of minefields and a German spy.
Engrossing desert adventure with plenty of suspense sequences borrowed from The Wages of Fear; long, but very well presented.

w T. J. Morrison, Christopher Landon d J. Lee-Thompson ph Gilbert Taylor m Leighton Lucas

John Mills, Sylvia Sims, Anthony Quayle, Harry Andrews

Ice Follies of 1939
US 1939 82m bw (Technicolor sequence)
MGM (Harry Rapf)

A Hollywood star goes east to help her old ice-skating friends put on a show.
The downright peculiar sight of these particular stars on ice is backed by good turns and practically no story.

w Florence Ryerson, Edgar Allan Woolf d Reinhold Schunzel ph Joseph Ruttenberg, Oliver T. Marsh m Roger Edens

Joan Crawford, James Stewart, Lew Ayres, Lewis Stone, Lionel Stander, Bess Ehrhardt, Charles D. Brown, the International Ice Follies

Ice Palace
US 1960   143m   Warnercolor
Cinemascope
Warner (Henry Blanke)

After World War I, two men set up a fishery business in Alaska, and their subsequent lives are tied up with the political development of the state.
Tedious saga from a bestseller, with entertaining incidents but no real grip.

w Harry Kleiner, novel Edna Ferber d Vincent Sherman ph Joseph Biroc m Max Steiner ad Malcolm Bert

Richard Burton, Robert Ryan, Martha Hyer, Carolyn Jones, Jim Backus, Ray Danton, Diane McBain, Karl Swenson

Ice Station Zebra
US 1968   148m   Metrocolor   Super Panavision
MGM / Filmways (James C. Pratt)

Russian and American agents speed towards the North Pole to recover a lost capsule containing vital military information.
Talky and unconvincingly staged spy adventure with a disappointing lack of action and a great many cold war platitudes.

w Douglas Heyes, Harry Julian Fink, novel Alistair MacLean d John Sturges ph Daniel L. Fapp m Michel Legrand

Rock Hudson, Patrick McGoohan, Ernest Borgnine, Jim Brown, Tony Bill, Lloyd Nolan, Gerald S. O'Loughlin, Alf Kjellin
    'It's terrible in such a familiar way that at some level it's pleasant. We learn to settle for so little, we moviegoers.'—Pauline Kael

AAN: Daniel L. Fapp

Ichabod and Mr Toad••
US 1949   68m   Technicolor
Walt Disney

Cartoon versions of stories by Washington Irving and Kenneth Grahame.
An uncomfortable double bill; the story of Ichabod, though well narrated by Basil

Rathbone, is macabre without being very interesting; The Wind in the Willows, however, is charmingly pictured, and Mr Toad is splendidly voiced by Eric Blore.

d Jack Kinney, Clyde Geronimi, James Algar supervisor Ben Sharpsteen

I'd Climb the Highest Mountain•
US 1951   88m   Technicolor
TCF (Lamar Trotti)

A Methodist preacher and his wife face the problems of life in a remote part of North Georgia.
Pleasant, rambling, adequately serious and old-fashioned family entertainment, well presented in Hollywood's medium style.

w Lamar Trotti, novel Corra Harris d Henry King ph Edward Cronjager m Sol Kaplan md Lionel Newman

Susan Hayward, William Lundigan, Rory Calhoun, Barbara Bates, Gene Lockhart, Lynn Bari, Ruth Donnelly, Alexander Knox

I'd Rather Be Rich•
US 1964   96m   Eastmancolor
U–I / Ross Hunter

To comfort her dying grandfather, an heiress introduces an eligible stranger as her fiancé . . . but the old man recovers and begins matchmaking.
Reasonably zesty remake of It Started with Eve, kept afloat by Chevalier's performance.

w Oscar Brodney, Leo Townsend, Norman Krasna d Jack Smight ph Russell Metty m Percy Faith

Maurice Chevalier, Sandra Dee, Robert Goulet, Andy Williams, Gene Raymond, Hermione Gingold, Charles Ruggles

An Ideal Husband•
GB 1947   96m   Technicolor
British Lion / London Films (Alexander Korda)

In the nineties, the career of a London diplomat is threatened by the reappearance of an old flame.
A slight, stiff play is swamped by the cast, the decor, and very garish colour, but there are moments of enjoyment along the way.

w Lajos Biro, play Oscar Wilde d Alexander Korda ph Georges Périnal m Arthur Benjamin ad Vincent Korda cost Cecil Beaton

Paulette Goddard, Hugh Williams, Michael Wilding, Diana Wynyard, C. Aubrey Smith, Constance Collier, Glynis Johns, Christine Norden

'The composing and cutting of this fine raw material is seldom above medium grade.'— *James Agee*

Idiot's Delight*
US 1939   105m   bw
MGM (Hunt Stromberg)

At the outbreak of World War II, in a hotel on the Swiss border, a hoofer with an all-girl troupe meets an old flame masquerading as a Russian countess.

Interesting but quite unsuccessful film version of a highly artificial play which had been carried off superbly by the Lunts but was now somewhat less well cast, though it did represent an early Hollywood challenge to Hitler. The flagwaving in fact made it more than a little boring.

w Robert E. Sherwood, from his play *d* Clarence Brown *ph* William Daniels *m* Herbert Stothart

Clark Gable, Norma Shearer, Edward Arnold, Charles Coburn, Burgess Meredith, Joseph Schildkraut, Laura Hope Crews, Skeets Gallagher, Pat Patterson, Fritz Feld

'The fun and excitement are still there, however filtered it may be.'—*Film Daily*

'The mood of the whole thing is forced and cheap—the coming world war staged by Maurice Chevalier.'—*Otis Ferguson*

'Exactly the same pseudo-qualities as *The Petrified Forest*: a moral pretentiousness, a kind of cellophaned intellectuality.'—*Graham Greene*

The Idle Class*
US 1922   20m approx   bw   silent
First National / Charles Chaplin

A tramp dreams of the rich life and is mistaken for the husband of a lady.
Rather slight later Chaplin without the full-blooded farcical elements which made him so popular around 1917.

wd Charles Chaplin *ph* Rollie Totheroh

Charles Chaplin, Edna Purviance, Mack Swain

The Idol
GB 1966   111m   bw
Embassy (Leonard Lightstone)

A divorced woman falls in love with her son's friend.
Stupefyingly boring generation-gap sex drama.

w Millard Lampell *d* Daniel Petrie *ph* Ken Higgins *m* Johnny Dankworth

Jennifer Jones, Michael Parks, John Leyton, Jennifer Hilary, Guy Doleman, Natasha Pyne

Idol of Paris
GB 1948   105m   bw
Premier (R. J. Minney)

In old Paris, a ragman's daughter becomes queen of the demi-mondaines.
Unintentionally hilarious copy of the Gainsborough period romances which had been so popular; much criticized because the leading ladies fight a duel with whips, but that's the least of its faults.

w Norman Lee, Stafford Dickens, Henry Ostrer, *novel* Paiva Queen of Love by Alfred Shirkauer *d* Leslie Arliss *ph* Jack Cox

Beryl Baxter, Christine Norden, Michael Rennie, Margaretta Scott, Keneth Kent, Henry Oscar, Miles Malleson, Andrew Osborn, Andrew Cruickshank

If . . .***
GB 1968   111m   Eastmancolor
Paramount / Memorial (Lindsay Anderson, Michael Medwin)

Discontent at a boys' public school breaks out into rebellion.
Allegorical treatment of school life with much fashionable emphasis on obscure narrative, clever cutting, variety of pace, even an unaccountable changing from colour to monochrome and vice versa. Intelligence is clearly at work, but it seems to have suffered from undigested gobs of Pinter, and the film as a whole makes no discernible point.

w David Sherwin d Lindsay Anderson ph Miroslav Ondricek *m* Marc Wilkinson *pd* Jocelyn Herbert

Malcolm McDowell, David Wood, Richard Warwick, Robert Swann, Christine Noonan, Peter Jeffrey, Arthur Lowe, Anthony Nicholls

'The school . . . is the perfect metaphor for the established system all but a few of us continue to accept.'—*David Wilson*

'It's something like the Writing on the Wall.'—*Lindsay Anderson*

'Combines a cold and queasy view of youth with a romantic view of violence.'—*New Yorker*

If I Had a Million**
US 1932   88m   bw
Paramount (Benjamin Glazer, Louis D. Lighton)

Various people each receive a million dollars from an eccentric who wants to test their reactions.
Interesting, dated multi-part comedy drama remembered chiefly for the brief sequence in which Laughton blows a raspberry to his boss and Fields chases road hogs. As an

entertainment it's patchy, lacking an overall style.

w Claude Binyon, Whitney Bolton, Malcolm Stuart Boylan, John Bright, Sidney Buchman, Lester Cole, Isabel Dawn, Boyce DeGaw, Walter de Leon, Oliver H. P. Garrett, Harvey Gates, Grover Jones, Ernst Lubitsch, Lawton Mackaill, Joseph L. Mankiewicz, William Slavens McNutt, Seton I. Miller, Tiffany Thayer, *story* Robert D. Andrews *d* Ernst Lubitsch, Norman Taurog, Stephen Roberts, Norman Z. McLeod, James Cruze, William A. Seiter, H. Bruce Humberstone

W. C. Fields, *Charles Laughton, May Robson,* Richard Bennett, Alison Skipworth, Gary Cooper, Wynne Gibson, George Raft, Jack Oakie, Frances Dee, Charles Ruggles, Mary Boland, Roscoe Karns, Gene Raymond, Lucien Littlefield

'It develops an obvious idea in an obvious way.'—*Time*

If I Had My Way*
US 1940 82m bw
Universal (David Butler)

Two vaudevillians help an orphan girl and open a new night club.
Quite likeable and very typical star vehicle of its period.

w William Conselman, James V. Kern d David Butler ph George Robinson m Frank Skinner

Bing Crosby, Charles Winninger, Gloria Jean, El Brendel, Allyn Joslyn, Donald Woods, Eddie Leonard, Claire Dodd, Blanche Ring

If I Were King*
US 1938 101m bw
Paramount

The 14th-century poet and rascal François Villon matches wits with Louis XI and leads an uprising of the people.
A story which we have grown used to seeing with music as *The Vagabond King* is here well presented but somehow rings hollow, with insufficient derring-do; it is the wrong kind of swashbuckling for its star, who is for once outacted by Rathbone in an unusual wily characterization.

w Preston Sturges d Frank Lloyd m Richard Hageman ph Theodor Sparkuhl

Ronald Colman, *Basil Rathbone,* Frances Dee, Ellen Drew, C. V. France, Heather Thatcher, Henry Wilcoxon, Sidney Toler

AAN: Richard Hageman; Basil Rathbone

If I'm Lucky
US 1945 79m bw
TCF (Brian Foy)

A singer runs for state governor and exposes corruption.
Lacklustre remake of *Thanks a Million*, with decidedly dispirited elements.

w Snag Werris, Robert Ellis, Helen Logan, George Bricker d Lewis Seiler ph Glen MacWilliams *songs* Edgar de Lange, Joseph Myrow *md* Emil Newman

Vivian Blaine, Perry Como, Carmen Miranda, Harry James, Phil Silvers, Edgar Buchanan, Reed Hadley

If It's Tuesday, This Must Be Belgium*
US 1969 98m De Luxe
UA / Wolper (Stan Margulies)

A group of American tourists have various adventures during a lightning tour of Europe.
Amusing comedy which does pretty well by a good idea.

w David Shaw d Mel Stuart ph Vilis Lapenieks m Walter Scharf

Suzanne Pleshette, Ian McShane, Mildred Natwick, Murray Hamilton, Michael Constantine, Sandy Baron, Norman Fell, Peggy Cass, Marty Ingels, Pamela Britton, Luke Halpin, Aubrey Morris

If Winter Comes
US 1948 97m bw
MGM (Victor Saville)

A sentimental idealist, unhappily married, finds himself at the mercy of village gossip when he takes in a pregnant girl.
Artificial romantic nonsense, unconvincingly staged and modernized from a very dated bestseller.

w Marguerite Roberts, Arthur Wimperis, *novel* A. S. M. Hutchinson d Victor Saville ph George Folsey m Herbert Stothart

Walter Pidgeon, Deborah Kerr, Janet Leigh, Angela Lansbury, Binnie Barnes, Dame May Whitty, Reginald Owen

If You Could Only Cook
US 1935 72m bw
Columbia

A young millionaire meets a poor girl and they get jobs as cook and butler.
Whimsical comedy-romance; thin but moderately beguiling.

w F. Hugh Herbert, Gertrude Purcell, Howard J. Green d William A. Seiter

Jean Arthur, Herbert Marshall, Leo Carrillo, Lionel Stander, Frieda Inescort
† This was the film which enabled Frank Capra to get out of his Columbia contract, because they accidentally promoted it in Europe as being directed by him.

If You Know Susie*
US 1948 90m bw
RKO

A vaudeville couple retire to his ancestral home in New England.
Mild family comedy capitalizing on the team established in *Show Business*.

w Warren Wilson, Oscar Brodney *d* Gordon Douglas *ph* Frank Redman

Eddie Cantor, Joan Davis, Allyn Joslyn, Bobby Driscoll, Charles Dingle

Ikiru*
Japan 1952 143m bw
Toho
aka: *Living; Doomed*

A clerk learns that he is dying and spends his last months creating a children's playground.
A moving and beautifully made personal drama which also gives an interesting background of modern Japan.

w Hideo Oguni, Shinobu Hashimoto, Akira Kurosawa *d Akira Kurosawa ph* Asaishi Nakai *m* Fumio Hayasaka

Takashi Shimura, Nobuo Kaneko, Kyoko Seki

I'll Be Seeing You**
US 1944 85m bw
David O. Selznick (Dore Schary)

A lady convict at home on parole for Christmas meets and falls for a shell-shocked soldier.
Schmaltzy, middle-American romantic drama with some nicely handled moments and plenty of talent on hand. In the Hollywood mainstream.

w Marion Parsonnet, *novel* Charles Martin *d William Dieterle ph Tony Gaudio m* Daniele Amfitheatrof

Ginger Rogers, Joseph Cotten, Shirley Temple, Spring Byington, Tom Tully, Chill Wills
'A sentimental, improbable picture, but unexpectedly rewarding in detail.'—*Richard Mallett, Punch*

I'll Cry Tomorrow*
US 1955 119m bw
MGM (Lawrence Weingarten)

Lillian Roth, a Broadway / Hollywood star of the early thirties, becomes an alcoholic.
Fictionalized biopic, pretty well done of the True Confessions kind.

w Helen Deutsch, Jay Richard Kennedy, *book* Lillian Roth, Gerold Frank *d* Daniel Mann *ph* Arthur E. Arling *m* Alex North

Susan Hayward, Richard Conte, Eddie Albert, Jo Van Fleet, Don Taylor, Ray Danton, Margo

'By emphasizing physical degradation in almost every frame, the film makes her less an object of acutely personal concern than a street casualty seen remotely from the top of a bar.'—*Alexander Walker*

AAN: Arthur E. Arling; Susan Hayward

I'll Get By
US 1950 86m Technicolor
TCF (William Perlberg)

Two song writers meet success, then join the marines and are reunited with their former girl friends.
Fair standard musical, a modernization of *Tin Pan Alley*.

w Mary Loos, Richard Sale *d* Richard Sale *ph* Charles G. Clarke *md* Lionel Newman

June Haver, Gloria de Haven, William Lundigan, Dennis Day, Harry James, Thelma Ritter

AAN: Lionel Newman

I'll Get You for This
GB 1950 83m bw

An American gambler in Italy goes after the gangsters who framed him. Second-grade star thick-ear. George Raft, Coleen Gray, Charles Goldner, Walter Rilla, Greta Gynt, Enzo Staiola. Written by George Callahan and William Rose, from the novel *High Stakes* by James Hadley Chase; directed by Joseph M. Newman; for Romulus. (US title: *Lucky Nick Cain*.)

I'll Give a Million*
US 1938 70m bw
TCF (Darryl F. Zanuck)

A millionaire becomes a tramp and disappears, letting it be known that he will give a fortune for genuine acts of kindness. Tramps are then royally entertained all over town.
Amusing depression comedy with satirical touches.

w Boris Ingster, Milton Sperling *d* Walter Lang *ph* Lucien Andriot *md* Louis Silvers

Warner Baxter, Peter Lorre, Marjorie Weaver, Jean Hersholt, John Carradine, J. Edward Bromberg, Lynn Bari, Fritz Feld, Sig Rumann

Ill Met by Moonlight
GB 1956 104m bw Vistavision
Rank / Vega (Michael Powell, Emeric Pressburger)
US title: *Night Ambush*

In Crete during the German occupation, British agents work with partisans to capture a German general.

Disappointingly dreary war adventure with too
many night locations, too little suspense and
characterization, and photography which
seems to be deliberately unattractive.

wd Michael Powell, Emeric Pressburger, *book*
W. Stanley Moss *ph* Christopher Challis
m Mikis Theodorakis

Dirk Bogarde, Marius Goring, David Oxley,
Cyril Cusack, John Cairney, Laurence Payne,
Wolfe Morris, Michael Gough

I'll Never Forget Whatshisname*
GB 1967 96m Technicolor
Universal / Scimitar (Michael Winner)

An advertising executive gives up power and
money for integrity on a small literary
magazine, but is won back by a mogul.
Vivid yet muddled tragi-comedy of the sixties,
with splashes of sex and violence in trendy
settings, a hero one really doesn't believe in,
and a title which seems to have no meaning
whatsoever.

w Peter Draper *d Michael Winner ph* Otto
Heller *m* Francis Lai

Oliver Reed, Orson Welles, Carol White,
Harry Andrews, Michael Hordern, Wendy
Craig, Marianne Faithfull

I'll See You in My Dreams*
US 1952 112m bw
Warner (Louis F. Edelman)

The domestic and professional life of
songwriter Gus Kahn.
Quiet-toned, well made, quite forgettable
musical.

w Melville Shavelson, Jack Rose *d* Michael
Curtiz *ph* Ted McCord *md* Ray Heindorf
ch Le Roy Prinz

Doris Day, Danny Thomas, Frank Lovejoy,
Patrice Wymore, James Gleason

I'll Take Romance
US 1937 85m bw
Columbia (Everett Riskin)

When an opera singer refuses to fulfil a South
American contract, her impresario kidnaps
her.
Moderate star vehicle.

w George Oppenheimer, Jane Murfin
d Edward H. Griffith *ph* Lucien Andriot
songs various

Grace Moore, Melvyn Douglas, Helen
Westley, Stuart Erwin, Margaret Hamilton,
Walter Kingsford, Esther Muir

I'll Take Sweden
US 1965 96m Technicolor
UA / Edward Small

A widowed oil company executive accepts a
Stockholm posting to remove his teenage
daughter from an unsuitable attachment.
Feeble comedy which unwisely attempts to be
with it, but is bogged down by amateurish
handling and wit-wise is sadly without it.

w Nat Perrin, Bob Fisher, Arthur Marx
d Frederick de Cordova *ph* Daniel L. Fapp
m Jimmy Haskell

Bob Hope, Tuesday Weld, Frankie Avalon,
Dina Merrill, Jeremy Slate, John Qualen,
Walter Sande

I'll Tell the World
US 1945 61m bw

A small-town sports announcer starts a lonely
hearts programme. Amiable second feature, a
reworking of the star's earlier *Advice to the
Lovelorn*. Lee Tracy, Brenda Joyce, Raymond
Walburn, June Preisser, Thomas Gomez.
Written by Henry Blankfort; directed by
Leslie Goodwins; for Universal.

Illegal*
US 1955 88m bw
Warner (Frank P. Rosenberg)

A disillusioned District Attorney becomes a
racketeer's lawyer but finally denounces him at
the cost of his own life.
Competent remake of *The Mouthpiece* (qv), a
good star melodrama.

w W. R. Burnett, James R. Webb, *story*
Frank J. Collins *d* Lewis Allen *ph* Peverell
Marley *m* Max Steiner

Edward G. Robinson, Nina Foch, Albert
Dekker, Hugh Marlowe, Jayne Mansfield,
Howard St John, Ellen Corby
  'Hard-hitting stuff in the old gangster
tradition.'—*MFB*

Illegal Entry
US 1949 84m bw

Undercover agents investigate a smuggling
racket. Routine, quite entertaining alleged
exposé. Howard Duff, George Brent, Marta
Toren, Tom Tully, Paul Stewart, Gar Moore.
Written by Joel Malone; directed by Frederick
de Cordova; for Universal-International.

Illegal Traffic
US 1938 67m bw

The FBI tracks down an organization devoted
to smuggling criminals away from danger.
Smart second feature based on J. Edgar
Hoover's *Persons in Hiding*. J. Carrol Naish,
Mary Carlisle, Robert Preston. Written by
Robert Yost, Lewis Foster and Stuart
Anthony; directed by Louis King; for
Paramount.

Illicit
US 1931   81m   bw

A disillusioned wife walks out on her husband
and seeks solace elsewhere. Undistinguished
weepie, which later became *Ex-Lady*. Barbara
Stanwyck, Ricardo Cortez, Joan Blondell,
Charles Butterworth. Written by Harvey
Thew; directed by Archie Mayo; for Warner.

The Illustrated Man*
US 1969   103m   Technicolor
Panavision
Warner / SKM (Howard B. Kreitsek, Ted
Mann)

A strange wanderer tells weird stories based
on the tattooed pictures which cover him from
tip to toe.
Oddball compendium based rather insecurely
on Ray Bradbury stories; in this form they
don't amount to much but the presentation is
assured.

w Howard B. Kreitsek *d* Jack Smight
ph Philip Lathrop *m* Jerry Goldsmith *ad* Joel
Schiller

Rod Steiger, Claire Bloom, Robert Drivas,
Don Dubbins, Jason Evers
'A curiously passionless affair – efficient
enough, meaty enough, but without poetry,
without charm, without beauty.'—*Philip Strick*
'A pretentious comic strip of maudlin and
muddled fantasies.'—*Judith Crist*

Illustrious Corpses*
Italy / France 1975   120m   Technicolor
PEA / UA (Alberto Grimaldi)
original title: *Cadaveri Eccellenti*

A right-wing conspiracy to arouse feelings
against dissidents is found to be behind the
murders of public figures.
Elegant police melodrama on an unlikely
political thesis.

w Francesco Rosi, Tonino Guerra, Lino
Jannuzzi, *novel* Il Contesto by Leonardo
Sciascia *d* Francesco Rosi *ph* Pasqualino de
Santis *m* Piero Piccioni

Lino Ventura, Alain Cuny, Maolo Bonacelli,
Marcel Bozzuffi, Max Von Sydow, Fernando
Rey, Charles Vanel, Tina Aumont
'Like watching layer after layer peeled off
some diseased flower until the poisoned root is
reached.'—*Michael Billington, Illustrated
London News*

I'm All Right Jack***
GB 1959   104m   bw
British Lion / Charter (Roy Boulting)

A world-innocent graduate takes a job in

industry; by starting at the bottom he
provokes a national strike.
Satirical farce which manages to hit most of its
widespread targets and finds corruption in
high, low and middle places. A not inaccurate
picture of aspects of British life in the fifties,
and a presage of the satire boom to come with
Beyond the Fringe and *That Was the Week
That Was.*

w Frank Harvey, John Boulting, *novel* Private
Life by *Alan Hackney* *d* John Boulting
ph Max Greene *m* Ken Hare

Ian Carmichael, Peter Sellers, Irene Handl,
Richard Attenborough, *Terry-Thomas*, Dennis
Price, Margaret Rutherford, Liz Fraser, *John
Le Mesurier*, Sam Kydd

I'm No Angel***
US 1933   88m   bw
Paramount (William Le Baron)

A carnival dancer gets off a murder charge,
moves into society and sues a man for breach
of promise.
The star's most successful vehicle, credited
with saving the fortunes of Paramount,
remains a highly diverting side show with
almost a laugh a minute. Released before the
Legion of Decency was formed, it also
contains some of Mae's fruitiest lines.

w Mae West *d* Wesley Ruggles *ph* Leo Tover
Mae West, Edward Arnold, Cary Grant,
Gregory Ratoff, Ralf Harolde, Kent Taylor,
Gertrude Michael
'The most freewheeling of all Mae's screen
vehicles, and the most satisfying of the lot.'—
James Robert Parish

Images
Eire 1972   101m   Technicolor
Panavision
Lions Gate / Hemdale (Tommy Thompson)

A semi-hysterical woman is confronted by the
images of her former lovers.
Pretentious psycho-drama which might have
made a good half-hour.

wd Robert Altman *ph* Vilmos Zsigismond
m John Williams

Susannah York, René Auberjonois, Marcel
Bozzuffi

AAN: John Williams

Imitation General
US 1958   88m   bw
MGM (William Hawks)

France 1944: when a general is killed, a
sergeant takes his place to preserve morale.
Odd, rather unpalatable war comedy-drama.

w William Bowers *d* George Marshall
ph George Folsey

Glenn Ford, Red Buttons, Taina Elg, Dean
Jones, Kent Smith

Imitation of Life**
US 1934 109m bw
Universal

A woman becomes rich through the pancake
recipe of her black servant, but the latter has a
tragic life because her daughter passes for
white.
Monumentally efficient tearjerker, generally
well done.

w William Hurlbut, *novel* Fannie Hurst
d John Stahl ph Merritt Gerstad *m* Heinz
Roemheld

Claudette Colbert, Warren William, *Louise
Beavers*, Ned Sparks, Rochelle Hudson, Fredi
Washington, Alan Hale, Henry Armetta
    'Classic, compulsively watchable rags-to-
riches-and-heartbreak weeper.'—*New Yorker,
1977*

AAN: best picture

Imitation of Life*
US 1959 124m Eastmancolor
U-I (Ross Hunter)

Glossy remake of the above with its heroine
now an actress; stunningly produced but dully
acted, making its racially sensitive plot seem
insincere.

w Eleanore Griffin, Allan Scott *d Douglas
Sirk ph* Russell Metty *m* Frank Skinner

Lana Turner, Juanita Moore, John Gavin,
Susan Kohner, Dan O'Herlihy, Sandra Dee,
Robert Alda

AAN: Juanita Moore; Susan Kohner

The Immigrant**
US 1917 20m approx bw silent
Mutual

A penniless immigrant befriends a girl on the
boat and later helps her in a café.
One of the most inventive early Chaplins, with
touches of sentiment and social comment
which for once only strengthen and do not
antagonize.

wd Charles Chaplin ph William C. Foster,
Rollie Totheroh

Charles Chaplin, Edna Purviance, Albert
Austin, Henry Bergman, Eric Campbell
    'In its roughness and apparent simplicity it is
as much a jewel as a story by O. Henry.'—
Photoplay

Immoral Tales
France 1974 103m Eastmancolor
Argos (Anatole Dauman)

Four bawdy stories, ranging from 1498 to
1970.
The usual sex portmantcau with a little more
strength in the detail and interest in human
behaviour than usual.

wd Walerian Borowczyk *ph* Bernard
Daillencourt, Guy Durban, Michel Zolat,
Noel Véry *m* Maurice Le Roux

Lise Danvers, Charlotte Alexandra, Paloma
Picasso, Florence Bellamy
    'You come out having learned something
about the waywardness of life and love and
having been taken on a mystery tour into the
present, the past, and the enigmatic
strangeness of womanhood.'—*Michael
Billington, Illustrated London News*

The Immortal Sergeant*
US 1943 90m bw
TCF (Lamar Trotti)

In the North African campaign, a battle-
toughened sergeant is killed after inspiring the
raw recruits under his command.
'Inspirational' war adventure, quite neatly
done but a shade embarrassed by its own
poetic leanings.

w Lamar Trotti, *novel* John Brophy *d* John
Stahl *ph* Arthur Miller *m* David Buttolph

Henry Fonda, Thomas Mitchell, Maureen
O'Hara, Allyn Joslyn, Reginald Gardiner,
Melville Cooper, Branwell Fletcher, Morton
Lowry
    'By the time the first soldier has bit the
sand, the film identifies itself: it is none other
than Hollywood's old friend the Foreign
Legion of Beau Geste vintage, jerked from the
shelf and clothed in a new uniform.'—*Time*

Impact
US 1949 111m bw
(UA) Harry M. Popkin

A woman and her lover plan the murder of
her rich industrialist husband, but things go
wrong and the husband survives under another
name . . .
Curiously elongated but watchable
melodrama, with the impression of a second
team doing its best.

w Dorothy Reid *d* Arthur Lubin *ph* Ernest
Laszlo

Brian Donlevy, Ella Raines, Charles Coburn,
Helen Walker

The Impatient Maiden
US 1932 78m bw

A romantic maidservant learns the difference between life and fantasy. Solidly made comedy-drama which doesn't seem to have inspired its director. Mae Clarke, Lew Ayres, Una Merkel, John Halliday, Andy Devine, Berton Churchill. Written by Richard Schayer and Winifred Dunn, from the novel *The Impatient Virgin* by Donald Henderson Clarke; directed by James Whale; for Universal.

The Impatient Years
US 1944 91m bw
Columbia

A soldier finds difficulty in adjusting to his civilian matrimonial state.
Thin star comedy.

w Virginia Van Upp *d* Irving Cummings *ph* Hal Mohr *m* Marlin Skiles

Jean Arthur, Lee Bowman, Charles Coburn, Edgar Buchanan, Harry Davenport, Grant Mitchell, Jane Darwell

The Imperfect Lady
US 1946 97m bw
Paramount (Karl Tunberg)
GB title: *Mrs Loring's Secret*

In nineties London, an MP marries a lady with a past.
Dusty melodrama, adequately produced.

w Karl Tunberg, *story* Ladislas Fodor *d* Lewis Allen *ph* John F. Seitz *m* Victor Young

Ray Milland, Teresa Wright, Cedric Hardwicke, Virginia Field, Anthony Quinn, Reginald Owen, Melville Cooper, George Zucco, Rhys Williams, Charles Coleman, Miles Mander, Edmund Breon, Frederick Worlock

The Impersonator*
GB 1961 64m bw
Bryanston / Herald (Anthony Perry)

Americans at a British air base are suspected when a murderous prowler strikes.
Well made second-feature thriller with effective locations, suspense sequences and village atmosphere.

wd Alfred Shaughnessy ph John Coquillon *m* de Wolfe

John Crawford, Jane Griffith, Patricia Burke, John Salew

The Importance of Being Earnest**
GB 1952 95m Technicolor
Rank / Javelin / Two Cities (Teddy Baird)

Two wealthy and eligible bachelors of the nineties have problems with their marriage prospects.

Disappointingly stagey rendering (when compared, say, with *Occupe-toi d'Amélie*) of Britain's most wondrously witty lighter-than-air comedy of manners. As a record of a theatrical performance, however, it is valuable.

w Anthony Asquith, *play* Oscar Wilde *d* Anthony Asquith *ph* Desmond Dickinson *m* Benjamin Frankel *ad Carmen Dillon*

Michael Redgrave, Michael Denison, Edith Evans, Margaret Rutherford, Joan Greenwood, Miles Malleson, Dorothy Tutin, Walter Hudd

'A more positive decision on style should have been taken. A film of this kind must be either an adaptation or a piece of filmed theatre. This one, being partially both, is not wholly either.'—*Gavin Lambert*

The Impossible Years
US 1968 98m Metrocolor Panavision
MGM / Marten (Lawrence Weingarten)

A university psychiatrist has trouble controlling his nubile 17-year-old daughter.
Wacky farce which veers between the tasteless and the ludicrous, and is never more than momentarily entertaining.

w George Wells, *play* Bob Fisher, Arthur Marx *d* Michael Gordon *ph* William H. Daniels *m* Don Costa

David Niven, Lola Albright, Chad Everett, Ozzie Nelson, Cristina Ferrare, Don Beddoe

'A comedy of the generation gap which didn't bridge it but fell right into it.'—*Gerald Garrett*

In a Lonely Place*
US 1950 93m bw
Columbia / Santana (Robert Lord)

An embittered Hollywood scriptwriter escapes a murder charge but loses his girl friend through his violent temperament.
Curious character melodrama which intrigues without satisfying.

w Andrew Solt, *novel* Dorothy B. Hughes *d* Nicholas Ray *ph* Burnett Gu¾ey *m* George Antheil

Humphrey Bogart, Gloria Grahame, Frank Lovejoy, Carl Benton Reid, Art Smith, Jeff Donnell

'It remains better than average, but lacks the penetration which would make it really interesting.'—*Gavin Lambert*

In a Year with 13 Moons
West Germany 1978 129m colour

Ordeals of a man who undergoes a sex change. Unattractive case history with expressionist decoration. Volker Spengler, Ingrid Caven, Gottfried John. Written and directed by Rainer Werner Fassbinder; for Tango / Project / Filverlag der Autoren.

In Celebration
GB 1974   131m   Eastmancolor
Ely Landau / Cinevision

Three sons travel north for their miner father's fortieth wedding anniversary.
Sharply observant but fairly predictable dramatics, plainly filmed.

w David Storey, from his play d Lindsay Anderson ph Dick Bush m Christopher Gunning

Alan Bates, James Bolam, Brian Cox, Constance Chapman, Bill Owen

In Cold Blood*
US 1967   134m   bw   Panavision
Columbia / Richard Brooks

An account of a real life crime in which an entire family was brutally murdered by wandering gunmen.
Unnecessarily complicated as narrative, and uncompromisingly brutal in treatment, this well-meaning film is hard to take in many ways.

wd Richard Brooks, book Truman Capote ph Conrad Hall m Quincy Jones

Robert Blake, Scott Wilson, John Forsythe, Paul Stewart, Gerald S. O'Loughlin, Jeff Corey
'It marks a slight step up for its director, best remembered for reducing Lord Jim to pablum and The Brothers Karamazov to pulp.'—John Simon

AAN: Richard Brooks (as writer); Richard Brooks (as director); Conrad Hall; Quincy Jones

In Enemy Country
US 1968   107m   Techniscope
Universal (Harry Keller)

In 1939 Paris, the French secret service evolves an elaborate four-year undercover plan.
Standard, overlong espionage melodrama with no surprises.

w Edward Anhalt, story Sy Bartlett d Harry Keller ph Loyal Griggs m William Lava

Tony Franciosa, Anjanette Comer, Guy Stockwell, Paul Hubschmid, Tom Bell, Harry Townes, Michael Constantine, John Marley

In God We Trust
US 1980   97m   Technicolor

A monk leaves his monastery to raise some ready cash. Dismal and tasteless attempt at religious satire. Marty Feldman, Peter Boyle, Louise Lasser, Richard Pryor, Wilfrid Hyde White. Written by Marty Feldman and Chris Allen; directed by Marty Feldman; for Universal. 'A rare achievement—a comedy with no laughs.'—Variety.

In Harm's Way*
US 1965   167m   bw   Panavision
Paramount / Sigma (Otto Preminger)

The American navy retaliates after Pearl Harbor.
Odd mix of all-star action, spectacle (mostly models) and personal romances, with a few interesting scenes; shorn of colour it seems rather half-hearted.

w Wendell Mayes, novel James Bassett d Otto Preminger ph Loyal Griggs m Jerry Goldsmith titles Saul Bass

John Wayne, Kirk Douglas, Patricia Neal, Tom Tryon, Paula Prentiss, Brandon de Wilde, Stanley Holloway, Burgess Meredith, Henry Fonda, Dana Andrews, Franchot Tone, Jill Haworth, George Kennedy, Hugh O'Brian, Carroll O'Connor, Patrick O'Neal, Slim Pickens, Bruce Cabot, Larry Hagman, James Mitchum
'Lacks even a touch of the touch.'—Stanley Kauffmann

AAN: Loyal Griggs

In Like Flint
US 1967   107m   De Luxe   Cinemascope
TCF (Saul David)

Top agent Derek Flint unmasks a subversive female spy ring which has kidnapped the President.
This sequel to Our Man Flint (qv) is silly rather than funny, a spy spoof which becomes irritatingly hard to take.

w Hal Fimberg d Gordon Douglas ph William Daniels m Jerry Goldsmith

James Coburn, Lee J. Cobb, Jean Hall, Andrew Duggan, Anna Lee
'It gently founders in yards of flat dialogue, lavishly uninteresting sets, fuzzy colour processing, and a supporting cast in which all the girls look alarmingly mass produced.'—MFB

In Love and War
US 1958   111m   Eastmancolor   Cinemascope
TCF (Jerry Wald)

Three men from different backgrounds join the US Marines and see service in the Pacific.

Self-conscious propaganda concoction of bare routine interest.

w Edward Anhalt, *novel* Anton Myrer *d* Philip Dunne *ph* Leo Tover *m* Hugo Friedhofer

Jeffrey Hunter, Robert Wagner, Bradford Dillman, Dana Wynter, Hope Lange, Sheree North, France Nuyen

In Name Only*
US 1939 94m bw
RKO (Pandro S. Berman)

A rich man falls in love but his wife refuses a divorce.The stars seem unhappy in this sombre matrimonial drama, but of its kind it's surprisingly well made.

w Richard Sherman, *novel* Memory of Love by Bessie Brewer *d* John Cromwell *ph* J. Roy Hunt *m* Roy Webb

Cary Grant, Carole Lombard, Kay Francis, Charles Coburn, Helen Vinson

'Shot with a refined taste for interior decoration . . . it is oversweetened with the material for tears.'—*Graham Greene*

In Old Arizona**
US 1929 95m bw
Fox

Adventures of the Cisco Kid.
Primitive sound western, a sensation in its day but now of purely historical interest.

w Tom Barry, *stories* O. Henry *d* Raoul Walsh, Irving Cummings *ph* Arthur Edeson

Warner Baxter, Edmund Lowe, Dorothy Burgess, J. Farrell MacDonald
† See also *The Cisco Kid.*

AA: Warner Baxter
AAN: best picture; Tom Barry; Raoul Walsh, Irving Cummings; Arthur Edeson

In Old California
US 1942 89m bw

A Boston pharmacist heads west towards gold rush California. Moderate star western with parsimonious budget. John Wayne, Binnie Barnes, Albert Dekker, Helen Parrish, Patsy Kelly, Edgar Kennedy, Dick Purcell, Charles Halton. Written by Gertrude Purcell and Frances Hyland; directed by William McGann; for Republic.

In Old Chicago***
US 1937 115m bw
TCF (Kenneth MacGowan)

Events leading up to the great Chicago fire include a torrid romance between a gambler and a café singer.

Spectacular melodrama which with its two-million-dollar budget was a deliberate attempt to outdo *San Francisco*, and only failed because the cast was less interesting. A splendid studio super-production.

w Lamar Trotti, Sonya Levien, *novel* We the O'Learys by Niven Busch *d* Henry King, *ph* Peverell Marley *m* Louis Silvers *sp* H. Bruce Humberstone, Daniel B. Clark, Fred Sersen, Louis J. Witte *ad* William Darling

Tyrone Power, Alice Faye, Don Ameche, *Alice Brady*, Andy Devine, Brian Donlevy, Phyllis Brooks, Tom Brown, Sidney Blackmer, Berton Churchill, Paul Hurst, Rondo Hatton, Eddie Collins

AA: Alice Brady
AAN: best picture; Niven Busch (original story); Louis Silvers

In Our Time*
US 1944 110m bw
Warner (Jerry Wald)

English girl marries Polish count and helps defy the Nazis.
Ambitious, would-be meaningful melodrama that doesn't quite come off.

w Ellis St Joseph, Howard Koch *d* Vincent Sherman *ph* Carl Guthrie *m* Franz Waxman

Ida Lupino, Paul Henreid, Nancy Coleman, *Nazimova*, Mary Boland, Victor Francen, Michael Chekhov

'The story starts a good many hares but prudently refrains from following them.'—*Richard Mallett, Punch*

In Person
US 1935 85m bw
RKO (Pandro S. Berman)

A glamorous but exhausted film star tries to escape her public by fleeing incognito to the country.
Mild star comedy.

w Allan Scott, *novel* Samuel Hopkins Adams *d* William A. Seiter *ph* Edward Cronjager *m* Roy Webb *songs* Oscar Levant, Dorothy Fields

Ginger Rogers, George Brent, Alan Mowbray, Grant Mitchell, Samuel S. Hinds, Spencer Charters

In Search of Gregory
GB 1969 90m Technicolor
Universal / Vic Films / Vera Films (Joe Janni, Daniele Senatore)

A girl attends her father's wedding to meet a mysterious guest named Gregory, whom she never quite contacts.

Irritatingly pretentious Pinterish puzzle-drama with apparently no hidden depths except the urge to be clever.

w Tonino Guerra, Lucile Laks d Peter Wood ph Otto Heller, Giorgio Tonti m Ron Grainer

Julie Christie, Michael Sarrazin, John Hurt, Adolfo Celi, Roland Culver, Tony Selby

'Moments in a vacuum: however lively the surface, the centre remains depressingly inert.'—MFB

In Search of the Castaways***
GB 1961 100m Technicolor
Walt Disney (Hugh Attwooll)

With the aid of an eccentric professor, three children seek their lost explorer father in some geographically fantastic regions of South America.
Engaging Victorian fantasy which starts realistically but builds up to sequences in the manner of The Wizard of Oz and concludes in Treasure Island vein. Jaunty juvenile fare.

w Lowell S. Hawley, novel Captain Grant's Children by Jules Verne d Robert Stevenson ph Paul Beeson m William Alwyn ad Michael Stringer

Maurice Chevalier, Hayley Mills, George Sanders, Wilfrid Hyde White, Wilfrid Brambell

'A thousand thrills . . . and Hayley Mills!'—publicity

In Society*
US 1944 74m bw
Universal (Edmund Hartmann)

Two incompetent plumbers ruin a mansion.
One of the better A & C romps, with little padding between the comedy highlights, though the trimmings are fearsomely dated.

w John Grant, Hal Finberg, Edmund L. Hartmann d Jean Yarbrough ph Jerome Ash m Edgar Fairchild

Bud Abbott, Lou Costello, Kirby Grant, Ann Gillis, Arthur Treacher, Steve Geray, George Dolenz, Marion Hutton

In the Cool of the Day
US 1962 91m Metrocolor Panavision
MGM (John Houseman)

The frail wife of a New York publisher dies in Greece after an affair with his colleague.
Travelogue with romantic asides; a pretty glum business.

w Meade Roberts, novel Susan Ertz d Robert Stevens ph Peter Newbrook m Francis Chagrin ad Ken Adam

Jane Fonda, Peter Finch, Arthur Hill, Angela Lansbury, Constance Cummings

In the French Style*
US / France 1962 105m bw
Columbia / Casanna / Orsay (Robert Parrish, Irwin Shaw)

An American girl in Paris has affairs with a young boy and with a divorced newspaperman.
Smooth, episodic, romantic character study, well made but with no perceptible dramatic point.

w Irwin Shaw d Robert Parrish ph Michel Kelber m Josef Kosma

Jean Seberg, Stanley Baker, Philippe Fouquet

In the Good Old Summertime*
US 1949 102m Technicolor
MGM (Joe Pasternak)

In a Chicago music store in 1906, a salesgirl corresponds through a dating service with a man who turns out to be the manager she detests.
Cheerful remake of The Shop around the Corner (qv), with agreeable music, garish colour and not much style.

w Albert Hackett, Frances Goodrich, Ivan Tors, play Miklos Laszlo d Robert Z. Leonard ph Harry Stradling md George Stoll ad Randell Duell ch Robert Alton

Judy Garland, Van Johnson, S. Z. Sakall, Spring Byington, Clinton Sundberg, Buster Keaton, Lilian Bronson

In the Heat of the Night**
US 1967 109m De Luxe
UA / Mirisch (Walter Mirisch)

In a small southern town, the bigoted and bombastic sheriff on a murder hunt grudgingly accepts the help of a black detective.
Overrated policier in which the personality clash is amusing (and was timely) but the murder puzzle is a complete throwaway.

w Sterling Silliphant d Norman Jewison ph Haskell Wexler m Quincy Jones

Sidney Poitier, Rod Steiger, Warren Oates, Quentin Dean, William Schallert

'A very nice film and a very good film and yes, I think it's good to see a black man and a white man working together . . . but it's not going to take the tension out of New York City; it's not going to stop the riots in Chicago.'—Rod Steiger
† Poitier subsequently starred in a couple of very inferior sequels, They Call Me Mister Tibbs and The Organization (both qv).

AA: best picture; Sterling Silliphant; Rod Steiger
AAN: Norman Jewison

In the Navy*
US 1941   86m   bw
Universal (Alex Gottlieb)

Two incompetents and a singing heart-throb are naval recruits.

A basically feeble follow-up to *Buck Privates* which outgrossed its predecessor and now stands as an interesting pointer to how mass entertainment has changed since 1941.

w John Grant, Arthur T. Horman *d* Arthur Lubin *ph* Joseph Valentine *songs* Gene de Paul, Don Raye

Bud Abbott, Lou Costello, Dick Powell, The Andrews Sisters, Claire Dodd, Dick Foran, Shemp Howard

In the Soup
GB 1936   72m   bw

A solicitor and his wife are forced to pose as their own servants. Undernourished star comedy, and this star's last screen appearance. Ralph Lynn, Judy Gunn, Morton Selten, Nelson Keyes, Bertha Belmore. Written by H. Fowler Mear, from a play by Ralph Lumley; directed by Henry Edwards; for Twickenham.

In This Our Life**
US 1942   101m   bw
Warner (David Lewis)

A neurotic girl steals her sister's husband, leaves him in the lurch, dominates her hapless family and is killed while on the run from the police.

Splendid star melodrama with good supporting acting and background detail.

w Howard Koch, *novel* Ellen Glasgow *d* John Huston *ph* Ernest Haller *m* Max Steiner

Bette Davis, Charles Coburn, Olivia de Havilland, Frank Craven, George Brent, Dennis Morgan, Billie Burke, Hattie McDaniel, Lee Patrick, Walter Huston (uncredited)

'No one is as good as Bette when she's bad!'—*publicity*

In Which We Serve****
GB 1942   114m   bw
Rank / Two Cities (Noel Coward)

Survivors from a torpedoed destroyer recall their life at sea and on leave.

Dated but splendid flagwaver; an archetypal British war film of almost limitless propaganda value.

w Noel Coward *d* Noel Coward, David Lean *ph* Ronald Neame *m* Noel Coward

Noel Coward, Bernard Miles, *John Mills,* Richard Attenborough, *Celia Johnson,* Kay Walsh, Joyce Carey, Michael Wilding, Penelope Dudley Ward, Kathleen Harrison, Philip Friend, George Carney, Geoffrey Hibbert, James Donald

'One of the screen's proudest achievements at any time and in any country.'—*Newsweek*

'Never at any time has there been a reconstruction of human experience which could touch the savage grandeur and compassion of this production.'—*Howard Barnes, New York Herald Tribune*

AAN: best picture; Noel Coward (as writer)

Inadmissible Evidence**
GB 1968   96m   bw
Paramount / Woodfall (Ronald Kinnoch)

A frustrated 40-year-old solicitor is on the verge of a nervous breakdown.

Interesting and surprisingly successful transcription of a difficult play which was virtually an anti-humanity soliloquy.

w John Osborne, from his play *d* Anthony Page *ph* Kenneth Hodges *m* Dudley Moore *ad* Seamus Flannery

Nicol Williamson, Eleanor Fazan, Jill Bennett, Peter Sallis, Eileen Atkins, Isobel Dean

'A play that was conceived as an increasingly bad dream has been made into a grittily detailed, naturalistic film.'—*Stanley Kauffmann*

Incendiary Blonde*
US 1945   112m   Technicolor
Paramount (Joseph Sistrom)

The life of twenties nightclub queen Texas Guinan.

Laundered biopic with guns, girls and gangsters as well as songs.

w Claude Binyon, Frank Butler *d* George Marshall *ph* Ray Rennahan *m* Robert Emmett Dolan

Betty Hutton, Arturo de Cordova, Charles Ruggles, Albert Dekker, Barry Fitzgerald, Mary Phillips, Bill Goodwin, Eduardo Ciannelli, Maurice Rocco

'It runs its noisy but high-minded course through steamy emotion, painful misunderstanding and dramatic self-sacrifice, winding up in the snow among the blood of dead gangsters. Have we ever seen gangsters in Technicolor before?'—*Richard Mallett, Punch*

AAN: Robert Emmett Dolan

Incident at Phantom Hill
US 1966   88m   Technicolor

Two men face desperate odds to reach one million dollars in gold. Full-blooded western programmer with useful performances. Robert Fuller, Dan Duryea, Jocelyn Lane, Claude Akins, Noah Beery Jnr. Written by Frank Nugent; directed by Earl Bellamy; for Universal.

Les Inconnus dans la Maison°
France 1941   94m   bw
Continental

An embittered ex-barrister saves his teenage daughter from a murder charge.
Unlikely melodrama remade as *Stranger in the House*; this version has more compelling writing and acting.

w Henri-Georges Clouzot, *novel* Georges Simenon *d* Henri Decoin *ph* Jules Kruger *m* Roland Manuel

Raimu, Juliette Faber, Jacques Baumer, Jean Tissier

The Incredible Journey**
US 1963   80m   Technicolor
Walt Disney (James Algar)

Two dogs and a cat, separated from their owners, escape and travel 250 miles home.
A novelty attraction which keeps going purely on its animal interest, which is considerable.

w James Algar, *book* Sheila Burnford *d* Fletcher Markle *ph* Kenneth Peach, Jack Couffer, Lloyd Beebe *m* Oliver Wallace

The Incredible Melting Man
US 1977   84m   Movielab
AIP / Quartet (Max J. Rosenberg)

The survivor of a space flight is rushed to hospital with radiation burns and an infection which causes his flesh to melt.
Unpleasant and nonsensical horror film with a few unintentional laughs and a plot borrowed from *The Quatermass Experiment*.

wd William Sachs *ph* Willy Curtis *m* Arlon Ober

Alex Rebar, Burr DeBenning, Myron Healey, Myron Aldredge

The Incredible Mr Limpet
US 1964   102m   Technicolor
Warner (John C. Rose)

A meek but patriotic clerk is turned down by the navy and turns into a fish. In this form he becomes a radar assistant to a warship.
Sentimental sub-Disney goo, part animated.

w Jameson Bewer, John C. Rose, *novel* Theodore Pratt *d* Arthur Lubin *ph* Harold Stine *m* Frank Perkins

Don Knotts, Andrew Duggan, Larry Keating, Jack Weston

The Incredible Sarah°
GB 1976   105m   Technicolor
Readers Digest (Helen M. Strauss)

The career of French actress Sarah Bernhardt up to the age of thirty-five.
Mildly pleasing old-fashioned biopic with remarkably unreliable detail and a regrettably bland approach to its fascinating subject.

w Ruth Wolff *d* Richard Fleischer *ph* Christopher Challis *m* Elmer Bernstein *pd* Elliot Scott

Glenda Jackson, Daniel Massey, Yvonne Mitchell, Douglas Wilmer, David Langton, Simon Williams, John Castle, Edward Judd, Peter Sallis

'An incredibly old-fashioned movie full of the most unforgettable moments you have ever tried to forget.'—*Andrew Sarris, Village Voice*

'A job lot of obligatory Hollywood platitudes strung together with all the skill of Captain Hook trying to thread a needle.'— *Benny Green, Punch*

The Incredible Shrinking Man**
US 1957   81m   bw
U-I (Albert Zugsmith)

After being caught in a radioactive mist, a man shrinks inexorably to micro-size.
Horrifyingly inevitable sci-fi with imaginative touches gracing a cheap production.

w Richard Matheson *d* Jack Arnold *ph* Ellis W. Carter *m* Joseph Gershenson *sp* Clifford Stine, Roswell A. Hoffman, Everett H. Bronssard

Grant Williams, Randy Stuart, April Kent, Paul Langton

'It opens up new vistas of cosmic terror.'— *Peter John Dyer*

The Indian Fighter
US 1955   88m   Technicolor
Cinemascope
UA / Bryna (William Schorr)

An Indian fighter protects a wagon train from the Sioux.
Simple-minded western with touches of philosophy and not much drive.

w Frank Davis, Ben Hecht *d* André de Toth *ph* Wilfrid M. Cline *m* Franz Waxman

Kirk Douglas, Elsa Martinelli, Walter Abel, Walter Matthau, Diana Douglas, Eduard Franz, Lon Chaney Jnr, Alan Hale Jnr, Elisha Cook Jnr

Indian Scout
US 1949   70m   bw

Episodes in the life of Davy Crockett. Minor western which hit the spot with small-town audiences, and in the late fifties, after the success of the Disney film, was reissued as *Davy Crockett, Indian Scout.* George Montgomery, Ellen Drew, Philip Reed, Noah Beery Jnr. Written by Richard Schayes; directed by Ford Beebe; for Edward Small.

Indiscreet**
GB 1958 100m Technicolor
Grandon (Stanley Donen)

An American diplomat in London falls in love with an actress but protects himself by saying he is married.

Affairs among the ultra rich, amusing when played by these stars but with imperfect production values which the alarmingly thin plot allows one too much time to consider.

w Norman Krasna, from his play Kind Sir *d* Stanley Donen *ph* Frederick A. Young *m* Richard Bennett, Ken Jones

Cary Grant, Ingrid Bergman, Phyllis Calvert, Cecil Parker, David Kossoff, Megs Jenkins
'One is often on the point of being bored, but one never is, quite.'—*Richard Roud*

'A film to which you would not hesitate to take your jeweller, your architect, your home decorator, your dressmaker and your domestic staff.'—*Alexander Walker*

Indiscretion of an American Wife*
Italy / US 1954 75m bw
David O. Selznick (Vittorio de Sica)
Alternative titles: *Terminus Station, Indiscretion*

An American woman and an Italian professor say goodbye in Rome's terminal station.
Strained attempt to re-do *Brief Encounter* against the busy background of a great railway station; moments of interest, but artificiality prevails, and the plot never gets up enough steam.

w Cesare Zavattini, Truman Capote, etc *d* Vittorio de Sica *ph* G. R. Aldo *m* Aldo Cicognini

Jennifer Jones, Montgomery Clift, Gino Cervi, Richard Beymer

Inferno**
US 1953 83m Technicolor 3-D
TCF (William Bloom)

When a millionaire breaks his leg in the desert, his wife and her lover leave him to die; but he contrives to catch up with them.
An outdoor melodrama which made better use of 3-D than any other film, suggesting the lone handicapped figure in the vast spaces; but the lovers are dull and the fire climax perfunctory.

w Francis Cockrell *d* Roy Baker *ph* Lucien Ballard *m* Paul Sawtell

Robert Ryan, William Lundigan, Rhonda Fleming

Inferno
Italy 1980 107m Technicolor

A New York apartment house is occupied by satanists who murder those who learn their secret. Absurdly overplotted and mainly incomprehensible shocker with some small pretensions to style. Leigh McCloskey, Irene Miracle, Eleonora Giorgi. Written and directed by Dario Argento; for TCF.

The Informer****
US 1935 91m bw
RKO (Cliff Reid)

An IRA leader is betrayed by a simple-minded hanger-on who wants money to emigrate; he is hounded by fellow rebels and his own conscience.
A tedious plot is turned into brilliant cinema by full-blooded acting and a highly stylized yet brilliantly effective *mise en scène* which never attempts reality.

w Dudley Nichols, *novel* Liam O'Flaherty *d* John Ford *ph* Joseph H. August *m* Max Steiner *ad* Van Nest Polglase

Victor McLaglen, Heather Angel, Margot Grahame, Una O'Connor, Wallace Ford, Preston Foster, J. M. Kerrigan, Joe Sawyer, Donald Meek
'As impressive as *Scarface*, or anything in the whole powerful literature redolent of fog and grime and dreariness which the Germans gave to the Americans.'—*Bardèche and Brasillach*

† An early British sound version was made in 1929 by Arthur Robison for BIP, with Lars Hansen and Lya de Putti.

AA: Dudley Nichols; John Ford; Max Steiner; Victor McLaglen
AAN: best picture

The Informers
GB 1963 104m bw
Rank (William MacQuitty)
US title: *Underworld Informers*

A police informer is murdered and his brother takes revenge.
Basic police melodrama, with clumsy script and jaded direction.

w Alun Falconer, *novel* Death of a Snout by Douglas Warner *d* Ken Annakin *ph* Reg Wyer *m* Clifton Parker

Nigel Patrick, Colin Blakely, Derren Nesbitt

L'Ingénue Libertine
France 1950 88m approx bw
Codo-Cinéma (Jean Velter)

A romantic girl lives in an imaginary world of
affairs, but can't bring herself to consummate
her marriage.

Minor period sex comedy which has the
distinction of being Britain's first 'X' film,
though the naughtiness is more implied than
stated.

w P. Laroche, *novel* Colette d Jacqueline
Audry ph Grignon m Vincent Scotto

Daniele Delorme, Frank Villard, Jean Tissier

Inherit the Wind•••
US 1960 127m bw
UA / Lomitas (Stanley Kramer)

A fictionalized account of the 1925 Scopes
'monkey trial', when a schoolmaster was
accused of teaching the theory of evolution.
Splendid theatrics with fine performances,
marred by boring subplots but enhanced by a
realistic portrait of a sweltering southern town.

w Nathan E. Douglas, Harold Jacob Smith,
play Jerome Lawrence, Robert E. Lee
d Stanley Kramer ph Ernest Laszlo m Ernest
Gold

Spencer Tracy, Fredric March, Florence
Eldridge, Gene Kelly, Dick York, Donna
Anderson, Harry Morgan, Elliott Reid,
Claude Akins

AAN: script; Ernest Laszlo; Spencer Tracy

The In-Laws
US 1979 103m Technicolor
Warner (Alan Arkin)

A timorous dentist and a CIA spy, whose
children are to marry, find themselves
unwillingly linked together in gunplay in a
South American republic.

Two charismatic actors can't fail to get some
laughs, but the extended script makes it a
bumpy ride.

w Andrew Bergman d Arthur Hiller
ph David M. Walsh m John Morris pd Pato
Guzman

Peter Falk, Alan Arkin, Richard Libertini,
Penny Peyser, Nancy Dussault

'It seems incapable either of adhering to the
conventions of a comedy-thriller plot or of
mustering sufficient invention to abandon plot
altogether for a farcical free-for-all.'—*Tim
Pulleine, MFB*

The Inn of the Sixth Happiness••
GB 1958 158m De Luxe Cinemascope
TCF (Mark Robson)

An English servant girl becomes a missionary
and spends many arduous years in China.
Romanticized biopic of Gladys Aylward, with
lots of children, a happy ending, and everyone
sensationally miscast. Somehow it all works,
even North Wales standing in for China.

w Isobel Lennart, *book* The Small Woman by
Alan Burgess d Mark Robson ph Frederick
A. Young m Malcolm Arnold

Ingrid Bergman, Curt Jurgens, Robert Donat,
Athene Seyler, Ronald Squire, Richard
Wattis, Moultrie Kelsall

AAN: Mark Robson

Inner Sanctum
The title was taken from a radio show
featuring mystery stories with a last minute
twist. The films were introduced rather oddly
by a misshapen head in a crystal ball on the
empty table of a boardroom. The head
belonged to David Hoffman, and he
introduced each film: 'This . . . is the inner
sanctum . . .' (The original reference was
presumably to the innermost working of the
human mind.) The films, made for Universal,
all starred Lon Chaney Jnr (who alternated as
hero and villain); they were among the most
boring and badly made second feature thrillers
of the forties.
1943: CALLING DR DEATH
1944: WEIRD WOMAN, DEAD MAN'S
EYES
1945: STRANGE CONFESSION (remake of
THE MAN WHO RECLAIMED HIS
HEAD), THE FROZEN GHOST
1946: PILLOW OF DEATH

Innocent Bystanders•
GB 1972 110m Eastmancolor
Sagittarius (George H. Brown)

The British secret service sends three agents to
trace a Russian traitor.
Confused and violent espionage thriller; rather
a waste of good production.

w James Mitchell d Peter Collinson ph Brian
Probyn m John Keating

Stanley Baker, Geraldine Chaplin, Dana
Andrews, Donald Pleasence

Innocent Sinners••
GB 1957 95m bw
Rank (Hugh Stewart)

A 13-year-old London girl builds a garden in
the rubble of a bombed church, and gets into
trouble with the police.
Likeable, slightly unfinished, mildy
astringent little human drama full of well-
observed character sketches.

w Neil Paterson, novel An Episode of Sparrows by Rumer Godden *d Philip Leacock ph* Harry Waxman *m* Philip Green

Flora Robson, Catherine Lacey, David Kossoff, Barbara Mullen, June Archer

The Innocents**
GB 1961 99m bw Cinemascope
TCF / Achilles (Jack Clayton)

In Victorian times, a spinster governess in a lonely house finds her young charges possessed by evil demons of servants now dead.
Elaborate revamping of Henry James' *The Turn of the Screw*, the ghosts being now (possibly) the figments of a frustrated woman's imagination. The frissons would have worked better on a normal-shaped screen, but the decor, lighting and general handling are exceptional.

w William Archibald, Truman Capote *d Jack Clayton ph* Freddie Francis *m* Georges Auric *ad Wilfrid Shingleton*

Deborah Kerr, Megs Jenkins, Pamela Franklin, Martin Stephens, Michael Redgrave, Peter Wyngarde

Innocents in Paris
GB 1953 102m bw
Romulus (Anatole de Grunwald)

British tourists spend a weekend in the gay city.
Strained compendium of anecdotes which misses an easy target.

w Anatole de Grunwald *d* Gordon Parry *ph* Gordon Lang *m* Josef Kosma

Alastair Sim, Margaret Rutherford, Jimmy Edwards, Claire Bloom, Laurence Harvey, Ronald Shiner

Innocents of Paris
US 1929 69m bw
Paramount

A Parisian junk dealer saves a boy's life and falls for his aunt.
Heavygoing and dated musical comedy which introduced Chevalier to world audiences.

w Ethel Doherty, Ernest Vajda *d* Richard Wallace *ph* Charles Lang *songs* Leo Robin, Richard A. Whiting

Maurice Chevalier, Sylvia Beecher, Russell Simpson, George Fawcett

Inquest*
GB 1939 60m bw
Charter (John Boulting)

A coroner has his suspicions as to who murdered the deceased.

Modest courtroom suspenser which marked the Boultings' first attempt (the second was *Suspect*) to raise the standard of second features.

w Francis Miller, *play* Michael Barringer *d* Roy Boulting

Elizabeth Allan, Herbert Lomas, Hay Petrie, Barbara Everest, Olive Sloane

Inserts*
GB 1975 117m De Luxe
UA / Film and General (Davina Belling, Clive Parsons)

In 1930 Hollywood, a fading silent queen and a has-been director take to drugs.
Curious, interesting semi-porno melodrama with Pinterish asides and an inaccurate but stimulating feel of the film city at its height.

wd John Byrum *ph* Denys Coop *md* Jessica Harper

Richard Dreyfuss, Jessica Harper, Veronica Cartwright, Bob Hoskins, Stephen Davies

   'The ludicrous plot and the painfully obvious symbolism make it tempting to interpret *Inserts* as a comedy. Yet to assume that a bad movie about the making of a bad movie is somehow good by virtue of its badness is to be guilty of a kind of mimetic fallacy.'—*Robert Asahina, New Leader*

Inside Daisy Clover*
US 1965 128m Technicolor
   Panavision
Warner / Pakula–Mulligan (Alan J. Pakula)

Tribulations of an adolescent movie star in thirties Hollywood.
Amusing, rather hysterical variant on *A Star Is Born*; agreeably wacky in spots, glum in others. Would have benefited from the greater permissiveness possible a few years later.

w Gavin Lambert, from his novel *d* Robert Mulligan *ph* Charles Lang Jnr *m* André Previn *ch* Herbert Ross *ad* Robert Clatworthy

Natalie Wood, Robert Redford, Ruth Gordon, Christopher Plummer, Roddy MacDowall

   'The movie is short on characters, detail, activity, dialogue, even music; it's as if it's so determined to be stylish and sophisticated that rather than risk vulgarity or banality, it eliminates almost everything.'—*Pauline Kael, 1968*

AAN: Ruth Gordon

Inside Out*
GB / West Germany 1975   97m
  Technicolor
Warner / Kettledrum (Judd Bernard)
TV title: *The Golden Heist*
aka: *Hitler's Gold*

A German ex-commandant of a POW camp
enlists the aid of Americans in a daring plan to
kidnap a Nazi war criminal from East
Germany and find buried Nazi loot.
Entertaining but very silly actioner with too
many changes of mood, though some
sequences please.

w Judd Bernard, Stephen Schneck d Peter
Duffell ph John Coquillon m Konrad Elfers

Telly Savalas, James Mason, Robert Culp,
Aldo Ray, Gunter Meisner, Adrian Hoven,
Charles Korvin, Richard Warner

The Inspector*
GB 1961   111m   De Luxe   Cinemascope
TCF (Mark Robson)
US title: *Lisa*

In 1946 a Dutch policeman rescues a Jewish
girl from an ex-Nazi and helps smuggle her to
Palestine.
Peripatetic melodrama with surface suspense
and subdued thoughts of ideology and race.
Moments of interest, but generally dully
developed and acted.

w Nelson Gidding, *novel* Jan de Hartog
d Philip Dunne ph Arthur Ibbetson
m Malcolm Arnold

Stephen Boyd, Dolores Hart, Leo McKern,
Hugh Griffith, Donald Pleasence, Harry
Andrews, Robert Stephens, Marius Goring
  'A sluggish mélange of melodrama,
romance, mystery and what the inactive might
call action.'—*Judith Crist*

An Inspector Calls**
GB 1954   79m   bw
British Lion / Watergate (A. D. Peters)

In 1912 a prosperous Yorkshire family is
visited by a mysterious inspector who proves
that each of them was partly responsible for
the death of a young girl.
Tactful, enjoyable record of a celebrated play
in its author's most typical manner.

w Desmond Davis, *play* J. B. Priestley d Guy
Hamilton ph Ted Scaife m Francis Chagrin
ad Joseph Bato

Alastair Sim, Jane Wenham, Arthur Young,
Olga Lindo, Brian Worth, Eileen Moore,
Bryan Forbes

Inspector Clouseau
GB 1968   105m   Eastmancolor
  Panavision
UA / Mirisch (Lewis J. Rachmil)

An incompetent French policeman is brought
to London to investigate the aftermath of the
Great Train Robbery.
Tiresome charade with all the jokes well
telegraphed, and a background of swinging
London.

w Tom and Frank Waldman d Bud Yorkin
ph Arthur Ibbetson m Ken Thorne

Alan Arkin, Delia Boccardo, Frank Finlay,
Patrick Cargill, Beryl Reid, Barry Foster

The Inspector General**
US 1949   101m   Technicolor
Warner (Jerry Wald)
aka: *Happy Times*

An assistant elixir salesman with a travelling
fair is mistaken by villagers for the dreaded
inspector general.
Well wrought but basically boring version of a
basically boring classic farce full of rhubarbing
Old Russians. Nice production and hilarious
moments do not quite atone for the dull
stretches.

w Philip Rapp, Harry Kurnitz, *play* Nikolai
Gogol d Henry Koster ph Elwood Bredell
songs Sylvia Fine m John Green ad Robert
Haas

Danny Kaye, Walter Slezak, Barbara Bates,
Elsa Lanchester, Gene Lockhart, Alan Hale,
Benny Baker, Walter Catlett

Inspector Hornleigh*
GB 1938   87m   bw
TCF (Robert T. Kane)

The Chancellor of the Exchequer's bag is
stolen.
First of three police comedy-dramas based on
a character created for the radio series
Monday Night at Eight by Hans Priwin. Not
bad, but the thinnest of the trio.

w Bryan Wallace, Gerald Elliott, Richard
Llewellyn d Eugene Forde ph Derrick
Williams

Gordon Harker, Alastair Sim, Hugh Williams,
Steve Geray, Wally Patch, Edward
Underdown, Gibb McLaughlin, Ronald Adam
  'The opening shots—the murder in the
squalid lodging and the stamp auction with the
rows of poker faces and the elaborately mute
bids—are not only good cinema, they are good
English cinema, as national as a shot, say,
from a Feyder, a de Mille or a Pommer.'—
Graham Greene

Inspector Hornleigh Goes to It°
GB 1940   87m   bw
TCF (Edward Black)
US title: *Mail Train*

Hornleigh and Bingham track down a fifth
columnist.
Zestful comedy thriller climaxing on an
express train: good fun for addicts of the
genre.

*w Val Guest, J. O. C. Orton, Frank Launder
d* Walter Forde *ph* John Cox *md* Louis Levy

Gordon Harker, Alastair Sim, Phyllis Calvert,
Edward Chapman, Charles Oliver, Raymond
Huntley, Percy Walsh, David Horne, Peter
Gawthorne

Inspector Hornleigh on Holiday°
GB 1939   87m   bw
TCF (Edward Black)

The inspector and his sergeant solve the death
of a fellow boarder at a seaside hotel.
Lively Hitchcockian comedy-thriller romp with
an excellent script and plenty of variety of
location.

*w Frank Launder, Sidney Gilliat, J. O. C.
Orton d* Walter Forde *ph* John Cox
md Louis Levy

Gordon Harker, Alastair Sim, Linden Travers,
Wally Patch, Edward Chapman, Philip
Leaver, Kynaston Reeves

Inspiration
US 1930   74m   bw
MGM

A French artists' model renounces her lover in
case she harms his career.
Inane romantic melodrama.

w Gene Markey *d* Clarence Brown
ph William Daniels

Greta Garbo, Robert Montgomery, Lewis
Stone, Marjorie Rambeau, Beryl Mercer,
John Miljan

The Intelligence Men
GB 1965   104m   Eastmancolor
Rank / Hugh Stewart
US title: *Spylarks*

Two incompetent spies blunder through a
series of adventures.
Inept and rather embarrassing big-screen
debut for two excellent television comedians.

w S. C. Green, R. M. Hills *d* Robert Asher
ph Jack Asher *m* Phillip Green

Eric Morecambe, Ernie Wise, William
Franklyn, April Olrich, Richard Vernon,
David Lodge, Warren Mitchell, Francis
Matthews

Intent to Kill°
GB 1958   89m   bw   Cinemascope
TCF / Zonic (Adrian Worker)

In a Montreal hospital, attempts are made on
the life of a South American dictator
recovering from a brain operation.
Solidly entertaining suspenser.

w Jimmy Sangster *d* Jack Cardiff
ph Desmond Dickinson *m* Kenneth V. Jones

Richard Todd, Betsy Drake, Herbert Lom,
Warren Stevens, Alexander Knox

Interference
US 1929   75m   bw

To prevent his wife from being blackmailed, a
dying man commits murder and turns himself
in. Dreary drama with the distinction of being
Paramount's first talking picture. William
Powell, Evelyn Brent, Clive Brook, Doris
Kenyon. Written by Ernest Pascal and Hope
Loring, from the play by Roland Pertwee and
Harold Dearden; directed by Lothar Mendes
and Roy Pomeroy; for Paramount.

Interiors°
US 1978   95m   Technicolor
UA / Jack Rollins-Charles H. Joffe

Everybody in a well-heeled American family
has problems.
Curious attempt by Woody Allen to make his
own version of the Bergmanesque psycho-
dramas he usually satirizes. Apparently this is
the real Woody, and the comedian was a
mask. Oh, well.

wd Woody Allen *ph* Gordon Willis *m* none

Kristin Griffith, Marybeth Hurt, Richard
Jordan, Diane Keaton, E. G. Marshall,
Geraldine Page, Maureen Stapleton, Sam
Waterston

AAN: script; direction; Geraldine Page;
Maureen Stapleton

'As dull as toothache and as predictable as a
metronome.'—*Barry Took, Punch*

Interlude
US 1957   89m   Technicolor
  Cinemascope
U-I (Ross Hunter)

An American girl in Munich falls in love with
an orchestral conductor but leaves him
because of his insane wife.
Dull remake of *When Tomorrow Comes* (qv),
with poor script and performances.

w Daniel Fuchs, Franklin Coen *d* Douglas
Sirk *ph* R. F. Schoengarth *m* Frank Skinner

Rossano Brazzi, June Allyson, Françoise
Rosay, Marianne Cook, Keith Andes, Jane
Wyatt

'Contains every cliché known to romantic fiction.'—*MFB*

Interlude*
GB 1968 113m Technicolor
Columbia / Domino (David Deutsch, Jack Hanbury)

A girl reporter falls for a celebrated orchestral conductor; they have an affair but he finally goes back to his wife.

Intermezzo remade for the swinging London set, quite agreeable in parts because of the acting but generally rather soggy.

w Lee Langley, Hugh Leonard d Kevin Billington ph Gerry Fisher m Georges Delerue pd Tony Woolard

Oskar Werner, Barbara Ferris, *Virginia Maskell*, *John Cleese*, Donald Sutherland, Nora Swinburne, Alan Webb

'If you laughed at *Brief Encounter* you will roar over this one.'—*Wilfrid Sheed*

'It's got all the schmaltz and none of the style of the tearjerkers of yesteryear.'—*Judith Crist, 1973*

Intermezzo***
US 1939 69m bw
David O. Selznick
GB title: *Escape to Happiness*

A renowned, married violinist has an affair with his musical protégée.

Archetypal cinema love story, Hollywoodized from a Swedish original but quite perfect in its brief, sentimental way.

w George O'Neil, *original scenario* Gosta Stevens, Gustav Molander d Gregory Ratoff ph Gregg Toland m Robert Henning, Heinz Provost m (score) Lou Forbes

Leslie Howard, *Ingrid Bergman*, John Halliday, Edna Best, Cecil Kellaway

'To one woman he gave his memories; to another he gave his dreams.'—*publicity*

AAN: Lou Forbes

International House*
US 1932 73m bw
Paramount

A weird variety of travellers are quarantined in a Shanghai hotel where a local doctor has perfected television.

Madcap farce which succeeds in hits and misses.

w Francis Martin, Walter de Leon, Lou Heifetz, Neil Brant d Edward Sutherland ph Ernest Haller

W. C. Fields, *George Burns*, *Gracie Allen*, Peggy Hopkins Joyce, Stuart Erwin, Sari

Matitza, Bela Lugosi, Edmund Breese, Lumsden Hare, Rose Marie, Rudy Vallee, Sterling Holloway, Cab Calloway and his band, Colonel Stoopnagle and Budd

'Constructed along the lines of a mammoth vaudeville show, the motivating story often is sidetracked entirely to permit a lot of unrelated hokum comedy.'—*Motion Picture Herald*

International Lady*
US 1941 102m bw
Edward Small

An FBI man falls for the lady Axis agent he is chasing.

Cliché-ridden melodrama partially saved by light comedy touches.

w Howard Estabrook d Tim Whelan ph Hal Mohr m Lucien Moraweck

George Brent, Basil Rathbone, Ilona Massey, Gene Lockhart, George Zucco, Francis Pierlot, Martin Kosleck, Marjorie Gateson

International Settlement
US 1938 75m bw
TCF (Darryl F. Zanuck)

An adventurer becomes involved in Shanghai gun-running during the war between China and Japan.

Brisk action romance with good technical credits.

w Lou Breslow, John Patrick d Eugene Forde ph Lucien Andriot md Samuel Kaylin

George Sanders, Dolores del Rio, June Lang, Dick Baldwin, Ruth Terry, John Carradine, Keye Luke, Harold Huber, Pedro de Cordoba

International Squadron*
US 1941 87m bw
Warner (Edmund Grainger)

A playboy becomes a fighting air ace.

Standard war story, quite well done; remake of *Ceiling Zero* (qv).

w Barry Trivers, *story* Frank Wead d Lewis Seiler ph Arthur Edeson

Ronald Reagan, James Stephenson, Julie Bishop, Cliff Edwards, Reginald Denny, Olympe Bradna, William Lundigan, John Ridgely

International Velvet
GB 1978 125m Metrocolor
MGM (Bryan Forbes)

A hostile orphan becomes an international horsewoman. Disappointing attempt to produce a sequel to 1944's *National Velvet*; none of it coheres, one is not clear to whom it is intended to appeal, and some of the dialogue is fearsome.

wd Bryan Forbes *ph* Tony Imi *m* Francis Lai *pd* Keith Wilson

Nanette Newman, Tatum O'Neal, Anthony Hopkins, Christopher Plummer, Peter Barkworth, Dinsdale Landen

The Internecine Project*
GB 1974 89m Eastmancolor
Maclean and Co / Lion International / Hemisphere (Barry Levinson, Andrew Donally)

A Harvard professor arranges the mutual extermination of four people who could spoil a politician's presidential chances.
Coldly murderous romp with plenty of style.

w Barry Levinson, Jonathan Lynn, *novel* Mort W. Elkind *d* Ken Hughes *ph* Geoffrey Unsworth *m* Roy Budd

James Coburn, Lee Grant, Harry Andrews, Ian Hendry, Michael Jayston, Keenan Wynn

Internes Can't Take Money*
US 1937 75m bw
Paramount (Benjamin Glazer)
GB title: *You Can't Take Money*

A hospital doctor persuades a gangster friend to help a woman find her missing child.
Quite interesting minor melodrama, first of the Dr Kildare series which was subsequently recast and restyled by MGM.

w Rian James, Theodore Reed, *story* Max Brand *d* Alfred Santell *ph* Theodor Sparkuhl *m* Gregory Stone

Joel McCrea, Barbara Stanwyck, Lloyd Nolan, Stanley Ridges, Lee Bowman, Irving Bacon

The Interns*
US 1962 130m bw
Columbia / Interns Co. / Robert Cohn

In an American hospital, newly qualified doctors have personal and career problems.
Birth, abortion, sudden death, drugs and women's lib all figure in this melodramatic compendium which succeeds well enough on its own level and spawned a sequel (*The New Interns*) and an unsuccessful TV series.

w Walter Newman, David Swift, *novel* Richard Frede *d* David Swift *ph* Russell Metty *m* Leith Stevens

Cliff Robertson, Michael Callan, James MacArthur, Nick Adams, Suzy Parker, Buddy Ebsen, Telly Savalas

Interpol
GB 1957 92m bw Cinemascope
Columbia / Warwick (Irving Allen, Albert R. Broccoli)
US title: *Pickup Alley*

The US Anti-Narcotics Squad trails across Europe the insane and ruthless leader of a drug ring.
Drearily routine thick ear electrified by one performance but not helped by wide screen.

w John Paxton *d* John Gilling *ph* Ted Moore *m* Richard Bennett

Victor Mature, Anita Ekberg, *Trevor Howard*, Bonar Colleano, Marne Maitland, Eric Pohlmann, Alec Mango, Peter Illing, Sidney Tafler

The Interrupted Journey
GB 1949 80m bw
Valiant (Anthony Havelock-Allan)

An author leaves his wife for another woman, changes his mind on the journey, pulls the communication cord and causes a train crash. Or does he?
Minor melodrama with expressionist tendencies and a dream explanation.
Interesting for its parts rather than its whole.

w Michael Pertwee *d* Daniel Birt *ph* Erwin Hillier

Richard Todd, Valerie Hobson, Christine Norden, Tom Walls, Ralph Truman, Vida Hope

Interrupted Melody
US 1955 106m Eastmancolor Cinemascope
MGM (Jack Cummings)

The story of Marjorie Lawrence, an Australian opera singer who fell victim to polio.
Standard biopic which jells less well than some.

w William Ludwig, Sonya Levien *d* Curtis Bernhardt *ph* Joe Ruttenberg, Paul Vogel *music supervisor* Saul Chaplin

Eleanor Parker, Glenn Ford, Roger Moore, Cecil Kellaway, Stephen Bekassy

AA: script
AAN: Eleanor Parker

Intimacy*
US 1965 87m bw
Goldstone (David Heilwell)

A businessman in need of a government contract tries to compromise the official concerned.

Unusual minor melodrama, interesting but not quite successful.

w Eva Wolas d Victor Stoloff ph Ted Saizis m Geordie Hormel

Barry Sullivan, Nancy Malone, Jack Ging, Joan Blackman, Jackie Shannon

Intimate Relations see Les Parents Terribles

The Intimate Stranger*
GB 1956   95m   bw
Anglo–Guild (Alec Snowden)
US title: *Finger of Guilt*

An American film producer in England is plagued by a strange girl who claims to have been his mistress.
Acceptable mystery thriller which holds the interest and has good detail.

w Peter Howard d Joseph Walton (Joseph Losey) m Trevor Duncan ph Gerald Gibbs

Richard Basehart, Mary Murphy, Mervyn Johns, Constance Cummings, Roger Livesey, Faith Brook

Into the Blue
GB 1950   83m   bw

A cheerful stowaway on a yacht helps the owners catch smugglers. Emaciated comedy which never gets going. Michael Wilding, Odile Versois, Jack Hulbert, Constance Cummings, Edward Rigby. Written by Pamela Wilcox Bower, Donald Taylor and Nicholas Phipps; directed by Herbert Wilcox; for Imperadio.

Intolerance***
US 1916   115m approx (24 fps)   bw
silent
D. W. Griffith

Four stories—including Belshazzar's feast and the massacre of St Bartholomew—of intolerance through the ages are intercut and linked by the image of a mother and her baby: 'out of the cradle, endlessly rocking'.
A massive enterprise of which audiences at the time and after were quite intolerant. Hard to take in parts, it rises to a fine climax as all the stories come to a head, including a modern one with a race between a car and train, and has been called 'the only film fugue'. At the time, by far the most expensive film ever made.

wd D. W. Griffith ph Billy Bitzer

Mae Marsh, Lillian Gish, Constance Talmadge, Robert Harron, Elmo Lincoln, Eugene Pallette

'A mad, brilliant, silly extravaganza. Perhaps the greatest movie ever made. In it one can see the source of most of the major traditions of the screen: the methods of Eisenstein and Von Stroheim, the Germans and the Scandinavians, and, when it's bad, de Mille.'—*New Yorker, 1980*

The Intruder*
GB 1953   84m   bw
British Lion / Ivan Foxwell

An ex-army officer surprises a burglar and recognizes his old commander who has been ill-served by society.
Watchable but rather mechanical compendium drama in which a series of cameos supposedly sum up the problems of life in post-war Britain.

w Robin Maugham, John Hunter, *novel* Line on Ginger by Robin Maugham d Guy Hamilton ph Ted Scaife m Francis Chagrin

Jack Hawkins, Michael Medwin, Hugh Williams, George Cole, Dennis Price, Dora Bryan

The Intruder*
US 1961   84m   bw
Filmgroup (Roger Corman)
GB title: *The Stranger*

A mild-mannered stranger arrives in a southern town and stirs up racist trouble. Cheaply-made social melodrama with many effective moments.

w Charles Beaumont, from his novel d Roger Corman ph Taylor Byars m Herman Stein

William Shatner, Frank Maxwell, Beverly Lunsford, Robert Emhardt, Jeanne Cooper, Leo Gordon, Charles Beaumont

Intruder in the Dust***
US 1951   87m   bw
MGM (Clarence Brown)

In a southern town, a boy and an old lady solve a mystery and prevent a black man from being lynched.
Excellent character drama which also offers vivid local colour, a murder puzzle and social comment. A semi-classic.

w Ben Maddow, novel William Faulkner d Clarence Brown ph Robert Surtees m Adolph Deutsch

Juano Hernandez, Elizabeth Patterson, David Brian, Claude Jarman Jnr, *Porter Hall*, Will Geer

'It is surely the years of range and experience which have given him a control of the medium so calm, sure and—apparently—

easy that he can make a complex story seem simple and straightforward.'—*Pauline Kael*

'A really good movie that is also and incidentally the first honestly worked out "racial" film I have seen.'—*Richard Winnington*

Invaders from Mars

US 1953 82m Cinecolor 3D
Edward L. Alperson

Martian invaders use hypnotized humans as saboteurs.
Poverty Row sci-fi partly redeemed by its erratic but talented designer who provides flashes of visual imagination.

w Richard Blake *d / pd William Cameron Menzies ph* John Seitz *m* Raoul Kraushaar

Helena Carter, Arthur Franz, Leif Erickson, Hillary Brooke

Invasion**

GB 1966 82m bw
AA / Merton Park (Jack Greenwood)

An English village is beset one night by invaders from outer space.
Understated, effective little suspenser, well done in all departments.

w Roger Marshall *d Alan Bridges ph* James Wilson *m* Bernard Ebbinghouse

Edward Judd, Valerie Gearon, Lyndon Brook, Yoko Tani, Tsai Chin, Barrie Ingham, Arthur Sharp

Invasion of the Body Snatchers****

US 1956 80m bw Superscope
Allied Artists / Walter Wanger

A small American town is imperceptibly taken over by an alien force.
Persuasive, thoroughly satisfying, low-budget science fiction, put across with subtlety and intelligence in every department.

w Daniel Mainwaring, *novel Jack Finney d Don Siegel ph* Ellsworth Fredericks *m* Carmen Dragon

Kevin McCarthy, Dana Wynter, Larry Gates, *King Donovan*, Carolyn Jones, Virginia Christine, Sam Peckinpah

'The world as they knew it was slipping away from them. Time was running out for the human race. And there was nothing to hold on to—except each other!'—*publicity*

Invasion of the Body Snatchers*

US 1978 115m Technicolor
UA / Robert H. Solo

Flashy updating of the 1956 classic, mistakenly set in a big city (San Francisco) and

confusingly unravelled, with nobody for the audience to empathize with. Its nicest effect is to have Kevin McCarthy repeat his old role in a cameo.

w W. D. Richter *d* Philip Kaufman
ph Michael Chapman *m* Denny Zeitlin
pd Charles Rosen

Donald Sutherland, Brooke Adams, Leonard Nimoy, Veronica Cartwright, Jeff Goldblum, Art Hindle, Lelia Goldoni, Kevin McCarthy, Don Siegel

Invasion Quartet

GB 1961 87m bw
MGM (Ronald Kinnoch)

An ill-assorted foursome of officers and a boffin take on the dangerous mission of silencing a Nazi gun trained on Dover.
A plot which could have been handled any way is played unsatisfactorily for farce, and all concerned are understandably uneasy.

w Jack Trevor Story, John Briley,
story Norman Collins *d* Jay Lewis
ph Geoffrey Faithfull, Gerald Moss *m* Ron Goodwin

Bill Travers, Spike Milligan, Grégoire Aslan, John Le Mesurier, Thorley Walters, Maurice Denham, Millicent Martin, Cyril Luckham

Invasion USA

US 1952 70m bw
Columbia (Albert Zugsmith)

A hypnotist in a New York bar gives a group of people a foretaste of what might happen to them under atomic attack.
Ludicrous, dangerous, hilarious low-budget exploitationer composed mainly of rubber rocks and old newsreels.

w Robert Smith *d* Alfred E. Green *ph* John L. Russell *m* Albert Glasser

Dan O'Herlihy, Gerald Mohr, Peggie Castle

Investigation of a Citizen above Suspicion*

Italy 1970 115m Technicolor
Vera (Daniele Senatore)

A successful police inspector kills his mistress and, paranoically considering himself above suspicion, plants clues leading to himself and even confesses the crime.
Fairly engrossing character study with political undertones; cinematically quite striking, too.

w Ugo Pirro, Elio Petri *d Elio Petri ph* Luigi Kuveiller *m* Ennio Morricone

Gian Maria Volonte, Florinda Bolkan, Salvo Randone, Gianni Santuccio

AAN: best foreign film; script

Invisible Agent*
US 1942   84m   bw
Universal (George Waggner)

Nazi and Japanese spies seek the secret of
invisibility from its inventor.
Lively fantasy thriller with a cast more
distinguished than it deserves.

w Curt Siodmak d Edwin L. Marin sp John
P. Fulton m Hans Salter

Cedric Hardwicke, Peter Lorre, Ilona Massey,
Jon Hall, Albert Basserman, J. Edward
Bromberg, John Litel

Invisible Boy
US 1957   89m   bw
MGM / Pan (Nicholas Nayfack)

A scientist allows his 10-year-old son to repair
a robot, which comes under the control of an
alien force.
Minor sci-fi utilizing the robot from *Forbidden
Planet.*

w Cyril Hume d Herman Hoffman
ph Harold Wellman m Les Baxter

Richard Eyer, Philip Abbott, Harold J. Stone,
Diane Brewster

The Invisible Man***
US 1933   71m   bw
Universal (Carl Laemmle Jnr)

A scientist discovers a means of making
himself invisible, but in the process becomes a
megalomaniac.
Superb blend of eccentric character comedy,
melodrama and trick photography in a
Hollywood English setting; remarkably
faithful to the spirit of the book. It made a star
of Claude Rains in his first film, even though
he is seen for only a couple of seconds.

w R. C. Sheriff, Philip Wylie, novel H. G.
Wells d James Whale ph Arthur Edeson
sp John P. Fulton

Claude Rains, Gloria Stuart, William
Harrigan, Henry Travers, E. E. Clive, Una
O'Connor, Forrester Harvey, Dudley Digges,
Holmes Herbert

'Taken either as a technical exercise or as a
sometimes profoundly moving retelling of the
Frankenstein fable, it is one of the most
rewarding of recent films.'—*William Troy*
† Sequels, successively less interesting, were
(all qv) *The Invisible Man Returns* (1940),
Invisible Woman (1941), *Invisible Agent*
(1942), *The Invisible Man's Revenge* (1944)
and *Abbott and Costello Meet the Invisible
Man* (1951). A TV series with an anonymous
hero was made by ATV in 1955; a Universal
one with David McCallum followed in 1975,
and was restructured as *The Gemini Man* in
1976.

The Invisible Man Returns
US 1940   81m   bw
Universal (Ken Goldsmith)

A man convicted of killing his brother uses the
secret of invisibility to find the real culprit.
Second in the series takes itself too seriously: a
slow starter which works its way to a strong
climax.

w Curt Siodmak, Lester Cole, Cedric
Belfrage d Joe May ph Milton Krasner
m Hans Salter, Frank Skinner sp John P.
Fulton

Vincent Price, Cedric Hardwicke, John
Sutton, Nan Grey, Cecil Kellaway, Alan
Napier, Forrester Harvey

The Invisible Man's Revenge
US 1944   77m   bw
Universal (Ford Beebe)

A psychopathic killer on the run takes refuge
with a doctor who has discovered the secret of
invisibility.
Curious reversion to the original story in that
the invisible man is now again the villain; but
otherwise there's no flavour at all to this
horror comic set in a phoney England.

w Bertram Millhauser d Ford Beebe m Hans
Salter sp John P. Fulton

Jon Hall, Leon Errol, John Carradine, Alan
Curtis, Evelyn Ankers, Gale Sondergaard,
Halliwell Hobbes

The Invisible Menace
US 1938   55m   bw

Murder at an army base brings strange
revelations of the past. Standard mystery in
which the star seems misplaced. Boris Karloff,
Regis Toomey, Marie Wilson, Henry Kolker.
Written by Crane Wilbur, from a play by
Ralph S. Zink; directed by John Farrow; for
Warner. (NB: Remade in 1943 as *Murder at
the Waterfront.*)

The Invisible Ray*
US 1936   79m   bw
Universal

A scientist discovers a superpowerful element
which makes him homicidal.
Slow-moving science fiction with a touch of
horror, and the pattern for its star's many later
roles as a sympathetic man who turns into a
monster. Interesting rather than stimulating.

w John Colton, story Howard Higgin, Douglas
Hodges d Lambert Hillyer ph George
Robinson m Franz Waxman sp John P.
Fulton

Boris Karloff, Bela Lugosi, Frances Drake, Frank Lawton, Walter Kingsford, Beulah Bondi, Violet Kemble Cooper, Nydia Westman

Invisible Stripes
US 1940 82m bw
Warner (Hal B. Wallis)

An ex-con finds it difficult to go straight.
By 1940 Warners must have been able to make rip-offs of *Angels with Dirty Faces* in their sleep, and this one, despite its cast, suggests that they did.

w Warren Duff, *book* Warden Lewis E. Lawes d Lloyd Bacon ph Ernest Haller m Heinz Roemheld

George Raft, Humphrey Bogart, William Holden, Flora Robson, Jane Bryan, Paul Kelly, Lee Patrick, Henry O'Neill, Moroni Olson

'It's a familiar cinematic yarn but strengthened by a zippy pace, excellent performances and direction.'—*Variety*

The Invisible Woman*
US 1941 72m bw
Universal (Burt Kelly)

A mad scientist turns a model invisible.
Screwball comedy with a deteriorating star at his hammiest: generally very laboured, but with some funny moments.

w Robert Lees, Fred Rinaldo, Gertrude Purcell d A. Edward Sutherland ph Elwood Bredell

John Barrymore, Charles Ruggles, Virginia Bruce, John Howard, Oscar Homolka, Donald MacBride, Edward Brophy, Shemp Howard, Margaret Hamilton, Maria Montez

Invitation
US 1952 81m bw
MGM (Lawrence Weingarten)

When a millionaire's daughter believes she is dying, revelations ensue about her beloved husband's original intentions.
Competently idiotic weepie with a happy ending.

w Paul Osborn, *story* Jerome Weidman d Gottfried Reinhardt ph Ray June m Bronislau Kaper

Dorothy McGuire, Van Johnson, Ruth Roman, Louis Calhern, Ray Collins, Michael Chekhov

'The dialogue is stagey and the treatment indeterminate, with overmuch reliance on the dubious emotional reinforcement of loud background music.'—*Penelope Houston*

Invitation to a Gunfighter*
US 1964 92m De Luxe
UA / Stanley Kramer (Richard Wilson)

A small-town tyrant hires a smooth gunfighter to keep down the farmers he has cheated.
Predictable, rather self-satisfied little western with a studio look. Smart script and performances.

w Elizabeth and Richard Wilson d Richard Wilson ph Joseph MacDonald m David Raksin

Yul Brynner, George Segal, Janice Rule, Pat Hingle

Invitation to Happiness
US 1939 95m bw
Paramount (Wesley Ruggles)

A society girl marries a prizefighter.
Routine star romantic drama.

w Claude Binyon d Wesley Ruggles ph Leo Tover m Frederick Hollander

Irene Dunne, Fred MacMurray, Charles Ruggles, Billy Cook, William Collier Snr, Marion Martin

Invitation to the Dance**
GB 1954 92m Technicolor
MGM (Arthur Freed)

Three stories in dance and mime.
Unsuccessful ballet film which closed its star's great period and virtually ended the heyday of the Hollywood musical. The simple fact emerged that European ballet styles were not Kelly's forte; yet there was much to enjoy in *Circus, Ring around the Rosy* and *The Magic Lamp*.

w, ch, d Gene Kelly ph Frederick A. Young m Jacques Ibert, André Previn, Rimsky-Korsakov ad Alfred Junge

Gene Kelly, Igor Youskevitch, Tommy Rall, Belita, Tamara Toumanova

The Ipcress File**
GB 1965 109m Techniscope
Rank / Steven / Lowndes (Harry Saltzman)

An intelligence man traces a missing scientist and finds that one of his own superiors is a spy.
The attempt to present a low-key James Bond (glasses, good at cookery, supermarket shopper) is frustrated by flashy direction and a confused plot. It did herald a new genre though the whole ambiance is now sadly dated, like an old copy of *The Sunday Times* Colour Supplement.

w Bill Canaway, James Doran, *novel* Len Deighton d Sidney J. Furie ph Otto Heller m John Barry ad Ken Adam

Michael Caine, Nigel Green, Guy Doleman, Sue Lloyd, Gordon Jackson
† Two sequels appeared starring 'Harry Palmer' (never named in the books): *Funeral in Berlin* and *Billion Dollar Brain* (both qv).

Irene
US 1940   101m   bw (colour sequence)
RKO / Imperator (Herbert Wilcox)

A New York Irish shopgirl moves into society.
Fairly dim picturization of the old musical: the cast does its best.

w Alice Duer Miller, *play* James H. Montgomery *d* Herbert Wilcox *ph* Russell Metty *md* Anthony Collins *songs* Harry Tierney, Joseph McCarthy

Anna Neagle, Ray Milland, Roland Young, Alan Marshal, May Robson, Billie Burke, Arthur Treacher, Marsha Hunt, Isabel Jewell, Ethel Griffies
   'This pre-camp version tries to be innocuously charming, and the effort is all too evident.'—*New Yorker, 1976*
† Previously filmed in 1926 with Colleen Moore.

AAN: Anthony Collins

Irish Eyes Are Smiling**
US 1944   90m   Technicolor
TCF (Damon Runyon)

The life and times of a nineties songwriter, Ernest R. Ball.
Standard musical biopic, handsomely mounted.

w Earl Baldwin, John Tucker Battle *d* Gregory Ratoff *ph* Harry Jackson *md* Alfred Newman, Charles Henderson

Dick Haymes, June Haver, Monty Woolley, Anthony Quinn, Beverly Whitney, Maxie Rosenbloom, Veda Ann Borg, Clarence Kolb

AAN: Alfred Newman, Charles Henderson

The Irish in Us
US 1935   84m   bw
Warner (Samuel Bischoff)

Adventures of three New York brothers.
Routine, good-natured star action frolic.

w Earl Baldwin *d* Lloyd Bacon *ph* George Barnes *md* Leo F. Forbstein

James Cagney, Pat O'Brien, Olivia de Havilland, Mary Gordon, Frank McHugh, Allen Jenkins, J. Farrell MacDonald, Thomas Jackson

Irma La Douce*
US 1963   146m   Technicolor
   Panavision
UA / Phalanx / Mirisch / Edward L. Alperson
   (Billy Wilder)

A Paris policeman falls for a prostitute and becomes her pimp.
A saucy yarn originally presented inventively as a small-scale stage musical becomes a tasteless yawn on the big screen, especially when presented at such length and without the songs. Minor compensations abound but are insufficient.

w Billy Wilder, I. A. L. Diamond *d* Billy Wilder *ph* Joseph La Shelle *md* André Previn *musical themes* Marguerite Monnot *ad* Alexander Trauner

Shirley Maclaine, Jack Lemmon, Lou Jacobi, Herschel Bernardi, Joan Shawlee, Bruce Yarnell

AA: André Previn
AAN: Joseph La Shelle; Shirley Maclaine

The Iron Curtain
US 1948   87m   bw
TCF (Sol C. Siegel)

A Russian official in Ottawa becomes disillusioned and reveals to the US authorities details of a spy ring.
Cold war biopic of Igor Gouzenko; not badly done in the semi-documentary mould.

w Milton Krims *d* William Wellman *ph* Charles G. Clarke *md* Alfred Newman, using Russian themes

Dana Andrews, Gene Tierney, Berry Kroeger, Edna Best

The Iron Duke*
GB 1934   88m   bw
Gaumont (Michael Balcon)

After Waterloo, the Duke of Wellington defeats a French scheme to discredit him.
A popular historical star vehicle of its time and a good example of British pre-war production in the Korda mould.

w Bess Meredith, play H. M. Harwood *d* Victor Saville *ph* Curt Courant

George Arliss, Gladys Cooper, Emlyn Williams, Ellaline Terriss, A. E. Matthews, Edmund Willard, Felix Aylmer

The Iron Glove
US 1954   77m   Technicolor

A staunch supporter of the Old Pretender meets friends and enemies in London at the court of George I. Stilted costume piece, unsuitably cast and flatly written. Robert Stack, Ursula Thiess, Richard Stapley, Alan Hale Jnr. Written by Jesse L. Lasky Jnr, De Vallon Scott and Douglas Heyes; directed by William Castle; for Columbia.

The Iron Horse*

US 1924   119m (24 fps)   bw   silent
Fox

A man seeking to avenge his father's murder
works on the first transcontinental railroad.
Archetypal western, very slow to start but with
an authentic cast of thousands.

w Charles Kenyon, John Russell d John Ford
ph George Schneidermann

George O'Brien, Madge Bellamy, Cyril
Chadwick, Fred Kohler

The Iron Maiden

GB 1962   98m   Eastmancolor
Anglo Amalgamated / GHW (Peter Rogers)
US title: *The Swinging Maiden*

An aircraft designer gets into trouble because
of his affection for traction engines.
Feeble attempt to duplicate the success of
Genevieve, this time starring a steamroller.
Very English.

w Vivian Cox, Leslie Bricusse d Gerald
Thomas ph Alan Hume m Eric Rogers

Michael Craig, Alan Hale Jnr, Jeff Donnell,
Cecil Parker, Noel Purcell, Roland Culver, the
Duke of Bedford, Anne Helm

The Iron Man

US 1931   73m   bw
Universal (Carl Laemmle Jnr)

A prizefighter is spurred on by his money-
hungry wife.
Competent, routine, ringside melodrama.

w Francis Edward Faragoh, *novel* W. R.
Burnett d Tod Browning ph Percy Hilburn

Lew Ayres, Jean Harlow, Robert Armstrong,
John Miljan, Eddie Dillon, Ned Sparks
† Remade in 1937 as *Some Blondes Are
Dangerous* and in 1951 under the original title.

The Iron Major

US 1943   85m   bw

The life of Frank Cavanaugh, football coach
and hero of World War I. Sub-standard
biopic. Pat O'Brien, Ruth Warrick, Robert
Ryan, Leon Ames. Written by Aben Kandel
and Warren Duff; directed by Ray Enright;
for RKO. 'A respectful, rather dull
picture . . . all the talk is in words of less than
one syllable.'—*James Agee.*

The Iron Mask*

US 1929   97m   bw   talking sequences,
sound and music score
(UA) Douglas Fairbanks

The true prince of France is kidnapped and
imprisoned, but the villains reckon without
D'Artagnan and the three musketeers.
Spirited star rendition of Dumas, the last big
silent costume drama of the twenties.

w W. Elton Thomas (Douglas Fairbanks),
novel Ten Years After by Alexandre Dumas
d Allan Dwan ph Henry Sharp pd Maurice
Leloir

Douglas Fairbanks, Nigel de Brulier, Belle
Bennett, Marguerite de la Motte

The Iron Mistress

US 1952   107m   Technicolor
Warner (Henry Blanke)

The life of westerner Jim Bowie and his
famous knife.
Stolid actioner with uninspired script and
performances.

w James R. Webb, *novel* Paul I. Wellman
d Gordon Douglas ph John Seitz m Max
Steiner

Alan Ladd, Virginia Mayo, Joseph Calleia,
Phyllis Kirk, Alf Kjellin, Douglas Dick, Tony
Caruso, George Voskovec

The Iron Petticoat

GB 1956   96m   Technicolor   Vistavision
Remus / Harry Saltzman (Betty E. Box)

An American air force officer persuades a
Russian lady flier of the advantages of the
western way of life.
Feeble imitation of *Ninotchka* with a saucy
star team which simply doesn't jell.

w Ben Hecht d Ralph Thomas ph Ernest
Steward

Bob Hope, Katharine Hepburn, James
Robertson Justice, Robert Helpmann, David
Kossoff, Alan Gifford, Paul Carpenter, Noelle
Middleton

'They seem amazed to find themselves in a
comedy that has no humour, and they go
through the motions grimly, like children at
dancing school, hoping it will all be over
soon.'—*William K. Zinsser*

Is Everybody Happy?

US 1929   80m   bw

The life of a clarinettist who rises from
poverty. Or, The Ted Lewis Story, a primitive
musical. Ted Lewis, Alice Day, Ann
Pennington, Lawrence Grant. Written by
Joseph Jackson and James A. Starr; directed
by Archie Mayo; for Warner.

Is Everybody Happy?

US 1943   73m   bw

A virtual remake of the above, with the star
fourteen years older; low-budget filler with a

few good numbers. Ted Lewis, Larry Parks, Michael Duane, Nan Gwyn. Written by Monte Brice; directed by Charles Barton; for Columbia.

Is Paris Burning?
France / US 1965   165m   Panavision   bw (colour sequence)
Paramount / Transcontinental / Marianne (Paul Graetz)

A multi-storied account of the 1944 liberation of Paris.
Muddled, scribbled, tedious and confusing attempt at a thinking man's all-star war epic.

w Francis Ford Coppola, Gore Vidal d René Clément ph Marcel Grignon m Maurice Jarre

Leslie Caron, Gert Frobe, Charles Boyer, Yves Montand, Orson Welles, Alain Delon, Jean-Pierre Cassel, Jean-Paul Belmondo, Kirk Douglas, Glenn Ford, Claude Dauphin, Daniel Gélin, Anthony Perkins, Simone Signoret, Robert Stack, George Chakiris

AAN: Marcel Grignon

Isadora*
GB 1968   138m   Eastmancolor Panavision
Universal (Robert and Raymond Hakim)
US title: *The Loves of Isadora*

Eccentric character dancer Isadora Duncan reflects on her crowded and unconventional life.
Ambitious and expensive but finally unsatisfactory biopic of a controversial figure of the twenties.

w Melvyn Bragg, Clive Exton d Karel Reisz ph Larry Pizer m Maurice Jarre pd Jocelyn Herbert ad Michael Seymour, Ralph Brinton

Vanessa Redgrave, Jason Robards Jnr, James Fox, Ivan Tchenko, John Fraser, Bessie Love
'A brave attempt at a daunting task.'—*Tom Milne*

AAN: Vanessa Redgrave

The Island*
Japan 1961   92m   bw
Kindai Eiga Kyokai (Kaneto Shindo)
original title: *Hadaka no Shima*

The quiet tenor of life for the only family inhabiting a tiny island is eventually broken by illness and death.
Slow, controlled, beautiful film in which not a single word of dialogue is spoken. The artificiality of this concept eventually diminishes its stature.

wd Kaneto Shindo ph Kiyoshi Kuroda m Hikaru Hayashi

Nobuko Otowa, Taiji Tonoyama, Shinji Tanaka, Masanori Horimoto
'A visual poem which mirrors tedium without ever inducing it.'—*MFB*

The Island
US 1980   114m   Technicolor
Universal (Richard Zanuck and David Brown)

A journalist is in fear of his life on a Caribbean island inhabited by the bloodthirsty descendants of seventeenth-century buccaneers.
Ridiculous shocker from the *Jaws* people; stupidly plotted and gruesome in detail.

w Peter Benchley, from his novel d Michael Ritchie ph Henri Decaë m Ennio Morricone

Michael Caine, David Warner, Angela Punch McGregor, Frank Middlemass, Dudley Sutton, Clyde Jeavons
'Suspense gives way to gut-level sadism aimed at the lowest common audience denominator.'—*Variety*

The Island at the Top of the World**
US 1974   93m   Technicolor
Walt Disney (Winston Hibler)

In 1907, a rich Englishman commissions an airship to take him to a mythical arctic Shangri-La in search of his lost son.
Generally brisk and effective adventure fantasy whose trick effects are sufficiently splendid to redeem a sag in the middle and an overplus of Viking chatter which has to be laboriously translated.

w John Whedon, *novel* The Lost Ones by Ian Cameron d Robert Stevenson ph Frank Phillips m Maurice Jarre pd Peter Ellenshaw sp Art Cruickshank, Danny Lee

Donald Sinden, David Hartman, Jacques Marin, Mako

Island in the Sky*
US 1953   109m   bw
Wayne–Fellows (Robert Fellows)

A transport plane makes a forced landing north of Greenland, and the crew must survive till help comes.
Well made outdoor suspenser shot in the California Sierras.

w Ernest K. Gann, from his novel d William Wellman ph Archie Stout m Emil Newman ad James Basevi

John Wayne, Lloyd Nolan, Walter Abel, Allyn Joslyn, Andy Devine, James Arness

Island in the Sun*
GB 1957 119m Technicolor
Cinemascope
TCF (Darryl F. Zanuck)

Sexual and racial problems erupt on a West Indian island.

Portmanteau romantic melodrama which generally misfires, especially in an attempt to parallel *Crime and Punishment*; but the cast is interesting.

w Alfred Hayes, *novel* Alec Waugh *d* Robert Rossen *ph* Frederick A. Young *m* Malcolm Arnold

James Mason, Joan Fontaine, Harry Belafonte, John Williams, Dorothy Dandridge, Joan Collins, Michael Rennie, Patricia Owens, Stephen Boyd, Basil Sydney, Diana Wynyard, Ronald Squire, John Justin

Island of Lost Men
US 1939 64m bw

An Oriental girl seeks her lost father in waterfront dives and finds him on a prison island. Adequate action programmer. Anna May Wong, Broderick Crawford, Anthony Quinn, J. Carrol Naish. Written by William R. Lipman and Horace McCoy; directed by Kurt Neumann; for Paramount.

Island of Lost Souls*
US 1932 74m bw
Paramount

On a remote South Sea island, mad Dr Moreau transforms animals into humans by vivisection.

Unchilling but interesting thriller with a rolling-eyed star performance.

w Waldemar Young, Philip Wylie, *story* The Island of Dr Moreau by H. G. Wells *d* Erle C. Kenton *ph* Karl Struss

Charles Laughton, Bela Lugosi, Richard Arlen, Kathleen Burke, Leila Hyams

Island of Lost Women
US 1958 72m bw

A newspaperman lands on a remote island where a scientist has retired from the world with his daughters. Unexciting hokum with more talk than action. Jeff Richards, Venetia Stevenson, John Smith, Alan Napier. Written by Ray Buffum; directed by Frank Tuttle; for Jaguar / Warner.

Island of Love
US 1963 101m Technicolor
Panavision
Warner / Belgrave (Morton da Costa)

A gangster finances a film providing his girl friend stars, but when it flops he chases the producers to a Greek island.

Dismally unfunny comedy wasting a talented cast.

w David R. Schwarz *d* Morton da Costa *ph* Harry Stradling *m* George Duning

Robert Preston, Tony Randall, Walter Matthau, Giorgia Moll

Island of Terror
GB 1966 89m Eastmancolor
Planet (Tom Blakeley)

On an Irish island, a scientist makes monsters who thrive on bone.

Horror hokum, moderately done.

w Edward Andrew Mann, Alan Ramsen *d* Terence Fisher *ph* Reg Wyer *m* Malcolm Lockyer *sp* John St John Earl

Peter Cushing, Edward Judd, Carole Gray, Eddie Byrne, Sam Kydd, Niall MacGinnis

Island of the Blue Dolphins
US 1964 93m Eastmancolor
U-I / Robert B. Radnitz

Two orphaned children grow up alone on a Californian island, protected by wild dogs. Pleasant if unconvincing family film based on a true story.

w Ted Sherdeman, Jane Klove, *novel* Scott O'Dell *d* James B. Clark *ph* Leo Tover *m* Paul Sawtell

Celia Kaye, Larry Dornasin, George Kennedy

Island of the Lost
US 1968 92m colour

An anthropologist sets sail for an uncharted island and is shipwrecked on it. Good-looking but singularly plotless action adventure. Richard Greene, Luke Halpin, Mark Hulswit. Written by Richard Carlson and Ivan Tors; directed by Richard Carlson; for Ivan Tors.

Islands in the Stream
US 1976 105m Metrocolor Panavision
Paramount (Peter Bart, Max Palevsky)

On a Bahamian island in 1940, an expatriate American artist welcomes his three sons and reflects on the futility of life.

Shapeless semi-autobiographical fragments culminating unpersuasively in an action climax of heroic self-sacrifice. A film on which no expense has been spared and which doesn't work at all.

w Denne Bart Petitclerc, *novel* Ernest Hemingway *d* Franklin Schaffner *ph* Fred J. Koenekamp *m* Jerry Goldsmith

George C. Scott, David Hemmings, Gilbert Roland, Susan Tyrell, Richard Evans, Claire Bloom, Hart Bochner, Julius Harris

'It is all too awful for words.'—*Benny Green, Punch*

AAN: photography

Isle of Fury
US 1936 60m bw

A fugitive from justice finds temporary peace on a South Sea island. Limp remake of *The Narrow Corner* (qv); its star later pretended he hadn't made it. Humphrey Bogart, Margaret Lindsay, Donald Woods. Written by Robert Andrews and William Jacobs; directed by Frank McDonald; for Warner.

Isle of Missing Men
US 1942 67m bw

Convicts on a prison island try to make a break. The very poor man's *Papillon*. Gilbert Roland, Helen Gilbert, John Howard. Written by Richard Oswald and Robert Chapin; directed by Richard Oswald; for Monogram.

Isle of the Dead**
US 1945 72m bw
RKO (*Val Lewton*)

On a Balkan island in 1912 a group of people shelter from the plague and fear that one of their number is a vampire.
Glum, ghoulish melodrama with some neatly handled shocks; quite different from any other horror film.

w Ardel Wray, Josef Mischel *d* Mark Robson *ph* Jack Mackenzie *m* Leigh Harline

Boris Karloff, Ellen Drew, Helene Thimig, Marc Cramer, Katherine Emery, Alan Napier, Jason Robards

Isn't It Romantic*
US 1948 87m bw
Paramount (Daniel Dare)

Romance hits the household of an ex-Civil War colonel in Indiana.
Pleasant but forgettable period semi-musical.

w Theodore Strauss, Josef Mischel, Richard Breen *d* Norman Z. McLeod *ph* Lionel Lindon *m* Joseph J. Lilley

Veronica Lake, Mona Freeman, Mary Hatcher, Roland Culver, Billy de Wolfe, Patric Knowles, Richard Webb, Kathryn Givney, Pearl Bailey

Isn't Life Wonderful?*
US 1924 88m (24 fps) bw silent
(UA) David Wark Griffith

The life of a family in post-war Germany.
An unpopular subject, and a grey-looking film, but the director shows a lot of his strength in it.

wd D. W. Griffith, *story* Geoffrey Moss

Carol Dempster, Neil Hamilton, Helen Lowell, Frank Puglia, Marcia Harris

Isn't Life Wonderful?*
GB 1952 83m Technicolor
ABP (Warwick Ward)

In 1902, drunken Uncle Willie runs a bicycle shop and manages to reconcile a lovers' quarrel.
Engaging, well cast family comedy.

w Brock Williams *d* Harold French *ph* Erwin Hillier *m* Philip Green *ad* Terence Verity

Donald Wolfit, Eileen Herlie, Cecil Parker, Eleanor Summerfield, Robert Urquhart, Cecil Trouncer

Istanbul
US 1956 84m Technicolor
       Cinemascope
U-I (Albert J. Cohen)

Various adventurers and an amnesiac girl seek stolen diamonds in Istanbul.
Dim remake of a flat-footed piece of thick ear called *Singapore*.

w Seton I. Miller, Barbara Gray, Richard Alan Simmons *d* Joseph Pevney *ph* William Daniels *m* Joseph Gershenson

Errol Flynn, Cornell Borchers, John Bentley, Torin Thatcher, Leif Erickson, Martin Benson, Vladimir Sokoloff, Werner Klemperer, Nat King Cole, Peggy Knudsen

It*
US 1927 72m (24 fps) bw silent
Famous Players-Lasky / Paramount (B. P. Schulberg)

A shopgirl tries to live by the tenets of Elinor Glyn's book, and finally marries her boss.
In its day a fast and funny spoof, and the years have not dealt too unkindly with it.

w Hope Loring, Louis D. Lighton, *adaptation* Elinor Glyn *d* Clarence Badger *ph* H. Kinley Martin

Clara Bow, Antonio Moreno, William Austin, Jacqueline Gadson, Gary Cooper, Elinor Glyn

It Ain't Hay
US 1943 79m bw
Universal (Alex Gottlieb)
GB title: *Money for Jam*

When a racehorse dies, a New York cabbie and his friend try to find a new one for the impecunious owners.

Formula Abbott and Costello with a small injection of sentiment and Runyonese. Not their best by a mile.

w Allen Boretz, John Grant, *story* Princess O'Hara by Damon Runyon *d* Erle C. Kenton *ph* Charles Von Enger *songs* Harry Revel, Paul Francis Webster

Bud Abbott, Lou Costello, Grace McDonald, Cecil Kellaway, Patsy O'Connor, Eugene Pallette, Shemp Howard, Eddie Quillan

It All Came True*
US 1940 97m bw
Warner (Mark Hellinger)

A gangster hides out in a boarding house and puts it back on its feet.
Competent New York fairy story full of sweetness and light.

w Michael Fessier, Lawrence Kimble, *story* Better Than Life by Louis Bromfield *d* Lewis Seiler *ph* Ernest Haller *m* Heinz Roemheld

Humphrey Bogart, Ann Sheridan, Jeffrey Lynn, Zasu Pitts, Una O'Connor, Jessie Busley, John Litel, Grant Mitchell, Felix Bressart

It Always Rains on Sunday***
GB 1947 92m bw
Ealing (Henry Cornelius)

An escaped convict takes refuge in his married mistress's house in East London.
Influential slumland melodrama, now dated— the stuff of every other television play—but at the time electrifyingly vivid and very well done.

w Angus Macphail, Robert Hamer, Henry Cornelius, *novel* Arthur La Bern d Robert Hamer ph Douglas Slocombe m Georges Auric

Googie Withers, John McCallum, Jack Warner, Edward Chapman, Susan Shaw, Sidney Tafler

It Came from beneath the Sea
US 1955 80m bw
Columbia / Sam Katzman (Charles Schneer)

A giant octopus half destroys San Francisco.
Tepid monster movie; special effects only fair.

w George Worthing Yates, Hal Smith *d* Robert Gordon *ph* Henry Freulich *md* Mischa Bakaleinikoff

Kenneth Tobey, Faith Domergue, Donald Curtis, Ian Keith

It Came from Outer Space**
US 1953 80m bw 3-D
U-I (William Alland)

A young astronomer sees a space ship land in the Arizona desert and tracks down the occupants who can adopt human appearance at will.
Quite bright science fiction, the first to use this theme of borrowing bodies and the first to utilize the western desert locations. 3-D adds a shock moment or two.

w Harry Essex, *story* Ray Bradbury *d* Jack Arnold *ph* Clifford Stine *m* Herman Stein *md* Joseph Gershenson

Richard Carlson, Barbara Rush, Charles Drake, Kathleen Hughes
'Desert was Arnold's favourite location, and he used it consistently to create a sense of strangeness and menace otherwise much restricted by his budgets.'—*Time Out, 1982*

It Could Happen to You
US 1939 73m bw

After a stag party, an advertising man finds a body in his car. Neat second-feature mystery.
Stuart Erwin, Gloria Stuart, Raymond Walburn, Douglas Fowley. Written by Allen Rivkin and Lou Breslow; directed by Alfred Werker; for TCF.

It Grows on Trees
US 1952 84m bw
U-I (Leonard Goldstein)

A housewife finds a money tree in her backyard.
Protracted fantasy comedy.

w Leonard Praskins, Barney Slater *d* Arthur Lubin *ph* Maury Gertsman *m* Frank Skinner

Irene Dunne (her last film), Dean Jagger, Joan Evans, Richard Crenna, Edith Meiser, Dee Pollock

It Had To Be You
US 1947 98m bw
Columbia / Don Hartman

A dizzy dame runs out on three prospective husbands and is pursued by an Indian.
Weak sex farce without the courage of its lack of convictions.

w Norman Panama, Melvin Frank *d* Don Hartman, Rudolph Maté *ph* Rudolph Maté *m* Heinz Roemheld *md* Morris Stoloff

Ginger Rogers, Cornel Wilde, Percy Waram, Spring Byington, Thurston Hall, Ron Randell

It Happened at the World's Fair
US 1962 104m Metrocolor Panavision
MGM / Ted Richmond

At the Seattle World's Fair, two crop-dusting pilots have romantic intrigues.
Routine star vehicles.

w Si Rose, Seaman Jacobs *d* Norman Taurog
ph Joseph Ruttenberg *m* Leith Stevens

Elvis Presley, Gary Lockwood, Joan O'Brien, Yvonne Craig, Ginny Tiu

It Happened Here**
GB 1963 99m bw
UA / Kevin Brownlow, Andrew Mollo

What might have happened if the Germans had invaded England in 1940.
A remarkable semi-professional reconstruction which took seven years to film and is totally convincing in detail, but unfortunately rather confused and padded as drama.

wd Kevin Brownlow, Andrew Mollo ph Peter Suschitsky *m* Jack Beaver

Sebastian Shaw, Pauline Murray, Fiona Lekland, Honor Fehrson
'For a grain of artistic truth, we can forgive even the grainy photography and wavering sound with which part of it is afflicted.'—*John Simon*

It Happened in Athens
US 1961 100m De Luxe Cinemascope
TCF (James S. Elliott)

At the first revival of the Olympic Games in 1896 a publicity-seeking actress announces that she will marry whoever wins the Marathon.
Witless extravagant romp, well mounted but adding up to zero.

w Laszlo Vadnay *d* Andrew Marton *ph* Curt Courant *m* Manos Hadjikis

Jayne Mansfield, Trax Colton, Bob Mathias

It Happened in Brooklyn*
US 1947 103m bw
MGM (Jack Cummings)

Young New Yorkers with musical talents find their way to fame.
Well-handled routine musical of its time.

w Isobel Lennart *d* Richard Whorf
ph Robert Planck *m* Johnny Green *songs* Jule Styne, Sammy Cahn

Frank Sinatra, Jimmy Durante, Kathryn Grayson, Peter Lawford, Gloria Grahame
'Aside from Sinatra and Durante the show amounts to practically nothing, but there is a general kindliness about it which I enjoyed.'—*James Agee*

It Happened on Fifth Avenue*
US 1947 115m bw
Allied Artists (Roy del Ruth)

A child of divorce finds amiable squatters in her millionaire father's house.

Curious, overlong, cheerful Capraesque comedy with the mildest of social pretensions.

w Everett Freeman, Frederick Stephani, Herbert Clyde Lewis *d* Roy del Ruth
ph Henry Sharp

Gale Storm, Ann Harding, Victor Moore, Charles Ruggles, Don Defore

AAN: script

It Happened One Night****
US 1934 105m bw
Columbia (Frank Capra)

A runaway heiress falls in love with the reporter who is chasing her across America.
Highly successful and influential romantic comedy, the first to use buses and motels as background and still come up sparkling; it remains superlative in patches, but overall has a faded, dated air.

w Robert Riskin, story Night Bus by Samuel Hopkins Adams *d Frank Capra ph* Joseph Walker *md* Louis Silvers

Clark Gable, Claudette Colbert, Walter Connolly, Roscoe Karns, Alan Hale, Ward Bond, Jameson Thomas, Arthur Hoyt
'It will be a long day before we see so little made into so much.'—*Otis Ferguson*
'Something to revive your faith in a medium which could belong among the great arts.'—*Robert Forsythe*
'We may look askance at Capra's sententious notions about the miserable rich and the happy poor, but there's no doubting the chord he struck in depression audiences.'—*Time Out, 1980*
† Remade 1956 (badly) as *You Can't Run away From It.*

AA: best picture; Robert Riskin; Frank Capra; Clark Gable; Claudette Colbert

It Happened One Sunday
GB 1943 99m bw

In Liverpool, a Canadian seaman falls for an Irish maid. Overlong romantic comedy with nowhere to go. Robert Beatty, Barbara White, Marjorie Rhodes, Ernest Butcher, Judy Kelly, Irene Vanbrugh. Written by Victor Skuzetsky, Friedrich Gotfurt and Stephen Black; directed by Karel Lamac; for ABPC.

It Happened to Jane
US 1959 98m Technicolor
  Cinemascope
Columbia / Arwin (Richard Quine)

A lady lobster dealer becomes involved in a battle with the railroad whose inefficiency affects her business.

Witless, wholesome farce which promises more than it delivers.

w Norman Karkov d Richard Quine
ph Charles Lawton Jnr m George Duning

Doris Day, Jack Lemmon, *Ernie Kovacs*, Steve Forrest

It Happened Tomorrow•••
US 1944 84m bw
(UA) Arnold Pressburger

A reporter meets an old man with the power to show him tomorrow's newspaper headlines, so that he always gets scoops—including his own death . . .
Engaging fantasy, flawlessly made and quietly very entertaining.

w *Dudley Nichols, René Clair d René Clair ph Archie Stout m Robert Stolz*

Dick Powell, Linda Darnell, Jack Oakie, *John Philliber*, Edgar Kennedy, Ed Brophy, George Cleveland, Sig Rumann
   'Students of cinematic style will find many shrewdly polished bits to admire and enjoy.'— *James Agee*

AAN: Robert Stolz

It Happens Every Spring
US 1949 80m bw
TCF (William Perlberg)

A chemistry teacher discovers a formula that makes baseballs repellent to wood.
Smartly produced but rather desperate fantasy comedy.

w Valentine Davies d Lloyd Bacon ph Joe MacDonald m Leigh Harline

Ray Milland, Jean Peters, Paul Douglas, Ed Begley, Ted de Corsia, Ray Collins, Jessie Royce Landis, Alan Hale Jnr

AAN: original story (Shirley W. Smith, Valentine Davies)

It Happens Every Thursday•
US 1953 80m bw
U-I (Anton Leader)

The new owner of a small-town newspaper becomes unpopular through his attempts to boost the circulation.
Pleasant comedy with amusing scenes.

w Dane Lussier d Joseph Pevney ph Russell Metty m Joseph Gershenson

Loretta Young, John Forsythe, Jimmy Conlin, Frank McHugh, Edgar Buchanan, Jane Darwell

It Shouldn't Happen to a Dog
US 1946 70m bw

A lady detective, her dog and a reporter solve a murder case more by good luck than good management. Acceptable comedy support.
Allyn Joslyn, Carole Landis, Margo Woode, Henry Morgan, Reed Hadley, John Alexander. Written by Eugene Ling and Frank Gabrielson; directed by Herbert I. Leeds; for TCF.

It Should Happen to You••
US 1954 87m bw
Columbia (Fred Kohlmar)

A slightly daffy New York model with an urge to be famous rents a huge billboard and puts her name on it.
Likeable comedy which starts brightly and slowly falls apart, disappointing considering the credentials of the talents involved and the satiric possibilities of the plot.

w *Ruth Gordon, Garson Kanin d George Cukor ph Charles Lang m Frederick Hollander*

Judy Holliday, Jack Lemmon, Peter Lawford, Michael O'Shea

It Shouldn't Happen to a Vet
GB 1976 93m Technicolor
EMI / Talent Associates / Readers Digest

Adventures of a Yorkshire vet just before World War II.
Competent sequel to *All Creatures Great and Small* (qv).

w Alan Plater, *books* James Herriot d Eric Till ph Arthur Ibbetson m Laurie Johnson

John Alderton, Colin Blakely, Lisa Harrow, Bill Maynard, Richard Pearson, Raymond Francis, John Barrett, Paul Shelley

It Started in Naples•
US 1960 100m Technicolor
   Vistavision
Paramount / Capri (Jack Rose)

A Philadelphia lawyer goes to Naples to settle his dead brother's affairs, and falls for his nephew's aunt.
Nicely made, formula romantic comedy which started life as a vehicle for Gracie Fields.

w Melville Shavelson, Jack Rose, Susi Cecchi d'Amico d Melville Shavelson ph Robert Surtees m Alessandro Cicognini

Clark Gable, Sophia Loren, Vittorio de Sica, Marietto, Paulo Carlini

It Started in Paradise
GB 1952 94m Technicolor
GFD / British Film Makers (Leslie Parkyn, Sergei Nolbandov)

The career of an ambitious dress designer.
Stilted and garishly coloured but often
amusing backstage melodrama of the fashion
world: a Hollywood-style star vehicle which
seems faintly surprising as a British product.

w Marghanita Laski d Compton Bennett
ph Jack Cardiff m Malcolm Arnold
ad Edward Carrick

Jane Hylton, Ian Hunter, Terence Morgan,
Muriel Pavlow, Brian Worth, *Martita Hunt,
Ronald Squire, Harold Lang*, Joyce Barbour,
Kay Kendall

It Started with a Kiss
US 1959 104m Metrocolor
  Cinemascope
MGM / Arcola (Aaron Rosenberg)

An army sergeant posted to Spain is
embarrassed when his wife follows him.
Flabby comedy with the emphasis on sex and
pratfalls.

w Charles Lederer d George Marshall
ph Robert Bronner m Jeff Alexander

Glenn Ford, Debbie Reynolds, Fred Clark,
Edgar Buchanan, Eva Gabor

It Started with Eve**
US 1941 93m bw
Universal (Joe Pasternak)

A dying millionaire wants to see his grandson
engaged, so a waitress obliges for an hour . . .
but the old man recovers.
Charming comedy which was probably the
star's best film; remade as *I'd Rather be Rich*
(qv).

w Norman Krasna, Leo Townsend d Henry
Koster ph Rudolph Maté md Charles Previn,
Hans Salter

Deanna Durbin, Charles Laughton, Robert
Cummings, Margaret Tallichet, Guy Kibbee,
Walter Catlett, Catherine Doucet

AAN: Charles Previn, Hans Salter

The Italian Job**
GB 1969 100m Eastmancolor
  Panavision
Paramount / Oakhurst (Michael Deeley)

Crooks stage a traffic jam in Turin in order to
pull off a bullion robbery.
Lively caper comedy which provides a good
measure of entertainment.

w Troy Kennedy Martin d Peter Collinson
ph Douglas Slocombe, Norman Warwick
m Quincy Jones

Michael Caine, Noel Coward, Benny Hill, Raf
Vallone, Tony Beckley, Rossano Brazzi,
Maggie Blye, Irene Handl, John Le Mesurier,
Fred Emney

It's a Big Country
US 1952 89m bw
MGM (Robert Sisk)

Seven stories show the diversity of the US and
the glory of being one of its citizens.
Stultifying flagwaver memorable chiefly as a
waste of good actors.

w William Ludwig, Helen Deutsch, George
Wells, Allen Rivkin, Dorothy Kingsley, Isobel
Lennart d Richard Thorpe, Don Weis, John
Sturges, Don Hartman, William Wellman,
Charles Vidor, Clarence Brown ph John
Alton, Ray June, William Mellor, Joseph
Ruttenberg m Bronislau Kaper, Rudolph G.
Kopp, David Raksin, David Rose

Ethel Barrymore, Keefe Brasselle, Nancy
Davis, Van Johnson, Gene Kelly, Janet Leigh,
Marjorie Main, Fredric March, George
Murphy, William Powell, S. Z. Sakall, Lewis
Stone, James Whitmore

It's a Boy
GB 1933 80m bw

A blackmailer claims to be a bridegroom's
long-lost illegitimate son. Heavy-footed
version of popular stage farce. Leslie Henson,
Edward Everett Horton, Heather Thatcher,
Alfred Drayton, Albert Burdon, Robertson
Hare, Wendy Barrie. Written by Austin
Melford, John Paddy Carstairs and L. H.
Gordon, from the play by Franz Arnold, Ernst
Bach and Austin Melford; directed by Tim
Whelan; for Gainsborough.

It's a Gift**
US 1934 73m bw
Paramount (William Le Baron)

A general store proprietor buys an orange
ranch by mail and transports his family to
California.
Roughly assembled comedy of disasters which
happens to show the star more or less at his
best, though the expected climax is lacking.

w Jack Cunningham, *story* W. C. Fields, J. P.
McEvoy d Norman Z. McLeod ph Henry
Sharp

W. C. Fields, Kathleen Howard, Jean
Rouverol, Julian Madison, Tommy Bupp,
Baby LeRoy

It's a Great Feeling*
US 1949 85m Technicolor
Warner (Alex Gottlieb)

No one will direct a Jack Carson movie, so he
has to do it himself.
Amiable studio farce with plenty of guest
appearances.

w Jack Rose, Mel Shavelson d David Butler
ph Wilfrid M. Cline m / ly Jule Styne, Sammy
Cahn

Jack Carson, Doris Day, Dennis Morgan, Bill
Goodwin, Gary Cooper, Joan Crawford, Errol
Flynn, Sidney Greenstreet, Danny Kaye,
Patricia Neal, Edward G. Robinson, Jane
Wyman, Eleanor Parker, Ronald Reagan

AAN: title song

It's a Mad Mad Mad Mad World••

US 1963 192m Technicolor Ultra
Panavision 70
UA / Stanley Kramer

An assortment of people including a frustrated
cop are overcome by greed when they hear of
buried loot.
Three hours of frantic chasing and violent
slapstick is too much even when done on this
scale and with this cast, but one must observe
that scene for scene it is extremely well done
and most of the players are in unusually good
form though they all outstay their welcome
and are upstaged by the stunt men.

w William and Tania Rose d Stanley Kramer
ph Ernest Laszlo m Ernest Gold stunts Carey
Loftin titles Saul Bass

Spencer Tracy, Jimmy Durante, Milton Berle,
Sid Caesar, Ethel Merman, Buddy Hackett,
Mickey Rooney, Dick Shawn, Phil Silvers,
Terry-Thomas, Jonathan Winters, Edie
Adams, Dorothy Provine, Eddie Anderson,
Jim Backus, William Demarest, Peter Falk,
Paul Ford, Leo Gorcey, Ben Blue, Edward
Everett Horton, Buster Keaton, Joe E.
Brown, Carl Reiner, the Three Stooges, Zasu
Pitts, Sterling Holloway, Jack Benny, Jerry
Lewis

'To watch on a Cinerama screen in full
colour a small army of actors inflict mayhem
on each other with cars, planes, explosives and
other devices for more than three hours with
stereophonic sound effects is simply too much
for the human eye and ear to respond to, let
alone the funny bone.'—Dwight MacDonald

AAN: Ernest Laszlo; Ernest Gold; title song
(m Ernest Gold, ly Mack David)

It's a Pleasure

US 1945 90m Technicolor

The career of an ice-skating couple is
interrupted when he takes to drink.
Unimpressive vehicle from the star's waning
years: the numbers are good but the rest very
soggy. Sonja Henie, Michael O'Shea, Marie
McDonald. Written by Lynn Starling and Eliot
Paul; directed by William A. Seiter; for
International / RKO.

It's a 2'6" above the Ground World

GB 1972 96m Eastmancolor
British Lion / Welbeck / Betty E. Box–Ralph
Thomas
Also known as: The Love Ban

A Roman Catholic couple go on the pill.
Smutty, not very funny sex comedy.

w Kevin Laffan, from his play d Ralph
Thomas ph Tony Imi m Stanley Myers

Nanette Newman, Hywel Bennett, Russell
Lewis, Simon Henderson, Milo O'Shea

It's a Wonderful Life••••

US 1946 129m bw
RKO / Liberty Films (Frank Capra)

A man is prevented from committing suicide
by an elderly angel, who takes him back
through his life to show him what good he has
done.
Superbly assembled small-town comedy drama
in a fantasy framework; arguably Capra's best
and most typical work.

w Frances Goodrich, Albert Hackett, Frank
Capra d Frank Capra ph Joseph Walker,
Joseph Biroc m Dmitri Tiomkin

James Stewart, Henry Travers, Donna Reed,
Lionel Barrymore, Thomas Mitchell, Beulah
Bondi, Frank Faylen, Ward Bond, Gloria
Grahame, H. B. Warner, Frank Albertson,
Samuel S. Hinds, Mary Treen

'One of the most efficient sentimental pieces
since A Christmas Carol.'—James Agee
'The most brilliantly made motion picture of
the 1940s, so assured, so dazzling in its use of
screen narrative.'—Charles Higham
'In its own icky, bittersweet way, it's terribly
effective.'—New Yorker, 1977

AAN: best picture; Frank Capra; James
Stewart

It's a Wonderful World••

US 1939 86m bw
MGM (Frank Davis)

Kidnapped by a suspected murderer, a girl
helps him track down the real criminal.
Madcap comedy mystery which now seems
much fresher and funnier than it did at the
time. A highlight of the crazy comedy cycle.

w Ben Hecht, Herman J. Mankiewicz d W. S.
Van Dyke II ph Oliver Marsh

Claudette Colbert, James Stewart, Guy
Kibbee, Nat Pendleton, Frances Drake, Edgar
Kennedy, Ernest Truex, Richard Carle,
Sidney Blackmer, Andy Clyde, Cliff Clark,
Hans Conried

'One of the few genuinely comic pictures in
a dog's age.'—Otis Ferguson

It's Alive
US 1974   91m   Technicolor
Warner / Larco (Larry Cohen)

A new-born baby turns out to be a vicious monster.
Exploitation horror flick in the worst of taste, with a good central performance.

wd Larry Cohen *ph* Fenton Hamilton
m Bernard Herrmann

John Ryan, Sharon Farrell, Andrew Duggan, Guy Stockwell, James Dixon, Michael Ansara

It's All Yours
US 1938   80m   bw

A millionaire leaves a fortune to his favourite secretary, hoping that it will make his nephew take notice of her. Unpersuasive romantic comedy with slightly crazy touches. Madeleine Carroll, Francis Lederer, Mischa Auer, Grace Bradley. Written by Mary C. McCall Jnr; directed by Elliott Nugent; for Columbia.

It's Always Fair Weather**
US 1955   101m   Eastmancolor
            Cinemascope
MGM (Arthur Freed)

In 1945 three army veterans vow to meet ten years on, but they find each other dull failures until they go on a wild spree.
Rather dejected New Yorkish comedy with musical sequences; some of it works very well, but the colour is crude and the wide screen doesn't help.

w / ly / m Betty Comden, Adolph Green
d Gene Kelly, Stanley Donen *ph* Robert Bronner *md* André Previn

Gene Kelly, Dan Dailey, Michael Kidd, Dolores Gray, Cyd Charisse

AAN: Betty Comden, Adolph Green (as writers); André Previn

It's Hard to Be Good
GB 1948   93m   bw
GFD / Two Cities

A demobbed war hero determines to spread peace and goodwill, but comes one cropper after another.
Well intended but somehow unprofessional comedy which irritates more than it amuses.

wd Jeffrey Dell *ph* Laurie Friedman
m Antony Hopkins

Jimmy Hanley, Anne Crawford, Raymond Huntley

It's in the Air*
GB 1938   86m   bw
ATP (Basil Dean)

Adventures of an accident-prone RAF recruit. Amiable star comedy with good situations and songs.

wd Anthony Kimmins *ph* Gordon Dines, Ronald Neame

George Formby, Garry Marsh, Polly Ward, Julien Mitchell, Jack Hobbs, Hal Gordon

It's in the Bag**
US 1945   87m   bw
(UA) Manhattan Productions
GB title: *The Fifth Chair*

The owner of a flea circus seeks a legacy hidden in one of five chairs which have been sold to a variety of people.
Patchily amusing, star-studded comedy which was also filmed as *Keep Your Seats Please* and *The Twelve Chairs*. Full enjoyment requires some knowledge of American radio characters.

w Jay Dratler, Alma Reville *d* Richard Wallace *ph* Russell Metty *m* Werner Heymann

Fred Allen, Binnie Barnes, *Jack Benny*, Robert Benchley, Don Ameche, Victor Moore, Rudy Vallee, William Bendix, Jerry Colonna
    'An untidy piece that doesn't make the most of itself but is full of fun.'—*Richard Mallett, Punch*

It's Love Again*
GB 1936   83m   bw
Gaumont (Michael Balcon)

A chorus girl poses as a socialite who has hit the headlines without ever existing.
Delightfully dated comedy musical.

w Lesser Samuels, Marian Dix, Austin Melford *d* Victor Saville *ph* Glen MacWilliams

Jessie Matthews, Robert Young, Sonnie Hale, Ernest Milton, Robb Wilton, Sara Allgood, Athene Seyler, Cyril Raymond.
    'Mr Saville has directed it with speed, efficiency and a real sense of the absurd.'—*Graham Greene*

It's Love I'm After*
US 1937   90m   bw
Warner

A beloved stage star couple fight like cat and dog behind the scenes.
Amusing romantic farce which has worn rather less well than might have been expected but does present two stars at their peak.

w Casey Robinson *d* Archie Mayo *ph* James Van Trees *m* Heinz Roemheld

Bette Davis, Leslie Howard, Olivia de Havilland, Patric Knowles, Eric Blore, George Barbier, Spring Byington, Bonita Granville, E. E. Clive

'One of the most delightful and diverting comedies the madcap cinema has yet turned out.'—*New York World Telegram*

'Proceeds like a somewhat deranged *Taming of the Shrew* . . . [BD and LH] are surrounded by that set of millionaires, valets and heiresses that were at one time as much of a convention in American comedy as the fops of Restoration theatre.'—*American Film Institute*

It's Never Too Late
GB 1956   95m   Eastmancolor

A mother considered dull by her family starts a new career as a scriptwriter. Acceptable but quite unexciting matinée comedy. Phyllis Calvert, Guy Rolfe, Susan Stephen, Patrick Barr, Delphi Lawrence, Sarah Lawson, Peter Hammond. Written by Edward Dryhurst, from the play by Felicity Douglas; directed by Michael McCarthy; for Park Lane / ABP.

It's Never Too Late to Mend
GB 1937   67m   bw

An evil squire schemes for the hand of the farmer's beautiful daughter. Archetypal melodrama of the 'Fie, Sir Jasper' school, mainly interesting in this version for the antics of its heavy-breathing star. *Tod Slaughter*, Marjorie Taylor, Jack Livesey, Lawrence Hanray. Written by H. F. Maltby, from the play by Charles Reade and Arthur Shirley; directed by David MacDonald; for George King.

It's Not Cricket
GB 1948   77m   bw
GFD / Gainsborough

Bowler-hatted officers catch a Nazi spy. Over-spoofed comedy which barely allows the stars a real chance.

w Lyn Lockwood, Bernard MacNab *d* Alfred Roome *ph* Gordon Lang *m* Arthur Wilkinson

Basil Radford, Naunton Wayne, Maurice Denham, Susan Shaw, Nigel Buchanan

It's Only Money
US 1962   84m   bw
Paramount / York / Jerry Lewis Productions (Paul Jones)

A TV repair mechanic hampers his detective friend in a search for a missing heir, which turns out to be himself.

Patchy mystery spoof with the star in rather better form than usual, and a memorable scene in which he is chased by an army of lawnmowers.

w John Fenton Murray *d* Frank Tashlin *ph* W. Wallace Kelley *m* Walter Scharf

Jerry Lewis, Zachary Scott, Joan O'Brien, Jesse White, Jack Weston

It's That Man Again**
GB 1942   84m   bw
GFD / Gainsborough (Edward Black)

The Mayor of Foaming-at-the-Mouth puts on a show to save a bombed theatre.

Smart, fast-moving comedy which no longer seems particularly funny in itself but is an invaluable record of the characters and wisecracks of a radio show which proved a prime morale booster during World War II.

w Howard Irving Young, *Ted Kavanagh d Walter Forde*

Tommy Handley, Jack Train, Greta Gynt, Dino Galvani, Dorothy Summers, Horace Percival, Sidney Keith, Clarence Wright

Ivan the Terrible**
USSR 1942–6   100m (part one), 88m (part two)   bw (some Agfacolor in part two)
Mosfilm
original title: *Ivan Groznyi*

The life of a 16th-century tsar.

A heavy-going film overflowing with grim, gloomy and superbly composed images: the plot is by the way, and part two (also known as *The Boyars' Plot*) is not up to the standard of part one, in which the coronation sequence alone is a masterpiece of cinema.

wd, ed Sergei Eisenstein ph Edouard Tissé (exteriors), Andrei Moskvin (interiors) *m Sergei Prokoviev ad Isaac Shpinel, L. Naumova*

Nikolai Cherkassov, Ludmilla Tselikovskaya, Serafima Birman

'A visual opera, with all of opera's proper disregard of prose-level reality . . . an extraordinarily bold experiment, fascinating and beautiful to look at.'—*James Agee*

Ivanhoe*
GB 1952   106m   Technicolor
MGM (Pandro S. Berman)

Derring-do among the knights of medieval England.

Tolerable, big-budget spectacular based on Sir Walter Scott's novel.

w Noel Langley, Aeneas Mackenzie
d Richard Thorpe
ph F. A. Young *m* Miklos Rozsa

Robert Taylor, Joan Fontaine, Elizabeth Taylor, Emlyn Williams, George Sanders, Robert Douglas, Finlay Currie, Felix Aylmer, Francis de Wolff, Guy Rolfe, Norman Wooland, Basil Sydney

AAN: best picture; F. A. Young; Miklos Rozsa

I've Got Your Number
US 1934 68m bw

Telephone service engineers help prove a girl innocent of burglary. Cheerful, fast-moving programmer typical of its studio at the time.
Joan Blondell, Pat O'Brien, Allen Jenkins, Glenda Farrell, Eugene Pallette. Written by Warren Duff and Sidney Sutherland; directed by Ray Enright; for Warner.

I've Lived Before
US 1956 82m bw
U–I (Howard Christie)

After a plane crash, the pilot recovers but believes himself to be another airman who died in 1918.
Dullish, talky drama which wastes its interesting reincarnation theme.

w Norman Jolley, William Talman d Richard Bartlett ph Maury Gertsman m Herman Stein

Jock Mahoney, Leigh Snowden, Ann Harding, John McIntire, Raymond Bailey, Jerry Paris

Ivy*
US 1947 99m bw
Universal (William Cameron Menzies)

In Edwardian society England, a lady poisoner gets her come-uppance.
Curiously ineffective period thriller in which the star is the elegant but artificial production design: the script is deadly dull.

w Charles Bennett, *novel* Mrs Belloc Lowndes *d Sam Wood ph Russell Metty* m Daniele Amfitheatrof *pd William Cameron Menzies*

Joan Fontaine, Herbert Marshall, Patric Knowles, Richard Ney, Cedric Hardwicke, Lucile Watson, Sara Allgood, Henry Stephenson, Rosalind Ivan, Lilian Fontaine, Una O'Connor, Isobel Elsom, Alan Napier, Paul Cavanagh, Gavin Muir, Norma Varden

'The real star is whoever was responsible for the dressing, setting, lighting and shooting, and that, I infer from past performance, is the producer, William Cameron Menzies.'—*James Agee*

J

J. W. Coop*
US 1971 112m Eastmancolor
Columbia / Robertson and Associates (Cliff Robertson)

After ten years in prison, a rodeo rider returns to his home town.
Well-made but rather inconsequential drama with attractive locations.

w Cliff Robertson, Gary Cartwright, Bud Shrake d Cliff Robertson ph Frank Stanley m Don Randi, Louie Shelton

Cliff Robertson, Cristina Ferrare, Geraldine Page,
R. G. Armstrong

Jabberwocky
GB 1977 101m Technicolor
Umbrella (John Goldstone, Sandy Lieberson)

A medieval cooper's apprentice is mistaken for a prince and slays the dragon which is terrorizing the neighbourhood.
An intellectual Carry On film, with very little more taste and a great deal more unpleasant imagery. Despite much re-editing, the laughs are very intermittent.

w Charles Alverson, Terry Gilliam d Terry Gilliam ph Terry Bedford m De Wolfe pd Roy Smith

Michael Palin, Max Wall, Deborah Fallender, Warren Mitchell, John Le Mesurier, Harry H. Corbett, Rodney Bewes, Bernard Bresslaw
'The constant emphasis on blood, excrement, dismemberment and filth ultimately becomes rather wearing.'—*Michael Billington, Illustrated London News*

Jack Ahoy
GB 1934 82m bw

An accident-prone naval rating routs bandits and wins the girl. Tailor-made star comedy with skilful moments. Jack Hulbert, Nancy O'Neil, Alfred Drayton, Tamara Desni. Written by Jack Hulbert, Leslie Arliss, Gerald Fairlie and Austin Melford; directed by Walter Forde; for Gaumont. 'Mr Hulbert is equal to all his occasions . . . his abounding energy and high spirits are never monotonous or wearisome.'—*E. V. Lucas, Punch.*

Jack of All Trades*
GB 1936 76m bw

A cheerful con man talks his way into a top job in an international firm. Odd amalgam of star comedy, musical numbers of the Astaire / Rogers type, shafts of satire from the original play, and finally some flat-footed farce. Certainly worth a look. Jack Hulbert, Gina Malo, Robertson Hare, Athole Stewart, Felix Aylmer, H. F. Maltby. Written by Jack Hulbert, Austin Melford and J. O. C. Orton, from the play *Youth at the Helm* by Paul Vulpuis; directed by Jack Hulbert and Robert Stevenson; for Gainsborough.

Jack of Diamonds
US / West Germany 1967 105m Metrocolor

A retired jewel thief introduces a brilliant pupil into society. Repetitive and rather glum comedy-drama which perks up occasionally. George Hamilton, Joseph Cotten, Marie Laforet, Maurice Evans, Wolfgang Preiss, Lilli Palmer, Carroll Baker, Zsa Zsa Gabor. Written by Jack de Witt and Sandy Howard; directed by Don Taylor; for Harris / Bavaria Atelier / MGM.

Jack Slade
US 1953 90m bw

A western gunman becomes a psychopathic killer. Cliché-ridden but rather brutish western, thought sensationally violent at the time. Mark Stevens, Dorothy Malone, Barton Maclane, John Litel, Paul Langton, Harry Shannon. Written by Warren Douglas; directed by Harold Schuster; for Allied Artists. (GB title: *Slade.*)

Jack the Giant Killer**
US 1961 94m Technicolor
Zenith / Edward Small (Robert E. Kent)

Demon Pendragon kidnaps the princess of Cornwall but she is rescued by a farmer's son. Very creditable fairy tale, with the right style and atmosphere assisted by vigorous acting, good pace and excellent trick effects. Unfortunately it turned out rather scary for a child audience and so fell between two stools.

w Orville Hampton, Nathan Juran   d Nathan Juran   ph David S. Horsley   m Paul Sawtell, Bert Shefter   sp Howard Anderson   ad Fernando Carere, Frank McCoy

Kerwin Mathews, Judi Meredith, *Torin Thatcher, Don Beddoe*, Walter Burke, Barry Kelley

Jack the Ripper
GB 1958   84m   bw
Mid Century (Baker and Berman)

In Victorian London the Ripper murders are finally attributed to a demented surgeon.
Flat and rather flabby treatment of a *cause célèbre,* saved by a reasonably convincing period look.

w Jimmy Sangster   d / ph Robert S. Baker, Monty Berman   m Stanley Black

Ewen Solon, Lee Patterson, Eddie Byrne, Betty McDowell, John Le Mesurier

Jackass Mail
US 1942   80m   bw
MGM (John Considine Jnr)

A horse thief marries the proprietress of a gambling saloon in the hope of hijacking her mail line, but she reforms him.
Boisterously conceived but anaemically scripted western comedy with the stars in full throttle.

w Lawrence Hazard   d Norman Z. McLeod   ph Clyde de Vinna   m David Snell, Earl Brent

Wallace Beery, Marjorie Main, J. Carrol Naish, Darryl Hickman, William Haade, Hobart Cavanaugh

'This time at least they are repeating their variation on the Min-and-Bill routine among companions whose resemblance to burlesque is as unabashed as their own.'—*Bosley Crowther, New York Times*

Jackboot Mutiny
Germany 1955   77m   bw
Arca-Ariston
original title: *Es Geschah am 20 Juli*

An account of the army officers' plot to assassinate Hitler.
Documentary-like treatment without much attempt at characterization. An important historical document nevertheless.

w W. P. Zibaso, Gustav Machaty   d G. W. Pabst   ph Kurt Hasse   m Johannes Weissenbach

Bernhard Wicki, Karl Ludwig Diehl, Carl Wery

The Jackpot**
US 1950   85m   bw
TCF (Samuel G. Engel)

A suburban husband finds that life becomes complicated when winning the jackpot on a radio quiz makes him a celebrity.
Modest, skilful comedy in Hollywood's best manner.

w Phoebe and Henry Ephron   d Walter Lang   ph Joseph La Shelle   md Lionel Newman

James Stewart, Barbara Hale, James Gleason, Fred Clark, Alan Mowbray, Patricia Medina, Natalie Wood, Tommy Rettig, Robert Gist, Lyle Talbot

Jack's the Boy*
GB 1932   91m   bw
Gainsborough (Michael Balcon)

The police commissioner's son proves his worth in rounding up a smash-and-grab gang.
Dated but lively farce which established its star as a British box office attraction of the thirties.

w W. P. Lipscomb   d Walter Forde   ph Leslie Rowson

Jack Hulbert, Cicely Courtneidge, Francis Lister, Winifred Shotter, Peter Gawthorne, Ben Field

'A riotously funny, good, clean, honest British picture.'—*Sydney Carroll, Sunday Times*

† The film in which Hulbert sang 'The Flies Crawled Up the Window' (*m* Vivian Ellis, *ly* Douglas Furber).

Jackson County Jail
US 1976   84m   Metrocolor
(UA) New World (Roger Corman)

A lady driver is hijacked, attacked, disbelieved by the local police, thrown into jail and raped by the jailer, whom she brains with a stool.
An exploitation piece with social pretensions which it in no way justifies: it is however quite competently entertaining in its mindlessly violent way.

w Donald Stewart   d Michael Miller   ph Bruce Logan   m Loren Newkirk

Yvette Mimieux, Tommy Lee Jones, Robert Carradine, Frederic Cook, Severn Darden, Howard Hesseman

Jacqueline*
GB 1956   93m   bw
Rank (George H. Brown)

A Belfast shipyard worker cannot stand heights, takes to drink, and is helped by his small daughter.

Convincing, well-made, realistically set domestic comedy-drama.

w Patric Kirwan, Liam O'Flaherty *d* Roy Baker *ph Geoffrey Unsworth m* Cedric Thorpe Davie

John Gregson, Kathleen Ryan, Jacqueline Ryan, Noel Purcell, Cyril Cusack, Marie Kean, Liam Redmond, Maureen Delany

Jaguar Lives
US 1979 90m Eastmancolor

Exploits of an international secret agent with skill in the martial arts. Flashy, violent, James Bond rip-off, years behind its time. Joe Lewis, Christopher Lee, Donald Pleasence, Capucine, Barbara Bach, Joseph Wiseman, Woody Strode, John Huston. Written by Yabo Yablonsky; directed by Ernest Pintoff; for Sandy Howard / Jaguar.

Jailhouse Rock*
US 1957 96m bw Cinemascope
MGM (Pandro S. Berman)

An ex-convict becomes a pop star. Reasonably competent star vehicle, sourer in tone than most.

w Guy Trosper *d* Richard Thorpe *ph* Robert Bronner *md* Jeff Alexander

Elvis Presley, Judy Tyler, Mickey Shaughnessy, Vaughn Taylor, Dean Jones

Jamaica Inn*
GB 1939 107m bw
Mayflower (Erich Pommer)

In old Cornwall, an orphan girl becomes involved with smugglers.
Stagey, stilted adventure story which never loses its studio feel or takes fire as a Hitchcock picture. The cast keeps it interesting.

w Sidney Gilliat, Joan Harrison, J. B. Priestley, *novel* Daphne du Maurier *d Alfred Hitchcock ph* Harry Stradling, Bernard Knowles *m* Eric Fenby

Charles Laughton, Maureen O'Hara, Leslie Banks, Robert Newton, Emlyn Williams, Wylie Watson, Marie Ney, Morland Graham
'I was irresistibly reminded of an all-star charity matinee.'—*Graham Greene*

Jamaica Run
US 1953 92m Technicolor
Paramount Pine–Thomas

A search for documents, which may apportion a great house to another branch of the family, leads to murder.
Plot-bound romantic mystery in period, with elements of a Caribbean *Rebecca*. Watchable medium-budget hokum.

wd Lewis R. Foster, *novel* Max Murray *ph* Lionel Lindon *m* Lucien Cailliet

Ray Milland, Arlene Dahl, Wendell Corey, Patric Knowles

Jane Eyre***
US 1943 96m bw
TCF (William Goetz)

In Victorian times, a harshly treated orphan girl becomes governess in a mysterious Yorkshire mansion with a brooding master. Sharply paced, reasonably faithful and superbly staged Hollywood version of Charlotte Brontë's archetypal romantic novel which stimulated so many imitations, including *Rebecca*.

w Aldous Huxley, Robert Stevenson, John Houseman *d* Robert Stevenson *ph* George Barnes *m* Bernard Herrmann *sp* Fred Sersen *ad* Wiard B. Ihnen, James Basevi

Joan Fontaine, Orson Welles, Margaret O'Brien, *Henry Daniell*, John Sutton, Agnes Moorehead, Elizabeth Taylor, Peggy Ann Garner, Sara Allgood, Aubrey Mather, Hillary Brooke, Edith Barrett, Ethel Griffies, Barbara Everest, *John Abbott*
'A careful and tame production, a sadly vanilla-flavoured Joan Fontaine, and Orson Welles treating himself to road operatic sculpturings of body, cloak and diction, his eyes glinting in the Rembrandt gloom, at every chance, like side orders of jelly.'—*James Agee*
'The essentials are still there; and the non-essentials, such as the gloom, the shadows, the ground mist, the rain and the storms, have been expanded and redoubled and magnified to fill up the gaps.'—*Richard Mallett, Punch*

Janice Meredith
US 1924 153m bw silent
Metro-Goldwyn / Cosmopolitan
GB title: *The Beautiful Rebel*

Vicissitudes of the coquettish daughter of a New Jersey family through the War of Independence.
Marathon melodrama not unlike *Gone with the Wind* in subject matter, but of no remaining interest.

w Lilly Hayward, *novel* Paul Leicester Ford *d* E. Mason Hopper *ad* Joseph Urban *music score* Deems Taylor

Marion Davies, Harrison Ford, Macklyn Arbuckle, Joseph Kilgour, George Nash, Tyrone Power Snr, May Vokes, W. C. Fields, Olin Howland

Janie

US 1944   106m   bw
Warner (Brock Pemberton)

The teenage daughter of a middle-class
American household gets into innocent
scrapes with the army.
Deafening tomboy farce.

w Agnes Christine Johnson, Charles Hoffman,
play Josephine Bentham, Herschel V.
Williams Jnr d Michael Curtiz ph Carl
Guthrie songs Lee David, Sammy Cahn, Jule
Styne

Joyce Reynolds, Robert Hutton, Ann
Harding, Edward Arnold, Robert Benchley,
Claire Foley, Hattie McDaniel
† Janie Gets Married, made the following year
and running 89m, had almost identical credits
except that Joan Leslie replaced Joyce
Reynolds and Dorothy Malone joined the
cast.

Japanese War Bride*

US 1952   94m   bw
TCF / Bernhard (Joseph Bernhard)

An officer wounded in Korea marries his
Japanese nurse and takes her home to
California.
Predictable domestic drama very similar to the
British Frieda, marginally interesting for
sociological reasons.

w Catherine Turney d King Vidor ph Lionel
Lindon m Emil Newman

Shirley Yamaguchi, Don Taylor, Cameron
Mitchell, Marie Windsor, James Bell, Louise
Lorimer

Jason and the Argonauts***

GB 1963   104m   Technicolor
Columbia / Charles H. Schneer

With help and hindrance from the gods, Jason
voyages in search of the Golden Fleece and
meets all kinds of monsters.
Rambling semi-classic mythological fantasy
which keeps its tongue firmly in its cheek and
provides a framework for some splendid stop-
frame animation.

w Jan Read, Beverly Cross d Don Chaffey
ph Wilkie Cooper m Bernard Herrmann
sp Ray Harryhausen

Todd Armstrong, Honor Blackman, Niall
MacGinnis, Andrew Faulds, Nancy Kovack

Jassy

GB 1947   102m   Technicolor
GFD / Gainsborough (Sydney Box)

A gypsy servant girl falls in love with her
master but is accused of murder.

Period romantic melodrama of the Man in
Grey school; poor of its kind despite high
production values.

w Dorothy and Campbell Christie, Geoffrey
Kerr, novel Norah Lofts d Bernard Knowles
ph Geoffrey Unsworth

Margaret Lockwood, Patricia Roc, Dennis
Price, Basil Sydney, Dermot Walsh, Nora
Swinburne, Linden Travers, Ernest Thesiger,
Cathleen Nesbitt, John Laurie, Jean Cadell,
Clive Morton

Java Head*

GB 1934   85m   bw
ATP (Basil Dean)

In 1850 Bristol, a shipbuilder forsakes his
Manchu wife for an English girl.
Rather obvious period melodrama with full-
blooded acting.

w Martin Brown, Gordon Wellesley
d J. Walter Ruben ph Bert Glennon

Anna May Wong, John Loder, Ralph
Richardson, Elizabeth Allan, Edmund
Gwenn, Herbert Lomas, George Curzon, Roy
Emerton

Jaws**

US 1975   125m   Technicolor
Panavision
Universal / Zanuck–Brown (William S.
Gilmore Jnr)

A man-eating shark causes havoc off the Long
Island coast.
In the exploitation-hungry seventies this film
took more money than any other. In itself,
despite genuinely suspenseful and frightening
sequences, it is a slackly narrated and
sometimes flatly handled thriller with an over-
abundance of dialogue and, when it finally
appears, a pretty unconvincing monster.

w Peter Benchley, Carl Gottlieb, novel Peter
Benchley d Steven Spielberg ph Bill Butler
m John Williams

Robert Shaw, Roy Scheider, Richard
Dreyfuss, Lorraine Gary, Murray Hamilton,
Carl Gottlieb

'A mind-numbing repast for sense-sated
gluttons. Shark stew for the stupefied.'—
William S. Pechter

'The opening sequences have few parallels
in modern cinema; like the shower scene in
Psycho they will haunt a whole generation.'—
Les Keyser, Hollywood in the Seventies

AA: John Williams
AAN: best picture

Jaws 2

US 1978   117m   Technicolor
Panavision
Universal / Richard Zanuck, David Brown
(Joe Alves)

Another man-eating shark menaces teenagers
in the Long Island resort of Amity.
Repetitive and feeble sequel aimed directly at
the popcorn market.

w Carl Gottlieb, Howard Sackler, Dorothy
Tristan d Jeannot Szwarc ph Michael Butler,
David Butler, Michael McGowan m John
Williams

Roy Scheider, Lorraine Gary, Murray
Hamilton, Joseph Mascolo, Colin Wilcox
  'A manipulation of the audience, in the best
sense of the term.'—Jeannot Szwarc, director

The Jayhawkers

US 1959   110m   Technicolor
Vistavision
Paramount / Panama and Frank

Before the Civil War, a farmer defeats a
militant posse of private raiders.
Unconvincing but rather unusual western, flat
patches alternating with striking ones.

w Melvin Frank, Joseph Petracca, Frank
Fenton,
 A. I. Bezzerides d Melvin Frank ph Loyal
Griggs m Jerome Moross

Fess Parker, Jeff Chandler, Nicole Maurey,
Henry Silva, Herbert Rudley

Jazz Comedy*

USSR 1934   93m   bw
Mosfilm
original title: Vesolye Rebyata

A shepherd is frequently mistaken for a
famous conductor.
Peripatetic comedy with many sight gags and
western slapstick: Russian comedy being still a
rare thing, it seems something of a revelation.

w Grigori Alexandrov, Nikolai Erdman, V.
Mass d Grigori Alexandrov ph Vladimir
Nilsen m Isaac Dunayevsky

Lubov Orlova, Leonid Utyosov, Maria
Strelkova

The Jazz Singer****

US 1927   89m   bw
Warner

A cantor's son makes it big in show business.
Archetypal Jewish weepie which became of
absorbing interest as the first talkie film (songs
and a few fragments of speech) and in its way,
surprisingly, is not half bad.

w Alfred A. Cohn, play Samson Raphaelson
d Alan Crosland ph Hal Mohr

Al Jolson, May McAvoy, Warner Oland,
Eugenie Besserer, Otto Lederer
  'A beautiful period piece, extravagantly
sentimental . . . yet entirely compelling in its
own conviction.'—NFT, 1969
  'The Jazz Singer definitely establishes the
fact that talking pictures are imminent.
Everyone in Hollywood can rise up and
declare that they are not, and it will not alter
the fact. If I were an actor with a squeaky
voice I would worry.'—Welford Beaton, The
Film Spectator

AAN: Alfred A. Cohn

The Jazz Singer

US 1953   107m   Technicolor
Warner (Louis F. Edelman)

Ill-considered, schmaltzy remake of the above.

w Frank Davis, Leonard Stern, Lewis Meltzer
d Michael Curtiz ph Carl Guthrie md Ray
Heindorf m Max Steiner

Danny Thomas, Peggy Lee, Mildred
Dunnock, Eduard Franz

AAN: Ray Heindorf; Max Steiner

The Jazz Singer

US 1980   115m   De Luxe
EMI / Jerry Leider

Oddly-timed reprise of the above, with doting
mum replaced by patient wife. A good basis
for a best-selling album, otherwise a pointless
enterprise.

w Herbert Baker, Stephen H. Foreman
d Richard Fleischer ph Isidore Mankofsky
m Leonard Rosenman pd Harry Horner

Neil Diamond, Laurence Olivier, Lucie
Arnaz, Catlin Adams, Sully Boyar
  'What is jazz to Neil Diamond and what is
Neil Diamond to jazz? Old title has nothing to
do with music on display here and would seem
meaningless to modern audiences.'—Variety

Jealousy

US 1929   66m   bw

A young artist is jealous of his wife's older
friend, and kills him. Turgid adaptation of a
two-character play; interesting only for its
cast, though the star died before it was
released. Jeanne Eagels, Fredric March,
Halliwell Hobbes, Henry Daniell. Written by
Garrett Fort and John D. Williams, from the
play by Louis Verneuil; directed by Jean De
Limur; for Paramount.

Jealousy*
US 1945   70m   bw

A failed writer, jealous of his wife's friendship with another man, is found murdered. Curious but interesting melodrama with much talent breaking through. Nils Asther, John Joder, Jane Randolph, Karen Morley. Written by Arnold Phillips, Gustav Machaty and Dalton Trumbo; directed by Gustav Machaty; music by Hans Eisler; for Republic. 'It is a sympathetic film, and in spite of its overall failure, contains enough sincerity and enough artistry to make most of the other films mentioned here look sick.'—*James Agee.*

Jeanne Eagels*
US 1957   114m   bw
Columbia (George Sidney)

A sideshow dancer becomes a Broadway star of the twenties but dies of drugs.
Well-upholstered but basically too conventional showbiz biopic.
w Daniel Fuchs, Sonya Levien, John Fante *d* George Sidney *ph* Robert Planck *m* George Duning
Kim Novak, Jeff Chandler, Agnes Moorehead, Charles Drake, Larry Gates, *Virginia Grey*

Jeannie*
GB 1941   101m   bw
GFD / Tansa (Marcel Hellman)
US title: *Girl in Distress*

A Scots girl comes into money and takes a European holiday.
Mildly astringent, generally amusing comedy which overcomes shaky production. Remade as *Let's Be Happy* in 1952.
w Anatole de Grunwald, Roland Pertwee, *play* Aimée Stuart *d* Harold French *ph* Bernard Knowles
Barbara Mullen, Michael Redgrave, *Albert Lieven*, Wilfrid Lawson, Kay Hammond, Edward Chapman, Googie Withers, Gus MacNaughton
'One of the easiest, sweetest of light comedies.'—*James Agee*

Jennie Gerhardt
US 1933   85m   bw
Paramount (B. P. Schulberg)

An unmarried mother is hard done by but gets the man she loves in the end.
Archetypal weepie, adequately put across.
w Josephine Lovett, Joseph M. March, S. K. Lauren, Frank Portos, *novel* Theodore Dreiser *d* Marion Gering *ph* Leon Shamroy

Sylvia Sidney, Donald Cook, Mary Astor, Edward Arnold, H. B. Warner, Theodor Von Eltz

Jennifer
US 1953   73m   bw
AA (Berman Swartz)

The lady housekeeper of a California mansion broods on the mysterious disappearance of her predecessor.
Slight, quietly effective suspenser with a let-down ending.
w Virginia Myers *d* Joel Newton *ph James Wong Howe m* Ernest Gold
Ida Lupino, Howard Duff, Robert Nicholas, Mary Shipp

Jeopardy
US 1952   69m   bw
MGM (Sol Baer Fielding)

A man on a camping holiday falls off a jetty and gets stuck in the timbers while the water rises; his wife frantically seeks help from an escaped convict.
Panic melodrama enjoyable for its clichés.
w Mel Dinelli *d* John Sturges *ph* Victor Milner *m* Dmitri Tiomkin
Barbara Stanwyck, Barry Sullivan, Ralph Meeker

Jeremiah Johnson**
US 1972   107m   Technicolor
      Panavision
Warner (Joe Wizan)

In the 1850s an ex-soldier becomes a mountain trapper.
Splendidly made if rather desultorily plotted adventure story with the feel of raw reality.
w John Milius, Edward Anhalt *d* Sydney Pollack *ph* Andrew Callaghan *m* John Rubinstein, Tim McIntire
Robert Redford, Will Geer, Allyn McLerie

Jeremy
US 1973   90m   De Luxe
UA / Kenasset (George Pappas)

A music student falls in love with a ballet dancer.
Sentimental love story with nothing positive to commend it, chiefly interesting because for commercial release it was blown up from 16mm.
wd Arthur Barron *ph* Paul Goldsmith *m* Lee Holdridge
Robby Benson, Glynnis O'Connor, Len Bari, Leonardo Cimino

Jericho
GB 1937 77m bw
Buckingham (Walter Futter, Max Schach)
US title: *Dark Sands*

A court-martialled officer pursues a
murderous deserter across Africa.
Lively star vehicle of its day.

w Frances Marion, George Barraud, Peter
Ruric, Robert N. Lee *d* Thornton Freeland
ph John W. Boyle

Paul Robeson, Henry Wilcoxon, Wallace
Ford, John Laurie, James Carew

The Jerk
US 1979 94m Technicolor
Universal / Aspen (Peter MacGregor-Scott)

An innocent white man brought up by black
sharecroppers goes out into the world and first
makes, then loses a fortune.
Hit-or-miss star vehicle with flashes of satire
and fallen aspirations to be a modern *Candide*.

w Steve Martin, Carl Gottlieb, Michael Elias
d Carl Reiner *ph* Victor J. Kemper *m* Jack
Elliott

Steve Martin, Bernadette Peters, Catlin
Adams, Bill Macy, Maurice Evans

'Goofy, dumb, innocent, loud,
uncoordinated, bashful and quite dirty.'—
Variety

The Jerusalem File
US / Israel 1971 96m Metrocolor
MGM / Sparta (Ram Ben Efraim)

American archaeologists in Jerusalem become
involved in Arab / Israeli espionage.
Muddled mixture of action and politics.

w Troy Kennedy Martin *d* John Flynn
ph Raoul Coutard *m* John Scott

Bruce Davison, Nicol Williamson, Donald
Pleasence, Ian Hendry

Jesse James**
US 1939 106m Technicolor
TCF (Nunnally Johnson)

After the Civil War, two brothers take to train
robbing when railroad employees harass their
family.
The life of an outlaw turns into family
entertainment when Hollywood bathes it in
sentiment, soft colour, family background and
warm humour. It works dangerously well, and
the action sequences are splendid.

w Nunnally Johnson *d* Henry King
ph George Barnes *md* Louis Silvers
ad William Darling, George Dudley

Tyrone Power, Henry Fonda, Nancy Kelly,
Jane Darwell, Randolph Scott, Henry Hull,
Slim Summerville, Brian Donlevy, J. Edward
Bromberg, John Carradine, Donald Meek
'An authentic American panorama.'—*New
York Times*
† Sequel 1940: *The Return of Frank James*.
Remake 1957: *The True Story of Jesse James*.

Jessica
France / Italy / US 1962 105m
Technicolor Panavision
UA / Ariane / Dear Film (Jean Negulesco)

The attractive midwife in a Sicilian village
causes the women to go on a sex strike.
Synthetic rustic naughtiness showing several
influences imperfectly assimilated.

w Edith Sommer, *novel* The Midwife of Pont
Clery by Flora Sundstrom *d* Jean Negulesco
ph Piero Portalupi *m* Mario Nascimbene

Angie Dickinson, Maurice Chevalier, Noel
Noel, Gabriele Ferzetti, Sylva Koscina, Agnes
Moorehead, Marcel Dalio

Jesus Christ Superstar*
US 1973 107m Technicolor Todd-AO
35
Universal (Norman Jewison, Robert
Stigwood)

Young tourists in Israel re-enact episodes of
the life of Christ.
Location-set fantasia based on the
phenomenally successful rock opera; some of
it works, but the original concept was a
theatrical one.

w Melvyn Bragg, Norman Jewison, *book* Tim
Rice *d* Norman Jewison *m* Andrew Lloyd
Webber *ph* Douglas Slocombe *md* André
Previn

Ted Neeley, Carl Anderson, Yvonne Elliman,
Barry Dennen
'One of the true fiascos of modern
cinema.'—*Paul D. Zimmerman*

AAN: André Previn

Jet over the Atlantic
US 1958 95m bw
Warner / Inter Continental (Benedict
Bogeaus)

A noble British passenger on a plane from
Madrid to New York has planted a gas bomb
in the luggage compartment.
Mechanical airborne suspenser with the usual
assortment of unconvincing types making
unconvincing gestures.

w Irving H. Cooper *d* Byron Haskin
ph George Stahl *m* Lou Forbes

Guy Madison, Virginia Mayo, George Raft, George Macready, Ilona Massey, Anna Lee, Margaret Lindsay, Venetia Stevenson, Mary Anderson, Brett Halsey, Frederic Worlock

Jet Pilot
US 1950–57   112m   Technicolor
Howard Hughes (Jules Furthman)

A Russian lady spy falls for an American pilot. Lamentably dull and stupid romantic actioner of which all concerned should be thoroughly ashamed, especially as it took seven years to complete and is not even technically competent.

w Jules Furthman d Josef Von Sternberg (and others) ph Winton C. Hoch m Bronislau Kaper

John Wayne, Janet Leigh, Jay C. Flippen, Paul Fix, Richard Rober, Roland Winters, Ivan Triesault, Hans Conried
'One of the most childish, tedious and futile cold war spy dramas yet concocted by a Hollywood screenwriter.'—*John Gillett*

Jet Storm*
GB 1959   99m   bw
British Lion / Britannia / Pendennis (Steven Pallos)

An airliner in flight from London to New York is discovered to have a bomb on board. All-star slice-of-life suspenser with competently handled dialogue and situations.

w Cy Endfield, Sigmund Miller d Cy Endfield ph Jack Hildyard m Thomas Rajna

Richard Attenborough, George Rose, Hermione Baddeley, Mai Zetterling, Diane Cilento, Stanley Baker, Harry Secombe, Virginia Maskell, Elizabeth Sellars, Sybil Thorndike, Bernard Braden, Cec Linder, David Kossoff

Les Jeux Interdits***
France 1952   84m   bw
Robert Dorfmann (Paul Joly)
aka: *Forbidden Games; The Secret Game*

In 1940, the little daughter of refugee parents sees her parents killed, and takes refuge with a peasant family, the small son of which helps her bury her dead puppy. They make a game of building a cemetery, which leads to a village feud . . .
Poignant anti-war tract which seemed a masterpiece at the time and is full of marvellous moments, but no longer holds up as a whole.

w *Jean Aurenche, Pierre Bost, novel* François Boyer d *René Clément* ph Robert Julliard m Narciso Yepes

Brigitte Fossey, Georges Poujouly, Amédée, Laurence Badie, Jacques Marin, Suzanne Courtal, Lucien Hubert
'A truly imposing achievement of blending several seemingly unrelated elements into a totally meaningful whole.'—*John Simon, 1967*
AA: best foreign film
AAN: François Boyer (original story)

Les Jeux Sont Faits*
France 1947   91m   bw
Films Gibe

Falling in love in Purgatory, two murdered people get a second chance to return to earth, but spend their time quarrelling. Somewhat despondent romantic fantasy with morsels of wit.

w Jean-Paul Sartre d Jean Delannoy ph Christian Matras m Georges Auric

Micheline Presle, Marcel Pagliero, Marguerite Moreno, Charles Dullin

Jew Suss**
GB 1934   109m   bw
Gaumont (Michael Balcon)
US title: *Power*

In old Wurttemberg, a Jew gains power to help his people, then finds he is Gentile. Interesting, heavy-handed historical satire on the pointlessness of race distinctions, made partly in answer to Nazi oppression in Germany.

w Dorothy Farnum, A. R. Rawlinson, *novel* Leon Feuchtwanger d Lothar Mendes

Conrad Veidt, Benita Hume, Frank Vosper, Cedric Hardwicke, Gerald du Maurier, Pamela Ostrer

Jew Suss*
Germany 1940   85m   bw
Terra

Celebrated travesty of the above, in which the Jew is wholly evil and rapes Aryan girls.

w Ludwig Metzger, Veit Harlan, Eberhard Wolfgang Möller d Veit Harlan ph Bruno Mondi m Wolfgang Zeller

Ferdinand Marian, Werner Krauss, Heinrich George, Kristina Söderbaum
'The epitome of anti-semitic propaganda . . . the most notorious film of the Third Reich and one which brought disgrace on almost everyone connected with it.'—*Georges Sadoul*
'Highly recommended for its artistic value and, to serve the politics of the State, recommended for young people.'—*Josef Goebbels*

Jewel Robbery*
US 1932   68m   bw
Warner

A jewel thief and a millionaire's wife fall in love in Vienna.
Good sparkling fun in the shadow of *Trouble in Paradise* (qv).

w Erwin Gelsey, *play* Ladislaus Fodor
d William Dieterle *ph* Robert Kurrle

William Powell, Kay Francis, Hardie Albright, André Luguet, Henry Kolker, Spencer Charters, Alan Mowbray, Helen Vinson, Lawrence Grant

Jezebel***
US 1938   104m   bw
Warner (Henry Blanke)

Before the Civil War, a southern belle stirs up trouble among the menfolk by her wilfulness and spite, but atones when a plague strikes.
Superb star melodrama, tossed to her in compensation for losing *Gone with the Wind*, and dealt with in high style by all concerned.

w Clements Ripley, Abem Finkel, John Huston, *play* Owen Davis Snr *d* William Wyler *ph* Ernest Haller *m* Max Steiner

Bette Davis, Henry Fonda, George Brent, Margaret Lindsay, Fay Bainter, Richard Cromwell, Donald Crisp, Henry O'Neill, John Litel, Spring Byington, Eddie Anderson, Gordon Oliver, Irving Pichel

'Its excellences come from many sources—good plotting and writing, a director and photographer who know how to make the thing flow along with dramatic pictorial effect, and a cast that makes its story a record of living people.'—*James Shelley Hamilton*
'Without the zing Davis gave it, it would have looked very mossy indeed.'—*Pauline Kael, 1968*

AA: Bette Davis; Fay Bainter
AAN: best picture; Ernest Haller; Max Steiner

Jigsaw
US 1949   72m   bw
(UA) Tower (The Danzigers)

An assistant District Attorney uncovers a mob stirring up racial hatred.
Undistinguished piece of do-goodery, curiously decorated by guest stars doing bit parts as a gesture of goodwill.

w Fletcher Markle, Vincent McConnor
d Fletcher Markle *ph* Don Malkames
m Robert Stringer

Franchot Tone, Jean Wallace, Myron McCormick, Marc Lawrence, Marlene Dietrich, Henry Fonda, John Garfield, Marsha Hunt, Leonard Lyons, Burgess Meredith

Jigsaw**
GB 1962   107m   bw   Cinemascope
British Lion / Britannia / Figaro (Val Guest)

Brighton policemen track down the murderer of a woman found in a lonely house on the beach.
Absorbing and entertaining little murder mystery which sustains its considerable length with interesting detail and plays as fair as can be with the audience. Excellent unassuming entertainment.

wd Val Guest, *play* Sleep Long My Love by Hilary Waugh *ph* Arthur Grant *m* none

Jack Warner, Ronald Lewis, *Michael Goodliffe*, Yolande Donlan, John Barron

Jim Thorpe, All-American
US 1951   105m   bw
Warner (Everett Freeman)
GB title: *Man of Bronze*

A Red Indian becomes a star footballer, but later succumbs to drink.
Adequate sporting biopic.

w Douglas Morrow, Everett Freeman
d Michael Curtiz *ph* Ernest Haller *m* Max Steiner

Burt Lancaster, Charles Bickford, Steve Cochran, Phyllis Thaxter, Dick Wesson

Jimmy the Gent*
US 1934   67m   bw
Warner (Robert Lord)

A racketeer supplies heirs for unclaimed estates.
Adequate star crime comedy.

w Bertram Millhauser *d* Michael Curtiz *ph* Ira Morgan *md* Leo F. Forbstein

Jimmy Cagney, Bette Davis, Alice White, Allen Jenkins, Arthur Hohl, Mayo Methot, Alan Dinehart, Hobart Cavanaugh, Ralf Harolde, Philip Reed, Joe Sawyer

'Fast and flip, rough and rowdy.'—*New York American*

Jitterbugs*
US 1943   75m   bw
TCF (Sol M. Wurtzel)

Laurel and Hardy help a nightclub singer to fight off gangsters.
The last Laurel and Hardy film to contain any good scenes, and almost the only one of their TCF films that did.

w Scott Darling *d* Mal St Clair *ph* Lucien Andriot

Stan Laurel, Oliver Hardy, Vivian Blaine, Bob Bailey, Douglas Fowley, Noel Madison, Lee Patrick

Jivaro

US 1953 91m Technicolor 3D
Paramount / William H. Pine, William C.Thomas
GB title: *Lost Treasure of the Amazon*

A mixed party of Americans follows a drunken treasure seeker into the jungle. Elementary treasure hunt adventure, hampered by studio foliage, bad script and half-hearted acting.

w Winston Miller, *story* David Duncan *d* Edward Ludwig *ph* Lionel Lindon *m* Gregory Stone

Fernando Lamas, Rhonda Fleming, Brian Keith, Lon Chaney Jnr, Marvin Miller, Richard Denning

Joan of Arc

US 1948 145m Technicolor
Walter Wanger

The last campaign of the Maid of Orleans. Strictly from Dullsville; one studio-set piece follows another, and a group of talented people clearly thought that prestige would sell itself without the hard work that goes into more commercial productions.

w Maxwell Anderson, Andrew Solt, *play* Joan of Lorraine by Maxwell Anderson *d* Victor Fleming *ph* Joe Valentine *m* Hugo Friedhofer *md* Emil Newman *ad* Richard Day

Ingrid Bergman, Jose Ferrer, George Coulouris, Francis L. Sullivan, Gene Lockhart, Ward Bond, John Ireland, Hurd Hatfield, Cecil Kellaway, George Zucco, J. Carrol Naish

'A bad film with one or two good things. It is childishly oversimplified, its battles *papier maché*, its heroine far too worldly, its spiritual content that of a chromo art calendar.'— *Herman G. Weinberg*

AA: Joe Valentine
AAN: Hugo Friedhofer; Ingrid Bergman; Jose Ferrer

Joan of Paris

US 1942 95m bw
TCF (David Hempstead)

A French resistance leader sacrifices herself so that Allied pilots can escape.
Well-made propaganda adventure dignified by excellent cast.

w Charles Bennett, Ellis St. Joseph, *story* Jacques Thery, Georges Kessel *d* Robert Stevenson *ph* Russell Metty *m* Roy Webb

Michele Morgan, Paul Henreid, Thomas Mitchell, Laird Cregar, May Robson, Alexander Granach, Alan Ladd

AAN: Roy Webb

Joanna

GB 1968 122m De Luxe Panavision
TCF / Laughlin (Michael S. Laughlin)

A girl art student comes to London and quickly finds the road to ruin.
Antediluvian rubbish tarted up with swinging London settings.

wd Michael Sarne *ph* Walter Lassally *m* Rod McKuen

Genevieve Waite, Christian Doermer, Calvin Lockhart, Donald Sutherland

'An unnecessarily protracted punishing of a very dead quadruped.'—*MFB*

The Job**

Italy 1961 90m bw
24 Horses Films (Alberto Soffientini)
original title; *Il Posto*

A teenage boy gets his first job, and progresses from office boy to clerk when a senior man dies.
Appealingly observant social comedy, very simple and extremely effective.

wd Ermanno Olmi *ph* Lamberto Caimi

Sandro Panzeri, Loredana Detto

'Rueful and funny and honest . . . the players have been encouraged not so much to act as to behave. Olmi stalks them like a naturalist, and the result is a small, unique and perfect achievement in film-making.'— *Penelope Houston, MFB*

Joe*

US 1970 107m De Luxe
Cannon (David Gil)

A construction worker in a bar meets a businessman who has just killed his daughter's drug addicted lover; they become buddies in their hatred of hippies.
Highly successful in America as a backlash against permissiveness, this rough-hewn opportunistic melodrama is vivid enough but moves in fits and starts.

w Norman Wexler *d / ph* John G. Avildsen *m* Bobby Scott

Peter Boyle, Dennis Patrick, Audrey Caire, Susan Sarandon

'A bad film disfigured by brute strokes of tendentiousness.'—*Penelope Gilliatt*
AAN: Norman Wexler

Joe Butterfly
US 1957   90m   Technicolor
Cinemascope
U-I (Aaron Rosenberg)

Shortly after World War II, American occupying troops are conned by a Japanese interpreter.
Dull comedy intent on healing old wounds.

w Sy Gomberg, Jack Sher, Marion Hargrove *d* Jesse Hibbs *ph* Irving Glassberg *m* Joseph Gershenson

Burgess Meredith, Audie Murphy, George Nader, Keenan Wynn, Fred Clark, John Agar, Charles McGraw

Joe Dakota
US 1957   90m   Technicolor
Cinemascope
U-I (Howard Christie)

A stranger appears in a western town in search of his Indian friend, who turns out to have been murdered by the townspeople so that they can share the profits from his oil well.
Feeble rip-off of *Bad Day at Black Rock*.

w William Talman, Norman Jolley *d* Richard Bartlett *ph* George Robinson *md* Joseph Gershenson

Jock Mahoney, Luana Patten, Charles McGraw, Barbara Lawrence, Claude Akins, Lee Van Cleef

Joe Kidd
US 1972   87m   Technicolor   Panavision
Universal / Malpaso (Sidney Beckerman)

A disreputable bounty hunter tracks down the leader of a tribe of Mexican bandits.
Rough and tumble star western with untenable moral attitudes.

w Elmore Leonard *d* John Sturges *ph* Bruce Surtees *m* Lalo Schifrin

Clint Eastwood, Robert Duvall, John Saxon, Don Stroud, James Wainwright

Joe Macbeth
GB 1955   90m   bw
Columbia / Frankovich (George Maynard)

A gangster is urged by his wife to rub out his boss.
Almost too bad to be funny, this effort to update Shakespeare has actors behaving as though they were stuck in treacle, and its gimmick quality is quickly dissipated by an indifferent production.

w Philip Yordan *d* Ken Hughes *ph* Basil Emmott *m* Trevor Duncan

Paul Douglas, Ruth Roman, Grégoire Aslan, Bonar Colleano, Sidney James

Joe Smith American°
US 1942   63m   bw
MGM (Jack Chertok)
GB title: *Highway to Freedom*

An aircraft factory worker with special knowledge is kidnapped by Nazis but leads the FBI to his captors.
Watchable propaganda thriller credited with easing Americans into a war mood.

w Allen Rivkin, *story* Paul Gallico *d* Richard Thorpe *ph* Charles Lawton Jnr

Robert Young, Marsha Hunt, Darryl Hickman, Harvey Stephens, Jonathan Hale, Noel Madison, Joseph Anthony
'Not a high-powered movie, it is a first rate die for the new propaganda models which Hollywood is readying for mass production.'—*Time*

Joey Boy
GB 1965   91m   bw
British Lion / Launder–Gilliat

In 1941, a group of petty crooks join the army.
Abysmal service comedy, incredibly cheap and tatty and the nadir of several of the talents involved.

wd Frank Launder *ph* Arthur Lavis *m* Philip Green

Harry H. Corbett, Stanley Baxter, Bill Fraser, Reg Varney, Percy Herbert, Lance Percival
'As visually shoddy as it is unfunny . . . the final shot (Corbett pulling a lavatory chain) is all too crudely apt.'—*MFB*

John and Julie
GB 1955   82m   Eastmancolor
Group Three (Herbert Mason)

Two children run away to see the coronation.
Genial little family comedy full of stock comic characters.

wd William Fairchild *ph* Arthur Grant *m* Philip Green

Colin Gibson, Leslie Dudley, Peter Sellers, Moira Lister, Wilfrid Hyde White, Sidney James, Andrew Cruickshank

John and Mary°
US 1969   92m   De Luxe   Panavision
TCF / Debrod (Ben Kadish)

Two New Yorkers have a one-night affair and cannot decide whether to continue.

Slight, disappointing sex comedy vehicle for
two stars who were very hot at the time.

w John Mortimer, *novel* Mervyn Jones
d Peter Yates *ph* Gayne Rescher *m* Quincy
Jones *pd* John Robert Lloyd

Dustin Hoffman, Mia Farrow, Michael Tolan,
Sunny Griffin, Tyne Daly

'The emphasis is not on action but on
acting, which although skilful and subtly
nuanced does not in this case amount to the
same thing as character.'—*Jan Dawson*

'Despite all the "now" sets and surfaces, it's
like an old comedy of the thirties—minus the
comedy.'—*Judith Crist*

John Goldfarb Please Come Home
US 1965   96m   De Luxe   Cinemascope
TCF / Steve Palmer / J. Lee-Thompson

An American spy pilot crashlands near the
palace of a Middle Eastern potentate at the
same time as a girl reporter arrives for an
interview.
Would-be satire on the cold war, anti-
feminism, American football, American /
Arab relations, etc. None of it works for a
minute, and the actors' desperation can be
plainly seen.

w William Peter Blatty d J. Lee-Thompson
ph Leon Shamroy *m* Johnny Williams

Shirley Maclaine, Richard Crenna, Peter
Ustinov, Fred Clark, Wilfrid Hyde White, Jim
Backus

John Loves Mary
US 1948   87m   bw
Warner

A GI returns home to get married, but
unfortunately, to help a friend, he has already
entered into a marriage of convenience.
Moderately amusing comedy with an excess of
complications.

w Phoebe and Henry Ephron, *play* Norman
Krasna d David Butler *ph* Peverell Marley
m David Buttolph

Ronald Reagan, Patricia Neal, Jack Carson,
Virginia Field

John Meade's Woman
US 1937   82m   bw

A timber industrialist marries a farm girl.
Solemn star drama. Edward Arnold, Francine
Larrimore, Gail Patrick, George Bancroft.
Written by Vincent Lawrence and Herman J.
Mankiewicz; directed by Richard Wallace; for
Paramount.

John Paul Jones
US 1959   126m   Technirama
Warner / Samuel Bronston

At the time of the American revolution a
young Scotsman rises to great heights in the
American navy.
Fragmented biopic with a succession of guest
stars which turn it into a charade almost as
silly as *The Story of Mankind*. On that level it
is not unentertaining.

wd John Farrow *ph* Michel Kelber *m* Max
Steiner

Robert Stack, Charles Coburn (as Benjamin
Franklin), Bette Davis (as Catherine the
Great), Marisa Pavan, Jean-Pierre Aumont,
Peter Cushing, Bruce Cabot, Macdonald
Carey

Johnny Allegro*
US 1949   81m   bw
Columbia (Irving Starr)
GB title: *Hounded*

A private eye eliminates a counterfeiter and
marries his wife.
Cheeky variation on the plot of *Gilda*, with
Macready repeating his role; later stages
borrow from *The Most Dangerous Game*. All
mildly diverting.

w Karen de Wolf, Guy Endore, James
Edward Grant d Ted Tetzlaff *ph* Joseph
Biroc *m* George Duning

George Raft, George Macready, Nina Foch,
Will Geer, Ivan Triesault

'Without any particular distinction, but
certainly not boring.'—*Richard Mallett, Punch*

Johnny Angel*
US 1945   79m   bw
RKO

A seaman solves the mystery of his father's
ship, found empty and adrift in the Gulf of
Mexico.
Very watchable mystery with plenty of plot
twists and efficient presentation.

w Steve Fisher d Edwin L. Marin *ph* Harry
J. Wild *m* Leigh Harline

George Raft, Claire Trevor, Signe Hasso,
Lowell Gilmore, Hoagy Carmichael, Marvin
Miller

Johnny Apollo
US 1940   93m   bw
TCF (Harry Joe Brown)

A well-heeled young man turns crook.
Moderate crime melo, impeccably turned out.

w Philip Dunne, Rowland Brown *d* Henry Hathaway *ph* Arthur Miller *m* Cyril Mockridge *md* Alfred Newman

Tyrone Power, Dorothy Lamour, Edward Arnold, Lloyd Nolan, Charles Grapewin, Lionel Atwill, Marc Lawrence, Jonathan Hale

Johnny Belinda**
US 1948 103m bw
Warner (Jerry Wald)

In a remote fishing community, a deaf mute girl is raped and the sympathetic local doctor is suspected of being the father of her baby.
Melodrama of the old school which in 1948 seemed oddly to mark a new permissiveness and made a big star of Jane Wyman; the production and locations were also persuasive.

w Irmgard Von Cube, Allen Vincent, *play* Elmer Harris *d Jean Negulesco ph* Ted McCord *m* Max Steiner *md* Leo F. Forbstein

Jane Wyman, Lew Ayres, Charles Bickford, Agnes Moorehead, Stephen McNally, Jan Sterling, Rosalind Ivan, Mabel Paige

AA: Jane Wyman
AAN: best picture; script; Jean Negulesco; Ted McCord; Max Steiner; Lew Ayres; Charles Bickford; Agnes Moorehead

Johnny Come Lately*
US 1943 97m bw
William Cagney
GB title: *Johnny Vagabond*

A travelling newspaperman is jailed for vagrancy in a small town and stays to expose corrupt politicians.
A turn-of-the-century folksy drama seemed an odd choice for a Cagney independent production, and it was not very persuasively made, but the star produced moments of his old charisma.

w John Van Druten, *novel* McLeod's Folly by Louis Bromfield *d* William K. Howard *ph* Theodor Sparkuhl *m* Leigh Harline

James Cagney, *Grace George*, Marjorie Main, Marjorie Lord, Hattie McDaniel, Edward McNamara, Bill Henry, Robert Barrat, George Cleveland, Margaret Hamilton, Lucien Littlefield, Irving Bacon

'The kind of business that might result if Jimmy Cagney, the immortal Hollywood movie star, had returned to play the lead in the annual production of his old high school's Masque and Film Club.'—*John T. McManus*

'The film does show a fatal commercial uneasiness and, I half suspect, radical loss or atrophy of cinematic judgment. But . . . there is a general ambience of hope and pleasure about the production which, regrettably, loses its glow.'—*James Agee*

AAN: Leigh Harline

Johnny Concho
US 1956 84m bw
UA / Kent (Frank Sinatra)

A coward runs Cripple Creek because he has a gunfighter brother, but when the latter is shot another gunman takes over.
Unexpected small-scale western, pleasantly made but no *High Noon*.

w David P. Harmon, Don McGuire *d* Don McGuire *ph* William Mellor *m* Nelson Riddle

Frank Sinatra, *William Conrad*, Phyllis Kirk, Wallace Ford, John Qualen

Johnny Cool*
US 1963 101m bw
UA / Chrislaw (William Asher)

A Sicilian bandit is sent to the US on a mission of vengeance.
Chilling gangster thriller, the callousness of which is apparently meant to be counterpointed by the humorous cameo appearances of several well-known faces. This does not work.

w Joseph Landon, *novel* John McPartland *d* William Asher *ph* Sam Leavitt *m* Billy May

Henry Silva, Elizabeth Montgomery, Jim Backus, Marc Lawrence, John McGiver, Sammy Davis Jnr, Mort Sahl, Telly Savalas, Joseph Calleia, Robert Armstrong, Douglass Dumbrille, Elisha Cook Jnr

Johnny Dark
US 1954 85m Technicolor
U-I (William Alland)

A motor company produces a new sports car designed by an employee, who drives it in a race.
Competent, unremarkable action melodrama tailor-made for its star.

w Franklin Coen *d* George Sherman *ph* Carl Guthrie *m* Joseph Gershenson

Tony Curtis, Piper Laurie, Don Taylor, Paul Kelly, Ilka Chase, Sidney Blackmer

Johnny Eager*
US 1941 107m bw
MGM (John W. Considine)

A gangster makes a play for a society girl.
Well-made, rather unattractive gangster melodrama.

w John Lee Mahin, James Edward Grant
d Mervyn Le Roy *ph* Harold Rosson
m Bronislau Kaper

Robert Taylor, *Van Heflin*, Lana Turner,
Edward Arnold, Robert Sterling, Patricia
Dane, Glenda Farrell, Henry O'Neill
   'The flaming drama of a high-born beauty
who blindly loved the most icy-hearted big
shot gangland ever knew!'—*publicity*

AA: Van Heflin

Johnny Frenchman
GB 1945   111m   bw
Ealing (S. C. Balcon)

Rivalry between the fishermen of Cornwall
and Brittany prevents the course of true love
from running smooth.
Rhubarbing extras and studio sets make this
an unreal and disappointing Ealing
melodrama, and all the actors look helpless.

w T. E. B. Clarke *d* Charles Frend *ph* Roy
Kellino *m* Clifton Parker

Françoise Rosay, Tom Walls, Patricia Roc,
Paul Dupuis, Ralph Michael, Frederick Piper,
Arthur Hambling

Johnny Got His Gun
US 1971   111m   colour
World Entertainments Ltd (Bruce
  Campbell)

In 1918 a soldier is so badly wounded as to
lose arms, legs, eyes, ears, mouth and nose,
and begs his doctors to kill him.
A horrifying and fascinating premise turns out
to have nowhere to go, at least not in this
talky treatment which the author has nurtured
too long.

wd Dalton Trumbo *ph* Jules Brenner
m Jerry Fielding

Timothy Bottoms, Jason Robards Jnr, Marsha
Hunt, Donald Sutherland, Kathy Fields,
Diane Varsi

Johnny Guitar*
US 1953   110m   Trucolor
Republic (Nicholas Ray)

In old Arizona, the proprietress of a gambling
saloon stakes a claim to valuable land and
incurs the enmity of a lady banker.
Weird Freudian western notable for a running
catfight between its lady protagonists; the title
character is decidedly secondary. Not exactly a
good movie, but memorable because it's
almost always over the top.

w Philip Yordan, *novel* Roy Chanslor
d Nicholas Ray *ph* Harry Stradling *m* Victor
Young

Joan Crawford, Mercedes McCambridge,
Sterling Hayden, Ernest Borgnine, Ward
Bond, John Carradine, Scott Brady
  'A very rum western, with cockeyed
feminist attitudes.'—*New Yorker, 1975*

Johnny Nobody
GB 1960   88m   bw   Warwickscope
Columbia / Viceroy (Irving Allen, Albert
  Broccoli)

A drunken Irish author challenges God to
strike him dead for blasphemy. When an
amnesiac shoots him, a nationwide religious
controversy begins, but the deed is found to
have a mercenary motive.
A mysterious rigmarole which irritates more
than it entertains.

w Patrick Kirwan, *story* The Trial of Johnny
Nobody by Albert Z. Carr *d* Nigel Patrick
ph Ted Moore *m* Ron Goodwin

Nigel Patrick, Aldo Ray, Yvonne Mitchell,
William Bendix, Cyril Cusack, Niall
MacGinnis, Bernie Winters, Noel Purcell,
Jimmy O'Dea
  'The more one thinks of it, the more one is
amazed that anyone should have thought a
plot and players as uniformly unlikely as these
could have worked out satisfactorily.'—*Peter
John Dyer, MFB*

Johnny Rocco
US 1958   83m   bw

The small son of a gangster is affected by his
father's notoriety. Awful sentimental
melodrama with tear-stained ending; for
connoisseurs of cliché. Richard Eyer, Stephen
McNally, Coleen Gray, Russ Conway. Written
by James O'Hanlon and Samuel F. Roeca;
directed by Paul Landres; for Allied Artists.

Johnny Stool Pigeon
US 1949   75m   bw
U-I (Aaron Rosenberg)

A detective releases a convict on condition
that he leads him to a drug smuggling gang.
Competent low budget addition to the
documentary police cycle.

w Robert L. Richards *d* William Castle
ph Maury Gertsman *m* Milton Schwarzwald

Howard Duff, Shelley Winters, Dan Duryea,
Gary Moore, Tony Curtis, John McIntire,
Barry Kelley, Leif Erickson

Johnny Tremain
US 1957   81m   Technicolor
Walt Disney

In 1773 Boston an apprentice silversmith joins the Sons of Liberty and helps start the War of Independence.
Schoolbook history with little vitality.

w Tom Blackburn, *novel* Esther Forbes
d Robert Stevenson *ph* Charles B. Boyle
m George Bruns

Hal Stalmaster, Luana Patten, Jeff York, Sebastian Cabot, Richard Beymer, Walter Sande

Johnny Trouble
US 1956 88m bw
Clarion (John H. Auer)

An elderly widow becomes involved with a boys' college and thinks she has found her lost grandson.
Sentimental, whimsical star vehicle.

w Charles O'Neal, David Lord *d* John H. Auer *ph* Peverell Marley *m* Frank de Vol

Ethel Barrymore, Stuart Whitman, Cecil Kellaway, Carolyn Jones, Jesse White

The Johnstown Flood*
US 1926 70m approx (24 fps) bw silent
Fox

A construction worker is warned by his girl friend of an approaching flood, in which she dies.
Curious melodrama with mild spectacle.

w Efrid Bingham, Robert Lord *d* Irving Cummings

George O'Brien, Janet Gaynor (her first film), Paul Panzer, George Harris

The Joker Is Wild*
US 1957 126m bw Vistavision
Paramount / Charles Vidor

Joe E. Lewis, a twenties nightclub singer, loses his voice after an attack by gangsters, and becomes a comedian.
Reasonably lively showbiz biopic in jaundiced vein; good atmosphere but far too long.

w Oscar Saul, *book* Art Cohn *d* Charles Vidor *ph* Daniel L. Fapp *m* Walter Scharf

Frank Sinatra, Mitzi Gaynor, Eddie Albert, Jeanne Crain, Beverly Garland, Jackie Coogan, Ted de Corsia

AA: song 'All the Way' (*m* Jimmy Van Heusen, *ly* Sammy Cahn)

The Jokers**
GB 1967 126m Technicolor
Universal / Adastra / Gildor / Scimitar (Maurice Foster, Ben Arbeid)

Two young brothers in London society plan to create a sensation by borrowing (and replacing) the crown jewels.
Bright suspense comedy which sums up the swinging London era pretty well and is generally amusing though it finally lacks aplomb.

w Dick Clement, Ian La Frenais d Michael Winner ph Ken Hodges *m* Johnny Pearson

Michael Crawford, Oliver Reed, Harry Andrews, *James Donald*, Daniel Massey, Michael Hordern, Gabriella Licudi, Frank Finlay, Warren Mitchell, Rachel Kempson, Peter Graves

A Jolly Bad Fellow*
GB 1964 95m bw
British Lion / Pax / Tower / Michael Balcon (Donald Taylor)
US title: *They All Died Laughing*

A brash chemistry don tries a new poison on his enemies.
Interesting but finally irritating comedy of murders with a punnish rather than a donnish script and only moments of genuine sub-Ealing hilarity.

w Robert Hamer, Donald Taylor, *novel* Don Among the Dead Men by C. E. Vulliamy
d Robert Hamer *ph* Gerald Gibbs *m* John Barry

Leo McKern, Janet Munro, Maxine Audley, Duncan Macrae, Dennis Price, Miles Malleson, Leonard Rossiter

Jolson Sings Again**
US 1949 96m Technicolor
Columbia (Sidney Buchman)

Al Jolson's later career and second marriage to a nurse he met while entertaining troops in World War II.
Breezy, routine, rather empty sequel to the following.

w Sidney Buchman *d* Henry Levin
ph William Snyder *md* Morris Stoloff, George Duning

Larry Parks, Barbara Hale, William Demarest, Ludwig Donath, Bill Goodwin, Tamara Shayne, Myron McCormick

AAN: Sidney Buchman; William Snyder; Morris Stoloff, George Duning

The Jolson Story****
US 1946 129m Technicolor
Columbia (Sidney Skolsky)

Asa Yoelson, son of a cantor, becomes Al Jolson, the great entertainer of the twenties; but showbiz success brings marital difficulties.

Whitewashed biopic in impeccable Hollywood style, with everything working shamelessly right, a new star in the leading role, perfect if unambitious production values, and a deluge of the best songs ever written.

w *Stephen Longstreet* d *Alfred E. Green, Joseph H. Lewis* ph Joseph Walker md Morris Stoloff

Larry Parks (using Jolson's own voice), *William Demarest, Evelyn Keyes, Ludwig Donath, Tamara Shayne*, Bill Goodwin, *Scotty Beckett*, John Alexander

'I have nothing in the world against this picture except that at least half of it seemed to me enormously tiresome.'—*James Agee*

AA: Morris Stoloff
AAN: Joseph Walker; Larry Parks; William Demarest

Jonathan Livingston Seagull*
US 1973   114m   De Luxe   Panavision
Paramount / JLS Partnership / Hall Bartlett

The life of a seagull who aims to fly faster than any of his peers and eventually arrives in a perfect world.
Weird 'family' fantasy based on a phenomenally successful book which clearly could not translate easily to the screen. The bird photography is much more successful than the mysticism.

w Richard Bach, from his book d Hall Bartlett ph *Jack Couffer* m Neil Diamond, Lee Holdridge ph Boris Leven

'A parable couched in the form of a nature film of overpowering beauty and strength in which, perhaps to our horror, we are forced to recognize ourselves in a seagull obsessed with the heights.'—*Michael Korda*
'It may be that the creature best qualified to review it is another seagull.'—*Benny Green, Punch*

AAN: Jack Couffer

The Jones Family
Less human, more farcical than the Hardy films (qv), this series was TCF's second feature answer to MGM's money-makers, and pleased a lot of people at the time. Pop was Jed Prouty, Mom was Spring Byington, Grandma was Florence Roberts, and the youngsters included Kenneth Howell, George Ernest, Billy Mahan, June Carlson and June Lang. The first script was from a play by Katharine Cavanaugh, and the principal director was Frank Strayer.

1936: EVERY SATURDAY NIGHT, EDUCATING FATHER, BACK TO NATURE
1937: OFF TO THE RACES, BORROWING TROUBLE, HOT WATER
1938: LOVE ON A BUDGET, TRIP TO PARIS, SAFETY IN NUMBERS, DOWN ON THE FARM
1939: EVERYBODY'S BABY, QUICK MILLIONS, THE JONES FAMILY IN HOLLYWOOD, TOO BUSY TO WORK
1940: ON THEIR OWN
† An earlier series with different actors was abandoned after two episodes: *Young as You Feel* (1931), *Business and Pleasure* (1932).

Joseph Andrews
GB 1977   104m   Eastmancolor
UA / Woodfall (Neil Hartley)

Adventures of a naïve 18th-century footman. Woebegone attempt to restage *Tom Jones*.

w Allan Scott, Chris Bryant d Tony Richardson ph David Watkin m John Addison pd Michael Annals

Peter Firth, Ann-Margret, Michael Hordern, Beryl Reid, Jim Dale, Peter Bull, John Gielgud, Hugh Griffith, Timothy West, Wendy Craig, Peggy Ashcroft, James Villiers, Karen Dotrice, Ronald Pickup

'Even the incidental pleasures cannot offset the sense of *déjà vu* which pervades this musty enterprise.'—*John Pym, MFB*
'The epic love story in which everybody has a great role and a big part.'—*publicity*

Josephine and Men
GB 1955   98m   Eastmancolor
Charter (John and Roy Boulting)

The three romances of a determined young woman.
Alarmingly thin, old-fashioned romantic comedy with all resolved in a country cottage. Nothing quite works, especially the colour.

w Nigel Balchin, Roy Boulting, Frank Harvey d Roy Boulting ph Gilbert Taylor m John Addison

Glynis Johns, *Jack Buchanan*, Donald Sinden, Peter Finch, Heather Thatcher, Ronald Squire

Josette
US 1938   73m   bw
TCF (Gene Markey)

A New Orleans coquette teases two men. Very minor musical, well enough presented but adding up to almost nothing.

w James Edward Grant d Allan Dwan ph John Mescall *songs* Harry Revel, Mack Gordon

Simone Simon, Don Ameche, Robert Young, Joan Davis, Bert Lahr, Paul Hurst, William Collier Snr, Lynn Bari, William Demarest

Jour de Fête•••
France 1948   87m   bw
Francinex

A village postman sees a film about the
efficiency of the American postal service and
decides to smarten himself up.
First, and some say best, of Tati's comedy
vehicles: two-thirds superb local colour, one-
third hilarious slapstick.

w Jacques Tati, Henri Marquet d Jacques
Tati ph Jacques Mercanton m Jean Yatove

Jacques Tati, Guy Decomble, Paul Fankeur,
Santa Relli

Le Jour Se Lève•••
France 1939   85m   bw
Sigma
aka: Daybreak

A murderer is besieged by police in his attic
room, remembers his past through the night,
and shoots himself.
A model of French poetic realism, and a
much-praised film which was almost destroyed
when it was bought for an American remake
(The Long Night).

w Jacques Viot, Jacques Prévert d Marcel
Carné ph Curt Courant, Philippe Agostini,
André Bac m Maurice Jaubert ad Alexander
Trauner

Jean Gabin, Jules Berry, Arletty, Jacqueline
Laurent
    'The man walks about his room, moves a
few things, lies on his bed, looks out of the
window, chain-smokes . . . and one is
genuinely interested in him all the time
(remembering afterwards that there exist
directors who contrive to be boring even when
they use fifteen characters in a motor car chase
crackling with revolver shots).'—Richard
Mallett, Punch

Journal of a Crime
US 1934   65m   bw

A woman shoots her husband's mistress and
gets amnesia before she can confess.
Melodramatic farrago which entertains by its
very excesses. Ruth Chatterton, Adolphe
Menjou, Claire Dodd, Douglass Dumbrille,
George Barbier. Written by F. Hugh Herbert
and Charles Kenyon; directed by William
Keighley; for Warner.

The Journey
US 1959   125m   Technicolor
MGM / Alby (Anatole Litvak)

During the 1956 Hungarian uprising, a busload
of international passengers is detained
overnight by a Russian major.

Pretentious, predictable and dull multi-
melodrama peopled by uninteresting
characters; different handling might have
made a Casablanca of it.

w George Tabori d Anatole Litvak ph Jack
Hildyard m Georges Auric

Yul Brynner, Deborah Kerr, Jason Robards
Jnr, Anouk Aimée, Robert Morley, E. G.
Marshall, Anne Jackson, David Kossoff, Kurt
Kasznar, Gerard Oury
    'Ten minutes of this and we know where we
are: we are back in the 1930s with Alfred
Hitchcock and that glamorous band of
international characters trapped in
Mitteleuropa.'—Steven Marcus

Journey for Margaret•
US 1942   81m   bw
MGM (B. P. Fineman)

An American correspondent brings home an
orphan from the London blitz.
Efficient tearful propaganda which
coincidentally made a star of little Margaret
O'Brien.

w David Hertz, William Ludwig, book
William L. White d W. S. Van Dyke ph Ray
June m Franz Waxman

Robert Young, Laraine Day, Margaret
O'Brien, Billy Severn, Fay Bainter, Signe
Hasso, Nigel Bruce, Halliwell Hobbes

Journey into Autumn•
Sweden 1954   86m   bw
Sandrews (Rune Waldekrantz)
original title: Kvinnodrom

Two business women visiting Gothenburg
have difficult relationships to settle.
Moody, impressionist sex drama which
succeeds by fits and starts.

wd Ingmar Bergman ph Hilding Bladh

Eva Dahlbeck, Harriet Andersson, Gunnar
Bjornstrand, Ulf Palme, Inga Landgre, Naima
Wifstrand
    'Scenes of austere anti-romanticism and
painful irony.'—Peter John Dyer, MFB

Journey into Fear•••
US 1942   71m   bw
RKO (Orson Welles)

A munitions expert finds himself in danger
from assassins in Istanbul, and has to be
smuggled home.
Highly enjoyable impressionist melodrama
supervised by Orson Welles and full of his
touches and excesses.

w Joseph Cotten, Orson Welles, novel Eric
Ambler d Norman Foster (and Orson Welles)
ph Karl Struss m Constantin Bakaleinikoff

Joseph Cotten, Dolores del Rio, Jack Moss, Orson Welles, Ruth Warrick, Agnes Moorehead

'Brilliant atmosphere, the nightmare of pursuit, eccentric encounters on the way, and when the shock comes it leaps at eye and ear.'—*William Whitebait*

† A 1976 remake, much heralded, was for obscure legal reasons hardly seen. Directed by Daniel Mann for New World, it starred Zero Mostel, Shelley Winters, Stanley Holloway, Vincent Price, Donald Pleasence, Sam Waterston, Joseph Wiseman, Scott Marlowe and Yvette Mimieux.

Journey to Shiloh
US 1966   101m   Techniscope

Seven young Texans leave home to fight in the Civil War. Episodic western which failed in its ambition to reach epic stature. James Caan, Michael Sarrazin, Brenda Scott, Paul Petersen, Don Stroud, Michael Burns, Michael Vincent, Harrison Ford, John Doucette, Noah Beery Jnr. Written by Gene Coon, from the novel *Fields of Honour* by Will Henry; directed by William Hale; for Universal.

Journey to the Center of the Earth***
US 1959   132m   De Luxe   Cinemascope
TCF (Charles Brackett)

An Edinburgh professor and assorted colleagues follow an explorer's trail down an extinct Icelandic volcano to the earth's centre. Enjoyable hokum which gets more and more fantastic but only occasionally misses its footing; it ends splendidly with the team being catapulted out of Stromboli on a tide of lava.

w Walter Reisch, Charles Brackett, novel Jules Verne *d* Henry Levin *ph* Leo Tover *m* Bernard Herrmann *ad* Lyle R. Wheeler, Franz Bachelin, Herman A. Blumenthal

James Mason, Arlene Dahl, Pat Boone, Peter Ronson, Diane Baker, Thayer David

'The attraction of a Jules Verne fantasy . . . is in the endearing contrast between the wildest adventures and the staidest Victorian propriety on the part of those undergoing them . . . There is about the whole film a good-natured enjoyment of its own excesses.'—*Penelope Houston*

Journey to the Far Side of the Sun*
GB 1969   99m   De Luxe   Cinemascope
Universal / Century 21 Productions (Gerry Anderson)

Alternative title: *Doppelganger*

An astronaut on a mission to a hitherto undetected planet discovers it to be an exact duplicate of Earth, and his own double returns in his place.

Intriguing, impeccably produced, but rather dull science fiction.

w Gerry and Sylvia Anderson, Donald James *d* Robert Parrish *ph* John Read *m* Barry Gray *sp* Harry Oakes *models* Derek Meddings

Ian Hendry, Roy Thinnes, Patrick Wymark, Lynn Loring, Herbert Lom, George Sewell, Ed Bishop

Journey Together*
GB 1944   95m   bw
RAF Film Unit

Trainee pilots receive instruction in England and America before going on their first bombing mission.

Modest wartime semi-documentary, pleasingly done.

w Terence Rattigan *d* John Boulting *ph* Harry Waxman *m* Gordon Jacob *pd* John Howell

Richard Attenborough, Jack Watling, David Tomlinson, Edward G. Robinson, Hugh Wakefield, Sebastian Shaw, Ronald Adam, Bessie Love

Journey's End*
GB 1930   120m   bw
Gainsborough–Welsh–Pearson–Tiffany (George Pearson)

France 1917: personal tensions mount as men die in the trenches.

Primitive early sound version (made in Hollywood because of better equipment) of a justly celebrated play first performed a year earlier. Cinematically uninteresting, with acting generally over the top, but it kept Whale and Clive in Hollywood where they shortly collaborated on *Frankenstein*.

w Joseph Moncure March, Gareth Gundrey, *play* R. C. Sheriff *d* James Whale *ph* Benjamin Kline

Colin Clive, Ian MacLaren, David Manners, Billy Bevan, Anthony Bushell, Robert Adair

'It has been transferred to the screen with the greatest possible tact and discretion.'—*James Agate*

'Hollywood has produced its first sex-appeal-less film. Mr George Pearson is to be congratulated on his restraint.'—*Punch*

'Almost painfully English . . . I cannot believe that the strangulated emotions which resulted can have meant much to audiences outside the English-speaking world.'—*Basil Wright, 1972*

Joy House

US 1964   98m   colour   Transcope

The husband of a wealthy American woman in France tries to kill her boy friend. Weird hothouse drama, an unsuccessful attempt to combine French and American styles. Jane Fonda, Alain Delon, Lola Albright. Written by René Clément, Pascal Jardin and Charles Williams; directed by René Clément; for Jacques Bar / MGM. (Aka: *The Love Cage*.)

Joy in the Morning

US 1965   103m   Metrocolor
MGM (Henry T. Weinstein)

Early episodes in the marriage of a poor teenage student.
Glutinous romantic drama, quite well made.

w Sally Benson, Alfred Hayes, Norman Lessing, *novel* Betty Smith d Alex Segal ph Ellsworth Fredericks m Bernard Herrmann

Richard Chamberlain, Yvette Mimieux, Arthur Kennedy, Oscar Homolka, Joan Tetzel, Sidney Blackmer

Joy of Living*

US 1938   90m   bw
RKO (Felix Young)

A practical-minded Broadway songstress succumbs to the charms of an aristocratic freewheeler.
Zany romantic comedy, not quite zippy enough to make one forget its irritating archness, but socio-historically very interesting, in the mould of *You Can't Take It with You*.

w Gene Towne, Allan Scott, Graham Baker d Tay Garnett ph Joseph Walker md Frank Tours

Irene Dunne, Douglas Fairbanks Jnr, Alice Brady, Guy Kibbee, Lucille Ball, Eric Blore, Jean Dixon, Warren Hymer, Billy Gilbert

Joyless Street*

Germany 1925   139m (24 fps)   bw
   silent
Sofar Film
original title: *Die Freudlose Gasse*

Problems of the inhabitants of a street in Vienna after World War I.
Realistic but studio-set melodrama which brought its director and Greta Garbo to international fame. In itself the film begins by stimulating and ends by boring.

w Willy Haas, *novel* Hugo Bettauer d G. W. Pabst ph Guido Seeber, Curt Oertel, Robert Lach

Asta Nielsen, Werner Krauss, *Greta Garbo*, Valeska Gert, Agnes Esterhazy

'Moments of searing pain, of mental anguish, of sheer unblemished beauty.'—*Paul Rotha, The Film Till Now*

Juarez**

US 1939   132m   bw
Warner (Hal. B. Wallis, Henry Blanke)

A revolutionary leader causes the downfall of Emperor Maximilian of Mexico.
Spectacular historical drama with many fine moments which do not quite coalesce into a dramatic whole, chiefly owing to the lack of a single viewpoint.

w John Huston, Wolfgang Reinhardt, Aeneas Mackenzie d William Dieterle ph Tony Gaudio m Erich Wolfgang Korngold

Brian Aherne, Bette Davis, Paul Muni, Claude Rains, John Garfield, Donald Crisp, Gale Sondergaard, Joseph Calleia, Gilbert Roland, Henry O'Neill, Pedro de Cordoba, Montagu Love, Harry Davenport

'A million dollars' worth of ballroom sets, regimentals, gauze shots and whiskers.'—*Otis Ferguson*

'Dramatically by far the most effective of Warners' biographical films of the thirties.'—*Graham Greene*

'Muni's big-star solemn righteousness is like a dose of medicine.'—*New Yorker, 1977*

'A story so momentous it required six Academy Award stars and a cast of 1,186 players!'—*publicity*

† Based vaguely on two novels: *The Phantom Crown* by Bertita Harding, and *Maximilian and Carlotta* by Franz Werfel.

AAN: Brian Aherne

Jubal

US 1955   101m   Technicolor
   Cinemascope
Columbia (William Fadiman)

A rancher's wife causes trouble when she falls in love with a wandering cowhand.
Solid sex western, moderately interestingly done.

w Russell S. Hughes, Delmer Daves, *novel* Jubal Troop by Paul Wellman d Delmer Daves ph Charles Lawton m David Raksin

Glenn Ford, Ernest Borgnine, Felicia Farr, Rod Steiger, Valerie French, Charles Bronson, Noah Beery Jnr

Jubilee*

GB 1978   104m   colour
Whaley-Malin / Megalovision

Queen Elizabeth I is transported by her astrologer into the latter part of the 20th century, and is appalled by what she sees. Outrageous dissection of modern urban life, full of black jokes: it has the right attitudes but is not free of a determination to shock at all costs.

w Derek Jarman and others *d* Derek Jarman *ph* Peter Middleton *m* Brian Eno

Jenny Runacre, Little Nell, Toyah Willcox, Jordan, Hermine Demoriane
    'One of the most intelligent and interesting films to be made in Britain in a long time.'— *Scott Meek, MFB*

Jubilee Trail*
US 1954 103m Trucolor
Republic (Joseph Kane)

Jealousy and murder by covered wagon en route from New Orleans to the California gold fields.
Bumpy adventure melodrama, generally quite entertaining.

w Bruce Manning, *novel* Gwen Bristow *d* Joseph Kane *ph* Jack Marta *m* Victor Young

Vera Hruba Ralston, Forrest Tucker, Joan Leslie, Pat O'Brien, John Russell, Ray Middleton

Judex**
France 1916 12 episodes totalling 5 hours approx bw silent
Gaumont

A Robin Hood type crimefighter destroys the empire of an evil banker.
Stylishly enjoyable serial from the maker of *Les Vampires* and *Fantômas*.

w Arthur Bernade, Louis Feuillade *d* Louis Feuillade

René Creste, Musidora, Yvette Andreyor, Louis Leubas
    † Another *Judex* serial was made in 1917, and in 1933 came a feature version directed by Maurice Champreux, with René Ferte. In 1963 Georges Franju directed another feature remake with Channing Pollock, and this was extremely well received.

The Judge Steps Out*
US 1947 91m bw
RKO
GB title: *Indian Summer*

A middle-aged judge leaves his wife and sets off on an aimless journey in the course of which he falls in love with a café proprietress. A pleasing human story, simply told in a

manner which at the time seemed more French than American.

w Boris Ingster, Alexander Knox *d* Boris Ingster *ph* Robert de Grasse *m* Constantin Bakaleinikoff

Alexander Knox, Ann Sothern, George Tobias, Sharyn Moffett

Judgment at Nuremberg**
US 1961 190m bw
UA / Roxlom (Stanley Kramer)

A fictionalized version of the 1948 trial of the Nazi leaders for crimes against humanity.
Interminable, heavy-going dramatic documentary expanded from a succinct TV play into a courtroom marathon with philosophical asides. All good stuff, but too much of it.

w Abby Mann, from his play *d* Stanley Kramer *ph* Ernest Laszlo *m* Ernest Gold *pd* Rudolph Sternad

Spencer Tracy, Marlene Dietrich, Burt Lancaster, Richard Widmark, *Maximilian Schell*, Judy Garland, Montgomery Clift, William Shatner, Edward Binns, Werner Klemperer, Torben Meyer, Alan Baxter, Ray Teal
    'Some believe that by tackling such themes Kramer earns at least partial remission from criticism. How much? 20 per cent off for effort?'—*Stanley Kauffmann*

AA: Abby Mann; Maximilian Schell
AAN: best picture; Stanley Kramer; Ernest Laszlo; Spencer Tracy; Judy Garland; Montgomery Clift

Judgment Deferred
GB 1951 88m bw
Group Three (John Baxter)

A collection of Dorset eccentrics brings to book the head of a dope smuggling ring who has framed one of their associates.
An unusual story can't compensate for stagey handling in this first disappointing production of a company set up by the National Film Finance Corporation to make low budget films with top talent.

w Geoffrey Orme, Barbara Emary, Walter Meade *d* John Baxter *ph* Arthur Grant

Hugh Sinclair, Helen Shingler, Abraham Sodaer, Leslie Dwyer, Joan Collins, Harry Locke, Elwyn Brook Jones, Bransby Williams, Maire O'Neill, Harry Welchman

Judith
US 1965 109m Technicolor
Panavision
Paramount / Cumulus / Command (Kurt Unger)

In 1947 Israel, loyalists rescue the wife of an
escaped war criminal and ask her to identify
him, but she takes her own revenge.
Glowering kibbutz adventures, well enough
made but adding up to neither one thing nor
the other, and rather confusing to non-Jews.

w Jon Michael Hayes, *story* Lawrence Durrell
d Daniel Mann *ph* John Wilcox *m* Sol
Kaplan *pd* Wilfrid Shingleton

Sophia Loren, Peter Finch, Jack Hawkins,
Hans Verner, André Morell

Judith of Bethulia
US 1913   42m (24 fps)   bw   silent
D. W. Griffith for Biograph

A widow in a city attacked by the Assyrians
courts their leader and beheads him.
Semi-biblical melodrama in Griffith's most
Victorian style.

w Frank Woods *d* D. W. Griffith *ph* Billy
Bitzer

Blanche Sweet, Henry B. Walthall, Lillian
Gish, Dorothy Gish, Lionel Barrymore, Mae
Marsh, Robert Harron

Juggernaut
GB 1936   64m   bw
Ambassador

A scientist lacking funds for his experiments
agrees to commit murder.
Tedious melodrama which wastes Karloff's
time.

w Cyril Campion, H. Fowler Mear, H.
Fraenkel *d* Henry Edwards *ph* Sidney Blythe

Boris Karloff, Mona Goya, Joan Wyndham,
Arthur Margetson, Anthony Ireland, Morton
Selten

Juggernaut**
GB 1974   110m   De Luxe   Panavision
United Artists / David E. Picker (Richard
   Alan Simmons)

A transatlantic liner is threatened by a mad
bomber.
Elaborate suspense spectacular, most of which
works pretty well.

w Richard Alan Simmons *d* Richard Lester
ph Gerry Fisher *m* Ken Thorne *pd* Terence
Marsh

Richard Harris, David Hemmings, Omar
Sharif, Anthony Hopkins, Ian Holm, Shirley
Knight, Roy Kinnear, Cyril Cusack, Freddie
Jones

'However unoriginal its basic ingredients, it
hardly ever slackens its pace or diverts
attention from its central premise.'—*Jonathan
Rosenbaum*

'Jaunty, cynical slapstick.'—*New Yorker*

The Juggler
US 1953   88m   bw
Columbia / Stanley Kramer

A Jewish refugee in Palestine has a horror of
being imprisoned, and runs away from a
transit camp with a small wandering boy.
Well-meaning cheapie, a curiously aimless
topical drama which fails to make any of its
several points.

w Michael Blankfort, from his novel
d Edward Dmytryk *ph* Roy Hunt *m* Georges
Antheil

Kirk Douglas, Milly Vitale, Paul Stewart, Joey
Walsh

Juke Girl
US 1942   90m   bw
Warner (Jack Saper, Jerry Wald)

Fruit workers in Florida get involved in
murder.
Hokum melodrama with all concerned
treading water.

w A. I. Bezzerides, *novel* Theodore Pratt
d Curtis Bernhardt *ph* Bert Glennon
m Adolph Deutsch

Ann Sheridan, Ronald Reagan, Richard
Whorf, Gene Lockhart, Faye Emerson,
George Tobias, Alan Hale, Howard da Silva,
Donald McBride, Fuzzy Knight, Willie Best

Jules et Jim**
France 1961   105m   bw   Franscope
Films du Carrosse / SEDIF (Marcel Berbert)

Before World War I, in Paris, a girl alternates
between a French and a German student, and
after the war they meet again to form a
constantly shifting triangle.
The plot bores before the end, but the
treatment is consistently interesting and the
acting almost equally so.

w François Truffaut, Jean Gruault,
novel Henri-Pierre Roche *d* François
Truffaut *ph* Raoul Coutard *m* Georges
Delerue

Oskar Werner, Jeanne Moreau, Henri Serre

'The sense is of a director intoxicated with
the pleasure of making films.'—*Penelope
Houston, MFB*

Julia**
US 1977   117m   Technicolor
TCF (Julien Derode)

Lillian Hellman reflects on the fortunes of her
friend Julia, filled with enthusiasm for
European causes and finally killed by the
Nazis.
Thoughtful, elegant patchwork of thirties
memories, a vehicle for actors and a subtle,
self-effacing director.

w Alvin Sargent, *book* Pentimento by Lillian Hellman *d* Fred Zinnemann *ph* Douglas Slocombe *m* Georges Delerue *ph* Carmen Dillon, Gene Callahan, Willy Holt

Jane Fonda, Vanessa Redgrave, Jason Robards Jnr, Maximilian Schell, Hal Holbrook, Rosemary Murphy, Cathleen Nesbitt, Maurice Denham

AA: script; Vanessa Redgrave; Jason Robards Jnr

AAN: best picture; Fred Zinnemann; Douglas Slocombe; Georges Delerue; Jane Fonda; Maximilian Schell

Julia Misbehaves
US 1948 99m bw
MGM (Everett Riskin)

An actress returns to her stuffy husband when her daughter is about to marry.
Desperate attempt to find a vehicle for a fading star team.

w William Ludwig, Arthur Wimperis, Harry Ruskin, *novel* The Nutmeg Tree by Margery Sharp *d* Jack Conway *ph* Joseph Ruttenberg *m* Adolph Deutsch

Greer Garson, Walter Pidgeon, Elizabeth Taylor, Peter Lawford, Cesar Romero, Lucile Watson, Nigel Bruce, Mary Boland, Reginald Owen, Ian Wolfe, Edmund Breon, Fritz Feld, Aubrey Mather, Henry Stephenson

Julie*
US 1956 97m bw
MGM / Arwin (Marty Melcher)

A concert pianist plans to murder his wife.
Wildly improbable but entertaining suspenser in which the lady finally has to assume control of an airplane.

wd Andrew Stone *ph* Fred Jackman Jnr *m* Leith Stevens

Doris Day, Louis Jourdan, Barry Sullivan, Frank Lovejoy, John Gallaudet
'Some of the dialogue reaches a fine pitch of banality.'—*MFB*

AAN: Andrew Stone (as writer); title song (*m* Leith Stevens, *ly* Tom Adair)

Juliet of the Spirits*
Italy / France 1965 145m Technicolor
Federiz / Francoriz (Clemente Fracassi)
original title: *Giulietta degli Spiriti*

A bored middle-aged woman finds she can conjure up spirits who lead her into a life of sensual gratification.
A fascinating patchwork of autobiographical flashbacks, the distaff side of *Eight and a Half*.

w Federico Fellini, Tullio Pinnelli, Brunello Rondi, Ennio Flaiano *d* Federico Fellini *ph* Gianni di Venanzo *m* Nino Rota

Giulietta Masina, Mario Pisu, Sandra Milo, Valentina Cortese, Sylva Koscina
'A kaleidoscope of fantasy, a series of cerebral inventions, of which only a few are artistically justified . . . an extravagant illusion, a huge confidence trick, with little new to say and an often pedantic way of saying it.'—*David Wilson, MFB*

Julius Caesar**
US 1953 121m bw
MGM (John Houseman)

Cassius and Brutus lead the conspirators who murder Caesar, but are themselves routed by Mark Antony.
Straightforward, rather leaden presentation of Shakespeare's play, lit by effective moments in the acting, but the sudden change from talk to battle is not smoothed over.

wd Joseph L. Mankiewicz *ph* Joseph Ruttenberg *m* Miklos Rozsa *ad* Cedric Gibbons, Edward Carfagno

John Gielgud, James Mason, Marlon Brando, Greer Garson, Deborah Kerr, Louis Calhern, Edmond O'Brien, George Macready, Michael Pate, John Hoyt, Alan Napier
'Greater than *Ivanhoe*!'—*publicity*
'Thrill to ruthless men and their goddess-like women in a sin-swept age!'—*publicity*
'Thrill to traitors and heroes, killings and conspiracies, passions and violence in Rome's most exciting age!'—*publicity*

AAN: best picture; Joseph Ruttenberg; Miklos Rozsa; Marlon Brando

Julius Caesar
GB 1969 116m Technicolor
          Panavision
Commonwealth United (Peter Snell)

Elementary production with a surprising number of faults and very few merits.

w Robert Furnival *d* Stuart Burge *ph* Ken Higgins *m* Michael Lewis *pd* Julia Trevelyan Oman

Richard Johnson, Jason Robards Jnr, *John Gielgud*, Charlton Heston, Robert Vaughn, Richard Chamberlain, Diana Rigg, Jill Bennett, Christopher Lee, Alan Browning, Andrew Crawford

AAN: Michael Lewis

Jumbo*

US 1962 124m Metrocolor Panavision
MGM (Joe Pasternak, Martin Melcher)
aka: *Billy Rose's Jumbo*

In 1910, the daughter of the owner of a shaky
circus prevents a take-over bid.
Hoary circus story with music. General effect
disappointing: the elephant steals the show.

w Sidney Sheldon, *play* Ben Hecht, Charles
MacArthur *d* Charles Walters *ph* William H.
Daniels *m* / *ly* Richard Rodgers, Lorenz
Hart *md* George Stoll *ch* Busby Berkeley

Doris Day, Jimmy Durante, Stephen Boyd,
Martha Raye, Dean Jagger

AAN: George Stoll

Jump for Glory

GB 1937 89m bw
Criterion (Douglas Fairbanks Jnr, Marcel
Hellman)
US title: *When Thief Meets Thief*

Adventures of a cat burglar who accidentally
kills his ex-partner.
Curious star comedy drama with pleasing
scenes.

w John Meehan Jnr, Harold French,
novel Gordon MacDonnell *d* Raoul Walsh
ph Cedric Williams

Douglas Fairbanks Jnr, Valerie Hobson, Alan
Hale, Edward Rigby, Barbara Everest, Jack
Melford, Anthony Ireland

Jump into Hell

US 1955 93m bw
Warner (David Weisbart)

Paratroops relieve a fort in Indo-China.
Mediocre semi-documentary war heroics.

w Irving Wallace *d* David Butler *ph* Peverell
Marley *m* David Buttolph

Jacques Sernas, Kurt Kasznar, Arnold Moss,
Peter Van Eyck, Pat Blake

Jumping Jacks*

US 1952 96m bw
Paramount / Hal B. Wallis

Two cabaret comedians join the paratroops.
Standard star farce, one of Martin and Lewis'
best.

w Robert Lees, Fred Rinaldo, Herbert Baker
d Norman Taurog *ph* Daniel L. Fapp
m Joseph J. Lilley

Dean Martin, *Jerry Lewis*, Mona Freeman,
Robert Strauss, Don Defore

June Bride

US 1948 97m bw
Warner (Henry Blanke)

Two bickering reporters are sent to cover a
small-town wedding.
Sloppily structured romantic farce in which
nothing ever comes together.

w Ranald MacDougall, *play* Feature for June
by Eileen Tighe, Graeme Lorimer
d Bretaigne Windust *ph* Ted McCord
m David Buttolph

Bette Davis, Robert Montgomery, Fay
Bainter, Tom Tully, Betty Lynn, Barbara
Bates, Jerome Cowan, Mary Wickes, Debbie
Reynolds

The Jungle Book*

US 1942 109m Technicolor
Alexander Korda (W. Howard Greene)
aka: *Rudyard Kipling's Jungle Book*

Growing up with animals in an Indian forest, a
boy forestalls the getaway of three thieves.
High-budgeted but rather boring live action
version with stiff-jointed model animals.

w Laurence Stallings, *stories* Rudyard Kipling
d Zoltan Korda, André de Toth *ph* Lee
Garmes, W. Howard Greene *m* Miklos Rozsa

Sabu, Joseph Calleia, John Qualen, Frank
Puglia, Rosemary de Camp

'More thrilling than the deeds of man . . .
more beautiful than the love of woman . . .
more wonderful than the dreams of
children!'—*publicity*

AAN: cinematography; Miklos Rozsa

Jungle Book*

US 1967 78m Technicolor
Walt Disney

Cartoon version relying less on action than on
songs and voices; patchily successful but no
classic.

d Wolfgang Reitherman *m* / *ly* Richard and
Robert Sherman, Terry Gilkyson
voices George Sanders, Phil Harris, Louis
Prima, Sebastian Cabot, Sterling Holloway

AAN: song 'The Bare Necessities' (*m* /
ly Terry Gilkyson)

Jungle Jim

When Johnny Weissmuller began to show his
middle-age spread, Columbia put him in a
jacket and more or less redid his Tarzan thing
in a series of second features which appeared
to be shot in producer Sam Katzman's back
garden and gradually indulged in wilder and
wilder plots. None of them has more than

curiosity value. Main scriptwriters were
Carroll Young, Dwight Babcock, Sam
Newman; main directors William Berke, Lee
Sholem, Spencer G. Bennet.

1948: JUNGLE JIM
1949: THE LOST TRIBE
1950: CAPTIVE GIRL, MARK OF THE
GORILLA, PYGMY ISLAND
1951: FURY OF THE CONGO, JUNGLE
MANHUNT
1952: JUNGLE JIM IN THE FORBIDDEN
LAND, VOODOO TIGER
1953: SAVAGE MUTINY, VALLEY OF
THE HEADHUNTERS, KILLER APE
1954: JUNGLE MANEATERS, CANNIBAL
ATTACK
1955: JUNGLE MOON MEN, DEVIL
GODDESS

The Jungle Princess*
US 1936 84m bw
Paramount (E. Lloyd Sheldon)

A British hunter is injured on a tropical island
and rescued by a native girl and her animal
retinue.
Dorothy Lamour's first film role cast her as the
female Tarzan she was to play (in a sarong, of
course) a dozen times again. This is strictly a
programmer, but after its success it was all
done again, rather better, as *Her Jungle Love*.

w Cyril Hume, Gerald Geraghty, Gouverneur
Morris *d* William Thiele *ph* Harry Fischbeck
md Boris Morros

Dorothy Lamour, Ray Milland, Akim
Tamiroff, Lynne Overman, Molly Lamont,
Hugh Buckler

'Poor Mr Lynne Overman is expected to
lend humorous relief to a film already richly
comic.'—*Graham Greene*

Junior Bonner*
US 1972 105m Movielab Todd-AO 35
ABC / Booth–Gardner / Joe Wizan / Solar

An ageing rodeo star returns to his home town
and finds his family in trouble.
Well-made, rather downcast and not very
interesting drama, remarkably gentle from this
director.

w Jeb Rosebrook *d* Sam Peckinpah
ph Lucien Ballard *m* Jerry Fielding

Steve McQueen, Ida Lupino, Robert Preston,
Joe Don Baker, Ben Johnson

Junior Miss*
US 1945 94m bw
TCF (William Perlberg)

A teenager causes trouble by meddling in the
lives of her family.
Amusing family comedy from a hit play.

w George Seaton, *play* Jerome Chodorov and
Joseph Fields, *and stories* Sally Benson
d George Seaton *ph* Charles Clarke *m* David
Buttolph

Peggy Ann Garner, Allyn Joslyn, Faye
Marlowe, Mona Freeman, Michael Dunne,
John Alexander

Juno and the Paycock*
GB 1930 85m bw
British International (John Maxwell)

During the Irish troubles of the early twenties,
tragedy comes to a poor Dublin family.
A plainly done film version of a modern classic
whose changes of mood would not in any case
have worked well on the screen.

w Alfred Hitchcock, Alma Reville, *play* Sean
O'Casey *d* Alfred Hitchcock *ph* Jack Cox

Sara Allgood, Edward Chapman, Maire
O'Neill, Sidney Morgan, John Laurie

'A film which completely justifies the
talkies.'—*James Agate*

Jupiter's Darling*
US 1954 96m Eastmancolor
   Cinemascope
MGM (George Wells)

Advancing on Rome, Hannibal falls in love
with the dictator's fiancée.
A splendid example of the higher lunacy, with
coloured elephants decorating an MGM
musical about the fall of the Roman Empire.
Small elements can be salvaged, and the gall is
enough to be divided into three parts.

w Dorothy Kingsley, *play* The Road to Rome
by Robert E. Sherwood *d* George Sidney
ph Paul C. Vogel, Charles Rosher *m* Burton
Lane *ly* Harold Adamson *ch* Hermes Pan
ad Cedric Gibbons, Uric McCleary

Esther Williams, Howard Keel, George
Sanders, Marge and Gower Champion,
Richard Haydn, William Demarest

Just a Gigolo
West Germany 1978 147m colour
Leguan (Rolf Thiele)

A young Prussian veteran of World War I
intends to succeed, but stumbles through the
Berlin underworld and is accidentally shot in a
street skirmish.
An international misadventure whose English
version is not only interminable and badly
dubbed but extremely clumsily made.

w Ennio de Concini, Joshua Sinclair *d* David
Hemmings *ph* Charly Steinberger *m* Gunther
Fischer *pd* Peter Rothe

David Bowie, Sydne Rome, Kim Novak,
Marlene Dietrich, David Hemmings, Maria
Schell, Curt Jurgens, Erika Pluhar
'It often goes for laughs it hasn't a hope of
getting; sometimes it aspires to tragic dignity
and looks truly inept. It would be kinder to
yourself and to everybody involved to
overlook it.'—*Time Out*

Just for You
US 1952   104m   Technicolor
Paramount (Pat Duggan)

A successful songwriter finds that his
troublesome teenage son is in love with his
own fiancée.
Tiresomely scripted, pleasantly played
romantic comedy with music.

w Robert Carson, *novel* Famous by Stephen
Vincent Benet *d* Elliott Nugent *ph* George
Barnes *md* Emil Newman *songs* Harry
Warren, Leo Robin

Bing Crosby, Jane Wyman, Bob Arthur, Ethel
Barrymore, Natalie Wood, Cora Witherspoon,
Regis Toomey

AAN: song 'Zing a Little Zong'

Just Imagine
US 1930   102m   bw
Fox

A man who dies in 1930 is revived in 1980 and
can't get used to the pace of life.
Famous fantasy which doesn't live up to its
reputation and can now be seen as hampered
by poor sets, script and acting. Futuristic sets
are few but choice.

d David Butler *w*, *songs* De Sylva, Brown,
Henderson *ch* Seymour Felix *ph* Ernest
Palmer

El Brendel, Maureen O'Sullivan, John
Garrick, Frank Albertson, Marjorie White,
Hobart Bosworth, Mischa Auer, Wilfred
Lucas

Just My Luck
GB 1957   86m   bw
Rank (Hugh Stewart)

A jeweller's assistant becomes involved in
horse racing.
Flat star vehicle.

w Alfred Shaughnessy *d* John Paddy
Carstairs *ph* Jack Cox *m* Philip Green

Norman Wisdom, Leslie Phillips, Margaret
Rutherford, Delphi Lawrence

Just Tell Me What You Want
US 1980   112m   Technicolor
Warner / Jay Presson Allen, Sidney Lumet

A powerful tycoon starts to weave plots when
one of his harem wants to go independent.
Thoroughly silly melodrama with a few
incidental humours.

w Jay Presson Allen, from her novel *d* Sidney
Lumet
ph Oswald Morris *m* Charles Strouse
pd Tony Walton

Ali MacGraw, Alan King, Myrna Loy,
Keenan Wynn, Tony Roberts, Dina Merrill,
Peter Weller
'Jay Presson Allen has adapted her trashy
novel into a trashy picture . . . Myrna Loy
looks as if she's constantly amazed at the kinds
of films getting made these days, and she's
absolutely right.'—*Variety*

Just You and Me, Kid
US 1979   93m   Metrocolor
Columbia / Irving Fein-Jerome M. Zeitman

An elderly comedian reluctantly takes care of
a naked teenager on the run from a dope
pusher.
Virtually a one-set comedy which quickly tires
the eye and ear; not a good idea despite the
veteran star.

w Oliver Hailey, Leonard Stern *d* Leonard
Stern *ph* David Walsh *m* Jack Elliott

George Burns, Brooke Shields, Burl Ives,
Lorraine Gary, John Schuck, Keye Luke,
Leon Ames, Ray Bolger, Carl Ballantine

Justice Est Faite*
France 1950   105m   bw
Silver Films

The personal lives of jurors in a mercy killing
case affect their verdict.
Absorbing courtroom drama with a message.

w Charles Spaak, André Cayatte *d* André
Cayatte *ph* Jean Bourgoin *m* Raymond
Legrand

Valentine Tessier, Claude Nollier, Jacques
Castelot, Michel Auclair

Justine
US 1969   116m   De Luxe   Panavision
TCF / Pandro S. Berman

In Alexandria in the thirties, the beautiful wife of a wealthy banker influences the lives of all who meet her.
Disastrous condensed version of a very unusual set of novels whose atmosphere has not translated at all well. The result is like a bad rehearsal for a film, which is not surprising in view of the number of producers variously involved. The author feared 'a sort of *Peyton Place* with camels', and got it.

w Lawrence B. Marcus, *novels* The Alexandria Quartet by Lawrence Durrell *d* George Cukor *ph* Leon Shamroy *m* Jerry Goldsmith

Anouk Aimée, Michael York, Dirk Bogarde, Anna Karina, John Vernon, George Baker, Philippe Noiret, Robert Forster, Jack Albertson, Michael Dunn, Barry Morse, Cliff Gorman, Severn Darden

'Could well stand as a model of what can happen when Hollywood gets to grips with a celebrated literary property.'—*David Wilson*

'Despite leaden forays into homosexuality, transvestitism, incest, and child prostitution, it remains as naively old-fashioned in its emotional and intellectual vocabulary as in its actual verbiage and cinematic technique.'—*John Simon*

K

Kagemusha**
Japan 1980 179m Eastmancolor
TCF / Toho (Akira Kurosawa)
aka: *The Double*; *Shadow Warrior*

On the death of a clan chief his place is taken
by the lookalike hired to overlook battlefields
while the chief is really busy elsewhere.
Fascinating Japanese epic centring on stately
ritual and court intrigue, with the occasional
battle for spectacular action; one of the
director's most impressive works.

w Akira Kurosawa, Masato Ide *d Akira
Kurosawa*
ph Kazuo Miyagawa, Asaiachi Nakai
m Shinichiro Ikebe

Tatsura Nakadai, Tsutomu Yamazaki, Kenichi
Hagiwara

AAN: best foreign film; art direction
BFA: direction; costume design

Kaleidoscope*
GB 1966 103m Technicolor
Warner / Winkast (Elliott Kastner)
Reissue title: *The Bank Breaker*

An American playboy breaks into a playing
card factory and marks the designs so that he
can win in every European casino.
Would-be swinging comedy-thriller which in
fact is entertaining only when it stops trying to
dazzle.

w Robert and Jane Howard-Carrington
d Jack Smight *ph Christopher Challis*
m Stanley Myers *ad Maurice Carter*

Warren Beatty, Susannah York, Clive Revill,
Eric Porter, Murray Melvin

'A "groovie movie" it certainly is, with a
battery of fashionable camera tricks,
kaleidoscopic dissolves, and virtually every
scene introduced from behind an irrelevant
piece of furniture.'—*David Wilson*

Kameradschaft*
Germany 1931 92m bw
Nerofilm
aka: *Comradeship*

On the Franco-German border French miners
are imprisoned below ground and Germans
burrow to free them.

Salutary message film with good dramatic
pointing.

w Laszlo Vajda, Karl Otten, Peter Martin
Lampel *d G. W. Pabst ph* Fritz Arno
Wagner, Robert Baberski

Ernst Busch, Alexander Granach, Fritz
Kampers, Gustav Puttjer

Kanal*
Poland 1956 97m bw
Film Polski (Stanislaw Adler)
aka: *They Loved Life*

In 1944, an anti-Nazi resistance group is
trapped in a sewer.
A suffocatingly unpleasant film to watch; its
message and technical excellence are
undoubted.

w Jerzy Stawinski, from his novel Kloakerne
d Andrzej Wajda *ph* Jerzy Lipman *m* Jan
Krenz

Teresa Izewska, Tadeusz Janczar, Emil
Kariewicz, Wienczylaw Glinski

Kangaroo
US 1952 84m Technicolor
TCF (Robert Bassler)

In old Australia, a con man pretends to be a
rancher's long lost heir, then complicates
things by falling in love with the rancher's
daughter.
Standard romantic action hokum.

w Harry Kleiner *d* Lewis Milestone
ph Charles G. Clarke *m* Sol Kaplan

Maureen O'Hara, Peter Lawford, Finlay
Currie, Richard Boone, Chips Rafferty,
Charles Tingwell

Kansas City Bomber
US 1972 99m Metrocolor
MGM / Levy–Gardner–Laven / Raquel
Welch (Marty Elfand)

A roller skating star finds time between affairs
to beat her rival in a big match.
Vulgar melodrama with good action scenes.

w Thomas Rickman, Calvin Clements
d Jerrold Freedman *ph* Fred Koenekamp
m Don Ellis

Raquel Welch, Kevin McCarthy, Norman
Alden, Jeanne Cooper

Kansas Raiders

US 1951   80m   Technicolor

During the Civil War, Jesse James joins
Quantrill's Raiders. Fast-moving, fairly violent
western only remotely based on fact. Audie
Murphy, Brian Donlevy, Marguerite
Chapman, Scott Brady, Tony Curtis, Richard
Arlen, James Best, Richard Long. Written by
Robert L. Richards; directed by Ray Enright;
for Universal-International.

Kapo

Italy / France 1960   115m   bw
Vides / Zebra / Francinex

A French Jewess survives the horrors of a Nazi
concentration camp and becomes camp guard.
Curious exploitation piece which turns tragedy
into melodrama, and doesn't even do that with
much flair.

w Franco Solinas, Gillo Pontecorvo d Gillo
Pontecorvo ph Goffredo Bellisario,
Alexander Sekulovic m Carlo Rustichelli

Susan Strasberg, Laurent Terzieff,
Emmanuelle Riva

Kate Plus Ten

GB 1938   81m   bw
Wainwright (Richard Wainwright)

A police inspector falls for the attractive
female leader of a bullion gang.
Curious comedy thriller with insufficient of
either commodity.

w Jack Hulbert, Jeffrey Dell, novel Edgar
Wallace d Reginald Denham ph Roy Kellino

Jack Hulbert, Genevieve Tobin, Noel
Madison, Francis L. Sullivan, Arthur
Wontner, Frank Cellier, Googie Withers,
Peter Haddon, Felix Aylmer, Leo Genn,
Edward Lexy

Kathleen

US 1941   88m   bw
MGM (George Haight)

A neglected daughter finds a new wife for her
widowed father.
One of the reasons for Shirley Temple's early
retirement.

w Mary McCall Jnr, story Kay Van Riper
d Harold S. Bucquet ph Sidney Wagner
m Franz Waxman

Shirley Temple, Herbert Marshall, Laraine
Day, Gail Patrick, Felix Bressart, Nella
Walker, Lloyd Corrigan

Kathy O

US 1958   99m   Eastmancolor
  Cinemascope
U-I (Sy Gomberg)

A temperamental child star befriends a lonely
columnist.
Overlong Hollywood comedy drama with
amusing moments.

w Jack Sher, Sy Gomberg d Jack Sher
ph Arthur E. Arling m Frank Skinner
songs Charles Tobias, Ray Joseph

Patty McCormack, Dan Duryea, Jan Sterling,
Sam Levene

Keep 'Em Flying

US 1941   86m   bw
Universal (Glenn Tryon)

Two incompetents in the Army Air Corps get
mixed up with identical twin girls.
A big moneymaker of its day, this comedy
now seems especially resistible.

w True Boardman, Nat Perrin, John Grant
d Arthur Lubin ph Joseph Valentine

Bud Abbott, Lou Costello, Martha Raye,
Carol Bruce, William Gargan, Dick Foran,
Charles Lang

Keep Fit*

GB 1937   82m   bw
ATP (Basil Dean)

A barber mistaken for an athlete finally excels
at sport and also catches a thief.
Good star vehicle with snappy songs and fast
comedy scenes.

w Anthony Kimmins, Austin Melford
d Anthony Kimmins ph Ronald Neame,
Gordon Dines

George Formby, Kay Walsh, Guy Middleton,
Gus McNaughton, Edmund Breon, George
Benson, C. Denier Warren, Hal Gordon, Hal
Walters, Leo Franklyn

Keep Smiling*

GB 1938   91m   bw
TCF (Robert T. Kane)
US title: Smiling Along

Problems of a touring concert party.
Pretty good star vehicle, though with
unfortunate signs of an attempt to glamorize
Our Gracie.

w Val Valentine, Rodney Ackland d Monty
Banks ph Max Greene

Gracie Fields, Roger Livesey, Mary Maguire,
Peter Coke, Jack Donohue, Tommy Fields,
Eddie Gray, Edward Rigby, Hay Petrie

Keep Your Powder Dry

US 1945   93m   bw
MGM (George Haight)

Three girls from different backgrounds join
the WACS.

Totally uninteresting and unconvincing female flagwaver.

w Mary C. McCall Jnr, George Bruce *d* Edward Buzzell *ph* Ray June *m* David Snell

Lana Turner, Laraine Day, Susan Peters, Agnes Moorehead, Bill Johnson, Natalie Schaefer, June Lockhart, Lee Patrick

Keep Your Seats Please*
GB 1936 82m bw
ATP (Basil Dean)

A prospective heir seeks a fortune hidden in one of six chairs.

Good star comedy on a theme later reworked in *It's in the Bag* (qv) and *The Twelve Chairs* (qv).

w Tom Geraghty, Ian Hay, Anthony Kimmins, *play* Twelve Chairs by Elie Ilf, Eugene Petrov *d* Monty Banks

George Formby, Florence Desmond, Alastair Sim, Gus McNaughton, Harry Tate

Keeper of the Flame*
US 1942 100m bw
MGM (Victor Saville)

A reporter befriends the widow of a politician and forces her to disclose her husband's guilty secret.

Well-acted but over-solemn melodrama which badly needs a sting in the tail.

w Donald Ogden Stewart, *novel* I. A. R. Wylie *d* George Cukor *ph* William Daniels *m* Bronislau Kaper

Spencer Tracy, Katharine Hepburn, Richard Whorf, Margaret Wycherly, Donald Meek, Stephen McNally, Audrey Christie, Frank Craven

'An expensive testimonial to Hollywood's inability to face a significant theme.'—*Time*

Keepers of Youth
GB 1931 70m bw
BIP

A young schoolmaster finds his fresh ideas make him unpopular, especially when he is found in a compromising position with the assistant matron.

Old-fashioned drama with a few lively scenes.

w Frank Launder, *play* Arnold Ridley *d* Thomas Bentley *ph* James Wilson, Bert Ford

Garry Marsh, Ann Todd, Robin Irvine, John Turnbull, O. B. Clarence, Mary Clare

Keeping Company
US 1940 80m bw

A young man announces his engagement but has trouble when his ex-girlfriend returns to town. Amiable family comedy which was announced to be the first of a series, but stayed lonely. Frank Morgan, Irene Rich, John Shelton, Ann Rutherford, Virginia Weidler, Dan Dailey, Gene Lockhart, Virginia Grey. Written by James Hill, Harry Ruskin and Adrian Scott; directed by S. Sylvan Simon; for MGM.

Kelly and Me
US 1956 86m Technicolor Cinemascope
U-I (Robert Arthur)

The ups and downs of a song and dance man and the dog who shares his act.

Mild vaudeville saga with totally predictable twists.

w Everett Freeman *d* Robert Z. Leonard *ph* Maury Gertsman *m* Joseph Gershenson

Van Johnson, Piper Laurie, Martha Hyer, Onslow Stevens

Kelly's Heroes
US / Yugoslavia 1970 143m
 Metrocolor Panavision
MGM / The Warriors / Avala (Irving Leonard)

During World War II, an American platoon abducts a German general and accidentally discovers the whereabouts of a fortune in gold. Crude slam-bang actioner for the obvious market.

w Troy Kennedy Martin *d* Brian G. Hutton *ph* Gabriel Figueroa *m* Lalo Schifrin *2nd unit* Andrew Marton

Clint Eastwood, Telly Savalas, Don Rickles, Donald Sutherland, Carroll O'Connor, Stuart Margolin, Dick Davalos

'Over two hours of consistently devastating explosions, pyrotechnics and demolition.'—*MFB*

'Made for no possible reason other than a chance to use the Yugoslav army at cut rates.'—*Judith Crist, 1973*

Kelly the Second
US 1936 71m bw

A determined lady trains a dimwitted prizefighter. Easy-going farce from a studio which knew how to make them; but this wasn't one of the best. Patsy Kelly, Guinn Williams, Charley Chase, Pert Kelton, Harold Huber. Written by Jack Jevne and Gordon Douglas; directed by Hal Roach; for MGM.

The Kennel Murder Case*
US 1933 73m bw
Warner

Philo Vance proves that an apparent suicide is really murder.

Complex murder mystery, very smartly handled and often cited as a classic of the genre; later remade as *Calling Philo Vance*.

w Robert N. Lee, Peter Milner, *novel* S. S. Van Dine *d* Michael Curtiz *ph* William Reese

William Powell, Mary Astor, Eugene Pallette, Ralph Morgan, Helen Vinson, Jack La Rue, Paul Cavanagh, Robert Barrat

'Players are cast so inevitably to type that the film is like a demonstration of the principles of running a stock company.'—*New Yorker, 1978*

'Stylistically a little gem.'—*Clive Hirschhorn*
† See also *Philo Vance*.

The Kentuckian
US 1955   104m   Technicolor
Cinemascope
UA / Hecht–Lancaster

A Kentucky backwoodsman takes his small son to settle in Texas.

Ambling mid-western with moments of interest.

w A. B. Guthrie Jnr, *novel* The Gabriel Horn by Felix Holt *d* Burt Lancaster *ph* Ernest Laszlo *m* Bernard Herrmann

Burt Lancaster, Dianne Foster, Diana Lynn, *Walter Matthau*, John McIntire, Una Merkel, John Carradine

Kentucky*
US 1938   95m   Technicolor
TCF (Gene Markey)

Horse-breeding rivalry prevents the smooth running of true love.

Harmless family entertainment, more professionally handled than its innumerable later imitations. Remade as *April Love*.

w Lamar Trotti, *novel* The Look of Eagles by John Taintor Foote *d* David Butler *ph* Ernest Palmer *md* Louis Silvers

Loretta Young, Richard Greene, Walter Brennan, Douglass Dumbrille, Karen Morley, Moroni Olsen, Russell Hicks

AA: Walter Brennan

La Kermesse Héroïque**
France 1935   115m   bw
Tobis
aka: *Carnival in Flanders*

When Spaniards invade a Flemish town in 1616, the men make themselves scarce and the women find other ways of conquering. Sprightly though overlong comedy which

seemed risqué at the time and therefore enjoyed international success.

w Charles Spaak, Jacques Feyder, *novel* Charles Spaak *d* Jacques Feyder *ph* Harry Stradling *m* Louis Beydts *ad* Lazare Meerson

Françoise Rosay, Louis Jouvet, Jean Murat, Alfred Adam, André Alerme

'A mixture of gay absurdity and shrewd comment, selecting its own pitch and holding it—comedy, you might say, self-contained.'—*Otis Ferguson*

'Everything fits perfectly into the pattern of cultured and sophisticated entertainment. Nowhere is there a false touch.'—*The Times, 1952*

Kes*
GB 1969   109m   Technicolor
UA / Woodfall (Tony Garnett)

In a northern industrial town, a boy learns about life from the fate of his pet bird.

'Realistic' family drama, full of the kind of merit that does not equate with entertainment: hard to take and harder to hear.

w Barry Hines, Ken Loach, Tony Garnet, *novel* A Kestrel for a Knave by Barry Hines *d* Ken Loach *ph* Chris Menges *m* John Cameron

David Bradley, Lynne Perrie, Colin Welland, Freddie Fletcher, Brian Glover

'There emerges a most discouraging picture of life in the industrial north . . . infinitely sad in its total implications, it is also immensely funny in much of its detail.'—*Brenda Davies*

The Kettles
The rustic couple evolved from characters in *The Egg and I* (qv); Marjorie Main and Percy Kilbride went on to play them in a cheap but very popular series for Universal, variously scripted and directed.

1949: MA AND PA KETTLE
1950: MA AND PA KETTLE GO TO TOWN
1951: MA AND PA KETTLE BACK ON THE FARM
1952: MA AND PA KETTLE AT THE FAIR
1953: MA AND PA KETTLE ON VACATION
1954: MA AND PA KETTLE AT HOME
1955: MA AND PA KETTLE AT WAIKIKI
1956: THE KETTLES IN THE OZARKS (Arthur Hunnicutt instead of Kilbride)
1957: THE KETTLES ON OLD MACDONALD'S FARM (Parker Fennelly instead of Kilbride)

The Key*
US 1934   71m   bw

In Ireland in the twenties, a British army
captain falls for the wife of an intelligence
officer. Heroics among the black and tans;
interesting but dated drama. William Powell,
Edna Best, Colin Clive, Hobart Cavanaugh,
Halliwell Hobbes, Henry O'Neill, Arthur
Treacher, Donald Crisp. Written by Laird
Doyle, from the play by R. Gore-Brown and
J. L. Hardy; directed by Michael Curtiz; for
Warner.

The Key*
GB 1958   134m   bw   Cinemascope
Columbia / Open Road (Carl Foreman)

World War II tugboat skippers, about to
embark on dangerous missions, pass on the
key to an apartment and a girl to go with it.
Rather foolish symbolic melodrama which
never makes its purpose clear but along the
way provides fragments of love story, chunks
of the supernatural and dollops of war action,
rather languidly assembled with great technical
competence but little real feeling. The talent
occasionally shows through.

w Carl Foreman, *novel* Stella by Jan de
Hartog d Carol Reed ph Oswald Morris
m Malcolm Arnold

William Holden, Sophia Loren, *Trevor
Howard*, Oscar Homolka, Kieron Moore

The Keyhole*
US 1933   69m   bw

A detective falls for the wife he is hired to
follow, then finds out that she isn't married at
all. Empty romantic drama with a few smart
lines, and sets by Anton Grot. Kay Francis,
George Brent, Glenda Farrell, Allen Jenkins,
Monroe Owsley. Written by Robert Presnell,
from a story by Alice Duer Miller; directed by
Michael Curtiz; for Warner.

Key Largo***
US 1948   101m   bw
Warner (Jerry Wald)

A returning war veteran fights gangsters on
the Florida keys.
Moody melodrama on similar lines to *To Have
and Have Not*: it sums up the post-war mood
of despair, allows several good acting
performances, and builds up to a pretty good
action climax.

w Richard Brooks, John Huston, *play* Maxwell
Anderson d John Huston ph Karl Freund
m Max Steiner

Humphrey Bogart, Lauren Bacall, *Claire
Trevor*, Edward G. Robinson, *Lionel
Barrymore*, Thomas Gomez, Marc Lawrence

'It's a confidently directed, handsomely shot
movie, and the cast go at it as if the nonsense
about gangsters and human dignity were high
drama.'—*New Yorker, 1977*
'A completely empty, synthetic work.'—
Gavin Lambert
AA: Claire Trevor

Key to the City
US 1950   101m   bw
MGM (Z. Wayne Griffin)

At a San Francisco convention, two mayors
get involved in several escapades and fall in
love.
Routine romantic comedy.

w Robert Riley Crutcher d George Sidney
ph Harold Rosson m Bronislau Kaper

Clark Gable, Loretta Young, Frank Morgan,
James Gleason, Marilyn Maxwell, Raymond
Burr, Lewis Stone, Raymond Walburn,
Pamela Britton

'A comedy made to measure . . . the script
concerns itself with wringing every possible
laugh from a number of stock situations.'—
Variety

The Keys of the Kingdom*
US 1944   137m   bw
TCF (Joseph L. Mankiewicz)

The life of a 19th-century Scottish priest in
China.
Studio-made missionary melodrama, a big hit
for its new star but otherwise an
undistinguished piece of work with a shuffling
pace and not much by way of climax.

w Joseph L. Mankiewicz, Nunnally Johnson,
novel A. J. Cronin d John M. Stahl
ph Arthur Miller m Alfred Newman
ad James Basevi, William Darling

Gregory Peck, Thomas Mitchell, Vincent
Price, Rose Stradner, Roddy McDowall,
Edmund Gwenn, Cedric Hardwicke, Peggy
Ann Garner, James Gleason, Anne Revere
'Long, earnest, long, worthy, interesting
and long.'—*Richard Mallett, Punch*
AAN: Arthur Miller; Alfred Newman;
Gregory Peck

Khartoum*
GB 1966   134m   Technicolor   Ultra
Panavision
UA / Julian Blaustein

The last years of General Gordon.
Dullish history book stuff which fails to
explain Gordon the man but occasionally
erupts into glowing action.

w Robert Ardrey d Basil Dearden
ph Edward Scaife, Harry Waxman m Frank
Cordell

Charlton Heston, Laurence Olivier, Ralph Richardson, Richard Johnson, Hugh Williams, Alexander Knox, Johnny Sekka, Nigel Green, Michael Hordern

'Academic accuracy and spectacular battles are unhappy partners.'—*MFB*

'Beautifully photographed, lavishly mounted, intelligently acted, but ultimately dull.'—*Sight and Sound*

AAN: Robert Ardrey

Kicking the Moon Around
GB 1938   78m   bw
Vogue (Howard Welsch)
US titles: *The Playboy; Millionaire Merry Go Round*

A millionaire goes into show business to establish a career for his singing protégée.
Mild, frothy comedy, dated but quite fluent.

w Angus McPhail, Roland Pertwee, Michael Hogan, Harry Fowler Mear   *d* Walter Forde
ph Francis Carver

Ambrose and his Orchestra, Evelyn Dall, Hal Thompson, Florence Desmond, Harry Richman, C. Denier Warren, Max Bacon

The Kid***
US 1921   52m approx (24 fps)   bw silent
First National / Charles Chaplin

A tramp brings up an abandoned baby, and later loses him to his mother; but there is a happy ending.
Sentimental comedy set in the slums. The comedy is very sparingly laid on, but the effect of the whole is much less painful than the synopsis would suggest, the production is comparatively smooth, the child actor is sensational, and the film contains much of the quintessential Chaplin.

wd Charles Chaplin   *ph* Rollie Totheroh
Charles Chaplin, Jackie Coogan, Edna Purviance

Kid Auto Races at Venice
US 1914   6m approx   bw   silent
Keystone / Mack Sennett

This much mentioned film is no more than a few candid camera shots of a children's car race on the California beach. It so happened that the young Charles Chaplin was called upon to liven up proceedings by causing a nuisance, and hastily conceived his tramp costume to do so. His fragments of comedy, primitive though they now seem, made him a star.

wd Henry Lehrman   *ph* Frank D. Williams

Kid Blue
US 1973   100m   De Luxe   Panavision
TCF / Marvin Schwarz Productions

In 1902 Texas a young outlaw tries to go straight.
Deliberately myth-deflating western with agreeably rich detail.

w Edwin Shrake   *d* James Frawley   *ph* Billy Williams   *m* Tim McIntyre, John Rubenstein
pd Joel Schiller

Dennis Hopper, Warren Oates, Peter Boyle, Ben Johnson, Lee Purcell, Janice Rule, Clifton James

A Kid for Two Farthings*
GB 1955   96m   Eastmancolor
London Films (Carol Reed)

Among the colourful characters of London's Petticoat Lane market moves a boy whose pet goat seems to have the magical power of a unicorn.
Whimsical character comedy-drama made with some style but too insubstantial and unconvincing to be affectionately remembered.

w Wolf Mankowitz   *d* Carol Reed   *ph* Ted Scaife   *m* Benjamin Frankel

Celia Johnson, Diana Dors, David Kossoff, Brenda de Banzie, Sidney Tafler, Primo Carnera, Joe Robinson

The Kid from Brooklyn
US 1946   114m   Technicolor
Samuel Goldwyn

A timid milkman becomes a prizefighter.
Yawn-provoking comedy, a remake of Harold Lloyd's *The Milky Way*; the first indication that Danny Kaye could be a bore.

w Grover Jones, Frank Butler, Richard Connell   *d* Norman Z. McLeod   *ph* Gregg Toland   *md* Carmen Dragon *songs* Jule Styne, Sammy Cahn

Danny Kaye, Virginia Mayo, Vera-Ellen, Steve Cochran, Eve Arden, Walter Abel, Lionel Stander, Fay Bainter, Clarence Kolb

The Kid from Left Field
US 1953   80m   bw

A big league basketball player is reduced to selling peanuts at the games, but passes on advice through his small son, who is appointed team manager. Half-hearted whimsy for addicts. Dan Dailey, Billy Chapin, Anne Bancroft, Lloyd Bridges, Ray Collins, Richard Egan. Written by Jack Sher; directed by Harmon Jones; for TCF.

The Kid from Spain**
US 1932 90m bw
Samuel Goldwyn

A simpleton is mistaken for a celebrated
bullfighter.
Charmingly dated star musical which, though
primitive in some respects, is a splendid
reminder of its period.

w William Anthony McGuire, Bert Kalmar,
Harry Ruby d Leo McCarey ph Gregg
Toland ch Busby Berkeley

Eddie Cantor, Lyda Roberti, Robert Young,
Ruth Hall, John Miljan, Noah Beery, J.
Carrol Naish, Stanley Fields, Betty Grable,
Paulette Goddard

Kid Galahad*
US 1937 101m bw
Warner (Samuel Bischoff)
TV title: Battling Bellhop

A bellhop is groomed as a prizefighter, and his
trainer grows jealous.
Good standard prizefight melodrama, remade
as The Wagons Roll at Night and later as Kid
Galahad with Elvis Presley (see below).

w Seton I. Miller, novel Francis Wallace
d Michael Curtiz ph Tony Gaudio m Heinz
Roemheld, Max Steiner

Edward G. Robinson, Bette Davis, Wayne
Morris, Jane Bryan, Humphrey Bogart, Harry
Carey

Kid Galahad
US 1962 96m De Luxe
UA / Mirisch (David Weisbart)

Tolerable light-hearted musical remake of the
above.

w William Fay d Phil Karlson ph Burnett
Guffey m Jeff Alexander

Elvis Presley, Lola Albright, Gig Young, Joan
Blackman, Charles Bronson, Ned Glass,
David Lewis, Robert Emhardt

Kid Glove Killer*
US 1942 73m bw
MGM (Jack Chertok)

A police laboratory scientist tracks down the
murderer of the mayor and finds his best
friend is the culprit.
Professional police suspenser of the kind now
tackled by television.

w John Higgins, Allen Rivkin d Fred
Zinnemann ph Paul C. Vogel m David Snell

Van Heflin, Lee Bowman, Marsha Hunt,
Samuel S. Hinds, Eddie Quillan

Kid Millions
US 1935 90m bw (Technicolor
  sequence)
Samuel Goldwyn

An East Side kid inherits a fortune and has the
time of his life.
Dated star musical with moments which still
please.

w George Oppenheimer, William Anthony
McGuire d Roy del Ruth ph Gregg Toland
m / ly Bert Kalmar, Harry Ruby ad Richard
Day

Eddie Cantor, Ethel Merman, Ann Sothern,
George Murphy, Warren Hymer

Kidnapped*
US 1938 90m bw
TCF

During the Jacobite rebellion a young boy is
sold by his wicked uncle as a slave, and is
helped by an outlaw.
Much altered version of a classic adventure
story, exciting enough in its own right, and
well made in the thirties tradition.

w Sonya Levien, Richard Sherman, Walter
Ferris, novel Robert Louis Stevenson
d Alfred L. Werker ph Bert Glennon
m Arthur Lange

Warner Baxter, Freddie Bartholemew, Arleen
Whelan, John Carradine, C. Aubrey Smith,
Nigel Bruce, Reginald Owen

Kidnapped*
GB 1959 95m Technicolor
Walt Disney (Hugh Attwooll)

A remake fairly faithful to the book, which
results in a few longueurs; but in general the
action is spirited.

wd Robert Stevenson ph Paul Beeson
m Cedric Thorpe Davie

Peter Finch, James MacArthur, Bernard Lee,
John Laurie, Finlay Currie, Niall MacGinnis,
Peter O'Toole, Miles Malleson, Oliver
Johnston, Duncan Macrae, Andrew
Cruickshank

Kidnapped*
GB 1971 107m Movielab Panavision
Omnibus (Frederick H. Brogger)

Remake incorporating sections of Catriona.
Not particularly exciting, but the acting helps.

w Jack Pulman d Delbert Mann ph Paul
Beeson m Roy Budd

Michael Caine, Lawrence Douglas, Trevor
Howard, Jack Hawkins, Donald Pleasence,
Gordon Jackson, Freddie Jones, Jack Watson

The Kidnappers*
GB 1953   95m   bw
Rank / Nolbandov–Parkyn
US title: *The Little Kidnappers*

In a Nova Scotian village at the turn of the
century a stern old man denies his young
grandchildren a pet, so they borrow a baby
and hide it in the woods.
Fairly pleasing and popular whimsy for family
audiences.

w Neil Paterson   *d* Philip Leacock   *ph* Eric
Cross   *m* Bruce Montgomery

Duncan Macrae, Vincent Winter, Jon Whiteley,
Theodore Bikel, Jean Anderson

The Kidnapping of the President*
Canada 1980   113m   De Luxe
Sefel (George Mendeluk, John Ryan)

Third-world terrorists devise a plot to bring
America to its knees by kidnapping the
president.
Spirited political thriller which suffers chiefly
from overlength.

w Richard Murphy, *novel* Charles Templeton
d George Mendeluk   *ph* Mike Malloy   *m* Paul
J. Zaza

Hal Holbrook, William Shatner, Van Johnson,
Ava Gardner, Miguel Fernandez, Cindy
Girling, Elizabeth Shepherd

Kiki
US 1931   96m   bw
UA / Mary Pickford (Joseph M. Schenck)

Long unseen star musical.

w Sam Taylor, *play* David Belasco   *d* Sam
Taylor   *ph* Karl Struss

Mary Pickford, Reginald Denny, Joseph
Cawthorne, Margaret Livingston

Kill or Cure
GB 1962   88m   bw
MGM (George H. Brown)

A series of murders at a nature clinic are
solved by a bumbling private detective.
Flatfooted and unprofessional murder farce
whose only pace is slow.

w David Pursall, Jack Seddon   *d* George
Pollock   *ph* Geoffrey Faithfull   *m* Ron
Goodwin

Terry-Thomas, Eric Sykes, Dennis Price,
Lionel Jeffries, Moira Redmond, David
Lodge, Ronnie Barker

Kill the Umpire
US 1950   78m   bw

An over-age baseball player can't get the
game out of his mind, and returns as an
argumentative umpire. Minor comedy of
presumed pleasure to sports addicts. William
Bendix, Una Merkel, Ray Collins, Gloria
Henry, William Frawley. Written by Frank
Tashlin; directed by Lloyd Bacon; for
Columbia.

The Killer Elite
US 1975   120m   De Luxe   Panavision
UA / Exeter–Persky Bright (Martin Baum,
   Arthur Lewis)

A private crime fighting organization handles
cases which the CIA prefers not to.
Smooth, fashionable violence which seems to
proclaim the end of a cycle.

w Marc Norman, Stirling Silliphant, *novel*
Monkey in the Middle by Robert Rostand
d Sam Peckinpah   *ph* Philip Lathrop   *m* Jerry
Fielding

James Caan, Robert Duvall, Arthur Hill, Gig
Young, Mako, Bo Hopkins, Burt Young, Tom
Clancy

'Merely a commercial chore.'—*Tom Milne*
   'A mysterious, elliptical, visually triumphant
film about personal survival in a world of
mean-minded machination.'—*Michael*
Billington, Illustrated London News

Killer Fish
France / Brazil 1978   101m   colour

The leader of a burglary gang hides their haul
in a dammed reservoir which he stocks with
piranha fish. Heavy-going underwater shocker,
with no fun while the fish are off-screen. Lee
Majors, Karen Black, Margaux Hemingway,
Marisa Berenson, James Franciscus. Written
by Michael Rogers; directed by Antonio
Margheriti; for Fawcett-Majors / Victoria /
   Filmar do Brazil. 'A slapdash actioner which
casts its rod in water so overfished of late that
it's amazing there's still anything down there
biting.'—*Variety.*

Killer McCoy
US 1947   104m   bw
MGM (Sam Zimbalist)

A prizefighter becomes involved in a murder.
Grade A production applied to a grade B
script.

w Frederick Hazlitt Brennan, Thomas
Lennon, George Bruce, George
Oppenheimer   *d* Roy Rowland   *ph* Joseph
Ruttenberg   *m* David Snell

Mickey Rooney, Ann Blyth, Brian Donlevy,
James Dunn, Tom Tully, Sam Levene, James
Bell, Gloria Holden

The Killer That Stalked New York
US 1950 75m bw
Columbia (Robert Cohn)
GB title: *Frightened City*

New York is on the alert for a girl smallpox carrier.
Absurdly-titled minor thriller, quite competent but wholly unsurprising.

w Harry Essex *d* Earl McEvoy *ph* Joseph Biroc *m* Hans Salter

Charles Korvin, Evelyn Keyes, William Bishop, Dorothy Malone, Lola Albright, Barry Kelley, Carl Benton Reid, Ludwig Donath

The Killers•••
US 1946 105m bw
U-I (Mark Hellinger)
TV title: *A Man Alone*

In a small sleazy town a gangster waits for two assassins to kill him, and we later find out why.
Elaborate tale of cross and double-cross, stunningly executed.

w Anthony Veiller, story Ernest Hemingway *d Robert Siodmak ph* Elwood Bredell *m* Miklos Rozsa

Burt Lancaster, Edmond O'Brien, Ava Gardner, Albert Dekker, Sam Levene, John Miljan, Virginia Christine, Vince Barnett, Charles D. Brown, Donald MacBride, Phil Brown, Charles McGraw, William Conrad
'About one tenth is Hemingway's, the rest is Universal-International's.'—*Richard Winnington*
'Seldom does a melodrama maintain the high tension that distinguishes this one.'—*Variety*
'There is nothing unique or even valuable about the picture, but energy combined with attention to form and detail doesn't turn up every day; neither does good entertainment.'—*James Agee*
† John Huston contributed to the script but is not credited.

AAN: Anthony Veiller; Robert Siodmak; Miklos Rozsa

The Killers•
US 1964 95m Pathecolor
U-I (Don Siegel)

Zesty, brutal remake intended for TV, but released theatrically because of its violence.

w Gene L. Coon *d* Don Siegel *ph* Richard L. Rawlings *m* Johnny Williams

John Cassavetes, Lee Marvin, Clu Gulager, Angie Dickinson, Ronald Reagan, Claude Akins

Killer's Kiss
US 1955 64m bw
UA / Stanley Kubrick

A prizefighter rescues a girl from her gangster lover, and is marked for death.
Tedious low-budget indie which first brought its director into notice.

w / d / ph Stanley Kubrick *m* Gerald Fried

Frank Silvera, Irene Kane, Jamie Smith

The Killers of Kilimanjaro
GB 1959 91m Technicolor
  Cinemascope
Columbia / Warwick (John R. Sloan)
US title: *Adamson of Africa*

A railroad engineer helps a girl find her lost father and fiancé.
Old-fashioned safari adventure full of action and animals.

w Richard Maibaum, Cyril Hume *d* Richard Thorpe *ph* Ted Moore *m* William Alwyn

Robert Taylor, Anne Aubrey, Grégoire Aslan, Anthony Newley

The Killing••
US 1956 83m bw
UA / Harris–Kubrick (J. B. Harris)

An ex-convict recruits helpers to steal two million dollars from a racetrack.
Incisive, entertaining, downbeat caper movie clearly influenced by *The Asphalt Jungle* and *Rififi*.

wd Stanley Kubrick, novel Clean Break by Lionel White *ph* Lucien Ballard *m* Gerald Fried

Sterling Hayden, Marie Windsor, Jay C. Flippen, Elisha Cook Jnr, Coleen Gray, Vince Edwards, Ted de Corsia, Joe Sawyer, Tim Carey
'The visual authority constantly dominates a flawed script.'—*Arlene Croce*
'The camera watches the whole shoddy show with the keen eye of a terrier stalking a pack of rats.'—*Time*

The Killing of a Chinese Bookie
US 1976 113m colour

A Los Angeles nightclub owner is prevailed upon by gangsters to pay off his debt by eliminating a troublesome Chinese. Another unendurable slab of Cassavetes pretentiousness; why he goes on trying, in the face of twenty years of public indifference, is beyond imagining. Ben Gazzara, Timothy Carey, Seymour Cassel, Morgan Woodward. Written and directed by John Cassavetes, for his own company.

The Killing of Sister George*
US 1969   138m   Metrocolor
Associates and Aldrich / Palomar

An ageing lesbian actress is fired from a TV
serial and her life collapses around her.
Heavily handled film version of an amusing
and moving play; everything is clumsily spelt
out, including the love scenes, and the
actresses are forced to repeat themselves.

w Lukas Heller, *play* Frank Marcus d Robert
Aldrich *ph* Joseph Biroc *m* Gerald Fried

Beryl Reid, Susannah York, *Coral Browne*,
Roland Fraser, Patricia Medina, Hugh
Paddick, Cyril Delevanti

'The play was second-rate, but with its nice
blend of the homely and the chilling, the
absurdist and the perverse, it had the quality
of a Kraft-Ebbing comic book. Aldrich and
Heller have turned this material into a
crawling tear-jerker, the lines spoken at a
speed adjusted to non-English or non-
language-speaking audiences.'—*John Simon*
'A clumpingly archaic piece of film-
making.'—*New Yorker, 1982*

Kim*
US 1950   112m   Technicolor
MGM (Leon Gordon)

The orphaned son of a British soldier in India
has adventures with his horseman friend who
belongs to the British secret service.
Colourful Boys' Own Paper high jinks, quite
lively but never convincing.

w Leon Gordon, Helen Deutsch, Richard
Schayer, *novel* Rudyard Kipling d Victor
Saville *ph* William Skall *m* André Previn

Errol Flynn, Dean Stockwell, Paul Lukas,
Robert Douglas, Thomas Gomez, Cecil
Kellaway, Arnold Moss, Reginald Owen

'Ornate, lavish, but curiously lacking in
genuine atmosphere, vitality or period
sense.'—*Penelope Houston*

Kind Hearts and Coronets***
GB 1949   106m   bw
Ealing

An impecunious heir eliminates eight
D'Ascoynes who stand between him and the
family fortune.
Witty, genteel black comedy well set in the
stately Edwardian era and quite deserving of
its reputation for wit and style; yet the effect is
curiously muffled and several opportunities
missed.

w *Robert Hamer, John Dighton, novel*
Noblesse Oblige by Roy Horniman *d Robert
Hamer ph* Douglas Slocombe

Dennis Price, Alec Guinness (in eight roles),
Valerie Hobson, Joan Greenwood, Miles
Malleson, Arthur Lowe

'A brilliant misfire for the reason that its
plentiful wit is literary and practically never
pictorial.'—*Richard Winnington*
'Enlivened with cynicism, loaded with
dramatic irony and shot through with a
suspicion of social satire.'—*Daily Telegraph*
'A film which can be seen and seen again
with undiminished pleasure.'—*Basil Wright,
1972*

Kind Lady*
US 1935   76m   bw
MGM / Lucien Hubbard
aka: *House of Menace*

A confidence trickster insinuates himself and
his criminal friends into the house of an invalid
lady.
Unusual but unconvincing melodrama with
overwrought leading performances.

w Bernard Schubert, *play* Edward Chodorov,
story Hugh Walpole d George B. Seitz
ph George Folsey *m* Edward Ward

Basil Rathbone, Aline MacMahon, Mary
Carlisle, Frank Albertson, Dudley Digges,
Doris Lloyd

Kind Lady*
US 1951   78m   bw
MGM (Armand Deutsch)

Edwardian-set remake of the above, rather
more subtly acted but failing to extract all
possible frissons.

w Jerry Davis, Edward Chodorov, Charles
Bennett d John Sturges *ph* Joseph
Ruttenberg *m* David Raksin

Maurice Evans, Ethel Barrymore, Angela
Lansbury, Keenan Wynn, Betsy Blair, John
Williams

'A curiously tame melodrama whose shocks,
when they do come, are muffled and
ineffectual.'—*Penelope Houston*

A Kind of Loving***
GB 1962   112m   bw
Anglo-Amalgamated / Waterhall / Vic Films
  (Joe Janni)

A young north country draughtsman is forced
into marriage, has to live with his dragon-like
mother in law, and finally sorts out a
relationship with his unhappy wife.
Blunt melodrama with strong kinship to
Saturday Night and Sunday Morning,
strikingly directed and photographed amid
urban grime and suburban conformity.

w Keith Waterhouse, Willis Hall, *novel* Stan
Barstow *d* John Schlesinger *ph* Denys Coop
m Ron Grainer

*Alan Bates, June Ritchie, Thora Hird, Bert
Palmer, Gwen Nelson*

King and Country*
GB 1964 86m bw
BHE (Norman Priggen, Joseph Losey)

In the trenches during World War I, a private
is courtmartialled and shot for desertion.
Neat cinematic treatment of a very downbeat
play.

w Evan Jones, *play* Hamp by John Wilson
d Joseph Losey *ph* Denys Coop *m* Larry
Adler *pd* Richard Macdonald

*Tom Courtenay, Dirk Bogarde, Leo McKern,
Barry Foster, James Villiers, Peter Copley*

The King and Four Queens
US 1956 86m De Luxe Cinemascope
UA / Russ / Field / Gabco (David
   Hempstead)

A cowboy braves the wrath of a lady
sharpshooter to gain gold and the hand of one
of her four daughters.
Tawdry sex western sporadically enlivened by
good-humoured playing.

w Margaret Fitts, Richard Alan Simmons
d Raoul Walsh *ph* Lucien Ballard *m* Alex
North

*Clark Gable, Eleanor Parker, Jo Van Fleet,
Jean Willes, Barbara Nichols, Sara Shane,
Roy Roberts*
  'A superficially cynical exercise in the rival
attractions of sex and money.'—*MFB*

The King and I*
US 1956 133m Eastmancolor
   Cinemascope 55
TCF (Charles Brackett)

Musical remake of *Anna and the King of Siam*
(qv), from the highly successful stage
production. The film is opulent in lush detail
but quite lacking in style.

w Ernest Lehman *d* Walter Lang *ph* Leon
Shamroy *m* Richard Rodgers *book / ly* Oscar
Hammerstein II *md* Alfred Newman, Ken
Darby *ad* Lyle Wheeler, John de Cuir

*Deborah Kerr, Yul Brynner, Rita Moreno,
Martin Benson, Alan Mowbray, Geoffrey
Toone, Terry Saunders*
  'Gaiety has something of a struggle to
survive.'—*Penelope Houston*
AA: Yul Brynner; Alfred Newman, Ken
Darby
AAN: best picture; Walter Lang; Leon
Shamroy; Deborah Kerr

The King and the Chorus Girl
US 1937 94m bw
Warner (Mervyn Le Roy)
GB title: *Romance Is Sacred*

A European prince on the spree falls for a
New York chorine.
Reasonably lively romantic comedy.

w Norman Krasna, Groucho Marx, from their
story Grand Passion *d* Mervyn Le Roy
ph Tony Gaudio *m* Werner Heymann

*Joan Blondell, Fernand Gravet, Edward
Everett Horton, Jane Wyman*

King Arthur Was a Gentleman
GB 1942 99m bw
GFD / Gainsborough (Edward Black)

A soldier becomes a hero when he believes he
has King Arthur's sword.
Not-too-successful attempt to turn a music hall
comedian into a figure of Chaplinesque
pathos.

w Val Guest, Marriott Edgar *d* Marcel
Varnel

*Arthur Askey, Evelyn Dall, Anne Shelton,
Max Bacon, Jack Train, Peter Graves, Vera
Frances, Ronald Shiner, Brefni O'Rourke*

King Creole
US 1958 116m bw Vistavision
(Paramount) Hal B. Wallis

A failed graduate becomes a singer in a New
Orleans night club, and gets involved with
gangsters.
Disagreeable crook melodrama turned into a
musical star vehicle.

w Herbert Baker, Michael V. Gazzo, *novel* A
Stone for Danny Fisher by Harold Robbins
d Michael Curtiz *ph* Russell Harlan
m Walter Scharf

*Elvis Presley, Carolyn Jones, Dean Jagger,
Walter Matthau, Dolores Hart, Paul Stewart*

A King in New York*
GB 1957 109m bw
Attica (Charles Chaplin)

A penniless European king finds himself at
odds with the American way of life.
Feeble Chaplin comedy from his anti-
American period; tedious dialogue and poor
physical production allow only momentary
flashes of the satire intended.

wd / m Charles Chaplin *ph* Georges Périnal

*Charles Chaplin, Michael Chaplin, Oliver
Johnson, Dawn Addams, Jerry Desmonde,
Harry Green, Maxine Audley, Sid James*
  'Unhappily he is a sadder and an older man;
the real punch is gone. His dethroned king is
an ironically apt image.'—*Marvin Felheim*

'Maybe the worst film ever made by a celebrated film artist.'—*New Yorker, 1977*

'It shows how the coming of sound was a curse to Chaplin; how its freedoms dissipated his strengths; how his attempts to exploit it intellectually and ideologically played to his weaknesses; how, in short, he was much more grievously hurt by history in art than by history in politics.'—*Stanley Kauffmann*

King Kong****
US 1933 100m bw
RKO (Merian C. Cooper)

A film producer on safari brings back a giant ape which terrorizes New York.
The greatest monster movie of all, a miracle of trick work and suspense, with some of the most memorable moments in film history.

w James Creelman, Ruth Rose, *story* Edgar Wallace *d* Merian C. Cooper, Ernest Schoedsack *ph* Edward Linden, Verne Walker, J. O. Taylor *sound effects* Murray Spivak *chief technician* Willis J. O'Brien *m* Max Steiner

Robert Armstrong, Fay Wray, Bruce Cabot, Frank Reicher

'Just amusing nonsense punctuated by such reflections as why, if the natives wanted to keep the monster on the other side of the wall, they should have built a door big enough to let him through.'—*James Agate*

AAN: photography

King Kong
US 1976 135m Metrocolor Panavision
Dino de Laurentiis

Semi-spoof remake with added sexual overtones; though launched on a massive wave of publicity, it lacks both the charm and the technical resources of its predecessor.

w Lorenzo Semple Jnr *d* John Guillermin *ph* Richard H. Kline *m* John Barry *pd* Dale Hennesy, Mario Chiari

Jeff Bridges, Charles Grodin, Jessica Lange, John Randolph, René Auberjonois, Julius Harris, Ed Lauter

'The one and original lovable monster is lost amid all the hydraulic manipulations in what now emerges as the story of a dumb blonde who falls for a huge plastic finger.'—*Judith Crist, Saturday Review*

'Even with colour, the settings of Kong II are no match for the rich black-and-white chiaroscuro of Kong I, with its echoes of artists like Gustave Doré and Max Ernst and its sensitivity to the emotional values of tone and texture.'—*Jack Kroll, Newsweek*

AAN: Richard H. Kline

King Lear*
GB / Denmark 1970 137m bw
Columbia / Filmways–Laterna (Michael Birkett)

Tragedy ensues when an old king prematurely divides his kingdom between his daughters. Miserably photographed in freezing Jutland, this is a deliberately downbeat version which despite its varied points of interest is extremely hard to sit through.

w William Shakespeare (a cut text) *d* Peter Brook *ph* Henning Kristiansen *m* none *pd* Georges Wakhevitch

Paul Scofield, Irene Worth, Alan Webb, Tom Fleming, Susan Engel, Cyril Cusack, Patrick Magee, Jack MacGowran

King of Alcatraz*
US 1938 56m bw
Paramount (William C. Thomas)

Convicts escape on a freighter, but one needs surgery. Pacy programmer with a stalwart cast.

w Irving Reis *d* Robert Florey *ph* Harry Fischbeck *md* Boris Morros

Gail Patrick, J. Carrol Naish, Lloyd Nolan, Harry Carey, Robert Preston, Anthony Quinn, Dennis Morgan, Porter Hall

King of Burlesque*
US 1936 88m bw
TCF (Kenneth MacGowan)

A vaudeville impresario overcomes his troubles.
Well-written musical with plenty of variety talent.

w James Seymour, Gene Markey, Harry Tugend *d* Sidney Lanfield *ph* Peverell Marley *songs* various

Warner Baxter, Alice Faye, Jack Oakie, Mona Barrie, Arline Judge, Dixie Dunbar, Gregory Ratoff, Herbert Mundin, *Fats Waller*, Kenny Baker

† Remade as *Hello Frisco Hello.*

King of Gamblers
US 1937 79m bw
Paramount
aka: *Czar of the Slot Machines*

A ruthless gangster loves a singer who loves a reporter who is out to expose him.
A muddled script mars this pacy lower-birth item.

w Doris Anderson *d* Robert Florey *ph* Harry Fischbeck *md* Boris Morros

Akim Tamiroff, Claire Trevor, Lloyd Nolan, Buster Crabbe, Porter Hall

King of Hearts

France / Italy 1966   110m   Eastmancolor
UA / Fildebroc / Montoro (Philippe de
  Broca)
original title: *Le Roi de Coeur*

In World War I, a Scottish soldier finds a
war-torn town occupied only by lunatics who
have escaped from the asylum and who want
to make him their king.
Heavy-handed whimsy which never catches
fire despite the talents involved.

w Daniel Boulanger *d* Philippe de Broca
ph Pierre Lhomme *m* Georges Delerue

Alan Bates, Geneviève Bujold, Jean-Claude
Brialy, Françoise Christophe, Pierre Brasseur,
Micheline Presle, Adolfo Celi, Julien Guiomar

King of Jazz***

US 1930   101m   Technicolor
Universal (Carl Laemmle Jnr)

Musical revue.
Stylish, spectacular, revelatory early musical: a
treasure trove.

*devised / d John Murray Anderson w Harry
Ruskin, Charles MacArthur pd Hal Mohr,
Ray Rennahan, Jerome Ash ad Herman Rose*

Paul Whiteman and his orchestra, John Boles,
Bing Crosby (with the Rhythm Boys), Laura
la Plante, Glenn Tryon, Slim Summerville,
Walter Brennan

King of Kings**

US 1927   155m approx (24 fps) (various
  versions)   bw   silent
(Pathé) Cecil B. de Mille

The life of Jesus, seen more or less from the
viewpoint of Mary Magdalene.
A patchy but frequently moving and pictorially
effective work, ranging from the sublime (the
first view of Jesus as a blind man regains his
sight) to the ridiculous ('Harness my zebras,
gift of the Nubian king!' says Mary Magdalene
in a sub-title).

w Jeanie Macpherson *d Cecil B. de Mille*
ph J. Peverell Marley

H. B. Warner, Jacqueline Logan, Joseph
Schildkraut (Judas), Ernest Torrence (Peter),
Victor Varconi (Pilate), Dorothy Cumming
(Mary, mother of Jesus), Rudolph Schildkraut
(Caiaphas)
'The most impressive of all motion
pictures.'—*Mordaunt Hall, New York Times*
'A picture which will tend to standardize the
world's conception of the New Testament . . .
de Mille has one of the best business minds in
pictures and making *King of Kings* was the
most brilliant stroke of his successful business
career.'—*Welford Beaton, The Film Spectator*

King of Kings*

US 1961   161m   Super Technirama
MGM / Samuel Bronston

The life of Jesus Christ.
Known in the trade as *I Was a Teenage Jesus*,
this good-looking but rather tedious film is
neither vulgar nor very interesting; a solemn,
decent, bible-in-pictures pageant.

w Philip Yordan *d* Nicholas Ray *ph* Franz
Planer, Manuel Berenger *m* Miklos Rozsa
ad Georges Wakhevitch

Jeffrey Hunter, Robert Ryan, Siobhan
McKenna, Frank Thring, Hurd Hatfield, Rip
Torn, Harry Guardino, Viveca Lindfors, Rita
Gam

The King of Marvin Gardens*

US 1972   104m   Eastmancolor
Columbia / BBS (Bob Rafaelson)

The host of a late night radio talk show gets
embroiled in his brother's schemes.
Thoughtful tragi-comedy overweighted by
talk, but with good performances.

w Jacob Brackman *d* Bob Rafaelson
ph Laszlo Kovacs

Jack Nicholson, Bruce Dern, Ellen Burstyn,
Julia Anne Robinson
'Indecipherable dark nonsense about
brothers and goals and the American dream.
An unqualified disaster.'—*New Yorker*
'Glum news from the people who made *Five
Easy Pieces*, which had a lot of good work in it
along with some pretentious flab. In their new
picture the flab has taken over.'—*Stanley
Kauffmann*

King of the Damned*

GB 1935   76m   bw
Gaumont (Michael Balcon)

On a South Seas convict settlement, harsh
treatment leads to mutiny.
A downright peculiar project for a British
studio at this time, but technically very
competent for those who like this kind of
thing.

w Charles Bennett, Sidney Gilliat, Noel
Langley, *play* John Chancellor *d* Walter
Forde *ph* Bernard Knowles *md* Louis Levy

Conrad Veidt, Helen Vinson, Noah Beery,
Cecil Ramage, Edmund Willard, Raymond
Lovell, Allan Jeayes, Percy Parsons

King of the Gypsies

US 1978   112m   Technicolor
Paramount / Dino de Laurentiis (Anna
  Gross)

A gypsy leader is denied the hand in marriage
of the daughter of a rival, so he kidnaps her.

Ethnic melodrama which despite its vigorous insistence on tradition—or perhaps because of it—plays like a mad musical without any songs.

w Frank Pierson, *novel* Peter Maas d Frank Pierson *ph* Sven Nykvist, Edward Lachman *m* David Grisman *pd* Gene Callahan

Sterling Hayden, Brooke Shields, Shelley Winters, Susan Sarandon, Judd Hirsch, Eric Roberts

King of the Khyber Rifles
US 1954   100m   Technicolor
Cinemascope
TCF (Frank Rosenberg)

In 1857 a British garrison in India is threatened by the forces of Kuuram Khan but saved by a half-caste officer.
Standard North-West Frontier adventure, old-fashioned and rather dull.

w Ivan Goff, Ben Roberts d Henry King *ph* Leon Shamroy *m* Bernard Herrmann

Tyrone Power, Terry Moore, Michael Rennie, Guy Rolfe, John Justin

King of the Roaring Twenties
US 1961   106m   bw
Warner / AA / Bischoff–Diamond
GB title: *The Big Bankroll*

A gambler, Arnold Rothstein, becomes powerful among twenties gangsters.
Routine crime drama, shoddily made.

w Jo Swerling d Joseph M. Newman *ph* Carl Guthrie *m* Franz Waxman

David Janssen, Dianne Foster, Mickey Rooney, Mickey Shaughnessy, Diana Dors, Dan O'Herlihy, Jack Carson, Keenan Wynn, William Demarest, Joseph Schildkraut, Regis Toomey, Murvyn Vye

'Superficial, shopworn biography of an infamous bookie.'—*MFB*

King of the Turf
US 1939   88m   bw

A gambler out of luck befriends a small boy who turns out to be his own son. Hard to take even at the time, this sentimental tarididdle does not bear later scrutiny. Adolphe Menjou, Dolores Costello, Walter Abel, Roger Daniel. Written and directed by George Bruce; for Edward Small.

King, Queen, Knave*
US / West Germany 1972   92m
Eastmancolor
Wolper / Maran (Lutz Hengst)

The wife of a Munich bookseller falls for his adolescent nephew.
Amusing, capriciously directed sex comedy.

w David Shaw, David Seltzer, *novel* Vladimir Nabokov d Jerzy Skolomowski *ph* Charly Steinberger *m* Stanley Myers

Gina Lollobrigida, David Niven, John Moulder-Brown, Mario Adorf, Carl Fox-Duering

King Rat**
US 1965   134m   bw
Columbia / Coleytown (James Woolf)

In Singapore's Changi Gaol during World War II an American corporal lives more comfortably than the other prisoners by shabby dealings with the camp guards.
Overlong but generally gripping character melodrama—'not a story of escape but a story of survival'.

wd Bryan Forbes, *novel* James Clavell *ph* Burnett Guffey *m* John Barry

George Segal, Tom Courtenay, John Mills, James Fox, Denholm Elliott, Todd Armstrong, Patrick O'Neal, James Donald, Alan Webb, Leonard Rossiter, Geoffrey Bayldon

AAN: Burnett Guffey

King Richard and the Crusaders
US 1954   113m   Warnercolor
Cinemascope
Warner (Henry Blanke)

During the Crusades, the dreaded Saladin arrives in England in disguise and falls in love with Lady Edith . . .
Crudely confected comic strip version of Sir Walter Scott's *The Talisman*, ineptly written and cast, with poor production values.

w John Twist d David Butler *ph* Peverell Marley *m* Max Steiner

Rex Harrison (as Saladin), Virginia Mayo, George Sanders, Laurence Harvey, Robert Douglas

'Do not adjust your set—the sound you hear is Sir Walter Scott turning in his grave.'—*Sunday Express*

King Solomon's Mines*
GB 1937   80m   bw
Gainsborough (Geoffrey Barkas)

Explorers in Africa persuade an exiled chief to help them find a diamond mine.
Rather somnolent though well-cast version of a favourite adventure novel, with a splendid final reel.

w Michael Hogan, A. R. Rawlinson, Roland Pertwee, Ralph Spence, Charles Bennett, *novel* H. Rider Haggard *d* Robert Stevenson *ph* Glen MacWilliams *m* Mischa Spoliansky

Cedric Hardwicke, *Paul Robeson*, Roland Young, John Loder, Anna Lee, Sydney Fairbrother, Robert Adams

'They kept the eye of the camera open for every form of wild and savage life and crammed it all into the picture, so one gets the impression that Allan Quartermain is delivering a lecture with illustrations rather than taking part in an adventure.'—*Richard Mallett, Punch*

King Solomon's Mines*
US 1950 102m Technicolor
MGM (Sam Zimbalist)

A remake which is largely travelogue with the merest trimmings of story.

w Helen Deutsch *d* Compton Bennett *ph* Robert Surtees

Stewart Granger, Deborah Kerr, Richard Carlson, Hugo Haas, Lowell Gilmore

AA: Robert Surtees
AAN: best picture

The King Steps Out*
US 1936 85m bw
Columbia (William Perlberg)

Emperor Franz Josef falls in love with the sister of the princess to whom he is betrothed. Rather heavy-handed romance with music, not in its director's best style but showing flashes of his decorative talent.

w Sidney Buchman, *operetta* Cissy by Herbert and Ernst Marischka *d* Josef Von Sternberg *ph* Lucien Ballard *songs* Fritz Kreisler, Dorothy Fields *ad* Stephen Goossen

Grace Moore, Franchot Tone, Walter Connolly, Raymond Walburn, Herman Bing, Victor Jory, Elizabeth Risdon, Nana Bryant, Frieda Inescort, Thurston Hall

'Josef Von Sternberg asked that it not be included in retrospectives of his work, but he really did make the damned thing.'—*New Yorker, 1977*

Kingdom of the Spiders
US 1977 95m colour
Arachnid / Dimension (Henry Fownes)

In an Arizona valley the death rate soars when tarantulas begin preying in groups on humans instead of singly on each other.
The spiders is coming, as Hitch might have remarked, and not even giant-size. Standard shudders, efficiently presented.

w Richard Robinson, Alan Caillou *d* John Cardos *ph* John Morrill, John Wheeler *md* Igo Kantor

William Shatner, Tiffany Bolling, Woody Strode, David MacLean

Kings Go Forth
US 1958 109m bw
UA / Ross–Eton (Frank Ross)

August 1944: two American soldiers fall out over a black French woman who is torn between them.
Heavy-going war melodrama, well enough done for those who can take it.

w Merle Miller, *novel* Joe David Brown *d* Delmer Daves *ph* Daniel Fapp *m* Elmer Bernstein

Frank Sinatra, Tony Curtis, Natalie Wood, Leora Dana, Karl Swenson

Kings of the Road
Germany 1975 176m bw

Two men on a bus talk of their past lives, their problems, their hopes and their fears.
Impossibly tedious two-hander which doubtless says something about life for those with the patience to sit it out. Ruediger Vogler, Hanns Zischler. Written and directed by Wim Wenders; for Wim Wenders Productions. (Original title: *Im Lauf der Zeit*.)

Kings of the Sun
US 1963 108m De Luxe Panavision
UA / Mirisch (Lewis J. Rachmil)

A Mayan tribe emigrates from Mexico to Texas and makes peace with the local Indian chief.
Ponderous dark age epic replete with human sacrifice, high-mindedness and solemn pauses. The actors and sets carry it as far as it will go.

w Elliot Arnold, James R. Webb *d* J. Lee-Thompson *ph* Joe MacDonald *m* Elmer Bernstein *ad* Alfred Ybarra

Yul Brynner, George Chakiris, Shirley Anne Field, Richard Basehart, Brad Dexter, Barry Morse

King's Rhapsody
GB 1955 93m Eastmancolor
  Cinemascope
Everest (Herbert Wilcox)

An exiled Ruritanian king leaves his mistress to return home to a political marriage.
Love versus duty in a ludicrously inept film of Ivor Novello's highly theatrical musical drama, cheaply made and killed stone dead by casting and wide screen.

w Pamela Bower, Christopher Hassall, A. P.
Herbert *d* Herbert Wilcox *ph* Max Greene

Errol Flynn, Anna Neagle, Patrice Wymore,
Martita Hunt, Finlay Currie

King's Row****
US 1941   127m   bw
Warner (David Lewis)

In a small American town during the early
years of the century, three children grow up
into a world of cruelty and madness.
Superb Hollywood melodrama, a Peyton Place
with great visual strength, haunting music and
a wholly absorbing if incredible plot.

w Casey Robinson, novel Henry Bellamann
*d Sam Wood ph James Wong Howe m Erich
Wolfgang Korngold pd William Cameron
Menzies*

Ann Sheridan, Robert Cummings, Ronald
Reagan, *Claude Rains,* Betty Field, Charles
Coburn, Nancy Coleman, *Maria Ouspenskaya,*
Harry Davenport, Judith Anderson, Karen
Verne
  'Half masterpiece and half junk.'—*James
Agate*
  'Out of the hushed strangeness of these
lives, and out of the shadows that hid their
shame, filmdom has fashioned a drama most
unusual, most touching and most
wonderful!'—*publicity*
  'Tranquilly accepting many varieties of
psychopathic behaviour as the simple facts of
life, this film has its own kind of sentimental
glow, yet the melodramatic incidents are
surprisingly compelling.'—*New Yorker, 1982*
  'One of the great melodramas, a veritable
Mount Rushmore of physical and emotional
cripples.'—*Time Out, 1981*

AAN: best picture; Sam Wood; James Wong
Howe

The King's Thief
US 1955   79m   Eastmancolor
  Cinemascope
MGM (Edwin H. Knopf)

The Duke of Brampton plots treason against
Charles II but a highwayman robs him of an
incriminating notebook.
Dismal swashbuckler with neither zest nor
style, just a cast of unhappy-looking actors.

w Charles Knopf *d* Robert Z. Leonard
ph Robert Planck *m* Miklos Rozsa

David Niven, Edmund Purdom, Ann Blyth,
George Sanders, Roger Moore

The King's Vacation
US 1933   62m   bw

A king abdicates to seek the simple life.

Pleasing fable with a few theatrical ironies.
George Arliss, Florence Arliss, Dick Powell,
Marjorie Gateson, Dudley Digges. Written by
Ernest Pascal and Maude T. Howell; directed
by John Adolfi; for Warner.

Kipps***
GB 1941   112m   bw
TCF (Edward Black)
US title: *The Remarkable Mr Kipps*

In 1906, a draper's assistant comes into money
and tries to crash society.
Charming, unassuming film of a well-loved
novel, later musicalized as *Half a Sixpence.*

w Sidney Gilliat, *novel* H. G. Wells *d Carol
Reed ph* Arthur Crabtree *m* Charles
Williams

Michael Redgrave, Phyllis Calvert, Diana
Wynyard, *Arthur Riscoe,* Max Adrian, Helen
Haye, Michael Wilding, Lloyd Pearson,
Edward Rigby, Hermione Baddeley, Frank
Pettingell, Beatrice Varley, Kathleen
Harrison, Felix Aylmer

Kismet
US 1930   90m   bw   65mm   Vitascope
Warner

An Oriental magician overcomes a wicked
vizier.
Rather tame filming of a spectacular which
belongs on the stage.

w Howard Estabrook, *play* Edward Knoblock
d John Francis Dillon *ph* John Seitz

Otis Skinner, Loretta Young, David Manners,
Mary Duncan, Sidney Blackmer, Fred
Sterling, Edmund Breese, Montagu Love

Kismet*
US 1944   100m   Technicolor
MGM (Everett Riskin)
TV title: *Oriental Dream*

Hollow and humourless but striking-looking
remake of the above.

w John Meehan, *d* William Dieterle
ph Charles Rosher *m* Herbert Stothart
ad Cedric Gibbons, Daniel B. Cathcart

Ronald Colman, Marlene Dietrich, James
Craig, Edward Arnold, Hugh Herbert, Joy
Ann Page, Florence Bates, Harry Davenport,
Hobart Cavanaugh, Robert Warwick

AAN: Charles Rosher; Herbert Stothart

Kismet
US 1955   113m   Eastmancolor
  Cinemascope
MGM (Arthur Freed)

Unlucky musical remake from the stage show
with Borodin music.

w Charles Lederer, Luther Davis, from their musical play *d* Vincente Minnelli *ph* Joseph Ruttenberg *ch* Jack Cole *ad* Cedric Gibbons, Preston Ames

Howard Keel, Ann Blyth, Dolores Gray, Vic Damone, Monty Woolley, Sebastian Cabot, Jay C. Flippen, Mike Mazurki, Jack Elam

The Kiss*
US 1929   64m approx (24 fps)   bw silent
MGM

A woman is accused of the murder of her jealous husband.
A wisp of a melodrama, enlivened by its star; otherwise only notable as MGM's last silent picture.

w Hans Kraly *d* Jacques Feyder *ph* William Daniels

Greta Garbo, Lew Ayres, Conrad Nagel, Holmes Herbert, Anders Randolf

Kiss and Make Up
US 1934   80m   bw
Paramount (B. P. Schulberg)

A Parisian beauty specialist forsakes a rich client for his loyal secretary.
Forgettable romantic comedy.

w Harlan Thompson, George Marion Jnr, *play* Stephen Bekeffi *d* Harlan Thompson *ph* Leon Shamroy

Cary Grant, Genevieve Tobin, Helen Mack, Edward Everett Horton, Lucien Littlefield, Mona Maris

Kiss and Tell*
US 1945   92m   bw
Columbia (Sol C. Siegel)

To protect another girl, an irrepressible teenager pretends to be pregnant.
Good-humoured farcical comedy which at the time was thought pretty shocking, especially with the infant darling of the thirties in the lead.

w F. Hugh Herbert, from his play *d* Richard Wallace *ph* Charles Lawton *m* Werner Heymann

Shirley Temple, Robert Benchley, Walter Abel, Jerome Courtland, Katherine Alexander, Porter Hall, Tom Tully

'All brilliantly characteristic of the worst anyone could think of American life.'—*James Agee*

A Kiss before Dying*
US 1956   94m   De Luxe   Cinemascope
UA / Crown (Robert Jacks)

A college boy kills women who get in his way.
Reasonably absorbing exercise in psychopathology which would have been more effective on a smaller screen.

w Lawrence Roman, *novel* Ira Levin *d* Gerd Oswald *ph* Lucien Ballard *m* Lionel Newman

Jeffrey Hunter, Joanne Woodward, Robert Wagner, Virginia Leith, *Mary Astor*, George Macready

The Kiss before the Mirror
US 1933   66m   bw

A lawyer defends a man who killed his wife from jealousy, then finds that the same thing is happening to him. Stilted drama which was thought stylish at the time but is now a disappointment from this director; miscast, too. Frank Morgan, Nancy Carroll, Gloria Stuart, Paul Lukas, Charles Grapewin. Written by William Anthony McGuire, from the play by Lazslo Fodor; directed by James Whale; for Universal. (NB: remade in 1938 as *Wives Under Suspicion*.)

A Kiss for Corliss
US 1949   88m   bw
UA / James Nasser
aka: *Almost a Bride*

A teenager develops a crush on a middle-aged roué.
Dismal sequel to *Kiss and Tell* in the shadow of *The Bachelor and the Bobby Soxer*.

w Howard Dimsdale *d* Richard Wallace *ph* Robert de Grasse *m* Werner Heymann

David Niven, Shirley Temple, Tom Tully, Darryl Hickman, Virginia Welles

'A disastrous teenage potboiler.'—*David Niven*

'I sometimes think that David Niven
Should not take all the parts he's given;
While of the art of Shirley Temple
I, for the moment, have had ample.'—*C. A. Lejeune*

A Kiss in the Dark
US 1949   87m   bw
Warner (Harry Kurnitz)

A concert pianist finds romance in a boarding house peopled with zany characters.
Paper-thin romantic comedy.

w Harry Kurnitz *d* Delmer Daves *ph* Robert Burks *m* Max Steiner

David Niven, Jane Wyman, Broderick Crawford, Maria Ouspenskaya, Victor Moore, Wayne Morris, Joseph Buloff, Curt Bois

Kiss Me Again**
US 1925   77m approx (24 fps)   bw
  silent
Warner

A bored wife is tempted to stray, but doesn't.
Excellent silent comedy from an old boulevard
farce, remade to less effect in the forties as
That Uncertain Feeling.

w Hans Kraly, *play* Divorcons by Victorien
Sardou, Emile de Najac *d Ernst Lubitsch*
ph Charles Von Enger

Marie Prévost, Monte Blue, John Roche,
Willard Louis, Clara Bow
  'Another sex masterpiece from the Attila of
Hollywood . . . Continental high comedy done
in the central European manner with
Germanic harshness and irony of attack.'—
Ted Shane, New Yorker
  'Perhaps the most exquisite light screen
comedy ever made on the subject of
l'amour.'—*Herman G. Weinberg*

Kiss Me Again
US 1931   74m   Technicolor

A French lieutenant and a cabaret singer chase
each other half across the world. Modest
musical from Victor Herbert's *Mademoiselle
Modiste*; popular at the time as a vehicle for
two-colour Technicolor. Walter Pidgeon,
Bernice Claire, Frank McHugh, Edward
Everett Horton. Written by Julien Josephson
and Paul Perez; directed by William A. Seiter;
for Warner. (GB title: *Toast of the Legion.*)

Kiss Me Deadly
US 1955   105m   bw
UA / Parklane (Robert Aldrich)

By helping a girl who is nevertheless
murdered, Mike Hammer prevents crooks
from stealing a case of radio-active material.
Curiously arty and excruciatingly boring
private eye thriller, a ripe piece of cinematic
cheese full of tilt shots and symbols: even the
titles read from down to up.

w A. I. Bezzerides *d* Robert Aldrich
ph Ernest Laszlo *m* Frank de Vol

Ralph Meeker, Albert Dekker, Cloris
Leachman, Paul Stewart, Juano Hernandez,
Wesley Addy, Maxene Cooper

Kiss Me Kate**
US 1953   111m   Anscocolor   3-D
MGM (Jack Cummings)

The married leading players of a musical
version of *The Taming of the Shrew* lead an
equally tempestuous life backstage.
Brisk, bright screen version of the Broadway
musical hit.

w Dorothy Kingsley, *play* Samuel and Bella
Spewack *d George Sidney ph* Charles
Rosher *m / ly Cole Porter md* André Previn,
Saul Chaplin *ch Hermes Pan*

Howard Keel, Kathryn Grayson, Ann Miller,
Keenan Wynn, Bobby Van, Tommy Rall,
James Whitmore, Bob Fosse, Kurt Kasznar
AAN: André Previn, Saul Chaplin

Kiss Me Stupid*
US 1964   124m   bw   Panavision
UA / Mirisch / Phalanx / (Billy Wilder)

A womanizing pop singer stops overnight in a
small California desert town and shows
interest in an unsuccessful songwriter in order
to get at his wife.
Draggy, tasteless, surprisingly unamusing
smoking room story, with the actors behaving
as though driven against their will (apart from
Dean Martin, ideally cast as the idol who gets
a headache if he doesn't have sex every night).
Some good wisecracks, but it should have
been much faster and funnier.

w Billy Wilder, I. A. L. Diamond, *play* L'oro
della fantasia by Anna Bonacci *d* Billy
Wilder *ph* Joseph La Shelle *m* André Previn
pd Alexander Trauner *songs* George and Ira
Gershwin

Dean Martin, Kim Novak, Ray Walston, Cliff
Osmond
  'A work of ferocious tastelessness . . .
Swiftian in its relentless disgust.'—*Peter
Barnes*

Kiss of Death**
US 1947   98m   bw
TCF (Fred Kohlmar)

A captured thief informs on his own gang, and
a psychopathic killer is sent to extract
vengeance.
Gloomy, well-made semi-location thriller
which descends into heavy melodrama.
Remade as *The Fiend Who Walked the West.*

w Ben Hecht, Charles Lederer *d* Henry
Hathaway *ph* Norbert Brodine *m* David
Buttolph

Victor Mature, Richard Widmark, Brian
Donlevy, Coleen Gray, Karl Malden, Taylor
Holmes
  'A tense, terrifying crime melodrama with
an unusually authentic seamy atmosphere.'—
New Yorker, 1980
  'Economy of narration enhances the
compactness and tautness of the whole and
achieves that rarity, a picture minus
unnecessary footage.'—*National Board of
Review*

'It illustrates a new and vigorous trend in US moviemaking. One of the best things that is happening in Hollywood is the tendency to move out of the studio—to base fictional pictures on fact, and to shoot them not in painted studio sets but in actual places.'—*James Agee*

AAN: original story (E. Lipsky); Richard Widmark

Kiss of the Vampire*

GB 1962 88m Eastmancolor
U-I / Hammer (Anthony Hinds)
US title: *Kiss of Evil*

In 1910 a Bavarian disciple of Dracula lures a British honeymoon couple.
This unsubtle variation on *Dracula* is handled in lively fashion, with a splendid climax in which assorted white-robed vampires are destroyed by bats.

w John Elder d *Don Sharp* ph Alan Hume m James Bernard

Noel Willman, Clifford Evans, Edward De Souza, Jennifer Daniel, Isobel Black

Kiss the Blood Off My Hands

US 1948 80m bw
Universal (Harold Hecht)
GB title: *Blood on My Hands*

A nurse helps a seaman on the run for murder.
Risible romantic melodrama in never-was London docks setting, with Newton large as life and twice as villainous.

w Leonardo Bercovici, *novel* Gerald Butler d Norman Foster ph Russell Metty m Miklos Rozsa

Joan Fontaine, Burt Lancaster, Robert Newton, Lewis Russell, Aminta Dyne

Kiss the Boys Goodbye*

US 1941 85m bw
Paramount

A Broadway producer falls for one of his chorines.
Moderately smart musical entertainment of its time.

w Harry Tugend, Dwight Taylor, *play* Clare Boothe d Victor Schertzinger m / ly Victor Schertzinger, Frank Loesser ph Ted Tetzlaff

Don Ameche, Mary Martin, Oscar Levant, Rochester, Raymond Walburn, Connie Boswell, Virginia Dale, Barbara Jo Allen, Elizabeth Patterson

Kiss the Bride Goodbye

GB 1944 89m bw

A runaway couple are unwittingly abetted by her uncle. Unsubtle family farce. Patricia Medina, Jimmy Hanley, Frederick Leister, Marie Lohr, Claud Allister, Ellen Pollock, Wylie Watson. Written by Jack Whittingham; directed by Paul Stein; for Butcher.

Kiss the Girls and Make Them Die

Italy 1966 106m Technicolor
Dino de Laurentiis
original title: *Si Tutte le Donne del Mondo . . .*

A rich industrialist has a plan to sterilize the whole male population of the world and restock it with his own mistresses, whom he keeps in suspended animation.
Patchy James Bond spoof.

w Jack Pulman, Dino Maiuri d Henry Levin, Dino Maiuri ph Aldo Tonti m Mario Nascimbene

Michael Connors, Dorothy Provine, Raf Vallone, Terry-Thomas

Kiss Them for Me

US 1957 105m Eastmancolor Cinemascope
TCF (Jerry Wald)

Three navy pilots spend a weekend's unofficial leave in San Francisco, and get into various kinds of trouble.
Based on a novel which also served as source for the musical *Hit the Deck*, this very heavy-footed comedy with serious asides is most unsuitably cast and generally ill-timed and unattractive.

w Julius Epstein, *novel* Shore Leave by Frederick Wakeman d Stanley Donen ph Milton Krasner m Lionel Newman

Cary Grant, Jayne Mansfield, Suzy Parker, Ray Walston, Larry Blyden, Leif Erickson, Werner Klemperer

Kiss Tomorrow Goodbye

US 1950 102m bw
(Warner) William Cagney

A violent criminal breaks jail and plans several daring robberies.
Surprisingly brutal star melodrama which failed to repeat the success of *White Heat*.

w Harry Brown, *novel* Horace McCoy d Gordon Douglas ph Peverell Marley m Carmen Dragon

James Cagney, Barbara Payton, Ward Bond, Luther Adler, Helena Carter, Steve Brodie, Rhys Williams, Barton MacLane, Frank Reicher, John Litel

'The mixture as before without an ingredient changed.'—*Otis Guernsey Jnr*

Kisses for My President
US 1964   113m   bw
Warner / Pearlayne (Curtis Bernhardt)

America's first woman president causes
problems for her husband.
Solidly-carpentered comedy with too few ideas
for its length.

w Claude Binyon, Robert G. Kane d Curtis
Bernhardt ph Robert Surtees m Bronislau
Kaper

Polly Bergen, Fred MacMurray, Arlene Dahl,
Eli Wallach, Edward Andrews

Kissin' Cousins
US 1963   96m   Metrocolor   Panavision
MGM / Four Leaf (Sam Katzman)

The USAF wants to build a missile base on
Smokey Mountain, and their PR man
discovers that one of the hillbillies is his
double.
A feeble production in every sense, even
below its star's usual standard.

w Gerald Drayson Adams, Gene Nelson
d Gene Nelson ph Ellis W. Carter md Fred
Karger

Elvis Presley, Arthur O'Connell, Glenda
Farrell, Jack Albertson

The Kissing Bandit
US 1948   102m   Technicolor
MGM (Joe Pasternak)

In old California, a young businessman finds
he is expected to keep up his bandit father's
criminal and romantic reputation.
Silly, witless musical which never settles into
gear; mocked by its star as Benny mocked *The
Horn Blows at Midnight.*

w Isabel Lennart, John Briard Harding
d Laslo Benedek ph Robert Surtees
m Georgie Stoll *songs* Nacio Herb Brown,
Earl Brent, Edward Heyman

Frank Sinatra, Kathryn Grayson, J. Carrol
Naish, Mildred Natwick, Mikhail Rasumny,
Billy Gilbert, Clinton Sundberg

Kitten with a Whip
US 1964   83m   bw

A girl escaped from reform school takes
refuge with a politician whose wife is away.
Over-the-top melodrama thought bannable at
the time. Ann-Margret, John Forsythe,
Patricia Barry, Ann Doran, Audrey Dalton.
Written and directed by Douglas Heyes, from
a book by Wade Miller; for Universal.

Kitty
GB 1928   90m (24 fps)   bw   silent
BIP / Burlington (Victor Saville)

A shopgirl loves a paralysed amnesiac, but his
mother interferes.
Uninteresting romantic melodrama, notable
only as Britain's first sound film: a few
dialogue sequences were quickly added for a
reissue in 1929.

w Violet Powell, Benn W. Levy,
novel Warwick Deeping d Victor Saville

John Stuart, Estelle Brody, Dorothy
Cumming, Marie Ault, Olaf Hytten

Kitty***
US 1945   103m   bw
Paramount (Karl Tunberg)

In 18th-century London, an aristocrat makes a
duchess of a guttersnipe.
Well-detailed period *Pygmalion* which works
much better than one would expect.

w Darrell Ware, Karl Tunberg, *novel*
Rosamund Marshall d Mitchell Leisen
ph Daniel L. Fapp m Victor Young

*Paulette Goddard, Ray Milland, Cecil
Kellaway, Constance Collier, Reginald Owen,*
Patric Knowles, Dennis Hoey, Sara Allgood,
Eric Blore, Gordon Richards, Michael Dyne
  'Enough sex, wit and urbane cynicism to
make one forget a footling ending.'—*Peter
John Dyer, MFB*

Kitty Foyle**
US 1940   108m   bw
RKO (Harry E. Edgington, David
  Hempstead)

A white-collar girl has a troubled love life.
Solid entertainment of its time, especially
aimed at ambitious young ladies.

w Dalton Trumbo, Donald Ogden Stewart,
novel Christopher Morley d Sam Wood
ph Robert de Grasse m Roy Webb

*Ginger Rogers, Dennis Morgan, James Craig,
Eduardo Ciannelli,* Ernest Cossart, Gladys
Cooper, Mary Treen

AA: Ginger Rogers
AAN: best picture; Dalton Trumbo, Donald
Ogden Stewart; Sam Wood

The Klansman
US 1974   112m   Technicolor
Paramount / Atlanta (William Alexander)

An Alabama sheriff confronts the Ku Klux
Klan.
Violent melodrama, all noise, brutality and
bad acting.

w Millard Kaufman, Samuel Fuller, *novel*
William Bradford Huie d Terence Young
ph Lloyd Ahern, Aldo Tonti m Stax
Organisation

Lee Marvin, Richard Burton, Cameron Mitchell,
O. J. Simpson, Lola Falana, David Huddleston, Luciana Paluzzi, Linda Evans
'There's not a shred of quality, dignity, relevance or impact in this yahoo-oriented bunk.'—*Variety*

Klondike Annie
US 1936 83m bw
Paramount (William Le Baron)

A torch singer on the run disguises herself as a missionary and revivifies a Klondike mission.
Laundered Mae West vehicle, from her fading period but not too bad.

w Mae West, Marion Morgan, George B. Dowell *d* Raoul Walsh *ph* George Clemens
Mae West, Victor McLaglen, Philip Reed, Helen Jerome Eddy, Harry Beresford, Harold Huber, Esther Howard

Klute•••
US 1971 114m Technicolor Panavision
Warner (Alan J. Pakula)

A policeman leaves the force to investigate the disappearance of a research scientist, and takes up with a call girl who is involved.
Excellent adult thriller with attention to detail and emphasis on character.

w Andy K. Lewis, Dave Lewis d Alan J. Pakula ph Gordon Willis *m* Michael Small
Jane Fonda, Donald Sutherland, Charles Cioffi, Roy Scheider, Rita Gam
AA: Jane Fonda
AAN: Andy K. Lewis, Dave Lewis

The Knack•••
GB 1965 84m bw
UA / Woodfall (Oscar Lewenstein)

A sex-starved young teacher lets one room of his house to a successful womanizer, another to an innocent girl from the north.
An excuse for an anarchic series of visual gags, a kaleidoscope of swinging London in which anything goes. Brilliantly done in the style of *A Hard Day's Night.*

w Charles Wood, *play* Ann Jellicoe *d Richard Lester ph David Watkin m* John Barry
Michael Crawford, Ray Brooks, Rita Tushingham, Donal Donnelly

Knave of Hearts•
GB 1954 103m bw
Transcontinental (Paul Graetz)
aka: *Monsieur Ripois et Son Nemesis*
US title: *Lover Boy*

A born philanderer confesses all his affairs to his wife.
Well-observed though strangely flat and disappointing sex comedy, something of a pioneer in its time and therefore perhaps too diffident in its approach.

w René Clément, Hugh Mills *d* René Clément *ph* Oswald Morris *m* Roman Vlad
Gérard Philipe, Margaret Johnston, Joan Greenwood, Natasha Parry, Valerie Hobson

Knickerbocker Holiday
US 1944 84m bw
UA / Harry Joe Brown / PCA

In old New Amsterdam, a one-legged tyrant finally sees the light.
Artificial musical from a famous stage original, with engaging moments including Charles Coburn singing 'September Song'.

w Thomas Lennon, from the 1938 stage musical (*m* Kurt Weill, *ly* Maxwell Anderson) based on Father Knickerbocker's History of New York by Washington Irving *d* Harry Joe Brown *ph* Phil Tammura *m* Werner Heymann
Charles Coburn, Nelson Eddy, Constance Dowling, Ernest Cossart, Shelley Winters, Otto Kruger
AAN: Werner Heymann

Knife in the Water•
Poland 1962 94m bw
ZRF Kamera (Stanislaw Zylewicz)
original title: *Noz w Wodzie*

A young couple ask a hitchhiker to spend a weekend on their yacht, and regret it.
Detached little melodrama in which the sex and violence hover beneath the surface. All very watchable, but in a minor key.

w Jerzy Skolimowski, Roman Polanski, Jakub Goldberg *d Roman Polanski ph* Jerzy Lipman *m* Krzystof Komeda
Leon Niemczyk, Jolanta Umecka, Zygmunt Malanowicz
AAN: best foreign film

Knight without Armour••
GB 1937 107m bw
London Films (Alexander Korda)

During the Russian Revolution of 1917, a widowed countess is helped to safety by a British translator.
Underrated romantic adventure with big production values and some splendid moments.

w Lajos Biro, Arthur Wimperis, Frances Marion, *novel* James Hilton *ph* Harry Stradling *d Jacques Feyder m* Miklos Rozsa

Robert Donat, Marlene Dietrich, Irene
Vanbrugh, Herbert Lomas, Austin Trevor,
Basil Gill, David Tree, John Clements,
Lawrence Hanray
 'A first class thriller, beautifully directed,
with spare and convincing dialogue and a
nearly watertight scenario.'—*Graham Greene*

Knights of the Round Table*
GB 1953   115m   Eastmancolor
  Cinemascope
MGM (Pandro S. Berman)

Lancelot, banished from King Arthur's court
for loving Guinevere, returns to defeat the evil
Modred.
Disappointingly flat, pageant-like adaptation
of the legends, with a few lively strands
insufficiently firmly drawn together.

w Talbot Jennings, Jan Lustig, Noel Langley
d Richard Thorpe *ph* Frederick A. Young,
Stephen Dade *m* Miklos Rozsa *ad* Alfred
Junge, Hans Peters

Robert Taylor, Mel Ferrer, Ava Gardner,
Anne Crawford, Stanley Baker, Felix Aylmer,
Robert Urquhart, Niall MacGinnis

Knights of the Teutonic Order*
Poland 1960   180m   Eastmancolor
  Dyaliscope
Studio Unit (Zygmunt Krol)

Teutonic knights pillage Poland on the pretext
of converting the inhabitants to Christianity;
when they kill a noblewoman, her daughter
swears revenge.
Medieval epic differing little from those of
Hollywood, but splendid to look at.

w Jerzy Stafan Stawinski, Aleksander Ford,
novel Henryk Sienkiewicz *d* Aleksander
Ford *ph* Mieczyslaw Jahoda *m* Kazimierz
Serocki

Urszula Modrzynska, Grazyna Staniszewska,
Andrzej Szalawski

Knock on Any Door*
US 1949   100m   bw
Columbia (Nicholas Ray)

A defence lawyer pleads with the jury for the
life of a slum boy on a murder charge.
Smartly-made but empty melodrama making
facile social points.

w Daniel Taradash, John Monks Jnr, *novel*
Willard Motley *d* Nicholas Ray *ph* Burnett
Guffey *m* George Antheil

Humphrey Bogart, John Derek, George
Macready, Allene Roberts

Knock on Wood**
US 1954   103m   Technicolor
Paramount (Norman Panama, Melvin
  Frank)

Stolen plans are hidden inside the dummy of
an unsuspecting ventriloquist.
Excellent star comedy with good script and
production (but some strange ideas of
London's geography).

wd Norman Panama, *Melvin Frank ph* Daniel
Fapp *songs* Sylvia Fine *m* Leith Stevens
ch Michael Kidd

Danny Kaye, Mai Zetterling, David Burns,
Torin Thatcher, Leon Askin, Abner
Biberman, Steve Geray

AAN: Norman Panama, Melvin Frank (script)

Knute Rockne, All American
US 1940   98m   bw
Warner (Robert Fellows)

The career of a famous Notre Dame football
coach.
Standard sporting biopic.

w Robert Buckner *d* Lloyd Bacon *ph* Tony
Gaudio

Pat O'Brien, Ronald Reagan, Gale Page,
Donald Crisp, Albert Basserman, John
Qualen, John Sheffield

Kongo
US 1932   86m   bw
MGM

An embittered African recluse takes revenge
on the daughter of his former enemy.
No-holds-barred melodrama which never
really exerts the right grip; a remake of the
Lon Chaney silent *West of Zanzibar.*

w Leon Gordon, *play* Chester de Vonde,
Kilbourn Gordon *d* William Cowen
ph Harold Rosson

Walter Huston, Lupe Velez, Virginia Bruce,
Conrad Nagel, C. Henry Gordon

Kotch*
US 1971   114m   Metrocolor
ABC / Kotch Company (Richard Carter)

An eccentric 72-year-old widower is at odds
with his family and helps a pregnant
babysitter.
Variously amusing, moving and sentimental,
this generally likeable film about a crotchety
grandpa is sustained by its star performance.

w John Paxton, *novel* Katherine Topkins
d Jack Lemmon *ph* Richard H. Kline
m Marvin Hamlisch

Walter Matthau, Deborah Winter, Felicia Farr,
Charles Aidman

AAN: Walter Matthau; song 'Life Is What You Make It' (*m* Marvin Hamlisch, *ly* Johnny Mercer)

Krakatoa, East of Java

US 1968   136m   Technicolor   Cinerama
ABC / Cinerama (Lester A. Sansom)

In 1883 the SS *Batavia Queen* leaves Singapore and is engulfed by the Krakatoa eruption. Mindless spectacular, technically quite impressive but with no dramatic interest whatsoever.

w Clifford Newton Gould, Bernard Gordon *d* Bernard Kowalski *ph* Manuel Berenguer *m* Frank de Vol *pd* / *sp* Eugene Lourié

Maximilian Schell, Diane Baker, Brian Keith, Rossano Brazzi, Barbara Werle, John Leyton, Sal Mineo, J. D. Cannon, Marc Lawrence

'Apparently designed to disprove the old adage, "they don't make them like that any more". At a conservative count it includes such sure-fire cinematic ingredients as hidden treasure, deep-sea divers with shattered lungs and claustrophobia, mutiny *and* fire on board ship, nuns, convicts, a lost orphan boy, girl divers and even a little striptease, climaxing in the biggest explosion and the greatest tidal wave known to history.'—*MFB*

Kramer versus Kramer***

US 1979   105m   Technicolor
Columbia / Stanley Jaffe (Richard C. Fischoff)

A divorced advertising executive gets temporary custody of his seven-year-old son. New-fashioned tearjerker, as slick as a colour supplement and catnip to the emotion-starved masses.

wd Robert Benton, *novel* Avery Corman *ph* Nestor Almendros *md* Erma E. Levin *pd* Paul Sylbert

Dustin Hoffman, Justin Henry, Meryl Streep, Jane Alexander, Howard Duff

'Pastel colours, a cute kid and a good script made this one of the most undeserved successes of the year: wall-to-wall sentiment.'—*Time Out*

AA: best picture; Robert Benton (as director); Dustin Hoffman; Meryl Streep; screen play adapted from another medium

The Kremlin Letter

US 1970   122m   De Luxe   Panavision
TCF (Carter de Haven, Sam Wiesenthal)

An American intelligence team is sent undercover to Moscow to retrieve an arms treaty mistakenly signed.
Tediously violent cold war mystifier: a few good performances do not make it worth unravelling.

w John Huston, Gladys Hill, *novel* Noel Behn *d* John Huston *ph* Ted Scaife *m* Robert Drasnin *pd* Ted Haworth

Richard Boone, Orson Welles, Bibi Andersson, Max Von Sydow, Patrick O'Neal, Ronald Radd, George Sanders, Dean Jagger, Nigel Green, Barbara Parkins, Lila Kedrova, Michael MacLiammoir, Sandor Eles, Niall MacGinnis, John Huston

'One of those all-star international spy sagas that trick out an indecipherably tortuous plot with a series of vignettes in which the pleasures of star-spotting are expected to compensate for any narrative longueurs.'—*Nigel Andrews*

'If you miss the first five minutes you miss one suicide, two executions, one seduction and the key to the plot!'—*publicity*

Kwaidan*

Japan 1964   164m   Eastmancolor
Tohoscope
Ninjin Club / Bungei

Four elegant ghost stories by Lafcadio Hearn. Visually a superb production; all the stories have merit, but *en masse* prove a bit much at one sitting.

w Yoko Mizuki *d* Masaki Kobayashi *ph* Yoshio Miyajima *m* Toru Takemitsu *ad* Shigemasa Toda

Rentaro Mikuni, Ganjiro Nakamura, Katsuo Nakamura

L

The L-Shaped Room*
GB 1962   142m   bw
British Lion / Romulus (James Woolf,
   Richard Attenborough)

A girl intending to have an abortion takes a
room in a London suburban house which is
none too clean but full of characters.
Watchable, mildly sensational low-life-
melodrama of the pre-swinging London era
when well-to-dos thought it amusing to live in
garrets. Hellishly overlong but enjoyable in
patches because of the professionalism with
which it is made.

w Bryan Forbes, *novel* Lynne Reid Banks
d Bryan Forbes ph Douglas Slocombe
m Brahms, John Barry

Leslie Caron, Tom Bell, *Brock Peters*, Cicely
Courtneidge, Bernard Lee, *Avis Bunnage*,
Patricia Phoenix, Emlyn Williams
  'It would be hard to imagine a more
unlikely, or commercially more sure-fire group
of lodgers living under a single roof than this
pregnant French girl, maladjusted negro,
lesbian actress, couple of prostitutes, and
unpublished writer who finally commits it all
to paper—shades of *I Am a Camera* as well as
A Taste of Honey.'—*MFB*

AAN: Leslie Caron

Laburnum Grove**
GB 1936   73m   bw
ATP (Basil Dean)

A suburban father reveals he is a forger.
Agreeable worm-turns comedy melodrama,
much copied since.

w Gordon Wellesley, Anthony Kimmins, *play*
J. B. Priestley d Carol Reed ph John W.
Boyle

Cedric Hardwicke, Edmund Gwenn, Victoria
Hopper, Ethel Coleridge, Katie Johnson,
Francis James
  'Here at last is an English film one can
unreservedly praise.'—*Graham Greene*

The Lacemaker
France / Switzerland / West Germany
   1977   107m   Eastmancolor
Action / FR3 / Citel / Janus (Yves Gasser)
original title: *La Dentellière*

An 18-year-old girl becomes ill and withdrawn
when her first affair breaks up.
Careful social character study, witty and
observant but in memory insufficiently
differentiated from numerous exploitation
pieces with similar plots.

w Pascal Lainé, Claude Goretta, *novel* Pascal
Lainé d Claude Goretta ph Jean Boffety
m Pierre Jansen

Isabelle Huppert, Yves Beneyton, Florence
Giorgetti, Anne Marie Düringer

Ladies Courageous
US 1944   88m   bw
Universal (Walter Wanger)

Girls ferry war planes from base to base for
the USAF. Absolutely predictable propaganda
potboiler.

w Norman Reilly Raine, Doris Gilbert d John
Rawlins ph Hal Mohr m Dmitri Tiomkin

Loretta Young, Geraldine Fitzgerald, Diana
Barrymore, Evelyn Ankers, Anne Gwynne,
Philip Terry, David Bruce, Lois Collier,
Samuel S. Hinds

Ladies in Love*
US 1936   97m   bw
TCF (B. G. De Sylva)

Man-hunting girls in Budapest form a joint
plan.
Amusing romantic nonsense.

w Melville Baker, *play* Ladislaus Bus-Fekete
d Edward H. Griffith ph Hal Mohr md Louis
Silvers

Janet Gaynor, Loretta Young, Constance
Bennett, Simone Simon, Don Ameche, Paul
Lukas, Tyrone Power, Alan Mowbray,
Wilfred Lawson, J. Edward Bromberg,
Virginia Field

Ladies in Retirement**
US 1941   92m   bw
Columbia

A housekeeper murders her employer for the
sake of her two mentally disturbed sisters.
Splendidly effective Grand Guignol, from a
well-written play but filmically quite
interesting. Remade with lots of gore as *The
Mad Room* (qv).

w Reginald Denham, Edward Percy, Garrett Fort, *play* Reginald Denham, Edward Percy *d Charles Vidor ph* George Barnes *m* Ernst Toch

Ida Lupino, Louis Hayward, Isobel Elsom, Edith Barrett, Elsa Lanchester, Emma Dunn

AAN: Ernst Toch

Ladies Love Brutes
US 1930 83m bw
Paramount

A gangster tries to improve himself to marry a socialite.
Uneasy comedy-drama with good moments.

w Waldemar Young, Herman J. Mankiewicz, *play* Pardon My Glove by Zoe Akins *d* Rowland V. Lee *ph* Harry Fischbeck

George Bancroft, Mary Astor, Fredric March, Margaret Quimby, Stanley Fields

Ladies' Man*
US 1931 70m bw
Paramount

A man of the world preys successfully on rich women until one grows jealous when her daughter falls for him.
Vivid, hard melodrama showing the blacker side of early thirties high society living.

w Herman J. Mankiewicz d Lothar Mendes *ph* Victor Milner

William Powell, Kay Francis, Carole Lombard, Gilbert Emery, Olive Tell

Ladies' Man
US 1947 90m bw

A poor farmer strikes oil, becomes a millionaire, and finds himself a prize for the ladies. Below-par comedy which wastes an agreeable cast. Eddie Bracken, Cass Daley, Virginia Welles, Spike Jones and his City Slickers. Written by Edmund Beloin, Jack Rose and Lewis Meltzer; directed by William D. Russell; for Paramount.

Ladies' Man
US 1961 106m Technicolor
Paramount / York (Jerry Lewis)

The adventures of an accident-prone houseboy at a Hollywood hotel for aspiring actresses.
Hit-or-miss collection of comic scraps which might have benefited from being put together on a less grandiose scale.

w Jerry Lewis, Bill Richmond *d* Jerry Lewis *ph* W. Wallace Kelley *m* Walter Scharf

Jerry Lewis, Helen Traubel, Jack Kruschen, Doodles Weaver, Gloria Jean

'Regression into infantilism cannot be carried much further than this.'—*MFB*

Ladies Must Live: see The Home Towners

Ladies of Leisure
US 1930 98m bw

A gold digger gets an attack of conscience and gives up her rich fiancé. Only fitfully interesting early Capra, with little sparkle in any department. Barbara Stanwyck, Lowell Sherman, Ralph Graves, Marie Prevost. Written by Milton Herbert Gropper and Jo Swerling; directed by Frank Capra; for Columbia.

Ladies of the Big House
US 1931 77m bw
Paramount

A married couple are framed on a murder charge and sent to prison.
Melodramatic nonsense in the wake of *The Big House.*

w Louis Weitzenkorn *d* Marion Gering *ph* David Abel

Sylvia Sidney, Gene Raymond, Wynne Gibson, Rockcliffe Fellows, Earle Foxe

Ladies Should Listen
US 1934 63m bw
Paramount (Douglas MacLean)

A knowledgeable switchboard operator helps a financier with his problems.
Moderately beguiling, instantly forgettable romantic frou-frou.

w Claude Binyon, Frank Butler, Guy Bolton *d* Frank Tuttle *ph* Harry Sharp

Cary Grant, Frances Drake, Edward Everett Horton, Rosita Morena, George Barbier, Nydia Westman, Charles Ray

Ladies They Talk About*
US 1933 69m bw
Warner

Trouble in a women's prison.
Entertaining comedy-melodrama which had some brushes with the Hays Office because of its frankly man-hungry characters.

w Sidney Sutherland, Brown Holmes, *play* Women in Prison by Dorothy Mackaye, Carlton Miles *d* Howard Bretherton, William Keighley *ph* John Seitz

Barbara Stanwyck, Lyle Talbot, Preston Foster, Dorothy Burgess, Lillian Roth, Maude Eburne, Ruth Donnelly, Harold Huber

Ladies Who Do
GB 1963 85m bw
British Lion / Bryanston / Fanfare (George H. Brown)

Charladies form a successful company from
tips they salvage from wastepaper baskets.
Mild farce sustained by familiar actors.

w Michael Pertwee d C. M. Pennington-
Richards ph Geoffrey Faithfull m Ron
Goodwin

Peggy Mount, Miriam Karlin, Robert Morley,
Harry H. Corbett, Dandy Nichols

The Lady and the Mob
US 1939 65m bw
Columbia (Fred Kohlmar)

A lady bank owner menaced by gangsters
forms her own mob.
Weak comedy.

w Richard Maibaum, Gertrude Purcell d Ben
Stoloff ph John Stumar

Fay Bainter, Ida Lupino, Lee Bowman, Henry
Armetta, Warren Hymer, Harold Huber

The Lady and the Monster
US 1944 86m bw
Republic (George Sherman)
aka: *Tiger Man*
GB title: *The Lady and the Doctor*

A scientist keeps alive the brain of a mortally
injured financier, and it comes to dominate
him.
Fair, over-padded version of a much filmed
thriller (see also *Donovan's Brain,
Vengeance*).

w Dane Lussier, Frederick Kohner, *novel*
Donovan's Brain by Curt Siodmak d George
Sherman ph John Alton m Walter Scharf

Erich Von Stroheim, Richard Arlen, Vera
Hruba Ralston, Mary Nash, Sidney Blackmer,
Helen Vinson

Lady and the Tramp**
US 1955 76m Technicolor
   Cinemascope
Walt Disney (Erdmann Penner)

A pedigree spaniel falls foul of two Siamese
cats and has a romantic adventure with a
mongrel who helps her.
Pleasant cartoon feature in Disney's cutest and
most anthropomorphic vein.

d Hamilton Luske, Clyde Geronomi, Wilfred
Jackson m Oliver Wallace

Lady Be Good*
US 1941 111m bw
MGM (Arthur Freed)

Married songwriters produce a musical.
Thin musical with good talent and tunes; very
little connection with the 1924 musical show.

w Jack McGowan, Kay Van Riper, John
McClain d Norman Z. McLeod ph George J.
Folsey, Oliver T. Marsh md George Stoll
songs various

Eleanor Powell, Robert Young, Ann Sothern,
Red Skelton, Dan Dailey, Virginia O'Brien,
Reginald Owen, John Carroll, Lionel
Barrymore, Jimmy Dorsey and his Orchestra

AA: song 'The Last Time I Saw Paris'
(*m* Jerome Kern, *ly* Oscar Hammerstein II)

Lady By Choice*
US 1934 78m bw
Columbia

A publicity-mad dancer adopts an old rummy
as a Mother's Day stunt.
Amusing sentimental comedy in the wake of
Lady for A Day.

w Jo Swerling, Dwight Taylor d David
Burton ph Ted Tetzlaff

Carole Lombard, May Robson, Walter
Connolly, Roger Pryor, Arthur Hohl,
Raymond Walburn, James Burke, Henry
Kolker

Lady Caroline Lamb*
GB 1972 123m Eastmancolor
   Panavision
EMI / GEC / Pulsar / Video
   Cinematographica (Fernando Ghia)

In 1805, impulsive Lady Caroline Ponsonby
marries William Lamb, later Lord Melbourne,
and then disgraces him by her wildness.
Pale, disappointing historical fiction with good
spots but no reverence for fact; slackly written
and handled, and not helped by the wide
screen.

wd Robert Bolt ph Oswald Morris
m Richard Rodney Bennett ad Carmen
Dillon

Sarah Miles, Jon Finch, Richard Chamberlain
(as Byron), Margaret Leighton, John Mills (as
Cobbett), *Ralph Richardson* (as George III),
Laurence Olivier (as Wellington)

Lady Chatterley's Lover
France 1955 101m / 84m (English
   version) bw
Regie du Film / Orsay Film (Gilbert Cohen-
   Séat)

The wife of a crippled and impotent mine-
owner has an affair with a coarse gamekeeper
and enjoys it.
Hilariously-po-faced transcription of a
notorious novel, of no cinematic interest
whatever.

w Gaston Bonheur, Philippe de Rothschild, Marc Allégret, *novel* D. H. Lawrence *d* Marc Allégret *ph* Georges Périnal *m* Joseph Kosma

Danielle Darrieux, Leo Genn, Erno Crisa

The Lady Consents
US 1936 76m bw
RKO (Edward Kaufman)

When a doctor's wife sees that he is in love with another woman, she makes it easy for him to get a divorce; but he finally comes back to her.
Unbelievable matinée drama for star fans.

w P. J. Wolfson, Anthony Veiller, *play* The Indestructible Mrs Talbot by P. J. Wolfson *d* Stephen Roberts *ph* J. Roy Hunt

Ann Harding, Herbert Marshall, Margaret Lindsay, Walter Abel, Edward Ellis, Hobart Cavanaugh, Ilka Chase

The Lady Eve***
US 1941 97m bw
Paramount (Paul Jones)

A lady cardsharper and her father are outsmarted on a transatlantic liner by a millionaire simpleton; she plans an elaborate revenge.
Hectic romantic farce, the first to show its director's penchant for mixing up sexual innuendo, funny men and pratfalls. There are moments when the pace drops, but in general it's scintillating entertainment, especially after viewing its weak remake *The Birds and the Bees* (qv).

wd Preston Sturges, *play* Monckton Hoffe *ph* Victor Milner *m* Leo Shuken, Charles Bradshaw

Barbara Stanwyck, Henry Fonda, Charles Coburn, Eugène Pallette, William Demarest, Eric Blore, Melville Cooper, Martha O'Driscoll, Janet Beecher, Robert Greig, Luis Alberni, Jimmy Conlin

'The whole theme, with all its variations of keys, is played to one end, to get laughs, and at several different levels it gets them.'— *National Board of Review*

'Preston Sturges, they tell me, is known in Hollywood as "the streamlined Lubitsch". This needn't put you off, because if he goes on producing films as lively as this one he will one day come to be known as Preston Sturges.'— *William Whitebait*

'This time Preston Sturges has wrapped you up another package that is neither very big nor very flashy, but the best fun in months.'—*Otis Ferguson*

'A mixture of visual and verbal slapstick, of high artifice and pratfalls . . . it represents the dizzy high point of Sturges' writing.'—*New Yorker, 1977*

AAN: Monckton Hoffe (original story)

Lady for a Day***
US 1933 95m bw
Columbia

Gangsters help an old apple seller to pose as a rich woman when her daughter visits.
Splendid sentimental comedy full of cinematic resource; the best translation of Runyon to the screen.

w Robert Riskin, *story* Madame La Gimp by Damon Runyon *d* Frank Capra *ph* Joseph Walker

May Robson, Warren William, Guy Kibbee, Glenda Farrell, Ned Sparks, Jean Parker, Walter Connolly, Nat Pendleton

AAN: best picture; Robert Riskin; Frank Capra; May Robson

Lady for a Night
US 1941 87m bw
Republic (Albert J. Cohen)

The lady owner of a gambling boat determines to break into society.
Moderate period comedy with a belated murder plot.

w Isabel Dawn, Boyce DeGaw *d* Leigh Jason *ph* Norbert Brodine *m* David Buttolph

Joan Blondell, John Wayne, Ray Middleton, Philip Merivale, Blanche Yurka, Edith Barrett, Leonid Kinskey, Montagu Love

The Lady from Cheyenne
US 1941 87m bw
Universal (Frank Lloyd)

In 1860 Wyoming, a schoolmistress fights for women's rights.
Mild western star romance.

w Kathryn Scola, Warren Duff *d* Frank Lloyd *ph* Milton Krasner *m* Frank Skinner

Loretta Young, Robert Preston, Gladys George, Edward Arnold, Frank Craven, Jessie Ralph, Spencer Charters, Alan Bridge

Lady from Louisiana
US 1941 84m bw
Republic (Bernard Vorhaus)

In old Mississippi, a lottery-owner's daughter falls in love with a lawyer employed to make her father's business illegal.
Curious pot-boiler containing everything but the kitchen stove, including murder and a raging storm.

w Vera Caspary, Guy Endore, Michael Hogan *d* Bernard Vorhaus *ph* Jack Marta *m* Cy Feuer

John Wayne, Ona Munson, Ray Middleton, Henry Stephenson, Helen Westley, Dorothy Dandridge, Jack Pennick

The Lady from Shanghai**
US 1948 87m bw
Columbia (Richard Wilson, William Castle)

A seaman becomes involved in the maritime wanderings of a crippled lawyer and his homicidal frustrated wife.

Absurd, unintelligible, plainly much cut and rearranged, this thriller was obviously left too much in Welles' hands and then just as unfairly taken out of them; but whole sequences of sheer brilliance remain, notably the final shoot-out in the hall of mirrors.

wd Orson Welles, *novel* If I Die Before I Wake by Sherwood King *ph* Charles Lawton Jnr *m* Heinz Roemheld

Orson Welles, Rita Hayworth, *Everett Sloane, Glenn Anders*, Ted de Corsia, Erskine Sanford, Gus Schilling

'The slurred social conscience of the hero leads him to some murky philosophizing, all of which with many individualities of diction clog the issue and the sound track. Sub-titles, I fear, would have helped.'—*Richard Winnington*

The Lady from Texas
US 1951 78m Technicolor

A Civil War widow is thought to be committable. Mild comedy of insanity, a pale shadow of *Harvey* whose star it borrows.
Josephine Hull, Mona Freeman, Howard Duff, Gene Lockhart, Craig Stevens, Ed Begley. Written by Gerald Drayson Adams and Connie Lee Bennett; directed by Joseph Pevney; for Universal-International.

The Lady Gambles
US 1949 99m bw
U-I (Michael Kraike)

A happy woman destroys her marriage when she becomes addicted to gambling.
Boring, overwrought, underplotted fiction for women.

w Lewis Meltzer, Oscar Saul *d* Michael Gordon *ph* Russell Metty *m* Frank Skinner

Barbara Stanwyck, Robert Preston, Stephen McNally, Edith Barrett, John Hoyt

'A kind of *Lost Weekend* of the gaming tables.'—*Ella Smith*

'The relentless drama of a woman driven to the depths of emotion by a craving beyond control!'—*publicity*

Lady Godiva
US 1955 89m Technicolor
U-I (Robert Arthur)

Lord Leofric tames a Saxon shrew but she suspects his motives and rides naked through the streets of Coventry to prove the loyalty of the Saxons.
Comic strip historical legend, reliably turned out for midwestern family audiences.

w Oscar Brodney, Harry Ruskin *d* Arthur Lubin *ph* Carl Guthrie *m* Joseph Gershenson

George Nader, Maureen O'Hara, Vic Morrow, Eduard Franz, Torin Thatcher

Lady Godiva Rides Again
GB 1951 90m bw
British Lion / London Films / Sidney Gilliat, Frank Launder

A waitress wins a local beauty contest and becomes a charm school starlet and later a stripteaser.
Disappointing satirical comedy with good credentials.

w Frank Launder, Val Valentine *d* Frank Launder *ph* Wilkie Cooper *m* William Alwyn

Pauline Stroud, Stanley Holloway, Diana Dors, Alastair Sim, George Cole, Dennis Price, John McCallum, Bernadette O'Farrell, Kay Kendall, Dora Bryan

The Lady Has Plans
US 1942 77m bw
Paramount (Fred Kohlmar)

A lady reporter in Lisbon is mistaken for a Nazi spy.
Competent fluff which veers between comedy and melodrama.

w Harry Tugend *d* Sidney Lanfield *ph* Charles Lang

Paulette Goddard, Ray Milland, Albert Dekker, Roland Young, Margaret Hayes, Cecil Kellaway, Addison Richards, Edward Norris

Lady Ice
US 1973 92m Technicolor Panavision
Tomorrow Entertainment (Harrison Starr)

An insurance investigator steals a diamond and goes into partnership with a gangster's daughter.
Unamusing Miami-based thriller.

w Alan Trustman, Harold Clemins *d* Tom Gries *ph* Lucien Ballard *m* Perry Botkin Jnr

Donald Sutherland, Jennifer O'Neil, Robert Duvall, Patrick Magee

Lady in a Cage
US 1964 97m bw
American Entertainments Corp. (Luther Davis)

A rich widow is trapped by roving marauders in her private elevator.
Unpleasant and boring suspenser with nasty details.

w Luther Davis *d* Walter Grauman *ph* Lee Garmes *m* Paul Glass *pd* Rudolf Sternad

Olivia de Havilland, James Caan, Ann Sothern, Jeff Corey

'The film parades its pretensions on a note of high-pitched hysteria.'—*MFB*

Lady in Cement
US 1968 93m De Luxe Panavision
TCF / Arcola / Millfield (Aaron Rosenberg)

A Florida private eye on his morning swim finds a dead blonde.
Routine private eye stuff with fashionable sex and violence added.

w Marvin H. Albert, Jack Guss *d* Gordon Douglas *ph* Joseph Biroc *m* Hugo Montenegro

Frank Sinatra, Raquel Welch, Richard Conte, Martin Gabel, Lainie Kazan, Pat Henry, Steve Peck

'While *Tony Rome* seemed to herald a return to the forties thriller, *Lady in Cement* marks nothing more exciting than a return to *Tony Rome*.'—*MFB*

The Lady in Question*
US 1940 81m bw
Columbia

A Parisian shopkeeper on a jury is responsible for getting a girl acquitted of a murder charge, but begins to worry when his son falls in love with her.
Stagey but quite satisfying Hollywood remake of the French drama *Gribouille*, with Raimy and Michele Morgan.

w Lewis Meltzer, *story* Marcel Achard *d* Charles Vidor *ph* Lucien Andriot *m* Lucien Moraweck

Brian Aherne, Rita Hayworth, Glenn Ford, Irene. Rich, George Coulouris, Lloyd Corrigan, Evelyn Keyes, Edward Norris, Curt Bois, Frank Reicher

The Lady in Red
US 1979 93m Metrocolor

The story of Dillinger's mistress. Okay but uninspired gangster drama from a fresh angle.
Pamela Sue Martin, Robert Conrad, Louise Fletcher, Robert Hogan, Rod Gist. Written by John Sayles; directed by Lewis Teague; for New World.

The Lady in the Car with Glasses and a Gun
France / US 1969 105m Eastmancolor Panavision
Lira Film / Columbia (Anatole Litvak)

An English secretary in Paris decides to drive to the coast but has various adventures which make her believe she is either mad or amnesiac.
Muddled, tedious suspenser with a totally implausible 'explanation'.

w Richard Harris, Eleanor Perry *d* Anatole Litvak *ph* Claude Renoir *m* Michel Legrand

Samantha Eggar, Oliver Reed, John McEnery, Stéphane Audran

Lady in the Dark**
US 1944 100m Technicolor
Paramount (Richard Blumenthal)

The editress of a fashion magazine is torn between three men, has worrying dreams, and takes herself to a psychoanalyst.
Lush, stylish and frequently amusing version of a Broadway musical, lacking most of the songs; despite its faults, an excellent example of studio spectacle and a very typical forties romantic comedy.

w Frances Goodrich, Albert Hackett, *play* Moss Hart *d* Mitchell Leisen *ph* Ray Rennahan *m* Kurt Weill *ly* Ira Gershwin *md* Robert Emmett Dolan *sp* Gordon Jennings *ad* Hans Dreier

Ginger Rogers, Warner Baxter, Ray Milland, Jon Hall, *Mischa Auer*, Mary Phillips, Barry Sullivan

'The minx in mink with a yen for men!'— *publicity*

AAN: Ray Rennahan; Robert Emmett Dolan

Lady in the Lake*
US 1946 103m bw
MGM (George Haight)

A private eye is assigned to find a missing wife . . .
Complex private eye yarn which makes the original Chandler dialogue sound childish by over-reliance on the subjective camera

method: we see the hero's face only when he looks in a mirror. An experiment that failed because it was not really understood.

w Steve Fisher, *novel* Raymond Chandler d Robert Montgomery ph Paul C. Vogel m David Snell

Robert Montgomery, Audrey Totter, Lloyd Nolan, Tom Tully, Leon Ames

Lady in the Morgue*
US 1938 70m bw
(GB title: *The Case of the Missing Blonde*)

A private eye investigates a suicide and uncovers three murders. Smart 'B' feature frequently cited as a model of its kind. Preston Foster, Frank Jenks, Patricia Ellis, Thomas Jackson. Written by Eric Taylor and Robertson White from the novel by Jonathan Latimer; directed by Otis Garrett; for Universal. (A previous film with the same characters, actors and director was *The Westland Case*.)

The Lady Is a Square
GB 1958 99m bw
ABP / Wilcox–Neagle

An impoverished socialite widow tries to keep her husband's symphony orchestra going and is helped by a pop singer.
Strained attempt to carry on the *Spring in Park Lane* tradition, with a few inspirations from Joe Pasternak and *One Hundred Men and a Girl*. Earnest performances, obvious jokes.

w Harold Purcell, Pamela Bower, Nicholas Phipps d Herbert Wilcox ph Gordon Dines md Wally Stott

Anna Neagle, Frankie Vaughan, Anthony Newley, Janette Scott, Wilfrid Hyde White

The Lady is Willing
GB 1933 74m bw

An ex-officer becomes a detective and takes his revenge on the financier who ruined him. Interesting comedy-melodrama with strong cast. Leslie Howard, Cedric Hardwicke, Binnie Barnes, Nigel Playfair, Nigel Bruce. Written by Guy Bolton, from the play by Louis Verneuil; directed by Gilbert Miller; for Columbia British.

The Lady Is Willing
US 1942 91m bw
Columbia (Mitchell Leisen)

A musical comedy star adopts a baby and falls in love with its pediatrician.
Dull mixture of light drama and heavy comedy, with all concerned ill at ease.

w James Edward Grant, Albert McCleery d Mitchell Leisen ph Ted Tetzlaff m W. Frank Harling

Marlene Dietrich, Fred MacMurray, Aline MacMahon, Stanley Ridges, Arline Judge, Marietta Canty

Lady Killer***
US 1933 76m bw
Warner (Henry Blanke)

A cinema usher turns to crime, flees to Hollywood, and becomes a movie star. Hectic slam-bang action comedy with melodramatic moments. Great fun.

w Ben Markson, *novel* The Finger Man by Rosalind Keating Shaffer d Roy del Ruth ph Tony Gaudio md Leo F. Forbstein

James Cagney, Mae Clarke, Leslie Fenton, Margaret Lindsay, Henry O'Neill, Willard Robertson, Raymond Hatton, Russell Hopton

'A kind of résumé of everything he has done to date in the movies.'—*New York Evening Post*

Lady L
France / Italy / US 1965   124m
    Eastmancolor   Panavision
Concordia / Champion / MGM (Carlo Ponti)

An 80-year-old lady recalls her romantic life from her youth as a Paris laundress. Unhappy, lumbering, styleless attempt to recapture several old forms, indifferently though expensively made and acted.

wd Peter Ustinov, *novel* Romain Gary ph Henri Alekan m Jean Françaix ad Jean D'Eaubonne, Auguste Capelier

Sophia Loren, David Niven, Paul Newman, Peter Ustinov, Claude Dauphin, Philippe Noiret, Michel Piccoli, Marcel Dalio, Cecil Parker, Eugène Deckers

Lady Luck
US 1946 97m bw
RKO (Warren Duff)

The daughter of a long line of ill-fated gamblers marries one and tries to reform him, but the reverse happens.
Tedious comedy drama.

w Lynn Root, Frank Fenton d Edwin L. Marin ph Lucien Andriot m Leigh Harline

Robert Young, Barbara Hale, Frank Morgan, James Gleason, Don Rice, Harry Davenport, Lloyd Corrigan

Lady on a Train*
US 1945 84m bw
Universal (Felix Jackson)

A girl arriving in New York by train sees a murder committed and can't make anyone believe her.
Cheerful mystery which starts in the right spirit but does not progress too satisfactorily.

w Edmund Beloin, Robert O'Brien, *novel* Leslie Charteris d Charles David ph Elwood Bredell m Miklos Rozsa

Deanna Durbin, Ralph Bellamy, David Bruce, Edward Everett Horton, George Coulouris, Allen Jenkins, Dan Duryea, Patricia Morison

The Lady Pays Off
US 1951 80m bw

A gambling schoolteacher agrees to pay off her debts by tutoring the casino owner's daughter. Flat and unprofitable romantic comedy-drama. Linda Darnell, Stephen McNally, Gigi Perreau, Virginia Field, Ann Codee. Written by Frank Gill Jnr and Albert J. Cohen; directed by Douglas Sirk; for Universal-International.

Lady of Burlesque*
US 1943 91m bw
Hunt Stromberg
GB title: *Striptease Lady*

A burlesque dancer solves a number of backstage murders.
Agreeable murder mystery with strong injections of comedy.

w James Gunn, *novel* The G-String Murders by Gypsy Rose Lee d William A. Wellman ph Robert de Grasse m Arthur Lange

Barbara Stanwyck, Michael O'Shea, J. Edward Bromberg, Iris Adrian, Gloria Dickson, Charles Dingle

AAN: Arthur Lange

Lady of the Tropics
US 1939 92m bw
MGM (Sam Zimbalist)

An American playboy in Saigon marries a half-caste girl but her former admirer prevents her from getting a passport.
Interminable romantic melodrama with stars apparently straight from the taxidermist.

w Ben Hecht d Jack Conway ph George Folsey m Franz Waxman

Robert Taylor, Hedy Lamarr, Joseph Schildkraut, Gloria Franklin, Ernest Cossart

Lady Possessed
US 1952 86m bw
Republic / Portland (James Mason)

An unbalanced woman imagines she is destined to take the place of a pianist's dead wife.

Weary melodramatic nonsense dating from Hollywood's first obsession with psychiatry.

w Pamela Kellino, James Mason, *novel* Del Palma by Pamela Kellino d William Spier, Roy Kellino ph Karl Struss m Nathan Scott

James Mason, June Havoc, Stephen Dunne, Fay Compton, Pamela Kellino, Steven Geray

Lady Scarface
US 1941 69m bw
RKO (Cliff Reid)

A police lieutenant captures a dangerous female gangster.
Weird gangster second feature with too many domestic comedy asides; notable only for the appearance in it of its dignified lead, fresh from *Rebecca*.

w Armand D'Usseau, Richard Collins d Frank Woodruff ph Nicholas Musuraca

Judith Anderson, Dennis O'Keefe, Frances Neal, Mildred Coles, Eric Blore, Marc Lawrence

Lady Sings the Blues*
US 1972 144m Eastmancolor
Panavision
Paramount / Motown / Weston / Furie (Jay Weston, James S. White)

The disastrous private life of blues singer Billie Holiday.
Old-fashioned showbiz biopic with new-fashioned drugs, sex and squalor.

w Terence McCloy, Chris Clark, Suzanne de Passe d Sidney J. Furie ph John Alonzo m Michel Legrand md Gil Askey

Diana Ross, Billy Dee Williams, Richard Pryor, James Callahan, Sid Melton

AAN: script; Gil Askey; Diana Ross

A Lady Takes a Chance
US 1943 86m bw
RKO (Frank Ross)
aka: *The Cowboy and the Girl*

A New York office girl on holiday in Oregon falls for a rodeo rider.
Slender star action romance.

w Robert Ardrey d William A. Seiter ph Frank Redman m Roy Webb

Jean Arthur, John Wayne, Charles Winninger, Phil Silvers, Mary Field, Don Costello, John Philliber, Grady Sutton, Hans Conried

The Lady Takes a Flyer
US 1958 95m Eastmancolor
Cinemascope

A pilot's wife finds that life at home is not

easy, especially with a baby. Heavy comedy or light drama; on either count a bore. Lana Turner, Jeff Chandler, Richard Denning, Chuck Connors, Andra Martin. Written by Danny Arnold; directed by William Alland; for Universal-International.

The Lady Takes a Sailor*
US 1949   99m   bw

A girl devoted to telling the truth insists on proving her story of a mysterious submarine which saved her after a sailing accident.
Curious romantic farce with echoes of the old slapstick tradition. Jane Wyman, Dennis Morgan, Eve Arden, Allyn Joslyn, Robert Douglas, William Frawley. Written by Everett Freeman; directed by Michael Curtiz; for Warner.

A Lady to Love
US 1930   92m   bw
MGM

An ageing grape grower spots an attractive waitress, sends her a marriage proposal by mail, but encloses a photo of his handsome foreman.
Rather primitive but well acted version of a subject later filmed more fluently under the title of the original play.

w Sidney Howard, from his play They Knew What They Wanted d Victor Seastrom
ph Merritt B. Gerstad

Edward G. Robinson, Vilma Banky, Robert Ames, Richard Carle

The Lady Vanishes****
GB 1938   97m   bw
Gaumont British / Gainsborough (Edward Black)

En route back to England by train from Switzerland, an old lady disappears and two young people investigate.
The disappearing lady trick brilliantly refurbished by Hitchcock and his screenwriters, who even get away with a horrid model shot at the beginning. Superb, suspenseful, brilliantly funny, meticulously detailed entertainment.

w Sidney Gilliat, Frank Launder, novel The Wheel Spins by Ethel Lina White d Alfred Hitchcock ph Jack Cox md Louis Levy

Margaret Lockwood, Michael Redgrave, Dame May Whitty, Paul Lukas, Basil Radford, Naunton Wayne, Catherine Lacey, Cecil Parker, Linden Travers, Googie Withers, Mary Clare, Philip Leaver

'If it were not so brilliant a melodrama, we should class it as a brilliant comedy.'—Frank S. Nugent

'No one can study the deceptive effortlessness with which one thing leads to another without learning where the true beauty of this medium is to be mined.'—Otis Ferguson

† Hitchcock was actually second choice as director. The production was ready to roll as Lost Lady, directed by Roy William Neill, with Charter and Caldicott already in place, when Neill became unavailable and Hitch stepped in.

The Lady Vanishes
GB 1979   97m   Eastmancolor Panavision
Rank / Hammer (Michael Carreras, Tom Sachs)

A remake of the above in which everything goes wrong: wrong shape, wrong actors, wrong style (or lack of it). Reasonable adherence to the original script can't save it.

w George Axelrod d Anthony Page
ph Douglas Slocombe m Richard Hartley
pd Wilfred Shingleton

Cybill Shepherd, Elliott Gould, Angela Lansbury, Herbert Lom, Arthur Lowe, Ian Carmichael, Gerald Harper, Jenny Runacre, Jean Anderson

Lady Windermere's Fan*
US 1925   80m (24 fps)   bw   silent
Warner

The mysterious Mrs Erlynne almost causes a scandal in London society.
Oscar Wilde's play transposed to the twenties, with the Lubitsch touch daringly displacing Wildean epigrams. Still more amusing than the sound remake, The Fan.

w Julien Josephson d Ernst Lubitsch
ph Charles Van Enger

Ronald Colman, May McAvoy, Irene Rich, Bert Lytell, Edward Martindel

'Lubitsch's best silent film, full of incisive details, discreet touches, nuances of gestures, where behaviour betrays the character and discloses the sentiment of the personages.'—Georges Sadoul

The Lady with a Lamp*
GB 1951   110m   bw
British Lion / Imperadio (Herbert Wilcox)

The life of Florence Nightingale and her work in reforming the nursing service in 19th-century England.
Solid biopic, not quite in accord with history.

w Warren Chetham Strode, play Reginald Berkeley d Herbert Wilcox ph Max Greene
m Anthony Collins ad William C. Andrews

Anna Neagle, Michael Wilding, Gladys
Young, Felix Aylmer, Julian D'Albie, Arthur
Young, Edwin Styles, Barbara Couper, Cecil
Trouncer, Rosalie Crutchley

'A slow, sedate, refined chronicle . . .
Herbert Wilcox is a good deal more at ease
with the balls and dinners, than with anything
that happens later.'—*Penelope Houston*

'It may please fans of Anna Neagle and
Michael Wilding, but not fans of Florence
Nightingale.'—*Richard Mallett, Punch*

Lady with a Past*
US 1932   80m   bw
RKO (Charles R. Rogers)
GB title: *Reputation*

A wealthy but shy girl almost accidentally
finds herself with a reputation as a scarlet
woman, and the men flock around her.
Moderately enjoyable star comedy drama.

w Horace Jackson, *novel* Harriet Henry
d Edward H. Griffith   *ph* Hal Mohr   *m* Max
Steiner

Constance Bennett, Ben Lyon, David
Manners, Astrid Allwyn, Merna Kennedy,
Blanche Frederici, Nella Walker

Lady with Red Hair*
US 1940   78m   bw
Warner (Edmund Grainger)

The life of actress Mrs Leslie Carter and her
association with impresario David Belasco.
Mildly interesting but unsatisfying biopic of a
lady scarcely remembered.

w Charles Kenyon, Milton Krims, N. Brewster
Morse, Norbert Faulkner   *d* Curtis Bernhardt
ph Arthur Edeson   *m* Heinz Roemheld

Miriam Hopkins, Claude Rains, Richard
Ainley, John Litel, Laura Hope Crews, Helen
Wesley, Mona Barrie, Victor Jory, Cecil
Kellaway, Fritz Leiber, Halliwell Hobbes

The Lady with the Little Dog*
USSR 1959   90m   bw
Lenfilm
original title: *Dama s Sobachkoi*

In Yalta at the turn of the century, an
unhappily married woman and a married man
start an affair which lasts secretly over the
years.
Modestly pleasing, subtly acted anecdote.

wd Josef Heifits, *story* Anton Chekhov
ph Andrei Moskvin, D. Meschiev   *m* Jiri
Sternwald

Ya Savvina, Alexei Batalov, Ala Chostakova

A Lady without Passport*
US 1950   84m   bw
MGM (Samuel Marx)

A secret service undercover man tracks down
aliens being smuggled into the US, and falls in
love with one of them.
Routine material, very well handled.

w Howard Dimsdale   *d* Joseph H. Lewis
ph Paul C. Vogel   *m* David Raksin

Hedy Lamarr, John Hodiak, James Craig,
George Macready, Steve Geray

The Ladykillers*
GB 1955   97m   Technicolor
Ealing (Seth Holt)

An old lady takes in a sinister lodger, who
with his four friends commits a robbery. When
she finds out, they plot to kill her, but are
hoist with their own petards.
Overrated comedy in poor colour; those who
made it quite clearly think it funnier than it is.

w William Rose   *d* Alexander Mackendrick
ph Otto Heller   *m* Tristam Cary

Alec Guinness, *Katie Johnson*, Peter Sellers,
Cecil Parker, Herbert Lom, Danny Green,
Jack Warner, Frankie Howerd, Kenneth
Connor

AAN: William Rose

The Lady's from Kentucky
US 1939   77m   bw

A racetrack gambler falls for a real lady.
Highly predictable and unpersuasive romance.
George Raft, Ellen Drew, Zasu Pitts, Hugh
Herbert. Written by Malcolm Stuart Boylan
and Rowland Brown; directed by Alexander
Hall; for Paramount.

A Lady's Morals
US 1930   75m   bw
MGM
GB title: *Jenny Lind*

The 'Swedish nightingale' learns that love is
more important than a singing career.
Cliché-strewn romance with music.

w Hans Kraly, Claudine West, John Meehan,
Arthur Richman   *d* Sidney Franklin

Grace Moore, Reginald Denny, Wallace
Beery, Jobyna Howland

Lafayette
France / Italy 1961   158m   Super
   Technirama 70
Copernic / Cosmos (Maurice Jacquin)

French officers help America in the
revolutionary war of 1776.
Nerveless international epic, interesting only
for its star cameos.

w Jean-Bernard Luc, Suzanne Arduini,
Jacques Sigurd, François Ponthier, Jean

Dréville, Maurice Jacquin *d* Jean Dréville
ph Claude Renoir, Roger Hubert *m* Steve
Laurent, Pierre Duclos

Michel Le Royer, Jack Hawkins, Orson
Welles, Howard St John, Vittorio de Sica,
Edmund Purdom, Jacques Castelot, Folco
Lulli

'It looks, sounds and smells like nothing so
much as the same old indigestible, ill-dubbed,
co-produced continental spectaculars which
have already turned the stomach in a whole
range of lesser screen ratios.'—*MFB*

Lafayette Escadrille

US 1957   93m   bw
Warner (William Wellman)
GB title: *Hell Bent for Glory*

Early in World War I, a young American joins
the French air force.
The director's valedictory film, on a subject
close to his heart, is a curiously disappointing,
flat and disjointed affair, partly salvaged by a
good period feel.

w A. S. Fleischmann *d* William A. Wellman
ph William Clothier m Leonard Rosenman

Tab Hunter, David Janssen, Clint Eastwood,
Will Hutchins, Paul Fix

The Lambeth Walk

GB 1939   84m   bw
CAPAD / Pinebrook (Anthony Havelock-
Allan)

A cockney bloke inherits a dukedom.
Mild screen version of a popular musical play
and a song which became a nationwide hit.

w Clifford Grey, John Paddy Carstairs,
Robert Edmunds, *play* Me and My Girl by
Louis Rose, Douglas Furber, Noel Gay
d Albert de Courville

Lupino Lane, Sally Gray, Seymour Hicks,
Enid Stamp Taylor, Wilfrid Hyde White,
Charles Heslop, Norah Howard

The Lamp Still Burns

GB 1943   90m   bw
GFD / Two Cities (Leslie Howard)

Adventures of wartime probationary nurses.
Understated wartime morale-builder, no
longer very interesting.

w Elizabeth Baron, Roland Pertwee, *novel*
One Pair of Feet by Monica Dickens
d Maurice Elvey *ph* Robert Krasker

Rosamund John, Stewart Granger, Godfrey
Tearle, Sophie Stewart, John Laurie,
Margaret Vyner, Cathleen Nesbitt, Joyce
Grenfell

Lancashire Luck

GB 1937   74m   bw

A poor girl's life is changed when her father
wins the pools. Modest comedy which started
its star's career. Wendy Hiller, George
Carney, Muriel George, Nigel Stock, George
Galleon. Written by A. R. Rawlinson, from a
story by Ronald Gow; directed by Henry Cass;
for Paramount British.

Lancelot and Guinevere*

GB 1962   117m   Eastmancolor
          Panavision
Emblem (Cornel Wilde)
US title: *Sword of Lancelot*

Sir Lancelot covets the wife of his beloved
King Arthur, but after Arthur's death she
takes the veil.
Decently made, rather tame transcription of
the legends, with all concerned doing quite
creditably but not brilliantly.

w Richard Schayer, Jefferson Pascal *d* Cornel
Wilde *ph* Harry Waxman *m* Ron Goodwin

Cornel Wilde, Jean Wallace, Brian Aherne,
George Baker, John Barrie

Lancer Spy*

US 1937   80m   bw
TCF

A German spy is captured and his English
double is sent back to replace him.
World War I yarn on the lines of *The Great
Impersonation* (qv). Excellent production and
a good beginning and end, but a slow middle.

w Philip Dunne, *novel* Marthe McKenna
d Gregory Ratoff *ph* Barney McGill
m Arthur Lange

George Sanders, Dolores del Rio, Peter Lorre,
Joseph Schildkraut, Virginia Field, Sig
Rumann, Fritz Feld

Land of the Pharaohs*

US 1955   105m   Warnercolor
          Cinemascope
Warner / Continental (Howard Hawks)

Pharaoh is obsessed with life after death and
builds a great pyramid for himself and his
treasures . . . but his wife is ambitious . . .
Unexpected, interesting excursion into
Ancient Egypt, distended by Cinemascope;
basically a macabre melodrama with a final
spectacular twist. The engineering details
would make a fascinating documentary.

w William Faulkner, Harry Kurnitz, H. Jack
Bloom *d* Howard Hawks *ph Lee Garmes,
Russell Harlan m Dmitri Tiomkin
ad Alexander Trauner*

Jack Hawkins, Joan Collins, Alexis Minotis, James Robertson Justice, Sidney Chaplin

'20,000 workers and technicians! 1,600 camels! 104 specially built barges! 9,753 players in one scene alone!'—*publicity*

'Her treachery stained every stone of the pyramid!'—*publicity*

The Land That Time Forgot*
GB 1974   91m   Technicolor
Amicus (John Dark)

In 1916, survivors from a torpedoed supply ship find themselves on a legendary island full of prehistoric monsters.
Lively old-fashioned adventure fantasy with good technical credits.

w James Cawthorne, Michael Moorcock, *novel* Edgar Rice Burroughs *d* Kevin Connor *ph* Alan Hume *m* Douglas Gamley *pd* Maurice Carter *sp* Derek Meddings, Roger Dicken

Doug McClure, John McEnery, Susan Penhaligon, Keith Barron, Anthony Ainley

The Land Unknown*
US 1957   78m   bw   Cinemascope
U-I (William Alland)

A plane is forced down into a strange Antarctic valley where dinosaurs still roam.
Efficient adventure fantasy on *King Kong* lines but without any of that film's panache.

w Laslo Gorog *d* Virgil Vogel *ph* Ellis Carter *m* Joseph Gershenson *sp* Roswell Hoffman, Fred Knoth, Orien Ernest, Jack Kevan

Jock Mahoney, Shawn Smith, William Reynolds, Henry Brandon

Land without Bread*
Spain 1932   27m   bw
Ramon Acin
aka: *Las Hurdes*

A famous documentary showing the poorest region of northern Spain, notable for some stunningly unpleasant images impeccably staged.

wd, ed Luis Bunuel *ph* Eli Lotar

Land without Music*
GB 1936   80m   bw
Capitol Films (Max Schach)
US title: *Forbidden Music*

The ruler of a Ruritanian country bans music because her subjects are too busy singing to make money. A revolutionary singer however wins the duchess's hand and reverses her decision.

Artless but attractively played operetta with the star in excellent form.

w Marian Dix, L. Du Garde Peach *d* Walter Forde *ph* John Boyle *m* Oscar Straus

Richard Tauber, Jimmy Durante, Diana Napier, June Clyde, Derrick de Marney, Esme Percy, George Hayes, Edward Rigby

Landfall
GB 1949   88m   bw
ABPC (Victor Skuzetzky)

A test pilot mistakenly believes that he accidentally sank a British submarine.
Second rate transcription of a popular novel.

w Talbot Jennings, Gilbert Gunn, Anne Burnaby, *novel* Nevil Shute *d* Ken Annakin

Michael Denison, Patricia Plunkett, Kathleen Harrison, David Tomlinson, Joan Dowling, Maurice Denham, A. E. Matthews, Margaretta Scott, Sebastian Shaw, Laurence Harvey

The Landlord*
US 1970   110m   De Luxe
United Artists / Mirisch / Carter (Norman Jewison)

A tycoon's son buys a tenement in Brooklyn's black ghetto, and conscience diverts him into improving the lot of his tenants.
Overlong satirical comedy, good on detail but short on structure.

w Bill Gunn, *novel* Kristin Hunter *d* Hal Ashby *ph* Gordon Willis *m* Al Kooper *pd* Robert Boyle

Beau Bridges, Lee Grant, Pearl Bailey, Diana Sands

'Bad taste from start to finish . . . not an avenue of offensiveness to any race is left unexplored.'—*Judith Crist*

AAN: Lee Grant

Landru
France / Italy 1962   115m   Eastmancolor
Rome-Paris / CC Champion (Carlo Ponti, Georges de Beauregard)
aka: *Bluebeard*

The true story of a furniture dealer who murdered women for financial gain, also treated by Chaplin in *Monsieur Verdoux*.

A curious artificial style has been adopted, making a tragi-comedy look like a farce which isn't very funny, and falls on very stony ground indeed despite the all star cast.

w Françoise Sagan *d* Claude Chabrol *ph* Jean Rabier *m* Pierre Jansen

Charles Denner, Michèle Morgan, Danielle Darrieux, Hildegarde Knef, Stéphane Audran, Catherine Rouvel

Larceny
US 1948 89m bw
Universal (Aaron Rosenberg)

A con man fleeces a war widow into paying for a memorial to her husband, but falls in love with her.

Drearily predictable melodrama.

w Herbert F. Margolis, Louis Markein, William Bowers novel The Velvet Fleece by Lois Ely, John Fleming d George Sherman ph Irving Glassberg m Leith Stevens

Joan Caulfield, John Payne, Dan Duryea, Shelley Winters, Dorothy Hart, Richard Rober, Dan O'Herlihy

Larceny Inc.
US 1942 95m bw
Warner (Jack Saper, Jerry Wald)

An ex-convict tries to rob a bank but finds that honesty pays best.

Tepid comedy-drama from the period when Warners were taming their gangster image.

w Everett Freeman, Edwin Gilbert, play The Night before Christmas by Laura and S. J. Perelman d Lloyd Bacon ph Tony Gaudio

Edward G. Robinson, Jane Wyman, Broderick Crawford, Anthony Quinn, Jack Carson, Edward Brophy, Harry Davenport, John Qualen, Barbara Jo Allen, Jackie Gleason, Grant Mitchell, Andrew Tombes

The Las Vegas Story
US 1952 88m bw
RKO (Robert Sparks)

When an investment broker and his new wife stop at Las Vegas, her shady past begins to emerge.

So-so programmer with some eccentric talents in average form, capped by a desert helicopter chase.

w Earl Felton, Harry Essex d Robert Stevenson ph Harry J. Wild m Constantin Bakaleinikoff

Jane Russell, Victor Mature, Vincent Price, Hoagy Carmichael, Colleen Miller, Brad Dexter, Jay C. Flippen

Lassie
The official Lassie series, made by MGM, was as follows:

1943: LASSIE COME HOME (qv)
1945: SON OF LASSIE (d S. Sylvan Simon with Peter Lawford, Donald Crisp, Nigel Bruce)
1946: COURAGE OF LASSIE (d Fred M. Wilcox with Elizabeth Taylor, Frank Morgan, Tom Drake)

1948: THE HILLS OF HOME[1] (d Fred M. Wilcox with Edmund Gwenn, Donald Crisp, Tom Drake)
1949: THE SUN COMES UP (d Richard Thorpe with Jeanette MacDonald, Lloyd Nolan)
1949: CHALLENGE TO LASSIE (d Richard Thorpe with Edmund Gwenn, Donald Crisp)
1951: THE PAINTED HILLS (d Harold F. Kress with Paul Kelly, Bruce Cowling)

† Later 'Lassie' features were taken from episodes of the long-running TV series.

[1](GB title: Master of Lassie)

Lassie Come Home*
US 1943 88m Technicolor
MGM (Samuel Marx)

A poor family is forced to sell its beloved dog, but she makes a remarkable journey to return to them.

First of the Lassie films and certainly the best: an old-fashioned heartwarmer.

w Hugo Butler, novel Eric Knight d Fred M. Wilcox ph Leonard Smith m Daniele Amfitheatrof

Roddy McDowall, Elizabeth Taylor, Donald Crisp, Edmund Gwenn, Dame May Whitty, Nigel Bruce, Elsa Lanchester, J. Pat O'Malley

'The late Eric Knight wrote this immortal essay in Doggery-Woggery. MGM finished it off.'—Richard Winnington

AAN: Leonard Smith

The Last Adventurers
GB 1937 77m bw

Adventures on board a fishing trawler. Acceptable low-budget outdoor drama. Niall MacGinnis, Linden Travers, Roy Emerton, Kay Walsh, Peter Gawthorne, Katie Johnson. Written by Denison Clift; directed by Roy Kellino; for Conway.

The Last American Hero*
US 1973 95m De Luxe Panavision
TCF / Wizan / Rojo (John Cutts, William Roberts)

The adventures of an illicit whisky distiller with a passion for fast cars.

Observant, amusing hillbilly comedy drama based on the early life of racing driver Junior Johnson.

w William Roberts d Lamont Johnson ph George Silano m Charles Fox

Jeff Bridges, Valerie Perrine, Geraldine Fitzgerald, Ned Beatty, Art Lund, Gary Busey † Reissue title: Hard Driver.

The Last Angry Man*
US 1959   100m   bw
Columbia (Fred Kohlmar)

An old doctor in a Brooklyn slum is made the subject of a TV documentary.
Self-confidently sentimental wallow which just about works.

w Gerald Green d Daniel Mann ph James Wong Howe m George Duning

Paul Muni, David Wayne, Betsy Palmer, Luther Adler, Dan Tobin, Robert F. Simon

AAN: Paul Muni

The Last Blitzkrieg
US 1959   84m   bw
Columbia / Sam Katzman

During the Battle of the Bulge a German leads a squad of American saboteurs.
Weakly pacifist, technically incompetent war adventure.

w Lou Morheim d Arthur Dreifuss ph Ted Scaife m Hugo de Groot

Van Johnson, Kerwin Mathews, Dick York, Larry Storch

The Last Bridge
Austria / Yugoslavia 1953   95m   bw
Cosmopol / UFUS (Carl Szokoll)

During World War II, a German nurse in Yugoslavia is captured by partisans and turns to their point of view.
Message melodrama, very ably put together with a bleakly tragic climax; but nothing at all new.

w Helmut Kautner, Norbert Kunze d Helmut Kautner ph Elio Carniel m Carl de Groof

Maria Schell, Bernhard Wicki, Barbara Rütting, Carl Möhner

The Last Chance*
Switzerland 1945   105m   bw
Praesens Film

In 1943 an Englishman and an American escape from a fascist camp in northern Italy and with the help of refugees cross the mountains into Switzerland.
Earnest propaganda piece which struck the spot at the time: cinematically rather plodding, but with some exciting scenes.

w Richard Schweitzer d Leopold Lindtberg ph Emil Berna m Robert Blum

E. G. Morrison, Ray Reagan, John Hoy, Luisa Rossi

The Last Command*
US 1955   110m   Trucolor
Republic (Frank Lloyd)

Jim Bowie returns to Texas in the 1830s and dies at the Alamo alongside other famous men.
Reasonably interesting western on a subject which has often figured but seldom worked.

w Warren Duff d Frank Lloyd ph Jack Marta m Max Steiner

Ernest Borgnine, Sterling Hayden, Anna Maria Alberghetti, Arthur Hunnicutt, Richard Carlson, J. Carrol Naish

The Last Days of Dolwyn*
GB 1949   95m   bw
London / BLPA (Anatole de Grunwald)
US title: *Woman of Dolwyn*

A Welsh valley is flooded to make a reservoir and a village has to be evacuated.
Interesting but rather stagey drama based on an actual 19th-century event, with personal melodrama added.

wd *Emlyn Williams* ph Otto Heller m John Greenwood

Edith Evans, Emlyn Williams, Richard Burton, Hugh Griffith, Barbara Couper, Allan Aynesworth

'The conventionally picturesque Welsh flavour and mounting probabilities apart, the treatment is stiff and episodic.'—*MFB*

The Last Days of Pompeii**
US 1935   96m   bw
RKO (Merian C. Cooper)

In ancient Pompeii, various personal dramas are submerged in the eruption of Vesuvius.
Starchy melodrama capped by a reel of spectacular disaster.

w Ruth Rose, Boris Ingster, *novel* Lord Lytton d Merian C. Cooper, Ernest Schoedsack ph Eddie Linden Jnr, J. Roy Hunt m Roy Webb sp *Vernon Walker, Harry Redmond*

Preston Foster, Basil Rathbone, Alan Hale, Dorothy Cooper

The Last Detail**
US 1973   104m   Metrocolor
Columbia / Acrobat / Persky–Bright (Gerald Ayres)

Two hardened naval petty officers escort a young recruit, sentenced for thieving, from Virginia to a New Hampshire jail, and give him a wild last night.
Foul-mouthed weekend odyssey, with a few well-observed moments for non-prudes.
Technically the epitome of Hollywood's most irritating seventies fashion, with fuzzy sound recording, dim against-the-light photography, and a general determination to show up the ugliness of everything around us.

w Robert Towne, *novel* Darryl Ponicsan
d Hal Ashby *ph* Michael Chapman
m Johnny Mandel

Jack Nicholson, Otis Young, Randy Quaid,
Clifton James, Carol Kane
  'Visually it is relentlessly lower-depths
gloomy, and the material, though often very
funny, is programmed to wrench your
heart.'—*New Yorker*

AAN: Robert Towne; Jack Nicholson; Randy
Quaid

The Last Dinosaur
US 1977   100m   colour
Rankin-Bass Productions

An oil-drilling team discovers a *tyrannosaurus
rex* while probing the polar oil-cap.
Inept monster saga with poorish special effects
from a Japanese team.

w William Overgard *d* Alex Grasshof, Tom
Kotani *ph* Shoshi Ueda *m* Maury Laws

Richard Boone, Joan Van Ark, Steven Keats

Last Embrace
US 1979   101m   Technicolor
UA (Michael Taylor, Dan Wigutow)

An investigator survives a number of attacks
on his life, though his wife is killed in the first
of them.
Hitchcockian mystery without the master's
zest or humour, though it leads to a pretty
exciting climax at Niagara Falls.

w David Shaber, *novel* The 13th Man by
Murray Teigh Bloom *d* Jonathan Demme
ph Tak Fujimoto *m* Miklos Rozsa

Roy Scheider, Janet Margolin, Sam Levene,
John Glover, Charles Napier, Christopher
Walken, Jacqueline Brookes
  'A case study of late seventies movie-
making which does everything in its power to
avoid taking risks.'—*John Pym, MFB*

The Last Flight°•••
US 1931   80m   bw
Warner

In 1919, four veteran American fliers stay on
in Paris in the hope of calming their shattered
physical and emotional states.
Fascinatingly offhand study on post-war
cynicism and the faint hope of a better world,
beautifully written and directed in a manner
more effective than *The Sun Also Rises*.

w *John Monk Saunders*, from his novel Single
Lady *d* William Dieterle *ph* Sid Hickox

Richard Barthelmess, Helen Chandler, David
Manners, John Mack Brown, *Elliott Nugent*,
Walter Byron

  'A narrative as tight and spare as a Racine
tragedy . . . unique in Hollywood of that time
in its persistent, calculated understatement.'—
Tom Milne, 1975

The Last Flight of Noah's Ark
US 1980   98m   Technicolor
Walt Disney

An impecunious pilot reluctantly flies an
orphanage worker and a cargo of animals
across the Pacific, only to be stranded with
them on a desert island.
It must have sounded like a good idea, but if it
was to work at all it needed much sharper
handling.

w Steven W. Carabatsos, Sandy Glass, George
Arthur Bloom, *story* The Gremlin's Castle by
Ernest K. Gann *d* Charles Jarrott *ph* Charles
F. Wheeler *m* Maurice Jarre

Elliott Gould, Geneviève Bujold, Ricky
Schroder, Tammy Lauren, Vincent Gardenia

The Last Gangster*
US 1937   81m   bw
MGM (J. J. Cohn)

A gangster is released from Alcatraz and plans
vengeance on his wife for deserting him.
Clean-cut star melodrama which suddenly
turns sentimental.

w John Lee Mahin *d* Edward Ludwig
ph William Daniels *montage Slavko
Vorkapitch*

Edward G. Robinson, Rose Stradner, James
Stewart, Lionel Stander, Douglas Scott, John
Carradine, Sidney Blackmer, Edward Brophy
  'A lot of water has flowed under the bridge
since *Little Caesar*, but Mr Robinson has
breasted the tides to make his impersonation
of a 1937 thug as persuasive as was his portrait
of a killer in that earlier classic of rats and
rackets.'—*Frank Nugent*

The Last Gentleman
US 1934   80m   bw

The career of a New England millionaire.
Pleasing star family drama. George Arliss,
Edna May Oliver, Ralph Morgan, Janet
Beecher, Charlotte Henry. Written by
Leonard Praskins; directed by Sidney
Lanfield; for Fox.

The Last Grenade
GB 1969   93m   Eastmancolor
Panavision
Cinerama / Dimitri de Grunwald / Josef
Shaftel

An army mercenary is betrayed by an ex-friend in the Congo and pursues him to Hong Kong.

Violent action melodrama with few redeeming qualities.

w Kenneth Ware, *novel* The Ordeal of Major Grigsby by John Sherlock d Gordon Flemyng ph Alan Hume m Johnny Dankworth

Stanley Baker, Alex Cord, Honor Blackman, Richard Attenborough, Rafer Johnson, Andrew Keir, Ray Brooks, Julian Glover, John Thaw

The Last Hard Men

US 1976   97m   De Luxe   Panavision
TCF / Belasco–Seltzer–Thatcher

A train robber breaks jail and sets out to revenge himself on the now-retired lawman who committed him.

Tough action adventure without much sense except to paint the end of the golden days of the west.

w Guerdon Trueblood, *novel* Gun Down by Brian Garfield d Andrew V. McLaglen ph Duke Callaghan m Jerry Goldsmith

Charlton Heston, James Coburn, Barbara Hershey, Christopher Mitchum, Michael Parks, Jorge Rivero, Thalmus Rasulala

'Script and direction seem equally tired.'—*Sight and Sound*

'The action proceeds slackly from one setpiece shoot-up to the next, barely providing the voltage for the two leads to expand their stereotyped roles into displays of star power.'—*Richard Combs, MFB*

Last Holiday*

GB 1950   88m   bw
ABPC / Watergate (Stephen Mitchell, A. D. Peters, J. B. Priestley)

A man with a short time to live has a thoroughly enjoyable and useful final fling.

Slight, amusing and moving comedy drama spoiled by an unnecessary double twist.

w J. B. Priestley d Henry Cass ph Ray Elton m Francis Chagrin

Alec Guinness, Kay Walsh, Beatrice Campbell, Grégoire Aslan, Bernard Lee, Wilfrid Hyde White, Helen Cherry, Sidney James, Muriel George

The Last Hunt*

US 1955   103m   Eastmancolor
   Cinemascope
MGM (Dore Schary)

Buffalo hunters fall out with each other.

Terse, brutish outdoor western with something

to say about old western myths and a famous ending in which the bad guy freezes to death while waiting to gun down the hero.

wd Richard Brooks ph Russell Harlan m Daniele Amfitheatrof

Stewart Granger, Robert Taylor, Debra Paget, Lloyd Nolan, Russ Tamblyn, Constance Ford

The Last Hurrah***

US 1958   125m   bw
Columbia (John Ford)

The political boss of a New England town fights his last campaign.

Enjoyable if disjointed melodrama, an old man's film crammed with cameo performances from familiar faces: important as one of Hollywood's great sentimental reunions.

w Frank Nugent, *novel* Edwin O'Connor d John Ford ph Charles Lawton Jnr

Spencer Tracy, Jeffrey Hunter, Dianne Foster, *Pat O'Brien, Basil Rathbone, Edward Brophy, Donald Crisp, James Gleason, John Carradine, Ricardo Cortez, Wallace Ford, Frank McHugh,* Frank Albertson, Anna Lee, Jane Darwell, Willis Bouchey, Basil Ruysdael

† A TV version was subsequently made with Carroll O'Connor.

The Last Journey*

GB 1935   66m   bw
Twickenham (Julius Hagen)

The driver of an express train, driven mad with jealousy, goes berserk.

Workmanlike little train suspenser with an exciting climax.

w John Soutar, H. Fowler Mear, *story* J. Jefferson Farjeon d Bernard Vorhaus

Godfrey Tearle, Hugh Williams, Julien Mitchell, Judy Gunn, Nelson Keys, Frank Pettingell, Olga Lindo, Sydney Fairbrother

The Last Laugh***

Germany 1924   73m approx (24 fps)
   bw   silent
UFA
original title: *Der Letzte Mann*

The old doorman of a luxury hotel is given the job of lavatory attendant but comes into a fortune and gets his revenge.

Ironic anecdote made important by its virtual abandonment of dialogue and whole-hearted adoption of the camera eye technique which gives some thrilling dramatic effects.

w Carl Mayer d F. W. Murnau ph Karl Freund

Emil Jannings, Max Hiller, Maly Delschaft, Hans Unterkirchen

'A marvellous picture—marvellous in its simplicity, its economy of effect, its expressiveness, and its dramatic power.'— *Life*

† A German remake of 1955 had Hans Albers in the lead and was of no interest.

The Last Married Couple in America
US 1979   102m   Technicolor
Universal / Cates Brothers

A Los Angeles couple resist the efforts of their friends to involve them in the swinging life.
Tolerable sex comedy of modern mores, a shade too long delayed after *Bob and Carol and Ted and Alice*.

w John Herman Shaner *d* Gilbert Cates *ph* Ralph Woolsey *m* Charles Fox *pd* Gene Callahan

Natalie Wood, George Segal, Richard Benjamin, Arlene Golonka, Arlan Arbus, Marilyn Sokol, Dom DeLuise, Valerie Harper

The Last Mile*
US 1932   84m   bw
World Wide (E. W. Hammons)

Tensions mount in jail as the execution of Killer Mears approaches.
Strident melodrama which works up quite a head of hysteria.

w Seton I. Miller, *play* John Wexley *d* Sam Bischoff *ph* Arthur Edeson

Preston Foster, Howard Phillips, George E. Stone, Noel Madison

The Last Mile
US 1959   81m   bw
UA / Vanguard (Milton Subotsky)

Even more hysterical remake, retaining the original period. A cheerless, though literally electrifying, entertainment.

w Milton Subotsky, Seton I. Miller *d* Howard W. Koch *ph* Joseph Brun *m* Van Alexander

Mickey Rooney, Clifford David, Frank Conroy, Frank Overton, Leon Janney

The Last Movie
US 1971   108m   Technicolor

Moviemakers go to Peru to film a western.
Muddled and pretentious melodrama following the success of *Easy Rider*. Dennis Hopper, Julie Adams, Rod Cameron, Daniel Ades, Michael Anderson Jnr. Written by Stewart Stern; directed by Dennis Hopper; for Universal.

The Last of Mrs Cheyney
US 1929   94m   bw
MGM

A confidence woman in British high society falls in love.
Old theatrical warhorse, much filmed but never very satisfactorily. (See below.)

w Hans Kraly, Claudine West, *play* Frederick Lonsdale *d* Sidney Franklin *ph* William Daniels

Norma Shearer, Basil Rathbone, George Barraud, Hedda Hopper, Maude Turner Gordon, Herbert Bunston

The Last of Mrs Cheyney
US 1937   98m   bw
MGM (Lawrence Weingarten)

Adequate, unexciting remake.

w Leon Gordon, Samson Raphaelson, Monckton Hoffe *d* Richard Boleslawski *ph* George Folsey *m* William Axt

Joan Crawford, Robert Montgomery, William Powell, Frank Morgan, Jessie Ralph, Nigel Bruce, Benita Hume, Melville Cooper, Sara Haden

† A further remake was *The Law and the Lady* (qv).

The Last of Sheila*
US 1973   123m   Technicolor
Warner (Herbert Ross)

A Hollywood star is killed by a hit-and-run driver; a year later her husband invites six friends to his yacht, and murders begin.
Confused, in-jokey showbiz whodunnit with flashes of interest.

w Stephen Sondheim, Anthony Perkins *d* Herbert Ross *ph* Gerry Turpin *m* Billy Goldenberg *ad* Ken Adam

Richard Benjamin, Dyan Cannon, James Coburn, James Mason, Joan Hackett, Ian MacShane, Raquel Welch

'The most teasing riddles for an audience are likely to be the real identities of the personalities being satirized.'—*MFB*

The Last of the Buccaneers
US 1950   79m   Technicolor

The story of Jean Lafitte, French privateer in the war of 1812. Cheerful low-budget swashbuckler. Paul Henreid, Jack Oakie, Karin Booth, Edgar Barrier, Mary Anderson, John Dehner. Written by Robert E. Kent; directed by Lew Landers; for Columbia.

The Last of the Comanches*
US 1953   85m   Technicolor
Columbia (Buddy Adler)
GB title: *The Sabre and the Arrow*

Survivors of an Indian raid take refuge in an abandoned mission until help arrives.
Competent western remake of *Sahara* (which was a remake of *The Lost Patrol*).

w Kenneth Gamet *d* André de Toth
ph Charles Lawton Jnr *m* George Duning

Broderick Crawford, Barbara Hale, Lloyd Bridges, Martin Milner

Last of the Fast Guns
US 1959   82m   Eastmancolor
Cinemascope

Rival gunfighters form a friendship but fall out over their mission. Mildly unusual western programmer. Gilbert Roland, Jock Mahoney, Linda Cristal, Eduard Franz, Lorne Greene, Carl Benton Reid. Written by David P. Harmon; directed by George Sherman; for Universal-International.

The Last of the Mohicans
US 1936   91m   bw
Edward Small

Incidents during colonial America's French–Indian war.
Vigorous if rough-and-ready western, later remade (poorly) as *Last of the Redmen* and as a Canadian TV series.

w Philip Dunne, John Balderston, Paul Perez, Daniel Moore, *novel* James Fenimore Cooper
d George B. Seitz *ph* Robert Planck *m* Roy Webb

Randolph Scott, Binnie Barnes, Bruce Cabot, Henry Wilcoxon, Heather Angel, Hugh Buckler

Last of the Red Hot Lovers*
US 1972   98m   Technicolor
Paramount (Howard W. Koch)

A middle-aged fish restaurateur feels the need for an extra-marital spree.
Modest, plainly-filmed sex comedy from a reliable stable.

w Neil Simon, from his play *d* Gene Saks
ph Victor J. Kemper *m* Neal Hefti

Alan Arkin, Paula Prentiss, Sally Kellerman, Renée Taylor

Last of the Secret Agents
US 1966   90m   Technicolor

Two odd job men are recruited as spies.
Pratfall comedy featuring a briefly existing comedy double act. Marty Allen, Steve Rossi, John Williams, Nancy Sinatra, Lou Jacobi, Theo Marcuse, Sig Rumann. Written by Mel Tolkin; directed by Norman Abbott; for Paramount.

The Last Outpost*
US 1935   75m   bw
Paramount (E. Lloyd Sheldon)

A British officer is captured by the Kurds and freed by an adventurer whose wife he covets.
Patchy, unusual adventure story with good moments.

w Philip MacDonald, *story* F. Britten Austin
d Charles Barton, Louis Gasnier *ph* Theodor Sparkuhl

Cary Grant, Claude Rains, Gertrude Michael, Kathleen Burke, Colin Tapley, Akim Tamiroff, Billy Bevan, Jameson Thomas

'Half of it is remarkably good and half of it quite abysmally bad. One can even put one's finger on the joins.'—*Graham Greene*

The Last Page
GB 1952   84m   bw

A bookseller is framed for the death of a blackmailer. Curious English mystery with American stars. George Brent, Marguerite Chapman, Diana Dors, Raymond Huntley, Peter Reynolds, Eleanor Summerfield. Written by Frederick Knott, from a play by James Hadley Chase; directed by Terence Fisher; for Hammer-Lippert. (US title: *Manbait*.)

The Last Picture Show**
US 1971   118m   bw
Columbia / LPS / BDS (Stephen J. Friedman)

Teenage affairs in a small Texas town in 1951, ending with the hero's embarkation for Korea and the closing of the tatty cinema.
Penetrating nostalgia with over-emphasis on sex; the detail is the attraction.

w Larry McMurty, Peter Bogdanovich *d* Peter Bogdanovich *ph* Robert Surtees *m* original recordings *pd* Polly Platt

Timothy Bottoms, Jeff Bridges, Cybill Shepherd, Ben Johnson, Cloris Leachman, Ellen Burstyn

'The most important work by a young American director since *Citizen Kane*.'—*Paul D. Zimmerman*

'So many things in it are so good that I wish I liked it more.'—*Stanley Kauffmann*

AA: Ben Johnson; Cloris Leachman
AAN: best picture; script; Peter Bogdanovich (as director); Robert Surtees; Jeff Bridges; Ellen Burstyn

The Last Posse
US 1953   73m   bw

Members of a thief-catching posse fall out on the way and return in disgrace. Stumbling little western, a poor return to the star after *All the King's Men*. Broderick Crawford, John Derek, Wanda Hendrix, Charles Bickford. Written by Seymour and Connie Lee, Bennett and Kenneth Gamet; directed by Alfred Werker; for Columbia.

The Last Remake of Beau Geste
US 1977   85m   Technicolor
Universal (William S. Gilmore Jnr)

The Geste brothers find themselves in the Foreign Legion after the theft of the Blue Water sapphire.
Woebegone spoof of a romantic original, with most of the jokes totally irrelevant to the purpose and seldom at all funny.

w Marty Feldman, Chris J. Allen *d* Marty Feldman *ph* Gerry Fisher *m* John Morris

Marty Feldman, Michael York, Ann-Margret, Peter Ustinov, Trevor Howard, James Earl Jones, Henry Gibson, Terry-Thomas, Roy Kinnear, Spike Milligan, Hugh Griffith, Irene Handl

'A ragbag of a film which looks like nothing so much as a Monty Python extravaganza in which inspiration has run dry and the comic timing gone sadly awry.'—*Tom Milne, MFB*

The Last Run*
US 1971   92m   Metrocolor   Panavision
MGM (Carter de Haven)

An ex-Chicago gangster retired to a Portuguese fishing village undertakes one last fatal job.
Well-made, rather uninteresting downbeat melodrama.

w Alan Sharp *d* Richard Fleischer *ph* Sven Nykvist *m* Jerry Goldsmith

George C. Scott, Tony Musante, Trish Van Devere

The Last Safari
GB 1967   110m   Technicolor
Paramount (Henry Hathaway)

A disillusioned white hunter takes on one last safari.
Dullsville adventure story with good animal photography redeeming some of the clichés.

w John Gay, *novel* Gilligan's Last Elephant by Gerald Hanley *d* Henry Hathaway *ph* Ted Moore *m* Johnny Dankworth

Stewart Granger, Kaz Garas, Gabriella Licudi, Johnny Sekka, Liam Redmond, Eugene Deckers

The Last Shot You Hear
GB 1970   90m   bw

Lovers plot murder, but the scheme backfires.
Unassuming mystery programmer from a West End success. Hugh Marlowe, Zena Walker, Patricia Haines, William Dysart, Thorley Walters. Written by Tim Shields, from the play *The Sound of Murder* by William Fairchild; directed by Gordon Hessler; for Lippert-TCF.

The Last Stage*
Poland 1947   110m   bw
Film Polski
original title: *Ostatni Etap*

Women suffer but one is finally rescued from the Nazi concentration camp at Auschwitz.
A dour, obsessive, horrifying record of human inhumanity, set in the actual camp and made by two former inmates.

w Wanda Jakubowska, Gerda Schneider *d* Wanda Jakubowska *ph* Borys Monastyrski *m* R. Palester

Huguette Faget, W. Bartowna, T. Gorecka

Last Summer*
US 1969   97m   Eastmancolor
Alsid / Francis (Alfred Crown, Sidney Beckerman)

Well-to-do teenagers have sexual adventures on a summer seaside holiday.
Striking off-beat melodrama with vividly sketched characters.

w Eleanor Perry, *novel* Evan Hunter *d* Frank Perry *ph* Gerald Hirschfeld *m* John Simon

Barbara Hershey, Richard Thomas, Bruce Davison, Cathy Burns, Ernesto Gonzales, Ralph Waite

AAN: Cathy Burns

The Last Sunset
US 1961   112m   Eastmancolor
U-I (Brynaprod) (Eugene Frenke, Edward Lewis)

A killer and his hunter learn a lot about each other before the final showdown.
Slow psycho-western with pretensions to tragedy.

w Dalton Trumbo, *novel* Showdown at Crazy Horse by Howard Rigsby *d* Robert Aldrich *ph* Ernest Laszlo *m* Ernest Gold

Rock Hudson, Kirk Douglas, Dorothy Malone, Carol Lynley, Joseph Cotten, Regis Toomey, Neville Brand

Last Tango in Paris*
France / Italy / US 1972   129m
Technicolor
Les Artistes Associés / PEA / UA (Alberto
Grimaldi)

A middle-aged man and a young French girl
have a doomed love affair.
Pretentious sex melodrama mainly notable for
being banned.

w Bernardo Bertolucci, Franco Arcalli
d Bernardo Bertolucci ph Vittorio Storaro
m Gato Barbieri

Marlon Brando, Maria Schneider, Jean-Pierre
Léaud
'An intense meditation on the realization of
mortality.'—Sight and Sound

AAN: Bernardo Bertolucci (as director);
Marlon Brando

The Last Time I Saw Archie
US 1961   98m   bw
UA / Mark VII / Manzanita / Talbot (Jack
Webb)

Adventures of a con man amid overage
civilian pilots at an army / air force base.
Patchy service comedy.

w William Bowers d Jack Webb ph Joe
MacDonald m Frank Comstock

Jack Webb, Robert Mitchum, Martha Hyer,
France Nuyen, Louis Nye, Jimmy Lydon,
Richard Arlen, Don Knotts, Robert Strauss,
Joe Flynn

The Last Time I Saw Paris
US 1954   116m   Technicolor
MGM (Jack Cummins)

A writer recalls his romance with a wealthy
American girl in Paris.
Dull romantic drama which very deadeningly
and predictably updates F. Scott Fitzgerald's
Babylon Revisited.

w Julius J. and Philip G. Epstein, Richard
Brooks d Richard Brooks ph Joseph
Ruttenberg m Conrad Salinger

Elizabeth Taylor, Van Johnson, Walter
Pidgeon, Donna Reed, Eva Gabor

Last Train from Gun Hill*
US 1959   98m   Technicolor   Vistavision
(Paramount) Hal B. Wallis / Bryna

A marshal tracks down the man who raped
and murdered his wife; it turns out to be the
son of an old friend.
Good suspense and action western culminating
in a *High Noon* situation.

w James Poe d John Sturges ph Charles Lang
Jnr m Dmitri Tiomkin

Kirk Douglas, Anthony Quinn, Earl
Holliman, Carolyn Jones, Brian Hutton

The Last Train from Madrid
US 1937   85m   bw
Paramount (George M. Arthur)

A variety of people escape the fighting in the
Spanish Civil War.
Tawdry topical melodrama with cliché
characters and situations.

w Louis Stevens, Robert Wyler d James
Hogan ph Harry Fischbeck md Boris Morros

Dorothy Lamour, Lew Ayres, Gilbert Roland,
Karen Morley, Lionel Atwill, Helen Mack,
Robert Cummings, Olympe Bradna, Anthony
Quinn, Lee Bowman, George Lloyd
'It is probably the worst film of the decade
and should have been the funniest.'—Graham
Greene
'Simply a topical and different background
for a glib little fiction.'—Frank S. Nugent

The Last Tycoon
US 1976   124m   Technicolor
Paramount / Academy / Sam Spiegel

The production head of a Hollywood studio in
the thirties has his troubles complicated when
he falls in love with a girl who reminds him of
his dead wife.
Astonishingly inept and boring big budget
all-star melodrama which doesn't even begin
promisingly (the scenes from supposed thirties
films are woefully inaccurate in style); it then
bogs down in interminable dialogue scenes,
leaving its famous cast all at sea.

w Harold Pinter, *novel* F. Scott Fitzgerald
d Elia Kazan ph Victor Kemper m Maurice
Jarre pd Eugene F. Callahan

Robert de Niro, Robert Mitchum, Tony
Curtis, Jeanne Moreau, Jack Nicholson, Ingrid
Boulting, Donald Pleasence, Ray Milland,
Dana Andrews, John Carradine
'So enervated it's like a vampire movie after
the vampires have left.'—New Yorker
'That the result is incoherent is no surprise;
that it is so hollow and visually graceless adds
a kind of wonder to the disappointment.'—
Sight and Sound
'The breathless reverence that informs the
movie kills it stone dead.'—Michael Billington,
Illustrated London News

The Last Valley
GB 1970   128m   Eastmancolor   Todd-
AO
ABC / Season / Seamaster (James Clavell)

In 1641 during the Thirty Years War a scholar
tries to defend a remote and prosperous Swiss
valley against a horde of mercenaries.

Big-scale historical action picture crammed
with pillage, torture, rape, death at the stake,
throat cutting and general carnage; reasonably
literate for all that, and convincingly set.

wd James Clavell, *novel* J. B. Pick
ph Norman Warwick *m* John Barry *ad* Peter
Mullins

Michael Caine, Omar Sharif, Florinda Bolkan,
Nigel Davenport, Per Oscarsson, Arthur
O'Connell, Brian Blessed

The Last Voyage*
US 1960   91m   Metrocolor
MGM / Andrew and Virginia Stone

A boiler room explosion causes an old
passenger liner to sink.
Spectacular if dramatically deficient actioner
for which a genuine liner (awaiting scrapping)
was sunk.

wd Andrew L. Stone ph Hal Mohr *m* Rudy
Schrager

Robert Stack, Dorothy Malone, Edmond
O'Brien, George Sanders, Woody Strode,
Jack Kruschen
    'A prolonged nerve stretcher.'—*MFB*

The Last Wagon
US 1956   99m   Eastmancolor
    Cinemascope
TCF (William B. Hawks)

A half breed wanted for murder joins an 1875
wagon train.
Heavy-going big-scale western.

w James Edward Grant, Delmer Daves, Gwen
Bagni *d* Delmer Daves *ph* Wilfrid Cline
m Lionel Newman

Richard Widmark, Felicia Farr, Tommy
Rettig, Susan Kohner, Ray Stricklyn, Nick
Adams, Carl Benton Reid

The Last Waltz
US 1978   115m   De Luxe
UA / Martin Scorsese, Jonathan Taplin

Rock documentary featuring the last concert
of The Band.
An occasion for specialists, very adequately
packaged.

d Martin Scorsese *pd* Boris Leven

The Last Warning*
US 1929   88m   bw
Universal

Murder backstage.
Shot as a silent film, with sound hurriedly
added, this remains a stylish comedy-thriller
with all the familiar ingredients of the
whodunnit.

w Alfred A. Cohn *d* Paul Leni *ph* Hal Mohr

Laura La Plante, Montagu Love, Roy D'Arcy,
John Boles, Mack Swain, Slim Summerville,
Margaret Livingston
† Remade in 1938 as *The House of Fear*, a
William Gargan second feature.

The Last Warning
US 1938   62m   bw
Universal

A private eye mystery.
Better-than-average second feature.

w Edmund L. Hartmann, *novel* The Dead
Don't Care by Jonathan Latimer *d* Albert S.
Rogell

Preston Foster, Joyce Compton, Frank Jenks

The Last Wave*
Australia 1977   106m   Atlab
(UA) Ayer / MacElroy / Derek Power

During a spell of freak weather, a lawyer has
recurrent dreams which give him the key to an
Aborigine prophecy about the world being
destroyed by flood . . .
Curious supernatural drama successfully
played as a mystery, with excellent
atmosphere and special effects.

w Peter Weir, Tony Morphett, Petru Popescu
d Peter Weir *ph* Russell Boyd *m* Charles
Wain *pd* Goran Warff

Richard Chamberlain, Olivia Hamnet,
Frederick Parslow

    'A Hitchcockian sense of minatory
dislocation.'—*Tim Pulleine, MFB*

The Last Word
US 1979   105m   colour

An Irish inventor by wily stratagems prevents
the demolition of the apartment block he
occupies. Oddly old-fashioned comedy drama
of little obvious appeal. Richard Harris, Karen
Black, Martin Landau, Biff McGuire. Written
by Michael Varhol, Greg Smith and Kit
Carson; directed by Roy Boulting; for Variety
International Pictures.

Last Year in Marienbad**
France / Italy 1961   94m   bw   Dyaliscope
Terra / Tamara / Cormoran / Precitel /
    Como / Argos / Cinetel / Silver / Cineriz

In a vast old-fashioned hotel, a man meets a
woman who may or may not have had an affair
with him the previous year in Marienbad—or
was it Frederiksbad?
A dreamy, elegant film which presents a
puzzle with no solution. It has its attractions
for film buffs and cryptogram addicts, but is
not for anyone who simply wants to be told a
story.

*w Alain Robbe-Grillet d Alain Resnais
ph* Sacha Vierny *m* Francis Seyrig
ad Jacques Saulnier

Delphine Seyrig, Giorgio Albertazzi, Sacha Pitoeff

'Clearly the film's creators know exactly what they want to do and have done it with complete success. Whether one responds to the result is entirely a matter of temperament.'—*John Russell Taylor, MFB*

AAN: Alain Robbe-Grillet

The Late Edwina Black*

GB 1951 78m bw
IFD / Elvey–Gartside
US title: *Obsessed*

When a schoolteacher's wife is found dead, the police have three suspects.
Adequately suspenseful Victorian thriller from a successful play.

w Charles Frank, David Evans, *play* William Dinner, William Morum *d* Maurice Elvey
ph Stephen Dade *m* Allan Gray

Geraldine Fitzgerald, David Farrar, *Roland Culver*, Jean Cadell, Mary Merrall, Harcourt Williams, Charles Heslop, Ronald Adam

The Late George Apley*

US 1946 96m bw
TCF (Fred Kohlmar)

The uneventful family life of a Boston blueblood.
Pleasant but tame family comedy-drama, solidly carpentered.

w Philip Dunne, *novel* John P. Marquand
d Joseph L. Mankiewicz *ph* Joseph La Shelle
m Cyril Mockridge

Ronald Colman, Edna Best, Vanessa Brown, Richard Haydn, Peggy Cummins, Charles Russell

The Late Show*

US 1977 93m Metrocolor
Warner (Robert Altman)

An ageing private eye in Los Angeles finds that his ex-partner's death and a lost cat have a complex connection.
A more-or-less engaging spoof of, or perhaps a valediction to, the private eye genre, with engaging scenes marred by poor colour and occasional excesses of violent action.

wd Robert Benton *ph* Chuck Rosher *m* Ken Wannberg

Art Carney, Lily Tomlin, Bill Macy, Ruth Nelson, Howard Duff, Joanna Cassidy, Eugene Roche

'On its own terms, it's perfectly executed. The squalid settings stink of decay; the spare pacing captures the tough style of Hammett prose; and the stylized use of blood puts some sting into murder.'—*Frank Rich, New York Post*

AAN: Robert Benton

Latin Lovers

US 1953 104m Technicolor
MGM (Joe Pasternak)

An heiress on holiday in Brazil looks for a man who will love her for herself alone.
Barren romantic drama, flatfooted and drawn out.

w Isobel Lennart *d* Mervyn Le Roy
ph Joseph Ruttenberg *m* George Stoll

Lana Turner, Ricardo Montalban, John Lund, Louis Calhern, Jean Hagen

Latin Quarter*

GB 1945 80m bw
British National
US title: *Frenzy*

In nineties Paris a mad sculptor murders his fiancée and hides her inside his latest exhibit. Artificial-looking but melodramatically effective thriller with a chilling climax and a detailed Dégas-period background.

wd Vernon Sewell *ph* Gunther Krampf, *play* l'Angoisse by Pierre Mills, Charles Vylars

Derrick de Marney, Joan Greenwood, Beresford Egan, Frederick Valk, Lily Kann, Martin Miller

Laugh with Max Linder**

France 1963 88m bw
Films Max Linder
original title: *En Compagnie de Max Linder*

Excerpts from three of the dapper comedian's most famous American comedies: *Be My Wife* (1921), *The Three Must Get Theres* (1922), *Seven Years' Bad Luck* (1923)
A compilation which must serve as a consensus of this almost forgotten comedian's work. The gag with a broken mirror in particular was borrowed by innumerable other comedians, notably the Marx Brothers in *Duck Soup*. Audiences new to Linder's work will find him not especially sympathetic but capable of many felicities. He wrote, produced and directed all three films.

compiler Maud Max Linder

Laughing Anne

GB 1953 90m Technicolor
Republic / Wilcox–Neagle

French Anne and her boxing lover are
characters of the Javanese waterfront; he kills
her after she has fallen for a sea captain.
Cheap and turgid adaptation of a Joseph
Conrad story; the author would not recognize
it. Studio settings put the lid on hilariously bad
work all round.

w Pamela Bower d Herbert Wilcox ph Max
Greene m Anthony Collins

Margaret Lockwood, Forrest Tucker, Ronald
Shiner, Wendell Corey, Robert Harris

Laughing Boy
US 1934 80m bw

A young Navajo brave marries an outcast
maiden. Misguided and absurd melodrama for
unsuitable stars. Ramon Novarro, Lupe Velez,
Chief Thunderbird, William Davidson.
Written by John Colton and John Lee Mahin,
from a novel by Oliver La Farge; directed by
W. S. Van Dyke; for MGM.

Laughing Gravy***
US 1931 20m bw

Stan and Ollie retrieve their dog when the
landlord throws it out into the snow. One of
the most endearing comedies of these stars,
and one of the simplest. Laurel and Hardy,
Charlie Hall. Written by H. M. Walker;
directed by James W. Horne; for Hal Roach.

The Laughing Policeman*
US 1973 112m De Luxe
TCF (Stuart Rosenberg)
GB title: An Investigation of Murder

A mad machine-gunner eludes the San
Francisco police.
Downbeat, semi-documentary police thriller
with pretensions. Too complex by half, with
an overplus of characterization, but the
location work is excellent.

w Thomas Rickman, novel Maj Sjowall, Per
Wahloo d Stuart Rosenberg ph David
Walsh m Charles Fox

Walter Matthau, Bruce Dern, Lou Gossett,
Albert Paulsen, Anthony Zerbe

Laughing Sinners
US 1931 71m bw

A girl with a past joins the Salvation Army.
Glum romance which however started an
effective star combination. Joan Crawford,
Clark Gable, Neil Hamilton, Marjorie
Rambeau, Guy Kibbee. Written by Bess
Meredyth and Martin Flavin; directed by
Harry Beaumont; for MGM.

Laughter**
US 1930 99m bw
Paramount (Herman J. Mankiewicz)

An ex-Follies girl marries a millionaire but
later goes on a spree with the composer she
once loved.
Sharply observed, before its time romantic
comedy reminiscent now of the later
Philadelphia Story in its attitudes to wealth
and love. A precursor of the smart crazy
comedies of the mid-thirties.

w Donald Ogden Stewart d Harry d'Abbabie
d'Arrast ph George Folsey

Fredric March, Nancy Carroll, Frank Morgan,
Glen Anders, Diane Ellis
  'One of the best talking pictures I have ever
seen.'—James Agate
  'A talkie with so fast a pace that it crowds
the comprehension of half the customers . . .
marked at intervals by superb dialogue and the
quick hand of a smart director.'—Pare Lorentz
  'A lovely sophisticated comedy.'—New
Yorker, 1977

AAN: Donald Ogden Stewart

Laughter in Paradise*
GB 1951 93m bw
ABPC (Mario Zampi)

An eccentric leaves in his will a fortune for
each of his relations providing they will
perform certain embarrassing or criminal acts.
A funny idea gets half-hearted treatment, but
the good bits are hilarious.

w Michael Pertwee, Jack Davies d Mario
Zampi ph William McLeod m Stanley Black

Alastair Sim, Joyce Grenfell, Hugh Griffith,
Fay Compton, John Laurie, George Cole,
Guy Middleton, Ronald Adam, Leslie Dwyer,
A. E. Matthews, Beatrice Campbell
† Remade 1972 as Some Will, Some Won't.

Laughter in the Dark*
GB / France 1969 104m De Luxe
UA / Woodfall / Winkast / Marceau (Neil
Hartley)

A wealthy art dealer is taken in by an
ambitious usherette and her lover, and after
being blinded in a car accident tries to kill
them.
Unsatisfactory adaptation of a novel with a
very specialized appeal: conventional swinging
London and Riviera settings only confuse the
spectator. Moments do work, though.

w Edward Bond, novel Vladimir Nabokov
d Tony Richardson ph Dick Bush
m Raymond Leppard ad Julia Trevelyan
Oman

Nicol Williamson, Anna Karina, Jean-Claude Drouot, Peter Bowles, Sian Phillips

'It fails to create the slightest interest in its trio of repulsive characters.'—*Philip Strick*

Laura****
US 1944 85m bw
TCF (Otto Preminger)

A beautiful girl is murdered . . . or is she? A cynical detective investigates.

A quiet, streamlined little murder mystery that brought a new adult approach to the genre and heralded the mature *film noir* of the later forties. A small cast responds perfectly to a classically spare script, and in Clifton Webb a new star is born.

w Jay Dratler, Samuel Hoffenstein, Betty Reinhardt, novel Vera Caspary d Otto Preminger ph Joseph La Shelle m David Raksin

Dana Andrews, Clifton Webb, Gene Tierney, Judith Anderson, *Vincent Price*, Dorothy Adams, James Flavin

'Everybody's favourite chic murder mystery.'—*New Yorker, 1977*

† Rouben Mamoulian directed some scenes before handing over to Preminger.

AA: Joseph La Shelle
AAN: script; Otto Preminger; Clifton Webb

The Laurel and Hardy Murder Case
US 1930 30m bw

Heirs to a fortune are menaced by a mad murderer. Empty spoof on *The Cat and the Canary* which affords little scope to Laurel and Hardy. Written by H. M. Walker; directed by James Parrott; for Hal Roach.

Laurel and Hardy's Laughing Twenties**
US 1965 90m bw
MGM / Robert Youngson

Excerpts from lesser comedians of the period—Max Davidson, Charlie Chase—are interspersed with highlights from Laurel and Hardy's silent two reelers.

A hilarious and craftsmanlike compilation, perhaps a little too long for its own good.

w, ed Robert Youngson commentator Jay Jackson *m* Skeets Alquist

† Films extracted include *Putting Pants on Philip, From Soup to Nuts, Wrong Again, The Finishing Touch, Liberty, Double Whoopee, Leave 'Em Laughing, You're Darn Tooting* and the custard pie climax from *The Battle of the Century*.

The Lavender Hill Mob****
GB 1951 78m bw
Ealing (Michael Truman)

A timid bank clerk conceives and executes a bullion robbery.

Superbly characterized and inventively detailed comedy, one of the best ever made at Ealing or in Britain.

w T. E. B. Clarke d Charles Crichton ph Douglas Slocombe m Georges Auric

Alec Guinness, Stanley Holloway, Sidney James, Alfie Bass, Marjorie Fielding, Edie Martin, John Gregson, Gibb McLaughlin

'Amusing situations and dialogue are well paced and sustained throughout: the climax is delightful.'—*MFB*

AA: T. E. B. Clarke
AAN: Alec Guinness

Law and Disorder*
GB 1958 76m bw
British Lion / Hotspur (Paul Soskin)

Crooks rally round a confederate about to be arrested, to prevent his son from learning of his father's real career.

Amusing, well-pointed caper on sub-Ealing lines.

w T. E. B. Clarke, novel Smuggler's Circuit by Denys Roberts *d* Charles Crichton *ph* Ted Scaife *m* Humphrey Searle

Michael Redgrave, Robert Morley, Joan Hickson, Lionel Jeffries, Ronald Squire, Elizabeth Sellars

Law and Disorder*
US 1975 102m Technicolor
Panavision
Memorial / Leroy Street / Ugo Fadsin
(William Richert)

New York suburbanites aghast at escalating violence form themselves into a vigilante patrol.

Bewilderingly uneven comedy drama which starts as satirical comedy and ends with one of the heroes dead and the other moralizing. Sporadically interesting, and certainly topical.

w Ivan Passer, William Richert, Kenneth Harris Fishman *d* Ivan Passer *ph* Arthur J. Ornitz *m* Andy Badale

Ernest Borgnine, Carroll O'Connor, Karen Black, Ann Wedgeworth, Leslie Ackerman, David Spielberg

The Law and Jake Wade*
US 1958 86m Metrocolor
Cinemascope
MGM (William Hawks)

A marshal helps an old outlaw friend to escape from jail, and lives to regret it.

Good standard western, enjoyable throughout but with no outstanding merits.

w William Bowers *d* John Sturges *ph* Robert Surtees

Robert Taylor, Richard Widmark, Patricia Owens, Robert Middleton, Henry Silva

Law and Order*
US 1932 80m bw

A cowboy becomes marshal and cleans up Tombstone. Drily effective fictionalization of Wyatt Earp's exploits, with a good star performance. *Walter Huston,* Harry Carey, Raymond Hatton, Russell Simpson, Russell Hopton. Written by *John Huston,* from the novel *Saint Johnson* by W. R. Burnett; directed by Edward L. Cahn; for Universal.

Law and Order
US 1953 80m Technicolor

Curious belated sequel to the above with Johnson moving on to tame Cottonwood; actual presentation rather dull. Ronald Reagan, Dorothy Malone, Preston Foster, Alex Nicol, Russell Johnson. Written by John and Gwen Bagni and D. D. Beauchamp; directed by Nathan Juran; for Universal-International.

The Law and the Lady
US 1951 104m bw
MGM (Edwin H. Knopf)

A couple of confidence tricksters inveigle themselves into the house of a vulgar millionairess, but one of them has an attack of conscience.

Dreary remake of *The Last of Mrs Cheyney* (qv) with the locale altered, the plot simplified, and the level of wit diluted.

w Leonard Spiegelgass, Karl Tunberg *d* Edwin H. Knopf *ph* George Folsey *m* Carmen Dragon

Greer Garson, Michael Wilding, Fernando Lamas, Marjorie Main, Hayden Rorke, Margalo Gillmore, Ralph Dumke

Law of the Lawless
US 1963 87m Techniscope
Paramount / A. C. Lyles

A judge arrives in a small western town to conduct the murder trial of a former friend. Jaded western of interest only for the producer's custom of packing the bit roles with former stars.

w Steve Fisher *d* William F. Claxton *ph* Lester Shorr

Dale Robertson, Yvonne de Carlo, William Bendix, Bruce Cabot, Barton MacLane, John Agar, Richard Arlen, Kent Taylor, Lon Chaney Jnr

Law of the Tropics
US 1941 76m bw
Warner (Ben Stoloff)

A café singer on the run from a murder charge marries a South American rubber plantation owner.

Hackneyed melodrama born from a mating of *Oil for the Lamps of China* and *Tropic Zone.*

w Charles Grayson *d* Ray Enright *ph* Sid Hickox *m* Howard Jackson

Constance Bennett, Jeffrey Lynn, Regis Toomey, Mona Maris, Frank Puglia, Thomas Jackson, Craig Stevens

The Lawless
US 1949 83m bw
Paramount / Pine–Thomas
GB title: *The Dividing Line*

The editor of a California small-town newspaper defends a Spanish boy who is being victimized by the racist element.

Well-meaning 'realistic' melodrama, unfortunately among the dullest of the socially conscious movies of this period.

w Geoffrey Homes *d* Joseph Losey *ph* Roy Hunt *m* Mahlon Merrick

Macdonald Carey, Gail Russell, John Sands, John Hoyt, Lee Patrick, Lalo Rios

The Lawless Breed
US 1952 83m Technicolor
U-I (William Alland)

The adventures and repentance of badman John Wesley Hardin.

Standard western programmer with the star in an unlikely role.

w Bernard Gordon *d* Raoul Walsh *ph* Irving Glassberg *m* Joseph Gershenson

Rock Hudson, Julie Adams, John McIntire, Dennis Weaver, Hugh O'Brian

A Lawless Street
US 1955 78m Technicolor
Columbia (Harry Joe Brown)

A marshal marries a dance hall entertainer, and loses interest in his job when she leaves him.

Enjoyable minor western.

w Kenneth Gamet, *novel* Marshal of Medicine Bend by Brad Ward *d* Joseph H. Lewis *ph* Ray Rennahan *m* Paul Sawtell

Randolph Scott, Angela Lansbury, Warner Anderson, Jean Parker, Wallace Ford, John Emery, James Bell, Ruth Donnelly, Michael Pate, Jeanette Nolan, Don Megowan

Lawman*
US 1970 99m Technicolor
UA / Scimitar (Michael Winner)

When a marshal tracks down drunken cowboys who have killed an old man, the townsfolk's resistance leads to a bloodbath.
Terse, violent western with a good cast.

w Gerald Wilson d Michael Winner ph Bob Paynter m Jerry Fielding

Burt Lancaster, Robert Ryan, Lee J. Cobb, Sheree North, Robert Duvall, Joseph Wiseman, John McGiver, Albert Salmi, J. D. Cannon

Lawrence of Arabia***
GB 1962 221m Technicolor Super Panavision 70
Columbia / Horizon (Sam Spiegel)

An adventurer's life with the Arabs, told in flashbacks after his accidental death in the thirties.
Sprawling epic which manages after four hours to give no insight whatever into the complexities of character of this mysterious historic figure, but is often spectacularly beautiful and exciting along the way.

w Robert Bolt d David Lean ph Frederick A. Young m Maurice Jarre pd John Box ad John Stoll

Peter O'Toole, Omar Sharif, Arthur Kennedy, Jack Hawkins, Donald Wolfit, Claude Rains, Anthony Quayle, Alec Guinness, Anthony Quinn, Jose Ferrer, Michel Ray, Zia Mohyeddin

'Grandeur of conception is not up to grandeur of setting.'—Penelope Houston

'Lean has managed to market epics as serious entertainment rather than as the spectacles they are.'—Time Out, 1980

AA: best picture; David Lean; Frederick A. Young; Maurice Jarre
AAN: Robert Bolt; Peter O'Toole; Omar Sharif

The Lawyer*
US 1970 120m Technicolor
Paramount (Brad Dexter)

An ambitious young Italian-American defence lawyer takes on a murder case.
Smartly-scripted, perfectly ordinary courtroom drama in a well-detailed western setting. The star subsequently played the same character in a TV series, Petrocelli.

w Sidney J. Furie, Harold Buchman d Sidney J. Furie ph Ralph Woolsey m Malcolm Dodds

Barry Newman, Harold Gould, Diana Muldaur, Robert Colbert, Kathleen Crowley, Booth Colman

Lawyer Man
US 1932 68m bw
Warner

An honest lawyer becomes corrupted by success.
Smart, cynical melodrama, dated but sufficiently fast-paced to remain interesting.

w Rian James, James Seymour, novel Max Trell d William Dieterle ph Robert Kurrle

William Powell, Joan Blondell, Helen Vinson, Alan Dinehart, Allen Jenkins, David Landau, Claire Dodd

Laxdale Hall
GB 1952 77m bw
Group Three (Alfred Shaughnessy)
US title: Scotch on the Rocks

MPs are sent to investigate a tiny Hebridean island which refuses to pay road tax.
Thin rehash of Whisky Galore put together without the Ealing style. Minor compensations can be found.

w John Eldridge, Alfred Shaughnessy d John Eldridge ph Arthur Grant m Frank Spencer

Raymond Huntley, Ronald Squire, Sebastian Shaw, Fulton Mackay, Kathleen Ryan, Kynaston Reeves

Le Mans*
US 1971 108m De Luxe Panavision
Solar / Cinema Center (Jack N. Reddish)

A sullen American enters for the 24-hour race.
Almost no plot and little documentary examination; what's left is a multitude of racing shots with Steve McQueen at the wheel.
For some this may be enough.

w Harry Kleiner d Lee H. Katzin ph Robert B. Hauser, René Gruissart Jnr m Michel Legrand

Steve McQueen, Siegfried Rauch, Elga Andersen, Ronald Leigh-Hunt

The League of Gentlemen***
GB 1960 112m bw
Rank / Allied Film Makers (Michael Relph)

An ex-army officer recruits high-class misfits with guilty secrets to help him in a bank robbery.
Delightfully handled comedy adventure, from the days (alas) when crime did not pay; a lighter ending would have made it a classic.

w Bryan Forbes, novel John Boland *d Basil
Dearden ph* Arthur Ibbetson *m* Philip Green

Jack Hawkins, Richard Attenborough, *Roger
Livesey, Nigel Patrick*, Bryan Forbes, Kieron
Moore, Terence Alexander, *Norman Bird*,
Robert Coote, Melissa Stribling, Nanette
Newman, Gerald Harper, Patrick Wymark,
David Lodge, Doris Hare, Lydia Sherwood

Lease of Life°
GB 1954   94m   Eastmancolor
Ealing (Jack Rix)

A poor clergyman is given a year to live, and
puts it to good use.
Somewhat depressing but well-acted drama
with excellent village atmosphere.

w Eric Ambler *d* Charles Frend *ph* Douglas
Slocombe *m* Alan Rawsthorne

Robert Donat, Kay Walsh, Adrienne Corri,
Denholm Elliott

The Leather Boys°
GB 1963   108m   bw   Cinemascope
British Lion / Garrick (Raymond Stross)

Two working-class teenagers marry for sex;
she becomes a drudge and he develops a
relationship with a homosexual motorcyclist.
Sharply-observed slice of low life which now
seems quite dated, the central figures no
longer being of the 'heroic' interest given them
at the time. Technically the film is tediously
and fashionably flashy.

w Gillian Freeman, *novel* Elliot George
d Sidney J. Furie *ph* Gerald Gibbs *m* Bill
McGuffie

Rita Tushingham, Dudley Sutton, Colin
Campbell, Gladys Henson

The Leather Saint
US 1955   86m   bw   Vistavision
Paramount (Norman Retchin)

To provide his parish hospital with medical
equipment, a Catholic priest becomes a
commercial prizefighter.
Unlikely piece of religiosity, not too badly
done.

w Norman Retchin, Alvin Ganzer *d* Alvin
Ganzer *ph* Haskell Boggs *md* Irvin Talbot

Paul Douglas, John Derek, Cesar Romero,
Ernest Truex, Jody Lawrance

Leathernecking
US 1930   80m   bw (colour sequence)
RKO (Louis Sarecky)
GB title: *Present Arms*

A Honolulu socialite falls for a marine, but
grows cool when she discovers that he is a

private and not an officer as he pretended.
Curiously cast, spasmodically funny non-
musical version of a Rodgers and Hart
Broadway hit.

w Alfred Jackson, Jane Murfin, *play* Present
Arms by Herbert Fields, Rodgers and Hart
d Edward Cline *ph* J. Roy Hunt *m* Oscar
Levant

Irene Dunne (her first role), Ken Murray,
Eddie Foy Jnr, Louise Fazenda, Ned Sparks,
Lilyan Tashman

Leave 'Em Laughing°
US 1928   20m   bw   silent

Stan has toothache, visits the dentist, and
accidentally causes all concerned to inhale an
overdose of laughing gas. The earlier
sequences are only mildly funny, but the
laughing finale is irresistible. Laurel and
Hardy, Edgar Kennedy, Charlie Hall. Written
by Hal Roach and Reed Heustis; directed by
Clyde Bruckman; for Hal Roach.

Leave Her to Heaven
US 1945   111m   Technicolor
TCF (William A. Bacher)

A selfish, jealous woman causes unhappiness
for those around her, even in her suicide.
No-holds-barred melodrama of the old school;
what seemed lush production at the time now
looks tatty.

w Jo Swerling, *novel* Ben Ames Williams
d John M. Stahl *ph* Leon Shamroy *m* Alfred
Newman

Gene Tierney, Cornel Wilde, Jeanne Crain,
Vincent Price, Mary Phillips, Ray Collins,
Gene Lockhart, Reed Hadley, Chill Wills

'The story's central idea might be plausible
enough in a dramatically lighted black and
white picture . . . but in the rich glare of
Technicolor, all its rental library
characteristics are doubly glaring.'—*James
Agee*
'The sum total of all human emotion!'—
publicity

AA: Leon Shamroy
AAN: Gene Tierney

Leaves from Satan's Book°
Denmark 1919   80m approx (24 fps)
  bw   silent
Nordisk

Episodes from the activities of Satan through
the ages: with Christ, the Inquisition, the
French Revolution and the Russian
Revolution.
Vaguely propagandist short-story compilation
with effective moments.

w Edgar Hoyer, Carl Dreyer, *novel* The Sorrows of Satan by Marie Corelli *d* Carl Dreyer *ph* George Schneevoigt

The Left Hand of God
US 1955 87m De Luxe Cinemascope
TCF (Buddy Adler)

China, 1947: a Catholic priest newly arrived in a small village proves to be an American flier on the run from a warlord; but he contrives to work a small 'miracle'.
Hollywood religiosity at its most contrived, put together without distinction; the players have a wary look.

w Alfred Hayes, *novel* William E. Barrett *d* Edward Dmytryk *ph* Franz Planer *m* Victor Young

Humphrey Bogart, Gene Tierney, Lee J. Cobb, E. G. Marshall, Agnes Moorehead

The Left Handed Gun*
US 1958 102m bw
Warner / Haroll (Fred Coe)

Billy the Kid sets out to shoot four men who have killed his friend.
'Method'-oriented western, efficiently made but somewhat downcast.

w Leslie Stevens, *TV play* Gore Vidal *d* Arthur Penn *ph* Peverell Marley *m* Alexander Courage

Paul Newman, John Dehner, Lita Milan, Hurd Hatfield

Left Right and Centre*
GB 1959 95m bw
British Lion / Launder and Gilliat

A TV personality becomes Tory candidate at a by-election.
Scrappy political comedy with the saving grace of a large number of comic talents.

w Sidney Gilliat, Val Valentine *d* Sidney Gilliat *ph* Gerald Gibbs *m* Humphrey Searle

Ian Carmichael, Alastair Sim, Patricia Bredin, Richard Wattis, Eric Barker, Gordon Harker, George Benson, Frederick Leister

The Legacy
GB 1978 102m colour
Columbia / Pethurst / Turman-Foster (David Foster)

An American designer goes to stay with her employer and finds herself in the middle of an occult murder plot.
Cliché-ridden screamer which will please the easily pleased.

w Jimmy Sangster, Patrick Tilley, Paul Wheeler *d* Richard Marquand *ph* Dick Bush, Alan Hume *m* Michael J. Lewis

Katharine Ross, Sam Elliot, John Standing, Ian Hogg, Margaret Tyzack, Charles Gray, Lee Montague, Hildegard Neil

The Legend of Hell House*
GB 1973 94m De Luxe
TCF / Academy (James H. Nicholson)

Four people arrive at a haunted house in which several psychic investigators have been killed.
Harrowing thriller, a less solemn but more frightening version of *The Haunting*.

w Richard Matheson, from his novel *d* John Hough *ph* Alan Hume *m* Brian Hodgson, Delia Derbyshire

Pamela Franklin, Roddy McDowall, Clive Revill, Gayle Hunnicutt, Roland Culver, Peter Bowles, Michael Gough
'One of the most absorbing, goose-fleshing and mind-pleasing ghost breaker yarns on film.'—*Judith Crist, 1977*

The Legend of Lobo*
US 1962 67m Technicolor
Walt Disney (James Algar)

The life of a forest wolf.
Anthropomorphic entertainment in which a dreaded animal becomes something of a hero and finally saves his mate from bounty hunters. Impeccably contrived, like a live-action *Bambi*.

w Dwight Hauser, James Algar, *story* Ernest Thompson Seton *d* James Algar *ph* Jack Couffer, Lloyd Beebe *m* Oliver Wallace

The Legend of Lylah Clare*
US 1968 130m Metrocolor Panavision
MGM / Robert Aldrich

A mad director brings an unknown actress to Hollywood because of her resemblance to a former star, his creation, who had died mysteriously.
Unintentionally risible melodrama with echoes of *Svengali* and *Sunset Boulevard*; not to the public's taste, or anyone else's, in the late sixties.

w Hugo Butler, Jean Rouverol, *TV play* Robert Thom, Edward de Blasio *d* Robert Aldrich *ph* Joseph Biroc *m* Frank de Vol

Peter Finch, Kim Novak, Ernest Borgnine, Coral Browne, Milton Seltzer, Rossella Falk, Gabriele Tinti, Valentina Cortesa, George Kennedy

Legend of the Lost
US 1957 107m Technirama
UA / Batjac / Robert Haggiag / Dear (Henry Hathaway)

Two adventurers and a slave girl seek a lost city in the Sahara.
Tediously vague and underplotted desert adventure with a few attractive moments.

w Robert Presnell Jnr, Ben Hecht *d* Henry Hathaway *ph* Jack Cardiff *m* A. F. Lavagnino

John Wayne, Sophia Loren, Rossano Brazzi

The Legend of the Seven Golden Vampires

GB / Hong Kong 1974   89m
  Eastmancolor   Panavision
Hammer–Shaw (Don Houghton, Vee King Shaw)

In 1904 Chungking, Professor Van Helsing finds his old enemy Dracula behind a Chinese vampire cult.
Hectic, outlandish mix of Hammer horror and Kung Fu; plenty of gusto but not much sense.

w Don Houghton *d* Roy Ward Baker *ph* John Wilcox, Roy Ford *m* James Bernard

Peter Cushing, David Chiang, Julie Ege, Robin Stewart, John Forbes Robertson

The Legend of Tom Dooley

US 1959   77m   bw
Columbia / Shpetner

At the end of the Civil War, Confederate youths take the law into their own hands and attack Unionists.
Youthful rebellion in historical mould, decently but rather dully delivered, based on a folk ballad.

w Stan Shpetner *d* Ted Post *ph* Gilbert Warrenton *m* Ronald Stein

Michael Landon, Richard Rust, Jo Morrow

The Lemon Drop Kid*

US 1951   91m   bw
Paramount (Robert A. Welch)

A gangster forces a bookie to find the money which he has lost on a horse through the bookie's incompetence.
Amusing Bob Hope / Runyon vehicle despite heavy sentiment about an old folks' home. The Santa Claus sequences are memorable.

w Edmund Hartman, Frank Tashlin, Robert O'Brien, *story* Damon Runyon *d* Sidney Lanfield *ph* Daniel L. Fapp *m* Victor Young

Bob Hope, Marilyn Maxwell, Lloyd Nolan, Jane Darwell, Andrea King, Fred Clark, Jay C. Flippen, William Frawley, Harry Bellaver

Lenin in October*

USSR 1937   111m   bw
Mosfilm
original title: *Lenin v Octiabrye*

The activities of Lenin during the revolution.
Stalwart propaganda piece, of solid but not outstanding cinematic interest.

w Alexei Kapler *d Mikhail Romm ph* Boris Volchok *m* Anatoli Alexandrov

Boris Shchukin

† The success of this film provoked *Lenin in 1918*, made in the following year (132m) by the same talents, with Cherkassov as Gorky. Many other Russian films on Lenin have followed.

Lenny**

US 1974   111m   bw
UA (Marvin Worth)

The career of obscene comedian Lenny Bruce and his struggles with the law.
Old-fashioned rags-to-riches-to-rags story, rampant with the new permissiveness.
Filmically extremely clever, emotionally hollow.

w Julian Barry, from his play *d Bob Fosse ph* Bruce Surtees *md* Ralph Burns *pd* Joel Schiller

Dustin Hoffman, Valerie Perrine, Jan Miner, Stanley Beck, Gary Morton,
  'For audiences who want to believe that Lenny Bruce was a saintly gadfly who was martyred for having lived before his time.'— *New Yorker*

AAN: best picture; Julian Barry; Bob Fosse; Bruce Surtees; Dustin Hoffman; Valerie Perrine

Leo the Last

GB 1969   104m   De Luxe
UA / Char / Wink / Boor (Irwin Winkler, Robert Chartoff)

An alienated aristocrat brings his retinue to a London slum and has an effect on most of the inhabitants.
Infuriating symbolic fantasy; only the writer-director (presumably) has any idea what it is about.

w William Stair, John Boorman *d* John Boorman *ph* Peter Suschitzky *m* Dred Myrow *pd* Tony Woollard

Marcello Mastroianni, Billie Whitelaw, Calvin Lockhart, Glenna Forster Jones, Graham Crowden, Gwen Ffrangcon Davies, David de Keyser, Vladek Sheybal, Kenneth J. Warren

Léon Morin, Priest*

France / Italy 1961   117m   bw
Rome-Paris Films (Georges de Beauregard)

During the German occupation of France a young widow finds herself falling in love with the young priest who is converting her to religion.

An intellectual romance, sharp and witty for the most part, with vivid wartime backgrounds.

wd Jean-Pierre Melville, *novel* Béatrix Beck *ph* Henri Decaë *m* Martial Solal, Albert Raisner

Jean-Paul Belmondo, Emmanuele Riva, Irène Tunc, Marielle Gozzi

The Leopard°°°

US / Italy 1963   205m   Technirama
Fox / Titanus / SNPC / GPC (Goffredo Lombardo)
original title: *Il Gattopardo*

The family life of an Italian nobleman at the time of Garibaldi.

Elaborate, complex family saga, painted like an old master with great care and attention to detail, but with not much chance outside Italy of delivering its original dramatic force. Visconti had asked for Lancaster, so TCF picked up the international release but couldn't make head or tail of it commercially; they even ruined its high quality by releasing a dubbed, shortened version in Cinemascope and De Luxe colour of poor standard.

wd Luchino Visconti, novel Giuseppe de Lampedusa *ph Giuseppe Rotunno m* Nino Rota *ad Mario Garbuglia*

Burt Lancaster, Claudia Cardinale, Alain Delon, Paolo Stoppa, Serge Reggiani, Leslie French

Leopard in the Snow

GB / Canada 1977   94m   Technicolor
Seastone / Leopard in the Snow
(W. Laurence Heisey)

A girl caught in a Cumberland blizzard is rescued by a mysterious stranger with a pet leopard. He turns out to be a disfigured racing driver, and she falls in love with him.

A deliberate cross between *Jane Eyre* and a shopgirl's romance, adequately produced for its intended audience.

w Anne Mather, Jill Hyem, *novel* Anne Mather *d* Gerry O'Hara *ph* Alfie Hicks *m* Kenneth V. Jones

Keir Dullea, Susan Penhaligon, Jeremy Kemp, Kenneth More, Billie Whitelaw

The Leopard Man°°

US 1943   59m   bw
RKO (*Val Lewton*)

Murders in a Mexican border town are attributed to an escaped leopard.

Effective minor piece in the Lewton horror gallery; poor plot countered by highly effective suspense sequences.

w Ardel Wray, Edward Dein, *novel* Black Alibi by Cornell Woolrich *d Jacques Tourneur ph* Robert de Grasse *m* Roy Webb

Dennis O'Keefe, Jean Brooks, Margo, James Bell, Isabel Jewell

Lepke

US 1974   110m   De Luxe   Panavision
Warner / AmeriEuro Pictures (Menahem Golan)

After World War I a small-time crook becomes head of Murder Incorporated. Violent but totally uninteresting gangster melodrama; fidelity to fact is not enough.

w Wesley Hau, Tamor Hoffs *d* Menahem Golan *ph* Andrew Davis *m* Ken Wannberg *pd* Jack Degovia

Tony Curtis, Anjanette Comer, Michael Callan, Warren Berlinger, Milton Berle, Gianni Russo

'A kosher version of *The Godfather*.'— *Verina Glaessner*

Les Girls: see under Girls

Les Miserables: see under Miserables

A Lesson in Love

Sweden 1953   95m   bw
Svensk Filmindustri

A gynaecologist and his wife grow bored and turn to other partners, but are reconciled. Slight comedy, surprisingly unsubtle for its creator, but passable.

wd Ingmar Bergman *ph* Martin Bodin, Bengt Nordwal *m* Dag Wiren

Gunnar Bjornstrand, Eva Dahlbeck, Harriet Andersson, Yvonne Lombard, Ake Grönberg

Let 'Em Have It°

US 1935   90m   bw
Edward Small
GB title: *False Faces*

The FBI go after criminals on a terror spree. Lively cops and robbers with some starkly effective moments.

w Joseph Moncure March, Elmer Harris *d* Sam Wood *ph* J. Peverell Marley, Robert Planck

Richard Arlen, Virginia Bruce, Alice Brady, Bruce Cabot, Harvey Stephens, Eric Linden, Joyce Compton, J. Farrell MacDonald

Let Freedom Ring
US 1939 100m sepia
MGM (Harry Rapf)

A westerner returns to his home town and
clears it of corruption.
Elementary Hollywood actioner with curious
credits, climaxed by Eddy singing *The Star
Spangled Banner*.

w Ben Hecht d Jack Conway ph Sidney
Wagner m Arthur Lange

Nelson Eddy, Victor McLaglen, Virginia
Bruce, Lionel Barrymore, H. B. Warner,
Raymond Walburn, Edward Arnold, Guy
Kibbee, Charles Butterworth, Billy Bevan

Let George Do It**
GB 1940 82m bw
Ealing (Basil Dearden)

A ukelele player accidentally goes to Bergen
instead of Blackpool and is mistaken for a spy.
Generally thought to be the best George
Formby vehicle, with plenty of pace, good
situations and catchy tunes.

w John Dighton, Austin Melford, Angus
MacPhail, Basil Dearden d Marcel Varnel
ph Gordon Dines, Ronald Neame

George Formby, Phyllis Calvert, Garry Marsh,
Romney Brent, Bernard Lee, Coral Browne,
Torin Thatcher, Hal Gordon

Let No Man Write My Epitaph
US 1960 106m bw
Columbia / Boris D. Kaplan

A slum boy wants to become a concert pianist
but falls in with gangsters.
Squalid, predictable melodrama without many
redeeming features.

w Robert Presnell Jnr, *novel* Willard Motley
d Philip Leacock ph Burnett Guffey
m George Duning

James Darren, Shelley Winters, Burl Ives,
Jean Seberg, Jeanne Cooper, Ricardo
Montalban, Ella Fitzgerald

Let the People Sing*
GB 1942 105m bw
British National (John Baxter)

An out-of-work comedian persuades a
drunken nobleman to join a protest against the
closing of a village hall.
A development of *The Good Companions*
which compares quite nicely with the Capra
films from across the water: naïve but
entertaining, with good star performances.

w John Baxter, Barbara K. Emery, Geoffrey
Orme, *novel J. B. Priestley d John Baxter*

Alastair Sim, Fred Emney, Edward Rigby,
Patricia Roc, Oliver Wakefield, Marian
Spencer, Olive Sloane, Gus McNaughton,
Charles Hawtrey

Let Us Be Gay
US 1930 79m bw

Divorcees meet again, many years later, in
Paris. Predictable star romance, now very
dated, like its title. Norma Shearer, Rod La
Rocque, Marie Dressler, Sally Eilers,
Raymond Hackett, Hedda Hopper. Written
by Frances Marion, from the play by Rachel
Crothers; directed by Robert Z. Leonard; for
MGM.

Let Us Live
US 1937 67m bw

An innocent taxi driver is convicted of
murder. Intense little melodrama which served
its purpose. Maureen O'Sullivan, Henry
Fonda, Ralph Bellamy. Written by Joseph F.
Dineen, Anthony Veiller and Allen Rivkin;
directed by John Brahm; for Columbia.

Let's Be Happy
GB 1957 107m Technicolor
    Cinemascope
ABP / Marcel Hellman

Footling musical remake of *Jeannie* (qv).

w Diana Morgan d Henry Levin ph Erwin
Hillier m Nicholas Brodszky md Louis Levy
songs Nicholas Brodszky, Paul Francis
Webster

Vera-Ellen, Tony Martin, Robert Flemyng,
Zena Marshall, Guy Middleton, Katherine
Kath, Jean Cadell, Gordon Jackson
'Success still eludes the Anglo-American
musical.'—*MFB*

Let's Be Famous
GB 1939 83m bw
Ealing (Michael Balcon)

A stage struck Irish lad and Lancashire lass
have various adventures in London.
Easy-going comedy introducing radio
personalities of the day.

w Roger MacDougall, Allan MacKinnon
d Walter Forde ph Ronald Neame, Gordon
Dines md Ernest Irving

Jimmy O'Dea, Betty Driver, Sonnie Hale,
Patrick Barr, Basil Radford, Milton Rosmer,
Garry Marsh

Let's Dance
US 1950 112m Technicolor
Paramount (Robert Fellows)

Show business partners reunite after five years of private life.
Tediously plotted musical with a couple of good numbers.

w Allan Scott, *story* Maurice Zolotow
d Norman Z. McLeod *ph* George Barnes
m Robert Emmett Dolan *songs* Frank Loesser

Fred Astaire, Betty Hutton, Roland Young, Ruth Warrick, Lucile Watson, Barton MacLane, Shepperd Strudwick, Melville Cooper, Harold Huber, George Zucco

Let's Do It Again
US 1953 95m Technicolor
Columbia (Oscar Saul)

A songwriter and his wife plan a divorce but call it off in the nick of time.
Tame musical remake of *The Awful Truth* (qv), pleasant enough but lacking style and punch.

w Mary Loos, Richard Sale d Alexander Hall *ph* Charles Lawton Jnr *m* George Duning *md* Morris Stoloff *songs* Lester Lee, Ned Washington

Jane Wyman, Ray Milland, Aldo Ray, Leon Ames

Let's Do It Again
US 1975 113m Technicolor
Warner / First Artists / Verdon (Melville Tucker, Pembroke J. Herring)

Three Atlanta workers conceive a zany plan to raise money for their church by hypnotizing a boxer into winning a big fight.
Lively but overlong farce reassembling the black talents of *Uptown Saturday Night*.

w Richard Wesley d Sidney Poitier
ph Donald M. Morgan *m* Curtis Mayfield

Sidney Poitier, Bill Cosby, Calvin Lockhart, John Amos, Denise Nicholas, Ossie Davis, Jimmy Walker

Let's Face It
US 1943 76m bw
Paramount (Fred Kohlmar)

A smart-alec soldier has a plot involving a ladies' health camp, but finds himself up to his neck in spies.
Tepid star comedy which unaccountably ditches almost all the numbers from the musical on which it was based.

w Harry Tugend, from the musical play by Dorothy and Herbert Fields and Cole Porter, based on the play Cradle Snatchers by Norma Mitchell and Russell Medcraft d Sidney Lanfield *ph* Lionel Lindon *songs* Cole Porter

Bob Hope, Betty Hutton, Eve Arden, Phyllis Povah, Dona Drake, Zasu Pitts, Marjorie Weaver, Raymond Walburn, Joe Sawyer

Let's Kill Uncle
US 1966 92m colour
Universal / William Castle

A boy is threatened by his wicked uncle, and retaliates.
Mildly intriguing black comedy, leadenly handled.

w Mark Rodger, *novel* Rohan O'Grady
d William Castle *ph* Harold Lipstein
m Herman Stein

Nigel Green, Mary Badham, Pat Cardi, Robert Pickering

Let's Live a Little
US 1948 85m bw
Eagle-Lion / United California Productions

An advertising agent falls for his lady psychiatrist, and after many vicissitudes they and their former partners make it to the altar.
Mild comedy which just about bubbles along despite a rather uncomfortable cast.

w Albert J. Cohen, Jack Harvey d Richard Wallace *ph* Ernest Laszlo *m* Werner Heymann

Hedy Lamarr, Robert Cummings, Anna Sten, Robert Shayne, Mary Treen

Let's Make It Legal
US 1951 77m bw

An attractive grandmother divorces her gambler husband and takes up with an old boy friend. Unremarkable but competent star comedy. Claudette Colbert, Zachary Scott, Macdonald Carey, Barbara Bates, Robert Wagner, Marilyn Monroe. Written by F. Hugh Herbert and I. A. L. Diamond; directed by Richard Sale; for TCF.

Let's Make Love*
US 1960 118m De Luxe Cinemascope
TCF (Jerry Wald)

A multi-millionaire, learning that he is to be burlesqued in a Broadway show, joins the cast as an actor.
Complex, moderately sophisticated, occasionally funny musical inspired by *On the Avenue* (qv); lively characterizations but poor numbers.

w Norman Krasna d George Cukor
ph Daniel L. Fapp *ch* Jack Cole *md* Lionel Newman, Earl H. Hagen *songs* Sammy Cahn, Jimmy Van Heusen

Yves Montand, Marilyn Monroe, Tony Randall, Wilfrid Hyde White, Frankie Vaughan, David Burns, and guests Bing Crosby, Gene Kelly, Milton Berle

AAN: Lionel Newman, Earl H. Hagen

Let's Scare Jessica to Death
US 1971   89m   colour
Paramount / Jessica Co

Back home after a nervous breakdown, our heroine is troubled by voices and visions, not to mention an ambulant corpse and a vampire or two.
Competent screamie.

w Norman Jonas, Ralph Rose   d John Hancock   ph Bob Baldwin   m Orville Stoeber

Zohra Lampert, Barton Heyman

The Letter*
US 1929   61m   bw
Paramount

Early talkie version of a solid piece of theatre. See below.

story and play W. Somerset Maugham   d Jean de Limur

Jeanne Eagels, O. P. Heggie, Reginald Owen, Herbert Marshall, Irene Browne

AAN: Jeanne Eagels

The Letter****
US 1940   95m   bw
Warner (Robert Lord)

A rubber plantation owner's wife kills a man in what seems to have been self-defence; but a letter from her proves it to have been a crime of passion, and becomes an instrument of blackmail.
Excellent performances and presentation make this the closest approximation on film to' reading a Maugham story of the Far East, though censorship forced the addition of an infuriating moral ending.

w Howard Koch, story W. Somerset Maugham   d William Wyler   ph Tony Gaudio   m Max Steiner

Bette Davis, Herbert Marshall, James Stephenson, Sen Yung, Frieda Inescort, Gale Sondergaard, Bruce Lester, Tetsu Komai
'The writing is taut and spare throughout . . . the unravelling of Maugham's story is masterly and the presentation visual and cinematic . . . the audience at the trade show did not move a finger.'—James Agate
† Herbert Marshall played the lover in the first version and the husband in the second.

AAN: best picture; William Wyler; Tony Gaudio; Max Steiner; Bette Davis; James Stephenson

Letter from an Unknown Woman****
US 1948   89m   bw
Universal (John Houseman)

A woman wastes her life in unrequited love for a rakish pianist.
Superior 'woman's picture' which gave its director his best chance in America to recreate his beloved Vienna of long ago. Hollywood production magic at its best.

w Howard Koch, novel Stefan Zweig   d Max Ophuls   ph Franz Planer   m Daniele Amfitheatrof   ad Alexander Golitzen

Joan Fontaine, Louis Jourdan, Mady Christians, Art Smith, Marcel Journet
'A film full of snow, sleigh bells, lights gleaming in ornamental gardens and trysts at night.'—Charles Higham, 1972
'It is fascinating to watch the sure deft means by which Ophuls sidetracks seemingly inevitable clichés and holds on to a shadowy, tender mood, half buried in the past. Here is a fragile filmic charm that is not often or easily accomplished.'—Richard Winnington
'Film narrative of a most skilled order.'—William Whitebait

Letter of Introduction*
US 1938   100m   bw
Universal (John M. Stahl)

A young actress is encouraged by an ageing star whom she does not know is her father.
Commercial melodrama with luxury trimmings, all very neatly packaged.

w Sheridan Gibney, Leonard Spiegelgass   d John M. Stahl   ph Karl Freund   m Charles Previn

Adolphe Menjou, Andrea Leeds, Edgar Bergen (and Charlie McCarthy), George Murphy, Eve Arden, Rita Johnson, Ernest Cossart, Ann Sheridan

A Letter to Three Wives**
US 1949   102m   bw
TCF (Sol C. Siegel)

Three wives on a picnic receive word from a friend that she has run off with one of their husbands.
Amusing short-story compendium which seemed more revelatory at the time than it does now, and paved the way for its writer-director's heyday.

wd Joseph L. Mankiewicz, novel John Klempner   ph Arthur Miller   m Alfred Newman

Jeanne Crain, Ann Sothern, Linda Darnell,
Jeffrey Lynn, Kirk Douglas, *Paul Douglas*,
Barbara Lawrence, Connie Gilchrist, Florence
Bates, Hobart Cavanaugh, and the voice of
Celeste Holm
'A peek into the other woman's male!'—
publicity
'A mere shadow of those acid Hollywood
comedies of the thirties . . . over-written and
under-directed . . . but it has a supply of
ironies and makes a certain alkaline comment
on present-day American customs and
manners.'—*Richard Winnington*
AA: Joseph L. Mankiewicz (as writer); Joseph
L. Mankiewicz (as director)
AAN: best picture

Letty Lynton
US 1932   84m   bw

When one lover is murdered, Letty turns to
another to prove her innocent. Bad girl drama
which established the star's box office appeal.
Joan Crawford, Robert Montgomery, Nils
Asther, May Robson, Lewis Stone. Written by
John Meehan and Wanda Tuchock; directed
by Clarence Brown; for MGM.

Les Liaisons Dangereuses*
France 1959   106m   bw
Films Marceau

Valmont and his wife compare notes on each
other's affairs.
Showy modernization of a notorious minor
classic.

w Roger Vailland, Roger Vadim, Claude
Brûlé, *novel* Choderlos de Laclos d Roger
Vadim ph Marcel Grignon m Jack Murray,
Thelonius Monk

Gérard Philipe, Jeanne Moreau, Annette
Vadim, Jeanne Valerie, Simone Renant, Jean-
Louis Trintignant
'A woman's picture par excellence.'—*John
Russell Taylor, MFB*

Libel*
GB 1959   100m   bw
MGM / Comet (Anatole de Grunwald)

An ex-POW baronet is accused of being an
impostor.
Old-fashioned courtroom spellbinder, quite
adequately done though occasionally creaky.

w Anatole de Grunwald, Karl Tunberg, *play*
Edward Wooll d Anthony Asquith
ph Robert Krasker m Benjamin Frankel

Dirk Bogarde, Olivia de Havilland, Paul
Massie, Wilfrid Hyde White, Robert Morley,
Anthony Dawson, Richard Wattis, Martin
Miller, Millicent Martin

Libeled Lady**
US 1936   98m   bw
MGM (Lawrence Weingarten)

An heiress sues a newspaper, and the editor
hires a friend to compromise her.
Lively four-star romantic comedy which sums
up its era as well as any.

w Maurine Watkins, Howard Emmett Rogers,
George Oppenheimer d Jack Conway
ph Norbert Brodine

Jean Harlow, Myrna Loy, Spencer Tracy,
William Powell, Walter Connolly, Charley
Grapewin, Cora Witherspoon, E. E. Clive,
Charles Trowbridge
'Handsomely mounted and produced,
lavishly costumed, cleverly written and artfully
directed, *Libeled Lady* is entirely worthy of
the noble comedians who head its cast.'—
Bland Johaneson, New York Daily Mirror
† Remade as *Easy to Wed* (qv); central
situation borrowed for *Man's Favorite Sport*
(qv).
AAN: best picture

The Liberation of L. B. Jones*
US 1970   102m   Technicolor
Columbia / Liberation Co (Ronald Lubin)

Racial murder is the result when a black
undertaker wants a divorce in a small
Tennessee town.
Violent, pointless but well-made melodrama
which really does not take matters much
further than *Intruder in the Dust*.

w Stirling Silliphant, Jesse Hill Ford, from
Ford's novel d William Wyler ph Robert
Surtees m Elmer Bernstein

Lee J. Cobb, Anthony Zerbe, Roscoe Lee
Browne, Lola Falana, Lee Majors, Barbara
Hershey, Yaphet Kotto, Arch Johnson, Chill
Wills
'With its genuinely ferocious climax it adds
up to probably the most powerful, if not the
most sophisticated, race-war film the
commercial studios have yet produced.'—
Nigel Andrews

Liberty**
US 1929   20m   bw   silent

Two convicts escape and have adventures high
on a construction site. Amusing gags are
succeeded by breathtaking thrills in the Harold
Lloyd style. Laurel and Hardy, James
Finlayson. Written by Leo McCarey and H.
M. Walker; directed by Leo McCary; for Hal
Roach.

Licensed to Kill

GB 1965   97m   Eastmancolor
Alistair Films (Estelle E. Richmond)
US title: *The Second Best Secret Agent in
the Whole Wide World*

The Foreign Office calls in agent Charles Vine
to protect a top international scientist.
Cheap copy of James Bond which wins no
laurels but produces a few efficient routine
thrills.

w Howard Griffiths, Lindsay Shonteff
d Lindsay Shonteff *ph* Terry Maher
m Bertram Chappell

Tom Adams, Veronica Hurst, Karel Stepanek,
Felix Felton, Peter Bull

Liebelei*

Austria 1932   85m   bw
Fred Lissa

A young army officer falls in love; but he is
killed in a duel and his girl commits suicide.
Semi-classic romantic novelette, like a warm-
up for *Letter from an Unknown Woman*.

w Hans Wilhelm, Kurt Alexander,
story Arthur Schnitzler *d* Max Ophuls
ph Franz Planer *m* Theo Macheber

Magda Schneider, Wolfgang Liebeneiner,
Luise Ullrich, Willy Eichberger, Gustaf
Gruendgens, Paul Hoerbiger
† A revised French version played as *Une
Histoire d'Amour*. The story had previously
been shot under the same title in Germany in
1927; and in the sixties Romy Schneider and
Alain Delon appeared in a French remake
called *Christine*.

Lies My Father Told Me

Canada 1975   102m   colour
Columbia / Pentimento / Pentacle (Anthony
Bedrich, Harry Gulkin)

Adventures of a poor Jewish boy and his
grandfather in Montreal in the twenties.
Effectively if rather dishonestly sentimental,
this is the kind of family picture for which
critics are always clamouring but which few
people in the seventies will pay to see.

w Ted Allan, from his book   *d* Jan Kadar
ph Paul Van der Linden   *m* Sol Kaplan

Yossi Yadin, Len Birman, Marilyn Lightstone,
Jeffrey Lynas

'Sentiment by numbers . . . a lovable child
awakening to discovery of the world; a
lovable, whimsical old grandfather; a lovable,
ne'er-do-well father; a lovable, long-suffering
mother; a lovable, broken-down horse;
lovable neighbours; a lovable whore across the
way. It all strives so hard to be lovable that
you want to scream.'—*David Robinson, The
Times*

† A British low-budgeter was made from the
same story in 1940, changing the venue to
Ireland and the race to Irish.
AAN: Ted Allan

Lt Robin Crusoe USN

US 1966   114m   Technicolor
Walt Disney (Bill Walsh, Ron Miller)

A navy pilot parachutes on to a Pacific island
and gets involved in the local women's lib
movement.
Slow-paced family comedy with very few
laughs.

w Bill Walsh, Don da Gradi   *d* Byron Paul
ph William Snyder   *m* Bob Brunner

Dick Van Dyke, Nancy Kwan, Akim Tamiroff

The Lieutenant Wore Skirts

US 1955   99m   Eastmancolor
    Cinemascope
TCF (Buddy Adler)

When a TV writer joins the service, his wife
enlists to be near him; but he is rejected on
medical grounds.
Raucous, tasteless farce which tries far too
hard to raise laughs.

w Albert Beich, Frank Tashlin   *d* Frank
Tashlin   *ph* Leo Tover   *m* Cyril Mockridge

Tom Ewell, Sheree North, Rita Moreno, Rick
Jason, Les Tremayne

The Life and Death of Colonel
Blimp***

GB 1943   163m   Technicolor
GFD / Archers (Michael Powell, Emeric
    Pressburger)
US title: *Colonel Blimp*

A British soldier survives three wars and falls
in love with three women.
Not the Blimp of the cartoon strip, but a
sympathetic figure in a warm, consistently
interesting if idiosyncratic love story against a
background of war. The Archers as usual
provide a sympathetic German lead (friend of
the hero); quite a coup in wartime.

wd Michael Powell, Emeric Pressburger
ph Jack Cardiff   *m* Allan Gray   *ad* Alfred
Junge

Roger Livesey, Anton Walbrook, Deborah
Kerr, Roland Culver, James McKechnie,
Albert Lieven, Arthur Wontner, A. E.
Matthews, David Hutcheson, Ursula Jeans,
John Laurie, Harry Welchman

'There is nothing brilliant about the picture,
but it is perceptive, witty and sweet-
tempered.'—*James Agee*

The Life and Times of Judge Roy Bean*
US 1972   124m   Technicolor
Panavision
National General / Famous Artists (John
  Foreman)

A fantasia on the famous outlaw judge of the
old west.
Sporadically entertaining but schematically
messy mixture of burlesqued folklore and
violent action, not in the same league as *Butch
Cassidy*.

w John Milius d John Huston ph Richard
Moore m Maurice Jarre

Paul Newman, Ava Gardner, Jacqueline
Bisset, Tab Hunter, Stacy Keach, Roddy
McDowall, Anthony Perkins, John Huston

AAN: song 'Marmalade, Molasses and Honey'
(*m* Maurice Jarre, *ly* A. and M. Byrne)

Life at the Top*
GB 1965   117m   bw
Columbia / Romulus (James Woolf)

Ten years after marrying into money, Joe
Lampton is dissatisfied, and he and his wife
both have affairs.
Rough-talking but basically predictable and
old-fashioned sequel to *Room at the Top*, a bit
compromised by having to reflect the sixties
London scene; the early Yorkshire sequences
are the best.

w Mordecai Richler d Ted Kotcheff
ph Oswald Morris m Richard Addinsell

Laurence Harvey, Jean Simmons, Honor
Blackman, Michael Craig, Donald Wolfit,
Margaret Johnston, Allan Cuthbertson,
Ambrosine Philpotts, Robert Morley, Nigel
Davenport, George A. Cooper
'Another thoroughly mean-spirited film of a
kind which has been taking root in the British
cinema.'—*Tom Milne*
† The character of Joe Lampton was later used
in a long running TV series called *Man at the
Top*, which sprouted a film of its own under
that title.

Life Begins
US 1932   72m   bw
Warner (Ray Griffith)
GB title: *Dream of Life*

A night in a maternity hospital.
Multi-melodrama later remade as *A Child Is
Born*. Passable.

w Earl Baldwin, *play* Mary McDougal
Axelson d James Flood ph James Van Trees

Loretta Young, Eric Linden, Aline
MacMahon, Preston Foster, Glenda Farrell,
Frank McHugh, Clara Blandick, Elizabeth
Patterson, Gilbert Roland

Life Begins at Eight Thirty*
US 1942   85m   bw
TCF (Nunnally Johnson)
GB title: *The Light of Heart*

A distinguished actor is reduced through drink
to being a street corner Santa Claus.
Diluted and sentimentalized version of an
agreeable play.

w Nunnally Johnson, *play* Emlyn Williams
d Irving Pichel ph Edward Cronjager
m Alfred Newman

Monty Woolley, Ida Lupino, Cornel Wilde,
Sara Allgood, Melville Cooper, J. Edward
Bromberg

Life Begins in College
US 1937   80m   bw

Three zanies save the honour of the college
football team. Another of the myriad college
football stories of the thirties, but this time
enlivened by comedians in the leads. The Ritz
Brothers, Joan Davis, Tony Martin, Gloria
Stuart, Fred Stone, Nat Pendleton. Written by
Karl Tunberg and Don Ettlinger; directed by
William A. Seiter; for TCF.

Life for Ruth*
GB 1962   91m   bw
Rank / Allied Film Makers (Michael Relph,
  Basil Dearden)

A little girl dies because her parents' religion
forbids blood transfusions.
Dramatized from the headlines, this little case
history is small beer as film-making, and not
exactly entertainment, but absorbing as a
comment on human behaviour.

w Janet Green, John McCormick d Basil
Dearden ph Otto Heller m William Alwyn
md Muir Mathieson

Michael Craig, Patrick McGoohan, Janet
Munro

A Life in the Balance*
US 1954   75m   bw
TCF / Panoramic (Leonard Goldstein)

A Mexican widower springs into action when
his young son is kidnapped by a murderer.
Taut little melodrama taking place during one
night in Mexico City; made with vigour on a
low budget.

w Robert Presnell Jnr, Leo Townsend
d Harry Horner
ph J. Gomez Urquiza m Raul Lavista

Ricardo Montalban, Anne Bancroft, Lee
Marvin

The Life of Emile Zola•••
US 1937   116m   bw
Warner (Henry Blanke)

The French writer intervenes in the case of
Alfred Dreyfus, condemned unjustly to
Devil's Island.
The box office success of this solidly-
carpentered piece of Hollywood history was
compounded in equal parts of star power and
the sheer novelty of having such a thing turn
up at the local Odeon.

w Norman Reilly Raine *story* Heinz Herald
and Geza Herczeg *d William Dieterle*
ph Tony Gaudio *m* Max Steiner *ad Anton
Grot*

Paul Muni, Joseph Schildkraut, Gale
Sondergaard, Gloria Holden, Donald Crisp,
Erin O'Brien Moore, John Litel, Henry
O'Neill, Morris Carnovsky, Ralph Morgan,
Louis Calhern, Robert Barrat, Vladimir
Sokoloff, Harry Davenport, Robert Warwick,
Walter Kingsford

'Along with *Louis Pasteur*, it ought to start
a new category—the Warner crusading films,
costume division.'—*Otis Ferguson*
'A grave story told with great dignity and
superbly played and produced.'—*Pare Lorentz*
'One of the fine ones which begin as a film
and end as an experience.'—*John Grierson*
'He plucked from the gutter a faded rose
and made an immortal masterpiece!'—
publicity

AA: best picture; script; Joseph Schildkraut
AAN: original story; William Dieterle; Max
Steiner; Paul Muni

A Life of Her Own
US 1950   108m   bw
MGM (Voldemar Vetluguin)

An innocent girl from Kansas becomes one of
New York's top models.
Road to ruin, American style, from the pages
of a women's magazine.

w Isabel Lennart *d* George Cukor
ph George Folsey *m* Bronislau Kaper

Lana Turner, Ray Milland, Tom Ewell, Louis
Calhern, Ann Dvorak, Barry Sullivan, Jean
Hagen

'This story belongs to the realms of soap
opera—extremely artificial, highly moral in
tone, and deliberately concocted to combine
luxurious settings with an elementary assault
on the audience's emotions.'—*MFB*

The Life of Jimmy Dolan
US 1933   85m   bw
Warner (Hal B. Wallis)
GB title: *The Kid's Last Fight*

An amiable wanderer is mistaken for a prize-
fighter wanted for murder.
Modest character romance, later remade as
They Made Me a Criminal.

w David Boehm, Erwin Gelsey, *play* Bertram
Millhauser, Beulah Marie Dix *d* Archie
Mayo *ph* Arthur Edeson

Douglas Fairbanks Jnr, Loretta Young, Aline
MacMahon, Guy Kibbee, Lyle Talbot, Fifi
D'Orsay, Harold Huber, George Meeker

The Life of Vergie Winters
US 1934   82m   bw
RKO (Pandro S. Berman)

A rising politician marries for position but
keeps watch over his mistress and their child.
Archetypal soap opera, a cross between *Stella
Dallas* and *Back Street.*

w Jane Murfin, *novel* Louis Bromfield
d Alfred Santell *ph* Lucien Andriot *m* Max
Steiner

Ann Harding, John Boles, Helen Vinson,
Frank Albertson, Lon Chaney Jnr, Sara
Haden, Ben Alexander, Donald Crisp

Life Upside Down•
France 1964   92m   bw
A.J. Films
original title: *La Vie à l'Envers*

A pleasant, ordinary young man discovers the
joy of being absolutely alone, and begins to
detach himself from his surroundings, ending
up in a barren flat and a private hospital ward.
Engaging semi-comic case history which
generates much sympathy for its eccentric
hero.

wd Alain Jessua ph Jacques Robin
m Jacques Loussier

Charles Denner, Anna Gaylor, Guy Saint-
Jean, Nicole Gueden

'The tone is civilized, quiet, infinitely
peaceful and often brilliantly funny.'—*Brenda
Davies, MFB*
'Amusing or disturbing depending on
whether it is viewed from the outside or the
inside, but perceptive and artistic whichever
way one views it.'—*John Simon*

Life with Father•
US 1947   118m   Technicolor
Warner (Robert Buckner)

Turn-of-the-century anecdotes of an irascible
well-to-do paterfamilias who won't be
baptized.
Well-upholstered screen version of a long
running play; oddly tedious considering the
talent involved.

w Donald Ogden Stewart, *play* Howard
Lindsay, Russel Crouse *d* Michael Curtiz
ph Peverell Marley, William V. Skall *m* Max
Steiner *ad* Robert Hass

William Powell, Irene Dunne, Edmund
Gwenn, Zasu Pitts, Elizabeth Taylor, Martin
Milner, Jimmy Lydon, Emma Dunn, Moroni
Olsen, Elizabeth Risdon
  'Everybody seems to be trying too hard . . .
the director is totally out of his element in this
careful, deadly version.'—*New Yorker, 1978*
† Censorship of the day absurdly clipped
Father's famous last line: 'I'm going to be
baptized, damn it!'

AAN: Peverell Marley, William V. Skall; Max
Steiner; William Powell

Lifeboat**
US 1944 96m bw
TCF (Kenneth MacGowan)

Survivors from a torpedoed passenger ship
include the U-Boat commander responsible.
Propaganda gimmick melodrama interesting
for the casting and for Hitchcock's response to
the challenge of filming in one cramped set.

w Jo Swerling, *story* John Steinbeck *d Alfred
Hitchcock ph* Glen MacWilliams *m* Hugo
Friedhofer

Tallulah Bankhead, Walter Slezak, Henry
Hull, John Hodiak, Canada Lee, William
Bendix, Mary Anderson, Heather Angel,
Hume Cronyn
  'The initial idea—a derelict boat and its
passengers as microcosm—is itself so artificial
that . . . it sets the whole pride and brain too
sharply to work on a tour de force for its own
sake.'—*James Agee*

AAN: John Steinbeck; Alfred Hitchcock;
Glen MacWilliams

Lift to the Scaffold*
France 1957 89m bw
Nouvelles Editions de Films (Jean Thuillier)
original title: *Ascenseur pour l'Echafaud*

An executive murders his employer but is
trapped in the building all night; meanwhile
his car is stolen and he is arrested for a murder
committed by the thief.
Complex, watchable suspenser with
pretensions.

w Roger Nimier, Louis Malle, *novel* Noel
Calef *d* Louis Malle *ph* Henri Decaë
m Miles Davis

Maurice Ronet, Jeanne Moreau, Georges
Poujouly, Yori Bertin, Lino Ventura
  'Cold, clever and rather elegant.'—*Penelope
Houston, MFB*

The Light across the Street
France 1955 99m bw
EGC / Fernand Rivers (Jacques Gauthier)
original title: *La Lumière d'en Face*

A lorry driver, injured in an accident,
becomes insanely jealous of his young wife.
Low-life melodrama tailored for the sultry
attractions of its new star.

w Louis Cahavance, René Masson, René
Lefèvre *d* Georges Lacombe *ph* Louis Page
m Norbert Glanzberg

Brigitte Bardot, Raymond Pellégrin, Roger
Pigaut, Claude Romain

The Light at the Edge of the World
US / Spain / Liechtenstein 1971   120m
  Eastmancolor Panavision
Bryna / Jet / Triumfilm (Kirk Douglas, Ilya
  Salkind)

A lighthouse keeper near Cape Horn resists a
band of wreckers.
Pretentious, disaster-prone version of a simple
adventure story; one wonders not so much
what went wrong as whether anything went
right in this international venture.

w Tom Rowe, *novel* Jules Verne *d* Kevin
Billington *ph* Henri Decaë *m* Piero Piccioni

Kirk Douglas, Yul Brynner, Samantha Eggar,
Jean-Claude Drouot, Fernando Rey, Renato
Salvatori

The Light in the Forest
US 1958 92m Technicolor
Walt Disney

Kidnapped by Indians as an infant, a teenager
is returned to his parents but finds the white
man's ways disturbing.
Modest frontier drama with a moral.

w Lawrence Edward Watkin, *novel* Conrad
Richter *d* Herschel Daugherty *ph* Ellsworth
Fredericks *m* Paul Smith

James MacArthur, Carol Lynley, Jessica
Tandy, Wendell Corey, Fess Parker, Joanne
Dru, Joseph Calleia

The Light in the Piazza
GB 1962 101m Metrocolor
  Cinemascope
MGM (Arthur Freed)

An American matron in Florence tries to
marry off her mentally retarded daughter to a
wealthy Italian.
Puzzling romantic drama in which one is never
quite sure why the characters behave as they
do; in the end all one appreciates is the tour of
northern Italy.

w Julius J. Epstein, *novel* Elizabeth Spencer *d* Guy Green *ph* Otto Heller *m* Mario Nascimbene

Olivia de Havilland, Yvette Mimieux, George Hamilton, Rossano Brazzi, Barry Sullivan

The Light that Failed*
US 1939 97m bw
Paramount

A London artist is going blind as the result of a war wound, and must finish the portrait of the little cockney whom he loves.
Nicely-made but rather boring star romance; no surprises in plot or performance.

w Robert Carson, *story* Rudyard Kipling *d* William Wellman *ph* Theodor Sparkuhl *m* Victor Young

Ronald Colman, Walter Huston, Ida Lupino, Dudley Digges, Muriel Angelus, Fay Helm
† Previously filmed in 1916 and 1923.

The Light Touch
US 1951 107m bw
MGM (Pandro S. Berman)

An elegant art thief tries to doublecross the gangster who employs him.
Elongated and witless romantic charade on European locations.

wd Richard Brooks, *story* Jed Harris, Tom Reed *ph* Robert Surtees *m* Miklos Rozsa

Stewart Granger, George Sanders, Pier Angeli, Kurt Kasznar, Larry Keating, Rhys Williams, Norman Lloyd, Mike Mazurki
'A comedy thriller which moves far too slowly for its imperfections to be overlooked.'—*Penelope Houston, MFB*

Light Up the Sky
GB 1960 90m bw
British Lion / Bryanston (Lewis Gilbert)

Life on a searchlight battery during World War II.
Wartime comedy-drama with accent on the laughs but adding dollops of tragedy and sentiment. A very patchy entertainment.

w Vernon Harris, *play* Touch It Light by Robert Storey *d* Lewis Gilbert *ph* John Wilcox *m* Douglas Gamley

Ian Carmichael, Tommy Steele, Benny Hill, Sydney Tafler, Victor Maddern, Harry Locke, Johnny Briggs, Dick Emery

Lightning Strikes Twice
US 1951 91m bw
Warner (Henry Blanke)

A woman decides to clear her lover of suspicion of murder, but later has her own doubts.

Silly melodrama with no credibility, little suspense, and too much talk.

w Lenore Coffee, *novel* Margaret Echard *d* King Vidor *ph* Sid Hickox *m* Max Steiner

Richard Todd, Ruth Roman, Mercedes McCambridge, Zachary Scott, Darryl Hickman, Frank Conroy, Kathryn Givney

Lights of New York***
US 1928 57m bw
Warner

A chorus girl becomes involved with gangsters.
The first '100 per cent all-talking' film, dramatically primitive but historically important.

w F. Hugh Herbert, Murray Roth *d* Bryan Foy *ph* E. B. DuPar

Helene Costello, Cullen Landis, Wheeler Oakman, Eugene Pallette, Tom Dugan, Gladys Brockwell, Mary Carr
'100 per cent crude.'—*Variety*

Lights of Old Broadway
US 1925 80m approx at 24 fps bw silent

Twin orphan girls find very different routes to happiness. One of the star's most popular vehicles. Marion Davies, Conrad Nagel, George K. Arthur, Julia Swayne Gordon. Written by Carey Wilson; directed by Monta Bell; for MGM.

Lights of Variety*
Italy 1950 94m bw
Film Capitolium (Alberto Lattuada)

A stage-struck young girl forsakes the manager of the troupe in which she found stardom for the bright lights of the city.
Tragi-comical backstage story in which the bits of detail are more entertaining than the plot.

w Federico Fellini *d* Alberto Lattuada *ph* Otello Martelli *m* Felice Lattuada

Peppino de Filippo, Carla del Poggio, Giulietta Masina, John Kitzmiller, Folco Lulli

The Likely Lads*
GB 1976 90m bw
EMI (Aida Young)

Two Geordie friends, with wife and mistress, go on a touring holiday.
Valuable as a record of an excellent and long-running TV series, this big screen version finds most of the humour regrettably broadened.

w Dick Clement, Ian La Frenais *d* Michael Tuchner *ph* Tony Imi *m* Mike Hugg

Rodney Bewes, James Bolam, Brigit Forsyth, Mary Tamm, Sheila Fearn, Zena Walker

A Likely Story
US 1947   88m   bw
RKO (Richard H. Berger)

A man thinks he has only a short time to live, and in trying to do his best for a girl friend gets mixed up with gangsters.
Even a star cast could not have made much of this zany comedy script.

w Bess Taffel *d* H. C. Potter *ph* Roy Hunt *m* Leigh Harline *md* Constantin Bakaleinikoff

Barbara Hale, Bill Williams, Lanny Rees, Sam Levene, Dan Tobin, Nestor Paiva

Li'l Abner*
US 1959   113m   Technicolor
   Vistavision
Paramount / Panama–Frank (Norman Panama)

The hillbilly town of Dogpatch, tagged the most useless community in America, fights being used as a test site for A-bombs.
Set-bound, intrinsically American, but bright and cheerful film of a stage show about Al Capp's famous comic strip characters.

wd Norman Panama, Melvin Frank from the musical show (*ly* Johnny Mercer, *words* Gene de Paul) *ph* Daniel L. Fapp *m* Gene de Paul *md* Joseph Lilley, Nelson Riddle *ch* Dee Dee Wood, Michael Kidd

Peter Palmer, Leslie Parrish, Billie Hayes, Howard St John, Stubby Kaye, Stella Stevens, Julie Newmar, Robert Strauss

AAN: Joseph Lilley, Nelson Riddle

The Lilac Domino
GB 1937   79m   bw

A Hungarian count is attracted at the gambling tables by a masked girl. Surprisingly undercast version of a popular operetta. June Knight, Michael Bartlett, Athene Seyler, Richard Dolman, S. Z. Sakall, Fred Emney, Jane Carr. Written by Basil Mason, Neil Gow, R. Hutter and Derek Neame, from the play by Rudolf Bernauer, E. Gatti and B. Jenbach; directed by Fred Zelnik; for Grafton-Capitol-Cecil.

Lilacs in the Spring
GB 1954   94m   Trucolor
Republic / Everest (Herbert Wilcox)
US title: *Let's Make Up*

During the London blitz a young actress is knocked unconscious and dreams of herself as Nell Gwyn, Queen Victoria and her own mother before waking up to deal with her personal problems.
Good-humoured theatrical charade deadened by poorish production and colour, strengthened by the star's game run-through of her staple characters. How Mr Flynn came to be involved is anybody's guess.

w Harold Purcell, from his play The Glorious Days *d* Herbert Wilcox *ph* Max Greene *m* Robert Farnon

Anna Neagle, Errol Flynn, Peter Graves, David Farrar, Kathleen Harrison

Lili*
US 1952   81m   Technicolor
MGM (Edwin H. Knopf)

A 16-year-old orphan girl joins a carnival and falls in love with the magician.
Romantic whimsy dependent entirely on treatment, which is sometimes heavy-handed. Charm, ballet and puppets are provided, but a little cheerful song and dance would not have been amiss.

w Helen Deutsch, *novel* Paul Gallico *d, ch* Charles Walters *ph* Robert Planck *m* Bronislau Kaper *ad* Cedric Gibbons, Paul Stroesse

Leslie Caron, Jean-Pierre Aumont, Mel Ferrer, Kurt Kasznar

'A lovely and beguiling little film, touched with the magic of romance.'—*Bosley Crowther*

AA: Bronislau Kaper
AAN: Helen Deutsch; Charles Walters; Robert Planck; Leslie Caron

Lilies of the Field*
US 1963   94m   bw
UA / Rainbow / Ralph Nelson

An itinerant black workman in New Mexico helps a group of German nuns to build a chapel.
Liberal, sentimental, under-dramatized little comedy with everyone coming to understand each other's point of view, so that the audience feels improved if not especially entertained.

w James Poe, *novel* William E. Barrett *d* Ralph Nelson *ph* Ernest Haller *m* Jerry Goldsmith

Sidney Poitier, Lilia Skala

AA: Sidney Poitier
AAN: best picture; James Poe; Ernest Haller; Lilia Skala

Liliom*
US 1930   94m   bw
Fox

A Budapest carnival man is killed in a fight but later comes back from heaven to see how his family is doing.
Ingeniously-staged fantasy, very dated but a lot more interesting than its musical remake *Carousel* (qv).

w S. N. Behrman, *play* Ferenc Molnar *d* Frank Borzage *ph* Chester Lyons *m* Richard Fall

Charles Farrell, Rose Hobart, Estelle Taylor, Lee Tracy, Walter Abel, Guinn Williams, H. B. Warner, Dawn O'Day (Anne Shirley)

Lilith*
US 1964 126m bw
Columbia / Centaur (Robert Rossen)

A trainee therapist at an asylum falls in love with a patient.
Strange, wistful, poetic and rather soporific character melodrama.

wd Robert Rossen, *novel* J. R. Salamanca *ph* Eugen Schufftan *m* Kenyon Hopkins *pd* Richard Sylbert

Warren Beatty, Jean Seberg, Peter Fonda, Kim Hunter, Anne Meacham, James Patterson, Jessica Walter, Gene Hackman
    'A remarkable attempt to dig a little deeper in an almost untilled field, and to throw some light on the relationship between madness and the creative imagination.'—*Tom Milne*

Lillian Russell**
US 1940 130m bw
TCF (Gene Markey)

The life and loves of the famous nineties entertainer.
Whitewashed biopic, extremely well made of its kind, and very typical.

w William Anthony McGuire *d* Irving Cummings *ph* Leon Shamroy *md* Alfred Newman

Alice Faye, Don Ameche, Edward Arnold, Warren William, Henry Fonda, Leo Carrillo, Helen Westley, Dorothy Peterson, Ernest Truex, Nigel Bruce, Claud Allister, Lynn Bari, Weber and Fields, Eddie Foy Jnr, Una O'Connor

Limbo*
US 1972 111m Technicolor
Universal (Linda Gottlieb)
aka: *Chained to Yesterday*

Women wait for their husbands to return from Vietnam.
Worthy but dramatically uninteresting multistoried semi-propaganda piece with an untried cast.

w Joan Silver, James Bridges *d* Mark Robson *ph* Charles Wheeler *m* Anita Kerr

Kate Jackson, Katherine Justice, Stuart Margolin, Hazel Medina, Kathleen Nolan

Limehouse Blues*
US 1935 65m bw
Paramount
aka: *East End Chant*

In London's shady quarter, an oriental roustabout tries to leave his jealous mistress for a girl with a shady past.
Artificial, atmospheric melodrama set in a never-never Limehouse redolent of *Broken Blossoms*. Interesting for its very excesses.

w Arthur Phillips, Cyril Hume, Grover Jones *d* Alexander Hall *ph* Harry Fischbeck

George Raft, Anna May Wong, Jean Parker, Kent Taylor, Billy Bevan

Limelight
GB 1935 80m bw
GFD / Herbert Wilcox

A chorus girl helps a street singer to become a star.
Highly predictable backstage musical drama which made a nine days wonder of 'The Street Singer'.

w Laura Whettier *d* Herbert Wilcox

Anna Neagle, *Arthur Tracy*, Jane Winton, Ellis Jeffreys, Muriel George
    'A syrupy concatenation to win all British hearts.'—*James Agate*

Limelight***
US 1952 144m bw
Charles Chaplin

A broken-down music hall comedian is stimulated by a young ballerina to a final hour of triumph.
Sentimental drama in a highly theatrical London East End setting. In other hands it would be very hokey, but Chaplin's best qualities, as well as his worst, are in evidence, and in a way the film sums up his own career.

w.d. m Charles Chaplin *ph* Karl Struss *ad* Eugene Lourié *photographic consultant* Rollie Totheroh

Charles Chaplin, *Claire Bloom, Buster Keaton*, Sydney Chaplin, Nigel Bruce, Norman Lloyd
    'From the first reel it is clear that he now wants to talk, that he *loves* to talk . . . where a development in the story line might easily be conveyed by a small visual effect, he prefers to make a speech about it . . . it is a disturbing rejection of the nature of the medium itself.'—*Walter Kerr*

'Surely the richest hunk of self-gratification since Huck and Tom attended their own funeral.'—*New Yorker, 1982*

AA: Charles Chaplin (for music)

The Lineup*
US 1958   86m   bw
Columbia (Frank Cooper)

San Francisco police trap a gunman who is also a drug contact.
Energetic, polished movie version of a popular TV series, *San Francisco Beat.*

w Stirling Silliphant d Don Siegel ph Hal Mohr m Mischa Bakaleinikoff

Warren Anderson, Robert Keith, Eli Wallach

The Lion
GB 1962   96m   De Luxe   Cinemascope
TCF (Samuel G. Engel)

An American lawyer goes to Africa to visit his ex-wife and their child.
Unabsorbing marital drama with child and animal interest.

w Irene and Louis Kamp, *novel* Joseph Kessel d Jack Cardiff ph Ted Scaife m Malcolm Arnold

William Holden, Trevor Howard, Capucine, Pamela Franklin
'The main fault must be attributed to the spiritless direction of Jack Cardiff, whose recent change of métier has resulted in the industry losing a great lighting cameraman.'—*John Gillett*

The Lion Has Wings*
GB 1939   76m   bw
Alexander Korda

A documentary drama tracing the steps leading up to the outbreak of war.
Once-inspiring propaganda piece, now regrettably hilarious. Valuable social history, though.

w Adrian Brunel, E. V. H. Emmett d Michael Powell, Brian Desmond Hurst, Adrian Brunel

Merle Oberon, Ralph Richardson, June Duprez, Robert Douglas, Anthony Bushell, Derrick de Marney, Brian Worth, Austin Trevor
'As a statement of war aims, one feels, this leaves the world beyond Roedean still expectant.'—*Graham Greene*

The Lion in Winter*
GB 1968   134m   Eastmancolor
Panavision
Avco Embassy / Haworth (Martin Poll)

Henry II and Eleanor of Aquitaine celebrate Christmas together and have a family row.
An acting feast for two principals and assorted supports, a talking marathon in which not all the talk is good, a smart comedy with sudden lapses into melodrama; stimulating in parts but all rather tiresome by the end, especially as there is not much medieval splendour.

w James Goldman, from his play d Anthony Harvey ph Douglas Slocombe m John Barry

Katharine Hepburn, Peter O'Toole, Jane Merrow, John Castle, Anthony Hopkins, Nigel Terry, Timothy Dalton
'He is not writing a factual movie about the Plantagenets but an interpretation in which he combines their language and ours.'—*Philip T. Hartung*

AA: James Goldman; John Barry; Katharine Hepburn
AAN: best picture; Anthony Harvey; Peter O'Toole

A Lion Is in the Streets*
US 1953   88m   Technicolor
Warner / William Cagney

An itinerant confidence trickster becomes a defender of the people, is nominated for governor, and becomes corrupt.
Busy melodrama which came a bit soon after *All the King's Men.*

w Luther Davis, *novel* Adria Locke Langley d Raoul Walsh ph Harry Stradling m Franz Waxman pd Wiard Ihnen

James Cagney, Barbara Hale, Anne Francis, Warner Anderson, John McIntire, Jeanne Cagney, Lon Chaney Jnr, Frank McHugh, Larry Keating, Onslow Stevens, James Millican, Sara Haden
'A headlong and dynamic drama which offers Mr Cagney one of his most colourful and meaningful roles.'—*Bosley Crowther*

Lipstick
US 1976   90m   Technicolor
Paramount / Dino de Laurentiis (Freddie Fields)

A girl is raped but gets nowhere in court until her sister lures the man to rape her too.
Franker but not very interesting extension of a fifties co-feature, with all the developments well telegraphed.

w David Rayfiel d Lamont Johnson ph Bill Butler m Michel Polnareff

Margaux Hemingway, Perry King, Anne Bancroft, Chris Sarandon, Mariel Hemingway, Robin Gammell

'One of *Lipstick*'s points is that voyeurism encourages senseless crime, but it unfortunately ignores its own lesson.'— *Marsha McCreadie, Films in Review*

The Liquidator*
GB 1965   104m   Metrocolor   Panavision
MGM / Leslie Elliott (Jon Pennington)

An ex-war hero is recruited by the secret service as an eliminator of security risks.
Fairly lively James Bond spoof which is never quite as funny as it imagines.

w Peter Yeldham, *novel* John Gardner   d Jack Cardiff   ph Ted Scaife   m Lalo Schifrin

Rod Taylor, Trevor Howard, *David Tomlinson*, Jill St John, Wilfrid Hyde White, Derek Nimmo, Eric Sykes, Akim Tamiroff

Lisbon
US 1956   90m   Trucolor   Naturama
Republic (Ray Milland)

An international crook negotiates an Iron Curtain prisoner's release, but the man's wife has other ideas.
Glossy international intriguer with smart performances.

w John Tucker Battle   d Ray Milland   ph Jack Marta   m Nelson Riddle

Ray Milland, *Claude Rains*, Maureen O'Hara, Yvonne Furneaux, Francis Lederer, Percy Marmont, Edward Chapman

The Lisbon Story
GB 1946   103m   bw

Spies in 1940 Lisbon rescue a French atom scientist. Flat filming of a musical show which kept Britons humming 'Pedro the Fisherman' throughout World War II. Patricia Burke, David Farrar, Walter Rilla, *Richard Tauber*, Austin Trevor, Harry Welchman. Written by Jack Whittingham, from the play by Harold Purcell and Harry Parr-Davies; directed by Paul Stein; for British National.

The List of Adrian Messenger**
US 1963   98m   bw
U-I / Joel (Edward Lewis)

An intelligence officer traps a mass murderer with a penchant for disguise.
Old-fashioned mystery thriller, as though Holmes and Watson were combating a modern Moriarty (and a rough-hewn production). The whole thing is camped up like an end-of-term treat, and as a further gimmick four guest stars allegedly appear under heavy disguise in cameo parts.

w Anthony Veiller, *novel* Philip MacDonald   d John Huston   ph Joe MacDonald   m Jerry Goldsmith

George C. Scott, Kirk Douglas, Clive Brook, Dana Wynter, Jacques Roux, Walter Tony Huston, Herbert Marshall, Bernard Archard, Gladys Cooper; and Robert Mitchum, Frank Sinatra, Burt Lancaster, Tony Curtis

Listen Darling
US 1938   70m   bw
MGM (Jack Cummings)

Children try to find their widowed mother a new husband.
Slight domestic comedy chiefly notable for its young talent.

w Elaine Ryan, Anne Morrison Chapin, *story* Katherine Brush   d Edwin L. Marin   ph Charles Lawton Jnr   m George Axt   md George Stoll

Mary Astor, Judy Garland, Freddie Bartholomew, Walter Pidgeon, Alan Hale, Scotty Beckett, Charley Grapewin, Barnett Parker, Gene Lockhart

Lisztomania
GB 1975   104m   colour   Panavision
Warner / VPS / Goodtimes (Roy Baird, David Puttnam)

The life of Liszt seen in terms of a modern pop performer.
The most excessive and obscene of all this director's controversial works, incapable of criticism on normal terms except that it seems unusually poor in production values.

wd Ken Russell   ph Peter Suschitsky   md John Forsyth

Roger Daltrey, Sara Kestelman, Paul Nicholas, Fiona Lewis, John Justin, Ringo Starr

'Ken Russell's first completely unmitigated catastrophe in several years . . . a welter of arbitrary gags, manic self-references and frantic exploitation-movie clichés.'—*Tony Rayns*

'Oscar Wilde once said "Each man kills the thing he loves", and the remark perfectly suits Ken Russell's film treatments of classical composers . . . he has bludgeoned into pulp some of the finest music civilization has produced.'—*Patrick Snyder*

The Little Ark
US 1971   86m   De Luxe   Panavision
Cinema Center / Robert B. Radnitz

Two war orphans and their pets, trapped in a flood, sail to safety in a houseboat.
Well-meaning, somewhat allegorical family film, too desultory to maintain interest and rather too frightening for children.

w Joanna Crawford, *novel* Jan de Hartog
d James B. Clark *ph* Austin Dempster,
Denys Coop *m* Fred Karlin

Theodore Bikel, Philip Frame, Genevieve
Ambas

AAN: song, 'Come Follow Follow Me'

Little Big Horn°
US 1951 86m bw
Lippert (Carl K. Hittleman)
GB title: *The Fighting Seventh*

A cavalry squad sets out to warn Custer about
Little Big Horn, but all the men are massacred
before Custer arrives.
Dour, impressive low-budget western.

wd Charles Marquis Warren ph Ernest Miller
m Paul Dunlap

Lloyd Bridges, John Ireland, Marie Windsor,
Reed Hadley, Hugh O'Brian, Wally Cassell,
King Donovan

Little Big Man°
US 1970 147m Technicolor
Panavision
Stockbridge / Hiller / Cinema Center (Stuart
Millar)

An aged veteran of the old west recounts his
life story—with elaborations.
A number of episodes varying from stark
tragedy to satirical farce are framed for no
good reason by the star in heavy disguise; the
intention is hard to guess but there are goodies
along the way.

w Calder Willingham, *novel* Thomas Berger
d Arthur Penn *ph Harry Stradling m* John
Hammond *pd* Dean Tavoularis

Dustin Hoffman, Martin Balsam, Faye
Dunaway, *Chief Dan George*, Richard
Mulligan, Jeff Corey

'A hip epic, with an amiable first hour. Then
the massacres and messages take over.'—*New
Yorker, 1976*

'A tangy and, I think, unique film with
American verve, about some of the things
American verve has done.'—*Stanley
Kauffmann*

A Little Bit of Heaven
US 1940 87m bw
Universal (Joe Pasternak)

A 12-year-old girl becomes a singing sensation
but runs into family opposition.
Predictable vehicle for a young star being built
up as a stop-gap Deanna Durbin.

w Daniel Taradash, Gertrude Purcell, Harold
Goldman, *story* Grover Jones *d* Andrew
Marton *ph* John Seitz *m* Charles Previn

Gloria Jean, Robert Stack, Hugh Herbert,
C. Aubrey Smith, Stuart Erwin, Nan Grey,
Eugene Pallette, Billy Gilbert, Butch and
Buddy

Little Boy Lost
US 1953 95m bw
Paramount (William Perlberg)

An American returns to Paris after the war to
find his wife dead and his small son missing.
Rather dull tearjerker.

wd George Seaton, *novel* Marghanita Laski
ph George Barnes *m* Victor Young

Bing Crosby, Claude Dauphin, Christian
Fourcade, Gabrielle Dorziat, Nicole Maurey

Little Caesar°°°°
US 1930 77m bw
Warner

The rise and fall of a vicious gangster.
Its central character clearly modelled on Al
Capone, this also has historical interest as
vanguard of a spate of noisy gangster films.
The star was forever identified with his role,
and the film, though technically dated, moves
fast enough to maintain interest over fifty
years later.

w Francis Faragoh, Robert E. Lee, *novel* W.
R. Burnett *d* Mervyn Le Roy *ph* Tony
Gaudio *m* Erno Rapee

Edward G. Robinson, Douglas Fairbanks Jnr,
Glenda Farrell, William Collier Jnr, Ralph
Ince, George E. Stone, Thomas Jackson,
Stanley Fields, Sidney Blackmer

'It has irony and grim humour and a real
sense of excitement and its significance does
not get in the way of the melodrama.'—
Richard Dana Skinner

AAN: Francis Faragoh, Robert E. Lee

The Little Colonel°°
US 1935 80m bw (colour sequence)
TCF (B. G. De Sylva)

In a southern household after the Civil War, a
little girl ends a family feud, plays Cupid to
her sister, routs a few villains and mollifies her
cantankerous grandfather.
First-class Temple vehicle, the first to boast an
expensive production.

w William Conselman, *novel* Annie Fellows
Johnson *d* David Butler *ph* Arthur Miller
md Arthur Lange

Shirley Temple, Lionel Barrymore, Evelyn
Venable, John Lodge, Bill Robinson, Hattie
McDaniel, Sidney Blackmer

Little Darlings
US 1980 92m Metrocolor

Teenage girls at a summer camp take bets on who will lose her virginity first. Crass and tasteless comedy with only prurient appeal.
Tatum O'Neal, Kristy McNichol, Krista Errickson, Armande Assante. Written by Kimi Peck and Dalene Young; directed by Ronald F. Maxwell; for Stephen J. Friedman / Paramount.

The Little Damozel
GB 1933   73m   bw

A gambler marries a young singer for a bribe, but falls in love with her. Lavender-tinted romance with music; notable as its star's first major role. Anna Neagle, James Rennie, Benita Hume, Athole Stewart, Alfred Drayton. Written by Donovan Pedelty, from the play by Monckton Hoffe; directed by Herbert Wilcox; for British and Dominions.

Little Fauss and Big Halsy
US 1970   99m   Movielab   Panavision
Paramount / Alfran / Furie (Albert S. Ruddy)

Two motor cycle track racers team up and have violent adventures round the country. Rather pointless capers in the wake of *Easy Rider*, neither interesting nor well done.

w Charles Eastman d Sidney J. Furie
ph Ralph Woolsey

Robert Redford, Michael J. Pollard, *Noah Beery Jnr*, Lauren Hutton
  'A sort of *Batman and Robin* on wheels.'—*Rex Reed*

The Little Foxes***
US 1941   116m   bw
Samuel Goldwyn

A family of schemers in post-Civil War days will stop at nothing to outwit each other. Superb film of a brilliant play; excellent to look at and listen to, with a compelling narrative line and memorable characters.

w *Lillian Hellman*, from her play d *William Wyler ph Gregg Toland m* Meredith Willson

Bette Davis, Herbert Marshall, Teresa Wright, Richard Carlson, *Charles Dingle, Dan Duryea, Carl Benton Reid, Patricia Collinge,* Jessica Grayson, Russell Hicks
  'One of the really beautiful jobs in the whole range of movie making.'—*Otis Ferguson*

  'No one knows better than Wyler when to shift the camera's point of view, when to cut, or how to relate the characters in one shot to those in the next . . . you never have to wonder where you are in a Wyler picture.'—*Arthur Knight*

AAN: best picture; Lillian Hellman; William Wyler; Meredith Willson; Bette Davis; Teresa Wright; Patricia Collinge

Little Friend
GB 1934   85m   bw

A girl is driven to attempt suicide by her parents' proposed divorce. Fairly well written but rather stilted domestic drama which maintained a small reputation. Nova Pilbeam, Matheson Lang, Lydia Sherwood, Arthur Margetson, Allan Aynesworth, Jean Cadell, Jimmy Hanley. Written by Margaret Kennedy, Christopher Isherwood and Berthold Viertel, from the novel by Ernst Lothar; directed by Berthold Viertel; for Gaumont.

The Little Giant
US 1933   74m   bw
Warner

At the end of Prohibition, a beer baron moves to California and tries to break into society. Disappointingly unfunny gangster comedy which never really gets going.

w Robert Lord, Wilson Mizner d Roy del Ruth ph Sid Hickox md Leo F. Forbstein

Edward G. Robinson, Mary Astor, Helen Vinson, Kenneth Thompson, Russell Hopton, Donald Dillaway

Little Giant
US 1946   91m   bw
Universal (Joseph Gershenson)
GB title: *On the Carpet*

Misadventures of a vacuum cleaner salesman. Curious, unsatisfactory Abbott and Costello comedy in which the boys play separate characters instead of working as a team. They should have waited for a better script before experimenting.

w Paul Jarrico, Richard Collins, Walter de Leon d William A. Seiter ph Charles van Enger m Edgar Fairchild

Bud Abbott, Lou Costello, Brenda Joyce, George Cleveland, Elena Verdugo

The Little Girl Who Lives Down the Lane
US / Canada / France 1976   94m   colour
Zev Braun / ICL / Filmedis-Filmel (Zev Braun)

A 13-year-old girl, when her father dies, is discovered to be keeping her mother's corpse in the cellar, and doesn't stop at more murders to keep her secret.
Tasteless piece of grand guignol, badly directed and over-acted.

w Laird Koenig, from his novel d Nicolas
Gessner ph Pene Verzier m Christian
Gaubert

Jodie Foster, Alexis Smith, Martin Sheen,
Scott Jacoby

† Originally intended as a TV movie.

The Little Hut
US 1957 90m Eastmancolor
MGM / Herbson S A (F. Hugh Herbert, Mark
  Robson)

A man, his wife and her lover are shipwrecked
on a desert island.
Sophisticated French farce which falls
resoundingly flat in this bowdlerized
Hollywood version in bilious colour, fatally
compromising itself at the beginning with a
'realistic' London prologue.

w F. Hugh Herbert, play André Roussin and
Nancy Mitford d Mark Robson ph Frederick
A. Young m Robert Farnon ad Elliot Scott

Stewart Granger, David Niven, Ava Gardner,
Walter Chiari, Finlay Currie, Jean Cadell

Little Man, What Now?*
US 1934 90m bw
Universal

Problems of Germany in the grip of
unemployment.
One of the studio's several 'sequels' to All
Quiet on the Western Front, poignant at the
time but now very dated.

w William Anthony McGuire, novel Hans
Fallada d Frank Borzage ph Norbert
Brodine

Margaret Sullavan, Douglass Montgomery,
Alan Hale, Muriel Kirkland, Alan Mowbray,
Mae Marsh

The Little Minister
US 1934 110m bw
RKO (Pandro S. Berman)

In 1840 Scotland, the gypsy girl with whom the
new pastor falls unsuitably in love is really the
local earl's wayward daughter.
Tedious film version of a cloyingly whimsical
play.

w Jane Murfin, Sarah Y. Mason, Victor
Heerman, play J. M. Barrie d Richard
Wallace ph Henry Gerrard m Max Steiner

Katharine Hepburn, John Beal, Alan Hale,
Donald Crisp, Lumsden Hare, Andy Clyde,
Beryl Mercer, Dorothy Stickney, Frank
Conroy, Reginald Denny
  'Although dear Babbie's elfin whimsies are
likely to cause teeth-gnashing among
unsympathetic moderns, Miss Hepburn plays

the part with likeable sprightliness and
charm.'—André Sennwald, New York Times

Little Miss Broadway
US 1938 70m bw
TCF (David Hempstead)

A small girl is adopted by the owner of a hotel
for vaudeville artistes.
One of the child star's more casual vehicles,
but quite pleasing.

w Harry Tugend, Jack Yellen d Irving
Cummings ph Arthur Miller md Louis
Silvers

Shirley Temple, George Murphy, Jimmy
Durante, Edna May Oliver, Phyllis Brooks,
George Barbier, Edward Ellis, Jane Darwell,
El Brendel, Donald Meek, Claude
Gillingwater, Russell Hicks
  'It can't be old age, but it does look like
weariness.'—New York Times

Little Miss Marker**
US 1934 80m bw
Paramount (B. P. Schulberg)
GB title: The Girl in Pawn

A cynical racetrack gambler is forced to adopt
a little girl, who not only softens him but saves
him from his enemies.
The twin appeals of Temple (a new hot
property) and Runyon made this a big hit of
its time.

w William R. Lipman, Sam Hellman, Gladys
Lehman, story Damon Runyon d Alexander
Hall ph Alfred Gilks

Shirley Temple, Adolphe Menjou, Dorothy
Dell, Charles Bickford, Lynne Overman,
Frank McGlynn Snr, Willie Best

† Remade as Sorrowful Jones (qv).

Little Miss Marker
US 1980 103m Technicolor
Universal (Jennings Lang)

Mainly glutinous remake of the above, with
acerbic asides from the star.

wd Walter Bernstein ph Philip Lathrop
m Henry Mancini

Walter Matthau, Julie Andrews, Tony Curtis,
Bob Newhart, Sara Stimson, Lee Grant, Brian
Dennehy

Little Murders
US 1971 108m De Luxe
TCF / Brodsky–Gould (Jack Brodsky)

A young photographer rises above all the
urban horror of New York life, but when his
wife is killed by a sniper he takes to violence.
This adaptation of an ultrablack comedy

would have worked better as a comic strip, for its characters are satirical puppets, and when played by human beings the whole thing seems violently silly.

w Jules Feiffer, from his play *d* Alan Arkin *ph* Gordon Willis *m* Fred Kaz

Elliot Gould, Marcia Rodd, Elizabeth Wilson, Vincent Gardenia, Alan Arkin

Little Nellie Kelly*
US 1940 100m bw
MGM (Arthur Freed)

The daughter of a New York Irish cop makes good on the stage.
Sentimental nostalgic vehicle for young Judy Garland, who plays both wife and daughter and sings plenty of standard melodies.

w Jack McGowan, *play* George M. Cohan *d* Norman Taurog *songs* George M. Cohan, Roger Edens, Lew Brown, Arthur Freed *ph* Ray June

Judy Garland, George Murphy, Charles Winninger, Douglas McPhail, Arthur Shields, Forrester Harvey

Little Old New York
US 1940 100m bw
TCF (Raymond Griffith)

The story of Robert Fulton and his invention of the steamboat.
Romantic hokum with a veneer of fact; good production.

w Harry Tugend, *play* Rida Johnson Young *d* Henry King *ph* Leon Shamroy *m* Alfred Newman

Alice Faye, Richard Greene, Fred MacMurray, Henry Stephenson, Brenda Joyce, Andy Devine, Fritz Feld, Ward Bond

The Little Prince
US 1974 89m Technicolor
Paramount / Stanley Donen

A small boy leaves the asteroid he rules to learn of life on earth.
A whimsical bestseller turns into an arch musical which falls over itself early on and never recovers; in any case it fatally lacks the common touch, though it has pleasing moments.

w Alan Jay Lerner, *novel* Antoine de St-Exupery *d Stanley Donen ph Christopher Challis m / ly* Frederick Loewe, Alan Jay Lerner *pd* John Barry

Richard Kiley, Steven Warner, *Bob Fosse*, Gene Wilder, Joss Ackland, Clive Revill, Victor Spinetti, Graham Crowden

'Handsome production cannot obscure limited artistic achievement.'—*Variety*
AAN: title song; musical adaptation (Angela Morley, Douglas Gamley)

The Little Princess**
US 1939 93m Technicolor
TCF (Gene Markey)

In Victorian London a little girl is left at a harsh school when her father goes abroad.
One of the child star's plushest vehicles, a charming early colour film complete with dream sequence and happy ending.

w Ethel Hill, Walter Ferris, *novel* Frances Hodgson Burnett *d* Walter Lang *ph Arthur Miller, William Skall md* Louis Silvers

Shirley Temple, Richard Greene, Anita Louise, Ian Hunter, Cesar Romero, Arthur Treacher, Mary Nash, Sybil Jason, Miles Mander, Marcia Mae Jones, Beryl Mercer, E. E. Clive

A Little Romance
US 1979 108m Technicolor
Warner / Orion (Patrick Kelley)

A French teenager elopes with an American girl, encouraged by a garrulous old pickpocket.
Treacly juvenile romance enriched by in-jokes and an enjoyably over-the-top star performance.

w Allan Burns, *novel* Patrick Cauvin *d* George Roy Hill *ph* Pierre William Glenn *m* Georges Delerue *pd* Henry Bumstead

Laurence Olivier, Diane Lane, Thelonious Bernard, Arthur Hill, Sally Kellerman, Broderick Crawford, David Dukes

Little Women***
US 1933 115m bw
RKO / David O. Selznick (Kenneth MacGowan)

The growing up of four sisters in pre-Civil War America.
Charming 'big picture' of its day, with excellent production and performances.

w Sarah Y. Mason, Victor Heerman, *novel* Louisa May Alcott *d George Cukor ph* Henry Gerrard *m* Max Steiner

Katharine Hepburn, Paul Lukas, Joan Bennett, Frances Dee, Jean Parker, *Spring Byington*, Edna May Oliver, Douglass Montgomery, Henry Stephenson, Samuel S. Hinds, John Lodge, Nydia Westman

'If to put a book on the screen with all the effectiveness that sympathy and good taste and careful artifice can devise is to make a fine motion picture, then *Little Women* is a fine picture.'—*James Shelley Hamilton*

'One of the most satisfactory pictures I have ever seen.'—*E. V. Lucas, Punch*

'A reminder that emotions and vitality and truth can be evoked from lavender and lace as well as from machine guns and precision dances.'—*Thornton Delehanty, New York Post*

AA: script

AAN: best picture; George Cukor

Little Women*
US 1949 122m Technicolor
MGM (Mervyn Le Roy)

Syrupy Christmas-card remake, notably lacking the light touch.

w Andrew Solt, Sarah Y. Mason, Victor Heerman d Mervyn Le Roy ph Robert Planck, Charles Schoenbaum m Adolph Deutsch (after Max Steiner)

June Allyson, Elizabeth Taylor, Peter Lawford, Margaret O'Brien, Janet Leigh, Mary Astor

'It will raise a smile and draw a tear from the sentimental.'—*MFB*

AAN: cinematography

The Little World of Don Camillo*
France / Italy 1952 106m bw
Rizzoli-Amato-Francinex (Giuseppe Amato)

In a small Italian village the parish priest and the communist mayor are in a constant state of amiable feud.
Slightly lethargic character comedy with a mild message for its times, popular enough to warrant several sequels.

w Julien Duvivier, René Barjavel, *novel* Giovanni Guareschi d Julien Duvivier ph Nicolas Hayer m Alessandro Cicognini

Fernandel, Gino Cervi, Sylvie, Manara, Vera Talqui, Franco Interlenghi

'Cute and cosy.'—*MFB*

The Littlest Rebel*
US 1935 70m bw
TCF (B. G. De Sylva)

A small southern girl persuades President Lincoln to release her father.
Charming, archetypal early Temple vehicle, very well produced.

w Edwin Burke, *play* Edward Peple d David Butler ph John Seitz m Cyril Mockridge

Shirley Temple, John Boles, Jack Holt, Karen Morley, *Bill Robinson*, Guinn Williams, Willie Best, Frank McGlynn Snr

Live a Little, Steal a Lot
US 1974 102m CFI
American International (Dominick Galate)

Jewel thieves go from success to success, but the police finally force them to strike a bargain and return the gems.
Elaborate but rather unattractive caper story based on the exploits of two real criminals.

w E. Arthur Kuhn d Marvin Chomsky ph Michael Hugo m Philip Lambro

Robert Conrad, Don Stroud, Donna Mills, Robyn Miller, Luther Adler, Paul Stewart

Live and Let Die*
GB 1973 121m Eastmancolor
UA / Eon (Harry Saltzman)

James Bond chases a black master criminal and becomes involved in West Indian Voodoo.
Standard tongue-in-cheek spy adventure with a new lightweight star and an air of *déjà vu*. Professional standards high.

w Tom Mankiewicz, *novel* Ian Fleming d Guy Hamilton ph Ted Moore m George Martin *titles* Maurice Binder

Roger Moore, Yaphet Kotto, Jane Seymour, Clifton James, David Hedison, Bernard Lee, Lois Maxwell

'Plot lines have descended further to the level of the old Saturday afternoon serial, and the treatment is more than ever like a cartoon.'—*Variety*

'A Bond movie is not made. It is packaged. Like an Almond Joy. So much coconut to this much chocolate and a dash of raisins.'—*Joseph Gelmis*

AAN: title song (*m* / *ly* Paul and Linda McCartney)

Live for Life
France / Italy 1967 130m Eastmancolor
UA / Ariane / Vides
original title: *Vivre pour Vivre*

A news reporter forsakes his wife for a fashion model.
Interminable and unoriginal romantic drama against Sunday supplement backgounds.

w Pierre Uytterhoeven, Claude Lelouch d, ph Claude Lelouch m Francis Lai

Yves Montand, Candice Bergen, Annie Forardot, Irene Tunc

'The overall effect is of *Gone with the Wind* remade by Jacopetti.'—*New Yorker*

The Live Ghost
US 1934 20m bw

Two reluctant sailors think they have murdered one of their mates. Somewhat unyielding material for Stan and Ollie, but still funnier than any of their rivals at the time. Laurel and Hardy, Walter Long, Arthur Housman. Written by H. M. Walker; directed by Charles Rogers; for Hal Roach.

Live, Love and Learn
US 1937   78m   bw
MGM (Harry Rapf)

A bohemian painter is tamed by marriage. Tiresome romantic trifle.

w Charles Brackett, Cyril Hume, Richard Maibaum d George Fitzmaurice ph Ray June m Edward Ward

Robert Montgomery, Rosalind Russell, Robert Benchley, Helen Vinson, Mickey Rooney, Monty Woolley, E. E. Clive, Maude Eburne

Live Now, Pay Later
GB 1962   104m   bw
(Regal) Woodlands / Jay Lewis (Jack Hanbury)

A credit store salesman is himself heavily in debt, and his private life is in ruins; but even after a chapter of unexpected and tragic events he remains irrepressibly optimistic.
A satirical farce melodrama which lets fly in too many directions at once and has a cumulatively cheerless effect despite funny moments.

w Jack Trevor Story, novel All on the Never Never by Jack Lindsay d Jay Lewis ph Jack Hildyard m Ron Grainer

Ian Hendry, John Gregson, June Ritchie, Geoffrey Keen, Liz Fraser

Lives of a Bengal Lancer**
US 1935   119m   bw
Paramount (Louis D. Lighton)

Adventures on the North-West Frontier. British army heroics are here taken rather solemnly, but the film is efficient and fondly remembered.

w Waldemar Young, John F. Balderston, Achmed Abdullah, Grover Jones, William Slavens McNut, book Francis Yeats-Brown d Henry Hathaway ph Charles Lang m Milan Roder

Gary Cooper, Franchot Tone, Richard Cromwell, Sir Guy Standing, C. Aubrey Smith, Monte Blue, Kathleen Burke, Colin Tapley, Douglass Dumbrille, Akim Tamiroff, Noble Johnson
'The best army picture ever made.'—Daily Telegraph

AAN: best picture; script; Henry Hathaway

The Living Desert**
US 1953   72m   Technicolor
Walt Disney (James Algar)

A light-hearted documentary showing the animals and insects which live in American desert areas. The aim is entertainment and Disney is not above faking, i.e. the famous sequence in which scorpions appear to do a square dance, but on its level the thing is brilliantly done.

w James Algar, Winston Hibler, Ted Sears d James Algar ph N. Paul Kenworthy Jnr, Robert H. Grandall m Paul Smith special processes Ub Iwerks
'The film has the same cosy anthropomorphism as a Disney cartoon and its facetious commentary and vulgar music score are typical of others in the series.'—Georges Sadoul
† The other 'True Life Adventures' were: Seal Island 49 (3 reels), Beaver Valley 50 (3 reels), Nature's Half Acre 51 (3 reels), Water Birds 52 (3 reels), Prowlers of the Everglades 53 (3 reels), The Vanishing Prairie 54, The African Lion 55, Secrets of Life 56, White Wilderness 58, Jungle Cat 60.

Living Free
GB 1972   92m   colour
Columbia / Open Road / High Road

On the death of Elsa the lioness, George and Joy Adamson capture her three cubs and transfer them for their own safety to Serengeti.
Sloppy sequel to Born Free, depending very heavily on the appeal of the cubs.

w Maurice Kaufman d Jack Couffer ph Wolfgang Suschitzky m Sol Kaplan

Susan Hampshire, Nigel Davenport, Geoffrey Keen

The Living Idol
Mexico / US 1956   100m   Eastmancolor Cinemascope
MGM (Albert Lewin)

A Mexican girl becomes possessed by the spirit of the jaguar to whom local maidens were once sacrificed.
Pretentious but rather enjoyable highbrow hokum of the heady kind expected from this producer.

wd Albert Lewin ph Jack Hildyard m Rodolpho Halffter

James Robertson Justice, Steve Forrest, Liliane Montevecchi

Living in a Big Way
US 1947   103m   bw
MGM (Pandro S. Berman)

A demobbed GI finds he can't get on with his rich selfish wife and opens up a charity home for the families of war casualties.

Odd mixture of comedy, drama and a few songs and dances, not forgetting a message or two. It mostly falls flat on its face.

w Gregory La Cava, Irving Ravetch d Gregory La Cava ph Harold Rosson m Lennie Hayton

Gene Kelly, Marie McDonald, Charles Winninger, Phyllis Thaxter, Spring Byington, Clinton Sundberg

Living It Up*
US 1954 95m Technicolor
Paramount / Hal B. Wallis (Paul Jones)

A suspected victim of radium poisoning is played up by the press into a national hero. Remake of *Nothing Sacred* with Lewis as Carole Lombard; deserves a mark for cheek.

w Jack Rose, Mel Shavelson d Norman Taurog ph Daniel Fapp

Dean Martin, Jerry Lewis, Janet Leigh, Edward Arnold, Fred Clark, Sheree North, Sig Rumann

Living on Velvet*
US 1935 77m bw
Warner (Edward Chodorov)

A happy-go-lucky aviator changes his life style when he narrowly escapes death in a crash. Reasonably interesting 'serious' drama of its period.

w Jerry Wald, Julius Epstein d Frank Borzage ph Sid Hickox md Leo F. Forbstein

George Brent, Kay Francis, Warren William, Helen Lowell, Henry O'Neill, Samuel S. Hinds, Russell Hicks, Edgar Kennedy

Lizzie
US 1957 81m bw
MGM / Bryna (Jerry Bresler)

Murder and rape turn a girl into a triple personality.
Preposterous cash-in on *The Three Faces of Eve*, too silly to be even funny.

w Mel Dinelli, *novel* The Bird's Nest by Shirley Jackson d Hugo Haas ph Paul Ivano m Leith Stevens

Eleanor Parker, Richard Boone, Joan Blondell, Hugo Haas
'Ruddy peculiar.'—*MFB*

Lloyd's of London**
US 1936 115m bw
TCF (Kenneth MacGowan)

A young messenger boy in the 18th century grows up to found a great insurance company. Thoroughly well mounted, if unconvincing and slightly boring, historical charade in which the Prince of Wales, Lord Nelson, Dr Johnson and other personages make guest appearances. An archetypal prestige film of its time which also turned out to be box office.

w Ernest Pascal, Walter Ferris, *book* Curtis Kenyon d Henry King ph Bert Glennon md Louis Silvers

Tyrone Power, Madeleine Carroll, George Sanders, Freddie Bartholomew, C. Aubrey Smith, Guy Standing, Virginia Field, Montagu Love, Gavin Muir, Miles Mander, Una O'Connor, E. E. Clive

'The name of England is so freely on the characters' lips that we recognize at once an American picture. These people live, make love, bear children all from the most patriotic motives, and it's all rather like London in coronation week.'—*Graham Greene*

Lock Up Your Daughters
GB 1969 103m Technicolor
Columbia / Domino (David Deutsch)

In 18th-century London an aristocratic rake and various lower orders are all in search of female companionship and get their wires crossed.
Noisy, vulgar, ill-acted version (without music) of a successful musical based on two old theatrical warhorses.

w Keith Waterhouse, Willis Hall, *play* Bernard Miles based on Rape upon Rape by Henry Fielding and The Relapse by John Vanbrugh d Peter Coe ph Peter Suschitsky m Ron Grainer pd Tony Woollard

Christopher Plummer, Roy Kinnear, Georgia Brown, Susannah York, Glynis Johns, Ian Bannen, Tom Bell, Elaine Taylor, Jim Dale, Kathleen Harrison, Roy Dotrice, Vanessa Howard, Fenella Fielding, Peter Bayliss, *Richard Wordsworth,* Peter Bull, Fred Emney
'Subtlety is neither required nor displayed.'—*Jack Ibberson*

The Locket
US 1946 85m bw
RKO

A *femme fatale* is bent on destroying men, and eventually we discover why.
Dark, confusing melodrama very typical of the immediate post-war years; it has little to say but says it dourly, even achieving flashbacks within flashbacks within flashbacks.

w Sheridan Gibney d John Brahm ph Nicholas Musuraca m Roy Webb

Laraine Day, Robert Mitchum, Brian Aherne,
Gene Raymond, Ricardo Cortez

The Lodger*
GB 1932 85m bw
Twickenham (Julius Hagen)
US title: *The Phantom Fiend*

The upstairs lodger is suspected of being Jack
the Ripper . . .
Modernized version of a story already tackled
by Hitchcock as a silent and to be done again
in costume in 1944. Not bad, for a minor
British film of the time.

w Ivor Novello, Miles Mander, Paul Rotha,
H. Fowler Mear, *novel* Mrs Belloc Lowndes
d Maurice Elvey *ph* Stanley Blythe, Basil
Emmott

Ivor Novello, Elizabeth Allan, A. W.
Baskomb, Jack Hawkins, Barbara Everest,
Peter Gawthorne, Kynaston Reeves

The Lodger*
US 1944 84m bw
TCF (Robert Bassler)

1880s version of the above in which the lodger
is Jack the Ripper.
Nicely mounted apart from some
anachronisms, but a little dull.

w Barre Lyndon *d* John Brahm *ph* Lucien
Ballard *m* Hugo Friedhofer

Laird Cregar, Merle Oberon, George Sanders,
Cedric Hardwicke, Sara Allgood, Aubrey
Mather, Queenie Leonard, Helena Pickard,
Lumsden Hare, Frederick Worlock

Logan's Run*
US 1976 118m Metrocolor Todd-AO
MGM (Saul David)

In the future, people try to escape from a
society which dooms everyone to death at
thirty.
Interesting and quite exciting fantasy
melodrama which mercifully moves instead of
preaching.

w David Zelag Goodman, novel William F.
Nolan *d* Michael Anderson *ph* Ernest
Laszlo *m* Jerry Goldsmith *pd* Dale Hennesy

Michael York, Richard Jordan, Jenny
Agutter, Roscoe Lee Browne, Farrah Fawcett-
Majors, Peter Ustinov, Michael Anderson Jnr
  'A science fiction film made by people who
don't understand science fiction for the
amusement of people who don't care one way
or the other.'—*S. Frank, L. A. Panorama*
  'It puts the future back two thousand
years.'—*Benny Green, Punch*
AAN: Ernest Laszlo

Lola*
France / Italy 1960 91m bw Franscope
Rome-Paris / Euro-International

A cabaret dancer in Nantes chooses between
three men.
A slight romance which was much admired for
its decoration and visual style, which reminded
many of Max Ophuls.

wd Jacques Demy ph Raoul Coutard
m Michel Legrand

Anouk Aimée, Jacques Harden, Marc Michel,
Elina Labourdette

Lola Montes*
France / Germany 1955 140m
    Eastmancolor Cinemascope
Gamma / Florida / Oska

The life of the famous courtesan and her
romance with the King of Bavaria, told in
diverting fragments by a circus ringmaster.
An elaborate, expensive and trickily presented
historical charade which confused the public
and bankrupted its production company; but
the various shorter versions released didn't
help.

w Max Ophuls, Annette Wademant, Franz
Geiger, *novel* Cécil Saint-Laurent *d Max
Ophuls ph* Christian Matras *m* Georges
Auric *ad* Jean d'Aubonne, Willy Schatz

Martine Carol, Anton Walbrook, Peter
Ustinov, Ivan Desny, Oskar Werner, Will
Quadflieg
  'If you want to know what form can really
do for content, rush along.'—*Derek Malcolm,
The Guardian, 1978*

Lolita**
GB 1962 152m bw
MGM / Seven Arts / AA / Anya / Transworld
(James B. Harris)

A middle-aged lecturer falls for a 14-year-old
girl and marries her mother to be near her.
Fitfully amusing but slightly plotted and very
lengthy screen version of a sensational novel in
which the heroine is only twelve, which makes
a difference. The flashback introduction and
various comic asides are pretentious and
alienating.

w Vladimir Nabokov, from his novel
d Stanley Kubrick *ph* Oswald Morris
m Nelson Riddle

James Mason, Shelley Winters, Sue Lyon,
Peter Sellers
  'The director's heart is apparently
elsewhere. Consequently, we face the problem
without the passion, the badness without the
beauty, the agony without the ecstasy.'—
Andrew Sarris

'A diluted *Blue Angel* with a teenage temptress instead of a tart.'—*Stanley Kauffmann*

'So clumsily structured that you begin to wonder whether what was shot and then cut out, whether the beginning was intended to be the end; and it is edited in so dilatory a fashion that after the first hour, almost every scene seems to go on too long.'—*Pauline Kael*

AAN: Vladimir Nabokov

Lolly Madonna XXX

US 1973 105m Metrocolor
MGM (Rodney Carr-Smith)
GB title: *The Lolly Madonna War*

Tennessee hillbilly farmers fight over a meadow.
Violent feudin' melodrama, technically accomplished but of limited interest to non-hillbillies.

w Rodney Carr-Smith, Sue Grafton, from her novel d Richard C. Sarafian ph Philip Lathrop m Fred Myrow

Rod Steiger, Robert Ryan, Scott Wilson, Jeff Bridges, Season Hubley

London After Midnight*

US 1927 approx 75m bw silent
MGM (Tod Browning)
GB title: *The Hypnotist*

A creepy house murder is solved by hypnotism, and a grinning monster proves to be a red herring.
Famous star thriller of which lamentably no prints survive; remade as *Mark of the Vampire*.

w Tod Browning, Waldemar Young d Tod Browning ph Merritt Gerstad

Lon Chaney, Marceline Day, Conrad Nagel, Henry B. Walthall, Polly Moran

London Belongs to Me**

GB 1948 112m bw
GFD / Individual (Frank Launder, Sidney Gilliat)
US title: *Dulcimer Street*

A young boy is arrested on a murder charge and his boarding-house friends rally to his defence.
Unconvincing but highly entertaining sub-Dickensian comedy-drama with a rousing finish and an abundance of character roles.

w Sidney Gilliat, J. B. Williams, *novel* Norman Collins d Sidney Gilliat ph Wilkie Cooper m Benjamin Frankel

Alastair Sim, Stephen Murray, Richard Attenborough, Fay Compton, Wylie Watson,
Susan Shaw, Ivy St Helier, Joyce Carey, Andrew Crawford, Eleanor Summerfield, Hugh Griffith, Gladys Henson

London Melody

GB 1937 75m bw
GFD / Herbert Wilcox
US title: *Girls in the Street*

A diplomat falls for a dancer.
Light but rather humourless musical drama.

w Florence Tranter, Monckton Hoffe
d Herbert Wilcox ph F. A. Young

Anna Neagle, Tullio Carminati, Robert Douglas, Horace Hodges

London Town*

GB 1946 126m Technicolor
GFD / Wesley Ruggles
US title: *My Heart Goes Crazy*

An understudy finally achieves stardom thanks to his daughter's schemes.
Disastrous and expensive attempt to make a major British musical without a single new idea. Tasteless, tawdry and sluggish, but it does record for posterity four of the star's sketches.

w Elliot Paul, Siegfried Herzig, Val Guest
d Wesley Ruggles ph Erwin Hiller

Sid Field, Greta Gynt, Kay Kendall, Tessie O'Shea, Claude Hulbert, Sonnie Hale, Mary Clare, Petula Clark, Jerry Desmonde

'I can't see the point of importing an American director and giving him all the time and money in the world to play with when we can make bad musicals on our own, and quicker.'—*Richard Winnington*

The Lone Hand

US 1953 80m Technicolor

A quiet western farmer is really a Pinkerton detective. Slightly unusual western in which the happy ending is not however in doubt. Joel McCrea, Barbara Hale, Alex Nicol, Charles Drake, James Arness. Written by Joseph Hoffman; directed by George Sherman; for Universal-International.

Lone Star

US 1952 90m bw
MGM (Z. Wayne Griffin)

Andrew Jackson enlists the aid of a Texas adventurer to persuade Sam Houston to change his mind about an agreement with Mexico.
Slow-moving semi-western, hard to follow for non-Americans. Production values quite high.

w Borden Chase, Howard Estabrook
d Vincent Sherman *ph* Harold Rosson
m David Buttolph

Clark Gable, Ava Gardner, Lionel
Barrymore, Broderick Crawford, Ed Begley,
Beulah Bondi, James Burke, William Farnum,
Lowell Gilmore, Moroni Olsen, Russell
Simpson, William Conrad

The Lone Wolf

The jewel thief turned sleuth was created by
Louis Joseph Vance and turned up in several
silent films. During the talkie period several
actors played Michael Lanyard; the role of his
valet passed from Raymond Walburn to Eric
Blore to Alan Mowbray. All the films were
made for Columbia, but only the first was
anything like a main feature.
1935: THE LONE WOLF RETURNS (*d* Roy
William Neill with Melvyn Douglas)
1938: THE LONE WOLF IN PARIS (*d*
Albert S. Rogell with Francis Lederer)
1939: THE LONE WOLF SPY HUNT
(*d* Peter Godfrey with Warren William)
1940: THE LONE WOLF STRIKES
(*d* Sidney Salkow with Warren William)
1941: THE LONE WOLF MEETS A LADY,
THE LONE WOLF TAKES A CHANCE,
THE LONE WOLF KEEPS A DATE (all as
above), SECRETS OF THE LONE WOLF
(*d* Edward Dmytryk; WW)
1943: ONE DANGEROUS NIGHT
(*d* Michael Gordon: WW), PASSPORT TO
SUEZ (*d* André de Toth: WW)
1946: THE NOTORIOUS LONE WOLF
(*d* D. Ross Lederman; with Gerald Mohr)
1947: THE LONE WOLF IN LONDON
(*d* Leslie Goodwins: GM), THE LONE
WOLF IN MEXICO (*d* D. Ross Lederman:
GM)
1949: THE LONE WOLF AND HIS LADY
(*d* John Hoffman: GM)

The Loneliness of the Long Distance Runner*
GB 1962   104m   bw
British Lion / Bryanston / Woodfall (Tony
    Richardson)

The only thing a Borstal boy does well is run,
and as he trains he thinks back to his
depressing life.
Rather pale study of a social outcast;
interesting scenes do not quite form a
compelling whole.

w Alan Sillitoe, from his short story *d* Tony
Richardson *ph* Walter Lassally *m* John
Addison

Tom Courtenay, Michael Redgrave, James
Bolam, Avis Bunnage, Alec McCowen, Joe
Robinson, Julia Foster

Lonely Are the Brave*
US 1962   107m   bw   Panavision
U-I / Joel (Edward Lewis)

The last of the cowboy rebels is no match for
pursuit by jeep and helicopter.
A strange, sad, rather moving fable, with very
good performances and action scenes, but a
shade too unrelenting in its downbeat tone to
become a popular classic.

w Dalton Trumbo, *novel* Brave Cowboy by
Edward Abbey *d* David Miller *ph* Philip
Lathrop *m* Jerry Goldsmith

Kirk Douglas, Walter Matthau, Gena
Rowlands, Michael Kane, Carroll O'Connor,
Karl Swenson, George Kennedy, Bill Raisch

The Lonely Man
US 1957   87m   bw   Vistavision
Paramount (Pat Duggan)

An outlaw hopes to regain social recognition
and contacts the son who abhors him.
Dullish psycho western.

w Harry Essex, Robert Smith *d* Henry Levin
ph Lionel Lindon *m* Van Cleave

Jack Palance, Anthony Perkins, Elaine Aiken,
Neville Brand, Lee Van Cleef, Elisha Cook
Jnr, Robert Middleton

Lonelyhearts*
US 1958   103m   bw
UA / Dore Schary

A young journalist finds himself engrossed,
appalled and sickened by his work on the
agony column.
Episodic, occasionally interesting but generally
too vaguely liberal; an intellectual reshaping of
a despairing novel. The producer as usual is
well meaning but doesn't quite make it.

w Dore Schary, *novel* Nathanael West
d Vincent J. Donehue *ph* John Alton
m Conrad Salinger

Montgomery Clift, Robert Ryan, Myrna Loy,
Dolores Hart, Maureen Stapleton

AAN: Maureen Stapleton

Lonesome*
US 1928   69m (24 fps)   bw   silent
Universal

Young lovers lose each other at Luna Park but
later discover that they are neighbours.
Amiable exploration of the life of city
workers, comparable with *The Crowd* but
showing a lighter touch.

w Edmund T. Lowe *d* Paul Fejos *ph* Gilbert
Warrenton

Glenn Tryon, Barbara Kent

The Long and the Short and the Tall*
GB 1960 105m bw
ABP / Michael Balcon
US title: *Jungle Fighters*

In Malaya during World War II a Japanese
scout is captured by a British patrol.
Stark war melodrama with the emphasis on
character. Vivid at the time, it now seems very
routine.

w Wolf Mankowitz, *play* Willis Hall *d* Leslie
Norman *ph* Erwin Hillier *m* Stanley Black

Laurence Harvey, Richard Todd, David
McCallum, Richard Harris, Ronald Fraser,
John Meillon, John Rees, Kenji Takaki

The Long Arm**
GB 1956 96m bw
Ealing (Tom Morahan)
US title: *The Third Key*

A Scotland Yard superintendent solves a
series of robberies.
Good straightforward police thriller with
careful detail.

*w Janet Green, Robert Barr d Charles Frend
ph* Gordon Dines *m* Gerbrand Schurmann

Jack Hawkins, Dorothy Alison, John Stratton,
Michael Brooke, Geoffrey Keen, Sidney
Tafler, Meredith Edwards, Ralph Truman,
Ursula Howells
'A generally efficient example of popular
British film-making.'—*MFB*

The Long Dark Hall
GB 1951 86m bw
British Lion / Five Oceans (Anthony
  Bushell)

A chorus girl is murdered and her married
lover is accused.
Miserable mystery with a trick ending, most
inappropriately cast.

w Nunnally Johnson, W. E. C. Fairchild
d Anthony Bushell, Reginald Beck *ph* Wilkie
Cooper *m* Benjamin Frankel

Rex Harrison, Lilli Palmer, Raymond
Huntley, Denis O'Dea, Anthony Bushell,
Henry Longhurst, Patricia Wayne, Meriel
Forbes, Brenda de Banzie, Anthony Dawson

The Long Day's Dying
GB 1968 95m Techniscope
Paramount / Junction Films

Three British paratroopers in Europe are cut

off from their unit and die pointlessly.
Violent, irritating anti-war film which
resurrects all the clichés and makes itself
unpleasant into the bargain.

w Charles Wood, *novel* Alan White *d* Peter
Collinson *ph* Brian Probyn *m* Malcolm
Lockyer *pd* Disley Jones

David Hemmings, Tom Bell, Tony Beckley,
Alan Dobie
'It is typical of all that is wrong with the film
that it should end on a frozen frame of a
soldier in the act of dying while heavily ironic
patriotic music swells on the sound track.'—
David Wilson

Long Day's Journey into Night**
US 1961 174m bw
Ely Landau

Connecticut 1912: days in the life of an ageing
actor, his drug addicted wife and their sons,
one of whom is an alcoholic and the other
Eugene O'Neill.
Heavy going, nicely handled, superbly acted
version of a play which can be a player's
triumph and certainly is here; but it still has
more effect in the theatre.

w Eugene O'Neill *d* Sidney Lumet *ph* Boris
Kaufman *m* André Previn *pd* Richard Sylbert

Ralph Richardson, Katharine Hepburn, Jason
Robards Jnr, *Dean Stockwell*
'Letting his players have their head, lighted
miraculously so that every flicker of emotion is
preserved, and pursuing them with Kaufman's
unobtrusive camera, Lumet illuminates the
play, line by line, and gives it all the impact of
a live performance.'—*Brenda Davies*
'A very great play has been not translated to
the screen but reverently put behind glass.'—
John Simon

AAN: Katharine Hepburn

The Long Duel
GB 1967 115m Technicolor
Panavision
Rank (Ken Annakin)

On the North-West Frontier in the twenties,
British officers disagree about handling the
natives, and one of them forms a strong regard
for the native leader.
Unconvincing cut-price Indian adventure with
little cohesion and less entertainment value.

w Peter Yeldham *d* Ken Annakin *ph* Jack
Hildyard *m* Patrick John Scott

Trevor Howard, Yul Brynner, Harry
Andrews, Charlotte Rampling, Virginia
North, Andrew Keir, Laurence Naismith,
Maurice Denham

'The dialogue seems to have been written by a computer fed a programme of execrable films on the same theme.'—*MFB*

The Long Good Friday*
GB 1980   105m   colour
Black Lion / Calendar (Barry Hanson)

A gangland boss faces violent reprisals from the competition.

Heavily melodramatic stylish updating of *Scarface* in a London East End setting. A critical success despite vicious detail and IRA plot involvement.

w Barrie Keefe d John Mackenzie ph Phil Meheux m Francis Monkman

Bob Hoskins, Helen Mirren, Dave King, Brian Hall, Eddie Constantine, Stephen Davis

The Long Goodbye
US 1973   111m   Technicolor
Panavision
UA / Lions Gate (Jerry Bick)

Philip Marlowe helps an eccentric friend who is suspected of murdering his wife.

Ugly, boring travesty of a well-respected detective novel, the apparent intention being to reverse the author's attitudes completely and to substitute dullness and incomprehensibility.

w Leigh Brackett, novel Raymond Chandler d Robert Altman ph Vilmos Zsigismond m John T. Williams

Elliott Gould, Nina Van Pallandt, Sterling Hayden, Mark Rydell, Henry Gibson

'Altman's fragmentation bomb blows up itself rather than the myths he has said he wants to lay to rest.'—*Sight and Sound*

'The trouble is that this Marlowe is an untidy, unshaven, semi-literate dimwit slob who could not locate a missing skyscraper and who would be refused service at a hot dog stand.'—*Charles Champlin*

'A spit in the eye to a great writer.'—*Michael Billington, Illustrated London News*

The Long Gray Line*
US 1955   138m   Technicolor
Cinemascope
Columbia (Robert Arthur)

The career of an athletics trainer at West Point.

Dim biopic, the kind of true life yarn that Americans like, produced in the cheerful, sentimental, sparring way that John Ford likes.

w Edward Hope, book Bring Up the Brass by Merty Maher d John Ford ph Charles Lawton Jnr m George Duning md Morris Stoloff

Tyrone Power, Maureen O'Hara, Donald Crisp, Ward Bond, Robert Francis, Betsy Palmer, Phil Carey, Harry Carey Jnr, Patrick Wayne, Sean McClory

'Its celebration of the codes and ideals of West Point vexatiously combines sentimental cosiness and a kind of religious awe.'—*Gavin Lambert*

The Long Hot Summer*
US 1958   118m   Eastmancolor
Cinemascope
TCF (Jerry Wald)

Conflict arises between a Mississippi town boss and a tenant farmer.

Busy Peyton Place-style family brawling saga with sex on the side, flabby as narrative but compulsive as character study.

w Irving Ravetch, Harriet Frank, stories William Faulkner d Martin Ritt ph Joseph La Shelle m Alex North

Orson Welles, Paul Newman, Joanne Woodward, Tony Franciosa, Lee Remick, Angela Lansbury

Long John Silver
Australia 1953   106m   Eastmancolor
Cinemascope
TI Pictures (Joseph Kaufman)

Back from Treasure Island, Silver and Hawkins plan a return visit with fresh clues to the treasure.

Cheaply produced, bitsy-piecy adventure fragments with no one to restrain the star from eye-rolling.

w Martin Rackin d Byron Haskin ph Carl Guthrie m David Buttolph

Robert Newton, Connie Gilchrist, Kit Taylor, Rod Taylor

The Long Long Trailer*
US 1954   96m   Anscocolor
MGM (Pandro S. Berman)

A construction engineer and his bride buy a trailer for their honeymoon, and wish they hadn't.

Disaster comedy with long bright periods and the inevitable saggy bits.

w Frances Goodrich, Albert Hackett, novel Clinton Twiss d Vincente Minnelli ph Robert Surtees m Adolph Deutsch

Lucille Ball, Desi Arnaz, Marjorie Main, Keenan Wynn, Moroni Olsen

Long Lost Father
US 1934   63m   bw
RKO

A restaurant owner saves his daughter from a theft charge.
Competent minor star drama.

w Dwight Taylor, *novel* G. B. Stern *d* Ernest B. Schoedsack *ph* Nicholas Musuraca *m* Max Steiner

John Barrymore, Helen Chandler, Donald Cook, Alan Mowbray, Claude King

The Long Memory
GB 1952 96m bw
Rank / Europa (Hugh Stewart)

An ex-con, framed for a murder he did not commit, plots revenge but instead uncovers a fresh crime.
Slow and dreary melodrama set largely on a barge, never rising to anything like excitement.

w Robert Hamer, Frank Harvey, *novel* Winston Clewes *d* Robert Hamer *ph* Harry Waxman *m* William Alwyn

John Mills, John McCallum, Elizabeth Sellars, Geoffrey Keen

The Long Night*
US 1947 97m bw
(RKO) Anatole Litvak

A young man shoots the seducer of his sweetheart and barricades himself in a room against the police.
Good-looking but empty remake of *Le Jour se Lève*.

w John Wexley, *story* Jacques Viot *d* Anatole Litvak *ph* Sol Polito *m* Dmitri Tiomkin

Henry Fonda, Barbara Bel Geddes, Vincent Price, Ann Dvorak, Queenie Smith

'This film faithfully reproduces the letter while altering the spirit of the original almost beyond recognition.'—*MFB*

'It would be interesting to see it on a double bill with its French original. Both films clearly rate themselves as tragedies; they are merely intelligent trash. But the old one is much more discreet with its self-pity and much more sharply edged.'—*James Agee*

Long Pants*
US 1927 58m (24 fps) bw silent
First National / Harry Langdon

A country bumpkin has trouble in the city.
Far from the best Langdon comedy, but funny in flashes.

w Arthur Ripley *d* Frank Capra *ph* Elgin Lessley

Harry Langdon, Gladys Brockwell, Alan Roscoe, Alma Bennett

The Long Riders
US 1980 99m Technicolor
UA / Huka (Tim Zinnemann)

The story of western outlaw brothers named Younger, Miller and James.
Well-worn territory with new-fangled violent detail. Not much of an attraction despite the gimmick of having the various anti-heroes played by real brothers.

w Bill Bryden, Steven Phillip Smith, Stacy Keach, James Keach *d* Walter Hill *ph* Ric Waite *m* Ry Cooder *pd* Jack T. Collis

Stacy Keach, James Keach, David Carradine, Keith Carradine, Robert Carradine, Dennis Quaid, Randy Quaid

The Long Ships
GB / Yugoslavia 1963 126m Technirama
Columbia / Warwick / Avila (Irving Allen)

A Viking adventurer and a Moorish prince fall out over a golden bell.
Stilted medieval epic with some visual compensations but more chat than action.

w Berkely Mather, Beverly Cross, *novel* Frank G. Bengtsson *d* Jack Cardiff *ph* Christopher Challis *m* Dusan Radic

Richard Widmark, Sidney Poitier, Russ Tamblyn, Rosanna Schiaffino, Oscar Homolka, Colin Blakely

The Long Voyage Home**
US 1940 104m bw
Walter Wanger

Merchant seamen on shore leave get drunk, philosophize and have adventures.
Stagey-looking but dramatically interesting amalgam of four one-act plays by Eugene O'Neill, with talent abounding.

w Dudley Nichols *d* John Ford *ph* Gregg Toland *m* Richard Hageman

John Wayne, Thomas Mitchell, Ian Hunter, Ward Bond, Barry Fitzgerald, Wilfrid Lawson, Mildred Natwick, John Qualen, Arthur Shields, Joe Sawyer

AAN: best picture; Dudley Nichols; Gregg Toland; Richard Hageman

The Long Wait
US 1954 93m bw
UA / Parklane (Lesser Samuels)

An amnesia victim returns home to solve a murder in which he was involved.
Flatulent version of a Mickey Spillane novel, over-plotted and inadequately motivated.

w Alan Green, Lesser Samuels *d* Victor Saville *ph* Franz Planer *m* Mario Castelnuovo Tedesco

Anthony Quinn, Charles Coburn, Gene Evans, Peggie Castle, Dolores Donlan

The Longest Day**
US 1962 169m bw Cinemascope
TCF (*Darryl F. Zanuck, Elmo Williams*)

A multi-faceted account of the landings in Normandy in June 1944.

Extraordinarily noisy war spectacular, enjoyable as a violent entertainment once one has caught all the threads, but emotionally unaffecting because every part is played by a star.

w Cornelius Ryan, Romain Gary, James Jones, David Pursall, Jack Seddon, *book* Cornelius Ryan *d* Andrew Marton, Ken Annakin, Bernhard Wicki *ph* Henri Persin, Walter Wottitz, Pierre Levent, Jean Bourgoin *m* Maurice Jarre, Paul Anka

John Wayne, Robert Mitchum, Henry Fonda, Robert Ryan, Rod Steiger, Robert Wagner, Paul Anka, Fabian, Tommy Sands, Richard Beymer, Mel Ferrer, Jeffrey Hunter, Sal Mineo, Roddy McDowall, Stuart Whitman, Steve Forrest, Eddie Albert, Edmond O'Brien, Red Buttons, Tom Tryon, Alexander Knox, Ray Danton, Ron Randell, Richard Burton, Donald Houston, Kenneth More, Peter Lawford, Richard Todd, Leo Genn, John Gregson, Sean Connery, Michael Medwin, Leslie Phillips, Irina Demich, Bourvil, Jean-Louis Barrault, Christian Marquand, Arletty, Curt Jurgens, Paul Hartmann, Gert Frobe, Wolfgang Preiss, Peter Van Eyck, Christopher Lee, Eugene Deckers, Richard Wattis

AA: photography
AAN: best picture

The Longest Yard
US 1974 122m Technicolor
Paramount / Long Road (Albert S. Ruddy)
GB title: *The Mean Machine*

Imprisoned for drunkenness and car theft, a football star is blackmailed into training a prison football team of hulking misfits.
Violent, meandering comedy-drama with murderous jokes but no narrative grip.

w Tracy Keenan Wynn *d* Robert Aldrich *ph* Joseph Biroc *m* Frank de Vol

Burt Reynolds, Eddie Albert, Ed Lauter, Michael Conrad, Jim Hampton

Look Back in Anger*
GB 1959 99m bw
ABP / Woodfall (Gordon L. T. Scott)

A bad-tempered young man with a grudge against life and the government runs a market stall, lives in a squalid flat, and has an affair with his wife's best friend.

Well-made version of a play whose sheer dreariness was theatrically stimulating but in terms of film realism becomes only depressing and stupid despite competence all round. It also set shoddy standards for its many less proficient imitators.

w Nigel Kneale, *play John Osborne d* Tony Richardson *ph* Oswald Morris *m* Chris Barber

Richard Burton, Mary Ure, Claire Bloom, Edith Evans, Gary Raymond, Glen Byam Shaw, Phyllis Neilson-Terry, Donald Pleasence, George Devine

Look Before You Love
GB 1948 96m bw

Romance in Rio for a girl of the embassy staff.
Abysmal romantic comedy with little of either commodity in evidence. Margaret Lockwood, Griffith Jones, Norman Wooland, Phyllis Stanley, Michael Medwin, Maurice Denham.
Written by Reginald Long; directed by Harold Huth; for Burnham / Rank.

Look for the Silver Lining*
US 1949 106m Technicolor
Warner (William Jacobs)

The life story of twenties stage star Marilyn Miller.
Harmless musical biopic with a sense of humour.

w Phoebe and Henry Ephron, Marian Spitzer, Bert Kalmar, Harry Ruby *d* David Butler *ph* Peverell Marley *md* Ray Heindorf

June Haver, *Ray Bolger, Charles Ruggles*, Gordon Macrae, Rosemary de Camp, S. Z. Sakall, Walter Catlett

AAN: Ray Heindorf

Look Up and Laugh*
GB 1935 82m bw
ATP (Basil Dean)

Market stallholders defy a big chain store.
Good star comedy with music.

w Gordon Wellesley, *story* J. B. Priestley *d* Basil Dean

Gracie Fields, Douglas Wakefield, Harry Tate, Alfred Drayton, Morris Harvey, Vivien Leigh, Robb Wilton

Looking for Mr Goodbar
US 1977 136m Metrocolor
Paramount (Freddie Fields)

A teacher of deaf children leads a sordid secret night life.

Exploitative and very boring sex melodrama which doesn't even make one believe in its central character.

wd Richard Brooks, *novel* Judith Rossner *ph* William A. Fraker *m* Artie Kane *ad* Edward Carfagno

Diane Keaton, Tuesday Weld, William Atherton, Richard Kiley

'Brooks has laid a windy jeremiad about permissive sex on top of fractured film syntax.'—*Judith Crist*

AAN: William A. Fraker; Tuesday Weld

Looking for Trouble
US 1933 77m bw

Two telephone engineers brawl over a girl. Early star vehicle, quite watchable. Spencer Tracy, Jack Oakie, Constance Cummings, Morgan Conway, Arline Judge. Written by Leonard Praskins and Elmer Harris; directed by William Wellman; for Darryl F. Zanuck / UA.

The Looking Glass War
GB 1969 107m Technicolor
   Panavision
Columbia / M. J. Frankovich (John Box)

The British secret service sends a young Pole into East Germany to find a top secret film. Jaundiced spy story which aims for irony and tragedy but becomes merely verbose and irritating.

wd Frank R. Pierson, *novel* John Le Carré *ph* Austin Dempster *m* Wally Scott

Christopher Jones, Pia Degermark, Ralph Richardson, Anthony Hopkins, Paul Rogers, Susan George, Ray McAnally, Robert Urquhart, Maxine Audley, Anna Massey

'There are a lot of incidental pleasures, but in the final analysis they only add up to half a film.'—*Nigel Andrews*

Looking on the Bright Side°
GB 1931 81m bw
ATP (Basil Dean)

A songwriter gets ideas above his station but eventually returns to the manicurist who loves him.

Dated but lively musical which helped confirm Gracie's stardom.

w Basil Dean, Archie Pitt, Brock Williams *d* Basil Dean

Gracie Fields, Richard Dolman, Julian Rose, Wyn Richmond

Loot°
GB 1970 101m Eastmancolor
Performing Arts Ltd (Arthur Lewis)

A crook hides his mother's body and uses the coffin to carry the proceeds of a robbery. Breakneck black farce which still can't move quite fast enough to cover up its bad taste, though well done by all concerned.

w Ray Galton, Alan Simpson, *play* Joe Orton *d* Silvio Narizzano *ph* Austin Dempster *m* Keith Mansfield, Richard Willing-Denton *ad* Anthony Pratt

Richard Attenborough, Lee Remick, Hywel Bennett, Milo O'Shea, Dick Emery

Lord Camber's Ladies
GB 1932 80m bw

A nobleman tries to murder his way out of a romantic tangle. Rather dull suspenser notable only for its stagey cast and the fact that Alfred Hitchcock produced it. Gerald du Maurier, Gertrude Lawrence, Benita Hume, Nigel Bruce, Clare Greet, A. Bromley Davenport. Written by Benn W. Levy, Edwin Greenwood and Gilbert Wakefield, from the novel *The Case of Lady Camber* by Horace Annesley Vachell; directed by Benn W. Levy; for BIP.

Lord Edgware Dies
GB 1934 81m bw

Hercule Poirot proves that an elderly nobleman was not killed by his young wife. Modest whodunnit: the intended series did not catch on. Austin Trevor, Jane Carr, Richard Cooper, John Turnbull, Michael Shepley. Written by H. Fowler Mear, from the novel by Agatha Christie; directed by Henry Edwards; for Twickenham.

Lord Jeff
US 1938 78m bw
MGM (Frank Davis)
GB title: *The Boy from Barnardo's*

A well-brought-up boy gets into trouble and is sent under supervision to a naval school. Adequate family film with absolutely no surprises.

w Bradford Roper, Val Burton, André Boehm *d* Sam Wood *ph* John Seitz *m* Edward Ward

Freddie Bartholomew, Mickey Rooney, Charles Coburn, Herbert Mundin, Terry Kilburn, Gale Sondergaard, Peter Lawford

Lord Jim°
GB 1964 154m Technicolor Super
   Panavision
Columbia / Keep (René Dupont)

Adventures of a sailor who prowls the Far East looking for truth; he helps enslaved natives, is raped by a tribal chief, and finally sacrifices his life.

Lush and very boring farrago of miscellaneous incident, with a central character about whose fate no one can care. However, an expensive production must have its points of interest, and the belated introduction of a gentleman villain gives a little edge.

wd Richard Brooks, *novel* Joseph Conrad *ph Frederick A. Young m* Bronislau Kaper *pd* Geoffrey Drake

Peter O'Toole, *James Mason*, Eli Wallach, Paul Lukas, Jack Hawkins, Daliah Lavi, Curt Jurgens, Akim Tamiroff

Lord Love a Duck*
US 1966 105m bw
UA / Charleston (George Axelrod)

A senior Los Angeles student practises hypnotism on his girl friend.
Rather sloppy satire on American culture and fancies, dressed up as crazy comedy; occasional laughs.

w Larry H. Johnson, George Axelrod, *novel* Al Hine *d* George Axelrod *ph* Daniel Fapp *m* Neal Hefti

Roddy McDowall, Tuesday Weld, Lola Albright, Ruth Gordon, Harvey Korman, Max Showalter

Lord of the Flies
GB 1963 91m bw
Allen–Hogdon Productions / Two Arts (Lewis M. Allen)

After a plane crash, a party of English schoolboys are stranded on an uncharted tropical island and gradually turn savage.
Semi-professional production of a semi-poetic novel which worked well on the printed page but on screen seems crude and unconvincing.

wd Peter Brook, *novel* William Golding *ph* Tom Hollyman, Gerald Feil *m* Raymond Leppard

James Aubrey, Tom Chapin, Hugh Edwards, Roger Elwin, Tom Gaman

Lord of the Rings*
US 1978 133m De Luxe
UA / Fantasy (Saul Zaentz)

In Middle Earth the Dark Lord loses a powerful ring, and a Hobbit tries to prevent him from getting it back.
Disappointingly stolid, overlong and confused cartoon version of a modern classic which may well deserve all those adjectives. Parts of it are charming, and the method of making cartoons from film of actors photographed in the ordinary way is certainly ingenious though it denies the cartoon characters their own full richness.

w Chris Conkling, Peter S. Beagle, *books* J. R. R. Tolkien *d* Ralph Bakshi *ph* Timothy Galfas

voices: Christopher Guard, John Hurt, William Squire, Michael Scholes

Lorna Doone**
GB 1934 90m bw
ATP (Basil Dean)

In 1625 on Exmoor, a farmer comes to love an outlaw's daughter who proves to be in reality a kidnapped heiress.
Simple, straightforward, effective version of the famous romance, with refreshing use of exteriors.

w Dorothy Farnum, Miles Malleson, Gordon Wellesley, *novel* R. D. Blackmore *d Basil Dean ph* Robert Martin

Victoria Hopper, John Loder, Margaret Lockwood, *Roy Emerton,* Edward Rigby, Mary Clare, Roger Livesey, George Curzon, D. A. Clarke-Smith, Lawrence Hanray, Amy Veness, Eliot Makeham

Lorna Doone
US 1951 89m Technicolor
Columbia (Edward Small)

Grotesque remake which treats the story like a cheap western.

w Jesse L. Lasky Jnr, Richard Schayer *d* Phil Karlson *ph* Charles Van Enger *m* George Duning

Barbara Hale, Richard Greene, Anne Howard, William Bishop, Carl Benton Reid, Ron Randell, Sean McClory, Onslow Stevens, Lester Matthews, John Dehner

Lost*
GB 1955 89m Technicolor
Rank (Vivian A. Cox)
US title: *Tears for Simon*

The police go on the trail of a stolen child.
Mildly effective semi-documentary police story, with good use of locations.

w Janet Green *d* Guy Green *ph* Harry Waxman *m* Benjamin Frankel

David Farrar, David Knight, Julia Arnall, Anthony Oliver, Thora Hird, Eleanor Summerfield, Marjorie Rhodes, Joan Sims

Lost and Found
US 1979 105m Technicolor
Columbia / Gordon (Melvin Frank)

A widowed American professor meets an English divorcee on a skiing holiday, but after marriage they prove to be incompatible.

Unattractive romantic comedy-drama which despite capable stars degenerates into a series of wounding slanging matches.

w Melvin Frank, Jack Rose *d* Melvin Frank *ph* Douglas Slocombe *m* John Cameron *pd* Trevor Williams

Glenda Jackson, George Segal, Maureen Stapleton, Paul Sorvino, John Cunningham, Hollis McLaren

Lost Angel*
US 1943 91m bw
MGM (Robert Sisk)

A lost little girl is adopted by a reporter. Good star vehicle for the sentimentally-inclined, with solid production and casting back-up.

w Isabel Lennart *d* Roy Rowland *ph* Robert Surtees *m* Daniele Amfitheatrof

Margaret O'Brien, James Craig, Marsha Hunt, Philip Merivale, Henry O'Neill, Donald Meek, Keenan Wynn

'A beautiful opportunity for true satire is offered and, I regret to say, thrown away. For our little Gulliver is rapidly decivilized by all the familiar bromidic palliatives: love, crooning, fairies and night clubs.'—*Richard Winnington*

Lost Boundaries*
US 1949 105m bw
Film Classics (Louis de Rochemont)

In a New Hampshire town in the forties, a beloved doctor and his wife are found to have negro blood.
Well-meaning but dramatically ineffective racial drama which meanders along allowing an occasional burst of genuine feeling to come through.

w Virginia Shaler, Eugene Ling *d* Alfred Werker *ph* William J. Miller *m* Louis Applebaum

Mel Ferrer, Beatrice Pearson, Richard Hylton, Susan Douglas, Canada Lee, Grace Coppin

'It cannot be said to betray its subject, but is, rather, unequal to it.'—*Gavin Lambert*

Lost Command
US 1966 128m Technicolor Panavision
Columbia / Red Lion (Mark Robson)

Adventures of a French paratroop regiment in Indo-China and Algeria.
Anti-war war adventure; noisy but scarcely inspired.

w Nelson Gidding, *novel* The Centurions by Jean Larteguy *d* Mark Robson *ph* Robert Surtees *m* Franz Waxman

Anthony Quinn, Alain Delon, George Segal, Michèle Morgan, Maurice Ronet, Claudia Cardinale, Grégoire Aslan, Jean Servais

The Lost Continent*
GB 1968 98m Technicolor
Hammer (Michael Carreras)

The captain of a tramp steamer illegally carries dynamite, and he and his passengers are stranded in a weird Sargasso Sea colony run by the Spanish Inquisition.
Hilariously imaginative hokum with splendid art direction and some of the grottiest monsters on film; but memorable moments do not quite add up to a classic of the genre.

w Michael Nash, *novel* Uncharted Seas by Dennis Wheatley *d* Michael Carreras *ph* Paul Beeson *m* Gerard Schurmann *sp* Robert A. Mattey, Cliff Richardson *ad* Arthur Lawson

Eric Porter, Hildegarde Neff, Suzanna Leigh, Tony Beckley, Nigel Stock, Neil McCallum, Jimmy Hanley, James Cossins, Victor Maddern

'One of the most ludicrously enjoyable bad films since *Salome Where She Danced*.'—*MFB*

Lost Honeymoon
US 1947 70m bw

An amnesiac GI fails to remember either his wife or his young family. Artificial comedy which the actors can't carry off. Franchot Tone, Ann Richards, Tom Conway. Written by Joseph Fields; directed by Leigh Jason; for Eagle-Lion.

Lost Horizon****
US 1937 130m (released at 118m) bw
Columbia (Frank Capra)

Escaping from an Indian revolution, four people are kidnapped by plane and taken to an idyllic civilization in a Tibetan valley, where the weather is always kind and men are not only gentle to each other but live to a very advanced age.
Much re-cut romantic adventure which leaves out some of the emphasis of a favourite Utopian novel but stands up pretty well on its own, at least as a supreme example of Hollywood moonshine, with perfect casting, direction and music. If the design has a touch of Ziegfeld, that's Hollywood.

w Robert Riskin, *novel* James Hilton *d* Frank Capra *ph* Joseph Walker *m* Dmitri Tiomkin *ad* Stephen Goosson

Ronald Colman, H. B. Warner, Thomas
Mitchell, Edward Everett Horton, Sam Jaffe,
Isabel Jewell, Jane Wyatt, Margo, John
Howard

'One of the most impressive of all thirties
films, a splendid fantasy which, physically and
emotionally, lets out all the stops.'—*John
Baxter, 1968*

'One is reminded of a British critic's
comment on *Mary of Scotland*, "the
inaccuracies must have involved tremendous
research".'—*Robert Stebbins*

'The best film I've seen for ages, but will
somebody please tell me how they got the
grand piano along a footpath on which only
one person can walk at a time with rope and
pickaxe and with a sheer drop of three
thousand feet or so?'—*James Agate*

'If the long dull ethical sequences had been
cut to the bone there would have been plenty
of room for the real story: the shock of
western crudity and injustice on a man
returned from a more gentle and beautiful way
of life.'—*Graham Greene*

† A 1943 reissue trimmed down the negative
still further, to 109 minutes; but in 1979 the
American Film Institute was busily restoring a
print of the original length.

AAN: best picture; Dmitri Tiomkin; H. B.
Warner

Lost Horizon*
US 1972 143m Panavision
Technicolor
Columbia / Ross Hunter

Torpid remake with a good opening followed
by slabs of philosophizing dialogue and an
unbroken series of tedious songs.

w Larry Kramer d Charles Jarrott ph Robert
Surtees m Burt Bacharach songs Burt
Bacharach, Hal David ad Preston Ames

Peter Finch, Liv Ullmann, Sally Kellerman,
Bobby Van, George Kennedy, Michael York,
Olivia Hussey, James Shigeta, John Gielgud,
Charles Boyer

'It will never play again outside of Shangri-
La.'—*Les Keyser, Hollywood in the Seventies*

Lost in a Harem**
US 1944 89m bw
MGM (George Haight)

Two travelling entertainers in the Middle East
get mixed up with a conniving sultan, who
hypnotizes them.
Lively, well-staged romp which shows the
comedians at their best and uses astute
borrowings from burlesque, pantomime, and
Hollywood traditions of fantasy and running
jokes.

w Harry Ruskin, John Grant, Harry Crane
d Charles Reisner ph Lester White m David
Snell

Bud Abbott, Lou Costello, Douglass
Dumbrille, Marilyn Maxwell, John Conte,
Jimmy Dorsey and his Orchestra

The Lost Man
US 1969 113m Technicolor
Panavision
Universal (Ernest B. Wehmeyer)

After a robbery, a crook is pursued by the
police and goes into hiding.
Odd Man Out made over as a vehicle for
polemics about civil rights for blacks: too
shiny, too long, too talky to have any grip.

wd Robert Alan Aurthur ph Jerry
Finnerman m Quincy Jones

Sidney Poitier, Joanna Shimkus, Al Freeman
Jnr, Michael Tolan, Leon Bibb, Richard
Dysart, David Steinberg, Paul Winfield

The Lost Moment*
US 1947 89m bw
U-I (Martin Gabel)

An American publisher goes to Venice to
recover love letters written by a famous poet
to a lady now aged 105.
Slightly absurd but memorable period drama
with a guilty secret eventually coming to light,
all put across with apparently deliberate
artificiality.

w Leonardo Bercovici, novel The Aspern
Papers by Henry James d Martin Gabel
ph Hal Mohr m Daniele Amfitheatrof

Robert Cummings, Susan Hayward, Agnes
Moorehead, Joan Lorring, Eduardo Ciannelli

'A compelling piece, highly stylized and
very personal, with a beautifully photographed
studio recreation of Venice.'—*NFT, 1973*

The Lost Patrol*
US 1934 74m bw
RKO (Cliff Reid)

A small British army group is lost in the
Mesopotamian desert under Arab attack.
Much-copied adventure story of a small patrol
under attack (compare *Sahara*, *Bataan* and
The Last of the Comanches for a start). The
original now seems pretty starchy but retains
moments of power.

w Dudley Nichols, story Patrol by Philip
MacDonald d John Ford ph Harold
Wenstrom m Max Steiner

Victor McLaglen, Boris Karloff, Wallace
Ford, Reginald Denny, J. M. Kerrigan, Billy
Bevan, Alan Hale

'Boiling passions in the burning sands!'—
publicity
† A silent British version was released in 1929,
written and directed by Walter Summers for
British Instructional, with Cyril McLaglen,
Sam Wilkinson and Terence Collier.
AAN: Max Steiner

The Lost People
GB 1949 89m bw
GFD / Gainsborough (Gordon Wellesley)

Displaced persons gather for comfort in a
disused German theatre.
Once again a very flat film has been unsuitably
made from an effective piece of theatre, with
all possible types present and all views
represented. Not on.

w Bridget Boland, from her play Cockpit
d Bernard Knowles *ph* Jack Asher *m* John
Greenwood

Richard Attenborough, Mai Zetterling,
Siobhan McKenna, Dennis Price, Maxwell
Reed, William Hartnell, Gerard Heinz,
Harcourt Williams, Marcel Poncin

The Lost Squadron*
US 1932 79m bw
RKO (David O. Selznick)

World War I pilots find work stunting for a
movie studio.
Unusual comedy-drama with several points of
interest.

w Herman J. Mankiewicz, Wallace Smith
d George Archainbaud *ph* Leo Tover,
Edward Cronjager *m* Max Steiner

Richard Dix, Mary Astor, Erich Von
Stroheim, Joel McCrea, Dorothy Jordan,
Hugh Herbert, Robert Armstrong

The Lost Weekend****
US 1945 101m bw
Paramount *(Charles Brackett)*

Two days in the life of a young dipsomaniac
writer.
Startlingly original on its release, this stark
little drama keeps its power, especially in the
scenes on New York streets and in a dipso
ward. It could scarcely have been more
effectively filmed.

*w Charles Brackett, Billy Wilder,
novel* Charles Jackson *d* Billy Wilder
ph John F. Seitz m Miklos Rozsa

Ray Milland, Jane Wyman, Philip Terry,
Howard da Silva, Frank Faylen
'I undershtand that liquor interesh; innerish;
intereshtsh are rather worried about thish film.
Thatsh tough.'—*James Agee*

'Most to be admired are its impressions of
bare dreadful truth: the real crowds in the real
streets as the hero-victim lugs his typewriter to
the pawnshop, the trains screaming overhead,
the awful night as he makes his escape from
the alcoholics' ward.'—*Dilys Powell*
AA: best picture; script; Billy Wilder (as
director); Ray Milland
AAN: John F. Seitz; Miklos Rozsa

The Lost World
US 1960 98m De Luxe Cinemascope
TCF / Saratoga (Irwin Allen)

Professor Challenger is financed by a
newspaper to confirm the report of prehistoric
life on a South African plateau.
Pitiful attempt to continue the success of
Journey to the Center of the Earth, with the
story idiotically modernized, unconvincing
monsters, a script which inserts conventional
romance and villainy, and fatal miscasting of
the central part.

w Irwin Allen, Charles Bennett, *novel* Sir
Arthur Conan Doyle *d* Irwin Allen
ph Winton C. Hoch *m* Bert Shefter, Paul
Sawtell

Claude Rains, *Michael Rennie*, David
Hedison, *Richard Haydn*, Fernando Lamas,
Jill St John, Ray Stricklyn
'Resembles nothing so much as a ride on a
rundown fairground Ghost Train.'—*MFB*

Lottery Lover
US 1935 80m bw

A shy sailor wins a lottery prize, an
introduction to a Folies Bergère star, but falls
in love with the public relations girl organizing
the stunt. Faded romantic comedy of little
surviving interest. Lew Ayres, Reginald
Denny, Pat Paterson, Sterling Holloway.
Written by Sig Herzic; directed by William
Thiele; for Fox.

Louisa*
US 1950 90m bw

A much-married man finds that both his
daughter and his mother have boy friend
trouble. Friendly generation gap comedy with
practised talent. Ronald Reagan, Spring
Byington, Charles Coburn, Ruth Hussey,
Edmund Gwenn, Piper Laurie, Scotty
Beckett. Written by Stanley Roberts; directed
by Alexander Hall; for Universal-
International.

Louisiana Purchase*
US 1941 98m Technicolor
Paramount (Harold Wilson)

Efforts are made to compromise a politician. Quite lively transcription of a Broadway musical success with elements of political satire including a climactic filibuster scene.

w Jerome Chodorov, Joseph Fields, play Morrie Ryskind songs Irving Berlin d Irving Cummings ph Harry Hallenberger, Ray Rennahan

Bob Hope, Vera Zorina, Victor Moore, Irene Bordoni, Dona Drake, Raymond Walburn, Maxie Rosenbloom, Frank Albertson, Donald MacBride, Andrew Tombes

AAN: Harry Hallenberger, Ray Rennahan

Louisiana Story*
US 1948   77m   bw
Standard Oil Company (Robert Flaherty)

In the Louisiana bayous a young native boy watches as oil drillers make a strike.
Quite beautiful but over-extended semi-documentary.

w Robert and Frances Flaherty d Robert Flaherty ph Richard Leacock m Virgil Thompson

Joseph Boudreaux, Lionel Leblanc, Frank Hardy

AAN: original story

Love*
US 1927   82m (24 fps)   bw   silent
MGM (Edmund Goulding)

Anna Karenina leaves her husband and child for Count Vronsky.
Marginally interesting first shot at a famous subject by a star who came back to it in 1935.

w Frances Marion, Lorna Moon, novel Leo Tolstoy d Edmund Goulding ph William Daniels m Ernst Luz ad Cedric Gibbons, Alexander Toluboff

Greta Garbo, John Gilbert, Brandon Hurst, Philippe de Lacy, George Fawcett, Emily Fitzroy
† An alternative happy ending was provided for exhibitors who wanted it.

Love Affair
US 1932   68m   bw
Columbia

An heiress falls for a flying instructor.
Mild romantic comedy drama.

w Jo Swerling, story Ursula Parrott d Thornton Freeland ph Ted Tetzlaff

Dorothy Mackaill, Humphrey Bogart, Jack Kennedy, Astrid Allwyn, Halliwell Hobbes, Barbara Leonard

Love Affair***
US 1939   89m   bw
RKO (Leo McCarey)

On a transatlantic crossing, a European man of the world meets a New York girl, but their romance is flawed by misunderstanding and physical accident.
The essence of Hollywood romance, and one of the most fondly remembered films of the thirties, perhaps because of the easy comedy sense of the first half.

w Delmer Daves, Donald Ogden Stewart, story Mildred Cram, Leo McCarey d Leo McCarey ph Rudolph Maté

Charles Boyer, Irene Dunne, Maria Ouspenskaya, Lee Bowman, Astrid Allwyn, Maurice Moscovitch
'Those excited over the mastery of form already achieved in pictures, will like to follow this demonstration of the qualities of technique and imagination the films must always have and keep on recruiting to their service . . . Clichés of situation and attitude are lifted almost beyond recognition by a morning freshness of eye for each small thing around.'—Otis Ferguson
'McCarey brought off one of the most difficult things you can attempt with film. He created a mood, rather than a story; he kept it alive by expert interpolations; he provided comedy when he needed comedy and poignancy when he needed substance; and he did it with the minimum of effort.'—Pare Lorentz
† Remade as An Affair to Remember (qv).

AAN: best picture; original story; Irene Dunne; Maria Ouspenskaya; song 'Wishing' (m / ly Buddy de Sylva)

Love and Bullets
US 1978   103m   Metrocolor
ITC (Pancho Kohner)

A gangster's mistress is brought back from Switzerland by a revengeful Phoenix cop.
Downbeat bang-bang with a high death rate and a glum finale; generally low-grade stuff.

w Wendell Mayes, John Melson d Stuart Rosenberg ph Fred Koenekamp m Lalo Schifrin pd John de Cuir

Charles Bronson, Jill Ireland, Rod Steiger, Henry Silva, Strother Martin, Bradford Dillman, Michael V. Gazzo
'A relatively dismaying example of the Lew Grade entertainment formula: as locations, production values and clichéd set-pieces proliferate, scripts increasingly look like shaggy dog stories desperately in search of a

point, and actors are left to do their own thing as characters disintegrate.'—*Richard Combs, MFB*

'Love and bullets my eye: embarrassment and tedium would be more like it.'—*Time Out*

Love and Death*
US 1975 85m De Luxe
UA / Jack Rollins, Charles H. Joffe

In 1812 Russia, a man condemned reviews the follies of his life.
Personalized comedy fantasia inspired by *War and Peace*, Ingmar Bergman and S. J. Perelman. Basically only for star fans.

wd Woody Allen *ph* Ghislain Cloquet *m* Prokofiev

Woody Allen, Diane Keaton, Georges Adel, Despo, Frank Adu

Love and Hisses*
US 1937 84m bw
TCF (Kenneth MacGowan)

A gossip columnist and a bandleader continue their feud.
Moderate sequel to *Wake Up and Live* (qv); it got by.

w Art Arthur, Curtis Kenyon *d* Sidney Lanfield *ph* Robert Planck *m* Louis Silvers

Walter Winchell, Ben Bernie and his orchestra, Joan Davis, Bert Lahr, Simone Simon, Ruth Terry

Love and Learn
US 1947 83m bw

Two impoverished songwriters are secretly helped by a rich girl. Tame comedy with few laughs. Jack Carson, Robert Hutton, Martha Vickers, Janis Paige, Otto Kruger. Written by Eugene Conrad, Francis Swann and I. A. L. Diamond; directed by Frederick de Cordova; for Warner.

Love and Pain and the Whole Damn Thing
US 1972 113m Eastmancolor
Columbia / Gus (Alan J. Pakula)

An asthmatic young American on holiday in Spain has an affair with an older woman suffering from an incurable disease.
Dreary doomed romance studiously treated as tourist comedy.

w Alvin Sargent *d* Alan J. Pakula
ph Geoffrey Unsworth *m* Michael Small

Maggie Smith, Timothy Bottoms

Love at First Bite*
US 1979 96m colour
Simon (Joel Freeman)

Count Dracula flees from the communists and settles in New York.
Energetic spoof, with jokes on the sexy side; good work all round.

w Robert Kaufman *d* Stan Dragoti
ph Edward Rosson *m* Charles Bernstein
pd Serge Krizman

George Hamilton, Susan St James, Richard Benjamin, Dick Shawn, Arte Johnson

Love Before Breakfast
US 1936 90m bw

Two Park Avenue beaux vie for a socialite.
Thinly plotted but quite amusing romantic comedy. Carole Lombard, Preston Foster, Cesar Romero, Janet Beecher, Bert Roach. Written by Herbert Fields, from the novel *Spinster Dinner* by Faith Baldwin; directed by Walter Lang; for Universal.

The Love Bug**
US 1968 107m Technicolor
Walt Disney (Bill Walsh)

An unsuccessful racing driver finds that his small private Volkswagen has a mind of its own.
Amusing, pacy period fantasy in the best Disney style.

w Bill Walsh, Don da Gradi *d* Robert Stevenson *ph* Edward Colman *m* George Bruns *sp* Eustace Lycett

David Tomlinson, Dean Jones, Michele Lee, Buddy Hackett, Joe Flynn, Benson Fong, Joe E. Ross

Love Crazy*
US 1941 100m bw
MGM (Pandro S. Berman)

When his wife threatens to divorce him, a businessman hatches all manner of crazy schemes, including disguising himself as his own sister.
Zany romantic comedy, over-stretched but with a fair share of hilarity.

w William Ludwig, Charles Lederer, David Hertz *d* Jack Cummings *ph* Ray June
m David Snell

William Powell, Myrna Loy, Gail Patrick, Jack Carson, Florence Bates, Sidney Blackmer, Vladimir Sokoloff, Donald MacBride, Sig Rumann, Sara Haden, Elisha Cook Jnr, Kathleen Lockhart

Love Eternal*
France 1943 111m bw
André Paulvé
original title: *L'Eternel Retour*

The love story of Tristan and Isolde.
This modernized version had a Teutonic look
and was respected rather than admired.

w Jean Cocteau d Jean Delannoy ph Roger
Hubert m Georges Auric ad Wakhevitch

Jean Marais, Madeleine Sologne, Jean Murat,
Yvonne de Bray

Love from a Stranger**
GB 1937 90m bw
Trafalgar (Max Schach)

A young woman realizes she may have
married a maniac.
Stalwart suspenser from a popular novel and
play.

w Frances Marion, *play* Frank Vosper, *story*
Philomel Cottage by Agatha Christie
d Rowland V. Lee ph Philip Tannura
m Benjamin Britten

Ann Harding, Basil Rathbone, Binnie Hale,
Bruce Seton, Jean Cadell, Bryan Powley, Joan
Hickson, Donald Calthrop

Love from a Stranger
US 1947 81m bw
Eagle Lion (James J. Geller)
GB title: *A Stranger Walked In*

Stilted period remake.

w Philip MacDonald d Richard Whorf
ph Tony Gaudio m Hans Salter

Sylvia Sidney, John Hodiak, Ann Richards,
John Howard, Isobel Elsom, Frederick
Worlock

The Love Goddesses**
US 1965 87m bw
Paramount / Walter Reade / Sterling

A light-hearted account of female sexuality on
the Hollywood screen.
Sharp-eyed compilation film which is worth a
dozen books on the subject.

pd Saul J. Turell, Graeme Ferguson m Percy
Faith narrator Carl King
† Clips include *Blonde Venus, Morocco, True
Heart Susie, Cleopatra* (1934), *Intolerance, The
Cheat, The Sheik, Blood and Sand, The
Sorrows of Satan, The Loves of Sunya, Diary
of a Lost Girl, Ecstasy, L'Atlantide, Peter the
Tramp, Cabin in the Cotton, Platinum Blonde,
Gold Diggers of 1933, No Man of Her Own,
Professional Sweetheart, Love Me Tonight, I'm
No Angel, Baby Face, They Won't Forget,
College Swing, Her Jungle Love, Gilda, A
Place in the Sun, Some Like it Hot.*

Love Happy*
US 1949 85m bw
Lester Cowan / Mary Pickford

A group of impoverished actors accidentally
gets possession of the Romanov diamonds.
The last dismaying Marx Brothers film, with
Harpo taking the limelight and Groucho
loping in for a couple of brief, tired
appearances. A roof chase works, but Harpo
tries too hard for sentiment, and the
production looks shoddy.

w Ben Hecht, Frank Tashlin, Mac Benoff
d David Miller ph William Mellor

Groucho, Harpo, Chico, Eric Blore, Ilona
Massey, Marilyn Monroe, Vera-Ellen

Love Has Many Faces
US 1964 104m Eastmancolor
Columbia / Jerry Bresler

A rich woman marries a beach boy and has an
affair with another, who is murdered.
Hilarious but unentertaining sex melodrama
built around an overage star.

w Marguerite Roberts d Alexander Singer
ph Joseph Ruttenberg m David Raksin

Lana Turner, Cliff Robertson, Hugh O'Brian,
Stefanie Powers, Ruth Roman, Virginia Grey
'For connoisseurs of perfectly awful
movies.'—*Judith Crist*

Love in a Goldfish Bowl
US 1961 88m Technicolor Panavision

On holiday in Honolulu, two teenagers get
into mischief. Tiresome youth-oriented family
comedy with pleasant backgrounds. Tommy
Sands, Fabian, Jan Sterling, Toby Michaels,
Edward Andrews, John McGiver. Written and
directed by Jack Sher; for Paramount / Jurow-
Shepherd.

Love in Exile
GB 1936 78m bw

A Ruritanian king is induced to abdicate but
fights back. Airy comedy with little general
appeal. Clive Brook, Helen Vinson, Mary
Carlisle, Will Fyffe, Ronald Squire, Tamara
Desni, Henry Oscar. Written by Herman
Mankiewicz, Roger Burford and Ernest Betts,
from the novel *His Majesty's Pajamas* by Gene
Markey; directed by Alfred L. Werker; for
Capitol.

Love in the Afternoon
US 1957 126m bw
AA (Billy Wilder)

The daughter of a private detective warns an
American philanderer in Paris that an enraged
husband is en route to shoot him.
Tired and dreary romantic sex comedy,
miscast and far too long. With the talent
around, there are of course a few
compensations.

w Billy Wilder, I. A. L. Diamond, *novel*
Claude Anet *d* Billy Wilder *ph* William
Mellor *m* Franz Waxman *ad* Alexander
Trauner

Gary Cooper, Audrey Hepburn, Maurice
Chevalier, John McGiver

Love Is a Ball
US 1962 112m Technicolor
Panavision
UA / Oxford / Gold Medal (Martin H. Poll)
GB title: *All This and Money Too*

A Riviera matchmaker recruits instructors to
train his star pupil, but one of them walks
away with the lady.
Forgettable comedy in which more effort goes
into the glamorous background than the script.

w David Swift, Tom and Frank Waldman,
novel The Grand Duke and Mr Pimm by
Lindsay Hardy *d* David Swift *ph* Edmond
Séchan *m* Michel Legrand

Glenn Ford, Charles Boyer, Hope Lange,
Ricardo Montalban, Telly Savalas, Ruth
McDevitt, Ulla Jacobsson

Love Is a Many Splendored Thing*
US 1955 102m De Luxe Cinemascope
TCF (Buddy Adler)

During the Korean War, a Eurasian lady
doctor in Hong Kong falls in love with a war
correspondent.
Self-admittedly sentimental soaper with a
tragic ending; the theme tune kept it popular
for years.

w John Patrick, *novel* Han Suyin *d* Henry
King *ph* Leon Shamroy *m* Alfred Newman

Jennifer Jones, William Holden, Torin
Thatcher, Isobel Elsom, Murray Matheson,
Virginia Gregg, Richard Loo

AA: Alfred Newman; title song (*m* Sammy
Fain, *ly* Paul Francis Webster)
AAN: best picture; Leon Shamroy; Jennifer
Jones

Love Is a Racket
US 1932 72m bw

A newspaperman covers up for a girl
suspected of murder, but she lets him down.
Jaundiced comedy-drama of Broadway night
life; quite effective. Douglas Fairbanks Jnr,
Frances Dee, Ann Dvorak, Lee Tracy, Lyle
Talbot, Warren Hymer. Written by Courtney
Terrett; directed by William Wellman; for
Warner.

Love Is News*
US 1937 78m bw
TCF (Earl Carroll, Harold Wilson)

An heiress marries a scoop-hunting reporter
just to show him how embarrassing publicity
can be.
Silly romantic comedy with plenty of laughs.

w Harry Tugend, Jack Yellen *d* Tay Garnett
ph Ernest Palmer

Tyrone Power, Loretta Young, Don Ameche,
Slim Summerville, Dudley Digges, Walter
Catlett, Jane Darwell, Stepin Fetchit, George
Sanders, Frank Conroy, Elisha Cook Jnr
† Remade as *Sweet Rosie O'Grady* and *That
Wonderful Urge*.

Love Letters*
US 1945 101m bw
Paramount (Hal B. Wallis)

A girl who has lost her memory through war
shock is threatened by more physical danger.
Oddly unexciting romantic melodrama
directed and designed in heavy but satisfying
style. Typical post-war depressive fare.

w Ayn Rand, *novel* Pity My Simplicity by
Chris Massie *d* William Dieterle *ph* Lee
Garmes *m* Victor Young

Jennifer Jones, Joseph Cotten, Ann Richards,
Gladys Cooper, Anita Louise, Cecil Kellaway,
Robert Sully, Byron Barr, Reginald Denny,
Lumsden Hare

AAN: Jennifer Jones; title song (*m* Victor
Young, *ly* Edward Heyman); Victor Young

Love, Life and Laughter*
GB 1934 83m bw
ATP (Basil Dean)

A film actress catches the eye of a Ruritanian
prince.
Lively star vehicle ranging from sentiment to
slapstick.

w Robert Edmunds *d* Maurice Elvey

Gracie Fields, John Loder, Norah Howard,
Allan Aynesworth, Esme Percy, Robb Wilton,
Fred Duprez, Horace Kenney, Veronica
Brady

The Love Lottery
GB 1953 83m Technicolor
Ealing (Monja Danischewsky)

A British film star is persuaded to offer
himself as first prize in a lottery.
Satirical farce which doesn't come off, mainly
owing to paucity of comedy ideas.

w Harry Kurnitz *d* Charles Crichton
ph Douglas Slocombe *m* Benjamin Frankel
pd Tom Morahan

David Niven, Herbert Lom, Peggy Cummins,
Anne Vernon, Charles Victor, Gordon
Jackson, Felix Aylmer, Hugh McDermott

The Love Machine
US 1971   110m   Eastmancolor
Columbia / Mike Frankovich

Megalomaniac TV reporter progresses to
network programme controller but is finally
undone by his vivid sex life.
Stodgy, silly melodrama from a bestseller
whose inspiration was well known in TV
circles.

w Samuel Taylor, *novel* Jacqueline Susann
d Jack Haley Jnr ph Charles Lang Jnr
m Artie Butler

John Philip Law, Dyan Cannon, Robert Ryan,
Jackie Cooper, David Hemmings, Shecky
Greene

Love Me Forever
US 1936   92m   bw
Columbia
GB title: *On Wings of Song*

A down and out singer makes good.
Fair star vehicle.

w Jo Swerling, Sidney Buchman d Victor
Schertzinger ph Joe Walker md Louis Silvers

Grace Moore, Leo Carillo, Robert Allen,
Spring Byington, Michael Bartlett, Thurston
Hall, Douglas Dumbrille, Luis Alberni

Love Me or Leave Me**
US 1955   122m   Eastmancolor
   Cinemascope
MGM (Joe Pasternak)

Twenties singer Ruth Etting is befriended by a
racketeer who pushes her to the top but drives
her to drink and despair in the process.
Agreeably bitter showbiz biopic which gives
the impression of being not too far from the
truth.

w Daniel Fuchs, Isabel Lennart d Charles
Vidor ph Arthur E. Arling md George Stoll
ad Cedric Gibbons, Urie McCleary

Doris Day, James Cagney, Cameron Mitchell,
Robert Keith, Tom Tully, Harry Bellaver,
Richard Gaines

AA: original story (Daniel Fuchs)
AAN: script; George Stoll; James Cagney;
song 'I'll Never Stop Loving You' (m Nicholas
Brodszky, ly Sammy Cahn)

Love Me Tender
US 1956   95m   bw   Cinemascope
TCF (David Weisbart)

Three brothers fall out over loot they have
brought home from the Civil War.
Odd western designed (perhaps after shooting
began) as Presley's introductory vehicle; he

sings four songs before getting shot, and
reappears in ghostly form at the end.

w Robert Buckner d Robert D. Webb
ph Leo Tover m Lionel Newman

Richard Egan, Debra Paget, Elvis Presley,
Robert Middleton, William Campbell, Neville
Brand, Mildred Dunnock, Bruce Bennett,
James Drury, Ken Clark, Barry Coe

Love Me Tonight****
US 1932   104m   bw
Paramount (Rouben Mamoulian)

A Parisian tailor accidentally moves into the
aristocracy.
The most fluently cinematic comedy musical
ever made, with sounds and words, lyrics and
music, deftly blended into a compulsively and
consistently laughable mosaic of sophisticated
nonsense; one better than the best of Lubitsch
and Clair.

w Samuel Hoffenstein, Waldemar Young,
George Marion Jnr d Rouben Mamoulian
ph Victor Milner songs Rodgers and Hart

Maurice Chevalier, Jeanette MacDonald,
Charles Butterworth, Charles Ruggles, Myrna
Loy, C. Aubrey Smith, Elizabeth Patterson,
Ethel Griffies, Blanche Frederici, Robert
Greig

'Gay, charming, witty, it is everything that
the Lubitsch musicals should have been but
never were.'—*John Baxter, 1968*
'With the aid of a pleasant story, a good
musician, a talented cast and about a million
dollars, he has done what someone in
Hollywood should have done long ago—he has
illustrated a musical score.'—*Pare Lorentz*
'It has that infectious spontaneity which
distinguishes the American musical at its
best.'—*Peter Cowie, 1970*
'A rich amalgam of filmic invention, witty
decoration and wonderful songs.'—*NFT, 1974*

Love Nest
US 1951   84m   bw

A writer and his wife invest in an apartment
building but find their tenants time-consuming.
Fairly lively comedy with varied talent.
William Lundigan, June Haver, Frank Fay,
Marilyn Monroe, Jack Paar, Leatrice Joy.
Written by I. A. L. Diamond, from a novel by
Scott Corbett; directed by Joseph Newman;
for TCF.

Love on the Dole***
GB 1941   100m   bw
British National (John Baxter)

Life among unemployed cotton workers in industrial Lancashire between the wars. Vividly characterized, old-fashioned social melodrama, well made on a low budget; a rare problem picture for Britain at this time.

w Walter Greenwood, Barbara K. Emery, Rollo Gamble, *novel Walter Greenwood d John Baxter*

Deborah Kerr, Clifford Evans, *George Carney*, Joyce Howard, Frank Cellier, Geoffrey Hibbert, *Mary Merrall*, Maire O'Neill, *Marjorie Rhodes*, A. Bromley Davenport, Marie Ault, Iris Vandeleur, Kenneth Griffith

Love on the Run°
US 1936   81m   bw
MGM (Joseph L. Mankiewicz)

Rival newspapermen help an heiress to escape an unwanted wedding and in the process uncover a ring of spies.
Harebrained star farce, smoothly assembled and still fairly funny.

w John Lee Mahin, Manuel Seff, Gladys Hurlbut *d* W. S. Van Dyke *ph* Oliver T. Marsh *m* Franz Waxman

Clark Gable, Joan Crawford, Franchot Tone, Reginald Owen, Mona Barrie, Ivan Lebedeff, William Demarest

'A slightly daffy cinematic item of absolutely no importance.'—*New York Times*

Love on the Run°
France 1978   95m   Eastmancolor

Antoine Doinel, separated from his family, is still having girl trouble. Amorous adventure of the character first glimpsed in *Les Quatre Cent Coups* and presumably based on the director; fair sophisticated fun for those who appreciate the joke. Jean-Pierre Leaud, Marie-France Pisier, Claude Jade, Rosy Varte. Written by François Truffaut and others; directed by François Truffaut; for Les Films du Carrosse.

Love on Wheels
GB 1932   87m   bw

A department store assistant becomes publicity-conscious. Zippy little comedy of its day. Jack Hulbert, Edmund Gwenn, Leonora Corbett, Gordon Harker, Percy Parsons, Roland Culver, Miles Malleson. Written by Victor Saville, Angus Macphail, Robert Stevenson and Douglas Furber; directed by Victor Saville; for Gainsborough.

The Love Parade°°
US 1929   112m   bw
Paramount (Ernst Lubitsch)

The prince of Sylvania marries.
Primitive sound operetta set among the idle European rich, with clear but faded instances of the Lubitsch touch.

w Ernest Vajda, Guy Bolton, *play* The Prince Consort by Leon Xanrof and Jules Chancel *d* Ernst Lubitsch *ph* Victor Milner *songs* Victor Schertzinger, Clifford Grey

Maurice Chevalier, Jeanette MacDonald, Lupino Lane, Lillian Roth, Edgar Norton, Lionel Belmore, Eugene Pallette

'The first truly cinematic screen musical in America.'—*Theodore Huff*

AAN: best picture; Ernst Lubitsch; Victor Milner; Maurice Chevalier

Love, Soldiers and Women
France / Italy 1953   96m   bw
Franco-London / Continental
original title: *Destinées*; US title: *Daughters of Destiny*

Three stories of women in war: Joan of Arc, Lysistrata, and a modern American war widow visiting her husband's grave.
Uninteresting patchwork with Lysistrata predictably stealing the show.

'Jeanne': *w* Jean Aurenche, Pierre Bost *d* Jean Delannoy *with* Michèle Morgan
'Elizabeth': *w* Sergio Amedei *d* Marcel Pagliero *with* Claudette Colbert, Eleanora Rossi Drago
'Lysistrata': *w* Jean Ferry, Henri Jeanson, Carlo Rim, *play* Aristophanes *d* Christian-Jaque *with* Martine Carol, Raf Vallone, Paolo Stoppa

Love Story
GB 1944   112m   bw
GFD / Gainsborough (Harold Huth)
US title: *A Lady Surrenders*

In Cornwall during World War II, a half-blind airman falls for a pianist with a weak heart.
Novelettish love story which became popular because of its Cornish Rhapsody.

w Leslie Arliss, Doreen Montgomery, Rodney Ackland, *novel* J. W. Drawbell *d* Leslie Arliss *ph* Bernard Knowles *m* Hubert Bath

Margaret Lockwood, Stewart Granger, Patricia Roc, Tom Walls, Reginald Purdell, Moira Lister

'A splendid, noble and fatuous piece.'—*C. A. Lejeune*

'In psychology and dialogue this is straight out of *Mabel's Weekly*.'—*Richard Winnington*

Love Story°
US 1970   100m   Movielab
Paramount (David Golden)

Two students marry; she dies.
A barrage of ripe old Hollywood clichés spiced with new-fangled bad language. In the circumstances, well enough made, and certainly astonishingly popular.

w Erich Segal, from his novelette *d* Arthur Hiller *ph* Dick Kratina *m* Bach, Mozart, Handel *md* Francis Lai

Ali MacGraw, Ryan O'Neal, Ray Milland, John Marley
    'Camille with bullshit.'—*Alexander Walker*

AAN: best picture; Erich Segal; Arthur Hiller; Francis Lai; Ali MacGraw; Ryan O'Neal; John Marley

Love That Brute
US 1950   85m   bw
TCF (Fred Kohlmar)

A ruthless Chicago gangleader is actually a softy, leaving his supposedly rubbed-out enemies in a comfortable cellar; a young governess persuades him to reform.
Rickety, dully-scripted gangster farce.

w Darrell Ware, John Lee Mahin, Karl Tunberg *d* Alexander Hall *ph* Lloyd Ahern *m* Cyril Mockridge

Paul Douglas, Jean Peters, Cesar Romero, Joan Davis, Arthur Treacher

Love Thy Neighbour
GB 1973   85m   Technicolor
EMI / Hammer (Roy Skeggs)

A prejudiced white worker has coloured neighbours.
Elongated screen version of the popular TV series in which the West Indians smile through all the insults and come out top in the end. It might have been worse, but not much.

w Vince Powell, Harry Driver *d* John Robins *ph* Moray Grant *m* Albert Elms

Jack Smethurst, Kate Williams, Rudolph Walker, Nina Baden-Semper, Bill Fraser, Charles Hyatt, Keith Marsh, Patricia Hayes, Arthur English

Love under Fire
US 1937   75m   bw
TCF (Nunnally Johnson)

A detective catches up with a lady jewel thief in Madrid during the Spanish Civil War.
Adequately entertaining but rather tasteless adventure comedy.

w Gene Fowler, Allen Rivkin, Ernest Pascal, *play* Walter Hackett *d* George Marshall *ph* Ernest Palmer *m* Arthur Lange

Loretta Young, Don Ameche, Frances Drake, Walter Catlett, John Carradine, Borrah Minevitch and his Rascals, Sig Rumann, Harold Huber, E. E. Clive, Katherine de Mille

Love with the Proper Stranger**
US 1964   100m   bw
Paramount / Boardwalk (Alan J. Pakula)

A musician tries to help his pregnant shopgirl friend get an abortion, but they decide to get married instead.
Oddly likeable comedy drama set on New York's Italian East Side, with an excellent location sense.

w Arnold Schulman *d* Robert Mulligan *ph* Milton Krasner *m* Elmer Bernstein

Steve McQueen, Natalie Wood, Tom Bosley, Edie Adams, Herschel Bernardi

AAN: Arnold Schulman; Milton Krasner; Natalie Wood

The Loved One*
US 1965   118m   bw
MGM / Filmways (Neil Hartley)

A young English poet in California gets a job at a very select burial ground.
A pointed satire on the American way of death has been allowed to get out of hand, with writer and actors alike laying it on too thick; but there are pleasantly waspish moments in a movie advertised as 'the motion picture with something to offend everybody'.

w Terry Southern, Christopher Isherwood, *novel* Evelyn Waugh *d* Tony Richardson *ph* Haskell Wexler *m* John Addison *pd* Rouben Ter-Arutunian

Robert Morse, John Gielgud, Rod Steiger, *Liberace,* Anjanette Comer, Jonathan Winters, Dana Andrews, Milton Berle, James Coburn, Tab Hunter, Margaret Leighton, Roddy McDowall, Robert Morley, Lionel Stander
    'Even a chaotic satire like this is cleansing, and it's embarrassing to pan even a bad movie that comes out against God, mother and country.'—*Pauline Kael, 1968*
    'A spineless farrago of collegiate gags.'—*Stanley Kauffmann*
    'A sinking ship that makes it to port because everyone on board is too giddy to panic.'—*New Yorker, 1978*

Lovely to Look At*
US 1952   102m   Technicolor
MGM (Jack Cummings)

Three Broadway producers inherit a Paris fashion house.

Lavish but dullish remake of *Roberta* (qv), in itself no great shakes as a storyline; again the fashions and the numbers are the thing.

w George Wells, Harry Ruby *d* Mervyn Le Roy *ph* George J. Folsey *m* Jerome Kern *ad* Cedric Gibbons, Gabriel Scognamillo

Howard Keel, Kathryn Grayson, Ann Miller, Red Skelton

A Lovely Way to Die
US 1968   98m   Techniscope
Universal (Richard Lewis)
GB title: *A Lovely Way to Go*

An ex-cop becomes bodyguard to a suspected murderess, but proves her innocent.
Offbeat mélange of caper comedy, black farce, private eye detection, courtroom drama, spectacular action and routine thick ear. Doesn't work.

w A. J. Russell *d* David Lowell Rich *ph* Morris Hartzband *m* Kenyon Hopkins

Kirk Douglas, Sylva Koscina, Eli Wallach, *Martyn Green*, Kenneth Haigh, Sharon Farrell

'The net result is rather as though Philip Marlowe had met Doris Day on his not very inspiring way to the forum.'—*MFB*

Lover Come Back**
US 1961   107m   Eastmancolor
U-I / Seven Pictures / Nob Hill / Arwin

Rival executives find themselves advertising a non-existent product.
Fairly sharp advertising satire disguised as a romantic comedy; the most entertaining of the Day-Hudson charmers.

w Stanley Shapiro, Paul Henning *d* Delbert Mann *ph* Arthur E. Arling *m* Frank de Vol

Doris Day, Rock Hudson, *Tony Randall*, Jack Oakie, Edie Adams

AAN: Stanley Shapiro, Paul Henning

The Lovers
GB 1972   89m   Eastmancolor
British Lion / Gildor (Maurice Foster)

A Manchester bank clerk with a prim girl friend finds it difficult to lose his virginity.
Well-written but rather arch comedy which seemed much funnier and fresher as a TV series.

w Jack Rosenthal *d* Herbert Wise *ph* Bob Huke *m* Carl Davis

Richard Beckinsale, Paula Wilcox, Joan Scott, Susan Littler, John Comer, Stella Moray, Nikolas Simmonds

Lovers and Other Strangers***
US 1969   104m   Metrocolor
ABC / David Susskind

After living together for eighteen months, Susan and Mike decide to get married, and find their parents have sex problems of their own.
Wise, witty and well acted sex farce, with many actors making the most of ample chances under firm directoral control.

w Renée Taylor, Joseph Bologna, David Zelag Goodman *d* Cy Howard *ph* Andrew Laszlo *m* Fred Karlin

Gig Young, Anne Jackson, Richard Castellano, Bonnie Bedelia, Michael Brandon, *Beatrice Arthur*, Robert Dishy, Harry Guardino, Diane Keaton, Cloris Leachman, Anne Meara, *Marian Hailey*

'An extremely engaging comedy.'—*Gillian Hartnoll*

AA: song 'For All We Know' (*m* Fred Karlin, *ly* Robb Wilson, Arthur James)
AAN: script; Richard Castellano

Lovers Courageous
US 1932   78m   bw

An unsuccessful playwright covets the admiral's daughter. Heavily-titled comedy with good performances of the period. Robert Montgomery, Madge Evans, Roland Young, Frederick Kerr, Reginald Owen, Halliwell Hobbes, Alan Mowbray. Written by Frederick Lonsdale; directed by Robert Z. Leonard; for MGM.

The Lovers of Lisbon*
France 1954   112m   bw
EGC / Hoche / Fides (Jacques Gauthier)
original title: *Les Amants du Tage*

A man who has killed his unfaithful wife is acquitted of murder, gets a job as a taxi driver in Lisbon, and falls for a rich Englishwoman who has killed her husband and is being pursued by a police inspector.
Pretentious tosh with a few compensations.

w Marcel Rivet, *novel* Joseph Kessel *d* Henri Verneuil *ph* Roger Hubert *m* Lucien Legrand

Daniel Gélin, Françoise Arnoul, Trevor Howard, Ginette Leclerc, Marcel Dalio

The Lovers of Toledo
Italy / France / Spain 1952   82m   bw
EGE / Lux / Athenea (Raymond Eger)

In 1825 a cruel police chief releases a political prisoner in return for the hand in marriage of his mistress.
Curiously unpersuasive period melodrama with good credits but too many international cooks.

w Claude Vermorel, *story* Le Coffre et le Revenant by Stendhal *d* Henri Decoin *ph* Michel Kelber *m* Jean-Jacques Grunenwald

Pedro Armendariz, Alida Valli, Gérard Landry, Françoise Arnoul

Loves of a Blonde*
Czechoslovakia 1965   82m   bw
Barrandov Studios
original title: *Lasky Jedne Plavovlasky*
aka: *A Blonde in Love*

A factory girl falls for a visiting musician but meets suspicion from his family when she pursues him.
Mild anecdote with excellent humorous detail which endeared it to international critics.

w Milos Forman, Jaroslav Papousek, Ivan Passer *d* Milos Forman *ph* Miroslav Ondricek *m* Evzen Illin

Hanna Brejchova, Vladimir Pucholt
    'It depends on an instinctive sense of timing and a consistent vision of life and people.'— *Georges Sadoul*

AAN: best foreign film

The Loves of Carmen
US 1948   99m   Technicolor
Columbia (Charles Vidor)

In 1820s Seville, a dragoon corporal is enslaved by a gypsy, kills her husband and becomes an outlaw.
Unrewarding version of the original much-filmed story, with both stars plainly wishing they were elsewhere.

w Helen Deutsch, *novel* Prosper Mérimée *d* Charles Vidor *ph* William Snyder *m* Mario Castelnuovo-Tedesco

Rita Hayworth, Glenn Ford, Victor Jory, Ron Randell, Luther Adler, Arnold Moss, Margaret Wycherly, Bernard Nedell

AAN: William Snyder

The Loves of Edgar Allan Poe
US 1942   67m   bw
TCF (Bryan Foy)

The famous writer marries his childhood sweetheart but becomes an alcoholic.
A curiosity which fails to bring out the bizarre truth and emerges as a stilted charade.

w Samuel Hoffenstein, Tom Reed *d* Harry Lachman *ph* Lucien Andriot *m* Emil Newman

John Shepperd, Linda Darnell, Virginia Gilmore, Jane Darwell, Frank Conroy, Henry Morgan

The Loves of Joanna Godden
GB 1947   89m   bw
Ealing (Sidney Cole)

On Romney Marsh at the turn of the century, a woman farmer has three suitors.
Dullish 'woman's picture'.

w H. E. Bates, Angus Macphail, *novel* Sheila Kaye-Smith *d* Charles Frend *ph* Douglas Slocombe *m* Ralph Vaughan Williams

Googie Withers, John McCallum, Jean Kent, Derek Bond, Chips Rafferty, Henry Mollison, Sonia Holm, Edward Rigby, Josephine Stuart
† Robert Hamer directed some scenes.

The Loves of Sunya
US 1927   80m (24 fps)   bw   silent
Swanson Producing Corporation

A yogi recognizes two young lovers as people he wronged in a previous existence, and warns them of impending disaster.
Star tosh of its period, unthinkable now as a screen attraction.

w Earle Brown, *play* The Eyes of Youth by Max Marcin, Charles Guernon *d* Albert Parker *ph* Dudley Murphy *ad* Hugo Ballin

Gloria Swanson, John Boles, Anders Randolph, Hush Miller, Florbelle Fairbanks, Raymond Hackett
† Previously filmed as *Eyes of Youth* with Clara Kimball Young.

Lovin' Molly*
US 1973   98m   Movielab
Stephen Friedman (David Golden)

In Texas between 1925 and 1945, two men friends and an accommodating lady have a shifting relationship.
Odd little drama compendium, with fragments told by each in turn; too slight in structure and substance for complete success, but interesting most of the way.

w Stephen Friedman, *novel* Leaving Cheyenne by Larry McMurtry *d* Sidney Lumet *ph* Edward Brown *m* Fred Hellerman

Blythe Danner, Anthony Perkins, Beau Bridges, Edward Binns, Susan Sarandon

Loving**
US 1970   90m   Eastmancolor
Columbia / Brooks Ltd (Don Devlin)

A commercial artist reaches crisis point with both his wife and his mistress.
Smart New Yorkish sex comedy, typical of many but better than most.

w Don Devlin, *novel* Brooks Wilson Ltd by J. M. Ryan *d* Irvin Kershner *ph* Gordon Willis *m* Bernardo Segall *pd* Walter Scott Herndon

George Segal, Eva Marie Saint, Sterling
Hayden, Keenan Wynn, Nancie Phillips, Janis
Young, David Doyle

Loving Couples*
Sweden 1964 118m bw
Sandrew (Rune Waldekranz)
original title: Älskande Par

Three expectant mothers think back over their
sex lives.
Superbly made, rather hollow diatribe against
sex, presented as a series of intricate
flashbacks. Along the way, there is much to
enjoy, but the result is not really a film of
importance.

w Mai Zetterling, David Hughes,
novel Froknarna von Pahlen by Agnes von
Krusenstjerna d Mai Zetterling ph Sven
Nykvist m Rodger Wallis

Harriet Andersson, Gunnel Lindblom, Anita
Bjork, Gunnar Bjornstrand, Eva Dahlbeck,
Frank Sundstrom, Inga Landgre
  '. . . that air of packaged neurosis so
peculiar to the Swedish cinema.'—Tom Milne,
MFB

Loving You
US 1957 101m Technicolor
Vistavision
Paramount / Hal B. Wallis

A press agent signs a young hillbilly singer to
give zest to her husband's band.
Empty-headed, glossy star vehicle.

w Herbert Baker, Hal Kanter d Hal Kanter
ph Charles Lang Jnr m Walter Scharf

Elvis Presley, Lizabeth Scott, Wendell Corey,
Dolores Hart, James Gleason

The Luck of Ginger Coffey*
Canada / US 1964 100m bw
Crawley / Roth–Kershner (Leon Roth)

An Irish layabout in Canada finds it difficult to
keep a job or protect his family.
Mildly interesting character study with good
background detail of Montreal.

w Brian Moore, from his novel d Irvin
Kershner ph Manny Wynn m Bernardo
Segall

Robert Shaw, Mary Ure, Liam Redmond

The Luck of the Irish*
US 1947 99m bw
TCF (Fred Kohlmar)

A New York newsman's love life is
complicated by a helpful leprechaun he meets
in Ireland.

Hollywood moonshine, second class: the will
and the players are there, but the script is not
funny enough.

w Philip Dunne, novel There Was a Little
Man by Constance and Guy Jones d Henry
Koster ph Joseph La Shelle m Cyril
Mockridge

Tyrone Power, Cecil Kellaway, Anne Baxter,
Lee J. Cobb, James Todd, Jayne Meadows, J.
M. Kerrigan, Phil Brown

AAN: Cecil Kellaway

Lucky Jim**
GB 1957 95m bw
British Lion / Charter (Roy Boulting)

At a provincial university, an accident-prone
junior lecturer has a disastrous weekend with
his girl friend and his professor.
Quite funny in its own right, this is a
vulgarization of a famous comic novel which
got its effects more subtly, with more sense of
place, time and character.

w Jeffrey Dell, Patrick Campbell, novel
Kingsley Amis d John Boulting ph Max
Greene

Ian Carmichael, Hugh Griffith, Terry-Thomas,
Sharon Acker, Jean Anderson, Maureen
Connell, Clive Morton, John Welsh, Reginald
Beckwith, Kenneth Griffith

Lucky Jordan
US 1942 83m bw
Paramount (Fred Kohlmar)

A con man is drafted and overcomes Nazi
agents.
Forgettable star cheapie.

w Darrell Ware, Karl Tunberg d Frank
Tuttle ph John F. Seitz m Adolph Deutsch

Alan Ladd, Helen Walker, Sheldon Leonard,
Marie McDonald, Mabel Paige, Lloyd
Corrigan, Dave Willock, Miles Mander
  'It's still cops and robbers, no matter how
you slice it . . . Mr Ware and Mr Tunberg are
not above dragging in mother love as the
reason the gangster changes from a selfish
killer to a patriot.'—Joseph Pihodna, New
York Herald Tribune

Lucky Lady
US 1975 118m De Luxe
TCF / Gruskoff / Venture (Michael Grusko¾)

A cabaret girl in 1930 Tijuana joins two
adventurers in smuggling liquor into the US by
boat.
Whatever can be done wrong with such a story
has been done, including irritatingly washed
out photography, kinky sex, and sudden

switches from farce to gore. None of it holds the interest for a single moment.

w Willard Huyck, Gloria Katz *d* Stanley Donen *ph* Geoffrey Unsworth *m* Ralph Burns *pd* John Barry

Liza Minnelli, Gene Hackman, Burt Reynolds, Michael Hordern, Geoffrey Lewis, Robby Benson

'A manic mess that tries to be all things to all people and ends up offering nothing to anyone.'—*Frank Rich*

'It sports its calculations on its sleeve like rhinestones.'—*Sight and Sound*

Lucky Me*
US 1954   100m   Warnercolor
Cinemascope
Warner (Henry Blanke)

Theatrical entertainers stranded in Florida get a lucky break.
Watchable, forgettable musical.

w James O'Hanlon, Robert O'Brien, Irving Elinson *d* Jack Donohue *ph* Wilfrid M. Cline *md* Ray Heindorf

Doris Day, Robert Cummings, Phil Silvers, Eddie Foy Jnr, Nancy Walker, Martha Hyer, Bill Goodwin, Marcel Dalio

'The first Cinemascope musical . . . pleasant, light-hearted, frothy entertainment.'—*MFB*

Lucky Night
US 1939   90m   bw
MGM (Louis D. Lighton)

An heiress goes out into the world to make a life for herself, and falls for a man she finds on a park bench.
Tedious pattern romance which did neither of its stars any good.

w Vincent Laurence, Grover Jones *d* Norman Taurog *ph* Ray June

Myrna Loy, Robert Taylor, Joseph Allen, Henry O'Neill, Douglas Fowley, Marjorie Main, Charles Lane, Bernard Nedell

Lucky Partners*
US 1940   101m   bw
RKO (George Haight)

Two strangers share a sweepstake ticket and fall in love.
A very thin comedy kept afloat by its stars.

w Allan Scott, John Van Druten, *story* Bonne Chance by Sacha Guitry *d* Lewis Milestone *ph* Robert de Grasse *m* Dmitri Tiomkin

Ronald Colman, Ginger Rogers, Jack Carson, Spring Byington, Cecilia Loftus, Harry Davenport

The Lucky Star*
Canada 1980   110m   colour
Tele Metropole International / Claude Leger

During World War II a Dutch Jewish boy studies wild west films and captures a German colonel.
Unusual and likeable family adventure story with an unnecessary downbeat ending.

w Max Fischer, Jack Rosenthal *d* Max Fischer *ph* Frank Tody *m* Art Philipps

Rod Steiger, Louise Fletcher, Brett Marx, Lou Jacobi, Helen Hughes

The Lucky Stiff
US 1948   101m   bw

A cabaret singer sentenced to death for murder is secretly reprieved but comes back as a 'ghost' to scare the real culprit into confession. Weird comedy-melodrama which seems to embarrass all concerned. Dorothy Lamour, Brian Donlevy, Claire Trevor, Irene Hervey. Written and directed by Lewis R. Foster, from a novel by Craig Rice; for Amusement Enterprises / UA.

Lucretia Borgia
France / Italy 1952   105m approx
Technicolor
Ariane / Filmsonor / Rizzoli

Cesare Borgia uses his beautiful sister as a political pawn.
Well-mounted but rather boring period barnstormer.

w Cécil Saint-Laurent, Jacques Sigurd, Christian-Jaque *d* Christian-Jaque *ph* Christian Matras *m* Maurice Thiriet

Martine Carol, Pedro Armendariz, Massimo Serato, Ventine Tessier

Lucy Gallant*
US 1955   104m   Technicolor
Vistavision
Paramount / Pine–Thomas

The success story of a dressmaker who comes to run a group of fashion shops but neglects her love life.
Efficient, smartly-handled woman's picture.

w John Lee Mahin, Winston Miller, *novel* The Life of Lucy Gallant by Margaret Cousins *d* Robert Parrish *ph* Lionel Lindon *m* Van Cleave

Jane Wyman, Charlton Heston, Claire Trevor, Thelma Rittcr, William Demarest, Wallace Ford, Tom Helmore, Mary Field

Ludwig*

Italy / France / West Germany 1972
186m Technicolor Panavision
Mega / Cinetel / Dieter Gessler / Divina
(Robert Gordon Edwards)

The 19th-century King of Bavaria becomes
involved in scandal and goes mad.
A stylish but historically questionable and
highly coloured view of events; it drags its
heels long before history did.

w Luchino Visconti, Enrico Medioli
d Luchino Visconti ph Armando Nannuzzi
md Franco Nannino

Helmut Berger, Romy Schneider, Trevor
Howard, Silvana Mangano, Helmut Griem,
Nora Ricci, Gert Frobe, John Moulder Brown

Lullaby of Broadway*

US 1951 92m Technicolor
Warner (William Jacobs)

The daughter of a faded Broadway star
becomes the new toast of the town.
Reasonably lively musical with solid
production values but little style or wit.

w Earl Baldwin d David Butler ph Wilfrid
Cline md Ray Heindorf

Doris Day, Billy de Wolfe, Gene Nelson,
Gladys George, Florence Bates, S. Z. Sakall

Lulu Belle

US 1948 87m bw

A selfish singer has a bad effect on one man
after another. Dreary melodrama with a
miscast star. Dorothy Lamour, George
Montgomery, Otto Kruger, Albert Dekker,
Glenda Farrell. Written by Everett Freeman,
from the play by Charles MacArthur and
Edward Shelton; directed by Leslie Fenton;
for Benedict Bogeaus / Columbia.

Lumière D'Eté*

France 1943 112m bw
Discina (Andre Paulvé)

The idle and decadent rich in a mountain hotel
are affected in various ways by workmen in
the valley below.
Unusual and generally interesting character
melodrama.

w Jacques Prévert, Pierre Laroche d Jean
Grémillion ph Louis Page m Roland Manuel

Madeleine Renaud, Pierre Brasseur,
Madeleine Robinson, Paul Bernard, Jane
Marken, Georges Marchal

La Luna

Italy 1979 142m Eastmancolor
TCF / Fiction Cinematografica (Giovanni
Bertolucci)

A singer has an incestuous relationship with
her teenage son.
Interminable catalogue of events few people
wanted to experience; the kindest description
would be 'pretentious claptrap'.

w Giuseppe and Bernardo Bertolucci, Clare
Peploe d Bernardo Bertolucci ph Vittorio
Storaro m operatic excerpts

Jill Clayburgh, Matthew Barry, Laura Betti,
Renato Salvatori, Fred Gwynne

Lunch on the Grass**

France 1959 91m Eastmancolor
Compagnie Jean Renoir
original title: Déjeuner sur l'Herbe

An international scientist hears the pipes of
pan, embarks on a country idyll and
impregnates a housemaid whom he later
marries.
Charming if overlong frolic with ideas, a
harking back to earlier Renoir themes such as
in Boudu Sauvé des Eaux.

wd Jean Renoir ph Georges Leclerc
m Joseph Kosma

Paul Meurisse, Catherine Rouvel, Fernand
Sardou, Ingrid Nordine
'A warm, loving, garrulous, undisciplined
film.'—Penelope Houston, MFB

Lure of the Wilderness

US 1952 92m Technicolor
TCF (Robert L. Jacks)

A man falsely accused of murder hides for
eight years in Georgia's Okefenokee swamp.
Remake of Swamp Water, with Walter
Brennan playing the same part. The plot
works fairly well still, but colour doesn't suit
the scenery.

w Louis Lantz, story Vereen Bell d Jean
Negulesco ph Edward Cronjager m Franz
Waxman

Jeffrey Hunter, Jean Peters, Walter Brennan,
Constance Smith, Jack Elam

Lured*

US 1947 102m bw
(UA) James Nasser
GB title: Personal Column

An American dancer stranded in London
helps Scotland Yard catch a killer.
Minor murder mystery with a pleasing cast.

w Leo Rosten, from the French film Pièges
d Douglas Sirk ph William Daniels m Michel
Michelet pd Nicolai Remisoff

Lucille Ball, George Sanders, Charles Coburn,
Boris Karloff, Cedric Hardwicke, Alan
Mowbray, George Zucco, Joseph Calleia,
Robert Coote, Alan Napier

Lust for a Vampire
GB 1970 95m Technicolor
Hammer (Harry Fine, Michael Style)

In 1830 an English writer discerns that a pupil in an exclusive mid-European girls' school is a reincarnated vampire.
Moderate Hammer horror.

w Tudor Gates, based on J. Sheridan Le Fanu's Carmilla d Jimmy Sangster ph David Muir m Harry Robinson

Ralph Bates, Michael Johnson, Barbara Jefford, Suzanna Leigh, Yutte Stensgaard, Mike Raven, Helen Christie

Lust for Gold
US 1949 90m bw
Columbia (S. Sylvan Simon)

A young man goes to Arizona to search for a lost gold mine discovered by his grandfather.
Moderate western drama consisting largely of flashback.

w Ted Sherdeman, Richard English, novel Thunder God's Gold by Barry Storm d S. Sylvan Simon ph Archie Stout m George Duning

Ida Lupino, Glenn Ford, Gig Young, William Prince, Edgar Buchanan, Will Geer, Paul Ford

Lust for Life**
US 1956 122m Metrocolor
Cinemascope
MGM (John Houseman)

The life of Vincent Van Gogh.
Fairly absorbing, not inaccurate, but somehow uninspiring biopic, probably marred by poor colour and wide screen; despite good work all round, it simply doesn't fall into a classic category.

w Norman Corwin, book Irving Stone d Vincente Minnelli ph F. A. Young, Russell Harlan m Miklos Rozsa ad Cedric Gibbons, Hans Peters, Preston Ames,

Kirk Douglas, Anthony Quinn (as Gauguin), James Donald, Pamela Brown, Everett Sloane, Niall MacGinnis, Noel Purcell, Henry Daniell, Lionel Jeffries, Madge Kennedy, Jill Bennett, Laurence Naismith
'Two hours of quite shattering and exciting entertainment.'—Alan Dent, Illustrated London News

AA: Anthony Quinn
AAN: Norman Corwin; Kirk Douglas

The Lusty Men*
US 1952 113m bw
RKO / Wald–Krasna (Jerry Wald)

Tensions lead to the death of one of a pair of rider friends on a rodeo tour.
Standard melodrama with semi-documentary detail and star performances.

w Horace McCoy, David Dortort d Nicholas Ray ph Lee Garmes m Roy Webb

Robert Mitchum, Arthur Kennedy, Susan Hayward, Arthur Hunnicutt

Luther*
GB 1973 112m Eastmancolor
American Express / Ely Landau / Cinevision

In 1525, the teachings of Luther culminate in the Peasants' Revolt.
Hard-to-watch filming by the American Film Theatre of a singularly theatrical play, and not a very good one at that. Some good acting.

w Edward Anhalt, play John Osborne d Guy Green ph Freddie Young m John Addison pd Peter Mullins

Stacy Keach, Patrick Magee, Hugh Griffith, Robert Stephens, Alan Badel, Julian Glover, Judi Dench, Leonard Rossiter, Maurice Denham

Luv
US 1967 95m Technicolor Panavision
Columbia / Jalem (Martin Manulis)

When a man prevents an old friend from jumping off the Brooklyn Bridge and brings him home, a sexual square dance develops.
A modern comedy that should have stayed in the theatre.

w Elliott Baker, play Murray Shisgal d Clive Donner ph Ernest Laszlo m Gerry Mulligan

Jack Lemmon, Peter Falk, Elaine May, Nina Wayne, Eddie Mayehoff, Paul Hartman, Severn Darden
'A light but incisive comedy about the patterns and language of love in a Freud-ridden society has become an inept and lethally unamusing film farce.'—MFB

Luxury Liner
US 1933 72m bw
Paramount

Stories of various passengers on a liner bound from New York to Bremerhaven.
Interesting minor multi-drama, like a rough sketch for Ship of Fools (qv).

w Gene Markey, Kathryn Scola, novel, Gina Kaus d Lothar Mendes ph Victor Milner

George Brent, Zita Johann, Vivienne Osborne, Alice White, Verree Teasdale, C. Aubrey Smith, Frank Morgan, Henry Wadsworth, Billy Bevan

Luxury Liner
US 1948 98m Technicolor
MGM (Joe Pasternak)

The captain of a liner has trouble with his
teenage daughter.
Minor shipboard musical with pleasing talents
applied.

w Gladys Lehmann, Richard Connell
d Richard Whorf ph Ernest Laszlo
md George Stoll

George Brent, Jane Powell, Lauritz Melchior,
Frances Gifford, Marina Koshetz, Xavier
Cugat, Richard Derr, Connie Gilchrist

Lydia*
US 1941 104m bw
Alexander Korda (Lee Garmes)

An ageing lady recalls her former beaux.
Pleasing remake of Carnet du Bal, with
excellent production values.

w Ben Hecht, Samuel Hoffenstein, story
Julien Duvivier, Laszlo Bus-Fekete d Julien
Duvivier ph Lee Garmes m Miklos Rozsa
pd Vincent Korda

Merle Oberon, Joseph Cotten, Alan Marshal,
Edna May Oliver, Hans Yaray, George
Reeves, John Halliday, Sara Allgood

AAN: Miklos Rozsa

Lydia Bailey
US 1952 89m Technicolor
TCF (Jules Schermer)

In 1802 a Boston lawyer visits Haiti to obtain
the signature of a wayward heiress, and
becomes involved in the negro fight against the
French.
Standard adventure romance with plenty of
excitements.

w Michael Blankfort, Philip Dunne, novel
Kenneth Roberts d Jean Negulesco ph Harry
Jackson m Hugo Friedhofer

Dale Robertson, Anne Francis, Charles
Korvin, William Marshall, Adeline de Walt
Reynolds

M•••
Germany 1931   118m   bw
Nero Film

A psychopathic murderer of children evades
the police but is caught by the city's criminals
who find his activities getting them a bad
name.
An unmistakable classic whose oddities are
hardly worth criticizing, this is part social
melodrama and part satire, but entirely
unforgettable, with most of its sequences
brilliantly staged.

*w Thea Von Harbou, Paul Falkenberg, Adolf
Jansen, Karl Vash d Fritz Lang ph* Fritz
Arno Wagner m Adolf Jansen *ad* Karl
Vollbrecht, Emil Hasler

Peter Lorre, Otto Wernicke, Gustav
Grundgens
    'Visual excitement, pace, brilliance of
surface and feeling for detail.'—*New Yorker,
1977*
† Of Lang's later work, *Fury* comes closest to
the feeling and style of *M*.

M•
US 1951   82m   bw
Columbia (Seymour Nebenzal)

Faithful but fated remake; without the heavy
expressionist techniques, the story seems
merely silly and the atmosphere is all wrong.

w Norman Reilly Raine, Leo Katcher
d Joseph Losey *ph* Ernest Laszlo *m* Michel
Michelet

David Wayne, Howard da Silva, Luther
Adler, Martin Gabel, Glenn Anders, Karen
Morley, Norman Lloyd, Walter Burke

Ma and Pa Kettle•
US 1949   75m   bw
U-I (Leonard Goldstein)

Pa Kettle wins a house in a contest and is
accused of cheating.
First of a series of low-budget comedies which,
based on characters from *The Egg and I* (qv),
had astonishing commercial success in
America. The standard varied from adequate
to painful.

w Herbert Margolis, Louis Morheim, Al
Lewis *d* Charles Lamont *ph* Maury
Gertsman *m* Milton Schwarzwald

Marjorie Main, Percy Kilbride, Richard Long,
Meg Randall
    'Not exactly Noel Coward.'—*Leonard
Maltin*
† For others in the series, see under *The
Kettles*.

Ma Nuit chez Maud•
France 1969   110m   bw
Films du Losange
aka: *My Night at Maud's*

A Catholic clerk in a small town falls in love
with an elegant divorcee but can't bring
himself to court her openly and marries
someone else.
Subdued, literate talk-piece which finally
exhausts rather than stimulates.

wd Eric Rohmer *ph* Nestor Almendros

Jean-Louis Trintignant, Françoise Fabian,
Marie-Christine Barault

AAN: best foreign film; Eric Rohmer (as
writer)

Macabre
US 1958   73m   bw
AA (William Castle)

When a small-town doctor's daughter is
kidnapped, he fears she may have been buried
alive in the cemetery.
Genuine but unsuccessful attempt to film a
horror comic; incredibly stodgy writing, acting
and direction put the lid on it.

w Robb White *d* William Castle *ph* Carl
Guthrie *m* Les Baxter

William Prince, Jim Backus, Jacqueline Scott,
Philip Tonge, Ellen Corby
    'A ghoulish but totally ineffective horror
piece, set mainly in undertakers' offices and an
atmosphere of graveyards and swirling fog.'—
MFB
† When first released, admission carried
insurance against death by fright. Some said it
should have been death by boredom.

Macao
US 1952   81m   bw
RKO (Alex Gottlieb)

A wandering American in the Far East helps a detective catch a gangster.
A few flashy decorative touches show the director's hand, otherwise this is routine, murky thick ear.

w Bernard C. Schoenfeld, Stanley Rubin
d Josef Von Sternberg (and Nicholas Ray)
ph Harry J. Wild m Anthony Collins

Robert Mitchum, Jane Russell, William Bendix, Gloria Grahame, Thomas Gomez

MacArthur the Rebel General*
US 1977   130m   Technicolor
Universal / Richard D. Zanuck, David Brown (Frank McCarthy)

The exploits of General MacArthur during the Pacific wars and his strained relationships with two presidents.
Sober, earnest political biography with war sequences; very well done but somehow unsympathetic.

w Hal Barwood, Matthew Robbins d Joseph Sargent ph Mario Tosi m Jerry Goldsmith

Gregory Peck, Dan O'Herlihy (as Roosevelt), Ed Flanders (as Truman), Ward Costello, Marj Dusay, Ivan Bonar
'A biopic that begins when its subject is sixty lacks roots—and in this case revelation.'—Judith Crist

Macbeth*
US 1948   89m   bw
Republic (Orson Welles)

A famous—or infamous—attempt to film Shakespeare in twenty-one days in papier mâché settings running with damp; further hampered by the use of a form of unintelligible bastard Scots. A few striking moments at the beginning remain; the rest should be silence.

d Orson Welles ph John L. Russell
m Jacques Ibert ad Fred Ritter

Orson Welles, Jeanette Nolan, Dan O'Herlihy, Roddy McDowall, Edgar Barrier, Robert Coote

Macbeth*
GB 1971   140m   Technicolor   Todd-AO 35
Playboy / Caliban (Andrew Braunsberg)

A sharpened and brutalized version; the blood swamps most of the cleverness and most of the poetry.

d Roman Polanski ph Gilbert Taylor m the Third Ear Band pd Wilfrid Shingleton

Jon Finch, Francesca Annis, Martin Shaw, Nicholas Selby, John Stride

McCabe and Mrs Miller
US 1971   120m   Technicolor
Panavision
Warner (David Foster, Mitchell Brower)

At the turn of the century a gambling gunfighter comes to a northwest mining town and uses his money to set up lavish brothels.
Obscurely scripted, muddy-coloured and harshly recorded western melodrama whose squalid 'realism' comes as close to fantasy as does The Wizard of Oz.

w Robert Altman, Brian Mackay, novel McCabe by Edmund Naughton d Robert Altman ph Vilmos Zsigmond pd Leon Ericksen

Warren Beatty, Julie Christie, René Auberjonois, Shelley Duvall, John Schuck
'A fleeting, diaphanous vision of what frontier life might have been.'—Pauline Kael
'Altman directed M*A*S*H, which wandered and was often funny; then Brewster McCloud, which wandered and was not funny; now this, which wanders and is repulsive. The thesis seems to be that if you take a corny story, fuzz up the exposition, vitiate the action, use a childishly ironic ending, and put in lots of profanity and nudity, you have Marched On with Time.'—Stanley Kauffmann
AAN: Julie Christie

The McConnell Story
US 1955   107m   Warnercolor
Cinemascope
Warner (Henry Blanke)
GB title: Tiger in the Sky

The career and accidental death of a jet ace of the Korean war.
Crude, obvious and saccharine biopic.

w Ted Sherdeman, Sam Rolfe d Gordon Douglas ph John Seitz, Ted McCord m Max Steiner

Alan Ladd, June Allyson, James Whitmore, Frank Faylen, Willis Bouchey

Macho Callahan
US 1970   100m   Movielab   Panavision
Avco / Felicidad (Bernard Kowalski, Martin C. Schute)

A vengeful cowboy annihilates all who stand in his way.
Squalid Mexican-made western with unremitting emphasis on violence.

w Clifford Newton Gould d Bernard Kowalski ph Gerry Fisher m Pat Williams

David Janssen, Lee J. Cobb, David Carradine, James Booth

MacKenna's Gold*
US 1969   136m   Technicolor   Super
   Panavision
Columbia / Highroad (Carl Foreman, Dmitri
   Tiomkin)

A dying Indian entrusts a sheriff with a map of
the legendary Valley of Gold, and when the
news breaks the map is in demand.
Curious serial-like western melodrama packed
with stars and pretensions above its station.
On a lower level, it is quite enjoyable.

w Carl Foreman, *novel* Will Henry d J. Lee-
Thompson ph Joseph MacDonald, Harold
Wellman m Quincy Jones pd Geoffrey
Drake

Gregory Peck, Omar Sharif, Telly Savalas,
Camilla Sparv, Keenan Wynn, Julie Newmar,
Ted Cassidy, Eduardo Ciannelli, Eli Wallach,
Edward G. Robinson, Raymond Massey,
Burgess Meredith, Anthony Quayle, Lee J.
Cobb
   'Preposterous hotch-potch of every cliché
known to the gold lust book.'—*MFB*
   'Twelve-year-olds of all ages might tolerate
it.'—*Judith Crist*
   'A western of truly stunning absurdity, a
thriving example of the old Hollywood maxim
about how to succeed by failing big.'—*Vincent
Canby*

The McKenzie Break*
GB 1970   106m   De Luxe
UA / Levy–Gardner–Laven

During World War II, German prisoners at a
Scottish camp stage an escape.
Effective little action suspenser.

w William Norton d Lamont Johnson
ph Michael Reed m Riz Ortolani

Brian Keith, Helmut Griem, Ian Hendry, Jack
Watson, Patrick O'Connell, Horst Janson

The Mackintosh Man*
GB 1973   99m   Technicolor
Warner / Newman–Foreman / John Huston

A government agent is sent to prison to
contact a criminal gang.
Convoluted but entertaining spy thriller with
good performances and action sequences.

w Walter Hill, *novel* The Freedom Trap by
Desmond Bagley d John Huston ph Oswald
Morris m Maurice Jarre

Paul Newman, James Mason, Dominique
Sanda, Nigel Patrick, Harry Andrews, Michael
Hordern, Ian Bannen, Peter Vaughan, Roland
Culver, Percy Herbert, Robert Lang, Leo
Genn

McLintock*
US 1963   127m   Technicolor
   Panavision
UA / Batjac (Michael Wayne)

A cattle baron can control a whole town but
not his termagant wife.
Sub-Ford western farce borrowed from *The
Taming of the Shrew*, with much fist-fighting
and mud-splattering, and rather too much chat
in between.

w James Edward Grant d Andrew V.
McLaglen ph William H. Clothier m Frank
de Vol

John Wayne, Maureen O'Hara, Yvonne de
Carlo, Patrick Wayne, Stefanie Powers, Chill
Wills, Bruce Cabot, Jack Kruschen

The McMasters
US 1969   90m   Technicolor
JayJen (Dimitri de Grunwald)

A black man returning home from the Civil
War gets unexpected help from a tough
landowner.
Racial western with black, white and red
points of view, all very violently expressed.

w Harold Jacob Smith d Alf Kjellin
ph Lester Shorr m Coleridge-Taylor
Parkinson

Brock Peters, Burl Ives, David Carradine,
Nancy Kwan, Jack Palance, Dane Clark, John
Carradine, I. Q. Jones, R. G. Armstrong

The Macomber Affair*
US 1947   89m   bw
(UA) Benedict Bogeaus (Casey Robinson)

The wife of a bullying big game hunter falls for
their guide.
Safari melodrama with a plot which has
become a cliché but seemed fresh enough at
the time. Goodish writing and acting.

w Casey Robinson, *story* The Short Happy
Life of Francis Macomber by Ernest
Hemingway d Zoltan Korda ph Karl Struss
m Miklos Rozsa

Gregory Peck, Joan Bennett, Robert Preston,
Reginald Denny, Carl Harbord, Jean Gillie
   'The best movie job on Hemingway to
date.'—*James Agee*

Macon County Line
US 1973   89m   Eastmancolor
Sam Arkoff / Max Baer

In mid-fifties Louisiana, a couple of hell-
raisers are harassed by a local sheriff, and
much bloodshed results.
Shapeless melodrama more or less in the wake
of *Easy Rider*; an unattractive film which
unaccountably had great box-office success.

w Max Baer, Richard Compton *d* Richard
Compton *ph* Daniel Lacambre *m* Stu Phillips

Alan Vint, Cheryl Waters, Geoffrey Lewis,
Joan Blackman, Jesse Vint, Max Baer

McQ
US 1974 111m Technicolor
  Panavision
Warner / Batjac / Levy–Gardner

A Seattle police detective goes after the
gangster who killed his friend.
Rambling, violent thriller with good sequences
but no cohesion.

w Lawrence Roman *d* John Sturges
ph Harry Stradling Jnr *m* Elmer Bernstein

John Wayne, Eddie Albert, Diana Muldaur,
Colleen Dewhurst, Clu Gulager, David
Huddleston, Julie Adams

McVicar
GB 1980 112m Eastmancolor

The true story of the escapes from prison of a
violent criminal who was subsequently
reformed and rehabilitated. Some smart
sequences don't prevent this from being an
exploitation item. Roger Daltrey, Adam
Faith, Cheryl Campbell, Billy Murray,
Georgina Hale. Written by John McVicar and
Tom Clegg; directed by Tom Clegg; for The
Who Films.

Mad About Men
GB 1954 90m Technicolor
GFD / Group Films (Betty Box)

By mutual agreement, a sports mistress and a
mermaid change places for a while.
Laborious rehash of *Miranda* with familiar
jokes.

w Peter Blackmore *d* Ralph Thomas
ph Ernest Steward *m* Benjamin Frankel

Glynis Johns, Donald Sinden, Anne
Crawford, Margaret Rutherford, Dora Bryan,
Nicholas Phipps, Irene Handl

Mad about Music*
US 1938 98m bw
Universal (Joe Pasternak)

A girl at a Swiss school adopts a personable
visitor as her father.
Pleasing star vehicle with charm and humour;
badly remade as *Toy Tiger* (qv).

w Bruce Manning, Felix Jackson *d* Norman
Taurog *ph* Joseph Valentine *m* / *ly* Harold
Adamson, Jimmie McHugh *m* Frank Skinner,
Charles Previn

Deanna Durbin, Herbert Marshall, Gail
Patrick, Arthur Treacher, Helen Parrish,
Marcia Mae Jones, William Frawley

AAN: original story (Marcella Burk, Frank
Kohner); Joseph Valentine; Frank Skinner,
Charles Previn

The Mad Doctor
US 1941 90m bw
Paramount (George Arthur)
GB title: *A Date with Destiny*

A doctor marries wealthy women and then
murders them.
Naïve melodrama of little interest except as a
vehicle for its star.

w Howard J. Green *d* Tim Whelan *ph* Ted
Tetzlaff *m* Victor Young

Basil Rathbone, Ellen Drew, John Howard,
Barbara Allen, Ralph Morgan, Martin
Kosleck

The Mad Doctor of Market Street
US 1942 61m bw

Shipwrecked people on a tropical island find
that one of their number is a dangerous
paranoiac. Dull and misleadingly titled
second-feature melodrama. Lionel Atwill, Nat
Pendleton, Una Merkel, Claire Dodd. Written
by Al Martin; directed by Joseph H. Lewis;
for Universal.

The Mad Genius
US 1931 81m bw
Warner

A crippled puppeteer adopts a boy and makes
him into a great dancer.
Curious variation on *Trilby*, filmed as *Svengali*
the previous year with much the same cast.
Not a great success: the script is dreadful.

w J. Grubb Alexander, Harvey Thew, *play*
The Idol by Martin Brown *d* Michael Curtiz
ph Barney McGill *ad* Anton Grot

John Barrymore, Marian Marsh, Donald
Cook, Luis Alberni, Carmel Myers, Charles
Butterworth, Boris Karloff, Frankie Darro

The Mad Ghoul
US 1943 65m bw
Universal (Ben Pivar)

A mad scientist needs fresh hearts to keep
alive the victims of his experiments with a
poison vapour.
Stagey, tasteless horror melodrama.

w Brenda Weisberg, Paul Gangelin,
story Hans Kraly *d* James Higan *ph* Milton
Krasner *md* Hans Salter

George Zucco, David Bruce, Evelyn Ankers,
Turhan Bey, Robert Armstrong, Charles
McGraw, Milburn Stone

Mad Love
US 1935 83m bw
MGM (John Considine Jnr)
GB title: *The Hands of Orlac*

A pianist loses his hands in an accident; a mad
surgeon, in love with the pianist's wife, grafts
on the hands of a murderer.
Absurd Grand Guignol done with great style
which somehow does not communicate itself in
viewer interest, only in cold admiration.

w Guy Endore, P. J. Wolfson, John
Balderston, *novel* The Hands of Orlac by
Maurice Renard *d* Karl Freund *ph* Chester
Lyons, Gregg Toland *m* Dmitri Tiomkin

Colin Clive, Peter Lorre, Frances Drake, Ted
Healy, Edward Brophy, Isabel Jewell, Sara
Haden

The Mad Magician
US 1954 72m bw
Columbia (Bryan Foy)

A magician's star-struck inventor murders his
employer and several others who stand
between him and the big time.
Hokey horror flick set in the eighties and
originally shown in 3-D.

w Crane Wilbur *d* John Brahm *ph* Bert
Glennon *m* Emil Newman

Vincent Price, Mary Murphy, Eva Gabor,
John Emery, Patrick O'Neal

The Mad Miss Manton*
US 1938 80m bw
RKO (Pandro S. Berman)

A zany socialite involves her friends in a
murder mystery.
Mildly funny comedy-thriller without too
much of either, but a good example of the
style of thirties craziness at its zenith.

w Philip G. Epstein *d* Leigh Jason
ph Nicholas Musuraca *m* Roy Webb

Barbara Stanwyck, Henry Fonda, Sam
Levene, Frances Mercer, Stanley Ridges,
Whitney Bourne, Hattie McDaniel, Miles
Mander

The Mad Room
US 1969 92m Berkey Pathecolor
Columbia / Norman Mauer

A companion kills her wealthy employer so
that her mentally retarded brother and sister
will have a home.
Tasteless remake of *Ladies in Retirement*, in
the brutalized vein which audicnces are
supposed by producers to want. In modern
dress and sharp locations, it succeeds only in
being nauseating.

w Bernard Girard, A. Z. Martin *d* Bernard
Girard *ph* Harry Stradling Jnr *m* Dave
Grusin

Stella Stevens, Shelley Winters, Skip Ward,
Carol Cole, Severn Darden

Mad Wednesday*
US 1947 77m bw
Howard Hughes

A middle-aged book-keeper is sacked and
goes on the town.
Woolly and unattractive farce which proved
something of a disaster for all the talents
concerned but historically is of considerable
interest. It begins with an excerpt from *The
Freshman* and continues to comic adventures
with a lion.

wd / pd Preston Sturges (re-edited by others)
ph Robert Pittack *m* Werner Richard
Heymann

Harold Lloyd, Jimmy Conlin, Raymond
Walburn, Franklin Pangborn, Al Bridge,
Margaret Hamilton, Edgar Kennedy

Madame Bovary
US 1949 114m bw
MGM (Pandro S. Berman)

A passionate girl marries a dull husband, takes
a lover, and commits suicide.
Dull, emasculated version of a classic.

w Robert Ardrey, *novel* Gustave Flaubert
d Vincente Minnelli *ph* Robert Planck
m Miklos Rozsa

Jennifer Jones, Van Heflin, James Mason,
Louis Jourdan, Christopher Kent, Gene
Lockhart, Gladys Cooper, John Abbott,
George Zucco
† Previously filmed in 1932 as *Unholy Love.*

Madame Butterfly
US 1932 88m bw
Paramount

A Japanese geisha commits hara kiri when an
American lieutenant passes her up for a
western girl.
Drearily modernized version of the opera
without its music; an odd idea to say the least.

w Josephine Lovett, Joseph M. March, *play*
David Belasco, John Luther Long *d* Marion
Gering *ph* David Abel *md* W. Franke
Harling

Sylvia Sidney, Cary Grant, Charlie Ruggles,
Sandor Kallay, Irving Pichel, Helen Jerome
Eddy
  'The long-drawn tragedy might be bearable
if it were expressed in music or poetry,
without any such embellishment it is apt to be
painfully pathetic.'—*The Times*

Madame Curie*
US 1944   124m   bw
MGM (Sidney Franklin)

The life and marriage of the woman who
discovered radium.
Dignified and rather dull biopic which well
exemplifies MGM's best production style of
the forties.

w Paul Osborn, Paul H. Rameau, *book* Eve
Curie *d* Mervyn Le Roy *ph* Joseph
Ruttenberg *m* Herbert Stothart *ad* Cedric
Gibbons, Paul Groesse

Greer Garson, Walter Pidgeon, Henry
Travers, Albert Basserman, Robert Walker,
C. Aubrey Smith, Dame May Whitty, Victor
Francen, Elsa Basserman, Reginald Owen,
Van Johnson
  'It achieves a notable triumph in making the
discovery of a new element seem almost as
glamorous as an encounter with Hedy
Lamarr.'—*C. A. Lejeune*

AAN: best picture; Joseph Ruttenberg;
Herbert Stothart; Greer Garson; Walter
Pidgeon

Madame De*
France / Italy 1953   102m   bw
Franco-London / Indus / Rizzoli
US title: *The Earrings of Madame de*

Tragic misunderstandings arise when a society
wife sells her earrings and tells her husband
she has lost them.
Elegant, rather heavy-handed but superbly
glossy extension of a fashionable novelette.

w Marcel Achard, Max Ophuls, Annette
Wademant, *novel* Louise de Vilmorin *d Max
Ophuls ph* Christian Matras *m* Oscar Straus,
Georges Van Parys *ad* Jean d'Eaubonne

Charles Boyer, Danielle Darrieux, Vittorio de
Sica, Lea di Lea, Jean Debucourt

Madame Dubarry**
Germany 1919   85m (24 fps)   bw   silent
Union-UFA
US title: *Passion*

The life and times of the glamorous courtesan
of Louis XV.
Milestone silent film which introduced to the
cinemas of America and Britain not only the
subtleties of the European cinema but the
more adaptable subtleties of a key director,
here dealing rather heavy-handedly with
material which he should later have re-used.

w Fred Orbing, Hans Kraly *d* Ernst Lubitsch
ph Theodor Sparkuhl

Pola Negri, Emil Jannings, Harry Liedtke,
Reinhold Schunzel

Madame Dubarry
US 1934   77m   bw

The life of the legendary courtesan at
Versailles. Utterly unpersuasive but
sometimes decorative historical charade.
Dolores del Rio, Reginald Owen, Victor Jory,
Anita Louise, Osgood Perkins, Verree
Teasdale. Written by Edward Chodorov;
directed by William Dieterle; for Warner.

Madame Rosa
France 1977   120m   Eastmancolor

An elderly Jewish prostitute runs an unofficial
nursery school and cares especially for a
fourteen-year-old Arab. Splendidly acted but
basically dreary fable twisted from a novel
which took the child's point of view. *Simone
Signoret,* Claude Dauphin, Samy Ben Youb.
Written and directed by Moshe Mizrahi, from
the novel by Emile Ajar; for Lira Films.
(Original title: *La Vie Devant Soi.*)

Madame Satan*
US 1930   105m   bw
MGM (C. B. de Mille)

When her husband strays, a socialite disguises
herself as a mysterious *femme fatale* and wins
him back.
Abysmal comedy in which both director and
principals appear frozen until the closing reels
present a crazy, spectacular party on a
dirigible which crashes but allows a happy
ending.

w Jeanie Macpherson *d* C. B. de Mille
ph Harold Rosson *m* Herbert Stothart

Kay Johnson, Reginald Denny, Lillian Roth,
Roland Young
  'A strange conglomeration of unreal
incidents that are sometimes set forth with no
little technical skill.'—*Mordaunt Hall, New
York Times*

Madame X*
US 1929   95m   bw
MGM
TV title: *Absinthe*

After an accidental death, a wealthy woman
disappears and goes down in the world; at a
subsequent murder trial she is defended by her
unrecognizing son.
Two silent versions (with Dorothy Donnelly
and Pauline Frederick) had been made of this
old theatrical warhorse; two sound versions
followed this one. The thing defies criticism.

w Willard Mack, *play* Alexandre Bisson
d Lionel Barrymore

Ruth Chatterton, Raymond Hackett, Mitchell
Lewis, Sidney Toler, Carroll Nye, Lewis
Stone, Richard Carle

'Works like this confound the reformers, elevate the name of pictures, and tell the world that there is an art in film making.'— *Variety*

AAN: Lionel Barrymore; Ruth Chatterton

Madame X*
US 1937 72m bw
MGM (James K. McGuinness)

Competent remake with an excellent cast.

w John Meehan *d* Sam Wood *ph* John B. Seitz *m* David Snell

Gladys George, John Beal, Warren William, Reginald Owen, Lynne Carver, Henry Daniell, Emma Dunn, Ruth Hussey, George Zucco

'A fine old play, dated and outmoded. Audiences will leave the theatre expecting to find the coachman with horse and buggy.'— *Variety*

Madame X
US 1965 100m Technicolor
Universal / Ross Hunter / Eltee

An elaborately dressed remake which suffered from a wooden lead; the more expensive the production, the more obvious the holes in the plot and the psychology.

w Jean Holloway *d* David Lowell Rich *ph* Russell Metty *m* Frank Skinner

Lana Turner, John Forsythe, Ricardo Montalban, *Constance Bennett*, Burgess Meredith, Keir Dullea, Virginia Grey, Warren Stevens

'One is free to enjoy a luxurious wallow in emotions that are all the more enjoyable for having no connection whatever with reality.'— *Brenda Davies*

Made for Each Other*
US 1938 90m bw
David O. Selznick

Problems of a lawyer and his new wife culminate in the near-death of their infant son. Smooth star tearjerker.

w Jo Swerling *d* John Cromwell *ph* Leon Shamroy *m* Hugo Friedhofer, David Buttolph, *theme* Oscar Levant *pd* William Cameron Menzies

Carole Lombard, James Stewart, Charles Coburn, Lucile Watson, Harry Davenport, Eddie Quillan, Esther Dale, Louise Beavers

Made for Each Other*
US 1971 107m De Luxe
TCF / Roy Townshend

Romance between two New Yorkers with inferiority complexes.
Elongated cabaret sketch, a Brooklynesque comedy of flashy brilliance but limited general interest.

w Renée Taylor, Joe Bologna *d* Robert B. Bean *ph* William Storz

Renée Taylor, Joe Bologna

Made in Heaven
GB 1953 81m Technicolor

Married couples compete for the Dunmow Flitch. Easy-going family comedy which aims to be liked. David Tomlinson, Petula Clark, Sonja Ziemann, A. E. Matthews, Charles Victor, Sophie Stewart, Richard Wattis, Athene Seyler. Written by William Douglas Home; directed by John Paddy Carstairs; for Fanfare / Rank.

Madeleine*
GB 1949 114m bw
GFD / David Lean / Cineguild (Stanley Haynes)

In Victorian Glasgow a well-to-do young woman is accused of murdering her lover, but the verdict is 'not proven'.
Dramatically 'dead' because of its ambiguous ending, this lavish and good-looking treatment of a *cause célèbre* was a mistake for all concerned, but its incidental pleasures are considerable.

w Nicholas Phipps, Stanley Haynes *d* David Lean *ph* Guy Green *w* William Alwyn *pd* John Bryan *costumes* Margaret Furse

Ann Todd, Leslie Banks, Elizabeth Sellars, Ivor Barnard, Ivan Desny, Norman Wooland, Edward Chapman, Barbara Everest, André Morell, Barry Jones, Jean Cadell, John Laurie, Eugene Deckers

Mademoiselle Docteur*
GB 1937 84m bw
Grafton / Trafalgar (Max Schach)

A German lady spy falls for a British agent. War melodrama vaguely based on fact and later remade as *Fraulein Doktor*.

w Jacques Natanson, Marcel Achard, Ernest Betts *d* Edmond Greville *ph* Otto Heller

Dita Parlo, John Loder, Erich Von Stroheim, Claire Luce, Gyles Isham, Clifford Evans, John Abbott

Mademoiselle Fifi*
US 1944 69m bw
RKO (Val Lewton)

During the Franco-Prussian war a stagecoach is held up because a prostitute, despite the urging of her fellow passengers, refuses to sleep with a Prussian officer. When she gives in, they shun her, and she kills him.
Interesting low budget version of a story which inspired many films.

w Josef Mischel, Peter Ruric, *stories* Boule de Suif / Mademoiselle Fifi by Guy de Maupassant *d* Robert Wise *ph* Harry Wild *m* Werner Heymann

Simone Simon, Kurt Kreuger, John Emery, Alan Napier, Jason Robards Sr, Norma Varden, Helen Freeman, Fay Helm

'There is a gallant, fervent quality about the whole picture, faults and all, which gives it a peculiar kind of life and likeableness, and which signifies that there is one group of men working in Hollywood who have neither lost nor taken care to conceal the purity of their hope and intention.'—*James Agee*

Madhouse*
GB 1974 92m Eastmancolor
AIP / Amicus (Milton Subotsky)

A reluctant horror actor makes a comeback and finds himself involved in a series of grisly murders.
In-jokey horror piece with clips from old AIP chillers; quite likeable.

w Greg Morrison, *novel* Devilday by Angus Hall *d Jim Clark ph* Ray Parslow *m* Douglas Gamley

Vincent Price, Peter Cushing, Robert Quarry, Adrienne Corri, Natasha Pyne, Linda Hayden, Barry Dennen

Madigan*
US 1968 100m Techniscope
Universal (Frank P. Rosenberg)

A Brooklyn police detective brings in a dangerous escaped criminal at the cost of his own life.
Lively, well-characterized police thriller with excellent locations.

w Henri Simoun, Abraham Polonsky, *novel* The Commissioner by Richard Dougherty *d Don Siegel ph* Russell Metty *m* Don Costa

Richard Widmark, Henry Fonda, Michael Dunn, Inger Stevens, Harry Guardino, James Whitmore, Susan Clark, Steve Ihnat, Don Stroud, Sheree North, Warren Stevens, Raymond St Jacques
† The character was later resurrected for a TV series also starring Richard Widmark.

Madison Avenue
US 1961 94m bw Cinemascope
TCF (Bruce Humberstone)

An advertising executive plans to revenge himself on his treacherous boss.
Predictable melodrama with an adequate plot but dismal acting and presentation.

w Norman Corwin, *novel* The Build-Up Boys by Jeremy Kirk *d* Bruce Humberstone *ph* Charles G. Clarke *m* Harry Sukman

Dana Andrews, Jeanne Crain, Eleanor Parker, Eddie Albert, Howard St John, Henry Daniell, Kathleen Freeman
'Simply nowhere near grand enough.'—*MFB*

Madness of the Heart
GB 1949 105m bw
GFD / Two Cities (Richard Wainwright)

A blind girl marries a French aristocrat and has to cope with a jealous neighbour.
Heavily disguised version of the *Rebecca* theme, with a happy ending after many alarums and excursions, most of them irrelevant. As film-making, very thin.

wd Charles Bennett, *novel* Flora Sandstrom *ph* Desmond Dickinson *m* Allan Gray

Margaret Lockwood, Paul Dupuis, Kathleen Byron, Maxwell Reed

Madonna of the Seven Moons
GB 1944 110m bw
GFD / Gainsborough (R. J. Minney)

Affected by childhood rape, a demure lady has a second life as a daring gypsy.
Novelettish balderdash killed stone dead by stilted presentation; but highly successful in its day.

w Roland Pertwee, Brock Williams, *novel* Margery Lawrence *d* Arthur Crabtree

Phyllis Calvert, Stewart Granger, Patricia Roc, Peter Glenville, John Stuart, Jean Kent, Nancy Price, Peter Murray Hill, Reginald Tate
'One of the most diverting British films of the forties.'—*Richard Roud*

The Madwoman of Chaillot*
GB 1969 142m Technicolor Panavision
Warner / Commonwealth United (Ely Landau)

An eccentric Parisian lady has equally eccentric friends, but her real life is in the past.
A highly theatrical whimsy which somewhat lacks humour, this should never have been considered as a film, certainly not as an all-star extravaganza; but it was, and it falls flat on its face in the first reel of tedious conversation.

w Edward Anhalt, *play* Jean Giraudoux *d* Bryan Forbes *ph* Claude Renoir, Burnett Guffey *m* Michael J. Lewis *pd* Ray Simm

Katharine Hepburn, Yul Brynner, Danny Kaye, Edith Evans, Charles Boyer, Claude Dauphin, John Gavin, Paul Henreid, Nanette Newman, Oscar Homolka, Margaret Leighton, Giulietta Masina, Richard Chamberlain, Donald Pleasence, Fernand Gravet

'One finds oneself too often longing for the drop of the curtain.'—*Brenda Davies*

'The intentions are honourable—defeat is inevitable.'—*Rex Reed*

'One of Giraudoux's less good and most fragile plays has been rewritten, bloated with inept contemporary references, drawn out to gigantic proportions of humourless vacuity, and peopled with a barrelful of nonacting stars.'—*John Simon*

Maedchen in Uniform*
Germany 1931   90m   bw
Deutsche Film- Gemeinschaft
aka: *Girls in Uniform*

A girl at a strict boarding school falls in love with one of the teachers and commits suicide. Famous early stab at lesbianism, remade in 1958 with Romy Schneider and Lilli Palmer. Interesting for content, not style.

w F. D. Andam, Christa Winsloe, *play* Gestern und Heute by Christa Winsloe *d* Leontine Sagan *ph* Reimar Kuntze *m* Hansen Milde-Meissner

Dorothea Wieck, Ellen Schwannecke, Hertha Thiele, Emilie Lunde

'At once a strident warning against the consequences of Hitler's regime and the first truly radical lesbian film.'—*Time Out, 1981*

The Maggie**
GB 1953   93m   bw
Ealing (Michael Truman)
US title: *High and Dry*

An American businessman is tricked into sending his private cargo to a Scottish island on an old puffer in need of repair. Mildly amusing comedy about the wily Scots; not the studio at its best, but pretty fair.

w William Rose   d Alexander Mackendrick ph Gordon Dines   *m* John Addison

Paul Douglas, *Alex Mackenzie*, James Copeland, Abe Barker, Dorothy Alison, Hubert Gregg, Geoffrey Keen, Andrew Keir, Tommy Kearins

Magic
US 1978   107m   Technicolor
Joseph E. Levine

A ventriloquist obsessed by his dummy is impelled to murder.
Pretentious and occasionally unpleasant version of an oft-told tale.

w William Goldman, from his novel *d* Richard Attenborough *ph* Victor J. Kemper *m* Jerry Goldsmith *pd* Terence Marsh

Anthony Hopkins, Ann-Margret, Burgess Meredith, Ed Lauter, E. J. Andre, David Ogden Stiers

'The gloomily withdrawn Hopkins has no vulgarity in his soul—nothing that suggests any connection with the world of entertainment—and the picture grinds along.'—*New Yorker*

The Magic Bow
GB 1946   106m   bw
GFD / Gainsborough

Episodes in the life of the violin virtuoso Paganini.
Poor costumer, dramatically and historically unpersuasive.

w Norman Ginsbury, Roland Pertwee *d* Bernard Knowles *ph* Jack Cox *violin solos Yehudi Menuhin*

Stewart Granger, Jean Kent, Phyllis Calvert, Dennis Price, Cecil Parker, Felix Aylmer, Frank Cellier, Marie Lohr, Henry Edwards

The Magic Box*
GB 1951   118m   Technicolor
Festival Films (Ronald Neame)

The life of William Friese-Greene, a British cinema pioneer who died in poverty.
A joint British film industry venture to celebrate the Festival of Britain, this rather downbeat and uneventful story takes on the nature of a pageant or a series of charades, with well-known people appearing to no good purpose. But it means well.

w Eric Ambler   *d* John Boulting   *ph* Jack Cardiff   *m* William Alwyn   *pd* John Bryan

Robert Donat, Margaret Johnson, Maria Schell, John Howard Davies, Renée Asherson, Richard Attenborough, Robert Beatty, Michael Denison, Leo Genn, Marius Goring, Joyce Grenfell, Robertson Hare, Kathleen Harrison, Jack Hulbert, Stanley Holloway, Glynis Johns, Mervyn Johns, Barry Jones, Miles Malleson, Muir Mathieson, A. E. Matthews, John McCallum, Bernard Miles, Laurence Olivier, Cecil Parker, Eric Portman, Dennis Price, Michael Redgrave, Margaret Rutherford, Ronald Shiner, Sybil Thorndike, David Tomlinson, Cecil Trouncer, Peter Ustinov, Kay Walsh, Emlyn Williams, Harcourt Williams, Googie Withers

The Magic Christian
GB 1970 95m Technicolor
Commonwealth United / Grand Films
(Dennis O'Dell)

An eccentric millionaire spends his wealth
deflating those who pursue money or power.
A series of variably funny but always
unpleasant sketches, climaxing with citizens
delving for spoils in a vat of blood and
manure. In its aim to be satirical, very typical
of its time.

w Terry Southern, Joseph McGrath, Peter
Sellers, *novel* Terry Southern d Joseph
McGrath ph Geoffrey Unsworth m Ken
Thorne pd Assheton Gorton

Peter Sellers, Ringo Starr, Richard
Attenborough, Laurence Harvey, Christopher
Lee, Spike Milligan, Yul Brynner, Roman
Polanski, Raquel Welch, Wilfrid Hyde White,
Fred Emney, John Le Mesurier, Dennis Price,
Patrick Cargill, John Cleese, Graham
Chapman

The Magic Face
US 1951 90m bw
Columbia (Mort Briskin, Robert Smith)

A brilliant German impersonator kills Hitler,
takes his place, and leads Germany
deliberately into defeat.
Hilariously unlikely anecdote 'as told to
William Shirer', performed with vigour but
handicapped by a shoddy production.

w Mort Briskin, Robert Smith d Frank
Tuttle ph Tony Braun m Herschel Burke
Gilbert

Luther Adler, Patricia Knight, Ilka Windish,
William L. Shirer

'If Shirer believed this story, then he must
be the only person in the world to do so.'—
Gavin Lambert

Magic Fire
US 1954 94m Trucolor
Republic (William Dieterle)

The life and loves of Richard Wagner.
Remarkably boring biopic with much music
but little story or characterization. Ugly colour
minimizes German locations.

w Bertita Harding, E. A. Dupont, David
Chantler d William Dieterle ph Ernest
Haller md Erich Wolfgang Korngold

Alan Badel, Yvonne de Carlo, Peter Cushing,
Frederick Valk, Carlos Thompson, Valentina
Cortesa

The Magic of Lassie
US 1978 99m colour
Jack Wrather (Bonita Granville)

A collie dog is sold but makes its way back
home.
Downright peculiar revamp of *Lassie Come
Home* with music and an ageing all-star cast.

w Jean Holloway, Richard B. Sherman,
Robert M. Sherman d Don Chaffey

James Stewart, Alice Faye, Mickey Rooney,
Pernell Roberts, Stephanie Zimbalist, Gene
Evans

AAN: song, 'When You're Loved'

The Magic Sword
US 1962 80m Eastmancolor
UA / Bert I. Gordon

The son of a well-meaning witch rescues a
princess from the clutches of an evil sorcerer.
Shaky medieval fantasy on too low a budget.

w Bernard Schoenfeld d Bert I. Gordon
ph Paul Vogel m Richard Markowitz sp Milt
Rice

Basil Rathbone, Estelle Winwood, Gary
Lockwood, Anne Helm

Magic Town
US 1947 103m bw
William A. Wellman (Robert Riskin)

An opinion pollster discovers a small town
which exactly mirrors the views of the USA at
large.
A bright Capraesque idea is extraordinarily
dully scripted, the production looks dim, and
all concerned are operating one degree under.

w Robert Riskin d William A. Wellman
ph Joseph Biroc m Roy Webb

James Stewart, Jane Wyman, Kent Smith,
Regis Toomey, Donald Meek

The Magician*
US 1926 approx 80m bw silent
MGM

A dabbler in the occult comes to grief when he
tries to influence a young girl.
A melodrama with interesting credits;
unfortunately no prints remain.

from the novel by Somerset Maugham d Rex
Ingram

Paul Wegener, Ivan Petrovitch, Alice Terry

The Magician of Lublin
West Germany / Israel 1979 114m
 colour
Geria-Golan-Globus (Harry N. Blum)

In 1901 an itinerant magician with an active
sex life dreams of being able really to fly.
Curious muddled fable with apparent
correspondences to the Christ story, like
Bergman's *The Face.* In the end it does not

confidently address itself to any audience, despite clever moments.

w Irving S. White, Menahem Golan *novel* Isaac Bashevis Singer *d* Menahem Golan *ph* David Gurfinkel *m* Maurice Jarre *pd* Jurgen Kiebach

Alan Arkin, Louise Fletcher, Valerie Perrine, Shelley Winters, Lou Jacobi, Warren Berlinger

'California Polish accents grapple with ham-fisted direction and a script of surpassing banality.'—*Sight and Sound*

The Magnet
GB 1950   79m   bw
Ealing (Sidney Cole)

A small boy steals a magnet and accidentally becomes a hero.
Very mild Ealing comedy, not really up to snuff.

w T. E. B. Clarke *d* Charles Frend *ph* Lionel Banes *m* William Alwyn

Stephen Murray, Kay Walsh, William Fox, Meredith Edwards, Gladys Henson, Thora Hird, Wylie Watson

The Magnetic Monster°
US 1953   75m   bw
UA / Ivan Tors

A new radio-active element causes 'implosions' of increasing size by drawing energy from the area around it.
Well-told low-budget sci-fi with the audience kept abreast of all developments; the undersea lab scenes are borrowed from an old German film, *Gold*.

w Curt Siodmak, Ivan Tors *d* Curt Siodmak *ph* Charles Van Enger *pd* George Van Marter

Richard Carlson, King Donovan, Jean Byron, Byron Foulger

The Magnificent Ambersons****
US 1942   88m   bw
RKO (Orson Welles)

A proud family loses its wealth and its control of the neighbourhood, and its youngest male member gets his come-uppance.
Fascinating period drama told in brilliant cinematic snippets; owing to studio interference the last reels are weak, but the whole is a treat for connoisseurs, and a delight in its fast-moving control of cinematic narrative.

wd Orson Welles, *novel* Booth Tarkington *ph* Stanley Cortez *m* Bernard Herrmann *ad* Mark-Lee Kirr

Joseph Cotten, Dolores Costello, Agnes Moorehead, Tim Holt, Anne Baxter, Ray Collins, Richard Bennett, Erskine Sanford, Donald Dillaway

'Rich in ideas that many will want to copy, combined in the service of a story that few will care to imitate.'—*C. A. Lejeune*

'Nearly every scene is played with a casual perfection which could only come from endless painstaking planning and rehearsals, and from a wonderful sense of timing.'—*Basil Wright, 1972*

† Previously filmed in 1925 as *Pampered Youth*.

AAN: best picture; Stanley Cortez; Agnes Moorehead

The Magnificent Brute
US 1936   77m   bw

A blast furnace boss becomes involved with stolen money. Star character drama; very predictable. Victor McLaglen, Binnie Barnes, Billy Burrud, William Hall, Jean Dixon. Written by Owen Francis, Lewis J. Foster and Bertram Millhauser; directed by John G. Blystone; for Universal.

Magnificent Doll
US 1946   95m   bw
Universal (Jack H. Skirball, Bruce Manning)

Dolly Madison, wife of the President, finds that traitor Aaron Burr is a memory from her own past.
Uneasy historical semi-fiction, badly cast and rather boring, yet with some sense of period style.

w Irving Stone *d* Frank Borzage *ph* Joseph Valentine *m* Hans Salter

Ginger Rogers, David Niven, Burgess Meredith, Stephen McNally, Peggy Wood, Robert Barrat

'No duller case has ever been made out for liberty.'—*Daily Mail*

'Some day the moviemakers will discover that they can make history wonderfully believable and exciting by just sticking roughly to the facts.'—*The Times*

The Magnificent Dope
US 1942   83m   bw
TCF (William Perlberg)

As a publicity stunt a success school brings the nation's most complete failure to New York, and he outsmarts them all.
Dim sub-Capra comedy.

w George Seaton *d* Walter Lang *ph* Peverell Marley *md* Emil Newman

Henry Fonda, Lynn Bari, Don Ameche,
Edward Everett Horton, George Barbier,
Frank Orth, Hobart Cavanaugh

The Magnificent Fraud
US 1939 78m bw

The president of a Latin American republic is
murdered, and an impersonator takes his
place. Sharply played dramatic hokum. Akim
Tamiroff, Lynne Overman, Patricia Morison,
Mary Boland. Written by Gilbert Gabriel and
Walter Ferris; directed by Robert Florey; for
Paramount.

The Magnificent Matador
US 1955 94m Eastmancolor
Cinemascope
Edward L. Alperson
GB title: *The Brave and the Beautiful*

A matador trains his illegitimate son to follow
in his footsteps but has a premonition of his
death in the ring.
Dreary bullfighting drama with romantic
interludes.

w Charles Lang *d* Budd Boetticher
ph Lucien Ballard *m* Raoul Kraushaar

Anthony Quinn, Maureen O'Hara, Manuel
Rojas, Richard Denning, Thomas Gomez,
Lola Albright

Magnificent Obsession**
US 1935 112m bw
Universal (John M. Stahl)

The playboy who is half-responsible for the
death of a woman's husband and for her own
blindness becomes a surgeon and cures her.
Absurd soaper which was phenomenally
popular and is certainly well done.

w George O'Neil, Sarah Y. Mason, Victor
Heerman, *novel Lloyd C. Douglas d John M.
Stahl ph* John Mescall *m* Franz Waxman

Irene Dunne, Robert Taylor, Ralph Morgan,
Sara Haden, Charles Butterworth, Betty
Furness, Arthur Hoyt, Gilbert Emery, Arthur
Treacher

Magnificent Obsession**
US 1954 108m Technicolor
Universal (*Ross Hunter*)

Glossy remake which sent Ross Hunter to the
commercial heights as a remaker of thirties
weepies. This one worked best.

w Robert Blees *d Douglas Sirk ph* Russell
Metty *m* Frank Skinner

Jane Wyman, Rock Hudson, Agnes
Moorehead, Barbara Rush, Otto Kruger,
Gregg Palmer, Paul Cavanagh, Sara Shane
AAN: Jane Wyman

The Magnificent Rebel
US 1960 94m Technicolor
Walt Disney (Peter V. Herald)

Episodes in the life of the young Beethoven.
Solid Disney biopic, shot in Vienna with good
period detail.

w Joanne Court *d* Georg Tressler *ph* Goran
Strindberg *md* Frederick Stark

Karl Boehm, Ernst Nadhering, Ivan Desny,
Gabriele Porks

The Magnificent Seven**
US 1960 138m De Luxe Panavision
UA / Mirisch–Alpha (John Sturges)

A Mexican village hires seven American
gunmen for protection against bandits.
Popular western based on the Japanese *Seven
Samurai*; good action scenes, but the rest is
verbose and often pretentious.

w William Roberts *d* John Sturges
ph Charles Lang Jnr *m Elmer Bernstein*

Yul Brynner, Steve McQueen, Robert Vaughn,
James Coburn, Charles Bronson, Horst
Buchholz, Eli Wallach, Brad Dexter, Vladimir
Sokoloff

AAN: Elmer Bernstein

The Magnificent Seven Deadly Sins
GB 1971 107m colour
Tigon (Graham Stark)

Compendium of comedy sketches, a very
variable ragbag of old jokes.

w Bob Larbey, John Esmonde, Dave
Freeman, Barry Cryer, Graham Chapman,
Graham Stark, Marty Feldman, Alan
Simpson, Ray Galton, Spike Milligan
d Graham Stark *ph* Harvey Harrison Jnr
m Roy Budd

Bruce Forsyth, Joan Sims, Roy Hudd, Harry
Secombe, Leslie Phillips, Julie Ege, Harry H.
Corbett, Ian Carmichael, Alfie Bass, Spike
Milligan, Ronald Fraser

The Magnificent Seven Ride
US 1972 100m De Luxe
UA / Mirisch (William A. Calihan)

Tired finale to a patchy series (*Return of the
Seven, Guns of the Magnificent Seven*) in
which the original leader returns to save a
Mexican village once again from bandits. Very
modest.

w Arthur Rowe *d* George McCowan *ph* Fred
Koenekamp *m* Elmer Bernstein

Lee Van Cleef, Stefanie Powers, Mariette
Hartley, Pedro Armendariz Jnr, Luke Askew

The Magnificent Two
GB 1967   100m   Eastmancolor
Rank (Hugh Stewart)

One of two incompetent travelling salesmen in a Latin American banana republic is persuaded to pose as a dead rebel leader. More or less a Bob Hope vehicle, adapted for the less realistic Morecambe and Wise with unhappy results: too few sight gags and a curious emphasis on violence. The third and last of their attempts to find film vehicles.

w S. C. Green, R. M. Hills, Michael Pertwee, Peter Blackmore d Cliff Owen ph Ernest Steward m Ron Goodwin

Eric Morecambe, Ernie Wise, Margit Saad, Cecil Parker, Virgilio Teixeira, Isobel Black, Martin Benson

The Magnificent Yankee°
US 1951   88m   bw
MGM (Armand Deutsch)
GB title: *The Man with Thirty Sons*

Episodes in the later life of Judge Oliver Wendell Holmes.
Vaguely well-meaning biopic without much dramatic sense.

w Emmet Lavery, from his play d John Sturges ph Joseph Ruttenberg m David Raksin

Louis Calhern, Ann Harding, Eduard Franz, Philip Ober, Richard Anderson, Edith Evanson

AAN: Louis Calhern

Magnum Force
US 1973   124m   Technicolor
Panavision
Warner / Malpaso (Robert Daley)

Inspector Harry Callahan has to track down his partner who is slaughtering gangsters in cold blood.
Toned-down sequel to *Dirty Harry*; the violence is still there but the hero no longer commits it.

w John Milius d Ted Post ph Frank Stanley m Lalo Schifrin

Clint Eastwood, Hal Holbrook, Mitch Ryan, Felton Perry, David Soul
    'A ragbag of western mythology and head-on thuggery.'—*Sight and Sound*

The Magus
GB 1968   116m   De Luxe   Panavision
TCF / Blazer (John Kohn, Jud Kinberg)

An English schoolmaster on a Greek island is influenced by the local magician.

Fashionable philosophical nonsense, an elaborate mystery with no solution; the kind of film that all concerned begin to wish they had never thought of, especially as the presentation has nothing like the panache required, so that not even the critics liked it.

w John Fowles, from his novel d Guy Green ph Billy Williams m Johnny Dankworth pd Don Ashton

Michael Caine, Anthony Quinn, Candice Bergen, Anna Karina, Paul Stassino, Julian Glover, George Pastell
    'Faintly ludicrous some of the time and painfully unexciting all of the time.'—*MFB*
    'This may not be the most misguided movie ever made, but it's in there pitching.'—*Rex Reed*
    'There's enough incoherence pretending to be enigma, sex play and chat about existentialism and self-discovery to make teenagers think they're having an experience; for grown-ups it's an ordeal.'—*Judith Crist*
    'It has much of the fascination of a Chinese puzzle, but it would have been infinitely more enthralling if it hadn't been quite so flatly acted and directed.'—*Michael Billington, Illustrated London News*

Mahler°
GB 1974   115m   Technicolor
Goodtimes Enterprises (Roy Baird)

Fantasia on the life and times of the Jewish composer.
Fairly successful Ken Russell musical biopic on the lines of his early BBC specials.

wd Ken Russell ph Dick Bush

Robert Powell, Georgiana Hale, Richard Morant, Lee Montague, Rosalie Crutchley, Benny Lee, David Collings
    'A piece of movie making that sets my pulses racing.'—*Michael Billington, Illustrated London News*
    'Whether the title of the opus happens to be *Strauss* or *Tchaikovsky* or *Elgar* or *Brubeck*, the real title is always *Russell*.'—*Benny Green, Punch*

Mahogany
US 1975   109m   colour   Panavision
Paramount / Nikor (Rob Cohen, Jack Ballard)

The love life of a model and fashion designer.
Virtually a Joan Crawford vehicle redesigned for a black heroine who creates her own clothes. Fairly hilarious.

w John Byrum d Berry Gordy ph David Watkin m Michael Masser

Diana Ross, Billy Dee Williams, Anthony
Perkins, Jean-Pierre Aumont, Nina Foch,
Beah Richards, Marisa Mell
'The level of silliness rises steadily.'—*Geoff
Brown*
    'Movies as frantically bad as *Mahogany* can
be enjoyed on at least one level; the spectacle
of a lot of people making fools of themselves.'
—*Time*
    'What *Mahogany* does so fascinatingly and
sometimes hilariously is to pilfer certain stock
clichés of 50's Hollywood and adapt them to a
black milieu.'—*Molly Haskell*

AAN: song 'Do You Know Where You're
Going To?' (*m* Michael Masser, *ly* Gerry
Goffin)

Maid of Salem*
US 1937   86m   bw
Paramount (Frank Lloyd)

In 1692 Salem, a young girl is accused of
witchcraft but saved by her lover.
Remarkably solemn period melodrama,
unfortunately betrayed by amiable but miscast
leads.

w Bradley King, Walter Ferris, Durward
Grinstead *d* Frank Lloyd *ph* Leo Tover
m Victor Young

Claudette Colbert, Fred MacMurray, Harvey
Stephens, Gale Sondergaard, Louise Dresser,
Edward Ellis, Beulah Bondi, Bonita Granville
    'Once the panic of witchcraft starts you are
carried along on a vicious crescendo of
madness and terror.'—*Stage*

The Maids
GB 1974   95m   Technicolor
Ely Landau / Cinevision

Two Paris maids evolve a sado-masochistic
ritual involving the death of their employer,
but never go through with it.
Unbalanced and dreary film version of an
essentially theatrical play.

w Robert Enders, Christopher Miles,
play Jean Genet *d* Christopher Miles
ph Douglas Slocombe *m* Laurie Johnson

Glenda Jackson, Susannah York, Vivien
Merchant, Mark Burns

Maid's Night Out
US 1937   65m   bw

A wealthy girl falls for the milkman, who is
really a rich man who thinks she's the maid.
Skittish second-feature comedy which helped
to build a new star. Joan Fontaine, Allan
Lane, Billy Gilbert, Cecil Kellaway, Hedda
Hopper. Written by Bert Granet; directed by
Ben Holmes; for RKO.

Maigret Sets a Trap*
France / Italy 1957   119m   bw
Intermondia / J. P. Guibert / Jolly Film

Maigret sets a policewoman as decoy for a
knife murderer . . .
Probably the best Maigret film, with excellent
Parisian atmosphere and excellent acting.

w Michel Audiard, *novel* Georges Simenon
d Jean Delannoy *ph* Louis Page *m* Paul
Misraki *ad* René Renoux

Jean Gabin, Annie Girardot, Jean Desailly,
Oliver Hussenot, Alfred Adam, Lino Ventura

Mail Order Bride
US 1963   83m   Metrocolor   Panavision
MGM (Richard E. Lyons)
GB title: *West of Montana*

An old westerner tries to find a bride for a
wild young man in his charge.
Mild western comedy drama; quite tolerable.

wd Burt Kennedy *ph* Paul C. Vogel
m George Bassman

Buddy Ebsen, Lois Nettleton, Keir Dullea,
Warren Oates, Marie Windsor

The Main Attraction
GB 1962   90m   Metrocolor
Seven Arts (John Patrick)

A wandering singer causes emotional
problems backstage at a circus.
Limp melodrama with the star miscast as a
fatal charmer.

w John Patrick *d* Daniel Petrie *ph* Geoffrey
Unsworth *m* Andrew Adorian

Pat Boone, Mai Zetterling, Nancy Kwan,
Yvonne Mitchell, John Le Mesurier

The Main Event
US 1979   112m   Technicolor
Warner / First Artists / Barwood (Jon
    Peters, Barbra Streisand)

A lady entrepreneur takes on a prizefighter.
Thin and very patchy comedy for confirmed
addicts of its star.

w Gail Parent, Andrew Smith *d* Howard
Zieff *ph* Mario Tosi *m* Michael Melvoin
pd Charles Rosen

Barbra Streisand, Ryan O'Neal, Paul Sand,
Whitman Mayo, James Gregory

Main Street: see I Married a Doctor

Main Street to Broadway*
US 1953   102m   bw
Lester Cowan Productions

After several reverses a young playwright sees
his work through to a Broadway opening

night; it fails, but he has learned several lessons.

Curious, flat attempt to show the public how Broadway works, with big stars playing themselves in cameo roles.

w Samson Raphaelson *d* Tay Garnett *ph* James Wong Howe

Tom Morton, Mary Murphy, Ethel Barrymore, Lionel Barrymore, Shirley Booth, Rex Harrison, Lilli Palmer, Helen Hayes, Henry Fonda, Tallulah Bankhead, Mary Martin, Louis Calhern, John Van Druten, Cornel Wilde, Joshua Logan, Agnes Moorehead, Gertrude Berg

Les Mains Sales
France 1951   103m   bw
Fernand Rivers
aka: *Dirty Hands*

A young communist intellectual, required to kill a traitor, finds he can do so only when he suspects the man of making love to his wife. Verbose and dull version of a play which had some international success as *Crime Passionel*.

wd Fernand Rivers, *play* Jean-Paul Sartre *ph* Jean Bachelet

Pierre Brasseur, Daniel Gélin, Claude Nollier

Maisie
US 1939   74m   bw
MGM (J. Walter Ruben)

Adventures of a Brooklyn showgirl.
Acceptable programmer which led to a series, all quite watchable and absolutely forgettable.

w Mary McCall Jnr, *novel* Dark Dame by Wilson Collinson *d* Edwin L. Marin *ph* Leonard Smith

Ann Sothern, Robert Young, Ian Hunter, Ruth Hussey, Anthony Allan (John Hubbard), Cliff Edwards

The succeeding titles, mostly written by Mary McCall and directed by Marin or Harry Beaumont or Roy del Ruth, were:

1940: CONGO MAISIE (with John Carroll; a remake of RED DUST), GOLD RUSH MAISIE (with Lee Bowman), MAISIE WAS A LADY (with Lew Ayres, Maureen O'Sullivan)
1941: RINGSIDE MAISIE (with George Murphy; GB title CASH AND CARRY)
1942: MAISIE GETS HER MAN (with Red Skelton; GB title SHE GOT HER MAN)
1943: SWING SHIFT MAISIE (with James Craig; GB title THE GIRL IN OVERALLS)
1944: MAISIE GOES TO RENO (with John Hodiak; GB title YOU CAN'T DO THAT TO ME)

1946: UP GOES MAISIE (with George Murphy; GB title UP SHE GOES)
1947: UNDERCOVER MAISIE (with Barry Nelson; GB title UNDERCOVER GIRL)

The Major and the Minor**
US 1942   100m   bw
Paramount (Arthur Hornblow Jnr)

A girl poses as a child in order to travel half fare on a train, and is helped by an officer who falls for her.
Moderately smart comedy showing the writer-director's emergent style. Remade as *You're Never Too Young* (qv).

w Charles Brackett, Billy Wilder *d* Billy Wilder *ph* Leo Tover *m* Robert Emmett Dolan

Ginger Rogers, Ray Milland, Rita Johnson, Robert Benchley, Diana Lynn, Edward Fielding, Frankie Thomas, Charles Smith
'The script seems to have been concocted after the title.'—*New Yorker, 1977*

Major Barbara***
GB 1941   121m   bw
Gabriel Pascal

The daughter of an armaments millionaire joins the Salvation Army but resigns when it accepts her father's donation.
Stagey but compulsive version of a play in which the author takes typical side swipes at anything and everything within reach, allowing for some gorgeous acting (and overacting) by an impeccable cast.

w Anatole de Grunwald, Gabriel Pascal, *play* Bernard Shaw *d* Gabriel Pascal, Harold French, David Lean *ph* Ronald Neame *m* William Walton

Wendy Hiller, Rex Harrison, Robert Morley, Robert Newton, Marie Lohr, Emlyn Williams, Sybil Thorndike, Deborah Kerr, David Tree, Felix Aylmer, Penelope Dudley Ward, Walter Hudd, Marie Ault, Donald Calthrop
'Shaw's ebullience provides an unslackening fount of energy . . . his all-star cast of characters are outspoken as no one else is in films except the Marx Brothers.'—*William Whitebait*

Major Dundee*
US 1965   134m   Eastmancolor
    Panavision
Columbia (Jerry Bresler)

A small group of men from a US cavalry post sets out to annihilate marauding Indians.
Large-scale, rough and ready western which rambles along in humourless vein but rises to some spectacularly bloodthirsty climaxes.

w Harry Julian Fink, Oscar Saul, Sam Peckinpah *d* Sam Peckinpah *ph* Sam Leavitt *m* Daniele Amfitheatrof

Charlton Heston, Richard Harris, Jim Hutton, James Coburn, Michael Anderson Jnr, Warren Oates, Senta Berger, Slim Pickens

A Majority of One
US 1961 156m Technicolor
Warner (Mervyn Le Roy)

A Jewish widow has a shipboard romance with a Japanese businessman.
Interminable stage-bound comedy-drama, boringly assembled and fatally compromised by the casting of stars who are neither Jewish nor Japanese.

w Leonard Spiegelgass, from his play *d* Mervyn Le Roy *ph* Harry Stradling *m* Max Steiner

Rosalind Russell, Alec Guinness, Ray Danton, Madlyn Rhue

AAN: Harry Stradling

Make a Wish
US 1937 75m bw
(RKO) Sol Lesser

A composer discovers a boy singer at a summer camp.
Acceptable family entertainment.

w Gertrude Berg, Bernard Schubert, Earle Snell *d* Kurt Neumann *ph* John Mescall *songs* Oscar Strauss *m* Hugo Riesnfeld

Basil Rathbone, Bobby Breen, Marion Claire, Leon Errol, Henry Armetta, Ralph Forbes, Donald Meek

AAN: Hugo Riesenfeld

Make Me a Star
US 1932 80m bw
Paramount (Lloyd Sheldon)

A grocery clerk goes to Hollywood and becomes a film star.
Modest remake of a silent success; see also *Merton of the Movies*.

w Sam Wintz, Walter de Leon, Arthur Kober, *novel* Merton of the Movies by Harry Leon Wilson *d* William Beaudine *ph* Allen Siegler

Stuart Erwin, Joan Blondell, Zasu Pitts, Ben Turpin, Florence Roberts; and Tallulah Bankhead, Clive Brook, Garry Cooper, Maurice Chevalier, Claudette Colbert, Fredric March, Jack Oakie, Charlie Ruggles, Sylvia Sidney

Make Me an Offer*
GB 1954 88m Eastmancolor
Group Three (W. P. Lipscomb)

An antique dealer has an ambition to own a famous vase.
Mildly pleasant Jewish comedy with interesting sidelights on the antique business.

w W. P. Lipscomb, *novel* Wolf Mankowitz *d* Cyril Frankel *ph* Denny Densham *m* John Addison

Peter Finch, Adrienne Corri, *Meier Tzelniker*, Rosalie Crutchley, Finlay Currie, *Ernest Thesiger*, Wilfrid Lawson, Alfie Bass

Make Mine Music**
US 1946 74m Technicolor
Walt Disney (Joe Grant)

A programme of cartoon shorts: JOHNNY FEDORA, ALL THE CATS JOIN IN, WITHOUT YOU, TWO SILHOUETTES, CASEY AT THE BAT, THE MARTINS AND THE COYS, BLUE BAYOU, AFTER YOU'VE GONE, WILLIE THE SINGING WHALE.

An insubstantial banquet, sometimes arty and sometimes chocolate boxy, which occasionally rises to the expected heights.

w various *d* various

'There is enough genuine charm and imagination and humour to make up perhaps one good average Disney short.'—*James Agee*

Make Way for Tomorrow**
US 1937 94m bw
Paramount (Leo McCarey)

An elderly couple are in financial difficulty and have to be parted because their children will not help.
Sentimental drama which had a devastating effect at the time but now seems oversimplified and exaggerated.

w Vina Delmar, *novel* The Years Are So Long by Josephine Lawrence *d* Leo McCarey *ph* William C. Mellor *m* George Antheil

Victor Moore, Beulah Bondi, Thomas Mitchell, Fay Bainter, Porter Hall, Barbara Read, Maurice Moscovitch, Elizabeth Risdon, Gene Lockhart

'The most brilliantly directed and acted film of the year.'—*John Grierson*
'A sense of misery and inhumanity is left vibrating in the nerves.'—*Graham Greene*

Make Your Own Bed
US 1944 82m bw

A detective and his girl friend pretend to be servants in order to protect an inventor from Nazis. Mirthless pratfall farce. Jack Carson, Jane Wyman, Irene Manning, Ricardo Cortez, Alan Hale, George Tobias. Written by Francis Swann and Edmund Joseph; directed by Peter Godfrey; for Warner.

Malaya*
US 1949 95m bw
MGM (Pandro S. Berman)
GB title: *East of the Rising Sun*

An adventurer attempts to smuggle rubber out
of Japanese-occupied Malaya.
Dour action melodrama, unworthy of its
considerable cast but watchable.

w Frank Fenton d Richard Thorpe
ph George Folsey m Bronislau Kaper

Spencer Tracy, James Stewart, Sidney
Greenstreet, John Hodiak, Valentina Cortesa,
Lionel Barrymore, Gilbert Roland

The Male Animal*
US 1942 101m bw
Warner (Wolfgang Reinhardt)

A dry college professor emancipates himself
when his wife becomes attracted to a football
star.
Stagebound but amusing college comedy with
pleasant humour and good performances.
Remade as *She's Working Her Way through
College* (qv).

w Julius J. and Philip G. Epstein, Stephen
Morehouse Avery, *play* James Thurber and
Elliott Nugent d Elliott Nugent ph Arthur
Edeson m Heinz Roemheld

Henry Fonda, Olivia de Havilland, Jack
Carson, Joan Leslie, Eugene Pallette, Don
Defore, Herbert Anderson, Hattie McDaniel

The Malta Story
GB 1953 103m bw
GFD / British Film Makers (Peter de
Sarigny)

An English flier is involved in the defence of
Malta during World War II.
Glib propaganda piece which is not very
excitingly written or characterized, and fails to
convince on any but the most elementary
level.

w William Fairchild, Nigel Balchin d Brian
Desmond Hurst ph Robert Krasker
m William Alwyn

Alec Guinness, Anthony Steel, Muriel
Pavlow, Jack Hawkins, Flora Robson, Renée
Asherson, Ralph Truman, Reginald Tate,
Hugh Burden

The Maltese Falcon**
US 1931 80m bw
Warner
TV title: *Dangerous Female*

After the death of his partner, private eye Sam
Spade is dragged into a quest for a priceless
statuette.

Excellent crime melodrama with smart pace
and performances. Remade as *Satan Met a
Lady* (1936); and see below.

w Maude Fulton, Lucien Hubbard, Brown
Holmes, *novel Dashiell Hammett d Roy del
Ruth ph* William Rees

Ricardo Cortez, Bebe Daniels, *Dudley Digges,*
Dwight Frye, Robert Elliott, Thelma Todd,
Oscar Apfel
'The best mystery thriller of the year.'—
New York Times
'A nice blend of humour, intelligence and
suspense.'—*Clive Hirschhorn, 1979*
'He's as fast on the draw as he is in the
drawing room!'—*publicity*

The Maltese Falcon**
US 1941 101m bw
Warner (Henry Blanke)

A remake which shows the difference between
excellence and brilliance; here every nuance is
subtly stressed, and the cast is perfection.

wd John Huston *ph* Arthur Edeson
m Adolph Deutsch

*Humphrey Bogart, Mary Astor, Sidney
Greenstreet, Elisha Cook Jnr, Barton
MacLane, Lee Patrick, Peter Lorre*, Gladys
George, *Ward Bond, Jerome Cowan*
'The first crime melodrama with finish,
speed and bang to come along in what seems
like ages.'—*Otis Ferguson*
'A work of entertainment that is yet so
skilfully constructed that after many years and
many viewings, it has the same brittle
explosiveness—and some of the same
surprise—that it had in 1941.'—*Pauline Kael,
1968*
'The trick which Mr Huston has pulled is a
combination of American ruggedness with the
suavity of the English crime school—a blend
of mind and muscle—plus a slight touch of
pathos.'—*Bosley Crowther, New York Times*
'Admirable photography of the sort in which
black and white gives full value to every detail,
every flicker of panic.'—*Francis Wyndham*

AAN: best picture; John Huston (as writer);
Sidney Greenstreet

Mambo
Italy / USA 1954 92m (English version),
    107m (Italian version) bw
Paramount / Ponti / De Laurentiis

A Venetian shopgirl loves a worthless
gambler, is romanced by a haemophiliac
count, and joins a dance troupe.
Patchy melodrama with plenty going on but no
grip.

w Guido Piovene, Ivo Perelli, Ennio de Concini, Robert Rossen *d* Robert Rossen *ph* Harold Rosson *m* Nino Rota, Francesco Lavagnino *sets* Andrei Andrejew *ch* Katherine Dunham

Silvana Mangano, Michael Rennie, Shelley Winters, Vittorio Gassman, Eduardo Cianelli, Mary Clare, Katherine Dunham and her troupe

Mame*
US 1974 131m Technicolor Panavision
Warner / ABC (Robert Fryer, James Cresson)

In 1928, a 10-year-old boy goes to live with his eccentric, sophisticated aunt.
Old-fashioned and rather bad film of a much overrated Broadway musical, inept in most departments but with occasional show-stopping moments.

w Paul Zandel, *play* Jerome Lawrence, Robert E. Lee, *book* Patrick Dennis *d* Gene Saks *ph* Philip Lathrop *m / ly* Jerry Herman *pd* Robert F. Boyle

Lucille Ball, Beatrice Arthur, Robert Preston, Bruce Davison, Jane Connell, Joyce Van Patten, John McGiver

'It makes one realize afresh the parlous state of the Hollywood musical, fighting to survive against misplaced superstars and elephantine budgets matched with minuscule imagination.'—*Geoff Brown*

'The cast seem to have been handpicked for their tone-deafness, and Lucille Ball's close-ups are shot blatantly out of focus.'—*Sight and Sound*

'So terrible it isn't boring; you can get fixated staring at it and wondering what Lucille Ball thought she was doing.'—*New Yorker, 1977*

Mammy*
US 1930 84m bw
Warner

Murder backstage at a minstrel show.
One of the star's better musicals.

w L. G. Rigby, Joseph Jackson *d* Michael Curtiz *ph* Barney McGill *m* Irving Berlin

Al Jolson, Lowell Sherman, Hobart Bosworth, Louise Dresser, Lee Moran

A Man, a Woman and a Bank
Canada 1979 101m CFI color

A civil engineer and a computer expert devise a foolproof way of robbing a bank. We have been here before, except that these days the criminals are allowed to get away with it.

Ho-hum. Donald Sutherland, Brooke Adams, Paul Mazursky. Written by Raynold Gideon, Bruce A. Evans and Stuart Margolin; directed by Noel Black; for Bennett / McNichol.

A Man About the House
GB 1947 95m bw
British Lion (Edward Black)

Two English ladies inherit an Italian villa and fall under the spell of the handsome handyman, who marries one of them and proceeds slowly to poison her.
Now clearly dull, at the time this seemed a fairly enterprising rehash of *Gaslight, Kind Lady* and *Rebecca*.

w J. B. Williams, Leslie Arliss *d* Leslie Arliss *ph* Tom Day

Margaret Johnston, Dulcie Gray, Kieron Moore, Felix Aylmer, Lilian Braithwaite

A Man About the House
GB 1974 90m colour
EMI / Hammer (Roy Skeggs)

Two young women, their male flatmate and their landlords combine forces to prevent the terrace from being razed for redevelopment.
Mild and rather exhausting sex comedy from the TV series, as relentlessly single-minded as a 'Carry On'.

w Johnnie Mortimer, Brian Cooke *d* John Robins *ph* Jimmy Allen *m* Christopher Gunning

Richard O'Sullivan, Paula Wilcox, Sally Thomsett, Yootha Joyce, Brian Murphy, Peter Cellier, Patrick Newell, Spike Milligan, Arthur Lowe

Man About Town*
US 1939 85m bw
Paramount (Arthur Hornblow Jnr)

A Broadway producer in London makes his girlfriend jealous.
Fairly amusing comedy-musical programmer.

w Morrie Ryskind *d* Mark Sandrich *ph* Ted Tetzlaff *md* Victor Young

Jack Benny, Dorothy Lamour, Edward Arnold, Binnie Barnes, Phil Harris, Eddie Anderson, Monty Woolley, Isabel Jeans, Betty Grable, E. E. Clive

Man Afraid
US 1957 84m bw Cinemascope

A priest is forced to kill a hoodlum in self-defence, and is then threatened by the dead man's psychopathic father. Heavy-going melodrama not helped at all by the very wide screen. George Nader, Phyllis Thaxter,

Harold J. Stone, Tim Hovey, Eduard Franz. Written by Herb Meadow; directed by Harry Keller; for Universal-International.

Man Alive

US 1945 70m bw

A husband thought to be dead comes back as a 'ghost' and frightens away his wife's new suitor. Curious and rather tasteless comedy. Pat O'Brien, Ellen Drew, Adolphe Menjou, Rudy Vallee, Jack Norton. Written by Edwin Harvey Blum; directed by Ray Enright; for RKO.

A Man Alone*

US 1955 96m Trucolor
Republic

A wandering gunman is framed by other badmen.

Solemn, slow-moving but generally interesting western, the star's first attempt at direction.

w John Tucker Battle d Ray Milland ph Lionel Lindon m Victor Young

Ray Milland, Mary Murphy, Ward Bond, Raymond Burr, Arthur Space, Lee Van Cleef, Alan Hale Jnr

A Man and a Woman**

France 1966 102m Eastmancolor
Les Films 13
aka: Un Homme et une Femme

A racing driver and a script girl, both of whose spouses are dead, meet while visiting their children, and an affair leads to marriage. Slight romantic drama so tricked out with smart images that it looks like a series of expensive commercials. A great box office success, but its director never again succeeded in this vein which he made his own.

w Claude Lelouch, Pierre Uytterhoven d Claude Lelouch ph Claude Lelouch m Francis Lai

Anouk Aimée, Jean-Louis Trintignant
'When in doubt, Lelouch's motto seems to be, use a colour filter or insert lyrical shots of dogs and horses; when in real doubt, use both.'—Tom Milne, MFB

'A slick item with all the Hollywood ingredients.'—John Simon

AA: Claude Lelouch, Pierre Uytterhoven
AAN: Claude Lelouch (as director); Anouk Aimée

Man at the Top*

GB 1973 87m Technicolor
Hammer / Dufton (Peter Charlesworth)

A pharmaceutical executive finds that his firm is marketing an unsafe drug.

Further adventures of the belligerent hero of Room at the Top (qv), this time following a popular television series. All very fashionable and predictable.

w Hugh Whitemore d Mike Vardy ph Bryan Probyn m Roy Budd

Kenneth Haigh, Nanette Newman, Harry Andrews, John Quentin, Charlie Williams

The Man Behind the Gun

US 1952 82m Technicolor

A cavalry officer is sent to quell a rebellion and helps to found Los Angeles. Cheerful western programmer. Randolph Scott, Patrice Wymore, Dick Wesson, Phil Carey. Written by John Twist; directed by Felix Feist; for Warner.

The Man Behind the Mask

GB 1936 79m bw

A mad scientist kidnaps a nobleman's daughter. Serial-like hokum with interesting credits. Hugh Williams, Maurice Schwarz, Jane Baxter, Donald Calthrop, Henry Oscar. Written by Ian Hay, Syd Courtenay, Jack Byrd and Stanley Haynes; directed by Michael Powell; for Joe Rock.

The Man Between*

GB 1953 101m bw
British Lion / London Films (Carol Reed)

Ivo Kern operates successfully as a West Berlin racketeer; love causes a softening of his attitudes and leads to his death.

Imitation Third Man with an uninteresting mystery and a solemn ending. Good acting and production can't save it.

w Harry Kurnitz d Carol Reed ph Desmond Dickinson m John Addison ad André Andreiev

James Mason, Hildegarde Neff, Claire Bloom, Geoffrey Toone, Ernst Schroeder

'A cold-hearted film about people with cold feet.'—Daily Express

A Man Called Gannon

US 1969 105m Technicolor

A wandering cowboy helps a widow rancher in her fight against encroaching cattlemen. Adequate remake of The Man Without a Star, which somehow had much more stature. Tony Franciosa, Michael Sarrazin, Judi West, Susan Oliver, John Anderson. Written by Gene Kearney, D. D. Beauchamp and Borden Chase; directed by James Goldstone; for Universal.

A Man Called Horse*
US 1970   114m   Technicolor
Panavision
Cinema Center / Sanford Howard

In 1825 an English aristocrat is captured by
Indians, lives with them and eventually
becomes their leader.
Harrowing account of tribal life and customs,
with much bloodshed and torture and most of
the dialogue in Indian. Occasionally
impressive but not exactly entertaining.

w Jack di Witt, *story* Dorothy M. Johnson
d Elliot Silverstein ph Robert Hauser
m Leonard Rosenman

Richard Harris, Judith Anderson, Jean
Gascon, Manu Tupou

† Sequel 1976: *The Return of a Man Called
Horse.*

The Man Called Noon
GB / Spain / Italy 1973   95m   Technicolor
Frontier / Montana / Finarco (Euan Lloyd)

A western gunslinger loses his memory.
Childish western melodrama in the violent
manner.

w Scot Finch, *novel* Louis L'Amour d Peter
Collinson ph John Cabrera m Luis Bacalov

Richard Crenna, Stephen Boyd, Rosanna
Schiaffino, Farley Granger

A Man Called Peter*
US 1955   119m   De Luxe   Cinemascope
TCF (Samuel G. Engel)

The life of Peter Marshall, a Scottish
clergyman who became chaplain to the US
Senate.
Careful but rather dreary biopic.

w Eleanore Griffin, *book* Catherine Marshall
d Henry Koster ph Harold Lipstein m Alfred
Newman

Richard Todd, Jean Peters, Marjorie
Rambeau, Jill Esmond, Les Tremayne,
Robert Burton

AAN: Harold Lipstein

A Man Could Get Killed*
US 1966   98m   Technicolor   Panavision
Universal / Cherokee (Ernest Wehmeyer)

An American businessman in Lisbon is
mistaken for a secret agent.
Minor thrill comedy with a confused plot and a
willing cast.

w T. E. B. Clarke, Richard Breen, *novel*
Diamonds Are Danger by David Walker
d Ronald Neame, Cliff Owen ph Gabor
Pogany m Bert Kaemfert

James Garner, Melina Mercouri, Sandra Dee,
Tony Franciosa, Robert Coote, Roland
Culver, Cecil Parker, Grégoire Aslan, Dulcie
Gray, Martin Benson, Niall MacGinnis

A Man for All Seasons****
GB 1966   120m   Technicolor
Columbia / Highland (Fred Zinnemann)

Sir Thomas More opposes Henry VIII's
divorce, and events lead inexorably to his
execution.
Irreproachable film version of a play which
has had its narrative tricks removed but stands
up remarkably well. Acting, direction, sets,
locations and costumes all have precisely the
right touch.

w Robert Bolt, from his play d Fred
Zinnemann ph Ted Moore m Georges
Delerue pd John Box

Paul Scofield, Wendy Hiller, Susannah York,
Robert Shaw, Orson Welles, Leo McKern,
Nigel Davenport, John Hurt, Corin Redgrave,
Cyril Luckham, Jack Gwyllim

AA: best picture; Robert Bolt; Fred
Zinnemann; Ted Moore; Paul Scofield
AAN: Wendy Hiller; Robert Shaw

Man Friday
GB 1975   115m   Eastmancolor
Panavision
Avco-Embassy / ITC / ABC / Keep Films
(Jules Buck)

The story of Robinson Crusoe told so that
Friday appears the more intelligent.
A pointless and not very entertaining exercise
which wears out its welcome very early.

w Adrian Mitchell d Jack Gold ph Alex
Phillips m Carl Davis

Peter O'Toole, Richard Roundtree

'Liberal intentions trail sadly through every
sequence and cause absurd fluctuations of
tone, since no one seems to have decided
whether laborious slapstick, heavy
portentousness or method acting is the best
vehicle for the message.'—*Jill Forbes*

The Man from Bitter Ridge
US 1955   80m   Technicolor

A special agent goes undercover to nail
stagecoach bandits, but himself comes under
suspicion. Adequate western programmer.
Lex Barker, Mara Corday, Stephen McNally,
Trevor Bardette, John Dehner. Written by
Lawrence Roman; directed by Jack Arnold;
for Universal-International.

The Man from Blankley's
US 1930   67m   bw
Warner

A drunken aristocrat goes to the wrong party
and teaches those present, and himself, a thing
or two.

Amusing star trifle, previously filmed as a
silent.

w Harvey Thew, Joseph Jackson, story F.
Anstey d Alfred E. Green ph James Van
Trees

John Barrymore, Loretta Young, William
Austin, Albert Gran, Emily Fitzroy

The Man from Colorado
US 1949   99m   Technicolor
Columbia (Jules Schermer)

A maladjusted Civil War veteran becomes a
western judge and rules by the gun.

Slightly unusual, watchable star western.

w Robert D. Andrews, Ben Maddow, Borden
Chase d Henry Levin ph William Snyder
m George Duning

Glenn Ford, William Holden, Ellen Drew,
Ray Collins, Edgar Buchanan, Jerome
Courtland, James Millican, Jim Bannon

'No more humour than a lawyer's shingle,
but it has suspense and some exciting shots of
fist fights and burning houses.'—Time

The Man from Dakota*
US 1940   75m   bw

A Yankee soldier is taken prisoner by the
south and becomes a spy. Good period action
piece. Wallace Beery, Dolores Del Rio, John
Howard, Donald Meek, H. B. Warner, Victor
Varconi. Written by Laurence Stallings, from
the novel by Mackinlay Kantor; directed by
Leslie Fenton; for MGM. (GB title: Arouse
and Beware.)

Man from Del Rio
US 1956   82m   bw
UA / Robert L. Jacks

A Mexican hobo becomes sheriff and forces
the local badman to leave town.

Modest, efficient, rather brutal little western.

w Richard Carr d Harry Horner ph Stanley
Cortez m Fred Steiner

Anthony Quinn, Katy Jurado, Peter Whitney,
Douglas Fowley

The Man from Down Under
US 1943   103m   bw

A veteran of World War I smuggles two
orphans back into Australia. Appallingly
indulgent sentimental star vehicle, a mistake

for all concerned. Charles Laughton, Binnie
Barnes, Donna Reed, Richard Carlson,
Horace McNally, Arthur Shields. Written by
Wells Root and Thomas Seller; directed by
Robert Z. Leonard; for MGM.

The Man from Laramie**
US 1955   104m   Technicolor
           Cinemascope
Columbia (William Goetz)

A wandering cowman seeks revenge on those
who killed his brother.

Grade A western with new-fangled touches of
brutality touching off the wide screen
spectacle.

w Philip Yordan, Frank Burt d Anthony
Mann ph Charles Lang Jnr m George
Duning md Morris Stoloff

James Stewart, Arthur Kennedy, Donald
Crisp, Cathy O'Donnell, Alex Nicol, Aline
MacMahon, Wallace Ford, Jack Elam

The Man from Morocco
GB 1944   116m   bw
ABP

Members of the international brigade are
captured and later sent by Vichy to build a
Sahara railway for the Germans; one escapes
to London with vital information.

Stilted, meandering and extremely
unconvincing melodrama with a star ill at ease.

w Warwick Ward, Edward Dryhurst,
Marguerite Steen, story Rudolph Cartier
d Max Greene ph Basil Emmott

Anton Walbrook, Margaretta Scott, Mary
Morris, Reginald Tate, Peter Sinclair, David
Horne

The Man from the Alamo*
US 1953   79m   Technicolor
U-I (Aaron Rosenberg)

A survivor of the Alamo is thought to be a
deserter but proves his story and exposes a
villain.

Satisfying western programmer.

w Steve Fisher, D. D. Beauchamp d Budd
Boetticher ph Russell Metty m Frank
Skinner

Glenn Ford, Victor Jory, Julia Adams, Hugh
O'Brian

The Man from the Diners' Club*
US 1963   96m   bw
Columbia / Dena / Ampersand

A clerk accidentally lets a credit card go to a
notorious gangster, and makes desperate
efforts to retrieve it.

Minor star comedy with funny moments surviving a slapdash script.

w Bill Blatty d Frank Tashlin ph Hal Mohr m Stu Philips

Danny Kaye, Telly Savalas, Martha Hyer, Cara Williams, Everett Sloane, George Kennedy

The Man from Uncle

This long-running one-hour TV series (1964-8) began as a spoof of James Bond, which was itself a spoof. Not much more serious or convincing than *Batman*, they caused a lot of people to suspend their disbelief. Robert Vaughn played Napoleon Solo, David McCallum Ilya Kuryakin, and Leo G. Carroll Mr Waverly. Several feature films were made up from various episodes, and did well in cinemas in some countries. They were: TO TRAP A SPY, THE SPY WITH MY FACE, THE KARATE KILLERS, THE SPY IN THE GREEN HAT, ONE OF OUR SPIES IS MISSING, THE HELICOPTER SPIES, HOW TO STEAL THE WORLD and ONE SPY TOO MANY.

A Man from Wyoming
US 1930 70m bw

A slow-speaking engineer joins the army, serves overseas and marries an ambulance driver. Uncertain star vehicle which helped to mould his screen character. Gary Cooper, June Collyer, Regis Toomey, E. H. Calvert, Morgan Farley. Written by John Weaver and Albert Shelby Le Vino; directed by Rowland V. Lee; for Paramount. 'Bad enough to be good entertainment if taken as farce.'—*New York Evening Post.*

The Man from Yesterday
US 1932 71m bw
Paramount

A man is reported missing in World War I, but years later his wife and her new fiancé find him in Switzerland, dying of gas poisoning. Enoch Arden rides again, and very boringly.

w Oliver H. P. Garrett d Berthold Viertel ph Karl Struss

Claudette Colbert, Clive Brook, Charles Boyer, Andy Devine, Alan Mowbray, Christian Rub

Man Hunt**
US 1941 98m bw
TCF (Kenneth MacGowan)

A big game hunter misses a shot at Hitler and is chased back to England by the Gestapo. Despite hilariously inaccurate English

backgrounds, this is perhaps its director's most vivid Hollywood thriller, though watered down in tone from the original novel.

w Dudley Nichols, *novel* Rogue Male by Geoffrey Household d Fritz Lang ph Arthur Miller m Alfred Newman

Walter Pidgeon, Joan Bennett, *George Sanders*, John Carradine, Roddy McDowall, Ludwig Stossel, Heather Thatcher, Frederick Worlock

'A tense and intriguing thriller that is both propaganda and exciting entertainment.'— *Paul M. Jensen, 1969*

'In its manipulation of these dark and intent forces on a checkerboard, it manages to take your breath away.'—*Otis Ferguson*
† Remade for TV in 1976 as *Rogue Male.*

The Man I Love
US 1946 76m bw
Warner (Arnold Albert)

A nightclub singer is involved with a mobster. Dreary little melodrama which never really gets going.

w Catherine Turney d Raoul Walsh ph Sid Hickox m Max Steiner

Ida Lupino, Robert Alda, Andrea King, Martha Vickers, Bruce Bennett, Alan Hale, Dolores Moran, John Ridgely

The Man I Married*
US 1940 79m bw
TCF (Raymond Griffith)
aka: *I Married a Nazi*

When an American couple take a European vacation, the wife is horrified to find her husband, who is of German parentage, agreeing with the Nazis.
Naïve but striking melodrama exploring attitudes of its time.

w Oliver H. P. Garrett, *novel* Swastika by Oscar Shisgall d Irving Pichel ph Peverell Marley m David Buttolph

Joan Bennett, Francis Lederer, Lloyd Nolan, Anna Sten, Otto Kruger, Maria Ouspenskaya, Ludwig Stossel, Johnny Russell

The Man in Grey**
GB 1943 116m bw
GFD / Gainsborough (Edward Black)

In Regency times, an aristocratic girl's love for her less fortunate friend is repaid by jealousy, treachery and murder.
Rather dully performed flashback costume melodrama which caught the public imagination in the middle of a dreary world war, especially as its evil leading characters

were played by stars who rapidly went right to the top. The several imitations which followed, including *The Wicked Lady, Jassy* and *Hungry Hill*, became known as the Gainsborough school.

w Margaret Kennedy, Leslie Arliss, Doreen Montgomery, *novel* Lady Eleanor Smith *d* Leslie Arliss *ph* Arthur Crabtree *m* Cedric Mallabey *ad* Walter Murton

James Mason, Margaret Lockwood, Phyllis Calvert, Stewart Granger, Helen Haye, Nora Swinburne, Raymond Lovell, Martita Hunt

'There was not a moment when I would not gladly have dived for my hat.'—*James Agate*

'All the time-tested materials: gypsy fortune-teller; scowling, black-browed villain; gushy diary kept by a doe-eyed girl who munches candied violets; fire-breathing adventuress who dotes on discord and low-cut gowns . . .'—*Time*

The Man in Half Moon Street
US 1944 91m bw
Paramount (Walter MacEwen)

A mysteriously handsome young scientist is actually a 90-year-old who has discovered a surgical method of preserving youth. Boring screen version of a play which was conceived in an almost romantic vein; Hollywood has taken it too literally.

w Charles Kenyon, *play* Barre Lyndon *d* Ralph Murphy *ph* Henry Sharp *m* Miklos Rozsa

Nils Asther, Helen Walker, Brandon Hurst, *Reinhold Schunzel*

† Remade in straight horror vein as *The Man Who Could Cheat Death* (qv).

The Man in the Attic
US 1953 82m bw

Remake of the much-remade *The Lodger,* this time with parsimonious production values and no style. Jack Palance, Constance Smith, Byron Palmer, Frances Bavier, Rhys Williams. Written by Robert Presnell Jnr and Barre Lyndon; directed by Hugo Fregonese; for TCF.

The Man in the Back Seat*
GB 1961 57m bw
Independent Artists (Julian Wintle, Leslie Parkyn)

Two robbers fail to separate a bookie from the locked bag chained to his wrist; at first taking him with them they finally kill him and are apparently haunted by him.

Taut, downbeat little crime thriller which won a few critical plaudits.

w Malcolm Hulke, Eric Paice *d* Vernon Sewell *ph* Reg Wyer *m* Stanley Black

Derren Nesbitt, Keith Faulkner, Carol White, Harry Locke

Man in the Dark*
US 1953 70m bw 3-D
Columbia (Wallace Macdonald)

A convict submits to a brain operation which will remove his criminal tendencies. Unfortunately it also removes his memory, and on his release he is bewildered when gangsters expect him to know where the loot is hidden.

Silly low-budgeter which is only notable as the 3-D film which most exploited the short-lived medium. Apart from a roller coaster ride, objects hurled at the audience include scissors, spiders, knives, forceps, fists and falling bodies.

w George Bricker, Jack Leonard *d* Lew Landers *ph* Floyd Crosby *md* Ross de Maggio

Edmond O'Brien, Audrey Totter, Ted de Corsia, Horace MacMahon

The Man in the Gray Flannel Suit*
US 1956 152m Eastmancolor Cinemascope
TCF (Darryl F. Zanuck)

A young New York executive is offered a demanding job but decides that his first loyalty is to his wife and children.

An amusingly accurate novel of Madison Avenue mores becomes a marathon emotional melodrama in which the mordant bits quickly give way to domestic problems and a guilt complex about a wartime affair, shown in lengthy flashback. It's all too much.

w Nunnally Johnson, *novel* Sloan Wilson *d* Nunnally Johnson *ph* Charles G. Clarke *m* Bernard Herrmann

Gregory Peck, Fredric March, Jennifer Jones, Ann Harding, *Arthur O'Connell, Henry Daniell*, Marisa Pavan, Lee J. Cobb, Keenan Wynn, Gene Lockhart, Gigi Perreau, Connie Gilchrist, Joseph Sweeney

The Man in the Iron Mask***
US 1939 119m bw
Edward Small

King Louis XIV keeps his twin brother prisoner.

Exhilarating swashbuckler based on a classic novel, with a complex plot, good acting and the three musketeers in full cry.

w George Bruce, novel Alexandre Dumas *d James Whale ph* Robert Planck *m* Lucien Moraweck

Louis Hayward, Warren William (as
D'Artagnan), Alan Hale, Bert Roach, Miles
Mander, Joan Bennett, Joseph Schildkraut,
Walter Kingsford, Marion Martin, Montagu
Love, Albert Dekker

'A sort of combination of The Prisoner of
Zenda and The Three Musketeers, with a few
wild west chases thrown in . . . not
unentertaining.'—Richard Mallett, Punch
† Remade 1976 as a TV movie with Richard
Chamberlain, and 1978 as The Fifth Musketeer
(qv).

AAN: Lucien Moraweck

The Man in the Middle*

GB 1964 94m bw Cinemascope
TCF / Pennebaker / Belmont (Walter
Seltzer)

In India during World War II, an American
lieutenant is indicted for murder and the
defence counsel is instructed to lose the case.
Courtroom melodrama with unusual angles;
quite intriguing, though the wide screen
doesn't help.

w Keith Waterhouse, Willis Hall, novel The
Winston Affair by Howard Fast d Guy
Hamilton ph Wilkie Cooper m John Barry

Robert Mitchum, Trevor Howard, Keenan
Wynn, Barry Sullivan, France Nuyen,
Alexander Knox

'For once Mitchum seems to have an excuse
for keeping his eyes at half mast.'—Judith
Crist

The Man in the Mirror

GB 1936 82m bw
JH Productions / Wardour (Julius Hagen)

A timid man's reflection steps out of the
mirror and organizes him.
Modest comedy with a pleasing star.

w F. McGrew Willis, Hugh Mills,
novel William Garrett d Maurice Elvey
ph Curt Courant

Edward Everett Horton, Geneviève Tobin,
Garry Marsh, Ursula Jeans, Alastair Sim,
Aubrey Mather, Felix Aylmer

Man in the Moon

GB 1960 99m bw
Allied Film Makers / Excalibur (Michael
Relph)

A man who earns his living as Mr Normal, a
human guinea pig for scientific research, is
chosen as the first astronaut.
Dated comedy which rather dismayingly turns
from mild satire to outright farce and fantasy.

w Michael Relph, Bryan Forbes d Basil
Dearden ph Harry Waxman m Philip Green

Kenneth More, Shirley Anne Field, Michael
Hordern, John Phillips, John Glyn-Jones,
Charles Gray, Norman Bird

The Man in the Net

US 1958 96m bw
UA / Mirisch-Jaguar (Walter Mirisch)

When a painter is accused of murdering his
wife, he goes into hiding and is helped by
children.
Extremely tedious and inept mystery, doubly
disappointing in view of the credits.

w Reginald Rose, novel Patrick Quentin
d Michael Curtiz ph John Seitz m Hans
Salter

Alan Ladd, Carolyn Jones, Diane Brewster,
John Lupton, Charles McGraw, Tom
Helmore, John Alexander

Man in the Saddle

US 1951 87m Technicolor

A small rancher is victimized by his wealthy
neighbour. Fairly lively western which
develops into a series of gunfights. Randolph
Scott, Alexander Knox, Joan Leslie, Ellen
Drew, Richard Rober. Written by Kenneth
Gamet; directed by André de Toth; for Harry
Joe Brown / Columbia. (GB title: The
Outcast.)

Man in the Shadow*

US 1957 80m bw Cinemascope
U-I (Albert Zugsmith)
GB title: Pay the Devil

The sheriff of a small western town
investigates a murder against the wishes of a
powerful local rancher.
Mini-social drama in which the honest man
wins out at last . . . and who would expect
anything different. A brooding melodrama
which delivers less than it promises.

w Gene L. Coon d Jack Arnold ph Arthur
E. Arling m Joseph Gershenson

Jeff Chandler, Orson Welles, Colleen Miller,
John Larch, Joe Schneider, Leo Gordon

The Man in the Sky*

GB 1956 87m bw
Ealing (Seth Holt)
US title: Decision against Time

A test pilot refuses to bale out when an engine
catches fire; his plight is interwoven with
scenes of his family, friends and associates.
Thin suspense drama with some effective
moments but too many irrelevant asides.

w William Rose, John Eldridge d Charles
Crichton ph Douglas Slocombe m Gerbrand
Schurmann

Jack Hawkins, Elizabeth Sellars, Walter
Fitzgerald, Eddie Byrne, John Stratton, Victor
Maddern, Lionel Jeffries, Donald Pleasence

The Man in the Trunk
US 1942   70m   bw

The ghost of a murder victim helps a young
attorney to nail the culprit. Slightly uneasy
spook comedy with a good star performance.

Raymond Walburn, Lynne Roberts, George
Holmes, J. Carrol Naish, Dorothy Peterson.
Written by John Larkin; directed by Malcolm
St Clair; for TCF.

The Man in the White Suit••••
GB 1951   81m   bw
Ealing (Sidney Cole)

A scientist produces a fabric that never gets
dirty and never wears out. Unions and
management are equally aghast.
Brilliant satirical comedy played as farce and
put together with meticulous cinematic
counterpoint, so that every moment counts
and all concerned give of their very best.

*w Roger Macdougall, John Dighton,
Alexander Mackendrick d Alexander
Mackendrick ph Douglas Slocombe
m Benjamin Frankel*

Alec Guinness, Joan Greenwood, Cecil Parker,
Vida Hope, *Ernest Thesiger,* Michael Gough,
Howard Marion Crawford, Miles Malleson,
George Benson, Edie Martin

'The combination of an ingenious idea, a
bright, funny and imaginative script, skilful
playing and perceptive brisk direction has
resulted once more in a really satisfying Ealing
comedy.'—*Richard Mallett, Punch*

AAN: script

Man in the Wilderness•
US 1971   105m   Technicolor
   Panavision
Warner / Wilderness (Sanford Howard)

In 1820 in the Canadian northwest, a fur
trapper is mauled by a grizzly and left for
dead, but he learns to survive and sets out for
revenge.
Endurance melodrama modelled after *A Man
Called Horse*; a bit stretched and only for the
hardened, but taking an agreeably unromantic
view of nature.

*w Jack di Witt d Richard Sara½an ph Gerry
Fisher m Johnny Harris*

Richard Harris, John Huston, John Bindon,
Prunella Ransome, Henry Wilcoxon, Ben
Carruthers

Man Made Monster•
US 1940   57m   bw
Universal (Jack Bernard)
GB title: *The Electric Man*

A scientist experiments with a man who is
impervious to electric shock, and turns him
into a walking robot.
A smart little semi-horror originally planned
for Karloff and Lugosi.

*w Joseph West d George Waggner
ph Elwood Bredell m Hans Salter
md Charles Previn sp John P. Fulton*

Lon Chaney Jnr, Lionel Atwill, Anne Nagel,
Frank Albertson, Samuel S. Hinds

Man of a Thousand Faces••
US 1957   122m   bw   Cinemascope
U-I (Robert Arthur)

The rise to fame of silent screen character
actor Lon Chaney.
Moderately commendable biopic with a strong
sense of period Hollywood, an excellent star
performance, but too much sudsy emoting
about deaf mute parents and an ungrateful
wife.

*w R. Wright Campbell, Ivan Goff, Ben
Roberts d Joseph Pevney ph Russell Metty
m Frank Skinner ad Alexander Golitzen*

James Cagney, Dorothy Malone, Robert
Evans (as Irving Thalberg), Roger Smith,
Marjorie Rambeau, Jane Greer, Jim Backus

AAN: script

Man of Aran••
GB 1934   75m   bw
Gainsborough (Michael Balcon)

The primitive life of crofting and fishing folk in
the west of Ireland.
A lowering documentary very typical of its
maker: highly impressive scene for scene, but
tedious as a whole; still, highly remarkable
that it was made at all for the commercial
cinema.

*w Robert and Frances Flaherty d Robert
Flaherty*

Colman King, Maggie Dirane (amateurs)

'In so far as it is a rendering of the efforts of
the Atlantic to overwhelm and demolish a wall
of rock, it is magnificent; but the human note
is inadequate and unnecessary.'—*E. V. Lucas,
Punch*

'However real, it would have made better
truth if it had been handled with more of the
art of fiction.'—*Otis Ferguson*

Man of Conquest
US 1939   99m   bw
Republic (Sol C. Siegel)

The life of western hero Sam Houston, who became president of Texas.
Competent action / domestic biopic.

w Wells Root, E. E. Paramore Jnr d George Nicholls Jnr ph Joseph H. August m Victor Young

Richard Dix, Joan Fontaine, Gail Patrick, Edward Ellis, Victor Jory, Robert Barrat, George Hayes, Ralph Morgan, Robert Armstrong, C. Henry Gordon, Janet Beecher

AAN: Victor Young

Man of La Mancha*
US 1972 132m De Luxe
UA / PEA (Arthur Hiller)

Arrested by the Inquisition and thrown into prison, Miguel de Cervantes relates the story of Don Quixote.
Unimaginative but generally good-looking attempt to recreate on the screen an essentially theatrical experience.

w Dale Wasserman, from his play d Arthur Hiller ph Goffredo Rotunno m Mitch Leigh ly Joe Darion md Laurence Rosenthal ad Luciano Damiani

Peter O'Toole, Sophia Loren, James Coco, Harry Andrews, John Castle, Brian Blessed
    'Needful of all the imagination the spectator can muster.'—Variety

AAN: Laurence Rosenthal

Man of Marble*
Poland 1978 165m colour
PRF / Zespol X (Andrzej Wajda)

Young film makers gather material on a political hero of the fifties.
An extended drama on the style of Citizen Kane but with much more relevance to contemporary history. A key film to students of Poland, but too specialized for general entertainment.

w Aleksander Scibor-Rylski d Andrzej Wajda ph Edward Klosinski m Andrzej Korzinski

Jerzy Radziwilowicz, Krystyna Janda, Michael Tarkowski, Tadeusz Lomnicki

Man of the Moment
GB 1935 82m bw

An engaged young man saves a girl from suicide and falls in love with her. Minor romantic comedy of predictable development.
Douglas Fairbanks Jnr, Laura La Plante, Claude Hulbert, Margaret Lockwood, Donald Calthrop, Monty Banks. Written by Roland Pertwee, Guy Bolton and A. R. Rawlinson, from a play by Yves Mirande; directed by Monty Banks; for Warner.

Man of the West
US 1958 100m De Luxe Cinemascope
UA / Ashton (Walter M. Mirisch)

In 1874 Arizona, a reformed gunman is cajoled by his old buddies to help them rob a bank.
Talkative, set-bound, cliché-ridden star western with minor compensations.

w Reginald Rose, novel Will C. Brown d Anthony Mann ph Ernest Haller m Leigh Harline

Gary Cooper, Lee J. Cobb, Julie London, Arthur O'Connell, Jack Lord, John Dehner, Royal Dano, Robert Wilke

Man on a String
US 1960 92m bw
Columbia / Louis de Rochemont
GB title: Confessions of a Counterspy

A Russian-born Hollywood producer is asked by the Russians to work as a spy but becomes a double agent.
Slightly unbelievable biopic about Boris Morros, rather childlike in its simplicity and not too entertaining either.

w John Kafka, Virginia Shaler, book Ten Years a Counterspy by Boris Morros d André de Toth ph Charles Lawton Jnr and others m George Duning

Ernest Borgnine, Kerwin Mathews, Colleen Dewhurst, Alexander Scourby, Glenn Corbett, Vladimir Sokoloff

Man on a Swing
US 1975 108m Technicolor
Paramount (Howard B. Jaffe)

Investigations into a murder are helped by a would-be medium.
Overlong and confused psycho-mystery with one stand-out performance.

w David Zelag Goodman d Frank Perry ph Adam Holender m Lalo Schifrin

Cliff Robertson, Joel Grey, Dorothy Tristan, Peter Masterson
    'Runs out of interest long before it runs out of film.'—Variety

Man on a Tightrope*
US 1953 105m bw
TCF (Robert L. Jacks)

A Czech circus owner has trouble with the communist authorities and tries to escape.
Adventure story with cold war pretensions which virtually kill it.

w Robert Sherwood d Elia Kazan ph Georg Krause m Franz Waxman

Fredric March, Cameron Mitchell, Adolphe Menjou, Gloria Grahame, Terry Moore, Richard Boone, John Dehner, Dorothea Wieck

Man on Fire
US 1957 95m bw
MGM (Sol C. Siegel)

When his wife divorces him, a middle-aged man refuses to hand over their son.
Low-key personal drama of very moderate interest and modest budget.

wd Ranald MacDougall *ph* Joseph Ruttenberg *m* David Raksin

Bing Crosby, Inger Stevens, Mary Fickett, E. G. Marshall

The Man on the Eiffel Tower°
US 1948 82m Anscocolor
A & T (Irving Allen)

A crazy killer defies Inspector Maigret to discover his identity.
Early independent production, an unsatisfactory crime melodrama with international talent and Paris locations. Some quirky acting carries it through.

w Harry Brown, *novel* A Battle of Nerves by Simenon *d* Burgess Meredith *ph* Stanley Cortez

Charles Laughton, Burgess Meredith, Franchot Tone, Robert Hutton, Jean Wallace, Patricia Roc, Wilfrid Hyde White, Belita

The Man on the Flying Trapeze°
US 1935 65m bw
Paramount (William Le Baron)
GB title: *The Memory Expert*

Adventures of an oppressed family man who is useful to his boss because of his prodigious memory.
Plotless rigmarole of shapeless comedy sketches, for star fans.

w Ray Harris, Sam Hardy, Jack Cunningham, Bobby Vernon, *story* Charles Bogle (W. C. Fields) *d* Clyde Bruckman *ph* Al Gilks

W. C. Fields, Kathleen Howard, Mary Brian, Grady Sutton, Vera Lewis, Lucien Littlefield, Oscar Apfel

The Man on the Roof°
Sweden 1976 109m Eastmancolor
Svensk Filmindustri (Per Berglund)
original title: *Mannen pa Taket*

A brutal policeman is murdered, and a rooftop sniper turns out to be the culprit.
Alternately vivid and lumbering police thriller with a regrettable tendency to moralize.

wd Bo Widerberg, *novel* The Abominable Man by Max Sjöwall, Max Wahlöös *ph* Odd Geir Saether, Per Kallberg, others *m* Björn Lindh

Carl Gustav Lindstedt, Gunnel Wadner, Hakan Serner, Sven Wollter

Man on the Run
GB 1949 82m bw

A deserter becomes innocently involved in a jewel robbery. Competent crime programmer.
Derek Farr, Joan Hopkins, Edward Chapman, Laurence Harvey, John Stuart. Written and directed by Lawrence Huntingdon; for ABPC.

Man Proof
US 1938 74m bw
MGM (Louis D. Lighton)

In trying to win back her man a woman discovers she really loves someone else.
Modest romantic comedy which leaves its stars at sea.

w Vincent Lawrence, Waldemar Young, George Oppenheimer, *novel* The Four Marys by Fanny Heaslip Lea *d* Richard Thorpe *ph* Karl Freund *m* Franz Waxman

Myrna Loy, Franchot Tone, Walter Pidgeon, Rosalind Russell, Nana Bryant, Ruth Hussey

The Man They Could Not Hang
US 1939 65m bw
Columbia

A scientist working on a mechanical heart causes the death of a volunteer student. He is executed, but his assistant restores him to life and he determines to murder those who convicted him.
Predictable horror hokum which set Karloff on his mad doctor cycle.

w Karl Brown *d* Nick Grinde *ph* Benjamin Kline *md* Morris Stoloff

Boris Karloff, Lorna Gray, Robert Wilcox, Roger Pryor, Don Beddoe, Byron Foulger

A Man to Remember°
US 1938 80m bw
RKO (Robert Sisk)

At a small-town doctor's funeral, his life is remembered by mourners.
Modestly effective family film.

w Dalton Trumbo, *novel* Failure by Katharine Haviland-Taylor *d* Garson Kanin *ph* J. Roy Hunt *m* Roy Webb

Edward Ellis, Anne Shirley, Lee Bowman, William Henry, Granville Bates

The Man Upstairs*
GB 1958   88m   bw
British Lion / ACT (Robert Dunbar)

A mild-mannered lodger becomes violent, injures a policeman, and barricades himself in his room.
Character melodrama reminiscent of both *Fourteen Hours* and *Le Jour se Lève*, but not so interesting as either.

w Alun Falconer *d* Don Chaffey *ph* Gerald Gibbs

Richard Attenborough, Bernard Lee, Donald Houston, Dorothy Alison, Maureen Connell, Kenneth Griffith, Virginia Maskell, Patricia Jessel

The Man Who Broke the Bank at Monte Carlo*
US 1935   67m   bw
TCF (Nunnally Johnson)

A Russian émigré becomes a taxi driver, wins a fortune at roulette, loses it all again, and returns happily to his cab.
Very mild, unconvincing and not very entertaining malarkey which rested squarely on its star, who carried it with aplomb.

w Nunnally Johnson *d* Stephen Roberts *ph* Ernest Palmer

Ronald Colman, Joan Bennett, Colin Clive, Nigel Bruce, Montagu Love, Frank Reicher, Ferdinand Gottschalk

The Man Who Came to Dinner***
US 1941   112m   bw
Warner (Jack Saper, Jerry Wald)

An acid-tongued radio celebrity breaks his hip while on a lecture tour, and terrorizes the inhabitants of the suburban home where he must stay for several weeks.
Delightfully malicious caricature of Alexander Woolcott which, though virtually confined to one set, moves so fast that one barely notices the lack of cinematic variety, and certainly provides more than a laugh a minute, especially for those old enough to understand all the references.

w Julius J. and Philip G. Epstein, *play George S. Kaufman, Moss Hart d* William Keighley *ph* Tony Gaudio *m* Frederick Hollander

Monty Woolley, Bette Davis, Ann Sheridan, *Jimmy Durante* (spoofing Harpo Marx), *Reginald Gardiner* (spoofing Noel Coward), Richard Travis, *Billie Burke, Grant Mitchell, Ruth Vivian, Mary Wickes*, George Barbier, Elisabeth Fraser

The Man Who Changed His Mind
GB 1936   66m   bw

A scientist dabbles in brain transplants. Mild British-style horror piece; not a success. Boris Karloff, Anna Lee, Donald Calthrop, John Loder, Frank Cellier, Cecil Parker. Written by John L. Balderston, L. DuGarde Peach and Sidney Gilliat; directed by Robert Stevenson; for Gainsborough. (US title: *The Man Who Lived Again*.)

The Man Who Cheated Himself
US 1950   81m   bw
TCF (Jack M. Warner)

A woman shoots her husband and her homicide detective lover covers up for her. Efficient crime melodrama.

w Seton I. Miller, Philip MacDonald *d* Felix Feist *ph* Russell Harlan *m* Louis Forbes

Lee J. Cobb, Jane Wyatt, John Dall, Terry Frost

The Man Who Could Cheat Death
GB 1959   83m   Technicolor
Paramount / Hammer (Anthony Nelson-Keys)

A surgeon looks 35 but is really 104, having had a series of gland operations performed on himself.
Vulgar, gory, gruesomely coloured Hammer version of a rather attractive play, previously filmed under its original title *The Man in Half Moon Street* (qv). The shocks are routine, and entertainment value is minimal.

w Jimmy Sangster, *play* Barre Lyndon *d* Terence Fisher *ph* Jack Asher *m* Richard Rodney Bennett

Anton Diffring, Hazel Court, Christopher Lee, Arnold Marle, Delphi Lawrence, Francis de Wolff

The Man Who Could Work Miracles***
GB 1936   82m   bw
London (Alexander Korda)

A city clerk discovers he has the power to work miracles (given him by sportive gods) and nearly causes the end of the earth. Slow-moving but rather pleasing variation on a simple theme.

w Lajos Biro, *story* H. G. Wells *d* Lothar Mendes *ph* Harold Rosson

Roland Young, Ralph Richardson, Ernest Thesiger, Edward Chapman, Joan Gardner, Sophie Stewart, Robert Cochrane, George Zucco, Lawrence Hanray, George Sanders

   'Sometimes fake poetry, sometimes unsuccessful comedy, sometimes farce, sometimes sociological discussion, without a spark of creative talent or a trace of film ability.'—*Graham Greene*

The Man Who Cried Wolf
US 1937   67m   bw

An actor continually confesses to crimes he
didn't commit in the hope that when he does
commit one he won't be believed. An
attractive idea rather poorly handled. Lewis
Stone, Tom Brown, Barbara Read, Marjorie
Main, Forrester Harvey. Written by Charles
Grayson and Sy Bartlett; directed by Lewis R.
Foster; for Universal.

The Man Who Fell to Earth°
GB 1976   138m   colour   Panavision
British Lion (Michael Deeley, Barry
   Spikings)

A visitor from another planet tries to colonize
Earth, but his powers are destroyed and he
ends an alcoholic cripple.
A weird piece of intellectual science fiction
made weirder by longueurs of all varieties:
obscure narrative, voyeuristic sex, pop music
and metaphysics. Not an easy film or a likeable
one, despite its great technical skill.

w Paul Mayersburg, *novel* Walter Tevis
d Nicolas Roeg *ph* Anthony Richmond
md John Phillips

David Bowie, Rip Torn, Candy Clark, Buck
Henry

'Once you have pierced through its glittering
veneer, you find only another glittering veneer
underneath.'—*Michael Billington, Illustrated
London News*

'There is a punch line, but it takes forever,
and great expectations slump away.'—*Charles
Champlin, L.A. News*

'You feel finally that all that has been
achieved has been to impose an aura of
mystery and enigma where essentially there is
none; to turn a simple tale into the sort of
accumulation of sensations that has become
fashionable.'—*David Robinson, The Times*

The Man Who Finally Died
GB 1962   100m   bw   Cinemascope
British Lion / Magna / White Cross (Norman
   Williams)

A German-born Englishman returns to
Bavaria for news of his father, and becomes
involved in a spy plot.
Busy adaptation of a TV serial with a
convoluted plot which might have been more
pacily developed and better explained.

w Lewis Greifer, Louis Marks *d* Quentin
Lawrence *ph* Stephen Dade *m* Philip Green

Stanley Baker, Peter Cushing, Mai Zetterling,
Eric Portman, Niall MacGinnis, Nigel Green,
Barbara Everest, Harold Scott

The Man Who Found Himself
US 1937   67m   bw
RKO (Cliff Reid)

A nurse helps a downcast doctor face his
problems and renew his enthusiasm for life.
Simple-minded programmer.

w J. Robert Bren, Edmund Hartman, G. V.
Atwater *d* Lew Landers *ph* Roy Hunt

John Beal, Joan Fontaine, Philip Huston, Jane
Walsh, George Irving

The Man Who Had His Hair Cut Short°
Belgium 1966   94m   bw
Belgian Cultural Ministry

A frustrated law clerk has an aberration after
attending an autopsy and meeting again an old
love.
Pessimistic case history with unpleasant details
often brilliantly recorded.

w Anna de Pagter, André Delvaux *d* André
Delvaux *ph* Ghislain Cloquet *m* Freddy
Devreese

Seene Rouffaer, Beata Tyszkiewicz, Hector
Camerlynck

The Man Who Had Power over Women
GB 1970   89m   Eastmancolor

A successful public relations man comes to
hate himself, his job and what it has done to
his marriage. Fashionable wallow in guilt and
luxury, not very convincingly done. Rod
Taylor, Carol White, James Booth, Penelope
Horner, Charles Korvin, Alexandra Stewart,
Keith Barron. Written by Alan Scott and
Chris Bryant, from the novel by Gordon
Williams; directed by John Krish; for
Kettledrum / Avco.

The Man Who Haunted Himself
GB 1970   94m   Technicolor
ABP / Excalibur (Michael Relph)

After recovering from a road accident, a staid
businessman finds that he has an evil
doppelganger who steals his wife and his job.
Mildly effective if inexplicable story idea
which served more suitably as a Hitchcock TV
half hour and here, despite adequate
production, outstays its welcome.

w Basil Dearden, Michael Relph, *story* The
Case of Mr Pelham by Anthony Armstrong
d Basil Dearden *ph* Tony Spratling
m Michael Lewis

Roger Moore, Hildegarde Neil, Olga-Georges
Picot, Anton Rodgers, Freddie Jones, Thorley
Walters, John Carson, John Welsh

The Man Who Knew Too Much***
GB 1934 84m bw
GFD / Gaumont British (Ivor Montagu)

A child is kidnapped by spies to ensure her father's silence, but he springs into action.
Splendid early Hitchcock which after a faded start moves into memorable sequences involving a dentist, an East End mission and the Albert Hall. All very stagey by today's standards, but much more fun than the expensive remake.

w A. R. Rawlinson, Charles Bennett, D. B. Wyndham Lewis, Edwin Greenwood, Emlyn Williams d Alfred Hitchcock ph Curt Courant m Arthur Benjamin

Leslie Banks, Edna Best, Peter Lorre, Nova Pilbeam, Frank Vosper, Hugh Wakefield, Pierre Fresnay

'The film's mainstay is its refined sense of the incongruous.'—Peter John Dyer, 1964

The Man Who Knew Too Much*
US 1956 120m Technicolor Vistavision
(Paramount) Alfred Hitchcock

Flaccid remake of the above, twice as long and half as entertaining, though it does improve after a very slow start.

w John Michael Hayes, Angus MacPhail d Alfred Hitchcock ph Robert Burks m Bernard Herrmann

James Stewart, Doris Day, Bernard Miles, Brenda de Banzie, Daniel Gelin, Ralph Truman, Mogens Wieth, Alan Mowbray, Hillary Brooke

AA: song 'Que Sera Sera' (m / ly Jay Livingston, Ray Evans)

The Man Who Loved Cat Dancing
US 1973 114m Metrocolor Panavision
MGM (Martin Poll, Eleanor Perry)

A runaway wife is kidnapped by train thieves and comes to love one of them.
Outdoor variation on No Orchids for Miss Blandish, remarkably lacking in any kind of entertainment value.

w Eleanor Perry, novel Marilyn Dunham d Richard Sarafian ph Harry Stradling Jnr m John Williams

Sarah Miles, Burt Reynolds, Lee J. Cobb, Jack Warden, George Hamilton, Bo Hopkins, Robert Donner, Jay Silverheels

'Any number of things have gone wrong with this peculiarly dreary western.'—Tom Milne

'Sarah Miles undergoes more perils than Pauline.'—Variety

The Man Who Loved Redheads
GB 1954 90m Eastmancolor
British Lion / London Films (Josef Somlo)

Throughout his career, a diplomat seeks women who resemble the redhead with whom in youth he had had an idyllic affair.
West End theatrical moonshine, poorly filmed in ugly colour but saved by the cast.

w Terence Rattigan, from his play Who Is Sylvia? d Harold French ph Georges Périnal m Benjamin Frankel

John Justin, Moira Shearer, Roland Culver, Gladys Cooper, Denholm Elliott, Harry Andrews, Patricia Cutts, Moira Fraser, Joan Benham, Jeremy Spenser

The Man Who Never Was**
GB 1955 102m De Luxe Cinemascope
TCF / André Hakim

In 1943, the British secret service confuses the Germans by dropping a dead man into the sea with false documents.
Mainly enjoyable true life war story marred by an emotional romantic sub-plot with a double twist but helped by an equally fictitious spy hunt which cheers up the last half hour.

w Nigel Balchin, book Ewen Montagu d Ronald Neame ph Oswald Morris m Alan Rawsthorne

Clifton Webb, Robert Flemyng, Gloria Grahame, Stephen Boyd, Laurence Naismith, Josephine Griffin

The Man Who Played God*
US 1932 81m bw
Warner
GB title: The Silent Voice

A musician goes deaf but finds satisfaction in helping a young student.
Stagey but effective star vehicle which Arliss also played as a silent film. Remade as Sincerely Yours (qv).

w Julian Josephson, Maude Howell, play The Silent Voice by Jules Eckert Goodman d John G. Adolfi ph James Van Trees

George Arliss, Violet Heming, Ivan Simpson, Bette Davis, Louise Closser Hale, Donald Cook, Ray Milland

The Man Who Reclaimed His Head*
US 1934 81m bw
Universal (Henry Henigson)

A writer who feels he has been betrayed and his brain sapped by his publisher takes a gruesome revenge.
Oddball period melodrama tailored rather unsuccessfully for a new star. Remade as Strange Confession (see Inner Sanctum).

w Jean Bart, Samuel Ornitz, *play* Jean Bart
d Edward Ludwig *ph* Merrit Gerstad

Claude Rains, Joan Bennett, Lionel Atwill,
Juanita Quigley, Henry O'Neill, Lawrence
Grant

The Man Who Shot Liberty Valance*
US 1962   122m   bw
Paramount / John Ford (Willis Goldbeck)

A tenderfoot becomes a hero for shooting a
bad man, but the shot was really fired by his
friend and protector.
Clumsy, obvious western with the director
over-indulging himself but providing some
good scenes in comedy vein.

w James Warner Bellah, Willis Goldbeck
d John Ford *ph* William H. Clothier *m* Cyril
Mockridge

James Stewart, John Wayne, Vera Miles, Lee
Marvin, Edmond O'Brien, Andy Devine,
Jeanette Nolan, John Qualen, Ken Murray,
Woody Strode, Lee Van Cleef, Strother
Martin, John Carradine
  'Like Queen Victoria, John Wayne has
become lovable because he stayed in the
saddle into a new era.'—*Pauline Kael*
  'A heavy-spirited piece of nostalgia.'—
Judith Crist, 1975
  'A film whose fascination lies less in what it
is itself than in what it reveals about the art of
its maker.'—*William S. Pechter*

The Man Who Talked Too Much
US 1940   75m   bw
Warner (Edmund Grainger)

A smart defence attorney gets the goods on a
gangster and decides to turn him in.
Below-par remake of *The Mouthpiece* (qv),
later filmed again as *Illegal* (qv).

w Walter de Leon, Tom Reed, *play* The
Mouthpiece by Frank J. Collins d Vincent
Sherman *ph* Sid Hickox

George Brent, Brenda Marshall, Richard
Barthelmess, Virginia Bruce, William
Lundigan, John Litel, George Tobias, Henry
Armetta, Alan Baxter

The Man Who Turned to Stone
US 1957   71m   bw

A girls' reformatory is taken over by a group
of zombie scientists born in the eighteenth
century. Cheap horror item with a few choice
moments for connoisseurs of the absurd.
Victor Jory, Ann Doran, Charlotte Austin,
William Hudson, Paul Cavanagh. Written by
Raymond T. Marcus; directed by Leslie
Kardos; for Clover / Columbia.

The Man Who Watched Trains Go By
GB 1952   80m   Technicolor
Raymond Stross
aka: *Paris Express*

A clerk steals money in order to fulfil his wish
of world travel, and this leads to murder.
Miscast minor Simenon, not exactly badly
made but with no spark of excitement or
suspense.

wd Harold French, *novel* Georges Simenon
ph Otto Heller *m* Benjamin Frankel

Claude Rains, Marius Goring, Marta Toren,
Anouk Aimée, Herbert Lom, Ferdy Mayne

The Man Who Understood Women
US 1959   105m   Eastmancolor
  Cinemascope
TCF (Nunnally Johnson)

An arrogant, exhibitionist film producer finally
alienates his long-suffering wife.
Something of an aberration, with good scenes
submerged in an unholy mixture of sharp
comedy and sentimental melodrama.

wd Nunnally Johnson, *novel* Colours of the
Day by Romain Gary *ph* Milton Krasner
m Robert Emmett Dolan

Henry Fonda, Leslie Caron, Myron
McCormick, Cesare Danova, Marcel Dalio,
Conrad Nagel, Harry Ellerbe
  'A pretentious extravaganza on a romantic
theme.'—*MFB*

The Man Who Would Be King*
US 1975   129m   colour   Panavision
Columbia / Allied Artists / Persky-Bright /
  Devon (John Foreman)

In India in the 1880s, two adventurers find
themselves accepted as kings by a remote
tribe, but greed betrays them.
After an ingratiating start this ambitious fable
becomes more predictable, and comedy gives
way to unpleasantness. Despite its sporadic
high quality, one does not remember it with
enthusiasm.

w John Huston, Gladys Hill, *story* Rudyard
Kipling d John Huston *ph* Oswald Morris
m Maurice Jarre *pd* Alexander Trauner

Sean Connery, Michael Caine, Christopher
Plummer (as Kipling), Saeed Jaffrey, Jack
May, Shakira Caine

AAN: script

The Man with a Cloak*
US 1951   81m   bw
MGM (Stephen Ames)

In 1848 New York, a mysterious stranger (who
turns out to be Edgar Allan Poe) helps a

young French girl to keep her inheritance. Curious domestic melodrama set on MGM's choicest sets; its playful literary allusion causes it to fall between suspense thriller and character drama, but the acting keeps one watching.

w Frank Fenton, *story* John Dickson Carr *d* Fletcher Markle *ph* George Folsey *m* David Raksin

Joseph Cotten, Barbara Stanwyck, Leslie Caron, Louis Calhern, Joe de Santis, Jim Backus, Margaret Wycherly

The Man with Bogart's Face

US 1980   106m   CFI color
TCF / Melvin Simon (Andrew J. Fenady)

An unremarkable private eye gets lots of assignments because he looks like Humphrey Bogart.
Amiably nostalgic romp, not too spoofy to be enjoyable for its own sake, but notably underproduced.

w Andrew J. Fenady, from his novel *d* Robert Day *ph* Richard C. Glouner *m* George Duning

Robert Sacchi, Misty Rowe, Michelle Phillips, Franco Nero, Olivia Hussey, Victor Buono, Herbert Lom, George Raft, Yvonne de Carlo, Jay Robinson, Mike Mazurki, Henry Wilcoxon, Victor Sen Yung

The Man with My Face

US 1951   77m   bw

A successful young man finds a double in his place at both home and office, and himself branded as an imposter. Intriguing yarn which deserved a better production. Barry Nelson, Lynn Ainley, John Harvey, Carole Matthews, Jack Warden. Written by Samuel W. Taylor, Edward J. Montagne, T. J. McGowan and Vincent Bogart, from a novel by Samuel W. Taylor; directed by Edward J. Montagne; for Edward F. Gardner / UA.

The Man with Nine Lives*

US 1940   73m   bw
Columbia
GB title: *Behind the Door*

A scientist believes he can cure cancer by freezing, but accidentally locks himself and his patients in an underground ice chamber for seven years, and goes berserk when thawed out.
Interesting, rather prophetic science fiction thriller which rather lacks the style required to put it over.

w *Karl Brown, story* Harold Shumate *d* Nick Grinde *ph* Benjamin Kline

Boris Karloff, Byron Foulger, Roger Pryor, Jo Ann Sayers

The Man with the Golden Arm*

US 1956   119m   bw
Otto Preminger

A Chicago poker dealer finally kicks the drug habit.
Sensational on its first release, with its cold turkey scenes, this now seems a muddled impressionist melodrama with echoes of the silent German cinema and much over-acting and miscasting all round. But Sinatra is good; and it *is* different . . .

w Walter Newman, Lewis Meltzer, *novel* Nelson Algren *d* Otto Preminger *ph* Sam Leavitt *m* Elmer Bernstein *pd* Joe Wright *titles* Saul Bass
Frank Sinatra, Kim Novak, Eleanor Parker, Darren McGavin, Arnold Stang, Robert Strauss, John Conte, Doro Merande, George E. Stone
'Nothing very surprising or exciting . . . a pretty plain and unimaginative look-see at a lower depths character.'—*Bosley Crowther*
'A very inferior film . . . the script is inexcusably clumsy, the sets are unbelievable and the casting is ridiculous.'—*Diana Willing, Films in Review*
'It has the same running time as *Citizen Kane* but it seems a whole lot longer.'—*Robert James*
AAN: Elmer Bernstein; Frank Sinatra

The Man with the Golden Gun*

GB 1974   125m   Eastmancolor
UA / Eon (Harry Saltzman, Albert R. Broccoli)

James Bond goes to the Far East to liquidate a professional assassin named Scaramanga.
Thin and obvious Bond extravaganza with conventional expensive excitements.

w Richard Maibaum, Tom Mankiewicz, *novel* Ian Fleming *d* Guy Hamilton *ph* Ted Moore, Oswald Morris *m* John Barry *pd* Peter Murton

Roger Moore, Christopher Lee, Britt Ekland, Maud Adams, Hervé Villechaize, Clifton James, Richard Loo, Marc Lawrence
'The script lacks satiric insolence and the picture grinds on humourlessly.'—*New Yorker*

The Man with the Gun*

US 1955   84m   bw
UA / Formosa (Sam Goldwyn Jnr)
GB title: *The Trouble Shooter*

A gunfighter in search of his estranged wife becomes lawman of a lawless town.
Modest, watchable western.

w N. B. Stone Jnr, Richard Wilson *d* Richard Wilson *ph* Lee Garmes *m* Alex North

Robert Mitchum, Jan Sterling, Karen Sharpe, Henry Hull, Emile Meyer, John Luplon

The Man with the Movie Camera**
USSR 1928   60m approx   bw   silent
VUFKU
original title: *Chelovek s Kinoapparatom*

A 'camera eye' documentary without any plot, showing, through a succession of street and interior scenes, all the tricks of which the instrument is capable; it takes a bow at the end.
Unique documentary which was understandably a sensation when it first appeared but now often seems merely quaint.

wd, ed Dziga Vertov *ph* Mikhail Kaufman

The Man with Two Faces*
US 1934   72m   bw
Warner

An actor takes revenge on a scoundrel who had preyed on his sister.
Pleasing melodrama hinging on disguise; the Hays Office surprisingly allowed the hero to get away with it.

w Tom Reed, Niven Busch, *play* The Dark Tower by George S. Kaufman, Alexander Woolcott *d* Archie Mayo *ph* Tony Gaudio

Edward G. Robinson, Mary Astor, Ricardo Cortez, Louis Calhern, Mae Clarke, John Eldredge

The Man Within*
GB 1947   88m   Technicolor
GFD / Production Film Service (Muriel and Sydney Box)
US title: *The Smugglers*

An orphan boy discovers that his mysterious new guardian is a smuggler.
Unconvincing period yarn which has managed to drain every vestige of subtlety from the novel, but at least looks good.

w Muriel and Sydney Box, *novel* Graham Greene *d* Bernard Knowles *ph* Geoffrey Unsworth *m* Clifton Parker

Michael Redgrave, Richard Attenborough, Jean Kent, Joan Greenwood
   'With more style this might have been rather good. Outside of life more private than I am normally party to I can't recall hearing so many men so often say, to other men, *I hate him!* or *I hate you!*'—James Agee

The Man without a Star*
US 1955   89m   Technicolor
U-I (Aaron Rosenberg)

A wandering cowboy helps settlers to put up barbed wire against an owner of vast cattle herds.
Conventional but entertaining star western.

w Borden Chase, D. D. Beauchamp, *novel* Dee Linford *d* King Vidor *ph* Russell Metty *m* Joseph Gershenson

Kirk Douglas, Jeanne Crain, Claire Trevor, William Campbell, Jay C. Flippen, Mara Corday, Richard Boone
   † Remade for TV as *A Man Called Gannon.*

Man, Woman and Sin
US 1927   85m approx at 24 fps   bw   silent

A reporter has an affair with his boss's mistress. Glossy romantic drama marking the first screen appearance of a sensational stage star; her effect on screen was more muted.
Jeanne Eagels, John Gilbert, Marc McDermott. Written by Alice Duer Miller; directed by Monta Bell; for MGM.

The Manchurian Candidate***
US 1962   126m   bw
UA / MC (Howard W. Koch)

A Korean war 'hero' comes back a brainwashed zombie triggered to kill a liberal politician, his control being his own monstrously ambitious mother.
Insanely plotted but brilliantly handled spy thriller, a mixture of Hitchcock, Welles and *All the King's Men.*

w George Axelrod, *novel* Richard Condon *d* John Frankenheimer *ph* Lionel Lindon *m* David Amram *pd* Richard Sylbert

Frank Sinatra, Laurence Harvey, Janet Leigh, James Gregory, Angela Lansbury, Henry Silva, John McGiver
   'The unAmerican film of the year.'—*Penelope Houston*
   'An intelligent, funny, superbly written, beautifully played, and brilliantly directed study of the all-embracing fantasy in everyday social, emotional and political existence.'—*Philip Strick, 1973*

AAN: Angela Lansbury

Mandalay
US 1934   65m   bw

A lady of the tropics murders her lover and pushes his body through a porthole. Steamy melodrama which the masses found absorbing.
Kay Francis, Ricardo Cortez, Lyle Talbot, Ruth Donnelly, Shirley Temple, Warner Oland, Lucien Littlefield, Reginald Owen. Written by Austin Parker and Charles Kenyon; directed by Michael Curtiz; for Warner.

Mandingo
US 1975 126m Technicolor
Dino de Laurentiis (Peter Herald)

On a slave breeding plantation in 1840
Louisiana, passions ride high.
Like *Gone with the Wind* with all the
characters on heat, this exuberant and
unpleasant melodrama goes several points
over the top from start to finish but proved to
have wide appeal for the groundlings, in the
Tobacco Road tradition of a wallow in other
people's depravities.

w Norman Wexler, *play* Jack Kirkland, *novel*
Kyle Onstott d Richard Fleischer ph Richard
H. Kline m Maurice Jarre pd Boris Leven

James Mason, Susan George, Perry King,
Richard Ward, Brenda Sykes, Ken Norton

Mandy***
GB 1952 93m bw
Ealing (Leslie Norman)
US title: *The Crash of Silence*

A little girl, born deaf, is sent to a special
school.
Carefully wrought and very sympathetic little
semi-documentary film in which all the adults
underplay in concession to a new child star
who alas did not last long at the top.

w Nigel Balchin, Jack Whittingham, *novel*
This Day Is Ours by Hilda Lewis d *Alexander
Mackendrick* ph Douglas Slocombe
m William Alwyn

Jack Hawkins, Terence Morgan, Phyllis
Calvert, *Mandy Miller*, Godfrey Tearle,
Dorothy Alison

Manèges*
France 1950 90m bw
Films Modernes-Discina (Emil Natan)
GB title: *The Wanton*

A scheming girl marries the middle-aged
owner of a riding school and, with her greedy
mother, milks him of his money.
A neat little melodrama with flashbacks so
arranged that the girl, paralysed in an
accident, seems for the first half to have an
angelic character.

w Jacques Sigurd d Yves Allégret ph Jean
Bourgoin

Simone Signoret, Bernard Blier, *Frank Villard*,
Jane Marken

Manhandled
US 1949 97m bw
Paramount / Pine–Thomas

The secretary of a bogus psychiatrist becomes
involved in a murder and finds herself in
danger from all comers.

Modest, overlong suspenser with adequate
production values.

w Lewis R. Foster, Whitman Chambers, *novel*
The Man Who Stole a Dream by L. S.
Goldsmith d Lewis R. Foster ph Ernest
Laszlo m David Chudnow

Dorothy Lamour, Dan Duryea, Sterling
Hayden, Irene Hervey, Harold Vermilyea,
Philip Reed, Alan Napier, Art Smith, Irving
Bacon

Manhattan***
US 1979 96m bw Panavision
UA / Jack Rollins / Charles H. Joffe

Episodes in the sex life of a TV comedy writer
with an obsession about New York.
As close to a summation of Woody Allen's
views and *oeuvre* as anybody needs; some
smart jabs about the lives we lead are
sometimes bogged down in earnestness and
half-comic despair.

w Woody Allen, Marshall Brickman
d Woody Allen ph Gordon Willis md Tom
Pierson

Woody Allen, Diane Keaton, Meryl Streep,
Mariel Hemingway, Michael Murphy

'Given that the identity of his films has
increasingly been determined by his
compulsion to talk about the things he finds
important, but also by his fear of having them
come out as anything but a joke, it is not
surprising that he has scarcely been able to
decide on a form for his "art": from the
anything-for-a-laugh skittering of his early
films, to the broad parodies and pastiches of
his middle period, to the recent confessional /
psychoanalytical mode.'—*Richard Combs,
MFB*

'A masterpiece that has become a film for
the ages by not seeking to be a film of the
moment.'—*Andrew Sarris*

Manhattan Melodrama**
US 1934 93m bw
MGM (David O. Selznick)

Two slum boys grow up friends, one as district
attorney and the other as a gangster.
Archetypal American situation drama (cf
Angels with Dirty Faces, Cry of the City, etc),
with the bad guy inevitably indulging in self-
sacrifice at the end. An all-star cast makes it
palatable in this case, though the film is
inevitably dated.

w Oliver H. P. Garrett, Joseph L.
Mankiewicz, *story* Arthur Caesar d W. S.
Van Dyke ph James Wong Howe

William Powell, Clark Gable, Myrna Loy, Leo
Carrillo, Nat Pendleton, George Sidney,
Isabel Jewell, Thomas E. Jackson

† *Manhattan Melodrama* gained some irrelevant fame as the movie John Dillinger was watching when he was cornered and shot.
AA: Arthur Caesar

Maniac
GB 1963   86m   bw   Hammerscope
Columbia / Hammer (Jimmy Sangster)

Murders by oxyacetylene torch in the Camargue, with the wrong lunatic going to the asylum.
Hammer's mark two plot, the shuddery murder mystery in which someone is not quite what he seems; feebly done in this case, with a fatally slow start.

w Jimmy Sangster   *d* Michael Carreras   *ph* Wilkie Cooper

Kerwin Mathews, Donald Houston, Nadia Gray, Justine Lord

The Manitou
US 1978   104m   CFI Color
Herman Weist / Melvin Simon (William Girdler)

A fake spiritualist finds his girl friend is possessed by the demon of a 400-year-old Indian.
Boring retread of *The Exorcist*.

w William Girdler, Jon Cedar, Tom Pope, *novel* Graham Masterton   *d* William Girdler   *ph* Michel Hugo   *m* Lalo Schifrin

Tony Curtis, Susan Strasberg, Michael Ansara, Stella Stevens, Jon Cedar, Ann Sothern, Burgess Meredith, Paul Mantee

Mannequin
US 1937   95m   bw
MGM (Joseph L. Mankiewicz)

The wife of a small-time crook gets a modelling job and falls for a shipping magnate.
Competent star melodrama about a working girl's harassments.

w Lawrence Hazard   *d* Frank Borzage   *ph* George Folsey   *m* Edward Ward

Joan Crawford, Spencer Tracy, Alan Curtis, Ralph Morgan, Mary Philips, Elizabeth Risdon, Leo Gorcey

AAN: song 'Always and Always' (*m* Edward Ward, *ly* Chet Forrest, Bob Wright)

Manon*
France 1949   96m   bw
Alcina (P. E. Decharme)

After the liberation, a girl who has been a collaborator becomes involved in the black market, passes from man to man, and ends up being shot by Arabs in the Sahara desert.
Oddball modernized version of *Manon Lescaut*, with post-war pessimism and the glamour of sin going hand in hand. Worth comparing with *Gilda*.

w H. G. Clouzot, J. Ferry, *novel* L'Abbé Prévost   *d* H. G. Clouzot   *ph* Armand Thirard   *m* Paul Misraki

Michel Auclair, Cécile Aubry, Serge Reggiani, Gabrille Dorziat
'A clever idea, handled cleverly, but without depth of feeling.'—*Penelope Houston*

Manon des Sources
France 1952   190m   bw
Films Marcel Pagnol

A Provençal girl who lives in the hills with her goats is thought to be a witch, and takes her revenge on the populace by stopping the water supply.
Insanely long idyll of the countryside with the writer-director unintentionally caricaturing himself.

wd Marcel Pagnol   *ph* Willy   *m* Raymond Legrand

Jacqueline Pagnol, Raymond Péllégrin, Henri Vibert
'Something of an endurance test for all but the most enthusiastic Pagnol admirers.'—*John Gillett, MFB*

Manpower*
US 1941   103m   bw
Warner (Mark Hellinger)

Power linesmen fall out over a nightclub hostess.
Yet another variation on *Tiger Shark*, with vivid fisticuff and storm sequences supporting the star performers.

w Richard Macaulay, Jerry Wald   *d* Raoul Walsh   *ph* Ernest Haller   *m* Adolph Deutsch

Edward G. Robinson, George Raft, Marlene Dietrich, Alan Hale, Frank McHugh, Eve Arden, Barton MacLane, Walter Catlett, Joyce Compton, Ward Bond
'The pace and cutting are those of the best gangster films . . . the climax outdoes anything the Lyceum may have known.'—*William Whitebait*

Man's Castle*
US 1933   75m   bw
Columbia

Romance blooms among the unemployed who live in a shanty town on the banks of the East River.
Depression moonshine which at the time was taken for realism; sociologically very interesting but very faded as entertainment.

w Jo Swerling, *play* Lawrence Hazard
d Frank Borzage *ph* Joseph August
m W. Franke Harling

Spencer Tracy, Loretta Young, Glenda
Farrell, Walter Connolly, Arthur Hohl,
Marjorie Rambeau, Dickie Moore-
  'Heavily sentimental yet magically
romantic.'—*New Yorker, 1977*

Man's Favourite Sport?*
US 1963   120m   Technicolor
Universal / Gibraltar / Laurel (Howard
  Hawks)

A star salesman of fishing tackle finds his bluff
called when he has to enter a fishing
competition.
Over-extended romantic farce drawn by the
director from memories of older and better
films, such as *Libeled Lady* and his own
Bringing Up Baby.
w John Fenton Murray *d* Howard Hawks
ph Russell Harlan *m* Henry Mancini

Rock Hudson, Paula Prentiss, Maria Perschy,
Charlene Holt, John McGiver, Roscoe Karns
  'Hawks' deadpan documentation of a
physical gag is as effective as ever, but the
overall pace of his direction is curiously
contemplative, as though he were savoring all
his past jokes for the last time.'—*Andrew
Sarris*

Manslaughter*
US 1922   80m approx (24 fps)   bw
  silent
Paramount / Famous Players (Cecil B. de
  Mille)

An idle rich girl accidentally kills a man while
driving, and is sent to prison, but falls for the
district attorney who convicted her.
De Mille was here testing out his *Ten
Commandments* format, with a long flashback
during the DA's speech to the idle rich of
ancient Rome. It worked like a charm at the
box office.
w Jeanie McPherson, *novel* Alice Duer
Miller *d* Cecil B. de Mille *ph* Alvin Wyckoff

Leatrice Joy, Thomas Meighan, Lois Wilson,
John Miltern

† A 1930 sound remake for Paramount was
directed by George Abbott, who also tried in
vain to modernize the screenplay (by omitting
the flashback). Claudette Colbert and Fredric
March starred.

Mantrap
US 1961   93m   bw   Panavision
Paramount / Tiger (Edmond O'Brien,
  Stanley Frazen)

An honest man is lured by an old Marine
friend into a hi-jack attempt which leads to the
death of his wife.
Rather uninteresting melodrama, played and
directed for more than it's worth.
w Ed Waters, *novel* Taint of the Tiger by John
D. Macdonald *d* Edmond O'Brien *ph* Loyal
Griggs *m* Leith Stevens

Jeffrey Hunter, David Janssen, Stella Stevens,
Hugh Sanders

Manuela*
GB 1957   95m   bw
British Lion / Ivan Foxwell
US title: *Stowaway Girl*

In a South American port, the engineer of a
tramp steamer smuggles aboard a half caste
girl, but it is the disillusioned captain who falls
in love with her.
Downbeat seafaring melodrama, fine for those
seeking a mood piece.
w William Woods, from his novel *d* Guy
Hamilton *ph* Otto Heller *m* William Alwyr

Trevor Howard, Elsa Martinelli, Pedro
Armendariz, Donald Pleasence

The Manxman
GB 1929   90m (24 fps)   bw   silent
British International (John Maxwell)

A fisherman thought drowned comes back to
find that his girl is expecting his best friend's
baby.
Stern romantic melodrama of virtually no
interest despite its director.
w Eliot Stannard, *novel* Hall Caine *d* Alfred
Hitchcock *ph* Jack Cox

Carl Brisson, Malcolm Keen, Anny Ondra,
Randle Ayrton, Clare Greet
† Previously filmed in 1916 with Henry Ainley
and Elizabeth Risdon.

Many Rivers to Cross*
US 1955   94m   Eastmancolor
  Cinemascope
MGM (Jack Cummings)

A trapper bound for Canada is helped by a
sharp-shooting girl, and in return he saves her
from marauding Indians.
Simple-minded, cheerful, quite refreshing
western compounded of equal parts comedy
and action.
w Harry Brown, Guy Trosper *d* Roy
Rowland *ph* John Seitz *m* Cyril Mockridge

Robert Taylor, Eleanor Parker, Victor
McLaglen, Josephine Hutchinson, Jeff
Richards, Russ Tamblyn, James Arness, Alan
Hale Jnr

Mara Maru
US 1952 98m bw
Warner (David Weisbart)

A Manila salvage expert locates a sunken
treasure and defeats crooks who are also in
pursuit of it.
Lethargic but pleasant-looking star vehicle
with a plot borrowed from *The Maltese
Falcon.*

w N. Richard Nash, Philip Yordan, Sidney
Harmon, Hollister Noble *d* Gordon Douglas
ph Robert Burks *m* Max Steiner

Errol Flynn, Ruth Rôman, Raymond Burr,
Paul Picerni, Richard Webb

The Marat / Sade°
GB 1966 116m De Luxe
UA / Marat Sade (Michael Birkett)
aka: *The Persecution and Assassination of
Jean-Paul Marat as performed by the
inmates of the Asylum of Charenton
under the direction of the Marquis de
Sade*

The title tells all, except that at the end the
inmates go berserk.
Fairly plain filming of an Old Vic *succès
d'estime* which it became fashionable to
announce that one had seen and understood.
The film makes no effort to attract the
unbeliever.

w Adrian Mitchell, *play* Peter Weiss *d* Peter
Brook *ph* David Watkin *m* Richard Peaslee

Glenda Jackson, Patrick Magee, Ian
Richardson, Michael Williams, Robert Lloyd,
Clifford Rose, Freddie Jones

Marathon Man°°
US 1976 126m Metrocolor
Paramount (Robert Evans, Sidney
Beckerman)

A vicious Nazi returns from Uruguay to New
York in search of diamonds which had been
kept for him by his now-dead brother, and is
outwitted by the young brother of an
American agent he has killed.
Complex mystery thriller which seems to have
things to mutter about freedom and
McCarthyism and Nazism, but finally settles
down to being a simple shocker with a nick-of-
time climax. The presentation is dazzling.

w William Goldman, from his novel *d* John
Schlesinger *ph* Conrad Hall *m* Michael
Small *pd* Richard MacDonald

Dustin Hoffman, *Laurence Olivier,* Roy
Scheider, William Devane, Marthe Keller,
Fritz Weaver, Marc Lawrence
'A film of such rich texture and density in its
construction, so fascinatingly complex in its

unfolding, so engrossing in its personalities,
and so powerful in its performance and pace
that the seduction of the senses has physical
force.'—*Judith Crist, Saturday Review*

'Fashionably violent . . . distinctly self-
conscious . . . conventionally moralistic . . .
and absolutely devoid of resonance.'—*Tom
Milne, MFB*

'If at the film's end, you have followed the
series of double and triple crosses, braved the
torture scenes, and still don't know what it was
about, you're bound to have company.'—*Paul
Coleman, Film Information*

'A Jewish revenge fantasy.'—*Pauline Kael*

'He has made a most elegant, bizarre,
rococo melodrama out of material which,
when you think about it, makes hardly any
sense at all.'—*Vincent Canby, New York
Times*

AAN: Laurence Olivier

March or Die
GB 1977 107m Technicolor
ITC / Associated General (Dick Richards,
Jerry Bruckheimer)

In 1918, tensions rise at a Foreign Legion
outpost threatened by Arabs.
Incredibly old-hat romantic melodrama of the
kind that was being spoofed forty years ago.
The considerable talent involved seems
unfortunately under instruction to take it
seriously.

w David Zelag Goodman *d* Dick Richards
ph John Alcott *m* Maurice Jarre

Gene Hackman, Terence Hill, Catherine
Deneuve, Max Von Sydow, Ian Holm, Marcel
Bozzuffi

† The writer and director more successfully
revived a different set of clichés in *Farewell
My Lovely.*

Mardi Gras
US 1958 107m De Luxe Cinemascope
TCF (Jerry Wald)

In New Orleans at holiday time, a film star
falls for a cadet.
Mindless musical using up available talent.

w Winston Miller, Hal Kanter *d* Edmund
Goulding *ph* Wilfrid M. Cline *md* Lionel
Newman

Pat Boone, Christine Carere, Sheree North,
Tommy Sands, Gary Crosby, Fred Clark,
Richard Sargent, Barrie Chase

AAN: Lionel Newman

Mare Nostrum°
US 1925 approx 110m bw silent
MGM

A Spanish captain loves a German spy. Tragic romantic melodrama, a major attraction of its time.

w Willis Goldbeck, *novel* Vicente Blasco Ibanez d Rex Ingram ph John Seitz

Antonio Moreno, Alice Terry

Margie*
US 1946 94m Technicolor
TCF (Walter Morosco)

A married woman reminisces about her college days, when she married the French teacher despite her tendency to lose her bloomers at the most embarrassing moments. Wholly pleasing nostalgia, very smartly and brightly handled.

w F. Hugh Herbert, *stories* Ruth McKinney, Richard Bransten d Henry King ph Charles Clarke md Alfred Newman

Jeanne Crain, Glenn Langan, *Alan Young*, Lynn Bari, Barbara Lawrence, Conrad Janis, Esther Dale

Margin for Error*
US 1943 74m bw
TCF (Ralph Dietrich)

Just before World War II, the Nazi consul in New York is murdered in his own office. Mildly intriguing whodunnit with the case solved by a Jewish cop.

w Lillie Hayward, *play* Clare Boothe Luce d Otto Preminger ph Edward Cronjager m Leigh Harline

Milton Berle, Joan Bennett, Otto Preminger, Carl Esmond, Howard Freeman, Poldy Dur, Hans Von Twardowski

Marguerite de la Nuit*
France / Italy 1955 126m Technicolor
SNEG / Gaumont Actualités / Cino del Duca (Léon Carré)

An octogenarian signs a pact with the devil in return for his lost youth; but when he has it he causes the death of the woman he loves. Expensive, sporadically interesting, but unpersuasive updating of *Faust*.

w Ghislaine Autant-Lara, Gabriel Arout d Claude Autant-Lara ph Jacques Natteau m René Cloërc

Michèle Morgan, Yves Montand, Jean-François Calvé, Massimo Girotti

Maria Marten, or The Murder in the Red Barn
GB 1935 67m bw
George King

A wicked Victorian squire kills his pregnant mistress and is haunted.
Stilted melodrama, ripely played, from a real-life case. (The villain's scalp is still exhibited in a museum at Bury St Edmunds.)

w Randall Faye d George King ph George Stretton

Tod Slaughter, Sophie Stewart, Eric Portman, Clare Greet

† Several versions had been made in silent days.

Marie Antoinette*
US 1938 149m bw
MGM (Hunt Stromberg)

The last days of the French court before the revolution.
Too slow by half, and so glamorized and fictionalized as to lack all interest, this long delayed production stands only as an example of MGM's expensive prestige movies of the thirties.

w Claudine West, Donald Ogden Stewart, Ernest Vajda d W. S. Van Dyke ph William Daniels *montage* Slavko Vorkapitch m Herbert Stothart ad Cedric Gibbons

Norma Shearer, Tyrone Power, John Barrymore, Robert Morley, Gladys George, Anita Louise, Joseph Schildkraut, Henry Stephenson, Reginald Gardiner, Peter Bull, Albert Dekker, Cora Witherspoon, Barnett Parker, Joseph Calleia, Henry Kolker, George Zucco, Henry Daniell, Harry Davenport, Barry Fitzgerald, Mae Busch, Robert Barrat
'A resplendent bore.'—*New Yorker, 1977*

AAN: Herbert Stothart; Norma Shearer; Robert Morley

La Marie du Port
France 1949 95m bw
Sacha Gordine

A Cherbourg restaurateur takes his mistress home for her father's funeral, and falls in love with her younger sister.
Slight romantic drama, well enough put over but not very memorable except for its slightly cynical mood.

w Louis Chavance, Marcel Carné, *novel* Georges Simenon d Marcel Carné ph Henri Alekan m Joseph Kosma

Jean Gabin, Blanchette Brunoy, Nicole Courcel, Claude Romain, Louis Cseigner, Jeanne Marken, Carette

Marie Octobre
France 1958 102m bw
Orex / SF / Abbey / Doxa (Lucien Viard)
US title: *Secret Meeting*

At a reunion dinner of a wartime resistance group, a traitor is exposed and killed.
Stultifying one-set talkfest employing Hitchcock's long-discarded ten-minute take.

w Julien Duvivier, Jacques Robert, *novel* Jacques Robert *d* Julien Duvivier *ph* Robert Le Fèbvre *m* Jean Yatove *ad* Georges Wakhevitch

Danielle Darrieux, Serge Reggiani, Bernard Blier, Paul Meurisse, Noel Roquevert, Lino Ventura, Paul Guers, Paul Frankeur

Marines Let's Go
US 1961 103m De Luxe Cinemascope
TCF (Raoul Walsh)

Marines fighting in Korea are granted leave in Japan.
Brawling tragi-farce with predictable characters, a long way after *What Price Glory*.

w John Twist, *story* Raoul Walsh *d* Raoul Walsh *ph* Lucien Ballard *m* Irving Gertz

Tom Tryon, David Hedison, Tom Reese, Linda Hutchins, William Tyler
'A typically noisy, insensitive and maudlin tribute to the American Marines.'—*MFB*

Marius**
France 1931 125m bw
Marcel Pagnol / Paramount

The son of a Marseilles waterfront café owner gives up his sweetheart to go to sea.
Celebrated character drama which succeeds through the realism and vitality of its people and their dialogue.

w *Marcel Pagnol*, from his play *d* Alexander Korda *ph* Ted Pahle *m* Francis Grammon

Raimu, Pierre Fresnay, Charpin, Orane Demazis

† Two sequels with the same players and from the same pen made this a famous trilogy. In *Fanny* (1932, 128m, *d* Marc Allégret) the heroine marries an old widower to give her baby a father. In *César* (1936, 117m, *d* Marcel Pagnol) Marius comes back twenty years later and is reunited with his family.
†† *Port of Seven Seas* (MGM 1938) was a hammy and stagey Hollywood compression of the trilogy. See also *Fanny* (1960) a dull version of the stage musical, with the songs removed.

Marjorie Morningstar
US 1958 123m Warnercolor
(Warner) United States Pictures (Milton Sperling)

A New York Jewish girl has great ambitions for herself but ends up a suburban housewife.
Stodgy 'woman's picture' with all talents somewhat uneasy in their assignments, mainly because the Jewish quality is imperfectly conveyed.

w Everett Freeman, *novel* Herman Wouk *d* Irving Rapper *ph* Harry Stradling *m* Max Steiner

Natalie Wood, Gene Kelly, Claire Trevor, Everett Sloane, Ed Wynn, Martin Milner, Carolyn Jones, George Tobias, Jesse White, Martin Balsam

AAN: song 'A Very Private Love' (*m* Sammy Fain, *ly* Paul Francis Webster)

The Mark*
GB 1961 127m bw Cinemascope
TCF / Raymond Stross / Sidney Buchman

A sexual psychopath finds on emerging from prison that his past still haunts him despite the help of his psychiatrist.
Worthy but evasive social drama which outstays its welcome but provides good performances.

w Sidney Buchman, Stanley Mann *d* Guy Green *ph* Douglas Slocombe *m* Richard Rodney Bennett

Stuart Whitman, Maria Schell, *Rod Steiger*, Brenda de Banzie, Maurice Denham, Donald Wolfit, Paul Rogers, Donald Houston
'There is seriousness and care, but neither boldness nor passion . . . no hint of the truly sordid is allowed to seep through.'—*MFB*

AAN: Stuart Whitman

The Mark of Cain
GB 1947 88m bw
GFD / Two Cities (W. P. Lipscomb)

The attractive housekeeper of a Manchester businessman is blamed when his brother accidentally poisons him.
Turgid period melodrama in which few opportunities are offered and none taken.

w Francis Crowdy, Christianna Brand, W. P. Lipscomb, *novel* Airing in a Closed Carriage by Joseph Shearing *d* Brian Desmond Hurst *ph* Erwin Hillier *m* Bernard Stevens

Sally Gray, Eric Portman, Patrick Holt, Dermot Walsh, Denis O'Dea, Edward Lexy, Miles Malleson

The Mark of the Hawk
US 1958 84m Technicolor Superscope

An educated African fights for the emergence of his people by peaceful means. Well-intentioned but muddled topical drama.
Sidney Poitier, Juano Hernandez, Eartha Kitt, John McIntire. Marne Maitland, Patrick

Allen. Written by H. Kenn Carmichael;
directed by Michael Audley; for Universal-
International.

Mark of the Vampire*
US 1935 61m bw
MGM (E. J. Mannix)

A policeman tries to solve an old murder in an
eerie house by hiring vaudeville performers to
pose as vampires.
Semi-spoof horror which is flawed by lack of
pace and a patchy script, but contains splendid
visual moments. A remake of the Lon Chaney
silent, *London After Midnight*.

w Guy Endore, Bernard Schubert d Tod
Browning ph James Wong Howe

Lionel Barrymore, Jean Hersholt, Elizabeth
Allan, Bela Lugosi, Carol Borland, Lionel
Atwill, Henry Wadsworth, Donald Meek,
Jessie Ralph, Ivan Simpson, Holmes Herbert

The Mark of Zorro*
US 1920 90m (24 fps) bw silent
Douglas Fairbanks

A Mexican Robin Hood carves his initial
wherever he turns up to harass the Spanish
invaders.
A little faded now, but this swashbuckler
opened up a whole new career for its star; the
1940 version clearly has more style.

w from the novel The Curse of Capistrano by
Johnston McCulley d Fred Niblo ph William
McGann m William Perry

Douglas Fairbanks, Marguerite de la Motte,
Noah Beery

The Mark of Zorro***
US 1940 94m bw
TCF (Raymond Griffith)

After being educated in Spain, Diego de Vega
returns to California and finds the country
enslaved and his father half-corrupted by
tyrants. Disguising himself as a masked bandit,
he leads the country to expel the usurpers.
Splendid adventure stuff for boys of all ages,
an amalgam of *The Scarlet Pimpernel* and
Robin Hood to which in this version the
director adds an overwhelming pictorial sense
which makes it stand out as the finest of all.

w John Tainton Foote, Garrett Fort, Bess
Meredyth d Rouben Mamoulian ph Arthur
Miller m Alfred Newman ad Richard Day,
Joseph C. Wright

*Tyrone Power, Basil Rathbone, J. Edward
Bromberg*, Linda Darnell, Eugene Pallette,
Montagu Love, Janet Beecher, Robert
Lowery

AAN: Alfred Newman

Marked Woman*
US 1937 96m bw
Warner (Lou Edelman)

A nightclub girl is persuaded to testify against
an underworld boss.
A twist on the usual run of gangster
melodramas, performed with the star's
accustomed intensity and presented with the
studio's usual panache.

w Robert Rossen, Abem Finkel d Lloyd
Bacon ph George Barnes m Heinz
Roemheld md Leo F. Forbstein

Bette Davis, Humphrey Bogart, Jane Bryan,
Eduardo Ciannelli, Isabel Jewell, Allen
Jenkins, Mayo Methot, Lola Lane, Henry
O'Neill
† Remade as *Lady Gangster*.

Marlowe*
US 1969 95m Metrocolor
MGM / Katzka–Berne–Cherokee /
  Beckerman (Sergei Petchnikoff)

Private eye Philip Marlowe is hired by a
nervous girl to find her missing brother.
The authentic Chandler atmosphere is caught
by this busy thriller, but there seems to be a
deliberate attempt to make a confusing plot
even more obscure, so that the end result is
more tiresome than amusing.

w Stirling Silliphant, *novel* The Little Sister by
Raymond Chandler d Paul Bogart
ph William H. Daniels m Peter Matz

*James Garner, Rita Moreno, Sharon Farrell,
Bruce Lee*, Gayle Hunnicutt, Carroll
O'Connor, William Daniels, Jackie Coogan
  'One does wonder whether the simple
human squalor of the Bogart–Chandler era
can ever be recaptured by an increasingly
meretricious Hollywood.'—*MFB*

Marnie*
US 1964 130m Technicolor
Universal / Geoffrey Stanley Inc (Alfred
  Hitchcock)

A rich man marries a kleptomaniac and cures
her, but a nightmare in her past makes her still
sexually frigid.
Psychodrama with background crime and
suspense, lethargically handled by the old
master, who alone knows what he saw in it in
the first place, as this heroine does not even
have fire under her ice. The production is
curiously artificial in many ways, from dummy
horses to backcloths to back projection.

w Jay Presson Allen, *novel* Winston Graham
d Alfred Hitchcock ph Robert Burks
m Bernard Herrmann pd Robert Boyle

Tippi Hedren, Sean Connery, Martin Gabel,
Diane Baker, Louise Latham

Maroc 7

GB 1967 91m Eastmancolor
Panavision

The lady editor of a top fashion magazine
doubles as a jewel thief and becomes involved
in Moroccan intrigue. Complex sub-Bond tale
of cross and double cross; hardly worth
following, really. Gene Barry, Elsa Martinelli,
Cyd Charisse, Leslie Phillips, Denholm
Elliott, Alexandra Stewart, Eric Barker,
Angela Douglas. Written by David Osborn;
directed by Gerry O'Hara; for Cyclone /
Rank.

Marooned*

US 1969 134m Technicolor
Panavision 70

Columbia / Frankovich–Sturges (Frank
Capra Jnr)

Three astronauts are stranded in space, and a
rescue mission gets under way.
Very heavy-going space suspenser with all
possible technical accomplishment but little
life of its own.

w Mayo Simon, novel Martin Caidin d John
Sturges ph Daniel Fapp pd Lyle R. Wheeler

Gregory Peck, Richard Crenna, David
Janssen, James Franciscus, Gene Hackman,
Lee Grant, Nancy Kovack, Mariette Hartley,
Scott Brady

'In something like the plight of Ironman
One, Sturges' work seems on the point of
slowing to a standstill as it drifts further into
projects of ever-increasing, self-effacing size
and anonymous technical dexterity.'—Richard
Combs

'It has all the zip, zest and zing of a moon
walk, and I suspect a computer fed a
dictionary could come up with better
dialogue.'—Judith Crist, 1973

AAN: Daniel Fapp

The Marquise of O*

West Germany / France 1976 107m
Eastmancolor

Janus / Films du Losange

At the end of the eighteenth century, during
the Russian invasion of an Italian town, a
noblewoman finds herself pregnant . . .
Careful novella with many ambiguities, more
concerned with what might have happened
than with what did. Interesting but
exasperating.

wd Eric Rohmer, story Heinrich von Kleist
ph Nestor Almendros m Roger Delmotte

Edith Clever, Bruno Ganz, Peter Luhr, Edda
Seippel

'Some may find it slow, sentimental, naïve
and old-fashioned; others leisurely, beautiful,
controlled and illuminating. I found it both
often at the same time.'—Alan Brien, Sunday
Times

'A bold, funny story becomes a formal,
tame film, like a historical work recreated for
educational TV.'—New Yorker, 1980

The Marriage Circle**

US 1924 78m (24 fps) bw silent
Warner

A bachelor on the loose becomes amorously
involved in two marriages.
Feather-light comedy of manners which began
a whole new American school, heavily
influenced by various European masters.

w Paul Bern, play Only a Dream by Lothar
Schmidt d Ernst Lubitsch ph Charles Van
Enger

Monte Blue, Florence Vidor, Marie Prevost,
Adolphe Menjou, Creighton Hale

'A vanished world of roses, kisses and
embraces, of whispers and sighs, of a woman's
shadowed arm encased in georgette beckoning
across a moonlit garden . . . and hand-kissing
all over the place.'—Herman G. Weinberg

'At once perfect cinematography and
perfect conventional drama.'—Iris Barry, The
Spectator

'So slim a plot, so hackneyed if you will, is
told with gaiety and a wit that lift it into the
very first rank of screen comedy.'—National
Board of Review

† Remade as One Hour with You, also by
Lubitsch.

The Marriage Go Round

US 1961 98m De Luxe Cinemascope
TCF (Leslie Stevens)

A Swedish girl suggests to a married American
professor that she borrow his body for mating
purposes, believing they would produce the
perfect child.
Silly, unfunny sex comedy.

w Leslie Stevens d Walter Lang ph Leo
Tover m Dominic Frontière

James Mason, Susan Hayward, Julie Newmar,
Robert Paige, June Clayworth

'As tedious as it is tasteless.'—Evening
Standard

'It offers James Mason, an actor who
couldn't crack a joke if it was a lichee nut, and
Susan Hayward, a bargain basement Bette
Davis whose lightest touch as a comedienne
would stun a horse.'—Time

Marriage Is a Private Affair
US 1943   116m   bw
MGM (Pandro S. Berman)

A spoilt rich girl becomes a petulant wife.
Abysmally slow, uninvolving and poorly acted
star fodder.

w David Hertz, Lenore Coffee, *novel* Judith
Kelly   d Robert Z. Leonard   ph Ray June
m Bronislau Kaper

Lana Turner, James Craig, John Hodiak,
Frances Gifford, Keenan Wynn, Natalie
Schaefer, Hugh Marlowe, Paul Cavanagh

The Marriage of a Young Stockbroker**
US 1971   95m   De Luxe
TCF / Laurence Turman

A stockbroker who finds his life and his
marriage dull tries voyeurism and extra-
marital sex.
Sardonic adult comedy of the battle between
the sexes, pretty lively from start to finish.

w *Lorenzo Semple Jnr, novel* Charles Webb
d Laurence Turman   ph Laszlo Kovacs
m Fred Karlin

Richard Benjamin, Joanna Shimkus, Elizabeth
Ashley, Adam West, Patricia Barry

The Marriage of Corbal
GB 1936   93m   bw

Before the French revolution, an aristocratic
lady tries to escape disaster by the right
marriage. Stilted adventure story with too
much talk. Nils Asther, Hugh Sinclair, Hazel
Terry, Noah Beery, Davy Burnaby. Written
by S. Fullman, from the novel *The Nuptials of
Corbal* by Rafael Sabatini; directed by Karl
Grune; for Capitol.

The Marriage of Maria Braun*
West Germany 1978   119m   Fujicolor
Albatros / Trio / WDR / FdA (Michael
Fengler)

Vicissitudes of a post-war bride who is
eventually blown up in a gas explosion.
A mixture of solemnity and irony which keeps
its basic points well concealed but, despite a
sometimes flagging pace, more or less
consistently entertains the eye.

w Peter Märthesheimer, Pea Fröhloch
d Rainer Werner Fassbinder   ph Michael
Ballhaus   m Peer Raben

Hanna Schygulla, Klaus Lowitsch, Ivan
Desny, Gottfried John

Marriage on the Rocks
US 1965   109m   Technicolor
Panavision
Warner / A-C / Sinatra (William H. Daniels)

An ad man and his wife decide to go to
Mexico for a divorce but once there change
their minds; she ends up accidentally married
to his best friend.
All this talent retreats fearfully from a witless,
tasteless script and slow handling. A dismal
comedy.

w Cy Howard   d Jack Donohue   ph William
H. Daniels   m Nelson Riddle

Frank Sinatra, Dean Martin, Deborah Kerr,
Cesar Romero, Hermione Baddeley, Tony
Bill, Nancy Sinatra, John McGiver

'A long, coarse, and nearly always unfunny
comedy, hammered together for no apparent
reason except to make money.'—*New Yorker*

The Marriage Playground
US 1929   70m   bw
Paramount

Children of divorced rich parents wander
round Europe in a group.
Slightly unusual drama of its day; sound
technique very thin.

w J. Walter Rubin, Doris Anderson, *novel*
The Children by Edith Wharton   d Lothar
Mendes   ph Victor Milner

Fredric March, Kay Francis, Mary Brian,
Lilyan Tashman, Huntley Gordon, Anita
Louise

Marry Me
GB 1949   97m   bw
GFD / Gainsborough (Betty Box)

Four stories of a marriage bureau.
A styleless portmanteau of anecdotes put over
by a clear second team.

w Lewis Gilbert, Denis Waldock   d Terence
Fisher   ph Ray Elton   d Clifton Parker

Derek Bond, Susan Shaw, Patrick Holt, Carol
Marsh, David Tomlinson, Zena Marshall, Guy
Middleton, Nora Swinburne, Jean Cadell,
Mary Jerrold

The Marrying Kind*
US 1952   93m   bw
Columbia (Bert Granet)

A couple seeking divorce tell their troubles to
a judge, and change their minds.
Smart, New Yorkish, tragi-comic star vehicle
which works pretty well.

w Ruth Gordon, Garson Kanin   d George
Cukor   ph Joseph Walker   m Hugo Friedhofer
Judy Holliday, Aldo Ray, Madge Kennedy,
Mickey Shaughnessy

La Marseillaise*
France 1937   145m   bw
Films La Marseillaise (Jean Renoir)

The story of the French revolution of 1789.
A rather disconnected epic which, despite a
few splendid scenes, never moved its
audiences to enthusiasm.

wd Jean Renoir *ph* Jean Bourgoin and
others *md* Joseph Kosma

Pierre Renoir, Lise Delemare, Louis Jouvet,
Leon Larive, Georges Spanelly, Elisa Ruis,
William Aguet

The Marseilles Contract
GB / France 1974   89m   Eastmancolor
Warner / AIP / Kettledrum / PECF (Judd
   Bernard)
US title: *The Destructors*

An American narcotics agent in Paris hires an
assassin to dispose of a drug smuggler.
Routine action melodrama with a jokey
atmosphere not sustained by a downbeat
script.

w Judd Bernard *d* Robert Parrish *ph*
Douglas Slocombe *m* Roy Budd

Michael Caine, Anthony Quinn, James
Mason, Alexandra Stewart, Marcel Bozzufi,
Maurice Ronet

Martin Luther*
US / Germany 1953   114m   bw
Louis De Rochemont / Lutheran Church
   Productions (Lothar Wolff)

The career and doubts of Martin Luther.
Frequently vivid, occasionally boring, small-
scale account of the first Protestant.

w Allan Sloane, Lothar Wolff, others *d* Irving
Pichel *ph* Joseph C. Brun *m* Mark Lothar

Niall MacGinnis, John Ruddock, Pierre
Lefèvre, Guy Verney, David Horne, Philip
Leaver, Irving Pichel, Alexander Gauge

AAN: Joseph C. Brun

Martin Roumagnac
France 1946   99m   bw
Alcina (Marc Le Pelletier)

The trial, with flashbacks, of a small-town
businessman who has murdered his mistress.
Wholly unabsorbing and ordinary story of a
crime passionnel, totally wasting its stars.

wd Georges Lacombe *ph* Roger Hubert
m Marcel Mirouze

Jean Gabin, Marlene Dietrich, Margo Lion,
Marcel Hérrand

Marty****
US 1955   91m   bw
UA / Hecht–Hill–Lancaster (Harold Hecht)

A 34-year-old Brooklyn butcher fears he will
never get a girl because he is unattractive, but

at a Saturday night dance he meets a girl with
similar fears. Unfortunately she is not
Italian . . .
The first of the filmed teleplays which in the
mid-fifties seemed like a breath of spring to
Hollywood (they were cheap) and also
brought in a new wave of talent. This is one of
the best, its new naturalistic dialogue falling
happily on the ear; but it has been so
frequently imitated since that its revolutionary
appearance is hard to imagine.

w Paddy Chayevsky, from his play *d Delbert
Mann ph Joseph La Shelle m* Roy Webb

*Ernest Borgnine, Betsy Blair, Esther Minciotti,
Joe Mantell*, Karen Steele, Jerry Paris

   'Something rare in the American cinema
today: a subtle, ironic and compassionate
study of ordinary human relationships.'—
Gavin Lambert

AA: best picture; Paddy Chayevsky; Delbert
Mann; Ernest Borgnine
AAN: Joseph La Shelle; Betsy Blair; Joe
Mantell

Mary Burns Fugitive*
US 1935   84m   bw
Paramount (Walter Wanger)

The innocent girl friend of a gangster is
convicted through circumstantial evidence,
escapes from prison and finds true love.
Competent meshing of well-tried thirties
elements, a good typical wish-fulfilment
melodrama of its time.

w Gene Towne, Graham Baker, Louis
Stevens *d* William K. Howard *ph* Leon
Shamroy

Sylvia Sidney, Melvyn Douglas, Alan Baxter,
Pert Kelton, Wallace Ford, Brian Donlevy,
Esther Dale

Mary Mary
US 1963   126m   Technicolor
Warner (Mervyn Le Roy)

A publisher falls in love again with his ex-wife
but finds she is being pursued by a film star.
Feeble film version of a lighter-than-air
Broadway success, with the actors paralysed
behind the footlights and the camera asleep in
the stalls.

w Richard L. Breen, *play* Jean Kerr
d Mervyn Le Roy *ph* Harry Stradling
m Frank Perkins

Debbie Reynolds, Barry Nelson, Michael
Rennie, Diane McBain

Mary of Scotland*
US 1936   123m   bw
RKO (Pandro S. Berman)

Mary Stuart refuses to give up her claim to the English throne, and is eventually executed. Sombre historical charade with splendid sets and atmosphere but suffering from script and performances that don't quite make it despite effort all round.

w Dudley Nichols, *play* Maxwell Anderson d John Ford *ph Joseph H. August* m Nathaniel Shilkret *ad Van Nest Polglase, Carroll Clark*

Katharine Hepburn, Fredric March, Donald Crisp, Florence Eldridge, Douglas Walton, John Carradine, Robert Barrat, Monte Blue, Moroni Olsen, Frieda Inescort, Alan Mowbray

'An unpromising and stagey play is fleshed out into a rich and confident exercise in filmcraft.'—*John Baxter, 1968*

'Events are walked through as though they were rooms in a museum, and closing time at three.'—*Otis Ferguson*

Mary Poppins***
US 1964 139m Technicolor
Walt Disney (Bill Walsh)

In Edwardian London a magical nanny teaches two slightly naughty children to make life enjoyable for themselves and others.
Sporadically a very pleasant and effective entertainment for children of all ages, with plenty of brightness and charm including magic tricks, the mixing of live with cartoon adventures, and just plain fun. It suffers, however, from a wandering narrative in the second half (when Miss Poppins scarcely appears) and from Mr Van Dyke's really lamentable attempt at Cockney.

w Bill Walsh, Don da Gradi, *novel* P. L. Travers d Robert Stevenson *ph* Edward Colman *m / ly Richard M. and Robert B. Sherman. pd* Tony Walton *sp Eustace Lycett, Peter Ellenshaw, Robert A. Mattey*

Julie Andrews, David Tomlinson, Glynis Johns, Dick Van Dyke, Reginald Owen, Ed Wynn, Matthew Garber, Karen Dotrice, Hermione Baddeley, Elsa Lanchester, Arthur Treacher, Jane Darwell

AA: Richard M. and Robert B. Sherman; Julie Andrews; song 'Chim Chim Cheree' AAN: best picture; script; Robert Stevenson; Edward Colman

Mary Queen of Scots
GB 1971 128m Technicolor
Panavision
Universal / Hal B. Wallis

The story of Mary Stuart's opposition to Elizabeth I, her imprisonment and execution.

Schoolbook history in which none of the characters comes to life; dramatic movement is almost entirely lacking despite the liberties taken with fact.

w John Hale *ph* Christopher Challis d Charles Jarrott *m* John Barry

Vanessa Redgrave, Glenda Jackson, Trevor Howard, Patrick McGoohan, Nigel Davenport

AAN: John Barry; Vanessa Redgrave

M*A*S*H***
US 1970 116m De Luxe Panavision
TCF / Aspen (Ingo Preminger, Leon Ericksen)

Surgeons at a mobile hospital in Korea spend what spare time they have chasing women and bucking authority.
Savage comedy of man's rebellion in the face of death, alternating sex farce with gory operation scenes; hailed as the great anti-everything film, and certainly very funny for those who can take it. It led to a television series which for once did not disgrace its original.

w Ring Lardner Jnr, *novel* Richard Hooker d Robert Altman *ph* Harold E. Stine m Johnny Mandel

Donald Sutherland, Elliott Gould, Tom Skerritt, Sally Kellerman, Robert Duvall, Jo Ann Pflug, René Auberjonois, Gary Burghof

'Bloody funny. A hyper-acute wiretap on mankind's death wish.'—*Joseph Morgenstern*

'The laughter is blood-soaked and the comedy cloaks a bitter and terrible truth.'—*Judith Crist*

'A foul-mouthed, raucous, anti-establishment comedy, combining gallows humour, sexual slapstick and outrageous satire.'—*Les Keyser, Hollywood in the Seventies*

AA: Ring Lardner Jnr
AAN: best picture; Robert Altman; Sally Kellerman

The Mask of Dijon
US 1946 73m bw

A conjuror becomes obsessed by hypnotism and takes to murder to prove his superiority. Heavy-going thriller with little discernible point. Erich Von Stroheim, Jeanne Bates, William Wright. Written by Arthur St Claire and Griffin Jay; directed by Lew Landers; for PRC.

The Mask of Dimitrios***
US 1944 99m bw
Warner (Henry Blanke)

A timid Dutch novelist is drawn into a Middle-Eastern intrigue with money at the centre of it.
Generally successful international intriguer, moodily shot in evocative sets, and remarkable for its time in that the story is not distorted to fit romantic stars: character actors bear the entire burden.

. w Frank Gruber, novel Eric Ambler d Jean Negulesco ph Arthur Edeson m Adolph Deutsch

Peter Lorre, Sidney Greenstreet, Zachary Scott, Faye Emerson, Victor Francen, Steven Geray, Florence Bates, Eduardo Ciannelli, Kurt Katch, John Abbott, Monte Blue

The Mask of Fu Manchu**
US 1932 70m bw
MGM

Nayland Smith and his party are caught and threatened with torture by the yellow terror. Highly satisfactory episode in the nefarious adventures of the master criminal, fast moving, humorous and very good to look at.

w John Willard, Edgar Woolf, Irene Kuhn, stories Sax Rohmer d Charles Brabin, Charles Vidor ph Tony Gaudio

Boris Karloff, Myrna Loy, Lewis Stone, Karen Morley, Charles Starrett, Jean Hersholt, Lawrence Grant

Mask of the Avenger
US 1951 83m Technicolor

During the Austro-Italian War, a count's son avenges his father's death and exposes a traitor. Very moderate swashbuckler on the lines of The Mark of Zorro. John Derek, Anthony Quinn, Jody Lawrence, Arnold Moss, Eugene Iglesias. Written by Jesse Lasky Jnr; directed by Phil Karlson; for Hunt Stromberg / Columbia.

Maskerade*
Austria 1935 87m bw

An inveterate ladies' man finds himself trapped. Charming romantic comedy. Anton Walbrook, Paula Wesseley, Olga Tscheshowa. Written and directed by Willi Forst; for Tobis / Sascha.

The Masque of the Red Death**
GB 1964 89m Pathecolor 'Scope
AIP / Alta Vista (George Willoughby)

A medieval Italian prince practises devil worship while the plague rages outside, but when he holds a ball, death is an uninvited guest.

Languorous, overstretched, often visually striking horror piece with some extremely effective touches among its longueurs.

w Charles Beaumont, R. Wright Campbell, story Edgar Allan Poe d Roger Corman ph Nicolas Roeg m David Lee ad Robert Jones costumes Laura Nightingale

Vincent Price, Hazel Court, Jane Asher, Patrick Magee, John Westbrook

Masquerade*
GB 1965 101m Eastmancolor
UA / Novus (Michael Relph)

To avert friction between Arab states the young heir to one of them is abducted by a British secret service agent; but one of the plotters has other fish to fry.
Quite a lively spy romp with a spectacular action climax, but the plot is simply too complicated.

w Michael Relph, William Goldman, novel Castle Minerva by Victor Canning d Basil Dearden ph Otto Heller m Philip Green pd Don Ashton

Cliff Robertson, Jack Hawkins, Charles Gray, Bill Fraser, Marisa Mell, Michel Piccoli, John Le Mesurier

Masquerade in Mexico
US 1945 96m bw
Paramount (Karl Tunberg)

A stranded showgirl is hired by a Mexican banker to entice a gigolo away from his wife. Talent-starved remake of Midnight (qv), which seems second-hand even if you don't know why.

w Karl Tunberg d Mitchell Leisen ph Lionel Lindon m Victor Young

Dorothy Lamour, Arturo de Cordova, Patric Knowles, Ann Dvorak, George Rigaud, Natalie Schafer, Mikhail Rasumny, Billy Daniels

The Master Gunfighter
US 1975 120m Metrocolor Panavision

In gold rush California, a mysterious avenger rights a variety of wrongs. Pretentious western which failed to advance the career of its somewhat over-confident creator. Tom Laughlin, Ron O'Neal, Lincoln Kilpatrick, Barbara Carrera. Written by Harold Lapland, from a Japanese film Goyokin written by Kei Tasaka and Hideo Gosha; directed by Tom Laughlin; for Avondale / Warner.

The Master of Ballantrae
GB 1953 89m Technicolor
Warner

Two brothers toss to decide which shall join Bonnie Prince Charlie's 1745 rebellion. Half-hearted version of a classic adventure novel.

w Herb Meadow, *novel* R. L. Stevenson *d* William Keighley *ph* Jack Cardiff *m* William Alwyn

Errol Flynn, Anthony Steel, Roger Livesey, Beatrice Campbell, Felix Aylmer, Mervyn Johns, Jacques Berthier, Yvonne Furneaux, Ralph Truman

'All that can be salvaged from this rather unforgivable Anglo-American junket are some pleasant exteriors.'—*Gavin Lambert*

Master of Bankdam°
GB 1947 105m bw
GFD / Holbein (Nat Bronsten, Walter Forde, Edward Dryhurst)

19th-century chronicles of a mill-owning Yorkshire family.
Archetypal 'trouble at t'mill' saga with moderate production, good acting and undeniably compulsive story.

w Edward Dryhurst, Moie Charles, *novel* Thomas Armstrong *d* Walter Forde *ph* Basil Emmott

Tom Walls, Anne Crawford, Dennis Price, Stephen Murray, Linden Travers, Jimmy Hanley, Nancy Price, David Tomlinson, Herbert Lomas

Master of the World
US 1961 104m Magnacolor
AIP / Alta Vista (James H. Nicholson, Anthony Carras)

In 1848 a mad inventor takes to the air in his magnificent flying machine in the hope of persuading men to stop war.
Aerial version of *Twenty Thousand Leagues under the Sea*, with cheap sets and much use of stock footage; some scenes however have a certain vigour.

w Richard Matheson, *novels* Jules Verne *d* William Witney *ph* Gil Warrenton *m* Les Baxter

Vincent Price, Charles Bronson, Henry Hull, Mary Webster, David Frankham

Masterson of Kansas
US 1955 73m Technicolor

The sheriff of Dodge City prevents an Indian uprising by saving an innocent man from the gallows. Unhistorical two-bit western. George Montgomery, Nancy Gates, James Griffith, Jean Willes. Written by Douglas Heyes; directed by William Castle; for Sam Katzman / Columbia.

Mata Hari°°
US 1932 92m bw
MGM

The career of the famous lady spy of World War I.
Elaborate melodrama, pictorially satisfying and generally more entertaining than might be supposed, with both star and supporting cast in rich thespian form.

w Benjamin Glazer, Leo Birinski, Doris Anderson, Gilbert Emery *d George Fitzmaurice ph* William Daniels

Greta Garbo, Ramon Novarro, Lionel Barrymore, Lewis Stone, C. Henry Gordon, Karen Morley, Blanche Frederici

The Match King
US 1932 80m bw

A world-famous match manufacturer gets into spectacular money difficulties. Thinly veiled biopic of Ivar Kreuger; not at all bad. *Warren William*, Lili Damita, Glenda Farrell, Harold Huber. Written by Houston Branch and Sidney Sutherland; directed by Howard Bretherton; for Warner.

The Matchmaker°
US 1958 101m bw Vistavision
Paramount (Don Hartman)

In New York at the turn of the century, a rich merchant decides to marry again but the matchmaker he consults has her own eye on him.
Cold and lifeless version of an amusing play which also served as the basis for the musical *Hello Dolly* (qv).

w John Michael Hayes, *play* Thornton Wilder *d* Joseph Anthony *ph* Charles Lang *m* Adolph Deutsch

Shirley Booth, Paul Ford, Anthony Perkins, Shirley Maclaine, Wallace Ford, Robert Morse, Perry Wilson

'Long static dialogue exchanges are further extended by frequent confidences expressed directly to the audience . . . but in spite of the general lack of pace, lightness and dimension there is still a great deal to enjoy.'—*Peter John Dyer*

Matilda
US 1978 105m Movielab
AIP / Albert S. Ruddy

A down-at-heel theatrical agent finds success with a boxing kangaroo.
Damon Runyon meets Walt Disney in an old-fashioned family audience picture for which there may no longer be an audience.

w Albert S. Ruddy, Timothy Galfas, *novel*
Paul Gallico *d* Daniel Mann *ph* Jack Woolf
pd Boris Leven

Elliott Gould, Robert Mitchum, Harry
Guardino, Clive Revill, Karen Carlson, Lionel
Stander, Art Metrano, Roy Clark

La Maternelle*
France 1932 89m bw
Photosonor

A maid in a nursery school becomes devoted
to the children and in particular to one who
causes trouble when her friend decides to
marry.
A touching drama of its day which now seems
rather primitive.

w Jean Benoit-Lévy *d* Jean Benoit-Lévy,
Marie Epstein *ph* Georges Asselin
m Edouard Flament

Madeleine Renaud, Paulette Elambert, Alice
Tissot, Mady Berry

The Mating Game
US 1959 96m Metrocolor
  Cinemascope
MGM (Philip Barry Jnr)

An income-tax inspector becomes involved in
the affairs of an unorthodox farming family.
Dismally unfunny adaptation for Americans of
a very English novel; everyone works hard to
no avail.

w William Roberts, *novel* The Darling Buds of
May by H. E. Bates *d* George Marshall
ph Robert Bronner *m* Jeff Alexander

Debbie Reynolds, Tony Randall, Paul
Douglas, Fred Clark, Una Merkel, Philip
Ober, Charles Lane, Philip Coolidge

'Every joke is driven past the point of
exhaustion.'—*MFB*

The Mating of Millie
US 1948 87m bw

A self-confident young woman wants to adopt
a small boy and tries to propel a bus driver
into a marriage of convenience. Amiable if
protracted romantic comedy with dashes of
sentiment and an obvious outcome. Glenn
Ford, Evelyn Keyes, Willard Parker, Jimmy
Hunt, Ron Randell. Written by Louella
MacFarlane and St Clair McKelway; directed
by Henry Levin; for Columbia.

The Mating Season
US 1950 101m bw
Paramount (Charles Brackett)

A factory draughtsman marries an
ambassador's daughter; his mother loses her
job and comes incognito to work for them as a
cook.

Uninteresting mechanical domestic comedy in
which the young folk are dull and the older
ones overplay.

w Walter Reisch, Charles Brackett, Richard
Breen *d* Mitchell Leisen *ph* Charles Lang

Gene Tierney, John Lund, Miriam Hopkins,
Thelma Ritter, Jan Sterling

AAN: Thelma Ritter

A Matter of Dignity*
Greece 1957 104m bw
Finos (Anis Nohra)
original title: *To Telefteo Psemma*

The daughter of a bankrupt family reluctantly
agrees to marry a millionaire, and the family's
false values lead to tragedy.
Rather offbeat melodrama with the director in
good form.

wd Michael Cacoyannis *ph* Walter Lassally
m Manos Hadjidakis

Ellie Lambetti, Georges Pappas, Athena
Michaelidou

A Matter of Life and Death****
GB 1946 104m Technicolor
GFD / Archers (Michael Powell, Emeric
  Pressburger)
US title: *Stairway to Heaven*

A pilot with brain damage after bailing out is
torn between this world and the next, but an
operation puts things to rights.
Outrageous fantasy which seemed more in
keeping after the huge death toll of a world
war, and in any case learned the Hollywood
lesson of eating its cake and still having it, the
supernatural elements being capable of
explanation. A mammoth technical job in the
heavenly sequences, it deserves full marks for
its sheer arrogance, wit, style and film flair.

wd Michael Powell, Emeric Pressburger
ph Jack Cardiff *m* Allan Gray *pd* Hein
Heckroth

*David Niven, Roger Livesey, Kim Hunter,
Marius Goring, Raymond Massey, Abraham
Sofaer*

'Powell and Pressburger seem to have
reached their heaven at last . . . an illimitable
Wembley stadium, surrounded by tinkly music
and mists, from which all men of insight, if
they were ever careless enough to get there,
would quickly blaspheme their way out.'—
Richard Winnington

'A dazzling mesh of visionary satire, post-
war politics and the mystical side of English
romanticism.'—*Tony Rayns, Time Out, 1979*

'Beautifully written, beautifully acted,
beautifully executed . . . you would think such

formidable merits would add up to quite a film—and darned if they don't.'—*Time Out*

'This film, whether or not you find its philosophy half-baked, is downright good cinema, doing things that couldn't be done in any other medium'—*Tribune*

'It compelled attention and created emotion.'—*Basil Wright, 1972*

A Matter of Time
US / Italy 1976   97m (originally 165m) Technicolor
(AIP) Jack H. Skirball, J. Edmund Grainger

An Italian country chambermaid is taught about life by a faded countess.
Interminable even in its abbreviated form, this woebegone fantasy is a tribute to his miscast daughter by a director who never had much sense of plot to begin with. It has to be seen to be believed.

w John Gay, *novel* The Film of Memory by Maurice Druon *d* Vincente Minnelli
ph Geoffrey Unsworth *m* Nino Oliviero

Liza Minnelli, Ingrid Bergman, Charles Boyer, Tina Aumont, Gabriele Ferzetti, Spiros Andros

'So hackneyed, inept and stupid as to be almost amusing.'—*John Simon, New York*

'So spectacularly crazy that if Minnelli could only persuade Mel Brooks to put his name on it, *A Matter of Time* might yet be the comedy sleeper of the year.'—*Frank Rich, New York Post*

A Matter of Who
GB 1961   92m   bw
MGM / Foray (Walter Shenson, Milton Holmes)

The World Health Organization tracks down a smallpox outbreak.
Curious blend of semi-documentary with suspense and comedy; not really a starter.

w Milton Holmes *d* Don Chaffey *ph* Erwin Hillier *m* Edwin Astley

Terry-Thomas, Sonja Ziemann, Alex Nicol, Guy Deghy, Richard Briers, Clive Morton, Geoffrey Keen, Martin Benson, Honor Blackman, Carol White

The Maverick Queen
US 1955   90m   Trucolor   Naturama

A lady rustler falls for a Pinkerton detective sent to arrest her. Tedious western in bilious colour. Barbara Stanwyck, Barry Sullivan, Scott Brady, Mary Murphy, Wallace Ford, Jim Davis. Written by Kenneth Gamet and DeVallon Scott, from the novel by Zane Grey; directed by Joe Kane; for Republic.

Maya
US 1966   91m   Technicolor   Panavision
MGM / King Brothers (Mary P. Murray, Herman King)

A teenage American boy arrives in India to visit his disillusioned father, who finally comes to understand him only after he has run away. Good-looking but otherwise uninteresting animal drama which served as the pilot for a TV series.

w John Fante *d* John Berry *ph* Gunter Senftleben *m* Riz Ortolani

Clint Walker, Jay North, I. S. Johar, Sajid Kahn

Mayerling
France / GB 1968   141m   Eastmancolor Panavision
Corona / Winchester (Robert Dorfmann)

In 1888 the heir to the Habsburg Empire is forced into a suicide pact with his mistress. Tedious dramatization of historical events which in 1936 had made a delicate French film but in these hands seems an endless and boring manipulation of doubtful events into turgid romance.

wd Terence Young, *novel* Claude Anet
ph Henri Alekan *m* Francis Lai *pd* Georges Wakhevitch

Omar Sharif, Catherine Deneuve, James Mason, Ava Gardner, James Robertson Justice, Genevieve Page, Ivan Desny, Maurice Teynac

The Mayor of 44th Street
US 1942   86m   bw
RKO (Cliff Reid)

Dance bands are threatened by hooligans demanding protection money.
Boring melodrama with music.

w Lewis R. Foster *d* Alfred E. Green
ph Robert de Grasse *songs* Mort Greene, Harry Revel

George Murphy, Anne Shirley, Richard Barthelmess, William Gargan, Joan Merrill, Millard Mitchell, Mary Wickes, Freddie Martin and band

AAN: song 'There's a Breeze on Lake Louise'

The Mayor of Hell*
US 1933   90m   bw
Warner

A racketeer becomes superintendent of a reform school, and it changes his life.
Moderate star vehicle with a plot that did yeoman service thereafter in Dead End Kids films.

w Edward Chodorov *d* Archie Mayo *ph* Barney McGill *m* Leo F. Forbstein

James Cagney, Madge Evans, Allen Jenkins, Dudley Digges, Frankie Darro

'Propaganda for nothing: like most of what comes out of Hollywood, it is entertaining trash.'—*Time*

† Remade in 1938 as *Crime School* with Humphrey Bogart, 1939 as *Hell's Kitchen* with Ronald Reagan.

Maytime**
US 1937 132m bw (sepia sequence) MGM (Hunt Stromberg)

An opera star falls in love with a penniless singer but her jealous impresario shoots him. Lush romantic musical which turns gradually into melodrama and ends in a ghostly reunion for the lovers. If that's what you like, it could scarcely be better done.

w Noel Langley, *operetta* Rida Johnson Young *d* Robert Z. Leonard *ph* Oliver T. Marsh *m* Sigmund Romberg *md* Herbert Stothart

Jeanette MacDonald, Nelson Eddy, John Barrymore, Herman Bing, Lynne Carver, Rafaela Ottiano, Paul Porcasi, Sig Rumann
† Shooting had begun in colour with Frank Morgan in Bing's part and Paul Lukas in Barrymore's; this footage, directed by Edmund Goulding, was abandoned on Irving Thalberg's death.

AAN: Herbert Stothart

The Maze
US 1953 81m bw 3-D Allied Artists (Richard Heermance)

The heir to a title also inherits a family curse and turns into a giant frog. Rather splendidly idiotic horror film which raises plenty of laughs but no frissons.

w Dan Ullman, *story* Maurice Sandoz *d* William Cameron Menzies *ph* Harry Neumann *m* Marlin Skiles

Richard Carlson, Veronica Hurst, Katherine Emery, Michael Pate, Lillian Bond, Hillary Brooke, Owen McGiveney

Me and Marlborough*
GB 1935 84m bw GFD / Gainsborough (Michael Balcon)

In Marlborough's army, a woman takes the place of her soldier husband to prove his innocence of spying. Curious period service farce, not quite a success but an interesting attempt at something different.

w Ian Hay, Marjorie Gaffney, *story* W. P. Lipscomb, Reginald Pound *d* Victor Saville

Cicely Courtneidge, Tom Walls, Barry McKay, Alfred Drayton

Me and My Gal*
US 1932 79m bw Fox
GB title: *Pier 13*

A cop on the beat romances a hashslinger and catches a crook. Pleasant little programmer, very evocative of its period.

w Arthur Kober *d* Raoul Walsh *ph* Arthur Miller

Spencer Tracy, Joan Bennett, George Walsh, Marion Burns, J. Farrell MacDonald, Noel Madison, Henry B. Walthall
† Remade in 1949 as *Pier 13*.

Me and My Pal*
US 1933 20m bw

Ollie becomes engrossed in a jigsaw puzzle and forgets to get married. Oddball star comedy which nearly comes off but simply doesn't provide enough jokes. Laurel and Hardy, James Finlayson, Eddie Dunn. Written by Stan Laurel; directed by Charles Rogers and Lloyd French; for Hal Roach.

Me and the Colonel
US 1958 110m bw Columbia / Court–Goetz (William Goetz)

In 1940 an anti-semitic Polish colonel is obliged to flee from France in the company of a Jewish refugee. Rather obvious war comedy with predictable but not very entertaining situations, sentiment, action and pathos. The stars cope well enough but the picture never picks up steam.

w S. N. Behrman, George Froeschel, *play* Franz Werfel *d* Peter Glenville *ph* Burnett Guffey *m* George Duning

Danny Kaye, Curt Jurgens, Nicole Maurey, Françoise Rosay, Akim Tamiroff, Martita Hunt, Alexander Scourby, Liliane Montevecchi, Ludwig Stossel

Me, Natalie*
US 1969 111m De Luxe Cinema Center (Stanley Shapiro)

An unattractive 18-year-old girl moves into Greenwich Village and learns to accept herself as she is. Basically very predictable but rather well done character study with excellent detail.

w A. Martin Zweiback *d* Fred Coe *ph* Arthur J. Ornitz *m* Henry Mancini

Patty Duke, James Farentino, Martin Balsam, Elsa Lanchester, Salome Jens, Nancy Marchand, Al Pacino

Mean Streets**
US 1973 110m Technicolor
Taplin–Perry–Scorsese (Jonathan T. Taplin)

Four young Italian-Americans use Tony's Bar as a base for drinking, brawling and hustling. Relentlessly sordid melodrama with a good eye for realistic detail.

w Martin Scorsese, Mardik Martin d Martin Scorsese ph Norman Gerard

Harvey Keitel, Robert de Niro, David Proval, Amy Robinson, Richard Romanus

'A thicker-textured rot than we have ever had in an American movie, and a deeper sense of evil.'—New Yorker

'Lacks a sense of story and structure . . . unless a film-maker respects the needs of his audience, he can't complain if that audience fails to show up.'—Variety

'Extraordinarily rich and distinguished on many levels.'—Joseph Gelmis

The Meanest Man in the World
US 1943 57m bw

An easy-going small-town lawyer finds that business picks up when he becomes tough and mean. Very minor star comedy with a muddled opening followed by strictly rationed laughs. Jack Benny, Priscilla Lane, Rochester, Edmund Gwenn, Anne Revere. Written by George Seaton and Allan House, from a play by George M. Cohan; directed by Sidney Lanfield; for TCF.

The Mechanic
US 1972 100m Technicolor
UA / Chartoff / Winkler / Carlino
reissue title: Killer of Killers

A professional assassin under contract to the Mafia makes his missions look like accidents. Violent thriller with a few pretensions, but too flashily made to be taken seriously.

w Lewis John Carlino d Michael Winner ph Richard Kline, Robert Paynter m Jerry Fielding

Charles Bronson, Jan-Michael Vincent, Keenan Wynn, Jill Ireland

A Medal for Benny*
US 1945 77m bw
Paramount (Paul Jones)

An old rustic is the centre of small town celebrations in honour of his dead war hero son.

Satirical-sentimental location drama, effective but not memorable.

w Frank Butler, original story John Steinbeck, Jack Wagner d Irving Pichel ph Lionel Lindon m Victor Young

Dorothy Lamour, Arturo de Cordova, J. Carrol Naish, Mikhail Rasumny, Charles Dingle, Frank McHugh, Grant Mitchell

AAN: original story; J. Carrol Naish

Medal for the General
GB 1944 99m bw

An old general takes in evacuees and finds a new interest in life. Uneventful character drama which seemed mildly pleasing at the time. Godfrey Tearle, Jeanne de Casalis, Morland Graham, Mabel Constanduros, John Laurie, Petula Clark. Written by Elizabeth Baron, from the novel by James Ronald; directed by Maurice Elvey; for British National.

Medea*
Italy / France / West Germany 1970
118m Eastmancolor
San Marco / Number One / Janus (Franco Rossellini, Marina Cicogna)

Jason brings back as his wife the high priestess of the Golden Fleece, but her adjustment is to say the least uncomfortable.
In modern terms the case history of a psychopath, this weird production plays like an opera without music, and seems to have been designed as a vehicle for its charismatic star.

wd Pier Paolo Pasolini, play Euripides ph Ennio Guarnieri

Maria Callas, Giuseppe Gentile, Laurent Terzieff, Massimo Girotti

The Medium*
Italy 1951 80m bw
Transfilm (Walter Lowendahl)

A fake medium feels a genuine manifestation, shoots at it and kills her assistant, but is still not sure whether he was responsible.
A filmic but not entirely satisfactory treatment of a modest but popular modern opera.

wd, m Gian-Carlo Menotti, his opera co-d Alexander Hammid ph Enzo Serafin

Marie Powers, Anna Maria Alberghetti, Leo Coleman

AAN: Gian-Carlo Menotti (for music)

Medium Cool**
US 1969 111m Technicolor
Paramount / H & J Pictures (Tully Friedman)

A TV news cameraman is made apathetic by the events around him.
Stimulating if overlong comment on the quality of life in the sixties, immaculately made and with a rather effective though obvious twist ending.

wd, ph Haskell Wexler m Mike Bloomfield *ad* Leon Ericksen

Robert Forster, Verna Bloom, Peter Bonerz, Marianna Hill, Sid McCoy

'A deeply moving questioning of America's violence and voyeurism.'—*Jan Dawson*

'I can't think of any film that tells one more about the texture of American life today.'—*Michael Billington, Illustrated London News*

The Medusa Touch*
GB / France 1978   109m   Technicolor
ITC / Bulldog / Citeca (Arnon Milchan, Elliott Kastner)

A novelist is haunted by the belief that he can cause disaster.
And he does, very predictably, while any intellectual excitement in the script is rapidly replaced by mere mayhem.
Different, but not exciting.

w John Briley, *novel* Peter Van Greenway *d* Jack Gold *ph* Arthur Ibbetson *m* Michael J. Lewis *sp* Doug Ferris

Richard Burton, Lee Remick, Lino Ventura, Harry Andrews, Alan Badel, Jeremy Brett, Michael Hordern, Gordon Jackson

Meet Danny Wilson
US 1951   83m   bw
U-I (Leonard Goldstein)

An overbearing crooner gets to the top with the help of gangsters.
Fairly abrasive star vehicle, almost amounting to self-parody.

w Don McGuire *d* Joseph Pevney *ph* Maury Gertsman *md* Joseph Gershenson

Frank Sinatra, Shelley Winters, Alex Nicol, Raymond Burr

Meet John Doe***
US 1941   123m   bw
Liberty Films (Frank Capra)

A tramp is hired to embody the common man in a phony political drive, and almost commits suicide.
Vividly staged but over-sentimental Capra extravaganza with high spots outnumbering low.

w Robert Riskin d Frank Capra ph George Barnes *m* Dmitri Tiomkin

Gary Cooper, *Barbara Stanwyck*, Edward Arnold, Walter Brennan, James Gleason, Spring Byington, Gene Lockhart, Rod la Rocque, Irving Bacon, Regis Toomey, Ann Doran, Warren Hymer, Andrew Tombes

'For the sake of a happy ending that would keep Gary Cooper alive, the meanings were so distorted that the original authors sued.'—*New Yorker, 1978*

'Capra is as skilled as ever in keeping things moving along briskly and dramatically.'—*National Board of Review*

AAN: original story (Richard Connell, Robert Presnell)

Meet Me after the Show*
US 1951   88m   Technicolor
TCF (George Jessel)

A musical star thinks she has discovered an affair between her husband and his glamorous backer.
Surprisingly bright routine musical.

w Mary Loos, Richard Sale *d Richard Sale ph Arthur E. Arling md* Lionel Newman *songs* Jule Styne, Leo Robin

Betty Grable, Macdonald Carey, Rory Calhoun, Eddie Albert, Irene Ryan

Meet Me at Dawn
GB 1946   99m   bw
TCF / Marcel Hellman
US title: *The Gay Duellist*

A professional duellist is commissioned to provoke a duel with a senator, but unwittingly hires the senator's daughter to play the injured party.
A totally laborious and artificial period comedy which never seems even to aspire to the style required.

w Lesley Storm, James Seymour, Maurice Cowan, *story* Le Tueur by Anatole Litvak, Marcel Achard *d* Thornton Freeland *ph* Gunther Krampf *m* Mischa Spoliansky

Hazel Court, William Eythe, Stanley Holloway, Margaret Rutherford, Basil Sydney, Irene Browne

Meet Me at the Fair
US 1952   87m   Technicolor
U-I (Albert J. Cohen)

In 1900, an orphan joins a travelling medicine show.
Mildly pleasing open-air comedy drama.

w Irving Wallace, *novel* The Great Companions by Gene Markey *d* Douglas Sirk *ph* Maury Gertsman *md* Joseph Gershenson

Diana Lynn, Dan Dailey, Hugh O'Brian, Chet Allen, Rhys Williams

Meet Me in Las Vegas

US 1956   112m   Eastmancolor
Cinemascope
MGM (Joe Pasternak)
GB title: *Viva Las Vegas!*

A gambler's luck changes when he grabs the hand of a passing ballerina.
Listless song-and dance extravaganza which wastes a great deal of talent.

w Isabel Lennart *d* Roy Rowland *ph* Robert Bronner *m* Georgie Stoll, Johnny Green *ly* Sammy Cahn *ch* Eugène Loring, Hermes Pan

Dan Dailey, Cyd Charisse, Agnes Moorehead, Lili Darvas, Paul Henreid, Oscar Karlweis, Lena Horne, Jerry Colonna, Frankie Laine
  'A large-scale musical of almost stupefying banality.'—*MFB*

AAN: Georgie Stoll, Johnny Green

Meet Me in St Louis***

US 1944   113m   Technicolor
MGM (Arthur Freed)

Scenes in the life of an affectionate family at the turn of the century.
Patchy but generally highly agreeable musical nostalgia with an effective sense of the passing years and seasons.

w Irving Brecher, Fred F. Finklehoffe, *novel* Sally Benson *d* Vincente Minnelli *ph* George Folsey *md* Georgie Stoll

Judy Garland, Margaret O'Brien, Tom Drake, Leon Ames, Mary Astor, Lucille Bremer, June Lockhart, *Harry Davenport*, Marjorie Main, Joan Carroll, Hugh Marlowe, Robert Sully, Chill Wills
  'A family group framed in velvet and tinsel . . . it has everything a romantic musical should have.'—*Dilys Powell, 1955*

AAN: script; George Folsey; Georgie Stoll; song 'The Trolley Song' (*m* / *ly* Ralph Blane, Hugh Martin)

Meet Me Tonight

GB 1952   85m   Technicolor
Rank / Anthony Havelock Allan

Three short Noel Coward plays: *Red Peppers, Fumed Oak, Ways and Means*.
Regrettably bald treatment of three playlets which have not lasted well. A thoroughly artificial evening.

w / *m* Noel Coward *d* Anthony Pelissier *ph* Desmond Dickinson

Ted Ray, Kay Walsh, Stanley Holloway, Betty Ann Davies, Nigel Patrick, Valerie Hobson

Meet Mr Penny

GB 1938   70m   bw

A meek clerk leads a revolt against a speculator who wants to build on allotments.
Early Ealing-style social comedy based on a radio character; of no abiding interest.
Richard Goolden, Vic Oliver, Fabia Drake, Kay Walsh, Patrick Barr, Hermione Gingold, Wilfrid Hyde-White. Written by Victor Kendall and Doreen Montgomery, from the character created by Maurice Moisiewicz; directed by David MacDonald; for British National.

Meet Mr Lucifer*

GB 1953   81m   bw
Ealing (Monja Danischewsky)

The Demon King in a tatty provincial pantomime dreams he is the devil preventing people from wasting time watching television.
Clean and occasionally amusing piece of topical satire on tellymania; but the prologue is funnier than the sketches.

w Monja Danischewsky, *play* Beggar My Neighbour by Arnold Ridley *d* Anthony Pelissier *ph* Desmond Dickinson *m* Eric Rogers

Stanley Holloway, Peggy Cummins, Jack Watling, Barbara Murray, Joseph Tomelty, Gordon Jackson, Jean Cadell, Kay Kendall, Ian Carmichael, Gilbert Harding, Charles Victor, Humphrey Lestocq

Meet Nero Wolfe*

US 1936   73m   bw
Columbia

A corpulent stay-at-home sleuth solves a disappearance and a murder.
The film debut of an engaging crime character, who oddly never made it to a series.

w Howard J. Green, Bruce Manning, Joseph Anthony, *novel* Fer de Lance by Rex Stout *d* Herbert Biberman *ph* Henry Freulich

Edward Arnold, Lionel Stander, Joan Perry, Rita Hayworth, Victor Jory, Nana Bryant, Walter Kingsford, John Qualen

Meet the People

US 1944   100m   bw
MGM (E. Y. Harburg)

A Broadway musical star proves she isn't snooty by taking a job in a shipyard.
Thin propaganda musical which wastes a fair amount of talent.

w S. M. Herzig, Fred Saidy, *play* Louis Lantz, Sol and Ben Barzman *d* Charles Reisner *ph* Robert Surtees *songs* various

Lucille Ball, Dick Powell, Virginia O'Brien,
Bert Lahr, Rags Ragland, June Allyson, Steve
Geray, Phil Regan, Spike Jones and his City
Slickers, Vaughn Monroe and his Orchestra

Meet the Stewarts
US 1942 74m bw

Newlyweds have trouble when he's poor and
she's used to rich living. Modest marital
comedy with young talent. William Holden,
Frances Dee, Grant Mitchell. Written by
Elizabeth Dunn and Karen de Wolf; directed
by Alfred E. Green; for Columbia.

Melba
GB 1953 113m Technicolor
Horizon (Sam Spiegel)

The life of the internationally famous
Australian opera singer of Victorian days.
Moderately interesting recreation of a woman
and an era, though dramatically rather stodgy.

w Harry Kurnitz d Lewis Milestone ph Ted
Scaife md Muir Mathieson ad André
Andreiev

Patrice Munsel, Robert Morley, Alec Clunes,
Martita Hunt, Sybil Thorndike, John
McCallum

Melody
GB 1971 106m Eastmancolor
Hemdale / Sagittarius / Goodtimes (David
    Puttnam)
aka: S.W.A.L.K.

Calf love at school causes jealousy between
two boys.
Tough-sentimental teenage comedy-drama of
little interest to adults.

w Alan Parker d Waris Hussein ph Peter
Suschitsky m Richard Hewson

Jack Wild, Mark Lester, Tracy Hyde

Melody Time*
US 1948 75m Technicolor
Walt Disney (Ben Sharpsteen)

An unlinked variety show of cartoon
segments.
A mainly mediocre selection with the usual
moments of high style: *Once upon a
Wintertime, Bumble Boogie, Johnny
Appleseed, Little Toot, Trees, Blame it on the
Samba, Pecos Bill.*

w various d various

'There seems to be an obvious connection
between the Disney artists' increasing
insipidity and their increasing talent for fright,
but I will leave it to accredited sado-
masochists to make the discovery.'—*James
Agee*

The Member of the Wedding*
US 1953 91m bw
Columbia / Stanley Kramer

A 12-year-old girl learns something about life
when her sister gets married and a young boy
dies.
Boringly contained in a kitchen set, this filmed
play has interesting characters but is really not
good enough for the talent involved.

w Edna and Edward Anhalt, *play* and *novel*
Carson McCullers d Fred Zinnemann ph Hal
Mohr m Alex North

Julie Harris, *Ethel Waters*, Brandon de Wilde,
Arthur Franz, Nancy Gates, James Edwards

AAN: Julie Harris

The Men***
US 1950 85m bw
Stanley Kramer
reissue title: *Battle Stripe*

Paraplegic war veterans are prepared for
civilian life; the fiancée of one of them helps
overcome his problems.
Vivid semi-documentary melodrama, at the
time rather shocking in its no-holds-barred
treatment of sexual problems.

w *Carl Foreman d Fred Zinnemann
ph* Robert de Grasse m Dmitri Tiomkin

*Marlon Brando, Teresa Wright, Everett
Sloane*, Jack Webb, Howard St John
  'A completely new experience between men
and women!'—*publicity*
  'Don't be misled into feeling that to see this
film is merely a duty; it is, simply, an
experience worth having.'—*Richard Mallett,
Punch*
  'I was afraid I was gonna die . . . now I'm
afraid I'm gonna live!'—*more publicity*

AAN: Carl Foreman

Men Are Not Gods
GB 1937 92m bw
London (Alexander Korda)

An actor playing Othello nearly strangles his
wife.
Tepid melodramatic attempt at a theme later
used in
A Double Life.

w G. B. Stern, Iris Wright d Walter Reisch
ph Charles Rosher

Miriam Hopkins, Sebastian Shaw, Rex
Harrison, Gertrude Lawrence, A. E.
Matthews, Val Gielgud, Laura Smithson

Men Are Such Fools
US 1938 69m bw

The worm turns when his wife threatens to

leave him for a singing career. Mediocre is the word for this threadbare drama. Wayne Morris, Humphrey Bogart, Priscilla Lane, Hugh Herbert, Penny Singleton. Written by Norman Reilly Raine and Horace Jackson; directed by Busby Berkeley; for Warner.

The Men in Her Life
US 1941   90m   bw
Columbia (Gregory Ratoff)

A former circus rider becomes a ballerina. Well-worn rags-to-riches romance of little interest.

w Frederick Kohner, Michael Wilson, Paul Trivers, *novel* Ballerina by Lady Eleanor Smith d Gregory Ratoff ph Harry Stradling, Arthur Miller md David Raksin

Loretta Young, Conrad Veidt, Dean Jagger, Eugenie Leontovich, Shepperd Strudwick, Otto Kruger, Paul Baratoff

Men in War
US 1957   104m   bw
Security (Sidney Harmon)

Korea 1950: an infantry platoon is cut off from HQ and tries to take an enemy-occupied hill. Stereotyped small-scale war heroics; the film makes its points but fails to entertain.

w Philip Yordan d Anthony Mann ph Ernest Haller m Elmer Bernstein

Robert Ryan, Robert Keith, Aldo Ray, Vic Morrow, James Edwardes, Sen Yung

Men in White
US 1934   80m   bw
MGM (Monta Bell)

An ambitious intern is in love with an attractive socialite who resents his devotion to duty.
Popular but obvious star drama.

w Waldemar Young, *play* Sidney Kingsley d Richard Boleslawski ph George Folsey

Clark Gable, Myrna Loy, Jean Hersholt, Elizabeth Allan, Otto Kruger, C. Henry Gordon, Wallace Ford

Men Must Fight
US 1933   73m   bw

War comes to New York in 1940. A forgotten pacifist tract which trod the same paths as did H. G. Wells; of historical interest only apart from a spectacular air raid climax. Robert Young, Diana Wynyard, May Robson, Phillips Holmes, Lewis Stone. Written by S. K. Lauren, Reginald Lawrence and C. Gardner Sullivan; directed by Edgar Selwyn; for MGM.

Men of Boys' Town
US 1941   106m   bw
MGM (John W. Considine Jnr)

Further adventures of Father Flanagan. Mushy sequel to *Boys' Town* (qv).

w James Kevin McGuinness d Norman Taurog ph Harold Rosson m Herbert Stothart

Spencer Tracy, Mickey Rooney, Bobs Watson, Larry Nunn, Lee J. Cobb, Mary Nash, Henry O'Neill, Darryl Hickman, Anne Revere

Men of the Fighting Lady
US 1954   80m   Anscocolor
MGM (Henry Berman)

Adventures of an aircraft carrier during the Korean War.
Tepid war actioner with a few effective semi-documentary sequences of naval tactics.

w Art Cohn d Andrew Marton ph George Folsey m Miklos Rozsa

Van Johnson, Walter Pidgeon, Louis Calhern, Dewey Martin, Keenan Wynn, Frank Lovejoy, Robert Horton

Men of Tomorrow
GB 1932   88m   bw
Paramount (Alexander Korda)

Oxford students have more than academic work on their minds.
Dim comedy-drama with an interesting cast.

w Arthur Wimperis, Anthony Gibbs, *play* Young Apollo by Anthony Gibbs d Leontine Sagan ph Bernard Browne

Maurice Braddell, Joan Gardner, Emlyn Williams, Merle Oberon, Robert Donat

Men of Two Worlds
GB 1946   109m   Technicolor
GFD / Two Cities (John Sutro)
US title: *Witch Doctor*
aka: *Kisenga, Man of Africa*

In Tanganyika, an educated native helps white men to counter the force of witch doctors and persuade tribes to leave an infected area. Earnest but totally unpersuasive semi-documentary shot in unconvincing sets and garish colour.

w Thorold Dickinson, Joyce Cary, E. Arnot Robertson, Herbert Victor d Thorold Dickinson ph Geoffrey Unsworth, Desmond Dickinson m Arthur Bliss

Eric Portman, Phyllis Calvert, Robert Adams, Orlando Martins, Arnold Marle, Cathleen Nesbitt, David Horne, Cyril Raymond

Men o'War*
US 1929 20m bw

Two sailors and two girls have adventures in a park. Simple-minded early talkie star comedy featuring their famous soda fountain routine.

Laurel and Hardy, James Finlayson. Written by H. M. Walker; directed by Lewis R. Foster; for Hal Roach.

Men of Yesterday
GB 1936 82m bw

Old army rivalries die down at a reunion. Dated but interesting drama with interpolated variety talent. Stewart Rome, Sam Livesey, Hay Petrie, Cecil Parker, with George Robey, Ella Shields, Will Fyffe, Dick Henderson. Written by Gerald Elliott and Jack Francis; directed by John Baxter; for UK Films.

Men with Wings
US 1938 106m Technicolor
Paramount (William Wellman)

Civil aviation pioneers fall out over a girl. Disappointing epic from the maker of *Wings*, with highly predictable story line, modest acting and ho-hum spectacle.

w Robert Carson d William Wellman ph W. Howard Greene m W. Franke Harling, Gerald Carbonara

Fred MacMurray, Ray Milland, Louise Campbell, Andy Devine, Lynne Overman, Porter Hall, Walter Abel, Virginia Weidler, Donald O'Connor

'To all women who love and admire the fearless heroes of the air, and who, with brave hearts, encourage them, hope, and pray for them.'—*director's dedication*

Men without Women
US 1930 77m bw
Fox

Men in a submarine are trapped on the ocean bed.

Early talkie action drama noted more for its credits than its accomplishment.

w Dudley Nichols d John Ford ph Joseph H. August

Kenneth MacKenna, Frank Albertson, Paul Page, Pat Somerset, Stuart Erwin, Warren Hymer, John Wayne

Menace
US 1934 58m bw

Murders follow the suicide of a mining engineer. Compact little dark house thriller with good stagey performances. Gertrude Michael, Paul Cavanagh, Henrietta Crosman, John Lodge, Ray Milland, Berton Churchill,

Halliwell Hobbes. Written by Chandler Sprague and Anthony Veiller, from a story by Philip MacDonald; directed by Ralph Murphy; for Paramount.

The Mephisto Waltz*
US 1971 109m De Luxe
TCF / QM Productions

A satanic concert pianist on the point of death wills his soul into the body of a journalist. Complex diabolical mumbo-jumbo with plenty of style.

w Ben Maddow, *novel* Fred Mustard Stewart d Paul Wendkos ph William W. Spencer m Jerry Goldsmith

Alan Alda, Jacqueline Bisset, Curt Jurgens, Barbara Parkins

The Mercenaries
GB 1968 100m Metrocolor Panavision
MGM / George Englund
US title: *Dark of the Sun*

In the Belgian Congo in 1960 a mercenary officer is ordered to bring back a fortune in diamonds by armoured train.
Basically an old-fashioned thriller about the hazards of a journey beset by brutish villains and damsels in distress, this unpleasant film is notable for the amount of sadistic action it crams into its running time.

w Quentin Werty, Adrian Spies, *novel* Dark of the Sun by Wilbur Smith d Jack Cardiff ph Edward Scaife m Jacques Loussier

Rod Taylor, Yvette Mimieux, Kenneth More, Jim Brown, Peter Carsten, André Morell, Guy Deghy, Calvin Lockhart, Alan Gifford

'The violence done to the human body is matched by violence done to the intelligence by a stock adventure story given a gloss of topicality and social insult.'—*Judith Crist*

Merrill's Marauders
US 1962 98m Technicolor
Cinemascope
Warner / US Pictures (Milton Sperling)

Adventures of a crack US army unit in 1942 Burma.
Physically exhausting war adventure with emphasis on hand-to-hand fighting and much bloodshed.

w Samuel Fuller, Milton Sperling d Samuel Fuller ph William Clothier m Howard Jackson

Jeff Chandler, Ty Hardin, Andrew Duggan, Peter Brown, Will Hutchins, Claude Akins

Merrily We Go to Hell
US 1932 78m bw
Paramount

A socialite marries a dipsomaniac journalist. Glum problem drama.

w Edwin Justin Mayer, *novel* I Jerry Take Thee Joan by Cleo Lucas *d* Dorothy Arzner *ph* David Abel

Sylvia Sidney, Fredric March, Adrienne Allen, Richard Gallagher, Florence Burton, Esther Howard, Kent Taylor

Merrily We Live*
US 1938 90m bw
Hal Roach

A zany family hires a chauffeur who is actually a famous writer posing as a tramp.
Quite likeable compound of *My Man Godfrey* and *You Can't Take It with You.*

w Eddie Moran, Jack Jevne *d* Norman Z. McLeod *ph* Norbert Brodine *md* Marvin Hatley

Constance Bennett, Brian Aherne, Billie Burke, Alan Mowbray, Patsy Kelly, Ann Dvorak, Tom Brown, Bonita Granville, Marjorie Rambeau, Clarence Kolb

AAN: Norbert Brodine; Billie Burke; title song (*m* Phil Craig, *ly* Arthur Quenzer)

Merry Andrew
US 1958 103m Metrocolor
Cinemascope
MGM / Sol C. Siegel

A stuffy teacher in search of an ancient statue joins a travelling circus.
Deliberately charming star comedy which plumps too firmly for whimsy and, despite its professionalism, provokes barely a smile, let alone a laugh.

w Isabel Lennart, I. A. L. Diamond, *story* Paul Gallico *d / ch* Michael Kidd *ph* Robert Surtees *m* Saul Chaplin *ly* Johnny Mercer

Danny Kaye, Pier Angeli, Baccaloni, Noel Purcell, Robert Coote, Patricia Cutts, Rex Evans, Walter Kingsford, Tommy Rall, Rhys Williams

Merry Go Round of 1938
US 1937 87m bw

Four vaudevillians adopt a small girl, and later head for Hollywood. Sentimental farce with zany moments and an encouraging cast. Jimmy Savo, Bert Lahr, Mischa Auer, Billy House, Alice Brady, Louise Fazenda. Written by Monte Brice and A. Dorian Atvos; directed by Irving Cummings; for Universal.

The Merry Monahans
US 1944 90m bw
Universal (Michael Fessier, Ernest Pagano)

Adventures of a family of vaudeville performers.
Acceptable backstage comedy drama with good atmosphere.

w Michael Fessier, Ernest Pagano *d* Charles Lamont *ph* Charles Van Enger *m* Hans Salter

Donald O'Connor, Jack Oakie, Rosemary de Camp, Peggy Ryan, Ann Blyth, Isabel Jewell, John Miljan

AAN: Hans Salter

The Merry Widow*
US 1925 111m (24 fps) bw silent
MGM (Irving Thalberg)

A bankrupt king orders a nobleman to woo a wealthy American widow.
An operetta without music (or dialogue) is usually a poor thing, but the director added a few unpredictable touches.

w Erich Von Stroheim, Benjamin Glazer, *operetta* Victor Leon, Leo Stein *d* Erich Von Stroheim *ph* Oliver Marsh, Ben Reynolds, William Daniels *m* William Axt, D. Mendoza

Mae Murray, John Gilbert, Roy D'Arcy, Tully Marshall

† The story goes that when reproved by Thalberg for wasting film stock on, for instance, endless shots of a wardrobe full of shoes, Von Stroheim remarked: 'The character has a foot fetish.' 'And you,' said Thalberg, 'have a footage fetish!'

The Merry Widow**
US 1934 99m bw
MGM

Patchy, but sometimes sparkling version.

w Samson Raphaelson, Ernest Vajda *d* Ernst Lubitsch *ph* Oliver T. Marsh *m* Franz Lehar

Maurice Chevalier, Jeanette MacDonald, Edward Everett Horton, Una Merkel, George Barbier, Donald Meek, Sterling Holloway, Shirley Ross

'It is Lubitsch; it is also Hollywood; it is the cream of the American bourgeois film. It is a charlotte russe.'—*Peter Ellis, New Masses*

The Merry Widow
US 1952 105m Technicolor
MGM (Joe Pasternak)

Chill, empty remake.

w Sonya Levien, William Ludwig *d* Curtis Bernhardt *ph* Robert Surtees

Fernando Lamas, Lana Turner, Richard Haydn, Una Merkel, Thomas Gomez, John Abbott

'Nothing has been omitted (except the spirit of the original).'—*MFB*

Merton of the Movies*
US 1947 82m bw
MGM

An innocent young man in Hollywood
becomes a star.

The plot and characterizations of this old
chestnut are resistible, but the Hollywood
background is well managed and convincing.

w George Wells, Lou Breslow, *novel* Henry
Leon Wilson *d* Robert Alton *ph* Paul C.
Vogel *m* David Snell

Red Skelton, Virginia O'Brien, Alan
Mowbray

A Message to Garcia*
US 1936 86m bw
TCF (Raymond Griffith)

During the Spanish–American war a Cuban
girl helps an American agent get through to
the rebel leader with a diplomatic message.

Agreeable embroidery of a historical incident:
good production values and entertaining star
performances.

w W. P. Lipscomb, Gene Fowler, *book*
Andrew S. Rohan *d* George Marshall
ph Rudolph Maté *m* Louis Silvers

Wallace Beery, Barbara Stanwyck, John
Boles, Alan Hale, Herbert Mundin, Mona
Barrie

Meteor
US 1979 107m Movielab Panavision
Palladium (Sandy Howard, Gabriel Katzka)

A huge meteor, preceded by dangerous
fragments, heads relentlessly towards
Earth . . .

Talkative disaster movie with occasional
moments of interest.

w Stanley Mann, Edmund H. North *d* Ronald
Neame *ph* Paul Lohmann *m* Laurence
Rosenthal *visual effects* Margo Anderson,
William Cruse

Sean Connery, Natalie Wood, Karl Malden,
Brian Keith, Martin Landau, Trevor Howard,
Henry Fonda, Joseph Campanella

Metropolis***
Germany 1926 120m approx (24 fps)
   bw silent
UFA

In the year 2000, the workers in a modernistic
city live underground and unrest is quelled by
the persuasion of a saintly girl, Maria; but a
mad inventor creates an evil Maria to incite
them to revolt.

Always somewhat overlong, and certainly
heavy-going in places, this futuristic fantasy

not only has many brilliant sequences which
created genuine excitement and terror, but it
inspired a great many Hollywood clichés to
come, notably the Frankenstein theme. The
BBC's version of the seventies, with an
electronic music sound track, is the most
satisfactory.

w *Thea Von Harbou* d *Fritz Lang* ph *Karl
Freund, Günther Rittau* sp *Eugen Schufftan*
ad *Otto Hunte, Erich Kettelhut, Karl
Vollbrecht*

Brigitte Helm, Alfred Abel, Gustav Fröhlich,
Rudolf Klein-Rogge, Fritz Rasp

'It goes too far and always gets away with
it.'—*New Yorker, 1978*

'A wonderful, stupefying folly.'—*New
Yorker, 1982*

Metropolitan*
US 1935 79m bw
TCF (Darryl F. Zanuck)

A capricious prima donna walks out of the
Metropolitan Opera and forms her own
company.

Earnest and well-made melodrama with song;
it earned critical plaudits but was a
disappointment at the box office.

w Bess Meredyth, George Marion Jnr
d Richard Boleslawski *ph* Rudolph Maté
md Alfred Newman

Lawrence Tibbett, Alice Brady, Virginia
Bruce, Cesar Romero, Thurston Hall, Luis
Alberni

Mexican Spitfire

A series of second feature comedies nominally
about a young businessman and his
temperamental Mexican wife (Donald Woods
and Lupe Velez), whose interest shifted firmly
to the young man's accident-prone uncle Matt
and his aristocratic boss Lord Epping, both of
whom were played by the rubber-legged
Ziegfeld comic Leon Errol at something near
the top of his form. The plots made little
sense, but the hectic situations provoked
hearty roars of laughter. The films were all
made by RKO, and all directed by Leslie
Goodwins.

1939: THE GIRL FROM MEXICO,
MEXICAN SPITFIRE
1940: MEXICAN SPITFIRE OUT WEST
1941: MEXICAN SPITFIRE'S BABY,
MEXICAN SPITFIRE AT SEA
1942: MEXICAN SPITFIRE SEES A
GHOST, MEXICAN SPITFIRE'S
ELEPHANT
1943: MEXICAN SPITFIRE'S BLESSED
EVENT

Michael and Mary
GB 1931   85m   bw

A husband thought dead for many years
returns to disturb his wife's second marriage.
Acceptable comedy from a popular stage play;
it headed its stars towards Hollywood.

Herbert Marshall, Edna Best, Elizabeth
Allan, Frank Lawton, D. A. Clarke-Smith.
Written by Angus MacPhail, Robert
Stevenson and Lajos Biro, from the play by
A. A. Milne; directed by Victor Saville; for
Gaumont.

Michael Shayne
The private eye created by Brett Halliday was
featured in several second features starring
Lloyd Nolan, mostly directed by Eugene
Forde for Fox. They were adequate time-
passers without too much sparkle.

1940: MICHAEL SHAYNE PRIVATE
DETECTIVE
1941: DRESSED TO KILL, JUST OFF
BROADWAY, THE MAN WHO
WOULDN'T DIE
1942: TIME TO KILL (a version of
Chandler's FAREWELL MY LOVELY),
BLUE WHITE AND PERFECT

The Michigan Kid
US 1947   70m   Cinecolor

Several people hunt for treasure stolen from a
stagecoach. Lower berth western. Jon Hall,
Victor McLaglen, Rita Johnson, Andy
Devine, Byron Foulger, Milburn Stone.
Written by Roy Chanslor, from a novel by
Rex Beach; directed by Ray Taylor; for
Universal.

Mickey One*
US 1965   93m   bw
Columbia / Florin / Tatira (Arthur Penn,
   Harrison Starr)

A nightclub entertainer runs away after an
orgy to find some meaning in his life.
Obscure symbolic melodrama whose flashes of
talent and interest needed firmer control.

w Alan Surgal d Arthur Penn ph Ghislain
Cloquet m Eddie Sauter pd George Jenkins

Warren Beatty, Hurd Hatfield, Alexandra
Stewart, Franchot Tone, Teddy Hart, Jeff
Corey

   'Arresting at first, it becomes more and
more bogged down by its own pretensions,
until one's main interest is simply in seeing it
through.'—MFB

Midas Run
US 1969   104m   Technicolor
Raymond Stross / MPI (Leon Chooluck)
GB title: A Run on Gold

An ageing secret service chief plans to hi-jack
a bullion shipment.
Incompetently handled caper story with
interest unwisely shifted for romantic purposes
to the plotter's recruits.

w James D. Buchanan, Ronald Austin, Berne
Giler d Alf Kjellin ph Ken Higgins m Elmer
Bernstein

Fred Astaire, Richard Crenna, Anne
Heywood, Ralph Richardson, Roddy
McDowall, Adolfo Celi, Maurice Denham,
Cesar Romero

Middle of the Night**
US 1959   118m   bw
Columbia (George Justin)

An elderly garment manufacturer falls in love
with a young girl.
Serious and moving examination of a human
predicament, shot against beautifully observed
New York backgrounds.

w Paddy Chayevsky, from his TV play
d Delbert Mann ph Joseph Brun m George
Bassman

Fredric March, Kim Novak, Glenda Farrell,
Jan Norris, Lee Grant

   'A work of greater cogency than his New
York play script and of deeper maturity than
his Marty.'—Time

   'The best of the TV transformations into
film.'—Stanley Kauffmann

The Middle Watch
GB 1930   112m   bw

Female guests on board ship have to be hidden
from the captain. Naval froth in primitive
talkie form; absurdly long but popular. Owen
Nares, Jacqueline Logan, Jack Raine, Dodo
Watts, Reginald Purdell. Written by Norman
Walker and Frank Launder, from the play by
Ian Hay and Stephen King-Hall; directed by
Norman Walker; for BIP. (NB: In 1940 ABPC
made a smoother version with Jack Buchanan,
Greta Gynt, David Hutcheson, Kay Walsh,
Fred Emney and Reginald Purdell [in the
same role]; directed by Thomas Bentley.)

Midnight
US 1934   80m   bw
Universal / All Star (Chester Erskine)
aka: Call It Murder

A District Attorney finds his own daughter on
the wrong side of the law.
Tepid family melodrama.

wd Chester Erskine, *play* Paul and Claire Sifton *ph* William Steiner

Sidney Fox, O. P. Heggie, Henry Hull, Humphrey Bogart, Margaret Wycherly, Lynne Overman, Richard Whorf, Cora Witherspoon

Midnight***
US 1939 95m bw
Paramount (Arthur Hornblow Jnr)

A girl stranded in Paris is hired by an aristocrat to seduce the gigolo paying unwelcome attention to his wife.
Sparkling sophisticated comedy which barely flags until a slightly disappointing ending; all the talents involved are in excellent form.

w Billy Wilder, Charles Brackett, story Edwin Justus Mayer, Franz Schultz *d Mitchell Leisen ph* Charles Lang *m* Frederick Hollander

Claudette Colbert, Don Ameche, *John Barrymore*, Francis Lederer, Mary Astor, Elaine Barrie, Hedda Hopper, Rex O'Malley
'Leisen's masterpiece, one of the best comedies of the thirties.'—*John Baxter, 1968*
'One of the authentic delights of the thirties.'—*New Yorker, 1976*
'It has the elements of an American *La Règle du Jeu*.'—*John Gillett*

Midnight Cowboy***
US 1969 113m De Luxe
UA / Jerome Hellman

A slightly dim-witted Texan comes to New York to offer his services as a stud for rich ladies, but spends a hard winter helping a tubercular con man.
Life in the New York gutter, brilliantly if not too accurately observed by a master showman with no heart.

w Waldo Salt, *novel* James Leo Herlihy *d John Schlesinger ph Adam Holender md* John Barry *pd* John Robert Lloyd

Jon Voight, Dustin Hoffman, Brenda Vaccaro, Sylvia Miles, John McGiver
'If only Schlesinger's directorial self-discipline had matched his luminous sense of scene and his extraordinary skill in handling actors, this would have been a far more considerable film.'—*Arthur Schlesinger Jnr (no relation)*
'A great deal besides cleverness, a great deal of good feeling and perception and purposeful dexterity.'—*Stanley Kauffmann*

AA: best picture; Waldo Salt; John Schlesinger
AAN: Dustin Hoffman; Jon Voight; Sylvia Miles

Midnight Episode
GB 1950 78m bw
Columbia / Triangle (Thomas Lageard)

An old busker stumbles over a dead body and a lot of money.
Tame British version of Raimu's French success *Monsieur La Souris*, saved only by its star performance.

w Rita Barisse, Reeve Taylor, Paul Vincent Carroll, David Evans, William Templeton *d* Gordon Parry *ph* Hone Glendining

Stanley Holloway, Natasha Parry, Leslie Dwyer, Reginald Tate, Meredith Edwards, Wilfrid Hyde White, Joy Shelton

Midnight Express*
GB 1978 121m Eastmancolor
Columbia / Casablanca (Alan Marshall, David Puttnam)

Tribulations of an American student arrested in Turkey for carrying hashish.
Misleadingly-titled wallow in prison atrocities, extremely well made but certainly not entertaining and with little discernible point.

w Oliver Stone, *memoir* Billy Hayes *d* Alan Parker *ph* Michael Seresin *m* Giorgio Moroder

Brad Davis, Randy Quaid, John Hurt, Irene Miracle, Bo Hopkins
'One of the ugliest sado-masochistic trips, with heavy homosexual overtones, that our thoroughly nasty movie age has yet produced.'—*Richard Schickel, Time*
'The film details all [the horrors] so relentlessly on one screaming note that it is rather like being hit in the gut until you no longer feel a thing.'—*Derek Malcolm, The Guardian*
'Muted squalor with a disco beat in the background, all packaged as social protest.'—*New Yorker, 1982*

AA: script; music
AAN: best picture; Alan Parker; John Hurt

Midnight Lace*
US 1960 108m Eastmancolor
Universal (Ross Hunter, Martin Melcher)

The wife of a rich Londoner is terrorized by threatening phone calls and voices in the fog.
Thoroughly silly rehash of *Gaslight* and *The Boy Who Cried Wolf*; its glamorous accoutrements can't fight a lack of humour or predictable plot development.

w Ivan Goff, Ben Roberts, *play* Matilda Shouted Fire by Janet Green *d* David Miller *ph* Russell Metty *m* Frank Skinner

Doris Day, Rex Harrison, John Gavin, Myrna Loy, Roddy McDowall, Herbert Marshall, Natasha Parry, John Williams, Anthony Dawson, Hermione Baddeley, Richard Ney, Rhys Williams, Doris Lloyd

The Midnight Man
US 1974 117m Technicolor
Universal / Norlan (Roland Kibbee, Burt Lancaster)

An ex-cop, paroled after killing his wife's lover, takes a job as security guard and runs into a murder case.
Muddled mystery with pretentious characterization and bouts of violence.

wd Roland Kibbee, Burt Lancaster, *novel* The Midnight Lady and the Mourning Man by David Anthony *ph* Jack Priestley *m* Dave Grusin

Burt Lancaster, Susan Clark, Cameron Mitchell, Morgan Woodward, Harris Yulin, Robert Quarry, Joan Lorring, Lawrence Dobin, Ed Lauter
'A thriller that has the impenetrability of Chandler but none of the flavour.'—*Tom Milne*
'Efficient enough but lifeless, and burdened with portentous sentiments about solitude, violence and the nature of the beast.'—*Sight and Sound*

Midnight Mary
US 1933 76m bw

A gangster's moll on trial for her life thinks back to her past. Intolerable now, but a hit of its year despite star miscasting. Loretta Young, Ricardo Cortez, Franchot Tone, Una Merkel, Andy Devine, Harold Huber. Written by Gene Markey and Anita Loos; directed by William Wellman; for MGM.

Midnight Patrol*
US 1933 20m bw

Incompetent policemen arrest their own chief as a burglar. Good standard star slapstick. Laurel and Hardy, Charlie Hall, Walter Plinge. Writer uncredited; directed by Lloyd French; for Hal Roach.

Midnight Taxi
US 1937 73m bw

A G-man becomes a taxi driver to rout a gang of counterfeiters. Competent, predictable crime programmer. Brian Donlevy, Frances Drake, Alan Dinehart, Sig Rumann, Gilbert Roland, Harold Huber, Lon Chaney Jnr. Written by Lou Breslow and John Patrick; directed by Eugene Forde; for TCF.

The Midshipmaid
GB 1932 84m bw

A naval commander loves the daughter of a politician out to effect navy cuts. Very modest comedy with music, a key step in the star's success story. Jessie Matthews, Frederick Kerr, Basil Sydney, Nigel Bruce, Claud Allister, John Mills, George Zucco. Written by Ian Hay and Stephen King-Hall, from their play; directed by Albert de Courville; for Gaumont.

Midshipman Easy
GB 1935 77m bw
ABP (Basil Dean, Thorold Dickinson)
US title: *Men of the Sea*

In 1790, young naval officers rescue a girl from Spanish bandits.
Stilted adventure story with interesting credits.

w Anthony Kimmins, *novel* Frederick Marryat *d* Carol Reed *ph* John W. Boyle

Hughie Green, Margaret Lockwood, Harry Tate, Robert Adams, Roger Livesey, Lewis Casson

A Midsummer Night's Dream***
US 1935 117m bw
Warner (Max Reinhardt)

Two pairs of lovers sort out their problems with fairy help at midnight in the woods of Athens.
Shakespeare's play is treated with remarkable respect in this super-glamorous Hollywood adaptation based on the Broadway production by Max Reinhardt. Much of it comes off, and visually it's a treat.

w Charles Kenyon, Mary McCall Jnr, *play* William Shakespeare *d* Max Reinhardt, William Dieterle *ph* Hal Mohr, Fred Jackman, Byron Haskin, H. F. Koenekamp *m* Mendelssohn *md* Erich Wolfgang Korngold *ch* Bronislawa Nijinska *ad* Anton Grot

James Cagney, Dick Powell, Jean Muir, Ross Alexander, Olivia de Havilland, Joe E. Brown, Hugh Herbert, Arthur Treacher, Frank McHugh, Otis Harlan, Dewey Robinson, *Victor Jory*, Verree Teasdale, *Mickey Rooney*, Anita Louise, Grant Mitchell, Ian Hunter, Hobart Cavanaugh
'The publicity push behind the film is tremendous—it is going to be a success or everyone at Warner Brothers is going to get fired.'—*Robert Forsythe*
'Its assurance as a work of film technique is undoubted.'—*John Baxter, 1968*
'Its worst contradiction lies in the way Warners first ordered up a whole batch of

foreign and high-sounding names to handle music, dances, general production—and then turned around and handed them empty vessels for actors.'—*Otis Ferguson*

'Three centuries in the making!'—*publicity*

AA: photography
AAN: best picture

Midway*

US 1976 131m Technicolor
Panavision Sensurround
Universal / Mirisch Corporation (Walter Mirisch)
GB title: *The Battle of Midway*

The tide turns for the Americans when the Japanese attack the Pacific island of Midway in 1942.

Noisy flagwaver with confused strategy and too many stars in small parts.

w Donald S. Sanford *d* Jack Smight
ph Harry Stradling Jnr *m* John Williams

Charlton Heston, Henry Fonda, Robert Mitchum, Glenn Ford, Edward Albert, James Coburn, Hal Holbrook, Toshiro Mifune, Robert Wagner, Robert Webber, Ed Nelson, James Shigeta, Monte Markham, Chris George, Glenn Corbett

'We are over-informed about the movements of every ship and plane, under-informed about how the battle was finally won, and positively swamped with tedious human interest.'—*Sight and Sound*

Mighty Joe Young*

US 1949 94m bw
RKO (Merian C. Cooper)

A little girl brings back from Africa a pet gorilla which grows to enormous size and causes a city to panic.

Rather tired comic-sentimental follow-up to *King Kong*, with a tedious plot and variable animation but a few endearing highlights.

w Ruth Rose *d* Ernest Schoedsack *ph* J. Roy Hunt *m* Roy Webb *sp* Willis O'Brien, Ray Harryhausen

Terry Moore, Ben Johnson, Robert Armstrong, Frank McHugh, Douglas Fowley

The Mikado*

GB 1939 91m Technicolor
GFD / G and S (Geoffrey Toye, Victor Somlo)

In Japan, a timid official is appointed Lord High Executioner and finds that his first intended victim is the Emperor's son, travelling incognito.

Agreeable film version of the classic Gilbert and Sullivan comic opera, with some of the D'Oyly Carte Company's most celebrated members in excellent form.

w Geoffrey Toye, *opera* W. S. Gilbert
m Arthur Sullivan *d* Victor Schertzinger
ph Bernard Knowles

Martyn Green, John Barclay, Sydney Granville, Kenny Baker, Jean Colin, Constance Willis

† The 1966 version by British Home Entertainment featured a later D'Oyly Carte company including John Reed but suffered from a frozen camera and flat lighting, so that little of the original vivacity and charm came over.

Mikey and Nicky

US 1976 118m colour
Paramount (Michael Hausman)

Two crooks are old friends, but one has been hired to kill the other . . .

Intolerable improvisatory sentimental melodrama. Who on earth shells out the money for pictures like this?

wd Elaine May *ph* Victor Kemper *m* John Strauss

Peter Falk, John Cassavetes, Ned Beatty, Sanford Meisner, Rose Arrick, Joyce Van Patten

'An impenetrable, ugly and almost unendurable mess.'—*Frank Rich, New York Post*

'A pretext for Falk and Cassavetes to indulge in one of those long, lugubrious Actors' Studio exercises that wore out its welcome with the last frame of *Husbands* and the first frame of *The Killing of a Chinese Bookie*.'—*Molly Haskell, Village Voice*

Mildred Pierce**

US 1945 113m bw
Warner (Jerry Wald)

A dowdy housewife leaves her husband, becomes the owner (through hard work) of a restaurant chain, and survives a murder case before true love comes her way.

A woman's picture par excellence, glossily and moodily photographed, with a star suffering in luxury on behalf of the most ungrateful daughter of all time.

w Ranald MacDougall, Catherine Turney, *novel* James M. Cain *d* Michael Curtiz
ph Ernest Haller *m* Max Steiner *ad* Anton Grot

Joan Crawford, Jack Carson, Zachary Scott, *Eve Arden, Ann Blyth*, Bruce Bennett,

George Tobias, Lee Patrick, Moroni Olsen
   'The kind of woman most men want—but
shouldn't have!'—*publicity*
   'Constant, lambent, virulent attention to
money and its effects, and more authentic
suggestions of sex than one hopes to see in
American films.'—*James Agee*

AA: Joan Crawford
AAN: best picture; script; Ernest Haller; Eve
Arden; Ann Blyth

The Milkman
US 1950 87m bw
Universal-International (Ted Richmond)

Two milkmen tangle with gangsters.
Odd little comedy which gets the benefit of the
doubt more by bringing its stars together than
by giving them anything to do.

w Albert Beich, James O'Hanlon, Martin
Ragaway, Leonard Stern *d* Charles Barton
ph Clifford Stine *m* Milton Rosen

Donald O'Connor, Jimmy Durante, Joyce
Holden, Piper Laurie, William Conrad, Paul
Harvey, Henry O'Neill

The Milky Way*
US 1936 88m bw
Paramount / Harold Lloyd (Edward
Sheldon)

A milkman becomes a prizefighter and
overcomes a gang of crooks.
Modest Harold Lloyd comedy towards the end
of his career; remade as *The Kid from
Brooklyn* (qv).

w Grover Jones, Frank Butler, Richard
Connell, *play* Lynn Root, Harry Clark
ph Alfred Gilks *d* Leo McCarey

Harold Lloyd, Adolphe Menjou, Verree
Teasdale, Helen Mack, William Gargan,
George Barbier, Lionel Stander
   'The work of many hands, all laid on
expertly.'—*Otis Ferguson*
   'One is more amazed than ever at the good
fortune of this youngish man whose chief
talent is not to act at all, to do nothing, to
serve as a blank wall for other people to scrawl
their ideas on.'—*Graham Greene*

The Milky Way*
France / Italy 1968 102m Eastmancolor
Greenwich / Medusa (Serge Silberman)

Two tramps set off on pilgrimage from Paris to
a Spanish shrine, and have various surprising
encounters.
A picaresque examination of Catholic
doctrine, full of surface interest but requiring
special knowledge for full appreciation.

w Luis Bunuel, Jean-Claude Carrière *d* Luis
Bunuel ph Christian Matras *m* Luis Bunuel

Laurent Terzieff, Paul Frankeur, Delphine
Seyrig, Edith Scon
   'A mere trifle wrapped in a triple cloak of
befuddling obscurantism.'—*John Simon*

Le Million****
France 1931 89m bw
Tobis (Frank Clifford)

An artist and an ingratiating crook search
Paris for a lost lottery ticket.
With its delicate touch, perfect sense of
comedy timing and infectious use of recitative
and song, this is superb screen entertainment
using most of the medium's resources.

wd René Clair, musical comedy Georges Berr,
M. Guillemaud *ph* Georges Périnal
*m Georges Van Parys, Armand Bernard,
Philippe Parès ad* Lazare Meerson

Annabella, René Lefèvre, *Paul Olivier*, Louis
Allibert, Vanda Gréville, Raymond Cordy
   'René Clair at his exquisite best; no one else
has ever been able to make a comedy move
with such delicate inevitability.'—*New Yorker,
1978*
† The style of this film was developed and
expanded in Hollywood by Lubitsch in *One
Hour with You* and by Mamoulian in *Love Me
Tonight.*

Million Dollar Baby
US 1941 100m bw
Warner (Hal B. Wallis, David Lewis)

A girl inherits a fortune and a lot of problems.
Very predictable but sometimes sprightly
comedy with a hard-working cast.

w Richard Macaulay, Jerry Wald, Casey
Robinson, *story* Miss Wheelwright Discovers
America by Leonard Spiegelgass *d* Curtis
Bernhardt *ph* Charles Rosher *m* Max Steiner

Priscilla Lane, Jeffrey Lynn, Ronald Reagan,
May Robson, Lee Patrick, Helen Westley,
George Barbier, John Qualen, Walter Catlett,
Nan Wynn

Million Dollar Duck
US 1971 92m Technicolor
Walt Disney (Bill Anderson)

A duck lays eggs with solid gold yolks, which
provoke interest from gangsters as well as the
government.
Minor Disney fantasy borrowed without
permission from *Mr Drake's Duck* (qv).

w Roswell Rogers *d* Vincent McEveety
ph William Snyder *m* Buddy Baker

Dean Jones, Sandy Dennis, Joe Flynn

Million Dollar Legs*
US 1932   64m   bw
Paramount

A mythical sport-ridden country decides to enter the Olympic Games.
The good gags in this film are weighted down by plodding treatment, and the general effect is more doleful than funny.

w Harry Myers, Nick Barrows, Joseph L. Mankiewicz d Edward Cline ph Arthur Todd

W. C. Fields, Jack Oakie, Andy Clyde, Lyda Roberti, Ben Turpin, Hugh Herbert, Billy Gilbert, George Barbier, Susan Fleming
'One of the silliest and funniest pictures ever made.'—*New Yorker, 1977*

Million Dollar Legs
US 1939   59m   bw
Paramount

College students back a favourite horse. Very modest collegiate comedy.

w Lewis Foster, Richard English d Nick Grinde ph Harry Fischbeck

Betty Grable, John Hartley, Donald O'Connor, Jackie Coogan, Buster Crabbe, Thurston Hall

Million Dollar Mermaid*
US 1952   115m   Technicolor
MGM (Arthur Hornblow Jnr)
GB title: *The One Piece Bathing Suit*

The story of Australian swimmer Annette Kellerman.
Inaccurate biopic with a *raison d'être* in its spectacular aquashow scenes, but nothing at all new in its script.

w Everett Freeman d Mervyn Le Roy
ph George J. Folsey md Adolph Deutsch
ch Busby Berkeley

Esther Williams, Victor Mature, Walter Pidgeon, David Brian, Jesse White, Maria Tallchief, Howard Freeman

AAN: George J. Folsey

The Million Pound Note*
GB 1954   91m   Technicolor
GFD / Group Films (John Bryan)
US title: *Man with a Million*

A man inherits a million dollars in the form of a single banknote and finds it difficult to spend.
Fairly pleasing period comedy which wears its one joke pretty thin but is nicely decorated and acted.

w Jill Craigie, *story* Mark Twain d Ronald Neame ph Geoffrey Unsworth m William Alwyn

Gregory Peck, Jane Griffiths, Ronald Squire, Joyce Grenfell, A. E. Matthews, Reginald Beckwith, Hartley Power, Wilfrid Hyde White

The Millionaire
US 1931   80m   bw

A bored millionaire retires and secretly buys a garage. Fairly deft star comedy which well satisfied depression audiences. *George Arliss, Florence Arliss,* Evalyn Knapp, David Manners, Noah Beery, J. Farrell MacDonald, James Cagney. Written by Julien Josephson and Booth Tarkington, from a story by Earl Derr Biggers; directed by John Adolfi; for Warner. (NB: Remade in 1947 as *That Way with Women* [qv].)

A Millionaire for Christy
US 1951   91m   bw
TCF (Bert Friedlob)

A lawyer's secretary is sent to Los Angeles to inform an heir of his good fortune, and decides to marry him.
Modest romantic comedy with plenty to be modest about.

w Ken Englund d George Marshall ph Harry Stradling m Victor Young

Eleanor Parker, Fred MacMurray, Richard Carlson, Douglass Dumbrille

The Millionairess*
GB 1960   90m   De Luxe   Cinemascope
TCF / Dimitri de Grunwald (Pierre Rouve)

The richest woman in the world falls for a poor Indian doctor.
Messy travesty of a Shavian comedy that was never more than a star vehicle to begin with. Hardly any of it works despite the star cast, who are mostly miscast.

w Wolf Mankowitz, *play* Bernard Shaw
d Anthony Asquith ph Jack Hildyard
m Georges Van Parys

Sophia Loren, Peter Sellers, Alastair Sim, Vittorio de Sica, Dennis Price, Gary Raymond, Alfie Bass, Miriam Karlin, Noel Purcell
'The result, lacking any sort of dramatic cohesion or continuity and seemingly planned less as a film than as a series of haphazard effects, is merely tiring.'—*Peter John Dyer*

Millions
GB 1936   70m   bw

A struggling composer is really the son of a millionaire. Fairly lively comedy of rival self-made men. Gordon Harker, Frank Pettingell, Richard Hearne, Jane Carr. Written by

Michael Barringer; directed by Leslie Hiscott; for Herbert Wilcox.

Millions like Us**
GB 1943   103m   bw
GFD / Gainsborough (Edward Black)

The tribulations of a family in wartime, especially of the meek daughter who goes into war work and marries an airman, who is killed.

Fragmentary but reasonably accurate picture of the Home Front during World War II; a little more humour would not have been out of place, but as propaganda it proved an effective weapon.

wd Frank Launder, Sidney Gilliat ph Jack Cox *md* Louis Levy

Patricia Roc, Gordon Jackson, Moore Marriott, Eric Portman, Anne Crawford, Basil Radford, Naunton Wayne, Joy Shelton, Megs Jenkins
  'There is an unsentimental warmheartedness which I hope we shall cling to and extend in filmed representations of the British scene.'— *Richard Winnington*
† The only picture Launder and Gilliat directed side by side on the floor.

Mimi
GB 1935   94m   bw

In a Paris garret, a poor girl dies after encouraging a playwright. *La Bohème* without the music; not a good idea. Douglas Fairbanks Jnr, Gertrude Lawrence, Diana Napier, Harold Warrender, Carol Goodner, Richard Bird. Written by Clifford Grey, Paul Merzbach, Jack Davies and Denis Waldock, from the novel *La Vie Bohème* by Henri Murger; directed by Paul Stein; for BIP.

Min and Bill**
US 1930   69m   bw
MGM

A boozy old waterfront character and his wife try to keep her daughter from being placed in care.

Well-remembered and much-loved character comedy which led to the even more successful *Tugboat Annie* with the same team.

w Frances Marion, Marion Jackson, *play* Dark Star by Lorna Moon *d* George Hill
ph Harold Wenstrom

Marie Dressler, Wallace Beery, Dorothy Jordan, Marjorie Rambeau, Donald Dillaway, Russell Hopton

AA: Marie Dressler

The Mind Benders*
GB 1963   113m   bw
Anglo–Amalgamated / Novus (Michael Relph)

A scientist undergoes an experiment aimed at depriving him of all sensation. It works too well; he becomes a sadist; and his colleagues can't reverse the process.
Matter-of-factly played hocus-pocus with spy asides; quite gripping while it's on, but in no way memorable.

w James Kennaway *d* Basil Dearden
ph Denys Coop *m* Georges Auric

Dirk Bogarde, John Clements, Mary Ure, Michael Bryant

The Mind of Mr Reeder*
GB 1939   75m   bw

An elderly government employee unmasks a forger and murderer. Entertaining crime comedy-drama which never quite realizes its potential. Will Fyffe, Kay Walsh, George Curzon, Chili Bouchier, John Warwick. Written by Bryan Edgar Wallace, Marjorie Gaffney and Michael Hogan, from the novel by Edgar Wallace; directed by Jack Raymond; for Grand National.

The Mind of Mr Soames
GB 1970   98m   Technicolor
Columbia / Amicus (Teresa Bolland)

A man who has lived in a coma for thirty years is cured but faces the world as a new-born infant.
Ill-advised attempt at science fiction with meaning; its earnestness becomes a bore.

w John Hale, Edward Simpson, *novel* Charles Eric Maine *d* Alan Cooke *ph* Billy Williams
m Michael Dress

Terence Stamp, Robert Vaughn, Nigel Davenport, Donal Donnelly, Christian Roberts, Vickery Turner, Scott Forbes

Mine Own Executioner***
GB 1947   108m   bw
London Films

A lay psychiatrist undertakes the care of a mentally disturbed war veteran, but fails to prevent him from murdering his wife.
When this film first appeared it seemed like the first adult drama featuring sophisticated people to emerge from a British studio. Time and television have blunted its impact, but it remains a well told suspense melodrama with memorable characters.

w Nigel Balchin, from his novel *d* Anthony Kimmins *ph* Wilkie Cooper *m* Benjamin Frankel

Burgess Meredith, Kieron Moore, Dulcie Gray, Barbara White, Christine Norden
'The first psychoanalytical film that a grown-up can sit through without squirming.'— *Richard Winnington*

Ministry of Fear***
US 1944   85m   bw
Paramount (Seton I. Miller)

During World War II in England, a man just out of a mental hospital wins a cake at a village fair and finds himself caught up in bewildering intrigues.

Little to do with the novel, but a watchable, well-detailed little thriller on Hitchcock lines, once you forgive the usual phoney Hollywood England.

w Seton I. Miller, *novel* Graham Greene d *Fritz Lang* ph *Henry Sharp* m Victor Young

Ray Milland, Marjorie Reynolds, Carl Esmond, Hillary Brooke, Dan Duryea, Percy Waram, Alan Napier, Erskine Sanford
'A crisp and efficiently made thriller with no pretension to intellectual content.'—*Paul Jensen*

The Miniver Story
GB 1950   104m   bw
MGM (Sidney Franklin)

Mrs Miniver faces the tribulations of post-war Britain.

Glum sequel to *Mrs Miniver*, with the dauntless heroine finally succumbing to a glossy but fatal disease. Well enough made, but very hard to take.

w Ronald Millar, George Froeschel d H. C. Potter ph Joseph Ruttenberg m Herbert Stothart

Greer Garson, Walter Pidgeon, Cathy O'Donnell, John Hodiak, Leo Genn, Reginald Owen, Henry Wilcoxon, William Fox, Anthony Bushell

Minnie and Moskowitz*
US 1971   115m   Technicolor
Universal (Al Rubin)

Two lonely Los Angeles misfits have a bumpy courtship.

Enjoyably aimless character comedy.

wd John Cassavetes ph Arthur J. Ornitz m Bob Harwood

Gena Rowlands, Seymour Cassel

Minstrel Man*
US 1944   70m   bw

A minstrel star seeks his long-lost daughter.

Interesting sidelights on old-time minstrel shows in a production somewhat less tatty than is usual from this company. Benny Fields, Gladys George, Roscoe Karns. Written by Irwin Franklin and Pierre Gendron; directed by Joseph H. Lewis; for PRC.

AAN: song, 'Remember Me to Carolina'.

The Miracle
Italy 1948   40m   bw
Tania Film (Roberto Rossellini)

A simple-minded peasant woman is seduced by a shepherd but believes her baby has been immaculately conceived.

Curious, rather unsatisfactory parable originally intended as part of a two-item tribute to the power of a star actress. (The other section, Cocteau's *The Human Voice*, was withdrawn for copyright reasons.)

w Tullio Pinelli, Roberto Rossellini, Federico Fellini d Roberto Rossellini ph Aldo Tonti m Renzo Rossellini

Anna Magnani, Federico Fellini
'Acting on a plane scarcely known to the cinema.'—*Sunday Times*

The Miracle
US 1959   121m   Technirama
Warner (Henry Blanke)

In Spain during the Peninsular War, a nun breaks her vows in order to follow a British soldier, and a statue of the Virgin Mary steps down to take her place.

And that's only the beginning in this very tall tale, full of heavy breathing, violent action and religiosity, from the old Max Reinhardt pageant. Quite incredible, and sloppily done.

w Frank Butler, *play* Karl Vollmoeller d Irving Rapper ph Ernest Haller m Elmer Bernstein

Carroll Baker, Roger Moore, Walter Slezak, Vittorio Gassman, Katina Paxinou, Dennis King, Isobel Elsom, Torin Thatcher

Miracle in Milan**
Italy 1951   101m   bw
PDS / ENIC

A foundling goes to live with the poor on the outskirts of Milan, and his erstwhile guardian returns from heaven to help them repel capitalists and fly away on broomsticks to a better land.

An unlikely fable which manages to avoid all the obvious pitfalls and sends one out of the cinema in a warm glow.

w Cesare Zavattini, Vittorio de Sica,
novel Toto il Buono by Cesare Zavattini
d *Vittorio de Sica* *ph* G. R. Aldo
m Alessandro Cicognini

Francesco Golisano, Brunella Bovo, Emma
Gramatica, Paolo Stoppa

Miracle in Soho
GB 1957 93m Eastmancolor
Rank (Emeric Pressburger)

A Soho roadworker falls for a barmaid.
Rudimentary romantic whimsy in an
unconvincing street set, with characters either
too voluble or just plain dull.

w Emeric Pressburger *d* Julian Amyes
ph Christopher Challis *m* Brian Easdale

John Gregson, Belinda Lee, Cyril Cusack

Miracle in the Rain**
US 1954 107m bw
Warner (Frank P. Rosenberg)

A plain New York girl falls for a soldier; when
he is killed in action, he keeps their
appointment on the church steps as a ghost.
Archetypal Hollywood schmaltz, half acute
observation of amusing types, half sentimental
whimsy, with a final supernatural touch of
eating your cake and having it.

w *Ben Hecht* *d* Rudolph Maté *ph* Russell
Metty *m* Franz Waxman

Jane Wyman, Van Johnson, Fred Clark,
Eileen Heckart, William Gargan

The Miracle Man
US 1932 85m bw
Paramount

A gang of crooks is reformed by a faith healer
they have exploited.
Adequate remake of the silent Lon Chaney
vehicle; no sparks this time.

w Waldemar Young, Samuel Hoffenstein, *play*
Frank L. Packard, George M. Cohan
d Norman Z. McLeod *ph* David Abel

Sylvia Sidney, Chester Morris, Irving Pichel,
John Wray, Robert Coogan, Hobart
Bosworth, Boris Karloff, Ned Sparks, Virginia
Bruce

The Miracle of Morgan's Creek****
US 1943 99m bw
Paramount (Preston Sturges)

Chaos results when a stuttering hayseed tries
to help a girl accidentally pregnant by a soldier
she met hazily at a dance.
Weird and wonderful one-man assault on the
Hays Office and sundry other American
institutions such as motherhood and politics;

an indescribable, tasteless, roaringly funny
mêlée, as unexpected at the time as it was
effective, like a kick in the pants to all other
film comedies.

wd *Preston Sturges* *ph* John Seitz *m* Leo
Shuken, Charles Bradshaw

Betty Hutton, Eddie Bracken, William
Demarest, Diana Lynn, Porter Hall, Akim
Tamiroff, Brian Donlevy, Alan Bridge
'Like taking a nun on a roller coaster.'—
James Agee
'This film moves in a fantastic and irreverent
whirl of slapstick, nonsense, farce, sentiment,
satire, romance, melodrama—is there any
ingredient of dramatic entertainment except
maybe tragedy and grand opera that hasn't
been tossed into it?'—*National Board of
Review*
'Bad taste or no bad taste, I thoroughly
enjoyed it.'—*Richard Mallett, Punch*
AAN: Preston Sturges (as writer)

The Miracle of Our Lady of Fatima
US 1952 102m Warnercolor
Warner (Bryan Foy)

An account of the 1917 appearance of the
Virgin Mary to three Portuguese peasant
children.
Poorly staged religious film which manages to
be less pro-Catholic than anti-communist, and
was clearly seen by Jack L. Warner as a means
of atoning for *Mission to Moscow*. A real cold
war piece.

w Crane Wilbur, James O'Hanlon *d* John
Brahm *ph* Edwin DuPar *m* Max Steiner
ad Edward Carrere

Gilbert Roland, Frank Silvera, Angela Clarke,
Jay Novello
AAN: Max Steiner

The Miracle of the Bells
US 1948 120m bw
Jesse L. Lasky

The death of a glamorous film star causes a
small-town miracle and a nationwide publicity
stunt.
One hopes that this oddity was intended as a
satire; as a straight entertainment it's more
than a little icky, and good production values
scarcely help.

w Ben Hecht, *novel* Russell Janney *d* Irving
Rapper *ph* Robert de Grasse *m* Leigh
Harline

Fred MacMurray, Alida Valli, Frank Sinatra,
Lee J. Cobb
'An offensive exhibition of vulgar
insensitivity.'—*MFB*

'I hereby declare myself the founding father of the Society for the Prevention of Cruelty to God.'—*James Agee*

The Miracle of the White Stallions*
US 1962   118m   Technicolor
Walt Disney (Peter V. Herald)
GB title: *The Flight of the White Stallions*

During World War II the Nazis occupy Vienna and the owner of the Spanish Riding School guides his stallions to safety.
Adequate family adventure fare with a dull hero but interesting backgrounds.

w A. J. Carothers *d* Arthur Hiller
ph Gunther Anders *m* Paul Smith

Robert Taylor, Lilli Palmer, Eddie Albert, Curt Jurgens

Miracle on Main Street*
US 1940   76m   bw
RKO / Jack Skirball

A cabaret dancer finds an abandoned baby but her plans are thwarted by the return of her husband.
Odd, interesting but flatly handled melodrama.

w Sam Ornitz, Boris Ingster, *story* Felix Jackson *d* Steve Sekely *ph* Charles Van Enger

Walter Abel, Margo, William Collier, Jane Darwell, Lyle Talbot, Wynne Gibson

Miracle on 34th Street***
US 1947   94m   bw
TCF (William Perlberg)
GB title: *The Big Heart*

A department store Santa Claus claims to be the real thing.
Mainly charming comedy fantasy which quickly became an American classic but does suffer from a few dull romantic stretches.

wd George Seaton, *story* Valentine Davies
ph Charles Clarke, Lloyd Ahern *m* Cyril Mockridge

Edmund Gwenn, Maureen O'Hara, John Payne, Natalie Wood, Gene Lockhart, Porter Hall, William Frawley, Jerome Cowan, Thelma Ritter

AA: George Seaton (as writer); Valentine Davies; Edmund Gwenn
AAN: best picture

The Miracle Woman*
US 1932   90m   bw
Columbia (Harry Cohn)

A lady evangelist turns confidence trickster.
Mild satirical drama inspired by the career of Aimée Semple Macpherson.

w Jo Swerling, *play* Bless You Sister by Robert Riskin, John Meehan *d* Frank Capra
ph Joseph Walker *m* uncredited

Barbara Stanwyck, Sam Hardy, David Manners, Beryl Mercer, Russell Hopton
'Such a beauty, well staged and handsomely lighted.'—*New Yorker, 1977*

The Miracle Worker*
US 1962   106m   bw
UA / Playfilms (Fred Coe)

The childhood of Helen Keller, taught by Annie Sullivan after being left blind, deaf and dumb in an illness.
A moving real-life story is given hysterical treatment and the good scenes have a hard task winning through; in any case a documentary might have been more persuasive.

w William Gibson, from his play *d* Arthur Penn *ph* Ernest Caparros *m* Laurence Rosenthal *ad* George Jenkins

Anne Bancroft, Patty Duke, Victor Jory, Inga Swenson, Andrew Prine, Beah Richards

AA: Anne Bancroft; Patty Duke
AAN: William Gibson; Arthur Penn

Miracles for Sale
US 1939   71m   bw

An illusionist catches a murderer. What could have been a smart mystery piece is sabotaged by stilted writing and direction, a muddled narrative style, and illusions which are patently faked by the camera. Robert Young, Florence Rice, Henry Hull, Frank Craven, Lee Bowman, William Demarest. Written by James Edward Grant, Marion Parsonnet and Harry Ruskin, from the novel *Death in a Top Hat* by Clayton Rawson; directed by Tod Browning; for MGM.

Mirage***
US 1965   109m   bw
U-I (Harry Keller)

During a New York power blackout, an executive falls to his death from a skyscraper and a cost accountant loses his memory.
Striking puzzler, rather slowly developed but generally effective and with a strong sense of place and timing.

w Peter Stone, *novel* Walter Ericson
d Edward Dmytryk *ph* Joe MacDonald
m Quincy Jones

Gregory Peck, Diane Baker, Walter Abel, *Walter Matthau*, Leif Erickson, Kevin McCarthy

Miranda*
GB 1947   80m   bw
GFD / Gainsborough

A doctor on holiday in Cornwall catches a
mermaid and takes her to London disguised as
an invalid.
Simple-minded comedy which scores a few
easy laughs on obvious targets.

w Peter Blackmore, from his play d Ken
Annakin ph Ray Elton m Temple Abady

Glynis Johns, Griffith Jones, Googie Withers,
Margaret Rutherford, David Tomlinson, Sonia
Holm, John McCallum
† Sequel 1949, *Mad about Men.*

The Mirror Crack'd*
GB 1980   105m   Technicolor
EMI / John Brabourne, Richard,Goodwin

Murders result from the making of an all-star
film in an English village.
After adventures on the Orient Express and
the Nile, this follow-up in the Agatha Christie
stakes seems somewhat subdued, but the
production is polished and the murder plot
compels attention.

w Jonathan Hales, Barry Sandler
novel Agatha Christie d Guy Hamilton
ph Christopher Challis m John Cameron
pd Michael Stringer

Angela Lansbury, Geraldine Chaplin,
Elizabeth Taylor, Rock Hudson, Tony Curtis,
Edward Fox, Kim Novak, Marella
Oppenheim, Charles Gray

Les Misérables****
US 1935   109m   bw
Twentieth Century (Darryl F. Zanuck)

Unjustly convicted and sentenced to years in
the galleys, Jean Valjean emerges to build up
his life again but is hounded by a cruel and
relentless police officer.
Solid, telling, intelligent version of a much-
filmed classic novel; in adaptation and
performance it is hard to see how this film
could be bettered.

w W. P. Lipscomb, *novel* Victor Hugo
d Richard Boleslawski ph Gregg Toland
m Alfred Newman

Fredric March, Charles Laughton, Cedric
Hardwicke, Rochelle Hudson, Frances Drake,
John Beal, Jessie Ralph, Florence Eldridge
  'A superlative effort, a thrilling, powerful,
poignant picture.'—*New York Evening Post*
  'Deserving of rank among the cinema's
finest achievements.'—*New York World
Telegram*

† Other versions of the story: 1909, 1913
(French); 1917 (William Farnum); 1923
(French: Gabriel Gabrio); 1929 as *The
Bishop's Candlesticks* (Walter Huston); 1934
(French: Harry Baur); 1946 (Italian: Gino
Cervi); 1952 (see below); 1956 (French: Jean
Gabin); 1978 (British: Richard Jordan).
AAN: best picture; Gregg Toland

Les Misérables**
US 1952   106m   bw
TCF (Fred Kohlmar)

Solemn remake, well done but lacking the
spark of inspiration.

w Richard Murphy d Lewis Milestone
ph Joseph La Shelle m Alex North

Michael Rennie, Robert Newton, Edmund
Gwenn, Debra Paget, Cameron Mitchell,
Sylvia Sidney, Elsa Lanchester, James
Robertson Justice, Joseph Wiseman, Rhys
Williams

The Misfits*
US 1961   124m   bw
United Artists / Seven Arts (Frank E. Taylor)

Cowboys gather in the Nevada desert to rope
wild mustangs, and a divorcee becomes
involved with one of them.
Ill-fated melodrama whose stars both died
shortly afterwards; a solemn, unattractive,
pretentious film which seldom stops wallowing
in self-pity.

w Arthur Miller d John Huston ph Russell
Metty m Alex North

Clark Gable, Marilyn Monroe, Montgomery
Clift, Eli Wallach, Thelma Ritter, James
Barton, Estelle Winwood, Kevin McCarthy

Miss Annie Rooney
US 1942   86m   bw
Edward Small

Poor Irish girl loves rich boy.
A totally routine offering for a teenage star;
no wonder she didn't make it.

w George Bruce d Edwin L. Marin
ph Lester White md Edward Paul

Shirley Temple, William Gargan, Guy Kibbee,
Dickie Moore, Peggy Ryan, Gloria Holden,
Jonathan Hale, Mary Field

Miss Grant Takes Richmond*
US 1949   87m   bw
Columbia (S. Sylvan Simon)
GB title: *Innocence Is Bliss*

A dumb secretary helps defeat crooks and
improve the local housing situation.
Mildly amusing star comedy.

w Nat Perrin, Devery Freeman, Frank Tashlin *d* Lloyd Bacon *ph* Charles Lawton Jnr *m* Heinz Roemheld *md* Morris Stoloff

Lucille Ball, William Holden, Janis Carter, James Gleason, Gloria Henry, Frank McHugh, George Cleveland
'One of the more delightful comedies of the season.'—*Lawrence J. Quirk*

Miss London Ltd
GB 1943 99m bw
GFD / Gainsborough (Edward Black)

An escort agency is formed to assist soldiers on leave.
Flagwaving light entertainment with popular performers of the time.

w Val Guest, Marriott Edgar *d* Val Guest

Arthur Askey, Anne Shelton, Evelyn Dall, Richard Hearne, Max Bacon, Jack Train, Peter Graves, Jean Kent

Miss Marple
Agatha Christie's inquisitive spinster detective was brought to the screen by director George Pollock and star Margaret Rutherford in four increasingly disappointing films for MGM.
1962: MURDER SHE SAID (qv)
1963: MURDER AT THE GALLOP
1964: MURDER MOST FOUL, MURDER AHOY
See also *The Mirror Crack'd*.

Miss Pacific Fleet
US 1935 76m bw

Two stranded show girls enter a popularity contest to win the fare back home. A comedy with little to laugh at. Glenda Farrell, Joan Blondell, Hugh Herbert, Allen Jenkins, Warren Hull, Guinn Williams. Written by Lucille Newmark, Peter Milne and Patsy Flick; directed by Ray Enright; for Warner.

Miss Pilgrim's Progress
GB 1949 82m bw

An American working girl in Britain helps to save a village from development. Wholly artificial and unendearing comedy. Yolande Donlan, Michael Rennie, Garry Marsh, Emrys Jones, Reginald Beckwith, Helena Pickard, Jon Pertwee. Written and directed by Val Guest; for Daniel M. Angel.

Miss Pinkerton*
US 1932 66m bw
Warner

A private nurse helps a police detective to solve a murder case.
Pleasing little mystery comedy.

w Lilyan Hayward, Niven Busch, *story* Mary Roberts Rinehart *d* Lloyd Bacon *ph* Barney McGill

Joan Blondell, George Brent, Mae Madison, John Wray, Ruth Hall, C. Henry Gordon, Elizabeth Patterson
† Remade as *The Nurse's Secret* (1946).

Miss Robin Hood
GB 1952 78m bw

A lady author pits her wits against crooks and saves an old lady's fortune. Disappointing star comedy with no build-up. Margaret Rutherford, Richard Hearne, Michael Medwin, Peter Jones, James Robertson Justice, Sidney James, Dora Bryan. Written by Val Valentine, Patrick Campbell and Geoffrey Orme; directed by John Guillermin; for Group 3.

Miss Sadie Thompson*
US 1953 91m Technicolor 3-D
Columbia (Lewis J. Rachmil)

Vigorous semi-musical remake of *Rain* (qv); a good star vehicle, but not otherwise notable.

w Harry Kleiner *d* Curtis Bernhardt *ph* Charles Lawton *md* George Duning

Rita Hayworth, Jose Ferrer, Aldo Ray, Russell Collins, Harry Bellaver

AAN: song 'Blue Pacific Blues' (*m* Lester Lee, *ly* Ned Washington)

Miss Susie Slagle's
US 1946 88m bw
Paramount (John Houseman)

Romances of nursing students in 1910 Baltimore.
Modest melodramatic potboiler.

w Anne Froelich, Hugo Butler, *novel* Augusta Tucker *d* John Berry *ph* Charles Lang Jnr *m* Daniele Amfitheatrof

Veronica Lake, Joan Caulfield, Sonny Tufts, Lillian Gish, Ray Collins, Billy de Wolfe, Bill Edwards, Roman Bohnen, Morris Carnovsky, Lloyd Bridges

Miss Tatlock's Millions*
US 1948 101m bw
Paramount (Charles Brackett)

A stunt man impersonates the idiot heir to a fortune.
Tasteless but quite funny comedy with a cast of eccentrics indulging in enjoyable fooling.

w Charles Brackett, Richard L. Breen *d* Richard Haydn *ph* Charles Lang Jnr *m* Victor Young

John Lund, Wanda Hendrix, Monty Woolley,
Barry Fitzgerald, Robert Stack, Ilka Chase,
Dorothy Stickney

Miss V from Moscow
US 1943 70m bw

A Russian spy impersonates a German spy in
Paris. Hilariously inept propaganda piece;
since the Cold War it has been retitled *Intrigue
in Paris*. Lola Lane, Noel Madison, Howard
Banks. Written by Arthur St Claire and
Sherman Lowe; directed by Albert Herman;
for PRC.

The Missing Juror
US 1944 71m bw

Members of a murder jury are killed off one
by one. Minor puzzle piece from the *I Love a
Mystery* series. Jim Bannon, Janis Carter,
George Macready. Written by Charles
O'Neal; directed by Budd Boetticher; for
Columbia.

The Missing Rembrandt
GB 1932 82m bw

Sherlock Holmes saves a lady's honour and
nails a blackmailer. Not the best of this
particular series, but Wontner is a Holmes to
relish. Arthur Wontner, Ian Fleming, Jane
Welsh, Miles Mander, Francis L. Sullivan.
Written by Cyril Twyford and H. Fowler
Mear, from the story *Charles Augustus
Milverton* by Arthur Conan Doyle; directed by
Leslie Hiscott; for Twickenham.

Mission to Moscow**
US 1943 112m bw
Warner (Robert Buckner)

The Russian career of US Ambassador Joseph
E. Davies.
Stodgy but fascinating wartime propaganda
piece viewing the Russians as warm-hearted
allies; in the later days of the McCarthy witch
hunt, Jack L. Warner regretted he had ever
allowed it to be made.

w Howard Koch, *book* Joseph E. Davies
d Michael Curtiz *ph* Bert Glennon *m* Max
Steiner

Walter Huston, Ann Harding, Oscar
Homolka, George Tobias, Gene Lockhart,
Eleanor Parker, Richard Travis, Helmut
Dantine, Victor Francen, Henry Daniell,
Barbara Everest, Dudley Field Malone,
Roman Bohnen, Maria Palmer, Moroni
Olsen, Minor Watson

'A mishmash: of Stalinism with New
Dealism with Hollywoodism with opportunism
with shaky experimentalism with mesmerism

with onanism, all mosaicked into a remarkable
portrait of what the makers of the film think
the Soviet Union is like—a great glad two-
million-dollar bowl of canned borscht,
eminently approvable by the Institute of Good
Housekeeping.'—*James Agee*

Mississippi*
US 1935 80m bw
Paramount (Arthur Hornblow Jnr)

A showboat singer has a cloud on his
reputation.
Mild period musical with occasional stops for
comedy.

w Herbert Fields, Claude Binyon, *story* Booth
Tarkington *d* Edward A. Sutherland
ph Charles Lang *m / ly* Rodgers and Hart

Bing Crosby, W. C. Fields, Joan Bennett, Gail
Patrick, Claude Gillingwater, John Miljan,
Queenie Smith

Mississippi Gambler
US 1953 98m Technicolor
U-I (Ted Richmond)

A showboat gambler has trouble with a bad
loser, but finally marries his sister.
Picturesque star melodrama with period
settings and not much meat in the story.

w Seton I. Miller *d* Rudolph Maté *ph* Irving
Glassberg *m* Frank Skinner

Tyrone Power, Piper Laurie, John McIntyre,
Julia Adams, Dennis Weaver

The Missouri Breaks
US 1976 126m De Luxe
UA / Elliott Kastner / Robert B. Sherman

Montana ranchers and rustlers fight over land
and livestock, and a hired killer shoots it out
with a horse thief.
Savage, dislikeable western with both stars
over the top.

w Thomas McGuane *d* Arthur Penn
ph Michael Butler *m* John Williams

Marlon Brando, Jack Nicholson, Randy
Quaid, Kathleen Lloyd, Frederic Forrest,
Harry Dean Stanton

'It is typical of the film's richness and
ambiguity that the title has about five possible
punning meanings.'—*Michael Billington,
Illustrated London News*

'Although listed as the director, Mr Penn
finds himself perched on Brando's knee and
manipulated as shamelessly as Edgar Bergen
used to waggle Charlie McCarthy.'—*Benny
Green, Punch*

'Nothing more than the self-conscious
cleverness of some merry prankster with a

blanket of scorn for all who don't share his flippancy.'—*William S. Pechter*

'A pair of million dollar babies in a five and ten cent flick.'—*Charles Champlin, Los Angeles Times*

'A picture of which it might be said they shouldn't make 'em like that any more . . . a picture that explains very little, including why anyone thought it a work that demanded to be made.'—*Robert Hatch, Nation*

Mr Ace
US 1946   84m   bw
Benedict Bogeaus

A rich, spoiled congresswoman is backed by a gangster but gets religion.
Odd star drama, perfunctorily made.

w Fred Finklehoffe d Edwin L. Marin
ph Karl Struss m Heinz Roemheld

Sylvia Sidney, George Raft, Stanley Ridges, Sara Haden, Jerome Cowan

Mr and Mrs Smith*
US 1941   95m   bw
RKO (Harry E. Edington)

A much-married couple discover that their marriage wasn't legal.
Smartish matrimonial comedy, surprisingly but not obviously directed by the master of suspense.

w Norman Krasna d Alfred Hitchcock
ph Harry Stradling m Edward Ward

Carole Lombard, Robert Montgomery, Gene Raymond, Jack Carson, Philip Merivale, Lucile Watson, William Tracy

'I doubt that your interest or amusement will last as long as the picture.'—*Otis Ferguson*

Mr Belvedere Goes to College*
US 1949   88m   bw
TCF (Samuel G. Engel)

A self-styled genius goes back to school and helps a college widow.
Flat follow up to *Sitting Pretty* (qv), with only a few laughs.

w Richard Sale, Mary Loos, Mary McCall Jnr
d Elliott Nugent ph Lloyd Ahern m Alfred Newman

Clifton Webb, Shirley Temple, Alan Young, Tom Drake, Jessie Royce Landis, Kathleen Hughes, Taylor Holmes

Mr Belvedere Rings the Bell*
US 1951   87m   bw
TCF (André Hakim)

Imperturbable Mr Belvedere enters an old folks' home under false pretences to test his theories of ageing.

A not unagreeable star vehicle for those who can stand the sentiment.

w Ranald MacDougall, *play* The Silver Whistle by Robert E. McEnroe d Henry Koster ph Joseph La Shelle m Cyril Mockridge

Clifton Webb, Joanne Dru, Hugh Marlowe, Zero Mostel, Doro Merande

Mr Billion*
US 1977   93m   De Luxe
TCF / Pantheon (Gabriel Katzka, Steve Bach, Ken Friedman)

An Italian garage mechanic becomes heir to a vast estate, providing he can get to San Francisco in time for the signing ceremony and outwit the villains trying to stop him.
Moderately engaging old-fashioned comedy-adventure.

w Ken Friedman, Jonathan Kaplan
d Jonathan Kaplan ph Matthew F. Leonetti
m Dave Grusin

Terence Hill, Valerie Perrine, Jackie Gleason, Slim Pickens, William Redfield, Chill Wills

Mr Blandings Builds His Dream House***
US 1948   84m   bw
RKO (Norman Panama, Melvin Frank)

A New York advertising man longs to live in the Connecticut countryside, but finds the way to rural satisfaction is hard.
It hasn't the lightness and brightness of the book, but this is a fun film for the middle-aged who like to watch three agreeable stars doing their thing.

w Norman Panama, Melvin Frank, novel Eric Hodgkin d H. C. Potter ph James Wong Howe m Leigh Harline md Constantin Bakaleinikoff

Cary Grant, Myrna Loy, Melvyn Douglas, Reginald Denny, Louise Beavers, Ian Wolfe, Harry Shannon, Nestor Paiva, Jason Robards

'A bulls-eye for middle-class middlebrows.'—*James Agee*

'I loved it. That was really a pleasure to make.'—*H. C. Potter, 1973*

Mister Buddwing
US 1966   99m   bw
MGM / DDD / Cherokee (Douglas Laurence, Delbert Mann)
GB title: *Woman without a Face*

An amnesiac wakes up in Central Park and goes in search of his identity.
Rather muddled melodrama in which the characters are so dull that by the time the flashbacks fall into place we scarcely care.

w Dale Wassermann, *novel* Buddwing by
Evan Hunter *d* Delbert Mann *ph* Ellsworth
Fredericks *m* Kenyon Hopkins

James Garner, Jean Simmons, Angela
Lansbury, Suzanne Pleshette, Katharine Ross,
George Voskovec, Jack Gilford, Joe Mantell,
Raymond St Jacques

Mister Cory
US 1957 92m Eastmancolor
  Cinemascope
U-I (Robert Arthur)

A small-time gangster leaves the Chicago
slums to seek fame and fortune among the
country-club set.
Modest star comedy drama.

wd Blake Edwards *ph* Russell Metty
m Joseph Gershenson

Tony Curtis, Martha Hyer, Charles Bickford,
Kathryn Grant

Mr Deeds Goes to Town***
US 1936 118m bw
Columbia (Frank Capra)

A small-town poet inherits a vast fortune and
sets New York on its heels by his honesty.
What once was fresh and charming now seems
rather laboured in spots, and the production is
parsimonious indeed, but the courtroom scene
still works, and the good intentions conquer
all.

w Robert Riskin, story Opera Hat by Clarence
Budington Kelland *d Frank Capra ph* Joseph
Walker *m* Adolph Deutsch *md* Howard
Jackson

Gary Cooper, Jean Arthur, Raymond
Walburn, Lionel Stander, Walter Catlett,
George Bancroft, Douglass Dumbrille, H. B.
Warner, Ruth Donnelly, *Margaret Seddon,
Margaret McWade*

'I have an uneasy feeling he's on his way
out. He's started to make pictures about
themes instead of people.'—*Alistair Cooke*
'Everywhere the picture goes, from the
endearing to the absurd, the accompanying
business is carried through with perfect zip and
relish.'—*Otis Ferguson*
'A comedy quite unmatched on the
screen.'—*Graham Greene*

AA: Frank Capra
AAN: best picture; Robert Riskin; Gary
Cooper

Mr Denning Drives North
GB 1951 93m bw
London Films (Anthony Kimmins, Stephen
  Mitchell)

A wealthy man accidentally kills a criminal in
love with his daughter; he hides the body,
which then disappears.
Initially suspenseful but finally disappointing
melodrama which seems to lack a twist or two.

w Alec Coppel *d* Anthony Kimmins *ph* John
Wilcox *m* Benjamin Frankel

John Mills, Phyllis Calvert, Sam Wanamaker,
Freda Jackson

Mr Dodd Takes the Air
US 1937 78m bw
Warner (Mervyn Le Roy)

A country cousin becomes a hit as a crooner.
Modest comedy for small towns.

w William Wister Haines, Elaine Ryan,
story Clarence Budington Kelland *d* Alfred
E. Green *ph* Arthur Edeson *songs* Al
Dubin, Harry Warren

Kenny Baker, Jane Wyman, Alice Brady,
Gertrude Michael, Frank McHugh, Luis
Alberni, Henry O'Neill, Harry Davenport

AAN: Al Dubin and Harry Warren for
'Remember Me'

Mr Drake's Duck**
GB 1950 85m bw
Daniel M. Angel / Douglas Fairbanks

A duck lays a uranium egg, and a gentleman
farmer finds himself at the centre of
international military disagreement.
Brisk and amusing minor comedy deploying
British comic types to good purpose.

wd Val Guest, radio play Ian Messiter
ph Jack Cox

Douglas Fairbanks Jnr, Yolande Donlan,
Wilfrid Hyde White, A. E. Matthews, Jon
Pertwee, Reginald Beckwith, Howard Marion-
Crawford, Peter Butterworth, Tom Gill

Mister 880**
US 1950 90m bw
TCF (Julian Blaustein)

An elderly counterfeiter perplexes the US
Secret Service.
Whimsical star comedy which moves along
cheerfully enough to be a good example of the
Hollywood programmer at its prime.

w Robert Riskin *d* Edmund Goulding
ph Joseph La Shelle *m* Sol Kaplan

Edmund Gwenn, Burt Lancaster, Dorothy
McGuire, Millard Mitchell

AAN: Edmund Gwenn

Mr Emmanuel*
GB 1944 97m bw
Two Cities (William Sistrom)

In 1936 an elderly Jew visits Germany in search of the mother of an orphan boy. Simply made but quite effective and unusual story giving Aylmer his only star part.

w Gordon Wellesley, Norman Ginsburg, *novel* Louis Golding d Harold French ph Otto Heller

Felix Aylmer, Greta Gynt, Walter Rilla, Peter Mullins, Ursula Jeans, Elspeth March, Meier Tzelniker

Mr Forbush and the Penguins*
GB 1971 101m Technicolor
EMI / PGI / Henry Trettin

A biologist is sent to the Antarctic to study penguins, and gets a new understanding of life.
Rather broken-backed animal film with a moral; pleasant enough, its two halves don't fit together.

w Anthony Shaffer, *novel* Graham Billey d Roy Boulting, *Arne Sucksdorff* ph Harry Waxman, Ted Scaife m John Addison

John Hurt, Hayley Mills, Tony Britton

Mr Hobbs Takes a Vacation*
US 1962 116m De Luxe Cinemascope
TCF (Jerry Wald)

A city dweller takes a seaside house for a family holiday, but it turns out to be a crumbling ruin.
Overlong, sloppy comedy which devotes too much time to teenage romance but manages occasional smiles.

w Nunnally Johnson, *novel* Edward Streeter d Henry Koster ph W. C. Mellor m Henry Mancini

James Stewart, Maureen O'Hara, Fabian, John Saxon, Marie Wilson, Reginald Gardiner, *John McGiver*

Mr Imperium
US 1951 87m Technicolor
MGM (Edwin H. Knopf)
GB title: *You Belong to My Heart*

An exiled king in Hollywood meets a famous film star with whom he once had a romance. Minor romantic drama with songs.

w Edwin Knopf, Don Hartman d Don Hartman ph George J. Folsey *songs* Harold Arlen m Bronislau Kaper

Lana Turner, Ezio Pinza, Marjorie Main, Barry Sullivan, Cedric Hardwicke, Debbie Reynolds

Mr Klein*
France / Italy 1976 123m Eastmancolor
Lira / Adel / Nova / Mondial Te-Fi
(Raymond Danon, Alain Delon)

In 1942 Paris, a prosperous antique dealer is mistaken for a mysterious Jew of the same name, and despite the danger gradually assumes his identity.
Complex Kafkaesque character study: occasionally arresting but generally rather glum.

w Franco Solinas d Joseph Losey ph Gerry Fisher m Egisto Macchi, Pierre Porte

Alain Delon, Jeanne Moreau, Suzanne Flon, Michael Lonsdale, Louis Seigner, Juliet Berto

Mr Lucky*
US 1943 98m bw
RKO (David Hempstead)

During World War II a gambling ship owner goes straight and instigates Bundles for Britain.
Unconvincing mixture of comedy and drama with the actors looking somewhat bewildered.

w Milton Holmes, Adrian Scott d H. C. Potter ph George Barnes m Roy Webb

Cary Grant, Laraine Day, Charles Bickford, Gladys Cooper, Alan Carney, Henry Stephenson, Paul Stewart, Walter Kingsford
'If it weren't for Cary Grant's persuasive personality the whole thing would melt away to nothing at all.'—*Philip G. Hartung*
† Remade 1950 as *Gambling House*.

Mr Majestyk*
US 1974 103m De Luxe
UA / Mirisch (Walter Mirisch)

A Colorado melon grower crosses swords with the local Mafia.
Violent but unexpectedly enjoyable action melodrama.

w Elmore Leonard d Richard Fleischer ph Richard Kline m Charles Bernstein

Charles Bronson, Al Lettieri, Linda Cristal, Lee Purcell, Paul Keslo

Mister Moses*
GB 1965 103m Technicolor
Panavision
UA / Frank Ross / Talbot

A quack doctor is the only person who can persuade an African tribe to move before their land is flooded, and he leads them to their promised land.
Adventure spectacle with naïve biblical parallels; quite agreeable.

w Charles Beaumont, Monja Danischewsky,
novel Max Catto d Ronald Neame
ph Oswald Morris *m* John Barry

Robert Mitchum, Carroll Baker, Ian Bannen,
Alexander Knox, Reginald Beckwith,
Raymond St Jacques

Mr Moto

The Japanese detective created by John P.
Marquand and played by Peter Lorre figured
in several above-average second features of
the late thirties, but the outbreak of war
caused him to vanish. The casts were
interesting, the TCF production excellent, and
the director usually Norman Foster. The 1965
attempt to revive the character with Henry
Silva was painfully boring.

1937: THINK FAST MR MOTO (with
Virginia Field, Sig Rumann), THANK YOU
MR MOTO (with Pauline Frederick, Sidney
Blackmer)
1938: MR MOTO'S GAMBLE (with Keye
Luke, Lynn Bari), MR MOTO TAKES A
CHANCE (with Rochelle Hudson, J. Edward
Bromberg), MYSTERIOUS MR MOTO
(with Henry Wilcoxon, Erik Rhodes)
1939: MR MOTO'S LAST WARNING (with
Ricardo Cortez, George Sanders, Robert
Coote, John Carradine), MR MOTO IN
DANGER ISLAND (with Jean Hersholt,
Warren Hymer), MR MOTO TAKES A
VACATION (with Joseph Schildkraut, Lionel
Atwill)
1965: THE RETURN OF MR MOTO

Mr Music*

US 1950 113m bw
Paramount (Robert L. Welch)

A college girl is employed to keep an idle
middle-aged songwriter's nose to the
grindstone.
Bland musical remake of *Accent on Youth*
(qv); pleasant performances, moments of
comedy, guest stars.

w Arthur Sheekman d Richard Haydn
ph George Barnes *songs* Johnny Burke,
James Van Heusen *ad* Hans Dreier, Earl
Hedrick

Bing Crosby, Nancy Olson, Charles Coburn,
Ruth Hussey, Marge and Gower Champion,
Peggy Lee, Groucho Marx

Mr Peabody and the Mermaid

US 1948 89m bw
U-I (Nunnally Johnson)

A middle-aged husband imagines an affair
with a mermaid.
Bone-headed quick-cash-in on *Miranda* (qv);
it never begins to work.

w Nunnally Johnson, *novel* Guy and
Constance Jones d Irving Pichel *ph* Russell
Metty *m* Robert Emmett Dolan

William Powell, Ann Blyth, Irene Hervey,
Andrea King, Clinton Sundberg

Mr Perrin and Mr Traill*

GB 1948 92m bw
GFD / Two Cities (Alexander Galperson)

A handsome young master at a boys' school
incurs the jealousy of an embittered colleague.
Flat, over-acted but mildly watchable
picturization of a well-known story.

w L. A. G. Strong, *novel* Hugh Walpole
d Lawrence Huntington *ph* Erwin Hillier
m Alan Gray

Marius Goring, David Farrar, Greta Gynt,
Edward Chapman, Raymond Huntley, Mary
Jerrold, Finlay Currie, Ralph Truman

Mister Quilp

GB 1975 119m Technicolor
  Panavision
Reader's Digest (Helen M. Straus)
aka: *The Old Curiosity Shop*

In 1840 London, an antique-shop owner is in
debt to a hunchback moneylender who has
designs on his business.
The novel, with its villainous lead, is a curious
choice for musicalizing, and in this treatment
falls desperately flat, with no sparkle of
imagination visible anywhere.

w Louis Kamp, Irene Kamp, *novel* The Old
Curiosity Shop by Charles Dickens d Michael
Tuchner *ph* Christopher Challis *m* Anthony
Newley *pd* Elliot Scott *md* Elmer Bernstein
ch Gillian Lynne

Anthony Newley, Michael Hordern, David
Hemmings, Sarah-Jane Varley, David
Warner, Paul Rogers, Jill Bennett

'Another soggy piece of family
entertainment from Reader's Digest, who
produced the toothless screen musicals of *Tom
Sawyer* and *Huckleberry Finn*.'—*Philip French*
'Dickens shorn of sentiment, melodrama or
love . . . Mr Newley's Quilp, a galvanized
Quasimodo on a permanent high, is something
of a strain to watch.'—*Michael Billington,
Illustrated London News*

Mr Ricco

US 1975 98m Panavision colour
MGM (Douglas Netter)

A defence counsel risks his life to prove his
black client innocent.
Complex urban action thriller with a tired,
ageing hero and impenetrable plot.

w Robert Hoban *d* Paul Bogart *ph* Frank Stanley *m* Chico Hamilton

Dean Martin, Eugene Roche, Thalmus Rasulala, Denise Nicholas, Cindy Williams, *Geraldine Brooks*, Frank Puglia

Mister Roberts**

US 1955   123m   Warnercolor
Cinemascope
Warner / Leland Hayward

Life aboard a World War II cargo ship yearning for action.
A mixture of comedy and sentimentality which has become an American minor classic as a play; this film version is a shambling affair but gets most of the effects over.

w Frank Nugent, Joshua Logan, *play* Thomas Heggen and Joshua Logan, *novel Thomas Heggen d* John Ford, Mervyn Le Roy *ph* Winton Hoch *m* Franz Waxman

Henry Fonda, James Cagney, William Powell, Jack Lemmon, Betsy Palmer, Ward Bond, Phil Carey, Ken Curtis, Harry Carey Jnr

AA: Jack Lemmon
AAN: best picture

Mr Robinson Crusoe

US 1932   76m   bw
Douglas Fairbanks

A playboy takes a bet that he could live alone on a desert island . . . but a girl turns up.
Mild adventure comedy with the star in subdued form.

w Douglas Fairbanks *d* Edward Sutherland *ph* Max Dupont *m* Alfred Newman

Douglas Fairbanks, William Farnum, Earle Browne, Maria Alba

Mr Sardonicus

US 1961   90m   bw
Columbia / William Castle

A surgeon is lured to an ex-girl friend's remote home to cure her sadistic husband's crippled face.
Flatly handled, boring semi-horror.

w Robb White *d* William Castle *ph* Burnett Guffey *m* Von Dexter

Ronald Lewis, Guy Rolfe, Audrey Dalton, Oscar Homolka

Mr Scoutmaster

US 1953   87m   bw
TCF

A TV personality wants to understand children and is persuaded to take over a scout troop.

A star vehicle which starts promisingly enough in the *Sitting Pretty* vein but quickly falls headlong into an abyss of sentimentality.

w Leonard Praskins, Barney Slater *d* Henry Levin *ph* Joseph La Shelle *m* Cyril Mockridge *md* Lionel Newman

Clifton Webb, Edmund Gwenn, George Winslow, Frances Dee, Veda Ann Borg

Mr Skeffington***

US 1944   127m   bw
Warner (Julius J. and Philip G. Epstein)

A selfish beauty finally turns to her discarded dull husband; when he is blind, he doesn't mind her faded looks.
Long, patchily made, but thoroughly enjoyable star melodrama.

w Julius J. and Philip G. Epstein, *novel* 'Elizabeth' *d* Vincent Sherman *ph* Ernest Haller *m* Franz Waxman

Bette Davis, Claude Rains, Walter Abel, Richard Waring, George Coulouris, John Alexander, Jerome Cowan

'An endless woman's page dissertation on What To Do When Beauty Fades.'—*James Agee*
'To call the film a good one would be to exaggerate; but entertaining and interesting, I insist, it is.'—*Richard Mallett, Punch*

AAN: Bette Davis; Claude Rains

Mr Skitch

US 1933   70m   bw

A Missouri family heads for California. Very passable star family entertainment. Will Rogers, Zasu Pitts, Florence Desmond, Rochelle Hudson. Written by Anne Cameron from her novel *Green Dice*; directed by James Cruze; for TCF.

Mr Smith Goes to Washington****

US 1939   130m   bw
Columbia (Frank Capra)

Washington's youngest senator exposes corruption in high places, almost at the cost of his own career.
Archetypal high-flying Capra vehicle, with the little man coming out top as he seldom does in life. Supreme gloss hides the corn, helter-skelter direction keeps one watching, and all concerned give memorable performances. A cinema classic.

w Sidney Buchman, story Lewis R. Foster *d Frank Capra ph Joseph Walker m Dmitri Tiomkin montage Slavko Vorkapich*

James Stewart, Claude Rains, Jean Arthur, Thomas Mitchell, Edward Arnold, Guy

Kibbee, Eugene Pallette, Beulah Bondi, *Harry Carey*, H. B. Warner, Astrid Allwyn, Ruth Donnelly, Charles Lane, Porter Hall
'More fun, even, than the Senate itself . . . not merely a brilliant jest, but a stirring and even inspiring testament to liberty and freedom.'—*Frank S. Nugent, New York Times*
'A totally compelling piece of movie-making, upholding the virtues of traditional American ideals.'—*NFT, 1973*
'Very good, beautifully done and extremely entertaining; long, but worth the time it takes.'—*Richard Mallett, Punch*
'More of the heartfelt than is good for the stomach.'—*New Yorker, 1977*

AA: Lewis R. Foster
AAN: best picture; Sidney Buchman; Frank Capra; Dmitri Tiomkin; James Stewart; Claude Rains; Harry Carey

Mr Soft Touch
US 1949 93m bw

A gangster is reformed at Christmas by a social worker. Dewy-eyed romance with Damon Runyonish asides; only for soft touches. Glenn Ford, Evelyn Keyes, John Ireland, Beulah Bondi, Percy Kilbride, Roman Bohnen. Written by Orin Jannings; directed by Henry Levin and Gordon Douglas; for Columbia. (GB title: *House of Settlement*.)

Mr Topaze
GB 1961 84m Eastmancolor
Cinemascope
TCF / Dimitri de Grunwald (Pierre Rouve)
US title: *I Like Money*

An honest ex-schoolmaster becomes prosperous when he joins some shady businessmen.
Predictable, sluggish character comedy, with a good actor unable to make it as a star. Or as a director.

w Pierre Rouve, *play* Topaze by Marcel Pagnol *d* Peter Sellers *ph* John Wilcox *m* Georges Van Parys

Peter Sellers, Herbert Lom, Leo McKern, Nadia Gray, Martita Hunt, John Neville, Billie Whitelaw, Michael Gough, Joan Sims, John Le Mesurier, Michael Sellers
'A film of minor pleasures and major inadequacies.'—*Penelope Houston, MFB*
† See also *Topaze* (1933).

Mr Winkle Goes to War
US 1944 80m bw
Columbia (Jack Moss)
GB title: *Arms and the Woman*

A middle-aged bank clerk joins the army and becomes a hero.
Agreeable, forgettable propaganda comedy-drama.

w Waldo Salt, George Corey, Louis Solomon, *novel* Theodore Pratt *d* Alfred E. Green *ph* Joseph Walker *m* Carmen Dragon, Paul Sawtell

Edward G. Robinson, Ruth Warrick, Ted Donaldson, Bob Haymes, Richard Lane, Robert Armstrong, Walter Baldwin

Mr Wong
A cheeseparing set of second features from Monogram, based on stories by Hugh Wiley. Boris Karloff was unsuitably cast as a Chinese detective, and in the last film he was replaced by Keye Luke. The films were directed by William Nigh.

1938: MR WONG DETECTIVE
1939: THE MYSTERY OF MR WONG, MR WONG IN CHINATOWN
1940: THE FATAL HOUR, DOOMED TO DIE (GB title: THE MYSTERY OF THE WENTWORTH CASTLE)
1941: PHANTOM OF CHINATOWN

Mr Wu*
US 1927 80m approx (24 fps) bw
silent
MGM

A Chinese villain kills his daughter when she wants to marry an Englishman.
Turgid outmoded melodrama from a stage success: purely a star vehicle.

w Lorna Moon, *play* Maurice Vernon, Harold Owen *d* William Nigh *ph* John Arnold

Lon Chaney, Louise Dresser, Anna May Wong, Ralph Forbes, Renee Adoree, Holmes Herbert

Mrs Fitzherbert
GB 1947 99m bw
British National

The Prince Regent secretly marries a Catholic widow.
Stilted, ill-cast historical charade.

w Montgomery Tully, *novel* Winifred Carter *d* Montgomery Tully *ph* James Wilson *m* Hans May

Peter Graves, Joyce Howard, Leslie Banks, Margaretta Scott

Mrs Gibbons' Boys
GB 1962 82m bw Byronscope

A widow plans to marry respectably for the sake of her three convict sons. Unattractive farce with clodhopping characters and too much slapstick. Kathleen Harrison, Lionel Jeffries, Diana Dors, John Le Mesurier, Frederick Bartman, David Lodge, Dick Emery, Eric Pohlmann, Milo O'Shea. Written by Peter Blackmore and Max Varnel, from the play by Joseph Stein and Will Glickman; directed by Max Varnel; for Byron / British Lion.

Mrs Mike
US 1949   99m   bw
Nassour / Huntingdon Hartford (Edward Gross)

A Mountie takes his new wife to live in the frozen northwest.
Predictable sentimental drama, well enough done to keep interest, but only just.

w Lewis Levitt, De Witt Bodeen *d* Louis King *ph* Joseph Biroc *m* Max Steiner

Dick Powell, Evelyn Keyes, J. M. Kerrigan, Angela Clarke

Mrs Miniver**
US 1942   134m   bw
MGM (Sidney Franklin)

An English housewife survives World War II.
This is the rose-strewn English village, Hollywood variety, but when released it proved a beacon of morale despite its false sentiment, absurd rural types and melodramatic situations. It is therefore beyond criticism, except that some of the people involved should have known better.

w Arthur Wimperis, George Froeschel, James Hilton, Claudine West, *novel* Jan Struther *d* William Wyler *ph* Joseph Ruttenberg *m* Herbert Stothart

Greer Garson, Walter Pidgeon, Teresa Wright, Richard Ney, Dame May Whitty, Henry Travers, Reginald Owen, Henry Wilcoxon, Helmut Dantine, Rhys Williams, Aubrey Mather

'That almost impossible feat, a war picture that photographs the inner meaning, instead of the outward realism of World War II.'— *Time*

AA: best picture; script; William Wyler; Joseph Ruttenberg; Greer Garson; Teresa Wright
AAN: Walter Pidgeon; Dame May Whitty; Henry Travers

Mrs O'Malley and Mr Malone*
US 1950   69m   bw
MGM (William H. Wright)

On a train to New York, a radio contest

winner and a lawyer help solve a murder.
Lively second feature farce.

w William Bowers *d* Norman Taurog *ph* Adolph Deutsch

Marjorie Main, James Whitmore, Ann Dvorak, Fred Clark, Dorothy Malone, Phyllis Kirk

Mrs Parkington
US 1944   124m   bw
MGM (Leon Gordon)

A lady's maid marries a miner who becomes wealthy, and pushes her way into society.
Thoroughly unconvincing three-generation drama, with a bewigged and powdered star giving the boot to her conniving relations. It has production values and nothing else.

w Robert Thoeren, Polly James, *novel* Louis Bromfield *d* Tay Garnett *ph* Joseph Ruttenberg *m* Bronislau Kaper

Greer Garson, Walter Pidgeon, Edward Arnold, Agnes Moorehead, Cecil Kellaway, Gladys Cooper, Frances Rafferty, Tom Drake, Peter Lawford, Dan Duryea, Hugh Marlowe, Selena Royle
† The heroine is shown having a romance with Edward VII when Prince of Wales; special scenes were shot for the European version substituting Cecil Kellaway, who played Edward, by Hugo Haas who played a European king of indeterminate origin.

AAN: Greer Garson; Agnes Moorehead

Mrs Pollifax—Spy
US 1970   110m   De Luxe
UA / Mellor (Frederick Brisson)

A respectable American matron offers her services to the CIA and sees active service in Albania.
Incredible comedy-dramatic vehicle for a star who won't give up. An obvious failure from the word go.

w C. A. McKnight, *novel* Dorothy Gilman *d* Leslie Martinson *ph* Joseph Biroc *m* Lalo Schifrin

Rosalind Russell, Darren McGavin
† C. A. McKnight was Rosalind Russell.

Mrs Pym of Scotland Yard
GB 1939   65m   bw

A lady detective exposes a fake spiritualist. A would-be series character bites the dust through plot malnutrition. Mary Clare, Edward Lexy, Nigel Patrick, Anthony Ireland, Irene Handl. Written by Fred Elles, Peggy Barwell and Nigel Morland, from the novel by Nigel Morland; directed by Fred Elles; for Hurley / Grand National.

Mrs Wiggs of the Cabbage Patch*
US 1934 80m bw
Paramount (Douglas MacLean)

Adventures of a poor family who live on the wrong side of the tracks in a broken down old shack.
A Depression fantasy of respectability and optimism, almost incredible to see now, although it plumbed the same never-never milieu as did Chaplin. Moments of comedy still please, but one does long for Mr Fields' delayed entry.

w William Slavens McNutt, Jane Storm, *novel* Alice Hegan Rice d Norman Taurog
ph Charles Lang

Pauline Lord, *Zasu Pitts, W. C. Fields*, Evelyn Venable, Kent Taylor, Charles Middleton, Donald Meek, Edith Fellows, Virginia Weidler, George Breakston
  'A nasty all's-right-with-the-world burlesque of poverty, with emotions to tug at such heartstrings as are worn dangling from the mouth.'—*Otis Ferguson*

Mrs Wiggs of the Cabbage Patch
US 1942 80m bw
Paramount

Curiously quick remake, almost word for word, but without the moments of inspiration.

w Doris Anderson, Jane Storm, William Slavens McNutt d Ralph Murphy ph Leo Tover

Fay Bainter, Hugh Herbert, Vera Vague, Barbara Britton, Carl Switzer, Moroni Olsen, Billy Lee

Mix Me a Person
GB 1961 116m bw
Wessex (Sergei Nolbandov)

A barrister's psychiatrist wife takes on one of his failures, a client condemned to death for murder.
Once it gets started, a routine suspense thriller with the wrong man convicted and an espresso bar background. Not a very good one, though.

w Ian Dalrymple, *novel* Jack Trevor Story
d Leslie Norman ph Ted Moore
songs Johnny Worth *md* Muir Mathieson

Anne Baxter, Donald Sinden, Adam Faith, Walter Brown, Glyn Houston

Mixed Company
US 1974 109m De Luxe
UA / Cornell (Melville Shavelson)

A basketball coach and his wife adopt several children of different races.

Room for One More and then some, but not very interesting.

w Melville Shavelson, Mort Lachman
d Melville Shavelson ph Stan Lazan m Fred Karlin pd Stan Jolley

Barbara Harris, Joseph Bologna, Lisa Gerritson, Arianne Heller

The Mob*
US 1951 87m bw
Columbia (Jerry Bresler)
GB title: *Remember That Face*

A policeman works undercover to catch a dockside racketeer.
Tough, lively thriller with effectively sustained mystery and a serial-like finale.

w William Bowers d Robert Parrish
ph Joseph Walker m George Duning

Broderick Crawford, Richard Kiley, Ernest Borgnine, Neville Brand, Charles Bronson

Moby Dick*
US 1930 75m bw
Warner

Captain Ahab returns minus a leg from fighting the white whale, and finds that his fiancée is too shocked to love him.
Mangled remake of a fine novel filmed in silent form as *The Sea Beast*.

w J. Grubb Alexander, *novel* Herman Melville d Lloyd Bacon ph Robert Kurrie

John Barrymore, Joan Bennett, Lloyd Hughes, May Boley, Walter Long

Moby Dick**
GB 1956 116m Technicolor
Warner / Moulin (John Huston)

A whaling skipper is determined to harpoon the white whale which robbed him of a leg.
Pretentious period adventure, rather too obsessed with symbolism and certainly too slowly developed, but full of interesting detail which almost outweighs the central miscasting.

w Ray Bradbury, John Huston, *novel* Herman Melville d John Huston ph Oswald Morris
m Philip Stainton

Gregory Peck, Richard Basehart, Friedrich Ledebur, Leo Genn, Orson Welles, James Robertson Justice, Harry Andrews, Bernard Miles, Noel Purcell, Edric Connor, Joseph Tomelty, Mervyn Johns
  'Interesting more often than exciting.'—*Variety*

Mockery
US 1927 75m approx at 24 fps bw
  silent

A noble peasant saves a countess from the
Russian revolution. Overly serious vehicle for
a star more at ease in melodrama. Lon
Chaney, Barbara Belford, Ricardo Cortez,
Emily Fitzroy. Written and directed by
Benjamin Christensen; for MGM.

The Model and the Marriage Broker
US 1952 103m bw
TCF (Charles Brackett)

A broker conceals her profession from a friend
but gets the friend fixed up.
Moderate, unsurprising comedy somewhat
overweighted by talent which can't express
itself.

w Charles Brackett, Walter Reisch, Richard
Breen d George Cukor ph Milton Krasner
m Cyril Mockridge

Thelma Ritter, Jeanne Crain, Scott Brady,
Zero Mostel, Michael O'Shea, Nancy Kulp

Model Wife
US 1941 78m bw

Young marrieds must pretend to be single in
order to keep their jobs. Tedious comedy.
Joan Blondell, Dick Powell, Charles Ruggles,
Lee Bowman, Lucile Watson. Written by
Charles Kaufman, Horace Jackson and Grant
Garrett; directed by Leigh Jason; for
Universal.

Modern Times***
US 1936 87m bw
Charles Chaplin

An assembly-line worker goes berserk but
can't get another job.
Silent star comedy produced in the middle of
the sound period; flashes of genius alternate
with sentimental sequences and jokes without
punch.

wd / m Charles Chaplin ph Rollie Totheroh,
Ira Morgan

Charles Chaplin, Paulette Goddard, Henry
Bergman, Chester Conklin, Tiny Sandford

'A feature picture made out of several one-
and two-reel shorts, proposed titles being *The
Shop, The Jailbird, The Singing Waiter*.'—*Otis
Ferguson*

Modesty Blaise
GB 1966 119m Technicolor
TCF / Modesty Blaise Ltd (Joseph Janni)

Female arch-agent Modesty Blaise defends a
shipload of diamonds against a sadistic master
criminal.
Comic-strip adventures made by people with
no sense of humour; Fu Manchu was much
more fun.

w Evan Jones, *comic strip* Peter O'Donnell,
Jim Holdaway d Joseph Losey ph Jack
Hildyard m Johnny Dankworth

Monica Vitti, Dirk Bogarde, Terence Stamp,
Harry Andrews, Michael Craig, Scilla Gabel,
Clive Revill, Rossella Falk, Joe Melia

Mogambo*
GB 1953 116m Technicolor
MGM (Sam Zimbalist)

The headquarters of a Kenyan white hunter is
invaded by an American showgirl and a British
archaeologist and his wife, and they all go off
on a gorilla hunt.
Amiable, flabby remake of *Red Dust*, with
direction scarcely in evidence and the gorillas
out-acting a genial cast.

w John Lee Mahin d John Ford ph Robert
Surtees, F. A. Young

Clark Gable, Ava Gardner, Grace Kelly,
Donald Sinden, Laurence Naismith, Philip
Stainton
† The story was also made as *Congo Maisie* in
1940.

AAN: Ava Gardner; Grace Kelly

Mohammed, Messenger of God
Lebanon 1976 182m Eastmancolor
Panavision
Filmco International (Moustapha Akkad)
aka: *The Message*

The life of the seventh-century religious
leader.
Predictably reverential and exceedingly
tedious religious epic, rather like a lesser de
Mille item and fatally handicapped by the
decision never to show Mohammed at all.

w H. A. L. Craig (with Arab advice)
d Moustapha Akkad ph Jack Hildyard
m Maurice Jarre pd Tambi Larsen, Maurice
Fowler

Anthony Quinn, Irene Papas, Michael Ansara,
Johnny Sekka, Michael Forest, André Morell

'For well over three hours this film
stumbles, staggers, lurches and bumbles
ahead, without any true rhythm, construction,
vision, or even bare minimum of craft.'—*John
Simon, New York*

Molly and Me
US 1945 76m bw
TCF

A cantankerous old man is tamed by his new
housekeeper.
Sentimental little star vehicle.

w Leonard Praskins d Lewis Seiler
ph Charles G. Clarke m Cyril Mockridge

Gracie Fields, Monty Woolley, Reginald Gardiner, Roddy McDowall, Natalie Schaefer, Edith Barrett

† This followed the more successful teaming of the stars in *Holy Matrimony*.

The Molly Maguires

US 1970   123m   Technicolor
Panavision
Paramount / Tamm (Martin Ritt, Walter Bernstein)

In the Pennsylvania coalmining district in the 1870s, an undercover detective exposes the leaders of a secret society.

Sober-sided and slow-moving account of actual events which also formed the basis for Conan Doyle's rather more entertaining *The Valley of Fear*. Expensive, nicely photographed, but unpersuasive and empty.

w Walter Bernstein *d* Martin Ritt *ph* James Wong Howe *m* Henry Mancini

Richard Harris, Sean Connery, Samantha Eggar, Frank Finlay, Anthony Zerbe, Bethel Leslie, Art Lund

'The film's vague sense of grievance and harrowing circumstances hangs in the air like the smoky pall cast up by the anthracite workings.'—*Richard Combs*

'A cold, dry and rather perfunctory film.'—*Arthur Schlesinger Jnr*

Moment by Moment

US 1979   105m   Technicolor
Panavision
Universal (Robert Stigwood)

A bored Beverly Hills wife has an affair with a young drifter.

Tedious proof that even the biggest new stars of the seventies can't carry a no-good picture.

wd Jane Wagner *ph* Philip Lathrop *m* Lee Holdridge *pd* Harry Horner

John Travolta, Lily Tomlin, Andra Akers, Bert Kramer, Debra Feuer

'Little more than an animated snapshot of its leading man, baring body and soul to various effect . . . truly terrible.'—*Gilbert Adair, MFB*

Moment of Danger

GB 1962   87m   bw

Thieves fall out and pursue each other to Malaga. Falling between the stools of thriller and character drama, this is a poor effort in either category. Trevor Howard, Dorothy Dandridge, Edmund Purdom, Michael Hordern, Paul Stassino. Written by David Osborn and Donald Ogden Stewart, from a novel by Donald MacKenzie; directed by Laslo Benedek; for ABPC / Douglas Fairbanks Jnr. (US title: *Malaga*.)

Moment to Moment

US 1966   108m   Technicolor
Universal (Mervyn Le Roy)

A housewife finds herself with a body on her hands.

Incredibly old-fashioned romantic / melodramatic malarkey set on the French Riviera but scarcely moving a step out of Hollywood. Lush settings made it marketable to women.

w John Lee Mahin, Alec Coppel *d* Mervyn Le Roy *ph* Harry Stradling *m* Henry Mancini

Jean Seberg, *Honor Blackman*, Sean Garrison, Arthur Hill, Grégoire Aslan

Mon Oncle*

France 1956   116m   Eastmancolor
Specta / Gray / Alterdel–Centaure (Louis Dolivet)

A small boy has less affection for his parents than for his vague, clumsy uncle.

Tiresomely long star vehicle, with Tati harping on his theory of detachment, ie keeping his comic character on the fringes of the action. It really doesn't work in a film of this length, and the jokes are thin.

w Jacques Tati, Jacques Lagrange *d* Jacques Tati *ph* Jean Bourgoin *m* Alain Romains, Franck Barcellini

Jacques Tati, Jean-Pierre Zola, Adrienne Servatie, Alain Becourt, Yvonne Arnaud

'Deft, elusive, full of heart.'—*Brenda Davies, MFB*

AA: best foreign film

Mondo Cane*

Italy 1961   105m   Technicolor
Cineriz
aka: *A Dog's Life*

A documentary of thirty sequences of violently eccentric human behaviour, including cannibalism, pig killing, a dog meal restaurant, etc.

Emetic exploitation piece, quite glibly assembled. Its huge commercial success made one worry for the world.

wd Gualtiero Jacopetti *ph* Antonio Climati, Benito Frattari

AAN: song 'More' (*m* Riz Ortolani, Nino Oliviero, *ly* Norman Newell)

Money from Home

US 1954   100m   Technicolor   3-D
Paramount / Hal Wallis

A racing tipster and an assistant veterinary surgeon find themselves in charge of a horse.
A comedy with two strokes against it: the stars, and that never-never gangster land which was already a terrible cliché in the early fifties.

w Hal Kanter, *story* Damon Runyon d George Marshall *ph* Daniel L. Sapp m Leigh Harline

Dean Martin, Jerry Lewis, Marjie Millar, Pat Crowley, Richard Haydn, Robert Strauss, Gerald Mohr, Sheldon Leonard

The Money Trap
US 1966 92m bw Panavision
MGM (Max E. Youngstein, David Karr)

A hard-up policeman turns to crime.
A cheap thriller decorated with waning stars; competent at the lowest level.

w Walter Bernstein, *novel* Lionel White d Burt Kennedy *ph* Paul C. Vogel m Hal Schaefer

Glenn Ford, Rita Hayworth, Elke Sommer, Ricardo Montalban, Joseph Cotten, Tom Reese, James Mitchum

Money, Women and Guns
US 1959 80m Eastmancolor
Cinemascope

A murdered prospector scrawls a will before dying; a detective investigates the beneficiaries. What could have been an effective western whodunnit is jinxed by erratic writing and direction. Jock Mahoney, Kim Hunter, Tim Hovey, Gene Evans, William Campbell, Lon Chaney Jnr, Tom Drake, James Gleason. Written by Montgomery Pittman; directed by Richard H. Bartlett; for Universal-International.

Monkey Business***
US 1931 81m bw
Paramount (Herman J. Mankiewicz)

Four ship's stowaways crash a society party and catch a few crooks.
The shipboard part of this extravaganza is one of the best stretches of Marxian lunacy, but after the Chevalier impersonations it runs out of steam. Who's grumbling?

w S. J. Perelman, Will B. Johnstone, Arthur Sheekman d Norman Z. McLeod *ph* Arthur L. Todd

Groucho, Chico, Harpo, Zeppo, Thelma Todd, Rockcliffe Fellowes, Ruth Hall, Harry Woods

Monkey Business*
US 1952 97m bw
TCF (Sol C. Siegel)

A chimpanzee in a research lab accidentally concocts an elixir of youth.
Remarkably laboured comedy by and with top people; it can't fail to have funny moments, but they are few and far between.

w Ben Hecht, Charles Lederer, I. A. L. Diamond d Howard Hawks *ph* Milton Krasner m Leigh Harline

Cary Grant, Ginger Rogers, *Charles Coburn, Marilyn Monroe*, Hugh Marlowe

A Monkey in Winter*
France 1962 103m bw Totalvision
CIPRA / Cité (Jacques Bar)
aka: *Une Singe en Hiver; It's Hot in Hell*

In a small Normandy resort, a hotel owner and a literary guest get drunk together and plan great fantasies, but finally return to their responsibilities.
Amiable, meandering star character comedy.

w François Boyer, *novel* Antoine Blondin d Henri Verneuil *ph* Louis Page m Michel Magne

Jean Gabin, Jean-Paul Belmondo, Suzanne Flon, Noel Roquevert, Paul Frankeur, Gabrielle Dorziat

Monkey on My Back
US 1957 93m bw
UA / Imperial / Edward Small

A Guadalcanal hero is given morphine to relieve malaria and becomes addicted.
Dreary case history sold as exploitation.

w Crane Wilbur, Anthony Veiller, Peter Dudley, from the experiences of Barney Ross d André de Toth *ph* Maury Gertsman m Paul Sawtell, Bert Shafter

Cameron Mitchell, Dianne Foster, Jack Albertson, Paul Richards

Monkeys Go Home
US 1966 101m Technicolor
Walt Disney (Ron Miller)

An American inherits a French olive farm and trains chimpanzees to harvest the crop.
Footling comedy with not much of an idea, let alone a plot.

w Maurice Tombragel, *novel* The Monkeys by G. K. Wilkinson d Andrew V. McLaglen *ph* William Snyder m Robert F. Brunner

Maurice Chevalier, Dean Jones, Yvette Mimieux, Bernard Woringer, Jules Munshin, Alan Carney

'Innocuous, extrovertly cheerful and good-humoured—and very dull.'—*MFB*

The Monolith Monsters
US 1957 77m bw
U–I (Howard Christie)

A meteorite lands in the desert and causes rocks to rise and expand, becoming toppling pillars which threaten a local community.
Dully-written science fiction with moderate special effects.

w Norman Jolley, Robert M. Fresco *d* John Sherwood *ph* Ellis Carter *md* Joseph Gershenson

Lola Albright, Grant Williams, Les Tremayne, Phil Harvey

Monsieur Beaucaire*
US 1946 93m bw
Paramount (Paul Jones)

King Louis XV's bumbling barber impersonates a court dandy.
What seemed a lively period burlesque has faded somewhat with age, but it still has its moments. Any relation between this and the silent Valentino film is quite accidental.

w Melvin Frank, Norman Panama *d* George Marshall *ph* Lionel Lindon *md* Robert Emmett Dolan

Bob Hope, Joan Caulfield, Patric Knowles, Marjorie Reynolds, Cecil Kellaway, Joseph Schildkraut, Reginald Owen, Constance Collier, Hillary Brooke, Douglass Dumbrille, Mary Nash

'Whether you yawn or rather wearily laugh depends chiefly on your chance state of mind.'—*James Agee*

Monsieur Hulot's Holiday***
France 1953 91m bw
Cady / Discina (Fred Orain)
original title: *Les Vacances de Monsieur Hulot*

An accident-prone bachelor arrives at a seaside resort and unwittingly causes havoc for himself and everyone else.
Despite lame endings to some of the jokes, this is a film to set the whole world laughing, Hulot himself being an unforgettable character and some of the timing magnificent. One feels that it could very nearly happen.

w Jacques Tati, Henri Marquet *d* Jacques Tati *ph* Jacques Mercanton, Jean Mouselle *m* Alain Romans

Jacques Tati, Nathalie Pascaud, Michèle Rolla, Valentine Camax

'The casual, amateurish air of his films clearly adds to their appeal: it also appears to explain their defects.'—*Penelope Houston, MFB*

AAN: script

Monsieur Verdoux**
US 1947 125m bw
Charles Chaplin

A bank cashier marries and murders rich women to support his real wife.
Interesting but unsatisfactory redrafting of the Landru case; the star is more dapper than funny, the moral is unconvincing, and the slapstick sequences too often raise yawns.

wd / m Charles Chaplin *ph* Rollie Totteroh

Charles Chaplin, Martha Raye, Isobel Elsom

'Even today it will seem a failure to anyone who has taken half a dozen lessons in film technique.'—*Andrew Sarris, 1970*

AAN: Charles Chaplin (as writer)

Monsieur Vincent*
France 1947 113m bw
EDIC / UGC

The life of 17th-century St Vincent de Paul, who gave up all worldly goods to devote his life to the poor.
Earnest, realistic Catholic biopic.

w Jean-Bernard Luc, Jean Anouilh *d* Leon Carré *ph* Claude Renoir *m* J. J. Grunenwald

Pierre Fresnay, Aimé Clairiond, Jean Debucourt, Lise Delemare

The Monster
US 1925 70m approx at 24 fps bw
silent

A scientist abducts passing motorists and uses them in his experiments at bringing the dead back to life. Typical star grotesquerie without much flair. Lon Chaney, Gertrude Olmstead, Hallam Cooley, Walter James. Written by Willard Mack and Albert Kenyon, from a play by Crane Wilbur; directed by Roland West; for MGM.

The Monster and the Girl
US 1940 64m bw
Paramount (Jack Moss)

A man is wrongfully executed and his brain is implanted in a gorilla, which goes on the rampage.
Curiously ineffectual considering its plot and cast, this little horror thriller seems to have been the first to use this particular situation, which became very well worn later.

w Stuart Anthony *d* Stuart Heisler *ph* Victor Milner *m* Sigmund Krumgold

Paul Lukas, Ellen Drew, Joseph Calleia, George Zucco, Robert Paige, Rod Cameron, Phillip Terry, Onslow Stevens, Gerald Mohr

Montana Moon
US 1930 88m bw

A wealthy rancher's spoiled daughter is about to leave for New York when she falls for a handsome cowboy. A long string of nothings with bursts of song; incompetent early talkie.

Joan Crawford, Johnny Mack Brown, Ricardo Cortez, Lloyd Ingraham, Cliff Edwards. Written by Sylvia Thalberg and Frank Butler; directed by Malcolm St Clair; for MGM.

Monte Carlo*
US 1930 94m bw
Paramount (Ernst Lubitsch)

A count passes himself off as a hairdresser to win a gambling lady.
Faded but charming romantic comedy with music, the first to show its director's sound style in full throttle, notably in the final 'Beyond the Blue Horizon' sequence.

w Ernest Vajda, *play* The Blue Coast by Hans Muller, *novel* Monsieur Beaucaire by Booth Tarkington *d* Ernst Lubitsch *ph* Victor Milner *m* W. Franke Harling *songs* Leo Robin, Richard Whiting *ad* Hans Dreier

Jack Buchanan, Jeanette MacDonald, Zasu Pitts, Tyler Brooke, Claud Allister, Lionel Belmore
'Very stylish and sly, not to be missed.'—
New Yorker, 1978

The Monte Carlo Story
Italy / US 1956 101m Technirama
Tatanus (Marcello Girosi)

A gambler looks for a rich wife, and finds instead a glamorous woman as penniless as himself: they become confidence tricksters but suffer a change of heart.
Lubitsch might have made something of it, but this is a flavourless pudding of a film and the stars can do nothing with it.

wd Samuel Taylor, *story* Marcello Girosi, Dino Risi *ph* Giuseppe Rotunno *m* Renzo Rossellini

Marlene Dietrich, Vittorio de Sica, Arthur O'Connell, Mischa Auer, Natalie Trundy, Jane Rose, Renato Rascel

Monte Walsh*
US 1970 108m Technicolor
Cinema Center (Hal Landis, Bobby Roberts)

Two ageing cowboys find life increasingly hard and hopeless; an old acquaintance kills one and is shot by the other.
'Realistic' western developed in leisurely style with the emphasis on character and on the real drudgery of frontier life.

w David Z. Goodman, Lukas Heller, *novel* Jack Schaefer *d* William A. Fraker *ph* David M. Walsh *m* John Barry

Lee Marvin, Jack Palance, Jeanne Moreau, Mitch Ryan, Jim Davis
'As boring a western as ever involved a bronco-busting scene that alone cost almost half a million dollars.'—*Judith Crist*

Monty Python and the Holy Grail**
GB 1975 90m Technicolor
EMI / Python (Monty) Pictures / Michael White (Mark Forstater)

King Arthur and his knights seek the Holy Grail.
Hellzapoppin-like series of linked sketches on a medieval theme; some slow bits, but often uproariously funny and with a remarkable visual sense of the middle ages.

w Graham Chapman, John Cleese, Terry Gilliam, Eric Idle, Michael Palin *d* Terry Gilliam, Terry Jones *ph* Terry Bedford *animation* Terry Gilliam *m* Neil Innes *pd* Roy Smith

Graham Chapman, John Cleese, Terry Gilliam, Eric Idle, Michael Palin
'The team's visual buffooneries and verbal rigmaroles are piled on top of each other with no attention to judicious timing or structure, and a form which began as a jaunty assault on the well-made revue sketch and an ingenious misuse of television's fragmented style of presentation, threatens to become as unyielding and unfruitful as the conventions it originally attacked.'—*Geoff Brown*

Monty Python's Life of Brian**
GB 1979 93m Eastmancolor
Hand Made Films (John Goldstone)

A contemporary of Jesus is mistaken for him and crucified.
Controversial middle-eastern romp which left its creators battered but extremely wealthy. In the face of such an onslaught of bad taste, criticism seems irrelevant.

written by and starring John Cleese, Graham Chapman, Eric Idle, Michael Palin, Terry Gilliam, Terry Jones *d* Terry Jones *ph* Peter Biziou *m* Geoffrey Burgon

The Moon and Sixpence***
US 1943   85m   bw (colour sequence)
Albert Lewin / David L. Loew (Stanley Kramer)

A stockbroker leaves his wife and family, spends some selfish years painting in Paris and finally dies of leprosy on a South Sea island.
Pleasantly literary adaptation of an elegant novel based on the life of Gauguin; a little stodgy in presentation now, but much of it still pleases.

w Albert Lewin, *novel* W. Somerset Maugham d Albert Lewin ph John Seitz m Dmitri Tiomkin

George Sanders, Herbert Marshall (as Maugham), *Steve Geray*, Doris Dudley, Elena Verdugo, Florence Bates, Heather Thatcher, Eric Blore, Albert Basserman
'An admirable film until the end, when it lapses into Technicolor and techni-pathos.'— *James Agate*

AAN: Dmitri Tiomkin

The Moon Is Blue*
US 1953   99m   bw
Otto Preminger

A spry young girl balances the attractions of a middle-aged lover against her young one.
Paper-thin comedy partly set on top of the Empire State Building (and thereafter in a dowdy set); mildly amusing in spots, it gained notoriety, and a Production Code ban, by its use of such naughty words as 'virgin' and 'mistress'.

w F. Hugh Herbert, from his play d Otto Preming · ph Ernest Laszlo m Herschel Burke Gilbert

Maggie McNamara, David Niven, William Holden, Tom Tully, Dawn Addams
'It adds nothing to the art of cinema and certainly does not deserve the attention it will get for flouting the Production Code.'—*Philip T. Hartung*

AAN: Maggie McNamara; title song (*m* Herschel Burke Gilbert, *ly* Sylvia Fine)

The Moon Is Down**
US 1943   90m   bw
TCF (Nunnally Johnson)

A Norwegian village resists the Nazis.
Sombre, talkative, intelligent little drama, the best of the resistance films, shot on the set of *How Green Was My Valley* (with snow covering).

w Nunnally Johnson, *novel* John Steinbeck d Irving Pichel ph Arthur Miller m Alfred Newman

Henry Travers, Cedric Hardwicke, Lee J. Cobb, Dorris Bowden, Margaret Wycherly, Peter Van Eyck, John Banner
'This may well be a true picture of Norway and its people. But it fails to strike fire, to generate passion. It leaves one feeling rather proud but also sad.'—*Bosley Crowther*

Moon over Burma
US 1940   76m   bw
Paramount

Jungle lumbermen fight over a stranded American entertainer.
Routine adventure romance climaxing in a forest fire.

w Frank Wead, W. P. Lipscomb, Harry Clark d Louis King ph William Mellor m Victor Young

Dorothy Lamour, Robert Preston, Preston Foster, Doris Nolan, Albert Basserman, Frederick Worlock, Addison Richards

Moon over Miami*
US 1941   92m   Technicolor
TCF (Harry Joe Brown)

Two sisters seek rich husbands in Florida.
Musical remake of *Three Blind Mice*, which was suspiciously similar to *Golddiggers of Broadway, The Greeks Had a Word for Them*, etc., and the later *How to Marry a Millionaire* and *Three Little Girls in Blue*. In short, a Hollywood standard, not too badly done.

w Vincent Lawrence, Brown Holmes d Walter Lang ph Peverell Marley, Leon Shamroy md Alfred Newman

Don Ameche, Betty Grable, Carole Landis, Charlotte Greenwood, Jack Haley, Cobina Wright Jnr, Robert Greig

Moon Pilot**
US 1961   98m   Technicolor
Walt Disney (Ron Miller)

A reluctant astronaut falls in love with a girl from outer space, who finally accompanies him on his mission.
Engaging science-fiction spoof with good performances.

w Maurice Tombragel, *serial* Robert Buckner d James Neilson ph William Snyder m Peter Smith sp Eustace Lycett

Edmond O'Brien, Tom Tryon, Brian Keith

The Moon Spinners*
GB 1964   119m   Technicolor
Walt Disney (Bill Anderson)

A young girl holidaying in Crete becomes involved with jewel robbers.

Teenage adventure against attractive locations; quite agreeable but overlong.

w Michael Dyne, *novel* Mary Stewart *d* James Neilson *ph* Paul Beeson *m* Ron Grainer

Hayley Mills, Peter McEnery, Eli Wallach, Joan Greenwood, John Le Mesurier, *Pola Negri*

Moon Zero Two
GB 1969 100m Technicolor
Hammer (Michael Carreras)

In 2021, the moon is being colonized and crooks are trying to get control of an asteroid. A self-acknowledged 'space western' which has a few bright ideas but suffers from a childish script.

w Michael Carreras, *story* Gavin Lyall, Frank Hardman, Martin Davidson *d* Roy Ward Baker *ph* Paul Beeson *m* Don Ellis

James Olson, Catherina Von Schell, Warren Mitchell, Ori Levy, Adrienne Corri, Dudley Foster, Bernard Bresslaw, Neil McCallum

'It's all just about bad enough to fill older audiences with nostalgia for the inspired innocence of Flash Gordon, or even the good old days of Abbott and Costello in outer space.'—*MFB*

Moonfleet*
US 1955 87m Eastmancolor
Cinemascope
MGM (John Houseman)

In Dorset in 1770 an orphan boy finds that his elegant guardian leads a gang of smugglers. Period gothic melodrama which nearly, but not quite, comes off; the script simply doesn't build to the right climax, and too many characters come to nothing. But there are splendid moments.

w Margaret Fitts, Jan Lustig, *novel* J. Meade Faulkner *d* Fritz Lang *ph* Robert Planck *m* Miklos Rozsa

Stewart Granger, Jon Whiteley, George Sanders, Joan Greenwood, Viveca Lindfors, Liliane Montevecchi, Melville Cooper, Sean McClory, John Hoyt, Alan Napier

Moonlight Sonata*
GB 1937 90m bw
Pall Mall (Lothar Mendes)

Stranded victims of a plane crash are affected by the art of a famous pianist.
Curious, slight, unexpected play-on-film designed to showcase the talent of Paderewski.

w Edward Knoblock, E. M. Delafield
d Lothar Mendes *ph* Jan Stallich

Ignace Paderewski, Eric Portman, *Marie Tempest*, Charles Farrell, Barbara Greene, Binkie Stuart

The Moonlighter
US 1953 77m bw 3-D
Warner (Joseph Bernhard)

A cattle rustler moves towards reforming.
Ho-hum western which offers its stars little to work with and was not even very exciting in 3-D.

w Niven Busch *d* Roy Rowland *ph* Bert Glennon *m* Heinz Roemheld

Fred MacMurray, Barbara Stanwyck, Ward Bond, William Ching, John Dierkes, Morris Ankrum

The Moonraker*
GB 1958 82m Technicolor
ABPC (Hamilton Inglis)

During the English Civil War, a noble highwayman smuggles the king's son into France.
Likeable swashbuckler which confines its second half to suspense at an inn, a who-is-it rather than a whodunnit. Good fun.

w Robert Hall, Wilfred Eades, Alistair Bell, *play* Arthur Watkyn *d* David MacDonald *ph* Laurie Johnson

George Baker, Sylvia Syms, Marius Goring, Peter Arne, Richard Leech, Clive Morton, Paul Whitsun-Jones, Gary Raymond, John Le Mesurier (as Cromwell), Patrick Troughton, Michael Anderson Jnr

Moonraker
GB 1979 126m Technicolor
Panavision
UA / Eon (Albert S. Broccoli)

James Bond investigates the disappearance of a space shuttle during a test flight.
Adventures in Venice, Rio and the upper Amazon; all very repetitive and no longer more than faintly amusing.

w Christopher Wood, *novel* Ian Fleming *d* Lewis Gilbert *ph* Jean Tournier *m* John Barry *pd* Ken Adam

Roger Moore, Lois Chiles, Michael Lonsdale, Richard Kiel, Geoffrey Keen, Lois Maxwell, Bernard Lee

'Conspicuously expensive production values but an unmistakably cut price plot.'—*Sight and Sound*

Moonrise*
US 1948 90m bw
Republic

A murderer's son is driven into violence by memories and fears of his childhood. Broody melodrama set against a remote village and swamp background; not a very interesting story, but memorable detail.

w Charles Haas d Frank Borzage ph John L. Russell m William Lava

Gail Russell, Dane Clark, Ethel Barrymore, Allyn Joslyn, Rex Ingram

The Moon's Our Home*
US 1936 80m bw
Paramount (Walter Wanger)

A headstrong actress marries an adventurer on impulse, and they both try to work it out. Light, bright romantic comedy with the zany tinge then in fashion.

w Isabel Dawn, Boyce DeGaw, novel Faith Baldwin d William A. Seiter ph Joseph Valentine

Margaret Sullavan, Henry Fonda, Beulah Bondi, Charles Butterworth, Margaret Hamilton, Dorothy Stickney, Lucien Littlefield

The Moonshine War
US 1970 100m Metrocolor Panavision
MGM / Filmways (James C. Pratt, Leonard Blair)

In Kentucky just before the repeal of prohibition, a corruptible revenue agent regrets bringing in a sadistic crook to help confiscate illegal whisky.
Downright peculiar hillbilly melodrama, neither straight nor satirical; interesting only in fits and starts.

w Elmore Leonard, from his novel d Richard Quine ph Richard H. Kline m Fred Karger

Patrick McGoohan, Richard Widmark, Alan Alda, Melodie Johnson, Will Geer

The Moonspinners see The Moon Spinners

Moontide*
US 1942 94m bw
TCF (Mark Hellinger)

A seaman cares for an unhappy waif.
A Hollywood attempt at romantic melodrama in the French manner. It looks good, and the cast is fine, but everything is just a bit too glum.

w John O'Hara, novel Willard Robertson d Archie Mayo ph Charles G. Clarke m Cyril Mockridge, David Buttolph

Jean Gabin, Ida Lupino, Claude Rains, Thomas Mitchell, Jerome Cowan, Sen Yung, Tully Marshall, Helen Reynolds

AAN: Charles G. Clarke

The Morals of Marcus
GB 1936 75m bw
Gaumont British (W. J. Locke)

A girl escapes from a Middle Eastern harem by stowing away with a British aristocrat. Feeble 'naughty' comedy, killed by lack of wit and pace.

w Guy Bolton, Miles Mander, play W. J. Locke d Miles Mander ph John W. Boyle

Lupe Velez, Ian Hunter, Adrienne Allen, Noel Madison, J. H. Roberts, H. F. Maltby

The More the Merrier***
US 1943 104m bw
Columbia (George Stevens)

In crowded Washington during World War II, a girl allows two men to share her apartment and falls in love with the younger one. Thoroughly amusing romantic comedy with bright lines and situations; remade less effectively as Walk Don't Run (qv).

w Robert Russell, Frank Ross, Richard Flournoy, Lewis R. Foster d George Stevens ph Ted Tetzlaff m Leigh Harline md Morris Stoloff

Jean Arthur, Joel McCrea, Charles Coburn, Richard Gaines, Bruce Bennett

'The gayest comedy that has come from Hollywood in a long time. It has no more substance than a watermelon, but is equally delectable.'—Howard Barnes

'Farce, like melodrama, offers very special chances for accurate observation, but here accuracy is avoided ten times to one in favour of the easy burlesque or the easier idealization which drops the bottom out of farce. Every good moment frazzles or drowns.'—James Agee

† Garson Kanin has claimed to have written virtually all the script.

AA: Charles Coburn
AAN: best picture; script; original story (Frank Ross, Robert Russell); George Stevens; Jean Arthur

Morgan—A Suitable Case for Treatment**
GB 1966 97m bw
British Lion / Quintra (Leon Clore)

A young woman determines to leave her talented but half-mad artist husband, who has a fixation on gorillas and behaves in a generally uncivilized manner.

Archetypal sixties marital fantasy, an extension of *Look Back in Anger* in the mood of swinging London. As tiresome as it is funny—but it *is* funny.

w David Mercer, from his play *d* Karel Reisz *ph* Larry Pizer, Gerry Turpin *m* Johnny Dankworth

Vanessa Redgrave, *David Warner*, Robert Stephens, Irene Handl, Newton Blick, Nan Munro

'Poor Morgan: victim of a satire that doesn't bite, lost in a technical confusion of means and ends, and emerging like an identikit photograph, all bits and pieces and no recognizable face.'—*Penelope Houston*

'The first underground movie made above ground.'—*John Simon*

'I think *Morgan* is so appealing to college students because it shares their self-view: they accept this mess of cute infantilism and obsessions and aberrations without expecting the writer and director to resolve it and without themselves feeling a necessity to sort it out.'—*Pauline Kael*

AAN: Vanessa Redgrave

Morning Departure*
GB 1950   102m   bw
Rank / Jay Lewis (Leslie Parkyn)
US title: *Operation Disaster*

Twelve men are caught in a trapped submarine, and only eight can escape.
Archetypal stiff-upper-lip service tragedy, which moves from briskness to a slow funereal ending.

w William Fairchild, *play* Kenneth Woolard *d* Roy Baker *ph* Desmond Dickinson

John Mills, Richard Attenborough, Nigel Patrick, Lana Morris, Peter Hammond, Helen Cherry, James Hayter, Andrew Crawford, George Cole, Michael Brennan, Wylie Watson, Bernard Lee, Kenneth More

Morning Glory***
US 1933   74m   bw
RKO (Pandro S. Berman)

A young actress comes to New York determined to succeed.
Marvellously evocative theatrical drama which provided a strong star part for a fresh young actress and surrounded her with accomplished thespians. Remade to much less effect as *Stage Struck* (qv).

w Howard J. Green, *play* Zoe Akins *d* Lowell Sherman *ph* Bert Glennon *m* Max Steiner

Katharine Hepburn, Douglas Fairbanks Jnr, Adolphe Menjou, Mary Duncan, C. Aubrey Smith, Don Alvarado

AA: Katharine Hepburn

Morocco***
US 1930   97m   bw
Paramount (Louis D. Lighton)

A cabaret singer arrives in Morocco and continues her wicked career by enslaving all the men in sight; but true love reaches her at last.
The star's first American film reveals her quintessence, and although wildly dated in subject matter remains a perversely enjoyable entertainment.

w Jules Furthman, *novel* Amy Jolly by Benno Vigny *d* Josef Von Sternberg *ph* Lee Garmes *m* Karl Hajos

Marlene Dietrich, Gary Cooper, Adolphe Menjou, Ullrich Haupt, Juliette Compton, Francis McDonald

'A cinematic pattern brilliant, profuse, subtle, and at almost every turn inventive.'—*Wilton A. Barrett*

'Enchantingly silly, full of soulful grand passions, drifting cigarette smoke, and perhaps a few too many pictorial shots of the Foreign Legion marching this way and that.'—*New Yorker, 1979*

AAN: Josef Von Sternberg; Lee Garmes; Marlene Dietrich

The Mortal Storm**
US 1940   100m   bw
MGM

A German family in the thirties is split by Nazism.
Solid anti-Nazi melodrama typical of the period before America entered the war; good performances outweigh unconvincing studio sets.

w Claudine West, George Froeschel, Andersen Ellis, *novel* Phyllis Bottome *d* Frank Borzage *ph* William Daniels *m* Edward Kane

Margaret Sullavan, Robert Young, James Stewart, Frank Morgan, Robert Stack, Bonita Granville, Irene Rich, Maria Ouspenskaya

'The love story of today with the popular stars of *The Shop Around the Corner*!'—*publicity*

† The film caused Goebbels to ban the showing of MGM pictures in all German territories.

Moscow Nights
GB 1935   75m   bw

A Russian girl sacrifices her virtue to save her lover from execution. Cardboard melodrama of pre-revolutionary Moscow; not by any means a classic. Laurence Olivier, Penelope Dudley Ward, Harry Baur, Robert Cochran, Morton Selten, Athene Seyler. Written by Erich Seipmann, from the novel by Pierre Benoit; directed by Anthony Asquith; for London Films / Capitol Films. (US title: *I Stand Condemned*.)

Mosquito Squadron
GB 1968   90m   De Luxe

In 1944, the RAF tries out bouncing bombs in a French offensive. Very minor and belated war heroics for double-billing. David McCallum, Suzanne Neve, David Buck, Dinsdale Landen, Charles Gray. Written by Donald Sanford and Joyce Perry; directed by Boris Sagal; for Lewis J. Rachmil / UA.

Moss Rose
US 1947   82m   bw
TCF (Gene Markey)

A Victorian chorus girl suspects her aristocratic admirer of being a murderer. Absurd, stilted mystery melodrama with a better-looking production than it deserves.

w Jules Furthman, Tom Reed *d* Gregory Ratoff *ph* Joe MacDonald *m* David Buttolph

Peggy Cummins, Victor Mature, Ethel Barrymore, Vincent Price

The Most Dangerous Game***
US 1932   63m   bw
(RKO) Merian C. Cooper
GB title: *The Hounds of Zaroff*

A mad hunter lures guests on to his island so that he can hunt them down like animals. Dated but splendidly shivery melodrama with moments of horror and mystery and a splendidly photographed chase sequence. Much imitated in curious ways, and not only by direct remakes such as *A Game of Death* and *Run for the Sun* (qv).

w James Creelman, story Richard Connell *d* Ernest B. Schoedsack, Irving Pichel *ph* Henry Gerrard *m* Max Steiner

Leslie Banks, Joel McCrea, Fay Wray, Robert Armstrong, Noble Johnson

The Most Dangerous Man in the World
GB 1969   99m   De Luxe   Panavision
TCF / APJAC (Mort Abrahams)
US title: *The Chairman*

A top scientist is sent by western intelligence on a mission into Red China, with a transmitter and a detonator implanted in his skull.

Wild Boys' Own Paper adventure which regrettably slows down in the middle for political philosophizing.

w Ben Maddow, *novel* The Chairman by Jay Richard Kennedy *d* J. Lee-Thompson *ph* Ted Moore *m* Jerry Goldsmith

Gregory Peck, Anne Heywood, Arthur Hill, Conrad Yama, Francisca Tu, Keye Luke, Alan Dobie, Ori Levy

Mother***
USSR 1926   90m approx (24 fps)   bw   silent
Mezhrabpom–Russ
original title: *Mat*

A mother incriminates her strike-breaking son, but realizes her error.
Propagandist social melodrama which is also brilliantly conceived and edited, with sequences matching those of Eisenstein.

w N. Zarkhi, V. I. Pudovkin, *novel* Maxim Gorky *d* V. I. Pudovkin *ph* A. Golovnia

Vera Baranovskaya, Nikolai Batalov
† Other versions appeared in 1920 and (*d* Mark Donskoi) 1955.

Mother Carey's Chickens
US 1938   82m   bw
RKO (Pandro S. Berman)

The tribulations of a small-town family in the nineties.
Modest domestic drama, not totally unpleasing.

w S. K. Lauren, Gertrude Purcell, *novel* Kate Douglas Wiggin *d* Rowland V. Lee *ph* Roy Hunt

Anne Shirley, Ruby Keeler, Fay Bainter, James Ellison, Walter Brennan, Donnie Dunagan, Frank Albertson, Alma Kruger, Jackie Moran, Virginia Weidler, Margaret Hamilton
† Remade 1963 as *Summer Magic*.

Mother Didn't Tell Me
US 1950   88m   bw
TCF (Fred Kohlmar)

A working girl marries a doctor and their off duty hours don't coincide.
Thin comedy.

wd Claude Binyon, *novel* The Doctor Wears Three Faces by Mary Baird *ph* Joseph La Shelle *m* Cyril Mockridge

Dorothy McGuire, William Lundigan, June Havoc, Gary Merrill, Jessie Royce Landis

Mother Is a Freshman
US 1948   80m   Technicolor

A mother goes to college and falls for the teacher with whom her daughter is infatuated. Thin romantic comedy lacking the piquancy at which it aims. Loretta Young, Van Johnson, Rudy Vallee, Barbara Lawrence, Betty Lynn, Robert Arthur. Written by Mary Loos and Richard Sale; directed by Lloyd Bacon; for TCF. (GB title: *Mother Knows Best*.)

Mother, Jugs and Speed
US 1976   98m   De Luxe   Panavision
TCF (Joseph R. Barbera)

Comic and tragic events in the lives of Los Angeles drivers of private commercial ambulances.
Black comedy of incidents ranging from farcical to sentimental, sometimes funny but basically unacceptable in either vein.

w Tom Mankiewicz *d* Peter Yates *ph* Ralph Woolsey *m* various *md* Joel Sill

Bill Cosby, Raquel Welch, Harvey Keitel, *Allen Garfield*, Bruce Davison, Larry Hagman

Mother Riley Meets the Vampire
GB 1952   74m   bw
Renown (John Gilling)
US title: *My Son the Vampire*

An old washerwoman accidentally catches a robot-wielding crook called The Vampire. Childish farce notable for Lucan's last appearance in his dame role, and Lugosi's last substantial appearance of any kind—two pros at the end of their tether.

w Val Valentine *d* John Gilling *ph* Stan Pavey *m* Linda Southworth

Arthur Lucan, Bela Lugosi, Dora Bryan, Richard Wattis
   'Stupid, humourless and repulsive.'—*MFB*

Mother Wore Tights*
US 1947   109m   Technicolor
TCF (Lamar Trotti)

Recollections of a vaudeville team and their growing family.
Well-mounted, reasonably charming family musical, one of the best of the many TCF examples of this genre.

w Lamar Trotti, *book* Miriam Young *d* Walter Lang *ph* Harry Jackson *md* Alfred Newman, Charles Henderson

Betty Grable, Dan Dailey, Mona Freeman, Connie Marshall, Vanessa Brown, Robert Arthur, Sara Allgood, William Frawley, Ruth Nelson

AA: Alfred Newman, Charles Henderson
AAN: Harry Jackson; song 'You Do' (*m* Josef Myrow, *ly* Mack Gordon)

Moulin Rouge
US 1934   69m   bw
(UA) Darryl F. Zanuck

The wife of a songwriter impersonates her own sister in order to revitalize her marriage and her stage career.
Predictable minor star vehicle, quite competently done.

w Nunnally Johnson, Henry Lehrman, *play* Lyon de Bri *d* Sidney Lanfield *ph* Charles Rosher *md* Alfred Newman *songs* Harry Warren, Al Dubin

Constance Bennett, Franchot Tone, Tullio Carminati, Helen Westley, Andrew Tombes, Hobart Cavanaugh

Moulin Rouge**
GB 1952   119m   Technicolor
Romulus (Jack Clayton)

Fictional biopic of Toulouse Lautrec.
The dramatic emphasis is on the love affairs of the dwarfish artist, but the film's real interest is in its evocation of 19th-century Montmartre, and especially in the first twenty-minute can can sequence. Nothing later can stand up to the exhilaration of this, and the film slowly slides into boredom.

w John Huston, Anthony Veiller, *novel* Pierre La Mure *d* John Huston *ph* Oswald Morris *m* Georges Auric *ad* Paul Sheriff

Jose Ferrer, Zsa Zsa Gabor, Katherine Kath, Colette Marchand

AAN: best picture; John Huston (as director); Jose Ferrer; Colette Marchand

The Mountain*
US 1956   105m   Technicolor
   Vistavision
Paramount (Edward Dmytryk)

After an airplane crash the wreck is difficult to reach. A young man sets off alone to loot it, and his elder brother follows to stop him.
An indeterminate production in which one believes neither the setting, the plot nor the characters, especially not with Vistavision making everything sharply unreal and the brothers seeming two generations apart.

w Ranald MacDougall, *novel* Henri Troyat *d* Edward Dmytryk *ph* Franz Planer *m* Daniele Amfitheatrof

Spencer Tracy, Robert Wagner, Claire Trevor, William Demarest, E. G. Marshall

The Mountain Eagle
GB 1926   72m approx (24 fps)   bw
   silent
Gainsborough / Emelka (Michael Balcon)
US title: *Fear o'God*

A young schoolmistress resists the attentions of a businessman, escapes to the mountains, and marries a recluse.

Unremarkable romantic drama; one of the lost Hitchcock films.

w Eliot Stannard *d* Alfred Hitchcock *ph* Baron Ventimiglia

Nita Naldi, Bernard Goetzke, Malcolm Keen

The Mountain Men

US 1980 102m Metrocolor Panavision

Two nineteenth-century trappers have adventures with Indians. Rumbustious, foulmouthed and lethargic western of the primitive kind; no possible interest. Charlton Heston, Brian Keith, Victoria Racino, Stephen Macht, John Glover. Written by Frazer Clarke Heston; directed by Richard Lang; for Martin Ransohoff / Columbia. 'It plays like a Sunn Classic four-waller uncomfortably spiced up with violence and profanity.'—*Variety*.

The Mountain Road

US 1960 102m bw
Columbia / William Goetz

In 1944 China, an American officer helps peasants against the Japanese.
Confused and rather dreary war adventure with pretensions.

w Alfred Hayes, *novel* Theodore White *d* Delbert Mann *ph* Burnett Guffey *m* Jerome Moross *md* Morris Stoloff

James Stewart, Lisa Lu, Glenn Corbett, Henry Morgan, Frank Silvera, James Best, Mike Kellin, Frank Maxwell, Alan Baxter

Mourning Becomes Electra*

US 1947 170m bw
RKO / Theatre Guild (Dudley Nichols)

Murder, doom and guilt affect a New England family at the end of the Civil War.
A mark for trying is all. This is a clearly fated attempt to film the unfilmable, a long and lugubrious updating of Sophocles with more than its share of risible moments.

wd Dudley Nichols, *play* Eugene O'Neill *m* Richard Hagemann *ph* George Barnes *ad* Albert D'Agostino

Michael Redgrave, Rosalind Russell, Katina Paxinou, Kirk Douglas, Raymond Massey, Nancy Coleman, Leo Genn

'A star cast fumbles with helpless and sometimes touching ineptitude.'—*Gavin Lambert*

'Within its own terms of mistaken reverence, a good, straight, deliberately unimaginative production.'—*James Agee*

AAN: Michael Redgrave; Rosalind Russell

The Mouse on the Moon

GB 1963 85m Eastmancolor
UA / Walter Shenson

The tiny duchy of Grand Fenwick discovers that its home-made wine makes excellent rocket fuel.
Piddling sequel to *The Mouse that Roared*, suffering from a hesitant script, too few jokes, and overacting.

w Michael Pertwee *d* Richard Lester *ph* Wilkie Cooper *m* Ron Grainer

Margaret Rutherford, Ron Moody, Bernard Cribbins, David Kossoff, Terry-Thomas, Michael Crawford

The Mouse that Roared**

GB 1959 85m Technicolor
Columbia / Open Road (Carl Foreman)

The tiny duchy of Grand Fenwick is bankrupt, and its minister decides to declare war on the United States, be defeated, and receive Marshall Aid.
Lively comedy which sounds rather better than it plays, but has bright moments.

w Roger Macdougall, Stanley Mann, *novel* Leonard Wibberley *d* Jack Arnold *ph* John Wilcox *m* Edwin Astley

Peter Sellers (playing three parts), Jean Seberg, David Kossoff, William Hartnell, Leo McKern, Macdonald Parke, Harold Kasket

'The kind of irrepressible topical satire whose artistic flaws become increasingly apparent but whose merits outlast them.'—*Peter John Dyer*

The Mouthpiece**

US 1932 90m bw
Warner (Lucien Hubbard)

A prosecuting counsel successfully turns to defence but becomes corrupt.
A hard-hitting and entertaining melodrama allegedly based on the career of William Fallon, a New York lawyer.

w Joseph Jackson, Earl Baldwin *d* James Flood, Elliott Nugent *ph* Barney McGill

Warren William, Sidney Fox, Aline MacMahon, John Wray, Ralph Ince, Guy Kibbee

Move

US 1970 88m De Luxe Panavision

A frustrated playwright writes pornography to make money; he moves to a larger apartment but his mind is full of fantasies. None of which are of much interest to the paying customers, the movie being drenched with self-pity.
Elliott Gould, Paula Prentiss, Genevieve

Waite, John Larch, Joe Silver. Written by Joel Lieber and Stanley Hart, from a novel by Joel Lieber; directed by Stuart Rosenberg; for TCF.

Move Over Darling**
US 1963 103m De Luxe Cinemascope
TCF / Arcola / Arwin (Aaron Rosenberg, Marty Melcher)

A wife who has spent five years shipwrecked on a desert island returns to find that her husband has just remarried.
Thin but fitfully amusing remake of *My Favorite Wife*; sheer professionalism gets it by.

w Hal Kanter, Jack Sher d Michael Gordon
ph Daniel L. Fapp m Lionel Newman

Doris Day, James Garner, Polly Bergen, Thelma Ritter, Chuck Connors, Fred Clark

Movie Crazy**
US 1932 82m bw
Harold Lloyd

A filmstruck young man is mistakenly invited to Hollywood for a film test.
The silent comedian is not quite at his best in this early sound comedy, but it contains his last really superb sequences and its picture of Hollywood is both amusing and nostalgic.

w Harold Lloyd and others d Clyde Bruckman ph Walter Lundin

Harold Lloyd, Constance Cummings

Movie Movie**
US 1978 106m part colour
ITC (Stanley Donen)

A pastiche of a thirties double bill, including a boxing yarn (*Dynamite Hands*) and a Busby-Berkeley style girlie show (*Baxter's Beauties of 1933*).
Unfortunately there weren't enough paying customers to appreciate the spoofs, which are pretty patchy anyway; but golden moments stay in the mind.

w Larry Gelbart, Sheldon Keller d Stanley Donen ph Chuck Rosher Jnr, Bruce Surtees
m Ralph Burns ch Michael Kidd

George C. Scott, Trish Van Devere, Red Buttons, Eli Wallach, Michael Kidd, Barbara Harris, Barry Bostwick, Art Carney, Jocelyn Brando

'*Camp*, which has to do with a switch of vision from one era to another, cannot be created, and where it is, as this and previous attempts testify, it is immediately swallowed in its own idiocy.'—*Richard Combs, MFB*

Moving Violation*
US 1976 91m De Luxe
TCF / Roger Corman

Small-town teenagers are pursued by the sheriff because they saw him commit a murder.
Old hat suspenser with a smart new line in thrills.

w David R. Osterhout, William Norton
d Charles S. Dubin ph Charles Correll
m Don Leake

Stephen McHattie, Kay Lenz, Eddie Albert, Lonnie Chapman, Will Geer

'Probably the most hair-raising pursuit sequences in the history of film.'—*Cleveland Amory*

Much Too Shy
GB 1942 92m bw
Columbia (Ben Henry)

A gormless handyman gets into trouble when the portraits of his lady clients are sold to an advertising agency with nude bodies added to them.
A slightly vulgar and talkative farce which restricts the star.

w Ronald Frankau d Marcel Varnel

George Formby, Kathleen Harrison, Hylda Bayley, Eileen Bennett, Joss Ambler, Jimmy Clitheroe

The Mudlark**
GB 1950 98m bw
TCF (Nunnally Johnson)

A scruffy boy from the docks breaks into Windsor Castle to see Queen Victoria and ends her fifteen years of seclusion.
A pleasant whimsical legend which could have done without the romantic interest, but which despite an air of unreality provides warm-hearted, well upholstered entertainment for family audiences.

w Nunnally Johnson, novel Theodore Bonnet
d Jean Negulesco ph Georges Périnal
m William Alwyn ad C. P. Norman

Alec Guinness, Irene Dunne, *Andrew Ray*, Anthony Steel, Constance Smith, *Finlay Currie, Edward Rigby*

The Mummy**
US 1932 72m bw
Universal (Stanley Bergerman)

An Egyptian mummy comes back to life and covets a young girl.
Strange dreamlike horror film with only fleeting frissons but plenty of narrative interest despite the silliest of stories and some fairly stilted acting.

*w John I. Balderston d Karl Freund
ph Charles Stumar*

Boris Karloff, Zita Johann, David Manners,
Arthur Byron, Edward Van Sloan

'It beggars description . . . one of the most
unusual talkies ever produced.'—*New York
Times*

'Editing very much in the Germanic style,
magnificent lighting and a superb performance
from Karloff make this a fantasy almost
without equal.'—*John Baxter, 1968*

'A love story that lived for three thousand
years!'—*publicity*

The Mummy*
GB 1959 88m Technicolor
Hammer (Michael Carreras)

A mummy brought back to England by
archaeologists wakes up and goes on the
rampage.
Typical Hammer vulgarization of a Hollywood
legend; starts slowly and unpleasantly, but
picks up speed and resource in the last half
hour.

*w Jimmy Sangster d Terence Fisher ph Jack
Asher m Frank Reizenstein*

Peter Cushing, Christopher Lee, Yvonne
Furneaux, Eddie Byrne, Felix Aylmer,
Raymond Huntley, John Stuart
† Hammer sequels, of little interest, were
Curse of the Mummy's Tomb (1964), *The
Mummy's Shroud* (1966) and *Blood from the
Mummy's Tomb* (1971).

The Mummy's Hand**
US 1940 67m bw
Universal (Ben Pivar)

The high priest of an evil sect revivifies an
Egyptian mummy and uses it to kill off
members of an archaeological expedition.
Semi-sequel to 1932's *The Mummy*,
economically using the same flashback. It
starts off in comedy vein, but the last half hour
is among the most scary in horror film history.

*w Griffin Jay, Maxwell Shane d Christy
Cabanne ph Elwood Bredell*

Dick Foran, Wallace Ford, *George Zucco*,
Cecil Kellaway, Peggy Moran, *Tom Tyler,
Eduardo Ciannelli*
† Sequels, of decreasing merit, were *The
Mummy's Tomb* (1942) (in which the heroes
of *The Mummy's Hand* are killed off), *The
Mummy's Ghost* (1944) and *The Mummy's
Curse* (1944). See also *Abbott and Costello
Meet the Mummy.*

The Muppet Movie**
GB 1979 97m Eastmancolor
ITC (Jim Henson)

Kermit the Frog and friends travel across
America to Hollywood and are offered a film
contract by Lew Lord, the famous impresario.
Technically an adroit transfer of the celebrated
puppets from their TV backstage milieu to a
wider canvas; but the latter tends to dwarf
them, the material is very variable, the guest
stars look embarrassed and the show goes on
too long.

*w Jerry Juhl, Jack Burns d James Frawley
ph Isidore Mankofsky pd Joel Schiller
m Paul Williams, Kenny Ascher*

Charles Durning, Edgar Bergen, Bob Hope,
Milton Berle, Mel Brooks, James Coburn,
Dom DeLuise, Elliott Gould, Cloris
Leachman, Telly Savalas, Orson Welles

Murder**
GB 1930 92m bw
British International (John Maxwell)

A girl is convicted of murder, but one of the
jurors sets out to prove her innocent.
Interesting early Hitchcock, a rare whodunnit
for him.

w Alma Reville, novel Enter Sir John *by
Clemence Dane and Helen Simpson d Alfred
Hitchcock ph Jack Cox*

Herbert Marshall, Nora Baring, Phyllis
Konstam, Edward Chapman, Miles Mander,
Esmé Percy, Donald Calthrop

Murder at Monte Carlo
GB 1934 70m bw
Warner (Irving Asher)

A professor is murdered for his roulette
system.
Modest second feature notable only as a
springboard for the career of its star.

*w John Hastings Turner, Michael Barringer,
novel* Tom Van Dyke *d Ralph Ince ph Basil
Emmott*

Errol Flynn, Eve Gray, Paul Graetz, Molly
Lamont, Ellis Irving

Murder at the Vanities*
US 1934 89m bw
Paramount (E. Lloyd Sheldon)

Murder backstage at the first night of Earl
Carroll's Vanities.
Curious, stylish mixture of musical numbers,
broad comedy and mystery. Dated, but fun.

*w Carey Wilson, Joseph Gollomb, Sam
Hellman d Mitchell Leisen ph Leo Tover*

Jack Oakie, Victor McLaglen, Carl Brisson,
Kitty Carlisle, Dorothy Stickney, Gertrude
Michael, Jessie Ralph, Gail Patrick

Murder at the Windmill
GB 1949 70m bw

At London's famous girlie show, a front row patron is murdered. Rather rushed-looking whodunnit with interesting detail. Garry Marsh, Jack Livesey, Jon Pertwee, Diana Decker, Jimmy Edwards, Eliot Makeham. Written and directed by Val Guest; for Daniel Angel and Nat Cohen.

Murder by Contract*
US 1958 81m bw
Columbia / Orbin (Leon Chooluck)

A professional killer makes a fatal mistake and is shot down by police.
Low-budgeter which seemed stark and original at the time, but television has familiarized its contents. Moody, contrasty photography and restrained style give it a minor distinction.

w Ben Simcoe d *Irving Lerner* ph *Lucien Ballard* m Perry Borkin

Vince Edwards, Philip Pine, Herschel Bernardi, Caprice Toriel
'Ice cold and completely unsentimental.'— *John Gillett*

Murder by Death*
US 1976 94m Metrocolor
Columbia / Ray Stark

Several (fictional) detectives are invited to stay at the home of a wealthy recluse, and mystery and murder follow.
Sometimes thin but generally likeable spoof of a longstanding genre; the stars seize their opportunities avidly, and the film does not outstay its welcome

w *Neil Simon* d Robert Moore ph David M. Walsh m Dave Grusin pd Stephen Grimes

Peter Falk, Alec Guinness, Peter Sellers, Truman Capote, Estelle Winwood, Elsa Lanchester, Eileen Brennan, James Coco, David Niven, Maggie Smith, Nancy Walker
'Plenty of scene-stealing actors but not many scenes worth stealing.'—*Michael Billington, Illustrated London News*
'Polished performances fail to compensate for a vacuous and frustratingly tortuous plot.'—*Sight and Sound*
'It seems to me that if you haven't watched the real Thin Man and the real Bogie in the real *Maltese Falcon* you won't see the joke; and if you have watched them, the joke is not good enough.'—*Dilys Powell, Sunday Times*

Murder by Decree
GB / Canada 1978 112m Metrocolor
Avco / Decree Productions / Saucy Jack
(Robert A. Goldstone)

Sherlock Holmes investigates the matter of Jack the Ripper and comes upon a Masonic conspiracy.
Interminably long and unpardonably muddled variation on this over-familiar theme, with halts for the performances of guest artists and no clear grip on narrative or character.

w John Hopkins d Bob Clark ph Reginald H. Morris m Carl Zittrer, Paul Zaza pd Harry Pottle

Christopher Plummer, James Mason, Anthony Quayle, David Hemmings, Susan Clark, John Gielgud, Donald Sutherland, Frank Finlay, Geneviève Bujold

Murder by the Clock
US 1931 76m bw
Paramount

Creepy goings on in an old house after the death of a dowager who has built herself a tomb from which she can escape if buried alive.
Tasteless chiller which had the distinction of being withdrawn from British circulation after public protests.

w Henry Myers, Rufus King, Charles Beahan, *play* Charles Beahan, *novel* Rufus King d Edward Sloman ph Karl Struss

Lilyan Tashman, William 'Stage' Boyd, Regis Toomey, Irving Pichel, Blanche Frederici, Walter McGrail

Murder He Says**
US 1945 91m bw
Paramount (E. D. Leshin)

An insurance salesman stays with a homicidal family of hillbillies.
A curious black farce which seems to be compounded of *Cold Comfort Farm* and *The Red Inn*. Very funny, and ahead of its time.

w Lou Breslow d George Marshall ph Theodor Sparkuhl

Fred MacMurray, Marjorie Main, Helen Walker, Peter Whitney, Jean Heather, Porter Hall, Mabel Paige

Murder in Reverse
GB 1945 88m bw

After long imprisonment for a supposed murder, a convict comes out and hunts down the victim, who isn't really dead. A reasonable crime entertainment of its day which seemed to introduce a new star; but it hasn't worn well. William Hartnell, Jimmy Hanley, Chili Bouchier, John Slater, Dinah Sheridan, Wylie Watson. Written and directed by Montgomery Tully, from a novel by 'Seamark'; for British National.

Murder in the Big House
US 1942   67m   bw

Two reporters uncover a murder ring in a
prison. Acceptable second feature which
catapulted its star to fame—at another studio.
Van Johnson, George Meeker, Faye Emerson,
Frank Wilcox. Written by Raymond Schrock;
directed by B. Reeves Eason; for Warner.
(NB: A previous 1936 version was called
Jailbreak and starred Craig Reynolds. *Murder
in the Big House* was reissued in 1945 as *Born
for Trouble*.)

Murder in the Cathedral
GB 1951   136m   bw
George Hoellering

The 12th-century struggle between Henry II
and his archbishop culminates in the
assassination of Becket in Canterbury
Cathedral.
Plainly filmed, slightly amateur version of the
celebrated verse play; scarcely a rewarding
cinematic experience.

wd George Hoellering, *play* T. S. Eliot
ph David Kosky   *m* Laszlo Lajtha   *ad* Peter
Pendrey

Father John Grosner, Alexander Gauge,
David Ward, George Woodbridge, Basil
Burton, Paul Rogers, Niall MacGinnis, Mark
Dignam, Leo McKern
   'A curious ordeal for the audience . . . a
no-man's-land between cinema and drama has
been discovered, rather than any extension of
either.'—*Gavin Lambert*

Murder in the Family
GB 1938   75m   bw

Who killed rich Aunt Octavia? Mild
whodunnit with interesting cast. Barry Jones,
Jessica Tandy, Evelyn Ankers, Donald Gray,
David Markham, Glynis Johns, Roddy
McDowall. Written by David Evans, from the
novel by James Ronald; directed by Al
Parker; for TCF.

Murder in the Fleet
US 1935   70m   bw
MGM (Lucien Hubbard)

Sabotage on a navy cruiser turns out to be the
work of a mad inventor.
Weak and confused mixture of melodrama and
comedy.

wd Edward Sedgwick   *ph* Milton Krasner

Robert Taylor, Jean Parker, Jean Hersholt,
Ted Healy, Una Merkel, Nat Pendleton,
Raymond Hatton, Donald Cook, Mischa Auer

Murder in Times Square
US 1943   72m   bw

An actor-playwright is suspected of four
theatrical murders. Standard detection work
with some slight claim to sophistication.
Edmund Lowe, Sidney Blackmer, Marguerite
Chapman, John Litel. Written by Stuart
Palmer and Paul Gangelin; directed by Lew
Landers; for Columbia.

Murder, Incorporated
US 1960   103m   bw   Cinemascope
TCF (Burt Balaban)

In the thirties, Anastasia and Lepke build up
their crime syndicate which spreads terror
through New York.
Tedious and poorly made gangster thriller,
unforgivable faults considering the many
admirable models it has to follow.

w Irve Tunick, Mel Barr   *d* Burt Balaban,
Stuart Rosenberg   *ph* Gayne Rescher
m Frank de Vol

Stuart Whitman, Mai Britt, Henry Morgan,
Peter Falk, David J. Stewart, Simon Oakland,
Morey Amsterdam
AAN: Peter Falk

The Murder Man*
US 1935   84m   bw
MGM (Harry Rapf)

A reporter commits murder and frames
someone else.
Good low-key melodrama with an interesting
cast.

w Tim Whelan, John C. Higgins   *d* Tim
Whelan   *ph* Lester White   *m* William Axt

Spencer Tracy, Virginia Bruce, Lionel Atwill,
James Stewart, Harvey Stephens, William
Collier Snr

Murder on the Orient Express**
GB 1974   131m   Technicolor
EMI / GW Films (John Brabourne, Richard
   Goodwin)

In the early thirties, Hercule Poirot solves a
murder on a snowbound train.
Reasonably elegant but disappointingly
slackly-handled version of a classic mystery
novel. Finney overacts and his all-star support
is distracting, while as soon as the train chugs
into its snowdrift the film stops moving too,
without even a dramatic 'curtain'.

w Paul Dehn, *novel* Agatha Christie   *d* Sidney
Lumet   *ph* Geoffrey Unsworth   *m* Richard
Rodney Bennett   *pd* Tony Walton

Albert Finney, *Ingrid Bergman*, Lauren
Bacall, Wendy Hiller, Sean Connery, Vanessa

Redgrave, Michael York, Martin Balsam,
Richard Widmark, Jacqueline Bisset, Jean-
Pierre Cassel, Rachel Roberts, George
Coulouris, *John Gielgud*, Anthony Perkins,
Colin Blakely, Jeremy Lloyd, Denis Quilley
    'Audiences appear to be so hungry for this
type of entertainment that maybe it hardly
matters that it isn't very good.'—*Judith Crist*

AA: Ingrid Bergman
AAN: Paul Dehn; Geoffrey Unsworth;
Richard Rodney Bennett; Albert Finney

Murder She Said*
GB 1961   87m   bw
MGM (George H. Brown)

An elderly spinster investigates after seeing a
woman strangled in a passing train.
Frightfully British and disappointingly tame
adaptation of an Agatha Christie character,
with only the star (who is somewhat miscast)
holding one's attention.

w David Pursall, Jack Seddon, *novel* 4.50 from
Paddington by Agatha Christie *d* George
Pollock *ph* Geoffrey Faithfull *m* Ron
Goodwin

Margaret Rutherford, Charles Tingwell, Muriel
Pavlow, Arthur Kennedy, James Robertson
Justice, Thorley Walters, Gerald Cross,
Conrad Phillips
† Thanks to Miss Rutherford's popularity,
three increasingly poor sequels were made:
Murder at the Gallop (1963), *Murder Most
Foul* (1964), *Murder Ahoy* (1964).

Murder without Crime
GB 1950   76m   bw

A blackmailer extracts money for a crime not
yet committed. Thin four-hander from a rather
mysterious West End success. Dennis Price,
Derek Farr, Joan Dowling, Patricia Plunkett.
Written and directed by J. Lee-Thompson,
from his play; for ABPC.

The Murderers Are Among Us*
Germany 1947   87m   bw
Defa
original title: *Die Mörder Sind Unter Uns*

In the ruins of Berlin several post-war
characters indulge in gloomy self-examination.
Almost a caricature of what one would expect
from a defeated people, this now-curious item
has a certain power of its own.

wd Wolfgang Staudte *ph* Friedl Behn-Grund,
Eugen Klagemann *m* Ernst Roters

Hildegard Knef, Ernst Fischer, Arno Paulsen

Murderer's Row
US 1966   108m   Technicolor
Columbia / Meadway—Claude / Euan Lloyd

Matt Helm tracks down an international villain
who has kidnapped an inventor.
Witless and uninventive spy spoof which drags
itself wearily along but never attempts an
explanation of its own title.

w Herbert Baker, *novel* Donald Hamilton
d Henry Levin *ph* Sam Leavitt *m* Lalo
Schifrin

Dean Martin, Ann-Margret, Karl Malden,
Camilla Sparv, James Gregory, Beverly
Adams, Tom Reese

Murders in the Rue Morgue*
US 1932   62m   bw
Universal (Carl Laemmle Jnr)

A series of grisly murders prove to be the
work of a trained ape.
A distant relation of the original story, mildly
interesting for its obvious Caligari influences,
but not very good in any way.

w Tom Reed, Dale Van Avery, John Huston,
story Edgar Allan Poe *d* Robert Florey
ph Karl Freund

Bela Lugosi, Sidney Fox, Leon Ames, Bert
Roach, Brandon Hurst

Murders in the Rue Morgue*
US 1971   86m   Foto Film Color
AIP

Poe's story is being presented at a Grand
Guignol theatre in Paris, and when murders
happen within the company Inspector Vidocq
comes to investigate.
Playfully plotted chiller which has more to do
with *The Phantom of the Opera* than with Poe.
A good time waster for addicts.

w Charles Wicking, Henry Slesar *d* Gordon
Hessler *ph* Manuel Berengier *m* Waldo de
Los Rios

Jason Robards Jnr, Herbert Lom, Lilli
Palmer, Adolfo Celi, Michael Dunn

Murders in the Zoo
US 1933   64m   bw

A jealous zoologist finds interesting ways to
murder any man who shows interest in his
wife. Modest time-passer with a rampant star.
Lionel Atwill, Charles Ruggles, Kathleen
Burke, John Lodge, Randolph Scott, Gail
Patrick. Written by Philip Wylie and Seton I.
Miller; directed by Edward Sutherland; for
Paramount.

Muriel*
France / Italy 1963   116m   Eastmancolor
Argos / Alpha / Eclair / Films de la Pléiade /
   Dear Films (Anatole Dauman)
aka: *Muriel, ou le Temps d'un Retour*

A widow and her stepson are both misled by memories of past loves.
Elusive character drama which, though over-generous in length, fails to satisfy.

w Jean Cayrol d Alain Resnais ph Sacha Vierny m Hans Werner Henze

Delphine Seyrig, Jean-Pierre Kérien, Nita Klein, Jean-Baptiste Thierrée

'One has to watch and listen with every nerve alert.'—Tom Milne, MFB

Murph the Surf
US 1975   101m   colour

Two Miami playboys steal a famous sapphire from a museum. Criminal autobiography based on fact; but it never settles down to being comedy or drama. Robert Conrad, Don Stroud, Donna Mills, Luther Adler. Written by E. Arthur Kean, from a story by Allan Dale Kuhn; directed by Marvin Chomsky; for AIP. (Aka: Live a Little, Steal a Lot.)

Murphy's War*
GB 1971   108m   Eastmancolor
    Panavision
Hemdale / Yates–Deeley (Michael Deeley)

A torpedoed British merchantman in Venezuela devotes himself to bombing a U-boat from a home-made plane.
Modest adventure story with the star in better form than the script.

w Stirling Silliphant, novel Max Catto d Peter Yates ph Douglas Slocombe m John Barry

Peter O'Toole, Sian Phillips, Philippe Noiret, Horst Janson

The Music Box****
US 1932   30m   bw

Two delivery men take a piano to a house at the top of a flight of steps. Quintessential Laurel and Hardy, involving almost all their aspects including a slight song and dance. With Billy Gilbert. Written by H. M. Walker; directed by James Parrott; for Hal Roach. AA: best short.

Music for Millions*
US 1944   117m   bw
MGM (Joe Pasternak)

A small girl helps her pregnant sister who is a member of Jose Iturbi's orchestra.
Dewy-eyed wartime musical, full of popular classics, sentimentality and child interest, all smoothly packaged. As an example of what the public wanted in 1944, quite an eye-opener.

w Myles Connelly d Henry Koster ph Robert Surtees md George Stoll

Margaret O'Brien, June Allyson, Jose Iturbi, Jimmy Durante, Marsha Hunt, Hugh Herbert, Henry Davenport, Connie Gilchrist
AAN: Myles Connelly

Music Hath Charms*
GB 1935   70m   bw
BIP (Walter C. Mycroft)

A dance band's broadcast has various effects on listeners.
Pleasing, modest portmanteau of sketches with music.

w Jack Davies, Courtney Territt, L. Du Garde Peach d Thomas Bentley, Alexander Esway, Walter Summers, Arthur Woods

Henry Hall and his Orchestra, Carol Goodner, W. H. Berry, Arthur Margetson, Antoinette Cellier, Billy Milton

Music in My Heart
US 1940   70m   bw

An alien singer wins the lead in a Broadway musical, which prevents him from being deported. Forgettable second feature which was its leading lady's last stepping stone before stardom. Rita Hayworth, Tony Martin, Edith Fellows, Alan Mowbray, George Tobias, Eric Blore, Andre Kostelanetz and his orchestra. Written by James Edward Grant; directed by Joseph Santley; for Columbia. AAN: song, 'It's a Blue World'.

Music in the Air
US 1934   85m   bw
Fox

An opera singer is torn between two men. Heavy-going light entertainment.

w Howard Young, Billy Wilder, play Oscar Hammerstein II, Jerome Kern ph Ernest Palmer d Joe May

Gloria Swanson, John Boles, Douglass Montgomery, June Lang, Al Shean, Reginald Owen, Joseph Cawthorn, Hobart Bosworth

Music Is Magic
US 1935   67m   bw

By a series of unexpected events, a young girl becomes a Hollywood star. Unpretentious and fairly snappy musical which still provides moments to enjoy. Alice Faye, Bebe Daniels, Ray Walker, Frank Mitchell, Jack Durant, Hattie McDaniel. Written by Edward Eliscu and Lou Breslow; directed by George Marshall; for TCF.

The Music Lovers*
GB 1970   123m   Eastmancolor
    Panavision
UA / Rossfilms (Roy Baird)

Homosexual composer Tchaikovsky is impelled to marry, loses his sponsor, drives his wife into an asylum and dies of cholera. Absurd fantasia on the life of a great composer, produced in a manner reminiscent of MGM's sillier musicals; up to a point hysterically (and unintentionally) funny, then rather sickening.

w Melvyn Bragg, *book* Beloved Friend by C. D. Bowen, Barbara Von Meck *d Ken Russell ph* Douglas Slocombe *md* André Previn

Richard Chamberlain, *Glenda Jackson, Christopher Gable*, Max Adrian, Isabella Telezynska, Maureen Pryor, Andrew Faulds
'Tchaikovsky has been made the excuse for a crude melodrama about sex.'—*Konstantin Bazarov*
'The story of a homosexual who married a nymphomaniac!'—*publicity*

The Music Man***
US 1962   151m   Technirama
Warner (Morton da Costa)

A confidence trickster persuades a small-town council to start a boys' band, with himself as the agent for all the expenses.
Reasonably cinematic, thoroughly invigorating transference to the screen of a hit Broadway musical. Splendid period 'feel', standout performances, slight sag in second half.

w Marion Hargrove, *book* Meredith Willson *d Morton da Costa ph* Robert Burks *md* Ray Heindorf *ch* Onna White *songs Meredith Willson*

Robert Preston, Shirley Jones, Buddy Hackett, *Hermione Gingold*, Pert Kelton, Paul Ford
AA: Ray Heindorf
AAN: best picture

Mustang Country
US 1976   79m   Technicolor
Universal (John Champion)

In 1925 Montana, a rancher comes out of retirement to help to round up a wild stallion. Mild outdoor yarn for family audiences.

wd John Champion *ph* J. Barry Herron *m* Lee Holdridge

Joel McCrea, Nika Mina, Robert Fuller, Patrick Wayne

The Mutations
GB 1974   92m   Eastmancolor
Columbia / Getty (Robert D. Weinbach)

A bio-chemist uses circus freaks in his experiments to find the perfect synthesis of plant and animal.

Tasteless horror film with little style of any kind.

w Robert D. Weinbach, Edward Mann *d* Jack Cardiff *ph* Paul Beeson *m* Basil Kirchin

Donald Pleasence, Tom Baker, Brad Harris, Julie Ege, Michael Dunn, Scott Antony, Jill Haworth, Lisa Collings

Mutiny in the Big House
US 1939   93m   bw

A chaplain is at the centre of a prison break, and tries to calm the mob. Archetypal cellblock movie, and not the worst of them. Charles Bickford, Barton Maclane. Written by Robert D. Andrews and Martin Mooney; directed by William Nigh; for Monogram.

The Mutiny of the Elsinore
GB 1937   79m   bw

A reporter on a sailing ship for a story finds himself in the middle of a mutiny. Very studio-bound seafaring adventure. Paul Lukas, Lyn Harding, Kathleen Kelly, Clifford Evans. Written by Walter Summers and Beaufoy Milton, from the novel by Jack London; directed by Roy Lockwood; for Argyle British.

Mutiny on the Bounty***
US 1935   135m   bw
MGM (Irving Thalberg, Albert Lewin)

An 18th-century British naval vessel sets off for South America but during a mutiny the captain is cast adrift and the mutineers settle in the Pitcairn Islands.
A still-entertaining adventure film which seemed at the time like the pinnacle of Hollywood's achievement but can now be seen to be slackly told, with wholesale pre-release editing very evident. Individual scenes and performances are however refreshingly well-handled.

w Talbot Jennings, Jules Furthman, Carey Wilson, *book* Charles Nordhoff, James Hall *d Frank Lloyd ph* Arthur Edeson *m* Herbert Stothart

Charles Laughton, Clark Gable, Franchot Tone, Movita, Dudley Digges, Henry Stephenson, Donald Crisp, Eddie Quillan, Francis Lister, Spring Byington, Ian Wolfe
'Incidents are made vivid in terms of the medium—the swish and pistol crack of the lash, the sweating lean bodies, the terrible labour, and the ominous judgment from the quarterdeck.'—*Otis Ferguson*

AA: best picture
AAN: script; Frank Lloyd; Herbert Stothart;
Charles Laughton; Clark Gable; Franchot
Tone

Mutiny on the Bounty
US 1962 185m Technicolor Ultra
Panavision 70
MGM / Arcola (Aaron Rosenberg)
Overlong and unattractive remake marred
principally by Brando's English accent and
various production follies, not to mention his
overlong and bloody death scene. The
shipboard sadism still works pretty well, but
after the landing in Tahiti boredom takes over.

w Charles Lederer d Lewis Milestone
ph Robert Surtees m Bronislau Kaper

Trevor Howard, Marlon Brando, Richard
Harris, Hugh Griffith, Tarita, Richard Haydn,
Percy Herbert, Duncan Lamont, Gordon
Jackson, Chips Rafferty, Noel Purcell
AAN: best picture; Robert Surtees; Bronislau
Kaper; song 'Follow Me' (m Bronislau Kaper,
ly Paul Francis Webster)

My American Uncle*
France 1980 126m Eastmancolor
Andrea Films / TFI (Philippe Dussart)
Original title: *Mon Oncle Américain*

Professor Henri Laborit explains the lives of
two men and a woman in terms of animal
behaviour.
Fascinatingly assembled but basically
pessimistic dissection of human life, in the
director's most meticulous style. The
American uncle is the piece of good luck
which may be just around the corner (but
probably isn't).

w Jean Gruault, from the works of Henri
Laborit d Alain Resnais ph Sacha Vierny
m Arié Dzierlatka

Gerard Depardieu, Nicole Garcia, Roger
Pierre, Henri Laborit
AAN: screenplay

My Blood Runs Cold
US 1965 108m bw Panavision
Warner (William Conrad)

A spoilt heiress meets a strange young man
who claims she is the reincarnation of a long
dead charmer; he turns out to be a madman
who has come across an old diary.
Initially intriguing but eventually exhausting
melodrama with a weak solution.

w John Mantley d William Conrad ph Sam
Leavitt m George Duning

Troy Donahue, Joey Heatherton, Barry
Sullivan, Jeanette Nolan
'Not all that bad, but not worth missing *I
Love Lucy* for either.'—*Leonard Maltin*

My Blue Heaven
US 1950 96m Technicolor
TCF (Sol C. Siegel)

A pair of troupers want a family, by adoption
if not otherwise.
Routine musical drenched in sentimentality.

w Lamar Trotti, Claude Binyon d Henry
Koster ph Alfred E. Arling m Alfred
Newman songs Harold Arlen

Betty Grable, Dan Dailey, Mitzi Gaynor,
David Wayne, Jane Wyatt, Una Merkel

My Brilliant Career*
Australia 1979 100m Eastmancolor
NSW Film Corporation / Margaret Fink

The daughter of an Australian bush farmer at
the turn of the century dreams of the world
beyond and writes a memoir.
Pleasing but very slow picture of a world gone
by.

w Eleanor Witcombe, *novel* Miles Franklin
d Gillian Armstrong ph Don McAlpine
m Nathan Waks

Judy Davis, Sam Neill, Wendy Hughes,
Robert Grubb, Max Cullen

BFA: Judy Davis

My Brother Jonathan
GB 1947 108m bw
ABP

The life of a small-town doctor who wanted to
be a great surgeon.
Unobjectionable, unexciting novel-on-film
with the typically British artificial studio look
of the time.

w Leslie Landau, Adrian Alington,
novel Francis Brett Young d Harold French
ph Derick Williams m Hans May

Michael Denison, Dulcie Gray, Ronald
Howard, Stephen Murray

My Brother Talks to Horses
US 1946 93m bw
MGM (Samuel Marx)

A boy who can talk to horses finds himself in
demand by racetrack gamblers.
Well-mounted but uninspired whimsy with a
fatal lack of pace.

w Morton Thomson, from his novel Joe the
Wounded Tennis Player d Fred Zinnemann
ph Joseph Ruttenberg m Rudolph Kopp

Butch Jenkins, Peter Lawford, Charlie
Ruggles, Edward Arnold, Beverly Tyler,
Spring Byington

My Brother's Keeper
GB 1948   91m   bw
GFD / Gainsborough (Anthony
   Darnborough)

Two convicts escape, handcuffed together; one
is violent, the other innocent.
Pre-*Defiant Ones* social melodrama, quite well
made but suffering from miscasting.

w Frank Harvey, *story* Maurice Wiltshire
d Alfred Roome, Roy Rich   *ph* Gordon Lang
m Clifton Parker

Jack Warner, George Cole, Jane Hylton,
David Tomlinson, Bill Owen, Raymond
Lovell, Yvonne Owen, Beatrice Varley

My Cousin Rachel*
US 1952   98m   bw
TCF (Nunnally Johnson)

A Cornish gentleman dies in Italy after
marrying a mysterious lady; when she comes
to England she arouses the hostility, and love,
of her husband's foster son.
Well-wrought but dramatically unsatisfactory
Victorian melodrama from a bestseller; plenty
of suspicion but no solution makes Rachel a
dull girl.

w Nunnally Johnson, *novel* Daphne du
Maurier   *d* Henry Koster   *ph* Joseph La
Shelle   *m* Franz Waxman

Olivia de Havilland, Richard Burton, John
Sutton, Audrey Dalton, Ronald Squire

AAN: Joseph La Shelle; Richard Burton

My Daughter Joy
GB 1950   81m   bw
Columbia / Gregory Ratoff
US title: *Operation X*

In order to cement a new trade pact, an
international financier plans to marry his
daughter to the son of an African sultan.
Turgid melodrama swamping some good
actors.

w Robert Thoeren, William Rose, *novel*
David Golder by Irene Neirowsky   *d* Gregory
Ratoff   *ph* Georges Périnal

Edward G. Robinson, Peggy Cummins, Nora
Swinburne, Richard Greene, Finlay Currie,
Gregory Ratoff, Ronald Adam, Walter Rilla,
James Robertson Justice, David Hutcheson

My Darling Clementine***
US 1946   98m   bw
TCF (Samuel G. Engel)

Wyatt Earp cleans up Tombstone and wipes
out the Clanton gang at the OK corral.
Archetypal western mood piece, full of
nostalgia for times gone by and crackling with
memorable scenes and characterizations.

w Samuel G. Engel, Winston Miller, *book*
Wyatt Earp, Frontier Marshal by Stuart N.
Lake   *d* John Ford   *ph* Joe MacDonald
m Cyril Mockridge

Henry Fonda, Victor Mature, Walter Brennan,
Linda Darnell, Cathy Downs, Tim Holt, Ward
Bond, *Alan Mowbray*, John Ireland, Jane
Darwell

'Every scene, every shot is the product of a
keen and sensitive eye.'—*Bosley Crowther*
'Considerable care has gone to its period
reconstruction, but the view is a poetic one.'—
Lindsay Anderson

My Dear Miss Aldrich
US 1937   73m   bw

The glamorous new owner of a newspaper
never agrees with its editor. Skilful light
comedy with good work all round. Maureen
O'Sullivan, Walter Pidgeon, Edna May
Oliver, Rita Johnson, Janet Beecher. Written
by Herman Mankiewicz; directed by George
B. Seitz; for MGM.

My Dear Secretary
US 1948   96m   bw

A secretary marries her boss and becomes
jealous of his new secretary. Slow-paced,
frivolous romantic comedy. Kirk Douglas,
Laraine Day, Keenan Wynn. Written and
directed by Charles Martin; for Cardinal /
UA.

My Dream Is Yours
US 1949   101m   Technicolor
Warner

A Hollywood talent scout discovers a new
singer.
Competent, forgettable musical.

w Harry Kurnitz, Dane Lussier   *d* Michael
Curtiz   *ph* Ernest Haller   *m* Harry Warren
ly Ralph Blane   *ch* Le Roy Prinz.

Doris Day, Jack Carson, Lee Bowman,
Adolphe Menjou, Eve Arden, S. Z. Sakall
† A remake of *Twenty Million Sweethearts*.

My Fair Lady***
US 1964   175m   Technicolor
   Super Panavision 70
CBS / Warner (Jack L. Warner)

Musical version of *Pygmalion*, about a flower
girl trained by an arrogant elocutionist to pass
as a lady.

Careful, cold transcription of a stage success; cinematically quite uninventive when compared with *Pygmalion* itself, but a pretty good entertainment.

w Alan Jay Lerner, *play* Pygmalion by Bernard Shaw *d* George Cukor *ph* Harry Stradling *m* Frederick Loewe *ch* Hermes Pan *ad* Gene Allen *costumes* Cecil Beaton

Rex Harrison, Audrey Hepburn, *Stanley Holloway*, Wilfrid Hyde White, Gladys Cooper, Jeremy Brett, Theodore Bikel, Isobel Elsom, Mona Washbourne, Walter Burke
   'The property has been not so much adapted as elegantly embalmed.'—*Andrew Sarris*

AA: best picture; George Cukor; Harry Stradling; Rex Harrison
AAN: Alan Jay Lerner; Stanley Holloway; Gladys Cooper

My Favorite Blonde***
US 1942   78m   bw
Paramount (Paul Jones)

A burlesque comic travelling by train helps a lady in distress and lives to regret it.
Smartly paced spy comedy thriller, one of its star's best vehicles.

w Don Hartman, Frank Butler, Melvin Frank, Norman Panama d Sidney Lanfield ph William Mellor *m* David Buttolph

Bob Hope, Madeleine Carroll, Gale Sondergaard, George Zucco, Lionel Royce, Walter Kingsford, Victor Varconi

My Favorite Brunette*
US 1947   87m   bw
Paramount (Daniel Dare)

A photographer gets mixed up with mobsters.
Pretty fair star vehicle which half-heartedly spoofs *Farewell My Lovely*.

w Edmund Beloin, Jack Rose *d* Elliott Nugent *ph* Lionel Lindon *m* Robert Emmett Dolan

Bob Hope, Dorothy Lamour, Peter Lorre, Lon Chaney Jnr, John Hoyt, Charles Dingle, Reginald Denny

My Favorite Spy
US 1942   86m   bw

The bandleader Kay Kyser has to postpone his honeymoon when he is called up and set to spy-catching. Fairly slick nonsense featuring a band popular at the time. Kay Kyser, Ginny Simms, Ish Kabibble, Ellen Drew, Jane Wyman. Written by Sig Herzig, William Bowers; directed by Tay Garnett; for RKO.

My Favorite Spy*
US 1951   93m   bw
Paramount (Paul Jones)

A burlesque comic is asked by the US government to pose as an international spy who happens to be his double.
Moderately funny star vehicle with more willing hands than good ideas. The chase finale however is worth waiting for.

w Edmund Hartmann, Jack Sher *d* Norman Z. McLeod *ph* Victor Milner *m* Victor Young

Bob Hope, Hedy Lamarr, Francis L. Sullivan, Arnold Moss, Mike Mazurki, Luis Van Rooten

My Favorite Wife***
US 1940   88m   bw
RKO (Leo McCarey)

A lady explorer returns after several shipwrecked years to find that her husband has married again.
A well-worn situation gets its brightest treatment in this light star vehicle.

w Sam and Bella Spewack, Leo McCarey d Garson Kanin ph Rudolph Maté *m* Roy Webb

Cary Grant, Irene Dunne, Randolph Scott, Gail Patrick, Ann Shoemaker, Donald MacBride
   'One of those comedies with a glow on it.'—*Otis Ferguson*
† Other variations (qv): *Too Many Husbands, Our Wife, Three for the Show, Move Over Darling.*
AAN: script; Roy Webb

My Foolish Heart*
US 1949   98m   bw
Samuel Goldwyn

A woman deceives her husband into thinking her forthcoming child is his.
A 'woman's picture' par excellence, and among the first to benefit from commercial plugging of a schmaltzy theme tune.

w Julius J. and Philip G. Epstein, *story* J. D. Salinger *d* Mark Robson *ph* Lee Garmes *m* Victor Young

Susan Hayward, Dana Andrews, Kent Smith, Robert Keith, Gigi Perreau, Lois Wheeler, Jessie Royce Landis
   'Obviously designed to pull the plugs out of the tear glands and cause the ducts to overflow.'—*Bosley Crowther, New York Times*
AAN: Susan Hayward; title song (*m* Victor Young, *ly* Ned Washington)

My Forbidden Past
US 1951 81m bw
RKO (Polan Banks)

A New Orleans beauty seeks vengeance when
her cousin prevents her marriage.
Stuffy period melodrama with vigorous
performances.

w Marion Parsonnet, *novel* Polan Banks
d Robert Stevenson *ph* Harry J. Wild
m Frederick Hollander *ad* Albert S.
D'Agostino

Ava Gardner, Melvyn Douglas, Robert
Mitchum, Janis Carter, Lucile Watson

My Friend Flicka*
US 1943 89m Technicolor
TCF

Adventures of a young boy and his pet colt.
Winsome boy-and-horse story, one of the most
popular family films of the forties. Sequel 1945
with virtually the same cast: *Thunderhead Son
of Flicka*.

w Mary O'Hara from her novel *d* Harold
Schuster *m* Alfred Newman

Roddy McDowall, Preston Foster, Rita
Johnson, James Bell, Jeff Corey

My Friend Irma*
US 1949 103m bw
Paramount / Hal B. Wallis

Dumb blonde Irma's con-man boy friend lends
her apartment to two soda jerks.
Comic strip humour responsible for the screen
debut of Martin and Lewis. Sequel 1950: *My
Friend Irma Goes West.*

w Cy Howard, Parke Levy, *radio show* Cy
Howard *d* George Marshall *ph* Leo Tover
m Roy Webb

Marie Wilson, John Lund, Diana Lynn, *Dean
Martin, Jerry Lewis*, Don Defore, Hans
Conried, Kathryn Givney

My Gal Sal*
US 1942 103m Technicolor
TCF (Robert Bassler)

The career and romances of songwriter Paul
Dreiser.
Conventional nineties musical biopic, more
vigorous and likeable than most.

w Seton I. Miller, Darrell Ware, Karl
Tunberg, *book* My Brother Paul by Theodore
Dreiser *d* Irving Cummings *ph* Ernest
Palmer *md* Alfred Newman

Rita Hayworth, Victor Mature, John Sutton,
Carole Landis, James Gleason, Phil Silvers,
Walter Catlett, Mona Maris, Frank Orth

AAN: Alfred Newman

My Geisha
US 1962 120m Technirama
Paramount / Steve Parker

A director makes a film in Japan; his wife
disguises herself as a geisha and gets the
leading role.
Silly, overstretched comedy with pretty
locations.

w Norman Krasna *d* Jack Cardiff
ph Shunichuro Nakao *m* Franz Waxman

Shirley Maclaine, Yves Montand, Robert
Cummings, Edward G. Robinson, Yoko Tani

My Girl Tisa***
US 1948 95m bw
United States Pictures (Milton Sperling)

An immigrant girl in New York in the nineties
falls for an aspiring politician, is threatened
with deportation but saved by the intervention
of Theodore Roosevelt.
Charming period fairy tale with excellent
background detail and attractive
performances.

w Allen Boretz, *play* Lucille S. Prumbs, Sara
B. Smith *d* Elliott Nugent *ph* Ernest Haller
m Max Steiner

*Lilli Palmer, Sam Wanamaker, Alan Hale,
Stella Adler*, Akim Tamiroff

My Learned Friend***
GB 1943 76m bw
Ealing (Robert Hamer)

A shady lawyer is last on a mad ex-convict's
murder list of those who helped get him
convicted.
Madcap black farce, plot-packed and generally
hilarious; the star's last vehicle, but one of his
best, with superbly timed sequences during a
pantomime and on the face of Big Ben.

w *John Dighton, Angus Macphail d* Basil
Dearden, Will Hay ph Wilkie Cooper
m Ernest Irving

Will Hay, Claude Hulbert, Mervyn Johns,
Ernest Thesiger, Charles Victor, Lloyd
Pearson, Maudie Edwards, G. H. Mulcaster,
Gibb McLaughlin

My Life with Caroline*
US 1941 81m bw
RKO (Lewis Milestone)

An understanding husband thinks his high-
spirited wife may be having an affair.
Very minor romantic comedy with an
agreeable air but no substance whatever.

w John Van Druten, Arnold Belgard *d* Lewis
Milestone *ph* Victor Milner *m* Werner
Heymann

Ronald Colman, Anna Lee, Reginald
Gardiner, Charles Winninger, Gilbert Roland

My Little Chickadee*
US 1939 83m bw
Universal (Lester Cowan)

A shady lady and an incompetent cardsharp
unmask a villain in the old west.
A clash of comedy personalities which is
affectionately remembered but in truth does
not play very well apart from the odd line.

w Mae West, W. C. Fields d Edward Cline
ph Joseph Valentine *m* Frank Skinner
md Charles Previn

Mae West, W. C. Fields, Joseph Calleia, Dick
Foran, Margaret Hamilton
'It obstinately refuses to gather
momentum.'—*The Times*
'A classic among bad movies . . . the satire
never really gets off the ground. But the
ground is such an honest mixture of dirt,
manure and corn that at times it is fairly
aromatic.'—*Pauline Kael, 1968*

My Love Came Back
US 1940 85m bw

A millionaire helps the career of a pretty
young violinist. Palatable comedy of its day,
promptly forgotten. Olivia de Havilland,
Jeffrey Lynn, Charles Winninger, Eddie
Albert, Spring Byington, S. Z. Sakall, Jane
Wyman. Written by Robert Buckner, Ivan
Goff and Earl Baldwin; directed by Curtis
Bernhardt; for Warner.

My Lucky Star*
US 1938 84m bw
TCF (Harry Joe Brown)

A shopgirl is innocently caught in a
compromising situation with the owner's son.
Fluffy comedy, acceptable as a background for
skating sequences.

w Harry Tugend, Jack Yellen *d* Roy del
Ruth *ph* John Mescall *songs* Mack Gordon,
Harry Revel *m* Louis Silvers

Sonja Henie, Richard Greene, Joan Davis,
Buddy Ebsen, Cesar Romero, Arthur
Treacher, George Barbier, Louise Hovick,
Billy Gilbert

My Man
US 1928 85m approx part talkie bw

A poor girl becomes a Broadway star.
Lachrymose and technically primitive debut
for the ebullient Fanny Brice; with Guinn
Williams, Edna Murphy. Written by Robert
Lord and Darryl F. Zanuck; directed by
Archie Mayo; for Warner.

My Man and I
US 1952 99m bw
MGM (Stephen Ames)

A Mexican farm labourer, proud of his
American citizenship, is drawn into trouble.
Eccentric melodrama in which all the native
Americans are whores, cheats or murderers;
well enough made but not very interesting.

w John Fante, Jack Leonard *d* William
Wellman *ph* William Mellor *m* David
Buttolph

Ricardo Montalban, Shelley Winters, Claire
Trevor, Wendell Corey

My Man Godfrey***
US 1936 90m bw
Universal (Gregory La Cava)

A zany millionaire family invite a tramp to be
their butler and find he is richer than they are.
Archetypal Depression concept which is also
one of the best of the thirties crazy
sophisticated comedies, though its pacing
today seems somewhat unsure.

*w Morrie Ryskind, Eric Hatch, Gregory La
Cava d Gregory La Cava ph* Ted Tetzlaff
m Charles Previn

*Carole Lombard, William Powell, Alice
Brady, Mischa Auer*, Eugene Pallette, Gail
Patrick, Alan Mowbray, Jean Dixon

AAN: best picture; script; Gregory La Cava
(as director); Carole Lombard; William
Powell; Alice Brady; Mischa Auer

My Man Godfrey
US 1957 92m Technicolor
    Cinemascope
U-I (Ross Hunter)

Tepid remake which without the period
background, and in unsuitable wide screen,
raises very few laughs.

w Everett Freeman, Peter Berneis, William
Bowers *d* Henry Koster *ph* William Daniels
m Frank Skinner

June Allyson, David Niven, Jessie Royce
Landis, Jay Robinson, Robert Keith, Martha
Hyer, Eva Gabor
'The butler did it! He made every lady in
the house oh so very happy!'—*publicity*

My Name Is Julia Ross**
US 1945 65m bw
Columbia

A girl is kidnapped and forced to impersonate
an heiress.
A very good second feature which has been
culted into a reputation beyond its worth,
though it is undeniably slick and entertaining.

w Muriel Roy Bolton, *novel* The Woman in Red by Anthony Gilbert *d* Joseph H. Lewis *ph* Burnett Guffey *md* Mischa Bakaleinikoff

Nina Foch, Dame May Whitty, George Macready, Roland Varno, Doris Lloyd

'A superior, well-knit thriller.'—*Don Miller*

'A likeable, unpretentious, generally successful attempt to turn good trash into decently artful entertainment.'—*James Agee*

My Old Dutch
GB 1934 82m bw

Ageing cockney parents see their son die a hero. Historically interesting sentimental wallow, built around a popular song; very primitive by most standards. Gordon Harker, Betty Balfour, Michael Hogan, Florrie Forde. Written by Bryan Wallace, Marjorie Gaffney, Mary Murillo and Michael Hogan; directed by Sinclair Hill; for Gainsborough. (NB: A 1915 version had starred the original singer, Albert Chevalier, with Florence Turner and Henry Edwards.)

My Outlaw Brother
US 1951 78m bw

A young man is shocked to find that his elder brother is a notorious bandit. Glum little semi-western, unpersuasively cast. Mickey Rooney, Robert Preston, Robert Stack, Wanda Hendrix. Written by Gene Fowler Jnr; directed by Elliott Nugent; for Eagle Lion.

My Own True Love
US 1948 84m bw
Paramount

A lonely man home from the war quarrels with his son over a girl twenty years younger than himself.
Minor romantic drama, competently but coldly presented.

w Arthur Kober, *novel* Yolanda Foldes *d* Compton Bennett *ph* Charles Lang *m* Robert Emmett Dolan

Phyllis Calvert, Melvyn Douglas, Philip Friend, Wanda Hendrix, Binnie Barnes

My Pal Gus
US 1952 84m bw
TCF (Stanley Rubin)

A business man has a five-year-old problem son and in sorting him out falls in love with his schoolteacher.
Unrewarding domestic drama with actors who look as though they would rather be somewhere else.

w Fay and Michael Kanin *d* Robert Parrish *ph* Leo Tover *m* Leigh Harline

Richard Widmark, Joanne Dru, Audrey Totter, George Winslow, Joan Banks, Regis Toomey, Ludwig Donath

My Reputation
US 1946 96m bw
Warner (Henry Blanke)

A widow is talked about for dispensing too soon with her weeds.
Dim drama, hastily shot on familiar sets with a reach-me-down script.

w Catherine Turney, *novel* Instruct My Sorrows by Clare Jaynes *d* Curtis Bernhardt *ph* James Wong Howe *m* Max Steiner

Barbara Stanwyck, George Brent, Warner Anderson, Lucile Watson, John Ridgely, Eve Arden, Jerome Cowan, Esther Dale, Scotty Beckett

My Sin
US 1931 79m bw

A drunken lawyer helps a woman who has shot her husband. Turgid melodrama which failed to make a screen idol of its star. Tallulah Bankhead, Fredric March. Harry Davenport, Scott Kolk, Ann Sutherland. Written by Owen David and Adelaide Heilbron, from the story by Frederick Jackson; directed by George Abbott; for Paramount.

My Sister Eileen*
US 1942 96m bw
Columbia (Max Gordon)

Two Ohio girls come to New York and live with some zany friends in a Greenwich Village basement apartment.
Rather strained high jinks which were, not surprisingly, later musicalized.

w Ruth McKinney, Joseph Fields, Jerome Chodorov, *book* Ruth McKinney *d* Alexander Hall *ph* Joseph Walker *md* Morris Stoloff

Rosalind Russell, Janet Blair, Brian Aherne, Allyn Joslyn, George Tobias, Elizabeth Patterson, June Havoc

AAN: Rosalind Russell

My Sister Eileen*
US 1955 108m Technicolor
Cinemascope
Columbia (Fred Kohlmar)

Musical version of the above, via a Broadway show. Watchable but hardly stimulating.

w Blake Edwards, Richard Quine, *play* Joseph Fields, Jerome Chodorov *d* Richard Quine *ph* Charles Lawton Jnr *m* George Duning *md* Morris Stoloff *ch Bob Fosse songs* Jule Styne, Leo Robin

Betty Garrett, Janet Leigh, Jack Lemmon, Bob Fosse, Kurt Kasznar, Horace MacMahon, Dick York

My Six Convicts*
US 1952 104m bw
Columbia / Stanley Kramer

A psychologist joins the staff of an American prison and gains the trust of six inmates.
Moderately interesting semi-documentary melodrama marred by a conventional prison break climax.

w Michael Blankfort, *book* Donald Powell Wilson *d* Hugo Fregonese *ph* Guy Roe *m* Dmitri Tiomkin

John Beal, *Millard Mitchell, Gilbert Roland*, Marshall Thompson, Regis Toomey

My Six Loves
US 1965 101m Technicolor
Vistavision
Paramount / Gant Gaither

A musical comedy star goes to the country for a rest and with the help of the local minister adopts six scruffy children.
Icky sentimental comedy for the easily pleased.

w John Fante, Joseph Calvelli, William Wood *d* Gower Champion *ph* Arthur E. Arling *m* Walter Scharf

Debbie Reynolds, David Janssen, Cliff Robertson, Eileen Heckart
'Enough to make you settle for cyclamates—or cyanide.'—*Judith Crist, 1973*

My Son John
US 1952 122m bw
Paramount (Leo McCarey)

An American Catholic family is horrified when its eldest son is revealed as a communist.
The lower depths of Hollywood's witch hunt cycle are marked by this Goldwynesque family saga, all sweetness and light, in which the commie son is treated as though he had rabies.
Purely as entertainment the plot is pretty choppy and defeats all attempts at acting.

w Myles Connelly, Leo McCarey *d* Leo McCarey *ph* Harry Stradling *m* Robert Emmett Dolan

Helen Hayes, Robert Walker, Dean Jagger, Van Heflin, Minor Watson, Frank McHugh, Richard Jaeckel

AAN: Leo McCarey (original story)

My Son My Son*
US 1940 117m bw
Edward Small

A man who becomes rich spoils his son and lives to regret it.
Solid narrative from a bestseller.

w Lenore Coffee, *novel* Howard Spring *d* Charles Vidor *ph* Harry Stradling *m* Edward Ward

Brian Aherne, Madeleine Carroll, Louis Hayward, Laraine Day, Henry Hull

My Teenage Daughter
GB 1956 100m bw
British Lion / Everest (Herbert Wilcox)
US title: *Teenage Bad Girl*

A widow's seventeen-year-old daughter meets an aggressive young man and ends up in court.
Predictable domestic drama, a tame British version of *Rebel without a Cause*.

w Felicity Douglas *d* Herbert Wilcox *ph* Max Greene

Anna Neagle, Sylvia Syms, Kenneth Haigh, Norman Wooland, Wilfrid Hyde White, Julia Lockwood, Helen Haye

My Uncle Antoine
Canada 1971 110m Eastmancolor

In a Quebec village a young boy reluctantly helps his undertaker uncle to deliver a coffin.
French-speaking comedy drama with a sour edge, as thoughts of death mar a family Christmas. Jacques Gagnon, Lyne Champagne, Jean Duceppe, Olivette Thibault. Written by Clément Perron; directed by Claude Jutra; for the National Film Board of Canada.

My Wife's Best Friend
US 1952 87m bw

A wife learns of her husband's infidelity, and imagines how Cleopatra, Joan of Arc and other historical figures might handle the situation. A sharp little comedy rather similar to *Unfaithfully Yours*. Anne Baxter, Macdonald Carey, Cecil Kellaway, Casey Adams, Catherine McLeod. Written by Isobel Lennart; directed by Richard Sale; for TCF.

My Wife's Family
GB 1931 80m bw

A wife thinks her husband has an illegitimate child. Archetypal British farce. This may be the best version; it was also made with Charlie Clapham in 1941 and with Ronald Shiner in 1956. Gene Gerrard, Muriel Angelus, Jimmy Godden, Amy Veness. Written by Fred

Duprez and Val Valentine, from the play by
Fred Duprez, Hal Stephens and Harry B.
Linton; directed by Monty Banks; for BIP.

My Wild Irish Rose
US 1947   101m   Technicolor
Warner

The ups and downs of Irish tenor Chauncey
Olcott and his encounters with Lillian Russell.
Inoffensive but not very exciting period
musical, rather lacking in humour.

w Peter Milne, *book* Rita Ilcott d David
Butler ph Arthur Edeson m Ray Heindorf,
Max Steiner ch Le Roy Prinz

Dennis Morgan, Arlene Dahl, Andrea King,
Alan Hale, George Tobias

AAN: Ray Heindorf, Max Steiner

Myra Breckinridge
US 1970   94m   De Luxe   Panavision
TCF (Robert Fryer)

After a sex change operation a film critic goes
to Hollywood to accomplish the deflation of
the American male.
A sharply satirical novel has been turned into
a sleazy and aimless picture which became a
watershed of permissiveness; after
international outcry it was shunned even by its
own studio. A few good laughs do emerge
from the morass, but even the old clips are
misused.

w Mike Sarne, David Giler, *novel* Gore Vidal
d Mike Sarne ph Richard Moore m Lionel
Newman

Mae West, Raquel Welch, John Huston, Rex
Reed, Jim Backus, John Carradine, Andy
Devine

'At last, the book that couldn't be written is
now the motion picture that couldn't be
made!'—*publicity*
'Whatever the novel may be like, it surely
cannot be this sort of witless, lip-smacking,
continuously inept cop-out.'—*John Simon*

The Mysterious Doctor
US 1942   57m   bw

Nazis strike at an English village by staging a
headless ghost. Risible propaganda hokum
which somehow earned an 'H' certificate. John
Loder, Eleanor Parker, Bruce Lester, Lester
Matthews, Forrester Harvey. Written by
Richard Weil; directed by Ben Stoloff; for
Warner.

Mysterious Intruder
US 1946   62m   bw

A private detective seeks a missing heiress.

Intriguing minor thriller, part of the *Whistler*
series. Richard Dix, Barton Maclane, Nina
Vale, Regis Toomey. Written by Eric Taylor;
directed by William Castle; for Columbia.

Mysterious Island*
GB 1961   101m   Technicolor
Columbia / Ameran (Charles Schneer)

Confederate officers escape by balloon and
join shipwrecked English ladies on a strange
island where they are menaced by prehistoric
monsters and helped by Captain Nemo.
Rambling, lively juvenile adventure with good
moments and excellent monsters.

w John Prebble, Dan Ullman, Crane Wilbur,
novel Jules Verne d Cy Endfield ph Wilkie
Cooper m Bernard Herrmann sp Ray
Harryhausen

Joan Greenwood, Michael Craig, Herbert
Lom, Michael Callan, Gary Merrill
† An early sound version was made by MGM
in 1929, directed by Lucien Hubbard. Despite
Technicolor and a cast which included Lionel
Barrymore it was judged unsatisfactory, and
concentrated less on stop-frame monsters than
on the submarine elements ignored in the
above but remade in *Captain Nemo and the
Underwater City* (qv).

The Mysterious Lady
US 1928   84m (24 fps)   bw   silent
MGM

A glamorous Russian spy has to save her lover
from execution as a traitor.
Threadbare star melodrama.

w Bess Meredyth d Fred Niblo ph William
Daniels

Greta Garbo, Conrad Nagel, Gustav Von
Seyffertitz

Mystery in Mexico
US 1948   65m   bw

An insurance detective disappears in Mexico;
another is sent to find him and uncovers a
complex plot. Fairly effective time-passer shot
on location. William Lundigan, Ricardo
Cortez, Jacqueline White, Tony Barrett.
Written by Lawrence Kimble; directed by
Robert Wise; for RKO.

Mystery Junction
GB 1951   67m   bw

Passengers stranded in a snowbound railway
station solve a mystery. One of the better
second features of its type. Sidney Tafler,
Barbara Murray, Pat Owens, Martin Benson.
Written and directed by Michael McCarthy;
for Anglo Amalgamated.

The Mystery of Edwin Drood*
US 1935   85m   bw
Universal

In a cathedral town, a drug- addicted choirmaster is his nephew's rival for the hand of Rosa Bud.
Fairly creditable attempt to deal with a famous unfinished novel. Slightly stilted, but good visuals and performances.

w John L. Balderston, Gladys Unger, Bradley King, Leopold Atlas, *novel* Charles Dickens d *Stuart Walker* ph George Robinson m Edward Ward

Claude Rains, Douglass Montgomery, Heather Angel, David Manners, E. E. Clive, Valerie Hobson

The Mystery of Marie Roget
US 1942   61m   bw
Universal (Paul Malvern)

A Parisian music hall star plots to kill her sister but herself disappears.
Ham-fisted, stilted mystery drama relying hardly at all on its original.

w Michael Jacoby, *story* Edgar Allan Poe d Phil Rosen ph Elwood Bredell m Hans Salter

Maria Montez, Patric Knowles, *Maria Ouspenskaya*, Lloyd Corrigan, John Litel, Edward Norris, Frank Reicher

The Mystery of Mr X
US 1934   84m   bw
MGM (Lawrence Weingarten)

In foggy London, a jewel thief protects himself by finding the murderer of several policemen.
Passable mystery, later remade as *The Hour of Thirteen*.

w Howard Emmett Rogers, Philip MacDonald, Monckton Hoffe, *novel* X vs Rex by Philip MacDonald d Edgar Selwyn ph Oliver T. Marsh

Robert Montgomery, Elizabeth Allan, Lewis Stone, Ralph Forbes, Henry Stephenson, Forrester Harvey

The Mystery of the Marie Celeste
GB 1935   80m   bw

A mad sailor kills his fellow crew members and jumps overboard. Unpersuasive solution to an unsolved mystery in a production which sounds more interesting than it is. Bela Lugosi, Shirley Grey, Arthur Margetson, Edmund Willard, Dennis Hoey. Written and directed by Denison Clift; for Hammer. (US title: *Phantom Ship*.)

The Mystery of the Wax Museum****
US 1933   77m   Technicolor
Warner (Henry Blanke)

A sculptor disfigured in a fire builds a wax museum by covering live victims in wax.
Archetypal horror material is augmented by a sub-plot about drug-running and an authoritative example of the wisecracking reporter school of the early thirties. The film is also notable for its highly satisfactory use of two-colour Technicolor and for its splendid art direction. Remade 1953 as *House of Wax* (qv).

w *Don Mullally, Carl Erickson, play* Charles S. Belden d *Michael Curtiz* ph Ray Rennahan ad Anton Grot

Lionel Atwill, Fay Wray, *Glenda Farrell, Frank McHugh*, Gavin Gordon, Allen Vincent, Edwin Maxwell

'Marvellously grisly chiller.'—*Judith Crist, 1977*

'Its most telling details are its horrific ones. The fire at the beginning, with lifelike figures melting into grisly ooze; night time in the city morgue, with a dead body suddenly popping up as a side effect of embalming fluid; chases through shadows as the ghoulish sculptor collects bodies for his exhibit; and the shock when Atwill's homemade wax face crumbles to the floor and exposes the hidden demon.'— *Tom Shales, The American Film Heritage, 1972*

Mystery Street*
US 1950   93m   bw
MGM (Frank E. Taylor)

Harvard medical scientists help solve a murder by examining the victim's bones.
Standard semi-documentary police thriller; well paced and quite entertaining.

w *Sidney Boehm, Richard Brooks* d John Sturges ph John Alton m Rudolph Kopp

Ricardo Montalban, Sally Forrest, Elsa Lanchester, Bruce Bennett, Marshall Thompson, Jan Sterling

AAN: Leonard Speigelgass (original story)

Mystery Submarine
GB 1962   92m   bw
British Lion / Britannia / Bertram Ostrer
US title: *Decoy*

A Nazi submarine is captured and sent out again with a British crew.
Routine war adventure.

w Hugh Woodhouse, Bertram Ostrer, Jon Manchip White d C. M. Pennington-Richards ph Stan Pavey m Clifton Parker

Edward Judd, James Robertson Justice, Laurence Payne, Albert Lieven

N

Naked Alibi
US 1954 85m bw
U-I (Ross Hunter)

The police track a homicidal baker to a
Mexican border town.
Modest police thriller which sags after it
crosses the border.

w Lawrence Roman d Jerry Hopper
ph Russell Metty m Joseph Gershenson

Sterling Hayden, Gene Barry, Gloria
Grahame, Marcia Henderson, Casey Adams,
Chuck Connors

The Naked and the Dead
US 1958 131m Technicolor RKOscope
RKO Teleradio / Gregjac (Paul Gregory)

Adventures of an army platoon in the Pacific
war.
Shorn of the four letter words which made the
novel notorious, this is a routine war film,
neither very good nor very bad.

w Denis and Terry Sanders, novel Norman
Mailer d Raoul Walsh ph Joseph La Shelle
m Bernard Herrmann

Aldo Ray, Cliff Robertson, Raymond Massey,
William Campbell, Richard Jaeckel, James
Best, Joey Bishop, Robert Gist, Jerry Paris,
L. Q. Jones

The Naked City****
US 1948 96m bw
Universal (Mark Hellinger)

New York police track down a killer.
Highly influential documentary thriller which,
shot on location in New York's teeming
streets, claimed to be giving an impression of
city life; actually its real mission was to tell an
ordinary murder tale with an impressive
accumulation of detail and humour. The
narrator's last words became a cliché: 'There
are eight million stories in the naked city. This
has been one of them.'

w Malvin Wald, Albert Maltz d Jules Dassin
ph William Daniels m Frank Skinner, Miklos
Rozsa md Milton Schwarzwald

Barry Fitzgerald, Don Taylor, Howard Duff,
Dorothy Hart, Ted de Corsia, Adelaide Klein

AA: William Daniels
AAN: original story (Malvin Wald)

The Naked Dawn
US 1956 82m Technicolor

A hired robber finds that his boss is not to be
trusted. Heavy-going Mexican western. Arthur
Kennedy, Eugene Iglesias, Betta St John.
Written by Nina and Herman Schneider;
directed by Edgar G. Ulmer; for Universal-
International.

Naked Earth
GB 1958 96m bw Cinemascope
TCF / Foray Films (Adrian Worker)

In 1895 a young Irish farmer goes to Africa to
grow tobacco, but moves on to crocodile
hunting.
Predictable and uninteresting epic of
endurance; not very convincing either.

w Milton Holmes d Vincent Sherman
ph Erwin Hillier

Richard Todd, Juliette Greco, John
Kitzmiller, Finlay Currie, Laurence Naismith,
Christopher Rhodes, Orlando Martins

The Naked Edge
GB 1961 100m bw
US / Pennebaker / Baroda (Walter Seltzer,
    George Glass)

A successful executive is suspected by his wife
of an old murder in which he testified against
the man who was convicted.
Dreary thriller which piles up red herrings in
shoals, then abandons them all for a razor-
and-bathroom finale.

w Joseph Stefano, novel First Train to
Babylon by Max Ehrlich d Michael
Anderson ph Erwin Hillier m William Alwyn

Gary Cooper, Deborah Kerr, Peter Cushing,
Eric Portman, Diane Cilento, Hermione
Gingold, Michael Wilding, Ronald Howard

The Naked Hills
US 1955 73m Pathecolor
Allied Artists / La Salle (Josef Shaftel)

Starting in 1849, a young prospector spends his life looking for gold.
Curious, mildly interesting saga with an obsession instead of a plot.

wd Josef Shaftel *ph* Frederick Gately *m* Herschel Burke Gilbert

David Wayne, Marcia Henderson, Keenan Wynn, James Barton, Jim Backus, Denver Pyle

The Naked Jungle*
US 1954 95m Technicolor
Paramount / George Pal (Frank Freeman Jnr)

In 1901 a young woman is married by proxy to a South American cocoa planter, and when she arrives at his jungle home she has to conquer not only him but an army of soldier ants.
Mixture of *Rebecca* elements with a more unusual kind of thrill; all quite watchable, and the ant scenes very effective.

w Philip Yordan, Ranald MacDougall, *story* Leiningen Versus the Ants by Carl Stephenson *d* Byron Haskin *ph* Ernest Laszlo *m* Daniele Amfitheatrof

Charlton Heston, Eleanor Parker, William Conrad, Abraham Sofaer, John Dierkes, Douglas Fowley

The Naked Maja
Italy / US 1959 112m Technirama
MGM / Titanus (Goffredo Lombardo)

Peasant Francisco Goya becomes a famous painter through the influence of the Duchess of Alba.
Boring and unconvincing biopic.

w Giorgio Prosperi, Norman Corwin, Albert Lewin, Oscar Saul *d* Henry Koster *ph* Giuseppe Rotunno *m* Francesco Lavagnino

Anthony Franciosa, Ava Gardner, Amedeo Nazzari, Gino Cervi, Lea Padovani, Massimo Serrato
'This travesty of Goya's life, country and period adds up to nothing more entertaining than a perfunctory, heavy-handed pageant.'— *MFB*

The Naked Prey*
US 1966 94m Technicolor Panavision
Paramount / Theodora / Sven Persson (Cornel Wilde)

In 1840, a white hunter becomes brutalized when a tribe hunts him down as though he were a lion.

Savage adventure story with bloodthirsty detail; unusual and certainly effective.

w Clint Johnston, Don Peters *d* Cornel Wilde *ph* I. A. R. Thompson *md* Andrew Tracy, from African folk music

Cornel Wilde, Gert Van Den Berg, Ken Gampu
'Overtones pretentious, but it tries.'—*Sight and Sound*

AAN: script

The Naked Runner
GB 1967 104m Techniscope
Warner / Artanis (Brad Dexter)

British intelligence conceive a plan to turn an innocent businessman into a spy killer.
Silly espionage thriller further marred by its director's penchant for making a zany composition of every frame.

w Stanley Mann, *novel* Francis Clifford *d* Sidney J. Furie *ph* Otto Heller *m* Harry Sukman

Frank Sinatra, Peter Vaughan, Derren Nesbitt, Nadia Gray, Toby Robins, Cyril Luckham, Edward Fox, Inger Stratton
'It might be a good movie to read by if there were light in the theatre.'—*Pauline Kael*

The Naked Spur*
US 1952 91m Technicolor
MGM (William H. Wright)

A bounty hunter has trouble getting his quarry back to base.
Standard big studio western shot in Colorado, with all characters motivated by greed.

w Sam Rolfe, Harold Jack Bloom *d* Anthony Mann *ph* William Mellor *m* Bronislau Kaper

James Stewart, Robert Ryan, Janet Leigh, Millard Mitchell

AAN: script

The Naked Street
US 1955 83m bw
Edward Small

A racketeer's daughter marries a worthless crook: her father saves him from the electric chair but he murders again.
Semi-documentary exposé melodrama about unpleasant people; reasonably proficient on its level.

w Maxwell Shane, Leo Katcher *d* Maxwell Shane *ph* Floyd Crosby *m* Emil Newman

Anthony Quinn, Anne Bancroft, Farley Granger, Peter Graves

The Naked Truth*
GB 1957   92m   bw
Rank / Mario Zampi
US title: *Your Past is Showing*

Celebrities band together to kill a blackmailer
who threatens to expose unsavoury aspects of
their lives.
Frenzied black farce, quite a lot of which
comes off.

w Michael Pertwee d Mario Zampi ph Stan
Pavey m Stanley Black

Peter Sellers, Terry-Thomas, Peggy Mount,
Dennis Price, Shirley Eaton, Georgina
Cookson

Nana*
US 1934   89m   bw
Samuel Goldwyn
GB title: *Lady of the Boulevards*

The high life and subsequent degradation of a
Parisian demi-mondaine in the nineties.
Stylish yet stolid slice of *le beau monde*,
intended to create a new star.

w Willard Mack, Harry Wagstaff Gribble,
novel Emile Zola d *Dorothy Arzner*
ph *Gregg Toland* m Alfred Newman

Anna Sten, Lionel Atwill, Phillips Holmes,
Richard Bennett, Mae Clarke, Muriel
Kirkland, Reginald Owen, Jessie Ralph

Nancy Drew
This series of second features starring Bonita
Granville as a teenage small-town detective
was moderately well received but quickly
forgotten. The character was created in novels
by Edward Stratemeyer and his daughter
Harriet Evans; the films were all directed by
William Clemens for Warners.

1938: NANCY DREW, DETECTIVE
1939: NANCY DREW, REPORTER;
NANCY DREW, TROUBLE SHOOTER;
NANCY DREW AND THE HIDDEN
STAIRCASE

Nancy Goes to Rio
US 1950   99m   Technicolor
MGM (Joe Pasternak)

Two actresses, mother and daughter, are both
after the same part.
Mild shipboard musical.

w Sidney Sheldon d Robert Z. Leonard
ph Ray June m George Stoll

Jane Powell, Ann Sothern, Carmen Miranda,
Barry Sullivan, Louis Calhern, Fortunio
Bonanova, Hans Conried

Nancy Steele Is Missing*
US 1938   85m   bw
TCF (Nunnally Johnson)

Crooks try to pass off a girl as the long lost
heir to a fortune.
Slightly unusual, well cast melodrama.

w Gene Fowler, Hal Long, *novel* C. F. Coe
d George Marshall ph Barney McGill
m David Buttolph

Victor McLaglen, Peter Lorre, June Lang,
Jane Darwell, John Carradine

The Nanny*
GB 1965   93m   bw
ABP / Hammer (Jimmy Sangster)

A ten-year-old boy hates his nanny, and with
good reason, for she is a neurotic murderess.
Muted Hammer experiment in
psychopathology, with too much equivocation
before the dénouement; the star's role allows
few fireworks, and the plot is rather
unpleasant.

w Jimmy Sangster, *novel* Evelyn Piper d Seth
Holt ph Harry Waxman m Richard Rodney
Bennett

Bette Davis, Jill Bennett, William Dix, James
Villiers, Wendy Craig, Pamela Franklin,
Maurice Denham

Nanook of the North*
US 1921   57m (1947 sound version)
   bw   silent
Revillon Freres

The life of an Eskimo and his family.
Primitive but trail-blazing documentary, hard
to sit through for modern audiences.

w, d, ph, ed Robert Flaherty
  'In a day of emotional and artistic
deliquescence on the screen, a picture with the
fresh strength and pictorial promise of *Nanook
of the North* is in the nature of a revolution.'—
Frances Taylor Patterson

† Nanook himself died of hunger on the ice
shortly after the film was released.

Napoleon***
France 1927   240m approx (24 fps)   bw
   (some colour)   silent
WESTI / Société Générale de Films

The early life of Napoleon.
A cinematic epic which, although brilliant in
most particulars, owes its greatest interest to
its narrative sweep, its flair for composition
and its use of triptych screens which at the end
combine to show one giant picture, the clear
precursor of Cinerama. In 1934 Gance revised
his film and added stereophonic sound.

w, d, ed Abel Gance ph various *m* Arthur Honegger

Albert Dieudonné, Antonin Artaud, Pierre Batcheff

Napoleon and Samantha
US 1972 91m Technicolor
Walt Disney (Winston Hibler)

When his old guardian dies, a small boy and his girl friend run away with their pet lion.

Patchy, episodic action drama for older children, with a very sleepy lion.

w Stewart Raffil *d* Bernard McEveety *ph* Monroe Askins *m* Buddy Baker

Michael Douglas, Will Geer

AAN: Buddy Baker

The Narrow Corner
US 1933 71m bw

On an eastern island, a man on the run for murder finds he can't escape his fate.
Mediocre adaptation of a Somerset Maugham novel in which very little happens; the added love interest doesn't help. Douglas Fairbanks Jnr, Ralph Bellamy, Dudley Digges, Arthur Hohl, Patricia Ellis. Written by Robert Presnell; directed by Alfred E. Green; for Warner. (Remade three years later as *Isle of Fury* [qv].)

The Narrow Margin***
US 1950 70m bw
RKO (Stanley Rubin)

Police try to guard a prosecution witness on a train from Chicago to Los Angeles.
Tight little thriller which takes every advantage of its train setting. What the trade used to call a sleeper, it gave more satisfaction than many a top feature.

w Earl Felton *d* Richard Fleischer *ph* George E. Diskant

Charles McGraw, Marie Windsor, Jacqueline White, Queenie Leonard

AAN: original story (Martin Goldsmith, Jack Leonard)

Nashville**
US 1975 161m Metrocolor Panavision
Paramount / ABC (Robert Altman)

A political campaign in Nashville organizes a mammoth pop concert to gain support.
Kaleidoscopic, fragmented, multi-storied musical melodrama, a mammoth movie which can be a bore or an inspiration according to taste. Certainly many exciting moments pass by, but the length is self-defeating.

w Joan Tewkesbury *d* Robert Altman *ph* Paul Lohmann *md* Richard Baskin

Geraldine Chaplin, David Arkin, Barbara Baxley, Ned Beatty, Karen Black, Keith Carradine, Henry Gibson, Keenan Wynn, Lily Tomlin, Ronee Blakley

'A gigantic parody . . . crammed with samples taken from every level of Nashville society, revealed in affectionate detail bordering on caricature in a manner that would surely delight Norman Rockwell.'—*Philip Strick*

'Wildly over-praised Altman, with all the defects we once looked on as marks of healthy ambitiousness: terrible construction, messy editing, leering jokes at its own characters, unending pomposity.'—*Time Out, 1980*

AA: song 'I'm Easy' (*m* / *ly* Keith Carradine)
AAN: best picture; Robert Altman; Lily Tomlin; Ronee Blakley

Nasty Habits*
GB 1976 92m Technicolor
Brut / Bowden (Robert Enders)

An abbess dies and the nuns vie for succession.
Satirical comedy rather obviously based on the Watergate scandals; initially amusing , but very tiresome by the end.

w Robert Enders, *novel* The Abbess of Crewe by Muriel Spark *d* Michael Lindsay-Hogg *ph* Douglas Slocombe *m* John Cameron

Glenda Jackson, Melina Mercouri, Genevieve Page, Sandy Dennis, Anne Jackson, Anne Meara, Edith Evans, Susan Penhaligon, Rip Torn, Eli Wallach, Jerry Stiller

'The sort of material just about fit for a half-hour TV sketch.'—*Richard Combs, MFB*

The National Health*
GB 1973 97m Eastmancolor
Columbia (Ned Sherrin, Terry Glinwood)

Life in the general men's ward of a large antiquated hospital.
Acerbic comedy from a National Theatre play which mixes tragedy and farce into a kind of *Carry on Dying*.

w Peter Nichols, from his play *d* Jack Gold *ph* John Coquillon *m* Carl Davis *pd* Ray Simm

Jim Dale, Lynn Redgrave, Eleanor Bron, Sheila Scott-Wilkinson, Donald Sinden, Colin Blakely, Clive Swift

National Lampoon's Animal House*
US 1978 109m Technicolor
Universal (Matty Simmons, Ivan Reitman)

On an American campus around 1962, scruffy newcomers challenge the elegant elite.
A ragbag of college gags, of interest only to those who have had the experience; but its success caused much imitation, especially in American television.

w Harold Ramis, Douglas Kenney, Chris Miller *d* John Landis *ph* Charles Correll *m* Elmer Bernstein

John Belushi, Tim Matheson, John Vernon, Donald Sutherland, Verna Bloom, Cesare Danova, Mary Louise Weller

National Velvet*
US 1944   125m   Technicolor
MGM (Pandro S. Berman)

Children train a horse to win the Grand National.
A big bestseller from another era; its flaws of conception and production quickly became evident.

w Theodore Reeves, Helen Deutsch, *novel* Enid Bagnold *d* Clarence Brown *ph* Leonard Smith *m* Herbert Stothart

Mickey Rooney, Elizabeth Taylor, *Anne Revere*, Donald Crisp, Angela Lansbury, Jackie Jenkins, Reginald Owen, Terry Kilburn, Norma Varden, Alec Craig, Arthur Shields, Dennis Hoey
† Sequel 1978: *International Velvet.*

AA: Anne Revere
AAN: Clarence Brown; Leonard Smith

Naughty But Nice
US 1939   90m   bw
Warner (Sam Bischoff)

A professor of classical music accidentally writes a popular song.
Mildly amusing comedy musical with all the tunes adapted from the classics (cf *That Night with You*).

w Jerry Wald, Richard Macaulay *d* Ray Enright *ph* Arthur L. Todd *songs* Harry Warren, Johnny Mercer

Dick Powell, Ann Sheridan, Ronald Reagan, Gale Page, Zasu Pitts, Jerry Colonna

Naughty Marietta**
US 1935   106m   bw
MGM (Hunt Stromberg)

A French princess goes to America and falls in love with an Indian scout.
Period operetta which set the seal of success on the MacDonald-Eddy team. In itself, dated but quite pleasing for those who like the genre.

w John Lee Mahin, Frances Goodrich, Albert Hackett, *operetta* Rida Johnson Young *d* W. S. Van Dyke *ph* William Daniels *m* Victor Herbert *ad* Cedric Gibbons

Jeanette MacDonald, Nelson Eddy, Frank Morgan, Elsa Lanchester, Douglass Dumbrille, Joseph Cawthorn, Cecelia Parker, Walter Kingsford
'When these two profiles come together to sing Ah Sweet Mystery of Life, it's beyond camp, it's in a realm of its own.'—*Judith Crist, 1977*
AAN: best picture

The Naughty Nineties
US 1945   72m   bw
Universal (Edward L. Hartmann, John Grant)

Two incompetents help an old showboat owner.
Dim star comedy apart from the team's rendition of their most famous routine, 'Who's On First'.

w Edmund L. Hartmann, John Grant, Edmund Joseph, Hal Fimburg *d* Jean Yarborough *ph* George Robinson

Bud Abbott, Lou Costello, Henry Travers, Alan Curtis, Rita Johnson, Joe Sawyer

The Navigator***
US 1924   63m approx (24 fps)   bw
silent
Metro-Goldwyn / Buster Keaton (Joseph M. Schenck)

A millionaire and his girl are the only people on a transatlantic liner marooned in mid-ocean.
A succession of hilarious sight gags: the star in top form.

w Jean Havez, Clyde Bruckman, J. A. Mitchell *d* Buster Keaton, Donald Crisp *ph* Elgin Lessley, Byron Houck

Buster Keaton, Kathryn McGuire
'Studded with hilarious moments and a hundred and one adroit gags.'—*Photoplay*

Navy Blues
US 1941   109m   bw
Warner (Jerry Wald)

Naval ratings get into trouble in Honolulu.
Undernourished musical comedy with not too much of either commodity.

w Jerry Wald, Richard Macaulay, Arthur T. Horman *d* Lloyd Bacon *ph* Tony Gaudio *ch* Seymour Felix *songs* Arthur Schwarz, Johnny Mercer

Ann Sheridan, Jack Oakie, Martha Raye, Jack
Haley, Herbert Anderson, Jack Carson,
Richard Lane, Jackie Gleason, Howard da
Silva

Nazarin*
Mexico 1958   94m   bw
Barbachano Ponce

A Catholic priest tries to take the teachings of
Christ literally, but is drastically
misunderstood.
A black atheistic satire pretty typical of its
director, but not among his most enjoyable
works.

w Julio Alejandro, Luis Bunuel, *novel* Benito
Perez Galdos *d Luis Bunuel ph* Gabriel
Figueroa

Francisco Rabal, Marga Lopez, Rita Macedo,
Ignacio Lopez Tarso

Nazi Agent*
US 1942   84m   bw
MGM (Irving Asher)

A German-American is forced by his Nazi
twin to help a group of German spies.
Modest suspenser with a plot twist similar to
The Great Impersonation and *Dead Ringer*.

w Paul Gangelin, John Meehan Jnr *d Jules
Dassin ph* Harry Stradling *m* Lennie Hayton

Conrad Veidt, Ann Ayars, Frank Reicher,
Dorothy Tree, Martin Kosleck

Necromancy
US 1973   83m   colour
Cinerama (Bert I. Gordon)

Two young people become involved in small-
town witchcraft.
Low-key, low-talent thriller overbalanced by
its star.

wd Bert I. Gordon *ph* Winton C. Hoch
m Fred Karger

Orson Welles, Pamela Franklin, Michael
Onthean, Lee Purcell

Ned Kelly
GB 1970   103m   Technicolor
UA / Woodfall (Neil Hartley)

The career of a 19th-century Australian
outlaw.
Obstinately unlikeable action picture with
some kind of message which never becomes
clear amid all the cleverness.

w Tony Richardson, Ian Jones *d* Tony
Richardson *ph* Gerry Fisher *m* Shel
Silverstein *pd* Jocelyn Herbert

Mick Jagger, Allen Bickford, Geoff Gilmour,
Mark McManus

Negatives*
GB 1968   98m   Eastmancolor
Crispin / Kettledrum (Judd Bernard)

Three people indulge in sexual fantasies
involving Dr Crippen and Baron Von
Richthofen.
Smoothly done but impenetrable psychological
poppycock: what is fact and what is fancy,
only the author knows.

w Peter Everett, Roger Lowry, *novel* Peter
Everett *d* Peter Medak *ph* Ken Hodges
m Basil Kirchin

Glenda Jackson, Peter McEnery, Diane
Cilento, Maurice Denham, Steven Lewis,
Norman Rossington

Nell Gwyn**
GB 1934   85m   bw
B and D (Herbert Wilcox)

The affair of Charles II and an orange seller.
Naïve, vivid account of a famous couple;
physically cheap and rather faded, but the best
film on the subject and one of the best
covering this period.

w *Miles Malleson d* Herbert Wilcox
ph F. A. Young

Anna Neagle, Cedric Hardwicke, Jeanne de
Casalis, Muriel George, Miles Malleson, Esmé
Percy, Moore Marriott

The Neptune Factor
Canada 1972   98m   De Luxe   Panavision
TCF / Quadrant / Bellevue–Pathe (Sanford
   Howard)
Later retitled: *The Neptune Disaster*

American oceanologists conduct an
experiment in underwater living.
Wet 'actioner' in which very little happens
except a few porthole views of magnified fish.

w Jack de Witt *d* Daniel Petrie *ph* Harry
Makin *m* Lalo Schifrin

Ben Gazzara, Walter Pidgeon, Yvette
Mimieux, Ernest Borgnine, Chris Wiggins

Neptune's Daughter*
US 1949   93m   Technicolor
MGM (Jack Cummings)

A lady bathing suit designer has a South
American romance.
Generally thought one of the better aquatic
musicals, and certainly very typical of them
and its studio at this time.

w Dorothy Kingsley *d* Edward Buzzell
ph Charles Rosher *m* George Stoll
songs Frank Loesser

Esther Williams, Red Skelton, Ricardo Montalban, Betty Garrett, Keenan Wynn, Xavier Cugat and his Orchestra, Mike Mazurki, Ted de Corsia, Mel Blanc

AA: song, 'Baby, It's Cold Outside'

The Net
GB 1953   86m   bw
Rank / Two Cities (Anthony Darnborough)
US title: *Project M7*

Tension among boffins in an aviation research station leads to murder and the discovery of a spy.
Low-key suspenser, quite adequately presented.

w William Fairchild, *novel* John Pudney
d Anthony Asquith ph Desmond Dickinson
m Benjamin Frankel

Phyllis Calvert, Noel Willman, Herbert Lom, James Donald, Robert Beatty, Muriel Pavlow, Walter Fitzgerald, Maurice Denham

Network**
US 1976   121m   Metrocolor
MGM / UA (Howard Gottfried, Fred Caruso)

A network news commentator begins to say what he thinks about the world and becomes a new messiah to the people and an embarrassment to his sponsors.
Overheated satire which in between its undoubted high points becomes noisy and tiresome, not helped by fuzzy photography. Its very existence in a commercial system, however, is as remarkable as its box-office success.

w *Paddy Chayevsky* d Sidney Lumet
ph Owen Roizman m Elliot Lawrence

Peter Finch, William Holden, Faye Dunaway, Robert Duvall, Wesley Addy, Ned Beatty, Beatrice Straight, John Carpenter

'The cast of this messianic farce take turns yelling at us soulless masses.'—*New Yorker*
'Too much of this film has the hectoring stridency of tabloid headlines.'—*Michael Billington, Illustrated London News*
† The theme was taken up a year later in the shortlived TV series *W.E.B.*

AA: Paddy Chayevsky; Peter Finch; Faye Dunaway; Beatrice Straight
AAN: best picture; Sidney Lumet; Owen Roizman; William Holden; Ned Beatty

Neutral Port
GB 1940   92m   bw

A merchant navy captain avenges the loss of his ship by sabotaging a German U-boat.
Unconvincing propaganda, rather stagily presented. Will Fyffe, Phyllis Calvert, Leslie Banks, Yvonne Arnaud, Hugh McDermott, Frederick Valk. Written by J. B. Williams and T. J. Morrison; directed by Marcel Varnel; for Gainsborough.

Nevada Smith*
US 1966   131m   Eastmancolor
  Panavision
Avco / Solar (Joe Levine, Henry Hathaway)

A cowboy takes a long revenge on the outlaws who murdered his parents.
Violent, sour, occasionally lively but frequently boring western melodrama on a well worn theme.

w John Michael Hayes, from the 'early life' of a character in The Carpetbaggers by Harold Robbins d Henry Hathaway ph Lucien Ballard m Alfred Newman

Steve McQueen, Karl Malden, Brian Keith, Suzanne Pleshette, Arthur Kennedy, Janet Margolin, Howard da Silva, Raf Vallone, Pat Hingle

Never a Dull Moment
US 1943   60m   bw

Three comedians prevent a nightclub owner from carrying out a robbery. The last thin vehicle for a famous comedy trio; even here they have their moments. The Ritz Brothers, Frances Langford, Mary Beth Hughes, George Zucco, Franklin Pangborn. Written by Mel Ronson and Stanley Roberts; directed by Edward Lilley; for Universal.

Never a Dull Moment
US 1950   89m   bw
RKO (Harriet Parsons)

A lady music critic marries a rodeo cowboy and finds life hard down on the ranch.
Very mild star programmer.

w Lou Breslow, Doris Anderson, *novel* Who Could Ask for Anything More? by Kay Swift d George Marshall ph Joseph Walker m Frederick Hollander md Constantin Bakaleinikoff

Irene Dunne, Fred MacMurray, William Demarest, Andy Devine, Gigi Perreau, Natalie Wood, Philip Ober, Jack Kirkwood

Never a Dull Moment
US 1967   100m   Technicolor
Walt Disney (Ron Miller)

An unsuccessful actor is mistaken for a notorious gangster.
Slapstick romp with vigour but not much flair.

w A. J. Carothers, *novel* John Godey *d* Jerry
Paris *ph* William Snyder *m* Robert F.
Brunner

Dick Van Dyke, Edward G. Robinson,
Dorothy Provine, Henry Silva, Joanna Moore,
Tony Bill, Slim Pickens, Jack Elam

Never Give a Sucker an Even Break*
US 1941 70m bw
Universal
GB title: *What a Man*

W. C. Fields dives off an aeroplane into the
lap of a young woman who has never seen a
man; she falls in love with him.
Stupefyingly inept in its scripting and pacing,
this comedy is often irresistibly funny because
of the anti-everything personality of its writer-
star. No one else could have got away with it,
or would have been likely to try.

w John T. Neville, Prescott Chaplin, *story* Otis
Criblecoblis (W. C. Fields) *d* Edward Cline
ph Charles Van Enger *m* Frank Skinner

W. C. Fields, Gloria Jean, Leon Errol, Butch
and Buddy, Franklin Pangborn, Anne Nagel,
Mona Barrie, Ann Miller, Margaret Dumont

Never Let Go
GB 1960 91m bw
Rank / Julian Wintle–Leslie Parkin (Peter de
Sarigny)

A travelling salesman has his car stolen and
stands up to the sadistic gang boss responsible.
Brutishly unattractive thriller, apparently
designed for the sole purpose of giving Peter
Sellers a villainous part.

w Alun Falconer *d* John Guillermin
ph Christopher Challis *m* John Barry

Richard Todd, Peter Sellers, Elizabeth Sellars,
Adam Faith, Carol White, Mervyn Johns,
Noel Willman

Never Let Me Go
GB 1953 94m bw
MGM (Clarence Brown)

After World War II an American
correspondent marries a Russian ballerina but
is later deported by the authorities.
Ho-hum romantic melodrama, quite
interestingly cast.

w Roland Millar, George Froeschel, *novel*
Came the Dawn by Roger Bax *d* Delmer
Daves *ph* Robert Krasker *m* Hans May

Clark Gable, Gene Tierney, Richard Haydn,
Belita, Bernard Miles, Kenneth More, Karel
Stepanek, Theodore Bikel, Frederick Valk

Never Love a Stranger
US 1958 93m bw
Harold Robbins / Allied Artists (Peter
Gettlinger)

A Catholic boy who has become a gangster
helps his Jewish friend who has become
assistant district attorney to trap a vicious
hoodlum.
The old *Manhattan Melodrama* theme is
dusted off once again, this time to very little
effect.

w Harold Robbins, Richard Day, *novel*
Harold Robbins *d* Robert Stevens *ph* Lee
Garmes *m* Raymond Scott

John Drew Barrymore, Steve McQueen,
Robert Bray, Lita Milan, R. G. Armstrong,
Salem Ludwig

Never on Sunday*
Greece 1959 97m bw
Lopert / Melinafilm (Jules Dassin)
original title: *Pote tin Kyriaki*

An American scholar in Greece is infatuated
by a prostitute and sets about improving her.
Amiable if rather shoddy variation on
Pygmalion: the star performance and the
music carried it, along with its own
naughtiness, to success.

wd Jules Dassin *ph* Jacques Natteau
m Manos Hadjidakis

Melina Mercouri, Jules Dassin, Georges
Foundas, Tito Vandis, Despo Diamantidou
'It barely stands scrutiny, but it
communicates cheerfulness, and this in itself is
no mean achievement.'—*Penelope Houston,
MFB*

AA: title song (Manos Hadjidakis)
AAN: direction; script; Melina Mercouri

Never Put it in Writing*
GB 1963 93m bw
MGM / Andrew Stone

A young executive tries to recover from the
mails an indiscreet letter he has written to his
boss.
Frantic hit-or-miss farcical comedy
distinguished by Dublin locations and cast.

wd Andrew Stone *ph* Martin Curtis *m* Frank
Cordell

Pat Boone, Fidelma Murphy, Reginald
Beckwith, John Le Mesurier, Colin Blakely

Never Say Die*
US 1939 80m bw
Paramount (Paul Jones)

A millionaire hypochondriac is convinced he is
dying.

Thin farce with Hope on the very brink of
stardom; some bright moments.

w Don Hartman, Frank Butler, Preston
Sturges d Elliott Nugent ph Leo Tover
md Boris Morros

Martha Raye, Bob Hope, Andy Devine, Alan
Mowbray, Gale Sondergaard, Sig Rumann,
Ernest Cossart, Monty Woolley, Christian
Rub

'The most enjoyable film for weeks . . .
consistently absurd . . . no dignity, no passion,
and a magnificent cast.'—Graham Greene

Never Say Goodbye
US 1946   97m   bw
Warner (William Jacobs)

A seven-year-old girl draws her divorced
parents back together.
Highly derivative romantic comedy mishmash
which did its star's career no good at all.

w James V. Kern, I. A. L. Diamond, Lewis
R. Foster, Ben and Norma Barzman d James
V. Kern ph Arthur Edeson m Frederick
Hollander

Errol Flynn, Eleanor Parker, Lucile Watson,
S. Z. Sakall, Donald Woods, Patti Brady,
Forrest Tucker, Hattie McDaniel

Never Say Goodbye
US 1955   96m   Technicolor
U-I (Albert J. Cohen)

In 1945 Berlin an American army doctor
marries a pianist who is later trapped in the
Russian zone; they meet years later in
America.
Romantic drama aimed at a female audience,
remade from This Love of Ours (qv).

w Charles Hoffman d Jerry Hopper
ph Maury Gertsman m Frank Skinner

Rock Hudson, George Sanders, Cornell
Borchers, Ray Collins, David Janssen

Never So Few
US 1959   124m   Metrocolor
Cinemascope
MGM / Canterbury (Edmund Grainger)

Adventures of World War II Americans
commanding Burmese guerrillas.
Jungle actioner with pauses for philosophizing;
well enough made but not very interesting.

w Millard Kaufman, novel Tom Chamales
d John Sturges ph William H. Daniels
m Hugo Friedhofer

Frank Sinatra, Gina Lollobrigida, Peter
Lawford, Steve McQueen, Paul Henreid,
Richard Johnson, Brian Donlevy, Charles
Bronson, Dean Jones

Never Steal Anything Small
US 1958   94m   Eastmancolor
Cinemascope
U-I (Aaron Rosenberg)

The reformation of a corrupt but sympathetic
dockers' union boss.
Curious semi-musical which doesn't come off
at all despite excellent credentials.

wd Charles Lederer, play The Devil's
Hornpipe by Rouben Mamoulian, Maxwell
Anderson ph Harold Lipstein m Allie
Wrubel ly Maxwell Anderson ch Hermes
Pan

James Cagney, Shirley Jones, Roger Smith,
Cara Williams, Nehemiah Persoff, Royal
Dano, Anthony Caruso

Never Take No for an Answer*
GB 1951   82m   bw
Anthony Havelock-Allan

A small boy goes to Rome to get permission
from the Pope to take his sick donkey to be
blessed in the church.
Slight, easy-going whimsy with attractive sunlit
locations.

w Paul and Pauline Gallico, novel The Small
Miracle by Paul Gallico d Maurice Cloche,
Ralph Smart ph Otto Heller m Nino Rota

Vittorio Manunta, Denis O'Dea, Guido
Cellano, Nerio Bernardi

'The main pleasures of this slender film are
visual ones.'—MFB

† Remade as a TV movie Small Miracle.

Never the Twain Shall Meet
US 1931   89m   bw

A young lawyer goes native when he falls for a
South Sea island girl. Stilted misalliance
melodrama, previously made in 1925 as a
silent with Bert Lytell and Anita Stewart; its
faded notions simply didn't survive sound.
Leslie Howard, Conchita Montenegro, Karen
Morley, C. Aubrey Smith. Written by Ruth
Cummings and Edwin Justus Mayer, from the
novel by Peter B. Kyne; directed by W. S.
Van Dyke; for MGM.

Never Too Late
US 1965   104m   Technicolor
Panavision
Warner / Lear–Yorkin (Norman Lear)

A well-to-do middle-aged housewife discovers
she is pregnant.
Predictable, rather hysterical domestic
comedy, flatly developed from a successful
play which offered two star parts for old
stagers.

w Sumner Arthur Long, from his play *d* Bud Yorkin *ph* Philip Lathrop *m* David Rose

Paul Ford, Maureen O'Sullivan, Connie Stevens, Jim Hutton, Lloyd Nolan, Henry Jones, Jane Wyatt

Never Wave at a WAC
US 1952 87m bw
Independent Artists (Frederick Brisson)
GB title: *The Private Wore Skirts*

A Washington hostess joins the WACs and finds she can't get beyond the rank of private. Pattern comedy, unconvincing in all respects but with a smattering of funny moments. Flagwaving takes over towards the end.

w Ken Englund *d* Norman Z. McLeod *ph* William Daniels *m* Elmer Bernstein

Rosalind Russell, Paul Douglas, Marie Wilson, William Ching, Leif Erickson, Arleen Whelan, Charles Dingle

The New Adventures of Get-Rich-Quick Wallingford
US 1931 76m bw

Exploits of an attractive go-getter. Reliable comedy of its day. William Haines, Jimmy Durante, Leila Hyams, Guy Kibbee. Written by Charles MacArthur, from the novel by G. R. Chester; directed by Sam Wood; for MGM.

The New Babylon*
USSR 1929 80m approx (24 fps) bw silent
Sovkino
original title: *Novyi Vavilon*

The rise and fall of the 1871 French commune, seen through the eyes of a girl department store worker.
Propagandist socio-historical melodrama, most interesting now for its sub-Eisenstein technique.

wd Leonid Trauberg, Grigori Kozintsev *ph* Andrei Moskvin, Yevgeni Mikhailov *m* Dmitri Shostakovich *ad* Yevgeni Enei

Yelena Kuzmina, Pyotr Sobelevsky, Sophie Magarill

The New Centurions*
US 1972 103m Eastmancolor Panavision
Columbia / Chartoff–Winkler
GB title: *Precinct 45: Los Angeles Police*

An old cop teaches a new one.
'Realistic' crime prevention saga which spawned the TV series *Police Story* and *Police Woman*. Well done within its limits.

w Stirling Silliphant, *novel* Joseph Wambaugh *d* Richard Fleischer *ph* Ralph Woolsey *m* Quincy Jones

George C. Scott, Stacy Keach, Jane Alexander, Rosalind Cash, Scott Wilson

New Faces*
US 1954 99m Eastmancolor Cinemascope
Edward L. Alperson (Leonard Sillman)

A revue goes on despite money problems. Five minutes of plot, ninety-five minutes of revue from the Broadway stage; mostly quite amusing, and chiefly notable for introducing Eartha Kitt with all her standards.

w various *d* Harry Horner *ph* Lucien Ballard *m* Raoul Kraushaar *revue deviser* John Murray Anderson

Eartha Kitt, Ronny Graham, Alice Ghostley, Robert Clary, Paul Lynde

The New Interns
US 1964 123m bw
Columbia (Robert Cohn)

Young doctors at a city hospital have trouble saving a rapist and his victim.
Unnecessary sequel to *The Interns*, its 'realism' requiring large pinches of salt.

w Wilton Schiller *d* John Rich *ph* Lucien Ballard *m* Earle Hagen

George Segal, Telly Savalas, Michael Callan, Dean Jones, Inger Stevens, Stefanie Powers, Lee Patrick

A New Kind of Love
US 1963 110m Technicolor
Paramount / Llenroc (Melville Shavelson)

An American dress designer in Paris is softened by a boorish newspaper columnist. Very thin sex comedy, dressed to kill but with nowhere to go.

wd Melville Shavelson *ph* Daniel Fapp *m* Leith Stevens

Paul Newman, Joanne Woodward, Maurice Chevalier, Thelma Ritter, George Tobias

AAN: Leith Stevens

The New Land see The Emigrants

A New Leaf*
US 1970 102m Movielab
Paramount / Aries / Elkins (Joe Manduke)

A middle-aged playboy, close to bankruptcy, thinks of acquiring a wealthy wife.
Agreeably mordant comedy which sparkles in patches rather than as a whole.

wd Elaine May, story The Green Heart by
Jack Ritchie *ph* Gayne Rescher *m* John
Mandel, Neal Hefti *pd* Richard Fried

Walter Matthau, Elaine May, Jack Weston,
George Rose, William Redfield, James Coco
  'Unashamedly a thirties fairy tale in
modern, but not fashionable, dress.'—*Jan
Dawson*

New Mexico
US 1952   78m   Anscocolor

A cavalry officer tries to make peace with the
Indians, but when an Indian child is
accidentally killed a savage war breaks out.
Standard western, not badly made. Lew
Ayres, Marilyn Maxwell, Robert Hutton,
Andy Devine, Raymond Burr, Jeff Corey.
Written by Max Trell; directed by Irving Reis;
for Irving Allen / United Artists.

New Moon*
US 1940   105m   bw
MGM (Robert Z. Leonard)

Romance in old French Louisiana.
Stalwart adaptation of an operetta previously
filmed in 1931 with Lawrence Tibbett and
Grace Moore.

w Jacques Deval, Robert Arthur *d* Robert Z.
Leonard *ph* William Daniels *m / ly* Sigmund
Romberg, Oscar Hammerstein

Jeanette MacDonald, Nelson Eddy, Mary
Boland, George Zucco, H. B. Warner,
Stanley Fields, Grant Mitchell

New Morals for Old
US 1932   77m   bw

John Van Druten's play *After All*, about the
generation gap in the London aristocracy, was
here rather unwisely translated to the
American middle class and emerged as a
decided curiosity. Robert Young, Myrna Loy,
Jean Hersholt, Lewis Stone, Laura Hope
Crews, Elizabeth Patterson. Written by Zelda
Sears and Wanda Tuchock; directed by
Charles Brabin; for MGM.

New Orleans*
US 1947   89m   bw
Jules Levey

How jazz was born, according to the movies.
Routine low-budgeter enlivened by a splendid
array of guest musicians.

w Elliot Paul, Dick Irving Hyland *d* Arthur
Lubin *ph* Lucien Andriot *md* Nathaniel
Finston

Louis Armstrong and his All Stars, Arturo de
Cordova, Dorothy Patrick, *Billie Holiday,
Meade Lux Lewis, Woody Herman* and his
Orchestra

New Wine
US 1941   89m   bw

Franz Schubert seeks the patronage of
Beethoven and sacrifices his love life to music.
Weirdly cast romantic drama, rather fumbling
in all departments. Alan Curtis (as Schubert!),
Ilona Massey, Albert Basserman, Binnie
Barnes, Sterling Holloway. Written by
Howard Estabrook and Nicholas Jory;
directed by Reinhold Schunzel; for Gloria /
UA. (GB title: *The Great Awakening*.)

New York Confidential
US 1955   87m   bw
Warner / Russel Rouse, Clarence Greene

The head of a crime syndicate is assassinated
by his own hired killer.
Unexciting 'realistic' thriller with the gangsters
presented as family and businessmen;
seventeen years later *The Godfather* did it
rather better.

w Clarence Greene, Russel Rouse *d* Russel
Rouse *ph* Edward Fitzgerald *m* Joseph
Mullendore *pd* Fernando Carrere

Broderick Crawford, Richard Conte, Anne
Bancroft, Marilyn Maxwell, Onslow Stevens,
J. Carrol Naish, Barry Kelley, Mike Mazurki,
Celia Lovsky

The New York Hat*
US 1912   10m approx (24 fps)   bw
silent
D. W. Griffith

A small-town minister is gossiped about when
he buys a hat for a young girl.
Influential early short story film with good
local backgrounds.

w Anita Loos *d D. W. Griffith ph* Billy
Bitzer

Mary Pickford, Lionel Barrymore, Lillian
Gish, Dorothy Gish, Robert Harron, Mack
Sennett, Mae Marsh

New York, New York*
US 1977   153m   Technicolor
Panavision
UA / Chartoff–Winkler (Gene Kirkwood)

In the late forties in New York, a single-
minded saxophonist fails to do right by his girl
friend, who becomes a Hollywood star.
A clever recreation of the big band era,
hampered by gross overlength, unattractive
characters and a pessimistic plot.

w Earl Mac Rauch, Mardik Martin *d* Martin
Scorsese *ph* Laszlo Kovacs *pd* Boris Leven
md Ralph Burns

Liza Minnelli, Robert de Niro, Lionel
Stander, Barry Primus

Newman's Law

US 1974   99m   Technicolor
Universal (Richard Irving)

A cop uses unconventional methods to trap drug smugglers.

Very routine police actioner, just above TV movie level.

w Anthony Wilson d Richard Heffron
ph Vilis Lapenieks m Robert Prince

George Peppard, Roger Robinson, Eugene Roche, Gordon Pinsent, Abe Vegoda

News Is Made at Night

US 1939   72m   bw

To boost circulation, a news editor pins a string of murders on a well-known gangster, and soon regrets it. Pacy crime comedy-drama, very acceptable as the lower half of a double bill. Preston Foster, Lynn Bari, Eddie Collins, Russell Gleason, George Barbier, Charles Halton. Written by John Larkin; directed by Alfred Werker; forTCF.

The Next Man

US 1976   107m   Technicolor
Artists Entertainment Complex (Martin Bregman)

A female assassin is hired to kill the Saudi Arabian Minister of State at the United Nations.

Fractured and uninteresting thriller in which all manner of cinematic styles obscure the storyline but point up the lack of narrative skill.

w Mort Fine, Alan R. Trustman, David M. Wolf, Michael Chapman d Richard C. Sarafian ph Michael Chapman m Michael Kamen pd Gene Callahan

Sean Connery, Cornelia Sharpe, Albert Paulsen, Adolfo Celi, Charles Cioffi

'The director takes forever to set up the film's premise, and then he lingers over interminable street festivals and lush scenery.'—Dave Pomeroy, Film Information

The Next of Kin***

GB 1942   102m   bw
Ealing (S. C. Balcon)

Careless talk causes loss of life in a commando raid.

A propaganda instructional film which was made so entertainingly that it achieved commercial success and remains an excellent example of how to make a bitter pill palatable.

w Thorold Dickinson, Basil Bartlett, Angus Macphail, John Dighton d Thorold Dickinson ph Ernest Palmer m William Walton

Mervyn Johns, Nova Pilbeam, Stephen Murray, Reginald Tate, Basil Radford, Naunton Wayne, Geoffrey Hibbert, Philip Friend, Mary Clare, Basil Sydney

'The detail everywhere is curious and surprising, with something of the fascination of a Simenon crime being unravelled.'—William Whitebait

Next Stop Greenwich Village*

US 1975   111m   Movielab
TCF (Paul Mazursky, Tony Ray)

In 1953 in a poor quarter of New York, a young Jew tries to stretch his wings.

A bumper bundle of Jewish clichés dressed up as autobiography, and switching abruptly from comedy to tragedy and back. Vivid, but not exactly entertaining.

wd Paul Mazursky ph Arthur Ornitz m Bill Conti

Lenny Baker, Shelley Winters, Ellen Greene, Lois Smith, Dori Brenner

'Some tartly comic observation, but the fragmented structure keeps the mixture inert.'—Sight and Sound

Next Time We Love

US 1936   87m   bw
Universal (Paul Kohner)
GB title: Next Time We Live

The wife of a war-correspondent has plenty of time for romance.

Romantic drama which badly needs an injection of comedy.

w Melville Baker, stories Ursula Parrott d Edward H. Griffith ph Joseph Valentine

Margaret Sullavan, Ray Milland, James Stewart, Grant Mitchell, Robert McWade

The Next Voice You Hear*

US 1950   83m   bw
MGM (Dore Schary)

God speaks to mankind on the radio, and the life of Joe Smith American is changed.

Soppy parable, the archetypal instance of Schary's reign of do-goodery at MGM. (He wrote a book about it, Case History of a Movie.) The idea is handled with deadly reverence, and falls quite flat, while the depiction of the inhabitants of American suburbia is depressing.

w Charles Schnee d William Wellman
ph William Mellor m David Raksin

James Whitmore, Nancy Davis, Lillian Bronson, Jeff Corey

'The sins of the American working man are singularly uninteresting and their obliteration seems scarcely to require the very voice of God.'—*Henry Hart*

Niagara●●●
US 1952 89m Technicolor
TCF (Charles Brackett)

While visiting Niagara Falls, a faithless wife is plotting to murder her husband, but he turns the tables.
Excellent suspenser with breathtaking locations; in the best Hitchcock class though slightly marred by the emphasis on Monroe's wiggly walk (it was her first big part).

w Charles Brackett, Walter Reisch, Richard Breen *d* Henry Hathaway *ph Joe MacDonald m* Sol Kaplan

Joseph Cotten, Jean Peters, *Marilyn Monroe,* Don Wilson, Casey Adams
'A masterly example of fluid screen narrative.'—*Charles Higham*
'It would have turned out a much better picture if James Mason had played the husband as I wanted. He has that intensity, that neurotic edge. He was all set to do it, but his daughter Portland said she was sick of seeing him die in his pictures.'—*Henry Hathaway*

Nice Girl?●
US 1941 95m bw
Universal (Joe Pasternak)

A teenager finds herself in demand by two older men.
Amusing romantic trifle supposed to mark the growing up of Universal's great teenage star.

w Richard Connell, Gladys Lehman
d William A. Seiter *ph* Joseph Valentine
md Charles Previn

Deanna Durbin, Franchot Tone, Robert Stack, Walter Brennan, Robert Benchley, Helen Broderick, Ann Gillis

A Nice Girl Like Me
GB 1969 91m Eastmancolor
Anglo Embassy / Partisan (Roy Millichip)

A sheltered young lady sets out to see life but keeps getting pregnant.
Insufferable romantic whimsy, made to look like a marathon TV commercial but never so interesting.

w Anne Piper, Desmond Davis *d* Desmond Davis *ph* Gil Taylor, Manny Wynn *m* Pat Williams

Barbara Ferris, Harry Andrews, Gladys Cooper, Joyce Carey, Bill Hinnant, James

Villiers, Christopher Guinee, Fabia Drake
'High-toned woman's magazine nostalgia.'—*MFB*

A Nice Little Bank That Should Be Robbed
US 1958 87m bw Cinemascope
TCF (Anthony Muto)
GB title: *How to Rob a Bank*

Two incompetent crooks rob a bank and buy a racehorse.
Feeble comedy, a sad waste of its stars.

w Sidney Boehm *d* Henry Levin *ph* Leo Tover *m* Lionel Newman

Mickey Rooney, Tom Ewell, Mickey Shaugnessy, Dina Merrill

Nicholas and Alexandra●
GB 1971 189m Eastmancolor
Panavision
Columbia / Horizon (Sam Spiegel)

The life of Tsar Nicholas II from 1904 to the execution of the family in 1918.
Inflated epic of occasional interest, mainly for its sets; generally heavy going.

w James Goldman, *book* Robert K. Massie
d Franklin Schaffner *ph Frederick A. Young
m* Richard Rodney Bennett *pd John Box*

Michael Jayston, Janet Suzman, Laurence Olivier, Jack Hawkins, Tom Baker, Harry Andrews, Michael Redgrave, Alexander Knox

AAN: best picture; Frederick A. Young; Richard Rodney Bennett; Janet Suzman

Nicholas Nickleby●●
GB 1947 108m bw
Ealing (John Croydon)

The adventures of a Victorian schoolmaster, deprived of his rightful fortune, who joins a band of travelling entertainers.
Quite tasteful and expert but too light-handed potted version of Dickens, which suffered by comparison with the David Lean versions.

w John Dighton, *novel* Charles Dickens
d Alberto Cavalcanti *ph* Gordon Dines
m Lord Berners

Derek Bond, *Cedric Hardwicke, Alfred Drayton, Sybil Thorndike,* Stanley Holloway, James Hayter, Sally Ann Howes, Jill Balcon, Cyril Fletcher, Fay Compton

The Nickel Ride
US 1975 110m De Luxe

A wheeler dealer in downtown Los Angeles learns that he is marked for elimination.
Unpleasant and entirely uninteresting low-life

crime melodrama. Jason Miller, Linda Haynes, Victor French, John Hillerman, Bo Hopkins. Written by Eric Roth; directed by Robert Mulligan; for TCF.

Nickelodeon*
US / GB 1976   122m   Metrocolor
Columbia / EMI / Chartoff–Winkler (Frank Marshall)

In 1910, various characters come together to make movies, finally attending the 1915 opening in Hollywood of *The Birth of a Nation*.

What should have been a hugely entertaining chunk of comic nostalgia is killed stone dead by embarrassed acting, poor timing, and a general lack of funny ideas, despite having so much to borrow from.

w W. D. Richter, Peter Bogdanovich d Peter Bogdanovich ph Laszlo Kovacs md Richard Hazard

Ryan O'Neal, Burt Reynolds, Tatum O'Neal, Brian Keith, Stella Stevens, John Ritter, Jane Hitchcock

'Ponderous slapstick and a pathetic parody of Harold Lloyd.'—*Sight and Sound*

'Another collection of scenes from other people's films.'—*Howard Kissel, Women's Wear Daily*

'The slightest familiarity with the early works of Hal Roach—not to mention D. W. Griffith, here pretentiously quoted—reveals how little Bogdanovich understands his vastly superior predecessors.'—*Robert Asahina, New Leader*

'The crudest, stupidest, unfunniest farce of this or any other year.'—*John Simon, New York*

The Niebelungen***
Germany 1924   bw   silent
Decla–Bioscop
Part One: 'Siegfried': 115m approx (24 fps)
Part Two: 'Kriemheld's Revenge': 125m approx (24 fps)

Siegfried kills a dragon and marries a princess of Burgundy but the fierce queen Brunhilde arranges his death. His widow marries Attila the Hun and they massacre the Burgundians. Stately, warlike legends are transformed into a slow, chilling, awe-inspiring sequence of films, the décor being of special interest. The films were conceived as a tribute to the German nation, and were among Hitler's favourites.

w Thea Von Harbou d Fritz Lang ph Carl Hoffman, Gunther Rittau ad Otto Hunte, Karl Vollbrecht, Erich Kettelhut

Paul Richter, Marguerite Schön, Theodor Loos, Hannah Ralph, Rudolph Klein-Rogge

Night after Night*
US 1932   70m   bw
Paramount

An ex-boxer seeking refinement buys a night club and falls for a socialite.

Dim little drama which is remembered for introducing Mae West to the screen with her famous line, 'Goodness had nothing to do with it'.

w Vincent Laurence, *novel* Single Night by Louis Bromfield d Archie Mayo ph Ernest Haller

George Raft, Constance Cummings, Wynne Gibson, *Mae West,* Alison Skipworth, Roscoe Karns, Louis Calhern

Night and Day*
US 1946   132m   Technicolor
Warner (Arthur Schwarz)

The life of Cole Porter.

Or rather, a fictitious story about a composer who happens to be called Cole Porter. A careful but undistinguished musical with pleasant moments.

w Charles Hoffman, Leo Townsend, William Bowers d Michael Curtiz ph Peverell Marley, William V. Skall m / ly Cole Porter md Max Steiner, Ray Heindorf ch Le Roy Prinz

Cary Grant, Alexis Smith, Monty Woolley, Mary Martin, Ginny Simms, Jane Wyman, Eve Arden, Victor Francen, Alan Hale, Dorothy Malone

AAN: Max Steiner, Ray Heindorf

Night and the City
GB 1950   101m   bw
TCF (Samuel G. Engel)

A crooked wrestling promoter is tracked down by an underworld gang.

A fated attempt to extend the success of *Naked City* in a London setting; the surface is accomplished enough, but the plot and characters are just plain dull, especially as little is seen of the police.

w Jo Eisinger, *novel* Gerald Kersh d Jules Dassin ph Max Greene m Benjamin Frankel

Richard Widmark, Gene Tierney, Googie Withers, Hugh Marlowe, Herbert Lom

'Brilliantly photographed, it is an example of neo-expressionist techniques at their most potent.'—*Richard Roud, 1964*

The Night Angel
US 1931   75m   bw

A Prague lawyer falls for the daughter of the brothel keeper he has sent to prison, and after killing a jealous suitor is himself accused of murder. Would-be Dietrichean high-style melodrama which did its stars no good at all and virtually ended Miss Carroll's career. Fredric March, Nancy Carroll, Alan Hale, Alison Skipworth, Katherine Emmett. Written and directed by Edmund Goulding; for Paramount.

A Night at Earl Carroll's
US 1940   63m   bw

When gangsters kidnap stars of Earl Carroll's nightclub, the restaurant staff put on their own show. Tinseltown time-passer which served a very small purpose. Ken Murray, J. Carrol Naish, Lilian Cornell, Blanche Stewart. Written by Lynn Starling; directed by Kurt Neumann; for Paramount.

A Night at the Opera****
US 1935   96m   bw
MGM (Irving Thalberg)

Three zanies first wreck, then help an opera company.
Certainly among the best of the Marxian extravaganzas, and the first to give them a big production to play with as well as musical interludes by other than themselves for a change of pace. The mix plays beautifully.
w George S. Kaufman, Morrie Ryskind d Sam Wood ph Merritt Gerstad md Herbert Stothart
Groucho, Chico, Harpo (Zeppo absented himself from here on), *Margaret Dumont*, Kitty Carlisle, Allan Jones, Walter Woolf King, *Sig Rumann*

Night Beat
GB 1948   91m   bw

Demobbed, a commando becomes a policeman and his friend becomes a crook.
Manhattan Melodrama, British style; no more than an adequate offering of its type. Anne Crawford, Maxwell Reed, Ronald Howard, Christine Norden, Hector Ross, Sidney James. Written by T. J. Morrison, Roland Pertwee and Robert Westerby; directed by Harold Huth; for BLPA.

Night Boat to Dublin
GB 1945   99m   bw
ABP (Hamilton Inglis)

An MI5 man saves an atom scientist from kidnapping.
Generally watchable low key thriller with familiar British ingredients.
w Lawrence Huntington, Robert Hall d Lawrence Huntington

Robert Newton, Raymond Lovell, Muriel Pavlow, Guy Middleton, Herbert Lom, Martin Miller, Marius Goring

Night Club Scandal
US 1937   74m   bw
Paramount

A society doctor murders his wife and incriminates her lover.
Smooth second feature remake of *Guilty as Hell*, chiefly notable for its star's last controlled performance.
w Lillie Hayward, play Riddle Me This by Daniel Rubin d Ralph Murphy ph Leo Tover
John Barrymore, Lynne Overman, Charles Bickford, Elizabeth Patterson, Evelyn Brent, Louise Campbell, J. Carrol Naish

Night Court
US 1932   90m   bw

A corrupt judge frames a girl on a prostitution charge. Tough star melodrama. Walter Huston, Lewis Stone, Anita Page, Phillips Holmes, Jean Hersholt. Written by Mark Hellinger, Bayard Veiller, Charles Beehan and Lenore Coffee; directed by W. S. Van Dyke; for MGM. (GB title: *Justice for Sale*).

The Night Digger
GB 1971   100m   colour

A frustrated spinster protects a handyman clearly guilty of murder, and runs away with him. How this came to be made at all when the Finney version of *Night Must Fall* had recently flopped is a mystery; it had so little box office appeal that it was barely released. Patricia Neal, Nicholas Clay, Pamela Browne, Jean Sanderson, Yootha Joyce, Peter Sallis, Graham Crowden. Written by Roald Dahl, from a story by Joy Cowley; directed by Alastair Reid; for MGM.

Night Flight*
US 1933   84m   bw
MGM (David O. Selznick)

The president of a civil airline insists that dangerous night flights must continue as a mark of progress.
Spurious, unsatisfactory, multi-star air melodrama lacking both narrative flow and the common touch.
w Oliver H. P. Garrett, stories Antoine de St Exupéry d Clarence Brown ph Oliver T. Marsh, Elmer Dyer, Charles Marshall
John Barrymore, Helen Hayes, Lionel Barrymore, Clark Gable, Robert Montgomery, Myrna Loy, William Gargan, C. Henry Gordon

'It is in the sense it conveys of human beings caught in the swift machinery of modern living that *Night Flight* soars above other pictures of its kind.'—*James Shelley Hamilton*

Night Games*
Sweden 1966   105m   bw
Sandrews (Lena Malmsjö)
original title: *Nattlek*

A 35-year-old man is sexually inhibited by memories of his dead mother's passions and perversions.
Curious Freudian parable apparently intended as a comment on the state of Europe.
Audiences found it merely peculiar.

wd Mai Zetterling, from her novel *ph* Rune Ericson *m* Jan Johansson, George Riedel

Ingrid Thulin, Keve Hjelm, Lena Brundin, Naima Wifstrand

'The best one can say is that it never lets up for a moment.'—*David Wilson, MFB*

Night Games
US 1980   100m   Technicolor

A neurotic Beverly Hills housewife is terrified of men. Crazy mix of case history, eroticism and suspense with insufficient of any to satisfy fans. Cindy Pickett, Joanna Cassidy, Barry Primus. Written by Anton Diether and Clarke Reynolds; directed by Roger Vadim; for Golden Harvest / Avco.

Night Hair Child
GB 1971   89m   Movielab
Leander / Harry Alan Towers (Graham Harris)

A 12-year-old boy makes sexual advances to his stepmother.
Corrupt voyeuristic weirdie which has to be seen to be believed.

w Trevor Preston   *d* James Killy   *ph* Harry Waxman   *m* Stelvio Cipriani

Mark Lester, Britt Ekland, Hardy Kruger, Harry Andrews, Lilli Palmer

Night Has a Thousand Eyes
US 1948   80m   bw
Paramount (André Boehm)

A vaudeville mentalist finds that he really does have the power to predict the future.
Predictable supernatural melodrama closely modelled on *The Clairvoyant* (qv); quite nicely made but simply not exciting.

w Barre Lyndon, Jonathan Latimer, *novel* Cornell Woolrich   *d* John Farrow   *ph* John F. Seitz   *m* Victor Young

Edward G. Robinson, Gail Russell, John Lund, Virginia Bruce, William Demarest, Richard Webb, Jerome Cowan

The Night Has Eyes*
GB 1942   79m   bw
ABP (John Argyle)
US title: *Terror House*

A young teacher disappears on the Yorkshire moors; her friend goes in search, and comes under the influence of a strange young man and his sinister housekeeper.
Stagey but effective little thriller, with oodles of fog and bog to help the suspense.

w Alan Kennington   *d* Leslie Arliss
ph Gunther Krampf   *m* Charles Williams

James Mason, Joyce Howard, *Wilfrid Lawson*, *Mary Clare*, Tucker McGuire, John Fernald
'Some ingenuity and not a little style.'—*The Times*

The Night Holds Terror*
US 1955   86m   bw
Columbia (Andrew Stone)

Three gunmen on the run kidnap a factory worker and hold him to ransom.
Effective, detailed, low-budget police melodrama; its plot may be over familiar now, but at the time it was refreshing and the whole film an intelligent exercise in suspense.

wd Andrew Stone *ph* Fred Jackman Jnr *m* Lucien Calliet

Jack Kelly, Hildy Parks, John Cassavetes, David Cross, Edward Marr, Jack Kruschen

A Night in Casablanca**
US 1946   85m   bw
David L. Loew

Three zanies rout Nazi refugees in a North African hotel.
The last authentic Marxian extravaganza; it starts uncertainly, builds to a fine sustained frenzy, then peters out in some overstretched airplane acrobatics.

w Joseph Fields, Roland Kibbee, Frank Tashlin   *d* Archie Mayo   *ph* James Van Trees   *m* Werner Janssen   *pd* Duncan Cramer

Groucho, Chico, Harpo, Sig Rumann, Lisette Verea, Charles Drake, Lois Collier, Dan Seymour
'It is beside the main point to add that it isn't one of their best movies; for the worst they might ever make would be better worth seeing than most other things I can think of.'—*James Agee*

A Night in Paradise
US 1946   84m   Technicolor
(Universal) Walter Wanger

Aesop falls in love at the court of King Croesus.
Deadly boring, unintentionally funny Arabian Nights farrago without the saving grace of action.

w Ernest Pascal, Emmet Lavery, *novel* Peacock's Feather by George S. Hellman *d* Arthur Lubin *ph* Hal Mohr *m* Frank Skinner

Merle Oberon, Turhan Bey, Thomas Gomez, Gale Sondergaard, Ray Collins, George Dolenz, John Litel, Ernest Truex, Jerome Cowan, Douglass Dumbrille

Night into Morning
US 1951 86m bw
MGM (Edwin H. Knopf)

A college professor loses his wife and son in an accident; despair drives him to drink and attempted suicide.
Well-made and well meaning melodrama whose virtual absence of plot makes it seem by the end merely maudlin.

w Karl Tunberg, Leonard Spiegelgass *d* Fletcher Markle *ph* George Folsey *m* Carmen Dragon

Ray Milland, Nancy Davis, John Hodiak, Lewis Stone, Jean Hagen, Rosemary de Camp

The Night Invader
GB 1942 81m bw

A Britisher in an occupied country is helped to capture a Nazi count. Propaganda potboiler for double billing. Anne Crawford, David Farrar, Carl Jaffe, Sybilla Binder, Marius Goring. Written by Brock Williams, Edward Dryhurst and Roland Pertwee, from the novel *Rendezvous with Death* by John Bentley; directed by Herbert Mason; for Warner.

The Night Is Young
US 1934 82m bw

A European archduke loves a ballerina. High-class musical which failed despite an intriguing cast and a Romberg and Hammerstein score. Evelyn Laye, Ramon Novarro, Una Merkel, Edward Everett Horton, Rosalind Russell, Charles Butterworth, Herman Bing, Henry Stephenson, Donald Cook. Written by Vicki Baum; directed by Dudley Murphy; for MGM.

Night Key
US 1937 67m bw
Universal

An inventor's idea is stolen by his former partner, and he takes an appropriate revenge. Low-key star melodrama: competent, but no great shakes.

w Tristam Tupper, John C. Moffit *d* Lloyd Corrigan *ph* George Robinson *m* Louis Forbes *make up* Jack Pierce

Boris Karloff, Jean Rogers, Warren Hull, Samuel S. Hinds, Alan Baxter, Ward Bond, Edwin Maxwell

The Night Life of the Gods
US 1935 75m bw

An inventor turns statues into people, and vice versa. Fantasy comedy from a well-known comic novel; interesting despite low level of invention. Alan Mowbray, Florine McKinney, Richard Carle, Peggy Shannon. Written by Barry Trivers, from Thorne Smith's novel; directed by Lowell Sherman; for Universal.

A Night Like This
GB 1932 74m bw

An Irish policeman breaks up a crooked gambling club. Minor Aldwych farce which hasn't worn well. Tom Walls, Ralph Lynn, Robertson Hare, Winifred Shotter, Mary Brough, Claude Hulbert. Written by Ben Travers, from his play; directed by Tom Walls; for British and Dominions.

Night Mail***
GB 1936 24m bw
GPO Film Unit

A 'film poem' showing the journey of the mail train from London to Glasgow.
One of the best and most influential of British documentaries: despite a few absurdities, it remains a pleasure to watch.

wd Basil Wright, Harry Watt ph J. Jones, H. E. Fowle m Benjamin Britten poem W. H. Auden *sound arrangements* Alberto Cavalcanti

Night Monster
US 1942 73m bw
Universal
GB title: *House of Mystery*

Murders are committed in a spooky house by a cripple who produces synthetic legs by self-hypnotism.
Stilted, creaky would-be thriller with a good cast and an impertinent plot.

w Clarence Upson Young *d* Ford Beebe *ph* Charles Van Enger

Ralph Morgan, Don Porter, Irene Hervey, Bela Lugosi, Lionel Atwill, Nils Asther, Leif Erickson, Frank Reicher

Night Moves*
US 1975 99m Technicolor
Warner / Hillier / Layton (Robert M. Sherman)

A private eye is engaged to find a runaway teenager.

Apparently a Chandlerish mystery, this is really a Pinterish audience-teaser with obsessions about communication and the meaning of life. A smart-ass entertainment for eager trendies.

w Alan Sharp *d* Arthur Penn *ph* Bruce Surtees *m* Michael Small *pd* George Jenkins

Gene Hackman, Jennifer Warren, Edward Binns, Harris Yulin, Kenneth Mars

'Beneath the complicated unravelling of a mystery, an anti-mystery, with the hero's detection registering as an evasion of his own problems; beneath a densely charted intrigue of betrayals and cross purposes, a cryptic void . . .'—*Jonathan Rosenbaum*

'A suspenseless suspenser . . . there's very little rhyme or reason for the plot's progression.'—*Variety*

'Rich and dense enough to set up reverberations long after one has left the cinema.'—*Michael Billington, Illustrated London News*

Night Must Fall**
US 1937 117m bw
MGM (Hunt Stromberg)

A bland young bellboy who is really a psychopathic murderer attaches himself to the household of a rich old lady.

Unconvincing but memorable Hollywood expansion of an effective British chiller.

w John Van Druten, *play* Emlyn Williams *d* Richard Thorpe *ph* Ray June *m* Edward Ward

Robert Montgomery, Rosalind Russell, *May Whitty*, Alan Marshal, Merle Tottenham, Kathleen Harrison, Matthew Boulton, E. E. Clive

'A pretty little murder play has made a long dim film.'—*Graham Greene*

'The most exhilarating shrouds of horror hang over it. It represents a provocative imagination, a skilled adapter, a sensitive director, a splendid acting job.'—*Bland Johaneson, New York Daily Mirror*

AAN: Robert Montgomery; May Whitty

Night Must Fall
GB 1964 105m bw
MGM (Albert Finney, Karel Reisz)

Dreary remake with a mannered star performance and the emphasis on axe murders. A mistake from beginning to end.

w Clive Exton *d* Karel Reisz *ph* Freddie Francis *m* Ron Grainer

Albert Finney, Susan Hampshire, Mona Washbourne, Sheila Hancock, Michael Medwin, Joe Gladwin, Martin Wyldeck

'Not so much a thriller as a typically humourless example of that overworked genre known as psychological drama . . . (Finney) constantly recalls a ventriloquist's dummy.'— *MFB*

The Night My Number Came Up*
GB 1954 94m bw
Ealing (Tom Morahan)

A man dreams that his plane will crash, and the dream begins to come true.

Intriguing little melodrama which badly lacks a twist ending and foxes itself by a flashback construction which leaves very little open to doubt. Production generally good.

w R. C. Sherriff *d* Leslie Norman *ph* Lionel Banes *m* Malcolm Arnold

Michael Redgrave, Alexander Knox, Sheila Sim, Denholm Elliott, Ursula Jeans, George Rose, Nigel Stock, Michael Hordern, Ralph Truman, Victor Maddern, Bill Kerr, Alfie Bass

Night Nurse*
US 1931 72m bw
Warner

A nurse uncovers a plot by other members of the household against her patient's children.

Fast-moving melodrama with solid star performances; just what the public wanted in 1931.

w Oliver H. P. Garrett, *novel* Dora Macy *d* William Wellman *ph* Chick McGill

Barbara Stanwyck, Ben Lyon, Joan Blondell, Clark Gable, Charles Winninger, Vera Lewis, Blanche Frederici, Charlotte Merriam

'A conglomeration of exaggerations, often bordering on serial dramatics.'—*Hollywood Reporter*

The Night of January 16th
US 1941 79m bw

A secretary is arrested for her boss's murder; but is he really dead? A stage thriller full of theatrical trickery becomes a very mundane film. Robert Preston, Ellen Drew, Nils Asther, Margaret Hayes. Written by Delmer Daves, Robert Pirosh and Eve Greene from a play by Ayn Rand; directed by William Clemens; for Paramount.

The Night of Nights
US 1939 86m bw

A once-famous Broadway writer, now a

drunk, tries to ensure his daughter's fame. Curious downbeat melodrama without the courage of its convictions, or the actors to give the right bravura performances. Pat O'Brien, Olympe Bradna, Reginald Gardiner, Roland Young. Written by Donald Ogden Stewart; directed by Lewis Milestone; for Paramount.

Night of the Demon***
GB 1957   87m   bw
Columbia / Sabre (Frank Bevis)
US title: *Curse of the Demon*

An occultist despatches his enemies by raising a giant medieval devil.
Despite dim work from the leads, this supernatural thriller is intelligently scripted and achieves several frightening and memorable sequences in the best Hitchcock manner.

w Charles Bennett, Hal E. Chester, *story* Casting the Runes by *M. R. James d Jacques Tourneur ph* Ted Scaife *m* Clifton Parker *ad* Ken Adam

Dana Andrews, Peggy Cummins, *Niall MacGinnis, Athene Seyler*, Brian Wilde, Maurice Denham, Ewan Roberts, Liam Redmond, Reginald Beckwith

Night of the Eagle**
GB 1961   87m   bw
Independent Artists (Albert Fennell)
US title: *Burn, Witch, Burn*

At a medical school, a jealous witch sets an evil force on her rival.
Pretty good supernatural thriller, let down by leading performances and sustained by character roles and solid production values in creepy sequences.

w Charles Beaumont, Richard Matheson, George Baxt, *novel* Conjure Wife by Fritz Leiber Jnr *d* Sidney Hayers *ph* Reg Wyer *m* William Alwyn

Margaret Johnston, Janet Blair, Peter Wyngarde, Anthony Nicholls, Reginald Beckwith, Kathleen Byron

The Night of the Following Day*
US 1969   100m   Technicolor
Universal / Gina (Hubert Cornfield)

A young girl arriving in Paris to stay with her father is kidnapped and held to ransom by an eccentric gang.
Straightforward suspense thriller with delusions of grandeur; the second half bogs down in pretentious talk and the end suggests that the whole thing was a dream.

w Hubert Cornfield, Robert Phippeny, *novel* The Snatchers by Lionel White *d Hubert Cornfield ph* Willy Kurant *m* Stanley Myers

Marlon Brando, Richard Boone, Rita Moreno, Pamela Franklin, Jess Hahn

Night of the Garter
GB 1933   86m   bw

A newly married man tries to retrieve an intimate gift from an old flame. One of the best-remembered comedies of Sydney Howard; with Winifred Shotter, Elsie Randolph, Austin Melford. Written by Austin Melford and Marjorie Gaffney, from the play *Getting Gertie's Garter* by Avery Hopwood and Wilson Collison; directed by Jack Raymond; for Herbert Wilcox.

The Night of the Generals**
GB 1967   148m   Technicolor
   Panavision
Columbia / Horizon / Filmsonor (Sam
   Spiegel)

A German intelligence agent tracks down a psychopathic Nazi general who started killing prostitutes in Warsaw during World War I. A curiously bumpy narrative which is neither mystery nor character study but does provide a few effective sequences and impressive performances. The big budget seems well spent.

w Joseph Kessel, Paul Dehn, *novel* Hans Helmut Hirst *d* Anatole Litvak *ph* Henri Decaë *m* Maurice Jarre *pd* Alexander Trauner

Peter O'Toole, *Omar Sharif, Tom Courtenay*, Donald Pleasence, Joanna Pettet, *Philippe Noiret*, Charles Gray, Coral Brown, John Gregson, Harry Andrews, Nigel Stock, Christopher Plummer, Juliette Greco
   'The "who" is obvious from the first and the "dunnit" interminable.'—*Judith Crist, 1973*
   'Lurid and vivid, if nothing else.'—*Robert Windeler*

The Night of the Grizzly
US 1966   102m   Techniscope
Paramount (Burt Dunne)

A Wyoming ex-sheriff kills a marauding bear and earns the respect of his son.
Stout-hearted family film, rather sluggishly made.

w Warren Douglas *d* Joseph Pevney *ph* Harold Lipstein, Loyal Griggs *m* Leith Stevens

Clint Walker, Martha Hyer, Keenan Wynn, Leo Gordon, Kevin Brodie, Nancy Kulp, Ellen Corby, Jack Elam, Ron Ely

The Night of the Hunter***
US 1955   93m   bw
UA / Paul Gregory

A psychopathic preacher goes on the trail of hidden money, the secret of which is held by two children.

Weird, manic fantasy in which evil finally comes to grief against the forces of sweetness and light (the children, an old lady, water, animals). Although the narrative does not flow smoothly there are splendidly imaginative moments, and no other film has ever quite achieved its texture.

w *James Agee, novel Davis Grubb   d Charles Laughton   ph Stanley Cortez   m* Walter Schumann

Robert Mitchum, Shelley Winters, Lillian Gish, Don Beddoe, Evelyn Varden, Peter Graves, James Gleason

'One of the most frightening movies ever made.'—*Pauline Kael, 1968*

'A genuinely sinister work, full of shocks and over-emphatic sound effects, camera angles and shadowy lighting.'—*NFT, 1973*

'One of the most daring, eloquent and personal films to have come from America in a long time.'—*Derek Prouse*

The Night of the Iguana***
US 1964   125m   bw
MGM / Seven Arts (Ray Stark)

A disbarred clergyman becomes a travel courier in Mexico and is sexually desired by a teenage nymphomaniac, a middle-aged hotel owner and a frustrated itinerant artist.

The author is most tolerable when poking fun at his own types, and this is a sharp, funny picture with a touch of poetry.

w *Anthony Veiller, play Tennessee Williams   d John Huston   ph Gabriel Figueroa   m* Benjamin Frankel   *ad* Stephen Grimes

Richard Burton, Deborah Kerr, Ava Gardner, Sue Lyon, *Grayson Hall, Cyril Delevanti*

'One man . . . three women . . . one night!'—*publicity*

'Whatever poetry it had seems to have leaked out.'—*New Yorker, 1982*

AAN: Gabriel Figueroa; Grayson Hall

Night of the Juggler
US 1980   100m   Technicolor

A New Yorker relentlessly pursues the kidnapper of his daughter. Average chase thriller with good location staging of car crashes. James Brolin, Cliff Gorman, Richard Castellano, Abby Bluestone. Written by Bill Norton Snr and Rick Natkin; directed by Robert Butler; for Columbia.

Night of the Lepus
US 1972   88m   Metrocolor
MGM (A. C. Lyles)

A serum meant to control a surplus of rabbits instead produces monster varieties four feet tall.

Tolerable sci-fi tailored to a very tired formula.

w *Don Holiday, Gene R. Kearney, novel* The Year of the Angry Rabbit by Russell Braddon *d* William F. Claxton *ph* Ted Voigtlander *m* Jimmie Haskell

Stuart Whitman, Rory Calhoun, Janet Leigh, Paul Fix, De Forrest Kelley

'For insomniacs with lax standards.'—*Judith Crist*

The Night of the Living Dead
US 1968   98m   bw

Flesh-eating zombies, activated by radiation from a space rocket, ravage the countryside. Gruesome horror comic with effective moments; the director was still doing the same schtick ten years later. Judith O'Dea, Duane Jones, Karl Hardman, Keith Wayne. Written by John A. Russo; directed by George A. Romero; for Image Ten. 'The best film ever made in Pittsburgh.'—*Anon.*

Night Owls*
US 1930   20m   bw

A policeman wanting to record an arrest bribes two tramps to burgle a house. The stars at their most hilariously incompetent, unable even to get through a doorway efficiently. Laurel and Hardy, Edgar Kennedy, James Finlayson. Written by Leo McCarey and H. M. Walker; directed by James Parrott; for Hal Roach.

Night Passage*
US 1957   90m   Technirama
U-I (Aaron Rosenberg)

A railroad worker entrusted with a payroll finds that the bandits trying to rob it are led by his own brother.

Obscurely titled and rather empty western providing standard excitements.

w *Borden Chase   d* James Neilson   *ph* William Daniels   *m* Dmitri Tiomkin

James Stewart, Audie Murphy, Dan Duryea, Brandon de Wilde, Dianne Foster

Night People*
US 1954   93m   Technicolor
  Cinemascope
TCF (Nunnally Johnson)

When a US corporal stationed in Berlin is kidnapped by the Russians, his influential father flies into action.

Curiously titled cold war suspenser which would have been more memorable if not in Cinemascope; the pace and talent are visible, but the wide screen and poor colour dissipate them.

wd Nunnally Johnson ph Charles G. Clarke m Cyril Mockridge

Gregory Peck, Broderick Crawford, Anita Bjork, Walter Abel, Rita Gam, Buddy Ebsen, Jill Esmond, Peter Van Eyck

'You have never really seen Gregory Peck until you see him in Cinemascope!'—*publicity*

'We didn't say nice people, we said *night people!*'—*publicity*

AAN: original story (Jed Harris, Tom Reed)

Night Plane from Chungking
US 1942   69m   bw
Paramount

Assorted international passengers are flown from Chungking to India, but one of their number is a German spy who will kill to get his hands on vital information.

A lower-case 'who is it' based on *Shanghai Express*. Not bad according to its lights.

w Earl Felton, Theodore Reeves, Lester Cole d Ralph Murphy ph Theodor Sparkuhl

Ellen Drew, Robert Preston, Otto Kruger, Steve Geray, Ernest Dorian, Tamara Geva, Sen Yung

The Night Porter
Italy 1973   118m   Technicolor
Lotar Films (Robert Gordon Edwards, Esa De Simone)

The wife of an opera conductor recognizes a hotel porter as the sadistic SS commandant of a concentration camp in which she spent the war years; they now resume a sado-masochistic love affair.

A downright deplorable film, with no cinematic skill or grace to excuse it; the visuals are as loathsome as the sound is indecipherable, and the sheer pointlessness of it is insulting.

w Liliana Cavani, Italo Moscati d Liliana Cavani ph Alfio Contini m Daniele Paris

Dirk Bogarde, Charlotte Rampling, Philippe Leroy, Gabriele Ferzetti, Isa Miranda

'Its claim to be saying something important is offensive, but the picture is too crudely trumped up to be a serious insult.'—*New Yorker*

Night Ride
GB 1937   70m   bw

Unemployed lorry drivers start an independent co-operative. Brisk action programmer. Julian Vedey, Wally Patch, Jimmy Hanley, Joan Ponsford. Written by Ralph Bettinson; directed by John Paddy Carstairs; for Paramount.

Night Song
US 1947   101m   bw
RKO (Harriet Parsons)

A wealthy socialite falls for a blind pianist and pretends to be blind also, and poor to boot. Silly, pretentious soaper, moodily photographed.

w Frank Fenton, Irving Hyland, De Witt Bodeen d John Cromwell ph Lucien Ballard m Leith Stevens

Dana Andrews, Merle Oberon, Hoagy Carmichael, Ethel Barrymore, Artur Rubenstein, Eugene Ormandy

The Night They Raided Minsky's**
US 1968   99m   De Luxe
UA / Tandem (Norman Lear)
GB title: *The Night They Invented Striptease*

Various human problems are posed and solved during a night at a burlesque theatre. Marvellous kaleidoscopic ragbag of brilliant fragments which unfortunately don't cohere in the mind into a really memorable film, though it gives detailed pleasure on every viewing.

w Arnold Schulman, Sidney Michaels, Norman Lear, book Rowland Barber d William Friedkin ph Andrew Laszlo m Charles Strouse pd William Eckart, Jean Eckar ch Danny Daniels narrator Rudy Vallee

Jason Robards, Britt Ekland, *Norman Wisdom*, Forrest Tucker, Joseph Wiseman, Bert Lahr, Harry Andrews, Denholm Elliott, Elliot Gould, Jack Burns

'The Fanny Brice country stunningly brought to life—every face a snapshot of yesterday.'—*Alexander Walker*

Night Tide
US 1961   84m   bw

A sailor falls in love with a fairground freak show girl who may be a real mermaid. Cheaply made and very derivative romantic fantasy which seemed to hold a promise never fulfilled. Dennis Hopper, Linda Lawson, Gavin Muir, Luana Anders. Written and directed by Curtis Harrington; for Virgo Films.

A Night to Remember•
US 1941 91m bw
Columbia (Samuel Bischoff)

A Greenwich Village mystery-writing couple try to solve a murder.
Reasonably sparkling comedy whodunnit with a zany tinge.

w Richard Flournoy, Jack Henley d Richard Wallace ph Joseph Walker m Werner Heymann md Morris Stoloff

Loretta Young, Brian Aherne, Jeff Donnell, William Wright, Sidney Toler, Gale Sondergaard, Donald MacBride, Lee Patrick, Blanche Yurka

A Night to Remember•••
GB 1958 123m bw
Rank (William Macquitty)

The story of the 1912 sea disaster when the *Titanic* struck an iceberg.
A major film enterprise featuring hundreds of cameos, none discernibly more important than the other. On this account the film seems alternately stiff and flabby as narrative, but there is much to enjoy and admire along the way, though the sense of awe is dissipated by the final model shots.

w *Eric Ambler, book* Walter Lord d *Roy Baker* ph *Geoffrey Unsworth* m William Alwyn

Kenneth More, Honor Blackman, Michael Goodliffe, David McCallum, George Rose, Anthony Bushell, Ralph Michael, John Cairney, Kenneth Griffith, Frank Lawton, Michael Bryant

'A worthy, long-drawn-out documentary, with noticeably more honesty about human nature than most films, but little shape or style.'—*Kenneth Cavender*

Night Train to Munich•••
GB 1940 93m bw
TCF (Edward Black)
aka: *Gestapo; Night Train*

A British agent poses as a Nazi in order to rescue a Czech inventor.
First-rate comedy suspenser obviously inspired by the success of *The Lady Vanishes* and providing much the same measure of thrills and laughs.

w *Frank Launder, Sidney Gilliat, novel* Report on a Fugitive by Gordon Wellesley d *Carol Reed* ph Otto Kanturek m Charles Williams md Louis Levy

Margaret Lockwood, *Rex Harrison, Basil Radford, Naunton Wayne*, Paul Henreid, Keneth Kent, Felix Aylmer, Roland Culver,

Eliot Makeham, Raymond Huntley, Wyndham Goldie

'A very nice triumph of skill and maturity in films, and thus a pleasure to have.'—*Otis Ferguson*

AAN: Gordon Wellesley

Night unto Night•
US 1949 85m bw
Warner (Owen Crump)

An epileptic scientist falls for a girl hallucinated by the ghost of her dead husband.
Cheerless nuthouse melodrama, one of the well-meant aberrations which Hollywood studios used to produce as a sop to conscience.

w Kathryn Scola, *novel* Philip Wylie d *Don Siegel* ph Peverell Marley m Franz Waxman

Ronald Reagan, Viveca Lindfors, Rosemary de Camp, Broderick Crawford, Osa Massen, Craig Stevens, Erskine Sanford

The Night Walker•
US 1964 86m bw
U-I / William Castle

The widow of a tough executive, killed and disfigured in an explosion, is haunted in her dreams not only by him but by a mysterious lover who turns up in reality.
Stiff and unconvincing but still fairly frightening low-budget shocker with a plot twist or two.

w *Robert Bloch* d William Castle ph Harold Stine m Vic Mizzy

Robert Taylor, *Barbara Stanwyck*, Lloyd Bochner, Rochelle Hudson, Judi Meredith, Hayden Rorke

Night Watch
GB 1973 98m Technicolor
Avco / Brut (David White)

A widow recovering from a nervous breakdown keeps seeing bodies in the night. Her friends try to help, but things are not quite what they seem.
Predictable coiled-spring shocker which goes curiously flat despite a star cast and lashings of blood. Perhaps we have all been here once too often.

w Tony Williamson, *play* Lucille Fletcher d Brian G. Hutton ph Billie Williams m John Cameron

Elizabeth Taylor, Laurence Harvey, Billie Whitelaw, Robert Lang, Tony Britton, Bill Dean

'It has all the trappings of a Joan Crawford vehicle of the forties, with numerous elegant dresses for Miss Taylor, an appropriately

unbecoming wardrobe for Miss Whitelaw, and
a set which is an art director's dream.'—
Brenda Davies

'Elizabeth Taylor's gowns are by Valentino,
her jewellery is by Van Cleef and Arpels, even
her kitchen is by Westinghouse. And she is
still going out of her mind.'—*Alexander
Walker*

Night without Sleep

US 1952   77m   bw
TCF (Robert Bassler)

A man reconstructs his drunken actions the
night before, and fears he has committed a
murder.
Dreary melodrama, all frayed tempers,
drunkenness and cigarette smoke.

w Frank Partos, Elick Moll   *d* Roy Baker
ph Lucien Ballard   *m* Cyril Mockridge

Gary Merrill, Linda Darnell, Hildegarde Neff,
Hugh Beaumont, Mae Marsh

Night World

US 1932   58m   bw

Characters with an assortment of problems
congregate in a nightclub. Tolerable slice-of-
life drama with interesting cast. Lew Ayres,
Boris Karloff, Mae Clarke, Russell Hopton,
Dorothy Revier, Bert Roach, Hedda Hopper.
Written by P. J. Wolfson and Allen Rivkin;
directed by Hobart Henley; for Universal.

The Nightcomers*

GB 1971   96m   Technicolor
Scimitar / Kastner–Kanter–Ladd (Michael
Winner)

How the ghost-ridden children in *The Turn of
the Screw* became evil; they became involved
in aberrant sexual activities between the
gardener and the housekeeper, and finally
murdered the former.
Despite its unexpected literariness this is
unpleasant and unconvincing nonsense with a
boring script punctuated by shock cuts and
very little period feel.

w Michael Hastings   *d* Michael Winner
ph Robert Paynter   *m* Jerry Fielding

Stephanie Beacham, Marlon Brando, Thora
Hird, Harry Andrews, Verna Harvey,
Christopher Ellis

Nightfall*

US 1956   78m   bw
Columbia (Ted Richmond)

The police and two bank robbers chase an
innocent artist who happens to know that the
loot is hidden in a Wisconsin snowdrift.
Occasionally stylish but obscurely narrated
suspenser.

w Stirling Silliphant, *novel* David Goodis
d Jacques Tourneur   *ph* Burnett Guffey
m George Duning

Anne Bancroft, Aldo Ray, Brian Keith, James
Gregory, Jocelyn Brando, Frank Albertson

Nighthawks

GB 1978   113m   Eastmancolor

The life of an actively homosexual
schoolteacher. Painful low-life drama with
many signs of its amateur status. Ken
Robertson and non-professionals. Written and
directed by Ron Peck and Paul Hallam; for
Nashburgh / Four Corner Films.

Nightmare

US 1942   81m   bw
Universal

A gambler in wartime London helps a
beautiful girl escape from Nazi spies.
Thin espionage thriller with a good sequence
or two and a smooth villain.

w Dwight Taylor, *novel* Escape by Philip
MacDonald   *d* Tim Whelan   *ph* George
Barnes   *m* Frank Skinner

Brian Donlevy, Diana Barrymore, *Gavin
Muir*, Henry Daniell, Hans Conried, Arthur
Shields

Nightmare*

US 1956   89m   bw
UA / Pine–Thomas / Shane (Maxwell
Shane)

A young musician is hypnotized into
committing a murder, and reconstructs his
actions with the help of his policeman brother-
in-law.
Lethargic remake of the ingenious *Fear in the
Night* (qv). Watchable.

wd Maxwell Shane, *novel* Cornell Woolrich
ph Joseph Biroc   *m* Herschel Burke Gilbert

Edward G. Robinson, Kevin McCarthy,
Virginia Christine, Connie Russell

Nightmare*

GB 1964   82m   bw   Hammerscope
U-I / Hammer (Jimmy Sangster)

18-year-old Janet still has nightmares after
seeing her mad mother kill her father six years
ago; brought home, even more frightening
visions afflict her.
Genuinely scary *Diabolique*-type mystery with
the usual Hammer borrowings put to good
use.

w Jimmy Sangster   *d* Freddie Francis   *ph* John
Wilcox   *m* Don Banks

Moira Redmond, David Knight, Brenda Bruce, John Welsh, *Jennie Linden*

Nightmare Alley**
US 1947   112m   bw
TCF (George Jessel)

A fairground barker becomes a successful confidence trickster dealing with the supernatural, but finally sinks to the depths. Unusual road to ruin melodrama, a striking oddity from Hollywood at the time, and still quite interesting and well done.

w Jules Furthman, novel William Lindsay Gresham   *d Edmund Goulding   ph Lee Garmes   m* Cyril Mockridge

Tyrone Power, Coleen Gray, Joan Blondell, *Taylor Holmes*, Helen Walker, Mike Mazurki, Ian Keith
  'The picture goes just short of all that might have made it very interesting . . . even so, two or three sharply comic and cynical scenes make it worth seeing.'—*James Agee*

Nightmare in the Sun*
US 1963   81m   De Luxe
Afilmco (Marc Lawrence, John Derek)

A rich man kills his wife and blames a hitch-hiker who has had a brief affair with her. Modest independent melodrama, quite interestingly made though not entirely effective.

w Ted Thomas   *d* Marc Lawrence   *ph* Stanley Cortez   *m* Paul Glass

John Derek, Ursula Andress, Arthur O'Connell, Aldo Ray

Nijinsky**
US 1980   125m   Metrocolor
Paramount / Hera (Harry Saltzman)

The rise and fall of a great dancer groomed for stardom in the Ballets Russes by the impresario Diaghilev.
Rather boringly scripted with the emphasis on homosexual love, this film finally survives through its electrifying personalities and its strong sense of period.

w Hugh Wheeler   *d* Herbert Ross   *ph* Douglas Slocombe   *md* John Lanchbery   *pd John Blezard*

Alan Bates, George de la Pena, Leslie Brown, *Alan Badel*, Colin Blakely, Ronald Pickup, Ronald Lacey, Jeremy Irons, Anton Dolin, Janet Suzman, Sian Phillips, members of the London Festival Ballet
  'The impression is left of a fascinating subject which proved too challenging for its makers, who settle eventually for what is

uncomfortably near *All About Eve* with Bette Davis in a dinner jacket and Anne Baxter in a jock strap.'—*Alan Brien, Sunday Times*

Nikki, Wild Dog of the North*
US 1961   74m   Technicolor
Walt Disney (Winston Hibler)

The life of a Canadian trapper's wolf dog. Pleasing 'true life fiction' which didn't quite reach top feature status.

w Ralph Wright, Winston Hibler, *novel* James Oliver Curwood   *d* Jack Couffer   *m* Oliver Wallace

Emile Genest, Jean Coutu

Nine Girls
US 1944   78m   bw
Columbia (Burt Kelly)

College girls are murdered in a sorority house. Cheapjack whodunnit with a cardboard look and feel.

w Karen de Wolff, Connie Lee, *play* Wilfred H. Pettit   *d* Leigh Jason   *ph* James Van Trees   *m* John Leopold

Ann Harding, Evelyn Keyes, Jinx Falkenberg, Anita Louise, Leslie Brooks, Lynn Merrick, Jeff Donnell, Nina Foch, Marcia Mae Jones, William Demarest

Nine Hours to Rama
GB 1962   125m   De Luxe   Cinemascope
TCF / Red Lion (Mark Robson)

Events leading to the assassination of Mahatma Gandhi.
Fictionalized, sensationalized and very dull, this multi-character drama holds interest only for snatches of acting and location backgrounds.

w Nelson Gidding, *novel* Stanley Wolpert   *d* Mark Robson   *ph* Arthur Ibbetson   *m* Malcolm Arnold

Jose Ferrer, Diane Baker, Robert Morley, J. S. Casshyap, Horst Buchholz, Harry Andrews
  'The only interesting line in the movie is the thick brown one visible on the inside of every white collar.'—*John Simon*

Nine Lives Are Not Enough
US 1941   63m   bw

A reporter solves a multi-murder in a boarding house. Lively second feature which moves at a commendable pace. Ronald Reagan, Howard da Silva, James Gleason, Ed Brophy, Faye Emerson, Peter Whitney, Charles Drake. Written by Fred Niblo Jnr; directed by A. Edward Sutherland; for Warner.

Nine Men*
GB 1943 68m bw

A sergeant and a handful of men in an old fort
hold off the Italians in the Libyan desert.

Sharp semi-documentary of the war which
paled against the mightier epics to follow. Jack
Lambert, Gordon Jackson, Frederick Piper,
Grant Sutherland, Bill Blewett. Written and
directed by Harry Watt; for Ealing.

Nine to Five*
US 1980 110m De Luxe
TCF / IPC (Bruce Gilbert)

Three office women plot to get rid of their
boss, and nearly make it.

Agreeable comedy somewhat reminiscent of
Sturges' *Unfaithfully Yours*.

w Colin Higgins, Patricia Resnick d Colin
Higgins ph Reynaldo Villalobos m Charles
Fox pd Dean Mitzner

Jane Fonda, Dolly Parton, Lily Tomlin,
Dabney Coleman, Sterling Hayden, Elizabeth
Fraser, Henry Jones

'An effective escapist feast with lotsa funny
physical schtick.'—*Variety*

AAN: best song (Dolly Parton)

1984*
GB 1955 91m bw
Holiday (N. Peter Rathvon)

Europe has become the fascist state of
Oceania, ruled by Big Brother; Winston Smith
yearns for the old days, and is brainwashed.

The famous prophecy of a dehumanized future
is followed with reasonable fidelity apart from
the defiant ending, but the novel is too literary
for cinematic success and the result is too
often both downbeat and boring.

w William P. Templeton, Ralph Bettinson,
novel George Orwell d Michael Anderson
ph C. Pennington Richards m Malcolm
Arnold

Michael Redgrave, Edmond O'Brien, Jan
Sterling, David Kossoff, Mervyn Johns,
Donald Pleasence

1941*
US 1979 118m Metrocolor Panavision
Columbia / Universal / A-Team (John
   Milius)

Just after Pearl Harbor, a stray Japanese
submarine terrorizes Hollywood.

Absurdly over-budgeted manic farce which
substitutes noise for wit and slapstick for
comedy; it fails on every level.

w Robert Zemeckis, Bob Gale d Steven
Spielberg ph William A. Fraker m John
Williams pd Dean Edward Mitzner

Dan Aykroyd, Ned Beatty, John Belushi,
Lorraine Gary, Murray Hamilton, Christopher
Lee, Tim Matheson, Toshiro Mifune, Warren
Oates, Robert Stack, Elisha Cook Jnr

'Aimed at young audiences, who deserve
better fun.'—*New Yorker*

'Its sheer relentless physicality, its
elaborately orchestrated pointlessness on
every other level, make it probably the purest
demonstration of what it means to have two of
the all-time commercial blockbusters to one's
record and one's hands firmly on the fantasy
machine.'—*Richard Combs, MFB*

'So overloaded with visual humour of rather
monstrous nature that the feeling emerges that
once you've seen ten explosions, you've seen
them all.'—*Variety*

'Spielberg intended it as "a stupidly
outrageous celebration of paranoia" . . .
audiences found it curiously unfunny and
elephantine.'—*Les Keyser, Hollywood in the
Seventies*

1900*
Italy / France / West Germany 1976
   320m Technicolor
TCF / PEA / Artistes Associés / Artemis
   (Alberto Grimaldi)
original title: *Novecento*

The political and personal vicissitudes of a
noble Italian family between 1900 and 1945.

Immensely long and heavy-going study of the
rise of fascism in the form of a family saga.
For specialists only.

w Bernardo Bertolucci, Franco Arcalli,
Giuseppe Bertolucci d Bernardo Bertolucci
ph Vittorio Stovaro m Ennio Morricone
ad Enzo Frigiero

Burt Lancaster, Robert de Niro, Gerard
Depardieu, Dominique Sanda, Donald
Sutherland, Sterling Hayden

'Exasperatingly uneven, but its most
powerful moments can't be matched by any
movie since *Godfather Two*.'—*Time*

'Bertolucci tried to write a 19th-century
novel on film: the result is appalling, yet it has
the grandeur of a classic visionary folly.'—*New
Yorker*

† The film was normally shown in two separate
parts.

99 and 44 / 100 Per Cent Dead
US 1974 98m De Luxe Panavision
TCF / Joe Wizan / Vashon
aka: *Call Harry Crown*

A losing gang boss hires a trouble shooter.

Violent gangster melodrama apparently
intended as a black comedy; if so, as clumsy as
its title.

w Robert Dillon   *d* John Frankenheimer
ph Ralph Woolsey   *m* Henry Mancini

Richard Harris, Edmond O'Brien, Bradford
Dillman, Ann Turkel, Chuck Connors,
Constance Ford

'Esthetically, commercially and morally, a
quintessential fiasco.'—*Variety*

† The title in fact spoofs an ad familiar to
Americans for a soap which was said to be '99
and 44 / 100 per cent pure'.

99 River Street*
US 1953   83m   bw
UA / Edward Small

A taxi driver becomes involved in a diamond
robbery.
Adequate thick ear with quite good detection
and action sequences.

w Robert Smith   *d Phil Karlson   ph* Franz
Planer

John Payne, Evelyn Keyes, Frank Faylen,
Brad Dexter, Peggie Castle

Ninotchka***
US 1939   110m   bw
MGM (Ernst Lubitsch)

A Paris playboy falls for a communist emissary
sent to sell some crown jewels.
Sparkling comedy on a theme which has been
frequently explored; delicate pointing and
hilarious character comedy sustain this version
perfectly until the last half hour, when it
certainly sags; but it remains a favourite
Hollywood example of this genre.

*w Charles Brackett, Billy Wilder, Walter
Reisch, story* Melchior Lengyel   *d Ernst
Lubitsch   ph William Daniels   m* Werner
Heymann

*Greta Garbo, Melvyn Douglas, Sig Rumann,
Alexander Granach, Felix Bressart*, Ina Claire,
Bela Lugosi

'The Lubitsch style, in which much was
made of subtleties—glances, finger
movements, raised eyebrows—has
disappeared. Instead we have a hard, brightly
lit, cynical comedy with the wisecrack
completely in control.'—*John Baxter, 1968*
'Garbo laughs!'—*publicity*
'Don't pronounce it—see it!'—*publicity*

AAN: best picture; script; story; Greta Garbo

The Ninth Configuration
US 1980   105m   Metrocolor

A new psychiatrist in a compound of military
misfits becomes the victim of a terror
campaign. Weirdly obscure would-be thriller
which only mystifies and annoys. Stacy Keach,

Scott Wilson, Jason Miller, Ed Flanders,
Neville Brand, Moses Gunn. Written, directed
and produced by William Peter Blatty; for
Lorimar.

No Blade of Grass
GB 1970   97m   Metrocolor   Panavision
MGM (Cornel Wilde)

Industrial pollution sets a destructive virus
ruining the crops of the world; anarchy
spreads through Britain and one family takes
refuge in the Lake District.
Apocalyptic sci-fi, moderately well done
though so humourless as to be almost funny.

w Sean Forestal, Jefferson Pascal, *novel* John
Christopher   *d* Cornel Wilde   *ph* H. A. R.
Thompson   *m* Burnell Whibley

Nigel Davenport, Jean Wallace, Patrick Holt,
John Hamill

No Deposit, No Return
US 1976   112m   Technicolor
Walt Disney (Ron Miller)

Airport confusion causes crooks to abduct
(unwittingly) a millionaire's grandchildren; the
millionaire gives chase.
Overlong and tedious action comedy which
makes little sense.

w Arthur Alsberg, Don Nelson   *d* Norman
Tokar   *ph* Frank Phillips   *m* Buddy Baker

David Niven, Darren McGavin, Don Knotts,
Herschel Bernardi, Barbara Feldon, John
Williams, Vic Tayback, Kim Richards

'Once again one is left wondering why there
should be such an unbridgeable gulf between
the brilliant professionalism and sometimes
innovative genius of the Disney animated
films, and the dull artlessness of the majority
of their live-action pictures.'—*Philip French,
The Times*

No Down Payment**
US 1957   105m   bw   Cinemascope
TCF (Jerry Wald)

Tension among smart suburban couples in a
Los Angeles housing development.
Lively domestic melodrama, very useful to
sociologists as a mirror of its times.

w Philip Yordan, novel John McPartland
d Martin Ritt   ph Joseph La Shelle   *m* Leigh
Harline

Joanne Woodward, Tony Randall, Sheree
North, Jeffrey Hunter, Cameron Mitchell,
Patricia Owens, Barbara Rush, Pat Hingle

No Funny Business
GB 1933   75m   bw
John Stafford

Two professional co-respondents are sent to
the Riviera; each mistakes the other as his
client.
Stagey farce, notable for its unlikely star
teaming and its hilariously dated style.

w Victor Hanbury, Frank Vosper, Dorothy
Hope d John Stafford, Victor Hanbury

Gertrude Lawrence, Laurence Olivier, Jill
Esmond, Edmund Breon, Gibb McLaughlin,
Muriel Aked

No Highway°°
GB 1951   98m   bw
TCF (Louis D. Lighton)
US title: *No Highway in the Sky*

During a transatlantic flight, a boffin works
out that the plane's tail is about to fall off from
metal fatigue.
The central premise of this adaptation from a
popular novel is fascinating, but the romantic
asides are a distraction and the characters
cardboard; the film still entertains through
sheer professionalism.

w R. C. Sherriff, Oscar Millard, Alec Coppel,
novel Nevil Shute d Henry Koster
ph Georges Périnal

James Stewart, Marlene Dietrich, Glynis
Johns, Jack Hawkins, Janette Scott, Elizabeth
Allan, Kenneth More, Niall MacGinnis,
Ronald Squire

No Leave, No Love
US 1946   118m   bw
MGM (Joe Pasternak)

Sailors on leave meet an English girl.
Witless, overlong musical extravaganza.

w Charles Martin, Leslie Karkos d Charles
Martin ph Harold Rosson, Robert Surtees
md Georgie Stoll

Van Johnson, Pat Kirkwood, Keenan Wynn,
Guy Lombardo and his Orchestra, Edward
Arnold, Marie Wilson, Leon Ames

No Limit°
GB 1935   79m   bw
ATP (Basil Dean)

A motor mechanic enters for the TT Races.
Lively star comedy with Isle of Man locations.

w Tom Geraghty, Fred Thompson,
story Walter Greenwood d Monty Banks

George Formby, Florence Desmond, Edward
Rigby, Jack Hobbs, Peter Gawthorne, Alf
Goddard

No Love for Johnnie°
GB 1960   111m   bw   Cinemascope
Rank / Five Star (Betty E. Box)

The personal and political problems of a
Labour MP.
Predictable but quite lively study of ambition
and frustration, with good cameos;
Cinemascope all but ruins its impact.

w Nicholas Phipps, Mordecai Richler, *novel*
Wilfred Fienburgh d Ralph Thomas
ph Ernest Steward m Malcolm Arnold

Peter Finch, Mary Peach, *Stanley Holloway*,
Donald Pleasence, Billie Whitelaw, Hugh
Burden, Rosalie Crutchley, Michael
Goodliffe, Mervyn Johns, Geoffrey Keen,
Paul Rogers, Dennis Price, Peter Barkworth,
Fenella Fielding, Gladys Henson

No Man Is an Island
US 1962   114m   Eastmancolor
U-I / Gold Coast (John Monks Jnr, Richard
   Goldstone)
GB title: *Island Escape*

After the Japanese attack on Guam, a
radioman finds refuge in a leper colony and
sets up his own resistance unit.
Unexceptional war adventure in the jungle.

wd John Monks Jnr, Richard Goldstone
ph Carl Kayser m Restie Umali

Jeffrey Hunter, Marshall Thompson, Barbara
Perez, Ronald Remy
   'Good clean fun for right-minded
teenagers.'—*MFB*

No Man of Her Own°
US 1932   98m   bw
Paramount

A big-time gambler marries a local girl on a
bet and tries to keep her innocent of his
activities.
Star romantic comedy drama, quite
professionally assembled and played.

w Maurine Watkins, Milton H. Gropper
d Wesley Ruggles ph Leo Tover

Clark Gable, Carole Lombard, Dorothy
Mackail, Grant Mitchell, George Barbier,
Elizabeth Patterson, J. Farrell MacDonald
   'Just about everything that the ordinary
picture fan looks for: drama, romance,
comedy, strong build-ups, exciting climaxes, a
fine line of human interest.'—*Film Daily*

No Man of Her Own°
US 1949   98m   bw
Paramount (Richard Maibaum)

A pregnant wanderer is involved in a train crash and assumes the identity of the wife of a dead passenger.
Glossy star melodrama, very watchable.

w Catherine Turney, Sally Benson, Mitchell Leisen d Mitchell Leisen ph Daniel L. Fapp m Hugo Friedhofer

Barbara Stanwyck, John Lund, Lyle Bettger, *Jane Cowl*, Phyllis Thaxter, Henry O'Neill, Richard Denning

No Minor Vices
US 1948 96m bw
(MGM) Enterprise

A doctor brings home an artist friend who proceeds to wreck his household.
Interminable thin comedy which gives no clue as to what the talent involved thought it was doing.

w Arnold Manoff d Lewis Milestone ph George Barnes m Franz Waxman

Dana Andrews, Lilli Palmer, Louis Jourdan, Jane Wyatt, Norman Lloyd

No More Ladies
US 1935 79m bw
MGM

A society girl thinks that by marrying a rake she can reform him.
Breezy sophisticated comedy which doesn't quite maintain its impetus.

w Donald Ogden Stewart, Horace Jackson, *play* A. E. Thomas d Edward H. Griffith, George Cukor ph Oliver T. Marsh m Edward Ward

Joan Crawford, Robert Montgomery, Franchot Tone, Charles Ruggles, Edna May Oliver, Gail Patrick, Reginald Denny, Arthur Treacher

No No Nanette
US 1930 90m approx bw with Technicolor sequences

A married bible publisher secretly helps three girls, who all visit him on the same day. Early talkie version of the rather naïve musical hit, with a priceless moment or two among the dross. Bernice Claire, Lucien Littlefield, Lilyan Tashman, Bert Roach, Zasu Pitts. Written by Howard Emmett Rogers, from the play by Otto Harbach and Frank Mandel; directed by Clarence Badger; for Warner.

No Orchids for Miss Blandish
GB 1948 102m bw
Renown (A. R. Shipman, Oswald Mitchell)

An heiress is kidnapped by gangsters and falls for their psychopathic leader.
Hilariously awful gangster movie from a bestselling shocker. Everyone concerned is all at sea, and the result is one of the worst films ever made.

wd St John L. Clowes, *novel* James Hadley Chase ph Gerald Gibbs

Jack La Rue, Linden Travers, Hugh McDermott, Walter Crisham, Lily Molnar, Zoe Gail

'This must be the most sickening exhibition of brutality, perversion, sex and sadism ever to be shown on a cinema screen . . . with pseudo-American accents the actors literally battle their way through a script laden with suggestive dialogue.'—*MFB*

† Remade as *The Grissom Gang* (qv).

No Parking
GB 1938 72m bw
Herbert Wilcox

A car park attendant is mistaken for an American killer.
Modest, entertaining star comedy.

w Gerald Elliott, *story* Carol Reed d Jack Raymond

Gordon Harker, Leslie Perrins, Irene Ware, Cyril Smith

No Peace among the Olives
Italy 1950 99m bw
Lux (Domenico Davanzati)

A young shepherd goes home after the war and finds himself at war again—against a local racketeer.
A rather crude melodrama comparable with the American *Thieves' Highway* and other *films noirs* of the time.

w Giuseppe de Santis and others d Giuseppe de Santis ph Pietro Portalupi m Goffredo Petrassi

Lucia Bose, Raf Vallone, Folco Lulli, Dante Maggio

No Place for Jennifer
GB 1949 90m bw

Divorcing parents think again when their twelve-year-old daughter runs away. Very predictable tearjerker which kept box offices busy in its day. Leo Genn, Rosamund John, Janette Scott, Beatrice Campbell, Guy Middleton, Anthony Nicholls, Jean Cadell. Written by J. Lee-Thompson, from the novel *No Difference to Me* by Phyllis Hambledon; directed by Henry Cass; for ABPC.

No Questions Asked
US 1951 80m bw
MGM (Nicholas Nayfack)

A young lawyer undertakes shady business and finds himself framed for murder.
Well made second feature on conventional lines.

w Sidney Sheldon d Harold Kress ph Harold Lipstein m Leith Stevens

Barry Sullivan, George Murphy, Arlene Dahl, Jean Hagen, William Reynolds, Mari Blanchard

No Resting Place
GB 1951 77m bw
Colin Lesslie

A wandering Irish tinker accidentally kills a man and is hounded by a Civil Guard.
Interesting attempt at realistic location drama, suffering from a dejected plot and unsympathetic characters.

w Paul Rotha, Colin Lesslie, Michael Orrom, novel Ian Niall d Paul Rotha ph Wolfgang Suschitsky m William Alwyn

Michael Gough, Noel Purcell, Jack McGowran

No Room at the Inn
GB 1948 82m bw
British National (Ivan Foxwell)

A monstrous woman half-starves evacuees and turns her house into a brothel.
Absurd melodrama from a play which was popular because it offered a full-blooded star performance. The film is less convincing but works pretty well on its level.

w Ivan Foxwell, Dylan Thomas, play Joan Temple d Dan Birt ph James Wilson

Freda Jackson, Joy Shelton, Hermione Baddeley, Joan Dowling, Harcourt Williams, Sydney Tafler, Frank Pettingell, Niall MacGinnis

No Sad Songs for Me
US 1950 89m bw
Columbia (Buddy Adler)

A young wife discovers she has only eight months to live, and spends it planning her husband's future.
Well-meant but rather icky melodrama featuring one of those beautiful illnesses that appear to have no physical effect.

w Howard Koch, novel Ruth Southard d Rudolph Maté ph Joseph Walker m George Duning

Margaret Sullavan, Wendell Corey, Viveca Lindfors, Natalie Wood, John McIntire

AAN: George Duning

No Sex Please, We're British°
GB 1973 91m Technicolor
Columbia / BHP (John R. Sloan)

A wrongly addressed parcel of dirty postcards causes chaos when it arrives at a bank.
Archetypal British farce with less plot than one might expect, but quite brightly performed.

w Anthony Marriott, Johnnie Mortimer, Brian Cooke, play Anthony Marriott, Alistair Foot d Cliff Owen ph Ken Hodges m Eric Rogers

Ronnie Corbett, Beryl Reid, *Arthur Lowe,* Ian Ogilvy, Susan Penhaligon, David Swift, Michael Bates, Gerald Sim

No Time for Comedy°
US 1940 93m bw
Warner (Robert Lord)

A playwright is depressed by the times and has lost the knack of making people laugh.
Smooth film version of a thoughtful romantic comedy play.

w Julius J. and Philip G. Epstein, play S. N. Behrman d William Keighley ph Ernest Haller m Heinz Roemheld

James Stewart, Rosalind Russell, Charles Ruggles, Genevieve Tobin, Allyn Joslyn, Clarence Kolb, Louise Beavers

No Time for Love°
US 1943 83m bw
Paramount (Mitchell Leisen)

A lady photographer falls for the foreman of a crew digging a tunnel under the Hudson.
Agreeable romantic slapstick farce.

w Claude Binyon d Mitchell Leisen ph Charles Lang Jnr m Victor Young

Claudette Colbert, Fred MacMurray, Ilka Chase, Richard Haydn, June Havoc, Marjorie Gateson, Bill Goodwin

No Time for Sergeants
US 1958 111m bw
Warner (Mervyn Le Roy)

Adventures of a hillbilly army conscript.
Heavy-handed adaptation of the stage success, a real piece of filmed theatre with not much sparkle to it.

w John Lee Mahin, play Ira Levin, novel Mac Hyman d Mervyn Le Roy ph Harold Rosson m Ray Heindorf

Andy Griffith, William Fawcett, Murray Hamilton, Nick Adams, Myron McCormick, Bartlett Robinson

No Trees in the Street
GB 1958 96m bw
ABP / Allegro (Frank Godwin)

Problems of a London slum family in the thirties.
Artificial and unconvincing attempt at a London *Love on the Dole*, dragged up and redigested in a later era when 'realism' was thought to be fashionable.

w Ted Willis, from his play *d* J. Lee-Thompson *ph* Gilbert Taylor *m* Laurie Johnson

Sylvia Syms, Herbert Lom, Joan Miller, Melvyn Hayes, Stanley Holloway, Liam Redmond, Ronald Howard, Carole Lesley, Lana Morris, Lily Kann

'Nothing remains but crude sensationalism and several moments of unconscious humour.'—*MFB*

No Way Out*
US 1950 106m bw
TCF (Darryl F. Zanuck)

A crook stirs up racial feeling against a black doctor in whose hands his brother has died.
Vivid, hard-hitting melodrama with a hospital background and a strong sociological flavour.

w Joseph L. Mankiewicz, Lesser Samuels
d Joseph L. Mankiewicz *ph Milton Krasner*
m Alfred Newman

Richard Widmark, Sidney Poitier, Linda Darnell, Stephen McNally, Harry Bellaver, Stanley Ridges, Ossie Davis, Ruby Dee

'A production designed solely for purposes of agitation and propaganda, unworthy of literary or cinematic consideration.'—*Henry Hart, Films in Review*

AAN: script

No Way to Treat a Lady*
US 1968 108m Technicolor
Paramount / Sol C. Siegel

A mass murderer of women who is also a master of disguise has a running battle with a police detective.
Curious mixture of star show-off piece, murder mystery, black farce, suspense melodrama and Jewish comedy. Bits of it come off very well, but it's a bumpy ride.

w John Gay, *novel* William Goldman *d* Jack Smight *ph* Jack Priestley *m* Stanley Myers

Rod Steiger, George Segal, Lee Remick, Eileen Heckart, Murray Hamilton, Michael Dunn

Noah's Ark**
US 1929 135m bw
Warner

The biblical story of Noah is paralleled, rather loosely, with a tragedy of World War I.

Naïve but fascinating Hollywood epic which in patches triumphantly overcomes the problems of the part-talkie period and is always fascinating to look at.

w Anthony Coldeway, Darryl F. Zanuck
d Michael Curtiz ph Hal Mohr, Barney McGill *ph* Anton Grot

Dolores Costello, Noah Beery, Louise Fazenda, Guinn Williams, Paul McAllister, Myrna Loy

'The sweetest love story ever told! The epic drama of the age! Drama with a world sweep, colossal and sublime!'—*publicity*

Nob Hill*
US 1945 95m Technicolor
TCF (André Daven)

In the gay nineties, a San Francisco saloon owner tries to step into society and win one of its most eligible young ladies.
Engaging period musical drama with all talents working well.

w Wanda Tuchock, Norman Reilly Raine
d Henry Hathaway *ph* Edward Cronjager
md Emil Newman, Charles Henderson

George Raft, Joan Bennett, Peggy Ann Garner, Vivian Blaine, Alan Reed, B. S. Pully, Edgar Barrier

Nobody Lives Forever
US 1946 100m bw
Warner (Robert Buckner)

A con man fleeces a rich widow, then falls in love with her.
Forgettable romantic melodrama.

w W. R. Burnett *d* Jean Negulesco
ph Arthur Edeson *m* Adolph Deutsch

John Garfield, Geraldine Fitzgerald, Walter Brennan, Faye Emerson, George Coulouris, George Tobias

Nobody Runs Forever*
GB 1968 101m Eastmancolor
Rank / Selmur (Betty E. Box)
US title: *The High Commissioner*

An Australian detective is sent to arrest the high commissioner in London on a charge of murdering his first wife.
Sub-Hitchcock thriller which comes to life in patches but has a plot and dialogue which obviously embarrass the actors.

w Wilfred Greatorex, *novel* The High Commissioner by Jon Cleary *ph* Ernest Steward *m* Georges Delerue

Rod Taylor, Christopher Plummer, Lilli Palmer, Camilla Sparv, Daliah Lavi, Clive Revill, Lee Montague, Calvin Lockhart, Derren Nesbitt, Leo McKern, Franchot Tone

Nobody's Perfect
US 1968   103m   Techniscope
Universal (Howard Christie)

An ex-naval officer returns to Japan to make amends for stealing a buddha.
Flatfooted comedy adventure.

w John D. F. Black, *novel* The Crows of Edwina Hill by Allan R. Bosworth d Alan Rafkin ph Robert H. Wyckoff m Irving Gertz

Doug McClure, Nancy Kwan, Steve Carlson, James Whitmore, David Hartman, Gary Vinson, James Shigeta

Nocturne*
US 1946   87m   bw
RKO (Joan Harrison)

A police detective investigates the death of a composer.
Amusingly self-mocking crime thriller, quite smoothly done in all departments.

w *Jonathan Latimer d Edwin L. Marin*
ph Harry J. Wild m Leigh Harline

George Raft, Lynn Bari, Virginia Huston, Joseph Pevney, Myrna Dell, Edward Ashley, Walter Sande, Mabel Paige

Non Stop New York
GB 1937   71m   bw
GFD / Gaumont

In 1940, gangsters on a transatlantic airliner try to kill a key witness.
Slightly futuristic thriller of its time, now hilariously dated but quite entertaining as well as giving a rare picture of air travel in the thirties.

w Curt Siodmak, Roland Pertwee, J. O. C. Orton, Derek Twist, *novel* Sky Steward by Ken Attiwill d Robert Stevenson

John Loder, Anna Lee, Francis L. Sullivan, Frank Cellier, Desmond Tester, Athene Seyler, Jerry Verno

None But the Brave
US 1965   105m   Technicolor
   Panavision
Warner / Eiga / Toho / Artanis (Frank Sinatra)

During World War II a plane carrying US Marines to the Pacific front crashlands on an island held by Japanese.
Anti-war melodrama in which the action scenes are more memorable than the admirable sentiments.

w John Twist, Katsuya Susaki d Frank Sinatra ph Harold Lipstein m Johnny Williams

Frank Sinatra, Clint Walker, Tommy Sands, Tony Bill, Brad Dexter

None But the Lonely Heart*
US 1944   113m   bw
RKO (David Hempstead)

In the thirties, a cockney drifter finds himself when he learns that his mother is dying.
Wildly astonishing moodpiece to come from Hollywood during World War II; its picture of East End low life is as rocky as its star performance, but it started Miss Barrymore on the west coast career which sustained her old age.

wd Clifford Odets, *novel* Richard Llewellyn
ph George Barnes m Hanns Eisler
md Constantin Bakaleinikoff

Cary Grant, *Ethel Barrymore*, June Duprez, Barry Fitzgerald, Jane Wyatt, George Coulouris, Dan Duryea, Konstantin Shayne, Morton Lowry, Helene Thimig

'A perplexing mixture of good and bad, authentic and phony.'—*Hermione Rich Isaacs, Theatre Arts*

AA: Ethel Barrymore
AAN: Hanns Eisler; Cary Grant

None Shall Escape*
US 1944   85m   bw
Columbia (Sam Bischoff)

The career of a Nazi officer shown as flashbacks from his trial as a war criminal.
Taut topical melodrama reflecting the mood of the time.

w Lester Cole d André de Toth ph Lee Garmes m Ernst Toch

Alexander Knox, Marsha Hunt, Henry Travers, Dorothy Morris, Richard Crane

AA: Lester Cole; original story (Alfred Neumann, Joseph Thau)

Noose
GB 1948   98m   bw
ABPC / Edward Dryhurst

A Soho black market gang is exposed.
Vivid though rather tatty film version of a West End play success.

w Richard Llewellyn, from his play
d Edmond T. Greville ph Hone Glendining
m Charles Williams

Nigel Patrick, Carole Landis, Derek Farr, Joseph Calleia, Stanley Holloway, Hay Petrie, John Slater

The Noose Hangs High
US 1948   77m   bw

Two window washers are hired by a crooked bookie who finds their incompetence hard to tolerate when they lose his winnings. Thin star comedy filled with the team's cornier routines, not too cleverly revived. Bud Abbott, Lou Costello, Leon Errol, Joseph Calleia, Murray Leonard, Cathy Downs, Mike Mazurki, Fritz Feld. Written by John Grant and Howard Harris; directed by Charles Barton; for Eagle-Lion. (A previous film of the same story was made in 1939 under the title *For Love or Money*, with June Lang, Robert Kent and Ed Brophy.)

Nora Prentiss*
US 1946   117m   bw
Warner (William Jacobs)

A doctor falls for a café singer who ruins his life.
Standard star melodrama aimed at women, and appreciated by them.

w N. Richard Nash, *story* Paul Webster, Jack Sobell   *d* Vincent Sherman   *ph* James Wong Howe   *m* Franz Waxman

Ann Sheridan, Kent Smith, Bruce Bennett, Robert Alda, Rosemary de Camp, John Ridgely, Wanda Hendrix

'A mouth like hers is just for kissing . . . not for telling!'—*publicity*

Norma Rae*
US 1979   114m   De Luxe   Panavision
TCF / Martin Ritt / Rose and Asseyev

A southern girl becomes an angry union organizer.
Well-intentioned and well-acted pamphlet of political enlightenment with an inevitably ambivalent attitude.

w Irving Ravetch, Harriet Frank Jnr   *d* Martin Ritt   *ph* John A. Alonzo   *m* David Shire
pd Walter Scott Herndon

Sally Field, Beau Bridges, Ron Leibman, Pat Hingle, Barbara Baxley

Norman, Is That You?
US 1976   92m   Metrocolor

Adulterous parents find that their son is a homosexual. Unattractive comedy roughly filmed and given a black ambience. Not worth buying a ticket. Redd Foxx, Pearl Bailey, Dennis Dugan, Michael Warren, Tamara Dobson. From the play by Ron Clark and Sam Bobrick; directed by George Schlatter; for George Schlatter / MGM.

The Norseman
US 1978   90m   Movielab
AIP / Charles B. Pierce / Fawcett Majors

A Viking heads across the sea to America in search of his long lost father.
Low grade hokum for the easily pleased.

wd Charles B. Pierce   *ph* Robert Bethard
m Jaime Mendoza-Nava

Lee Majors, Cornel Wilde, Mel Ferrer, Jack Elam, Chris Connelly

The North Avenue Irregulars
US 1978   99m   Technicolor

A Presbyterian minister becomes an undercover agent for the FBI, helping to expose a crooked gambling syndicate. Very heavy comedy which seems to find itself much funnier than the audience does. Edward Herrmann, Barbara Harris, Susan Clark, Karen Valentine, Michael Constantine, Cloris Leachman, Patsy Kelly, Douglas Fowley, Alan Hale Jnr. Written by Don Tait, from the novel by the Rev. Albert Fay Hill; directed by Bruce Bilson; for Disney. (GB title: *Hill's Angels*.)

North by Northwest****
US 1959   136m   Technicolor
   Vistavision
MGM (Alfred Hitchcock)

A businessman is mistaken for a spy, and enemy agents then try to kill him because he knows too much.
Delightful chase comedy-thriller with a touch of sex, a kind of compendium of its director's best work, with memories of *The 39 Steps*, *Saboteur* and *Foreign Correspondent* among others.

w Ernest Lehman   *d* Alfred Hitchcock
ph Robert Burks   *m* Bernard Herrmann

Cary Grant, Eva Marie Saint, James Mason Leo G. Carroll, Martin Landau, Jessie Royce Landis, Adam Williams

'It is only when you adopt the basic premise that Cary Grant could not possibly come to harm that the tongue in Hitchcock's cheek becomes plainly visible.'—*Hollis Alpert, Saturday Review*

AAN: Ernest Lehman

North Dallas Forty
US 1979   118m   Metrocolor
Paramount (Frank Yablans)

The gruelling life of a professional football player, laced with drugs, sex and alcohol.
Well made but generally unattractive, the kind of movie for which one wouldn't expect to find an audience.

w Frank Yablans, Ted Kotcheff, Peter Gent, *novel* Peter Gent   *d* Ted Kotcheff   *ph* Paul Lohmann   *m* John Scott   *pd* Alfred Sweeney

Nick Nolte, Mac Davis, Charles Durning, Dayle Haddon, Bo Swenson

North Sea Hijack
GB 1979   100m   Technicolor
Universal / Cinema Seven (Mo Rothman)
US title: *ffoulkes*

A British oil rig in the North Sea is held for ransom.
Asinine *Boy's Own Paper* adventure story with the very minimum of thrills and a totally miscast hero.

w Jack Davies, from his novel Esther, Ruth and Jennifer d Andrew V. McLaglen
ph Tony Imi m Michael J. Lewis pd Maurice Carter

Roger Moore, Anthony Perkins, James Mason, Michael Parks, David Hedison, Jack Watson, George Baker, Faith Brook

North Star*
US 1943   105m   bw
Samuel Goldwyn (William Cameron Menzies)
aka: *Armored Attack*

A Russian village defends itself against the Nazi onslaught.
Highly artificial propaganda piece later disowned by its makers and retitled. Good acting can't make its mark when the Russian steppes become a never-never land.

w Lillian Hellmann d Lewis Milestone
ph James Wong Howe m Aaron Copland

Anne Baxter, Farley Granger, Jane Withers, Dana Andrews, Walter Brennan, Erich Von Stroheim, Dean Jagger, Ann Harding, Carl Benton Reid, Walter Huston

'Putting American villagers into Russian costumes and calling them by Russian names is never going to deceive this old bird.'—*James Agate*
'Its failure is the case history of every Hollywood film that steps out of its scope.'—*Richard Winnington*
'Something to be seen more in sorrow than in anger and more in the attitude of the diagnostician in any emotion at all.'—*James Agee*

AAN: Lillian Hellmann; James Wong Howe; Aaron Copland

North to Alaska*
US 1960   122m   De Luxe   Cinemascope
TCF (Henry Hathaway)

In 1900, two successful gold prospectors have woman trouble.
Good-natured brawling adventure story which

could do with cutting but is certainly the type of action movie they don't make 'em like any more.

w John Lee Mahin, Martin Rackin, Claude Binyon, *play* Birthday Gift by Ladislas Fodor
d Henry Hathaway ph Leon Shamroy
m Lionel Newman

John Wayne, Stewart Granger, Fabian, Capucine, Ernie Kovacs, Mickey Shaughnessy, Karl Swenson, Joe Sawyer, John Qualen

North to the Klondike
US 1942   60m   bw

Gold hunters protect the rights of a girl who has made a strike. Typical economy size programme filler with a studio look and a stalwart cast. Broderick Crawford, Lon Chaney Jnr, Andy Devine, Evelyn Ankers, Keye Luke. Written by Clarence Upson Young, Lew Sarecky, George Bricker and William Castle; directed by Erle C. Kenton; for Universal.

Northern Pursuit*
US 1943   94m   bw
Warner (Jack Chertok)

A Mountie tracks a stranded Nazi pilot through the Canadian wastes.
Rather unusual star actioner, not badly done.

w Frank Gruber, Alvah Bessie d Raoul Walsh ph Sid Hickox m Adolph Deutsch

Errol Flynn, Helmut Dantine, Julie Bishop, John Ridgely, Gene Lockhart, Tom Tully, Bernard Nedell

Northwest Frontier***
GB 1959   129m   Eastmancolor
Cinemascope
Rank / Marcel Hellman
US title: *Flame Over India*

In 1905 an English officer during a rebellion escorts a young Hindu prince on a dangerous train journey.
Thoroughly enjoyable Boys' Own Paper adventure story with excellent set pieces and a spot-the-villain mystery.

w *Robin Estridge d J. Lee-Thompson*
ph Geoffrey Unsworth m Mischa Spoliansky

Kenneth More, Lauren Bacall, Herbert Lom, Ursula Jeans, Wilfrid Hyde White, I. S. Johar, Eugene Deckers, Ian Hunter

'*Northwest Frontier* seems to have borrowed its eccentric engine from *The General*, its hazardous expedition from *Stagecoach* and its background of tribal violence from *The Drum*.'—*Penelope Houston*

Northwest Mounted Police*
US 1940   125m   Technicolor
Paramount (Cecil B. de Mille)

A Texas Ranger seeks a fugitive in Canada.
Typical big-scale action concoction by de
Mille, but in this case none of it's very
memorable and the detail is poor.

w Alan Le May, Jesse Lasky Jnr, C. Gardner
Sullivan d Cecil B. de Mille ph Victor
Milner, Howard Greene m Victor Young

Gary Cooper, Paulette Goddard, Madeleine
Carroll, Preston Foster, Robert Preston,
George Bancroft, Lynne Overman, Akim
Tamiroff, Walter Hampden, Lon Chaney Jnr,
Montagu Love, George E. Stone
    'Two hours of colour, killing, kindness and
magnificent country.'—Otis Ferguson
    'A movie in the grand style. God's own
biggest trees and mountains for prop and
backdrop; staunch courage and lofty aims
among the good people; cunning and
treachery lurking within the sinister forces; the
ominous note of doom finally stifled by the
fortitude of noble men.'—Time

AAN: Victor Milner, Howard Greene; Victor
Young

Northwest Outpost
US 1947   91m   bw
Republic (Allan Dwan)
GB title: End of the Rainbow

Adventures of California cavalrymen.
Milk-and-water adventures in a forgettable
operetta.

w Elizabeth Meehan, Richard Sale d Allan
Dwan ph Reggie Lanning m Rudolf Friml

Nelson Eddy, Ilona Massey, Hugo Haas, Elsa
Lanchester

Northwest Passage***
(Part One, Rogers' Rangers)
US 1940   126m   Technicolor
MGM (Hunt Stromberg)

Colonial rangers fight it out with hostile
Indians.
Part Two was never made, but no one seemed
to mind that the characters in Part One never
got round to seeking the titular sea route. The
adventures depicted had the feel of historical
actuality, and the star was well cast.

w Lawrence Stallings, Talbot Jennings, novel
Kenneth Roberts d King Vidor ph Sidney
Wagner, William V. Skall m Herbert Stothart

Spencer Tracy, Robert Young, Ruth Hussey,
Walter Brennan, Nat Pendleton, Robert
Barrat, Lumsden Hare, Donald MacBride
    'Half men, half demons, warriors such as

the world has never known . . . they lived with
death and danger for the women who
hungered for their love!'—publicity

AAN: Sidney Wagner, William V. Skall

Norwood
US 1969   95m   Technicolor
Paramount / Hal B. Wallis

A Vietnam veteran returns to his Texas home
but feels restless and decides to become a
radio singer.
A rather ordinary film about an innocent
abroad, neither very funny nor very moving.

w Marguerite Roberts d Jack Haley Jnr
ph Robert B. Hauser m Al de Lory

Glen Campbell, Kim Darby, Joe Namath,
Carol Lynley, Pat Hingle, Tisha Sterling, Dom
De Luise, Jack Haley, Cass Daley, Gil Lamb

Nosferatu***
Germany 1921   72m approx (24 fps)   bw
Prana

Count Dracula goes to Bremen and is
destroyed by sunlight.
An unofficial treatment of the Bram Stoker
novel, with a terrifying count and several
splendid moments. It took its director to
Hollywood.

w Henrik Galeen d F. W. Murnau ph Fritz
Arno Wagner ad Albin Grau

Max Schreck, Gustav Von Wangenheim,
Greta Schroeder, Alexander Granach

Not as a Stranger**
US 1955   135m   bw
UA / Stanley Kramer

A medical student has professional and
personal struggles.
Earnest filming of a bestseller, with all the
actors too old for their parts.

w Edna and Edward Anhalt, novel Morton
Thompson d Stanley Kramer ph Franz
Planer m George Antheil pd Rudolph
Sternad

Robert Mitchum, Olivia de Havilland,
Broderick Crawford, Frank Sinatra, Gloria
Grahame, Charles Bickford, Myron
McCormick, Lon Chaney Jnr, Jesse White,
Henry Morgan, Lee Marvin, Virginia
Christine

Not Now, Darling
GB 1972   97m   Eastmancolor

A furrier gets into a complicated situation
when he arranges for his mistress to have a
cheap mink coat. Interminable film version (in
Multivista, a shoot-and-edit equivalent to TV

taping which gives a dingy look and can only
work in a single set) of a West End farce
which wasn't marvellous to begin with. Leslie
Phillips, Ray Cooney, Moira Lister, Julie Ege,
Joan Sims, Derren Nesbitt, Barbara Windsor,
Jack Hulbert, Cicely Courtneidge, Bill Fraser.
Written by John Chapman, from the play by
Ray Cooney; directed by Ray Cooney and
David Croft; for LMG / Sedgemoor / Not
Now Films.

Not of This Earth**
US 1957 72m bw
AA (Roger Corman)

An alien comes to earth in human form in
search of blood which may save his planet.
Modestly budgeted minor sci-fi; ruthless,
original and competent.

w *Charles Griffith, Mark Hanna d Roger
Corman ph* John Mescall *m* Ronald Stein

Paul Birch, Beverly Garland, Morgan Jones

Not So Dumb
US 1929   80m approx at 24 fps   bw
   silent

A naïve girl throws a big party in the hope of
advancing her boy friend's career. Popular
comedy of its time. Marion Davies, Elliott
Nugent, Raymond Hackett, Franklin
Pangborn, Julia Faye. Written by Wanda
Tuchock and Edwin Justus Mayer, from the
play *Dulcy* by George S. Kaufman and Marc
Connolly; directed by King Vidor; for MGM.
(NB: Previously made as *Dulcy* by Warner in
1923, directed by Sidney Franklin, with
Constance Talmadge.)

Not with My Wife You Don't
US 1966   119m   Technicolor
Warner / Fernwood / Reynard (Norman
   Panama, Joel Freeman)

A Korean war veteran is furious when an old
rival turns up in London and again makes eyes
at his wife.
Extraordinarily flat star comedy of cross and
double cross among friends.

w *Norman Panama, Larry Gelbart, Peter
Barnes d* Norman Panama *ph* Charles Lang,
Paul Beeson *m* Johnny Williams

Tony Curtis, George C. Scott, Virna Lisi,
Carroll O'Connor, Richard Eastham
   'About as frothy as a tin of dehydrated
milk.'—*MFB*
   'It has all the verve, subtlety and
sophistication of its title.'—*Judith Crist*

Nothing But the Best**
GB 1964   99m   Eastmancolor
Anglo Amalgamated / Domino (David
   Deutsch)

An ambitious clerk learns to fight his way to
the top by cheek and one-upmanship.
Hard, skilful, rather unattractive comedy with
interesting social comments on its time.

w *Frederic Raphael d Clive Donner
ph* Nicolas Roeg *m* Ron Grainer *ad* Reece
Pemberton

Alan Bates, Denholm Elliott, Harry Andrews,
Millicent Martin, Pauline Delany

Nothing But the Night*
GB 1972   90m   Eastmancolor
Rank / Charlemagne (Anthony Nelson
   Keys)

The trustees of an orphanage die off
mysteriously, and it seems that the orphans
themselves are responsible.
Convoluted murder mystery with horror
elements and a twist hardly worth waiting for;
earnest performances help.

w *Brian Hayles, novel* John Blackburn
d Peter Sasdy *ph* Ken Talbot *m* Malcolm
Williamson

Christopher Lee, Peter Cushing, Diana Dors,
Georgia Brown, Keith Barron, John Robinson

Nothing But Trouble
US 1945   70m   bw
MGM (B. F. Ziedman)

A chef and butler accidentally prevent a
poison plot against a young king.
Feebly-devised star comedy, their last for a big
studio.

w *Russel Rouse, Ray Golden d* Sam Taylor
ph Charles Salerno Jnr *m* Nathaniel Shilkret

Stan Laurel, Oliver Hardy, Mary Boland,
Henry O'Neill, David Leland

Nothing Personal
US 1980   97m   Movielab

A professor and a lady lawyer try to stop seal
hunting. The subject is an unsuitable starting
point for a thin and zany comedy which gets
nowhere and stays there. Donald Sutherland,
Suzanne Somers, Larence Dane, Roscoe Lee
Browne. Written by Robert Kaufman;
directed by George Bloomfield; for David M.
Perlmutter / AIP.

Nothing Sacred****
US 1937   77m   Technicolor
David O. Selznick

A girl thought to be dying of a rare disease is
built up by the press into a national heroine;
but the diagnosis was wrong.
Hollywood's most bitter and hilarious satire,
with crazy comedy elements and superb
wisecracks; a joy.

w Ben Hecht, story Letter to the Editor by James H. Street *d* William Wellman *ph* W. Howard Greene *m* Oscar Levant

Carole Lombard, Fredric March, Walter Connolly, Charles Winninger, Sig Rumann, Frank Fay, Maxie Rosenbloom, Margaret Hamilton, Hedda Hopper, Monty Woolley, Hattie McDaniel, Olin Howland, John Qualen † Refashioned in 1953 as a stage musical, *Hazel Flagg*, with music by Jule Styne; this in turn became a Martin and Lewis comedy *Living It Up* (Jerry Lewis in the Carole Lombard part).

Notorious***
US 1946 101m bw
RKO (Alfred Hitchcock)

In Rio, a notorious lady marries a Nazi renegade to help the US government but finds herself falling in love with her contact.
Superb romantic suspenser containing some of Hitchcock's best work.

w Ben Hecht d Alfred Hitchcock ph Ted Tetzlaff *m* Roy Webb

Cary Grant, Ingrid Bergman, Claude Rains, Louis Calhern, Leopoldine Konstantin, Reinhold Schunzel

'Velvet smooth in dramatic action, sharp and sure in its characters, and heavily charged with the intensity of warm emotional appeal.'—*Bosley Crowther*

'The suspense is terrific.'—*New Yorker, 1976*

'A film in the supercharged American idiom which made *Casablanca* popular.'—*Hermione Rich Isaacs, Theatre Arts*

AAN: Ben Hecht; Claude Rains

The Notorious Landlady
GB 1962 127m bw
Columbia / Kohlr ar / Quine (Fred Kohlmar)

An American diplomat in London takes rooms with a murder suspect; after many mysterious happenings he helps to clear her.
Flatly whimsical goings on in comical old London, complete with fog and eccentrics. The actors all try hard but are deflated by the script.

w Larry Gelbart, Richard Quine *d* Richard Quine *ph* Arthur E. Arling *m* George Duning

Kim Novak, Jack Lemmon, Fred Astaire, Lionel Jeffries, Estelle Winwood, Maxwell Reed

La Notte*
Italy / France 1960 121m bw
Nepi / Sofitedip / Silver

A moderately successful novelist and his wife begin to question their marriage and their life. Slow but engaging character drama set during one night in Milan.

w Michelangelo Antonioni, Ennio Flaiano, Antonio Guerra *d Michelangelo Antonioni ph* Gianni di Venanzo *m* Giorgio Gaslini

Marcello Mastroianni, Jeanne Moreau, Monica Vitti, Bernhard Wicki

Nous Sommes Tous les Assassins*
France 1952 108m bw
UGC
aka: *Are We All Murderers?*

An illiterate youth is taught to kill during the war; afterwards he kills again for money and is sent for execution.
A solemn sermon on capital punishment, and a powerful though rather glib one.

w André Cayatte, Charles Spaak *d* André Cayatte *ph* Jean Bourgoin

Marcel Mouloudji, Raymond Péllégrin, Antoine Balpêtre, Claude Laydu

Les Nouveaux Messieurs*
France 1928 135m approx (24 fps) bw silent
Albatros / Séquance

A glamorous dancer forsakes a count for a rising trade union official.
Lengthy political satire which caused a few headlines when first released.

w Charles Spaak, Jacques Feyder, *play* Robert de Flers, Francis de Grosset *d* Jacques Feyder *ph* Georges Périnal, Maurice Defassiaux *ad* Lazare Meerson

Albert Préjean, Gaby Morlay, Henri Roussel

Now About These Women . . .*
Sweden 1964 80m Eastmancolor
Svensk Filmindustri
aka: *All These Women*

A critic comes to stay with a famous cellist whose biography he is writing, but his efforts are hampered by all the women in the house. Virtually indescribable black farce comedy which doesn't really work, yet, as always with this director, is continually of interest.

w Erland Josephson, Ingmar Bergman *d* Ingmar Bergman *ph* Sven Nykvist *m* Erik Nordgren

Jarl Kulle, Georg Funkquist, Eva Dahlbeck, Karen Kavli, Harriet Andersson, Bibi Andersson, Gertrud Fridh

Now and Forever*
US 1934 82m bw
Paramount (Louis D. Lighton)

A jewel thief and his mistress are taught a thing or two by his small daughter.
Odd mixture of comedy and drama which was box office at the time but seems pretty dated after nearly fifty years, though technically very smooth.

w Vincent Lawrence, Sylvia Thalberg
d Henry Hathaway ph Harry Fischbeck

Gary Cooper, Carole Lombard, Shirley Temple, Guy Standing, Charlotte Granville, Gilbert Emery, Henry Kolker

'Expertly contrived to furnish first-rate entertainment.'—*Thornton Delehanty, New York Post*

Now Barabbas ...
GB 1949   87m   bw
Warner / Anatole de Grunwald
aka: *Now Barabbas Was a Robber*

Stories of men in prison.
Thinly intercut dramas; from a stage success.

w Anatole de Grunwald, *play* William Douglas Home d Gordon Parry ph Otto Heller

Richard Greene, Cedric Hardwicke, William Hartnell, Kathleen Harrison, Leslie Dwyer, Richard Burton, Kenneth More, Ronald Howard, Stephen Murray, Beatrice Campbell, Betty Ann Davies, Alec Clunes

Now I'll Tell
US 1934   72m   bw
Fox (Winfield Sheehan)
GB title: *When New York Sleeps*

The story of Arnold Rothstein, gambler-racketeer of the twenties, as told by his widow.
Competent crime / domestic programmer.

wd Edwin Burke ph Ernest Palmer m Hugo Friedhofer

Spencer Tracy, Helen Twelvetrees, Hobart Cavanaugh, Alice Faye, G. P. Huntley Jnr, Shirley Temple, Leon Ames

'In spite of the breezy sequences with which it starts, it quickly gets improbable and goes from bad to maudlin.'—*Otis Ferguson*

Now Voyager***
US 1942   117m   bw
Warner (Hal B. Wallis)

A dowdy frustrated spinster takes the psychiatric cure and embarks on a doomed love affair.
A basically soggy script still gets by, and how, through the romantic magic of its stars, who were all at their best; and suffering in mink went over very big in wartime.

w Casey Robinson, *novel* Olive Higgins Prouty d Irving Rapper ph Sol Polito m Max Steiner

Bette Davis, Claude Rains, Paul Henreid, Gladys Cooper, John Loder, Bonita Granville, Ilka Chase, Lee Patrick, Charles Drake, Franklin Pangborn

'If it were better, it might not work at all. This way, it's a crummy classic.'—*New Yorker, 1977*

AA: Max Steiner
AAN: Bette Davis; Gladys Cooper

Now You See Him Now You Don't
US 1972   88m   Technicolor
Walt Disney

Two students discover an elixir of invisibility and help prevent a gangster from taking over the college.
Flat Disney frolic with fair trick effects.

w Joseph L. McEveety d Robert Butler
ph Frank Phillips m Robert F. Brunner
sp Eustace Lycett, Danny Lee

Kurt Russell, Cesar Romero, Joe Flynn, Jim Backus, William Windom, Edward Andrews, Richard Bakalyan

Nowhere to Go
GB 1958   87m   bw
Ealing (Eric Williams)

A thief escapes from prison but can get no help from the underworld and is accidentally shot after being sheltered by a socialite.
Glum character melodrama which fails to sustain interest despite the best intentions.

w Seth Holt, Ken Tynan, *book* Donald MacKenzie d Seth Holt ph Paul Beeson
m Dizzy Reece

George Nader, Maggie Smith, Bernard Lee, Geoffrey Keen, Andree Melly, Bessie Love, Howard Marion Crawford

The Nude Bomb
US 1980   94m   Technicolor

An incompetent secret agent chases a missile-launching villain. Curious and unsatisfactory attempt to revive a twenty-year-old TV situation comedy minus half its personnel.
Don Adams, Sylvia Kristel, Dana Elcar, Rhonda Fleming, Andrea Howard, Norman Lloyd. Written by Arne Sultan, Bill Dana and Leonard B. Stern; directed by Clive Donner; for Universal. 'Fans of the vidshow will derive much more enjoyment by crowding round their television sets with a bowl of popcorn watching *Get Smart* re-runs.'—*Variety*.

Number Seventeen*
GB 1932 63m bw
BIP (John Maxwell)

A girl jewel thief reforms and helps the police track down her former gang.

Minor Hitchcock thriller largely confined to a single interior until the final train chase, which despite obvious models remains exhilarating.

w Alfred Hitchcock, Alma Reville, Rodney Ackland, *play* J. Jefferson Farjeon *d Alfred Hitchcock ph* Jack Cox

Leon M. Lion, Anne Grey, John Stuart, Donald Calthrop, Barry Jones, Garry Marsh
† The same play had been filmed as a silent in 1928 by Geza Bolvary, with Guy Newall; it was shot in Germany.

The Nun and the Sergeant
US 1962 74m bw
UA / Springfield

In Korea, a tough sergeant commanding a 'dirty dozen' mission is joined by a schoolgirl and a nun.

Minor war adventure, moderately well done but highly unconvincing.

w Don Cerveris d Franklin Adreon ph Paul Ivano m Jerry Fielding

Anna Sten, Robert Webber, Leo Gordon, Hari Rhodes

The Nun's Story***
US 1959 151m Technicolor
Warner (Henry Blanke)

A Belgian girl joins a strict order, endures hardship in the Congo, and finally returns to ordinary life.

The fascinating early sequences of convent routine are more interesting than the African adventures, but this is a careful, composed and impressive film with little Hollywood exaggeration.

w Robert Anderson, book Kathryn C. Hulme d Fred Zinnemann ph Franz Planer m Franz Waxman

Audrey Hepburn, Peter Finch, Edith Evans, Peggy Ashcroft, Dean Jagger, Mildred Dunnock, Patricia Collinge, Beatrice Straight

'A major directorial achievement . . . the best study of the religious life ever made in the American cinema.'—*Albert Johnson, Film Quarterly*

AAN: best picture; Robert Anderson; Fred Zinnemann; Franz Planer; Franz Waxman; Audrey Hepburn

Nurse Edith Cavell
US 1939 98m bw

The story of a British nurse executed as a spy during World War I; previously filmed in 1930 as *Dawn* with Sybil Thorndike. This is a moderately touching but uninspired treatment. Anna Neagle, George Sanders, May Robson, Edna May Oliver, Alan Marshal. Written by Michael Hogan from the novel *Dawn* by Reginald Berkeley; directed by Herbert Wilcox; for Imperator / RKO. AAN: music by Anthony Collins.

Nurse on Wheels
GB 1963 86m bw
Anglo Amalgamated / GHW (Peter Rogers)

Adventures of a young District Nurse.
Part sentimental, part Carry On; watchable of its curious kind.

w Norman Hudis, *novel* Nurse Is a Neighbour by Joanna Jones d Gerald Thomas ph Alan Hume m Eric Rogers

Juliet Mills, Ronald Lewis, Joan Sims, Raymond Huntley, Athene Seyler

The Nursemaid Who Disappeared
GB 1939 86m bw

A domestic agency hides a gang of kidnappers. Fairly pleasing mystery of the old school. Arthur Margetson, Peter Coke, Lesley Brook, Edward Chapman, Coral Browne, Martita Hunt. Written by Paul Gangelin and Connery Chappell, from the novel by Philip MacDonald; directed by Arthur Woods; for Warner.

The Nutty Professor
US 1963 107m Technicolor
Paramount / Jerry Lewis (Ernest D. Glucksman)

An eccentric chemistry professor discovers an elixir which turns him into a pop idol.
Long dreary comedy which contains patches of its star at somewhere near his best; but even *Dr Jekyll and Mr Hyde* is funnier.

w Jerry Lewis, Bill Richmond d Jerry Lewis ph W. Wallace Kelley m Walter Scharf

Jerry Lewis, Stella Stevens, Howard Morris, Kathleen Freeman

O. Henry's Full House**
US 1952   117m   bw
TCF (André Hakim)
GB title: *Full House*

John Steinbeck introduces five stories by O. Henry.

Modelled on the success of *Quartet* (qv), this compendium was less successful because these turn-of-the-century tales of New York depend less on character than on the sting in the tail; but the cast and production were lavish.

m Alfred Newman

THE COP AND THE ANTHEM *w* Lamar Trotti *d* Henry Koster *ph* Lloyd Ahern
Charles Laughton, David Wayne, Marilyn Monroe
THE CLARION CALL *w* Richard Breen *d* Henry Hathaway *ph* Lucien Ballard
Dale Robertson, Richard Widmark
THE LAST LEAF *w* Ivan Goff, Ben Roberts *d* Jean Negulesco *ph* Joe MacDonald
Anne Baxter, Jean Peters, Gregory Ratoff
THE RANSOM OF RED CHIEF
w Nunnally Johnson *d* Howard Hawks *ph* Milton Krasner
Fred Allen, Oscar Levant
THE GIFT OF THE MAGI *w* Walter Bullock *d* Henry King *ph* Joe MacDonald
Jeanne Crain, Farley Granger

O.H.M.S.
GB 1936   86m   bw
Gaumont (Geoffrey Barkas)
US title: *You're in the Army Now*

British forces fighting in China are joined by an American gangster on the run, who dies a hero.
Stiff-upper-lip adventure of no particular interest.

w Bryan Edgar Wallace, Austin Melford, A. R. Rawlinson, Lesser Samuels, Ralph Bettinson *d* Raoul Walsh *ph* Roy Kellino

John Mills, Wallace Ford, Anna Lee, Frank Cellier, Grace Bradley, Frederick Leister

O Lucky Man**
GB 1973   174m   Eastmancolor
Warner / Memorial / Sam (Michael Medwin, Lindsay Anderson)

The odyssey of a trainee salesman who after a while as an international financier settles down to be a do-gooder.
Modern revue-style version of *Candide / Decline and Fall*; very hit or miss in style and effect, and hellishly overlong, but with good things along the way.

w David Sherwin *d* Lindsay Anderson *ph* Miroslav Ondricek *m Alan Price pd* Jocelyn Herbert

Malcolm McDowell, Arthur Lowe, Ralph Richardson, Rachel Roberts, Helen Mirren, Mona Washbourne, Dandy Nichols
'A sort of mod *Pilgrim's Progress*.'—*New Yorker*

O.S.S.*
US 1946   107m   bw
Paramount

American spies are parachuted into France in 1943.
Espionage heroics with an unhappy ending and a slight documentary flavour. Not bad of its kind.

w Richard Maibaum *d Irving Pichel ph* Lionel Lindon *m* Daniele Amfitheatrof, Heinz Roemheld

Alan Ladd, Geraldine Fitzgerald, Patric Knowles, John Hoyt, Don Beddoe

Oasis
France / Germany 1956   100m approx
   Eastmancolor   Cinemascope
TCF / Roxy / Criterion (Gerd Oswald, Luggi
   Waldleitner)

An ex-pilot gets involved with two attractive women who are smuggling gold across the Sahara.
Glum romantic adventure.

w Joseph and Georges Kessel *d* Yves Allégret *ph* Roger Hubert *m* Paul Misraki

Pierre Brasseur, Michèle Morgan, Cornell Borchers, Grégoire Aslan

Objective Burma*
US 1944 142m bw
Warner (Jerry Wald)

Exploits of an American platoon in the Burma campaign.
Overlong but vivid war actioner which caused a diplomatic incident by failing to mention the British contribution.

w Ranald MacDougall, Lester Cole, Alvah Bessie d *Raoul Walsh* ph James Wong Howe m Franz Waxman

Errol Flynn, James Brown, William Prince, George Tobias, Henry Hull, Warner Anderson, John Alwin
'At the rate Errol Flynn and co. knock off the Japanese, it may make you wonder why the war need outlast next weekend.'—*Time*
AAN: original story (Alvah Bessie); Franz Waxman

The Obliging Young Lady
US 1941 80m bw

A secretary escorts a wealthy child out of town while her parents wrangle over custody.
Tedious comedy with interest occasionally provided by the supporting cast. Joan Carroll, Ruth Warrick, Edmond O'Brien, Eve Arden, Franklin Pangborn, Marjorie Gateson, John Miljan, George Cleveland. Luis Alberni, Charles Lane. Written by Frank Ryan and Bert Granet; directed by Richard Wallace; for RKO.

The Oblong Box
GB 1969 95m Eastmancolor
AIP (Gordon Hessler)

One of two 19th-century brothers is mysteriously disfigured and buried alive; he recovers and runs amok.
Nastily effective horror film with a frail story but good background detail.

w Lawrence Huntington d *Gordon Hessler* ph John Coquillon m Harry Robinson

Vincent Price, Christopher Lee, Alastair Williamson, Hilary Dwyer, Peter Arne, Maxwell Shaw, Rupert Davies
'A pervasive aura of evil.'—*MFB*

Obsession
GB 1948 98m bw
GFD / Independent Sovereign
US title: *The Hidden Room*

A doctor decides to kill his wife's lover by imprisoning him in a lonely cellar while he accumulates enough acid to destroy all traces of his body.

Implausible, overstretched thriller, carefully enough done to be bearable.

w Alec Coppel, from his play A Man About a Dog d Edward Dmytryk ph C. Pennington Richards m Nino Rota

Robert Newton, Sally Gray, Phil Brown, Naunton Wayne

Obsession*
US 1976 98m Technicolor Panavision
Columbia (Robert S. Bremson)

A widower with guilt feelings meets the double of his dead wife and is drawn into a strange plot.
Hitchcockian adventure with a few unwise attempts at seriousness, à la *Don't Look Now*. Generally entertaining, skilled and quite rewarding.

w Paul Schrader d Brian de Palma ph Vilmos Zsigmond m Bernard Herrmann

Cliff Robertson, Geneviève Bujold, John Lithgow, Sylvia Williams, Wanda Blackman, Patrick McNamara
'An unholy mess. Intended as an *hommage* to Hitchcock . . . it attitudinizes [also] towards the old-fashioned tearjerker and towards the sophisticated European film, with cultural references strewn like breadcrumbs along the way of Hansel and Gretel . . .'—*John Simon, New York*
'Merely a mannered cerebral exercise without any emotional underpinning or unconscious feeling of its own.'—*Andrew Sarris, Village Voice*
AAN: Bernard Herrmann

Occupe-Toi d'Amélie***
France 1949 95m bw
Lux (Louis Wipf)
aka: *Keep an Eye on Amelia*

A Parisian cocotte agrees to go through a mock marriage ceremony with her lover's best friend to fool his uncle: but the ceremony turns out to be real.
Hilarious and superbly stylized adaptation of a period boulevard farce: the play starts in a theatre, showing the audience, but gradually cinema technique takes over. Acting, timing and editing are all impeccable, and the production stands as a model of how such things should be done.

w Jean Aurenche, Pierre Bost, play Georges Feydeau d *Claude Autant-Lara* ph André Bac m René Cloërc

Danielle Darrieux, Jean Desailly, Bourvil, Carette, Grégoire Aslan

'Even those who do not respond to the artificialities of French vaudeville will admire the ingenuity and elegance of treatment.'— *Gavin Lambert, MFB*

'Most people, I think, could see it with considerable enjoyment even twice on the same evening.'—*Richard Mallett, Punch*

Ocean's Eleven*
US 1960 128m Technicolor
Panavision
Warner / Dorchester (Lewis Milestone)

A gang of friends plan to rob a Las Vegas casino.
Self-indulgent and overlong caper comedy which marked Hollywood's entry into a subsequently much overworked field. In this case the plot stops all too frequently for guest spots and in-jokes.

w Harry Brown, Charles Lederer *d* Lewis Milestone *ph* William H. Daniels *m* Nelson Riddle

Frank Sinatra, Peter Lawford, Sammy Davis Jnr, Richard Conte, Dean Martin, Angie Dickinson, Cesar Romero, Joey Bishop, Patrice Wymore, Akim Tamiroff, Henry Silva, Ilka Chase

The October Man**
GB 1947 98m bw
GFD / Two Cities (Eric Ambler)

After an accident which causes a head injury and subsequent depression, a lonely man staying at a small hotel is suspected of a local murder.
Nice blend of character study, mystery and suspense, with excellent attention to suburban detail.

w Eric Ambler *d* Roy Baker *ph* Erwin Hillier
John Mills, Joan Greenwood, Edward Chapman, Kay Walsh, Catherine Lacey, Joyce Carey, Adrianne Allen, Felix Aylmer

'This film of psychological suspense tells its complicated story with complete clarity, but it is mainly to be noted for its settings.'—*Basil Wright, 1972*

October Moth
GB 1959 54m bw

A mentally retarded farmhand goes berserk after causing a fatal car crash. Unattractive and singularly pointless little melodrama which neither edifies nor entertains. Lana Morris, Lee Patterson, Peter Dynely, Robert Cawdron. Written and directed by John Kruse; for Independent Artists.

The Odd Couple**
US 1968 105m Technicolor
Panavision
Paramount (Howard W. Koch)

A fussy divorce-shocked newswriter moves in with his sloppy sportscaster friend, and they get on each other's nerves.
Straight filming of a funny play which sometimes seems lost on the wide screen, but the performances are fine.

w Neil Simon, from his play *d* Gene Saks *ph* Robert B. Hauser *m* Neal Hefti

Jack Lemmon, Walter Matthau, John Fiedler, Herb Edelman, David Sheiner, Larry Haines, Monica Evans, Carole Sheely, Iris Adrian

AAN: Neil Simon

Odd Man Out***
GB 1946 115m bw
GFD / Two Cities (Carol Reed)
US title: *Gang War*

An IRA gunman, wounded and on the run in Belfast, is helped and hindered by a variety of people.
Superbly crafted but rather empty dramatic charade, visually and emotionally memorable but with nothing whatever to say.

w F. L. Green, R. C. Sherriff, *novel* F. L. Green *d* Carol Reed *ph* Robert Krasker *m* William Alwyn

James Mason, Robert Newton, Kathleen Ryan, F. J. McCormick, Cyril Cusack, Robert Beatty, Fay Compton, Dan O'Herlihy, Denis O'Dea, Maureen Delany, Joseph Tomelty, William Hartnell

'The story seems to ramify too much, to go on too long, and at its unluckiest to go arty. Yet detail by detail *Odd Man Out* is made with great skill and imaginativeness and with a depth of ardour that is very rare.'—*James Agee*

'Quite simply the most imaginative film yet produced in England, comparable with *Quai des Brumes* and *Le Jour se Lève*.'—*William Whitebait, New Statesman*

Odds against Tomorrow*
US 1959 96m bw
UA / Harbel (Robert Wise)

Three crooks plan to rob a bank, but two of them cause the enterprise to fail because of their own racist hatreds.
Sour, glossy crime thriller with elementary social significance.

w John O. Killens, Nelson Gidding, *novel* John P. McGivern *d* Robert Wise *ph* Joseph Brun *m* John Lewis

Robert Ryan, Harry Belafonte, *Ed Begley*, Shelley Winters, Gloria Grahame, Will Kuluva, Kim Hamilton

'An efficient but unnecessarily portentous thriller.'—*Penelope Houston*

The Odessa File**
GB 1974 129m Eastmancolor
Panavision
Columbia / Domino / Oceanic (John Woolf)

In 1963, a young German reporter tracks down a gang of neo-Nazis.

Elaborate but uninvolving suspenser with several excellent cliffhanging sequences and a let-down climax.

w Kenneth Ross, George Markstein, *novel* Frederick Forsyth *d* Ronald Neame *ph* Oswald Morris *m* Andrew Lloyd Webber *pd* Rolf Zeherbauer

Jon Voight, Maria Schell, Maximilian Schell, Mary Tamm, Derek Jacobi, Peter Jeffrey, *Noel Willman*

'As resistible a parcel of sedative entertainment as ever induced narcolepsy in a healthy man.'—*Benny Green, Punch*

Odette*
GB 1950 123m bw
Herbert Wilcox

A Frenchwoman with an English husband spies for the French resistance, is caught and tortured.

Deglamorized true life spy story with emotional moments let down by generally uninspired handling, also by the too well-known image of its star, who however gives a remarkable performance.

w Warren Chetham Strode, *book* Jerrard Tickell *d* Herbert Wilcox *ph* Max Greene *m* Anthony Collins

Anna Neagle, Trevor Howard, Peter Ustinov, Marius Goring

'As a work of art, pretty flat . . . though innumerable people will find it moving and impressive, they will have done the work themselves.'—*Richard Mallett, Punch*

Odongo
GB 1956 85m Technicolor
Cinemascope

A collector of animals for zoos runs into various kinds of trouble during an African safari. Elementary jungle adventure centring on a small Sabu-like jungle boy. For the now extinct family audience. Macdonald Carey, Rhonda Fleming, Juma, Eleanor Summerfield, Francis de Wolff, Earl Cameron. Written and directed by John Gilling; for Warwick / Columbia.

Of Human Bondage**
US 1934 83m bw
(RKO)

A well-to-do Englishman is brought down by his infatuation with a sluttish waitress.

This version of the famous novel brought Bette Davis to prominence but is not otherwise any better than the others.

w Lester Cohen, *novel* W. Somerset Maugham *d* John Cromwell *ph* Henry W. Gerrard *m* Max Steiner

Leslie Howard, Bette Davis, Frances Dee, Reginald Owen, Reginald Denny, Kay Johnson, Alan Hale

'A totally obtuse concoction, serving only to demonstrate how untalented an actress Bette Davis was before she perfected those camp mannerisms.'—*John Simon, 1967*

Of Human Bondage*
US 1946 105m bw
Warner (Henry Blanke)

Good-looking but thoroughly dull remake.

w Catherine Turney *d* Edmund Goulding *ph* Peverell Marley *m* Erich Wolfgang Korngold

Paul Henreid, Eleanor Parker, Alexis Smith, Edmund Gwenn, Patric Knowles, Janis Paige, Henry Stephenson

Of Human Bondage
GB 1964 99m bw
MGM / Seven Arts (James Woolf)

Disastrous remake with both star roles miscast.

w Bryan Forbes *d* Henry Hathaway, Ken Hughes *ph* Oswald Morris *m* Ron Goodwin *pd* John Box

Laurence Harvey, Kim Novak, Nanette Newman, Roger Livesey, Jack Hedley, Robert Morley, Siobhan McKenna, Ronald Lacey

Of Human Hearts*
US 1938 100m bw
MGM (John Considine Jnr)

A 19th-century idyll of middle America and especially of a preacher and his wayward son. Curious all-American moral fable, splendidly made and acted.

w Bradbury Foote, *novel* Benefits Forgot by Honoré Morrow *d* Clarence Brown *ph* Clyde de Vinna *m* Herbert Stothart

Walter Huston, James Stewart, Beulah Bondi, Gene Reynolds, Charles Coburn, Guy Kibbee, John Carradine, Gene Lockhart, Ann Rutherford

AAN: Beulah Bondi

Of Love and Desire
US 1963 97m De Luxe
New World (Victor Stoloff)

An engineer in Mexico takes up with the
boss's nymphomaniac sister.
Unwise sensationalist vehicle for an ageing
leading lady who is past such carryings on.

w Laslo Gorag, Richard Rush d Richard
Rush ph Alex Phillips m Ronald Stein

Merle Oberon, Steve Cochran, John Agar,
Curt Jurgens

Of Mice and Men***
US 1939 107m bw
Hal Roach (Lewis Milestone)

An itinerant worker looks after his mentally
retarded cousin, a giant who doesn't know his
own strength.
A strange and unexpected tragedy which has
strength and is very persuasively made but
seems somehow unnecessary.

w Eugene Solow, novel John Steinbeck
d Lewis Milestone ph Norbert Brodine
m Aaron Copland

Burgess Meredith, Lon Chaney Jnr, Betty
Field, Charles Bickford, Roman Bohnen, Bob
Steele, Noah Beery Jnr

AAN: best picture; Aaron Copland

Off Limits
US 1953 89m bw
Paramount (Harry Tugend)
GB title: Military Policemen

A boxing manager trains a young fighter in
the military police.
Flat star comedy.

w Hal Kanter, Jack Sher d George Marshall
ph Peverell Marley m Van Cleave

Bob Hope, Mickey Rooney, Marilyn Maxwell,
Marvin Miller

Off the Dole
GB 1935 89m bw

An amateur detective catches burglars. Artless
comedy shot on a minuscule budget; it helped
to make George Formby a star. With Beryl
Formby, Constance Shotter, Dan Young.
Written and directed by Arthur Mertz; for
Mancunian.

The Offence*
GB 1972 113m De Luxe
United Artists / Tantallon (Denis O'Dell)

A tough police inspector bullies a suspected
child molester.
Tortuous psychological study on the fringe of
hysteria; good performances.

w John Hopkins, from his play This Story of
Yours d Sidney Lumet ph Gerry Fisher
m Harrison Birtwhistle

Sean Connery, Trevor Howard, Ian Bannen,
Vivien Merchant

Oh Dad, Poor Dad, Mamma's Hung You in the Closet and I'm Feelin' So Sad
US 1966 86m Technicolor
Paramount / Seven Arts (Ray Stark, Stanley
Rubin)

A dead father helps his son to get married
despite his mother's influence to the contrary.
Zany black comedy which never really worked
on the stage, let alone the screen.

w Ian Bernard, play Arthur Kopit d Richard
Quine ph Geoffrey Unsworth m Neal Hefti

Rosalind Russell, Jonathan Winters, Robert
Morse, Hugh Griffith, Barbara Harris, Lionel
Jeffries, Cyril Delevanti, Hiram Sherman

Oh, God*
US 1977 104m Technicolor
Warner (Jerry Weintraub)

A bewildered supermarket manager is enlisted
by God to prove to the world that it can only
work if people try.
Overlong but generally amiable reversion to
the supernatural farces of the forties: its
success seems to show that people again need
this kind of comfort.

w Larry Gelbart, novel Avery Corman d Carl
Reiner ph Victor Kemper m Jack Elliott

George Burns, John Denver, Ralph Bellamy,
Donald Pleasence, Teri Garr, William
Daniels, Barnard Hughes, Paul Sorvino, Barry
Sullivan, Dinah Shore, Jeff Corey, David
Ogden Stiers
'Undeniably funny and almost impossible to
dislike.'—Tom Milne, MFB

AAN: Larry Gelbart

Oh God Book Two
US 1980 94m Technicolor

God enlists a child to remind people that he is
still around. Crass sequel with sentiment
replacing jokes. George Burns, Suzanne
Pleshette, David Birney, Louanne, Howard
Duff, Hans Conried, Wilfrid Hyde White.
Written by Josh Greenfield, Hal Goldman,
Fred S. Fox, Seaman Jacobs and Melissa
Miller; directed by Gilbert Cates; for Warner.

Oh Heavenly Dog
US 1980 103m De Luxe

A private eye is reincarnated as a dog and
solves his own murder. Witless fantasy

comedy, an uncredited remake of *You Never Can Tell* which also rates as a Benji movie with curious additions of sex and profanity. A total muddle. Chevy Chase, Jane Seymour, Omar Sharif, Robert Morley, Alan Sues. Written by Rod Browning and Joe Camp; directed by Joe Camp; for Mulberry Square / TCF.

Oh Men! Oh Women!

US 1957 90m Eastmancolor
Cinemascope
TCF (Nunnally Johnson)

A psychoanalyst discovers that his wife is involved with two of his patients.
Scatty Broadway comedy which strains the patience.

wd Nunnally Johnson, *play* Edward Chodorov *ph* Charles G. Clarke *m* Cyril Mockridge

David Niven, Ginger Rogers, Dan Dailey, Barbara Rush, Tony Randall

'The ugliest sort of fun.'—*Observer*
'Cinemascope discovers a solution to the problem of filling its wide screen; the characters spend most of their time full length on the psychoanalyst's couch.'—*Sunday Times*

Oh Mr Porter°°°°

GB 1937 84m bw
GFD / Gainsborough (Edward Black)

The stationmaster of an Irish halt catches gun-runners posing as ghosts.
Marvellous star comedy showing this trio of comedians at their best, and especially Hay as the seedy incompetent. The plot is borrowed from *The Ghost Train*, but each line and gag brings its own inventiveness. A delight of character comedy and cinematic narrative.

w Marriott Edgar, Val Guest, J. O. C. Orton, *story* Frank Launder *d* Marcel Varnel *ph* Arthur Crabtree *md* Louis Levy

Will Hay, Moore Marriott, Graham Moffatt, Dave O'Toole, Dennis Wyndham

'That rare phenomenon: a film comedy without a dud scene.'—*Peter Barnes, 1964*
'Behind it lie the gusty uplands of the British music hall tradition, whose rich soil the British film industry is at last beginning to exploit.'—*Basil Wright*

Oh Rosalinda!

GB 1955 105m Technicolor
Cinemascope
ABP / Powell and Pressburger

A playboy in four-power Vienna plays a practical joke on four officers and the flirtatious wife of one of them.

Lumbering attempt to modernize *Die Fledermaus*, unsuitably wide-screened and totally lacking the desired Lubitsch touch. A monumental step in the decline of these producers, and a sad stranding of a brilliant cast.

wd Michael Powell, Emeric Pressburger
ph Christopher Challis *m* Johann Strauss
ad Hein Heckroth

Anton Walbrook, Michael Redgrave, Anthony Quayle, Mel Ferrer, Dennis Price, Ludmilla Tcherina

Oh What a Lovely War°°

GB 1969 144m Technicolor
Panavision
Paramount / Accord (Brian Duffy, Richard Attenborough)

A fantasia with music on World War I.
A brave all-star attempt which comes off only in patches; the pier apparatus from the stage show really doesn't translate, the piece only works well when it becomes cinematic, as in the recruiting song and the final track-back from the graves. But there are many pleasures, as well as yawns, along the way.

w Len Deighton, *stage show* Joan Littlewood, Charles Chilton *d* Richard Attenborough *ph* Gerry Turpin *m* various *md* Alfred Ralston *pd* Don Ashton

Ralph Richardson, Meriel Forbes, John Gielgud, Kenneth More, John Clements, Paul Daneman, Joe Melia, Jack Hawkins, John Mills, Maggie Smith, Michael Redgrave, Laurence Olivier, Susannah York, Dirk Bogarde, Phyllis Calvert, Vanessa Redgrave

'This musical lampoon is meant to stir your sentiments, evoke nostalgia, and make you react to the obscenity of battles and bloodshed, and apparently it does all that for some people.'—*New Yorker, 1977*
'A naïve, sentimental, populist affair, using many (too many) clever devices yet making the same old simplistic statements.'—*John Simon*

Oh You Beautiful Doll°

US 1949 93m Technicolor
TCF (George Jessel)

Fred Fisher wants to write opera but is more successful with pop songs.
Standard turn of the century biopic, very pleasantly handled and performed.

w Albert and George Lewis *d* John M. Stahl *ph* Harry Jackson *md* Alfred Newman

S. Z. Sakall, Mark Stevens, June Haver, *Charlotte Greenwood*, Jay C. Flippen, Gale Robbins

Oil for the Lamps of China*
US 1935 98m bw
Warner (Robert Lord)

The career in China of an American oil
company representative.
Adequate general audience picture from a
bestseller.

w Laird Doyle, novel Alice Tisdale Hobart
d Mervyn Le Roy ph Tony Gaudio m Heinz
Roemheld md Leo F. Forbstein

Pat O'Brien, Josephine Hutchinson, Jean
Muir, Lyle Talbot, Arthur Byron, John
Eldredge, Henry O'Neill, Donald Crisp
  'Far above average in performance,
direction and content.'—John Baxter, 1968
† Remade 1941 as Law of the Tropics.

Okay America
US 1932 80m bw

A brash reporter saves a politician's daughter
from kidnapping. Okay melodrama remade in
1939 as Risky Business. Lew Ayres, Maureen
O'Sullivan, Louis Calhern, Walter Catlett,
Edward Arnold. Written by William Anthony
McGuire; directed by Tay Garnett; for
Universal. (GB title: Penalty of Fame.)

Okay for Sound*
GB 1937 85m bw
GFD / Gainsborough (Edward Black)

The Crazy Gang runs amok in a film studio.
Patchy farce with music hall talents of the
time.

w Marriott Edgar, Val Guest, R. P. Weston,
Bert Lee d Marcel Varnel ph Jack Cox
md Louis Levy

Bud Flanagan, Chesney Allen, Jimmy Nervo,
Teddy Knox, Charlie Naughton, Jimmy Gold,
Fred Duprez, Enid Stamp-Taylor, Graham
Moffatt, Meinhart Maur, H. F. Maltby, Peter
Dawson, The Radio Three, The Sherman
Fisher Girls

Oklahoma!**
US 1955 143m Technicolor Todd-AO
Magna / Rodgers and Hammerstein (Arthur
Hornblow Jnr)

A cowboy wins his girl despite the intervention
of a sinister hired hand.
Much of the appeal of the musical was in its
simple timeworn story and stylized sets; the
film makes the first merely boring and the
latter are replaced by standard scenery, not
even of Oklahoma. The result is efficient
rather than startling or memorable.

w Sonya Levien, William Ludwig, 'book'
Oscar Hammerstein, play Green Grow the
Rushes by Lynn Riggs d Fred Zinnemann
ph Robert Surtees songs Richard Rodgers,
Oscar Hammerstein II m Robert Russell
Bennett, Jay Blackton, Adolph Deutsch
pd Oliver Smith

Gordon Macrae, Shirley Jones, Rod Steiger,
Gloria Grahame, Charlotte Greenwood, Gene
Nelson, Eddie Albert

AA: music score
AAN: Robert Surtees; Robert Russell
Bennett, Jay Blackton, Adolph Deutsch

Oklahoma Crude*
US 1973 111m Technicolor
Columbia / Stanley Kramer

In 1913, a drifting oil man stops to help a girl
develop her rig.
Dour, downbeat melodrama with restricted
action and much bad language; within its lights
quite entertaining, but odd.

w Marc Norman d Stanley Kramer
ph Robert Surtees m Henry Mancini
pd Alfred Sweeney

Faye Dunaway, George C. Scott, John Mills,
Jack Palance, Woodrow Parfrey

The Oklahoma Kid**
US 1939 80m bw
Warner (Samuel Bischoff)

During the settlement of the Cherokee Strip a
cowboy avenges the unjust lynching of his
father.
Competent but slightly disappointing star
western memorable for the clash in this guise
of its protagonists, more usually seen as
gangsters.

w Warren Duff, Robert Buckner, Edward E.
Paramore d Lloyd Bacon ph James Wong
Howe m Max Steiner

James Cagney, Humphrey Bogart, Rosemary
Lane, Donald Crisp, Harvey Stephens,
Charles Middleton, Edward Pawley, Ward
Bond
  'There's something entirely disarming about
the way he has tackled horse opera, not
pretending for a minute to be anything but
New York's Jimmy Cagney all dressed up as a
Robin Hood of the old west.'—Frank Nugent

The Oklahoman
US 1956 78m De Luxe Cinemascope

A widowed doctor becomes the subject of
gossip when he takes an Indian girl for his
housekeeper. Rather curious domestic western
which erupts into action sequences but devotes
too much time to talk and romance. Joel
McCrea, Barbara Hale, Brad Dexter, Gloria

Talbott, Michael Pate. Written by Daniel B. Ullman; directed by Francis D. Lyon; for Walter Mirisch / Allied Artists.

Old Acquaintance**
US 1943   110m   bw
Warner (Henry Blanke)

Two jealous lady novelists interfere in each other's love lives.
A dated but rather splendid battle of the wild cats, with two stars fighting their way through a plush production and a rather overlong script.

w John Van Druten, Lenore Coffee, *play* John Van Druten *d* Vincent Sherman *ph* Sol Polito *m* Franz Waxman

Bette Davis, Miriam Hopkins, Gig Young, John Loder, Dolores Moran, Philip Reed, Roscoe Karns, Anne Revere

'The odd thing is that the two ladies and the director can make the whole business look fairly intelligent, detailed and plausible; and that on the screen such trash can seem, even, mature and adventurous.'—*James Agee*

'Trashy fun, on an unusually literate level.'—*New Yorker, 1978*

Old Bill and Son
GB 1940   96m   bw

Too old for active duty, a veteran follows his son to Flanders. Ineffective screen version of a popular newspaper strip. Morland Graham, John Mills, Mary Clare, Renée Houston, Rene Ray, Roland Culver. Written by Bruce Bairnsfather and Ian Dalrymple, from Bairnsfather's cartoons; directed by Ian Dalrymple; for Legeran Films.

Old Bones of the River*
GB 1938   90m   bw
GFD / Gainsborough (Edward Black)

A teacher in Africa accidentally quells a native rising.
Tediously funny star comedy; enough said.

w Marriott Edgar, Val Guest, J. O. C. Orton *character* Edgar Wallace *d* Marcel Varnel *ph* Arthur Crabtree *m* Louis Levy *ad* Vetchinsky

Will Hay, Moore Marriott, Graham Moffatt, Robert Adams, Jack Livesey

Old Boyfriends*
US 1978   103m   Technicolor
Edward R. Pressman Productions (Paul Schrader)

A divorcee survives a nervous breakdown and goes on a journey of her past life to find out where she went wrong.

Low-key and somehow rather flat romantic odyssey, with interesting sequences and characters muted by the director's jaundiced eye.

w Paul and Leonard Schrader *d* Joan Tewkesbury *ph* William A. Fraker *m* David Shire

Talia Shire, Richard Jordan, John Belushi, Keith Carradine, John Houseman, Buck Henry, Bethel Leslie

The Old Curiosity Shop*
GB 1934   95m   bw
BIP / Wardour

The lives of a gambler and his granddaughter are affected by a miserly dwarf.
Heavy-going Dickens novel given reasonably rich production and well enough acted; sentimentality prevented a remake until the unsuccessful *Mister Quilp* (qv) in 1975.

w Margaret Kennedy, Ralph Neale, *novel* Charles Dickens *d* Thomas Bentley

Hay Petrie, Ben Webster, Elaine Benson, Beatrice Thompson, Gibb McLaughlin, Reginald Purdell, Polly Ward

The Old Dark House****
US 1932   71m   bw
Universal (Carl Laemmle Jnr)

Stranded travellers take refuge in the house of a family of eccentrics.
Marvellous horror comedy filled with superb grotesques and memorable lines, closely based on a Priestley novel but omitting the more thoughtful moments. A stylist's and connoisseur's treat.

w Benn W. Levy, R. C. Sherriff, *novel* Benighted by *J. B. Priestley d* James Whale *ph* Arthur Edeson

Melvyn Douglas, Charles Laughton, Raymond Massey, Boris Karloff, Ernest Thesiger, Eva Moore, Gloria Stuart, Lilian Bond, Brember Wills, John Dudgeon (Elspeth Dudgeon)

'An unbridled camp fantasy directed with great wit.'—*Charles Higham*

'Each threat as it appears is revealed to be burlap and poster paint . . . despite storm, attempted rape and a remarkable final chase, the film is basically a confidence trick worked with cynical humour by a brilliant technician.'—*John Baxter, 1968*

'Basically a *jeu d'esprit* in which comedy of manners is edged into tragedy of horrors, the film never puts a foot wrong.'—*Tom Milne, MFB, 1978*

Old English
US 1930   87m   bw

In order to provide for his grandchildren, a financier makes certain illegal arrangements which involve his prearranged death.

Satisfying pattern play arranged for its star.

George Arliss, Leon Janney, Doris Lloyd, Betty Lawford, Ivan Simpson. Written by Walter Anthony and Maude Howell, from the play by John Galsworthy; directed by Alfred E. Green; for Warner.

The Old-Fashioned Way*
US 1934 74m bw
Paramount / (William Le Baron)

Adventures of The Great McGonigle and his troupe of travelling players.

Period comedy tailored for its star and incorporating fragments of *The Drunkard.* Not so funny as it might be, but essential for students.

w Garnett Weston, Jack Cunningham, Charles Bogle (W. C. Fields) *d* William Beaudine *ph* Benjamin Reynolds *m* Harry Revel

W. C. Fields, Joe Morrison, Judith Allen, Jan Duggan, Jack Mulhall, Baby Leroy

Old Hutch
US 1936 80m bw

An idler finds a fortune but can't spend it because everybody knows he hasn't worked for years. Satisfactory star comedy. Wallace Beery, Elizabeth Patterson, Eric Linden, Cecilia Parker, Donald Meek, Virginia Grey. Written by George Kelly; directed by J. Walter Ruben; for MGM.

Old Iron
GB 1939 80m bw

A shipping magnate disowns his son for marrying against his will, but a car accident reconciles them. Very boring drama, an odd choice for this star, who can't cope with it. Tom Walls, Eva Moore, Cecil Parker, Richard Ainley, David Tree, Enid Stamp-Taylor. Written by Ben Travers; directed by Tom Walls; for TW Productions / British Lion.

The Old Maid**
US, 1939 95m bw
Warner (Henry Blanke)

When her suitor is killed in the Civil War, an unmarried mother lets her childless cousin bring up her daughter as her own.

A 'woman's picture' par excellence, given no-holds-barred treatment by all concerned but a little lacking in surprise.

w Casey Robinson, *play* Zoe Akins, *novel* Edith Wharton *d* Edmund Goulding *ph* Tony Gaudio *m* Max Steiner *md* Leo F. Forbstein

Bette Davis, Miriam Hopkins, George Brent, Jane Bryan, Donald Crisp, Louise Fazenda, Henry Stephenson, Jerome Cowan, William Lundigan, Rand Brooks

'It is better than average and sticks heroically to its problem, forsaking all delights and filling a whole laundry bag with wet and twisted handkerchiefs.'—*Otis Ferguson*

'The picture isn't bad, but it trudges along and never becomes exciting.'—*New Yorker, 1977*

The Old Man and the Sea*
US 1958 89m Technicolor
Warner / Leland Hayward

An old fisherman dreams of hooking a great fish.

Expensive but poor-looking and stultifyingly dull one-character drama with variable production effects, a low key *Moby Dick.* Interesting but not effective.

w Ernest Hemingway, from his novel *d* John Sturges *ph* James Wong Howe, Floyd Crosby, Tom Tutweiler, Lamar Boren *m* Dmitri Tiomkin

Spencer Tracy, Felipe Pazos, Harry Bellaver

'A literary property about as suited for the movie medium as *The Love Song of J. Alfred Prufrock.'*—*Time*

'A strange amalgam of practically unassisted acting, good camerawork and editing, and a lot of special effects.'—*Ernest Callenbach, Film Quarterly*

AA: Dmitri Tiomkin
AAN: James Wong Howe; Spencer Tracy

Old Mother Riley

This Irish washerwoman with flailing arms and a nice line in invective was a music hall creation of Arthur Lucan, a variation of a pantomime dame. His wife Kitty Macshane played Mother Riley's daughter, and despite personal difficulties they were top of the bill for nearly 30 years. The films were very cheaply made and the padding is difficult to sit through, but Lucan at his best is a superb comedian: they were made for small independent companies such as Butcher's and usually directed by Maclean Rogers.

1937: OLD MOTHER RILEY
1938: OLD MOTHER RILEY IN PARIS
1939: OLD MOTHER RILEY MP, OLD MOTHER RILEY JOINS UP
1940: OLD MOTHER RILEY IN BUSINESS, OLD MOTHER RILEY'S GHOSTS
1941: OLD MOTHER RILEY'S CIRCUS
1942: OLD MOTHER RILEY IN SOCIETY

1943: OLD MOTHER RILEY DETECTIVE
1944: OLD MOTHER RILEY AT HOME
1945: OLD MOTHER RILEY
HEADMISTRESS
1947: OLD MOTHER RILEY'S NEW
VENTURE
1949: OLD MOTHER RILEY'S JUNGLE
TREASURE
1952: MOTHER RILEY MEETS THE
VAMPIRE

Old Yeller*

US 1957 83m Technicolor
Walt Disney

The love of a boy for his dog.
Archetypal family movie set in a remote rural
area.

w Fred Gipson, William Tubberg, *novel* Fred
Gipson d Robert Stevenson *ph* Charles P.
Boyle *m* Oliver Wallace

Dorothy McGuire, Fess Parker, Tommy Kirk,
Kevin Corcoran, Jeff York, Chuck Connors

The Oldest Profession

France / West Germany / Italy 1967
115m Eastmancolor

Six sketches about prostitution. Very variable
portmanteau, with moments of interest
towards the end. Michele Mercier, Elsa
Martinelli, Jeanne Moreau, Jean-Claude
Brialy, Raquel Welch, Nadia Gray, Anna
Karina. Written by Ennio Flaiano, Daniel
Boulanger, Georges and André Tabet, Jean
Aurenche, Jean-Luc Godard; directed by
Franco Indovina, Mauro Bolognini, Philippe
de Broca, Michel Pfleghar, Claude Autant-
Lara, Jean-Luc Godard; for Gibe / Francoriz /
Rialto / Rizzoli.

Oliver!***

GB 1968 146m Technicolor
Panavision 70
Columbia / Warwick / Romulus (John
Woolf)

A musical version of *Oliver Twist.*
The last, perhaps, of the splendid film musicals
which have priced themselves out of existence;
it drags a little in spots but on the whole it
does credit both to the show and the original
novel, though eclipsed in style by David
Lean's straight version.

w Vernon Harris, *play* Lionel Bart, *novel*
Charles Dickens d Carol Reed ph Oswald
Morris m Lionel Bart md John Green
pd John Box ch Onna White

Ron Moody, Oliver Reed, Harry Secombe,
Mark Lester, Shani Wallis, *Jack Wild,* Hugh

Griffith, Joseph O'Conor, Leonard Rossiter,
Hylda Baker, Peggy Mount, Megs Jenkins
  'Only time will tell if it is a great film but it
is certainly a great experience.'—*Joseph*
Morgenstern
  'There is a heightened discrepancy between
the romping jollity with which everyone goes
about his business and the actual business
being gone about . . . such narrative elements
as the exploitation of child labour, pimping,
abduction, prostitution and murder combine
to make *Oliver!* the most non-U subject ever
to receive a U certificate.'—*Jan Dawson*
AA: best picture; Carol Reed; John Green
AAN: Vernon Harris; Oswald Morris; Ron
Moody; Jack Wild

Oliver the Eighth

US 1933 20m bw

Ollie goes on a blind date, and the lady turns
out to be homicidal. Star farce which never
quite rises to the occasion; pleasant fooling but
no more. Laurel and Hardy, Mae Busch, Jack
Barty. Written by anon; directed by Lloyd
French; for Hal Roach.

Oliver Twist****

GB 1948 116m bw
GFD / Cineguild (Ronald Neame)

A foundling falls among thieves but is rescued
by a benevolent old gentleman.
Simplified, brilliantly cinematic version of a
voluminous Victorian novel, beautiful to look
at and memorably played, with every scene
achieving the perfect maximum impact.

w *David Lean, Stanley Haynes, novel Charles*
Dickens d David Lean ph Guy Green
m Arnold Bax pd John Bryan

Alec Guinness, Robert Newton, Francis L.
Sullivan, John Howard Davies, Kay Walsh,
Anthony Newley, Henry Stephenson, Mary
Clare, Gibb McLaughlin, Diana Dors
  'A thoroughly expert piece of movie
entertainment.'—*Richard Winnington*

Oliver's Story

US 1978 92m Technicolor
Paramount (David V. Picker)

A sequel to *Love Story,* showing how Oliver
succumbed to depression but finally found
another girl friend.
Love means never having to watch this trendy
rubbish.

w Erich Segal, John Korty d John Korty
ph Arthur Ornitz *m* Francis Lai, Lee
Holdridge

Ryan O'Neal, Candice Bergen, Nicola Pagett,
Edward Binns, Ray Milland

Olly Olly Oxen Free

US 1978   93m   Metrocolor
Rico Lion (Richard A. Colla)

A junkyard proprietress helps two young
children to launch a decrepit hot-air balloon.
Simpleminded children's adventure with a
surprising star.

w Eugene Poinc *d* Richard A. Colla
ph Gayne Rescher *m* Bob Alcivar *pd* Peter
Wooley

Katharine Hepburn, Kevin McKenzie, Dennis
Dimster

Los Olvidados*

Mexico 1951   88m   bw
Utramar / Oscar Dancigers
aka: *The Young and the Damned*

A good boy is contaminated by the young
thugs in Mexico City's slums, and both he and
his tormentor die violently.
Sober but penetrating analysis of social
conditions leading to violence. The film was
widely acclaimed, yet its very proficiency and
excellent photography tend to glamorize its
subject. Compare, however, the Hollywood
resolutions of *Dead End*, on a similar subject.

w Luis Bunuel, Luis Alcoriza, Oscar
Dancigers *d* Luis Bunuel *ph* Gabriel
Figueroa *m* Gustavo Pitaluga

Alfonso Mejia, Miguel Inclan, Estela Inda,
Roberto Cobo

Olympische Spiele***

Germany 1936   Part 1, 118m; Part 2,
107m   bw
Leni Riefenstahl

An account of the Berlin Olympic Games.
This magnificent film is in no sense a mere
reporting of an event. Camera movement,
photography and editing combine with music
to make it an experience truly olympian,
especially in the introductory symbolic
sequence suggesting the birth of the games. It
was also, dangerously, a hymn to Nazi
strength.

d, ed Leni Riefenstahl *assistant* Walter
Ruttman *ph* Hans Ertl, Walter Franz and 42
others *m* Herbert Windt
   'Here is the camera doing superbly what
only the camera can do: refashioning the
rhythms of the visible; of the moment seen.'—
Dilys Powell

The Omaha Trail

US 1942   62m   bw
The laying of train track across the west causes
Indian wars. Brisk second feature western with

good production values. James Craig, Dean
Jagger, Edward Ellis, Chill Wills, Donald
Meek, Pamela Blake, Howard da Silva.
Written by Jesse Lasky Jnr and Hugo Butler;
directed by Edward Buzzell; for MGM.

Omar Khayyam

US 1956   101m   Technicolor
Vistavision
Paramount (Frank Freeman Jnr)

The Persian poet and philosopher defends his
Shah against the Assassins.
Clean but dull Arabian Nights fantasy with
pantomime sets and no humour.

w Barre Lyndon *d* William Dieterle
ph Ernest Laszlo *m* Victor Young

Cornel Wilde, Michael Rennie, Raymond
Massey, John Derek, Yma Sumac, Sebastian
Cabot, Debra Paget

The Omega Man*

US 1971   98m   Technicolor   Panavision
Warner / Walter Seltzer

In 1977 a plague resulting from germ warfare
has decimated the world's population; in Los
Angeles, one man wages war against
loathsome carriers of the disease.
'Realistic' version of a novel which was about
vampires taking over, and was previously
filmed unsatisfactorily as *The Last Man on
Earth*. This nasty version rises to a few good
action sequences but is bogged down by talk in
between.

w John William Corrington and Joyce M.
Corrington, *novel* I am Legend by Richard
Matheson *d* Boris Sagal *ph* Russell Metty
m Ron Grainer

Charlton Heston, Rosalind Cash, Anthony
Zerbe

The Omen**

US 1976   111m   De Luxe   Panavision
TCF (Harvey Bernhard)

The adopted child of an ambassador to Great
Britain shows unnerving signs of being
diabolically inspired.
Commercially successful variation on *The
Exorcist*, quite professionally assembled and
more enjoyable as entertainment than its
predecessor.

w David Seltzer *d Richard Donner ph* Gil
Taylor *m* Jerry Goldsmith

Gregory Peck, Lee Remick, David Warner,
Billie Whitelaw, Leo McKern, Harvey
Stevens, Patrick Troughton, Anthony
Nicholls, Martin Benson
   'A cut above the rest in that it has an

ingenious premise, a teasingly labyrinthine development, a neat sting in its tail, and enough confidence in its own absurdities to carry them off.'—*David Robinson, The Times*
† See *Damien: Omen II* and *The Final Conflict*.

AA: Jerry Goldsmith
AAN: song '*Ave Satani*'

On a Clear Day You Can See For Ever*
US 1970   129m   Technicolor
  Panavision
Paramount (Howard Koch)

A psychiatric hypnotist helps a girl to stop smoking, and finds that in trances she remembers previous incarnations.
Romantic musical which tries, and fails, to substitute wispy charm for its original Broadway vitality. There are compensations.

w Alan Jay Lerner, from his play d Vincente Minnelli ph Harry Stradling m Burton Lane

Barbra Streisand, Yves Montand, Bob Newhart, Larry Blyden, Jack Nicholson, Simon Oakland

On an Island with You
US 1948   104m   Technicolor
MGM (Joe Pasternak)

A film actress on location in the South Seas is chased by a naval officer.
Below par musical which far outstays its welcome.

w Dorothy Kingsley, Dorothy Cooper, Charles Martin, Hans Wilhelm d Richard Thorpe ph Charles Rosher md George Stoll

Esther Williams, Peter Lawford, Jimmy Durante, Ricardo Montalban, Cyd Charisse, Xavier Cugat and his Orchestra

On Approval***
GB 1943   80m   bw
(GFD) Clive Brook

An Edwardian duke and an American heiress plan a chaperoned trial marriage in a remote Scottish castle.
Sparkling comedy of manners made even more piquant by careful casting and mounting; a minor delight.

w *Clive Brook, Terence Young, play Frederick Lonsdale d Clive Brook*

Clive Brook, Beatrice Lillie, Googie Withers, Roland Culver, O. B. Clarence, Lawrence Hanray, Hay Petrie
'Totally diverting, highly cinematic.'—*NFT, 1974*
'There has probably never been a richer, funnier anthology of late-Victorian mannerisms.'—*Time*

'I enjoyed it so thoroughly that I have to fight off superlatives.'—*James Agee*
† Also filmed in 1930 by Tom Walls for Herbert Wilcox, with Walls, Yvonne Arnaud, Winifred Shotter and Edmund Breon.

On Borrowed Time*
US 1939   98m   bw
MGM (Sidney Franklin)

An old man refuses to die and chases Death up the apple tree.
Amiable, very American fantasy with much sentiment and several effective moments.

w Alice Duer Miller, Frank O'Neill, Claudine West, *novel* Lawrence Edward Watkin
d Harold S. Bucquet ph Joseph Ruttenberg m Franz Waxman

Lionel Barrymore, Bobs Watson, Beulah Bondi, *Cedric Hardwicke* (as Mr Brink), Una Merkel, Ian Wolfe, Philip Terry, Eily Malyon
'A weird, wild, totally unpredictable fantasy with dream sequences more like Bunuel than anything in the cinema.'—*John Russell Taylor, 1965*

On Dangerous Ground
US 1951   82m   bw
RKO (John Houseman)

A tough cop falls in love with the blind sister of a mentally defective murderer.
Pretentious Hollywood *film noir* in the Gabin manner, partly redeemed by its glossy surface.

w A. I. Bezzerides, *novel* George Butler
d Nicholas Ray ph George E. Diskant
m Bernard Herrmann

Robert Ryan, Ida Lupino, Ward Bond, Ed Begley, Cleo Moore, Charles Kemper

On Her Majesty's Secret Service**
GB 1969   140m   Technicolor
  Panavision
UA / Eon / Danilaq (Harry Saltzman, Albert R. Broccoli)

James Bond tracks down master criminal Blofeld in Switzerland.
Perhaps to compensate for no Sean Connery and a tragic ending, the producers of this sixth Bond opus shower largesse upon us in the shape of no fewer than four protracted and spectacular climaxes. Splendid stuff, but too much of it, and the lack of a happy centre does show.

w Richard Maibaum, *novel* Ian Fleming
d Peter Hunt ph Michael Reed, Egil Woxholt, Roy Ford, John Jordan m John Barry pd Syd Cain

George Lazenby, Diana Rigg, Telly Savalas, Ilse Steppat, Gabriele Ferzetti, Yuri Borienko, Bernard Lee, Lois Maxwell

On Moonlight Bay**
US 1951　95m　Technicolor
Warner (William Jacobs)

Family crises, to do with growing up and
young love, in a 1917 Indiana town.
Pleasant musical, competently made, from the
Penrod stories, with the emphasis switched to
big sister.

w Melville Shavelson, Jack Rose, *stories*
Booth Tarkington　d Roy del Ruth　ph Ernest
Haller　md Ray Heindorf

Doris Day, Gordon Macrae, Leon Ames,
Rosemary de Camp, Billy Gray
† See also *By the Light of the Silvery Moon*, a
companion piece.

On Our Merry Way*
US 1948　107m　bw
Benedict Bogeaus, Burgess Meredith
aka: *A Miracle Can Happen*

A reporter is urged by his wife to dig up some
human interest stories.
Frail compendium of anecdotes which barely
work.

w Laurence Stallings, *story* Arch Oboler
d King Vidor, Leslie Fenton　ph Joseph
August, Gordon Avil, John Seitz, Edward
Cronjager　m Heinz Roemheld　md David
Chudnow, Skitch Henderson

Burgess Meredith, Paulette Goddard, Fred
MacMurray, Hugh Herbert, James Stewart,
Dorothy Lamour, Victor Moore, Henry
Fonda, William Demarest

On the Avenue**
US 1937　89m　bw
TCF (Gene Markey)

An heiress rages because she is being satirized
in a revue, but later falls in love with the star.
Bright musical which keeps moving and uses
its talents wisely.

w Gene Markey, William Conselman　d Roy
del Ruth　ph Lucien Andriot　m / ly Irving
Berlin　ch Seymour Felix

Dick Powell, Madeleine Carroll, The Ritz
Brothers, George Barbier, Alice Faye, Walter
Catlett, Joan Davis, E. E. Clive
† Revamped as *Let's Make Love* (qv).

On the Beach**
US 1959　134m　bw
United Artists / Stanley Kramer

When most of the world has been devastated
by atomic waste, an American atomic
submarine sets out to investigate.
Gloomy prophecy which works well in spasms
but is generally too content to chat rather than
imagine. A solid prestige job nevertheless.

w John Paxton, James Lee Barrett, *novel*
Nevil Shute　d Stanley Kramer　ph Giuseppe
Rotunno, Daniel Fapp　m Ernest Gold
pd Rudolph Sternad

Gregory Peck, Ava Gardner, Fred Astaire,
Anthony Perkins, Donna Anderson, John
Tate, Lola Brooks
'Its humanism is clearly of the order that
seeks the support of a clamorous music score.
The characters remain little more than
spokesmen for timid ideas and Salvation Army
slogans, their emotions hired from a
Hollywood prop room; which is all pretty
disturbing in a film about nothing less than the
end of the world.'—*Robert Vas*
AAN: Ernest Gold

On the Beat
GB 1962　105m　bw
Rank (Hugh Stewart)

A Scotland Yard car park attendant manages
to capture some crooks and become a
policeman.
Busy but flat comedy vehicle, never very
likeable.

w Jack Davies　d Robert Asher　ph Geoffrey
Faithfull　m Philip Green

Norman Wisdom, Jennifer Jayne, Raymond
Huntley, David Lodge

On the Buses
GB 1971　88m　Technicolor
EMI / Hammer (Ronald Woolfe, Ronald
　Chesney)

Women drivers cause trouble at a bus depot.
Grotesque, ham-handed farce from a TV
series which was sometimes funny; this is
merely vulgar.

w Ronald Woolfe, Ronald Chesney　d Harry
Booth　ph Mark MacDonald　m Max Harris

Reg Varney, Doris Hare, Anna Karen,
Michael Robbins, Stephen Lewis
† *Mutiny on the Buses* followed in 1972 and
Holiday on the Buses in 1973. Both were
deplorably witless.

On the Double*
US 1961　92m　Technicolor　Panavision
Paramount / Dena–Capri (Jack Rose)

During World War II, an American private is
asked to impersonate a British intelligence
officer.
From the plot and the talents it seems one
might start laughing at this while still in the
queue, but in fact most of it goes sadly awry
and it never quite comes to the boil.

w Jack Rose, Melville Shavelson *d* Melville Shavelson *ph* Harry Stradling, Geoffrey Unsworth *m* Leith Stevens

Danny Kaye, Dana Wynter, Wilfrid Hyde White, Diana Dors, Margaret Rutherford, Allan Cuthbertson, Jesse White

On the Fiddle*
GB 1961 97m bw
Anglo-Amalgamated / S. Benjamin Fisz
US title: *Operation Snafu*

A wide boy and a slow-witted gypsy have comic and other adventures in the RAF. Curious mixture of farce and action, more on American lines than British, but quite entertainingly presented.

w Harold Buchman, *novel* Stop at a Winner by R. F. Delderfield *d* Cyril Frankel *ph* Ted Scaife *m* Malcolm Arnold

Alfred Lynch, Sean Connery, Cecil Parker, Wilfrid Hyde White, Kathleen Harrison, Alan King, Eleanor Summerfield, Eric Barker, Terence Longdon, John Le Mesurier, Harry Locke

On the Night of the Fire*
GB 1939 94m bw
GFD / G & S (Josef Somlo)
US title: *The Fugitive*

A barber kills the blackmailer of his wife. Dour little drama, rather unusual for pre-war British studios.

w Brian Desmond Hurst, Terence Young, *novel* F. L. Green *d* Brian Desmond Hurst *ph* Gunther Krampf

Ralph Richardson, Diana Wynyard, Romney Brent, Mary Clare, Henry Oscar, Frederick Leister

On the Riviera**
US 1951 90m Technicolor
TCF (Sol C. Siegel)

A cabaret artist is persuaded to pose as a philandering businessman.
Remake of *Folies Bergère* and *That Night in Rio* (see also *On the Double*); disliked at the time and accused of tastelessness, it now seems smarter and funnier than comparable films of its era.

w Valentine Davies, Phoebe and Henry Ephron *d* Walter Lang *ph* Leon Shamroy *m* Alfred Newman

Danny Kaye, Corinne Calvet, Gene Tierney, Marcel Dalio, Jean Murat

AAN: Alfred Newman

On the Threshold of Space
US 1956 96m Eastmancolor Cinemascope
TCF (William Bloom)

The USAF medical corps explores human reactions at high altitudes.
Semi-documentary flagwaver with dreary domestic asides; very dated now, and of no particular nostalgic interest.

w Simon Wincelberg, Francis Cockrill *d* Robert D. Webb *ph* Joe MacDonald *m* Lyn Murray

Guy Madison, Virginia Leith, John Hodiak, Dean Jagger, Warren Stevens

On the Town****
US 1949 98m Technicolor
MGM (*Arthur Freed*)

Three sailors enjoy twenty-four hours' leave in New York.
Most of this brash location musical counts as among the best things ever to come out of Hollywood; the serious ballet towards the end tends to kill it, but it contains much to be grateful for.

w Betty Comden, Adolph Green, *ballet* Fancy Free by Leonard Bernstein *d / ch* Gene Kelly, Stanley Donen *ph* Harold Rosson *md* Lennie Hayton, Roger Edens *songs* various

Gene Kelly, Frank Sinatra, Jules Munshin, Vera-Ellen, Betty Garrett, Ann Miller, Tom Dugan, Florence Bates, Alice Pearce

'A film that will be enjoyed more than twice.'—*Lindsay Anderson*

'So exuberant that it threatens at moments to bounce right off the screen.'—*Time*

'The speed, the vitality, the flashing colour and design, the tricks of timing by which motion is fitted to music, the wit and invention and superlative technical accomplishment make it a really exhilarating experience.'—*Richard Mallett, Punch*

AA: Lennie Hayton, Roger Edens

On the Waterfront***
US 1954 108m bw
Columbia / Sam Spiegel

After the death of his brother, a young stevedore breaks the hold of a waterfront gang boss.
Intense, broody dockside thriller with 'method' performances; very powerful of its kind, and much imitated.

w Budd Schulberg, from his novel *d* Elia Kazan *ph* Boris Kaufman *m* Leonard Bernstein *ad* Richard Day

Marlon Brando, Eva Marie Saint, *Lee J. Cobb*, Rod Steiger, Karl Malden, Pat Henning, Leif Erickson, James Westerfield, John Hamilton

'An uncommonly powerful, exciting and imaginative use of the screen by gifted professionals.'—*New York Times*

'A medley of items from the Warner gangland pictures of the thirties, brought up to date.'—*Steven Sondheim, Films in Review*

† Sample dialogue: 'Charlie, oh Charlie, you don't understand. I coulda had class. I coulda been a contender.'

AA: best picture; Budd Schulberg; Elia Kazan; Boris Kaufman; Richard Day; Marlon Brando; Eva Marie Saint
AAN: Leonard Bernstein; Lee J. Cobb; Rod Steiger; Karl Malden

On with the Show
US 1929 98m Technicolor (two-colour)
Warner

Crude early talkie musical revue with historical interest.

w Robert Lord, *play* Shoestring by Humphrey Pearson *d* Alan Crosland *ph* Tony Gaudio *songs* Grant Clarke, Harry Akst

Betty Compson, Louise Fazenda, Sally O'Neil, Joe E. Brown, Ethel Waters, Arthur Lake

On Your Toes*
US 1939 94m bw
Warner (Robert Lord)

Backstage jealousies at the ballet.
Smooth film version of a top Broadway show of its time.

w Jerry Wald, Richard Macaulay, *play* George Abbott *d* Ray Enright *ph* James Wong Howe, Sol Polito *m* / *ly* Richard Rodgers, Lorenz Hart

Vera Zorina, Eddie Albert, Alan Hale, Frank McHugh, James Gleason, Donald O'Connor, Gloria Dickson

Once a Crook
GB 1941 81m bw

A publican with a shady past helps his son who is in trouble with the law. Low-key character comedy for two stars who would benefit from a greater tendency to farce. Gordon Harker, Sydney Howard, Frank Pettingell, Carla Lehmann, Bernard Lee, Kathleen Harrison, Cyril Cusack. Written by Roger Burford, from the play by Evadne Price and Ken Attiwill; directed by Herbert Mason; for TCF.

Once a Jolly Swagman*
GB 1948 100m bw
GFD / Wessex (Ian Dalrymple)
US title: *Maniacs on Wheels*

A factory worker becomes a speedway rider. Competent sporting drama of no particular interest.

w William Rose, Jack Lee *d* Jack Lee *ph* H. E. Fowle *m* Bernard Stevens

Dirk Bogarde, Renée Asherson, Bonar Colleano, Bill Owen

Once a Sinner
GB 1950 80m bw

A girl with a shady past finds her husband is being threatened by her ex-partner. Uninteresting character melodrama which defeats its lightweight stars. Pat Kirkwood, Jack Watling, Joy Shelton, Sidney Tafler, Thora Hird. Written by David Evans, from the novel *Irene* by Ronald Marsh; directed by Lewis Gilbert; for John Argyle / Butcher.

Once a Thief
US 1965 107m bw Panavision
MGM / Cipra / RN / Fred Engel (Jacques Bar)

An ex-convict is hounded by a vengeful cop. Glum crime melodrama gleamingly photographed but otherwise quite routine.

w Zekial Marko *d* Ralph Nelson *ph* Robert Burks *m* Lalo Schifrin

Alain Delon, Ann-Margret, Van Heflin, Jack Palance, John David Chandler

Once in Paris
US 1978 100m TVC color

A naïve American writer is introduced to the delights of Paris by a worldly chauffeur and an amorous British noblewoman. A movie that adds up to very little, but pleases along the way. Wayne Rogers, Gayle Hunnicutt, Jack Lenoir, Philippe Hart, Tanya Lopert. Written and directed by Frank D. Gilroy, for his own company.

Once in a Lifetime**
US 1933 80m approx bw
Universal

How a script was sold in old-time Hollywood. Half good-humoured, half-scathing satire on Hollywood; technique dated, content still amusing.

w Seton I. Miller, *play* Moss Hart, George S. Kaufman *d* Russell Mack *ph* George Robinson

Jack Oakie, Sidney Fox, Aline MacMahon, Russell Hopton, Zasu Pitts, Louise Fazenda, Gregory Ratoff, Onslow Stevens

Once Is Not Enough

US 1975 122m Movielab Panavision
Paramount / Sujac / Aries (Howard W. Koch)
aka: *Jacqueline Susann's Once Is Not Enough*

The daughter of a movie producer is corrupted by his circle.
Old-fashioned jet-set melodrama with new-fashioned sexual novelties.

w Julius J. Epstein, *novel* Jacqueline Susann *d* Guy Green *ph* John A. Alonzo *m* Henry Mancini *pd* John de Cuir

Kirk Douglas, Alexis Smith, David Janssen, George Hamilton, Melina Mercouri, Gary Conway, Brenda Vaccaro, Deborah Raffin

AAN: Brenda Vaccaro

Once More My Darling

US 1949 92m bw
Universal (Joan Harrison)

A young girl is romantically pursued by an older man.
Tame comedy.

w Robert Carson *d* Robert Montgomery *ph* Franz Planer *m* Elizabeth Firestone

Robert Montgomery, Ann Blyth, Jane Cowl, Taylor Holmes, Charles McGraw

Once More with Feeling

GB 1960 92m Technicolor
Columbia / Stanley Donen

The volatile private life of an orchestral conductor.
Thin comedy from a West End play, something between a shouting match and a fashion show.

w Harry Kurnitz, from his play *d* Stanley Donen *ph* Georges Périnal *md* Muir Mathieson *pd* Alexander Trauner

Yul Brynner, Kay Kendall, Geoffrey Toone, Maxwell Shaw, Mervyn Johns, Martin Benson, Gregory Ratoff

Once Upon a Dream

GB 1948 84m bw

An officer's wife has a romantic dream about her husband's batman, and comes to believe it true. Very wispy comedy which does none of its principals any good. Googie Withers, Griffith Jones, Guy Middleton, Raymond Lovell, Hubert Gregg. Written by Patrick Kirwan and Victor Katona; directed by Ralph Thomas; for Triton / Rank.

Once Upon a Honeymoon*

US 1942 116m bw
RKO (Leo McCarey)

An American radio correspondent and an ex-burlesque queen cheat the Nazis—and her husband—in Europe during World War II.
Smooth but curious mixture of comedy and drama, a satisfactory but unmemorable star vehicle.

w Sheridan Gibney, Leo McCarey *d* Leo McCarey *ph* George Barnes *m* Robert Emmett Dolan

Cary Grant, Ginger Rogers, Walter Slezak, Albert Dekker, Albert Bassermann, Ferike Boros, Harry Shannon

'The attempt to play for both laughs and significance against a terrifying background of Nazi aggression is on the whole a little disappointing.'—*Newsweek*

Once Upon a Time*

US 1944 89m bw
Columbia (Louis Edelman)

A luckless producer makes a sensation out of a boy and his dancing caterpillar.
Thin whimsical comedy, too slight to come off given such standard treatment, but with nice touches along the way.

w Lewis Meltzer, Oscar Saul, *radio play* My Client Curley by Norman Corwin, Lucille F. Herrmann *d* Alexander Hall *ph* Franz Planer *m* Frederick Hollander

Cary Grant, Janet Blair, James Gleason, Ted Donaldson, Howard Freeman, William Demarest, Art Baker, John Abbott

'There just isn't enough material here for a full-length feature.'—*Philip T. Hartung*
'It would be nice to see some screen fantasy if it were done by anyone with half a heart, mind and hand for it. But when the studios try to make it, duck and stay hid till the mood has passed.'—*James Agee*

Once Upon a Time in the West*

Italy / US 1969 165m Techniscope
Paramount / Rafran / San Marco (Fulvio Morsella)

A lonely woman in the old west is in danger from a band of gunmen.
Immensely long and convoluted epic western marking its director's collaboration with an American studio and his desire to make serious statements about something or other. Beautifully made, empty, and very violent.

w Sergio Leone, Sergio Donati *d* Sergio Leone *ph* Tonino Delli Colli *m* Ennio Morricone

Henry Fonda, Claudia Cardinale, Jason Robards, Charles Bronson, Gabriele Ferzetti, Keenan Wynn, Paolo Stoppa, Lionel Stander, Jack Elam, Woody Strode

The One and Only
US 1978   98m   Movielab
Paramount / First Artists (Steve Gordon, David V. Picker)

A stage-struck egomaniac finds success at the expense of happiness with his wife.
Uneasy mixture of farce and sentiment intended as a star vehicle, but not a very successful one.

w Steve Gordon d Carl Reiner ph Victor J. Kemper m Patrick Williams

Henry Winkler, Kim Darby, Gene Saks, William Daniels, Polly Holiday, Herve Villechaize, Harold Gould, Richard Lane

One Day in the Life of Ivan Denisovich*
GB 1971   105m   Eastmancolor
Group W / Leontes / Norsk (Caspar Wrede)

Life in a Siberian labour camp in 1950.
A fairly successful book adaptation, as far as mere pictures can cope with the harrowing detail.

w Ronald Harwood, novel Alexander Solzhenitsyn d Caspar Wrede ph Sven Nykvist m Arne Nordheim

Tom Courtenay, Espen Skjonberg, James Maxwell, Alfred Burke, Eric Thompson, Matthew Guinness
'The film's general air of earnestness deflects rather than stimulates involvement.'—David Wilson

One Desire
US 1955   94m   Technicolor
U-I (Ross Hunter)

The romantic career of the lady owner of a gambling saloon.
Tawdry nineties drama which never really gets going.

w Lawrence Roman, Robert Blees, novel Tacey Cromwell by Conrad Richter d Jerry Hopper ph Maury Gertsman m Frank Skinner md Joseph Gershenson

Anne Baxter, Rock Hudson, Julia Adams, Natalie Wood, Barry Curtis, William Hopper, Carl Benton Reid
'The standards of writing and characterization belong to a Victorian servant girl's paper-covered romance.'—MFB

One Exciting Night
GB 1944   89m   bw

A singing welfare worker averts a plan to steal a Rembrandt. Very ho-hum stuff for a very popular but histrionically untried star. Vera Lynn, Donald Stewart, Mary Clare, Frederick Leister, Richard Murdoch. Written by Howard Irving Young, Peter Fraser, Margaret Kennedy and Emery Bonnet; directed by Walter Forde; for Columbia British.

One Eyed Jacks
US 1961   141m   Technicolor
Vistavision
Paramount / Pennebaker (Frank P. Rosenberg)

An outlaw has a running battle with an old friend.
Grossly self-indulgent western controlled (unwisely) by its star, full of solemn pauses and bouts of violence.

w Guy Trosper, Calder Willingham, novel The Authentic Death of Hendry Jones by Charles Neider d Marlon Brando ph Charles Lang Jnr m Hugo Friedhofer

Marlon Brando, Karl Malden, Pina Pellicier, Katy Jurado, Slim Pickens, Ben Johnson, Timothy Carey, Elisha Cook Jnr

AAN: Charles Lang Jnr

One Flew over the Cuckoo's Nest***
US 1975   134m   De Luxe
UA / Fantasy Films (Paul Zaentz, Michael Douglas)

A cheerful immoralist imprisoned for rape is transferred for observation to a state mental hospital.
Wildly and unexpectedly commercial film of a project which had lain dormant for fourteen years, this amusing and horrifying film conveniently sums up anti-government attitudes as well as make love not war and all that. It's certainly impossible to ignore.

w Laurence Hauben, Bo Goldman, novel Ken Kesey d Milos Forman ph Haskell Wexler m Jack Nitzche pd Paul Sylbert

Jack Nicholson, Louise Fletcher, William Redfield, Will Sampson, Brad Dourif, Christopher Lloyd
'Lacks the excitement of movie art, but the story and the acting make the film emotionally powerful.'—New Yorker

AA: best picture; script; Milos Forman; Jack Nicholson; Louise Fletcher
AAN: Haskell Wexler; Jack Nitzche; Brad Dourif

One Foot in Heaven*
US 1941   108m   bw
Warner (Robert Lord, Irving Rapper)

The small-town doings of a methodist minister.

Slow but pleasing chronicle, nicely assembled.

w Casey Robinson, *biography* (of his father) Hartzell Spence d Irving Rapper ph Charles Rosher m Max Steiner

Fredric March, Martha Scott, Beulah Bondi, Gene Lockhart, Elizabeth Fraser, Harry Davenport, Laura Hope Crews, Grant Mitchell, Moroni Olsen, Ernest Cossart, Jerome Cowan

'A clean, sweet, decent picture.'—*Cecilia Ager*

AAN: best picture

One Foot in Hell
US 1960 89m De Luxe Cinemascope
TCF (Sydney Boehm)

The sheriff of a small western town is secretly plotting revenge on the townsfolk for their long-ago treatment of his wife.

Unusual western suspenser with plenty of violent action and an extremely equivocal hero.

w Aaron Spelling, Sydney Boehm d James B. Clark ph William C. Mellor m Dominic Frontière

Alan Ladd, Dan O'Herlihy, Don Murray, Dolores Michaels, Barry Coe, Larry Gates, John Alexander

One Good Turn
US 1931 20m bw

Two odd job men see their benefactress rehearsing a play, and think she is really being evicted. Moderate star comedy with nice moments. Laurel and Hardy, Mary Carr, Billy Gilbert. Written by H. M. Walker; directed by James W. Horne; for Hal Roach.

One Hour with You***
US 1932 84m bw
Paramount (*Ernst Lubitsch*)

The affairs of a philandering Parisian doctor. Superbly handled comedy of manners in Lubitsch's most inventive form, handled by a most capable cast. Unique entertainment of a kind which is, alas, no more.

w *Samson Raphaelson, play* Only a Dream by Lothar Schmidt d *George Cukor, Ernst Lubitsch ph* Victor Milner m *Oscar Straus, Richard Whiting ly* Leo Robin ad Hans Dreier

Maurice Chevalier, Jeanette MacDonald, Genevieve Tobin, Roland Young, Charles Ruggles, George Barbier

'A brand new form of musical entertainment . . . he has mixed verse, spoken and sung, a smart and satiric musical background, asides to the audience, and sophisticated dialogue, as well as lilting and delightful songs . . . The result is something so delightful that it places the circle of golden leaves jauntily upon the knowing head of Hollywood's most original director.'—*Philadelphia Inquirer*

† A remake of Lubitsch's silent success *The Marriage Circle*.

AAN: best picture

One Hundred and One Dalmatians***
US 1961 79m Technicolor
Walt Disney

The dogs of London help save puppies which are being stolen for their skins by a cruel villainess.

Disney's last really splendid feature cartoon, with the old flexible style cleverly modernized and plenty of invention and detail in the story line. The London backgrounds are especially nicely judged.

w Bill Peet, *novel* Dodie Smith d Wolfgang Reitherman, Hamilton S. Luske, Clyde Geronimi

120 Days of Sodom
Italy / France 1975 117m Technicolor

After the Italian campaign of 1944, four local dignitaries marry each other's daughters, withdraw with a bevy of nubile girls to a mountain retreat, and tell each other sado-masochistic sexual adventures. Thoroughly revolting and much banned piece with no perceptible point but a good deal of emetic detail. Paolo Bonacelli, Giorgio Cataldi, Uberto P. Quintavalle, Aldo Valetti. Written and directed by Pier Paolo Pasolini, from the novel by the Marquis de Sade; for PEA / PAA.

One Hundred Men and a Girl***
US 1937 84m bw
Universal (*Joe Pasternak*)

A young girl persuades a great conductor to form an orchestra of unemployed musicians. Delightful and funny musical fable, an instance of the Pasternak formula of sweetness and light at its richest and best.

w *Bruce Manning, Charles Kenyon, Hans Kraly d Henry Koster ph* Joseph Valentine m Charles Previn *songs* various

Deanna Durbin, Adolphe Menjou, Leopold Stokowski, Alice Brady, Mischa Auer, Eugene Pallette, Billy Gilbert, Alma Kruger, Jed Prouty, Frank Jenks, Christian Rub

AA: Charles Previn
AAN: best picture; original story (Hans Kraly)

100 Rifles*
US 1969 109m De Luxe
TCF / Marvin Schwartz

In war-torn Mexico, a black American sheriff and his prisoner become involved in a girl's fight for vengeance after her father's death. Blood-soaked adventure with plenty of tough action and tight pace. A little too purposeful in its unpleasantness to be very entertaining.

w Clair Huffaker, Tom Gries, *novel* Robert MacLeod d *Tom Gries* ph Cecilio Paniagua m Jerry Goldsmith

Jim Brown, Raquel Welch, Burt Reynolds, Fernando Lamas, Dan O'Herlihy, Hans Gudegast

One in a Million**
US 1937 94m bw
TCF (Raymond Griffith)

The daughter of a Swiss innkeeper becomes an Olympic ice-skating champion.
Sonja Henie's film debut shows Hollywood at its most professional, making entertainment out of the purest moonshine with considerable injections of novelty talent.

w Lenore Praskins, Mark Kelly d Sidney Lanfield ph Edward Cronjager md Louis Silvers

Sonja Henie, Don Ameche, *The Ritz Brothers*, Jean Hersholt, Ned Sparks, Arline Judge, Dixie Dunbar, Borrah Minnevitch and his Rascals, Montagu Love

One Is a Lonely Number*
US 1972 97m Metrocolor
MGM (Stan Margulies)

When her husband leaves her, a woman tries to develop new interests.
Satirical sentimental view of American divorce, with interesting moments.

w David Seltzer, *novel* Rebecca Morris d Mel Stuart ph Michel Hugo m Michel Legrand

Trish Van Devere, Monte Markham, Melvyn Douglas, Janet Leigh

One Little Indian
US 1973 91m Technicolor
Walt Disney (Winston Hibler)

A cavalry corporal escapes from jail and falls in with a ten-year-old Indian.
Sentimental semi-western, a bit dull for Disney apart from a camel.

w Harry Spalding d Bernard McEveety ph Charles F. Wheeler m Jerry Goldsmith

James Garner, Vera Miles, Pat Hingle, Morgan Woodward, John Doucette

One Man's Way
US 1964 105m bw

A crime reporter becomes a priest. Rather self-conscious biography of Norman Vincent Peale, adequately assembled but containing no surprises. Don Murray, Diana Hyland, William Windom, Virginia Christine, Carol Ohmart. Written by Eleanore Griffin and John W. Bloch, from the book *Minister to Millions* by Arthur Gordon; directed by Denis Sanders; for UA.

One Million BC*
US 1940 80m bw
Hal Roach
GB title: *Man and His Mate*
aka: *The Cave Dwellers*

Life between warring tribes of primitive man in the stone age.
Impressive-looking but slow-moving grunt-and-groan epic originally based on D. W. Griffith's *Man's Genesis* and on which Griffith did some work. The totally unhistoric dinosaurs (which had disappeared long before man arrived) are impressively concocted by magnifying lizards.

w Mickell Novak, George Baker, Joseph Frickert d Hal Roach, Hal Roach Jnr, D. W. Griffith ph Norbert Brodine m Werner R. Heymann

Victor Mature, Carole Landis, Lon Chaney Jnr, John Hubbard, Nigel de Brulier, Conrad Nagel

AAN: Werner R. Heymann

One Million Years BC*
GB 1966 100m Technicolor
Hammer (Michael Carreras)

A vague remake of the above, with animated monsters. Not badly done, with some lively action.

w Michael Carreras d Don Chaffey ph Wilkie Cooper m Mario Nascimbene

John Richardson, Raquel Welch, Robert Brown, Percy Herbert, Martine Beswick
  'Very easy to dismiss the film as a silly spectacle; but Hammer production finesse is much in evidence and Don Chaffey has done a competent job of direction. And it is all hugely enjoyable.'—*David Wilson*

One Minute to Zero
US 1952 105m bw
RKO (Edmund Grainger)

In Korea a US colonel is evacuating American
civilians but is forced to bomb refugees.
Flat war film with Something To Say and the
star at his most humourless.

w Milton Krims, William Haines d Tay
Garnett ph William E. Snyder m Constantin
Bakaleinikoff

Robert Mitchum, Ann Blyth, William Talman,
Charles McGraw, Richard Egan

One More River*
US 1934 88m bw
Universal (James Whale)
GB title: Over the River

A wife runs away from her husband, and he
sets detectives on her and her lover.
Old-fashioned, well made picturization of a
novel.

w R. C. Sherriff, novel John Galsworthy
d James Whale ph John Mescall m W.
Franke Harling

Colin Clive, Diana Wynyard, C. Aubrey
Smith, Jane Wyatt, Lionel Atwill, Mrs Patrick
Campbell, Frank Lawton, Reginald Denny,
Henry Stephenson, Alan Mowbray,
E. E. Clive

'Taste, elegance, narrative drive and a
deliberate nostalgia for the Galsworthy
period.'—Peter John Dyer, 1966

One More Spring*
US 1935 87m bw
Fox (Winfield Sheehan)

Three strangers, in reduced circumstances due
to the Depression, meet in Central Park and
pool their resources.
Topical serio-comedy which looks pretty dated
but still serves as a summation of American
mid-thirties attitudes.

w Edwin Burke, novel Robert Nathan
d Henry King ph John Seitz md Arthur
Lange

Janet Gaynor, Warner Baxter, Walter Woolf
King, Grant Mitchell, Jane Darwell, Roger
Imhof, John Qualen, Dick Foran, Stepin
Fetchit

One More Time
GB 1969 93m De Luxe
UA / Chrislaw–Tracemark (Milton Ebbins)

More crime-solving adventures of Salt and
Pepper.
Even less funny than before; see Salt and
Pepper.

w Michael Pertwee d Jerry Lewis ph Ernest
Steward m Les Reed

Peter Lawford, Sammy Davis Jnr, Esther
Anderson, Maggie Wright

One More Tomorrow*
US 1946 89m bw
Warner (Henry Blanke)

A wealthy playboy marries a left-wing
photographer and buys up her magazine.
An interesting but dated play fails to come to
life because neither cast nor director seem to
understand what it's about.

w Charles Hoffman, Catherine Turney, Julius
J. and Philip G. Epstein, play The Animal
Kingdom by Philip Barry d Peter Godfrey
ph Bert Glennon d Max Steiner

Ann Sheridan, Dennis Morgan, Jack Carson,
Alexis Smith, Jane Wyman, Reginald
Gardiner, John Loder, Marjorie Gateson

One More Train to Rob
US 1971 108m Technicolor
Universal (Robert Arthur)

A train robber comes out of prison and warily
takes up with his old partners.
Undistinguished western which tries to be
funny and serious at the same time.

w Don Tait, Dick Nelson d Andrew V.
McLaglen ph Alric Edens m David Shire

George Peppard, Diana Muldaur, John
Vernon, France Nuyen, Steve Sandor

One New York Night*
US 1935 80m bw
MGM (Bernard Hyman)
GB title: The Trunk Mystery

A young farmer in Manhattan on a visit finds a
body in the hotel room next to his.
Slick comedy thriller very typical of its date
and studio.

w Frank Davis play Edward Childs Carpenter
d Jack Conway

Franchot Tone, Una Merkel, Steffi Duna,
Conrad Nagel, Charles Starrett, Harold Huber
'A comedy of astonishing intelligence and
finish . . . it ought to take its place
immediately with the classics.'—Graham
Greene

One Night in Lisbon
US 1941 97m bw
Paramount (Edward H. Griffith)

During World War II an American flier falls
for a British socialite who is being used by the
government as a decoy for spies.

Flabby romantic comedy-drama which mostly wastes a good cast.

w Virginia Van Upp, *play* There's Always Juliet by John Van Druten *d* Edward H. Griffith *ph* Bert Glennon *m* Sigmund Krumgold

Madeleine Carroll, Fred MacMurray, Edmund Gwenn, Patricia Morison, Billie Burke, John Loder, Dame May Whitty, Reginald Denny, Billy Gilbert

One Night in the Tropics
US 1940 69m bw
Universal (Leonard Spiegelgass)

Holidays on a Caribbean island lead to a double wedding.
Very lightweight comedy-musical notable only for introducing Abbott and Costello.

w Gertrude Purcell, Charles Grayson, *play* Love Insurance by Earl Derr Biggers *d* A. Edward Sutherland *ph* Joseph Valentine *md* Charles Previn *songs* Oscar Hammerstein II, Jerome Kern, Otto Harbach, Dorothy Fields

Allan Jones, Nancy Kelly, Bud Abbott, Lou Costello, Robert Cummings, Leo Carillo, Peggy Moran, Mary Boland

One Night of Love**
US 1934 95m bw
Columbia (Harry Cohn)

An opera star rebels against her demanding teacher.
Light classical musical which was a surprising box office success and brought Hollywood careers for Lily Pons, Gladys Swarthout, Miliza Korjus, etc.

w Dorothy Speare, Charles Beahan, S. K. Lauren, James Gow, Edmund North *d* Victor Schertzinger *ph* Joseph Walker *songs* Victor Schertzinger, Gus Kahn *m* Louis Silvers *md* Pietro Cimini

Grace Moore, Tullio Carminati, Lyle Talbot, Mona Barrie, Nydia Westman, Jessie Ralph, Luis Alberni, Jane Darwell

AA: Victor Schertzinger, Gus Kahn (as songwriters)
AAN: best picture; direction; Louis Silvers; Grace Moore

One Night With You
GB 1948 92m bw

An English girl and an Italian tenor, stranded by a train failure, are taken for forgers.
Rather frantic but occasionally amusing Italian-set comedy. Nino Martini, Patricia Roc, Hugh Wakefield, Bonar Colleano, Guy

Middleton, Stanley Holloway, Irene Worth, Charles Goldner. Written by Caryl Brahms and S. J. Simon; directed by Terence Young; for Two Cities / Rank.

One of Our Aircraft Is Missing*
GB 1941 102m bw
British National (Michael Powell, Emeric Pressburger)

A bomber is grounded after a raid and its crew is helped by the Dutch resistance.
Efficient propaganda piece which starts vigorously but gets bogged down in talk.

wd Michael Powell, Emeric Pressburger
ph Ronald Neame

Godfrey Tearle, Eric Portman, Hugh Williams, Bernard Miles, Hugh Burden, Emrys Jones, Googie Withers, Pamela Brown, Peter Ustinov, Joyce Redman, Hay Petrie, Robert Helpmann, Alec Clunes

AAN: script

One of Our Dinosaurs Is Missing*
US 1975 94m Technicolor
Walt Disney (Bill Walsh)

In the 1920s a strip of secret microfilm is smuggled out of China and hidden in a dinosaur's skeleton in the Natural History Museum.
Unexceptionable family comedy with everyone trying hard; somehow it just misses, perhaps because it is told through talk rather than cinematic narrative.

w Bill Walsh, *novel* The Great Dinosaur Robbery by David Forrest *d* Robert Stevenson *ph* Paul Beeson *m* Ron Goodwin

Helen Hayes, Peter Ustinov, Derek Nimmo, Clive Revill, Joan Sims, Bernard Bresslaw, Roy Kinnear, Deryck Guyler, Richard Pearson

One Rainy Afternoon*
US 1935 79m bw

In a cinema one afternoon, a gigolo kisses the wrong girl. Rather heavy-handed light comedy with interesting credentials. Francis Lederer, Ida Lupino. Written by Stephen Morehouse Avery and Maurice Hamline from a play by Emeric Pressburger and René Pujal ; directed by Rowland V. Lee; for Pickford-Lasky.

One Summer Love
US 1976 97m colour Panavision

A young man leaves mental hospital for his Connecticut home, only to find everyone there nuttier than he is. Over-the-top melodrama. Beau Bridges, Susan Sarandon,

Mildred Dunnock, Michael B. Miller. Written by N. Richard Nash; directed by Gilbert Cates; for AIP. (Aka: *Dragonfly*.)

One Sunday Afternoon**

US 1933   93m   bw
Paramount (Louis D. Lighton)

In 1910, a Brooklyn dentist feels he has married the wrong girl, but discovers that his choice was the right one.

Pleasant period comedy drama which was twice remade; as *The Strawberry Blonde* (qv) and see below.

w William Slavens McNutt, Grover Jones, *play* James Hagan   *d* Stephen Roberts
ph Victor Milner

Gary Cooper, Frances Fuller, Fay Wray, Neil Hamilton, Roscoe Karns
  'Still pitched in stage tempo and unfolds haltingly.'—*Variety*

One Sunday Afternoon

US 1948   90m   Technicolor
Warner (Jerry Wald)

Pleasant but undistinguished musical remake of the above.

w Robert L. Richards   *d* Raoul Walsh   *ph* Sid Hickox, Wilfrid M. Cline   *md* Ray Heindorf
ad Anton Grot

Dennis Morgan, Dorothy Malone, Janis Paige, Don Defore, Ben Blue
  'A lackadaisical and uninspired jaunt down memory lane.'—*New Yorker, 1978*

The One That Got Away**

GB 1957   111m   bw
Rank (Julian Wintle)

A German flier, Franz Von Werra, is captured and sent to various British prisoner-of-war camps, from all of which he escapes.
True-life biopic, developed in a number of suspense and action sequences, all very well done.

w Howard Clewes, *book* Kendal Burt, James Leasor   *d* Roy Baker   *ph* Eric Cross
m Hubert Clifford

Hardy Kruger, Michael Goodliffe, Colin Gordon, *Alec McCowen*

One Third of a Nation*

US 1939   79m   bw
Federal Theatre (Dudley Murphy)

A shopgirl persuades a landlord to tear down his dangerous slums and put up good buildings.
Naïve do-goodery, not too persuasively managed.

w Dudley Murphy, Oliver H. P. Garrett, *play* Arthur Arent   *d* Dudley Murphy   *ph* William Mellor

Sylvia Sidney, Leif Erickson, Myron McCormick, Hiram Sherman, Sidney Lumet, Percy Waram

One Touch of Venus*

US 1948   82m   bw
Universal / Lester Cowan

In a fashionable department store, a statue of Venus comes to life and falls for a window dresser.
Pleasant satirical comedy, watered down from the Broadway original.

w Harry Kurnitz, Frank Tashlin, *play* S. J. Perelman, Ogden Nash   *d* William A. Seiter
ph Franz Planer   *songs* Kurt Weill
ad Bernard Herzbrun, Emrich Nicholson

Ava Gardner, Robert Walker, Eve Arden, Dick Haymes, Olga San Juan, Tom Conway

One, Two, Three***

US 1961   115m   bw   Panavision
United Artists / Mirisch / Pyramid (Billy Wilder)

An executive in West Berlin is trying to sell Coca Cola to the Russians while preventing his boss's daughter from marrying a communist.
Back to *Ninotchka* territory, but this time the tone is that of a wild farce which achieves fine momentum in stretches but also flags a lot in between, teetering the while on the edge of taste.

w Billy Wilder, I. A. L. Diamond, *play* Ferenc Molnar   *d* Billy Wilder   *ph* Daniel Fapp   *m* André Previn

James Cagney, Horst Buchholz, Arlene Francis, Pamela Tiffin, Lilo Pulver, Howard St John, Leon Askin
  'A sometimes bewildered, often wonderfully funny exercise in nonstop nuttiness.'—*Time*
  'This first-class featherweight farce is a serious achievement.'—*Stanley Kauffmann*

AAN: Daniel Fapp

One Way Passage*

US 1932   69m   bw
Warner (Robert Lord)

On an ocean voyage, a dying girl falls in love with a crook going home to face a life sentence.
Pattern melodrama which stood Hollywood in good stead.

w Wilson Mizner, Joseph Jackson, Robert Lord   *d* Tay Garnett   *ph* Robert Kurrie

William Powell, Kay Francis, Frank McHugh,
Aline MacMahon, Warren Hymer, Herbert
Mundin, Roscoe Karns, Stanley Fields
† Remade as *'Til We Meet Again* (qv).

AA: original story (Robert Lord)

One Way Pendulum
GB 1964   85m   bw
UA / Woodfall (Michael Deeley)

A suburban clerk leads a dream existence; his
son teaches speak-your-weight machines to
sing, while he sets an imaginary murder trial in
motion.
A nonsense play (which has many adherents)
resists the literalness of the camera eye.

w N. F. Simpson, from his play   *d* Peter
Yates   *ph* Denys Coop   *m* Richard Rodney
Bennett

Eric Sykes, George Cole, Peggy Mount,
Alison Leggatt, Mona Washbourne

One Way Street
US 1950   79m   bw
U-I / Leonard Goldstein (Sam Goldwyn Jnr)

A disillusioned doctor steals a fortune and
hides out in a Mexican village, where he
regains his self-respect.
Thin and pointless melodrama.

w Lawrence Kimble   *d* Hugo Fregonese
ph Maury Gertsman   *m* Frank Skinner

James Mason, Marta Toren, Dan Duryea,
William Conrad, King Donovan, Jack Elam
'It is reported that James Mason chooses his
own parts, and if this is true I have to report
that he is a glutton for punishment.'—*Daily
Herald*
'One of the dullest, most stupid films of the
year.'—*Sunday Pictorial*

One Wild Oat
GB 1951   78m   bw

An old flame tries to blackmail a highly
respectable solicitor. Modest film version of a
popular West End farce. Robertson Hare,
Stanley Holloway, Sam Costa, Andrew
Crawford, Vera Pearce, Robert Moreton,
Irene Handl. Written by Vernon Sylvaine and
Lawrence Huntingdon, from the play by
Vernon Sylvaine; directed by Charles
Saunders; for Coronet / Eros.

Onibaba°
Japan 1964   104m   bw   Tohoscope
Kindai Eiga Kyokai / Tokyo Eiga
aka: *The Hole*

In medieval times on a remote marshy plain,
mother and daughter live by killing stray

soldiers and selling their armour, until
daughter takes one for a lover and mother
becomes jealous.
A kind of original horror legend is told by this
strange, compelling piece with its frequent
moments of nastiness. It remains, perhaps
mercifully, unique.

wd Kaneto Shindo   *ph* Kiyomi Juroda
m Hikaru Hayashi

Nobuko Otowa, Jitsuko Yoshimura, Kei Sato

The Onion Field
US 1979   126m   Eastmancolor
Black Marble (Walter Coblenz)

Two policemen are shot at by a manic killer,
and the one who survives finds that he is
suspected of cowardice and has to resign from
the force.
Well meaning but lumbering case history. The
author must carry the blame, as for once the
picture was made exactly on his terms.

w Joseph Wambaugh, from his novel
d Harold Becker   *ph* Charles Rosher
m Eumir Depdato   *pd* Brian Eatwell

John Savage, James Woods, Franklyn Seales,
Ted Danson, Ronny Cox, David Huffman

Onionhead
US 1958   110m   bw
Warner (Jules Schermer)

Adventures of a ship's cook in the US
Coastguard.
Service comedy that must have seemed funnier
in the US than in Britain.

w Nelson Gidding, *novel* Weldon Hill
d Norman Taurog   *ph* Harold Rosson
md Ray Heindorf

Andy Griffith, Felicia Farr, Walter Matthau,
Erin O'Brien, Joe Mantell, Ray Danton,
Roscoe Karns, James Gregory, Tige Andrews
† An attempt to cash in on the success of *No
Time for Sergeants*.

Only Angels Have Wings**
US 1939   121m   bw
Columbia (Howard Hawks)

Tension creeps into the relationships of the
men who fly cargo planes over the Andes
when a stranded showgirl sets her cap at the
boss.
For an action film this is really too restricted
by talk and cramped studio sets, and its theme
was more entertainingly explored in *Red Dust*.
Still, it couldn't be more typical of the Howard
Hawks film world, where men are men and
women have to be as tough as they are.

w Jules Furthman, *story* Howard Hawks
d Howard Hawks *ph* Joseph Walker, Elmer
Dyer *m* Dmitri Tiomkin *md* Morris Stoloff

Cary Grant, Jean Arthur, Rita Hayworth,
Richard Barthelmess, Thomas Mitchell, Sig
Rumann, Victor Kilian, John Carroll, Allyn
Joslyn

'All these people did the best they could
with what they were given—but look at it.'—
Otis Ferguson

The Only Game in Town

US 1969   113m   De Luxe
TCF (Fred Kohlmar)

A Las Vegas chorus girl and a piano player
have an unhappy life because of his gambling
fever.

Uninteresting two-header from a play that
didn't make it; no light relief, no action, and
not even very good acting.

w Frank D. Gilroy, from his play *d* George
Stevens *ph* Henri Decaë *m* Maurice Jarre

Elizabeth Taylor, Warren Beatty, Charles
Braswell, Hank Henry

'It epitomizes the disaster the studio and
star systems foist on films . . . the only two-
character tale around to cost $11 million.'—
Judith Crist

Only the Valiant

US 1950   105m   bw
William Cagney

A tough cavalry officer in a lonely fort wins a
battle against Indians.

Standard top-of-the-bill western; competent
but not very gripping.

w Edmund H. North, Harry Brown *d* Gordon
Douglas *ph* Lionel Lindon *m* Franz Waxman

Gregory Peck, Ward Bond, Gig Young, Lon
Chaney Jnr, Barbara Payton, Neville Brand

Only Two Can Play***

GB 1962   106m   bw
British Lion / Vale (Launder and Gilliat)

A much married assistant librarian in a Welsh
town has an abortive affair with a councillor's
wife.

Well characterized and generally diverting
'realistic' comedy which slows up a bit towards
the end but contains many memorable
sequences and provides its star's last good
character performance.

w Bryan Forbes, novel That Uncertain Feeling
by *Kingsley Amis d Sidney Gilliat ph* John
Wilcox *m* Richard Rodney Bennett
ad Albert Witherick

Peter Sellers, Mai Zetterling, Virginia Maskell,
Richard Attenborough, Raymond Huntley,
John Le Mesurier, *Kenneth Griffith*

Only When I Larf*

GB 1968   103m   Eastmancolor
Paramount / Beecord (Len Deighton, Brian
  Duffy, Hugh Attwooll)

The adventures of three confidence tricksters.
Quite likeable but unmemorable 'with it'
comedy of the sixties; the tricks are more
amusing than the characterization.

w John Salmon, *novel* Len Deighton *d* Basil
Dearden *ph* Anthony Richmond *m* Ron
Grainer

Richard Attenborough, David Hemmings,
Alexandra Stewart, Nicholas Pennell, Melissa
Stribling, Terence Alexander, Edric Connor,
Calvin Lockhart, Clifton Jones

Only Yesterday

US 1933   105m   bw

An unmarried mother is seduced twice by the
same man. One that Ross Hunter didn't get
around to remaking . . . and a good job too.
Margaret Sullavan, John Boles, Billie Burke,
Reginald Denny, Edna May Oliver, Benita
Hume. Written by William Hurlbut, George
O'Neill and Arthur Richman; directed by John
M. Stahl; for Universal.

Ooh, You Are Awful*

GB 1972   97m   Eastmancolor
British Lion / Quintain (E. M. Smedley
  Aston)
US title: *Get Charlie Tully*

A London con man seeks a fortune, the clue
to which is tattooed on the behind of one of
several girls.

Amusing star vehicle with plenty of room for
impersonations and outrageous jokes.

w John Warren, John Singer *d Cliff Owen*
ph Ernest Stewart *m* Christopher Gunning

Dick Emery, Derren Nesbitt, Ronald Fraser,
Pat Coombs, William Franklyn, Brian Oulton,
Norman Bird

Open City**

Italy 1945   101m   bw
Minerva
original title: *Roma, Città Aperta*

Italian underground workers defy the Nazis in
Rome towards the end of the war.

A vivid newsreel quality is achieved by this
nerve-stretching melodrama in which all the
background detail is as real as care could make
it.

w Sergio Amidei, Federico Fellini *d Roberto Rossellini ph* Ubaldo Arata *m* Renzo Rossellini

Aldo Fabrizzi, *Anna Magnani*, Marcello Pagliero, Maria Michi

AAN: script

Open Season

US / Spain / Switzerland 1974   104m
  Eastmancolor   Panavision
Impala / Arpa (George H. Brown, Jose S.
  Vicuna)

Three young criminals hunt human prey, but one of their victims takes his own revenge.
Rough, flashy, violent melodrama which pretends to have something to say but in fact is merely sensationalist.

w David Osborn, Liz Charles Williams
d Peter Collinson *ph* Fernando Arribas
m Ruggero Cini

Peter Fonda, Cornelia Sharp, John Phillip Law, Richard Lynch, Albert Mendoza, William Holden
'Both patience and the plot line are severely strained by the artiness Collinson frequently indulges, with frozen shots to mark the moments of truth and a meaningless punctuation throughout of long shots, angles and flashes.'—*Tom Milne*
'An offensive, gamy potboiler.'—*Variety*

Opening Night

US 1978   144m   Metrocolor
Faces Distribution (Al Ruban)

A Broadway actress is on the point of a nervous breakdown.
Interminable addition to the director's list of unwatchable personal films.

wd John Cassavetes *ph* Al Ruban *m* Bo Horwood

Gena Rowlands, Ben Gazzara, John Cassavetes, Joan Blondell, Paul Stewart, Zohra Lampert, Laura Johnson
'Shrill, puzzling, depressing and overlong.'—*Variety*

L'Opéra de Quat' Sous see Die Dreigroschenoper

Operation Amsterdam*

GB 1958   104m   bw
Rank / Maurice Cowan

In 1940 spies are sent into Holland to prevent the invading Germans from finding Amsterdam's stock of industrial diamonds.
Semi-documentary war adventure, well mounted and played.

w Michael McCarthy, John Eldridge, *book* Adventure in Diamonds by David Walker
d Michael McCarthy ph Reg Wyer, *m* Philip Green

Peter Finch, Tony Britton, Eva Bartok, Alexander Knox, Malcolm Keen, Tim Turner, John Horsley, Melvyn Hayes, Christopher Rhodes

Operation CIA

US 1965   90m   bw

An agent is rushed to Saigon to find a secret message which was never delivered. Crude thick-ear with a few suspenseful moments.
Burt Reynolds, John Hoyt, Daniele Aubry, Kieu Chinh, Cyril Collick. Written by Bill S. Ballinger and Peer J. Oppenheimer; directed by Christian Nyby; for Allied Artists.

Operation Crossbow*

GB 1965   116m   Metrocolor   Panavision
MGM / Carlo Ponti
aka: *The Great Spy Mission*

In World War II, trained scientists are parachuted into Europe to destroy the Nazi rocket-making plant at Peenemunde.
Unlikely, star-packed war yarn with more passing tragedy than most, all obliterated by a shoot-em-up James Bond finale.

w Robert Imrie (Emeric Pressburger), Derry Quinn, Ray Rigby *d* Michael Anderson
ph Erwin Hillier *m* Ron Goodwin

George Peppard, Tom Courtenay, John Mills, Sophia Loren, Lilli Palmer, Anthony Quayle, Patrick Wymark, Jeremy Kemp, Paul Henreid, Trevor Howard, Sylvia Sims, Richard Todd

Operation Daybreak

US 1975   119m   Technicolor
Warner / Howard R. Schuster / American
  Allied (Carter de Haven)

In 1941, Czech patriots kill the hated Nazi Heydrich and are hunted down.
Curiously-timed evocation of wartime resistance adventures, too realistic for the squeamish and certainly not very entertaining despite a fair level of professionalism.

w Ronald Harwood, *novel* Seven Men at Daybreak by Alan Burgess *d* Lewis Gilbert
ph Henri Decaë *m* David Hentschel

Timothy Bottoms, Martin Shaw, Joss Ackland, Nicola Pagett, Anthony Andrews, Anton Diffring, Carl Duering, Diana Coupland

Operation Eichmann
US 1961   94m   bw

After the war, the Nazi who exterminated six million Jews escapes from Europe but is eventually recaptured. Crude exploitation item designed to cash in on Eichmann's trial, a documentary on which would have been much more interesting. Werner Klemperer (as Eichmann), Ruta Lee, Donald Buka, John Banner. Written by Lewis Copley; directed by R. G. Springsteen; for Allied Artists.

Operation Kid Brother
Italy 1967   105m   Techniscope

007's brother defeats an international mastermind with the help of a Scottish archery team. Very elementary James Bond spoof, with a confusing array of old and new elements but less than the required minimum of style. Neil Connery (Sean's kid brother), Daniela Bianchi, Adolfo Celi, Bernard Lee, Lois Maxwell, Agata Flori. Written by Paolo Levi, Vincenzo Mannino and Carlo Tritto; directed by Alberto de Martino; for Dario Sabatello. (Aka: *OK Connery*.) 'A grotesque parody of a parody . . . bad enough to be hysterically funny.'—*MFB*.

Operation Mad Ball*
US 1957   105m   bw
Columbia (Jed Harris)

American troops in Normandy are forbidden to fraternize with nurses, but a clandestine dance is arranged.
Madcap army farce which keeps promising to be funnier than it is.

w Arthur Carter, Jed Harris, Blake Edwards, *play* Arthur Carter *d Richard Quine*
ph Charles Lawton Jnr *m* George Duning

Jack Lemmon, Ernie Kovacs, Kathryn Grant, Mickey Rooney, James Darren, Arthur O'Connell

Operation Pacific
US 1950   109m   bw
Warner (Louis F. Edelmann)

Adventures of a submarine commander in the Pacific war.
Routine war heroics, tolerably done but overstretched.

wd George Waggner *ph* Bert Glennon
m Max Steiner

John Wayne, Patricia Neal, Ward Bond, Scott Forbes, Phil Carey, Paul Picerni, William Campbell, Martin Milner

Operation Petticoat*
US 1959   124m   Eastmancolor
Universal / Granart (Robert Arthur)

During World War II, a crippled submarine is refloated by fair means and foul, and a party of nurses is taken aboard.
Flabby comedy with good moments, but not many.

w Stanley Shapiro, Maurice Richlin *d* Blake Edwards *ph* Russell Harlan *m* David Rose

Cary Grant, Tony Curtis, Joan O'Brien, Dina Merrill, Gene Evans, Arthur O'Connell, Richard Sargent

'Grant is a living lesson in getting laughs without lines.'—*Variety*

AAN: script

Operation St Peter's
Italy 1968   100m   colour

Three thieves steal Michelangelo's *Pietà* and sell it for forty dollars to an American gangster. Rather surprisingly watchable comedy chase, with the star parodying his past roles. Edward G. Robinson, Lando Buzzanca, Heinz Ruhmann, Jean-Claude Brialy. Written by Ennio de Concini, Adriano Baracco, Roberto Gianviti and Lucio Fulci; directed by Lucio Fulci; for Turi Vasile / Paramount.

Operation Secret
US 1952   108m   bw
Warner (Henry Blanke)

A traitor in the French resistance movement shoots a colleague, and the wrong man is accused.
Belated World War II adventure which gives the impression of having been discarded by Errol Flynn.

w James R. Webb, Harold Medford *d* Lewis Seiler *ph* Ted McCord *m* Roy Webb

Cornel Wilde, Steve Cochran, Paul Picerni, Karl Malden

Operation Thunderbolt*
Israel 1977   117m   Eastmancolor
     Panavision
GS Films (Menahem Golan, Yoram Globus)
aka: *Entebbe: Operation Thunderbolt*

An account of the rescue of Israeli hostages from terrorists who have hijacked their plane to Entebbe.
Victory at Entebbe and *Raid on Entebbe* were made with all-star casts for American television. This home-grown account of a famous deed is more modest yet more authoritative.

w Clarke Reynolds *d* Menahem Golan *ph* Adam Greenberg *m* Dov Seltzer

Klaus Kinski, Assaf Dayan, Ori Levy, Yehoram Geon, Mark Heath

Operator 13

US 1933 86m bw

MGM / Cosmopolitan (Lucien Hubbard)

GB title: *Spy 13*

During the Civil War an actress becomes a Union spy.

Elaborate period romance with action highlights.

w Harry Thew, Zelda Sears, Eve Greene *d* Richard Boleslawski *ph George Folsey m* William Axt

Marion Davies, Gary Cooper, Jean Parker, Katherine Alexander, Ted Healy, Russell Hardie, Henry Wadsworth, Douglass Dumbrille

AAN: George Folsey

The Opposite Sex

US 1956 116m Metrocolor

Cinemascope

MGM (Joe Pasternak)

A New York socialite divorces her unfaithful husband but finally takes him back.

Softened, musicalized version of *The Women* (qv); very patchy, shapeless, and not nearly sharp enough.

w Fay and Michael Kanin, *play* Clare Boothe *d* David Miller *ph* Robert Bronner *m* Nicholas Brodszky *songs* Nicholas Brodszky, Sammy Cahn

June Allyson, Dolores Gray, Joan Collins, Ann Sheridan, Agnes Moorehead, Joan Blondell, Barbara Jo Allen, Charlotte Greenwood

The Optimists of Nine Elms*

GB 1973 110m Eastmancolor

Cheetah / Sagittarius (Adrian Gaye, Victor Lyndon)

Children of a London slum make friends with an old busker.

Gentle, sentimental, quite well-observed piece of wistful melancholia, falsified by its star performance.

wd Anthony Simmons, from his novel *co-w* Tudor Gates *ph* Larry Pizer *m* George Martin

Peter Sellers, Donna Mullane, John Chaffey, David Daker, Marjorie Yates

The Oracle

GB 1952 83m bw

Group Three (Colin Lesslie)

A reporter discovers that a village well in Ireland contains an oracle which can predict the future.

Weak sub-Ealing comedy which aims to please and gets a few laughs. All very British.

w Patrick Campbell *d* C. M. Pennington-Richards *ph* Wolfgang Suschitsky *m* Temple Abady

Robert Beatty, Virginia McKenna, Mervyn Johns, Gilbert Harding

Orca—Killer Whale

US 1977 92m Technicolor Panavision

Famous Films / Dino de Laurentiis (Luciano Vincenzoni)

Off Newfoundland, a killer whale takes revenge for its mate's death.

A rather unpleasant attempt to mix horror and thrills with ecology: not very entertaining, and not for the squeamish.

w Luciano Vincenzoni, Sergio Donati *d* Michael Anderson *ph* Ted Moore, J. Barry Herron *m* Ennio Morricone

Richard Harris, Charlotte Rampling, Will Sampson, Keenan Wynn

'The biggest load of cod imaginable.'—*Philip Bergson, Sunday Times*

'There are more thrills to be had in the average dolphinarium.'—*Sight and Sound*

Orchestra Wives**

US 1942 97m bw

TCF (William Le Baron)

A small-town girl marries the singer of a travelling swing band.

Fresh and lively musical of its period, full of first-class music and amusing backstage backbiting.

w Karl Tunberg, Darrell Ware *d* Archie Mayo *ph* Lucien Ballard *md* Alfred Newman

Ann Rutherford, George Montgomery, Lynn Bari, *Glenn Miller and his Orchestra,* Carole Landis, Jackie Gleason

AAN: song 'I've Got a Girl in Kalamazoo' (*m* Harry Warren, *ly* Mack Gordon)

Orders Are Orders

GB 1954 78m bw

Group 3 (Donald Taylor)

Flabby update of *Orders Is Orders* with an interesting cast below par.

w Donald Taylor, Geoffrey Orme *d* David Paltenghi *ph* Arthur Grant *m* Stanley Black

Peter Sellers, Brian Reece, Sid James, Tony Hancock, Margot Grahame, Raymond Huntley, Maureen Johnson, June Thorburn, Bill Fraser

Orders Is Orders
GB 1933 88m bw
Gaumont British (Michael Balcon)

An army barracks is disrupted when an American film company gets permission to work there.
Breezy farce which pleased at the time.

w Leslie Arliss, Sidney Gilliat, *play* Ian Hay, Anthony Armstrong d Walter Forde ph Glen MacWilliams

Charlotte Greenwood, James Gleason, Cedric Hardwicke, Cyril Maude, Ian Hunter, Ray Milland, Jane Carr, Donald Calthrop, Eliot Makeham, Wally Patch, Finlay Currie

Orders to Kill°
GB 1958 111m bw
British Lion / Lynx (Anthony Asquith, Anthony Havelock-Allan)

During World War II a bomber pilot undertakes a mission to parachute into occupied France and kill a double agent, who turns out afterwards to have been innocent.
Strong, hard-to-take but well made war story about the effect of war on conscience.

w Paul Dehn d Anthony Asquith
ph Desmond Dickinson m Benjamin Frankel
Paul Massie, Irene Worth, James Robertson Justice, *Leslie French*, Eddie Albert, Lillian Gish, John Crawford, Jacques Brunius, Lionel Jeffries

The Oregon Trail
US 1959 86m De Luxe Cinemascope

A New York reporter in 1846 is sent to cover a westward trek. Prototype settlers vs Indians western with all the expected incident. Fred MacMurray, William Bishop, Nina Shipman, Gloria Talbot, Henry Hull, John Carradine, Elizabeth Patterson. Written by Louis Vittes and Gene Fowler Jnr; directed by Gene Fowler Jnr; for TCF.

The Organization
US 1971 108m De Luxe
UA / Mirisch (Walter Mirisch)

San Francisco policemen combat an international drug smuggling organization.
The third and weakest adventure of Virgil Tibbs, black policeman of *In the Heat of the Night*. Absolutely routine.

w James R. Webb d Don Medford
ph Joseph Biroc m Gile Melle

Sidney Poitier, Barbara McNair, Sheree North, Gerald S. O'Loughlin

Orphans of the Storm°
US 1921 124m (24 fps) bw silent
D. W. Griffith

Two sisters are caught up in the French revolution of 1789.
Half melodrama, half epic, this celebrated film survives chiefly by its careful attention to historical detail and by the excitement of its crowd scenes.

w D. W. Griffith, *play* Adolph Ennery
d D. W. Griffith ph Henrick Sartov

Lillian Gish, Dorothy Gish, Joseph Schildkraut, Lucille La Verne, Morgan Wallace, Frank Puglia, Creighton Hale
'There is scarcely a scene or an effect in the entire production that is not beautiful to look upon, and there is scarcely a moment that is not charged with intense dramatic power.'— *Robert E. Sherwood, Life*

Orphée°°°
France 1949 112m bw
André Paulvé 1 / Films du Palais Royal

Death, represented by a princess, falls in love with Orpheus, a poet, and helps him when he goes into hell in pursuit of his dead love.
Fascinating poetic fantasy which may have been finally unintelligible but was filled to overflowing with memorable scenes and cinematic tricks, from the entry to the hereafter through a mirror to intercepted code messages such as 'L'oiseau compte avec ses doigts'. The closest the cinema has got to poetry.

wd Jean Cocteau, from his play ph Nicolas Hayer m Georges Auric ad Jean d'Eaubonne
Jean Marais, François Périer, Maria Casarès, Marie Déa, Edouard Dermithe, Juliette Greco
'It is a drama of the visible and the invisible . . . I interwove many myths. Death condemns herself in order to help the man she is duty bound to destroy. The man is saved but Death dies: it is the myth of immortality.'—*Jean Cocteau*
† See the sequel *Le Testament d'Orphée*.

The Oscar°
US 1966 118m Pathecolor
Paramount / Greene–Rouse

On the night of the Academy Awards his friend recalls a heel's rise to stardom.
Squalid, sensationalist account of Hollywood mores; one nopes it isn't quite true.

w Harlan Ellison, Russel Rouse, Clarence Greene, *novel* Richard Sale *d* Russel Rouse *ph* Joseph Ruttenberg *m* Percy Faith

Stephen Boyd, Elke Sommer, Tony Bennett, Eleanor Parker, Milton Berle, Joseph Cotten, Jill St John, Edie Adams, Ernest Borgnine, Ed Begley, Walter Brennan, Broderick Crawford, James Dunn, Peter Lawford, Edith Head, Hedda Hopper, Merle Oberon, Bob Hope, Frank Sinatra

'This is the sort of film that only Hollywood could make, and on that level it is preposterously enjoyable.'—*David Wilson*

'That true movie rarity—a picture that attains a perfection of ineptitude quite beyond the power of words to describe.'—*Richard Schickel*

Oscar Wilde**
GB 1959 96m bw
Vantage (William Kirby)

Scandal strikes Oscar Wilde through his involvement with Lord Alfred Douglas.

Competent, well acted version of well-known events of the nineties, with Morley in his original stage role; generally more satisfactory than *The Trials of Oscar Wilde* which was shot simultaneously.

w Jo Eisinger *d* Gregory Ratoff *ph* Georges Périnal *m* Kenneth V. Jones

Robert Morley, John Neville, Phyllis Calvert, *Ralph Richardson*, Dennis Price, Alexander Knox, Edward Chapman, Martin Benson, Robert Harris, Henry Oscar, William Devlin

O'Shaughnessy's Boy
US 1935 88m bw

A circus performer is reunited with the son his wife took away in childhood. Shameless sentiment which failed to repeat for its stars the success of *The Champ*. Wallace Beery, Jackie Cooper, Leona Maricle, Sara Haden, Henry Stephenson, Spanky MacFarland. Written by Leonard Praskins and Otis Garrett; directed by Richard Boleslawski; for MGM.

Ossessione*
Italy 1942 135m bw
ICI

A wanderer falls for the wife of an innkeeper and they murder him, but fate takes a hand. Unofficial remake of *The Postman Always Rings Twice*, barely released outside Italy. A powerful melodrama credited with starting the neo-realist school.

w Antonio Pietrangeli, Giuseppe de Santis, Gianni Puccini, Luchino Visconti, Mario Alicata *d Luchino Visconti ph* Aldo Tonti, Domenico Scala *m* Giuseppe Rosati

Massimo Girotti, Clara Calamai, Elio Marcuzzo

† Other versions: *Le Dernier Tournant* (France 1939); *The Postman Always Rings Twice* (US 1945).

Othello*
US / France 1951 91m bw
Mercury / Films Marceau

Shakespeare's play as rearranged by Orson Welles at the start of his European wanderings; modest budget, flashes of brilliance, poor technical quality, variable acting. Not really the best way to film Shakespeare.

w Orson Welles, *play* William Shakespeare *d* Orson Welles *ad* Alexander Trauner

Orson Welles, Micheal MacLiammoir, Fay Compton, Robert Cook, Suzanne Cloutier, Michael Laurence, Hilton Edwards, Doris Dowling

Othello*
GB 1965 166m Technicolor Panavision
BHE (Richard Godwin)

A record of the National Theatre production, disappointing in terms of cinema but a valuable record of a famous performance.

d Stuart Burge *ph* Geoffrey Unsworth *md* Richard Hampton

Laurence Olivier, Frank Finlay, Joyce Redman, Maggie Smith, Derek Jacobi, Robert Lang, Anthony Nicholls

AAN: Laurence Olivier; Frank Finlay; Joyce Redman; Maggie Smith

The Other*
US 1972 100m De Luxe
TCF / Rex-Benchmark (Tom Tryon)

A boy insists that his dead twin is responsible for several unexplained deaths.

Subtle family ghost story for intellectuals; a bit pretentious and restrained for popular success.

w Tom Tryon, from his novel *d* Robert Mulligan *ph* Robert Surtees *m* Jerry Goldsmith *pd* Albert Brenner

Uta Hagen, Diana Muldaur, Chris Connelly, Victor French

The Other Love
US 1947 96m bw
Enterprise (David Lewis)

At a Swiss sanatorium, a lady concert pianist who is dying falls in love with her doctor.
Fairly icky 'woman's picture' with uncomfortable performances.

w Ladislas Fodor, Harry Brown, *story* Erich Maria Remarque *d* André de Toth *ph* Victor Milner *m* Miklos Rozsa

Barbara Stanwyck, David Niven, Richard Conte, Gilbert Roland, Joan Lorring, Lenore Aubert

Other Men's Women
US 1931 70m bw

A train driver falls for his partner's wife.
Stilted heavy-breathing melodrama. Grant Withers, James Cagney, Mary Astor, Joan Blondell, Regis Toomey. Written by William K. Wells; directed by William A. Wellman; for Warner.

The Other Side of Midnight
US 1977 166m De Luxe Panavision
TCF / Frank Yablans, Martin Ransohoff (Howard W. Koch Jnr)

Before and after World War II a young Parisienne courts an American flyer, but her tycoon husband eventually exacts a grim revenge on both of them.
Turgid and interminable adaptation of a best-seller, with no likeable characters and several unpleasant sequences.

w Herman Raucher, Daniel Taradash, *novel* Sidney Sheldon *d* Charles Jarrott *ph* Fred J. Koenekamp *m* Michel Legrand *pd* John De Cuir

Marie-France Pisier, John Beck, Susan Sarandon, Raf Vallone, Clu Gulager, Christian Marquand

'After 166 minutes the feeling that one has actually lived through it all is a little too real for comfort.'—*David Badder, MFB*

'A fatuous, money-spinning film from the fatuous, money-spinning book.'—*New Yorker*

'Right down to the nonsense title, this epic of schlock restores the era of *Now Voyager* . . . the movie equivalent of a good bad read.'—*Time Out*

The Other Side of the Mountain
US 1975 102m Technicolor
Universal / Filmways / Larry Peerce (Edward S. Feldman)
GB title: *A Window to the Sky*

A girl skiing champion is paralysed by polio.
Maudlin tearjerker based on a real case; altogether too much of a good thing.

w David Seltzer, *book* A Long Way Up by E. G. Valens *d* Larry Peerce *ph* David M. Walsh *m* Charles Fox

Marilyn Hassett, Beau Bridges, Belinda Montgomery, Nan Martin, William Bryant, Dabney Coleman

AAN: song 'Richard's Window' (*m* Charles Fox, *ly* Norman Gimbel)

The Other Side of the Mountain Part Two
US 1977 99m Technicolor
Universal / Filmways (Edward S. Feldman)

Crippled skier Jill Kinmont becomes a teacher and falls in love again.
More true-life weepie material spun out from the first successful film; the sequel is quickly forgettable.

w Douglas Day Stewart *d* Larry Peerce *ph* Ric Waite *m* Lee Holdridge

Marilyn Hassett, Timothy Bottoms, Nan Martin, Belinda J. Montgomery

Otley**
GB 1968 91m Technicolor
Columbia / Open Road (Bruce Cohn Curtis)

An inoffensive Londoner falls in with spies and murderers.
Semi-spoof comedy thriller taking in James Bondery and the swinging London set.
Generally pretty funny, but not entirely certain of its own motives.

w Ian La Frenais, Dick Clement, *novel* Martin Waddell *d* Dick Clement *ph* Austin Dempster *m* Stanley Myers

Tom Courtenay, Romy Schneider, Alan Badel, James Villiers, Leonard Rossiter, Freddie Jones, James Bolam, Fiona Lewis

Our Betters*
US 1933 83m bw
RKO (David O. Selznick)

An American woman in London finds her titled husband is unfaithful and sets about causing society scandals.
Dimly adapted West End success makes an interesting but unamusing film.

w Jane Murfin, Harry Wagstaff Gribble, *play* W. Somerset Maugham *d* George Cukor *ph* Charles Rosher *md* Max Steiner

Constance Bennett, Violet Kemble Cooper, Alan Mowbray, Gilbert Roland, Phoebe Foster, Charles Starrett, Grant Mitchell, Anita Louise, Minor Watson, Hugh Sinclair

'One of those familiar dreams of high life in which we are asked to admire even while we condemn the superb immorality of our almost godlike betters.'—*The Times*

Our Blushing Brides see Our Dancing Daughters

Our Daily Bread*
US 1934   80m   bw
King Vidor

A young couple in the Depression inherit a
broken-down farm and make it work.
A rather drab sequel to *The Crowd*, with an
irrigation ditch finale in clear imitation of
Eisenstein.

w Elizabeth Hill, *story* King Vidor *d* King
Vidor *ph* Robert Planck *m* Alfred Newman

Karen Morley, Tom Keene, John Qualen,
Barbara Pepper, Addison Richards

'With the arrival of the ditchdigging
sequence, all that has gone before seems but
buildup for this compelling climax.'—*Eileen
Bowser, Film Notes, 1969*
† Vidor so desperately wanted to make the
film that, discovering its theme to be
unpopular with sponsors, he pawned
everything he owned to finance it.

Our Dancing Daughters*
US 1928   86m approx (24 fps)   bw
   silent
MGM / Cosmopolitan (Hunt Stromberg)

A wild young socialite knows when to stop,
and makes a good marriage; her friend doesn't
and falls to her death while drunk.
Mild exploitation piece of its time which swept
Joan Crawford to stardom after her dance in
her underwear.

w Josephine Lovett *d* Harry Beaumont
ph George Barnes

Joan Crawford, Johnny Mack Brown, Dorothy
Sebastian, Anita Page, Nils Asther
† Sequels: *Our Modern Maidens* (silent, 1929)
with JC, Rod La Rocque, Douglas Fairbanks
Jnr, Anita Page, w Josephine Lovett; *Our
Blushing Brides* (sound, 1930) with JC, Robert
Montgomery, Anita Page, Dorothy Sebastian,
Raymond Hackett, w Bess Meredyth and John
Howard Lawson. Neither was remarkable.
AAN: Josephine Lovett; George Barnes.

Our Fighting Navy
GB 1937   75m   bw

In South America, a British naval captain
saves the consul's daughter from a
revolutionary. Tuppenny blood heroics,
unconvincingly staged. Robert Douglas, H. B.
Warner, Noah Beery, Richard Cromwell,
Hazel Terry, Esme Percy. Written by
'Bartimeus', Guy Pollock, H. T. Bishop,
Gerald Elliott and Harrison Owens; directed
by Norman Walker; for Herbert Wilcox. (US
title: *Torpedoed*.)

Our Hearts Were Young and Gay*
US 1944   81m   bw
Paramount (Sheridan Gibney)

Two well-to-do flappers of the twenties find
fun and romance in Paris.
A pleasant, undemanding piece of nostalgia
based on a popular biography; in 1946 a less
successful sequel, *Our Hearts Were Growing
Up*, involved the young ladies with bootleggers
at Princeton.

w Sheridan Gibney, *book* Cornelia Otis
Skinner, Emily Kimbrough *d* Lewis Allen
ph Theodor Sparkuhl *m* Werner Heymann

Gail Russell, Diana Lynn, Charles Ruggles,
Dorothy Gish, Beulah Bondi, James Brown,
Bill Edwards, Jean Heather

Our Hospitality**
US 1923   70m approx (24 fps)   bw
   silent
Metro / Buster Keaton (Joseph M. Schenck)

Around 1850, a southerner returns home to
claim his bride and finds himself in the middle
of a blood feud.
Charming rather than hilarious star comedy
with a splendid ancient train and at least one
incredible stunt by the star.

w Jean Havez, Joseph Mitchell, Clyde
Bruckman *d* Buster Keaton, Jack Blystone
ph Elgin Lessley, Gordon Jennings

Buster Keaton, Natalie Talmadge, Joe Keaton,
Buster Keaton Jnr

Our Little Girl
US 1935   63m   bw
TCF (Edward Butcher)

A doctor's daughter brings her parents
together.
One of the child star's thinner and more
sentimental vehicles.

w Stephen Morehouse Avery, Allen Rivkin,
Jack Yellen, *story* Heaven's Gate by Florence
Leighton Pfalzgraf *d* John Robertson
ph John Seitz *md* Oscar Bradley

Shirley Temple, Joel McCrea, Rosemary
Ames, Lyle Talbot, Erin O'Brien-Moore

Our Man Flint*
US 1965   108m   De Luxe   Cinemascope
TCF (Saul David)

An American secret agent and super stud
fights an organization bent on controlling the
world through its weather.
Comic strip imitation of James Bond; in its
wild way the first instalment scored a good
many laughs, but the sequel, *In Like Flint*
(qv), quickly ended the series.

w Hal Fimberg, Ben Starr *d* Daniel Mann *ph* Daniel L. Fapp *m* Jerry Goldsmith

James Coburn, Lee J. Cobb, Gila Golan, Edward Mulhare, Benson Fong, Sigrid Valdis
'Despite the fact that everyone from designers to actors seems to be having a ball, the film somehow goes over the edge of parody—ultimately it looks suspiciously like a case of wish-fulfilment.'—*John Gillett*

Our Man in Havana*
GB 1959 112m bw Cinemascope
Columbia / Kingsmead (Carol Reed)

A British vacuum cleaner salesman in Havana allows himself to be recruited as a spy, and wishes he hadn't.
The wry flavour of the novel does not really translate to the screen, and especially not to the wide screen, but a few lines and characters offer compensation.

w Graham Greene, from his novel *d* Carol Reed *ph* Oswald Morris *m* Hermanos Deniz Cuban Rhythm Band

Alec Guinness, *Noel Coward*, Burl Ives, Maureen O'Hara, Ernie Kovacs, *Ralph Richardson*, Jo Morrow, Paul Rogers, Grégoire Aslan, Duncan Macrae
'The main weakness is the absence of economic, expressive cutting and visual flow. As a result . . . stretches of dialogue become tedious to watch; and the essential awareness of the writer's shifting tensions yields disappointingly to the easier mannerisms of any conventional comedy-thriller.'—*Peter John Dyer*

Our Miss Brooks
US 1955 85m bw

A lady teacher finds that the professor to whom she is engaged is tied to mother's apron strings. Verbose comedy considerably less funny than the TV series from which it was spun off. Eve Arden, Gale Gordon, Robert Rockwell, Don Porter, Jane Morgan, Richard Crenna, Nick Adams. Written by Al Lewis and Joseph Quillan; directed by Al Lewis; for Warner.

Our Miss Fred*
GB 1972 96m Technicolor
EMI / Willis World Wide (Josephine Douglas)

In World War II France, an actor escapes in women's clothes when his troupe is captured by the Nazis.
A carefully nurtured vehicle for Britain's top female impersonator somehow doesn't come off; celluloid both constrains his range and reveals his inadequacies.

w Hugh Leonard *d* Bob Kellett *ph* Dick Bush *m* Peter Greenwell

Danny La Rue, Alfred Marks, Lance Percival, Lally Bowers, Frances de la Tour, Walter Gotell

Our Modern Maidens see Our Dancing Daughters

Our Mother's House*
GB 1967 105m Metrocolor
MGM / Filmways (Jack Clayton)

When mother dies, seven children, who don't want to go to an orphanage, bury her in the garden. Then their ne'er-do-well father turns up.
Unpleasant and rather boring melodrama, too silly to have much dramatic impact.

w Jeremy Brooks, Haya Harareet, *novel* Julian Gloag *d* Jack Clayton *ph* Larry Pizer *m* Georges Delerue

Dirk Bogarde, Margaret Brooks, Pamela Franklin, Mark Lester, Yootha Joyce, Anthony Nicholls
'The children begin to display an alarming variety of accents . . . and when Dirk Bogarde enters, doing a rich Bill Sykes act as the long lost wicked father to a predominantly genteel family, the whole structure collapses.'—*Tom Milne*

Our Neighbours the Carters
US 1939 85m bw

A small-town pharmacist is so poor that he considers an offer from a wealthy friend to adopt one of his children. A small-town saga of smiles and tears, much appreciated at the time. Frank Craven, Genevieve Tobin, Edmund Lowe. Written by S. K. Lauren and Renaud Hoffman; directed by Ralph Murphy; for Paramount.

Our Relations*
US 1936 65m bw
Hal Roach / Stan Laurel Productions

Two sailors entrusted with a diamond ring get mixed up with their long lost and happily married twin brothers.
A fast-moving comedy which contains some of Laurel and Hardy's most polished work as well as being their most satisfying production.

w Richard Connell, Felix Adler, Charles Roger, Jack Jevne, *story* The Money Box by W. W. Jacobs *d* Harry Lachman *ph* Rudolph Maté

Stan Laurel, Oliver Hardy, James Finlayson, Alan Hale, Sidney Toler, Daphne Pollard, Iris Adrian, Noel Madison, Ralf Harolde, *Arthur Housman*

Our Town**
US 1940 90m bw
Principal Artists / Sol Lesser

Birth, life and death in a small New
Hampshire community.

One of the main points of the play, the
absence of scenery, is abandoned in this screen
version, and the graveyard scene has to be
presented as a dream, but the film retains the
narrator and manages to make points of its
own while absorbing the endearing qualities
which made the play a classic.

w Thornton Wilder, Frank Craven, Harry
Chantlee, *play* Thornton Wilder *d Sam
Wood* *ph* Bert Glennon *m* Aaron Copland
pd William Cameron Menzies

Frank Craven, William Holden, *Martha Scott,
Thomas Mitchell, Fay Bainter, Guy Kibbee,
Beulah Bondi,* Stuart Erwin
'You can nearly smell things cooking, and
feel the night air.'—*Otis Ferguson*

AAN: best picture; Aaron Copland; Martha
Scott

Our Very Own
US 1950 93m bw
Samuel Goldwyn

A girl is shocked to discover that she is
adopted.
Another Goldwyn foray into chintzy, middle-
class, small-town America, but not a winning
example.

w F. Hugh Herbert *d* David Miller *ph* Lee
Garmes *m* Victor Young *ad* Richard Day

Ann Blyth, Farley Granger, Joan Evans, Jane
Wyatt, Ann Dvorak, Donald Cook, Natalie
Wood, Gus Schilling, Phyllis Kirk

Our Vines Have Tender Grapes*
US 1945 105m bw
MGM (Robert Sisk)

Life in a Norwegian farm community in
southern Wisconsin.
Unexceptionable family picture produced in
MGM's best manner.

w Dalton Trumbo, *novel* George Victor
Martin *d* Roy Rowland *ph* Robert Surtees
m Bronislau Kaper

Edward G. Robinson, Margaret O'Brien,
James Craig, Agnes Moorehead, Jackie
'Butch' Jenkins, Morris Carnovsky, Frances
Gifford, Sara Haden

Our Wife*
US 1931 20m bw

Stan helps Ollie to elope. Good standard star
comedy with a rather disappointing third

sequence as three people try to get into a car
designed for one. Laurel and Hardy, James
Finlayson, Jean London. Written by H. M.
Walker; directed by James W. Horne; for Hal
Roach.

Our Wife
US 1941 95m bw
Columbia (John M. Stahl)

A composer is romantically torn between a
lady scientist and his own ex-wife.
Middling romantic comedy of a kind very
familiar at the time.

w P. J. Wolfson, *play* Lillian Day by Lyon
Mearson *d* John M. Stahl *ph* Franz Planer
m Leo Shuken

Melvyn Douglas, Ruth Hussey, Ellen Drew,
Charles Coburn, John Hubbard, Harvey
Stephens

Out of Season*
GB 1975 90m Technicolor
EMI / Lorimar (Robert Enders, Merv
Adelson)

One winter in an English seaside resort, an old
love is rekindled.
Restrained sexual fireworks in the old French
manner, well enough done with excellent
atmosphere but a shade overlong and marred
by the need to indulge in modern tricks such
as a deliberately ambiguous ending.

w Reuben Bercovitch, Eric Bercovici *d Alan
Bridges* *ph* Arthur Ibbetson *m* John
Cameron

Cliff Robertson, Vanessa Redgrave, Susan
George, Edward Evans

Out of the Blue
US 1947 86m bw

A Greenwich village artist thinks a girl who
has passed out in his apartment is dead, and
tries to hide the body. Tasteless and very
unfunny farce. George Brent, Carole Landis,
Ann Dvorak, Turhan Bey, Virginia Mayo,
Elizabeth Patterson, Julia Dean, Richard
Lane. Written by Vera Caspary, Walter
Bullock and Edward Eliscu; directed by Leigh
Jason; for Eagle Lion.

Out of the Clouds*
GB 1954 88m Eastmancolor
Ealing (Michael Relph, Basil Dearden)

Several personal stories mesh against a
background of London airport during a fog.
A dull compendium of stories with a
background of documentary detail which is
now fascinating because it's so dated.

w John Eldridge, Michael Relph d Michael
Relph, Basil Dearden ph Paul Beeson
m Richard Addinsell

Anthony Steel, Robert Beatty, David Knight,
Margo Lorenz, James Robertson Justice,
Eunice Gayson, Isabel Dean, Gordon Harker,
Bernard Lee, Michael Howard, Marie Lohr,
Esme Cannon, Abraham Sofaer

'The film relies considerably on small-time
players and marginal incidents; the detail,
however, never looks like adding up to a
satisfactory whole.'—*Penelope Houston*

Out of the Fog*
US 1941 86m bw
Warner (Henry Blanke)

Gangsters move in to terrorize an innocent
Brooklyn family.
Standard exploration of a situation which
became routine.

w Robert Rossen, Jerry Wald, Richard
Macaulay, *play* The Gentle People by Irwin
Shaw d Anatole Litvak ph James Wong
Howe

Ida Lupino, John Garfield, Thomas Mitchell,
Eddie Albert, George Tobias, Aline
MacMahon, Jerome Cowan, John Qualen,
Leo Gorcey

Out of the Past**
US 1947 97m bw
RKO (Warren Duff)
GB title: *Build My Gallows High*

A private detective is hired by a hoodlum to
find his homicidal girl friend; he does, and falls
in love with her.
Moody *film noir* with Hollywood imitating
French models; plenty of snarling and a death-
strewn climax.

w Geoffrey Homes, from his novel Build My
Gallows High d Jacques Tourneur
ph Nicholas Musuraca m Roy Webb

Robert Mitchum, Jane Greer, Kirk Douglas,
Rhonda Fleming, Richard Webb, Steve
Brodie, Virginia Huston, Dickie Moore

'Is this not an outcrop of the national
masochism induced by a quite aimless, newly
industrialized society proceeding rapidly on its
way to nowhere?'—*Richard Winnington*

'Mitchum is so sleepily self-confident with
the women that when he slopes into clinches
you expect him to snore in their faces.'—
James Agee

Out of this World
US 1945 96m bw
Paramount (Sam Coslow)

A Western Union messenger becomes a hit
crooner and a national phenomenon.
Very mild comedy with the gimmick that Bing
Crosby dubbed the singing.

w Walter de Leon, Arthur Phillips d Hal
Walker ph Stuart Thompson m Victor
Young

Eddie Bracken, Veronica Lake, Diana Lynn,
Cass Daley, Parkyakarkus, Donald MacBride,
Florence Bates, Carmen Cavallero

The Out of Towners*
US 1970 98m Movielab
Paramount / Jalem (Paul Nathan)

An executive and his wife fly into New York
for an interview, but their encounter with the
city is a mounting series of traumatic disasters.
A love-hate relationship with a city
demonstrated by a resident is something of an
in-joke and becomes increasingly hysterical
and unsympathetic, but there are bright
moments in this company.

w Neil Simon d Arthur Hiller ph Andrew
Laszlo m Quincy Jones

Jack Lemmon, Sandy Dennis

Outback*
Australia 1970 109m Technicolor
NIT / Group W (George Willoughby)

A young teacher becomes involved in the
rougher side of life in a remote Australian
village.
A convincingly brutal picture of a community
whose interests range from homosexuality to a
bloody kangaroo hunt.

w Evan Jones, *novel* Wake in Fright by
Kenneth Cook d Ted Kotcheff ph Brian
West m John Scott

Gary Bond, Donald Pleasence, Chips Rafferty

Outcast Lady
US 1934 79m bw

A spoilt rich girl goes from man to man but
helps her drunken brother. Modest remake of
the Garbo vehicle A Woman of Affairs.
Constance Bennett, Hugh Williams, Mrs
Patrick Campbell, Elizabeth Allan, Henry
Stephenson, Leo G. Carroll. Written by Zoe
Akins, from the novel *The Green Hat* by
Michael Arlen; directed by Robert Z.
Leonard; for MGM. (GB title: *A Woman of
the World*.)

An Outcast of the Islands**
GB 1951 102m bw
London Films (Carol Reed)

A shiftless trader finds a secret Far Eastern trading post where he can be happy – but even here he becomes an outcast.
An interesting but not wholly successful attempt to dramatize a complex character study. It looks great and is well acted.

w William Fairchild, *novel* Joseph Conrad
d Carol Reed *ph* John Wilcox *m* Brian Easdale
Trevor Howard, Ralph Richardson, Kerima, Robert Morley, Wendy Hiller, George Coulouris, Frederick Valk, Wilfrid Hyde White, Betty Ann Davies
'The script is so overwhelmed by the narrative itself that the characters and relationships fail to crystallize . . . while the handling is often intelligent, ingenious, and has its effective moments, no real conception emerges.'—*Gavin Lambert*

The Outcasts of Poker Flat
US 1937 68m bw
RKO (Robert Sisk)
Four undesirables are run out of town and stuck in a mountain cabin during a snowstorm.
Overstretched anecdote with a predictably downbeat finale and not much action.

w John Twist, Harry Segall, *story* Bret Harte
d Christy Cabanne *ph* Robert de Grasse
Preston Foster, Jean Muir, Van Heflin

The Outcasts of Poker Flat
US 1952 80m bw
TCF (Julian Blaustein)
Good-looking but equally undramatic remake of the above.

w Edmund H. North *d* Joseph M. Newman
ph Joseph La Shelle *m* Hugo Friedhofer
Dale Robertson, Anne Baxter, Cameron Mitchell, Miriam Hopkins

The Outfit
US 1973 103m Metrocolor
MGM (Carter de Haven)
A criminal just out of prison finds himself in danger from the Syndicate.
Unattractive rehash of *Point Blank* with much gratuitous violence.

wd John Flynn, *novel* Richard Stark *ph* Bruce Surtees *m* Jerry Fielding
Robert Duvall, Karen Black, Robert Ryan, Joe Don Baker, Timothy Carey, Richard Jaeckel, Sheree North, Marie Windsor, Jane Greer, Elisha Cook Jnr
'A nice profusion of Hollywood character actors makes up for the overall lack of drive.'—*Sight and Sound*

The Outlaw°
US 1943 126m bw
Howard Hughes
Billy the Kid, Doc Holliday and Pat Garrett meet up at a way station and quarrel over a half-breed girl.
Half-baked western with much pretentious chat and the main interest squarely focused on the bosom of the producer's new discovery.
This aspect kept censorship ballyhoo going for six years before the film was finally released in truncated form, and audiences found it not worth the wait, though it does look good.

w Jules Furthman *d* Howard Hughes
ph Gregg Toland *md* Victor Young
Jack Beutel, Jane Russell, Thomas Mitchell, Walter Huston

Outlaw Blues
US 1977 101m Technicolor
Warner / Fred Weintraub–Paul Heller (Steve Tisch)
An ex-con finds that a singing star has stolen his song.
Fashionable comedy-melodrama with no great entertainment value despite action scenes towards the end.

w B. W. L. Norton *d* Richard T. Heffron
ph Jules Brenner *m* Charles Bernstein
Peter Fonda, Susan Saint James, John Crawford, James Callahan, Michael Lerner

The Outlaw Josey Wales°
US 1976 135m De Luxe Panavision
Warner / Malpaso (Robert Daley)
A westerner gradually avenges the death of his wife at the hands of bandits.
Bloodthirsty actioner in the star's usual mould; likely to prove unintentionally funny for hardened addicts.

w Phil Kaufman, Sonia Chernus, *novel* Gone to Texas by Forrest Carter *d* Clint Eastwood
ph Bruce Surtees *m* Jerry Fielding
Clint Eastwood, Chief Dan George, Sondra Locke, John Vernon, Bill McKinney
'If only the actors hadn't got in the way of the scenery, it would have been a very beautiful film indeed.'—*Benny Green, Punch*
AAN: Jerry Fielding

Outpost in Morocco
US 1949 92m bw
Joseph N. Ermolieff
A romantic Foreign Legion officer falls for the daughter of an enemy Arab.

Despite authentic locations and the co-operation of the Legion this is a stolid piece of work, too dull even for children's matinees.

w Charles Grayson, Paul de St Columbe
d Robert Florey ph Lucien Andriot

George Raft, Akim Tamiroff, Marie Windsor, John Litel, Eduard Franz

Outrage
US 1950   75m   bw
Filmmakers (Collier Young)

A girl who has been raped is almost unhinged by the experience.
Well-meaning low-budgeter, thin in entertainment value.

w Ida Lupino, Collier Young, Marvin Wald
d Ida Lupino ph Archie Stout m Paul Sawtell md Constantin Bakaleinikoff
pd Harry Horner

Mala Powers, Tod Andrews, Robert Clarke, Raymond Bond, Lilian Hamilton

'An unconvincing mixture of sensationalism, sentiment and half-baked sociology.'—MFB

The Outrage*
US 1964   97m   bw   Panavision
MGM / Harvest / February / Ritt / Kayos (A. Ronald Lubin)

Conflicting views of a western murder.
Wildly ineffective remake of Rashomon, with everyone strangely overacting and little sense of the west as it is normally depicted.

w Michael Kanin d Martin Ritt ph James Wong Howe m Alex North

Paul Newman, Edward G. Robinson, Laurence Harvey, Claire Bloom, William Shatner, Albert Salmi

The Outriders
US 1950   93m   Technicolor
MGM (Richard Goldstone)

Three Confederate soldiers escape from a yankee prison camp.
Competent star western with solid production values.

w Irving Ravetch d Roy Rowland ph Charles Schoenbaum m André Previn

Joel McCrea, Arlene Dahl, Barry Sullivan, Claude Jarman Jnr, Ramon Novarro

The Outsider
GB 1931   93m   bw

A 'quack' osteopath is finally able to make a surgeon's crippled daughter walk. Cast-iron theatre and a fairly successful quota quickie which was also released in America. Harold Huth, Joan Barry, Norman McKinnel, Frank Lawton, Mary Clare. Written by Harry

Lachman and Alma Reville, from the play by Dorothy Brandon; directed by Harry Lachman; for Cinema House / MGM.

The Outsider
GB 1939   90m   bw

Sturdy remake of the above. George Sanders, Mary Maguire, Frederick Leister, Peter Murray Hill, Kathleen Harrison. Written by Dudley Leslie; directed by Paul Stein; for ABPC.

The Outsider
US 1961   108m   bw
U-I (Sy Bartlett)

Ira Hayes, a simple Red Indian, becomes a war hero but cannot reconcile himself to living in a white society.
Prolonged biopic which proves a shade too much for an eager star; it's all earnest and mildly interesting but not cinematically compulsive.

w Stewart Stern d Delbert Mann ph Joseph La Shelle m Leonard Rosenman

Tony Curtis, James Franciscus, Bruce Bennett, Gregory Walcott, Vivian Nathan, Edmund Hashim, Stanley Adams

Outward Bound*
US 1930   82m   bw
Warner

Passengers on a strange liner discover that they are all dead and heading for purgatory.
Early sound version of a popular twenties play which does not translate too well to cinematic forms and now seems very dated apart from a couple of performances; remade as Between Two Worlds (qv).

w J. Grubb Alexander, play Sutton Vane
d Robert Milton ph Hal Mohr

Leslie Howard, Douglas Fairbanks Jnr, Alec B. Francis, Helen Chandler, Beryl Mercer, Alison Skipworth, Montagu Love, Dudley Digges

Over She Goes*
GB 1937   74m   bw

An old friend helps a nobleman to thwart a blackmailer. Lively comedy vehicle for a forgotten star. Stanley Lupino, Laddie Cliff, Gina Malo, Clare Luce, Max Baer, Sally Gray, Syd Walker. Written by Elizabeth Meehan and Hugh Brooke, from the play by Stanley Lupino; directed by Graham Cutts; for ABPC.

Over the Moon
GB 1937   78m   Technicolor
London Films (Alexander Korda)

A poor girl comes into a fortune but this does not help her romance with a proud young doctor.
Insubstantial comedy which turns itself into a European travelogue before petering out.

w Anthony Pelissier, Arthur Wimperis, Alec Coppel d Thornton Freeland ph Harry Stradling m Mischa Spoliansky

Merle Oberon, Rex Harrison, Ursula Jeans, Robert Douglas, Louis Borell, Zena Dare, Peter Haddon, David Tree

Over Twenty-One

US 1945   102m   bw
Columbia (Sidney Buchman)

A famous lady screenwriter copes with wartime domestic problems while her husband is off at the war.
Thin star comedy based on Ruth Gordon's play about her own predicament; not for the wider audience, and not very good anyway.

w Sidney Buchman, play Ruth Gordon d Alexander Hall ph Rudolph Maté m Marlin Skiles

Irene Dunne, Alexander Knox, Charles Coburn, Jeff Donnell, Lee Patrick, Phil Brown, Cora Witherspoon

The Overlanders**

Australia 1946   91m   bw
Ealing (Ralph Smart)

In 1943 a drover saves a thousand head of cattle from the Japanese by taking them two thousand miles across country.
Attractive, easy-going semi-western, the first and best of several films made by Ealing Studios in Australia.

wd Harry Watt ph Osmond Borradaile m John Ireland

Chips Rafferty, John Heyward, Daphne Campbell

Overlord*

GB 1975   83m   bw
EMI / Jowsend (James Quinn)

An eighteen-year-old is called up in early 1944 and killed in the D-Day landings.
Semi-documentary recreating a time in history (with much aid from newsreels) but making no discernible point. Interesting, though.

w Stuart Cooper, Christopher Hudson d Stuart Cooper ph John Alcott m Paul Glass

Brian Stirner, Davyd Harries, Nicholas Ball, Julie Neesam

Owd Bob*

GB 1938   78m   bw
GFD / Gainsborough (Edward Black)
US title: To the Victor

A Cumberland farmer's faithful dog is accused of killing sheep.
Sentimental yarn with good location backgrounds; the plot was later reused as Thunder in the Valley.

w Michael Hogan, J. B. Williams, novel Alfred Olivant d Robert Stevenson ph Jack Cox md Louis Levy

Will Fyffe, John Loder, Margaret Lockwood, Moore Marriott, Graham Moffatt, Wilfred Walter, Elliot Mason

The Owl and the Pussycat*

US 1970   96m   Eastmancolor
  Panavision
Columbia / Rastar (Ray Stark)

A bookstore assistant reports a fellow tenant for prostitution, and when she is evicted she moves in with him.
Wacky, bawdy double act which starts promisingly but outstays its welcome. A solid step forward in permissiveness, with kinky behaviour as well as four-letter words.

w Buck Henry, play Bill Manhoff d Herbert Ross ph Harry Stradling, Andrew Laszlo m Richard Halligan

Barbra Streisand, George Segal, Robert Klein. Allen Garfield
'If computers ever turn out romantic comedies, the results will look like this.'— Stanley Kauffmann

The Ox-Bow Incident**

US 1943   75m   bw
TCF (Lamar Trotti)
GB title: Strange Incident

A cowboy is unable to prevent three wandering travellers being unjustly lynched for murder.
Stark lynch law parable, beautifully made but very depressing.

w Lamar Trotti, novel Walter Van Tilburg Clark d William Wellman ph Arthur Miller m Cyril Mockridge

Henry Fonda, Henry Morgan, Jane Darwell, Anthony Quinn, Dana Andrews, Mary Beth Hughes, William Eythe, Harry Davenport, Frank Conroy
'Realism that is as sharp and cold as a knife.'—Frank S. Nugent, New York Times
'Very firm, respectable, and sympathetic; but I still think it suffers from rigor artis.'— James Agee

AAN: best picture

P

P.J.
US 1967 109m Techniscope
Universal (Edward J. Montagne)
GB title: *New Face in Hell*

A down-at-heel private eye takes a job as
bodyguard to a boorish businessman.
Routine thick-ear with a predictable turnabout
plot.

w Philip Reisman Jnr *d* John Guillermin
ph Loyal Griggs *m* Neal Hefti

George Peppard, Gayle Hunnicutt, Raymond
Burr, Susan St James, Coleen Gray, Jason
Evers, Wilfrid Hyde White, Severn Darden

'Enough action to keep you from noticing
that the plot doesn't make any sense.'—*Judith
Crist*

Pacific Blackout
US 1942 76m bw
Paramount (Sol C. Siegel)

An inventor escapes from jail and proves his
innocence during a practice air raid blackout.
Minor melo which proved profitably topical,
being released shortly after the Japanese
attack on Pearl Harbor.

w Lester Cole, W. P. Lipscomb *d* Ralph
Murphy *ph* Theodor Sparkuhl

Robert Preston, Martha O'Driscoll, Philip
Merivale, Eva Gabor, Louis Jean Heydt,
Thurston Hall

Pacific Destiny
GB 1956 97m Eastmancolor
Cinemascope
James Lawrie

Experiences of a British colonial servant in the
South Seas.
Pleasant episodic drama which needed a firmer
hand all round.

w Richard Mason, *autobiography* A Pattern
of Islands by Sir Arthur Grimble *d* Wolf
Rilla *ph* Martin Curtis *m* James Bernard

Denholm Elliott, Susan Stephen, Michael
Hordern

Pacific Rendezvous
US 1942 76m bw

A coding expert breaks up an enemy spy ring.
Competent propaganda potboiler, rehashed
from the rather smarter *Rendezvous*, which
was set one war earlier. Lee Bowman, Jean
Rogers, Mona Maris, Carl Esmond, Paul
Cavanagh, Blanche Yurka. Written by Harry
Kurnitz, P. J. Wolfson, George Oppenheimer;
directed by George Sidney; for MGM.

The Pack
US 1977 99m colour

Abandoned dogs on a remote island turn on
holidaymakers. *The Birds* becomes *The Dogs*;
competently made but unsurprising thriller.
Joe Don Baker, Hope Alexander Willis,
Richard B. Shull, R. G. Armstrong. Written
and directed by Robert Clouse, from the novel
by Dave Fisher; for Warner.

Pack Up Your Troubles*
US 1931 68m bw
Hal Roach

Two World War I veterans try to look after
their late pal's orphan daughter.
Patchy comedy vehicle in which too many gags
are not fully thought out or timed.

w H. M. Walker *d* George Marshall, Ray
McCarey *ph* Art Lloyd

Stan Laurel, Oliver Hardy, Donald Dillaway,
Mary Carr, Charles Middleton, Dick Cramer,
James Finlayson, Tom Kennedy, Billy Gilbert

Pack Up Your Troubles*
US 1939 75m bw

Exploits in Flanders of three zany soldiers.
Good slapstick antics in an unfamiliar venue.
The Ritz Brothers, Jane Withers, Joseph
Schildkraut, Lynn Bari, Stanley Fields.
Written by Lou Breslow and Owen Francis;
directed by H. Bruce Humberstone; for TCF.
(GB title: *We're In the Army Now*.)

The Pad, and How to Use It*
US 1966 86m Technicolor
Universal (Ross Hunter)

A shy young man has his first date.
Pleasant, odd little comedy apparently made
in emulation of *The Knack*.

w Thomas C. Ryan, Benn Starr, *play* The Private Ear by Peter Shaffer *d* Brian C. Hutton *ph* Ellsworth Fredericks *m* Russ Garcia

Brian Bedford, James Farentino, Julie Sommars, Edy Williams, Nick Navarro

Paddy O'Day
US 1935   73m   bw

An Irish child emigrates to America to find that her mother has died. One of the more satisfactory vehicles for a child star maintained by the studio as an antidote to the cuter antics of Shirley Temple. *Jane Withers,* Pinky Tomlin, Rita Hayworth, Jane Darwell, Francis Ford. Written by Lou Breslow and Edward Eliscu; directed by Lewis Seiler; for TCF.

Paddy the Next Best Thing
US 1933   75m   bw
Fox

Adventures of an Irish tomboy in New York. Modest star comedy from a popular play.

w Edwin Burke, *play* Gertrude Page *d* Harry Lachman *ph* John Seitz

Janet Gaynor, Warner Baxter, Walter Connolly, Harvey Stephens, Margaret Lindsay

Padre Padrone**
Italy 1977   113m   Eastmancolor
Radiotelevisione Italia (Tonino Paoletti)
aka: *Father and Master*

The author recounts how he grew up with a violent and tyrannical father.
A vivid chunk of autobiography with food for thought on several levels, and a clever piece of film-making to boot.

wd Paolo Taviani, Vittorio Taviani,
book Gavino Ledda *ph* Mario Masini
md Egisto Macchi

Omero Antonutti, Saverio Marconi, Marcella Michelangeli

The Pagan
US 1929   85m approx   bw

A South Sea islander falls for the daughter of a white trader. Highly commercial star vehicle apparently made as an afterthought to *White Shadows in the South Seas.* Ramon Novarro, Renee Adoree, Dorothy Janis, Donald Crisp. Written by Dorothy Farnum; directed by W. S. Van Dyke; for MGM.

Pagan Love Song
US 1950   76m   Technicolor
MGM (Arthur Freed)

An American schoolteacher marries a Tahitian girl.

Very mild musical potboiler using familiar talents.

w Robert Nathan, Jerry Davis *d* Robert Alton *ph* Charles Rosher *m* Harry Warren *ly* Arthur Freed

Esther Williams, Howard Keel, Rita Moreno, Minna Gombell

Page Miss Glory*
US 1935   90m   bw
Warner / Cosmopolitan

A con man wins a beauty contest with a composite photograph of a non-existent girl. Amusing comedy-musical, unjustly forgotten.

w Delmer Daves, Robert Lord, *play* Joseph Schrank, Philip Dunning *d* Mervyn Le Roy *ph* George Folsey *m / ly* Harry Warren, Al Dubin

Dick Powell, Marion Davies, Frank McHugh, Pat O'Brien, Mary Astor, Lyle Talbot, Patsy Kelly, Allen Jenkins, Barton MacLane

Pagliacci*
GB 1936   92m   colour

A jealous clown kills his wife and her lover. A surprising British enterprise of the time which did fairly well at the box office, presumably because of the colour. Richard Tauber, Steffi Duna, Diana Napier, Arthur Margetson, Esmond Knight, Jerry Verno. Written by Monckton Hoffe, John Drinkwater, Roger Burford and Ernest Betts, from the opera by Ruggiero Leoncavallo; directed by Karl Grune; for Trafalgar. (US title: *A Clown Must Laugh.*)

Paid*
US 1930   80m   bw
MGM
GB title: *Within the Law*

A woman sent to prison unjustly plots revenge on those responsible.
Reliable melodrama with the heroine eventually forgiving and forgetting.

w Charles MacArthur, Lucien Hubbard, *play* Within the Law by Bayard Veiller *d* Sam Wood *ph* Charles Rosher

Joan Crawford, Kent Douglass, Robert Armstrong, Marie Prévost, John Miljan, Polly Moran

Paid in Full
US 1949   105m   bw
Paramount / Hal B. Wallis

A woman is responsible for the death of her sister's child, and becomes pregnant herself in

the knowledge that giving birth will be fatal to her.
Stolid, contrived tearjerker.

w Robert Blees, Charles Schnee d William Dieterle ph Leo Tover m Victor Young

Lizabeth Scott, Diana Lynn, Robert Cummings, Eve Arden, Ray Collins, Frank McHugh, Stanley Ridges, Louis Jean Heydt

Paint Your Wagon*
US 1969 164m Technicolor
Panavision 70
Paramount / Alan Jay Lerner (Tom Shaw)

During the California Gold Rush, two prospectors set up a Mormon menage with the same wife.
Good-looking but uncinematic and monumentally long version of an old musical with a new plot and not much dancing. There are minor pleasures, but it really shouldn't have been allowed.

w Paddy Chayevsky, *musical play* Alan Jay Lerner, Frederick Loewe d Joshua Logan ph William A. Fraker md Nelson Riddle pd John Truscott

Lee Marvin, Clint Eastwood, Jean Seberg, Harve Presnell, Ray Walston

'One of those big movies in which the themes are undersized and the elements are juggled around until nothing fits together right and even the good bits of the original show you started with are shot to hell.'—*Pauline Kael*

AAN: Nelson Riddle

Painted Boats
GB 1945 63m bw

Romance among the bargees. Excessively thin location drama, which nevertheless has an early place in the Ealing tradition. Jenny Laird, Bill Blewett, Robert Griffith, May Hallatt. Written by Louis MacNeice and Michael McCarthy; directed by Charles Crichton; for Ealing. (US title: *The Girl on the Canal*.)

The Painted Veil*
US 1934 84m bw
MGM (Hunt Stromberg)

In China, a doctor's wife gives up her lover to join her husband fighting an epidemic.
Soulful melodrama which seemed much more acceptable in this version than in the summer stock style remake *The Seventh Sin*.

w John Meehan, Salka Viertel, Edith Fitzgerald, *novel* W. Somerset Maugham d Richard Boleslawski ph William Daniels m Herbert Stothart

Greta Garbo, George Brent, Herbert Marshall, Warner Oland, Jean Hersholt

Painting the Clouds with Sunshine
US 1951 86m Technicolor
Warner (William Jacobs)

Three singing sisters go to Las Vegas in search of rich husbands.
Yet another revamp of the original *Gold Diggers* (qv), and not a very lively one.

w Henry Clark, Roland Kibbee, Peter Milne d David Butler ph Wilfred Cline

Virginia Mayo, Gene Nelson, Dennis Morgan, S. Z. Sakall, Lucille Norman, Tom Conway

Paisà*
Italy 1946 115m bw
Foreign Film Productions / OFI

Six episodes in the Battle of Italy between 1943 and 1945.
More important historically than dramatically, *Paisà* was always a somewhat disappointing experience, especially as the earlier episodes are stronger than the later ones. Like *Open City*, it was partly improvised and had a gritty documentary quality.

w Federico Fellini, Roberto Rossellini d Roberto Rossellini ph Otello Martelli m Renzo Rossellini

William Tubbs, Gar Moore, Maria Michi and non-professionals

AAN: script

The Pajama Game***
US 1957 101m Warnercolor
Warner / George Abbott

Workers in a pajama factory demand a pay rise, but their lady negotiator falls for the new boss.
Brilliantly conceived musical on an unlikely subject, effectively concealing its Broadway origins and becoming an expert, fast-moving, hard-hitting piece of modern musical cinema.

w *George Abbott, Richard Bissell, book* Seven and a Half Cents by Richard Bissell d *Stanley Donen, ph* Harry Stradling *songs* Richard Adler, Jerry Ross *ch* Bob Fosse

Doris Day, John Raitt, *Eddie Foy Jnr*, Reta Shaw, Carol Haney

Pal Joey**
US 1957 109m Technicolor
Columbia / Essex–Sidney (Fred Kohlmar)

The rise of a nightclub entertainer who is also a heel.
Smart musical which begins very brightly indeed but slides off alarmingly into conventional sentiment.

w Dorothy Kingsley, *play* John O'Hara, *stories* John O'Hara *d* George Sidney *ph* Harold Lipstein *songs Richard Rodgers, Lorenz Hart*

Frank Sinatra, Rita Hayworth, Kim Novak, Bobby Sherwood, Hank Henry, Elizabeth Patterson, Barbara Nichols

The Paleface***
US 1948 91m Technicolor
Paramount (Robert L. Welch)

Calamity Jane undertakes an undercover mission against desperadoes, and marries a timid dentist as a cover.
Splendid wagon train comedy western with the stars in excellent form. Sequel, *Son of Paleface* (qv); remake, *The Shakiest Gun in the West* (1968).

w Edmund Hartman, Frank Tashlin *d* Norman Z. McLeod *ph* Ray Rennahan *m* Victor Young

Bob Hope, Jane Russell, Robert Armstrong, Iris Adrian, Robert Watson, Jack Searle, Joe Vitale, Clem Bevans, Charles Trowbridge

AA: song 'Buttons and Bows' (*m* Jay Livingston, *ly* Ray Evans)

The Palm Beach Story***
US 1942 88m bw
Paramount (Paul Jones)

The wife of a penurious engineer takes off for Florida to set her sights on a millionaire.
Flighty comedy, inconsequential in itself, but decorated with scenes, characters and zany touches typical of its creator, here at his most brilliant if uncontrolled.

wd Preston Sturges *ph* Victor Milner *m* Victor Young

Claudette Colbert, Joel McCrea, Rudy Vallee, Mary Astor, Sig Arno, Robert Warwick, Torben Meyer, Jimmy Conlin, William Demarest, Jack Norton, Robert Greig, Roscoe Ates, Chester Conklin, Franklin Pangborn, Alan Bridge, *Robert Dudley*
  'Surprises and delights as though nothing of the kind had been known before . . . farce and tenderness are combined without a fault.'— *William Whitebait*

Palm Springs
US 1936 74m bw

An elderly Englishman becomes a gambler in order to give his daughter the appropriate upbringing. Slight romantic comedy which gave a young Englishman a foothold in Hollywood. David Niven, Sir Guy Standing, Frances Langford, Ernest Cossart, Spring Byington. Written by Joseph Fields; directed by Aubrey Scotto; for Paramount. (GB title: *Palm Springs Affair.*)

Palm Springs Weekend
US 1963 100m Technicolor
Warner (Michael Hoey)

Various holidaymakers at Palm Springs get romantically involved.
Youth-oriented farce, better produced than most but basically a depressing experience.

w Earl Hanmer Jnr *d* Norman Taurog *ph* Harold Lipstein *m* Frank Perkins

Troy Donahue, Ty Hardin, Connie Stevens, Stefanie Powers, Robert Conrad, Jack Weston, Andrew Duggan

Palmy Days
US 1932 77m bw
Samuel Goldwyn

Shady fortune tellers find a willing stooge.
Dated star comedy.

w Eddie Cantor, Mornie Ryskind, David Greenman *d* A. Edward Sutherland *ph* Gregg Toland *ch* Busby Berkeley

Eddie Cantor, Charlotte Greenwood, Charles Middleton, George Raft, Walter Catlett

Pan-Americana*
US 1945 85m bw
RKO (Sid Rogell)

A New York magazine sends editors around South America to choose the prettiest girl of each nation.
Slick, mindless musical with good numbers.

w Laurence Kimble *d* John H. Auer *ph* Frank Redman *md* Constantin Bakaleinikoff *ch* Charles O'Curran

Audrey Long, Philip Terry, Robert Benchley, Eve Arden, Ernest Truex, Marc Cramer

Panama Hattie
US 1942 79m bw
MGM (Arthur Freed)

A showgirl in Panama helps to capture Nazis.
Dim film version of a Broadway musical, stripped of most of its music and more like a *Maisie* comedy.

w Jack McGowan, Wilkie Mahoney, *musical play* Herbert Fields, B. G. De Sylva, Cole Porter *d* Norman Z. McLeod *ph* George Folsey *md* George Stoll

Ann Sothern, Dan Dailey, Red Skelton, Marsha Hunt, Rags Ragland, Virginia O'Brien, Alan Mowbray, Ben Blue, Carl Esmond

Pancho Villa
Spain 1972   93m   Technicolor
Granada Films (Bernard Gordon)
In 1916 Villa is rescued from execution and
starts a reign of terror.
Mexican banditry played half for laughs and
half for real; not a successful compromise.

w Julian Halevy d Eugenio Martin
ph Allejandro Ulloa m Anton Garcia-Abril
Telly Savalas, Clint Walker, Chuck Connors

Pandora and the Flying Dutchman*
GB 1950   122m   Technicolor
Romulus (Albert Lewin)
A cold but beautiful American woman in
Spain falls for a mystery man who turns out to
be a ghostly sea captain; she dies so as to be
with him.
Pretentious, humourless, totally unpersuasive
fantasy of the kind much better done in
Portrait of Jennie. The writer-director wears
Omar Khayyam's moving finger to the bone,
and the actors look thoroughly unhappy; even
the colour is a bit thick.

wd Albert Lewin ph Jack Cardiff m Alan
Rawsthorne ad John Bryan
James Mason, Ava Gardner, Harold
Warrender, Nigel Patrick, Sheila Sim, Mario
Cabre, John Laurie, Pamela Kellino, Marius
Goring
'Conspicuous in its confident assumption of
scholarship and its utter poverty of
imagination and taste.'—*C. A. Lejeune*
'It might have been enjoyably silly but for
Lewin's striving to be classy and an air of
third-rate decadence that hangs about it. This
is an Anglo-American co-production and one
of the occasions, I think, when we might be
generous and let Hollywood have all the
credit.'—*Richard Winnington*

Pandora's Box*
Germany 1929   97m approx (24 fps)
  bw   silent
Nero Film
original title: *Die Büchse der Pandora*
aka: *Lulu*
A woman murders her lover, becomes a
prostitute, and is murdered in London by Jack
the Ripper.
Oddball fantasy on a few favourite German
themes: very watchable, and benefiting from
its star performance.

w G. W. Pabst, Laszlo Wajda, *plays* Erdgeist
and Pandora's Box by Franz Wedekind d G.
W. Pabst ph Günther Krampf

Louise Brooks, Fritz Kortner, Franz Lederer,
Gustav Diessi
† Remade in Austria in 1962 as *No Orchids
for Lulu*, with Nadja Tiller.

Panic Button
US 1963   98m   bw
A hasbeen film star is hired by gangsters to
star in a film which must lose money; but it
wins the Venice Festival award. Artless and
padded comedy with good moments provided
by an intriguing cast. Maurice Chevalier,
Akim Tamiroff, Jayne Mansfield, Eleanor
Parker, Michael Connors. Written by Hal
Biller; directed by George Sherman; for
Gorton Associates.

The Panic in Needle Park
US 1971   110m   De Luxe
Gadd Productions (Dominick Dunne)
Drug addiction problems in a New York
ghetto.
Vivid, intimate but overlong and
unsympathetic account of a junkie and his
mistress.

w Joan Didion, John Gregory Dunne, *novel*
James Mills d Jerry Schatzberg ph Adam
Holender m none
Al Pacino, Kitty Winn, Adam Vint, Richard
Bright, Kiel Martin

Panic in the Streets***
US 1950   96m   bw
TCF (Sol C. Siegel)
On the New Orleans waterfront, public health
officials seek a carrier of bubonic plague.
Semi-documentary suspenser in the *Naked
City* manner; location Hollywood at its best.

w Richard Murphy, Edward and Edna Anhalt
d Elia Kazan ph Joe MacDonald m Alfred
Newman
Richard Widmark, Jack Palance, Paul
Douglas, Barbara Bel Geddes, Zero Mostel
'A model of what an action story should be
. . . every department is admirably
handled.'—*Richard Mallett, Punch*
AA: original story (Edward and Edna Anhalt)

Panic in Year Zero*
US 1962   93m   bw   Cinemascope
AIP (Lou Rusoff, Arnold Houghland)
Adventures of a family on a fishing trip in the
mountains when Los Angeles is blasted by a
nuclear attack.
Mildly interesting catalogue of predictable
events—thugs, looting, fear of fall-out—in a
simple-minded script finishing with a hopeful
meeting of the UN.

w Jay Simms, John Morton *d* Ray Milland
ph Gil Warrenton *m* Les Baxter

Ray Milland, Jean Hagen, Frankie Avalon,
Joan Freeman

Panique*
France 1946   98m   bw
Filmsonor

A respectable man knows who committed a
murder, and the murderer cunningly swings
the blame onto him.
Careful suspenser with a twist ending.

w Charles Spaak, Julien Duvivier,
novel Georges Simenon *d* Julien Duvivier
ph Nicolas Hayer

Michel Simon, Viviane Romance, Paul
Bernard

   'Whether you like it or not, you may be
forced to agree that it's a near-perfect
movie.'—*Pauline Kael, 1972*

The Panther's Claw
US 1942   73m   bw

Thatcher Colt solves a blackmail case which
ends in murder. Unassuming but efficient
second-feature mystery. Sidney Blackmer,
Byron Foulger, Rick Vallin. Written by
Martin Mooney and Athony Abbott; directed
by William Beaudine; for PRC.

Papa's Delicate Condition
US 1963   98m   Technicolor
Paramount / Amro (Jack Rose)

At the turn of the century in a small Texas
town an amiable family man gets into scrapes
when he drinks too much.
Basically pleasing period comedy which suffers
from slow, stiff treatment.

w Jack Rose, *book* Corinne Griffith *d* George
Marshall *ph* Loyal Griggs *m* Joseph J. Lilley

Jackie Gleason, Glynis Johns, Charles
Ruggles, Charles Lane, Laurel Goodwin,
Juanita Moore, Elisha Cook Jnr, Murray
Hamilton

AA: song 'Call Me Irresponsible' (*m* James
Van Heusen, *ly* Sammy Cahn)

The Paper Chase**
US 1973   111m   De Luxe   Panavision
TCF (Robert C. Thompson, Rodrick Paul)

A Harvard law graduate falls in love with the
divorced daughter of his tetchiest professor.
A thoughtful analysis of attitudes to learning
turns into just another youth movie.

wd James Bridges, *novel* John Jay Osborn Jnr
ph Gordon Willis *m* John Williams

Timothy Bottoms, Lindsay Wagner, *John
Houseman*, Graham Bickel

   'A slightly unfocused account of conformism
and milk-mild rebellion on the campus.'—
Sight and Sound

   'A worthy film which engages the eye and
the brain.'—*Benny Green, Punch*

AA: John Houseman
AAN: James Bridges (as writer)

Paper Lion
US 1968   105m   colour

The training of a professional football player.
Rather single-minded sporting biography from
a book by George Plimpton. Alan Alda,
Lauren Hutton, David Doyle, Sugar Ray
Robinson. Written by Lawrence Roman;
directed by Alex March; for United Artists.

Paper Moon**
US 1973   103m   bw
Paramount / Saticoy (Peter Bogdanovich)

In the American midwest in the thirties, a
bible salesman and a plain little girl make a
great con team.
Unusual but overrated comedy, imperfectly
adapted from a very funny book, with careful
but disappointing period sense and
photography. A lot more style and gloss was
required.

w Alvin Sargent, *novel* Addie Pray by *Joe
David Brown* *d* Peter Bogdanovich
ph Laszlo Kovacs *m* popular songs and
recordings

Ryan O'Neal, Tatum O'Neal, Madeleine
Kahn, John Hillerman

   'I've rarely seen a film that looked so unlike
what it was about.'—*Stanley Kauffmann*

   'At its best the film is only mildly amusing,
and I'm not sure I could recall a few
undeniable highlights if pressed on the
point.'—*Gary Arnold*

AA: Tatum O'Neal
AAN: Alvin Sargent; Madeleine Kahn

Paper Orchid
GB 1949   86m   bw

A girl reporter is suspected of murdering an
actor. Mystery programmer which did not
displease. Hugh Williams, Hy Hazell, Sidney
James, Garry Marsh, Andrew Cruickshank,
Ivor Barnard, Walter Hudd. Written by Val
Guest, from the novel by Arthur La Bern;
directed by Roy Baker; for Ganesh /
Columbia.

Paper Tiger
GB 1975   99m   Technicolor
Maclean and Co (Euan Lloyd)

An ageing Englishman becomes tutor to the son of the Japanese ambassador in a Pacific state, and finds he has to live his heroic fantasies in reality.

Uneasy adventure comedy drama which might, given more skilled handling, have been much better than it is.

w Jack Davies d Ken Annakin ph John Cabrera m Roy Budd

David Niven, Toshiro Mifune, Hardy Kruger, Ando, Ivan Desny, Irene Tsu, Miiko Taka, Ronald Fraser, Jeff Corey

'Makes no demands, except on 99 minutes of our time.'—*Michael Billington, Illustrated London News*

Papillon*
US 1973   150m   Technicolor
Panavision
Papillon Partnership / Corona / General Production Co (Robert Dorfmann)

Filmed autobiography of life on Devil's Island. Overlong and rather dreary film of a bestseller; it determinedly rubs the audience's nose in ordure from the start, and the final successful escape is one try too many.

w Dalton Trumbo, Lorenzo Semple Jnr, *book* Henri Charrière d Franklin Schaffner
ph Fred Koenekamp m Jerry Goldsmith

Steve McQueen, Dustin Hoffman, Don Gordon, Anthony Zerbe, George Coulouris, Woodrow Parfrey

'A 2½-hour epic trampling the corn growing round the theme of man's inhumanity to man.'—*Sight and Sound*

'Papillon offers torture as entertainment but winds up making entertainment a form of torture . . . a tournament of brutality unrelieved by imagination.'—*Paul D. Zimmermann*

'So overloaded with details that the stars are almost lost in exposition, repetition and unfocused drama.'—*Judith Crist, 1977*

'So solemn one would think it the story of a pope at the very least.'—*New Yorker, 1980*

AAN: Jerry Goldsmith

The Paradine Case**
US 1947   115m   bw
Selznick

A barrister falls in love with his client, a murder suspect who, it turns out, is actually guilty.

A stodgy and old-fashioned script is given gleaming treatment; this and the acting make it seem better thirty years later than it did on release.

w David O. Selznick, *novel* Robert Hichens
d Alfred Hitchcock ph Lee Garmes m Franz Waxman

Gregory Peck, *Alida Valli*, Ann Todd, Louis Jourdan, *Charles Laughton*, Charles Coburn, Ethel Barrymore, Leo G. Carroll

'This is the wordiest script since the death of Edmund Burke.'—*James Agee*

'The characters and their problems don't make much imprint on a viewer; if you can't remember whether you've seen the picture or not, chances are you did and forgot it.'—*New Yorker, 1976*

AAN: Ethel Barrymore

Paradise Alley
US 1978   107m   Technicolor
Universal / Force Ten (John F. Roach, Ronald A. Suppa)

The adventures of three wrestling brothers in New York's Hell's Kitchen during the forties. Fashionable update of the *City for Conquest* school, not in itself very interesting despite amusing bits.

wd Sylvester Stallone ph Laszlo Kovacs
m Bill Conti pd John W. Corso

Sylvester Stallone, Kevin Conway, Anne Archer, Joe Spinell, Armand Assante, Lee Canalito

Paradise for Three
US 1937   78m   bw

A businessman goes to Germany to find out how the workers live. An interesting premise leads inevitably into a flimsy romantic comedy. Robert Young, Frank Morgan, Mary Astor, Edna May Oliver, Florence Rice, Reginald Owen, Henry Hull, Sig Rumann, Herman Bing. Written by George Oppenheimer and Harry Ruskin; directed by Edward Buzzell; for MGM. (GB title: *Romance for Three*.)

Paradise for Two
GB 1937   77m   bw

A millionaire posing as a reporter is asked to pose as a millionaire. Cheerful comedy-romance. Jack Hulbert, Patricia Ellis, Arthur Riscoe, Googie Withers, Sidney Fairbrother, Wylie Watson, David Tree. Written by Robert Stevenson and Arthur Macrae; directed by Thornton Freeland; for Korda / Denham.

The Parallax View*
US 1974   102m   Technicolor
  Panavision
Paramount / Gus / Harbour / Doubleday
  (Alan J. Pakula)

Witnesses to a political assassination are
systematically killed, despite the efforts of a
crusading journalist.
Stylish, persuasive political thriller with a
downbeat ending; the villains win.

w David Giler, Lorenzo Semple Jnr, *novel*
Loren Singer d Alan J. Pakula ph Gordon
Willis m Michael Small

Warren Beatty, Paula Prentiss, William
Daniels, Hume Cronyn, Walter McGinn

'Pakula at his best . . . the test sequence is
one of the most celebrated, manipulating the
audience as it bombards Beatty's psyche.'—
Les Keyser, Hollywood in the Seventies
  'It is terribly important to give an audience a
lot of things they may not get as well as those
they will, so that finally the film does take on a
texture and is not just simplistic
communication.'—*Alan J. Pakula*

Paramount on Parade*
US 1930   102m   bw   (Technicolor
  sequence)
Paramount (Elsie Janis)

A revue featuring Paramount contract stars.
A ragged affair by any standard, but worth a
look for a couple of Chevalier's numbers.

w various d Dorothy Arzner, Otto Brower,
Edmund Goulding, Victor Heerman, Edwin
H. Knopf, Rowland V. Lee, Ernst Lubitsch,
Lothar Mendes, Victor Schertzinger, Edward
Sutherland, Frank Tuttle ph Harry Fischbeck,
Victor Milner m various

Richard Arlen, Jean Arthur, George
Bancroft, Clara Bow, Nancy Carroll, Ruth
Chatterton, Maurice Chevalier, Gary Cooper,
Leon Errol, Kay Francis, Harry Green, Mitzi
Green, Dennis King, Fredric March, Nino
Martini, Jack Oakie, Charles 'Buddy' Rogers,
Lillian Roth, Fay Wray, Clive Brook, Warner
Oland, Eugene Pallette, William Powell

Paranoiac*
GB 1963   80m   bw   Cinemascope
U-I / Hammer (Anthony Hinds)

An heiress is saved from a suicide attempt by a
young man claiming to be her dead brother.
A complex maze of disguise, mistaken
identity, family curses and revelations of
something nasty in the woodshed, out of
Psycho by *Taste of Fear*. Not very good in
itself, but interesting in its borrowings.

w Jimmy Sangster d Freddie Francis
ph Arthur Grant m Elisabeth Lutyens

Oliver Reed, Janette Scott, Alexander
Davion, Sheila Burrell, Liliane Brousse,
Maurice Denham, John Bonney

Les Parapluies de Cherbourg**
France / West Germany 1964   92m
  Eastmancolor
Parc / Madeleine / Beta
aka: *The Umbrellas of Cherbourg*

A shopgirl loves a gas station attendant. He
goes on military service; she finds she is
pregnant and marries for security. Years later
they meet briefly by accident.
Unexpected, charming, pretty successful
screen operetta with only sung dialogue.
Careful acting and exquisite use of colour and
camera movement paste over the thinner
sections of the plot.

wd Jacques Demy ph Jean Rabier m Michel
Legrand ad Bernard Evein

Catherine Deneuve, *Anne Vernon*, Nino
Castelnuovo

'Poetic neo-realism.'—*Georges Sadoul*
  'We are told that in Paris the opening night
audience wept and the critics were ecstatic. It
would have made a little more sense the other
way round.'—*John Simon*

AAN: script; Michel Legrand; song, 'I Will
Wait for You'

Pardners
US 1956   88m   Technicolor   Vistavision
Paramount (Paul Jones)

An incompetent idiot goes west and
accidentally cleans up the town.
Stiff western star burlesque, a remake of
Rhythm on the Range.

w Sidney Sheldon d Norman Taurog
ph Daniel Fapp songs Sammy Cahn, Jimmy
Van Heusen

Dean Martin, Jerry Lewis, Agnes Moorehead,
Lori Nelson, John Baragrey, Jeff Morrow,
Lon Chaney Jnr

Pardon My Past*
US 1945   88m   bw
Columbia

A man unwittingly takes on the problems of
his double, a shady playboy.
Amusing mistaken identity comedy.

w Earl Felton, Karl Kamb d Leslie Fenton
ph Russell Metty m Dmitri Tiomkin

Fred MacMurray, Marguerite Chapman,
Akim Tamiroff, Rita Johnson, William
Demarest, Harry Davenport

Pardon Us°
US 1931 55m bw
Hal Roach
aka: *Jailbirds*

Two zany bootleggers find themselves in and out of prison.
Patchy star comedy which finds the boys on the whole not in quite their best form.

w H. M. Walker *d* James Parrott *ph* Jack Stevens

Stan Laurel, Oliver Hardy, Wilfred Lucas, Walter Long, James Finlayson

The Parent Trap°
US 1961 129m Technicolor
Walt Disney (George Golitzen)

Twin daughters of separated parents determine to bring the family together again.
Quite bright but awesomely extended juvenile romp.

wd David Swift, *novel* Das Doppelte Lottchen by Erich Kastner *ph* Lucien Ballard *m* Paul Smith

Hayley Mills, Maureen O'Hara, Brian Keith, Charles Ruggles, Leo G. Carroll, Una Merkel, Joanna Barnes, Cathleen Nesbitt, Ruth McDevitt, Nancy Kulp

Les Parents Terribles°°
France 1948 98m bw
Sirius

Life with a family in which the children are as neurotic as the parents.
Alternately hilarious and tragic, this is a fascinating two-set piece of filmed theatre, with every performance a pleasure.

wd Jean Cocteau, from his play *ph* Michel Kelber *m* Georges Auric *ad* Christian Bérard, Guy de Gastyne

Jean Marais, Yvonne de Bray, Gabrielle Dorziat, Marcel André, Josette Day

† In 1953 a curious and unsatisfactory British version was made by Charles Frank under the title *Intimate Relations,* with Marian Spencer, Russell Enoch, Ruth Dunning, Harold Warrender and Elsy Albiin.

Paris
US 1929 88m part colour

An American stage star, her fiancé, her partner and her mother-in-law-to-be converge on the Champs Elysées. Shaky musical with interesting talent, but bereft of its original Cole Porter score. Irene Bordoni, Jack Buchanan, Louise Closser Hale, Jason Robards. Written by Hope Loring; directed by Clarence Badger; for Warner.

Paris after Dark
US 1943 85m bw

In wartime Paris a doctor leads the resistance forces. Propaganda potboiler, quite neatly made and cast. George Sanders, Philip Dorn, Brenda Marshall, Marcel Dalio, Madeleine LeBeau. Written by Howard Buchman; directed by Leonide Moguy; for TCF. (GB title: *The Night Is Ending.*)

Paris Blues°
US 1961 98m Technicolor
UA / Pennebaker / Diane / Jason / Monica / Monmouth (Sam Shaw)

Two jazz musicians have romantic problems in Paris.
Semi-serious mini-drama with emphasis on the music; one is not quite sure what the actors thought they were up to.

w Jack Sher, Irene Kamp, Walter Bernstein, *novel* Harold Flender *d* Martin Ritt *ph* Christian Matras *m* Duke Ellington

Paul Newman, Joanne Woodward, Sidney Poitier, Louis Armstrong, Diahann Carroll, Serge Reggiani, Barbara Laage

AAN: Duke Ellington

Paris Calling
US 1941 95m bw
Universal / Charles K. Feldman

When the Nazis invade Paris, a woman discovers that her husband is a traitor.
Totally predictable flagwaver.

w Benjamin Glazer, Charles Kaufmann *d* Edwin L. Marin *ph* Milton Krasner *m* Richard Hageman

Elisabeth Bergner, Basil Rathbone, Randolph Scott, Gale Sondergaard, Lee J. Cobb, Eduardo Ciannelli, Charles Arnt

Paris Holiday°
US 1957 101m Technirama
UA / Tolda (Bob Hope)

An American comedian meets a French one in Paris, and both have narrow escapes because their script contains the clue to a gang of counterfeiters.
Amiable location romp with the stars in pretty good form.

w Edmund Beloin, Dean Riesner *d* Gerd Oswald *ph* Roger Hubert *m* Joseph J. Lilley

Bob Hope, Fernandel, Anita Ekberg, Martha Hyer, André Morell, Maurice Teynac, Jean Murat, Preston Sturges

Paris Honeymoon
US 1935 85m bw

An American in Paris persuades his fiancée to forget a French nobleman. Candy floss musical for star fans. Bing Crosby, Franciska Gaal, Akim Tamiroff. Written by Frank Butler and Don Hartman; directed by Frank Tuttle; for Paramount.

Paris in Spring
US 1935 81m bw

Four visitors change partners in the romantic city. Predictable romance with good ingredients. Mary Ellis, Tullio Carminati, Lynne Overman, Ida Lupino. Written by Samuel Hoffenstein, Franz Schulz and Keene Thompson, from the play by Dwight Taylor; directed by Lewis Milestone; for Paramount. (GB title: *Paris Love Song*.)

Paris Model
US 1953 88m bw

Stories involving four copies of the same Paris gown. Depressing dramatic package with production values at a low ebb and some pleasant talents going awry. Paulette Goddard, Eva Gabor, Marilyn Maxwell, Barbara Lawrence, Tom Conway, Leif Erickson, Florence Bates, Cecil Kellaway, Robert Hutton. Written by Robert Smith; directed by Alfred E. Green; for Albert Zugsmith / Columbia.

Paris Qui Dort*
France 1923 40m approx (24 fps) bw
   silent
Films Diamant
aka: *The Crazy Ray*

A mad scientist invents a ray which brings everyone but six people in Paris to a halt. Mildly entertaining semi-professional comedy showing several of its director's most engaging traits.

wd, ed René Clair *ph* Maurice Défassiaux, Paul Guichard

Henri Rollan, Albert Préjean, Marcel Vallée, Madeleine Rodrigue

Paris Underground
US 1945 97m bw
(UA) Constance Bennett
GB title: *Madame Pimpernel*

Two women caught in Paris when the Nazis invade continue their resistance activities. Artificial and not very exciting flagwaver.

w Boris Ingster, Gertrude Purcell, *novel* Etta Shiber *d* Gregory Ratoff *ph* Lee Garmes *m* Alexander Tansman

Constance Bennett, Gracie Fields, George Rigaud, Kurt Kreuger, Leslie Vincent

'Mainly trash, involving enough handsome young men, in various poses of gallant gratitude, to satisfy Mae West in her prime.'— *James Agee*

AAN: Alexander Tansman

Paris When It Sizzles
US 1963 110m Technicolor
Paramount (Richard Quine, George Axelrod)

A film writer tries out several script ideas with his secretary as heroine and himself as hero or villain.

As a French film called *La Fête à Henriette* this was a charming whimsy, but Hollywood made it heavy-handed and boring, especially as no one in it seems to be having much fun.

w George Axelrod, *screenplay* Julien Duvivier, Henri Jeanson *d* Richard Quine *ph* Charles Lang Jnr *m* Nelson Riddle

William Holden, Audrey Hepburn, Grégoire Aslan, Noel Coward, Raymond Bussières
   'The new script embalms the original instead of reviving it.'—*Stanley Kauffmann, New Republic*

Park Row
US 1952 83m bw
UA / Samuel Fuller

Conflict breaks out between two newspapers in 1886 New York.
Earnest but flat low-budgeter of a rather unusual kind.

wd Samuel Fuller *ph* Jack Russell *ad* Ray Robinson

Gene Evans, Mary Welch, Herbert Hayes, Forrest Taylor

Parnell*
US 1937 96m bw
MGM (John M. Stahl)

A 19th-century Irish politician comes to grief through his love for a married woman.
Well made but miscast biopic, a resounding thud at the box office.

w John Van Druten, S. N. Behrman, *play* Elsie T. Schauffler *d* John M. Stahl *ph* Karl Freund *m* William Axt

Clark Gable, Myrna Loy, Edmund Gwenn, Edna May Oliver, Alan Marshal, Donald Crisp, Billie Burke, Berton Churchill, Donald Meek, Montagu Love, George Zucco
   'A singularly pallid, tedious and unconvincing drama.'—*Frank Nugent*
   'Poor though the picture may be, it is pleasing to think how clean a film magnate's wish-fulfilments are, how virginal and high-

minded the tawdry pathetic human past becomes when the Mayers and Goldwyns turn the magic ring.'—*Graham Greene*

Parrish
US 1961   137m   Technicolor
Warner (Delmer Daves)

A young tobacco plantation worker has an ample sex life and the luck to become boss.
Predictable trudge through scenes from a bestselling novel, less offensive than most such adaptations.

wd Delmer Daves, *novel* Mildred Savage *ph* Harry Stradling *m* Max Steiner

Troy Donahue, Claudette Colbert, Karl Malden, Dean Jagger, Connie Stevens, Diane McBain, Sharon Hugueny

The Parson of Panamint
US 1941   84m   bw
Paramount (Harry Sherman)

A gold rush mountain town is corrupted by success until a two-fisted parson puts things right.
Middling western morality play.

w Harold Shumate, Adrian Scott, *novel* Peter B. Kyne *d* William McGann *ph* Russell Harlan *m* Irwin Talbot

Charles Ruggles, Ellen Drew, Philip Terry, Joseph Schildkraut, Henry Kolker, Janet Beecher, Paul Hurst

Une Partie de Campagne***
France 1936   40m   bw
Pierre Braunberger
aka: *A Day in the Country*

Around 1880, a Parisian tradesman and his family picnic one Sunday in the country, and one of the daughters falls in love.
An unfinished film which was much admired for its local colour, like an impressionist picture come to life.

wd Jean Renoir, *story* Guy de Maupassant *ph* Claude Renoir, Jean Bourgoin *m* Joseph Kosma

Sylvie Bataille, Georges Darnoul, Jane Marken, Paul Temps

Une Partie de Plaisir*
France 1975   100m   colour
La Boétie / Sunchild / Gerico (André Genoves)

The analysis of a divorce.
Bitter comedy drama, with the director's usual scriptwriter playing out his own life story. A little too incestuous for its own good, but with striking moments.

w Paul Gegauff *d* Claude Chabrol *ph* Jean Rabier

Paul Gegauff, Danielle Gegauff, Paula Moore, Michel Valette

The Party*
US 1968   98m   De Luxe   Panavision
UA / Mirisch / Geoffrey (Blake Edwards)

An accident-prone Indian actor is accidentally invited to a swank Hollywood party and wrecks it.
Would-be Tatiesque comedy of disaster, occasionally well-timed but far too long for all its gloss.

w Blake Edwards, Tom and Frank Waldman *d* Blake Edwards *ph* Lucien Ballard *m* Henry Mancini *pd* Fernando Carrere

Peter Sellers, Claudine Longet, Marge Champion, Fay McKenzie, Steve Franken, Buddy Lester

'One thing the old movie makers did know is that two reels is more than enough of this stuff.'—*Wilfred Sheed*

'It is only rarely that one laughs or even smiles; mostly one just chalks up another point for ingenuity.'—*Tom Milne*

Party Girl
US 1958   98m   Metrocolor
Cinemascope
MGM / Euterpe (Joe Pasternak)

In twenties Chicago, a lawyer wins a girl from a gangster.
Heavy-handed Scarface-style saga which at one time won a curious reputation for being a satire.

w George Wells *d* Nicholas Ray *ph* Robert Bronner *m* Jeff Alexander

Robert Taylor, Cyd Charisse, Lee J. Cobb, John Ireland, Kent Smith, Claire Kelly, Corey Allen

The Party's Over
GB 1963   94m   bw
Tricastle (Anthony Perry)

An American girl joins a group of Chelsea beatniks and dies in a fall from a balcony; her father investigates.
Tasteless and boring swinging London trash which became notorious when its producers (Rank) disowned it because it features a party at which a man makes love to a dead girl. An unattractive display of moral squalor.

w Marc Behm *d* Guy Hamilton *ph* Larry Pizer *m* John Barry

Oliver Reed, Eddie Albert, Ann Lynn, Louise Sorel

Passage Home
GB 1955   102m   bw
GFD / Group Films (Julian Wintle)

In 1931, tensions run high on a merchant ship when the captain accepts an attractive girl as passenger from South America.
Obvious melodrama complete with drunken captain and storm at sea; not badly done if it must be done at all.

w William Fairchild, *novel* Richard Armstrong d Roy Baker ph Geoffrey Unsworth m Clifton Parker

Peter Finch, Anthony Steel, Diane Cilento, Cyril Cusack, Geoffrey Keen, Hugh Griffith, Duncan Lamont, Bryan Forbes, Gordon Jackson, Michael Craig

Passage West
US 1951   81m   Technicolor

Religious pioneers headed west are menaced by escaped convicts. Entertaining minor western. John Payne, Dennis O'Keefe, Arleen Whelan, Peter Hanson. Written by Lewis R. Foster and Nedrick Young; directed by Lewis R. Foster; for Pine-Thomas / Paramount.

Passage to Marseilles*
US 1944   110m   bw
Warner (Hal B. Wallis)

Convicts escape from Devil's Island and join the Free French.
A rare example of a film boasting flashbacks within flashbacks within flashbacks, this confusing if sometimes entertaining all-star saga is done to death by its unconvincing flagwaving endpapers which prevent it from being at all comparable with *Casablanca*, as was clearly intended.

w Casey Robinson, Jack Moffitt, *story* Charles Nordhoff, James Hall ph James Wong Howe d Michael Curtiz m Max Steiner

Humphrey Bogart, Michèle Morgan, Claude Rains, Philip Dorn, Sidney Greenstreet, Peter Lorre, Helmut Dantine, George Tobias, John Loder, Victor Francen, Eduardo Ciannelli
   'Invincibly second rate.'—*Richard Mallet, Punch*

Passenger*
Poland 1963   63m   bw   Dyaliscope
Kadr
original title: *Pasazerka*

A German woman on a liner sees a woman she thinks she recognizes, and realizes that it is one of her charges when she was an official in a concentration camp.

Minor but effective character drama, in essence an investigation of guilt. The director died during its making, so some scenes are replaced by still photographs.

wd Andrzej Munk, *play* Zofia Posmysz-Piasecka ph Krzysztof Winiewicz

Aleksandra Slaska, Anna Ciepielewska

The Passenger*
Italy / France / Spain 1975   119m
   Metrocolor
MGM / CCC / Concordia / CIPI (Carlo Ponti)
aka: *Profession: Reporter*

A TV reporter in a desert hotel changes identities with a dead man and finds he is now an African gun runner being drawn irresistibly towards his own death.
Pretty much in the style of *Blow Up*, but this time with no frills of fashion or nudity to bring the public in. After this, Antonioni was given up by the commercial cinema.

w Mark Peploe, Peter Wollen, Michelangelo Antonioni d Michelangelo Antonioni ph Luciano Tovoli md Ivan Vandor

Jack Nicholson, Maria Schneider, Jenny Runacre, Ian Hendry
   'A film of real romance, depth and power . . . the very quintessence of cinema.'—*Michael Billington, Illustrated London News*

The Passing of the Third Floor Back*
GB 1935   90m   bw
Gaumont (Ivor Montagu)

A Christ-like visitor stays at a London boarding house and changes the lives of the inmates.
Competent film version of a famous, sentimental, dated play.

w Michael Hogan, Alma Reville, *play* Jerome K. Jerome d Berthold Viertel ph Curt Courant

Conrad Veidt, René Ray, Anna Lee, Frank Cellier, Mary Clare, Beatrix Lehmann, Cathleen Nesbitt, Sara Allgood
   'The pious note has been toned down, the milk of human kindness has been agreeably watered, and the types in the small London private hotel are observed with malicious realism.'—*Graham Greene*

Passion
US 1954   84m   Technicolor

Jealousy erupts between ranchers in Spanish California. Peculiarly titled western of no merit whatsoever. Yvonne de Carlo, Cornel Wilde, Raymond Burr, Lon Chaney Jnr, Rodolfo Acosta, John Qualen. Written by

Beatrice A. Dresher and Joseph Leytes;
directed by Allan Dwan; for Benedict
Bogeaus / RKO.

The Passionate Friends••
GB 1948 91m bw
GFD / Cineguild (Eric Ambler)
US title: *One Woman's Story*

A woman marries an older man, then meets
again her young lover.
A simple and obvious dramatic situation is
tricked out with flashbacks and the inimitable
high style of its director to make a satisfying
entertainment.

w Eric Ambler, *novel* H. G. Wells *d* David
Lean *ph Guy Green m* Richard Addinsell

Ann Todd, Trevor Howard, Claude Rains,
Betty Ann Davies, Isabel Dean, Arthur
Howard, Wilfrid Hyde White

The Passionate Stranger
GB 1956 97m part bw, part
  Eastmancolor
British Lion / Beaconsfield (Peter Rogers,
  Gerald Thomas)
US title: *A Novel Affair*

A lady novelist bases a character on her virile
chauffeur; he reads the book and thinks she
fancies him.
Feeble comedy, half of it consisting of a
dramatization of the heroine's very dull novel.

w Muriel and Sydney Box *d* Muriel Box
ph Otto Heller *m* Humphrey Searle

Ralph Richardson, Margaret Leighton, Carlo
Justini, Patricia Dainton, Marjorie Rhodes,
Thorley Walters, Frederick Piper

Passionate Summer
GB 1958 104m Eastmancolor
Rank / Kenneth Harper

A divorced headmaster at a Jamaican school is
loved by three women.
Silly melodrama with splendid backgrounds
ruined by poor colour.

w Joan Henry, *novel* The Shadow and the
Peak by Richard Mason *d* Rudolph Cartier
ph Ernest Steward *m* Angelo Lavagnino

Virginia McKenna, Bill Travers, Yvonne
Mitchell, Alexander Knox, Ellen Barrie, Carl
Mohner.
'The climactic hurricane does little to dispel
the overall feeling of emotional suffocation.'—
MFB

Passport to Pimlico••••
GB 1949 84m bw
Ealing (E. V. H. Emmett)

Part of a London district is discovered to
belong to Burgundy, and the inhabitants find
themselves free of rationing restrictions.
A cleverly detailed little comedy which
inaugurated the best period of Ealing, its
preoccupation with suburban man and his
foibles. Not exactly satire, but great fun, and
kindly with it.

w T. E. B. Clarke d Henry Cornelius
ph Lionel Banes *m Georges Auric*

Stanley Holloway, *Margaret Rutherford,* Basil
Radford, Naunton Wayne, Hermione
Baddeley, John Slater, Paul Dupuis, Jane
Hylton, Raymond Huntley, Betty Warren,
Barbara Murray, Sidney Tafler

AAN: T. E. B. Clarke

The Password Is Courage•
GB 1962 116m bw
MGM / Andrew and Virginia Stone

In Europe during World War II, Sgt-Major
Charles Coward has a career of escapes and
audacious anti-Nazi exploits.
Lively, slightly over-humorous account of one
man's war, well mounted and shot entirely on
location.

wd Andrew L. Stone, *biography* John Castle
ph David Boulton

Dirk Bogarde, Maria Perschy, Alfred Lynch,
Nigel Stock, Reginald Beckwith

'The experiences are, it seems, mainly true
but they do not seem so.'—*Guardian*

Pastor Hall•
GB 1940 97m bw
Charter (John Boulting)

The story of German village pastor Niemoller,
who in 1934 was shot for denouncing the
Nazis.
A courageous film of its time, not very
interesting dramatically or cinematically.

w Leslie Arliss, Haworth Bromley, Anna
Reiner, *play* Ernst Toller *d* Roy Boulting
ph Max Greene

Wilfrid Lawson, Nova Pilbeam, Seymour
Hicks, Marius Goring, Percy Walsh, Brian
Worth, Peter Cotes, Hay Petrie

Pat and Mike••
US 1952 95m bw
MGM (Lawrence Weingarten)

A small-time sports promoter takes on a
female intellectual multi-champion.
A comedy which amuses because of its star
playing, but doesn't really develop. All very
easy going, with guest appearances from
sporting personalities.

w Ruth Gordon, Garson Kanin *d* George Cukor *ph* William Daniels *m* David Raksin

Spencer Tracy, Katharine Hepburn, Aldo Ray, William Ching, Sammy White, Jim Backus, Phyllis Povah

AAN: script

Pat Garrett and Billy the Kid
US 1973   106m   Metrocolor   Panavision
MGM (Gordon Carroll)

Blood-spattered version of a western legend, with violence always to the fore, accentuated by the impossibility of listening to the dialogue because of poor direction and recording.

w Rudolph Wurlitzer *d* Sam Peckinpah *ph* John Coquillon *m* Bob Dylan

James Coburn, Kris Kristofferson, Bob Dylan, Richard Jaeckel, Katy Jurado, Slim Pickens, Chill Wills, Jason Robards Jnr

'A sombre, intense, downbeat essay on the truth behind the legend and the legend behind the truth.'—*Sight and Sound*

'Shows what Peckinpah can do when he doesn't put his mind to it.'—*Stanley Kauffmann*

'A rash adventure in inadvertent self-parody.'—*William S. Pechter*

A Patch of Blue*
US 1966   105m   bw   Panavision
MGM / Pandro S. Berman

A blind girl who lives in a slum is helped by a negro with whom she falls in love without realizing his colour.

Polished tearjerker with racial overtones; nicely done for those who can take it.

wd Guy Green, *novel* Be Ready with Bells and Drums by Elizabeth Kata *ph* Robert Burks *d* Jerry Goldsmith

Sidney Poitier, Elizabeth Hartman, Shelley Winters, Wallace Ford, Ivan Dixon, Elizabeth Fraser, John Qualen

AA: Shelley Winters
AAN: Robert Burks; Jerry Goldsmith; Elizabeth Hartman

Pather Panchali**
India 1955   115m   bw
Government of West Bengal

In a small Bengal village, the son of a would-be writer grows up in poverty and tragedy before setting off with what remains of the family to seek a living in Benares.

A remarkable first film of a director now famous, showing that people are much the same though the details of their daily lives may be different. The pace may be slow but the content is mainly absorbing.

wd Satyajit Ray, novels Bhibuti Bashan Bannerjee *ph* Subrata Mitra *m* Ravi Shankar

Kanu Bannerjee, Karuna Bannerjee, Uma Das Gupta, Subir Bannerjee, Chunibala

Paths of Glory****
US 1957   86m   bw
UA / Bryna (James B. Harris)

In 1916 in the French trenches, three soldiers are courtmartialled for cowardice.

Incisive melodrama chiefly depicting the corruption and incompetence of the high command; the plight of the soldiers is less interesting. The trench scenes are the most vivid ever made, and the rest is shot in genuine castles, with resultant difficulties of lighting and recording; the overall result is an overpowering piece of cinema.

w Stanley Kubrick, Calder Willingham, Jim Thompson, *novel* Humphrey Cobb *d Stanley Kubrick ph* Georg Krause *m* Gerald Fried

Kirk Douglas, Adolphe Menjou, George Macready, Wayne Morris, Richard Anderson, Ralph Meeker, Timothy Carey

'A bitter and biting tale, told with stunning point and nerve-racking intensity.'—*Judith Crist*

'Beautifully performed, staged, photographed, cut and scored.'—*Colin Young*

Patrick the Great*
US 1945   88m   bw
Universal (Howard Benedict)

An actor whose career is waning is jealous of his young son.

Slick teenage family comedy, virtually a one-man show for O'Connor.

w Jane Hall, Bertram Millhauser, Dorothy Bennett, Frederick and Ralph Block *d* Frank Ryan *ph* Frank Redman *m* Hans Salter

Donald O'Connor, Donald Cook, Peggy Ryan, Frances Dee, Eve Arden, Thomas Gomez, Gavin Muir, Andrew Tombes

The Patriot**
US 1928   110m approx (24 fps)   bw
silent
Paramount

Mad Czar Paul I is assassinated by his chief adviser for the good of the state.

Historical melodrama with a good many comedy touches: the director makes the most of both aspects, but they don't in the end hang together despite bravura acting.

w Hans Kraly, *novel* Alfred Neumann *d Ernst Lubitsch ph* Bert Glennon *ad* Hans Dreier

Emil Jannings, Lewis Stone, Florence Vidor, Neil Hamilton

'I believe this picture the most suggestive we ever ran. Just another reason why we need censorship. Small-town exhibitors need clean pictures.'—*Ohio exhibitor's report in Motion Picture Herald*

AA: Hans Kraly

AAN: best picture; Ernst Lubitsch; Lewis Stone

The Patsy*

US 1927   80m approx (24 fps)   bw
silent
MGM
GB title: *The Politic Flapper*

Tired of being taken for granted, a girl puts on a surprising show for her family.
Amusing comedy which, in sound, might have made Miss Davies a bigger star than she ever became.

w Agnes Christine Johnson, *play* Barry Connors *d* King Vidor

Marion Davies, Marie Dressler, Lawrence Gray, Del Henderson, Jane Winton

'Marion Davies is in my opinion Filmland's Funniest Female, the only one I would mention in the same breath as Charlie Chaplin.'—*A. P. Herbert, Punch*

The Patsy

US 1964   101m   Technicolor
Paramount / Jerry Lewis (E. J. Glicksman)

Hollywood executives try to mould a bellboy to replace a deceased comedian.
A few mildly funny scenes scarcely atone for a long raucous comedy in which the star upstages his betters.

wd Jerry Lewis *ph* Wallace Kelley *m* David Raksin

Jerry Lewis, Everett Sloane, Peter Lorre, John Carradine, Phil Harris, Hans Conried

Patterns***

US 1956   88m   bw
UA / Jed Harris, Michael Myerberg
GB title: *Patterns of Power*

The tough boss of a New York corporation forces a showdown between a young executive and the older ineffectual man who he hopes will resign.
Tense little boardroom melodrama with domestic asides, one of the best of the filmed TV plays of the mid-fifties.

w Rod Serling, from his play   *d* Fielder Cook
ph Boris Kaufman

Van Heflin, Everett Sloane, Ed Begley, Beatrice Straight, Elizabeth Wilson

Patton***

US 1969   171m   De Luxe   Dimension 150
TCF (Frank McCarthy)
GB title: *Patton—Lust for Glory*

World War II adventures of an aggressive American general.
Brilliantly handled wartime character study which is also a spectacle and tries too hard to have it both ways, but as a piece of film-making is hard to beat.

w Francis Ford Coppola, Edmund H. North
d Franklin Schaffner *ph* Fred Koenekamp
m Jerry Goldsmith

George C. Scott, Karl Malden, Michael Bates, Stephen Young, Michael Strong, Frank Latimore

'Here is an actor so totally immersed in his part that he almost makes you believe he is the man himself.'—*John Gillett*

AA: best picture; script; Franklin Schaffner; George C. Scott

AAN: Fred Koenekamp; Jerry Goldsmith

Paula

US 1952   80m   bw
Columbia (Buddy Adler)
GB title: *The Silent Voice*

A barren wife causes a boy's deafness in an accident; she cures and adopts him.
Adequate woman's picture, a vehicle for a star and a luxuriant wardrobe.

w James Poe, William Sackheim   *d* Rudolph
Maté *ph* Charles Lawton Jnr   *m* George Duning

Loretta Young, Kent Smith, Alexander Knox, Tommy Rettig

The Pawnbroker**

US 1965   114m   bw
Landau–Unger (Worthington Miner)

A Jew in slummy New York is haunted by his experiences in Nazi prison camps.
Engrossing, somewhat over-melodramatic character study, generally well done.

w David Friedkin, Morton Fine, *novel* Edward Lewis Wallant *d* Sidney Lumet *ph* Boris Kaufman *m* Quincy Jones

Rod Steiger, Brock Peters, Geraldine Fitzgerald, Jaime Sanchez, Thelma Oliver, Juano Hernandez

AAN: Rod Steiger

Pay or Die!*

US 1960   109m   bw
Allied Artists (Richard Wilson)

In 1906, a New York Italian police detective forms a special squad to combat the Black Hand.
Tough, convincing period melodrama.

w Richard Wilson, Bertram Millhauser
d Richard Wilson ph Lucien Ballard
m David Raksin ad Fernando Carrere

Ernest Borgnine, Alan Austin, Zohra Lampert, Robert F. Simon, Renata Vanni

Payday
US 1972 103m colour
Cinerama / Pumice / Fantasy (Ralph J. Gleason)

An over-age pop singer has personal problems which erupt into violence.
Well made, dislikeable melodrama.

w Don Carpenter d Daryl Duke ph Richard C. Glouner md Ed Bogas

Rip Torn, Ahna Capri, Elayne Heilveil, Michael C. Gwynn

Payment Deferred°
US 1932 75m bw
MGM

A man desperate for money poisons his wealthy nephew.
Watchable photographed play.

w Ernest Vajda, Claudine West, play Jeffrey Dell d Lothar Mendes ph Merritt Gerstad

Charles Laughton, Maureen O'Sullivan, Ray Milland, Dorothy Peterson, Veree Teasdale, Billy Bevan, Halliwell Hobbes

Payment on Demand°
US 1951 90m bw
RKO / Jack H. Skirball

A happy wife and mother is appalled when her husband asks for a divorce.
A star suffers her way through luxury to a happy ending; good enough stuff for its intended audience.

w Bruce Manning, Curtis Bernhardt d Curtis Bernhardt ph Leo Tover m Victor Young

Bette Davis, Barry Sullivan, Jane Cowl, Kent Taylor, Betty Lynn, John Sutton, Frances Dee, Otto Kruger

'An absolutely typical Joan Crawford picture except that Bette Davis happens to be in the Joan Crawford part.'—*Richard Mallett, Punch*

Payroll°
GB 1961 105m bw
Anglo Amalgamated / Lynx (Norman Priggen)

Small-time crooks snatch £100,000, but after the getaway things begin to go wrong.
Tense, vivid, thoroughly predictable *Rififi*-style thriller, handled with solid professionalism.

w George Baxt, novel Derek Bickerton
d Sidney Hayers ph Ernest Steward m Reg Owen

Michael Craig, Billie Whitelaw, Françoise Prévost, Kenneth Griffith, William Lucas, Tom Bell, Barry Keegan, Joan Rice, Glyn Houston

Peck's Bad Boy
US 1934 70m bw

Adventures of a well-intentioned but accident-prone boy in a midwestern town. Old-fashioned American juvenile classic, modestly well done. Jackie Cooper, Jackie Searle, Dorothy Peterson, Thomas Meighan, Written by Bernard Schubert and Marguerite Roberts from the story by G. W. Peck; directed by Edward Cline; for Sol Lesser / TCF. (Previously made in 1921 with Jackie Coogan.)

Peeper
US 1975 87m De Luxe Panavision
TCF / Chartoff–Winkler (Ron Buck)

In 1947 Los Angeles, a poor British private eye gets into trouble when he seeks a man's lost daughter.
Semi-spoofing Chandleresque caper which is never quite funny or quite thrilling enough.

w W. D. Richter, novel Deadfall by Keith Laumer d Peter Hyams ph Earl Rath m Richard Clements

Michael Caine, Natalie Wood, Kitty Winn, Thayer David, Liam Dunn

'Flimsy whimsy.'—*Variety*

Peeping Tom
GB 1959 109m Eastmancolor
Anglo Amalgamated / Michael Powell

A film studio focus puller is obsessed by the lust to murder beautiful women and photograph the fear on their faces.
Thoroughly disagreeable suspenser, a kind of compendium of the bad taste the director showed in flashes during his career.

w Leo Marks d Michael Powell ph Otto Heller m Brian Easdale

Carl Boehm, Moira Shearer, Anna Massey, Maxine Audley, Esmond Knight, Michael Goodliffe, Shirley Ann Field, Jack Watson

'Of enormous and deserved reputation.'—*Time Out, 1982*

Peg of Old Drury*
GB 1935 76m bw
Herbert Wilcox / B & D

The romance of 18th-century actress Peg
Woffington with David Garrick.
Primitive but vivacious historical romp with
adequate star performances.

w Miles Malleson, *play* Masks and Faces by
Charles Reade, Tom Taylor d Herbert
Wilcox ph F. A. Young

Anna Neagle, Cedric Hardwicke, Jack
Hawkins, Margaretta Scott, Hay Petrie

Peg o'My Heart
US 1933 89m bw

To the concern of his family, an English
nobleman falls for an Irish colleen. Half-
hearted version of a famous lavender-tinted
stage hit previously filmed in the twenties with
its original star Laurette Taylor; but by 1933
its time was past. Marion Davies, Onslow
Stevens, Alan Mowbray, Robert Greig, Irene
Browne, J. Farrell MacDonald, Juliette
Compton. Written by Frances Marion, from
the play by J. Hartley Manners; directed by
Robert Z. Leonard; for MGM.

Peking Express
US 1951 90m bw
Paramount / Hal B. Wallis

In communist China, an assortment of people
are aboard a train which is diverted by
outlaws.
Pot-boiling remake of *Shanghai Express* (qv);
an adequate time-passer.

w John Meredyth Lucas d William Dieterle
ph Charles Lang m Dmitri Tiomkin

Joseph Cotten, Corinne Calvet, Edmund
Gwenn, Marvin Miller
　'Lacks flavour or distinction.'—*Leonard
Maltin*

The Penalty
US 1941 81m bw
MGM (Jack Chertok)

The son of a gangster is regenerated by farm
life and turns against his father.
Antediluvian sweetness and light which wastes
a good cast.

w Harry Ruskin, John C. Higgins d Harold S.
Bucquet ph Harold Rosson

Edward Arnold, Lionel Barrymore, Marsha
Hunt, Robert Sterling, Gene Reynolds

Pendulum*
US 1969 102m Technicolor
Columbia / Pendulum (Stanley Niss)

A convicted murderer and rapist is freed on
appeal and kills the wife of the detective who
arrested him.
Heavy-going police melodrama, efficient but
not very interesting.

w Stanley Niss d George Schaefer ph Lionel
Lindon m Walter Scharf

George Peppard, Jean Seberg, Richard Kiley,
Charles McGraw, Robert F. Lyons, Madeleine
Sherwood

Penelope
US 1966 98m Metrocolor Panavision
MGM / Euterpe (Joe Pasternak, Arthur
　Loew Jnr)

The wife of a bank vice-president is a bank
robber and kleptomaniac.
Would be cute comedy which only sickens one
for wasting its talent.

w George Wells, *novel* E. V. Cunningham
d Arthur Hiller ph Harry Stradling
m Johnny Williams

Natalie Wood, Ian Bannen, Dick Shawn,
Peter Falk, Jonathan Winters, Lila Kedrova,
Lou Jacobi, Norma Crane, Arthur Malet,
Jerome Cowan

Penn of Pennsylvania
GB 1941 79m bw
British National (Richard Vernon)
US title: *The Courageous Mr Penn*

Persecuted Quakers leave England for
America.
Stodgily fictionalized history.

w Anatole de Grunwald, *book* William Penn
by C. E. Vulliamy d Lance Comfort

Clifford Evans, Deborah Kerr, Denis
Arundell, Aubrey Mallalieu, Henry Oscar,
Max Adrian

Pennies from Heaven
US 1936 81m bw

A wanderer protects a homeless little girl from
the truant officer. Mild star musical, lucky
enough to have a hit title song. Bing Crosby,
Edith Fellows, Madge Evans, Louis
Armstrong and his band. Written by
Katherine Leslie Moore, William Rankin and
Jo Swerling; directed by Norman Z. McLeod;
for Columbia.

Penny Paradise
GB 1938 72m bw

A tugboat captain thinks he has won the
football pools; but the coupon wasn't posted.
An old, old story, put over with modest
effectiveness. Edmund Gwenn, Betty Driver,

Jimmy O'Dea, Marie O'Neill, Jack Livesey.
Written by Tommy Thompson, W. L. Meade
and Thomas Browne; directed by Carol Reed;
for ATP.

Penny Points to Paradise
GB 1951   77m   bw

A pools winner takes cash but nearly loses it
to a forger. Abysmally made comedy, only
interesting as an early teaming of the Goons.
Harry Secombe, Peter Sellers, Spike Milligan,
Alfred Marks, Bill Kerr, Freddie Frinton,
Paddy O'Neil. Written by John Ormonde;
directed by Tony Young; for Advance /
Adelphi.

Penny Princess
GB 1952   94m   Technicolor
Rank / Conquest (Frank Godwin)

A New York shopgirl inherits a tiny European
state and boosts its economy by marketing a
mixture of cheese and schnapps.
Thin, spoofy comedy with mild moments of
fun.

wd Val Guest *ph* Geoffrey Unsworth
m Ronald Hamner

Dirk Bogarde, Yolande Donlan, A. E.
Matthews, Anthony Oliver, Edwin Styles,
Reginald Beckwith, Kynaston Reeves, Peter
Butterworth, Laurence Naismith, Mary Clare,
Desmond Walter-Ellis

Penny Serenade*
US 1941   120m   bw
Columbia (Fred Guiol)

Courtship, marriage and the death of two
children are recollected by a woman
contemplating divorce.
Well-played but uneasy film which veers
suddenly and disconcertingly from light
comedy into tragedy.

w Morrie Ryskind *d* George Stevens
ph Joseph Walker *m* W. Franke Harling

Cary Grant, Irene Dunne, Beulah Bondi,
Edgar Buchanan, Ann Doran

'To make something out of very little, and
that so near at hand, is one of the tests of
artistry.'—*Otis Ferguson*
'A tear compeller showing how Cary Grant
and Irene Dunne lose first their own baby and
then the one they adopt. Which, as Lady
Bracknell would certainly have observed,
looks like carelessness.'—*James Agate*

AAN: Cary Grant

Penthouse*
US 1933   90m   bw

When he outlives his usefulness to the
underworld, a lawyer is framed for murder.
Sprightly murder comedy-drama which plays
like a try-out for *The Thin Man*. Warner
Baxter, Myrna Loy, C. Henry Gordon, Nat
Pendleton, Charles Butterworth, George E.
Stone. Written by Frances Goodrich and
Albert Hackett; directed by W. S. Van Dyke;
for Hunt Stromberg / MGM. (GB title:
Crooks in Clover.)

The Penthouse
GB 1967   96m   Eastmancolor
Paramount / Tahiti (Harry Fine)

Illicit lovers in an unfinished block of flats are
terrorized by intruders.
Thoroughly objectionable and unpleasant
melodrama with no attractive characters and
no attempt to explain itself.

wd Peter Collinson, *play* The Meter Man by J.
Scott Forbes *ph* Arthur Lavis *m* John
Hawkesworth

Suzy Kendall, Terence Morgan, Tony
Beckley, Norman Rodway, Martine Beswick
'Pornography in Pinter's clothing.'—*MFB*

The People against O'Hara*
US 1951   102m   bw
MGM (William H. Wright)

An ex-alcoholic defence lawyer sacrifices
himself to prove his client's innocence.
Formula drama, well made and entertainingly
performed, with snatches of bright dialogue.

w John Monks Jnr, *novel* Eleanor Lipsky
d John Sturges *ph* John Alton *m* Carmen
Dragon

Spencer Tracy, Diana Lynn, Pat O'Brien,
John Hodiak, James Arness, Arthur Shields,
Eduardo Ciannelli, Louise Lorimer

The People Next Door
US 1970   93m   De Luxe
Avco Embassy (Herb Brodkin)

Suburban parents have trouble with their
drug-addicted teenage daughter.
Hysterical melodrama with good credentials.

w J. P. Miller, from his TV play *d* David
Greene *ph* Gordon Willis *m* Don Sebesky

Eli Wallach, Julie Harris, Hal Holbrook,
Cloris Leachman, Stephen McHattie,
Nehemiah Persoff
'As unlovely a picture of suburban living as
one is likely to see.'—*Judith Crist*

People on Sunday*

Germany 1929 72m approx (24 fps)
    bw   silent
Filmstudio 1929
original title: *Menschen am Sonntag*

Two couples spend a day in Berlin's countryside.
Influential semi-documentary with fascinating credits.

w Billy Wilder, Curt Siodmak *d* Robert Siodmak, Fred Zinnemann, Edgar G. Ulmer *ph* Eugen Schüfftan

Brigitte Borchert, Christl Ehlers, Annie Schreyer

The People That Time Forgot

GB 1977   90m   Technicolor
AIP / Amicus (John Dark)

Major McBride tries to rescue his old friend from a prehistoric island on which he disappeared in 1916.
Tepid sequel to *The Land That Time Forgot*: even the dinosaurs don't rise to the occasion.

w Patrick Tilley *d* Kevin Connor *ph* Alan Hume *m* John Scott *pd* Maurice Carter

Patrick Wayne, Sarah Douglas, Dana Gillespie, Doug McClure, Thorley Walters, Shane Rimmer, Tony Britton

People Will Talk**

US 1951   110m   bw
TCF (Darryl F. Zanuck)

A surgeon's unorthodox psychological methods cause jealousy among his colleagues, especially when he falls in love with a pregnant patient.
Oddly entertaining jumble of melodrama, comedy, romance, speeches and a little mystery, all quite typical of its director.

wd Joseph L. Mankiewicz, *play* Dr Praetorius by Curt Goetz *ph* Milton Krasner *md* Alfred Newman

Cary Grant, Jeanne Crain, Finlay Currie, Hume Cronyn, Walter Slezak, Sidney Blackmer, Basil Ruysdael

'A picture so mature and refreshingly frank as to hold that an erring young woman might be rewarded with a wise and loving mate is most certainly a significant milestone in the moral emancipation of American films.'—*New York Times*

Pepe

US 1960   195m   Eastmancolor
    Cinemascope
Columbia / George Sidney (Jacques Gelman)

A Mexican peasant in Hollywood gets help from the stars.
Feeble and seemingly endless extravaganza in which the boring stretches far outnumber the rest, and few of the guests have anything worthwhile to do.

w Dorothy Kingsley, Claude Binyon
d George Sidney *ph* Joe MacDonald
md Johnny Green

Cantinflas, Dan Dailey, Shirley Jones, Ernie Kovacs, Jay North, William Demarest, Michael Callan, Maurice Chevalier, Bing Crosby, Richard Conte, Bobby Darin, Sammy Davis Jnr, Jimmy Durante, Zsa Zsa Gabor, Judy Garland, Hedda Hopper, Joey Bishop, Peter Lawford, Janet Leigh, Jack Lemmon, Kim Novak, André Previn, Donna Reed, Debbie Reynolds, Greer Garson, Edward G. Robinson, Cesar Romero, Frank Sinatra, Billie Burke, Tony Curtis, Dean Martin, Charles Coburn

AAN: Joe MacDonald; Johnny Green; song, 'Faraway Part of Town' (*m* André Previn, *ly* Dory Langdon)

Pépé le Moko**

France 1936   90m   bw
Paris Film

A Parisian gangster lives in the Algerian casbah where the police can't get at him; but love causes him to emerge and be shot.
Romantic melodrama modelled on the American gangster film but with a decided poetic quality of its own: the Americans promptly paid it the compliment of remaking it as the not-too-bad *Algiers*.

w Henri Jeanson, Roger d'Ashelbe,
novel Roger d'Ashelbe (Henri La Barthe)
d Julien Duvivier *ph* Jules Kruger *m* Vincent Scotto *ad* Jacques Krauss

Jean Gabin, Mireille Ballin, Gabriel Gabrio, Lucas Gridoux

'One of the most compelling of all French films.'—*New Yorker, 1977*

'Perhaps there have been pictures as exciting on the thriller level . . . but I cannot remember one which has succeeded so admirably in raising the thriller to a poetic level.'—*Graham Greene*

Percy

GB 1971   103m   Eastmancolor
Anglo EMI / Welbeck (Betty E. Box)

After an unfortunate accident, a young man undergoes a successful penis transplant, and sets out to discover who the donor was.
Barrage of phallic jokes, some quite funny, but mostly as witless as the whole idea.

w Hugh Leonard, *novel* Raymond Hitchcock
d Ralph Thomas *ph* Ernest Steward *m* Ray
Davies

Hywel Bennett, Elke Sommer, *Denholm
Elliott*, Britt Ekland, Cyd Hayman

Percy's Progress
GB 1974   101m   Eastmancolor
EMI (Betty E. Box)

A chemical causes impotence in all males
except the owner of the first transplanted
penis.
Percy dug deep, but this is really the bottom of
the barrel.

w Sid Colin *d* Ralph Thomas *ph* Tony Imi
m Tony Macauley

Leigh Lawson, Elke Sommer, Denholm
Elliott, Judy Geeson, Harry H. Corbett,
Vincent Price, Adrienne Posta, Julie Ege,
James Booth

A Perfect Couple*
US 1979   112m   De Luxe
TCF / Lions Gate (Robert Altman)

A middle-aged Greek much dependent on his
family meets a jazz singer through a dating
service.
A free-speaking update of *Marty*, featuring the
Altman repertory company; intelligent
sequences are muffled by the familiar Altman
messiness of approach.

w Robert Altman, Allan Nicholls *d* Robert
Altman *ph* Edmond L. Koons *md* Tom
Pierson, Tony Berg

Paul Dooley, Marta Heflin, Titos Vandis,
Belita Moreno, Henry Gibson, Dimitra Arliss

Perfect Day*
US 1929   20m   bw

Various problems delay a family's departure
for a picnic. Technically a most adept star
comedy but its repetition can annoy. Laurel
and Hardy, Edgar Kennedy. Written by Hal
Roach, Leo McCarey and H. M. Walker;
directed by James Parrott; for Hal Roach.
(NB: The picnic was originally to have
occupied the second reel, but the departure
gags swelled to occupy the entire footage.)

Perfect Friday*
GB 1970   95m   Eastmancolor
London Screenplays / Sunnymede (Dimitri
   de Grunwald)

A bank manager engages aristocratic help to
rob his own bank.
Middling comedy caper.

w Anthony Greville-Bell, J. Scott Forbes
d Peter Hall *ph* Alan Hume *m* Johnny
Dankworth *pd* Terence Marsh

Stanley Baker, Ursula Andress, David
Warner, Patience Collier, T. P. McKenna,
David Waller, Joan Benham, Julian Orchard

The Perfect Furlough
US 1958   93m   Eastmancolor
   Cinemascope
U-I (Robert Arthur)
GB title: *Strictly for Pleasure*

To help morale at a remote Arctic army unit,
one of the men is selected to enjoy the perfect
leave in Paris on behalf of the others.
Amiable farce which entertains while it's on
but is quickly forgotten.

w Stanley Shapiro *d* Blake Edwards
ph Philip Lathrop *m* Frank Skinner

Tony Curtis, Janet Leigh, Elaine Stritch,
Keenan Wynn, Troy Donahue, King
Donovan, Linda Cristal

The Perfect Gentleman
US 1935   73m   bw

A retired officer helps an actress make a
comeback. Genial comedy which didn't quite
work well enough to make an English variety
star popular on both sides of the Atlantic.
Cicely Courtneidge, Frank Morgan, Heather
Angel, Herbert Mundin, Henry Stephenson.
Written by Edward Childs Carpenter; directed
by Tim Whelan; for MGM. (GB title: *The
Imperfect Lady*.)

The Perfect Marriage
US 1946   88m   bw
Paramount / Hal B. Wallis

On their tenth wedding anniversary, a happy
couple have a row and start divorce
proceedings.
Wispy comedy, unmemorable and rather
tiresome.

w Leonard Spiegelgass, *play* Samson
Raphaelson *d* Lewis Allen *ph* Russell Metty
m Frederick Hollander

David Niven, Loretta Young, Eddie Albert,
Nona Griffith, Virginia Field, Jerome Cowan,
Rita Johnson, Charles Ruggles, Nana Bryant,
Zasu Pitts
'Another film about disillusionment and
reconciliation in a mansion with constant
evening dress.'—*Sunday Times*

The Perfect Specimen
US 1937   98m   bw
Warner (Harry Joe Brown)

The grandmother of a rich young man brings him up uncontaminated by the world, but when a girl crashes her car into his fence he proves fitted to deal with the situation. Fantasticated comedy a long way after *Mr Deeds* and too slow by half.

w Norman Reilly Raine, Lawrence Riley, Brewster Morse, Fritz Falkenstein, Samuel Hopkins Adams *d* Michael Curtiz *ph* Charles Rosher

Errol Flynn, Joan Blondell, Hugh Herbert, Edward Everett Horton, May Robson, Dick Foran, Beverly Roberts, Allen Jenkins

Perfect Strangers**
GB 1945 102m bw
MGM / London Films (Alexander Korda)
US title: *Vacation from Marriage*

A downtrodden clerk and his dowdy wife go to war, and come back unrecognizably improved. Pleasant comedy with good actors; but the turnabout of two such caricatures really strains credibility.

w Clemence Dane, Anthony Pelissier *d* Alexander Korda *ph* Georges Périnal

Robert Donat, Deborah Kerr, Glynis Johns, Ann Todd, Roland Culver, Elliot Mason, Eliot Makeham, Brefni O'Rourke, Edward Rigby

'War is supposed to be the catalyst, the sportsman's bracer; and the film's chief weakness is its failure to show the briefly exalted couple sinking back, uncontrollably, under their peacetime stone.'—*James Agee*
AA: original story (Clemence Dane)

Perfect Strangers
US 1950 87m bw
Warner (Jerry Wald)
GB title: *Too Dangerous to Love*

Two jurors on a murder case fall in love. Talkative, unlikely, and rather boring potboiler.

w Edith Sommer, *play* Ladies and Gentlemen by Charles MacArthur, Ben Hecht *d* Bretaigne Windust *ph* Peverell Marley *m* Leigh Harline

Ginger Rogers, Dennis Morgan, Thelma Ritter, Margalo Gillmore, Howard Freeman, Alan Reed, Paul Ford, George Chandler

Perfect Understanding*
GB 1933 80m bw
Gloria Swanson British Pictures Ltd

A couple agree to marry on condition that they will never disagree with each other. Silly comedy with a unique star combination looking acutely uncomfortable.

w Miles Malleson, Michael Powell *d* Cyril Gardner *ph* Curt Courant

Gloria Swanson, Laurence Olivier, John Halliday, Nigel Playfair, Michael Farmer, Genevieve Tobin, Nora Swinburne

The Perfect Woman*
GB 1949 89m bw
GFD / Two Cities (George and Alfred Black)

A girl changes places with her inventor uncle's robot woman.
Described as a romp, this is in fact a pretty good farce, very fast moving and well played after the usual expository start.

w George Black, Bernard Knowles, J. B. Boothroyd, *play* Wallace Geoffrey, Basil Mitchell *d* Bernard Knowles *ph* Jack Hildyard *m* Arthur Wilkinson

Patricia Roc, Nigel Patrick, Stanley Holloway, David Hurst, Miles Malleson, Irene Handl

Performance*
GB 1970 105m Technicolor
Warner / Goodtimes (Donald Cammell)

A vicious gangster moves in with an ex-pop star.
Dense, Pinterish melodrama about alter egos; not really worth the trouble it takes, but superficially very flashily done.

w Donald Cammell *d* Nicolas Roeg, Donald Cammell *ph* Nicolas Roeg *m* Jack Nitzche *md* Randy Newman

James Fox, Mick Jagger, Anita Pallenberg, Michèle Breton, Stanley Meadows, Allan Cuthbertson

'A humourless, messy mixture of crime and decadence and drug-induced hallucination.'— *New Yorker, 1980*

'You don't have to be a drug addict, pederast, sado-masochist or nitwit to enjoy it, but being one or more of these things would help.'—*John Simon*

Perilous Holiday
US 1946 89m bw

A newly acquainted couple become involved with counterfeiters in Mexico City. Passable comedy-crime programme filler. Pat O'Brien, Ruth Warrick, Alan Hale, Minna Gombell. Written by Robert Carson and Roy Chanslor; directed by Edward H. Griffith; for Columbia.

A Perilous Journey
US 1953 87m bw
Republic (.V. J. O'Sullivan)

A party of women sail to the California goldfields to sell themselves into marriage. Reasonably lively action drama.

w Richard Wormser, *novel* The Golden Tide by Virgie Roe *d* R. G. Springsteen *ph* Jack Marta *m* Victor Young

Vera Ralston, David Brian, Charles Winninger, Scott Brady, Virginia Grey, Ben Cooper

The Perils of Pauline*
US 1947 96m Technicolor
Paramount (Sol C. Siegel)

The career of silent serial queen Pearl White. An agreeable recreation of old time Hollywood, with plenty of slapstick chases but a shade too much sentiment also.

w P. J. Wolfson *d* George Marshall *ph* Ray Rennahan *md* Robert Emmett Dolan

Betty Hutton, John Lund, Billy de Wolfe, William Demarest, Constance Collier, Frank Faylen, William Farnum, Paul Panzer, Snub Pollard, Creighton Hale, Chester Conklin, James Finlayson, Hank Mann, Bert Roach, Francis McDonald, Chester Clute
'People who can accept such stuff as solid gold have either forgotten a lot, or never knew first-rate slapstick when they saw it, twenty or thirty years ago, when it was one of the wonders of the world.'—*James Agee*
AAN: song 'I Wish I Didn't Love You So' (*m* / *ly* Frank Loesser)

Period of Adjustment
US 1962 122m bw Panavision
MGM / Marten (Lawrence Weingarten)

A Korean War veteran has the shakes and his sexual adequacy is effected, as his wife furiously discovers.
Comedy of maladjustment, tolerably witty but unsuitably widescreened.

w Isabel Lennart, *play* Tennessee Williams *d* George Roy Hill *ph* Paul bc. Vogel *m* Lyn Murray

Tony Franciosa, Jane Fonda, Jim Hutton, Lois Nettleton

Permission to Kill
US / Austria 1975 97m Technicolor
  Panavision
Warner / Sascha (Paul Mills)

British agents try to stop a communist returning home from the west.
Prolonged, confusing and boring spy melodrama in which everyone looks understandably glum.

w Robin Estridge, from his novel *d* Cyril Frankel *ph* Freddie Young *m* Richard Rodney Bennett

Bekim Fehmiu, Dirk Bogarde, Ava Gardner, Timothy Dalton, Frederic Forrest
'Pretentious political mishmash.'—*MFB*

Perri**
US 1957 75m Technicolor
Walt Disney (Winston Hibler)

The life of a squirrel.
Disney's first True Life Fantasy, in which live footage of animals is manipulated against artificial backgrounds to produce an effect as charming and unreal as a cartoon.

w Ralph Wright, Winston Hibler, *novel* Felix Salten *d* Ralph Wright *ph* various *m* Paul Smith
AAN: Paul Smith

Persecution
GB 1974 96m Eastmancolor
Fanfare / Tyburn (Kevin Francis)

A rich American woman in England is hated by her son and fearful that her murky past will be revealed.
Rich but not engrossing nonsense, somewhat à la *Baby Jane*, with hazy script and stolid production.

w Robert B. Hutton, Rosemary Wootten *d* Don Chaffey *ph* Ken Talbot *m* Paul Ferris

Lana Turner, Ralph Bates, Olga Georges-Picot, Trevor Howard, Suzan Farmer, Ronald Howard, Patrick Allen
'Gives off the unmistakable odour of damp mothballs.'—*Michael Billington, Illustrated London News*

Persona**
Sweden 1966 81m bw
Svensk Filmindustri (Lars-Owe Carlberg)

A nurse begins to identify with her mentally ill patient, and herself has a nervous breakdown. Intense clinical study presented in a very complex cinematic manner which tends to obscure the main theme while providing endless fascination for cinéastes.

wd Ingmar Bergman *ph* Sven Nykvist *m* Lars Johan Werle, *Liv Ullmann, Bibi Andersson, Gunnar Bjornstrand*
'Reactions have ranged from incomprehension to irritation with what is dismissed as a characteristic piece of self-indulgence on Bergman's part—Bergman talking to himself again.'—*David Wilson, MFB*
'A puzzling, obsessive film that Bergman seems not so much to have worked out as to have torn from himself.'—*New Yorker, 1977*

Personal Affair

GB 1953   83m   bw

Rank / Two Cities (Anthony Darnborough)

A schoolmaster and his neurotic wife run into trouble when a girl pupil develops a crush on him.

Preposterous domestic drama making much ado about nothing.

w Lesley Storm, from her play d Anthony Pelissier ph Reg Wyer m William Alwyn

Leo Genn, Gene Tierney, Glynis Johns, Pamela Brown

Personal Property*

US 1937   84m   bw

MGM (John W. Considine Jnr)

GB title: *The Man in Possession*

An American widow in England, in financial straits, falls for the bailiff sent to keep an eye on her.

Moderate star comedy which still amuses.

w Hugh Mills, Ernest Vajda, *play* The Man in Possession by H. M. Harwood d W. S. Van Dyke II ph William Daniels m Franz Waxman

Jean Harlow, Robert Taylor, Reginald Owen, Una O'Connor, Henrietta Crosman, E. E. Clive, Cora Witherspoon, Barnett Parker

Persons in Hiding*

US 1939   71m   bw

Paramount

A bored girl absconds with gangsters and becomes a public enemy.

Interesting programmer which led to several sequels using the same book as source; this one was vaguely inspired by the story of Bonnie and Clyde.

w William R. Lipman, Horace McCoy, *book* J. Edgar Hoover d Louis King ph Harry Fischbeck m Boris Morros

Patricia Morison, J. Carrol Naish, Lynne Overman, William Henry, Helen Twelvetrees, William Frawley

'A little on the tame side, but distinguished by the presence of a crooked and merciless heroine.'—*Graham Greene*

Persons Unknown*

Italy 1958   105m   bw

Lux / Vides / Cinecittà (Franco Cristaldi)

original title: *I Soliti Ignoti;* US title: *Big Deal on Madonna Street*

Adventures of a gang of incompetent thieves, who get arrested more often than they get away, and finally, elaborately drill through a

wall into the bank . . . only to find it's the wrong wall and they are in another room of the same flat.

Spoof black comedy working up to an elaborate take-off of *Rififi*; a great success in Italy and the USA, mildly received elsewhere.

w Age Scarpelli, Suso Cecchi d'Amico, Mario Monicelli d Mario Monicelli ph Gianni di Venanzo m Piero Umiliani

Vittorio Gassman, Renato Salvatori, Toto, Marcello Mastroianni, Memmo Carotenuto, Carla Gravina, Rosanna Rory

Pete 'n Tillie*

US 1972   100m   Technicolor Panavision

Universal (Julius J. Epstein)

The tragi-comic marriage of two eccentrics.

Curious: plain drama treated as comedy, with surprisingly satisfactory results, but not an example to be followed.

w Julius J. Epstein, *novel* Witch's Milk by Peter de Vries d Martin Ritt ph John Alonzo m John T. Williams

Walter Matthau, Carol Burnett, Geraldine Page, René Auberjonois, Barry Nelson, Henry Jones

'For the most part an amusing, moving, sentimental comedy. The wisecracks stay on this side of human possibility – that is, we don't feel, as we do so often with Neil Simon, that the characters have private gag writers in their homes.'—*Stanley Kauffmann*

AAN: Julius J. Epstein; Geraldine Page

Pete Kelly's Blues*

US 1955   95m   Warnercolor Cinemascope

Warner (Jack Webb)

Jazz musicians in the twenties get involved with gangsters.

Minor cult film, mainly for the score; dramatically it is not exactly compelling.

w Richard L. Breen d Jack Webb ph Hal Rosson ph Harper Goff m Sammy Cahn, Ray Heindorf, Arthur Hamilton, Matty Matlock

Jack Webb, Edmond O'Brien, Janet Leigh, Peggy Lee, Andy Devine, *Ella Fitzgerald,* Lee Marvin, Martin Milner

'Concerned with striking attitudes and establishing an atmosphere rather than developing anything very coherent in the way of narrative . . . one remains aware of an over-deliberate straining after effect.'—*Penelope Houston*

AAN: Peggy Lee

Peter Ibbetson*

US 1935 85m bw
Paramount (Louis D. Lighton)

Childhood sweethearts meet again as adults,
are separated when he is imprisoned for her
husband's murder, but are reunited in heaven.
Downright peculiar romantic fantasy, even
more oddly cast, but extremely well produced.

w Vincent Lawrence, Waldemar Young,
Constance Collier, *novel* George du Maurier
d Henry Hathaway ph Charles Lang m Ernst
Toch

Gary Cooper, Ann Harding, Ida Lupino, John
Halliday, Douglass Dumbrille, Virginia
Weidler, Dickie Moore, Doris Lloyd
'A triumph of surrealist thought.'—*André
Breton*
'One of the world's ten best films.'—*Luis
Bunuel*

AAN: Ernst Toch

Peter Pan***

US 1953 76m Technicolor
Walt Disney

Three London children are taken into
fairyland by a magic flying boy who cannot
grow up.
Solidly crafted cartoon version of a famous
children's play; not Disney's best work, but
still miles ahead of the competition.

supervisor Ben Sharpsteen d Wilfred Jackson,
Clyde Geronomi, Hamilton Luske

The Peterville Diamond

GB 1942 85m bw
Warner (A. H. Salomon)

A bored wife revives her husband's interest by
cultivating the advances of a jewel thief.
Modest comedy-drama, smoothly presented:
the same play formed the basis of Dieterle's
Jewel Robbery.

w Brock Williams, Gordon Wellesley,
play Jewel Robbery by Ladislas Fodor
d Walter Forde ph Basil Emmott md Jack
Beaver

Anne Crawford, Donald Stewart, Renee
Houston, Oliver Wakefield, Charles Heslop,
William Hartnell, Felix Aylmer, Charles
Victor

Pete's Dragon

US 1977 127m Technicolor
Walt Disney (Ron Miller, Jerome
Courtland)

In Maine in 1900, a nine-year-old boy escapes
from grasping foster-parents with his pet
dragon, which no one but himself can see.
A kind of juvenile rewrite of *Harvey*. The
dragon is drawn (rather poorly) and the
human characters are not exactly three-
dimensional. A long way from *Mary Poppins*.

w Malcolm Marmorstein, *story* Seton
I. Miller, S. S. Field d Don Chaffey
ph Frank Phillips *anim* Ken Anderson
md Irwin Kostal songs Al Kasha, Joel
Hirschhorn ch Onna White

Sean Marshall, Mickey Rooney, Jim Dale,
Helen Reddy, Red Buttons, Shelley Winters,
Jim Backus, Joe E. Ross, Ben Wrigley
'For a Disney film it's terribly badly made,
in parts so clumsy that it looks like the work of
the Burbank Amateur Camera Club.'—*Barry
Took, Punch*

AAN: music; song, 'Candle on the Water'

The Petrified Forest**

US 1936 83m bw
Warner (Henry Blanke)

Travellers at a way station in the Arizona
desert are held up by gangsters.
Rather faded melodrama (it always was),
which is important to Hollywood for
introducing such well used figures as the poet
idealist hero and the gangster anti-hero, and
for giving Bogart his first meaty role.
Otherwise, the settings are artificial, the acting
theatrical, the development predictable and
the dialogue pretentious.

w Charles Kenyon, Delmer Daves,
play Robert E. Sherwood d Archie Mayo
ph Sol Polito md Leo F. Forbstein

Leslie Howard, Bette Davis, *Humphrey
Bogart,* Genevieve Tobin, Dick Foran, Joe
Sawyer, Porter Hall, Charley Grapewin
'Drama slackens under the weight of Mr
Sherwood's rather half-baked philosophy.'—
Alistair Cooke
'There is good dramatic material here, but
Mr Sherwood doesn't see his play as certain
things happening, but as ideas being
expressed, "significant" cosmic ideas. . . . Life
itself, which crept in during the opening scene,
embarrassed perhaps at hearing itself so
explicitly discussed, crept out again, leaving us
only with the symbols, the too pasteboard
desert, the stunted cardboard studio trees.'—
Graham Greene
† Remade as *Escape in the Desert* (qv).

Petticoat Fever

US 1936 80m bw
MGM (Frank Davis)

A girl and her stuffy fiancé crash land their
plane in sub-Arctic Labrador and are helped
by a wireless operator who has not seen a
woman for two years.

Pert, slightly unusual comedy which comes off pretty well.

w Harold Goldman, *play* Mark Reed
d George Fitzmaurice *ph* Ernest Haller
m William Axt

Robert Montgomery, Myrna Loy, Reginald Owen, Winifred Shotter

The Petty Girl
US 1950 88m Technicolor
Columbia (Nat Perrin)
GB title: *Girl of the Year*

A calendar artist takes a staid college professor as his model, and causes a scandal. Witless comedy musical which barely lingers in the memory.

w Nat Perrin, *story* Mary McCarthy *d* Henry Levin *ph* William Snyder *m* George Duning
songs Harold Arlen, Johnny Mercer

Robert Cummings, Joan Caulfield, Melville Cooper, Elsa Lanchester, Audrey Long, Mary Wickes, Frank Orth

Petulia*
US 1968 105m Technicolor
Warner / Petersham (Raymond Wagner)

A doctor's life is disrupted by his meeting and loving a kooky girl who has family problems. Swinging London melodrama which happens to be set in San Francisco. All very flashy, and occasionally arresting or well acted, but adding up to nothing.

w Lawrence B. Marcus, *novel* Me and the Arch Kook Petulia by John Haase *d* Richard Lester *ph* Nicolas Roeg *m* John Barry

George C. Scott, Julie Christie, Richard Chamberlain, Joseph Cotten, Arthur Hill, Shirley Knight, Kathleen Widdoes, Pippa Scott

'A sad and savage comment on the ways we waste our time and ourselves in upper-middle-class America.'—*Richard Schickel*

'A soulless, arbitrary, attitudinizing piece of claptrap.'—*John Simon*

Peyton Place**
US 1957 157m De Luxe Cinemascope
TCF (Jerry Wald)

Sex, frustration and violence ferment under the placid surface of a small New England town.
Well-made film of what was at the time a scandalous bestseller, one of the first to reveal those nasty secrets of 'ordinary people'.

w John Michael Hayes, *novel* Grace Metalious *d* Mark Robson *ph* William Mellor *m* Franz Waxman

Lana Turner, Arthur Kennedy, Hope Lange, Lee Philips, Lloyd Nolan, Diane Varsi, Russ Tamblyn, Terry Moore, Barry Coe, David Nelson, Betty Field, Mildred Dunnock, Leon Ames, Lorne Greene

AAN: best picture; John Michael Hayes; Mark Robson; William Mellor; Lana Turner; Arthur Kennedy; Hope Lange; Diane Varsi; Russ Tamblyn

Phaedra*
US / Greece 1961 116m bw
UA / Melinafilm (Jules Dassin)

A tycoon's wife falls in love with her stepson. Ludicrous, awesomely folly-filled attempt to modernize and sex up Greek tragedy.

wd Jules Dassin *ph* Jacques Natteau *m* Mikis Theodorakis

Melina Mercouri, Anthony Perkins, Raf Vallone, Elizabeth Ercy

'Unfortunately unforgettable.'—*John Simon*

Phantom Lady**
US 1944 87m bw
Universal (Joan Harrison)

A man is accused of murder and his only alibi is a mysterious lady he met in a bar.
Odd little thriller which doesn't really hold together but is made for the most part with great style.

w Bernard C. Schoenfeld, *novel* William Irish *d* Robert Siodmak *ph* Woody Bredell
m Hans Salter

Franchot Tone, Alan Baxter, Ella Raines, Elisha Cook Jnr, Fay Helm, Andrew Tombes

The Phantom Light
GB 1934 75m bw

Wreckers try to scare off a new lighthouse keeper. Effective minor comedy-thriller with good credentials. Gordon Harker, Binnie Hale, Ian Hunter, Donald Calthrop, Milton Rosmer, Herbert Lomas. Written by Austin Melford and Ralph Smart, from the play *The Haunted Light* by Evadne Price and Joan Roy Byford; directed by Michael Powell; for Gainsborough.

Phantom of Crestwood*
US 1932 77m bw
RKO (David O. Selznick)

Murder strikes when a blackmailer assembles her victims.
Lively mystery with spoof elements.

w Bartlett Cormack, J. Walter Ruben
d J. Walter Ruben *ph* Henry Gerrard *m* Max Steiner

Ricardo Cortez, H. B. Warner, Anita Louise, Karen Morley, Pauline Frederick, Robert McWade, Skeets Gallagher

Phantom of Paris
US 1931   73m   bw

A magician proves by a complex plan that he did not kill his fiancée's father. Unusual but tortuous thriller which fails to thrill. John Gilbert, Leila Hyams, Ian Keith, C. Aubrey Smith, Lewis Stone, Jean Hersholt. Written by Bess Meredyth, John Meehan and Edwin Justus Mayer; directed by John S. Robertson; for MGM.

Phantom of the Opera***
US 1926   94m (24 fps)   bw (Technicolor sequence)   silent
Universal

A disfigured man in a mask abducts the prima donna of the Paris Opera House to his lair in the sewers below.
Patchy but often splendid piece of Grand Guignol which not only provided its star with a famous role but was notable for its magnificent visual style.

w Raymond Shrock, Elliot Clawson, *novel* Gaston Leroux   *d* Rupert Julian *ph* Charles Van Enger, Virgil Miller   *ad* Dan Hall

Lon Chaney, Mary Philbin, Norman Kerry, Gibson Gowland

The Phantom of the Opera**
US 1943   92m   Technicolor
Universal (George Waggner)

This version is more decorous and gentlemanly, with much attention paid to the music, but it certainly has its moments.

w Erich Taylor, Samuel Hoffenstein, *d* Arthur Lubin   *ph* Hal Mohr, W. Howard Greene   *m* Edward Ward   *ad* John B. Goodman, Alexander Golitzen

Claude Rains, Nelson Eddy, Susanna Foster, Edgar Barrier, Leo Carrillo, J. Edward Bromberg, Jane Farrar, Hume Cronyn

AA: Hal Mohr, W. Howard Greene; John B. Goodman, Alexander Golitzen

Phantom of the Opera
GB 1962   90m   Technicolor
U-I / Hammer (Anthony Hinds)

Stodgy remake with the accent on shock.

w John Elder   *d* Terence Fisher   *ph* Arthur Grant   *m* Edwin Astley

Herbert Lom, Edward de Souza, Heather Sears, Thorley Walters, Michael Gough, Ian Wilson, Martin Miller, John Harvey, Miriam Karlin

'The only shock is that the British, who could have had a field day with this antique, have simply wafted it back with a lick and a promise.'—*New York Times*

Phantom of the Paradise*
US 1974   91m   Movielab
TCF / Pressman Williams (Edward R. Pressman)

A modern satirical remake of *Phantom of the Opera* in rock opera terms, set in a pop music palace. Not bad in spots, but it doesn't really know where it's going.

wd Brian de Palma   *ph* Larry Pizer   *m* Paul Williams   *pd* Jack Fisk

Paul Williams, William Finley, Jessica Harper, George Memmoli, Gerrit Graham

'Too broad in its effects and too bloated in style to cut very deeply as a parody . . . closer to the anything goes mode of a *Mad* magazine lampoon.'—*Richard Combs*

AAN: Paul Williams

Phantom of the Rue Morgue
US 1954   84m   Warnercolor   3-D
Warner (Henry Blanke)

In old Paris, a killer of pretty girls turns out to be an ape.
Dull revamping of a rather dull story, with boring characters and little horror.

w Harold Medford, James R. Webb, *story* Murders in the Rue Morgue by Edgar Allan Poe   *d* Roy del Ruth   *ph* Peverell Marley   *m* David Buttolph

Karl Malden, Claude Dauphin, Steve Forrest, Patricia Medina, Allyn McLerie, Dolores Dorn

The Phantom President*
US 1932   78m   bw
Paramount

A fast-talking quack doubles for a lacklustre presidential candidate.
A likely but in fact unsuccessful film debut for a famous Broadway star: many points of interest.

w Walter de Leon, Harlan Thompson *d* Norman Taurog   *ph* David Abel *songs* Richard Rodgers, Lorenz Hart

George M. Cohan, Claudette Colbert, Jimmy Durante, George Barbier, Sidney Toler, Jameson Thomas, Paul Hurst, Alan Mowbray

'For anyone who cares about American theatrical history, it's an indispensable record of Cohan's style.'—*New Yorker, 1978*

The Phantom Tollbooth**
US 1969 90m Metrocolor
MGM / Animation Visual Arts

A bored boy goes through a magic tollbooth to land beyond his wildest imagination, rescues Rhyme and Reason, and defeats the Demons of Ignorance.

Ambitious and well-devised, though rather slow-starting, cartoon feature which falls in style somewhere between *Alice in Wonderland* and *The Wizard of Oz* but is more intellectual than either and would be beyond the reach of most children. Discerning adults may have a ball.

w Chuck Jones, Sam Rosen, *novel* Norton Juster *d* Chuck Jones, Abe Levitow *ph* Maurice Noble

Butch Patrick

Phase IV
GB 1973 84m Technicolor
Paramount / Alced (Paul B. Radin)

In the Arizona desert, ants attack a scientific installation.

Oddly effective if repulsive science fiction; the ants are all the more unpleasant because they stay the normal size.

w Mayo Simon *d* Saul Bass *ph* Dick Bush *m* Brian Gascoyne

Nigel Davenport, Lynne Frederick, Michael Murphy, Alan Gifford

The Phenix City Story*
US 1955 100m bw
Allied Artists (Sam Bischoff, David
    Diamond)

A young lawyer fights the racketeers who control his town.

Goodish example of the semi-documentary melodramas of small-town corruption which swarmed out of Hollywood following the Kefauver investigations.

w Crane Wilbur, Dan Mainwaring *d* Phil Karlson *ph* Harry Neumann *m* Harry Sukman

Richard Kiley, *Edward Andrews*, John McIntire, Kathryn Grant

Phffft
US 1954 91m bw
Columbia (Fred Kohlmar)

The title refers to the sound of an expiring match; the story tells of a couple who get

divorced and try to find out what they have been missing.

Champagne comedy with no bubbles.

w George Axelrod *d* Mark Robson *ph* Charles Lang *m* Frederick Hollander

Jack Lemmon, Judy Holliday, Kim Novak, Jack Carson, Luella Gear, Donald Randolph, Donald Curtis, Merry Anders

The Philadelphia Story****
US 1940 112m bw
MGM (Joseph L. Mankiewicz)

A stuffy heiress, about to be married for the second time, turns human and returns gratefully to number one.

Hollywood's most wise and sparkling comedy, with a script which is even an improvement on the original play. Cukor's direction is so discreet you can hardly sense it, and all the performances are just perfect.

w Donald Ogden Stewart, play Philip Barry d George Cukor ph Joseph Ruttenberg m Franz Waxman ad Cedric Gibbons

Katharine Hepburn, Cary Grant, James Stewart, Ruth Hussey, Roland Young, John Halliday, Mary Nash, Virginia Weidler, John Howard, Henry Daniell

'There are just not enough superlatives sufficiently to appreciate this show.'— *Hollywood Reporter*

'An exceptionally bright job of screenplay writing . . . though films like this do little to advance the art of motion pictures, they may help to convince some of the more discerning among cultural slugabeds that when movies want to turn their hand to anything, they can turn it.'—*Otis Ferguson*

AA: Donald Ogden Stewart; James Stewart
AAN: best picture; George Cukor; Katharine Hepburn; Ruth Hussey

Philo Vance

The smooth sleuth created by S. S. Van Dine was a popular film hero of the thirties, for several different companies and with several different actors. As a series it was very variable indeed.

1929: THE CANARY MURDER CASE (Paramount: William Powell); THE GREENE MURDER CASE (Paramount: William Powell)
1930: THE BISHOP MURDER CASE (MGM: Basil Rathbone); THE BENSON MURDER CASE (Paramount: William Powell)
1933: THE KENNEL MURDER CASE (qv) (Warner: William Powell)

1934: THE DRAGON MURDER CASE
(Warner: Warren William)
1935: THE CASINO MURDER CASE
(MGM: Paul Lukas)
1936: THE GARDEN MURDER CASE
(MGM: Edmund Lowe)
1937: NIGHT OF MYSTERY (Paramount:
Grant Richards)
1937: THE SCARAB MURDER CASE
(British: Wilfrid Hyde White)
1939: THE GRACIE ALLEN MURDER
CASE (Paramount: Warren William);
CALLING PHILO VANCE (Warner: James
Stephenson)
1947: PHILO VANCE RETURNS (PRC:
William Wright); PHILO VANCE'S
GAMBLE (PRC: Alan Curtis); PHILO
VANCE'S SECRET MISSION (PRC: Alan
Curtis)

Phone Call from a Stranger
US 1952 96m bw
TCF (Nunnally Johnson)

Of four airplane acquaintances, only one
survives a crash; he visits the families of the
others.
Four stories with an unlikely link. (The
compendium craze, which had started in 1948
with *Quartet,* was now straining itself.)
Nothing to remember except Miss Davis.

w Nunnally Johnson d Jean Negulesco
ph Milton Krasner m Franz Waxman

Bette Davis, Gary Merrill, Michael Rennie,
Shelley Winters, Keenan Wynn, Evelyn
Varden, Warren Stevens, Craig Stevens

'A cinematic party line on which several
conversations are going at once, none of them
coming across very distinctly.'—*Time*

Piccadilly*
GB 1929 105m (24 fps) bw silent
BIP (E. A. Dupont)

A club owner's fiancée is accused of killing his
Chinese mistress.
Sub-Edgar Wallace melodrama, no longer
watchable with a straight face.

w Arnold Bennett d E. A. Dupont
ph Werner Brandes

Gilda Gray, Anna May Wong, Jameson
Thomas, Cyril Ritchard, Ellen Pollock,
Charles Laughton, Debroy Somers and his
Band

Piccadilly Incident*
GB 1946 102m bw
ABP (Herbert Wilcox)

During World War II, a girl believed drowned
returns from the front to find her husband
remarried.

The Enoch Arden theme again, and the first of
the Wilcox-Neagle 'London' films, though
untypically a melodrama with a sad ending.
Efficient enough for its chosen audience.

w Nicholas Phipps d Herbert Wilcox ph Max
Greene

Anna Neagle, Michael Wilding, Michael
Laurence, Frances Mercer, Coral Browne, A.
E. Matthews, Edward Rigby, Brenda Bruce

Piccadilly Jim*
US 1936 100m bw
MGM (Harry Rapf)

A cartoonist helps his father to marry by
making the bride's stuffy family objects of
ridicule.
Amiable comedy with a diverting London
setting.

w Charles Brackett, Edwin Knopf, *novel* P.
G. Wodehouse d Robert Z. Leonard
ph Joseph Ruttenberg m William Axt

Robert Montgomery, Madge Evans, Frank
Morgan, Billie Burke, Eric Blore, Robert
Benchley, Ralph Forbes, Cora Witherspoon,
E. E. Clive

Piccadilly Third Stop
GB 1960 90m bw
Rank / Sydney Box / Ethiro (Norman
    Williams)

A smooth crook seduces the daughter of an
eastern ambassador in London to gain entry to
the embassy and rob it.
Boring and rather unpleasant thriller partly
redeemed by a final chase through the
Underground.

w Leigh Vance d Wolf Rilla ph Ernest
Steward m Philip Green

Terence Morgan, Yoko Tani, John Crawford,
William Hartnell, Mai Zetterling, Dennis
Price, Ann Lynn

Pick a Star
US 1937 67m bw
Hal Roach / MGM

An innocent girl in Hollywood achieves
stardom with the help of a publicity man.
Perfectly awful Cinderella story with
interesting glimpses behind the studio scenes
and (if you can wait that long) a couple of
good Laurel and Hardy sequences.

w Richard Flournoy, Arthur Vernon Jones,
Thomas J. Dugan d Edward Sedgwick
ph Norbert Brodine

Rosina Lawrence, Jack Haley, Patsy Kelly,
Mischa Auer, *Stan Laurel, Oliver Hardy,*
Charles Halton, Lyda Roberti

Pick Up
US 1951 78m bw
Columbia (Hugo Haas)

A lonely middle-aged man falls for a tart who is interested only in his money.
Modest variation on *The Blue Angel*, the first of several second features made by Haas to feature himself as a second Emil Jannings. They got progressively more maudlin.

wd Hugo Haas *ph* Paul Ivano

Hugo Haas, Beverly Michaels, Allan Nixon, Howard Chamberlin

Pickup on South Street*
US 1953 80m bw
TCF (Jules Schermer)

A pickpocket steals a girl's wallet and finds himself up to his neck in espionage.
Over-rich mixture of crime, violence and anti-communism, smartly made without being very interesting.

wd Samuel Fuller *ph* Joe MacDonald
m Leigh Harline

Richard Widmark, Jean Peters, *Thelma Ritter*, Richard Kiley

† Remade 1968 as *Capetown Affair*.

AAN: Thelma Ritter

The Pickwick Papers*
GB 1952 115m bw
George Minter (Bob McNaught)

Various adventures of the Pickwick Club culminate in Mrs Bardell's suit for breach of promise.
Flatly conceived and loosely constructed Dickensian comedy; good humour and lots of well-known faces do not entirely atone for lack of artifice.

wd Noel Langley *ph* Wilkie Cooper
m Antony Hopkins *ad* Fred Pusey

James Hayter, James Donald, Donald Wolfit, Hermione Baddeley, Hermione Gingold, Kathleen Harrison, *Nigel Patrick*, Alexander Gauge, Lionel Murton

Picnic**
US 1956 113m Technicolor
Cinemascope
Columbia (Fred Kohlmar)

A brawny wanderer causes sexual havoc one summer in a small American town.
Seminal melodrama setting new directions for Hollywood and illustrating the side of life the Hardy family never showed. Generally quite compulsive despite some overacting.

w Daniel Taradash, *play William Inge*
d Joshua Logan *ph* James Wong Howe
m George Duning *pd* Jo Mielziner
ad William Flannery

William Holden, Kim Novak, Rosalind Russell, *Susan Strasberg*, Arthur O'Connell, Cliff Robertson, Betty Field, Verna Felton, Reta Shaw

'Mr Logan's idea of an outing in the corn country includes a choir of at least a hundred voices, a camera so alert that it can pick up the significance of the reflection of a Japanese lantern in a pool (futility, wistfulness, the general transience of life, as I get it) and a sound track let loose in the most formidable music I've heard in my time at the movies.'—*New Yorker*

AAN: best picture; Joshua Logan; George Duning; Arthur O'Connell

Picnic at Hanging Rock*
Australia 1975 115m Eastmancolor
Picnic Productions / Australia Film
Corporation (Hal and Jim McElroy)

In 1900, schoolgirls set out for a picnic; some disappear and are never found.
An intriguing but finally irritating puzzle with no answer; the atmosphere is nicely calculated, but as in *L'Avventura* the whole thing outstays its welcome.

w Cliff Green, *novel* Joan Lindsay *d* Peter Weir *ph* Russell Boyd *m* Bruce Smeaton

Rachel Roberts, Dominic Guard, Helen Morse, Jacki Weaver, Vivean Gray, Kirsty Child

'Atmospherically vivid, beautifully shot, and palpably haunting.'—*Michael Billington, Illustrated London News*

Picture Mommy Dead
US 1966 88m Pathecolor
Embassy / Berkeley (Bert I. Gordon)

A girl who has been hospitalized following the death of her mother in a fire returns home to find, apparently, that her father's new wife is trying to kill her.
Twist-ending shocker with tired stars, from the tag end of the *Baby Jane* cycle.

w Robert Sherman *d* Bert I. Gordon
ph Ellsworth Fredericks *m* Robert Drasnin

Don Ameche, Martha Hyer, Zsa Zsa Gabor, Susan Gordon, Maxwell Reed, Signe Hasso, Wendell Corey

The Picture of Dorian Gray**
US 1945 110m bw (Technicolor
inserts)
MGM (Pandro S. Berman)

A Victorian gentleman keeps in the attic a picture of himself, which shows his age and depravity while he stays eternally young.
Elegant variation on *Dr Jekyll and Mr Hyde*, presented in portentous style which suits the subject admirably.

wd Albert Lewin, *novel* Oscar Wilde
ph Harry Stradling *m* Herbert Stothart

George Sanders, Hurd Hatfield, Donna Reed, Angela Lansbury, Peter Lawford
'Respectful, earnest, and, I'm afraid, dead.'—*James Agee*
'Loving and practised hands have really improved Wilde's original, cutting down the epigrammatic flow . . . and rooting out all the preciousness which gets in the way of the melodrama.'—*Richard Winnington*
AA: Harry Stradling
AAN: Angela Lansbury

The Picture Snatcher**
US 1933 77m bw
Warner

An ex-racketeer just out of prison becomes a scandal photographer.
Lively star vehicle, interesting for period detail.
w Allen Rivkin, P. J. Wolfson *d* Lloyd Bacon *ph* Sol Polito *md* Leo F. Forbstein

James Cagney, Ralph Bellamy, Patricia Ellis, Alice White, Ralf Harolde, Robert Emmett O'Connor, Robert Barrat
'A vulgar but generally funny collection of blackouts.'—*Time*
'Fast, snappy, tough and packed with action.'—*New York Herald Tribune*
† Remade 1947 as *Escape from Crime*, with Richard Travis.

A Piece of the Action
US 1977 135m Metrocolor
Warner / First Artists / Verdon (Melville Tucker)

Crooks are blackmailed into helping rebellious adolescents.
A black version, at immense length, of the hoodlum comedies in which the Dead End Kids so often featured. Not badly made, but out of date without being nostalgic.
w Charles Blackwell, *story* Timothy March *d* Sidney Poitier *ph* Don Morgan *m* Curtis Mayfield

Sidney Poitier, James Earl Jones, Bill Cosby, Denise Nicholas, Hope Clarke, Tracy Reed, Jason Evers, Marc Lawrence

The Pied Piper**
US 1942 86m bw
TCF (Nunnally Johnson)

An elderly man who hates children finds himself smuggling several of them out of occupied France.
Smart, sentimental, occasionally funny war adventure.

w Nunnally Johnson, *novel* Nevil Shute
d Irving Pichel *ph* Edward Cronjager
m Alfred Newman

Monty Woolley, Anne Baxter, Roddy McDowall, Otto Preminger, J. Carrol Naish, Lester Matthews, Jill Esmond, Peggy Ann Garner

AAN: best picture; Edward Cronjager; Monty Woolley

The Pied Piper
GB 1971 90m Eastmancolor
Panavision
Sagittarius / Goodtimes (David Puttnam, Sanford Lieberson)

In 1349 a strolling minstrel rids Hamelin of a plague of rats.
Paceless, slightly too horrific, and generally disappointing fantasy, especially from this director; poor sets and restricted action.
w Jacques Demy, Mark Peploe, Andrew Birkin *d* Jacques Demy *ph* Peter Suschitsky *m* Donovan *pd* Assheton Gorton

Donovan, Donald Pleasence, Michael Hordern, Jack Wild, Diana Dors, John Hurt

Pierre of the Plains
US 1942 66m bw

Adventures of a cheerful trapper in Canada's northwest territory. Unashamed second-feature version of a play which its producer, Edgar Selwyn, had written in 1907 and which had been filmed in 1918 (as *Hearts of the Wild*) and in 1922 (as *Over the Border*). (Selwyn was the man who once merged with Goldfish to form Goldwyn, a name which Goldfish then kept.) John Carroll, Ruth Hussey, Bruce Cabot, Reginald Owen, Henry Travers, Evelyn Ankers. Written by Bertram Millhauser and Laurence Kimble; directed by George B. Seitz; for MGM.

The Pigeon That Took Rome
US 1962 101m bw Panavision
Paramount / Llenroc (Melville Shavelson)

American undercover agents are smuggled into Rome during the German occupation.
Heavy-going war comedy-drama with bright sequences countered by too little wit and too many voluble Italians.
wd Melville Shavelson, *novel* The Easter Dinner by Donald Downes *ph* Daniel Fapp *m* Alessandro Cicognini

Charlton Heston, Elsa Martinelli, Brian Donlevy, Harry Guardino, Baccaloni

Pigskin Parade
US 1936 93m bw
TCF (Bogart Rogers)
GB title: *Harmony Parade*

A country farmer becomes a college football hero.
Livelier-than-average college comedy.

w Harry Tugend, Jack Yellen, William Conselman *d* David Butler *ph* Arthur Miller *md* David Buttolph

Stuart Erwin, Patsy Kelly, Jack Haley, Johnny Downs, Betty Grable, Arline Judge, Dixie Dunbar, Judy Garland, Tony Martin, Elisha Cook Jnr

AAN: Stuart Erwin

The Pilgrim*
US 1923   38m approx (24 fps)   bw silent
First National

An escaped convict disguises himself as a minister and does a few good deeds.
Star comedy with more sentiment than laughter.

wd Charles Chaplin *ph* Rollie Totheroh

Charles Chaplin, Edna Purviance, Kitty Bradbury, Mack Swain

Pillars of the Sky
US 1956   95m   Technicolor
Cinemascope
U-I (Robert Arthur)
GB title: *The Tomahawk and the Cross*

An indian scout and a missionary help bring peace between cavalry and indians.
Modest western, adequately done.

w Sam Rolfe *d* George Marshall *ph* Harold Lipstein *m* Joseph Gershenson

Jeff Chandler, Dorothy Malone, Ward Bond, Keith Andes, Lee Marvin, Sydney Chaplin, Michael Ansara, Willis Bouchey

Pillow Talk**
US 1959   110m   Eastmancolor
Cinemascope
Universal / Arwin (Ross Hunter, Martin Melcher)

Two people who can't stand each other fall in love via a party line.
Slightly elephantine romantic comedy which nevertheless contains a number of funny scenes and was notable for starting off the Hudson-Day partnership and a run of similar comedies which survived the sixties.

w Stanley Shapiro, Maurice Richlin *d* Michael Gordon *ph* Arthur E. Arling *m* Frank de Vol

Doris Day, Rock Hudson, Tony Randall, Thelma Ritter, Nick Adams, Julia Meade, Allen Jenkins, Marcel Dalio, Lee Patrick

AA: Stanley Shapiro, Maurice Richlin
AAN: Frank de Vol; Doris Day; Thelma Ritter

Pillow to Post
US 1945   96m   bw
Warner (Alex Gottlieb)

A girl poses as a soldier's wife to get a hotel room.
World War II comedy on a familiar theme (*The More the Merrier, Standing Room Only, The Doughgirls*, etc). Uninspired.

w Charles Hoffman, *play* Pillar to Post by Rose Simon Kohn *d* Vincent Sherman *ph* Wesley Anderson *m* Frederick Hollander

Ida Lupino, Sidney Greenstreet, William Prince, Stuart Erwin, Ruth Donnelly, Barbara Brown, Frank Orth

Pilot Number Five
US 1943   71m   bw
MGM (B. P. Fineman)

A pilot in the South Pacific volunteers for a desperate mission because—we learn in flashback—he hates fascists.
Rather unpalatable propaganda encased in dim drama.

w David Hertz *d* George Sidney *ph* Paul C. Vogel *m* Lennie Hayton

Franchot Tone, Gene Kelly, Marsha Hunt, Van Johnson, Alan Baxter, Dick Simmons, Steve Geray

Pimpernel Smith**
GB 1941   121m   bw
British National (Leslie Howard)
US titles: *Mister V; The Fighting Pimpernel*

A professor of archaeology goes into war-torn Europe to rescue refugees.
The Scarlet Pimpernel unassumingly and quite effectively brought up to date, with memorable scenes after a slow start.

w Anatole de Grunwald, Roland Pertwee, Ian Dalrymple *d* Leslie Howard *ph* Max Greene *m* John Greenwood

Leslie Howard, Mary Morris, Francis L. Sullivan, Hugh McDermott, Raymond Huntley, Manning Whiley, Peter Gawthorne, David Tomlinson

Pin Up Girl
US 1944   83m   Technicolor
TCF (William Le Baron)

A Washington secretary becomes a national celebrity when she meets a navy hero.
Adequate star flagwaver, mildly interesting for its new streamlined set designs.

w Robert Ells, Helen Logan, Earl Baldwin
d Bruce Humberstone *ph* Ernest Palmer
md Emil Newman, Charles Henderson
songs James V. Monaco, Mack Gordon
ch Hermes Pan *ad* James Basevi, Joseph C.
Wright

Betty Grable, John Harvey, Martha Raye, Joe
E. Brown, Eugene Pallette, Dave Willcock,
Charles Spivak and his Orchestra
'A spiritless blob of a musical, and a
desecration of a most inviting theme.'—*Bosley
Crowther*

The Pink Jungle
US 1968   104m   Techniscope
Universal / Cherokee (Stan Margulies)

A photographer and his model are stranded in
a South American village and become
involved in a diamond hunt.
Curious mixture of adventure and light
comedy that works only in patches.

w Charles Williams, *novel* Snake Water by
Alan Williams *d* Delbert Mann *ph* Russell
Metty *m* Ernie Freeman
James Garner, Eva Renzi, George Kennedy,
Nigel Green, Michael Ansara, George Rose
'Another backlot cheapie.'—*Robert
Windeler*

The Pink Panther**
US 1963   113m   Technirama
UA / Mirisch (Martin Jurow)

An incompetent *surêté* inspector is in
Switzerland on the trail of a jewel thief called
The Phantom.
Sporadically engaging mixture of pratfalls,
Raffles, and Monsieur Hulot, all dressed to
kill and quite palatable for the uncritical.
Inspector Clouseau later became a cartoon
character and also provoked five sequels: *A
Shot in the Dark, Inspector Clouseau, The
Return of the Pink Panther, The Pink Panther
Strikes Again* and *The Revenge of the Pink
Panther.*

w Maurice Richlin, Blake Edwards *d* Blake
Edwards *ph* Philip Lathrop *m* Henry
Mancini *ad* Fernando Carrere *animation* De
Patie-Freleng
David Niven, Peter Sellers, Capucine, Claudia
Cardinale, Robert Wagner, Brenda de Banzie,
Colin Gordon
AAN: Henry Mancini

The Pink Panther Strikes Again*
GB 1976   103m   De Luxe   Panavision
United Artists / Amjo (Blake Edwards)

After a nervous breakdown, Chief Inspector
Dreyfus builds up a vast criminal organization

devoted to the extermination of Inspector
Clouseau.
Zany pratfall farce with signs of
overconfidence since the success of *The Return
of the Pink Panther.* But some gags are funny,
despite a rather boring star.

w Frank Waldman, Blake Edwards *d* Blake
Edwards *ph* Harry Waxman *m* Henry
Mancini
Peter Sellers, Herbert Lom, Colin Blakely,
Leonard Rossiter, Lesley-Anne Down, Burt
Kwouk
AAN: song, 'Come To Me' (*ly* Don Black,
m Henry Mancini)

Pink String and Sealing Wax*
GB 1945   89m   bw
Ealing (S. C. Balcon)

In 1880 Brighton, a publican's wife plans to
have her husband poisoned.
Unusual, carefully handled period crime
melodrama which needed a slightly firmer
grip.

w Diana Morgan, Robert Hamer, *play* Roland
Pertwee *d* Robert Hamer *ph* Stanley Pavey
m Norman Demuth
Googie Withers, Mervyn Johns, Gordon
Jackson, Sally Ann Howes, Mary Merrall,
John Carol, Catherine Lacey, Gary Marsh

Pinky**
US 1949   102m   bw
TCF (Darryl F. Zanuck)

In the American south, a negro girl who
passes for white has romantic problems.
Rather blah problem picture which seemed
brave at the time; a highly professional piece
of work nevertheless.

w Philip Dunne, Dudley Nichols, *novel*
Quality by Cid Ricketts Summer *d* Elia
Kazan *ph* Joe MacDonald *m* Alfred
Newman
Jeanne Crain, Ethel Barrymore, Ethel Waters,
William Lundigan, Basil Ruysdael, Nina Mae
McKinney, Frederick O'Neal, Evelyn Varden
AAN: Jeanne Crain; Ethel Barrymore; Ethel
Waters

Pinocchio****
US 1940   77m   Technicolor
Walt Disney

The blue fairy breathes life into a puppet,
which has to prove itself before it can turn into
a real boy.
Charming, fascinating, superbly organized and
streamlined cartoon feature without a single
second of boredom.

supervisors Ben Sharpsteen, Hamilton Luske
m / ly Leigh Harline, Ned Washington, Paul J. Smith

'A film of amazing detail and brilliant conception.'—*Leonard Maltin*

'A work that gives you almost every possible kind of pleasure to be got from a motion picture.'—*Richard Mallett, Punch*

'The limits of the animated cartoon have been blown so wide open that some of the original wonder of pictures has been restored.'—*Otis Ferguson*

AA: Leigh Harline (*m*); song 'When You Wish Upon a Star' (*m* Leigh Harline, *ly* Ned Washington)

Piranha°
US 1978 92m Metrocolor
New World (Roger Corman, Jeff Schechtman, Jon Davison)

A mad doctor's stock of man-eating fish is accidentally released into the local rivers. Slightly spoofy thriller with a high death rate and a better than usual script. On the whole, an improvement on *Jaws*.

w John Sayles *d* Joe Dante *ph* Jamie Anderson *m* Pino Danaggio *sp* Jon Berg

Bradford Dillman, Heather Menzies, Kevin McCarthy, Bruce Gordon, Barbara Steele, Keenan Wynn, Dick Miller

The Pirate°°
US 1948 102m Technicolor
MGM (Arthur Freed)

In a West Indian port, a girl imagines that a wandering player is a famous pirate, who in fact is her despised and elderly suitor.
Minor MGM musical with vivid moments and some intimation of the greatness shortly to come; all very set-bound, but the star quality is infectious.

w Albert Hackett, Frances Goodrich, *play* S. N. Behrman *d* Vincente Minnelli *ph* Harry Stradling *m / ly* Cole Porter *md* Lennie Hayton

Gene Kelly, Judy Garland, Walter Slezak, Gladys Cooper, Reginald Owen, George Zucco, *the Nicholas Brothers*

AAN: Lennie Hayton

Pirates of Blood River°
GB 1961 84m Technicolor
   Hammerscope
Hammer (Anthony Nelson Keys)

Pirates in search of gold terrorize a Huguenot settlement.
Land-locked blood and thunder for tough schoolboys.

w John Hunter, John Gilling *d* John Gilling
ph Arthur Grant

Christopher Lee, Andrew Keir, Kerwin Mathews, Glenn Corbett, Peter Arne, Oliver Reed, Marla Landi, Michael Ripper

Pirates of Tortuga
US 1961 97m De Luxe Cinemascope

In the 17th-century Caribbean, a privateer is ordered by the king to go undercover and rout Sir Henry Morgan. Listless swashbuckler with inferior talent. Ken Scott, Dave King, Letitia Roman, John Richardson, Robert Stephens, Edgar Barrier. Written by Melvin Levy, Jesse L. Lasky Jnr and Pat Silver; directed by Robert D. Webb; for Sam Katzman / TCF.

Pirates of Tripoli
US 1955 72m Technicolor

A pirate captain comes to the aid of an oriental princess. More akin to the Arabian Knights than Blackbeard, but not bad for a double-biller. Paul Henreid, Patricia Medina, Paul Newland, John Miljan, Lillian Bond. Written by Allen March; directed by Felix Feist; for Sam Katzman / Columbia.

The Pit and the Pendulum°
US 1961 85m Pathecolor Panavision
AIP / Alta Vista (Roger Corman)

Lovers plan to drive her brother mad; he responds by locking them in his torture chamber.
The centrepiece only is borrowed from Poe; the rest is lurid but mostly ineffective. Still, its commercial success started the Poe cycle of the sixties.

w Richard Matheson *d* Roger Corman
ph Floyd Crosby *m* Les Baxter

Vincent Price, Barbara Steele, John Kerr

'As in *House of Usher*, the quality of the film is its full-blooded feeling for Gothic horror—storms and lightning, mouldering castles and cobwebbed torture chambers, bleeding brides trying to tear the lids from their untimely tombs.'—*David Robinson*

Pitfall
US 1948 85m bw
Samuel Bischoff

An insurance investigator proves easy prey for a grasping woman.
Modest suspenser, quite efficiently made.

w Jay Dratler, from his novel *d* André de Toth *ph* Harry Wild *md* Louis Forbes

Dick Powell, Lizabeth Scott, Jane Wyatt, Raymond Burr, John Litel, Byron Barr, Ann Doran

Pittsburgh
US 1942   91m   bw
Universal (Charles K. Feldman)

A coal miner's daughter has two loves, all of
them trying to improve their social status as
Pittsburgh becomes a world centre of steel
production.
Routine melodrama ending as a flagwaver,
and allowing none of its stars any opportunity.

w Kenneth Gamet, Tom Reed d Lewis Seiler
ph Robert de Grasse m Hans Salter

Marlene Dietrich, Randolph Scott, John
Wayne, Frank Craven, Louise Allbritton,
Shemp Howard, Ludwig Stossel, Thomas
Gomez

A Place in the Sun°°
US 1951   122m   bw
Paramount / George Stevens

A poor young man, offered the chance of a
rich wife, allows himself to be convicted and
executed for the accidental death of his former
fiancée.
Overblown, overlong and over-praised
melodrama from a monumental novel of social
guilt; sometimes visually striking, this version
alters the stresses of the plot and leaves no
time for sociological detail. A film so clearly
intended as a masterpiece could hardly fail to
be boring.

w Michael Wilson, Harry Brown, novel An
American Tragedy by Theodore Dreiser
d George Stevens ph William C. Mellor
m Franz Waxman ad Hans Dreier, Walter
Tyler

Montgomery Clift, Elizabeth Taylor, Shelley
Winters, Anne Revere, Keefe Brasselle, Fred
Clark, Raymond Burr, Frieda Inescort,
Shepperd Strudwick, Kathryn Givney, Walter
Sande

'An almost incredibly painstaking work . . .
mannered enough for a very fancy Gothic
murder mystery. This version gives the story a
modern setting, but the town is an
arrangement of symbols of wealth, glamour
and power versus symbols of poor, drab
helplessness—an arrangement far more
suitable to the thirties than to the fifties.'—
Pauline Kael

AA: script; George Stevens; William C.
Mellor; Franz Waxman
AAN: best picture; Montgomery Clift; Shelley
Winters

A Place of One's Own°°
GB 1944   92m   bw
GFD / Gainsborough (R. J. Minney)

In Edwardian times, an old house is taken
over by an elderly couple, and their young
companion is possessed by the spirit of a
murdered girl.
Charming little ghost story, not quite detailed
enough to be totally effective.

w Brock Williams, novel Osbert Sitwell
d Bernard Knowles ph Stephen Dade
m Hubert Bath md Louis Levy

James Mason, Barbara Mullen, Margaret
Lockwood, Dennis Price, Helen Haye,
Michael Shepley, Dulcie Gray, Moore
Marriott

'A fine piece of work . . . gripping,
marvellous, outstanding, eerie, perky,
beautiful, lovely and different.'—C. A.
Lejeune
'One comes away with an impression of
elegance which has not so far been frequent in
the British cinema.'—Dilys Powell

A Place to Go
GB 1963   86m   bw
British Lion / Excalibur (Michael Relph,
   Basil Dearden)

A young man depressed by his urban
environment turns to crime.
Panorama of London low life, efficiently
varied and well made but not in any way
memorable. It Always Rains on Sunday,
fifteen years earlier, wears better.

w Michael Relph, Clive Exton, novel Bethnal
Green by Michael Fisher d Basil Dearden
ph Reg Wyer m Charles Blackwell

Rita Tushingham, Mike Sarne, Doris Hare,
John Slater, Bernard Lee, Barbara Ferris, Roy
Kinnear

The Plague of the Zombies°
GB 1965   91m   Technicolor
Hammer (Anthony Nelson Keys)

A voodoo-practising Cornish squire raises
zombies from the dead and uses them to work
his tin mine.
They don't explain why he didn't simply hire
the living; apart from that this is Hammer on
its better side, with a charming elderly hero
and good suspense sequences.

w Peter Bryan d John Gilling ph Arthur
Grant m James Bernard

André Morell, John Carson, Diane Clare,
Brook Williams, Jacqueline Pearce, Alex
Davion, Michael Ripper

'Visually the film is splendid . . . the script
manages several offbeat strokes.'—MFB

The Plainsman**
US 1936   113m   bw
Paramount / Cecil B. de Mille

The life of Wild Bill Hickok and his friends
Buffalo Bill and Calamity Jane.
Standard big-scale thirties western; narrative
lumpy, characters idealized, spectacle
impressive, technical credits high.

w Waldemar Young, Lynn Riggs, Harold
Lamb d Cecil B. de Mille ph Victor Milner,
George Robinson m George Antheil
md Boris Morros

Gary Cooper, James Ellison, Jean Arthur,
Charles Bickford, Helen Burgess, Porter Hall,
Paul Harvey, Victor Varconi

'Certainly the finest western since The
Virginian; perhaps the finest western in the
history of the film.'—Graham Greene
† The story was remade as a TV movie in
1966, with Don Murray.

The Plainsman and the Lady
US 1946   84m   bw

In 1847, the Pony Express is threatened by
stagecoach owners. Moderate western for
family consumption. William Elliott, Gail
Patrick, Vera Ralston, Joseph Schildkraut.
Written by Richard Wormser; directed by
Joseph Kane; for Republic.

Le Plaisir*
France 1952   97m   bw
Stera / CCFC

Three stories by Guy de Maupassant, about
the search for pleasure: 'Le Masque', 'La
Maison Tellier', 'Le Modèle'.
Stylish but rather subdued compendium, with
no highlights to stay in the memory.

w Jacques Natanson, Max Ophuls d Max
Ophuls ph Christian Matras, Philippe
Agostini m Joe Hajos

Claude Dauphin, Gaby Morlay; Madeleine
Renaud, Danielle Darrieux, Ginette Leclerc,
Jean Gabin, Pierre Brasseur; Simone Simon,
Daniel Gélin

'An attractive theme tune, good
performances, and the pleasure itself of
virtuosity.'—Gavin Lambert, MFB

Planet of the Apes***
US 1968   119m   De Luxe   Panavision
TCF / Apjac (Mort Abrahams)

Astronauts caught in a time warp land on a
planet which turns out to be Earth in the
distant future, when men have become beasts
and the apes have taken over.
Stylish, thoughtful science fiction which starts
and finishes splendidly but suffers from a sag
in the middle. The ape make-up is great.

w Michael Wilson, Rod Serling,
novel Monkey Planet by Pierre Boulle
d Franklin Schaffner ph Leon Shamroy
m Jerry Goldsmith

Charlton Heston, Roddy McDowall, Kim
Hunter, Maurice Evans, James Whitmore,
James Daly, Linda Harrison

'One of the most telling science fiction films
to date.'—Tom Milne
† Sequels, in roughly descending order of
interest, were BENEATH THE PLANET OF
THE APES (1969), ESCAPE FROM THE
PLANET OF THE APES (1970),
CONQUEST OF THE PLANET OF THE
APES (1972) and BATTLE FOR THE
PLANET OF THE APES (1973). A TV series
followed in 1974, and a cartoon series in 1975.

AAN: Jerry Goldsmith

The Planter's Wife
GB 1952   91m   bw
Rank / Pinnacle (John Stafford)
US title: Outpost in Malaya

Malaya under the terrorists. A wife is planning
to leave but changes her mind after she and
her husband defend their home in a siege.
Superficial studio-bound melodrama unworthy
of its subject but a good star vehicle.

w Peter Proud, Guy Elmes d Ken Annakin
ph Geoffrey Unsworth m Allan Gray

Claudette Colbert, Jack Hawkins, Ram
Gopal, Jeremy Spenser, Tom Macauley,
Helen Goss

Platinum Blonde*
US 1931   92m   bw
Columbia

A newspaper reporter falls for an heiress.
Limp romantic comedy with interesting
performances: the film which established Jean
Harlow.

w Robert Riskin, Jo Swerling, story Harry E.
Chandler, Doug Churchill d Frank Capra
ph Joseph Walker

Robert Williams, Loretta Young, Jean
Harlow, Halliwell Hobbes, Reginald Owen

Platinum High School
US 1960   96m   bw

A father investigates his son's death at a
military academy for rich juvenile delinquents.
Hilarious serial-like melodrama with the worm
turning to some effect. Mickey Rooney, Dan
Duryea, Terry Moore, Warren Berlinger,
Yvette Mimieux, Conway Twitty, Elisha Cook
Jnr, Richard Jaeckel. Written by Robert
Smith; directed by Charles Haas; for Albert
Zugsmith / MGM. (GB title: Rich, Young and
Deadly.)

Play Dirty*
GB 1969   118m   Technicolor
Panavision
UA / Lowndes (Harry Saltzman)

During World War II, a squad of ex-criminals is given the job of destroying an enemy oil depot in North Africa.

Small-scale Dirty Dozen with would-be ironic twists; well made entertainment for the stout-hearted.

w Lotte Colin, Melvyn Bragg   d André de Toth   ph Edward Scaife   m Michel Legrand

Michael Caine, Nigel Davenport, Nigel Green, Harry Andrews, Bernard Archard, Daniel Pilon

Play It Again Sam*
US 1972   86m   Technicolor   Panavision
Paramount / APJAC / Rollins–Joffe (Arthur P. Jacobs)

A neurotic film critic is abandoned by his wife and seeks fresh companionship, with help from the shade of Humphrey Bogart.

Random comedy for star fans, mainly quite lively and painless.

w Woody Allen, from his play   d Herbert Ross   ph Owen Roizman   m Billy Goldenberg

Woody Allen, Diane Keaton, Jerry Lacy, Susan Anspach

Play It as It Lays
US 1972   94m   Technicolor   Panavision

An unsuccessful actress takes stock of her wrecked life. With-it melodrama which audiences preferred to be without. Anthony Perkins, Tuesday Weld, Tammy Grimes, Adam Roarke, Ruth Ford. Written by Joan Didion and John Gregory Dunne, from the novel by Joan Didion; directed by Frank Perry; for Universal.

Play Misty for Me*
US 1971   102m   Technicolor
Universal / Malpaso (Robert Daley)

A radio disc jockey is pestered by a girl who turns out to be homicidally jealous.

Smartly made if over-extended psycho melodrama with good suspense sequences and a fair quota of shocks.

w Jo Heims, Dean Reisner   d Clint Eastwood   ph Bruce Surtees   m Dee Barton

Clint Eastwood, Jessica Walter, Donna Mills, John Larch

Players
US 1979   120m   Metrocolor
Paramount (Robert Evans)

A pro tennis player is trained for top stardom by a sculptress with a mysterious past.

Entirely uninvolving romantic drama stretched around a Wimbledon match; slickness does not compensate for a gaping hole at the centre.

w Arnold Schulman   d Anthony Harvey   ph James Crabe   m Jerry Goldsmith   pd Richard Sylbert

Ali MacGraw, Dean-Paul Martin, Maximilian Schell, Pancho Gonzalez

Playgirl
US 1954   85m   bw

A small-town girl becomes a good-time girl in the big city. Totally unsurprising melodrama. Shelley Winters, Barry Sullivan, Colleen Miller, Gregg Palmer, Richard Long, Kent Taylor. Written by Robert Blees; directed by Joseph Pevney; for Universal-International.

Playmates*
US 1941   96m   bw
RKO (Cliff Reid)

For the sake of a lucrative radio contract, John Barrymore agrees to turn bandleader Kay Kyser into a Shakespearian actor.

Barrymore's last film is a weird comedy concoction, awesome in its waste of his talents but fairly funny in a high school kind of way.

w James V. Kern   d David Butler   ph Frank Redman   songs James Van Heusen, Johnny Burke

Kay Kyser and his Band, *John Barrymore,* Ginny Simms, Lupe Velez, May Robson, Patsy Kelly, Peter Lind Hayes, George Cleveland

Playtime*
France 1968   152m   Eastmancolor
70mm
Specta Films (René Silvera)

Hulot and a group of American tourists are bewildered by life in an airport, a business block and a restaurant.

Incredibly extended series of sketches, none of which is devastatingly funny. The irritation is that the talent is clearly there but needs control.

w Jacques Tati, Jacques Lagrange   d Jacques Tati   ph Jean Badal, Andreas Winding   m Francis Lemarque   pd Eugene Roman

Jacques Tati, Barbara Dennek, Jacqueline Lecomte, Henri Piccoli

'Tati still seems the wrong distance from his audience: not so far that we cannot see his gifts, not close enough so that they really touch.'—*Stanley Kauffmann*

'How sad that the result of all this, though it includes a great deal of intermittent pleasure, comes at times so dangerously close to boredom.'—*Brenda Davies, MFB*

'A series of brilliant doodles by an artist who has earned the right to indulge himself on such a scale.'—*Alexander Walker*

Plaza Suite*
US 1971   114m   Technicolor
Paramount (Howard B. Koch)

Three sketches set in the same suite at New York's Plaza Hotel, with Walter Matthau appearing in all three but in different character.

A highly theatrical entertainment which was bound to seem flattened on the screen, but emerges with at least some of its laughs intact.

w Neil Simon, from his play   *d* Arthur Hiller
ph Jack Marta   *m* Maurice Jarre

Walter Matthau, Maureen Stapleton, Barbara Harris, Lee Grant, Louise Sorel

Please Believe Me
US 1950   87m   bw
MGM (Val Lewton)

An English girl inherits an American ranch and is chased by a millionaire, a con man and a lawyer.

Dullsville comedy which failed to establish its star in America.

w Nathaniel Curtis   *d* Norman Taurog
ph Robert Planck   *m* Hans Salter

Deborah Kerr, Robert Walker, Mark Stevens, Peter Lawford, James Whitmore, Spring Byington

Please Don't Eat the Daisies
US 1960   111m   Metrocolor   Panavision
MGM (Joe Pasternak)

The family of a drama critic move to the country.

Thin, obvious comedy, all dressed up but with nowhere to go.

w Isobel Lennart, *book* Jean Kerr   *d* Charles Walters   *ph* Robert Bronner   *m* David Rose

Doris Day, David Niven, Janis Paige, Spring Byington, Patsy Kelly, Richard Haydn, Jack Weston, John Harding, Margaret Lindsay

Please Murder Me
US 1956   78m   bw
DCA (Donald Hyde)

An attorney defends an accused murderess, at great cost to himself.

Adequate Poverty Row suspenser with a foreseeable trick ending.

w Al C. Ward, Donald Hyde   *d* Peter Godfrey   *ph* Allen Stensvold

Angela Lansbury, Raymond Burr, Dick Foran, John Dehner, Lamont Johnson, Denver Pyle

Please Sir
GB 1971   101m   Eastmancolor
Rank / LWL / Leslie Grade (Andrew Mitchell)

The masters and pupils of Fenn Street school go on an annual camp.

Grossly inflated, occasionally funny big-screen version of the TV series.

w John Esmonde, Bob Larbey   *d* Mark Stuart
ph Wilkie Cooper   *m* Mike Vickers

John Alderton, Deryck Guyler, Joan Sanderson, Noel Howlett, Eric Chitty, Richard Davies

Please Turn Over
GB 1959   87m   bw

A teenager writes a sexy best-seller clearly featuring her family and friends. Acceptable but uninspired comedy from a West End success. Ted Ray, Jean Kent, Leslie Phillips, Joan Sims, Julia Lockwood, Charles Hawtrey, Lionel Jeffries. Written by Norman Hudis, from the play *Book of the Month* by Basil Thomas; directed by Gerald Thomas; for Beaconsfield / Anglo Amalgamated.

The Pleasure Garden
GB / Germany 1925   74m approx (24 fps)
bw   silent
Gainsborough / Emelka (Michael Balcon, Erich Pommer)

A chorus girl marries a rich colonial who goes native.

Boring melodrama with a few touches typical of its director, whose first film it is.

w Eliot Stannard, *novel* Oliver Sandys
d Alfred Hitchcock   *ph* Baron Ventigmilia

Virginia Valli, John Stuart, Miles Mander, Carmelita Gerghty

The Pleasure Girls
GB 1965   88m   bw
Compton Tekli

Girl flatmates in London have trouble with their boy friends.

The road to ruin sixties style, hackneyed but quite well observed.

wd Gerry O'Hara   *ph* Michael Reed
m Malcolm Lockyer

Ian McShane, Francesca Annis, Tony Tanner, Klaus Kinski, Mark Eden, Suzanna Leigh

The Pleasure of His Company
US 1961   114m   Technicolor
Paramount / Perlberg–Seaton

An ageing playboy arrives unexpectedly in San
Francisco for his daughter's wedding.
Tame family comedy, very flatly adapted from
the stage; dressed to kill, but with no narrative
or cinematic drive.

w Samuel Taylor, *play* Samuel Taylor,
Cornelia Otis Skinner d George Seaton
ph Robert Burks m Alfred Newman

Fred Astaire, Lilli Palmer, Debbie Reynolds,
Charles Ruggles, Tab Hunter, Gary Merrill,
Harold Fong
    'Smart comedy in its most diluted form.'—
MFB

The Pleasure Seekers
US 1964   107m   De Luxe   Cinemascope
TCF (David Weisbart)

Three girls in Madrid find boy friends.
Dim remake of *Three Coins in the Fountain,*
adequate but unstimulating on all levels.

w Edith Sommer d Jean Negulesco
ph Daniel L. Fapp m Lionel Newman,
Alexander Courage

Ann-Margret, Tony Franciosa, Carol Lynley,
Gene Tierney, Brian Keith, Gardner McKay,
Isobel Elsom

AAN: Lionel Newman, Alexander Courage

The Plough and the Stars*
US 1936   72m   bw
RKO (Cliff Reid, Robert Sisk)

In 1916, a Dublin marriage is threatened by
the husband's appointment as commander of
the citizen army.
Rather elementary film version of the play
about the Troubles; interesting for effort
rather than performance, and for the talent
involved.

w Dudley Nichols, *play* Sean O'Casey d John
Ford ph Joseph August m Roy Webb

Barbara Stanwyck, Preston Foster, Barry
Fitzgerald, Denis O'Dea, Eileen Crowe, F. J.
McCormick, Arthur Shields, Una O'Connor,
Moroni Olsen, J. M. Kerrigan, Bonita
Granville

Plunder*
GB 1930   98m   bw

Two society friends turn jewel thieves to help
an heiress. Primitive talkie version of a Ben
Travers farce which veered towards
melodrama but had a successful stage revival
at the National Theatre in 1978; valuable as a
record of the original performances. Tom

Walls, Ralph Lynn, Robertson Hare, Winifred
Shotter, Sydney Lynn, Ethel Coleridge.
Written by W. P. Lipscomb; directed by Tom
Walls; for Herbert Wilcox / British and
Dominions.

Plunder of the Sun*
US 1953   81m   bw
Warner (Robert Fellows)

Various criminal elements seek buried
treasure among the Mexican Aztec ruins.
Interestingly located, well made,
unconvincingly scripted melodrama, yet
another borrowing from *The Maltese Falcon.*

w Jonathan Latimer, *novel* David Dodge
d John Farrow ph Jack Draper m Antonio
D. Conde

Glenn Ford, Diana Lynn, Francis L. Sullivan,
Patricia Medina, Sean McClory, Douglass
Dumbrille, Eduardo Noriega

The Plunderers
US 1947   87m   bw

An undercover cavalry officer becomes friends
with an outlaw who saves his life. Routine
western, just about watchable. Rod Cameron,
Ilona Massey, Adrian Booth. Written by
Gerald Geraghty and Gerald Drayson Adams;
directed by Joseph Kane; for Republic.

The Plunderers
US 1960   94m   bw
Allied Artists / August (Joseph Pevney)

In the old west, four juvenile delinquents take
over a town.
The Wild One in period dress. Nothing in
particular.

w Bob Barbash d Joseph Pevney ph Eugene
Polito m Leonard Rosenman

Jeff Chandler, John Saxon, Ray Sticklyn,
Roger Torrey, Dee Pollock, Marsha Hunt,
Dolores Hart, Jay C. Flippen, James
Westerfield

Plymouth Adventure*
US 1952   105m   Technicolor
MGM (Dore Schary)

The Pilgrim Fathers sail from Plymouth on the
Mayflower and spend their first months ashore
on the coast of America.
Well-meaning schoolbook history, totally
unconvincing and very dull despite obvious
effort all round. One or two of the actors have
their moments.

w Helen Deutsch, *novel* Ernest Gebler
d Clarence Brown ph William Daniels
m Miklos Rozsa

Spencer Tracy, Gene Tierney, Van Johnson, Leo Genn, Dawn Addams

'It demonstrates how Hollywood can dull down as well as jazz up history.'—*Judith Crist, 1973*

Pocket Money

US 1972 100m Technicolor
First Artists / Coleytown (John Foreman)

Two slow-thinking Arizona cowboys try to make money herding cattle.
Peculiar modern western comedy drama which doesn't work.

w Terry Malick, *novel* Jim Kane by J. K. S. Brown d Stuart Rosenberg *ph* Laszlo Kovacs *m* Alex North

Paul Newman, Lee Marvin, Strother Martin, Kelly Jean Peters, Wayne Rogers

Pocketful of Miracles

US 1961 136m Technicolor
Panavision
UA / Franton (Frank Capra)

Kindly gangsters help an old apple seller to persuade her long lost daughter that she is a lady of means.
Boring, overlong remake of *Lady for a Day*, showing that Capra's touch simply doesn't work on the wide screen, that his themes are dated anyway, and that all the fine character actors in Hollywood are a liability unless you find them something to do.

w Hal Kanter, Harry Tugend, *scenario* Robert Riskin, *story* Damon Runyon d Frank Capra *ph* Robert Bronner *m* Walter Scharf

Bette Davis, Glenn Ford, Hope Lange, Arthur O'Connell, Peter Falk, Thomas Mitchell, Edward Everett Horton, Sheldon Leonard, Barton MacLane, Jerome Cowan, Fritz Feld, Snub Pollard, David Brian, Ann-Margret, John Litel, Jay Novello, Willis Bouchey, George E. Stone, Mike Mazurki, Jack Elam, Mickey Shaughnessy, Peter Mann, Frank Ferguson

'The effect is less one of whimsy than of being bludgeoned to death with a toffee apple.'—*Peter John Dyer*
'The story has enough cracks in it for the syrup to leak through.'—*Playboy*

AAN: title song (*m* James Van Heusen, *ly* Sammy Cahn); Peter Falk

Poet's Pub

GB 1949 79m bw
GFD / Aquila

A rowing blue takes over a Tudor inn and discovers a priceless jewelled gauntlet, the wearer of which is kidnapped during the performance of a pageant.
Very thin, naive treatment of a whimsical novel. The last film to use the Independent Frame process.

w Diana Morgan, *novel* Eric Linklater d Frederick Wilson *ph* George Stretton *m* Clifton Parker

Derek Bond, Rona Anderson, Barbara Murray, Leslie Dwyer, Joyce Grenfell

Poil de Carotte*

France 1932 94m bw

A small boy is picked on by his ageing mother to the point where he attempts suicide.
Country melodrama which made its director's name but seems a little faded now despite bravura sequences.

w Jules Renard d Julien Duvivier *ph* Thirard Monniot

Harry Baur, Robert Lynen, Catherine Fontenoy

Point Blank*

US 1967 92m Metrocolor Panavision
MGM / Judd Bernard, Irwin Winkler

A gangster takes an elaborate revenge on his cheating partner.
Extremely violent gangster thriller, well shot on location and something of a cult, but with irritating pretentiousness and obscure plot points.

w Alexander Jacobs, David Newhouse, Rafe Newhouse, *novel* The Hunter by Richard Stark d John Boorman *ph* Philip Lathrop *m* Johnny Mandel

Lee Marvin, Angie Dickinson, Keenan Wynn, Carroll O'Connor, Lloyd Bochner, Michael Strong, John Vernon, Sharon Acker

†*The Outfit* (qv) is a kind of sequel / reprise.

Poison Pen*

GB 1939 79m bw
ABP (Walter C. Mycroft)

A village community is set at odds by a writer of vindictive anonymous letters.
Effective minor drama, with good location atmosphere.

w Doreen Montgomery, William Freshman, N. C. Hunter, Esther McCracken, *play* Richard Llewellyn d Paul Stein

Flora Robson, Reginald Tate, Robert Newton, Ann Todd, Geoffrey Toone, Belle Chrystal, Edward Chapman, Edward Rigby

'A lamentably artificial piece.'—*Richard Mallett, Punch*

Polly of the Circus
US 1932 72m bw
MGM

A trapeze artiste falls for the local minister,
but incurs disapproval from his bishop.
Elementary romance reminiscent of silent
drama.

w Carey Wilson, *play* Margaret Mayo
d Alfred Santell ph George Barnes

Marion Davies, Clark Gable, C. Aubrey
Smith, Raymond Hatton, David Landau,
Maude Eburne, Guinn Williams, Ray Milland

Pollyanna*
US 1960   134m Technicolor
Walt Disney (George Golitzen)

A 12-year-old orphan girl cheers up the
grumps of the small town where she comes to
live.
Well cast but overlong and rather humourless
remake of a children's classic from an earlier
age.

wd David Swift, *novel* Eleanor Porter
ph Russell Harlan m Paul Smith ad Carroll
Clark, Robert Clatworthy

Hayley Mills, Jane Wyman, Karl Malden,
Nancy Olson, Adolphe Menjou, Donald
Crisp, Agnes Moorehead, Richard Egan,
Kevin Corcoran, James Drury, Reta Shaw,
Leora Dana

'Even Hayley Mills can neither prevent one
from sympathizing with the crusty aunts,
hermits, vicars and hypochondriacs who get so
forcibly cheered up, nor from feverishly
speculating whether films like this don't run
the risk of inciting normally kind and gentle
people into certain excesses of violent crime –
child murder, for instance.'—*MFB*

Pony Express*
US 1953   101m Technicolor
Paramount (Nat Holt)

In 1860 Buffalo Bill Cody and Wild Bill
Hickok are sent to establish pony express
stations across California.
Standard western which tells a factual tale
adequately if rather slowly.

w Charles Marquis Warren d Jerry Hopper
ph Ray Rennahan m Paul Sawtell

Charlton Heston, Forrest Tucker, Rhonda
Fleming, Jan Sterling

Pony Soldier
US 1952   82m Technicolor
TCF (Samuel G. Engel)
GB title: *MacDonald of the Canadian
Mounties*

The mounties settle the hash of Canadian
Indian renegades who have been causing
trouble on the American border.
Mediocre outdoor adventure.

w John C. Higgins d Joseph M. Newman
ph Harry Jackson m Alex North

Tyrone Power, Cameron Mitchell, Robert
Horton, Thomas Gomez, Penny Edwards,
Adeline de Walt Reynolds

Pool of London
GB 1950 85m bw
Ealing (Michael Relph)

A smuggling sailor gets involved in murder.
Routine semi-documentary police thriller with
locations in London docks decorating a
standard piece of thick ear.

w Jack Whittingham, John Eldridge d Basil
Dearden ph Gordon Dines m John Addison

Bonar Colleano, Susan Shaw, Earl Cameron,
Renée Asherson, Moira Lister, Max Adrian,
James Robertson Justice, Joan Dowling
'Done with such imagination, humour and
visual attractiveness as to hold the pleased
attention of all who like to use their eyes and
their ears.'—*Richard Mallett, Punch*

Poor Cow*
GB 1967   101m Eastmancolor
Anglo Amalgamated / Vic / Fenchurch (Joe
Janni)

The dismal life of a young London mother
who lives in squalor with her criminal
husband.
Television-style fictional documentary
determined to rub one's nose in the mire.
Innovative and occasionally striking but not
very likeable.

w Nell Dunn, Ken Loach, *novel* Nell Dunn
d Ken Loach ph Brian Probyn m Donovan

Carol White, Terence Stamp, John Bindon,
Kate Williams, Queenie Watts
'A superficial, slightly patronizing excursion
into the nether realms of social realism.'—*Jan
Dawson*

Poor Little Rich Girl*
US 1936 79m bw
TCF (Darryl F. Zanuck)

A child is separated from her father and joins
a radio singing act.
Pleasing star vehicle with all the expected
elements, adapted from a Mary Pickford
vehicle of 1917.

w Sam Hellman, Gladys Lehman, Harry
Tugend d Irving Cummings ph John Seitz
songs Mack Gordon, Harry Revel

Shirley Temple, Jack Haley, Alice Faye, Gloria Stuart, Michael Whalen, Sara Haden, Jane Darwell, Claude Gillingwater, Henry Armetta

Pope Joan
GB 1972 132m Eastmancolor Panavision
Big City Productions / Kurt Unger
aka: *The Devil's Imposter*

The legend of a 9th-century German semi-prostitute who discovered a vocation to preach and was made Pope.
Uninspiring pageant, brutish and rather silly, full of would-be medieval sensationalism.

w John Briley *d* Michael Anderson *ph* Billy Williams *m* Maurice Jarre *pd* Elliott Scott

Liv Ullmann, Trevor Howard, Olivia de Havilland, Maximilian Schell, Keir Dullea, Robert Beatty, Franco Nero, Patrick Magee

Popeye
US 1980 114m colour
Paramount / Disney (Robert Evans)

Popeye returns to Sweethaven in search of the father who abandoned him.
Lamentable attempt by an ill-chosen director to humanize and sentimentalize a celebrated cartoon character who doesn't get into the expected physical action until the film is nearly over.

w Jules Feiffer, from characters created by E. C. Segar *d* Robert Altman *ph* Giuseppe Rotunno *m / ly* Harry Nilsson *pd* Wolf Kroeger

Robin Williams, Shelley Duvall, Ray Walston, Paul Dooley

Popi*
US 1969 113m De Luxe
UA / Leonard Films (Herbert B. Leonard)

Adventures of a cheerful inhabitant of New York's Puerto Rican ghetto.
Ethnic comedy-drama of the kind that has since found its way in abundance into American TV series. Very competently done for those who like it, e.g. Puerto Ricans.

w Tina and Lester Pine *d* Arthur Hiller *ph* Ross Lowell *m* Dominic Frontière

Alan Arkin, Rita Moreno, Miguel Alejandro, Ruben Figuero

'An appropriately disenchanted view of an immigrant's struggling ambitions in the Promised Land.'—*Richard Combs*

Poppy*
US 1936 74m bw
Paramount (Paul Jones)

An itinerant medicine-seller sets up his stall in a small town where his daughter falls in love with the mayor's son.
Clumsily but heavily plotted vehicle for W. C. Fields, who as usual has great moments but seems to rob the show of its proper pace.

w Waldemar Young, Virginia Van Upp, *play* Dorothy Donnelly *d* A. Edward Sutherland *ph* William Mellor *m* Frederick Hollander

W. C. Fields, Rochelle Hudson, Richard Cromwell, Granville Bates, Catherine Doucet, Lynne Overman, Maude Eburne

'Antique hokum trussed up for a Fields vehicle.'—*Literary Digest*

Porgy and Bess*
US 1959 138m Technicolor Todd-AO
Samuel Goldwyn

A slum girl falls in love with a crippled beggar.
Negro opera about the inhabitants of Catfish Row; full of interest for music lovers, but not lending itself very readily to screen treatment.

w N. Richard Nash, *libretto* Du Bose Heyward, *play* Porgy by Du Bose and Dorothy Heyward *d* Otto Preminger *ph* Leon Shamroy *m* George Gershwin *m* André Previn, Ken Darby *ch* Hermes Pan

Sidney Poitier, Dorothy Dandridge, Sammy Davis Jnr, Pearl Bailey, Brock Peters, Diahann Carroll, Clarence Muse

AA: André Previn, Ken Darby
AAN: Leon Shamroy

Pork Chop Hill*
US 1959 97m bw
United Artists / Melville / Lewis Milestone

The Americans in Korea take a vital hill but the colonel in command finds it difficult to hold.
Ironic war film with vivid spectacle separated by much talk.

w James R. Webb *d* Lewis Milestone *ph* Sam Leavitt *m* Leonard Rosenman *pd* Nicolai Remisoff

Gregory Peck, Harry Guardino, George Shibata, Woody Strode, James Edwards, Rip Torn, George Peppard, Barry Atwater, Robert Blake

Porridge*
GB 1979 93m Eastmancolor
Black Lion / Witzend

Old lags at Slade Prison try to arrange an escape for a first offender.
Genial expansion of a successful TV series to the big screen; alas, as usual the material is stretched to snapping point, and the welcome

irony of the original becomes sentimentality.
Still, the film is a valuable record of
memorable characters.

w Dick Clement, Ian La Frenais d Dick
Clement ph Bob Huke md Terry Oates

*Ronnie Barker, Richard Beckinsale, Fulton
Mackay, Brian Wilde, Peter Vaughan,*
Geoffrey Bayldon, Julian Holloway

Port of New York*
US 1949 82m bw
Eagle Lion (Aubrey Schenck)

A woman narcotics smuggler determines to
betray her colleagues to the authorities.
Good routine semi-documentary thick ear,
notable for an early appearance by Yul
Brynner as villain-in-chief.

w Eugene Ling d Laslo Benedek ph George
E. Diskant w Sol Kaplan

Scott Brady, Richard Rober, K. T. Stevens,
Yul Brynner

Port of Seven Seas*
US 1938 81m bw
MGM (Henry Henigson)

Love on the Marseilles waterfront.
Stagey Hollywoodization of Pagnol's *Marius*
trilogy: some vigour shows through.

w Preston Sturges d James Whale ph Karl
Freund m Franz Waxman

Wallace Beery, Frank Morgan, Maureen
O'Sullivan, John Beal, Jessie Ralph, Cora
Witherspoon

Porte des Lilas*
France / Italy 1957 95m bw
Filmsonor / Rizzoli (Jacques Plante)
aka: *Gate of Lilacs*

A gangster on the run shelters in a poor
quarter of Paris, but his treachery is his
undoing.
Atmospheric comedy-drama put across with
the expected style but providing very little to
smile at.

w René Clair, Jean Aurel, *novel* La Grande
Ceinture by René Fallet d René Clair
ph Robert Le Fèbvre m Georges Brassens

Pierre Brasseur, Georges Brassens, Henri
Vidal, Dany Carrel, Raymond Bussières,
Amedée, Alain Bouvette

Les Portes de la Nuit*
France 1946 106m bw
Pathé Cinema
aka: *Gates of Night*

Various people in post-war Paris are drawn
into a pattern woven by Destiny—who appears
as a melancholy tramp.
A polished piece of post-war gloom, and the
archetype of all *films noirs* of the period. The
beginning, also, of its director's decline.

w Jacques Prévert d Marcel Carné
ph Philippe Agostini m Joseph Kosma
ad Alexander Trauner

Pierre Brasseur, Yves Montand, Nathalie
Nattier, Serge Reggiani, Jean Vilar, Saturnin
Fabre, Mady Berry, Dany Robin
† One of the few films to have been based on a
ballet—*Le Rendezvous* by Prévert. Oddly
enough its realistic scenes of daily life are
among its most successful elements.

Portnoy's Complaint
US 1972 101m Technicolor
  Panavision
Warner / Chehnault (Ernest Lehman)

A young New York Jewish boy has mother
and masturbation problems.
Foolhardy attempt to film a fashionably
sensational literary exercise; one of
Hollywood's last attempts – thank goodness –
to be 'with it'.

wd Ernest Lehman, *novel* Philip Roth
ph Philip Lathrop m Michel Legrand

Richard Benjamin, Karen Black, Lee Black,
Jack Somack, Jill Clayburgh, Jeannie Berlin

'The spectator is forced into the doubly
uncomfortable position of a voyeur who can't
actually see anything.'—*Jan Dawson*

Portrait from Life
GB 1948 90m bw
GFD / Gainsborough (Antony
  Darnborough)
US title: *The Girl in the Painting*

In an art gallery, a German professor
recognizes a portrait as that of his daughter,
lost during the war in Germany, and after a
search discovers her to have been an amnesiac
under the protection of a leading Nazi.
Tolerable melodrama with similarities to *The
Seventh Veil* (the girl has to choose between
four men).

w Frank Harvey Jnr, Muriel and Sydney Box
d Terence Fisher ph Jack Asher m Benjamin
Frankel

Mai Zetterling, Robert Beatty, Guy Rolfe,
Herbert Lom, Patrick Holt

Portrait in Black*
US 1960 113m Eastmancolor
U-I / Ross Hunter

An elderly shipping tycoon is murdered by his wife and doctor, but they are blackmailed. Absurd old-fashioned melodrama of dark doings among the idle rich. Quite entertaining for addicts.

w Ivan Goff, Ben Roberts *d* Michael Gordon *ph* Russell Metty *m* Frank Skinner

Lana Turner, Anthony Quinn, Richard Basehart, Anna May Wong, Lloyd Nolan, Sandra Dee, John Saxon, Ray Walston, Virginia Grey
'Connoisseurs of the higher tosh should find it irresistible.'—*Penelope Houston*

Portrait of a Mobster
US 1961 108m bw
Warner

The career of twenties gangster Dutch Schultz. Over-familiar, warmed over racketeering stuff with no particular edge or style.

w Howard Browne *d* Joseph Pevney *ph* Eugene Polito *m* Max Steiner

Vic Morrow, Leslie Parrish, Peter Breck, Ray Danton (repeating as Legs Diamond), Norman Alden, Ken Lynch

Portrait of Clare
GB 1950 98m bw
ABPC (Leslie Landau)

In 1900, a woman looks back on her three marriages.
High school novelette for easily pleased female audiences.

w Leslie Landau, Adrian Arlington, *novel* Francis Brett Young *d* Lance Comfort *ph* Gunther Krampf *ad* Don Ashton

Margaret Johnston, Richard Todd, Robin Bailey, Ronald Howard, Mary Clare, Marjorie Fielding, Anthony Nicholls, Lloyd Pearson

Portrait of Jennie***
US 1948 86m bw (tinted sequence)
David O. Selznick
GB title: *Jennie*

A penniless artist meets a strange girl who seems to age each time he sees her; they fall in love and he discovers that she has long been dead, though she finally comes to life once more during a sea storm like the one in which she perished.
A splendid example of the higher Hollywood lunacy: a silly story with pretensions about life and death and time and art, presented with superb persuasiveness by a first-class team of actors and technicians.

w Peter Berneis, Paul Osborn, Leonard Bernovici, *novel* Robert Nathan *d* William Dieterle *ph* Joseph August *m* Dmitri Tiomkin, after Debussy

Jennifer Jones, Joseph Cotten, Ethel Barrymore, David Wayne, Lillian Gish, Henry Hull, Florence Bates
'Though the story may not make sense, the pyrotechnics, joined to the dumbfounded silliness, keep one watching.'—*New Yorker 1976*

AAN: Joseph August

The Poseidon Adventure**
US 1972 117m De Luxe Panavision
TCF / Kent (Irwin Allen)

A luxury liner is capsized, and trapped passengers have to find their way to freedom via an upside down world.
Tedious disaster movie which caught the public fancy and started a cycle. Spectacular moments, cardboard characters, flashes of imagination.

w Stirling Silliphant, Wendell Mayes, *novel* Paul Gallico *ph* Harold Stine *d* Ronald Neame *m* John Williams *pd* William Creber

Gene Hackman, Ernest Borgnine, Shelley Winters, Red Buttons, Carol Lynley, Leslie Nielson, Arthur O'Connell, Pamela Sue Martin, Roddy McDowall, Eric Shea, Jack Albertson, Stella Stevens
'The script is the only cataclysm in this waterlogged *Grand Hotel*.'—*New Yorker*
† See also: *Beyond the Poseidon Adventure.*

AA: song 'The Morning After' (*m / ly* Al Kasha, Joel Hirschhorn)
AAN: Harold Stine; John Williams; Shelley Winters

Posse**
US 1975 93m Technicolor Panavision
Paramount / Bryna (Kirk Douglas)

A US marshal seeking higher office vows to capture a railroad bandit, but the tables are smartly turned.
Unusual minor western, quite pleasing in all departments and neither mindless nor violent.

w William Roberts, Christopher Knopf *d* Kirk Douglas *ph* Fred Koenekamp *m* Maurice Jarre

Kirk Douglas, Bruce Dern, Bo Hopkins, James Stacy, Luke Askey, David Canary

Posse from Hell
US 1961 89m Technicolor

Four killers escape from jail and take over a

town. Moderate western programmer with more violence than usual. Audie Murphy, John Saxon, Zohra Lampert, Vic Morrow, Robert Keith. Written by Clair Huffaker; directed by Herbert Coleman; for Universal / International.

Possessed*
US 1931 76m bw
MGM

A factory girl goes to New York in search of riches.
Reasonably gutsy Depression melodrama which moves at a fair pace.

w Lenore Coffee, *play* The Mirage by Edgar Selwyn d Clarence Brown ph Oliver T. Marsh

Joan Crawford, Clark Gable, Wallace Ford, Skeets Gallagher, Frank Conroy, Marjorie White, John Miljan
'Lots of luxury; lots of charm; lots of smooth talk about courage and marriage and what women want.'—*James R. Quirk*

Possessed*
US 1947 108m bw
Warner (Jerry Wald)

An emotionally unstable nurse marries her employer but retains a passionate love for an engineer whom she kills when he does not respond.
Extremely heavy, almost Germanic, flashback melodrama with everyone tearing hammer and tongs at the rather ailing script. Fun if you're in that mood, and an interesting example of the American *film noir* of the forties.

w Silvia Richards, Ranald MacDougall, *novel* One Man's Secret by Rita Weiman d Curtis Bernhardt ph Joseph Valentine m Franz Waxman

Joan Crawford, Raymond Massey, Van Heflin, Geraldine Brooks, Stanley Ridges, John Ridgely, Moroni Olsen
'Acting with bells on.'—*Richard Winnington*
'Miss Crawford performs with the passion and intelligence of an actress who is not content with just one Oscar.'—*James Agee*
AAN: Joan Crawford

The Possession of Joel Delaney*
US 1971 108m Eastmancolor
ITC / Haworth (George Justin)

A wealthy New York divorcee tries to save her brother from death at the hands of a Puerto Rican occult group who believe in ritual murder and demonic possession.
Unpleasant, frightening and overlong horror

film with some kind of message struggling to get out but precious little entertainment value.

w Matt Robinson, Grimes Grice, *novel* Ramona Stewart d Waris Hussein ph Arthur J. Ornitz m Joe Ragoso

Shirley Maclaine, Perry King, Lisa Kohane, David Ellacott
'Some see the film as a political allegory; I see it as a piece of political tosh.'—*Michael Billington, Illustrated London News*

The Postman Always Rings Twice*
US 1946 113m bw
MGM (Carey Wilson)

A guilty couple murder her husband but get their come-uppance.
Pale shadow of *Double Indemnity,* efficient but not interesting or very suspenseful.

w Harry Ruskin, Niven Busch, *novel* James M. Cain d Tay Garnett ph Sidney Wagner m George Bassman

Lana Turner, John Garfield, Cecil Kellaway, Hume Cronyn, Leon Ames, Audrey Totter, Alan Reed
'It was a real chore to do *Postman* under the Hays Office, but I think I managed to get the sex across.'—*Tay Garnett*

Postman's Knock*
GB 1961 88m bw
MGM (Ronald Kinnoch)

A village postman is transferred to London, finds life and work bewildering, but captures some crooks and ends up a hero.
Mildly amusing star vehicle rising to good comic climaxes.

w John Briley, Jack Trevor Story d Robert Lynn ph Gerald Moss m Ron Goodwin

Spike Milligan, Barbara Shelley, Wilfrid Lawson

Pot Luck*
GB 1936 71m bw

A Scotland Yard inspector enlists the aid of department store staff to recover a stolen Chinese vase. Surprisingly not from a stage original, this action farce gets better as it goes along and finds time for a quick spoof of *The Old Dark House.* Tom Walls, Ralph Lynn, Robertson Hare, Diana Churchill, Gordon James, Martita Hunt. Written by Ben Travers; directed by Tom Walls; for Gainsborough.

Pot o' Gold
US 1941 87m bw
(UA) James Roosevelt
GB title: *The Golden Hour*

A radio giveaway show finds work for idle
musicians.
Thin Capraesque comedy which needed more
determined handling.

w Walter de Leon *d* George Marshall *ph* Hal
Mohr *md* Lou Forbes

James Stewart, Paulette Goddard, Horace
Heidt, Charles Winninger, Mary Gordon,
Frank Melton, Jed Prouty

Powder River
US 1953 77m Technicolor

A marshal finds that an embittered doctor is
the killer he is seeking. Satisfactory
programmer, more of a suspense drama than a
western. Rory Calhoun, Cameron Mitchell,
Corinne Calvet, Penny Edwards, Carl Betz,
John Dehner. Written by Geoffrey Holmes,
from a novel by Stuart Lake; directed by Louis
King; for TCF.

Powder Town
US 1942 79m bw

A scientist in a munitions plant comes into
conflict with a tough foreman. Propaganda
action programmer. Victor McLaglen,
Edmond O'Brien, June Havoc. Written by
David Boehm and Vicki Baum from a novel
by Max Brand; directed by Rowland V. Lee;
for RKO.

The Power*
US 1967 109m Metrocolor
  Cinemascope
MGM / George Pal

Scientists researching into human endurance
are menaced by one of their number who has
developed the ability to kill by will power.
Interesting but finally unexciting and
exasperating science fiction which badly lacks
a gimmick one can actually see.

w John Gay, *novel* Frank M. Robinson
d Byron Haskin *ph* Ellsworth Fredericks
m Miklos Rozsa

Michael Rennie, George Hamilton, Suzanne
Pleshette, Nehemiah Persoff, Earl Holliman,
Arthur O'Connell, Aldo Ray, Barbara
Nichols, Yvonne de Carlo, Richard Carlson,
Gary Merrill, Ken Murray, Miiko Taka, Celia
Lovsky
  'The movie takes itself very seriously. We
don't have to.'—*Robert Windeler*

The Power and the Glory*
US 1933 76m bw
Fox (Jesse L. Lasky)

The flashback story of a tycoon who rose from
nothing and was corrupted by power.
Often noted as a forerunner of *Citizen Kane*,
this is in fact a disappointing film with a very
thin script and a general sense of aimlessness.
'Presented in narratage' meant that the
characters voice their unspoken thoughts.
Most interesting for its credits.

w Preston Sturges *d* William K. Howard
ph James Wong Howe *m* Louis de Francesco

Spencer Tracy, Colleen Moore, Ralph
Morgan, Helen Vinson

The Power and the Prize*
US 1956 98m bw Cinemascope
MGM (Nicholas Nayfack)

An ambitious company executive is criticized
by his president for wanting to marry a
European refugee, but the other executives
support him.
Unconvincing big business fairy tale which
passes the time competently enough, though
Taylor is a humourless hero.

w Robert Ardrey, *novel* Howard Swiggett
d Henry Koster *ph* George Folsey
m Bronislau Kaper

Robert Taylor, Elizabeth Mueller, Mary
Astor, Burl Ives, Charles Coburn, Cedric
Hardwicke

Power of the Press
US 1943 63m bw

The owner of a New York paper kills to
maintain its isolationist line. Hard-hitting
melodrama which overdoes the propaganda.
Lee Tracy, Guy Kibbee, Otto Kruger, Gloria
Dickson. Written by Samuel Fuller and
Robert D. Andrews; directed by Lew
Landers; for Columbia.

Power Play
GB / Canada 1978 109m colour
Robert Cooper / Canada United Kingdom
  (Christopher Dalton)

In a mythical country, a tank commander joins
the leaders of a coup d'état only to
doublecross them.
Uninteresting mixture of violent action and
verbosity.

wd Martyn Burke *ph* Ousama Rawi *m* Ken
Thorne

Peter O'Toole, David Hemmings, Donald
Pleasence, Barry Morse

The Powers Girl
US 1942 92m bw
UA / Charles R. Rogers
GB title: *Hello Beautiful*

Girls come to New York to become models for John Robert Powers.
Extremely thin and forgettable musical.

w Edwin Moran, Harry Segall, *book* John Robert Powers d Norman Z. McLeod
ph Stanley Cortez *md* Louis Silvers

George Murphy, Anne Shirley, Carole Landis, Alan Mowbray (as Powers), Dennis Day, Benny Goodman and his Orchestra, Mary Treen

Practically Yours
US 1944 89m bw
Paramount (Mitchell Leisen)

A war hero comes back after being supposed dead, and finds himself with a fiancée he never met.
Silly romantic comedy which never gets going.

w Norman Krasna d Mitchell Leisen
ph Charles Lang Jnr *m* Victor Young

Claudette Colbert, Fred MacMurray, Gil Lamb, Cecil Kellaway, Robert Benchley, Rosemary de Camp, Tom Powers, Jane Frazee

Prelude to Fame
GB 1950 88m bw
Rank / Two Cities (Donald B. Wilson)

The health of a child musical prodigy is endangered by an ambitious woman who pushes him to the top.
Banal drama with classical music, generally overacted by the adults.

w Robert Westerby, *story* Young Archimedes by Aldous Huxley d Fergus McDonell
ph George Stretton

Jeremy Spenser, Guy Rolfe, Kathleen Ryan, Kathleen Byron, James Robertson Justice, Henry Oscar, Rosalie Crutchley

The Premature Burial
US 1961 81m Eastmancolor
  Panavision
AIP (Roger Corman)

A man afraid of being buried alive suffers just that fate, but later comes to and wreaks revenge on his tormentors.
Gloomy Gothic horror based vaguely on Edgar Allan Poe: the ultimate in graveyard ghoulishness.

w Charles Beaumont, Ray Russell d Roger Corman *ph* Floyd Crosby *m* Ronald Stein
ad Daniel Haller

Ray Milland, Heather Angel, Hazel Court, Richard Ney, Alan Napier, John Dierkes

Premiere
GB 1938 71m bw

The principal backer of a stage show is shot during the first performance. Slightly unusual mystery drama. John Lodge, Judy Kelly, Joan Marion, Hugh Williams, Edmund Breon, Steven Geray, Edward Chapman. Written by F. McGrew Willis; directed by Walter Summers; for ABPC.

Presenting Lily Mars*
US 1943 104m bw
MGM (Joe Pasternak)

A girl from the sticks hits it big on Broadway. No, the plot wasn't new, but some of the numbers were nice.

w Richard Connell, Gladys Lehman, *novel* Booth Tarkington d Norman Taurog
ph Joseph Ruttenberg *md* George Stoll

Judy Garland, Van Heflin, Fay Bainter, Richard Carlson, Martha Eggerth, Spring Byington, Bob Crosby and his band, Tommy Dorsey and his band

The President's Analyst*
US 1967 104m Technicolor
  Panavision
Paramount / Panpiper (Stanley Rubin)

A psychiatrist who has been asked to treat the President is pursued by spies of every nationality.
Wild political satirical farce which finally unmasks as its chief villain the telephone company. Laughs along the way, but it's all rather too much.

wd Theodore J. Flicker ph William A. Fraker *m* Lalo Schifrin *ph* Pato Guzman

James Coburn, Godfrey Cambridge, Severn Darden, Joan Delaney, Pat Harrington, Eduard Franz, Will Geer

The President's Lady*
US 1953 96m bw
TCF (Sol C. Siegel)

An account of the early career of Andrew Jackson, a lawyer whose frail wife died shortly after he became president.
Well-produced political historical romance.

w John Patrick, *novel* Irving Stone *d* Henry Levin *ph* Leo Tover *m* Alfred Newman

Charlton Heston, Susan Hayward, John McIntire, Fay Bainter, Carl Betz
  'History plays a curious second fiddle to love's old sweet song.'—*New York Times*

Pressure Point*
US 1962 89m bw
UA / Larcas / Stanley Kramer

A black prison psychiatrist has longstanding trouble with a violent racist inmate.

Curious, quite compelling case history, told in pointless and confusing flashback; sharply made and photographed, melodramatically acted.

w Hubert Cornfield, S. Lee Pogositin
d Hubert Cornfield ph Ernest Haller
m Ernest Gold

Sidney Poitier, Bobby Darin, Peter Falk, Carl Benton Reid

Prestige
US 1932 71m bw

A woman follows her fiancé to a Malayan prison colony where he is on the staff, and finds he has become an alcoholic. Tediously stilted romantic melodrama which seems at least twice as long as its actual running time. Ann Harding, Melvyn Douglas, Adolphe Menjou, Guy Bates Post, Clarence Muse. Written by Francis Edwards Faragoh, from the novel *Lips of Steel* by Harry Hervey; directed by Tay Garnett; for RKO.

Pretty Baby*
US 1950 92m bw
Warner (Harry Kurnitz)

A girl finds it easier to get a seat on the subway if she is carrying a (dummy) baby, but gets into complications when she meets a baby food king.
Silly but quite pleasant comedy variation on *Bachelor Mother.*

w Everett Freeman, Harry Kurnitz
d Bretaigne Windust *ph* Peverell Marley
m David Buttolph

Betsy Drake, Edmund Gwenn, Dennis Morgan, Zachary Scott, William Frawley

Pretty Baby
US 1978 109m Metrocolor
Paramount (Louis Malle)

A 12-year-old girl grows up in a New Orleans brothel.
Tedious elaboration of a sensational subject; neither good art nor good commerce.

w Polly Platt, Louis Malle *d* Louis Malle
ph Sven Nykvist *md* Jerry Wexler

Keith Carradine, Susan Sarandon, Brooke Shields, Francis Faye, Antonio Fargas

AAN: Jerry Wexler

Pretty Ladies
US 1925 70m at 24 fps bw silent

The husband of a Broadway actress leaves her for a chorus girl. Heavy-going melodrama with a star who later turned comedienne and a couple of stars-to-be playing bits. Zasu Pitts,

Tom Moore, Norma Shearer, Lilyan Tashman, Conrad Nagel, George K. Arthur, Myrna Loy, Joan Crawford. Written by Adela Rogers St John; directed by Monta Bell; for MGM.

Pretty Maids All in a Row*
US 1971 95m Metrocolor
MGM (Gene Roddenberry)

High school girl students are being murdered by their guidance counsellor.
Uneasy murder comedy with few laughs, casting its star as a most unlikely villain. An interesting if unsuccessful attempt to be different.

w Gene Roddenberry, *novel* Francis Pollini
d Roger Vadim *ph* Charles Rosher *m* Lalo Schifrin

Rock Hudson, Angie Dickinson, Telly Savalas, Roddy McDowall, Keenan Wynn

Pretty Poison**
US 1968 89m De Luxe
TCF / Lawrence Turman / Mollino (Marshal Backlar, Noel Black)

A psychotic arsonist enlists the aid of a teenager but soon discovers she is kinkier than he and has murder in mind.
Bizarre black comedy-melodrama, quite successfully mixed and served.

w Lorenzo Semple Jnr, *novel* She Let Him Continue by Stephen Geller *d Noel Black*
ph David Quaid *m* Johnny Mandel

Anthony Perkins, Tuesday Weld, Beverly Garland, John Randolph, Dick O'Neill, Clarice Blackburn

Pretty Polly
GB 1967 102m Techniscope
Universal / George W. George, Frank Granat
US title: *A Matter of Innocence*

On a world tour with her vulgar aunt, a timid maiden finds romance in Singapore.
Slight romantic fable decked out with travel guide backgrounds and at odds with the cynicism of the short story from which it originates.

w Keith Waterhouse, Willis Hall, *story* Noel Coward *d* Guy Green *ph* Arthur Ibbetson
m Michel Legrand

Hayley Mills, Trevor Howard, Shashi Kapoor, Brenda de Banzie, Dick Patterson, Peter Bayliss, Patricia Routledge, Dorothy Alison

'It came and went this winter, leaving a slight trace of camphor and old knitting needles.'—*Wilfrid Sheed*

Pride and Prejudice***
US 1940 116m bw
MGM (Hunt Stromberg)

An opinionated young lady of the early 19th-century wins herself a rich husband she had at first despised for his pride.

A pretty respectable version of Jane Austen's splendid romantic comedy, with a generally excellent cast; full of pleasurable moments.

w Aldous Huxley, Jane Murfin, *play* Helen Jerome, *novel Jane Austen d Robert Z. Leonard ph* Karl Freund *m* Herbert Stothart

Laurence Olivier, Greer Garson, Edmund Gwenn, Mary Boland, Melville Cooper, Edna May Oliver, Karen Morley, Frieda Inescort, Bruce Lester, Edward Ashley, Ann Rutherford, Maureen O'Sullivan, E. E. Clive, Heather Angel, Marsha Hunt

'The most deliciously pert comedy of old manners, the most crisp and crackling satire in costume that we can remember ever having seen on the screen.'—*Bosley Crowther*

'Animated and bouncing, the movie is more Dickens than Austen; once one adjusts to this, it's a happy and carefree viewing experience.'—*New Yorker, 1980*

'Five charming sisters on the gayest, merriest manhunt that ever snared a bewildered bachelor! Girls! take a lesson from these husband hunters!'—*publicity*

The Pride and the Passion*
US 1957 131m Technicolor
Vistavision
UA / Stanley Kramer

In 1810 Spain a British naval officer helps Spanish guerrillas, by reactivating an old cannon, to win their fight against Napoleon.
Stolid, miscast adventure spectacle, its main interest being the deployment of the gun across country by surging throngs of peasants.

w Edna and Edward Anhalt, *novel* The Gun by C. S. Forester *d* Stanley Kramer *ph* Franz Planer *m* Georges Antheil

Cary Grant, Sophia Loren, Frank Sinatra, Theodore Bikel, John Wengraf, Jay Novello, Philip Van Zandt

'The whirr of the cameras often seems as loud as the thunderous cannonades. It evidently takes more than dedication, co-operative multitudes and four million dollars to shoot history in the face.'—*Time*

The Pride of St Louis
US 1952 93m bw
TCF (Jules Schermer)

The life of baseball star Dizzy Dean, who injured himself and became a commentator.
Sporting biopic of clearly restricted interest; modestly well done.

w Herman J. Mankiewicz *d* Harmon Jones *ph* Leo Tover *m* Arthur Lange

Dan Dailey, Joanne Dru, Richard Haydn, Richard Crenna, Hugh Sanders

AAN: original story (Guy Trosper)

Pride of the Marines*
US 1945 120m bw
Warner (Jerry Wald)
GB title: *Forever in Love*

The story of Marine Al Schmid, blinded while fighting the Japanese.
Over-dramatic, sudsy biopic which is well enough mounted to carry quite an impact in the flagwaving Hollywood style.

w Albert Maltz *d* Delmer Daves *ph* Peverell Marley *m* Franz Waxman

John Garfield, Eleanor Parker, Dane Clark, John Ridgely, Rosemary de Camp, Ann Doran, Warren Douglas, Tom D'Andrea

'Long drawn out and never inspired, but very respectably honest and dogged.'—*James Agee*

AAN: Albert Maltz

The Pride of the Yankees*
US 1942 128m bw
Samuel Goldwyn

The story of baseball star Lou Gehrig, who died of amytropic lateral sclerosis at the height of his powers.
Standard sporting biopic ending on Gehrig's famous speech to the crowd; emotion covers the film's other deficiencies.

w Jo Swerling, Herman J. Mankiewicz, *story* Paul Gallico *d* Sam Wood *ph* Rudolph Maté *m* Leigh Harline *pd* William Cameron Menzies

Gary Cooper, Teresa Wright, Babe Ruth, Walter Brennan, Dan Duryea, Elsa Janssen, Ludwig Stossel, Virginia Gilmore

AAN: best picture; script; Paul Gallico; Rudolph Maté; Leigh Harline; Gary Cooper; Teresa Wright

Prime Cut
US 1972 91m Technicolor Panavision
Cinema Center (Joe Wizan)

A Kansas gangster incurs the wrath of his Chicago bosses, and a hired killer is sent to eliminate him.
Gory cat-and-mouse chase melodrama with no interest save its excesses.

w Robert Dillon *d* Michael Ritchie *ph* Gene Polito *m* Lalo Schifrin

Gene Hackman, Lee Marvin, Angel Tompkins, Sissy Spacek

The Prime Minister*
GB 1940 109m bw
Warner (Max Milder)

Episodes in the life of Disraeli.
Modestly budgeted historical pageant notable only for performances.

w Brock Williams, Michael Hogan *d* Thorold Dickinson

John Gielgud, Diana Wynyard, Will Fyffe, Stephen Murray, Owen Nares, Fay Compton (as Queen Victoria), Lyn Harding, Leslie Perrins

The Prime of Miss Jean Brodie*
GB 1969 116m De Luxe
TCF (Robert Fryer)

A sharp-minded Edinburgh schoolmistress of the thirties is a bad influence on her more easily-swayed pupils.
Interesting but slackly handled and maddeningly played character drama.

w Jay Presson Allen, *novel* Muriel Spark *d* Ronald Neame *ph* Ted Moore *m* Rod McKuen *pd* John Howell

Maggie Smith, Robert Stephens, Pamela Franklin, Celia Johnson, Gordon Jackson, Jane Carr

'The novel lost a good deal in its stage simplification, and loses still more in its movie reduction of that stage version.'—*John Simon*

AA: Maggie Smith
AAN: song 'Jean' (*m* / *ly* Rod McKuen)

The Primrose Path
US 1940 92m bw
RKO (Gregory La Cava)

The youngest of a family of shanty-town prostitutes falls in love with an honest hamburger stand proprietor.
Downright peculiar melodrama for its day and age, and not very entertaining either, spending most of its time being evasive.

w Allan Scott, Gregory La Cava, *play* Robert Buckner, Walter Hart, *novel* February Hill by Victoria Lincoln *d* Gregory La Cava *ph* Joseph H. August *m* Werner Heymann

Ginger Rogers, Joel McCrea, Marjorie Rambeau, Henry Travers, Miles Mander, Queenie Vassar, Joan Carroll

'The story isn't good enough, the direction isn't sincere enough, to give any pain to the

lumps in the throat which its designers obviously had in mind.'—*Richard Mallett, Punch*

AAN: Marjorie Rambeau

The Prince and the Pauper*
US 1937 118m bw
Warner (Robert Lord)

In Tudor London, young Edward VI changes places with a street urchin who happens to be his double.
Well-produced version of a famous story; it never quite seems to hit the right style or pace, but is satisfying in patches.

w Laird Doyle, *novel* Mark Twain *d* William Keighley *ph* Sol Polito *m* Erich Wolfgang Korngold

Errol Flynn, Claude Rains, Billy and Bobby Mauch, Henry Stephenson, Barton MacLane, Alan Hale, Eric Portman, Montagu Love (as Henry VIII), Lionel Pape, Halliwell Hobbes, Fritz Leiber

The Prince and the Pauper*
Panama 1977 121m Technicolor Panavision
International Film Production / Ilya and Alexander Salkind
US title: *Crossed Swords*

Young Edward VI changes place with a beggar, who helps to expose a traitor.
Moderately well-made swashbuckler with an old-fashioned air, not really helped by stars in cameo roles or by the poor playing of the title roles.

w George MacDonald Fraser, *novel* Mark Twain *d* Richard Fleischer *ph* Jack Cardiff *m* Maurice Jarre *pd* Anthony Pratt

Mark Lester, Oliver Reed, Raquel Welch, Ernest Borgnine, George C. Scott, Rex Harrison, David Hemmings, Charlton Heston (as Henry VIII), Harry Andrews, Murray Melvin, Julian Orchard

The Prince and the Showgirl*
GB 1957 117m Technicolor
Warner / Marilyn Monroe Productions (Laurence Olivier)

In London for the 1911 coronation, a Ruritanian prince picks up a chorus girl and they come to understand and respect each other.
Heavy-going comedy, rich in production values but weak in dramatic style and impact.

w Terence Rattigan, from his play The Sleeping Prince *d* Laurence Olivier *ph* Jack

Cardiff *m* Richard Addinsell *pd* Roger
Furse *ad* Carmen Dillon

Laurence Olivier, Marilyn Monroe, Sybil
Thorndike, Richard Wattis, Jeremy Spenser,
Esmond Knight, Rosamund Greenwood,
Maxine Audley

Prince of Foxes*
US 1949   107m   bw
TCF (Sol. C. Siegel)

A wandering adventurer in medieval Italy gets
mixed up with the Borgias.
Good-looking historical fiction with a slight
edge to it.

w Milton Krims, *novel* Samuel Shellabarger
d Henry King *ph* Leon Shamroy *m* Alfred
Newman

Tyrone Power, Orson Welles, Wanda
Hendrix, Felix Aylmer, Everett Sloane,
Katina Paxinou, Marina Berti

'Plot, counterplot, action and vengeance.'—
MFB

'This pretentious chapter of pseudo-history
never rises above the merely spectacular,
hovers mostly around the conventionally
banal, and descends once to the unpardonably
crude.'—*Richard Mallett, Punch*

AAN: Leon Shamroy

Prince of Pirates
US 1953   80m   Technicolor

A young prince of the Netherlands turns pirate
when his brother allies with the Spanish
invader. Fast-moving costume potboiler with
lavish use of action scenes from *Joan of Arc*.
John Derek, Barbara Rush, Carla Balenda,
Whitfield Connor, Edgar Barrier. Written by
John O'Dea and Samuel Newman; directed by
Sidney Salkow; for Columbia.

Prince of Players*
US 1955   102m   De Luxe   Cinemascope
TCF (Philip Dunne)

Episodes in the life of actor Edwin Booth,
brother of the man who killed Abraham
Lincoln.
Earnest but ham-fisted biopic more notable, as
a Hollywood entertainment, for its dollops of
straight Shakespeare than for any dramatic
interest.

w Moss Hart, *book* Eleanor Ruggles *d* Philip
Dunne *ph* Charles G. Clarke *m* Bernard
Herrmann

Richard Burton, Eva Le Gallienne, Maggie
McNamara, John Derek, Raymond Massey,
Charles Bickford, Elizabeth Sellars, Ian Keith

Prince Valiant*
US 1954   100m   Technicolor
Cinemascope
TCF (Robert L. Jacks)

The son of the exiled king of Scandia seeks
King Arthur's help against the usurper, and
becomes involved in a court plot.
Agreeable historical nonsense for teenagers,
admittedly and sometimes hilariously from a
comic strip.

w Dudley Nichols, *comic strip* Harold Foster
d Henry Hathaway *ph* Lucien Ballard
m Franz Waxman

Robert Wagner, James Mason, Debra Paget,
Janet Leigh, Sterling Hayden, Victor
McLaglen, Donald Crisp, Brian Aherne,
Barry Jones, Primo Carnera

The Prince Who Was a Thief
US 1951   88m   Technicolor
U-I (Leonard Goldstein)

An Arabian Nights prince is lost as a baby and
brought up by thieves, but finally fights back
to his rightful throne.
Given the synopsis, any viewer can write the
script himself. Standard eastern western romp.

w Gerald Drayson Adams, Aeneas
Mackenzie,
story Theodore Dreiser *d* Rudolph Maté
ph Irving Glassberg *m* Hans Salter

Tony Curtis, Piper Laurie, Everett Sloane,
Jeff Corey

The Princess and the Pirate*
US 1944   94m   Technicolor
Samuel Goldwyn (Don Hartman)

An impostor is on the run from a vicious
pirate.
Typical star costume extravaganza with fewer
laughs than you'd expect.

w Don Hartman, Melville Shavelson, Everett
Freeman *d* David Butler *ph* William Snyder,
Victor Milner *m* David Rose

Bob Hope, Virginia Mayo, Victor McLaglen,
Walter Slezak, Walter Brennan, Marc
Lawrence, Hugo Haas, Maude Eburne

AAN: David Rose

Princess Charming
GB 1934   78m   bw

A Ruritanian revolution forces a princess to
escape in disguise. Light operetta with an
intriguing cast. Evelyn Laye, Yvonne Arnaud,
George Grossmith, Max Miller, Henry
Wilcoxon, Ivor Barnard, Francis L. Sullivan.
Written by L. DuGarde Peach, Arthur
Wimperis and Lauri Wylie, from the play

Alexandra by F. Martos; directed by Maurice Elvey; for Gainsborough.

The Princess Comes Across*
US 1936   76m   bw
Paramount (Arthur Hornblow Jnr)

A starstruck Brooklyn girl makes a transatlantic liner voyage disguised as a princess, and finds herself involved in a murder mystery.

Zany comedy thriller with plenty of jokes.

w Walter de Leon, Frances Martin, Frank Butler, Don Hartman, Philip MacDonald, *novel* Louis Lucien Rogger   *d* William K. Howard   *ph* Ted Tetzlaff   *m* Phil Boutelje

Carole Lombard, Fred MacMurray, Alison Skipworth, Douglass Dumbrille, William Frawley, Porter Hall, George Barbier, Lumsden Hare, Sig Rumann, Mischa Auer, Tetsu Komai

Princess of the Nile
US 1954   71m   Technicolor

An Egyptian princess of the middle ages leads her country against the invasion of a bedouin prince. Lethargic costume piece with hopelessly miscast actors. Debra Paget, Michael Rennie, Jeffrey Hunter, Dona Drake, Edgar Barrier, Jack Elam, Lee Van Cleef. Written by Gerald Drayson Adams; directed by Harmon Jones; for TCF.

Princess O'Rourke
US 1943   94m   bw
Warner (Hal B. Wallis)

An ace pilot falls for a princess and causes diplomatic complications.

Very thin wartime comedy with a propaganda ending involving Franklin Roosevelt.

wd Norman Krasna   *ph* Ernest Haller   *m* Frederick Hollander

Olivia de Havilland, Robert Cummings, Charles Coburn, Jack Carson, Jane Wyman, Harry Davenport, Gladys Cooper, Minor Watson, Curt Bois

AA: Norman Krasna (as writer)

Prison without Bars
GB 1938   80m   bw

The newest inmate of a reform school for girls vies with the superintendent for the love of the doctor. Basically paperback trash, this film of a notorious original was shot in three languages, but the English version at least omitted the lesbianism, except by implication. Cinematically it was without style. Edna Best, Corinne Luchaire, Barry K. Barnes, Mary

Morris, Lorraine Clewes, Martita Hunt, Glynis Johns. Written by Hans Wilhelm, Margaret Kennedy and Arthur Wimperis, from the play by Kaus, Eis and Koveloff; directed by Brian Desmond Hurst; for Alexander Korda / Irving Asher.

The Prisoner*
GB 1955   91m   bw
(Columbia) Facet / London Independent Producers (Vivian A. Cox)

In a European totalitarian state, a Cardinal is tortured and brainwashed.

Virtually a two-character talkpiece from an offbeat play which should have stayed in the theatre.

w Bridget Boland, from her play   *d* Peter Glenville   *ph* Reg Wyer   *m* Benjamin Frankel

Alec Guinness, Jack Hawkins, Wilfrid Lawson, Kenneth Griffith, Ronald Lewis, Raymond Huntley

The Prisoner of Second Avenue*
US 1975   98m   Technicolor   Panavision
Warner (Melvin Frank)

A New York clerk and his wife are driven to distraction by the problems of urban living.

Gloomier-than-usual (from this author) collection of one-liners which almost turns into a psychopathic melodrama and causes its amiable leading players to overact horrendously.

w Neil Simon, from his play   *d* Melvin Frank   *ph* Philip Lathrop   *m* Marvin Hamlisch

Jack Lemmon, Anne Bancroft, Gene Saks, Elizabeth Wilson

The Prisoner of Shark Island**
US 1936   95m   bw
TCF (Darryl F. Zanuck)

The story of the doctor who treated the assassin of President Lincoln.

Well-mounted historical semi-fiction with excellent detail.

w Nunnally Johnson   d John Ford   ph Bert Glennon   md Louis Silvers

Warner Baxter, Gloria Stuart, Joyce Kay, Claude Gillingwater, Douglas Wood, Harry Carey, Paul Fix, John Carradine

'A powerful film, rarely false or slow, maintaining the relentless cumulative pressure, the logical falling of one thing into another, until the audience is included in the movement and carried along with it in some definite emotional life that is peculiar to the art of motion pictures at its best.'—*Otis Ferguson*

Prisoner of War
US 1954   81m   bw
MGM (Henry Berman)

Life in a communist prison camp in Korea.
Sensational propaganda, reduced to comic
strip level.

w Allen Rivkin d Andrew Marton ph Robert
Planck m Jeff Alexander

Ronald Reagan, Steve Forrest, Dewey Martin,
Oscar Homolka, Robert Horton, Paul
Stewart, Henry Morgan, Stephen Bekassy
  'It presents its catalogue of horrors in a
manner unworthy of the cause it attempts to
uphold.'—*John Gillett*

The Prisoner of Zenda**
US 1937   101m   bw
David O. Selznick

An Englishman on holiday in Ruritania finds
himself helping to defeat a rebel plot by
impersonating the kidnapped king at his
coronation.
A splendid schoolboy adventure story is
perfectly transferred to the screen in this
exhilarating swashbuckler, one of the most
entertaining films to come out of Hollywood.

w *John Balderston, Wills Root, Donald Ogden
Stewart, novel Anthony Hope d John
Cromwell ph James Wong Howe m Alfred
Newman*

*Ronald Colman, Douglas Fairbanks Jnr,
Madeleine Carroll, David Niven, Raymond
Massey, Mary Astor, C. Aubrey Smith*, Byron
Foulger, Montagu Love
  'The most pleasing film that has come along
in ages.'—*New York Times*
  'One of those rare movies that seem, by
some magic trick, to become more fascinating
and beguiling with each passing year.'—*John
Cutts, 1971*
  † Previously filmed in 1913 and 1922.

AAN: Alfred Newman

The Prisoner of Zenda*
US 1952   100m   Technicolor
MGM (Pandro S. Berman)

A costly scene-for-scene remake which only
goes to show that care and discretion are no
match for the happy inspiration of the original.

w John Balderston, Noel Langley d Richard
Thorpe ph Joseph Ruttenberg m *Alfred
Newman*

Stewart Granger, James Mason, Deborah
Kerr, Robert Coote, Robert Douglas, Jane
Greer, Louis Calhern, Francis Pierlot, Lewis
Stone

The Prisoner of Zenda
US 1979   108m   Technicolor
Universal (Walter Mirisch)

Palpably uneasy version of the above which
teeters between comedy and straight romance,
with barely a moment of real zest creeping in.
The star is way off form in both roles.

w Dick Clement, Ian La Frenais d Richard
Quine ph Arthur Ibbetson m Henry
Mancini pd John J. Lloyd

Peter Sellers, Lynne Frederick, Lionel
Jeffries, Elke Sommer, Gregory Sierra, Stuart
Wilson, Jeremy Kemp, Catherine Schell,
Simon Williams, Norman Rossington, John
Laurie
  'Flatly directed, leadenly unfunny.'—*Paul
Taylor, MFB*

Prisoners of the Casbah
US 1953   78m   Technicolor

An Eastern princess and her lover take refuge
from the evil Grand Vizier in the Casbah, a
haven for outcasts. Inept sword and sandal
actioner; you can almost smell the Turkish
delight. Gloria Grahame, Cesar Romero,
Turhan Bey, Nestor Paiva. Written by
DeVallon Scott; directed by Richard Bare; for
Sam Katzman / Columbia.

Private Affairs
US 1940   74m   bw

A girl with problems seeks out the father she
has never met. Thin comedy with a pleasant
cast. Nancy Kelly, Robert Cummings, Roland
Young, Hugh Herbert, Montagu Love,
Jonathan Hale. Written by Charles Grayson,
Leonard Spigelgass and Peter Milne, from a
story by Walter Green; directed by Albert S.
Rogell; for Universal.

The Private Affairs of Bel Ami*
US 1947   119m   bw
UA / David L. Loew (Ray Heinz)

In nineties Paris, a career journalist climbs to
fame over the ruined lives of his friends.
Tame and stuffy adaptation of an incisive
novel, rather poorly produced.

wd Albert Lewin, *novel* Guy de Maupassant
ph Russell Metty m Darius Milhaud

George Sanders, Angela Lansbury, Ann
Dvorak, Frances Dee, John Carradine, Hugo
Haas, Marie Wilson, Albert Basserman,
Warren William

Private Angelo
GB 1949   106m   bw
Pilgrim (Peter Ustinov)

An Italian soldier hates war and spends World War II on the run from both sides.
Listless satirical comedy that just isn't funny enough.

w Peter Ustinov, Michael Anderson, *novel* Eric Linklater *d* Peter Ustinov *ph* Erwin Hillier

Peter Ustinov, Godfrey Tearle, Robin Bailey, Maria Denis, Marjorie Rhodes, James Robertson Justice, Moyna McGill

Private Buckaroo
US 1942 68m bw

The difficulties of putting on shows for soldiers. Slaphappy second feature worth preserving for the talent. The Andrews Sisters, Harry James and his Orchestra, Joe E. Lewis, Donald O'Connor, Peggy Ryan, Huntz Hall, Ernest Truex, Shemp Howard. Written by Edmund Kelso and Edmund James; directed by Edward Cline; for Universal.

The Private Files of J. Edgar Hoover*
US 1978 112m Movielab
AIP / Larco (Larry Cohen)

The supposedly true facts of the career of the longtime head of the FBI.
Unreliable exposé with some interesting bits.

wd Larry Cohen *ph* Paul Glickman *m* Miklos Rozsa

Broderick Crawford, Jose Ferrer, Michael Parks, Ronee Blakely, Rip Torn, Celeste Holm, Dan Dailey, Raymond St Jacques, Howard Da Silva, June Havoc, John Marley, Andrew Duggan, Lloyd Nolan

Private Izzy Murphy
US 1926 80m approx at 24 fps bw silent

A Jewish boy loves a Catholic girl. Dreary variant on *Abie's Irish Rose*, popular enough for a 1927 sequel called *Sailor Izzy Murphy*. George Jessel, Patsy Ruth Miller, Vera Gordon. Written by Philip Lonergan; directed by Lloyd Bacon; for Warner.

The Private Life of Don Juan
GB 1934 90m bw
London Films (Alexander Korda)

In 17th-century Spain, the famous lover fakes death and makes a comeback in disguise.
Lacklustre frolic by an overage star through dismal sets. The production was meant to extend the success of *The Private Life of Henry VIII*, but totally failed to do so.

w Lajos Biro, Frederick Lonsdale, *play* Henri Bataille *d* Alexander Korda *ph* Georges Périnal *m* Ernst Toch

Douglas Fairbanks, Merle Oberon, Binnie Barnes, Benita Hume, Joan Gardner, Melville Cooper, Athene Seyler, Owen Nares
'One of those ideas that never really take off.'—*New Yorker, 1977*

The Private Life of Henry VIII***
GB 1933 97m bw
London Films (*Alexander Korda*)

How Henry beheaded his second wife and acquired four more.
This never was a perfect film, but certain scenes are very funny and its sheer sauciness established the possibility of British films making money abroad, as well as starting several star careers. It now looks very dated and even amateurish in parts.

w Lajos Biro, Arthur Wimperis *d* Alexander Korda *ph* Georges Périnal *m* Kurt Schroeder

Charles Laughton, Elsa Lanchester, Robert Donat, Merle Oberon, Binnie Barnes, Franklin Dyall, Miles Mander, Wendy Barrie, Claud Allister, Everly Gregg

AA: Charles Laughton
AAN: best picture

The Private Life of Sherlock Holmes***
GB 1970 125m De Luxe Panavision
UA / Phalanx / Mirisch / Sir Nigel (Billy Wilder)

A secret Watson manuscript reveals cases in which Sherlock Holmes became involved with women.
What started as four stories is reduced to two, one brightly satirical and the other no more than a careful and discreet recreation, with the occasional jocular aside, of the flavour of the stories themselves. A very civilized and pleasing entertainment except for the hurried rounding-off which is a let-down.

w Billy Wilder, I. A. L. Diamond *d* Billy Wilder *ph* Christopher Challis *m* Miklos Rozsa *ad* Alexander Trauner

Robert Stephens, Colin Blakely, Genevieve Page, Clive Revill, Christopher Lee, Catherine Lacey, Stanley Holloway
'Affectionately conceived and flawlessly executed.'—*NFT, 1974*

Private Lives*
US 1931 92m bw
MGM (Albert Lewin)

Ex-marrieds desert their intended new spouses to try each other again.
An essentially theatrical comedy, and a great one, seems somewhat slow-witted on film.

w Hans Kraly, Richard Schayer, *play* Noel Coward *d* Sidney Franklin *ph* Ray Binger

Norma Shearer, Robert Montgomery, Reginald Denny, Una Merkel, Jean Hersholt.

The Private Lives of Elizabeth and Essex**
US 1939   106m   Technicolor
Warner (Robert Lord)

Elizabeth I falls in love with the Earl of Essex, but events turn him into a rebel and she has to order his execution.
Unhistorical history given the grand treatment; a Hollywood picture book, not quite satisfying dramatically despite all the effort.

w Norman Reilly Raine, Aeneas Mackenzie, *play* Elizabeth the Queen by Maxwell Anderson *d* Michael Curtiz *ph* Sol Polito *m* Erich Wolfgang Korngold

Bette Davis, Errol Flynn, Olivia de Havilland, Donald Crisp, Vincent Price, Alan Hale, Henry Stephenson, Henry Daniell, Leo G. Carroll, Nanette Fabray, Robert Warwick, John Sutton
'A rather stately, rigorously posed and artistically technicolored production.'—*Frank S. Nugent*

AAN: Sol Polito; Erich Wolfgang Korngold

Private Number
US 1936   80m   bw
TCF (Raymond Griffith)
GB title: *Secret Interlude*

A wealthy young man keeps a secret of his marriage to a housemaid.
Warmed-over class melodrama previously filmed in 1930 as *Common Clay*. Adequate within its lights.

w Gene Markey, William Conselman, *play* Common Clay by Cleves Kinkead *d* Roy del Ruth *ph* Peverell Marley *m* Louis Silvers

Loretta Young, Robert Taylor, Basil Rathbone, Patsy Kelly, Marjorie Gateson, Paul Harvey, Monroe Owsley, John Miljan

Private Potter
GB 1962   89m   bw
MGM / Ben Arbeid

A young soldier is court-martialled for cowardice but claims he had a vision of god.
Stilted morality play, unpersuasively made and acted.

w Ronald Harwood, from his TV play *d* Caspar Wrede *ph* Arthur Lavis *m* George Hall

Tom Courtenay, Mogens Wieth, Ronald Fraser, James Maxwell, Ralph Michael, Brewster Mason

The Private Secretary
GB 1935   70m   bw

A clerical gentleman is duped into protecting a rich young idler from his creditors. Moderately effective filming of a popular stage farce from a German original. Edward Everett Horton, Barry Mackay, Judy Gunn, Oscar Asche, Sydney Fairbrother, Alastair Sim, Michael Shepley. Written by Arthur Macrae, George Broadhurst and H. Fowler Mear, from the play by Van Moser; directed by Henry Edwards; for Twickenham.

The Private War of Major Benson
US 1955   105m   Technicolor
            Cinemascope
U-I (Howard Pine)

A soldier with outspoken views is sent to cool off as commander of a military academy run by an order of nuns.
Cute and sentimental nonsense with unlikely situations, a martinet becoming soft-centred and a happy-ever-after finale.

w William Roberts, Richard Alan Simmons *d* Jerry Hopper *ph* Harold Lipstein *m* Joseph Gershenson

Charlton Heston, Julie Adams, Tim Hovey, William Demarest, Tim Considine, Sal Mineo, Nana Bryant, Milburn Stone, Mary Field

AAN: original story (Bob Mosher, Joe Connelly)

Private Worlds*
US 1935   84m   bw
Paramount (Walter Wanger)

Romance among the doctors at a mental hospital.
Melodrama treated with what was at the time unexpected seriousness.

w Lynn Starling, *novel* Phyllis Bottome *d* Gregory La Cava *ph* Leon Shamroy *m* Heinz Roemheld

Claudette Colbert, Charles Boyer, Joel McCrea, Joan Bennett, Helen Vinson, Esther Dale, Samuel S. Hinds

AAN: Claudette Colbert

A Private's Affair
US 1959   92m   De Luxe   Cinemascope
TCF (David Weisbart)

Three army recruits form a close harmony trio and get into various scrapes.
Thin service comedy for the 'new' youth audience.

w Winston Miller *d* Raoul Walsh *ph* Charles G. Clarke *m* Cyril Mockridge

Sal Mineo, Christine Carere, Barry Coe, Barbara Eden, Gary Crosby, Terry Moore, Jim Backus, Jessie Royce Landis

Private's Progress***
GB 1956 97m bw
British Lion / Charter (Roy Boulting)

An extremely innocent young national serviceman is taught a few army dodges and becomes a dupe for jewel thieves.
Celebrated army farce with satirical pretensions; when released it had something to make everyone in Britain laugh.

w Frank Harvey, John Boulting, novel Alan Hackney d John Boulting ph Eric Cross m John Addison

Ian Carmichael, Terry-Thomas, Richard Attenborough, Dennis Price, Peter Jones, William Hartnell, Thorley Walters, Ian Bannen, Jill Adams, Victor Maddern, Kenneth Griffith, Miles Malleson, John Le Mesurier

Privilege*
GB 1967 103m Technicolor
Universal / Worldfilm / Memorial (John Heyman)

The publicity campaign for a pop star turns him into a religious messiah.
Rather hysterical fable for our time, undeniably forceful in spots and yawnful in others.

w Norman Bogner, story Johnny Speight d Peter Watkins ph Peter Suschitzky m Mike Leander

Paul Jones, Jean Shrimpton, Mark London, Max Bacon, Jeremy Child, James Cossins, Victor Henry

'Everything in it goes wrong, and one can do little but catalogue the failures.'—MFB

The Prize***
US 1963 135m Metrocolor Panavision
MGM / Roxbury (Pandro S. Berman)

In Stockholm during the Nobel Prize awards, a drunken American author stumbles on a spy plot.
Whatever the original novel is like, the film is a Hitchcock pastiche which works better than most Hitchcocks: suspenseful, well characterized, fast moving and funny from beginning to end.

w Ernest Lehman, novel Irving Wallace d Mark Robson ph William Daniels m Jerry Goldsmith

Paul Newman, Elke Sommer, Edward G. Robinson, Diane Baker, Kevin McCarthy, Leo G. Carroll, Micheline Presle

A Prize of Arms
GB 1961 105m bw
British Lion / Interstate (George Maynard)

An ex-army officer and an explosives expert plan to steal an army payroll.
Standard, pacy caper melodrama offering nothing at all new.

w Paul Ryder d Cliff Owen ph Gilbert Taylor m Robert Sharples

Stanley Baker, Tom Bell, Helmut Schmid, John Phillips

A Prize of Gold
GB 1955 100m Technicolor
Columbia / Warwick (Phil C. Samuel)

An American army sergeant in Berlin decides to steal a cargo of Nazi loot.
Routine caper thriller with sentimental leanings.

w Robert Buckner, John Paxton, novel Max Catto d Mark Robson ph Ted Moore m Malcolm Arnold

Richard Widmark, Mai Zetterling, Nigel Patrick, George Cole, Donald Wolfit, Andrew Ray, Joseph Tomelty, Karel Stepanek

The Prizefighter and the Lady
US 1933 102m bw
MGM (Hunt Stromberg)
GB title: Every Woman's Man

A boxer falls for a high class gangster's girl.
Plodding romantic melodrama, popular because it starred a real boxer.

w John Meehan, John Lee Mahin d W. S. Van Dyke ph Lester White m David Snell

Myrna Loy, Max Baer, Otto Kruger, Walter Huston, Jack Dempsey, Primo Carnera

AAN: original story (Frances Marion)

The Prodigal
US 1955 115m Eastmancolor Cinemascope
MGM (Charles Schnee)

The son of a Hebrew farmer falls for the high priestess of a pagan cult.
Wildly apocryphal 'biblical' story of obvious expensiveness but no merit.

w Maurice Zimm d Richard Thorpe ph Joseph Ruttenberg m Bronislau Kaper

Lana Turner, Edmund Purdom, Louis Calhern, James Mitchell, Walter Hampden, Francis L. Sullivan, Joseph Wiseman, Audrey Dalton, Taina Elg, Neville Brand, Cecil Kellaway

'A few lines of dialogue derive from the Bible; the rest is pure Hollywood, but

Hollywood in its mood of sham solemnity when even the unintentional jokes are not funny.'—*MFB*

The Producers*
US 1967 88m Pathecolor
Avco / Springtime / MGM / Crossbow
·(Sidney Glazier)

A Broadway producer seduces elderly widows to obtain finance for his new play, sells 25000 per cent in the expectation that it will flop, and is horrified when it succeeds.

Dismally unfunny satire except for the play itself, *Springtime for Hitler*, which is neatly put down. This has, however, become a cult film, so that criticism is pointless.

wd Mel Brooks *ph* Joseph Coffey *m* John Morris

Zero Mostel, Gene Wilder, Kenneth Mars, Estelle Winwood, Renee Taylor, Dick Shawn

'Over and over again promising ideas are killed off, either by over-exposure or bad timing.'—*Tom Milne*

'An almost flawless triumph of bad taste, unredeemed by wit or style.'—*Arthur Schlesinger Jnr*

AA: Mel Brooks (as writer)
AAN: Gene Wilder

Professional Soldier
US 1936 75m bw
TCF (Darryl F. Zanuck)

A kidnapper befriends the young prince who is his victim.
Predictable, polished family film.

w Gene Fowler, Howard Willis Smith, *story* Damon Runyon *d* Tay Garnett *ph* Rudolph Maté *m* Louis Silvers

Victor McLaglen, Freddie Bartholemew, Constance Collier, Gloria Stuart, Michael Whalen

Professional Sweetheart
US 1933 70m bw
RKO (Merian C. Cooper)
GB title: *Imaginary Sweetheart*

A radio 'purity girl' seeks some real life romance.
Modestly smart comedy of no lasting merit.

w Maurine Watkins *d* William Seiter *ph* Edward Cronjager *m* Max Steiner

Ginger Rogers, Betty Furness, Gregory Ratoff, Sterling Holloway, Frank McHugh, Zasu Pitts, Allen Jenkins, Norman Foster, Edgar Kennedy, Franklin Pangborn

The Professionals**
US 1966 123m Technicolor
Panavision
Columbia / Pax (Richard Brooks)

Skilled soldiers of fortune are hired by a millionaire rancher to get back his kidnapped wife.
Strong-flavoured star western with good suspense sequences.

wd Richard Brooks, *novel* A Mule for the Marquesa by Frank O'Rourke *ph* Conrad Hall *m* Maurice Jarre

Burt Lancaster, Lee Marvin, Robert Ryan, Jack Palance, Ralph Bellamy, Claudia Cardinale, Woody Strode

'After the *Lord Jim* excursion, it is good to see Brooks back on his own professional form, filming the tight, laconic sort of adventure which usually seems to bring out the best in Hollywood veterans.'—*Penelope Houston*

'It has the expertise of a cold old whore with practised hands and no thoughts of love.'—*Pauline Kael, 1968*

AAN: Richard Brooks (as writer and as director); Conrad Hall

Professor Beware*
US 1938 93m bw
Paramount

A staid professor finds himself on the run across America in pursuit of an Egyptian artefact.
Slow-starting comedy with only moments of the comedian at his best.

w Delmer Daves, Jack Cunningham, *story* Crampton Harris, Francis M. and Marian B. Cockrell *d* Elliott Nugent *ph* Archie Stout

Harold Lloyd, Phyllis Welch, Raymond Walburn, Lionel Stander, William Frawley, Thurston Hall, Cora Witherspoon, Sterling Holloway

Project X*
US 1968 97m Technicolor
Paramount / William Castle

In the year 2118, a man is scientifically induced to think he lives in the 1960s so that he can recover a lost secret.
Fearsomely complex science fiction, cheaply made but on the whole intriguingly imagined.

w Edmund Morris, *novels* Leslie P. Davies *d* William Castle *ph* Harold Stine *m* Van Cleave

Christopher George, Greta Baldwin, Henry Jones, Monte Markham, Harold Gould

The Promise

GB 1969 98m Eastmancolor
Commonwealth United / Howard and
Wyndham

Two young men and a girl share a flat after the
1942 siege of Leningrad; thirteen years later,
their dreams of life considerably modified,
they meet again and change partners.
Talky and too carefully budgeted screen
version of a somewhat pretentious play.

w Michael Hayes, *play* Aleksei Arbuzov
d Michael Hayes ph Brendan Stafford
m Iwan Williams pd William McCrow

Ian McKellen, John Castle, Susan Macready,
Mary Jones, David Mettheim

Promise at Dawn

US / France 1970 102m De Luxe
Avco / Nathalie (Jules Dassin)

The boyhood of novelist Romain Gary and the
last years of his fearsome Russian Jewish
actress mother with whom he traipses around
Europe.
Scrappy star vehicle and unnecessary biopic in
a variety of indulgent styles.

w Jules Dassin, *play* First Love by Samuel
Taylor d Jules Dassin ph Jean Badal
m Georges Delerue

Melina Mercouri, Assef Dayan

Promise Her Anything

GB 1966 97m Technicolor
Seven Arts (Stanley Rubin)

A mail order movie maker falls for a young
French widow in the next flat.
Scatty comedy set in Greenwich Village and
aiming in vain for a kind of frantic bohemian
charm, with a baby as deus ex machina.

w William Peter Blatty d Arthur Hiller
ph Douglas Slocombe m Lynn Murray

Warren Beatty, Leslie Caron, Hermione
Gingold, Lionel Stander, Robert Cummings,
Keenan Wynn, Cathleen Nesbitt

Promises in the Dark

US 1979 115m Metrocolor
Warner / Orion (Jerome Hellman)

A young girl dies of cancer.
Depressing and not particularly well done case
history, a curious enterprise in view of the
hundreds of television movies relentlessly
exploring the same field.

w Loring Mandel d Jerome Hellman
ph Adam Holender m Leonard Rosenman

Marsha Mason, Ned Beatty, Susan Clark,
Michael Brandon, Kathleen Beller, Paul
Clemens

Prophecy

US 1979 102m Movielab Panavision
Paramount (Robert L. Rosen)

In rural Maine, mercury poisoning produces
huge animal mutants.
Unpleasant ecological shocker with no
particular talent in evidence.

w David Seltzer d John Frankenheimer
ph Harry Stradling Jnr m Leonard
Rosenman pd William Craig Smith

Talia Shire, Robert Foxworth, Armand
Assante, Richard Dysart

Prosperity

US 1932 90m bw

Mothers-in-law disagree about the marriage of
their children. Reliable comedy of the
depression, marking the last teaming of its
popular stars. *Marie Dressler, Polly Moran,*
Anita Page, Norman Foster, Henry Armetta.
Written by Eve Greene and Zelda Sears;
directed by Sam Wood; for MGM.

Prostitute

GB 1980 96m colour
Kestrel (Tony Garnett)

A provincial tart moves into the West End.
Downbeat, supposedly realistic documentary
drama which ends up being depressing but not
in the least titillating.

w Tony Garnett ph Charles Stewart m The
Gangsters

Eleanor Forsythe, Kate Crutchley, Kim
Lockett, Nancy Samuels

The Proud and Profane

US 1956 112m bw Vistavision
Paramount (William Perlberg)

In the Pacific War a Roman Catholic widow
falls for a tough Lieutenant Colonel. ('My
pleasure is physical; my men call me The
Beast.')
Unlikely romantic melodrama with a certain
amount of plain speaking, otherwise routine.

wd George Seaton, *novel* The Magnificent
Bastards by Lucy Herndon Crockett ph John
F. Warren m Victor Young

William Holden, Deborah Kerr, Thelma
Ritter, Dewey Martin, William Redfield

The Proud Ones

US 1956 94m Eastmancolor
Cinemascope
TCF (Robert L. Jacks)

A marshal cleans up a crooked town despite
the hazards of his own physical disability and a
deputy who hates him.

Entertaining though rather foolishly scripted western.

w Edmund North, Joseph Patracca d Robert D. Webb ph Lucien Ballard m Lionel Newman

Robert Ryan, Jeffrey Hunter, Virginia Mayo, Robert Middleton

The Proud Rebel
US 1958 103m Technicolor
MGM / Sam Goldwyn Jnr

After the Civil War, a southerner wanders the Yankee states in search of a doctor to cure his mute son; he falls for a lady farmer and his son finds his voice at a crucial moment.
Pretty dim family western for pretty dim families; everything happens precisely according to plan.

w Joseph Patracca, Lillie Hayward d Michael Curtiz ph Ted McCord m Jerome Moross

Alan Ladd, Olivia de Havilland, David Ladd, Dean Jagger, Cecil Kellaway, Dean Stanton, Henry Hull, John Carradine, James Westerfield

The Proud Valley*
GB 1939 76m bw
Ealing (Sergei Nolbandov)

A black stoker helps unemployed Welsh miners reopen their pits.
Neat little propaganda drama.

w Roland Pertwee, Louis Golding, Jack Jones d Pen Tennyson ph Roy Kellino, Glen MacWilliams m Ernest Irving

Paul Robeson, Edward Chapman, Edward Rigby, *Rachel Thomas*, Simon Lack, Clifford Evans, Allan Jeayes

Providence*
France / Switzerland 1977 107m Eastmancolor
Action Film / Société Française de Production / FR3 / Citel (Philippe Dussart)

A famous writer, dying, spends a painful night in unpleasant and sometimes fantastic recollections of his sons and their women; but the reality, when they come to lunch next day, is somewhat different.
Despite its cast and other credits, this is a repellent and not too well acted study in the lack of communication, told at undue length and in turgid colour.

w David Mercer d Alain Resnais ph Ricardo Aronovitch m Miklos Rozsa ad Jacques Saulnier

John Gielgud, Dirk Bogarde, Ellen Burstyn, David Warner, Elaine Stritch

'The movie is peculiarly fastidious and static: you feel as if it were going to dry up and blow away.'—*New Yorker*

The Prowler*
US 1951 92m bw
Horizon (Sam Spiegel)

A discontented wife thinks she sees a prowler and calls a cop; they have an affair and murder her husband.
Another variant on *Double Indemnity* and *The Postman Always Rings Twice*; the script is terse and the actors well-handled.

w Hugo Butler d Joseph Losey ph Arthur Miller m Lyn Murray

Van Heflin, Evelyn Keyes, John Maxwell, Katharine Warren
'A rivetingly cool, clean thriller.'—*NFT, 1973*

Prudence and the Pill*
GB 1968 92m De Luxe
TCF / Kenneth Harper, Ronald Kahn

A girl borrows her mother's contraceptive pills and replaces them with aspirin, causing no end of complications.
Self-consciously naughty sex comedy with a long dénouement and some stiff patches to affect one's enjoyment of the brighter moments.

w Hugh Mills, from his play d Fielder Cook ph Ted Moore m Bernard Ebbinghouse

David Niven, Deborah Kerr, Edith Evans, Keith Michell, Robert Coote, Irina Demick, Joyce Redman, Judy Geeson
'Everybody winds up pregnant to clutter the earth, apparently, with people as obnoxious as their progenitors.'—*Judith Crist*

Psyche 59
GB 1964 94m bw
Columbia / Troy / Schenck (Philip Hazelton)

A wife recovers from blindness after realizing that her husband is in love with her sister.
Pretentious melodrama with stuffy dialogue, pompous direction and irritating characters.

w Julian Halevy, *novel* Françoise de Ligneris d Alexander Singer ph Walter Lassally m Kenneth V. Jones

Patricia Neal, Curt Jurgens, Samantha Eggar, Ian Bannen, Beatrix Lehmann

Psycho***
US 1960 109m bw
Shamley / Alfred Hitchcock

At a lonely motel vicious murders take place and are attributed to the manic mother of the young owner.

Curious shocker devised by Hitchcock as a tease and received by most critics as an unpleasant horror piece in which the main scene, the shower stabbing, was allegedly directed not by Hitchcock but by Saul Bass. After enormous commercial success it achieved classic status over the years; despite effective moments of fright, it has a childish plot and script, and its interest is that of a tremendously successful confidence trick, made for very little money by a TV crew.

w Joseph Stefano, *novel* Robert Bloch *d Alfred Hitchcock* (and *Saul Bass*) *ph* John L. Russell *m Bernard Herrmann*

Anthony Perkins, Vera Miles, John Gavin, Janet Leigh, John McIntire, Martin Balsam, Simon Oakland

'Probably the most visual, most cinematic picture he has ever made.'—*Peter Bogdanovich*

'I think the film is a reflection of a most unpleasant mind, a mean, sly, sadistic little mind.'—*Dwight MacDonald*

'Don't give away the ending—it's the only one we have!'—*publicity*

† When asked by the press what he used for the blood in the bath, Mr Hitchcock said: 'Chocolate sauce'.

AAN: Alfred Hitchcock; John L. Russell; Janet Leigh

Psychomania
GB 1972 91m Technicolor
Benmar (Andrew Donally)

A Hells Angels motor cyclist commits suicide and returns from the dead an invulnerable monster.
Arrant nonsense of the macabre sort, sometimes irresistibly amusing.

w Armand d'Usseau *d* Don Sharp *ph* Ted Moore *m* David Whitaker

George Sanders, Nicky Henson, Beryl Reid, Robert Hardy

The Psychopath
GB 1966 83m Techniscope
Paramount / Amicus (Milton Subotsky)

Men are found dead in London, each with a doll beside him.
Complicated horror thriller in which the actors go further over the top the more the plot winds down.

w Robert Bloch *d* Freddie Francis *ph* John Wilcox *m* Philip Martell

Patrick Wymark, Margaret Johnston, John Standing, Alexander Knox, Judy Huxtable, Don Borisenko, Thorley Walters, Colin Gordon

PT 109
US 1963 140m Technicolor
Panavision
Warner (Brian Foy)

Adventures of president-to-be John F. Kennedy when he was a naval lieutenant in the Pacific during World War II.
Extraordinarily protracted and very dull action story which seems to have been overawed by its subject.

w Richard L. Breen *d* Leslie H. Martinson *ph* Robert Surtees *m* William Lava, David Buttolph

Cliff Robertson, Ty Hardin, James Gregory, Robert Blake

Public Deb Number One
US 1940 80m bw

A waiter spanks a spoiled society girl at a communist rally, and accepts a job which makes him a capitalist. Lively comedy packed with familiar faces. Brenda Joyce, George Murphy, Ralph Bellamy, Elsa Maxwell, Mischa Auer, Charles Ruggles, Maxie Rosenbloom, Berton Churchill, Franklin Pangborn, Hobart Cavanaugh, Lloyd Corrigan, Elisha Cook Jnr. Written by Karl Tunberg and Darrell Ware; directed by Gregory Ratoff; for TCF.

The Public Enemy***
US 1931 84m bw
Warner
GB title: *Enemies of the Public*

Two slum boys begin as bootleggers, get too big for their boots, and wind up dead.
Although it doesn't flow as a narrative, this early gangster film still has vivid and startling scenes and was most influential in the development of the urban American crime film.

w Kubec Glasmon, John Bright *d William Wellman ph Dev* Jennings *m* David Mendoza

James Cagney, Edward Woods, Jean Harlow, Joan Blondell, Beryl Mercer, Donald Cook, Mae Clarke, Leslie Fenton

'The real power of *The Public Enemy* lies in its vigorous and brutal assault on the nerves and in the stunning acting of James Cagney.'—*James Shelley Hamilton*

'A postscript said that the producers wanted to "depict honestly an environment that exists today in certain strata of American life, rather than glorify the hoodlum or the criminal". The film had a different effect: Cagney was playful and dynamic, and so much more appealing than the characters opposed to him that

audiences rooted for him in spite of
themselves.'—*Martin Quigley Jnr, 1970*
AAN: Kubec Glasmon, John Bright

Public Enemy's Wife

US 1935 78m bw
Warner (Sam Bischoff)
GB title: *G-Man's Wife*

Lower-berth gangster thrills culminating in a
chase climax; neatly enough done.

w Abem Finkel, Harold Buckley, *story* David
O. Selznick, P. J. Wolfson *ph* Ernest Haller
d Nick Grinde

Pat O'Brien, Margaret Lindsay, Robert
Armstrong, Cesar Romero, Dick Foran, Dick
Purcell

† Remade as *Bullets for O'Hara* (1942).

Public Hero Number One

US 1935 89m bw
MGM (Lucien Hubbard)

A G-man goes undercover to track down the
Purple Gang.
Moderate thick ear dating from the time when
studios tried to smother public outcry against
gangster films by presenting the cop as the
hero.

w Wells Root *d* J. Walter Ruben *ph* Gregg
Toland

Chester Morris, Jean Arthur, Joseph Calleia,
Lionel Barrymore, Paul Kelly, Lewis Stone,
Paul Hurst
    'The best picture on criminal life I've
seen.'—*Otis Ferguson*

Pufnstuf

US 1970 98m Technicolor
Universal / Krofft Enterprises

A dejected boy is led by his talking flute on a
talking boat to Living Island, full of strange
but friendly animals in fear of an incompetent
witch.
Amalgam of a TV series using life-size puppets
to project a mildly pleasing variation on *The
Wizard of Oz*, without quite achieving the
right blend of wit and charm.

w John Fenton Murray, Si Rose
d Hollingsworth Morse *ph* Kenneth Peach
m Charles Fox *ad Alexander Golitzen*

Jack Wild, Billie Hayes, Martha Raye, Mama
Cass

Pulp*

GB 1972 95m colour
UA / Klinger–Caine–Hodges (Michael
Klinger)

An ex-funeral director now living in the
Mediterranean as a successful pulp fiction
writer gets involved with gangsters and
weirdos.
Occasionally funny pastiche which sorely lacks
shape and is sustained by guest appearances
and zany ideas.

wd Mike Hodges ph Ousama Rawi
m George Martin

Michael Caine, *Mickey Rooney*, Lizabeth
Scott, Lionel Stander, Nadia Cassini, Al
Lettieri, Dennis Price
    'Various eccentrics act out their "turns", but
never quite lift a light comedy-thriller through
the more playful and productive inversions of
parody.'—*Richard Combs*

The Pumpkin Eater***

GB 1964 118m bw
Columbia / Romulus (James Woolf)

A compulsive mother (of eight children) finds
her third marriage rocking when she gets
evidence of her husband's affairs.
Brilliantly made if basically rather irritating
kaleidoscope of vivid scenes about silly
people, all quite recognizable as sixties
Londoners; very well acted.

w Harold Pinter, *novel* Penelope Mortimer
d Jack Clayton ph Oswald Morris m Georges
Delerue

Anne Bancroft, Peter Finch, James Mason,
Maggie Smith, Cedric Hardwicke, Richard
Johnson, Eric Porter
    'There never was a film so rawly
memorable.'—*Evening Standard*
    'It is solid, serious, intelligent, stylish. It is
also, for the most part, quite dead.'—*The
Times*
AAN: Anne Bancroft

The Punch and Judy Man*

GB 1962 96m bw
(ABP) Macconkey (Gordon L. T. Scott)

A seaside children's entertainer tries and
fails to establish himself as an important
citizen.
Melancholy comedy of failure which did not
please its star's adherents and indeed just
missed the style it was seeking.

w Philip Oakes, Tony Hancock *d* Jeremy
Summers *ph* Gilbert Taylor *m* Derek Scott,
Don Banks

Tony Hancock, Sylvia Syms, Ronald Fraser,
Barbara Murray, John Le Mesurier, Hugh
Lloyd

Puppet on a Chain*
GB 1970 98m Technicolor
Big City (Kurt Unger)

An American Interpol agent hunts down drug smugglers in Amsterdam.

Sadistic adventure thriller, a toughened version of James Bond, climaxing in a splendid boat chase through Amsterdam.

w Alistair MacLean, Don Sharp, Paul Wheeler, *novel* Alistair MacLean *d* Geoffrey Reeve, *Don Sharp ph* Jack Hildyard, Skeets Kelly *m* Piero Piccioni

Sven Bertil Taube, Barbara Parkins, Patrick Allen, Alexander Knox, Vladek Sheybal
'One suspects that a marionette also sat in for Alistair MacLean.'—*Judith Crist*

The Purple Gang
US 1960 85m bw

In Detroit during prohibition a gang of juvenile delinquents become as powerful as the gangsters. Unpleasant detail mars this cops-and-robbers subject; twenty years later it would have been even more of a shocker, but it's bad enough as it is. Robert Blake, Barry Sullivan, Elaine Edwards, Marc Cavell, Jody Lawrance, Susie Marquette, Paul Dubov. Written by Jack DeWitt; directed by Frank McDonald; for Allied Artists.

The Purple Heart*
US 1944 99m bw
TCF (Darryl F. Zanuck)

American prisoners of war in Japan are tried and executed.

Relentlessly sombre flagwaver, extremely persuasively presented.

w Jerome Cady, Darryl F. Zanuck *d* Lewis Milestone *ph* Arthur Miller *m* Alfred Newman

Dana Andrews, Richard Conte, Farley Granger, Kevin O'Shea, Sam Levene, Don Barry, Richard Loo
'It is unusually edged, well organized and solidly acted. But I feel extremely queasy watching fiction—especially persuasive fiction—which pretends to clarify facts that are not clear, and may never become so.'—*James Agee*

The Purple Mask
US 1955 82m Technicolor
Cinemascope
U-I (Howard Christie)

In 1802 Paris the Royalist resistance to Napoleon is led by the mysterious Purple Mask, who also disguises himself as a foppish dandy.

Cheeky rewrite of *The Scarlet Pimpernel*, with plenty of gusto but not much style.

w Oscar Brodney *d* Bruce Humberstone *ph* Irving Glassberg *m* Joseph Gershenson

Tony Curtis, Dan O'Herlihy, Colleen Miller, Gene Barry, Angela Lansbury, George Dolenz, John Hoyt
'Sir Percy, one feels, would have personally conducted this lot to the guillotine.'—*MFB*

The Purple Plain*
GB 1954 100m Technicolor
GFD / Two Cities (John Bryan)

During the Burma campaign, a Canadian squadronleader regains his shattered nerves during an arduous trek across country.

Psychological study and eastern adventure combined; not the best of either, but a potent crowd-puller.

w Eric Ambler, *novel* H. E. Bates *d* Robert Parrish *ph* Geoffrey Unsworth *m* John Veale

Gregory Peck, Maurice Denham, Win Min Than, Lyndon Brook, Brenda de Banzie, Bernard Lee, Anthony Bushell, Ram Gopal

Pursued*
US 1947 101m bw
(Warner) United States (Milton Sperling)

A revenge-seeking cowboy accidentally causes a tragedy in his adopted family.

Glum, good-looking revenge western.

w Niven Busch *d* Raoul Walsh *ph James Wong Howe m* Max Steiner

Robert Mitchum, Teresa Wright, Judith Anderson, Dean Jagger, Alan Hale, Harry Carey Jnr

The Pursuit of Happiness
US 1934 75m bw
Paramount (Arthur Hornblow Jnr)

In 1776 Connecticut a Puritan maid falls for a Hessian soldier.

Mildly pleasing romantic comedy centring on the ancient practice of 'bundling' in which betrothed couples might sleep together fully clothed.

w Stephen Morehouse Avery, Jack Cunningham, J. P. McEvoy, Virginia Van Upp, *play* Lawrence Langner, Armina Marshall *d* Alexander Hall *ph* Karl Struss

Francis Lederer, Joan Bennett, Charles Ruggles, Mary Boland, Walter Kingsford, Minor Watson

The Pursuit of Happiness*
US 1970 98m Eastmancolor
Columbia / TA Films / Norton–Simon
(David Susskind)

A New York college dropout is sent to prison after a hit and run accident.
Smooth, watchable but empty youth movie.

w Sidney Carroll, George L. Sherman *d* Robert Mulligan *ph* Dick Kratina *m* Dave Grusin

Michael Sarrazin, Barbara Hershey, Robert Klein, Ruth White, E. G. Marshall, Arthur Hill

Pushover*
US 1954   91m   bw
Columbia (Jules Schermer)

An honest policeman involves himself in murder for loot.
Another variation on *Double Indemnity*, smoothly carpentered as the first appearance of newly-groomed star Kim Novak. The events of a night were familiar and watchable.

w Roy Huggins, *novels* The Night Watch by Thomas Walsh, Rafferty by William S. Ballinger *d* Richard Quine *ph* Lester B. White *m* Arthur Morton

Fred MacMurray, Kim Novak, Phil Carey, Dorothy Malone, E. G. Marshall

Putting Pants on Philip*
US 1927   20m   bw   silent

A respectable man meets his randy Scottish nephew who wears nothing under his kilt.
Early star comedy, allegedly their first as a team but before their more recognizable characteristics had developed. Not at all bad in its way, though developing into one long chase. Laurel and Hardy, Sam Lufkin, Harvey Clark. Written by H. M. Walker; directed by Clyde Bruckman; for Hal Roach.

Puzzle of a Downfall Child
US 1970   104m   Technicolor
Universal / Newman—Foreman

Fantasy reminiscences of a top fashion model.
Pretentious, fashionable, seemingly interminable collage of sex and high living.

w Adrian Joyce *d* Jerry Schatzberg *ph* Adam Holender *m* Michael Small

Faye Dunaway, Barry Primus, Viveca Lindfors, Barry Morse, Roy Scheider

Pygmalion****
GB 1938   96m   bw
Gabriel Pascal

A professor of phonetics takes a bet that he can turn a cockney flower seller in six months into a lady who can pass as a duchess.
Perfectly splendid Shavian comedy of bad manners, extremely well filmed and containing memorable lines and performances; subsequently turned into the musical *My Fair Lady* (qv). One of the most heartening and adult British films of the thirties.

w Anatole de Grunwald, W. P. Lipscomb, Cecil Lewis, Ian Dalrymple, *play* Bernard Shaw *d* Anthony Asquith, Leslie Howard *ph* Harry Stradling *m* Arthur Honegger

Leslie Howard, Wendy Hiller, Wilfrid Lawson, Scott Sunderland, Marie Lohr, David Tree, Esmé Percy, Everley Gregg, Jean Cadell

'An exhibition of real movie-making – of a sound score woven in and out of tense scenes, creating mood and tempo and characterization.'—*Pare Lorentz*

AAN: best picture; script; Bernard Shaw; Leslie Howard; Wendy Hiller

Q Planes**
GB 1939 82m bw
Harefield / London Films (Irving Asher,
Alexander Korda)
US title: *Clouds over Europe*

A secret ray helps spies to steal test aircraft
during proving flights.
Lively comedy thriller distinguished by a droll
leading performance.

w Ian Dalrymple, Brock Williams, Jack
Whittingham, Arthur Wimperis *d* *Tim
Whelan* *ph* Harry Stradling *md* Muir
Mathieson

Ralph Richardson, Laurence Olivier, Valerie
Hobson, George Merritt, George Curzon, Gus
McNaughton, David Tree

Quackser Fortune Has a Cousin in the Bronx*
US 1970 90m Eastmancolor
UMC (John H. Cushingham)

An Irish layabout strikes up an acquaintance
with an American student.
Likeable if plotless Dublin comedy, pleasantly
photographed.

w Gabriel Walsh *d* Waris Hussein *ph* Gil
Taylor *m* Michael Dress

Gene Wilder, Margot Kidder, Eileen Colgen,
Seamus Ford

Quadrophenia
GB 1979 120m Eastmancolor

A drama of bitter rivalry between Mods and
Rockers on the Brighton beaches in 1964.
What passes for a successful musical at the end
of the seventies is typified by this violent,
screaming and wholly unattractive amalgam of
noise, violence, sex and profanity. The Who,
Kate Williams, Michael Elphick. Written by
Dave Humphries, Martin Stellman and Franc
Roddam; directed by Franc Roddam; for
Polytel.

Quai des Brumes***
France 1938 89m bw
Rabinovitch
US title: *Port of Shadows*

An army deserter rescues a girl from crooks
but is killed before they can escape.

Artificial, set-bound, but at the time wholly
persuasive melodrama which became one of
the archetypal French films of the thirties, its
doomed lovers syndrome not being picked up
by Hollywood until after World War II.

w Jacques Prévert, novel Pierre MacOrlan
*d Marcel Carné ph Eugen Schüfftan
m Maurice Jaubert ad Alexander Trauner*
*Jean Gabin, Michèle Morgan, Michel Simon,
Pierre Brasseur*

'Unity of space, time and action give the
film a classical finish.'—*Georges Sadoul*
† The plot was in fact almost identical with
that of *Pépé le Moko.* The romantic pessimism
of these films, plus *Le Jour Se Lève,* so suited
the mood of France that Vichy officials later
said: 'If we have lost the war it is because of
Quai des Brumes.'

Quai des Orfèvres*
France 1947 105m bw
Majestic

A music hall artiste is accused of murdering
the man he took to be seducing his mistress.
The equivalent of many a British Scotland
Yard thriller, but a good one, with excellent
acting, atmosphere and suspense.

w Henri-Georges Clouzot, Jean Ferry,
novel Legitime Défense by Stanislas-André
Steeman *d Henri-Georges Clouzot
ph* Armand Thirard *m* Francis Lopez

Louis Jouvet, Bernard Blier, Suzy Delair,
Pierre Larquey, Simone Rennant
'The wonder of *Quai des Orfèvres* is the way
Clouzot has pricked it with life.'—*Guardian*
'A stunningly well made entertainment.'—
New Yorker, 1982

Quality Street*
US 1937 84m bw
RKO (Pandro S. Berman)

When an officer returns from the Napoleonic
wars, he does not recognize his sweetheart,
whose beauty has faded, so she masquerades
as her own capricious niece.
Fairly successful attempt to capture on screen
the essence of Barrie whimsy; everyone tries
hard, anyway.

w Mortimer Offner, Allan Scott, *play* J. M. Barrie *d* George Stevens *ph* Robert de Grasse *m* Roy Webb

Katharine Hepburn, Franchot Tone, Fay Bainter, Eric Blore, Cora Witherspoon, Estelle Winwood, Florence Lake, Joan Fontaine

'It is strictly a self-propelled picture, tearing breathlessly, even hysterically, through Barrie's quizzical account of a man-hunt. . . . But we were exhausted by the intensity of Miss Hepburn's concentration on it. Her Phoebe needs a neurologist far more than a husband. Such flutterings and jitterings and twitchings, such hand-wringings and mouth-quiverings, such runnings-about and eyebrow-raisings have not been on the screen in many a moon.'—*Frank Nugent, New York Times*
† Previously made by MGM in 1927 (silent), with Marion Davies and Conrad Nagel; directed by Sidney Franklin.
AAN: Roy Webb

Quantez
US 1957   80m   Eastmancolor   Cinemascope

Robbers hiding for the night in a frontier town become involved in an Indian attack. Curious, slow-paced attempt to redo *The Gunfight* with inferior materials; not a profitable experience.
Fred MacMurray, Dorothy Malone, James Barton, Sydney Chaplin, John Gavin, John Larch, Michael Ansara. Written by R. Wright Campbell; directed by Harry Keller; for Universal-International.

The Quare Fellow
GB 1962   90m   bw
BLC / Bryanston (Anthony Havelock-Allan)

Life in a Dublin prison when two men are to be hanged, as experienced by a new young warder.
Watered-down version of a rumbustious stage tragi-comedy, with not much but the gloom left.
wd Arthur Dreifuss, *play* Brendan Behan *ph* Peter Hennessey *m* Alexander Faris

Patrick McGoohan, Sylvia Syms, Walter Macken, Dermot Kelly, Hilton Edwards

Quartet***
GB 1948   120m   bw
GFD / Gainsborough (Anthony Darnborough)

Four stories introduced by the author. This entertaining production began the compendium fashion (*Full House, Phone Call from a Stranger*, etc) and is fondly

remembered, though all the stories had softened endings and the middle two did not work very well as drama. Subsequent Maugham compilations were *Trio* and *Encore* (both qv).

w R. C. Sherriff, *stories* W. *Somerset Maugham m* John Greenwood

THE FACTS OF LIFE   *d* Ralph Smart *ph* Ray Elton

Basil Radford, Naunton Wayne, Mai Zetterling, Jack Watling, James Robertson Justice

THE ALIEN CORN   *d* Harold French *ph* Ray Elton

Dirk Bogarde, Françoise Rosay, Raymond Lovell, Honor Blackman, Irene Browne

THE KITE   *d* Arthur Crabtree *ph* Ray Elton

George Cole, Hermione Baddeley, Susan Shaw, Mervyn Johns, Bernard Lee

THE COLONEL'S LADY   *d* Ken Annakin *ph* Reg Wyer

Cecil Parker, Linden Travers, Nora Swinburne, Ernest Thesiger, Felix Aylmer, Henry Edwards, Wilfrid Hyde White

Quatermass and the Pit**
GB 1967   97m   Technicolor
Hammer / Anthony Nelson Keys
US title: *Five Million Years to Earth*

Prehistoric skulls are unearthed during London Underground excavations, and a weird and deadly force makes itself felt.
The third film of a Quatermass serial is the most ambitious, and in many ways inventive and enjoyable, yet spoiled by the very fertility of the author's imagination: the concepts are simply too intellectual to be easily followed in what should be a visual thriller. The climax, in which the devil rears over London and is 'earthed', is satisfactorily harrowing.
w Nigel Kneale, from his TV serial   *d* Roy Ward Baker *ph* Arthur Grant *m* Tristam Cary

Andrew Keir, James Donald, Barbara Shelley, Julian Glover, Duncan Lamont, Edwin Richfield, Peter Copley

The Quatermass Experiment**
GB 1955   82m   bw
Exclusive / Hammer (Anthony Hinds)
US title: *The Creeping Unknown*

When a rocketship returns from space, two of its three crew members have disappeared and the third is slowly taken over by a fungus which thrives on blood.

Intelligent science fiction based on a highly successful BBC TV serial; the film version is generally workmanlike despite its obvious low budget.

w Richard Landau, Val Guest, *serial Nigel Kneale d* Val Guest *ph* Jimmy Harvey

Brian Donlevy, Jack Warner, Margia Dean, *Richard Wordsworth,* David King Wood, Thora Hird, Gordon Jackson

Quatermass II**
GB 1957 85m bw
Hammer (Anthony Hinds)
US title: *Enemy from Space*

A research station operating under military secrecy is supposed to be making synthetic foods, but is in fact an acclimatization centre for invaders from outer space.
Simplified version of a TV serial, a bit stodgy in the talk scenes, but building into sequences of genuine alarm and based on an idea of lingering persuasiveness.

w Nigel Kneale, Val Guest, *serial Nigel Kneale d Val Guest ph* Gerald Gibbs
m James Bernard

Brian Donlevy, John Longden, Sidney James, Bryan Forbes, William Franklyn, Charles Lloyd Pack, Percy Herbert, Tom Chatto

Quebec
US 1951 85m Technicolor

The wife of the loyalist governor of Quebec is in love with the leader of the rebels. Ho-hum period actioner with some pretty backgrounds and not much personality. Corinne Calvet, John Barrymore Jnr, Barbara Rush, Patric Knowles, John Hoyt, Arnold Moss. Written by Alan Le May; directed by George Templeton; for Paramount.

Queen Bee*
US 1955 95m bw
Columbia (Jerry Wald)

A wealthy woman has a compulsion to dominate everyone around her.
Claustrophobic southern-set melodrama obviously created for its star.

wd Ranald MacDougall, *novel* Edna Lee
ph Charles Lang *m* George Duning
md Morris Stoloff

Joan Crawford, Barry Sullivan, Betsy Palmer, John Ireland, Lucy Marlow, William Leslie, Fay Wray

AAN: Charles Lang

Queen Christina****
US 1933 101m bw
MGM (Walter Wanger)

The queen of 17th-century Sweden, distressed at the thought of a political marriage, goes wandering through her country in men's clothes and falls in love with the new Spanish ambassador.
The star vehicle par excellence, superb to look at and one of its star's most fondly remembered films. Historically it's nonsense, but put across with great style.

w Salka Viertel, H. M. Harwood, S. N. Behrman d Rouben Mamoulian ph William Daniels m Herbert Stothart

Greta Garbo, John Gilbert, Ian Keith, Lewis Stone, C. Aubrey Smith, Reginald Owen, Elizabeth Young

'Garbo, as enchanting as ever, is still enveloped by her unfathomable mystery.'— *Photoplay*
'An unending series of exceptional scenes.'—*Modern Screen*
† The leading male role was announced in turn for Leslie Howard, Franchot Tone, Nils Asther, Bruce Cabot and Laurence Olivier: Garbo turned them all down.

Queen Elizabeth*
France 1912 35m approx (24 fps) bw
   silent
Histrionic Film
original title: *Les Amours de la Reine Elisabeth*

Scenes from the life of the queen.
Abysmally boring now, this film is important in several ways. It is our best record of Sarah Bernhardt. It was immensely successful throughout the world. It made cinema interesting to all classes, not just the hoi polloi. It made the fortunes of Adolph Zukor, who bought it cheaply and went on to found Paramount Pictures. (Bernhardt is said to have remarked to him: 'You have put me in pickle for all time!')

w Eugene Moreau d Henri Desfontaines, Louis Mercanton

Sarah Bernhardt, Lou Tellegen

Queen Kelly**
US 1928 100m approx (24 fps)
   (unfinished version) bw silent
United Artists / Joseph Kennedy

A convent girl goes to the bad, is ill-used by a prince, becomes a white slave in Africa but finally inherits a fortune.
Sexually-oriented extravaganza, the last great folly of its director but never finished by him. Various versions exist: in all of them individual scenes are more entertaining than the whole. Extracts were shown in *Sunset Boulevard*.

wd Erich Von Stroheim *ph* Gordon Pollock,
Paul Ivano, Ben Reynolds *m* Adolf Tandler
ad Harry Miles

Gloria Swanson, Walter Byron, Seena Owen

Queen of Atlantis see L'Atlantide

Queen of Hearts*
GB 1936 80m bw
ATP (Basil Dean)

A working girl poses as a socialite and wins a
matinee idol.
Stalwart romantic comedy with its star slightly
more glamorized than usual.

w Clifford Grey, H. F. Maltby, Douglas
Furber, Anthony Kimmins, Gordon
Wellesley *d* Monty Banks

Gracie Fields, John Loder, Enid Stamp
Taylor, Fred Duprez, Edward Rigby, Hal
Gordon

The Queen of Spades***
GB 1948 96m bw
ABP / World Screen Plays (Anatole de
  Grunwald)

A Russian officer tries to wrest from an
ancient countess the secret of winning at cards,
in return for which he has sold his soul to the
devil; but she dies of fright and haunts him.
Disappointingly slow-moving but splendidly
atmospheric recreation of an old Russian story
with all the decorative stops out; the chills
when they come are quite frightening, the
style is impressionist and the acting suitably
extravagant.

w Rodney Ackland, Arthur Boys,
novel Alexander Pushkin *d* Thorold
Dickinson *ph* Otto Heller *m* Georges Auric
ad Oliver Messel

Anton Walbrook, Edith Evans, Ronald
Howard, Yvonne Mitchell, Mary Jerrold

Queen of the Mob*
US 1940 61m bw
Paramount

A murderess and her three sons are captured
by the FBI.
Pacy crime melodrama from the *Persons in
Hiding* series, based on the exploits of Ma
Barker.

w Horace McCoy, William R. Lippmann
d James Hogan *ph* Theodor Sparkuhl

Blanche Yurka, Ralph Bellamy, Jack Carson,
Richard Denning, Paul Kelly, J. Carrol Naish,
Jeanne Cagney, William Henry, James Seay,
Hedda Hopper

The Queen's Guards
GB 1960 112m Technicolor
  Cinemascope
TCF / Imperial (Michael Powell)

Reminiscences during trooping the colour of
father and son guardsmen.
Incredibly old-fashioned family melodrama
complete with skeleton in family closet;
despite its date it has a decidedly pre-war air,
except that it might have been more smartly
done then.

w Roger Milner *d* Michael Powell *ph* Gerald
Turpin *m* Brian Easdale

Raymond Massey, Daniel Massey, Robert
Stephens, Ursula Jeans, Judith Stott,
Elizabeth Shepherd, Duncan Lamont, Ian
Hunter, Jack Watling

  'This flagwaving museum piece would be
distressing if it weren't so inept . . . [the
actors] battle manfully with dialogue and
characters as dated as a Crimean cavalry
charge. The film could scarcely be taken as a
tribute to the Guards except, just possibly, by
elderly aunts in Cheltenham.'—*MFB*

Queimada!
France / Italy 1968 132m De Luxe
PEA / PPA (Alberto Grimaldi)
aka: *Burn!*

A diplomat is sent to a Caribbean island to
break the Portuguese sugar monopoly and
becomes involved with revolutionaries.
An indigestible attempt to combine adventure
with the film of ideas; very tedious.

w Franco Solinas, Giorgio Arlorio *d* Gillo
Pontecorvo *ph* Marcello Gatti *m* Ennio
Morricone

Marlon Brando, Renato Salvatori, Norman
Hill, Evaristo Marquez

Quentin Durward*
GB 1955 101m Eastmancolor
  Cinemascope
MGM (Pandro S. Berman)
aka: *The Adventures of Quentin Durward*

An elderly English lord sends his nephew to
woo a French lady on his behalf; but the boy
falls in love with her himself.
Haphazardly constructed and produced, but
quite enjoyable, period romp, with a bold
black villain and several rousing set pieces
including a final set-to on bell ropes.

w Robert Ardrey, *novel* Sir Walter Scott
d Richard Thorpe *ph* Christopher Challis
m Bronislau Kaper

Robert Taylor, Kay Kendall, Robert Morley, Alec Clunes, Marius Goring, Wilfrid Hyde White, Ernest Thesiger, Duncan Lamont, Harcourt Williams, Laya Raki, George Cole

Quest for Love*
GB 1971 90m Eastmancolor
Rank / Peter Rogers Productions (Peter Eton)

After an explosion during an experiment, a young physicist finds himself living a different life, in love with a dying girl; returning to normal, he finds the girl and saves her.
Pleasing variation on *Berkeley Square*, quite well staged and played.

w Terence Feely, *story* Random Quest by John Wyndham, Ralph Thomas *ph* Ernest Steward *m* Eric Rogers

Tom Bell, Joan Collins, Denholm Elliott, Laurence Naismith, Lyn Ashley

Quick before It Melts
US 1964 97m Metrocolor Panavision
MGM / Biography (Douglas Lawrence, Delbert Mann)

A journalist is sent to cover a naval enterprise in the Antarctic, and gets a scoop despite his shyness.
Noisy service comedy with precious little plot.

w Dale Wasserman, *novel* Philip Benjamin *d* Delbert Mann *ph* Russell Harlan *m* David Rose

George Maharis, Robert Morse, Anjanette Comer, James Gregory, Howard St John, Janine Gray, Michael Constantine
'The combination of romantic dalliance, service high jinks and hectic journalism remains uniformly flat all through.'—*MFB*

The Quick Gun
US 1964 88m Techniscope

A gunfighter gets an icy welcome when he returns home to claim his father's farm.
Standard western with the hero redeemed and elected sheriff at the end. Audie Murphy, Merry Anders, James Best, Ted de Corsia, Walter Sande, Frank Ferguson. Written by Robert E. Kent; directed by Sidney Salkow; for Admiral / Columbia.

Quick Let's Get Married
US 1965 100m colour
Golden Eagle (William Marshall)
aka: *The Confession, Seven Different Ways*

The voice of a sneak thief in a ruined church is taken by an unwed mother as a miracle.
Downright peculiar mishmash wasting interesting stars; an independent production by Rogers and husband in Jamaica.

w Allen Scott *d* William Dieterle *ph* Robert Bronner *m* Michael Colicchio

Ginger Rogers, Ray Milland, Barbara Eden, Walter Abel, Cecil Kellaway, Elliott Gould, Michael Ansara, David Hurst

Quick Millions**
US 1931 69m bw
Fox

An ambitious truck driver becomes a ruthless racketeer.
Fast-moving, otherwise naïve early gangster melodrama notable for Tracy's first star performance.

w Courtney Terrett, Rowland Brown, John Wray *d* Rowland Brown *ph* Joseph August

Spencer Tracy, Marguerite Churchill, Sally Eilers, Robert Burns, John Wray, George Raft

Quicksand
US 1950 79m bw

A garage mechanic gets involved in crime for the sake of an unworthy girl. Lower-case melodrama of no notable merit. Mickey Rooney, Jeanne Cagney, Barbara Bates, Peter Lorre. Written by Robert Smith; directed by Irving Pichel; for Mort Briskin / UA.

The Quiet American**
US 1957 122m bw
UA / Figaro (Joseph L. Mankiewicz)

An American in Saigon has naïve ideas for ending the war; he saves the life of a journalist who for various reasons becomes jealous and is duped into betraying the American to the communists.
Semi-successful excursion into the territory of Graham Greene, who as in *Brighton Rock* has allowed his ironic ending to be totally re-emphasized, here making the film anti-communist instead of anti-American.

wd *Joseph L. Mankiewicz, novel* Graham Greene *ph* Robert Krasker *m* Mario Nascimbene

Michael Redgrave, Audie Murphy, Claude Dauphin, Giorgia Moll, Bruce Cabot, Fred Sadoff, Richard Loo

The Quiet Man***
US 1952 129m Technicolor
Republic / Argosy (John Ford, Merian C. Cooper)

An Irish village version of *The Taming of the Shrew*, the tamer being an ex-boxer retired to the land of his fathers and in need of a wife.
Archetypal John Ford comedy, as Irish as can

be, with everything but leprechauns and the Blarney Stone on hand. Despite some poor sets the film has a gay swing to it, much brawling vigour and broad comedy, while the actors all give their roistering best.

w Frank Nugent, story Maurice Walsh d John Ford ph Winton C. Hoch, Archie Stout m Victor Young

John Wayne, Maureen O'Hara, Barry Fitzgerald, Victor McLaglen, Ward Bond, Mildred Natwick, Francis Ford, Arthur Shields, Eileen Crowe, Sean McClory, Jack McGowran

   'Ford's art and artifice . . . are employed to reveal a way of life—stable, rooted, honourable, purposeful in nature's way, and thereby rhythmic. Everyone is an individual, yet everyone and everything has a place.'— *Henry Hart, Films in Review*

AA: John Ford; Winton C. Hoch, Archie Stout
AAN: best picture; Frank Nugent; Victor McLaglen

Quiet Please, Murder*
US 1943   70m   bw
TCF (Ralph Dietrich)
Nazis and art thieves cause a high death rate in a public library.
Unusual, stylish second feature.

wd John Larkin ph Joe MacDonald m Emil Newman

George Sanders, Kurt Katch, Gail Patrick, Richard Denning, Lynne Roberts, Sidney Blackmer, Byron Foulger

Quiet Wedding***
GB 1940   80m   bw
Paramount / Conqueror (Paul Soskin)
Middle-class wedding preparations are complicated by family guests.
A semi-classic British stage comedy is admirably filmed with a splendid cast.

w Terence Rattigan, Anatole de Grunwald, play Esther McCracken d Anthony Asquith

Margaret Lockwood, Derek Farr, *A. E. Matthews, Marjorie Fielding, Athene Seyler, Peggy Ashcroft,* Margaretta Scott, Frank Cellier, Roland Culver, Jean Cadell, David Tomlinson, Bernard Miles
† Remade as *Happy is The Bride* (qv).

Quiet Weekend
GB 1946   92m   bw
Associated British
The Royds spend a weekend at their country cottage and get involved with poachers.

Trivial and poorly-made sequel, not up to the standard of *Quiet Wedding* as a comic study of British types.

w Victor Skuzetsky, play Esther McCracken d Harold French ph Eric Cross

Derek Farr, Marjorie Fielding, George Thorpe, Frank Cellier

The Quiller Memorandum*
GB 1966   105m   Eastmancolor
Panavision
Rank / Ivan Foxwell / Carthay
A British secret service man is sent to Berlin to combat a neo-Nazi organization.
Disappointingly thin but smooth and watchable spy story.

w Harold Pinter, novel The Berlin Memorandum by Adam Hall (Elleston Trevor) d Michael Anderson ph Erwin Hillier m John Barry

George Segal, Max Von Sydow, Alec Guinness, Senta Berger, George Sanders, Robert Helpmann, Robert Flemyng

   'In disposing of most of the storyline Pinter has virtually thrown out the baby with the bathwater; all that remains is a skeleton plot which barely makes sense and is totally lacking in excitement.'—*Brenda Davies*

   'Harold Pinter wrote the screenplay and for each word of dialogue there has to be a separate scene involving several different camera angles, which is perhaps why they asked him to do it as the story is pretty thin.'—*J. A., Illustrated London News*

Quintet
US 1979   118m   De Luxe
TCF / Lions Gate (Robert Altman)
In an icebound city of the future, citizens play a death game and a survivor hunts down a killer who plays for real.
Dismayingly pretentious claptrap which did its star's career no good at all.

w Frank Barhydt, Robert Altman, Patricia Resnick d Robert Altman ph Jean Boffety m Tom Pierson pd Leon Ericksen

Paul Newman, Vittorio Gassman, Fernando Rey, Bibi Andersson, Brigitte Fossey, Nina Van Pallandt

Quo Vadis**
US 1951   171m   Technicolor
MGM (Sam Zimbalist)
A Roman commander under Nero falls in love with a Christian girl and jealous Poppea has them both thrown to the lions.

Spectacular but stagey and heavy-handed Hollywood version of a much-filmed colossus which shares much of its plot line with *The Sign of the Cross*. Three hours of solemn tedium with flashes of vigorous acting and a few set pieces to take the eye; but the sermonizing does not take away the bad taste of the emphasis on physical brutality.

w John Lee Mahin, S. N. Behrman, Sonya Levien *d* Mervyn Le Roy *ph* Robert Surtees, William V. Skall *m* Miklos Rozsa *ad* Cedric Gibbons, Edward Carfagno, William Horning

Robert Taylor, Deborah Kerr, *Peter Ustinov, Leo Genn, Patricia Laffan*, Finlay Currie, Abraham Sofaer, Marina Berti, Buddy Baer, Felix Aylmer, Nora Swinburne, Ralph Truman, Norman Wooland

'In making this film, MGM feel privileged to add something of permanent value to the cultural treasure house of mankind . . .'— *publicity*

'Ancient Rome is going to the dogs, Robert Taylor is going to the lions, and Peter Ustinov is going crazy!'—*publicity*

AAN: best picture; Robert Surtees, William V. Skall; Miklos Rozsa; Peter Ustinov; Leo Genn

R

RPM (Revolutions Per Minute)
US 1970   97m   colour
Columbia / Stanley Kramer

At an American college, a middle-aged
professor teaches liberal ideas.
Dim, thankfully forgotten addition to the
Strawberry Statement cycle.

w Erich Segal *d* Stanley Kramer *ph* Michel
Hugo, Perry Botkin Jnr *m* Barry de Vorzon

Anthony Quinn, Ann-Margret, Gary
Lockwood, Paul Winfield, Alan Hewitt

Rabbit, Run
US 1970   94m   Technicolor   Panavision
Warner

A man leaves his pregnant wife for a
prostitute.
Uninteresting sex melodrama without any of
the wit which distinguishes the book; hard to
sit through.

w Howard B. Kreitsek, *novel* John Updike
d Jack Smight *ph* Philip Lathrop *m* Ray
Burton, Brian King

James Caan, Anjanette Comer, Arthur Hill,
Jack Albertson, Carrie Snodgress

The Rabbit Trap*
US 1959   76m   bw
UA / Canon (Harry Kleiner)

A hardworking draughtsman finally defies his
boss and completes his holiday with his family.
Watchable minor drama just about marking
the end of Hollywood's infatuation with TV
plays which had begun with *Marty*; the moral
and family problems of ordinary people were
beginning to prove a shade lacking in
excitement.

w J. P. Miller, from his TV play *d* Philip
Leacock *ph* Irving Glassberg *m* Jack
Marshall

Ernest Borgnine, Bethel Leslie, David Brian,
Kevin Corcoran

Race with the Devil
US 1975   88m   De Luxe
TCF / Saber / Maslansky (Wes Bishop)

Holidaymakers witness a black mass and are
pursued by the diabolists.

Silly melodrama which resolves into a wild car
chase and much violence.

w Lee Frost, Wes Bishop *d* Jack Starrett
ph Robert Jessup *m* Leonard Rosenman

Peter Fonda, Warren Oates, Loretta Swit,
Lara Parker, R. G. Armstrong

The Racers
US 1955   112m   De Luxe   Cinemascope
TCF (Julian Blaustein)
GB title: *Such Men Are Dangerous*

A Monte Carlo Rally contestant is financed by
an attractive lady gambler.
Routine racing car melodrama, totally
unmemorable but impersonally efficient.

w Charles Kaufman, *novel* Hans Ruesch
d Henry Hathaway *ph* Joe MacDonald
m Alex North

Kirk Douglas, Bella Darvi, Gilbert Roland,
Cesar Romero, Lee J. Cobb, Katy Jurado,
Charles Goldner, George Dolenz

Rachel and the Stranger*
US 1948   92m   bw
RKO (Richard H. Berger)

A western farmer feels real love for his wife
for the first time when an attractive stranger
seems likely to take her away from him.
Modestly appealing romantic drama in a
western setting.

w Martin Rackin, *novel* Howard Fast
d Norman Foster *ph* Maury Gertsman
m Roy Webb *md* Constantin Bakaleinikoff

Loretta Young, Robert Mitchum, William
Holden, Gary Gray, Tom Tully, Sara Haden,
Frank Ferguson

Rachel, Rachel**
US 1968   101m   Eastmancolor
Warner / Kayos (Paul Newman)

Events in the life of a middle-aged
schoolmistress in a small New England town.
Appealing and freshly observed study of a
limited personality in a small community.

w Stewart Stern, *novel* A Jest of God by
Margaret Laurence *d* Paul Newman
ph Gayne Rescher *m* Jerome Moross

Joanne Woodward, Estelle Parsons, James Olson, Kate Harrington, Donald Moffat, Geraldine Fitzgerald, Bernard Barrow

'It could all very easily degenerate into a woman's weepy; and the fact that it doesn't is due largely to Newman's refusal to treat Manawaka as another Peyton Place.'—*Jan Dawson*

'It tends to verge on dullness, but something always saves it.'—*John Simon*

AAN: best picture; Stewart Stern; Joanne Woodward; Estelle Parsons

The Rack
US 1956   100m   bw
MGM (Arthur M. Loew Jnr)

A veteran of the Korean War is courtmartialled for collaborating with the enemy under torture.
Dullish courtroom melodrama overstretched from a TV play.

w Stewart Stern   *TV play* Rod Serling
d Arnold Laven   *ph* Paul Vogel   *m* Adolph Deutsch

Paul Newman, Walter Pidgeon, Edmond O'Brien, Lee Marvin, Cloris Leachman, Wendell Corey

The Racket*
US 1951   88m   bw
RKO / Edmund Grainger

Police break up the empire of a powerful gangster.
Oddly timed and rather weak remake of the 1928 film; glossy but very old-fashioned in treatment.

w William Wister Haines, *play* Bartlett Cormack   *d* John Cromwell   *ph* George E. Diskant   *m* Constantin Bakaleinikoff

Robert Ryan, Robert Mitchum, Ray Collins, Lizabeth Scott, William Talman

Radio Parade of 1935
GB 1934   96m   bw with colour sequence

Amateur talent makes it big for a radio station. Historically interesting revue which unfortunately requires its comic lead to play straight. Will Hay, Helen Chandler, Clifford Mollison, Davy Burnaby, The Western Brothers, Alfred Drayton, Lily Morris, Nellie Wallace, Clapham and Dwyer, Claude Dampier, Ronald Frankau, Ted Ray, Beryl Orde, Stanelli. Written by Jack Davies, Paul Perez, Arthur Woods and James Bunting; directed by Arthur Woods; for BIP.

Rafferty and the Gold Dust Twins
US 1975   92m   Technicolor   Panavision
Warner / Gruskoff-Venture-Linson

A drifter encounters two female vagrants who force him at gunpoint to drive them to New Orleans and get him into various adventures. Indulgent and unattractive 'road' movie which despite occasional amusing incident gets nowhere very slowly.

w John Kaye   *d* Dick Richards   *ph* Ralph Woolsey   *m* Artie Butler

Alan Arkin, Sally Kellerman, MacKenzie Phillips, Alex Rocco, Charlie Martin Smith, Harry Dean Stanton, John McLiam

Raffles*
US 1940   72m   bw
Samuel Goldwyn

Raffles the famous cricketer is also a compulsive and daring amateur thief. Slight, modernized version of the turn-of-the-century stories; very palatable, but it could have been better.

w John Van Druten, Sydney Howard, *novel* Raffles the Amateur Cracksman by E. W. Hornung   *d* Sam Wood   *ph* Gregg Toland   *m* Victor Young

David Niven, Olivia de Havilland, *Dudley Digges*, May Whitty, Douglas Walton, Lionel Pape, E. E. Clive, Peter Godfrey
† This was virtually a scene-for-scene remake of the 1930 Goldwyn version starring Ronald Colman, Kay Francis and Alison Skipworth. It was written by Sidney Howard and directed by George Fitzmaurice.

Rage
US 1966   103m   Technicolor
Columbia / Joseph M. Schenck / Cinematografico Jalisco (Gilberto Gazcon)

A drunken doctor finds a new will to live during a difficult journey to avert a rabies epidemic.
Pattern melodrama with no surprises, but gripping most of the way.

w Teddi Sherman, Gilberto Gazcon, Fernando Mendez   *d* Gilberto Gazcon   *ph* Rosalio Solano   *m* Gustavo Cesar Carreon

Glenn Ford, Stella Stevens, David Reynoso, Armando Silvestre

Rage
US 1972   99m   De Luxe   Panavision
Warner (Fred Weintraub)

A father takes revenge when his son dies after a chemical warfare accident.
Well-meaning but turgid and boring melodrama.

w Philip Friedman, Dan Kleinman *d* George C. Scott *ph* Fred Koenekamp *m* Lalo Schifrin .

George C. Scott, Richard Basehart, Martin Sheen, Barnard Hughes, Stephen Young
'Sluggish, tired and tiring.'—*Variety*

Rage at Dawn
US 1955 86m Technicolor

Detectives stage a fake train robbery to attract the evil Reno brothers. Very moderate western programmer. Randolph Scott, Forrest Tucker, J. Carrol Naish, Mala Powers, Edgar Buchanan, Ray Teal. Written by Horace McCoy; directed by Tim Whelan; for Nat Holt / RKO.

Rage in Heaven
US 1941 82m bw
MGM (Gottfried Reinhardt)

An unstable millionaire becomes jealous of his wife and arranges his own death so that her supposed lover will be suspected.
Stilted melodrama with the stars more or less at sea.

w Christopher Isherwood, Robert Thoeren, *novel* James Hilton *d* W. S. Van Dyke II *ph* Oliver T. Marsh *m* Bronislau Kaper

Robert Montgomery, Ingrid Bergman, George Sanders, Lucile Watson, Oscar Homolka, Philip Merivale, Matthew Boulton, Aubrey Mather
'Nothing happens but the obvious, and that only after a long and confused struggle.'—*Otis Ferguson*

The Rage of Paris*
US 1938 78m bw
Universal (B. G. De Sylva)

Confidence tricksters invest their money in a French girl who is out to nail a millionaire.
If memory serves right, an amusingly amoral trifle in the best style of its year.

w Bruce Manning, Felix Jackson *d* Henry Koster

Danielle Darrieux, Douglas Fairbanks Jnr, Louis Hayward, Mischa Auer, Helen Broderick, Harry Davenport, Samuel S. Hinds, Mary Martin (in a bit part)

A Rage to Live
US 1965 101m bw Panavision
UA / Mirisch (Lewis J. Rachmil)

The unhappy college and married life of a nymphomaniac.
Well made but deliberately 'daring' case history which becomes too obvious and silly.

w John T. Kelley, *novel* John O'Hara *d* Walter Grauman *ph* Charles Lawton *m* Nelson Riddle

Suzanne Pleshette, Bradford Dillman, Ben Gazzara, Peter Graves, Bethel Leslie, James Gregory, Ruth White
'Stuff like this needs the exuberance of grand opera; sadly, all it gets here is a blue note.'—*MFB*

Raggedy Ann and Andy*
US 1977 85m Movielab Panavision
Lester Osterman (Richard Horner)

Toys come to life and have their own adventures while their owner is absent.
Attractive fully animated cartoon feature in which only the central story is lacking in pace and humour.

w Patricia Thackray, Max Wilk, *stories* Johnny Gruelle *d Richard Williams*

Raging Bull*
US 1980 119m colour
UA / Chartoff-Winkler

The rise to fame of an unlikeable middle-weight boxer, based on the autobiography of Jake La Motta.
Powerfully made but very violent and alienating ringside melodrama.

w Paul Schrader, Mardik Martin *d Martin Scorsese* *ph* Michael Chapman *m* from library sources *pd* Gene Rudolf

Robert De Niro, Cathy Moriarty, Joe Pesci, Frank Vincent, Nicholas Colasanto
'Scorsese makes pictures about the kind of people you wouldn't want to know.'—*Variety*
AA: editing (Thelma Schoonmaker); Robert De Niro
AAN: best film; best direction; Cathy Moriarty; Joe Pesci
BFA: editing

The Raging Moon*
GB 1970 111m Technicolor
EMI (Bruce Cohn Curtis)
aka: *Long Ago Tomorrow*

A love affair develops between two inmates of a home for the physically handicapped.
Appealing romantic drama which nearly became a big commercial success.

wd Bryan Forbes, novel Peter Marshall *ph* Tony Imi *m* Stanley Myers

Malcolm McDowell, Nanette Newman, Georgia Brown, Bernard Lee, Gerald Sim, Michael Flanders

The Raging Tide
US 1951 93m bw
U-I (Aaron Rosenberg)

A San Francisco gangster stows away on a
fishing trawler and redeems himself when he
perishes saving the life of a fisherman.
Fearfully old-fashioned seafaring melodrama,
rather well made.

w Ernest K. Gann, from his novel Fiddler's
Green d George Sherman ph Russell Metty
m Frank Skinner

Richard Conte, Charles Bickford, Shelley
Winters, Stephen McNally, Alex Nicol, Jesse
White, John McIntire

The Ragman's Daughter
GB 1972 94m Technicolor
TCF / Penelope (Harold Becker)

A Nottingham layabout falls in love with an
exciting middle-class girl; they fail to
overcome parental opposition and she is killed
in a road accident.
Wispy drama framed in pointless flashbacks;
done on the cheap, it never seems to get
anywhere and even fails to use its locations to
advantage.

w Alan Sillitoe, from his short story d Harold
Becker ph Michael Seresin m Kenny Clayton

Simon Rouse, Victoria Tennant, Patrick
O'Connell, Leslie Sands

The Raid*
US 1954 83m Technicolor
TCF (Robert L. Jacks)

In 1864 six confederate soldiers escape from a
union prison, and from a Canadian refuge
carry out a revenge raid on a small Vermont
town.
Interesting little action drama, crisply
characterized and plotted, and based on a
historical incident.

w Sidney Boehm, story Affair at St Albans by
Herbert Ravenal Sass d Hugo Fregonese
ph Lucien Ballard m Roy Webb

Van Heflin, Anne Bancroft, Richard Boone,
Lee Marvin, Tommy Rettig, Peter Graves,
Douglas Spencer, Will Wright, John Dierkes

Raid on Rommel
US 1971 99m Technicolor
Universal (Harry Tatelman)

In North Africa during World War II, a
British officer releases prisoners of war and
leads them in an assault on Tobruk.
Dispirited low-budget actioner apparently first
intended for television.

w Richard Bluel d Henry Hathaway ph Earl
Rath m Hal Mooney

Richard Burton, John Colicos, Clinton Greyn,
Wolfgang Preiss

The Raiders
US 1964 75m Technicolor

Cattle drovers enlist the aid of famous western
characters to persuade the railroad company
to extend its line through dangerous country.
Slightly oddball western with endearing
moments amid the miscalculations. Robert
Culp (as Wild Bill Hickok), Judi Meredith (as
Calamity Jane), James McMullan (as Buffalo
Bill Cody). Brian Keith, Alfred Ryder, Simon
Oakland. Written by Gene L. Coon; directed
by Herschel Daugherty; for Revue /
Universal.

Rails into Laramie
US 1954 81m Technicolor

Railway construction is hampered in Laramie
by a saloon keeper who keeps the workers too
happy. Solid co-feature western, quite
enjoyable. John Payne, Dan Duryea, Mari
Blanchard, Barton Maclane, Harry Shannon,
Lee Van Cleef. Written by D. D. Beauchamp
and Joseph Hoffman; directed by Jesse Hibbs;
for Universal-International.

The Railway Children***
GB 1970 108m Technicolor
EMI (Robert Lynn)

Three Edwardian children and their mother
move into Yorkshire when their father is
imprisoned as a spy, and have adventures on
the railway line while helping to prove his
innocence.
Fresh and agreeable family film with many
pleasing touches to compensate for its
meandering plot.

wd Lionel Jeffries, novel E. Nesbit ph Arthur
Ibbetson m Johnny Douglas

Dinah Sheridan, William Mervyn, Jenny
Agutter, Bernard Cribbins, Iain Cuthbertson,
Gary Warren, Sally Thomsett

Rain*
US 1932 92m bw
(UA)

Stranded passengers in Pago Pago during an
epidemic include a prostitute and a missionary
who lusts after her.
Early talkie version of a much filmed story;
interesting but not very entertaining now that
the sensational aspects have worn off.

w Maxwell Anderson, *play* John Colton, Clemence Randolph, *story* W. Somerset Maugham d Lewis Milestone *ph* Oliver T. Marsh *m* Alfred Newman

Joan Crawford, Walter Huston, William Gargan, Beulah Bondi, Matt Moore, Guy Kibbee, Walter Catlett

† Other versions: *Sadie Thompson* (1928) with Gloria Swanson; *Miss Sadie Thompson* (1953) (qv).

The Rain People
US 1969 101m Technicolor
Warner / American Zoetrope (Bart Patton, Ronald Colby)

A depressed housewife leaves home, drives across country, and picks up a mentally retarded hitch-hiker who tries to protect her.
Slow, pretentious character drama which strains after art but only presents an unedifying study of failure.

wd Francis Ford Coppola *ph* Wilmer Butler *m* Ronald Stein

Shirley Knight, James Caan, Robert Duvall, Tom Aldredge, Marya Zimmet
'The rain people are people made of rain and when they cry they disappear because they cry themselves away.'—*sample dialogue*

Rainbow Island
US 1944 95m Technicolor
Paramount (I. D. Leshin)

A white girl brought up by her doctor father on a Pacific island is pursued by three sailors escaping from the Japanese.
Cheerful spoof of the sarong cycle with the star seeing the joke; otherwise a silly service farce with South Sea trimmings.

w Walter de Leon, Seena Owen, Arthur Phillips *d* Ralph Murphy *ph* Karl Struss *m* Roy Webb

Dorothy Lamour, Eddie Bracken, Gil Lamb, Barry Sullivan, Forrest Orr, Anne Revere, Reed Hadley, Marc Lawrence

The Rainbow Jacket
GB 1954 99m Technicolor
Ealing (Michael Relph)

A boy jockey is blackmailed into losing a big race.
Disappointing racecourse drama which packs in all the expected ingredients.

w T. E. B. Clarke *d* Basil Dearden *ph* Otto Heller *m* William Alwyn

Kay Walsh, Bill Owen, Edward Underdown, Robert Morley, Wilfrid Hyde White, Charles Victor, Honor Blackman, Sidney James

The Rainmaker
US 1956 121m Technicolor
 Vistavision
Paramount / Hal B. Wallis (Paul Nathan)

In 1913 Kansas, a fake rainmaker has more success melting the heart of a confirmed spinster.
Such a whimsical play is too talky to make a good movie, especially as the actors are over-age, their performances are mannered, the dialogue seems interminable and the production is too stagey.

w N. Richard Nash, from his play *d* Joseph Anthony *ph* Charles Lang Jnr *m* Alex North

Katharine Hepburn, Burt Lancaster, Wendell Corey, Lloyd Bridges, Earl Holliman, Cameron Prud'homme, Wallace Ford

AAN: Alex North; Katharine Hepburn

The Rains Came***
US 1939 103m bw
TCF (Darryl F. Zanuck)

High-class parasites in India during the Raj redeem themselves when a flood disaster strikes.
Wholly absorbing disaster spectacular in which the characterization and personal plot development are at least as interesting as the spectacle, and all are encased in a glowingly professional production.

w Philip Dunne, Julien Josephson, *novel* Louis Bromfield *d* Clarence Brown *ph* Arthur Miller *m* Alfred Newman *sp* Fred Sersen

Myrna Loy, *George Brent*, Tyrone Power, Brenda Joyce, *Maria Ouspenskaya, Joseph Schildkraut*, H. B. Warner, Nigel Bruce, Mary Nash, Jane Darwell, Marjorie Rambeau, Henry Travers
'It would be difficult to improve on the direction, the outbreak of the monsoon, a curtain billowing in the breeze, a lamp casting the shadow of lattice work against white silk, servants scattering for cover . . .'—*Charles Higham, 1972*

AAN: Alfred Newman

The Rains of Ranchipur
US 1955 104m Eastmancolor
 Cinemascope
TCF (Frank Ross)

Dismal remake of *The Rains Came*, with bored actors and inferior production, all the character of the original being wiped out by badly processed wide-screen spectacle.

w Merle Miller *d* Jean Negulesco *ph* Milton Krasner *m* Hugo Friedhofer

Lana Turner, Fred MacMurray, Richard
Burton, Joan Caulfield, Eugenie Leontovich,
Michael Rennie

Raintree County
US 1958   166m   Technicolor
   Panavision (Camera 65)
MGM (David Lewis)

During the Civil War a southern belle gets the
man she thinks she wants, but subsequently
finds life as a schoolmaster's wife boring.

Dreary attempt by MGM to out-do *Gone with
the Wind*, with neither characters nor plot one
third as interesting and the production values
merely expensive.

w Millard Kaufman, *novel* Ross Lockridge
d Edward Dmytryk ph Robert Surtees
m Johnny Green

Montgomery Clift, Elizabeth Taylor, Eva
Marie Saint, Nigel Patrick, Lee Marvin, Rod
Taylor, Agnes Moorehead, Walter Abel,
Jarma Lewis, Tom Drake, Gardner McKay,
Rhys Williams

AAN: Johnny Green; Elizabeth Taylor

Raise the Roof
GB 1930   77m   bw

An actress is bribed to sabotage a touring
show. Early talkie which retains surprising
freshness. Betty Balfour, Maurice Evans, Jack
Raine, Sam Livesey, Ellis Jeffreys. Writer
uncredited; directed by Walter Summers; for
BIP.

Raise the Titanic!
US 1980   122m   De Luxe
Lord Grade / Martin Starger (William Frye)

Assorted Americans try to recover rare
minerals from the wreck of the ship which
sank in the North Atlantic in 1912.
Heavy-going exploiter with little action and
even less plot.

w Adam Kennedy, Eric Hughes, *novel* Clive
Cussler d Jerry Jameson ph Matthew F.
Leonetti *second unit ph* Rex Metz *underwater
ph* Bob Steadman m John Barry pd John F.
DeCuir

Jason Robards, Richard Jordan, Alec
Guinness, David Selby, Anne Archer, J. D.
Cannon

'Hits new depths hitherto unexplored by the
worst of Lew Grade's overloaded ark
melodramas. This one wastes a potentially
intriguing premise with dull scripting, a
lacklustre cast, laughably phony trick work
and clunky direction that makes *Voyage of the
Damned* seem inspired by comparison.'—
Variety

A Raisin in the Sun*
US 1961   128m   bw
Columbia / Paman—Doris (David Susskind,
   Philip Rose)

The life of a struggling black family in a
cramped Chicago flat.
Earnest but claustrophobic play-on-film which
long outstays its welcome but contains good
performances.

w *Lorraine Hansberry*, from her play
d Daniel Petrie ph Charles Lawton Jnr
m Laurence Rosenthal

Sidney Poitier, Ruby Dee, Claudia McNeil,
Diana Sands, Ivan Dixon, John Fielder, Lou
Gossett

Raising the Wind
GB 1961   91m   colour

Misadventures of students at a music academy.
A Carry On in all but name, from the same
stable; good moments among the dross. James
Robertson Justice, Leslie Phillips, Kenneth
Williams, Sidney James, Paul Massie, Liz
Fraser, Eric Barker, Jennifer Jayne, Geoffrey
Keen, Esma Cannon. Written by Bruce
Montgomery; directed by Gerald Thomas; for
GHW / Anglo Amalgamated.

The Rake's Progress*
GB 1945   123m   bw
GFD / Individual (Frank Launder, Sidney
   Gilliat)
US title: *Notorious Gentleman*

The career of a cheerful ne'er-do-well playboy
of the thirties.
The road to ruin played for light comedy, with
silly endpapers in which, quite out of
character, the rake becomes a war hero.
Generally good production, witty script.

w Frank Launder, Sidney Gilliat, *story* Val
Valentine d Sidney Gilliat ph Wilkie
Cooper m William Alwyn pd David
Rawnsley

Rex Harrison, Lilli Palmer, Margaret
Johnston, Godfrey Tearle, Griffith Jones, Guy
Middleton, Jean Kent, Marie Lohr, Garry
Marsh, David Horne, Alan Wheatley

Rally Round the Flag Boys
US 1958   106m   De Luxe   Cinemascope
TCF (Leo McCarey)

A small community protests at the siting
nearby of a missile base.
Raucous service and sex comedy which
becomes frenetic without ever being very
funny.

w Claude Binyon, Leo McCarey, *novel* Max Shulman *d* Leo McCarey *ph* Leon Shamroy *m* Cyril Mockridge

Paul Newman, Joanne Woodward, Joan Collins, Jack Carson, Dwayne Hickman, Tuesday Weld, Gale Gordon, Murvyn Vye

Ramona
US 1936   90m   Technicolor
TCF (Sol M. Wurtzel)

A half-breed girl and an Indian chief's son combat the greed of white pioneers.
Old-fashioned, stuffy adventure romance, much filmed in silent days.

w Lamar Trotti, *novel* Helen Hunt Jackson *d* Henry King *ph* William Skall, Chester Lyons *m* Alfred Newman

Loretta Young, Don Ameche, Kent Taylor, Pauline Frederick, Jane Darwell, Katherine de Mille, Victor Kilian, John Carradine

Rampage
US 1963   98m   Technicolor
Warner Seven Arts / Talbot (William Fadiman)

Two white hunters love the same girl; one releases a tiger to harm the other, but it escapes.
Silly, unconvincing, old-style melodrama in which even the animals seem to overact.

w Robert Holt, Marguerite Roberts, *novel* Alan Caillou *d* Phil Karlson *ph* Harold Lipstein *m* Elmer Bernstein

Robert Mitchum, Jack Hawkins, Elsa Martinelli, Sabu, Emile Genest

Ramrod
US 1947   94m   bw
UA (Harry Sherman)

A predatory lady ranch owner hires a tough foreman and her ruthlessness causes several deaths and a stampede.
Ho-hum minor western with fading stars.

w Jack Moffit, Graham Baker, Cecile Kramer, *story* Luke Short *d* André de Toth *ph* Russell Harlan *m* Adolph Deutsch

Veronica Lake, Joel McCrea, Preston Foster, Charles Ruggles, Donald Crisp, Arleen Whelan, Lloyd Bridges

Rancho De Luxe
US 1974   95m   De Luxe
UA / EK (Anthony Ray)

Cheerful cattle rustlers go on a binge and end up in prison.
Modern anti-everything western; it's anti-entertainment as well.

w Thomas McGuane *d* Frank Perry *ph* William A. Fraker *m* Jimmy Buffett

Sam Waterston, Jeff Bridges, Elizabeth Ashley, Charlene Dallas, Clifton James, Slim Pickens

Rancho Notorious
US 1952   89m   Technicolor
RKO / Fidelity (Howard Welsch)

A cowboy seeking revenge for his girl friend's murder follows a clue to a lonely ranch run by a saloon singer.
Curious western which seems to have been intended as another *Destry Rides Again* but is made in a hard inflexible style which prevents it from appealing.

w Daniel Taradash *d* Fritz Lang *ph* Hal Mohr *m* Emil Newman

Marlene Dietrich, Arthur Kennedy, Mel Ferrer, Gloria Henry, William Frawley, Jack Elam

'Every quality you might ask of a western is in lavish supply—except entertainment value.'—*Alton Cook*

Random Harvest***
US 1942   126m   bw
MGM (Sidney Franklin)

A shell-shocked officer in the 1914–18 war escapes from an asylum, marries a music hall singer and is idyllically happy until a shock makes him remember that he is the head of a noble family. His wife, whom he does not now remember, dutifully becomes his secretary and years later another shock brings memory and happiness back.
A silly enough story works remarkably well in this rather splendid, no holds barred, roses round the door romance in Hollywood's best style with incomparable stars. A triumph of the Peg's Paper syndrome, and hugely enjoyable because it is done so enthusiastically.

w Claudine West, George Froeschel, Arthur Wimperis, *novel* James Hilton *d* Mervyn Le Roy *ph* Joseph Ruttenberg *m* Herbert Stothart

Ronald Colman, Greer Garson, Susan Peters, Philip Dorn, Reginald Owen, Henry Travers, Margaret Wycherly, Bramwell Fletcher, Arthur Margetson

'I would like to recommend this film to those who can stay interested in Ronald Colman's amnesia for two hours and who could with pleasure eat a bowl of Yardley's shaving soap for breakfast.'—*James Agee*

'A strangely empty film . . . its characters are creatures of fortune, not partisans in determining their own fates.'—*Bosley Crowther, New York Times*

'It is cast with pearly players in every part. Its pedigreed plot is savoured with just the right mixture of ups and downs, ecstasy and well-bred anguish, implausibility and psyche. And it moves towards its climax with the measured tread and nicely timed emotional bumps of a Hearst Cosmopolitan serial. It is perhaps the clearest example of the year of how a studio possessing lion's shares of movie-making capital and ingratiating talent can mate these two to synthesize a magnificent neuter, which will predictably bring in vast box office returns with which to produce more neuters.'—*John McManus, PM*

AAN: best picture; script; Mervyn Le Roy; Herbert Stothart; Ronald Colman; Susan Peters

Ransom*
US 1955   104m   bw
MGM (Nicholas Nayfack)

A rich man takes desperate measures to rescue his son from a kidnapper.
Solid but overlong suspenser, virtually a vehicle for a star at his twitchiest and most dogged.

w Cyril Hume, Richard Maibaum *d* Alex Segal *ph* Arthur E. Arling *m* Jeff Alexander

Glenn Ford, Donna Reed, Leslie Nielsen, Juano Hernandez, Robert Keith
'He faced a decision that someday may be yours to make!'—*publicity*

Ransom*
GB 1975   98m   Eastmancolor
Lion International (Peter Rawley)
aka: *The Terrorists*

A British ambassador to Scandinavia is kidnapped by terrorists and a Norwegian security chief gives chase.
Topical but unconvincing action thriller with unfamiliar detail; builds up to exciting sequences but is quickly forgotten.

w Paul Wheeler *d* Caspar Wrede *ph* Sven Nykvist *m* Jerry Goldsmith

Sean Connery, Ian McShane, Norman Bristow, John Cording, Isabel Dean, William Fox, Robert Harris

Rapture
US / France 1965   104m   bw
International Classics / TCF (Christian Ferry)

A mentally unstable girl has a tragic romance with a fugitive murderer.
Gloomy all the way, and if it's art it needs explaining.

w Stanley Mann, *novel* Rapture in My Rags by Phyllis Hastings *d* John Guillermin *ph* Marcel Grignon

Patricia Gozzi, Dean Stockwell, Melvyn Douglas, Gunnel Lindblom

The Rare Breed
US 1966   97m   Technicolor   Panavision
Universal (William Alland)

An English bull is taken by its woman owner to St Louis to breed with American longhorns, and various frictions are caused among the ranchers.
Amusing western idea which misses fire by not coming down firmly as either drama or comedy; it does however pass the time amiably enough.

w Ric Hardman *d* Andrew V. McLaglen *ph* William H. Clothier *m* Johnny Williams

James Stewart, Maureen O'Hara, Brian Keith, Juliet Mills, Don Galloway, David Brian, Jack Elam, Ben Johnson

Rashomon***
Japan 1951   83m   bw
Daiei
aka: *In the Woods*

In medieval Japan, four people have different versions of a violent incident when a bandit attacks a nobleman in the forest.
Indescribably vivid in itself, and genuinely strange (one of the versions is told by a ghost), *Rashomon* reintroduced Japanese films to the world market and was remade (badly) in Hollywood as *The Outrage*.

wd Akira Kurosawa, *story* Inside a Bush by Ryunosuke Akutagawa *ph* Kazuo Matsuyama *m* Takashi Matsuyama

Toshiro Mifune, Machiko Kyo, Masayuki Mori, Takashi Shimura
'A masterpiece, and a revelation.'—*Gavin Lambert, MFB*
AA: best foreign film

Raskolnikov*
Germany 1923   80m approx (at 24 fps)
bw   silent
Neumann (Robert Wiene)

A student kills a pawnbroker and is hounded by a police inspector until he confesses.
Interesting adaptation of *Crime and Punishment* with some of the expressionist aspects of the same director's *The Cabinet of Dr Caligari*.

wd Robert Wiene ph Willy Godberger
ad Andre Andreyev

Gregory Khmara, Michael Tarkhanov, Pavel
Pavlov, Vera Toma

Rasputin and the Empress*
US 1932   133m   bw
MGM (Irving Thalberg)
GB title: *Rasputin the Mad Monk*

The story of the last years of the Russian
court, when a sinister monk gained influence
over the empress.

An unhappy film which was besieged by
lawsuits and never generated much drama of
its own despite starring the three Barrymores,
who all seemed to be acting in separate rooms.
Production values are the most impressive
thing about it.

w Charles MacArthur *d* Richard Boleslawski
ph William Daniels *m* Herbert Stothart

John Barrymore, Ethel Barrymore, Lionel
Barrymore, Diana Wynyard, Ralph Morgan,
C. Henry Gordon, Edward Arnold, Jean
Parker, Gustav Von Seyffertitz, Anne Shirley
(Dawn O'Day)

AAN: Charles MacArthur

The Rat*
GB 1937   72m   bw

A Parisian thief takes the blame for murder,
but is saved by the socialite who loves him.
Rather smart talkie version of a well-worn
theatrical hit, previously filmed in 1925 as a
silent, with Ivor Novello as star. Anton
Walbrook, Ruth Chatterton, Rene Ray,
Beatrix Lehmann, Felix Aylmer, Mary Clare.
Written by Hans Rameau, Marjorie Gaffney,
Miles Malleson and Romney Brent, from the
play by Ivor Novello and Constance Collier;
directed by Jack Raymond; for Herbert
Wilcox.

The Rat Race*
US 1960   105m   Technicolor
Paramount / Perlberg–Seaton

A young jazz musician and a dance hall
hostess share a flat and face the adversities of
New York.

A kind of sour fairy tale of the big city which
has neither enough jokes nor enough incident
but purveys the kind of charm that grows on
one despite oneself.

w Garson Kanin, from his play *d* Robert
Mulligan *ph* Robert Burks *m* Elmer
Bernstein

Tony Curtis, Debbie Reynolds, Jack Oakie,
Kay Medford, Don Rickles

'The New Yorkers of *The Rat Race* – noisy
soft-hearted landlady, philosophical bartender,
backchatting taxi driver – are as familiar as the
settings of shabby apartment house and quiet
little bar across the street. Film makers no
longer need to invent here – they simply move
in for a few weeks.'—*Penelope Houston*

Rationing
US 1943   93m   bw

A small-town shopkeeper is frustrated by
wartime restrictions. Amiable comedy for
established stars. Wallace Beery, Majorie
Main, Donald Meek, Howard Freeman,
Connie Gilchrist. Written by William Lipman,
Grant Garrett and Harry Ruskin; directed by
Willis Goldbeck; for MGM.

Raton Pass
US 1951   84m   bw

A greedy wife swindles her husband out of his
share in their ranch. Unusual western
melodrama; quite entertaining. Dennis
Morgan, Patricia Neal, Steve Cochran, Scott
Forbes, Dorothy Hart. Written by Tom
Blackburn and James Webb; directed by
Edwin L. Marin; for Warner. (GB title:
Canyon Pass.)

Rattle of a Simple Man
GB 1964   95m   bw
Sydney Box (William Gell)

A shy football supporter in London spends the
night with a tart for a bet.
Archetypal farcical situation with sentiment
added to string it out to twice its proper
length. Production values modest but
adequate.

w Charles Dyer, from his play *d* Muriel Box
ph Reg Wyer *m* Stanley Black

Harry H. Corbett, *Diane Cilento,* Thora Hird,
Charles Dyer

The Raven*
US 1935   61m   bw
Universal

A doctor obsessed by Poe-inspired torture
devices transforms a gangster on the run into a
hideous mutant.
Silly but quite effective horror film with
memorable sequences.

w David Boehm *d* Lew Landers *ph* Charles
Stumar *md* Gilbert Kurland

Bela Lugosi, Boris Karloff, Samuel S. Hinds,
Irene Ware, Lester Matthews

The Raven*
US 1963   86m   Pathecolor   Panavision
AIP / Alta Vista (Roger Corman)

Two 15th-century conjurors fight a deadly duel of magic.

The rather splendid duel is a long time coming; the preliminaries are largely confined to chat in a single set, and the random jokes do not quite atone for the boredom.

w Richard Matheson *d* Roger Corman *ph* Floyd Crosby *m* Les Baxter

Vincent Price, Peter Lorre, Boris Karloff, Hazel Court, Jack Nicholson

Raw Edge
US 1956 76m Technicolor

A convict escapes and seeks revenge on the gang that sent him up. Tense, fairly adult western. Rory Calhoun, Yvonne de Carlo, Mara Corday, Rex Reason, Neville Brand. Written by Harry Essex and Robert Hill; directed by John Sherwood; for Universal-International.

Raw Deal
US 1948 78m bw

A convict is helped by his girl friend to escape, and the police chase them across country. Fairly violent crime melodrama which holds the attention. Dennis O'Keefe, Claire Trevor, Marsha Hunt, John Ireland, Raymond Burr. Written by Leopold Atlas and John C. Higgins; directed by Anthony Mann; for Reliance / Eagle Lion.

Raw Wind in Eden
US 1958 93m Eastmancolor
Cinemascope
U-I (William Alland)

A model is stranded on a Sardinian island, and falls in love with a mysterious American who turns out to be a disillusioned millionaire. Wish-fulfilment woman's picture with the occasional relief of a smart line.

w Elizabeth and Richard Wilson *d* Richard Wilson *ph* Enzo Serafin *m* Hans Salter

Esther Williams, Jeff Chandler, Carlos Thompson, Rossana Podesta, Eduardo de Filippo, Rik Battaglia

Rawhide**
US 1950 86m bw
TCF (Samuel G. Engel)
TV title: *Desperate Siege*

Four escaped convicts terrorize a stagecoach stop.

Good suspense western with excellent technical credits.

w Dudley Nichols *d* Henry Hathaway *ph* Milton Krasner *m* Sol Kaplan

Tyrone Power, Susan Hayward, Hugh Marlowe, Jack Elam, Dean Jagger, George Tobias, Edgar Buchanan, Jeff Corey

The Razor's Edge*
US 1946 146m bw
TCF (Darryl F. Zanuck)

A well-to-do young man spends the years between the wars first idling, then looking for essential truth.

The novel was an empty parable with amusing trimmings. In the film the trimmings seem less amusing, but the presentation is glossy.

w Lamar Trotti, *novel* W. Somerset Maugham *d* Edmund Goulding *ph* Arthur Miller *m* Alfred Newman *ad* Richard Day, Nathan Juran

Tyrone Power, Gene Tierney, *Clifton Webb, Herbert Marshall,* John Payne, Anne Baxter, Lucile Watson, Frank Latimore, Elsa Lanchester, Fritz Kortner

'I like Somerset Maugham when he's looking through keyholes or down cracks, not at vistas.'—*Richard Winnington*

AA: Anne Baxter
AAN: best picture; Clifton Webb

Reach for Glory*
GB 1962 86m bw
Columbia / Blazer (John Kohn, Jud Kinberg)

During World War II, evacuee boys play war games and a German refugee is accidentally killed.

Grim and unpalatable parable, competently rather than excitingly made.

w John Rae, from his novel The Custard Boys *d* Philip Leacock *ph* Bob Huke *m* Bob Russell

Kay Walsh, Harry Andrews, Michael Anderson Jnr, Oliver Grimm, Alexis Kanner, Martin Stephenson, Richard Vernon

Reach for the Sky*
GB 1956 135m bw
Rank / Pinnacle (Daniel M. Angel)

Douglas Bader loses both legs in a 1931 air crash, learns to walk on artificial limbs and flies again in World War II.

Box office exploitation of one man's personal heroism, adequately but not inspiringly put together with many stiff upper lips and much jocular humour.

wd Lewis Gilbert, *book* Paul Brickhill *ph* Jack Asher *m* John Addison

Kenneth More, Muriel Pavlow, Lyndon Brook, Lee Patterson, Alexander Knox, Dorothy Alison, Sydney Tafler, Howard Marion Crawford

Reaching for the Moon
US 1931   90m   bw
United Artists (Douglas Fairbanks)

On a transatlantic liner, a new cocktail has a sensational effect on a mild-mannered hero.
Very flimsy comedy with songs and some athletic stunts for its hero.

,wd Edmund Goulding *ph* Ray June
song Irving Berlin

Douglas Fairbanks, Bebe Daniels, Edward Everett Horton, Claud Allister, Jack Mulhall, Bing Crosby

Reaching for the Sun
US 1941   90m   bw

A clam digger who needs an outboard motor goes to work in a Detroit car plant. Easygoing comedy, too muted to recommend itself widely. Joel McCrea, Ellen Drew, Eddie Bracken, Albert Dekker. Written by W. L. River from a novel by Wessel Smitter; directed by William Wellman; for Paramount.

Ready Willing and Able
US 1937   93m   bw
Warner (Samuel Bischoff)

Two songwriters import an English leading lady for their new show.
Lightweight star musical with no outstanding qualities except a number in which girls dance on the keys of a huge typewriter.

w Sig Herzig, Jerry Wald, Warren Duff
d Ray Enright *ph* Sol Polito *ch* Bobby Connelly *songs* Johnny Mercer, Richard Whiting

Ruby Keeler, Ross Alexander, Lee Dixon, Wini Shaw, Jane Wyman, Allen Jenkins

The Real Glory*
US 1939   96m   bw
Samuel Goldwyn

Soldiers of fortune help the American Army to quell a terrorist uprising in the Philippines just after the Spanish-American War.
Well made Gunga Dinnery.

w Jo Swerling, Robert R. Presnell *d* Henry Hathaway *ph* Rudolph Maté *m* Alfred Newman *ad* James Basevi

Gary Cooper, David Niven, Broderick Crawford, Andrea Leeds, Reginald Owen, Kay Johnson, Russell Hicks, Vladimir Sokoloff

'The same sort of picture as *Gunga Din*.'— *Richard Mallett, Punch*
'Recommended to adolescents of all ages.'—*New Statesman*

'In times like these, we question the wisdom of rattling the bones in Yankee imperialism's closet.'—*Daily Worker*

Reap the Wild Wind**
US 1942   124m   Technicolor
Paramount / Cecil B. de Mille

Seafaring salvage engineers fight over a southern belle.
Georgia-set period adventure; intended as another *Gone with the Wind*, it simply doesn't have the necessary, but on its level it entertains solidly, climaxing with the famous giant squid fight.

w Alan le May, Jesse Lasky Jnr *d* Cecil B. de Mille *ph* Victor Milner, Dewey Wrigley, William V. Skall *m* Victor Young *ad* Hans Dreier, Roland Anderson

Ray Milland, John Wayne, *Paulette Goddard*, Raymond Massey, Robert Preston, Lynne Overman, Susan Hayward, Charles Bickford, Walter Hampden, Louise Beavers, Martha O'Driscoll, Hedda Hopper

'The essence of all his experience, the apogee of all his art, and as jamfull a motion picture as has ever played two hours upon a screen.'—*Howard Barnes, New York Herald Tribune*

AAN: photography

Rear Window***
US 1954   112m   Technicolor
Alfred Hitchcock

A news photographer, confined to his room by a broken leg, sees a murder committed in a room on the other side of the court.
Artificial but fairly gripping suspenser of an unusual kind; with such restricted settings, all depends on the script and the acting, and they generally come up trumps.

w John Michael Hayes, novel Cornell Woolrich *d Alfred Hitchcock ph* Robert Burks *m* Franz Waxman

James Stewart, Grace Kelly, Raymond Burr, Judith Evelyn, Wendell Corey, Thelma Ritter

AAN: John Michael Hayes; Alfred Hitchcock; Robert Burks

Rebecca****
US 1940   130m   bw
David O. Selznick

The naïve young second wife of a Cornish landowner is haunted by the image of his glamorous first wife Rebecca.
The supreme Hollywood entertainment package, set in Monte Carlo and Cornwall, with generous helpings of romance, comedy, suspense, melodrama and mystery, all

indulged in by strongly-drawn characters, and directed by the new English wizard for the glossiest producer in town, from a novel which sold millions of copies. It really couldn't miss, and it didn't.

w Robert E. Sherwood, Joan Harrison, novel Daphne du Maurier d Alfred Hitchcock ph George Barnes m Franz Waxman

Laurence Olivier, Joan Fontaine, George Sanders, Judith Anderson, Nigel Bruce, Gladys Cooper, Florence Bates, Reginald Denny, C. Aubrey Smith, Melville Cooper, Leo G. Carroll, Leonard Carey

'Hitchcock fans will have to put up with a surprising lack of the characteristic Hitchcock improvisations in the way of salty minor personages and humorous interludes, and satisfy themselves with a masterly exhibition of the Hitchcock skill in creating suspense and shock with his action and his camera.'— *National Board of Review*

AA: best picture; George Barnes
AAN: script; Alfred Hitchcock; Franz Waxman; Laurence Olivier; Joan Fontaine; Judith Anderson

Rebecca of Sunnybrook Farm
US 1938 80m bw
TCF (Raymond Griffith)

A child performer becomes a pawn in the fight to exploit her talents on radio.
Unrecognizable revamping of a famous story makes a very thin star vehicle.

w Karl Tunberg, Don Ettlinger, novel Kate Douglas Wiggin d Allan Dwan ph Arthur Miller m Arthur Lange songs various

Shirley Temple, Randolph Scott, Jack Haley, Gloria Stuart, Phyllis Brooks, Helen Westley, Slim Summerville, Bill Robinson

The Rebel*
GB 1960 105m Technicolor
Associated British (W. A. Whitaker)
US title: *Call Me Genius*

A suburban businessman goes to Paris to become an artist.
A kind of farcical *The Moon and Sixpence,* insufficiently well tailored to the requirements of a very specialized comic, but occasionally diverting none the less.

w Alan Simpson, Ray Galton d Robert Day ph Gilbert Taylor m Frank Cordell

Tony Hancock, George Sanders, Paul Massie, Margit Saad, Grégoire Aslan, Dennis Price, Irene Handl, Mervyn Johns, Peter Bull, John Le Mesurier, Nanette Newman, Oliver Reed, John Wood

'The more prosaic the setting, the funnier Hancock seems; transplanted into a conventionally silly screen art world, he is submerged among the other grotesques.'— *Penelope Houston*

Rebel in Town
US 1956 78m bw

A bank robber accidentally kills a small boy and is hunted down by the father. Surprisingly stark western with no particular merit. John Payne, John Smith, Ruth Roman, J. Carrol Naish, Ben Cooper. Written by Danny Arnold; directed by Alfred Werker; for Bel Air / UA.

The Rebel Son
GB 1939 90m bw
London Films Omnia (E. C. Molinier, Charles David)

A Tartar leader's son falls in love with the daughter of the opposing leade..
Resistible grafting of the Romeo and Juliet story into the barbarians of the Steppes, with much carousing and threatened violence surrounding a good central performance. It includes much footage from a 1936 French film, *Taras Bulba.*

w Adrian Brunel, story Gogol d Alexis Granowsky and Adrian Brunel ph Franz Planer and Bernard Browne

Harry Baur, Patricia Roc, Roger Livesey, Anthony Bushell, Joan Gardner

Rebel without a Cause**
US 1955 111m Warnercolor
Cinemascope
Warner (David Weisbart)

The adolescent son of a well-to-do family gets into trouble with other kids and the police. The first film to suggest that juvenile violence is not necessarily bred in the slums, this somewhat dreary melodrama also catapulted James Dean to stardom as the prototype fifties rebel.

w Stewart Stern d Nicholas Ray ph Ernest Haller m Leonard Rosenman

James Dean, Natalie Wood, Jim Backus, Sal Mineo, Ann Doran, Dennis Hopper

AAN: original story (Nicholas Ray); Natalie Wood; Sal Mineo

Reckless
US 1935 96m bw
MGM (David O. Selznick)

A theatrical agent loves the glamorous star he represents, but she marries a drunken millionaire.

Remarkably flat backstage melodrama with music, based on the life of Libby Holman.

w P. J. Wolfson *d* Victor Fleming *ph* George Folsey *songs* various

Jean Harlow, William Powell, Franchot Tone, May Robson, Ted Healy, Nat Pendleton, Rosalind Russell, Henry Stephenson

The Reckless Moment*
US 1949   82m   bw
Columbia (Walter Wanger)

A woman accidentally kills her daughter's would-be seducer, and is then trailed by a blackmailer.
Uninteresting melodrama electrified by Ophuls' direction, which might have been applied to something more worthwhile.

w Henry Garson, R. W. Soderborg, *novel* The Blank Wall by Elizabeth Sanxay Holding *d Max Ophuls ph* Burnett Guffey *m* Hans Salter *md* Morris Stoloff

Joan Bennett, James Mason, Geraldine Brooks, Henry O'Neill, Shepperd Strudwick
  'Swift, sure narrative and solidly pleasurable detail.'—*Richard Winnington*

The Reckoning**
GB 1969   108m   Technicolor
Columbia / Ronald Shedlo (Hugh Perceval)

A tough London executive with a Liverpool-Irish background has a brutal streak and a self-destructive urge, but goes on narrowly averting misfortune.
Interesting melodrama of a man disgusted with both bourgeois and working-class values; slickly made and fast-moving.

w John McGrath, *novel* The Harp That Once by Patrick Hall *d Jack Gold ph Geoffrey Unsworth m* Malcolm Arnold

Nicol Williamson, Rachel Roberts, Paul Rogers, Zena Walker, Ann Bell, Gwen Nelson, J. G. Devlin

The Red Badge of Courage**
US 1951   69m   bw
MGM (Gottfried Reinhardt)

A youth called up during the Civil War gets his first taste of battle.
Fresh, poetic, but dramatically unsatisfactory filming of a classic American novel. The story of its production is fascinatingly told in *Picture,* a book by Lillian Ross.

wd John Huston, *novel* Stephen Crane *ph* Harold Rosson *m* Bronislau Kaper

Audie Murphy, Bill Mauldin, Douglas Dick, Royal Dano, John Dierkes, Andy Devine, Arthur Hunnicutt

Red Ball Express
US 1952   83m   bw
U-I (Aaron Rosenberg)

A supply column runs from the Normandy beachhead to Patton's army on the outskirts of Paris.
Standard war adventure, not too convincingly mounted but providing the usual excitements.

w John Michael Hayes *d* Budd Boetticher *ph* Maury Gertsman

Jeff Chandler, Sidney Poitier, Alex Nicol, Judith Braun, Hugh O'Brian, Jack Kelly, Jack Warden

The Red Beret
GB 1953   88m   Technicolor
Warwick (Irving Allen, Albert R. Broccoli)
US title: *Paratrooper*

In 1940, an American with a guilt complex joins the British paratroopers.
Routine war action flagwaver; good battle scenes, rubbish in between.

w Richard Maibaum, Frank Nugent, *book* Hilary St George Saunders *d* Terence Young *ph* John Wilcox *m* John Addison

Alan Ladd, Susan Stephen, Leo Genn, Harry Andrews, Donald Houston, Anthony Bushell, Patric Doonan, Stanley Baker, Lana Morris

The Red Danube
US 1950   119m   bw
MGM (Carey Wilson)

In occupied Vienna, citizens are being returned to Russia against their will.
Tedious and silly Red-baiting cold war charade.

w Gina Kaus, Arthur Wimperis, *novel* Vespers in Vienna by Bryan Marshall *d* George Sidney *ph* Charles Rosher *m* Miklos Rozsa

Ethel Barrymore, Walter Pidgeon, Janet Leigh, Peter Lawford, Francis L. Sullivan, Angela Lansbury, Louis Calhern, Melville Cooper

The Red Desert*
Italy / France 1964   116m   Eastmancolor
Duemila / Federiz (Angelo Rizzoli)
original title: *Il Deserto Rosso*

A wife suffers from depression, and a brief affair with her husband's friend doesn't help.
Elongated character study, very talkative but rather decoratively designed with the same subtle use of colour in an urban landscape as was seen later in *Blow Up.*

w Michelangelo Antonioni, Tonino Guerra *d Michelangelo Antonioni ph* Carlo di Palma *m* Giovanni Chionetti

Monica Vitti, Richard Harris, Carlos Chionetti
'The beauty is stationary, painterly; and the arresting image precisely arrests and retards the already moribund thrust of the film.'— *John Simon*

Red Dust***
US 1932 86m bw
MGM

On a rubber plantation in Indo-China, the overseer is pursued by his engineer's bride but himself falls for a stranded prostitute.
Vigorous romantic melodrama with echoes of *Rain;* remade as *Congo Maisie* (1940) and *Mogambo* (1954).

w John Lee Mahin, *play* Wilson Collison
d *Victor Fleming* ph Harold Rosson

Clark Gable, Jean Harlow, Mary Astor, Gene Raymond, Donald Crisp, Tully Marshall, Forrester Harvey
'Gable and Harlow have full play for their curiously similar sort of good-natured toughness.'—*Time*
'Sure fire fun. Done so expertly it almost overcomes the basic script shortcomings.'—*Variety*
'He treated her rough—and she loved it!'—*publicity*
† The Gable role was first announced for John Gilbert.
†† Scenes showing the shooting of *Red Dust* are included in *Bombshell.*

Red Garters**
US 1954 91m Technicolor
Paramount (Pat Duggan)

Various familiar types congregate in the western town of Paradise Lost, and settle matters by the Code of the West.
Amusing western musical spoof slightly deadened by its pretty but finally boring theatrically stylized scenery. Songs are catchy, performances good natured.

w *Michael Fessier* d George Marshall
ph *Arthur E. Arling* m Joseph J. Lilley
songs Jay Livingston, Ray Evans

Rosemary Clooney, Guy Mitchell, Gene Barry, Jack Carson, Pat Crowley, Cass Daley, Frank Faylen, Reginald Owen
'A musical of considerable freshness and gaiety.'—*MFB*

Red Headed Woman*
US 1932 74m bw
MGM

A shopgirl marries the boss but is rejected in his social circles.

Unconvincing but occasionally entertaining melodrama.

w Anita Loos, *novel* Katharine Brush d Jack Conway ph Harold Rosson

Jean Harlow, Chester Morris, Lewis Stone, Leila Hyams, Una Merkel, Henry Stephenson, Charles Boyer, May Robson

The Red House*
US 1947 100m bw
Sol Lesser

A moody farmer's guilty obsession with an old house in the woods is that he murdered his parents in it.
Psycho-like suspense melodrama, too extended for comfort and too restricting for the actors, but effective in spurts.

wd Delmer Daves, *novel* George Agnew Chamberlain ph Bert Glennon m Miklos Rozsa

Edward G. Robinson, Judith Anderson, Lon McCallister, Allene Roberts, Rory Calhoun, Julie London, Ona Munson

The Red Inn*
France 1951 95m bw
Memnon
original title: *L'Auberge Rouge*

In 1833, stagecoach travellers stay at a remote inn, where the owners intend to rob and murder them.
Extreme black farce which manages to be pretty funny for those who can take this kind of thing: even the survivors of the night's massacre fall down a ravine.

w *Jean Aurenche, Pierre Bost* d Claude Autant-Lara ph André Bac m René Cloërc ad Max Douy

Fernandel, Françoise Rosay, Carette, Grégoire Aslan

Red Line 7000
US 1965 110m Technicolor
Paramount / Laurel (Howard Hawks)

The career and loves of a stock car racer.
Very routine romantic actioner full of the director's favourite situations but failing to find any fresh slant.

w George Kirgo d Howard Hawks ph Milton Krasner m Nelson Riddle

James Caan, Laura Devon, Gail Hire, Charlene Holt, John Robert Crawford

The Red Light
US 1949 83m bw
UA / Pioneer (Roy Del Ruth)

An industrialist tracks down his brother's murderer.

Competent routine detection piece with engaging clues.

w George Callahan d Roy Del Ruth ph Bert Glennon m Dmitri Tiomkin

George Raft, Virginia Mayo, Raymond Burr, Gene Lockhart, Henry Morgan, Arthur Franz

Red Mountain

US 1951 84m Technicolor
Paramount / Hal B. Wallis

A Confederate captain joins Quantrell's Raiders but is horrified by their brutality. Fast-moving action western.

w John Meredyth Lucas, George W. George, George F. Slavin d William Dieterle ph Charles Lang Jnr m Franz Waxman

Alan Ladd, Lizabeth Scott, Arthur Kennedy, John Ireland, Jeff Corey, James Bell

Red Planet Mars

US 1952 87m bw
UA / Donald Hyde, Anthony Veiller

Americans and Russians both tune in to Mars and learn that it is a powerful Christian planet; the news causes first panic, then a religious revival and a determination to live more harmoniously on earth.

Lunatic farrago that has to be seen to be believed.

w Anthony Veiller, John L. Balderston d Harry Horner ph Joseph Biroc m Mahlon Merrick md David Chudnow ad Charles D. Hall

Herbert Berghof, Peter Graves, Andrea King, Marvin Miller

The Red Pony

US 1949 88m Technicolor
Republic (Lewis Milestone)

When his pet pony dies after an illness, a farmer's son loses faith in his father. Sincere but rather obvious little fable which although capably made does not make inspiring film drama.

w John Steinbeck d Lewis Milestone ph Tony Gaudio m Aaron Copland pd Nicolai Remisoff

Myrna Loy, Robert Mitchum, Peter Miles, Louis Calhern, Shepperd Strudwick, Margaret Hamilton

Red River**

US 1948 133m bw
UA / Monterey (Howard Hawks)

How the Chisholm Trail was developed as a cattle drive.

Brawling western, a bit serious and long drawn out but with splendid action sequences.

w Borden Chase, Charles Schnee d Howard Hawks ph Russell Harlan m Dmitri Tiomkin

John Wayne, Montgomery Clift, Joanne Dru, Walter Brennan, Colleen Gray, John Ireland, Noah Beery Jnr, Harry Carey Jnr

AAN: original story (Borden Chase)

Red Salute*

US 1935 78m bw
Edward Small
aka: *Runaway Daughter*; GB title: *Arms and the Girl*

A college girl with communist leanings takes a cross country trip with an American soldier. Odd little romantic comedy modelled on *It Happened One Night*; it was picketed for its inconsequential attitude to politics.

w Humphrey Pearson, Manuel Seff d Sidney Lanfield ph Robert Planck

Barbara Stanwyck, Robert Young, Hardie Albright, Cliff Edwards, Ruth Donnelly, Gordon Jones, Henry Kolker

The Red Shoes****

GB 1948 136m Technicolor
GFD / The Archers *(Michael Powell, Emeric Pressburger)*

A girl student becomes a great ballet star but commits suicide when torn between love and her career.

Never was a better film made from such a penny plain story so unpersuasively written and performed; the splendour of the production is in the intimate view it gives of life backstage in the ballet world with its larger-than-life characters. The ballet excerpts are very fine, and the colour discreet; the whole film is charged with excitement.

wd Michael Powell, Emeric Pressburger ph Jack Cardiff m Brian Easdale pd Hein Heckroth

Anton Walbrook, Moira Shearer, Marius Goring, Robert Helpmann, Albert Basserman, Frederick Ashton, Leonide Massine, Ludmilla Tcherina, Esmond Knight
  'In texture, like nothing the British cinema has ever seen.'—*Time Out, 1981*

AA: Brian Easdale
AAN: best picture; original story (Michael Powell, Emeric Pressburger)

Red Skies of Montana

US 1952 99m Technicolor
TCF (Samuel G. Engel)
aka: *Smoke Jumpers*

Tension among firefighting crews in the mountains of Montana.
Adequate, routine action melodrama with semi-documentary touches.

w Harry Kleiner *d* Joseph M. Newman *ph* Charles G. Clarke *m* Sol Kaplan

Richard Widmark, Jeffrey Hunter, Constance Smith, Richard Boone, Richard Crenna

Red Sky at Morning
US 1970 113m Technicolor
Universal / Hal Wallis

During World War II the family of an officer on active service find life in New Mexico not what they've been used to.
Peyton Place by any other name, well produced but of little real interest.

w Marguerite Roberts, *novel* Richard Bradford *d* James Goldstone *ph* Vilmos Zsigismond *m* Billy Goldenberg

Claire Bloom, Richard Thomas, Richard Crenna, Catherine Burns, Desi Arnaz Jnr, John Colicos, Harry Guardino

Red Sun
France / Italy / Spain 1971 108m
Eastmancolor
Corona / Oceania / Balcazar (Robert Dorfman)

In 1870 Arizona, an outlaw is forced to accompany a Japanese samurai to recover a ceremonial sword which his partner has stolen.
Unusual but generally ineffective western with a fashionable international cast.

w Lair Koenig, D. B. Petitclerc, W. Roberts, L. Roman *d* Terence Young *ph* Henri Alekan *m* Maurice Jarre

Charles Bronson, Toshiro Mifune, Alain Delon, Ursula Andress, Capucine
'A nice exotic item ruined by suburban direction.'—*Sight and Sound*

Red Sundown
US 1956 81m Technicolor

A gunslinger becomes a deputy and tames a lawless town. Elementary western action piece, not unentertaining. Rory Calhoun, Martha Hyer, Dean Jagger, Robert Middleton, James Millican, Grant Williams. Written by Martin Berkeley; directed by Jack Arnold; for Universal-International.

The Red Tent*
Italy / USSR 1970 121m Technicolor
Paramount / Vides / Mosfilm (Franco Cristaldi)

The story of General Nobile's ill-fated 1928 expedition by dirigible to the Arctic.
Stiffly-conceived international spectacular with one striking sequence but not much good cheer.

w Ennio de Concini, Richard Adams *d* Mikhail Kalatozov *ph* Leonid Kalashnikov *m* Ennio Morricone

Peter Finch, Sean Connery, Hardy Kruger, Claudia Cardinale, Mario Adorf, Massimo Girotti

Red Tomahawk
US 1967 80m Technicolor

The small town of Deadwood is caught up in the aftermath of Little Big Horn. Talkative western filled with old faces, as is this producer's wont. Howard Keel, Joan Caulfield, Broderick Crawford, Scott Brady, Wendell Corey, Richard Arlen, Tom Drake. Written by Steve Fisher; directed by R. G. Springsteen; for A. C. Lyles / Paramount.

Red Wagon
GB 1933 107m bw

Passions mount in a travelling circus. Gypsies and jealousies are the ingredients of a melodrama aimed at the international market.
It failed. Charles Bickford, Raquel Torres, Greta Nissen, Don Alvarado, Anthony Bushell, Paul Graetz, Jimmy Hanley, Frank Pettingell. Written by Roger Burford, Edward Knoblock and Arthur Woods, from the novel by Lady Eleanor Smith; directed by Paul Stein; for BIP.

Redbeard*
Japan 1965 165 bw Tohoscope
Toho-Kurosawa
original title: *Akahige*

Problems of a 19th-century doctor.
Almost a Japanese version of *The Citadel*:
Kurosawa himself called it 'a monument to goodness in man'. Rather heavy-going, but sporadically compelling.

w Masato Ide, Hideo Oguni, Akira Kurosawa, *novel* Shugoro Yamamoto *d* Akira Kurosawa *ph* A. Nakai, T. Saito *m* M. Sato

Toshiro Mifune, Yuzo Kayama
'A three-hour excursion into nineteenth-century hospital soap opera; a mediocre enough script, but beautifully directed and flawlessly acted.'—*John Simon*

Redemption
US 1930 82m bw

A man thought dead commits suicide rather

than interrupt his wife's new life. Elaborate but unsuccessful talkie debut of a waning star; very hard going. John Gilbert, Renee Adoree, Eleanor Boardman, Conrad Nagel. Written by Dorothy Farnum and Edwin Justus Mayer, from *The Living Corpse* by Leo Tolstoy; directed by Fred Niblo; for MGM.

Reflection of Fear
US 1971   90m   Eastmancolor
Columbia (Howard B. Jaffe)

A retarded teenage girl kills her mother and her grandmother.
Psycho thriller of little interest or suspense.

w Edward Hume, Lewis John Carlino, *novel* Go to Thy Deathbed by Stanton Forbes *d* William A. Fraker *ph* Laszlo Kovacs *m* Fred Myrow

Robert Shaw, Mary Ure, Signe Hasso, Sondra Locke, Mitch Ryan

Reflections in a Golden Eye*
US 1967   108m   Technicolor
Warner Seven Arts (Ray Stark)

Repressions at a peacetime army camp in Georgia. A private soldier rides nude on horseback, a major has the hots for him, the major's wife has an affair with their neighbour, whose wife has cut off her nipples with garden shears.
A film as idiotic as its story line, but smoothly marshalled so that at least it's more amusing than boring.

w Chapman Mortimer, Gladys Hill, *novel* Carson McCullers *d John Huston ph Aldo Tonti pd* Stephen Grimes *m* Toshiro Mayuzumi

Marlon Brando, Elizabeth Taylor, Brian Keith, Julie Harris, Robert Forster, Zorro David
'One feels trapped in a huge overheated hothouse containing nothing but common snapdragons.'—*John Simon*
'Nothing more than nutty people and pseudo porn.'—*Judith Crist*
'Pedestrian, crass, and uninvolving to the point of repellence.'—*John Simon*

The Reformer and the Redhead*
US 1950   90m   bw
MGM (Norman Panama, Melvin Frank)

A small-town reform candidate abandons his crooked protector and wins under his own steam, helped by the daughter of the zoo superintendent.
Scatty sub-Capra comedy with a lightweight script but good production and playing.

wd Norman Panama, Melvin Frank *ph* Ray June *m* David Raksin

Dick Powell, June Allyson, Cecil Kellaway, David Wayne, Ray Collins, Robert Keith, Marvin Kaplan

La Règle du Jeu***
France 1939   113m   bw
La Nouvelle Edition Française
aka: *The Rules of the Game*

A count organizes a weekend shooting party which results in complex love intrigues among servants as well as masters.
Celebrated satirical comedy with a uniquely bleak outlook.

w Jean Renoir, Carl Koch d Jean Renoir ph Jean Bachelet, Alain Renoir *m* Joseph Kosma, Roger Desormières *ad* Eugène Lourié, Max Douy

Marcel Dalio, Nora Gregor, Jean Renoir, Mila Parély, Julien Carette, Gaston Modot, Roland Toutain
'It is a question of panache, of preserving a casual indifference to the workings of fate.'—*The Times*
'How brilliantly Renoir focuses the confusion! The rather fusty luxury of the chateau, the constant mindless slaughter of wild animals, the minuets of adultery and seduction, the gavottes of mutual hatred or mistrust. . .'—*Basil Wright, 1972*
† The film was originally banned as indicting the corruption of France, and during the war the negative was destroyed during an air raid; but eventually a full version was pieced together from various materials.

The Reincarnation of Peter Proud
US 1974   104m   Technicolor
Avco Embassy / Bing Crosby (Frank P. Rosenberg)

A history professor is troubled by recurring dreams of his former existence.
Hysterical psychic melodrama which pretty well ruins its own chances by failing to explain its plot.

w Max Ehrlich, from his novel *d* J. Lee-Thompson *ph* Victor J. Kemper *m* Jerry Goldsmith

Michael Sarrazin, Jennifer O'Neill, Margot Kidder, Cornelia Sharpe, Paul Hecht
'It may well be the silliest approach to the subject in any medium . . . all flashbacks trampling the action with the finesse of a rogue elephant.'—*Tom Milne*

The Reivers*
US 1970   111m   Technicolor
   Panavision
Cinema Center / Duo / Solar (Irving Ravetch)

In Mississippi at the turn of the century a hired hand borrows the new family auto for a trip into Memphis with the grandson of the family and a black stablehand.

Pleasant but insubstantial yarn of more gracious days; most attractive to look at, it entertains gently without ever reaching a point.

w Irving Ravetch, Harriet Frank Jnr, *novel* William Faulkner *d* Mark Rydell *ph Richard Moore m* John Williams

Steve McQueen, Sharon Farrell, Will Geer, Rupert Crosse, Mitch Vogel, Michael Constantine, Juano Hernandez, Clifton James

AAN: John Williams; Rupert Crosse

Relentless
US 1948 93m Technicolor

A cowboy framed for murder must clear himself before the posse catches up with him.

Brisk western copy of *The 39 Steps*. Robert Young, Marguerite Chapman, Willard Parker, Barton Maclane, Will Wright. Written by Winston Miller; directed by George Sherman; for Columbia.

The Reluctant Debutante*
US 1958 96m Metrocolor
Cinemascope
MGM / Avon (Pandro S. Berman)

A noble couple have difficulty in steering their American-educated daughter through the intricacies of the London season.

A slight but pleasing British comedy has become a rather strident example of lend-lease, but still affords minor pleasures.

w William Douglas Home, from his play *d* Vincente Minnelli *ph* Joseph Ruttenberg *md* Eddie Warner *ad* Jean d'Aubonne

Rex Harrison, Kay Kendall, Sandra Dee, Peter Myers, Angela Lansbury, John Saxon, Diane Clare

The Reluctant Dragon**
US 1941 72m Technicolor
Walt Disney

A tour of the Disney Studios affords some glimpses of how cartoons are made.

Amiable pot-pourri of cartoon shorts (*Baby Weems, How to Ride a Horse* and the title story) linked by a studio tour of absorbing interest.

w various *d* Alfred Werker (live action), various

Robert Benchley, Frances Gifford, Nana Bryant

Reluctant Heroes*
GB 1951 80m bw
Byron (Henry Halstead)

Comedy of national servicemen and their misdemeanours.

Simple-minded army farce which was popular for years as play and film.

w Colin Morris, from his play *d* Jack Raymond

Brian Rix, Ronald Shiner, Derek Farr, Christine Norden, Larry Noble

The Reluctant Widow
GB 1950 91m bw
Rank / Two Cities (Gordon Wellesley)

During the Napoleonic wars a governess is co-opted as a spy.

Thin romantic drama which despite nice art direction never really sparks into life.

w Gordon Wellesley, J. B. Boothroyd, *novel* Georgette Heyer *d* Bernard Knowles *ph* Jack Hildyard *ad Carmen Dillon*

Jean Kent, Guy Rolfe, Kathleen Byron, Paul Dupuis, Lana Morris, Julian Dallas, Peter Hammond, Andrew Cruickshank

Remains to be Seen
US 1953 88m bw
MGM (Arthur Hornblow Jnr)

The manager of an apartment house finds a dead body, and before the police arrive someone sticks a knife into it.

Flabby comedy-thriller giving the cast little to work on.

w Sidney Sheldon, *play* Howard Lindsay, Russel Crouse *d* Don Weis *ph* Robert Planck *md* Jeff Alexander

June Allyson, Van Johnson, Angela Lansbury, Louis Calhern, John Beal, Dorothy Dandridge

The Remarkable Andrew*
US 1942 80m bw
Paramount (Richard Blumenthal)

A young municipal bookkeeper is framed by local politicians but helped by the ghost of Andrew Jackson and friends.

Pleasant, rather faded, whimsical comedy which also managed to be propaganda for the war effort.

w Dalton Trumbo *d* Stuart Heisler *ph* Theodor Sparkuhl *m* Victor Young

William Holden, Ellen Drew, Brian Donlevy, Rod Cameron, Richard Webb, Porter Hall, Frances Gifford, Nydia Westman, Montagu Love

'About all that comes through in the

juxtaposition of these lithograph characters over modern Shale City is Franklin's delight over the electric light and Jackson's alarm over the radio.'—*John McManus, PM*

The Remarkable Mr Pennypacker

US 1958 87m Technicolor
Cinemascope
TCF (Charles Brackett)

A Pennsylvania businessman leads two lives with two separate families.
Feeble and obvious period comedy of bigamy; very few laughs.

w Walter Reisch, *play* Liam O'Brien *d* Henry Levin *ph* Milton Krasner *m* Leigh Harline

Clifton Webb, Dorothy McGuire, Charles Coburn, Ray Stricklyn, Jill St John, Ron Ely, David Nelson

Rembrandt****

GB 1937 85m bw
London Films (Alexander Korda)

Episodes in the life of the 17th-century painter.
Austerely comic, gently tragic character piece, superbly staged and photographed, with a great performance at its centre.

w Lajos Biro, June Head, Carl Zuckmayer d Alexander Korda

Charles Laughton, Elsa Lanchester, Gertrude Lawrence, Edward Chapman, Walter Hudd, Roger Livesey, Herbert Lomas, Allan Jeayes, Sam Livesey, Raymond Huntley, John Clements

'Amazingly full of that light which the great master of painting subdued to his supreme purpose.'—*James Agate*
'The film is ruined by lack of story and continuity: it has no drive. Like *The Private Life of Henry the Eighth* it is a series of unrelated tableaux.'—*Graham Greene*

Remember?

US 1939 83m bw
MGM (Milton Bren)

A newly married couple do not get on, so a friend gives them a potion which makes them lose their memories and fall in love all over again.
Silly, witless comedy which did no good for anyone concerned.

w Corey Ford, Norman Z. McLeod
d Norman Z. McLeod *ph* George Folsey
m Edward Ward

Robert Taylor, Greer Garson, Lew Ayres, Billie Burke, Reginald Owen, George Barbier, Henry Travers, Richard Carle, Laura Hope Crews, Halliwell Hobbes, Sig Rumann

Remember Last Night?**

US 1936 80m bw
Universal

Socialites with hangovers find that murder was committed during their party.
Ingenious but overlong mixture of styles: farce, *Thin Man* comedy, murder mystery, satire, fantasy. Very well worth looking at.

w Harry Clark, Dan Totheroh, Doris Malloy, *novel* The Hangover Murders by Adam Hobhouse *d* James Whale *ph* Joseph Valentine *m* Franz Waxman

Robert Young, Edward Arnold, Arthur Treacher, Constance Cummings, Robert Armstrong, Sally Eilers, Reginald Denny, Ed Brophy, Jack La Rue, Gustav Von Seyffertitz, Gregory Ratoff

'Parodying the detective thriller in a dazzling cascade of gags, this brilliant divertissement eventually takes off into pure surrealism.'—*Tom Milne, MFB, 1974*

Remember My Name*

US 1978 94m De Luxe
Lion's Gate (Robert Altman)

After twelve years in prison, a woman takes calm revenge on the man who allowed her to take the blame for his crime.
Basically reminiscent of a Barbara Stanwyck vehicle of the forties, this interesting film is finally too concerned to strike on all levels, including satire, social awareness and fashionable pessimism.

wd Alan Rudolph *ph* Tak Fujimoto

Geraldine Chaplin, Anthony Perkins, Moses Gunn, Berry Berenson, Jeff Goldblum

Remember the Day*

US 1941 86m bw
TCF (William Perlberg)

An elderly schoolteacher recollects her past life.
Pleasant sentimental drama, very well mounted.

w Tess Schlesinger, Frank Davis, Allan Scott, *play* Philo Higley *d* Henry King *ph* George Barnes *m* Alfred Newman

Claudette Colbert, John Payne, Shepperd Strudwick, Jane Seymour, Anne Revere, Frieda Inescort

Remember the Night*

US 1940 94m bw
Paramount (Mitchell Leisen)

An assistant district attorney takes a lady shoplifter home with him for Christmas.

Eccentric but winning blend of comedy, romance and drama, deftly mixed by master chefs.

w Preston Sturges d Mitchell Leisen ph Ted Tetzlaff *m* Frederick Hollander

Barbara Stanwyck, Fred MacMurray, Beulah Bondi, Elizabeth Patterson, Sterling Holloway, Paul Guilfoyle, Willard Robertson

Remorques*
France 1941 80m bw
MAIC
US title: *Stormy Waters*

A tugboat captain falls in love with a mysterious woman but remains faithful to his invalid wife.
Effective, minor, romantic melodrama.

w Jacques Prévert, André Cayatte, *novel* Roger Vercel *d* Jean Grémillon *ph* Armand Thirard, Louis Née *m* Roland Manuel

Jean Gabin, Michèle Morgan, Madeleine Renaud, Fernand Ledoux

Rendezvous
US 1935 106m bw
MGM (Lawrence Weingarten)

A decoding expert breaks an enemy spy ring. Agreeable light romantic comedy drama with an espionage plot.

w Bella and Samuel Spewack, *novel* Black Chamber by Herbert Yardley *d* William K. Howard *ph* William Daniels *m* William Axt

William Powell, Rosalind Russell, Binnie Barnes, Lionel Atwill, Cesar Romero, Samuel S. Hinds, Henry Stephenson, Frank Reicher

Rendezvous with Annie
US 1946 89m bw

An American soldier in England goes absent without leave to see his wife in New York, an exploit which later nearly loses him a fortune. An engaging comedy idea filmed with insufficient wit, this gets by on charm. Eddie Albert, Faye Marlowe, C. Aubrey Smith. Written by Mary Loos and Richard Sale; directed by Allan Dwan; for Republic.

Renegades
US 1930 84m bw

A disgraced French officer becomes a hero of the Foreign Legion. Satisfying romantic melodrama of its period. Warner Baxter, Myrna Loy, Bela Lugosi, Noah Beery, C. Henry Gordon, Gregory Gaye. Written by Jules Furthman from a novel by André Armandy; directed by Victor Fleming; for Fox.

Renegades
US 1946 88m Technicolor

An outlaw's son tries in vain to go straight. Unsurprising but efficient bill-topping western of its day. Evelyn Keyes, Larry Parks, Willard Parker, Edgar Buchanan. Written by Melvin Levey and Francis Faragoh; directed by George Sherman; for Columbia.

Rentadick
GB 1972 94m Eastmancolor
Rank / Paradine / Virgin (Ned Sherrin)

Incompetent private eyes become involved in the battle for a deadly nerve gas.
Ineffective crazy comedy which never takes shape, preferring to aim barbs of satire in all directions.

w John Cleese, Graham Chapman *d* Jim Clark *ph* John Coquillon *m* Carl Davis

James Booth, Richard Briers, Julie Ege, Donald Sinden, Roy Kinnear

Repeat Performance*
US 1947 93m bw
Eagle Lion / Aubrey Schenck

People in trouble find they can repeat the previous year.
Adequate flashback fantasy, very dated now.

w Walter Bullock *d* Alfred L. Werker *ph* Lew O'Connell *m* George Antheil

Louis Hayward, Joan Leslie, Tom Conway, Richard Basehart, Virginia Field

Report to the Commissioner
US 1974 112m Metrocolor
UA / M. J. Frankovich
GB title: *Operation Undercover*

A policeman's son follows in father's footsteps but finds life around Times Square dismaying. Realistic, concerned crime melodrama with nothing very new to say.

w Abby Mann, Ernest Tidyman, *novel* James Mills *d* Milton Katselas *ph* Mario Tosi *m* Elmer Bernstein

Michael Moriarty, Yaphet Kotto, Susan Blakely, Hector Elizondo, Tony King, Michael McGuire

'A clear also-ran in the police thriller stakes.'—*Verina Glaessner*

'A bit too full of sweat and frenzy.'—
Michael Billington, Illustrated London News

The Reptile*
GB 1966 90m Technicolor
Hammer (Anthony Nelson Keys)

A Cornish village is terrified by several mysterious and unpleasant deaths; it turns out that the daughter of the local doctor, victim of a Malayan sect, periodically turns into a deadly snake.

Silly horror story most effectively filmed as a mixture of chills, detection and good characterization.

w John Elder d John Gilling ph Arthur Grant *m* Don Banks

Noel Willman, Jennifer Daniel, Ray Barrett, Jaqueline Pearce, Michael Ripper, John Laurie, Marne Maitland

Repulsion**
GB 1965   105m   bw
Compton / Tekli (Gene Gutowski)

A Belgian manicurist in London is driven by pressures into neurotic withdrawal; terrified above all by sex, she locks herself up in her gloomy flat and murders her boy friend and landlord when they try to approach her.

Weird, unmotivated but undeniably effective Grand Guignol in the form of a case history; little dialogue, which is just as well as the director at that time clearly had no ear for the language.

w Roman Polanski, Gerard Brach *d Roman Polanski ph Gilbert Taylor m* Chico Hamilton

Catherine Deneuve, Ian Hendry, John Fraser, Patrick Wymark, Yvonne Furneaux

Requiem for a Heavyweight*
US 1962   87m   bw
Columbia (David Susskind)
GB title: *Blood Money*

The last bouts of a prizefighter who will not realize his career is over.

Tough, effective melodrama, extremely well acted.

w Rod Serling, from his TV play *d Ralph Nelson ph Arthur J. Ornitz m* Laurence Rosenthal

Anthony Quinn, *Jackie Gleason, Mickey Rooney*, Julie Harris, Stan Adams, Madame Spivy, Jack Dempsey, Cassius Clay

The Rescuers*
US 1977   77m   Technicolor
Walt Disney (Ron Miller)

The Mouse Rescue Aid Society volunteer to bring back a girl lost in a swamp.

Feature-length cartoon which, while by no means as bad as some of Disney's very routine seventies product, still seems light years away from his classics of the thirties.

w various, from stories by Margery Sharp *d* Wolfgang Reitherman, John Lounsbery, Art Stevens

'The people who really need rescuing are the Disney animators and cameramen.'—*Time Out*

'It's no *Snow White* but there are long moments when its inventiveness and skill are entirely captivating. I have only this one lingering doubt: if you are going to put this amount of effort into a movie shouldn't you have more at the end than a snappy collection of 330,000 drawings and a bill for six million dollars?'—*Barry Took, Punch*

AAN: song, 'Someone's Waiting for You'

The Restless Breed
US 1957   81m   Eastmancolor by Pathé

The son of a secret service agent arrives in a frontier town to avenge his father's death. Standard star western full of expected elements. Scott Brady, Anne Bancroft, Jay C. Flippen, Jim Davis, Rhys Williams. Written by Steve Fisher; directed by Allan Dwan; for Edward L. Alperson.

The Restless Years
US 1959   86m   bw   Cinemascope

A small-town dressmaker tries to prevent her daughter from discovering that she is illegitimate. Antediluvian sudser with second-string talent. John Saxon, Sandra Dee, Margaret Lindsay, Luana Patten, Virginia Grey. Written by Edward Anhalt, from the play *Teach Me How to Cry* by Patricia Joudry; directed by Helmut Kautner; for Universal-International.

Resurrection
US1931   81m   bw
Universal

In 1870s Russia, a peasant girl is seduced by a prince and bears his child.
Unremarkable version of a much-filmed melodrama.

w Finis Fox, *novel* Leo Tolstoy *d* Edwin Carewe *ph* Robert B. Kurrle, Al Green *m* Dmitri Tiomkin

Lupe Velez, John Boles, Nance O'Neil, William Keighley, Rose Tapley
† See also: *We Live Again.*

Retreat, Hell!
US 1952   95m   bw
(Warner) United States (Milton Sperling)

Adventures of a Marine unit in the Korean War.
Standard war film.

w Milton Sperling, Ted Sherdeman *d* Joseph H. Lewis *ph* Warren Lynch *m* William Lava

Frank Lovejoy, Richard Carlson, Anita
Louise, Russ Tamblyn

Return from the Ashes*
GB 1965   104m   bw   Panavision
UA / Mirisch (J. Lee-Thompson)

A woman returns from Dachau to find that her
husband is living with her step-daughter and
that they plan to murder her.
Broken-backed thriller melodrama, the first
half of which is quite irrelevant to the second.
The whole is modestly inventive for those who
don't mind a mixture of *Enoch Arden, Psycho*
and *Dial M for Murder* with a touch of the
concentration camps and a background of
post-war misery.

w Julius J. Epstein, *novel* Hubert Monteilhet
d J. Lee-Thompson *ph Christopher Challis*
m Johnny Dankworth

Ingrid Thulin, Maximilian Schell, Samantha
Eggar, Herbert Lom

Return from Witch Mountain
US 1978   93m   Technicolor
Walt Disney (Ron Miller, Jerome
   Courtland)

A brother and sister from outer space come
back to earth for a vacation and are used by
crooks for their own purposes.
Acceptable sequel to *Escape from Witch
Mountain*, with improved special effects.

w Malcolm Marmorstein d John Hough
ph Frank Phillips *m* Lalo Schifrin *sp* Eustace
Lycett, Art Cruickshank, Danny Lee

Bette Davis, Christopher Lee, Ike Eisenmann,
Kim Richards, Jack Soo

The Return of a Man Called Horse*
US 1976   125m   De Luxe   Panavision
UA / Sandy Howard / Richard Harris

The English nobleman of *A Man Called Horse*
goes back to the west to save his adopted
Indian tribe from extinction.
Another 'realistic' action adventure with
torture highlights; nicely made, but not for the
squeamish.

w Jack de Witt d Irvin Kershner *ph Owen
Roizman m Laurence Rosenthal*

Richard Harris, Gale Sondergaard, Geoffrey
Lewis, Bill Lucking, Jorge Luke
   'Maintains a tidy balance between nausea
and boredom.'—*Judith Crist*
† At 17 minutes, this pre-title sequence must
be the longest so far.

The Return of Bulldog Drummond
GB 1934   71m   bw

Drummond forms a society to oust crooked
foreigners from Britain. Good Drummond
exploit with traces of the original Fascism.
Ralph Richardson, Ann Todd, Francis L.
Sullivan, Claud Allister, Joyce Kennedy.

Written and directed by Walter Summers,
from the novel *The Black Gang* by 'Sapper';
for BIP.

The Return of Dr X*
US 1939   62m   bw
Warner (Bryan Foy)

A modern vampire terrorizes the city.
Minor thriller which doesn't get going till the
last reel; only notable for Bogart's appearance
as the monster. Nothing to do with *Dr X*.

w Lee Katz, *novel* The Doctor's Secret by
William J. Makin d Vincent Sherman *ph* Sid
Hickox *m* Bernhard Kaun

Dennis Morgan, Rosemary Lane, Wayne
Morris, Humphrey Bogart, Olin Howland,
John Litel

The Return of Dracula*
US 1958   77m   bw
UA / Gramercy (Jules V. Levy, Arthur
   Gardner)
GB title: *The Fantastic Disappearing Man*

A European vampire makes his way to an
American small town in the guise of a refugee
Iron Curtain painter.
Quite nicely made low-budget horror film with
a good balance of the supernatural and the
ordinary.

w Pat Fielder d Paul Landres *ph* Jack
McKenzie *m* Gerald Fried

Francis Lederer, Norman Eberhardt, Ray
Stricklyn, Jimmie Baird, John Wengraf

The Return of Frank James*
US 1940   92m   Technicolor
TCF (Darry F. Zanuck)

A sequel to *Jesse James* (qv).
Moody, nicely photographed western in which
Jesse's brother avenges his murder.

w Sam Hellman d *Fritz Lang* *ph* George
Barnes, William V. Skall *m* David Buttolph

Henry Fonda, Gene Tierney, Jackie Cooper,
Henry Hull, John Carradine, J. Edward
Bromberg, Donald Meek, Eddie Collins,
George Barbier
   'I doubt if any character was ever as lily
white as that of Frank James here, but that is a
present from the Hays Office to you, and
anyway the part is played by Henry Fonda.
Durn if I don't like that boy.'—*Otis Ferguson*

The Return of October
US 1948   89m   Technicolor

A girl's inheritance is contested on the
grounds that she thinks a horse is the
reincarnation of her Uncle Willie. Thin
whimsy which leaves its stars with egg on their
faces. Glenn Ford, Terry Moore, Dame May
Whitty, James Gleason, Albert Sharpe.
Written by Norman Panama and Melvin
Frank; directed by Joseph H. Lewis; for
Columbia. (GB title: *A Date with Destiny*.)

The Return of Peter Grimm
US 1935   82m   bw

A strong-minded family man returns as a
ghost to see how his family is getting on
without him. Fairly satisfying fantasy with
good performances. Lionel Barrymore, Helen
Mack, Edward Ellis, Donald Meek. Written
by Francis Edwards Faragoh from the play by
David Belasco; directed by George Nicholls
Jnr; for RKO. (Previously filmed in 1925 with
Alec B. Francis and Janet Gaynor.)

The Return of the Bad Men
US 1948   90m   bw
RKO (Nat Holt)

A farmer tries to reform the female leader of a
terrorist outlaw gang, but she is killed in a
bank raid.
Standard, well shot western which contrives to
introduce a number of well-known historical
bandits.

w Charles O'Neal, Jack Netteford, Luci Ward
d Ray Enright *ph* J. Roy Hunt *m* Roy
Webb *md* Constantin Bakaleinikoff

Randolph Scott, Robert Ryan, Anne Jeffreys,
Jacqueline White, Steve Brodie

Return of the Frontiersman
US 1950   74m   Technicolor

A man escapes from prison to prove himself
innocent of the bank robbery for which he was
convicted. Goodish double-bill western with
no surprises. Gordon Macrae, Julie London,
Rory Calhoun, Fred Clark, Edwin Rand.
Written by Edna Anhalt; directed by Richard
Bare; for Warner.

The Return of the Pink Panther*
GB 1974   113m   De Luxe   Panavision
UA / Jewel / Pimlico / Mirisch / Geoffrey
   (Blake Edwards)

When the Pink Panther diamond – national
treasure of the Eastern state of Lugash – is
once again stolen, bungling Inspector
Clouseau is called in.

Rehash of jokes from *The Pink Panther* (qv),
not bad in parts but a rather tedious whole.

w Frank Waldman, Blake Edwards *d* Blake
Edwards *ph* Geoffrey Unsworth *m* Henry
Mancini

Peter Sellers, Christopher Plummer, Herbert
Lom, Catherine Schell, Peter Arne, Peter
Jeffrey, Grégoire Aslan, David Lodge,
Graham Stark

'The film never comes fully to the boil, but
simmers in a series of self-contained, self-
destructing little set pieces.'—*Richard Combs*

'The first film in history to be upstaged by its
own credit titles.'—*Benny Green, Punch*

The Return of the Scarlet Pimpernel*
GB 1937   94m   bw
London Films (Alexander Korda, Arnold
   Pressburger)

Sir Percy Blakeney saves his wife and other
French aristos from the guillotine.
Predictable, stylish revolutionary romance,
much thinner in plot and performance than its
predecessor.

w Lajos Biro, Arthur Wimperis, Adrian
Brunel *d* Hans Schwarz

Barry K. Barnes, Sophie Stewart, Margaretta
Scott, James Mason, *Henry Oscar,* Francis
Lister, Anthony Bushell

The Return of the Seven
US 1966   95m   Technicolor   Panavision
UA / Mirisch / CB (Ted Richmond)

The seven gunmen, slightly reconstituted, fight
again to rescue some kidnapped farmers.
The mixture as before (see *The Magnificent
Seven*); adequate but scarcely inspired.

w Larry Cohen *d* Burt Kennedy *ph* Paul
Vogel *m* Elmer Bernstein

Yul Brynner, Robert Fuller, Julian Mateos,
Warren Oates, Claude Akins, Virgilio
Texeira, Emilio Fernandez, Jordan
Christopher

AAN: Elmer Bernstein

The Return of the Terror
US 1934   65m   bw

A scientist feigns insanity to avoid prosecution
for murder, and escapes to his old sanatorium,
where murder strikes again. Barnstorming
murder mystery borrowing its title and nothing
else from Edgar Wallace. John Halliday, Mary
Astor, Lyle Talbot, Frank McHugh, Irving
Pichel, J. Carrol Naish. Written by Eugene
Solow and Peter Milne; directed by Howard
Bretherton; for Warner.

The Return of the Vampire*
US 1943   69m   bw
Columbia (Sam White)

Dracula reappears amid the London blitz.
Şurprisingly well made and complexly plotted
horror film; it looks good and only lacks
humour. The wolf man, however, is a
regrettable intrusion.

w Griffin Jay d Lew Landers ph John
Stumar, L. J. O'Connell m Mario
Castelnuovo-Tedesco md Morris Stoloff

Bela Lugosi, Nina Foch, Frieda Inescort,
Miles Mander, Matt Willis, Roland Varno,
Ottola Nesmith

Return to Macon County
US 1975   89m   Movielab
AIP / Macon Service Company (Eliot
  Schick)

In the fifties, two wandering youths pick up a
waitress and have serious trouble with a manic
policeman in America's unfriendliest area.
Slam-bang sequel to Macon County Line,
rather unintentionally comic.

wd Richard Compton ph Jacques Marquette
m Robert O. Ragland

Nick Nolte, Don Johnson, Robin Mattson,
Robert Viharo

Return to Paradise*
US 1953   109m   Technicolor
UA / Aspen (Theron Warth)

A peace seeker settles on a tiny South Sea
island and leaves when his wife dies; he
returns after World War II with his daughter.
Curious idyll, slow but not displeasing.

w Charles Kaufman, novel James Michener
d Mark Robson ph Winton Hoch m Dmitri
Tiomkin

Gary Cooper, Barry Jones, Roberta Haynes,
Moira MacDonald

Return to Peyton Place*
US 1961   122m   De Luxe   Cinemascope
TCF / API (Jerry Wald)

Constance Mackenzie's daughter writes a
novel about Peyton Place and falls in love with
the publisher.
More closets are unlocked, more skeletons fall
out; for addicts, the sequel does not
disappoint, and it's all very glossy.

w Ronald Alexander d Jose Ferrer
ph Charles G. Clarke m Franz Waxman

Jeff Chandler, Carol Lynley, Eleanor Parker,
Mary Astor, Robert Sterling, Luciana Paluzzi,
Brett Halsey, Tuesday Weld

'Enough soap suds to pollute the Mississippi
along with the mind.'—Judith Crist, 1973

Return to Yesterday
GB 1940   68m   bw

A bored Hollywood star seeks anonymity in a
seaside repertory company. Mild comedy, not
without interest. Clive Brook, Anna Lee,
Dame May Whitty, Hartley Power, Milton
Rosmer, David Tree, Olga Lindo. Written by
Robert Stevenson, Margaret Kennedy, Roland
Pertwee and Angus MacPhail, from the play
Goodness How Sad by Robert Morley;
directed by Robert Stevenson; for Ealing.

Reunion in France
US 1943   104m   bw
MGM (Joseph L. Mankiewicz)
GB title: Mademoiselle France

A selfish Parisian dress designer gradually
realizes that her world has changed when the
Nazis invade and she is asked to help an
American flier.
Action flagwaver which tries also to be a
woman's picture and goes pretty soppily about
it.

w Jan Lustig, Marvin Borowsky, Marc
Connelly, story Ladislas Bus-Fekete d Jules
Dassin ph Robert Planck m Franz Waxman

Joan Crawford, John Wayne, Philip Dorn,
Reginald Owen, Albert Basserman, John
Carradine, Ann Ayars, J. Edward Bromberg,
Henry Daniell, Moroni Olsen, Howard da
Silva

'Miss Crawford isn't making all the sacrifices
implied in the script . . . Dressing like a
refugee is certainly not in her contract.'—New
York Herald Tribune

Reunion in Vienna*
US 1933   100m   bw
MGM

A long-exiled nobleman tries to take up an old
romance even though the lady is married.
Lacklustre adaptation of a play which must
have style; the performances remain
interesting.

w Ernest Vajda, Claudine West, play Robert
E. Sherwood d Sidney Franklin ph George
Folsey

John Barrymore, Diana Wynyard, Frank
Morgan, May Robson, Eduardo Ciannelli,
Una Merkel, Henry Travers

AAN: George Folsey

Revenge
GB 1971   89m   Eastmancolor
Rank / Peter Rogers Productions (George H.
  Brown)

When children are raped and murdered in a north country town, two men take the law into their own hands.

Crude melodrama set in Cold Comfort Farm country; efficient but unrewarding.

w John Kruse d Sidney Hayers ph Ken Hodges m Eric Rodgers

Joan Collins, Sinead Cusack, James Booth, Ray Barrett, Kenneth Griffith

The Revenge of Frankenstein
GB 1958   89m   Technicolor
Columbia / Hammer (Anthony Hinds)

Baron Frankenstein evades the guillotine and makes a new creature with the brain of a homicidal dwarf.

Dullish horror farrago with a few indications of quirkish humour.

w Jimmy Sangster, Hurford Janes d Terence Fisher ph Jack Asher m Leonard Salzedo

Peter Cushing, Michael Gwynn, Oscar Quitak, Francis Matthews, Eunice Gayson, John Welsh, Lionel Jeffries, Richard Wordsworth, Charles Lloyd Pack, John Stuart, Arnold Diamond

† This second Hammer Frankenstein set the tone for the rest; see *The Curse of Frankenstein*.

The Revenge of the Pink Panther
US 1978   98m   Technicolor   Panavision
UA / Blake Edwards

Inspector Clouseau tracks down a drug-smuggling industrialist.

Feeble addition to a series which was always too pleased with itself.

w Frank Waldman, Ron Clarke, Blake Edwards d Blake Edwards ph Ernie Day m Henry Mancini

Peter Sellers, Herbert Lom, Robert Webber, Dyan Cannon, Burt Kwouk, Paul Stewart, Robert Loggia, Graham Stark

The Revengers
US 1972   108m   De Luxe   Panavision
Cinema Center / Martin Rackin

A rancher gathers a posse to hunt down the Indians who have allegedly murdered his wife and family.

Standard major western with a dismal script which echoes *The Dirty Dozen* and *The Wild Bunch*: sometimes repulsive, seldom exciting.

w Wendell Mayes d Daniel Mann ph Gabriel Torres m Pino Calvi

William Holden, Ernest Borgnine, Susan Hayward, Woody Strode, Roger Hanin

The Revolt of Mamie Stover
US 1956   93m   Eastmancolor
Cinemascope
TCF (Buddy Adler)

A dance hall girl leaves San Francisco for Honolulu, makes money there but reforms for love of a rich novelist.

Absurdly bowdlerized and boring film version of a novel about a sleazy prostitute; hardly worth making at all in this form, especially as the cast seems well capable of a raunchier version.

w Sidney Boehm, *novel* William Bradford Huie d Raoul Walsh ph Leo Tover m Hugo Friedhofer

Jane Russell, Agnes Moorehead, Richard Egan, Joan Leslie

The Revolutionary
US 1970   101m   Technicolor
(UA) Pressman–Williams (Edward R. Pressman)

Episodes in the life of a revolutionary, from distributing leaflets to attempted assassination. A rather casual study of one man's radicalism, in no particular time or place; no doubt of great interest to other revolutionaries.

w Hans Konigsberger d Paul Williams ph Brian Probyn m Michael Small

Jon Voight, Jennifer Salt, Robert Duvall

The Reward
US 1965   92m   De Luxe   Cinemascope
TCF / Aaron Rosenberg

A mixed group of adventurers set out across the desert to capture a murderer; but thieves fall out.

Pretentious and talky melodrama which quickly scuttled its director's chances in Hollywood. Little action, obvious outcome, attractive Death Valley locations.

w Serge Bourguignon, Oscar Mullard, *novel* Michael Barrett d Serge Bourguignon ph Joe MacDonald m Elmer Bernstein

Max Von Sydow, Efrem Zimbalist Jnr, Yvette Mimieux, Gilbert Roland, Emilio Fernandez, Henry Silva

Rhapsody
US 1954   116m   Technicolor
MGM (Lawrence Weingarten)

A wealthy woman affects the lives of two quite different musicians, each of whom has his weakness.

Tedious romantic drama which vainly attempted a smart veneer but boasted a splendid musical sound track.

w Fay and Michael Kanin, *novel* Maurice
Guest by Henry Handel Richardson
d Charles Vidor *ph* Robert Planck
md Johnny Green, Bronislau Kaper
pianist Claudio Arrau *violinist* Michael Rabin

Elizabeth Taylor, Vittorio Gassman, John
Ericson, Louis Calhern, Michael Chekhov,
Barbara Bates, Celia Lovsky, Richard
Hageman

Rhapsody in Blue**
US 1945 139m bw
Warner (Jesse L. Lasky)

The life story of composer George Gershwin.
No more trustworthy on factual matters than
other Hollywood biopics of its era, this rather
glum saga at least presented the music and the
performers to excellent advantage.

w Howard Koch, Elliot Paul *d* *Irving Rapper*
ph Sol Polito *md* Ray Heindorf, Max Steiner
ch Le Roy Prinz *ad* Anton Grot, John
Hughes

Robert Alda, Joan Leslie, Alexis Smith,
Charles Coburn, Julie Bishop, *Albert
Basserman, Oscar Levant, Herbert Rudley*,
Rosemary de Camp, Morris Carnovsky, *Al
Jolson, Paul Whiteman*, George White, Hazel
Scott

AAN: Ray Heindorf, Max Steiner

Rhino
US 1964 91m Metrocolor
MGM / Ivan Tors (Ben Chapman)

A scientist working with white rhinos is joined
by an unscrupulous big game hunter.
Inoffensive African adventure.

w Art Arthur, Arthur Weiss *d* Ivan Tors
ph Sven Persson, Lamar Boren *m* Lalo
Schifrin

Harry Guardino, Robert Culp, Shirley Eaton

Rhodes of Africa*
GB 1936 91m bw
Gaumont (Geoffrey Barkas)
US title: *Rhodes*

A rough-hewn diamond miner becomes Prime
Minister of Cape Colony.
Heavy-going but generally interesting
historical drama shot on location.

w Michael Barringer, Leslie Arliss, Miles
Malleson, *book* Sarah Millin *d* Berthold
Viertel

Walter Huston, Oscar Homolka, Basil Sydney,
Peggy Ashcroft, Frank Cellier, Bernard Lee,
Lewis Casson

'Solid, worthy, humourless, it unrolls its
eleven well-bred reels with all the technical
advantages of 1936.'—*Graham Greene*

Rhubarb
US 1951 94m bw
Paramount (Perlberg–Seaton)

A millionaire leaves his fortune, including a
baseball team, to a wild ginger cat, which
means problems for his publicity agent.
Typical scatty farce of the early fifties, held
together by the splendid performance of the
disdainful feline in the title role rather than by
any special merit in the handling.

w Dorothy Reid, Francis Cockrill, *novel*
H. Allen Smith *d* Arthur Lubin *ph* Lionel
Lindon *m* Van Cleave

Ray Millan.i, Jan Sterling, Gene Lockhart,
William Frawley

Rhythm on the Range*
US 1936 87m bw
Paramount (Benjamin Glazer)

A hired hand saves the boss's daughter when
she is kidnapped by local badmen.
Easy-going musical comedy with a western
background, later remade as *Pardners* (qv).

w John C. Moffett, Sidney Salkow, Walter de
Leon, Francis Martin *d* Norman Taurog
ph Karl Struss *songs* various

Bing Crosby, Martha Raye, Frances Farmer,
Bob Burns, Lucile Watson, Samuel S. Hinds,
George E. Stone, Warren Hymer

'Bing Crosby as a cowboy; Bing Crosby
crooning a prize bull to sleep on a freight car;
Bing Crosby more than ever like Walt
Disney's Cock Robin; it needs some stamina
to be a film reviewer.'—*Graham Greene*

Rhythm on the River*
US 1940 92m bw
Paramount (William Le Baron)

A song writer employs 'ghosts' to produce his
music and lyrics; they discover this fact and go
into business for themselves.
Cheerful musical with strong billing.

w Dwight Taylor, Billy Wilder, Jacques Théry
d Victor Schertzinger *ph* Ted Tetzlaff
m Johnny Burke, James V. Monaco

*Bing Crosby, Mary Martin, Basil Rathbone,
Oscar Levant*, Oscar Shaw, Charley
Grapewin, William Frawley

AAN: song 'Only Forever'

Rich and Strange*
GB 1932 83m bw
BIP (John Maxwell)
US title: *East of Shanghai*

A young couple come into money and take a
trip around the world.
Slight, agreeable early talkie with a few
Hitchcock touches.

w Alma Reville, Val Valentine, Alfred
Hitchcock, *novel* Dale Collins *d Alfred
Hitchcock ph* Jack Cox, Charles Martin
m Hal Dolphe

Henry Kendall, Joan Barry, Percy Marmont,
Betty Amann, Elsie Randolph

The Rich Are Always with Us
US 1932   73m   bw
Warner (Sam Bischoff)

A socialite determines on a divorce but her
new love is annoyed by her concern for her
ex-husband.
Cocktail drama of a kind which totally
disappeared from the screen.

w Austin Parker, *novel* E. Pettit *d* Alfred E.
Green *ph* Ernest Haller *m* W. Franke
Harling

Ruth Chatterton, George Brent, John Miljan,
Bette Davis, Adrienne Dore, Mae Madison,
Robert Warwick

Rich Kids
US 1979   96m   Technicolor

An adolescent boy and girl are mildly
corrupted by the behaviour of their parents.
Spasmodically interesting comedy-drama
which seems ill at ease among the rich and
alternates between exploitation, satire and
whimsy. Trini Alvarado, Jeremy Levy,
Kathryn Walker, John Lithgow, Terry Kiser,
David Selby. Written by Judith Ross; directed
by Robert M. Young; for Robert Altman /
Lion's Gate / UA.

Rich Man, Poor Girl
US 1938   72m   bw

Consternation takes a white-collar family
when a millionaire takes a fancy to one of its
daughters. Unexciting comedy-drama vaguely
modelled on *You Can't Take It With You.* Lew
Ayres, Ruth Hussey, Robert Young, Don
Castle, Guy Kibbee, Lana Turner, Rita
Johnson. Written by Joseph Fields and Jerome
Chodorov, from a play by Edith Ellis; directed
by Reinhold Schunzel; for MGM.

Rich Man's Folly
US 1931   80m   bw
Paramount

A rich man has no time for his children.
Curious updating of Dickens' *Dombey and
Son;* not really a success.

w Grover Jones, Edward Paramore Jnr
d John Cromwell *ph* David Abel

George Bancroft, Frances Dee, Robert Ames,
Juliette Compton, Dorothy Peterson

Rich, Young and Pretty
US 1951   95m   Technicolor
MGM (Joe Pasternak)

A Texas rancher takes his young daughter to
Paris, where she meets her real mother.
Moderate musical.

w Dorothy Cooper, Sidney Sheldon
d Norman Taurog *ph* Robert Planck
m Nicholas Brodszky *ly* Sammy Cahn
ch Nick Castle

Danielle Darrieux, Wendell Corey, Jane
Powell, Fernando Lamas, Vic Damone

AAN: song 'Wonder Why' (*m* Nicholas
Brodszky, *ly* Sammy Cahn)

Richard III•••
GB 1955   161m   Technicolor
   Vistavision
London Films (Laurence Olivier)

Shakespeare's play about Richard Crookback,
his seizure of the throne and his defeat at
Bosworth.
Theatrical but highly satisfying filming of a
splendidly melodramatic view of history.
Interesting but not fussy camera movement,
delightful sets (followed by a disappointingly
'realistic' battle) and superb performances.

w William Shakespeare (adapted by Laurence
Olivier, Alan Dent, with additions)
d Laurence Olivier ph Otto Heller *ph* Roger
Furse *m William Walton ad Carmen Dillon*

Laurence Olivier, Claire Bloom, *Ralph
Richardson, Cedric Hardwicke,* Stanley Baker,
Alec Clunes, John Gielgud, Mary Kerridge,
Pamela Brown, Michael Gough, Norman
Wooland, Helen Haye, Patrick Troughton,
Clive Morton, Andrew Cruickshank

AAN: Laurence Olivier

The Richest Girl in the World
US 1934   76m   bw

A millionairess changes places with her
secretary to find a man who will love her for
herself. Rose-coloured romance, remade in
1944 as *Bride by Mistake.* Miriam Hopkins,
Joel McCrea, Fay Wray, Henry Stephenson,
Reginald Denny, Beryl Mercer. Written by
Norman Krasna; directed by William A.
Seiter; for RKO. AAN: Norman Krasna.

The Riddle of the Sands•
GB 1978   102m   Eastmancolor
   Panavision
Rank / Worldmark (Drummond Challis)

In 1901 a British yachtsman in the North Sea
hits upon a German trial invasion.

Rather too placid adaptation of a semi-classic adventure story in which too little happens to make a rousing action film; points of interest along the way, though.

w Tony Maylam, John Bailey, *novel* Erskine Childers *d* Tony Maylam *ph* Christopher Challis *m* Howard Blake *ph* Hazel Peiser

Michael York, Simon MacCorkindale, Jenny Agutter, Alan Badel, Jurgen Andersen

Ride a Crooked Trail
US 1958 88m Eastmancolor
Cinemascope

A crook takes refuge in a small town and becomes its honest marshal. One we've heard before, and seen better done. Audie Murphy, Walter Matthau, Gia Scala, Henry Silva. Written by Borden Chase; directed by Jesse Hibbs; for Universal-International.

The Ride Back*
US 1957 79m bw
UA / Associates and Aldrich (William Conrad)

A lawman arrests an outlaw wanted for murder, but has the problem of getting him back to base.
Slightly offbeat low-budget western, well enough done if it had to be done at all.

w Anthony Ellis *d* Allen H. Miner *ph* Joseph Biroc *m* Frank de Vol

Anthony Quinn, William Conrad, George Trevino, Lita Milan

Ride beyond Vengeance
US 1966 100m Technicolor
Columbia / Tiger / Goodson / Todman / Sentinel / Fenady

A young westerner, accused of cattle rustling and branded, vows revenge.
Dourly brutal but studio-bound and very padded western; if there is any entertainment value it doesn't emerge for more than a few moments.

w Andrew J. Fenady, *novel* The Night of the Tiger by Al Dewlen *d* Bernard McEveety *ph* Lester Shorr *m* Richard Markowitz

Chuck Connors, Michael Rennie, Kathryn Hays, Claude Akins, Bill Bixby, Paul Fix, Gary Merrill, Joan Blondell, Gloria Grahame, Ruth Warrick, Arthur O'Connell, Frank Gorshin, James MacArthur
† Probably intended as a TV movie and found too violent.

Ride Clear of Diablo
US 1954 80m Technicolor

A young man seeking vengeance on his father's murderer becomes deputy to a sheriff hired to kill him too. Lively enough star western. Audie Murphy, Dan Duryea, Susan Cabot, Abbe Lane, Russell Johnson, Paul Birch, Jack Elam. Written by George Zuckerman; directed by Jesse Hibbs; for Universal-International.

Ride 'Em Cowboy
US 1941 82m bw
Universal (Alex Gottlieb)

Two hot dog vendors find themselves working on an Arizona dude ranch.
Slick but routine comedy star vehicle with no outstanding sequences.

w True Boardman, John Grant *d* Arthur Lubin *ph* John W. Boyle *m* Frank Skinner *songs* Don Raye, Gene de Paul

Bud Abbott, Lou Costello, Dick Foran, Anne Gwynne, Samuel S. Hinds, Richard Lane, Johnny Mack Brown, Ella Fitzgerald

Ride Lonesome
US 1959 73m Eastmancolor
Cinemascope

A bounty hunter catches a killer as bait to trap the criminal's brother against whom he plots vengeance. Mildly suspenseful western, rather lost on the wide screen. Randolph Scott, Karen Steele, Pernell Roberts, James Best, James Coburn, Lee Van Cleef. Written by Burt Kennedy; directed by Budd Boetticher; for Columbia.

Ride the High Country**
US 1962 94m Metrocolor
Cinemascope
MGM (Richard E. Lyons)
GB title: *Guns in the Afternoon*

Two retired lawmen help transport gold from a mining camp to the bank, but one has ideas of his own.
Thoughtful western graced by ageing star presences; generally well done.

w N. B. Stone Jnr *d* Sam Peckinpah *ph* Lucien Ballard *m* George Bassman

Joel McCrea, Randolph Scott, Edgar Buchanan, Mariette Hartley, James Drury
'A nice little conventional unconventional western.'—*Stanley Kauffmann*

Ride the High Iron
US 1957 74m bw

A war veteran gets into the seamier side of public relations. Curious little urban melodrama with a high moral tone, like a cut-price *Sweet Smell of Success*. Don Taylor, Raymond Burr, Sally Forrest. Written by Milton Gelman; directed by Dòn Weis; for Columbia.

Ride the Man Down
US 1952   90m   Trucolor

The death of a rancher sets off a bitter fight for his lands. Flat and uninteresting western melodrama. Brian Donlevy, Ella Raines, Rod Cameron, Forrest Tucker, Barbara Britton, James Bell, Chill Wills, J. Carrol Naish, Jim Davis. Written by Mary McCall Jnr; directed by Joe Kane; for Republic.

Ride the Pink Horse*
US 1947   101m   bw
U-I

An ex-serviceman visits a New Mexican town in search of the gangster who killed his buddy. Dour, complex melodrama with a certain amount of style but not enough substance.

w Charles Lederer, *novel* Dorothy B. Hughes
d Robert Montgomery *ph* Russell Metty
m Frank Skinner

Robert Montgomery, Wanda Hendrix, Andrea King, Thomas Gomez, Fred Clark, Art Smith

AAN: Thomas Gomez

Ride the Wild Surf
US 1964   101m   Eastmancolor
Columbia / Jana (Jo and Art Napoleon)

Surf riders go to Hawaii and find romance. Pleasant, overlong, open air fun and games.

w Jo and Art Napoleon *d* Don Taylor
ph Joseph Biroc *m* Stu Phillips

Fabian, Shelley Fabares, Tab Hunter, Barbara Eden

The Ride to Hangman's Tree
US 1967   90m   Technicolor

Three bandits never quite manage to reform. Easy-going western, played on the light side in a vein later developed in *Butch Cassidy and the Sundance Kid*. Jack Lord, James Farentino, Don Galloway, Melody Johnson, Richard Anderson. Written by Luci Ward, Jack Natteford and William Bowers; directed by Alan Rafkin; for Universal.

Ride, Vaquero
US 1953   90m   Anscocolor
MGM (Stephen Ames)

Ranchers settling in New Mexico after the Civil War cause some natives to turn bandit; one of them has a mysterious American associate called Rio.

Very mildly interesting western with the stars rather swamping a humourless script.

w Frank Fenton *d* John Farrow *ph* Robert Surtees *m* Bronislau Kaper

Robert Taylor, Ava Gardner, Howard Keel, Anthony Quinn, Charlita

Rider on a Dead Horse
US 1962   72m   bw

A prospector murders one partner for his gold and tries to pin the blame on the other. Watchable minor western with good use of location. John Vyvyan, Bruce Gordon, Kevin Hagen, Lisa Lu. Written by Stephen Longstreet; directed by Herbert L. Strock; for Allied Artists.

Riders of Vengeance
US 1952   80m   Technicolor

During the California gold rush, a prospector takes revenge on a local dictator. Standard western themes against a colourful background. Richard Conte, Barbara Britton, Viveca Lindfors, Hugh O'Brian, Morris Ankrum, William Reynolds, Dennis Weaver. Written by Polly James and Lillie Hayward; directed by Lesley Selander; for Universal-International. (GB title: *The Raiders*.)

Riders to the Stars*
US 1954   81m   Color Corporation
UA / Ivan Tors

Rocket scientists investigate the problems of cosmic bombardment.
Enjoyably straightforward science fiction with no monsters or political problems; it has decided historic interest as a record of what scientists in 1954 thought rocket travel would be like.

w Curt Siodmak *d* Richard Carlson
ph Stanley Cortez *m* Harry Sukman

Richard Carlson, Herbert Marshall, William Lundigan, Dawn Addams, Martha Hyer, Robert Karnes, Lawrence Dobkin

Riding High
US 1943   88m   Technicolor
Paramount (Fred Kohlmar)
GB title: *Melody Inn*

A burlesque queen goes home to Arizona and helps ranchers by performing at a dude ranch. Dim formula musical with exuberance but neither wit nor style.

w Walter de Leon, Arthur Phillips, Art Arthur, *play* Ready Money by James Montgomery *d* George Marshall *ph* Karl Struss, Harry Hallenberger *md* Victor Young

Dorothy Lamour, Dick Powell, Victor Moore, Gil Lamb, Cass Daley, Bill Goodwin, Rod Cameron, Glenn Langan, Andrew Tombes, Tim Ryan, Douglas Fowley, Milt Britton and his Band

Riding High*
US 1950 112m bw
Paramount (Frank Capra)

An easygoing racing man forsakes the chance of wealth to train his beloved horse for the Imperial Derby.
The director's familiar ingredients—farce, sentimentality, fast cutting, nice people and a lot of noise—seem a shade too tried and tested in this remake of his 1934 success *Broadway Bill*. Despite the cast, the result is only moderately entertaining.

w Robert Riskin *d* Frank Capra *ph* George Barnes, Ernest Laszlo *m* James Van Heusen *ly* Johnny Burke

Bing Crosby, Coleen Gray, Charles Bickford, Raymond Walburn, James Gleason, Oliver Hardy, Frances Gifford, William Demarest, Ward Bond, Clarence Muse, Percy Kilbride, Harry Davenport, Margaret Hamilton, Douglass Dumbrille, Gene Lockhart

Riding Shotgun
US 1954 75m Warnercolor

A shotgun stagecoach guard carries on a long vendetta against an outlaw. Routine western excitements, played mainly indoors. Randolph Scott, Wayne Morris, Joan Weldon, Joe Sawyer, James Millican, Charles Bronson, James Bell. Written by Tom Blackburn; directed by André de Toth; for Warner.

Riff Raff
US 1935 90m bw
MGM (Irving Thalberg)

A con man and his wife end up on the wrong side of the law.
Modest comedy drama that never quite sparks.

w Frances Marion, H. W. Haneman, Anita Loos *d* Robert Z. Leonard *m* Edward Ward

Jean Harlow, Spencer Tracy, Joseph Calleia, Una Merkel, Mickey Rooney, Victor Kilian, J. Farrell MacDonald

Riff Raff*
US 1947 80m bw
RKO

A dying man hands a Panama City con man a map to valuable oil deposits, and various shady people are after it.

Rather heavy but well made comedy-drama with some striking scenes.

w Martin Rackin *d* Ted Tetzlaff *ph* George E. Diskant *m* Roy Webb

Pat O'Brien, Walter Slezak, Anne Jeffreys, Percy Kilbride, Jerome Cowan

Rififi**
France 1955 116m bw
Indus / Pathé / Prima
original title: *Du Rififi chez les Hommes*

After an elaborate raid on a jewellery store, thieves fall out and the caper ends in bloodshed.
A film with much to answer for, in the form of hundreds of imitations showing either detailed accounts of robberies (*Topkapi, Gambit*) or gloomy looks at the private lives of criminals. At the time it seemed crisp and exciting, and the 25-minute silent robbery sequence is quite something.

w René Wheeler, Jules Dassin, Auguste le Breton, *novel* Auguste le Breton *d* Jules Dassin *ph* Philippe Agostini *m* Georges Auric

Jean Servais, Carl Mohner, Robert Manuel, Marie Sabouret, Perlo Vita (Jules Dassin)
† Several 'sequels' were made using the word *rififi* (criminal argot for 'trouble') in the title, but in plot terms they were entirely unrelated.

The Right Approach
US 1961 92m bw Cinemascope
TCF (Oscar Brodney)

A Hollywood opportunist tries to make it as a star.
A potentially witty Hollywood story is sabotaged by a style which is as naïve as it is dismal; and Mr Vaughan's hopes of stardom unfairly ended right here.

w Fay and Michael Kanin, *play* Garson Kanin *d* David Butler *ph* Sam Leavitt *m* Dominic Frontière

Frankie Vaughan, Martha Hyer, Juliet Prowse, Gary Crosby, David MacLean, Jesse White, Jane Withers

Right Cross
US 1950 90m bw
MGM (Armand Deutsch)

A boxing champion injures his hand and has to abandon his career.
Rather dull sporting melodrama with a Mexican background, saved by good production values.

w Charles Schnee *d* John Sturges *ph* Norbert Brodine *m* David Raksin

Dick Powell, June Allyson, Lionel Barrymore, Ricardo Montalban

The Right to Live
US 1935 75m bw

Someone in the family mercifully kills a crippled war hero. Uninspired rendering of Somerset Maugham's play *The Sacred Flame*, previously filmed under its own title in 1929 (with Pauline Frederick, Henrietta Crosman, George Brent). Colin Clive, Josephine Hutchinson, Peggy Wood, C. Aubrey Smith, Leo G. Carroll, Halliwell Hobbes. Written by Ralph Block; directed by William Keighley; for Warner. (GB title: *The Sacred Flame*.)

The Ring
US 1952 79m bw
King Brothers

A young Mexican becomes a prizefighter in the hope of winning greater respect for Mexican-Americans.
Well-meant low-budget programmer.

w Irving Shulman *d* Kurt Neumann
ph Russell Harlan *m* Herschel Burke Gilbert

Gerald Mohr, Lalo Rios, Rita Moreno, Robert Arthur

Ring of Bright Water*
GB 1969 107m Technicolor
Palomar / Brightwater (Joseph Strick)

A civil servant buys a pet otter and moves to a remote cottage in the western Highlands.
Disneyesque fable for animal lovers, from a bestselling book.

w Jack Couffer, Bill Travers, *book* Gavin Maxwell *d* Jack Couffer *ph* Wolfgang Suschitsky *m* Frank Cordell

Bill Travers, Virginia McKenna, Peter Jeffrey, Roddy McMillan, Jameson Clark

Ring of Fear
US 1954 88m Warnercolor
Cinemascope
Warner / Wayne–Fellows (Robert M. Fellows)

A homicidal maniac returns to the circus where he used to work and causes various 'accidents'.
Tediously predictable circus melodrama with a curious but not very likeable cast.

w Paul Fix, Philip MacDonald, James Edward Grant *d* James Edward Grant *ph* Edwin DuPar *m* Emil Newman, Arthur Lange

Clyde Beatty, Pat O'Brien, Mickey Spillane, Sean McClory, Marion Carr, John Bromfield, Pedro Gonzalez Gonzalez, Emett Lynn

Ring of Fire
US 1961 90m Metrocolor
MGM / Andrew and Virginia Stone

An Oregon sheriff is kidnapped by teenage delinquents but manages to lead them into both a police trap and a forest fire.
Outdoor action thriller with a plot which is ludicrously unconvincing in detail, though the fire scenes impress.

wd Andrew L. Stone *ph* William H. Clothier
m Duane Eddy

David Janssen, Joyce Taylor, Frank Gorshin, Joel Marston

Ring of Spies*
GB 1963 90m bw
British Lion (Leslie Gilliatt)
US title: *Ring of Treason*

How the Portland spy ring was tracked down.
Documentary drama, rather less intriguing, somehow, than the actual facts; but the sheer thought of spies in the suburbs keeps interest going.

w Frank Launder, Peter Barnes *d* Robert Tronson *ph* Arthur Lavis

Bernard Lee, Margaret Tyzack, David Kossoff, Nancy Nevinson, William Sylvester

The Ringer*
GB 1952 78m bw
BL / London (Hugh Perceval)

A dangerous criminal known only as The Ringer threatens to kill the crooked lawyer responsible for his sister's death.
Artful old-fashioned mystery, quite well restaged, and in fact the best extant example of filmed Wallace.

w Val Valentine, *novel* and *play* Edgar Wallace *d* Guy Hamilton *ph* Ted Scaife
m Malcolm Arnold

Donald Wolfit, Mai Zetterling, Herbert Lom, Greta Gynt, William Hartnell, Norman Wooland
† The play was also filmed in 1931 with Patrick Curwen, Franklin Dyall and Gordon Harker; and in 1938 as *The Gaunt Stranger* (qv).

Rings on Her Fingers*
US 1942 85m bw
TCF (Milton Sperling)

The front girl for a couple of confidence tricksters falls in love with their first victim.
Lively comedy which drags into drama in its second half.

w Ken Englund *d* Rouben Mamoulian
ph George Barnes *m* Cyril Mockridge

Gene Tierney, Henry Fonda, Laird Cregar, Spring Byington, Shepperd Strudwick, Frank Orth, Henry Stephenson, Marjorie Gateson

Rio
US 1939 78m bw
Universal

A crooked financier escapes from Devil's Island to join his wife in Rio, only to find she has been unfaithful.
Modest but well made melodrama.

w Stephen Morehouse Avery, Frank Partos, Edwin Justus Mayer, Abem Kandel, Jean Negulesco d John Brahm ph Hal Mohr m Frank Skinner md Charles Previn

Basil Rathbone, Victor McLaglen, Sigrid Gurie, Robert Cummings, Leo Carrillo, Billy Gilbert, Irving Bacon, Irving Pichel

Rio Bravo**
US 1959 141m Technicolor
Warner (Howard Hawks)

A wandering cowboy and a drunken sheriff hold a town against outlaws.
Cheerfully overlong and slow-moving western in which everybody, including the director, does his thing. All very watchable for those with time to spare, but more a series of revue sketches than an epic.

w Jules Furthman, Leigh Brackett d Howard Hawks ph Russell Harlan m Dmitri Tiomkin
John Wayne, Dean Martin, Ricky Nelson, Angie Dickinson, Walter Brennan, Ward Bond, John Russell, Pedro Gonzalez Gonzalez, Claude Akins, Harry Carey Jnr, Bob Steele
† More or less remade in 1966 as El Dorado and in 1970 as Rio Lobo.

Rio Conchos*
US 1964 107m De Luxe Cinemascope
TCF (David Weisbart)

Two thousand rifles are stolen from an army command port and traced to the hide-out of a former Confederate colonel who wants to continue the Civil War.
Good standard western which shares much of its story line with The Comancheros.

w Clair Huffaker, Joseph Landon d Gordon Douglas ph Joe MacDonald m Jerry Goldsmith

Richard Boone, Edmond O'Brien, Stuart Whitman, Tony Franciosa

Rio Grande*
US 1950 105m bw
Republic (John Ford, Merian C. Cooper)

A Cavalry unit on the Mexican border in the 1880s conducts a vain campaign against marauding Indians.
Thin Ford western on his favourite theme, with too many pauses for song, too many studio sets, and too little plot. Aficionados, however, will find much to admire.

w James Kevin McGuinness, story James Warner Bellah d John Ford ph Bert Glennon, Archie Stout m Victor Young

John Wayne, Maureen O'Hara, Ben Johnson, Claude Jarman Jnr, Harry Carey Jnr, Chill Wills, J. Carrol Naish, Victor McLaglen

Rio Lobo*
US 1970 114m Technicolor
Cinema Center (Howard Hawks)

A union colonel near the end of the Civil War recovers a gold shipment and exposes a traitor.
Rambling western with traces of former glory, enjoyable at least for its sense of humour.

w Leigh Brackett, Burton Wohl d Howard Hawks ph William Clothier m Jerry Goldsmith

John Wayne, Jorge Rivero, Jennifer O'Neill, Jack Elam, Victor French, Chris Mitchum, Mike Henry

Rio Rita
US 1929 135m bw and Technicolor
RKO (William Le Baron)

Romance on a ranch near the Mexican border.
Very early talkie version of a popular Broadway operetta of the twenties; historical interest only.

w Luther Reed, Russell Mack, book Guy Bolton, Fred Thomson, as produced by Florenz Ziegfeld d Luther Reed ph Robert Kurle, Lloyd Knetchel md Victor Baravalle songs Harry Tierney, Joe McCarthy

Bebe Daniels, John Boles, Bert Wheeler, Robert Woolsey, Dorothy Lee, Don Alvarado, George Renavent

Rio Rita
US 1942 91m bw
MGM (Pandro S. Berman)

Flat-footed remake bringing in Nazi spies; poor comedy even by Abbott and Costello standards.

w Richard Connell, Gladys Lehman d S. Sylvan Simon ph George J. Folsey m Herbert Stothart

Bud Abbott, Lou Costello, John Carroll, Kathryn Grayson, Tom Conway, Barry Nelson

Riot
US 1968   98m   Technicolor
Paramount / William Castle

While the warden is away, thirty-five convicts
take over a state penitentiary and are violently
subdued.
Strikingly bloody melodrama set in an actual
prison in Arizona; well made, but less
entertaining than Cagney and Raft used to be.

w James Poe, *novel* Frank Elli d Buzz Kulik
ph Robert B. Hauser m Christopher Komeda

Gene Hackman, Jim Brown, Ben Carruthers,
Mike Kellin, Gerald O'Loughlin, Clifford
David

Riot in Cell Block Eleven*
US 1954   80m   bw
Allied Artists / Walter Wanger

In a big American prison three convicts seize
their guards, free the other prisoners and
barricade themselves in their block.
Socially concerned low-budgeter, quite nicely
made and persuasive of the need for prison
reform.

w *Richard Collins d Don Siegel ph* Russell
Harlan m Herschel Burke Gilbert

Neville Brand, *Emile Meyer*, Frank Faylen,
Leo Gordon, Robert Osterloh, Paul Frees,
Don Keefer
  'As a compassionate, angry, unsensational
account of an episode of violence it makes
considerably more impact than many of the
overblown melodramas currently in
fashion.'—*Penelope Houston*

Riptide*
US 1934   90m   bw
MGM (Irving Thalberg)

A British diplomat weds a Manhattan chorus
girl, but she later falls for an old flame.
Elegantly set, star-packed drawing-room
drama which somehow didn't click.

wd Edmund Goulding ph Ray June
m Herbert Stothart

Norma Shearer, Robert Montgomery, Herbert
Marshall, Mrs Patrick Campbell, Skeets
Gallagher, Ralph Forbes, Lilyan Tashman,
Helen Jerome Eddy, George K. Arthur,
Halliwell Hobbes

The Rise and Fall of Legs Diamond
US 1960   101m   bw
Warner / United States (Milton Sperling)

The career of a New York hoodlum of the
twenties.
Inspired, like *King of the Roaring Twenties*, by
the TV success of *The Untouchables*, this was
part of a brief attempt by Warners to
recapture its pre-war gangster image. Alas,
stars and style were equally lacking.

w Joseph Landon d Budd Boetticher
ph Lucien Ballard m Leonard Rosenman

Ray Danton, Karen Steele, Elaine Stewart,
Jesse White, Simon Oakland, Robert Lowery,
Warren Oates, Judson Pratt

The Rise and Rise of Michael Rimmer
GB 1970   101m   Technicolor
Warner / David Frost (Harry Fine)

An efficiency expert takes over an advertising
agency and is soon an MP, a cabinet minister,
and PM.
Satirical comedy which quickly goes overboard
and is only occasionally funny; it does,
however, mark the final death throes of the
swinging sixties, and the changeover to *Monty
Python*.

w Peter Cook, John Cleese, Kevin Billington,
Graham Chapman d Kevin Billington
ph Alex Thompson m John Cameron

Peter Cook, John Cleese, Arthur Lowe,
Denholm Elliott, Ronald Fraser, Vanessa
Howard, George A. Cooper, Harold Pinter,
James Cossins, Roland Culver, Dudley Foster,
Julian Glover, Dennis Price, Ronnie Corbett

Rise and Shine
US 1941   93m   bw
TCF (Mark Hellinger)

A dumb but brilliant football player is
kidnapped by the other side.
Drab collegiate comedy, disappointing
considering the credits.

w Herman J. Mankiewicz, *novel* My Life and
Hard Times by James Thurber d Allan Dwan
ph Edward Cronjager m Emil Newman
songs Leo Robin, Ralph Rainger

Linda Darnell, Jack Oakie, George Murphy,
Walter Brennan, Milton Berle, Sheldon
Leonard, Donald Meek, Ruth Donnelly,
Donald MacBride, Raymond Walburn, Emma
Dunn

Rising Damp
GB 1980   98m   colour
ITC / Black Lion (Roy Skeggs)

The amorous and conniving landlord of a slum
boarding house develops a passion for one of
his tenants.
A useful reminder of a TV sitcom worth
remembering, but handicapped by restriction
of action, paucity of plot and the overlength
usual in film versions of such things, not to
mention the premature death of its original
co-star Richard Beckinsale.

w Eric Chappell *d* Joe McGrath *ph* Frank Watts *m* David Lindup

Leonard Rossiter, Frances de la Tour, Don Warrington, Denholm Elliott, Christopher Strauli

The Rising of the Moon
Eire 1957 81m bw
Warner / Four Provinces (Lord Killanin)

Three Irish short stories.
Curiously dull John Ford portmanteau with the Abbey players.

w Frank Nugent, *stories* Frank O'Connor, Malcolm J. McHugh, Lady Gregory *d* John Ford *ph* Robert Krasker *m* Eamonn O'Gallagher *narrator* Tyrone Power

Maureen Connell, Eileen Crowe, Cyril Cusack, Maureen Delany, Donald Donelly, Frank Lawton, Edward Lexy, Jack MacGowran, Denis O'Dea, Jimmy O'Dea, Noel Purcell

The Ritz*
US 1976 90m Technicolor
Warner / Courtyard (Denis O'Dell)

A comedy of mistaken identities in a gay New York turkish bath.
An adaptation of a stage success which doesn't seem nearly as funny as it thinks it is; but some of it does work.

w Terrance McNally, from his play *d* Richard Lester *ph* Paul Wilson *m* Ken Thorne *pd* Phillip Harrison

Jack Weston, Rita Moreno, Jerry Stiller, Kaye Ballard, Bessie Love, George Coulouris, F. Murray Abrahams, Treat Williams

The River*
India 1951 87m Technicolor
Oriental / International / Theatre Guild (Kenneth McEldowney)

Episodes in the life of a small English community living on the banks of the Ganges.
A slight and surprising work from this director, superbly observed and a pleasure to watch but dramatically very thin.

w Rumer Godden, Jean Renoir, *novel* Rumer Godden *d* Jean Renoir *ph* Claude Renoir *m* M. A. Partha Sarathy *pd* Eugene Lourié

Nora Swinburne, Esmond Knight, Arthur Shields, Adrienne Corri
† Renoir's assistant was Satyajit Ray.

River Lady
US 1948 78m Technicolor
The beautiful owner of a Mississippi gambling

boat tries to buy up all her rivals. Routine romantic drama. Yvonne de Carlo, Rod Cameron, Dan Duryea, Helena Carter, Lloyd Gough, Florence Bates, John McIntire. Written by D. D. Beauchamp and William Bowers; directed by George Sherman; for Universal-International.

River of No Return*
US 1954 91m Technicolor
        Cinemascope
TCF (Stanley Rubin)

During the California gold rush a widower and his 10-year-old son encounter a saloon singer with a gold claim.
Cheerful, clichéd star western designed to exploit the splendours of early Cinemascope, and very adequate for this purpose.

w Frank Fenton *d* Otto Preminger *ph* Joseph La Shelle *m* Cyril Mockridge *md* Lionel Newman

Robert Mitchum, Marilyn Monroe, Tommy Rettig, Rory Calhoun, Murvyn Vye

The River's Edge
US 1956 87m Eastmancolor
        Cinemascope
TCF (Benedict Bogeaus)

A fugitive bank robber forces a farmer to guide him over the mountains into Mexico.
Sluggish open-air character melodrama.

w Harold J. Smith *d* Allan Dwan *ph* Harold Lipstein *m* Lou Forbes

Ray Milland, Anthony Quinn, Debra Paget, Byron Foulger

River's End
US 1930 74m bw

A Mountie dies chasing his man, who then impersonates him. Popular, contrived, outdoor thriller, previously filmed in 1922 with Lewis Stone, and subsequently in 1940 with Dennis Morgan (this version became known as *Double Identity*). Charles Bickford, Evalyn Knapp, J. Farrell MacDonald, Zasu Pitts, David Torrence. Written by Charles Kenyon, from the story by James Oliver Curwood; directed by Michael Curtiz; for Warner.

The Road Back**
US 1937 97m bw
Universal (James Whale)

After World War I, German soldiers go home to problems and disillusion.
A major work, intended as a sequel to *All Quiet on the Western Front*. Despite impressive sequences, it doesn't quite reach inspiring heights.

w R. C. Sherriff, Charles Kenyon, *novel* Erich Maria Remarque *d James Whale ph John Mescall, George Robinson m* Dmitri Tiomkin *ad* Charles D. Hall

Richard Cromwell, John King, Slim Summerville, Andy Devine, Barbara Read, Louise Fazenda, Noah Beery Jnr, Lionel Atwill, John Emery, Etienne Girardot, Spring Byington, Laura Hope Crews

'They call it an all-star cast and that means there isn't a single player of any distinction to be picked out of the herd. . . . It might be funny if it wasn't horrifying. This is America seeing the world in its own image.'—*Graham Greene*

† The film is said to have been extensively reshot after protests from the German consul in Los Angeles. No 35mm negative now exists, as it reverted to Remarque and was lost.

Road House
GB 1934   76m   bw

A girl on a murder charge is helped by a famous actress who is really her mother. Stock melodrama with a good script and popular players. Violet Loraine, Gordon Harker, Emlyn Williams, Hartley Power, Stanley Holloway, Marie Lohr, Geraldo and his band. Written by Austin Melford and Leslie Arliss, from the play by Walter Hackett; directed by Maurice Elvey; for Gaumont.

Road House*
US 1948   95m   bw
TCF (Edward Chodorov)

A road house owner is jealous of his manager and frames him for murder.
Dated but watchable *film noir* of its era, with all characters cynical or homicidal.

w Edward Chodorov *d* Jean Negulesco *ph* Joseph La Shelle *m* Cyril Mockridge

Richard Widmark, Ida Lupino, Cornel Wilde, Celeste Holm

Road Show*
US 1941   86m   bw
Hal Roach

A young man wrongly committed to an insane asylum escapes with another inmate and joins a travelling circus.
Engaging scatty comedy on familiar Roach lines which suffers from lame pacing but manages some likeable moments.

w Arnold Beldard, Harry Langdon, Mickell Novak, *novel* Eric Hatch *d* Gordon Douglas *ph* Norbert Brodine *m* George Stoll

John Hubbard, Adolphe Menjou, Carole Landis, Patsy Kelly, George E. Stone

Road to Denver*
US 1955   90m   Trucolor

An honest ranch hand gets into trouble when he tries to help his lawless brother. Uninspired western which just about passes the time. John Payne, Lee J. Cobb, Skip Homeier, Mona Freeman, Ray Middleton, Andy Clyde, Lee Van Cleef. Written by Horace McCoy and Allen Rivkin; directed by Joe Kane; for Republic.

The Road to Glory*
US 1936   103m   bw
TCF (Darryl F. Zanuck)

Adventures of a French regiment in World War I.
Meticulously produced war movie which bears comparison with *All Quiet on the Western Front.*

w Joel Sayre, William Faulkner *d* Howard Hawks *ph* Gregg Toland *m* Louis Silvers

Fredric March, Warner Baxter, Lionel Barrymore, June Lang, Gregory Ratoff, Victor Kilian, John Qualen, Julius Tannen, Leonid Kinskey

Road to Mandalay
US 1926   77m at 24 fps   bw   silent

Two eastern planters quarrel over a girl. Potboiling star vehicle. Lon Chaney, Lois Moran, Owen Moore, Henry B. Walthall. Written by Elliott Clawson and Herman Mankiewicz; directed by Tod Browning; for MGM.

The Road to Salina
France / Italy 1971   96m   colour
   Panavision

The proprietress of a roadside café recognizes a drifter as her long-lost son. Boring emotional drama stymied by the multi-language problem. Rita Hayworth, Mimsy Farmer, Robert Walker Jnr, Ed Begley, Sophie Hardy. Written by Georges Lautner, Pascal Jardin and Jack Miller; directed by Georges Lautner; for Robert Dorfmann.

Road to Singapore
US 1931   70m   bw

A doctor's wife is caught with her lover, and her life falls to pieces. Tensions among the oriental upper crust: very dated and not very convincing. William Powell, Louis Calhern, Doris Kenyon, Marian Marsh, Alison Skipworth. Written by J. Grubb Alexander, from a play by Roland Pertwee; directed by Alfred E. Green; for Warner.

THE 'ROAD' SERIES:

Road to Singapore*
US 1940   84m   bw
Paramount (Harlan Thompson)

Two rich playboys swear off women until they quarrel over a Singapore maiden.
The first Hope–Crosby–Lamour 'road' picture is basically a light romantic comedy and quite forgettable; the series got zanier as it progressed.

w Don Hartman, Frank Butler, *story* Harry Hervey d Victor Schertzinger ph William C. Mellor m Victor Young

Bing Crosby, Bob Hope, Dorothy Lamour, Charles Coburn, Judith Barrett, Anthony Quinn, Jerry Colonna

Road to Zanzibar**
US 1941   92m   bw
Paramount (Paul Jones)

The trio on safari in Africa, with *Hellzapoppin* gags breaking in and an anything-goes atmosphere.

w Frank Butler, Don Hartman d Victor Schertzinger ph Ted Tetzlaff m Victor Young *songs* Johnny Burke, Jimmy Van Heusen

Hope, Crosby, Lamour, Una Merkel, Eric Blore, Luis Alberni, Douglass Dumbrille
'The funniest thing I've seen on the screen in years. Years.'—*Otis Ferguson*

Road to Morocco**
US 1942   83m   bw
Paramount (Paul Jones)

Hollywood Arab palaces, a captive princess, topical gags and talking camels.

w Frank Butler, Don Hartman d David Butler ph William C. Mellor md Victor Young *songs* Johnny Burke, Jimmy Van Heusen

Hope, Crosby, Lamour, Anthony Quinn, Dona Drake

AAN: script

Road to Utopia**
US 1945   89m   bw
Paramount (Paul Jones)

The California gold rush, with all the previous gag styles in good order, capped by a cheeky epilogue and constant explanatory narration by Robert Benchley.

w Norman Panama, Melvin Frank d Hal Walker ph Lionel Lindon m Leigh Harline *songs* Johnny Burke, Jimmy Van Heusen

Hope, Crosby, Lamour, Douglass Dumbrille, Hillary Brooke, Jack La Rue

AAN: script

Road to Rio**
US 1947   100m   bw
Paramount (Daniel Dare)

Guest stars are given their head, plot intrudes again in the shape of a hypnotized heiress, and the style is more constrained (but still funny).

w Edmund Beloin, Jack Rose d Norman Z. McLeod ph Ernest Laszlo md Robert Emmett Dolan *songs* Johnny Burke, Jimmy Van Heusen

Hope, Crosby, Lamour, Gale Sondergaard, Frank Faylen, the Wiere Brothers, the And.ews Sisters
'Enough laughs to pass the time easily and to remind you how completely, since sound came in, the American genius for movie comedy has disintegrated.'—*James Agee*

AAN: Robert Emmett Dolan

Road to Bali*
US 1952   91m   Technicolor
Paramount (Harry Tugend)

In and around the South Seas, with colour making the sets obvious and the gags only tediously funny. The team's zest was also flagging.

w Frank Butler, Hal Kanter, William Morrow d Hal Walker ph George Barnes md Joseph J. Lilley *songs* Johnny Burke, Jimmy Van Heusen

Hope, Crosby, Lamour, Murvyn Vye, Peter Coe

Road to Hong Kong
GB 1962   91m   bw
UA / Melnor (Norman Panama)

Curious, slightly dismal-looking attempt to continue the series in a British studio and on a low budget. A few good gags, but it's all very tired by now, and the space fiction plot makes it seem more so.

w Norman Panama, Melvin Frank d Melvin Frank ph Jack Hildyard m Robert Farnon pd Roger Furse

Hope, Crosby, Lamour, Joan Collins, Robert Morley, Walter Gotell, Felix Aylmer and guests Peter Sellers, David Niven, Frank Sinatra, Dean Martin, Jerry Colonna

Roadhouse Nights*
US 1930   71m   bw
Paramount

A reporter exposes a gangster operating from a country nightclub.
Experimental mingling of elements which later become very familiar.

w Garrett Fort, *story* Ben Hecht d Hobart Henley ph William Steiner

Helen Morgan, Charles Ruggles, Fred Kohler,
Jimmy Durante, Fuller Mellish Jnr

The Roaring Twenties***
US 1939   106m   bw
Warner (Hal B. Wallis)

A World War I veteran returns to New York,
innocently becomes involved in bootlegging,
builds up an empire and dies in a gang war.
Among the last of the Warner gangster cycle,
this was perhaps the best production of them
all, despite the familiar plot line: stars and
studio were in cracking form.

w Jerry Wald, Richard Macaulay, Robert
Rossen, *story* Mark Hellinger d *Raoul Walsh,
Anatole Litvak ph Ernest Haller m* Heinz
Roemheld

James Cagney, Humphrey Bogart, Priscilla
Lane, Jeffrey Lynn, Gladys George, Frank
McHugh, Paul Kelly, Elizabeth Risdon

Rob Roy the Highland Rogue
GB 1953   81m   Technicolor
Walt Disney (Perce Pearce)

After the defeat of the clans in the 1715
rebellion, their leader escapes and after
several adventures is granted a royal pardon.
A kind of Scottish Robin Hood, so stiffly acted
and made that it might as well—or better—be
a cartoon.

w Lawrence E. Watkin d Harold French
ph Guy Green m Cedric Thorpe Davie

Richard Todd, Glynis Johns, James Robertson
Justice, Michael Gough, Finlay Currie,
Geoffrey Keen, Archie Duncan

Robbers' Roost
US 1955   82m   De Luxe

An honest cowboy is employed by cattle
rustlers and strives to clear his name. Fair
western programmer. George Montgomery,
Richard Boone, Sylvia Findley, Bruce
Bennett, Peter Graves, Warren Stevens,
William Hopper. Written by John O'Dea,
Sidney Salkow and Maurice Geraghty, from a
novel by Zane Grey; directed by Sidney
Salkow; for Leonard Goldstein / UA.

Robbery*
GB 1967   113m   Eastmancolor
Joseph E. Levine / Oakhurst (Michael
Deeley, Stanley Baker)

Criminals conspire to rob the night mail train
from Glasgow.
Heavy-going fictionalized account of the
famous train robbery of 1963; best seen as
standard cops and robbers, with some good
chase sequences.

w Edward Boyd, Peter Yates, George
Markstein d *Peter Yates ph* Douglas
Slocombe m Johnny Keating

Stanley Baker, James Booth, Frank Finlay,
Joanna Pettet, Barry Foster, William
Marlowe, Clinton Greyn, George Sewell

Robbery under Arms
GB 1957   99m   Eastmancolor
Rank (Joe Janni)

In 19th-century Australia, two farming
brothers join the notorious outlaw Captain
Starlight.
Howlingly dull film version of a semi-classic
adventure novel; a rambling story with no
unity of viewpoint is saved only by excellent
photography.

w Alexander Baron, W. P. Lipscomb, *novel*
Rolf Boldrewood d Jack Lee ph Harry
Waxman m Matyas Seiber

Peter Finch, David McCallum, Ronald Lewis,
Maureen Swanson, Jill Ireland, Laurence
Naismith, Jean Anderson

The Robe**
US 1953   135m   Technicolor
  Cinemascope
TCF (Frank Ross)

Followers and opponents of Jesus are affected
by the robe handed down by him at his
crucifixion.
The first film in Cinemascope was,
surprisingly, a biblical bestseller, but the
crowded Roman sets hid most of the flaws in
the process. The film itself was competent and
unsurprising in the well-tried *Sign of the Cross*
manner.

w Philip Dunne, *novel* Lloyd C. Douglas
d Henry Koster ph Leon Shamroy m Alfred
Newman

Richard Burton, Jean Simmons, Michael
Rennie, *Victor Mature*, Jay Robinson, Torin
Thatcher, Dean Jagger, Richard Boone, Betta
St John, Jeff Morrow, Ernest Thesiger, Dawn
Addams

AAN: best picture; Leon Shamroy; Richard
Burton

Roberta*
US 1935   105m   bw (Technicolor
  sequence)
RKO (Pandro S. Berman)

An American inherits a Parisian fashion
house.
Thin and remarkably flatly-handled musical
romance of the old school, charged only by the
occasional appearances in supporting roles of
Astaire and Rogers, then on the brink of
stardom.

w Jane Murfin, Sam Mintz, Allan Scott, *play*
Otto Harbach, *book* Gowns by Roberta by
Alice Duer Miller *d* William A. Seiter
ph Edward Cronjager *m Jerome Kern*
md Max Steiner *ch* Fred Astaire *ad* Van
Nest Polglase

Irene Dunne, *Fred Astaire, Ginger Rogers,*
Randolph Scott, Helen Westley, Claire Dodd,
Victor Varconi, Torben Meyer
† Remade as *Lovely to Look At* (qv).

AAN: song 'Lovely to Look At'

Robin and Marian*
US 1976   107m   Technicolor
Columbia / Rastar (Dennis O'Dell)

Robin Hood returns from the Crusades and
finds conditions in Britain depressing; he
finally conquers the evil Sheriff but dies in the
attempt.
A kind of serious parody of medieval life,
after the fashion of *The Lion in Winter* but
much glummer; in fact, nothing to laugh at at
all.

w James Goldman *d* Richard Lester
ph David Watkin *m* John Barry *pd* Michael
Stringer

Sean Connery, Audrey Hepburn, Robert
Shaw, Ronnie Barker, Nicol Williamson,
Richard Harris, Denholm Elliott, Kenneth
Haigh, Ian Holm, Bill Maynard, Esmond
Knight, Peter Butterworth
'Surface realism only hides a core of mush,
suddenly revealed when the hero and heroine
settle down for love-making in a field of
corn.'—*Geoff Brown*
'Whimsical jokiness is a bit hard to reconcile
with the final plunge into sacrificial
romance.'—*Michael Billington, Illustrated
London News*

Robin and the Seven Hoods*
US 1964   123m   Technicolor
 Panavision
Warner / PC (Howard W. Koch, William H.
 Daniels)

A spoof of the Robin Hood legend set in
gangland Chicago of the twenties.
Too flabby by far to be as funny as it thinks it
is, this farrago of cheerful jokes has effective
moments and lively routines, but most of them
are nearly swamped by flat treatment and the
wide screen.

w David Schwartz *d* Gordon Douglas
ph William H. Daniels *m* Nelson Riddle
songs Sammy Cahn, James Van Heusen

Frank Sinatra, Dean Martin, Bing Crosby,
Sammy Davis Jnr, Peter Falk, Barbara Rush,
Edward G. Robinson, Victor Buono, Barry
Kelley, Jack La Rue, Allen Jenkins, Sig
Rumann, Hans Conried

AAN: Nelson Riddle; song 'My Kind of
Town' (*m* James Van Heusen, *ly* Sammy
Cahn)

Robin Hood**
US 1922   127m approx   (24 fps)   bw
 silent
Douglas Fairbanks

Robin Hood combats Prince John and the
Sheriff of Nottingham.
An elaborate version of the legend which
featured some of Hollywood's most celebrated
sets and allowed the star to perform a
selection of exhilarating stunts.

w Douglas Fairbanks *d* Allan Dwan
ph Arthur Edeson *ad* Wilfrid Buckland, Irvin
J. Martin

Douglas Fairbanks, Wallace Beery, Alan
Hale, Enid Bennett
'The high water mark of film production. It
did not grow from the bankroll, it grew from
the mind.'—*R. E. Sherwood*
'A story book picture, as gorgeous and
glamorous a thing in innumerable scenes as
the screen has yet shown . . . thrilling
entertainment for the whole family group.'—
National Board of Review
† See also *The Adventures of Robin Hood* and
The Story of Robin Hood and his Merrie Men.

Robin Hood
US 1973   83m   Technicolor
Walt Disney (Wolfgang Reitherman)

Alarmingly poor cartoon feature with all the
characters 'played' by animals; songs
especially dim and treatment quite lifeless.

w Larry Clemmons, Ken Anderson, others
d Wolfgang Reitherman *voices* Brian
Bedford, Peter Ustinov, Terry-Thomas, Phil
Harris, Andy Devine, Pat Buttram

AAN: song 'Love' (*m* George Bruns, *ly* Floyd
Huddleston)

Robin Hood of El Dorado*
US 1936   86m   bw

Joaquin Murieta turns bandit to avenge
himself on the men who killed his wife.
Whitewashed biopic of a notorious western
desperado, played mainly for action and light
relief. Warner Baxter, Bruce Cabot, Margo,
Eric Linden, J. Carrol Naish, Ann Loring.
Written by William Wellman, Melvin Levy
and Joseph Calleia; directed by William
Wellman; for MGM.

Robinson Crusoe and the Tiger
Mexico 1969   110m   Eastmancolor

Simple but extremely handsome version of the
famous story, with the addition of a tiger

which Crusoe takes as a pet. Hugo Stieglitz,
Ahui. Written by Mario Marzac and Rene
Cardona Jnr, from the novel by Daniel Defoe;
directed by Rene Cardona Jnr; for Avant /
Avco Embassy.

Robinson Crusoe on Mars**

US 1964   110m   Techniscope
Paramount / Devonshire (Aubrey Schenck)

An astronaut lands on Mars and learns to
survive until rescue comes.
Remarkably close to Defoe (Man Friday being
a refugee in an interplanetary war) this is an
absorbing, entertaining and well-staged piece
of science fiction, strikingly shot in Death
Valley.

w Ib Melchior, John C. Higgins d Byron
Haskin ph Winton C. Hoch m Van Cleave
sp Lawrence Butler ad Hal Pereira, Arthur
Lonergan

Paul Mantee, Adam West, Vic Lundin

Robinson Crusoeland

France / Italy 1950   98m   bw
Sirius / Franco-London / Fortezza
aka: Atoll K; Escapade; Utopia

Stan and Ollie inherit an island in the Pacific,
but uranium is discovered on it.
Laurel and Hardy's last film is a dispiriting
mess, and the less said about it the better.

w unknown, d Leo Joannon, John Berry
ph Armand Thirard, Louis Née m Paul
Misraki

Stan Laurel, Oliver Hardy, Suzy Delair

Rocco and his Brothers**

Italy / France 1960   180m   bw
Titanus / Les Films Marceau (Goffredo
   Lombardo)

A peasant family moves into Milan, and each
of its five brothers has his problems.
Massive portmanteau of realistic stories, a bit
hard to take despite its undoubted brilliance.

w Luchino Visconti, Suso Cecchi d'Amico,
Vasco Pratolini d Luchino Visconti
ph Giuseppe Rotunno m Nino Rota

Alain Delon, Renato Salvatori, Annie
Girardot, Katina Paxinou, Roger Hanin,
Paolo Stoppa, Suzy Delair, Claudia Cardinale

Rock a Bye Baby

US 1958   107m   Technicolor
Vistavision
Paramount (Jerry Lewis)

A film star asks her devoted schoolday
admirer to look after her triplets by a secret
marriage.
Tasteless jazzing-up of The Miracle of
Morgan's Creek by talents distinctly
unsympathetic.

wd Frank Tashlin ph Haskell Boggs
m Walter Scharf

Jerry Lewis, Marilyn Maxwell, Reginald
Gardiner, Salvatore Baccaloni, Hans Conried,
Isobel Elsom, James Gleason, Isa Moore,
Connie Stevens

Rock around the Clock*

US 1956   74m   bw
Columbia (Sam Katzman)

A band playing a new form of jive—rock 'n
roll—becomes a nationwide sensation.
A cheap second feature with guest artists, this
cheerful little movie deserved at least a
footnote in the histories because it spotlights
the origins and the leading purveyors of rock
'n roll. It also caused serious riots in several
countries. A sequel in 1957, Don't Knock the
Rock, was merely cheap.

w Robert E. Kent, James B. Gordon d Fred
F. Sears ph Benjamin H. Kline

Bill Haley and the Comets, the Platters, Little
Richard, Tony Martinez and his Band,
Freddie Bell and the Bellboys, Johnny
Johnson, Alan Freed, Lisa Gaye, Alix Talton

The Rocket Man

US 1954   79m   bw

A visitor from outer space gives a magic ray
gun to an orphan boy and tells him to use it
only for good. Elementary fantasy with
amusing moments. Charles Coburn, George
'Foghorn' Winslow, Spring Byington, Anne
Francis, John Agar. Written by Lenny Bruce
and Jack Henley; directed by Oscar Rudolph;
for TCF.

Rockets Galore

GB 1958   94m   Technicolor
Rank / Relph and Dearden
US title: Mad Little Island

The Scottish island of Todday resists the
installation of a rocket-launching site.
Amiable but disappointingly listless sequel to
Whisky Galore.

w Monja Danischewsky d Michael Relph
ph Reg Wyer m Cedric Thorpe Davie

Jeannie Carson, Donald Sinden, Roland
Culver, Noel Purcell, Ian Hunter, Duncan
Macrae, Jean Cadell, Carl Jaffe, Gordon
Jackson, Catherine Lacey

Rocketship XM*

US 1950   79m   bw
Lippert (Kurt Neumann)

An expedition to the moon lands by accident
on Mars.
The first post-war space adventure is sheer

hokum, quite likeable for its cheek though not for its cheap sets.

wd Kurt Neumann *ph* Karl Struss *m* Ferde Grofe

Lloyd Bridges, Osa Massen, John Emery, Hugh O'Brian

The Rocking Horse Winner°
GB 1949 90m bw
Rank / Two Cities (John Mills)

A boy discovers he can predict winners while riding an old rocking horse; his mother's greed has fatal results.

A very short story is fatally over-extended and becomes bathetic; but the production is solid and the film deserves a mark for trying.

wd Anthony Pelissier, *story* D. H. Lawrence *ph* Desmond Dickinson *m* William Alwyn *ad* Carmen Dillon

John Mills, Valerie Hobson, John Howard Davies, Ronald Squire, Hugh Sinclair, Cyril Smith

Rocky°°
US 1976 119m Technicolor
UA / Chartoff-Winkler (Gene Kirkwood)

A slightly dimwitted Philadelphia boxer makes good.

Pleasantly old-fashioned comedy-drama with rather unattractive characters in the modern manner. Despite the freshness, on the whole *Marty* is still preferable.

w Sylvester Stallone *d John G. Avildsen* *ph* James Crabe *m* Bill Conti

Sylvester Stallone, Burgess Meredith, Talia Shire, Burt Young, Carl Weathers, Thayer David

AA: best picture; John G. Avildsen
AAN: Sylvester Stallone (as writer); song 'Gotta Fly Now' (*m* Bill Conti, *ly* Carol Connors, Ayn Robbins); Sylvester Stallone (as actor); Burgess Meredith; Talia Shire; Burt Young

Rocky II
US 1979 119m Technicolor
UA / Irwin Winkler, Robert Chartoff

After success comes failure; then Rocky marries his sweetheart and works for another big fight.

Over-inflated but under-nourished sequel with absolutely nothing new to offer.

wd Sylvester Stallone *ph* Bill Butler *m* Bill Conti

Sylvester Stallone, Talia Shire, Burt Young, Carl Weathers, Burgess Meredith

Rocky Mountain
US 1950 83m bw
Warner (William Jacobs)

A Confederate horseman gets involved in an Indian war.

Routine star western with unusual tragic ending.

w Winston Miller, Alan le May *d* William Keighley *ph* Ted McCord *m* Max Steiner

Errol Flynn, Patrice Wymore, Scott Forbes, Guinn Williams, Slim Pickens

Roger Touhy, Gangster
US 1944 73m bw

An associate of Al Capone is finally cornered by the FBI. Unsurprising, competent cops-and-robbers melodrama, based more or less on fact. Preston Foster, Victor McLaglen, Lois Andrews, Kent Taylor, Anthony Quinn, Henry Morgan. Written by Crane Wilbur and Jerry Cady; directed by Robert Florey; for TCF. (GB title: *The Last Gangster*.)

Rogue Cop
US 1954 92m bw
MGM (Nicholas Nayfack)

A police detective is on the payroll of a crime syndicate.

Uncompelling star melodrama.

w Sidney Boehm, *novel* William P. McGivern *d* Roy Rowland *ph* John Seitz *m* Jeff Alexander

Robert Taylor, George Raft, Janet Leigh, Steve Forrest, Anne Francis

'Another of the sour, disillusioned crime stories which have recently been coming into fashion.'—*Penelope Houston*

AAN: John Seitz

The Rogue Song°
US 1930 115m Technicolor
MGM (Lionel Barrymore)

A bandit wins the hand of a Russian princess. Primitive early sound operetta, not salvaged by a few Laurel and Hardy scenes added as an afterthought.

w Frances Marion, John Colton, *operetta* Gypsy Love by Franz Lehar, Robert Bodansky *d* Lionel Barrymore, Hal Roach *ph* Percy Hilburn, C. Edgar Schoenbaum *m* Dmitri Tiomkin

Laurence Tibbett, Catherine Dale Owen, Florence Lake, Judith Voselli, Nance O'Neill, Stan Laurel, Oliver Hardy
† No print was known to exist, but in 1980 the sound track was issued on record.

AAN: Laurence Tibbett

Rogue's March
US 1953 84m bw
MGM (Leon Gordon)

A British army officer is unjustly accused of
espionage but becomes a hero in India.
Victorian comedy adventure set on a never-
never frontier. Not much.

w Leon Gordon d Allan Davis ph Paul C.
Vogel m Alberto Columbo

Peter Lawford, Richard Greene, Janice Rule,
Leo G. Carroll, John Abbott, Patrick Aherne

Rogues of Sherwood Forest*
US 1950 80m Technicolor
Columbia (Fred M. Packard)

Robin Hood's son helps the barons to force
the signing of Magna Carta.
Satisfactory action adventure.

w George Bruce d Gordon Douglas
ph Charles Lawton Jnr m Heinz Roemheld,
Arthur Morton

John Derek, Diana Lynn, George Macready,
Alan Hale, Paul Cavanagh, Lowell Gilmore,
Billy House

Rogues' Regiment
US 1948 86m bw
U-I

An intelligence man joins the French Foreign
Legion in Saigon to track down an ex-Nazi.
Keen but rather muddled actioner.

w Robert Buckner d Robert Florey
ph Maury Gertsman m Daniele Amfitheatrof

Dick Powell, Marta Toren, Vincent Price,
Stephen McNally

Rollerball*
US 1975 129m Technicolor Scope
UA / Norman Jewison

In the 21st century an ultra-violent game is
used to release the anti-social feelings of the
masses.
A one-point parable, and an obvious point at
that, is stretched out over more than two
hours of violence in which the rules of the
game are not even explained. A distinctly
unlikeable film.

w William Harrison d Norman Jewison
ph Douglas Slocombe md André Previn
pd John Box

James Caan, John Houseman, Ralph
Richardson, Maud Adams, John Beck, Moses
Gunn

   'A classic demonstration of how several
millions of dollars can be unenjoyably
wasted.'—Jonathan Rosenbaum

Rollercoaster
US 1977 118m Technicolor
   Panavision Sensurround
Universal (Jennings Lang)

A saboteur blows up rollercoasters if his
blackmail demands are not met.
Limp, unsuspenseful, would-be spectacular in
which a stalwart cast struggles with inane
dialogue and situations.

w Richard Levinson, William Link d James
Goldstone ph David M. Walsh m Lalo
Schifrin

George Segal, Timothy Bottoms, Richard
Widmark, Susan Strasberg, Harry Guardino,
Henry Fonda

Le Roman d'un Tricheur*
France 1936 83m bw
Cinéas
aka: The Story of a Cheat

A reformed elderly cardsharp writes his
memoirs.
First person singular comedy, a tour de force
in which only the narrator speaks, the rest use
pantomime only.

wd Sacha Guitry ph Marcel Lucien

Sacha Guitry, Marguerite Moreno, Serge
Grave

Roman Holiday**
US 1953 118m bw
Paramount (William Wyler)

A princess on an official visit to Rome slips
away incognito and falls in love with a
newspaperman.
Wispy, charming, old-fashioned romantic
comedy shot in Rome and a little obsessed by
the locations; one feels that a studio base
would have resulted in firmer control of the
elements. The stars, however, made it
memorable.

w Ian McLellan Hunter, John Dighton
d William Wyler ph Franz Planer, Henri
Alekan m Georges Auric

Gregory Peck, Audrey Hepburn, Eddie
Albert, Hartley Power, Harcourt Williams

   'While Capra, or in a different way
Lubitsch, could have made something wholly
enjoyable from it, it would seem that Wyler's
technique is now too ponderously inflexible for
such lightweight material.'—MFB

AA: original story (Ian McLellan Hunter);
Audrey Hepburn
AAN: best picture; script; William Wyler;
photography; Eddie Albert

Roman Scandals**
US 1933 93m bw
Samuel Goldwyn

A troubled young man dreams himself back in
ancient Rome.

Musical farce which is not only pretty
entertaining on its own account but remains
interesting for a number of reasons; as its
star's best vehicle, for its Depression
bookends, as a spoof on *The Sign of the Cross*
and the inspiration of scores of other comedies
in which the heroes dreamed themselves back
into other times. Note also the musical
numbers, the chariot race finale, and the rare
appearance of Ruth Etting.

w William Anthony McGuire, George
Oppenheimer, Arthur Sheekman, Nat Perrin,
story George S. Kaufman, Robert E.
Sherwood *d* Frank Tuttle *chariot
sequence* Ralph Cedar *ph* Gregg Toland
m Alfred Newman *ch* Busby Berkeley
songs various

Eddie Cantor, Gloria Stuart, Ruth Etting,
Edward Arnold, Alan Mowbray, Verree
Teasdale

The Roman Spring of Mrs Stone*
GB 1961 104m Technicolor
Warner Seven Arts / AA (Louis de
Rochemont)

A widowed American actress in Rome begins
to drift into lassitude and moral decline.

Vivien Leigh gets degraded again in this
rambling novella complete with mysterious
dark stranger waiting at the end. Nice to look
at, and occasionally compelling, but
unsuccessful as a whole.

w Gavin Lambert, *novel* Tennessee Williams
d José Quintero *ph* Harry Waxman
m Richard Addinsell *pd* Roger Furse
ad Herbert Smith

Vivien Leigh, Warren Beatty, Lotte Lenya,
Jeremy Spenser, Coral Browne, Ernest
Thesiger

AAN: Lotte Lenya

Romance*
US 1930 76m bw
MGM

A clergyman falls in love with the opera singer
mistress of an industrialist.

Simple-minded romantic drama with the star
not at her best; but an interesting example of
'high class' romance of the time.

w Bess Meredyth, Edwin Justus Mayer,
play Edward Sheldon *d* Clarence Brown
ph William Daniels

Greta Garbo, Lewis Stone, Gavin Gordon,
Elliott Nugent, Clara Blandick, Florence
Lake, Henry Armetta

AAN: Clarence Brown; Greta Garbo

Romance in Manhattan
US 1934 78m bw

A New York girl helps a Czech immigrant to
find work in the metropolis. Slim, sentimental
movie novelette without a touch of
sophistication. Ginger Rogers, Francis
Lederer, Arthur Hohl, J. Farrell MacDonald,
Eily Malyon, Donald Meek. Written by Jane
Murfin and Edward Kaufmann; directed by
Stephen Roberts; for RKO.

Romance in the Dark
US 1938 78m bw

A famous baritone helps a singing servant to
get famous. Musical romance for the carriage
trade, with apparently more comedy asides
than were originally intended. Gladys
Swarthout, John Boles, John Barrymore,
Claire Dodd, Fritz Field, Curt Bois. Written
by Frank Partos and Anne Morrison Chapin;
directed by H. C. Potter; for Paramount.

Romance of a Horse Thief
US / Yugoslavia 1971 100m Technicolor
Allied Artists / Jadran / Emmanuel L. Wolf
(Gene Gutowski)

In a Polish village in 1904 there is dismay
when horses are commandeered by Cossacks
for service in the Russo-Japanese war.
Nostalgic Jewish drama which ends up rather
like *Fiddler on the Roof* without the music.

w David Opatoshu, based on his father's
novel *d* Abraham Polonsky *ph* Piero
Portalupsisic *m* Mort Shuman

Yul Brynner, Eli Wallach, Jane Birkin, Oliver
Tobias, Lainie Kazan, David Opatoshu

The Romance of Rosy Ridge
US 1947 103m bw
MGM (Jack Cummings)

After the Civil War, farmers make their own
peace.

Mild period romance with everything settled
by a betrothal.

w Lester Cole, *novel* Mackinlay Kantor
d Roy Rowland *ph* Sidney Wagner
m George Bassman

Van Johnson, Thomas Mitchell, Janet Leigh,
Selena Royle, Marshall Thompson, Dean
Stockwell

'Rustic charm spread through it like
molasses.'—*Douglas Eames*

Romance on the High Seas*
US 1948   99m   Technicolor
Warner (Alex Gottleib, George Amy)
GB title: *It's Magic*

Various romances mesh on an ocean voyage.
Lightweight musical which introduces Doris
Day and generally manages to keep afloat.

w Julius J. and Philip G. Epstein, I. A. L.
Diamond *d* Michael Curtiz *ph* Elwood
Bredell *m* Ray Heindorf *songs* Jule Styne,
Sammy Cahn

Jack Carson, Janis Paige, Don Defore, Doris
Day, Oscar Levant, S. Z. Sakall, Eric Blore,
Franklin Pangborn, Fortunio Bonanova

AAN: Ray Heindorf; song 'It's Magic' (*m* Jule
Styne, *ly* Sammy Cahn)

Romanoff and Juliet*
US 1961   103m   Technicolor
U-I / Pavla (Peter Ustinov)

Both Americans and Russians woo the tiny
country of Concordia, and war threatens while
the ambassadors' children fall in love.
Despite the author's wit this pattern comedy
became something of a bore as a stylized stage
piece, and the film is not smartly enough
handled to be anything but a yawn; the
humour never becomes cinematic.

wd Peter Ustinov, from his play *ph* Robert
Krasker *m* Mario Nascimbene *ad* Alexander
Trauner

Peter Ustinov, Sandra Dee, John Gavin,
Akim Tamiroff, Tamara Shayne, John
Phillips, Alix Talton, Peter Jones

The Romantic Age
GB 1949   86m   bw

A precocious French student sets her cap at
the art teacher. Fluffy farce in which all the
adults behave like children; not well regarded.
Mai Zetterling, Hugh Williams, Margot
Grahame, Petula Clark, Carol Marsh,
Raymond Lovell, Paul Dupuis. Written by
Edward Dryhurst and Peggy Barwell, from a
novel by Serge Weber; directed by Edmond T.
Greville; for Pinnacle - Rank. (US title:
Naughty Arlette.)

The Romantic Englishwoman*
GB 1975   116m   Eastmancolor
Dial / Meric–Matalon (Daniel M. Angel)

A discontented woman, holidaying at Baden
Baden, falls in love with a stranger while her
husband completes a novel on the same
theme.
Almost as ambiguous as *Last Year in
Marienbad*, this annoying film wastes good

actors in a script which hovers uncertainly
between fantasy, melodrama and reality,
intending one supposes to make humourless
and obvious comparisons between romance
and life.

w Tom Stoppard, Thomas Wiseman,
novel Thomas Wiseman *d* Joseph Losey
ph Gerry Fisher *m* Richard Hartley

Glenda Jackson, Michael Caine, Helmut
Berger, Marcus Richardson, Kate Nelligan,
René Kolldehoff, Michel Lonsdale

'The central trio bite off their lines, play
deviously with hypocrisies and humiliations,
and seem slightly aware that they're creations
by artifice out of artificiality.'—*Penelope
Houston*

'An itsy-bitsy, fragmented film that seems
less than the sum of its parts.'—*Michael
Billington, Illustrated London News*

Rome Adventure
US 1962   119m   Warnercolor

A pretty American librarian goes to Rome to
learn about love, and does. Sluggish and
overstretched travelogue with dollops of arch
romance; hard to take. Suzanne Pleshette,
Troy Donahue, Angie Dickinson, Rossano
Brazzi, Constance Ford, Chad Everett.
Written and directed by Delmer Daves; for
Warner. (GB title: *Lovers Must Learn*.)

Rome Express***
GB 1932   94m   bw
Gaumont (Michael Balcon)

Thieves and blackmail victims are among the
passengers on an express train.
Just a little faded now as sheer entertainment,
this remains the prototype train thriller from
which *The Lady Vanishes, Murder on the
Orient Express* and a hundred others are all
borrowed; it also spawned a myriad movies in
which strangers are thrown together in
dangerous situations. Technically it still works
very well, though the script needs
modernizing.

w Clifford Grey, Sidney Gilliat, Frank Vosper,
Ralph Stock *d* Walter Forde *ph* Gunther
Krampf

Conrad Veidt, Gordon Harker, Esther
Ralston, Joan Barry, Harold Huth, Cedric
Hardwicke, Donald Calthrop, Hugh Williams,
Finlay Currie, Frank Vosper, Muriel Aked,
Eliot Makeham

'A first class craftsman's job.'—*Basil Wright*
† Remade 1948 as *Sleeping Car to Trieste* (qv).

Romeo and Juliet*
US 1936   127m   bw
MGM (Irving Thalberg)

Hollywood Shakespeare with a super production and a rather elderly cast. Not entertaining in the strict sense, but full of interest.

w Talbot Jennings d George Cukor
ph William Daniels m Herbert Stothart
ad Cedric Gibbons

Leslie Howard, Norma Shearer, John Barrymore, Basil Rathbone, Edna May Oliver, Henry Kolker, C. Aubrey Smith, Violet Kemble-Cooper, Robert Warwick, Virginia Hammond, Reginald Denny, Ralph Forbes, Andy Devine, Conway Tearle

'Unimaginative, coarse-grained, a little banal, it is frequently saved—by Shakespeare—from being a bad film.'— *Graham Greene*

'It is impossible to realize how bad this film was unless you reflect on how good it might have been.'—*Alberto Cavalcanti*

AAN: best picture; Norma Shearer; Basil Rathbone

Romeo and Juliet
GB 1954 138m Technicolor
Rank / Verona (Joe Janni, Sandro Ghenzi)

Good-looking but extremely boring version shot on Italian locations with quite unacceptable leads.

wd Renato Castellani ph Robert Krasker
m Roman Vlad

Laurence Harvey, Susan Shentall, Aldo Zollo, Enzo Fiermonte, Flora Robson, Mervyn Johns, Sebastian Cabot, Lydia Sherwood, Giulio Garbinetti, Nietta Zocchi, Bill Travers, Norman Wooland, John Gielgud as prologue speaker

Romeo and Juliet*
GB 1968 152m Technicolor
Paramount / BHE / Verona / Dino de Laurentiis (Anthony Havelock-Allan, John Brabourne, Richard Goodwin)

The with-it version for modern youngsters; unfortunately the admirably rapid style does not suit the verse, and long before the much-deferred end the thing becomes just as tiresome as the other versions.

w Franco Brusati, Masolino D'Amico
d Franco Zeffirelli ph Pasquale de Santis
m Nino Rota

Leonard Whiting, Olivia Hussey, John McEnery, Michael York, Pat Heywood, Milo O'Shea, Paul Hardwick, Natasha Parry, Antonio Pierfederici, Esmeralda Ruspoli, Bruce Robinson, Roberto Bisacco, Laurence Olivier as prologue speaker

'A large gold watch should be tossed to Zeffirelli for his part in reversing the movies' reputation for emasculating the classics.'— *Newsweek*

AA: Pasquale de Santis
AAN: best picture; Franco Zeffirelli

La Ronde***
France 1950 100m bw
Sacha Gordine

In 1900 Vienna, an elegant compère shows that love is a merry-go-round: prostitute meets soldier meets housemaid meets master meets married woman meets husband meets midinette meets poet meets actress meets officer meets prostitute meets soldier . . . Superb stylized comedy with a fine cast, subtle jokes, rich decor and fluent direction; not to mention a haunting theme tune.

w Jacques Natanson, Max Ophuls,
novel Arthur Schnitzler d Max Ophuls
ph Christian Matras m Oscar Straus

Anton Walbrook, Simone Signoret, Serge Reggiani, Simone Simon, Daniel Gélin, Danielle Darrieux, Fernand Gravey, Odette Joyeux, Jean-Louis Barrault, Isa Miranda, Gérard Philipe

'One of the most civilized films to have come from Europe in a long time.'—*Gavin Lambert, MFB*

'A film that drags on and on by what seems like geometric progression.'—*John Simon, 1968*

AAN: script

La Ronde
France 1964 110m Eastmancolor
Franscope
Robert and Raymond Hakim

Vulgarization of the above, reset in Paris in 1913. The lack of a compère vastly reduces the number of jokes.

w Jean Anouilh d Roger Vadim ph Henri Decaë m Michel Magne

Marie Dubois, Claude Giraud, Anna Karina, Jean-Claude Brialy, Jane Fonda, Maurice Ronet, Catherine Spaak, Bernard Noel, Francine Bergé, Jean Sorel

Rookery Nook**
GB 1930 76m bw
British and Dominions (Herbert Wilcox)

A nervous husband on holiday tries to hide a runaway girl who has asked for protection against her stepfather.
Primitive talkie technique cannot entirely conceal the brilliance of the original Aldwych farce team in their most enduring vehicle.

w *Ben Travers,* from his play d Tom Walls

Ralph Lynn, Tom Walls, Robertson Hare, Winifred Shotter, Mary Brough, Ethel Coleridge, Griffith Humphreys, Margot Grahame

Rookies
US 1927   75m at 24 fps   bw   silent

Army adventures of a tough sergeant and a bumbling recruit. Popular comedy of its day which established the new team of Karl Dane and George K. Arthur; also with Marceline Day, Louise Lorraine, Tom O'Brien. Written by Byron Morgan; directed by Sam Wood; for MGM.

Room at the Top***
GB 1958   117m   bw
Remus (John and James Woolf)

An ambitious young clerk causes the death of his real love but manages to marry into a rich family.
Claimed as the first British film to take sex seriously, and the first to show the industrial north as it really was, this melodrama actually cheats on both counts but scene for scene is vivid and entertaining despite a weak central performance.

w *Neil Paterson, novel* John Braine d *Jack Clayton ph Freddie Francis m* Mario Nascimbene

Laurence Harvey, *Simone Signoret,* Heather Sears, Donald Wolfit, Ambrosine Philpotts, Donald Houston, Raymond Huntley, John Westbrook, Allan Cuthbertson, Hermione Baddeley, Mary Peach
 'A drama of human drives and torments told with maturity and precision.'—*Stanley Kauffmann*

AA: Neil Paterson; Simone Signoret
AAN: best picture; Jack Clayton; Laurence Harvey; Hermione Baddeley

Room for One More
US 1952   95m   bw
Warner (Henry Blanke)

A married couple adopt several underprivileged children.
Slightly mawkish family movie redeemed by star performances.

w Jack Rose, Melville Shavelson d Norman Taurog ph Robert Burks m Max Steiner

Cary Grant, Betsy Drake, Lurene Tuttle, Randy Stuart, George Winslow

Room Service*
US 1938   78m   bw
RKO (Pandro S. Berman)

Penniless theatricals find ways of staying in a hotel until they can find a backer.
Claustrophobic Broadway farce unsuitably adapted for the Marx Brothers, who are constrained by having to play characters with a passing resemblance to human beings.

w Morrie Ryskind, *play* John Murray, Allen Boretz d William A. Seiter ph Russell Metty m Roy Webb

Groucho, Chico, Harpo, Lucille Ball, *Donald MacBride,* Frank Albertson, Ann Miller, Philip Loeb
 'It should also be noted . . . that there is a scene in which a turkey is chased around a room. Not everybody will care for this.'—*MFB*
† Remade as *Step Lively* (qv).

Rooney*
GB 1958   88m   bw
Rank (George H. Brown)

Adventures of a bachelor Irish dustman. Moderately charming, though unconvincing, Dublin comedy.

w Patrick Kirwan, *novel* Catherine Cookson d George Pollock ph Christopher Challis m Philip Green

John Gregson, Barry Fitzgerald, Muriel Pavlow, June Thorburn, Noel Purcell, Marie Kean, Liam Redmond, Jack MacGowan, Eddie Byrne

Rooster Cogburn*
US 1975   108m   Technicolor
   Panavision
Universal (Paul Nathan)

An elderly marshal after a gang of outlaws is helped by the Bible-thumping daughter of a priest.
Disappointing western too obviously patterned after *True Grit* and *The African Queen.* Having had the idea for outrageous star casting, the producers obviously decided erroneously that the film would make itself.

w Martin Julien d Stuart Millar ph Harry Stradling Jnr m Laurence Rosenthal

John Wayne, Katharine Hepburn, Anthony Zerbe, Richard Jordan, John McIntyre, Strother Martin
 'Like one of those infuriating exhibition bouts in which two resilient old pros bob, weave and spar without ever landing any punches.'—*Michael Billington, Illustrated London News*
† 'Martin Julien' allegedly covers the writing talents of Hal Wallis, his wife Martha Hyer, and some friends.

The Root of All Evil

GB 1946   110m   bw

A jilted woman becomes unscrupulous in
business in order to get even with her ex-
boyfriend. Incredible farrago with a star ill at
ease. Phyllis Calvert, Michael Rennie, John
McCallum, Moore Marriott, Brefni O'Rourke,
Hazel Court, Edward Rigby. Written and
directed by Brock Williams, from the novel by
J. S. Fletcher; for Gainsborough.

The Roots of Heaven*

US 1958   125m   Eastmancolor
   Cinemascope
TCF / Darryl F. Zanuck

A white man in central Africa dedicates
himself to prevent the slaughtering of
elephants.
Curiously patchy version of a novel which was
a strange choice for filming; so many side
issues are introduced that at times it takes on
the look of another jolly safari adventure.

w Romain Gary, Patrick Leigh-Fermor,
novel Romain Gary d John Huston
ph Oswald Morris m Malcolm Arnold

Trevor Howard, Juliette Greco, Errol Flynn,
Eddie Albert, Orson Welles, Paul Lukas,
Herbert Lom, Grégoire Aslan, Friedrich
Ledebur, Edric Connor

'The Huston who did *Sierra Madre* would
have lighted his cigar with this script.'—
Stanley Kauffmann

Rope**

US 1948   80m   Technicolor
Transatlantic (Sidney Bernstein, Alfred
   Hitchcock)

Two homosexuals murder a friend for the
thrill of it and conceal his body in a trunk from
which they serve cocktails to a party including
his father and girl friend.
An effective piece of Grand Guignol on the
stage, this seemed rather tasteless when set in
a New York skyscraper, especially when the
leading role of the investigator was miscast
and Hitch had saddled himself with the ten-
minute take, a short-lived technique which
made the entire action (set in one room)
cinematically continuous (and dizzy-making).
Of considerable historic interest, nevertheless.

w Arthur Laurents, *play* Patrick Hamilton
d Alfred Hitchcock ph Joseph Valentine,
William V. Skall md Leo F. Forbstein
theme François Poulenc

James Stewart, John Dall, Farley Granger,
Joan Chandler, Cedric Hardwicke, Constance
Collier, Edith Evanson, Douglas Dick

Rope of Sand*

US 1949   105m   bw
Paramount (Hal B. Wallis)

Various factions seek hidden diamonds in a
prohibited South African area.
Ham-fisted adventure story which suggests at
times that a violent parody of *Casablanca* was
intended. The stars carry it through.

w Walter Doniger d William Dieterle
ph Charles Lang m Franz Waxman

Burt Lancaster, Paul Henreid, Claude Rains,
Peter Lorre, Corinne Calvet, Sam Jaffe

Rosalie*

US 1938   118m   bw
MGM (William Anthony McGuire)

A college football hero falls for an incognito
Balkan princess.
Ambitious light musical with a wispy plot but
satisfying numbers.

w William Anthony McGuire, *play* William
Anthony McGuire, Guy Bolton d W. S. Van
Dyke ph Oliver T. Marsh m Herbert
Stothart *songs* Cole Porter

Nelson Eddy, Eleanor Powell, Frank Morgan,
Ray Bolger, Ilona Massey, Reginald Owen,
Edna May Oliver, Jerry Colonna

The Rose

US 1979   134m   De Luxe
TCF (Tony Ray)

Drink and drugs cause the decline and death
of a famous rock singer.
An unattractive, hysterical, foul-mouthed
show business biopic roughly based on Janis
Joplin, this does afford an undisciplined
nightclub talent a role to get her teeth into.

w Bill Kerby, Bo Goodman d Mark Rydell
ph Vilmos Zsigmond md Paul A. Rothchild
pd Richard MacDonald

Bette Midler, Alan Bates, Frederic Forrest,
Harry Dean Stanton, Barry Primus

Rose Marie*

US 1936   113m   bw
MGM (Hunt Stromberg)

A Canadian Mountie gets his man—and a
lady.
Backwoods romance from a stage success,
filmed mostly on location and quite
successfully.

w Frances Goodrich, Albert Hackett, Alice
Duer Miller, *play* Otto Harbach, Oscar
Hammerstein II d W. S. Van Dyke
ph William Daniels md Herbert Stothart
songs various

Nelson Eddy, Jeanette MacDonald, James
Stewart, Reginald Owen, Allan Jones, Gilda
Gray, George Regas, Alan Mowbray, Robert
Greig, Una O'Connor, David Niven, Herman
Bing
† Previously filmed in 1928—and see below.

Rose Marie
US 1954   115m   Technicolor
  Cinemascope
MGM (Mervyn Le Roy)

Dull remake with stodgy handling and poor
sets.

w Ronald Millar d Mervyn Le Roy ph Paul
C. Vogel md Georgie Stoll ch Busby
Berkeley

Howard Keel, Ann Blyth, Fernando Lamas,
Bert Lahr, Marjorie Main, Ray Collins

Rose of Washington Square**
US 1939   86m   bw
TCF (Nunnally Johnson)

Tribulations of a Broadway singer in love with
a worthless husband.
Revamping of the Fanny Brice story; smartly
done, but the material interpolated for Jolson
is what makes the film notable.

w Nunnally Johnson d Gregory Ratoff
ph Karl Freund m Louis Silvers
songs various

Alice Faye, Tyrone Power, *Al Jolson, Hobart
Cavanaugh*, William Frawley, Joyce Compton,
Louis Prima and his band

The Rose Tattoo
US 1955   117m   bw   Vistavision
Paramount / Hal B. Wallis

A Sicilian woman on the gulf coast is
tormented by the infidelity of her dead
husband, but a brawny truckdriver makes her
forget him.
Heavily theatrical material, unsuited to the big
screen for all the powerful acting (or perhaps
because of it).

w John Michael Hayes, play Tennessee
Williams d Daniel Mann ph James Wong
Howe m Alex North

Anna Magnani, Burt Lancaster, Marisa
Pavan, Ben Cooper, Virginia Grey, Jo Van
Fleet
  'The boldest story of love you have ever
been permitted to see!'—publicity

AA: James Wong Howe; Anna Magnani
AAN: best picture; Alex North; Marisa Pavan

Roseanna McCoy
US 1949   89m   bw
Samuel Goldwyn

In old Virginia the Hatfields and the McCoys
continue their feud with tragic results.
Hillbilly Romeo and Juliet saga, a shade too
cornfed despite the credits.

w John Collier d Irving Reis ph Lee Garmes
m David Buttolph

Joan Evans, Farley Granger, Charles
Bickford, Raymond Massey, Richard
Basehart, Aline MacMahon

Rosebud
US 1975   126m   Eastmancolor
  Panavision
UA / Otto Preminger

Five girls of wealthy families are kidnapped by
the Palestine Liberation Army.
Overlong topical suspenser which goes awry
by not being very suspenseful, and by packing
in too many irrelevant satirical jibes.

w Erik Lee Preminger, novel Joan
Hemingway, Paul Bonnecarrere d Otto
Preminger ph Denys Coop m Laurent
Petitgerard titles Saul Bass

Peter O'Toole, Richard Attenborough, Cliff
Gorman, Claude Dauphin, John V. Lindsay,
Peter Lawford, Raf Vallone, Adrienne Corri

Roseland*
US 1977   103m   color
Cinema Shares / Merchant Ivory (Ismail
  Merchant)

Generation after generation, the lonely and
the loving come to a New York ballroom.
Pleasantly intentioned slice-of-life drama
which is rather slackly written and handled,
with unprofessionalism showing through at
several points.

w Ruth Prawer Jhabvala d James Ivory
ph Ernest Vincze m Michael Gibson

Geraldine Chaplin, Teresa Wright, Lou
Jacobi, Don de Natale, Louise Kirkland,
Helen Gallagher, Joan Copeland, Conrad
Janis, Lilia Skala, Christopher Walken

Rosemary's Baby**
US 1968   137m   Technicolor
Paramount / William Castle

After unwittingly becoming friendly with
diabolists, an actor's wife is impregnated by
the Devil.
Seminal gothic melodrama which led in due
course to the excesses of *The Exorcist*; in itself
well done in a heavy-handed way, the book
being much more subtle.

wd Roman Polanski, novel Ira Levin
ph William Fraker m Krzysztof Komeda
pd Richard Sylbert

Mia Farrow, John Cassavetes, Ruth Gordon, Sidney Blackmer, Patsy Kelly, Ralph Bellamy, Maurice Evans, Angela Dorian, Elisha Cook, Charles Grodin

AA: Ruth Gordon
AAN: Roman Polanski (as writer)

Rosie
US 1967 98m Techniscope
Universal / Ross Hunter (Jacque Mapes)

A rich woman spends wildly and her daughters try to have her committed to safeguard their inheritance.
Hopelessly muddled comedy drama which flits from one mood to the other without making a success of either.

w Samuel Taylor, *play* Ruth Gordon, *French original* Les Joies de la Famille by Philippe Heriat *d* David Lowell Rich *ph* Clifford Stine *m* Lyn Murray

Rosalind Russell, Brian Aherne, Sandra Dee, Vanessa Brown, Audrey Meadows, James Farentino, Leslie Nielsen, Margaret Hamilton, Reginald Owen, Juanita Moore, Virginia Grey
'A mawkish mixture of *Auntie Mame* and *King Lear.'—MFB*

Rotten to the Core
GB 1965 88m bw
Panavision
BL / Tudor (The Boulting Brothers)

Ex-convicts plan an army payroll robbery.
Routine caper comedy, unsuitably widescreened, with a few good jokes along the way.

w Jeffrey Dell, Roy Boulting, John Warren, Len Heath *d* John Boulting *ph* Freddie Young *m* Michael Dress

Anton Rodgers, *Thorley Walters,* Eric Sykes, Kenneth Griffith, Charlotte Rampling, Ian Bannen, Avis Bunnage, Raymond Huntley
† The original title, *Rotten to the Corps,* was more apt but plainly seemed too subtle.

Le Rouge et le Noir*
France / Italy 1954 170m approx
Eastmancolor
Franco London / Documento
aka: *Scarlet and Black*

A carpenter's son becomes a private tutor, seduces his master's wife and is sent to study for the priesthood . . .
Massive attempt to conquer an unfilmable novel. Some enjoyable scenes and decor are the best it can offer.

w Jean Aurenche, Pierre Bost, Claude Autant-Lara, *novel* Stendhal *d* Claude Autant-Lara *ph* Michel Kelber *m* René Cloërc *ad* Max Douy

Gérard Philipe, Danielle Darrieux, Antonella Lualdi, Jean Martinelli

The Rough and the Smooth
GB 1959 99m bw
Renown (George Minter)
US title: *Portrait of a Sinner*

An archaeologist about to marry the niece of a press lord falls for a mysterious nymphomaniac.
Preposterous melodrama about unreal people; its very excesses become enjoyable for those who can stay the course.

w Audrey Erskine-Lindop, Dudley Leslie, *novel* Robin Maugham *d* Robert Siodmak *ph* Otto Heller *md* Muir Mathieson

Tony Britton, Nadja Tiller, William Bendix, Natasha Parry, Norman Wooland, Donald Wolfit, Tony Wright, Adrienne Corri, Joyce Carey
'The script is never even on nodding terms with life, and tries to make up for this deficiency by a candidly explosive vocabulary which gives the production a weirdly old-fashioned air.'—*MFB*

Rough Cut
US 1980 112m Movielab
Paramount / David Merrick

A retiring Scotland Yard inspector spars with a jewel thief and finally changes sides.
Dated comedy which required a much lighter touch in all departments.

w Francis Burns, *novel* Touch the Lion's Paw by Derek Lambert *d* Don Siegel
ph Frederick Young *m* Nelson Riddle, from Duke Ellington themes *pd* Ted Haworth

Burt Reynolds, Lesley Anne Down, David Niven, Timothy West, Patrick Magee, Joss Ackland
'All surface smartness without a single structural idea.'—*Richard Combs, MFB*

Rough Night in Jericho
US 1967 97m Techniscope
Universal (Martin Rackin)

A stagecoach man rids a cattle town of a villain.
Totally uninteresting star western with glum performances.

w Sidney Boehm, Marvin H. Albert, *novel* The Man in Black by Marvin H. Albert
d Arnold Laven *ph* Russell Metty *m* Don Costa

George Peppard, Dean Martin, Jean Simmons, John McIntire, Slim Pickens, Don Galloway, Brad Weston

Rough Shoot*
GB 1952 86m bw
Raymond Stross
US title: *Shoot First*

A retired US officer in Dorset thinks he has
shot a poacher—but the dead man is a spy,
and someone else shot him.
Minor Hitchcock-style thriller with a climax in
Madame Tussaud's. Generally efficient and
entertaining.

w Eric Ambler, novel Geoffrey Household
d Robert Parrish ph Stan Pavey *m* Hans May

Joel McCrea, Evelyn Keyes, Marius Goring,
Roland Culver, Frank Lawton, Herbert Lom

Roughly Speaking*
US 1945 117m bw
Warner (Henry Blanke)

Oddball, overlong domestic comedy drama
about father's wild and impractical schemes.

w Louise Randall Pierson, from her book
d Michael Curtiz *ph* Joseph Walker *m* Max
Steiner

Rosalind Russell, Jack Carson, Robert
Hutton, Jean Sullivan, Alan Hale, Donald
Woods, Andrea King, Ray Collins, Kathleen
Lockhart

The Rounders
US 1965 85m Metrocolor Panavision
MGM (Richard E. Lyons)

Two modern cowboys mean to settle down but
never get around to it.
Pale comedy western which never gets going.

wd Burt Kennedy, *novel* Max Evans *ph* Paul
C. Vogel *m* Jeff Alexander

Henry Fonda, Glenn Ford, Chill Wills, Sue
Anne Langdon, Edgar Buchanan

Roustabout
US 1964 101m Techniscope
Hal B. Wallis

A wandering tough guy joins a travelling
carnival.
Dreary star vehicle momentarily salvaged by
its co-star.

w Allan Weiss, Anthony Lawrence *d* John
Rich *ph* Lucien Ballard *m* Joseph L. Lilley

Elvis Presley, Barbara Stanwyck, Sue Ann
Langdon, Joan Freeman, Leif Erickson

Roxie Hart**
US 1942 72m bw
TCF (Nunnally Johnson)

A twenties showgirl confesses for the sake of
publicity to a murder of which she is innocent.

Crowded Chicago burlesque which now seems
less funny than it did but is full of smart
moments.

w Nunnally Johnson, play Chicago by Maurine
Watkins *d William Wellman ph* Leon
Shamroy *m* Alfred Newman

Ginger Rogers, George Montgomery,
Adolphe Menjou, Lynne Overman, Nigel
Bruce, Spring Byington, Sara Allgood,
William Frawley

'A masterpiece of form, of ensemble acting,
of powerhouse comedy and scripting.'—*NFT,
1974*

† The play was also filmed in 1927 under its
original title, with Phyllis Haver.

Royal African Rifles
US 1954 75m Cinecolor

In British East Africa in 1914, a lieutenant
tracks down a consignment of stolen guns.
Mini-budget *Boys Own Paper* heroics; quite
enjoyable on its level. Louis Hayward,
Veronica Hurst, Michael Pate, Angela
Greene, Steve Geray, Bruce Lester. Written
by Dan Ullman; directed by Lesley Selander;
for Allied Artists. (GB title: *Storm over
Africa*.)

The Royal Bed
US 1931 74m bw

The king and queen of a European country
lead their own private lives. Insufficient wit
graces this would-be daring romantic drama
from a Broadway hit. Mary Astor, Lowell
Sherman, Nance O'Neill, Anthony Bushell,
Robert Warwick. Written by J. Walter Ruben,
from the play *The Queen's Husband* by Robert
E. Sherwood; directed by Lowell Sherman; for
RKO. (GB title: *The Queen's Husband*.)

Royal Cavalcade
GB 1935 104m bw

A chronicle of the events of the reign of King
George V. Thoroughly embarrassing jubilee
tribute, of historical interest only. Marie Lohr,
Hermione Baddeley, Esme Percy, John Mills,
Reginald Gardiner, Syd Walker, Seymour
Hicks, Owen Nares, Matheson Lang, George
Robey, Florrie Forde, many others. Written
by Marjorie Deans; directed by Marcel
Varnel, Thomas Bentley, Herbert Brenon,
Norman Lee, Walter Summers and Will
Kellino; for BIP.

A Royal Divorce
GB 1938 85m bw

Napoleon Bonaparte in 1809 marries a widow
whose reputation isn't exactly spotless. Heavy
comedy or light drama, take your pick; not

exactly riveting as either. Pierre Blanchar, Ruth Chatterton, Frank Cellier, Carol Goodner, George Curzon, John Laurie, Jack Hawkins. Written by Miles Malleson, from the novel *Josephine* by Jacques Thery; directed by Jack Raymond; for Herbert Wilcox.

The Royal Family of Broadway*
US 1930 82m bw
Paramount
GB title: *Theatre Royal*

The off-stage escapades of a famous family of actors.
Fairly funny lampoon of the Barrymores, primitively staged and very talky but still entertaining for those in the joke.

w Herman J. Mankiewicz, Gertrude Purcell, *play* George S. Kaufman, Edna Ferber *d* George Cukor, Cyril Gardner *ph* George Folsey

Fredric March, Henrietta Crosman, Ina Claire, Mary Brian, Charles Starrett, Frank Conroy

'Lionel does not come into the burlesque at all, and I can quite believe that he is the most damaged of the entire family.'—*James Agate*

'Stagebound and awkward, but great fun anyway.'—*New Yorker, 1977*

AAN: Fredric March

Royal Flash
GB 1975 118m Technicolor
TCF / Two Roads (David V. Picker, Denis O'Dell)

A Victorian bully and braggart has various adventures in Europe and Ruritania.
A rather unsatisfactory romp which takes pot shots at every 19th-century person and object in the encyclopaedia, but is never as funny as it intends to be.

w George Macdonald Fraser, from his novel *d* Richard Lester *ph* Geoffrey Unsworth *m* Ken Thorpe *ph* Terence Marsh

Malcolm McDowall, Oliver Reed, Alan Bates, Florinda Bolkan, Britt Ekland, Lionel Jeffries, Tom Bell, Joss Ackland, Leon Greene, Richard Hurndall, Alastair Sim, Michael Hordern

The Royal Hunt of the Sun
GB 1969 121m Technicolor
Security Pictures (Eugene Frenke, Philip Yordan)

How the Spanish soldier Pizarro on his South American trek overcame the Inca god-king Atahualpa.
Deadly literal rendering with nothing to replace the play's theatrical splendour, resembling nothing so much as an opera without the music.

w Philip Yordan, *play* Peter Shaffer *d* Irving Lerner *ph* Roger Barlow, Marc Wilkinson

Robert Shaw, Christopher Plummer, Nigel Davenport, Michael Craig, Leonard Whiting, Andrew Keir, James Donald, Percy Herbert, Alexander Davion

A Royal Scandal
US 1945 94m bw
TCF (Ernst Lubitsch)
GB title: *Czarina*

The illicit loves of Catherine the Great.
Censored romps around some chilly court sets; very few moments of interest, and none of the style of the silent version *Forbidden Paradise*.

w Edwin Justus Mayer, *play* Lajos Biro, Melchior Lengyel *d* Otto Preminger *ph* Arthur Miller *m* Alfred Newman

Tallulah Bankhead, Charles Coburn, Anne Baxter, William Eythe, Vincent Price, Mischa Auer, Sig Rumann, Vladimir Sokoloff

'Nothing is one-tenth well enough done, and all the laughs are played for at their cheapest, far down the ramp.'—*James Agee*

Royal Wedding
US 1951 93m Technicolor
MGM (Arthur Freed)
GB title: *Wedding Bells*

Journalists congregate in London for the royal wedding.
Thin musical with acceptable numbers.

w Alan Jay Lerner *d* Stanley Donen *ph* Robert Planck *md* Johnny Green *songs* Alan Jay Lerner, Burton Lane

Fred Astaire, Jane Powell, Sarah Churchill, Peter Lawford, Keenan Wynn

AAN: song 'Too Late Now' (*m* Burton Lane, *ly* Alan Jay Lerner)

Ruby Gentry
US 1952 82m bw
Joseph Bernhard / King Vidor

A tempestuous girl, brought up as a boy in the Carolina swamps, has a love-hate relationship with a local aristocrat, revenges herself on the people who scorn her, loses her lover in a swamp shooting, and becomes a sea captain.
Richly absurd sex melodrama typical of its director and star yet not very entertaining.

w Sylvia Richards *d* King Vidor *ph* Russell Harlan *m* Heinz Roemheld *ad* Dan Hall

Jennifer Jones, Charlton Heston, Karl Malden, Josephine Hutchinson

Ruggles of Red Gap**
US 1935 90m bw
Paramount (Arthur Hornblow Jnr)

A British butler has a startling effect on the family of an American rancher who takes him out west.

A famous comedy which seemed hilarious at the time but can now be seen as mostly composed of flat spots; the performances however are worth remembering.

w Walter de Leon, Harlan Thompson, Humphrey Pearson, *novel* Harry Leon Wilson d Leo McCarey ph Alfred Gilks

Charles Laughton, Mary Boland, Charles Ruggles, Zasu Pitts, Roland Young, Leila Hyams, James Burke, Maude Eburne, Lucien Littlefield

'A sane, witty, moving and quite unusual picture of Anglo-American relations.'—*C. A. Lejeune*

'The most heart-warming comedy of the season . . . there is about it a sympathetic and even a patriotic quality which is touching.'— *Literary Digest*

'The archetypal film they don't make any more, partly because comedy has now grown too raucous to favour the quiet drollery of players like Charlie Ruggles and Mary Boland, partly because even McCarey himself had trouble after the thirties separating sentiment from sentimentality.'—*Time Out, 1980*

† Remade as *Fancy Pants* (qv).

AAN: best picture

Rulers of the Sea*
US 1939 96m bw
Paramount (Frank Lloyd)

Problems surround the first steamship voyage across the Atlantic.
Well-made period action drama.

w Talbot Jennings, Frank Cavett, Richard Collins d Frank Lloyd ph Theodor Sparkuhl, Archie Stout m Richard Hageman

Douglas Fairbanks Jnr, Margaret Lockwood, Will Fyffe, Montagu Love, George Bancroft, Mary Gordon, Alan Ladd

The Ruling Class*
GB 1971 155m De Luxe
Keep Films (Jules Buck, Jack Hawkins)

The fetishistic Earl of Gurney is succeeded by his mad son Jack who believes he is God.
An overlong satirical play with brilliant patches is hamfistedly filmed but boasts some bright performances. The hits are as random as the misses, however.

w Peter Barnes, from his play d Peter Medak ph Ken Hodges m John Cameron

Peter O'Toole, Harry Andrews, *Arthur Lowe, Alastair Sim,* Coral Browne, Michael Bryant

'This irritating and unsatisfying film is worth being irritated and unsatisfied by.'—*Stanley Kauffmann*

AAN: Peter O'Toole

Rumba*
US 1935 71m bw
Paramount (William Le Baron)

A society girl has a yen for a Broadway hoofer.
Streamlined star vehicle which attempts to recapture the success of *Bolero* (qv).

w Howard J. Green d Marion Gering ph Ted Tetzlaff

Carole Lombard, George Raft, Margo, Lynne Overman, Monroe Owsley, Iris Adrian, Gail Patrick, Samuel S. Hinds, Jameson Thomas

Run for Cover*
US 1955 92m Technicolor Vistavision
Paramount (William H. Pine)

An ex-convict becomes innocently involved in a train robbery.
Adequate star western.

w William C. Thomas, *story* Harriet Frank Jnr, Irving Ravetch d Nicholas Ray ph Daniel Fapp md Howard Jackson

James Cagney, Viveca Lindfors, John Derek, Jean Hersholt, Grant Withers, Ernest Borgnine, Jack Lambert

Run for the Sun
US 1956 99m Technicolor Superscope
UA / Russ–Field (Harry Tatelman)

Crashlanding in the Mexican jungle, a disillusioned author and a lady journalist find themselves at the mercy of renegade Nazis.
Tame remake of *The Most Dangerous Game* with Count Zaroff replaced by Lord Haw-Haw. Sluggish plot development mars the action.

w Dudley Nichols, Roy Boulting d Roy Boulting ph Joseph La Shelle m Fred Steiner

Richard Widmark, Jane Greer, Trevor Howard, Peter Van Eyck

A Run for Your Money*
GB 1949 83m bw
Ealing (Leslie Norman)

Welsh Rugby supporters have various adventures on their one day in London.
Slight, bright, British chase comedy with characterizations as excellent as they are expected.

w Richard Hughes, Charles Frend, Leslie Norman d Charles Frend ph Douglas Slocombe m Ernest Irving

Alec Guinness, Meredith Edwards, Moira
Lister, Donald Houston, Hugh Griffith, Clive
Morton, Joyce Grenfell

Run of the Arrow
US 1956 85m Technicolor RKOscope
Global (Samuel Fuller)

An ex-Civil War soldier is captured by Indians
and accepted by them, but sickened by their
violence.
Bloody little western in the accustomed Fuller
vein of unpleasantness.

wd Samuel Fuller *ph* Joseph Biroc *m* Victor
Young

Rod Steiger, Sarita Montiel, Charles Bronson,
Tim McCoy, Ralph Meeker

Run Silent Run Deep*
US 1958 93m bw
UA / Hecht–Hill–Lancaster (William Schorr)

Antagonisms flare up between the officers of a
US submarine in Tokyo Bay during World
War II.
Competent, unsurprising war actioner trading
on its stars.

w John Gay *d* Robert Wise *ph* Russell
Harlan *m* Franz Waxman

Clark Gable, Burt Lancaster, Jack Warden,
Brad Dexter, Nick Cravat, Joe Maross, H. M.
Wynant
   'Mostly good sea fights. Otherwise it's damn
the torpedoes, half speed ahead.'—*Time*

Run Wild, Run Free*
GB 1969 98m Technicolor
Columbia / Irving Allen (John
Danischewsky)

A mute boy living on Dartmoor gains self-
confidence through the love of animals.
Rather vaguely developed family film with
agreeable sequences.

w David Rook, from his novel The White
Colt, *d* Richard C. Sarafian *ph* Wilkie
Cooper *m* David Whitaker

John Mills, Sylvia Syms, Mark Lester,
Bernard Miles, Gordon Jackson, Fiona
Fullerton

The Runaround*
US 1946 100m bw
Universal (Joseph Gershenson)

Two rival detectives are hired to find a missing
heiress.
Peripatetic comedy on the lines of *It Happened
One Night*; unexpectedly enjoyable.

w Arthur T. Horman, Sam Hellman
d Charles Lamont *ph* George Robinson
m Frank Skinner

Rod Cameron, Broderick Crawford, Ella
Raines, Samuel S. Hinds, Frank McHugh,
George Cleveland

The Runaway Bus*
GB 1954 78m bw
Eros / Conquest–Guest (Val Guest)

Passengers at London Airport are fogbound,
and a relief bus driver takes some of them to
Blackbushe. Incognito among them are
robbers and detectives . . .
Vaguely plotted variation on *The Ghost Train*,
with fair production, a good smattering of
jokes, and a hilarious view of a great airport in
its earlier days.

wd Val Guest *ph* Stan Pabey *m* Ronald
Binge

Frankie Howerd, Margaret Rutherford,
George Coulouris, Petula Clark, Terence
Alexander, Toke Townley, Belinda Lee

The Runner Stumbles
US 1979 110m CFI color
Melvin Simon Productions (Stanley
Kramer)

In the mid-twenties, a Catholic priest is
accused of the murder of a nun for whom he
had felt a strong romantic attraction.
Musty exhumation of a genuine case which has
little dramatic interest and even less wider
significance. Good acting does not atone.

w Milan Stiff, from his play *d* Stanley
Kramer *ph* Laszlo Kovacs *m* Ernest Gold
pd Alfred Sweeney Jnr

Dick Van Dyke, Kathleen Quinlan, Maureen
Stapleton, Ray Bolger, Tammy Grimes, Beau
Bridges
   'The reanimated corpse of middlebrow
Hollywood pretension . . . funereal pacing,
portentous low angles and symbolic
overkill.'—*Paul Taylor, MFB*

The Running Man*
GB 1963 103m Technicolor
Panavision
Columbia / Peet (Carol Reed, John R.
Sloan)

A private airline pilot fakes an accident and
disappears, leaving his wife to collect the
insurance and meet him in Spain.
Flabby, expensive suspenser; both plot and
character take a back seat to scenic views.

w John Mortimer, *novel* The Ballad of the
Running Man by Shelley Smith *d* Carol Reed
ph Robert Krasker *m* William Alwyn

Laurence Harvey, Alan Bates, Lee Remick,
Felix Aylmer, Eleanor Summerfield, Allan
Cuthbertson

'There seems to be something about the panoramic screen that seduces film-makers into filling it with irrelevant local colour and drawing the whole proceedings out to a length that matches its width.'—*Brenda Davies*

Running Scared
GB 1972 98m Technicolor Panavision
Paramount / Wigan / Hemmings / O'Toole (Gareth Wigan)

A university student is generally condemned for allowing his friend to commit suicide; eventually he takes his own life.
Depressing and rather pointless exercise in death wish complicated by a doomed love affair.

w Clive Exton, David Hemmings, *novel* Gregory MacDonald *d* David Hemmings *ph* Ernest Day *m* Michael J. Lewis

Robert Powell, Gayle Hunnicutt, Barry Morse, Stephanie Bidmead, Edward Underdown, Maxine Audley, Georgia Brown

Russian Roulette
US 1975 90m Eastmancolor
ITC / Elliott Kastner / Bulldog

Real and fake secret agents shoot it out when the Russian premier is about to visit Vancouver.
Fast-moving but impossible to follow location thriller which resolves itself into a series of chases.

w Tom Ardies, Stanley Mann, Arnold Margolin, *novel* Kosygin is Coming by Tom Ardies *d* Lou Lombardo *ph* Brian West *m* Michael J. Lewis

George Segal, Gordon Jackson, Denholm Elliott, Cristina Raines, Richard Romanus, Louise Fletcher, Nigel Stock
'A stale, mechanical espionage caper that wastes its star.'—*Kevin Thomas*

The Russians Are Coming, The Russians Are Coming*
US 1966 126m De Luxe Panavision
UA / Mirisch (Norman Jewison)

Russian submariners make a forced landing on a Connecticut holiday island and cause panic.
'Daring' cold war comedy which turns out to be of the most elementary and protracted nature, saved from boredom only by a few cameos.

w William Rose, *novel* The Off-Islanders by Nathaniel Benchley *d* Norman Jewison *ph* Joseph Biroc *m* Johnny Mandel

Carl Reiner, Eva Marie Saint, Alan Arkin, John Philip Law, Paul Ford, Tessie O'Shea, Brian Keith, Jonathan Winters, Theodore Bikel, Ben Blue
'Rather amiable, though the film, like its title, seems to repeat most things twice.'—*Sight and Sound*
'Why the crazy title? If we told you, you'd only laugh!'—*publicity*

AAN: best picture; William Rose; Alan Arkin

Ruthless*
US 1948 104m bw
Eagle Lion / Arthur S. Lyons

A conniver breaks several lives on his way to the top.
Rich melodrama with some entertaining moments.

w S. K. Lauren, Gordon Kahn, *novel* Prelude to Night by Dayton Stoddert *d* Edgar G. Ulmer *ph* Bert Glennon *m* Werner Janssen

Zachary Scott, Sidney Greenstreet, Diana Lynn, Louis Hayward, Martha Vickers, Lucille Bremer, Edith Barrett, Raymond Burr, Dennis Hoey

RX Murder
GB 1958 85m bw Cinemascope

The doctor of a small seaside resort has had four wives die on him. Could it be murder?
Modest mystery with an obvious outcome.
Marius Goring, Rick Jason, Lisa Gastoni, Mary Merrall, Vida Hope, Phyllis Neilson-Terry, Frederick Leister, Nicholas Hannen.
Written and directed by Derek Twist, from the novel *The Deeds of Dr Deadcert* by Joan Fleming; for TCF. (GB release title: *Family Doctor*.)

Ryan's Daughter**
GB 1970 206m Metrocolor
    Panavision 70
MGM / Faraway (Anthony Havelock-Allan)

1916 Ireland: a village schoolmaster's wife falls for a British officer.
A modestly effective pastoral romantic melodrama, stretched on the rack of its director's meticulous film-making technique and unnecessarily big budget. A beautiful, impressive, well-staged and well-acted film, but not really four hours' worth of drama.

w Robert Bolt *d* David Lean *ph* Frederick A. Young *m* Maurice Jarre *pd* Stephen Grimes (who created an entire village)

Sarah Miles, Robert Mitchum, Chris Jones, John Mills, Trevor Howard, Leo McKern
'Instead of looking like the money it cost to make, the film feels like the time it took to shoot.'—*Alexander Walker*

AA: Frederick A. Young; John Mills
AAN: Sarah Miles

S

SOS Pacific*
GB 1959 91m bw
Rank / Sydney Box (John Nasht, Patrick Filmer-Sankey)

Survivors of a Pacific plane crash await rescue on a small island which is the site of an imminent H-bomb test.
Satisfactory open-air thick ear with strongly deployed types and a suspense climax.

w Robert Westerby d Guy Green ph Wilkie Cooper

Eddie Constantine, Pier Angeli, John Gregson, Richard Attenborough, Eva Bartok, Clifford Evans, Jean Anderson, Cec Linder

Saadia
US 1953 87m Technicolor
MGM (Albert Lewin)

A young French doctor in the Sahara has trouble with the local witch doctor.
Pretentious and ill-considered multi-national romance from the champion of Omar's Rubaiyat.

wd Albert Lewin, novel Echec au Destin by Francis D'Autheville ph Christopher Challis m Bronislau Kaper

Cornel Wilde, Mel Ferrer, Rita Gam, Michel Simon, Wanda Rotha, Cyril Cusack, Marcel Poncin, Peter Bull

Sabotage***
GB 1936 76m bw
Gaumont British (Michael Balcon, Ivor Montagu)
US title: A Woman Alone

The proprietor of a small London cinema is a dangerous foreign agent.
Unattractively plotted but fascinatingly detailed Hitchcock suspenser with famous sequences and a splendidly brooding melodramatic atmosphere.

w Charles Bennett, Ian Hay, Helen Simpson, E. V. H. Emmett, novel The Secret Agent by Joseph Conrad d Alfred Hitchcock ph Bernard Knowles md Louis Levy

Oscar Homolka, Sylvia Sidney, John Loder, Desmond Tester, Joyce Barbour, Matthew Boulton

'Tightly packed, economical, full of invention and detail.'—NFT, 1961

Saboteur***
US 1942 108m bw
Universal (Frank Lloyd, Jack H. Skirball)

A war worker unjustly suspected of sabotage flees across the country and unmasks a spy ring.
Flawed Hitchcock action thriller, generally unsatisfactory in plot and pace but with splendid sequences at a ball, in Radio City Music Hall, and atop the Statue of Liberty.

w Peter Viertel, Joan Harrison, Dorothy Parker, story Alfred Hitchcock d Alfred Hitchcock ph Joseph Valentine m Frank Skinner md Charles Previn

Robert Cummings, Priscilla Lane, Otto Kruger, Alan Baxter, Alma Kruger, Norman Lloyd

The Saboteur, Code Name Morituri*
US 1965 122m bw
TCF / Arcola / Colony (Aaron Rosenberg)

In 1942 a German pacifist working for the allies is actually a German spy.
Dreary as a whole, suspenseful in snatches, this shipboard melodrama is full of irrelevancies and is in any case played much more seriously than the matter demands.

w Daniel Taradash, novel Werner Jeorg Kosa d Bernhard Wicki ph Conrad Hall m Jerry Goldsmith

Yul Brynner, Marlon Brando, Trevor Howard, Janet Margolin

AAN: Conrad Hall

Sabre Jet
US 1953 96m Cinecolor

A US Air Force colonel in Korea has trouble with his career-hunting wife as well as with the enemy. Propaganda cheapie with a few stirring aerial moments. Robert Stack, Coleen Gray, Richard Arlen, Julie Bishop, and Leon Ames, Amanda Blake. Written by Dale Eunson and Katherine Albert; directed by Louis King; for Krueger Productions / UA.

Sabrina*
US 1954 113m bw
Paramount (Billy Wilder)
GB title: *Sabrina Fair*

The chauffeur's daughter is wooed by both her brother employers.
Superior comedy, rather uneasily cast.

w Billy Wilder, *play* Samuel Taylor *d* Billy Wilder *ph* Charles Lang Jnr *m* Frederick Hollander

Humphrey Bogart, William Holden, Audrey Hepburn, Walter Hampden, John Williams, Martha Hyer, Joan Vohs, Marcel Dalio
  'This is never less than a glittering entertainment, but somehow a certain measure of lead has found its way into the formula.'—*Time*

AAN: Billy Wilder (as writer and director); Charles Lang Jnr; Audrey Hepburn

The Sad Sack
US 1957 98m bw Vistavision
Paramount (Paul Nathan)

Adventures of an army misfit.
Resistible star comedy.

w Edmund Beloin, Nate Monaster, *cartoon* George Baker *d* George Marshall *ph* Loyal Griggs *m* Walter Scharf

Jerry Lewis, David Wayne, Phyllis Kirk, Peter Lorre, Joe Mantell, Gene Evans, George Dolenz, Liliane Montvecchi, Shepperd Strudwick

Saddle the Wind*
US 1958 84m Metrocolor
  Cinemascope
MGM (Armand Deutsch)

A reformed gunman's young brother gets into bad company.
Modestly effective, humourless western drama.

w Rod Serling *d* Robert Parrish *ph* George J. Folsey *m* Jeff Alexander

Robert Taylor, John Cassavetes, Julie London, Donald Crisp, Charles McGraw, Royal Dano, Richard Erdman

Saddle Tramp
US 1950 76m Technicolor

A wandering cowboy adopts four orphan children and after various adventures marries the eldest of them. Mild family western for star fanciers. Joel McCrea, Wanda Hendrix, John Russell, John McIntire, Jeanette Nolan, Russell Simpson. Written by Harold Shumate; directed by Hugo Fregonese; for Universal-International.

Sadie McKee*
US 1934 88m bw
MGM (Lawrence Weingarten)

A maid at various times loves her master, a young ne'er-do-well, and a middle-aged millionaire.
Solidly carpentered millgirl's romance of the period.

w John Meehan, *story* Vina Delmar
d Clarence Brown *ph* Oliver T. Marsh

Joan Crawford, Franchot Tone, Gene Raymond, Edward Arnold, Esther Ralston, Jean Dixon, Leo Carrillo, Akim Tamiroff
  'The stuff the fans cry for.'—*Hollywood Reporter*

Sadie Thompson*
US 1928 95m (24 fps) bw silent
Gloria Swanson

In the South Seas, a fire-and-brimstone missionary is attracted to a prostitute.
Steamy, much-filmed melodrama (see *Rain, Miss Sadie Thompson*). This version has long been unavailable for revaluation.

w G. Gardner Sullivan, *story* Rain by W. Somerset Maugham *d* Raoul Walsh *ph* George Barnes, Robert Kurrle *ad* William Cameron Menzies

Gloria Swanson, Lionel Barrymore, Blanche Frederici, Charles Lane, Florence Midgley, Raoul Walsh
  'It's stirring and ironic and funny. You couldn't ask more.'—*Photoplay*

AAN: George Barnes; Gloria Swanson

Safari
GB 1956 91m Technicolor
  Cinemascope
Warwick (Adrian Worker)

A white hunter falls in love with the wife of his employer and luckily the latter is killed by the Mau Mau.
Feeble adventure story exploiting political tensions.

w Anthony Veiller *d* Terence Young *ph* John Wilcox, Fred Ford, Ted Moore *m* William Alwyn

Victor Mature, Janet Leigh, Roland Culver, John Justin, Earl Cameron, Liam Redmond, Orlando Martins

The Safecracker
GB 1958 96m bw
MGM / Coronado (David E. Rose)

A safecracker is released to help in a commando raid during World War II.

One-twelfth of a dirty dozen, with a long indecisive lead-up and not much pull as drama or comedy.

w Paul Monash, *story* Rhys Davies *d* Ray Milland *ph* Gerald Gibbs *m* Richard Rodney Bennett

Ray Milland, Barry Jones, Jeanette Sterke, Victor Maddern, Ernest Clark, Cyril Raymond, Melissa Stribling

Safety Last°°°
US 1923   70m (24 fps)   bw   silent
Harold Lloyd

A small-town boy goes to the big city and to impress his girl friend enters a contest to climb a skyscraper.
Marvellous star comedy which set a new standard not only in sight gags but in the comedy-thrill stunts which became Lloyd's stock-in-trade.

w Harold Lloyd, Sam Taylor, Tim Whelan, Hal Roach *d* Sam Taylor, Fred Newmeyer *ph* Walter Lundin

Harold Lloyd, Mildred Davis, Noah Young

The Saga of Anatahan
Japan 1953   90m   bw

During the Pacific war, castaways on a remote island kill each other for the sake of one woman. A curious footnote to its director's career, this mannered film is entirely in Japanese with English commentary, and does not recommend itself to western audiences. Written and directed by Josef Von Sternberg; for Daiwa productions.

Sahara°°
US 1943   97m   bw
Columbia

During the retreat from Tobruk a group of men of mixed nationality find water for themselves and harass the Nazis.
Good, simple war actioner with a realistic feel and strong characters deployed in melodramatic situations.

w John Howard Lawson, Zoltan Korda *d* *Zoltan Korda* *ph* Rudolph Maté *m* Miklos Rozsa

Humphrey Bogart, Bruce Bennett, Lloyd Bridges, Rex Ingram, J. Carrol Naish, Dan Duryea, Kurt Kreuger
  'It borrows, chiefly from the English, a sort of light-alloy modification of realism which makes the traditional Hollywood idiom seem as obsolete as a minuet.'—*James Agee*

AAN: Rudolph Maté; J. Carrol Naish

Saigon
US 1947   93m   bw
Paramount (P. J. Wolfson)

Veteran airmen in Saigon are offered half a million to help in a robbery.
Tired studio-set star actioner.

w P. J. Wolfson, Arthur Sheekman *d* Leslie Fenton *ph* John Seitz *m* Robert Emmett Dolan

Alan Ladd, Veronica Lake, Douglas Dick, Wally Cassell, Luther Adler, Morris Carnovsky, Mikhail Rasumny

Sail a Crooked Ship
US 1961   88m   bw
Columbia / Philip Barry Jnr

A shipowner unwittingly takes on a crew of crooks intending to use the boat as a getaway after a bank robbery.
Flimsy comedy sustained by a star comedian.

w Ruth Brooks Flippen, Bruce Geller, *novel* Nathaniel Benchley *d* Irving Brecher *ph* Joseph Biroc *m* George Duning

Robert Wagner, *Ernie Kovacs,* Dolores Hart, Carolyn Jones, Frank Gorshin

Sailing Along
GB 1938   90m   bw
Gaumont-British

A girl barge hand meets an impresario and becomes a dancing star.
Rather deadly British musical romance with the star not at her best, the supporting talents wasted, and a generally heavy hand in evidence.

wd Sonnie Hale *ph* Glen MacWilliams *m* / *ly* Arthur Johnston, Maurice Sigler *ad* Alfred Junge

Jessie Matthews, Roland Young, Barry Mackay, Jack Whiting, Noel Madison, Alastair Sim, Athene Seyler, Frank Pettingell

Sailor Beware
US 1952   103m   bw
Paramount / Hal B. Wallis

Martin and Lewis in the navy.
Unlovable star antics.

w James Allardice, Martin Rackin, *play* Kenyon Nicholson, Charles Robinson *d* Hal Walker *ph* Daniel L. Fapp *m* Joseph J. Lilley

Dean Martin, Jerry Lewis, Corinne Calvet, Marion Marshall, Robert Strauss, Leif Erickson

Sailor Beware*
GB 1956   80m   bw
Romulus (Jack Clayton)
US title: *Panic in the Parlor*

A young sailor has trouble with his mother-in-law-to-be.
Plain but adequate film version of a successful lowbrow stage farce about an archetypal female dragon.

w Philip King and Falkland L. Cary, from their play *d* Gordon Parry *ph* Douglas Slocombe *m* Peter Akister

Peggy Mount, Esma Cannon, Cyril Smith, Shirley Eaton, Ronald Lewis

The Sailor Takes a Wife
US 1945   91m   bw

A sailor on leave gets married and finds he has acquired a few problems. Rather self-consciously cute sentimental comedy, proficiently staged. June Allyson, Robert Walker, Reginald Owen, Hume Cronyn, Eddie Anderson, Audrey Totter, Gerald Oliver Smith. Written by Anne Chapin and Whitfield Cook, from a play by Chester Erskine; directed by Richard Whorf; for MGM.

The Sailor Who Fell from Grace with the Sea
GB 1976   105m   Technicolor
AVCO / Sailor Company (Martin Poll)

A precocious boy interferes with his widowed mother's affair with a sailor by castrating the latter.
Weird and unattractive sex fantasy set in Dartmouth of all places and not helped by tiresome sex scenes.

wd Lewis John Carlino, *novel* Gogo No Eiko by Mishima Yukio *ph* Douglas Slocombe *m* John Mandel

Sarah Miles, Kris Kristofferson, Jonathan Kahn, Margo Cunningham, Earl Rhodes

'Like the act of love, this film must be experienced from beginning to end!'— *publicity*

'This everyday tale of torture, scopophilia, copulation, masturbation, dismemberment and antique dealing deserves to be traded back to the Japs and made required viewing for timorous kamikaze pilots.'—*Benny Green, Punch*

The Sailor's Return
GB 1978   100m   colour

A Victorian seaman returns to his native village with a black bride, and opens a pub. Lame-paced and highly predictable yarn of prejudice and doomed love, assembled with almost no cinematic flair. Tom Bell, Shope Sodeinde, Elton Charles, Mick Ford, Clive Swift. Written by James Saunders from the novel by David Garnett; directed by Jack Gold; for Euston Films. (As a theatrical film it found no takers, and in GB was first shown on television in 1980.)

Sailors Three**
GB 1940   86m   bw
Ealing (Culley Forde)
US title: *Three Cockeyed Sailors*

Drunken sailors capture a German battleship by mistake.
Low service comedy which keeps moving, is brightly played and reaches a good standard. Sequel: *Fiddlers Three* (qv).

w Angus Macphail, John Dighton, Austin Melford *d* Walter Forde *ph* Gunther Krampf *md* Ernest Irving

Tommy Trinder, Claude Hulbert, Michael Wilding, Carla Lehmann, Jeanne de Casalis, James Hayter, John Laurie

The Saint
Leslie Charteris' famous character, the reformed British gentleman crook who becomes a Robin Hood of crime, has been most popular in the long-running sixties TV series starring Roger Moore. The films which featured him never seemed to hit quite the right note, and now seem slow. All but one were made for RKO, who later switched allegiance to THE FALCON (qv).

1938: THE SAINT IN NEW YORK
1939: THE SAINT STRIKES BACK, THE SAINT IN LONDON
1940: THE SAINT'S DOUBLE TROUBLE, THE SAINT TAKES OVER
1941: THE SAINT IN PALM SPRINGS, THE SAINT'S VACATION
1943 (Republic): THE SAINT MEETS THE TIGER
1954: THE SAINT'S GIRL FRIDAY

Louis Hayward played the role in the first and last; Hugh Sinclair in VACATION and TIGER; George Sanders in the rest.

St Benny the Dip
US 1951   79m   bw
Danzigers
GB title: *Escape If You Can*

Gamblers learn to escape the law by dressing as priests, but circumstance converts them to good works.
Unfunny comedy notable only for its cast.

w John Roeburt *d* Edgar G. Ulmer *ph* Don Malkames *m* Robert Stringer

Freddie Bartholemew, Roland Young, Dick Haymes, Lionel Stander, Nina Foch

St Ives
US 1973 93m Technicolor
Warner (Pancho Kohner, Stanley Kanter)

An ex-police reporter gets involved in a complex murder puzzle.
Soporific suspenser with every tired situation in the book.

w Barry Beckerman, *novel* The Procane Chronicle by Oliver Bleeck *d* J. Lee-Thompson *ph* Lucien Ballard *m* Lalo Schifrin

Charles Bronson, Harry Guardino, John Houseman, Jacqueline Bisset, Maximilian Schell, Harris Yulin, Dana Elcar, Elisha Cook Jnr

'Much cross-cutting of the sort where the only events you care less about than the ones you cut from are the ones you cut to.'—*John Simon*

Saint Jack
US 1979 115m colour
New World / Shoals Creek / Playboy / Copa de Oro (Roger Corman)

An American wanderer in Singapore finds his metier as a pimp.
Whimsical, loquacious black comedy which failed to set its wavering director back on the firm ground he needed.

w Peter Bogdanovich, Howard Sackler, Paul Theroux, *novel* Paul Theroux *d* Peter Bogdanovich *ph* Robby Muller *m* various

Ben Gazzara, Denholm Elliott, James Villiers, Joss Ackland, Rodney Bewes, Mark Kingston, Lisa Lu, George Lazenby, Peter Bogdanovich

Saint Joan
GB 1957 110m bw
Otto Preminger

Glumly assembled screen version of the brilliantly argumentative play about the Maid of Orleans. Plenty of talent, but neither wit nor style.

w Graham Greene, *play* Bernard Shaw *d* Otto Preminger *ph* Georges Périnal *m* Mischa Spoliansky *pd* Roger Furse

Jean Seberg, Anton Walbrook, Richard Widmark, John Gielgud, Felix Aylmer, Harry Andrews, Richard Todd

St Louis Blues*
US 1939 92m bw
Paramount (Jeff Lazarus)

A Broadway musical star finds new fame down south.
Moderate star entertainment with good guest artists.

w John C. Moffitt, Malcolm Stuart Boylan, Frederick Hazlitt Brennan *d* Raoul Walsh *ph* Theodor Sparkuhl *songs* Frank Loesser, Burton Lane

Dorothy Lamour, Lloyd Nolan, Tito Guizar, Jerome Cowan, Jessie Ralph, William Frawley, the King's Men, Matty Melneck and his Orchestra

The St Louis Kid
US 1934 67m bw
Warner (Sam Bischoff)
GB title: *A Perfect Weekend*

A hot-headed truck driver takes the side of milk farmers in a trade dispute.
Modest star action comedy with a fair amount to amuse.

w Seton I. Miller, Warren Duff *d* Ray Enright *ph* Sid Hickox

James Cagney, Patricia Ellis, Hobart Cavanaugh, Spencer Charters, Addison Richards

St Martin's Lane**
GB 1938 85m bw
Mayflower (Erich Pommer)
US title: *Sidewalks of London*

A middle-aged busker falls in love with a brilliant girl dancer who becomes a star.
Well-made romantic drama with star performances and interesting theatrical background.

w Clemence Dane *d* Tim Whelan *ph* Jules Kruger *m* Arthur Johnson

Charles Laughton, Vivien Leigh, Rex Harrison, Tyrone Guthrie, Larry Adler, Gus MacNaughton

The St Valentine's Day Massacre
US 1967 99m De Luxe Panavision
TCF / Los Altos (Roger Corman)

The twenties gang war between Al Capone and Bugs Moran.
The director's first big studio film is disappointing; stagey, poorly developed, unconvincing-looking and overacted.

w Howard Browne *d* Roger Corman *ph* Milton Krasner *m* Fred Steiner *md* Lionel Newman

Jason Robards Jnr, George Segal, Ralph Meeker, Jean Hale, Clint Ritchie, Joseph Campanella, Richard Bakalyan, David Canary, Bruce Dern, Harold J. Stone, Kurt Kreuger, John Agar, Alex D'Arcy

The Sainted Sisters
US 1948   89m   bw
Paramount (Richard Maibaum)

Two New York con girls find themselves taken in by the inhabitants of the small town in which they are hiding out.
Unfunny period comedy which misses on all cylinders.

w Harry Clark d William D. Russell
ph Lionel Lindon m Van Cleave

Veronica Lake, Joan Caulfield, Barry Fitzgerald, William Demarest, George Reeves, Beulah Bondi, Chill Wills, Darryl Hickman

'Lake, Caulfield, and a swarm of clichés, pleasantly kidded in a manner derived from Preston Sturges.'—*James Agee*

Saints and Sinners
GB 1948   85m   bw

An ex-convict comes back to his home town to prove that those who condemned him were fools or knaves. Curious slice of Irish whimsy mixed with Ealing comedy; not very satisfactory. Kieron Moore, Christine Norden, Sheila Manahan, Michael Dolan, Maire O'Neill, Noel Purcell. Written by Paul Vincent Carroll and Leslie Arliss; directed by Leslie Arliss; for London Films / BLPA.

Sally
US 1930   c. 90m   Technicolor
Warner

A waitress makes it to the lights of Broadway.
Lightweight musical play, previously filmed in 1925 with Colleen Moore and Leon Errol, here the basis of an elaborate colour production with its original star, who however did not take too kindly to the camera.

w Waldemar Young, *play* Guy Bolton and Jerome Kern d John Francis Dillon ph Dev Jennings, E. E. Schoenbaum ch Larry Ceballos

Marilyn Miller, Joe E. Brown, Alexander Grey, T. Roy Barnes, Pert Kelton, Ford Sterling.

Sally and St Anne
US 1952   90m   bw
U-I (Leonard Goldstein)

When an Irish-American family is threatened with eviction, the daughter appeals to St Anne for help.
Whimsical comedy, quite nimbly performed.

w James O'Hanlon, Herb Meadow
d Rudolph Maté ph Irving Glassberg
m Frank Skinner

Ann Blyth, Edmund Gwenn, Hugh O'Brian, John McIntire, Jack Kelly

Sally in Our Alley*
GB 1931   77m   bw
ATP / Basil Dean

Poor girl loves wounded soldier.
Early talkie drama with music which made Gracie Fields a star and gave her a theme song.

w Miles Malleson, Archie Pitt, Alma Reville, *play* The Likes of 'Er by Charles McEvoy d Maurice Elvey

Gracie Fields, Ian Hunter, Florence Desmond, Ivor Barnard

Sally, Irene and Mary
US 1938   72m   bw
TCF (Gene Markey)

Three girls try to break into show business.
Simple-minded romantic comedy-musical, well enough done.

w Harry Tugend, Jack Yellen d William A. Seiter ph Peverell Marley md Arthur Lange

Alice Faye, Tony Martin, Fred Allen, Jimmy Durante, Gregory Ratoff, Joan Davis, Marjorie Weaver, Gypsy Rose Lee

Sally of the Sawdust
US 1925   78m at 24 fps   bw   silent

A circus juggler and faker tries to prevent his daughter from discovering that she is adopted.
Silent version of the stage hit *Poppy*, remade under its own title in 1936 (qv). In both versions W. C. Fields takes over the whole show (not to one's entire satisfaction) and the director's name in this case should not lead one to expect a film of significance, as he seems to have been glad of the work. With Carol Dempster, Alfred Lunt, Effie Shannon, Erville Anderson. Written by Forrest Halsey, from the play by Dorothy Donnelly; directed by D. W. Griffith; for Paramount / United Artists.

Salome
US 1923   80m at 24 fps   bw   silent

Almost unendurable as an entertainment, this stylized silent provided a famous role for its star against backgrounds in Aubrey Beardsley style, and is much illustrated in film histories. The *New Yorker* commented on a 1980 revival: 'The movie looks better in stills than when one actually sees it, but a folly like this should probably be experienced.' Nazimova, Mitchell Lewis, Nigel de Brulier, Based on Aubrey Beardsley's drawings and Oscar

Wilde's play; sets and costumes by Natacha Rambova; directed by Charles Bryant; for Nazimova.

Salome
US 1953 103m Technicolor
Columbia / Beckworth (Buddy Adler)

Princess Salome of Galilee eludes her licentious stepfather, falls in love with a secret Christian, and leaves home when her dancing fails to save the life of John the Baptist. Distorted biblical hokum with an interesting cast frozen into unconvincing attitudes.

w Harry Kleiner, Jesse Lasky Jnr d William Dieterle ph Charles Lang m George Duning md Daniele Amfitheatrof ad John Meehan

Rita Hayworth, Charles Laughton, Stewart Granger, Judith Anderson, Cedric Hardwicke, Alan Badel, Basil Sydney, Maurice Schwartz, Rex Reason, Arnold Moss
'The supreme screen achievement of our time!'—*publicity*

Salome Where She Danced*
US 1945 90m Technicolor
Universal (Walter Wanger, Alexander Golitzen)

During the Austro-Prussian war a dancer is suspected of being a spy and flees to Arizona, where she affects the lives of the citizenry. Absurdly plotted and stiffly played romantic actioner whose sheer creakiness made it a minor cult film.

w Laurence Stallings, *story* Michael J. Phillips d Charles Lamont ph Hal Mohr, W. Howard Green m Edward Ward

Yvonne de Carlo, Rod Cameron, Albert Dekker, David Bruce, Walter Slezak, Marjorie Rambeau, J. Edward Bromberg, Abner Biberman, John Litel, Kurt Katch
'I gratefully salute it as the funniest dead-pan parody I have ever seen.'—*James Agee*

Saloon Bar*
GB 1940 76m bw
Ealing (Michael Balcon)

A murder is solved during an evening in a pub.
Amusing, well-made little suspenser from a West End success.

w Angus MacPhail, John Dighton, *play* Frank Harvey d Walter Forde ph Ronald Neame md Ernest Irving

Gordon Harker, Elizabeth Allen, Mervyn Johns, Joyce Barbour, Anna Konstam, Judy Campbell, Norman Pierce, Alec Clunes, Felix Aylmer, Mavis Villiers, Torin Thatcher, O. B. Clarence

Salt and Pepper
GB 1968 101m De Luxe
UA / Chrislaw / Tracemark (Milton Ebbins)

Soho nightclub proprietors solve a murder. Infuriating throwaway star vehicle set in the dregs of swinging London. The sequel, *One More Time* (1970), was quite unnecessary.

w Michael Pertwee d Richard Donner ph Ken Higgins m Johnny Dankworth

Sammy Davis Jnr, Peter Lawford, Michael Bates, Ilona Rodgers, John Le Mesurier, Graham Stark, Ernest Clark

Saludos Amigos*
US 1943 43m Technicolor
Walt Disney

Donald Duck has various South American adventures with a parrot named Joe Carioca. Basically a naïve implementation of the good neighbour policy, but with flashes of brilliant animation and some mingling of live-action with cartoon.

Production supervisor Norman Ferguson

'Self-interested, belated ingratiation embarrasses me, and Disney's famous cuteness, however richly it may mirror national infantilism, is hard on my stomach.'—*James Agee*

AAN: music (Edward J. Plumb, Paul J. Smith, Charles Wolcott); title song (m Charles Wolcott, ly Ned Washington)

Salute John Citizen
GB 1942 98m bw
British National (Wallace Orton)

A clerk and his family suffer cheerfully through the blitz.
Modest, competent propaganda piece.

w Clemence Dane, Elizabeth Baron, *novel* Mr Bunting at War by Robert Greenwood d Maurice Elvey

Edward Rigby, Stanley Holloway, George Robey, Mabel Constanduros, Jimmy Hanley, Dinah Sheridan, Peggy Cummins, Stewart Rome

Salute for Three
US 1943 75m bw

An all-girl orchestra opens a canteen for servicemen. Modest, middling propaganda musical with minimum talents. Betty Jane Rhodes, Macdonald Carey, Dona Drake and her orchestra, Marty May, Lorraine and Rognan. Written by Davis Anderson, Curtis Kenyon, Hugh Wedlock Jnr and Howard Snyder; directed by Ralph Murphy; for Paramount.

Salute to the Marines
US 1943   101m   Technicolor
MGM (John Considine Jnr)

A sergeant-major struggles to get his family
out of the Philippines when the Japs attack.
Recruiting poster heroics with comedy
interludes.

w Wells Root, George Bruce, *story* Robert
Andrews *d* S. Sylvan Simon *ph* Charles
Schoenbaum, W. Howard Green *m* Lennie
Hayton

Wallace Beery, Fay Bainter, Marilyn
Maxwell, William Lundigan, Keye Luke,
Reginald Owen, Ray Collins, Noah Beery,
Russell Gleason

The Salvation Hunters**
US 1925   65m (24 fps)   bw   silent
Academy Photoplays (Josef Von
   Sternberg, George K. Arthur)

Among the mud flats of San Pedro, a boy wins
his girl from a brute.
Mini-budgeted minor classic whose very
artiness and pretentiousness were keys to its
director's later development.

wd Josef Von Sternberg ph Josef Von
Sternberg, Edward Gheller

George K. Arthur, Georgia Hale, Bruce
Guerin
   'Audience reaction was: even *our* lives are
not so drab as this, and if they are we don't
want to know about it. Asked to comment on
the failure of a film he had praised so highly,
Chaplin said, "Well, you know I was only
kidding. They all take everything I say so
seriously. I thought I'd praise a bad picture
and see what happened." '—*Richard Griffith
and Arthur Mayer, The Movies*

Salvatore Giuliano*
Italy 1961   125m   bw
Lux / Vides / Galatea (Franco Cristaldi)

The bullet-ridden body of key Sicilian Mafia
leader Giuliano triggers flashbacks to his
complex and brutal career.
Vivid, sometimes obscure, politically oriented
melodrama based on fact. Undoubtedly a local
classic, but not an easy film to appreciate.

w Francesco Rosi, Suso Cecchi d'Amico, Enzo
Provenzale, Franco Solinas *d Francesco Rosi
ph* Gianni di Venanzo *m* Piero Piccioni

Frank Wolff, Salvo Randone, Federico Zardi
   'Epic reportage in the twentieth-century
manner of a society reminiscent of some
backward corner of the nineteenth century.'—
Peter John Dyer, MFB

The Salzburg Connection
US 1972   93m   De Luxe   Panavision
TCF (Ingo Preminger)

An American lawyer on holiday in Salzburg
finds himself suspected by spies of both sides.
Turgid, routine action thriller with attractive
locations.

w Oscar Millard, *novel* Helen MacInnes
d Lee H. Katzin *ph* Wolfgang Treu
md Lionel Newman

Barry Newman, Anna Karina, Maria
Brandauer, Karen Jensen, Wolfgang Preiss
   'So dull you can't tell the CIA agents from
the neo-Nazis or double agents—or the inept
actors from the blocks and stones in the
handsome Austrian locales.'—*Judith Crist*

Sam Whiskey
US 1969   96m   De Luxe
UA / Brighton (Jules Levy, Arthur Gardner,
   Arnold Laven)

An itinerant gambler is paid to recover a
fortune in gold bars from the bottom of a
Colorado river.
Easy-going but rather slackly-handled western.

w William W. Norton *d* Arnold Laven
ph Robert Moreno *m* Herschel Burke Gilbert

Burt Reynolds, Clint Walker, Ossie Davis,
Angie Dickinson, Rick Davis, William
Schallert

Same Time, Next Year*
US 1978   119m   colour
Universal / Walter Mirisch, Robert Mulligan

An illicit affair is carried on for twenty-five
years, the couple confining themselves to one
annual meeting in a hotel.
Careful film version of a smash Broadway
comedy; the flimsiness of the premise is well
concealed, but it remains a one-set play.

w Bernard Slade, from his play *d* Robert
Mulligan *ph* Robert Surtees *m* Marvin
Hamlisch *pd* Henry Bumstead

Ellen Burstyn, Alan Alda
AAN: Bernard Slade; Robert Surtees; Ellen
Burstyn; song, 'The Last Time I Felt Like
This'

Sammy Going South*
GB 1963   128m   Eastmancolor
   Cinemascope
Bryanston (Hal Mason)
US title: *A Boy Ten Feet Tall*

A 10-year-old boy is orphaned in Port Said
and hitch-hikes to his aunt in Durban.
Disappointing family-fodder epic in which the
mini-adventures follow each other too
predictably.

w Denis Cannan, *novel* W. H. Canaway
d Alexander Mackendrick *ph* Erwin Hillier
m Tristam Cary

Fergus McClelland, Edward G. Robinson,
Constance Cummings, Harry H. Corbett

Samson and Delilah
US 1949 128m Technicolor
Paramount / Cecil B. de Mille

Delilah, rejected by religious strong man
Samson, cuts his hair and delivers him to his
enemies.
Absurd biblical hokum, stodgily narrated and
directed, monotonously photographed and
edited, and notable only for the 30-second
destruction of the temple at the end.

w Jesse L. Lasky Jnr, Fredric M. Frank
d Cecil B. de Mille *ph* George Barnes
m Victor Young *ad* Hans Dreier, Walter
Tyler

Hedy Lamarr, Victor Mature, Angela
Lansbury, George Sanders, Henry Wilcoxon,
Olive Deering, Fay Holden, Russ Tamblyn

'To ignore so enormous, over-coloured,
over-stuffed, flamboyant an "epic" would be
almost as absurd as taking it seriously.'—
Richard Mallett, Punch

'Perhaps de Mille's survival is due to the fact
that he decided in his movie nonage to ally
himself with God as his co-maker and get his
major scripts from the Bible, which he has
always handled with the proprietary air of a
gentleman fondling old love letters.'—*New
Yorker*

AAN: George Barnes; Victor Young

San Antone
US 1952 90m bw

During the Civil War a Texas rancher
antagonizes an army lieutenant. Very routine,
competent western without any moment of
inspiration. Rod Cameron, Forrest Tucker,
Arleen Whelan, Katy Jurado, Rodolfo
Acosta. Written by Steve Fisher, from the
novel *Golden Herd* by Curt Carroll; directed
by Joe Kane; for Republic.

San Antonio*
US 1945 109m Technicolor
Warner (Robert Buckner)

A cowboy incurs the jealousy of a saloon
owner.
Typically thinly-plotted Warner star western
which works well enough sequence by
sequence, climaxing with a fight in the
deserted Alamo.

w Alan le May, W. R. Burnett *d* David
Butler *ph* Bert Glennon *m* Max Steiner

Errol Flynn, Alexis Smith, Paul Kelly, Victor
Francen, S. Z. Sakall, John Litel, Florence
Bates, Robert Shayne, Monte Blue, Robert
Barrat

AAN: song 'Some Sunday Morning' (*m* Ray
Heindorf, M. K. Jerome, *ly* Ted Koehler)

San Demetrio London*
GB 1943 105m bw
Ealing (Robert Hamer)

In 1940, the survivors of a crippled tanker
bring it back home.
Rather flat and dated propaganda piece which
seemed much more vivid at the time.

w Robert Hamer, Charles Frend, *story*
F. Tennyson Jesse *d* Charles Frend
ph Ernest Palmer, Roy Kellino *m* John
Greenwood

Walter Fitzgerald, Mervyn Johns, Ralph
Michael, Robert Beatty, Charles Victor,
Frederick Piper, Gordon Jackson

San Diego I Love You*
US 1944 83m bw
Universal (Michael Fessier, Ernest Pagano)

A family travels to San Diego to promote
father's inventions.
Pleasing, easy-come-easy-go comedy full of
memorable incident and characterization.

w Michael Fessier, Ernest Pagano *d* Reginald
Le Borg *ph* Hal Mohr *m* Hans Salter

Louise Allbritton, Edward Everett Horton,
Jon Hall, Eric Blore, *Buster Keaton*, Irene
Ryan

San Francisco****
US 1936 117m bw
MGM (John Emerson, Bernard Hyman)

The loves and career problems of a Barbary
Coast saloon proprietor climax in the 1906
earthquake.
Incisive, star-packed, superbly-handled
melodrama which weaves in every kind of
appeal and for a finale has some of the best
special effects ever conceived.

w Anita Loos, story Robert Hopkins *d* W. S.
Van Dyke *ph* Oliver T. Marsh *m* Edward
Ward *md* Herbert Stothart *montage John
Hoffman*

*Clark Gable, Spencer Tracy, Jeanette
MacDonald, Jack Holt, Jessie Ralph*, Ted
Healy, Shirley Ross, Al Shean, Harold
Huber

'Prodigally generous and completely
satisfying.'—*Frank S. Nugent*

'She fell in love with the toughest guy on the
toughest street in the world!'—*publicity*

AAN: best picture; Robert Hopkins;
W. S. Van Dyke; Spencer Tracy

The San Francisco Story*
US 1952   90m   bw
Warner / Fidelity–Vogue (Howard Welsch)

In 1856, a wanderer bound for China stops in
San Francisco to get involved in politics.
Lively melodrama with good period feel.

w D. D. Beauchamp, *novel* Richard Summers
d Robert Parrish ph John Seitz m Emil
Newman

Joel McCrea, Yvonne de Carlo, Sidney
Blackmer, Florence Bates

San Quentin*
US 1937   70m   bw
Warner (Sam Bischoff)

A convict's sister loves the warden.
Standard tough prison melodrama,
competently done.

w Peter Milne, Humphrey Cobb, *story* John
Bright, Robert Tasker d Lloyd Bacon ph Sid
Hickox m Heinz Roemheld, David Raksin

Pat O'Brien, Ann Sheridan, Humphrey
Bogart, Barton MacLane, Joseph Sawyer,
Veda Ann Borg

San Quentin
US 1946   66m   bw

A convict starts a movement for the
rehabilitation of prisoners after release, but
despite himself is caught up in a prison break.
Tolerable support of a familiar kind. Lawrence
Tierney, Barton Maclane, Marian Carr,
Raymond Burr, Joe Devlin. Written by
Lawrence Kimble, Arthur A. Ross and
Howard J. Green; directed by Gordon
Douglas; for RKO.

Sanctuary
US 1960   90m   bw   Cinemascope
TCF (Richard D. Zanuck)

The governor's daughter is seduced by a
bootlegger, and her life goes from one tragedy
to another.
Confused adaptation of unadaptable material,
full of pussyfoot daring but little sense.

w James Poe, *novel* William Faulkner d Tony
Richardson ph Ellsworth Fredericks m Alex
North

Lee Remick, Bradford Dillman, Yves
Montand, Odetta, Harry Townes, Howard St
John, Reta Shaw, Strother Martin

The Sand Pebbles*
US 1966   193m   De Luxe   Panavision
TCF / Argyle / Solar (Robert Wise)

In 1926 an American gunboat patrolling the
Yangtze river gets involved with Chinese
warlords.
Confused action blockbuster with Vietnam
parallels for those who care to pick them up;
pretty thinly stretched entertainment despite
the tons of explosive.

w Robert Anderson, *novel* Richard
McKenna d Robert Wise ph Joseph
MacDonald m Jerry Goldsmith

Steve McQueen, Candice Bergen, Richard
Attenborough, Richard Crenna, Marayat
Andriane, Mako, Larry Gates. Simon
Oakland

'If it had been done twenty years ago, it
would have been fast and unpretentious, with
some ingeniously faked background shots . . .
and we would never have asked for larger
historical meanings.'—*Pauline Kael*

AAN: best picture; Joseph MacDonald; Jerry
Goldsmith; Steve McQueen; Mako

Sanders of the River*
GB 1935   98m   bw
London (Alexander Korda)

Problems of a British colonial servant in
keeping peace among the tribes.
Much-caricatured African adventure of the
very old school, helped by Robeson's
personality.

w Lajos Biro, Jeffrey Dell, Arthur Wimperis
d Zoltan Korda

Leslie Banks, Paul Robeson, Nina Mae
McKinney, Robert Cochran

Sandokan the Great
Italy / France / Spain 1963   114m
   Techniscope

The son of the Sultan of Borneo wages jungle
war against the oppressive British. A curious
mixture of Tarzan and Robin Hood, this
character appeared in several adventures
before expiring; the first chapter is the best, or
least worst. Steve Reeves, Genevieve Grad,
Rik Battaglia, Andrea Bosic. Written by
Fulvio Gicca and Umberto Lenzi, from the
novel by Emilio Salgari; directed by Umberto
Lenzi; for Filmes / CCF / Ocean.

The Sandpiper
US 1965   116m   Metrocolor   Panavision
MGM / Filmways (John Calley)

An artist lives with her illegitimate son in a
Monterey beach shack; when she is forced to
send the boy to school he attracts the attention
of the minister in charge.
Absurd novelettish love story basically copied
from *The Garden of Allah;* pretty seascapes
are the most rewarding aspect.

w Dalton Trumbo, Michael Wilson
d Vincente Minnelli *ph* Milton Krasner
m Johnny Mandel

Elizabeth Taylor, Richard Burton, Eva Marie
Saint, Charles Bronson, Robert Webber

'Straight Louisa May Alcott interlarded with
discreet pornographic allusions.'—*John Simon*

'Sex-on-the-sand soap opera.'—*Robert
Windeler*

AA: song 'The Shadow of Your Smile'
(*m* Johnny Mandel, *ly* Paul Francis Webster)

Sands of Iwo Jima*
US 1949 109m bw
Republic (Edmund Grainger)

During World War II in the Pacific, a tough
sergeant of marines moulds raw recruits into
fighting men but is himself shot by a sniper.

Celebrated star war comic, still quite hypnotic
in its flagwaving way.

w Harry Brown, James Edward Grant
d Allan Dwan *ph* Reggie Lanning *m* Victor
Young

John Wayne, John Agar, Adele Mara, Forrest
Tucker, Arthur Franz, Julie Bishop, Richard
Jaeckel

'The battle sequences are terrifyingly real
. . . but the personal dramatics make up a
compendium of war-picture clichés.'—*Variety*

'Say what you like about the sentimental
flavour of war pictures such as this, there's no
denying they keep you in your seat.'—*Richard
Mallett, Punch*

AAN: Harry Brown (original story); John
Wayne

Sands of the Desert
GB 1960 92m Technicolor

A diminutive travel agent goes out to
investigate a desert holiday camp which has
suffered from sabotage. Limp star comedy
with poor studio work and meandering script.

Charlie Drake, Peter Arne, Sarah Branch,
Raymond Huntley, Peter Illing, Harold
Kasket. Written and directed by John Paddy
Carstairs; for Associated British.

Sands of the Kalahari
GB 1965 119m Technicolor
  Panavision
Pendennis (Cy Endfield, Stanley Baker)

Survivors of a plane crash trek across the
desert and are menaced by baboons and each
other.

Hysterical melodrama with predictable heebie-
jeebies by all concerned and the baddie finally
left to the mercy of the monkeys. For
hardened sensationalists.

wd Cy Endfield, *novel* William Mulvihill
ph Erwin Hillier *m* Johnny Dankworth

Stanley Baker, Stuart Whitman, Harry
Andrews, Susannah York, Theodore Bikel,
Nigel Davenport, Barry Lowe

The Sandwich Man*
GB 1966 95m Eastmancolor
Rank / Titan (Peter Newbrook)

In the course of a walking day around London
a sandwich man encounters many of his
eccentric acquaintances.

Spurned when it was first released, this
comedy variety show, mostly in mime, can
now be seen to be of a kind popularized by
TV, and may have been simply ahead of its
time. It certainly seems funnier than it did.

w Michael Bentine, Robert Hartford-Davis
d Robert Hartford-Davis *ph* Peter
Newbrook *m* Mike Vickers

Michael Bentine, Dora Bryan, Suzy Kendall,
Norman Wisdom, Harry H. Corbett, Bernard
Cribbins, Ian Hendry, Stanley Holloway, Alfie
Bass, Diana Dors, Ron Moody, Wilfrid Hyde
White, Donald Wolfit, Max Bacon, Fred
Emney, Frank Finlay, Peter Jones, Michael
Medwin, Ronnie Stevens, John Le Mesurier,
Sidney Tafler, John Junkin, Warren Mitchell

Sangaree
US 1953 95m Technicolor 3-D
Paramount / Pine–Thomas

Trouble ensues when a plantation owner wills
his wealth to the son of a slave.

Period skullduggery rather hammily
presented.

w David Duncan, *novel* Frank G. Slaughter
d Edward Ludwig *ph* Lionel Lindon, W.
Wallace Kelley *m* Lucien Caillet

Fernando Lamas, Arlene Dahl, Patricia
Medina, Francis L. Sullivan, Charles Korvin,
Tom Drake, John Sutton, Willard Parker,
Lester Matthews

Santa Fe
US 1951 89m Technicolor

After the Civil War, the eldest of four
westbound brothers tries to prevent the others
from becoming outlaws.

Regulation star western, with action sequences
a litte under par. Randolph Scott, Jerome
Courtland, Janis Carter, Peter Thompson,
John Archer, Warner Anderson, Roy
Roberts. Written by Kenneth Gamet; directed
by Irving Pichel; for Harry Joe Brown /
Columbia.

Santa Fe Passage
US 1954 89m Trucolor

An Indian-hating scout with a bad record is
hired to transport arms to Santa Fe. Rough-
and-ready brawling western with very little
going for it. John Payne, Rod Cameron, Faith
Domergue, Slim Pickens, Leo Gordon.
Written by Lillie Hayward; directed by
William Witney; for Republic.

Santa Fe Trail**
US 1940 110m bw
Warner (Robert Fellows)

A cavalry officer is responsible for the final
capture of John Brown.
The most solemn western from star or studio
has impressive patches amid routine
excitements.

w Robert Buckner *d Michael Curtiz ph* Sol
Polito *m* Max Steiner

Errol Flynn, Olivia de Havilland, Raymond
Massey, Ronald Reagan, Alan Hale, Van
Heflin, Gene Reynolds, Henry O'Neill
  'A thousand miles of danger with a
thousand thrills a mile!'—*publicity*

Santee
US 1972 93m colour
Vagabond (Deno Paoli, Edward Platt)

A boy goes west to find his father and
befriends the bounty hunter who has killed
him.
Personable, violent western with adequate
style and performances.

w Brand Bell *d* Gene Nelson *ph* Donald
Morgan *m* Don Randi

Glenn Ford, Michael Burns, Dana Wynter,
Jay Silverheels, Harry Townes, John Larch

Santiago
US 1956 92m Warnercolor
  Cinemascope
Warner (Martin Rackin)
GB title: *The Gun Runner*

A Mississippi paddle-boat sets out for Cuba
with a consignment of guns for the rebels.
Stiff period actioner of no particular merit.

w Martin Rackin, John Twist *d* Gordon
Douglas *ph* John Seitz *m* David Buttolph

Alan Ladd, Rossana Podesta, Lloyd Nolan,
Chill Wills, Paul Fix, L. Q. Jones, Frank de
Kova

The Saphead*
US 1920 70m (24 fps) bw silent
Metro / Buster Keaton

A shy young man reads a manual on how to
win the modern girl.
Interesting early star comedy: quite winning in
its way, but without the spectacular moments
which were a feature of his later films.

w June Mathis, *play* The New Henrietta by
Winchell Smith, Victor Mapes *d* Herbert
Blache *ph* Harold Wenstrom

Buster Keaton, Beula Booker, William H.
Crane, Irving Cummings

Sapphire**
GB 1959 92m Eastmancolor
Rank / Artna (Michael Relph)

Scotland Yard solves the murder of a coloured
music student.
Efficient police thriller with a strong race
angle.

w Janet Green *d* Basil Dearden *ph* Harry
Waxman *m* Philip Green

Nigel Patrick, Michael Craig, Yvonne
Mitchell, Paul Massie, Bernard Miles, Olga
Lindo, Earl Cameron, Gordon Heath, Robert
Adams
  'A dandy murder mystery—taut, tantalizing
and beautifully done.'—*Judith Crist, 1980*

Saps at Sea
US 1940 60m bw
Hal Roach

Olly needs a rest after working in a horn
factory, so he and Stan take a boating holiday
but are kidnapped by a gangster.
Disappointing star comedy with gags too few
and too long drawn out.

w Charles Rogers, Harry Langdon, Gil Pratt,
Felix Adler *d* Gordon Douglas *ph* Art
Lloyd *m* Marvin Hatley

Stan Laurel, Oliver Hardy, James Finlayson,
Dick Cramer, Ben Turpin

Saraband for Dead Lovers*
GB 1948 96m Technicolor
Ealing (Michael Relph)
US title: *Saraband*

The tragic love affair of Konigsmark and
Sophie Dorothea, wife of the Elector of
Hanover who later became George I of
England.
Gloomy but superb-looking historical love
story; it just misses being a memorable film.

w John Dighton, Alexander Mackendrick,
novel Helen Simpson *d* Basil Dearden,
Michael Relph *ph Douglas Slocombe*
m Alan Rawsthorne

Stewart Granger, Joan Greenwood, Françoise
Rosay, Flora Robson, Peter Bull

'Suspense, romance, interest and excitement in full measure.'—*MFB*

The Saracen Blade
US 1954   76m   Technicolor

In the thirteenth century a young Italian crusader devotes himself to avenging the murder of his father. Cut-price swashbuckler full of unintentional laughs and therefore quite watchable. Ricardo Montalban, Betta St John, Rick Jason, Carolyn Jones, Michael Ansara. Written by DeVallon Scott and Worthing Yates, from the novel by Frank Yerby; directed by William Castle; for Sam Katzman / Columbia.

Sarah and Son
US 1930   85m   bw
Paramount

A widow seeks the baby her husband took away from her.
Mother love saga; soppy but with good credits.

w Zoe Akins, *novel* Timothy Shea
d Dorothy Arzner *ph* Charles Lang

Ruth Chatterton, Fredric March, Fuller Mellish Jnr, Gilbert Emery, Doris Lloyd

AAN: Ruth Chatterton

Saratoga*
US 1937   102m   bw
MGM (Bernard H. Hyman)

A bookmaker helps the daughter of a horse breeder.
Forgettable racetrack drama notable chiefly as the last film of Jean Harlow who died before it was completed.

w Anita Loos, Robert Hopkins *d* Jack Conway *ph* Ray June *m* Edward Ward

Clark Gable, Jean Harlow, Lionel Barrymore, Frank Morgan, Walter Pidgeon, Una Merkel, Cliff Edwards, George Zucco, Jonathan Hale
'Glib, forthright, knowing and adroit.'— *Time*

Saratoga Trunk*
US 1943   135m   bw
Warner (Hal B. Wallis)

A notorious woman comes back to New Orleans and falls for a cowboy helping a railroad combine against their rivals.
Curious, unsatisfactory, miscast and overlong film version of a bestseller; there are enjoyable sequences, but it simply fails to come alive.

w Casey Robinson, *novel* Edna Ferber
d Sam Wood *ph* Ernest Haller *m* Max Steiner *ph* Joseph St Amaad

Ingrid Bergman, Gary Cooper, Flora Robson, Jerry Austin, Florence Bates, John Warburton, John Abbott, Curt Bois, Ethel Griffies
'It lacks a logical pattern of drama and character . . . a piece of baggage labelled solely for the stars.'—*Bosley Crowther*

AAN: Flora Robson

Saskatchewan
US 1954   87m   Technicolor
U-I (Aaron Rosenberg)
GB title: *O'Rourke of the Royal Mounted*

A mountie helps the lady survivor of an Indian attack.
Standard star actioner.

w Gil Doud *d* Raoul Walsh *ph* John Seitz
m Joseph Gershenson

Alan Ladd, Shelley Winters, J. Carrol Naish, Hugh O'Brian, Robert Douglas, Richard Long, Jay Silverheels

The Satan Bug*
US 1965   114m   De Luxe   Panavision
UA / Mirisch / Kappa (John Sturges)

At a top-secret desert research station, one scientist is a traitor, and a deadly virus has been stolen for use by a mad millionaire.
Slow-moving, portentous, gadget-filled actioner which looks good but seldom stimulates.

w James Clavell, Edward Anhalt,
novel Alistair MacLean *d* John Sturges
ph Robert Surtees *m* Jerry Goldsmith

George Maharis, Richard Basehart, Anne Francis, Dana Andrews, Ed Asner

Satan Met a Lady*
US 1936   74m   bw
Warner (Henry Blanke)

Various crooks and a private detective pursue a rare artifact.
Perversely rewritten version of *The Maltese Falcon* (qv). Fascinating but not really successful

w Brown Holmes *w* William Dieterle
ph Arthur Edeson *m* Leo F. Forbstein

Bette Davis, Warren William, Alison Skipworth, Arthur Treacher, Wini Shaw, Marie Wilson, Porter Hall
'One lives through it in constant expectation of seeing a group of uniformed individuals appear suddenly from behind the furniture and take the entire cast into protective custody.'—*Bosley Crowther*

Satan Never Sleeps

US / GB 1962   126m   De Luxe
  Cinemascope
TCF / Leo McCarey
GB title: *The Devil Never Sleeps*

In the late forties in China, Catholic
missionaries defy the communists.
Failed anti-Red imitation of *Inn of the Sixth
Happiness* with the priests from *Going My
Way*. Has to be seen to be believed.

w Claude Binyon, Leo McCarey *d* Leo
McCarey *ph* Oswald Morris *m* Richard
Rodney Bennett

Clifton Webb, William Holden, France
Nuyen, Weaver Lee, Athene Seyler, Martin
Benson
   'For all its superficial smirk of piety, this is
just a prurient, soft-soapy and holy water
version of the spicy story about the lonely
missionary and the beautiful native girl.'—
Time

The Satanic Rites of Dracula

GB 1973   88m   Technicolor
Hammer (Roy Skeggs)
US title: *Dracula is Alive and Well and
  Living in London*

When vampires infest London, a property
speculator proves to be Dracula himself.
Intriguingly plotted screamer with more
mystery than horror.

w Don Houghton *d* Alan Gibson *ph* Brian
Probyn *m* John Cacavas

Peter Cushing, Christopher Lee, Michael
Coles, William Franklyn, Freddie Jones,
Richard Vernon, Patrick Barr

Satellite in the Sky

GB 1956   85m   Warnercolor
  Cinemascope
Warner / Tridelta / Danziger

A rocketship is ordered to lose a tritonium
bomb in space, but the device attaches itself to
the side of the ship.
Boringly talkative low-budget science fiction
with ideas beyond its station but not enough
talent to put them over.

w John Mather, J. T. McIntosh, Edith Dell
d Paul Dickson *ph* Georges Périnal *m* Albert
Elms

Kieron Moore, Lois Maxwell, Donald Wolfit,
Bryan Forbes, Jimmy Hanley, Alan Gifford

Saturday Island

GB 1951   102m   Technicolor
Coronado (David E. Rose)
US title: *Island of Desire*

In 1943 a supply boat is torpedoed and a
Canadian nurse finds romance on a desert
island with a US marine and a one-armed
RAF pilot.
Unlikely, conversational, old-fashioned love
story.

wd Stuart Heisler, *novel* Hugh Brooke
ph Oswald Morris *m* William Alwyn

Linda Darnell, Tab Hunter, Donald Gray

Saturday Night and Sunday Morning••••

GB 1960   89m   bw
Bryanston / Woodfall (Harry Salzman, Tony
  Richardson)

A Nottingham factory worker is dissatisfied
with his lot, gets into trouble through an affair
with a married woman, but finally settles for
convention.
Startling when it emerged, this raw working-
class melodrama, with its sharp detail and
strong comedy asides, delighted the mass
audience chiefly because of its strong central
character thumbing his nose at authority.
Matching the mood of the times, and
displaying a new attitude to sex, it transformed
British cinema and was much imitated.

w Alan Sillitoe, *from his novel* *d* Karel Reisz
ph Freddie Francis *m* Johnny Dankworth

Albert Finney, Shirley Anne Field, *Rachel
Roberts*, Bryan Pringle, Norman Rossington,
Hylda Baker

Saturday Night Fever•

US 1978   119m   Movielab
Paramount / Robert Stigwood (Milt Felsen)

Italian roughnecks in Brooklyn live for their
Saturday night disco dancing, and one of them
falls in love with a girl who makes him realize
there are better things in life.
Foul-mouthed, fast-paced slice of life which
plays like an updated version of *Marty* except
that all the characters seem to have crawled
from under stones. The slick direction, fast
editing and exciting dance numbers do
something to take away the sour taste.

w Norman Wexler, *story* Nik Cohn *d* John
Badham *ph* Ralf D. Bode *songs* Barry,
Robin and Maurice Gibb (and others),
performed by the Bee Gees *ed* David
Rawlins *pd* Charles Bailey

John Travolta, Karen Lynn Gorney, Barry
Miller, Joseph Cali, Paul Pape, Bruce
Ornstein
   'A stylish piece of contemporary
anthropology, an urban safari into darkest
America, a field study of the mystery cults

among the young braves and squaws growing up in North Brooklyn.'—*Alan Brien, Sunday Times*

AAN: John Travolta

Saturday Night Out
GB 1963   96m   bw

Five sailors spend an overnight leave in London. Portmanteau drama in which all elements are equally uninteresting. Bernard Lee, Heather Sears, John Bonney, Francesca Annis, Erika Remberg, Colin Campbell, David Lodge. Written by Donald and Derek Ford; directed by Robert Hartford-Davis; for Compton-Tekli.

Saturday's Children
US 1940   101m   bw
Warner (Henry Blanke)

An impractical young inventor marries an ambitious young woman, but depressed finances lead to discord.
Glum, dated rehash of a 1929 silent; watchable but not compelling.

w Julius J. and Philip G. Epstein, *play* Maxwell Anderson *d* Vincent Sherman *ph* James Wong Howe

John Garfield, Claude Rains, Anne Shirley, Lee Patrick, George Tobias, Roscoe Karns, Elizabeth Risdon, Berton Churchill

† The story was also made in 1935 as *Maybe It's Love*, with Ross Alexander, Henry Travers and Gloria Stuart; William McGann directed without flair.

Saturn Three
GB 1980   87m   colour
ITC / Transcontinental (Stanley Donen)

A maniac builds a robot on a remote space station, and they both go berserk.
Rather unpleasant blend of space fiction, horror and suspense, with some nasty detail and a general feeling that the actors wish they were elsewhere.

w Martin Amis, *story* John Barry *d* Stanley Donen *ph* Billy Williams *m* Elmer Bernstein *pd* Stuart Craig

Kirk Douglas, Farrah Fawcett, Harvey Keitel, Ed Bishop

Satyricon*
Italy / France 1969   129m   De Luxe Panavision
UA / PAA / PEA (Alberto Grimaldi)
aka: *Fellini Satyricon*

Sexual adventures of a Roman student. Garish, sporadically enjoyable sketches on a very thin thread of plot: a more benevolent version of the usual Fellini nightmare.

w Federico Fellini, Bernardino Zapponi *d* Federico Fellini *ph* Giuseppe Rotunno *m* Nino Rota, Ilhan Mimaroglu, Tod Dockstader, Andrew Rudin *pd* Danilo Donati

Martin Potter, Hiram Keller, Salvo Randone, Max Born

'A picaresque satire in fragments . . . a series of tableaux which carry the poetry visually at the price of coherence.'—*Mike Wallington, MFB*

'Part of the gradual decomposition of what once was one of the greatest talents in film history . . . a gimcrack, shopworn nightmare.'—*John Simon*

AAN: Federico Fellini (as director)

Le Sauvage
France / Italy 1978   107m   Eastmancolor
Lira / PAI (Raymond Danon)

A business executive has opted out of life to be alone on a desert island, but on his last night in the city accidentally helps a runaway heiress who follows him.
A promising and amusing start is squandered in the tedious island sequences of this patchy romantic comedy, which does however leave one with a sense of freshness and optimism rare in the cinema of the seventies.

w Jean-Paul Rappeneau, Elizabeth Rappeneau, Jean-Loup Dabadie *d* Jean-Paul Rappeneau *ph* Pierre Lhomme *m* Michel Legrand

Yves Montand, Catherine Deneuve, Luigi Vannucchi, Dana Wynter

The Savage
US 1952   95m   Technicolor
Paramount (Mel Epstein)

A white boy grows up with Indians and later suffers from divided loyalties.
Solemn, rather tedious but well produced western.

w Sidney Boehm, *novel* L. L. Foreman *d* George Marshall *ph* John F. Seitz *m* Paul Sawtell

Charlton Heston, Susan Morrow, Peter Hanson, Joan Taylor, Richard Rober, Don Porter

The Savage Eye*
US 1959   68m   bw
City Film Corporation (Ben Maddow, Joseph Strick, Sidney Meyers)

An unhappily married young woman takes a jaundiced view of life around her in Los Angeles.

The wisp of plot is merely an excuse to present a documentary exposé of the seamier side of life in America's most eccentric city, with its faith healers and revellers. Much of it is fascinating, though the film is not a cohesive whole and the would-be poetic commentary falls on its face.

wd, ed Ben Maddow, Joseph Strick, Sidney Meyers *m* Leonard Rosenman

Barbara Baxley, Gary Merrill, Herschel Bernardi

The Savage Guns
US / Spain 1961   83m   Metrocolor
    Cinemascope

After the Civil War, an American rancher settles in Mexico but finds his pacifist principles tested by bandits. Unappealing, stodgy western with the Hammer horror team rather curiously cast as co-producers. Richard Basehart, Don Taylor, Alex Nicol, Jose Nieto, Fernando Rey. Written by Edmund Morris (?Jimmy Sangster); directed by Michael Carreras; for Capricorn / Tecisa / MGM.

The Savage Innocents
GB / France / Italy 1960   107m   Super
    Technirama 70
Joseph Janni / Magic Film / Playart / Gray
    Films (Maleno Malenotti)

Trials of an Eskimo and his wife in Canada's frozen north.

Conscientious, determined and very boring account of Eskimo life played by actors talking pidgin English. Not a success despite the magnificent photography.

w Nicholas Ray, *novel* Top of the World by Hans Ruesch *d* Nicholas Ray, Baccio Bandini *ph* Aldo Tonti, Peter Hennessy *m* Angelo Lavagnino

Anthony Quinn, Yoko Tani, Marie Yang, Peter O'Toole, Carlo Justini, Anna May Wong, Lee Montague, Ed Devereaux

Savage Messiah*
GB 1972   103m   Metrocolor
MGM / Russ–Arts (Ken Russell)

The life together (1910–14) of the 18-year-old painter Gaudier and 38-year-old Sophie Brzeska.

Intense, fragmentary art film about two eccentrics; would have better suited TV.

w Christopher Logue, *book* H. S. Ede *d* Ken Russell *ph* Dick Bush *m* Michael Garrett *pd* Derek Jarman

Dorothy Tutin, Scott Anthony, Helen Mirren, Lindsay Kemp, Michael Gough, John Justin

Savage Pampas
Spain / Argentina / US 1967   108m
    Eastmancolor   Superpanorama
Jaime Prados–Dasa–Sam Bronston

In 19th-century Argentina the commander of an isolated fort finds that a bandit is bribing his men to desert.

Densely plotted semi-western, sometimes good to look at but slow and lugubrious.

w Hugo Fregonese, John Melson *d* Hugo Fregonese *ph* Marcel Berenguer *m* Waldo de los Rios

Robert Taylor, Ron Randell, Ty Hardin, Rosenda Monteros, Marc Lawrence

Savage Sam*
US 1962   104m   Technicolor
Walt Disney (Bill Anderson)

The youngest son of a homesteading family has a troublesome dog which redeems itself by tracking down Apaches.

Folksy boy-and-dog western, good of its kind, with adequate suspense and scenery.

w Fred Gipson, William Tunberg *d* Norman Tokar *ph* Edward Colman *m* Oliver Wallace

Brian Keith, Tommy Kirk, Kevin Corcoran, Dewey Martin, Jeff York

'A cadet edition of the best of Ford.'—*MFB*

Savage Wilderness
US 1956   98m   Technicolor
    Cinemascope
Columbia (William Fadiman)
GB title: *The Last Frontier*

An Indian-hating fort commander puts himself and his charges in jeopardy.

Standard western with good performances and excellent action scenes.

w Philip Yordan, Russell S. Hughes, *novel* The Gilded Rooster by Richard Emery Roberts *d* Anthony Mann *ph* William Mellor *m* Leigh Harline

Victor Mature, *Robert Preston*, Guy Madison, Anne Bancroft, James Whitmore, Peter Whitney

Savages
US 1972   106m   colour
Angelika / Merchant–Ivory (Joseph Saleh)

Forest wanderers take over a deserted mansion and begin to feel its civilizing influence.

Mild fable which needed a Bunuel to do it justice; a few lively moments.

w George Swift Trow, Michael O'Donoghue
d James Ivory *ph* Walter Lassally *m* Joe
Raposo

Louis Stadlen, Anne Francine, Thayer David,
Salome Jens, Neil Fitzgerald

Save the Tiger*
US 1972 100m Movielab
Paramount / Jalem / Filmways / Cirandinha
(Steve Shagan)

A middle-aged businessman regrets the slack
morality of modern America.
Self-adulatory drama which really has little
point but gets a few marks for meaning well
and for vivid scenes.

w Steve Shagan *d* John G. Avildsen *ph* Jim
Crabe *m* Marvin Hamlisch

Jack Lemmon, Jack Gilford, Laurie
Heineman, Norman Burton, Thayer David
'A scathing indictment of the US, of
materialism, war, marriage—the works.
Wordy, literate and deeply felt.'—*NFT, 1974*

AA: Jack Lemmon
AAN: Steve Shagan; Jack Gilford

Sawdust and Tinsel*
Sweden 1953 95m bw
Svensk Filmindustri
aka: *The Naked Night;* original title:
Gycklarnas Afton

The owner of a travelling circus leaves his
mistress for his separated wife, and is
challenged to fight by the mistress's new lover.
Powerfully-made yet rather pointless
melodrama about unpleasant people.

wd Ingmar Bergman ph Sven Nykvist
m Karl-Birger Blomdahl

Harriet Andersson, Ake Grönberg, Hasse
Ekman, Annika Tretow
'One of the extremely rare instances of a
film's elements all blending perfectly.'—*John
Simon*

The Saxon Charm
US 1948 88m bw
Universal (Joseph Sistrom)

A Broadway impresario dominates the lives of
those around him.
Rather heavy-going comedy drama which
could have done with more malicious wit;
allegedly based on Jed Harris.

wd Claude Binyon, *novel* Frederick
Wakeman *ph* Milton Krasner *m* Walter
Scharf

Robert Montgomery, Susan Hayward, John
Payne, Audrey Totter, Henry Morgan, Harry
Von Zell, Cara Williams, Chill Wills, Heather
Angel

Say Hello to Yesterday
GB 1970 92m Eastmancolor
Josef Shaftel (William Hill)

A middle-aged married woman goes to
London for shopping and is pursued by a
strange young man whom she allows to seduce
her.
Unattractive 'with it' romantic drama with a
swinging London setting, a long way after
Brief Encounter.

w Alvin Rakoff, Peter King *d* Alvin Rakoff
ph Geoffrey Unsworth *m* Riz Ortolani

Jean Simmons, Leonard Whiting, *Evelyn
Laye*, John Lee, Jack Woolgar

Say It with Songs
US 1929 89m bw
Warner

A radio singer accidentally kills a man and is
jailed for manslaughter.
Miscalculated star vehicle with a few good
moments among the sentiment and
melodrama.

w Darryl F. Zanuck, Joseph Jackson, Harvey
Gates *d* Lloyd Bacon *ph* Lee Garmes

Al Jolson, Davey Lee, Marian Nixon, Fred
Kohler, Holmes Herbert

Say One for Me
US 1959 117m De Luxe Cinemascope
TCF / Bing Crosby (Frank Tashlin)

Adventures of a parish priest in New York's
theatrical quarter.
Unconvincing, unattractive imitation of *Going
My Way* which counters bad taste with
religiosity.

w Robert O'Brien *d* Frank Tashlin *ph* Leo
Tover *songs* Sammy Cahn, James Van
Heusen *md* Lionel Newman

Bing Crosby, Robert Wagner, Debbie
Reynolds, Ray Walston, Les Tremayne,
Connie Gilchrist, Frank McHugh, Joe Besser,
Sebastian Cabot

AAN: Lionel Newman

Sayonara**
US 1957 147m Technirama
Goetz Pictures–Pennebaker (William Goetz)

An American air force major in Tokyo after
the war falls in love with a Japanese actress.
A lush travelogue interrupted by two
romances, one tragic and one happy. A great
success at the time, though mainly of interest
to Americans; now vaguely dated.

w Paul Osborn, *novel* James A. Michener
d Joshua Logan *ph Ellsworth Fredericks*
m Franz Waxman *ad* Ted Haworth

Marlon Brando, Miyoshi Umeki. Miiko Taka,
Red Buttons, Ricardo Montalban, Patricia
Owens, Kent Smith, Martha Scott, James
Garner

AA: Miyoshi Umeki; Red Buttons
AAN: best picture; Paul Osborn; Joshua
Logan; Ellsworth Fredericks; Marlon Brando

Scalawag
US / Italy 1973 93m Technicolor
Bryna / Inex–Oceania (Anne Douglas)

Mexico 1840: a one-legged pirate and a boy try
to trace a hidden treasure.
Flagrant reworking of *Treasure Island*, heavily
overdone by stars and rhubarbing extras alike.

w Albert Maltz, Sid Fleischman *d* Kirk
Douglas *ph* Jack Cardiff *m* John Cameron

Kirk Douglas, Mark Lester, Neville Brand,
David Stroud, Lesley-Anne Down, Phil
Brown

The Scalphunters*
US 1968 102m De Luxe Panavision
UA / Bristol / Norlan (Levy–Gardner–Laven)

An old cowboy and a black ex-slave track
down a gang who kill Indians for their scalps.
Vigorous, aimless, likeable comedy western
with the emphasis on brawling.

w William Norton *d* Sydney Pollack
ph Duke Callaghan, Richard Moore *m* Elmer
Bernstein

Burt Lancaster, Ossie Davis, Telly Savalas,
Shelley Winters, Nick Cravat, Paul Picerni

'It is the sort of frolic where bodies litter the
ground, but you know they'll get up and draw
their pay. And where even a villain can crack
a joke without losing face.'—*Robert Ottaway*

Scandal at Scourie
US 1953 90m Metrocolor
MGM (Edwin H. Knopf)

The wife of the Protestant reeve of a Scottish-
Canadian Protestant community adopts a
Catholic child.
Sentimental whimsy with no holds barred, but
with rather jaded acting and production.

w Norman Corwin, Leonard Spiegelgass, Karl
Tunberg *d* Jean Negulesco *ph* Robert
Planck *m* Daniele Amfitheatrof

Greer Garson, Walter Pidgeon, Agnes
Moorehead, Arthur Shields, Philip Ober,
Donna Corcoran

A Scandal in Paris*
US 1946 100m bw
UA / Arnold Pressburger
aka: *Thieves' Holiday*

Adventures of Vidocq, a 19th-century rogue
who became Paris chief of police.
The actors look uneasy in their costumes, and
the sets are cardboard, but there is fun to be
had from this light comedy-drama.

w Ellis St Joseph *d* Douglas Sirk *ph* Guy
Roe *m* Hans Eisler

George Sanders, Signe Hasso, Carole Landis,
Akim Tamiroff, Gene Lockhart

Scandal Sheet
US 1931 77m bw

A newspaper editor with principles prints
scandal involving his wife. Dated star drama.
George Bancroft, Kay Francis, Regis Toomey,
Clive Brook. Written by Vincent Lawrence
and Max Marcin; directed by John Cromwell;
for Paramount.

Scandal Sheet
US 1939 67m bw

A ruthless publisher sacrifices himself to save
his son. Uninteresting star quickie. Otto
Kruger, Ona Munson, Edward Norris. Written
by Joseph Carole; directed by Nick Grinde;
for Columbia.

Scandal Sheet
US 1952 81m bw
Columbia (Edward Small)
GB title: *The Dark Page*

An editor has to allow his star reporter to
expose a murderer—himself.
Obvious, reasonably holding melodrama with
familiar characters.

w Ted Sherdeman, Eugene Ling, James Poe,
novel Samuel Fuller *d* Phil Karlson
ph Burnett Guffey *m* George Duning

Broderick Crawford, John Derek, Donna
Reed, Rosemary de Camp, Henry O'Neill,
Henry Morgan

Scandalous John
US 1971 117m Technicolor
Walt Disney (Bill Walsh)

The elderly owner of a derelict ranch resists all
efforts to close him up.
Unsatisfactory Disney attempt to capture a
more adult audience than usual; overlong,
repetitious and dreary.

w Bill Walsh, Don da Gradi, *novel* Richard
Gardner *d* Robert Butler *ph* Frank Phillips
m Rod McKuen

Brian Keith, Alfonso Arau, Michele Carey,
Rick Lenz, Henry Morgan, Simon Oakland

The Scapegoat*
GB 1959 92m bw
MGM / Du Maurier–Guinness (Dennis Van Thal)

A quiet bachelor on a French holiday is tricked into assuming the identity of a lookalike aristocrat who wants to commit a murder.
Disappointing adaptation of a good story, with much evidence of re-cutting and an especially slack middle section.

w Gore Vidal, Robert Hamer, *novel* Daphne du Maurier *d* Robert Hamer *ph* Paul Beeson *m* Bronislau Kaper

Alec Guinness, Bette Davis, Irene Worth, Nicole Maurey, Pamela Brown, Geoffrey Keen

The Scar
US 1948 83m bw
Eagle–Lion (Bryan Foy, Paul Henreid)
aka: *Hollow Triumph*

A fugitive kills his psychoanalyst double and takes his place, but is caught for the double's crimes.
Cheap suspense thriller with no suspense and no surprises.

w Daniel Fuchs, *novel* Murray Forbes *d* Steve Sekely *ph* John Alton *m* Sol Kaplan

Joan Bennett, Paul Henreid, Eduard Franz, Leslie Brooks, John Qualen, Mabel Paige, Herbert Rudley

Scaramouche**
US 1952 115m Technicolor
MGM (Carey Wilson)

A young man disguises himself as an actor to avenge the death of his friend at the hands of a wicked marquis.
Cheerful swashbuckler set in French revolutionary times, first filmed in the twenties with Ramon Novarro. MGM costume production at somewhere near its best.

w Ronald Millar, George Froeschel, *novel* Rafael Sabatini *d* George Sidney *ph* Charles Rosher *m* Victor Young *ad* Cedric Gibbons, Hans Peters

Stewart Granger, Mel Ferrer, Eleanor Parker, Janet Leigh, Henry Wilcoxon, Nina Foch, Lewis Stone, Robert Coote, Richard Anderson

Scarecrow*
US 1973 112m Technicolor
Panavision
Warner (Robert M. Sherman)

Two of the world's losers hitch-hike across America.

Well-shot but eventually dreary parable of friendship, a pedestrian *Easy Rider*.

w Garry Michael White *d* Jerry Schatzberg *ph* Vilmos Zsigmond *m* Fred Myrow

Gene Hackman, Al Pacino
'Here's a picture that manages to abuse two American myths at once—the Road and the Male Pair.'—*Stanley Kauffmann*

Scared Stiff
US 1953 108m bw
Paramount (Hal B. Wallis)

Nightclub entertainers get involved with a girl who has inherited a spooky castle off the Cuban coast.
Stretched-out remake of *The Ghost Breakers*; the last half hour, being closest to the original, is the most nearly funny.

w Herbert Baker, Walter de Leon *d* George Marshall, Ed Simmons, Norman Lear *ph* Ernest Laszlo *md* Joseph J. Lilley

Dean Martin, Jerry Lewis, Lizabeth Scott, Carmen Miranda, George Dolenz, Dorothy Malone, William Ching, Jack Lambert

The Scarf
US 1951 86m bw
UA / Gloria (I. G. Goldsmith)

A man escapes from a lunatic asylum and proves himself innocent of the crime for which he was committed.
Glum and pretentious murder mystery with a pictorial style to match its flowery dialogue.

wd E. A. Dupont *ph* Franz Planer *m* Herschel Burke Gilbert

John Ireland, Mercedes McCambridge, Emlyn Williams, James Barton, Lloyd Gough, Basil Ruysdael

Scarface****
US 1932 99m bw
Howard Hughes
aka: *The Shame of a Nation*

The life and death of a Chicago gangster of the twenties.
Obviously modelled on Al Capone, with an incestuous sister thrown in, this was perhaps the most vivid film of the gangster cycle, and its revelling in its own sins was not obscured by the subtitle, *The Shame of a Nation*.

w Ben Hecht, Seton I. Miller, John Lee Mahin, W. R. Burnett, Fred Pasley, *novel* Armitage Traill *d Howard Hawks ph* Lee Garmes, L. W. O'Connell *m* Adolph Tandler, Gus Arnheim

Paul Muni, Ann Dvorak, George Raft, Boris Karloff, Osgood Perkins, Karen Morley, C. Henry Gordon, Vince Barnett, Henry Armetta, Edwin Maxwell

'More brutal, more cruel, more wholesale than any of its predecessors.'—*James Shelley Hamilton*

'Because it was so close to the actual events, it possesses a kind of newsreel quality which cannot be recaptured or imitated. It vibrates with the impact of things that were real and deeply felt.'—*National Film Theatre programme, 1961*

The Scarface Mob*
US 1958   96m   bw
Desilu (Quinn Martin)

Al Capone's empire thrives while he is in Alcatraz, and prohibition agent Eliot Ness recruits a tough squad to fight the gangsters. Though released theatrically, this was in effect a pilot film for the successful TV series *The Untouchables*, well enough done within its limits.

w Paul Monash, *novel* The Untouchables by Eliot Ness d Phil Karlson ph Charles Straumer m Wilbur Hatch

Robert Stack, Neville Brand, Keenan Wynn, Barbara Nichols, Joe Mantell, Pat Crowley, Bruce Gordon, Paul Picerni, Abel Fernandez

Scarlet Angel
US 1952   81m   Technicolor
U-I (Leonard Goldstein)

A saloon hostess presents herself to a wealthy family as their dead son's wife.
Modest, satisfactorily plotted woman's picture with action interludes.

w Oscar Brodney d Sidney Salkow ph Russell Metty m Joseph Gershenson

Yvonne de Carlo, Rock Hudson, Richard Denning, Henry O'Neill, Amanda Blake

The Scarlet Blade*
GB 1963   82m   Technicolor
    Hammerscope
Hammer (Anthony Nelson Keys)
US title: *The Crimson Blade*

In 1648, a Cromwellian colonel plans to hang every royalist rebel.
Adequate swashbuckler.

wd John Gilling ph Jack Asher m Gary Hughes

Lionel Jeffries, Oliver Reed, Jack Hedley, June Thorburn, Duncan Lamont

The Scarlet Coat
US 1955   99m   Eastmancolor
    Cinemascope
MGM (Nicholas Nayfack)

During the American War of Independence,

an American officer deserts to the British in order to unmask a traitor.
Rather talky historical actioner with too much time spent on friendship and romance.

w Karl Tunberg d John Sturges ph Paul C. Vogel m Conrad Salinger

Cornel Wilde, Michael Wilding, George Sanders, Anne Francis, Robert Douglas, Bobby Driscoll, John McIntire

Scarlet Dawn*
US 1932   76m   bw
Warner (Hal Wallis)

During the Russian revolution, an exiled aristocrat loves a serving maid.
Heavy-going romantic drama distinguished by stylish direction and sets.

w Niven Busch, Erwin Gelsey, Douglas Fairbanks Jnr, *novel* Revolt by Mary McCall Jnr d William Dieterle ph Ernest Haller ad Anton Grot

Douglas Fairbanks Jnr, Nancy Carroll, Lilyan Tashman, Guy Kibbee, Sheila Terry, Frank Reicher

The Scarlet Empress***
US 1934   109m   bw
Paramount

A fantasia on the love life of Catherine the Great.
A marvellous, overwhelming, dramatically insubstantial but pictorially brilliant homage to a star; not to everyone's taste, but a film to remember.

w Manuel Komroff d *Josef Von Sternberg* ph *Bert Glennon* md W. Franke Harling, John M. Leipold, Milan Roder ad Hans Dreier, Peter Ballbusch, Richard Kollorsz

Marlene Dietrich, John Lodge, Sam Jaffe, Louise Dresser, C. Aubrey Smith, Gavin Gordon, Jameson Thomas

'She's photographed behind veils and fishnets, while dwarfs slither about and bells ring and everybody tries to look degenerate.'—*New Yorker, 1975*

'A ponderous, strangely beautiful, lengthy and frequently wearying production.'—*Mordaunt Hall, New York Times*

The Scarlet Hour
US 1955   93m   bw   Vistavision
Paramount (Michael Curtiz)

A bored wife persuades her lover to turn thief; her husband misconstrues the situation and is accidentally killed.
Complex suspenser designed to introduce new talent; rather too smooth, and pretty boring.

w Rip van Ronkel, Frank Tashlin, Meredyth Lucas *d* Michael Curtiz *ph* Lionel Lindon *m* Leith Stevens

Carol Ohmart, Tom Tryon, James Gregory, Jody Lawrance, E. G. Marshall, *Elaine Stritch*

The Scarlet Letter*
US 1926   90m (24 fps)   bw   silent
MGM / Jury

In Puritan New England, the mother of an illegitimate child wears the scarlet A (for adulteress) for years rather than reveal that her lover was the village priest.
Celebrated 17th-century melodrama, quite powerfully made in the best silent tradition, but of little intrinsic interest for modern audiences.

w Frances Marion, *novel* Nathaniel Hawthorne *d* Victor Sjostrom *ph* Henrik Sartov   *ad* Cedric Gibbons

Lillian Gish, Lars Hanson, Karl Dane, Henry B. Walthall

† Other versions include the following: US 1910, US 1911, US 1913, US 1917, US 1920, GB 1922, US 1934, Germany 1971, US (TV) 1979

The Scarlet Pimpernel***
GB 1934   98m   bw
London Films (Alexander Korda)

In the early days of the French revolution, an apparently foppish Englishman leads a daring band in rescuing aristocrats from the guillotine.
First-class period adventure with a splendid and much imitated plot, strong characters, humour and a richly detailed historical background.

w Robert E. Sherwood, Sam Berman, Arthur Wimperis, Lajos Biro, *novel* Baroness Orczy *d* Harold Young

Leslie Howard, Merle Oberon, Raymond Massey, Nigel Bruce, Bramwell Fletcher, Anthony Bushell, Joan Gardner, Walter Rilla
'One of the most romantic and durable of all swashbucklers.'—*New Yorker, 1976*
'A triumph for the British film world.'— *Sunday Times*

Scarlet Street**
US 1946   103m   bw
(Universal) Walter Wanger (Fritz Lang)

A prostitute is murdered by her client and her pimp is executed for the crime.
Daring but rather gloomy Hollywood melodrama, the first in which a crime went unpunished (though the culprit was shown

suffering remorse). Interesting and heavily Teutonic, but as entertainment not a patch on the similar but lighter *The Woman in the Window*, which the same team had made a year previously.

w Dudley Nichols, *play* La Chienne by George de la Fouchardière (filmed by Jean Renoir in 1932) *d* Fritz Lang *ph* Milton Krasner *m* Hans Salter *ad* Alexander Golitzen

Edward G. Robinson, Joan Bennett, Dan Duryea, Jess Barker, Margaret Lindsay, Rosalind Ivan, Samuel S. Hinds, Arthur Loft
'The director unerringly chooses the right sound and image to assault the spectator's sensibilities.'—*C. A. Lejeune*

The Scarlet Thread
GB 1950   84m   bw

Jewel thieves take refuge in a Cambridge college. Flabby melodrama featuring emergent young talent. Kathleen Byron, Laurence Harvey, Sidney Tafler, Arthur Hill, Dora Bryan. Written by A. R. Rawlinson, from a play by A. R. Rawlinson and Moie Charles; directed by Lewis Gilbert; for Nettlefold / Butcher.

Scars of Dracula
GB 1970   96m   Technicolor
Hammer / EMI (Aida Young)

A young man on the run finds himself an unwitting guest of Count Dracula.
Overpadded vampire saga, its few effective moments stemming directly from the original novel.

w John Elder   *d* Roy Ward Baker *ph* Moray Grant *m* James Bernard

Christopher Lee, Dennis Waterman, Christopher Matthews, Jenny Hanley, Patrick Troughton, Michael Gwynn, Bob Todd

Scattergood Baines
US 1941   69m   bw

The new owner of a small-town hardware store takes an interest in his fellow men. First of several second features featuring the exploits of a likeable busybody. *Guy Kibbee,* Carol Hughes, John Archer, Emma Dunn. Written by Michael L. Simmons and Edward T. Lowe, from the stories by Clarence Budington Kelland; directed by Christy Cabanne; for RKO. (The succeeding episodes were as follows: *Scattergood Pulls the Strings,* 1941; *Scattergood Meets Broadway,* 1941; *Scattergood Rides High,* 1942; *Scattergood Survives a Murder,* 1942; *Cinderella Swings It,* 1943.)

Scavenger Hunt
US 1979   116m   De Luxe
TCF / Melvin Simon

A rich man leaves a fortune to the member of his family who can collect most of the useless objects in a list provided.

Depressing cheapjack imitation of Kramer's *It's a Mad Mad Mad Mad World*, which itself was not free from fault.

w Steven A. Vail, Henry Harper *d* Michael Schultz *ph* Ken Lamkin *m* Billy Goldenberg

Richard Benjamin, James Coco, Scatman Crothers, Cloris Leachman, Cleavon Little, Roddy McDowall, Robert Morley, Richard Mulligan, Tony Randall, Dirk Benedict, Vincent Price

'Loud, obnoxious, and above all unfunny.'—*Variety*

School for Husbands
GB 1937   71m   bw
Wainwright (Richard Wainwright)

A romantic novelist annoys the husbands of his adoring fans.

Would-be champagne comedy which bubbles pretty well for most of its length.

w Frederick Jackson, Gordon Aherry, Austin Melford, *play* Frederick Jackson *d* Andrew Marton *ph* Phil Tannura

Rex Harrison, Henry Kendall, Romney Brent, Diana Churchill, June Clyde

School for Scoundrels*
GB 1960   94m   bw
ABP / Guardsman (Hal E. Chester)

A failure reports to the College of One-Upmanship and his life is transformed.

Amusing trifle, basically a series of sketches by familiar comic actors.

w Patricia Mayes, Hal E. Chester, *books* Stephen Potter *d* Robert Hamer *ph* Erwin Hillier *m* John Addison

Ian Carmichael, Alastair Sim, Terry-Thomas, Janette Scott, Dennis Price, Peter Jones, Edward Chapman, John Le Mesurier

School for Secrets
GB 1946   108m   bw
Rank / Two Cities (George H. Brown, Peter Ustinov)
US title: *Secret Flight*

The boffins who invented radar find themselves in a little war action of their own.

An unsatisfactory entertainment which, with the best intentions, shuffles between arch comedy, character drama, war action and documentary, doing less than justice to any of these aspects.

wd Peter Ustinov

Ralph Richardson, Raymond Huntley, Richard Attenborough, Marjorie Rhodes, John Laurie, Ernest Jay, David Tomlinson, Finlay Currie

Schweik's New Adventures
GB 1943   84m   bw

An unassuming Czechoslovakian writer gently kids the Nazi occupiers and manages to save some of his friends from the concentration camp. Curious English attempt to film a popular Czechoslovakian character; it made mildly effective wartime propaganda, though few went to see it. Lloyd Pearson, George Carney, Julien Mitchell, Richard Attenborough, Margaret McGrath. Written by Karel Lamac and Con West, from the novel by Jaroslav Hasek; directed by Karel Lamac; for Eden Films.

Scorpio
US 1972   114m   Technicolor
UA / Scimitar (Walter Mirisch)

CIA agents doublecross each other.

Incredibly complex spy thriller in which it's difficult to know, or care, who's following whom. The brutalities, however, are capably staged.

w David W. Rintels, Gerald Wilson
d Michael Winner *ph* Robert Paynter
m Jerry Fielding

Burt Lancaster, Alain Delon, Paul Scofield, John Colicos, Gayle Hunnicutt, J. D. Cannon
'Strictly zoom and thump.'—*Sight and Sound*

Scotland Yard
US 1941   68m   bw
TCF (Sol M. Wurtzel)

The Nazis capture a London banker and use his double to turn funds over to them.

Outlandish spy melodrama which certainly keeps the interest.

w Samuel G. Engel, John Balderston, *play* Deniston Clift *d* Norman Foster *ph* Virgil Miller *m* Emil Newman

Nancy Kelly, Edmund Gwenn, Henry Wilcoxon, John Loder, Melville Cooper, Gilbert Emery, Norma Varden

Scott of the Antarctic**
GB 1948   111m   Technicolor
Ealing (Sidney Cole)

After long preparation, Captain Scott sets off on his ill-fated 1912 expedition to the South Pole.

The stiff-upper-lip saga par excellence;
inevitable knowledge of the end makes it
pretty downbeat, and the actors can only be
sincere; but the snowscapes, most of them
artificial, are fine.

w Ivor Montagu, Walter Meade, Mary Hayley
Bell *d* Charles Frend *ph* Geoffrey Unsworth,
Jack Cardiff, Osmond Borradaile *m* Ralph
Vaughan Williams

John Mills, James Robertson Justice, Derek
Bond, Harold Warrender, Reginald Beckwith,
Kenneth More, James McKechnie, John
Gregson

The Scoundrel**

US 1935 74m bw
Paramount (Ben Hecht, Charles MacArthur)

A famous writer dies; his ghost comes back to
find the meaning of love.
Unique thirties supernatural melodrama with
barbs of dated wit despatched by a splendid
cast. Nonsense, but great nonsense.

wd Ben Hecht, Charles MacArthur ph Lee
Garmes *m* George Antheil

Noel Coward, Alexander Woolcott, Julie
Haydon, Stanley Ridges, Eduardo Ciannelli
    'An unmistakeable whiff from a gossip
column world which tries hard to split the
difference between an epigram and a
wisecrack.'—*William Whitebait*

AA: original story
AAN: script

Scram!*

US 1932 20m bw

Two vagrants are ordered out of town but by a
series of misadventures are found drunk with
the judge's wife. Generally sprightly star
comedy culminating in a marathon laughing
session. Laurel and Hardy, Arthur Housman,
Rychard Cramer, Vivien Oakland. Written by
H. M. Walker; directed by Ray McCarey; for
Hal Roach.

Scream and Scream Again*

GB 1969 94m Eastmancolor
AIP / Amicus (Milton Subotsky)

Murders are traced to superhuman composite
beings created by a mad scientist.
Energetic and well-staged though rather
humourless shocker.

w Christopher Wicking, *novel* The
Disorientated Man by Peter Saxon *d* Gordon
Hessler *ph* John Coquillon *m* David
Whittaker *ad* Don Mingaye

Vincent Price, Christopher Lee, Peter
Cushing, Alfred Marks, Anthony Newlands,
David Lodge

Screaming Mimi

US 1958 79m bw

After being sexually assaulted a dancer comes
to believe she has committed murder . . . and
later we learn that she has. Sub-Freudian
melodrama on the comic strip level. Anita
Ekberg, Phil Carey, Harry Townes, Gypsy
Rose Lee, Romney Brent, Alan Gifford.
Written by Robert Blees, from the book by
Frederic Brown; directed by Gerd Oswald; for
Sage / Columbia.

Scrooge*

GB 1935 78m bw
Twickenham (Julius Hagen, Hans Brahm)

A miser reforms after ghosts haunt him on
Christmas Eve.
Acceptable unambitious version with
interesting performances.

w Seymour Hicks, H. Fowler Mear,
novel Charles Dickens *d* Henry Edwards
ph Sidney Blythe, William Luff

Seymour Hicks, Donald Calthrop (Cratchit),
Athene Seyler, Oscar Asche, Barbara Everest,
Maurice Evans, C. V. France, Marie Ney

Scrooge***

GB 1951 86m bw
Renown (Brian Desmond Hurst)

By far the best available version of the classic
parable; casting, art direction, pace and
general handling are as good as can be.

w Noel Langley *d Brian Desmond Hurst*
ph C. Pennington-Richards *m* Richard
Addinsell

Alastair Sim, Mervyn Johns, Kathleen
Harrison, Jack Warner, Michael Hordern,
Hermione Baddeley, George Cole, Miles
Malleson

Scrooge*

GB 1970 113m Technicolor
Panavision
Cinema Center / Waterbury (Richard H.
Solo)

Dim musical version, darkly coloured and
quite lost on the wide screen; but it has its
macabre moments of trick photography.

w / m / ly Leslie Bricusse *d* Ronald Neame
ph Oswald Morris *pd* Terry Marsh

Albert Finney, Michael Medwin, Alec
Guinness, Edith Evans, Kenneth More, David
Collings, Laurence Naismith, Kay Walsh

AAN: song 'Thank You Very Much' (*m / ly*
Leslie Bricusse); music

Scudda Hoo, Scudda Hay
US 1948   98m   Technicolor
TCF (Walter Morosco)
GB title: *Summer Lightning*

A farmer's son is less interested in girls than in
the welfare of his two mules.
Antediluvian rural romance for the simple-
minded.

wd F. Hugh Herbert, *novel* George Agnew
Chamberlain *ph* Ernest Palmer *m* Cyril
Mockridge

June Haver, Lon McCallister, Walter
Brennan, Anne Revere, Natalie Wood,
Robert Karnes, Henry Hull, Tom Tully,
Marilyn Monroe

Scum
GB 1979   97m   Eastmancolor

Injustices in a Borstal institution lead to a riot.
Gorily overstated view of boys' prison life
from the inside, with the camera gloating over
each violent close-up. (The original TV play
had been made, then banned, by the BBC.)
Ray Winstone, Mick Ford, Julian Firth, John
Blundell. Written by Roy Minton; directed by
Alan Clarke; for Berwick Street Films.

The Sea Bat
US 1930   69m   bw

Mexican fishermen compete to kill a deadly
sting-ray. The *Jaws* of its time; box office
hokum. Charles Bickford, Raquel Torres, Nils
Asther, John Miljan, Gibson Gowland, Boris
Karloff. Written by Bess Meredyth and John
Howard Lawson; directed by Wesley Ruggles;
for MGM.

The Sea Chase*
US 1955   117m   Warnercolor
   Cinemascope
Warner (John Farrow)

In 1939 a German freighter tries to make it
from Sydney harbour back to Germany.
Unusual but not very compelling naval
melodrama, chiefly because the leads are
miscast.

w James Warner Bellah, John Twist, *novel*
Andrew Geer *d* John Farrow *ph* William
Clothier *m* Roy Webb

John Wayne, Lana Turner, David Farrar, Lyle
Bettger, Tab Hunter, James Arness, Dick
Davalos, John Qualen

   'A film compounded of monotonously
familiar ingredients.'—*Penelope Houston*

Sea Devils
US 1937   88m   bw

Exploits of the ice patrols of the US Coast
Guard. Flagwaving action hokum for popular
stars. Victor McLaglen, Preston Foster, Ida
Lupino, Donald Woods. Written by Frank
Wead, John Twist and P. J. Wolfson; directed
by Ben Stoloff; for RKO.

Sea Devils
GB 1953   90m   Technicolor
Coronado (David E. Rose)

Spies prevent Napoleon's invasion of England.
Cheerful, forgettable swashbuckler.

w Borden Chase *d* Raoul Walsh *ph* Wilkie
Cooper *m* Richard Addinsell

Yvonne de Carlo, Rock Hudson, Maxwell
Reed, Denis O'Dea, Michael Goodliffe,
Bryan Forbes, Ivor Barnard, Arthur Wontner

Sea Fury
GB 1958   97m   bw
Rank (Benjamin Fisz)

Rivalry strikes up between an old and a young
sailor on tugboats plying between Spain and
England.
Shapeless, leery melodrama with strong
performances and an exciting storm-at-sea
climax.

w John Kruse, Cy Endfield *d* Cy Endfield
ph Reg Wyer *m* Philip Green

Stanley Baker, Victor McLaglen, Luciana
Paluzzi, Grégoire Aslan, Francis de Wolff,
David Oxley, Rupert Davies, Robert Shaw

The Sea Gull*
GB 1968   141m   Technicolor
Warner / Sidney Lumet

Loves and hates on a 19th-century Russian
estate.
Rather heavily star-studded, but certainly
proficient film version of a Chekhov favourite.

w Moura Budberg, *play* Anton Chekhov
d Sidney Lumet *ph* Gerry Fisher *m* none
pd Tony Walton

James Mason, Simone Signoret, Vanessa
Redgrave, David Warner, Harry Andrews,
Ronald Radd, Eileen Herlie, Kathleen
Widdoes, Denholm Elliott, Alfred Lynch

   'The camera cannot capture the hollowness
of space, the oppressive immoveableness of a
seemingly harmless enclosure, stasis settling
on everything like a fine, corrosive dust.'—
John Simon

   'They stand side by side. Young and old.
Rich and poor. They gather together for a
single purpose. Survival.'—*publicity*

The Sea Hawk***
US 1940 122m bw
Warner (Hal B. Wallis, Henry Blanke)

Elizabeth I encourages one of her most able captains to acts of piracy against the Spanish.
Wobbly-plotted but stirring and exciting seafaring actioner, with splendid battle and duel scenes.

w Seton I. Miller, Howard Koch d Michael Curtiz ph Sol Polito m Erich Wolfgang Korngold ad Anton Grot

Errol Flynn, Flora Robson, Brenda Marshall, Henry Daniell, Claude Rains, Donald Crisp, Alan Hale, Una O'Connor, James Stephenson, Gilbert Roland, William Lundigan
  'Endless episodes of court intrigue tend to diminish the effect of the epic sweep of the high seas dramatics.'—Variety

AAN: Erich Wolfgang Korngold

The Sea of Grass
US 1947 131m bw
MGM (Pandro S. Berman)

A cattle tycoon is so obsessed by his work that he alienates his family.
Brooding, overlong semi-western with an unexpected cast.

w Marguerite Roberts, Vincent Lawrence, novel Conrad Richter d Elia Kazan ph Harry Stradling m Herbert Stothart

Spencer Tracy, Katharine Hepburn, Melvyn Douglas, Phyllis Thaxter, Robert Walker, Edgar Buchanan, Harry Carey, Ruth Nelson, James Bell
  'In spite of all the sincerity and talent involved, an epically dreary film.'—Time

Sea of Lost Ships
US 1953 85m bw

The US Coast Guard saves a passenger ship from an iceberg. Scrappy, semi-documentary account punctuated by rough action highlights.
Walter Brennan, John Derek, Wanda Hendrix, Richard Jaeckel, Barton Maclane, Darryl Hickman. Written by Steve Fisher; directed by Joe Kane; for Republic.

Sea of Sand*
GB 1958 98m bw
Rank / Tempean (Robert Baker, Monty Berman)
US title: Desert Patrol

Just before Alamein an Eighth Army desert group plans to destroy one of Rommel's last petrol dumps.
Good standard war suspenser.

w Robert Westerby d Guy Green ph Wilkie Cooper m Clifton Parker

Richard Attenborough, John Gregson, Vincent Ball, Percy Herbert, Michael Craig, Barry Foster, Andrew Faulds, Dermot Walsh

The Sea Shall Not Have Them
GB 1954 93m bw
Eros / Daniel M. Angel

Survivors of a seaplane crash await rescue in a dinghy.
Rather dim computerized compendium of flashback mini-dramas.

w Lewis Gilbert, Vernon Harris d Lewis Gilbert ph Stephen Dade m Malcolm Arnold

Dirk Bogarde, Michael Redgrave, Bonar Colleano, Jack Watling, Anthony Steel, Nigel Patrick, James Kenney, Sidney Tafler, George Rose

Sea Wife
GB 1957 82m De Luxe Cinemascope
TCF / Sumar (André Hakim)

Survivors of a shipwreck near Singapore in 1942 are rescued, not before the bosun has fallen in love with the only lady, not knowing she is a nun.
Flashbacked, uncertain, intermittently effective film of a popular minor novel.

w George K. Burke, novel Sea Wyf and Biscuit by J. M. Scott d Bob McNaught ph Ted Scaife m Kenneth V. Jones, Leonard Salzedo

Richard Burton, Joan Collins, Basil Sydney, Cy Grant

The Sea Wolf**
US 1941 90m bw
Warner (Henry Blanke)

Survivors of a ferry crash in San Francisco Bay are picked up by a psychopathic freighter captain who keeps them captive.
Much filmed action suspenser which in this version looks great but overdoes the talk.

w Robert Rossen, novel Jack London d Michael Curtiz ph Sol Polito m Erich Wolfgang Korngold

Edward G. Robinson, Alexander Knox, Ida Lupino, John Garfield, Gene Lockhart, Barry Fitzgerald, Stanley Ridges, David Bruce, Howard da Silva
  'A Germanic, powerful work almost devoid of compromise.'—Charles Higham, 1972
† Other versions appeared in 1913, with Hobart Bosworth; in 1920, with Noah Beery; in 1925, with Ralph Ince; in 1930, with Milton Sills; in 1950 (as Barricade, turned into a

western), with Raymond Massey; in 1958 (as *Wolf Larsen*), with Barry Sullivan; and in 1975 (Italian), as *Wolf of the Seven Seas*, with Chuck Connors.

The Sea Wolves*
GB-US-Switzerland 1980   122m   Eastmancolor
Richmond-Lorimar-Varius (Euan Lloyd)

In 1943, elderly British territorials living in India dispose of a Nazi transmitter in neutral Goa.
Mildly larkish *Boy's Own Paper* adventure with a somewhat geriatric air; an interesting 1980 throwback to the films of 1950.

w Reginald Rose *novel* Boarding Party by James Leasor *d* Andrew McLaglen *ph* Tony Imi *m* Roy Budd

Gregory Peck, Roger Moore, Trevor Howard, David Niven, Barbara Kellerman, Patrick MacNee, Patrick Allen, Bernard Archard, Faith Brook, Martin Benson, Allan Cuthbertson, Kenneth Griffith, Donald Houston, Glyn Houston, Percy Herbert, Patrick Holt, Terence Longdon, John Standing, Michael Medwin

'As a genre—the arterio-sclerotic war movie—it'll never catch on.'—*Time Out*

Seagulls over Sorrento
GB 1954   92m   bw
MGM (John and Roy Boulting)
US title: *Crest of the Wave*

Life on a naval research station on a small Scottish island.
A long-running British service comedy has been Americanized to little effect, but it remains just about watchable.

w Frank Harvey, Roy Boulting, *play* Hugh Hastings *d* John and Roy Boulting *ph* Gilbert Taylor *m* Miklos Rozsa

Gene Kelly, John Justin, Bernard Lee, Sidney James, Jeff Richards, Patric Doonan, Patrick Barr

Seal Island see The Living Desert

Sealed Verdict
US 1948   83m   bw
Paramount (Robert Fellows)

An American officer in Germany falls in love with the ex-girl friend of a Nazi war criminal.
Routine melodrama, as boring as it sounds.

w Jonathan Latimer, *novel* Lionel Shapiro *d* Lewis Allen *ph* Leo Tover *m* Hugo Friedhofer

Ray Milland, Florence Marly, Broderick Crawford, John Hoyt, John Ridgely, Ludwig Donath

Seance on a Wet Afternoon*
GB 1964   121m   bw
Rank / Allied Film Makers (Richard Attenborough, Bryan Forbes, Jack Rix)

A fake medium persuades her husband to kidnap a child so that she can become famous by revealing its whereabouts in a trance.
Overlong character melodrama in which the suspense is better than the psychopathology. A mannered performance from the lady, a false nose from the gentleman, and a general air of gloom.

wd Bryan Forbes *ph* Gerry Turpin *m* John Barry

Kim Stanley, Richard Attenborough, Nanette Newman, Patrick Magee

AAN: Kim Stanley

The Search*
US / Switzerland 1948   105m   bw
MGM / Praesens Film (Lazar Wechsler)

An American soldier in Germany cares for a war orphan.
Vivid semi-documentary post-war drama which falls down in its elementary dramatics but sent audiences home wiping away tears.

w Richard Schweizer, David Wechsler, Paul Jarrico *d* Fred Zinnemann *ph* Emil Berna *m* Robert Blum

Montgomery Clift, Aline MacMahon, Ivan Jandl, Wendell Corey

AA: original story (Richard Schweizer, David Wechsler)
AAN: script; Fred Zinnemann; Montgomery Clift

The Search for Bridey Murphy*
US 1956   84m   bw   Vistavision
Paramount (Pat Duggan)

A Colorado businessman and amateur hypnotist finds a lady neighbour so good a subject that he is able to delve into her previous incarnation as a long-dead Irish peasant.
Adequately presented with alienation effects, but mainly consisting of two-shots and fuzzy flashbacks, this treatment of an actual case (subsequently discredited) works up to a fine pitch of frenzy when the subject seems unable to come back from her previous life.

wd Noel Langley, *book* Morey Bernstein *ph* John F. Warren *m* Irving Talbot

Teresa Wright, Louis Hayward, Kenneth Tobey, Nancy Gates, Richard Anderson

The Searchers**
US 1956   119m   Technicolor   Vistavision
Warner / C. V. Whitney (Merian C. Cooper)

A Confederate war veteran tracks down the Indians who have slaughtered his brother and sister-in-law and carried off their daughter. Desultory, easy-going, good-looking western in typical Ford style; a bit more solemn than usual.

w Frank S. Nugent, *novel* Alan le May *d* John Ford *ph* Winton C. Hoch *m* Max Steiner

John Wayne, Jeffrey Hunter, Natalie Wood, Vera Miles, Ward Bond, John Qualen, Henry Brandon, Antonio Moreno

The Searching Wind*
US 1946   107m   bw
Paramount (Hal B. Wallis)

Affairs of an American diplomat in Europe during the thirties.
Earnest melodrama which would have been better timed six years earlier. Excellent production, though.

w Lillian Hellman, from her play *d* William Dieterle *ph* Lee Garmes *m* Victor Young *ad* Hans Drier, Franz Bachelin

Robert Young, Sylvia Sidney, Ann Richards, Douglas Dick, Dudley Digges, Albert Basserman, Dan Seymour

The Seashell and the Clergyman*
France 1928   30m approx (24 fps)   bw
    silent
(Producer unknown)

A clergyman is afflicted by sexual torments. Celebrated surrealist short with memorable images and a great deal of confusion.

w Antonin Artaud *d* Germaine Dulac *ph* Paul Guichard

Alix Allin

† In GB the film was banned by the censor with the famous comment: 'It is so cryptic as to have no apparent meaning. If there is a meaning, it is doubtless objectionable.'

Sebastian
GB 1968   100m   Eastmancolor
Paramount / Maccius (Herb Brodkin,
    Michael Powell)

An Oxford professor and code expert is appointed to the secret service.
Mildly spoofy spy yarn: style but not much substance.

w Gerald Vaughan-Hughes *d* David Greene *ph* Gerry Fisher *m* Jerry Goldsmith *pd* Wilfred Shingleton

Dirk Bogarde, *John Gielgud,* Lilli Palmer, Susannah York, Janet Munro, Margaret Johnston, Nigel Davenport, Ronald Fraser

'One of the problems with this kind of movie is the enormous pressure put on the audience to have a good time over practically nothing.'—*Renata Adler*

Second Best Bed
GB 1938   74m   bw

A magistrate is suspected of adultery. Cheerful star comedy with a touch of sophistication. Tom Walls, Jane Baxter, Veronica Rose, Carl Jaffe, Greta Gynt. Written by Ben Travers; directed by Tom Walls; for Capitol.

Second Chance
US 1953   82m   Technicolor   3-D
RKO (Edmund Grainger)

In South America, a professional killer stalks a gangster's moll.
Comic strip antics with a climax on a stalled cable car.

w Oscar Millard, Sidney Boehm, *story* D. M. Marshman Jnr *d* Rudolph Maté *ph* William Snyder *m* Roy Webb

Robert Mitchum, Linda Darnell, Jack Palance, Reginald Sheffield, Roy Roberts

Second Chorus
US 1941   84m   bw
Paramount (Boris Morros)

Two trumpeters and their lady manager hit Broadway.
Mild musical.

w Elaine Ryan, Ian McClellan Hunter, Frank Cavett *d* H. C. Potter *ph* Theodor Sparkuhl *songs* various *m* Artie Shaw

Fred Astaire, Burgess Meredith, Paulette Goddard, Charles Butterworth, Artie Shaw and his Band, Frank Melton, Jimmy Conlon

AAN: Artie Shaw; song 'Love of my Life' (*m* Artie Shaw, *ly* Johnny Mercer)

Second Fiddle
US 1939   86m   bw
TCF (Gene Markey)

A Minnesota skating schoolteacher goes to Hollywood and becomes a star.
Routine star vehicle.

w Harry Tugend *d* Sidney Lanfield *ph* Leon Shamroy *md* Louis Silvers

Sonja Henie, Tyrone Power, Edna May Oliver, Rudy Vallee, Mary Healy, Lyle Talbot, Alan Dinehart

AAN: song 'I Poured My Heart into a Song' (*m / ly* Irving Berlin)

The Second Greatest Sex

US 1955   87m   Technicolor
   Cinemascope
U-I (Albert J. Cohen)

Western women emulate Lysistrata to stop
their men from feuding.
Flat attempt to cash in on *Seven Brides for
Seven Brothers*; some good acrobatic dancing
but no style.

w Charles Hoffman *d* George Marshall
ph Wilfrid M. Cline *md* Joseph Gershenson
ch Lee Scott

Jeanne Crain, George Nader, Bert Lahr, Kitty
Kallen, Paul Gilbert, Keith Andes, Mamie
Van Doren, Tommy Rall

Second Honeymoon

US 1937   79m   bw
TCF (Raymond Griffith)

A man tries to win back his ex-wife.
Moderate star romantic comedy.

w Kathryn Scola, Darrell Ware, *story* Philip
Wylie *d* Walter Lang *ph* Ernest Palmer
m David Buttolph

Tyrone Power, Loretta Young, Stuart Erwin,
Claire Trevor, Marjorie Weaver, Lyle Talbot,
J. Edward Bromberg

The Second Mrs Tanqueray

GB 1952   75m   bw
Vandyke (Roger Proudlock)

A Victorian society widower marries a
notorious lady.
Stiff-backed penny-pinching version of an
interestingly antiquated play.

play Arthur Wing Pinero *d* Dallas Bower

Pamela Brown, Hugh Sinclair, Ronald Ward,
Virginia McKenna, Andrew Osborn

The Second Time Around

US 1961   99m   De Luxe   Cinemascope
TCF / Cummings / Harman (Jack
   Cummings)

In 1912 Arizona, a widow stands for sheriff
and has plenty of choice for a husband.
Light-hearted western fun mixed with family
sentimentality.

w Oscar Saul, Cecil Van Heusen, *novel*
Richard Emery Roberts *d* Vincent Sherman
ph Ellis W. Carter *m* Gerald Fried

Debbie Reynolds, Steve Forrest, Andy
Griffith, Juliet Prowse, Thelma Ritter, Ken
Scott, Isobel Elsom

'Keep a lemon handy for sucking to ward off
an attack of the terminal cutesies.'—*Judith
Crist, 1973*

Seconds**

US 1966   106m   bw
Paramount / Joel / Gibraltar (Edward
   Lewis)

A secret organization sells a special service to
the jaded rich; apparent death followed by
physical rejuvenation.
An intriguing half-hour is followed by a glum
new life for our hero, capped by a horrifying
finale in which, dissatisfied, he learns he is to
become one of the corpses necessary to the
organization's continuance.

w Lewis John Carlino, *novel* David Ely
d John Frankenheimer *ph* James Wong Howe
m Jerry Goldsmith *titles* Saul Bass

Rock Hudson, *John Randolph, Will Geer*,
Salome Jens, Jeff Corey, Richard Anderson,
Murray Hamilton, Wesley Addy

AAN: James Wong Howe

The Secret Agent**

GB 1936   83m   bw
Gaumont British (Michael Balcon, Ivor
   Montagu)

A reluctantly recruited spy is ordered to kill a
man.
Unsatisfactory in casting and writing, this
Hitchcock suspenser nevertheless has many
typically amusing moments.

w Charles Bennett, *play* Campbell Dixon,
story Ashenden by Somerset Maugham
d Alfred Hitchcock *ph* Bernard Knowles
md Louis Levy

John Gielgud, Robert Young, *Peter Lorre*,
Madeleine Carroll, Percy Marmont, Lilli
Palmer, Florence Kahn

'As uncommon as it is unsentimentally
cruel.'—*Peter John Dyer, 1964*

'Many sequences which show Hitchcock at
his very best: the fake funeral, the murder on
the mountainside, the riverside café, and the
climax in a chocolate factory.'—*NFT, 1961*

'How unfortunate it is that Mr Hitchcock, a
clever director, is allowed to produce and even
to write his own films, though as a producer he
has no sense of continuity and as a writer he
has no sense of life. His films consist of a
series of small "amusing" melodramatic
situations: the murderer's button dropped on
the baccarat board; the strangled organist's
hands prolonging the notes in the empty
church; the fugitives hiding in the bell tower
when the bell begins to swing. Very
perfunctorily he builds up to these tricky
situations . . . and then drops them.'—
Graham Greene

The Secret beyond the Door
US 1948 98m bw
Universal / Walter Wanger (Fritz Lang)

An heiress marries a moody millionaire with a
death fixation, and comes to think of herself as
his next potential victim.
Silly melodrama with much chat and little
suspense.

w Sylvia Richards, *story* Rufus King d Fritz
Lang ph Stanley Cortez m Miklos Rozsa

Joan Bennett, Michael Redgrave, Anne
Revere, Barbara O'Neil, Natalie Schaefer,
Paul Cavanagh

'A dog-wagon *Rebecca* with a seasoning of
psychiatrics.'—*Otis L. Guernsey Jnr*
'Lang gets a few wood-silky highlights out of
this sow's ear, but it is a hopeless job and a
worthless movie.'—*James Agee*

The Secret Bride
US 1935 63m bw
Warner
GB title: *Concealment*

A District Attorney is secretly married to the
daughter of the politician he is trying to
convict.
Dismal melodrama, tritely scripted.

w Tom Buckingham, F. Hugh Herbert, Mary
McCall Jnr, *play* Concealment by Leonard
Ide d William Dieterle ph Ernest Haller

Barbara Stanwyck, Warren William, Glenda
Farrell, Grant Mitchell, Arthur Byron, Henry
O'Neill, Douglass Dumbrille

Secret Ceremony
GB 1969 109m Eastmancolor
Universal / World Films / Paul M. Heller
(John Heyman, Norman Priggen)

A prostitute mothers a young girl with a
strange past.
Nuthouse melodrama for devotees of the
director.

w George Tabori, *short story* Marco Denevi
d Joseph Losey ph Gerry Fisher m Richard
Rodney Bennett

Elizabeth Taylor, Robert Mitchum, Mia
Farrow, Pamela Brown, Peggy Ashcroft

'This piece of garbage is so totally ridiculous
that I can't imagine why anyone would want to
be in it, let alone see it.'—*Rex Reed*

Secret Command
US 1944 92m bw
Columbia (Phil L. Ryan)

An ex-foreign correspondent goes undercover
at a shipyard to track down saboteurs.
Routine wartime thick ear.

w Roy Chanslor, *story* The Saboteurs by John
and Ward Hawkins d Eddie Sutherland
ph Franz Planer m Paul Sawtell

Pat O'Brien, Carole Landis, Chester Morris,
Ruth Warrick, Barton MacLane, Tom Tully,
Wallace Ford, Howard Freeman

The Secret Fury
US 1950 86m bw
RKO (Jack H. Skirball, Bruce Manning)

A successful pianist is deliberately driven
insane by her fiancé.
Derivative melodrama of no great interest.

w Lionel House d Mel Ferrer ph Leo Tover
m Roy Webb md Constantin Bakaleinikoff

Claudette Colbert, Robert Ryan, Jane Cowl,
Paul Kelly, Philip Ober, Elizabeth Risdon,
Doris Dudley

The Secret Garden*
US 1949 92m bw (Technicolor
sequence)
MGM (Clarence Brown)

An orphan girl goes to stay with her moody
uncle and brightens up the lives of those
around her.
Subdued, richly produced, rather likeable
Victorian fable with the same moral as *The
Bluebird* and *The Wizard of Oz*: happiness is
in your own back yard.

w Robert Ardrey, *novel* Frances Hodgson
Burnett d Fred M. Wilcox ph Ray June
m Bronislau Kaper

Margaret O'Brien, Herbert Marshall, Gladys
Cooper, Elsa Lanchester, Dean Stockwell,
Brian Roper

'Uneven, but oddly and unexpectedly
interesting.'—*Richard Mallett, Punch*

The Secret Heart
US 1946 97m bw
MGM (Edwin H. Knopf)

A widow has problems with her emotionally
disturbed daughter.
Old-fashioned woman's picture.

w Rose Franken, William Brown Meloney
d Robert Z. Leonard ph George Folsey
m Bronislau Kaper

Claudette Colbert, Walter Pidgeon, June
Allyson, Robert Sterling, Marshall Thompson,
Elizabeth Patterson, Richard Derr, Patricia
Medina

' "There are three things you can't hide,"
says Walter Pidgeon in one of his bantering
moments; "love, smoke, and a man riding a
camel." I would add a fourth—that old MGM
touch.'—*Richard Winnington*

The Secret Invasion
US 1964   98m   De Luxe   Panavision
UA / San Carlos (Gene Corman)

During World War II five convicted criminals
become commandos.
Cut price *Dirty Dozen*, quite well made and
exciting.

w R. Wright Campbell   d Roger Corman
ph Arthur E. Arling   m Hugo Friedhofer

Stewart Granger, Raf Vallone, Henry Silva,
Mickey Rooney, Edd Byrnes, William
Campbell, Peter Coe

The Secret Life of an American Wife**
US 1968   92m   De Luxe
TCF / Charlton (George Axelrod)

A bored suburban housewife sets out to
seduce a movie star.
Sympathetic comedy of sixties suburban
manners.

wd George Axelrod   ph Leon Shamroy
m Billy May

Walter Matthau, Anne Jackson, Patrick
O'Neal, Edy Williams
  'Both a first-class satire on American mores
and a compassionate study of wish-
fulfilment.'—*NFT, 1970*

The Secret Life of Walter Mitty**
US 1947   110m   Technicolor
Samuel Goldwyn

A mother's boy dreams of derring-do, and
eventually life catches up with fiction.
This pleasantly remembered star comedy,
though it never had much to do with Thurber,
can now be seen to have missed most of its
opportunities, though the nice moments do
tend to compensate.

w Ken Englund, Everett Freeman, story
James Thurber   d Norman Z. McLeod
ph Lee Garmes   m David Raksin

Danny Kaye, Virginia Mayo, Boris Karloff,
Florence Bates, Fay Bainter, *Thurston Hall*,
Ann Rutherford, Gordon Jones, Reginald
Denny

Secret Mission
GB 1942   94m   bw
GFD / Marcel Hellman / Excelsior

During World War II four British Intelligence
officers are landed in occupied France to
discover the truth about German defences.
Stilted war suspenser.

w Anatole de Grunwald, Basil Bartlett,
Terence Young   d Harold French   ph Bernard
Knowles   m Mischa Spoliansky

Hugh Williams, Carla Lehmann, James
Mason, Roland Culver, Nancy Price, Michael
Wilding, Percy Walsh

The Secret of Blood Island
GB 1964   84m   Technicolor
U-I / Hammer

A girl parachutist secret agent is smuggled into
a Japanese POW camp and out again.
Absurd blood and thunder, almost perversely
enjoyable—but not quite.

w John Gilling   d Quentin Lawrence   ph Jack
Asher   m James Bernard

Barbara Shelley, Jack Hedley, Charles
Tingwell, Bill Owen, Lee Montague

The Secret of Convict Lake*
US 1951   83m   bw
TCF (Frank P. Rosenberg)

In the 1870s, escaped convicts take over a
California town.
Brooding, snowy, set-bound western
melodrama; predictable but watchable.

w Oscar Saul   d Michael Gordon   ph Leo
Tover   m Sol Kaplan   md Lionel Newman

Glenn Ford, Gene Tierney, Ann Dvorak,
Ethel Barrymore, Zachary Scott, Barbara
Bates, Cyril Cusack, Jeanette Nolan, Ruth
Donnelly

The Secret of Madame Blanche
US 1933   85m   bw

The woman who takes the blame for murder
committed by a young man is the mother he
never knew. Or, *Madame X* unofficially
revisited: all-stops-out melodrama very typical
of its time. Irene Dunne, Phillips Holmes,
Lionel Atwill, Douglas Walton, Jean Parker,
Una Merkel. Written by Frances Goodrich
and Albert Hackett; directed by Charles
Brabin; for MGM.

The Secret of My Success
GB 1965   105m   Metrocolor   Panavision
MGM / Andrew and Virginia Stone

A village policeman follows his mother's
dictum that he should not think ill of others,
and accidentally goes from success to success.
Flabby portmanteau comedy full of in-jokes
and flat-footed farce; satire is not evident.

wd Andrew L. Stone   ph David Boulton
m Lucien Caillet and others   md Roland Shaw

James Booth, Lionel Jeffries, *Amy Dalby*,
Stella Stevens, Honor Blackman, Shirley
Jones, Joan Hickson

The Secret of St Ives
US 1949   76m   bw

During the Napoleonic War, a French prisoner-of-war escapes from Edinburgh Castle, only to be accused of murder. Modest swashbuckler with a somewhat lacklustre atmosphere. Richard Ney, Vanessa Brown, Henry Daniell, Aubrey Mather. Written by Eric Taylor, from the story by Robert Louis Stevenson; directed by Phil Rosen; for Columbia.

The Secret of Santa Vittoria*
US 1969 140m Technicolor
Panavision
UA / Stanley Kramer

In 1945 an Italian village hides its wine from the occupying Germans.
Expected, exhausting epic comedy with everyone talking at once.

w William Rose, Ben Maddow, *novel* Robert Crichton d Stanley Kramer ph Giuseppe Rotunno m Ernest Gold

Anthony Quinn, Anna Magnani, Virna Lisi, Hardy Kruger, Sergio Franchi, Renato Rascel
'A brainless farrago of flying rolling pins and rotten vegetables, filled with the kind of screaming, belching, eye-rolling fictional Italians only Stanley Kramer could invent.'— *Rex Reed*

AAN: Ernest Gold

The Secret of Stamboul
GB 1936 93m bw

An English adventurer foils a Turkish revolution. Pale rendering of a full-blooded best-seller. Valerie Hobson, Frank Vosper, James Mason, Kay Walsh, Peter Haddon. Written by Richard Wainwright, Howard Irving Young and Noel Langley, from the novel *The Eunuch of Stamboul* by Dennis Wheatley; directed by Andrew Marton; for Wainwright. (NB: Reissue title: *The Spy in White*.)

The Secret of the Blue Room
US 1933 66m bw

An heiress's three suitors all volunteer to spend the night in the haunted room of her mansion. Murderous malarkey without the courage of its convictions. Lionel Atwill, Gloria Stuart, Paul Lukas, Edward Arnold, Onslow Stevens, Robert Barrat, Elizabeth Patterson. Written by William Hurlbut; directed by Kurt Neumann; for Universal. (NB: Remade in 1938 as *The Missing Guest* and in 1944 as *Murder in the Blue Room*.)

The Secret of the Incas
US 1954 101m Technicolor
Paramount (Mel Epstein)

Various adventurers seek a priceless Inca jewel.
Boys' Own Paper yarn which sounds a good deal more exciting than it is: too much talk and a few choice studio backcloths drop the tension alarmingly, and the script lacks humour and conciseness.

w Ranald MacDougall, Sidney Boehm d Jerry Hopper ph Lionel Lindon m David Buttolph

Charlton Heston, Robert Young, Thomas Mitchell, Nicole Maurey, Yma Sumac, Glenda Farrell, Michael Pate

The Secret of the Loch
GB 1934 80m bw
ABFD / Bray Wyndham

A diver thinks he finds a prehistoric monster in Loch Ness.
Mildly amusing exploitation item following the 1934 rebirth of interest in the old legend.

w Charles Bennett, Billie Bristow d Milton Rosmer

Seymour Hicks, Nancy O'Neil, Gibson Gowland, Frederick Peisley, Rosamund John, Ben Field

The Secret Partner*
GB 1961 91m bw
MGM (Michael Relph)

A blackmailing dentist is visited by a mysterious hooded stranger who forces him to rob one of his businessman victims.
Complex puzzle thriller, neatly made in sub-Hitchcock style.

w David Pursall, Jack Seddon d Basil Dearden ph Harry Waxman m Philip Green

Stewart Granger, Haya Harareet, Bernard Lee, Hugh Burden, Melissa Stribling, Norman Bird, Conrad Philips

The Secret People*
GB 1951 96m bw
Ealing (Sidney Cole)

European refugees in London during the thirties become members of a ring of anarchists.
Downbeat political melodrama which pleased neither the masses nor the highbrows, despite plaudits for sensitive direction and performances.

w Thorold Dickinson, Wolfgang Wilhelm d *Thorold Dickinson* ph Gordon Dines m Roberto Gerhard

Valentina Cortese, Serge Reggiani, Audrey Hepburn, Charles Goldner, Megs Jenkins, Irene Worth, Athene Seyler, Reginald Tate

'The tension and power of the film make it one of the most remarkable British productions for some time.'—*Penelope Houston*

'That *Secret People*, despite the creative agonies recorded by Mr Lindsay Anderson [in a book on the making of the film] should turn out to be a confused, unco-ordinated spy thriller concealing a tentative message deep down below some strained effects of style is another tragedy of British film hopes.'—*Richard Winnington*

The Secret Six*
US 1931   83m   bw
MGM

A syndicate of businessmen finance two reporters to get evidence against a gang of bootleggers.
Solidly carpentered gangster thriller.

w Frances Marion *d* George Hill *ph* Harold Wenstrom

Wallace Beery, Lewis Stone, Clark Gable, John Mack Brown, Jean Harlow, Marjorie Rambeau, Paul Hurst, Ralph Bellamy, John Miljan

The Secret War of Harry Frigg
US 1967   109m   Techniscope
Universal / Albion (Hal E. Chester)

In 1943 a private engineers the escape of five captured generals.
Unattractive war comedy; slow, uninventive and overlong.

w Peter Stone, Frank Tarloff *d* Jack Smight *ph* Russell Metty *m* Carlo Rustichelli

Paul Newman, *John Williams*, Sylva Koscina, Andrew Duggan, Tom Bosley, Charles D. Gray, Vito Scotti, James Gregory

The Secret Ways*
US 1961   112m   bw
U-I / Heath (Richard Widmark)

An American reporter is recruited to rescue a scholar from communist Hungary.
Pretentious Iron Curtain melodrama, quite good to look at but overlong and no *Third Man.*

w Jean Hazelwood, *novel* Alistair MacLean *d* Phil Karlson *ph* Max Greene *m* Johnny Williams

Richard Widmark, Sonja Ziemann, Charles Regnier, Walter Rilla, Howard Vernon, Senta Berger

Secrets of a Secretary
US 1931   76m   bw

A social secretary discovers that her ex-husband is blackmailing her employer's daughter. *Peg's Paper* romance of a heroine who rises above her many problems. Claudette Colbert, Herbert Marshall, George Metaxas, Mary Boland, Berton Churchill. Written by Dwight Taylor and Charles Brackett; directed by George Abbott; for Paramount.

Secrets of a Soul**
Germany 1926   95m (24 fps)   bw   silent
UFA / Hans Neumann

A chemist develops a knife phobia, has hallucinations, and tries to cut his wife's throat.
A lesson in elementary psychology which was innovatory at the time and survives as cinema for its stylish and impressionist use of visual techniques.

w Colin Ross, Hans Neumann, G. W. Pabst *d* G. W. Pabst *ph* Guido Seeber, Curt Oertel, Robert Lach

Werner Krauss, Jack Trevor, Ruth Weyher, Pawel Pawlow

The Seduction of Joe Tynan*
US 1979   107m   Technicolor
Universal (Martin Bregman)

A young senator alienates his wife when he sacrifices his principles for advancement.
Fairly arresting political character drama with strong narrative and acting

w Alan Alda *d* Jerry Schatzberg *ph* Adam Holender *m* Bill Conti

Alan Alda, Barbara Harris, Meryl Streep, *Melvyn Douglas,* Rip Torn, Carrie Nye, Charles Kimbrough

See Here Private Hargrove*
US 1944   102m   bw
MGM (George Haight)

Adventures of a raw recruit in the US army.
Standard transcription of a humorous bestseller which did its best to make the war painless for Americans.

w Harry Kurnitz, *book* Marion Hargrove *d* Wesley Ruggles *ph* Charles Lawton *m* David Snell

Robert Walker, Donna Reed, Robert Benchley, Keenan Wynn, Bob Crosby, Ray Collins, Chill Wills, Grant Mitchell
† Sequel 1945: *What Next, Corporal Hargrove?*

See My Lawyer
US 1945   67m   bw

Comedians try to get out of a nightclub

commitment by insulting the customers. Thin vehicle for a team that wasn't going anywhere: too many variety acts got in their way. Ole Olsen, Chic Johnson, Grace McDonald, Franklin Pangborn, Alan Curtis, Noah Beery Jnr, Ed Brophy. Written by Edmund L. Hartmann and Stanley Davis; directed by Edward Cline; for Universal.

The Seekers

GB 1954 90m Eastmancolor
GFD / Fanfare (George H. Brown)
US title: *Land of Fury*

In 1820 a British sailor and his family emigrate to New Zealand.
Stilted epic which never gains the viewer's sympathy or interest.

w William Fairchild *d* Ken Annakin
ph Geoffrey Unsworth *m* William Alwyn

Jack Hawkins, Glynis Johns, Inia Te Wiata, Noel Purcell, Kenneth Williams, Laya Raki

Seems Like Old Times°

US 1980 102m Metrocolor
Columbia / Ray Stark

An innocently involved bank robber takes refuge with his ex-wife, a lady lawyer married to the district attorney.
Nostalgic farce which doesn't quite live up to the old skills and often bogs down in talk. Funny moments, though.

w Neil Simon *d* Jay Sandrich *ph* David M. Walsh *m* Marvin Hamlisch *pd* Gene Callahan

Goldie Hawn, Chevy Chase, Charles Grodin, Robert Guillaume, Harold Gould, George Grizzard

The Sellout

US 1951 82m bw
MGM (Nicholas Nayfack)

A newspaper editor exposes a corrupt administration.
Competent melodrama with no surprises.

w Charles Palmer *d* Gerald Mayer *ph* Paul Vogel *m* David Buttolph

Walter Pidgeon, John Hodiak, Audrey Totter, Thomas Gomez, Everett Sloane, Cameron Mitchell, Karl Malden, Paula Raymond

The Sellout

GB / Italy 1975 102m colour
Warner / Oceanglade / Amerifilm (Josef Shaftel)

Russians and Americans lure a double agent to Jerusalem in order to eliminate him.

Unsmiling spy melodrama with a complex plot, a bagful of clichés and some unnecessarily unpleasant violence.

w Judson Kinberg, Murray Smith *d* Peter Collinson *ph* Arthur Ibbetson *m* Mike Green, Colin Frechter

Richard Widmark, Oliver Reed, Gayle Hunnicutt, Sam Wanamaker, Vladek Sheybal, Ori Levy, Assef Dayan

Seminole

US 1953 86m Technicolor

A West Point graduate goes to Florida to make peace with the Indians. Slightly unusual but not very interesting semi-western with the usual clichés. Rock Hudson, Anthony Quinn, Barbara Hale, Richard Carlson, Hugh O'Brian, Russell Johnson, Lee Marvin, James Best. Written by Charles K. Peck Jnr; directed by Budd Boetticher; for Universal-International.

Semi-Tough°

US 1977 107m De Luxe
UA / David Merrick

The manager's daughter decides between two star members of a football team.
Rambling satiric comedy which takes jabs at various states of mind in America today, notably the fashionable forms of self-help therapy. Much of it comes off quite well.

w Walter Bernstein, *novel* Dan Jenkins *d* Michael Ritchie *ph* Charles Rosher Jnr *m* Jerry Fielding

Burt Reynolds, Kris Kristofferson, Jill Clayburgh, Bert Convy, Robert Preston, Lotte Lenya, Roger E. Mosley

The Senator Was Indiscreet°

US 1947 95m bw
U-I (Nunnally Johnson)
GB title: *Mr Ashton Was Indiscreet*

A foolish politician determines to become president and hires a press agent.
Satirical political farce which hurls its shafts wide and doesn't seem to mind how few of them hit.

w Charles MacArthur, *story* Edwin Lanham *d* George S. Kaufman *ph* William Mellor *m* Daniele Amfitheatrof

William Powell, Ella Raines, Peter Lind Hayes, Ray Collins, Arleen Whelan, Allen Jenkins, Hans Conried, Charles D. Brown

Send Me No Flowers°

US 1964 100m Technicolor
U-I / Martin Melcher (Harry Keller)

A hypochondriac mistakenly thinks he is dying and tries to provide another spouse for his wife.

A timeworn farcical situation is handled in the glossy Doris Day manner; it all starts quite brightly but gradually fizzles out.

w Julius Epstein, *play* Norman Barrasch, Carroll Moore *d* Norman Jewison *ph* Daniel Fapp *m* Frank de Vol *ad* Alexander Golitzen, Robert Clatworthy

Doris Day, Rock Hudson, Tony Randall, Paul Lynde, Clint Walker, Hal March, Edward Andrews

Sensation
GB 1936 67m bw

A village barmaid is murdered and only our reporter hero sees the wider implications.

Presentable murder mystery. John Lodge, Diana Churchill, Francis Lister, Joan Marion, Margaret Vyner, Athene Seyler, Richard Bird. Written by Dudley Leslie, Marjorie Deans and William Freshman, from the play *Murder Gang* by Basil Dean and George Munro; directed by Brian Desmond Hurst; for BIP. 'The genuine situation is lost in false trials, in an absurd love story, in humour based on American films, and in the complete unreality of the "murder gang".'—*Graham Greene*.

Sensations of 1945
US 1944 87m bw
Andrew L. Stone

Father and son disagree over the handling of their publicity agency.

Slim plot holds together a ragbag of variety acts, some quite choice.

w Dorothy Bennett *d* Andrew L. Stone *ph* Peverell Marley, John Mescall *md* Mahlon Merrick

Eleanor Powell, W. C. Fields, Sophie Tucker, Dennis O'Keefe, Eugene Pallette, C. Aubrey Smith, Lyle Talbot, Dorothy Donegan, Cab Calloway and his band, Woody Herman and his band

AAN: Mahlon Merrick

Senso°
Italy 1953 115m Technicolor
Lux
aka: *The Wanton Countess* (cut version)

In 1866 Venice a noblewoman falls in love with an officer of the invading Austrian army, but finally denounces him.

The melodramatic plot is less important than the portrait of a period, for this is an expensive film in the grand style, often breathtaking to look at.

w Luchino Visconti, Suso Cecchi d'Amico and others *story* Camilla Botto *d* Luchino Visconti *ph* G. R. Aldo, Robert Krasker *m* Anton Bruckner *ad* Ottavio Scotti

Alida Valli, Farley Granger, Massimo Girotti, Christian Marquand

Sentimental Journey
US 1946 94m bw
TCF (Walter Morosco)

An actress who knows she is dying arranges for a little orphan girl to take her place in her husband's affections.

Hollywood's most incredible three-handkerchief picture; nicely made, but who dared to write it?

w Samuel Hoffenstein, Elizabeth Reinhardt, *story* Nelia Gardner White *d* Walter Lang *ph* Norbert Brodine *m* Cyril Mockridge

Maureen O'Hara, John Payne, William Bendix, Cedric Hardwicke, Glenn Langan, Mischa Auer, Connie Marshall, Kurt Kreuger

'In twenty years of filmgoing I can't remember being so slobbered at: the apotheosis of the weepie.'—*Richard Winnington*

† Remade as *The Gift of Love* (qv).

The Sentinel
US 1976 92m Technicolor
Universal / Jeffrey Konvitz

A disturbed girl in an old apartment house is haunted by walking corpses: the house turns out to be the gateway to hell and her boy friend its appointed sentinel.

Vulgarly modish rip-off of several fashionable themes, notably *Rosemary's Baby* and *The Exorcist*.

w Michael Winner, Jeffrey Konvitz, *novel* Jeffrey Konvitz *d* Michael Winner *ph* Dick Kratina *m* Gil Melle

Chris Sarandon, Cristina Raines, Martin Balsam, John Carradine, Jose Ferrer, Ava Gardner, Arthur Kennedy, Burgess Meredith, Sylvia Miles, Deborah Raffin, Eli Wallach, Jerry Orbach

'Moral or ironic points are hard to discern in the eye-wrenching flux of a Michael Winner movie, which drifts and zooms across its polished people and places in a continual caressing motion, as crudely excitatory as any sex movie when the climaxes are approaching.'—*Richard Combs, MFB*

'A man with a face that looks like chicken giblets, a naked whore with a mouse on her thigh, a cat devouring a canary and Sylvia Miles in a tight leotard—these are some of the highlights of *The Sentinel*, a perfect film for those who like to slow down and look at traffic accidents.'—*Janet Maslin, Newsweek*

Separate Tables**
US 1958 98m bw
UA / Hecht–Hill–Lancaster (Harold Hecht)

Emotional tensions among the boarders at a British seaside guest house.
The genteel melodramas seem less convincing on the Hollywood screen than they did on the London stage, but the handling is thoroughly professional.

w Terence Rattigan, John Gay, *play* Terence Rattigan *d* Delbert Mann *m* David Raksin *ph* Charles Lang

Burt Lancaster, Rita Hayworth, *David Niven*, Deborah Kerr, *Wendy Hiller, Gladys Cooper, Cathleen Nesbitt, Felix Aylmer*, Rod Taylor, Audrey Dalton, *May Hallatt*

AA: David Niven; Wendy Hiller
AAN: best picture; script; Charles Lang; David Raksin; Deborah Kerr

September Affair
US 1950 104m bw
Paramount (Hal B. Wallis)

Two married people fall in love and a plane crash in which they are reported dead gives them their chance.
Turgid romantic melodrama, not very well made despite the background tour of Capri; what made it a hit was the playing of the old Walter Huston record of the title song.

w Robert Thoeren *d* William Dieterle *ph* Charles B. Lang *m* Victor Young

Joseph Cotten, Joan Fontaine, Françoise Rosay, Jessica Tandy, Robert Arthur, Jimmy Lydon
'A smooth surface mirrors the film's essential superficiality.'—*Penelope Houston*

September Storm
US 1960 110m De Luxe
Cinemascope 3-D
TCF / Alco (Edward L. Alperson)

A New York model and two adventurers search for sunken treasure off an uncharted Mediterranean island.
Thin actioner originally intended to marry 3-D and Cinemascope, but failed to do so.

w W. R. Burnett, *novel* The Girl in the Red Bikini by Steve Fisher *d* Byron Haskin *ph* Jorge Stahl Jnr, Lamar Boren *m* Edward L. Alperson Jnr

Joanne Dru, Mark Stevens, Robert Strauss

Sequoia
US 1934 73m bw

A girl living in the High Sierras defends wild animals from hunters. Refreshingly unusual outdoor drama with good location photography. Jean Parker, Russell Hardie, Samuel S. Hinds, Paul Hurst. Written by Ann Cunningham, Sam Arnstrong and Carey Wilson; directed by Chester Franklin; photographed by Chester Lyons; for MGM. 'It was unlikely that either Miss Parker or the deer would eat the puma, but I hung on hoping that the puma would eat the deer or Miss Parker.'—*James Agate.*

Serenade
US 1956 121m Warnercolor
Warner (Henry Blanke)

A vineyard worker becomes a successful opera singer and is desired by two women.
Cliché success story with plot taking second place to singing.

w Ivan Goff, Ben Roberts, John Twist, *novel* James M. Cain *d* Anthony Mann *ph* Peverell Marley *md* Ray Heindorf *songs* Nicholas Brodszky

Mario Lanza, Joan Fontaine, Sarita Montiel, Vincent Price, Joseph Calleia, Harry Bellaver, Vince Edwards, Silvio Minciotti

The Sergeant
US 1968 108m Technicolor
Warner / Robert Wise (Richard Goldstone)

France, 1952. In a dreary army camp, a tough army sergeant with a guilt complex is brought face to face with his own homosexuality.
Well-made but very ponderous and limited melodrama which could have been told in half the time.

w Dennis Murphy, from his novel *d* John Flynn *ph* Henri Persin *m* Michel Mayne

Rod Steiger, John Philip Law, Frank Latimore, Ludmila Mikael

Sergeant Deadhead
US 1965 89m CFI colour

An army sergeant is accidentally sent into orbit and undergoes a personality change. Clumsy comedy partially redeemed by its supporting players. Frankie Avalon, Deborah Walley, Fred Clark, Cesar Romero, Eve Arden, Gale Gordon, Buster Keaton, Harvey Lembeck, John Ashley. Written by Louis M. Heyward; directed by Norman Taurog; for AIP.

Sergeant Madden
US 1939   90m   bw
MGM (J. Walter Ruben)

A policeman's son becomes a gangster.
Routine crime melodrama with sentimental
trimmings, quite untypical of its director.

w Wells Root, *story* A Gun in His Hand by
William A. Ulman   d Josef Von Sternberg
ph John Seitz   m William Axt

Wallace Beery, Tom Brown, Alan Curtis,
Laraine Day, Fay Holden, Marc Lawrence,
Marion Martin

Sgt Pepper's Lonely Hearts Club Band
US 1978   111m   Technicolor
   Panavision
Universal / Robert Stigwood (Dee Anthony)

A family band finds a new sound despite the
activities of villains.
Oddball hotch-potch of middle-aged comedy
and youth nostalgia with an American small-
town setting. Some moments please, but most
of it simply doesn't gell.

w Henry Edwards   d Michael Schultz
ph Owen Roizman   m various (mostly the
Beatles)   pd Brian Eatwell

Peter Frampton, Barry Gibb, Robin Gibb,
Maurice Gibb, George Burns, Frankie
Howerd, Donald Pleasence, Paul Nicholas,
Sandy Farina, Alice Cooper, Steve Martin,
Earth Wind and Fire

'Another of those films which serve as
feature-length screen advertising for an
album.'—*Variety*

Sergeant Rutledge*
US 1960   111m   Technicolor
Warner / John Ford (Willis Goldbeck,
   Patrick Ford)

In 1881 a black army sergeant is on trial for
rape and murder, but his defence counsel
reveals the real culprit.
Flashback western; not the director's best, but
generally of some interest.

w James Warner Bellah, Willis Goldbeck
d John Ford   ph Bert Glennon   m Howard
Jackson

Woody Strode, Jeffrey Hunter, Constance
Towers, Willis Bouchey, Billie Burke,
Carleton Young, Juano Hernandez, Mae
Marsh

Sergeant Steiner
West Germany 1979   115m
   Eastmancolor   Panavision
Palladium / Rapidfilm (Arlene Sellers, Alex
   Winitsky)

The German sergeant hero of *Cross of Iron*
survives the Western Front and involvement in
an anti-Hitler conspiracy.
Somewhat bloodless though interesting sequel
to an exceptionally nasty war film, with an
international cast aiming at better box office.

w Tony Williamson   d Andrew McLaglen
ph Tony Imi   m Peter Thomas

Richard Burton, Robert Mitchum, Curt
Jurgens, Rod Steiger, Helmut Griem, Michael
Parks

Sergeant York**
US 1941   134m   bw
Warner (Jesse L. Lasky)

The story of a gentle hillbilly farmer who
became a hero of World War I.
Standard real-life fiction given the big
treatment; a key Hollywood film of its time in
several ways.

w Abem Finkel, Harry Chandler, Howard
Koch, John Huston   d Howard Hawks
ph Arthur Edeson   m Max Steiner

Gary Cooper, Joan Leslie, Walter Brennan,
George Tobias, David Bruce, Stanley Ridges,
Margaret Wycherly, Dickie Moore, Ward
Bond

'I hardly think the effect is any different
from that of a parade, with colours and a
band; it is stirring and it is too long; there are
too many holdups and too many people out of
step, and your residue of opinion on the
matter is that it will be nice to get home and
get your shoes off.'—*Otis Ferguson*

'It has all the flavour of true Americana, the
blunt and homely humour of backwoodsmen
and the raw integrity peculiar to simple
folk.'—*Bosley Crowther, New York Times*

AA: Gary Cooper
AAN: best picture; script; Howard Hawks;
Sol Polito; Max Steiner; Walter Brennan;
Margaret Wycherly

Sergeants Three
US 1961   112m   Technicolor
   Panavision
(UA) Essex–Claude (Frank Sinatra)

Just after the Civil War three cavalry
sergeants, with the help of an ex-slave bugler,
dispose of some hostile Indians.
High-spirited but exhausting parody of *Gunga
Din*, with bouts of unfunny bloodthirstiness
separated by tedious slabs of dialogue.

w W. R. Burnett   d John Sturges   ph Winton
Hock, Carl Guthrie   m Billy May

Frank Sinatra, Dean Martin, Peter Lawford,
Sammy Davis Jnr, Joey Bishop, Henry Silva,
Ruta Lee

'The participants have a better time than the onlookers.'—*Judith Crist, 1973*

Serial*
US 1980   91m   Movielab
Paramount / Sidney Beckerman

Well-heeled Californians in a high suburban community go in for various cults and fashions.
Amusing satire on everything from *Peyton Place* to *Bob and Carol and Ted and Alice*. Just a little late in coming, that's all.

w Rich Eustis, Michael Elias, *novel* Cyra McFadden *d* Bill Persky *ph* Rexford Metz *m* Lalo Schifrin

Martin Mull, Tuesday Weld, Jennifer McAllister, Sam Chew Jnr, Sally Kellerman, Nita Talbot, Bill Macy, Christopher Lee, Pamela Bellwood, Peter Bonerz, Tom Smothers

Serious Charge
GB 1959   99m   bw
Alva (Mickey Delamar)

A small-town troublemaker, accused by his priest of being responsible for the death of a young girl, amuses himself by accusing the priest of making homosexual advances.
A sensational play of its time makes a dull film despite earnest performances.

w Guy Elmes, Mickey Delamar, *play* Philip King *d* Terence Young *ph* Georges Périnal *m* Leighton Lucas

Anthony Quayle, Andrew Ray, Sarah Churchill, Irene Browne, Percy Herbert, Cliff Richard

The Serpent
France / Italy / Germany 1974   124m colour
Films La Boetie (Henri Verneuil)

A top KGB official defects to the west.
Complicated, humourless, multi-lingual spy capers.

w Henri Verneuil, Gilles Perrault, *novel* Pierre Nord *d* Henri Verneuil *ph* Claude Renoir *m* Ennio Morricone

Yul Brynner, Henry Fonda, Dirk Bogarde, Philippe Noiret, Farley Granger, Virna Lisi

The Serpent's Egg*
West Germany / US 1977   120m Eastmancolor
Rialto-Dino de Laurentiis

An American trapeze artist has a hard time in Berlin at the time of Hitler's rise to power.
More of a curate's egg, really, with a poor

leading performance and too many lapses into nastiness, but much incidental interest of the kind one associates with the director.

wd Ingmar Bergman *ph* Sven Nykvist *m* Rolf Wilhelm *pd* Rolf Zehetbauer

David Carradine, Liv Ullmann, Gert Frobe, James Whitmore, Heinz Bennent
'A crackpot tragedy: everything is strained, insufficient, underfelt.'—*New Yorker*

Serpico*
US 1973   130m   Technicolor
Paramount / Artists Entertainment Complex / Dino de Laurentiis (Martin Bregman)

A New York cop reveals police corruption and is eventually forced to leave the country.
A harrowing true story played with authentic gloom and violence.

w Waldo Salt, Norman Wexler, *book* Peter Maas *d* Sidney Lumet *ph* Arthur J. Ornitz *m* Mikis Theodorakis

Al Pacino, John Randolph, Jack Kehoe, Biff McGuire
'There's nothing seriously wrong with *Serpico* except that it's unmemorable, and not even terribly interesting while it's going on.'—*Stanley Kauffmann*

AAN: script; Al Pacino

The Servant**
GB 1963   116m   bw
Elstree / Springbok (Joseph Losey, Norman Priggen)

A rich, ineffectual young man is gradually debased and overruled by his sinister manservant and his sexy 'sister'.
Acclaimed in many quarters on its first release, this downbeat melodrama now seems rather naïve and long drawn out; its surface gloss is undeniable, but the final orgy is more risible than satanic.

w Harold Pinter, *novel* Robin Maugham *d* Joseph Losey *ph* Douglas Slocombe *m* Johnny Dankworth

Dirk Bogarde, James Fox, Sarah Miles, Wendy Craig, Catherine Lacey, Richard Vernon
'Moodily suggestive, well acted, but petering out into a trickle of repetitious unmeaningful nastiness.'—*John Simon*

Servants' Entrance
US 1934   88m   bw
Fox

A maid falls in love with a chauffeur.
Upstairs downstairs style comedy drama; passable.

w Samson Raphaelson, *novel* Sigrid Boo
d Frank Lloyd *ph* Hal Mohr *m* Arthur Lange

Janet Gaynor, Lew Ayres, Walter Connolly,
G. P. Huntley Jnr, Sig Rumann, Louise
Dresser, Astrid Allwyn, Ned Sparks

Service De Luxe
US 1938   85m   bw

Adventures of the members of a super-
secretarial agency. Very tolerable but
uninspired comedy which doesn't really allow
its acting talent full rein. Constance Bennett,
Vincent Price, Charles Ruggles, Helen
Broderick, Mischa Auer, Halliwell Hobbes.
Written by Gertrude Purcell and Leonard
Spiegelgass; directed by Rowland V Lee; for
Universal.

Service for Ladies
GB 1932   93m   bw
Paramount (Alexander Korda)
US title: *Reserved for Ladies*

A waiter has a way with his rich lady clients.
Tenuous satirical comedy, a variation on the
American silent *The Grand Duchess and the
Waiter.*

w Eliot Crawshay-Williams, Lajos Biro, *novel*
The Head Waiter by Ernst Vajda
d Alexander Korda

Leslie Howard, George Grossmith, Benita
Hume, Elizabeth Allan, Morton Selten, Cyril
Ritchard, Martita Hunt, Merle Oberon

The Set Up•••
US 1949   72m   bw
RKO (Richard Goldstone)

An ageing boxer refuses to pull his last fight,
and is beaten up by gangsters.
One of the most brilliant little *films noirs* of
the late forties; thoroughly studio-bound, yet
evoking a brilliant feeling for time and place.
Photography, direction, editing, acting are all
of a piece.

w Art Cohn, *poem* Joseph Moncure March
d Robert Wise *ph* Milton Krasner
md Constantin Bakaleinikoff

Robert Ryan, Audrey Totter, George Tobias,
Alan Baxter, Wallace Ford

Seven Angry Men•
US 1954   90m   bw
Allied Artists (Vincent M. Fennelly)

In Kansas, John Brown determines to abolish
slavery by violence.
Low-budget, intensely felt little biopic of the
celebrated 19th-century fanatic and his sons.

w Daniel B. Ullman d Charles Marquis
Warren *ph* Ellsworth Fredericks *m* Carl
Brandt

Raymond Massey, Jeffrey Hunter, Larry
Pennell, Debra Paget, Leo Gordon, John
Smith, James Best, Dennis Weaver

Seven Beauties•
Italy 1975   115m   Technicolor
Medusa (Lina Wertmuller, Giancarlo
   Giannini, Arrigo Colombo)
original title: *Pasqualino Settebellezze*

An incorrigible survivor manages to get
through the rigours of World War II and
scarcely notices the damage to his honour.
Candide-like mixture of farce and satire with
the addition of a good deal of unpleasantness.
Less meaningful abroad than on its home
ground.

wd Lina Wertmuller *ph* Tonino delli Colli
m Enzo Jannacci

Giancarlo Giannini, Fernando Rey, Shirley
Stoler, Piero di Iorio

AAN: Lina Wertmuller (as writer and as
director); Giancarlo Giannini

Seven Brides for Seven Brothers••
US 1954   104m   Anscocolor
   Cinemascope
MGM (Jack Cummings)

In the old west, seven hard-working brothers
decide they need wives, and carry off young
women from the villages around.
Disappointingly studio-bound western musical,
distinguished by an excellent score and some
brilliant dancing, notably the barn-raising
sequence.

w Frances Goodrich, Albert Hackett, *story*
Sobbin' Women by Stephen Vincent Benet
d Stanley Donen *ph* George Folsey
ch Michael Kidd *songs* Johnny Mercer, Gene
de Paul *m* Adolph Deutsch, Saul Chaplin

Howard Keel, Jane Powell, Jeff Richards,
Russ Tamblyn, Tommy Rall, Howard Petrie,
Marc Platt, Jacques d'Amboise, Matt Mattox

AA: Adolph Deutsch, Saul Chaplin
AAN: best picture; script; George Folsey

Seven Cities of Gold•
US 1955   103m   De Luxe   Cinemascope
TCF (Robert D. Webb, Barbara McLean)

In 1796, a Spanish expedition sets out from
Mexico to annex California, but with it goes
Father Junipero Serra . . .
A semi-historical, semi-religious western
which ends up not being much of anything but
has interesting sequences.

w Richard L. Breen, John C. Higgins, *novel*
Isabelle Gibson Ziegler *d* Robert D. Webb
ph Lucien Ballard *m* Hugo Friedhofer

Michael Rennie, Richard Egan, Anthony
Quinn, Rita Moreno, Jeffrey Hunter, Eduardo
Noriega, John Doucette

Seven Days in May***
US 1964 120m bw
Seven Arts / Joel / John Frankenheimer
  (Edward Lewis)

An American general's aide discovers that his
boss intends a military takeover because he
considers the President's pacifism traitorous.
Absorbing political mystery drama marred
only by the unnecessary introduction of a
female character. Stimulating entertainment.

w Rod Serling, *novel* Fletcher Knebel, Charles
W. Bailey II *d* John Frankenheimer
ph Ellsworth Fredericks *m* Jerry Goldsmith

Kirk Douglas, Burt Lancaster, *Fredric March*,
Ava Gardner, Martin Balsam, *Edmond
O'Brien*, George Macready, John Houseman

'A political thriller which grips from start to
finish.'—*Penelope Houston*

'It is to be enjoyed without feelings of guilt,
there should be more movies like it, and there
is nothing first class about it.'—*John Simon*

'In the best tradition of the suspense thriller,
with the ultimate thrill our awareness of its
actual potential.'—*Judith Crist*

AAN: Edmond O'Brien

Seven Days Leave
US 1929 83m bw
Paramount (Louis D. Lighton)
GB title: *Medals*

A London charlady 'adopts' a soldier, and
both their lives are changed.
Sentimental melodrama which suited the times
and confirmed Cooper's stardom.

w John Farrow, Dan Totheroh, *play* The Old
Lady Shows Her Medals by J. M. Barrie
d Richard Wallace *ph* Charles Lang
songs Frank Loesser, Jimmy McHugh

Gary Cooper, Beryl Mercer, Daisy Belmore,
Nora Cecil, Tempe Piggott, Arthur Hoyt,
Basil Radford

Seven Days Leave
US 1942 87m bw
RKO (Tim Whelan)

In order to inherit a hundred thousand dollars,
a soldier must marry within a week.
Cheerful frivolity featuring radio stars of the
time.

w William Bowers, Ralph Spence, Curtis
Kenyon, Kenneth Earl *d* Tim Whelan
ph Robert de Grasse *md* Roy Webb

Lucille Ball, Victor Mature, Harold Peary,
Mary Cortes, Ginny Simms, Ralph Edwards,
Peter Lind Hayes, Marcy McGuire, Wallace
Ford

Seven Days to Noon**
GB 1950 94m bw
London Films (The Boulting Brothers)

A professor engaged on atomic research
threatens to blow up London unless his work
is brought to an end.
Persuasively understated suspense piece which
was subsequently much copied, so that it now
seems rather obvious.

w Frank Harvey, Roy Boulting, Paul Dehn,
James Bernard *d* John Boulting *ph* Gilbert
Taylor *m* John Addison

*Barry Jones, Olive Sloane, André Morell, Joan
Hickson*, Sheila Manahan, Hugh Cross,
Ronald Adam, Marie Ney

'A first rate thriller that does not pretend to
a serious message, but yet will leave a query in
the mind.'—*Richard Winnington*

AA: script

The Seven Deadly Sins*
France / Italy 1952 150m bw
Franco London / Costellazione

The master of ceremonies introduces seven
stories and an epilogue.
Among the most successful compendiums of
its kind, partly because of cast and credits and
partly because it came when French
naughtiness was appealing to a wide
international audience.

w Jean Aurenche, Pierre Bost, Roberto
Rossellini, Leo Joannon, Carlo Rim, Diego
Fabbri, Liana Ferri, Eduardo de Filippo,
Charles Spaak, Turi Vaselle, René Wheeler
d Eduardo de Filippo, Jean Dréville, Yves
Allégret, Roberto Rossellini, Carlo Rim,
Claude Autant-Lara, Georges Lacombe

Gérard Philipe, Isa Miranda, Eduardo de
Filippo, Noel-Noel, Louis de Funès, Viviane
Romance, Frank Villard, Henri Vidal,
Michèle Morgan, Françoise Rosay

711 Ocean Drive*
US 1950 102m bw
Columbia (Frank N. Seltzer)

A wireless expert is drawn into the bookie
racket.
Overlong but vigorous crime exposé
melodrama with excellent location sequences,
notably a climax on Hoover Dam.

w Richard English, Francis Swann *d Joseph H. Newman ph* Franz Planer *m* Sol Kaplan

Edmond O'Brien, Joanne Dru, Otto Kruger, Don Porter, Sammy White, Dorothy Patrick, Barry Kelley, Howard St John

Seven Faces of Dr Lao*
US 1964   100m   Metrocolor
MGM / George Pal

An elderly Chinaman with a penchant for spectacular disguise solves the problems of a western desert town.
A pleasant idea and excellent production are submerged in a sloppily sentimental and verbose script.

w Charles G. Finney, from his novel *d* George Pal *ph* Robert Bronner *m* Leigh Harline *make up* William Tuttle

Tony Randall, Arthur O'Connell, John Ericson, Barbara Eden, Noah Beery Jnr, Lee Patrick, Minerva Urecal, John Qualen

Seven Footsteps to Satan
US 1929   70m   bw

A rich recluse plays an elaborate and macabre joke on his niece and nephew. Richly-designed but dramatically disappointing haunted house spoof. Thelma Todd, Creighton Hale, Sheldon Lewis, Ivan Christie, Sojin. Written by Richard Bee; directed by Benjamin Christensen; for Warner.

Seven Golden Men*
Italy / France / Spain 1965   91m
Eastmancolor

Seven master criminals plot to rob a bank of its gold. Simple-minded but slickly handled caper story with many visual pleasures. Rossana Podesta, Philippe Leroy, Gastone Moschin, Gabriele Tinti. Written and directed by Marco Vicario; for Atlantica / PUF / Asfilm / Warner. (A sequel, *Seven Golden Men Strike Again*, was less successful.)

Seven Hills of Rome
US / Italy 1957   104m   Technirama
MGM / Titanus (Lester Welch)

An American singer in Italy is pursued by the fiancée with whom he has quarrelled.
Thin travelogue with several halts for the star to sing; production very patchy.

w Art Cohn, Giorgio Prosperi *d* Roy Rowland *ph* Tonino Delli Colli *md* George Stoll

Mario Lanza, Renato Rascel, Marisa Allasio, Peggie Castle

Seven Keys to Baldpate*
US 1935   69m   bw
RKO

An old theatrical warhorse also filmed in 1926 and 1947. None is as amusing as a good stage production.

play George M. Cohan, *story* Earl Derr Biggers *d* William Hamilton, Edward Killy *ph* Robert de Grasse

Gene Raymond, Margaret Callahan, Eric Blore, Grant Mitchell, Moroni Olsen, Henry Travers

The Seven Little Foys*
US 1955   95m   Technicolor   Vistavision
Paramount (Jack Rose)

The story of a family vaudeville act.
Routine showbiz biopic, a little heavy on the syrup.

w Melville Shavelson, Jack Rose *d* Melville Shavelson *ph* John F. Warren *md* Joseph J. Lilley

Bob Hope, Milly Vitale, George Tobias, Angela Clarke, Herbert Heyes, *James Cagney* as George M. Cohan

AAN: script

Seven Men from Now
US 1956   78m   Warnercolor
Batjac (Andrew V. McLaglen, Robert E. Morrison)

A sheriff seeks revenge when his wife is killed by bandits.
Good western programmer.

w Burt Kennedy *d* Budd Boetticher *ph* William H. Clothier *m* Henry Vars

Randolph Scott, Gail Russell, Lee Marvin, Walter Reed, Don Barry, John Larch

The Seven Minutes
US 1971   102m   De Luxe
TCF (Russ Meyer)

A bookseller is arrested for distributing an obscene novel, and many people are unexpectedly involved in the court case.
A fascinating piece of old-fashioned hokum, full of 'daring' words and cameo performances.

w Richard Warren Lewis, *novel* Irving Wallace *d* Russ Meyer *ph* Fred Mandl *m* Stu Philips

Wayne Maunder, Marianne MacAndrew, Yvonne de Carlo, Phil Carey, Jay C. Flippen, Edy Williams, Lyle Bettger, Ron Randell, David Brian, Charles Drake, John Carradine, Harold J. Stone

Seven Nights in Japan
GB / France 1976   104m   Eastmancolor
EMI–Marianne (Lewis Gilbert)

The heir to the British throne has shore leave in Tokyo and falls in love with a geisha.
Tediously daring romance with a banal script which seems over impressed by its own barely-existent controversial qualities.

w Christopher Wood d Lewis Gilbert
ph Henri Decaë m David Hentschel

Michael York, Hidemi Aoki, James Villiers, Peter Jones, Charles Gray

The Seven Per Cent Solution
US 1976   114m   Technicolor
Universal (Herbert Ross)

Dr Watson lures Sherlock Holmes to Vienna so that Professor Freud can cure him of persecution complex and cocaine addiction.
Drearily serious spoof with only a glimmer of the required style and a totally miscast Holmes.

w Nicholas Meyer, from his novel d Herbert Ross ph Oswald Morris m John Addison pd Ken Adam

Nicol Williamson, Robert Duvall, Alan Arkin, Vanessa Redgrave, Laurence Olivier, Jeremy Kemp, Samantha Eggar, Joel Grey, Charles Gray, Georgia Brown, Regine
'Sorrily botched all-star extravaganza.'—Sight and Sound
'Comes into the category of hit and myth . . . A heavyweight spoof in which Sherlock Holmes is placed under hypnosis by Sigmund Freud. The audience is then placed under hypnosis by director Herbert Ross.'—Michael Billington, Illustrated London News

AAN: script

Seven Samurai***
Japan 1954   155m   bw
Toho (Shojiro Motoki)
original title: Shichi-nin no Samurai

16th-century villagers hire samurai to defend their property against an annual raid by bandits.
Superbly strange, vivid and violent medieval adventure which later served as the basis for the western The Magnificent Seven.

w Akira Kurosawa, Shinobu Hashimoto, Hideo Oguni d Akira Kurosawa ph Asaichi Nakai m Fumio Hayasaka

Toshiro Mifune, Takashi Shimura, Kuninori Kodo
'It is as sheer narrative, rich in imagery, incisiveness and sharp observation, that it makes its strongest impact . . . It provides a fascinating display of talent, and places its director in the forefront of creative film-makers of his generation.'—Gavin Lambert, Sight and Sound
'This, on the surface, is a work of relentless, unmitigated action, as epic as any film ever made, and, again on the surface, sheer entertainment. Yet it is also an unquestionable triumph of art.'—John Simon

Seven Seas to Calais
US / Italy 1962   103m   Eastmancolor
Cinemascope
MGM / Adelphia

In 1577, Sir Francis Drake follows the Spanish treasure route.
Ho-hum swashbuckler with a background of schoolboy history.

w Filippo Sanjust d Rudolph Maté ph Giulio Gianini m Franco Mannino

Rod Taylor, Keith Michell, Irene Worth, Anthony Dawson, Basil Dignam

Seven Sinners*
GB 1936   70m   bw
Gaumont (Michael Balcon)
US title: Doomed Cargo

Gunrunners wreck trains to cover traces of murder.
Fascinatingly dated comedy suspenser with excellent sub-Hitchcock sequences, the whole thing having a strong flavour of The 39 Steps.

w Frank Launder, Sidney Gilliat, L. DuGarde Peach, Austin Melford, play The Wrecker by Arnold Ridley, Bernard Merivale d Albert de Courville

Edmund Lowe, Constance Cummings, Thomy Bourdelle, Henry Oscar, Felix Aylmer, Allan Jeayes, O. B. Clarence

Seven Sinners*
US 1940   86m   bw
Universal (Joe Pasternak)
GB title: Café of Seven Sinners

A cabaret singer is deported from several South Sea islands for causing too many fights among the naval officers.
Ho-hum hokum with an amiable cast and a good-natured final free-for-all.

w John Meehan, Harry Tugend d Tay Garnett ph Rudolph Maté m Frank Skinner

Marlene Dietrich, John Wayne, Albert Dekker, Broderick Crawford, Mischa Auer, Billy Gilbert, Oscar Homolka, Anne Lee, Samuel S. Hinds
'Nothing to worry about, unless you happen to be in the theatre, watching it go from fairly good to worse than worse.'—Otis Ferguson

Seven Sweethearts
US 1942   98m   bw
MGM (Joe Pasternak)

Seven daughters must marry in sequence,
eldest first.
Period musical frou-frou inspired by *Pride and
Prejudice*. So light it almost floats.

w Walter Reisch, Leo Townsend *d* Frank
Borzage *ph* George Folsey *m* Franz Waxman

Kathryn Grayson, Marsha Hunt, Van Heflin,
Cecelia Parker, S. Z. Sakall, Peggy Moran,
Isobel Elsom, Diana Lewis, Donald Meek,
Louise Beavers

Seven Thieves*
US 1960   102m   bw   Cinemascope
TCF (Sidney Boehm)

An elderly crook conceives a last plan to rob
the Monte Carlo casino.
Routine caper story, efficiently presented with
some humour.

w Sidney Boehm, *novel* Lions at the Kill by
Max Catto *d* Henry Hathaway *ph* Sam
Leavitt *m* Dominic Frontière

Edward G. Robinson, Rod Steiger, Joan
Collins, Eli Wallach, Michael Dante,
Alexander Scourby, Berry Kroeger, Sebastian
Cabot
  'Christ, it was supposed to be a fun film, and
Steiger is far, far from having a sense of
humour.'—*Henry Hathaway*

The Seven-Ups
US 1973   103m   TVC   De Luxe
TCF / Philip D'Antoni

Gangsters are hunted down by a secret force
of the New York police.
Formulary realistic rough stuff in the wake of
The French Connection.

w Albert Ruben, Alexander Jacobs *d* Philip
D'Antoni *ph* Urs Furrer *m* Don Ellis

Roy Scheider, Victor Arnold, Jerry Leon,
Tony Lo Bianco, *Richard Lynch*

Seven Waves Away
GB 1956   95m   bw
Columbia / Copa (John R. Sloan)
US title: *Abandon Ship*

After the sinking of a luxury liner, the officer
in charge of a lifeboat has to make life or
death decisions.
Initially gripping but finally depressing open
sea melodrama derived from *Souls at Sea* and
later remade for TV as *The Last Survivors*.

wd Richard Sale *ph* Wilkie Cooper *m* Arthur
Bliss

Tyrone Power, Mai Zetterling, Lloyd Nolan,
Stephen Boyd, Moira Lister, James Hayter,
Marie Lohr, Moultrie Kelsall, Noel Willman,
Gordon Jackson, Clive Morton, John Stratton
  'Eventually one is bludgeoned into a
grudging admiration for the film's staying
power.'—*Peter John Dyer*

Seven Ways from Sundown
US 1960   87m   Eastmancolor

A Texas Ranger befriends an outlaw, but has
twinges of conscience. Straightforward
character western with the inevitable shootout
finale. Audie Murphy, Barry Sullivan, Venetia
Stevenson, John McIntire, Kenneth Tobey.
Written by Clair Huffaker; directed by Harry
Keller; for Universal-International.

Seven Women*
US 1966   100m   Metrocolor   Panavision
MGM / John Ford / Bernard Smith

In 1935, an isolated Chinese mission staffed by
American women is overrun by bandits.
Dusty melodrama which might have appealed
in the thirties but was quite out of tune with
the sixties. Well enough made and acted, but a
strange choice for Ford's last film.

w Janet Green, John McCormick, *story*
Chinese Finale by Norah Lofts *d* John Ford
ph Joseph La Shelle *m* Elmer Bernstein

Anne Bancroft, Flora Robson, Margaret
Leighton, Sue Lyon, Mildred Dunnock, Betty
Field, Anna Lee, Eddie Albert, Mike
Mazurki, Woody Strode, Irene Tsu

The Seven Year Itch*
US 1955   105m   De Luxe   Cinemascope
TCF (Charles K. Feldman, Billy Wilder)

A married man has a fling with the girl
upstairs.
An amusing theatrical joke, with dream
sequences like revue sketches, is really all at
sea on the big screen, especially as the affair
remains unconsummated, but direction and
performances keep the party going more or
less.

w Billy Wilder, George Axelrod, *play* George
Axelrod *d* Billy Wilder *ph* Milton Krasner
m Alfred Newman

Tom Ewell, Marilyn Monroe, Sonny Tufts,
Evelyn Keyes, Robert Strauss, Oscar
Homolka, Marguerite Chapman, Victor
Moore

1776*
US 1972   141m   Eastmancolor
  Panavision
Columbia / Jack L. Warner

The thirteen American colonies prepare to declare their independence of Great Britain. Plain, low-key filming of the successful Broadway musical showing the domestic lives of the historical figures concerned. Splendid moments alternate with stretches of tedium.

w Peter Stone, from his play d Peter Hunt ph Harry Stradling Jnr m / ly Sherman Edwards ad George Jenkins

William Daniels, Howard da Silva, Ken Howard, Donald Madden, Blythe Danner

AAN: Harry Stradling Jnr

Seventh Cavalry
US 1956 75m Technicolor
Columbia / Scott–Brown

An officer accused of cowardice volunteers to bring back General Custer's body after Little Big Horn.
Lively co-feature with a good traditional action climax.

w Peter Packer d Joseph H. Lewis ph Ray Rennahan m Mischa Bakaleinikoff

Randolph Scott, Barbara Hale, Jay C. Flippen, Jeanette Nolan, Frank Faylen

The Seventh Cross**
US 1944 112m bw
MGM (Pandro S. Berman)

Seven Germans escape from a concentration camp, and the Nazis threaten to execute them all. Just one escapes.
Impressive melodrama, brilliantly limiting its escape / suspense story to studio sets. Old-style Hollywood production at its best; but a rather obviously contrived story.

w Helen Deutsch, novel Anna Seghers d Fred Zinnemann ph Karl Freund m Roy Webb ad Cedric Gibbons, Leonid Vasian

Spencer Tracy, Signe Hasso, Hume Cronyn, Jessica Tandy, Agnes Moorehead, Felix Bressart, George Macready, George Zucco

AAN: Hume Cronyn

The Seventh Dawn
GB 1964 123m Technicolor
UA / Holden / Charles K. Feldman (Karl Tunberg)

In the early fifties a Malayan rubber planter finds that his best friend is a leading terrorist.
Doom-laden romantic adventure drama with a lot of suffering and too little entertainment value.

w Karl Tunberg, novel The Durian Tree by Michael Keon d Lewis Gilbert ph Freddie Young m Riz Ortolani

William Holden, Tetsuro Tamba, Capucine,

Susannah York, Michael Goodliffe, Allan Cuthbertson, Maurice Denham

'Echoes of The Ugly American, Love Is a Many-Splendored Thing, and many another adventure East of Sumatra, with every character running absolutely true to form.'— MFB

'An interminable melange of political, racial and romantic clichés, with performances and dialogue as overripe as the jungle setting.'— Judith Crist, 1973

Seventh Heaven**
US 1927 93m approx (24 fps) bw
  silent
Fox

A Paris sewer worker shelters a street waif, marries her and after idyllic happiness goes off to war, returning blinded.
All softness, sweetness and light, a very typical—and attractive—film of its director and a big influence on Hollywood's European period.

w Benjamin Glazer, play Austin Strong d Frank Borzage ph Ernest Palmer, J A. Valentine

Janet Gaynor, Charles Farrell, Gladys Brockwell, David Butler

AA: Benjamin Glazer; Frank Borzage; Janet Gaynor
AAN: best picture

Seventh Heaven*
US 1937 102m bw
TCF (Raymond Griffith)

Dewy-eyed remake; the mood is antediluvian but the production impresses.

w Melville Baker d Henry King ph Merritt Gerstad m Louis Silvers ad William Darling

James Stewart, Simone Simon, Jean Hersholt, Gale Sondergaard, J. Edward Bromberg, Gregory Ratoff, John Qualen, Victor Kilian, Sig Rumann, Mady Christians

The Seventh Seal***
Sweden 1957 95m bw
Svensk Filmindustri (Allan Ekelund)
original title: Det Sjunde Inseglet

Death comes for a knight, who challenges him to a game of chess while he tries to show illustrations of goodness in mankind: but Death takes them all away in the end.
A modestly budgeted minor classic which, because of its international success and its famous shots, is seldom analysed in detail. In fact its storyline is meandering and apparently pointless, and it is kept going by its splendid cinematic feel and its atmosphere is that of a dark world irrationally sustained by religion.

*wd Ingmar Bergman ph Gunnar Fischer
m* Erik Nordgren

Max Von Sydow, Bengt Ekerot, Gunnar
Bjornstrand, Nils Poppe, Bibi Andersson,
Gunnel Lindblom

'The most extraordinary mixture of beauty
and lust and cruelty, Odin-worship and
Christian faith, darkness and light.'—*Alan
Dent, Illustrated London News*

The Seventh Sin

US 1957 94m bw Cinemascope
MGM (David Lewis)

A faithless wife accompanies her bacteriologist
husband to fight a Chinese cholera epidemic,
and regains her self-respect.
Tatty remake of a Garbo vehicle which was
dated even in 1934. (See *The Painted Veil*.)

w Karl Tunberg, *novel* The Painted Veil by
Somerset Maugham *d* Ronald Neame
ph Ray June *m* Miklos Rozsa

Eleanor Parker, Bill Travers, George Sanders,
Jean-Pierre Aumont, Françoise Rosay

The Seventh Survivor

GB 1941 75m bw

Survivors of a shipwreck gather in a lighthouse
and discover that one of them is a Nazi agent.
Adequate mystery potboiler, comparable with
Hitchcock's talkier *Lifeboat*. Linden Travers,
Austin Trevor, John Stuart, Martita Hunt,
Frank Pettingell, Jane Carr, Felix Aylmer,
Wally Patch, Henry Oscar. Written by
Michael Barringer; directed by Leslie Hiscott;
for British National.

The Seventh Veil***

GB 1945 94m bw
Theatrecraft / Sydney Box / Ortus

A concert pianist is romantically torn between
her psychiatrist, her guardian, and two other
fellows.
A splendid modern melodrama in the tradition
of *Jane Eyre* and *Rebecca*; it set the seal of
moviegoing approval on psychiatry, classical
music, and James Mason, and it is the most
utter tosh.

*w Muriel and Sydney Box d Compton
Bennett ph Reg Wyer m Benjamin Frankel*

James Mason, Ann Todd, Herbert Lom,
Albert Lieven, Hugh McDermott, Yvonne
Owen, David Horne, Manning Whiley

'An example of the intelligent, medium-
priced picture made with great technical polish
which has represented for Hollywood the
middle path between the vulgar and the
highbrow.'—*Spectator*

'A popular film that does not discard taste
and atmosphere.'—*Daily Mail*
'A rich, portentous mixture of Beethoven,
Chopin, Kitsch and Freud.'—*Pauline Kael,
1968*
'An odd, artificial, best sellerish kind of
story, with reminiscences of *Trilby* and *Jane
Eyre* and all their imitations down to
Rebecca.'—*Richard Mallett, Punch*

AA: script

The Seventh Victim*

US 1943 71m bw
RKO (*Val Lewton*)

A girl goes to New York in search of her
sister, who is under the influence of Satanists.
Much praised but in effect rather boring little
thriller, with rather stately acting and
ponderous direction and dialogue. Censorship
made the plot so obscure that it's difficult to
follow.

w Charles O'Neal, De Witt Bodeen *d* Mark
Robson *ph* Nicholas Musuraca *m* Constantin
Bakaleinikoff

Kim Hunter, Tom Conway, Jean Brooks,
Hugh Beaumont, Erford Gage, Isabel Jewell,
Evelyn Brent
'It is the almost oppressive mood, the
romantic obsession with death-in-life, which
dominates the film.'—*NFT, 1973*
† Note the use in the first scene of the
staircase from *The Magnificent Ambersons*.

The Seventh Voyage of Sinbad*

US 1958 89m Technicolor
Columbia / Morningside (Charles Schneer)

Sinbad seeks a roc's egg which will restore his
fiancée from the midget size to which an evil
magician has reduced her.
Lively fantasy with narrative drive and
excellent effects.

w Kenneth Kolb *d* Nathan Juran *ph* Wilkie
Cooper *m* Bernard Herrmann *sp Ray
Harryhausen*

Kerwin Mathews, Kathryn Grant, Torin
Thatcher, Richard Eyer, Alec Mango

A Severed Head*

GB 1970 98m Technicolor
Columbia / Winkast (Alan Ladd Jnr)

A wine merchant has a long-standing affair
which he thinks is secret, but is annoyed when
his wife tries the same game.
Unwisely boisterous screen version of a slyly
academic novel; tolerably sophisticated for
those who don't know the original.

w Frederic Raphael, *novel* Iris Murdoch
d Dick Clement *ph* Austin Dempster
m Stanley Myers *pd* Richard Macdonald

Lee Remick, Richard Attenborough, Ian Holm, Claire Bloom, Jennie Linden, Clive Revill

Sex and the Single Girl
US 1964   114m   Technicolor
Warner / Richard Quine / Reynard (William T. Orr)

A journalist worms his way into the life of a lady sexologist in order to unmask her—but guess what.
Coy sex comedy with noise substituting for wit and style, all pretence being abandoned in a wild chase climax.

w Joseph Heller, David R. Schwarz, *book* Helen Gurley Brown d Richard Quine
ph Charles Lang Jnr m Neal Hefti

Natalie Wood, Tony Curtis, Henry Fonda, Lauren Bacall, Mel Ferrer, Fran Jeffries, Edward Everett Horton, Otto Kruger
  'For those willing to devote two hours of their lives to a consideration of Natalie Wood's virginity.'—*Judith Crist, 1973*

Sextette*
US 1978   91m   Metrocolor
Briggs and Sullivan (Warren G. Toub)

The honeymoon of a Hollywood film star is interrupted by her previous husbands.
An amazing last stab at her old métier by an 86-year-old ex-star. It doesn't work, of course, and most of it is embarrassing, but the attempt is in itself remarkable.

w Herbert Baker, *play* Mae West d Ken Hughes ph James Crabe m Artie Butler

Mae West, Tony Curtis, Ringo Starr, Dom de Luise, Timothy Dalton, George Hamilton, Alice Cooper, Rona Barrett, Walter Pidgeon, George Raft

Sexton Blake and the Hooded Terror
GB 1938   70m   bw

A millionaire is unmasked as the head of a criminal gang. Rather unyielding series melodrama, chiefly interesting for the casting of Tod Slaughter as Blake's Moriarty. George Curzon, Tod Slaughter, Greta Gynt, Charles Oliver, David Farrar. Written by A. R. Rawlinson; directed by George King; for George King. (NB: Other Sexton Blake movies, all cheaply made by British independents, include six 1928 two-reelers starring Langhorne Burton; *Sexton Blake and the Bearded Doctor* and *Sexton Blake and the Mademoiselle*, both 1935, both with Curzon; *Meet Sexton Blake* and *The Echo Murders*, both 1943, both with David Farrar; and *Murder on Site Three*, 1963, with Geoffrey Toone.)

Shack Out on 101*
US 1955   80m   bw
AA / William F. Broidy

A waitress at a café near a research establishment unmasks two spies.
Modest suspenser which seemed at the time to have some fresh and realistic attitudes.

w Ed and Mildred Dein d Ed Dein ph Floyd Crosby m Paul Dunlap

Frank Lovejoy, Lee Marvin, Keenan Wynn, Terry Moore, Whit Bissell

Shadow in the Sky
US 1951   78m   bw
MGM (William H. Wright)

A shell-shocked marine moves from a psychiatric hospital to live with his sister. Low-key drama, plainly but quite well done, though of little continuing interest.

w Ben Maddow d Fred M. Wilcox
ph George Folsey m Bronislau Kaper

Ralph Meeker, Nancy Davis, James Whitmore, Jean Hagen

Shadow of a Doubt***
US 1943   108m   bw
Universal (Jack H. Skirball)

A favourite uncle comes to visit his family in a small Californian town. He is actually on the run from police, who know him as the Merry Widow murderer.
Hitchcock's quietest film is memorable chiefly for its depiction of small-town life; but the script is well written and keeps the suspense moving slowly but surely.

w *Thornton Wilder, Sally Benson, Alma Reville, story* Gordon McDonell d *Alfred Hitchcock* ph Joe Valentine m Dmitri Tiomkin

Joseph Cotten, Teresa Wright, Hume Cronyn, Macdonald Carey, Patricia Collinge, Henry Travers, Wallace Ford
  'Some clever observation of rabbity white-collar life which, in spite of a specious sweetness, is the best since *It's a Gift*.'—*James Agee*
† Remade in 1959 as *Step Down to Terror*, with Charles Drake.

AAN: original story

Shadow of a Woman
US 1946   78m   bw

A woman suspects her husband of trying to murder his son by a former marriage. Poor melodrama on *Love from a Stranger* lines.
Andrea King, Helmut Dantine, Don McGuire, Richard Erdman, William Prince.

Written by Whitman Chambers and C.
Graham Baker; directed by Joseph Santley;
for Warner.

Shadow of the Cat
GB 1961   79m   bw
U-I / BHP

A cat appears to wreak vengeance on those
who murdered its mistress.
Tolerable old dark house shocker with an
amusing theme not too well sustained.

w George Baxt d John Gilling ph Alec
Grant m Mikis Theodorakis

André Morell, William Lucas, Barbara
Shelley, Conrad Phillips, Alan Wheatley,
Vanda Godsell, Richard Warner, Freda
Jackson

Shadow of the Eagle
GB 1950   92m   bw

In 1770, a Russian envoy to Venice falls for
the princess he is supposed to kidnap. Limp
swashbuckler based on a deservedly shadowy
corner of European history. Richard Greene,
Valentina Cortese, Greta Gynt, Binnie
Barnes, Charles Goldner, Walter Rilla.
Written by Doreen Montgomery and Hagar
Wilde; directed by Sidney Salkow; for
Anthony Havelock-Allan / Valiant.

Shadow on the Wall
US 1949   84m   bw
MGM (Robert Sisk)

A child is traumatized by the accidental
witnessing of the murder of her unpleasant
stepmother.
Forgettable melodramatic suspenser.

w William Ludwig d Pat Jackson ph Ray
June m André Previn

Ann Sothern, Zachary Scott, Gigi Perreau,
Nancy Davis, Kristine Miller, John McIntire

The Shadow on the Window
US 1957   73m   bw
Columbia (Jonie Taps)

Three teenage thugs break into a lonely house,
murder its owner and hold a girl hostage.
Routine crime programmer, rather boringly
unravelled.

w Leo Townsend, David Harmon d William
Asher ph Kit Carson m George Duning

Betty Garrett, Phil Carey, John Barrymore
Jnr, Corey Allen, Gerald Saracini

Shadows*
US 1959   81m   bw
Cassavetes / Cassel / Maurice McEndree

Two blacks and their sister find their identities
in Manhattan.
16mm realistic drama which began a new and
essentially dreary trend of grainily true-life
pictures with improvised dialogue and little
dramatic compression.

w the cast d John Cassavetes ph Erich
Kollmar m Charles Mingus

Ben Carruthers, Leila Goldoni, Hugh Hurd,
Rupert Crosse, Anthony Ray

  'I don't so much object to its mindlessness
as to its formlessness, regardless of the
practical excuses that may be advanced for its
rambling incoherence.'—*William S. Pechter*

  'A picture of startling immediacy and
shocking power.'—*Robert Hatch, Nation*

Shady Lady
US 1945   90m   bw

An elderly cardsharp is persuaded to help the
district attorney nab others of his kind.
Poorish comedy which offers its star little
support. Charles Coburn, Ginny Simms,
Robert Paige, Martha O'Driscoll, Alan Curtis.
Written by Curt Siodmak, Gerald Geraghty
and M. M. Musselman; directed by George
Waggner; for Universal.

Shaft*
US 1971   100m   Metrocolor
MGM / Shaft Productions (Joel Freeman)

A black private eye finds himself at odds with
a powerful racketeer.
Violent, commercial action thriller which
spawned two sequels and a tele-series as well
as stimulating innumerable even more violent
imitations.

w Ernest Tidyman, John D. F. Black
d Gordon Parks ph Urs Furrer m Isaac
Hayes

Richard Roundtree, Moses Gunn, Charles
Cioffi, Christopher St John

  'Relentlessly supercool dialogue, all
throwaway colloquialisms and tough
Chandlerian wisecracks.'—*MFB*

AA: title song (m / ly Isaac Hayes)
AAN: Isaac Hayes (musical score)

Shaft in Africa
US 1973   112m   Metrocolor   Panavision
(MGM) Shaft Productions (Roger Lewis)

Shaft is kidnapped by an Ethiopian emir who
wants him to track down a gang of slavers.
More miscellaneous violence, rather shoddily
assembled, with a few good jokes.

w Stirling Silliphant d John Guillermin
ph Marcel Grignon m Johnny Pate

Richard Roundtree, Frank Finlay, Vonetta
McGee

Shaft's Big Score
US 1972 105m Metrocolor Panavision
MGM / Shaft Productions (Richard Lewis, Ernest Tidyman)

Shaft avenges the death of a friend and comes up against the numbers racket.

Violent footage and an incomprehensible plot.

w Ernest Tidyman d Gordon Parks ph Urs Furrer m Gordon Parks

Richard Roundtree, Moses Gunn, Drew Bundini Brown, Joseph Mascolo

The Shaggy DA
US 1976 92m Technicolor
Walt Disney (Ron Miller)

A magic ring enables a young lawyer to become a talking dog and thus expose corruption.

Rather feeble sequel to *The Shaggy Dog*, with overtones of Watergate.

w Don Tait d Robert Stevenson ph Frank Phillips m Buddy Baker sp Eustace Lycett, Art Cruickshank, Danne Lee

Dean Jones, Tim Conway, Suzanne Pleshette, Jo Anne Worley, Vic Tayback, Keenan Wynn, Dick Van Patten

The Shaggy Dog*
US 1959 101m bw
Walt Disney (Bill Walsh)

A small boy turns into a big shaggy dog and catches some crooks.

Simple-minded, overlong Disney comedy for kids and their indulgent parents; good laughs in the chase scenes.

w Bill Walsh, Lillie Hayward, *novel* The Hound of Florence by Felix Salten d Charles Barton ph Edward Colman m Paul Sawtell

Fred MacMurray, Jean Hagen, Tommy Kirk, Cecil Kellaway, Annette Funicello, Tim Considine, Kevin Corcoran, Alexander Scourby

Shake Hands with the Devil*
Eire 1959 110m bw
UA / Troy / Pennebaker (Michael Anderson)

In 1921 Dublin a surgeon is the secret leader of the IRA, and comes to cherish violence as an end rather than a means.

Downbeat action melodrama, politically very questionable but well made.

w Ivan Goff, Ben Roberts, *novel* Rearden Connor d Michael Anderson ph Erwin Hillier m William Alwyn

James Cagney, Glynis Johns, Don Murray, Dana Wynter, Michael Redgrave, Sybil Thorndike, Cyril Cusack, Niall MacGinnis, Richard Harris, Ray McAnally, Noel Purcell

Shakedown
US 1950 80m bw
U-I (Ted Richmond)

A ruthless press photographer becomes a blackmailer.

Routine crime melodrama, adequately done.

w Alfred Lewis, Martin Goldsmith d Joseph Pevney ph Irving Glassberg m Joseph Gershenson

Howard Duff, Brian Donlevy, Anne Vernon, Peggy Dow, Lawrence Tierney, Bruce Bennett

The Shakedown
GB 1959 92m bw
Rank / Alliance / Ethiro (Norman Williams)

A Soho vice boss photographs prominent people in compromising situations and blackmails them.

A semi-remake set in the squalid London so beloved of film makers at the time, before it became 'swinging'. Of no interest or entertainment value.

w Leigh Vance d John Lemont ph Brendan J. Stafford m Philip Green

Terence Morgan, Hazel Court, Donald Pleasence, Bill Owen, Robert Beatty, Harry H. Corbett, Gene Anderson, Eddie Byrne

The Shakiest Gun in the West
US 1967 101m Techniscope
Universal (Edward J. Montagne)

A cowardly dentist becomes a western hero.

Dreary farce, an unsubtle remake of *The Paleface*.

w Jim Fritzell, Everett Greenbaum d Alan Rafkin ph Andrew Jackson m Vic Mizzy

Don Knotts, Barbara Rhoades, Jackie Coogan, Don Barry

Shalako
GB 1968 118m Technicolor Franscope
Kingston / Dimitri de Grunwald (Euan Lloyd)

New Mexico, 1880: a cowboy acts as guide to European aristocratic big game hunters, but the Indians become annoyed and attack.

A cute idea is given routine treatment; though packed with stars, the action never becomes very exciting despite incidental brutalities.

w J. J. Griffith, Hal Hopper, Scot Finch, *novel* Louis L'Amour d Edward Dmytryk ph Ted Moore m Robert Farnon

Sean Connery, Brigitte Bardot, Jack Hawkins, Stephen Boyd, Peter Van Eyck, Honor Blackman, Eric Sykes, Alexander Knox, Woody Strode, Victor French

Shall We Dance?**
US 1937   116m   bw
RKO (Pandro S. Berman)

Dancing partners pretend to be married but
are not; until they both get the same idea.
A light musical which was full of good things
but nevertheless began the decline of Astaire-
Rogers films; repetition was obvious, as was
ostentation for its own sake, and the audience
was expecting too much.

w Allan Scott, Ernest Pagano d Mark
Sandrich ph David Abel m / ly George and
Ira Gershwin md Nathaniel Shilkret ad Van
Nest Polglase

Fred Astaire, Ginger Rogers, Edward Everett
Horton, Eric Blore, Harriet Hoctor, Jerome
Cowan, Ketti Gallian, Ann Shoemaker

AAN: song 'They Can't Take That Away
From Me'

Shampoo*
US 1975   110m   Technicolor
Columbia / Persky–Bright / Vista (Warren
   Beatty)

A Beverly Hills hairdresser seduces his most
glamorous clients.
Ugly little sex farce with few laughs but much
dashing about and bad language. Its setting on
election eve 1968 has made some people think
it a political satire.

w Robert Towne, Warren Beatty d Hal
Ashby ph Laszlo Kovacs m Paul Simon

Warren Beatty, Julie Christie, Lee Grant,
Goldie Hawn, Jack Warden, Tony Bill, Jay
Robinson

'It has the bursting-with-talent but fuzziness-
of-effect aspect of a movie made by a group of
friends for their own amusement.'—*Richard
Combs*

AA: Lee Grant
AAN: script; Jack Warden

Shamus
US 1972   98m   Eastmancolor
Columbia / Robert M. Weitman

A private eye is hired by a wealthy man to
recover stolen jewels and find a murderer.
A forties retread with seventies violence;
junky stuff, with a few laughs for buffs who
can spot the in-jokes.

w Barry Beckerman d Buzz Kulik ph Victor
J. Kemper m Jerry Goldsmith

Burt Reynolds, Dyan Cannon, John Ryan, Joe
Santos, Giorgio Tozzi, Ron Weyland

'Very hectic, very vividly New York and as
idiotic as Reynolds' physical resiliency.'—
Judith Crist

Shane*
US 1953   118m   Technicolor
Paramount (George Stevens, Ivan Moffat)

A mysterious stranger helps a family of
homesteaders.
Archetypal family western, but much slower
and statelier than most, as though to
emphasize its own quality, which is evident
anyway.

w A. B. Guthrie Jnr, *novel* Jack Schaefer
d George Stevens ph Loyal Griggs m Victor
Young

Alan Ladd, Jean Arthur, Van Heflin, *Jack
Palance*, Brandon de Wilde, Ben Johnson,
Edgar Buchanan, Emile Meyer, Elisha Cook
Jnr, John Dierkes

'A kind of dramatic documentary of the
pioneer days of the west.'—*MFB*
'Westerns are better when they're not too
self-importantly self-conscious.'—*New Yorker,
1975*
'Stevens managed to infuse a new vitality, a
new sense of realism into the time-worn story
through the strength and freshness of his
visuals.'—Arthur Knight

AA: Loyal Griggs
AAN: best picture; A. B. Guthrie Jnr; George
Stevens; Jack Palance; Brandon de Wilde

Shanghai
US 1935   77m   bw
Paramount (Walter Wanger)

A visiting American lady falls in love with a
half caste.
Romantic drama programmer.

w Gene Towne, Graham Baker, Lynn
Starling d James Flood ph James Van Trees

Loretta Young, Charles Boyer, Warner
Oland, Alison Skipworth, Fred Keating,
Charles Grapewin, Walter Kingsford

Shanghai Express*
US 1932   84m   bw
Paramount

A British officer and his old flame meet on a
train which is waylaid by Chinese bandits.
Superbly pictorial melodrama which set the
pattern for innumerable train movies to come,
though none matched its deft visual quality
and few sketched in their characters so neatly.
Plot and dialogue are silent style, but
refreshingly so.

w Jules Furthman d Josef Von Sternberg
ph Lee Garmes m W. Franke Harling
ad Hans Dreier

Marlene Dietrich, Clive Brook, Warner Oland,
Anna May Wong, Eugene Pallette, Lawrence

Grant, Louise Closser Hale, Gustav Von
Seyffertitz
'A limited number of characters, all
meticulously etched, highly atmospheric sets
and innumerable striking photographic
compositions.'—*Curtis Harrington, 1964*
AA: Lee Garmes
AAN: best picture; Josef Von Sternberg

The Shanghai Gesture*
US 1941 90m bw
Arnold Pressburger (Albert de Courville)

The proprietress of a Shanghai gambling
casino taunts her ex-husband by showing him
his daughter in a state of degradation; but he
proves that the girl is her daughter also.
An ancient theatrical shocker was completely
bowdlerized and chopped into nonsense for
the screen; but the director's hand showed in
the handling of the vast casino set.

w Josef Von Sternberg, Geza Herczeg, Karl
Vollmoeller, Jules Furthman, *play* John
Colton d *Josef Von Sternberg* ph Paul Ivano
m Richard Hageman *ad Boris Leven*

Ona Munson, Victor Mature, Walter Huston,
Gene Tierney, Albert Basserman, Phyllis
Brooks, Maria Ouspenskaya, Eric Blore, Ivan
Lebedeff, Mike Mazurki
'The effect of a descent into a maelstrom of
iniquity.'—*Curtis Harrington, 1962*
'In spite of all the changes necessitated by
the Hays Office, seldom have decadence and
sexual depravity been better suggested on the
screen.'—*Richard Roud, 1966*
'Hilariously, awesomely terrible.'—*New
Yorker, 1977*
AAN: Richard Hageman

The Sharkfighters
US 1956 72m Technicolor
Cinemascope
(UA) Formosa (Samuel Goldwyn Jnr)

To save the lives of fliers forced down into the
sea, navy scientists experiment with a shark
repellent.
Straightforward semi-documentary with
suspenseful action sequences.

w Lawrence Roman, John Robinson d Jerry
Hopper ph Lee Garmes m Jerome Moross

Victor Mature, Karen Steele, James Olson,
Claude Akins

Shark's Treasure*
US 1974 95m De Luxe
UA / Symbol (Cornel Wilde)

Treasure hunters seek buried gold in the
Caribbean where sharks abound.
Fairly thrilling action hokum.

wd Cornel Wilde ph Jack Atcheler, Al
Giddings
m Robert O. Ragland

Cornel Wilde, Yaphet Kotto, John Neilson,
David Canary, Cliff Osmond
'Wilde maintains his reputation for making
the most likeable bad movies around.'—*Tom
Milne*

She*
US 1935 89m bw
RKO (Merian C. Cooper)

Ancient papers lead a Cambridge professor
and his friends to the lost city where dwells a
queen who cannot die—until she falls in love.
The producers have the right spirit for this
Victorian fantasy, but tried too hard to
emulate the mood of their own *King Kong*,
and it was a mistake to transfer the setting
from Africa to the Arctic. One for
connoisseurs, though.

w Ruth Rose, Dudley Nichols, *novel* H. Rider
Haggard d Irving Pichel, Lansing G. Holden
ph J. Roy Hunt m Alfred Newman

Randolph Scott, Nigel Bruce, Helen Gahagan
'To an unrepentant Haggard fan it does
sometimes seem to catch the thrill as well as
the childishness of his invention.'—*Graham
Greene*

She
GB 1965 105m Technicolor
Hammerscope
ABP / Hammer (Aida Young)

Flat, uninventive and tedious remake which
reverts to Africa but does nothing else right; it
ignores the essential Cambridge prologue and
ignores all suggestions of fantasy.

w David T. Chantler d Robert Day ph Harry
Waxman m James Bernard

Peter Cushing, Ursula Andress, Christopher
Lee, John Richardson, Bernard Cribbins,
André Morell, Rosenda Monteros
'The stagey decor of Kor is in the art deco
style of Radio City Music Hall, and you keep
expecting the Rockettes to turn up . . . the
picture is deadly slow, and the lovebirds could
try anyone's patience, but camp like this is a
rarity.'—*New Yorker, 1976*

She Couldn't Say No
US 1952 89m bw
RKO (Robert Sparks)
GB title: *Beautiful But Dangerous*

An heiress returns to the town of her
childhood to distribute anonymous gifts to
those who had helped her.

Moderate Capraesque comedy which doesn't quite come off.

w D. D. Beauchamp, William Bowers, Richard Flournoy *d* Lloyd Bacon *ph* Harold J. Wild *m* Roy Webb

Jean Simmons, Robert Mitchum, Arthur Hunnicutt, Edgar Buchanan, Wallace Ford, Raymond Walburn

She Didn't Say No!
GB 1958   97m   Technicolor
ABP (Sergei Nolbandov)

A young Irish widow has five illegitimate children, each by a different father.
Coyly daring comedy full of stage Oirishisms and obvious jokes, a few of which work.

w T. J. Morison, Una Troy, from her novel We Are Seven *d* Cyril Frankel *ph* Gilbert Taylor *m* Tristam Cary

Eileen Herlie, Jack MacGowran, Perlita Neilson, Niall MacGinnis, Ian Bannen

She Done Him Wrong***
US 1933   68m   bw
Paramount (William Le Baron)

A lady saloon keeper of the Gay Nineties falls for the undercover cop who is after her.
As near undiluted Mae West as Hollywood ever came: fast, funny, melodramatic and pretty sexy; also a very atmospheric and well-made movie.

w Mae West, from her play Diamond Lil (with help on the scenario from Harry Thew, John Bright) *d* Lowell Sherman *ph* Charles Lang *songs* Ralph Rainger

Mae West, Cary Grant, Owen Moore, Gilbert Roland, Noah Beery, David Landau, Rafaela Ottiano, Rochelle Hudson, Dewey Robinson

AAN: best picture

She Gets Her Man*
US 1945   73m   bw
Universal (Warren Wilson)

A country girl in New York tracks down a blowgun murderer.
Disarming mystery farce which tries every slapstick situation known to gag writers, and gets away with it.

w Warren Wilson, Clyde Bruckman *d* Erle C. Kenton *ph* Jerry Ash

Joan Davis, William Gargan, Leon Errol, Milburn Stone, Russell Hicks

She Loves Me Not*
US 1934   85m   bw
Paramount (Benjamin Glazer)

A showgirl murder witness takes refuge in a men's college.
Larky musical farce later remade as *True to the Army* and *How to be Very Very Popular*; this first version is perhaps the most nearly amusing.

w Ben Glazer, *novel* Edward Hope, *play* Howard Lindsay *d* Elliott Nugent *ph* Charles Lang *songs* various

Bing Crosby, Miriam Hopkins, Kitty Carlisle, Edward Nugent, Lynne Overman, Henry Stephenson, Warren Hymer, George Barbier

AAN: song 'Love in Bloom'

She Married an Artist
US 1938   78m   bw

A wife becomes jealous of her husband's models. Very mild romantic comedy. John Boles, Francis Drake, Albert Dekker. Written by Avery Strakosch, Delmer Daves and Gladys Lehman; directed by Marion Gering; for Columbia.

She Married Her Boss
US 1935   90m   bw

A secretary marries her boss and finds herself taken for granted. Pleasant but rather thin romantic comedy with amiable stars. Claudette Colbert, Melvyn Douglas, Raymond Walburn, Edith Fellows, Jean Dixon, Katherine Alexander. Written by Sidney Buchman; directed by Gregory La Cava; for Columbia.

She Shall Have Murder
GB 1950   90m   bw

A law clerk helps to solve the murder of an elderly client. Old-fashioned light comedy whodunnit, the equivalent of reading a Crime Club thriller. Rosamund John, Derrick de Marney, Mary Jerrold, Felix Aylmer, Joyce Heron, Beatrice Varley. Written by Allan Mackinnon, from a novel by Delano Ames; directed by Daniel Birt; for Concanen / IFD.

She Wolf of London
US 1946   61m   bw

A girl thinks she must be the family werewolf. Risibly inept semi-horror melodrama with a highly implausible solution and poor production. June Lockhart, Don Porter, Sara Haden, Lloyd Corrigan, Dennis Hoey, Martin Kosleck. Written by George Bricker; directed by Jean Yarbrough; for Universal. (GB title: *The Curse of the Allenbys*.)

She Wore a Yellow Ribbon**
US 1949   103m   Technicolor
RKO / Argosy (John Ford, Meridan C.
  Cooper)

Problems of a cavalry officer about to retire.
Fragmentary but very enjoyable western with
all Ford ingredients served piping hot.

w Frank Nugent, Laurence Stallings, *story*
James Warner Bellah   *d John Ford*
ph Winton C. Hoch   m Richard Hageman

John Wayne, Joanne Dru, John Agar, Ben
Johnson, Harry Carey Jnr, Victor McLaglen,
Mildred Natwick, George O'Brien, Arthur
Shields

AA: Winton C. Hoch

She Wouldn't Say Yes
US 1945   87m   bw

A lady psychiatrist falls for the subject of an
experiment. Star comedy vehicle which falls
rather flat. Rosalind Russell, Lee Bowman,
Charles Winninger, Adele Jergens. Written by
Laslo Gorog, William Thiele, Virginia Van
Upp, John Jacoby and Sarett Tobias; directed
by Alexander Hall; for Columbia.

She Wrote the Book
US 1946   72m   bw

A lady professor imagines herself to be the
glamorous femme fatale heroine of a lurid
novel. Adventures of a female Walter Mitty;
one of the star's better comedies. Joan Davis,
Mischa Auer, Jack Oakie, Kirby Grant, John
Litel, Gloria Stuart, Thurston Hall. Written by
Warren Wilson and Oscar Brodney; directed
by Charles Lamont; for Universal.

The Sheep Has Five Legs*
France 1954   96m   bw
Raoul Ploquin
original title: *Le Mouton a Cinq Pattes*

A town seeking publicity tries to bring
together the five quintuplet grandsons of its
oldest inhabitant.
Mildly saucy star vehicle which was in fact
most notable for introducing Fernandel to an
international audience.

w Albert Valentin   *d* Henri Verneuil
ph Armand Thirard   *m* Georges Van Parys

Fernandel, Françoise Arnoul, Delmont,
Paulette Dubost, Louis de Funès

AAN: original story

The Sheepman*
US 1958   91m   Metrocolor
  Cinemascope
MGM (Edmund Grainger)

A tough sheep farmer determines to settle in a
cattle town.
Easy-going western with humorous moments.

w William Bowers, James Edward Grant
d George Marshall   *ph* Robert Bronner
m Jeff Alexander

Glenn Ford, Shirley Maclaine, Leslie Nielsen,
Mickey Shaughnessy, Edgar Buchanan

AAN: script

The Sheik*
US 1921   73m (24 fps)   bw   silent
Famous Players-Lasky / George Melford

An English heiress falls for a desert chieftain.
Archetypal romantic tosh which set the seal on
Valentino's superstardom.

w Monte M. Katterjohn, *novel* E. M. Hull
d George Melford   *ph* William Marshall

Rudolph Valentino, Agnes Ayres, Adolphe
Menjou, Walter Long, Lucien Littlefield
  'A photoplay of tempestuous love between a
madcap English beauty and a bronzed Arab
chief!'—*publicity*
† *Son of the Sheik*, released in 1926, was even
more popular.

The Sheik Steps Out
US 1937   68m   bw
Republic (Herman Schlom)

A modern sheik has a riotous time in the big
city.
Uninventive spoof of the Valentino myth.

w Adele Buffington, Gordon Kahn   *d* Irving
Pichel   *ph* Jack Marta   *md* Alberto Columbo

Ramon Novarro, Lola Lane, Gene Lockhart,
Kathleen Burke, Stanley Fields

Shenandoah**
US 1965   105m   Technicolor
Universal (Robert Arthur)

How the American Civil War affected the lives
of a Virginia family.
Surprisingly hard-centred and moving semi-
western for the family; excellent performances
and well-controlled mood.

w *James Lee Barrett   d Andrew V. McLaglen*
ph William Clothier   *m* Frank Skinner
md Joseph Gershenson

James Stewart, Rosemary Forsyth, Doug
McClure, Glenn Corbett, Katharine Ross,
Philip Alford

The Sheriff of Fractured Jaw
GB 1958   103m   Eastmancolor
  Cinemascope
TCF / Daniel M. Angel

A London gunsmith in the old west accidentally becomes a hero.

Tame, predictable comedy with a clear lack of invention.

w Arthur Dales *d* Raoul Walsh *ph* Otto Heller *m* Robert Farnon

Kenneth More, Jayne Mansfield, Robert Morley, Ronald Squire, David Horne, Henry Hull, Eynon Evans, Bruce Cabot, William Campbell

Sherlock Holmes

The innumerable Sherlock Holmes films are noted in *Filmgoer's Companion*, and in this volume the appropriate films are listed under their own titles including the modernized dozen made in the forties by Universal, starring Basil Rathbone as Holmes and Nigel Bruce as Watson. These followed on from Fox's two period pieces, THE HOUND OF THE BASKERVILLES and THE ADVENTURES OF SHERLOCK HOLMES (qv). The series started and ended somewhat lamely but several of the episodes remain highly enjoyable, for performances and dialogue rather than plot or pacing. All but the first were directed by Roy William Neill.

1942: SHERLOCK HOLMES AND THE VOICE OF TERROR (*d* John Rawlins *with* Reginald Denny, Thomas Gomez); SHERLOCK HOLMES AND THE SECRET WEAPON* (with Lionel Atwill as Moriarty) 1943: SHERLOCK HOLMES IN WASHINGTON* (*with* Henry Daniell, George Zucco); SHERLOCK HOLMES FACES DEATH** (*with* Halliwell Hobbes, Dennis Hoey) 1944: SHERLOCK HOLMES AND THE SPIDER WOMAN** (*with* Gale Sondergaard, Dennis Hoey); THE SCARLET CLAW** (*with* Gerald Hamer); THE PEARL OF DEATH** (*with* Miles Mander, Dennis Hoey, Rondo Hatton) 1945: THE HOUSE OF FEAR* (*with* Aubrey Mather, Dennis Hoey); THE WOMAN IN GREEN* (*with* Henry Daniell as Moriarty); PURSUIT TO ALGIERS (*with* Martin Kosleck) 1946: TERROR BY NIGHT* (*with* Alan Mowbray), DRESSED TO KILL (GB title: SHERLOCK HOLMES AND THE SECRET CODE; *with* Patricia Morison)

Sherlock Holmes*
US 1932 68m bw
Fox

Moriarty brings Chicago gangsters into London.

Interesting but rather unsatisfactory Holmes adventure.

w Bertram Milhauser *d* William K. Howard *ph* George Barnes

Clive Brook, Reginald Owen, Ernest Torrence, Miriam Jordan, Alan Mowbray, Herbert Mundin

Sherlock Junior**
US 1924 45m (24 fps) bw   silent
Metro / Buster Keaton (Joseph M. Schenck)

A film projectionist, unjustly accused of stealing a watch, has dreams of being a great detective.

Fast-moving, gag-filled comedy which ranks among its star's best.

w Clyde Bruckman, Jean Haves, Joseph Mitchell *d, ed* Buster Keaton *ph* Elgin Lessley, Bryon Houck

Buster Keaton, Kathryn McGuire, Ward Crane, Joseph Keaton

She's Working Her Way through College
US 1952   101m   Technicolor
Warner (William Jacobs)

A burlesque queen goes to college and brings out the beast in an English professor.

Limp and vulgar musical remake of a well-liked play and film; just about gets by as a lowbrow timekiller.

w Peter Milne, *play* The Male Animal by James Thurber, Elliott Nugent *d* Bruce Humberstone *ph* Wilfrid Cline *md* Ray Heindorf *ch* Le Roy Prinz *songs* Sammy Cahn, Vernon Duke

Virginia Mayo, Ronald Reagan, Don Defore, Gene Nelson, Phyllis Thaxter, Patrice Wymore

† Sequel 1953: *She's Back on Broadway.*

Shine on Harvest Moon*
US 1944   112m   bw (Technicolor sequence)
Warner (William Jacobs)

The life and times of vaudeville singer Nora Bayes.

Standard ragtime biopic, very adequately made.

w Sam Hellman, Richard Weil, Francis Swan, James Kern *d* David Butler *ph* Arthur Edeson *md* Heinz Roemheld

Ann Sheridan, Dennis Morgan, Jack Carson, Irene Manning, S. Z. Sakall, Marie Wilson, Robert Shayne

The Shining*
GB 1980 119m (general release; cut from
  première length of 146m)   colour
Warner / Stanley Kubrick

Under the influence of a desolate hotel where
murders had occurred, a caretaker goes
berserk and threatens his family.
Uninteresting ghost story sparked by
meticulous detail and sets but finally vitiated
by overlength and an absurdly over-the-top
star performance.

w Stanley Kubrick, Diane Johnson
novel Stephen King *d* Stanley Kubrick
ph John Alcott *m* Bela Bartok (on record)
pd Roy Walker

Jack Nicholson, Shelley Duvall, Danny Lloyd,
Barry Nelson, Scatman Crothers, Philip Stone
  'The truly amazing question is why a
director of Kubrick's stature would spend his
time and effort on a novel that he changes so
much it's barely recognizable, taking away
whatever originality it possessed while
emphasizing its banality. The answer
presumably is that Kubrick was looking for a
"commercial" property he could impose his
own vision on, and Warners, not having
learned its lesson with *Barry Lyndon*, was silly
enough to let him do it.'—*Variety*

The Shining Hour
US 1938 76m bw

A nightclub dancer marries a gentleman
farmer, but has trouble with his family.
Overcast melodrama with insufficient basic
interest in the characters. Joan Crawford,
Melvyn Douglas, Margaret Sullavan, Robert
Young, Fay Bainter, Allyn Joslyn, Hattie
McDaniel. Written by Ogden Nash and Jane
Murfin, from the play by Keith Winter;
directed by Frank Borzage; for MGM.

Shining Victory
US 1941 80m bw
Warner (Robert Lord)

A psychiatrist is torn between love and duty.
Adequate romantic programmer.

w Howard Koch, Ann Froelick, *play* Jupiter
Laughs by A. J. Cronin *d* Irving Rapper
ph James Wong Howe *m* Max Steiner

James Stephenson, Geraldine Fitzgerald,
Donald Crisp, Barbara O'Neil, Montagu
Love, Sig Rumann

Ship Ahoy
US 1942 95m bw
MGM (Jack Cummings)

On a trip to Puerto Rico, a tap dancer is
enlisted as a spy.
Tepid musi-comedy.

w Harry Clark *d* Eddie Buzzell *ph* Leonard
Smith *md* George Stoll *ad* Merrill Pye

Eleanor Powell, Red Skelton, Bert Lahr,
Virginia O'Brien, William Post Jnr, James
Cross

Ship of Fools*
US 1965 150m bw
Columbia / Stanley Kramer

In 1933 a German liner leaves Vera Cruz for
Bremerhaven with a mixed bag of passengers.
Ambitious, serious, quite fascinating slice-of-
life shipboard multi-melodrama. Capable
mounting, memorable performances and a
bravura finale erase memories of padding and
symbolic pretensions.

w Abby Mann, novel Katherine Anne Porter
d Stanley Kramer ph Ernest Laszlo m Ernest
Gold

Vivien Leigh, Simone Signoret, Oskar Werner,
Heinz Ruhmann, Jose Ferrer, Lee Marvin,
Elizabeth Ashley, Michael Dunn, George
Segal, Jose Greco, Charles Korvin, Alf
Kjellin, Werner Klemperer, John Wengraf,
Lilia Skala, Karen Verne
  'When you're not being hit over the head
with the symbolism, you're being punched in
the stomach by would-be inventive camera
work while the music score unremittingly fills
your nostrils with acrid exhalations.'—*John
Simon*

AA: Ernest Laszlo
AAN: best picture; Abby Mann; Simone
Signoret; Oskar Werner; Michael Dunn

The Ship That Died of Shame
GB 1955 91m bw
Ealing (Michael Relph, Basil Dearden)

The wartime crew of a motor gunboat buy the
vessel and go into postwar business as
smugglers.
Thin and rather obvious melodramatic fable.

w John Whiting, Michael Relph, Basil
Dearden, *novel* Nicholas Monsarrat
d Michael Relph, Basil Dearden ph Gordon
Dines m William Alwyn

Richard Attenborough, George Baker, Bill
Owen, Virginia McKenna, Roland Culver,
Bernard Lee, Ralph Truman, John Chandos
  'A sentimental fantasy tacked on to a
basically conventional thriller.'—*Penelope
Houston*

Shipbuilders
GB 1943 89m bw

A cavalcade of the problems of a Clydeside
tycoon in the thirties. Plodding propaganda
piece ending with masters and unions working
for Britain. Clive Brook, Morland Graham,

Finlay Currie, Maudie Edwards. Written by Gordon Wellesley, Stephen Potter and Reginald Pound; directed by John Baxter; for British National.

Shipmates Forever
US 1935   124m   bw

An admiral's son disappoints his dad by preferring song and dance to the navy. Very stretched light musical without any overpowering talents. Dick Powell, Ruby Keeler, Lewis Stone, Ross Alexander, Eddie Acuff, Dick Foran. Written by Delmer Daves; directed by Frank Borzage; for Warner.

Ships with Wings*
GB 1941   103m   bw
Ealing (S. C. Balcon)

Aircraft carriers prepare for World War II. Historically interesting, dramatically insubstantial flagwaver.

w Sergei Nolbandov, Patrick Kirwan, Austin Melford, Diana Morgan d Sergei Nolbandov ph Max Greene, Eric Cross, Roy Kellino m Geoffrey Wright

John Clements, Leslie Banks, Jane Baxter, Ann Todd, Basil Sydney, Edward Chapman, Hugh Williams, Frank Pettingell, Michael Wilding

Shipyard Sally
GB 1939   79m   bw

A barmaid persuades a shipyard ôwner to reopen. Sub-Ealing style comedy with music which manages to bring in management and man as well as waving a flag or two. Gracie Fields, Sydney Howard, Morton Selten, Norma Varden, Oliver Wakefield. Written by Karl Tunberg and Don Ettlinger; directed by Monty Banks; for TCF.

The Shiralee*
GB 1957   99m   bw
Ealing (Jack Rix)

An Australian swagman leaves his wife and takes to the road with his small daughter. Episodic character comedy-drama throwing a fairly sharp light on the Australian scene.

w Neil Paterson, Leslie Norman, novel D'Arcy Niland d Leslie Norman ph Paul Beeson m John Addison

Peter Finch, Dana Wilson, Elizabeth Sellars, George Rose, Russell Napier, Nial MacGinnis, Tessie O'Shea

Shock
US 1946   70m   bw
TCF

A girl in a hotel sees a murder committed, and an elaborate plan is concocted to silence her. Flat treatment ruins a good suspense situation.

w Eugene Ling d Alfred Werker ph Glen MacWilliams, Joe MacDonald m David Buttolph

Vincent Price, Lynn Bari, Frank Latimore, Annabel Shaw

'Extreme improbabilities and a general lack of finish.'—MFB

Shock Corridor
US 1963   101m   bw (colour sequence)
Leon Fromkess / Sam Firks (Samuel Fuller)

A journalist gets himself admitted to a mental asylum to solve the murder of an inmate. Sensational melodrama, a cinematic equivalent of the yellow press, and on that level quite lively.

wd Samuel Fuller ph Stanley Cortez m Paul Dunlap

Peter Breck, Constance Towers, Gene Evans, James Best, Hari Rhodes, Philip Ahn

Shock Treatment
US 1964   94m   bw
Warner (Aaron Rosenberg)

Murders are committed in a mental institution. Tasteless thriller, not even very arresting as a yarn.

w Sidney Boehm d Denis Sanders ph Sam Leavitt m Jerry Goldsmith

Lauren Bacall, Roddy MacDowall, Carol Lynley, Ossie Davis, Stuart Whitman, Douglass Dumbrille

The Shocking Miss Pilgrim
US 1946   85m   Technicolor
TCF (William Perlberg)

In 1894 Boston, a lady typist (stenographer) fights for women's rights.
Period comedy with music; not nearly as sharp as it thinks it is.

wd George Seaton ph Leon Shamroy ad James Basevi, Boris Leven songs George and Ira Gershwin

Betty Grable, Dick Haymes, Anne Revere, Allyn Joslyn, Gene Lockhart, Elizabeth Patterson, Arthur Shields, Elizabeth Risdon

The Shoes of the Fisherman**
US 1968   157m   Metrocolor   Panavision
MGM (George Englund)

After twenty years as a political prisoner, a Russian bishop becomes Pope.
Predigested but heavy-going picturization of a bestseller; big budget, big stars, big hopes. In

fact a commercial dud, with plenty of superficial interest but more dramatic contrivance than religious feeling.

w John Patrick, James Kennaway, *novel* Morris West *d Michael Anderson ph Erwin Hiller m* Alex North *ad Edward Carfagno, George W. Davis*

Anthony Quinn, David Janssen, Laurence Olivier, Oskar Werner, John Gielgud, Barbara Jefford, Leo McKern, Vittorio de Sica, Clive Revill, Paul Rogers
'A splendidly decorated curate's egg.'— *MFB*

AAN: Alex North

Shoeshine**
Italy 1946   90m   bw
Paolo W. Tamburella
original title: *Sciuscià*

In Nazi-occupied Rome two shoeshine boys become involved in black marketeering, with tragic consequences.
Not especially rewarding to watch now, this was a key film in the development of Italian neo-realism.

w Cesare Zavattini, Sergio Amidei, Adolfe Franci, C. G. Viola *d Vittorio de Sica ph* Anchise Brizzi, Elio Paccara

Franco Interlenghi, Rinaldo Smordoni
'It is filled in every scene with an awareness of the painful complexity of even simple evil.'—*James Agee*

AAN: script

Shoot the Pianist*
France 1960   80m   bw   Dyaliscope
Films de la Pléiade (Pierre Braunberger)
original title: *Tirez sur le Pianiste*

A bar-room piano player becomes involved with gangsters and his girl friend is killed.
Fair copy of an American *film noir*, not especially interesting except for its sharp observation.

w Marcel Moussy, François Truffaut, *novel* Down There by David Goodis *d François Truffaut ph* Raoul Coutard *m* Jean Constantin, Georges Deleru

Charles Aznavour, Nicole Berger, Marie Dubois, Michèle Mercier, Albert Rémy
'Pictorially it is magnificent, revealing Truffaut's brilliant control over his images; emotionally, it is all a little jejeune.'—*John Gillett, MFB*

The Shooting
US 1966   82m   De Luxe
Santa Clara (Jack Nicholson, Monte Hellman)

An ex-bounty hunter is trailed by a hired killer.
Simplistic semi-professional western which achieves some power despite poor technical quality and a deliberately obscure ending.

w Adrien Joyce *d* Monte Hellman *ph* Gregory Sandor *m* Richard Markowitz

Warren Oates, Will Hutchins, Jack Nicholson, Millie Perkins

Shooting Stars*
GB 1928   80m (24 fps)   bw   silent
British Instructional (H. Bruce Woolf)

The wife of a film star puts real bullets in a prop gun but her lover is killed by mistake.
Late silent drama with comedy touches: its main interest lies in its behind-the-scenes background and in the emergence of a new director.

w John Orton, Anthony Asquith *d* Anthony Asquith, A. V. Bramble

Annette Benson, Brian Aherne, Donald Calthrop, Wally Patch, Chili Bouchier

The Shootist**
US 1976   100m   Technicolor
Panavision
Paramount / Frankovich-Self

In 1901, a dying ex-gunfighter arrives in a small town to set his affairs in order.
Impressive semi-western melodrama, very well written and acted all round; the kind of solidly entertaining and thoughtful movie one imagined they didn't make any more.

w *Miles Hood Swarthout, Scott Hale, novel* Glendon Swarthout *d Don Siegel ph* Bruce Surtees *m* Elmer Bernstein

John Wayne, Lauren Bacall, James Stewart, Ron Howard, Bill McKinney, Richard Boone, John Carradine, Scatman Crothers, Harry Morgan, Hugh O'Brian, Sheree North
'Just when it seemed that the western was an endangered species, due for extinction because it had repeated itself too many times, Wayne and Siegel have managed to validate it once more.'—*Arthur Knight*
'Watching this film is like taking a tour of Hollywood legends.'—*Frank Rich*

Shootout
US 1971   94m   Technicolor
Universal (Hal B. Wallis)

After seven years in prison, a bank robber seeks out his betrayer.
Routine, flatly-handled revenge western.

w Marguerite Roberts, *novel* The Lone Cowboy by Will James *d* Henry Hathaway *ph* Earl Rath *m* Dave Grusin

Gregory Peck, Pat Quinn, Robert F. Lyons, Susan Tyrell, Jeff Corey, James Gregory, Rita Gam

Shootout at Medicine Bend
US 1957   87m   bw

Three ex-soldiers clean up a corrupt community. Entertaining western programmer. Randolph Scott, James Craig, Angie Dickinson, James Garner, Gordon Jones. Written by John Tucker Battle and D. D. Beauchamp; directed by Richard Bare; for Warner.

The Shop around the Corner**
US 1940   97m   bw
MGM (Ernst Lubitsch)

In a Budapest shop, the new floorwalker and a girl who dislikes him find they are pen pals. Pleasant period romantic comedy which holds no surprises but is presented with great style.

w *Samson Raphaelson,* play Nikolaus Laszlo d *Ernst Lubitsch* ph William Daniels m Werner Heymann

James Stewart, Margaret Sullavan, *Frank Morgan,* Joseph Schildkraut, Sara Haden, *Felix Bressart,* William Tracy
  'It's not pretentious but it's a beautiful job of picture-making, and the people who did it seem to have enjoyed doing it just as much as their audiences will enjoy seeing it.'—*James Shelley Hamilton*
  'An agreeably bittersweet example of light entertainment.'—*Charles Higham, 1972*
  'One of the most beautifully acted and paced romantic comedies ever made in this country.'—*New Yorker, 1978*
† Remade as *In The Good Old Summertime* (qv).

The Shop at Sly Corner
GB 1946   92m   bw
Pennant (George King)
US title: *Code of Scotland Yard*

An antique dealer who is also a fence kills a blackmailer in order to shield his daughter. Competent but stagey version of a West End success, giving full rein to a bravura star performance.

w *Katherine Strueby, play* Edward Percy d George King

Oscar Homolka, Muriel Pavlow, Derek Farr, Manning Whiley, Kenneth Griffith, Kathleen Harrison, Garry Marsh, Irene Handl

The Shop on Main Street*
Czechoslovakia 1965   128m   bw
Ceskoslovensky Film
original title: *Obchod na Korze*; aka: *The Shop on the High Street*

During the German invasion of Czechoslovakia, a well-meaning carpenter tries to shield an old Jewish lady, but his own rough treatment kills her.
A rather obvious sentimental fable, developed at too great length, but with bravura acting.

w Ladislav Grosman, Jan Kadar, Einar Klos d Jan Kadar, Einar Klos ph Vladimir Novotny m Zdenek Liska

Ida Kaminska, Jozef Kroner, Hana Slivkova, Martin Holly
  'Overlong, derivative, ploddingly directed.'—*John Simon*
AA: best foreign film
AAN: Ida Kaminska

Shopworn Angel*
US 1928   90m approx   bw   part-talkie
Paramount (Louis D. Lighton)

A showgirl meets a naïve young soldier off to war and forsakes her man about town.
Hard-boiled, soft-centred romantic drama remade as below and later as *That Kind of Woman* (qv).

w Howard Estabrook, Albert Shelby Le Vino, *play* Private Pettigrew's Girl by Dana Burnet d Richard Wallace ph Charles Lang

Nancy Carroll, Gary Cooper, Paul Lukas, Emmett King

Shopworn Angel*
US 1938   85m   bw
MGM (Joseph L. Mankiewicz)

Smooth, close remake of the above.

w Waldo Salt d H. C. Potter ph Joseph Ruttenberg m Edward Ward *montage* Slavko Vorkapitch

Margaret Sullavan, James Stewart, Walter Pidgeon, Hattie McDaniel, Sam Levene

Short Cut to Hell
US 1957   89m   bw   Vistavision
Paramount (A. C. Lyles)

A racketeer hires a gunman to commit a double murder, then doublecrosses him.
Rough and ready remake of *This Gun for Hire* (qv), less arresting than the original.

w Ted Berkeman, Raphael Blau, W. R. Burnett, *novel* A Gun for Sale by Graham Greene d James Cagney ph Haskell Boggs md Irvin Talbot

Robert Ivers, Georgeann Johnson, William Bishop, Murvyn Vye

A Shot in the Dark*
US 1964   101m   De Luxe   Panavision
UA / Mirisch / Geoffrey (Blake Edwards)

A woman is accused of shooting her lover; accident-prone Inspector Clouseau investigates.

Further adventures of the oafish, Tatiesque clodhopper from *The Pink Panther*; mildly funny for those in the mood for pratfalls.

w Blake Edwards, William Peter Blatty *d* Blake Edwards *ph* Christopher Challis *m* Henry Mancini *pd* Michael Stringer

Peter Sellers, Elke Sommer, George Sanders, Herbert Lom, Tracy Reed, Graham Stark

Shotgun
US 1954   81m   Technicolor print

A deputy marshal avenges the death of his boss. Rather violent western with a few unusual angles. Sterling Hayden, Zachary Scott, Yvonne de Carlo, Guy Prescott, Robert Wilke. Written by Clark E. Reynolds and Rory Calhoun; directed by Lesley Selander; for Allied Artists.

Should Ladies Behave?
US 1933   90m   bw

A young girl falls for her aunt's lover. Brittle comedy of manners which transferred poorly from Broadway with a star well over the top. Alice Brady, Lionel Barrymore, Conway Tearle, Katherine Alexander, Halliwell Hobbes, Mary Carlisle. Written by Sam and Bella Spewack, from the play *The Vinegar Tree* by Paul Osborn; directed by Harry Beaumont; for MGM.

Should Married Men Go Home?
US 1928   20m   bw   silent

Tribulations on the golf course end in a mud-slinging contest. Goodish star slapstick, but the preliminary domestic scene is the funniest. Laurel and Hardy, Edgar Kennedy. Written by Leo McCarey, James Parrott and H. M. Walker, directed by *d* James Parrott; for Hal Roach.

Shoulder Arms*
US 1918   24m (24 fps)   bw   silent
Charles Chaplin / First National

A soldier in the trenches dreams of winning the war single-handedly.
A comedy which meant a great deal at the time of its release but now provides precious little to laugh at.

wd Charles Chaplin *ph* Rollie Totheroh

Charles Chaplin, Edna Purviance, Sydney Chaplin, Henry Bergman, Albert Austin

The Shout*
GB 1978   87m   colour
Rank / Recorded Picture (Jeremy Thomas)

A man who may be mad claims that, like the old aborigine magicians, he can kill by shouting.
Curiously gripping but ultimately pointless fable, very well done to little purpose.

w Michael Austin, Jerzy Skolimovsky, *story* Robert Graves *d* Jerzy Skolimovsky *ph* Mike Molloy *m* Rupert Hine, Anthony Banks, Michael Rutherford

Alan Bates, Susannah York, John Hurt, Robert Stephens, Tim Curry

Shout at the Devil*
GB 1976   147m   Technicolor
  Panavision
Tonav (Michael Klinger)

In 1913 Zanzibar, a hard-drinking American and an old Etonian Englishman join forces to rout a brutal German commissioner who resents their poaching ivory in his territory. The main characters are respectively repellent, effete, and just plain nasty, but the action scenes are vivid and the production is mainly notable as an expensive old-fashioned British film made at a time when there were few British films of any kind.

w Wilbur Smith, Stanley Price, Alastair Reid, *novel* Wilbur Smith *d* Peter Hunt *ph* Mike Reed *m* Maurice Jarre

Lee Marvin, Roger Moore, Barbara Parkins, René Kolldehoff, Ian Holm, Karl Michael Vogler, Maurice Denham, Jean Kent, Robert Lang, Murray Melvin, George Coulouris
'Elephantine plod through the action highlights of a best seller.'—*Sight and Sound*

Show Business***
US 1944   92m   bw
RKO (Eddie Cantor)

The careers of four friends in vaudeville. Lively low-budget period musical which probably presents the best picture of what old-time vaudeville was really like; a lot of fun when the plot doesn't get in the way.

w Joseph Quillan, Dorothy Bennett *d* Edwin L. Marin *ph* Robert de Grasse, Vernon L. Walker *m* George Duning *md* Constantin Bakaleinikoff *ch* Nick Castle

Eddie Cantor, Joan Davis, George Murphy, Constance Moore, Don Douglas, Nancy Kelly
'Bits of archaic vaudeville which give off a moderately pleasant smell of peanuts and cigar smoke.'—*James Agee*

The Show Goes On
GB 1937   93m   bw
ABFD (Basil Dean)

A mill girl becomes a star singer with the help of a dying composer.

An attempt to turn Gracie Fields into a serious performer, this was not much enjoyed by her fans.

w Austin Melford, Anthony Kimmins, E. G. Valentine d Basil Dean

Gracie Fields, Owen Nares, Edward Rigby, John Stuart, Horace Hodges, Amy Veness, Cyril Rutchard

The Show-Off
US 1934 80m bw

A girl's blundering new husband alienates his in-laws and nearly wrecks his brother-in-law's career. Surefire satirical comedy-drama from a Broadway staple, this low-budget item gave MGM a new star. *Spencer Tracy*, Madge Evans, Clara Blandick, Henry Wadsworth, Grant Mitchell, Lois Wilson. Written by Herman Mankiewicz from the play by George Kelly; directed by Charles Riesner; for MGM. (NB: The play had been filmed twice in silent days by Paramount, and turned up again in 1946 as a Red Skelton vehicle.)

Show of Shows**
US 1929 128m Technicolor
Warner (Darryl F. Zanuck)

A big musical show put on by Warner contract artists.
Primitive early talkie, of vital historical interest but mostly photographed from a seat in the stalls.

w / m various d John G. Adolfi ph Barney McGill

Frank Fay, H. B. Warner, Monte Blue, Lupino Lane, Ben Turpin, Chester Morris, Ted Lewis and his band, Georges Carpentier, Patsy Ruth Miller, Beatrice Lillie, Winnie Lightner, Irene Bordoni, Myrna Loy, Douglas Fairbanks Jnr, John Barrymore, Betty Compson

'Colour photography of the crudest, most garish kind, the resulting impression being that a child of seven has been let loose with a shilling box of paints.'—*James Agate*

Show People
US 1928 80m at 24 fps bw silent

A naïve young actress makes it in Hollywood. Historically important comedy with cameo appearances by many stars of the time. Marion Davies, William Haines. Written by Wanda Tuchock, Agnes Christine Johnson and Lawrence Stallings; directed by *King Vidor*; for MGM.

Show Them No Mercy*
US 1935 76m bw
TCF (Raymond Griffith)
GB title: *Tainted Money*

Kidnappers are rounded up by G-men.
Lively crime thriller typical of its time.

w Kubec Glasmon, Henry Lehrman d George Marshall ph Bert Glennon m David Buttolph

Rochelle Hudson, Cesar Romero, Bruce Cabot, Edward Norris, Edward Brophy, Warren Hymer

'Direct, surely dramatic, inevitable and full of terror.'—*Otis Ferguson*

Showboat***
US 1936 110m bw
Universal (Carl Laemmle Jnr)

Lives and loves of the personnel on an old-time Mississippi showboat.
Great style and excellent performances mark this version, which still suffers from longueurs in the middle followed by the rapid passage of many years to provide a happy ending.

w Oscar Hammerstein II, from his book for the Broadway musical from Edna Ferber's novel d James Whale ph John Mescall m Jerome Kern ly Oscar Hammerstein II

Irene Dunne, Allan Jones, Helen Morgan, Paul Robeson, Charles Winninger, Hattie McDaniel, Donald Cook, Sammy White

'For three quarters of its length good entertainment: sentimental, literary, but oddly appealing.'—*Graham Greene*
† A primitive talkie version of *Showboat*, now lost, was made in 1929.

Showboat**
US 1951 108m Technicolor
MGM (Arthur Freed)

Vigorous remake with good ensemble dancing; otherwise inferior to the 1936 version.

w John Lee Mahin d George Sidney ph Charles Rosher md Conrad Salinger, Adolph Deutsch ch Robert Alton

Kathryn Grayson, *Howard Keel*, Ava Gardner, William Warfield, *Joe E. Brown*, Robert Sterling, Marge and Gower Champion, Agnes Moorehead

AAN: Charles Rosher; Conrad Salinger; Adolph Deutsch

The Showdown
US 1950 86m bw

A trail boss seeks revenge on his brother's killer. Routine western with a touch of mystery. Wild Bill Elliott, Marie Windsor, Walter Brennan, Henry Morgan, William

Ching, Rhys Williams. Written by Richard Wormser and Dan Gordon; directed by Darrell and Stuart McGowan; for Republic.

Showdown
US 1963   79m   Technicolor

Two wandering cowboys become involved with a criminal. Below-par western with little action and rather boring characters. Audie Murphy, Charles Drake, Harold J. Stone, Kathleen Crowley, Skip Homeier, L. Q. Jones, Strother Martin. Written by Bronson Howitzer; directed by R. G. Springsteen; for Universal.

Showdown
US 1972   99m   Technicolor   Todd-AO 35
Universal (George Seaton)

A sheriff finds that his old friend is leader of an outlaw gang.
Routine star western adequately done.

w Theodore Taylor d George Seaton
ph Ernest Laszlo m David Shire

Rock Hudson, Dean Martin, Susan Clark, Donald Moffat, Don McLiam

Showdown at Abilene
US 1956   80m   Technicolor

A shellshocked Civil War veteran, returning home to find his girl married, reluctantly takes a job as sheriff. Fairly lively western remade eleven years later as *Gunfight in Abilene*. Jock Mahoney, David Janssen, Martha Hyer, Lyle Bettger, Grant Williams. Written by Bernie Giler, from the novel *Gun Shy* by Clarence Upson Young; directed by Charles Haas; for Universal-International.

Showgirl in Hollywood
US 1930   80m   bw and Technicolor

A girl singer is spotted and trained for movie stardom. Naïve look behind the studio scenes, historically fascinating but dramatically dull. Alice White, Jack Mulhall, Blanche Sweet, Ford Sterling, John Miljan, Herman Bing. Written by Harvey Thew and James A. Starr, from the novel *Hollywood Girl* by J. P. McEvoy; directed by Mervyn LeRoy; for Warner.

The Shrike
US 1955   88m   bw
U-I (Aaron Rosenberg)

A brilliant theatre man has a nervous breakdown because his wife is a vindictive harpy.
Theatrical two-hander, aridly filmed, of little interest except to show that both stars are capable of sustained emotional acting.

w Ketti Frings, *play* Joseph Kramm d Jose Ferrer ph William Daniels m Frank Skinner *titles Saul Bass*

Jose Ferrer, June Allyson, Joy Page, Jacqueline de Wit, Kendall Clark
'The film is unvaryingly paced, the result, one feels, of a respectable but far from invigorating honesty of purpose.'—*MFB*

The Shuttered Room
GB 1967   110m   Technicolor
Warner / Troy-Schenck (Philip Hazelton)

Returning to her childhood home on an island off the New England coast, a girl and her husband are subjected to terror and violence. Stretched out suspenser which looks good and is carefully made but fails in its effort to combine the menace of teenage yobboes with that of the monster lurking upstairs.

w D. B. Ledrov, Nathaniel Tanchuck, *story* H. P. Lovecraft, August Derleth d David Greene ph Ken Hodges m Basil Kirchin

Gig Young, Carol Lynley, Flora Robson, Oliver Reed, William Devlin

Une Si Jolie Petite Plage*
France 1948   91m   bw
CICC (Emile Darbon)
aka: *Such a Pretty Little Beach*

A murderer returns to the small seaside town where he spent his childhood, befriends the maid at the hotel, and after a few days kills himself.
A melancholy anecdote which works both as a character study and pictorially.

w Jacques Sigurd d Yves Allégret ph Henri Alekan m Maurice Thiriet

Gérard Philipe, Jean Servais, *Madeleine Robinson*, Jane Marken, Carette
'Shows fine craftsmanship and is beautifully sensitive to place and atmosphere.'—*Gavin Lambert, MFB*

Side Street
US 1950   83m   bw
MGM (Sam Zimbalist)

A petty thief finds himself involved with big-time crooks.
Well-made but rather boring crime melodrama with an excellent car chase finale.

w Sidney Boehm d Anthony Mann
ph Joseph Ruttenberg m Lennie Hayton

Farley Granger, Cathy O'Donnell, James Craig, Paul Kelly, Jean Hagen, Edmon Ryan, Paul Harvey

Sidewalks of New York*
US 1931   73m   bw
MGM (Lawrence Weingarten)

The playboy owner of some tenement
apartments falls in love with the daughter of
one of the tenants.

Interesting rather than wholly successful early
sound comedy which marked the beginning of
Keaton's decline; he was not allowed full
control and the comedy scenes are thinly
spaced.

w George Landy, Paul Gerard Smith, Eric
Hatch, Robert E. Hopkins d Jules White,
Zion Myers ph Leonard Smith

Buster Keaton, Anita Page, Cliff Edwards,
Frank Rowan

The Siege of Pinchgut
GB 1959   104m   bw
Ealing (Eric Williams)
US title: *Four Desperate Men*

Escaped convicts take over a small island in
Sydney harbour.

Disappointingly obvious location melodrama
with routine excitements.

w Harry Watt, Jon Cleary d Harry Watt
ph Gordon Dines m Kenneth V. Jones

Aldo Ray, Heather Sears, Neil McCallum,
Victor Maddern, Carlo Justini

The Siege at Red River
US 1954   86m   Technicolor
TCF / Panoramic (Leonard Goldstein)

During the American Civil War a Confederate
agent behind northern lines defeats a
treacherous helper and escapes to the south.

Modest, generally watchable, and quite
forgettable western.

w Sidney Boehm d Rudolph Maté
ph Edward Cronjager m Lionel Newman

Van Johnson, Joanne Dru, Richard Boone,
Milburn Stone, Jeff Morrow, Craig Hill

The Siege of Sidney Street*
GB 1960   92m   bw   Dyaliscope
Midcentury (Robert S. Baker, Monty
   Berman)

An account of the anarchists who infiltrated
London in 1912.

Detailed but not dramatically absorbing
historical reconstruction with unsatisfactory
fictional trimmings.

w Jimmy Sangster, Alexander Baron d /
ph Robert S. Baker, Monty Berman
m Stanley Black

Peter Wyngarde, Donald Sinden, Nicole
Berger, Kieron Moore, Leonard Sachs, Tutte
Lemkow

The Siege of the Saxons
GB 1963   85m   Technicolor
Columbia / Ameran (Jud Kinberg)

When King Arthur is ill, the Saxons plot his
overthrow but are foiled by a handsome
outlaw.

Comic strip adventure with action highlights
borrowed from older and better films.

w John Kohn, Jud Kinberg d Nathan Juran
ph Wilkie Cooper, Jack Willis m Laurie
Johnson

Ronald Lewis, Janette Scott, Ronald Howard,
Mark Dignam, John Laurie, Richard Clarke,
Jerome Willis

The Sign of Four
GB 1932   75m   bw

Sherlock Holmes clears up a mystery including
a hidden fortune, a secret pact, revenge from
the east, and a pygmy who blows poison darts
through a pipe. Very acceptable version of the
famous story, previously filmed as a silent.
Arthur Wontner, Ian Hunter, Isla Bevan,
Miles Malleson, Herbert Lomas, Roy
Emerton. Written by W. P. Lipscomb, from
the novel by Sir Arthur Conan Doyle; directed
by Rowland V. Lee and Graham Cutts; for
ATP.

The Sign of the Cross***
US 1932   123m   bw
Paramount (Cecil B. de Mille)

In the days of Nero, a Roman officer is
converted to Christianity.

A heavily theatrical play becomes one of de
Mille's most impressive films, the genuine
horror of the arena mingling with the
debauched humour of the court. A wartime
prologue added in 1943 prolongs the film
without improving it.

w Waldemar Young, Sidney Buchman, *play*
Wilson Barrett d Cecil B. de Mille ph Karl
Struss m Rudolph Kopp

Fredric March, Elissa Landi, *Charles
Laughton, Claudette Colbert*, Ian Keith, Harry
Beresford, Arthur Hohl, Nat Pendleton

'A beautiful film to watch . . . a triumph of
popular art.'—*Charles Higham, 1972*

'However contemptible one may find de
Mille's moralizing, it is impossible not to be
impressed by *The Sign of the Cross*.'—*John
Baxter, 1968*

'De Mille's bang-them-on-the-head-with-
wild-orgies-and-imperilled-virginity style is at
its ripest.'—*New Yorker, 1976*

'Preposterous, but the laughter dies on the
lips.'—*NFT, 1974*

'A picture which will proudly lead all the

entertainment the screen has ever seen.'—
publicity

'This slice of "history" has it all: Laughton's
implicitly gay Nero fiddling away while an
impressive miniature set burns, Colbert
bathing up to her nipples in asses' milk,
Christians and other unfortunates thrown to a
fearsome menagerie, much suggestive slinking
about in Mitchell Leisen's costumes, much
general debauchery teetering between the
sadistic and the erotic. Not for people with
scruples.'—*Geoff Brown, Time Out, 1980*

AAN: Karl Struss

The Sign of the Pagan
US 1954   92m   Technicolor
Cinemascope
U-I (Albert J. Cohen)

Attila the Hun is defeated by the Romans.
Historic horse opera, rather cheaply done.

w Oscar Brodney, Barre Lyndon *d* Douglas
Sirk *ph* Russell Metty *m* Frank Skinner,
Hans Salter

Jeff Chandler, Jack Palance, Rita Gam,
Ludmilla Tcherina, Jeff Morrow, George
Dolenz, Eduard Franz, Alexander Scourby

The Sign of the Ram
US 1948   84m   bw
Columbia (Irving Cummings Jnr)

A selfish invalid interferes in her family's
affairs.
Stultifying melodrama in the wake of *Guest in
the House*, devised for the unfortunate Miss
Peters who was crippled after an accident.
Poor production values don't help.

w Charles Bennett *d* John Sturges
ph Burnett Guffey *m* Hans Salter

Susan Peters, Alexander Knox, Peggy Ann
Garner, May Whitty

Signpost to Murder
US 1967   74m   bw   Panavision
MGM / Martin (Lawrence Weingarten)

A convicted murderer escapes after ten years
and a lonely wife promises to help him.
Tricksy mystery set in a never-never English
village.

w Sally Benson, *play* Monte Doyle *d* George
Englund *ph* Paul C. Vogel *m* Lyn Murray

Joanne Woodward, Stuart Whitman, Edward
Mulhare, Alan Napier, Murray Matheson

The Silence*
Sweden 1963   96m   bw
Svensk Filmindustri
original title: *Tystnaden*

Of two women in a large hotel in a foreign city
where the military are dominant, one
masturbates while the other sleeps with a
barman.
Bergman may know what this was all about,
but it's a certainty that no one else did: so
everyone thought it must be very clever and
went to see it. Superficially, as usual, it is
careful and fascinating.

wd Ingmar Bergman ph Sven Nykvist
m from Bach

Ingrid Thulin, Gunnel Lindblom

'There is not enough forward thrust, not
enough momentum to unite the specific points,
the complementary but discrete images. The
pearls are there, but the string is too weak to
hold them.'—*John Simon*

Le Silence est d'Or*
France 1947   99m   bw
Pathé / RKO Radio

In 1906 a comedian becomes a film producer
and as a result falls into an affair with a young
girl.
Somehow not an important film, but quite a
delightful one, especially for its local colour
and for the combination of Clair and Chevalier
up to their old tricks.

wd René Clair ph Armand Thirard
m Georges Van Parys

Maurice Chevalier, François Périer, Marcelle
Derrien

The Silencers*
US 1966   103m   Technicolor
Columbia / Irving Allen (Jim Schmerer)

Adventures of a sexy secret agent.
Or, James Bond sent up rotten. Plenty of fun
along the way, with in-jokes and characters
like Lovey Kravezit, but the plot could have
done with more attention, and the sequels
(*Murderers Row, The Ambushers, Wrecking
Crew*) were uncontrolled disaster areas.

w Oscar Saul, *novel* Donald Hamilton *d* Phil
Karlson *ph* Burnett Guffey *m* Elmer
Bernstein

Dean Martin, Stella Stevens, Victor Buono,
Daliah Lavi, Cyd Charisse, Robert Webber,
James Gregory, Nancy Kovack

The Silent Battle
GB 1939   84m   bw

A French agent battles revolutionaries in the
Balkans. Unconvincing spy stuff with an
uncertain tone. Rex Harrison, Valerie
Hobson, John Loder, Muriel Aked, John
Salew, George Devine. Written by Wolfgang

Wilhelm and Rodney Ackland, from the novel by Jean Bommart; directed by Herbert Mason; for Anthony Havelock-Allan / Pinebrook.

Silent Dust*
GB 1947   82m   bw
ABP / Independent Sovereign

A baronet builds a memorial to his son who has apparently been killed in action, but the son turns up and proves to be an absolute bounder.
Effective stage melodrama, quite neatly filmed.

w Michael Pertwee, *play* The Paragon by Roland and Michael Pertwee *d* Lance Comfort *ph* Wilkie Cooper *m* Georges Auric
Sally Gray, Derek Farr, Stephen Murray, Nigel Patrick, Seymour Hicks

The Silent Enemy
GB 1958   112m   bw
Romulus (Bertram Ostrer)

The World War II exploits of a naval frogman in the Mediterranean.
Stereotyped naval underwater adventures, adequately presented.

wd William Fairchild *ph* Egil Woxholt, Otto Heller *m* William Alwyn
Laurence Harvey, John Clements, Michael Craig, Dawn Addams, Sidney James, Alec McCowen, Nigel Stock

The Silent Flute
US 1978   95m   colour
Volare (Richard St Johns)

In a martial arts tournament, a hero is chosen to challenge the wizard Zetan.
Curiously mystical adventure allegory with an unhelpful title. Not too bad for those in the mood.

w Stirling Silliphant, Stanley Mann *d* Richard Moore *ph* Ronnie Taylor *m* Bruce Smeaton
Jeff Cooper, David Carradine, Roddy McDowall, Christopher Lee, Eli Wallach

Silent Movie*
US 1976   87m   De Luxe
TCF / Crossbow (Michael Hertzberg)

An alcoholic producer gets the idea that a silent movie would be a great novelty, and tries to get stars to take part.
Fairly lively spoof with the talents concerned in variable form. The shortage of laughter made it a hit in the seventies, but at no time does it approach the Keaton or Laurel and Hardy level.

w Mel Brooks, Ron Clark, Rudy de Luca, Barry Levinson *d* Mel Brooks *ph* Paul Lohmann *m* John Morris
Mel Brooks, Marty Feldman, Dom De Luise, Bernardette Peters, Sid Caesar, Harold Gould, Fritz Feld, Harry Ritz, Henny Youngman *guest stars* Anne Bancroft, Paul Newman, Burt Reynolds, James Caan, Liza Minnelli, Marcel Marceau

The Silent Partner
US 1978   105m   colour
Carolco (Garth H. Drabinsky)

A bank teller foils an attempted raid and steals the money himself.
A suspense thriller of a familiar kind; it might have been entertaining but elects instead to be unpleasant.

w Curtis Hanson, *novel* Think of a Number by Anders Bodelson *d* Daryl Duke *ph* Stephen Katz *m* Oscar Peterson
Christopher Plummer, Elliott Gould, Susannah York, Celine Lomez, Michael Kirby

The Silent Passenger
GB 1935   75m   bw

Lord Peter Wimsey clears a man of a murder charge. Not an unappealing presentation of Dorothy Sayers' famous detective, though he is presented as too much the silly ass and the story is weak. Peter Haddon, John Loder, Mary Newland, Austin Trevor, Donald Wolfit, Leslie Perrins, Robb Wilton. Written by Basil Mason; directed by Reginald Denham; for Phoenix.

Silent Running*
US 1971   90m   Technicolor
Universal / Michel Gruskoff / Douglas Trumbull

Members of a space station crew in 2001 are space gardening to replenish nuclear-devasted earth.
Sombre futuristic fantasy, well made but slow and muddled in development.

w Deric Washburn, Mike Cimino, Steve Bocho *d* Douglas Trumbull *ph* Charles F. Wheeler *m* Peter Schickele
Bruce Dern, Cliff Potts, Ron Rifkin, Jesse Vint

The Silent Witness
US 1932   73m   bw

A man confesses to murder in order to protect his son. Solid courtroom stuff of its day, built for a new star who never quite made it. Lionel Atwill, Helen Mack, Greta Nissen, Bramwell

Fletcher, Alan Mowbray. From the play by Jack de Leon and Jack Celestin; directed by Marcel Varnel; for Fox.

Silk Stockings*
US 1957 116m Metrocolor
Cinemascope
MGM (Arthur Freed)

A Russian composer in Paris agrees to write music for a Hollywood film; a lady commissar is sent to get him back.
Musical rewrite of *Ninotchka* via a Broadway show; good moments but generally very stretched.

w Leonard Gershe, Leonard Spiegelgass, *play* George S. Kaufman, Leueen McGrath, Abe Burrows, *original play* Melchior Lengyel d Rouben Mamoulian ph Robert Bronner m / ly Cole Porter md André Previn

Fred Astaire, Cyd Charisse, Peter Lorre, Janis Paige, George Tobias, Jules Munshin, Joseph Buloff

The Silken Affair
GB 1956 96m bw
Dragon (Fred Feldkamp)

An accountant decides to live it up, and finds himself on trial for manipulating the firm's books.
Unsatisfactory mix of comedy and fantasy, with a dim plot and virtually no comic ideas.

w Robert Lewis Taylor d Roy Kellino ph Gilbert Taylor m Peggy Stuart

David Niven, Genevieve Page, Wilfrid Hyde White, Ronald Squire, Beatrice Straight, Howard Marion Crawford, Dorothy Alison

Silken Skin*
France 1964 118m bw
Films du Carrosse / SEDIF
original title: *La Peau Douce*

A middle-aged married man leaves his wife for an attractive young girl, but the latter leaves him and his wife shoots him.
Carefully balanced mixture of comedy and melodrama which rings almost every possible change on the theme of adultery and does so with wit.

w François Truffaut, Jean-Louis Richard d François Truffaut ph Raoul Coutard m Georges Delerue

Jean Desailly, Françoise Dorléac, Nelly Benedetti

Silver Bears
GB 1977 113m Technicolor
EMI / Raleigh (Martin Schute)

A Las Vegas money man invests money in various European outlets and makes a killing. Extraordinarily complex financial jape which tries the patience of all but financiers.

w Peter Stone, *novel* Paul Erdman d Ivan Passer ph Anthony Richmond m Claude Bolling

Michael Caine, Louis Jourdan, Cybill Shepherd, Stephane Audran, David Warner, Tom Smothers, Martin Balsam, Charles Gray

Silver Blaze
GB 1937 70m bw

Sherlock Holmes clears a racehorse of having killed its trainer. Not the best of the Holmes series, but this is a very satisfying Holmes.
Arthur Wontner, Ian Fleming, Lyn Harding, Judy Gunn, Lawrence Grossmith, Arthur Macrae. Written by Arthur Macrae and H. Fowler Mear, from the story by Sir Arthur Conan Doyle; directed by Thomas Bentley; for Twickenham. (US title: *Murder at the Baskervilles*.)

The Silver Chalice
US 1955 142m Warnercolor
Cinemascope
Warner (Victor Saville)

Adventures of a slave freed by Luke the apostle to fashion a chalice to hold the cup used at the Last Supper.
Po-faced biblical hokum, slower and deadlier than most, with howlingly bad casting and direction. On reflection, interesting things are being attempted with limbo set design, but in this sea of boredom the attempt only raises an eyebrow.

w Lesser Samuels, *novel* Thomas B. Costain d Victor Saville ph William V. Skall m Franz Waxman pd *Rolf Gerard*

Paul Newman, Pier Angeli, Jack Palance, Virginia Mayo, Walter Hampden, Joseph Wiseman, Alexander Scourby, Lorne Greene, Michael Pate, E. G. Marshall

AAN: William V. Skall; Franz Waxman

Silver City
US 1951 90m Technicolor

A mining assayer helps a farmer and his daughter protect the ore found on their land. Standard western programmer with plenty of action. Yvonne de Carlo, Edmond O'Brien, Barry Fitzgerald, Richard Arlen, Gladys George, Laura Elliot, Edgar Buchanan, John Dierkes. Written by Frank Gruber, from a story by Luke Short; directed by Byron Haskin; for Nat Holt / Paramount. (GB title: *High Vermilion*.)

The Silver Darlings
GB 1947   84m   bw

Hebridean islanders take to herring fishing as a last chance to avoid emigration. Uneventful island mood piece which lacks the poetic quality which might have made it memorable.
Clifford Evans, Helen Shingler, Carl Bernard, Norman Shelley, Simon Lack, Hugh Griffith. Written by Clarence Elder, from the novel by Neil Gunn; directed by Clarence Elder and Clifford Evans; for Holyrood.

Silver Dollar*
US 1932   84m   bw
Warner

A poor farmer goes to Colorado for the gold rush, strikes it rich, and learns that money doesn't bring happiness.
Packed biopic of one H. A. W. Tabor, an excellent star vehicle.

w Carl Erickson, Harvey Thew   *d* Alfred E. Green   *ph* James Van Trees

Edward G. Robinson, Bebe Daniels, Aline MacMahon, Jobyna Howland, Robert Warwick, Russell Simpson

Silver Dream Racer
GB 1980   111m   Eastmancolor
   Panavision
Rank / David Wickes (Rene Dupont)

A garage mechanic becomes a racing motorcyclist and is killed at the peak of success.
One wonders who can have thought there was any box office appeal in this cliché-ridden, derivative, flashily made update of the Road to Ruin.

wd David Wickes   *ph* Paul Beeson   *m* David Essex

David Essex, Beau Bridges, Cristina Raines, Harry H. Corbett, Lee Montague, Clark Peters.

'Watching this grotesque hotch-potch of implausible characters being shunted through improbable situations is uncannily akin to being assaulted by a non-stop stream of TV commercials.'—*Tom Milne, MFB*

The Silver Fleet*
GB 1943   87m   bw
GFD / Archers (Michael Powell, Emeric
   Pressburger, Ralph Richardson)

In occupied Holland, a shipping magnate destroys his new U-boat and himself and his Nazi mentors with it.
Slow-starting, rather stilted melodrama which when it gets into its stride provides good acting and gripping propaganda.

wd Vernon Sewell, Gordon Wellesley

Ralph Richardson, Esmond Knight, Googie Withers, Beresford Egan, Frederick Burtwell, Kathleen Byron

Silver Lode
US 1954   80m   Technicolor print

A respected citizen of Silver Lode proves that the marshal who rides into town on his wedding day to accuse him of murder is a civilian bent on revenge. Broody little western melodrama, not half bad. John Payne, Dan Duryea, Lizabeth Scott, Dolores Moran, Emile Meyer, Robert Warwick. Written by Karen de Wolf; directed by Allan Dwan; for Benedict Bogeaus / RKO.

Silver Queen
US 1942   80m   bw
UA / Harry Sherman

A chivalrous western gambler rescues a girl from the wiles of a villain.
Standard romantic melodrama mainly set in saloons.

w Bernard Schubert, Cecile Kramer   *d* Lloyd Bacon   *ph* Russell Harlan   *m* Victor Young

George Brent, Priscilla Lane, Bruce Cabot, Lynne Overman, Eugene Pallette, Janet Beecher, Guinn Williams, Roy Barcroft

AAN: Victor Young

Silver River
US 1948   110m   bw
Warner (Owen Crump)

A ruthless gambler becomes powerful but loses everything because of his character defects.
Meandering western drama with a few good highlights dissipated by long chunks of character building and a rehash of the David and Bathsheba story.

w Stephen Longstreet, Harriet Frank Jnr   *d* Raoul Walsh   *ph* Sid Hickox   *m* Max Steiner

Errol Flynn, Ann Sheridan, Thomas Mitchell, Bruce Bennett, Tom D'Andrea, Barton Maclane, Monte Blue, Alan Bridge

Silver Streak*
US 1976   113m   De Luxe
TCF / Martin Ransohoff, Frank Yablans

On a trans-continental train, a young publisher discovers a murder and is at the mercy of the culprits.
Rather like an update of a Bob Hope comedy-thriller with a whiff of sex, this amiable spoof

goes on too long, brings in a second comic too
late, and ends with fashionable but irrelevant
violence.

w Colin Higgins *d* Arthur Hiller *ph* David
M. Walsh *m* Henry Mancini *pd* Alfred
Sweeney

Gene Wilder, Jill Clayburgh, Richard Pryor,
Patrick McGoohan, Ned Beatty, Clifton
James, Ray Walston, Richard Kiel

'Nineteen-seventies performers are trapped
in this fake thirties mystery comedy, which is
so inept you can't even get angry.'—*New
Yorker*

Simba
GB 1955 99m Eastmancolor
GFD / Group Film (Peter de Sarigny)

An English farmer in Kenya fights the Mau
Mau.
Savagely topical melodrama which tends to
cheapen a tragic situation.

w John Baines *d* Brian Desmond Hurst
ph Geoffrey Unsworth *m* Francis Chagrin

Dirk Bogarde, Donald Sinden, Virginia
McKenna, Basil Sydney, Marie Ney, Joseph
Tomelty, Earl Cameron, Orlando Martins

Simon*
US 1980 97m Technicolor
Warner / Orion (Louis A. Stroller, Martin
Bregman)

Corrupt scientists brainwash a psychology
professor into thinking he's from another
planet.
Solemn comic fantasy which doesn't seem to
make much of a point and only superficially
entertains, but is well made and well acted.

wd Marshall Brickman *ph* Adam Holender
m Stanley Silverman *pd* Stuart Wurtzel

Alan Arkin, Madeleine Kahn, Austin
Pendleton, Judy Graubert, William Finley,
Fred Gwynne

Simon and Laura*
GB 1955 91m Technicolor Vistavision
GFD / Group Films (Teddy Baird)

The actors who play husband and wife in a TV
series are married in reality and hate each
other, a fact that shows in the live Christmas
episode.
Adequate film of a reasonably sophisticated
West End comedy; good lines and
performances.

w Peter Blackmore, *play* Alan Melville
d Muriel Box *ph* Ernest Steward
m Benjamin Frankel

Peter Finch, Kay Kendall, Ian Carmichael,
Alan Wheatley, Richard Wattis, Muriel
Pavlow, Maurice Denham, Hubert Gregg

The Sin of Madelon Claudet
US 1931 74m bw
MGM
GB title: *The Lullaby*

A mother is separated from her illegitimate
baby.
Sob stuff for a rising star: hilarious now.

w Charles MacArthur, *play* Eward Knoblock
d Edgar Selwyn

Helen Hayes, Robert Young, Neil Hamilton,
Lewis Stone, Marie Prevost, Cliff Edwards,
Jean Hersholt, Karen Morley

AA: Helen Hayes

Sin Town
US 1942 74m bw
Universal (George Waggner)

Two confidence tricksters arrive in a western
town and solve a murder.
Members of the studio repertory company in a
passable western discarded by Marlene
Dietrich.

w Gerald Geraghty, W. Scott Darling,
Richard Brooks *d* Ray Enright *m* Hans
Salter

Constance Bennett, Broderick Crawford, Leo
Carrillo, Anne Gwynne, Patric Knowles,
Andy Devine, Ward Bond, Ralf Harolde

Sinbad and the Eye of the Tiger
GB 1977 113m Metrocolor
Columbia / Andor (Charles H. Schneer, Ray
Harryhausen)

Sinbad frees a city from a wicked woman's
spell.
Lumpish sequel to a sequel: even the animated
monsters raise a yawn this time.

w Beverly Cross *d* Sam Wanamaker *ph* Ted
Moore *m* Roy Budd *sp* Ray Harryhausen

Patrick Wayne, Taryn Power, Jane Seymour,
Margaret Whiting, Patrick Troughton

Sinbad the Sailor
US 1947 117m Technicolor
RKO (Stephen Ames)

Sinbad sets off on his eighth voyage to find the
lost treasure of Alexander.
Well-staged but humourless Arabian Nights
swashbuckler.

w John Twist *d* Richard Wallace *ph* George
Barnes *m* Roy Webb

Douglas Fairbanks Jnr, Walter Slezak, Maureen O'Hara, Anthony Quinn, George Tobias, Jane Greer, Mike Mazurki, Sheldon Leonard

Since You Went Away***
US 1944   172m   bw
David O. Selznick

When hubby is away at the war, his wife and family adopt stiff upper lips.

Elaborate flagwaving investigation of the well-heeled American home front in World War II, with everyone brimming with goodwill and not a dry eye in the place. Absolutely superbly done, if it must be done at all, and a symposium of Hollywood values and techniques of the time.

w David O. Selznick, book Margaret Buell Wilder d John Cromwell ph Stanley Cortez, Lee Garmes m Max Steiner pd William L. Pereira

Claudette Colbert, Joseph Cotten, Jennifer Jones, Shirley Temple, Agnes Moorehead, Monty Woolley, Lionel Barrymore, Guy Madison, Robert Walker, Hattie McDaniel, Craig Stevens, Keenan Wynn, Albert Basserman, Nazimova, Lloyd Corrigan

'A deft, valid blend of showmanship, humour, and yard-wide Americanism.'—*James Agee*

'The whole litany of that middle-class synthetic emotionalism, meticulously annotated over a decade by tough and sentimental experts, has been procured for us.'—*Richard Winnington*

'A rather large dose of choking sentiment.'—*Bosley Crowther*

'It is not an average US reality. It is an average US dream.'—*Time*

AA: Max Steiner
AAN: best picture; Stanley Cortez; Claudette Colbert; Jennifer Jones; Monty Woolley

Sincerely Yours
US 1955   115m   Warnercolor
Warner (Henry Blanke)

A concert pianist goes deaf and retires to his penthouse, but with the help of binoculars lipreads the humble folk below. Helping them anonymously gives him courage to have an operation.

Absurd updating for a modern non-star of a creaky old George Arliss vehicle *The Man Who Played God*.

w Irving Wallace d Gordon Douglas ph William H. Clothier m adviser George Liberace

Liberace, Joanne Dru, Dorothy Malone, Alex Nicol, William Demarest

Sinful Davey
GB 1968   95m   Eastmancolor
Panavision
UA / Mirisch / Webb (William N. Graf)

In 1821 a young Scotsman determines to become a criminal like his father, but falls in love.

Thin imitation of *Tom Jones*, highly implausible but played with some zest:

w James R. Webb, based on the autobiography of David Haggart d John Huston ph Ted Scaife, Freddie Young m Ken Thorne pd Stephen Grimes

John Hurt, Pamela Franklin, Nigel Davenport, Ronald Fraser, Robert Morley, Maxine Audley, Noel Purcell

Sing As We Go***
GB 1934   80m   bw
ATP (Basil Dean)

An unemployed millgirl gets various holiday jobs in Blackpool.

A splendid, pawky star vehicle which is also the best picture we have of industrial Lancashire in the thirties. Great fun.

w J. B. Priestley, Gordon Wellesley d Basil Dean

Gracie Fields, John Loder, *Frank Pettingell*, Dorothy Hyson, Stanley Holloway

'We have an industrial north that is bigger than Gracie Fields running around a Blackpool fun fair.'—*C. A. Lejeune*

Sing Baby Sing*
US 1936   87m   bw
TCF (Darryl F. Zanuck)

A drunken Shakespearian actor sets his sights on a night club singer.

Reasonably hilarious take-off on the John Barrymore-Elaine Barrie affair, with several Fox contractees fooling to the top of their bent with the help of good musical numbers.

w Milton Sperling, Jack Yellen, Harry Tugend d Sidney Lanfield ph Peverell Marley songs various md Louis Silvers

Alice Faye, Adolphe Menjou, Gregory Ratoff, Patsy Kelly, Ted Healy, The Ritz Brothers, Montagu Love, Dixie Dunbar

AAN: song 'When Did You Leave Heaven?' (*ly* Walter Bullock, *m* Richard Whiting)

Sing, Boy, Sing
US 1958   91m   bw   Cinemascope
TCF (Henry Ephron)

A rock and roll star comes close to a nervous breakdown because of an unscrupulous manager and a revivalist grandfather.
Fairly painless vehicle for a singing star.

w Claude Binyon d Henry Ephron
ph William C. Mellor m Lionel Newman

Tommy Sands, Edmond O'Brien, John McIntire, Lili Gentle, Nick Adams, Josephine Hutchinson

Sing You Sinners**
US 1938 88m bw
Paramount (Wesley Ruggles)

The adventures of a happy-go-lucky family and their racehorse.
Cheerful family musical with amiable cast and good tunes.

w Claude Binyon d Wesley Ruggles ph Karl Struss md Boris Morros songs James V. Monaco, Johnny Burke

Bing Crosby, Donald O'Connor, Fred MacMurray, Elizabeth Patterson, Ellen Drew, John Gallaudet

The Singer Not the Song
GB 1960 132m colour Cinemascope
Rank (Roy Baker)

In an isolated Mexican town a priest defies an outlaw who oddly respects him.
Lengthy character drama with little action or humour but a great deal of moody introspection and a suggestion of homosexuality.

w Nigel Balchin, novel Audrey Erskine Lindop d Roy Baker ph Otto Heller
m Philip Green

John Mills, Dirk Bogarde, Mylene Demongeot, John Bentley, Laurence Naismith, Eric Pohlmann

'A rewarding film, as startling as a muffled scream from the subconscious.'—Peter John Dyer

The Singing Fool**
US 1928 110m bw
Warner

A successful singer goes on the skids when his small son dies.
Early talkie musical, a sensation because of its star's personality, but a pretty maudlin piece of drama.

w C. Graham Baker, play Leslie S. Barrows d Lloyd Bacon ph Byron Haskin songs Lew Brown, Ray Henderson, B. G. De Sylva

Al Jolson, Davey Lee, Betty Bronson, Josephine Dunn, Arthur Housman

'Obvious and tedious as the climax is, when the black-faced comedian stands before the camera and sings "Sonny Boy" you know the man is greater, somehow, than the situation, the story or the movie.'—Pare Lorentz

Singin' in the Rain****
US 1952 102m Technicolor
MGM (Arthur Freed)

When talkies are invented, the reputation of one female star shrivels while another grows.
Brilliant comic musical, the best picture by far of Hollywood in transition, with the catchiest tunes, the liveliest choreography, the most engaging performances and the most hilarious jokes of any musical.

w Adolph Green, Betty Comden d / ch Gene Kelly, Stanley Donen ph Harold Rosson
m Nacio Herb Brown md Lennie Hayton
ly Arthur Freed

Gene Kelly, Donald O'Connor, Debbie Reynolds, Millard Mitchell, Jean Hagen, Rita Moreno, Cyd Charisse, Douglas Fowley

'Perhaps the most enjoyable of all movie musicals.'—New Yorker, 1975

AAN: Lennie Hayton; Jean Hagen

The Singing Kid
US 1936 83m bw
Warner (Robert Lord)

A cocky night club singer takes a talented juvenile under his wing.
Routine star vehicle most notable for a string of standards sung by him right after the credits.

w Warren Duff, Pat C. Flick d William Keighley ph George Barnes md Leo F. Forbstein songs E. Y. Harburg, Harold Arlen

Al Jolson, Sybil Jason, Allen Jenkins, Lyle Talbot, Edward Everett Horton, Beverly Roberts, Claire Dodd

The Singing Marine
US 1937 107m bw

A marine singer wins a talent contest and success goes to his head. Light musical of very little interest save two dance sequences by Busby Berkeley. Dick Powell, Doris Weston, Jane Darwell, Hugh Herbert, Lee Dixon, Dick Wesson, Allen Jenkins, Jane Wyman, Larry Adler. Written by Delmer Daves; directed by Ray Enright; for Warner.

The Singing Nun
US 1966 98m Metrocolor Panavision
MGM (Jon Beck)

Adventures of a nun who takes her music to
the outside world.
Icky musical drama based on a true character.

w Sally Benson, John Furia d Henry Koster
ph Milton Krasner md Harry Sukman
songs Soeur Sourire

Debbie Reynolds, Greer Garson, Ricardo
Montalban, Agnes Moorehead, Chad Everett,
Katharine Ross, Ed Sullivan, Juanita Moore

AAN: Harry Sukman

Sink the Bismarck**•**
GB 1960   97m   bw   Cinemascope
TCF / John Brabourne

In 1941, Britain's director of naval operations
arranges the trapping and sinking of
Germany's greatest battleship.
Tight little personal drama which would have
been better on a standard screen, as its ships
are plainly models and much of the footage
stretched-out newsreel. Nevertheless, a good
example of the stiff-upper-lip school.

w Edmund H. North d Lewis Gilbert
ph Christopher Challis m Clifton Parker
md Muir Mathieson

Kenneth More, Dana Wynter, Karel Stepanek,
Carl Mohner, Laurence Naismith, Geoffrey
Keen, Michael Hordern, Maurice Denham,
Esmond Knight

Sinner's Holiday
US 1930   55m   bw
Warner

A fairground barker loves the daughter of a
penny arcade owner, but is framed by her
brother.
Early talkie quickie using Bradway talent, and
introducing James Cagney to the screen. It still
has vigour if little else.

w Harvey Thew, George Rosener,
play Penny Arcade by Marie Baumer d John
G. Adolfi ph Ira Morgan

Grant Withers, Evalyn Knapp, James Cagney,
Joan Blondell, Lucille La Verne, Warren
Hymer, Noel Madison

The Sins of Rachel Cade
US 1960   123m   Technicolor
Warner (Henry Blanke)

An American missionary nurse in the Belgian
Congo falls in love with a crashed flier and has
a baby.
Romantic melodrama which starts like *The
Nun's Story* and ends like Peg's Paper;
competent on its level.

w Edward Anhalt, *novel* Charles Mercer
d Gordon Douglas ph Peverell Marley
m Max Steiner

Angie Dickinson, Roger Moore, Peter Finch,
Errol John, Woody Strode, Juano Hernandez,
Frederick O'Neal, Mary Wickes

Sir Henry at Rawlinson's End
GB 1980   71m   bw

A grossly eccentric English aristocrat lays a
family ghost. Weirdly isolated, semi-
professional comedy with elements of
everything from Ealing to Monty Python.
Trevor Howard, Patrick Magee, Denise
Coffey, J. G. Devlin. Written by Vivien
Stanshall and Steve Roberts from Stanshall's
radio play; directed by Steve Roberts; for
Charisma.

Siren of Atlantis see L'Atlantide

Siren of Bagdad
US 1953   72m   Technicolor

A travelling magician helps reinstate a
deposed sultan. Flippant oriental extravaganza
aiming at the Hope–Crosby style but falling
sadly short of it. Paul Henreid, Patricia
Medina, Hans Conried, Charlie Lung. Written
by Robert E. Kent; directed by Richard
Quine; for Same Katzman / Columbia.

Sirocco
US 1951   98m   bw
Columbia / Santana (Robert Lord)

In 1925 Damascus, an American runs guns for
the rebels.
Tedious romantic drama in the *Casablanca*
vein but with none of the magic.

w A. I. Bezzerides, Hans Jacoby, *novel* Coup
de Grâce by Joseph Kessel d Curtis
Bernhardt ph Burnett Guffey m George
Antheil

Humphrey Bogart, Marta Toren, Lee J. Cobb,
Everett Sloane, Gerald Mohr, Zero Mostel,
Onslow Stevens

Sister Kenny*
US 1946   116m   bw
RKO

The career of a nurse who instigated treatment
for polio.
Standard, well-done biopic.

w Dudley Nichols, Alexander Knox, Mary
McCarthy d Dudley Nichols ph George
Barnes m Alexander Tansman

Rosalind Russell, Alexander Knox, Dean
Jagger, Philip Merivale, Beulah Bondi,
Dorothy Peterson
† From the autobiography of Australian nurse
Mary Kenny: *And They Shall Walk*.

AAN: Rosalind Russell

The Sisters*
US 1938 98m bw
Warner (Hal B. Wallis)

The marriages of three sisters from a small Montana town.

Well-made potboiler for women; it even brings in the San Francisco earthquake, and the star teaming is piquant to say the least.

w Milton Krims, *novel* Myron Brinig
d Anatole Litvak ph Tony Gaudio m Max Steiner

Bette Davis, Errol Flynn, Anita Louise, Ian Hunter, Donald Crisp, Beulah Bondi, Jane Bryan, Alan Hale, Dick Foran, Henry Travers, Patric Knowles, Lee Patrick, Harry Davenport

Sitting Pretty*
US 1933 85m bw
Paramount (Charles R. Rogers)

Two songwriters strike it rich in Hollywood.

Cheerful comedy musical, interesting for its backgrounds.

w Jack McGowan, S. J. Perelman, Lou Breslow d Harry Joe Brown ph Milton Krasner *songs* Mack Gordon, Harry Revel

Jack Oakie, Jack Haley, Ginger Rogers, Thelma Todd, Gregory Ratoff, Lew Cody, Harry Revel, Mack Gordon

Sitting Pretty***
US 1948 84m bw
TCF (Samuel G. Engel)

A young couple acquire a most unusual male baby sitter, a self-styled genius who sets the neighbourhood on its ears by writing a novel about it.

Out of the blue, a very funny comedy which entrenched Clifton Webb as one of Hollywood's great characters and led to two sequels, *Mr Belvedere Goes to College* and *Mr Belvedere Rings the Bell* (qv).

w F. Hugh Herbert, *novel* Belvedere by Gwen Davenport d Walter Lang ph Norbert Brodine m Alfred Newman

Clifton Webb, Robert Young, Maureen O'Hara, *Richard Haydn*, Louise Allbritton, Ed Begley, Randy Stuart, Larry Olsen

AAN: Clifton Webb

Sitting Target
GB 1972 92m Metrocolor
MGM (Barry Kulick)

A violent killer escapes from jail and seeks revenge on those who 'shopped' him.

Rough, tough action thriller; passes the time for hardened addicts.

w Alexander Jacobs, *novel* Lawrence Henderson d Douglas Hickox ph Ted Scaife m Stanley Myers pd Jonathan Barry

Oliver Reed, Jill St John, Edward Woodward, Frank Finlay, Ian McShane, Freddie Jones, Robert Beatty

Situation Hopeless But Not Serious
US 1965 97m bw
Paramount / Castle (Gottfried Reinhardt)

In 1944, two American fliers are captured by a friendly, lonely mild-mannered German, who keeps them in his cellar and hasn't the heart to tell them when the war is over . . .

Flat little comedy which leaves a talented cast no room for manoeuvre.

w Silvia Reinhardt, *novel* The Hiding Place by Robert Shaw d Gottfried Reinhardt ph Kurt Hasse m Harold Byrne

Alec Guinness, Robert Redford, Mike Connors, Anita Hoefer

Six Black Horses
US 1962 80m Eastmancolor

A girl hires a gunslinger and a horse thief to escort her across Indian territory. Rather glum western programmer. Audie Murphy, Dan Duryea, Joan O'Brien, George Wallace, Roy Barcroft. Written by Burt Kennedy; directed by Harry Keller; for Universal-International.

Six Bridges to Cross
US 1955 96m bw
U-I (Aaron Rosenberg)

The criminal career of a young hoodlum in Boston in the thirties.

Public Enemy reprise with a sentimental veneer, smooth but uninteresting.

w Sidney Boehm, *novel* They Stole Two and a Half Million Dollars and Got Away with It by Joseph F. Dineen d Joseph Pevney ph William Daniels m Joseph Gershenson

Tony Curtis, George Nader, Julie Adams, Jay C. Flippen, Sal Mineo, Jan Merlin

Six Day Bike Rider
US 1934 69m bw
Warner (Sam Bischoff)

One of life's failures impresses his girl by entering a cycling contest.

One of the star's stronger comedy vehicles.

w Earl Baldwin d Lloyd Bacon ph Warren Lynch

Joe E. Brown, Maxine Doyle, Frank McHugh, Gordon Westcott

Six Hours to Live
US 1932   78m   bw

A scientist revives a diplomat for six hours so
that his murderer can be traced. Fanciful
hokum set at a Geneva peace conference.
Warner Baxter, John Boles, Miriam Jordan,
Irene Ware, George Marion. From the story
by Gordon Morris and Morton Barteaux;
directed by William Dieterle; for Fox.

Six Lessons from Madame La Zonga
US 1941   62m   bw

A Cuban nightclub proprietress causes mix-
ups on a pleasure boat. Witless vehicle for two
stars popular at another studio in the *Mexican
Spitfire* series. Lupe Velez, Leon Errol,
William Frawley, Helen Parrish, Charles
Lang, Eddie Quillan, Quinn Williams. Written
by Stanley Rubin, Marion Orth, Larry Rhine
and Ben Chapman; directed by John Rawlins;
for Universal.

Six of a Kind*
US 1934   69m   bw
Paramount

Comic adventures of six people driving across
America.
Minor comedy which doesn't come off as a
whole but adequately displays the talents of its
stars.
w Walter de Leon, Harry Ruskin *d* Leo
McCarey *ph* Henry Sharp *m* Ralph Rainger

Charles Ruggles, Mary Boland, W. C. Fields,
Alison Skipworth, George Burns, Gracie
Allen
  'Another pleasing film . . . it reminds the
Englishman of *Three Men in a Boat.*'—*E. V.
Lucas, Punch*

633 Squadron*
GB 1964   94m   Technicolor   Panavision
UA / Mirisch (Cecil F. Ford)

In 1944 Mosquito aircraft try to collapse a cliff
overhanging a munitions factory in a
Norwegian fjord.
Standard war heroics with enough noise and
disorder to keep most audiences hypnotized.
w James Clavell, Howard Koch, *novel*
Frederick E. Smith *d* Walter Grauman
ph Ted Scaife, John Wilcox *m* Ron Goodwin

Cliff Robertson, George Chakiris, Maria
Perschy, Harry Andrews, Donald Houston,
Michael Goodliffe

Sixty Glorious Years**
GB 1938   95m   Technicolor
Imperator (Herbert Wilcox)
US title: *Queen of Destiny*

Scenes from the life of Queen Victoria.
A stately pageant apparently composed of
material which couldn't be fitted into the
previous year's black-and-white success
Victoria the Great. Fascinating, though the
camerawork is not very nimble.

w Robert Vansittart, Miles Malleson, Charles
de Grandcourt *d* Herbert Wilcox
ph Frederick A. Young

Anna Neagle, Anton Walbrook, C. Aubrey
Smith, Walter Rilla, Charles Carson, Felix
Aylmer, Lewis Casson

† The two films were edited together in 1943
to make a new selection called *Queen Victoria*,
and in the process the original negatives were
accidentally destroyed, so that both films now
have to be printed from unattractive dupes.

Skateboard
US 1977   95m   Technicolor

A small-time theatrical agent in trouble builds
up a professional skateboard team.
Unsatisfactory exploitation item which devotes
more time to its plot than to its sport. Allen
Garfield, Kathleen Lloyd, Leif Garrett,
Richard Van Der Wyk. Written by Richard A.
Wolf, George Gage; directed by George
Gage; for Universal.

The Ski Raiders
US 1972   90m   Technicolor   Panavision
Warner (Edward L. Rissien)
aka: *Snow Job*

An alpine ski instructor devises a scheme to
rob a bank.
Very medium caper thriller with a
breathtaking opening sequence.
w Ken Kolb, Jeffrey Bloom *d* George
Englund *ph* Gabor Pogany, Willy Bogner
m Jacques Loussier

Jean Claude Killy, Cliff Potts, Vittorio de
Sica, Daniele Gaubert

Skidoo
US 1968   98m   Technicolor   Panavision
Paramount / Sigma (Otto Preminger)

Active and reformed gangsters get involved
with hippies and preach universal love.
Abysmal mishmash with top talent abused;
clearly intended as satirical farce, but in fact
one of the most woebegone movies ever made.

w Doran William Cannon *d* Otto Preminger
ph Leon Shamroy *m* Harry Nilsson

Jackie Gleason, Carol Channing, Groucho
Marx, Frankie Avalon, Fred Clark, Michael
Constantine, Frank Gorshin, John Philip Law,

Peter Lawford, Burgess Meredith, George
Raft, Cesar Romero, Mickey Rooney
'Unspeakable.'—*Michael Billington,
Illustrated London News*

The Skin Game
GB 1932 85m bw
BIP (John Maxwell)

A landowner hates his self-made neighbour.
Stiff picturization of a well-known stage play.

w Alfred Hitchcock, Alma Reville, *play* John
Galsworthy d Alfred Hitchcock ph Jack Cox

Edmund Gwenn, John Longden, Jill Esmond,
C. V. France, Helen Haye, Phyllis Konstam,
Frank Lawton

The Skin Game*
US 1971 102m Technicolor
Panavision
Warner / Cherokee (Harry Keller)

A white and a black con man have near
escapes in many a western town.
Amusing comedy western with good pace and
a few shafts of wit.

w Peter Stone, Richard Alan Simmons d Paul
Bogart ph Fred Koenekamp m David Shire

James Garner, Lou Gossett, Susan Clark,
Brenda Sykes, Ed Asner, Andrew Duggan,
Henry Jones, Neva Patterson

Skippy*
US 1931 88m bw
Paramount

The young son of a local health inspector
makes friends in the slums.
Standard, blameless family entertainment.

w Joseph L. Mankiewicz, Norman McLeod,
comic strip Percy Crosby d Norman Taurog
ph Karl Struss

Jackie Cooper, Robert Coogan, Mitzi Green,
Jackie Searl, Willard Robertson

AA: Norman Taurog
AAN: best picture; script; Jackie Cooper

Skirts Ahoy
US 1952 105m Technicolor
MGM (Joe Pasternak)

Three girls join the navy and get their men.
Musical recruiting poster, quite devoid of
interest.

w Isobel Lennart d Sidney Lanfield
ph William Mellor m Harry Warren ly Ralph
Blane ch Nick Castle

Esther Williams, Vivian Blaine, Joan Evans,
Barry Sullivan, Keefe Brasselle, Dean Miller,
Debbie Reynolds, Bobby Van, Billy Eckstine

The Skull
GB 1965 83m Techniscope
Paramount / Amicus (Milton Subotsky)

The skull of the Marquis de Sade haunts two
antiquarians.
Clodhopping horror with very visible wires.

w Milton Subotsky, *story* Robert Bloch
d Freddie Francis ph John Wilcox
m Elisabeth Lutyens

Peter Cushing, Christopher Lee, Patrick
Wymark, Jill Bennett, Nigel Green, Michael
Gough, George Coulouris

Skullduggery
US 1969 105m Technicolor
Panavision
Universal (Saul David)

Archaeologists and adventurers clash on a trek
in New Guinea.
Fashionable oddball adventure about the
discovery of an unspoiled primitive tribe; the
elements don't jell.

w Nelson Gidding d Gordon Douglas
ph Robert Moreno m Oliver Nelson

Burt Reynolds, Susan Clark, Roger C.
Carmel, Paul Hubschmid, Chips Rafferty,
Alexander Knox, Edward Fox, Wilfrid Hyde
White, Rhys Williams

Sky Devils
US 1931 89m bw
Caddo / Howard Hughes

Two draft dodgers find themselves heroes of
the Army Air Corps in World War I France.
Little-seen but unremarkable adventure
comedy in the Flagg and Quirt tradition.

w Joseph Moncure March, Edward
Sutherland d Edward Sutherland ph Tony
Guadio md Alfred Newman ch Busby
Berkeley

Spencer Tracy, William Boyd, Ann Dvorak,
George Cooper, Billy Bevan, Forrester
Harvey

Sky Full of Moon
US 1952 73m bw
MGM (Sidney Franklin Jnr)

A rodeo cowboy wins money and a showgirl in
Las Vegas.
Ambling comedy with an agreeable air of
innocence.

wd Norman Foster ph Ray June m Paul
Sawtell

Carleton Carpenter, Jan Sterling, Keenan
Wynn

Sky Riders*
US 1976 91m De Luxe Todd-AO 35
TCF (Terry Morse Jnr)

In Athens, the family of an American
businessman is kidnapped by terrorists and
rescued by hang gliders led by a soldier of
fortune.
Old-fashioned actioner with new-fashioned
political concern.

w Jack de Witt, Stanley Mann, Gary Michael
White, Hall T. Sprague, Bill McGaw
d Douglas Hickox ph Ousama Rawi m Lalo
Schifrin

James Coburn, Susannah York, Robert Culp,
Charles Aznavour, Werner Pochath, Kenneth
Griffith, Harry Andrews

Sky West and Crooked
GB 1965 102m Eastmancolor
Rank / John Mills (Jack Hanbury)
US title: *Gypsy Girl*

A mentally retarded girl falls in love with a
gypsy.
Eccentric rural melodrama with echoes of
Cold Comfort Farm and *Les Jeux Interdits*.
Interesting, but scarcely a runaway success.

w Mary Hayley Bell, John Prebble d John
Mills ph Arthur Ibbetson m Malcolm Arnold

Hayley Mills, Ian McShane, Laurence
Naismith, *Geoffrey Bayldon*, Annette Crosbie,
Norman Bird
'Behind the overwhelming feyness of it all
lurk assumptions which in cold blood look
almost sinister.'—*MFB*

Skyjacked*
US 1972 101m Metrocolor Panavision
MGM / Walter Seltzer

A Boeing 707 on a flight from Los Angeles to
Minneapolis is forced by a mad bomber to fly
to Moscow.
Shamelessly hackneyed aeroplane adventure
with quite enjoyable elements.

w Stanley R. Greenberg, *novel* Hijacked by
David Harper d John Guillermin ph Harry
Stradling Jnr m Perry Botkin Jnr

Charlton Heston, Yvette Mimieux, James
Brolin, Claude Akins, Jeanne Crain, Rosey
Grier, Walter Pidgeon, Leslie Uggams

Skylark
US 1941 94m bw
Paramount (Mark Sandrich)

A wife decides on her fifth anniversary that
she is tired of being secondary to her
husband's career, and needs a fling.

Formula matrimonial comedy; plenty of talent
but no sparkle.

w Z. Myers, *play* Samson Raphaelson d Mark
Sandrich ph Charles Lang m Victor Young

Claudette Colbert, Ray Milland, Brian
Aherne, Binnie Barnes, Walter Abel, Grant
Mitchell, Mona Barrie, Ernest Cossart

The Sky's the Limit
GB 1937 79m bw

A sacked aircraft designer suddenly finds
himself in demand. Amiable star musical. Jack
Buchanan, Mara Loseff, William Kendall,
David Hutcheson, H. F. Maltby, Athene
Seyler, Sara Allgood. Written by Jack
Buchanan and Douglas Furber; directed by
Lee Garmes and Jack Buchanan; for Jack
Buchanan.

The Sky's the Limit*
US 1943 89m bw
RKO (David Hempstead)

A flier on leave meets and falls for a news
photographer.
Thin musical with incidental compensations.

w Frank Fenton, Lynn Root d Edward H.
Griffith ph Russell Metty m Leigh Harline
md Leo F. Forbstein

Fred Astaire, Joan Leslie, *Robert Benchley*,
Robert Ryan, Elizabeth Patterson

AAN: Leigh Harline; song 'My Shining Hour'
(m Harold Arlen, ly Johnny Mercer)

Skyscraper Souls
US 1932 100m bw

In an office building, several personal
dilemmas interlock. Portmanteau drama in the
Grand Hotel mould, and quite comparable.
Warren William, Maureen O'Sullivan, Verree
Teasdale, Gregory, Ratoff, Jean Hersholt,
Norman Foster, Anita Page, George Barbier,
Wallace Ford, Hedda Hopper. Written by C.
G. Sullivan and Elmer Harris, from the book
by Faith Baldwin; directed by Edgar Selwyn;
for MGM.

Slander
US 1956 81m bw
MGM (Armand Deutsch)

Revelations about a film star in a scandal
magazine lead to blackmail and murder.
Unlikely melodrama, routinely assembled,
based on the Confidential Magazine lawsuits.

w Jerome Weidman d Roy Rowland
ph Harold J. Marzerati m Jeff Alexander

Van Johnson, Ann Blyth, Steve Cochran,
Marjorie Rambeau, Harold J. Stone

Slap Shot*
US 1977 124m Technicolor
Universal / Robert J. Wunsch, Stephen Friedman

The wily player-coach of a fading ice hockey team finds ways, including dirty play, of keeping it going.
Violent, foul-mouthed comedy which works as it goes but leaves a bad taste in the mouth.

w Nancy Dowd d George Roy Hill ph Victor Kemper, Wallace Worsley md Elmer Bernstein

Paul Newman, Michael Ontkean, Lindsay Crouse, Jennifer Warren, Strother Martin

'Fast, noisy, profane . . . gets you laughing, all right, but you don't necessarily enjoy yourself.'—*New Yorker*

'Both indulgent and moralizing, the self-consciously racy script ends up looking merely opportunistic.'—*Time Out*

Slattery's Hurricane
US 1949 87m bw
TCF (William Perlberg)

Loves of a storm-spotting pilot with the US Weather Bureau in Florida.
Forgettable programmer with good storm sequences.

w Herman Wouk, Richard Murphy, *novel* Herman Wouk d André de Toth ph Charles G. Clarke m Cyril Mockridge

Richard Widmark, Linda Darnell, Veronica Lake, John Russell, Gary Merrill, Walter Kingsford

Slaughter
US 1972 90m De Luxe Todd-AO 35
AIP / Slaughter United (Monroe Sachson)

A black Vietnam veteran hunts down the underworld syndicate which killed his mother and father.
Hectic crime yarn with a pitilessly violent hero and not enough style to relieve the unappetizing monotony.

w Mark Hanna, Don Williams d Jack Starrett ph Rosanio Solano m Luchi de Jesus

Jim Brown, Rip Torn, Don Gordon, Cameron Mitchell

'The cast perform their trigger-happy tasks with all the passionate conviction of a team of well-oiled robots.'—*Jan Dawson*

Slaughter on Tenth Avenue
US 1957 103m bw
U-I (Albert Zugsmith)

The New York DA's office investigates union murders on the docks.
Uninteresting imitation of *On the Waterfront*.

w Lawrence Roman, *novel* The Man Who Rocked the Boat by William J. Keating, Richard Carter d Arnold Laven ph Fred Jackman m Richard Rodgers

Richard Egan, Jan Sterling, Dan Duryea, Julie Adams, Walter Matthau, Charles McGraw, Sam Levene, Mickey Shaughnessy, Harry Bellaver

Slaughter Trail
US 1952 78m Cinecolor

Three outlaws cause trouble between white man and Indian. Rough-hewn western strung together by verses of a ballad. Brian Donlevy, Gig Young, Virginia Grey, Andy Devine, Robert Hutton. Written by Sid Kuller; directed by Irving Allen; for RKO.

Slaughterhouse Five*
US 1972 104m Technicolor
Universal / Vanadas (Paul Monash)

A suburban optometrist has nightmare space / time fantasies involving Nazi POW camps and a strange futuristic planet.
Interesting but infuriating anti-war fantasy for intellectuals.

w Stephen Geller, *novel* Kurt Vonnegut Jnr d George Roy Hill ph Miroslav Ondricek m J. S. Bach, performed by Glen Gould pd Henry Bumstead

Michael Sacks, Ron Leibman, Eugène Roche, Sharon Gans, Valerie Perrine, Sorrell Booke, John Dehner

'A lot of good makings in this picture; but very little is made.'—*Stanley Kauffmann*

Slaughter's Big Rip-Off
US 1973 93m Movielab Todd-AO 35
AIP (Monroe Sachson)

Still on the run from gangsters who have killed his best friend, Slaughter violently disposes of a number of adversaries.
More routine black violence, a rampage of senseless brutality against sunny Los Angeles backgrounds.

w Charles Johnson d Gordon Douglas ph Charles Wheeler m Jim Brown, Fred Wesley

Jim Brown, Ed MacMahon, Brock Peters, Don Stroud

Slave Girl
US 1947 79m Technicolor
U-I (Michael Fessier, Ernest Pagano)

In the early 1800s, a diplomat is sent to Tripoli to ransom sailors held by the power-mad potentate.
Criticism would be superfluous: when the film was finished it was obviously so bad that executives ordered the addition of a talking camel and other *Hellzapoppin*-type jokes in order to turn it into a comedy.

w Michael Fessier, Ernest Pagano *d* Charles Lamont *ph* George Robinson, W. Howard Greene *m* Milton Rosen

George Brent, Yvonne de Carlo, Albert Dekker, Broderick Crawford, Lois Collier, Andy Devine, Carl Esmond, Arthur Treacher

Slave Girls
GB 1966 95m Technicolor
Cinemascope
Hammer (Aida Young)
US title: *Prehistoric Women*

A hunter seeking white rhinoceros finds himself in a lost valley ruled by a tribe of women.
Feebly preposterous comic strip farrago without the saving grace of humour.

wd Michael Carreras *ph* Michael Reed *m* Carlo Mantelli

Michael Latimer, Martine Beswick, Edina Ronay

Slaves
US 1969 110m Eastmancolor
Slaves Company / Theatre Guild / Walter Reade (Philip Langner)
In 1850 Kentucky a slave stands up for his rights and plans escape.
Well-meaning but muddled and old-fashioned melodrama, hardly well enough done to raise comparison with *Gone with the Wind*.

wd Herbert J. Biberman *ph* Joseph Brun *m* Bobby Scott

Stephen Boyd, Ossie Davis, Dionne Warwick, Shepperd Strudwick, Nancy Coleman, David Huddleston, Gale Sondergaard

Sleep My Love*
US 1948 96m bw
(UA) Mary Pickford (Charles 'Buddy' Rogers)
A man plots to murder his wife, but is foiled.
Thin suspenser, rather splendidly photographed in the expressionist manner.

w St Clair McKelway, *novel* Leo Rosten *d* Douglas Sirk *ph* Joseph Valentine *m* Rudy Schrager

Claudette Colbert, Don Ameche, Robert Cummings, Rita Johnson, George Coulouris, Hazel Brooks, Keye Luke

Sleeper*
US 1973 88m De Luxe
UA / Charles Rollins, Charles Joffe (Jack Greenberg)
A health food store owner is deep frozen after an operation and wakes two hundred years in the future.
Predictable star vehicle with an agreeable string of bright gags.

w Woody Allen, Marshall Brickman *d* Woody Allen *ph* David M. Walsh *m* Woody Allen *pd* Dale Hennesy

Woody Allen, Diane Keaton, John Beck, Mary Gregory
'Verbal and visual gags rain down like hailstones.'—*Michael Billington, Illustrated London News*

The Sleeping Beauty*
US 1959 75m Technirama 70
Walt Disney (Ken Peterson)
Rather stodgy, unwisely Cinemascoped feature cartoon of the old legend; very fashionable and detailed, but somehow lifeless.

d Clyde Geronomi *md* George Bruns *pd* Don da Gradi, Ken Anderson

AAN: George Bruns

Sleeping Car
GB 1933 82m bw
A woman on the run pretends to marry a sleeping car attendant, then finds they really are married. Artificial comedy with interesting cast from London stage. Madeleine Carroll, Ivor Novello, Laddie Cliff, Kay Hammond, Claud Allister, Stanley Holloway. Written by Franz Schultz; directed by Anatole Litvak; for Gaumont.

The Sleeping Car Murders*
France 1965 95m bw Cinemascope
PECF (Julien Derode)
original title: *Compartiment Tueurs*
When the overnight express from Marseilles reaches Paris, a girl is found dead in the sleeping car.
Rather long-winded whodunnit with an unlikely solution: a good pace helps, however, as do skilful borrowings from American police films of the forties.

wd Costa-Gavras, *novel* Sebastien Japrisot *ph* Jean Tournier *m* Michel Magne

Yves Montand, Simone Signoret, Pierre Mondy, Catherine Allégret, Jacques Pérrin, Jean-Louis Trintignant, Michel Piccoli

Sleeping Car to Trieste*
GB 1948 95m bw
GFD / Two Cities (George H. Brown)

Spy melodrama, a slow-starting but generally entertaining remake of *Rome Express* (qv).

w Allan Mackinnon *d* John Paddy Carstairs *ph* Jack Hildyard *m* Benjamin Frankel

Albert Lieven, Jean Kent, David Tomlinson, David Hutcheson, Rona Anderson, Paul Dupuis, Finlay Currie, *Alan Wheatley*, Derrick de Marney, Grégoire Aslan, Hugh Burden

The Sleeping Cardinal
GB 1931 84m bw

Sherlock Holmes exposes a smuggling ring. Slow-paced but interesting adaptation, vaguely based on *The Empty House*. Arthur Wontner, Ian Fleming, Norman McKinnel, Jane Welsh, Louis Goodrich. Written by Cyril Twyford and H. Fowler Mear, from stories by Sir Arthur Conan Doyle; directed by Leslie Hiscott; for Twickenham.

The Sleeping City**
US 1950 85m bw
U-I (Leonard Goldstein)

A policeman disguises himself as a medical student to learn more about a murder in a general hospital.
A location melodrama of modest excellence.

w Jo Eisinger *d* George Sherman *ph* William Miller *m* Frank Skinner

Richard Conte, Richard Taber, Coleen Gray, John Alexander, Peggy Dow, Alex Nicol

The Sleeping Tiger
GB 1954 89m bw
Anglo-Amalgamated / Insignia (Victor Hanbury)

A psychiatrist overpowers a criminal and takes him home as a guinea pig; the criminal then falls in love with the psychiatrist's wife.
Turgid and unconvincing melodrama, a thoroughgoing bore.

w Harold Buchman, Carl Foreman, *novel* Maurice Moiseiwitch *d* Joseph Losey *ph* Harry Waxman *m* Malcolm Arnold

Dirk Bogarde, Alexander Knox, Alexis Smith, Hugh Griffith, Maxine Audley, Glyn Houston, Billie Whitelaw

'There is a splendour about this film, which has one of the most absurdly extravagant plots on record, and never flinches from it.'—*Gavin Lambert*

The Slender Thread*
US 1966 98m bw
Paramount / Athene (Stephen Alexander)

A volunteer social worker tries to prevent a woman from committing suicide while police track her down from their phone conversations.
Acceptable star melodrama, curiously artificially styled.

w Stirling Silliphant *d* Sydney Pollack *ph* Loyal Griggs *m* Quincy Jones

Anne Bancroft, Sidney Poitier, Steven Hill, Telly Savalas

Sleuth**
GB 1972 139m colour
Palomar (Morton Gottlieb)

A successful thriller writer invents a murder plot which rebounds on himself.
Well-acted version of a highly successful piece of stage trickery; despite hard work all round it seems much less clever and arresting on the screen, and the tricks do show.

w Anthony Shaffer, from his play *d* Joseph L. Mankiewicz *ph* Oswald Morris *m* John Addison

Laurence Olivier, Michael Caine

AAN: Joseph L. Mankiewicz; John Addison; Laurence Olivier; Michael Caine

A Slight Case of Larceny
US 1952 71m bw

Garage proprietors find a way of tapping their rivals' supply of petrol. Laboured comedy for two rather tiresome stars. Mickey Rooney, Eddie Bracken, Elaine Stewart, Marilyn Erskine, Douglas Fowley. Written by Jerry Davis; directed by Don Weis; for MGM.

A Slight Case of Murder***
US 1938 85m bw
Warner (Sam Bischoff)

When a beer baron tries to go legitimate his colleagues attempt to kill him, but end up shooting each other.
Amusing black farce, remade to less effect as *Stop, You're Killing Me* (qv).

w Earl Baldwin, Joseph Schrank, *play* Damon Runyon, Howard Lindsay *d* Lloyd Bacon *ph* Sid Hickox
m M. K. Jerome, Jack Scholl

Edward G. Robinson, Jane Bryan, Willard Parker, *Ruth Donnelly*, Allen Jenkins, John Litel, Harold Huber, Edward Brophy, Bobby Jordan

'The complications crazily mount, sentiment never raises its ugly head, a long nose is made at violence and death.'—*Graham Greene*

Slightly French
US 1948   81m   bw

A film director in trouble passes off a Bowery-born carnival dancer as an exotic French star. Rather tedious comedy which lively performances can't sustain. Dorothy Lamour, Don Ameche, Janis Carter, Jeanne Manet, Willard Parker. Written by Karen de Wolf; directed by Douglas Sirk; for Columbia.

Slightly Honorable
US 1940   85m   bw
(UA) Walter Wanger (Tay Garnett)

Lawyer partners set out to break a crime syndicate.
Fair crime thriller which can't decide whether it's comedy or drama.
w John Hunter Lay, Robert Tallman, Ken Englund, *novel* Send Another Coffin by F. G. Presnell *d* Tay Garnett *ph* Merritt Gerstad *m* Werner Janssen

Pat O'Brien, Broderick Crawford, Edward Arnold, Eve Arden, Claire Dodd, Ruth Terry, Bernard Nedell, Alan Dinehart, Douglass Dumbrille, Ernest Truex

Slightly Scarlet
US 1956   92m   Technicolor   Superscope
(RKO) Benedict Bogeaus

The mayor's secretary loves the leader of a criminal gang.
Competent but uninteresting crime romance.
w Robert Blees, *novel* James A. Cain *d* Allan Dwan *ph* John Alton *m* Louis Forbes

Arlene Dahl, John Payne, Rhonda Fleming, Kent Taylor, Ted de Corsia
'So complicated that it is difficult to sort out which characters are supposed to be sympathetic.'—*MFB*

Slim
US 1937   85m   bw

Electric linesmen argue about their work and their women. A reworking of *Tiger Shark* which itself later became *Manpower*; competent action stuff. Pat O'Brien, Margaret Lindsay, Henry Fonda, Stuart Erwin, J. Farrell MacDonald, Jane Wyman. Written by William Wister Haines; directed by Ray Enright; for Warner.

Slim Carter
US 1957   82m   Eastmancolor

A playboy is signed up by a Hollywood studio and required to change his image. Curious sentimental comedy which might have worked with stronger casting. Jock Mahoney, Julie Adams, Tim Hovey, William Hopper, Ben Johnson, Barbara Hale. Written by Montgomery Pitman; directed by Richard H. Bartlett; for Universal-International.

The Slipper and the Rose°
GB 1976   146m   Technicolor   Panavision
Paradine Co-Productions (David Frost, Stuart Lyons)

The story of Cinderella.
The elements are charming, but the treatment is fussy yet uninventive and the film is immensely overlong and lacking in magic and wit. Alas, not the renaissance of the family film that was hoped for.
w Bryan Forbes, Robert and Richard Sherman *d* Bryan Forbes *ph* Tony Imi *songs* Robert and Richard Sherman *pd* Ray Simm

Richard Chamberlain, Gemma Craven, Kenneth More, Michael Hordern, Edith Evans, Annette Crosbie, Margaret Lockwood, *Christopher Gable*, Julian Orchard, Lally Bowers, John Turner
'The tunes, I'm afraid, go in one ear and out the other; and, as Dr Johnson said of *Paradise Lost*, no man wished it a minute longer.'—*Michael Billington, Illustrated London News*
AAN: music; song, 'He Danced with Me'

Slither°
US 1972   96m   Metrocolor
MGM / Talent Associates / Jack Sher

An ex-con, some gangsters, and a few mobile homes are involved in a chase across California for some hidden loot.
Wackily with-it comedy-thriller ranging from violence to slapstick, the former always undercut into the latter. Pretty funny, once you get the idea.
w W. D. Richter *d* Howard Zieff *ph* Laszlo Kovacs *m* Tom McIntosh

James Caan, Peter Boyle, Sally Kellerman, Louise Lasser

Slow Dancing in the Big City
US 1978   110m   Technicolor
UA / CIP (Michael Levee, John G. Avildsen)

A New York newspaper columnist is affected by a dying eight-year-old drug addict and an ailing girl ballet dancer.

Warners in the thirties might have got away with this corn, but in 1978, played against a realistic backdrop, it seems merely silly and indigestible, its title as pretentious as its use of four-letter words.

w Barra Grant *d* John G. Avildsen *ph* Ralf D. Bode *m* Bill Conti

Paul Sorvino, Anne Ditchburn, Nicholas Coster, Anita Dangler

'The earnestness and shamelessness of the director are so awesome that if the picture fails as romance, it succeeds as camp.'—*New Yorker*

The Small Back Room**

GB 1949   106m   bw
London Films / The Archers
US title: *Hour of Glory*

A bomb expert with a lame foot and a drink problem risks his life dismantling a booby bomb and returns to his long-suffering girl friend.

Rather gloomy suspense thriller with ineffective personal aspects but well-made location sequences and a fascinating background of boffins at work in post-war London.

wd Michael Powell, Emeric Pressburger
ph Christopher Challis m Brian Easdale

David Farrar, Kathleen Byron, Jack Hawkins, Leslie Banks, Robert Morley, Cyril Cusack

Small Change*

France 1976   105m   Eastmancolor
Films du Carosse / Artistes Associés
(Marcel Berbert, Roland Thenot)
original title: *L'Argent de Poche*

Linked incidents affecting a class of small boys in provincial France.

Competent if rather ordinary little portmanteau which one can't imagine adults actually paying to see.

w François Truffaut, Susan Schiffman *d* François Truffaut *ph* Pierre-William Glenn *m* Maurice Jaubert

Geory Desmouceaux, Philippe Goldman, Claudio Deluca

A Small Circle of Friends

US 1980   112m   Technicolor

Adventures of Harvard men at the end of the sixties. Comedy, sex, politics and melodrama are all ploughed into this tiresome and predictable mixture. Brad Davis, Karen Allen, Jameson Parker, Shelley Long, John Friedrich. Written by Ezra Sacks; directed by Rob Cohen; for United Artists. 'Sacks'

recreation of his college days relies on a mistaken belief that an audience will love his characters as much as they love each other.'— *John Pym, MFB.*

Small Town Girl*

US 1936   90m   bw
MGM (Hunt Stromberg)

A girl traps a handsome stranger into offering marriage when he's drunk, then sets out to win him when he's sober.

Thin but adequate romantic comedy, a good example of MGM's production line of the mid-thirties, with established star and character players helping upcoming talents.

w John Lee Mahin, Edith Fitzgerald, *novel* Ben Ames Williams *d* William A. Wellman *ph* Oliver Marsh, Charles Rosher *m* Edward Ward

Janet Gaynor, Robert Taylor, James Stewart, Binnie Barnes, Frank Craven, Elizabeth Patterson, Lewis Stone, Andy Devine, Isabel Jewell, Charley Grapewin, Robert Greig, Agnes Ayres

Small Town Girl*

US 1953   93m   Technicolor
MGM (Joe Pasternak)

Musical remake of the above.

Willing hands make the most of it, but the songs are not the best.

w Dorothy Cooper, Dorothy Kingsley *d* Leslie Kardos *ph* Joseph Ruttenberg *songs* Leo Robin, Nicholas Brodszky *md* André Previn *ch* Busby Berkeley

Jane Powell, Farley Granger, *Bobby Van*, Ann Miller, Robert Keith, Billie Burke, S. Z. Sakall, Fay Wray, Nat King Cole

AAN: song, 'My Flaming Heart'

A Small Town in Texas

US 1976   96m   colour

An ex-convict returns to his hometown seeking revenge on those who framed him. Unpleasant shock thriller with much violence. Susan George, Timothy Bottoms, Bo Hopkins, Art Hindle. Written by William Norton; directed by Jack Starrett; for AIP.

The Small Voice*

GB 1948   83m   bw
British Lion / Constellation (Anthony Havelock-Allan)
US title: *Hideout*

Escaped convicts hold up a playwright and his wife in their country cottage.

Gripping, well-characterized version of a very
well worn plot.

w Derek Neame, Julian Orde, *novel* Robert
Westerby *d* Fergus McDoneli

James Donald, Valerie Hobson, Howard
Keel, David Greene, Michael Balfour, Joan
Young

The Small World of Sammy Lee
GB 1962   107m   bw
Bryanston / Seven Arts / Ken Hughes
  (Frank Godwin)

A small-time Soho crook tries desperately to
raise money to pay off threatening bookies.
Overlong 'realist' comedy-melodrama based
on a TV play and filled with low-life
'characters'; vivid but cursed with a tedious
hero.

wd Ken Hughes, from his TV play
ph Wolfgang Suschitzky *m* Kenny Graham
ad Seamus Flannery

Anthony Newley, Julia Foster, Robert
Stephens, Wilfrid Brambell, Warren Mitchell,
Miriam Karlin, Kenneth J. Warren

The Smallest Show on Earth*
GB 1957   81m   bw
British Lion / Launder and Gilliat (Michael
  Relph)
US title: *Big Time Operators*

Two young marrieds inherit a decayed cinema
and make it pay.
Amiable caricature comedy with plenty of
obvious jokes and a sentimental attachment to
old cinemas but absolutely no conviction, little
plot, and a very muddled sense of the line
between farce and reality.

w William Rose, John Eldridge *d* Basil
Dearden *ph* Douglas Slocombe *m* William
Alwyn

Bill Travers, Virginia McKenna, Margaret
Rutherford, Bernard Miles, Peter Sellers,
Leslie Phillips, Francis de Wolff

Smart Girls Don't Talk
US 1948   81m   bw

A society girl rats on her gangster boy friend
after her brother has been killed. Flatly
handled underworld melodrama, as
uninteresting as its cast. Virginia Mayo, Bruce
Bennett, Robert Hutton, Richard Rober, Tom
D'Andrea. Written by William Sackheim;
directed by Richard Bare; for Warner.

Smart Money
US 1931   90m   bw
Warner

A gambler hits the big time but finally goes to
jail.
Rather ordinary crime drama, a distinct
letdown for its star after *Little Caesar*.

w Kubec Glasmon, John Bright, Lucien
Hubbard, Joseph Jackson *d* Alfred E. Green
ph Robert Kurrie

Edward G. Robinson, James Cagney, Evalyn
Knapp, Ralf Harolde, Noel Francis, Margaret
Livingstone, Boris Karloff, Billy House
† This film marks the only teaming of
Robinson and Cagney.

AAN: script

Smart Woman
US 1948   93m   bw
Monogram (Hal E. Chester)

A crafty lady lawyer becomes romantically
involved with a crusading district attorney.
What to Monogram was a high-class
production would have been a very routine
programmer from anyone else.

w Alvah Bessie, Louise Morheim, Herbert
Margolis *d* Edward A. Blatt *ph* Stanley
Cortez *m* Louis Gruenberg *md* Constantin
Bakaleinikoff

Constance Bennett, Brian Aherne, Barry
Sullivan, Michael O'Shea, James Gleason,
Otto Kruger, Isobel Elsom, Taylor Holmes,
John Litel

Smash and Grab
GB 1937   76m   bw

A detective's wife helps him track down a
criminal mastermind. Agreeable star comedy.
Jack Buchanan, Elsie Randolph, Arthur
Margetson, Antony Holles, Zoe Wynn,
Edmund Willard, David Burns. Written by
Ralph Spence; directed by Tim Whelan; for
Jack Buchanan / GFD.

Smash-up, The Story of a Woman
US 1947   113m   bw
Universal-International (Walter Wanger)
GB title: *A Woman Destroyed*

The story of a lady alcoholic.
Tedious distaff side of *The Lost Weekend*.

w John Howard Lawson *d* Stuart Heisler
ph Stanley Cortez *m* Daniele Amfitheatrof

Susan Hayward, Lee Bowman, Eddie Albert,
Marsha Hunt, Carl Esmond, Carleton Young,
Charles D. Brown

AAN: original story (Dorothy Parker, Frank
Cavett); Susan Hayward

Smashing Time
GB 1967 96m Eastmancolor
Paramount / Partisan / Carlo Ponti (Ray
  Millichip)

Two north country girls have farcical
adventures in swinging London, including
paint squirting and pie throwing.
Horrendous attempt to turn two unsuitable
actresses into a female Laurel and Hardy;
plenty of coarse vigour but no style or
sympathy.

w George Melly d Desmond Davis
ph Manny Wynn m John Addison

Rita Tushingham, Lynn Redgrave, Ian
Carmichael, Anna Quayle, Michael York,
Irene Handl, Jeremy Lloyd

Smile*
US 1975 113m De Luxe
UA (Michael Ritchie)

A bird's eye view of the Young Miss America
pageant in a small California town.
A witty series of sketches in the form of a
drama-documentary or satirical mosaic. Highly
polished fun for those who can stay the course.

w Jerry Belson d Michael Ritchie ph Conrad
Hall m various

Bruce Dern, Barbara Feldon, Michael Kidd,
Geoffrey Lewis, Nicholas Pryor

 'A beady, precise, technically skilful
movie.'—Michael Billington, Illustrated
London News

Smiles of a Summer Night**
Sweden 1955 105m bw
Svensk Filmindustri
original title: Sommarnattens Leende

A country lawyer meets again a touring actress
who was once his mistress, and accepts an
invitation for him and his young wife to stay at
her mother's country home for a weekend.
Comedy of high period manners with an
admirable detached viewpoint and elegant
trappings. It later formed the basis of Stephen
Sondheim's A Little Night Music, a stage
musical which was later filmed.

wd Ingmar Bergman ph Gunnar Fischer
m Erik Nordgren

Gunnar Bjornstrand, Eva Dahlbeck, Ulla
Jacobsson, Harriet Andersson, Margit
Carlquist, Naima Wifstrand, Jarl Kulle

Smiley*
GB 1956 97m Technicolor
  Cinemascope
TCF / London Films (Anthony Kimmins)

An adventurous Australian boy has various

adventures and finally gets the bicycle he
wants.
An open-air 'William'-type story for children,
quite nicely made and generally refreshing.
Smiley Gets a Gun was a less effective sequel.

w Moore Raymond, Anthony Kimmins
d Anthony Kimmins ph Ted Scaife, Russ
Wood m William Alwyn

Colin Petersen, Ralph Richardson, Chips
Rafferty, John McCallum

The Smiling Ghost
US 1941 71m bw

A girl reporter solves a haunted house
mystery. Moderate comedy chiller with plenty
going on. Alexis Smith, Wayne Morris,
Brenda Marshall, Alan Hale, Willie Best,
David Bruce, Helen Westley, Richard Ainley.
Written by Kenneth Gamet; directed by Lewis
Seiler; for Warner.

Smilin' Through**
US 1932 97m bw
MGM (Irving Thalberg)

Three generations of complications follow
when a Victorian lady is accidentally killed by
a jealous lover on her wedding day.
Archetypal sentimental romantic drama,
wholly absorbing to the mass audience and
extremely well done; originally a 1922 Norma
Talmadge vehicle.

w Ernest Vajda, Claudine West, Donald
Ogden Stewart, J. B. Fagan, play Jane Cowl,
Jane Murfin d Sidney Franklin ph Lee
Garmes

Norma Shearer, Leslie Howard, Fredric
March, O. P. Heggie, Ralph Forbes, Beryl
Mercer

 'A sensitive and beautiful production
distinguished by excellent settings and rich
photography.'—New York Mirror

AAN: best picture

Smilin' Through*
US 1941 100m Technicolor
MGM (Victor Saville)

Flat but adequate remake of the above.

w Donald Ogden Stewart, John Balderston
d Frank Borzage ph Leonard Smith
m Herbert Stothart

Jeanette MacDonald, Gene Raymond, Brian
Aherne, Ian Hunter, Frances Robinson,
Patrick O'Moore

The Smiling Lieutenant***
US 1931 88m bw
Paramount (Ernst Lubitsch)

A Viennese guards officer leaves his mistress to become consort to a visiting princess.
A sophisticated soufflé in Lubitsch's best style, naughty but quite nice, with visual effects largely replacing dialogue.

w Ernest Vajda, Samson Raphaelson, *operetta* A Waltz Dream *d Ernst Lubitsch ph* George Folsey *m* Oscar Straus *md* Adolph Deutsch

Maurice Chevalier, Miriam Hopkins, Claudette Colbert, Charles Ruggles, George Barbier, Elizabeth Patterson

'All the shrewd delights that were promised in *The Love Parade* all realized with an economy and sureness that give it a luster which no other American-made comedy satire has achieved. One must look to *Le Million* to find its peer.'—*Richard Watts, New York Post*

AAN: best picture

Smokey and the Bandit*
US 1977 97m Technicolor
Universal / Rastar (Robert L. Levy)

A Georgia bootlegger on a mission picks up a girl in distress and is chased by her irate sheriff fiancé.
Frantic chase comedy full of car crashes and low lines: a surprise box office smash.

w James Lee Barrett, Charles Shyer, Alan Mandel *d* Hal Needham *ph* Bobby Byrne *m* Bill Justis, Jerry Reed, Art Feller

Burt Reynolds, Jackie Gleason, Sally Field, Jerry Reed, Mike Henry, Pat McCormick, Paul Williams

Smokey and the Bandit II
US 1980 101m Technicolor
Universal / Rastar / Mort Engelberg
GB title: *Smokey and the Bandit Ride Again*

A trucker is hired to take a pregnant elephant to the Republican convention.
More mindless chasing and crashing, with even less wit than before and rather more wholesale destruction.

w Jerry Belson, Brock Yates *d* Hal Needham *ph* Michael Butler *md* Snuff Garrett

Burt Reynolds, Jackie Gleason, Sally Field, Jerry Reed, Dom DeLuise, Paul Williams

Smoky
US 1946 87m Technicolor
TCF (Robert Bassler)

An especially independent horse virtually runs the ranch on which he lives.
Family saga of the great outdoors, well enough assembled.

w Dwight Cummings, Lillie Hayward, Dorothy Yost, *novel* Will James *d* Louis King *ph* Charles Clarke *m* David Raksin *md* Emil Newman

Fred MacMurray, Anne Baxter, Burl Ives, Bruce Cabot, Esther Dale

† The story was also made by Fox in 1933 with Victor Jory, and in 1966 with Fess Parker.

SNAFU
US 1945 85m bw
Columbia
GB title: *Welcome Home*

Middle-class parents rescue their difficult 15-year-old son from the army, then wish they hadn't.
Predictable, well-greased comedy of a rebellious teenager.

w Louis Solomon, Harold Buchman, from their play *d* Jack Moss *ph* Franz Planer *m* Paul Sawtell

Robert Benchley, Vera Vague, Conrad Janis, Nanetta Parks

† The title can be bowdlerized as 'Situation Normal, All Fouled Up'.

The Snake Pit**
US 1948 108m bw
TCF (Anatole Litvak, Robert Bassler)

A girl becomes mentally deranged and has horrifying experiences in an institution.
A headline-hitting film which made a stirring plea for more sympathetic treatment of mental illness. Very well made, and arrestingly acted, but somehow nobody's favourite movie.

w Frank Partos, Millen Brand, *novel* Mary Jane Ward *d Anatole Litvak ph* Leo Tover *m* Alfred Newman

Olivia de Havilland, Leo Genn, Mark Stevens, Celeste Holm, Glenn Langan, Leif Erickson, Beulah Bondi, Lee Patrick, Natalie Schaefer

'A film of superficial veracity that requires a bigger man than Litvak; a good film with bad things.'—*Herman G. Weinberg*

AAN: best picture; script; Anatole Litvak; Alfred Newman; Olivia de Havilland

The Sniper**
US 1952 87m bw
Columbia / Stanley Kramer (Edna and Edward Anhalt)

A psychopath kills a succession of blondes with a high-powered rifle.
Semi-documentary police drama which was quite startling and influential when released but seems quite routine now.

w Harry Brown *d Edward Dmytryk ph* Burnett Guffey *m* George Antheil

Adolphe Menjou, Arthur Franz, Gerald Mohr, Richard Kiley, Frank Faylen, Marie Windsor

AAN: original story (Edna and Edward Annalt)

The Snorkel
GB 1958 80m bw
Columbia / Hammer (Michael Carreras)

A man murders his wife and is given away by his observant young stepdaughter.
Tenuous suspenser which outstays its welcome.

w Peter Myers, Jimmy Sangster, Anthony Dawson *d* Guy Green *ph* Jack Asher

Peter Van Eyck, Mandy Miller, William Franklyn, Grégoire Aslan

Snow Treasure
US 1968 95m Eastmancolor
Sagittarius (Irving Jacoby)

In Nazi-occupied Norway a teenage boy finds gold hidden in the snow; an underground agent helps him get it to safety.
Curiously undernourished but attractively made adventure film.

w Irving Jacoby, Peter Hansen, *novel* Marie McSwigan *d* Irving Jacoby *ph* Sverre Bergli *m* Egil Monn-Iversen

James Franciscus, Paul Anstad, Paoul Oyen, Randi Borch

Snow White and the Seven Dwarfs••••
US 1937 82m Technicolor
Walt Disney

Disney's first feature cartoon, a mammoth enterprise which no one in the business thought would work. The romantic leads were wishy-washy but the splendid songs and the marvellous comic and villainous characters turned the film into a world-wide box office bombshell which is almost as fresh today as when it was made.

w Ted Sears, Otto Englander, Earl Hurd, Dorothy Ann Blank, Richard Creedon, Dick Richard, Merrill de Maris, Webb Smith, from the fairy tale by the brothers Grimm *supervising director David Hand m* Frank Churchill, Leigh Harline, Paul Smith *songs* Larry Morey, Frank Churchill

'The first full-length animated feature, the turning point in Disney's career, a milestone in film history, and a great film.'—*Leonard Maltin*

'Sustained fantasy, the animated cartoon grown up.'—*Otis Ferguson*

AAN: Frank Churchill, Leigh Harline, Paul Smith

Snow White and the Three Stooges•
US 1961 107m De Luxe Cinemascope (TCF) Chanford (Charles Wick)
GB title: *Snow White and the Three Clowns*

The old story retold as a vehicle for a champion skater and three veteran clowns.
Surprisingly tolerable as a holiday attraction, once you get over the shock.

w Noel Langley, Elwood Ullman *d* Walter Lang *ph* Leon Shamroy *m* Lyn Murray *ad* Jack Martin Smith, Maurice Ransford

Carol Heiss, Moe Howard, Larry Fine, Joe de Rita, Edson Stroll, Patricia Medina, Guy Rolfe, Buddy Baer, Edgar Barrier

Snowball Express
US 1972 99m Technicolor
Walt Disney (Ron Miller)

An insurance accountant inherits a dilapidated skiing hotel in the Colorado Rockies.
Uninspired family comedy with slapstick on the snow slopes.

w Don Tait, Jim Parker, Arnold Margolin, *novel* Château Bon Vivant by Frankie and John O'Rear *d* Norman Tokar *ph* Frank Phillips *m* Robert F. Brunner

Dean Jones, Nancy Olson, Henry Morgan, Keenan Wynn, Mary Wickes, Johnny Whittaker

'As wholesome and bland as that old American favourite the peanut butter and jelly sandwich.'—*MFB*

Snowbound
GB 1948 87m bw
Gainsborough

Various people congregate at a ski hut in the Swiss Alps; all are after buried Nazi loot.
A rather foolish story which provides little in the way of action but at least assembles a fine crop of character actors.

w David Evans, Keith Campbell, *novel* The Lonely Skier by Hammond Innes *d* David MacDonald *ph* Stephen Dade

Robert Newton, Dennis Price, Herbert Lom, Stanley Holloway, Marcel Dalio, Mila Parely, Guy Middleton

The Snows of Kilimanjaro••
US 1952 117m Technicolor
TCF (Darryl F. Zanuck)

A hunter lies wounded in Africa and while waiting for help looks back over his life and loves.
Hollywood version of a portable Hemingway, with reminiscences of several novels stirred into a lush and sprawling mix of action and

romance, open spaces and smart salons. A big popular star film of its time, despite constricted and unconvincing characters.

w Casey Robinson, *story* Ernest Hemingway d Henry King ph Leon Shamroy m Bernard Herrmann

Gregory Peck, Susan Hayward, Ava Gardner, Hildegard Neff, Leo G. Carroll, Torin Thatcher, Marcel Dalio
'A naïve kind of success story with a conventional boy-meets-lots-of-girls plot.'— *Karel Reisz*

'The succinct and vivid qualities associated with Hemingway are rarely evoked, and what has been substituted is for the most part meandering, pretentious and more or less maudlin romance.'—*Newsweek*

AAN: Leon Shamroy

So Big*
US 1932 80m bw
Warner (Lucien Hubbard)

A schoolteacher marries a farmer, has trouble with her son, falls in love with a sculptor.
Watchable, superficial, top-talented adaptation of a best-seller, first filmed in 1925 with Colleen Moore.

w J. Grubb Alexander, Robert Lord, *novel* Edna Ferber d William Wellman ph Sid Hickox m W. Franke Harling

Barbara Stanwyck, George Brent, Dickie Moore, Guy Kibbee, Bette Davis, Hardie Albright

So Big
US 1953 101m bw
Warner (Henry Blanke)

By the time this inflated remake came along, the story was just too corny despite careful production.

w John Twist d Robert Wise ph Ellsworth Fredericks m Max Steiner

Jane Wyman, Sterling Hayden, Richard Beymer, Nancy Olson, Steve Forrest, Elizabeth Fraser, Martha Hyer

So Dark the Night*
US 1946 71m bw
Columbia

A detective tracks down a murderer whom he finds to be himself.
Smart second feature with a likeable leading performance.

w Aubrey Wisberg, Martin Berkeley, Dwight Babcock d Joseph H. Lewis m Hugo Friedhofer

Steven Geray, Ann Codee, Micheleine Cheirel

So Dear to My Heart*
US 1948 84m Technicolor
Walt Disney

Life on a country farm in 1903.
Live action nostalgia with a few cartoon segments; well enough done, but mainly appealing to well brought up children.

w John Tucker Battle, *novel* Midnight and Jeremiah by Sterling North d Harold Schuster ph Winton C. Hoch m Paul Smith

Burl Ives, Beulah Bondi, Harry Carey, Luana Patten, Bobby Driscoll

AAN: song 'Lavender Blue' (m Eliot Daniel, ly Larry Morey)

So Ends Our Night*
US 1941 120m bw
(UA) David L. Loew, Albert Lewin

Refugees from Nazi Germany are driven from country to country and meet persecution everywhere.
Worthy but rather drab and unfocused melodrama from the headlines.

w Talbot Jennings, *novel* Flotsam by Erich Maria Remarque d John Cromwell ph William Daniels m Louis Gruenberg

Fredric March, Margaret Sullavan, Glenn Ford, Frances Dee, Anna Sten, Erich Von Stroheim, Joseph Cawthorn, Leonid Kinskey, Alexander Granach, Sig Rumann
'It ought to be a great picture but it isn't.'— *Archer Winsten, New York Post*

AAN: Louis Gruenberg

So Evil My Love*
US 1948 100m bw
Paramount (Hal B. Wallis)

A missionary's widow is enticed into a life of crime and immorality by a scoundrelly artist.
Curious Victorian melodrama with a Wildean flavour; doesn't quite come off.

w Leonard Spiegelgass, Ronald Miller, *novel* Joseph Shearing d Lewis Allen ph Max Greene m Victor Young, William Alwyn

Ray Milland, Ann Todd, Geraldine Fitzgerald, Leo G. Carroll, Raymond Huntley, Martita Hunt, Moira Lister, Raymond Lovell, Muriel Aked, Finlay Currie, Hugh Griffith

So Goes My Love
US 1946 88m bw
(U-I) Jack H. Skirball / Bruce Manning
GB title: *A Genius in the Family*

The domestic life of inventor Hiram Maxim. Formula period family film with pleasant moments.

w Bruce Manning, James Clifden *d* Frank Ryan *ph* Joseph Valentine *m* Hans Salter

Myrna Loy, Don Ameche, Rhys Williams, Bobby Driscoll, Richard Gaines

So Little Time
GB 1952 88m bw
ABP / Mayflower (Aubrey Baring, Maxwell Setton)

In occupied Belgium an aristocratic lady falls in love with a Nazi colonel.
Doomed love story with musical accompaniment; tolerable but slow.

w John Cresswell *d* Compton Bennett *ph* Oswald Morris *m* Robert Gill

Marius Goring, Maria Schell, Gabrielle Dorziat, Barbara Mullen

So Long at the Fair*
GB 1950 86m bw
Rank / Gainsborough / Sydney Box (Betty E. Box)

During the 1889 Paris Exposition a girl books into a hotel with her brother, and next day finds that he has totally disappeared and his existence is denied by all concerned.
Straightforward version of an old yarn which has turned up in such varied forms as *The Lady Vanishes* and *Bunny Lake is Missing*. This modest production is pleasant enough but badly lacks drive.

w Hugh Mills, Anthony Thorne *d* Terence Fisher, Anthony Darnborough *ph* Reginald Wyer *m* Benjamin Frankel *ad* Cedric Dawe

Jean Simmons, Dirk Bogarde, David Tomlinson, Marcel Poncin, Cathleen Nesbitt, Honor Blackman, Betty Warren, Felix Aylmer, André Morell

So Proudly We Hail*
US 1943 125m bw
Paramount (Mark Sandrich)

The self-sacrifice of war nurses in the Pacific.
Fairly harrowing and well-meant but studio-bound and unconvincing flagwaver.

w Allan Scott *d* Mark Sandrich *ph* Charles Lang *m* Miklos Rozsa

Claudette Colbert, Paulette Goddard, Veronica Lake, George Reeves, Barbara Britton, Walter Abel, Sonny Tufts, John Litel
'Probably the most deadly accurate picture ever made of what war looks like through the lenses of a housewives' magazine romance.'— *James Agee*
'The stars are devotedly, almost gallantly, deglamorized and dishevelled but they cannot

escape the smell of studio varnish.'—*Richard Winnington*

AAN: Allan Scott; Charles Lang; Paulette Goddard

So Red the Rose*
US 1935 82m bw
Paramount (Douglas MacLean)

The life of a southern family during the Civil War.
Quiet, pleasing historical romance.

w Laurence Stallings, Maxwell Anderson, Edwin Justus Mayer, *novel* Stark Young *d* King Vidor *ph* Victor Milner *m* W. Franke Harling

Margaret Sullavan, Randolph Scott, Walter Connolly, Elizabeth Patterson, Janet Beecher, Robert Cummings

So This Is London
GB 1939 89m bw

An American magnate visits his English rival, and romance springs up between their children. Brightish comedy with a fair scattering of funny lines. Robertson Hare, Alfred Drayton, George Sanders, Berton Churchill, Fay Compton, Carla Lehmann, Stewart Granger, Ethel Revnell, Gracie West. Written by William Conselman, Ben Travers, Tom Phipps and Douglas Furber; directed by Thornton Freeland; for TCF.

So This Is Love
US 1953 101m Technicolor
Warner (Henry Blanke)
GB title: *The Grace Moore Story*

Events leading up to Grace Moore's debut at the Metropolitan Opera in 1928.
Acceptable musical biopic full of the usual Hollywood contrivances.

w John Monks Jnr, from Grace Moore's autobiography *d* Gordon Douglas *ph* Robert Burks *md* Ray Heindorf, Max Steiner *ch* Le Roy Prinz *ad* Edward Carrere

Kathryn Grayson, Merv Griffin, Joan Weldon, Walter Abel, Rosemary de Camp, Jeff Donnell, Douglas Dick, Mabel Albertson, Fortunio Bonanova

So This Is New York*
US 1948 78m bw
Stanley Kramer / Enterprise

In 1919 some country cousins who have come into money have a big time in the gay city.
Curious, sporadically effective, silent-style comedy which doesn't quite come off.

w Carl Foreman, Herbert Baker, *novel* The Big Town by Ring Lardner *d* Richard Fleischer *ph* Jack Russell *m* Dmitri Tiomkin

Henry Morgan, Rudy Vallee, Hugh Herbert, Bill Goodwin, Virginia Grey, Dona Drake, Leo Gorcey

So This Is Paris
US 1955　96m　Technicolor
U-I (Albert J. Cohen)

Three American sailors on leave in Paris meet girls and help war orphans.
Very thin imitation of *On the Town*, bogged down by sentimentality and lack of sparkle. The musical numbers, however, are not bad.

w Charles Hoffman *d* Richard Quine *ph* Maury Gertsman *md* Joseph Gershenson *ch* Gene Nelson, Lee Scott

Tony Curtis, Gloria de Haven, Gene Nelson, *Corinne Calvet*, Paul Gilbert, Mara Corday, Allison Hayes

So Well Remembered*
GB 1947　114m　bw
(RKO) Alliance (Adrian Scott)

The ambitious daughter of a mill-owner marries a rising politician but almost ruins his life.
Rather routine treatment of a three-decker north country novel; humdrum incident and unsympathetic characters, but full of minor British virtues.

w John Paxton, *novel* James Hilton *d* Edward Dmytryk *ph* Frederick A. Young

John Mills, Martha Scott, Trevor Howard, Patricia Roc, Richard Carlson

Soak the Rich*
US 1935　74m　bw
Paramount (Ben Hecht, Charles MacArthur)

A rebellious rich girl is cured when she is rescued from kidnapping.
Smartly written social comedy-melodrama.

wd Ben Hecht, Charles MacArthur *ph* Leon Shamroy

Walter Connolly, John Howard, Mary Taylor, Lionel Stander, Ilka Chase

Society Doctor
US 1935　63m　bw
MGM (Lucien Hubbard)
GB title: *After Eight Hours*

A doctor's modern ideas incur hostility: he goes into private practice, but returning to the hospital is wounded by a gangster and supervises his own operation under spinal anaesthetic.

Melodramatic hokum with most attention going to the second male lead, the young and rising Robert Taylor.

w Sam Marx, Michael Fessier, *novel* The Harbor by Theodore Reeves *d* George B. Seitz *ph* Lester White *m* Oscar Radin

Chester Morris, Virginia Bruce, Robert Taylor, Billie Burke, Raymond Walburn, Henry Kolker, William Henry

Sodom and Gomorrah
Italy / France 1962　154m　colour
Titanus / S. N. Pathe (Gottfredo Lombardo)

Lot and the Hebrews become involved in a Helamite plan to take over the rich sinful cities of Sodom and Gomorrah.
Dreary biblical blood-and-thunder; an international muddle, tedious in the extreme outside a few hilariously misjudged moments.

w Hugo Butler, Giorgio Prosperi *d* Robert Aldrich *ph* Silvano Ippoliti, Cyril Knowles *m* Miklos Rozsa *ad* Ken Adam

Stewart Granger, Stanley Baker, Pier Angeli, Anouk Aimée, Rossana Podesta

Soft Beds, Hard Battles
GB 1973　107m　colour
Rank / Charter (John Boulting)
US title: *Undercovers Hero*

Inhabitants of a Paris brothel help to win World War II.
Ragbag of poor sketches and dirty jokes, with the star in several ineffective roles including Hitler.

w Leo Marks, Roy Boulting *d* Roy Boulting *ph* Gil Taylor *m* Neil Rhoden

Peter Sellers, Lila Kedrova, Curt Jurgens, Gabriella Licudi, Jenny Hanley

Sol Madrid
US 1968　90m　Metrocolor　Panavision
MGM / Gershwin–Kastner (Hall Bartlett)
GB title: *The Heroin Gang*

An undercover narcotics agent is assigned to track down an elusive Mafia executive.
Humdrum, predictable, brutishly violent international crime caper.

w David Karp, *novel* Fruit of the Poppy by Robert Wilder *d* Brian G. Hutton *ph* Fred Koenekamp *m* Lalo Schifrin

David McCallum, Telly Savalas, Stella Stevens, Ricardo Montalban, Rip Torn, Pat Hingle, Paul Lukas, Perry Lopez, Michael Ansara

Solaris**
USSR 1972　165m　Sovcolor　'Scope
Mosfilm

A psychologist is sent to investigate the many deaths in a space station orbiting a remote planet.

Heavy-going but highly imaginative space fiction in which the menaces are ghosts materialized from the subjects' guilty pasts. The technology is superbly managed, but the whole thing is humourless.

w Andrei Tarkovsky, Friedrich Gorenstein, *novel* Stanislaw Lem d Andrei Tarkovsky ph Vadim Yusov m Eduard Artemyev

Natalya Bondarchuk, Donatas Banionis, Yuri Yarvet

Soldier Blue*
US 1970 114m Technicolor
Panavision
Avco (Gabriel Katzka, Harold Loeb)

A paymaster's detachment of the US cavalry is attacked by Indians seeking gold, and two white survivors trek through the desert.

Extremely violent 'anti-violence' western with a particularly nauseating climax following clichés all the way. From a director with pretensions.

w John Gay, *novel* Arrow in the Sun by Theodore V. Olsen d Ralph Nelson ph Robert Hauser m Roy Budd

Candice Bergen, Peter Strauss, Donald Pleasence

'One is more likely to be sickened by the film itself than by the wrongs it tries to right.'—*Tom Milne*

Soldier in the Rain
US 1963 87m bw
AA / Cedar / Solar (Martin Jurow)

Two army sergeants have wild plans for their demob, but one dies.

Curious sentimental tragi-comedy which misfires on all cylinders.

w Blake Edwards, Maurice Richlin, *novel* William Goldman d Ralph Nelson ph Philip Lathrop m Henry Mancini

Steve McQueen, Jackie Gleason, Tuesday Weld, Tony Bill, Tom Poston, Ed Nelson, John Hubbard

Soldier of Fortune*
US 1955 96m De Luxe Cinemascope
TCF (Buddy Adler)

When a photographer disappears in Red China, his wife comes to Hong Kong to institute a search, enlists the aid of an amiable smuggler.

Cheerful Boys' Own Paper adventure romance with attractive locations and some silly anti-Red dialogue.

w Ernest K. Gann, from his novel d Edward Dmytryk ph Leo Tover m Hugo Friedhofer

Clark Gable, Susan Hayward, Gene Barry, Alex D'Arcy, Michael Rennie, Tom Tully, Anna Sten, Russell Collins, Leo Gordon

'A very good adventure film but not one of the Gable smashes.'—*Hollywood Reporter*

Soldiers of the King
GB 1933 80m bw

A guards lieutenant causes trouble when he wants to marry a music hall star. Sprightly star vehicle with all talents in good form. Cicely Courtneidge, Edward Everett Horton, Anthony Bushell, Frank Cellier, Dorothy Hyson, Leslie Sarony. Written by J. O. C. Orton, Jack Hulbert and W. P. Lipscomb; directed by Maurice Elvey; for Gainsborough.

Soldiers Three
US 1951 87m bw
MGM (Pandro S. Berman)

Adventures of three roistering British officers on the North-West Frontier.

A kind of unofficial remake of *Gunga Din* without the title character; one suspects it was meant seriously and found to be so bad that the only way out was strenuously to play it for laughs.

w Marguerite Roberts, Tom Reed, Malcolm Stuart Boylan d Tay Garnett ph William Mellor m Adolph Deutsch

Stewart Granger, David Niven, Robert Newton, Walter Pidgeon, Cyril Cusack, Greta Gynt, Frank Allenby, Robert Coote, Dan O'Herlihy

'Kipling fans will probably have a fit but my guess is that it will have most people in fits of laughter.'—*Daily Mail*

The Solid Gold Cadillac**
US 1956 99m bw
Columbia (Fred Kohlmar)

A very minor stockholder upsets the crooked board of a large corporation.

Vaguely Capraesque comedy which begins brightly but peters out; performances sustain passing interest.

w Abe Burrows, *play* George S. Kaufman, Howard Teichmann d Richard Quine ph Charles Lang m Cyril Mockridge

Judy Holliday, Paul Douglas, *John Williams, Fred Clark*, Hiram Sherman, Neva Patterson, Ralph Dumke, Ray Collins, Arthur O'Connell

The Solitaire Man
US 1933 68m bw

Crooks doublecross each other on a Paris–
London aeroplane. Smart little comedy with
top talent. Herbert Marshall, Elizabeth Allan,
Mary Boland, Lionel Atwill, May Robson,
Ralph Forbes. Written by James Kevin
McGuinness, from the play by Bella and
Samuel Spewack; directed by Jack Conway;
for MGM.

Solomon and Sheba*
US 1959   142m   Super Technirama 70
UA / Edward Small (Ted Richmond)

When David names his younger son as heir,
his older son plots revenge.
Dullish biblical spectacle, alternating between
pretentiousness and cowboys and Indians.

w Anthony Veiller, Paul Dudley, George
Bruce d King Vidor ph Frederick A. Young
m Mario Nascimbene ad Richard Day, Alfred
Sweeney

Yul Brynner, Gina Lollobrigida, George
Sanders, Marisa Pavan, David Farrar, John
Crawford, Laurence Naismith, Alejandro
Rey, Harry Andrews

Sombrero
US 1953   103m   Technicolor
MGM (Jack Cummings)

Two Mexican villages feud over the burial
place of a famous poet.
Rather self-consciously unusual musical which
never catches fire but certainly keeps one
watching its incredible mixture of music and
melodrama.

w Norman Foster, Josefina Niggli, from her
novel A Mexican Village d Norman Foster
ph Ray June m Leo Arnaud

Ricardo Montalban, Pier Angeli, Yvonne de
Carlo, Nina Foch, Cyd Charisse, Rick Jason,
Jose Greco, Thomas Gomez, Kurt Kasznar,
Walter Hampden, John Abbott

'Staggering is the only word for the hokum
of this extraordinary film.'—*Gavin Lambert*

Some Call It Loving
US 1973   103m   Technicolor
Pleasant Pastures / James B. Harris

A young man buys a 'sleeping beauty' at a fair
but is sorry when he wakes her up.
Fashionable fantasy, amplified from a slender,
winning short story.

wd James B. Harris, *story* Sleeping Beauty by
John Collier ph Mario Tosi m Richard
Hazard

Zalman King, Carol White, Tisa Farrow,
Richard Pryor, Veronica Anderson

Some Came Running
US 1959   136m   Metrocolor
Cinemascope
MGM / Sol C. Siegel

A disillusioned writer returns after service to
his home town and takes up with a gambler
and a prostitute.
Strident and rather pointless melodrama with
solid acting and production values.

w John Patrick, Arthur Sheekman, *novel*
James Jones d Vincente Minnelli ph William
H. Daniels m Elmer Bernstein

Frank Sinatra, Dean Martin, Shirley Maclaine,
Martha Hyer, Arthur Kennedy, Nancy Gates,
Leora Dana

AAN: song 'To Love and Be Loved'
(*m* James Van Heusen, *ly* Sammy Cahn);
Shirley Maclaine; Martha Hyer; Arthur
Kennedy

Some Girls Do
GB 1969   93m   Eastmancolor
Rank / Ashdown (Betty E. Box)

Bulldog Drummond traces the sabotage of a
supersonic airliner to a gang of murderous
women.
Abysmal spoof melodrama in the swinging
sixties mould; a travesty of a famous
character.

w David Osborn, Liz Charles-Williams
d Ralph Thomas ph Ernest Steward
m Charles Blackwell

Richard Johnson, Daliah Lavi, Bebi Loncar,
James Villiers, Sydne Rome, Robert Morley,
Maurice Denham, Florence Desmond, Ronnie
Stevens

Some Kind of a Nut
US 1969   89m   De Luxe
UA / Mirisch / TFT / DFI (Walter Mirisch)

When a bank teller grows a beard because of
an unsightly bee sting, he is thought to be
flouting authority and his whole life changes.
Laboured, cliché-ridden anti-establishment
comedy, a waste of the talent involved.

wd Garson Kanin ph Burnett Guffey, Gerald
Hirschfeld m Johnny Mandel

Dick Van Dyke, Angie Dickinson, Rosemary
Forsyth, Zohra Lampert, Elliot Reid, Dennis
King

Some Like It Hot
US 1939   65m   bw
Paramount

A sideshow owner runs out of money.
Very mild comedy, one of several which
helped to establish Hope's star potential.

w Lewis R. Foster, *play* Wilkie C. Mahoney, Ben Hecht, Gene Fowler *d* George Archainbaud *ph* Karl Struss

Bob Hope, Shirley Ross, Una Merkel, Gene Krupa, Richard Denning

† The play, *The Great Magoo*, was previously filmed in 1934 as *Shoot the Works*.

Some Like It Hot•••
US 1959   122m   bw
UA / Mirisch (Billy Wilder)

Two unemployed musicians accidentally witness the St Valentine's Day Massacre and flee to Miami disguised as girl musicians. Overstretched but sporadically very funny comedy which constantly flogs its central idea to death and then recovers with a smart line or situation. It has in any case become a milestone of film comedy.

w Billy Wilder, I. A. L. Diamond *d* Billy Wilder *ph* Charles Lang Jnr *m* Adolph Deutsch

Jack Lemmon, Tony Curtis, Marilyn Monroe, Joe E. Brown, George Raft, Pat O'Brien, Nehemiah Persoff, George E. Stone, Joan Shawlee

AAN: script; Billy Wilder (as director); Charles Lang Jnr; Jack Lemmon

Some People
GB 1962   93m   Eastmancolor
Vic Films (James Archibald)

Troublesome teenage factory workers are helped by a church organist and become model citizens.

Bland propaganda for the Duke of Edinburgh's Award scheme for young people, quite acceptably presented, with pop music ad lib.

w John Eldridge *d* Clive Donner *ph* John Wilcox *m* Ron Grainer

Kenneth More, Ray Brooks, Annika Wells, David Andrews, Angela Douglas, David Hemmings, Harry H. Corbett

Some Will, Some Won't
GB 1969   90m   Technicolor
ABP / Transocean (Giulio Zampi)

In order to inherit under an eccentric will, four people have to perform tasks out of character. Thin remake of *Laughter in Paradise* (qv); funny moments extremely few.

w Lew Schwarz *d* Duncan Wood *ph* Harry Waxman *m* Howard Blake

Ronnie Corbett, Thora Hird, Michael Hordern, Leslie Phillips, Barbara Murray,

James Robertson Justice, Dennis Price, Wilfrid Brambell, Eleanor Summerfield, Arthur Lowe

Somebody Killed Her Husband
US 1978   96m   Movielab
Columbia / Melvin Simon (Martin Poll)

The title tells what happened when an unhappily married young mother falls in love. Very thin suspense comedy which starts as it ends, uncertainly.

w Reginald Rose *d* Lamont Johnson *ph* Andrew Laszlo, Ralf D. Bode *m* Alex North *ph* Ted Haworth

Farrah Fawcett-Majors, Jeff Bridges, John Wood, Tammy Grimes, John Glover, Patricia Elliott

Somebody Loves Me
US 1952   97m   Technicolor
Paramount / Perlberg-Seaton

First successful in San Francisco at earthquake time, Blossom Seeley climbs to Broadway success with her partner Benny Fields, then retires to become his wife. Adequate, unsurprising star musical of the second or third rank.

wd Irving Brecher *ph* George Barnes *songs* Jay Livingston, Ray Evans

Betty Hutton, Ralph Meeker, Robert Keith, Adele Jergens, Billie Bird, Sid Tomack, Ludwig Stossel

Somebody Up There Likes Me•
US 1956   112m   bw
MGM (Charles Schnee)

An East Side kid with reform school experience becomes middleweight boxing champion of the world.
A sentimental fantasia on the life of Rocky Graziano, expertly blending violence, depression, prizefight sequences and fake uplift.

w Ernest Lehman *d* Robert Wise *ph* Joseph Ruttenberg *m* Bronislau Kaper

Paul Newman, Pier Angeli, Everett Sloane, Eileen Heckart, Sal Mineo, Joseph Buloff, Harold J. Stone, Robert Loggia

AA: Joseph Ruttenberg

Someone at the Door
GB 1936   74m   bw

The new owner of a spooky house invents a murder which seems to come true. Derivative but quite amusing comedy thriller. Billy Milton, Aileen Marson, Noah Beery, Edward

Chapman, Hermione Gingold, John Irwin.
Written by Jack Davies and Marjorie Deans,
from the play by Dorothy and Campbell
Christie; directed by Herbert Brenon; for BIP.
(NB: Remade in 1950 with Michael Medwin,
Yvonne Owen and Garry Marsh; directed by
Francis Searle; for Hammer.)

Someone behind the Door
France 1971 97m colour

A brain surgeon takes a psychopathic patient
home and tries to make him commit murder.
Adequate but somehow unexciting suspenser.
Charles Bronson, Anthony Perkins, Jill
Ireland. Written by Mark Boehm and Jacques
Robert; directed by Nicolas Gessner; for Lira
Film. (Aka: *Two Minds for Murder*.)

Something Big
US 1971 108m Technicolor
Cinema Center / Stanmore and Penbar
  (Andrew V. McLaglen)

A retiring cavalry colonel has a last battle with
his old enemy.
Wry serio-comic western in the Ford tradition.

w James Lee Barrett *d* Andrew V. McLaglen
ph Harry Stradling Jnr *m* Marvin Hamlisch

Dean Martin, Brian Keith, Honor Blackman,
Carol White, Ben Johnson, Albert Salmi,
Denver Pyle

Something for Everyone*
US 1970 110m colour
National General (John Flaxman)
GB title: *Black Flowers for the Bride*

A young con man insinuates himself into the
household of a widowed Austrian countess.
Unusual black comedy which doesn't quite
come off.

w Hugh Wheeler, *novel* The Cook by Harry
Kressing *d* Harold Prince *ph* Walter
Lassally *m* John Kander

Angela Lansbury, Michael York, Anthony
Corlan, Heidelinde Weis

'Nothing much for anyone, actually.'—*New
Yorker*

Something for the Birds
US 1952 81m bw
TCF (Samuel G. Engel)

An elderly fraud is of help to a Washington
girl trying to save a bird sanctuary.
Derivative, competent but slightly boring
political whimsy on Capra lines.

w I. A. L. Diamond, Boris Ingster *d* Robert
Wise *ph* Joseph La Shelle *m* Sol Kaplan

Edmund Gwenn, Victor Mature, Patricia
Neal, Larry Keating, Christian Rub

Something for the Boys
US 1944 87m Technicolor
TCF (Irving Starr)

A southern plantation is turned into a retreat
for army wives.
Modest musical, vaguely based on a Broadway
success.

w Robert Ellis, Helen Logan, Frank
Gabrielson, *musical comedy* Cole Porter,
Herbert and Dorothy Fields *d* Lewis Seiler
ph Ernest Palmer *title song* Cole Porter *other
songs* Harold Adamson, Jimmy McHugh

Carmen Miranda, Michael O'Shea, Vivian
Blaine, Phil Silvers, Sheila Ryan, Perry Como,
Glenn Langan, Cara Williams

Something in the Wind
US 1948 89m bw
U-I (Joseph Sistrom)

A lady disc jockey is mistaken for her aunt,
who has been seeing too much for the heirs'
liking of a wealthy old man.
Poorish star musical comedy.

w Harry Kurnitz, William Bowers *d* Irving
Pichel

Deanna Durbin, Donald O'Connor, John
Dall, Charles Winninger, Helena Carter

Something Money Can't Buy
GB 1952 82m bw
Rank / Vic (Joe Janni)

After World War II a young couple find
civilian life difficult and dreary, but finally
start a catering and secretarial business.
Weakly contrived comedy which makes
nothing of its possibilities and is limply
handled all round.

w Pat Jackson, James Lansdale Hodson *d* Pat
Jackson *ph* C. Pennington-Richards *m* Nino
Rota

Patricia Roc, Anthony Steel, A. E. Matthews,
Moira Lister, David Hutcheson, Michael
Trubshawe, Diane Hart, Charles Victor,
Henry Edwards

Something of Value
US 1957 113m bw
MGM (Pandro S. Berman)

A young African with many English friends is
initiated into the Kikuyu.
An attempt to see all sides in the case of the
African ritual murders of the fifties;
bloodthirsty and unconvincing as well as dull.

wd Richard Brooks, *novel* Robert Ruark
ph Russell Harlan *m* Miklos Rozsa

Rock Hudson, Sidney Poitier, Dana Wynter,
Wendy Hiller, Robert Beatty, Juano
Hernandez, William Marshall, Walter
Fitzgerald, Michael Pate

Something to Live For
US 1952 89m bw
Paramount (George Stevens)

A commercial artist member of Alcoholics
Anonymous falls for a dipsomaniac actress but
refuses to break up his marriage.
Glossy romantic melodrama with some style
but no depth; the casting makes it seem like a
sequel to *The Lost Weekend.*

w Dwight Taylor d George Stevens
ph George Barnes m Victor Young

Ray Milland, Joan Fontaine, Teresa Wright,
Richard Derr, Douglas Dick
'The victory over alcohol becomes a
somewhat woebegone business.'—*Penelope
Houston*

Something Wild
US 1961 112m bw
(UA) Prometheus (George Justin)

A girl's life and attitudes change after she is
raped, and she moves in with a garage
mechanic.
A bit of a wallow, with much method acting
but no clear analysis of the central
relationship.

w Jack Garfein, Alex Karmel, *novel* Mary
Ann by Alex Karmel d Jack Garfein
ph Eugene Schufftan m Aaron Copland
ad Richard Day

Carroll Baker, Ralph Meeker, Mildred
Dunnock, Charles Watts, Martin Kosleck,
Jean Stapleton

Sometimes a Great Notion*
US 1971 114m Technicolor
  Panavision
Universal / Newman–Foreman
GB title: *Never Give an Inch*

In a small Oregon township, trouble is caused
by an independent family of lumberjacks.
Freewheeling but unsatisfactorily eccentric
comedy-melodrama which never quite jells but
has flashes of individuality.

w John Gay, *novel* Ken Kesey d Paul
Newman ph Richard Moore m Henry
Mancini

Paul Newman, Henry Fonda, Lee Remick,
Michael Sarrazin, Richard Jaeckel, Linda
Lawson, Cliff Potts

AAN: song 'All His Children' (m Henry
Mancini, *ly* Alan and Marilyn Bergman);
Richard Jaeckel

Somewhere I'll Find You*
US 1942 108m bw
MGM (Pandro S. Berman)

Brother war correspondents quarrel over a girl
and later find her in Indo-China smuggling
Chinese babies to safety.
Absurd but satisfactory star vehicle of the
second rank, with the theme designed to
prepare America for war.

w Marguerite Roberts, *story* Charles
Hoffman d Wesley Ruggles ph Harold
Rosson m Bronislau Kaper

Clark Gable, Lana Turner, Robert Sterling,
Patricia Dane, Reginald Owen, Lee Patrick,
Charles Dingle, Rags Ragland, William Henry

Somewhere in England
GB 1940 79m bw
Mancunian (John E. Blakeley)

High jinks among army recruits staging a
show.
One of a series of misshapen and badly made
regional comedies which afflicted British
cinemas in the forties and should be
mentioned for their immense popularity, their
new-style vulgarity (later to be refined by the
Carry On series) and their highly popular
stars.

w Arthur Mertz, Rodney Parsons d John E.
Blakeley

Frank Randle, Harry Korris, Robbie Vincent,
Winki Turner, Dan Young
† Subsequently released, or allowed to escape,
between 1941 and 1949 were *Somewhere in
Camp, Somewhere on Leave, Somewhere in
Civvies* and *Somewhere in Politics.*

Somewhere in the Night*
US 1946 111m bw
TCF (Anderson Lawler)

An amnesiac war veteran tries to discover his
true identity and discovers he is a crook with
much-wanted information.
Overlong suspenser with a tentative *film noir*
atmosphere. A few nice touches partly atone
for a tediously conversational plot.

w Howard Dimsdale, Joseph L. Mankiewicz,
story The Lonely Journey by Marvin
Borowsky d Joseph L. Mankiewicz
ph Norbert Brodine m David Buttolph

John Hodiak, Nancy Guild, Lloyd Nolan,
Richard Conte, Josephine Hutchinson, *Fritz
Kortner*

The Son-Daughter
US 1932 79m bw

True love among the San Francisco Chinese is affected by warring Tongs. Ill-advised oriental romance which failed to please. Ramon Novarro, Helen Hayes, Lewis Stone, Warner Oland, Ralph Morgan, H. B. Warner, Louise Closser Hale. Written by Claudine West, Leon Gordon and John Goodrich, from a play by David Belasco and George Scarborough; directed by Clarence Brown; for MGM.

Son of a Gunfighter
US / Spain 1964   90m   Metrocolor
Cinemascope

A young westerner stalks the outlaw responsible for his mother's death. Tolerable international western. Russ Tamblyn, Kieron Moore, James Philbrook, Fernando Rey. Written by Clarke Reynolds; directed by Paul Landres; for Lester Welch / Zurbano / MGM.

Son of Ali Baba
US 1952   75m   Technicolor
U-I (Leonard Goldstein)

A cadet of the military academy outwits a wicked caliph.
Routine Arabian Nights hokum.

w Gerald Drayson Adams d Kurt Neumann
ph Maury Gertsman m Joseph Gershenson

Tony Curtis, Piper Laurie, Susan Cabot, Victor Jory

Son of Captain Blood
Italy / Spain 1962   95m   Eastmancolor
Dyaliscope

Captain Blood's son routs his father's enemies. Lively swashbuckler with the original star's son rather unhappily cast. Sean Flynn, Ann Todd, Jose Nieto, John Kitzmiller. Written by Mario Caiano; directed by Tullio Demichelli; for Harry Joe Brown / CCM / BP.

Son of Dr Jekyll
US 1951   77m   bw

Dr Jekyll's son worries about developing a split personality, but discovers that his father's supposed friend Dr Lanyon is the nigger in the woodpile. Irresistibly silly elaboration of a famous story; no thrills but several good unintentional laughs. Louis Hayward, Alexander Knox, Jody Lawrance, Lester Matthews, Paul Cavanagh, Gavin Muir, Rhys Williams. Written by Mortimer Braus and Jack Pollexfen; directed by Seymour Friedman; for Columbia.

Son of Dracula*
US 1943   80m   bw
Universal (Ford Beebe)

A mysterious stranger named Alucard, with a penchant for disappearing in puffs of smoke, turns up on a southern plantation.
Stolid series entry with a miscast lead; nicely handled moments.

w Eric Taylor d Robert Siodmak ph George Robinson m Hans Salter

Lon Chaney Jnr, Louise Allbritton, Robert Paige, Samuel S. Hinds, Evelyn Ankers, Frank Craven, J. Edward Bromberg
† The title cheats: he isn't the son of, but the old man himself . . .

Son of Frankenstein***
US 1939   99m   bw
Universal (Rowland V. Lee)

The old baron's son comes home and starts to dabble, with the help of a broken-necked and vindictive shepherd.
Handsomely mounted sequel to Bride of Frankenstein and the last of the classic trio. The monster is less interesting, but there are plenty of other diversions, including the splendid if impractical sets.

w Willis Cooper d Rowland V. Lee
ph George Robinson m Frank Skinner
ad Jack Otterson

Basil Rathbone, Boris Karloff, Bela Lugosi, Lionel Atwill, Josephine Hutchinson, Donnie Dunagan, Emma Dunn, Edgar Norton, Lawrence Grant

Son of Fury*
US 1942   102m   bw
TCF (William Perlberg)

An 18th-century Englishman is deprived of his inheritance, flees to a South Sea island but comes back seeking restitution.
Elaborate costumer which suffers from loss of suspense during the central idyll. Much to enjoy along the way.

w Philip Dunne, novel Benjamin Blake by Edison Marshall d John Cromwell ph Arthur Miller m Alfred Newman

Tyrone Power, Gene Tierney, George Sanders, Frances Farmer, Roddy McDowall, John Carradine, Elsa Lanchester, Dudley Digges, Harry Davenport, Halliwell Hobbes
† Remade as Treasure of the Golden Condor (qv).

Son of Kong*
US 1933   69m   bw
RKO (Merian C. Cooper)

After Kong has wrecked New York, producer Carl Denham flees from his creditors and finds more monsters on the old island.

Hasty sequel to the splendid *King Kong*; the results were so tame and unconvincing that the film was sold as a comedy, but it does have a few lively moments after four reels of padding.

w Ruth Rose *d* Ernest B. Schoedsack *ph* Eddie Linden, Vernon Walker, J. O. Taylor *m* Max Steiner *sp* Willis O'Brien

Robert Armstrong, Helen Mack, Frank Reicher, John Marston, Victor Wong

Son of Monte Cristo*
US 1940 102m bw
(UA) Edward Small

The masked avenger who quashes a dictatorship in 1865 Lichtenstein is none other than the son of Edmond Dantes.
Cheerful swashbuckler of the second class.

w George Bruce *d* Rowland V. Lee *ph* George Robinson *m* Edward Ward

Louis Hayward, Joan Bennett, George Sanders, Florence Bates, Lionel Royce, Montagu Love, Clayton Moore, Ralph Byrd

Son of Paleface*
US 1952 95m Technicolor
(Paramount) Bob Hope (Robert L. Welch)

A tenderfoot and a government agent compete for the attentions of a lady bandit.
Gagged-up sequel to *The Paleface*; much of the humour now seems self-conscious and dated in the *Road* tradition which it apes, but there are still moments of delight.

w Frank Tashlin, Joseph Quillan, Robert L. Welch *d* Frank Tashlin *ph* Harry J. Wild *m* Lyn Murray

Bob Hope, Roy Rogers, Jane Russell, Trigger, Douglass Dumbrille, Harry Von Zell, Bill Williams, Lloyd Corrigan

AAN: song 'Am I in Love' (*m / ly* Jack Brooks)

Son of Robin Hood
GB 1958 77m Eastmancolor
  Cinemascope
TCF / Argo (George Sherman)

Robin's daughter joins with the Regent's brother to overthrow the Black Duke.
Empty-headed romp, more or less in the accepted tradition.

w George George, George Slavin *d* George Sherman *ph* Arthur Grant *m* Leighton Lucas

David Hedison, June Laverick, David Farrar, Marius Goring, Philip Friend, Delphi Lawrence, George Coulouris, George Woodbridge

Son of Sinbad*
US 1955 88m Technicolor Superscope
RKO (Robert Sparks)

Sinbad and Omar Khayyam are imprisoned by the Caliph but escape with the secret of green fire.
Arabian Nights burlesque, mainly quite bright, with the forty thieves played by harem girls.

w Aubrey Wisberg, Jack Pollexfen *d* Ted Tetzlaff *ph* William Snyder *m* Victor Young

Dale Robertson, Vincent Price, Sally Forrest, Lili St Cyr, Mari Blanchard, Leon Askin, Jay Novello

The Son of the Sheik*
US 1926 74m at 24 fps bw silent

Ahmed protects a dancing girl from a band of renegades.
Tongue-in-cheek desert romp which was probably its star's best film. He plays a dual role of father and son.

w Frances Marion, George Marion Jnr, Frederick Gresac *d* George Fitzmaurice *m* (1934 sound version) Jack Ward

Rudolph Valentino, Vilma Banky, Agnes Ayres

The Song and Dance Man
US 1936 72m bw

A vaudeville dancer goes on the skids but turns up when his former partner needs him.
Hokey backstage drama with interesting detail.
Paul Kelly, Claire Trevor, Michael Whalen, Ruth Donelly, James Burke. Written by Maude Fulton, from a play by George M. Cohan; directed by Allan Dwan; for TCF

A Song Is Born*
US 1948 113m Technicolor
Samuel Goldwyn

Flat remake of *Ball of Fire* (qv), graced by an array of top-flight musical talent.

w Harry Tugend *d* Howard Hawks *ph* Gregg Toland *m* Hugo Friedhofer *md* Emil Newman *songs* Don Raye, Gene de Paul

Danny Kaye, Virginia Mayo, Hugh Herbert, Steve Cochran, Felix Bressart, J. Edward Bromberg, Mary Field, Ludwig Stossel, Louis Armstrong, Charlie Barnet, Benny Goodman, Lionel Hampton, Tommy Dorsey, Mel Powell

The Song of Bernadette**
US 1943 156m bw
TCF (William Perlberg)

A peasant girl has a vision of the Virgin Mary
at what becomes the shrine of Lourdes.
Hollywood religiosity at its most commercial;
but behind the lapses of taste and truth is an
excellent production which was phenomenally
popular and created a new star.

w George Seaton, *novel* Franz Werfel
d *Henry King* ph *Arthur Miller* m Alfred
Newman *ad James Basevi, William Darling*

Jennifer Jones, William Eythe, Charles
Bickford, Vincent Price, Lee J. Cobb, Gladys
Cooper, Anne Revere, Roman Bohnen,
Patricia Morison, Aubrey Mather, Charles
Dingle, Mary Anderson, Edith Barrett, Sig
Rumann

'A tamed and pretty image, highly
varnished, sensitively lighted, and exhibited
behind immaculate glass, the window at once
of a shrine and of a box office.'—*James Agee*

'It contains much to conciliate even the
crustiest and most prejudiced objector.'—
Richard Mallett, Punch

AA: Arthur Miller; Alfred Newman; Jennifer
Jones
AAN: best picture; George Seaton; Henry
King; Charles Bickford; Gladys Cooper; Anne
Revere

Song of Ceylon°°
GB 1934   40m   bw
Ceylon Tea Board (John Grierson)

A pictorial, almost sensuous, but not very
informative documentary in four sections:
'The Buddha', 'The Virgin Island', 'The
Voices of Commerce', 'The Apparel of a
God'. Its influence was immense.

wd, ph Basil Wright m Walter Leigh

Song of Freedom*
GB 1936   80m   bw
Hammer (J. Fraser Passmore)

A black London docker becomes an opera
singer, then goes to Africa to free the tribe of
which he has discovered himself to be the
head.
A weird fable but a good star vehicle and a
surprisingly smart production for the time.

w Fenn Sherie, Ingram d'Abbes, Michael
Barringer, Philip Lindsay d J. Elder Wills

Paul Robeson, Elizabeth Welch, George
Mosart, Esmé Percy

Song of Love*
US 1947   118m   bw
MGM (Clarence Brown)

The story of Clara and Robert Schumann and
their friend Johannes Brahms.

Dignified musical biopic which unfortunately
falls into most of the pitfall clichés of the
genre. Dull it may be, but it looks good and
the music is fine.

w Ivan Tors, Irmgard Von Cube, Allen
Vincent, Robert Ardrey d Clarence Brown
ph Harry Stradling md Bronislau Kaper
ad Cedric Gibbons *piano* Artur Rubenstein

Katharine Hepburn, Paul Henreid, Robert
Walker, Henry Daniell, Leo G. Carroll, Else
Janssen, Gigi Perreau

'This is how Brahms and the Schumanns
might very possibly have acted if they had
realized that later on they would break into
the movies.'—*Time*

Song of Norway*
US 1970   141m   De Luxe
   Super Panavision 70
ABC / Andrew and Virginia Stone

A fantasia on the life of Grieg.
Multinational hodgepodge, mostly in the
Sound of Music style but with everything from
cartoons to Christmas cracker backgrounds.
Quite watchable, and the landscapes are
certainly splendid.

wd Andrew Stone *ph* Davis Boulton *stage
musical* Milton Lazarus *(book)* Robert
Wright, George Forrest *(m / ly)*

Toralv Maurstad, Florence Henderson,
Christina Schollin, Frank Poretta, Harry
Secombe, Edward G. Robinson, Robert
Morley, Elizabeth Larner, Bernard Archard,
Oscar Homolka, Richard Wordsworth

Song of Russia
US 1944   107m   bw
MGM (Joe Pasternak)

An American symphony conductor is in
Russia when hostilities begin, and watches the
citizens' war effort with admiration.
A terrible big-budget film which followed the
wartime propaganda line but five years later
was heavily criticized by the Unamerican
Activities Committee (for the wrong reasons).

w Paul Jarrico, Richard Collins d Gregory
Ratoff ph Harry Stradling m Herbert
Stothart

Robert Taylor, Susan Peters, John Hodiak,
Robert Benchley, Felix Bressart, Michael
Chekhov, Darryl Hickman

'Film makers have evolved a new tongue—
the broken accent deriving from no known
language to be used by foreigners on all
occasions.'—*Richard Winnington*

'MGM performs the neatest trick of the
week by leaning over backward in Russia's
favour without once swaying from right to
left.'—*Newsweek*

Song of Scheherezade
US 1947 107m Technicolor
Universal (Edward Kaufman)

In 1865 naval cadet Rimsky-Korsakov falls in
love with a dancer.
Yet another composer takes a drubbing in this
dull and unconvincing hodgepodge.

wd Walter Reisch *ph* Hal Mohr, William V.
Skall *md* Miklos Rozsa *ch* Tilly Losch
ad Jack Otterson

Yvonne de Carlo, Jean-Pierre Aumont, Brian
Donlevy, Eve Arden, Charles Kullman, John
Qualen, Richard Lane, Terry Kilburn

Song of Songs*
US 1933 89m bw
Paramount (Rouben Mamoulian)

A German peasant girl falls for a sculptor but
marries a lecherous baron.
Pretentious romantic nonsense, made fairly
palatable by the director's steady hand.

w Leo Birinsky, Samuel Hoffenstein, *play*
Edward Sheldon, *novel* Das hohe Lied by
Herman Sudermann w Rouben Mamoulian
ph Victor Milner *m* Karl Hajos, Milien
Rodern *ad* Hans Dreier

Marlene Dietrich, Brian Aherne, Lionel
Atwill, Alison Skipworth, Hardie Albright
  'An ornate and irresistible slice of outright
hokum.'—*Peter John Dyer, 1966*

Song of Surrender
US 1949 93m bw
Paramount (Richard Maibaum)

In turn-of-the-century New England, a
sophisticated visitor from New York falls for
the wife of the museum curator.
Ho-hum romantic drama, well enough
presented.

w Richard Maibaum *d* Mitchell Leisen
ph Daniel L. Fapp *m* Victor Young

Wanda Hendrix, Claude Rains, Macdonald
Carey, Andrea King, Henry Hull, Elizabeth
Patterson, Art Smith

Song of the Islands*
US 1942 75m Technicolor
TCF (William Le Baron)

On a South Sea island, the daughter of an
Irish beachcomber falls for the son of an
American cattle king.
Wispy musical with agreeable settings and
lively songs.

w Joseph Schrank, Robert Pirosh, Robert
Ellis, Helen Logan *d* Walter Lang *ph* Ernest
Palmer *md* Alfred Newman *songs* various

Betty Grable, Victor Mature, Jack Oakie,
Thomas Mitchell, *Hilo Hattie*, Billy Gilbert,
George Barbier

Song of the South*
US 1947 94m Technicolor
Walt Disney (Perce Pearce)

On a long-ago southern plantation, small boys
listen to the Brer Rabbit stories from an
elderly black servant.
Too much Uncle Remus and not enough Brer
Rabbit, we fear, but children liked it. The
cartoons were actually very good.

w Dalton Raymond *d* Harve Foster
ph Gregg Toland *m* Daniele Amfitheatrof,
Paul J. Scott, Charles Wolcott *cartoon
credits* various

Ruth Warrick, Bobby Driscoll, James Baskett,
Luana Patten, Lucile Watson, Hattie
McDaniel
  'The ratio of live to cartoon action is
approximately two to one, and that is the ratio
of the film's mediocrity to its charm.'—*Bosley
Crowther*
AA: song 'Zip a Dee Do Dah' (*m* Allie
Wrubel, *ly* Ray Gilbert)
AAN: Daniele Amfitheatrof, Paul J. Scott,
Charles Wolcott

A Song to Remember**
US 1945 113m Technicolor
Columbia (Louis F. Edelman)

The life and death of Chopin and his liaison
with George Sand.
Hilarious classical musical biopic which was
unexpectedly popular and provoked a flood of
similar pieces. As a production, not at all bad,
but the script . . .

w Sidney Buchman *d* Charles Vidor *ph* Tony
Gaudio *md* Miklos Rozsa, Morris Stoloff
piano José Iturbi *ad* Lionel Banks, Van Nest
Polglase

Cornel Wilde, Merle Oberon, Paul Muni,
Stephen Bekassy, Nina Foch, George
Coulouris, Sig Arno, Howard Freeman,
George Macready
  'It is the business of Hollywood to shape the
truth into box-office contours.'—*Richard
Winnington*
  'As infuriating and funny a misrepresentation
of an artist's life and work as I have seen.'—
James Agee

AAN: original story (Ernest Marischka); Tony
Gaudio; Miklos Rozsa, Morris Stoloff; Cornel
Wilde

Song without End
US 1960   142m   Eastmancolor
Cinemascope
Columbia (William Goetz)

The life and loves of Franz Liszt.

What worked at the box office for Chopin failed disastrously for Liszt; famous people are turned into papier maché dullards. Again, the production is elegance itself.

w Oscar Millard d Charles Vidor, George Cukor ph James Wong Howe md Morris Stoloff, Henry Sukman piano Jorge Bolet ad Walter Holscher

Dirk Bogarde, Capucine, Genevieve Page, Patricia Morison, Ivan Desny, Martita Hunt, Lyndon Brook, Alex Davion (as Chopin)

AA: Morris Stoloff, Henry Sukman

Sons and Lovers***
GB 1960   103m   bw   Cinemascope
TCF / Company of Artists / Jerry Wald

A Nottingham miner's son learns about life and love.

Well-produced and generally absorbing, if unsurprising, treatment of a famous novel.

w Gavin Lambert, T. E. B. Clarke, novel D. H. Lawrence d Jack Cardiff ph Freddie Francis m Mario Nascimbene

Dean Stockwell, Trevor Howard, Wendy Hiller, Mary Ure, Heather Sears, William Lucas, Donald Pleasence, Ernest Thesiger

'An album of decent Edwardian snapshots.'—Peter John Dyer

AA: Freddie Francis
AAN: best picture; script; Jack Cardiff; Trevor Howard; Mary Ure

Sons o'Guns
US 1936   79m   bw

A Broadway dancer in uniform finds himself accidentally enlisted and sent to France.

Among the better comedies of this star. Joe E. Brown, Joan Blondell, Eric Blore, Wini Shaw, Robert Barrat. Written by Julius J. Epstein and Jerry Wald; directed by Lloyd Bacon; for Warner.

The Sons of Katie Elder*
US 1965   122m   Technicolor
Panavision
Paramount / Hal B. Wallis (Paul Nathan)

At Katie Elder's funeral, her four troublesome wandering sons find themselves on the verge of further trouble.

Sluggish all-star western with predictable highlights.

w Allan Weiss, William H. Wright, Harry Essex d Henry Hathaway ph Lucien Ballard m Elmer Bernstein

John Wayne, Dean Martin, Michael Anderson Jnr, Earl Holliman, Martha Hyer, Jeremy Slate, James Gregory, George Kennedy, Paul Fix

Sons of the Desert****
US 1934   68m   bw
Hal Roach
GB title: Fraternally Yours

Stan and Ollie want to go to a Chicago convention, but kid their wives that they are going on a cruise for health reasons.

Archetypal Laurel and Hardy comedy, unsurpassed for gags, pacing and sympathetic characterization.

w Frank Craven, Byron Morgan d William A. Seiter ph Kenneth Peach

Stan Laurel, Oliver Hardy, Charlie Chase, Mae Busch, Dorothy Christie

Sorcerer
US 1977   121m   Technicolor
Universal / Film Properties International (William Friedkin)
GB title: Wages of Fear

Volunteers are needed to drive nitro-glycerine to an outpost in the South American jungle.

Why anyone should have wanted to spend twenty million dollars on a remake of The Wages of Fear, do it badly, and give it a misleading title is anybody's guess. The result is dire.

w Walon Green, novel Georges Arnaud (and the film by Henri-Georges Clouzot) d William Friedkin ph John M. Stephens, Dick Bush m various pd John Box

Roy Scheider, Bruno Cremer, Francisco Rabal, Amidou, Ramon Bieri

The Sorcerers
GB 1967   85m   Eastmancolor
Tigon / Curtwel / Global (Patrick Curtis, Tony Tenser)

An old couple find a way of regaining their youth through hypnotizing a young man to do their bidding.

Rather slight but oddly memorable horror film, with an elegant old lady becoming the real monster.

w Michael Reeves, Tom Baker, John Burke d Michael Reeves ph Stanley Long m Paul Ferris

Boris Karloff, *Catherine Lacey,* Ian Ogilvy, Elizabeth Ercy, Victor Henry, Susan George, Meier Tzelniker

Sorrell and Son
GB 1933 97m bw

When his wife leaves them, a man devotes his life to his worthless son. Fair picturization of a popular novel. H. B. Warner, Hugh Williams, Winifred Shotter, Margot Grahame, Donald Calthrop, Louis Hayward. Written by Lydia Hayward, from the novel by Warwick Deeping; directed by Jack Raymond; for Herbert Wilcox / B and D.

Sorrowful Jones
US 1949 88m bw
Paramount (Robert L. Welch)

A racetrack tout unofficially adopts an orphan girl.
Heavy-going sentimental comedy peopled by comic gangsters, a remake of *Little Miss Marker* with the emphasis changed.

w Melville Shavelson, Edmund Hartmann, Jack Rose, *story* Damon Runyon *d* Sidney Lanfield *ph* Daniel L. Fapp *m* Robert Emmett Dolan

Bob Hope, Lucille Ball, William Demarest, Bruce Cabot, Thomas Gomez, Tom Pedi, Houseley Stevenson, Mary Jane Saunders

Sorry Wrong Number**
US 1948 89m bw
Paramount (Hal B. Wallis, Anatole Litvak)

A bedridden neurotic woman discovers she is marked for murder and tries to summon help. Artificial but effective suspenser, extended from a radio play.

w Lucille Fletcher, from her play *d* Anatole Litvak *ph* Sol Polito *m* Franz Waxman

Barbara Stanwyck, Burt Lancaster, Ann Richards, Wendell Corey, Ed Begley, Harold Vermilyea, Leif Erickson, William Conrad

AAN: Barbara Stanwyck

Souls at Sea*
US 1937 93m bw
Paramount (Henry Hathaway)

In a 19th-century shipwreck an intelligence officer must save himself, and his mission, at the cost of other lives, and is courtmartialled. A lively seafaring melodrama produced on a fairly impressive scale.

w Grover Jones, Dale Van Every *d* Henry Hathaway *ph* Charles Lang Jnr *m* Milan Roder, W. Franke Harling *md* Boris Morros

Gary Cooper, George Raft, Frances Dee, Henry Wilcoxon, Harry Carey, Olympe Bradna, Robert Cummings, Porter Hall, George Zucco, Virginia Weidler, Joseph Schildkraut, Gilbert Emery

AAN: Milan Roder, W. Franke Harling

The Sound and the Fury
US 1959 117m Eastmancolor
Cinemascope
TCF / Jerry Wald

A once proud southern family has sunk low in finance and moral stature, and a stern elder son tries to do something about it. Heavy melodrama with performances to match.

w Irving Ravetch, Harriet Frank Jnr, *novel* William Faulkner *d* Martin Ritt *ph* Charles G. Clarke *m* Alex North

Yul Brynner, Joanne Woodward, Margaret Leighton, Stuart Whitman, Ethel Waters, Jack Warden, Françoise Rosay, John Beal, Albert Dekker

'A fourth carbon copy of Chekhov in Dixie.'—*Stanley Kauffmann*

The Sound Barrier**
GB 1952 118m bw
London Films (David Lean)
US title: *Breaking the Sound Barrier*

An aircraft manufacturer takes risks with the lives of his family and friends to prove that the sound barrier can be broken. Riveting, then topical, melodrama with splendid air sequences; a bit upper crust, but with well-drawn characters.

w Terence Rattigan *d* David Lean *ph* Jack Hildyard *m* Malcolm Arnold

Ralph Richardson, Nigel Patrick, Ann Todd, John Justin, Dinah Sheridan, Joseph Tomelty, Denholm Elliott

AAN: Terence Rattigan

The Sound of Music***
US 1965 172m De Luxe Todd-AO
TCF / Argyle (Robert Wise)

In 1938 Austria, a trainee nun becomes governess to the Trapp family, falls in love with the widower father, and helps them all escape from the Nazis.
Slightly muted, very handsome version of an enjoyably old-fashioned stage musical with splendid tunes.

w Ernest Lehman, *book* Howard Lindsay, Russel Crouse *d* Robert Wise *ph* Ted

*McCord m / ly Richard Rodgers, Oscar
Hammerstein II md Irwin Kostal pd Boris
Leven*

Julie Andrews, Christopher Plummer, Richard
Haydn, Eleanor Parker, *Peggy Wood*, Anna
Lee, Marni Nixon

'. . . sufficient warning to those allergic to
singing nuns and sweetly innocent children.'—
John Gillett

AA: best picture; Robert Wise; Irwin Kostal
AAN: Ted McCord; Julie Andrews; Peggy
Wood

Sound Off

US 1952 83m Supercinecolor
Columbia (Jonie Taps)

An entertainer is recruited into the army and
has predictable difficulties.
Dishevelled service farce with funny moments.

w Blake Edwards, Richard Quine *d* Richard
Quine *ph* Ellis Carter *m* Morris Stoloff

Mickey Rooney, Anne James, Sammy White,
John Asher, Gordon Jones

Sounder*

US 1972 105m De Luxe Panavision
TCF / Radnitz–Mattel (Robert B. Radnitz)

During the thirties Depression, black
sharecroppers in the deep south endure
various tribulations.
Well made liberated family movie . . . but not
very exciting.

w Lonnie Elder III, *novel* William H.
Armstrong *d* Martin Ritt *ph* John Alonzo
m Taj Mahal

Paul Winfield, Cicely Tyson, Kevin Hooks,
Carmen Mathews, James Best, Taj Mahal

AAN: best picture; Lonnie Elder III; Paul
Winfield; Cicely Tyson

Sous les Toits de Paris*

France 1930 92m bw
Tobis (Frank Clifford)

A Parisian street singer falls in love with a girl,
fights her lover, and proves himself innocent
of theft.
Surprisingly serious and darkly lit little
comedy-drama which, while well enough
directed, hardly seems to merit its classic
status.

wd René Clair ph Georges Périnal
m Armand Bernard *pd* Lazare Meerson

Albert Préjean, Pola Illery, Gaston Modot,
Edmond Gréville

South American George

GB 1941 93m bw

An unsuccessful singer poses as a South
American opera star. Not among the star's
best. George Formby, Linden Travers, Enid
Stamp-Taylor, Jacques Brown, Felix Aylmer.
Written by Leslie Arliss, Norman Lee and
Austin Melford; directed by Marcel Varnel;
for Ben Henry / Columbia.

South of Algiers

GB 1952 95m Technicolor
ABP / Mayflower (Aubrey Baring, Maxwell
   Setton)
US title: *The Golden Mask*

Archaeologists and thieves search the Sahara
for a priceless mask.
Schoolboy adventure story with a
straightforward plot and plenty of local colour.

w Robert Westerby *d* Jack Lee *ph* Oswald
Morris *m* Robert Gill

Van Heflin, Wanda Hendrix, Eric Portman,
Charles Goldner, Jacques François, Jacques
Brunius, Alec Mango, Marne Maitland

South of St Louis

US 1948 88m Technicolor

Before the Civil War starts, southern farmers
are plagued by Union guerrillas. Pretty good
western with plenty of action. Joel McCrea,
Zachary Scott, Victor Jory, Douglas Kennedy,
Dorothy Malone, Alexis Smith, Alan Hale.
Written by Zachary Gold and James R. Webb;
directed by Ray Enright; for Milton Sperling /
   Warner.

South of Suez

US 1940 85m bw

A diamond miner falls for the daughter of a
man he is accused of murdering. Watchable
melodrama with pleasing actors, George
Brent, Brenda Marshall, George Tobias,
James Stephenson, Lee Patrick, Eric Blore,
Cecil Kellaway. Written by Barry Triver;
directed by Lewis Seiler; for Warner.

South of Tahiti

US 1941 75m bw

Four adventurers drift ashore on a tropical
island. Penny-pinching hokum without even
the colour to make it watchable. Brian
Donlevy, Maria Montez, Broderick Crawford,
Andy Devine, Henry Wilcoxon, H. B.
Warner. Written by Gerald Geraghty; directed
by George Waggner; for Universal. (GB title:
White Savage.)

South Pacific**

US 1958 170m Technicolor Todd-AO
Magna / S. P. Enterprises (Buddy Adler)

In 1943 an American navy nurse on a South Pacific island falls in love with a middle-aged French planter who becomes a war hero. Overlong, solidly produced film of the musical stage hit, with great locations, action climaxes and lush photography (also a regrettable tendency to use alarming colour filters for dramatic emphasis).

w Paul Osborn, Richard Rodgers, Oscar Hammerstein II, Joshua Logan, *stories* Tales of the South Pacific by James A. Michener d Joshua Logan *ph* Leon Shamroy *m / ly* Richard Rodgers, Oscar Hammerstein II *md* Alfred Newman, Ken Darby *ch* Le Roy Prinz

Mitzi Gaynor, Rossano Brazzi, Ray Walston, John Kerr, France Nuyen, Juanita Hall

AAN: Leon Shamroy; Alfred Newman, Ken Darby

South Riding**
GB 1937 91m bw
London Films (Alexander Korda, Victor Saville)

A schoolmistress in a quiet Yorkshire dale exposes crooked councillors and falls for the depressed local squire.
Dated but engrossing multi-drama from a famous novel; a good compact piece of film-making.

w Ian Dalrymple, Donald Bull, *novel* Winifred Holtby *d* Victor Saville

Ralph Richardson, Edna Best, Edmund Gwenn, Ann Todd, Glynis Johns, John Clements, Marie Lohr, Milton Rosmer, Edward Lexy

South Sea Sinner
US 1950 88m bw

On a South Sea island, a fugitive from justice is blackmailed by a café owner. Hackneyed elements are strung together without much flair in this routine melodrama. Macdonald Carey, Shelley Winters, Luther Adler, Helena Carter, Frank Lovejoy, Art Smith, Liberace. Written by Joel Malone and Oscar Brodney; directed by Bruce Humberstone; for Universal-International. (GB title: *East of Java*.)

South Sea Woman
US 1953 99m bw
Warner (Sam Bischoff)
aka: *Pearl of the South Pacific*

Adventures of a fight-loving marine in the Pacific war.
Unlovable mixture of brawling, romancing and war-winning.

w Edwin Blum, *play* William M. Rankin *d* Arthur Lubin *ph* Ted McCord *m* David Buttolph

Burt Lancaster, Virginia Mayo, Chuck Connors, Arthur Shields, Barry Kelley, Leon Askin

The Southern Star*
GB / France 1968 105m Techniscope
Columbia / Eurofrance / Capitole

In French West Africa in 1912, a penniless American finds a huge diamond which several crooks are after.
Quite a likeable adventure romp, with good suspense sequences and convincing jungle settings.

w David Pursall, Jack Seddon, *novel* Jules Verne *d* Sidney Hayers *ph* Raoul Coutard *m* Georges Garvarentz

George Segal, Ursula Andress, Orson Welles, Ian Hendry, Michael Constantine, Johnny Sekka, Harry Andrews

A Southern Yankee*
US 1948 90m bw
MGM (Paul Jones)
GB title: *My Hero*

During the Civil War a southern bellboy masquerades as a spy and finds himself behind enemy lines.
A rather feeble reworking of Buster Keaton's *The General*, with some excellent gags supervised by the master himself.

w Harry Tugend *d* Edward Sedgwick *ph* Ray June *m* David Snell

Red Skelton, Brian-Donlevy, Arlene Dahl, George Coulouris, Lloyd Gough, John Ireland, Minor Watson, Charles Dingle

The Southerner***
US 1945 91m bw
(UA) David Loew, Robert Hakim

Problems of penniless farmers in the deep south.
Impressive, highly pictorial outdoor drama, more poetic than *The Grapes of Wrath* and lacking the acting strength.

wd Jean Renoir, *novel* Hold Autumn in Your Hand by George Sessions Perry *ph* Lucien Andriot *m* Werner Janssen

Zachary Scott, Betty Field, *Beulah Bondi*, J. Carrol Naish, Percy Kilbride, Blanche Yurka, Norman Lloyd
'I cannot imagine anybody failing to be spellbound by this first successful essay in Franco-American screen collaboration.'— *Richard Winnington*

'You can smell the earth as the plough turns it up; you can sense the winter and the rain and the sunshine.'—*C. A. Lejeune*
† Some sources state that the script was by William Faulkner.

AAN: Jean Renoir (as director); Werner Janssen

Soylent Green*
US 1973   97m   Metrocolor   Panavision
MGM (Walter Seltzer, Russell Thatcher)

In 2022, the population of New York exists in perpetual heat on synthetic foods; a policeman hears from his elderly friend about an earlier time when things were better.
Lively futuristic yarn with a splendid climax revealing the nature of the artificial food; marred by narrative incoherence and by direction which fails to put plot points clearly across.

w Stanley R. Greenberg, *novel* Make Room, Make Room by Harry Harrison *d* Richard Fleischer *ph* Richard H. Kline *m* Fred Myrow

Charlton Heston, *Edward G. Robinson*, Leigh Taylor-Young, Chuck Connors, Brock Peters, Joseph Cotten

The Space Children
US 1958   71m   bw   VistaVision

Children at a rocket testing site sabotage equipment on the instructions of a strange pulsating object. Naïve moral fable, not badly done on its level. Adam Williams, Peggy Webber, Michel Ray, Jackie Coogan. Written by Bernard Schoenfeld; directed by Jack Arnold; for William Alland / Paramount.

The Spaceman and King Arthur
GB 1979   93m   Technicolor

An astronaut and his robot accidentally land themselves back at the court of King Arthur. Mindless but occasionally funny rewrite of Mark Twain's *A Connecticut Yankee*. Dennis Dugan, Jim Dale, Ron Moody, Kenneth More, John Le Mesurier, Rodney Bewes, Robert Beatty. Written by Don Tait; directed by Russ Mayberry; for Walt Disney. (US title:*Unidentified Flying Oddball.*)

Spanish Affair
US 1958   92m   Technicolor   Vistavision
Paramount / Nomad (Bruce Odlum)

An American architect in Madrid falls in love with his interpreter and is pursued by her lover.

Curiously plotless excuse for a travelogue, lushly photographed but not exactly gripping.

w Richard Collins *d* Don Siegel *ph* Sam Leavitt *m* Daniele Amfitheatrof

Richard Kiley, Carmen Sevilla, Jose Guardiola

Spanish Fly
GB 1975   86m   Technicolor

An Englishman in Majorca tries to improve a purchase of local wine by putting an aphrodisiac in it, with predictable results. Crude, tatty comedy by people who should know better. Terry-Thomas, Leslie Phillips, Graham Armitage, Frank Thornton, Sue Lloyd. Written by Robert Ryerson; directed by Bob Kellett; for Winkle / EMI.

The Spanish Gardener
GB 1956   97m   Technicolor   Vistavision
Rank (John Bryan)

The British consul in Spain is annoyed when his young son develops a strong friendship with the gardener.
Slow, understated study in human relationships which doesn't come off; any sexual relevance is well concealed.

w Lesley Storm, John Bryan, *novel* A. J. Cronin *d* Philip Leacock *ph* Christopher Challis *m* John Veale

Dirk Bogarde, Michael Hordern, Jon Whiteley, Cyril Cusack, Geoffrey Keen, Maureen Swanson, Lyndon Brook, Josephine Griffin, Bernard Lee, Rosalie Crutchley

The Spanish Main*
US 1945   101m   Technicolor
RKO (Robert Fellows)

In the Caribbean, the fiancée of the Spanish viceroy is kidnapped by a pirate who determines to tame her before marrying her. Slightly tongue-in-cheek pirate hokum; generally good value for the easily amused.

w George Worthing Yates, Herman J. Mankiewicz *d* Frank Borzage *ph* George Barnes *m* Hanns Eisler *md* Constantin Bakaleinikoff

Paul Henreid, Maureen O'Hara, Binnie Barnes, Walter Slezak, John Emery, Barton MacLane, J. M. Kerrigan, Nancy Gates, Fritz Leiber, Jack La Rue, Mike Mazurki, Victor Kilian

AAN: George Barnes

Spare a Copper*
GB 1940   77m   bw

A police war reservist catches saboteurs. One of the last good Formby comedies, with everything percolating as it should. George Formby, Dorothy Hyson, Bernard Lee, John Warwick, John Turnbull, George Merritt. Written by Roger MacDougall, Austin Melford and Basil Dearden; directed by John Paddy Carstairs; for Ealing.

Spare the Rod
GB 1961 93m bw
British Lion / Bryanston / Weyland (Victor Lyndon)

At an East End school, a novice master wins the confidence of tough pupils.
A British *Blackboard Jungle*, paving the way for *To Sir with Love*; not exciting on its own account.

w John Cresswell, *novel* Michael Croft *d* Leslie Norman *ph* Paul Beeson *m* Laurie Johnson

Max Bygraves, Geoffrey Keen, Donald Pleasence, Richard O'Sullivan, Betty McDowall, Eleanor Summerfield, Mary Merrall

Sparrows Can't Sing
GB 1962 94m bw
Elstree / Carthage

Returning after two years at sea, a sailor searches for his wife and threatens vengeance on her lover.
Relentlessly caricatured cockney comedy melodrama, too self-conscious to be effective, and not at all likeable anyway.

w Stephen Lewis, Joan Littlewood *d* Joan Littlewood *ph* Mac Greene *m* James Stevens

James Booth, Barbara Windsor, Roy Kinnear, Avis Bunnage, George Sewell, Barbara Ferris, Murray Melvin, Arthur Mullard

Spartacus**
US 1960 196m Super Technirama 70
U-I / Bryna (Edward Lewis)

The slaves of ancient Rome revolt and are quashed.
Long, well-made, downbeat epic with deeper than usual characterization and several bravura sequences.

w Dalton Trumbo, *novel* Howard Fast *d* Stanley Kubrick *ph* Russell Metty *m* Alex North *pd* Alexander Golitzen

Kirk Douglas, Laurence Olivier, Charles Laughton, Tony Curtis, Jean Simmons, Peter Ustinov, John Gavin, Nina Foch, Herbert Lom, John Ireland, John Dall, Charles McGraw, Woody Strode

'Everything is depicted with a lack of imagination that is truly Marxian.'—*Anne Grayson*
'A lot of first-rate professionals have pooled their abilities to make a first-rate circus.'—*Stanley Kauffmann*
'One comes away feeling rather revolted and not at all ennobled.'—*Alan Dent, Illustrated London News*
AA: Russell Metty; Peter Ustinov
AAN: Alex North

Spawn of the North**
US 1938 110m bw
Paramount (Albert Lewin)

In 1890s Alaska, American fishermen combat Russian poachers.
Solidly carpentered all-star action melodrama, a sizzler of its day. Remade 1953 as *Alaska Seas*.

w Talbot Jennings, Jules Furthman *d* Henry Hathaway *ph* Charles Lang *m* Dmitri Tiomkin

George Raft, Henry Fonda, Dorothy Lamour, *John Barrymore*, Akim Tamiroff, Louise Platt, Lynne Overman, Fuzzy Knight, Vladimir Sokoloff, Duncan Renaldo, John Wray

'This film has something which the cinema of bygone days used to supply as a matter of course—action and thrills, the quickened pulse and the lump in the throat.'—*Basil Wright*

Speak Easily*
US 1932 83m bw
MGM (Lawrence Weingarten)

A professor inherits a Broadway musical and falls for the lure of the bright lights.
Interesting Keaton talkie at the point of his decline.

w Ralph Spence, Lawrence E. Johnson, *novel* Footlights by Clarence Budington Kelland *d* Edward Sedgwick *ph* Harold Wentstrom

Buster Keaton, Jimmy Durante, Hedda Hopper

Special Delivery
US 1976 99m De Luxe
TCF / Bing Crosby Productions (Richard Berg)

Three disabled Vietnam veterans rob a bank, and the consequences are complicated.
Unremarkable suspenser which takes itself too seriously.

w Don Gazzaniga *d* Paul Wendkos *ph* Harry Stradling Jnr *m* Lalo Schifrin

Bo Svenson, Cybill Shepherd, Michael C. Gwynne, Vic Tayback, Sorrell Booke

The Speckled Band
GB 1931   90m   bw

Sherlock Holmes saves an heiress from a
horrible death. Limp and overstretched
version of Conan Doyle's story, interesting
only for the actors. Raymond Massey, Athole
Stewart (as Watson), Lyn Harding (as Rylott),
Angela Baddeley, Nancy Price. Written by W.
P. Lipscomb; directed by Jack Raymond; for
Herbert Wilcox / B and D.

The Specter of the Rose*
US 1946   90m   bw
Republic

A schizophrenic ballet dancer lives his role
and nearly murders his wife.
A rather hilarious bid for culture: hard to sit
through without laughing, but unique.

wd Ben Hecht   ph Lee Garmes   m Georges
Antheil

Viola Essen, Ivan Kirov, Michael Chekhov

Spellbound
GB 1940   82m   bw
Pyramid Amalgamated (R. Murray Leslie)
aka: *Passing Clouds*; US title: *The Spell of
Amy Nugent*

A young man is in despair when his fiancée
dies, and nearly goes mad when a medium
materializes her from the dead.
Very odd, very naïve, but somehow rather
winning.

w Miles Malleson, *novel* The Necromancers by
Robert Benson   d John Harlow

Derek Farr, Vera Lindsay, Frederick Leister,
Hay Petrie, Diana King, Felix Aylmer

Spellbound***
US 1945   111m   bw
David O. Selznick

The new head of a mental institution is an
impostor and an amnesiac; a staff member
falls in love with him and helps him recall the
fate of the real Dr Edwardes.
Enthralling and rather infuriating
psychological mystery; the Hitchcock touches
are splendid, and the stars shine magically, but
the plot could have stood a little more
attention.

w Ben Hecht, Angus MacPhail, *novel* The
House of Dr Edwardes by Francis Beeding
d Alfred Hitchcock   ph George Barnes   dream
sequence Salvador Dali   m Miklos Rozsa
ad James Basevi

Ingrid Bergman, Gregory Peck, Leo G.
Carroll, Michael Chekhov, Rhonda Fleming,
John Emery, Norman Lloyd, Steve Geray

'Just about as much of the id as could be
safely displayed in a Bergdorf Goodman
window.'—*James Agee*
'Bergman's apple-cheeked sincerity has
rarely been so out of place as in this confection
whipped up by jaded chefs.'—*New Yorker,
1976*

AA: Miklos Rozsa
AAN: best picture; Alfred Hitchcock; George
Barnes; Michael Chekhov

Spencer's Mountain*
US 1963   121m   Technicolor
   Panavision
Warner (Delmer Daves)

Life in rural America in the thirties with a
poor quarry worker and his family of nine.
Sentimental rose-tinted hokum which later
became TV's *The Waltons*. Expertly
concocted, Hollywood style.

wd Delmer Daves, *novel* Earl Hanmer Jnr
ph Charles Lawton, H. F. Koenekamp
m Max Steiner

Henry Fonda, Maureen O'Hara, James
MacArthur, Donald Crisp, Wally Cox, Mimsy
Farmer, Lilian Bronson

Spendthrift
US 1936   80m   bw

A millionaire playboy runs out of cash. Mild
romantic comedy. Henry Fonda, Pat Paterson,
Mary Brian, George Barbier, Ed Brophy.
Written by Raoul Walsh and Bert Hanlon;
directed by Raoul Walsh; for Paramount.

The Spider and the Fly
GB 1949   95m   bw
GFD / Maxwell Setton, Aubrey Baring

In 1913 a Parisian safecracker constantly
outwits an inspector of the Sûreté, but war
brings changes.
Coldly ironic comedy drama which really,
regrettably, doesn't work.

w Robert Westerby   d Robert Hamer
ph Geoffrey Unsworth   m Georges Auric

Eric Portman, Guy Rolfe, Nadia Gray,
George Cole, Edward Chapman, John Carol,
Maurice Denham
'Not sufficiently exciting for a thriller, not
quite sharp enough for a real drama of
character.'—*Gavin Lambert, MFB*

The Spider's Stratagem*
Italy 1970   97m   Eastmancolor
Radiotelevisione Italiana / Red Film
   (Giovanni Bertolucci)

Revisiting the village in the Po valley where
his father was murdered by fascists in 1936,

our gradually disillusioned hero learns that his father was really a traitor executed by his own men.

Elaborately mysterious puzzle play for intellectuals, with infinite shades of meaning which few will bother to explore. The atmosphere, however, is superbly caught.

w Bernardo Bertolucci, Eduardo de Gregorio, Marilu Parolini, *story* The Theme of the Traitor and the Hero by Jorge Luis Borges *d* Bernardo Bertolucci *ph* Vittorio Storaro, Franco di Giacomo

Giulio Brogi, Alida Valli, Tino Scotti, Pino Campanini

Spies of the Air

GB 1940 73m bw
British Consolidated (K. C. Alexander)
reissue title: *Law and Disorder*

A solicitor unmasks saboteurs using portable radios to direct bombers.

Thin, tolerable comedy thriller using most of the talents of *This Man is News*.

w Roger MacDonald *d* David MacDonald

Barry K. Barnes, Alastair Sim, Diana Churchill, Edward Chapman, Austin Trevor, Leo Genn, Roger Livesey

The Spikes Gang

US 1974 96m De Luxe
UA / Mirisch / Duo / Sanford

Three boys shelter a bank robber and join his gang.

Doom-laden, violent western with a few comic lines.

w Irving Ravetch, Harriet Frank Jnr, *novel* The Bank Robber by Giles Tippette *d* Richard Fleischer *ph* Brian West *m* Fred Karlin

Lee Marvin, Gary Grimes, Ron Howard, Charles Martin Smith, Arthur Hunnicutt, Noah Beery Jnr

Spinout

US 1966 93m Metrocolor Panavision
MGM / Euterpe (Joe Pasternak)
GB title: *California Holiday*

A carefree touring singer agrees to drive an experimental car in a road race.

Mild star musical which at least stays in the open air.

w Theodore J. Flicker, George Kirgo *d* Norman Taurog *ph* Daniel L. Fapp *md* Georgie Stoll

Elvis Presley, Shelley Fabares, Carl Betz, Cecil Kellaway, Diane McBain, Deborah Walley, Jack Mullaney, Will Hutchins, Una Merkel

The Spiral Road

US 1962 145m Eastmancolor
U-I (Robert Arthur)

In 1936 Java, an atheist medical man fights a leprosy epidemic and eventually becomes a missionary.

A long slog through jungle / religious clichés, with a hilariously miscast star and an almost Victorian script.

w John Lee Mahin, Neil Paterson, *novel* Jan de Hartog *d* Robert Mulligan *ph* Russell Harlan *m* Jerry Goldsmith

Rock Hudson, Burl Ives, Geoffrey Keen, Gena Rowlands, Will Kuluva, Neva Patterson, Philip Abbott

The Spiral Staircase***

US 1945 83m bw
RKO (Dore Schary)

A small town in 1906 New England is terrorized by a psychopathic killer of deformed girls.

Archetypal old dark house thriller, superbly detailed and set during a most convincing thunderstorm. Even though the identity of the villain is pretty obvious, this is a superior Hollywood product.

w Mel Dinelli, *novel* Some Must Watch by Ethel Lina White *d* Robert Siodmak *ph* Nicholas Musuraca *m* Roy Webb *ad* Albert S. D'Agostino, Jack Okey

Dorothy McGuire, George Brent, Kent Smith, Ethel Barrymore, Rhys Williams, Rhonda Fleming, Gordon Oliver, Sara Allgood, James Bell

'A nice, cosy and well-sustained atmosphere of horror.'—C. A. Lejeune

AAN: Ethel Barrymore

The Spiral Staircase

GB 1975 89m Technicolor
Warner / Raven (Peter Shaw)

Modernized remake of the above using virtually the same script, and apparently determined to prove how badly it can be presented.

w Allan Scott, Chris Bryant *d* Peter Collinson *ph* Ken Hodges *m* David Lindup

Jacqueline Bisset, Christopher Plummer, Sam Wanamaker, Mildred Dunnock, Gayle Hunnicutt, Sheila Brennan, Elaine Stritch, John Ronane, Ronald Radd, John Phillip Law

'I don't think this needless remake is going to set anyone's flesh creeping, except at the vulgar flashiness of the whole enterprise.'— *Michael Billington, Illustrated London News*

The Spirit Is Willing
US 1966   100m   Technicolor
Paramount / William Castle

A family finds that its holiday home is haunted
by the ghosts of a *crime passionel.*
Overlong, overlayed and witless farce with
virtually no opportunity well taken.

w Ben Starr, *novel* The Visitors by Nathaniel
Benchley *d* William Castle *ph* Hal Stine
m Vic Mizzy

Sid Caesar, Vera Miles, John McGiver, Cass
Daley, John Astin, Mary Wickes, Jesse White

The Spirit of St Louis*
US 1957   135m   Warnercolor
   Cinemascope
Warner (Leyland Hayward)

In 1927 Charles Lindbergh flies a specially
constructed plane 3,600 miles nonstop New
York to Paris in 33½ hours.
Impeccably in its period, this needlessly
Cinemascoped reconstruction can scarcely
avoid dull patches since for long stretches its
hero is on screen solo apart from a fly, and his
monologues become soporific.

w Billy Wilder, Wendell Mayes, *book* Charles
Lindbergh *d* Billy Wilder *ph* Robert Burks,
Peverell Marley *m* Franz Waxman

James Stewart, Murray Hamilton, Marc
Connelly

The Spirit of the Beehive*
Spain 1973   98m   Eastmancolor
Elias Querejeta

In 1940 in a remote village, two children see a
travelling film show of Frankenstein, and their
imaginations run riot; or do they?
Sensitive story of childish imagination,
reminiscent of *Jeux Interdits* and yet very
much its own vision.

w Francisco J. Querejeta *d* Victor Erice
ph Luis Cuadrado *m* Luis de Pablo

Fernando Fernan Gomez, Teresa Gimpera,
Ana Torrent, Isabel Telleria

Spite Marriage*
US 1929   77m (24 fps)   bw   silent
MGM / Buster Keaton (Lawrence
   Weingarten)

A tailor's assistant loves an actress, who
marries him to spite someone else.
For a Keaton comedy from his great period,
this is remarkably thin on invention, and its
pleasures, though undeniable, are minor.

w Richard Schayer, Lew Lipton *d* Edward
Sedgwick *ph* Reggie Lanning

Buster Keaton, Dorothy Sebastian, Edward
Earle, Leila Hyams

Spitfire*
US 1934   88m   bw
RKO (Pandro S. Berman)

An Ozark mountain girl believes herself to be
a faith healer and is driven from the
community.
Curious star melodrama with effective
moments.

w Jane Murfin, *play* Trigger by Lula Vollmer
d John Cromwell *ph* Edward Cronjager
m Max Steiner

Katharine Hepburn, Robert Young, Ralph
Bellamy, Martha Sleeper, Louis Mason
'The picture would suggest that Katharine
Hepburn is condemned to elegance, doomed
to be a lady for the rest of her natural life, and
that her artistry does not extend to the
interpretation of the primitive or the uncouth.
That her producers have not bothered to give
her a scenario of any interest or quality is
another aspect of the situation.'—*The New
Yorker*

Splendor
US 1935   77m   bw
Samuel Goldwyn

The son of a once-wealthy Park Avenue
family marries a poor girl.
Dated romantic drama.

w Rachel Crothers, from her play *d* Elliott
Nugent *ph* Gregg Toland *md* Alfred
Newman

Joel McCrea, Miriam Hopkins, Helen
Westley, Katherine Alexander, David Niven,
Paul Cavanagh, Billie Burke, Arthur Treacher
'A model of dramatic exposition, but it
suffers from inaction and its theme is too
commonplace.'—*New York Times*

Splendor in the Grass*
US 1961   124m   Technicolor
Warner / NBI (Elia Kazan)

Adolescent love in a small Kansas town in the
twenties.
Impressive though curiously unmemorable
addition to a nostalgic young sex cycle which
was already played out; production and
performances well up to scratch.

w William Inge *d* Elia Kazan *ph* Boris
Kaufman *m* David Amram

Natalie Wood, Warren Beatty, Pat Hingle,
Audrey Christie, Barbara Loden, Zohra
Lampert, Sandy Dennis
'Less like a high-school version of *Summer
and Smoke* than [like] an Andy Hardy story
with glands.'—*Stanley Kauffmann*

AA: William Inge
AAN: Natalie Wood

Splinters
GB 1929 82m bw

Soldiers at the front in 1915 form a concert party. Easy-going crowd-pleaser of its time.
Nelson Keys, Sidney Howard, Lew Lake, Hal Jones. Written by W. P. Lipscomb; directed by Jack Raymond; for Herbert Wilcox / B and D. (NB: Sequels, of roughly the same standard, included *Splinters in the Navy*, 1931, and *Splinters in the Air*, 1937; both with Sidney Howard.)

The Split
US 1968 90m Metrocolor Panavision
MGM / Spectrum (Robert Chartoff, Irwin Winkler)

A black criminal plans to rob the Los Angeles Coliseum during a football match.
Busy, brutal crime thriller, well enough done but totally unsympathetic.

w Robert Sabaroff, *novel* The Seventh by Richard Stark *d* Gordon Flemyng *ph* Burnett Guffey *m* Quincy Jones

Jim Brown, Diahann Carroll, Ernest Borgnine, Julie Harris, Gene Hackman, Jack Klugman, Warren Oates, James Whitmore, Donald Sutherland

Split Second
US 1953 85m bw
RKO (Edmund Grainger)

An escaped convict hides out with four hostages in an Arizona ghost town which has been cleared in preparation for an atom bomb test.
Routine suspenser.

w William Bowers, Irving Wallace *d* Dick Powell *ph* Nicholas Musuraca *m* Roy Webb

Stephen McNally, Alexis Smith, Jan Sterling, Keith Andes, Arthur Hunnicutt, Paul Kelly, Richard Egan, Robert Paige

The Spoilers*
US 1930 86m bw
Paramount

In Alaska during the gold rush, crooked government officials begin despoiling the richest claims.
Early talkie version of a famous brawling saga.

w Bartlett Cormack, Agnes Brand Leahy, *novel* Rex Beach *d* Edward Carewe *ph* Harry Fischbeck

Gary Cooper, William 'Stage' Boyd, Betty Compson, Kay Johnson, Harry Green, Slim Summerville

The Spoilers**
US 1942 87m bw
Universal (Frank Lloyd)

Two adventurers in the Yukon quarrel over land rights and a saloon entertainer.
Well-packaged mixture of saloon brawls, romance and adventure, much filmed as a silent.

w Lawrence Hazard, Tom Reed *d* Ray Enright *ph* Milton Krasner *m* Hans Salter *ad* Jack Otterson

Marlene Dietrich, Randolph Scott, John Wayne, Margaret Lindsay, Harry Carey, Richard Barthelmess, George Cleveland, Samuel S. Hinds

The Spoilers*
US 1955 82m Technicolor
U-I (Ross Hunter)

Adequate, unmemorable remake of the above.

w Oscar Brodney, Charles Hoffman *d* Jesse Hibbs *ph* Maury Gertsman *m* Joseph Gershenson

Anne Baxter, Jeff Chandler, Rory Calhoun, Barbara Britton, Carl Benton Reid, Ray Danton, John McIntire, Raymond Walburn, Wallace Ford

The Sport of Kings
GB 1931 98m bw

A strict JP inherits a bookie business. Heavy-going adaptation of a stage comedy warhorse, which nevertheless paved the way for many screen farces of the thirties. Leslie Henson, Gordon Harker, Hugh Wakefield, Dorothy Boyd. Written by Angus MacPhail, from the play by Ian Hay; directed by Victor Saville; for Gainsborough.

Spring and Port Wine
GB 1970 101m Technicolor
EMI / Memorial (Michael Medwin)

A Lancashire family runs into trouble when stern father insists that teenage daughter should eat a meal she refuses.
A popular old-fashioned stage comedy which simply doesn't work on film, partly from being set in a too-real town (Bolton) and partly because of a miscast lead.

w Bill Naughton, from his play *d* Peter Hammond *ph* Norman Warwick *m* Douglas Gamley *pd* Reece Pemberton

James Mason, Diana Coupland, Susan George, Rodney Bewes, Hannah Gordon, Adrienne Posta, Arthur Lowe

Spring in Park Lane**
GB 1948 92m bw
British Lion / Herbert Wilcox

A diamond merchant's niece falls for a
footman who just happens to be an
impoverished lord in disguise.

Flimsy but highly successful romantic comedy
which managed to get its balance right and is
still pretty entertaining, much more so than its
sequel *Maytime in Mayfair*.

w Nicholas Phipps, play Come Out of the
Kitchen by Alice Duer Miller *d Herbert
Wilcox ph* Max Greene *m* Robert Farnon

*Anna Neagle, Michael Wilding, Tom Walls,
Nicholas Phipps*, Peter Graves, Marjorie
Fielding, *Nigel Patrick*, Lana Morris

'A never-failing dream of Olde Mayfaire
and its eternally funny butlers and maids, its
disguised lords and ladies.'—*Richard
Winnington*

Spring Meeting
GB 1940 93m bw

In Ireland, an impecunious widow wants her
son to marry the daughter of an old flame.

Staid film version of a comedy whose
characters turned up again in *Treasure Hunt*.
Nova Pilbeam, Basil Sydney, Henry Edwards,
Sarah Churchill, Michael Wilding, *Margaret
Rutherford*, Enid Stamp Taylor, Hugh
McDermott. Written by Walter C. Mycroft
and Norman Lee, from the play by M. J.
Farrell and John Perry; directed by Walter C.
Mycroft; for ABPC.

Spring Parade*
US 1940 89m bw
Universal (Joe Pasternak)

A single baker's assistant falls for a prince.
Pleasing, artificial Austrian frou-frou with star
and support in good escapist form.

w Bruce Manning, Felix Jackson, *story* Ernst
Marischka *d* Henry Koster *ph* Joseph
Valentine *m* Robert Stolz *md* Charles Previn

Deanna Durbin, Robert Cummings, S. Z.
Sakall, Mischa Auer, Henry Stephenson,
Anne Gwynne, Butch and Buddy

AAN: Joseph Valentine; Charles Previn; song
'Waltzing in the Clouds' (*m* Robert Stolz,
ly Gus Kahn)

Spring Reunion
US 1956 79m bw
UA / Bryna (Jerry Bresler)

College classmates fall in love all over again at
a reunion fifteen years later.

Romantic fiction for the middle-aged,
performed with bare competence.

wd Robert Pirosh *ph* Harold Lipstein
m Herbert Spencer, Earle Hagen

Betty Hutton, Dana Andrews, Jean Hagen,
Robert Simon, James Gleason, Laura La
Plante, Irene Ryan

Springfield Rifle
US 1952 93m Warnercolor
Warner (Louis E. Edelman)

A Union officer gets himself cashiered, joins
the Confederates as a spy, and unmasks a
traitor.

Stolid Civil War western with Grade A
production but not much individuality.

w Charles Marquis Warren, Frank Davis
d André de Toth *ph* Edwin DuPar *m* Max
Steiner

Gary Cooper, Phyllis Thaxter, David Brian,
Lon Chaney Jnr, Paul Kelly, Phil Carey,
James Millican, Guinn Williams

Springtime in the Rockies
US 1942 91m Technicolor
TCF (Darryl F. Zanuck)

Romances blossom on a mountain holiday.
Flimsily-plotted, studio-bound, absolutely
routine musical.

w Walter Bullock, Ken Englund *d* Irving
Cummings *ph* Ernest Palmer *m* Alfred
Newman *songs* Mack Gordon, Harry Warren

Betty Grable, John Payne, Carmen Miranda,
Edward Everett Horton, Cesar Romero,
Charlotte Greenwood, Frank Orth, Harry
James and his Music Makers

Spy for a Day
GB 1939 71m bw

A farm hand is discovered to be the exact
double of a spy. The only screen vehicle for
this 'gormless' comedian, and not a bad one.
Duggie Wakefield, Paddy Browne, Jack Allen,
Albert Lieven, Nicholas Hannen, Gibb
McLaughlin. Written by Anatole de
Grunwald, Hans Wilhelm, Emeric
Pressburger, Ralph Block and Tommy
Thompson, from a story by Stacy Aumonier;
directed by Mario Zampi; for Two Cities.

Spy Hunt*
US 1950 74m bw
Universal (Ralph Dietrich)
GB title: *Panther's Moon*

Secret microfilm is stowed in the collar of one
of two panthers being transported out of
Europe by train for circus use.
Slick minor espionage thriller.

w George Zuckerman, Leonard Lee, *novel*
Panther's Moon by Victor Canning *d* George
Sherman, *ph* Irving Glassberg *m* Walter
Scharf *md* Joseph Gershenson

Howard Duff, Marta Toren, Philip Friend,
Robert Douglas, Philip Dorn, Walter Slezak,
Kurt Kreuger

The Spy in Black**
GB 1939 82 bw
Harefield / Alexander Korda (Irving Asher)
US title: *U-Boat 29*

In the Orkneys in 1917, German spies don't
trust each other.
Unusual romantic melodrama which provided
an unexpectedly interesting romantic team.

w Emeric Pressburger, Roland Pertwee, *novel*
J. Storer Clouston *d* Michael Powell
ph Bernard Browne *m* Miklos Rosza

Conrad Veidt, Valerie Hobson, Hay Petrie,
Helen Haye, Sebastian Shaw, Marius Goring,
June Duprez, Athole Stewart, Cyril Raymond

Spy of Napoleon
GB 1936 101m bw

A dancer saves Louis Napoleon from
assassination. Solidly mounted period piece
without much sense of humour. Richard
Barthelmess, Dolly Haas, Frank Vosper,
Francis L. Sullivan, Lyn Harding, Henry
Oscar. Written by L. DuGarde Peach,
Frederick Merrick and Harold Simpson;
directed by Maurice Elvey; for Twickenham.

The Spy Who Came in from the Cold**
GB 1966 112m bw
Paramount / Salem (Martin Ritt)

A British master spy is offered a chance to get
even with his East German opponent by being
apparently sacked, disillusioned, and open for
recruitment.
The old undercover yarn with trimmings of
such sixties malaises as death wish, anti-
establishmentism and racial problems. As a
yarn, quite gripping till it gets too downbeat,
but very harshly photographed.

w Paul Dehn, Guy Trosper, *novel* John Le
Carré *d* Martin Ritt *ph* Oswald Morris
m Sol Kaplan *pd* Tambi Larsen

Richard Burton, Claire Bloom, *Oskar Werner*,
Peter Van Eyck, Sam Wanamaker, Rupert
Davies, George Voskovec, Cyril Cusack,
Michael Hordern, Robert Hardy, Bernard
Lee, Beatrix Lehmann
AAN: Richard Burton

The Spy Who Loved Me
GB 1977 125m Eastmancolor
Panavision
UA / Eon (Albert R. Broccoli)

James Bond and a glamorous Russian spy
combine forces to track down and eliminate a
megalomaniac shipping magnate with an
undersea missile base.
Witless spy extravaganza in muddy colour,
with the usual tired chases and pussyfoot
violence but no new gimmicks except a seven-
foot villain with steel teeth.

w Christopher Wood, Richard Maibaum,
novel Ian Fleming *d* Lewis Gilbert
ph Claude Renoir *m* Marvin Hamlisch
pd Ken Adam

Roger Moore, Barbara Bach, Curt Jurgens,
Richard Kiel, Caroline Munro, Walter Gotell,
Bernard Lee, Lois Maxwell, George Baker,
Desmond Llewellyn, Edward De Souza,
Sydney Tafler
'The film, bearing no relation to its nominal
source, seems to do nothing more than
anthologize its forerunners.'—*Tim Pulleine,
MFB*

AAN: Marvin Hamlisch; song, 'Nobody Does
It Better'

The Spy with a Cold Nose
GB 1966 93m Eastmancolor
Paramount / Associated London / Embassy
(Robert Porter)

A fashionable vet is blackmailed by MI5 into
inserting a radio transmitter into a bulldog.
Rather painful, overacted and overwritten
farce full of obvious jokes masquerading as
satire.

w Ray Galton, Alan Simpson *d* Daniel
Petrie *ph* Kenneth Higgins *m* Riz Ortolani
Lionel Jeffries, Laurence Harvey, Daliah Lavi,
Eric Sykes, Eric Portman, Colin Blakely,
Denholm Elliott, Robert Flemyng, Paul Ford,
Bernard Lee, June Whitfield, Bernard
Archard

S•P•Y•S
GB 1974 100m Technicolor
Dymphana / C-W / American Film
Properties (Irwin Winkler, Robert
Chartoff)

Clumsy CIA agents in Paris come across a list
of KGB agents in China.
Surprisingly dull and unfashionable parade of
comic spy clichés; the talents involved
obviously intended something closer to
M*A*S*H.

w Malcolm Marmorstein, Lawrence J. Cohen, Fred Freeman *d* Irwin Kershner *ph* Gerry Fisher *m* John Scott

Elliott Gould, Donald Sutherland, Zouzou, Joss Ackland, Kenneth Griffith, Vladek Sheybal

'Seems to have arrived several years too late to find its true niche.'—*Sight and Sound*

Squadron Leader X
GB 1942 100m bw
RKO (Victor Hanbury)

A Nazi hero poses as a British pilot but has difficulty getting back home.
Tall war story with dreary romantic trimmings.

w Wolfgang Wilhelm, Miles Malleson
d Lance Comfort

Eric Portman, Ann Dvorak, Walter Fitzgerald, Barry Jones, Henry Oscar, Beatrice Varley

The Squall
US 1929 105m bw

A Hungarian gypsy girl attracts all the male members of a farming family, and causes trouble. Perfectly awful melodrama made worse by early sound techniques. Myrna Loy, Alice Joyce, Loretta Young, Richard Ticker, Carroll Nye, Zasu Pitts, Harry Cording. Written by Bradley King, from the play by Jean Bart; directed by Alexander Korda; for Warner.

The Square Jungle
US 1955 85m bw
U-I (Albert Zugsmith)

A conceited boxer gets his come-uppance.
Tailor-made studio co-feature.

w George Zuckerman *d* Jerry Hopper *ph* George Robinson *m* Heinz Roemheld

Tony Curtis, Ernest Borgnine, Pat Crowley, Jim Backus, Paul Kelly

The Square Peg*
GB 1958 89m bw
Rank (Hugh Stewart)

An army recruit finds he is the double of a German general.
Slam-bang star slapstick, shorter than usual and with a few jokes that can't fail.

w Jack Davies *d* John Paddy Carstairs *ph* Jack Cox *m* Philip Green

Norman Wisdom, Edward Chapman, Campbell Singer, Hattie Jacques, Brian Worth, Terence Alexander

The Squaw Man
US 1931 106m bw
MGM (Cecil B. de Mille)
GB title: *The White Man*

An Indian maiden saves the life of a British aristocrat, bears his child and commits suicide.
Third outing for a hoary miscegenation drama filmed in 1914 with Dustin Farnum and Red Wing, and in 1918 with Elliott Dexter and Ann Little. This talkie version sank without trace.

w Lucien Hubbard, Lenore Coffee, *play* Edwin Milton Royle *d* Cecil B. de Mille *ph* Harold Rosson *m* Herbert Stothart

Warner Baxter, Lupe Velez, Charles Bickford, Eleanor Boardman, Roland Young, Paul Cavanagh, Raymond Hatton

The Squeaker*
GB 1937 77m bw
London Films (Alexander Korda)
US title: *Murder on Diamond Row*

A dangerous diamond fence is unmasked by a discredited policeman.
Typical Edgar Wallace who-is-it, performed with old-fashioned bravura.

w Edward O. Berkman, Bryan Wallace, *novel* Edgar Wallace *d* William K. Howard

Edmund Lowe, Sebastian Shaw, Ann Todd, Tamara Desni, Alastair Sim, Robert Newton, Allan Jeayes, Stewart Rome
† Previously filmed in 1930, directed by Edgar Wallace for British Lion; with Percy Marmont, Eric Maturin, Anne Grey and Nigel Bruce.

The Squeeze
GB 1977 107m Technicolor
Warner / Martinat (Stanley O'Toole)

An alcoholic ex-cop rescues his ex-wife from kidnappers.
Sleazy action thriller which despite efficient production goes over the top in its search for unpleasant detail.

w Leon Griffiths, *novel* David Craig *d* Michael Apted *ph* Dennis Lewiston *m* David Hentschel

Stacy Keach, David Hemmings, Stephen Boyd, Edward Fox, Carol White, Freddie Starr

Squibs*
GB 1935 77m bw

A cockney flowergirl wins a sweepstake.
Acceptable sound version of a series of rather naïve silents which pleased the crowds in the early twenties with the same star: they were

Squibs, Squibs MP, Squibs' Honeymoon and *Squibs Wins the Calcutta Sweep. Betty Balfour,* Gordon Harker, Stanley Holloway, Margaret Yarde, Michael Shepley. Written by Michael Hogan and H. Fowler Mear, from the play by Clifford Seyler and George Pearson; directed by Henry Edwards; for Twickenham.

Squirm
US 1976   92m   Movielab
AIP / The Squirm Company (Edgar
  Lansbury, Joseph Beruh)

A power cable cut in a storm turns worms into maneaters.
Revolting shocker with a few funny moments for those who can take it.

wd Jeff Lieberman *ph* Joseph Mangine
m Robert Prince

John Scardino, Patricia Pearcy, R. A. Dow, Jean Sullivan

Stablemates
US 1938   89m   bw

A broken-down vet saves a stableboy's racehorse. Sentimental comedy vehicle for two masters of the surreptitious tear. Wallace Beery, Mickey Rooney, Margaret Hamilton, Minor Watson, Marjorie Gateson. Written by Reginald Owen and William Thiele; directed by Sam Wood; for MGM.

Stage Door•••
US 1937   93m   bw
RKO (Pandro S. Berman)

Life in a New York theatrical boarding house for girls.
Melodramatic, sharply comedic, always fascinating slice of stagey life from a Broadway hit; the performances alone make it worth preserving.

w Morrie Ryskind, Anthony Veiller, play Edna Ferber, George S. Kaufman d Gregory La Cava ph Robert de Grasse m Roy Webb ad Van Nest Polglase

Katharine Hepburn, Ginger Rogers, Adolphe Menjou, Gail Patrick, Constance Collier, Andrea Leeds, Lucille Ball, Samuel S. Hinds, Jack Carson, Franklin Pangborn, Eve Arden
  'It is a long time since we have seen so much feminine talent so deftly handled.'—*Otis Ferguson*
  'Zest and pace and photographic eloquence.'—*Frank S. Nugent, New York Times*
  'A rare example of a film substantially improving on a stage original and a

remarkably satisfying film on all levels.'—*NFT, 1973*

AAN: best picture; script; Gregory La Cava; Andrea Leeds

Stage Door Canteen•
US 1943   132m   bw
Sol Lesser (Barnett Briskin)

How the stars in New York entertained the armed forces during World War II.
Nothing as a film, mildly interesting as sociology and for some rarish appearances.

w Delmer Daves *d* Frank Borzage *ph* Harry Wild *m* Freddie Rich *pd* Harry Horner

Cheryl Walker, Lon McCallister, Judith Anderson, Tallulah Bankhead, Ray Bolger, Katherine Cornell, Helen Hayes, George Jessel, Alfred Lunt, Harpo Marx, Yehudi Menuhin, Elliott Nugent, Cornelia Otis Skinner, Ethel Waters, May Whitty, William Demarest, Gracie Fields, Katharine Hepburn, Gertrude Lawrence, Ethel Merman, Merle Oberon, Johnny Weissmuller, Edgar Bergen, Jane Cowl, Lynn Fontanne, Paul Muni, Gypsy Rose Lee, George Raft, etc; Count Basie, Benny Goodman, Xavier Cugat, Guy Lombardo, Kay Kyser and their bands
  'A nice harmless picture for the whole family, and a goldmine for those who are willing to go to it in the wrong spirit.'—*James Agee*

AAN: Freddie Rich; song 'We Mustn't Say Goodbye' (*m* Johnny Monaco, *ly* Al Dubin)

Stage Fright•
GB 1950   110m   bw
Warner / ABPC (Alfred Hitchcock)

A man is on the run for a backstage murder, and his girl friend takes a job as maid to the great star he says is responsible.
Creaky Hitchcock thriller in which you can see all the joins and the stars seem stuck in treacle; but a few of the set pieces work well enough.

w Whitfield Cook, *novel* Man Running by Selwyn Jepson *d* Alfred Hitchcock *ph* Wilkie Cooper *m* Leighton Lucas

Marlene Dietrich, Jane Wyman, Richard Todd, Alastair Sim, Michael Wilding, Sybil Thorndike, Kay Walsh, Miles Malleson

Stage Struck
US 1936   95m   bw
Warner (Robert Lord)

Young people put on a show and become instant hits.

Dim musical oddly shorn of production numbers.

w Tom Buckinham, Pat C. Flick, Robert Lord *d / ch* Busby Berkeley *ph* Byron Haskin *m* Leo F. Forbstein *songs* Harold Arlen, E. Y. Harburg

Dick Powell, Joan Blondell, Jeanne Madden, the Yacht Club Boys, Warren William, Frank McHugh

Stage Struck**
US 1957   95m   Technicolor
RKO (Stuart Millar)

A young actress comes to New York intent on stardom . . .
Careful, slightly arid remake of *Morning Glory* marred by a tiresome central performance; good theatrical detail.

w Ruth and Augustus Goetz, *play* Zoe Akins *d* Sidney Lumet *ph* Franz Planer *m* Alex North *ad* Kim Edgar Swados

Susan Strasberg, Henry Fonda, Herbert Marshall, *Joan Greenwood*, Christopher Plummer

Stage to Thunder Rock
US 1964   89m   Techniscope
Paramount / A. C. Lyles

An ageing sheriff takes a bank robber back to jail by stagecoach.
Acceptable lower-berth western with the producer's usual roster of half-forgotten character actors.

w Charles Wallace *d* William F. Claxton *ph* W. Wallace Kelley *m* Paul Dunlap

Barry Sullivan, Marilyn Maxwell, Scott Brady, Keenan Wynn, Allan Jones, Lon Chaney Jnr, John Agar, Wanda Hendrix, Anne Seymour, Robert Lowery

Stagecoach****
US 1939   99m   bw
(UA) Walter Wanger

Various western characters board a stagecoach in danger from an Indian war party.
What looked like a minor western with a plot borrowed from Maupassant's *Boule de suif*, became a classic by virtue of the firm characterization, restrained writing, exciting climax and the scenery of Monument Valley. Whatever the reasons, it damn well works.

w Dudley Nichols, *story* Stage to Lordsburg by Ernest Haycox *d* John Ford *ph* Bert Glennon, Ray Binger *m* Richard Hageman, W. Frank Harling, John Leopold, Leo Shuken, Louis Gruenberg *md* Boris Morros

Claire Trevor, John Wayne, Thomas Mitchell, George Bancroft, Andy Devine, Berton Churchill, Louise Platt, John Carradine, Donald Meek, Tim Holt, Chris-Pin Martin
'Grand Hotel on wheels.'—*New Yorker, 1975*
'The basic western, a template for everything that followed.'—*John Baxter, 1968*
'A motion picture that sings a song of camera.'—*Frank S. Nugent, New York Times*

AA: music; Thomas Mitchell
AAN: best picture; John Ford; Bert Glennon; Ray Binger

Stagecoach
US 1966   114m   De Luxe   Cinemascope
TCF / Martin Rackin

Absolutely awful remake of the above; costly but totally spiritless, miscast and uninteresting.

w Joseph Landon *d* Gordon Douglas *ph* William H. Clothier *m* Jerry Goldsmith

Ann-Margret, Alex Cord, Bing Crosby, Van Heflin, Slim Pickens, Robert Cummings, Stefanie Powers, Michael Connors, Red Buttons, Keenan.Wynn

Staircase*
US / France 1969   101m   De Luxe
   Panavision
TCF / Stanely Donen

The problems of two ageing homosexual hairdressers.
Unsatisfactorily opened-out and over-acted version of an effective two-handler play. Oddly made in France, so that the London detail seems all wrong.

w Charles Dyer, from his play *d* Stanley Donen *ph* Christopher Challis *m* Dudley Moore

Richard Burton, Rex Harrison, Cathleen Nesbitt, Beatrix Lehmann
'The shape is smashed . . . no longer a graceful duet, it becomes a waddling tale, spattered with ugliness, that falls into the biggest sentimental trap for homosexual material: it pleads for pity.'—*Stanley Kauffmann*

Stakeout on Dope Street*
US 1958   83m   bw
Warner (Andrew J. Fenady)

Three young men find a briefcase containing heroin and are attacked by the gangsters who lost it.
Lively little crime morality, uneven but worth a look.

w Irwin Schwartz, Irvin Kershner, Andrew J. Fenady *d* Irvin Kershner *ph* Mark Jeffrey *m* Richard Markowitz

Yale Wexler, Jonathon Haze, Morris Miller, Abby Dalton

Stalag 17**
US 1953 120m bw
Paramount (Billy Wilder)

Comedy and tragedy for American servicemen in a Nazi prisoner-of-war camp.

High jinks, violence and mystery in a sharply calculated mixture; an atmosphere quite different from the understated British films on the subject.

w Billy Wilder, Edwin Blum, *play* Donald Bevan, Edmund Trzinski *d* Billy Wilder *ph* Ernest Laszlo *m* Franz Waxman

William Holden, Don Taylor, Otto Preminger, *Robert Strauss*, Harvey Lembeck, Richard Erdman, Peter Graves, Neville Grand, Sig Rumann
'A facility for continuous rapid-fire action which alternately brings forth the laughs and tingles the spine.'—*Otis L. Guernsey Jnr*
'Raucous and tense, heartless and sentimental, always fast-paced, it has already been assigned by critics to places on their lists of the year's ten best movies.'—*Life*

AA: William Holden
AAN: Billy Wilder (as director), Robert Strauss

The Stalking Moon*
US 1968 109m Technicolor
Panavision
National General / Stalking Moon Company (Alan J. Pakula)

An ageing scout escorts home a white woman who has escaped from the Indians, and kills a murderous Apache.

Slow, thoughtful western with effective moments.

w Alvin Sargent, *novel* Theodore V. Olsen *d* Robert Mulligan *ph* Charles Lang *m* Fred Karlin

Gregory Peck, Eva Marie Saint, Robert Forster, Frank Silvera

Stallion Road
US 1947 97m bw
Warner (Alex Gottlieb)

An outbreak of anthrax threatens a racing stable.

Routine romantic drama with sporting background.

w Stephen Longstreed *d* James V. Kern *ph* Arthur Edeson *m* Frederick Hollander

Ronald Reagan, Alexis Smith, Zachary Scott, Peggy Knudsen, Patti Brady, Harry Davenport, Frank Puglia

Stamboul Quest
US 1934 88m bw
MGM (Walter Wanger)

During World War I, Germany's most notorious lady spy falls for an American medical student.

Modest variation on the true story twice filmed as *Fraülein Doktor*; standard Hollywood values.

w Herman J. Mankiewicz *d* Sam Wood *ph* James Wong Howe *m* Herbert Stothart

Myrna Loy, George Brent, Lionel Atwill, C. Henry Gordon, Douglass Dumbrille, Mischa Auer.

The Stand at Apache River
US 1953 77m Technicolor

Apaches attack a reservation when the army won't listen to reason. Conventional western with sympathy for the Indians. Stephen McNally, Julie Adams, Hugh Marlowe, Hugh O'Brian, Jack Kelly. Written by Arthur Ross; directed by Lee Sholem; for Universal-International.

Stand by for Action
US 1943 109m bw
MGM (Robert Z. Leonard, Orville O. Dull)
GB title: *Cargo of Innocents*

A Harvard graduate learns the realities of war on an old destroyer.

Studio-bound war heroics slurping into sentiment.

w George Bruce, Herman J. Mankiewicz, John L. Balderston *d* Robert Z. Leonard *ph* Charles Rosher *m* Lennie Hayton

Robert Taylor, Charles Laughton, Brian Donlevy, Walter Brennan, Marilyn Maxwell, Henry O'Neill

Stand In*
US 1937 90m bw
Walter Wanger

An efficiency expert is sent to save a Hollywood studio from bankruptcy.

Amusing satire which could have done with sharper scripting and firmer control but is pleasantly remembered.

w Gene Towne, Graham Baker, *serial* Clarence Budington Kelland *d* Tay Garnett *ph* Charles G. Clarke *m* Heinz Roemheld

Leslie Howard, Joan Blondell, Humphrey Bogart, Alan Mowbray, Marla Shelton, C. Henry Gordon, Jack Carson, Tully Marshall

Stand Up and Be Counted*
US 1971 99m Eastmancolor
Columbia / Mike Frankovich

An international woman journalist returns to
Denver and becomes involved in women's lib.
A glamoured-up flirtation with a fashionable
theme, quite nicely done but instantly dated—
and sociologically interesting.

w Bernard Slade d Jackie Cooper ph Fred
Koenekamp m Ernie Wilkins

Jacqueline Bisset, Stella Stevens, Steve
Lawrence, Gary Lockwood, *Loretta Swit*, Lee
Purcell, Madlyn Rhue

Stand Up and Cheer*
US 1934 80m bw
Fox (Winfield Sheehan)

The new US Secretary of Amusement
attempts to shake the country's Depression
blues by staging a mammoth revue.
Naïve propaganda, but the whole world was
swept away to cloud nine—by Shirley Temple.

w Ralph Spence, Will Rogers, Philip Klein
d Hamilton McFadden ph Ernest Palmer
md Arthur Lange

Warner Baxter, Madge Evans, Nigel Bruce,
Stepin Fetchit, Frank Melton, Lila Lee, Ralph
Morgan, James Dunn, *Shirley Temple*, John
Boles, George K. Arthur
  'Impossible to file it away in an ordinary
drawer marked 'Stinkers'. This one is extra, it
is super, and it butters itself very thickly with
the most obvious sort of topical
significance.'—*Otis Ferguson*

Stand Up and Fight*
US 1939 99m bw
MGM (Mervyn Le Roy)

A southern aristocrat comes into conflict with
a stagecoach operator used as transportation
for stolen slaves.
Superior star action piece with plenty of
vigorous brawls.

w James M. Cain, Jane Murfin, Harvey
Ferguson d W. S. Van Dyke II ph Leonard
Smith m William Axt

Wallace Beery, Robert Taylor, Florence Rice,
Helen Broderick, Charles Bickford, Barton
MacLane, Charley Grapewin, John Qualen

Stand Up Virgin Soldiers
GB 1977 90m Technicolor
Warner / Greg Smith / Maidenhead

More sexual adventures of National
Servicemen in Singapore in 1950.

The Virgin Soldiers had a certain authenticity
behind the fooling; this is a bawdy romp, and
not a very efficient one.

w Leslie Thomas, from his novel d Norman
Cohen ph Ken Hodges m Ed Welch

Nigel Davenport, Robin Askwith, George
Layton, Robin Nedwell, Warren Mitchell,
John Le Mesurier, Edward Woodward, Irene
Handl

Standing Room Only*
US 1944 83m bw
Paramount (Paul Jones)

Hotel rooms being hard to find in wartime
Washington, a resourceful secretary hires out
herself and her boss as a servant couple.
Moderate romantic farce with a few good
laughs.

w Darrell Ware, Karl Tunberg d Sidney
Lanfield ph Charles Lang m Robert Emmett
Dolan

Paulette Goddard, Fred MacMurray, Edward
Arnold, Roland Young, Hillary Brooke,
Porter Hall, Clarence Kolb, Anne Revere

Stanley and Livingstone**
US 1939 101m bw
TCF (Kenneth MacGowan)

An American journalist goes to Africa to find
a lost Victorian explorer.
A prestige picture which played reasonably
fair with history and still managed to please
the masses.

w Philip Dunne, Julien Josephson d Henry
King ph George Barnes m Alfred Newman
ad Thomas Little

Spencer Tracy, Cedric Hardwicke, Richard
Greene, Nancy Kelly, Walter Brennan,
Charles Coburn, Henry Hull, Henry Travers,
Miles Mander, Holmes Herbert
  'Sound, worthy, interesting.'—*Richard
Mallett, Punch*
  'Most of the film consists of long shots of
stand-ins moving across undistinguished
scenery. . . . Mr Tracy is always a human
being, but Sir Cedric is an elocution lesson, a
handclasp.'—*Graham Greene*

The Star*
US 1952 91m bw
TCF / Bert E. Friedlob

A once famous Hollywood star is financially
and psychologically on her uppers.
A movie apparently tailor-made for its star
turns out to be a disappointingly plotless
wallow.

w Katherine Albert, Dale Eunson d Stuart
Heisler ph Ernest Laszlo m Victor Young

Bette Davis, Sterling Hayden, Natalie Wood, Warner Anderson, Minor Watson

'The story of every woman who ever climbed the stairway to the stars—and found herself at the bottom looking up!'—*publicity*

AAN: Bette Davis

Star!**

US 1968 194m De Luxe Todd-AO
TCF / Robert Wise (Saul Chaplin)

Revue artist Gertrude Lawrence rises from poverty to international stardom and a measure of happiness.
Elephantiasis finally ruins this patient, detached, generally likeable recreation of a past theatrical era. In the old Hollywood style, it would probably have been even better on a smaller budget; but alas the star would still have been ill at ease with the drunken termagant scenes.

w William Fairchild *d* Robert Wise *ph* Ernest Laszlo *md* Lennie Hayton *ch* Michael Kidd *pd* Boris Leven

Julie Andrews, Richard Crenna, Michael Craig, *Daniel Massey* (as Noel Coward), John Collin, Robert Reed, Bruce Forsyth, Beryl Reid, Jenny Agutter
† Short version: *Those Were the Happy Days*.

AAN: Ernest Laszlo; Lennie Hayton; title song (*m* James Van Heusen, *ly* Sammy Cahn); Daniel Massey

Star Dust*

US 1940 85m bw
TCF (Kenneth MacGowan)

A talent scout discovers a new Hollywood star.
Light, amusing studio comedy, a pleasing addition to Hollywood mythology.

w Robert Ellis, Helen Logan *d* Walter Lang *ph* Peverell Marley *m* David Buttolph

Linda Darnell, John Payne, Roland Young, Charlotte Greenwood, William Gargan, Mary Beth Hughes, Donald Meek, Jessie Ralph

A Star Is Born***

US 1937 111m Technicolor
David O. Selznick

A young actress meets Hollywood success and marries a famous leading man, whose star wanes as hers shines brighter.
Abrasive romantic melodrama which is also the most accurate study of Hollywood ever put on film.

w Dorothy Parker, Alan Campbell, Robert Carson, story William A. Wellman, based partly on *What Price Hollywood* (1932) (qv)

d William A. Wellman *ph* W. Howard Greene *m* Max Steiner

Janet Gaynor, Fredric March, Adolphe Menjou, Lionel Stander, Andy Devine, May Robson, Owen Moore, Franklin Pangborn
'Good entertainment by any standards.'—*Frank S. Nugent, New York Times*
'A peculiar sort of masochistic self-congratulatory Hollywood orgy.'—*New Yorker, 1975*
'The first colour job that gets close to what colour must eventually come to: it keeps the thing in its place, underlining the mood and situation of the story rather than dimming everything else out in an iridescent razzle-dazzle.'—*Otis Ferguson*

AA: original story; W. Howard Greene
AAN: best picture; script; William A. Wellman; Janet Gaynor; Fredric March

A Star Is Born**

US 1954 181m Technicolor
Cinemascope
Warner (Sidney Luft)

Musical version of the above which begins very strongly and has two splendid performances, but suffers in the second half from a lack of writing strength and heavy post-production cutting. The numbers add very little except length.

w Moss Hart *d* George Cukor *ph* Sam Leavitt *md* Ray Heindorf

Judy Garland, James Mason, Charles Bickford, Jack Carson, Tommy Noonan, Amanda Blake, Lucy Marlow
'Maintains a skilful balance between the musical and the tear jerker.'—*Penelope Houston*

AAN: Ray Heindorf; song 'The Man that Got Away' (*m* Harold Arlen, *ly* Ira Gershwin); Judy Garland; James Mason

A Star Is Born*

US 1976 140m Metrocolor
Warner / Barwood / First Artists (Barbra Streisand, Jon Peters)

Interminable remake set in the pop world amid screaming crowds and songs at high decibel level; also an insufferable piece of showing off by the star. But some of the handling has style.

w John Gregory Dunne, Joan Didion, Frank Pierson *d* Frank Pierson *ph* Robert Surtees *md* Paul Williams *pd* Polly Platt

Barbra Streisand, Kris Kristofferson, Paul Mazursky, Gary Busey

'A clear case for the monopolies commission.'—*Michael Billington, Illustrated London News*

'A bore is starred.'—*Village Voice*

AA: song 'Evergreen' (*m* Barbra Streisand, *ly* Paul Williams)

AAN: Robert Surtees; Roger Kellaway (music underscoring)

The Star Maker*
US 1939 94m bw
Paramount (Charles R. Rodgers)

A songwriter makes the big time by organizing kid acts.
Pleasant minor musical based on the career of Gus Edwards.

w Frank Butler, Don Hartman, Arthur Caesar *d* Roy del Ruth *ph* Karl Struss

Bing Crosby, Louise Campbell, Linda Ware, Ned Sparks, Laura Hope Crews, Janet Waldo, Walter Damrosch

Star of Midnight**
US 1935 90m bw
RKO (Pandro S. Berman)

A New York attorney solves the disappearance of a leading lady.
Wisecracking, debonair murder mystery modelled on *The Thin Man*.

w Howard J. Green, Anthony Veiller, Edward Kaufman *d* Stephen Roberts *ph* J. Roy Hunt *m* Max Steiner

William Powell, Ginger Rogers, Paul Kelly, Gene Lockhart, Ralph Morgan, Leslie Fenton, J. Farrell MacDonald

'It is all suavity and amusement, pistol shots and cocktails.'—*Graham Greene*

'One of the best sophisticated comedy-mysteries in a period full of such films.'—*NFT, 1973*

The Star Spangled Girl
US 1971 92m colour
Paramount (Howard W. Koch)

A sweet old-fashioned girl is fought for by two young radicals.
Unamusingly 'with it' comedy from an unsuccessful play.

w Arnold Margolin, Jim Parker, *play* Neil Simon *d* Jerry Paris *ph* Sam Leavitt *m* Charles Fox

Sandy Duncan, Tony Roberts, Todd Susman, Elizabeth Allen

Star Spangled Rhythm***
US 1942 99m bw
Paramount (Joseph Sistrom)

The doorman of Paramount Studios pretends to his sailor son that he is a big producer.
Frenetic farce involving most of the talent on Paramount's payroll and culminating in an 'impromptu' show staged for the navy. A good lighthearted glimpse of wartime Hollywood.

w Harry Tugend *d* George Marshall *ph* Leo Tover, Theodor Sparkuhl, *md* Robert Emmett Dolan *songs* Johnny Mercer, Harold Arlen

Betty Hutton, Eddie Bracken, *Victor Moore, Walter Abel,* Anne Revere, Cass Daley, Gil Lamb, Macdonald Carey, Bob Hope, Bing Crosby, Paulette Goddard, Veronica Lake, Dorothy Lamour, Vera Zorina, Fred MacMurray, Ray Milland, Lynne Overman, Franchot Tone, Dick Powell, *Walter Dare Wahl and Co, Cecil B. de Mille, Preston Sturges,* Alan Ladd, Rochester, Katherine Dunham, Susan Hayward

AAN: Robert Emmett Dolan; song 'Black Magic' (*m* Harold Arlen, *ly* Johnny Mercer)

Star Trek: The Motion Picture
US 1979 132m Metrocolor Panavision
Paramount (Gene Roddenberry)

In the twenty-third century, Admiral Kirk resumes command of the *Enterprise* to combat an alien force.
And a surprisingly boring one. Vast sets and big-screen solemnity hardly make this more enjoyable than some of the TV episodes which got more tricks and philosophical fun into one-third of the length.

w Harold Livingstone, Alan Dean Foster *d* Robert Wise *ph* Richard H. Kline, Richard Yuricich *m* Jerry Goldsmith *pd* Harold Michelson

William Shatner, Leonard Nimoy, DeForest Kelley, Stephen Collins, Persis Khambatta

Star Wars***
US 1977 121m Technicolor
Panavision
TCF / Lucasfilm (Gary Kurtz)

A rebel princess in a distant galaxy escapes, and with the help of her robots and a young farmer overcomes the threatening forces of evil.
Flash Gordon rides again, but with timing so impeccably right that the movie became a phenomenon and one of the top grossers of all time. In view of the hullaballoo, some disappointment may be felt with the actual experience of watching it . . . but it's certainly good harmless fun, put together with style and imagination.

wd George Lucas ph Gilbert Taylor *m* John Williams *pd* John Barry *sp* many and various

Mark Hamill, Harrison Ford, Carrie Fisher, Peter Cushing, Alec Guinness, Anthony Daniels (See Threepio), Kenny Baker (Artoo Detoo), Dave Prowse (Darth Vader)

'A great work of popular art, fully deserving the riches it has reaped.'—*Time*

'Acting in this movie I felt like a raisin in a giant fruit salad. And I didn't even know who the coconuts or the canteloups were.'—*Mark Hamill*

'He intended his film, Lucas confesses, for a generation growing up without fairy tales. His target audience was fourteen years and younger. . . It was a celebration, a social affair, a collective dream, and people came again and again, dragging their friends and families with them.'—*Les Keyser, Hollywood in the Seventies*

'The loudness, the smash and grab editing and the relentless pacing drive every idea from your head, and even if you've been entertained you may feel cheated of some dimension—a sense of wonder, perhaps.'— *New Yorker, 1982*

AA: John Williams

AAN: best picture; script; direction; Alec Guinness

The Star Witness*
US 1931 68m bw
Warner

An old man witnesses a crime and threatened by gangsters.
Pacy melodrama with good performances.

w Lucien Hubbard *d* William Wellman *ph* James Van Trees

Walter Huston, Chic Sale, Grant Mitchell, Frances Starr, Sally Blane

AAN: Lucien Hubbard

Stardust Memories*
US 1980 88m bw
UA / Jack Rollinson, Charles H. Joffe

An increasingly melancholy comedian attends a retrospective of his work and is plagued by real and imaginary fears.
A plainly autobiographical work which, while amusing and moving in spots, makes it doubtful that the writer / director / star can even now shake off his obsessions.

wd Woody Allen *ph* Gordon Willis *m* Dick Hyman

Woody Allen, Charlotte Rampling, Jessica Harper, Marie-Christine Barrault, Tony Roberts, Helen Hanft

'Its posturing pyrotechnics seem more the symptom of a crisis than its controlled expression.'—*Gilbert Adair, MFB*

Stars and Stripes Forever*
US 1952 89m Technicolor
TCF (Lamar Trotti)
GB title: *Marching Along*

In the 1890s John Philip Sousa, a bandmaster who wants to write ballads, finds success as a writer of marches.
Low-key musical biopic with predictably noisy numbers.

w Lamar Trotti, from Sousa's autobiography *d* Henry Koster *ph* Charles G. Clarke *md* Alfred Newman

Clifton Webb, Debra Paget, Robert Wagner, Ruth Hussey, Finlay Currie, Roy Roberts, Lester Matthews

The Stars Are Singing
US 1952 99m Technicolor
Paramount (Irving Asher)

A Polish refugee girl illegally enters the US and becomes an opera star.
Painless Cinderella fantasy in which everybody sings.

w Liam O'Brien *d* Norman Taurog *ph* Lionel Lindon *md* Victor Young

Anna Maria Alberghetti, Lauritz Melchior, Rosemary Clooney, Fred Clark, Mikhail Rasumny

Stars in My Crown*
US 1950 89m bw
MGM (William H. Wright)

A two-gun parson brings peace to a Tennessee town after the Civil War.
Sentimental family western, quite pleasantly made and performed.

w Margaret Fitts, *novel* Joe David Brown *d* Jacques Tourneur *ph* Charles Schoenbaum *m* Adolph Deutsch

Joel McCrea, Ellen Drew, Dean Stockwell, Juano Hernandez, James Mitchell, Lewis Stone, Alan Hale, Amanda Blake

The Stars Look Down**
GB 1939 110m bw
Grafton (Isadore Goldschmidt)

The son of a coal miner struggles to become an MP.
Economically but well made social drama from a popular novel, with good pace and backgrounds.

w J. B. Williams, A. J. Cronin, *novel* A. J. Cronin *d* Carol Reed *ph* Max Greene *m* Hans May

Michael Redgrave, Margaret Lockwood, Edward Rigby, Emlyn Williams, Nancy Price, Allan Jeayes, Cecil Parker, Linden Travers

'Dr Cronin's mining novel has produced a very good film—I doubt whether in England we have ever produced a better.'—*Graham Greene*

Stars over Broadway
US 1935   89m   bw
Warner (Sam Bischoff)

Agent turns hotel porter into radio star.
Unremarkable musical, with unusual talent.

w Jerry Wald, Julius J. Epstein, Pat C. Flick *d* William Keighley *ph* George Barnes *md* Leo F. Forbstein *ch* Busby Berkeley, Bobby Connolly *songs* Harry Warren, Al Dubin

James Melton, Jane Froman, Pat O'Brien, Jean Muir, Frank McHugh, Marie Wilson, Frank Fay

Start the Revolution without Me*
US 1969   90m   Technicolor
Warner / Norbud (Norman Lear)

Two sets of twins get mixed up at the court of Louis XVI.
Historical spoof of the kind subsequently made familiar by Mel Brooks; the script might have suited Abbott and Costello better than these two actors.

w Fred Freeman, Lawrence J. Cohen *d* Bud Yorkin *ph* Jean Tournier *m* John Addison

Donald Sutherland, Gene Wilder, Hugh Griffith, Jack McGowran, Billie Whitelaw, Victor Spinetti, Ewa Aulin

Starting Over*
US 1979   106m   Movielab
Paramount / Century Associates (Alan J. Pakula, James L. Brooks)

A divorced man nearly goes back to his wife but finally plumps for a nursery school teacher.
Plain-speaking sex comedy-drama with accomplished stars giving rather more than the script is worth.

w James L. Brooks, *novel* Dan Wakefield *d* Alan J. Pakula *ph* Sven Nykvist *m* Marvin Hamlisch *pd* George Jenkins

Burt Reynolds, Jill Clayburgh, Candice Bergen, Charles Durning, Austin Pendleton

State Fair**
US 1933   98m   bw
Fox (Winfield Sheehan)

Dad wants his prize pig to win at the fair, but the younger members of his family have romance in mind.

Archetypal family film, much remade but never quite so pleasantly performed.

w Paul Green, Sonya Levien, *novel* Phil Stong *d* Henry King *ph* Hal Mohr *md* Louis de Francesco

Will Rogers, Janet Gaynor, Lew Ayres, Sally Eilers, Norman Foster, Louise Dresser, Frank Craven, Victor Jory, Hobart Cavanaugh
'A pungent, good-humoured motion picture.'—*Pare Lorentz*
'Vigour, freshness and sympathy abound in its admittedly idealized fantasy treatment of small-town life.'—*Charles Higham, 1972*

AAN: best picture; script

State Fair**
US 1945   100m   Technicolor
TCF (William Perlberg)
TV title: *It Happened One Summer*

Musical remake with an amiable cast and a rousing score.

w / ly Oscar Hammerstein II *d* Walter Lang *ph* Leon Shamroy *m* Richard Rodgers *md* Alfred Newman

Charles Winninger, Jeanne Crain, Dana Andrews, Vivian Blaine, Dick Haymes, Fay Bainter, Frank McHugh, Percy Kilbride, Donald Meek
'Surely the sort of theme that clamours for movie treatment. But no, say Twentieth Century Fox: let's make the fair look like a night club. Let's look around for stars of pristine nonentity. Let's screw the camera down to the studio floor. The result, "an epic that sings to the skies . . . with glorious, glamorous new songs".'—*Richard Winnington*

AA: song 'It Might As Well Be Spring'
AAN: Alfred Newman

State Fair
US 1962   118m   De Luxe   Cinemascope
TCF (Charles Brackett)

Dullsville modernized version, condescending towards the rurals and peopled by unattractive youngsters.

w Richard Breen *d* Jose Ferrer *ph* William C. Mellor *md* Alfred Newman

Pat Boone, Alice Faye, Tom Ewell, Pamela Tiffin, Ann-Margret, Bobby Darin, Wally Cox

State of the Union***
US 1948   110m   bw
(MGM) Liberty Films (Frank Capra)
GB title: *The World and His Wife*

An estranged wife rejoins her husband when he is running for president.

Brilliantly scripted political comedy which unfortunately goes soft at the end but offers stimulating entertainment most of the way.

w Anthony Veiller, Myles Connelly, *play Howard Lindsay, Russel Crouse d Frank Capra ph* George J. Folsey *m* Victor Young

Spencer Tracy, Katharine Hepburn, Adolphe Menjou, Van Johnson, Angela Lansbury, Lewis Stone, Howard Smith, Raymond Walburn, Charles Dingle

'A triumphant film, marked all over by Frank Capra's artistry.'—*Howard Barnes*

State Secret°°
GB 1950   104m   bw
British Lion / London (Frank Launder, Sidney Gilliat)
US title: *The Great Manhunt*

In a Ruritanian country, spies pursue a surgeon, the only man who knows that the dictator is dead.
Hitchcockian chase comedy-thriller which is well detailed and rises to the heights on occasion.

wd Sidney Gilliat *ph* Robert Krasker *m* William Alwyn

Douglas Fairbanks Jnr, Glynis Johns, Herbert Lom, Jack Hawkins, Walter Rilla, Karel Stepanek, Carl Jaffe

'An admirably fast-moving diversion in the Hitchcock tradition.'—*Richard Mallett, Punch*

State's Attorney°
US 1932   79m   bw

A prosecuting counsel nearly pays the penalty for arrogance. Good star melodrama. John Barrymore, Jill Esmond, William Boyd, Helen Twelvetrees. Written by Rowland Brown and Gene Fowler; directed by George Archainbaud; for RKO. (GB title: *Cardigan's Last Case.*)

Station Six Sahara
GB 1962   101m   bw
British Lion / CCC / Artur Brauner (Victor Lyndon)

Five men working on a remote Saharan pipeline quarrel over the favours of an American girl whose car crashes nearby.
Raging old-fashioned melodrama with the courage of its lack of convictions.

w Bryan Forbes, Brian Clemens *d* Seth Holt *ph* Gerald Gibbs *m* Ron Grainer

Carroll Baker, Ian Bannen, Peter Van Eyck, Denholm Elliott, Mario Adorf, Jorg Felmy, Biff McGuire

Station West
US 1948   91m   bw
RKO (Robert Sparks)

A saloon queen is the secret head of a gang of gold robbers.
Predictable but well made western patterned after *Destry Rides Again.*

w Frank Fenton, Winston Miller, *novel* Luke Short *d* Sidney Lanfield *ph* Harry J. Wild *m* Heinz Roemheld

Dick Powell, Jane Greer, Agnes Moorehead, Burl Ives, Tom Powers, Gordon Oliver, Steve Brodie, Guinn Williams, Raymond Burr, Regis Toomey

The Statue
US 1970   89m   Eastmancolor
Cinerama / Josef Shaftel (Anis Nohra)

A languages professor is embarrassed when his sculptress wife makes an immense nude statue of him—with someone else's private parts.
Strained phallic comedy which doesn't even make the most of its one joke.

w Alec Coppel, Denis Norden *d* Rod Amateau *ph* Piero Portalupi *m* Riz Ortolani

David Niven, Virna Lisi, Robert Vaughn, Ann Bell, John Cleese, Hugh Burden

Stay Away Joe
US 1968   102m   Metrocolor   Panavision
MGM (Douglas Lawrence)

An Indian rodeo rider returns to his reservation, makes several romantic conquests, and helps a government rehabilitation scheme.
Thin if surprising vehicle for a singing star; all rather tedious.

w Michael A. Hoey, *novel* Dan Cushman *d* Peter Tewkesbury *ph* Fred Koenekamp *m* Jack Marshall

Elvis Presley, Burgess Meredith, Joan Blondell, Katy Jurado, Thomas Gomez, Henry Jones, L. Q. Jones

Stay Hungry
US 1976   102m   De Luxe
UA / Outov (Harold Schneider, Bob Rafaelson)

The heir to an Alabama estate annoys the locality by assembling a curious bunch of friends and making unexpected use of his money.
Rather obvious and pointless fable; well made but not very stimulating.

w Charles Gaines, Bob Rafaelson, *novel* Charles Gaines *d* Bob Rafaelson *ph* Victor Kemper *m* Bruce Langhorne, Byron Berline

Jeff Bridges, Sally Field, Arnold Schwarzenegger, R. G. Armstrong, Robert Englund, Roger E. Mosley

Steamboat Bill Jnr*
US 1928   71m (24 fps)   bw   silent
UA / Buster Keaton / Joseph Schenck

A student takes over his father's old Mississippi steamboat, and wins the daughter of his rival.
Rather flat comedy redeemed by a magnificent cyclone climax.

w Carl Harbaugh, Buster Keaton d Charles Riesner ph J. Devereaux Jennings, Bert Haines

Buster Keaton, Ernest Torrence, Marion Byron

Steamboat Round the Bend*
US 1935   80m   bw
TCF (Sol M. Wurtzel)

A Mississippi steamboat captain defeats his rival and finds evidence to clear his nephew of a murder charge.
Rather heavily-scripted star vehicle which sacrifices fun for atmosphere but is often good to look at.

w Dudley Nichols, Lamar Trotti, *novel* Ben Lucien Berman d *John Ford* ph George Schneiderman m Samuel Kaylin

Will Rogers, Anne Shirley, Eugene Pallette, John McGuire, Irvin S. Cobb, Berton Churchill, Stepin Fetchit, Roger Imhof, Raymond Hatton

Steel
US 1979   101m   Movielab
Columbia / Panzer / Davis / Fawcett-Majors (Lee Majors)

When a construction boss is killed, his daughter vows to complete his last project.
Flashy, foul-mouthed, but basically old-fashioned hokum climaxing in a race to complete before foreclosure.

w Leigh Chapman d Steve Carver ph Roger Shearman m Michael Colombier pd Ward Preston

Lee Majors, Jennifer O'Neill, Art Carney, George Kennedy, Harris Yulin, Terry Kiser, Richard Lynch, Albert Salmi

The Steel Bayonet
GB 1957   85m   bw   Hammerscope
(UA) Hammer (Michael Carreras)

During the assault on Tunis a battle-weary platoon holds a farm against enemy attack.

Dreary cliché-ridden war melodrama peopled by all the usual types.

w Howard Clewes d Michael Carreras ph Jack Asher m Leonard Salzedo

Leo Genn, Kieron Moore, Michael Medwin, Robert Brown, Michael Ripper, John Paul, Bernard Horsfall

Steel Town
US 1952   84m   Technicolor
U-I (Leonard Goldstein)

A steel president's nephew joins the company as a furnace hand.
Routine drama with an unusual background.

w Gerald Drayson Adams, Lou Breslow d George Sherman ph Charles P. Boyle m Joseph Gershenson

Ann Sheridan, John Lund, Howard Duff, James Best, Nancy Kulp

The Steel Trap*
US 1952   85m   bw
TCF / Thor (Bert E. Friedlob)

An assistant bank manager steals half a million dollars from the vault but is troubled by conscience and manages to put it back before the loss is discovered.
Solidly competent little suspenser with plenty of movement.

wd *Andrew Stone* ph Ernest Laszlo m Dmitri Tiomkin

Joseph Cotten, Teresa Wright, Jonathan Hale, Walter Sande

Steelyard Blues
US 1972   92m   Technicolor
Warner / S. B. Productions (Tony Bill, Michael and Julia Phillips)

An ex-con and his call-girl friend are an embarrassment to his DA brother.
Bits and pieces of anti-establishment comedy are tacked on to a thin plot; a few of them work.

w David S. Ward d Alan Myerson ph Laszlo Kovacs, Steven Larner m Nick Gravenites

Donald Sutherland, Jane Fonda, Peter Boyle, Howard Hesseman

Stella Dallas*
US 1925   110m approx (24 fps)   bw   silent
Samuel Goldwyn

An uncouth woman loses both husband and daughter.
Standard weepie complete with 'out into the cold cold snow' ending, but handled here with tact and discretion. A seminal film of its time.

w Frances Marion, *novel* Olive Higgins Prouty *d* Henry King *ph* Arthur Edeson

Belle Bennett, Ronald Colman, Lois Moran, Jean Hersholt, Douglas Fairbanks Jnr, Alice Joyce

Stella Dallas*
US 1937 106m bw
Samuel Goldwyn

Fashionable remake with excellent talent; 1937 audiences came to sneer and stayed to weep.

w Victor Heerman, Sara Y. Mason *d* King Vidor *ph* Rudolph Maté *m* Alfred Newman

Barbara Stanwyck, John Boles, Anne Shirley, Barbara O'Neil, Alan Hale, Marjorie Main, Tim Holt

AAN: Barbara Stanwyck; Anne Shirley

Step Down to Terror
US 1959 76m bw
U-I (Joseph Gershenson)
GB title: *The Silent Stranger*

A man returns to his home town and is discovered to be a psychopathic killer on the run.
Dismal reworking of *Shadow of a Doubt*; strictly second feature stuff.

w Mel Dinelli, Czenzi Ormonde, Chris Cooper *d* Harry Keller *ph* Russell Metty *m* Joseph Gershenson

Charles Drake, Coleen Miller, Rod Taylor, Josephine Hutchinson, Jocelyn Brando

Step Lively*
US 1944 88m bw
RKO (Robert Fellows)

Gleaming musical remake of *Room Service* (qv); all very efficient if witless.

w Warren Duff, Peter Milne *d* Tim Whelan *ph* Robert de Grasse *md* Constantin Bakaleinikoff *songs* Jule Styne, Sammy Cahn

Frank Sinatra, George Murphy, Adolphe Menjou, Gloria de Haven, Anne Jeffreys, Walter Slezak, Eugene Pallette

The Stepford Wives*
US 1974 115m TVC
Fadsin / Palomar (Edgar J. Sherick)

A new wife in a commuter village outside New York finds all her female friends too good to be true . . . because their husbands have had them replaced by computerized models.
An attractive idea which needs a much lighter and pacier touch but entertains in patches and shows agreeable sophistication.

w William Goldman, *novel* Ira Levin *d* Bryan Forbes *ph* Owen Roizman *m* Michael Small *pd* Gene Callahan

Katharine Ross, Paula Prentiss, Nanette Newman, Peter Masterson, Patrick O'Neal, Tina Louise, William Prince

'It was hard to tell Katharine Ross playing a robot from Katharine Ross playing a normal housewife.'—*Les Keyser, Hollywood in the Seventies*

Steptoe and Son
GB 1972 98m Technicolor
EMI / Associated London Films (Aida Young)

Harold gets married, mislays his wife but thinks he is a father.
Strained attempt to transfer the TV rag-and-bone comedy (which in the US became *Sanford and Son*) to the big screen. Not the same thing at all.

w Ray Galton, Alan Simpson *d* Cliff Owen *ph* John Wilcox *m* Roy Budd, Jack Fishman

Wilfrid Brambell, Harry H. Corbett, Carolyn Seymour, Arthur Howard, Victor Maddern
† *Steptoe and Son Ride Again*, which followed in 1973, was even more crude and out of character.

The Sterile Cuckoo
US 1969 107m Technicolor
Paramount / Boardwalk (Alan J. Pakula)
GB title: *Pookie*

A talkative but insecure college girl has her first sexual adventures.
Rather tiresome comedy drama with good scenes; general handling far too restrained.

w Alvin Sargent, *novel* John Nicholson *d* Alan J. Pakula *ph* Milton Krasner *m* Fred Karlin

Liza Minnelli, Tim McIntire, Wendell Burton, Austin Green, Sandra Faison

AAN: song 'Come Saturday Morning' (*m* Fred Karlin, *ly* Dory Previn); Liza Minnelli

Stevie*
US / GB 1978 102m Technicolor
First Artists / Grand Metropolitan (Robert Enders)

An account of the uneventful life of poetess Stevie Smith, lived out mainly in a London suburb under the fear of death.
Claustrophobic showcase for a whimsical lady; interesting for some specialized audiences.

w Hugh Whitemore, from his play *d* Robert Enders *ph* Freddie Young *m* Marcus Gowers

Glenda Jackson, Mona Washbourne, Trevor Howard, Alec McCowen

Stiletto

US 1969   99m   Berkey–Pathe
Avco / Harold Robbins (Norman Rosemont)

A wealthy playboy racing driver is in fact a Mafia executioner.

Dreary, violent, fashionable Mafioso melodrama with international jet set trimmings.

w A. J. Russsell, *novel* Harold Robbins *d* Bernard Kowalski *ph* Jack Priestly *m* Sid Ramin

Alex Cord, Britt Ekland, Barbara McNair, Patrick O'Neal, Joseph Wiseman, John Dehner, Eduardo Ciannelli, Roy Scheider

The Sting**

US 1973   129m   Technicolor
Universal / Richard Zanuck, David Brown
  (Tony Bill, Michael S. Phillips)

In twenties Chicago, two con men stage an elaborate revenge on a big time gangster who caused the death of a friend.

Bright, likeable, but overlong, unconvincingly studio-set and casually developed comedy suspenser cashing in on star charisma but riding to enormous success chiefly on its tinkly music and the general lack of simple entertainment.

w David S. Ward   *d George Roy Hill*
ph Robert Surtees   *m Scott Joplin* (arranged by Marvin Hamlisch) *ad* Henry Bumstead

Paul Newman, *Robert Redford*, Robert Shaw, Charles Durning, Ray Walston, Eileen Brennan

'A visually claustrophobic, mechanically plotted movie that's meant to be a roguishly charming entertainment.'—*New Yorker*

'It demonstrates what can happen when a gifted young screenwriter has the good fortune to fall among professionals his second time out.'—*Judith Crist*

'A testament to the value of blue eyes and bright smiles.'—*Les Keyser, Hollywood in the Seventies*

AA: best picture; David S. Ward; George Roy Hill; Marvin Hamlisch
AAN: Robert Surtees; Robert Redford

Stir Crazy

US 1980   111m   Metrocolor
Columbia / Hannah Weinstein

Two New Yorkers heading for California to try their luck are wrongly convicted of a bank robbery but plan escape from prison.

Extended farce giving rather too free rein to its stars' potential for mugging, and polishing up every prison gag in the book.

w Bruce Jay Friedman   *d* Sidney Poitier *ph* Fred Schuler   *m* Tom Scott   *pd* Alfred Sweeney

Gene Wilder, Richard Pryor, George Stanford Brown, Jobeth Williams

A Stitch in Time

GB 1963   94m   bw
Rank (Hugh Stewart)

A butcher's boy goes into hospital and falls for a nurse.

Thin star slapstick; all one can say is that it's marginally preferable to Jerry Lewis.

w Jack Davies   *d* Robert Asher   *ph* Jack Asher   *m* Philip Green

Norman Wisdom, Edward Chapman, Jerry Desmonde, Jeanette Sterke, Jill Melford

Stolen Face

GB 1952   72m   bw

Via plastic surgery a girl criminal is given another face, which produces a different kind of trouble. Quickie melodrama which proved fairly popular because of its Hollywood stars. Paul Henreid, Lizabeth Scott, André Morell, Susan Stephen, Mary Mackenzie, Arnold Ridley. Written by Martin Berkeley and Richard Landau; directed by Terence Fisher; for Hammer-Lippert.

Stolen Holiday

US 1937   82m   bw

A model marries a fortune hunter to protect him from the law. Slightly unusual romantic drama based on the career of Alexander Stavisky. *Claude Rains,* Kay Francis, Ian Hunter, Alison Skipworth, Charles Halton, Alex D'Arcy. Written by Casey Robinson; directed by Michael Curtiz; for Warner.

Stolen Hours

GB 1963   97m   De Luxe
UA / Mirisch / Barbican (Denis Holt)

An American divorcee with only a year to live falls in love with her surgeon.

Tired remake of *Dark Victory*; pleasant Cornish backgrounds.

w Jessamyn West   *d* Daniel Petrie   *ph* Harry Waxman   *m* Mort Lindsey

Susan Hayward, Michael Craig, Diane Baker, Edward Judd, Paul Rogers

Stolen Kisses*
France 1968   91m   Eastmancolor
Films du Carrosse / Artistes Associés
   (Marcel Berbert)
original title: *Baisers Volés*

An ineffective young man can find neither
work nor love.

A pleasing, rather sad little comedy which has
almost the feel of a Keaton; but one is not
quite sure at the end what its creator intended.

w François Truffaut, Claude de Givray,
Bernard Revon *d* François Truffaut
ph Denys Clerval *m* Antoine Duhamel

Jean-Pierre Léaud, Delphine Seyrig, Michel
Lonsdale, Claude Jade

AAN: best foreign film

A Stolen Life*
GB 1939   91m   bw
(Paramount) Orion (Anthony Havelock-
   Allan)

In Brittany, a woman deceives her husband by
exchanging identities with her dead twin.
An actress's showcase, quite satisfactorily
mounted.

w Margaret Kennedy, George Barraud, *novel*
Karel J. Benes *d* Paul Czinner *ph* Philip
Tannura *m* William Walton

Elisabeth Bergner, Michael Redgrave, Wilfrid
Lawson, Richard Ainley, Mabel Terry-Lewis,
Clement McCallin

A Stolen Life*
US 1946   107m   bw
Warner (Bette Davis)

Enjoyable if slightly disappointing remake
with New England backgrounds.

w Catherine Turney *d* Curtis Bernhardt
ph Sol Polito, Sid Hickox *m* Max Steiner

Bette Davis, Glenn Ford, Dane Clark, Walter
Brennan, Charles Ruggles, Bruce Bennett,
Peggy Knudsen, Esther Dale
   'A distressingly empty piece of show-off.'—
Bosley Crowther
   'What I'm waiting for is a film about
beautiful identical quintuplets who all love the
same man.'—*Richard Winnington*

The Stone Killer*
US 1973   Ṣ_m   Technicolor
Columbia / Dino de Laurentiis (Michael
   Winner)

A brutal Los Angeles police detective takes on
the Mafia.
Fast-moving amalgam of chases and violence
with a downbeat hero.

w Gerald Wilson, *novel* A Complete State of
Death by John Gardner *d* Michael Winner
ph Richard Moore *m* Roy Budd

Charles Bronson, Martin Balsam, Ralph
Waite, David Sheiner, Norman Fell
   'Film-making as painting by numbers.'—
Sight and Sound

The Stooge*
US 1951   100m   bw
Paramount / Hal B. Wallis

In 1930 a conceited song and dance man fails
to realize that his moronic stooge is the act's
real attraction.
Typical, and particularly resistible, Martin and
Lewis concoction: whenever one thinks of
laughing, a dollop of sentimentality comes
along and promptly quashes the idea.

w Fred Finkelhoffe, Martin Rackin *d* Norman
Taurog *ph* Daniel L. Fapp *m* Joseph J. Lilley

Dean Martin, Jerry Lewis, Polly Bergen,
Marie McDonald, Eddie Mayehoff, Marion
Marshall, Richard Erdman

Stop Press Girl
GB 1949   78m   bw

A girl finds she has the unconscious power to
bring all machinery to a halt. Weary comedy
which has nowhere to go after its first silly
idea. Sally Ann Howes, Gordon Jackson,
Basil Radford, Naunton Wayne, James
Robertson Justice, Sonia Holm, Nigel
Buchanan, Kenneth More. Written by Basil
Thomas and T. J. Morrison; directed by
Michael Barry; for Aquila / Rank.

Stop You're Killing Me*
US 1953   86m   Warnercolor
Warner (Louis F. Edelman)

At the end of prohibition a beer baron decides
to go straight, but finds his house filled with
the corpses of rival gangsters.
Frantic remake of *A Slight Case of Murder*
with a few musical numbers added; all rather
messy.

w James O'Hanlon *d* Roy del Ruth *ph* Ted
McCord *md* Ray Heindorf

Broderick Crawford, Claire Trevor, Virginia
Gibson, Bill Hayes, Sheldon Leonard, Joe
Vitale, Howard St John, Henry Morgan,
Margaret Dumont

Stopover Tokyo
US 1957   100m   Eastmancolor
   Cinemascope
TCF (Walter Reisch)

An American spy in Tokyo seeks to capture a communist undercover man.

Sprawling espionage stuff with frequent halts for scenic tours.

w Richard L. Breen, Walter Reisch, *novel* John P. Marquand *d* Richard L. Breen *ph* Charles G. Clarke *m* Paul Sawtell

Robert Wagner, Joan Collins, Edmond O'Brien, Ken Scott, Larry Keating

Stories from a Flying Trunk
GB 1979   88m   Technicolor
EMI / Sands (John Brabourne, Richard Goodwin)

Three Hans Andersen stories are performed by stop frame animation and by ballet dancers dressed as vegetables.

Lugubrious attempt to repeat the success of *Tales of Beatrix Potter;* moments to make one smile, but on the whole a depressing experience.

wd Christine Edzard *m* Gioacchino Rossini *ph* Robin Browne, Brian West

Murray Melvin, Ann Firbank, Johanna Sonnex, Tasneem Maqsood

The Stork Club
US 1945   98m   bw
Paramount (B. G. De Sylva)

A nightclub hat-check girl saves an elderly millionaire from drowning.

Very light comedy with music, a great ad for a once famous night haunt.

w B. G. De Sylva, John McGowan *d* Hal Walker *ph* Charles Lang Jnr *md* Robert Emmett Dolan

Betty Hutton, Barry Fitzgerald, Don Defore, Robert Benchley, Bill Goodwin, Iris Adrian, Mary Young, Mikhail Rasumny

Storm at Daybreak
US 1932   80m   bw

A fanciful reconstruction of events leading up to the Sarajevo assassination which precipitated World War I. Unlikely melodrama with stars forced to overact; still, a rich and historically interesting slice of ham. Walter Huston, Kay Francis, Nils Asther, Phillips Holmes, Eugene Pallette, C. Henry Gordon, Jean Parker. Written by Bertram Millhauser, from a play by Sandor Hunyady; directed by Richard Boleslawski; for MGM.

Storm Center
US 1956   87m   bw
Columbia / Phoenix (Julian Blaustein)

A small-town librarian is dismissed when she refuses to remove a communist book from the shelves.

Formula anti-McCarthy melodrama originally designed for Mary Pickford's comeback; not very absorbing and rather dingily produced.

w Daniel Taradash Elick Moll *d* Daniel Taradash *ph* Burnett Guffey *m* George Duning

Bette Davis, Brian Keith, Kim Hunter, Paul Kelly, Joe Mantell

Storm Fear
US 1955   88m   bw
(UA) Theodora (Cornel Wilde)

Three fugitives from justice hide in a mountain cabin, but all meet violent deaths.

Gloomy, strenuous melodrama, partly shot outdoors.

w Horton Foote, *novel* Clinton Seeley *d* Cornel Wilde *ph* Joseph La Shelle *m* Elmer Bernstein

Cornel Wilde, Jean Wallace, Dan Duryea, Lee Grant, Steven Hill, Dennis Weaver

Storm in a Teacup*
GB 1937   87m   bw
Alexander Korda / Victor Saville

A national sensation ensues when a Scottish provost fines an old lady for not licensing her dog, and she refuses to pay.

Early Ealing-type comedy, a bit emaciated by later standards.

w Ian Dalrymple, Donald Bull, *play* Sturm in Wasserglass by Bruno Frank *d* Ian Dalrymple, Victor Saville *ph* Max Greene *m* Frederic Lewis

Vivien Leigh, Rex Harrison, Cecil Parker, Sara Allgood, Ursula Jeans, Gus McNaughton, Arthur Wontner

Storm over Asia*
USSR 1928   93m approx (24 fps)   bw silent
Mezhrabpomfilm
original title: *Potomok Chingis-Khana*; aka: *The Heir to Genghis Khan*

A Mongolian trapper is discovered to be descended from Genghis Khan and made puppet emperor of a Soviet province.

Curious yarn without much discernible point though with the usual patches of propagandizing. It certainly looks good.

w Osip Brik *d* V. I. Pudovkin *ph* A. L. Golovnya

I. Inkizhinov, Valeri Inkizhinov, A. Dedintsev

Storm over Lisbon
US 1944   86m   bw
Republic (George Sherman)

An international spy mastermind runs a
Lisbon night club and sells documents to the
highest bidder.
Feeble copy of *Casablanca*.

w Doris Gilbert, Dane Lussier d George
Sherman ph John Alton m Walter Scharf

Vera Hruba Ralston, Erich Von Stroheim,
Richard Arlen, Eduardo Ciannelli, Otto
Kruger, Robert Livingston, Mona Barrie,
Frank Orth

Storm over the Nile
GB 1955   107m   Technicolor
   Cinemascope
Independent / London (Zoltan Korda)

Feeble remake of *The Four Feathers* (qv),
using most of that film's action highlights
stretched out to fit the wide screen.

w R. C. Sherriff d Terence Young ph Ted
Scaife, Osmond Borradaile m Benjamin
Frankel

Anthony Steel, Laurence Harvey, Ronald
Lewis, Ian Carmichael, James Robertson
Justice, Mary Ure, Geoffrey Keen, Jack
Lambert, Ferdy Mayne, Michael Hordern
   'The material appears not so much dated as
fossilized within its period.'—*Penelope
Houston*

Storm over Tibet
US 1951   87m   bw
Columbia / Summit (Ivan Tors, Laslo
   Benedek)

An explorer steals a holy mask which brings
bad luck.
Slight adventure yarn ingeniously built around
an old German documentary.

w Ivan Tors, Sam Mayer d Andrew Marton
ph George E. Diskant, Richard Angst
m Arthur Honegger

Rex Reason, Diana Douglas, Myron Healey

Storm Warning*
US 1950   93m   bw
Warner (Jerry Wald)

A New York model goes south to visit her
sister, and finds that her brother-in-law is an
oversexed brute and a Ku Klux Klan killer.
Heavy melodrama disguised as a social
document; sufficiently arresting for its
purposes.

w Daniel Fuchs, Richard Brooks d Stuart
Heisler ph Carl Guthrie m Daniele
Amfitheatrof

Ginger Rogers, Doris Day, *Steve Cochran*,
Ronald Reagan, Hugh Sanders, Raymond
Greenleaf, Ned Glass

Stormy Weather
GB 1935   74m   bw

A top executive foils a blackmail racket in
Chinatown. Very presentable vehicle for the
Aldwych team of farceurs. Tom Walls, Ralph
Lynn, Robertson Hare, Yvonne Arnaud,
Gordon James, Graham Moffatt. Written by
Ben Travers, from his play; directed by Tom
Walls; for Gainsborough.

Stormy Weather***
US 1943   77m   bw
TCF (Irving Mills)

A backstage success story lightly based on the
career of Bill Robinson.
Virtually a high-speed revue with all-black
talent, and what talent! The production is
pretty slick too.

w Frederick Jackson, Ted Koehler d Andrew
Stone ph Leon Shamroy, Fred Sersen
md Benny Carter ch Clarence Robinson

*Bill Robinson, Lena Horne, Fats Waller, Ada
Brown, Cab Calloway,* Katherine Dunham
and her Dancers, Eddie Anderson, Flournoy
Miller, *The Nicholas Brothers*, Dooley Wilson

The Story of a Woman
US / Italy 1969   101m   Technicolor
Universal / Westward (Leonardo Bercovici)

A Swedish girl pianist in Rome falls in love
with a fashionable doctor, then back in
Sweden meets an American diplomat.
Intermezzo-type romantic drama with colour
supplement trappings. Tolerable of its kind.

wd Leonardo Bercovici ph Piero Portalupi
m John Williams

Robert Stack, Bibi Andersson, James
Farentino, Annie Girardot, Frank Sundstrom

The Story of Adèle H*
France 1975   98m   Eastmancolor
Films du Carrosse / Artistes Associés
   (Marcel Berbert, Claude Miller)

In 1863, the daughter of Victor Hugo follows
her lover to Nova Scotia.
Surprisingly slow and stilted version of a true
story, though with a few of the expected
subtleties.

w François Truffaut, Jean Gruault, Suzanne
Schiffman d François Truffaut ph Nestor
Almendros m Maurice Jaubert

Isabelle Adjani, Bruce Robinson, Sylvia
Marriott

AAN: Isabelle Adjani

The Story of Alexander Graham Bell**
US 1939   97m   bw
TCF (Kenneth MacGowan)
GB title: *The Modern Miracle*

The inventor of the telephone marries a deaf
girl.
Acceptable history lesson with dullish
principals but excellent production.

w Lamar Trotti   *d* Irving Cummings   *ph* Leon
Shamroy   *m* Louis Silvers

Don Ameche, Henry Fonda, Loretta Young,
Charles Coburn, Gene Lockhart, Spring
Byington, Bobs Watson

The Story of Dr Wassell*
US 1944   140m   Technicolor
Paramount / Cecil B. de Mille

The adventures of a naval doctor who
heroically saved men during the Pacific war.
Long, slogging, glamorized account of real
events which is typical de Mille and very
unconvincing physically, but keeps one
watching simply as a story.

w Alan le May, Charles Bennett, *book* James
Hilton   *d* Cecil B. de Mille   *ph* Victor Milner,
William Snyder   *m* Victor Young

Gary Cooper, Laraine Day, Signe Hasso,
Dennis O'Keefe, Carol Thurston, Carl
Esmond, Paul Kelly, Stanley Ridges
   'The director has taken a true story of
heroism . . . and jangled it into a cacophony
of dancing girls, phoney self-sacrifice and
melodramatic romance.'—*Howard Barnes*
   'To be regretted beyond qualification. It
whips the story into a nacreous foam of lies
whose speciousness is only the more painful
because Mr de Mille is so obviously free from
any desire to alter the truth except for what he
considers to be its own advantage.'—*James
Agee*

The Story of Esther Costello*
GB 1957   103m   bw
Columbia / Romulus (James Woolf)
US title: *The Golden Virgin*

A blind Irish deaf mute girl is adopted by an
American socialite and her plight becomes an
international cause.
Rich melodrama develops from this unlikely
premise and the star enjoys it hugely.

w Charles Kaufman, *novel* Nicholas
Monsarrat   *d* David Miller   *ph* Robert
Krasker   *m* Georges Auric

Joan Crawford, Heather Sears, Rossano
Brazzi, Ron Randell, Lee Patrick, Fay
Compton, John Loder, Denis O'Dea, Sidney
James, Maureen Delany

The Story of GI Joe**
US 1945   108m   bw
(UA) Lester Cowan (David Hall)
aka: *War Correspondent*

Journalist Ernie Pyle follows fighting men into
the Italian campaign.
Slow, convincing, sympathetic war film with
good script and performances; not by any
means the usual action saga.

w Leopold Atlas, Guy Endore, Philip
Stevenson, *book Ernie Pyle d William A.
Wellman ph Russell Metty m* Ann Ronell,
Louis Applebaum

Burgess Meredith, Robert Mitchum, Freddie
Steele, Wally Cassell, Jimmy Lloyd, Jack
Reilly
   'It is humorous, poignant and tragic, an
earnestly human reflection of a stern life and
the dignity of man.'—*Thomas M. Pryor*
   'A tragic and eternal work of art.'—*James
Agee*
   'One of the best films of the war.'—*Richard
Mallett, Punch*

AAN: script; music score; song 'Linda' (*m /
ly* Ann Ronell); Robert Mitchum

The Story of Gilbert and Sullivan*
GB 1953   109m   Technicolor
British Lion / London Films (Frank Launder,
Sidney Gilliat)

In 1875 a young composer named Arthur
Sullivan and a librettist named William Gilbert
come together under the auspices of Rupert
D'Oyly Carte and write the Savoy Operas.
Light, accurate, well-cast and well-produced
Victorian musical which somehow fails to
ignite despite the immense talent at hand.

w Sidney Gilliat, Leslie Baily   *d* Sidney
Gilliat   *ph* Christopher Challis   *md* Sir
Malcolm Sargent   *pd* Hein Heckroth

Robert Morley, Maurice Evans, Peter Finch,
Eileen Herlie, Dinah Sheridan, Isabel Dean,
Wilfrid Hyde White, Muriel Aked

The Story of Louis Pasteur***
US 1936   85m   bw
Warner (Henry Blanke)

How the eminent 19th-century French scientist
overcomes obstacles in finding cures for
various diseases.
Adequate biopic which caused a sensation and
started a trend; some of the others were better
but this was the first example of Hollywood
bringing schoolbook history to box office life.

w Sheridan Gibney, Pierre Collins   *d William
Dieterle ph* Tony Gaudio   *m* Bernhard Kaun,
Heinz Roemheld

Paul Muni, Josephine Hutchinson, Anita Louise, Donald Woods, Fritz Leiber, Henry O'Neill, Porter Hall, Akim Tamiroff, Walter Kingsford

'What should be vital and arresting has been made hollow and dull . . . we are tendered something that is bright and stagey for something out of life.'—*Otis Ferguson*

'More exciting than any gangster melodrama.'—*C. A. Lejeune*

AA: script; Paul Muni
AAN: best picture

The Story of Mankind
US 1957   100m   Technicolor
Warner / Cambridge (Irwin Allen)

A heavenly tribunal debates whether to allow man to destroy himself, and both the Devil and the Spirit of Man cite instances from history.
Hilarious charade, one of the worst films ever made, but full of surprises, bad performances, and a wide range of stock shots.

w Irwin Allen, Charles Bennett, *book* Henrik Van Loon d Irwin Allen ph Nicholas Musuraca m Paul Sawtell

Ronald Colman, Vincent Price, Cedric Hardwicke, the Marx Brothers, Hedy Lamarr, Agnes Moorehead, Reginald Gardiner, Peter Lorre, Virginia Mayo, Charles Coburn, Francis X. Bushman

The Story of Molly X
US 1949   82m   bw

When a criminal is killed, his wife masterminds the gang to find out who killed him. Silly melodrama, generally ineptly presented. June Havoc, John Russell, Dorothy Hart, Elliott Lewis, Connie Gilchrist. Written and directed by Crane Wilbur; for Universal / International.

The Story of Robin Hood and his Merrie Men
GB 1952   84m   Technicolor
Walt Disney (Perce Pearce)

When Prince John starts a ruthless taxation campaign, Robert Fitzooth turns outlaw. Fairly competent but quite forgettable version of the legend, softened for children.

w Laurence E. Watkin d Ken Annakin ph Guy Green m Clifton Parker

Richard Todd, Joan Rice, James Hayter, Hubert Gregg, James Robertson Justice, Martita Hunt, Peter Finch

The Story of Ruth
US 1960   132m   De Luxe   Cinemascope
TCF (Samuel G. Engel)

Ruth becomes the favourite of a pagan king but eventually flees to Israel.
Tedious, portentous bible-in-pictures, of virtually no interest or entertainment value.

w Norman Corwin d Henry Koster
ph Arthur E. Arling m Franz Waxman

Elana Eden, Peggy Wood, Viveca Lindfors, Stuart Whitman, Tom Tryon, Jeff Morrow, Thayer David, Eduard Franz

The Story of Seabiscuit
US 1949   98m   Technicolor
Warner (William Jacobs)
GB title: *Pride of Kentucky*

The success story of a racehorse.
Blue grass vapidities, the kind of family entertainment that drove the families away.

w John Taintor Foote d David Butler
ph Wilfrid Cline md David Buttolph

Shirley Temple, Barry Fitzgerald, Lon McCallister, Rosemary de Camp, Donald McBride, Pierre Watkin

The Story of Shirley Yorke
GB 1948   92m   bw

A nobleman tries to blame his wife's nurse for her death by poison. Lethargic version of a play previously filmed as *Lord Camber's Ladies* (qv). Derek Farr, Dinah Sheridan, Margaretta Scott, John Robinson, Barbara Couper, Valentine Dyall. Written by A. R. Rawlinson, Maclean Rogers and Kathleen Butler, from the play *The Case of Lady Camber* by H. A. Vachell; directed by Maclean Rogers; for Butcher's.

The Story of Temple Drake*
US 1933   71m   bw
Paramount

A neurotic southern flapper is abducted by gangsters, and likes it.
Deliberately shocking melodrama of its time, restructured from a notorious book later filmed under its own title. Very dated, but interesting.

w Oliver H. P. Garrett, *novel* Sanctuary by William Faulkner d Stephen Roberts ph Karl Struss

Miriam Hopkins, Jack La Rue, William Gargan, William Collier Jnr, Irving Pichel, Guy Standing, Elizabeth Patterson, Florence Eldridge

The Story of Three Loves
US 1953   122m   Technicolor
MGM (Sidney Franklin)

Three love stories concerning the passengers on a transatlantic liner.

Three bits of old-fashioned kitsch, one tragic, one whimsical, one melodramatic, all rather slow and dull though well produced.

w John Collier, Jan Lustig, George Froeschel *d* Gottfried Reinhardt, Vincente Minnelli *ph* Charles Rosher, Harold Rosson *m* Miklos Rozsa

Ethel Barrymore, James Mason, Moira Shearer, Pier Angeli, Leslie Caron, Kirk Douglas, Farley Granger, Agnes Moorehead, Zsa Zsa Gabor

The Story of Vernon and Irene Castle**
US 1939 93m bw
RKO (George Haight, Pandro S. Berman)

The story of a husband and wife dance team who had their first success in Paris and became influential international celebrities before he was killed as a flier in World War I. Pleasant understated musical with very agreeable dance sequences and a firm overall style. The last of the main stream of Astaire-Rogers musicals.

w Richard Sherman, Oscar Hammerstein II, Dorothy Yost, *books* Irene Castle *d* H. C. Potter *ph* Robert de Grasse *md* Victor Baravalle *ch* Hermes Pan *ad* Van Nest Polglase

Fred Astaire, Ginger Rogers, Edna May Oliver, Walter Brennan, Lew Fields, Etienne Girardot, Donald MacBride

The Story of Will Rogers
US 1950 109m Technicolor
Warner (Robert Arthur)

A wild west performer becomes a Ziegfeld star and pop philosopher.
Bland, unshaped biopic of one of American show business's best loved figures, who died in an air crash in 1935.

w Frank Davis, Stanley Roberts *d* Michael Curtiz *ph* Wilfrid M. Cline *md* Victor Young

Will Rogers Jnr, Jane Wyman, James Gleason, Eddie Cantor (as himself), Carl Benton Reid

The Story on Page One
US 1960 123m bw Cinemascope
TCF / Company of Artists (Jerry Wald)

A lawyer undertakes the defence of a woman who with her lover is charged with the murder of her husband.
Long drawn out and not very interesting courtroom drama, performed and presented with some style.

wd Clifford Odets *ph* James Wong Howe *m* Elmer Bernstein

Rita Hayworth, Tony Franciosa, Gig Young, Mildred Dunnock, Hugh Griffith, Sanford Meisner, Alfred Ryder

Stowaway*
US 1936 86m bw
TCF (Earl Carroll, Harold Wilson)

The orphan daughter of a Shanghai missionary stows away on an American pleasure ship. Very good star vehicle in which Shirley performs some of her best musical numbers.

w William Conselman, Arthur Sheekman, Nat Perrin *d* William A. Seiter *ph* Arthur Miller *md* Louis Silvers *songs* Mack Gordon, Harry Revel

Shirley Temple, Robert Young, Alice Faye, Eugene Pallette, Helen Westley, Arthur Treacher, J. Edward Bromberg, Astrid Allwyn

La Strada*
Italy 1954 94m bw
Ponti / de Laurentiis
aka: *The Road*

A half-witted peasant girl is sold to an itinerant strong man and ill-used by him. Curious attempt at a kind of poetic neo-realism, saved by style and performances.

w Federico Fellini, Ennio Flaiano, Tullio Pinelli *d* Federico Fellini *ph* Otello Martelli *m* Nino Rota

Giulietta Masina, Anthony Quinn, Richard Basehart

AA: best foreign film
AAN: script

Straight on Till Morning
GB 1972 96m Technicolor
EMI / Hammer (Roy Skeggs)

A Liverpool girl in London meets a dangerous psychotic.
Unattractive suspenser, wildly directed.

w Michael Peacock *d* Peter Collinson *ph* Brian Probyn *m* Roland Shaw

Rita Tushingham, Shane Briant, Tom Bell, Annie Ross, James Bolam

Straight, Place and Show*
US 1938 66m bw

Three pony-ride proprietors impersonate Russian jockeys to save a race. Lively, unpretentious vehicle for three zanies, with a further bonus in its lead singer. The Ritz Brothers, Ethel Merman, Richard Arlen, Phyllis Brooks, George Barbier, Sidney Blackmer. Written by M. M. Musselman and

Allen Rivkin, from a play by Damon Runyon and Irving Caesar; directed by David Butler; for TCF. (GB title: *They're Off.*)

Straight Time
US 1978   114m   Technicolor
Warner / First Artist / Sweetwall (Stanley Beck, Tim Zinnemann)

A psychotic parolee fails to go straight.
Unappetizing social melodrama with an irresolute leading performance.

w Alvin Sargent, Edward Bunker, Jeffrey Boam, *novel* No Beast So Fierce by Edward Bunker *d* Ulu Grosbard *ph* Owen Roizman *m* David Shire

Dustin Hoffman, Theresa Russell, Gary Busey, Harry Dean Stanton
'One leaves the theatre hoping the character will die painfully and slowly in a hail of bullets.'—*Variety*

Strait Jacket
US 1963   92m   bw
Columbia / William Castle

A woman who murdered her faithless husband with an axe is released twenty years later, and more axe murders occur.
Dull and unattractive shocker in which all concerned lean over backwards to conceal the trick ending.

w Robert Bloch *d* William Castle *ph* Arthur E. Arling *m* Van Alexander

Joan Crawford, Diane Baker, Leif Erickson, Howard St John, Rochelle Hudson, George Kennedy

The Strange Affair
GB 1968   106m   Techniscope
Paramount (Howard Harrison, Stanley Mann)

A young London policeman finds that his superiors are almost as corrupt as the villains.
Stylishly made melodrama of despair, with a sexy nymphet heroine straight from swinging London. It all leaves a sour taste in the mouth.

w Stanley Mann, *novel* Bernard Toms *d David Greene ph* Max Thompson *m* Basil Kirchin

Michael York, Jeremy Kemp, Susan George, Jack Watson, George A. Cooper

Strange Bedfellows
US 1965   99m   Technicolor
U-I / Panama–Frank (Melvin Frank)

An American executive in London nearly divorces his fiery Italian wife.
Frantic sex comedy with picture postcard background; fatiguing rather than funny, but with minor compensations.

w Melvin Frank, Michael Pertwee *d* Melvin Frank *ph* Leo Tover *m* Leigh Harline

Rock Hudson, Gina Lollobrigida, Gig Young, Edward Judd, Howard St John, Arthur Haynes, Dave King, Terry-Thomas
'The grind of predictable situations is further afflicted by considerable lapses in taste.'—*MFB*

Strange Boarders*
GB 1938   79m   bw
GFD / Gainsborough (Edward Black)

A police detective postpones his honeymoon to book into a boarding house and discover which of the guests is a spy.
Quite engaging comedy-thriller in the Hitchcock mould, with entertaining performances and incidents.

w A. R. Rawlinson, Sidney Gilliatt, *novel* The Strange Boarders of Paradise Crescent by E. Phillips Oppenheim *d* Herbert Mason *ph* Jack Cox

Tom Walls, Renee Saint-Cyr, Leon M. Lion, Googie Withers, C. V. France, Ronald Adam, Irene Handl, George Curzon, Martita Hunt

Strange Cargo*
US 1940   105m   bw
MGM (Joseph L. Mankiewicz)

Eight convicts escape from Devil's Island and are influenced by a Christ-like fugitive.
One of Hollywood's occasional lunacies; one doubts whether even the author knew the point of this cockamamy parable, but it was well produced and acted.

w Lawrence Hazard, *novel* Not Too Narrow, Not Too Deep by Richard Sale *d* Frank Borzage *ph* Robert Planck *m* Franz Waxman

Clark Gable, Joan Crawford, Ian Hunter, Peter Lorre, Paul Lukas, Albert Dekker, J. Edward Bromberg, Eduardo Ciannelli, Frederick Worlock
'Even the most hardened mystics may blush.'—*New Yorker, 1978*

The Strange Case of Doctor RX
US 1942   66m   bw

A mysterious murderer eliminates criminals whom the law can't touch. Inept semi-horror which wastes a good cast, as did the same author's *Night Monster*. Lionel Atwill, Patric Knowles, Anne Gwynne, Samuel S. Hinds, Shemp Howard, Mona Barrie, Paul Cavanagh, Mantan Moreland. Written by Clarence Upson Young; directed by William Nigh; for Universal.

Strange Conquest: see The Crime of Dr Hallet

The Strange Death of Adolf Hitler*
US 1943   74m   bw
Universal

A stage impressionist murders the Führer and takes his place, steering Germany deliberately into losing the war.

One of the more eccentric curios of World War II, especially from a mundane studio like Universal. Once one recovers from the shock of its existence, the thing is moderately well done. See also *The Magic Face.*

w Fritz Kortner d James Hogan m Hans Salter

Ludwig Donath, Gale Sondergaard, Fritz Kortner, George Dolenz

The Strange Door*
US 1951   81m   bw
U-I (Ted Richmond)

A young nobleman, passing through the one-way door of a castle, finds himself the prisoner of a madman.

Torture-chamber suspenser, adequately if rather tediously developed, with most of its interest reposing in the cast.

w Jerry Sackheim, *story* The Sire de Maletroit's Door by Robert Louis Stevenson d Joseph Pevney ph Irving Glassberg m Joseph Gershenson

Charles Laughton, Boris Karloff, Michael Pate, Sally Forrest, Richard Stapley, Alan Napier

Strange Evidence
GB 1932   71m   bw

When an invalid dies, his adulterous wife is suspected. Mildly interesting quickie whodunnit. Leslie Banks, Carol Goodner, George Curzon, Frank Vosper, Norah Baring, Diana Napier. Written by Miles Malleson, from a story by Lajos Biro; directed by Robert Milton; for Alexander Korda / Paramount.

Strange Interlude**
US 1932   110m   bw
MGM (Irving Thalberg)
GB title: *Strange Interval*

Problems of an unfulfilled wife and her lover. Surprising film version of a very heavy modern classic, complete with asides to the audience; very dated now, but a small milestone in Hollywood's development.

w Bess Meredyth, C. Gardner Sullivan, *play* Eugene O'Neill d Robert Z. Leonard ph Lee Garmes

Norma Shearer, Clark Gable, May Robson, Alexander Kirkland, Ralph Morgan, Robert Young, Maureen O'Sullivan, Henry B. Walthall

'A cinematic novelty to be seen by discerning audiences.'—*Film Weekly*

'More exciting than a thousand "action" movies.'—*Pare Lorentz*

'The film in which you hear the characters think!'—*publicity*

Strange Intruder
US 1957   78m   bw
AA (Lindsley Parsons)

A psychopathic ex-POW menaces the children of his dead friend's wife.

Gloomy second feature melodrama, rather well presented.

w David Evans, Warren Douglas, *novel* Helen Fowler d Irving Rapper ph Ernest Haller m Paul Dunlap

Edmund Purdom, Ida Lupino, Ann Harding, Jacques Bergerac, Carl Benton Reid

Strange Lady in Town
US 1955   118m   Warnercolor
    Cinemascope
Warner (Mervyn Le Roy)

Adventures of a woman doctor in 1880 Santa Fe.

Quaint western drama which is never any more convincing than its star.

w Frank Butler d Mervyn Le Roy ph Harold Rosson m Dmitri Tiomkin

Greer Garson, Dana Andrews, Cameron Mitchell, Lois Smith, Walter Hampden

The Strange Love of Martha Ivers**
US 1946   116m   bw
Paramount / Hal B. Wallis

A murderous child becomes a wealthy woman with a spineless lawyer husband; the melodrama starts when an ex-boy friend returns to town.

Irresistible star melodrama which leaves no stone unturned; compulsive entertainment of the old school.

w Robert Rossen d Lewis Milestone ph Victor Milner m Miklos Rozsa

Barbara Stanwyck, Van Heflin, Kirk Douglas, Lizabeth Scott, Judith Anderson, Roman Bohnen

'Fate drew them together and only murder can part them!'—*publicity*

'Whisper her name!'—*publicity*

AAN: original story (Jack Patrick)

The Strange Love of Molly Louvain
US 1932   74m   bw

The mother of an illegitimate child has men competing for her attentions, including a gangster, a reporter and a young innocent.
Pattern melodrama which suited the masses.
Ann Dvorak, Richard Cromwell, Lee Tracy, Leslie Fenton, Guy Kibbee, Evalyn Knapp, Frank McHugh. Written by Erwin Gelsey and Brown Holmes, from a play by Maurine Watkins; directed by Michael Curtiz; for Warner.

The Strange One*
US 1957   99m   bw
Columbia / Sam Spiegel
GB title: *End as a Man*

A sadistic cadet causes trouble at a southern military college.
A weird and unsavoury but rather compelling melodrama which unreels like a senior version of *Tom Brown's Schooldays*.

w Calder Willingham, from his novel End as a Man d Jack Garfein ph Burnett Guffey m Kenyon Hopkins

Ben Gazzara, George Peppard, Mark Richman, Pat Hingle, Arthur Storch, Paul Richards, Geoffrey Horne, James Olson
'The film's brilliance is in its persuasive depiction of a highly controversial, artificially organized world; its failure is to make any dramatic statement about it.'—*MFB*

The Strange Woman
US 1946   100m   bw
(UA) Hunt Stromberg (Jack Chertok)

A scheming woman plays with the lives of three men.
Star wish-fulfilment; otherwise a hammy costume piece.

w Herb Meadows, *novel* Ben Ames Williams d Edgar G. Ulmer ph Lucien Andriot m Carmen Dragon

Hedy Lamarr, George Sanders, Louis Hayward, Gene Lockhart, Hillary Brooke

The Stranger*
US 1946   95m   bw
(RKO) Sam Spiegel

An escaped Nazi criminal marries an American woman and settles in a Connecticut village.
Highly unconvincing and artificial melodrama enhanced by directorial touches, splendid photography and no-holds-barred climax involving a church clock.

w Anthony Veiller, *story* Victor Trivas, Decia Dunning d Orson Welles ph Russell Metty m Bronislau Kaper

Edward G. Robinson, Orson Welles, Loretta Young, Philip Merivale, Richard Long, Konstantin Shayne
'Some striking effects, with lighting and interesting angles much relied on.'—*Bosley Crowther*
'A film of confused motivations and clumsy effects.'—*Basil Wright, 1972*
AAN: original story

Stranger at My Door
US 1956   85m   bw
Republic (Sidney Picker)

A gunman takes refuge in the house of a preacher who tries to convert him.
Odd, sentimental little western morality play, not badly presented.

w Barry Shipman d William Witney ph Bud Thackery m Dale Butts

Macdonald Carey, Skip Homeier, Patricia Medina, Louis Jean Heydt

The Stranger Came Home
GB 1954   80m   bw

After being assaulted in the Far East, a financier loses his memory and does not return home until three years later, when murder ensues. Muddled mystery quickie, only notable as the film which persuaded its star to retire. Paulette Goddard, William Sylvester, Patrick Holt, Paul Carpenter, Russell Napier, Alvys Maben. Written by Michael Carreras, from the novel *Stranger at Home* by George Sanders; directed by Terence Fisher; for Exclusive. (US title: *The Unholy Four*.)

A Stranger in My Arms
US 1958   88m   bw   Cinemascope
U-I (Ross Hunter)

A test pilot falls in love with his dead friend's widow and helps her face up to her in-laws.
Dreary romantic drama.

w Peter Berneis, *novel* And Ride a Tiger by Robert Wilder d Helmut Kautner ph William Daniels m Joseph Gershenson

June Allyson, Jeff Chandler, *Mary Astor*, Sandra Dee, Charles Coburn, Conrad Nagel, Peter Graves

Stranger on the Third Floor*
US 1940   64m   bw
RKO (Lee Marcus)

A reporter finds that he was wrong in the well-intentioned testimony which helps convict an innocent man for murder.
Stylish B feature with a striking dream scene and a curious fleeting performance by Lorre as the real murderer.

w Frank Partos *d* Boris Ingster *ph* Nicholas Musuraca *m* Roy Webb

Margaret Tallichet, Peter Lorre, John McGuire, Charles Waldron, Elisha Cook Jnr, Charles Halton, Ethel Griffies

The Stranger Wore a Gun
US 1953 83m Technicolor 3-D

An honest adventurer finds that the man who once saved his life has become a stagecoach robber. Routine western with many objects hurled at the audience to show off the 3-D process. Randolph Scott, George Macready, Claire Trevor, Joan Weldon, Lee Marvin, Ernest Borgnine, Alfonso Bedoya. Written by Kenneth Gamet; directed by André de Toth; for Columbia.

The Stranger's Hand
GB 1953 85m bw
British Lion / John Stafford, Peter Moore
aka: *Mano della Straniero*

A schoolboy is due to meet his father in Venice, but the father is kidnapped by enemy agents.
Rather tentative suspense thriller with a vague plot which seems to defeat an excellent cast.

w Guy Elmes, Giorgio Bassani, *story* Graham Greene *d* Mario Soldati *ph* Enzo Serafin *m* Nino Rota

Trevor Howard, Richard O'Sullivan, Francis L. Sullivan, Alida Valli, Eduardo Ciannelli, Richard Basehart, Stephen Murray

Strangers May Kiss
US 1931 82m bw
MGM

A sophisticated wife takes love and fidelity lightly.
Dated romantic drama.

w John Meehan, *novel* Ursula Parrott *d* George Fitzmaurice *ph* William Daniels

Norma Shearer, Robert Montgomery, Neil Hamilton, Marjorie Rambeau, Irene Rich

Strangers on a Train***
US 1951 101m bw
Warner (Alfred Hitchcock)

A tennis star is pestered on a train by a psychotic who wants to swap murders, and proceeds to carry out his part of the bargain. This quirky melodrama has the director at his best, sequence by sequence, but the story is basically unsatisfactory. It makes superior suspense entertainment, however.

w Raymond Chandler, Czenzi Ormonde, *novel* Patricia Highsmith *d* Alfred Hitchcock *ph* Robert Burks *m* Dmitri Tionkin *md* Ray Heindorf

Farley Granger, *Robert Walker*, Ruth Roman, Leo G. Carroll, Patricia Hitchcock, *Marion Lorne*, Howard St John, Jonathan Hale, Laura Elliott

'You may not take it seriously, but you certainly don't have time to think about anything else.'—*Richard Mallett, Punch*
† Remade 1970 as *Once You Kiss A Stranger*.

AAN: Robert Burks

The Stranger's Return
US 1933 89m bw

An old farmer disapproves of his granddaughter's affair with a married man. An American view of Cold Comfort Farm country, too heavy to click at the box office. Lionel Barrymore, Miriam Hopkins, Franchot Tone, Beulah Bondi, Stuart Erwin, Irene Hervey. Written by Brown Holmes and Phil Stong; directed by King Vidor; for MGM.

Strangers When We Meet*
US 1960 117m Technicolor Cinemascope
Columbia / Bryna (Richard Quine)

A successful architect starts an affair with a beautiful married neighbour.
Beverly Hills soap opera with lots of romantic suffering in luxury. Lumpy but generally palatable.

w Evan Hunter, from his novel *d* Richard Quine *ph* Charles Lang Jnr *m* George Duning

Kirk Douglas, Kim Novak, *Ernie Kovacs, Walter Matthau,* Barbara Rush, Virginia Bruce, Helen Gallagher, Kent Smith

The Strangler
US 1963 80m bw
AA

An obese lab technician murders nurses who help his hated mother.
Modest, lively shocker.

w Bill S. Ballinger *d* Burt Topper *ph* Jacques Marquette *m* Marlin Skiles

Victor Buono, David McLean, Ellen Corby, Diane Sayer

The Stranglers of Bombay
GB 1959 81m bw Megascope
Columbia / Hammer (Anthony Hinds)

In 1826 travellers are waylaid and sacrificially killed by a cult of stranglers.

Semi-historical parade of atrocities, repellent but scarcely exciting.

w David Z. Goodman *d* Terence Fisher *ph* Arthur Grant *m* James Bernard

Guy Rolfe, Allan Cuthbertson, Andrew Cruickshank, Marne Maitland, Jan Holden, George Pastell, Paul Stassino

Strategic Air Command
US 1955   114m   Technicolor
Vistavision
Paramount (Samuel J. Briskin)

A baseball player is recalled to air force duty. Sentimental flagwaver featuring the newest jets of the fifties.

w Valentine Davies, Beirne Lay Jnr *d* Anthony Mann *ph* William Daniels *m* Victor Young

James Stewart, June Allyson, Frank Lovejoy, Barry Sullivan, Alex Nicol, Bruce Bennett, Jay C. Flippen, James Millican, James Bell

AAN: original story (Beirne Lay Jnr)

The Stratton Story
US 1949   106m   bw
MGM (Sam Wood)

An amateur baseball enthusiast becomes a famous professional, but suffers an accident which involves the amputation of a leg. Mild sentimental biopic, well made but not very interesting.

w Douglas Morrow, Guy Trosper *d* Sam Wood *ph* Harold Rosson *m* Adolph Deutsch

James Stewart, June Allyson, Frank Morgan, Agnes Moorehead, Bill Williams

AA: original story (Douglas Morrow)

Straw Dogs
GB 1971   118m   Eastmancolor
Talent Associates / Amerbroco (Daniel Melnick)

In a Cornish village, a mild American university researcher erupts into violence when taunted by drunken villagers who commit sustained assaults on himself and his wife.
Totally absurd, poorly contrived, hilariously overwritten Cold Comfort Farm melodrama with fa.cical violence.

w David Zelag Goodman, Sam Peckinpah, *novel* The Siege of Trencher's Farm by Gordon M. Williams *d* Sam Peckinpah *ph* John Coquillon, *m* Jerry Fielding

Dustin Hoffman, Susan George, Peter Vaughan, David Warner, T. P. McKenna, Colin Welland

AAN: Jerry Fielding

The Strawberry Blonde**
US 1941   97m   bw
Warner (William Cagney)

A dentist in turn-of-the-century Brooklyn wonders whether he married the right woman. Pleasant period comedy drama, a remake of *One Sunday Afternoon* (qv).

w Julius J. and Philip G. Epstein *d* Raoul Walsh *ph* James Wong Howe *m* Heinz Roemheld

James Cagney, Olivia de Havilland, *Rita Hayworth, Alan Hale,* George Tobias, Jack Carson, Una O'Connor, George Reeves

'It not only tells a very human story, it also creates an atmosphere, recreates a period.'— *New York Sun*

AAN: Heinz Roemheld

Strawberry Roan
GB 1944   84m   bw

A farmer weds a showgirl who ruins his life. Rather glum rural drama with some style but little entertainment value. William Hartnell, Carol Raye, Walter Fitzgerald, Sophie Stewart, John Ruddock, Wylie Watson, Petula Clark. Written by Elizabeth Baron, from the novel by A. G. Street; directed by Maurice Elvey; for British National.

The Strawberry Statement
US 1970   109m   Metrocolor
MGM / Robert Chartoff, Irwin Winkler

Student rebels occupy a university administration building.
One of a short-lived group of student anti-discipline films of the early seventies, and about the most boring.

w Israel Horowitz, *novel* James Simon Kunen *d* Stuart Hagmann *ph* Ralph Woolsey *m* Ian Freebairn Smith

Bruce Davison, Kim Darby, Bud Cort, Murray MacLeod

Street Angel*
US 1928   101m   bw   part-talkie
Fox

An unwilling prostitute becomes a circus artiste.
A sentimental and tawdry tale becomes a vehicle for good typical work by director and stars.

w Marion Orth *play* Lady Cristallinda by Monckton Hoffe *d* Frank Borzage *ph* Ernest Palmer, Paul Ivano *ad* Harry Oliver

Janet Gaynor, Charles Farrell, Henry Armetta, Guido Trento

'A thing of beauty is a joy for ever . . .'—
publicity

AAN: Ernest Palmer; Janet Gaynor

Street Corner
GB 1953   94m   bw
Rank / LIP / Sydney Box
US title: *Both Sides of the Law*

Days in the lives of the women police of
Chelsea.
Patter-plotted female *Blue Lamp*; just about
watchable.

w Muriel and Sydney Box d Muriel Box
ph Reg Wyer m Temple Abady

Rosamund John, Anne Crawford, Peggy
Cummins, Terence Morgan, Barbara Murray,
Sarah Lawson, Ronald Howard, Eleanor
Summerfield, Michael Medwin

Street of Chance
US 1930   78m   bw
Paramount

A New York gambler gets his come-uppance.
Dullish family melodrama with gangsters as *dei
ex machina*.

w Howard Estabrook, Lenore Coffee d John
Cromwell ph Charles Lang

William Powell, Kay Francis, Regis Toomey,
Jean Arthur

AAN: script

Street of Shame*
Japan 1956   85m   bw
Daiei (Masaichi Nagata)
original title: *Akasen Chitai*

Stories of women in a Tokyo brothel.
Unremarkable material executed with the style
expected of the director.

w Masashige Narusawa d Kenji Mizoguchi
ph Kazuo Miyagawa m Toshiro Mayazumi

Machiko Kyo, Ayako Wakao, Aiko Mimasu

Street Scene*
US 1931   80m   bw
Samuel Goldwyn

In a New York slum street on a hot summer
night, an adulterous woman is shot by her
husband.
Slice-of-life drama from an influential play;
never much of a film, and very dated.

w Elmer Rice, from his play d King Vidor
ph George Barnes m Alfred Newman

Sylvia Sidney, William Collier Jnr, Max
Mantor, David Landau, Estelle Taylor,
Russell Hopton

'Whenever the camera starts to focus on two
or three characters, the plot thickens and

Street Scene flies out the window; petty
domestic tragedy supplants the original slice-
of-life conception.'—*National Board of Review*

The Street with No Name*
US 1948   93m   bw
TCF

An FBI man goes undercover to unmask a
criminal gang.
The oldest crime plot in the world, applied
with vigour to the documentary realism of *The
House on 92nd Street* and built around the *Kiss
of Death* psychopathic character created by
Richard Widmark.

w Harry Kleiner d William Keighley ph *Joe
MacDonald* m Lionel Newman

Richard Widmark, Mark Stevens, Lloyd
Nolan, Barbara Lawrence, Ed Begley

† Remade 1955 as *House of Bamboo*.

A Streetcar Named Desire**
US 1951   122m   bw
Charles K. Feldman / Elia Kazan

A repressed southern widow is raped and
driven mad by her brutal brother-in-law.
Reasonably successful, decorative picture from
a highly theatrical but influential play; unreal
sets and atmospheric photography vaguely
Sternbergian.

w Tennessee Williams, from his play d Elia
Kazan ph Harry Stradling m Alex North
ad Richard Day

Vivien Leigh, Marlon Brando, Kim Hunter,
Karl Malden

AA: Vivien Leigh; Kim Hunter; Karl Malden
AAN: best picture; Tennessee Williams; Elia
Kazan; Harry Stradling; Alex North; Marlon
Brando

Streets of Laredo
US 1949   92m   Technicolor
Paramount (Robert Fellows)

Two of three bandit friends become Texas
Rangers.
Adequate star western, a remake of *The Texas
Rangers*.

w Charles Marquis Warren d Leslie Fenton
ph Ray Rennahan m Victor Young

William Holden, William Bendix, Macdonald
Carey, Mona Freeman

Strictly Dishonourable
US 1951   94m   bw
MGM (Melvin Frank, Norman Panama)

A young girl falls in love with a rakish Italian
opera star; he is such a sentimentalist that he
marries her.

Emasculated sentimental version of the sharp Preston Sturges comedy.

wd Norman Panama, Melvin Frank *ph* Ray June *m* Lennie Hayton

Ezio Pinza, Janet Leigh, Millard Mitchell, Maria Palmer

† Previously filmed in 1931 by Universal, with Paul Lukas, Sidney Fox and Lewis Stone.

Strictly Unconventional: see The Circle

Strike***
USSR 1924   70m approx (24 fps)   bw
  silent
Goskino / Proletkult

A 1912 strike of factory workers is brutally put down by the authorities.
Brilliant propaganda piece with superbly cinematic sequences.

wd Sergei M. Eisenstein ph Edouard Tissé, Vassili Khvatov

Grigori Alexandrov, Maxim Strauch, Mikhail Gomarov

Strike Me Pink*
US 1936   104m   bw
Samuel Goldwyn

A timid amusement park owner is threatened by crooks.
Acceptable star comedy with music.

w Frank Butler, Walter de Leon, Francis Martin *d* Norman Taurog *ph* Gregg Toland, Merritt Gerstad *m* Alfred Newman *songs* Harold Arlen, Lew Brown

Eddie Cantor, Sally Eilers, Ethel Merman, William Frawley, Parkyakarkus

Strike Up the Band*
US 1940   120m   bw
MGM (Arthur Freed)

A high-school band takes part in a nationwide radio contest.
Rather tiresomely high-spirited musical with the stars at the top of their young form.

w Fred Finklehoffe, John Monks Jnr *d* / *ch* Busby Berkeley *ph* Ray June *md* Georgie Stoll, Roger Edens

Judy Garland, Mickey Rooney, Paul Whiteman and his Orchestra, June Preisser, William Tracy, Larry Nunn

AAN: Georgie Stoll, Roger Edens; song 'Our Love Affair' (*m* / *ly* Roger Edens, Georgie Stoll)

The Strip*
US 1951   85m   bw
MGM (Joe Pasternak)

A band drummer is accused of the murder of a racketeer.
Minor mystery melodrama intriguingly set on Sunset Strip, with jazz accompaniment.

w Allen Rivkin *d* Leslie Kardos *ph* Robert Surtees *m* George Stoll

Mickey Rooney, Sally Forrest, William Demarest, James Craig, Kay Brown; and Louis Armstrong, Earl Hines, Jack Teagarden

AAN: song 'A Kiss To Build a Dream On' (*m* / *ly* Bert Kalmar, Harry Ruby, Oscar Hammerstein II)

The Stripper*
US 1963   95m   bw   Cinemascope
TCF (Jerry Wald)
GB title: *Woman of Summer*

An ageing beauty queen returns to her Kansas hometown and has an affair with a 19-year-old garage hand.
Downbeat character melodrama typical of its time and its author; competent but sterile and rather tedious.

w Meade Roberts, *play* A Loss of Roses by William Inge *d Franklin Schaffner ph* Ellsworth Fredericks *m* Jerry Goldsmith

Joanne Woodward, Richard Beymer, *Claire Trevor*, Carol Lynley, Robert Webber, Louis Nye, Gypsy Rose Lee, Michael J. Pollard

Stromboli
Italy 1949   107m   bw
RKO / Be-Ro (Roberto Rossellini)

A Lithuanian refugee accepts the protection of marriage to an Italian fisherman, but resents the barrenness and hostility of her life, especially when the local volcano erupts.
Sloppy melodrama with pretensions, interesting but not even attractive to the eye.

w Roberto Rossellini and others *d* Roberto Rossellini *ph* Otello Martelli *m* Renzo Rossellini

Ingrid Bergman, Mario Vitale, Renzo Cesana
† The international version was cut to 81m.

The Strong Man*
US 1926   75m approx (24 fps)   bw
  (colour sequence)   silent
First National / Harry Langdon

A war veteran returns and searches the city for his female penfriend.
Quite charming star comedy, probably Langdon's best.

w Frank Capra, Arthur Ripley, Hal Conklin, Robert Eddy *d* Frank Capra *ph* Elgin Lessley, Glenn Kershner

Harry Langdon, Gertrude Astor, Tay Garnett

Stronger than Desire
US 1939   82m   bw

A lawyer's wife gets into trouble and lets him try an innocent man for her crime. Fast remake of *Evelyn Prentice*; a good half-bill.

Walter Pidgeon, Virginia Bruce, Ann Dvorak, Lee Bowman, Rita Johnson, Ilka Chase. Written by David Hertz and William Ludwig; directed by Leslie Fenton; for MGM.

The Strongest Man in the World
US 1976   92m   Technicolor
Walt Disney (Bill Anderson)

An accident in a science lab gives a student superhuman strength.
Formula comedy for older children.

w Joseph L. McEveety, Herman Groves *d* Vincent McEveety *ph* Andrew Jackson *m* Robert F. Brunner

Kurt Russell, Joe Flynn, Eve Arden, Cesar Romero, Phil Silvers, Dick Van Patten, Harold Gould, William Schallert, James Gregory, Roy Roberts, Fritz Feld, Raymond Bailey, Eddie Quillan, Burt Mustin

Strongroom*
GB 1961   80m   bw
Bryanston / Theatrecraft (Guido Coen)

Two car breakers plan a once-for-all bank robbery but get involved with potential murder when their hostages get locked in. Suspenseful second feature with gloss and pace.

w Max Marquis, René Harris *d* Vernon Sewell *ph* Basil Emmott *m* Johnny Gregory

Colin Gordon, Ann Lynn, Derren Nesbitt, Keith Faulkner

The Struggle*
US 1931   88m   bw
UA / D. W. Griffith

A New Yorker goes to the bad on bootleg liquor.
The director's last film reveals many of his old skills allied to a Victorian tract.

w Anita Loos, John Emerson *d* D. W. Griffith *ph* Joseph Ruttenberg

Hal Skelly, Zita Johann, Charlotte Wynters, Jackson Halliday

The Stud
GB 1978   90m   colour
Brent Walker / Artoc (Edward D. Simons)

A millionaire's wife installs her lover as manager of a discotheque, but he becomes bored and wants a place of his own.
Life among the unpleasant rich. A surprise box office success, richly undeserved.

w Jackie Collins, from her novel *d* Quentin Masters *ph* Peter Hannan *m* Biddu

Joan Collins, Oliver Tobias, Sue Lloyd, Mark Burns, Doug Fisher, Walter Gotell
  'Watching it is rather like being buried alive in a coffin stuffed with back numbers of *Men Only*.'—*Alan Brien*

The Student Prince
US 1954   107m   Anscocolor
  Cinemascope
MGM (Joe Pasternak)

A prince studies in Heidelberg and falls for a barmaid.
Ruritanian operetta, lumpishly filmed, with Mario Lanza providing only the voice of the hero as he got too fat to play the part.

w William Ludwig, Sonya Levien, *play* Old Heidelberg by Wilhelm Meyer-Foerster *operetta* Dorothy Donnelly *d* Richard Thorpe *ph* Paul C. Vogel *m* Sigmund Romberg *md* George Stoll

Edmund Purdom, Ann Blyth, John Williams, Edmund Gwenn, S. Z. Sakall, John Ericson, Louis Calhern, Betta St John, Evelyn Varden
† Without the music, the play had been filmed at MGM in 1926, with Ramon Novarro and Norma Shearer under Ernst Lubitsch's direction.

The Studio Murder Mystery
US 1929   62m   bw

An actor is murdered on a film set. Primitive talkie comedy mystery now interesting only for its studio backgrounds. Neil Hamilton, Florence Eldridge, Warner Oland, Eugene Pallette, Fredric March, Doris Hill, Chester Conklin. Written by Frank Tuttle, from a magazine serial by the Edingtons; directed by Frank Tuttle; for Paramount.

Studs Lonigan
US 1960   95m   bw

The growing up of an unlettered Chicago Irishman in the twenties. Rough-and-ready version of a celebrated novel, not a bad try but insufficiently detailed to be any kind of classic. Christopher Knight, Jack Nicholson, Frank Gorshin. Written by Philip Yordan, from the novel by James T. Farrell; directed by Irving Lerner; for Philip Yordan.

A Study in Terror*
GB 1965   95m   Eastmancolor
Compton—Tekli / Sir Nigel (Henry E. Lester)
Sherlock Holmes discovers the identity of Jack the Ripper.

A reasonably good Holmes pastiche marred by a surfeit of horror and over-riotous local colour; quite literate, but schizophrenic.

w Donald and Derek Ford, *novel* Ellery Queen d James Hill ph Desmond Dickinson m John Scott ad Alex Vetchinsky

John Neville, Donald Houston, John Fraser, Robert Morley, Cecil Parker, Anthony Quayle, Barbara Windsor, Adrienne Corri, Judi Dench, Frank Finlay, Barry Jones, Kay Walsh, Georgia Brown

The Stunt Man°
US 1978 129m Metrocolor
Melvin Simon (Richard Rush)

A Vietnam veteran on the run from the police finds refuge as a star stunt man for a sinister film director.
Overlong, curious, but sometimes compelling melodrama which entertains on the surface while its actual aims are harder to fathom.

w Lawrence B. Marcus *novel* Paul Brodeur d Richard Rush ph Mario Tosi m Dominic Frontière

Peter O'Toole, Steve Railsback, Barbara Hershey, Allen Goorwitz, Alex Rocco, Sharon Farrell

AAN: screenplay; Richard Rush; Peter O'Toole

The Subject Was Roses°
US 1968 107m Metrocolor
MGM (Edgar Lansbury)

A young war veteran finds he can't communicate with his parents, and vice versa.
Photographed play notable for its performances.

w Frank D. Gilroy, from his play d Ulu Grosbard ph Jack Priestley

Patricia Neal, Jack Albertson, Martin Sheen, Don Saxon, Elaine Williams

AA: Jack Albertson
AAN: Patricia Neal

Submarine Command
US 1951 87m bw
Paramount (John Farrow, Joseph Sistrom)

A submarine officer who considers himself a coward becomes a hero in Korea.
Very routine soul-searching actioner.

w Jonathan Latimer d John Farrow ph Lionel Lindon m David Buttolph

William Holden, Don Taylor, Nancy Olsen, William Bendix, Moroni Olsen, Peggy Webber

Submarine X-I
GB 1967 90m Eastmancolor
UA / Mirisch (John C. Champion)

A submarine commander in World War II trains men to attack the *Lindendorf* in midget submarines.
Belated quota quickie, routine in every department.

w Donald S. Sanford, Guy Elmes d William Graham ph Paul Beeson

James Caan, Norman Bowler, David Sumner

The Subterraneans
US 1960 89m Metrocolor
  Cinemascope
MGM (Arthur Freed)

The love affairs of San Francisco bohemians.
A boring oddity with lashings of eccentric behaviour and sexual hang-ups; MGM venturing very timidly outside its field.

w Robert Thom, *novel* Jack Kerouac d Ranald MacDougall ph Joseph Ruttenberg m André Previn

George Peppard, Leslie Caron, Janice Rule, Roddy McDowall, Anne Seymour, Jim Hutton

Subway in the Sky
GB 1958 87m bw
Sydney Box (John Temple-Smith, Patrick Filmer-Sankey)

A Berlin cabaret star finds her landlady's ex-husband, a deserter, hiding in her apartment and sets out to prove his innocence of drug smuggling.
Tedious photographed play with precious few points of dramatic interest.

w Jack Andrews, *play* Ian Main d Muriel Box ph Wilkie Cooper m Mario Nascimbene

Hildegarde Neff, Van Johnson, Katherine Kath, Cec Linder, Albert Lieven, Edward Judd

A Successful Calamity
US 1931 75m bw

A millionaire discovers the true worth of his family when he pretends to be poor. Good star vehicle which pleases despite its predictability.
George Arliss, Mary Astor, Evalyn Knapp, Grant Mitchell, William Janney. Written by Maude Howell, Julien Josephson and Austin Parker, from the play by Clare Kummer; directed by John G. Adolfi; for Warner.

Such Good Friends°
US 1971 102m Movielab
Paramount / Sigma (Otto Preminger)

A successful man has a mysterious illness and his wife enlists help from his friends. Satirical parable which alternates between sex comedy and medical exposé; generally heavy-going but with good moments.

w Elaine May, *novel* Lois Gould *d* Otto Preminger *ph* Gayne Rescher *m* Thomas Z. Shepherd

Dyan Cannon, James Coco, Jennifer O'Neil, Nina Foch, Laurence Luckinbill, Ken Howard, Burgess Meredith, Louise Lasser, Sam Levene, Rita Gam, Nancy Guild

Sudden Fear°•
US 1952   111m   bw
RKO / Joseph Kaufman

A playwright heiress finds that her husband is plotting to kill her.
Archetypal star suspenser, glossy and effectively climaxed.

w Lenore Coffee, Robert Smith *d* David Miller *ph* Charles Lang Jnr *m* Elmer Bernstein

Joan Crawford, Jack Palance, Gloria Grahame, Bruce Bennett, Mike Connors

AAN: Charles Lang Jnr; Joan Crawford; Jack Palance

Suddenly°
US 1954   75m   bw
UA / Robert Bassler

Gunmen take over a suburban house and plan to assassinate the President who is due to pass by.
Moderately effective minor suspenser with rather too much psychological chat.

w Richard Sale *d* Lewis Allen *ph* Charles G. Clarke *m* David Raksin

Frank Sinatra, Sterling Hayden, James Gleason, Nancy Gates, Kim Charney

Suddenly It's Spring
US 1947   87m   bw
Paramount (Claude Binyon)

A WAC captain comes home to find that her husband wants a divorce.
Tired romantic comedy with no fizz at all.

w Claude Binyon *d* Mitchell Leisen *ph* Daniel L. Fapp *m* Victor Young

Paulette Goddard, Macdonald Carey, Fred MacMurray, Arleen Whelan, Lillian Fontaine, Frank Faylen, Victoria Horne

Suddenly Last Summer°
GB 1959   114m   bw
Columbia / Horizon (Sam Spiegel)

A homosexual poet's young cousin goes mad when she sees him raped and murdered by beach boys.
Arty flashback talk-piece from a one-act play, padded out with much sub-poetic mumbo jumbo; it takes too long to get to the revelation, which is ambiguously presented anyway.

w Gore Vidal, *play* Tennessee Williams *d* Joseph L. Mankiewicz *ph* Jack Hildyard *m* Buxton Orr, Malcolm Arnold *pd* Oliver Messel

Katharine Hepburn, Elizabeth Taylor, Montgomery Clift, Albert Dekker, Mercedes McCambridge, Gary Raymond

  'A short play turns into a ludicrous, lumbering horror movie.'—*New Yorker, 1978*
  'I loathe this film, I say so candidly. To my mind it is a decadent piece of work, sensational, barbarous and ridiculous.'—*C. A. Lejeune, Observer*
  ↗ 'A wholly admirable rendering into film of a work at once fascinating and nauseating, brilliant and immoral.'—*Arthur Knight*

AAN: Katharine Hepburn; Elizabeth Taylor

Suez°
US 1938   104m   bw
TCF (Darryl F. Zanuck)

The career of French engineer Ferdinand de Lesseps, who built the Suez Canal.
Superbly mounted but rather undramatic fictionalized biopic.

w Philip Dunne, Julien Josephson *d* Allan Dwan *ph* Peverell Marley *md* Louis Silvers

Tyrone Power, Annabella, Loretta Young, J. Edward Bromberg, Joseph Schildkraut, Henry Stephenson, Sidney Blackmer, Maurice Moscovitch, Sig Rumann, Nigel Bruce, Miles Mander, George Zucco, Leon Ames, Rafaela Ottiano

AAN: Peverell Marley; Louis Silvers

Sugarfoot
US 1951   80m   Technicolor

Two men meet on a train for Prescott, Arizona, and each determines to make the town his own. Unusual but fatally sluggish western. Randolph Scott, Raymond Massey, Adele Jergens, S. Z. Sakall, Robert Warwick, Arthur Hunnicutt. Written by Russell Hughes, from a novel by Clarence Budington Kelland; directed by Edwin L. Marin; for Warner. (TV title: *Swirl of Glory*.)

Sugarland Express°•
US 1974   110m   Technicolor
Panavision
Universal (Richard Zanuck, David Brown)

A convict's wife persuades him to escape because their baby is being adopted, and they inadvertently leave behind them a trail of destruction, ending in tragedy.
Mainly comic adventures with a bitter aftertaste, very stylishly handled.

w Hal Barwood, Matthew Robbins *d* Steven Spielberg *ph* Vilmos Zsigmond *m* John Williams

Goldie Hawn, Ben Johnson, Michael Sacks, William Atherton

'*Ace in the Hole* meets *Vanishing Point*.'— *Sight and Sound*

The Suitor°
France 1962 85m bw
CAPAC
original title: *Le Soupirant*

A nervous young man makes several attempts to get married.
The most successful feature of Pierre Etaix, a student of Tati: his jokes are more polished but in the end his own personality seems rather lacking.

w Pierre Etaix, Jean-Claude Carrière *d* Pierre Etaix *m* Pierre Levant

Pierre Etaix, Laurence Lignères, France Arnell

The Sullivans°
US 1944 111m bw
TCF (Sam Jaffe)
Reissue title: *The Fighting Sullivans*

Five sons of the same family are killed in World War II.
Inspirational true story which had a wide appeal.

w Mary C. McCall Jnr *d* Lloyd Bacon *ph* Lucien Andriot *m* Alfred Newman

Anne Baxter, Thomas Mitchell, Selena Royle, Edward Ryan, Trudy Marshall, John Campbell, James Cardwell, John Alvin, George Offerman Jnr, Roy Roberts

AAN: original story (Jules Schermer, Edward Doherty)

Sullivan's Travels°°°°
US 1941 90m bw
Paramount (Paul Jones)

A Hollywood director tires of comedy and goes out to find real life.
Marvellously sustained tragi-comedy which ranges from pratfalls to the chain gang and never loses its grip or balance.

wd Preston Sturges *ph* John Seitz *m* Leo Shuken

Joel McCrea, Veronica Lake, Robert Warwick, William Demarest, Franklin Pangborn, Porter Hall, Byron Foulger, Eric Blore, Robert Greig, Torben Meyer, *Jimmy Conlin*, Margaret Hayes

'A brilliant fantasy in two keys—slapstick farce and the tragedy of human misery.'— *James Agee*
'The most witty and knowing spoof of Hollywood movie-making of all time.'—*Film Society Review*
'Reflecting to perfection the mood of wartime Hollywood, it danced on the grave of thirties social cinema.'—*Eileen Bowser, 1969*

Summer and Smoke
US 1961 118m Technicolor Vistavision
Paramount / Hal B. Wallis

In a small Mississippi town in 1916, the minister's spinster daughter nurses an unrequited love for the local rebel.
Wearisome screen version, in hothouse settings, of a pattern play about earthly and spiritual love.

w James Poe, Meade Roberts, *play* Tennessee Williams *d* Peter Glenville *ph* Charles Lang Jnr *m* Elmer Bernstein *ad* Walter Tyler

Geraldine Page, Laurence Harvey, Una Merkel, John McIntire, Pamela Tiffin, Rita Moreno, Thomas Gomez, Casey Adams, Earl Holliman, Lee Patrick, Malcolm Atterbury

AAN: Elmer Bernstein; Geraldine Page; Una Merkel

Summer Holiday°°
US 1948 92m Technicolor
MGM (Arthur Freed)

Life for a small-town family at the turn of the century.
Musical version of a famous play: excellent individual numbers, warm playing and sympathetic scenes, but a surprising lack of overall style.

w Frances Goodrich, Albert Hackett, Ralph Blane, *play* Ah Wilderness by Eugene O'Neill *d* Rouben Mamoulian *ph* Charles Schoenbaum *md* Lennie Hayton *songs* Harry Warren, Ralph Blane *ch* Charles Walters

Walter Huston, Mickey Rooney, Frank Morgan, Agnes Moorehead, Butch Jenkins, Selena Royle, Marilyn Maxwell, Gloria de Haven, Anne Francis

† The film was finished in 1946 and held back because it seemed unlikely to succeed.

Summer Holiday*
GB 1962   109m   Technicolor
Cinemascope
ABP / Ivy (Kenneth Harper)

Four young London Transport mechanics
borrow a double decker bus for a continental
holiday.
Pacy, location-filmed youth musical with
plenty of general appeal.

w Peter Myers, Ronnie Cass d Peter Yates
ph John Wilcox md Stanley Black

Cliff Richard, Lauri Peters, Melvyn Hayes,
Una Stubbs, Teddy Green, Ron Moody,
Lionel Murton, David Kossoff

Summer Interlude*
Sweden 1950   97m   bw
Svensk Filmindustri (Alan Ekelund)
original title: Sommarlek

A prima ballerina remembers a happy summer
she spent with a boy who was tragically killed.
Melancholy romance quite typical of its
creator but with less density of meaning than
usual.

w Ingmar Bergman, Herbert Grevenius
d Ingmar Bergman ph Gunnar Fischer, Bengt
Jarnmark m Erik Nordgren

Maj-Britt Nilsson, Birger Malmsten, Alf
Kjellin

Summer Magic*
US 1963   104m   Technicolor
Walt Disney (Ron Miller)

Children help their widowed mother in 1912
Boston.
Amiable remake of Mother Carey's Chickens,
irreproachably presented.

w Sally Benson d James Neilson ph William
Snyder m Buddy Baker songs the Sherman
Brothers

Hayley Mills, Burl Ives, Dorothy McGuire,
Darren McGavin, Deborah Walley, Una
Merkel, Eddie Hodges, Michael J. Pollard

AAN: William Snyder

Summer of '42*
US 1971   103m   Technicolor
Warner (Richard Alan Roth)

Adolescents make sexual explorations on a
New England island in 1942.
Well-observed indulgence in the new
permissiveness.

w Herman Raucher d Robert Mulligan
ph Robert Surtees m Michel Legrand

Jennifer O'Neill, Gary Grimes, Jerry Houser,
Oliver Conant, Lou Frizell

AA: Michel Legrand
AAN: Herman Raucher; Robert Surtees

Summer of the Seventeenth Doll
US / Australia 1959   94m   bw
UA / Hecht–Hill–Lancaster (Leslie Norman)
US title: Season of Passion

Two cane-cutters on their annual city lay-off
have woman trouble.
Miscast and unsatisfactory rendering of a good
play; the humour has evaporated.

w John Dighton, play Ray Lawler d Leslie
Norman ph Paul Beeson m Benjamin
Frankel

Ernest Borgnine, John Mills, Angela
Lansbury, Anne Baxter, Vincent Ball

A Summer Place
US 1959   130m   Technicolor
Warner (Delmer Daves)

Romantic summer adventures of teenagers
and their elders on an island off the coast of
Maine.
Sex among the idle rich: a routine piece of
Hollywood gloss, bowdlerized from a
bestseller.

wd Delmer Daves, novel Sloan Wilson
ph Harry Stradling m Max Steiner

Richard Egan, Dorothy McGuire, Sandra
Dee, Arthur Kennedy, Troy Donahue,
Constance Ford, Beulah Bondi

Summer Stock*
US 1950   109m   Technicolor
MGM (Joe Pasternak)
GB title: If You Feel Like Singing

A theatre troupe takes over a farm for
rehearsals, and the lady owner gets the bug.
Likeable but halting musical with the star's
weight problems very obvious.

w George Wells, Sy Gomberg d Charles
Walters ph Robert Planck md Johnny
Green ch Nick Castle

Judy Garland, Gene Kelly, Gloria de Haven,
Carleton Carpenter, Eddie Bracken, Phil
Silvers, Hans Conried
† June Allyson was to have starred, but
became pregnant.

Summer Storm*
US 1944   106m   bw
UA (Seymour Nebenzal)

In 1912 Russia, a provincial judge falls for a
local mancatcher.
One of Hollywood's occasional aberrations, an
attempt to do something very European in
typical west coast style. An interesting failure.

w Rowland Leigh, *story* The Shooting Party by Anton Chekhov *d* Douglas Sirk *ph* Archie Stout *md* Karl Hajos

George Sanders, Linda Darnell, *Edward Everett Horton,* Anna Lee, Hugo Haas, John Philiber, Sig Rumann, André Charlot

'There are bits of acting and photography which put it as far outside the run of American movies as it laudably tries to be. But most of it had for me the sporty speciousness of an illustrated drugstore classic.'—*James Agee*

AAN: Karl Hajos

Summer Wishes, Winter Dreams*
US 1973 88m Technicolor
Columbia / Rastar (Jack Brodsky)

A neurotic New York housewife goes to pieces when her mother dies but finds a new understanding of her husband when she accompanies him on a trip to the World War II battlefields.
Menopausal melodrama, well observed but disappointingly wispy and underdeveloped.

w Stewart Stern *d* Gilbert Cates *ph* Gerald Hirschfeld *m* Johnny Mandel

Joanne Woodward, Martin Balsam, Sylvia Sidney, Dori Brenner, Win Forman

AAN: Joanne Woodward; Sylvia Sidney

Summer with Monika*
Sweden 1952 97m bw
Svensk Filmindustri (Allan Ekelund)

A wild, restless girl defies her parents and goes off with her boy friend for an island holiday. Her subsequent pregnancy and motherhood don't in the least suit her, and the father is left alone with the baby.
Probably truthful but rather glum and unsophisticated drama of young love; not among Bergman's most interesting films.

w Ingmar Bergman, *novel* Per Anders Fogelstrom *ph* Gunnar Fischer *m* Erik Nordgren

Harriet Andersson, Lars Ekborg

Summertime***
US 1955 99m Eastmancolor
Ilya Lopert / Alexander Korda
GB title: *Summer Madness*

An American spinster has a holiday in Venice and becomes romantically involved.
Delightful, sympathetic travelogue with dramatic asides, great to look at and hinging on a single superb performance.

w David Lean, H. E. Bates, *play* The Time of the Cuckoo by Arthur Laurents *d* David Lean *ph* Jack Hildyard *m* Sandro Cicogini

Katharine Hepburn, Rossano Brazzi, Isa Miranda, Darren McGavin, Mari Aldon, André Morell

'The eye is endlessly ravished.'—*Dilys Powell*

AAN: David Lean; Katharine Hepburn

Summertree
US 1971 88m Eastmancolor
Warner / Bryna (Kirk Douglas)

A bored student learns about life and becomes a Vietnam casualty.
Well-made, rather tedious character study; good social observation.

w Edward Hume, Stephen Yafa, *play* Ron Cowen *d* Anthony Newley *ph* Richard C. Glouner *m* David Shire

Michael Douglas, Brenda Vaccaro, Jack Warden, Barbara Bel Geddes

The Sun Also Rises**
US 1957 129m Eastmancolor
          Cinemascope
TCF (Darryl F. Zanuck)

In Paris after World War I an impotent journalist meets a nymphomaniac lady of title, and they and their odd group of friends have various saddening adventures around Europe.
Not a bad attempt to film a difficult novel, though Cinemascope doesn't help and the last half hour becomes turgid. *The Last Flight* (qv) conveyed the same atmosphere rather more sharply.

w Peter Viertel, *novel* Ernest Hemingway *d* Henry King *ph* Leo Tover *m* Hugo Friedhofer

Tyrone Power, Ava Gardner, *Errol Flynn*, Eddie Albert, Mel Ferrer, Robert Evans, Juliette Greco, Gregory Ratoff, Marcel Dalio, Henry Daniell

The Sun Never Sets
US 1939 98m bw
Universal (Rowland V. Lee)

Two brothers in the African colonial service prevent a munitions baron from plunging the world into war.
Stiff upper lip melodrama, very dated.

w W. P. Lipscomb *d* Rowland V. Lee *ph* George Robinson *m* Frank Skinner *md* Charles Previn

Basil Rathbone, Douglas Fairbanks Jnr, Virginia Field, Lionel Atwill, Barbara O'Neil, C. Aubrey Smith, Melville Cooper

The Sun Shines Bright**
US 1953   92m   bw
Republic / Argosy (John Ford, Merian C.
 Cooper)

Forty years after the Civil War, the judge of a
Kentucky town still has trouble quelling the
Confederate spirit.
Mellow anecdotes of time gone by, scrappily
linked but lovingly polished; a remake of a
Will Rogers vehicle *Judge Priest.*

w Lawrence Stallings, *stories* Irwin S. Cobb
d John Ford *ph* Archie Stout *m* Victor Young

Charles Winninger, Arleen Whelan, John
Russell, Stepin Fetchit, Milburn Stone, Grant
Withers, Russell Simpson
 'Passages of quite remarkable poetic feeling
. . . alive with affection and truthful
observation.'—*Lindsay Anderson*

Sun Valley Serenade*
US 1941   86m   bw
TCF (Milton Sperling)

The band manager at an Idaho ice resort takes
care of a Norwegian refugee.
Simple-minded musical which still pleases
because of the talent involved.

w Robert Ellis, Helen Logan   *d* H. Bruce
Humberstone *ph* Edward Cronjager
songs Mack Gordon, Harry Warren   *m* Emil
Newman

Sonja Henie, *Glenn Miller and his Orchestra*,
John Payne, *Milton Berle*, Lynn Bari, Joan
Davis, *The Nicholas Brothers*, Dorothy
Dandridge

AAN: Edward Cronjager; Emil Newman;
song 'Chattanooga' (*m* Harry Warren,
ly Mack Gordon)

Sunburn
GB / US 1979   98m   Technicolor
Hemdale / Bind Films (David Korda)

An insurance investigator hires a model to act
as his wife while he trails a suspected murderer
in Acapulco.
All sun and skin and swirling cameras, this
entire movie is a seventies cliché, but it
provides some fitful amusement.

w John Daly, Stephen Oliver, James Booth,
novel The Bind by Stanley Ellin   *d* Richard C.
Sarafian *ph* Alex Phillips Jnr   *m* John
Cameron

Farrah Fawcett, Charles Grodin, Art Carney,
Joan Collins, William Daniels, John
Hillerman, Eleanor Parker, Keenan Wynn

Sunday, Bloody Sunday***
GB 1971   110m   De Luxe
UA / Vectia (Joseph Janni)

A young designer shares his sexual favours
equally between two loves of different sexes, a
Jewish doctor and a lady executive.
Stylishly made character study with
melodramatic leanings, rather self-conscious
about its risky subject but, scene by scene,
both adult and absorbing, with an
overpowering mass of sociological detail about
the way we live.

w Penelope Gilliatt   *d* John Schlesinger
ph Billy Williams   *m* Ron Geesin   *pd* Luciana
Arrighi

Glenda Jackson, Peter Finch, Murray Head,
Peggy Ashcroft, Maurice Denham, Vivian
Pickles, Frank Windsor, Tony Britton, Harold
Goldblatt

AAN: Penelope Gilliatt; John Schlesinger;
Glenda Jackson; Peter Finch

Sunday Dinner for a Soldier*
US 1944   86m   bw
TCF (Walter Morosco)

A poor family living on a derelict Florida
houseboat scrape together enough money to
invite a soldier for a meal.
Sentimental little flagwaving romance, quite
sympathetically presented and agreeably
underacted.

w Wanda Tuchock, Melvin Levy   *d* Lloyd
Bacon *ph* Joe MacDonald   *m* Alfred
Newman

Anne Baxter, John Hodiak, Charles
Winninger, Anne Revere, Connie Marshall,
Chill Wills, Bobby Driscoll, Jane Darwell
 'Simple, true and tender, the best
propaganda America has put out in the
current year.'—*Richard Winnington*
 'Their eyes met! Their lips questioned!
Their arms answered!'—*publicity*

Sunday in New York*
US 1963   105m   Metrocolor
MGM / Seven Arts (Everett Freeman)

Complications in the love life of a brother and
sister, each of whom thinks the other is very
moral.
Fresh, fairly adult sex comedy with New York
backgrounds.

w Norman Krasna, from his play   *d* Peter
Tewkesbury *ph* Leo Tover   *m* Peter Nero

Cliff Robertson, Rod Taylor, Jane Fonda,
Robert Culp, Jo Morrow, Jim Backus

Sundays and Cybèle*
France 1962   110m   bw   Franscope
Terra / Fides / Orsa / Trocadéro (Romain
Pinès)
original title: *Cybèle ou les Dimanches de
Ville d'Avray*

An amnesiac ex-pilot strikes up a friendship with an abandoned 12-year-old girl, but the relationship is misunderstood and ends in tragedy.

A fashionable film of its time which now has little to offer: its director's reputation sagged alarmingly when he went to Hollywood.

w Serge Bourgignon, Antoine Tudal, *novel* Bernard Echasseriaux *d* Serge Bourgignon *ph* Henri Decaë *m* Maurice Jarre

Hardy Kruger, Nicole Courcel, Patricia Gozzi, Daniel Ivernel

'Studied charm and a creakingly melodramatic dénouement take the place of any serious attempt to probe the characters or situation . . . the film is so busily preoccupied with being as attractive, visually and sentimentally, as it possibly can, that it never has time to consider what it is being attractive about.'—*Tom Milne, MFB*

'Uneven but highly meritorious . . . a near-triumph of the intelligently mobile camera.'—*John Simon*

AA: best foreign film
AAN: script: Maurice Jarre

Sundown
US 1941 91m bw
Walter Wanger

The adopted daughter of an Arab trader assists British troops in Africa during World War II.

Artificial-looking romantic actioner with good cast.

w Barre Lyndon *d* Henry Hathaway *ph* Charles Lang *m* Miklos Rozsa

Gene Tierney, Bruce Cabot, George Sanders, Harry Carey, Joseph Calleia, Cedric Hardwicke, Carl Esmond, Reginald Gardiner

AAN: Charles Lang; Miklos Rozsa

The Sundowners**
GB / Australia 1960 133m Technicolor
Warner (Gerry Blatner)

In the twenties an Irish sheepdrover and his family travel from job to job in the Australian bush.

Easygoing, often amusing but lethargically developed family film with major stars somewhat ill at ease. Memorable sequences.

w Isabel Lennart, *novel* Jon Cleary *d* Fred Zinnemann *ph* Jack Hildyard *m* Dmitri Tiomkin

Robert Mitchum, Deborah Kerr, *Glynis Johns*, Peter Ustinov, Michael Anderson Jnr, Dina Merrill, *Wylie Watson*, Chips Rafferty

'For all Zinnemann's generous attention to character, the hints of longing, despair and indomitable spirit, the overall impression remains one of sheer length and repetition and synthetic naturalism.'—*Richard Winnington*

AAN: best picture; Isabel Lennart; Fred Zinnemann; Deborah Kerr; Glynis Johns

Sunny*
US 1930 81m bw
Warner

A showgirl falls for a rich young man.

Tinny early musical notable for its star.

w Humphrey Pearson, Henry McCarthy, *musical play* Otto Harbach, Oscar Hammerstein II, Jerome Kern *ph* Ernest Haller *d* William A. Seiter

Marilyn Miller, Lawrence Grey, Jack Donahue, Mackenzie Ward, O. P. Heggie

Sunny*
US 1941 97m bw
RKO / Imperator (Herbert Wilcox)

Adequate remake of the above.

w Sig Herzig *d* Herbert Wilcox *ph* Russell Metty *m* Anthony Collins

Anna Neagle, Ray Bolger, John Carroll, Edward Everett Horton, Frieda Inescort, Grace and Paul Hartman

AAN: Anthony Collins

Sunny Side Up*
US 1929 80m bw
Fox

A slum girl falls for the son of a rich Southampton family.

Typical early musical of the softer kind; rewarding for those who can project themselves back.

w / m / ly B. G. De Sylva, Lew Brown, Ray Henderson *d* David Butler *ph* Ernest Palmer

Janet Gaynor, Charles Farrell, El Brendel, Marjorie White, Sharon Lynn

Sunnyside*
US 1919 27m approx (24 fps) bw
silent
First National / Charles Chaplin

The overworked odd job man at a country hotel has a pastoral dream.

Very mildly funny star comedy which was intended as a satire on the D. W. Griffith / Charles Ray type of rural drama then popular. It doesn't work in this vein either.

wd Charles Chaplin *ph* Rollie Totheroh

Charles Chaplin, Edna Purviance, Tom Wilson, Albert Austin, Henry Bergman

Sunrise**
US 1927   97m (24 fps)   bw   silent
Fox

A villager in love with a city woman tries to kill his wife but then repents and spends a happy day with her.
Lyrical melodrama, superbly handled: generally considered among the finest Hollywood productions of the twenties.

w Carl Meyer, *novel* A Trip to Tilsit by Hermann Sudermann *d* F. W. Murnau *ph* Karl Struss, Charles Rosher *m* (sound version) Hugo Riesenfeld

Janet Gaynor, George O'Brien, Margaret Livingston
'It is filled with intense feeling and in it is embodied an underlying subtlety . . . exotic in many ways for it is a mixture of Russian gloom and Berlin brightness.'—*Mordaunt Hall, New York Times*
'Not since the earliest, simplest moving pictures, when locomotives, fire engines and crowds in streets were transposed to the screen artlessly and endearingly, when the entranced eye was rushed through tunnels and over precipices on runaway trains, has there been such joy in motion as under Murnau's direction.'—*Louise Bogan, The New Republic*
AA: Karl Struss, Charles Rosher; Janet Gaynor

Sunrise at Campobello*
US 1960   143m   Technicolor
Warner / Dore Schary

The early life of Franklin Roosevelt, including his battle against polio and return to politics.
Static filming of a rather interesting Broadway success and of a memorable performance.

w Dore Schary, from his play *d* Vincent J. Donehue *ph* Russell Harlan *m* Franz Waxman

Ralph Bellamy, Greer Garson, Ann Shoemaker, Hume Cronyn, Jean Hagen

AAN: Greer Garson

Sunset Boulevard***
US 1950   110m   bw
Paramount (Charles Brackett)

A luckless Hollywood scriptwriter goes to live with a wealthy older woman, a slightly dotty and extremely possessive relic of the silent screen.
Incisive melodrama with marvellous moments but a tendency to overstay its welcome; the first reels are certainly the best, though the last scene is worth waiting for and the malicious observation throughout is a treat.

w Charles Brackett, Billy Wilder, D. M. Marshman Jnr *d* Billy Wilder *ph* John F. Seitz *m* Franz Waxman

Gloria Swanson, William Holden, Erich Von Stroheim, Fred Clark, Nancy Olson, Jack Webb, Lloyd Gough, Cecil B. de Mille, H. B. Warner, Anna Q. Nilsson, Buster Keaton, Hedda Hopper
'That rare blend of pungent writing, expert acting, masterly direction and unobtrusively artistic photography which quickly casts a spell over an audience and holds it enthralled to a shattering climax.'—*New York Times (T.M.P.)*
'Miss Swanson's performance takes her at one bound into the class of Boris Karloff and Tod Slaughter.'—*Richard Mallett, Punch*
'A weird, fascinating motion picture about an art form which, new as it is, is already haunted by ghosts.'—*Otis L. Guernsey Jnr, New York Herald Tribune*

AA: script; Franz Waxman
AAN: best picture; Billy Wilder (as director); John F. Seitz; Gloria Swanson; William Holden; Erich Von Stroheim; Nancy Olson

The Sunshine Boys*
US 1975   111m   Metrocolor
MGM / Rastar (Ray Stark)

Two feuding old vaudeville comedians come together for a television spot, and ruin it.
Over-extended sketch in which one main role is beautifully underplayed, the other hammed up, and the production lacks any kind of style. The one-liners are good, though.

w Neil Simon, from his play *d* Herbert Ross *ph* David M. Walsh *md* Harry V. Lojewski

Walter Matthau, *George Burns*, Richard Benjamin, Carol Arthur
'It's just shouting, when it needs to be beautifully timed routines.'—*New Yorker*
'They feud with ill-matched resources, and the movie's visual delights vanish with the title sequence.'—*Sight and Sound*

AA: George Burns
AAN: Neil Simon; Walter Matthau

Sunshine Susie
GB 1931   87m   bw

A banker pretends to be a clerk in order to court a typist. Viennese-set comedy which worked at the time but quickly dated. Renate Muller, Jack Hulbert, Owen Nares, Morris Harvey, Sybil Grove. Written by Angus MacPhail, Robert Stevenson, Victor Saville and Noel Wood-Smith, from the play *The Private Secretary* by Franz Schultz; directed by Victor Saville; for Gainsborough.

Sunstruck

Australia 1972 92m Eastmancolor
Immigrant (Jack Neary, James Grafton)

A shy Welsh schoolmaster emigrates to the
Australian outback.

Simple-minded, uninspired, predictable family
comedy for star fans.

w Stan Mars *d* James Gilbert *ph* Brian West
m Peter Knight

Harry Secombe, Maggie Fitzgibbon, John
Meillon, Dawn Lake

The Super Cops

US 1974 94m Metrocolor

Two New York cops are suspended for
breaking too many rules, but wage their
private war on crime. Low-life crime
melodrama which plays effectively enough as a
lighter-hearted *Serpico*. Ron Leibman, David
Selby, Sheila Frazier, Pat Hingle, Dan Frazer.
Written by Lorenzo Semple Jnr, from the
book by L. H. Whittemore; directed by
Gordon Parks Jnr; for St Regis Films / UA.

Superfly

US 1972 98m Technicolor
Warner (Sig Shore)

The New York adventures of black cocaine
peddlers.

'Sensational' comedy with violence in which
the pushers exit laughing. Tedious and
deplorable.

w Philip Fenty *d* Gordon Parks *ph* James
Signorelli *m* Jeff Alexander

Ron O'Neal, Carl Lee, Sheila Frazier
'It suggests that New York is now nothing
more than a concrete junkieyard.'—*Philip
Strick*

Superman

US / GB 1978 142m colour Panavision
Warner / Alexander Salkind (Pierre
Spengler)

A baby saved from the planet Krypton when it
explodes grows up as a newspaperman and
uses his tremendous powers to fight evil and
support the American way.

Long, lugubrious and only patchily
entertaining version of the famous comic strip,
with far too many irrelevant preliminaries and
a misguided sense of its own importance.

w Mario Puzo, David Newman, Robert
Benton, Leslie Newman *d* Richard Donner
ph Geoffrey Unsworth *m* John Williams
pd John Barry *sp* various

Christopher Reeve, Marlon Brando, Margot
Kidder, Jackie Cooper, Glenn Ford, Phyllis
Thaxter, Trevor Howard, Gene Hackman,
Ned Beatty, Susannah York, Valerie Perrine

'Though one of the two or three most
expensive movies made to date, it's cheesy-
looking, and the plotting is so hit or miss that
the story never seems to get started; the
special effects are far from wizardly and the
editing often seems hurried and jerky just at
the crucial points.'—*New Yorker*

'The epitome of supersell.'—*Les Keyser,
Hollywood in the Seventies*

† Reprehensible records were set by Brando
getting three million dollars for a ten-minute
performance (and then suing for a share of the
gross); and by the incredible 7½-minute credit
roll at the end.

AAN: John Williams

Superman II

US 1980 127m Technicolor
Warner / Alexander Salkind (Pierre
Spengler)

Three renegade Kryptonians threaten Earth
with a space bomb.

Half the first episode was devoted to a creaky
and unnecessary setting up of plot and
characters. This sequel is all the better for
diving straight into action, but a classic it isn't,
even of the comic strip kind.

w Mario Puzo, David Newman, Leslie
Newman *d* Richard Lester *ph* Geoffrey
Unsworth, Robert Paynter *m* Ken Thorne

Christopher Reeve, Gene Hackman, Ned
Beatty, Jackie Cooper, Sarah Douglas,
Margot Kidder, Valerie Perrine, Susannah
York, Terence Stamp, Jack O'Halloran, E. G.
Marshall

Supernatural*

US 1933 67m bw
Paramount

A girl is possessed by the soul of a dead
murderess.

Mad doctor nonsense, interestingly but not
very successfully styled.

w Harvey Thew, Brian Marlow *d* Victor
Halperin *ph* Arthur Martinelli

Carole Lombard, H. B. Warner, Randolph
Scott, Vivienne Osborne, Alan Dinehart

Support Your Local Gunfighter

US 1971 92m De Luxe
UA / Cherokee / Brigade (Burt Kennedy)

A con man jumps a train at a small mining
town and is mistaken for a dreaded gunfighter.

Disappointing sequel to the following; just a couple of good jokes.

w James Edward Grant *d* Burt Kennedy *ph* Harry Stradling Jnr *m* Jack Elliott, Allyn Ferguson

James Garner, Suzanne Pleshette, Joan Blondell, Jack Elam, Chuck Connors, Harry Morgan, Marie Windsor, Henry Jones, John Dehner

Support Your Local Sheriff**
US 1968   92m   Technicolor
UA / Cherokee (William Bowers)

Gold is found near a western village, and the resulting influx of desperate characters causes problems for the sheriff.
Amusing comedy, drawing on many western clichés.

w William Bowers *d* Burt Kennedy *ph* Harry Stradling Jnr *m* Jeff Alexander

James Garner, Joan Hackett, Walter Brennan, Jack Elam, Henry Morgan, Bruce Dern, Henry Jones

'It rejuvenates a stagnating genre by combining just the right doses of parody and affectionate nostalgia.'—*Jan Dawson*

Suppose They Gave a War and Nobody Came
US 1969   114m   De Luxe
Engel–Auerbach / ABC (Fred Engel)

Three accident-prone PROs try to give the army a good name in a town which wishes it would go away; they eventually cause panic by arriving at a dance in a tank.
Muddled farce which may have hoped to be satire.

w Don McGuire, Hal Captain *d* Hy Averback *ph* Burnett Guffey *m* Jerry Fielding

Tony Curtis, Brian Keith, Ernest Borgnine, Ivan Dixon, Suzanne Pleshette, *Tom Ewell*, Bradford Dillman, Arthur O'Connell, Robert Emhardt, John Fiedler, Don Ameche

Surprise Package
GB 1960   100m   bw
Columbia / Stanley Donen

An American gangster is deported to the same Mediterranean island as an exiled European king, whose crown gets stolen.
Flat and feeble comedy which defeats its stars.

w Harry Kurnitz, *novel* Art Buchwald *d* Stanley Donen *ph* Christopher Challis *m* Benjamin Frankel

Yul Brynner, Noel Coward, Mitzi Gaynor, Bill Nagy, Eric Pohlmann, George Coulouris, Warren Mitchell

Susan and God*
US 1940   117m   bw
MGM (Hunt Stromberg)
GB title: *The Gay Mrs Trexel*

A flighty society woman gets religion but fails to practise what she preaches.
Unusual comedy-drama for MGM to tackle, but a fairly successful one for high class audiences.

w Anita Loos, *play* Rachel Crothers *d* George Cukor *ph* Robert Planck *m* Herbert Stothart

Joan Crawford, Fredric March, Ruth Hussey, John Carroll, Rita Hayworth, Nigel Bruce, Bruce Cabot, Rita Quigley, Rose Hobart, Constance Collier, Gloria de Haven, Marjorie Main

Susan Lenox, Her Fall and Rise*
US 1931   76m   bw
MGM (Paul Bern)
GB title: *The Rise of Helga*

A farm girl flees to the city when her father tries to marry her off to a brute.
Moderate star melodrama with the star somewhat miscast.

w Wanda Tuchock, *novel* David Graham Phillips *d* Robert Z. Leonard *ph* William Daniels

Greta Garbo, Clark Gable, Jean Hersholt, John Miljan, Alan Hale

Susan Slade
US 1961   116m   Technicolor
Warner (Delmer Daves)

An engineer brings his family back to San Francisco from Chile, and his teenage daughter runs into problems of the heart.
Stilted, busy sudser.

w Delmer Daves, *novel* Doris Hume *d* Delmer Daves *ph* Lucien Ballard *m* Max Steiner

Connie Stevens, Troy Donahue, Dorothy McGuire, Lloyd Nolan, Brian Aherne, Natalie Schaefer, Grant Williams, Bert Convy, Kent Smith

Susan Slept Here
US 1954   98m   Technicolor
RKO (Harriet Parsons)

The Hollywood scriptwriter of a film about youth problems agrees to look after a delinquent teenage girl.
Skittish, would-be piquant comedy; quite unattractive.

w Alex Gottlieb *d* Frank Tashlin *ph* Nicholas Musuraca *md* Leigh Harline

Dick Powell, Debbie Reynolds, Anne Francis, Glenda Farrell, Alvy Moore, Horace MacMahon

AAN: song 'Hold My Hand'

Susannah of the Mounties*
US 1939 78m bw
TCF (Kenneth MacGowan)

A little girl who is the only survivor of a wagon train massacre is looked after by the Canadian Mounties.
Adequate star action romance, Shirley's last real success.

w John Taintor Foote, Philip Dunne d Sidney Lanfield ph Bert Glennon m Louis Silvers

Shirley Temple, Randolph Scott, Margaret Lockwood, J. Farrell MacDonald, Maurice Moscovitch, Moroni Olsen, Victor Jory

The Suspect*
US 1944 84m bw
Universal

A henpecked husband kills his wife and is blackmailed.
Efficient studio-bound suspenser with theatrically effective acting.

w Bertram Millhauser, novel James Ronald d Robert Siodmak ph Paul Ivano m Frank Skinner

Charles Laughton, Henry Daniell, Rosalind Ivan, Ella Raines, Molly Lamont, Dean Harens

'High marks for tension, local colour, story.'—William Whitebait

Suspect*
GB 1960 81m bw
The Boulting Brothers / British Lion

Government research chemists find a traitor in their midst.
Entertaining but fairly routine spy melodrama, shot on an experimental low budget but confined to lower berth bookings.

w Nigel Balchin, from his novel Sort of Traitors d Roy and John Boulting ph Max Greene m John Wilkes

Tony Britton, Virginia Maskell, Peter Cushing, Ian Bannen, Raymond Huntley, Donald Pleasence, Thorley Walters, Spike Milligan, Kenneth Griffith

'A better standard of second feature film is badly needed, but the way to do it is not by making pictures which look as though they have strayed from TV.'—Penelope Houston

Suspicion**
US 1941 99m bw
RKO

A sedate young girl marries a playboy, and comes to suspect that he is trying to murder her.
Rather artificial and stiff Hitchcock suspenser, further marred by an ending suddenly switched to please the front office. Full of the interesting touches one would expect.

w Samson Raphaelson, Alma Reville, Joan Harrison, novel Before the Fact by Francis Iles d Alfred Hitchcock ph Harry Stradling m Franz Waxman

Joan Fontaine, Cary Grant, Nigel Bruce, Cedric Hardwicke, May Whitty, Isabel Jeans, Heather Angel, Leo G. Carroll

'The fact that Hitchcock throws in a happy end during the last five minutes, like a conjuror explaining his tricks, seems to me a pity; but it spoils the film only in retrospect, and we have already had our thrills.'—William Whitebait, New Statesman

AA: Joan Fontaine
AAN: best picture; Franz Waxman

Suspiria*
Italy 1976 97m Eastmancolor Technovision
Seda Spettacoli (Claudio Argento)

A young American dance student arrives at dead of night at a continental academy where murder is the order of the day.
Psycho meets The Exorcist, with no holds barred: a genuinely scary thriller with gaudy visuals and a screaming sound track. A pyrotechnic display for those who can take it.

w Dario Argento, Dario Nicolodi d Dario Argento ph Luciano Tovoli m Dario Argento

Jessica Harper, Alida Valli, Joan Bennett, Stefania Casini, Udo Kier

'Thunderstorms and explicitly grotesque murders pile up as Argento happily abandons plot mechanics to provide a bravura display of his technical skill.'—Time Out

Sutter's Gold
US 1936 75m bw

During the California gold rush an immigrant has to fight for his rights when a strike starts on his land. Patchily arresting western which by costing much more than it should started the exit of Carl Laemmle from the chairman's office. Edward Arnold, Lee Tracy, Binnie Barnes, Katherine Alexander, Addison Richards, Montagu Love, John Miljan. Written by Jack Kirkland, Walter Woods and George O'Neil; directed by James Cruze; for Universal. (Most of the action footage was reused in a 1939 quickie, Mutiny on the Blackhawk.)

Suzy*
US 1936   95m   bw
MGM (Maurice Revnes)

A French air ace of World War I marries an
American showgirl; they then find that her
former husband, thought dead, is still alive.
Proficient star comedy-drama with romance,
action, comedy and a complex plot. A
showcase for its stars.

w Dorothy Parker, Alan Campbell, Horace
Jackson, Lenore Coffee, *novel* Herbert
Gorman d George Fitzmaurice ph Ray June
m William Axt

Jean Harlow, Cary Grant, Franchot Tone,
Benita Hume, Lewis Stone

AAN: song 'Did I Remember' (*m* Walter
Donaldson, *ly* Harold Adamson)

Svengali**
US 1931   81m   bw
Warner

In nineties Paris, a hypnotist turns a girl into a
great opera singer but she does not reciprocate
his love.
Victorian fantasy melodrama with a great
grotesque part for the star and interesting
artwork.

w J. Grubb Alexander, *novel* Trilby by
George du Maurier d Archie Mayo
ph Barney McGill

John Barrymore, Marian Marsh, Luis Alberni,
Lumsden Hare, Donald Crisp, Paul Porcasi
  'Barrymore never needed occult powers to
be magnetic, but interest flags when he's
offscreen.'—*New Yorker, 1978*

AAN: Barney McGill

Svengali
GB 1954   82m   Eastmancolor
Renown / Alderdale (Douglas Pierce)

Flatulent remake which does have the virtue
of following the original book illustrations but
is otherwise unpersuasive.

wd Noel Langley ph Wilkie Cooper
m William Alwyn ad Fred Pusey

Donald Wolfit, Hildegarde Neff, Terence
Morgan, Derek Bond, Paul Rogers, David
Kossoff, Hubert Gregg, Noel Purcell, Alfie
Bass, Harry Secombe

Swallows and Amazons
GB 1974   92m   Eastmancolor
EMI / Theatre Projects (Richard Pilbrow)

In the twenties four children have adventures
in the Lake District.
Mild family film, great to look at but lacking in
real excitement or style.

w David Wood, *novel* Arthur Ransome
d Claude Whatham ph Denis Lewiston
m Wilfred Josephs

Virginia McKenna, Ronald Fraser, Simon
West, Sophie Neville, Zanna Hamilton,
Stephen Grenville

Swamp Water**
US 1941   90m   bw
TCF (Irving Pichel)
GB title: *The Man Who Came Back*

A fugitive holds out for years in the
Okefenokee swamp, and affects the lives of
the local township.
A strange little story, not very compelling as
drama but with striking photography and
atmosphere. Remade more straightforwardly
as *Lure of the Wilderness* (qv).

w Dudley Nichols, *story* Vereen Bell d Jean
Renoir ph Peverell Marley m David Buttolph

Walter Huston, Walter Brennan, Anne
Baxter, Dana Andrews, Virginia Gilmore,
John Carradine, Eugene Pallette, Ward Bond,
Guinn Williams
  'So bad it's terrific.'—*Otis Ferguson*

The Swan*
US 1956   108m   Eastmancolor
   Cinemascope
MGM (Dore Schary)

In 1910 Hungary, a girl of noble stock is
groomed to marry the crown prince.
Interesting chiefly for a typical Hollywood
reaction to a news event; about to lose their
top star to a real life prince, MGM dusted off
this old and creaky property for her last film.
The star cast can't make much of it and the
treatment is very heavy.

w John Dighton, *play* Ferenc Molnar
d Charles Vidor ph Robert Surtees
m Bronislau Kaper ad Cedric Gibbons,
Randall Duell

Grace Kelly, Alec Guinness, Louis Jourdan,
Agnes Moorehead, Jessie Royce Landis, Brian
Aherne, Leo G. Carroll, *Estelle Winwood*,
Robert Coote
  'Balancing between artificial comedy and a
no less artificial romantic theme, the film
ultimately requires considerably greater finesse
and subtlety in the handling.'—*Penelope
Houston*

Swanee River**
US 1939   84m   Technicolor
TCF (Darryl F. Zanuck)

The life and loves of Stephen Foster.
Attractive, unsurprising family film in rich
early colour, sparked by Jolson as E. P.
Christy.

w John Taintor Foote, Philip Dunne *d* Sidney Lanfield *ph* Bert Glennon *md* Louis Silvers

Don Ameche, *Al Jolson*, Andrea Leeds, Felix Bressart, Russell Hicks

AAN: Louis Silvers

The Swarm
US 1978 116m Technicolor
Panavision
Warner (Irwin Allen)

African killer bees menace the US.
Very obvious all-star disaster movie with risible dialogue. A box office flop, probably because several TV movies had already tackled the same subject.

w Stirling Silliphant, *novel* Arthur Herzog *d* Irwin Allen *ph* Fred J. Koenekamp *m* Jerry Goldsmith *sp* L. B. Abbott, Van Der Veer, Howard Jensen

Michael Caine, Katharine Ross, Richard Widmark, Richard Chamberlain, Olivia de Havilland, Fred MacMurray, Ben Johnson, Lee Grant, Jose Ferrer, Patty Duke Astin, Slim Pickens, Bradford Dillman, Henry Fonda, Cameron Mitchell

'You could pass it all off as a sick joke, except that it cost twelve million dollars, twenty-two million bees, and several years of someone's life.'—*Guardian*

'The story is of a banality matched only by the woodenness of the acting.'—*Barry Took, Punch*

Swashbuckler*
US 1976 101m Technicolor
Panavision
Universal / Elliott Kastner (Jennings Lang)
GB title: *The Scarlet Buccaneer*

Rival pirates help a wronged lady.
Uninspired reworking of some old Errol Flynn ideas; the idea was pleasant, but the old style is sadly lacking.

w Jeffrey Bloom *d* James Goldstone *ph* Philip Lathrop *m* John Addison *pd* John Lloyd

Robert Shaw, James Earl Jones, Peter Boyle, Geneviève Bujold, Beau Bridges, Geoffrey Holder

'This tacky pastepot job can't make up its mind whether it's serious, tongue-in-cheek, satirical, slapstick, burlesque, parody or travesty; but be assured it is all of the above.'—*Variety*

'The talented cast is left to play living statues, immobilized by dumb dialogue and awkward action.'—*Judith Crist*

Sweeney!*
GB 1976 89m Technicolor
EMI / Euston (Ted Childs)

Scotland Yard's Flying Squad investigates a suicide and uncovers an elaborate political blackmail scheme.
Enjoyable big screen version of a pacy, violent TV cop show.

w Ranald Graham *d* David Wickes *ph* Dusty Miller *m* Denis King

John Thaw, Dennis Waterman, Barry Foster, Ian Bannen, Colin Welland, Michael Coles, Joe Melia

Sweeney Todd, the Demon Barber of Fleet Street*
GB 1936 68m bw
George King

A barber kills his customers and makes them into 'mutton pies' for sale at the shop next door.
Decent version of a famous old melodrama; stilted as film-making, but preserving a swaggering star performance.

w Frederick Hayward, H. F. Maltby, *play* George Dibdin-Pitt

Tod Slaughter, Bruce Seton, Eve Lister, Stella Rho, Ben Soutten

Sweet Adeline
US 1935 85m bw
Warner (Edward Chodorov)

In the nineties, the daughter of a beer garden owner attracts the attention of a composer and becomes a Broadway star.
Unexceptional, and quite forgotten, adaptation of a pleasant, old-fashioned Broadway musical.

w Erwin S. Gelsey, *play* Jerome Kern, Oscar Hammerstein II, Harry Armstrong, Dick Gerard *d* Mervyn Le Roy *m / ly* Jerome Kern, Oscar Hammerstein II *ph* Sol Polito *ch* Bobby Connolly *ad* Robert Haas

Irene Dunne, Donald Woods, Ned Sparks, Hugh Herbert, Wini Shaw, Louis Calhern, Nydia Westman, Joseph Cawthorn

Sweet Bird of Youth*
US 1962 120m Metrocolor
Cinemascope
MGM / Roxbury (Pandro S. Berman)

A Hollywood drifter brings an ageing glamour star back to his home town, but runs into revenge from the father of a girl he had seduced.
Emasculated version of an overwrought play with the author's usual poetic squalor;

comatose patches alternate with flashes of good acting and diverting dialogue, but the wide screen and heavy colour don't direct the attention.

wd Richard Brooks, *play* Tennessee Williams *ph* Milton Krasner *m* Harold Gellman *md* Robert Armbruster

Paul Newman, Geraldine Page, *Ed Begley*, Mildred Dunnock, Rip Torn, Shirley Knight, Madeleine Sherwood

AA: Ed Begley
AAN: Geraldine Page; Shirley Knight

Sweet Charity*
US 1969   149m   Technicolor Panavision 70
Universal (Robert Arthur)

A New York taxi dancer dreams of love.
A revue-type musical bowdlerized from Fellini's *Le notti di Cabiria* accords ill with real New York locations, especially as its threads of plot come to nothing; but behind the camera are sufficient stylists to ensure striking success with individual numbers.

w Peter Stone, *play* Neil Simon *d* Robert Fosse *ph* Robert Surtees *m* Cy Coleman *ly* Dorothy Fields *md* Joseph Gershenson

Shirley Maclaine, Ricardo Montalban, John McMartin, *Chita Rivera*, Paula Kelly, Stubby Kaye, Sammy Davis Jnr

  'The kind of platinum clinker designed to send audiences flying towards the safety of their television sets.'—*Rex Reed*

AAN: Cy Coleman (as music director)

Sweet Music
US 1934   100m   bw

An orchestra leader and a girl singer spar a lot but finally make it up. The slimmest of stories stretches over a few good numbers and some snappy dialogue; but it's all too long. Rudy Vallee, Ann Dvorak, Ned Sparks, Helen Morgan, Allen Jenkins, Alice White, Robert Armstrong. Written by Jerry Wald, Carl Erickson and Warren Duff; directed by Alfred E. Green; for Warner.

Sweet November
US 1968   113m   Technicolor
Warner Seven Arts / Jerry Gershwin, Elliott Kastner

An English tycoon in New York meets a girl who takes a new lover every month because she hasn't long to live.
Irritating exercise in eccentric sentimentality, not helped by twitchy stars.

w Herman Raucher *d* Robert Ellis Miller *ph* Daniel L. Fapp *m* Michel Legrand

Anthony Newley, Sandy Dennis, Theodore Bikel, Burr de Benning

The Sweet Ride
US 1967   110m   De Luxe   Panavision
TCF (Joe Pasternak)

Surfers and drop-outs on a California beach have woman trouble.
Teenage melodrama, well produced but abysmal of content.

w Tom Mankiewicz, *novel* William Murray *d* Harvey Hart *ph* Robert B. Hauser *m* Pete Rugolo

Jacqueline Bisset, Tony Franciosa, Michael Sarrazin, Bob Denver, Michael Wilding

Sweet Rosie O'Grady*
US 1943   79m   Technicolor
TCF (William Perlberg)

A Police Gazette reporter tries to uncover the past of a musical comedy star.
Pleasant nineties musical with plenty of zest but a lack of good numbers. A typical success of the war years.

w Ken Englund *d* Irving Cummings *ph* Ernest Palmer *ch* Hermes Pan *songs* Mack Gordon, Harry Warren *ad James Basevi, Joseph C. Wright*

Betty Grable, Robert Young, Adolphe Menjou, Reginald Gardiner, Virginia Grey, Phil Regan, Sig Rumann, Hobart Cavanaugh, Alan Dinehart
† Remake of *Love Is News*; remade as *That Wonderful Urge*.

Sweet Smell of Success***
US 1957   96m   bw
UA / Norma / Curtleigh (James Hill)

A crooked press agent helps a megalomaniac New York columnist break up his sister's marriage.
Moody, brilliant, Wellesian melodrama put together with great artificial style; the plot matters less than the photographic detail and the skilful manipulation of decadent characters, bigger than life-size.

w Clifford Odets, Ernest Lehman *d Alexander Mackendrick ph James Wong Howe m Elmer Bernstein ad* Edward Carrere

Burt Lancaster, *Tony Curtis*, Martin Milner, Sam Levene, Susan Harrison, Barbara Nichols, *Emile Meyer*
  'A sweet slice of perversity, a study of dollar and power worship.'—*Pauline Kael*

Sweet William
GB 1980 90m Eastmancolor

A London girl discovers that her American lover is constantly unfaithful. A situation in search of a story makes this slight piece with its wry observations rather less memorable than the average TV play. Sam Waterston, Jenny Agutter, Anna Massey, Daphne Oxenford, Arthur Lowe, Geraldine James. Written by Beryl Bainbridge, from her novel; directed by Claude Whatham; for Kendon.

Sweethearts**
US 1938 120m Technicolor
MGM (Hunt Stromberg)

Two stars of the musical stage never stop fighting each other.
The lightest and most successful of the MacDonald / Eddy musicals, with an excellent script, production and cast.

w Dorothy Parker, Alan Campbell d W. S. Van Dyke ph Oliver Marsh m Victor Herbert md Herbert Stothart

Jeanette MacDonald, Nelson Eddy, Frank Morgan, Ray Bolger, Florence Rice, Mischa Auer, Fay Holden, Reginald Gardiner, Herman Bing, Allyn Joslyn, Raymond Walburn, Lucile Watson, Gene Lockhart

AA: Oliver Marsh
AAN: Herbert Stothart

The Swimmer**
US 1968 94m Technicolor
Columbia / Horizon / Dover (Frank Perry, Roger Lewis)

A man clad only in trunks swims his way home via the pools of his rich friends, and arrives home to find that his success is a fantasy.
Strange but compelling fable, too mystifying for popular success, about the failure of the American dream. Annoyingly inexplicit, but well made and sumptuously photographed in a variety of Connecticut estates.

w Eleanor Perry, short story John Cheever d Frank Perry, Sydney Pollack ph David L. Quaid m Marvin Hamlisch

Burt Lancaster, Janice Rule, Kim Hunter, Diana Muldaur, Cornelia Otis Skinner, Marge Champion

Swing Fever
US 1943 80m bw

A bandleader uses hypnotism to train a boxer. Witless farrago with sprightly musical numbers. Kay Kyser and his band, Marilyn Maxwell, Nat Pendleton, William Gargan, Lena Horne. Written by Nat Perrin and Warren Wilson; directed by Tim Whelan; for MGM.

Swing High Swing Low**
US 1937 97m bw
Paramount (Arthur Hornblow Jnr)

A talented trumpeter goes on a bender but is rescued by his wife.
Backstage comedy-drama, a beautifully cinematic version of a very tedious story also filmed as *Dance of Life* (1929) and *When My Baby Smiles at Me* (1948).

w Virginia Van Upp, Oscar Hammerstein II, play Burlesque by George Manker Walters, Arthur Hopkins d Mitchell Leisen ph Ted Tetzlaff m Victor Young md Boris Morros

Carole Lombard, Fred MacMurray, Charles Butterworth, Jean Dixon, Dorothy Lamour, Harvey Stephens, Franklin Pangborn, Anthony Quinn

'Enough concentrated filmcraft to fit out half a dozen of those gentlemen who are always dashing around in an independent capacity making just the greatest piece of cinema ever.'—*Otis Ferguson*

Swing Time**
US 1936 103m bw
RKO (Pandro S. Berman)

A dance team can't get together romantically because he has a commitment to a girl back home.
Satisfactory but unexciting musical vehicle for two stars at the top of their professional and box-office form.

w Howard Lindsay, Allan Scott d George Stevens ph David Abel md Nathaniel Shilkret songs Jerome Kern, Dorothy Fields

Fred Astaire, Ginger Rogers, Victor Moore, Helen Broderick, Eric Blore, Betty Furness, Georges Metaxa

AA: song 'The Way You Look Tonight'

Swing Your Lady*
US 1937 77m bw
Warner (Sam Bischoff)

A promoter gets involved in the problems of a hillbilly wrestler.
Minor comedy with some laughs.

w Joseph Scrank, Maurice Leo, story Toehold on Artemus by H. R. Marsh d Ray Enright ph Arthur Edeson m Adolph Deutsch

Humphrey Bogart, Louise Fazenda, Nat Pendleton, Frank McHugh, Penny Singleton, Allen Jenkins, Ronald Reagan, The Weaver Brothers and Elviry

The Swinger
US 1966 81m Technicolor
Paramount / George Sidney

When a girl writer's wholesome stories are rejected, she pretends to have a naughty past. With-it comedy which audiences preferred to be without.

w Lawrence Roman *d* George Sidney *ph* Joseph Biroc *m* Marty Paich

Ann-Margret, Tony Franciosa, Robert Coote, Yvonne Romain, Horace MacMahon, Nydia Westman

'A hectically saucy mixture of lechery, depravity, perversion, voyeurism and girlie magazines . . . a heavy, witless pudding.'— *MFB*

The Swiss Family Robinson
US 1940 93m bw
(RKO) Gene Towne, Graham Baker

A shipwrecked family builds a new home on a desert island.
Pleasing low-budgeter.

w Gene Towne, Graham Baker, Walter Ferris, *novel* Johann Wyss *d* Edward Ludwig *ph* Nicholas Musuraca

Thomas Mitchell, Edna Best, Freddie Bartholemew, Tim Holt, Terry Kilburn
'In outlook, dialogue and manner it is frankly old-fashioned.'—*MFB*

The Swiss Family Robinson*
GB 1960 126m Technicolor
  Panavision
Walt Disney (Bill Anderson, Basil Keys)

Quite pleasing comedy adventure from the children's classic.

w Lowell S. Hawley *d* Ken Annakin *ph* Harry Waxman *m* William Alwyn

John Mills, Dorothy McGuire, James MacArthur, Tommy Kirk, Kevin Corcoran, Janet Munro, Sessue Hayakawa, Cecil Parker

Swiss Miss*
US 1938 73m bw
(MGM) Hal Roach

Two mousetrap salesmen in Switzerland run into trouble with a cook, a gorilla and two opera singers.
Operetta style vehicle which constrains its stars, since their material is somewhat below vintage anyway. Not painful to watch, but disappointing.

w James Parrott, Felix Adler, Charles Nelson *d* John G. Blystone *ph* Norbert Brodine

Stan Laurel, Oliver Hardy, Walter Woolf King, Della Lind, Eric Blore

The Swissmakers
Switzerland 1978 108m Eastmancolor

Cases of a department investigating applicants for naturalization. Amusing satirical comedy which presumably has more bite in its home territory. Walo Luond, Emil Steinberger, Beatrice Kessler. Written by Rolf Lyssy and Christa Maerker; directed by Rolf Lyssy; for Lyssy / Rex / Willora / Schoch / Ecco.

The Sword and the Rose
GB 1952 91m Technicolor
Walt Disney (Perce Pearce)

The romantic problems of young Mary Tudor. Unhistorical charade not quite in the usual Disney vein, and not very good.

w Laurence E. Watkin, *novel* When Knighthood Was in Flower by Charles Major *d* Ken Annakin *ph* Geoffrey Unsworth *m* Clifton Parker

Richard Todd, Glynis Johns, James Robertson Justice, Michael Gough, Jane Barrett, Peter Copley, Rosalie Crutchley, Jean Mercure, D. A. Clarke-Smith

The Sword in the Stone**
US 1963 80m Technicolor
Walt Disney (Ken Peterson)

In the Dark Ages, a young forest boy named Wart becomes King Arthur.
Feature cartoon with goodish sequences but disappointingly showing a flatness and economy of draughtsmanship.

w Bill Peet, *novel* The Once and Future King by T. H. White *d* Wolfgang Reitherman *m* George Bruns *songs* The Sherman Brothers

AAN: George Bruns

Sword of Ali Baba
US 1965 81m Technicolor

Ali Baba is forced from the royal court to become a king of thieves. Cut-rate programme filler utilizing great chunks of *Ali Baba and the Forty Thieves* (twenty-one years older), with one actor, Frank Puglia, playing the same role in both films. Peter Mann, Jocelyn Lane, Peter Whitney, Gavin McLeod. Written by Edmund Hartmann and Oscar Brodney; directed by Virgil Vogel; for Universal.

Sword of Monte Cristo
US 1951 80m Supercinecolor

Virtuous rebels and a villainous minister all seek the fabulous treasure of Monte Cristo. Rubbishy sequel apparently shot in somebody's back garden by people only recently acquainted with film techniques. George Montgomery, Paula Corday, Berry

Kroeger, Robert Warwick, William Conrad.
Written and directed by Maurice Geraghty;
for Edward L. Alperson.

Sword of Sherwood Forest
GB 1960 80m Technicolor Megascope
Columbia / Hammer / Yeoman (Richard
    Greene, Sidney Cole)

Robin Hood reveals the villainy of the Sheriff
of Nottingham and the Earl of Newark.
This big-screen version of a popular TV series
makes a rather feeble addition to the legend,
but the actors try hard.

w Alan Hackney d Terence Fisher ph Ken
Hodges m Alan Hoddinott

Richard Greene, Peter Cushing, Richard
Pasco, Niall MacGinnis, Jack Gwyllim, Sarah
Branch, Nigel Green

Sylvia
US 1964 115m bw
Paramount / Joseph E. Levine

A millionaire with a mysterious fiancée hires a
detective to discover the truth about her past.
Improbable story of a high-minded prostitute,
sluggishly narrated and variably acted.

w Sidney Boehm, novel E. V. Cunningham
d Gordon Douglas ph Joseph Ruttenberg
m David Raksin

Carroll Baker, George Maharis, Peter
Lawford, Joanne Dru, Ann Sothern, Viveca
Lindfors, Edmond O'Brien, Aldo Ray

Sylvia and the Ghost*
France 1944 93m bw
Ecran Français / André Paulvé
Original title: Sylvie et la Fantôme

A sixteen-year-old girl lives in her father's
castle and is friendly with the ghost of a man
killed in a duel fought for love of her
grandmother.
Melancholy comedy which despite some
charming moments somehow misses the
expected style which would have made it a
minor classic.

w Jean Aurenche, play Alfred Adam
d Claude Autant-Lara ph Philippe Agostini
m René Cloerc

Odette Joyeux, François Périer, Jacques Tati,
Louis Salou, Jean Desailly
    'A charming film, written, handled and
acted with wit, feeling and a beautiful lightness
of touch.'—Gavin Lambert

Sylvia Scarlett*
US 1935 94m bw
RKO (Pandro S. Berman)

A girl masquerades as a boy in order to escape
to France with her crooked father.
Strange, peripatetic English comedy-adventure
which failed to ring any bells but preserves
aspects of interest.

w Gladys Unger, John Collier, Mortimer
Offner, novel Compton Mackenzie d George
Cukor ph Joseph August m Roy Webb

Katharine Hepburn, Cary Grant, Edmund
Gwenn, Brian Aherne, Lennox Pawle
    'It seems to go wrong in a million directions,
but it has unusually affecting qualities.'—New
Yorker, 1978
    'A sprawling and ineffective essay in
dramatic chaos.'—Richard Watts Jnr, New
York Herald Tribune
    'A tragic waste of time and screen talent.'—
Eileen Creelman, New York Sun
    'A much more polished comedy than most,
and consistently engaging.'—Winston Burdett,
Brooklyn Daily Eagle

La Symphonie Pastorale*
France 1946 105m bw
Les Films Gibe

A Swiss pastor takes in an orphan child who
grows up to be a beautiful girl and causes
jealousy between himself and his son.
Curious mountain tragedy, a great visual
pleasure with its symbolic use of snow and
water.

w Jean Delannoy, Jean Aurenche,
novel André Gide d Jean Delannoy
ph Armand Thirard m Georges Auric

Pierre Blanchar, Michèle Morgan

Symphony of Six Million
US 1932 94m bw
RKO (Pandro S. Berman)
GB title: Melody of Life

A doctor drags himself from New York's
slums to Park Avenue, but feels guilty and
demoralized when he can't save the life of his
own father.
Monumental tearjerker, not badly done.

w Bernard Schubert, J. Walter Ruben, novel
Fannie Hurst d Gregory La Cava ph Leo
Tover m Max Steiner

Irene Dunne, Ricardo Cortez, Gregory
Ratoff, Anna Appel, Noel Madison, Julie
Haydon

Synanon
US 1965 106m bw
Columbia / Richard Quine
GB title: Get Off My Back

Stories of the inmates of a voluntary
Californian institution for the rehabilitation of
drug addicts.
Well-intentioned but rather dreary case
histories, unconvincingly dramatized. The
house and its leader subsequently came in for
much press criticism.

w Ian Bernard, S. Lee Pogostin *d* Richard
Quine *ph* Harry Stradling *m* Neal Hefti

Edmond O'Brien (as Chuck Dederich), Chuck
Connors, Stella Stevens, Alex Cord, Eartha
Kitt, Richard Conte, Barbara Luna
'The real drug addicts who appear in the
background are plumpish, greyish and utterly
ordinary; but the fictional ones are
glamorously handsome, and lead lives which
are full of throbbing emotion and upset.'—
Tom Milne, MFB

The System
US 1953   90m   bw
Warner (Sam Bischoff)

A crime leader is softened by love, and allows
himself to be convicted.
Strange nonsense inspired by the Kefauver
investigations into American society; neither
edifying nor entertaining.

w Jo Eisinger *d* Lewis Seiler *ph* Edwin
DuPar *m* David Buttolph

Frank Lovejoy, Joan Weldon, Bob Arthur,
Paul Picerni, Don Beddoe

The System
GB 1964   90m   bw
British Lion / Bryanston / Kenneth Shipman
US title: *The Girl-Getters*

Seaside layabouts have a system for collecting
and sharing rich girl visitors, but one of the
latter traps the leader at his own game.
Adequate sexy showcase for some looming
talents; all very unattractive, but smoothly
directed in a number of imitated styles.

w Peter Draper *d Michael Winner ph* Nicolas
Roeg *m* Stanley Black

Oliver Reed, Jane Merrow, Barbara Ferris,
Julia Foster, Ann Lynn, Guy Dolcman,
Andrew Ray, David Hemmings, John
Alderton, Derek Nimmo, Harry Andrews
'A modest, skilful, charming,
inconsequential, and fairly dishonest little
picture, to be enjoyed and deprecated in
roughly equal measure.'—*John Simon*

T

T. R. Baskin
US 1971 89m Technicolor
Paramount (Peter Hyams)
GB title: *A Date with a Lonely Girl*

A businessman in Chicago meets an unhappy girl who tells him her story of loneliness and lack of communication.
Intolerable self-pitying mishmash with no place to go.

w Peter Hyams *d* Herbert Ross *ph* Gerald Hirschfeld *m* Jack Elliott

Candice Bergen, Peter Boyle, James Caan, Marcia Rodd, Erin O'Reilly

Taggart
US 1965 85m Technicolor print

A young western squatter avenges his parents' murder but finds himself pursued by three professional gunslingers. Tough adult western, quite well made. Tony Young, Dan Duryea, Dick Foran, Emile Meyer, Elsa Cardenas, Jean Hale, David Carradine. Written by Robert Creighton Williams, from the novel by Louis L'Amour; directed by R. G. Springsteen; for Universal.

Tabu*
US 1931 80m bw
Colorart Synchrotone

The life of a young Tahitian pearl fisherman. The plot is used only to bring together the elements of a superb travelogue, but the conflicts between the aims of the two directors are clearly seen.

wd F. W. Murnau, Robert Flaherty *ph* Floyd Crosby, Robert Flaherty *m* Hugo Riesenfeld

AA: Floyd Crosby

Tail Spin
US 1938 83m bw
TCF (Harry Joe Brown)

The interwoven private lives of lady civilian air pilots.
Predictable romantic goings on; a tear, a smile, a song, etc.

w Frank Wead *d* Roy del Ruth *ph* Karl Freund *m* Louis Silvers

Alice Faye, Constance Bennett, Joan Davis, Nancy Kelly, Charles Farrell, Jane Wyman, Kane Richmond, Wally Vernon, Harry Davenport

Take a Giant Step
US 1958 100m bw
UA / Sheila / Hecht–Hill–Lancaster (Julius J. Epstein)

A young black person brought up in a white town feels ill at ease and runs into adolescent troubles.
Well-meaning racial drama with good detail but no real feeling.

w Louis S. Peterson, Julius J. Epstein *d* Philip Leacock *ph* Arthur Arling *m* Jack Marshall

Johnny Nash, Estelle Hemsley, Ruby Dee, Frederick O'Neal

Take a Girl Like You
GB 1970 101m Eastmancolor
Columbia / Albion (Hal E. Chester)

A north country girl comes to teach in London and has man trouble.
Old-fashioned novelette with sex trimmings and neither zest nor humour.

w George Melly, *novel* Kingsley Amis *d* Jonathan Miller *ph* Dick Bush *m* Stanley Myers

Hayley Mills, Oliver Reed, Noel Harrison, Sheila Hancock, John Bird, Aimi MacDonald

Take a Letter, Darling**
US 1942 94m bw
Paramount (Fred Kohlmar)
GB title: *Green-Eyed Woman*

A woman executive hires a male secretary.
Smartish romantic comedy.

w Claude Binyon *d* Mitchell Leisen *ph* John Mescall *m* Victor Young

Rosalind Russell, Fred MacMurray, Macdonald Carey, Constance Moore, Cecil Kellaway, Charles Arnt, Kathleen Howard, Dooley Wilson

AAN: John Mescall; Victor Young

Take Care of My Little Girl
US 1951   93m   Technicolor
TCF (Julian Blaustein)

A university freshwoman gets into trouble
with her sorority.
Ho-hum exposé of college conventions, of
routine interest at best.

w Julius J. and Philip G. Epstein, *novel* Peggy
Goodwin *d* Jean Negulesco *ph* Harry
Jackson *m* Alfred Newman

Jeanne Crain, Mitzi Gaynor, Dale Robertson,
Jean Peters, Jeffrey Hunter
   'As is customary in college pictures, it
appears that Tri U recruits most of its strength
from the chorus.'—*Penelope Houston*

Take It or Leave It
US 1944   68m   bw

A sailor enters a quiz show to raise money for
his expectant wife. Thin link for a string of old
movie clips which form the questions; all from
Fox films of course. Phil Baker, Phil Silvers,
Edward Ryan, Marjorie Massow; with clips of
Shirley Temple, the Ritz Brothers, Betty
Grable, Alice Faye, Sonja Henie, Ai Jolson,
etc. Written by Harold Buchman, Snag Werris
and Mac Benoff; directed by Ben Stoloff; for
TCF.

Take Her, She's Mine*
US 1963   98m   De Luxe   Cinemascope
TCF (Henry Koster)

A lawyer protects his teenage daughter from
boys and causes.
Routine Hollywood family comedy with some
laughs and an agreeable cast.

w Nunnally Johnson, *play* Phoebe and Henry
Ephron *d* Henry Koster *ph* Lucien Ballard
m Jerry Goldsmith

James Stewart, Sandra Dee, Robert Morley,
Audrey Meadows, Philippe Forquet, John
McGiver

Take Me High
GB 1973   90m   Technicolor
EMI (Kenneth Harper)

A bank manager helps an unsuccessful
restaurant to launch a new hamburger.
Jaded youth musical with no dancing but some
zip and bounce to commend it to mums and
dads if not to its intended young audience.

w Christopher Penfold *d* David Askey
ph Norman Warwick *m* / *songs* Tony Cole

Cliff Richard, Debbie Watling, Hugh Griffith,
George Cole, Anthony Andrews, Richard
Wattis

Take Me Out to the Ball Game***
US 1949   93m   Technicolor
MGM (Arthur Freed)
GB title: *Everybody's Cheering*

A woman takes over a baseball team and the
players are antagonistic.
Lively, likeable nineties comedy musical which
served as a trial run for *On the Town* and in its
own right is a fast-moving, funny, tuneful
delight with no pretensions.

w Harry Tugend, George Wells *d* Busby
Berkeley *ph* George Folsey *md* Adolph
Deutsch *songs* Betty Comden, Adolph Green,
Roger Edens

Gene Kelly, Frank Sinatra, Esther Williams,
Betty Garrett, Jules Munshin, Edward Arnold,
Richard Lane, Tom Dugan

Take Me to Town
US 1953   81m   Technicolor
U-I (Ross Hunter)

The three sons of a backwoods widower
import a vaudeville artiste as their new
mother.
Old-fashioned family schmaltz containing
every known cliché professionally stitched into
the plot.

w Richard Morris *d* Douglas Sirk *ph* Russell
Metty *m* Joseph Gershenson

Ann Sheridan, Sterling Hayden, Philip Reed,
Lee Patrick, Lee Aaker, Harvey Grant, Dusty
Henley

Take My Life**
GB 1947   79m   bw
GFD / Cineguild (Anthony Havelock-Allan)

A man is suspected of murdering an ex-girl
friend, and his wife journeys to Scotland to
prove him innocent.
Hitchcock-style thriller with excellent detail
and performances.

w Winston Graham, Valerie Taylor *d* Ronald
Neame *ph* Guy Green *m* William Alwyn

Hugh Williams, Greta Gynt, Marius Goring,
Francis L. Sullivan, Rosalie Crutchley, Henry
Edwards, Ronald Adam

Take My Tip
GB 1937   74m   bw
Gaumont-British

Lord Pilkington gets his revenge on a
confidence trickster when they meet at a
Dalmatian hotel.
Reasonably lively comedy musical adapted for
the stars.

w Sidney Gilliat, Michael Hogan, Jack Hulbert *d* Herbert Mason *ph* Bernard Knowles *songs* Sam Lerner, Al Goodheart, Al Hoffman

Jack Hulbert, Cicely Courtneidge, Frank Cellier, Harold Huth, Frank Pettingell, Robb Wilton, H. F. Maltby

Take One False Step°
US 1949 94m bw
U-I (Chester Erskine)

An innocent middle-aged man who has befriended a girl is hunted by the police when she is murdered.
Fairly absorbing and well-cast chase thriller in a minor key.

w Irwin Shaw, Chester Erskine, *story* Night Call by Irwin and David Shaw *d* Chester Erskine *ph* Franz Planer *m* Walter Scharf

William Powell, Shelley Winters, Marsha Hunt, Dorothy Hart, James Gleason, Felix Bressart, Art Baker, Sheldon Leonard

Take the High Ground
US 1953 101m Anscocolor
MGM (Dore Schary)

A tough sergeant trains army conscripts for action in Korea.
Very routine flagwaver.

w Millard Kaufman *d* Richard Brooks *ph* John Alton *m* Dmitri Tiomkin

Richard Widmark, Karl Malden, Carleton Carpenter, Elaine Stewart, Russ Tamblyn, Jerome Courtland, Steve Forrest, Robert Arthur

AAN: Millard Kaufman

Take the Money and Run
US 1968 85m Technicolor
Palomar (Charles H. Joffe)

A social misfit becomes a bungling crook.
A torrent of middling visual gags, not the star's best vehicle.

wd Woody Allen *ph* Lester Shorr *m* Marvin Hamlisch

Woody Allen, Janet Margolin, Marcel Hillaire

The Taking of Pelham 123°
US 1974 104m Technicolor
Panavision
UA / Palomar / Palladium (Gabriel Katzka)

Four ruthless gunmen hold a New York subway train to ransom and have an ingenious plan for escape.
Entertaining crime caper made less enjoyable by all the fashionable faults; the script is deliberately hard to follow and full of four

letter words, the sound track hard to hear, and the visuals ugly.

w Peter Stone, *novel* John Godey *d* Joseph Sargent *ph* Owen Roizman *m* David Shire

Walter Matthau, Robert Shaw, Martin Balsam, Hector Elizondo, Earl Hindman, James Broderick

'Full of noise and squalling and dirty words used for giggly shock effects.'—*New Yorker*

Taking Off°°
US 1971 92m Movielab
Universal (Alfred W. Crown, Michael Hausman)

Suburban parents seek their errant daughter among the hippies, and gradually lose their own inhibitions.
Slight, formless, but amusing revue-style comment by a Czech director on the American scene.

w Milos Forman, John Guare, Jean-Claude Carrière, John Klein *d* Milos Forman *ph* Miroslav Ondricek

Lynn Carlin, Buck Henry, Linnea Heacock

A Tale of Five Cities
GB 1951 99m bw
Grand National (Alexander Paal)
US title: A Tale of Five Women

An amnesiac American seeks clues to his past in Rome, Vienna, Paris, Berlin and London.
Tedious pattern drama remarkable only for its then untried cast.

w Patrick Kirwan, Maurice J. Wilson *d* Montgomery Tully *ph* Gordon Lang *m* Hans May

Bonar Colleano, Gina Lollobrigida, Barbara Kelly, Lana Morris, Anne Vernon, Eva Bartok

A Tale of Two Cities°°
US 1936 121m bw
MGM (David O. Selznick)

A British lawyer sacrifices himself to save another man from the guillotine.
Richly detailed version of the classic melodrama, with production values counting more than the acting.

w W. P. Lipscomb, S. N. Behrman, *novel* Charles Dickens *d* Jack Conway *ph* Oliver T. Marsh *m* Herbert Stothart

Ronald Colman, Elizabeth Allan, Basil Rathbone, Edna May Oliver, Blanche Yurka, Reginald Owen, Henry B. Walthall, Donald Woods, Walter Catlett, H. B. Warner, Claude Gillingwater, Fritz Leiber

'His love challenged the flames of revolution!'—*publicity*

† Originally prepared at Warners for Leslie Howard.

AAN: best picture

A Tale of Two Cities*
GB 1958   117m   bw
Rank (Betty E. Box)

Modest but still costly remake with good moments but a rather slow pace.

w T. E. B. Clarke d Ralph Thomas
ph Ernest Steward m Richard Addinsell

Dirk Bogarde, Dorothy Tutin, Christopher Lee, Athene Seyler, Rosalie Crutchley, Ernest Clark, Stephen Murray, Paul Guers, Donald Pleasence, Ian Bannen, Cecil Parker, Alfie Bass

'Serviceable rather than imaginative.'—
MFB

A Talent for Loving
US 1969   101m   colour

Two generations of an international jet-setting family have woman trouble. Little-seen melodrama apparently disowned by those who made it. Richard Widmark, Cesar Romero, Topol, Genevieve Page. From the novel by Richard Condon; directed by Richard Quine; for Walter Shenson / Paramount.

Tales from the Crypt*
GB 1972   92m   Eastmancolor
Metromedia / Amicus (Milton Subotsky)

Five people get lost in catacombs and are shown the future by a sinister monk who turns out to be Satan.
Fair ghoulish fun; a quintet of stories with a recognizable Amicus link.

w Milton Subotsky, from comic strips by William Gaines d Freddie Francis
ph Norman Warwick m Douglas Gamley

Ralph Richardson, Geoffrey Bayldon, Peter Cushing, Joan Collins, Ian Hendry, Robin Phillips, Richard Greene, Barbara Murray, Roy Dotrice, Nigel Patrick, Patrick Magee

Tales of Beatrix Potter**
GB 1971   90m   Technicolor
EMI (Richard Goodwin)
US title: *Peter Rabbit and the Tales of Beatrix Potter*

Children's stories danced by the Royal Ballet in animal masks.
A charming entertainment for those who can appreciate it, though hardly the most direct way to tell these stories.

w Richard Goodwin, Christine Edward
d Reginald Mills ph Austin Dempster

m John Lanchbery ch Frederick Ashton
masks Rotislav Doboujinsky pd Christine Edward

The Tales of Hoffman**
GB 1951   127m   Technicolor
British Lion / London / Michael Powell, Emeric Pressburger

The poet Hoffman, in three adventures, seeks the eternal woman and is beset by eternal evil.
Overwhelming combination of opera, ballet, and rich production design, an indigestible hodgepodge with flashes of superior talent.

wd Michael Powell, Emeric Pressburger
ph Christopher Challis m *Jacques Offenbach*
pd *Hein Heckroth*

Robert Rounseville, Robert Helpmann, Pamela Brown, Moira Shearer, Frederick Ashton, Leonide Massine, Ludmilla Tcherina, Ann Ayars, Mogens Wieth; music conducted by Sir Thomas Beecham with the Royal Philharmonic Orchestra

'The most spectacular failure yet achieved by Powell and Pressburger, who seem increasingly to dissipate their gifts in a welter of aimless ingenuity.'—*Gavin Lambert*

'An art director's picnic: I marvelled without being enthralled.'—*Richard Mallett, Punch*

Tales of Manhattan**
US 1942   118m   bw
TCF (Boris Morros, Sam Spiegel)

Separate stories of a tail coat, which passes from owner to owner.
The stories are all rather disappointing in their different veins, but production standards are high and a few of the stars shine. A sequence starring W. C. Fields was deleted before release.

w Ben Hecht, Ferenc Molnar, Donald Ogden Stewart, Samuel Hoffenstein, Alan Campbell, Ladislas Fodor, Laslo Vadnay, Laszlo Gorog, Lamar Trotti, Henry Blankfort d *Julien Duvivier* ph Joseph Walker m Sol Kaplan

Charles Boyer, Rita Hayworth, Thomas Mitchell, Eugene Pallette; Ginger Rogers, Henry Fonda, Cesar Romero, Gail Patrick, Roland Young; *Charles Laughton*, Elsa Lanchester, Victor Francen, Christian Rub; *Edward G. Robinson*, George Sanders, James Gleason, Harry Davenport; Paul Robeson, Ethel Waters, Eddie Anderson

† Duvivier was clearly chosen to make this film because of his success with the similar *Carnet de Bal*; he and Boyer went on to make the less successful *Flesh and Fantasy* on similar lines.

Tales of Terror*
US 1962 90m Pathecolor Panavision
AIP (Roger Corman)

'Morella': a dying girl discovers the
mummified body of her mother. 'The Black
Cat': a henpecked husband kills his wife and
walls up the body. 'The Facts in the Case of M
Valdemar': an old man is hypnotized at the
moment of death.
Tolerable short story compendium, rather
short on subtlety and style.

w Richard Matheson, *stories* Edgar Allan Poe
d Roger Corman ph Floyd Crosby m Les
Baxter

Vincent Price, *Peter Lorre*, Basil Rathbone,
Debra Paget

Tales That Witness Madness
GB 1973 90m colour
Paramount / Amicus (Milton Subotsky,
  Norman Priggen)

Five ghostly tales linked by an old bookshop.
Extreme example of the Amicus
compendiums.

w Jay Fairbank d Freddie Francis
ph Norman Warwick m Bernard
Ebbinghouse

Jack Hawkins, Donald Pleasence, Georgia
Brown, Donald Houston, Suzy Kendall, Peter
McEnery, Joan Collins, Michael Jayston, Kim
Novak, Michael Petrovitch, Mary Tamm

Talk About a Stranger*
US 1952 65m bw
MGM (Richard Goldstone)

In a small town, gossip is unjustly aroused
over a mysterious stranger who is suspected of
various crimes.
Unusual though rather naïve second feature,
directed for more than its worth.

w Margaret Fitts, *novel* Charlotte Armstrong
d David Bradley ph John Alton m David
Buttolph

George Murphy, Nancy Davis, Lewis Stone,
Billy Gray, Kurt Kasznar

Talk About Jacqueline
GB 1942 84m bw

A girl is mistaken for her naughtier sister.
Thin, very British comedy with nowhere to go.
Hugh Williams, Carla Lehmann, Joyce
Howard, Roland Culver, John Warwick, Mary
Jerrold, Guy Middleton, Max Adrian. Written
by Roland Pertwee and Marjorie Deans, from
a novel by Katherine Holland; directed by
Harold French; for Excelsior / Marcel
Hellman.

Talk of the Devil
GB 1936 78m bw

An impersonator pins a crooked deal on a
magnate, who kills himself. Glum drama
chiefly notable as the first film to be shot at
Pinewood Studios. Ricardo Cortez, Sally
Eilers, Basil Sydney, Randle Ayrton, Charles
Carson. Written by Carol Reed, George
Barraud and Anthony Kimmins; directed by
Carol Reed; for B and D.

The Talk of the Town***
US 1942 118m bw
Columbia (George Stevens, Fred Guiol)

A girl loves both a suspected murderer and the
lawyer who defends him.
Unusual mixture of comedy and drama,
delightfully handled by three sympathetic
stars.

w Irwin Shaw, Sidney Buchman d George
Stevens ph Ted Tetzlaff m Frederick
Hollander

Roland Colman, Cary Grant, Jean Arthur,
Edgar Buchanan, Glenda Farrell, Charles
Dingle, Emma Dunn, Rex Ingram
  'A rip-roaring, knock-down-and-drag-out
comedy about civil liberties.'—*John T.
McManus*
  'Well tuned and witty, at its best when it
sticks to the middle ground between farce and
melodrama. The chief fault of the script is its
excessive length and the fact that a standard
lynching mob climax is followed by a
prolonged anti-climax.'—*Newsweek*
  'I can't take my lynching so lightly, even in a
screwball. Still, I am all for this kind of
comedy and for players like Arthur and Grant,
who can mug more amusingly than most
scriptwriters can write.'—*Manny Farber*

AAN: best picture; original story (Sidney
Harmon); script; Ted Tetzlaff; Frederick
Hollander

Tall, Dark and Handsome
US 1941 78m bw

In 1929 Chicago, a gangster aspires to be a
gentleman. Moderate crime comedy. Cesar
Romero, Virginia Gilmore, Charlotte
Greenwood, Milton Berle, Sheldon Leonard.
Written by Karl Tunberg and Darrell Ware;
directed by H. Bruce Humberstone; for TCF.

The Tall Headlines
GB 1952 100m bw
Grand National / Raymond Stross
aka: *The Frightened Bride*

A family is affected when the eldest son is
executed for murder.

Glum, boring, badly cast, badly written and generally inept melodrama.

w Audrey Erskine Lindop (from her novel), Dudley Leslie *d* Terence Young *ph* C. M. Pennington-Richards *m* Hans May

Flora Robson, Michael Denison, Mai Zetterling, Jane Hylton, André Morell, Dennis Price, Mervyn Johns, Naunton Wayne

'A falsity which will surely surprise even those familiar with the conventions of British middle-class cinema.'—*Lindsay Anderson*

Tall in the Saddle
US 1944   87m   bw
RKO (Robert Fellows)

The newly-arrived ranch foreman finds that his boss has been murdered.
Quite a watchable, and forgettable, mystery western.

w Michael Hogan, Paul J. Fix *d* Edwin L. Marin *ph* Robert de Grasse *m* Roy Webb *md* Constantin Bakaleinikoff

John Wayne, Ella Raines, Ward Bond, George 'Gabby' Hayes, Audrey Long, Elizabeth Risdon, Don Douglas, Paul Fix, Russell Wade

Tall Man Riding
US 1955   83m   Warnercolor

An adventurer feuds with a rancher but in the end marries his daughter. Unremarkable star western. Randolph Scott, Robert Barrat, Dorothy Malone, Peggie Castle, John Dehner. Written by Joseph Hoffman; directed by Lesley Selander; for Warner.

The Tall Men*
US 1955   122m   De Luxe   Cinemascope
TCF (William A. Bacher, William B. Hawks)

After the Civil War, two Texans head north for the Montana goldfields.
Solid star western.

w Sidney Boehm, Frank Nugent, *novel* Clay Fisher *d* Raoul Walsh *ph* Leo Tover *m* Victor Young

Clark Gable, Jane Russell, Robert Ryan, Cameron Mitchell, Juan Garcia, Harry Shannon, Emile Meyer

'A big action feast and value for anyone's money.'—*Newsweek*

Tall Story
US 1960   91m   bw
Warner / Mansfield (Joshua Logan)

A college basketball player faces various kinds of trouble when he marries.
Dislikeable campus comedy with leading players miscast.

w Julius J. Epstein, *novel* The Homecoming Game by Howard Nemoor *d* Joshua Logan *ph* Ellsworth Fredericks *m* Cyril Mockridge

Anthony Perkins, Jane Fonda, Ray-Walston, Anne Jackson, Marc Connelly, Murray Hamilton, Elizabeth Patterson

The Tall Stranger
US 1957   83m   De Luxe   Cinemascope

Cared for by wagon train pioneers after being mysteriously shot, a rancher tries to help them settle. Fair star western with some tough action. Joel McCrea, Virginia Mayo, Barry Kelley, Michael Ansara, Whit Bissell. Written by Christopher Knopf, from a story by Louis L'Amour; directed by Thomas Carr; for Allied Artists.

The Tall T*
US 1957   78m   Technicolor
Columbia / Scott–Brown (Harry Joe Brown)

Three bandits hold up a stagecoach and take a hostage, but are outwitted by a rancher.
Good small-scale suspense western with plenty of action and a blood-spattered finale.

w Burt Kennedy *d* Budd Boetticher *ph* Charles Lawton Jnr *m* Heinz Roemheld

Randolph Scott, Richard Boone, Maureen O'Sullivan, Arthur Hunnicutt, Skip Homeier, John Hubbard, Henry Silva

The Tall Target**
US 1951   78m   bw
MGM (Richard Goldstone)

A discredited police officer tries to stop the assassination of Abraham Lincoln on a train to Washington.
Lively period suspenser with excellent attention to detail and much of the attraction of *The Lady Vanishes*. The plot slightly relaxes its hold before the end.

w George Worthing Yates, Art Cohn *d* Anthony Mann *ph* Paul C. Vogel *ad* Cedric Gibbons, Eddie Imazu

Dick Powell, Adolphe Menjou, Paula Raymond, Marshall Thompson, *Ruby Dee*, Richard Rober, Will Geer, Florence Bates

'An intelligent minor picture which makes good use of its material.'—*MFB*

Tamahine
GB 1962   95m   Technicolor
   Cinemascope
ABP (John Bryan)

The headmaster of a boys' school is visited by his glamorous half-caste Polynesian cousin.
Simple-minded school comedy with predictable situations.

w Denis Cannan, *novel* Thelma Niklaus
d Philip Leacock *ph* Geoffrey Unsworth
m Malcolm Arnold

John Fraser, Nancy Kwan, Dennis Price,
Derek Nimmo, Justine Lord, James Fox,
Coral Browne, Michael Gough, Allan
Cuthbertson

The Tamarind Seed*
GB 1974 125m Eastmancolor
  Panavision
Jewel / Lorimar / Pimlico (Ken Wales)

While holidaying in Barbados, a British widow
falls for a Russian military attaché.
Old-fashioned romance which turns into a
mild spy caper. A well-heeled time-passer.

w Blake Edwards, *novel* Evelyn Anthony
d Blake Edwards *ph* Frederick A. Young
m John Barry

Julie Andrews, Omar Sharif, Sylvia Syms,
Dan O'Herlihy, Anthony Quayle, Oscar
Homolka

'A painless timekiller, but one wishes Miss
Andrews didn't always give the impression
that she had just left her horse in the
hallway.'—*Michael Billington, Illustrated
London News*

The Taming of the Shrew*
US 1967 122m Technicolor
  Panavision
Columbia / Royal / FAI (Richard
  McWhorter)

Petruchio violently tames his shrewish wife.
Busy version of one of Shakespeare's more
proletarian comedies; the words in this case
take second place to violent action and rioting
colour.

w Suso Cecchi d'Amico, Paul Dehn, Franco
Zeffirelli d Franco Zeffirelli *ph* Oswald
Morris, Luciano Trasatti *m* Nino Rota

Richard Burton, Elizabeth Taylor, Michael
York, Michael Hordern, Cyril Cusack, Alfred
Lynch, Natasha Pyne, Alan Webb, Victor
Spinetti

'As entertainment *Kiss Me Kate* is infinitely
better but then Cole Porter was a real artist
and Burton is a culture vulture.'—*Wilfrid
Sheed*
'The old warhorse of a comedy has been
spanked into uproarious life.'—*Hollis Alpert*

Tammy and the Bachelor*
US 1957 89m Technicolor
  Cinemascope
U-I (Ross Hunter)
GB title: *Tammy*

A backwoods tomboy falls for a stranded flier.
Whimsical romance for middle America,
which started Hollywood's last series of
proletarian family appeal before the family
was entirely forsaken for four letter words.

w Oscar Brodney, from stories by Cid Ricketts
Summer d Joseph Pevney *ph* Arthur E.
Arling *m* Frank Skinner *md* Joseph
Gershenson

Debbie Reynolds, Walter Brennan, Leslie
Nielsen, Mala Powers, Fay Wray, Sidney
Blackmer, Mildred Natwick

Tammy and the Doctor
US 1963 88m Eastmancolor
U-I / Ross Hunter

Tammy leaves her riverboat to accompany an
old lady who needs an operation in the big
city.
More artless family fodder.

w Oscar Brodney d Harry Keller *ph* Russell
Metty *m* Frank Skinner

Sandra Dee, Peter Fonda, Macdonald Carey,
Beulah Bondi, Margaret Lindsay, Reginald
Owen, Adam West

'The aura of simple religion and naïve
philosophy remains singularly charmless.'—
MFB

Tammy and the Millionaire
US 1967 88m Technicolor

Tammy becomes a private secretary in the big
city. A re-edit from four half-hour TV shows;
not at all watchable. Debbie Watson, Donald
Woods, Dorothy Green, Denver Pyle, Frank
McGrath. Written by George Tibbles; directed
by Sidney Miller, Leslie Goodwins and Ezra
Stone; for Universal.

Tammy Tell Me True
US 1961 97m Eastmancolor
U-I (Ross Hunter)

Tammy gets a college education and charms
all comers.
Sugar-coated sequel to the original.

w Oscar Brodney d Harry Keller *ph* Clifford
Stine *m* Percy Faith

Sandra Dee, John Gavin, Charles Drake,
Virginia Grey, *Beulah Bondi*, Julia Meade,
Cecil Kellaway, Edgar Buchanan

'The heroine appears to be not so much
old-fashioned as positively retarded.'—*MFB*

Tampico
US 1944 75m bw
TCF (Robert Bassler)

A tanker captain picks up survivors from a torpedoed ship and finds himself involved with spies.
Very minor action melodrama, efficiently made.

w Kenneth Gamet, Fred Niblo Jnr, Richard Macaulay d Lothar Mendes ph Charles G. Clarke m David Raksin

Edward G. Robinson, Lynn Bari, Victor McLaglen, Marc Lawrence, E. J. Ballentine, Mona Maris

Tanganyika
US 1954 81m Technicolor
A 1900 settler finds that the African colony of his choice is terrorized by a murderer. Curious blend of outdoor action and who-is-it; not at all bad. Van Heflin, Howard Duff, Ruth Roman, Jeff Morrow, Joe Comadaore. Written by Richard Alan Simmons and William Sackheim; directed by André de Toth; for Universal-International.

Tangier
US 1946 74m bw
A dancer hunts for the Nazi war criminal responsible for her father's death. You can tell returns had been bad from the fact that the queen of Technicolor was sentenced to monochrome, and in a two-bit Casablanca. Maria Montez, Kent Taylor, Robert Paige, Sabu, Preston Foster, Louise Allbritton, Reginald Denny, J. Edward Bromberg. Written by M. M. Musselman and Monty Collins; directed by George Waggner; for Universal-International.

The Tanks Are Coming
US 1951 90m bw
A tough sergeant learns humility during the race to Berlin. Tedious war drama which tries in vain to interest us in non-characters. Steve Cochran, Paul Picerni, Mari Aldon, Harry Bellaver, Philip Carey. Written by Robert Hardy Andrews; directed by D. Ross Lederman and Lewis Seiler; for Warner.

Tap Roots
US 1948 109m Technicolor
Universal-International (Walter Wanger)
A southern family tries to remain neutral in the Civil War.
Minor Gone with the Wind saga, quite expensively produced but not very exciting.
w Alan le May, novel James Street d George Marshall ph Winton C. Hoch, Lionel Lindon m Frank Skinner

Susan Hayward, Van Heflin, Boris Karloff, Julie London, Whitfield Connor

Tarantula
US 1955 80m bw
U-I (William Alland)
Scientists working on an artificial food become grossly misshapen, and an infected spider escapes and grows to giant size.
Moderate monster hokum with the desert setting which became a cliché; the grotesque faces are more horrific than the spider, which seldom seems to touch the ground.
w Robert M. Fresco, Martin Berkeley d Jack Arnold ph George Robinson m Joseph Gershenson

Leo G. Carroll, John Agar, Mara Corday, Nestor Paiva

Taras Bulba*
US 1962 124m Eastmancolor
Panavision
UA / H-H / Avala (Harold Hecht)
A cossack leader has bitter disagreements with his rebellious son.
Violent action epic based on a well-worn story; plenty of spectacular highlights.
w Waldo Salt, Karl Tunberg, novel Nicolai Gogol d J. Lee-Thompson ph Joe MacDonald m Franz Waxman pd Edward Carrere

Yul Brynner, Tony Curtis, Christine Kaufmann, Sam Wanamaker, Guy Rolfe, George Macready, Vladimir Sokoloff, Abraham Sofaer
'Now! Add a motion picture to the wonders of the world!'—publicity
AAN: Franz Waxman

Target Zero
US 1955 93m bw
Warner (David Weisbart)
An infantry patrol in Korea is cut off behind enemy lines.
Routine battle exploits with a highly unlikely superimposed romance.
w Sam Rolfe d Harmon Jones ph Edwin DuPar m David Buttolph

Richard Conte, Charles Bronson, Richard Stapley, Chuck Connors, L. Q. Jones, Peggie Castle

Targets*
US 1967 90m Pathecolor
(Paramount) Peter Bogdanovich

An elderly horror film star confronts and disarms a mad sniper at a drive-in movie. Oddball melodrama apparently meant to contrast real and fantasy violence; it doesn't quite work despite effective moments, and the low budget shows.

wd Peter Bogdanovich *ph* Laszlo Kovacs

Boris Karloff, Tim O'Kelly, James Brown, Sandy Baron

The Tarnished Angels

US 1957 91m bw Cinemascope
U-I (Albert Zugsmith)

A reporter falls in with a self-torturing family of circus air aces.
Unsatisfactory attempt to reunite the talents of *Written on the Wind*; a dull story, very boringly presented.

w George Zuckerman, *novel* Pylon by William Faulkner *d* Douglas Sirk *ph* Irving Glassberg *m* Frank Skinner *md* Joseph Gershenson

Rock Hudson, Robert Stack, Dorothy Malone, Jack Carson, Robert Middleton

The Tartars

Italy 1960 105m Technicolor
Totalscope
Lux (Riccardo Gualino)

Viking settlers on the Russian steppes fight Tartar invaders.
Action-packed comic strip.

d Richard Thorpe *ph* Amerigo Genarelli *m* Renzo Rossellini

Orson Welles, Victor Mature, Folco Lulli, Arnoldo Foa

Tarzan

The talkie *Tarzans* began with Johnny Weissmuller and tailed off from there. (See *Filmgoer's Companion* for the silents.) The 1932 version more or less followed the original Edgar Rice Burroughs novel, and all the MGM entries had a special vivid quality about them, but subsequently the productions, usually produced under the aegis of Sol Lesser, tailed off towards the standard of the TV series of the sixties starring Ron Ely.

1932: TARZAN THE APE MAN** (MGM: Weissmuller with Maureen O'Sullivan: *d* W. S. Van Dyke: 99m)
1933: TARZAN THE FEARLESS (Principal: Buster Crabbe: *d* Robert Hill: 73m)
1934: TARZAN AND HIS MATE*** (MGM: Weissmuller with Maureen O'Sullivan: *d* Cedric Gibbons: 105m)
  'Certainly one of the funniest things you'll ever see.'—*Otis Ferguson*

1935: THE NEW ADVENTURES OF TARZAN (Burroughs: Herman Brix: *d* Edward Kull: 75m)
1936: TARZAN ESCAPES** (MGM: Weissmuller with Maureen O'Sullivan: *d* Richard Thorpe: 95m)
1938: TARZAN'S REVENGE (Sol Lesser: Glenn Morris: *d* D. Ross Lederman: 70m); TARZAN AND THE GREEN GODDESS (Principal: Herman Brix: *d* Edward Kull: 72m: largely a re-edit of NEW ADVENTURES)
1939: TARZAN FINDS A SON (MGM: Weissmuller with O'Sullivan: Richard Thorpe: 90m)
1941: TARZAN'S SECRET TREASURE (MGM: Weissmuller with O'Sullivan: *d* Richard Thorpe: 81m)
1942: TARZAN'S NEW YORK ADVENTURE (MGM: Weissmuller with O'Sullivan: *d* Richard Thorpe: 71m)
1943: TARZAN TRIUMPHS (RKO: Weissmuller: *d* William Thiele: 78m); TARZAN'S DESERT MYSTERY (RKO: Weissmuller: *d* William Thiele: 70m)
1945: TARZAN AND THE AMAZONS (RKO: Weissmuller: *d* Kurt Neumann: 76m)
1946: TARZAN AND THE LEOPARD WOMAN (RKO: Weissmuller: *d* Kurt Neumann: 72m)
1947: TARZAN AND THE HUNTRESS (RKO: Weissmuller: *d* Kurt Neumann: 72m)
1948: TARZAN AND THE MERMAIDS (RKO: *d* Robert Florey: Weissmuller: 68m)
1949: TARZAN'S MAGIC FOUNTAIN (RKO: Lex Barker: *d* Lee Sholem: 73m)
1950: TARZAN AND THE SLAVE GIRL (RKO: Lex Barker: *d* Lee Sholem: 74m)
1951: TARZAN'S PERIL (RKO: Lex Barker: *d* Byron Haskin: 79m)
1952: TARZAN'S SAVAGE FURY (RKO: Lex Barker: *d* Cy Endfield: 80m)
1953: TARZAN AND THE SHE-DEVIL (RKO: Lex Barker: *d* Kurt Neumann: 76m)
1955: TARZAN'S HIDDEN JUNGLE (RKO: Gordon Scott: *d* Harold Schuster: 73m)
1957: TARZAN AND THE LOST SAFARI (colour) (MGM: Gordon Scott: *d* Bruce Humberstone: 84m)
1958: TARZAN'S FIGHT FOR LIFE (colour) (MGM: Gordon Scott: *d* Bruce Humberstone: 86m)
1959: TARZAN'S GREATEST ADVENTURE (colour) (MGM: Gordon Scott: *d* John Guillermin: 90m)
1959: TARZAN THE APE MAN (colour: remake of the original story) (MGM: Denny Miller: *d* Joseph Newman: 82m)

1960: TARZAN THE MAGNIFICENT (colour) (Paramount: Gordon Scott: *d* Robert Day: 88m)
1962: TARZAN GOES TO INDIA (colour) (MGM: Jock Mahoney: *d* John Guillermin: 86m)
1963: TARZAN'S THREE CHALLENGES (colour) (MGM: Jock Mahoney: *d* Robert Day: 92m)
1966: TARZAN AND THE VALLEY OF GOLD (colour) (NatGen: Mike Henry: Robert Day: 90m)
1967: TARZAN AND THE GREAT RIVER (colour) (Paramount: Mike Henry: *d* Robert Day: 88m)
1968: TARZAN AND THE JUNGLE BOY (colour) (Paramount: Mike Henry: *d* Robert Day: 90m)
1981: TARZAN THE APE MAN (colour) (MGM: Miles O'Keefe; *d* John Derek; 112m). A debased version with the emphasis on the undressed Jane played by Bo Derek.

Task Force
US 1949   116m   bw (Technicolor sequences)
Warner (Jerry Wald)

An admiral about to retire recalls his struggle to promote the cause of aircraft carriers. Stilted and long-drawn-out flagwaver with too much chat and action highlights borrowed from wartime newsreel.

wd Delmer Daves   *ph* Robert Burks, Wilfrid M. Cline   *m* Franz Waxman

Gary Cooper, Walter Brennan, Jane Wyatt, Wayne Morris, Julie London, Bruce Bennett, Stanley Ridges, Jack Holt

A Taste of Excitement
GB 1968   99m   Eastmancolor
Trio Films (George Willoughby)

An English girl holidaying on the Riviera suspects that someone is trying to kill her. Standard frightened lady / 'they won't believe me' mystery with enough twists to satisfy addicts.

w Brian Carton, Don Sharp, *novel* Waiting for a Tiger by Ben Healey   *d* Don Sharp   *ph* Paul Beeson

Eva Renzi, David Buck, Peter Vaughan, Sophie Hardy, Paul Hubschmid, Kay Walsh

Taste of Fear°°
GB 1961   82m   bw
Columbia / Hammer (Jimmy Sangster)
US title: *Scream of Fear*

A crippled heiress visits her long-lost father and is haunted by his corpse.

Smartly tricked-out sub-Hitchcock screamer with sudden shocks among the Riviera settings and a plot which Hammer borrowed from *Les Diaboliques* and used again and again.

w Jimmy Sangster   *d* Seth Holt   *ph* Douglas Slocombe   *m* Clifton Parker

Susan Strasberg, Ann Todd, Ronald Lewis, Christopher Lee, Leonard Sachs
  'All those creaking shutters, flickering candles, wavering shadows and pianos playing in empty rooms still yield a tiny frisson.'—
Penelope Houston

A Taste of Honey°°°
GB 1961   100m   bw
British Lion / Bryanston / Woodfall (Tony Richardson)

Adventures of a pregnant Salford teenager, her sluttish mother, black lover and homosexual friend.
Fascinating offbeat comedy drama with memorable characters and sharply etched backgrounds.

w Shelagh Delaney, Tony Richardson, *play* Shelagh Delaney   *d* Tony Richardson   *ph* Walter Lassally   *m* John Addison

Rita Tushingham, Dora Bryan, Murray Melvin, Robert Stephens, Paul Danquah
  'Tart and lively around the edges and bitter at the core.'—*Peter John Dyer*

Taste the Blood of Dracula
GB 1969   95m   Technicolor
Hammer (Aida Young)

A depraved peer involves three Victorian businessmen in the reactivation of Dracula. Latterday vampire saga, initially lively but mainly dreary.

w John Elder   *d* Peter Sasdy   *ph* Arthur Grant   *m* James Bernard

Christopher Lee, Geoffrey Keen, Gwen Watford, Linda Hayden, Peter Sallis, Anthony Corlan, John Carson, Ralph Bates

The Tattered Dress
US 1957   93m   bw   Cinemascope
U-I (Albert Zugsmith)

While conducting a murder defence, a criminal lawyer annoys a vindictive small-town sheriff, who plots revenge.
Silly melodrama which rapidly loses interest after a promising start.

w George Zuckerman   *d* Jack Arnold   *ph* Carl Guthrie   *m* Frank Skinner

Jeff Chandler, Jack Carson, Jeanne Crain, Gail Russell, George Tobias, Edward Andrews, Philip Reed

Tawny Pipit *
GB 1944 85m bw
GFD / Two Cities (Bernard Miles)

The life of a village in wartime is disrupted
when two rare birds nest in a local meadow.
Pleasant, thin little comedy, a precursor of the
Ealing school.

w Bernard Miles *d* Bernard Miles, Charles
Saunders

Bernard Miles, Rosamund John, Níall
MacGinnis, Jean Gillie, Christopher Steele,
Lucie Mannheim, Brefni O'Rourke, Marjorie
Rhodes
    'Almost unimaginably genteel.'—*James
Agee*
    'Not quite dry enough for the epicures nor
sweet enough for the addicts.'—*C. A. Lejeune*

Taxi!
US 1932 68m bw
Warner (Robert Lord)

Independent cab drivers defy a powerful trust.
Sassy comedy drama with plenty going on.

w Kubec Glasmon, John Bright, *play* The
Blind Spot by Kenyon Nicholson *d* Roy del
Ruth *ph* James Van Trees *md* Leo Forbstein

James Cagney, Loretta Young, George E.
Stone, Guy Kibbee, David Landau, Leila
Bennett, Matt McHugh
    'A sordid but amusing observation on minor
metropolitan endeavours.'—*Time*

Taxi
US 1952 77m bw
TCF (Samuel G. Engel)

A taxi driver helps a young mother find her
husband, and falls for her himself.
Practised sentimental guff, Hollywoodized
from the French film *Sans Laisser d'Adresse*.

w D. M. Marshman Jnr, Daniel Fuchs
d Gregory Ratoff *ph* Milton Krasner
m Leigh Harline

Dan Dailey, Constance Smith, Neva
Patterson, Blanche Yurka, Walter Woolf King

The Taxi Dancer
US 1926 64m at 24 fps bw silent

A Virginia girl in the big city rises from
dime-a-dance joints to the big time. Mildly
suggestive star melodrama which promises
more than it gives. Joan Crawford, Owen
Moore, Douglas Gilmore, Marc McDermott,
Gertrude Astor. Written by A. P. Younger
and Robert Terry Shannon; directed by Harry
Millarde; for MGM.

Taxi Driver * * *
US 1976 114m Metrocolor
Columbia / Italo–Judeo (Michael and Julia
Philips)

A lonely Vietnam veteran becomes a New
York taxi driver and allows the violence and
squalor around him to explode in his mind.
The epitome of the sordid realism of the
seventies, this unlovely but brilliantly made
film haunts the mind and paints a most vivid
picture of a hell on earth. Unfortunately the
plot in the latter stages makes no sense.

w Paul Schraeder *d* Martin Scorsese
ph Michael Chapman *m* Bernard Herrmann

Robert de Niro, Jodie Foster, Cybill Shepherd,
Peter Boyle, Leonard Harris, Harvey Keitel
    'I don't question the truth of this material. I
question Scorsese's ability to lift it out of the
movie gutters into which less truthful directors
have trampled it.'—*Stanley Kauffmann*
† Schraeder says the story was modelled after
the diaries of would-be assassin Arthur
Bremer.

AAN: best picture; Bernard Herrmann;
Robert de Niro; Jodie Foster

Taza, Son of Cochise
US 1954 79m Technicolor

Peace-loving Taza succeeds his dad and tries
not to be influenced by Geronimo. Routine
pro-Indian western. Rock Hudson (as Taza),
Barbara Rush, Gregg Palmer, Bart Roberts,
Morris Ankrum. Written by George
Zuckerman and Gerald Drayson Adams;
directed by Douglas Sirk; for Universal-
International.

Tea and Sympathy
US 1956 122m Metrocolor
  Cinemascope
MGM (Pandro S. Berman)

A sensitive teenage schoolboy is scorned by
his tougher classmates, but his housemaster's
wife takes him in hand . . .
Overblown and bowdlerized version of a quiet
little Broadway play; impeccable production
values, but no spark.

w Robert Anderson (and the Hays office),
from his play *d* Vincente Minnelli *ph* John
Alton *m* Adolph Deutsch

Deborah Kerr, *John Kerr*, Leif Erickson,
Edward Andrews, Darryl Hickman
    'Even the most daring story can be brought
onto the screen when done with courage,
honesty and good taste.'—*publicity*
    '. . . mounted for the screen as if it were a
precious *objet d'art* in danger from rioting but

miraculously saved. Besides being archaic, the film is a prodigiously silly fable, pulling the realities with which it deals dishonestly, systematically out of whack.'—*Parker Tyler*

Tea for Two*
US 1950   97m   Technicolor
Warner (William Jacobs)

A nearly bankrupt financier promises his niece 25,000 dollars for her new musical show if she can say no to every question for twenty-four hours.
Tinkly, quite amusing light musical which has little to do with *No No Nanette* on which it is allegedly based.

w Henry Clark d David Butler ph Wilfrid Cline md Ray Heindorf

Doris Day, Gordon Macrae, Gene Nelson, Eve Arden, Billy de Wolfe, S. Z. Sakall, Bill Goodwin, Patrice Wymore

Teacher's Pet*
US 1957   120m   bw   Vistavision
Paramount / Perlberg–Seaton (William Perlberg)

A tough city editor falls for a lady professor of journalism and enrols as a student.
Overlong one-joke comedy which quickly reneges on its early promise; but the principals play up divertingly.

w Fay and Michael Kanin d George Seaton ph Haskell Boggs m Roy Webb

Clark Gable, Doris Day, Gig Young, Mamie Van Doren, Nick Adams

AAN: Fay and Michael Kanin; Gig Young

The Teahouse of the August Moon*
US 1956   123m   Metrocolor
Cinemascope
MGM (Jack Cummings)

Okinawa 1944: a wily interpreter helps American troops succumb to the oriental way of life.
Adequate, well-acted screen version of a Broadway comedy which succeeded largely because of its theatricality. A few good jokes remain.

w John Patrick, from his play d Daniel Mann ph John Alton m Saul Chaplin

Marlon Brando, Glenn Ford, Eddie Albert, *Paul Ford*, Michiko Kyo, Henry Morgan

The Teckman Mystery
GB 1954   90m   bw
British Lion / London Films / Corona (Josef Somlo)

An author commissioned to write the biography of a dead airman finds him very much alive and his own life in danger.
Peripatetic spy story with the twists expected of this author; all quite enjoyable.

w Francis Durbridge, James Matthews, *BBC serial* Francis Durbridge d Wendy Toye ph Jack Hilyard m Clifton Parker

Margaret Leighton, John Justin, Michael Medwin, Meier Tzelniker, Roland Culver, George Coulouris, Raymond Huntley, Duncan Lamont

Teenage Rebel
US 1956   94m   bw   Cinemascope
TCF (Charles Brackett)

A wealthy California woman is visited by her teenage daughter from a former marriage; the girl proceeds to make difficulties for everyone.
The first film in black-and-white Cinemascope is a tedious drama of unreal people.

w Walter Reisch, Charles Brackett, *play* Edith Sommer d Edmund Goulding ph Joe MacDonald m Leigh Harline

Ginger Rogers, Michael Rennie, Mildred Natwick, Betty Lou Keim, Warren Berlinger, Louise Beavers, Irene Hervey

Teheran
GB 1947   86m   bw

A correspondent in Iran foils an assassination plot. Low-key blood and thunder; passable time-filler. Derek Farr, Marta Labarr, Manning Whiley, John Slater, John Warwick. Written by Akos Tolnay and William Freshman; directed by William Freshman and Giacomo Gentilomo; for Pendennis. (US title: *The Plot to Kill Roosevelt*.)

Telefon
US 1977   103m   Metrocolor
MGM (James B. Harris)

A Russian agent is instructed to seek out and destroy a ring of hard liners who are opposing detente with the west.
Moderately watchable espionage capers with a slightly new twist.

w Peter Hyams, Stirling Silliphant, *novel* Walter Wager d Don Siegel ph Michael Butler m Lalo Schifrin

Charles Bronson, Lee Remick, Donald Pleasence, Tyne Daly, Alan Badel, Patrick Magee, Sheree North

Tell England
GB 1931   88m   bw

In 1914, school chums join up and mostly die at Gallipoli. Even the most patriotic audiences ended up roaring with laughter at this stiff-upper-lip charade. Carl Harbord, Fay Compton, Tony Bruce, Dennis Hoey, Gerald Rawlinson, Wally Patch. Written by Anthony Asquith, from the novel by Ernest Raymond; directed by Anthony Asquith and Gerald Barkas; for British Instructional. (US title: *The Battle of Gallipoli*.)

Tell It to the Marines
US 1926   75m at 24 fps   bw   silent

A marine sergeant has an eventful time during training and in the Philippines. Lively war action piece with a more or less straight role for its star. Lon Chaney, William Haines, Eleanor Boardman, Carmel Myers, Warner Oland. Written by Richard Schayer; directed by George Hill; for MGM.

Tell Me a Riddle
US 1980   90m   CFI color

A dying old woman, long a recluse, is reconciled with her family. Adequate if not exciting treatment of a very downbeat subject. Lila Kedrova, Melvyn Douglas, Brooke Adams, Dolores Dorn, Lili Valenty, Zalman King. Written by Joyce Eliason and Alev Lytle, from the novel by Tillie Olsen; directed by Lee Grant; for Godmother / Filmways.

Tell Me That You Love Me, Junie Moon
US 1969   113m   Technicolor
Paramount / Sigma (Otto Preminger)

A disfigured girl, a homosexual paraplegic and an introvert epileptic set up house together. Absurd tragicomedy which remains disturbingly icky in conception and execution.

w Marjorie Kellogg, from her novel   *d* Otto Preminger   *ph* Boris Kaufman   *m* Philip Springer

Liza Minnelli, Ken Howard, Robert Moore, Kay Thompson, Leonard Frey, James Coco, Fred Williamson

'Like seeing a venerated senior citizen desperately trying to show he's in love with today by donning see-through clothes.'— *Michael Billington, Illustrated London News*

'It slushes us with sentimentality to the point past compassion.'—*Judith Crist*

Tell No Tales**
US 1938   68m   bw
MGM (Edward Chodorov)

A managing editor seeks a big scoop to save his newspaper, and solves a kidnap-murder case.

Intriguingly written and handled second feature, with excellent pace, performance and entertainment value.

w Lionel Houser   *d* Leslie Fenton   *ph* Joseph Ruttenberg   *m* William Axt

Melvyn Douglas, Louise Platt, Gene Lockhart, Douglass Dumbrille, Zeffie Tilbury, Halliwell Hobbes

'Full of excellent detail, and the smallest part is a genuine character. Add these qualities to its pace and excitement and you have something well worth seeing.'—*Richard Mallett, Punch*

Tell Them Willie Boy is Here*
US 1969   97m   Technicolor
Universal (Philip A. Waxman)

In 1909 an Indian turned cowboy comes up against old prejudices and is pursued into the desert after an accidental death.
Boringly predictable story of white man's guilt, very professionally made.

wd Abraham Polonsky, *novel* Willie Boy by Harry Lawton   *ph* Conrad Hall   *m* Dave Grusin

Robert Redford, Robert Blake, Katharine Ross, Susan Clark, Barry Sullivan, Charles McGraw, Charles Aidman, John Vernon

Tempest
Italy / France / Yugoslavia 1958   123m
 Technirama
(Paramount) Dino de Laurentiis / Gray /
 S. N Pathe / Bosnia

Adventures of a Russian ensign banished by Catherine the Great.
Expensive but sloppy epic which fails to generate much interest.

w Louis Peterson, Alberto Lattuada, Ivo Perelli, *novel* The Captain's Daughter by Alexander Pushkin   *d* Alberto Lattuada   *ph* Aldo Tonti   *m* Piero Piccioni

Van Heflin, Geoffrey Horne, Silvana Mangano, Oscar Homolka, Viveca Lindfors, Robert Keith, Vittorio Gassman, Finlay Currie, Agnes Moorehead, Helmut Dantine, Laurence Naismith

Temptation
US 1946   92m   bw
Universal (Edward Small)

An archaeologist's wife takes to poisoning both her husband and her blackmailing lover. Hoary Edwardian melodrama, unpersuasively restaged.

w Robert Thoeren, *novel* Bella Donna by Robert Hichens   *d* Irving Pichel   *ph* Lucien Ballard   *m* Daniele Amfitheatrof

Merle Oberon, George Brent, Charles Korvin, Paul Lukas, Lenore Ulric, Arnold Moss, Ludwig Stossel, Gavin Muir, Ilka Gruning, André Charlot

Temptation Harbour
GB 1946   104m   bw
ABP (Victor Skutesky)

A railway signalman finds and keeps stolen money.
Well-presented but boringly predictable melodrama with an overwrought leading performance set against yards of studio fog.

w Victor Skutesky, Frederic Gotfurt, Rodney Ackland, *novel* Newhaven/Dieppe by Georges Simenon d Lance Comfort

Robert Newton, Simone Simon, William Hartnell, Marcel Dalio, Margaret Barton, Edward Rigby, Joan Hopkins, Charles Victor, Kathleen Harrison

The Temptress*
US 1927   80m (24 fps)   bw   silent
MGM

An immoral woman drives men to disgrace, murder and suicide.
No-holds-barred melodrama which, being Garbo's second American film, fully confirmed her stardom.

w Dorothy Farnum d Mauritz Stiller, Fred Niblo

Greta Garbo, Antonio Moreno, Lionel Barrymore, Roy D'Arcy, Marc McDermott

'10'*
US 1979   122m   Metrocolor   Panavision
Columbia / Orion (Blake Edwards, Tony Adams)

A sex-mad middle-aged composer marks his girls from one to ten according to their performance.
Randy farce which struck some, but not all, audiences as the funniest thing since sliced bread.

wd Blake Edwards ph Frank Stanley m Henry Mancini pd Rodger Maus

Dudley Moore, Julie Andrews, Bo Derek, Robert Webber, Dee Wallace, Sam Jones

The Ten Commandments**
US 1923   150m approx (24 fps)
   part Technicolor   silent
Paramount / Famous Players–Lasky (Cecil B. de Mille)

Moses leads the Israelites into the promised land in modern San Francisco; a story of two brothers shows the power of prayer and truth.

The two halves in fact are totally disconnected; but this is a de Mille spectacular and therefore beyond reproach, while as a Hollywood milestone it cannot be denied a place in the Hall of Fame.

w Jeanie MacPherson d Cecil B. de Mille
ph Bert Glennon and others (*colour,* Ray Renahan)

Theodore Roberts, Richard Dix, Rod la Rocque, Edythe Chapman, Leatrice Joy, Nita Naldi

'It will last as long as the film on which it is recorded.'—*James R. Quirk, Photoplay*

The Ten Commandments*
US 1956   219m   Technicolor
   Vistavision
Paramount / Cecil B. de Mille (Henry Wilcoxon)

The life of Moses and his leading of the Israelites to the Promised Land.
Popular but incredibly stilted and verbose bible-in-pictures spectacle. A very long haul along a monotonous route, with the director at his pedestrian worst.

w Aeneas Mackenzie, Jesse L. Lasky Jnr, Jack Gariss, Frederic M. Frank d Cecil B. de Mille ph Loyal Griggs m Elmer Bernstein

Charlton Heston, Yul Brynner, Edward G. Robinson, Anne Baxter, Nina Foch, Yvonne de Carlo, John Derek, H. B. Warner, Henry Wilcoxon, Judith Anderson, John Carradine, Douglass Dumbrille, Cedric Hardwicke, Martha Scott, Vincent Price, Debra Paget

'De Mille not only moulds religion into a set pattern of Hollywood conventions; he has also become an expert at making entertainment out of it.'—*Gordon Gow, Films and Filming*
'The result of all these stupendous efforts? Something roughly comparable to an eight-foot chorus girl—pretty well put together, but much too big and much too flashy. . . . What de Mille has really done is to throw sex and sand into the moviegoers' eyes for almost twice as long as anyone else has ever dared to.'—*Time*
'What a story it tells! What majesty it encompasses! What loves it unveils! What drama it unfolds!'—*publicity*

AAN: best picture; Loyal Griggs

Ten Days in Paris
GB 1939   82m   bw
Columbia (Jerome J. Jackson)
US titles: *Missing Ten Days / Spy in the Pantry*

An amnesiac wakes up in Paris and finds he has been involved in espionage activities. Modest, quite likeable little comedy suspenser.

w John Meehan Jnr, James Curtis, *novel* The Disappearance of Roger Tremayne by Bruce Graeme *d* Tim Whelan *ph* Otto Kanturek *m* Miklos Rozsa

Rex Harrison, Karen Verne, Leo Genn, Joan Marion, Anthony Holles, John Abbott, Hay Petrie

Ten Gentlemen from West Point°°
US 1942 104m bw
TCF (William Perlberg)

Adventures in Indian territory, and back at West Point, of the first recruits to that military academy in the early 1800s.
Likeable mixture of comedy and flagwaving adventure, with excellent production values and a dominating performance.

w Richard Maibaum, George Seaton *d* Henry Hathaway *ph* Leon Shamroy *m* Alfred Newman

Laird Cregar, George Montgomery, Maureen O'Hara, John Sutton, Shepperd Strudwick, Victor Francen, Harry Davenport, Ward Bond, Douglass Dumbrille, Ralph Byrd, Louis Jean Heydt

AAN: Leon Shamroy

Ten Little Indians°
GB 1966 91m bw
Tenlit (Harry Alan Towers)

Ten people, including two servants invited to a remote house in the Austrian Alps are murdered one by one.
Fair copy of a classic whodunnit.

w Peter Yeldham, Harry Alan Towers, *novel* Agatha Christie *d* George Pollock *ph* Ernest Steward *m* Malcolm Lockyer

Wilfrid Hyde White, Dennis Price, Stanley Holloway, Leo Genn, Shirley Eaton, Hugh O'Brian, Daliah Lavi, Fabian, Mario Adorf, Marianne Hoppe

† Made also in 1945 and 1975, as *And Then There Were None* (qv).

Ten North Frederick°
US 1958 102m bw Cinemascope
TCF (Charles Brackett)

At the funeral of a local politico, his family and friends think back to the events of his life.
Small beer, but a generally adult and entertaining family drama despite a miscast lead.

wd Philip Dunne, novel John O'Hara *ph* Joe MacDonald *m* Leigh Harline

Gary Cooper, Geraldine Fitzgerald, Diane Varsi, Stuart Whitman, Suzy Parker, Tom Tully, Ray Stricklyn, John Emery

Ten Rillington Place°
GB 1970 111m Eastmancolor
Columbia / Filmways (Basil Appleby)

An account of London's sordid Christie murders of the forties.
Agreeably seedy reconstruction of a *cause célèbre*, carefully built around the star part of a murderous aberrant landlord. Too long, however, and finally too lacking in detail.

w Clive Exton, *book* Ludovic Kennedy *d* Richard Fleischer *ph* Denys Coop *m* Johnny Dankworth

Richard Attenborough, *John Hurt*, Judy Geeson, Pat Heywood, Isobel Black, Geoffrey Chater, André Morell, Robert Hardy

Ten Seconds to Hell
US 1959 93m bw
Hammer / Seven Arts (Michael Carreras)

Bomb disposal experts in post-war Berlin quarrel over a girl.
Boring, harsh, hollow melodrama, so artificially constructed that no one can possibly care who gets exploded.

w Robert Aldrich, Teddi Sherman, *novel* The Phoenix by Lawrence Bachmann *d* Robert Aldrich *ph* Ernest Laszlo *m* Kenneth V. Jones

Jack Palance, Jeff Chandler, Martine Carol, Robert Cornthwaite, Dave Willock, Wesley Addy

Ten Tall Men
US 1951 97m Technicolor
Columbia / Norma (Harold Hecht)

A Foreign Legion patrol prevents a Riff attack.
Comic strip adventures, efficiently handled.

w Roland Kibbee, Frank Davis *d* Willis Goldbeck *ph* William Snyder *m* David Buttolph

Burt Lancaster, Gilbert Roland, Kieron Moore, John Dehner, Jody Lawrance, George Tobias, Mike Mazurki

10.30 pm Summer
US / Spain 1966 85m Technicolor
UA / Jorill / Argos (Jules Dassin, Anatole Litvak)

The neurotic Greek wife of an Englishman travelling in Spain becomes obsessed with a murderer on the run.

Preposterously overwrought romantic melodrama.

w Jules Dassin, Marguerite Duras, *novel* Marguerite Duras d Jules Dassin ph Gabor Pogany m Christobel Hallfter

Peter Finch, Melina Mercouri, Romy Schneider, Julian Mateos

Ten Thousand Bedrooms

US 1956   114m   Metrocolor
      Cinemascope
MGM (Joe Pasternak)

An American millionaire finds romance when he buys a Rome hotel.
Old-fashioned, unfunny comedy sadly lacking pace and style.

w Laslo Vadnay, Art Cohn, William Ludwig, Leonard Spiegelgass d Richard Thorpe ph Robert Bronner m George Stoll *songs* Nicholas Brodszky, Sammy Cahn

Dean Martin, Eva Bartok, Anna Maria Alberghetti, Walter Slezak, Paul Henreid, Jules Munchin, Marcel Dalio

Ten Wanted Men

US 1955   80m   Technicolor

A rancher and his family are besieged by bandits in a lady's house. Rather elementary but efficient and good-looking western programmer. Randolph Scott, Jocelyn Brando, Richard Boone, Alfonso Bedoya, Donna Martell, Skip Homeier. Written by Kenneth Gamet, from a story by Irving Ravetch and Harriet Frank Jnr; directed by Bruce Humberstone; for Harry Joe Brown / Columbia.

Ten Who Dared

US 1960   92m   Technicolor
Walt Disney (James Algar)

In 1869 a scientific expedition sets out to chart the Colorado River.
Tedious and unconvincing adventures.

w Lawrence E. Watkin, from the journal of Major John Wesley Powell d William Beaudine ph Gordon Avil m Oliver Wallace

Brian Keith, John Beal, James Drury, R. G. Armstrong, Ben Johnson, L. Q. Jones

The Tenant

France 1976   126m   Eastmancolor
Paramount / Marianne (Andrew
      Braunsberg)
Original title: *Le Locataire*

A displaced person becomes convinced that his fellow lodgers are out to murder him.
Rather like a male version of the same

director's *Repulsion*, this wearisome case history shows the total dissipation of whatever talent he once had.

w Gerard Brach, Roman Polanski, *novel* Roland Topor d Roman Polanski ph Sven Nykvist m Philippe Sarde

Roman Polanski, Melvyn Douglas, Isabelle Adjani, Shelley Winters, Jo Van Fleet, Lila Kedrova, Claude Dauphin

'It does not seem to have been designed as self-parody, but it certainly comes across that way.'—*Janet Maslin, Newsweek*

'A long-winded exercise in tedium and morbidity.'—*Kevin Thomas, LA Times*

Tender Comrade

US 1943   101m   bw
RKO (David Hempstead)

Lady welders whose husbands are fighting men keep their chins up during World War II.
Dim tearjerker.

w Dalton Trumbo d Edward Dmytryk ph Russell Metty m Leigh Harline

Ginger Rogers, Robert Ryan, Ruth Hussey, Patricia Collinge, Mady Christians, Kim Hunter, Jane Darwell

Tender Is the Night*

US 1961   146m   De Luxe   Cinemascope
TCF (Henry T. Weinstein)

Adventures around Europe between the wars of a rich American psychiatrist who has married his patient.
Patchy, fairly literal transcription of a patently unfilmable novel about defiantly unreal people in what would now be the jet set. About half the result is superficially entertaining.

w Ivan Moffat, *novel* F. Scott Fitzgerald d Henry King ph Leon Shamroy m Bernard Herrmann

Jennifer Jones, Jason Robards Jnr, *Joan Fontaine, Tom Ewell*, Cesare Danova, Jill St John, Paul Lukas

AAN: title song (m Sammy Fain, *ly* Paul Francis Webster)

The Tender Trap*

US 1955   111m   Eastmancolor
      Cinemascope
MGM (Lawrence Weingarten)

A smart New York agent has a way with women which annoys his friend; but Casanova gets his come-uppance when he sets his sights on an apparently naïve young actress.
Thin comedy with agreeable moments, not helped by the wide screen.

w Julius J. Epstein, *play* Max Shulman, Robert Paul Smith *d* Charles Walters *ph* Paul Vogel *m* Jeff Alexander

Frank Sinatra, Debbie Reynolds, David Wayne, Celeste Holm, Lola Albright, Carolyn Jones

AAN: title song (*m* James Van Heusen, *ly* Sammy Cahn)

Tenderloin

US 1928 88m bw

A dancer is accused of stealing a fortune and finds gangsters suddenly interested in her. Primitive part-talkie (15 minutes of dialogue), unspeakably hammy to listen to though visually it had some inventiveness. Dolores Costello, Conrad Nagel, Mitchell Lewis, George E. Stone, Dan Wolheim. Written by Edward T. Lowe, from a story by Darryl Zanuck; directed by Michael Curtiz; for Warner.

Tennessee Champ

US 1954 75m Anscocolor

The Lord helps a religious boxer to win a few fights. Tedious sentimental square ring melodrama. Earl Holliman, Dewey Martin, Keenan Wynn, Shelley Winters, Yvette Dugay. Written by Art Cohn; directed by Fred M. Wilcox; for MGM.

Tennessee Johnson*

US 1943 102m bw

MGM (J. Walter Ruben)

GB title: *The Man on America's Conscience*

The rise and the problems of President Andrew Johnson.

Sincere, straightforward, well-produced historical drama which failed to set the Thames—or the Hudson—on fire.

w John Balderston, Wells Root *d* William Dieterle *ph* Harold Rosson *m* Herbert Stothart

Van Heflin, Ruth Hussey, Lionel Barrymore, Marjorie Main, Regis Toomey, Montagu Love, Porter Hall, Charles Dingle, J. Edward Bromberg

'Dieterle's customary high-minded, high-polished mélange of heavy touches and intelligent performances.'—*James Agee*

Tennessee's Partner

US 1955 87m Technicolor

A gambling queen and a tenderfoot are involved in a double cross which leads to murder. Predictable western from a story by Bret Harte. Ronald Reagan, John Payne,

Rhonda Fleming, Colleen Gray. Written by Milton Krims, D. D. Beauchamp, Graham Baker and Teddi Sherman; directed by Allan Dwan; for RKO.

Tension

US 1950 91m bw

MGM (Robert Sisk)

A chemist plans the perfect murder of his wife's lover, loses his nerve, then finds himself suspected when the man is murdered after all. Disappointing suspenser which starts well but outstays its welcome.

w Allen Rivkin *d* John Berry *ph* Harry Stradling *m* André Previn

Richard Basehart, Audrey Totter, Barry Sullivan, Cyd Charisse, Lloyd Gough, Tom d'Andrea

Tension at Table Rock

US 1956 93m Technicolor

When a stagecoach station owner is killed, a gunman takes care of his small son and at the same time rids a town of outlaws. All the clichés are in this one, fairly neatly amassed in corners labelled *High Noon, Hondo* and *Shane*. Written by Winston Miller, from a novel by Frank Gruber; directed by Charles Marquis Warren; for RKO.

Tentacles

Italy 1976 102m Technicolor

Technovision

Esse Cinematografica (E. F. Doria)

A deadly menace which leaves its victims as skeletons washed up on the California beach turns out to be a giant octopus . . .

Dreary *Jaws* rehash. Sadly there is no element of spoofing, it's all deadly serious.

w Jerome Max, Tito Carpi, Steve Carabatsos, Sonia Molteni *d* Oliver Hellman (Sonia Assonitis) *ph* Roberto d'Ettore Piazzoli *m* S. W. Cipriani

Shelley Winters, John Huston, Bo Hopkins, Henry Fonda, Claude Akins, Cesare Danova, Delia Boccardo

Tenth Avenue Angel

US 1948 74m bw

MGM (Ralph Wheelwright)

The little daughter of poor parents loses her faith in life.

Icky sentimental piece for a waning child star.

w Angna Enters, Craig Rice, Harry Ruskin, Eleanore Griffin *d* Roy Rowland *ph* Robert Surtees *m* Rudolph G. Kopp

Margaret O'Brien, Angela Lansbury, George
Murphy, Phyllis Thaxter, Rhys Williams,
Warner Anderson, Audrey Totter, Connie
Gilchrist

The Tenth Man
GB 1936   68m   bw

A wife shows faith in her husband even though
she knows him to be a crook. Stock film
version of one of Somerset Maugham's less
pungent plays. John Lodge, Antoinette
Cellier, Aileen Marson, Clifford Evans,
George Graves. Written by Geoffrey Kerr,
Dudley Leslie, Marjorie Deans and Jack
Davies; directed by Brian Desmond Hurst; for
BIP.

The Tenth Victim
Italy / France 1965   92m   Technicolor
Avco / CC Champion / Concordia (Carlo
  Ponti)

In the 21st century murder is legalized to avoid
birth control and war, and ten killings bring a
fabulous prize.
Science fiction satire which just about gets by.

w Tonina Guerra, Giorgio Salvioni, Ennio
Flaiano, Elio Petri, *story* The Seventh Victim
by Robert Sheckley *d* Elio Petri *ph* Gianni di
Venanzo *m* Piero Piccioni

Ursula Andress, Marcello Mastroianni, Elsa
Martinelli, Massimo Serato

Teresa**
US 1951   101m   bw
MGM (Arthur M. Loew)

A soldier with mother problems brings home
an Italian bride.
Careful, sensitive, intelligent variation on a
problem frequently considered by films of this
period (*Frieda, Fräulein, Japanese War Bride*).

w Stewart Stern *d* Fred Zinnemann
ph William J. Miller *m* Louis Applebaum

Pier Angeli, John Ericson, Patricia Collinge,
Richard Bishop, Peggy Ann Garner, Ralph
Meeker, Bill Mauldin

AAN: original story (Arthur Hayes, Stewart
Stern)

Term of Trial*
GB 1962   130m   bw
Romulus (James Woolf)

An unsuccessful schoolmaster is accused of
rape by a nymphomaniac schoolgirl he has
scorned.
Rather flabby 'adult' drama, too schematic to
be really interesting despite the best that
acting can do.

wd Peter Glenville, *novel* The Burden of
Proof by James Barlow *ph* Oswald Morris
m Jean-Michel Demase *ad* Antony Woolard

Laurence Olivier, Sarah Miles, Simone
Signoret, Hugh Griffith, Terence Stamp,
Roland Culver, Frank Pettingell, Thora Hird,
Dudley Foster, Norman Bird

La Terra Trema*
Italy 1948   160m   bw
Universalia

The life of a Sicilian fisherman and his family.
Seriously intended, carefully composed semi-
documentary stressing the economic problems
of the simple life. A commercial disaster: even
the Italians couldn't understand the accents of
the local actors.

wd Luchino Visconti *ph* G. R. Aldo
m Luchino Visconti, Willy Ferrero

A Terrible Beauty
GB 1960   90m   bw
UA / Raymond Stross
US title: *Night Fighters*

In a north Irish village, the IRA revive their
activities on the outbreak of World War II.
Heavily Oirish melodrama with a muddled
message.

w Robert Wright Campbell, *novel* Arthur
Roth *d* Tay Garnett *ph* Stephen Dade
m Cedric Thorpe Davie

Robert Mitchum, Anne Heywood, Dan
O'Herlihy, Cyril Cusack, Richard Harris,
Marianne Benet

The Terror
US 1928   82m approx   bw
Warner

A mysterious killer lurks in the cellars of a
country house.
Primitive talkie which attempted a few new
styles but showed that more were needed, also
that some silent actors could not make the
transfer.

w Harvey Gates, *novel* and *play* Edgar
Wallace *d* Roy del Ruth *ph* Barney McGill

May McAvoy, Edward Everett Horton,
Louise Fazenda, Alec B. Francis, John Miljan,
Frank Austin

'The only terrible thing about this talkie
Terror is its unnatural slowness . . . the
characters speak as if they were dictating
important letters.'—A. P. Herbert, *Punch*
† The first film without a single subtitle: all the
credits were spoken.
†† *Return of the Terror* (US 1934) has little to
do with it.

The Terror
GB 1938   73m   bw

Stilted remake of the above. Wilfrid Lawson,
Arthur Wontner, Alastair Sim, Linden
Travers, Bernard Lee, Henry Oscar. Written
by William Freshman; directed by Richard
Bird; for BIP.

The Terror
US 1963   81m   Pathecolor
AIP / Filmgroup (Roger Corman, Francis
 Ford Coppola)

A baron lives for twenty years in a creepy
castle, mourning the death of his wife . . .
Shoddy horror improvised over a weekend on
the set of *The Raven.* It looks it.

w Leo Gordon, Jack Hill *d* Roger Corman
ph John Nickolaus *m* Ronald Stein

Boris Karloff, Jack Nicholson, Sandra Knight,
Dorothy Neumann

Terror Aboard
US 1933   70m   bw

Gruesome murders occur during a pleasure
cruise. Fair murder mystery. Charles Ruggles,
John Halliday, Shirley Grey, Neil Hamilton,
Verree Teasdale, Jack La Rue. Written by
Harvey Thew and Manuel Seff; directed by
Paul Sloane; for Paramount.

Terror in a Texas Town*
US 1958   81m   bw
UA / Frank N. Seltzer

A Swedish seaman arrives in a small western
town and avenges the death of his brother.
Stylish second feature western, a genuine
sleeper which holds the interest throughout.

w Ben L. Perry *d Joseph H. Lewis ph Ray
Rennahan m* Gerald Fried

Sterling Hayden, Sebastian Cabot, Carol
Kelly, Eugene Martin, Ned Young

Terror in the Haunted House
US 1958   81m   bw

A bride finds that her honeymoon mansion is
one about which she has been having recurring
nightmares. The plot has everything, even an
axe murderer, but the treatment is soporific.
Gerald Mohr, Cathy O'Donnell, William
Ching, John Qualen, Barry Bernard. Written
by Robert C. Dennis; directed by Harold
Daniels; for Howco. (Alternative title: *My
World Dies Screaming.*)

Terror in the Wax Museum
US 1973   94m   De Luxe
Bing Crosby Productions / Fenady
 Associates (Andrew J. Fenady)

In Victorian London a waxworks owner is
murdered . . .
Cheaply produced murder mystery (even the
waxworks can't stand still) with horror asides
and a cast of elderly hams.

w Jameson Brewer *d* George Fenady
ph William Jurgensen *m* George Duning

Ray Milland, Broderick Crawford, Elsa
Lanchester, Louis Hayward, John Carradine,
Shani Wallis, Maurice Evans, Patric Knowles

The Terror of the Tongs
GB 1960   79m   Technicolor
Hammer / Merlin (Kenneth Hyman)

In 1910 Hong Kong a merchant avenges the
death of his daughter at the hands of a
villainous secret society.
Gory melodrama with dollops of screams,
torture and vaguely orgiastic goings-on.

w Jimmy Sangster *d* Anthony Bushell
ph Arthur Grant *m* James Bernard

Geoffrey Toone, Christopher Lee, Yvonne
Monlaur, Brian Worth, Richard Leech

Terror Train
Canada 1980   97m   De Luxe

Participants in a wild party aboard a train are
decimated by a mysterious psychotic. Shocks
and blood in the Carpenter tradition,
adequately mounted. Ben Johnson, Jamie Lee
Curtis, David Copperfield, Hart Bochner.
Written by T. Y. Drake; directed by Roger
Spottiswoode; for Astral.

Tess*
France-GB 1979   180m   colour
Renn-Burrill (Claude Berri)

A peasant girl tries to prove her noble heritage
but finds herself with an illegitimate child.
Solid, unexciting version of a classic Wessex
novel; a hard sell for 1980 audiences.

w Roman Polanski, Gerard Brach, John
Brownjohn *novel* Tess of the D'Urbervilles
by Thomas Hardy *d* Roman Polanski
ph Geoffrey Unsworth, Ghislain Cloquet
m Philippe Sarde *pd* Pierre Guffroy

Nastassia Kinski, Leigh Lawson, Peter Firth,
John Collin, David Markham, Richard
Pearson

 'It emerges without a hint of what might
have drawn Polanski to the material.'—*Sight
and Sound*

AA: Geoffrey Unsworth, Ghislain Cloquet;
art direction (Pierre Guffroy, Jack Stevens);
costume design (Anthony Powell)
AAN: best film; Roman Polanski; Philippe
Sarde
BFA: best photography

Tess of the Storm Country
US 1932　80m　bw
Fox

A retired sea captain's daughter loves the lord of the manor.
Antiquated tushery first filmed as a Mary Pickford silent.

w S. N. Behrman, Sonya Levien, Rupert Hughes, *novel* Grace Miller White d Alfred Santell ph Hal Mohr

Janet Gaynor, Charles Farrell, Dudley Digges, June Clyde, George Meeker

Test Pilot**
US 1938　118m　bw
MGM (Louis D. Lighton)

A brilliant but unpredictable test pilot is helped by his wife and his self-sacrificing friend.
A big box-office star vehicle of its time, still interesting as a highly efficient product.

w Waldemar Young, Vincent Lawrence, *story* Frank Wead d Victor Fleming ph Ray June m Franz Waxman

Clark Gable, Myrna Loy, Spencer Tracy, Lionel Barrymore, Samuel S. Hinds, Marjorie Main, Gloria Holden

'The picture is so noisy with sure-fire elements—box office cast, violent excitement, glycerine tears and such—that it may be hard to keep the ear attuned to the quieter, more authentically human things in it.'—*James Shelley Hamilton*

AAN: best picture; Frank Wead

Le Testament d'Orphée*
France 1959　83m　bw
Editions Cinégraphiques (Jean Thuillier)
aka: *The Testament of Orpheus*

The poet, as an 18th-century man, dies, enters space time, is revived, and seeks his identity.
Rather like a melancholy madman's *Alice in Wonderland*, this bizarre jumble has its fascinations but misses by a mile the arresting qualities of *Orphée*.

wd Jean Cocteau ph Roland Pointoizeau m Georges Auric and others

Jean Cocteau, Edouard Dermithe, Maria Casarès, François Périer, Henri Crémieux, Yul Brynner, Jean-Pierre Léaud, Daniel Gélin, Jean Marais, Pablo Picasso, Charles Aznavour

The Testament of Dr Mabuse**
Germany 1933　122m　bw
Nero (Fritz Lang)

A sequel to *Dr Mabuse the Gambler*: the criminal mastermind dies in an asylum, and his assistant takes over his identity.
Fast-moving penny dreadful, alleged by its director to be a denouncing of the doctrines of Hitler, but showing little evidence of being more than a very slick entertainment.

w Thea Von Harbou, Fritz Lang d Fritz Lang ph Fritz Arno Wagner m Hans Erdmann ad Karl Vollbrecht, Emil Hassler

Rudolf Klein-Rogge, Otto Wernicke, Gustav Diesl

† On arrival in America Lang claimed that 'slogans of the Third Reich have been put into the mouths of criminals in the film'. Yet his wife, who co-scripted it, stayed behind as a confirmed Nazi.

The Texan
US 1930　79m　bw
Paramount

The Llano Kid absolves his bandit past.
Early sound western, an interesting curiosity.

w Daniel Nathan Rufin, *story* The Double-Dyed Deceiver by O. Henry d John Cromwell ph Victor Milner

Gary Cooper, Fay Wray, Emma Dunn, Oscar Apfel

The Texans
US 1938　92m　bw
Paramount (Lucien Hubbard)

Problems of the post-Civil War years include new railroads, the Ku Klux Klan, and the new cattle drive routes.
Formula western with fairly well staged excitements backing a routine romantic triangle.

w Bertram Millhauser, Paul Sloane, William Wister Haines d James Hogan ph Theodor Sparkuhl m Gerard Carbonara

Joan Bennett, Randolph Scott, May Robson, Walter Brennan, Robert Cummings, Raymond Halton, Robert Barrat, Francis Ford

Texas
US 1941　94m　bw.(released in sepia)
Columbia (Sam Bischoff)

Two veteran Civil War southerners head for Texas to set up a cattle business.
Western vehicle for two young stars, now very ordinary-looking.

w Horace McCoy, Lewis Meltzer, Michael Blankfort d George Marshall ph George Meehan

William Holden, Glenn Ford, Claire Trevor, George Bancroft, Edgar Buchanan, Don Beddoe, Andrew Tombes, Addison Richards

'While spoofing a little along the way, it observes the etiquette and tradition of an accepted cinema form. It has rough riding, cattle rustling, shooting and a story that leaves out only the Indian raid and the rescue by the US Cavalry.'—*Christian Science Monitor*

Texas across the River

US 1966 101m Techniscope
Universal (Harry Keller)

A Texan, an Indian and a Spanish nobleman on the run from jealous rivals have various adventures.
Sloppy western which seems to have had jokes added when someone realized it wasn't good enough to be taken seriously.

w Wells Root, Harold Greene, Ben Starr *d* Michael Gordon *ph* Russell Metty *m* Frank de Vol *md* Joseph Gershenson

Dean Martin, Alain Delon, Joey Bishop, Rosemary Forsyth, Tina Marquard, Peter Graves, Andrew Prine, Michael Ansara

Texas Carnival

US 1951 77m Technicolor
MGM (Jack Cummins)

A fairground showman is mistaken for a millionaire and runs up debts.
Very thin comedy musical relying entirely on its stars.

w Dorothy Kingsley *d* Charles Walters *ph* Robert Planck *m* Harry Warren *ly* Dorothy Fields *ch* Hermes Pan

Esther Williams, Red Skelton, Howard Keel, Ann Miller, Paula Raymond, Keenan Wynn, Tom Tully

Texas Lady

US 1955 85m Technicolor Superscope
RKO (Nat Holt)

A lady newspaper owner runs an anti-corruption campaign.
Mild family western.

w Horace McCoy *d* Tim Whelan *ph* Ray Rennahan *m* Paul Sawtell

Claudette Colbert, Barry Sullivan, Grey Walcott, James Bell, Horace MacMahon, Ray Collins, Walter Sande, Douglas Fowley

The Texas Rangers*

US 1936 95m bw
Paramount (King Vidor)

Three wandering ne'er-do-wells break up; two

join the Texas Rangers and hunt down the third, who is an outlaw.
Pleasantly remembered star western, later remade as *The Streets of Laredo* (qv).

w Louis Stevens *d* King Vidor *ph* Edward Cronjager

Fred MacMurray, Jack Oakie, Lloyd Nolan, Jean Parker, Edward Ellis

† *The Texas Rangers Ride Again* was released in 1940, with the rangers going undercover to catch outlaws; it was only a second feature, with John Howard and Jack Oakie. Another film called *The Texas Rangers* came from Columbia in 1952 and had a similar plot to the original; otherwise it was a shoddy piece of work in Supercinecolor, with George Montgomery and Jerome Courtland.

Thank God It's Friday

US 1978 89m Metrocolor
Columbia / Motown / Casablanca (Rob Cohen)

Problems of a disc jockey in a Hollywood disco.
Routine youth programmer, rather like *Rock Around the Clock* twenty years after.

w Barry Armyan Bernstein *d* Robert Klane *ph* James Crabe *pd* Tom H. John *m* various

Valerie Landsburg, Terri Nunn, Chick Vennera, Donna Summer, The Commodores

AA: song, 'Last Dance'

Thank You, Jeeves*

US 1936 57m bw
TCF (Sol M. Wurtzel)

A valet helps prevent his master from becoming involved in gun-running.
Competent second feature notable as Niven's first leading role; also one of the very few attempts to film Wodehouse.

w Joseph Hoffman, Stephen Gross, *story* P. G. Wodehouse *d* Arthur Greville Collins *ph* Barney McGill *m* Samuel Kaylin

David Niven, Arthur Treacher, Virginia Field, Lester Matthews, Colin Tapley

Thank Your Lucky Stars***

US 1943 127m bw
Warner (Mark Hellinger)

Eddie Cantor and his double get involved in planning a patriotic show.
All-star wartime musical with some unexpected turns and a generally funny script.

w Norman Panama, Melvin Frank, James V. Kern d David Butler ph Arthur Edeson md Leo F. Forbstein ch Le Roy Prinz songs Frank Loesser, Arthur Schwartz

Eddie Cantor, Dennis Morgan, Joan Leslie,
Edward Everett Horton, S. Z. Sakall,
Humphrey Bogart, Jack Carson, *Bette Davis*,
Olivia de Havilland, *Errol Flynn*, John
Garfield, Alan Hale, Ida Lupino, *Ann*
Sheridan, Dinah Shore, George Tobias, Spike
Jones and his City Slickers, Willie Best, Hattie
McDaniel

'The loudest and most vulgar of the current
musicals, it is also the most fun, if you are
amused when show people kid their own
idiom.'—*James Agee*

'An all-star show with the conspicuous
flavour of amateur night at the studio.'—*New*
York Times

AAN: song 'They're Either Too Young or
Too Old'

Thanks a Million**
US 1935   87m   bw
TCF (Darryl F. Zanuck)

A crooner runs for governor.
Smart, amusing political musical.

w Nunnally Johnson   d Roy del Ruth
ph Peverell Marley   songs Arthur Johnston,
Gus Kahn   *m Arthur Lange*

Dick Powell, Fred Allen, Ann Dvorak, Patsy
Kelly, Phil Baker, Paul Whiteman and his
band, the Yacht Club Boys, Benny Baker,
Raymond Walburn, Alan Dinehart

Thanks for Everything*
US 1938   70m   bw
TCF (Darryl F. Zanuck)

Mr Average American is discovered,
promoted and merchandized.
Very acceptable satirical comedy of the
advertising world.

w Harry Tugend   d William A. Seiter
ph George Meehan   m Abe Meyer

Adolphe Menjou, Jack Haley, Jack Oakie,
Arleen Whelan, Tony Martin, Binnie Barnes,
George Barbier
   'The funniest film I can remember seeing for
many months, with something of the old
Kaufman touch.'—*Graham Greene*

Thanks for the Memory*
US 1938   75m   bw
Paramount

A smart novelist has trouble with his marriage.
Light, agreeable domestic comedy on familiar
lines.

w Lynn Starling, play Up Pops the Devil by
Frances Goodrich, Albert Hackett   *d George*
Archainbaud   *ph Karl Struss   m Boris Morros*

Bob Hope, Shirley Ross

Thark*
GB 1932   79m   bw
British and Dominion (Herbert Wilcox)

The heir to an old mansion spends a night in it
to prove it is not haunted.
Very funny Aldwych farce, plainly transferred
to the screen with the original stage team
intact. One's only regret is that it peters out at
the end.

w Ben Travers, from his play   d Tom Walls
ph F. A. Young

Ralph Lynn, Tom Walls, Robertson Hare,
Mary Brough, Claude Hulbert, Gordon James

That Brennan Girl
US 1946   97m   bw

A young mother neglects her baby for the sake
of a good time. Absurdly padded-out moral
tract. Mona Freeman, James Dunn, William
Marshall, June Duprez. Written by Doris
Anderson; directed by Alfred Santell; for
Republic.

That Certain Age*
US 1938   95m   bw
Universal (Joe Pasternak)

A girl gets a crush on an older man.
Pleasant, well-cast star musical for the family.

w Bruce Manning   d Edward Ludwig
ph Joseph Valentine   songs Jimmy McHugh,
Harold Adamson

Deanna Durbin, Melvyn Douglas, Jackie
Cooper, Irene Rich, Nancy Carroll, John
Halliday, Juanita Quigley, Jackie Searl,
Charles Coleman

AAN: song 'My Own'

That Certain Feeling
US 1956   102m   Technicolor
   Vistavision
Paramount (Melvin Frank, Norman
   Panama)

An arrogant comic strip artist loses his touch
and hires a 'ghost'—the ex-husband of his
secretary / fiancée.
Arid comedy from a mild Broadway play,
totally miscast and lacking any kind of
interest.

w Norman Panama, Melvin Frank, I. A. L.
Diamond, William Altman, *play* King of
Hearts by Jean Kerr, Eleanor Brooke
d Norman Panama, Melvin Frank   ph Loyal
Griggs   *m Joseph J. Lilley*

Bob Hope, George Sanders, Eva Marie Saint,
Pearl Bailey, Al Capp

That Certain Woman*
US 1937 91m bw
Warner (Hal B. Wallis)

A gangster's widow goes straight but runs into complex marriage trouble.
Self-sacrifice and mother love are rewarded by two convenient deaths and a happy ending in this routine romantic melodrama remade from a silent success.

wd Edmund Goulding, from his original screen play The Trespasser *ph* Ernest Haller *m* Max Steiner

Bette Davis, Henry Fonda, Ian Hunter, Anita Louise, Donald Crisp, Katherine Alexander, Mary Philips, Minor Watson

That Cold Day in the Park
Canada 1969 115m Eastmancolor
(Commonwealth United) Donald Factor / Robert Altman / Leon Mirrell

A spinster invites a lonely wandering boy into her home, makes him a prisoner and becomes possessively jealous.
A companion piece to *The Collector*, rather better done for those who like morbid psychology.

w Gillian Freeman, *novel* Richard Miles *d* Robert Altman *ph* Laszlo Kovacs *m* Johnny Mandel

Sandy Dennis, Michael Burns, Suzanne Benton, Luana Anders, John Garfield Jnr
'About as pretentious, loathsome and stupid as a film can get.'—*John Simon*

That Dangerous Age
GB 1949 98m bw
London Films (Gregory Ratoff)
US title: *If This Be Sin*

Recovering from a breakdown, a KC discovers that his daughter wants to marry a man with whom his wife once had an affair.
Purple patch melodrama which sympathetic actors can't quite freshen up.

w Gene Markey, *play* Autumn by Margaret Kennedy and Ilya Surgutchoff *d* Gregory Ratoff *ph* Georges Périnal *m* Mischa Spoliansky

Roger Livesey, Myrna Loy, Peggy Cummins, Richard Greene, Elizabeth Allan, Gerard Heinz, Jean Cadell, G. H. Mulcaster

That Darn Cat!*
US 1965 116m Technicolor
Walt Disney (Bill Walsh, Ron Miller)

A troublesome cat inadvertently helps to trail bank robbers.

Overlong but generally pleasing small-town comedy with well-paced sequences and a fascinating feline hero.

w The Gordons, Bill Walsh, *novel* Undercover Cat by the Gordons *d* Robert Stevenson *ph* Edward Colman *m* Bob Brunner

Hayley Mills, Dean Jones, Dorothy Provine, Roddy McDowall, Neville Brand, Elsa Lanchester, William Demarest, Frank Gorshin, Grayson Hall, Ed Wynn

That Forsyte Woman*
US 1949 114m Technicolor
MGM (Leon Gordon)
GB title: *The Forsyte Saga*

The wife of an Edwardian man of property falls in love with her niece's fiancé.
Moderately successful American attempt to film the first part of a very British novel sequence; so genteel, however, that it becomes dull.

w Jan Lustig, Ivan Tors, James B. Williams, *novel* A Man of Property by John Galsworthy *d* Compton Bennett *ph* Joseph Ruttenberg *m* Bronislau Kaper

Greer Garson, *Errol Flynn*, Robert Young, Janet Leigh, Walter Pidgeon, Harry Davenport, Aubrey Mather

That Funny Feeling
US 1965 92m Technicolor
U-I (Harry Keller)

A maid pretends she lives in her boss's apartment.
Makeshift romantic comedy which barely takes the attention even while it's on.

w David R. Schwarz *d* Richard Thorpe *ph* Clifford Stine *m* Joseph Gershenson

Sandra Dee, Bobby Darin, Donald O'Connor, Nita Talbot, Larry Storch, Leo G. Carroll, James Westerfield

That Girl from Paris
US 1936 105m bw
RKO (Pandro S. Berman)

A Paris opera singer falls for a swing band leader and stows away on a transatlantic liner to be near him.
Comedy-accented musical romance: not bad but not memorable.

w P. J. Wolfson, Dorothy Yost, Jane Murfin *d* Leigh Jason *ph* J. Roy Hunt *m* Edward Heyman *md* Nathaniel Shilkret

Lily Pons, Gene Raymond, Jack Oakie, Herman Bing, Lucille Ball, Mischa Auer, Frank Jenks

That Hagen Girl
US 1947   83m   bw
Warner (Alex Gottlieb)

A girl is convinced she is the illegitimate
daughter of her teacher.
Stale teenage drama with odd anti-
establishment overtones.

w Charles Hoffman, *novel* Edith Kneipple
Roberts d Peter Godfrey ph Karl Freund
m Franz Waxman

Shirley Temple, Ronald Reagan, Rory
Calhoun, Lois Maxwell, Dorothy Peterson,
Charles Kemper, Conrad Janis, Harry
Davenport

That Hamilton Woman**
US 1941   128m   bw
London Films (Alexander Korda)
GB title: *Lady Hamilton*

The affair of Lord Nelson and Emma
Hamilton.
Bowdlerized version of a famous misalliance;
coldly made but quite effective scene by scene,
with notable performances.

w Walter Reisch, R. C. Sherriff d Alexander
Korda ph Rudolph Maté m Miklos Rozsa

*Laurence Olivier, Vivien Leigh, Gladys
Cooper*, Alan Mowbray, Sara Allgood, Henry
Wilcoxon, Halliwell Hobbes

AAN: Rudolph Maté

That Kind of Woman
US 1959   92m   bw
Paramount / Ponti–Girosi

World War II remake of *Shopworn Angel*
(qv); rather well made but basically dated and
dull.

w Walter Bernstein d Sidney Lumet ph Boris
Kaufman m Daniele Amfitheatrof

Sophia Loren, Tab Hunter, George Sanders,
Jack Warden, Barbara Nicholas, Keenan
Wynn

'The romantic reunion of Tab Hunter and
Sophia Loren resembles nothing so much as a
sea scout given a luxury liner for Christmas.'—
Peter John Dyer

That Lady
GB 1955   100m   Eastmancolor
   Cinemascope
TCF / Atlanta (Sy Bartlett)

A noble widow at the court of Philip II of
Spain loves a minister but incurs the king's
jealous hatred.
Tepid historical romance which never flows as
a film should.

w Anthony Veiller, Sy Bartlett, *novel* Kate
O'Brien d Terence Young ph Robert
Krasker m John Addison

Olivia de Havilland, Gilbert Roland, *Paul
Scofield*, Françoise Rosay, Dennis Price,
Anthony Dawson, Robert Harris, Peter Illing,
Christopher Lee

'Somehow, somewhere, one feels,
something went very wrong.'—*MFB*

That Lady in Ermine
US 1948   89m   Technicolor
TCF (Ernst Lubitsch)

Two generations of European noblewomen
learn to repel invaders.
Cheerless musical comedy which never gets
started, what with the director dying during
production and unsuitable stars lost in tinselly
sets; the result can have appealed to no one.

w Samson Raphaelson d Ernst Lubitsch, Otto
Preminger ph Leon Shamroy *songs* Leo
Robin, Frederick Hollander

Betty Grable, Douglas Fairbanks Jnr, Cesar
Romero, Walter Abel, Reginald Gardiner,
Harry Davenport

AAN: song 'This Seems to be the Moment'
(*m* Frederick Hollander, *ly* Leo Robin)

That Lucky Touch
GB 1975   93m   Technicolor
Rank / Gloria (Dimitri de Grunwald)

During NATO war games in Brussels, a lady
correspondent falls for an arms dealer.
Dim romantic farce which gives the impression
of emanating from a dog-eared script written
for the kind of stars who no longer shine.

w John Briley, *story* Moss Hart d Christopher
Miles ph Douglas Slocombe m John Scott

Roger Moore, Susannah York, Lee J. Cobb,
Shelley Winters, Jean-Pierre Cassel, Raf
Vallone, Sydne Rome, Donald Sinden

That Man Bolt
US 1973   103m   Technicolor
Universal (Bernard Schwarz)

Adventures of a professional black courier
skilled in the martial arts.
Black Kung Fu hokum from a major company;
tolerable of its debased kind.

w Quentin Werty, Charles Johnson d Henry
Levin, David Lowell Rich ph Gerald Perry
Finnerman m Charles Bernstein

Fred Williamson, Bryon Webster, Miko
Mayama, Teresa Graves

'Gives every indication of having been
devised by a computer fed with a variety of
ingredients currently thought to guarantee box
office success.'—*John Raisbeck, MFB*

That Man from Rio

France / Italy 1964 120m Eastmancolor
Ariane / Artistes Associés / Dear Film /
  Vides (Alexander Mnouchkine, Georges
  Danciger)
original title: *L'Homme de Rio*

An airforce pilot finds himself helping his girl
friend in a worldwide search for stolen
statuettes.
Elaborate mock thriller which is never quite as
much fun as those involved seem to think. It
provoked several inferior sequels.

w J. P. Rappeneau, Ariane Mnouchkine,
Daniel Boulanger, Philippe de Broca
d Philippe de Broca *ph* Edmond Séchan
m Georges Delerue

Jean-Paul Belmondo, Jean Servais, Françoise
Dorléac, Adolfo Celi, Simone Renant
  'Fantasy takes over, with Belmondo
outdoing Fairbanks in agility, Lloyd in
cliffhanging, and Bond in indestructibility.'—
Brenda Davies, MFB

AAN: script

That Midnight Kiss

US 1949 98m Technicolor
MGM (Joe Pasternak)

An unknown becomes a great singing star.
Simple-minded vehicle for the first appearance
of Mario Lanza.

w Bruce Manning, Tamara Hovey *d* Norman
Taurog *ph* Robert Surtees *m* Bronislau
Kaper

Kathryn Grayson, Ethel Barrymore, Jose
Iturbi, Mario Lanza, Keenan Wynn, J. Carrol
Naish, Jules Munshin, Thomas Gomez,
Marjorie Reynolds

That Night*

US 1957 88m bw
Galahad (Himan Brown)

An overwhelmed TV writer has a heart attack,
and recovers after a series of medical setbacks.
Impressive minor case history, hardly
entertainment but quite arresting.

w Robert Wallace, Burton J. Rowles *d* John
Newland *ph* Maurice Hartzband *m* Mario
Nascimbene

John Beal, Augusta Dabney, Shepperd
Strudwick, Ralph Murphy

That Night in Rio*

US 1941 90m Technicolor
TCF (Fred Kohlmar)

A nightclub entertainer is paid to impersonate
a lookalike count, but this causes
complications with the countess.

Zippy musical based on a story first used in
Folies Bergère (qv) and later in *On the Riviera*
(qv).

w George Seaton, Bess Meredyth, Hal Long,
play Rudolph Lothar, Hans Adler *d* Irving
Cummings *ph* Leon Shamroy *songs* Mack
Gordon, Harry Warren

Don Ameche, Alice Faye, Carmen Miranda,
S. Z. Sakall, J. Carrol Naish, Curt Bois,
Leonid Kinskey, Maria Montez

That Obscure Object of Desire*

France / Spain 1978 103m Eastmancolor
Greenwich / Galaxie / In Cine (Serge
  Silberman)

A middle-aged gentleman suffers continual
humiliations from the girl he loves.
Unrecognizable remake of a novel previously
filmed as a vehicle for Dietrich and Bardot.
Despite the tricking out with surrealist touches
(the girl is played by two different actresses) it
is not one of Bunuel's best, and amuses only
on the surface.

w Luis Bunuel, Jean-Claude Carrière,
novel La Femme et le Pantin by Pierre Louys
d Luis Bunuel *ph* Edmond Richard *m* from
Richard Wagner

Fernando Rey, Carole Bouquet, Angela
Molina, Julien Bertheau

AAN: script

That Riviera Touch

GB 1966 98m Eastmancolor
Rank (Hugh Stewart)

Two tourists in the south of France get mixed
up with jewel thieves.
Disappointing star comedy ending in a
surfboard chase.

w S. C. Green, R. M. Hills, Peter Blackmore
d Cliff Owen *ph* Otto Heller *m* Ron
Goodwin

Eric Morecambe, Ernie Wise, Suzanne Lloyd,
Paul Stassino, Armand Mestral

That Touch of Mink**

US 1962 99m Eastmancolor
  Panavision
U-I / Granley / Arwin / Nob Hill (Stanley
  Shapiro, Martin Melcher)

Bachelor tycoon pursues virginal secretary.
Jaded sex comedy (or what passed for it in
nudge-nudge 1962) enlivened by practised star
performances and smart timing.

w Stanley Shapiro, Nate Monaster *d* Delbert
Mann *ph* Russell Metty *m* George Duning

Cary Grant, Doris Day, Gig Young, Audrey
Meadows, Dick Sargent, *John Astin*

'Too often there's a hampering second-hand air about situation and joke. Throughout, the determination is to keep faith with the American sex mythology at all costs.'—*Jack Pitman, Variety*

AAN: script

That Uncertain Feeling*
US 1941 84m bw
(UA) Sol Lesser (Ernst Lubitsch)

A wife with insomnia and hiccups befriends a wacky concert pianist who proceeds to move into her home.
Although Lubitsch had made this story before, as the silent *Kiss Me Again*, the elements didn't really jell in this version, which seemed silly rather than funny.

w Donald Ogden Stewart, Walter Reisch, *play* Divorçons by Victorien Sardou, Emile de Najac *d Ernst Lubitsch ph* George Barnes *m* Werner Heymann *pd* Alexander Golitzen

Merle Oberon, Melvyn Douglas, Burgess Meredith, Alan Mowbray, Olive Blakeney, Harry Davenport, Eve Arden, Sig Rumann

AAN: Werner Heymann

That Way With Women
US 1947 84m bw
Warner (Charles Hoffman)

A millionaire amuses himself by playing Cupid to a young couple.
Routine remake of *The Millionaire*: just about watchable.

w Leo Townsend *d* Frederick de Cordova *ph* Ted McCord *m* Frederick Hollander

Sidney Greenstreet, Dane Clark, Martha Vickers, Alan Hale, Craig Stevens, Barbara Brown

That Woman Opposite
GB 1957 83m bw
Monarch (William Gell)
US title: *City after Midnight*

In a small French town, a killer returns to silence a witness.
Slow-paced semi-mystery, reasonably well done.

wd Compton Bennett, *story* The Emperor's Snuff Box by John Dickson Carr *ph* Lionel Banes *m* Stanley Black

Phyllis Kirk, Dan O'Herlihy, Wilfrid Hyde White, Petula Clark, Jack Watling, William Franklyn, Margaret Withers

That Wonderful Urge
US 1948 82m bw
TCF (Fred Kohlmar)

A newspaperman is forced into marriage with a publicity-shy heiress.
Tepid romantic comedy, a remake of *Love Is News* (qv).

w Jay Dratler *d* Robert B. Sinclair *ph* Charles Clarke *m* Cyril Mockridge

Gene Tierney, Tyrone Power, Reginald Gardiner, Arleen Whelan, Lucile Watson, Gene Lockhart, Porter Hall, Taylor Holmes

That'll Be the Day*
GB 1973 91m Technicolor
EMI / Goodtimes (David Puttnam, Sanford Lieberson)

In 1958, a young drifter becomes a fairground worker, and eventually walks out on his wife and family to become a pop star.
Spirited return to British realism, with well-sketched cameos, a likeable dour viewpoint, and a cheerful pop music background.

w Ray Connolly *d* Claude Whatham *ph* Peter Suschitsky *md* Neil Aspinall, Keith Moon

David Essex, Ringo Starr, Rosemary Leach, James Booth, Billy Fury, Keith Moon, Rosalind Ayres
'As insubstantial as one of its own attempts at a statement.'—*Tony Rayns*

That's a Good Girl*
GB 1933 83m bw

A man about town seeks ways of making money. Archetypal vehicle for a debonair song and dance man. *Jack Buchanan,* Elsie Randolph, Dorothy Hyson, Garry Marsh, Vera Pearce, William Kendall. Written by Douglas Furber, Donovan Pedelty and Jack Buchanan; directed by Jack Buchanan; for Herbert Wilcox.

That's Entertainment**
US 1974 137m Metrocolor 70mm (blown up) / scope
MGM (Daniel Melnick, Jack Haley Jnr)

Fred Astaire, Gene Kelly, Elizabeth Taylor, James Stewart, Bing Crosby, Liza Minnelli, Donald O'Connor, Debbie Reynolds, Mickey Rooney and Frank Sinatra introduce highlights from MGM's musical past.
A slapdash compilation which was generally very big at the box office and obviously has fascinating sequences, though the narration is sloppily sentimental and the later wide-screen sequences let down the rest.

wd Jack Haley Jnr *ph* various *m* various

principal stars as above plus Judy Garland, Esther Williams, Eleanor Powell, Clark Gable, Ray Bolger

'While many ponder the future of MGM, none can deny that it has one hell of a past.'—*Variety*

'It is particularly gratifying to get the key sequences from certain movies without having to sit through a fatuous storyline.'—*Michael Billington, Illustrated London News*

That's Entertainment Part Two**
US 1976 133m Metrocolor 70mm
(blown up) / scope
MGM (Saul Chaplin, Daniel Melnick)

More of the above, introduced by Fred Astaire and Gene Kelly, with comedy and drama sequences as well as musical.

d Gene Kelly *titles* Saul Bass *ph* various

principal stars as above plus Jeanette MacDonald, Nelson Eddy, the Marx Brothers, Laurel and Hardy, Jack Buchanan, Judy Garland, Ann Miller, Mickey Rooney, Oscar Levant, Louis Armstrong, etc.

That's My Boy
US 1951 98m bw
Paramount / Hal B. Wallis (Cy Howard)

An athletic father tries to press his hypochondriac teenage son into the same mould.
American college comedy of no international interest.

w Cy Howard *d* Hal Walker *ph* Lee Garmes *m* Leigh Harline

Dean Martin, Jerry Lewis, Eddie Mayehoff, Ruth Hussey, Polly Bergen, John McIntire

That's My Wife*
US 1929 20m bw silent

Stan dresses up as Ollie's wife to impress his rich uncle. Lesser-known star comedy which well sustains its basic joke and includes some splendidly timed farce in a restaurant. Laurel and Hardy, Vivien Oakland, William Courtright. Written by Leo McCarey and H. M. Walker; directed by Lloyd French; for Hal Roach.

That's Right, You're Wrong*
US 1939 91m bw
RKO (David Butler)

A band leader gets a Hollywood contract but is hated by the studio head.
Typical of the nonsense musicals featuring Kay Kyser and his radio Kollege of Musical Knowledge. The movie background and self-spoofing made this first attempt one of the best.

w William Conselman, James V. Kern *d* David Butler *ph* Russell Metty *m* George Duning *songs* various

Kay Kyser, Adolphe Menjou, Lucille Ball, Dennis O'Keefe, May Robson, Edward Everett Horton, Ish Kabibble, Ginny Simms, Roscoe Karns, Moroni Olsen, Hobart Cavanaugh, Sheilah Graham, Hedda Hopper

That's the Spirit
US 1943 87m bw

A ghost comes back to tell his actress wife he didn't desert her as she thought. Rather heavy comedy of the *Here Comes Mr Jordan* school. Jack Oakie, Peggy Ryan, June Vincent, Gene Lockhart, Andy Devine, Arthur Treacher, Irene Ryan, Buster Keaton. Written by Michael Fessier and Ernest Pagano; directed by Charles Lamont; for Universal.

Theatre of Blood*
GB 1973 102m De Luxe
UA / Cineman (John Kohn, Stanley Mann)

A Shakespearean actor uses appropriate murder methods on the various critics who have ridiculed his performances.
Spoof horror picture which goes too far with some sick visuals; the idea and some of the performances are fine.

w Anthony Greville-Bell *d* Douglas Hickox *ph* Wolfgang Suschitzky *m* Michael J. Lewis *pd* Michael Seymour

Vincent Price, Diana Rigg, Ian Hendry, Harry Andrews, Coral Browne, Robert Coote, Jack Hawkins, Michael Hordern, Arthur Lowe, Robert Morley, Dennis Price, Diana Dors, Joan Hickson, Renée Asherson, Milo O'Shea, Eric Sykes

Theatre Royal
GB 1943 92m bw

A revue and a theatre are saved by a sentimental prop man. Shapeless star comedy with music; not their best. Bud Flanagan and Chesney Allen, Peggy Dexter, Lydia Sherwood, Horace Kenney, Marjorie Rhodes, Finlay Currie. Written by Bud Flanagan, Austin Melford and Geoffrey Orme; directed by John Baxter; for British National.

Their First Mistake**
US 1932 20m bw

Ollie decides to improve his marriage by adopting a baby, only to find that his wife has left him. Sublimely silly but endearing star comedy with brilliant passages of imbecilic conversation followed by well-timed farce. Laurel and Hardy, Mae Busch. Written by H. M. Walker; directed by George Marshall (who also plays a bit); for Hal Roach.

Their Purple Moment
US 1928   20m   bw   silent

Stan and Ollie go out on the town, only to discover that Stan's wife has replaced his money with grocery coupons. Minor star comedy with efficient but predictable restaurant scenes ending in a pie fight. Laurel and Hardy, Anita Garvin, Kay Deslys. Written by H. M. Walker; directed by James Parrott; for Hal Roach.

Them!•••
US 1954   94m   bw
Warner (David Weisbart)

Atomic bomb radiation causes giant ants to breed in the New Mexico desert.
Among the first, and certainly the best, of the post-atomic monster animal cycle, this durable thriller starts with several eerie desert sequences and builds up to a shattering climax in the Los Angeles sewers. A general air of understatement helps a lot.

w Ted Sherdeman, *story* George Worthing Yates   d Gordon Douglas   ph Sid Hickox   m Bronislau Kaper

Edmund Gwenn, James Whitmore, Joan Weldon, James Arness, Onslow Stevens

'I asked the editor: How does it look? And he said: Fine. I said: Does it look honest? He said: As honest as twelve foot ants can look.'—*Gordon Douglas*

Them Thar Hills••
US 1934   20m   bw

Stan and Ollie go camping, drink from a well full of moonshine whisky, and get drunk with another camper's wife. Consistently funny star comedy culminating in a tit-for-tat routine which was reprised in *Tit for Tat* the following year. Laurel and Hardy, Charlie Hall, Mae Busch, Billy Gilbert. Written by Stan Laurel and H. M. Walker; directed by Charles Rogers; for Hal Roach.

Theodora Goes Wild•
US 1936   94m   bw
Columbia (Everett Riskin)

A small-town girl writes a titillating bestseller. Mildly crazy comedy which helped develop the trend for stars performing undignified antics but today seems rather slow and dated.

w *Sidney Buchman*, *story* Mary McCarthy   d Richard Boleslawski   ph Joseph Walker   m Morris Stoloff

Irene Dunne, Melvyn Douglas, Thomas Mitchell, Thurston Hall, Rosalind Keith, Spring Byington, Elizabeth Risdon, Nana Bryant

AAN: Irene Dunne

There Ain't No Justice
GB 1939   83m   bw

A young boxer refuses to throw a fight. Minor sporting drama, well praised at the time but later forgotten. Jimmy Hanley, Edward Rigby, Mary Clare, Edward Chapman, Phyllis Stanley, Michael Wilding. Written by Pen Tennyson, James Curtis and Sergei Nolbandov; directed by Pen Tennyson; for Ealing.

There Goes My Heart
US 1938   91m   bw
Hal Roach

A reporter is assigned to track down a runaway heiress.
Very pale imitation of *It Happened One Night*.

w Jack Jevne, Eddie Moran   d Norman Z. McLeod   ph Norbert Brodine   m Marvin Hatley

Fredric March, Virginia Bruce, Patsy Kelly, Nancy Carroll, Eugene Pallette, Claude Gillingwater, Arthur Lake, Harry Langdon, Etienne Girardot

AAN: Marvin Hatley

There Goes the Bride
GB 1980   91m   Eastmancolor
Lonsdale (Martin Schute, Ray Cooney)

A harassed advertising executive suffers hallucinations about a lifesize cardboard cut-out of a twenties flapper.
Embarrassingly witless and plotless revamp of innumerable better comedies in the *Topper* tradition; it has to be seen to be believed.

w Terence Marcel, Ray Cooney *play* Ray Cooney and John Chapman   d Terence Marcel   ph James Devis   m Harry Robinson   pd Peter Mullins

Tom Smothers, Twiggy, Sylvia Syms, Martin Balsam, Michael Whitney, Geoffrey Sumner, Hermione Baddeley, Phil Silvers, Broderick Crawford, Jim Backus

'The whole thing would be laughable if it weren't so unfunny.'—*Gilbert Adair, MFB*

There Is Another Sun
GB 1951   95m   bw

A fairground wall of death rider turns to crime. Glum quickie which was oddly popular. Maxwell Reed, Susan Shaw, Laurence Harvey, Hermione Baddeley, Leslie Dwyer. Written by Guy Morgan; directed by Lewis Gilbert; for Butcher's.

There Was a Crooked Man*
GB 1960   107m   bw
UA / Knightsbridge (John Bryan)

An ex-safecracker outwits the crooked mayor of an industrial town.
Semi-happy attempt to humanize a knockabout clown; good supporting performances and production.

w Reuben Ship d Stuart Burge ph Arthur Ibbetson m Kenneth V. Jones

Norman Wisdom, Andrew Cruickshank, Alfred Marks, Susannah York, Reginald Beckwith

There Was a Crooked Man*
US 1970   126m   Technicolor
  Panavision
Warner Seven Arts (Joseph L. Mankiewicz)

In 1883 Arizona a murderer tries to escape from jail and recover hidden loot but is constantly thwarted by the sheriff who arrested him, now a warden.
Curious black comedy melodrama with lots of talent going nowhere in particular; hard to endure as a whole but with entertaining scenes.

w David Newman, Robert Benton d Joseph L. Mankiewicz ph Harry Stradling Jnr m Charles Strouse ad Edward Carrere

Kirk Douglas, Henry Fonda, Hume Cronyn, Warren Oates, Burgess Meredith, John Randolph, Arthur O'Connell, Martin Gabel, Alan Hale

There's a Girl in My Soup*
GB 1970   96m   Eastmancolor
Columbia / Ascot (John Boulting)

A randy TV personality finds himself outplotted by a waif he picks up.
Flimsy screen version of a long-running sex comedy; some laughs, but the star is uncomfortably miscast.

w Terence Frisby, from his play d Roy Boulting ph Harry Waxman m Mike D'Abo

Peter Sellers, Goldie Hawn, Tony Britton, Nicky Henson, John Comer, Diana Dors, Judy Campbell

There's Always Tomorrow
US 1956   84m   bw
Universal (Ross Hunter)

A married man falls for another woman. Very flat variation on *Brief Encounter*, with stars going through mechanical paces.

w Bernard Schoenfeld, *story* Ursula Parrott d Douglas Sirk ph Russell Metty m Herman Stein, Heinz Roemheld

Barbara Stanwyck, Fred MacMurray, Joan Bennett, Pat Crowley, William Reynolds, Gigi Perreau, Jane Darwell

† Previously made by Universal in 1934 with Frank Morgan and Binnie Barnes.

There's Magic in Music
US 1941   80m   bw

An ex-burlesque girl gets her break entertaining at a summer camp. Fair exhibition ground for young musical talent.
Allan Jones, Susanna Foster, Diana Lynn, Margaret Lindsay, Lynne Overman, Grace Bradley, William Collier Snr. Written and directed by Andrew L. Stone; for Paramount.

There's No Business like Show Business**
US 1954   117m   De Luxe   Cinemascope
TCF (Sol C. Siegel)

The life and times of a family of vaudevillians.
Mainly entertaining events and marvellous tunes make up this very Cinemascoped musical, in which the screen is usually filled with six people side by side.

w Phoebe and Henry Ephron d Walter Lang ph Leon Shamroy m / ly Irving Berlin ad John de Cuir, Lyle Wheeler m Lionel Newman, Alfred Newman

Ethel Merman, Dan Dailey, Marilyn Monroe, Donald O'Connor, Johnny Ray, Mitzi Gaynor, Hugh O'Brian, Frank McHugh

AAN: original story (Lamar Trotti); Lionel Newman, Alfred Newman

There's That Woman Again
US 1938   75m   bw

A district attorney is hampered by his meddlesome spouse. Half-hearted follow-up to *There's Always a Woman*; the *McMillan and Wife* of its day. Melvyn Douglas, Virginia Bruce, Margaret Lindsay, Stanley Ridges, Gordon Oliver, Tom Dugan, Don Beddoe. Written by Philip G. Epstein, James Edward Grant and Ken Englund; directed by Alexander Hall; for Columbia.

These Dangerous Years
GB 1957   92m   bw
British Lion / Anna Neagle
US title: *Dangerous Youth*

A Liverpool teenage gang leader is called up
and becomes a better guy.
Dim drama with music marking the debut of a
singing star.

w John Trevor Story d Herbert Wilcox
ph Gordon Dines m Stanley Black

Frankie Vaughan, George Baker, Carole
Lesley, Jackie Lane, Katherine Kath, Eddie
Byrne, Kenneth Cope

These Thousand Hills
US 1958 96m Eastmancolor
    Cinemascope
TCF (David Weisbart)

A successful cattle rancher finds that his best
friend is a rustler.
Large-scale but somehow unimpressive
western variant on *The Virginian*, cluttered
with sub-plots.

w Alfred Hayes, *novel* A. B. Guthrie Jnr
d Richard Fleischer ph Charles G. Clarke
m Leigh Harline

Richard Egan, Stuart Whitman, Don Murray,
Lee Remick, Albert Dekker, Harold J. Stone,
Patricia Owens

These Three**
US 1936 93m bw
Samuel Goldwyn

A lying schoolgirl accuses two
schoolmistresses of scandalous behaviour.
Bowdlerized version of a famous play (instead
of lesbianism we have extra-marital affairs). It
worked well enough at the time but now seems
dated; oddly enough when the play was filmed
full strength in 1962 it didn't work at all.

w Lillian Hellman, from her play *The
Children's Hour* d William Wyler ph Gregg
Toland m Alfred Newman

Merle Oberon, Miriam Hopkins, Joel
McCrea, *Bonita Granville*, Catherine Doucet,
Alma Kruger, Marcia Mae Jones, Margaret
Hamilton, Walter Brennan

AAN: Bonita Granville

These Wilder Years
US 1956 91m bw
MGM (Jules Schermer)

A wealthy industrialist returns to his home
town to trace his illegitimate son.
Modest sentimental drama with practised
stars.

w Frank Fenton d Roy Rowland ph George
Folsey m Jeff Alexander

James Cagney, Barbara Stanwyck, Walter
Pidgeon, Betty Lou Keim, Don Dubbins,
Edward Andrews

They All Kissed the Bride
US 1942 86m bw
Columbia (Edward Kaufman)

A woman executive falls in love with the
crusading writer who is out to expose working
conditions in her company.
No surprises are expected or provided in this
very ho-hum romantic comedy.

w P. J. Wolfson d Alexander Hall ph Joseph
Walker m Werner Heyman md Morris
Stoloff

Joan Crawford, Melvyn Douglas, Roland
Young, Billie Burke, Allen Jenkins, Andrew
Tombes, Helen Parrish, Mary Treen

AAN: Joan Crawford

They Call Me Mister Tibbs!
US 1970 108m De Luxe
UA / Mirisch (Herbert Hirshman)

A San Francisco police lieutenant suspects a
crusading local minister of murder.
Flat, dispirited police melodrama with
irrelevant domestic asides, a long way after *In
the Heat of the Night* which introduced the
main character. (*The Organization* was the
third and last in the so-called series.)

w Alan R. Trustman, James R. Webb
d Gordon Douglas ph Gerald Finnerman
m Quincy Jones

Sidney Poitier, Martin Landau, Barbara
McNair, Anthony Zerbe, Jeff Corey, Juano
Hernandez, Ed Asner

They Came by Night
GB 1939 72m bw

A jeweller pretends to be a crook in order to
lure the men who killed his brother. Smart
little suspense yarn. Will Fyffe, Phyllis
Calvert, Anthony Hulme, George Merritt,
Athole Stewart, John Glyn Jones. Written by
Frank Launder, Sidney Gilliatt, Michael
Hogan and Roland Pertwee; directed by Harry
Lachman; for TCF.

They Came to a City*
GB 1944 77m bw
Ealing (Sidney Cole)

Assorted people find themselves outside the
gates of a mysterious city.
The *Outward Bound* format applied to post-
war reconstruction, with characters deciding
what kind of a world they want. Good talk
and good acting, but not quite cinema.

w Basil Dearden, Sidney Cole, *play* J. B.
Priestley d Basil Dearden

Googie Withers, John Clements, Raymond Huntley, Renée Gadd, A. E. Matthews, Mabel Terry-Lewis, *Ada Reeve*, Norman Shelley, Frances Rowe

They Came to Blow Up America
US 1973 73m bw

An FBI man of German parentage goes to Nazi Germany and trains with a group of saboteurs, who are arrested when they set foot in the US. Tolerable propaganda potboiler.

George Sanders, Anna Sten, Ward Bond, Dennis Hoey, Sig Rumann, Ludwig Stossel. Written by Aubrey Wisberg; directed by Edward Ludwig; for TCF.

They Came to Cordura*
US 1959 123m Technicolor
  Cinemascope
Columbia / Goetz–Baroda (William Goetz)

In 1916 Mexico, six American military heroes are recalled to base, but the hardships of the journey reveal their true colours.
Watchable adventure epic, not so arresting as was intended but quite professional.

w Ivan Moffat, Robert Rossen, *novel* Glendon Swarthout *d* Robert Rossen *ph* Burnett Guffey *m* Elie Siegmeister

Gary Cooper, Rita Hayworth, Van Heflin, Richard Conte, Tab Hunter, Michael Callan, Dick York, Robert Keith

They Came to Rob Las Vegas*
Spain / France / Germany / Italy 1969
  128m Techniscope
Warner / Isasi / Capitoli / Eichberg / Franca

Criminals ambush a security truck in the Nevada desert.
Long-winded, flashily directed, gleamingly photographed, occasionally lively, frequently violent, finally tedious caper melodrama with a multi-lingual cast.

w Anthony Isasi, Jo Eisinger *d* Anthony Isasi *ph Juan Gelpi m* Georges Gavarentz

Jack Palance, Lee J. Cobb, Elke Sommer, Gary Lockwood, Georges Geret, Jean Servais

They Dare Not Love
US 1941 76m bw
Columbia (Sam Bischoff)

An Austrian prince flees the Nazis, but they force him to return and he has to leave his fiancée in America.
Curiously naïve romantic propaganda from this director; not at all memorable.

w Charles Bennett, Ernest Vajda *d* James Whale *ph* Franz Planer *m* Morris Stoloff

George Brent, Martha Scott, Paul Lukas, Egon Brecher, Roman Bohnen, Edgar Barrier, Frank Reicher

They Died with Their Boots On**
US 1941 140m bw
Warner (Robert Fellows)

The life of General Custer and his death at Little Big Horn.
It seems it all happened because of an evil cadet who finished up selling guns to the Indians. Oh, well! The first half is romantic comedy, the second steels itself for the inevitable tragic outcome, but it's all expertly mounted and played in the best old Hollywood style.

w Wally Kline, Aeneas Mackenzie *d Raoul Walsh ph Bert Glennon m* Max Steiner

Errol Flynn, Olivia de Havilland, Arthur Kennedy, Charles Grapewin, Anthony Quinn, Sidney Greenstreet, Gene Lockhart, Stanley Ridges, John Litel, Walter Hampden, Regis Toomey, Hattie McDaniel

They Drive by Night**
GB 1938 84m bw
Warner (Jerome Jackson)

An ex-convict is helped by lorry drivers to solve the silk stocking murders of which he is suspected.
Excellent, little-seen British suspenser of the Hitchcock school.

w Derek Twist, novel James Curtis *d* Arthur Woods *ph* Basil Emmott

Emlyn Williams, Ernest Thesiger, Anna Konstam, Allan Jeayes, Antony Holles, Ronald Shiner
  'Dialogue, acting and direction put this picture on a level with the French cinema.'— *Graham Greene*

They Drive by Night**
US 1940 97m bw
Warner (Mark Hellinger)
GB title: *The Road to Frisco*

A truck driver loses his brother in an accident, and in an attempt to improve his lot becomes involved with a scheming murderess.
Solid melodramatic entertainment which borrows the second half of its plot from *Bordertown*.

w Jerry Wald, Richard Macaulay, *novel* Long Haul by A. I. Bezzerides *d Raoul Walsh ph* Arthur Edeson *md* Adolph Deutsch

George Raft, Humphrey Bogart, *Ann Sheridan, Ida Lupino*, Gale Page, Alan Hale, Roscoe Karns, John Litel, Henry O'Neill, George Tobias

They Flew Alone*
GB 1941 103m bw
RKO / Imperator (Herbert Wilcox)
US title: *Wings and the Woman*

The story of Amy Johnson and Jim Mollison,
married flying pioneers of the thirties.
Adequate fictionalized history with interesting
historical detail.

w Miles Malleson *d* Herbert Wilcox

Anna Neagle, Robert Newton, Edward
Chapman, Nora Swinburne, Joan Kemp-
Welch, Charles Carson, Brefni O'Rourke

They Gave Him a Gun
US 1937 94m bw
MGM (Harry Rapf)

Despite the efforts of his friend, a war-
hardened veteran turns to crime and comes to
a sticky end.
Dullish moral melodrama with its stars looking
as though stuck in glue.

w Cyril Hume, Richard Maibaum, Maurice
Rapf, *novel* William Joyce Cowan
d W. S. Van Dyke II *ph* Harold Rosson

Spencer Tracy, Franchot Tone, Gladys
George, Edgar Dearing, Mary Treen, Cliff
Edwards

They Go Boom
US 1929 20m bw

Stan's nocturnal efforts to cure Ollie's cold
nearly bring down the house about their ears.
Average, rather protracted star comedy.
Laurel and Hardy, Charlie Hall. Written by
Leo McCarey and H. M. Walker; directed by
James Parrott; for Hal Roach.

They Got Me Covered*
US 1943 93m bw
Samuel Goldwyn

An incompetent foreign correspondent
inadvertently breaks up a spy ring in
Washington.
One of Hope's better and most typical
comedy-thriller vehicles.

w Harry Kurnitz *d* David Butler *ph* Rudolph
Maté *m* Leigh Harline

Bob Hope, Dorothy Lamour, Otto Preminger,
Lenore Aubert, Eduardo Ciannelli, Marion
Martin, Donald Meek, Donald MacBride,
Walter Catlett, John Abbott, Florence Bates,
Philip Ahn

They Knew Mr Knight
GB 1945 93m bw

A clerk and his family become rich, then poor,

through listening to a speculator. Slightly
oddball domestic drama reminiscent of
Priestley's *Angel Pavement*. Mervyn Johns,
Alfred Drayton, Nora Swinburne, Joyce
Howard, Joan Greenwood, Olive Sloane,
Peter Hammond. Written by Norman Walker
and Victor MacClure, from the novel by
Dorothy Whipple; directed by Norman
Walker; for IP / GHW.

They Knew What They Wanted**
US 1940 96m bw
RKO (Erich Pommer)

A waitress agrees by mail to marry a
California-Italian vineyard owner, but is
aghast when she arrives to discover that he
sent his handsome foreman's photograph.
First-rate minor drama, expertly handled by
stars and production team alike.

w Robert Ardrey, *play* Sidney Howard
d Garson Kanin *ph* Harry Stradling
m Alfred Newman

*Charles Laughton, Carole Lombard, William
Gargan*, Harry Carey, Frank Fay
† Previous versions include *The Secret Love*
(1928) with Pola Negri and *A Lady to Love*
(1930) with Vilma Banky (and Edward G.
Robinson).
   'For dialogue, acting, background and film
creation it's a honey.'—*Otis Ferguson*

AAN: William Gargan

They Live by Night*
US 1948 96m bw
RKO

A young man imprisoned for an accidental
killing escapes with two hardened criminals
and is forced to take part in their crimes.
Well-made if basically uninteresting
melodrama with a draggy romantic interest; its
'fealistic' yet impressionist style drew attention
on its first release, and it was remade in the
seventies as *Thieves like Us* (qv).

w Charles Schnee *d* Nicholas Ray *ph* George
E. Diskant *m* Leigh Harline

Farley Granger, Cathy O'Donnell, Howard da
Silva

They Made Me a Criminal*
US 1939 92m bw
Warner (Benjamin Glazer)

When he thinks he has killed a boxing
opponent, a young man flees to the west and
settles on a farm.
Competent remake of *The Life of Jimmy
Dolan*, a tribute to the American way.

w Sig Herzig d Busby Berkeley ph James
Wong Howe m Max Steiner

John Garfield, Claude Rains, Gloria Dickson,
May Robson, Billy Halop, Bobby Jordan, Leo
Gorcey, Huntz Hall, Gabriel Dell, Ann
Sheridan

They Made Me a Fugitive*
GB 1947   104m   bw
Warner / Alliance (Nat Bransten, James
   Carter)
US title: *I Became a Criminal*

An ex-RAF pilot is drawn into black
marketeering. Framed for a killing, he escapes
from Dartmoor and takes revenge on the gang
leader.
Deliberately squalid thriller which began a
fashion for British realism, but now seems
only momentarily entertaining.

w Noel Langley, *novel* A Convict Has
Escaped by Jackson Budd d Alberto
Cavalcanti ph Otto Heller

Trevor Howard, Sally Gray, *Griffith Jones*,
René Ray, Mary Merrall, Vida Hope, Ballard
Berkeley, Phyllis Robins

They Met in Bombay*
US 1941   86m   bw
MGM (Hunt Stromberg)

Jewel thieves on the run in the East fall in
love.
A rather unusual romantic comedy chase
which provides pretty satisfactory star
entertainment.

w Edwin Justus Mayer, Anita Loos, Leon
Gordon d Clarence Brown ph William
Daniels m Herbert Stothart

Clark Gable, Rosalind Russell, Peter Lorre,
Reginald Owen, Jessie Ralph, Matthew
Boulton, Eduardo Ciannelli, Luis Alberni

They Met in the Dark
GB 1943   104m   bw

A Blackpool theatrical agent is really a master
spy. Elementary spy romance with a richly
villainous performance from *Tom Walls*. Joyce
Howard, James Mason, Phyllis Stanley,
Edward Rigby, Ronald Ward, David Farrar.
Written by Anatole de Grunwald, Miles
Malleson, Basil Bartlett, Victor MacClure and
James Seymour, from the novel *The Vanishing
Corpse* by Anthony Gilbert; directed by Karel
Lamac; for Marcel Hellman / Rank.

They Might be Giants*
US 1972   88m   Technicolor
Universal / Paul Newman, John Foreman

A lawyer imagines he is Sherlock Holmes, and
is taken in hand by Dr Mildred Watson.
Curious fantasy comedy which rather
tentatively satirizes modern life and the need
to retreat into unreality. Mildly pleasing
entertainment for intellectuals.

w James Goldman, from his play d Anthony
Harvey ph Victor Kemper m John Barry

George C. Scott, Joanne Woodward, Jack
Gilford, Lester Rawlins

They Only Kill Their Masters*
US 1972   98m   Metrocolor
MGM (William Belasco)

A village police chief doggedly solves a series
of murders.
Atmospheric, serio-comic murder mystery
with a cast of old hands.

w Lane Slate d James Goldstone ph Michel
Hugo m Perry Botkin Jnr

James Garner, Katharine Ross, Hal
Holbrook, June Allyson, Harry Guardino,
Tom Ewell, Peter Lawford, Ann Rutherford,
Chris Connelly, Edmond O'Brien, Art
Metrano, Arthur O'Connell

They Rode West
US 1954   84m   Technicolor

A cavalry doctor at a frontier fort gets into
trouble by trying to help the Indians. Western
programmer whose sights are higher than its
achievement. Robert Francis, Donna Reed,
May Wynn, Phil Carey, Onslow Stevens, Jack
Kelly. Written by De Vallon Scott and Frank
Nugent; directed by Phil Karlson; for
Columbia.

They Shall Have Music
US 1939   105m   bw
Samuel Goldwyn
GB title: *Melody of Youth*

Jascha Heifetz conducts a charity concert to
help a music school for slum children.
Formula family film given the best possible
production.

w John Howard Lawson, Irmgard Von Cube
d Archie Mayo ph Gregg Toland md Alfred
Newman

Joel McCrea, Jascha Heifetz, Andrea Leeds,
Gene Reynolds, Walter Brennan, Porter Hall,
Terry Kilburn, Diana Lynn (Dolly Loehr)

AAN: Alfred Newman

They Shoot Horses, Don't They?*
US 1969   129m   De Luxe   Panavision
Palomar / Chartoff–Winkler–Pollack

Tragedy during a six-day marathon dance contest in the early thirties.
An unrelievedly harrowing melodrama about dreary people, confused by 'flashforwards' but full of skilled technique, entertaining detail, and one brilliant performance.

w James Poe, Robert E. Thompson, *novel* Horace McCoy d *Sydney Pollack* ph *Philip Lathrop* m John Green md John Green, Albert Woodbury pd Harry Horner

Gig Young, Jane Fonda, Susannah York, Michael Sarrazin, Red Buttons, Bonnie Bedelia, Bruce Dern

AA: Gig Young
AAN: script; John Green, Albert Woodbury; Sydney Pollack; Jane Fonda; Susannah York

They Were Expendable*
US 1945   135m   bw
MGM (John Ford, Cliff Reid)

Life in and around motor torpedo boats in the Pacific War.
Long drawn out flagwaver with some nice moments.

w Frank Wead, *book* William L. White d John Ford ph Joseph H. August m Herbert Stothart

John Wayne, Robert Montgomery, Donna Reed, Jack Holt, Ward Bond, Marshall Thompson, Leon Ames, Cameron Mitchell, Jeff York

   'For what seems at least half its dogged, devoted length all you have to watch is men getting on or off PT boats and other men watching them do so. But this is made so beautiful and so real that I could not feel one foot of the film was wasted.'—*James Agee*

They Were Not Divided*
GB 1951   102m   bw
Rank / Two Cities (Earl St John)

The life of a Guards officer is paralleled with that of his American friend; they both die on a reconnaissance during the advance on Berlin.
Odd mixture of barrack room comedy, semi-documentary action, propaganda and the most appalling sentimentality. No one questioned it at the box office, though.

wd Terence Young ph Harry Waxman m Lambert Williamson

Edward Underdown, Ralph Clanton, Helen Cherry, Stella Andrews, Michael Brennan, Michael Trubshaw, R.S.M. Brittain

   'It is a rather curious experience to see a film made with all the best trappings of realism containing so many of the clichés of the studio.'—*Gavin Lambert*

They Were Sisters
GB 1945   115m   bw
GFD / Gainsborough (Harold Huth)

The problems of three married sisters.
Flatly handled multi-melodrama, the chief attraction being 'wicked' James Mason as a sadist.

w Roland Pertwee, *novel* Dorothy Whipple d Arthur Crabtree ph Jack Cox m Louis Levy

James Mason, Phyllis Calvert, Dulcie Gray, Hugh Sinclair, Anne Crawford, Peter Murray Hill, Pamela Kellino

They Who Dare
GB 1953   107m   Technicolor
British Lion / Mayflower

During World War II a group of British soldiers are sent on a raiding expedition to Rhodes.
Grimmish war actioner with plenty of noise but not much holding power.

w Robert Westerby d Lewis Milestone ph Wilkie Cooper m Robert Gill

Dirk Bogarde, Denholm Elliott, Akim Tamiroff, Gérard Oury, Eric Pohlmann, Alec Mango

They Won't Believe Me*
US 1947   95m   bw
RKO (Joan Harrison)

A playboy finds himself on trial for murder because of his philandering with three women.
Unusual suspenser with Hitchcock touches; quite neatly packaged, complete with twist ending.

w Jonathan Latimer d Irving Pichel ph Harry J. Wild m Roy Webb

Robert Young, Susan Hayward, Rita Johnson, Jane Greer, Tom Powers, Don Beddoe, Frank Ferguson

They Won't Forget***
US 1937   94m   bw
Warner (Mervyn Le Roy)

The murder of a girl in a southern town leads to a lynching.
Finely detailed social drama, a classic of American realism; harrowing to watch.

w *Robert Rossen, Aben Kandel, novel* Death in the Deep South by Ward Greene d *Mervyn Le Roy* ph Arthur Edeson, Warren Lynch m Adolph Deutsch md Leo F. Forbstein

Claude Rains, Gloria Dickson, Edward Norris, Otto Kruger, Allyn Joslyn, Linda Perry, Elisha Cook Jnr, Lana Turner, Cy Kendall, Elizabeth Risdon

'Not only an honest picture, but an example of real movie-making.'—*Pare Lorenz*

Thicker than Water
US 1924 20m bw silent

Ollie spends his savings on a grandfather clock which is promptly destroyed by a passing truck. Well made but slightly tiresome star comedy, the last short ever made featuring Stan and Ollie. Laurel and Hardy, Daphne Pollard, James Finlayson. Written by Stan Laurel; directed by James W. Horne; for Hal Roach.

The Thief°
US 1952 86m bw
Harry M. Popkin (Clarence Greene)

A nuclear physicist is on the run from the FBI, who suspect him of being a spy.
Curious attempt to produce a thriller with no dialogue whatever; parts are well done, but the strain eventually shows, as the makers are not quite clever enough to flesh out the trickery with human interest.

w Clarence Greene, Russel Rouse *d* Russel Rouse *ph* Sam Leavitt *m* Herschel Gilbert

Ray Milland, Martin Gabel, Rita Gam, Harry Bronson, John McKutcheon

AAN: Herschel Gilbert

The Thief of Baghdad°°°°
GB 1940 109m Technicolor
London Films (Alexander Korda)

A boy thief helps a deposed king thwart an evil usurper.
Marvellous blend of magic, action and music, the only film to catch on celluloid the overpowering atmosphere of the Arabian Nights.

w Miles Malleson, Lajos Biro *d* Michael Powell, Ludwig Berger, Tim Whelan *ph* Georges Périnal, Osmond Borradaile *m* Miklos Rozsa *sp* Lawrence Butler

Conrad Veidt, Sabu, John Justin, June Duprez, Morton Selten, Miles Malleson, *Rex Ingram*, Mary Morris
'The true stuff of fairy tale.'—*Basil Wright*
'Both spectacular and highly inventive.'—*NFT, 1969*
'Magical, highly entertaining, and now revalued by Hollywood moguls Lucas and Coppola.'—*Time Out, 1980*

AA: Georges Périnal, Osmond Borradaile
AAN: Miklos Rozsa

Thief of Damascus
US 1952 78m Technicolor
Columbia / Sam Katzman

The wicked ruler of Damascus is deposed by his own general, in league with Sinbad, Aladdin, and Scheherezade.
Mindless bosh, interesting only for its liberal use of scenes from *Joan of Arc*; the mind boggles at the costume compromise.

w Robert E. Kent *d* Will Jason *ph* Ellis W. Carter *m* Mischa Bakaleinikoff

Paul Henreid, Lon Chaney Jnr, Jeff Donnell, John Sutton, Elena Verdugo

The Thief Who Came to Dinner
US 1973 105m De Luxe
Warner / Tandem (Bud Yorkin)

A computer analyst determines to become a jewel thief.
Tedious comedy aping the *Raffles* school but saddled with a complex plot and listless script.

w Walter Hill, *novel* Terence L. Smith *d* Bud Yorkin *ph* Philip Lathrop *m* Henry Mancini

Ryan O'Neal, Jacqueline Bisset, Warren Oates, Jill Clayburgh, Charles Cioffi

Thieves' Highway°°
US 1949 94m bw
TCF (Robert Bassler)

A truck driver tracks down the racketeers who cheated and maimed his father.
Glossy, highly professional thick ear shedding a convincing light into one of America's less salubrious corners.

w A. I. Bezzerides, from his novel Thieves' Market *d* Jules Dassin *ph* Norbert Brodine *m* Alfred Newman

Richard Conte, Valentina Cortesa, Lee J. Cobb, Jack Oakie, Millard Mitchell, Joseph Pevney, Barbara Lawrence, Hope Emerson

Thin Ice°
US 1937 78m bw
TCF (Raymond Griffith)
GB title: *Lovely to Look At*

A skating instructress at an Alpine resort falls in love with a visiting prince.
Light-hearted musical vehicle for Hollywood's newest novelty—a skating star.

w Boris Ingster, Milton Sperling, *novel* Der Komet by Attila Orbok *d* Sidney Lanfield *ph* Robert Planck, Edward Cronjager *md* Louis Silvers

Sonja Henie, Tyrone Power, Arthur Treacher, Raymond Walburn, Joan Davis, Sig Rumann, Alan Hale, Melville Cooper

The Thin Man°°°°
US 1934 93m bw
MGM (Hunt Stromberg)

In New York over Christmas, a tipsy detective with his wife and dog solves the murder of an eccentric inventor.

Fast-moving, alternately comic and suspenseful mystery drama developed in brief scenes and fast wipes. It set a sparkling comedy career for two stars previously known for heavy drama, it was frequently imitated, and it showed a wisecracking, affectionate married relationship almost for the first time.

w *Frances Goodrich, Albert Hackett, novel Dashiell Hammett d W. S. Van Dyke* ph James Wong Howe m William Axt

William Powell, Myrna Loy, Maureen O'Sullivan, Nat Pendleton, Minna Gombell, Edward Ellis, Porter Hall, Henry Wadsworth, William Henry, Harold Huber, Cesar Romero, Edward Brophy

'A strange mixture of excitement, quips and hard-boiled sentiment . . . full of the special touches that can come from nowhere but the studio, that really make the feet a movie walks on.'—*Otis Ferguson*

† Sequels, on the whole of descending merit, included the following, all made at MGM with the same star duo: 1936: *After the Thin Man* (110m). 1939: *Another Thin Man* (102m). 1941: *Shadow of the Thin Man* (97m). 1944: *The Thin Man Goes Home* (100m). 1947: *Song of the Thin Man* (86m).

AAN: best picture; script; W. S. Van Dyke; William Powell

The Thin Red Line
US 1964   99m   bw   Cinemascope
Security / ACE (Sidney Harmon)

Raw recruits land on Guadalcanal and most of them are killed.
Weary, routine, realistic war drama.

w Bernard Gordon, *novel* James Jones d Andrew Marton ph Manuel Berenguer m Malcolm Arnold

Keir Dullea, Jack Warden, James Philbrook, Kieron Moore

The Thing**
US 1951   87m   bw
RKO / Winchester (Howard Hawks)
GB title: *The Thing from Another World*

A US scientific expedition in the Arctic is menaced by a ferocious being they inadvertently thaw out from a spaceship.
Curiously drab suspense shocker mainly set in corridors, with insufficient surprises to sustain its length. It does, however, contain the first space monster on film, and is quite nimbly made, though it fails to use the central gimmick from its original story.

w Charles Lederer, *story* Who Goes There by J. W. Campbell Jnr d Christian Nyby (with mysterious help, either Hawks or Orson Welles) ph Russell Harlan m Dmitri Tiomkin

Robert Cornthwaite, Kenneth Tobey, Margaret Sheridan, Bill Self, Dewey Martin, James Arness (as the thing)

'There seems little point in creating a monster of such original characteristics if he is to be allowed only to prowl about the North Pole, waiting to be destroyed by the superior ingenuity of the US Air Force.'—*Penelope Houston*

'A monster movie with pace, humour and a collection of beautifully timed jabs of pure horror.'—*NFT, 1967*

Things Are Looking Up
GB 1935   78m   bw

A circus horsewoman has to pose as her schoolmistress sister. Lively star vehicle for an oddly matched team. Cicely Courtneidge, Max Miller, Mary Lawson, Dick Henderson, Dick Henderson Jnr, Judy Kelly. Written by Stafford Davies and Con West; directed by Albert de Courville; for Gaumont.

Things to Come****
GB 1936   113m   bw
London Films (Alexander Korda)

War in 1940 is followed by plague, rebellion, a new glass-based society, and the first rocketship to the moon.
Fascinating, chilling and dynamically well-staged vignettes tracing mankind's future. Bits of the script and acting may be wobbly, but the sets and music are magnificent, the first part of the prophecy chillingly accurate, and the whole mammoth undertaking almost unique in film history.

w H. G. Wells, from his book The Shape of Things to Come d / pd William Cameron Menzies ph Georges Périnal m Arthur Bliss sp Harry Zech, Ned Mann ad Vincent Korda

Raymond Massey, Edward Chapman, Ralph Richardson, Margaretta Scott, Cedric Hardwicke, Sophie Stewart, Derrick de Marney, John Clements

'An amazingly ingenious technical accomplishment, even if it does hold out small hope for our race . . . the existence pictured is as joyless as a squeezed grapefruit.'—*Don Herold*

'A leviathan among films . . . a stupendous spectacle, an overwhelming, Dorean, Jules Vernesque, elaborated *Metropolis*, staggering to eye, mind and spirit, the like of which has never been seen and never will be seen again.'—*The Sunday Times*

The Third Day

US 1965   119m   Technicolor
Panavision
Warner (Jack Smight)

An amnesiac learns that he is a rich unpopular tycoon facing a major crisis.
Glum melodrama which suggests domestic mystery but provides only interminable chat.

w Burton Wohl, Robert Presnell Jnr, *novel* Joseph Hayes   d Jack Smight   ph Robert Surtees   m Percy Faith

George Peppard, Elizabeth Ashley, Roddy McDowall, Herbert Marshall, Mona Washbourne, Robert Webber, Charles Drake, Sally Kellerman, Arte Johnson, Vincent Gardenia

Third Finger Left Hand

US 1940   96m   bw
MGM (John W. Considine Jnr)

A lady fashion editor fends off unwanted suitors by saying she is already married, but a commercial artist trumps this card by claiming to be the long lost husband of her invention.
Cheerful but overstretched romantic comedy.

w Lionel Houser   d Robert Z. Leonard
ph George Folsey   m David Snell

Myrna Loy, Melvyn Douglas, Lee Bowman, Bonita Granville, Raymond Walburn, Felix Bressart, Sidney Blackmer

The Third Generation

West Germany 1979   111m   colour

A Berlin executive becomes the victim of a gang of terrorists. Realistic melodrama, curiously muted in its satire and its anger, watchable more as an entertainment than as a polemic. Volker Spengler, Bulle Ogier, Harry Baer, Eddie Constantine. Written, directed, photographed and produced by Rainer Werner Fassbinder; for Tango / Project / FDA.

The Third Man****

GB 1949   100m   bw
British Lion / London Films / David O.
Selznick / Alexander Korda (Carol Reed)

An unintelligent but tenacious writer of westerns arrives in post-war Vienna to join his old friend Harry Lime, who seems to have met with an accident . . . or has he?
Totally memorable and irresistible romantic thriller. Stylish from the first to the last, with inimitable backgrounds of zither music and war-torn buildings pointing up a then-topical black market story full of cynical characters but not without humour. Hitchcock with feeling, if you like.

w Graham Greene   d Carol Reed   ph Robert Krasker   m Anton Karas

Joseph Cotten, Trevor Howard, Alida Valli, Orson Welles, Bernard Lee, Wilfrid Hyde White, Ernst Deutsch, Siegfried Breuer, Erich Ponto, Paul Hoerbiger

'Sensitive and humane and dedicated, [Reed] would seem to be enclosed from life with no specially strong feelings about the stories that come his way other than that they should be something he can perfect and polish with a craftsman's love.'—*Richard Winnington*

'Crammed with cinematic plums which could do the early Hitchcock proud.'—*Time*

AA: Robert Krasker
AAN: Carol Reed

Third Man on the Mountain

GB 1959   103m   Technicolor
Walt Disney (Bill Anderson)

In 1865 a Swiss dishwasher dreams of conquering the local mountain, and befriends a distinguished mountaineer.
Handsomely photographed boys' adventure story.

w Eleanore Griffin, *novel* Banner in the Sky by James Ramsay Ullman   d Ken Annakin   ph Harry Waxman, *George Tairraz*   m William Alwyn

James MacArthur, Michael Rennie, Janet Munro, James Donald, Herbert Lom, Laurence Naismith, Walter Fitzgerald, Nora Swinburne

The Third Secret

GB 1964   103m   bw   Cinemascope
TCF / Hubris (Robert L. Joseph)

A psychiatrist apparently commits suicide; a patient who has relied on his strength finds the truth by interviewing other patients.
Pretentious package of short stories, only one of which is relevant to the frame (yet another one featuring Patricia Neal was shot but discarded); full of philosophical conversations on a Thames mudbank and other absurdities, but well enough put together.

w Robert L. Joseph   d Charles Crichton
ph Douglas Slocombe   m Richard Arnell

Stephen Boyd, *Pamela Franklin*, Jack Hawkins, Richard Attenborough, Rachel Kempson, Diane Cilento, Paul Rogers, Freda Jackson

'An unappealing and irritatingly muddled scribble of a film, thoroughly lacking in suspense, veracity and justification.'—*MFB*

The Third Voice••
US 1959   80m   bw   Cinemascope
TCF (Maury Dexter, Hubert Cornfield)

A woman kills her wealthy lover and an
accomplice impersonates him through a series
of complex negotiations.
Superstylish minor thriller, with a plot
fascinating as it unfolds and a climax which is
only a slight letdown.

wd Hubert Cornfield, *novel* All the Way by
Charles Williams *ph* Ernest Haller *m* Johnny
Mandel

Edmond O'Brien, Laraine Day, Julie London

Thirteen Ghosts
US 1960   88m   bw (colour sequence)
Columbia / William Castle

A penniless scholar inherits a haunted house.
Childish thriller for which the audience was
issued with a 'ghost viewer' (anaglyph
spectacles) so that they could see the 'spirits'.
The gimmick was called Illusion-O.

w Robb White *d* William Castle *ph* Joseph
Biroc *m* Von Dexter

Charles Herbert, Jo Morrow, Martin Milner,
Rosemary de Camp, Donald Woods, Margaret
Hamilton

Thirteen Hours by Air•
US 1936   80m   bw
Paramount (E. Lloyd Sheldon)

A transcontinental plane is hijacked by an
ex-convict.
Solidly carpentered minor thriller which is also
an interesting record of the early days of
commercial aviation.

w Bogart Rogers, Kenyon Nicholson
d Mitchell Leisen *ph* Theodor Sparkhul

Fred MacMurray, Joan Bennett, Zasu Pitts,
Alan Baxter, Fred Keating, Brian Donlevy,
John Howard, Ruth Donnelly, Dean Jagger

13 Rue Madeleine•
US 1946   95m   bw
TCF (Louis de Rochemont)

Four trained American espionage agents
locate a Nazi rocket site in France.
Semi-documentary spy stuff in the tradition of
The House on 92nd Street but rather less
satisfactory despite excellent technique.

w John Monks Jnr, Sy Bartlett *d* Henry
Hathaway *ph* Norbert Brodine *m* David
Buttolph *md* Alfred Newman

James Cagney, Annabella, Richard Conte,
Frank Latimore, Walter Abel, Melville
Cooper, Sam Jaffe, Blanche Yurka

'Far and away the roughest, toughest spy
chase yet gleaned from the bulging files of the
OSS.'—*Time*
'I stole the plot of *The Virginian* and used it.
I'd always wanted to make that story
anyway.'—*Henry Hathaway*

13 West Street•
US 1962   80m   bw
Columbia / Ladd Enterprises

An engineer is attacked on the street by
teenage hoodlums and becomes obsessed by
revenge.
Competent, darkly photographed, rather
dislikeable little thriller, a kind of trial run for
Death Wish.

w Bernard Schoenfeld, Robert Presnell Jnr
d Philip Leacock *ph* Charles Lawton Jnr
m George Duning

Alan Ladd, Rod Steiger, Dolores Dorn,
Michael Callan, Kenneth MacKenna,
Margaret Hayes

Thirteen Women
US 1932   73m   bw

One of thirteen boarding school graduates is
trying to murder the others. Thin mystery
which wastes its cast. Ricardo Cortez, Irene
Dunne, Myrna Loy, Jill Esmond, Florence
Eldridge, Julie Haydon, Marjorie Gateson, C.
Henry Gordon. Written by Bartlett Cormack,
from a novel by Tiffany Thayer; directed by
George Archainbaud; for RKO.

The Thirteenth Chair
US 1929   85m   bw

A medium holds a seance to unmask a
murderer. Effective though now very dated
chiller from a Broadway hit. Margaret
Wycherly, Bela Lugosi, Holmes Herbert,
Conrad Nagel, Leila Hyams. Written by
Elliott Clawson, from the play by Bayard
Veiller; directed by Tod Browning; for MGM.
(NB: The same studio remade the vehicle in
1936 with Dame May Whitty, Henry Daniell,
Holmes Herbert—again—Elissa Landi and
Lewis Stone; the director was George B.
Seitz.)

The Thirteenth Guest•
US 1932   70m   bw
Monogram (M. H. Hoffman)

A haunted house, a will at midnight, and a
frightened lady.
Archetypal comedy thriller, shot on Poverty
Row but still watchable.

w Francis Hyland, Arthur Hoerl, *novel*
Armitage Traill *d* Albert Ray *ph* Harry
Neumann, Tom Galligan

Ginger Rogers, Lyle Talbot, J. Farrell
MacDonald, James Eagles, Eddie Phillips,
Erville Alderson

The Thirteenth Letter*
US 1951 85m bw
TCF (Otto Preminger)

A small French-Canadian town suffers from an
outbreak of poison pen letters.
Moderate transcription of a memorable
French film, *Le Corbeau*; in this version the
events seem all too predictable and the
performances dull.

w Howard Koch *d* Otto Preminger
ph Joseph La Shelle *m* Alex North

Charles Boyer, Linda Darnell, Constance
Smith, Michael Rennie, Françoise Rosay,
Judith Evelyn

–30–
US 1959 96m bw
Warner / Mark VII (Jack Webb)
GB title: *Deadline Midnight*

A night in the newsroom of a paper
preoccupied with scoops.
Not very dramatic, oddly titled and rather
pretentious newspaper melodrama confined
largely to one set.

w William Bowers *d* Jack Webb *ph* Edward
Colman *m* Ray Heindorf

Jack Webb, William Conrad, David Nelson,
Whitney Blake, James Bell, Nancy Valentine

Thirty Day Princess*
US 1934 74m bw
Paramount (B. P. Schulberg)

An actress is hired to impersonate a princess
who gets mumps while visiting New York in
hope of a loan.
Modest comedy which needed a wittier script
but is stylishly played.

w Preston Sturges, Frank Partos, *novel*
Clarence Budington Kelland *d* Marion
Gering *ph* Leon Shamroy

Sylvia Sidney, Cary Grant, Edward Arnold,
Henry Stephenson, Vince Barnett, Edgar
Norton, Lucien Littlewood

Thirty Is a Dangerous Age, Cynthia
GB 1967 84m Technicolor
Columbia / Walter Shenson

A timid nightclub pianist has trouble with
women but sells his first musical.

Mild star vehicle for a very mild star, basically
a few thin sketches, frantically overdirected.

w Dudley Moore, Joe McGrath, John Wells
d Joe McGrath *ph* Billy Williams *m* Dudley
Moore *titles* Richard Williams

Dudley Moore, Eddie Foy Jnr, Suzy Kendall,
John Bird, Duncan Macrae, Patricia
Routledge, John Wells

The Thirty-Nine Steps***
GB 1935 81m bw
Gaumont British (Ivor Montagu)

A spy is murdered; the man who has
befriended her is suspected, but eludes the
police until a chase across Scotland produces
the real villains.
Marvellous comedy thriller with most of the
gimmicks found not only in Hitchcock's later
work but in anyone else's who has tried the
same vein. It has little to do with the original
novel, and barely sets foot outside the studio,
but it makes every second count, and is
unparalleled in its use of timing, atmosphere
and comedy relief.

w Charles Bennett, Alma Reville, novel John
Buchan *d Alfred Hitchcock ph Bernard
Knowles m* Hubert Bath, Jack Beaver
md Louis Levy

Robert Donat, Madeleine Carroll, Godfrey
Tearle, Lucie Mannheim, Peggy Ashcroft,
John Laurie, *Wylie Watson, Helen Haye,*
Frank Cellier
   'A narrative of the unexpected—a
humorous, exciting, dramatic, entertaining,
pictorial, vivid and novel tale told with a fine
sense of character and a keen grasp of the
cinematic idea.'—*Sydney W. Carroll*
   'A miracle of speed and light.'—*Otis
Ferguson*

The Thirty-Nine Steps*
GB 1960 93m Eastmancolor
Rank (Betty E. Box)

Just to show that stars and story aren't
everything, this scene-for-scene remake muffs
every opportunity for suspense or general
effectiveness, and is practically a manual on
how not to make a thriller.

w Frank Harvey *d* Ralph Thomas *ph* Ernest
Steward *m* Clifton Parker

Kenneth More, Taina Elg, Barry Jones, Faith
Brook, Brenda de Banzie, Duncan Lamont,
James Hayter, Michael Goodliffe, Reginald
Beckwith

The Thirty-Nine Steps*
GB 1978 102m Eastmancolor
Rank / Norfolk International (James Kenelm
   Clarke)

Eager-to-please remake which goes back to the original period and more or less the original story, but rather spoils itself by a cliffhanger climax on the face of Big Ben, absurdly borrowed from Will Hay's *My Learned Friend*.

w Michael Robson, d Don Sharp ph John Coquillon m Ed Welch ph Harry Pottle

Robert Powell, Karen Dotrice, John Mills, Eric Porter, David Warner, George Baker, Ronald Pickup, Timothy West, Donald Pickering, Andrew Keir, Robert Flemyng, Miles Anderson

Thirty Seconds over Tokyo**
US 1944   138m   bw
MGM (Sam Zimbalist)

How the first American attack on Japan was planned.
Sturdy World War II action flagwaver, with Tracy guesting as Colonel Dolittle.

w Dalton Trumbo d Mervyn Le Roy
ph Harold Rosson, Robert Surtees m Herbert Stothart

Spencer Tracy, Van Johnson, Robert Walker, Phyllis Thaxter, Tim Murdock, Don Defore, Robert Mitchum

'All of the production involving planes and technical action is so fine that the film has the tough and literal quality of an air force documentary.'—*Bosley Crowther, New York Times*

'A big studio, big scale film, free of artistic pretensions, it is transformed by its not very imaginative but very dogged sincerity into something forceful, simple and thoroughly sympathetic.'—*James Agee*

AAN: Harold Rosson, Robert Surtees

Thirty-Six Hours*
US 1964   115m   bw   Panavision
MGM / Perlberg–Seaton / Cherokee
   (William Perlberg)

In 1944 an American major is kidnapped by the Nazis and after drugging is made to think that the war is over.
Well-detailed spy suspenser.

wd George Seaton, *stories* Roald Dahl, Carl K. Hittleman ph Philip Lathrop m Dmitri Tiomkin

James Garner, Rod Taylor, Eva Marie Saint, Werner Peters, John Banner

This above All*
US 1942   110m   bw
TCF (Darryl F. Zanuck)

A surgeon's daughter on active service during World War II falls in love with a conscientious objector who is also an army deserter: he proves his bravery during an air raid.
Superior studio-set war romance.

w R. C. Sheriff, *novel* Eric Knight d Anatole Litvak ph Arthur Miller m Alfred Newman

Tyrone Power, Joan Fontaine, Thomas Mitchell, Henry Stephenson, Nigel Bruce, Gladys Cooper, Philip Merivale, Alexander Knox, Melville Cooper

AAN: Arthur Miller

This Angry Age
Italy 1957   104m   Technirama

A French widow in Indo-China struggles to keep her rice fields going despite her family's waning interest. Curious international production which suffers from the audience's lack of interest in the central situation. Moments of interest and even beauty, though.

Silvana Mangano, Jo Van Fleet, Anthony Perkins, Alida Valli, Richard Conte, Nehemiah Persoff. Written by Irwin Shaw, René Clément, Ivo Perelli and Diego Fabbri, from the novel *Barrage Contre Le Pacifique* by Marguerite Duras; directed by René Clément; for Dino de Laurentiis. (Alternative title: *The Sea Wall*. Original title: *La Diga sul Pacifico*.)

This Could Be the Night
US 1957   104m   bw   Cinemascope
MGM (Joe Pasternak)

A schoolteacher becomes secretary to a gangster in his Broadway night club.
Unlikely romantic melodrama with music, like a more solemn *Guys and Dolls*.

w Isabel Lennart, *story* Cornelia Baird Gross d Robert Wise ph Russell Harlan m George Stoll

Jean Simmons, Paul Douglas, Tony Franciosa, Julie Wilson, Joan Blondell, J. Carrol Naish, Zasu Pitts

This Day and Age*
US 1933   98m   bw
Paramount / Cecil B. de Mille

During a youth week, boys put a gangster on trial and by his own methods force him to confess to murder.
A curious aberration for de Mille, this fairly powerful movie was condemned in some quarters as an incitement to fascism.

w Bartlett Cormack d Cecil B. de Mille
ph Peverell Marley m Howard Jackson, L. W. Gilbert, Abel Baer

Charles Bickford, Richard Cromwell, Judith Allen, Harry Green, Ben Alexander

'Loaded with that power which excites emotional hysteria . . . should stimulate audiences to the same pitch of enthusiasm as it did the preview crowd.'—*Motion Picture Herald*

'A strange tale from the Hollywood hills . . . the technical work is beyond reproach, but the story is excessively melodramatic.'—*Mordaunt Hall, New York Times*

This Earth Is Mine
US 1959   124m   Technicolor
   Cinemascope
U-I / Vintage (Casey Robinson, Claude Heilman)

A French-American vineyard owner in California brings out his granddaughter from England in the hope that she will consolidate his dynasty.
Solidly efficient film of a solidly efficient novel.

w Casey Robinson, *novel* The Cup and the Sword by Alice Tisdale Hobart *d* Henry King *ph* Winton Hoch, Russell Metty *m* Hugo Friedhofer

Jean Simmons, *Claude Rains*, Rock Hudson, Dorothy McGuire, Kent Smith, Anna Lee, Ken Scott

This England
GB 1941   84m   bw

Landowner and labourer express contrary views through five periods of English history. Unintentionally hilarious charade with all concerned left with egg on their faces. With propaganda like this, it's a wonder we still won the war. John Clements, Emlyn Williams, Constance Cummings, Frank Pettingell, Roland Culver, Esmond Knight, Morland Graham, Leslie French. Written by Emlyn Williams, A. R. Rawlinson and Bridget Boland; directed by David MacDonald; for British National.

This Gun for Hire***
US 1942   81m   bw
Paramount (Richard M. Blumenthal)

A professional killer becomes involved in a fifth columnist plot.
Efficient Americanization of one of its author's more sombre entertainments. The melodrama has an authentic edge and strangeness to it, and it established the star images of both Ladd and Lake, as well as being oddly downbeat for a Hollywood product of this jingoistic time.

w Albert Maltz, W. R. Burnett, *novel* A Gun for Sale by *Graham Greene* *d* Frank Tuttle *ph* John Seitz *m* David Buttolph

Alan Ladd, Veronica Lake, Robert Preston, *Laird Cregar*, Tully Marshall, Mikhail Rasumny, Marc Lawrence

This Happy Breed**
GB 1944   114m   Technicolor
GFD / Two Cities / Cineguild (Noel Coward, Anthony Havelock-Allan)

Life between the wars for a London suburban family.
Coward's domestic epic is unconvincingly written and largely miscast, but sheer professionalism gets it through, and the decor is historically interesting.

w David Lean, Ronald Neame, Anthony Havelock-Allan, *play* Noel Coward *d David Lean ph Ronald Neame*

Robert Newton, Celia Johnson, Stanley Holloway, John Mills, Kay Walsh, Amy Veness, Alison Leggatt

'Nearly two hours of the pleasure of recognition, which does not come very far up the scale of aesthetic values.'—*Richard Mallett, Punch*

This Happy Feeling
US 1958   92m   Eastmancolor
   Cinemascope
U-I (Ross Hunter)

An ageing actor is invigorated by a mild affair with his secretary.
Flat romantic comedy: the bubbles obstinately refuse to rise.

wd Blake Edwards, *play* For Love or Money by F. Hugh Herbert *ph* Arthur E. Arling *m* Frank Skinner

Curt Jurgens, Debbie Reynolds, John Saxon, Alexis Smith, *Mary Astor, Estelle Winwood*

This Is My Affair**
US 1937   102m   bw
TCF (Kenneth MacGowan)
GB title: *His Affair*

When President McKinley is assassinated, one of his top undercover agents is suspected of being a criminal, and threatened with execution.
Jolly good romantic melodrama with excellent period trappings; Hollywood of the thirties at its routine best.

w Allen Rivkin, Lamar Trotti *d* William A. Seiter *ph* Robert Planck *md* Arthur Lange

Robert Taylor, Barbara Stanwyck, Victor McLaglen, Brian Donlevy, Sidney Blackmer,

John Carradine, Sig Rumann, Alan Dinehart,
Douglas Fowley
   'The best American melodrama of the year
. . . admirable acting, quick and cunning
direction . . . a sense of doom, of almost
classic suspense.'—*Graham Greene*

This Is My Love
US 1954   91m   Technicolor

A sensitive young writer gives up everything to
help her sister and crippled husband run a
restaurant. Weird, miscast melodrama which
ends with Cinderella murdering the ugly sister.
Linda Darnell, Faith Domergue, Dan Duryea,
Rick Jason. Written by Hagar Wilde and
Hugh Brooke; directed by Stuart Heisler; for
RKO.

This Is My Street
GB 1963   94m   bw
Anglo-Amalgamated / Adder (Jack
Hanbury)

A Battersea wife has a fling with her mother's
lodger.
Unremarkable low-life drama.

w Bill MacIlwraith, *novel* Nan Maynard
d Sidney Hayers *ph* Alan Hume *m* Eric
Rogers

June Ritchie, Ian Hendry, Avice Landon,
Meredith Edwards, Madge Ryan, John Hurt,
Mike Pratt, Tom Adams

This Is the Army**
US 1943   121m   Technicolor
Warner (Jack L. Warner, Hal B. Wallis)

Army recruits put on a musical revue.
Mammoth musical flagwaver.

w Casey Robinson, Claude Binyon *d* Michael
Curtiz *ph* Bert Glennon, Sol Polito
songs Irving Berlin *m* Ray Heindorf

George Murphy, Joan Leslie, Irving Berlin,
George Tobias, Alan Hale, Charles
Butterworth, Rosemary de Camp, Dolores
Costello, Una Merkel, Stanley Ridges, Ruth
Donnelly, Kate Smith, Frances Langford,
Gertrude Niesen, Ronald Reagan, Joe Louis

AA: Ray Heindorf

This Is The Life
US 1943   87m   bw

A young girl singer gets a crush on an older
man. Lively youth musical from better-
mannered days. Donald O'Connor, Susanna
Foster, Peggy Ryan, Patric Knowles, Louise
Allbritton, Dorothy Peterson, Jonathan Hale.
Written by Wanda Tuchock, from the play
Angela Is 22 by Fay Wray and Sinclair Lewis;
directed by Felix Feist; for Universal.

This Island Earth**
US 1955   86m   Technicolor
U-I (William Alland)

Scientists at a mysterious research station are
really visitors from a planet in outer space, to
which they kidnap brilliant minds who they
hope can help them.
Absorbing science fiction mystery with
splendid special effects and only one mutant
monster to liven the last reels.

w Franklin Coen, Edward G. O'Callaghan,
novel Raymond F. Jones *d* Joseph Newman
ph / *sp* Clifford Stine, David S. Horsley
m Joseph Gershenson *ad* Alexander
Golitzen, Richard H. Riedel

Jeff Morrow, Faith Domergue, Rex Reason,
Lance Fuller, Russell Johnson, Robert
Nicholas, Karl Lindt

This Land Is Mine*
US 1943   103m   bw
RKO (Jean Renoir, Dudley Nichols)

A European village fights for freedom under
occupying Nazis, and a schoolmaster becomes
a hero.
Rather superfluous flagwaver with good
performances wasted in a totally predictable
and rather uninspiring script which gives the
director little scope.

w Dudley Nichols *d* Jean Renoir *ph* Frank
Redman *m* Lothar Perl

Charles Laughton, Maureen O'Hara, George
Sanders, Walter Slezak, Una O'Connor, Kent
Smith, Philip Merivale, Thurston Hall, George
Coulouris
   'Directed with the same Zolaesque
intensity, the same excited obsession with
locomotives, the same exquisite pictorial
sense, that informed *La Bête Humaine.*'—
Guardian
   'Dull, prolix and unamusing.'—*James Agate*
   'You cannot afford to dislocate or
internationalize your occupied country; or to
try to sell it to Americans by making your
citizens as well fed, well dressed and
comfortably idiomatic as Americans; or to
treat the show to the corrupted virtuosities of
studio lighting and heavy ballet
composition.'—*James Agee*

This Love of Ours
US 1945   90m   bw
U-I (Edward Dodds)

A jealous doctor leaves his wife but years later
saves her from an unhappy second marriage.
Stupid romantic melodrama with characters in
whose idiotic behaviour one can take no
interest. Remade as *Never Say Goodbye* (qv).

w Bruce Manning, John Klorer, Leonard Lee, *play* Comè Prima Meglio di Prima by Luigi Pirandello *d* William Dieterle *ph* Lucien Ballard *m* Hans Salter

Merle Oberon, Charles Korvin, Claude Rains, Carl Esmond, Jess Barker, Harry Davenport, Ralph Morgan, Fritz Leiber

'About as captivating as a funeral dirge.'— *Thomas M. Pryor, New York Times*

'A juicy example of masochistic team work . . . my favourite bad film in two years.'— *Richard Winnington*

AAN: Hans Salter

This Man in Paris
GB 1939   86m   bw

A London reporter in Paris exposes a counterfeiting gang. Slightly disappointing sequel to the spruce *This Man Is News*; no more were made. Barry K. Barnes, Valerie Hobson, Alastair Sim, Edward Lexy, Garry Marsh. Written by Allan McKinnon and Roger MacDougall; directed by David MacDonald; for Pinebrook. 'Five years have passed since *The Thin Man*, and this particular uxurious relationship of loving insults, hygienic sex, and raillery from twin beds is period enough for *Punch*.'—*Graham Greene*.

This Man Is Dangerous
GB 1941   82m   bw

A police inspector's son solves the case of a fake doctor and a mysterious nursing home. Nostalgically innocent crime caper; still quite entertaining. James Mason, Mary Clare, Margaret Vyner, Gordon McLeod, Frederick Valk. Written by John Argyle and Edward Dryhurst, from the novel *They Called Him Death* by David Hume; directed by Lawrence Huntington; for Rialto. (Aka: *The Patient Vanishes*.)

This Man Is Mine
GB 1946   103m   bw

A family invites a Canadian soldier for Christmas. Moderate heartwarmer which still exudes a patriotic sentimental glow. Tom Walls, Glynis Johns, Jeanne de Casalis, Hugh McDermott, Nova Pilbeam, Barry Morse. Written by Doreen Montgomery, Nicholas Phipps, Reginald Beckwith, Mabel Constanduros, Val Valentine and David Evans, from the play *A Soldier for Christmas* by Reginald Beckwith; directed by Marcel Varnel; for Columbia.

This Man Is News**
GB 1938   77m   bw
(Paramount) Pinebrook (Anthony Havelock-Allan)

A reporter tracks down jewel thieves. Thoroughly brisk and lively comedy-thriller on *Thin Man* lines. (See *This Man in Paris*.)

w Allan MacKinnon, Roger Macdougall, Basil Dearden *d* David MacDonald

Barry K. Barnes, Valerie Hobson, Alastair Sim, John Warwick, Garry Marsh

This Man's Navy
US 1945   100m   bw

Two old navy men compare their sons' exploits, especially in the matter of how many submarines destroyed. Easy-going star flagwaver. Wallace Beery, James Gleason, Tom Drake, Noah Beery, Selena Royle. Written by Borden Chase; directed by William Wellman; for MGM.

This Modern Age
US 1931   68m   bw
MGM

The socialite child of divorced parents goes to Paris to stay with her sophisticated mother. Mildly daring melodrama typical of its star and year.

w Sylvia Thalberg, Frank Butler, *story* Mildred Cram *d* Nick Grinde *ph* Charles Rosher

Joan Crawford, Pauline Frederick, Monroe Owsley, Neil Hamilton, Hobart Bosworth, Emma Dunn

This Property Is Condemned*
US 1966   110m   Technicolor
Paramount / Seven Arts / Ray Stark (John Houseman)

Sexual adventures of a tubercular but beautiful girl in her mother's boarding house in a Mississippi town.
The Tennessee Williams mixture as before, quite well done but almost entirely resistible.

w Francis Ford Coppola, Fred Coe, Edith Sommer, *play* Tennessee Williams *d* Sydney Pollack *ph* James Wong Howe *m* Kenyon Hopkins

Natalie Wood, Robert Redford, Mary Badham, Kate Reid, Charles Bronson, Jon Provost, John Harding, Alan Baxter, Robert Blake

This Sporting Life**
GB 1963   134m   bw
Rank / Independent Artists (Karel Reisz)

A tough miner becomes a successful rugby player, but his inner crudeness and violence keep contentment at bay.

Skilful movie-making around an unattractive hero in dismal settings; for all the excellent detail, we do not care sufficiently for the film to become any kind of classic.

w David Storey d *Lindsay Anderson*
ph *Denys Coop* m Roberto Gerhard

Richard Harris, Rachel Roberts, Alan Badel, William Hartnell, Colin Blakely, Vanda Godsell, Arthur Lowe

AAN: Richard Harris; Rachel Roberts

This Thing Called Love*
US 1941 98m bw
Columbia (William Perlberg)
GB title: *Married But Single*

A lady executive insists on proving that marriage is best if the partners start out just good friends.
Amusing comedy which at the time seemed a little saucy, and got itself banned by the Legion of Decency.

w George Seaton, Ken Englund, P. J. Wolfson d Alexander Hall ph Joseph Walker m Werner Heyman md Morris Stoloff

Rosalind Russell, Melvyn Douglas, Binnie Barnes, Allyn Joslyn, Gloria Dickson, Lee J. Cobb, Gloria Holden, Don Beddoe
'One of those laborious forties comedies in which the independent-minded woman has no common sense.'—*New Yorker, 1979*

This Time for Keeps
US 1947 105m Technicolor
MGM (Joe Pasternak)

The son of a famous singer falls in love with a swimming star.
Dim star musical with no outstanding sequences.

w Gladys Lehman d Richard Thorpe ph Karl Freund *songs* various

Esther Williams, Jimmy Durante, Lauritz Melchior, Johnnie Johnston, Xavier Cugat and his Orchestra
'The money spent on this production might easily have kept Mozart and Schubert alive and busy to the age of sixty, with enough left over to finance five of the best movies ever made. It might even have been invested in a good movie musical.'—*James Agee*

This Was a Woman
GB 1948 104m bw

A paranoid wife, prevented from running the lives of her offspring, tries to poison her husband. Intolerable, interminable melodrama; a stage event makes a very stagey

film. Sonia Dresdel, Barbara White, Walter Fitzgerald, Cyril Raymond, Marjorie Rhodes, Emrys Jones. Written by Val Valentine, from the play by Joan Morgan; directed by Tim Whelan; for Excelsior.

This Was Paris
GB 1941 88m bw

Spies suspect each other in Paris just before the Nazi occupation. Unpersuasive studio-bound potboiler. Ben Lyon, Ann Dvorak, Griffith Jones, Robert Morley, Harold Huth, Mary Maguire. Written by Brock Williams and Edward Dryhurst; directed by John Harlow; for Warner.

This Week of Grace
GB 1933 92m bw

An unemployed factory girl goes into service. Very typical but underproduced star vehicle. Gracie Fields, Frank Pettingell, Henry Kendall, John Stuart, Douglas Wakefield, Minnie Rayner. Written by H. Fowler Mear and Jack Marks; directed by Maurice Elvey; for Real Art.

This Woman Is Dangerous
US 1952 97m bw
Warner (Robert Sisk)

A woman gangster goes blind and falls in love with her doctor.
Glossy hokum without much dramatic movement; strictly for star fans.

w Geoffrey Homes, George Worthing Yates d Felix Feist ph Ted McCord m David Buttolph

Joan Crawford, David Brian, Dennis Morgan, Mari Aldon, Phil Carey

This Woman Is Mine
US 1941 92m bw

Fur traders fall out over a beautiful stowaway. Fairly well-produced but unexciting period drama. Franchot Tone, John Carroll, Walter Brennan, Carol Bruce, Nigel Bruce, Leo G. Carroll, Sig Rumann. Written by Seton I. Miller, from the novel *I, James Lewis* by Gilbert Wolff Gabriel; directed by Frank Lloyd; for Universal.

The Thomas Crown Affair**
US 1968 102m De Luxe Panavision
UA / Mirisch / Simkoe / Solar (Norman Jewison)

A bored property tycoon masterminds a bank robbery and is chased by a glamorous insurance investigator.

Not so much a movie as an animated colour supplement, this glossy entertainment makes style its prime virtue, plays cute tricks with multiple images and has a famous sexy chess game, but is not above being boring for the rest of the way.

w Alan R. Trustman *d Norman Jewison ph Haskell Wexler m* Michel Legrand *ad Robert Boyle*

Steve McQueen, Faye Dunaway, Paul Burke, Jack Weston, Yaphet Kotto

'Jewison and Wexler seem to have gone slightly berserk, piling up tricks and mannerisms until the film itself sinks out of sight, forlorn and forgotten.'—*Tom Milne*

'A glimmering, empty film reminiscent of an *haute couture* model—stunning on the surface, concave and undernourished beneath.'—*Stefan Kanter*

AA: song 'The Windmills of Your Mind' (*m* Michel Legrand, *ly* Alan and Marilyn Bergman)
AAN: Michel Legrand

Thoroughbreds Don't Cry
US 1937   80m   bw

Jockeys fight for the chance to ride a valuable English horse. Ho-hum racetrack yarn significant as the first teaming of two young stars. Mickey Rooney, Judy Garland, Ronald Sinclair, Sophie Tucker, C. Aubrey Smith. Written by Lawrence Hazard, J. Walter Ruben and Eleanor Griffin; directed by Alfred E. Green; for MGM.

Thoroughly Modern Millie*
US 1967   138m   Technicolor
Universal (Ross Hunter)

In the twenties, a young girl comes to New York, becomes thoroughly modern, falls for her boss, and has various adventures unmasking a white slave racket centring on a Chinese laundry.
Initially most agreeable but subsequently very patchy spoof of twenties fads and films, including a Harold Lloyd thrill sequence which just doesn't work and a comedy performance from Beatrice Lillie which does. Tunes and performances are alike variable.

w Richard Morris *d* George Roy Hill *ph Russell Metty ad* Alexander Golitzen, George Webb *m* Elmer Bernstein *md* André Previn, Joseph Gershenson *ch* Joe Layton *songs* various

Julie Andrews, Mary Tyler Moore, *John Gavin*, James Fox, Carol Channing, *Beatrice Lillie*, Jack Soo, Pat Morita, Anthony Dexter

'What a nice 65-minute movie is buried therein!'—*Judith Crist*

AA: Elmer Bernstein
AAN: André Previn, Joseph Gershenson; title song (*m* James Van Heusen, *ly* Sammy Cahn); Carol Channing

Those Calloways
US 1964   131m   Technicolor
Walt Disney (Winston Hibler)

Adventures of a marsh trapper and his family who live near a Maine village and try to protect wild geese from hunters. Predictable family saga with pleasant backgrounds.

w Louis Pelletier, *novel* Swift Water by Paul Annixter *d* Norman Tokar *ph* Edward Colman *m* Max Steiner

Brian Keith, Vera Miles, Brandon de Wilde, Walter Brennan, Ed Wynn, Linda Evans, Philip Abbott, John Larkin, John Qualen

Those Daring Young Men in Their Jaunty Jalopies
US / Italy / France 1969   125m
   Technicolor   Panavision
Paramount / Dino de Laurentiis / Marianne (Ken Annakin, Basil Keys)
GB title: *Monte Carlo or Bust*

Accidents befall various competitors in the Monte Carlo Rally.
Rough-edged imitation of *The Great Race* and *Those Magnificent Men in Their Flying Machines*, much feebler than either but with the waste of a big budget well in evidence.

w Jack Davies, Ken Annakin *d* Ken Annakin *ph* Gabor Pogany *m* Ron Goodwin

Peter Cook, Dudley Moore, Tony Curtis, Bourvil, Walter Chiari, Terry-Thomas, Gert Frobe, Susan Hampshire, Jack Hawkins, Eric Sykes

Those Endearing Young Charms
US 1945   81m   bw

An air corps mechanic loves a shopgirl. Nothing to remember about this light star time-passer. Robert Young, Laraine Day, Bill Williams, Ann Harding, Marc Cramer, Anne Jeffries. Written by Jerome Chodorov, from the play by Edward Chodorov; directed by Lewis Allen; for RKO. 'Well played, well directed, and not quite interesting enough to be worth the time it takes.'—*James Agee.*

Those Kids from Town
GB 1941   82m   bw

An earl takes in a group of noisy cockney kids evacuated from the city. Sentimental wartime crowdpleaser, not especially good but a fairly rare record of one aspect of the war. Shirley

Lenner, Jeanne de Casalis, Percy Marmont, Maire O'Neill, George Cole, Charles Victor. Written by Adrian Arlington, from his novel *These Our Strangers*; directed by Lance Comfort; for British National.

Those Magnificent Men in Their Flying Machines, or How I Flew from London to Paris in 25 hours and 11 Minutes**
GB 1965   133m   Technicolor   Todd-AO
TCF (Stan Marguilies, Jack Davies)

In 1910, a newspaper owner sponsors a London to Paris air race.
Long-winded, generally agreeable knockabout comedy with plenty to look at but far too few jokes to sustain it.

w Jack Davies, Ken Annakin *d Ken Annakin*
ph Christopher Challis m Ron Goodwin
pd Tom Morahan

Sarah Miles, Stuart Whitman, Robert Morley, Eric Sykes, Terry-Thomas, James Fox, Alberto Sordi, Gert Frobe, Jean-Pierre Cassel, Karl Michael Vogler, Irina Demich, Benny Hill, Flora Robson, Sam Wanamaker, Red Skelton, Fred Emney, Cicely Courtneidge, Gordon Jackson, John Le Mesurier, Tony Hancock, William Rushton

'There is many a likely gag, but none that survives the second or third reprise. It could have been a good bit funnier by being shorter: the winning time is 25 hours 11 minutes, and by observing some kind of neo-Aristotelian unity the film seems to last exactly as long.'— *John Simon*

AAN: script

Those Were the Days*
GB 1934   80m   bw
BIP (Walter C. Mycroft)

In the nineties, a magistrate seeks out his teenage stepson in a music hall.
Lively comedy which is valuable as giving the screen's best recreation of an old-time music hall.

w Fred Thompson, Frank Miller, Frank Launder, Jack Jordan, *play* The Magistrate by Arthur Wing Pinero *d Thomas Bentley*
ph Otto Kanturek *md* Idris Lewis

Will Hay, John Mills, Iris Hoey, Angela Baddeley, Claud Allister, George Graves, Jane Carr, H. F. Maltby

Those Were the Days
US 1940   74m   bw
Paramount (J. Theodore Reed)
GB title: *Good Old Schooldays*

During their 40th anniversary celebrations, a married couple look back to their courtship days at college.
Pleasant, light, nostalgic escapades.

w Don Hartman, *stories* George Fitch
d J. Theodore Reed *ph* Victor Milner

William Holden, Bonita Granville, Ezra Stone, Judith Barrett, Vaughan Glazer, Lucien Littlefield, Richard Denning

Those Wonderful Movie Cranks*
Czechoslovakia 1978   88m   colour
Barrandov (Jan Suster)

A travelling conjuror at the turn of the century introduces short cinema films into his act, and solves his woman trouble meanwhile.
Charming melancholy comedy which adds a little to art as well as to history.

w Oldrich Vlcek, Jiri Menzel *d Jiri Menzel*
ph Jaromir Sofr *m* Jiri Sust

Rudolf Hrusinsky, Vlasta Fabianova, Blazena Holisova

A Thousand Clowns*
US 1965   115m   bw
UA / Harell (Fred Coe)

A New Yorker who has abdicated from work leads a cheerful, useless life with his young nephew, but the school board have their doubts.
Imitative nonconformist comedy with frequent reminiscences of older, better plays such as *You Can't Take It with You*. Good lines occasionally make themselves felt, but the overall effect is patchy, the lead is miscast, and the location montages only emphasize the basic one-room set.

w Herb Gardner, from his play *d* Fred Coe
ph Arthur J. Ornitz *m* Don Walker

Jason Robards, Martin Balsam, Barry Gordon, Barbara Harris, *William Daniels*, Gene Saks

AA: Martin Balsam
AAN: best picture; Herb Gardner; Don Walker

Thousands Cheer*
US 1943   126m   Technicolor
MGM (Joe Pasternak)

An army base stages an all-star variety show.
Ho-hum studio extravaganza with some good numbers.

w Paul Jarrico, Richard Collins *d* George Sidney *ph* George Folsey *md* Herbert Stothart *songs* various

Kathryn Grayson, Gene Kelly, John Boles, Mary Astor, Jose Iturbi, Kay Kyser and his

Orchestra, Lionel Barrymore, Margaret
O'Brien, June Allyson, Mickey Rooney, Judy
Garland, Red Skelton, Eleanor Powell, Bob
Crosby and his Orchestra, Lena Horne, Frank
Morgan

'A thoroughly routine musical distinguished
only by Gene Kelly with nothing to use his
talents on, a terrible piece of trash by
Shostakovich, and the unpleasant sight of Jose
Iturbi proving he is a real guy by playing the
sort of boogie woogie anyone ought to be able
to learn through a correspondence course.'—
James Agee

AAN: George Folsey; Herbert Stothart

Three Bites of the Apple

US 1966 98m Metrocolor Panavision
MGM (Alvin Ganzer)

An English travel courier wins a lot of money
in a Rome casino, and nearly loses it all.
Very dull comedy perked up by attractive
locations.

w George Wells *d* Alvin Ganzer *ph* Gabor
Pogany *m* Eddy Manson

David McCallum, Sylva Koscina, Tammy
Grimes, Harvey Korman, Aldo Fabrizi

Three Blind Mice*

US 1938 75m bw
TCF (Raymond Griffith)

Three Kansas girls in the big city seek rich
husbands.
Mild comedy remade as *Three Little Girls in
Blue* and *How to Marry a Millionaire*, and not
all that different from any of the *Gold Diggers*
comedy musicals.

w Brown Holmes, Lynn Starling *d* William
A. Seiter *ph* Ernest Palmer

Loretta Young, Joel McCrea, David Niven,
Stuart Erwin, Marjorie Weaver, Pauline
Moore, Binnie Barnes, Jane Darwell, Leonid
Kinskey

Three Brave Men*

US 1956 88m bw Cinemascope
TCF (Herbert B. Swope Jnr)

A civilian employee in the US Navy is
suspended as a security risk and it takes a
lawsuit to set things straight.
Semi-factual anti-McCarthy drama proving
that America is a great place to live—when
you're winning. Good courtroom scenes.

wd Philip Dunne, *articles* Anthony Lewis
ph Charles G. Clarke *m* Hans Salter

Ray Milland, Ernest Borgnine, Nina Foch,
Dean Jagger, Frank Lovejoy, Edward
Andrews, Frank Faylen, James Westerfield,
Joseph Wiseman

The Three Caballeros***

US 1945 70m Technicolor
Walt Disney (Norman Ferguson)

A programme of shorts about South America,
linked by Donald Duck as a tourist.
Rapid-fire mélange of fragments supporting
the good neighbour policy, following the
shorter *Saludos Amigos* of 1943. The
kaleidoscopic sequences and the combination
of live action with cartoon remain of absorbing
interest.

w various *d* various *m* Edward Plumb, Paul
J. Smith, Charles Wolcott

† Stories include Pablo the Penguin, Little
Gauchito, a Mexican sequence and some
adventures with Joe Carioca.

AAN: Edward Plumb, Paul J. Smith, Charles
Wolcott

Three Came Home**

US 1950 106m bw
TCF (Nunnally Johnson)

In 1941 writer Agnes Newton Keith tries to
escape from Borneo but is interned and ill-
used by the Japanese.
Well-made, harrowing war adventure.

w Nunnally Johnson, *book* Agnes Newton
Keith *d* Jean Negulesco *ph* Milton Krasner
m Hugo Friedhofer *md* Lionel Newman

Claudette Colbert, Patric Knowles, Sessue
Hayakawa, Florence Desmond, Sylvia
Andrew, Phyllis Morris

Three Cases of Murder*

GB 1954 99m bw
British Lion / Wessex / London Films (Ian
Dalrymple, Hugh Perceval)

'In the Picture': a painting comes to life. 'You
Killed Elizabeth': a man suspects himself of
his faithless fiancée's murder. 'Lord
Mountdrago': the foreign secretary dreams of
killing an MP he hates.
Unlinked compendium, in which the first and
third stories are quite interesting and well
done, the second very commonplace.

w Donald Wilson, Sidney Caroll, Ian
Dalrymple (original stories Roderick
Wilkinson, Brett Halliday, W. Somerset
Maugham) *d* Wendy Toye, David Eady,
George More O'Ferrall *ph* Georges Périnal
m Doreen Carwithen

Alan Badel, Hugh Pryse, Leueen MacGrath,
Elizabeth Sellars, John Gregson, Emrys Jones,
Orson Welles, André Morell

Three Cheers for the Irish

US 1940 100m bw
Warner (Sam Bischoff)

An Irishman's daughter causes family trouble when she falls for a Scot.

Pleasant, unpretentious but overlong romantic comedy.

w Richard Macaulay, Jerry Wald *d* Lloyd Bacon *ph* Charles Rosher

Thomas Mitchell, Priscilla Lane, Dennis Morgan, Alan Hale, Virginia Grey, Irene Hervey, William Lundigan

Three Coins in the Fountain**
US 1954   102m   De Luxe   Cinemascope
TCF (Sol C. Siegel)

Three American girls find romance in Rome.

An enormous box office hit, the pattern of which was frequently repeated against various backgrounds; it was actually remade in Madrid as *The Pleasure Seekers*. In itself a thin entertainment, but the title song carried it.

w John Patrick, *novel* John H. Secondari *d* Jean Negulesco *ph* Milton Krasner *m* Victor Young *song Jule Styne, Sammy Cahn*

Clifton Webb, Dorothy McGuire, Louis Jourdan, Jean Peters, Rossano Brazzi, Maggie McNamara, Howard St John, Kathryn Givney, Cathleen Nesbitt

AA: Milton Krasner; title song
AAN: best picture

Three Comrades**
US 1938   98m   bw
MGM (Joseph L. Mankiewicz)

In twenties Germany, three friends find life hard but derive some joy from their love for a high-spirited girl who is dying of tuberculosis.

Despairing romance becomes a sentimental tearjerker with all the stops out; immaculately produced and very appealing to the masses, but prevented by censorship from being the intended indictment of Nazi Germany. The final scene in which the two surviving comrades are joined in the churchyard by their ghostly friends still packs a wallop.

w F. Scott Fitzgerald, Edward A. Paramore, *novel* Erich Maria Remarque *d* Frank Borzage *ph* Joseph Ruttenberg *m* Franx Waxman

Margaret Sullavan, Robert Taylor, Robert Young, Franchot Tone, Guy Kibbee, Lionel Atwill, Henry Hull, Charley Grapewin

'A remarkably high combination of talents has made it all very impressive and moving— good writing, a good man at the camera, good actors, and presiding over them a good director . . . such unforgettable bits as the pursuit of the boy who shot Gottfried, a glimpse from under the muffling blanket of the girl's stricken face, the startling downswoop of the camera's eye upon the girl getting up from bed to remove the burden of her illness from those who love her. These are high moments in a film full of beauty.'—*National Board of Review*

'A love story, beautifully told and consummately acted, but so drenched in hopelessness and heavy with the aroma of death, of wasted youth in a world of foggy shapes and nameless menaces, that its beauty and strength are often clouded and betrayed.'—*Time*

AAN: Margaret Sullavan

Three Cornered Moon*
US 1933   72m   bw
Paramount

A newly-poor Depression family has trouble finding work.

Slightly screwball romantic comedy, a predecessor of *You Can't Take It with You*; the humour now seems very faded, but it was a signpost of its day.

w S. K. Lauren, Ray Harris *d* Elliott Nugent *ph* Leon Shamroy

Claudette Colbert, Mary Boland, Richard Arlen, Wallace Ford, Lyda Roberti, Tom Brown, Hardie Albright

Three Daring Daughters
US 1948   115m   Technicolor
MGM (Joe Pasternak)
GB title: *The Birds and the Bees*

Three girls are dismayed to hear that their mother is remarrying.

Cheerful comedy with music, but nothing to write home about.

w Albert Mannheimer, Frederick Kohner, Sonya Levien, John Meehan *d* Fred M. Wilcox

Jeanette MacDonald, Jose Iturbi, Jane Powell, Anne Todd, Mary Elinor Donahue, Larry Adler, Edward Arnold, Harry Davenport, Moyna MacGill

Three Days of the Condor**
US 1975   118m   Technicolor
Panavision
Paramount/ Dino de Laurentiis / Wildwood (Stanley Schneider)

An innocent researcher for a branch of the CIA finds himself marked for death by assassins employed by another branch.

Entertaining New York-based thriller which shamelessly follows most of the twists of *The

39 Steps. It is just possible to follow its complexities, and the dialogue is smart.

w Lorenzo Semple Jnr, David Rayfiel, novel Six Days of the Condor by James Grady *d Sydney Pollack ph* Owen Roizman *m* Dave Grusin

Robert Redford, Faye Dunaway, Cliff Robertson, Max Von Sydow, John Houseman, Walter McGinn

Three Faces East*
US 1930 71m bw
Warner (Darryl F. Zanuck)

The butler to the British war minister is a German spy, and the German nurse sent to help him is really a British agent . . .
Slow, melodramatic remake of 1926 silent, later turned into a Karloff vehicle, *British Intelligence* (qv).

w Oliver H. P. Garrett, Arthur Caesar, *play* Anthony Paul Kelly *d* Roy del Ruth *ph* Chick McGill

Constance Bennett, Erich Von Stroheim, Anthony Bushell, William Holden

The Three Faces of Eve**
US 1957 95m bw Cinemascope
TCF (Nunnally Johnson)

A psychiatrist discovers that a female patient has three distinct personalities: a drab housewife, a good time girl and a mature sophisticated woman.
Alistair Cooke introduces this tall tale as if he believed it; as presented, it is entertaining but not very convincing. Its box office success was sufficient to start a schizophrenia cycle.

w Nunnally Johnson, *book* Corbett H. Thigpen MD, Hervey M. Cleckley MD *d* Nunnally Johnson *ph* Stanley Cortez *m* Robert Emmett Dolan

Joanne Woodward, Lee J. Cobb, David Wayne, Nancy Kulp, Edwin Jerome

AA: Joanne Woodward

Three Faces West
US 1940 79m bw
Republic (Sol C. Siegel)

A dust bowl community is helped by an Austrian doctor fleeing from the Nazis, but his daughter is followed by a Nazi suitor.
Unusual modern western, blandly told.

w F. Hugh Herbert, Joseph Moncure March, Samuel Ornitz *d* Bernard Vorhaus *ph* John Alton *m* Victor Young

John Wayne, Charles Coburn, Sigrid Gurie, Roland Varno, Spencer Charters, Sonny Bupp

Three for Bedroom C
US 1952 74m Natural Color
Brenco (Edward L. Alperson Jnr)

Confusion reigns on a train when a film star takes a compartment booked for a Harvard scientist.
Inept farce which never rises above mediocrity and coasts along well below it.

wd Milton H. Bren *ph* Ernest Laszlo *m* Heinz Roemheld

Gloria Swanson, Fred Clark, James Warren, Hans Conried, Steve Brodie, Margaret Dumont

Three for Jamie Dawn
US 1956 81m bw
AA (Hayes Goetz)

A crooked lawyer bribes three members of a murder jury.
Minor courtroom melodrama, limply developed.

w John Klempner *d* Thomas Carr *ph* Duke Green *m* Walter Scharf

Laraine Day, Ricardo Montalban, Richard Carlson, June Havoc

Three for the Show*
US 1955 93m Technicolor
Cinemascope
Columbia (Jonie Taps)

A married Broadway star finds that her first husband is still alive.
Adequate musical remake of *Too Many Husbands* (qv); not bad, not good.

w Edward Hope, Leonard Stern, *play* Too Many Husbands by W. Somerset Maugham *d* H. C. Potter *ph* Arthur E. Arling *ch* Jack Cole *songs* various

Betty Grable, Jack Lemmon, Marge Champion, Gower Champion, Myron McCormick, Paul Harvey

Three Girls about Town*
US 1942 71m bw
Columbia

Three sisters in New York find a corpse in their hotel bedroom.
A funny 'B' picture: fast paced and lively from start to finish.

w Richard Carroll *d* Leigh Jason *ph* Franz Planer

Joan Blondell, Binnie Barnes, Janet Blair, John Howard, Robert Benchley, Eric Blore, Una O'Connor

Three Godfathers*
US 1948   106m   Technicolor
MGM / Argosy (John Ford)

Three outlaws escaping across the desert take charge of an orphan baby.
'Orrible sentimental parable partly redeemed by splendid scenery.

w Laurence Stallings, Frank S. Nugent, *story* Frank B. Kyne   *d* John Ford   *ph* Winton Hoch   *m* Richard Hageman

John Wayne, Pedro Armendariz, Harry Carey Jnr, Ward Bond

† The story also appeared in 1909 as *Bronco Billy and the Baby*; in 1916 as *Three Godfathers*, with Harry Carey; in 1920 as *Marked Men*, with Harry Carey; in 1929 as *Hell's Heroes*, with Charles Bickford; in 1936 as *Three Godfathers*, with Chester Morris; and in 1975 as a TV movie, *The Godchild*, with Jack Palance.

Three Guys Named Mike
US 1951   90m   bw
MGM (Armand Deutsch)

An accident-prone air hostess has three suitors.
Inconsequential romantic comedy which shows the effort of stretching its thin material to feature length.

w Sidney Sheldon, *story* Ruth Brooks Flippen   *d* Charles Walters   *ph* Paul Vogel   *m* Bronislau Kaper

Jane Wyman, Barry Sullivan, Van Johnson, Howard Keel, Phyllis Kirk, Jeff Donnell

Three Hearts for Julia
US 1943   90m   bw

A reporter courts his wife all over again when she threatens to divorce him. One of those thin romantic comedies which sent its male lead back to the theatre. Melvyn Douglas, Ann Sothern, Lee Bowman, Felix Bressart, Reginald Owen, Richard Ainley. Written by Lionel Houser; directed by Richard Thorpe; for MGM.

The 300 Spartans*
US 1962   114m   De Luxe   Cinemascope
TCF (Rudolph Maté, George St George)

Sparta leads the ancient Greek states against Persia's attack at Thermopylae.
Quite a lively epic with some dignity.

w George St George   *d* Rudolph Maté   *ph* Geoffrey Unsworth   *m* Manos Hadjikakis

Richard Egan, Ralph Richardson, David Farrar, Diane Baker, Barry Coc, Donald Houston, Kieron Moore, John Crawford, Robert Brown

Three Husbands
US 1950   76m   bw
UA / Gloria (I. G. Goldsmith)

Three husbands receive letters from a dead friend claiming that he had affairs with each of their wives.
Silly copy of *A Letter to Three Wives*, with neither style nor sophistication.

w Vera Caspary, Edward Eliscu   *d* Irving Reis   *ph* Franz Planer   *m* Herschel Burke Gilbert

Emlyn Williams, Eve Arden, Howard da Silva, Ruth Warrick, Shepperd Strudwick, Vanessa Brown, Billie Burke, Jonathan Hale

Three in the Attic
US 1968   90m   Pathecolor
AIP - Hermes (Richard Wilson)

A college Casanova is locked in an attic by three girls who seduce him by rota until he cries for mercy.
One of the first outspoken comedies of the sexual revolution, but not a particularly funny one.

w Stephen Yafa, from his novel Paxton Quigley's Had the Course   *d* Richard Wilson   *ph* J. Burgi Contner   *m* Chad Stuart

Chris Jones, Yvette Mimieux, Judy Pace, Maggie Turett, Nan Martin

Three into Two Won't Go*
GB 1969   100m   Technicolor
Universal (Julian Blaustein)

An executive has an affair with a girl hitch-hiker who later moves into his house to his wife's astonishment.
Palatable sex drama with good performances, rather flabbily written and directed.

w Edna O'Brien, *novel* Andrea Newman   *d* Peter Hall   *ph* Walter Lassally   *m* Francis Lai

Rod Steiger, Claire Bloom, Judy Geeson, Peggy Ashcroft, Paul Rogers

Three Little Girls in Blue
US 1946   90m   Technicolor
TCF (Mack Gordon)

Musical remake of *Three Blind Mice* (qv); adequate and quite forgettable.

w Valentine Davies   *d* Bruce Humberstone   *ph* Ernest Palmer   *songs* Mack Gordon, Joseph Myrow

June Haver, George Montgomery, Vivian Blaine, Celeste Holm, Vera-Ellen, Frank Latimore, Charles Smith, Charles Halton

Three Little Words*
US 1950   102m   Technicolor
MGM (Jack Cummings)

The careers of songwriters Bert Kalmar and Harry Ruby.
Disappointingly ordinary musical in which two witty people are made to seem dull, and the plot allows Fred Astaire only one dance.

w George Wells *d* Richard Thorpe *ph* Harry Jackson *md* André Previn *ch* Hermes Pan *songs* Bert Kalmar, Harry Ruby and various collaborators

Fred Astaire, Red Skelton, Vera-Ellen, Arlene Dahl, Keenan Wynn, Gale Robbins, Gloria de Haven, Phil Regan, *Debbie Reynolds*

AAN: André Previn

The Three Lives of Thomasina
GB 1963   97m   Technicolor
Walt Disney

In a Scottish village in 1912, a vet finds that his methods are no match for a local girl who treats animals by giving them love.
Syrupy film for children: the animals are the main interest and one of them narrates . . .

w Robert Westerby, *novel* Thomasina by Paul Gallico *d* Don Chaffey *ph* Paul Beeson *m* Paul Smith

Susan Hampshire, Patrick McGoohan, Karen Dotrice, Vincent Winter, Laurence Naismith, Finlay Currie, Wilfrid Brambell

Three Loves Has Nancy
US 1938   69m   bw
MGM (Norman Krasna)

A jilted bride takes her time about her next selection.
Adequate star comedy.

w Bella and Sam Spewack, George Oppenheimer, David Hertz *d* Richard Thorpe *ph* William Daniels

Janet Gaynor, Robert Montgomery, Franchot Tone, Guy Kibbee, Claire Dodd, Reginald Owen, Charley Grapewin, Emma Dunn, Cora Witherspoon

The Three Maxims
GB 1937   87m   bw
GFD / Pathé Consortium (Herbert Wilcox)

Two trapezists love the girl member of the team, and the situation leads to attempted murder.
Effective Paris-set treatment of a well worn theme (see *Trapeze*).

w Herman Mankiewicz *d* Herbert Wilcox

Anna Neagle, Tullio Carminati, Leslie Banks, Horace Hodges

Three Men in a Boat
GB 1956   94m   Eastmancolor Cinemascope
Romulus (Jack Clayton)

In the 1890s, misadventures befall three men holidaying on the Thames.
Flabby burlesque of a celebrated comic novel whose style is never even approached.

w Hubert Gregg, Vernon Harris, *novel* Jerome K. Jerome *d* Ken Annakin *ph* Eric Cross *m* John Addison *ad* John Howell

David Tomlinson, Jimmy Edwards, Laurence Harvey, Shirley Eaton, Robertson Hare, Jill Ireland, Lisa Gastoni, Martita Hunt, A. E. Matthews, Ernest Thesiger, Adrienne Corri
† A previous version in 1933 starred William Austin, Edmond Breon and Billy Milton; directed by Graham Cutts for ATP.

Three Men on a Horse*
US 1936   85m   bw
Warner (Sam Bischoff)

A timid Brooklynite finds he can always pick winners, and gangsters get interested.
Smooth New Yorkish comedy which pleased at the time.

w Laird Doyle, *play* John Cecil Holm, George Abbott *d* Mervyn Le Roy *ph* Sol Polito

Frank McHugh, Sam Levene, Joan Blondell, Guy Kibbee, Carol Hughes, Allen Jenkins, Edgar Kennedy, Eddie Anderson, Harry Davenport

The Three Mesquiteers
A three-man cowboy team who operated in popular B features at the Hopalong Cassidy level. The make-up of the team varied: the actors most often found in it were John Wayne, Max Terhune, Bob Livingston, Ray Corrigan, Bob Steele, Rufe Davis, Tom Tyler, Raymond Hatton, Duncan Renaldo and Jimmy Dodd. The first film was made for RKO, all the rest for Republic: most frequent directors were George Sherman, Mack V. Wright, Joseph Kane, John English and Lester Orlebeck.

1935: POWDERSMOKE RANGE, THE THREE MESQUITEERS
1936: GHOST TOWN, GOLD, ROARIN' LEAD
1937: RIDERS OF THE WHISTLING SKULL, HIT THE SADDLE, GUNSMOKE RANCH, COME ON COWBOYS, RANGE DEFENDERS, HEART OF THE

ROCKIES, THE TRIGGER TRIO, WILD HORSE RODEO
1938: THE PURPLE VIGILANTES, CALL THE MESQUITEERS, CALL OF THE MESQUITEERS, OUTLAWS OF SONORA, RIDERS OF THE BLACK HILLS, HEROES OF THE HILLS, PALS OF THE SADDLE, OVERLAND STAGE RAIDERS, SANTA FE STAMPEDE, RED RIVER RANGE
1939: THE NIGHT RIDERS, THREE TEXAS STEERS, WYOMING OUTLAW, NEW FRONTIER, THE KANSAS TERRORS, COWBOYS FROM TEXAS
1940: HEROES OF THE SADDLE, PIONEERS OF THE WEST, COVERED WAGON DAYS, ROCKY MOUNTAIN RANGERS, OKLAHOMA RENEGADES, UNDER TEXAS SKIES, THE TRAIL BLAZERS, LONE STAR RAIDERS
1941: PRAIRIE PIONEERS, PALS OF THE PECOS, SADDLEMATES, GANGS OF SONORA, OUTLAWS OF THE CHEROKEE TRAIL, GAUCHOS OF EL DORADO, WEST OF CIMARRON
1942: CODE OF THE OUTLAW, RIDERS OF THE RANGE, WESTWARD HO, THE PHANTOM PLAINSMAN, SHADOWS ON THE SAGE, VALLEY OF HUNTED MEN
1943: THUNDERING TRAILS, THE BLOCKED TRAIL, SANTA FE SCOUTS, RIDERS OF THE RIO GRANDE

The Three Musketeers**
US 1939   73m   bw
TCF
GB title: *The Singing Musketeer*

A burlesque of the familiar story with pauses for song.
A very satisfactory entertainment with all concerned in top form.

w M. M. Musselman, William A. Drake, Sam Hellman   *d Allan Dwan   ph* Peverell Marley

Don Ameche, the Ritz Brothers, Binnie Barnes, *Joseph Schildkraut*, Lionel Atwill, Miles Mander, Gloria Stuart, Pauline Moore, John Carradine

The Three Musketeers***
US 1948   125m   Technicolor
MGM (Pandro S. Berman)

High-spirited version of the famous story, with duels and fights presented like musical numbers. Its vigour and inventiveness is a pleasure to behold.

w Robert Ardrey   *d George Sidney   ph* Robert Planck   *m* Herbert Stothart

Gene Kelly, Lana Turner, June Allyson, Frank Morgan, Van Heflin, Angela Lansbury, Vincent Price, Keenan Wynn, John Sutton, Gig Young, Robert Coote, Reginald Owen, Ian Keith, Patricia Medina

'A heavy, rough-housing mess. As Lady de Winter, Lana Turner sounds like a drive-in waitress exchanging quips with hotrodders, and as Richelieu, Vincent Price might be an especially crooked used car dealer. Angela Lansbury wears the crown of France as though she had won it at a county fair.'—*New Yorker, 1980*

AAN: Robert Planck

The Three Musketeers (The Queen's Diamonds)**
Panama 1973   107m   Technicolor
Film Trust (Alex Salkind)

Jokey version with realistic blood; despite very lively highlights it wastes most of its high production cost by not giving its plot a chance; but money was saved by issuing the second half separately as *The Four Musketeers* (*The Revenge of Milady*). The latter section was less attractive.

w George MacDonald Fraser   *d Richard Lester   ph David Watkin   m* Michel Legrand   *pd* Brian Eatwell

Michael York, Oliver Reed, Richard Chamberlain, Frank Finlay, Raquel Welch, Geraldine Chaplin, Spike Milligan, Faye Dunaway, Charlton Heston, Christopher Lee, Jean-Pierre Cassel

'It's one dragged-out forced laugh. No sweep, no romance, no convincing chivalric tradition to mock.'—*Stanley Kauffmann*

Three on a Match
US 1932   63m   bw
Warner (Sam Bischoff)

Three schoolgirl friends meet again in the big city, after which their paths cross melodramatically.
Predictable, watchable multi-story dramatics with an ironic twist: remade in 1938 as *Broadway Musketeers*.

w Lucien Hubbard   *d Mervyn Le Roy   ph* Sol Polito

Joan Blondell, Bette Davis, Ann Dvorak, Warren William, Grant Mitchell, Lyle Talbot, Humphrey Bogart, Glenda Farrell, Clara Blandick

Three Ring Circus
US 1954   103m   Technicolor
   Vistavision
Paramount / Hal B. Wallis

Ex-army veterans join a circus.
The mixture as before from Martin and Lewis:
variety acts interspersed with sentiment and
heavy mugging.

w Don McGuire, Joseph Pevney ph Loyal
Griggs d Joseph Pevney m Walter Scharf

Dean Martin, Jerry Lewis, Joanne Dru, Zsa
Zsa Gabor, Wallace Ford, Sig Rumann, Gene
Sheldon, Nick Cravat, Elsa Lanchester

Three Sailors and a Girl
US 1953 95m Technicolor
Warner (Sammy Cahn)

A ship's funds are unofficially invested in a
musical show.
Undernourished comedy musical.

w Roland Kibbee, Devery Freeman, *play* The
Butter and Egg Man by George S. Kaufman
d Roy del Ruth ph Carl Guthrie
songs Sammy Fain, Sammy Cahn

Jane Powell, Gordon Macrae, Gene Nelson,
Sam Levene, George Givot, Veda Ann Borg

Three Secrets*
US 1949 98m bw
(Warner) US Pictures (Milton Sperling)

Three women wait anxiously to find out whose
child survived a plane crash.
Well-made, formula woman's picture.

w Martin Rackin, Gina Kaus d *Robert Wise*
ph Sid Hickox m Davis Buttolph

Eleanor Parker, Patricia Neal, Ruth Roman,
Frank Lovejoy, Leif Erickson, Ted de Corsia,
Edmon Ryan, Larry Keating

The Three Sisters*
GB 1970 165m Eastmancolor
Alan Clore Films

At the turn of the century, three fatherless
sisters dream of abandoning Russian
provincial life for the big city.
Filmed Chekhov, better than most but still
lacking cinematic vigour.

translator Moura Budberg d Laurence
Olivier ph Geoffrey Unsworth m William
Walton

Laurence Olivier, Joan Plowright, Jeanne
Watts, Louise Purnell, Derek Jacobi, Alan
Bates, Ronald Pickup

Three Smart Girls**
US 1936 86m bw
Universal (Joe Pasternak)

Three sisters bring their parents back together.
Pleasant, efficient family film which made a
world star of Deanna Durbin.

w Adele Comandini, Austin Parker d Henry
Koster ph Joseph Valentine md Charles
Previn

Deanna Durbin, Barbara Read, Nan Grey,
Charles Winninger, Binnie Barnes, Ray
Milland, Alice Brady, Mischa Auer, Ernest
Cossart, Hobart Cavanaugh
'Idiotically tuned in to happiness, but it isn't
boring.'—*New Yorker, 1978*

AAN: best picture; script

Three Smart Girls Grow Up*
US 1939 87m bw
Universal (Joe Pasternak)

A girl helps her sisters to find beaus.
More of the above, quite palatable but
inevitably warmed over.

w Bruce Manning, Felix Jackson d Henry
Koster ph Joe Valentine

Deanna Durbin, Helen Parrish, Nan Grey,
Charles Winninger, Robert Cummings,
William Lundigan, Ernest Cossart, Nella
Walker
'The white feminine room which the three
sisters share, the quilted beds, the little furry
jackets over the pajamas—the whole
upholstery is so virginal that it evokes little
twitters of nostalgia from the stalls. Pillow
fights and first love and being sent to bed
without any dinner—the awkward age has
never been so laundered and lavendered and
laid away.'—*Graham Greene*

Three Strangers*
US 1946 92m bw
Warner (Wolfgang Reinhardt)

A sweepstake ticket brings fortune and
tragedy to three ill-assorted people.
Humdrum pattern play: the stars work hard to
bring a little magic to it.

w John Huston, Howard Koch d Jean
Negulesco ph Arthur Edeson m Adolph
Deutsch

Sidney Greenstreet, Peter Lorre, Geraldine
Fitzgerald, Joan Lorring, Robert Shayne,
Marjorie Riordan, Arthur Shields

Three Stripes in the Sun
US 1955 93m bw
Columbia (Fred Kohlmar)
GB title: *The Gentle Sergeant*

After World War II, a Japanese-hating
sergeant in the US occupation forces helps a
poverty-stricken orphanage.
Predictable sentimentality based on fact, with
good background detail.

wd Richard Murphy, *articles* E. J. Kelly
ph Burnett Guffey *m* George Duning

Aldo Ray, Phil Carey, Dick York, Chuck
Connors, Mitsuko Kimura

3.10 to Yuma**
US 1957 92m bw
Columbia (David Heilwell)

A sheriff has to get his prisoner on to a train
despite the threatening presence of the
prisoner's outlaw friends.
Tense, well-directed but rather talky low-
budget western: excellent performances and
atmosphere flesh out an unconvincing physical
situation.

w Halsted Welles *d Delmer Daves*
ph Charles Lawton Jnr *m* George Duning
Glenn Ford, Van Heflin, Felicia Farr, Leora
Dana, Henry Jones, Richard Jaeckel, Robert
Emhardt

'A vivid, tense and intelligent story about
probable people, enhanced by economical
writing and supremely efficient direction and
playing.'—*Guardian*

Three Violent People
US 1956 100m Eastmancolor
Vistavision
Paramount (Hugh Brown)

Brother ranchers quarrel over the wife of one
of them, an ex-saloon hostess.
Characterless 'character' western, a long way
after *Duel in the Sun*.

w James Edward Grant *d* Rudolph Maté
ph Loyal Griggs *m* Walter Scharf
Charlton Heston, Anne Baxter, *Gilbert
Roland*, Tom Tryon, Bruce Bennett, Forrest
Tucker, Elaine Stritch, Barton MacLane

The Three Weird Sisters
GB 1948 82m bw
British National (Louis H. Jackson)

Three old maids in a Welsh village plot to kill
their rich half-brother but are swept away by a
flood.
All-stops-out melodrama which doesn't quite
work and is generally remembered, if at all,
for the last third of its writing team.

w Louise Birt, David Evans, Dylan Thomas,
novel Charlotte Armstrong *d* Dan Birt
Nancy Price, Mary Clare, Mary Merrall, Nova
Pilbeam, Raymond Lovell, Anthony Hulme

Three Wise Fools
US 1946 90m bw
MGM (William Wright)

Three crusty old gents adopt an orphan, who
softens them.
Antediluvian whimsy without the expected
fun, remade from a silent.

w John McDermott, James O'Hanlon, *play*
Austin Strong *d* Edward Buzzell
Margaret O'Brien, Lionel Barrymore, Thomas
Mitchell, Edward Arnold, Lewis Stone, Jane
Darwell, Harry Davenport, Cyd Charisse

Three Wise Girls
US 1932 80m approx bw
Columbia

Three small-town girls gain wisdom in New
York.
Three millgirls' romances for the price of one.
Adequate, predictable romantic fodder of its
time.

w Robert Riskin, Agnes C. Johnson
d William Beaudine *ph* Ted Tetzlaff
Jean Harlow, Mae Clarke, Walter Byron,
Marie Prevost, Andy Devine, Natalie
Moorhead, Jameson Thomas

Three Women*
US 1924 60m approx (24 fps) bw
silent
Warner

A rake charms three women, each for a
different purpose.
Subtle satirical comedy; not one of the
director's masterpieces, but with enough barbs
to keep one watching.

w Ernst Lubitsch, Hans Kraly, from The Lilie
by Yolanthe Marees *d Ernst Lubitsch*
ph Charles Van Enger
Lew Cody, Pauline Frederick, May McAvoy,
Marie Prevost

Three Women
US 1977 123m De Luxe Panavision
TCF / Lion's Gate (Robert Altman)

Three women come to California for different
reasons; when their problems become
insurmountable they rely on each other.
Tiresomely somnambulistic multi-character
drama, half a satire, half a wallow, and never
an entertainment.

wd Robert Altman *ph* Charles Rosher
m Gerald Busby
Sissy Spacek, Janice Rule, Shelley Duvall,
Robert Fortier, Ruth Nelson, John Cromwell,
Sierra Pecheur

The Three Worlds of Gulliver
US / Spain 1959 100m Technicolor
Columbia / Morningside (Charles Schneer)

Gulliver's adventures in Lilliput and Brobdingnag.

Flat treatment of marvellous material, with all the excitement squeezed out of it and not even much pizazz in the trick photography.

w Arthur Ross, Jack Sher *d* Jack Sher *ph* Wilkie Cooper *m* Bernard Herrmann *sp* Ray Harryhausen

Kerwin Mathews, Basil Sydney, Mary Ellis, Jo Morrow, June Thorburn, Grégoire Aslan, Charles Lloyd Pack, Martin Benson

Thrill of a Romance
US 1945 105m Technicolor
MGM (Joe Pasternak)

A lady swimmer falls for a returning serviceman.

Empty musical vehicle with nothing memorable about it except the waste of time and money.

w Richard Connell, Gladys Lehmann *d* Richard Thorpe *ph* Harry Stradling *md* George Stoll

Esther Williams, Van Johnson, Lauritz Melchior, Frances Gifford, Henry Travers, Spring Byington, Tommy Dorsey

The Thrill of it All*
US 1963 104m Eastmancolor
U-I / Ross Hunter / Arwin (Ross Hunter, Marty Melcher)

The wife of a gynaecologist becomes an advertising model, and work pressures disrupt her marriage.

Glossy matrimonial farce which starts brightly but eventually flags and becomes exhausting. Its better jokes linger in the memory.

w Carl Reiner *d* Norman Jewison *ph* Russell Metty *m* Frank de Vol

Doris Day, James Garner, Arlene Francis, Edward Andrews, Reginald Owen, Zasu Pitts, Elliot Reid

'Pleasantly reminiscent of some of the screwball comedies of the thirties.'—*MFB*

Throne of Blood*
Japan 1957 105m bw
Toho (Akira Kurosawa, Sojiro Motoki)
original title: *Kumonosu-Jo*

A samurai, spurred on by his wife and an old witch, murders his lord at Cobweb Castle.

A Japanese version of *Macbeth* with a savage and horrifying final sequence. The whole film is a treat to look at.

w Hideo Oguni, Shinobu Hashimoto, Ryuzo Kikushima, Akira Kurosawa, from Shakespeare's play *d* Akira Kurosawa *ph* Asaichi Nakai *m* Masaru Sato

Toshiro Mifune, Isuzu Yamada

'Its final impression is of a man who storms into a room with an impassioned speech to deliver and then discovers that he has forgotten what he came to say.'—*Kenneth Cavander, MFB*

Through a Glass Darkly*
Sweden 1961 91m bw
Svensk Filmindustri

Four unfulfilled people on a remote island fail to communicate with each other or to understand what God is.

It sounds like a parody Bergman film, and it almost is. The same themes were carried through in *Winter Light* and *The Silence*.

wd Ingmar Bergman *ph* Sven Nykvist *m* Bach

Harriet Andersson, Gunnar Bjornstrand, Max Von Sydow, Lars Passgard

AA: best foreign film
AAN: Ingmar Bergman (as writer)

Through Different Eyes
US 1943 65m bw

A veteran DA cites an old murder case to illustrate the dangers of circumstantial evidence. Neat and peppy crime programme filler. Frank Craven, Donald Woods, Vivian Blaine, Mary Howard, Jerome Cowan. Written by Samuel G. Engel; directed by Thomas Z. Loring; for TCF.

Thumb Tripping*
US 1972 94m De Luxe
Avco (Robert Chartoff, Irwin Winkler)

A boy and a girl hitch-hiker in California have a variety of violent adventures.

Tail end of the *Easy Rider* fashion, with odd moments of interesting detail.

w Don Mitchell, from his novel *d* Quentin Masters *ph* Harry Stradling Jnr *m* Bob Thompson

Michael Burns, Meg Foster, Marianna Hill, Bruce Dern

Thunder
US 1929 90m at 24 fps bw silent

A train driver has trouble with his sons. Almost forgotten star melodrama, his last silent one, made when his health was already failing. Lon Chaney, James Murray, George Duryea, Phyllis Haver. Written by Byron Morgan and Ann Price; directed by William Nigh; for MGM.

Thunder Afloat
US 1939 95m bw

Rival boat owners vie for a 1918 navy
contract, and the winner finds he has been
trapped into enlisting. Rumbustious Flagg-
and-Quirt style comedy, good enough value
for the undemanding. Wallace Beery, Chester
Morris, Virginia Grey, Douglass Dumbrille,
Regis Toomey, Henry Victor, Jonathan Hale.
Written by Ralph Wheelwright, Wells Root
and Harvey Haislip; directed by George B.
Seitz; for MGM.

Thunder Bay*
US 1953   102m   Technicolor
U-I (Aaron Rosenberg)

An engineer is convinced that oil can be raised
from the Louisiana sea-bed.
Well-produced outdoor actioner.

w Gil Doud, John Michael Hayes d Anthony
Mann ph William Daniels m Frank Skinner

James Stewart, Joanne Dru, Dan Duryea, Jay
C. Flippen, Anthony Moreno, Gilbert Roland,
Marcia Henderson

Thunder Below
US 1932   71m   bw

A wife loves her husband's best friend. Dreary
melodrama with a star already seen to be box
office poison. Tallulah Bankhead, Charles
Bickford, Paul Lukas. From a novel by
Thomas Rourke; directed by Richard Wallace;
for Paramount.

Thunder in the City
GB 1937   88m   bw
Atlantic (Akos Tolnay, Alexander Esway)

An American salesman in London helps a
penniless duke promote a non-existent metal.
Mild satire on British and American
idiosyncrasies, now very faded.

w Robert Sherwood, Abem Kandel, Akos
Tolnay d Marion Gering ph Al Gilks
m Miklos Rozsa

Edward G. Robinson, Lulu Deste, Ralph
Richardson, Nigel Bruce, Constance Collier,
Arthur Wontner

Thunder in the East
US 1951   98m   bw
Paramount (Everett Riskin)

When India becomes independent in 1947, an
American wanting to sell arms clashes with the
peace-loving chief of a principality, but the
arms are needed when rebels attack.
Artificial and boring action melodrama with
platitudinous conversations.

w Jo Swerling, novel Rage of the Vulture by
Alan Moorehead d Charles Vidor ph Lee
Garmes m Hugo Friedhofer

Alan Ladd, Charles Boyer, Deborah Kerr,
Corinne Calvet, Cecil Kellaway

Thunder in the Sun
US 1958   81m   Technicolor
Seven Arts / Carollton (Clarence Greene)

In 1847 an Indian scout guides a group of
Basques to California with their vines.
Overwritten and melodramatic wagon train
story.

wd Russel Rouse ph Stanley Cortez m Cyril
Mockridge

Susan Hayward, Jeff Chandler, Jacques
Bergerac, Blanche Yurka, Carl Esmond

A Thunder of Drums*
US 1961   97m   Metrocolor
   Cinemascope
MGM (Robert J. Enders)

Trouble with Apaches at a frontier post in
1870.
Solid, unexciting first feature western, some
way after Ford.

w James Warner Bellah d Joseph Newman
ph William Spencer m Harry Sukman

Richard Boone, George Hamilton, Arthur
O'Connell, Luana Patten, Richard
Chamberlain, Charles Bronson

Thunder on the Hill
US 1951   84m   bw
U-I (Michael Kraike)
GB title: Bonaventure

In Norfolk, a nun solves a murder mystery
during a flood.
Modest whodunnit with an unusual
background but not much suspense.

w Oscar Saul, André Solt, play Bonaventure
by Charlotte Hastings d Douglas Sirk
ph William Daniels m Hans Salter

Claudette Colbert, Ann Blyth, Robert
Douglas, Anne Crawford, Philip Friend,
Gladys Cooper, John Abbott, Connie
Gilchrist, Gavin Muir

Thunder over the Plains
US 1953   82m   Warnercolor

After the Civil War, a Union officer is posted
with his family to the southwest territory, and
finds tension. Busy but uninvolving western
programmer with a reliable star. Randolph
Scott, Phyllis Kirk, Lex Barker, Charles
McGraw, Elisha Cook Jnr, Fess Parker.
Written by Russell Hughes; directed by André
de Toth; for Warner.

Thunder Road*
US 1958 92m bw
UA / DRM

Hillbilly bootleggers defy a Chicago gangster.
Downbeat but actionful crime melodrama with
an unusual background and plenty of car
chases.

w James Arlee Philips, Walter Wise d Arthur
Ripley ph Alan Stensvold m Jack Marshall

Robert Mitchum, Gene Barry, Jacques
Aubuchon, Keely Smith

Thunder Rock***
GB 1942 112m bw
Charter Films (John Boulting)

A journalist disgusted with the world of the
thirties retires to a lighthouse on Lake
Michigan and is haunted by the ghosts of
immigrants drowned a century before.
Subtle adaptation of an impressive and topical
anti-isolationist play, very well acted and
presented.

w Jeffrey Dell, Bernard Miles, play Robert
Ardrey d Roy Boulting ph Mutz Greenbaum
(Max Greene) m Hans May

Michael Redgrave, Lilli Palmer, Barbara
Mullen, James Mason, Frederick Valk,
Frederick Cooper, Finlay Currie, Sybilla
Binder

'Boldly imaginative in theme and
treatment.'—Sunday Express
'More interesting technically than anything
since Citizen Kane.'—Manchester Guardian

Thunderball**
GB 1965 132m Technicolor
Panavision
UA / Eon / Kevin McClory

James Bond goes underwater.
Commercially the most successful Bond, but
certainly not the best despite a plethora of
action sequences.

w Richard Maibaum, John Hopkins, novel Ian
Fleming d Terence Young ph Ted Moore
m John Barry

Sean Connery, Adolfo Celi, Claudine Auger,
Luciana Paluzzi, Rik Van Nutter, Bernard
Lee, Lois Maxwell, Martine Beswick

'The screenplay stands on tiptoe at the
outermost edge of the suggestive and gazes
yearningly down into the obscene.'—John
Simon

Thunderbird Six
GB 1968 90m Techniscope
UA / AP / Century 21 (Gerry and Sylvia
Anderson)

International Rescue combats the Black
Phantom.
Bright, suspenseful puppetoon based on the
TV series.

w Gerry and Sylvia Anderson d David Lane
ph Harry Oakes m Barry Gray ad Bob Bell

'Holds some charm for adults, or at least for
those who enjoy playing with miniature
trains.'—MFB

Thunderbirds
US 1942 79m Technicolor
TCF (Lamar Trotti)

Problems of Arizona flight instructors during
World War II.
Very minor flagwaver.

w Lamar Trotti d William A. Wellman
ph Ernest Palmer m David Buttolph

Gene Tierney, Preston Foster, John Sutton,
Jack Holt, May Whitty, George Barbier,
Richard Haydn, Reginald Denny, Ted North

Thunderbirds
US 1952 99m bw
Republic (John H. Auer)

An Oklahoma unit covers itself in glory during
World War II.
Scrappy, noisy war actioner with much
newsreel footage.

w Mary McCall Jnr d John H. Auer
ph Reggie Lanning m Victor Young

John Derek, John Barrymore Jnr, Mona
Freeman, Ward Bond, Gene Evans

Thunderbolt**
US 1929 94m bw
Paramount

A gangster is caught, tried, and repents.
Gloomy melodrama with interesting style and
credits.

w Jules Furthman, Herman J. Mankiewicz
d Josef Von Sternberg ph Henry Gerrard

George Bancroft, Fay Wray, Richard Arlen,
Tully Marshall, Eugénie Besserer

AAN: George Bancroft

Thunderbolt and Lightfoot*
US 1974 115m De Luxe Panavision
UA / Malpaso (Robert Daley)

A bank robber escapes prison, disguises
himself as a preacher, befriends a young
drifter, and discovers that a new building
stands on the spot where the loot is hidden.
Violent melodrama reworking an ancient
comedy situation; well made on its level.

wd Michael Cimino *ph* Frank Stanley *m* Dee Barton

Clint Eastwood, Jeff Bridges, George Kennedy, Geoffrey Lewis, Catherine Bach

AAN: Jeff Bridges

Thunderhead, Son of Flicka*
US 1945 78m Technicolor
TCF (Robert Bassler)

More where *My Friend Flicka* came from. Unexceptionable family film with excellent outdoor photography.

w Dwight Cummins, Dorothy Yost, *novel* Mary O'Hara *d* Louis King *ph* Charles Clarke *m* Cyril Mockridge

Roddy McDowall, Preston Foster, Rita Johnson, James Bell, Carleton Young

Thunderstorm
GB 1955 88m bw
Hemisphere / Binnie Barnes

A Spanish fisherman rescues a mysterious girl from a derelict yacht and falls in love with her although the villagers regard her as a witch. Heady stuff on a low budget, quite smoothly done for lovers of peasant drama.

w George St George, Geoffrey Holmes *d* John Guillermin *ph* Manuel Berenguer *m* Paul Misraki

Linda Christian, Carlos Thompson, Charles Korvin

Thursday's Child
GB 1942 81m bw

A child from an ordinary family has success in films and it goes to her head. Predictable domestic drama with some good moments, but rather overpraised at the time. Sally Ann Howes, Wilfrid Lawson, Kathleen O'Regan, Eileen Bennett, Stewart Granger, Felix Aylmer. Written by Donald Macardle and Rodney Ackland, from the novel by Donald Macardle; directed by Rodney Ackland; for ABPC.

THX 1138*
US 1970 95m Technicolor / scope
Warner / American Zoetrope (Francis Ford Coppola,
     Lawrence Sturhahn)

In a future society, computer programmed and emotionless, an automated human begins to break the rules.
Orwellian science fiction; a thoughtful, rather cold affair which is always good to look at.

w George Lucas, Walter Murch *d* George Lucas *ph* Dave Meyers, Albert Kihn *m* Lalo Schifrin

Robert Duvall, Donald Pleasence, Pedro Colley, Maggie McOmie, Ian Wolfe

Thy Soul Shall Bear Witness*
Sweden 1920 70m approx (24 fps) bw
     silent   Svensk Filmindustri
original title: *Korkarlen;* aka: *The Phantom Carriage*

A drunkard is knocked senseless, retraces his misspent life, hears the carriage of death approaching and returns to his family. Old-fashioned moralistic saga which hit the right note at the time and has scenes which still impress.

wd Victor Sjostrom, *novel* Selma Lagerlöf *ph* J. Julius Jaenzon

Victor Sjostrom, Hilda Borgstrom, Astrid Holm
† Remade in France in 1939 by Julien Duvivier, as *La Charette Fantôme*, with Pierre Fresnay and Louis Jouvet; and again in Sweden in 1958 as *Korkarlen*, by Arne Mattson.

Tiara Tahiti*
GB 1962 100m Eastmancolor
Rank / Ivan Foxwell

An up-from-the-ranks colonel and an aristocratic smoothie captain continue their antipathy in peacetime Tahiti, where one is nearly murdered and the other gets his comeuppance.
Uneasy mixture of light comedy and character drama; enjoyable in parts, but flabbily assembled and muddily photographed.

w Geoffrey Cotterell, Ivan Foxwell, *novel* Geoffrey Cotterell *d* William T. Kotcheff *ph* Otto Heller *m* Philip Green

John Mills, James Mason, Herbert Lom, Claude Dauphin, Rosenda Monteros

Tick, Tick, Tick . . .*
US 1969 100m Metrocolor Panavision
MGM / Nelson-Barrett (Ralph Nelson,
     James Lee Barrett)

The first black sheriff in a southern community has trouble with murder and rape cases. Socially conscious suspenser, well enough made from predictable elements and leading surprisingly to an upbeat ending.

w James Lee Barrett *d* Ralph Nelson *ph* Loyal Griggs *m* Jerry Stynes

Jim Brown, George Kennedy, Fredric March, Lynn Carlin, Don Stroud, Clifton James

A Ticket to Tomahawk*
US 1950 90m Technicolor
TCF (Robert Bassler)

A stagecoach line defies the new western railroad.

Would-be satirical western which doesn't quite have the stamina and after some pleasing touches settles for dullness.

w Mary Loos d Richard Sale ph Harry Jackson m Cyril Mockridge

Anne Baxter, Dan Dailey, Rory Calhoun, Walter Brennan, Charles Kemper, Connie Gilchrist, Arthur Hunnicutt, Sen Yung

Tickle Me
US 1965 90m De Luxe Panavision
AA (Ben Schwalb)

An unemployed rodeo star accepts a job at a health ranch and helps a girl escape from villains after hidden treasure.

Wispy star vehicle with an unexpected haunted ghost town climax.

w Elwood Ullman, Edward Bernds d Norman Taurog ph Loyal Griggs m Walter Scharf

Elvis Presley, Julia Adams, Jocelyn Lane, Jack Mullaney, Merry Anders, Connie Gilchrist

A Ticklish Affair
US 1963 95m Metrocolor Panavision
MGM / Euterpe (Joe Pasternak)

A naval commander in San Diego falls for a widow with several children.

Thin romantic comedy with too many juvenile antics.

w Ruth Brooks Flippen d George Sidney ph Milton Krasner m George Stoll, Robert Van Eyps

Shirley Jones, Gig Young, Red Buttons, Carolyn Jones, Edgar Buchanan

Tiger Bay**
GB 1959 105m bw
Rank / Wintle–Parkyn (John Hawkesworth)

A Polish seaman in Cardiff kills his faithless girl friend and kidnaps a child who proves more than a match for him.

Generally very proficient police chase melodrama with strong characterizations: a considerable box office success of its time.

w John Hawkesworth, Shelley Smith d J. Lee-Thompson ph Eric Cross m Laurie Johnson

Hayley Mills, John Mills, Horst Buchholz, Megs Jenkins, Anthony Dawson, Yvonne Mitchell

Tiger in the Smoke*
GB 1956 94m bw
Rank (Leslie Parkyn)

Ex-commando criminals comb London for hidden loot and threaten a young girl.

Odd little melodrama with a complex plot and a different, Graham Greene-like atmosphere.

w Anthony Pelissier, novel Marjorie Allingham d Roy Baker ph Geoffrey Unsworth m Malcolm Arnold

Tony Wright, Muriel Pavlow, Donald Sinden, Bernard Miles, Alec Clunes, Laurence Naismith, Christopher Rhodes, Kenneth Griffith, Beatrice Varley

The Tiger Makes Out*
US 1967 94m Technicolor
Columbia / Elan (George Justin)

A middle-aged New York postman takes revenge on society by kidnapping a young girl—who rather enjoys the experience.

Semi-surrealist comedy misguidedly extended from a two-character play; frantic pace prevents more than a few effective moments.

w Murray Shisgal, from his play d Arthur Hiller ph Arthur J. Ornitz m Milton Rogers

Eli Wallach, Anne Jackson, Bob Dishy, David Burns, Charles Nelson Reilly

Tiger Shark*
US 1932 80m bw
Warner

A tuna fisherman who has lost a hand to a shark marries the daughter of an old friend, finds she loves someone else, and is conveniently killed by another shark.

Vivid melodrama with a plot partly borrowed from Moby Dick and itself partly borrowed by innumerable other Warner films including Kid Galahad, The Wagons Roll at Night, Slim and Manpower.

w Wells Root, story Tuna by Houston Branch d Howard Hawks ph Tony Gaudio

Edward G. Robinson, J. Carrol Naish, Zita Johann

A Tiger Walks*
US 1963 91m Technicolor
Walt Disney (Ron Miller)

In a small western town, a tiger escapes from the circus.

A splendid animal and a happy ending help to make this a pretty good film for children.

w Lowell S. Hawley, novel Ian Niall d Norman Tokar ph William Snyder m Buddy Baker

Sabu, Brian Keith, Vera Miles, Pamela Franklin, Kevin Corcoran, Edward Andrews, Una Merkel, Frank McHugh

'The Disney message runs true to form—
grown-ups should practise what they preach
and children are right about animals.'—*MFB*

Tight Spot
US 1955   97m   bw
Columbia (Lewis J. Rachmil)

A material witness in the trial of a gangster is
released from prison in the custody of an
attorney.
Fairly routine crime melodrama with
unexciting star performances.

w William Bowers, *play* Dead Pigeon by
Leonard Kantor d Phil Karlson ph Burnett
Guffey m Morris Stoloff

Edward G. Robinson, Ginger Rogers, Brian
Keith, Lorne Greene, Lucy Marlow,
Katherine Anderson

Till Death Us Do Part*
GB 1968   100m   Eastmancolor
British Lion / Associated London Films (Jon
  Pennington)

From the thirties to the sixties with loud-
mouthed, bigoted Londoner Alf Garnett.
Unremarkable and frequently misguided
opening-up of a phenomenally successful TV
series, adapted for the US as *All in the Family*
The original cast wades cheerfully enough
through a bitty script; the sequel, *The Alf
Garnett Saga*, defeated them.

w Johnny Speight d Norman Cohen
ph Harry Waxman m Wilfrid Burns

Warren Mitchell, Dandy Nichols, Anthony
Booth, Una Stubbs, Liam Redmond, Bill
Maynard, Sam Kydd, Brian Blessed

Till the Clouds Roll By**
US 1946   137m   Technicolor
MGM (Arthur Freed)

The life and times of composer Jerome Kern.
Better-than-average biopic with better-than-
average tunes and stars.

w Myles Connolly, Jean Holloway d Richard
Whorf ph Harry Stradling, George J. Folsey
md Lennie Hayton

Robert Walker, Judy Garland, Lucille
Bremer, Van Heflin, Mary Nash, Dinah
Shore, Van Johnson, *June Allyson*, Tony
Martin, Kathryn Grayson, *Lena Horne, Frank
Sinatra, Virginia O'Brien*
   'A little like sitting down to a soda fountain
de luxe atomic special of maple walnut on
vanilla on burnt almond on strawberry on
butter pecan on coffee on raspberry sherbert
on tutti frutti with hot fudge, butterscotch,

marshmallow, filberts, pistachios, shredded
pineapple, and rainbow sprills on top, go
double on the whipped cream.'—*James Agee*

Till the End of Time*
US 1946   105m   bw
RKO

Three returning GIs find romance and
problems in their small town.
Downbeat variation on *The Best Years of Our
Lives* with a theme tune which puts words to a
Chopin Polonaise.

w Allen Rivkin d Edward Dmytryk ph Harry
J. Wild m Leigh Harline

Dorothy McGuire, Guy Madison, Robert
Mitchum

'Til We Meet Again
US 1939   99m   bw
Warner (David Lewis)

On a ship bound from Hong Kong to San
Francisco, a dying woman falls for a crook
about to be executed.
Stolid remake of *One Way Passage* (qv).

w Warren Duff, *story* Robert Lord d Edmund
Goulding ph Tony Gaudio m Ray Heindorf

Merle Oberon, George Brent, Frank
McHugh, Pat O'Brien, Geraldine Fitzgerald,
Eric Blore, Binnie Barnes, Henry O'Neill,
George Reeves

Till We Meet Again
US 1936   87m   bw

Former sweethearts find themselves both
spies, but on opposing sides. Unconvincing but
climactically suspenseful romantic drama.
Herbert Marshall, Gertrude Michael, Lionel
Atwill. Written by Edwin Justus Mayer,
Franklin Coen and Brian Marlow from a play
by Alfred Davis; directed by Robert Florey;
for Paramount.

Till We Meet Again
US 1944   88m   bw
Paramount (David Lewis)

A French nun helps an American aviator
escape from the Nazis.
Very moderate, nicely photographed,
romantic war actioner.

w Lenore Coffee, *play* Alfred Maury d Frank
Borzage ph Theodor Sparkuhl m David
Buttolph

Ray Milland, Barbara Britton, Walter Slezak,
Lucile Watson, Konstantin Shayne, Vladimir
Sokoloff, Mona Freeman

Tillie and Gus*
US 1933 61m bw
Paramount (Douglas MacLean)

Two middle-aged cardsharps return home, help their niece and nephew win an inheritance, and come first in a paddleboat race.
Jumbled comedy with good moments and a rousing climax.

w Walter de Leon, Francis Martin d Francis Martin ph Benjamin Reynolds

W. C. Fields, Alison Skipworth, Baby Le Roy, Jacqueline Wells, Clifford Jones, Clarence Wilson, Edgar Kennedy, Barton MacLane

Tillie's Punctured Romance*
US 1914 60m approx (24 fps) bw silent
Keystone / Mack Sennett

A country maid falls for a con man who steals her money; but she finally gets her revenge.
Museum piece comedy which no longer irritates the funny bone but has clear historical interest.

w Hampton Del Ruth, play Tillie's Nightmare by Edgar Smith d Mack Sennett

Marie Dressler, Charles Chaplin, Mabel Normand, Mack Swain

Tilly of Bloomsbury
GB 1940 83m bw

The daughter of a boarding house keeper falls for a rich young man. Basically a millgirl's romance, remembered for one final drunk scene for the star comedian. Sydney Howard, Jean Gillie, Henry Oscar, Athene Seyler, Michael Wilding, Kathleen Harrison, Michael Denison, Martita Hunt, Athole Stewart. Written by Nils Hostius and Jack Marks, from the play by Ian Hay; directed by Leslie Hiscott; for Hammersmith. (Previous versions: 1921, with Tom Reynolds and Edna Best, for Samuelson; 1931, with Sydney Howard and Phyllis Konstam, for Sterling.)

Timberjack
US 1954 94m Trucolor

A young man seeks his father's killer among forest lumberjacks. Resiliently cast action story of no great interest. Sterling Hayden, Vera Ralston, Adolphe Menjou, David Brian, Hoagy Carmichael, Chill Wills, Jim Davis, Elisha Cook Jnr. Written by Allen Rivkin, from the novel by Dan Cushman; directed by Joe Kane, for Republic.

Timbuktu
US 1959 92m bw

A gun runner quells a desert revolt in the French Sudan during World War II. Leaden-footed melodrama full of stock characters despite its complex plot. Yvonne de Carlo, Victor Mature, George Dolenz, John Dehner, Marcia Henderson. Written by Anthony Veiller; directed by Jacques Tourneur; for Edward Small.

Time after Time*
US 1980 112m Metrocolor Panavision
Warner / Orion (Charles Jaffe)

Jack the Ripper escapes via H. G. Wells' time machine from Victorian London to modern San Francisco; Wells gives chase and eventually projects him into limbo.
Amusing fantasy for those with light literary inclinations, marred by too much gore and a wandering middle section.

wd Nicholas Meyer, story Karl Alexander and Steve Hayes ph Paul Lohmann m Miklos Rozsa pd Edward Carfagno

Malcolm McDowell, David Warner, Mary Steenburgen, Charles Cioffi, Kent Williams

Time Bomb*
GB 1952 72m bw
MGM (Richard Goldstone)
US title: Terror on a Train

A saboteur places a bomb on a goods train travelling from the north of England to Portsmouth.
Tolerable suspenser padded out with domestic asides.

w Ken Bennett d Ted Tetzlaff ph Frederick A. Young m John Addison

Glenn Ford, Anne Vernon, Maurice Denham, Harcourt Williams, Harold Warrender, Bill Fraser, John Horsley, Victor Maddern

Time Flies*
GB 1944 88m bw
GFD / Gainsborough (Edward Black)

A professor invents a time machine and takes his friends back to the court of Good Queen Bess.
Very passable star farce.

w J. O. C. Orton, Ted Kavanaugh, Howard Irving Young d Walter Forde ph Basil Emmott md Louis Levy

Tommy Handley, Felix Aylmer, Evelyn Dall, George Moon, Moore Marriott, Graham Moffatt, John Salew, Olga Lindo. Stephane Grappelly

A Time for Killing

US 1967 83m Pathecolor Panavision
Columbia / Sage Western (Harry Joe
Brown)
GB title: *The Long Ride Home*

Confederate prisoners escape from a Union
fort and the commander sets off in pursuit.
Fairly savage western with Something to Say
about the corruption of war.

w Halsted Welles, *novel* Southern Blade by
Nelson and Shirley Wolford d Phil Karlson
ph Kenneth Peach m Mundell Lowe

Glenn Ford, George Hamilton, Inger Stevens,
Max Baer, Paul Petersen, Timothy Carey,
Todd Armstrong

A Time for Loving

GB 1971 104m colour
London Screen Plays / Mel Ferrer

Short romantic comedies set at different times
in the same Paris flat.
Portmanteau ooh-la-la, quite neat but pitifully
undernourished; certainly no *Plaza Suite*.

w Jean Anouilh d Christopher Miles
ph Andreas Winding m Michel Legrand
pd Theo Meurisse

Joanna Shimkus, Mel Ferrer, Britt Ekland,
Philippe Noiret, Lila Kedrova, Robert Dhery,
Michael Burns

Time Gentlemen Please

GB 1952 83m bw
Group Three (Herbert Mason)

A lazy tramp is the one blot on a prize-
winning English village.
Artificial, thinly scripted and overlit sub-
Ealing comedy with familiar characters and
situations.

w Peter Blackmore, *novel* Nothing to Lose by
R. J. Minney d Lewis Gilbert ph Wilkie
Cooper m Antony Hopkins

Eddie Byrne, Hermione Baddeley, Jane
Barrett, Robert Brown, Raymond Lovell,
Marjorie Rhodes, Dora Bryan, Thora Hird,
Sidney James, Edie Martin, Ivor Barnard,
Sidney Tafler

'Quite a nice little picture.'—*Karel Reisz*

Time in the Sun***

Mexico 1933 60m bw
Marie Seton

Unfinished fragments of Eisenstein's
incomplete *Que Viva Mexico*, snippets from
which were later released in various forms.
This is the longest and presumably best
version, with splendidly pictorial sequences of
peasant and Indian life culminating with *Death
Day*, all skulls and fireworks. Clearly the work
of a master, though if completed the film
might well have been a bore.

w Marie Seton, Paul Burnford d Sergei
Eisenstein ph Edouard Tissé

Time Limit*

US 1957 95m bw
UA / Richard Widmark, William Reynolds

During the Korean war an officer is
courtmartialled for suspected collaboration.
Suspenseful talk piece from a somewhat
intellectualized play.

w Henry Denker, *play* Henry Denker, Ralph
Berkey d *Karl Malden* ph Sam Leavitt
m Fred Steiner

Richard Widmark, Richard Basehart, Dolores
Michaels, June Lockhart, Carl Benton Reid,
Martin Balsam, Rip Torn
  'The tightly constructed story leads logically
and unfalteringly to a tense climax.'—*Lindsay
Anderson*

Time Lock*

GB 1957 73m bw
Romulus (Peter Rogers)

A small boy is trapped in a bank vault just as
it is being locked for the weekend.
Acceptable expansion of a Canadian TV
suspenser.

w Peter Rogers, *play* Arthur Hailey d Gerald
Thomas ph Peter Hennessy m Stanley Black

Robert Beatty, Betty McDowall, Vincent
Winter, Lee Patterson, Alan Gifford, Robert
Ayres

The Time Machine*

US 1960 103m Metrocolor
MGM / Galaxy (George Pal)

A Victorian scientist builds a machine which
after some trial and error transports him into
the year 802701.
Surprisingly careful recreation of a period, and
an undeniably charming machine, go for little
when the future, including the villainous
Morlocks, is so dull.

w David Duncan, *novel* H. G. Wells
d George Pal ph Paul C. Vogel m Russell   ℓ
Garcia ad George W. Davis, William Ferrari

Rod Taylor, Yvette Mimieux, Alan Young,
Sebastian Cabot, Tom Helmore, Whit Bissell,
Doris Lloyd

The Time of Their Lives*

US 1946 82m bw
Universal (Val Burton)

Revolutionary ghosts haunt a country estate. Unusual, quite effective Abbott and Costello vehicle with the comedians not playing as a team.

w Val Burton, Walter de Leon, Bradford Ropes, John Grant *d* Charles Barton *ph* Charles Van Enger *m* Milton Rosen

Bud Abbott, Lou Costello, Marjorie Reynolds, Binnie Barnes, Gale Sondergaard, John Shelton

The Time of Your Life*
US 1948 109m bw
William Cagney

A group of lovable eccentrics spend much of their time philosophizing in a San Francisco bar.
Not really a film at all, this essence of Saroyan contains much to enjoy or to annoy. The performances are pretty good.

w Nathaniel Curtis, *play William Saroyan*
d H. C. Potter *ph* James Wong Howe
m Carmen Dragon

James Cagney, William Bendix, Wayne Morris, Jeanne Cagney, Gale Page, Broderick Crawford, *James Barton*, Ward Bond, Paul Draper, James Lydon, Richard Erdman, Natalie Schaefer

'They have done so handsomely by Saroyan that in the long run everything depends on how much of Saroyan you can take.'—*Time*

Time out of Mind
US 1947 88m bw
Universal-International (Robert Siodmak)

The housekeeper's daughter finances music studies for the master's ungrateful son.
Silly romantic melodrama with few visible compensations.

w Abem Finkel, Arnold Phillips, *novel* Rachel Field *d* Robert Siodmak *ph* Maury Gertsman *m* Miklos Rozsa

Phyllis Calvert, Robert Hutton, Ella Raines, Eddie Albert, Leo G. Carroll

The Time, the Place and the Girl
US 1946 105m Technicolor
Warner (Alex Gottlieb)

Two nightclub owners have problems.
Lightweight musical, indistinguishable from a dozen others.

w Francis Swann, Agnes Christine Johnson, Lynn Starling *d* David Butler *ph* William V. Skall *m* Arthur Schwartz

Dennis Morgan, Jack Carson, Janis Paige, Martha Vickers, S. Z. Sakall, Alan Hale, Donald Woods, Angela Greene, Florence Bates

AAN: song 'A Girl in Calico' (*m* Arthur Schwartz, *ly* Leo Robin)

A Time to Love and a Time to Die*
US 1958 132m Eastmancolor
Cinemascope
U-I (Robert Arthur)

During World War II, a German officer on his last leave solves problems at home but is killed on his return to the front.
Interesting but preachy and generally misguided attempt, by the studio which made *All Quiet on the Western Front* and *The Road Back*, to repeat the dose in colour and wide screen.

w Orin Jannings, *novel* Erich Maria Remarque *d* Douglas Sirk *ph* Russell Metty *m* Miklos Rozsa

John Gavin, Lilo Pulver, Keenan Wynn, Jock Mahoney, Thayer David, Agnes Windeck, Erich Maria Remarque

The Time Travelers*
US 1964 84m Pathecolor
AIP / Dobie (William Redlin)

Scientists venture 107 years into the future, and on escaping find themselves in a time trap.
Ingenious and lively low-budget science fiction with a sobering ending.

wd Ib Melchior ph William Zsigismond
m Richard La Salle

Preston Foster, Phil Carey, Merry Anders, John Hoyt, Joan Woodbury

Time without Pity*
GB 1957 88m bw
Harlequin (John Arnold, Anthony Simmons)

An alcoholic arrives in London to seek new evidence which will prevent his son from being executed for murder.
Heavy-going, introspective, hysterical, downbeat melodrama which takes itself with a seriousness which is almost deadly.

w Ben Barzman *play* Someone Waiting by Emlyn Williams *d* Joseph Losey *ph* Freddie Francis *m* Tristam Cary

Michael Redgrave, Alec McCowen, Leo McKern, Renée Houston, Ann Todd, Peter Cushing, Paul Daneman, Lois Maxwell, George Devine, Richard Wordsworth, Joan Plowright

'It hammers home its effects with the concentration of a heavyweight out for the kill.'—*Philip Oakes*

Timetable*
US 1955 79m bw
(UA) Mark Stevens

An insurance investigator is assigned to a train robbery which he actually committed himself. Concise suspenser with good script and treatment.

w Aben Kandel *d* Mark Stevens *ph* Charles Van Enger *m* Walter Scharf

Mark Stevens, Felicia Farr, King Calder, Wesley Addy

Times Square

US 1980   113m   Technicolor
EMI / Robert Stigwood

Two ill-matched teenage girls form a shabby nightclub act and soon have New York by its ears.

Sometimes sharply made but generally unpleasant urban fairy story with suicide as the end, like a cross between *Saturday Night Fever* and *Midnight Cowboy*. Among a number of forgettable songs is one called 'Pissing in the River'.

w Jacob Brackman *story* Alan Moyle and Leanne Unger

d Alan Moyle *ph* James A. Contner *m* Blue Weaver

Tim Curry, Trini Alvarado, Robin Johnson, Peter Coffield, Herbert Berghof, David Margulies

Times Square Playboy: see The Home Towners

The Tin Drum*

West Germany / France 1979   142m   Eastmancolor
UA / Franz Seitz / Bioskop / GGB 14 KG / Hallelujah / Artemis / Argos / Jadran / Film PolskiOriginal title: *Die Blechtrommel*

Not caring for the world he is growing up in, a small boy determines to remain a child.

Fairly brilliantly made version of a labyrinthine satire; the emphasis on sex and scatological detail, however, eventually defeats its own objects.

w Jean-Claude Carrière, Franz Seitz, Volker Schlöndorff, *novel* Gunter Grass *d* Volker Schlöndorff *ph* Igor Luther *m* Maurice Jarre *pd* Nicos Perakis

David Bennent, Mario Adorf, Angela Winkler, Daniel Olbrychski

Tin Pan Alley***

US 1940   95m   bw
TCF (Kenneth MacGowan)

During World War I and after, two dancing girls love the same composer.

Archetypal musical, full of Broadway clichés, razzmatazz and zip. Remade 1950 as *I'll Get By*, not to such peppy effect.

w Robert Ellis, Helen Logan *d* Walter Lang *ph* Leon Shamroy *ch* Seymour Felix *songs* Mack Gordon, Harry Warren *m* Alfred Newman

Alice Faye, Betty Grable, John Payne, Jack Oakie, Allen Jenkins, Esther Ralston, The Nicholas Brothers, John Loder, Elisha Cook Jnr

AA: Alfred Newman

The Tin Star*

US 1957   93m   bw   Vistavision
Paramount / Perlberg–Seaton

An ex-sheriff turned bounty hunter helps a new young sheriff to catch bandits.

Dignified and well-characterized western with customary pleasures.

w Dudley Nichols *d* Anthony Mann *ph* Loyal Griggs *m* Elmer Bernstein

Henry Fonda, Anthony Perkins, Betsy Palmer, Michel Ray, Neville Brand, John McIntire

AAN: original story (Barney Slater, Joel Kane); script

The Tingler

US 1959   82m   bw
Columbia / William Castle

Fear (it says here) can create on the spinal column a parasite removable only by screaming. A scientist isolates it and it runs amok in a silent cinema.

Ridiculous shocker with generally dull handling but effective moments.

w Robb White *d* William Castle *ph* Wilfrid Cline *m* Von Dexter

Vincent Price, Judith Evelyn, Darryl Hickman, Patricia Cutts
   'The sheer effrontery of this piece of hokum is enjoyable in itself.'—*MFB*

Tip on a Dead Jockey

US 1957   99m   bw
MGM (Edwin H. Knopf)
GB title: *Time for Action*

A flier loses his nerve and turns international smuggler, but reforms.

Gloomy, pedestrian star melodrama, dully cast.

w Charles Lederer, *novel* Irwin Shaw *d* Richard Thorpe *ph* George J. Folsey *m* Miklos Rozsa

Robert Taylor, Dorothy Malone, Gia Scala, Martin Gabel, Marcel Dalio, Jack Lord

Titanic*
US 1953 98m bw
TCF (Charles Brackett)

Personal dramas aboard the *Titanic* in 1912
come to a head as the ship hits an iceberg.
An excellent example of studio production is
squandered on a dim script which arouses no
excitement.

w Charles Brackett, Walter Reisch, Richard
Breen d Jean Negulesco ph Joe MacDonald
m Sol Kaplan ad Lyle Wheeler, Maurice
Ransford

Clifton Webb, Barbara Stanwyck, Robert
Wagner, Audrey Dalton, Thelma Ritter,
Brian Aherne, Richard Basehart, Allyn Joslyn

AA: script

The Titfield Thunderbolt***
GB 1952 84m Technicolor
Ealing (Michael Truman)

When a branch railway line is threatened with
closure, the villagers take it over as a private
concern.
Undervalued on its release in the wake of
other Ealing comedies, this now seems among
the best of them as well as an immaculate
colour production showing the England that is
no more; the script has pace, the whole thing
is brightly polished and the action works up to
a fine climactic frenzy.

w T. E. B. Clarke d Charles Crichton
ph Douglas Slocombe m Georges Auric

Stanley Holloway, George Relph, John
Gregson, Godfrey Tearle, Edie Martin,
Naunton Wayne, Gabrielle Brune, Hugh
Griffith, Sidney James, Jack McGowran,
Ewan Roberts, Reginald Beckwith

Tit for Tat*
US 1934 20m bw

Adjoining shopkeepers violently settle an old
difference. Archetypal late star comedy:
brilliant timing, but the warmth and sympathy
have begun to ebb. Laurel and Hardy, Charlie
Hall, Mae Busch. Written by Stan Laurel;
directed by Charles Rogers; for Hal Roach.
AAN: best short.

T-Men*
US 1947 96m bw
Eagle Lion (Aubrey Schenck)

Treasury Department detectives trail a gang of
counterfeiters.
Tough, well-made crime melodrama which still
packs a punch in the traditional vein.

w John C. Higgins d Anthony Mann ph John
Alton m Paul Sawtell

Dennis O'Keefe, Alfred Ryder, Mary Meade,
Wallace Ford, June Lockhart, Charles
McGraw, Jane Randolph, Art Smith

To Be or Not to Be****
US 1942 99m bw
(Alexander Korda) Ernst Lubitsch

Warsaw actors get involved in an underground
plot and an impersonation of invading Nazis,
including Hitler.
Marvellous free-wheeling entertainment which
starts as drama and descends through romantic
comedy and suspense into farce; accused of
bad taste at the time, but now seen as an
outstanding example of Hollywood
moonshine, kept alight through sheer talent
and expertise.

w Edwin Justus Mayer, story Ernst Lubitsch,
Melchior Lengyel d Ernst Lubitsch
ph Rudolph Maté m Werner Heymann
ad Vincent Korda

Jack Benny, Carole Lombard, Robert Stack,
Stanley Ridges, Felix Bressart, Lionel Atwill,
Sig Rumann, Tom Dugan, Charles Halton

'As effective an example of comic
propaganda as *The Great Dictator* and far
better directed.'—*Charles Higham, 1972*
'Based on an indiscretion, but undoubtedly
a work of art.'—*James Agee*
'In any other medium it would be
acknowledged as a classic to rank with *The
Alchemist* or *A Modest Proposal.*'—*Peter
Barnes*
'Lubitsch's comic genius and corrosive wit
are displayed at every turn.'—*John Baxter*
'The actual business at hand . . . is nothing
less than providing a good time at the expense
of Nazi myth . . . Lubitsch distinguishes the
film's zanier moments with his customary
mastery of sly humour and innuendo, and
when the story calls for outright melodrama he
is more than equal to the occasion.'—
Newsweek

AAN: Werner Heymann

To Catch a Thief*
US 1955 97m Technicolor Vistavision
Paramount / Alfred Hitchcock

A famous cat burglar who has retired to the
Riviera catches a thief who is imitating his old
style.
Very slow, floppy and rather boring
entertainment enlivened by the scenery and
the odd Hitchcock touch.

w John Michael Hayes, novel David Dodge
d Alfred Hitchcock ph Robert Burks m Lyn
Murray

Cary Grant, Grace Kelly, *Jessie Royce Landis,*
John Williams, Charles Vanel, Brigitte Auber
  'Billed as a comedy-mystery, it stacks up as
a drawn-out pretentious piece that seldom hits
the comedy level.'—*Variety*
AA: Robert Burks

To Each His Own••
US 1946   100m   bw
Paramount (Charles Brackett)
During World War II, a middle-aged woman
in London meets the soldier who is her own
illegitimate and long-since-adopted-son.
The woman's picture par excellence, put
together with tremendous Hollywood flair and
extremely enjoyable to watch.

*w Charles Brackett, Jacques Théry d Mitchell
Leisen ph* Daniel L. Fapp *m Victor Young
ad* Hans Dreier, Roland Anderson

Olivia de Havilland, John Lund, Roland
Culver, Mary Anderson, Philip Terry, Bill
Goodwin, Virginia Welles, Virginia Horne
  'Paramount proudly brings to the screens of
America one of the three great love stories of
all time!'—*publicity*
AA: Olivia de Havilland
AAN: original story (Charles Brackett)

To Find a Man•
US 1971   93m   Eastmancolor
Columbia / Rastar (Irving Pincus)
The spoiled daughter of a rich family becomes
pregnant and is helped by a young chemist.
Quiet, well-made minor drama about
maturity, with good small-town atmosphere.

w Arnold Schulman, novel S. J. Wilson
d Buzz Kulik *ph* Andy Laszlo *m* David Shire

Pamela Martin, Darrell O'Connor, *Lloyd
Bridges*, Phyllis Newman, Tom Ewell, Tom
Bosley

To Have and Have Not••
US 1945   100m   bw
Warner (Howard Hawks)
An American charter boat captain in
Martinique gets involved with Nazis.
Fairly routinely made studio adventure
notable for first pairing of Bogart and Bacall,
as an imitation of *Casablanca*, and for its
consistent though not outstanding
entertainment value. Remade later as *The
Breaking Point* (qv) and *The Gun Runners*
(qv), and not dissimilar from *Key Largo* (qv).

w Jules Furthman, William Faulkner, novel
Ernest Hemingway *d Howard Hawks ph* Sid
Hickox *m* Franz Waxman (uncredited)
md Leo F. Forbstein

Humphrey Bogart, Lauren Bacall, Walter
Brennan, Hoagy Carmichael, Dolores Moran,
Sheldon Leonard, Dan Seymour, Marcel
Dalio
  'Remarkable for the ingenuity and industry
with which the original story and the
individualities of Ernest Hemingway have
been rendered down into Hollywood basic.'—
Richard Winnington
  'Sunlight on the lattice, sex in the corridors,
a new pianist at the café, pistol shots, the fat
sureté man coming round after dark.'—
William Whitebait

To Hell and Back
US 1955   106m   Technicolor
        Cinemascope
U-I (Aaron Rosenberg)
The war career of America's most decorated
infantryman.
Routine war story which happens to be about
a fellow who later became a film star.

w Gil Doud, book Audie Murphy *d* Jesse
Hibbs *ph* Maury Gertsman *m* Joseph
Gershenson

Audie Murphy, Marshall Thompson, Charles
Drake, Gregg Palmer, Jack Kelly, Paul
Picerni, Susan Kohner
  'The emotion is congealed and there is no
real personal response to the anguish of
war.'—*John Gillett*

To Kill a Clown
GB 1971   104m   De Luxe
Palomar (Theodore Sills)

A painter and his wife move to a New England
isle and are menaced by a crippled Vietnam
veteran and his vicious dogs.
Pretentious, politically oriented rehash of *The
Most Dangerous Game* (qv), carefully made
but too slow for suspense.

w George Bloomfield, I. C. Rapoport, novel
Master of the Hounds by Algis Budrys
d George Bloomfield *ph* Walter Lassally
m Richard Hill, John Hawkins

Alan Alda, Blythe Danner, Heath Lamberts,
Eric Clavering

To Kill a Mockingbird••
US 1962   129m   bw
U-I (Alan Pakula)
A lawyer in a small southern town defends a
black man accused of murder.
Familiar dollops of social conscience, very well
presented with a child interest and excellent
atmosphere, but a mite overlong.

w Horton Foote, *novel* Harper Lee *d Robert Mulligan ph* Russell Harlan *m* Elmer Bernstein

Gregory Peck, Mary Badham, Philip Alford, John Megna, Frank Overton, Rosemary Murphy, Ruth White, Brock Peters

AA: script; Gregory Peck
AAN: best picture; Robert Mulligan; Russell Harlan; Elmer Bernstein; Mary Badham

To Mary With Love
US 1936 87m bw

A businessman thinks back affectionately over ten years of married life. Harmless romantic comedy-drama. Warner Baxter, Myrna Loy, Ian Hunter, Claire Trevor, Jean Dixon. Written by Richard Sherman and Howard Ellis Smith; directed by John Cromwell; for TCF.

To Paris with Love
GB 1954 78m Technicolor
GFD / Two Cities (Anthony Darnborough)

A middle-aged widower and his son go to Paris on holiday and devise matrimonial plans for each other.
Thin, disappointing taradiddle which is short but seems long.

w Robert Buckner *d* Robert Hamer *ph* Reg Wyer *m* Edwin Astley

Alec Guinness, Vernon Gray, Odile Versois, Jacques François, Elina Labourdette, Austin Trevor

'The general impression is somehow too aimless, too muted.'—*Gavin Lambert*

To Please a Lady*
US 1950 91m bw
MGM (Clarence Brown)

A ruthless midget-car racer falls for the lady journalist who is hounding him.
Good action programmer with no frills.

w Barre Lyndon, Marge Decker *d* Clarence Brown *ph* Harold Rosson *m* Bronislau Kaper

Clark Gable, Barbara Stanwyck, Adolphe Menjou, Will Geer, Roland Winters, Emory Parnell, Frank Jenks

To Sir with Love
GB 1967 105m Technicolor
Columbia (James Clavell)

A West Indian teacher comes to a tough East End school.
Sentimental non-realism patterned after *The Blackboard Jungle* but much softer; its influence led to a TV situation comedy, *Please Sir.*

w James Clavell, *novel* E. R. Braithwaite *d* James Clavell *ph* Paul Beeson *m* Ron Grainer

Sidney Poitier, Christian Roberts, Judy Geeson, Suzy Kendall, Lulu, Faith Brook, Geoffrey Bayldon, Patricia Routledge

'The sententious script sounds as if it has been written by a zealous Sunday school teacher after a particularly exhilarating boycott of South African oranges.'—*MFB*

To the Devil a Daughter
GB / Germany 1975 93m Technicolor
EMI / Hammer–Terra Filmkunst (Roy Skeggs)

An occult novelist is asked to take care of a girl who has been 'promised' to a group of Satanists.
Confusingly told, high camp diabolic thriller.

w Chris Wicking, *novel* Dennis Wheatley *d* Peter Sykes *ph* David Watkin *m* Paul Glass

Richard Widmark, Christopher Lee, Denholm Elliott, Honor Blackman, Michael Goodliffe, Anthony Valentine, Derek Francis, Nastassja Kinski

To the Ends of the Earth**
US 1948 107m bw
Columbia (Sidney Buchman)

A government agent follows a world-wide trail after a narcotics gang.
Thoroughly riveting conventional thriller, nicely made and photographed.

w Jay Richard Kennedy *d* Robert Stevenson *ph* Burnett Guffey *m* George Duning

Dick Powell, Signe Hasso, Ludwig Donath, Vladimir Sokoloff, Edgar Barrier

To the Shores of Tripoli
US 1942 82m Technicolor
TCF (Milton Sperling)

A cocky playboy becomes a tough marine.
Despite the title, this modest flagwaver with romantic trimmings never moves out of the San Diego training grounds.

w Lamar Trotti *d* Bruce Humberstone *ph* Edward Cronjager *m* Alfred Newman

Maureen O'Hara, John Payne, Randolph Scott, Nancy Kelly, William Tracy, Maxie Rosenbloom, Henry Morgan, Russell Hicks, Minor Watson

AAN: cinematography

To the Victor
US 1948 100m bw
Warner (Jerry Wald)

French collaborators stand trial for war
crimes.
Glum melodrama with inadequate cast.

w Richard Brooks *d* Delmer Daves
ph Robert Burks *m* David Buttolph

Dennis Morgan, Viveca Lindfors, Bruce
Bennett, Victor Francen, Dorothy Malone,
Tom d'Andrea, Eduardo Ciannelli, Joseph
Buloff, Luis Van Rooten, William Conrad

To What Red Hell
GB 1929 100m bw
A young epileptic kills a prostitute and is
protected by his mother. Unpalatable
melodrama which failed to be as significant as
it wished. Sybil Thorndike, John Hamilton,
Bramwell Fletcher, Janice Adair. Written by
Leslie Hiscott, from the play by Percy
Robinson; directed by Edwin Greenwood; for
Strand / Twickenham.

The Toast of New Orleans
US 1950 97m Technicolor
MGM (Joe Pasternak)
A Bayou villager becomes a star of the New
Orleans opera.
Very ordinary setting for a new singing star.

w Sy Gomberg, George Wells *d* Norman
Taurog *ph* William Snyder *md* George Stoll
ch Eugene Loring

Kathryn Grayson, David Niven, Mario Lanza,
J. Carrol Naish, James Mitchell, Richard
Hageman, Clinton Sundberg, Sig Arno

AAN: song 'Be My Love' (*m* Nicholas
Brodszky, *ly* Sammy Cahn)

The Toast of New York**
US 1937 109m bw
RKO (Edward Small)
A 19th-century medicine showman becomes a
notorious Wall Street financier.
Smart biopic of Jim Fisk; good entertainment
with accomplished production.

w Dudley Nichols, John Twist, Joel Sayre
d Rowland V. Lee *ph* Peverell Marley
m Nathaniel Shilkret

Edward Arnold, Cary Grant, Frances Farmer,
Jack Oakie, Donald Meek, Clarence Kolb,
Thelma Leeds

Tobacco Road***
US 1941 84m bw
TCF (Jack Kirkland, Harry H. Oshrin)
Poor whites in Georgia are turned off their
land.
This bowdlerized version of a sensational book

and play has superbly orchestrated farcical
scenes separated by delightfully pictorial
quieter moments: it isn't what was intended,
but in its own way it's quite marvellous.

w Nunnally Johnson, novel Erskine Caldwell,
play Jack Kirkland *d John Ford ph* Arthur
Miller *m David Buttolph*

Charley Grapewin, Elizabeth Patterson, Dana
Andrews, Gene Tierney, *Marjorie Rambeau*,
Ward Bond, William Tracy, Zeffie Tilbury,
Slim Summerville, Grant Mitchell, Russell
Simpson, Spencer Charters

Tobruk
US 1967 110m Techniscope
Universal / Corman / Gibraltar (Gene
Corman)
During the North African war, a British major
and some German Jews try to blow up the
Nazi fuel bunkers.
Routine war adventure, quite tough and
spectacular but undistinguished.

w Leo V. Gordon *d* Arthur Hiller *ph* Russell
Harlan *m* Bronislau Kaper

Rock Hudson, George Peppard, Nigel Green,
Guy Stockwell, Jack Watson, Liam Redmond,
Leo Gordon, Norman Rossington, Percy
Herbert

Toby Tyler*
US 1959 96m Technicolor
Walt Disney (Bill Walsh)
In 1910, a young orphan runs away to join a
travelling circus in the midwest, and with the
help of a chimp becomes a famous star.
Acceptable, predictable family fare.

w Bill Walsh, Lillie Hayward, *novel* James
Otis Kaler *d* Charles Barton *ph* William
Snyder *m* Buddy Baker

Kevin Corcoran, Henry Calvin, Gene
Sheldon, Bob Sweeney, James Drury

Today We Live*
US 1933 113m bw
MGM (Howard Hawks)
During World War I, an aristocratic English
girl and her three lovers all find themselves at
the front, and two fail to return.
Stilted romantic melodrama with imposing
credentials.

w Edith Fitzgerald, Dwight Taylor, William
Faulkner, *story* Turnabout by William
Faulkner *d* Howard Hawks *ph* Oliver T.
Marsh

Joan Crawford, Gary Cooper, Robert Young,
Franchot Tone, Roscoe Karns, Louise Closser
Hale, Rollo Lloyd

The Todd Killings*
US 1970 93m Technicolor Panavision
National General (Barry Shear)

In a small American town, a 23-year-old boy
starts out on a rampage of rape and murder.
Violent psychological melodrama, based on
fact, with inventive direction.

w Dennis Murphy, Joe L. Oliansky d Barry
Shear ph Harold E. Stine m Leonard
Rosenman

Robert F. Lyons, Richard Thomas, Belinda
Montgomery, Barbara Bel Geddes, Gloria
Grahame

'The most striking of the many recent film
versions of the souring of the American
dream.'—Tony Rayns

Together Again
US 1944 93m bw
Columbia (Virginia Van Upp)

The widow of a New England mayor
commissions a statue in his honour.
The title refers to the reteaming of the stars
who were so popular in Love Affair and When
Tomorrow Comes, which is a sign of the lack
of invention elsewhere. A comedy without
laughs.

w Virgina Van Upp, F. Hugh Herbert
d Charles Vidor ph Joseph Walker
m Werner Heymann

Charles Boyer, Irene Dunne, Charles Coburn,
Mona Freeman, Jerome Courtland, Elizabeth
Patterson, Charles Dingle, Walter Baldwin

Tokyo Joe
US 1949 88m bw
Columbia / Santana (Robert Lord)

A former nightclub owner returns to postwar
Japan to reclaim his fortune and his ex-wife.
Dispirited star melodrama.

w Cyril Hume, Bertram Millhauser d Stuart
Heisler ph Charles Lawton Jnr m George
Antheil

Humphrey Bogart, Florence Marly, Alexander
Knox, Sessue Hayakawa, Lora Lee Michel,
Jerome Courtland

Tolable David*
US 1921 80m approx (24 fps) bw
 silent
First National / Inspiration

A quiet farming community is disrupted by
three marauding convicts, who are finally
despatched by the peace-loving youngest son.
Fresh, sympathetic David-and-Goliath story
which was a huge popular success on its
release.

w Edmund Goulding, Henry King,
novel Joseph Hergesheimer d Henry King
ph Henry Cronjager

Richard Barthelmess, Gladys Hulette, Ernest
Torrence, Warner Richmond

'It is sentimental in places, but not sloppy. It
is bucolic, but its rusticity is not rubbed in . . .
it is restrained, imaginatively suggestive when
not briefly literal. For all these reasons it is
stimulating.'—New York Times

† Columbia remade the story in 1931 with
Richard Cromwell, but its time had passed.

Tom Brown's Schooldays*
US 1940 86m bw
(RKO) The Play's the Thing (Gene Towne,
 Graham Baker)

Tom Brown finds life at Rugby brutal, but
helps to become a civilizing influence.
Pretty lively Hollywood version of a rather
unattractive semi-classic.

w Walter Ferris, Frank Cavell, novel Thomas
Hughes d Robert Stevenson ph Nicholas
Musuraca m Anthony Collins

Jimmy Lydon, Cedric Hardwicke, Billy Halop,
Freddie Bartholemew, Gale Storm, Josephine
Hutchinson

Tom Brown's Schooldays
GB 1951 96m bw
Renown (George Minter)

Unexciting remake featuring one surprisingly
strong performance.

w Noel Langley d Gordon Parry ph C.
Pennington-Richards m Richard Addinsell

Robert Newton, John Howard Davies, Diana
Wynyard, Francis de Wolff, Kathleen Byron,
Hermione Baddeley, James Hayter, Rachel
Gurney, Amy Veness, Max Bygraves, Michael
Hordern, John Charlesworth, John Forrest

'An odd mixture of the brutal and the
solemnly improving.'—Richard Mallett, Punch

Tom, Dick and Harry**
US 1940 86m bw
RKO (Robert Sisk)

A girl daydreams about her three boy friends,
but can't make up her mind.
Brightly-handled comedy which became a
minor classic but does seem to have faded a
little. Remade as The Girl Most Likely (qv).

w Paul Jarrico d Garson Kanin ph Merrit
Gerstad m Roy Webb

Ginger Rogers, Burgess Meredith, Alan
Marshal, George Murphy, Phil Silvers, Joe
Cunningham, Jane Seymour, Lenore
Lonergan

'Foot by foot the best made picture of this year.'—*Otis Ferguson*

AAN: Paul Jarrico

Tom Horn

US 1979 97m Technicolor Panavision
Warner / Solar / First Artists (Fred Weintraub)

An ex-cavalry scout gets a job as a stock detective, is framed for murder, and allows himself to be hanged.

Curious pessimistic and unsatisfactory semi-western in which the star was found to have lost his old charisma after being too long away.

w Thomas McGuane, Bid Shrake, from the alleged autobiography of Tom Horn
d William Wiard *ph* John Alonzo *m* Ernest Gold

Steve McQueen, Linda Evans, Richard Farnsworth, Billy Green Bush, Slim Pickens, Elisha Cook Jnr.

'Imagine a film that opens up with dialogue that can't be heard at all, then proceeds to build up to a fist fight that's never seen, that cuts away to sunsets to fill in other scenes that have no dramatic point, that presents a meal where the sound of knives and forks drowns out what's being said, and you have just the beginning of what's wrong with *Tom Horn.*'—*Variety*

Tom Jones***

GB 1963 129m Eastmancolor
UA / Woodfall (Tony Richardson)

In 18th-century England a foundling is brought up by the squire and marries his daughter after many adventures.

Fantasia on Old England, at some distance from the original novel, with the director trying every possible jokey approach against a meticulously realistic physical background. Despite trade fears, the *Hellzapoppin* style made it an astonishing box offce success (the sex helped), though it quickly lost its freshness and was much imitated.

w John Osborne, *novel* Henry Fielding
d Tony Richardson *ph* Walter Lassally, Manny Wynn *m* John Addison *pd* Ralph Brinton

Albert Finney, Susannah York, Hugh Griffith, Edith Evans, Joan Greenwood, Diane Cilento, George Devine, Joyce Redman, David Warner, Wilfrid Lawson, Freda Jackson, Rachel Kempson

'Uncertainty, nervousness, muddled method . . . desperation is writ large over it.'—*Stanley Kauffmann*

'Much of the time it looks like a home movie, made with sporadic talent by a group with more enthusiasm than discipline.'—*Tom Milne*

'It is as though the camera had become a method actor: there are times when you wish you could buy, as on certain juke boxes, five minutes' silence . . . Obviously a film which elicits such lyric ejaculations from the reviewers cannot be all good.'—*John Simon*

AA: best picture; John Osborne; Tony Richardson; John Addison

AAN: Albert Finney; Hugh Griffith; Edith Evans; Diane Cilento; Joyce Redman

Tom Sawyer

US 1973 103m De Luxe Panavision
UA / Readers Digest (Arthur P. Jacobs)

Reverential, rather tediously over-produced version for family audiences of the seventies, with brief songs and real Mississippi locations.

w / m / ly Richard and Robert Sherman
d Don Taylor *ph* Frank Stanley *md* John Williams *pd* Philip Jefferies

Johnnie Whitaker, Celeste Holm, Warren Oates, Jeff East, Jodie Foster

AAN: Richard and Robert Sherman; John Williams

Tom Thumb*

GB 1958 98m Eastmancolor
MGM / Galaxy (George Pal)

A tiny forest boy outwits a couple of thieves. Slight musical built round the legend of a two-inch boy; good trickwork and songs make it a delightful film for children.

w Ladislas Fodor *d* George Pal *ph* Georges Périnal *m* Douglas Gamley, Kenneth V. Jones *sp* Tom Howard

Russ Tamblyn, Jessie Matthews, Peter Sellers, Terry-Thomas, Alan Young, June Thorburn, Ian Wallace

Tomahawk

US 1951 82m Technicolor

An Indian scout helps the Sioux to get their territory rights. Competent small-scale western. Van Heflin, Yvonne De Carlo, Alex Nicol, Preston Foster, Jack Oakie, Tom Tully, Rock Hudson. Written by Silvia Richards and Maurice Geraghty; directed by George Sherman; for Universal-International. (GB title: *Battle of Powder River.*)

The Tomb of Ligeia**

GB 1964 81m Eastmancolor
Cinemascope
American International (Roger Corman)

A brooding Victorian metamorphoses his dead wife into a cat, then into the beautiful Lady Rowena.
Complex but rather fascinating horror suspenser which rejogs familiar elements into something new; the best of the Corman Poes.

*w Robert Towne, story Edgar Allan Poe
d Roger Corman ph Arthur Grant
m Kenneth V. Jones*

Vincent Price, Elizabeth Shepherd, John Westbrook, Oliver Johnson, Richard Johnson, Derek Francis

Tombstone (The Town Too Tough to Die)
US 1942　80m　bw

How Wyatt Earp cleaned up the town. Lacklustre low-budget version of a famous story. Richard Dix, Frances Gifford, Kent Taylor, Edgar Buchanan, Don Castle, Victor Jory. Written by Albert Shelby Le Vino and Edward E. Paramore; directed by William McGann; for Paramount.

Tommy*
GB 1975　108m　colour
Hemdale / Robert Stigwood

A deaf, dumb and blind child is eventually cured and becomes a rock celebrity. Mystical rock opera screened with the director's usual barrage of effects and an ear-splitting score. Of occasional interest.

*w Ken Russell, from the opera by Pete Townshend and the Who　d Ken Russell
ph Dick Bush, Ronnie Taylor　m Pete Townshend and the Who*

Roger Daltrey, Ann-Margret, Oliver Reed, Elton John, Eric Clapton, Keith Moon

AAN: Ann-Margret

Tomorrow at Ten*
GB 1962　80m　bw
Mancunian (Tom Blakeley)

A crook kidnaps a small boy and locks him up with a time bomb while he makes his demands in person. When the kidnapper is killed, the police have to hunt against time.
Tense second feature, well acted and efficiently done.

w Peter Millar, James Kelly　d Lance Comfort ph Basil Emmott m Bernie Fenton

Robert Shaw, John Gregson, Alec Clunes, Alan Wheatley, Ernest Clark, Kenneth Cope

Tomorrow Is Another Day
US 1951　90m　bw

An ex-convict is soon on the run for a crime

he didn't commit. Miserable melodrama apparently left over from John Garfield days. Steve Cochran, Ruth Roman, Lurene Tuttle, Bobby Hyatt, Ray Teal. Written by Guy Endore and Art Cohn; directed by Felix Feist; for Warner.

Tomorrow Is Forever*
US 1945　105m　bw
RKO–International (David Lewis)

A man supposed dead in the war returns with an altered face to find his wife has remarried. Enoch Arden rides again in a rampant woman's picture which is well enough made to be generally entertaining.

w Lenore Coffee　d Irving Pichel　ph Joe Valentine m Max Steiner

Orson Welles, Claudette Colbert, George Brent, Lucile Watson, Richard Long, Natalie Wood

Tomorrow Never Comes
Canada / GB 1977　109m　colour
Rank / Classic / Montreal Trust / Neffbourne (Michael Klinger, Julian Melzack)

A jealous lover shoots a caller at his girl's beach cabana and a police siege begins. Far from the class of *Le Jour Se Lève*, this is an exploitative and violent melodrama which need never have been made.

*w David Pursall, Jack Seddon, Sydney Banks
d Peter Collinson ph François Protat m Roy Budd*

Oliver Reed, Susan George, Raymond Burr, Stephen McHattie, John Ireland, Donald Pleasence, John Osborne, Cec Linder

Tomorrow the World*
US 1944　86m　bw
UA / Lester Cowan

A college professor adopts his orphaned German nephew, who turns out to be an ardent 12-year-old Nazi.
Adequate, predictable screen version of a once-topical play.

w Ring Lardner Jnr, Leopold Atlas, play
James Gow, Armand D'Usseau *d* Leslie Fenton *ph* Henry Sharp *m* Louis Applebaum

Fredric March, Betty Field, *Skip Homeier*, Agnes Moorehead, Joan Carroll

Tomorrow We Live
GB 1942　85m　bw
British Aviation (George King)
US title: *At Dawn We Die*

French villagers help a spy escape to Britain. Minor flagwaver marred by cheap sets.

w Anatole de Grunwald, Katherine Strueby
d George King

John Clements, Greta Gynt, Hugh Sinclair,
Judy Kelly, Godfrey Tearle, Yvonne Arnaud,
Bransby Williams

Tonight and Every Night
US 1945   92m   Technicolor
Columbia (Victor Saville)

The lives and loves of London showgirls
during the blitz.

Ludicrous concoction looking nothing like
London and certainly nothing like the
Windmill, the theatre to which it allegedly
pays tribute. There are some tolerable
numbers along the way.

w Lesser Samuels, Abem Finkel, *play* Heart
of a City by Lesley Storm   *d* Victor Saville
ph Rudolph Maté   *md* Morris Stoloff, Marlin
Skiles

Rita Hayworth, Lee Bowman, Janet Blair,
Marc Platt, Leslie Brooks, Dusty Anderson,
Florence Bates, Ernest Cossart

AAN: Morris Stoloff, Marlin Skiles; song
'Anywhere' (*m* Jule Styne, *ly* Sammy Cahn)

Tonight Is Ours
US 1933   76m   bw

A Balkan princess falls for a commoner in
Paris. One of the master's less sparkling plays
gets the heavy Hollywood treatment. Fredric
March, Claudette Colbert, Alison Skipworth,
Paul Cavanagh, Arthur Byron, Ethel Griffies.
Written by Edwin Justus Mayer, from the play
by Noel Coward; directed by Stuart Walker;
for Paramount.

Tonight or Never
US 1931   80m   bw
Samuel Goldwyn

A prima donna falls for a man she thinks is a
Venetian gigolo, but he turns out to be an
impresario from New York.

Flimsy comedy which turned out to be its
star's last vehicle of any consequence for
twenty years.

w Ernest Vajda, *play* Lily Hatvany   *d* Mervyn
Le Roy   *ph* Gregg Toland   *md* Alfred
Newman

Gloria Swanson, Melvyn Douglas (debut),
Ferdinand Gottschalk, Robert Greig, Alison
Skipworth, Boris Karloff

Tonight We Raid Calais
US 1943   70m   bw

A British agent lands in occupied France to
pave the way for a bombing raid. Adequate

low-budget morale booster. John Sutton,
Annabella, Lee J. Cobb, Beulah Bondi,
Blanche Yurka, Howard Da Silva, Marcel
Dalio. Written by Waldo Salt; directed by
John Brahm; for TCF.

Tonight We Sing*
US 1953   109m   Technicolor
TCF (George Jessel)

Sol Hurok stifles his own talent to become a
great musical impresario.

Blameless uppercrust biopic, with plenty of
well-staged guest talent.

w Harry Kurnitz, George Oppenheimer
d Mitchell Leisen   *ph* Leon Shamroy
md Alfred Newman   *ch* David Lichine

David Wayne, Anne Bancroft, Ezio Pinza
(Chaliapin), Roberta Peters, Tamara
Toumanova (Pavlova), Isaac Stern (Eugene
Ysaye), Jan Peerce

Tonka
US 1958   97m   Technicolor
Walt Disney

A Sioux Indian tames a magnificent white
horse, and after many adventures is reunited
with him at Little Big Horn.
Unremarkable and overlong adventure story.

w Lewis R. Foster, Lillie Hayward, *novel*
Comanche by David Appel   *d* Lewis R.
Foster   *ph* Loyal Griggs

Sal Mineo, Phil Carey, Jerome Courtland,
Rafael Campos, H. M. Wynant

Tons of Money
GB 1930   97m   bw

An inventor poses as his own cousin, and in
this guise achieves instant success. A long-
running stage farce makes a grimly overlong
movie. Ralph Lynn, Yvonne Arnaud, Mary
Brough, Robertson Hare, Gordon James,
Madge Saunders. Written by Herbert
Wilcox and Ralph Lynn, from the play by
Will Evans and Arthur Valentine; directed
by Tom Walls; for Herbert Wilcox /
B and D.

Tony Draws a Horse
GB 1950   91m   bw

How to deal with a naughty boy causes
mounting disagreement in the family. Very
theatrical farce which on screen seems merely
silly. Cecil Parker, Anne Crawford, Derek
Bond, Barbara Murray, Mervyn Johns,
Edward Rigby. Written by Brock Williams,
from the play by Lesley Storm; directed by
John Paddy Carstairs; for Pinnacle / GFD.

Tony Rome*

US 1967 111m De Luxe Panavision
TCF / Arcola / Millfield (Aaron Rosenberg)

A seedy Miami private eye runs into murder when he guards a millionaire's daughter.
Complex old-fashioned murder mystery decorated with the new amorality and fashionable violence. Tolerable for its backgrounds and professional expertise.
Sequel: *Lady in Cement* (qv).

w Richard L. Breen, *novel* Miami Mayhem by Marvin H. Albert d Gordon Douglas ph Joe Biroc m Billy May

Frank Sinatra, Jill St John, Richard Conte, Gena Rowlands, Simon Oakland, Jeffrey Lynn, Lloyd Bochner, Sue Lyon

Too Hot to Handle*

US 1938 105m bw
MGM (Lawrence Weingarten)

Adventures of a scoop-seeking newsreel cameraman.
Boisterous comedy-melodrama with as many sags as highlights but generally making a cheerful star entertainment.

w Laurence Stallings, John Lee Mahin d Jack Conway ph Harold Rosson m Franz Waxman

Clark Gable, Myrna Loy, Walter Connolly, Walter Pidgeon, Leo Carrillo, Johnny Hines, Virginia Weidler

'It's like an old-fashioned serial . . . no one can call it dull.'—*Howard Barnes*

'Breathlessly paced, witty, and violent, this is one of the more acid comedies to have been produced by the Thirties.'—*John Baxter*

Too Hot to Handle

GB 1960 100m Eastmancolor
ABP / Wigmore (Selim Cattan)

Two Soho strip club owners join forces to hunt down a blackmailer.
Rotten, hilarious British gangster film set in a totally unreal underworld and very uncomfortably cast.

w Herbert Kretzmer d Terence Young
ph Otto Heller m Eric Spear

Leo Genn, Jayne Mansfield, Karl Boehm, Danik Patisson, Christopher Lee, Patrick Holt

Too Late Blues

US 1961 100m bw
Paramount (John Cassavetes)

A jazz musician falls for a neurotic girl and has fears of going commercial.
Uninteresting professional feature from a director whose reputation was made with the amateur *Shadows*.

w John Cassavetes, Richard Carr d John Cassavetes ph Lionel Lindon m David Raksin

John Cassavetes, Stella Stevens, Bobby Darin, Everett Chambers, Nick Dennis, Rupert Crosse, Vince Edwards

Too Late for Tears

US 1949 99m bw
(UA) Hunt Stromberg

A lady bluebeard disposes of both husbands and boyfriends.
Silly melodrama, poorly cast.

w Roy Huggins d Byron Haskin ph William Mellor m Dale Butts

Lizabeth Scott, Don Defore, Arthur Kennedy, Dan Duryea, Kristine Miller, Barry Kelley

Too Late the Hero*

US 1969 144m Technicolor 70mm
Associates and Aldrich / Palomar

In World War II the Japanese hold one end of a small Pacific island, British and Americans the other.
Semi-cynical, long and bloody war adventure of competence but no great merit.

w Robert Aldrich, Lukas Heller d Robert Aldrich ph Joseph Biroc m Gerald Fried

Michael Caine, Cliff Robertson, Ian Bannen, Henry Fonda, Harry Andrews, Denholm Elliott, Ronald Fraser, Percy Herbert

Too Many Crooks*

GB 1958 87m bw
Rank / Mario Zampi

Incompetent crooks plot a kidnapping.
Agreeable farce with black edges and an excellent chase sequence.

w Michael Pertwee d Mario Zampi ph Stan Pavey m Stanley Black

Terry-Thomas, George Cole, Brenda de Banzie, Bernard Bresslaw, Sidney James, Joe Melia, Vera Day, John Le Mesurier

Too Many Girls

US 1940 85m bw
RKO (Harry Edgington, George Abbott)

The father of a wealthy co-ed hires four football heroes to protect her.
Witless nonsense, flabbily derived from a Broadway show.

w John Twist, *play* George Marion Jnr, Richard Rodgers, Lorenz Hart d George Abbott ph Frank Redman *songs* Rodgers and Hart

Lucille Ball, Desi Arnaz, Richard Carlson, Ann Miller, Eddie Bracken, Frances Langford, Harry Shannon

† The film on which Ball and Arnaz first met.

Too Many Husbands*
US 1940   84m   bw
Columbia (Wesley Ruggles)
GB title: *My Two Husbands*

Allegedly drowned on a boat cruise, a man turns up again after his wife has remarried.
Modest variation on a familiar theme, professional but unexciting; later remade as *Three for the Show* (qv).

w Claude Binyon, *play* Home and Beauty by W. Somerset Maugham *d* Wesley Ruggles *ph* Joseph Walker *m* Frederick Hollander

Jean Arthur, Melvyn Douglas, Fred MacMurray, Harry Davenport, Dorothy Peterson, Melville Cooper, Edgar Buchanan

Too Much Too Soon*
US 1958   121m   bw
Warner (Henry Blanke)

Young actress Diana Barrymore goes to Hollywood to look after her alcoholic father John, but mild success goes to her head and she too turns to drink.
Rather dismal and murkily photographed account of an absorbing real-life situation; one performance holds the first half together.

wd Art Napoleon, *memoirs* Diana Barrymore *ph* Nicholas Musuraca, Carl Guthrie *m* Ernest Gold *ad* George James Hopkins

Dorothy Malone, *Errol Flynn*, Efrem Zimbalist Jnr, Neva Patterson, Martin Milner, Ray Danton, Murray Hamilton

Too Young to Kiss
US 1951   89m   bw
MGM (Sam Zimbalist)

A girl pianist poses as an infant prodigy, and falls for the impresario who wants to adopt her.
Dull conveyor belt comedy.

w Frances Goodrich, Albert Hackett *d* Robert Z. Leonard *ph* Joseph Ruttenberg *m* Johnny Green

June Allyson, Van Johnson, Gig Young, Paula Corday, Larry Keating, Hans Conried

Too Young to Love
GB 1959   89m   bw
Rank / Welbeck (Herbert Smith)

A 15-year-old prostitute is brought before a Brooklyn juvenile court.

Tepid filming of a popular exploitation play of the fifties, mysteriously made in England.

w Sydney and Muriel Box, *play* Pick Up Girl by Elsa Shelley *d* Muriel Box *ph* Gerald Gibbs *m* Bruce Montgomery

Thomas Mitchell, Pauline Hahn, Joan Miller, Austin Willis, Jess Conrad, Bessie Love, Alan Gifford

Top Banana*
US 1953   100m   Color Corporation
Roadshow / Harry M. Popkin

A TV comedian invites an attractive salesgirl to join his show.
A wisp of plot is the excuse for a revue, and the interest is in the old-time burlesque acts, some of which survive the generally shoddy treatment.

w Gene Towne *d* Alfred E. Green *ph* William Bradford *m / ly* Johnny Mercer

Phil Silvers, Rose Marie, Danny Scholl, Jack Albertson

Top Hat****
US 1935   100m   bw
RKO (Pandro S. Berman)

The path of true love is roughened by mistaken identities.
Marvellous Astaire-Rogers musical, with a more or less realistic London supplanted by a totally artificial Venice, and show stopping numbers in a style which is no more separated by amusing plot complications lightly handled by a team of deft *farceurs*.

w Dwight Taylor, Allan Scott *d* Mark Sandrich *ph* David Abel, Vernon Walker *m / ly* Irving Berlin *ch* Hermes Pan *ad* Van Nest Polglase, Carroll Clark

Fred Astaire, Ginger Rogers, Edward Everett Horton, Helen Broderick, Eric Blore, Erik Rhodes

'In 25 years *Top Hat* has lost nothing of its gaiety and charm.'—*Dilys Powell, 1960*

AAN: best picture; song 'Cheek to Cheek'

Top Man
US 1943   74m   bw

When an officer is recalled to active duty his teenage son becomes head of the family.
Lively little putting-on-a-show comedy musical which established a new young star. *Donald O'Connor*, Richard Dix, Peggy Ryan, Lillian Gish, Susanna Foster, Anne Gwynne. Written by Zachary Gold; directed by Charles Lamont; for Universal.

Top o'the Morning
US 1949 100m bw
Paramount (Robert L. Welch)

Investigations follow the theft of the Blarney Stone.
More Irish whimsy from the *Going My Way* stars.

w Edmund Beloin, Richard Breen *d* David Miller *ph* Lionel Lindon *m* James Van Heusen

Bing Crosby, Barry Fitzgerald, Ann Blyth, Hume Cronyn, Eileen Crowe, John McIntire

Top Secret*
GB 1952 94m bw
ABP (Mario Zampi)
US title: *Mr Potts Goes to Moscow*

A sanitary engineer, mistaken for a spy, is kidnapped to Moscow when his blueprints are taken for atomic secrets.
Farcical satire full of chases and lavatory humour; much of it comes off nicely.

w Jack Davies, Michael Pertwee d Mario Zampi ph Stan Pavey m Stanley Black

George Cole, Oscar Homolka, Nadia Gray, Frederick Valk, Wilfrid Hyde White, Geoffrey Sumner, Ronald Adam

Top Secret Affair*
US 1956 100m bw
Warner / United States (Martin Rackin)
GB title: *Their Secret Affair*

A female news publisher tries to discredit a military diplomat but falls in love with him.
Curious comedy adaptation of a rather heavy novel, moderately skilled in all departments.

w Roland Kibbee, Allan Scott, *novel* Melville Goodwin USA by John P. Marquand *d* H. C. Potter *ph* Stanley Cortez *m* Roy Webb

Kirk Douglas, Susan Hayward, Jim Backus, Paul Stewart, John Cromwell, Roland Winters

Topaz*
US 1969 124m Technicolor
Universal / Alfred Hitchcock

In 1962 the CIA enlists a French agent to break up a Russian spy ring.
Oddly halting, desultory and unconvincing spy thriller shot mainly in flat TV style, with just a few short sequences in its director's better manner. A measure of its unsatisfactoriness is that three different endings were shot and actually used at various points of release.

w Samuel Taylor, *novel* Leon Uris *d* Alfred Hitchcock *ph* Jack Hildyard *m* Maurice Jarre

Frederick Stafford, John Forsythe, John Vernon, *Roscoe Lee Browne*, Dany Robin, Karin Dor, Michel Piccoli, Philippe Noiret

'A larger, slower, duller version of the spy thrillers he used to make in the thirties.'—*New Yorker, 1975*

Topaze*
US 1933 78m bw
(RKO) David O. Selznick

A simple schoolmaster allows himself to be exploited.
Interesting little comedy with the star playing against type: remade as *Mr Topaze* (qv).

w Benn W. Levy, *play* Marcel Pagnol *d* Harry d'Abbadie d'Arrast *ph* Lucien Andriot *m* Max Steiner

John Barrymore, Myrna Loy, Jobyna Howland, Jackie Searl

Topkapi*
US 1964 119m Technicolor
UA / Filmways (Jules Dassin)

International thieves try to rob the Istanbul museum.
Light-hearted caper story which gets out of control because of the variety of styles and accents, the director's impression that his wife can do no wrong, and the general slowness and lack of wit; but there are bright moments, colourful backgrounds, and a final suspense sequence in the *Rififi* manner.

w Monja Danischewsky, *novel* The Light of Day by Eric Ambler *d* Jules Dassin *ph* Henri Alekan *m* Manos Hadjidakis

Melina Mercouri, Maximilian Schell, Peter Ustinov, Robert Morley, Akim Tamiroff, Gilles Segal, Jess Hahn

AA: Peter Ustinov

Topper**
US 1937 96m bw
Hal Roach

A stuffy banker is haunted by the ghosts of his sophisticated friends the Kirbys, who are visible only to him.
Influential supernatural farce, still pretty funny and deftly acted though a shade slow to get going.

w Jack Jevne, Eric Hatch, Eddie Moran, *novel* The Jovial Ghosts by Thorne Smith *d* Norman Z. McLeod *ph* Norbert Brodine *md* Arthur Morton

Cary Grant, Constance Bennett, Roland Young, Billie Burke, Alan Mowbray, Eugene Pallette, Arthur Lake, Hedda Hopper

AAN: Roland Young

Topper Returns***
US 1941   87m   bw
Hal Roach

A girl ghost helps Topper solve her own murder.

Spirited supernatural farce which spoofs murder mysteries, spooky houses, frightened servants, dumb cops, etc, in a pacy, accomplished and generally delightful manner.

w Jonathan Latimer, Gordon Douglas, with additional dialogue by Paul Gerard Smith
d Roy del Ruth ph Norbert Brodine
m Werner Heyman

Roland Young, Joan Blondell, Eddie Anderson, Carole Landis, Dennis O'Keefe, *H. B. Warner*, Billie Burke, *Donald McBride*, Rafaela Ottiano

Topper Takes a Trip*
US 1939   85m   bw
Hal Roach

Ghostly Mrs Kirby helps Topper to save his wife from a Riviera philanderer.

Mildly pleasant follow-up, with a dog replacing Cary Grant who had become too expensive.

w Eddie Moran, Jack Jevne, Corey Ford
d Norman Z. McLeod ph Norbert Brodine

Constance Bennett, Roland Young, Billie Burke, Alan Mowbray, Verree Teasdale, Franklin Pangborn, Alexander D'Arcy

Tora! Tora! Tora!*
US 1970   144m   De Luxe   Panavision
TCF (Elmo Williams)

A reconstruction from both sides of the events leading up to Pearl Harbor.

Immense, largely studio-bound, calcified war spectacle with much fidelity to the record but no villains and no hero, therefore no drama and no suspense.

w Larry Forrester, Hideo Oguni, Ryuzo Kikushima d Richard Fleischer, Ray Kellogg, Toshio Masuda, Kinji Fukasaku ph Charles F. Wheeler and Japanese crews m Jerry Goldsmith sp L. B. Abbott, Art Cruickshank

Martin Balsam, Joseph Cotten, James Whitmore, Jason Robards, Edward Andrews, Leon Ames, George Macready, Soh Yamamura, Takahiro Tamura

'One of the least stirring and least photogenic historical epics ever perpetrated on the screen.'—*Gary Arnold*

AAN: Charles F. Wheeler

Torch Singer
US 1933   72m   bw
Paramount (Albert Lewis)
aka: *Broadway Singer*

An unwed mother supports her child by singing in night clubs.

Banal melodrama.

w Lenore Coffee, Lynn Starling, *play* Mike by Grace Perkins d Alexander Hall ph Karl Struss

Claudette Colbert, Ricardo Cortez, David Manners, Lyda Roberti, Baby LeRoy, Florence Roberts, Ethel Griffies, Helen Jerome Eddy

Torch Song
US 1953   90m   Technicolor
MGM (Henry Berman, Sidney Franklin Jnr)

A temperamental musical comedy star falls for a blind pianist.

Ossified star vehicle which looks great but is too often unintentionally funny.

w John Michael Hayes, Jan Lustig, *story* Why Should I Cry? by I. A. R. Wylie d Charles Walters ph Robert Planck m Adolph Deutsch

Joan Crawford, Michael Wilding, Gig Young, Marjorie Rambeau, Henry Morgan, Dorothy Patrick

'Here is Joan Crawford all over the screen, in command, in love and in color.'—*Otis L. Guernsey Jnr*

AAN: Marjorie Rambeau

Torchy Blane
Glenda Farrell played the hard-boiled girl reporter and Barton MacLane the tough police inspector who puts up with her in seven out of the nine second features made by Warners in the late thirties. The characters were created in short stories by Frederick Nebel, and the films were mostly directed by William Beaudine or Frank McDonald.

1936: SMART BLONDE
1937: FLY AWAY BABY, THE ADVENTUROUS BLONDE
1938: BLONDES AT WORK, TORCHY BLANE IN PANAMA (with Lola Lane, Paul Kelly), TORCHY GETS HER MAN
1939: TORCHY BLANE IN CHINATOWN, TORCHY RUNS FOR MAYOR, TORCHY PLAYS WITH DYNAMITE (with Jane Wyman, Allen Jenkins)

Torn Curtain**
US 1966   119m   Technicolor
Universal / Alfred Hitchcock

A defector who is really a double agent is embarrassed when his girl friend follows him into East Germany.
Patchy Hitchcock with some mechanically effective suspense sequences, a couple of efforts at something new, a few miscalculations, some evidence of carelessness, and a little enjoyable repetition of old situations.

w Brian Moore d Alfred Hitchcock ph John F. Warren m John Addison

Paul Newman, Julie Andrews, *Wolfgang Kieling*, Ludwig Donath, Lila Kedrova, Hans-Joerg Felmy, Tamara Toumanova

Torpedo Run*
US 1958 98m Metrocolor
    Cinemascope
MGM (Edmund S. Grainger)

A US submarine in World War II destroys a Japanese aircraft carrier in Tokyo Bay.
Well-staged potboiler with excellent action sequences marred slightly by excessive platitudinizing.

w Richard Sale, William Wister Haines d Joseph Pevney ph George J. Folsey

Glenn Ford, Ernest Borgnine, Diane Brewster, Dean Jones

The Torrent*
US 1925 75m (24 fps) bw silent
MGM (Hunt Stromberg)

Spanish sweethearts are parted by a domineering mother, and the girl consoles herself by becoming a Paris prima donna.
Adequate emotional vehicle of its day which happened to be Garbo's first American film.

w Dorothy Farnum, *novel* Vicente Blasco Ibanez d Monta Bell ph William Daniels

Ricardo Cortez, Greta Garbo, Gertrude Olmsted, Edward Connelly, Lucien Littlefield

Torrid Zone**
US 1940 88m bw
Warner (Mark Hellinger)

In Central America, a banana plantation manager is tricked by his boss into staying on, and helps a wandering showgirl as well as foiling bandits.
Enjoyable, fast-paced hokum with a plot borrowed from both *The Front Page* and *Red Dust*.

w Richard Macaulay, Jerry Wald d William Keighley ph James Wong Howe m Adolph Deutsch

James Cagney, Pat O'Brien, Ann Sheridan, Helen Vinson, Andy Devine, Jerome Cowan, George Tobias, George Reeves

Tortilla Flat*
US 1942 106m bw
MGM (Sam Zimbalist)

The problems of poor Mexican half-breeds in California.
Expensive but unappealing variation on *The Grapes of Wrath*, with none of the cast quite getting under the skin of their parts, and no sense of reality, rather that of a musical without music.

w John Lee Mahin, Benjamin Glazier, *novel* John Steinbeck d Victor Fleming ph Sidney Wagner m Franz Waxman

Spencer Tracy, Hedy Lamarr, John Garfield, Frank Morgan, Akim Tamiroff, Connie Gilchrist, John Qualen, Sheldon Leonard, Donald Meek, Allen Jenkins, Henry O'Neill

AAN: Frank Morgan

Torture Garden*
GB 1967 93m Technicolor
Columbia / Amicus (Milton Subotsky)

Five fairground visitors are told their future by the mysterious Dr Diablo.
Crude but effective horror portmanteau including one story about the resurrection of Edgar Allan Poe.

w Robert Bloch d Freddie Francis
ph Norman Warwick m Don Banks, James Bernard

Burgess Meredith, Jack Palance, Peter Cushing, Beverly Adams, Michael Bryant, John Standing

The Touch*
Sweden / US 1970 112m Eastmancolor
ABC / Cinematograph AB (Lars/Owe
    Carlburg)

The wife of a provincial surgeon falls in love with an archaeologist.
Freedom versus security: the Bergman treatment is given to a familiar love story, but the expected finesse is lacking.

wd Ingmar Bergman ph Sven Nykvist m Jan Johansson

Bibi Andersson, Elliott Gould, Max Von Sydow

Touch and Go
GB 1955 85m Technicolor
Ealing (Seth Holt)
US title: *The Light Touch*

A family has doubts about its decision to emigrate to Australia.
Very mild comedy which fails to engage sympathy because the characters don't seem real.

w William Rose *d* Michael Truman
ph Douglas Slocombe *m* John Addison

Jack Hawkins, Margaret Johnston, June
Thorburn, John Fraser, Roland Culver, Alison
Leggatt, James Hayter

A Touch of Class••
GB 1973   106m   Technicolor
Panavision
Avco / Brut / Gordon Films (Melvin Frank)

A married American businessman in London
has a hectic affair with a dress designer.
Amiable and very physical sex farce with
hilarious highlights and a few longueurs
between; the playing keeps it above water.

w Melvin Frank, Jack Rose *d* Melvin Frank
ph Austin Dempster *m* John Cameron

Glenda Jackson, George Segal, Paul Sorvino,
Hildegarde Neil
    'Machine-tooled junk.'—*William S. Pechter*
    'Brightly performed and quite engaging until
it fades into vapid variations on a one-joke
theme.'—*Sight and Sound*

AA: Glenda Jackson
AAN: best picture; script; John Cameron;
song, 'All That Love Went to Waste'
(*m* George Barrie, *ly* Sammy Cahn)

Touch of Evil••
US 1958   95m or 114m   bw
U-I (Albert Zugsmith)

A Mexican narcotics investigator
honeymooning in a border town clashes with
the local police chief over a murder.
Overpoweringly atmospheric melodrama
crammed with Wellesian touches, but very
cold and unsympathetic, with rather restrained
performances (especially his) and a plot which
takes some following. Hardly the most
auspicious return to Hollywood for a
wanderer, but now becoming a cult classic.

wd Orson Welles, novel Badge of Evil by Whit
Masterson *ph Russell Metty m* Henry
Mancini

Charlton Heston, Orson Welles, Janet Leigh,
Marlene Dietrich, Akim Tamiroff, Joseph
Calleia, Ray Collins, Dennis Weaver
    'Pure Orson Welles and impure balderdash,
which may be the same thing.'—*Gerald
Weales, Reporter*

A Touch of Larceny•
GB 1959   92m   bw
Paramount / Ivan Foxwell

A naval commander mysteriously disappears
in the hope that he will be branded a traitor
and can sue for libel.

Fairly amusing light comedy with lively
performances.

w Roger MacDougall, Guy Hamilton, Ivan
Foxwell, *novel* The Megstone Plot by Andrew
Garve *d* Guy Hamilton *ph* John Wilcox
m Philip Green

James Mason, Vera Miles, George Sanders,
Robert Flemyng, Ernest Clark, Duncan
Lamont, Peter Barkworth
    'A beguilingly polished comedy, reminiscent
in its style, urbanity and sheen of the sort of
thing Lubitsch was doing in the 30s.'—*Daily
Mail*

A Touch of Love
GB 1969   107m   Eastmancolor
Amicus / Palomar (Milton Subotsky)
US title: *Thank You All Very Much*

A pregnant London student tries to get an
abortion but later decides against it.
Curious bid for serious drama by horror
producers; all very conscientious but rather
dreary.

w Margaret Drabble, from her novel The
Millstone *d* Waris Hussein *ph* Peter
Suschitsky *m* Michael Dress

Sandy Dennis, Ian McKellen, Michael Coles,
John Standing, Eleanor Bron

A Touch of the Sun
GB 1956   80m   bw
Eros / Raystro (Raymond Stross)

A hall porter is left a fortune but after living it
up for a while returns to his old hotel which is
on the rocks.
Limp comedy vehicle.

w Alfred Shaughnessy *d* Gordon Parry
ph Arthur Grant *m* Eric Spear

Frankie Howerd, Ruby Murray, Dorothy
Bromiley, Gordon Harker, Reginald
Beckwith, Richard Wattis, Dennis Price,
Alfie Bass, Willoughby Goddard

Touchez pas au Grisbi•
France / Italy 1953   90m approx   bw
Del Duca / Antares
aka: *Honour among Thieves; Hands Off
the Loot*

Two crooks succeed in stealing a consignment
of gold, but that's only the start of their
worries.
Smooth underworld hokum, with a slightly
comic attitude implied if not stated.

w Jacques Becker, Maurice Griffe,
novel Albert Simonin *d* Jacques Becker
ph Pierre Montazel *m* Jean Wiener

Jean Gabin, Jeanne Moreau, Gaby Basset, Daniel Cauchy, Marilyn Buferd, Lino Ventura, René Dary

Toughest Man in Arizona
US 1952 90m Trucolor
Republic (Sidney Picker)

In 1861 a US marshal falls in love with the wife of an outlaw.
Easy-going, pleasant western aimed at the top half of a double bill.

w John K. Butler d R. G. Springsteen
ph Reggie Lanning m Dale Butts

Vaughn Monroe, Joan Leslie, Edgar Buchanan, Victor Jory, Jean Parker, Henry Morgan

Tovarich••
US 1937 98m bw
Warner (Robert Lord)

A royal Russian husband and wife flee the revolution to Paris and take jobs as servants in an eccentric household.
A lively comedy of its time; though many of the jokes now seem obvious, the playing preserves its essential quality.

w Casey Robinson, *play adaptation Robert E. Sherwood, original* Jacques Deval d Anatole Litvak ph Charles Lang m Max Steiner

Claudette Colbert, Charles Boyer, Basil Rathbone, Anita Louise, Melville Cooper, Isabel Jeans, Maurice Murphy, Morris Carnovsky, Gregory Gaye, Montagu Love, Fritz Feld

'The most exciting screen event of all time!'—*publicity*

'A yarn of charming and finely shaded characterizations. Both humour and heart appeal spring from intimate acquaintance with the background and motives of each player.'—*Variety*

Toward the Unknown
US 1956 115m Warnercolor
Warnerscope
Warner / Toluca (Mervyn Le Roy)
GB title: *Brink of Hell*

An over-age officer takes part in the X2 experiments with rocket-firing aircraft.
Humourless flagwaver, very forgettable.

w Beirne Lay Jnr d Mervyn Le Roy
ph Harold Rosson m Paul Baron

William Holden, Lloyd Nolan, Virginia Leith, Charles McGraw, Murray Hamilton, L. Q. Jones, James Garner, Paul Fix, Karen Steele

Towed in a Hole•••
US 1932 20m bw

Two would-be fishermen wreck the boat they have just bought. Brilliant star farce, filled with wonderfully lunatic dialogues and freshly-conceived slapstick. Laurel and Hardy.
Written by Stan Laurel; directed by George Marshall; for Hal Roach.

Tower of London••
US 1939 92m bw
Universal (Rowland V. Lee)

With the help of Mord the executioner, Richard Crookback kills his way to the throne but is destroyed at Bosworth.
The Shakespearean view of history played as a horror comic: despite an overall lack of pace, spirited scenes and good performances win the day.

w Robert N. Lee d Rowland V. Lee
ph George Robinson m Charles Previn

Basil Rathbone, Boris Karloff, Barbara O'Neil, Ian Hunter, Vincent Price, Nan Grey, John Sutton, Leo G. Carroll, Miles Mander

Tower of London•
US 1962 79m bw
AIP / Admiral (Gene Corman)

A variation on the same events, with Price graduating from Clarence to Crookback, and the addition of ghostly visions. All very cheap, but occasionally vivid melodrama, despite intrusive American accents.

w Leo V. Gordon, Amos Powell, James B. Gordon d Roger Corman ph Arch Dalzell m Michael Anderson

Vincent Price, Michael Pate, Joan Freeman, Robert Brown, Justice Eatson, Sara Salby, Richard McCauly, Bruce Gordon

The Tower of Terror
GB 1941 78m bw

British and German agents clash in a lighthouse tended by a mad keeper. Lurid penny-dreadful, quite amusing in its way.
Wilfrid Lawson, Movita, Michael Rennie, Morland Graham, George Woodbridge.
Written by John Argyle and John Reinhart; directed by Lawrence Huntington; for ABPC.

The Towering Inferno•••
US 1974 165m De Luxe Panavision
TCF / Warner (Irwin Allen)

The world's tallest building is destroyed by fire on the night of its inauguration.
Showmanlike but relentlessly padded disaster spectacular, worth seeing for its cast of stars, its sheer old-fashioned expertise, and its special effects.

w Stirling Silliphant, *novels* The Tower by Richard Martin Stern, The Glass Inferno by Thomas M. Scortia, Frank M. Robinson *d* John Guillermin, Irwin Allen *ph* Fred Koenekamp, Joseph Biroc *m* John Williams *sp* Bill Abbott *pd* William Creber

Paul Newman, Steve McQueen, William Holden, Faye Dunaway, Fred Astaire, Susan Blakely, Richard Chamberlain, Robert Vaughn, Jennifer Jones, O. J. Simpson, Robert Wagner

'Several generations of blue-eyed charmers act their roles as if each were under a separate bell jar.'—*Verina Glaessner*

'Each scene of someone horribly in flames is presented as a feat for the audience's delectation.'—*New Yorker*

'The combination of Grade A spectacle and B-picture characters induces a feeling of sideline detachment.'—*Michael Billington, Illustrated London News*

AA: photography; song 'We May Never Love Like This Again' (*m / ly* Al Kasha, Joel Hirschhorn)

AAN: best picture; John Williams; Fred Astaire

A Town Called Bastard
GB 1971 97m Technicolor Franscope
Benmar / Zurbano (Ben Fisz)
aka: *A Town Like Hell*

Mexican revolutionaries massacre a priest and his congregation and take over the town. Ten years later a widow arrives seeking vengeance.
Sadistic western with an opening massacre followed by twenty-two killings (count 'em).
Pretty dull otherwise.

w Richard Aubrey *d* Robert Parrish *ph* Manuel Berenguer *m* Waldo de Los Rios

Robert Shaw, Stella Stevens, Telly Savalas, Martin Landau, Michael Craig, Fernando Rey, Dudley Sutton

A Town like Alice**
GB 1956 117m bw
Rank / Vic Films (Joseph Janni)
US title: *The Rape of Malaya*

Life among women prisoners of the Japanese in Malaya, especially one who is finally reunited with her Australian lover.
Genteelly harrowing war film, formlessly adapted from the first part of a popular novel; a big commercial success of its day.

w W. P. Lipscomb, Richard Mason, *novel* Nevil Shute *d* Jack Lee *ph* Geoffrey Unsworth *m* Matyas Seiber

Virginia McKenna, Peter Finch, Takagi, Marie Lohr, Maureen Swanson, Jean Anderson, Renée Houston, Nora Nicholson

Town on Trial*
GB 1956 96m bw
Columbia / Marksman (Maxwell Setton)

A police inspector solves the murder of a girl after a tennis club dance in a British country town.
Straightforward murder mystery shot in Weybridge, with a wide variety of suspects having something to hide; settings and characters are quite realistic and also a little dreary.

w Ken Hughes, Robert Westerby *d* John Guillermin *ph* Basil Emmott *m* Tristam Cary

John Mills, Charles Coburn, Derek Farr, Barbara Bates, Alec McCowen, Geoffrey Keen, Elizabeth Seal, Margaretta Scott, Fay Compton

Town without Pity*
US / Switzerland / Germany 1961 103m bw
UA / Mirisch / Osweg / Gloria (Gottfried Reinhardt)

A German girl is raped and four American soldiers are accused; the defence counsel's wiles lead to the girl's suicide.
Dour drama with overpowering expressionist technique but not much real sympathy, interest or surprise.

w Silvia Reinhardt, George Hurdalek, *novel* The Verdict by Manfred Gregor *d* Gottfried Reinhardt *ph* Kurt Hasse *m* Dmitri Tiomkin

Kirk Douglas, E. G. Marshall, Christine Kaufmann, Barbara Rutting, Robert Blake, Richard Jaeckel

AAN: title song (*m* Dmitri Tiomkin, *ly* Ned Washington)

Toy Tiger
US 1956 88m Technicolor Cinemascope
U-I (Howard Christie)

The imaginative small son of a widow 'adopts' her business friend as his father.
Flat sentimental comedy off the studio's conveyor belt, a remake of *Mad about Music*.

w Ted Sherdeman *d* Jerry Hopper *ph* George Robinson *m* Joseph Gershenson

Jeff Chandler, Laraine Day, Tim Hovey, Cecil Kellaway, Richard Haydn, David Janssen

The Toy Wife*
US 1938 95m bw
MGM (Merian C. Cooper)
GB title: *Frou Frou*

In the early 19th century in Louisiana, a flirtatious girl causes jealousy and tragedy.

Another bid in the *Jezebel / Gone with the Wind* stakes, this handsome production proved a commercial misfire and hastened the end of its star's career.

w Zoe Akins *d* Richard Thorpe *ph* Oliver T. Marsh *m* Edward Ward

Luise Rainer, Melvyn Douglas, Robert Young, Barbara O'Neil, H. B. Warner, Alma Kruger, Walter Kingsford

Toys in the Attic*
US 1963 90m bw Panavision
UA / Claude / Mirisch

In a shabby New Orleans home, two ageing spinsters struggle to look after their ne'er-do-well brother.
Play into film doesn't go in this case, but the script and acting are interesting.

w James Poe, play Lillian Hellman d George Roy Hill *ph* Joseph Biroc *m* George Duning *ad* Cary Odell

Geraldine Page, Wendy Hiller, Dean Martin, Yvette Mimieux, Gene Tierney, Larry Gates

Track of the Cat*
US 1954 102m Warnercolor
Cinemascope
Warner / Wayne–Fellows / Batjac (Robert Fellows)

In the northern California backwoods one winter in the 1880s a farming family is menaced by a marauding mountain lion.
With the lion a symbol of evil, this is real Cold Comfort Farm country and despite good intentions all round becomes irresistibly funny before the end, largely because everyone moves and speaks so s-l-o-w-l-y. The bleached colour is interesting but would suit only snowy settings.

w A. I. Bezzerides, *novel* Walter Van Tilburg Clark *d William A. Wellman ph William H. Clothier m* Roy Webb

Robert Mitchum, Diana Lynn, Beulah Bondi, Teresa Wright, Tab Hunter, Philip Tonge, William Hopper, Carl Switzer
'Cinemascope's first genuine weirdie . . . the script is redolent of Eugene O'Neill, and to its presentation the director brings a touch of Poe . . . Despair hangs in the air like a curse . . . unfortunately ambition overreaches itself, and the film topples over into barnstorming melodrama.'—*MFB*

Trackdown
US 1976 98m De Luxe
UA / Essaness (Bernard Schwarz)

A Montana rancher follows his sister to Los Angeles and avenges her ill-treatment there by gangsters.
Routine action thriller with fashionable realism and violence.

w Paul Edwards *d* Richard T. Heffron *ph* Gene Polito *m* Charles Bernstein

Jim Mitchum, Karen Lamm, Anne Archer, Erik Estrada, Cathy Lee Crosby, Vince Cannon

Trade Winds
US 1939 93m bw
Walter Wanger

A girl who thinks she has committed murder flees to the Far East, and a cynical detective is sent to bring her back. Guess what happens.
Smartly written mixture of comedy, drama, mystery and travelogue which comes off only in spots; it needed a firmer hand.

w Dorothy Parker, Alan Campbell, Frank R. Adams *d* Tay Garnett *ph* Rudolph Maté *m* Alfred Newman

Fredric March, Joan Bennett, Ralph Bellamy, Ann Sothern, Sidney Blackmer, Thomas Mitchell, Robert Elliott

Trader Horn*
US 1930 120m bw
MGM

An experienced African trader overcomes tribal hostility.
Primitive talkie for which second units were sent to Africa amid much publicity hoo-ha. After fifty years, nothing of interest remains to be seen.

w Richard Schayer, Dale Van Every, Thomas Neville, *novel* Alfred Aloysius Horn, Etheldreda Lewis *d* W. S. Van Dyke *ph* Clyde de Vinna

Harry Carey, Edwina Booth, Duncan Renaldo, Mutia Omoolu, C. Aubrey Smith
AAN: best picture

Trader Horn
US 1973 105m Metrocolor
MGM (Lewis J. Rachmil)

Pitiful remake patched together largely from stock footage.

w William Norton, Edward Harper *d* Reza Badiyi *ph* Ronald W. Browne *m* Shelly Manne

Rod Taylor, Anne Heywood, Jean Sorel
'Laughably inept . . . it cannot face word of mouth for long.'—*Variety*

Traffic
France / Italy 1970 96m Eastmancolor
Corona / Gibe / Selenia (Robert Dorfman)

The designer of a camping car has various little accidents on the way from the works to a show.

Rambling comedy with understated jokes and an almost invisible star.

w Jacques Tati, Jacques Legrange d Jacques Tati (with Bert Haanstra) ph Edouard Van Den Enden, Marcel Weiss m Charles Dumont

Jacques Tati

The Trail of '98*
US 1928   90m at 24 fps   bw   silent

San Franciscans leave their homes for the Klondike gold rush. Impressive spectacular while it stays outdoors; not so good when the plot takes over. Dolores Del Rio, Ralph Forbes, Harry Carey, Karl Dane, Tully Marshall. Written by Waldmar Young and Ben Glazer, from the novel by Robert W. Service; directed by Clarence Brown; for MGM.

The Trail of the Lonesome Pine*
US 1936   102m   Technicolor
Paramount (Walter Wanger)

A hillbilly girl goes back home when her brother is killed in a family feud.

Antediluvian Ozarkian melodrama, notable as the first outdoor film to be shot in three-colour Technicolor.

w Grover Jones, Horace McCoy, Harvey Thew, novel John Fox Jnr d Henry Hathaway ph Howard Green m Hugo Friedhofer, Gerrard Carbonara

Sylvia Sidney, Fred MacMurray, Henry Fonda, Fred Stone, Nigel Bruce, Beulah Bondi, Robert Barrat, Spanky McFarland, Fuzzy Knight

'Unnatural as it is, the colour does no serious damage to the picture. This moldy bit of hokum . . . takes movies back to the days of their childhood.'—Newsweek

† The story was first filmed in 1915 by Cecil B. de Mille.

AAN: song 'A Melody from the Sky' (m Louis Alter, ly Sidney Mitchell)

Trail Street
US 1947   84m   bw

Wheat is planted in Kansas by the early settlers. Pretty good, unpretentious western. Randolph Scott, Robert Ryan, Anne Jeffreys, Billy House, George 'Gabby' Hayes. Written by Norman Houston and Gene Lewis; directed by Ray Enright; for Nat Holt / RKO.

The Train**
US 1964   140m   bw
UA / Ariane / Dear (Jules Bricken)

In 1944, the French resistance tries to prevent the Nazis from taking art treasures back to Germany on a special train.

Proficient but longwinded suspense actioner with spectacular sequences; a safe bet for train enthusiasts.

w Franklin Coen, Frank Davis, Walter Bernstein d John Frankenheimer ph Jean Tournier, Walter Wottitz m Maurice Jarre

Burt Lancaster, Paul Scofield, Jeanne Moreau, Michael Simon, Wolfgang Preiss, Suzanne Flon

'Extraordinarily good in many of its parts but rather disappointing as a whole . . . its greatest virtue is an almost overpowering physical realism.'—Moira Walsh, America

AAN: script

Train of Events
GB 1949   89m   bw
Ealing (Michael Relph)

Portmanteau of stories à la Friday the 13th or Dead of Night, linked by a train disaster.

A rather mechanical entertainment, proficiently made.

w Basil Dearden, T. E. B. Clarke, Ronald Millar, Angus MacPhail d Basil Dearden, Charles Crichton, Sidney Cole ph Lionel Banes, Gordon Dines m Leslie Bridgewater

Valerie Hobson, John Clements, Jack Warner, Gladys Henson, Peter Finch, Irina Baronova, Susan Shaw, Patric Doonan, Joan Dowling, Laurence Payne, Mary Morris

The Train Robbers
US 1973   92m   Technicolor   Panavision
Warner / Batjac (Michael Wayne)

A widow asks three gunmen to help her clear her husband's name by retrieving gold he had stolen.

Shaggy dog western, sadly lacking in comic situation and detail.

wd Burt Kennedy ph William Clothier
m Dominic Frontière

John Wayne, Ann-Margret, Rod Taylor, Ben Johnson, Bobby Vinton, Christopher George

The Traitor*
GB 1957   88m   bw
New Realm (E. J. Fancey)

At the annual reunion of a resistance group, the host announces that one of their number was a traitor.

Heavy-handed theatrical melodrama, helped by a stout plot and some directional flair.

wd Michael McCarthy ph Bert Mason m Jackie Brown

Donald Wolfit, Robert Bray, Jane Griffiths, Carl Jaffe, Anton Diffring, Oscar Quitak, Rupert Davies, John Van Eyssen

The Traitors*
GB 1962 69m bw
Ello (Jim O'Connelly)

A top scientist is killed and MI5 springs into action.
Commendable second feature with narrative virtues absent in most big films.

w Jim O'Connelly d Robert Tronson ph Michael Reed m Johnny Douglas

Patrick Allen, James Maxwell, Ewan Roberts, Zena Walker

Traitor's Gate
GB 1965 80m bw
Columbia / Summit (Ted Lloyd)

A London businessman organizes a gang to steal the Crown Jewels.
Modest caper melodrama, routine but watchable.

w John Sansom, novel Edgar Wallace d Freddie Francis ph Denys Coop

Albert Lieven, Gary Raymond, Margot Trooger, Klaus Kinski, Catherina Von Schell, Edward Underdown

The Tramp*
US 1915 20m approx (24 fps) bw silent
Mutual

A tramp saves a girl from crooks, is wounded and cared for by her, deliriously happy—until her lover arrives.
Fairly funny star comedy, the first with sentimental touches and the origin of the into-the-sunset fade-out.

wd Charles Chaplin ph Rollie Totheroh

Charles Chaplin, Edna Purviance, Bud Jamison, Leo White, Lloyd Bacon

Tramp Tramp Tramp*
US 1926 65m approx (24 fps) bw silent
Harry Langdon

Harry enters a cross-country walking contest in order to impress his girl.
Well-staged peripatetic comedy, the star's first feature.

w Frank Capra, Tim Whelan, Hal Conklin, Gerald Duffy, Murray Roth, J. Frank Holliday d Harry Edwards

Harry Langdon, Joan Crawford, Alec B. Francis

Transatlantic Merry Go Round
US 1934 92m bw

Romantic misunderstandings on an ocean liner. Patchy comedy with some good scenes.
Jack Benny, Nancy Carroll, Gene Raymond, Sydney Howard. Written by Joseph Moncure March, Harry W. Conn and Leon Gordon; directed by Ben Stoloff; for United Artists.

Trans-Europe Express*
France 1966 90m bw
Como Film (Samy Halfon)

Film-makers on a train invent a violent plot and then find life aping it.
A theme beloved of Hollywood is treated intellectually, and almost succeeds in attracting all classes.

wd Alain Robbe-Grillet ph Willy Kurant m Verdi

Jean-Louis Trintignant, Marie-France Pisier, Nadine Verdier, Christian Barbier, Charles Millot, Alain Robbe-Grillet

The Trap*
US 1958 84m Technicolor
Paramount / Parkwood–Heath (Melvin Frank, Norman Panama)
GB title: *The Baited Trap*

A lawyer helps a vicious killer to escape into Mexico, but the plan backfires.
Reasonably tense action thriller with desert backgrounds.

w Richard Alan Simmons, Norman Panama d Norman Panama ph Daniel L. Fapp m Irvin Talbot

Richard Widmark, Lee J. Cobb, Earl Holliman, Tina Louise, Carl Benton Reid, Lorne Green

The Trap
GB / Canada 1966 106m Eastmancolor Panavision
Parallel (George H. Brown)

In nineteenth-century British Columbia a rough trapper takes a wife, who at first is terrified of him but nurses him when he is hurt . . .
Primitive open air melodrama with good action sequences; well made but hardly endearing.

w David Osborn *d* Sidney Hayers *ph* Robert Krasker *m* Ron Goodwin

Oliver Reed, Rita Tushingham, Rex Sevenoaks, Barbara Chilcott

Trapeze**

US 1956 105m De Luxe Cinemascope
UA / Hecht–Lancaster (James Hill)

A circus partnership almost breaks up when a voluptuous third member is engaged. Concentrated, intense melodrama filmed almost entirely within a French winter circus and giving a very effective feel, almost a smell, of the life therein. Despite great skill in the making, however, the length is too great for a wisp of plot that goes back to *The Three Maxims* and doubtless beyond.

w James R. Webb *d* Carol Reed *ph* Robert Krasker *m* Malcolm Arnold

Burt Lancaster, Tony Curtis, Gina Lollobrigida, Thomas Gomez, Johnny Puleo, Katy Jurado, Sidney James

Traveller's Joy

GB 1949 78m bw

A divorced couple, stranded in Sweden by lack of funds, have to take joint action. Mild topical comedy from a popular play. Googie Withers, John McCallum, Yolande Donlan, Maurice Denham, Geoffrey Sumner, Colin Gordon, Dora Bryan. Written by Allan MacKinnon and Bernard Quayle, from the play by Arthur Macrae; directed by Ralph Thomas; for Gainsborough / Rank.

The Travelling Executioner*

US 1970 95m Metrocolor Panavision
MGM (Jack Smight)

In 1918 an ex-carnival showman travels the American south with his portable electric chair and charges a hundred dollars per execution, but falls for one of his proposed victims. Oddball fable without apparent moral; neither fantastic nor funny enough.

w Garrie Bateson *d* Jack Smight *ph* Philip Lathrop *m* Jerry Goldsmith

Stacy Keach, Mariana Hill, Bud Cort, Graham Jarvis

Travels with My Aunt*

US 1972 109m Metrocolor Panavision
MGM (Robert Fryer, James Cresson)

A staid bank accountant is landed in a series of continental adventures by his eccentric life-loving aunt.
Busy but fairly disastrous adaptation of a delightful novel, ruined by ceaseless chatter,

lack of characterization, shapeless incident and an absurdly caricatured central performance.

w Jay Presson Allen, Hugh Wheeler, *novel* Graham Greene *d* George Cukor *ph* Douglas Slocombe *m* Tony Hatch *pd* John Box

Maggie Smith, *Alec McCowen*, Lou Gossett, Robert Stephens, Cindy Williams
  'It seems to run down before it gets started.'—*New Yorker, 1977*

AAN: Douglas Slocombe; Maggie Smith

Tread Softly Stranger*

GB 1958 91m bw
Alderdale (George Minter)

In a north country town, two brothers in love with the same girl rob a safe.
Hilarious murky melodrama full of glum faces, with a well-worn trick ending; rather well photographed.

w George Minter, Denis O'Dell, *play* Jack Popplewell *d* Gordon Parry *ph* Douglas Slocombe *m* Tristam Cary

George Baker, Terence Morgan, Diana Dors, Wilfrid Lawson, Patrick Allen, Jane Griffith, Joseph Tomelty, Norman Macowan

Treasure Hunt

GB 1952 79m bw
Romulus (Anatole de Grunwald)

The eccentric middle-aged members of an Irish family find their father's fortune is missing.
Theatrical comedy with some charm and humour, but very much a photographed play.

w Anatole de Grunwald, *play* M. J. Perry *d* John Paddy Carstairs *ph* C. Pennington-Richards *m* Mischa Spoliansky

Jimmy Edwards, *Martita Hunt, Athene Seyler*, Naunton Wayne, June Clyde, Susan Stephen, Brian Worth

Treasure Island**

US 1934 105m bw
MGM (Hunt Stromberg)

An old pirate map leads to a long sea voyage, a mutiny, and buried treasure.
Nicely mounted Hollywood version of a classic adventure story, a little slow in development but meticulously produced.

w John Lee Mahin, novel Robert Louis Stevenson *d* Victor Fleming *ph* Ray June, Clyde de Vinna, Harold Rosson *m* Herbert Stothart

Wallace Beery, Jackie Cooper, Lewis Stone, *Lionel Barrymore*, Otto Kruger, Douglass Dumbrille, Nigel Bruce, Chic Sale

'The first three-quarters is so lively and well established in its mood as to make the whole quite worth going to.'—*Otis Ferguson*

Treasure Island*
GB 1950 96m Technicolor
Walt Disney (Perce Pearce)

Cheerful Disney remake, poor on detail but transfixed by a swaggeringly overplayed and unforgettable leading performance.

w Lawrence Edward Watkin *d* Byron Haskin *ph* F. A. Young *m* Clifton Parker *pd* Thomas Morahan

Robert Newton, Bobby Driscoll, Walter Fitzgerald, Basil Sydney, Denis O'Dea, Geoffrey Wilkinson, Ralph Truman
'Serviceable rather than imaginative.'—*Lindsay Anderson*

Treasure Island
GB / France / Germany / Spain 1971
 95m colour
Massfilms / FDL / CCC / Eguiluz (Harry Alan Towers)

Spiritless and characterless international remake with poor acting, production and dubbing.

w Wolf Mankowitz, O. W. Jeeves (Welles) *d* John Hough *ph* Cicilio Paniagua *m* Natal Massara

Orson Welles, Kim Burfield, Lionel Stander, Walter Slezak, Rik Battaglia

The Treasure of Lost Canyon
US 1952 82m Technicolor
U-I (Leonard Goldstein)

A small boy robbed of his inheritance finds it with the help of a country doctor who turns out to be his uncle.
Modest juvenile adventure, rather boringly narrated.

w Brainerd Duffield, Emerson Crocker, *story* by Robert Louis Stevenson *d* Ted Tetzlaff *ph* Russell Metty *m* Joseph Gershenson

William Powell, Julia Adams, Charles Drake, Rosemary de Camp, Henry Hull, Tommy Ivo

Treasure of Matecumbe
US 1976 116m Technicolor
Walt Disney (Bill Anderson)

Two boys seek buried gold in the Florida keys.
Cheerful adventure tale with a few nods to *Treasure Island*; all very competent in the Disney fashion.

w Don Tait *d* Vincent McEveety *ph* Frank Phillips *m* Buddy Baker

Robert Foxworth, Joan Hackett, Peter Ustinov, Vic Morrow, Jane Wyatt, Johnny Duran, Billy Attmore

The Treasure of Pancho Villa
US 1955 96m Technicolor Superscope
RKO / Edmund Grainger

Mexico 1915: an American adventurer becomes involved with the revolutionary Pancho Villa; both seek a gold consignment but it is buried in an avalanche.
Modestly well made, routine action drama.

w Niven Busch *d* George Sherman *ph* William Snyder *m* Leith Stevens

Rory Calhoun, Shelley Winters, *Gilbert Roland*, Joseph Calleia

Treasure of San Teresa
GB 1959 81m bw
Orbit (John Nasht, Patrick Filmer-Sankey)

An American secret service agent finds Nazi loot in a Czech convent.
Roughly-made, watchable actioner.

w Jack Andrews, Jeffrey Dell *d* Alvin Rakoff *ph* Wilkie Cooper *m* Philip Martell

Eddie Constantine, Dawn Addams, Marius Goring, Christopher Lee, Walter Gotell

Treasure of the Golden Condor
US 1952 93m Technicolor
TCF (Jules Buck)

A young Frenchman flees to the South Seas but returns to discredit his wicked uncle.
Ineffectual remake of *Son of Fury* (qv) with Guatemalan backgrounds and no punch at all.

wd Delmer Daves *ph* Edward Cronjager *m* Sol Kaplan

Cornel Wilde, Finlay Currie, Constance Smith, George Macready, Walter Hampden, Anne Bancroft, Fay Wray, Leo G. Carroll

The Treasure of the Sierra Madre**
US 1948 126m bw
Warner (Henry Blanke)

Three gold prospectors come to grief through greed.
Well-acted but partly miscast action fable on the oldest theme in the world; rather tedious and studio-bound for a film with such a high reputation.

wd John Huston, *novel* B. Traven *ph* Ted McCord *m* Max Steiner *md* Leo F. Forbstein

Humphrey Bogart, *Walter Huston*, Tim Holt, Alfonso Bedoya, John Huston, Bruce Bennett, Barton MacLane
'This bitter fable is told with cinematic integrity and considerable skill.'—*Henry Hart*

'The faces of the men, in close-up or in a group, achieve a kind of formal pattern and always dominate the screen.'—*Peter Ericsson*

'One of the very few movies made since 1927 which I am sure will stand up in the memory and esteem of qualified people alongside the best of the silent movies.'—*James Agee*

AA: John Huston (as writer and director); Walter Huston
AAN: best picture

A Tree Grows in Brooklyn••••
US 1945 128m bw
TCF (Louis D. Lighton)

Life for an Irish family with a drunken father in New York's teeming slums at the turn of the century.
A superbly-detailed studio production of the type they don't make any more: a family drama with interest for everybody.

w Tess Slesinger, Frank Davis, novel Betty Smith d Elia Kazan ph Leon Shamroy m Alfred Newman

Peggy Ann Garner, James Dunn, Dorothy McGuire, Joan Blondell, Lloyd Nolan, Ted Donaldson, James Gleason, Ruth Nelson, John Alexander, Adeline de Walt Reynolds, Charles Halton

'He tells a maximum amount of story with a minimum of film. Little touches of humour and human understanding crop up throughout.'—*Frank Ward, NBR*

AA: James Dunn
AAN: script

The Tree of Wooden Clogs•
Italy 1978 186m Gevacolor
RAI / GPC

In nineteenth-century Lombardy the lives of four peasant families are interwined.
Sensitive, novel-like investigation of times gone by; never very exciting but certainly never dull, despite the limits of 16mm and a non-professional cast.

w, d, ph Ermanno Olmi m from Bach

Trent's Last Case
GB 1952 90m bw
Wilcox–Neagle (Herbert Wilcox)

A journalist suspects that the death of a tycoon was murder.
Desultory version of a famous novel, with none of the original style and a few naïveties of its own.

w Pamela Bower, novel E. C. Bentley d Herbert Wilcox ph Max Greene m Anthony Collins

Michael Wilding, Margaret Lockwood, Orson Welles, John McCallum, Miles Malleson

Trial•
US 1955 109m bw
MGM (Charles Schnee)

A young lawyer defends a Mexican boy accused of rape and murder.
Stereotyped but pacy and watchable racial drama with political overtones, Our Hero having to resist bigots, Commies *and* McCarthyites.

w Don M. Mankiewicz, from his novel d Mark Robson ph Robert Surtees m Daniele Amfitheatrof

Glenn Ford, Dorothy McGuire, Arthur Kennedy, John Hodiak, Katy Jurado, Rafael Campos, Juano Hernandez, Robert Middleton, John Hoyt

AAN: Arthur Kennedy

The Trial•
France / Italy / West Germany 1962
120m bw
Paris Europa / FICIT / Hisa
original title: *Le Procès*

Joseph K is tried and condemned for an unspecified crime.
Kafka's nightmares tend to go on too long, and this film of one of them is no exception, despite its pin-screen prologue by Alexeieff and its inventive setting in the old Gare d'Orsay. Once again Welles the magician badly needs a Hollywood studio behind him.

wd, ed Orson Welles ph Edmond Richard m Jean Ledrut pd Jean Mandarut

Orson Welles, Jeanne Moreau, Anthony Perkins, Madeleine Robinson, Elsa Martinelli, Suzanne Flon, Akim Tamiroff, Romy Schneider

'The elaboration of scale and decor is as boring as in any biblical spectacular and for the same reason: because it is used without mind or feeling, not to bring out meaning but to distract us from asking for it.'—*Dwight MacDonald*

Trial by Combat
GB 1976 90m Technicolor
Warner / Combat (Fred Weintraub, Paul Heller)
aka: *Choice of Weapons*

An apparently harmless secret society of 'medieval knights' rededicates itself to the ritual execution of criminals who have escaped the law.

A rare specimen of comic macabre apparently inspired by the TV series *The Avengers*. Sadly, not much of it really works.

w Julian Bond, Steven Rossen, Mitchell Smith *d* Kevin Conner *ph* Alan Hume *m* Frank Cordell *pd* Edward Marshall

John Mills, Donald Pleasence, Peter Cushing, Barbara Hershey, David Birney, Margaret Leighton, Brian Glover

The Trial of Mary Dugan
US 1929 120m bw

Prosecution and defence counsel both change their feelings towards the girl on trial for murder. A cast-iron audience pleaser, this adapted stage play was the studio's first all-talking picture. It wouldn't stand the test of time. Norma Shearer, H. B. Warner, Raymond Hackett, Lewis Stone, Lilyan Tashman. Written by Bayard Veiller (and Becky Gardner) from his play; directed by Bayard Veiller; for MGM. (A 1940 remake directed by Norman Z. McLeod starred Laraine Day, Tom Conway, Robert Young, John Litel and Frieda Inescort, but was not a particular success.)

The Trials of Oscar Wilde**°
GB 1960 123m Super Technirama 70
Warwick / Viceroy (Harold Huth)
US title: *The Man with the Green Carnation*

Oscar Wilde fatally sues the Marquis of Queensberry for libel, and loses; he is then prosecuted for sodomy.
Plush account of a fascinating event; narrative drive is unfortunately lacking, but one is left with interesting performances.

wd Ken Hughes *ph* Ted Moore *m* Ron Goodwin *ad* Ken Adam, Bill Constable

Peter Finch, Yvonne Mitchell, *John Fraser*, Lionel Jeffries, *Nigel Patrick*, James Mason, Emrys Jones, Maxine Audley, Paul Rogers, James Booth

Tribute°
Canada 1980 122m colour
TCF / Joel B. Michaels, Garth B. Drabinsky

A Broadway press agent comes to know his son by his divorced wife just as he comes to know of his own fatal illness.
Satisfactory screen treatment of a play which is really a vehicle for a charismatic star.

w Bernard Slade, from his play *d* Bob Clark *ph* Reginald H. Morris *m* various

Jack Lemmon, Lee Remick, Robby Benson, Colleen Dewhurst, Kim Cattrall, John Marley

AAN: Jack Lemmon

Tribute to a Bad Man
US 1956 95m Eastmancolor Cinemascope
MGM (Sam Zimbalist)

A Wyoming horse breeder is callous in his treatment of rustlers, and wins the woman he wants when he becomes more understanding.
Somewhere behind an unsympathetic story and hesitant development lies a convincing picture of life in the old west.

w Michael Blankfort, *story* Jack Schaefer *d* Robert Wise *ph* Robert Surtees *m* Miklos Rozsa

James Cagney, Irene Papas, Don Dubbins, Stephen McNally, Vic Morrow, Royal Dano, Lee Van Cleef

Trio°
GB 1950 91m bw
Rank / Gainsborough (Antony Darnborough)

Following *Quartet* (qv), three more stories from Somerset Maugham: 'The Verger', 'Mr Knowall', and 'Sanatorium'.
An enjoyable package, unpretentiously handled but with full weight to the content.

w W. Somerset Maugham, R. C. Sherriff, Noel Langley, *stories* W. Somerset Maugham *d* Ken Annakin, Harold French *ph* Reg Wyer, Geoffrey Unsworth *m* John Greenwood *ad* Maurice Carter

James Hayter, Kathleen Harrison, Michael Hordern, Felix Aylmer; *Nigel Patrick*, Anne Crawford, Naunton Wayne, Wilfrid Hyde White; Michael Rennie, Jean Simmons, *John Laurie, Finlay Currie*, Roland Culver, Betty Ann Davies, Raymond Huntley, André Morell

The Trip°
US 1967 85m Pathecolor
AIP (Roger Corman)

A director of TV commercials tries LSD and has hallucinations.
Much-banned plotless wallow, the ultimate opt-out movie; well done for those who can take it.

w Jack Nicholson *d* Roger Corman *ph* Arch Dalzell *psychedelic effects* Peter Gardiner *montage* Dennis Jakob

Peter Fonda, Susan Strasberg, Bruce Dern, Salli Sachse, Dennis Hopper

Triple Cross
GB 1967 140m colour
Warner / Cineurop (Fred Feldkamp)

A small-time crook imprisoned on Jersey at the start of World War II offers to spy for the Nazis but reports to the English.

Ho-hum biopic of double agent Eddie Chapman; effective scenes merely interrupt the general incoherence.

w René Hardy, *book* The Eddie Chapman Story by Frank Owen d Terence Young ph Henri Alekan m Georges Garvarentz

Christopher Plummer, Yul Brynner, Trevor Howard, Romy Schneider, Gert Frobe, Claudine Auger

Triple Echo*
GB 1972   94m   colour
Hemdale / Senta (Graham Cottle)

In 1942, a soldier's wife welcomes another soldier to her farm for tea; he deserts and poses as her sister.

Foolish story which would possibly have worked as a TV play but hardly justifies a film despite the talent on hand.

w Robin Chapman, *novel* H. E. Bates d Michael Apted ph John Coquillon m Marc Wilkinson

Glenda Jackson, Brian Deacon, Oliver Reed

The Triumph of Sherlock Holmes*
GB 1935   84m   bw

Sherlock Holmes solves a murder stemming from enmity between Pennsylvania coal miners. Solidly satisfying adaptation of Conan Doyle's *The Valley of Fear*, with more of Moriarty added. Arthur Wontner, Ian Fleming, Lyn Harding, Jane Carr, Leslie Perrins, Michael Shepley. Written by H. Fowler Mear; directed by Leslie Hiscott; for Twickenham.

Triumph of the Will****
Germany 1936   120m   bw
Leni Riefenstahl / Nazi Party

The official record of the Nazi party congress held at Nuremberg in 1934.

A devastatingly brilliant piece of film-making—right from the opening sequence of Hitler descending from the skies, his plane shadowed against the clouds. The rally scenes are a terrifying example of the camera's power of propaganda. After World War II it was banned for many years because of general fears that it might inspire a new Nazi party.

d, ed Leni Riefenstahl ph Sepp Allgeier and 36 assistants m Herbert Windt

Tripoli
US 1950   95m   Technicolor

In 1805 the United States sends marines to rout the Barbary pirates. Not a superior actioner, but it passed the time. John Payne, Maureen O'Hara, Howard Da Silva, Philip Reed, Grant Withers, Lowell Gilmore. Written by Winston Miller; directed by Will Price; for Pine-Thomas / Paramount.

Tropic Holiday
US 1938   78m   bw

A Hollywood scriptwriter finds romance in Mexico. Musical time-filler with a bit of everything and not much of anything. Ray Milland, Dorothy Lamour, Bob Burns, Martha Raye, Binnie Barnes, Tito Guizar. Written by Don Hartman, Frank Butler, John C. Moffett and Duke Atteberry; directed by Theodore Reed; for Paramount.

Tropic Zone
US 1953   94m   Technicolor

In a banana port a man wanted by the police saves a plantation from being taken over by crooks. Tropical thick-ear, not entirely unendurable. Written and directed by Lewis R. Foster, from a novel by Tom Gill; for Pine-Thomas / Paramount.

Trog
GB 1970   91m   Technicolor
Warner / Herman Cohen

A man-ape is discovered in a pothole and trained by a lady scientist.

Ridiculous semi-horror film which degrades its star.

w Aben Kandel d Freddie Francis ph Desmond Dickinson m John Scott

Joan Crawford, Michael Gough, Bernard Kay, David Griffin

The Trojan Women*
US 1971   111m   Eastmancolor
Josef Shaftel (Michael Cacoyannis, Anis Nohra)

Troy has fallen to the Greeks and its women bemoan their fate.

And oh, how they bemoan! Even with this cast, Greek tragedy does not fill the big screen.

w Michael Cacoyannis, *play* Euripides d Michael Cacoyannis ph Alfio Contini m Mikis Theodorakis

Katharine Hepburn, Vanessa Redgrave, Geneviève Bujold, Irene Papas, Patrick Magee, Brian Blessed, Pauline Letts

Trooper Hook
US 1957 92m bw
UA / Sol Baer Fielding

A woman prisoner of the Indians has a half-breed son and becomes an outcast when returned to her people.
Peculiar western with good moments, but generally very slow and downbeat.

w Charles Marquis Warren, David Victor, Herbert Little Jnr, *story* Jack Schaefer d Charles Marquis Warren *ph* Ellsworth Fredericks *m* Gerald Fried

Barbara Stanwyck, Joel McCrea, Earl Holliman, Edward Andrews, John Dehner, Susan Kohner, Royal Dano

Trottie True*
GB 1949 98m Technicolor
GFD / Two Cities (Hugh Stewart)
US title: *The Gay Lady*

Adventures of a Gaiety girl who married a lord.
Self-conscious period comedy which could have been highly diverting but manages only to be sporadically charming in a whimsically amateurish way.

w C. Denis Freeman, *novel* Caryl Brahms, S. J. Simon d Brian Desmond Hurst *ph* Harry Waxman *m* Benjamin Frankel *ad* Ralph Brinton

Jean Kent, James Donald, Hugh Sinclair, Bill Owen, Andrew Crawford, Lana Morris

Trouble along the Way
US 1953 110m bw
Warner (Melville Shavelson)

A famous football coach is co-opted to help a bankrupt college but some of his methods are not quite above board.
American college comedy with dollops of religiosity—a double threat.

w Melville Shavelson, Jack Rose d Michael Curtiz *ph* Archie Stout *m* Max Steiner

John Wayne, Donna Reed, Charles Coburn, Tom Tully, Sherry Jackson, Marie Windsor
'No opportunites for a laugh or a tear are missed by the entire cast.'—*MFB*

Trouble for Two*
US 1936 75m bw
MGM (Louis D. Lighton)
GB title: *The Suicide Club*

A European prince in London for an arranged wedding gets involved with an ingenious organization for murder.
Light-hearted, black-edged Victorian literary spoof which starts nicely but can't quite keep up the pace.

w Manuel Seff, Edward Paramore Jnr, *stories* New Arabian Nights by Robert Louis Stevenson d J. Walter Rubin *ph* Charles G. Clarke *m* Franz Waxman

Robert Montgomery, Rosalind Russell, *Reginald Owen*, Frank Morgan, *Louis Hayward*, E. E. Clive, Walter Kingsford

Trouble in Paradise***
US 1932 86m bw
Paramount (Ernst Lubitsch)

Jewel thieves insinuate themselves into the household of a rich Parisienne, and one falls in love with her.
A masterpiece of light comedy, with sparkling dialogue, innuendo, great performances and masterly cinematic narrative. For connoisseurs, it can't be faulted, and is the masterpiece of American sophisticated cinema.

w *Samson Raphaelson, Grover Jones, play* The Honest Finder by Laszlo Aladar d *Ernst Lubitsch ph* Victor Milner *m* W. Franke Harling

Herbert Marshall, Miriam Hopkins, Kay Francis, Edward Everett Horton, Charles Ruggles, C. Aubrey Smith, Robert Greig, Leonid Kinskey

'One of the gossamer creations of Lubitsch's narrative art . . . it would be impossible in this brief notice to describe the innumerable touches of wit and of narrative skill with which it is unfolded.'—*Alexander Bakshy*

'A shimmering, engaging piece of work . . . in virtually every scene a lively imagination shines forth.'—*New York Times*

'An almost continuous musical background pointed up and commented on the action. The settings were the last word in modernistic design.'—*Theodor Huff, 1948*

Trouble in Store*
GB 1953 85m bw
GFD / Two Cities (Maurice Cowan)

A stock assistant causes chaos in a department store.
First, simplest and best of the Wisdom farces.

w John Paddy Carstairs, Maurice Cowan, Ted Willis d John Paddy Carstairs *ph* Ernest Steward *m* Mischa Spoliansky

Norman Wisdom, Jerry Desmonde, Margaret Rutherford, Moira Lister, Derek Bond, Lana Morris, Megs Jenkins, Joan Sims

Trouble in the Glen
GB 1954 91m Trucolor
Republic / Wilcox–Neagle (Stuart Robertson)

An Argentinian laird in a Scottish glen causes ill-feeling.

Heavy-handed Celtic comedy whose predictability and sentimentality could have been forgiven were it not for the most garish colour ever seen.

w Frank S. Nugent, *novel* Maurice Walsh *d* Herbert Wilcox *ph* Max Greene *m* Victor Young

Margaret Lockwood, Orson Welles, Forrest Tucker, Victor McLaglen, John McCallum, Eddie Byrne, Archie Duncan, Moultrie Kelsall

The Trouble with Angels
US 1966   112m   Pathecolor
Columbia / William Frye

Two mischievous new pupils cause trouble at a convent school.

Fun with the nuns, for addicts only.

w Blanche Hanalis, *novel* Life with Mother Superior by Jane Trahey *d* Ida Lupino *ph* Lionel Lindon *m* Jerry Goldsmith

Rosalind Russell, Hayley Mills, June Harding, Marge Redmond, Binnie Barnes, Gypsy Rose Lee, Camilla Sparv, Mary Wickes, Margalo Gillmore

'A relentless series of prankish escapades.'—*MFB*

The Trouble with Girls
US 1969   105m   Metrocolor   Panavision
MGM (Lester Welch)

In the twenties the manager of a travelling chautauqua (educational medicine show) gets involved in a small-town murder.

Curious vehicle for a very bored singing star, with some interesting background detail.

w Arnold and Lois Peyser, *novel* The Chautauqua by Day Keene, Dwight Babcock *d* Peter Tewksbury *ph* Jacques Marquette *m* Billy Strange

Elvis Presley, Marlyn Mason, Nicole Jaffe, Sheree North, Edward Andrews, John Carradine, Vincent Price, Joyce Van Patten

The Trouble with Harry**
US 1955   99m   Technicolor   Vistavision
(Paramount) Alfred Hitchcock

In the New England woods, various reasons cause various people to find and bury the same body.

Black comedy which never quite, despite bright moments, catches the style of the book; however, it is finely performed and the autumnal backgrounds are splendid.

w John Michael Hayes, *novel* Jack Trevor Story *d* Alfred Hitchcock *ph* Robert Burks *m* Bernard Herrmann

Edmund Gwenn, Mildred Natwick, John Forsythe, Shirley Maclaine, Mildred Dunnock

The Trouble with Women
US 1947   80m   bw

A psychology professor thinks women enjoy being treated rough; a lady reporter tests his theories. Silly romantic comedy. Ray Milland, Brian Donlevy, Teresa Wright, Rose Hobart, Charles Smith, Iris Adrian, Lloyd Bridges. Written by Arthur Sheekman, from a story by Ruth McKenney; directed by Sidney Lanfield; for Paramount.

True as a Turtle
GB 1956   96m   Eastmancolor
Rank (Peter de Sarigny)

Honeymooners join a variety of friends on a yacht crossing the Channel, and get involved in smuggling.

Artless, undemanding comedy for those who like messing about in boats.

w Jack Davies, John Coates, Nicholas Phipps *d* Wendy Toye *ph* Reg Wyer *m* Robert Farnon

John Gregson, June Thorburn, Cecil Parker, *Elvi Hale*, Keith Michell, Avice Landone

True Confession**
US 1937   85m   bw
Paramount (Albert Lewin)

A fantasy-prone girl confesses to a murder she didn't commit, and her upright lawyer husband defends her.

Archetypal crazy comedy with fine moments despite longueurs and a lack of cinematic inventiveness. Remade as *Cross My Heart* (qv).

w Claude Binyon, *play* Mon Crime by Louis Verneuil, George Berr *d* Wesley Ruggles *ph* Ted Tetzlaff *m* Frederick Hollander

Carole Lombard, Fred MacMurray, *John Barrymore*, Una Merkel, Porter Hall, Edgar Kennedy, Lynne Overman, Fritz Feld, *Irving Bacon*

'The best comedy of the year.'—*Graham Greene*

The True Glory****
GB / US 1945   90m   bw
Ministry of Information / Office of War Information

The last year of the war, retold by edited newsreels: D-Day to the Fall of Berlin.

A magnificent piece of reportage, worth a dozen fiction films in its exhilarating Shakespearean fervour, though the poetic commentary does occasionally go over the top. One of the finest of all compilations.

w Eric Maschwitz, Arthur Macrae, Jenny Nicholson, Gerald Kersh, Guy Trosper d Carol Reed, Garson Kanin research Peter Cusick m William Alwyn

'Dwarfs all the fiction pictures of the year.'—*Richard Mallett, Punch*

'Bold, welcome but inadequate use of blank verse; much more successful use of many bits of individualized vernacular narration, unusually free of falseness. Very jab-paced, energetic cutting; intelligent selection of shots, of which several hundred are magnificent.'—*James Agee*

True Grit*

US 1969 128m Technicolor
Paramount / Hal B. Wallis (Paul Nathan)

In the old west, a young girl wanting to avenge her murdered father seeks the aid of a hard-drinking old marshal.

Disappointingly slow-moving and uninventive semi-spoof western with a roistering performance from a veteran star, who won a sentimental Oscar for daring to look fat and old.

w Marguerite Roberts, novel Charles Portis d Henry Hathaway ph Lucien Ballard m Elmer Bernstein

John Wayne, Kim Darby, Glen Campbell, Dennis Hopper, Jeremy Slate, Robert Duvall, Strother Martin, Jeff Corey

'Readers may remember it as a book about a girl, but it's a film about John Wayne.'— *Stanley Kauffmann*

'There is a slight consistent heightening or lowering into absurdity, but there is also a strong feeling for the unvarnished preposterousness of everyday existence.'— *John Simon*

† *Rooster Cogburn* featured more adventures of the Wayne character, who also showed up on TV in 1978 in the guise of Warren Oates

AA: John Wayne
AAN: title song (*m* Elmer Bernstein, *ly* Don Black)

True Heart Susie*

US 1919 62m approx (24 fps) bw
   silent
D. W. Griffith / Artcraft

A country girl sells her cow to send her boy friend to college, but he is ungrateful.
Lavender-flavoured rustic romance, with the director at his most sentimental. But of its kind it is carefully done.

wd D. W. Griffith, story Marion Fremont ph Billy Bitzer

Lillian Gish, Robert Harron, Clarine Seymour

The True Story of Jesse James

US 1956 92m Eastmancolor
   Cinemascope
TCF (Herbert Swope Jnr)
GB title: *The James Brothers*

After the Civil War, Jesse and Frank James become outlaws and train robbers.
Fairly slavish remake of *Jesse James*, without the style.

w Walter Newman d Nicholas Ray ph Joe MacDonald m Leigh Harline

Robert Wagner, Jeffrey Hunter, Hope Lange, Agnes Moorehead, John Carradine, Alan Hale Jnr, Alan Baxter

Trunk Crime

GB 1939 51m bw

A student goes mad and tries to bury his enemy alive. Now dated, but at the time a smart little programme-filler by an enterprising young producer-director team. Manning Whiley, Barbara Everest, Hay Petrie, Thorley Walters. Written by Francis Miller, from the play by Edward Percy and Reginald Denham; directed by Roy Boulting; produced by John Boulting; for Charter.

The Truth about Women

GB 1957 107m Eastmancolor
British Lion / Beaconsfield (Sydney Box)

An old roué recounts to his son-in-law his early amorous adventures.
Tedious charade with neither wit nor grace.

w Muriel and Sydney Box d Muriel Box ph Otto Heller m Bruce Montgomery

Laurence Harvey, Julie Harris, Diane Cilento, Mai Zetterling, Eva Gabor, Michael Denison, Derek Farr, Roland Culver, Wilfrid Hyde White, Christopher Lee, Marius Goring, Thorley Walters, Ernest Thesiger, Griffith Jones

The Truth about Spring*

GB 1964 102m Technicolor
U-I / Quota Rentals (Alan Brown)

The bored nephew of a millionaire cruising in the Caribbean jumps at the chance to join friends on a scruffy yacht, but they all get involved with pirates.
Pleasing family film with good scenery and a friendly cast.

w James Lee Barrett, *novel* H. de Vere Stacpoole *d* Richard Thorpe *ph* Ted Scaife *m* Robert Farnon

Hayley Mills, James MacArthur, David Tomlinson, Lionel Jeffries, John Mills, Harry Andrews, Niall MacGinnis

Try and Get Me*
US 1951   92m   bw
(UA) Robert Stillman
GB title: *The Sound of Fury*

Two men are arrested for kidnapping and murder, and a journalist stirs the small town to lynch fury.
Harrowing, relentless melodrama, possibly the best on this subject.

w Jo Pagano, from his novel The Condemned *d* Cyril Endfield *ph* Guy Roe *m* Hugo Friedhofer

Frank Lovejoy, Lloyd Bridges, Kathleen Ryan, Richard Carlson, Katherine Locke, Adele Jergens, Art Smith
'The characterization and the handling of the drama are remarkable, at times reaching a complexity rare in films of this type.'—*Gavin Lambert*
'A strange, uncomfortable, sometimes brutal and depressing picture.'—*Richard Mallett, Punch*

The Trygon Factor*
GB 1966   88m   Technicolor
Rank / Rialto Film / Preben Phillipsen (Ian Warren)

Bogus nuns plan a million pound bank raid.
When you get used to its mixture of styles, this Anglo-German production is pretty good imitation Edgar Wallace, with bags of mystery and melodramatic goings-on involving larger than life characters most of whom come to sticky ends.

w Derry Quinn, Stanley Munro, Kingsley Amis *d* Cyril Frankel *ph* Harry Waxman *m* Peter Thomas

Stewart Granger, Susan Hampshire, Cathleen Nesbitt, Robert Morley, James Culliford, Brigitte Horney, Sophie Hardy, James Robertson Justice

Tudor Rose*
GB 1936   78m   bw
GFD / Gainsborough (Michael Balcon)
US title: *Nine Days a Queen*

The brief life and reign of Lady Jane Grey.
Modestly well made historical textbook.

w Robert Stevenson, Miles Malleson *d* Robert Stevenson *ph* Max Greene *m* Louis Levy

Cedric Hardwicke, Nova Pilbeam, John Mills, Felix Aylmer, Leslie Perrins, Frank Cellier, Desmond Tester, Gwen Frangcon Davies, Sybil Thorndike, Martita Hunt, Miles Malleson, John Laurie
'There is not a character, not an incident in which history has not been altered for the cheapest of reasons.'—*Graham Greene*

Tugboat Annie**
US 1933   88m   bw
MGM (Harry Rapf)

An elderly waterfront lady and her boozy friend smooth out the path of young love.
Hilarious and well-loved comedy vehicle for two great stars of the period.

w Zelda Sears, Eve Greene, *stories* Norman Reilly Raine *d* Mervyn Le Roy *ph* Gregg Toland

Marie Dressler, Wallace Beery, Robert Young, Maureen O'Sullivan, Willard Robertson, Paul Hurst

Tulsa*
US 1949   88m   Technicolor
Eagle–Lion (Walter Wanger)

The daughter of a cattle owner builds an oil empire.
Splendid Hollywood hokum of the second grade, very predictable but well-oiled.

w Frank Nugent, Curtis Kenyon *d* Stuart Heisler *ph* Winton Hoch *m* Frank Skinner

Susan Hayward, Robert Preston, Pedro Armendariz, Lloyd Gough, Chill Wills, Ed Begley
'Like a damp fuse, it produces a loud bang at the end of a long splutter.'—*Time*
'Meet Cherokee Lansing . . . half wildcat . . . half angel . . . all woman!'—*publicity*

Tumbleweeds**
US 1925   80m (24 fps)   bw   silent
United Artists / William S. Hart

A wandering cowboy helps a family of settlers.
The same plot as *Shane* works wonders in the last film of William S. Hart, which has the apparently authentic flavour of the old west.

w C. Gardner Sullivan, *story* Hal G. Evarts *d* King Baggott *ph* Joseph August

William S. Hart, Barbara Bedford, Lucien Littlefield, Monte Collins
† Reissued in 1939 with an added eight-minute introduction by Hart, showing how the west has changed.

Tunes of Glory**
GB 1960   107m   Technicolor
UA / Knightsbridge (Albert Fennell)

The new disciplinarian CO of a highland regiment crosses swords with his lax, hard-drinking predecessor.

Wintry barracks melodrama, finely acted and well made with memorable confrontation scenes compensating for a somewhat underdeveloped script.

w James Kennaway, from his novel *d Ronald Neame ph* Arthur Ibbetson

Alec Guinness, John Mills, Susannah York, Dennis Price, Kay Walsh, *Duncan Macrae,* Gordon Jackson, John Fraser, Allan Cuthbertson

AAN: James Kennaway

The Tunnel*
GB 1935   94m   bw
Gaumont (Michael Balcon)
US title: *Transatlantic Tunnel*

Crooked finances mar the completion of an undersea tunnel to America.
A rare example of British science fiction.

w Curt Siodmak, L. DuGarde Peach, Clemence Dane, *novel* Bernard Kellerman *d* Maurice Elvey *ph* Gunther Krampf *m* Louis Levy

Richard Dix, Leslie Banks, Madge Evans, Helen Vinson, C. Aubrey Smith, George Arliss, Walter Huston, Basil Sydney, Jimmy Hanley

The Tunnel of Love
US 1958   98m   bw   Cinemascope
MGM / Joseph Fields

A husband applying to adopt an orphan thinks he may, while drunk, have seduced the glamorous orphan agency official.
Tasteless and not very funny comedy, somewhat miscast.

w Joseph Fields, *play* Joseph Fields, Peter de Vries, *novel* Peter de Vries *d* Gene Kelly *ph* Robert Bronner

Richard Widmark, Doris Day, Gig Young, Gia Scala, Elizabeth Fraser, Elizabeth Wilson

Turkey Time
GB 1933   73m   bw

Family indiscretions come out at Christmas time. Vehicle for fruity characterizations by the popular Aldwych team, but not very strong as a farce. Tom Walls, Ralph Lynn, Robertson Hare, Dorothy Hyson, Mary Brough, Norma Varden. Written by Ben Travers, from his play; directed by Tom Walls; for Gaumont.

Turksib*
USSR 1929   60m approx (24 fps)   bw   silent
Vostok Kino

The making of the Turkestan–Siberia railway.
A highly fluent and pictorial documentary with an especially famous climax as the men struggle to lay the last rails and meet a deadline.

w Victor Turin and others *d* Victor Turin *ph* Yevgeni Slavinsky, Boris Frantzisson

Turn Back the Clock
US 1933   80m   bw

A man dreams of changing places with his rich friend. Unusual, quite pleasing comedy-drama. Lee Tracy, Otto Kruger, Mae Clarke, C. Henry Gordon, George Barbier. Written by Edgar Selwyn and Ben Hecht; directed by Edgar Selwyn; for MGM.

Turn of the Tide*
GB 1935   80m   bw
British National (John Corfield)

A feud between two fishing families ends in marriage.
Low-key, location-set action drama with a moral. The film which brought J. Arthur Rank into the business, which he saw had religious possibilities.

w L. DuGarde Peach, J. O. C. Orton, *novel* Three Fevers by Leo Walmsley *d* Norman Walker

Geraldine Fitzgerald, John Garrick, Niall MacGinnis, J. Fisher White, Joan Maude, Sam Livesey, Wilfrid Lawson, Moore Marriott

Turn the Key Softly
GB 1953   81m   bw
GFD / Chiltern (Maurice Cowan)

The problems of three women released from prison.
Soppy formula multi-drama with contrived and uninteresting plots and characters.

w Jack Lee, Maurice Cowan, *novel* John Brophy *d* Jack Lee *ph* Geoffrey Unsworth *m* Mischa Spoliansky

Yvonne Mitchell, Terence Morgan, Joan Collins, Kathleen Harrison, Thora Hird, Dorothy Alison, Glyn Houston, Geoffrey Keen, Clive Morton

Turnabout*
US 1940   83m   bw
Hal Roach

A benevolent god enables a quarrelsome couple to change bodies and see how they like it.

'The man's had a baby instead of the lady', said the ads. Well, not quite, but it did seem pretty daring at the time, and it still provides a hilarious moment or two.

w Mickell Novak, Berne Giler, John McLain, *novel* Thorne Smith *d* Hal Roach *ph* Norbert Brodine *m* Arthur Morton

Adolphe Menjou, John Hubbard, Carole Landis, Mary Astor, Verree Teasdale, Donald Meek, William Gargan, Joyce Compton

Turned Out Nice Again
GB 1941　81m　bw

An employee teaches an underwear firm to move with the times. Tolerable star comedy from his late period. George Formby, Peggy Bryan, Edward Chapman, Elliot Mason, Mackenzie Ward, O. B. Clarence. Written by Austin Melford, John Dighton and Basil Dearden, from the play *As You Are* by Hugh Mills and Wells Root; directed by Marcel Varnel; for ATP.

The Turners of Prospect Road
GB 1947　88m　bw

A taxi driver's family greyhound wins a big race. Uneasily cast domestic comedy drama. Wilfrid Lawson, Jeanne de Casalis, Maureen Glynne, Helena Pickard, Leslie Perrins, Peter Bull. Written by Victor Katona and Patrick Kirwan; directed by Maurice J. Wilson; for Grand National.

The Turning Point
US 1952　85m　bw
Paramount (Irving Asher)

A young lawyer is appointed by the state governor to smash a crime syndicate. Familiar exposé drama of its time, quite crisply done.

w Warren Duff *w* William Dieterle *ph* Lionel Lindon *md* Irwin Talbot

William Holden, Alexis Smith, Edmond O'Brien, Tom Tully, Ray Teal

The Turning Point*
US 1977　119m　De Luxe
TCF / Hera (Nora Kaye)

The American Ballet Theatre visits Oklahoma City, and its ageing star revisits an ex-colleague, now a housewife.
Posh person's soap opera, rather boringly made and interesting only for its performances, which are certainly vivid.

w Arthur Laurents *d* Herbert Ross *ph* Robert Surtees *m* John Lanchbery *pd* Albert Brenner

Anne Bancroft, Shirley Maclaine, Mikhail Baryshnikov, Leslie Browne, Tom Skerritt, Martha Scott, Marshall Thompson
'A backstage musical dressed up with smart cultural trimmings.'—*Alan Brien*
'We get a glimpse of something great in the movie—Mikhail Baryshnikov dancing—and these two harpies out of the soaps block the view.'—*New Yorker, 1978*

AAN: best picture; Herbert Ross; Robert Surtees; Anne Bancroft; Shirley Maclaine; Mikhail Baryshnikov; Leslie Browne

Twelve Angry Men****
US 1957　95m　bw
(UA) Orion–Nova (Henry Fonda, Reginald Rose)

A murder case jury about to vote guilty is convinced otherwise by one doubting member. Though unconvincing in detail, this is a brilliantly tight character melodrama which is never less than absorbing to experience. Acting and direction are superlatively right, and the film was important in helping to establish television talents in Hollywood.

w Reginald Rose, from his play *d Sidney Lumet ph Boris Kaufman m* Kenyon Hopkins

Henry Fonda, Lee J. Cobb, E. G. Marshall, Jack Warden, Ed Begley, Martin Balsam, John Fiedler, Jack Klugman, George Voskovec, Robert Webber, Edward Binns, Joseph Sweeney

AAN: best picture; Reginald Rose; Sidney Lumet

The Twelve Chairs
US 1970　93m　Movielab
UMC / Crossbow (Michael Hertzberg)

A Russian bureaucrat chases twelve dining chairs, in one of which is hidden the family jewels.
Tedious Mel Brooks romp with not too many laughs, from a yarn better handled in *Keep Your Seats Please* and *It's in the Bag,* from both of which he might have learned something about comedy timing.

w Mel Brooks, *novel* Ilf and Petrov *d* Mel Brooks *ph* Dorde Nikolic *m* John Morris

Ron Moody, Frank Langella, Dom De Luise, Bridget Brice, Diana Coupland, Mel Brooks
'In the end it runs out of both steam and jokes.'—*Michael Billington, Illustrated London News*

Twelve Good Men
GB 1936　64m　bw

A convict escapes to murder the jury who convicted him. Solidly carpentered suspenser. Henry Kendall, Nancy O'Neill, Percy Parsons, Morland Graham, Bernard Miles. Written by *Sidney Gilliat* and *Frank Launder* from the novel *Murders in Praed Street* by John Rhode; directed by Ralph Ince; for Warner.

Twelve O'Clock High•••
US 1949 132m bw
TCF (Darryl F. Zanuck)

During World War II, the commander of a US bomber unit in Britain begins to crack under the strain.

Absorbing character drama, justifiably a big box office success of its day, later revived as a TV series. All production values are excellent.

w Sy Bartlett, Beirne Lay Jnr d Henry King ph Leon Shamroy m Alfred Newman

Gregory Peck, Hugh Marlowe, Gary Merrill, Millard Mitchell, Dean Jagger, Robert Arthur, Paul Stewart, John Kellogg

AA: Dean Jagger
AAN: best picture; Gregory Peck

Twentieth Century•••
US 1934 91m bw
Columbia

A temperamental Broadway producer trains an untutored actress, but when a star she proves a match for him.

Though slightly lacking in pace, this is a marvellously sharp and memorable theatrical burlesque, and the second half, set on the train of the title, reaches highly agreeable peaks of insanity.

w Ben Hecht, Charles MacArthur, play Napoleon of Broadway by Charles Bruce Millholland *d Howard Hawks ph Joseph August*

John Barrymore, Carole Lombard, Roscoe Karns, Walter Connolly, Ralph Forbes, *Etienne Girardot,* Charles Lane, Edgar Kennedy

'Notable as the first comedy in which sexually attractive, sophisticated stars indulged in their own slapstick instead of delegating it to their inferiors.'—*Andrew Sarris, 1963*

'In the role of Jaffe John Barrymore fits as wholly and smoothly as a banana in a skin.'—*Otis Ferguson*

Twenty Million Miles to Earth
US 1957 82m bw
Columbia (Charles Schneer)

An American rocket ship returning from Venus breaks open and a scaly monster escapes into the Mediterranean and is cornered in the Roman coliseum.

Cheeseparing monster fiction which doesn't wake up till the last five minutes, and looks pretty silly even then.

w Bob Williams, Chris Knopf d Nathan Juran ph Irving Lippmann m Mischa Bakaleinikoff sp Ray Harryhausen

William Hopper, Joan Taylor, Frank Puglia, John Zaremba

Twenty Million Sweethearts
US 1934 89m bw
Warner

Singing radio sweethearts are kept apart because of their images.

Thin musical with moderate numbers, remade as *My Dream Is Yours*.

w Warren Duff, Harry Sauber d Ray Enright ph Sid Hickox songs Harry Warren, Al Dubin

Dick Powell, Ginger Rogers, Pat O'Brien, the Mills Brothers, Ted Fio Rito and his band, the Radio Rogues, Allen Jenkins, Grant Mitchell

Twenty Mule Team•
US 1940 84m bw
MGM (J. Walter Ruben)

Rivalry among the borax miners in Death Valley.

Adequate semi-western with an unusual theme and setting.

w Robert C. DuSoe, Owen Atkinson d Richard Thorpe ph Clyde De Vinna m David Snell

Wallace Beery, Leo Carrillo, Marjorie Rambeau, Anne Baxter, Douglas Fowley, Berton Churchill, Noah Beery Jnr, Arthur Hohl, Clem Bevans, Charles Halton, Minor Watson

The Twenty Questions Murder Mystery
GB 1949 95m bw

A killer taunts the police with clues sent to a radio quiz show. Somewhat heavy comedy mystery with interest arising from the broadcasting background. Robert Beatty, Rona Anderson, Clifford Evans, Edward Lexy, Olga Lindo, Richard Dimbleby, Jack Train, Stewart MacPherson, Daphne Padel, Norman Hackforth, Jeanne de Casalis. Written by Patrick Kirwan and Victor Katona; directed by Paul Stein; for Pax-Pendennis.

Twenty Thousand Leagues under the Sea••
US 1954 122m Technicolor
   Cinemascope
Walt Disney

Victorian scientists at sea are wrecked and
captured by the mysterious captain of a
futuristic submarine.
Pretty full-blooded adaptation of a famous
yarn, with strong performances and convincing
art and trick work.

w Earl Felton, *novel Jules Verne d Richard
Fleischer ph* Franz Planer, Franz Lehy, Ralph
Hammeras, Till Gabbani *m* Paul Smith
ad John Meehan

Kirk Douglas, James Mason, Paul Lukas,
Peter Lorre, Robert J. Wilke, Carlton Young,
Ted de Corsia

Twenty Thousand Years in Sing Sing**
US 1932   77m   bw
Warner (Robert Lord)

A tough criminal escapes from prison but his
girl kills a man during the attempt, and he
takes the blame.
Dated but fast-moving and still-powerful crime
melodrama, remade to less effect as *Castle on
the Hudson* (qv).

w Wilson Mizner, Brown Holmes,
book Lewis E. Lawes *d Michael Curtiz
ph* Barney McGill *m* Bernhard Kaun

Spencer Tracy, Bette Davis, Arthur Byron,
Lyle Talbot, Louis Calhern, Warren Hymer,
Sheila Terry, Edward McNamara

Twenty-Four Hours of a Woman's Life
GB 1952   90m   Technicolor
ABPC (Ivan Foxwell)
US title: *Affair in Monte Carlo*

A young widow tries to reform an inveterate
gambler, but he kills himself.
Stilted, over-literary romantic melodrama with
philosophical dialogue, flashback framing and
Riviera settings.

w Warren Chetham Strode, *novel* Stefan
Zweig *d* Victor Saville *ph* Christopher
Challis *m* Robert Gill, Philip Green

Merle Oberon, Leo Genn, Richard Todd,
Stephen Murray, Peter Illing, Isabel Dean

29 Acacia Avenue
GB 1945   83m   bw

Young people are having a good time when
their parents return unexpectedly from
holiday. Popular domestic comedy of its day.
Gordon Harker, Betty Balfour, Carla
Lehmann, Jimmy Hanley, Jill Evans, Hubert
Gregg, Dinah Sheridan, Henry Kendall, Guy
Middleton. Written by Muriel and Sydney
Box, from the play by Mabel and Denis
Constanduros; directed by Henry Cass; for
Boca / Columbia.

Twenty-One Days*
GB 1937   75m   bw
London Films (Alexander Korda)
aka: *The First and the Last*

A barrister's brother accidentally kills a man
and lets an old eccentric take the blame.
Watchable but very stilted melodrama with
interesting early performances by Olivier and
Leigh and a few good moments.

w Graham Greene, *play* John Galsworthy
d Basil Dean *ph* Jan Stallich

Laurence Olivier, Vivien Leigh, Leslie Banks,
Hay Petrie, Francis L. Sullivan, Esmé Percy,
Robert Newton, Victor Rietti

'I wish I could tell the extraordinary story
that lies behind this shelved and resurrected
picture, a story involving a theme song, and a
bottle of whisky, and camels in Wales.
Meanwhile let one guilty man, at any rate,
stand in the dock, swearing never to do it
again. . .'—*Graham Greene*
† The film was not shown until 1940.

Twenty-Three Paces to Baker Street*
US 1956   103m   Eastmancolor
         Cinemascope
TCF (Henry Ephron)

A blind playwright in a pub overhears a
murder plot and follows the trail to the bitter
end despite attacks on his life.
Sufficiently engrossing murder mystery with a
weird idea of London's geography: the hero's
Portman Square apartment has a balcony
overlooking the Thames two miles away.
Perhaps this is part of the script's light touch.

w Nigel Balchin, *novel* Philip MacDonald
d Henry Hathaway *ph* Milton Krasner
m Leigh Harline

Van Johnson, Vera Miles, *Cecil Parker*,
Patricia Laffan, Maurice Denham, *Estelle
Winwood*, Liam Redmond

Twice round the Daffodils
GB 1962   89m   bw
Anglo Amalgamated / GHW (Peter Rogers)

Comic and serious episodes in the lives of
male patients at a TB sanatorium.
Acceptable broadening, almost in *Carry On*
style, of a modestly successful play.

w Norman Hudis, *play* Ring for Catty by
Patrick Cargill, Jack Beale *d* Gerald Thomas
ph Alan Hume *m* Bruce Montgomery

Juliet Mills, Donald Sinden, Donald Houston,
Kenneth Williams, Ronald Lewis, Joan Sims,
Andrew Ray, Lance Percival, Jill Ireland,
Sheila Hancock, Nanette Newman

Twice Two
US 1933 20m bw

Stan and Ollie have each married the other's twin sister. . . . Strained and laboured trick comedy in which neither the double exposures nor the gags quite come off. Laurel and Hardy. Written by Stan Laurel; directed by James Parrott; for Hal Roach.

Twilight for the Gods
US 1958 120m Eastmancolor
U-I (Gordon Kay)

The captain of an old sailing ship takes her for a last voyage from Mexico to Tahiti.
Dull and miscast adventure story lacking the spark of the original novel; watchable only for the travelogue elements.

w Ernest K. Gann, from his novel d Joseph Pevney ph Irving Glassberg m David Raskin md Joseph Gershenson

Rock Hudson, Cyd Charisse, Arthur Kennedy, Leif Erickson, Charles McGraw, Ernest Truex, Richard Haydn, Wallace Ford, Celia Lovsky, Vladimir Sokoloff
'Rock Hudson has difficulty in suggesting a dedicated seaman who has served under sail for thirty years.'—*MFB*

The Twilight Hour
GB 1944 85m bw

A nobleman's gardener turns out to be the amnesiac father of the girl about to marry into the family. Plodding and very predictable drama with popular cast. Mervyn Johns, Basil Radford, Marie Lohr, A. E. Matthews, Lesley Brook, Grey Blake. Written by Jack Whittingham, from a novel by Arthur Valentine; directed by Paul Stein; for British National.

Twilight of Honor
US 1963 115m bw Panavision
MGM / Perlsea
GB title: *The Charge Is Murder*

A young small-town lawyer defends a neurotic no-good on a murder charge.
Modest courtroom melodrama in which the detail is better than the main plot.

w Henry Denker, *novel* Al Dewlen d Boris Sagal ph Philip Lathrop m John Green

Richard Chamberlain, *Claude Rains,* Joey Heatherton, Nick Adams, Joan Blackman, James Gregory, Pat Buttram, Jeanette Nolan

AAN: Nick Adams

Twilight's Last Gleaming
US / West Germany 1977 146m
 Technicolor
Lorimar / Bavaria Studios (Helmut Jedele)

An ex-general commandeers an atomic missile plant and blackmails the president into telling some political truths.
Suspense thriller, fairly incompetent on its level and with ideas above its station. A distinctly overlong and unlikeable entertainment.

w Ronald M. Cohen, Edward Huebsch, *novel* Viper Three by Walter Wager d Robert Aldrich ph Robert Hauser m Jerry Goldsmith

Burt Lancaster, Richard Widmark, Charles Durning, Melvyn Douglas, Paul Winfield, Burt Young, Joseph Cotten, Roscoe Lee Brown, Gerald S. O'Loughlin, Charles Aidman

Twin Beds*
US 1942 84m bw
Edward Small

A married couple are embarrassed by the antics of a drunken neighbour.
Slight pretext for a pretty funny old-fashioned farce.

w Curtis Kenyon, Kenneth Earl, E. Edwin Moran, *play* Margaret Mayo, Edward Salisbury Field d Tim Whelan ph Hal Mohr m Dmitri Tiomkin

George Brent, Joan Bennett, *Mischa Auer,* Una Merkel, Glenda Farrell, Ernest Truex, Margaret Hamilton, Charles Coleman

The Twinkle in God's Eye
US 1955 73m bw
Republic (Mickey Rooney)

A parson rebuilds a church in a western town where his father was killed by Indians.
Amiable if unlikely western drama with the star more convincing than one might expect.

w P. J. Wolfson d George Blair ph Bud Thackery m Van Alexander

Mickey Rooney, Hugh O'Brian, Colleen Gray, Michael Connors, Don Barry

Twinky
GB 1969 98m Technicolor
Rank / World Film Services (Clive Sharp)
US title: *Lola*

A 16-year-old London schoolgirl marries a dissolute 40-year-old American author.
Dreary sex comedy drama, the fag end of London's swinging sixties.

w Norman Thaddeus Vane *d* Richard Donner *ph* Walter Lassally *m* John Scott

Charles Bronson, Susan George, Trevor Howard, Michael Craig, Honor Blackman, Robert Morley, Jack Hawkins

Twins of Evil

GB 1971   87m   Eastmancolor
Rank / Hammer (Harry Fine, Michael Style)

Identical Austrian twins become devotees of a vampire cult.
Vampire-chasing Puritans add a little flavour to a routine Hammer horror.

w Tudor Gates *d* John Hough *ph* Dick Bush *m* Harry Robinson

Madeleine and Mary Collinson, Peter Cushing, Kathleen Byron, Dennis Price, Isobel Black

Twist around the Clock

US 1961   83m   bw
Columbia / Sam Katzman

An astute manager discovers a small-town dance called the twist and promotes it nationally.
Rock around the Clock revisited, with an even lower budget and fewer shreds of talent.

w James B. Gordon *d* Oscar Rudolph *ph* Gordon Avil *md* Fred Karger

Chubby Checker, the Marcels, Dion, John Cronin, Mary Mitchell

A Twist of Sand

GB 1968   91m   De Luxe
UA / Christina (Fred Engel)

An ill-matched set of criminals seek hidden diamonds on Africa's skeleton coast.
Pattern melodrama of thieves falling out, quite nicely put together but with performances too high pitched.

m Marvin H. Albert, *novel* Geoffrey Jenkins *d* Don Chaffey *ph* John Wilcox *m* Tristam Cary

Richard Johnson, Honor Blackman, Roy Dotrice, Peter Vaughan, Jeremy Kemp

Twisted Nerve

GB 1968   118m   Eastmancolor
British Lion / Charter (John Boulting)

A rich, disturbed young man disguises himself as a retarded teenager in order to kill his hated stepfather.
Absurd, unpleasant, longwinded and naïvely scripted shocker, rightly attacked because it asserted that brothers of mongoloids are apt to become murderers. A long way behind the worst Hitchcock.

w Leo Marks, Roy Boulting *d* Roy Boulting *ph* Harry Waxman *m* Bernard Herrmann

Hayley Mills, Hywel Bennett, Phyllis Calvert, Billie Whitelaw, Frank Finlay, *Barry Foster*, Salmaan Peer

'Curious and in some respects disagreeable . . . never thrilling enough to reach the Hitchcock level and without sufficient medical credibility to be taken seriously as a case history.'—*Michael Billington, Illustrated London News*

Two a Penny

GB 1967   98m   Eastmancolor
World Wide (Frank R. Jacobson)

An idle art student becomes involved in the drug racket but finally sees the light.
Naïve religious propaganda sponsored by the Billy Graham movement and featuring the evangelist in a cameo. A curiosity.

w Stella Linden *d* James F. Collier *ph* Michael Reed *m* Mike Leander

Cliff Richard, Dora Bryan, Ann Holloway, Avril Angers, Geoffrey Bayldon, Peter Barkworth

Two against the World

US 1936   64m   bw
Warner (Bryan Foy)
GB title: *The Case of Mrs Pembroke*

A gutter newspaper unnecessarily digs up a sordid murder case and causes the suicide of two people involved.
Remake of *Five Star Final* with the interest boringly shifted to the do-gooders who *don't* want to publish the story.

w Michel Jacoby, *play* Louis Weitzenkorn *d* William McGann *ph* Sid Hickox *m* Heinz Roemheld

Humphrey Bogart, Beverly Roberts, Helen MacKellar, Henry O'Neill, Linda Perry, Virginia Brissac

Two and Two Make Six

GB 1961   89m   bw
Bryanston / Prometheus (Monja Danischewsky)

Two motor cycling couples almost accidentally swap partners.
Reasonably fresh little romantic comedy.

w Monja Danischewsky *d* Freddie Francis *ph* Desmond Dickinson, Ronnie Taylor *m* Norrie Paramor

George Chakiris, Janette Scott, Alfred Lynch, Jackie Lynch, Malcolm Keen, Ambrosine Philpotts, Bernard Braden

The Two Faces of Dr Jekyll
GB 1960 88m Technicolor Megascope
Hammer (Anthony Nelson-Keys)
US title: *House of Fright*

A variation on the much-filmed story: the
schizo's evil half is the more handsome.
Surprisingly flat and tedious remake.

w Wolf Mankowitz, *novel* Robert Louis
Stevenson d Terence Fisher ph Jack Asher
m David Heneker, Monty Norman

Paul Massie, Dawn Addams, Christopher Lee,
David Kossoff, Francis de Wolff

Two-Faced Woman*
US 1941 90m bw
MGM (Gottfried Reinhardt)

A ski instructress who fears she may be losing
her publisher husband to another woman
poses as her own more vivacious twin sister.
The failure of this scatterbrained comedy is
alleged to be the reason for Garbo's
premature retirement. Looked at half a
century later, it is no great shakes but
harmless and eager to please; what sabotages
it is a shoddy production and flagging pace.

w S. N. Behrman, Salka Viertel, George
Oppenheimer, *play* Ludwig Fulda d George
Cukor ph Joseph Ruttenberg m Bronislau
Kaper

Greta Garbo, Melvyn Douglas, *Constance
Bennett*, Roland Young, Robert Sterling, Ruth
Gordon, George Cleveland
  'It is almost as shocking as seeing your
mother drunk.'—*Time*

Two Flags West*
US 1950 92m bw
TCF (Casey Robinson)

Sixty Confederate prisoners of war are granted
an amnesty and go west to fight the Indians.
Laboured but good-looking Civil War western.

w Casey Robinson d Robert Wise ph Leon
Shamroy m Hugo Friedhofer

Joseph Cotten, Jeff Chandler, Linda Darnell,
Cornel Wilde, Dale Robertson, Jay C.
Flippen, Noah Beery Jnr, Harry Von Zell
  'Its period reconstruction is remarkable.'—
Gavin Lambert

Two for the Road*
GB 1966 113m De Luxe Panavision
TCF / Stanley Donen

An architect and his wife motoring through
France recall the first twelve years of their
relationship.
Fractured, fashionable light romantic comedy
dressed up to seem of more significance than

the gossamer thing it really is; and some of the
gossamer has a Woolworth look.

w Frederic Raphael d Stanley Donen
ph Christopher Challis m Henry Mancini

Albert Finney, Audrey Hepburn, Eleanor
Bron, William Daniels, Claude Dauphin

AAN: Frederic Raphael

Two for the Seesaw
US 1962 120m bw Panavision
UA / Seesaw / Mirisch / Argyle / Talbot
  (Robert Wise)

A New York dance instructress has a
tempestuous affair with an Omaha attorney on
the verge of divorce.
Serious comedy or light drama, meticulously
detailed but immensely long for its content
and too revealing of its stage origins.

w Isabel Lennart, *play* William Gibson
d Robert Wise ph Ted McCord m André
Previn ad Boris Leven

Robert Mitchum, Shirley Maclaine

AAN: Ted McCord; song 'Second Chance'
(*m* André Previn, *ly* Dory Langdon)

Two Girls and a Sailor**
US 1944 124m bw
MGM (Joe Pasternak)

The title says it all.
Loosely-linked wartime musical jamboree with
first-class talent; a lively entertainment of its
type.

w Richard Connell, Gladys Lehman
d Richard Thorpe ph Robert Surtees
m George Stoll *songs* various

June Allyson, Gloria de Haven, Van Johnson,
Xavier Cugat and his Orchestra, *Jimmy
Durante*, Tom Drake, Lena Horne, Carlos
Ramirez, Harry James and his Orchestra, Jose
Iturbi, *Gracie Allen*, Virginia O'Brien, Albert
Coates

AAN: script

Two Girls on Broadway
US 1940 73m bw

A song and dance man breaks up a sister act.
Acceptable lower-case vaudeville musical
which rewrites the already wispy plot of
Broadway Melody. George Murphy, Joan
Blondell, Lana Turner, Kent Taylor, Wallace
Ford, Lloyd Corrigan. Written by Joseph
Fields and Jerome Chodorov; directed by S.
Sylvan Simon; for MGM. (GB title: *Choose
Your Partner*.)

Two Guys from Milwaukee
US 1946 90m bw

A young Balkan prince goes incognito in Brooklyn and befriends a cab driver.
Rumbustious comedy with an amiable cast and gag guest appearances. Dennis Morgan, Jack Carson, Joan Leslie, Janis Paige, S. Z. Sakall, Franklin Pangborn. Written by I. A. L. Diamond and Charles Hoffman; directed by David Butler; for Warner. (GB title: *Royal Flush*.)

Two Guys from Texas
US 1948   86m   Technicolor

Two vaudevillians find themselves on the run from crooks. Little more than a peg on which to hang some clowning and a few musical numbers. Dennis Morgan, Jack Carson, Dorothy Malone, Penny Edwards, Fred Clark, Gerald Mohr, Forrest Tucker. Written by I. A. L. Diamond and Allen Boretz; directed by David Butler; for Warner. (GB title: *Two Texas Knights*.)

The Two-Headed Spy*
GB 1958   93m   bw
Columbia (Hal E. Chester)

A bogus Nazi worms his way into the Gestapo hierarchy.
Adequate, not too exciting biopic of Colonel Alex Schottland; standard production values.

w James O'Donnell d André de Toth ph Ted Scaife m Bernard Schurmann

Jack Hawkins, Gia Scala, Alexander Knox, Erik Schumann, Felix Aylmer, Laurence Naismith, Donald Pleasence, Kenneth Griffith

Two Lane Blacktop
US 1971   103m   Technicolor   scope
Universal / Michael S. Laughlin

In the American southwest, the aimless owners of two souped-up cars have an interminable race.
Occasionally arresting, generally boring eccentricity by a big studio looking for another *Easy Rider*.

w Rudolph Wurlitzer, Will Corry d Monte Hellman ph Jack Deerson m Billy James

James Taylor, Warren Oates, Laurie Bird, Dennis Wilson

Two Left Feet
GB 1963   93m   bw
British Lion / Roy Baker (Leslie Gilliat)

A callow 19-year-old has girl trouble.
Ponderous sex comedy with no apparent purpose but some well observed scenes.

w Roy Baker, John Hopkins, *novel* In My Solitude by David Stuart Leslie d Roy Baker ph Wilkie Cooper m Philip Green

Michael Crawford, Nyree Dawn Porter, Julia Foster, David Hemmings, Dilys Watling, David Lodge, Bernard Lee

Two Loves
US 1961   100m   Metrocolor
    Cinemascope
MGM / Julian Blaustein
GB title: *Spinster*

An American teacher in New Zealand teaches Maoris and whites and falls for two men.
Pretentious romantic drama with unspeakable dialogue and eccentric characters.

w Ben Maddow, *novel* Sylva Ashton Warner d Charles Walters ph Joseph Ruttenberg m Bronislau Kaper

Shirley Maclaine, Jack Hawkins, Laurence Harvey, Nobu McCarthy

Two Minute Warning
US 1976   115m   Technicolor
    Panavision
Universal / Filmways (Edward S. Feldman)

A sniper terrifies the crowd at a championship football game.
Smartly directed but weakly plotted and scripted disaster movie: the mystery gunman remains a mystery at the end.

w Edward Hume, *novel* George LaFountaine d Larry Peerce ph Gerald Hirschfeld m Charles Fox

Charlton Heston, John Cassavetes, Martin Balsam, Beau Bridges, David Janssen, Marilyn Hassett, Jack Klugman, Gena Rowlands, Walter Pidgeon, Brock Peters, Mitch Ryan

'Even by the standards of exploitation movies, this film is an unusually dehumanizing experience. Not only does it exist solely for its gore, but it reduces the victims to the dimensions of plastic ducks at a shooting gallery.'—*Frank Rich, New York Post*

The Two Mrs Carrolls
US 1945 (released 1947)   99m   bw
Warner (Mark Hellinger)

A psychopathic artist paints his wives as the Angel of Death, then murders them with poisoned milk.
Stilted film of an old warhorse of a play, unhappily cast but working up some last-minute tension.

w Thomas Job, *play* Martin Vale d Peter Godfrey ph Peverell Marley m Franz Waxman

Barbara Stanwyck, Humphrey Bogart, Alexis Smith, Nigel Bruce, Isobel Elsom, Pat O'Moore, Peter Godfrey

Two Mules for Sister Sara
US 1969   116m   Technicolor
Panavision
Universal / Malpaso (Martin Rackin)

A wandering cowboy kills three men trying to rape a nun, but she is not what she seems.
Vaguely unsatisfactory western with patches of nasty brutality leading to an action-packed climax.

w Albert Maltz, Budd Boetticher d Don Siegel ph Gabriel Figueroa, Gabriel Torres m Ennio Morricone

Clint Eastwood, Shirley Maclaine, Manolo Fabregas, Alberto Morin

Two of a Kind
US 1951   75m   bw
Columbia (William Dozier)

A man is picked up by a glamorous girl who involves him in an elaborate scheme to defraud an elderly couple.
Modest suspenser.

w Lawrence Kimble, James Grunn d Henry Levin ph Burnett Guffey m George Duning

Edmond O'Brien, Lizabeth Scott, Terry Moore, Alexander Knox, Griff Barnett, Virginia Brissac

Two on a Guillotine*
US 1965   107m   bw   Panavision
Warner (William Conrad)

An illusionist arranges to be chained into his coffin at his funeral but promises to return from the dead.
Longwinded and unconvincing shocker with some effectively scary sequences.

w Henry Slesar, John Kneubuhl d William Conrad ph Sam Leavitt m Max Steiner

Connie Stevens, Dean Jones, Cesar Romero, Parley Baer, Virginia Gregg, Connie Gilchrist, John Hoyt

Two People
US 1973   100m   Technicolor
Universal (Robert Wise)

An army deserter returns home and falls for a fashion photographer.
Solemn, inconsequential topical drama which made no impact whatever.

w Richard de Roy d Robert Wise ph Gerald Hirschfeld m David Shire

Peter Fonda, Lindsay Wagner, Estelle Parsons, Alan Fudge
    'Sluggish pacing, lifeless looping and terminally ludicrous dialogue eventually turn the film into a travesty of its own form.'— *Variety*

Two Rode Together
US 1961   109m   Technicolor
Columbia / John Ford / Shpetner

An army commander and a tough marshal negotiate with Comanches for the return of prisoners.
Substandard Ford, moderately good-looking but uninteresting of plot and dreary of development.

w Frank Nugent, *novel* Will Cook d John Ford ph Charles Lawton Jnr m George Duning

James Stewart, Richard Widmark, Shirley Jones, Linda Cristal, Andy Devine, John McIntire

Two Seconds*
US 1932   68m   bw
Warner

In the last two seconds of his life a criminal reviews the events leading up to his execution.
Competent, pacy crime melodrama.

w Harvey Thew, *play* Elliott Lester d Mervyn Le Roy ph Sol Polito

Edward G. Robinson, Preston Foster, Vivienne Osborne, J. Carrol Naish, Guy Kibbee, Adrienne Dare
    'A film that compels attention.'—*Mordaunt Hall, New York Times*

Two Sisters from Boston*
US 1946   112m   bw
MGM (Joe Pasternak)

Two girls visiting New York find work in a Bowery saloon.
Nicely-detailed turn-of-the-century musical with pleasant talent.

w Myles Connolly d Henry Koster ph Robert Surtees md Charles Previn songs Sammy Fain, Ralph Freed

June Allyson, Kathryn Grayson, Lauritz Melchior, Jimmy Durante, Peter Lawford, Ben Blue

Two Smart People
US 1946   93m   bw
MGM (Ralph Wheelright)

A con man on parole in New Orleans is chased by a lady crook in search of his hidden loot.
Dog-eared comedy drama.

w Ethel Hill, Leslie Charteris d Jules Dassin ph Karl Freund m George Bassman

Lucille Ball, John Hodiak, Lloyd Nolan, Hugo Haas, Lenore Ulric, Elisha Cook Jnr, Lloyd Corrigan, Vladimir Sokoloff

Two Tars****
US 1928 20m bw silent

Two sailors in an old banger cause a traffic jam and a consequent escalation of violence.

Marvellous elaboration of a tit-for-tat situation, with the stars already at their technical best. Laurel and Hardy, Edgar Kennedy, Charley Rogers. Written by Leo McCarey and H. M. Walker; directed by James Parrott; for Hal Roach.

2001: A Space Odyssey***
GB 1968 141m Metrocolor Panavision
MGM / Stanley Kubrick (Victor Lyndon)

From ape to modern space scientist, mankind has striven to reach the unattainable.

A lengthy montage of brilliant model work and obscure symbolism, this curiosity slowly gathered commercial momentum and came to be cherished by longhairs who used it as a trip without LSD.

w Stanley Kubrick, Arthur C. Clarke, *story* The Sentinel by Arthur C. Clarke d Stanley Kubrick ph Geoffrey Unsworth, John Alcott m various classics pd Tony Masters, Harry Lange, Ernie Archer ad John Hoesli

Gary Lockwood, Keir Dullea, William Sylvester, Leonard Rossiter, Robert Beaty, Daniel Richter

'Somewhere between hypnotic and immensely boring.'—*Renata Adler*

'Morally pretentious, intellectually obscure and inordinately long . . . intensely exciting visually, with that peculiar artistic power which comes from obsession . . . a film out of control, an infuriating combination of exactitude on small points and incoherence on large ones.'—*Arthur Schlesinger Jnr*

'The satire throughout is tepid and half-hearted, and tends to look like unintended stupidity.'—*John Simon*

AAN: script; Stanley Kubrick

Two Thousand Women
GB 1944 97m bw
GFD / Gainsborough (Edward Black)

Two pilots try to rescue British women from a French concentration camp.

Routine mix of laughter and tears; hardly an outstanding film of its time, but mildly entertaining.

wd Frank Launder ph Jack Cox md Louis Levy

Phyllis Calvert, Flora Robson, Patricia Roc, Renée Houston, Anne Crawford, Jean Kent, James McKechnie, Reginald Purdell, Robert Arden, Thora Hird, Dulcie Gray, Carl Jaffe, Muriel Aked

Two Tickets to Broadway
US 1951 106m Technicolor
RKO (Jerry Wald)

Small-town college girl finds romance and success in the big city.

Very mild musical with TV studio backdrop.

w Sid Silvers, Hal Kanter d James V. Kern ph Edward Cronjager, Harry J. Wild m Walter Scharf

Janet Leigh, Eddie Bracken, Gloria de Haven, Tony Martin, Barbara Lawrence, *Joe Smith and Charlie Dale*

Two Tickets to London
US 1943 78m bw

A sailor accused of aiding an enemy submarine escapes and finds the true villain.

Routine wartime thick-ear. Alan Curtis, Michele Morgan, C. Aubrey Smith, Barry Fitzgerald, Dooley Wilson, Mary Gordon. Written by Tom Reed; directed by Edwin L. Marin; for Universal.

Two Way Stretch**
GB 1960 87m bw
British Lion / Shepperton (M. Smedley Aston)

Three convicts break jail to rob a maharajah.

Amusing comedy with good performances and situations, unofficially borrowed in part from *Convict 99*.

w John Warren, Len Heath d Robert Day ph Geoffrey Faithfull m Ken Jones

Peter Sellers, *Lionel Jeffries*, Wilfrid Hyde White, Bernard Cribbins, David Lodge, Maurice Denham, Beryl Reid, Liz Fraser, Irene Handl, George Woodbridge

Two Weeks in Another Town*
US 1962 107m Metrocolor
 Cinemascope
MGM (John Houseman)

An ex-alcoholic film director gets his comeback chance in Rome but is plagued by old memories.

Self-indulgent melodrama with entertaining patches for *cinéastes*, especially those who saw *The Bad and the Beautiful*.

w Charles Schnee, *novel* Irwin Shaw d Vincente Minnelli ph Milton Krasner m David Raksin

Kirk Douglas, Edward G. Robinson, Cyd Charisse, Daliah Lavi, George Hamilton, Claire Trevor, Rosanna Schiaffino, James Gregory, George Macready

Two Weeks with Love*
US 1950   92m   Technicolor
MGM (Jack Cummings)

Adventures on a family summer holiday at the turn of the century.
Pleasant family musical.

w John Larkin, Dorothy Kingsley d Roy Rowland ph Al Gilks m Georgie Stoll

Jane Powell, Ricardo Montalban, Louis Calhern, Ann Harding, Phyllis Kirk, Debbie Reynolds, Carleton Carpenter, Clinton Sundberg

Two Women*
Italy / France 1960   110m   bw
Champion / Marceau / Cocinor / SGC (Carlo Ponti)
original title: *La Ciociara*

During the Allied bombing of Rome a woman and her daughter travel arduously south and have a hard time at the hands of invading soldiers.
Rather hysterical character drama allowing for a splendid top-note performance from its star.

w Cesare Zavattini, Vittorio de Sica, *novel* Alberto Moravia d Vittorio de Sica ph Gabor Pogany m Armando Trovaioli

Sophia Loren, Eleonora Brown, Jean-Paul Belmondo, Raf Vallone

AA: Sophia Loren

Two Years before the Mast*
US 1946   98m   bw
Paramount

In the mid-19th century, a writer becomes a sailor to expose bad conditions.
Well-made but unconvincing-looking picturization of a famous book.

w Seton I. Miller, George Bruce, *book* Richard Henry Dana d John Farrow ph Ernest Laszlo m Victor Young

Alan Ladd, Brian Donlevy, William Bendix, Barry Fitzgerald, Howard da Silva, Albert Dekker, Luis Van Rooten, Darryl Hickman

Two's Company
GB 1936   74m   bw

An earl's son loves the daughter of an American millionaire. Not particularly successful hands-across-the-sea comedy.
Gordon Harker, Ned Sparks, Mary Brian, Patric Knowles, Robb Wilton, Morton Selten. Written by Tom Geraghty. Roland Pertwee, J. B. Morton, John Paddy Carstairs and Tim Whelan, from the novel *Romeo and Julia* by Sidney Horler; directed by Tim Whelan; for Paul Soskin / B and D.

Tycoon
US 1947   129m   Technicolor
RKO

An engineer is hired to drive a tunnel through the Andes, and starts a feud with his boss when he falls in love with his daughter.
Boring, studio-set action saga with too many stops for romance.

w Borden Chase, John Twist d Richard Wallace ph Harry J. Wild m Leigh Harline

John Wayne, Cedric Hardwicke, Laraine Day, James Gleason, Judith Anderson, Anthony Quinn, Grant Withers

Typhoon
US 1940   70m   Technicolor
Paramount (Anthony Veiller)

On a Dutch Guianan island, two sailors find a girl who has been a castaway since childhood. One of Lamour's several sarongers, quite entertaining in its way and commendably brisk.

w Allen Rivkin d Louis King ph William Mellor m Frederick Hollander

Dorothy Lamour, Robert Preston, Lynne Overman, J. Carrol Naish, Frank Reicher
   'One of the most emphatically silly pictures I ever saw in my life.'—*Richard Mallet, Punch*
   'The gem of pure, pellucid silliness.'—*James Agate*

U

Ugetsu Monogatari*
Japan 1953 94m bw
Daiei (Masaichi Nagata)

During a 16th century civil war two potters
find a way of profiteering, but their ambitions
bring disaster on their families.

Unique mixture of action, comedy and the
supernatural, with strong, believable
characters participating and a delightfully
delicate touch in script and direction. On its
first release it began to figure in many best ten
lists, but quickly seemed to fade from public
approbation.

w Matsutaro Kawaguchi, from 17th-century
collection by Akinara Ueda, Tales of a Pale
and Mysterious Moon after the Rain d Kenji
Mizoguchi ph Kazuo Miyagawa m Fumio
Hayasaka

Masayuki Mori, Machiko Kyo, Sakae Ozawa,
Mitsuko Mito

The Ugly American
US 1962 120m Eastmancolor
U-I / George Englund

A publisher is made ambassador to a south-
east Asian state.

Self-dating anti-communist drama which was
muddled and boring when new.

w Stewart Stern, novel William J. Lederer,
Eugene Burdick d George Englund
ph Clifford Stine m Frank Skinner

Marlon Brando, Eiji Okada, Sandra Church,
Pat Hingle, Arthur Hill, Jocelyn Brando,
Kukrit Pramoj

The Ugly Dachshund*
US 1965 93m Technicolor
Walt Disney (Winston Hibler)

A dachshund bitch fosters among its puppies
an orphan Great Dane.

Cheerful, fast-moving animal farce.

w Albert Aley, novel G. B. Stern d Norman
Tokar ph Edward Colman m George Bruns

Dean Jones, Suzanne Pleshette, Charles
Ruggles, Kelly Thordsen, Parley Baer, Mako,
Charles Lane

The Ultimate Warrior
US 1975 94m Technicolor
Warner (Fred Weintraub, Paul Heller)

In AD 2012 New York is ruled by a gangster,
the atmosphere is poisoned, and the only hope
is a new community on an island off North
Carolina.

Curious pretentious fantasy without the
courage of its convictions or much
entertainment value.

wd Robert Clouse ph Gerald Hirschfeld
m Gil Melle

Yul Brynner, Max Von Sydow, Joanna Miles,
William Smith, Richard Kelton, Stephen
McHattie

'Less a prophetic vision than a kind of
thick-ear West Side Story.'—Richard Combs

Ulysses*
Italy 1954 103m Technicolor
Lux Film / Ponti–de Laurentiis (Fernando
Cinquini)

Ulysses and his crew sail under the curse of
Cassandra, and encounter Circe, the sirens
and the cyclops.

Peripatetic adventure yarn not too far after
Homer; narrative style uncertain but highlights
good.

w Franco Brusati, Mario Camerini, Ennio de
Concini, Hugh Gray, Ben Hecht, Ivo Perelli,
Irwin Shaw, poem The Odyssey by Homer
d Mario Camerini ph Harold Rosson
m Alessandro Cicognini

Kirk Douglas, Silvana Mangano, Anthony
Quinn, Rosanna Podesta

Ulysses*
GB 1967 132m bw Panavision
Walter Reade (Joseph Strick)

Twenty-four hours in Dublin with a young
poet and a Jewish newspaper man.

A pleasant enough literary exercise, a decent
précis of an unmanageably prolix classic novel,
this specialized offering would have passed
unnoticed were it not for its language, which
got it banned in many places but now seems
mild indeed.

w Joseph Strick, Fred Haines, *novel* James Joyce *d Joseph Strick ph Wolfgang Suschitsky m* Stanley Myers

Maurice Roeves, Milo O'Shea, Barbara Jefford, T. P. McKenna, Anna Manahan, Maureen Potter

'No amount of pious invoking of Joyce's name can disguise the fact that a cheaply produced film is being sold at exorbitant prices so that someone can make his boodle off "culture".'—*John Simon*

'An act of homage in the form of readings from the book plus illustrated slides.'—*Pauline Kael*

'A facile and ludicrous reduction.'—*Stanley Kauffmann*

AAN: script

Ulzana's Raid
US 1972 103m Technicolor
Universal / Carter de Haven / Robert Aldrich

An ageing Indian fighter and a tenderfoot officer lead a platoon sent out to counter a murderous Apache attack.
Bloodthirsty, reactionary western with unpleasant shock moments.

w Alan Sharp *d* Robert Aldrich *ph* Joseph Biroc *m* Frank de Vol

Burt Lancaster, Bruce Davison, Jorge Luke, Richard Jaeckel, Lloyd Bochner

Umberto D**
Italy 1952 89m bw
Dear Films

A retired civil servant can barely afford his rent but won't part with his dog.
Downbeat, immensely moving study of old age in a society which fails to provide for it.

w Cesare Zavattini, Vittorio de Sica
d Vittorio de Sica ph G. R. Aldo
m Alessandro Cicognini

Carlo Battista

AAN: Cesare Zavattini (original story)

Unaccustomed As We Are
US 1929 20m bw silent

Ollie takes a friend home to dinner, but his wife walks out, leaving him to get into all kinds of trouble. The team's first sound comedy, rather hesitant in its use of the new medium. The story was later reworked as the last half hour of *Blockheads*. Laurel and Hardy, Edgar Kennedy, Mae Busch, Thelma Todd. Written by Leo McCarey and H. M. Walker; directed by Lewis R. Foster; for Hal Roach.

Uncensored
GB 1942 108m bw
GFD / Gainsborough (Edward Black)

In Brussels during the Nazi occupation, the leader of a toe-the-line paper secretly leads the patriots.
Unconvincing underground melodrama with stilted presentation and performances.

w Wolfgang Wilhelm, Terence Rattigan, Rodney Ackland, *novel* Oscar Millard
d Anthony Asquith *ph* Arthur Crabtree
m Hans May

Eric Portman, Phyllis Calvert, Griffith Jones, Raymond Lovell, Peter Glenville, Irene Handl, Carl Jaffe, Felix Aylmer

Uncertain Glory
US 1944 102m bw
Warner (Robert Buckner)

During World War II, a French playboy sacrifices himself for his country.
Tame star vehicle needing more action and less philosophy.

w Laszlo Vadnay, Max Brand *d* Raoul Walsh *ph* Sid Hickox *m* Adolph Deutsch

Errol Flynn, Paul Lukas, Jean Sullivan, Lucile Watson, Faye Emerson, James Flavin, Douglass Dumbrille, Dennis Hoey

Unchained
US 1955 75m bw
Warner / Hall Bartlett

A new governor experiments with a prison without bars.
Decent documentary drama which reaches no great heights.

wd Hall Bartlett, *book* Prisoners Are People by Kenyon J. Scudder *ph* Virgil Miller *m* Alex North

Chester Morris, Elroy Hirsch, Barbara Hale, Todd Duncan, Johnny Johnston, Peggy Knudsen, Jerry Paris, John Qualen

AAN: title song (*m* Alex North, *ly* Hy Zarek)

Uncle Silas*
GB 1947 103m bw
GFD / Two Cities (Josef Somlo, Laurence Irving)
US title: *The Inheritance*

A young Victorian heiress finds herself menaced by her uncle and his housekeeper.
Slow-starting but superbly made period suspenser; unfortunately the characters are all sticks.

w Ben Travers, *novel* Sheridan Le Fanu
d Charles Frank

Jean Simmons, Derrick de Marney, Katina
Paxinou, Derek Bond, Esmond Knight,
Sophie Stewart, Manning Whiley, Reginald
Tate, Marjorie Rhodes

Unconquered
US 1947   146m   Technicolor
Paramount / Cecil B. de Mille

An 18th-century English convict girl is
deported to the American colonies and suffers
various adventures before marrying a Virginia
militiaman.
Cardboard epic, expensive and noisy but
totally unpersuasive despite cannon, arrows,
fire and dynamite.

w Charles Bennett, Frederic M. Frank, Jesse
Lasky Jnr, *novel* Neil H. Swanson d Cecil B.
de Mille ph Ray Rennahan m Victor Young

Paulette Goddard, Gary Cooper, Boris
Karloff, Howard da Silva, Cecil Kellaway,
Ward Bond, Katherine de Mille, Henry
Wilcoxon, C. Aubrey Smith, Victor Varconi,
Virginia Grey, Porter Hall, Mike Mazurki
'De Mille bangs the drum as loudly as ever
but his sideshow has gone cold on us.'—
Richard Winnington
'A five-million dollar celebration of Gary
Cooper's virility, Paulette Goddard's
femininity, and the American frontier
spirit.'—*Time*
'I bought this woman for my own . . . and
I'll kill the man who touches her!'—*publicity*

The Undefeated
US 1969   119m   De Luxe   Panavision
TCF (Robert L. Jacks)

After the Civil War, two colonels from
opposite sides meet on the Rio Grande.
Sprawling, lethargic star western with
moments of glory.

w James Lee Barrett d Andrew V. McLaglen
ph William H. Clothier m Hugo Montenegro

John Wayne, Rock Hudson, Lee Meriwether,
Tony Aguilar, Roman Gabriel

Under Capricorn
GB 1949   117m   Technicolor
Transatlantic (Sidney Bernstein, Alfred
 Hitchcock)

In Australia in 1830 an English immigrant
stays with his cousin Henrietta, who has
become a dipsomaniac because of her
husband's cruelty.
Cardboard 'woman's picture' with elements of
Rebecca, shot with vestiges of Hitch's ten-
minute take. A pretty fair disaster.

w James Bridie, *novel* Helen Simpson
d Alfred Hitchcock ph Jack Cardiff, Paul
Beeson, Ian Craig m Richard Addinsell

Ingrid Bergman, Joseph Cotten, Michael
Wilding, Margaret Leighton, Jack Watling,
Cecil Parker, Denis O'Dea

Under Milk Wood*
GB 1971   88m   Technicolor
Timon (Hugo French, Jules Buck)

Life in the Welsh village of Llareggub, as seen
by the poet's eye.
Attractive but vaguely unsatisfactory screen
rendering of an essentially theatrical event
(originally a radio play); everything is much
too literal, a real place instead of a fantasy.

wd Andrew Sinclair, *play Dylan Thomas*
ph Bob Huke m Brian Gascoigne

Richard Burton, Elizabeth Taylor, Peter
O'Toole, Glynis Johns, Vivien Merchant, Sian
Phillips, Victor Spinetti, Rachel Thomas,
Angharad Rees, Ann Beach

Under My Skin
US 1949   86m   bw
TCF (Casey Robinson)

A crooked jockey is idolized by his son and
finally reforms rather than disillusion the boy.
Hokey sentimental melodrama with racetrack
backgrounds.

w Casey Robinson, *short story* My Old Man
by Ernest Hemingway d Jean Negulesco
ph Joseph La Shelle m Daniele Amfitheatrof

John Garfield, Micheline Presle, Luther
Adler, Orley Lindgren, Ann Codee

Under Ten Flags
US 1960   92m   bw
Paramount / Dino de Laurentiis

In World War II, a German surface raider in
disguise menaces British shipping.
Muddled naval epic with too many allegiances.

w Vittorio Petrilli, Duilio Coletti, Ulrich
Mohr, William Douglas Home d Duilio
Coletti, Silvio Narizzano ph Aldo Tonti
m Nino Rota

Van Heflin, Charles Laughton, John Ericson,
Mylène Demongeot, Cecil Parker, Folco Lulli,
Alex Nicol, Liam Redmond

Under the Gun
US 1950   83m   bw

A racketeer is jailed and tries to escape.
Lower-case prison adventure without much
conviction. Richard Conte, Audrey Totter,

John McIntire, Sam Jaffe, Shepperd
Strudwick, Written by George Zuckerman;
directed by Ted Tatzlaff; for Universal-
International.

Under the Pampas Moon
US 1935   78m   bw

A gaucho leader recovers his stolen horse.

Amiable modern adventure set in Argentina.
Warner Baxter, Ketti Gallian, Rita Hayworth,
Jack La Rue, J. Carrol Naish. Written by
Ernest Pascal and Bradley King; directed by
James Tinling; for Fox.

Under the Red Robe*
GB 1937   82m   bw
(TCF) Robert T. Kane

A hell-raising nobleman is persuaded by
Cardinal Richelieu to unmask the ringleader
of an anti-monarchist conspiracy.
Smart, unusual swashbuckler on the lines of
The Prisoner of Zenda, modestly but quite
effectively made.

w Lajos Biro, Philip Lindsay, J. L. Hodson,
novel Stanley J. Weyman   *d* Victor Sjostrom
ph Georges Périnal

Conrad Veidt, Raymond Massey, Annabella,
Romney Brent, Sophie Stewart, Wyndham
Goldie, Lawrence Grant

Under the Yum Yum Tree
US 1963   110m   Eastmancolor
Columbia / Sonnis / Swift (Frederick
Brisson)

Two college students have a trial marriage in
an apartment block with a lecherous landlord.
Coy, non-erotic and extremely tedious comedy
which runs out of jokes after reel one.

w Lawrence Roman, David Swift   *d* David
Swift   *ph* Joseph Biroc   *m* Frank de Vol

Jack Lemmon, Carol Lynley, Dean Jones,
Imogene Coca, Edie Adams, Paul Lynde,
Robert Lansing

Under Two Flags*
US 1936   111m   bw
TCF (Raymond Griffith)

A dashing French Foreign Legionnaire is
helped by a café girl.
Despite a highly predictable plot (of *Destry
Rides Again*) this was a solidly-produced epic
with a nice deployment of star talent.

w W. P. Lipscomb, Walter Ferris, *novel*
'Ouida'   *d* Frank Lloyd   *ph* Ernest Palmer
m Louis Silvers

Ronald Colman, Claudette Colbert, Rosalind
Russell, Victor McLaglen, J. Edward
Bromberg, Nigel Bruce, Herbert Mundin,
Gregory Ratoff, C. Henry Gordon, John
Carradine, Onslow Stevens

'How Ouida would have loved the abandon
of this picture, the thirty-two thousand rounds
of ammunition shot off into the Arizona
desert, the cast of more than ten thousand, the
five thousand pounds which insured the stars
against camel bites . . . and, in the words of
the programme, a fort two hundred feet
square, an Arabian oasis with eight full-sized
buildings, a forest of transplanted date palms,
two Arabian cities, a horse market and a
smaller fort.'—*Graham Greene*

'Love as burning as Sahara's sands!'—
publicity

Under Your Hat*
GB 1940   79m   bw
Grand National (Jack Hulbert)

Film stars chase spies and recover a stolen
carburettor.
Light-hearted adaptation of a stage musical,
showing the stars in their best film form.

w Rodney Ackland, Anthony Kimmins,
play Jack Hulbert, Archie Menzies, Geoffrey
Kerr, Arthur Macrae   *d* Maurice Elvey

Jack Hulbert, Cicely Courtneidge, Austin
Trevor, Leonora Corbett, Cecil Parker, H. F.
Maltby, Glynis Johns, Charles Oliver

Undercover
GB 1943   80m   bw

Yugoslavian partisans fight the Nazis. A rather
obviously English cast doesn't help to make
this flagwaver convincing. Tom Walls, Michael
Wilding, Mary Morris, John Clements,
Godfrey Tearle, Robert Harris, Rachel
Thomas. Written by John Dighton, Monja
Danischewsky, Sergei Nolbandov and Sergei
Sokulich; directed by Sergei Nolbandov; for
Ealing.

Undercover Girl
US 1950   80m   bw

A New York policewoman goes undercover to
avenge her father's murder. Rather tedious
crime programmer. Alexis Smith, Scott Brady,
Richard Egan, Gladys George, Edmon Ryan,
Gerald Mohr. Written by Harry Essex;
directed by Joseph Pevney; for Universal-
International.

Undercover Man*
US 1949   89m   bw
Columbia (Robert Rossen)

US treasury agents indict a gang leader for tax evasion.

Good semi-documentary crime melodrama based on the Al Capone case.

w Sidney Boehm, Malvin Wald d Joseph H. Lewis ph Burnett Guffey m George Duning

Glenn Ford, Nina Foch, Barry Kelley, James Whitmore, David Wolf, Esther Minciotti

Undercurrent*
US 1946   116m   bw
MGM (Pandro S. Berman)

A professor's daughter marries an industrialist and is frightened and finally endangered by the mystery surrounding his brother.

Overlong suspenser with solid performances and production values; a variation on *Gaslight*.

w Edward Chodorov, *story* Thelma Strabel d Vincente Minnelli ph Karl Freund m Herbert Stothart

Katharine Hepburn, Robert Taylor, Robert Mitchum, Edmund Gwenn, Marjorie Main, Jayne Meadows, Clinton Sundberg, Dan Tobin

'The indigestible plot, full of false leads and unkept promises, is like a woman's magazine serial consumed at one gulp.'—*Time*

Underground
US 1941   95m   bw
Warner (William Jacobs)

Underground leaders in Germany during World War II send out radio messages under the noses of the Nazis.

Forgotten actioner, quite solidly made.

w Charles Grayson d Vincent Sherman ph Sid Hickox m Adolph Deutsch

Jeffrey Lynn, Philip Dorn, Karen Verne, Mona Maris, Frank Reicher, Martin Kosleck, Ilka Gruning

Underground
US 1970   100m   De Luxe
UA / Levy–Gardner–Laven

An American paratrooper joins a French resistance group to kidnap a Nazi general. Routine war actioner.

w Ron Bishop, Andy Lewis d Arthur H. Nader ph Ken Talbot m Stanley Myers

Robert Goulet, Danièle Gaubert, Laurence Dobkin, Carl Duering

The Underpup
US 1939   81m   bw

A slum girl wins a country holiday among rich folk who ignore her. Light comedy-drama with music which seemed about to launch a rival to Deanna Durbin. Gloria Jean, Robert Cummings, Nan Grey, C. Aubrey Smith, Beulah Bondi, Virginia Weidler, Raymond Walburn, Margaret Lindsay. Written by Grover Jones; directed by Richard Wallace; for Joe Pasternak / Universal.

Undertow
US 1949   70m   bw

An ex-racketeer proves his innocence when a big-time gambler is murdered. Stock suspense crime story, not at all memorable. Scott Brady, John Russell, Dorothy Hart, Peggy Dow, Bruce Bennett. Written by Arthur T. Horman and Lee Loeb; directed by William Castle; for Universal-International.

Underwater Warrior
US 1958   91m   bw   Cinemascope

A naval reserve commander trains frogmen. Dry semi-documentary drama, unlikely to win any recruits. Dan Dailey, Ross Martin, James Gregory, Claire Kelly. Written by Gene Levitt; directed by Andrew Marton; for Ivan Tors / MGM.

Underworld*
US 1927   82m (24 fps)   bw   silent
Paramount
GB title: *Paying the Penalty*

A gangster is rescued from prison by his moll and his lieutenant, and when he realizes they are in love he allows them to escape when the law closes in.

An innovative film in its time, this melodrama was the first to look at crime from the gangsters' point of view. Its main appeal now lies in its lush direction.

w Ben Hecht, Robert N. Lee, Josef Von Sternberg d Josef Von Sternberg ph Bert Glennon ad Hans Dreier

George Bancroft, Evelyn Brent, Clive Brook, Larry Semon

† The film was a great international success and had an influence on the pessimistic French school of the thirties.

AA: Ben Hecht

Underworld USA*
US 1960   99m   bw
Columbia / Globe (Samuel Fuller)

A young gangster takes elaborate revenge for the killing of his father.

Violent syndicate melodrama with a semi-documentary veneer and some brutal scenes. Well done but heavy going.

wd Samuel Fuller ph Hal Mohr m Harry
Sukman

Cliff Robertson, Beatrice Kay, Larry Gates,
Dolores Dorn, *Robert Emhardt*, Paul Dubov,
Richard Rust

The Undying Monster*
US 1943 63m bw
TCF
GB title: *The Hammond Mystery*

A curse hangs over the English ancestral home
of the Hammonds.
Silly but well-photographed and directed
minor horror on wolf man lines.

w Lillie Hayward, Michel Jacoby,
novel Jessie D. Kerruish *d John Brahm
ph Lucien Ballard m* Emil Newman, David
Raksin

James Ellison, John Howard, Heather Angel,
Bramwell Fletcher, Heather Thatcher, Eily
Malyon, Halliwell Hobbes, Aubrey Mather

Unearthly Stranger*
GB 1963 75m bw
Independent Artists (Julian Wintle, Leslie
Parkyn, Albert Fennell)

Scientists working on a time-space formula
find that the bride of one of them is an alien in
search of their secret.
Surprisingly effective minor science fiction, in
some ways all the better for its modest,
TV-style production values.

w Rex Carlton d John Krish ph Reg Wyer
m Edward Williams

John Neville, Gabriella Licudi, Philip Stone,
Jean Marsh, Patrick Newell, Warren Mitchell

Uneasy Terms
GB 1948 91m bw

Detective Slim Callaghan proves that a
blackmail victim is not a murderer. The film
which proved that the British simply can't
make crime movies on the American model.
Michael Rennie, Moira Lister, Faith Brook,
Joy Shelton, Nigel Patrick, Paul Carpenter,
Barry Jones. Written by Peter Cheyney, from
his novel; directed by Vernon Sewell; for
British National.

Unexpected Father
US 1939 78m bw

A dancer looks after his late partner's baby.
Genial comedy introducing a baby star who
was popular until she got out of diapers. Baby
Sandy, Mischa Auer, Dennis O'Keefe, Shirley
Ross, Mayo Methot. Written by Leonard
Spiegelgass and Charles Grayson; directed by

Charles Lamont; for Universal. (GB title:
Sandy Takes a Bow.)

Unexpected Uncle
US 1941 67m bw

An elderly steel tycoon gives everything up to
become a tramp and play Cupid. Money-is-
not-everything fable, entirely dependent on
amiable performances. Charles Coburn, Anne
Shirley, James Craig, Ernest Truex, Russell
Gleason, Jed Prouty. Written by Delmer
Daves and Noel Langley, from the novel by
Eric Hatch; directed by Peter Godfrey; for
RKO.

The Unfaithful*
US 1947 109m bw
Warner (Jerry Wald)

A wife gets involved in a murder while her
husband is out of town.
Glossy romantic melodrama, an unofficial
remake of *The Letter*.

w David Goodis, James Gunn *d* Vincent
Sherman *ph* Ernest Haller *m* Max Steiner

Ann Sheridan, Zachary Scott, Lew Ayres, Eve
Arden, Steve Geray, Jerome Cowan, John
Hoyt
  'If she were yours, would you forgive?'—
publicity

Unfaithfully Yours**
US 1948 105m bw
TCF (Preston Sturges)

An orchestral conductor believes his wife is
unfaithful, and while conducting a concert
thinks of three different ways of dealing with
the situation.
A not entirely happy mixture of romance,
farce, melodrama and wit, but in general a
pretty entertaining concoction and the last
major film of its talented writer-director.

wd Preston Sturges ph Victor Milner
m Alfred Newman

Rex Harrison, Linda Darnell, Barbara
Lawrence, Rudy Vallee, Kurt Kreuger, Lionel
Stander, *Edgar Kennedy, Al Bridge*, Julius
Tannen, Torben Meyer, Robert Greig
  'Harrison discovers more ways of tripping
over a telephone cable than one can count,
and his efforts to falsify evidence through a
recalcitrant tape recorder are as funny as
anything thought up by Clair in *A Nous La
Liberté* or by Chaplin in *Modern Times*.'—
Basil Wright, 1972

Unfinished Business
US 1941 95m bw
Universal (Gregory La Cava)

A wife has thoughts that she should have
married her husband's brother.
Smooth but disappointing romantic comedy;
the detail is good enough, but it sadly lacks
drive.

w Eugene Thackery d Gregory La Cava
ph Joseph Valentine m Franz Waxman

Irene Dunne, Robert Montgomery, Eugene
Pallette, Preston Foster, Walter Catlett, June
Clyde, Phyllis Barry, Esther Dale, Samuel S.
Hinds
  'Once sentiment gets the upper hand, reach
for the exit.'—*Otis Ferguson*

The Unfinished Dance
US 1947   101m   Technicolor
MGM (Joe Pasternak)

The young star of a ballet school becomes
jealous of a talented newcomer, and causes
her injury in an accident.
The delicacies of the French original, *La Mort
du Cygne*, give way to standard Hollywood
hokum and produce an accomplished but
totally uninteresting film.

w Myles Connolly, *story* Paul Morand
d Henry Koster ph Robert Surtees
md Herbert Stothart

Margaret O'Brien, Cyd Charisse, Karin
Booth, Danny Thomas, Esther Dale
  'The same old story, with pathos, humour
and ballet substituted for pathos, humour and
chorus girls.'—*MFB*

The Unforgiven*
US 1960   125m   Technicolor
Panavision
UA / James Productions / Hecht–Hill–
Lancaster (James Hill)

A rancher's daughter is suspected of being an
Indian orphan, and violence results.
Good-looking, expensive but muddled racist
western, hard to enjoy.

w Ben Maddow, *novel* Alan le May d John
Huston ph *Franz Planer* m Dmitri Tiomkin

Burt Lancaster, Audrey Hepburn, Audie
Murphy, Lillian Gish, Charles Bickford, Doug
McClure, John Saxon, Joseph Wiseman,
Albert Salmi
  'How much strain can a director's reputation
take? Of late, John Huston seems to have
been trying to find out. I think he has carried
the experiment too far with *The Unforgiven*
. . . a work of profound phoniness, part adult
western, part that *Oklahoma!* kind of folksy
Americana.'—*Dwight MacDonald*
  'Ludicrous . . . a hodgepodge of crudely
stitched sententiousness and lame story-
conference inspirations.'—*Stanley Kauffmann*

The Unguarded Hour*
US 1936   87m   bw

A blackmailed woman has evidence to free a
man accused of murder, but dare not reveal it.
Twisty suspense thriller with a rather splendid
cast. Franchot Tone, Loretta Young, Roland
Young, Henry Daniell, Jessie Ralph, Lewis
Stone, Dudley Digges, E. E. Clive, Robert
Greig, Aileen Pringle. Written by Howard
Emmett Rogers and Leon Gordon, from the
play by Ladislas Fodor / Bernard Merivale;
directed by Sam Wood; for MGM.

The Unguarded Moment
US 1956   85m   Technicolor
U-I (Gordon Kay)

A schoolmistress who receives anonymous
love notes from a psychotic pupil is discredited
by his even more unbalanced father.
Well-meaning but boring melodrama with the
star attractively out of her usual element.

w Herb Meadow, Larry Marcus, *story*
Rosalind Russell d Harry Keller ph William
Daniels m Herman Stein

Esther Williams, George Nader, John Saxon,
Edward Andrews, Jack Albertson

Unholy Partners*
US 1941   95m   bw
MGM (Samuel Marx)

The editor of a sensational newspaper has to
accept finance from a gangster, but friction
results when the newspaper exposes some of
the gangster's activities.
Agreeable twenties melodrama with two solid
stars battling it out.

w Earl Baldwin, Lesser Samuels, Bartlett
Cormack d Mervyn Le Roy ph George
Barnes m David Snell

Edward G. Robinson, Edward Arnold,
Laraine Day, Marsha Hunt, William T. Orr,
Don Beddoe, Charles Dingle, Walter
Kingsford, Marcel Dalio

The Unholy Three*
US 1925   76m approx (24 fps)   bw
silent
MGM

A ventriloquist, a dwarf and a strong man
carry out a series of crimes which end in
murder.
Curious melodrama which set its star and
director off on a series of seven more and even
weirder eccentricities.

w Waldemar Young, *story* Clarence Robbins
d Tod Browning ph David Kesson

Lon Chaney, Harry Earles, Victor McLaglen,
Mae Busch, Matt Moore
† A talkie remake (Chaney's last film)
appeared in 1930 (70m) with Earles, Lila Lee,
Elliott Nugent and John Miljan.

The Unholy Night
US 1929 94m bw

A strangler is caught in the London fog.
Clumsy and talkative early talkie, chiefly
interesting for its cast. Lionel Barrymore,
Roland Young, Boris Karloff, John Loder,
Natalie Moorhead, Ernest Torrence, Polly
Moran, John Miljan. Written by Ben Hecht;
directed by Lionel Barrymore; for MGM.

The Unholy Wife
US 1957 94m Technicolor RKOscope
RKO (John Farrow)

A bored wife shoots a friend in mistake for her
husband but is sentenced for the accidental
death of her mother-in-law.
Totally uninteresting melodrama in the
Double Indemnity style, professionally made
but turgid.

w Jonathan Latimer *d* John Farrow
ph Lucien Ballard *m* Daniele Amfitheatrof

Diana Dors, Rod Steiger, Tom Tully, Beulah
Bondi, Marie Windsor, Arthur Franz, Luis
Van Rooten

The Uninvited**
US 1944 98m bw
Paramount (Charles Brackett)

A girl returns to her family house and is
haunted by her mother's spirit, which seems to
be evil.
One of the cinema's few genuine ghost stories,
and a good one, though encased in a rather
stiff production; it works up to a fine pitch of
frenzy.

w Dodie Smith, *novel* Uneasy Freehold by
Dorothy Macardle *d* Lewis Allen *ph* Charles
Lang *m* Victor Young

Ray Milland, Ruth Hussey, *Gail Russell*,
Donald Crisp, Cornelia Otis Skinner, Dorothy
Stickney, Barbara Everest, Alan Napier
'Thirty-five first-class jolts, not to mention a
well-calculated texture of minor frissons.'—
James Agee
'Still manages to ice the blood with its
implied horrors . . . you can almost smell the
ghostly mimosa.'—*Peter John Dyer, 1966*
† British critics of the time congratulated the
director on not showing the ghosts: in fact the
visible manifestations had been cut by the
British censor.

AAN: Charles Lang

Union Depot
US 1932 68m bw

The fortunes of several people clash in a
railway station. Pale but moderately
interesting imitation of *Grand Hotel*. Douglas
Fairbanks Jnr, Joan Blondell, Alan Hale,
Frank McHugh, George Rosener, Guy
Kibbee, David Landau. Written by Kenyon
Nicholson and Walter De Leon, from the play
by Gene Fowler, Douglas Durkin and Joe
Laurie; directed by Alfred E. Green; for
Warner. (GB title: *Gentleman for a Day*.)

Union Pacific**
US 1939 133m bw
Paramount / Cecil B. de Mille

Indians and others cause problems for the
railroad builders.
Standard big-scale western climaxing in a
spectacular wreck; not exactly exciting, but
very watchable.

w Walter de Leon, C. Gardner Sullivan, Jesse
Lasky Jnr *d* Cecil B. de Mille *ph* Victor
Milner, Dewey Wrigley *m* John Leipold,
Sigmund Krumgold *ad* Hans Dreier, Roland
Anderson

Barbara Stanwyck, Joel McCrea, Akim
Tamiroff, Robert Preston, Lynne Overman,
Brian Donlevy, Robert Barrat, Anthony
Quinn, Stanley Ridges, Henry Kolker, Evelyn
Keyes, Regis Toomey
'This latest de Mille epic contains all the
excelsior qualities we expect of his work—that
sense of a Salvationist drum beating round the
next corner—but it is never as funny as *The
Crusades* and he has lost his touch with
crowds.'—*Graham Greene*
'Excitement is the dominant emotion, with
swift succession of contrasting materials and
episodes, grim and gay, often furious,
sometimes funny. The narrative and action
take hold at the start and never let go.'—
Motion Picture Herald

Union Station**
US 1950 80m bw
Paramount (Jules Schermer)

Kidnappers nominate a crowded railroad
station as their ransom collection point.
Compelling little thriller modelled after *Naked
City*, with real locations and plenty of
excitement.

w Sidney Boehm, *novel* Thomas Walsh
d Rudolph Maté *ph* Daniel L. Fapp *m* David
Buttolph, Heinz Roemheld *md* Irvin Talbot

William Holden, *Barry Fitzgerald*, Nancy
Olson, *Lyle Bettger*, Jan Sterling, Allene
Roberts

Universal Soldier
GB 1971 96m colour
Appaloosa / Ionian (Frank J. Schwarz,
    Donald L. Factor)

A mercenary returns to London but can't
escape his past.
Solemnly meaningful melodrama on a tight
budget.

wd Cy Endfield *ph* Tony Imi *m* Philip
Goodhand-Tait

George Lazenby, Edward Judd, Benito
Carruthers, Germaine Greer, Rudolph Walker

The Unknown
US 1927 65m bw silent

A fake armless wonder has his arms
amputated to please a girl who can't stand the
touch of a man's hand. (She then changes her
mind.) Weird melodrama which even this
contortionist star can't save. Lon Chaney,
Joan Crawford, Norman Kerry. Written by
Waldemar Young; directed by Tod Browning;
for MGM.

The Unknown
US 1946 70m bw

An amnesiac heiress returns to her family
mansion. Twisty creeper in the *I Love a
Mystery* series; not bad for a second feature.
Karen Morley, Jeff Donnell, Jim Bannon.
Written by Malcolm Stuart Boylan and Julian
Harmon; directed by Henry Levin; for
Columbia.

The Unknown Man
US 1951 86m bw
MGM (Robert Thomsen)

A civil court lawyer of high principles
successfully undertakes a criminal case, finds
his client was really guilty, and sets matters
straight.
Contrived but entertaining morality with
standard production and performances.

w Ronald Millar, George Froeschel
d Richard Thorpe *ph* William Mellor
m Conrad Salinger

Walter Pidgeon, Ann Harding, Lewis Stone,
Barry Sullivan, Keefe Brasselle, Eduard
Franz, Richard Anderson, Dawn Addams

Unman, Wittering and Zigo
GB 1971 102m colour
Paramount / Mediarts (Gareth Wigan)

A nervous schoolmaster discovers that his
predecessor was murdered by the boys.
Macabre school story which overreaches itself
and peters out.

w Simon Raven, *TV play* Giles Cooper
d John Mackenzie *ph* Geoffrey Unsworth
m Michael J. Lewis

David Hemmings, Douglas Wilmer, Hamilton
Dyce, Carolyn Seymour

Unmarried
US 1939 66m bw

An ex-boxer, shy of marriage, raises an
orphan boy. Modest domestic drama notable
as one of the rare non-western appearances of
its star. Buck Jones, Donald O'Connor, Helen
Twelvetrees. Written by Lillie Hayward, Brian
Marlow and Grover Jones; directed by Kurt
Nuemann; for Paramount. (GB title: *Night
Club Hostess*.)

An Unmarried Woman*
US 1977 124m Movielab
TCF (Paul Mazursky, Tony Ray)

A sophisticated New York woman is deserted
by her husband, fights with her daughter, and
takes up with two men.
Frank, well observed depiction of one woman
in New York's new society; as modern as all
get out but not very attractive.

wd Paul Mazursky ph Arthur J. Ornitz
m Bill Conti *ph* Pato Guzman

Jill Clayburgh, Alan Bates, Michael Murphy,
Cliff Gorman, Pat Quinn, Kelly Bishop

AAN: best picture; script; Jill Clayburgh

Unpublished Story
GB 1942 91m bw
Columbia / Two Cities (Anthony Havelock-
    Allan)

A reporter exposes the Nazis behind a pacifist
organization.
Ho-hum formula flagwaver with generally
stilted production.

w Anatole de Grunwald, Patrick Kirwan
d Harold French *ph* Bernard Knowles
m Nicholas Brodzky

Valerie Hobson, Richard Greene, Basil
Radford, Roland Culver, Brefni O'Rourke,
Miles Malleson, George Carney, André
Morell

The Unseen
US 1945 82m bw
Paramount

A London governess comes to suspect that
dark deeds have taken place in the empty
house next door.
Period suspenser with good atmosphere but an
insubstantial plot.

w Hagar Wilde, Raymond Chandler *d* Lewis Allen *ph* John Seitz *m* Ernst Toch

Joel McCrea, Gail Russell, Herbert Marshall, Richard Lyon, Nona Griffith

† The film seems to have been a hurried attempt to repeat and combine the previous year's success, *Gaslight* and *The Uninvited*.

The Unsinkable Molly Brown*
US 1964 128m Metrocolor Panavision
MGM / Marten (Lawrence Weingarten)

Western orphan Molly Brown grows up determined to become a member of Denver society.
Semi-western comedy-musical about a real lady who wound up surviving the *Titanic*.
Bouncy and likeable but not at all memorable.

w Helen Deutsch, *musical play* Richard Morris *d* Charles Walters *ph* Daniel L. Fapp *md* Robert Armbruster *ad* George W. Davis, Preston Ames

Debbie Reynolds, Harve Presnell, *Ed Begley*, Jack Krischen, Hermione Baddeley, Martita Hunt

AAN: Daniel L. Fapp; Robert Armbruster; Debbie Reynolds

The Unsuspected*
US 1947 103m bw
Warner (Charles Hoffman)

A writer-producer of radio crime shows commits a murder and is forced to follow the clues on air.
Sleek, new look mystery thriller with a disappointing plot which gives its interesting cast little to do, and allows itself to peter out in chases.

w Ranald MacDougall, *novel* Charlotte Armstrong *d* Michael Curtiz *ph* Woody Bredell *m* Franz Waxman *ad* Anton Grot

Claude Rains, Joan Caulfield, Audrey Totter, Constance Bennett, Michael North, Hurd Hatfield, Fred Clark

Untamed
US 1955 109m Technicolor
Cinemascope
TCF (Bert E. Friedlob, William A. Bacher)

A Dutchman and an Irish girl meet again on a Boer trek to South Africa, and survive Zulu attacks.
A long and involved epic-style plot provides standard excitements and predictable romantic complications.

w Talbot Jennings, Michael Blankfort, Frank Fenton, *novel* Helga Moray *d* Henry King *ph* Leo Tover *m* Franz Waxman

Tyrone Power, Susan Hayward, Richard Egan, John Justin, Agnes Moorehead, Rita Moreno, Hope Emerson, Brad Dexter, Henry O'Neill

'A not unenjoyable essay in hokum.'—*MFB*

Untamed Frontier
US 1952 78m Technicolor
U-I (Leonard Goldstein)

The son of an unpopular Texan landowner commits murder.
Stolid minor western.

w Gerald Drayson Adams, Gwen and John Bagni *d* Hugo Fregonese *ph* Charles P. Boyle *m* Hans Salter

Joseph Cotten, Shelley Winters, Scott Brady, Suzan Ball, Minor Watson

Until They Sail
US 1957 95m bw Cinemascope
MGM (Charles Schnee)

Four New Zealand sisters have wartime romances.
Solid 'woman's picture', well enough presented.

w Robert Anderson, *novel* James A. Michener *d* Robert Wise *ph* Joseph Ruttenberg *m* David Raksin

Jean Simmons, Joan Fontaine, Paul Newman, Piper Laurie, Charles Drake, Wally Cassell, Sandra Dee

Up for the Cup
GB 1931 76m bw

A Yorkshireman gets into trouble when he comes to London for the Cup Final. Slap-happy star farce which pleased the public.
Sydney Howard, Joan Wyndham, Stanley Kirk, Sam Livesey, Moore Marriott. Written by Con West, R. P. Weston and Bert Lee; directed by Jack Raymond; for Herbert Wilcox / B and D. (The same star appeared in *Up for the Derby* in the following year; and in 1950 the original, with much the same script, was refashioned for Albert Modley; it was also directed by Jack Raymond.)

Up from the Beach*
US 1965 98m bw Cinemascope
TCF / Panoramic (Christian Ferry)

Just after D-Day, GIs have trouble in a Normandy village.
A kind of subdued sequel to *The Longest Day*, well made for war action addicts, but barely memorable.

w Stanley Mann, Claude Brule, *novel* Epitaph for an Enemy by George Barr *d* Robert Parrish *ph* Walter Wottitz *m* Edgar Cosma

Cliff Robertson, Red Buttons, Françoise
Rosay, Marius Goring, Irina Demick,
Broderick Crawford, James Robertson Justice,
Slim Pickens

Up in Arms**
US 1944 106m Technicolor
Samuel Goldwyn

A hypochondriac joins the army.
Loose, generally pleasant introductory vehicle
for Danny Kaye.

w Don Hartman, Robert Pirosh, Allen
Boretz d Elliott Nugent ph Ray Rennahan
md Ray Heindorf, Louis Forbes

Danny Kaye, Dinah Shore, Constance
Dowling, Dana Andrews, Louis Calhern, Lyle
Talbot

AAN: song 'Now I Know' (*m* Harold Arlen,
ly Ted Koehler); Ray Heindorf, Louis Forbes

Up in Central Park
US 1948 88m bw
U-I

In turn-of-the-century New York, an Irish girl
becomes involved in a crooked political set up.
Stiff and unyielding star musical.

w Karl Tunberg d William A. Seiter
ph Milton Krasner *songs* Sigmund Romberg

Deanna Durbin, Vincent Price, Dick Haymes,
Albert Sharpe, Tom Powers

Up in Mabel's Room
US 1944 77m bw

A flustered professor has to retrieve
incriminating evidence from an old flame's
room. Antediluvian bedroom farce which
keeps several ardent innocents working
happily. Dennis O'Keefe, Mischa Auer,
Marjorie Reynolds, Gail Patrick. Written by
Tom Reed from the play by Wilson Collinson
and Otto Harbach; directed by Allan Dwan;
for Edward Small. 'As horrible, and
wonderful, as watching a Gopher Prairie
dramatic club play a mail order farce (6m,
6f).'—*James Agee.*

Up in the Cellar
US 1970 94m Movielab
AIP (William J. Immerman)

A dejected freshman tries various schemes to
revenge himself on the college president.
Youth satire aimed at a number of targets
which quickly became obsolete; mildly
interesting sociologically.

wd Theodore J. Flicker, *novel* The Late Boy
Wonder by Angus Hall *ph* Earl Roth *m* Don
Randi

Wes Stern, Joan Collins, Larry Hagman, Judy
Pace

Up in the World
GB 1956 91m bw
Rank (Hugh Stewart)

A window cleaner becomes friendly with a boy
millionaire.
Slow and unattractive comedy star vehicle.

w Jack Davies, Henry Blyth, Peter
Blackmore d John Paddy Carstairs ph Jack
Cox m Philip Green

Norman Wisdom, Martin Carida, Jerry
Desmonde, Maureen Swanson, Ambrosine
Philpotts, Colin Gordon

Up Periscope
US 1959 111m Technicolor
Warnerscope
Warner / Lakeside (Aubrey Schenck)

During World War II a submarine frogman is
landed on a Pacific island to steal a Japanese
code book.
Stock adventure story given stock
presentation.

w Richard Landau, *novel* Robb White
d Gordon Douglas ph Carl Guthrie m Ray
Heindorf

James Garner, Edmond O'Brien, Alan Hale
Jnr, Carleton Carpenter

Up Pompeii
GB 1971 90m Technicolor

A wily slave outwits Nero and escapes the
eruption of Vesuvius.
Yawnmaking spinoff of a lively TV comedy
series: the jokes just lie there, and die there.

w Sid Colin d Bob Kellett ph Ian Wilson
m Carl Davis

Frankie Howerd, Patrick Cargill, Michael
Hordern, Barbara Murray, Lance Percival,
Bill Fraser, Adrienne Posta
† Sequels: *Up the Front, Up the Chastity Belt*
(qv).

Up the Chastity Belt*
GB 1971 94m Technicolor
EMI / Associated London Films (Ned
Sherrin)

Medieval adventures of the serf Lurkalot and
his master Sir Coward de Custard.
Patchy pantomime which doesn't always have
the courage of its own slapdash vulgarity.

w Sid Colin, Ray Galton, Alan Simpson
d Bob Kellett ph Ian Wilson m Carl Davis

Frankie Howerd, Graham Crowden, Bill
Fraser, Roy Hudd, Hugh Paddick, Anna
Quayle, Eartha Kitt, Dave King, Fred Emney

Up the Creek*
GB 1958 83m bw Hammerscope
Byron (Henry Halsted)

A none-too-bright naval lieutenant is assigned
command of a broken-down shore
establishment.
Cheeky remake of *Oh Mr Porter*. Jokes fair,
atmosphere cheerful and easy-going.

wd Val Guest *ph* Arthur Grant

David Tomlinson, Peter Sellers, Wilfrid Hyde
White, Vera Day, Tom Gill, Michael
Goodliffe, Reginald Beckwith, Lionel Jeffries
† Sequel: *Further Up the Creek*.

Up the Down Staircase*
US 1967 124m Technicolor
Warner / Pakula–Mulligan

Problems of a schoolteacher in one of New
York's tough sections.
Earnest, well-acted, not very likeable
melodrama.

w Tad Mosel, *novel* Bel Kaufman *d* Robert
Mulligan *ph* Joseph Coffey *m* Fred Karlin

Sandy Dennis, Patrick Bedford, Eileen
Heckart, Ruth White, Jean Stapleton, Sorrel
Booke, Roy Poole

Up the Front
GB 1972 89m Technicolor
EMI / Associated London Films (Ned
Sherrin)

A footman is hypnotized into enlisting in
World War I and has an enemy 'plan' tattooed
on his buttocks.
Threadbare end-of-the-pier romp.

w Sid Colin, Eddie Braben *d* Bob Kellett
ph Tony Spratling *m* Patrick Greenwell
ad Seamus Flannery

Frankie Howerd, Bill Fraser, Zsa Zsa Gabor,
Stanley Holloway, Hermione Baddeley,
Robert Coote, Lance Percival, Dora Bryan

Up the Junction
GB 1967 119m Techniscope
Paramount / BHE (Anthony Havelock–Allan,
John Brabourne)

A well-off girl crosses London's river to live
among the workers of Clapham.
Socially obsolete sensationalism based on a
television semi-documentary. An irritating
heroine moves hygienically among
motorbikes.

w Roger Smith, *book* Nell Dunn *d* Peter
Collinson *ph* Arthur Lavis *m* Mike Hugg,
Manfred Mann

Suzy Kendall, Dennis Waterman, Adrienne
Posta, Maureen Lipman, Michael Gothard,
Liz Fraser, Hylda Baker, Alfie Bass

Up the River
US 1930 80m bw
Fox

An ex-convict is threatened with exposure, but
his two pals escape to help him.
Very minor comedy with interesting credits.

w Maurine Watkins *d* John Ford *ph* Joseph
August

Spencer Tracy, Warren Hymer, Claire Luce,
Humphrey Bogart, William Collier Snr

Up the Sandbox
US 1972 98m Technicolor
Barwood / First Artists (Robert Chartoff,
Irwin Winkler)

A professor's wife finds she is pregnant again
and fantasizes about her future life.
Muddled comedy-drama with little point and
less entertainment value.

w Paul Zindel, *novel* Anne Richardson
Roiphe *d* Irwin Kershner *ph* Gordon Willis,
Andy Marton *m* Billy Goldenberg *ad* Harry
Horner

Barbra Streisand, David Selby, Ariane Heller,
Jane Hoffman
'A magical mystery tour through the picture
book mind of one Manhattan housewife.'—
Richard Combs

Up Tight
US 1968 104m Technicolor
Paramount / Marlukin (Jules Dassin)

A black street cleaner betrays his criminal pals
for money and is hunted down by them.
Ponderous black remake of *The Informer*, too
schematic to make any dramatic or human
impression.

w Jules Dassin, Ruby Dee, Julian Mayfield
d Jules Dassin *ph* Boris Kaufman *m* Booker
T. Jones *pd* Alexander Trauner

Raymond St Jacques, Ruby Dee, Julian
Mayfield, Frank Silvera, Roscoe Lee Browne,
Juanita Moore

Upperworld
US 1934 75m bw

A society-conscious wife drives her husband
into the arms of a girl from the Bronx. Smooth
romantic melodrama with a murder angle;
dated but enjoyable. Warren William, Mary
Astor, Ginger Rogers, Andy Devine, J. Carrol
Naish, Henry O'Neill. Written by Ben
Markson, from a story by Ben Hecht; directed
by Roy del Ruth; for Warner.

Upstairs and Downstairs
GB 1959   101m   Eastmancolor
Rank (Betty E. Box)

Newlyweds have trouble with maids and au pair girls.

Glossy, cheerful, empty-headed domestic comedy.

w Frank Harvey, *novel* Ronald Scott Thorn
d Ralph Thomas ph Ernest Steward

Michael Craig, Anne Heywood, Mylène Demongeot, James Robertson Justice, Sidney James, Daniel Massey, Claudia Cardinale, Joan Hickson, Joan Sims

Uptown Saturday Night*
US 1974   104m   Technicolor
Warner / Verdon / First Artists (Melville Tucker)

Three friends pursue crooks who have inadvertently stolen a winning lottery ticket.

Witless but high-spirited star comedy for blacks, with a variety of sordid backgrounds.

w Richard Wesley d Sidney Poitier ph Fred J. Koenekamp m Tom Scott

Sidney Poitier, Bill Cosby, Harry Belafonte, Flip Wilson, Roscoe Lee Browne, Richard Pryor, Rosalind Cash, Paula Kelly

'If it had been filmed with a white cast this collection of atrophied comedy routines would have been indistinguishable from a Monogram farce of the forties.'—*David McGillivray*

The Upturned Glass*
GB 1947   86m   bw
GFD / Triton (Sydney Box, James Mason)

A Harley Street surgeon murders the woman responsible for the death of the girl he loved.

Rather pointless psychopathology with an ill-explained title; an interesting example of a top star not knowing what's best for him.

w Jon P. Monaghan, Pamela Kellino
d Lawrence Huntington ph Reg Wyer
m Bernard Stevens

James Mason, Pamela Kellino, Rosamund John, Ann Stephens, Henry Oscar, Morland Graham, Brefni O'Rourke

'The psychology is genuine; so too is the tension; the camera plays some good quiet tricks.'—*William Whitebait*

Urban Cowboy
US 1980   135m   Movielab   Panavision
Paramount (Robert Evans, Irving Azoff)

A rural Texan finds it difficult to succeed in the big city.

Unpleasant and uninteresting star melodrama with a plot vaguely reminiscent of the first part of *An American Tragedy*.

w James Bridges, *novel* Aaron Latham
d James Bridges ph Ray Villalobos
m various songs pd Stephen Grimes

John Travolta, Debra Winger, Scott Glenn, Madolyn Smith

'A fatuous vehicle for John Travolta, requiring him to stride (stiffly and expressionlessly) through various macho torments . . . the two-hour-plus running time, incorporating a wealth of cliché characters, is excruciatingly protracted.'—*Tom Milne, MFB*

V

The Vagabond King
US 1956 88m Technicolor Vistavision
Paramount (Pat Duggan)

The life and loves of French medieval poet
and rebel François Villon.
Shiny, antiseptic studio-set remake of an old
musical warhorse.

w Ken Englund, Noel Langley, *operetta*
Rudolf Friml d Michael Curtiz ph Robert
Burks *md* Victor Young, *songs* Rudolf Friml

Oreste, Kathryn Grayson, Rita Moreno,
Walter Hampden, Leslie Nielsen, Cedric
Hardwicke, William Prince

† A 1930 version with Dennis King is lost.
Non-musical versions of the story include
1928's *The Beloved Rogue* with John
Barrymore, and 1938's *If I Were King* with
Ronald Colman.

The Valachi Papers
France / Italy 1972 127m Technicolor
Euro France / de Laurentiis Intermarco
   (Dino de Laurentiis)

A convicted gangster talks to an FBI agent
about his life in the Mafia.
Rough, violent gangster melodrama, none the
better for being based on actual events.

w Stephen Geller, *book* Peter Maas
d Terence Young ph Aldo Tonti m Riz
Ortolani

Charles Bronson, Fred Valleca, Gerald S.
O'Loughlin, Lino Ventura, Walter Chiari,
Amedeo Nazzari, Joseph Wiseman

Valdez Is Coming
US 1970 90m De Luxe
UA / Norlan / Ira Steiner

A Mexican confronts a rancher who has
double-crossed him.
Simply-conceived western which doesn't quite
manage to be the classic intended.

w Roland Kibbee, David Rayfiel d Edwin
Sherin ph Gabor Pogany m Charles Gross

Burt Lancaster, Susan Clark, Jon Cypher,
Barton Heyman, Frank Silvera

Valentino
US 1951 105m Technicolor
Columbia (Edward Small)

An Italian immigrant to the US becomes a
world-famous romantic film star but dies
young.
Disastrously flat attempt to recapture the feel
of Hollywood in the twenties as a background
to a flatulent romance.

w George Bruce d Lewis Allen ph Harry
Stradling m Heinz Roemheld

Anthony Dexter, Eleanor Parker, Richard
Carlson, Patricia Medina, Joseph Calleia,
Dona Drake, Lloyd Gough, Otto Kruger

'One can almost see the decorated border
round the words . . . it mixes fact, speculation,
needless inaccuracy and bathos.'—*Gavin
Lambert*

'The dialogue is unbelievably ham, the
"entirely imaginary" story commonplace; the
players deserve sympathy.'—*Richard Mallett,
Punch*

Valentino*
GB 1977 127m De Luxe
UA / Aperture / Chartoff–Winkler (Harry
   Benn)

Reporters quiz celebrities at a star's funeral,
and his eccentric life unfolds.
Sensationalist 'exposé' of Valentino's rise to
fame, with excellent period detail but no
sympathy for its subject.

w Ken Russell, Mardik Martin, *book* Brad
Steiger, Chaw Mank d Ken Russell ph Peter
Suschitzky m Ferde Grofe, Stanley Black
ad Philip Harrison

Rudolf Nureyev, Leslie Caron, Michelle
Phillips, Carol Kane, Felicity Kendal, Huntz
Hall, David de Keyser, Alfred Marks, Anton
Diffring, Jennie Linden, John Justin

Valerie
US 1957 80m bw
UA / Hal R. Makelim

A western rancher is accused of wounding his
wife and murdering her parents.
Curious little *Rashomon*-like courtroom
melodrama, quite well made and acted.

w Leonard Heidemann, Emmett Murphy
d Gerd Oswald ph Ernest Laszlo m Albert
Glasser

Anita Ekberg, Sterling Hayden, Anthony
Steel, John Wengraf

The Valiant
GB / Italy 1961   89m   bw
(UA) BHP / Euro International

During World War II, a battleship in
Alexandria harbour is mined, and the captain
tries desperately to avert disaster.
Ill-made war fodder, of no interest at any
level.

w Keith Waterhouse, Willis Hall d Roy
Baker ph Wilkie Cooper, Egil Woxholt
m Christopher Whelen

John Mills, Ettore Manni, Robert Shaw, Liam
Redmond, Ralph Michael, Colin Douglas,
Dinsdale Landen

Valiant Is the Word for Carrie
US 1936   110m   bw
RKO (Wesley Ruggles)

A childless woman devotes her life to orphan
children.
Tedious soap opera.

w Claude Binyon, *novel* Barry Benefield
d Wesley Ruggles ph Leo Tover

Gladys George, John Howard, Dudley
Digges, Arline Judge, Harry Carey, Isabel
Jewell

AAN: Gladys George

The Valley of Decision*
US 1945   119m   bw
MGM (Edwin H. Knopf)

In old Pittsburgh, an Irish housemaid marries
the master's son.
Trouble at t' mill epic romance, American
style; starrily cast but not excitingly made.

w John Meehan, Sonya Levien, *novel* Marcia
Davenport d Tay Garnett ph Joseph
Ruttenberg m Herbert Stothart

Greer Garson, Gregory Peck, Lionel
Barrymore, Donald Crisp, Preston Foster,
Gladys Cooper, Marsha Hunt, Reginald
Owen, Dan Duryea, Jessica Tandy, Barbara
Everest, Marshall Thompson

AAN: Herbert Stothart; Greer Garson

Valley of Eagles
GB 1951   86m   bw

A Swedish scientist chases into Lapland after
his wife and her lover who have stolen an
important formula. Unconvincing scenery
mars what might have been an unusual
adventure drama. Jack Warner, John
McCallum, Nadia Gray, Anthony Dawson,

Mary Laura Wood, Christopher Lee. Written
by Paul Tabori, Nat Bronsten and Terence
Young; directed by Terence Young; for
Independent Sovereign / GFD.

The Valley of Gwangi
US 1968   95m   Technicolor
Warner / Morningside (Charles H. Schneer)

Cowboys and scientists discover prehistoric
monsters in a 'forbidden' Mexican valley.
Tedious adventure yarn enhanced by good
special effects.

w William E. Bast d James O'Connelly
ph Erwin Hillier m Jerome Moross sp Ray
Harryhausen

Richard Carlson, Laurence Naismith, James
Franciscus, Gila Golan, Freda Jackson

Valley of Song
GB 1953   74m   bw

Members of a Welsh valley choir nearly come
to blows over the interpretation of *The
Messiah*. Neat, Ealing-style comedy from a
well-known radio play. Mervyn Johns, Clifford
Evans, Maureen Swanson, John Fraser,
Rachel Thomas, Rachel Roberts, Kenneth
Williams. Written by Cliff Morgan and Phil
Park, from the play *Choir Practice* by Cliff
Morgan; directed by Gilbert Gunn; for ABPC.

Valley of the Dolls*
US 1967   123m   De Luxe   Panavision
TCF / Red Lion (David Weisbart)

An innocent young actress is corrupted by
Broadway and Hollywood, and takes to drugs.
Cliché-ridden but good-looking road-to-ruin
melodrama from a bitchy bestseller;
production values high, but the whole thing
goes over the top at the end.

w Helen Deutsch, Dorothy Kingsley, *novel*
Jacqueline Susann d Mark Robson
ph William H. Daniels m André Previn
md John Williams ad Jack Martin Smith,
Richard Day

Barbara Parkins, Patty Duke, Susan Hayward,
Paul Burke, Sharon Tate, Martin Milner,
Tony Scotti, Charles Drake, Alex Davion, Lee
Grant, Robert H. Harris
  'A skilfully deceptive imitation of a real
drama . . . on a closer look the characters turn
out to be images that have almost nothing to
do with people.'—*Christian Science Monitor*
AAN: John Williams

Valley of the Giants
US 1938   79m   Technicolor

A lumberman fights pirates to preserve his

beloved redwoods. Routine outdoor thick-ear to which colour lent the semblance of freshness. Wayne Morris, Claire Trevor, Frank McHugh, Alan Hale, Donald Crisp, Charles Bickford. Written by Seton I. Miller and Michael Fessier, from the novel by Peter B. Kyne; directed by William Keighley; for Warner.

Valley of the Kings
US 1954   86m   Eastmancolor
MGM

Archaeologists fight looters in the tomb of a Pharaoh.
Thin as drama, with little action or suspense and dispirited acting, this hokum piece nevertheless benefits from splendid locations.

w Robert Pirosh, Karl Tunberg d Robert Pirosh ph Robert Surtees m Miklos Rozsa

Robert Taylor, Eleanor Parker, Carlos Thompson, Kurt Kasznar, Victor Jory

Valley of the Sun
US 1942   79m   bw
RKO (Graham Baker)

A government spy in old Arizona outwits a crooked Indian agent.
Cheapjack western with nothing to commend it.

w Horace McCoy, *story* Clarence Budington Kelland d George Marshall ph Harry J. Wild m Paul Sawtell

James Craig, Lucille Ball, Dean Jagger, Billy Gilbert, Cedric Hardwicke, Peter Whitney, Tom Tyler, Antonio Moreno, George Cleveland

Value for Money
GB 1955   93m   Technicolor   Vistavision
Rank / Group Films (Sergei Nolbandov)

A Yorkshire businessman determines to broaden his outlook, and falls in love with a London showgirl.
Highly undistinguished north country romantic farce which wastes a good production and cast.

w R. F. Delderfield, William Fairchild, *novel* Derick Boothroyd d Ken Annakin ph Geoffrey Unsworth m Malcolm Arnold

John Gregson, Diana Dors, Susan Stephen, Derek Farr, Frank Pettingell, Jill Adams, *Ernest Thesiger*, Charles Victor, Joan Hickson

Vampira
GB 1974   88m   colour
Columbia / Jack H. Wiener
US title: *Old Dracula*

A vampire count lures beauty-contest winners to his castle and uses their blood to revive his dead wife.
Would-be spoof which falls flat on its fangs.

w Jeremy Lloyd d Clive Donner ph Tony Richmond m David Whitaker

David Niven, Teresa Graves, Peter Bayliss, Jennie Linden, Linda Hayden, Nicky Henson, Bernard Bresslaw, Veronica Carlson

The Vampire
US 1957   74m   bw
UA / Gardner–Levy

A research scientist takes bat essence and becomes a vampire.
Silly attempt to turn a legend into science fiction: more risible than sinister.

w Pat Fielder d Paul Landres ph Jack Mackenzie m Gerald Fried

John Beal, Coleen Gray, Kenneth Tobey, Lydia Reed

The Vampire Bat
US 1933   71m   bw
Majestic (Phil Goldstone)

A mad doctor kills townsfolk in search of 'blood substitute'.
Primitive but vigorous low budget chiller.

w Edward Lowe d Frank Strayer ph Ira Morgan

Lionel Atwill, Fay Wray, Melvyn Douglas, Maude Eburne, George E. Stone, Dwight Frye, Lionel Belmore

Vampire Circus
GB 1971   87m   colour
Hammer (Wilbur Stark)

In 1825 a plague-ridden village is visited by a circus of animal vampires.
Silly but quite inventive horror thriller.

w Judson Kinberg d Robert Young ph Moray Grant m Philip Martell ad Scott MacGregor

Adrienne Corri, Laurence Payne, Thorley Walters, John Moulder Brown, Elizabeth Seal, Lynne Frederick, Robert Tayman, Robin Hunter

The Vampire Lovers
GB 1970   91m   Technicolor
Hammer / AIP (Harry Fine, Michael Style)

A lady vampire worms her way into several noble households.
Reasonably close retelling of Sheridan Le Fanu's *Carmilla*, complete with lesbian love scenes. Adequate production but not much spirit.

w Tudor Gates, Harry Fine, Michael Styles *story* 'Carmilla' by Sheridan Le Fanu *d* Roy Ward Baker *ph* Moray Grant *m* Harry Robinson

Ingrid Pitt, Peter Cushing, Pippa Steele, Madeleine Smith, George Cole, Dawn Addams, Douglas Wilmer, Kate O'Mara

Vampyr••
Germany / France 1931   83m   bw
Tobis Klangfilm / Carl Dreyer
aka: *The Strange Adventure of David Gray*

A young man staying in a remote inn suspects that he is surrounded by vampires and has a dream of his own death.
Vague, misty, virtually plotless but occasionally frightening and always interesting to look at, this semi-professional film long since joined the list of minor classics for two scenes: the hero dreaming of his own death and the villain finally buried by flour in a mill.

w Christen Jul, Carl Dreyer, *story* 'Carmilla' by Sheridan Le Fanu *d* Carl Dreyer *ph* Rudolph Maté, Louis Née *m* Wolfgang Zeller

Julian West, Sybille Schmitz, Maurice Schutz, Jan Hieronimko

Vanessa, Her Love Story
US 1935   76m   bw
MGM (David O. Selznick)

When her husband becomes insane, a Victorian lady falls for a gypsy.
Very dated romance which finished Helen Hayes's star career, for thirty years at least.

w Lenore Coffee, *novel* Hugh Walpole *d* William K. Howard *ph* Ray June

Helen Hayes, Robert Montgomery, May Robson, Otto Kruger, Lewis Stone, Henry Stephenson, Violet Kemble-Cooper, Jessie Ralph

The Vanishing American
US 1925   110m at 24 fps   bw   silent

A history of the American Indian. Solid western epic, now of historical interest only. Richard Dix, Lois Wilson, Noah Beery, Malcolm McGregor, Charles Stevens. From a story by Zane Grey; directed by George B. Seitz; for Paramount.

The Vanishing Corporal•
France 1962   106m   bw
Films du Cyclope
original title: *Le Caporal Epinglé*

After several attempts, three Frenchmen succeed in escaping from a detention camp.

Symbolic World War II drama told in mainly comic terms. Not one of its director's great films, but a warm and assured one.

w Jean Renoir, Guy Lefranc *d* Jean Renoir *ph* Georges Leclerc *m* Joseph Kosma

Jean-Pierre Cassel, Claude Brasseur, Claude Rich, O. E. Hasse

Vanishing Point•
US 1971   107m   De Luxe
TCF / Cupid (Norman Spencer)

An ex-racing driver who delivers cars for a living becomes hepped up on benzedrine and leads police a rare chase through the Nevada desert.
Strange, fashionable action suspenser which is better to look at than to understand.

w Guillermo Cain *d* Richard Sarafin *ph* John A. Alonzo *md* Jimmy Brown

Barry Newman, Cleavon Little, Dean Jagger, Victoria Medlin, Paul Koslo, Bob Donner
   'Uncomfortably reminiscent of *Easy Rider* as an odyssey through an unknown America in its discovery of strange alliances and unpredictable hostilities.'—*Tom Milne*

The Vanishing Virginian
US 1941   97m   bw
MGM (Edwin H. Knopf)

A conservative Virginian finds that he harbours suffragettes in his household.
Life with Father in another setting; rather yawn-provoking.

w Jan Fortune, *novel* Rebecca Yancey Williams *d* Frank Borzage *ph* Charles Lawton Jnr *m* David Snell

Frank Morgan, Spring Byington, Kathryn Grayson, Elizabeth Patterson, Louise Beavers

The Vanquished
US 1953   84m   Technicolor

After the Civil War, a returning Confederate officer finds corruption in his home town.
Uninspiring semi-western. John Payne, Jan Sterling, Colleen Gray, Lyle Bettger, Willard Parker, Roy Gordon. Written by Winston Miller, Frank Moss and Lewis R. Foster, from a novel by Karl Brown; directed by Edward Ludwig; for Pine-Thomas / Paramount.

Variety••
Germany 1925   104m (24 fps)   bw
   silent
UFA
aka: *Vaudeville*

An ageing acrobat seduces a young girl and later kills another man who is interested in her.

Crude, vivid backstage story, inventively presented to overcome the dullness and tawdriness of the plot.

w E. A. Dupont, Leo Birinsky, *novel* Frederick Hollander *d* E. A. Dupont *ph* Karl Freund

Emil Jannings, Lya de Putti, Maly Delschaft, Warwick Ward

'A continually roving lens seizes the best angle for every detail, expression and scene.'—*Leon Moussinac*

Variety Girl
US 1947 83m bw
Paramount (Daniel Dare)

Of all the young hopefuls arriving in Hollywood, one girl becomes a star.
The slightest of excuses for a tour of the Paramount studios, with all the contract stars doing bits. It doesn't add up to much.

w Edmund Hartmann, Frank Tashlin, Monte Brice, Robert Welch *d* George Marshall *ph* Lionel Lindon, Stuart Thompson *md* Joseph J. Lilley, Troy Saunders

Mary Hatcher, Olga San Juan, De Forrest Kelley, Glenn Tryon; and Bob Hope, Bing Crosby, Gary Cooper, Ray Milland, Alan Ladd, Barbara Stanwyck, Paulette Goddard, Dorothy Lamour, Veronica Lake, Sonny Tufts, Joan Caulfield, William Holden, Lizabeth Scott, Burt Lancaster, Gail Russell, Diana Lynn, Sterling Hayden, Robert Preston, William Bendix, Barry Fitzgerald, Billy de Wolfe, George Pal Puppetoons, Cecil B. de Mille, Mitchell Leisen, George Marshall, Spike Jones and his City Slickers, etc.

Variety Jubilee
GB 1942 92m bw

Two generations in the life of a music hall.
Naïve romance with fascinating appearances by some famous names of variety. Lesley Brook, Ellis Irving, Reginald Purdell, George Robey, Charles Coborn, Ella Retford, Wilson Keppel and Betty, The Ganjou Brothers and Juanita, Slim Rhyder, Betty Warren as Florrie Forde; Marie Lloyd Jnr as Marie Lloyd; Tom Finglass as Eugene Stratton; John Rorke as Gus Elen. Written by Kathleen Butler; directed by Maclean Rogers; for Butcher's.

Varsity Show
US 1937 80m bw
Warner (Louis F. Edelman)

Collegians stage a revue.
Mild musical.

w Warren Duff, Richard Macaulay, Jerry Wald, Sig Herzig *d* William Keighley *ph* Sol Polito, George Barnes *ch* Busby Berkeley *songs* Richard Whiting, Johnny Mercer

Dick Powell, Priscilla Lane, Rosemary Lane, Fred Waring and his Pennsylvanians, Buck and Bubbles, Johnny 'Scat' Davis, Ted Healy

Vault of Horror*
GB 1973 86m Eastmancolor
Metromedia / Amicus (Milton Subotsky)

Five men trapped in the basement of a skyscraper tell of their recurring dreams.
All-star horror omnibus, plainly but well staged.

w Milton Subotsky, *stories* William Gaines *d* Roy Ward Baker *ph* Denys Coop *m* Douglas Gamley

Daniel Massey, Anna Massey, Terry-Thomas, Glynis Johns, Curt Jurgens, Dawn Addams, Michael Craig, Edward Judd, Tom Baker, Denholm Elliott

The Velvet Touch*
US 1948 97m bw
(RKO) Independent Artists

A famous actress murders her producer and is struck by conscience but allows a detective to find his own way to the truth.
Solid murder melodrama with an excellent theatrical atmosphere.

w Leo Rosten *d* John Gage *ph* Joseph Walker *m* Leigh Harline

Rosalind Russell, Leo Genn, Sidney Greenstreet, Claire Trevor, Leon Ames, Frank McHugh

Vendetta
US 1950 84m bw
RKO / Howard Hughes

The daughter of an esteemed Corsican family takes vengeance on her father's enemies.
Outmoded ethnic melodrama with nothing to recommend it.

w W. R. Burnett, *novel* Columba by Prosper Mérimée *d* Mel Ferrer *ph* Franz Planer, Al Gilks *m* Roy Webb *md* Constantin Bakaleinikoff

Faith Domergue, George Dolenz, Donald Buka, Hilary Brooke, Nigel Bruce, Joseph Calleia, Hugo Haas

The Venetian Affair
US 1966 92m Metrocolor Panavision
MGM / Jerry Thorpe

A reporter investigates the death in Venice of an American diplomat.

Uninteresting and complicated spy thriller with pleasant locations.

w E. Jack Neuman, *novel* Helen MacInnes d Jerry Thorpe *ph* Milton Krasner, Enzo Serafin *m* Lalo Schifrin

Robert Vaughn, Karl Boehm, Elke Sommer, Ed Asner, Boris Karloff, Felicia Farr, Roger C. Carmel,Luciana Paluzzi, Joe de Santis

Venetian Bird*
GB 1952 95m bw
Rank / British Film Makers (Betty E. Box)
US title: *The Assassin*

A private detective goes to Venice to reward a wartime partisan, who turns out to have become a notorious criminal.
Standard action fare with a nod to *The Third Man* but not much excitement or sense of place.

w Victor Canning, from his novel *d* Ralph Thomas *ph* Ernest Steward *m* Nino Rota

Richard Todd, Eva Bartok, John Gregson, George Coulouris, Margot Grahame, Walter Rilla, Sidney James

Vengeance
GB / Germany 1962 83m bw
CCC / Raymond Stross
aka: *The Brain*

After a fatal accident, the brain of a tycoon is kept alive and persuades a doctor to find his murderer.
Twisty remake of *Donovan's Brain* (qv), not too badly done.

w Robert Stewart, Philip Mackie *d* Freddie Francis *ph* Bob Hulke *m* Ken Jones

Anne Heywood, Peter Van Eyck, Cecil Parker, Bernard Lee, Maxine Audley, Jeremy Spenser, Miles Malleson

The Vengeance of Fu Manchu
GB 1967 92m Eastmancolor
Anglo Amalgamated / Harry Alan Towers

The Yellow Peril plans a crime syndicate to counter Interpol, and creates a double for Nayland Smith . . .
Limp addition to a series which started well, but was subsequently robbed of period flavour.

w Harry Alan Towers, *novels* Sax Rohmer d Jeremy Summers *ph* John Von Kotze *m* Malcolm Lockyer

Christopher Lee, Douglas Wilmer, Tony Ferrer, Tsai Chin, Howard Marion Crawford, Wolfgang Kieling

The Vengeance of She
GB 1967 101m Technicolor
Hammer (Aida Young)

A girl is possessed by the spirit of long-dead Queen Ayesha.
Grotesquely unpersuasive reincarnation melodrama, a long long way from its inspiration.

w Peter O'Donnell *d* Cliff Owen *ph* Wolfgang Suschitzky *m* Mario Nascimbene

John Richardson, Olinka Berova, Edward Judd, Colin Blakely, Derek Godfrey, Noel Willman, André Morell, Jill Melford

Vengeance Valley
US 1951 82m Technicolor
MGM (Nicholas Nayfack)

A western rancher keeps his foster-brother's misdeeds from their father.
Well-made character western, a little short on action.

w Irving Ravetch, *novel* Luke Short d Richard Thorpe *ph* George Folsey *m* Rudolph G. Kopp

Burt Lancaster, Robert Walker, Ray Collins, Joanne Dru, Sally Forrest, John Ireland, Carleton Carpenter, Ted de Corsia

Vera Cruz***
US 1953 94m Technicolor Superscope
UA / Hecht–Hill–Lancaster (James Hill)

Adventurers in 1860 Mexico become involved in a plot against Emperor Maximilian.
Terse, lively western melodrama with unusual locations and comedy and suspense touches.
Great outdoor entertainment.

w *Roland Kibbee, James R. Webb, Borden Chase d Robert Aldrich ph Ernest Laszlo m Hugo Friedhofer*

Gary Cooper, Burt Lancaster, Denise Darcel, Cesar Romero, George Macready, Sarita Montiel, Ernest Borgnine, Morris Ankrum, Charles Bronson

The Verdict*
US 1946 86m bw
Warner (William Jacobs)

A retired Scotland Yard inspector continues to work on a case which vexes him.
Victorian murder mystery with very unconvincing Hollywood sets and curious casting, but rather nicely detailed.

w Peter Milne, *novel* The Big Bow Mystery by Israel Zangwill *d* Don Siegel *ph* Ernest Haller *m* Frederick Hollander

Sidney Greenstreet, Peter Lorre, Joan Lorring, George Coulouris, Rosalind Ivan, Paul Cavanagh, Arthur Shields

Vertigo**
US 1958   128m   Technicolor
Vistavision
(Paramount) Alfred Hitchcock

A detective with a fear of heights is drawn into
a complex plot in which a girl he loves
apparently falls to her death. Then he meets
her double . . .
Double identity thriller which doesn't really
hang together but has many sequences in
Hitchcock's best style despite central
miscasting.

w Alec Coppel, Samuel Taylor, *novel* D'entre
les Morts by Pierre Boileau, Thomas
Narcejac *d Alfred Hitchcock ph Robert
Burks m Bernard Herrmann*

James Stewart, Kim Novak, Barbara Bel
Geddes, Tom Helmore, Henry Jones

The Very Edge
GB 1962   89m   bw   Cinevision
British Lion / Garrick / Raymond Stross

An obsessive young man menaces a mother-
to-be.
Rather unpleasant suspenser, adequately
presented.

w E. J. Howard d Cyril Frankel ph Bob
Huke m David Lee

Anne Heywood, Richard Todd, Jack Hedley.
Jeremy Brett, Nicole Maurey, Barbara
Mullen, Maurice Denham, William Lucas

Very Important Person**
GB 1961   98m   bw
Rank / Independent Artists (Julian Wintle,
Leslie Parkyn)
US title: *A Coming-Out Party*

A senior British scientist is caught by the Nazis
and has to be rescued.
Very satisfactory British comedy with a few
suspense scenes; POW fare with a difference.

w *Jack Davies d* Ken Annakin *ph* Ernest
Steward *m* Reg Owen

James Robertson Justice, Stanley Baxter, Leslie
Phillips, Eric Sykes, Richard Wattis, Colin
Gordon

A Very Special Favor*
US 1965   105m   Technicolor
Universal / Lankershim (Robert Arthur)

A Frenchman with a spinster daughter asks an
American lawyer to 'initiate' her.
Tasteless, smirking comedy with several funny
scenes, glossily photographed in the lap of
luxury and interesting in its early use of
homosexuality as a comedy subject.

w Nate Monaster, Stanley Shapiro d Michael
Gordon *ph Leo Tover m* Vic Mizzy

Rock Hudson, Charles Boyer, Leslie Caron,
Nita Talbot, Dick Shawn, *Walter Slezak*, Larry
Storch

The Very Thought of You
US 1944   99m   bw
Warner (Jerry Wald)

Problems of a wartime marriage.
Tepid romantic potboiler.

w Alvah Bessie, Delmer Daves d Delmer
Daves *ph* Bert Glennon *m* Franz Waxman

Dennis Morgan, Eleanor Parker, Dane Clark,
Faye Emerson, Beulah Bondi, Henry Travers,
William Prince, Andrea King

Vessel of Wrath***
GB 1938   93m   bw
Mayflower (Erich Pommer)
US title: *The Beachcomber*

In the Dutch East Indies, the missionary's
spinster sister falls for a drunken
beachcomber.
First-rate character comedy, remade as *The
Beachcomber* (qv).

w Bartlett Cormack, B. Van Thal, *story W.
Somerset Maugham d* Erich Pommer

Charles Laughton, Elsa Lanchester, Robert
Newton, Tyrone Guthrie, Dolly Mollinger,
Eliot Makeham

The Vicar of Bray
GB 1937   68m   bw

The ex-tutor of Charles I persuades him to
pardon a traitor. Mild historical fable with
song; in its way quite refreshing. Stanley
Holloway, Hugh Miller, Margaret Vyner,
Felix Aylmer, Esmond Knight, Garry Marsh.
Written by H. Fowler Mear; directed by
Henry Edwards; for Twickenham.

Vice Squad
US 1953   88m   bw
UA / Jules Levy, Arthur Gardner
GB title: *The Girl in Room 17*

A police captain tracks down two bank
robbers who have killed a cop.
A day in the life of a police captain, quite
watchable but scarcely engrossing.

w Lawrence Roman, *novel* Harness Bull by
Leslie T. White *d* Arnold Laven *ph* Joseph
C. Biroc *m* Herschel Burke Gilbert

Edward G. Robinson, Paulette Goddard, K.
T. Stevens, Porter Hall, Adam Williams,
Edward Binns, Lee Van Cleef

Vice Versa*

GB 1947 111m bw
Rank / Two Cities (Peter Ustinov, George H. Brown)

A magic stone enables an unhappy Victorian boy to change places with his pompous father. Funny moments can't disguise the fact that this overlong comedy is a bit of a fizzle, its talented creator not being a film-maker. A pity, as British films have so rarely entered the realms of fancy.

w Peter Ustinov, *novel* F. Anstey d Peter Ustinov

Roger Livesey, Kay Walsh, Anthony Newley, *James Robertson Justice*, David Hutcheson, Petula Clark, Joan Young
'A repository of English oddities.'—*John Russell Taylor*

The Vicious Circle*

GB 1957 84m bw
Romulus (Peter Rogers)
US title: *The Circle*

An actress is found dead in Dr Latimer's flat and the weapon turns up in the boot of his car . . .
Entertaining whodunnit from a TV serial.

w Francis Durbridge, from his serial The Brass Candlestick d Gerald Thomas ph Otto Heller m Stanley Black

John Mills, Derek Farr, Noelle Middleton, Roland Culver, Wilfrid Hyde White, Mervyn Johns, René Ray, Lionel Jeffries, Lisa Daniely

Vicki*

US 1953 85m bw
TCF (Leonard Goldstein)

A girl model is murdered, and her sister proves that her boy friend is innocent, despite the efforts of a brutal detective.
Very competent if uninspired remake of *I Wake Up Screaming* (qv).

w Dwight Taylor d Harry Horner ph Milton Krasner m Leigh Harline

Jeanne Crain, Jean Peters, Richard Boone, Elliott Reid, Casey Adams, Alex D'Arcy, Carl Betz, Aaron Spelling

Victim***

GB 1961 100m bw
Rank / Allied Film Makers / Parkway (Michael Relph)

A barrister with homosexual inclinations tracks down a blackmailer despite the risk to his own reputation.

A plea for a change in the law is very smartly wrapped up as a murder mystery which allows all aspects to be aired, and the London locations are vivid.

w Janet Green, John McCormick d Basil Dearden ph Otto Heller m Philip Green

Dirk Bogarde, Sylvia Syms, John Barrie, Norman Bird, Peter McEnery, Anthony Nicholls, Dennis Price, *Charles Lloyd Pack*, Derren Nesbitt, John Cairney, Hilton Edwards, Peter Copley, Donald Churchill, Nigel Stock

Victoria the Great***

GB 1937 112m bw (Technicolor sequence)
British Lion / Imperator / Herbert Wilcox

Episodes in the life of Queen Victoria.
A decent film with all the British virtues, and a milestone in the cinema of its time. Script and performances are excellent; production sometimes falters a little.

w Robert Vansittart, Miles Malleson, plays Victoria Regina by Laurence Housman d Herbert Wilcox ph F. A. Young, William V. Skall m Anthony Collins

Anna Neagle, Anton Walbrook, H. B. Warner, Walter Rilla, Mary Morris, C. V. France, Charles Carson, Felix Aylmer, Derrick de Marney
'The effect of the final colour reel is to make the picture look like something enamelled on pottery and labelled "A Present from Blackpool".'—*James Agate*

The Victors*

GB 1963 175m bw Panavision
Columbia / Open Road (Carl Foreman)

World War II adventures of an American infantry platoon.
Patchy compendium with moral too heavily stressed but plenty of impressive scenes and performances along the way. The mixture of realism and irony, though, doesn't really mix.

w Carl Foreman, *novel* The Human Kind by Alexander Baron d Carl Foreman ph Christopher Challis m Sol Kaplan

George Peppard, George Hamilton, Albert Finney, Melina Mercouri, Eli Wallach, Vince Edwards, Rosanna Schiaffino, James Mitchum, *Jeanne Moreau*, Elke Sommer, Senta Berger, Peter Fonda, Michael Callan
'Doggerel epic.'—*John Coleman*
'War has revealed Mr Foreman as a pompous bore.'—*John Simon*
'Having made a point through an image it continually feels the need to state it all over again by way of dialogue.'—*Penelope Houston*

Victory*
US 1940 77m bw
Paramount (Anthony Veiller)

A Dutch East Indies recluse rescues a girl and is menaced by three villains who think he is wealthy.
Curious, ineffective but occasionally compelling attempt to translate the untranslatable to the screen.

w John L. Balderston, *novel* Joseph Conrad
d John Cromwell *ph* Leo Tover *m* Frederick Hollander

Fredric March, Betty Field, *Cedric Hardwicke*, Sig Rumann, Margaret Wycherly, Jerome Cowan, Fritz Feld, Rafaela Ottiano

'There is achieved a combination of amateur theatricals and earnest emptiness of motive and motion that will throw a blanket of reminiscent affection around this solemn, unusual and exotic buffoonery.'—*Otis Ferguson*

'A mood of impending doom and horror more than makes up for its slow and deliberate action . . . a fine and penetrating motion picture melodrama.'—*New York World Telegram*

Victory
US 1981 117m Metrocolor Panavision
Lorimar / Victory Company / Tom Stern (Freddie Fields)
alternative and GB release title: *Escape to Victory*

A German POW camp in 1943 houses many international football stars. A Nazi officer sees propaganda in a game against a German side, but the allies make it an opportunity for escape.
Flabby and unconvincing POW story with agreeably old-fashioned values sacrificed to trendy casting and a silly ending.

w Evan Jones, Yabo Yablonsky *d* John Huston *ph* Gerry Fisher *m* Bill Conti *pd* J. Dennis Washington

Sylvester Stallone, Michael Caine, Pele, Bobby Moore, Max Von Sydow, George Mikell, Daniel Massey

'Even readers of the *Boy's Own Paper* might have blenched . . . ludicrous beyond belief.'—*Tom Milne, MFB*

Victory through Air Power***
US 1943 65m Technicolor
Walt Disney

The history of aviation and the theories of Major Alexander de Seversky.
What was thought by many to be propaganda was in fact a demonstration of Disney's own

fascination with the theories of a controversial figure. The cartoon segments are put together with the studio's accustomed brilliance.

w various *d* H. C. Potter (live action), various *m* Edward J. Plumb, Paul J. Smith, Oliver J. Wallace

AAN: Edward J. Plumb, Paul J. Smith, Oliver J. Wallace

The View from Pompey's Head*
US 1955 97m Eastmancolor Cinemascope
TCF (Philip Dunne)
GB title: *Secret Interlude*

A New York lawyer returns on a case to the small town of his youth, and falls in love again with his old sweetheart.
Routine Marquand-type novelette, long on atmosphere and short on plot.

wd Philip Dunne, *novel* Hamilton Basso
ph Joe MacDonald *m* Elmer Bernstein

Richard Egan, Dana Wynter, Cameron Mitchell, *Sidney Blackmer, Marjorie Rambeau*

A View from the Bridge
France 1961 117m bw
Transcontinental (Paul Graetz)
original title: *Vu du Pont*

A longshoreman on the New York waterfront has passionate feelings for his wife's niece, and these erupt when she announces her engagement.
Solemn, self-examining melodrama, poorly adapted from the stage.

w Norman Rosten, *play* Arthur Miller
d Sidney Lumet *ph* Michel Kelber
m Maurice Leroux

Raf Vallone, Maureen Stapleton, Carol Lawrence, Jean Sorel, Raymond Péllégrin, Morris Carnovsky, Harvey Lembeck, Vincent Gardenia

† The film was shot in several languages.

Vigil in the Night
US 1940 96m bw
RKO (George Stevens)

Two nurses are attracted to the same doctor; one dies during an epidemic.
Dull, downbeat romantic melodrama with a miscast lead.

w Fred Guiol, P. J. Wolfson, Rowland Leigh, *novel* A. J. Cronin *d* George Stevens
ph Robert de Grasse *m* Alfred Newman

Carole Lombard, Anne Shirley, Brian Aherne, Julien Mitchell, Robert Coote, Peter Cushing, Ethel Griffies

The Viking Queen
GB 1967   91m   Technicolor
Warner / Hammer (John Temple-Smith)

During the first century AD, the queen of the Iceni tries to keep peace with the occupying Romans but has trouble with hot-headed Druids.

Stuff and nonsense from the Dark Ages; light should not have been shed upon it.

w Clarke Reynolds d Don Chaffey
ph Stephen Dade m Gary Hughes

Don Murray, Carita, Donald Houston, Andrew Keir, Patrick Troughton, Adrienne Corri, Niall MacGinnis, Wilfrid Lawson, Nicola Pagett

The Vikings•••
US 1958   116m   Technirama
UA / KD Productions (Jerry Bresler)

Two Viking half-brothers quarrel over the throne of Northumbria.

Slightly unpleasant and brutal but extremely well-staged and good-looking epic in which you can almost feel the harsh climate. Fine colour, strong performances, natural settings, vivid action, and all production values as they should be.

w Calder Willingham, novel The Viking by Edison Marshall d Richard Fleischer ph Jack Cardiff m Mario Nascimbene credit titles United Productions of America narrator Orson Welles

Kirk Douglas, Tony Curtis, Ernest Borgnine, Janet Leigh, Alexander Knox, Frank Thring, James Donald, Maxine Audley, Eileen Way

Villa Rides!
US 1968   125m   Technicolor
  Panavision
Paramount (Ted Richmond)

1912 Mexico: an American pilot who has been gun-running for the rebels is pressed into more active service.

Bang-bang actioner which pauses too often for reflection and local colour.

w Robert Towne, Sam Peckinpah d Buzz Kulik ph Jack Hildyard m Maurice Jarre ad Ted Howarth

Yul Brynner, Robert Mitchum, Charles Bronson, Grazia Bucetta, Herbert Lom, Alexander Knox, Fernando Rey

Village of Daughters
GB 1961   86m   bw
MGM (George H. Brown)

An unemployed commercial traveller in an Italian village finds himself choosing a bride for a successful emigré.

Voluble, gesticulating minor comedy.

w David Pursall, Jack Seddon d George Pollock ph Geoffrey Faithfull m Ron Goodwin

Eric Sykes, Warren Mitchell, Scilla Gabel, Carol White, Grégoire Aslan, John Le Mesurier

Village of the Damned••
GB 1960   78m   bw
MGM (Ronald Kinnoch)

Children born simultaneously in an English village prove to be super-intelligent and deadly beings from another planet.

Modestly made but absorbing and logical science fiction, cleanly presented.

w Stirling Silliphant, Wolf Rilla, Geoffrey Barclay, novel The Midwich Cuckoos by John Wyndham d Wolf Rilla ph Geoffrey Faithfull m Ron Goodwin

George Sanders, Barbara Shelley, Michael Gwynn, Martin Stephens, Laurence Naismith
† Sequel: Children of the Damned (qv).

Villain
GB 1971   98m   Technicolor   Panavision
EMI / Kastner / Ladd / Kanter

The come-uppance of a cowardly, sadistic, homosexual East End gang boss with a mother fixation.

Very unpleasant and unentertaining British low life shocker, plainly inspired by White Heat.

w Dick Clement, Ian La Frenais, novel The Burden of Proof by James Barlow d Michael Tuchner ph Christopher Challis m Jonathan Hodge

Richard Burton, Ian MacShane, Nigel Davenport, Joss Ackland, Cathleen Nesbitt, Donald Sinden, T. P. McKenna, Fiona Lewis

The Villain
US 1979   89m   Metrocolor
Columbia / Rastar (Paul Maslansky, Mort Engelberg)
GB title: Cactus Jack

An incompetent outlaw rides from one disaster to another.

No doubt amusing in conception, this attempt to put the cartoon character Wile E. Coyote into human form lamentably misfires, six minutes being an ideal length for that kind of comedy.

w Robert G. Kane d Hal Needham
ph Bobby Byrne m Bill Justis

Kirk Douglas, Arnold Schwarzenegger, Ann-Margret, Paul Lynde, Ruth Buzzi, Jack Elam, Strother Martin

'Timing is entirely absent from this limp, laughless fiasco, as is any evidence of imagination . . . desperation is the keynote.'— *Paul Taylor, MFB*

The Villain Still Pursued Her*
US 1940   66m   bw
(RKO) Harold B. Franklin

An innocent family suffers at the hands of a villainous landlord.
Clumsy burlesque of old time melodrama, interesting that it was done at all and with this cast.

w Elbert Franklin d Edward Cline ph Lucien Ballard m Frank Tours

Buster Keaton, Alan Mowbray, Anita Louise, Hugh Herbert, Joyce Compton, Margaret Hamilton, Billy Gilbert

The Vintage
US 1957   92m   Metrocolor
   Cinemascope
MGM (Edwin H. Knopf)

Two fugitives from justice cause trouble when they become grape pickers.
Steamy drama with an unconvincing French setting; a Hollywood aberration.

w Michael Blankfort, *novel* Ursula Keir
d Jeffrey Hayden ph Joseph Ruttenberg
m David Raksin

Mel Ferrer, John Kerr, Michèle Morgan, Pier Angeli, Theodore Bikel, Leif Erickson

The Violent Enemy
GB 1968   98m   Eastmancolor
Trio / Group W. (Wilfrid Eades)

An IRA explosives expert escapes from a British jail but quarrels with his leaders.
Dullish political melodrama needlessly rubbing salt in old wounds.

w Edmund Ward, *novel* A Candle for the Dead by Hugh Marlowe d Don Sharp
ph Alan Hume m John Scott

Tom Bell, Ed Begley, Susan Hampshire, Noel Purcell, Michael Standing

The Violent Men*
US 1955   96m   Technicolor
   Cinemascope
Columbia (Lewis J. Rachmil)
GB title: *Rough Company*

A crippled cattle baron drives small landowners from his valley, while his wife has an affair with his younger brother.

So much snarling goes on that this seems like a gangster film in fancy dress, but it does hold the attention.

w Harry Kleiner, *novel* Donald Hamilton
d Rudolph Maté ph Burnett Guffey,
W. Howard Greene m Max Steiner

Edward G. Robinson, Barbara Stanwyck, Glenn Ford, Brian Keith, Dianne Foster, May Wynn, Warner Anderson, Basil Ruysdael

The Violent Ones*
US 1967   90m   Eastmancolor
Madison / Harold Goldman

In a small Mexican town, three American hobos are interrogated after the rape and murder of a local girl.
Rather well shot murder mystery with emphasis on character, leading to a desert chase climax.

w Doug Wilson, Charles Davis d Fernando Lamas ph Fleet Southcott m Martin Skiles

Fernando Lamas, Aldo Ray, David Carradine, Tommy Sands

Violent Playground
GB 1958   108m   bw
Rank (Michael Relph)

A junior liaison officer in the Liverpool slums falls in love with the sister of a fire-raiser.
'Realistic' melodrama sabotaged by an entirely schematic and predictable plot; enervatingly dull until the siege climax.

w James Kennaway d Basil Dearden ph Reg Wyer m Philip Green

Stanley Baker, Anne Heywood, David McCallum, Peter Cushing, John Slater, Clifford Evans

Violent Saturday*
US 1955   90m   De Luxe   Cinemascope
TCF (Buddy Adler)

Crooks move quietly into a small town with the intention of robbing the bank.
Interesting little melodrama which the wide screen robs of its proper tension. Adequate presentation and performance.

w Sidney Boehm d Richard Fleischer
ph Charles G. Clarke m Hugo Friedhofer

Richard Egan, Victor Mature, Stephen McNally, Sylvia Sidney, Virginia Leith, Tommy Noonan, Lee Marvin, Margaret Hayes, J. Carrol Naish, Ernest Borgnine

Violette Nozière*
France / Canada 1977   122m
   Eastmancolor
Filmel / Cinevideo (Roger Morand)

In 1933 Paris, an eighteen-year-old girl leads a double life, gets syphilis, poisons her parents and is convicted of murder.
Oddly erratic but interesting recapitulation of a famous French murder case, not quite typical of its director.

w Odile Barski, Herve Bromberger, Frederic Grendel d Claude Chabrol ph Jean Rabier m Pierre Jansen pd Jacques Brizzio

Isabelle Huppert, Jean Carmier, Stephane Audran, Bernadette Lafont

The VIPs**

GB 1963 119m Metrocolor Panavision
MGM (Anatole de Grunwald)

Passengers at London Airport are delayed by fog and spend the night at a hotel.
Multi-story compendium cunningly designed to exploit the real-life Burton–Taylor romance. In itself, competent rather than stimulating.

w Terence Rattigan d Anthony Asquith ph Jack Hildyard m Miklos Rozsa

Richard Burton, Elizabeth Taylor, Maggie Smith, Rod Taylor, *Margaret Rutherford*, Louis Jourdan, Elsa Martinelli, Orson Welles, Linda Christian, Dennis Price, Richard Wattis, David Frost, Robert Coote, Joan Benham, Michael Hordern, Lance Percival, Martin Miller
'If Mr Rattigan's Aunt Edna still goes to the pictures she should like his latest offering, especially if she has a good lunch first.'— *Brenda Davies*

AA: Margaret Rutherford

The Virgin and the Gypsy*

GB 1970 95m colour
Kenwood / Dimitri de Grunwald (Kenneth Harper)

A Midlands clergyman's daughter falls in love with a gypsy fortune teller.
Slow, sensitive, stylish picturization of a Lawrence novella, with generally good performances.

w *Alan Plater, story D. H. Lawrence*
d *Christopher Miles* ph Robert Huke m Patrick Gowers pd Terence Knight

Joanna Shimkus, Franco Nero, Honor Blackman, Michael Burns, Maurice Denham, Fay Compton, Kay Walsh, Norman Bird

Virgin Island

GB 1958 94m Eastmancolor
British Lion / Countryman (Leon Clore, Graham Tharp)

A young couple set up house on a tiny Caribbean island.
Pleasant comedy slowed down by lack of plot and too much conversation.

w Philip Rush, Pat Jackson, *book* Our Virgin Island by Robb White d Pat Jackson ph Freddie Francis m Clifton Parker

Virginia Maskell, John Cassavetes, Sidney Poitier, Isabel Dean, Colin Gordon

The Virgin Queen*

US 1955 92m De Luxe Cinemascope
TCF (Charles Brackett)

The relationship of Queen Elizabeth I and Sir Walter Raleigh.
Unhistorical charade, quite pleasantly made and worth noting for its star performance.

w Harry Brown, Mindret Lord d Henry Koster ph Charles G. Clarke m Franz Waxman

Bette Davis, Richard Todd, Joan Collins, Herbert Marshall, Jay Robinson, Dan O'Herlihy, Robert Douglas, Romney Brent

The Virgin Soldiers**

GB 1969 96m Technicolor
Columbia / Carl Foreman (Leslie Gilliat, Ned Sherrin)

Serio-comic adventures of recruits in the British army in 1960 Singapore.
Autobiographical fragments, mostly from below the belt, sharply observed and often very funny.

w John Hopkins, novel Leslie Thomas d John Dexter ph Ken Higgins m Peter Greenwell

Hywel Bennett, Nigel Patrick, *Lynn Redgrave*, Nigel Davenport, *Rachel Kempson*, Michael Gwynn, Tsai Chin
'A kind of monstrous mating of *Private's Progress* and *The Family Way*, with bits of *The Long and the Short and the Tall* thrown in for good measure.'—*David Pirie*
† Sequel 1977: *Stand Up Virgin Soldiers*.

The Virgin Spring*

Sweden 1959 87m bw
Svensk Filmindustri (Allan Ekelund)
original title: *Jungfrukällan*

When her murderers are killed, a spring bubbles up from the spot where a young maiden met her death.
Stark and rather lovely filming of a medieval legend, with heavy symbolism and a strong pictorial sense.

w Ulla Isaakson d Ingmar Bergman ph Sven Nykvist m Erik Nordgren

Max Von Sydow, Brigitta Valberg, Gunnel Lindblom, Brigitta Pettersson

AA: best foreign film

Virginia City*
US 1940 121m bw
Warner (Robert Fellows)

A dance hall girl is really a southern spy helping a rebel colonel to steal a gold shipment from her Yankee boy friend.

Lumpy western in Warner's best budget but worst manner: the stars look unhappy and the plot progresses in fits and starts.

w Robert Buckner d Michael Curtiz ph Sol Polito m Max Steiner

Errol Flynn, Randolph Scott, Miriam Hopkins, Humphrey Bogart, Frank McHugh, Alan Hale, Guinn Williams, John Litel, Moroni Olsen, Russell Hicks, Douglass Dumbrille

The Virginian*
US 1929 95m bw
Paramount (Louis D. Lighton)

A stalwart ranch foreman has to see his best friend hanged for rustling, and defeats the local bad man.

Standard western with famous clichés, e.g. 'Smile when you say that . . .'

w Edward E. Paramore Jnr, Howard Estabrook, novel Owen Wister d Victor Fleming ph J. Roy Hunt

Gary Cooper, Walter Huston, Richard Arlen, Mary Brian, Chester Conklin, Eugene Pallette

The Virginian
US 1946 90m Technicolor
Paramount

Forgettable remake of the above.

w Frances Goodrich, Albert Hackett d Stuart Gilmore ph Harry Hallenberger m Daniele Amfitheatrof

Joel McCrea, Brian Donlevy, Sonny Tufts, Barbara Britton, William Frawley, Henry O'Neill, Fay Bainter

Viridiana**
Spain / Mexico 1961 91m bw
Uninci / Films 59 / Gustavo Alatriste (Munoz Suay)

A novice about to take her vows is corrupted by her wicked uncle and installs a load of beggars in his house.

Often hilarious surrealist melodrama packed with shades of meaning, most of them sacrilegious. A fascinating film to watch.

w Luis Bunuel, Julio Alajandro d Luis Bunuel ph José F. Agayo

Silvia Pinal, Francisco Rabal, Fernando Rey

'One of the cinema's few major philosophical works.'—Robert Vas

The Virtuous Bigamist see Four Steps in the Clouds

The Virtuous Sin
US 1930 81m bw
Paramount
GB title: Cast Iron

A girl tries to help her student husband when war takes him away from bacteriology.

Stilted romantic drama.

w Martin Brown, Louise Long, novel Lajos Zilahy d George Cukor, Louis Gasnier ph David Abel

Walter Huston, Kay Francis, Kenneth MacKenna, Paul Cavanagh

The Visit
US 1964 100m bw Cinemascope
TCF / Deutschefox / Cinecittà / Dear Film / Films du Siècle / PECF (Julien Derode, Anthony Quinn)

A millionairess offers a fortune to her home town, providing someone will kill her ex-lover.

A realistic production ill befits an essentially theatrical play, and all the effort goes for nothing.

w Ben Barzman, play Friedrich Durrenmatt d Bernhard Wicki ph Armando Nannuzzi m Hans-Martin Majewski

Ingrid Bergman, Anthony Quinn, Paolo Stoppa, Hans-Christian Blech, Valentina Cortesa, Irina Demick, Claude Dauphin, Eduardo Ciannelli

Visit to a Chief's Son
US 1974 92m De Luxe Panavision
UA / Robert Halmi

An American anthropologist and his son hope to film the rituals of an African tribe.

Minor adventure film with a happy resolution, based on a photomontage by the producer, a Life photographer.

w Albert Ruben d Lamont Johnson ph Ernest Day m Francis Lai

Robert Mulligan, Johnny Sekka, John Philip Hodgdon

Visit to a Small Planet
US 1959 101m bw
Paramount / Wallis–Hazen

A young man from outer space takes a look at Earth and falls in love.
A satirical play disastrously adapted for the moronic comedy of an unsuitable star.

w Edmund Beloin, Henry Garson, *play* Gore Vidal *d* Norman Taurog *ph* Loyal Griggs *m* Leigh Harline

Jerry Lewis, Joan Blackman, Earl Holliman, Fred Clark, John Williams, Jerome Cowan, Gavin Gordon, Lee Patrick

Les Visiteurs du Soir*
France 1942   110m   bw
André Paulvé
aka: *The Devil's Envoys*

The devil sends messengers to earth to corrupt two lovers, but he fails: even though he turns them to stone, their hearts still beat.
Made during the Occupation, this stately medieval fable was intended to be significant: the devil was Hitler, and the heartbeat that of France. Perhaps because it is so conscious of hidden meanings, it moves rather stiffly but is often beautiful to behold.

w Jacques Prévert, Pierre Laroche *d Marcel Carné ph* Roger Hubert *m* Joseph Kosma, Maurice Thiriet *ad* Alexandre Trauner, Georges Wakhevitch

Arletty, *Jules Berry*, Marie Déa, Alain Cuny, Fernand Ledoux, Marcel Herrand

I Vitelloni
Italy / France 1953   109m   bw
Peg / Cité (Lorenzo Pegoraro)
aka: *Spivs*

In a small Italian resort, aimless young people get into various kinds of trouble.
Interesting in its realistic detail, this sharply observed slice of life is long enough for its basic purposelessness to become apparent.

w Federico Fellini, Ennio Flaiano, Tullio Pinelli *d* Federico Fellini *ph* Otello Martelli, Tasatti, Carlini *m* Nino Rota

Franco Fabrizi, Franco Interlenghi, Eleonora Ruffo, Alberto Sordi

AAN: script

Viva Knievel
US 1977   104m   Technicolor
   Panavision

Evel Knievel becomes involved with drug smugglers. Abysmal attempt to turn a stuntman into an actor; a most ramshackle vehicle. Evel Knievel, Gene Kelly, Lauren Hutton, Leslie Nielsen, Red Buttons, Cameron Mitchell, Marjoe Gortner. Written

by Antonio Santillan and Norman Katkov; directed by Gordon Douglas; for Warner. 'A paste-and-scissors B picture of quite breathtaking inanity.'—*Financial Times*.

Viva Las Vegas
US 1964   85m   Metrocolor
MGM (Jack Cummins, George Sidney)
GB title: *Love in Las Vegas*

A sports car racer has fun in the gambling city. Tolerable star musical.

w Sally Benson *d* George Sidney *ph* Joseph Biroc *md* George Stoll

Elvis Presley, Ann-Margret, Cesare Danova, William Demarest, Nicky Blair, Jack Carter

Viva Maria!
France / Italy 1965   120m
   Eastmancolor   Panavision
Novelles Editions / Artistes Associés / Vides
   (Oscar Dancigers, Louis Malle)

An Irish anarchist girl arrives in Central America and joins a group of strolling players. All show and no substance, this is a colour supplement of a film, neither fish, flesh nor good red herring.

w Louis Malle, Jean-Claude Carrière *d* Louis Malle *ph* Henri Decaë *m* Georges Delerue *ad* Bernard Evein

Jeanne Moreau, Brigitte Bardot, George Hamilton, Paulette Dubost, Claudio Brook

Viva Max
US 1969   93m   Eastmancolor
Commonwealth United / Mark Carliner

A Mexican general marches his troops into Texas and seizes the Alamo.
Flat comedy with mildly amusing passages but too much noise, bluster and sentiment.

w Elliott Baker, *novel* James Lehrer *d* Jerry Paris *ph* Jack Richards *m* Hugo Montenegro

Peter Ustinov, *John Astin*, Pamela Tiffin, Jonathan Winters, Keenan Wynn, Henry Morgan, Alice Ghostley

Viva Villa**
US 1934   110m   bw
MGM (David O. Selznick)

The career of a Mexican rebel.
Gutsy action drama with some smoothing over of fact in the name of entertainment. A big, highly competent production of its year.

w Ben Hecht d Jack Conway ph James Wong Howe, Charles G. Clarke m Herbert Stothart

Wallace Beery, Fay Wray, Leo Carrillo, Donald Cook, Stuart Erwin, George E. Stone, Joseph Schildkraut, Henry B. Walthall, Katherine de Mille

'A strange poem of violence.'—*John Baxter, 1968*

'A glorified horse opera . . . the spectator's excitement is incited by the purely physical impact of the furious riding and war sequences, by the frequent sadism, and by the lively musical score.'—*Irving Lerner*

AAN: best picture; script

Viva Zapata**
US 1952   113m   bw
TCF (Darryl F. Zanuck)

A Mexican revolutionary is finally betrayed by a friend.
Moody, good-looking star vehicle taking a romanticized but glum view of history.

w John Steinbeck *d* Elia Kazan *ph* Joe MacDonald *m* Alex North *md* Alfred Newman

Marlon Brando, Jean Peters, Joseph Wiseman, Anthony Quinn, Arnold Moss, Margo, *Frank Silvera*

AA: Anthony Quinn
AAN: John Steinbeck; Alex North; Marlon Brando

Vivacious Lady*
US 1938   90m   bw
RKO (George Stevens)

A nightclub singer marries a botany professor and has trouble with his parents.
Pleasant romantic comedy for two popular stars.

w P. J. Wolfson, Ernest Pagano *d* George Stevens *ph* Robert de Grasse *m* Roy Webb

Ginger Rogers, James Stewart, Charles Coburn, Beulah Bondi, James Ellison, Frances Mercer, Franklin Pangborn, Grady Sutton, Jack Carson

AAN: Robert de Grasse

Vogues of 1938*
US 1937   108m   Technicolor
Walter Wanger
reissue title: *All This and Glamour Too*

Rival fashion houses compete at the Seven Arts Ball.
A fashion show with threads of plot, interesting for clothes and cast, all working hard.

w Bella and Samuel Spewack *d* Irving Cummings *ph* Ray Rennahan *m* Victor Young *md* Boris Morros *ch* Seymour Felix

Joan Bennett, Walter Baxter, Helen Vinson, Mischa Auer, Alan Mowbray, Jerome Cowan, Alma Kruger, Marjorie Gateson, Penny Singleton, Hedda Hopper

AAN: song 'That Old Feeling' (*m* Sammy Fain, *ly* Lew Brown)

The Voice in the Mirror
US 1958   102m   bw   Cinemascope

A reformed alcoholic thinks back on his past life. Glum case history of no particular point or persuasiveness. Richard Egan, Julie London, Walter Matthau, Arthur O'Connell, Troy Donahue, Mae Clarke, Ann Doran. Written by Larry Marcus; directed by Harry Keller; for Universal-International.

A Voice in the Wind
US 1944   85m   bw

Two refugees from the Nazis meet again and die on a remote island. Pretentious romantic claptrap, fascinating only for a few of the impressionist effects it contrives on the lowest of budgets. Francis Lederer, Sigrid Gurie, J. Carrol Naish. Written by Frederick Torberg; directed by *Arthur Ripley*; for Arthur Ripley.
'Like a mid-thirties French melodrama drenched in the Rembrandt-and-molasses manner of German films of the early to middle twenties. Even within those terms it is much less good than it might be, solemn, unimaginative, thinly detailed; but it is also richly nostalgic if you have any feeling for bad period art.'—*James Agee*.

The Voice of Bugle Ann*
US 1936   70m   bw
MGM (John Considine Jnr)

When a dog is killed its embittered owner seeks revenge.
Old-fashioned country tale, rather heavy-going but emotionally strong.

w Harvey Gates, Samuel Hoffenstein, *novel* Mackinlay Kantor *d* Richard Thorpe *ph* Ernest Haller

Lionel Barrymore, Maureen O'Sullivan, Eric Linden, Dudley Digges, Spring Byington, Charley Grapewin
'A very fine movie indeed.'—*Pare Lorentz*

The Voice of Merrill
GB 1952   84m   bw
Tempean (Robert Baker, Monty Berman)
US title: *Murder Will Out*

Three men are suspected of murder but one becomes a potential victim.
Complicated murder thriller which intrigues but hardly satisfies.

wd John Gilling *ph* Monty Berman *m* Frank Cordell

Valerie Hobson, James Robertson Justice, Edward Underdown, Henry Kendall, Garry Marsh, Sam Kydd

The Voice of the Turtle**
US 1948 103m bw
Warner (Charles Hoffman)
aka: *One for the Book*

A girl shares her apartment with a soldier on leave.

A three-character play is smoothly filmed, slightly broadened, and burnished till its pale wit glows nicely.

w John Van Druten, from his play *d* Irving Rapper *ph* Sol Polito *m* Max Steiner

Eleanor Parker, Ronald Reagan, *Eve Arden*, Wayne Morris, Kent Smith

Voices
GB 1973 91m Technicolor
(Hemdale) Warden (Robert Enders)

A young couple in an old country house are haunted by the voice of their dead son.
Twisty little ghost story which would have been more effective at one third of its length.

w George Kirgo, Robert Enders, *play* Richard Lortz *d* Kevin Billington *ph* Geoffrey Unsworth *m* Richard Rodney Bennett

Gayle Hunnicutt, David Hemmings

Voltaire*
US 1933 72m bw
Warner (Ray Griffith)

The life and times of the 18th-century French wit.
One of the better Arliss charades, because the film is as stagey as his performance.

w Paul Green, Maude T. Howell, *novel* George Gibbs, E. Laurence Dudley *d* John Adolfi *ph* Tony Gaudio

George Arliss, Doris Kenyon, Margaret Lindsay, Reginald Owen, Alan Mowbray, David Torrence, Douglass Dumbrille, Theodore Newton

Von Richthofen and Brown
US 1971 97m De Luxe
UA / Roger Corman (Gene Corman)
GB title: *The Red Baron*

During World War I, a Canadian pilot takes on Germany's air ace.
The airplanes are nice, but the film is grounded by plot and dialogue.

w John and Joyce Corrington *d* Roger Corman *ph* Michael Reed *m* Hugo Friedhofer

John Phillip Law, Don Stroud, Barry Primus, Karen Huston, Corin Redgrave, Hurd Hatfield

Von Ryan's Express**
US 1965 117m De Luxe Cinemascope
TCF (Saul David)

In an Italian POW camp during World War II, an unpopular American captain leads English prisoners in a train escape.
Exhilarating action thriller with slow spots atoned for by nail-biting finale, though the downbeat curtain mars the general effect.

w Wendell Mayes, Joseph Landon, *novel* Davis Westheimer *d* Mark Robson *ph* William H. Daniels, Harold Lipstein *m* Jerry Goldsmith

Frank Sinatra, Trevor Howard, Sergio Fantoni, Edward Mulhare, Brad Dexter, John Leyton, Wolfgang Preiss, James Brolin, Adolfo Celi

Voyage of the Damned*
GB 1976 155m Eastmancolor
ITC / Associated General (Robert Fryer)

In 1939, a ship leaves Hamburg for Cuba with Jewish refugees; but Cuba won't take them.
High-minded, expensive, but poorly devised rehash of *Ship of Fools*, with too many stars in cameos and not enough central plot.

w Steve Shagan, David Butler, *book* Gordon Thomas, Max Morgan-Witts *d* Stuart Rosenberg *ph* Billy Williams *m* Lalo Schifrin

Faye Dunaway, Max Von Sydow, Oskar Werner, Malcolm McDowell, James Mason, Orson Welles, Katharine Ross, Ben Gazzara, Lee Grant, Sam Wanamaker, Julie Harris, Helmut Griem, Luther Adler, Wendy Hiller, Nehemiah Persoff, Maria Schell, Fernando Rey, Donald Houston, Jose Ferrer, Denholm Elliott, Janet Suzman

'Not a single moment carries any conviction.'—*New Yorker*

'The movie stays surprisingly distanced and impersonal, like a panning shot that moves too quickly for all the details to register.'—*Charles Champlin, Los Angeles Times*

'With a story that is true (or thereabouts), tragic in its detail and implications, and about which it is impossible to take a neutral attitude, you feel an absolute bounder unless you give it the thumbs up.'—*Barry Took, Punch*

AAN: script; Lalo Schifrin; Lee Grant

Voyage to the Bottom of the Sea*
US 1961   105m   De Luxe   Cinemascope
TCF / Windsor (Irwin Allen)

USN Admiral Nelson takes scientists in his
futuristic atomic submarine to explode a belt
of radiation.
Childish but sometimes entertaining science
fiction which spawned a long-running TV
series.

w Irwin Allen, Charles Bennett d Irwin
Allen ph Winton Hoch, John Lamb m Paul
Sawtell, Bert Shefter ad J. M. Smith, Herman
A. Blumenthal

Walter Pidgeon, Robert Sterling, Joan
Fontaine, Peter Lorre, Barbara Eden, Michael
Ansara, Henry Daniell, Regis Toomey,
Frankie Avalon

The Vulture
GB 1967   92m   bw

A family curse transforms a scientist into a
giant vulture. Incredible nonsense—incredible
that anyone should try to get away with it. Fun
for those who like to watch actors in trouble.
Robert Hutton, Akim Tamiroff, Broderick
Crawford, Diane Clare. Written and directed
by Lawrence Huntington; for Lawrence
Huntington Productions.

W

W
US 1973 95m De Luxe
Bing Crosby Productions (Mel Ferrer)

A young wife is threatened by her psychotic first husband.
Tedious rehash of several frightened lady themes, all rather sick.

w Gerald di Pego, James Kelly *d* Richard Quine *ph* Gerry Hirschfeld *m* Johnny Mandell

Twiggy, Michael Witney, Eugene Roche, Dirk Benedict, John Vernon

The W Plan*
GB 1930 105m bw
BIP / Wardour (Victor Saville)

A British spy helps destroy Germany's secret tunnels.
Slightly fantasticated spy / war action which was a big popular success at the time.

w Victor Saville, Miles Malleson, Frank Launder, *novel* Graham Seton *d* Victor Saville *ph* F. A. Young, Werner Brandes

Brian Aherne, Madeleine Carroll, Gordon Harker, Gibb McLaughlin, George Merritt, Mary Jerrold

'Fast, spectacular action, fine acting and notably realistic war scenes.'—*NFT, 1971*

W. C. Fields and Me
US 1976 112m Technicolor
Universal (Jay Weston)

The rise to Hollywood fame of alcoholic comedian W. C. Fields.
Untruthful and rather boring biopic, with minor compensations.

w Bob Merrill, *book* Carlotta Monti *d* Arthur Hiller *ph* David M. Walsh *m* Henry Mancini *pd* Robert Boyle

Rod Steiger, Valerie Perrine, John Marley, Jack Cassidy (as John Barrymore), Paul Stewart (as Ziegfeld), Billy Barty, Bernadette Peters

'Steiger's impersonation largely keeps pace with the overriding vulgarity of the enterprise.'—*Sight and Sound*
'A stupid and pointless slander.'—*Judith Crist*

'Just the sort of memorial Fields might have wished for Baby Leroy.'—*Les Keyser, Hollywood in the Seventies*

WW and the Dixie Dancekings
US 1975 94m TVC
TCF (Stanley S. Canter)

In a southern state in the 1950s, a crook uses a travelling band as an alibi and stays to promote them.
Combination of *American Graffiti* and *Easy Rider*, either tiresome or tolerable according to one's mood. Very flashy, anyway.

w Thomas Rickman *d* John G. Avildsen *ph* Jim Crabe *m* Dave Grusin

Burt Reynolds, Art Carney, Conny Van Dyke, Jerry Reed, Ned Beatty

Wabash Avenue*
US 1950 92m Technicolor
TCF (William Perlberg)

During the Chicago World's Fair of 1892, a shimmy dancer is pursued by two men.
Bright rehash of *Coney Island* (qv), with solid tunes and performances.

w Harry Tugend, Charles Lederer *d* Henry Koster *ph* Arthur E. Arling *md* Lionel Newman

Betty Grable, Victor Mature, Phil Harris, Reginald Gardiner, Margaret Hamilton, James Barton, Barry Kelley

AAN: song 'Wilhelmina' (*m* Josef Myrow, *ly* Mack Gordon)

The Wackiest Ship in the Army
US 1960 99m Technicolor
Cinemascope
Columbia / Fred Kohlmar

In the South Pacific during World War II a decrepit sailing ship with an inexperienced crew manages to confuse Japanese patrols and land a scout behind enemy lines.
Slapstick war comedy with fragments of action; effect rather muddled.

wd Richard Murphy, *story* Herbert Carlson *ph* Charles Lawton *m* George Duning

Jack Lemmon, Ricky Nelson, John Lund, Chips Rafferty, Tom Tully, Joby Baker, Warren Berlinger, Richard Anderson

Waco
US 1966 85m Technicolor

A gunfighter is hired to straighten out a
corrupt town. Routine western programmer
with familiar faces in cameo parts. Howard
Keel, Jane Russell, Wendell Corey, Brian
Donlevy, John Smith, Gene Evans, DeForest
Kelley, Terry Moore, John Agar, Richard
Arlen, Robert Lowery, Willard Parker, Fuzzy
Knight. Written by Steve Fisher, from the
novel *Emporia* by Harry Sanford and Max
Lamb; directed by R. G. Springsteen; for
A. C. Lyles / Paramount.

The Wages of Fear●●●
France / Italy 1953 140m bw
Filmsonor / CICC / Vera
original title: *Le Salaire de la Peur*

The manager of a Central American oilfield
offers big money to drivers who will take
nitro-glycerine into the jungle to put out an oil
well fire.
After too extended an introduction to the less
than admirable characters, this fascinating film
resolves itself into a suspense shocker with one
craftily managed bad moment after another.

wd Henri-Georges Clouzot, *novel* Georges
Arnaud *ph* Armand Thirard *m* Georges
Auric

Yves Montand, Folco Lulli, Peter Van Eyck,
Charles Vanel, Vera Clouzot, William Tubbs
  'As skilful as, in its preoccupation with
violence and its unrelieved pessimism, it is
unlikeable.'—*Penelope Houston, Sight and
Sound*
  'It has some claim to be the greatest
suspense thriller of all time; it is the suspense
not of mystery but of Damocles' sword.'—
Basil Wright, 1972
† See *Sorcerer*, a lamentable remake.

Wagonmaster●●
US 1950 86m bw
RKO / Argosy (John Ford, Merian C.
Cooper)

Adventures of a Mormon wagon train
journeying towards Utah in 1879.
Low-key Ford western, essentially a collection
of incidents, fondly and enjoyably presented.

w Frank Nugent, Patrick Ford *d* John Ford
ph Bert Glennon *m* Richard Hageman

Ben Johnson, Joanne Dru, Harry Carey Jnr,
Ward Bond, Charles Kemper, Alan Mowbray,
Jane Darwell, Russell Simpson
  'The feel of the period, the poetry of space
and of endeavour, is splendidly
communicated.'—*Lindsay Anderson*

  'What emerges at the end is nothing less
than a view of life itself, the view of a
poet.'—*Patrick Gibbs, 1965*

The Wagons Roll at Night
US 1941 83m bw
Warner (Harlan Thompson)

The sweetheart of a circus owner makes a pass
at the new young lion-tamer.
Dull remake of *Kid Galahad* (qv), whose plot
was borrowed from *Tiger Shark* (qv). Warners
were good at this kind of retreading, but
gradually poor quality began to show.

w Fred Niblo Jnr, Barry Trivers *d* Ray
Enright *ph* Sid Hickox *m* Heinz Roemheld

Humphrey Bogart, Sylvia Sidney, Eddie
Albert, Joan Leslie, Sig Rumann, Cliff Clark,
Frank Wilcox

Waikiki Wedding●
US 1937 89m bw
Paramount (Arthur Hornblow Jnr)

A press agent in Hawaii promotes a Pineapple
Queen contest.
Light-hearted, empty-headed musical very
typical of this studio . . . except that this one is
quite good.

w Frank Butler, Walter de Leon, Don
Hartman, Francis Martin *d* Frank Tuttle
ph Karl Struss *m* Leo Shukin *md* Boris
Morros

Bing Crosby, Shirley Ross, Bob Burns,
Martha Raye, George Barbier, Leif Erickson,
Grady Sutton, Granville Bates, Anthony
Quinn

AA: song 'Sweet Leilani' (*m* / *ly* Harry
Owens)

Wait til the Sun Shines, Nellie●
US 1952 108m Technicolor
TCF (George Jessel)

The life of a small-town barber, from marriage
through tragedy to retirement.
Amiable, leisurely family drama with pleasant
settings; small beer, but oddly compulsive.

w Allan Scott, *novel* Ferdinand Reyher
d Henry King *ph* Leon Shamroy *m* Alfred
Newman

David Wayne, Jean Peters, Hugh Marlowe,
Albert Dekker, Alan Hale Jnr, Helene
Stanley

Wait until Dark●●
US 1967 108m Technicolor
Warner Seven Arts (Mel Ferrer)

A photographer unwittingly smuggles a drug-filled doll into New York, and his blind wife, alone in their flat, is terrorized by murderous crooks in search of it.
Sharp suspenser with shock moments, from a successful play; in this case the claustrophobic atmosphere helps, though a lack of light relief makes itself felt.

w Robert and Jane Howard-Carrington, play Frederick Knott d Terence Young ph Charles Lang m Henry Mancini ad George Jenkins

Audrey Hepburn, Alan Arkin, Richard Crenna, Efrem Zimbalist Jnr, Jack Weston

AAN: Audrey Hepburn

Wake Island*
US 1942 78m bw
Paramount (Joseph Sistrom)

During World War II, marines fight to hold an American base on a small Pacific island.
Terse, violent flagwaver, well done within its limits.

w W. R. Burnett, Frank Butler d John Farrow ph Theodor Sparkuhl, William C. Mellor m David Buttolph

Brian Donlevy, Macdonald Carey, Robert Preston, William Bendix, Albert Dekker, Walter Abel, Mikhail Rasumny, Rod Cameron, Barbara Britton

'Hollywood's first intelligent, honest and completely successful attempt to dramatize the deeds of an American force on a fighting front.'—*Newsweek*

AAN: best picture; script; John Farrow; William Bendix

Wake Me When It's Over
US 1960 126m De Luxe Cinemascope
TCF / Mervyn Le Roy

Soldiers holding a Pacific island build a de luxe hotel from surplus war material.
Aptly-titled army farce on the lines of *The Teahouse of the August Moon* but constructed from inferior material. Yawningly tedious.

w Richard Breen, *novel* Howard Singer d Mervyn Le Roy ph Leon Shamroy m Cyril Mockridge

Ernie Kovacs, Dick Shawn, Jack Warden, Margo Moore, Nobu McCarthy, Don Knotts, Robert Emhardt

Wake of the Red Witch**
US 1948 106m bw
Republic (Edmund Grainger)

The owner and captain of a ship settle their differences to seek treasure on an East Indian island.

Rattling good action yarn told in flashback, with adequate production and performances.

w Harry Brown, Kenneth Gamet, *novel* Garland Roark d Edward Ludwig ph Reggie Lanning m Nathan Scott

John Wayne, *Luther Adler,* Gail Russell, Gig Young, Adele Mara, Eduard Franz, Grant Withers, Henry Daniell, Paul Fix, Dennis Hoey

Wake Up and Dream
US 1946 92m Technicolor
TCF (Walter Morosco)

A little girl is determined to find her brother who is missing in action in World War II.
Ambitious but unappealing whimsy which descends into sentimentality; either way it bewildered audiences and critics.

w Elick Moll, *novel* The Enchanted Voyage by Robert Nathan d Lloyd Bacon ph Harry Jackson m Cyril Mockridge md Emil Newman

June Haver, John Payne, Connie Marshall, Charlotte Greenwood, John Ireland, Clem Bevans, Lee Patrick

Wake Up and Live*
US 1937 91m bw
TCF (Kenneth MacGowan)

Success and failure in the radio world as a commentator and a bandleader fight a verbal duel in public.
Fast-moving spoof in which something is always happening, and usually something funny.

w Harry Tugend, Jack Yellen, *book* Dorothea Brande d Sidney Lanfield ph Edward Cronjager m Louis Silvers

Walter Winchell, Ben Bernie and his band, Alice Faye, Jack Haley, Patsy Kelly, Ned Sparks, Grace Bradley, Walter Catlett, Joan Davis, Douglas Fowley, Miles Mander, Etienne Girardot

Walk a Crooked Mile
US 1948 91m bw
Columbia (Edward Small)

British and American agents investigate the leakage of atomic secrets.
Moderate semi-documentary spy thriller.

w George Bruce d Gordon Douglas ph George Robinson m Paul Sawtell

Louis Hayward, Dennis O'Keefe, Louise Allbritton, Carl Esmond, Raymond Burr, Onslow Stevens

Walk a Crooked Path
GB 1969   88m   Eastmancolor
Hanover (John Brason)

A housemaster at a boys' school is accused of
homosexuality.
Po-faced melodrama in a minor key;
reasonably effective but not exciting.

w Barry Perowne d John Brason ph John
Taylor m Leslie Bridgewater

Tenniel Evans, Faith Brook, Christopher Coll,
Patricia Haines, Pat Endersby, Margery
Mason, Peter Copley

Walk, Don't Run*
US 1966   114m   Technicolor
   Panavision
Columbia / Granley (Sol C. Siegel)

In Tokyo during the Olympics accommodation
is hard to find, and two men move in with a
girl.
Witless reprise of *The More the Merrier*,
notable only for the Tokyo backgrounds and
for Cary Grant's farewell appearance.

w Sol Saks d Charles Walters ph Harry
Stradling m Quincy Jones

Cary Grant, Samantha Eggar, Jim Hutton,
John Standing, Miiko Taka

'Too long as are most comedies today, it
seems to take its title far too literally; but
there are several very funny sequences, a
jaunty score, and the unflawed elegance of Mr
Grant.'—*Arthur Knight*

Walk East on Beacon*
US 1952   98m   bw
Columbia (Louis de Rochemont)
GB title: *The Crime of the Century*

The FBI exposes communist spies in the US.
Fast-moving semi-documentary spy thriller
modelled on the same producer's *The House
on 92nd Street*.

w Leo Rosten d Alfred Werker ph Joseph
Brun m Louis Applebaum

George Murphy, Finlay Currie, Virginia
Gilmore, Karel Stepanek, Louisa Horton

A Walk in the Spring Rain
US 1969   98m   Technicolor   Panavision
Columbia / Pingee (Stirling Silliphant)

A college lecturer's wife, on holiday in the
mountains, falls in love with a local man.
Romance for the middle-aged, nicely done if
lacking in surprise.

w Stirling Silliphant, *novel* Rachel Maddox
d Guy Green ph Charles B. Lang m Elmer
Bernstein

Ingrid Bergman, Anthony Quinn, Fritz
Weaver, Katherine Crawford

'Not one line or scene is believably written
or acted and the direction is so lazy it appears
to have been mailed in during the postal
strike.'—*Richard Roud*

A Walk in the Sun***
US 1946   117m   bw
Lewis Milestone Productions

The exploits of a single army patrol during the
Salerno landings of 1943, on one vital
morning.
Vivid war film in a minor key, superbly
disciplined and keenly acted.

w *Robert Rossen, novel* Harry Brown d *Lewis
Milestone ph Russell Harlan m* Fredric
Efrem Rich

Dana Andrews, Richard Conte, Sterling
Holloway, John Ireland, George Tyne,
Herbert Rudley, Richard Benedict, Norman
Lloyd, Lloyd Bridges, Huntz Hall

'Concerned with the individual rather than
the battlefield, the film is finely perceptive,
exciting, and very moving.'—*Penelope
Houston*

'A swiftly overpowering piece of work.'—
Bosley Crowther

'A notable war film, if not the most notable
war film to come from America.'—*Richard
Winnington*

'After nearly two hours one is sorry when it
ends.'—*Richard Mallett, Punch*

Walk like a Dragon
US 1960   95m   bw
Paramount / James Clavell

In 1870 San Francisco, a cowboy sets free a
Chinese slave girl but incurs racial intolerance
when he takes her home.
Curious 'liberated' western which gets itself in
a muddle and doesn't come off at all.

w James Clavell, Dan Mainwaring d James
Clavell ph Loyal Griggs m Paul Dunlap

Jack Lord, James Shigeta, Nobu McCarthy,
Mel Tormé, Josephine Hutchinson, Rodolfo
Acosta

Walk on the Wild Side
US 1962   114m   bw
Columbia / Famous Artists (Charles K.
   Feldman)

In the thirties, a penniless farmer finds the girl
he once loved working in a New Orleans
brothel.
A brilliant title sequence heralds the dreariest
and most verbose of self-conscious

melodramas, quite missing the sensational effect promised by the advertising.

w John Fante, Edmund Morris, *novel* Nelson Algren d Edward Dmytryk ph Joe MacDonald m Elmer Bernstein *credits Saul Bass*

Jane Fonda, Capucine, Barbara Stanwyck, Laurence Harvey, Anne Baxter, Richard Rust

'Since the film prides itself in calling a spade a spade, it is surprising to find all concerned reacting to their material as though they were up to their waists in a quagmire.'—*MFB*

'A side of life you never expected to see on the screen!'—*publicity*

AAN: title song (*m* Elmer Bernstein, *ly* Mack David)

Walk Softly Stranger
US 1950 81m bw
RKO (Robert Sparks)

A crook on the run falls for a crippled girl, who promises to wait for him.
Dismal love-conquers-all melodrama.

w Frank Fenton d Robert Stevenson ph Harry J. Wild m Frederick Hollander

Alida Valli, Joseph Cotten, Spring Byington, Paul Stewart, Jack Paar, Jeff Donnell, John McIntire

Walk the Proud Land
US 1956 88m Technicolor Cinemascope
U-I (Aaron Rosenberg)

An Indian agent persuades the army to use less violent methods.
Fair standard western with a thoughtful and sympathetic attitude.

w Gil Doud, Jack Sher d Jesse Hibbs ph Harold Lipstein m Joseph Gershenson

Audie Murphy, Anne Bancroft, Pat Crowley, Robert Warwick, Charles Drake, Tommy Rall, Jay Silverheels

Walkabout*
Australia 1970 100m Eastmancolor
Max L. Raab / Si Litvinoff

A man kills himself in the desert and his small children trek among the aborigines to safety.
Eerily effective contrast of city with native life, a director's and photographer's experimental success.

w Edward Bond, *novel* James Vance Marshall d / ph Nicolas Roeg m John Barry

Jenny Agutter, Lucien John, David Gimpell

The Walking Dead*
US 1936 66m bw
Warner (Louis F. Edelman)

A man is revived after electrocution and takes revenge on his enemies.
Dour but well mounted horror thriller in a shadowy style very typical of its director.

w Ewart Adamson, Peter Milne, Robert Adams, Lillie Hayward d *Michael Curtiz* ph Hal Mohr

Boris Karloff, Edmund Gwenn, Marguerite Churchill, Ricardo Cortez, Barton MacLane, Warren Hull, Henry O'Neill

Walking My Baby Back Home*
US 1953 95m Technicolor
U-I (Ted Richmond)

Ex-army musicians hit on a combination of symphonic and dixieland jazz.
The lightest of light musicals, this highly polished offering remains mildly pleasing though thinly written throughout.

w Don McGuire, Oscar Brodney d Lloyd Bacon ph Irving Glassberg md Joseph Gershenson

Donald O'Connor, Janet Leigh, Buddy Hackett, Lori Nelson, Scat Man Crothers, Kathleen Lockhart, George Cleveland, John Hubbard

The Walking Stick*
GB 1970 101m Metrocolor Panavision
MGM / Winkast (Alan Ladd Jnr)

A repressed girl polio victim falls reluctantly in love with a painter who involves her in his criminal schemes.
Slow moving character romance which has its heart in the right place but too often promises suspense which never comes, and is made in a chintzy cigarette commercial style.

w George Bluestone, *novel* Winston Graham d Eric Till ph Arthur Ibbetson m Stanley Myers

David Hemmings, Samantha Eggar, Phyllis Calvert, Ferdy Mayne, Emlyn Williams, Francesca Annis, Dudley Sutton

Walking Tall*
US 1973 125m De Luxe
Bing Crosby Productions (Mort Briskin)

A Tennessee farmer-sheriff meets violence with violence and becomes a local hero.
True story of an American vigilante, made with modest competence; its great commercial success may have been due to the support of the righteous, or of those who revel in violence.

w Mort Briskin *d* Phil Karlson *ph* Jack Marta *m* Walter Scharf

Joe Don Baker, Elizabeth Hartman, Gene Evans, Noah Beery Jnr

'A terrifying image of Nixon's silent majority at work.'—*Gareth Jones*

'It generates a primitive, atavistic sort of power: it awakens more apprehension and dredges up more complicated and contradictory emotions than one anticipates.'—*Gary Arnold*

† Sequel 1976: *Part Two Walking Tall.* (GB title: *Legend of the Lawman.*) 1977: *Walking Tall: Final Chapter*

Wall of Noise
US 1963   112m   bw
Warner (Joseph Landon)

A racehorse trainer falls for the boss's wife. Complex but predictable melodrama of the old school, adequately presented and performed.

w Joseph Landon, *novel* Daniel Michael Stein *d* Richard Wilson *ph* Lucien Ballard *m* William Lava

Suzanne Pleshette, Ty Hardin, Dorothy Provine, Ralph Meeker, Simon Oakland, Murray Matheson, Robert F. Simon

Wallflower
US 1948   77m   bw

Two sisters chase the same man; the less aggressive gets him. So-so comedy on familiar lines. Joyce Reynolds, Janis Paige, Robert Hutton, Edward Arnold, Jerome Cowan, Barbara Brown. Written by Phoebe and Henry Ephron, from the play by Reginald Denham and Mary Orr; directed by Frederick de Cordova; for Warner.

The Walls of Jericho
US 1948   106m   bw
TCF (Lamar Trotti)

An influential small-town newspaperman is undermined by his vindictive wife. Filmed novel of standard competence but minimum interest, ending in a courtroom scene.

w Lamar Trotti, *novel* Paul Wellman *d* John M. Stahl *ph* Arthur Miller *m* Cyril Mockridge

Cornel Wilde, Linda Darnell, Anne Baxter, Kirk Douglas, Ann Dvorak, Marjorie Rambeau, Henry Hull, Colleen Townsend

The Waltz King
US 1963   95m   Technicolor
Walt Disney (Peter V. Herald)

The life of young Johann Strauss in 1850s Vienna.
Medium-budget international family musical, tolerably well done.

w Maurice Tombragel *d* Steve Previn *ph* Gunther Anders *md* Helmuth Froschauer

Kerwin Mathews, Brian Aherne, Senta Berger, Peter Kraus, Fritz Eckhardt

The Waltz of the Toreadors*
GB 1962   105m   Technicolor
Rank / Wintle–Parkyn (Peter de Sarigny)

A lecherous retired general finds his past creeping up on him and loses his young mistress to his son.
Lukewarm adaptation of a semi-classic comedy, disastrously translated to English settings and characters.

w Wolf Mankowitz, *play* Jean Anouilh *d* John Guillermin *ph* John Wilcox *m* Richard Addinsell *pd* Wilfrid Shingleton

Peter Sellers, Margaret Leighton, Dany Robin, John Fraser, Cyril Cusack, Prunella Scales

Waltz Time
GB 1933   82m   bw

Things are not what they seem to be at a Viennese masked ball. Pleasant but slight musical comedy vaguely derived from *Die Fledermaus.* Evelyn Laye, Fritz Schultz, Gina Malo, Jay Laurier, Frank Titterton. Written by A. P. Herbert; directed by William Thiele; for Gaumont.

Waltz Time
GB 1945   100m   bw

At a Viennese ball, an Empress poses as her masked friend to win a philandering count. Rather plodding operetta which also has an unattributed allegiance to *Die Fledermaus.* Carol Raye, Peter Graves, Patricia Medina, Thorley Walters, Richard Tauber, Harry Welchman, George Robey, Anne Ziegler, Webster Booth. Written by Montgomery Tully, Jack Whittingham, Henry C. James and Karl Rossier; directed by Paul Stein; for British National.

Waltzes from Vienna
GB 1933   80m   bw
GFD / Gaumont
US title: *Strauss's Great Waltz*

A romance of the Strausses.
There is very little music and very little Hitchcock in this extremely mild romantic comedy.

w Alma Reville, Guy Bolton, *play* Guy
Bolton *d* Alfred Hitchcock

Jessie Matthews, Esmond Knight, Frank
Vosper, Fay Compton, Edmund Gwenn,
Robert Hale, Hindle Edgar

The Wanderers
US 1979   117m   Technicolor

In 1963, teenage street gangs fight in the
Bronx. A bad boys' *American Graffiti*, all
violence and unpleasantness. Ken
Wahl, John Friedrich, Karen Allen, Tonie
Kalem, Linda Manz. Written by Rose and
Philip Kaufman, from the novel by Richard
Price; directed by Philip Kaufman; for PSO /
Polyc.

The Wandering Jew*
GB 1933   111m   bw
Gaumont / Twickenham (Julius Hagen)

A Jew is condemned to live forever, but dies
in the Spanish Inquisition.
Ambitious fantasy which comes off pretty well
for those in the mood, but was a curious
choice for a British studio at the time.

w H. Fowler Mear, *play* E. Temple Thurston
d Maurice Elvey

Conrad Veidt, Marie Ney, Basil Gill, Anne
Grey, Dennis Hoey, John Stuart, Peggy
Ashcroft, Francis L. Sullivan, Felix Ayler,
Abraham Sofaer

Wanted for Murder*
GB 1946   103m   bw
Marcel Hellman

A man, obsessed with the fact that his father
was the public hangman, becomes a murderer
himself.
Curiously stagey melodrama with intermittent
use of London backgrounds; an interesting
curiosity.

w Emeric Pressburger, Rodney Ackland,
Maurice Cowan *d* Lawrence Huntington
ph Max Greene *m* Mischa Spoliansky

Eric Portman, Dulcie Gray, Derek Farr,
Roland Culver, Stanley Holloway, Barbara
Everest, Bonar Colleano, Kathleen Harrison
'A pleasant and unpretentious thriller of the
second or third grade.'—*James Agee*

The War against Mrs Hadley*
US 1942   86m   bw
MGM (Irving Asher)

A Washington matron tries to ignore the war
and preserve her social life.
Efficient little propaganda piece with a middle-
aged heroine.

w George Oppenheimer *d* Harold S. Bucquet
ph Karl Freund *m* David Snell

Fay Bainter, Edward Arnold, Richard Ney,
Jean Rogers, Sara Allgood, Spring Byington,
Van Johnson, Isobel Elsom, Halliwell
Hobbes, Miles Mander, Frances Rafferty,
Connie Gilchrist
'If this film is, as some have labelled it, the
American *Mrs Miniver*, then some of us must
have grave illusions about our own (or the
English) way of life.'—*Bosley Crowther*

AAN: George Oppenheimer

War and Peace**
US / Italy 1956   208m   Technicolor
    Vistavision
Carlo Ponti / Dino de Laurentiis

A Russian family's adventures at the time of
Napoleon's invasion.
Despite miscasting and heavy dubbing, the
pictorial parts of this précis of a gargantuan
novel are powerful and exciting enough; the
human side drags a little.

w Bridget Boland, Robert Westerby, King
Vidor, Mario Camerini, Ennio de Concini, Ivo
Perelli, *novel* Leo Tolstoy *d King Vidor*,
(battle scenes) *Mario Soldati ph Jack Cardiff*,
(battle scenes) *Aldo Tonti m* Nino Rota
ad Mario Chiari

Audrey Hepburn, Henry Fonda, Mel Ferrer,
Herbert Lom, John Mills, Oscar Homolka,
Wilfrid Lawson, Vittorio Gassman, Anita
Ekberg, Helmut Dantine, Milly Vitale, Barry
Jones
'The film has no more warmth than pictures
in an art gallery.'—*Philip T. Hartung*

AAN: King Vidor; Jack Cardiff

War and Peace***
USSR 1967   507m   Sovcolor   'Scope
    70mm
Mosfilm

An immensely long Russian version with some
of the most magnificently spectacular battle
scenes ever filmed. A treat for the eyes
throughout, and perhaps less taxing than
reading the novel, which it follows
punctiliously.

w Sergei Bondarchuk, Vasili Solovyov
d Sergei Bondarchuk ph Anatoli Petritsky
m Vyacheslav Ovchinnikov

Lyudmila Savelyeva, Sergei Bondarchuk,
Vyacheslav Tikhonov
† The film was five years in production and
cost forty million dollars.

AA: best foreign film

The War between Men and Women
US 1972 105m Technicolor
Panavision
National General / Jalem / Llenroc / 4D
(Danny Arnold)

A half-blind cartoonist marries a divorcee and is troubled by her ex-husband.
Semi-serious comedy vaguely based on Thurber, but not so that you'd notice, apart from the blind hero; generally neither funny nor affecting.

w Mel Shavelson, Danny Arnold, based on the writings of James Thurber d Melville Shavelson ph Charles F. Wheeler m Marvin Hamlisch pd Stan Jolley

Jack Lemmon, Barbara Harris, Jason Robards Jnr, Herb Edelman, Lisa Gerritsen

War Hunt
US 1961 83m bw
TD Enterprises (Terry Sanders)

Korea 1953: a kill-crazy private is befriended by a war orphan but finally has to be shot.
Vaguely commendable but not very expert indictment of the realities of war.

w Stanford Whitmore d Denis Sanders ph Ted McCord m Bud Shank

John Saxon, Robert Redford, Sidney Pollack, Charles Aidman, Tommy Matsuda

The War Lord**
US 1965 121m Technicolor
Panavision
Universal / Court (Walter Seltzer)

An officer of the Duke of Normandy has trouble with Druids and the law of *droit de seigneur*.
Complex medieval melodrama with an air of fantasy about it; generally likeably strange, but the production should have been more stylized and fanciful.

w John Collier, Millard Kaufman, *play* The Lovers by Leslie Stevens d Franklin Schaffner ph Russell Metty m Jerome Moross ad Alexander Golitzen, Henry Bumstead

Charlton Heston, Richard Boone, Rosemary Forsyth, Maurice Evans, Guy Stockwell, Niall MacGinnis, Henry Wilcoxon, James Farentino

The War Lover
GB 1962 105m bw
Columbia / Arthur Hornblow Jnr

In 1943, a Flying Fortress commander based in East Anglia has the wrong ideas about women and war.
Solemn character drama punctuated by aerial battles.

w Howard Koch, *novel* John Hersey d Philip Leacock ph Bob Huke m Richard Addinsell

Steve McQueen, Shirley Anne Field, Robert Wagner, Gary Cockrell, Michael Crawford

The War of the Worlds*
US 1952 85m Technicolor
Paramount / George Pal

Terrifying aliens invade Earth via the American midwest.
Spectacular battle scenes are the mainstay of this violent fantasy, which goes to pieces once the cardboard characters open their mouths.

w Barre Lyndon, *novel* H. G. Wells d Byron Haskin ph George Barnes ad Hal Pereira, Albert Nozaki

Gene Barry, Ann Robinson, Les Tremayne, Bob Cornthwaite, Sandra Giglio

The War Wagon**
US 1967 99m Technicolor Panavision
Universal / Batjac (Marvin Schwartz)

Two cowboys and an Indian plan to ambush the gold wagon of a crooked mining contractor.
Exhilarating but simply-plotted action western with strong comedy elements and a cast of old reliables.

w Clair Huffaker, from his novel Badman d Burt Kennedy ph William H. Clothier m Dmitri Tiomkin

John Wayne, Kirk Douglas, Howard Keel, Robert Walker, Keenan Wynn, Bruce Cabot, Gene Evans, Bruce Dern
'It all works splendidly.'—MFB

The Ware Case*
GB 1938 79m bw
Ealing / Capad (S. C. Balcon)

A nobleman is suspected of murdering his wife's rich brother.
Courtroom melodrama twice filmed as a silent; stagey but reasonably compelling in its way.

w Robert Stevenson, Roland Pertwee, E. V. H. Emmett, *play* G. P. Bancroft d Robert Stevenson ph Ronald Neame m Ernest Irving

Clive Brook, Jane Baxter, Barry K. Barnes, C. V. France, Francis L. Sullivan, Frank Cellier, Edward Rigby, Peter Bull, Athene Seyler, Ernest Thesiger
† Previous versions had been made in 1917 (with Matheson Lang) and 1930 (with Stewart Rome).

Warlock*
US 1959 123m De Luxe Cinemascope
TCF (Edward Dmytryk)

The cowardly citizens of a small western town hire a gunman as their unofficial marshal. Overlong, talkative and somewhat pretentious star western with good sequences.

w Robert Alan Aurthur, *novel* Oakley Hall d Edward Dmytryk *ph* Joe MacDonald *m* Leigh Harline

Henry Fonda, Richard Widmark, Anthony Quinn, Dorothy Malone, Dolores Michaels, Wallace Ford, Tom Drake, Richard Arlen, Regis Toomey, Don Beddoe, De Forrest Kelley

Warlords of Atlantis
GB 1978   96m   Technicolor
EMI / John Dark, Kevin Connor

Victorian sea scientists discover a lost land under the Mediterranean.
Predictable compote of monsters and unwearable costumes, without a trace of wit in the script. For infants only.

w Brian Hayles d Kevin Connor *ph* Alan Hume *m* Mike Vickers *pd* Elliot Scott

Doug McClure, Peter Gilmore, Shane Rimmer, Lea Brodie, Michael Gothard

A Warm December
GB / US 1972   101m   Technicolor
First Artists / Verdon (Melville Tucker)

A widowed American doctor in London falls for a mysterious African girl who turns out to be the dying niece of a diplomat.
Weird mishmash of *Love Story, Brief Encounter* and *Dark Victory*, getting the worst of all worlds.

w Lawrence Roman d Sidney Poitier *ph Paul Beeson* m Coleridge-Taylor Parkinson

Sidney Poitier, Esther Anderson, George Baker, Johnny Sekka, Earl Cameron

Warning Shot*
US 1966   100m   Technicolor
Paramount / Bob Banner (Buzz Kulik)

While looking for a psychopathic killer, a cop shoots dead a man who draws a gun on him. But the dead man's gun cannot be found, and the officer is suspended . . .
Watchable mystery decked out with guest stars; possibly intended as a TV movie.

w Mann Rubin, *novel* 711—Officer Needs Help by Whit Masterson d Buzz Kulik *ph* Joseph Biroc *m* Jerry Goldsmith

David Janssen, Lillian Gish, Ed Begley, Keenan Wynn, Sam Wanamaker, Eleanor Parker, Stefanie Powers, Walter Pidgeon, George Sanders, George Grizzard, Steve Allen, Carroll O'Connor, Joan Collins

Warpath
US 1951   93m   Technicolor
Paramount (Nat Holt)

An ex-army captain tracks down the outlaws who murdered his girl.
Goodish standard western.

w Frank Gruber d Byron Haskin *ph* Ray Rennahan *m* Paul Sawtell

Edmond O'Brien, Dean Jagger, Forrest Tucker, Harry Carey Jnr, Wallace Ford, Polly Bergen

Warn that Man
GB 1943   82m   bw

A fake nobleman is used in a plot to kidnap the prime minister. Lively comedy spy stuff with a hard-working cast. Gordon Harker, Raymond Lovell, Finlay Currie, Philip Friend, Jean Kent, Frederick Cooper. Written by Vernon Sylvaine and Lawrence Huntington, from the play by Vernon Sylvaine; directed by Lawrence Huntington; for ABPC.

Warning to Wantons
GB 1948   104m   bw

A nobleman takes in a flirtatious girl and finds she causes trouble for him and his family. Interminable comedy-drama made even duller by the Independent Frame production method, which cut cos's but restricted movement. Harold Warrender, Anne Vernon, David Tomlinson, Sonia Holm, Marie Burke, Judy Kelly. Written by Donald B. Wilson and James Laver, from the novel by Mary Mitchell; directed by Donald B. Wilson; for Aquila / GFD.

The Warriors
US 1979   94m   Movielab
Paramount (Laurence Gordon)

A New York street gang runs into trouble when making a cross-city journey.
A sick exploitation movie about urban violence, poorly made into the bargain.

w David Shaber, Walter Hill, *novel* Sol Yurick d Walter Hill *ph* Andrew Laszlo *m* Barry de Vorzon

Michael Beck, James Remar, Thomas Waites, Dorsey Wright, Brian Tyler, David Harris

Washington Masquerade
US 1932   92m   bw

A high-minded senator is corrupted by a worthless girl. Solid star melodrama. Lionel Barrymore, Karen Morley, Nils Asther, C. Henry Gordon, William Collier Snr. Written by John Meehan and Samuel Blythe, from the

play *The Claw* by Henri Bernstein; directed by
Charles Brabin; for MGM. (GB title: *Mad
Masquerade*.)

Washington Story
US 1952   82m   bw
MGM (Dore Schary)
GB title: *Target for Scandal*

A lady reporter goes to Washington to expose
corruption, but falls for an honest
congressman.
Standard flagwaver which takes itself a shade
too seriously.

wd Robert Pirosh *ph* John Alton *m* Conrad
Salinger

Van Johnson, Patricia Neal, Louis Calhern,
Sidney Blackmer, Philip Ober, Patricia
Collinge, Elizabeth Patterson, Moroni Olsen

Watch on the Rhine**
US 1943   114m   bw
Warner (Hal B. Wallis)

A German refugee and his family are pursued
by Nazi agents in Washington.
Talky play doesn't make much of a film,
though the talk is good talk and the
performances outstanding; but it made a
prestige point or two for Hollywood.

w Dashiell Hammett, *play* Lillian Hellman
d Herman Shumlin *ph* Merritt Gerstad, Hal
Mohr *m* Max Steiner

Paul Lukas, Bette Davis, Lucile Watson,
George Coulouris, Donald Woods, Geraldine
Fitzgerald, Beulah Bondi, Henry Daniell

AA: Paul Lukas
AAN: best picture; script; Lucile Watson

The Watchmaker of St Paul*
France 1973   105m   Eastmancolor
Lira (Raymond Danon)
original title: *L'Horlorgier de St Paul*

A watchmaker's tranquil life is shattered when
he learns that his son is wanted for murder.
Solid character drama with careful writing and
acting.

w Jean Aurenche, Pierre Bost, Bertrand
Tavernier, *novel* L'Horloger D'Everton by
Georges Simenon *d* Bertrand Tavernier
ph Pierre William Glenn *m* Philippe Sarde

Philippe Noiret, Jean Rochefort, Sylvain
Rougerie, Christine Pascal

The Water Babies
GB / Poland 1978   92m   colour
Ariadne / Studio Miniatur Filmowych (Peter
Shaw)

An 1850 chimney sweep evades his pursuers
by jumping into a pool, where he becomes
involved in an underwater adventure.
The live action bookends are strangely
subdued, the animated middle totally
characterless and seeming to bear little
relation to the rest. A considerable
disappointment.

w Michael Robson, *novel* Charles Kingsley
d Lionel Jeffries *ph* Ted Scaife *m* Phil
Coulter

James Mason, Billie Whitelaw, Bernard
Cribbins, Joan Greenwood, David Tomlinson,
Tommy Pender

Water Birds see The Living Desert

Waterfront
GB 1950   80m   bw
GFD / Conqueror
US title: *Waterfront Women*

A drunken ship's fireman comes back to
Liverpool after many years and causes trouble.
Unintentionally funny melodrama which gives
the actors a lot of trouble.

w John Brophy, Paul Soskin, *novel* John
Brophy *d* Michael Anderson *ph* Harry
Waxman *md* Muir Mathieson

Robert Newton, Richard Burton, Kathleen
Harrison, Susan Shaw, Avis Scott, Kenneth
Griffith

Waterhole Three
US 1967   100m   Techniscope
Paramount

Sheriff, crooks and a gambler seek buried
loot.
Rather irritatingly immoral western with a
hero who defines rape as assault with a
friendly weapon; in between it tries hard for
the ballad style.

w Joseph Steck, Robert R. Young *d* William
Graham *ph* Robert Burks *m* Dave Grusin

James Coburn, Carroll O'Connor, Margaret
Blye, Claude Akins, Joan Blondell, Timothy
Carey

Waterloo*
Italy / USSR 1970   132m   Technicolor
Panavision
Columbia / DDL / Mosfilm (Dino de
Laurentiis)

Historical events leading up to the 1815 battle.
The battle forms the last hour of this historical
charade, and looks both exciting and splendid,
though confusion is not avoided. The rest is a
mixed blessing.

w H. A. L. Craig, Sergei Bondarchuk
d Sergei Bondarchuk ph Armando Nannuzzi
m Nino Rota *pd* Mario Garbuglia

Rod Steiger, Christopher Plummer, Orson
Welles, Jack Hawkins, Virginia McKenna,
Dan O'Herlihy, Rupert Davies, Ian Ogilvy,
Michael Wilding

Waterloo Bridge*
US 1931   72m   bw
Universal (Carl Laemmle Jnr)

An army officer marries a ballerina; when he
is reported missing his family ignore her and
she sinks into prostitution.
One for the ladies, who lapped it up.

w Tom Reed, Benn W. Levy, *play* Robert E.
Sherwood *d* James Whale *ph* Arthur Edeson

Mae Clarke, Kent Douglass, Doris Lloyd,
Ethel Griffies, Enid Bennett, Frederick Kerr,
Bette Davis

Waterloo Bridge**
US 1940   103m   bw
MGM (Sidney Franklin)

Lush, all-stops-out remake of the above; for
yet another version see *Gaby*.

w S. N. Behrman, Hans Rameau, George
Froeschel *d* Mervyn Le Roy *ph Joseph
Ruttenberg m* Herbert Stothart

Vivien Leigh, Robert Taylor, Lucile Watson,
Virginia Field, Maria Ouspenskaya, C.
Aubrey Smith, Steffi Duna
'The director uses candlelight and rain more
effectively than he does the actors.'—*New
Yorker, 1977*

AAN: Joseph Ruttenberg; Herbert Stothart

Waterloo Road
GB 1944   76m   bw
GFD / Gainsborough (Edward Black)

A soldier whose wife is enamoured of a petty
crook absents himself to settle matters.
What at the time seemed cheerful realism now
seems chronically forced, but amusing
moments can still be found.

w Sidney Gilliat, *story* Val Valentine
d Sidney Gilliat *ph* Jack Cox *md* Louis Levy

John Mills, Stewart Granger, Joy Shelton,
Alastair Sim, Beatrice Varley, Alison Leggatt,
Jean Kent
'The harsh rattle of trains over a viaduct,
the clamour of the street market, the wailing
of sirens and the crash of bombs are the
accompaniment of this wartime love story.'—
Richard Winnington

'Unpretentious, credible, continuously
entertaining and just the right length.'—
Richard Mallett, Punch

Watermelon Man
US 1970   100m   Technicolor
Columbia / Johanna (John B. Bennett)

A bigoted insurance salesman wakes up one
morning to find he has turned into a black
man.
Spasmodically funny racial comedy,
compromised by the impossibility of a black
man playing white even with heavy make-up.

w Herman Raucher *d* Melvin Van Peebles
ph W. Wallace Kelley *m* Melvin Van Peebles

Godfrey Cambridge, Estelle Parsons, Howard
Caine, Mantan Moreland

Watusi
US 1959   85m   Technicolor
MGM (Al Zimbalist)

Harry Quartermain retraces his father's
footsteps to King Solomon's Mines.
Skilful re-use of *King Solomon's Mines*
footage; acceptable Boys' Own Paper stuff.

w James Clavell *d* Kurt Neumann *ph* Harold
E. Wellman

George Montgomery, Taina Elg, David
Farrar, Rex Ingram, Dan Seymour

Waxworks*
Germany 1924   62m approx (24 fps)
   bw   silent
Neptun-Film
original title: *Das Wachsfigurenkabinett*

A young poet in a fairground waxwork
museum concocts stories about Haroun al
Raschid, Ivan the Terrible and Jack the
Ripper.
The form later became familiar in such horror
films as *Torture Garden* and *Tales from the
Crypt*, but here the emphasis is not on horror
but on grotesquerie, and indeed the idea is
somewhat more entertaining than the rather
plodding execution.

w Henrik Galeen *d Paul Leni ph* Helmar
Lerski *ad* Paul Leni, Ernst Stern, Alfred
Junge

William Dieterle, Emil Jannings, Conrad
Veidt, Werner Krauss

The Way Ahead***
GB 1944   115m   bw
GFD / Two Cities (John Sutro, Norman
   Walker)
US title: *Immortal Battalion*

Adventures of a platoon of raw recruits during
World War II.

Memorable semi-documentary originally intended as a training film; the warm humour of the early scenes, however, never leads quite naturally into the final action and tragedy.

w Eric Ambler, Peter Ustinov *d Carol Reed ph* Guy Green *m* William Alwyn

David Niven, Stanley Holloway, Raymond Huntley, *William Hartnell*, James Donald, John Laurie, Leslie Dwyer, Hugh Burden, Jimmy Hanley, Renée Asherson, Penelope Dudley Ward, Reginald Tate, Leo Genn, Mary Jerrold, Peter Ustinov

Way Back Home
US 1932 81m bw

Problems of a Maine preacher.
Unintentionally hilarious farrago of dark deeds in a small town, from a radio serial.
Phillips Lord, Bette Davis, Effie Palmer, Bennett Kilpack, Frank Albertson, Mrs Phillips Lord. Written by Jane Murfin; directed by William A. Seiter; for RKO.

Way Down East**
US 1920 110m approx (24 fps) bw with colour sequence silent
D. W. Griffith

A country girl is seduced; her baby dies; her shame is revealed; but a kindly farmer rescues her from drowning and marries her.
Old-fashioned tearjerker impeccably mounted and very typical of its director in its sentimental mood. The ice floe sequence is famous for its excitement and realism.

w Anthony Paul Kelly, Joseph R. Grismer, D. W. Griffith, *play* Lottie Blair Parker *d D. W. Griffith ph* Billy Bitzer, Henrik Sortov

Lillian Gish, Richard Barthelmess, Lowell Sherman, Creighton Hale

Way Down East
US 1935 85m bw
TCF (Winfield Sheehan)

Tedious and unwise remake.

w Howard Estabrook, William Hurlbut *d* Henry King

Rochelle Hudson, Henry Fonda, Slim Summerville, Edward Trevor, Margaret Hamilton, Andy Devine, Spring Byington, Russell Simpson, Sara Haden

Way for a Sailor
US 1930 83m bw
MGM

Adventures of a tough seafarer and a pet seal.
Thin vehicle for a declining star whose talkie voice was at odds with his image.

w Laurence Stallings, W. L. River, *novel* Albert Richard Wetjen *d* Sam Wood *ph* Percy Hilburn

John Gilbert, Wallace Beery, Leila Hyams, Jim Tully, Polly Moran, Doris Lloyd

Way of a Gaucho
US 1952 91m Technicolor
TCF (Philip Dunne)

An Argentine gaucho joins the militia and fights Indians.
Mildly interesting western-in-disguise.

w Philip Dunne, *novel* Herbert Childs *d* Jacques Tourneur *ph* Harry Jackson *m* Sol Kaplan

Rory Calhoun, Gene Tierney, Richard Boone, Hugh Marlowe, Everett Sloane, Enrique Chaico

The Way of All Flesh*
US 1928 94m (24 fps) bw silent
Paramount

A respectable man leaves his wife, goes to the dogs, and is too ashamed to come back.
Star character drama, most watchable now when it goes over the top.

d Victor Fleming

Emil Jannings

AA: Emil Jannings
AAN: best picture
† Remade 1940 with Akim Tamiroff.

Way Out West****
US 1937 66m bw
Hal Roach (Stan Laurel)

Laurel and Hardy come to Brushwood Gulch to deliver the deed to a gold mine.
Seven reels of perfect joy, with the comedians at their very best in brilliantly-timed routines, plus two song numbers as a bonus.

w Jack Jevne, Charles Rogers, James Parrott, Felix Adler d James Horne ph Art Lloyd, Walter Lundin *m* Marvin Hatley

Stan Laurel, Oliver Hardy, James Finlayson, Sharon Lynne, Rosina Lawrence

'Not only one of their most perfect films, it ranks with the best screen comedy anywhere.'—*David Robinson, 1962*

'The film is leisurely in the best sense; you adjust to a different rhythm and come out feeling relaxed as if you'd had a vacation.'— *New Yorker, 1980*

AAN: Marvin Hatley

The Way to Love
US 1933 80m bw
Paramount (Benjamin Glazer)

A would-be Paris tourist guide works as a pavement hawker and helps a showgirl evade her knife-thrower partner.

Thin star vehicle with a few pleasant moments.

w Gene Fowler, Benjamin Glazer *d* Norman Taurog *ph* Charles Lang *m* / *ly* Ralph Rainger, Leo Robin

Maurice Chevalier, Edward Everett Horton, Ann Dvorak, Arthur Pierson, Minna Gombell, Blanche Frederici, Douglass Dumbrille, John Miljan

The Way to the Gold

US 1957   94m   bw   Cinemascope
TCF (David Weisbart)

An ex-convict seeks hidden loot but is pursued by competitors.

Gloomy, self-pitying melodrama.

w Wendell Mayes, *novel* Wilber Steele *d* Robert D. Webb *ph* Leo Tover *m* Lionel Newman

Jeffrey Hunter, Sheree North, Barry Sullivan, Walter Brennan, Ruth Donnelly, Neville Brand

The Way to the Stars****

GB 1945   109m   bw
Two Cities (Anatole de Grunwald)
US title: *Johnny in the Clouds*

World War II as seen by the guests at a small hotel near an airfield.

Generally delightful comedy drama suffused with tragic atmosphere but with very few flying shots, one of the few films which instantly bring back the atmosphere of the war in Britain for anyone who was involved.

w Terence Rattigan, Anatole de Grunwald *poem* John Pudney *d* Anthony Asquith *ph* Derrick Williams *m* Nicholas Brodszky

John Mills, Rosamund John, Michael Redgrave, Douglass Montgomery, Basil Radford, Stanley Holloway, Joyce Carey, Renée Asherson, Felix Aylmer, Bonar Colleano, Trevor Howard, Jean Simmons

'Not for a long time have I seen a film so satisfying, so memorable, or so successful in evoking the precise mood and atmosphere of the recent past.'—*Richard Mallett, Punch*

'Humour, humanity, and not a sign of mawkishness . . . a classic opening sequence, with the camera wandering through an abandoned air base, peering in at each detail in the nissen huts, the sleeping quarters, the canteens, noting all the time a procession of objects each of which will have its own special significance in the action of the film.'—*Basil Wright, 1972*

Way Way Out

US 1966   105m   De Luxe   Cinemascope
TCF / Coldwater / Jerry Lewis (Malcolm Stuart)

In 1994 a weather expert on the moon has woman trouble.

Dismal sex farce with an unusual backdrop; painful to sit through.

w William Bowers, Laslo Vadnay *d* Gordon Douglas *ph* William H. Clothier *m* Lalo Schifrin

Jerry Lewis, Connie Stevens, Robert Morley, Dick Shawn, Anita Ekberg, Dennis Weaver, Howard Morris, Brian Keith

The Way We Were**

US 1973   118m   Eastmancolor
Panavision
Columbia / Rastar (Ray Stark)

The romance and marriage of an upper-crust young novelist and a Jewish bluestocking girl, from college to Hollywood in the thirties, forties and fifties.

Instant nostalgia for Americans, some fun and a lot of boredom for everybody is provided by this very patchy star vehicle which makes a particular mess of the McCarthy witch hunt sequence but has undeniable moments of vitality.

w Arthur Laurents, from his novel *d* Sydney Pollack *ph* Harry Stradling Jnr *m* Marvin Hamlisch

Barbra Streisand, Robert Redford, Patrick O'Neal, Viveca Lindfors, Bradford Dillman, Lois Chiles, Allyn Ann McLerie, Herb Edelman, Murray Hamilton

'Not one moment of the picture is anything but garbage under the gravy of false honesty.'—*Stanley Kauffmann*

AA: Marvin Hamlisch; title song (*m* Marvin Hamlisch, *ly* Alan and Marilyn Bergman)
AAN: Harry Stradling Jnr; Barbra Streisand

The Way West*

US 1967   122m   De Luxe   Panavision
UA / Harold Hecht

Hazards of a wagon train between Missouri and Oregon in 1843.

Semi-spectacular western which looks good but falls apart dramatically, especially in its insistence on a sub-plot about a most unlikely nymphet.

w Ben Maddow, Mitch Lindemann, *novel* A. B. Guthrie Jnr *d* Andrew V. McLaglen *ph* William H. Clothier *m* Bronislau Kaper

Kirk Douglas, Robert Mitchum, Richard Widmark, Lola Albright, Michael Witney, Sally Field, Stubby Kaye, Jack Elam

'A jerk's idea of an epic; big stars, big landscapes, bad jokes, folksy-heroic music to plug up the holes, and messy hang-ups.'— *Pauline Kael*

The Wayward Bus
US 1957 89m bw Cinemascope
TCF (Charles Brackett)

A landslide strands an assortment of bus passengers in a lonely farmhouse . . .
. . . but not the old dark house, unfortunately: this lot does nothing but talk, and the plot never really forms.

w Ivan Moffat, *novel* John Steinbeck d Victor Vicas ph Charles G. Clarke m Leigh Harline

Dan Dailey, Jayne Mansfield, Joan Collins, Rick Jason, Dolores Michaels, Larry Keating, Betty Lou Keim

We Are Not Alone*
US 1939 112m bw
Warner (Henry Blanke)

A man having an innocent affair is accused of murdering his wife.
Gloomy, well-acted drama with a rather uneasy English setting.

w James Hilton, Milton Krims, *novel* James Hilton d Edmund Goulding ph Tony Gaudio m Max Steiner

Paul Muni, Jane Bryan, Flora Robson, Raymond Severn, Una O'Connor, Henry Daniell, Montagu Love, James Stephenson, Cecil Kellaway

We Dive at Dawn
GB 1943 98m bw
GFD / Gainsborough (Edward Black)

World War II adventures of a British submarine disabled in the Baltic.
Fairly routine war suspenser.

w J. P. Williams, Val Valentine, Frank Launder d Anthony Asquith ph Jack Cox

John Mills, Eric Portman, Reginald Purdell, Niall MacGinnis, Joan Hopkins, Josephine Wilson, Jack Watling

We Faw Down
US 1928 20m bw silent

Stan and Ollie have an evening out, but their lies to their wives become apparent. Moderate star comedy, later elaborated in *Sons of the Desert*. Laurel and Hardy, Bess Flowers, Vivien Oakland. Written by H. M. Walker; directed by Leo McCarey; for Hal Roach.

We Joined the Navy
GB 1962 105m Eastmancolor
Cinemascope
Dial / Daniel M. Angel

A carefree naval commander and three cadets get involved in the affairs of a small Mediterranean country.
Desperate naval farce which sinks from script malnutrition in reel two.

w Arthur Dales, *novel* John Winton d Wendy Toye ph Otto Heller m Ron Grainer

Kenneth More, Lloyd Nolan, Mischa Auer, Joan O'Brien, Jeremy Lloyd, Dinsdale Landen, Derek Fowlds

We Live Again*
US 1934 85m bw
Samuel Goldwyn

A Russian prince is brought up in the country and falls in love with a servant girl whose life later takes a downward path.
Beautifully made but dramatically uninteresting version of a Russian classic.

w Preston Sturges, Maxwell Anderson, Leonard Praskins, *novel* Resurrection by Leo Tolstoy d Rouben Mamoulian ph Gregg Toland m Alfred Newman

Fredric March, Anna Sten, Jane Baxter, C. Aubrey Smith, Ethel Griffies, Jessie Ralph, Sam Jaffe

We Were Dancing
US 1942 93m bw
MGM (Robert Z. Leonard, Orville Dull)

A Polish princess elopes from her engagement party with a gigolo.
Leaden romantic comedy produced in high style.

w Claudine West, Hans Rameau, George Froeschel, partly based on the play Tonight at 8.30 by Noel Coward d Robert Z. Leonard ph Robert Planck m Bronislau Kaper

Norma Shearer, Melvyn Douglas, Gail Patrick, Lee Bowman, *Marjorie Main*, Reginald Owen, Alan Mowbray, Florence Bates, Sig Rumann, Dennis Hoey, Heather Thatcher, Connie Gilchrist

We Were Strangers*
US 1949 105m bw
Columbia / Horizon (Sam Spiegel)

Cuban rebels in the thirties plan to assassinate a politician and have to build a tunnel through a cemetery.
Well-made but very downbeat adventure story, too cheerless to be exciting.

w Peter Viertel, John Huston, *novel* Rough
Sketch by Robert Sylvester *d John Huston*
ph Russell Metty *m* Georges Antheil

John Garfield, Jennifer Jones, Pedro
Armendariz, Gilbert Roland, Wally Cassell,
Ramon Novarro, David Bond, Jose Perez

'There is so much about this film I cannot
swallow—the implausibilities of detail, the
convention of broken accents, the literary
conversaziones, the naïve doctrines of
revolution . . . [but] it continues to haunt the
mind and has therefore had its say.'—*Richard
Winnington*

The Weaker Sex
GB 1948   84m   bw

Day-to-day problems of a well-to-do war
widow. Mild suburban comedy which sparkled
more on stage, with such curtain lines as:
'Quick, the fishmonger's got fish!' Ursula
Jeans, Cecil Parker, Joan Hopkins, Derek
Bond, Lana Morris, Thora Hird, John Stone.
Written by Esther McCracken and Paul
Soskin, from the play *No Medals* by Esther
McCracken; directed by Roy Baker; for Paul
Soskin / Two Cities.

The Weapon
GB 1956   81m   bw   Superscope 235
Penclean (Frank Bevis)

A boy finds a loaded revolver on a bomb site
and mistakenly thinks he has killed someone
with it.
Standard suspenser with a cast worthy of
something more interesting.

w Fred Freiburger *d* Val Guest *ph* Reg
Wyer *m* James Stevens

Lizabeth Scott, Steve Cochran, George Cole,
Herbert Marshall, Nicole Maurey, Jon
Whiteley, Laurence Naismith

The Web*
US 1947   87m   bw
U-I

A financier hires a young lawyer as his
bodyguard and lures him into committing
murder.
Modestly well staged and glossy thriller.

w William Bowers, Bertram Millhauser
d Michael Gordon *ph* Irving Glassberg
m Hans Salter

Edmond O'Brien, Vincent Price, Ella Raines,
William Bendix

The Webster Boy
GB 1961   83m   bw
Emmet Dalton
US title: *Middle of Nowhere*

A teenager suffers at the hands of a sadistic
schoolmaster.
Curious, totally unbelievable melodrama.

w Ted Allen *d* Don Chaffey *ph* Gerald
Gibbs *m* Wilfrid Joseph

Richard O'Sullivan, John Cassavetes, David
Farrar, Elizabeth Sellars, Niall MacGinnis

A Wedding*
US 1978   125m   De Luxe
TCF / Lion's Gate (Thommy Thompson,
   Robert Altman)

Two families converge for a fashionable
wedding, but the day is beset by calamities.
Wide-ranging satirical comedy which despite
excellent moments goes on far too long, is
rather too black, and is sabotaged by the
director's *penchant* for having fourteen people
talking at the same time. An exhausting
experience.

w John Considine, Patricia Resnick, Allan
Nicholls, Robert Altman *d* Robert Altman
ph Charles Rosher *md* Tom Walls

Carol Burnett, Paul Dooley, Amy Stryker,
Mia Farrow, Peggy Ann Garner, Lillian Gish,
Nina Van Pallandt, Vittorio Gassman,
Howard Duff, Desi Arnaz Jnr, Dina Merrill,
Geraldine Chaplin, Viveca Lindfors, Lauren
Hutton, John Cromwell

The Wedding March**
US 1928   196m approx (24 fps)   bw
   silent
Paramount / Celebrity

A Habsburg prince loves a poor girl but is
forced to marry a crippled princess, who dies;
he is then murdered by the poor girl's enraged
defender.
A marathon dose of Stroheim's favourite
subject, sex, with some violence and a few
fetishes thrown in. Full of fascinating touches,
but desperately overlong, it was originally
released in two parts, but failed to draw.

w Harry Carr, Erich Von Stroheim *d* Erich
Von Stroheim *ph* Hal Mohr, Ben Reynolds
ad Erich Von Stroheim, Richard Day

Erich Von Stroheim, Fay Wray, Zasu Pitts,
Matthew Betz, Maude George, Cesare
Gravina, George Fawcett

'A pitilessly authentic portrait of decadent
Imperialist Austria.'—*Georges Sadoul*
'The slowness, heaviness, mindlessness of
this temple of unnaturalness through which
man passes as through a forest of clichés defied
description.'—*John Simon, 1967*
† In 1975 there was published a pictorial
record, *The Complete Wedding March*, by
Herman G. Weinberg.

The Wedding Night*
US 1935 83m bw
Samuel Goldwyn

A Connecticut author causes tragedy when he takes an interest in the local Polish immigrant farmers and especially in the daughter of one of them.
Interesting and unusual but slightly tediously told drama.

w Edith Fitzgerald d King Vidor ph Gregg Toland m Alfred Newman

Gary Cooper, Anna Sten, Sig Rumann, Helen Vinson, Ralph Bellamy, Esther Dale

Wedding Present*
US 1936 81m bw
Paramount (B. P. Schulberg)

A pair of crack newspaper reporters take their jobs and themselves lightly.
Whimsical star comedy with some funny scenes.

w Joseph Anthony, *story* Paul Gallico d Richard Wallace ph Leon Shamroy

Cary Grant, Joan Bennett, George Bancroft, Conrad Nagel, Gene Lockhart, William Demarest, Edward Brophy

Wedding Rehearsal
GB 1932 84m bw
Ideal / Alexander Korda

A Guards officer foils his grandmother's plans to get him married by finding suitors for all the young ladies offered.
Frail comedy with unsure technique.

w Lajos Biro, Arthur Wimperis d Alexander Korda

Roland Young, George Grossmith, John Loder, Lady Tree, Wendy Barrie, Maurice Evans, Joan Gardner, Merle Oberon, Kate Cutler, Edmund Breon

Wee Willie Winkie**
US 1937 99m bw
TCF (Gene Markey)

A small girl becomes the mascot of a British regiment in India.
Vaguely based on a Kipling tale, this was the most expensive Temple vehicle and a first-rate family action picture with sentimental asides.

w Ernest Pascal, Julien Josephson, *story* Rudyard Kipling d John Ford ph Arthur Miller m Alfred Newman

Shirley Temple, Victor McLaglen, C. Aubrey Smith, June Lang, Michael Whalen, Cesar Romero, Constance Collier, Gavin Muir

Weekend at the Waldorf*
US 1945 130m bw
MGM (Arthur Hornblow Jnr)

Four stories about guests at New York's largest hotel.
Disguised version of *Grand Hotel,* with the same stories twisted; the talent at hand, however, is serviceable rather than inspiring.

w Sam and Bella Spewack d Robert Z. Leonard ph Robert Planck md Johnny Green

Ginger Rogers, Walter Pidgeon, Van Johnson, Lana Turner, Robert Benchley, Edward Arnold, Constance Collier, Leon Ames, Warner Anderson, Phyllis Thaxter, Keenan Wynn, Porter Hall, Samuel S. Hinds, George Zucco, Xavier Cugat

Weekend in Havana
US 1941 80m Technicolor
TCF (William Le Baron)

A shopgirl in Havana falls for a shipping executive.
Routine Fox musical showcasing familiar talents: adequate wartime escapist fare.

w Karl Tunberg, Darrell Ware d Walter Lang ph Ernest Palmer md Alfred Newman

Alice Faye, John Payne, Carmen Miranda, Cesar Romero, Cobina Wright Jnr, George Barbier, Sheldon Leonard, Leonid Kinskey

Weekend with Father
US 1951 83m bw
U-I (Ted Richmond)

A widow and a widower fall in love when taking their respective children to a summer camp.
Mechanical comedy of upsets and embarrassments.

w Joseph Hoffman d Douglas Sirk ph Clifford Stine m Frank Skinner

Van Heflin, Patricia Neal, Gigi Perreau, Virginia Field, Richard Denning

Weird Woman
US 1944 64m bw

A professor brings home from the South Seas a wife who seems to bring murder in her wake.
Stiff and stilted thriller from an interesting original; one of the disappointing *Inner Sanctum* series. Lon Chaney, Evelyn Ankers, Anne Gwynne, Ralph Morgan, Elizabeth Risdon. Written by Brenda Weisberg, from the novel *Conjure Wife* by Fritz Leiber; directed by Reginald Le Borg; for Universal.

Welcome Danger*
US 1929   110m   bw
Harold Lloyd

The meek son of a police chief gets involved in a tong war.

Moderate early talkie comedy showing the star in some trouble with pace and dialogue.

w Clyde Bruckman, Lex Neal, Felix Adler, Paul Gerard Smith d Clyde Bruckman
ph Walter Lundin, Henry Kohler

Harold Lloyd, Barbara Kent, Noah Young, Charles Middleton

Welcome Home Soldier Boys
US 1972   92m   De Luxe

Four war veterans go home and start a wave of violence. Clumsily brutal anti-war tract which merely repels. Joe Don Baker, Paul Koslo, Alan Vint, Billy Green Bush. Written by Guerdon Trueblood; directed by Richard Crompton; for TCF.

Welcome Mr Washington
GB 1944   90m   bw

A US sergeant in an English village falls for a local lady. Mild plea for harmony between allies; rather embarrassing to watch even at the time. Barbara Mullen. Donald Stewart, Peggy Cummins, Graham Moffatt, Martita Hunt. Written by Jack Whittingham, from a novel by Noel Streatfeild; directed by Leslie Hiscott; for British National / Shaftesbury.

Welcome Stranger
US 1947   107m   bw
Paramount (Sol C. Siegel)

A genial young doctor fills in for a crusty old one on vacation in a small town.

Formula sentimental comedy, one of several reuniting the stars of Going My Way.

w Arthur Sheekman d Elliott Nugent
ph Lionel Lindon m Robert Emmett Dolan

Bing Crosby, Barry Fitzgerald, Joan Caulfield, Wanda Hendrix, Frank Faylen, Elizabeth Patterson, Robert Shayne, Percy Kilbride

Welcome to Hard Times*
US 1967   103m   Metrocolor
MGM / Max E. Youngstein, David Carr
GB title: Killer on a Horse

A small western town arms itself against a mysterious bandit.

Curiously likeable, almost symbolic suspense western which has a good start and middle but not much idea how to end.

wd Burt Kennedy, novel E. L. Doctorow
ph Harry Stradling Jnr m Harry Sukman

Henry Fonda, Janice Rule, Keenan Wynn, Janis Paige, John Anderson, Warren Oates, Fay Spain, Edgar Buchanan, Aldo Ray, Lon Chaney Jnr, Elisha Cook Jnr

Welcome to LA*
US 1976   106m   De Luxe
Lion's Gate / Robert Altman

A young composer in Los Angeles has a varied sex life.

Fragmentary, vaguely mystical, momentarily interesting, frequently confusing slice of life as seen through misty glasses.

wd Alan Rudolph ph Dave Myers m Richard Baskin

Keith Carradine, Sally Kellerman, Geraldine Chaplin, Harvey Keitel, Lauren Hutton, Viveca Lindfors, Sissy Spacek, Denver Pyle

'The supposedly free-form, improvisational dynamics of an Altman movie have here become a strictly choreographed ballet.'— Richard Combs, MFB

Welcome to the Club
GB 1970   88m   bw
Welcome (Sam Lomberg)

Hiroshima 1945; an American Quaker sergeant upsets military protocol.
Pale satirical comedy shot in Copenhagen.

w Clement Biddle Wood, from his novel
d Walter Shenson ph Mikael Salomon
m Ken Thomas

Brian Foley, Jack Warden, Lee Meredith, Andy Jarrett

The Well*
US 1951   85m   bw
Cardinal / Harry M. Popkin (Clarence Greene, Leo Popkin)

A black child falls down a well, and the town unites to save her.
Forceful high-pitched melodrama, cut to a do-gooder pattern which became very familiar.

w Russel Rouse, Clarence Greene d Leo Popkin, Russel Rouse ph Ernest Laszlo
m Dmitri Tiomkin

Richard Rober, Henry Morgan, Barry Kelley, Christine Larson

AAN: script

The Well Groomed Bride*
US 1946   75m   bw
Paramount (Fred Kohlmar)

A naval officer searches San Francisco for a magnum of champagne with which to launch a ship.
Thin but cheerful star comedy.

w Claude Binyon, Robert Russell *d* Sidney Lanfield *ph* John F. Seitz *m* Roy Webb

Ray Milland, Olivia de Havilland, Sonny Tufts, James Gleason, Constance Dowling, Percy Kilbride, Jean Heather

We'll Meet Again
GB 1942 84m bw

A girl singer suffers while her boy friend loves another. Unassuming star vehicle for the Forces' Sweetheart. Vera Lynn, Geraldo, Patricia Roc, Ronald Ward, Donald Gray, Frederick Leister. Written by James Seymour and Howard Thomas; directed by Phil Brandon; for Columbia.

Wells Fargo*
US 1937 115m bw
Paramount (Frank Lloyd)

How the express delivery service was built up. Large-scale, entertaining western with overmuch emphasis on domestic issues.

w Paul Schofield, Gerald Geraghty, John Boland, *story* Stuart N. Lake *d* Frank Lloyd *ph* Theodor Sparkuhl *m* Victor Young

Joel McCrea, Bob Burns, Frances Dee, Lloyd Nolan, Henry O'Neill, Mary Nash, Ralph Morgan, John Mack Brown, Porter Hall, Clarence Kolb

Went the Day Well?**
GB 1942 92m bw
Ealing (S. C. Balcon)
US title: *Forty-eight Hours*

Villagers resist when German paratroopers invade an English village and the squire proves to be a quisling.
Could-it-happen melodrama which made excellent wartime propaganda; generally well staged.

w Angus MacPhail, John Dighton, Diana Morgan, *story* Graham Greene *d Alberto Cavalcanti ph* Willie Cooper *m* William Walton

Leslie Banks, Elizabeth Allen, Frank Lawton, Basil Sydney, Valerie Taylor, Mervyn Johns, Edward Rigby, Marie Lohr, C. V. France, David Farrar

We're Going to Be Rich
US 1938 80m bw

In the South African goldfields in 1880, a singer leaves her worthless husband for a publican. First American attempt to take over Our Gracie; it didn't work, but the damage was done. Gracie Fields, Victor McLaglen, Brian Donlevy, Coral Browne, Gus

McNaughton. Written by Monty Banks, Rohama Siegel and Sam Hellman; directed by Monty Banks; for TCF.

We're No Angels*
US 1954 106m Technicolor Vistavision
Paramount (Pat Duggan)

Three escaped Devil's Island convicts help a downtrodden storekeeper and his family to outwit a scheming relative.
Whimsical, overstretched period comedy suffering from miscasting but with some pleasantries along the way.

w Ranald MacDougall, *play* La Cuisine des Anges by Albert Husson *d* Michael Curtiz *ph* Loyal Griggs *m* Frederick Hollander

Humphrey Bogart, *Peter Ustinov*, Aldo Ray, Joan Bennett, Basil Rathbone, Leo G. Carroll, John Smith

We're Not Dressing*
US 1934 77m bw
Paramount (Benjamin Glazer)

A spoiled heiress shipwrecked on a Pacific island is tamed by an easy-going sailor.
Pleasant, madly dated, light-hearted variation on a much-filmed play, resolving itself into a series of comic turns.

w Horace Jackson, Francis Martin, George Marion Jnr, *play* The Admirable Crichton by J. M. Barrie *d* Norman Taurog *ph* Charles Lang *songs* Harry Revel, Mack Gordon

Bing Crosby, Carole Lombard, George Burns, Gracie Allen, Leon Errol, Ethel Merman, Jay Henry, Ray Milland

We're Not Married*
US 1952 85m bw
TCF (Nunnally Johnson)

Six couples find that they were never legally married.
Amiable, smartly-played compendium of sketches on a familiar theme.

w Nunnally Johnson *d* Edmund Goulding *ph* Leo Tover *m* Cyril Mockridge

Ginger Rogers, Fred Allen, Victor Moore, Paul Douglas, Eve Arden, Marilyn Monroe, David Wayne, Louis Calhern, Zsa Zsa Gabor, Mitzi Gaynor, Eddie Bracken, James Gleason, Jane Darwell

The Werewolf
US 1956 80m bw
Columbia / Clover (Sam Katzman)

In a small mountain town, a victim of radiation exposure periodically becomes a werewolf and is hounded down.

Absurd and tedious thriller which wastes an interesting background.

w Robert E. Kent, James B. Gordon *d* Fred F. Sears *ph* Edwin Linden *m* Mischa Bakaleinikoff

Steven Ritch, Don McGowan, Joyce Holden

Werewolf of London*
US 1935   75m   bw
Universal (Stanley Bergerman)

Werewolves fight for a rare Tibetan flower with curative properties.
Patchy horror film which lurches from excellent suspense scenes to tedious chunks of superfluous dialogue. In many ways a milestone in the history of its kind.

w Robert Harris *d* Stuart Walker *ph* Charles Stumar *m* Karl Hajos

Henry Hull, Warner Oland, Valerie Hobson, Spring Byington, Lester Matthews, Zeffie Tilbury, Ethel Griffies

West Eleven
GB 1963   93m   bw
(ABP) Daniel M. Angel (Vivian Cox)

A young London drifter is offered £10,000 to commit murder.
Dingy but not very convincing 'realist' melodrama with a jazzy style which induces weariness.

w Keith Waterhouse, Willis Hall, *novel* The Furnished Room by Laura del Rivo *d* Michael Winner *ph* Otto Heller *m* Stanley Black, Acker Bilk

Alfred Lynch, Eric Portman, Kathleen Harrison, Diana Dors, Kathleen Breck, Freda Jackson, Finlay Currie, Harold Lang

West of Shanghai
US 1937   64m   bw

Fugitives in the Far East are saved by the self-sacrifice of a Chinese war lord.
Unpersuasive melodrama remade from *The Bad Man* (1930), heavily depending on a star performance. Boris Karloff, Beverly Roberts, Ricardo Cortez, Gordon Oliver, Vladimir Sokoloff. Written by Crane Wilbur; directed by John Farrow; for Warner.

West of Zanzibar
US 1928   70m at 24 fps   bw   silent

A paralysed magician turned ivory trader settles an old score. Corny star vehicle remade in 1932 as *Kongo*, with Walter Huston. Lon Chaney, Lionel Barrymore, Jacqueline Gadsden, Mary Nolan. Written by Waldemar Young and Elliott Clawson; directed by Tod Browning; for MGM.

West Point of the Air
US 1935   90m   bw
MGM (Monta Bell)

The army sergeant father of an air cadet has great hopes for him.
Routine sentimental flagwaver.

w James J. McGuinness, John Monk Saunders, Frank Wead, Arthur J. Beckhard *d* Richard Rosson *ph* Clyde de Vinna, Charles A. Marshall, Elmer Dyer

Wallace Beery, Robert Young, Maureen O'Sullivan, Lewis Stone, James Gleason, Rosalind Russell, Russell Hardie, Henry Wadsworth, Robert Taylor

West Point Story*
US 1950   107m   bw
Warner (Louis F. Edelman)
GB title: *Fine and Dandy*

A Broadway producer stages a show at the military academy.
Thin and rather tedious musical saved by its irrepressible star.

w John Monks Jnr, Charles Hoffman, Irving Wallace *d* Roy del Ruth *ph* Sid Hickox *md* Ray Heindorf *songs* Sammy Cahn, Jule Styne

James Cagney, Virginia Mayo, Doris Day, Gordon Macrae, Gene Nelson, Alan Hale Jnr, Roland Winters, Jerome Cowan

AAN: Ray Heindorf

West Side Story***
US 1961   155m   Technicolor
    Panavision 70
(UA) Mirisch / Seven Arts (Robert Wise)

The Romeo and Juliet story in a New York dockland setting.
The essentially theatrical conception of this entertainment is nullified by determinedly realistic settings which make much of it seem rather silly, but production values are fine and the song numbers electrifying.

w Ernest Lehman, *play* Arthur Laurents, after Shakespeare *d* Robert Wise, Jerome Robbins *ph* Daniel L. Fapp *m* Leonard Bernstein *ly* Stephen Sondheim *pd* Boris Leven

Natalie Wood (sung by Marni Nixon), Richard Beymer (sung by Jimmy Bryant), Russ Tamblyn, *Rita Moreno*, George Chakiris

AA: best picture; Robert Wise, Jerome Robbins; Daniel L. Fapp; Rita Moreno; George Chakiris
AAN: Ernest Lehman; musical direction (Saul Chaplin, Johnny Green, Sid Ramin, Irwin Kostal)

Westbound

US 1959 69m Warnercolor

A stagecoach manager is entrusted with Californian gold, which attracts assorted villains. Stalwart star western which served its purpose. Randolph Scott, Virginia Mayo, Karen Steele, Andrew Duggan, Michael Pate. Written by Berne Giler; directed by Budd Boetticher; for Warner.

Western Union**

US 1941 94m Technicolor
TCF (Harry Joe Brown)

Politicians and crooks hamper the laying of cross country cables.
First rate western with familiar excitements.

w Robert Carson, *novel* Zane Grey d Fritz Lang ph Edward Cronjager m David Buttolph

Randolph Scott, Robert Young, Dean Jagger, Virginia Gilmore, Slim Summerville, John Carradine, Chill Wills, Barton MacLane.

'It is impossible to know what clichés the director may have prevented, but it is enough and too much to see those he left in.'—*Otis Ferguson*

The Westerner**

US 1940 99m bw
Samuel Goldwyn

Judge Roy Bean comes to grief through his love for Lily Langtry.
Moody melodramatic western with comedy touches; generally entertaining, the villain more so than the hero.

w Jo Swerling, Niven Busch, *story* Stuart N. Lake d William Wyler ph Gregg Toland m Dmitri Tiomkin

Gary Cooper, *Walter Brennan*, Doris Davenport, Fred Stone, Paul Hurst, Chill Wills, Charles Halton, Forrest Tucker, Dana Andrews, Lilian Bond, Tom Tyler

AA: Walter Brennan
AAN: Stuart N. Lake

Westward Ho the Wagons

US 1956 85m Technicolor
Cinemascope
Walt Disney (Bill Walsh)

A wagon train defends itself against Indians.
Slow and simple-minded family western.

w Tom Blackburn d William Beaudine ph Charles Boyle m George Bruns

Fess Parker, Kathleen Crowley, Jeff York, David Stollery, Sebastian Cabot, George Reeves

Westward Passage

US 1932 73m bw
RKO (David O. Selznick)

A wealthy girl weds a poor novelist but wants the rich full life for their children.
Dogged romantic drama with only the casting of interest.

w Bradley and Humphrey King, *novel* Margaret Ayer Barnes d Robert Milton ph Lucien Andriot m Max Steiner

Ann Harding, Laurence Olivier, Zasu Pitts, Irving Pichel, Juliette Compton, Florence Roberts

Westward the Women*

US 1951 118m bw
MGM (Dore Schary)

In the 1850s an Indian scout leads 150 Chicago women to meet husbands in California.
Good-looking episodic western, apparently intended mainly to amuse but seldom rising to the occasion.

w Charles Schnee d William Wellman ph William Mellor m Jeff Alexander

Robert Taylor, Denise Darcel, John McIntire, Marilyn Erskine, Hope Emerson, Lenore Lonergan, Julie Bishop

Westworld**

US 1973 89m Metrocolor Panavision
MGM (Paul N. Lazarus III)

In a millionaire holiday resort which recreates the past, a western badman robot goes berserk and relentlessly attacks two visitors.
Unusual and amusing but under-produced melodrama with slipshod story development and continuity, atoned for by memorable moments and underlying excitement.

wd Michael Crichton ph Gene Polito m Fred Karlin ad Herman Blumenthal

Yul Brynner, Richard Benjamin, James Brolin, Norman Bartold, Alan Oppenheimer

The Wet Parade*

US 1932 122m bw
MGM (Hunt Stromberg)

A politician points to the corruption caused by prohibition.
Sociologically interesting melodrama.

w John Lee Mahin, *novel* Upton Sinclair d Victor Fleming ph George Barnes

Walter Huston, Myrna Loy, Neil Hamilton, Lewis Stone, Jimmy Durante, Wallace Ford, Dorothy Jordan, John Miljan, Robert Young

We've Never Been Licked
US 1943   103m   bw

A young American raised in Japan finds
himself on the wrong side after Pearl Harbor.
Shoddy flagwaver, low on talent and
inspiration. Richard Quine, Anne Gwynne,
Noah Beery Jnr, Harry Davenport, Martha
O'Driscoll, William Frawley, Robert
Mitchum. Written by Norman Reilly Raine
and Nick Grinde; directed by John Rawlins;
for Walter Wanger / Universal. (GB title:
Texas to Tokyo.)

What a Way to Go*
US 1963   111m   De Luxe   Cinemascope
TCF / APJAC / Orchard (Arthur P. Jacobs)

An immensely rich girl tells her psychiatrist
how all her husbands proved not only
successful but accident-prone.
Wild, mainly agreeable, star-and-gag-laden
black comedy which starts on too high a note
and fails to sustain.

w Betty Comden, Adolph Green d J. Lee-
Thompson ph Leon Shamroy md Nelson
Riddle ly Comden and Green songs Jule
Styne

Shirley Maclaine, Bob Cummings, Dick Van
Dyke, Robert Mitchum, Gene Kelly, Dean
Martin, Paul Newman, Reginald Gardiner,
Margaret Dumont

What a Woman
US 1943   90m   bw

An author's agent gets into romantic
escapades with her writers. Ho-hum romantic
comedy, quickly forgotten. Rosalind Russell,
Brian Aherne, Willard Parker, Ann Savage,
Alan Dinehart. Written by Therese Lewis and
Barry Trivers; directed by Irving Cummings;
for Columbia. (Aka: *The Beautiful Cheat.*)

What Became of Jack and Jill?
GB 1971   90m   De Luxe
Palomar / Amicus (Milton Subotsky)

A young man tries to hasten his grandmother's
death but she has the last laugh.
Feeble suspenser with a dim ending.

w Roger Marshall, *novel* The Ruthless Ones
by Laurence Moody d Bill Bain ph Gerry
Turpin m Carl Davis

Vanessa Howard, Paul Nicholas, Mona
Washbourne, Peter Copley, Peter Jeffrey

What Changed Charley Farthing
GB 1975   101m   Eastmancolor
Patina–Hidalgo (Tristam Cones)

A philandering sailor has adventures in Cuba.

Weirdly ineffective comedy actioner which
never gets started and should never have been
thought of.

w David Pursall, Jack Seddon, *novel* Mark
Hebdon d Sidney Hayers ph Graham Edgar
m Angela Arteaga

Doug McClure, Lionel Jeffries, Warren
Mitchell, Hayley Mills, Dilys Hamlett,
Fernando Sancho

What Did You Do in the War, Daddy?
US 1966   115m   De Luxe   Panavision
UA / Mirisch / Geoffrey (Owen Crump,
Blake Edwards)

In 1943, an Italian town surrenders readily to
the Americans providing its wine festival and
football match can take place.
Silly war comedy with insufficient jokes for its
wearisome length. The performances are
bright enough.

w William Peter Blatty d Blake Edwards
ph Philip Lathrop m Henry Mancini

James Coburn, Dick Shawn, Sergio Fantoni,
Giovanni Ralli, Aldo Ray, Harry Morgan,
Carroll O'Connor, Leon Askin

What Price Glory?*
US 1952   111m   Technicolor
TCF (Sol. C. Siegel)

In 1917 France Captain Flagg and Sergeant
Quirt spar for the same girl.
Stagey remake of the celebrated silent film and
play; watchable if not exactly inspired.

w Phoebe and Henry Ephron, *play* Maxwell
Anderson, Lawrence Stallings d John Ford
ph Joe MacDonald m Alfred Newman

James Cagney, Dan Dailey, Corinne Calvet,
William Demarest, Robert Wagner, Marisa
Pavan, James Gleason

What Price Hollywood?*
US 1932   87m   bw
RKO (Pandro S. Berman)

A waitress becomes a film star with the help of
a drunken director who later commits suicide.
Fairly trenchant early study of the mores of
the film city, later revamped as *A Star Is Born*.

w Jane Murfin, Ben Markson, Gene Fowler,
Rowland Brown, *story* Adela Rogers St John
d George Cukor ph Charles Rosher m Max
Steiner *montage* Slavko Vorkapitch

Constance Bennett, Lowell Sherman, Neil
Hamilton, Gregory Ratoff, Brooks Bendict,
Louise Beavers, Eddie Anderson
'Many of the scenes are like sketches for the
later versions, but this film has its own

interest, especially because of its glimpses into the studio life of the time.'—*New Yorker, 1977*

AAN: Adela Rogers St John

Whatever Happened to Aunt Alice?*
US 1969   101m   Metrocolor
Associates and Aldrich / Palomar

A genteel widow murders her housekeepers for their private incomes.
Ladylike shocker with some black humour and good performances.

w Theodore Apstein, *novel* The Forbidden Garden by Ursula Curtiss d Lee H. Katzin ph Joseph Biroc m Gerald Fried

Geraldine Page, Ruth Gordon, Rosemary Forsyth, Robert Fuller, Mildred Dunnock

Whatever Happened to Baby Jane?*
US 1962   132m   bw
Warner Seven Arts / Associates and Aldrich (Robert Aldrich)

In middle age, a demented ex-child star lives in an old Hollywood mansion with her invalid sister, and tension leads to murder.
Famous for marking the first time Hollywood's ageing first ladies stooped to horror, and followed by *Hush Hush Sweet Charlotte* and the other *Whatevers*, this dreary looking melodrama only occasionally grabs the attention and has enough plot for about half its length. The performances, however, are striking.

w Lukas Heller, *novel* Henry Farrell d Robert Aldrich ph Ernest Haller m Frank de Vol

Bette Davis, Joan Crawford, Victor Buono, Anna Lee
'It goes on and on, in a light much dimmer than necessary, and the climax, when it belatedly arrives, is a bungled, languid mingling of pursuers and pursued . . .'—*New Yorker*

AAN: Ernest Haller; Bette Davis; Victor Buono

What's Good for the Goose
GB 1969   104m   Eastmancolor
Tigon (Tony Tenser, Norman Wisdom)

An assistant bank manager falls for a girl hitch-hiker and tries to recover his youth.
Embarrassing attempt to build a sexy vehicle for a star whose sentimental mugging always appealed mainly to children.

w Norman Wisdom d Menahem Golan ph William Brayne m Reg Tilsley

Norman Wisdom, Sally Geeson, Sally Bazeley, Derek Francis, Terence Alexander

What's New Pussycat?
US / France 1965   108m   Technicolor
UA / Famous Artists (Charles K. Feldman)

A fashion editor is distracted by beautiful girls.
Zany sex comedy with many more misses than hits, a product of the wildly swinging sixties when it was thought that a big budget and stars making fools of themselves would automatically ensure a success.

w Woody Allen d Clive Donner ph Jean Badal m Burt Bacharach

Peter O'Toole, Peter Sellers, Woody Allen, Ursula Andress, Romy Schneider, Capucine, Paula Prentiss
'Unfortunately for all concerned, to make something enjoyably dirty a lot of taste is required.'—*John Simon*

AAN: title song (*m* Burt Bacharach, *ly* Hal David)

What's So Bad About Feeling Good?
US 1965   94m   Technicolor
Universal (George Seaton)

A 'happy virus' is carried into New York by a toucan, and affects the lives of various people.
Flimsy pretext for a comedy, further hampered by a less than sparkling script. The actors have their moments.

w George Seaton, Robert Pirosh d George Seaton ph Ernesto Caparros m Frank de Vol

George Peppard, Mary Tyler Moore, Dom De Luise, John McMartin, Susan St James, Don Stroud, Charles Lane

What's the Matter with Helen?*
US 1971   101m   De Luxe
Filmways / Raymax (George Edwards, James C. Pratt)

In 1934 Hollywood, two women run a dancing school for child stars; one of them is a killer.
More *Baby Jane* melodramatics, quite lively and with interesting period detail.

w Henry Farrell d Curtis Harrington ph Lucien Ballard m David Raksin pd Eugene Lourié

Debbie Reynolds, Shelley Winters, Micheal MacLiammoir, Dennis Weaver, Agnes Moorehead
'A cast of seasoned troupers cannot quite alter the impression that they are all working to revive a stiff.'—*Bruce Williamson*

What's Up, Doc?**
US 1972   94m   Technicolor
Warner / Saticoy (Peter Bogdanovich)

In San Francisco, an absent-minded young

musicologist is troubled by the attentions of a dotty girl who gets him involved with crooks and a series of accidents.

Madcap comedy, a pastiche of several thirties originals. Spectacular slapstick and willing players are somewhat let down by exhausted patches and a tame final reel.

w Buck Henry, David Newman, Robert Benton d Peter Bogdanovich ph Laszlo Kovacs m Artie Butler pd Polly Pratt

Barbra Streisand, Ryan O'Neal, Kenneth Mars, Austin Pendleton, Madeleine Kahn, Mabel Albertson, Sorrell Booke

'A comedy made by a man who has seen a lot of movies, knows all the mechanics, and has absolutely no sense of humour. Seeing it is like shaking hands with a joker holding a joy buzzer: the effect is both presumptuous and unpleasant.'—*Jay Cocks*

'It's all rather like a 19th-century imitation of Elizabethan blank verse drama.'—*Stanley Kauffmann*

'It freely borrows from the best screen comedy down the ages but has no discernible style of its own.'—*Michael Billington, Illustrated London News*

The Wheeler Dealers
US 1963   106m   Metrocolor   Panavision
MGM / Filmways (Martin Ransohoff)
GB title: *Separate Beds*

A Texas tycoon with a flair for the stock market sets Wall Street agog by manipulating a mysterious and non-existent new product. Fun for financiers, but barely worth following for the rest. A slick, loud, hollow show.

w G. J. W. Goodman, Ira Wallach d Arthur Hiller ph Charles Lang Jnr m Frank de Vol

James Garner, Lee Remick, Phil Harris, Chill Wills, Jim Backus, Louis Nye, John Astin

When a Man Loves
US 1927   83m at 24 fps   bw   silent with synchronized music

A hero escapes from a prison ship and gives his all for love of a worthless woman. Freely adapted version of *Manon Lescaut*, successful because of the real-life romance of the stars.

John Barrymore, Dolores Costello, Warner Oland, Stuart Holmes, Holmes Herbert. Written by Bess Meredyth; directed by Alan Crosland; for Warner.

When a Stranger Calls
US 1979   97m   colour

A policeman determinedly chases a baby-murdering maniac. Middling screamer extended from a short, *The Sitter*; a passive

midsection separates a suspenseful start and finish. Charles Durning, Tony Beckley, Carol Kane, Colleen Dewhurst, Rachel Roberts. Written by Steve Feke and Fred Walton; directed by Fred Walton; for Melvin Simon / UA.

When Dinosaurs Ruled the Earth
GB 1969   100m   Technicolor
Hammer (Aida Young)

In prehistoric times, a girl is swept out to sea by a cyclone and adopted by a dinosaur. Sequel to *One Million Years BC*, all very silly but tolerably well done.

wd Val Guest ph Dick Bush m Mario Nascimbene sp Jim Danforth

Victoria Vetri, Patrick Allen, Robin Hawdon, Patrick Holt, Imogen Hassall

When Eight Bells Toll*
GB 1971   94m   Eastmancolor
   Panavision
Winkast (Elliott Kastner)

A naval secret service agent investigates the pirating of gold bullion ships off the Scottish coast.

Acceptable kill-happy thriller: humourless James Bondery graced by splendid Scottish landscapes.

w Alistair MacLean, from his novel d Etienne Perier ph Arthur Ibbetson m Wally Stott

Anthony Hopkins, Robert Morley, Corin Redgrave, Jack Hawkins, Ferdy Mayne, Derek Bond, Nathalie Delon

When I Grow Up*
US 1951   90m   bw
Horizon (S. P. Eagle)

A boy about to run away changes his mind after reading his grandfather's diaries. Pleasant, sentimental family film with an unusual approach.

wd Michael Kanin ph Ernest Laszlo
m Jerome Moross

Bobby Driscoll, Robert Preston, Charley Grapewin, Martha Scott, Ralph Dumke

When in Rome
US 1952   78m   bw
MGM (Clarence Brown)

A gangster in Rome steals a priest's clothes and is accepted in his place.

Typically American religious comedy, nicely made but straying somewhat over the top when the gangster reforms and becomes a monk.

w Charles Schnee, Dorothy Kingsley, Robert Buckner *d* Clarence Brown *ph* William Daniels *m* Carmen Dragon

Van Johnson, Paul Douglas, Joseph Calleia, Carlo Rizzo, Tudor Owen, Aldo Silvani, Dono Nardi

When Knights Were Bold
GB 1929   80m at 24 fps   bw   silent

An incompetent heir dreams that he lives in medieval times. Naïve romp which pleased at the time. Nelson Keys, Miriam Seeger, Eric Bransby Williams. Written by Tim Whelan and Herbert Wilcox, from a play by Charles Marlow; directed by Tim Whelan; for Herbert Wilcox. (Remade in 1936 with Jack Buchanan, Fay Wray and Garry Marsh; for Max Schach.)

When Ladies Meet*
US 1933   73m   bw
RKO

A successful lady novelist falls in love with her married publisher.
Smartish comedy of manners which still has a sting.

w John Meehan, Leon Gordon, *play* Rachel Crothers *d* Harry Beaumont *ph* Ray June

Ann Harding, Robert Montgomery, *Myrna Loy, Alice Brady*, Frank Morgan, Margaret Burton, Luis Alberni

When Ladies Meet
US 1941   108m   bw
MGM (Robert Z. Leonard, Orville O. Dull)

Over-produced and very talkative remake of the above.

w S. K. Lauren, Anita Loos *d* Robert Z. Leonard *ph* Robert Planck *m* Bronislau Kaper

Joan Crawford, Robert Taylor, Greer Garson, Spring Byington, Herbert Marshall, Rafael Strom, Olaf Hytten

When My Baby Smiles at Me
US 1948   98m   Technicolor
TCF (George Jessel)

A vaudevillian goes on the skids but is saved by his wife.
Routine musical handling of a dreary drama previously filmed as *Dance of Life* (1929) and *Swing High Swing Low* (qv).

w Lamar Trotti, *play* Burlesque by George Manker Walters, Arthur Hopkins *d* Walter Lang *ph* Harry Jackson *md* Alfred Newman

Betty Grable, Dan Dailey, Jack Oakie, June Havoc, Richard Arlen, James Gleason, Jean Wallace

AAN: Alfred Newman; Dan Dailey

When Strangers Marry*
US 1944   67m   bw
Monogram
aka: *Betrayed*

A young bride in New York discovers that she may have married a murderer.
Much-praised second feature: a bit stodgy now, but still entertaining.

w Philip Yordan, Dennis Cooper *d* William Castle *ph* Ira Morgan *m* Dmitri Tiomkin

Dean Jagger, Kim Hunter, Robert Mitchum, Neil Hamilton, Lou Lubin, Milt Kibbee, Dewey Robinson

'The obviousness of the low budget is completely overcome by the solid craftsmanship of the direction, script, music, editing and performances.'—*Don Miller*
'Taking it as a whole I have seldom for years now seen one hour so energetically and sensibly used in a film.'—*James Agee*

When the Daltons Rode*
US 1940   80m   bw
Universal

Adventures of the Dalton Gang.
Good standard western with whitewashed bad men for heroes.

w Harold Shumate, Stuart Anthony, Lester Cole *d* George Marshall *ph* Hal Mohr *m* Frank Skinner

Randolph Scott, Kay Francis, Brian Donlevy, Andy Devine, George Bancroft, Stuart Erwin

When the Legends Die*
US 1972   105m   De Luxe
Sagoponack (Stuart Millar)

A young Indian boy, frustrated by life on the reservations, is helped by an old rodeo rider who becomes his guardian.
Dour modern western, rather stylishly done and an eloquent plea for freedom, but dramatically uncompelling.

w Robert Dozier, *novel* Hal Borland *d* Stuart Millar *ph* Richard Kline *m* Glenn Paxton

Richard Widmark, Frederic Forrest, Luana Anders, Vito Scotti

When Time Ran Out
US 1980   109m   Technicolor
Panavision
Warner / Irwin Allen

Inhabitants of a South Sea island are threatened by a volcano.
Incredibly inept disaster movie, with all clichés on hand in the characters of some downcast actors.

w Carl Foreman, Stirling Silliphant, *novel* The Day the World Ended by Max Morgan Witts and Gordon Thomas *d* James Goldstone *ph* Fred J. Koenekamp *m* Lalo Schifrin

Paul Newman, Jacqueline Bisset, William Holden, Edward Albert, Burgess Meredith, Valentina Cortesa, Red Buttons, Alex Carras, Ernest Borgnine, James Franciscus

'Disaster movies don't come any more disastrous than this.'—*Tom Milne, MFB*

When Tomorrow Comes••
US 1939   82m   bw
Universal (John M. Stahl)

A waitress falls for a concert pianist with a mad wife.

Fascinating star romantic drama, a successful follow-up to *Love Affair*; full of clichés, but impeccably set and acted. The stuff that Hollywood dreams were made of.

w Dwight Taylor, *story* James M. Cain *d John M. Stahl ph* John Mescall *m* Charles Previn

Charles Boyer, Irene Dunne, Barbara O'Neil, Nydia Westman, Onslow Stevens

† The same story was remade twice in 1956, as *Serenade* and *Interlude*, and in 1968 as *Interlude* (all qv).

When We Are Married••
GB 1942   98m   bw
British National (John Baxter)

In 1890s Yorkshire, three couples celebrating their silver wedding are told they were never legally married.

A very funny play smartly filmed with a superb cast of character actors.

w Austin Melford, Barbara K. Emery, *play J. B. Priestley d* Herbert Mason

Raymond Huntley, Marian Spencer, Lloyd Pearson, Olga Lindo, Ernest Butcher, Ethel Coleridge, Sydney Howard, Barry Morse, Lesley Brook, Marjorie Rhodes, Charles Victor, Cyril Smith, George Carney

When Willie Comes Marching Home•
US 1949   82m   bw
TCF (Fred Kohlmar)

During World War II, events suddenly transform a small-town air training instructor into a war hero.

Awkwardly paced comedy which could have been much funnier but does amuse in fits and starts.

w Mary Loos, Richard Sale *d* John Ford *ph* Leo Tover *m* Alfred Newman

Dan Dailey, Colleen Townshend, Corinne Calvet, William Demarest, Evelyn Varden, James Lydon, Mae Marsh, Lloyd Corrigan

AAN: original story (Sy Gomberg)

When Worlds Collide
US 1951   82m   Technicolor
Paramount (George Pal)

Another planet is found to be rushing inevitably towards earth, but before the collision a few people escape in a space ship. Stolid science fiction with a spectacular but not marvellous climax following seventy minutes of inept talk.

w Sidney Boehm, *novel* Philip Wylie, Edwin Balmer *d* Rudolph Maté *ph* John Seitz, W. Howard Greene *m* Leith Stevens

Richard Derr, Barbara Rush, Larry Keating, Peter Hanson, John Hoyt

AAN: John Seitz, W. Howard Greene

When You're in Love•
US 1937   110m   bw
Columbia (Everett Riskin)
GB title: *For You Alone*

A European opera singer takes on a husband in order to get into the United States.
Pleasing musical star vehicle with comedy touches.

wd Robert Riskin *ph* Joseph Walker *md* Alfred Newman

Grace Moore, Cary Grant, Aline MacMahon, Henry Stephenson, Thomas Mitchell, Catherine Doucet, Luis Alberni, Emma Dunn

Where Angels Go, Trouble Follows
US 1968   95m   Eastmancolor
Columbia / William Frye

Nuns from a convent school take pupils to a California youth rally, and learn a thing or two.
Peripatetic comedy, rather frantically assembled; a sequel to *The Trouble with Angels*.

w Blanche Hanalis *d* James Neilson *ph* Sam Leavitt *m* Lalo Schifrin

Rosalind Russell, Stella Stevens, Binnie Barnes, Mary Wickes, Milton Berle, Arthur Godfrey, Robert Taylor, Van Johnson, Susan St James

Where Danger Lives
US 1950   84m   bw
RKO (Irving Cummings Jnr)

A doctor falls in love with a murderous patient and is drawn into her schemes.

Standard *film noir* of its time, competent
enough in its depressing way.

w Charles Bennett *d* John Farrow
ph Nicholas Musuraca *m* Roy Webb

Faith Domergue, Robert Mitchum, Claude
Rains, Maureen O'Sullivan, Charles Kemper

Where Do We Go from Here?*
US 1945   77m   Technicolor
TCF (William Perlberg)

A writer stumbles on a genie who takes him
through periods of American history,
including a voyage with Christopher
Columbus.
Well-staged and rather funny charade with at
least one memorable song.

w Morrie Ryskind *d* Gregory Ratoff
ph Leon Shamroy *songs* Kurt Weill, Ira
Gershwin

Fred MacMurray, June Haver, Joan Leslie,
Gene Sheldon, Anthony Quinn, Carlos
Ramirez, Fortunio Bonanova, Alan Mowbray,
Herman Bing, Otto Preminger
   'Nine parts heavy facetiousness to one part
very good fun.'—*James Agee*

Where Does it Hurt?
US 1971   88m   colour
Josef Shaftel (Rod Amateau, William
   Schwarz)

Adventures of a profiteering hospital
administrator.
Dislikeable, plodding smut in the form of
black comedy.

wd Rod Amateau, *novel* The Operator by
Budd Robinson, Rod Amateau *ph* Brick
Marquard *m* Keith Allison

Peter Sellers, Jo Ann Pflug, Rick Lenz, Eve
Druce

Where Eagles Dare**
GB 1969   155m   Metrocolor
   Panavision 70
MGM / Winkast (Elliott Kastner)

During World War II, seven British
paratroopers land in the Bavarian Alps to
rescue a high-ranking officer from an
impregnable castle.
Archetypal schoolboy adventure, rather
unattractively photographed but containing a
sufficient variety of excitements.

w Alistair MacLean, from his novel *d* Brian
G. Hutton *ph* Arthur Ibbetson,
H. A. R. Thompson *m* Ron Goodwin

Richard Burton, Clint Eastwood, Mary Ure,
Patrick Wymark, Michael Hordern, Donald
Houston, Peter Barkworth, Robert Beatty

Where It's At
US 1969   106m   De Luxe
UA / Frank Ross

The owner of a Las Vegas gambling hotel tries
to make his son take an interest in the
business.
Flaccid comedy drama which belies its credits.

wd Garson Kanin *ph* Burnett Guffey
m Benny Olsen

David Janssen, Rosemary Forsyth, Robert
Drivas, Brenda Vaccaro

Where Love Has Gone*
US 1964   114m   Techniscope
Paramount / Embassy (Joseph E. Levine)

A middle-aged man is appalled to hear that his
teenage daughter has killed her mother's
lover.
Squalid, glossy pulp fiction lightly based on the
Lana Turner case, distinguished only by the
game performances of its leading ladies.

w John Michael Hayes, *novel* Harold Robbins
d Edward Dmytryk *ph* Joe MacDonald
m Walter Scharf

Susan Hayward, Bette Davis, Mike Connors,
Joey Heatherton, Jane Greer, George
Macready
   'A typical Robbins pastiche of newspaper
clippings liberally shellacked with sentiment
and glued with sex.'—*Newsweek*

AAN: title song (*m* James Van Heusen,
ly Sammy Cahn)

Where No Vultures Fly*
GB 1951   107m   Technicolor
Ealing (Leslie Norman)
US title: *Ivory Hunter*

Adventures of an East African game warden.
Pleasantly improving family film, nicely shot
on location; a sequel, *West of Zanzibar,* was
less impressive.

w W. P. Lipscomb, Ralph Smart, Leslie
Norman *d* Harry Watt *ph* Geoffrey
Unsworth *m* Alan Rawsthorne

Anthony Steele, Dinah Sheridan, Harold
Warrender, Meredith Edwards
   'These expeditional films are really
journalistic jobs. You get sent out to a country
by the studio, stay as long as you can without
getting fired, and a story generally crops
up.'—*Harry Watt*

Where the Boys Are
US 1960   99m   Metrocolor
   Cinemascope
MGM / Euterpe (Joe Pasternak)

Four college girls spend the Easter vacation near a Florida military post in search of conquests.
Mindless, frothy youth musical, quite smoothly done.

w George Wells, *novel* Glendon Swarthout
d Henry Levin *ph* Robert Bronner
m George Stoll

George Hamilton, Dolores Hart, Paula Prentiss, Jim Hutton, Yvette Mimieux, Connie Francis, Frank Gorshin, Chill Wills, Barbara Nichols

Where the Sidewalk Ends
US 1950 95m bw
TCF (Otto Preminger)

A tough policeman accidentally kills a suspect and tries to implicate a gang leader.
Gloomy *policier* with curious moral values.

w Rex Connor (Ben Hecht), *novel* William L. Stuart *d* Otto Preminger *ph* Joseph La Shelle *m* Cyril Mockridge

Dana Andrews, Gene Tierney, Gary Merrill, Bert Freed, Tom Tully, Karl Malden, Ruth Donnelly, Craig Stevens, Robert Simon

Where the Spies Are
GB 1965 113m Metrocolor Panavision
MGM / Val Guest

A country doctor is bribed to become a spy by the promise of a car he greatly covets.
Patchy spy adventure which never settles into a comfortable style but provides occasional entertainment along its bumpy way.

w Wolf Mankowitz, Val Guest, *novel* Passport to Oblivion by James Leasor
d Val Guest *ph* Arthur Grant *m* Mario Nascimbene

David Niven, Françoise Dorleac, Nigel Davenport, John Le Mesurier, Ronald Radd, Cyril Cusack, Eric Pohlmann

Where There's a Will*
GB 1936 81m bw
Gainsborough (Edward Black, Sidney Gilliat)

A seedy education expert sponges on his rich relations but redeems himself by rounding up gangsters at a Christmas party.
Rather slapdash star comedy with very good scenes along the way.

w Will Hay, Robert Edmunds, Ralph Spence
d William Beaudine *ph* Charles Van Enger
md Louis Levy

Will Hay, Hartley Power, Gibb McLaughlin, Graham Moffatt, Norma Varden, Gina Malo

Where There's Life
US 1947 75m bw
Paramount

A timid New Yorker turns out to be heir to the throne of a Ruritanian country, and is harassed by spies of both sides.
Mild star comedy with slow patches.

w Allen Boretz, Melville Shavelson *d* Sidney Lanfield *ph* Charles Lang Jnr *m* Irwin Talbot

Bob Hope, Signe Hasso, William Bendix, George Coulouris

Where Were You When the Lights Went Out?*
US 1968 94m Metrocolor Panavision
MGM (Everett Freeman, Martin Melcher)

New York's famous electrical blackout in 1965 has its effect on the life of a musical comedy star.
Cheerful sex farce with intriguing beginnings; the later confinement to one set is just a bit harmful.

w Everett Freeman, Karl Tunberg, *play* Claude Magnier *d* Hy Averback
ph Ellsworth Fredericks *m* Dave Grusin

Doris Day, Terry-Thomas, Patrick O'Neal, Robert Morse, Lola Albright, Jim Backus, Ben Blue

Where's Charley?*
GB 1952 97m Technicolor
Warner

An Oxford undergraduate impersonates the rich aunt of his best friend.
Slow and rather stately musical version of the famous farce *Charley's Aunt*, unsatisfactorily shot on a mixture of poor sets and sunlit Oxford locations; worth cherishing for the ebullient performance of its over-age star.

w John Monks Jnr, *play* Brandon Thomas (via stage musical, *book* George Abbott *m* Frank Loesser) *d* David Butler *ph* Erwin Hillier
ch Michael Kidd

Ray Bolger, Robert Shackleton, Mary Germaine, Allyn McLerie, Margaretta Scott, Horace Cooper

Where's Jack?*
GB 1968 119m Eastmancolor
Paramount / Oakhurst (Stanley Baker)

In 18th-century London Jack Sheppard becomes a romantic highwayman at the behest of underworld leader Jonathan Wild.
Deliberately unromantic, squalid and 'realistic' period piece which takes no hold on the fancy despite the considerable care which was obviously taken in all departments.

w Rafe and David Newhouse d James Clavell ph John Wilcox m Elmer Bernstein pd Cedric Dawe

Tommy Steele, Stanley Baker, Fiona Lewis, Alan Badel, Dudley Foster, Sue Lloyd, Noel Purcell

Where's Poppa?*
US 1970 82m De Luxe
Jerry Tokovsky / Martin Worth

A Jewish lawyer's aged mother constantly harms his love life, and he considers various means of getting rid of her.
Much-censored black comedy which might have been funnier in a complete form. Even so, it has its moments.

w Robert Klane, from his novel d Carl Reiner ph Jack Priestly m Jack Elliott

George Segal, Ruth Gordon, Trish Van Devere, Ron Leibman

Where's That Fire?*
GB 1939 73m bw
TCF (Edward Black)

An incompetent village fire brigade accidentally saves the crown jewels from thieves.
Routine but not despicable star comedy, long thought lost; flat patches are well separated by hilarious sequences.

w Marriott Edgar, Val Guest, J. O. C. Orton d Marcel Varnel ph Arthur Crabtree

Will Hay, Moore Marriott, Graham Moffatt, Peter Gawthorne, Eric Clavering, Charles Hawtrey

W.H.I.F.F.S.
US 1975 92m Technicolor Panavision
Brut (C. O. Erickson)
GB title: C.A.S.H.

An impotent army veteran finds that a criminal career, helped by stolen army gas, helps his sex life.
Over-the-top comedy with vaguely anti-war and anti-pollution leanings.

w Malcolm Marmorstein d Ted Post ph David M. Walsh m John Cameron

Elliott Gould, Eddie Albert, Harry Guardino, Godfrey Cambridge, Jennifer O'Neill
† Rather typical of the film was its ambiguous catch line: 'The biggest bang in history!'
AAN: song, 'Now That We're in Love'

While I Live
GB 1947 85m bw
Edward Dryhurst
Reissue title: The Dream of Olwen.

A Cornishwoman believes an amnesiac girl to be the reincarnation of her dead sister.
Silly melodrama which achieved phenomenal popularity, despite poor production, because of its haunting theme tune The Dream of Olwen by Charles Williams.

w John Harlow, Doreen Montgomery, play This Same Garden by Robert Bell d John Harlow ph F. A. Young m Charles Williams

Tom Walls, Sonia Dresdel, Carol Raye, Clifford Evans, Patricia Burke, John Warwick, Edward Lexy

While the City Sleeps
US 1956 100m bw Superscope
RKO (Bert Friedlob)

Three chief executives of a newspaper empire are pitted against each other in a search for a murder scoop.
Star-packed but leaden-paced news bureau melodrama; a major disappointment considering the talent.

w Casey Robinson, novel The Bloody Spur by Charles Einstein d Fritz Lang ph Ernest Laszlo m Herschel Burke Gilbert

Dana Andrews, George Sanders, Ida Lupino, Sally Forrest, Thomas Mitchell, Rhonda Fleming, Vincent Price, Howard Duff, James Craig, Robert Warwick, John Barrymore Jnr

The Whip Hand
US 1951 82m bw
RKO (Lewis J. Rachmil)

A fisherman finds himself unwelcome in a lonely town run by ex-Nazi, now communist, bacteriologists.
Preposterous, pretentious anti-communist low-budgeter, mildly enjoyable for its sheer gall.

w George Bricker, Frank L. Moss d / pd William Cameron Menzies ph Nicholas Musuraca m Paul Sawtell

Elliott Reid, Carla Balenda, Edgar Barrier, Raymond Burr

Whiplash
US 1948 90m bw
Warner (William Jacobs)

A painter becomes a prizefighter.
Hokey, unpersuasive romantic melodrama.

w Maurice Geraghty, Harriet Frank Jnr d Lewis Seiler ph Peverell Marley m Franz Waxman

Dane Clark, Alexis Smith, Zachary Scott, Eve Arden, Jeffrey Lynn, S. Z. Sakall, Alan Hale, Douglas Kennedy

Whipsaw*
US 1935 88m bw
MGM (Harry Rapf)

A G-man infiltrates a gang by wooing its girl member.
Fairly snappy romantic drama which further established both its stars.

w Howard Emmett Rogers d Sam Wood ph James Wong Howe m William Axt

Spencer Tracy, Myrna Loy, Harvey Stephens, Clay Clements, William Harrigan

Whirlpool*
US 1950 98m bw
TCF (Otto Preminger)

A girl is accused of a murder committed by her hypnotist, who has willed himself out of a hospital bed.
Silly murder melodrama; glossy production makes it entertaining.

w Lester Barstow, Andrew Solt, novel Guy Endore d Otto Preminger ph Arthur Miller m David Raksin

Gene Tierney, Jose Ferrer, Richard Conte, Charles Bickford, Barbara O'Neil, Eduard Franz, Fortunio Bonanova

'It is sometimes difficult to discover from Miss Tierney's playing whether she is or is not under hypnosis.'—MFB

† Lester Barstow=Ben Hecht.

Whirlpool
GB 1959 95m Eastmancolor
Rank (George Pitcher)

A killer escapes in Cologne; his girl friend separates from him and gets a lift down the Rhine in a barge; the trip reforms her and she betrays her lover.
Modestly attractive travelogue with the burden of a very boring melodrama.

w Lawrence P. Bachmann d Lewis Allen ph Geoffrey Unsworth m Ron Goodwin

Juliette Greco, O. W. Fischer, William Sylvester, Marius Goring, Muriel Pavlow

Whisky Galore****
GB 1948 82m bw
Ealing (Monja Danischewsky)
US title: Tight Little Island

During World War II, a ship full of whisky is wrecked on a small Hebridean island, and the local customs and excise man has his hands full.
Marvellously detailed, fast-moving, well-played and attractively photographed comedy which firmly established the richest Ealing vein.

w Compton Mackenzie, Angus Macphail, novel Compton Mackenzie d Alexander Mackendrick ph Gerald Gibbs m Ernest Irving

Basil Radford, Joan Greenwood, Jean Cadell, Gordon Jackson, James Robertson Justice, Wylie Watson, John Gregson, Morland Graham, Duncan Macrae, Catherine Lacey, Bruce Seton, Henry Mollinson, Compton Mackenzie, A. E. Matthews

'Brilliantly witty and fantastic, but wholly plausible.'—Sunday Chronicle

The Whisperers*
GB 1966 106m bw
UA / Seven Pines (Michael S. Laughlin, Ronald Shedlo)

An old lady hears voices and is put upon by her son, her wandering husband, and various others.
Interesting but cold and finally unsatisfactory character melodrama; even the acting, though in a sense admirable, is too genteel.

w Bryan Forbes, novel Robert Nicolson d Bryan Forbes ph Gerry Turpin m John Barry

Edith Evans, Eric Portman, Avis Bunnage, Nanette Newman, Gerald Sim, Ronald Fraser

AAN: Edith Evans

Whispering Smith*
US 1948 88m Technicolor
Paramount (Mel Epstein)

A government agent investigating robberies finds his friend is implicated.
Fairly entertaining detective western.

w Frank Butler, Karl Lamb, novel Frank H. Spearman d Leslie Fenton ph Ray Rennahan m Adolph Deutsch

Alan Ladd, Robert Preston, Brenda Marshall, Donald Crisp, William Demarest, Fay Holden, Murvyn Vye, Frank Faylen

The Whistle at Eaton Falls*
US 1951 96m bw
Columbia (Louis de Rochemont)
GB title: Richer than the Earth

The story of a strike at a small-town plastics factory.
Reasonably absorbing semi-documentary with a final 'solution' which rather evades the issues.

w Lemist Esler, Virginia Shaler d Robert Siodmak ph Joseph Brun m Louis Applebaum

Lloyd Bridges, Dorothy Gish, Carleton Carpenter, Murray Hamilton, James Westerfield, Lenore Lonergan

Whistle Down the Wind*

GB 1961 99m bw

Rank / Allied Film Makers / Beaver (Richard
  Attenborough)

Three north country children think a murderer
on the run is Jesus Christ.

Charming allegorical study of childhood
innocence, extremely well made, amusing, and
avoiding sentimentality.

w Keith Waterhouse, Willis Hall, *novel* Mary
Hayley Bell *d* Bryan Forbes *ph* Arthur
Ibbetson *m* Malcolm Arnold

Hayley Mills, Bernard Lee, Alan Bates,
Norman Bird, Elsie Wagstaff, Alan Barnes

The Whistler

Originally a radio series of suspense stories
introduced by someone whistling the theme
tune, this was turned into a fairly workmanlike
series of second features quite unrelated to
each other except for the leading actor,
Richard Dix, who alternated as hero and
villain, and William Castle, who directed or
produced most of them.

1944: THE WHISTLER, THE MARK OF
THE WHISTLER
1945: THE POWER OF THE WHISTLER
1946: THE VOICE OF THE WHISTLER
1947: MYSTERIOUS INTRUDER, THE
SECRET OF THE WHISTLER, THE 12th
HOUR
1948: THE RETURN OF THE WHISTLER

Whistling in the Dark*

US 1941 77m bw

MGM (George Haight)

A radio detective is kidnapped by a criminal
who wants him to devise a perfect murder
which will then be pinned on him.

Scatty comedy-thriller which, though it now
seems slow to start, was popular enough to
warrant two sequels (*Whistling in Brooklyn,
Whistling in Dixie*).

w Robert McGonigle, Harry Clark, Albert
Mannheimer, *play* Laurence Gross, Edward
Childs Carpenter *d* S. Sylvan Simon
ph Sidney Wagner *m* Bronislau Kaper

Red Skelton, Conrad Veidt, Ann Rutherford,
Virginia Grey, Eve Arden, Rags Ragland,
Don Douglas, Lloyd Corrigan

† The play was previously filmed in 1933 with
Ernest Truex, and this version is now shown
on TV as *Scared*.

The White Angel*

US 1935 91m bw

Warner (Henry Blanke)

The life of Florence Nightingale.

Starchy biopic; the Victorian atmosphere is
never quite caught.

w Mordaunt Shairp, Michael Jacoby
d William Dieterle *ph* Tony Gaudio

Kay Francis, Ian Hunter, Donald Woods,
Nigel Bruce, Donald Crisp, Henry O'Neill,
Billy Mauch, Halliwell Hobbes

White Banners*

US 1938 88m bw

Warner (Henry Blanke)

A social worker tries to solve the problems of
a troubled family.

Moderate middle-class drama.

w Lenore Coffee, Cameron Rogers, Abem
Finkel, *novel* Lloyd C. Douglas *d* Edmund
Goulding *ph* Charles Rosher *m* Max Steiner

Fay Bainter, Claude Rains, Jackie Cooper,
Bonita Granville, Henry O'Neill, James
Stephenson, Kay Johnson

AAN: Fay Bainter

The White Buffalo

US 1977 97m Technicolor

Dino de Laurentiis (Pancho Kohner)

Wild Bill Hickok and Chief Crazy Horse join
forces to kill a marauding white buffalo.

Ridiculous symbolic western, not helped by
the very artificial looking beast of the title.

w Richard Sale, from his novel *d* J. Lee
Thompson *ph* Paul Lohmann *m* John Barry

Charles Bronson, Jack Warden, Will
Sampson, Kim Novak, Clint Walker, Stuart
Whitman, John Carradine, Slim Pickens, Cara
Williams, Douglas Fowley

'The dried husk of a *Moby Dick* allegory
seems to be rattling around here amidst all the
other dead wood.'—*Jonathan Rosenbaum,
MFB*

White Cargo*

US 1942 90m bw

MGM (Victor Saville)

White rubber planters are driven mad with
desire for a scheming native girl.

Antediluvian melodrama previously filmed in
1930. Good for laughing at, and the star
looked great as Tondelayo.

w Leon Gordon, from his play and *novel*
Hell's Playground by Vera Simonton
d Richard Thorpe *m* Bronislau Kaper

Hedy Lamarr, Walter Pidgeon, Richard
Carlson, Frank Morgan, Bramwell Fletcher,
Richard Ainley, Reginald Owen

† There was also a British version in 1929 (silent) with Leslie Faber and Gypsy Rhouma; and a few months later it emerged with added dialogue.

White Christmas*
US 1954   120m   Technicolor
Vistavision
Paramount (Robert Emmett Dolan)

Two entertainers boost the popularity of a winter resort run by an old army buddy.
Humdrum musical lifted only by its stars; a revamp of *Holiday Inn,* which was much better.

w Norman Krasna, Norman Panama, Melvin Frank d Michael Curtiz ph Loyal Griggs *songs* Irving Berlin

Bing Crosby, Danny Kaye, Rosemary Clooney, Vera-Ellen, Dean Jagger, Mary Wickes, Sig Rumann, Grady Sutton

AAN: 'Count Your Blessings Instead of Sheep'

The White Cliffs of Dover*
US 1944   126m   bw
MGM (Sidney Franklin)

An American girl who marries into the British aristocracy loses a husband in World War I and a son in World War II.
Tearful flagwaver with some entertaining scenes in the first half and the general sense of an all-stops-out production.

w Claudine West, Jan Lustig, George Froeschel, *poem* Alice Duer Miller d Clarence Brown ph George Folsey m Herbert Stothart

Irene Dunne, Alan Marshal, Frank Morgan, May Whitty, Roddy McDowall, C. Aubrey Smith, Gladys Cooper, Peter Lawford, Van Johnson

'A long, earnest, well-intentioned, over-emotionalized cliché.'—*Richard Mallett, Punch*

'This sterling silver picture . . . is such a tribute to English gentility as only an American studio would dare to make.'—*New York Times*

AAN: George Folsey

White Corridors*
GB 1951   102m   bw
GFD / Vic (Joseph Janni, John Croydon)

Life in a small Midlands hospital.
Competent multi-drama which found a big audience.

w Jan Read, Pat Jackson, *novel* Yeoman's Hospital by Helen Ashton d Pat Jackson ph C. Pennington-Richards

James Donald, Googie Withers, Godfrey Tearle, Petula Clark, Jack Watling, Moira Lister, Barry Jones, Megs Jenkins, Basil Radford

'This quality of professionalism is comparatively rare in British films.'—*Gavin Lambert*

White Cradle Inn
GB 1947   83m   bw
British Lion / Peak Films
US title: *High Fury*

A Swiss hotel owner adopts a refugee boy and is menaced by her ne'er-do-well husband, who finally sacrifices himself for the boy.
Unimpressive little drama which wastes its cast, but provides beautiful scenery.

w Harold French, Lesley Storm d Harold French ph Deric Williams

Madeleine Carroll, Michael Rennie, Ian Hunter, Anne Marie Blanc, Michael McKeag

The White Dawn
US 1976   110m   Movielab
Paramount / American Film Properties (Martin Ransohoff)

In 1900, survivors from a whaling ship are cared for by Eskimos, who turn on them when nature proves unkind.
Unpleasant fable with lots of bitter weather and subtitled Eskimos. Scarcely an entertainment, and its message is mumbled.

w James Houston, Tom Rickman d Philip Kaufman ph Michael Chapman m Henry Mancini

Warren Oates, Timothy Bottoms, Lou Gossett, Eskimo cast

White Feather*
US 1955   100m   Technicolor
Cinemascope
TCF / Panoramic (Robert L. Jacks)

A cavalry colonel tries to hold back gold prospectors until the Cheyenne have moved on to their new reservations.
Old-fashioned cowboys and (sympathetic) Indians, very efficiently done.

w Delmer Daves, Leo Townsend d Robert Webb ph Lucien Ballard m Hugo Friedhofer

Robert Wagner, John Lund, Jeffrey Hunter, Debra Paget, Eduard Franz, Noah Beery Jnr, Hugh O'Brian, Virginia Leith, Emile Meyer

White Heat***
US 1949   114m   bw
Warner (Louis F. Edelman)

A violent, mother-fixated gangster gets his comeuppance when a government agent is infiltrated into his gang.

This searing melodrama reintroduced the old Cagney and then some: spellbinding suspense sequences complemented his vivid and hypnotic portrayal.

w Ivan Goff, Ben Roberts, *story* Virginia Kellogg *d* Raoul Walsh *ph* Sid Hickox *m* Max Steiner

James Cagney, Edmond O'Brien, *Margaret Wycherly*, Virginia Mayo, Steve Cochran, John Archer

'The most gruesome aggregation of brutalities ever presented under the guise of entertainment.'—*Cue*

'In the hurtling tabloid traditions of the gangster movies of the thirties, but its matter-of-fact violence is a new post-war style.'—*Time*

AAN: Virginia Kellogg

The White Hell of Pitz Palu*
Germany 1929   approx 90m   bw

Mountaineers have a difficult ascent of Pitz Palu. Classic semi-documentary, noted for its pictorial compositions more than its dramatic qualities. Written and directed by G. W. Pabst and Dr Arnold Fank; for UFA. 'An astonishing and, to me, wildly terrifying film.'—*James Agate*.

White Savage
US 1943   75m   Technicolor
Universal (George Waggner)
GB title: *White Captive*

The queen of a beautiful South Sea island has trouble with shark hunters and crooks after her mineral deposits.

Self-admitted hokum strung loosely and colourfully around its star: big box office in the middle of the war.

w Richard Brooks *d* Arthur Lubin *ph* Lester White, William Snyder *m* Frank Skinner

Maria Montez, Jon Hall, Sabu, Thomas Gomez, Sidney Toler, Paul Guilfoyle, Turhan Bey, Don Terry

White Shadows in the South Seas*
US 1927   88m (sound version)   bw
MGM

An alcoholic doctor in Tahiti finds happiness with a native girl until he is killed by white colonials.

Rather boring melodrama illuminated by superb photography.

w Ray Doyle, Jack Cunningham, *book* Frederick J. O'Brien *d* W. S. Van Dyke (and Robert Flaherty) *ph* Clyde de Vinna and others (including Flaherty)

Monte Blue, Raquel Torres

AA: Clyde de Vinna

The White Sister
US 1933   110m   bw
MGM (Hunt Stromberg)

When her lover is reported killed in the war, an Italian noblewoman takes the veil . . . but he comes back.

Tiresome romantic drama from another age, a big prestige production of its time.

w Donald Ogden Stewart, *novel* F. Marion Crawford, Walter Hackett *d* Victor Fleming *ph* William Daniels *m* Herbert Stothart

Helen Hayes, Clark Gable, Lewis Stone, Louise Closser Hale, May Robson, Edward Arnold

White Tie and Tails
US 1946   81m   bw

A butler left in charge of the house gets ideas above his station. Modest comedy which lacks the required high style. Dan Duryea, Ella Raines, William Bendix, Richard Gaines, Clarence Kolb, Frank Jenks. Written by Bertram Millhauser, from the novel *The Victoria Docks at Eight* by Rufus King and Charles Leakon; directed by Charles Barton; for Universal.

The White Tower
US 1950   98m   Technicolor
RKO (Sid Rogell)

Various people have personal reasons for climbing an Alpine mountain.

Pretentiously symbolic melodrama with some good action sequences and curiously stilted performances.

w Paul Jarrico, *novel* James Ramsay Ullman *d* Ted Tetzlaff *ph* Ray Rennahan *m* Roy Webb

Glenn Ford, Claude Rains, Alida Valli, Oscar Homolka, Cedric Hardwicke, Lloyd Bridges, June Clayworth

'The main interest is a curiosity as to who will fall over which precipice when.'—*Penelope Houston*

The White Unicorn
GB 1947   97m   bw
GFD / John Corfield (Harold Huth)
US title: *Bad Sister*

In a home for delinquent girls, the worst offender exchanges reminiscences with the warden.
Peg's Paper melodrama in complex flashback form.

w Robert Westerby, A. R. Rawlinson, Moie Charles, *novel* Flora Sandstrom *d* Bernard Knowles *ph* Reg Wyer *m* Bretton Byrd

Margaret Lockwood, Joan Greenwood, Ian Hunter, Dennis Price, Guy Middleton, Catherine Lacey, Mabel Constanduros, Paul Dupuis

White Witch Doctor
US 1953   96m   Technicolor
TCF (Otto Lang)

A nurse in the Congo converts a gold-seeking adventurer.
Stale hokum in which the animals are the most interesting feature.

w Ivan Goff, Ben Roberts, *novel* Louise A. Stinetorf *d* Henry Hathaway *ph* Leon Shamroy *m* Bernard Herrmann

Susan Hayward, Robert Mitchum, Walter Slezak, Timothy Carey

White Woman
US 1933   68m   bw
Paramount

A cockney overseer in the Malaysian jungle takes back a cabaret singer as his bride.
Risible melodrama with an obvious outcome.

w Norman Reilly Raine, Frank Butler *d* Stuart Walker *ph* Harry Fischbeck

Charles Laughton, Carole Lombard, Kent Taylor, Charles Bickford, Percy Kilbride, Charles Middleton, James Bell
† Remade as *Island of Lost Men*.

White Zombie**
US 1932   74m   bw
American Securities Corporation (Edward Halperin)

Haitian zombies work a sugar mill for a white schemer.
Genuinely eerie horror film with a slow, stagey, out-of-this world quality coupled with an interesting sense of composition.

w Garnett Weston *d* Victor Halperin *ph* Arthur Martinelli *md* Abe Meyer

Bela Lugosi, Madge Bellamy, John Harron, Joseph Cawthorn
'A Gothic fairy tale filled with dreamlike imagery, traditional symbols, echoes of Romanticism, and (probably unintentional) psychosexual overtones.'—*Carlos Clarens*

'For those absolutely dedicated to gothic silliness.'—*New Yorker, 1977*

Who?
GB 1974   93m   Eastmancolor
British Lion / Hemisphere / Maclean

An American scientist is captured by the Russians after a car crash and returned six months later as a somewhat suspect android.
So-what mixture of character drama and James Bondery; aiming clearly at no particular audience, it failed to get a release.

w John Gould, *novel* Algis Budrys *d* Jack Gold *ph* Petrus Schloemp *m* John Cameron

Elliott Gould, Trevor Howard, Joseph Bova, Ed Grover, James Noble, Lyndon Brook

Who Done It?
US 1942   77m   bw
Universal (Alex Gottlieb)

Soda jerks in a New York radio station catch a murderer.
So-so comedy thriller, fatally lacking atmosphere (and good jokes).

w Stanley Roberts, Edmund Joseph, John Grant *d* Erle C. Kenton *ph* Charles Van Enger *m* Frank Skinner

Bud Abbott, Lou Costello, William Gargan, Louise Allbritton, Patric Knowles, Don Porter, Jerome Cowan, William Bendix, Mary Wickes, Thomas Gomez

Who Done It?
GB 1956   85m   bw
Ealing (Michael Relph, Basil Dearden)

An ice-rink sweeper sets up as a private eye and captures a ring of spies.
Lively but disappointing film debut for a star comic whose screen personality proved too bland.

w T. E. B. Clarke *d* Basil Dearden *ph* Otto Heller *m* Philip Green

Benny Hill, Belinda Lee, David Kossoff, Garry Marsh, Ernest Thesiger, Thorley Walters

Who Goes There?
GB 1952   85m   bw
British Lion / London Films (Anthony Kimmins)
US title: *The Passionate Sentry*

In a Grace and Favour house near St James' Palace, a guardsman is involved in a trail of romantic intrigue.
Very British romantic farce, dully and quickly filmed from a West End success.

w John Dighton, from his play *d* Anthony
Kimmins *ph* John Wilcox, Ted Scaife
m Muir Mathieson

Peggy Cummins, Valerie Hobson, George
Cole, Nigel Patrick, A. E. Matthews, Anthony
Bushell

Who Is Harry Kellerman and Why Is He Saying These Terrible Things About Me?
US 1971   108m   De Luxe
Cinema Center (Ulu Grosbard, Herb
Gardner)

A New York composer is persecuted by a
mysterious figure which turns out to be
himself.
Wild, shapeless, satirical psycho-comedy-
melodrama. Not very good.

w Herb Gardner *d* Ulu Grosbard *ph* Victor
Kemper *pd* Harry Horner

Dustin Hoffman, Barbara Harris, Jack
Warden, David Burns, Gabriel Dell, Dom De
Luise

AAN: Barbara Harris

Who Is Killing the Great Chefs of Europe?*
US 1978   112m   Metrocolor
Warner / Aldrich / Lorimar (Merv Adelson,
Lee Rich, William Aldrich)
GB title: *Too Many Chefs*

A fast food entrepreneur in London finds
himself at the centre of a series of grisly
murders.
Unusual and lighthearted black comedy
against the background of international
gastronomy.

w Peter Stone, *novel* Nan and Ivan Lyons
d Ted Kotcheff *ph* John Alcott *m* Henry
Mancini

George Segal, Jacqueline Bisset, *Robert
Morley*, Jean-Pierre Cassel, Philippe Noiret,
Jean Rochefort, Madge Ryan

Who Killed Mary What's Her Name?
US 1971   90m   De Luxe
Cannon (George Manasse)

An ex-boxer determines to solve the murder
of a prostitute.
Old-fashioned whodunnit with something to
say grafted on every five minutes: an
unsatisfactory mix.

w John O'Toole *d* Ernest Pintoff *ph* Greg
Sandor *m* Gary McFarland

Red Buttons, Alice Playten, Sylvia Miles, Sam
Waterston

Who Slew Auntie Roo?
GB 1972   91m   Movielab
AIP / Hemdale (John Pellatt)

A madwoman menaces two orphan children.
Pointless and slenderly plotted adaptation of
Hansel and Gretel, crude in all departments.

w Robert Blees, Jimmy Sangster *d* Curtis
Harrington *ph* Desmond Dickinson *m* Ken
Jones

Shelley Winters, Ralph Richardson, Mark
Lester, Lionel Jeffries, Chloe Franks, Hugh
Griffith, Rosalie Crutchley, Pat Heywood
'Not content with being a delicate fantasy of
childish nightmare, it tries to add a totally
inappropriate seasoning of Grand Guignol.'—
Tom Milne

Who Was That Lady?*
US 1960   115m   bw
Columbia / Ansark / George Sidney
(Norman Krasna)

A professor seen kissing a student persuades a
friend to tell his wife that they are both FBI
agents on duty. Foreign spies believe
them . . .
Agreeably wacky comedy with a strained and
prolonged middle section leading to a totally
zany climax.

w Norman Krasna, from his play *d* George
Sidney *ph* Harry Stradling *m* André Previn

Tony Curtis, Dean Martin, Janet Leigh, James
Whitmore, John McIntire, Barbara Nichols,
Larry Keating

The Whole Town's Talking*
US 1935   86m   bw
Columbia (Lester Cowan)
GB title: *Passport to Fame*

A gangster finds it convenient occasionally to
pose as his double, a meek little clerk.
Pleasingly neat comedy, well staged and acted.

w Jo Swerling, Robert Riskin, *novel* W. R.
Burnett *d* John Ford *ph* Joseph August

Edward G. Robinson, Jean Arthur, Arthur
Hohl, Wallace Ford, Arthur Byron, Donald
Meek, Edward Brophy, Etienne Girardot
'A lively and satisfactory combination of
farce and melodrama.'—*Richard Watts Jnr*

The Whole Truth*
GB 1958   84m   bw
Columbia / Romulus (Jack Clayton)

A jealous husband poses as a detective in
order to murder his wife and incriminate a film
producer.
A filmed play, but quite a solidly carpentered
murder thriller with a couple of neat twists.

w Jonathan Latimer, *play* Philip Mackie
d John Guillermin *ph* Wilkie Cooper
m Mischa Spoliansky

Stewart Granger, George Sanders, Donna
Reed, Gianna Maria Canale

Who'll Stop the Rain?

US 1978   125m   colour
UA / Gabriel Katzka, Herb Jaffe
GB title: *Dog Soldiers*

A Vietnam veteran takes to smuggling heroin
into the US, but gets his wife and friend
involved with gangsters.
Heavy-going, downbeat character drama with
action sequences; well enough done, but the
kind of movie that does nothing for anybody.

w Judith Roscoe, *book* Dog Soldiers by
Robert Stone *d* Karel Reisz *ph* Richard H.
Kline *m* Laurence Rosenthal

Nick Nolte, Tuesday Weld, Michael Moriarty,
Anthony Zerbe, Richard Masur, David
Opatoshu, Roy Sharkey, Gail Strickland

'Just another ambition-downer, a wasted
effort to make something meaningful out of
wasted lives.'—*Richard Schickel, Time*

Wholly Moses

US 1980   109m   Metrocolor   Panavision

A shepherd hears God talking to Moses, and
thinks he himself has been ordained to set his
people free. Inept and tasteless biblical spoof
which must set back by about ten years the
reputations of all connected with it. Dudley
Moore, James Coco, Paul Sand, Jack Gilford,
Dom DeLuise, John Houseman, Madeleine
Kahn. Written by Guy Thomas; directed by
Gary Weis; for David Begelman / Columbia.
'Deadly dullness of both writing and execution
render pointless any attempt to single out
blame for misfire, which leaves many talented
performers flailing about in desperate attempts
to generate laughs.'—*Variety.*

Whoopee*

US 1930   94m   Technicolor
Samuel Goldwyn, Florenz Ziegfeld

A timid young man is catapulted into various
adventures.
Early sound musical from a popular Broadway
show, later remade as *Up in Arms* (qv).

w William Conselman, *musical play* William
Anthony McGuire, *play* The Nervous Wreck
by Owen Davis *d* Thornton Freeland *ph* Lee
Garmes, Ray Rennahan, Gregg Toland
ch Busby Berkeley

Eddie Cantor, Eleanor Hunt, Paul Gregory,
Jack Rutherford, Ethel Shutta

Who's Afraid of Virginia Woolf?***

US 1966   129m   bw
Warner (Ernest Lehman)

A college professor and his wife have an
all-night shouting match and embarrass their
guests.
As a film of a play, fair to middling; as a
milestone in cinematic permissiveness, very
important; as an entertainment, sensational
for those in the mood.

w Ernest Lehman, *play Edward Albee d* Mike
Nichols *ph* Haskell Wexler *m* Alex North

*Richard Burton, Elizabeth Taylor, George
Segal, Sandy Dennis*
    'A magnificent triumph of determined
audacity.'—*Bosley Crowther*
    'One of the most scathingly honest
American films ever made.'—*Stanley
Kauffmann*
    'You are cordially invited to George and
Martha's for an evening of fun and games!'—
publicity

AA: Haskell Wexler; Elizabeth Taylor; Sandy
Dennis
AAN: best picture; Ernest Lehman; Mike
Nichols; Alex North; Richard Burton; George
Segal

Who's Been Sleeping in My Bed?

US 1963   103m   Technicolor
    Panavision
Paramount / Amro (Jack Rose)

A TV matinee idol finds he is a sex symbol
also in his private life.
Coy bedroom farce with no real action but a
smattering of jokes.

w Jack Rose *d* Daniel Mann *ph* Joseph
Ruttenberg *m* George Duning

Dean Martin, Elizabeth Montgomery, Martin
Balsam, Jill St John, Richard Conte, Carol
Burnett, Louis Nye, Yoko Tani, Elizabeth
Fraser

Who's Got the Action?

US 1962   93m   Technicolor   Panavision
Paramount / Amro (Jack Rose)

A bored wife and her law partner husband
have remarkable success betting on horses.
Badly cast and rather slow comedy with flashes
of wit.

w Jack Rose, *novel* Four Horse Players Are
Missing by Alexander Rose *d* Daniel Mann
ph Joseph Ruttenberg *m* George Duning

Dean Martin, Lana Turner, Eddie Albert,
Walter Matthau, Nita Talbot, Margo, Paul
Ford, John McGiver

Who's Minding the Mint?*
US 1967   97m   Technicolor
Columbia / Norman Maurer

An employee of the US mint and his friends
find a means of printing bills at night.
Smartly-made action comedy with good
performances.

w R. S. Allen, Harvey Bullock d Howard
Morris ph Joseph Biroc m Lalo Schifrin

Jim Hutton, Dorothy Provine, Milton Berle,
Joey Bishop, Bob Denver, Walter Brennan,
Victor Buono, Jack Gilford

Who's Minding the Store?*
US 1963   90m   Technicolor
Paramount / York / Jerry Lewis (Paul
Jones)

An accident-prone young man gets a job in a
department store.
Better-than-average star comedy, slapstick
being allowed precedence over sentimentality.

w Frank Tashlin, Harry Tugend d Frank
Tashlin ph W. Wallace Kelley m Joseph J.
Lilley

Jerry Lewis, Jill St John, Agnes Moorehead,
John McGiver, Ray Walston, Nancy Kulp

Why Shoot the Teacher?
Canada 1976   99m   colour
WSTT / Fraser Films (Lawrence Hertzog)

In 1935 a school teacher finds a chilly
reception when he settles in a Saskatchewan
village.
Unsatisfactory but occasionally quite
entertaining comedy-drama which hovers
around the *Cold Comfort Farm* mark.

w James Defilice, *novel* Max Braithwaite
d Silvio Narizzano ph Marc Champion
m Ricky Hyslop

Bud Cort, Samantha Eggar, Chris Wiggins,
Gary Reineke

Why We Fight***
US War Office 1942–5 (*Frank Capra*) bw

A series of feature-length compilations for
primary showing to the armed forces, these
were superbly vigorous documentaries which
later fascinated the public at large. Editing,
music and diagrams were all used to punch
home the message. Individual titles were:

'Prelude to War' (53m) w Eric Knight,
Anthony Veiller d Frank Capra
'The Nazis Strike' (42m) w as above d as
above
'Divide and Conquer' (58m) w Anthony
Veiller, Robert Heller d Frank Capra, Anatole
Litvak

'The Battle of Britain' (54m) wd Anthony
Veiller
'The Battle of Russia' (80m) w Anthony
Veiller, Robert Heller, Anatole Litvak,
d Anatole Litvak
'The Battle of China (60m) w Eric Knight,
Anthony Veiller d Frank Capra, Anatole
Litvak
'War Comes to America' (70m) w Anthony
Veiller d Anatole Litvak

All had editing by *William Hornbeck*, music
by *Dmitri Tiomkin* and commentary by *Walter
Huston*.

Why Worry?*
US 1923   60m   approx (24 fps)   bw
silent   Hal Roach - Harold Lloyd

A hypochondriac is cured when he gets mixed
up in a South American revolution.
Moderate star comedy with highlights well
spaced out.

d Sam Taylor, Fred Newmeyer

Harold Lloyd, Jobyna Ralston, Leo White

Wicked as They Come
GB 1956   94m   bw
Columbia / Film Locations (Maxwell
Setton)
US title: *Portrait in Smoke*

A beauty contest winner from the slums makes
money and luxury her goal.
Busy melodrama which interests without
edifying.

wd Ken Hughes co-w Robert Westerby,
Sigmund Miller ph Basil Emmott m Malcolm
Arnold

Arlene Dahl, Herbert Marshall, Phil Carey,
Michael Goodliffe, David Kossoff, Sidney
James, Ralph Truman, Faith Brook

The Wicked Lady*
GB 1945   104m   bw
GFD / Gainsborough (R. J. Minney)

In the days of Charles II, Lady Skelton
befriends a highwayman and takes to crime.
The most commercially successful of the
Gainsborough costume charades because of its
atmosphere of gloomy sin. Dramatically turgid
and surprisingly poorly acted and directed, but
with good period detail. It had to be reshot for
America because of the ladies' décolletage.

wd Leslie Arliss, *novel* The Life and Death of
the Wicked Lady Skelton by Magdalen King-
Hall ph Jack Cox m Hans May md Louis
Levy

Margaret Lockwood, James Mason, Griffith
Jones, Patricia Roc, Michael Rennie, Enid
Stamp-Taylor, Felix Aylmer, Martita Hunt,
David Horne
    'A mixture of hot passion and cold suet
pudding.'—*Manchester Guardian*
    'Rather dull and juvenile in its
determination to be daring.'—*Richard Mallett,
Punch*

A Wicked Woman

US 1934   71m   bw
MGM (Harry Rapf)
A woman kills her drunken husband to protect
her children, later confesses and is exonerated.
The tail end of the mother love saga, better
made than most.

w Florence Ryerson, Zelda Sears, *novel* Anne
Austin *d* Charles Brabin *ph* Lester White
Mady Christians, Charles Bickford, Betty
Furness, William Henry, Jackie Searle, Robert
Taylor, Paul Harvey

The Wicker Man*

GB 1973   86m   Eastmancolor
British Lion (Peter Snell)
A policeman flies to a remote Scottish isle to
investigate the death of a child, and finds
himself in the hands of diabolists.
Old-fashioned but remarkably well made scare
story, with effective shock moments.

w Anthony Shaffer *d* Robin Hardy *ph* Harry
Waxman *m* Paul Giovanni *ad* Seamus
Flannery
Edward Woodward, Britt Ekland, Christopher
Lee, Ingrid Pitt, Diane Cilento
    'An encouraging achievement for those who
had begun to despair of the British cinema.'—
David McGillivray

Wife, Doctor and Nurse*

US 1937   84m   bw
TCF (Raymond Griffith)
A romantic triangle as the title suggests.
Agreeable fluff with a mildly surprising end
(for 1937) suggesting a *ménage à trois*.

w Kathryn Scola, Darrell Ware, Lamar Trotti
d Walter Lang *ph* Edward Cronjager
m Arthur Lange
Loretta Young, Warner Baxter, Virginia
Bruce, Jane Darwell, Sidney Blackmer,
Maurice Cass, Minna Gombell, Elisha Cook
Jnr, Lon Chaney Jnr

Wife, Husband and Friend*

US 1939   80m   bw
TCF (Nunnally Johnson)

A man sabotages his wife's efforts to become a
professional singer.
Modestly agreeable romantic comedy later
remade as *Everybody Does It* (qv).

w Nunnally Johnson, *story* James M. Cain
d Gregory Ratoff *ph* Ernest Palmer *m* David
Buttolph
Loretta Young, Warner Baxter, Binnie
Barnes, Cesar Romero, George Barbier,
J. Edward Bromberg, Eugene Pallette,
Helen Westley

The Wife Takes a Flyer

US 1942   86m   bw
Columbia (B. P. Schulberg)
GB title: *A Yank in Dutch*
A Dutchwoman whose husband is in the
asylum takes in a fugitive USAF pilot in his
place although a Nazi officer is billeted on the
household.
Downright peculiar World War II comedy
which at the time seemed the height of bad
taste—and no laughs.

w Gina Kaus, Jay Dratler *d* Richard Wallace
ph Franz Planer *m* Werner Heyman
Joan Bennett, Franchot Tone, Allyn Joslyn,
Cecil Cunningham, Lloyd Corrigan, Georgia
Caine
    'Kicks in the pants, belching, and
exaggerated face-making are lifted from
burlesque to decorate this feeble attempt.'—
New York Post

Wife versus Secretary*

US 1936   88m   bw
MGM (Hunt Stromberg)
A publisher's wife starts to believe rumours
about his attention to his secretary.
Practised star comedy drama which provided
thoroughly satisfactory entertainment of a
kind the cinema seems to have forgotten.

w Norman Krasna, Alice Duer Miller, John
Lee Mahin, *novel* Faith Baldwin *d* Clarence
Brown *ph* Ray June *m* Herbert Stothart,
Edward Ward
Clark Gable, Myrna Loy, Jean Harlow, May
Robson, George Barbier, James Stewart,
Hobart Cavanaugh
    'See this picture if you enjoy the spectacle of
three clever stars shining for all they are
worth.'—*Film Weekly*

The Wilby Conspiracy*

GB 1975   105m   De Luxe
UA / Optimus / Baum–Dantine (Stanley
Sopel)
A British mining engineer is persuaded to help

a black revolutionary in his flight from Cape Town to Johannesburg.
Reasonably exciting political chase thriller with a sufficiency of twists and action sequences; philosophy is present but secondary.

w Rod Amateau, Harold Nebenzal, *novel* Peter Driscoll d Ralph Nelson *ph* John Coquillon m Stanley Myers

Sidney Poitier, Michael Caine, Nicol Williamson, Prunella Gee, Saeed Jaffrey, Persis Khambatta

The Wild Affair*
GB 1965   87m   bw
Seven Arts (Richard Patterson)

An office Christmas party nearly turns into an orgy.
Curious little comedy drama which plays almost like the Road to Ruin and has an attractive but miscast leading lady. Interesting elements.

wd John Krish, *novel* The Last Hours of Sandra Lee by William Sansom *ph* Arthur Ibbetson m Martin Slavin

Nancy Kwan, Terry-Thomas, Jimmy Logan, Bud Flanagan, Betty Marsden, Gladys Morgan, Paul Whitsun-Jones, Donald Churchill, Victor Spinetti

The Wild and the Innocent
US 1959   85m   Eastmancolor
Cinemascope

A trapper is torn between a mountain girl and a city tart. Oddly old-fashioned western, like *The Gold Rush* without laughs. Audie Murphy, Joanne Dru, Gilbert Roland, Sandra Dee, Jim Backus, Peter Breck. Written by Sy Gomberg and Jack Sher; directed by Jack Sher; for Universal-International.

The Wild and the Willing
GB 1962   112m   bw
Rank / Box–Thomas (Betty E. Box)
US title: *Young and Willing*

A troublesome student at a provincial university seduces the wife of his professor. Watchable sex melodrama with an interesting background on which no one seems to have quite enough grip; 'realism' is simply there to be exploited.

w Nicholas Phipps, Mordecai Richler, *play* The Tinker by Laurence Dobie, Robert Sloman d Ralph Thomas *ph* Ernest Steward m Norrie Paramor

Virginia Maskell, Paul Rogers, Ian McShane, Samantha Eggar, John Hurt, Catherine Woodville, John Standing, Jeremy Brett

Wild and Wonderful
US 1963   88m   Eastmancolor
U-I / Harold Hecht

A French film star poodle makes friends with an American gambler.
Amiable zany comedy in a set-bound Gay Paree.

w Larry Markes, Michael Morris, Waldo Salt d Michael Anderson *ph* Joseph La Shelle m Morton Stevens

Tony Curtis, Christine Kaufmann, Larry Storch, Marty Ingels, Jacques Aubuchon, Jules Munshin

The Wild Angels*
US 1966   85m   Pathecolor   Panavision
AIP (Roger Corman)

A Californian motorcycle gang is run on semi-religious, ritualistic, Nazi lines.
Much-banned melodrama, cheaply made but vigorously handled and of some interest on social and historical levels.

w Charles B. Griffith d Roger Corman *ph* Richard Moore m Mike Curb

Peter Fonda, Nancy Sinatra, Bruce Dern, Michael J. Pollard

Wild Bill Hickok Rides
US 1941   81m   bw

Wild Bill helps a homesteader keep his land.
Oddly cast, rather naïve little western.
Constance Bennett, Bruce Cabot, Warren William, Ward Bond, Howard da Silva.
Written by Charles Grayson, Paul Gerard Smith and Raymond Schrock; directed by Ray Enright; for Warner.

The Wild Blue Yonder
US 1952   98m   bw
Republic (Herbert J. Yates)
GB title: *Thunder Across the Pacific*

Incidents in the lives of bomber pilots in the Pacific during World War II.
Routine action flagwaver.

w Richard Tregaskis d Allan Dwan *ph* Reggie Lanning m Victor Young

Wendell Corey, Vera Hruba Ralston, Forrest Tucker, Phil Harris, Walter Brennan, Ruth Donnelly

Wild Boys of the Road*
US 1933   88m   bw
Warner (Robert Presnell)
GB title: *Dangerous Days*

Boys of poor families take to the road in gangs.

Vivid social melodrama of its day, now rather overstated.

w Earl Baldwin *d* William Wellman *ph* Arthur Todd

Frankie Darro, Rochelle Hudson, Edwin Philips, Arthur Hohl

The Wild Bunch***
US 1969   145m   Technicolor Panavision 70
Warner Seven Arts / Phil Feldman

In 1914, Texas bandits are ambushed by an old enemy and die bloodily in defence of one of their number against a ruthless Mexican revolutionary.
Arguably the director's best film, and one which set a fashion for blood-spurting violence in westerns. Undeniably stylish, thoughtful, and in places very exciting.

w Walon Green, Sam Peckinpah *d* Sam Peckinpah *ph* Lucien Ballard *m* Jerry Fielding *ad* Edward Carrere

William Holden, Ernest Borgnine, Robert Ryan, Edmond O'Brien, Warren Oates, Jaime Sanchez, Ben Johnson, Strother Martin, L. Q. Jones, Albert Dekker

'A western that enlarged the form aesthetically, thematically, demonically.'— *Stanley Kauffmann, 1972*
'We watch endless violence to assure us that violence is not good.'—*Judith Crist, 1976*

AAN: script; Jerry Fielding

The Wild Country
US 1970   100m   Technicolor
Walt Disney (Ron Miller)

In the late 1880s a farmer buys a dilapidated Wyoming ranch and falls foul of a local rancher who controls the water supply.
Predictable family western in the familiar Disney style.

w Calvin Clements Jnr, Paul Savage, *novel* Little Britches by Ralph Moody *d* Robert Totten *ph* Frank Phillips *m* Robert Bronner

Steve Forrest, Vera Miles, Jack Elam, Ronny Howard, Morgan Woodward

The Wild Geese
GB 1978   134m   Eastmancolor
Rank / Richmond (Euan Lloyd)

Adventures of four British mercenaries in a central African state.
All-star blood and guts with a few breezy touches in the script.

w Reginald Rose, *novel* Daniel Carney *d* Andrew V. McLaglen *ph* Jack Hildyard *m* Roy Budd

Roger Moore, Richard Burton, Richard Harris, Hardy Kruger, Stewart Granger, Jack Watson, Frank Finlay, Kenneth Griffith, Barry Foster, Jeff Corey, Ronald Fraser, Percy Herbert, Patrick Allen, Jane Hylton

Wild Geese Calling
US 1941   77m   bw
TCF (Harry Joe Brown)

A young adventurer in Oregon weds the girl friend of a conniving gambler.
Minor semi-western which never really finds a style.

w Horace McCoy, *novel* Stewart Edward White *d* John Brahm *ph* Lucien Ballard *m* Alfred Newman

Joan Bennett, Henry Fonda, Warren William, Ona Munson, Barton MacLane, Russell Simpson, Iris Adrian

Wild Harvest
US 1947   92m   bw
Paramount (Robert Fellows)

A romantic triangle develops among wheat harvesters on the western plains.
Standard star hokum.

w John Monks Jnr *d* Tay Garnett *ph* John F. Seitz *m* Hugo Friedhofer

Alan Ladd, Dorothy Lamour, Robert Preston, Lloyd Nolan, Dick Erdman, Allen Jenkins, Will Wright

Wild in the Country
US 1961   114m   De Luxe   Cinemascope
TCF / Company of Artists (Jerry Wald)

A rebellious hillbilly is involved with three women.
Weird confection designed to show the star in all his facets.

w Clifford Odets, *novel* The Lost Country by J. R. Salamanca *d* Philip Dunne *ph* William C. Mellor *m* Kenyon Hopkins

Elvis Presley, Hope Lange, Tuesday Weld, Millie Perkins, John Ireland, Gary Lockwood
'One can't help feeling he was better off prior to this misguided bid for class.'—*MFB*

Wild in the Sky
US 1971   83m   colour
AIP / Bald Eagle (William T. Naud, Dick Gautier)

Three young offenders skyjack a B52 jet bomber.
Black comedy melodrama, uncontrolled but with some engaging absurdities.

w William T. Naud, Dick Gautier *d* William T. Naud *ph* Thomas E. Spalding *m* Jerry Styner

Brandon de Wilde, Keenan Wynn, Dick Gautier, Tim O'Connor, James Daly, Robert Lansing

Wild in the Streets*
US 1968 97m Perfectcolor
AIP (Jack Cash)

In the imminent future, a pop singer becomes president and launches a campaign for teenage emancipation.
Satirical melodrama with a profusion of wild gags, some of which hit the target.

w Robert Thom d Barry Shear ph Richard Moore m Les Baxter

Shelley Winters, Chris Jones, Diane Varsi, Hal Holbrook, Millie Perkins

'Blatant, insensitive, crummy-looking . . . enjoyable at a pop, comic-strip level.'—*New Yorker, 1977*

Wild Is the Wind
US 1957 114m bw Vistavision
Paramount / Hal B. Wallis

A widowed Italian sheep rancher in Nevada marries his wife's sister from Italy, but she falls for his adopted son.
Intense Cold Comfort Farm melodrama with a strong similarity to *They Knew What They Wanted*; the strain shows, and the performances are tiresomely noisy.

w Arnold Schulman d George Cukor ph Charles Lang Jnr m Dmitri Tiomkin

Anna Magnani, Anthony Quinn, Tony Franciosa, Dolores Hart, Joseph Calleia

AAN: title song (m Dmitri Tiomkin, ly Ned Washington); Anna Magnani; Anthony Quinn

The Wild North
US 1951 97m Anscocolor
MGM (Stephen Ames)

A mountie gets his man but needs his help getting back to base.
Standard adventure story with avalanche and wolf attacks.

w Frank Fenton d Andrew Marton ph Robert Surtees m Bronislau Kaper

Stewart Granger, Wendell Corey, Cyd Charisse

The Wild One**
US 1954 79m bw
Columbia / Stanley Kramer

Hoodlum motorcyclists terrorize a small town.
Brooding, compulsive, well-made little melodrama which was much banned because there was no retribution. As a narrative it does somewhat lack dramatic point.

w John Paxton, *story* The Cyclists' Raid by Frank Rooney d Laslo Benedek ph Hal Mohr m Leith Stevens

Marlon Brando, Lee Marvin, Mary Murphy, Robert Keith, Jay C. Flippen

'That streetcar man has a new desire!—*publicity*
† 'What are you rebelling against?' 'What've you got?—sample dialogue.
†† Sharpness of photography was achieved by the Garutso lens.

The Wild Party
US 1956 81m bw
UA / Security (Sidney Harmon)

An ex-football player and some Los Angeles layabouts plot a kidnap.
Unpleasant melodrama laced with sex, violence and loud music.

w John McPartland d Harry Horner ph Sam Leavitt m Buddy Bregman

Anthony Quinn, Carol Ohmart, Jay Robinson, Arthur Franz, Nehemiah Persoff, Kathryn Grant, Paul Stewart

The Wild Party
US 1974 91m Movielab
AIP / Edgar Lansbury, Joseph Beruh (Ismail Merchant)

In 1929, a silent film comedian on the skids throws a party to show his latest movie.
Evocative of its period but virtually confined to a single set which becomes boring, this collection of unlikely events and tedious people has only obvious points to make and its final descent into tragedy is not compelling.

w Walter Marks, *poem* Joseph Moncure March d James Ivory ph Walter Lassally m Larry Rosenthal

James Coco, Raquel Welch, Perry King, Tiffany Bolling, Royal Dano, David Dukes, Dena Dietrich

'Seems to promise a pointillist precision about its characters and milieu which it never quite delivers.'—*Jonathan Rosenbaum*

Wild River*
US 1960 115m De Luxe Cinemascope
TCF (Elia Kazan)

In 1933 a Tennessee Valley Authority inspector incurs the wrath of a local matriarch who will not leave her valley even though it is to be flooded.
Interesting liberal-minded sociological drama marred by an added love story, as the similar *Last Days of Dolwyn* was marred by melodrama. Well made but somehow unmemorable.

w Paul Osborn, *novels* Borden Deal, William Bradford Huie *d* Elia Kazan *ph* Ellsworth Fredericks *m* Kenyon Hopkins

Montgomery Clift, *Jo Van Fleet*, Lee Remick, Albert Salmi, Jay C. Flippen, James Westerfield, Bruce Dern

Wild Rovers

US 1971   132m   Metrocolor
Panavision 70
MGM / Geoffrey (Blake Edwards, Ken Wales)

A middle-aged cowboy, depressed with the state of his life, joins with a younger man to become a bank robber.
Fashionable, derivative, quite unsuccessful western tragi-comedy mixing in shades of every director from Ford to Peckinpah.

wd Blake Edwards *ph* Philip Lathrop
m Jerry Goldsmith

William Holden, Ryan O'Neal, Karl Malden, Lynn Carlin, Tom Skerritt, Joe Don Baker, Rachel Roberts, Leora Dana, Moses Gunn
'An existentialist western which will not do much for existentialism, the western, or the box office.'—*Charles Champlin, Los Angeles Times*

Wild Strawberries***

Sweden 1957   93m   bw
Svensk Filmindustri (Allan Ekelund)
original title: *Smultronstället*

An elderly professor has a nightmare and thinks back over his long life.
A beautifully paced and acted, but somewhat obscure piece of probing symbolism.

wd Ingmar Bergman *ph* Gunnar Fischer
m Erik Nordgren

Victor Sjostrom, Ingrid Thulin, Gunnar Bjornstrand, Bibi Andersson, Naima Wifstrand, Jullan Kindahl
'The work of a man obsessed by cruelty, especially spiritual cruelty, trying to find some resolution.'—*Kenneth Cavander, MFB*
AAN: script

The Wildcats of St Trinian's

GB 1980   91m   Technicolor
Wildcat (E. M. Smedley-Aston)

The awful schoolgirls get unionized, and kidnap an Arab's daughter to gain attention. Crude and belated tailpiece to a series which was never very satisfactory. (See *The Belles of . . .* , *Blue Murder at . . .* , *The Pure Hell of . . .* , *The Great St Trinian's Train Robbery*.)

wd Frank Launder *ph* Ernest Steward
m James Kenelm Clarke

Sheila Hancock, Michael Hordern, Joe Melia, Thorley Walters, Rodney Bewes, Maureen Lipman, Ambrosine Philpotts

Will Penny**

US 1967   109m   Technicolor
Paramount / Fred Engel / Walter Seltzer / Tom Gries

A middle-aged cowpuncher falls foul of a family of maniacal cut-throats.
Realistically spare, laconic, uncomforting western with a curiously melodramatic set of villains.

wd Tom Gries *ph* Lucien Ballard *m* David Raksin

Charlton Heston, Joan Hackett, Donald Pleasence, Lee Majors, Bruce Dern, Anthony Zerbe, Clifton James, Ben Johnson

Will Success Spoil Rock Hunter?

US 1957   95m   Eastmancolor
Cinemascope
TCF (Frank Tashlin)
GB title: *Oh! For a Man!*

A timid advertising executive is touted for a publicity stunt as the world's greatest lover.
A too-wild satire on TV commercials: less frenzied direction and gag-writing would have prised more humour from the situations.

w Frank Tashlin, *play* George Axelrod
d Frank Tashlin *ph* Joe MacDonald *m* Cyril Mockridge

Jayne Mansfield, Tony Randall, Betsy Drake, Joan Blondell, John Williams, Henry Jones, Mickey Hargitay

Willard*

US 1971   95m   De Luxe
Cinerama / Bing Crosby (Mort Briskin)

A shy, withdrawn young man breeds and trains rats to kill his enemies.
Modest, rather unusual suspenser which builds well after a slow start; only horrifying to people who can't stand rats. A sequel, *Ben* (qv), later appeared.

w Gilbert Ralston, *novel* Ratman's Notebooks by Stephen Gilbert *d* Daniel Mann
ph Robert B. Hauser *m* Alex North *rat trainer* Moe de Sesso

Bruce Davison, Elsa Lanchester, Ernest Borgnine, Sondra Locke, Michael Dante, J. Pat O'Malley

Willie and Phil

US 1980   116m   De Luxe
TCF (Paul Mazursky, Tony Ray)

Two men and a woman enjoy a variable

ménage à trois throughout the seventies.
Curious attempt at an American *Jules et Jim*;
not badly done if you have to do it, but why
do it?

wd Paul Mazursky *ph* Sven Nykvist
m Claude Bolling

Michael Ontkean, Margot Kidder, Ray
Sharkey

Willy Wonka and the Chocolate
Factory*
US 1971   100m   Technicolor
David Wolper

A boy wins a tour of the local chocolate
factory and finds himself in the power of a
magician.
Semi-satiric Grimms Fairy Tale pastiche which
looks good but never seems quite happy with
itself.

w Roald Dahl, from his novel *d* Mel Stuart
ph Arthur Ibbetson *songs* Leslie Bricusse,
Anthony Newley *md* Walter Scharf
ad Harper Goff

Gene Wilder, Jack Albertson, Peter Ostrum,
Roy Kinnear, Aubrey Woods

AAN: Walter Scharf

Wilson***
US 1944   154m   Technicolor
TCF (Darryl F. Zanuck)

The rise and fall of an American president.
Admirably careful biopic which raises no
particular excitement but entertains and
instructs on various levels.

*w Lamar Trotti d Henry King ph Leon
Shamroy m Alfred Newman ad James
Basevi, Wiard Ihnen*

Alexander Knox, Charles Coburn, Cedric
Hardwicke, Geraldine Fitzgerald, Thomas
Mitchell, Ruth Nelson, William Eythe,
Vincent Price, Mary Anderson, Ruth Ford,
Sidney Blackmer, Stanley Ridges, Eddie Foy
Jnr, Charles Halton, Thurston Hall, J. M.
Kerrigan, Francis X. Bushman

'Not without tedium, but worth seeing as an
enormous expensive curiosity.'—*Richard
Mallett, Punch*

'Rich with the sense of movement and
multitude.'—*Daily Sketch*

AA: Lamar Trotti; Leon Shamroy
AAN: best picture; Henry King; Alfred
Newman; Alexander Knox

Winchester 73**
US 1950   92m   bw
U-I (Aaron Rosenberg)

Long-time enemies settle an old grudge.
Entertaining, popular, hard-riding, hard-
shooting western of the old school.

w Robert L. Richards, Borden Chase, *story*
Stuart N. Lake *d Anthony Mann ph William
Daniels m* Frank Skinner *md* Joseph
Gershenson

James Stewart, Shelley Winters, Dan Duryea,
Stephen McNally, Millard Mitchell, Charles
Drake, John McIntire, Will Geer, Jay C.
Flippen, Rock Hudson, Tony Curtis, John
Alexander, Steve Brodie

The Wind*
US 1927   75m (sound version 1928)   bw
MGM

A sheltered Virginia girl goes to live on the
rough and windy Texas prairie, marries a man
she doesn't love and kills a would-be rapist.
Heavy melodrama with a strong visual sense.

w Frances Marion, *novel* Dorothy
Scarborough *d* Victor Sjostrom *ph* John
Arnold

Lillian Gish, Lars Hanson, Montagu Love,
Dorothy Cummings

'So penetrating is the atmosphere that one
can almost feel the wind itself and taste the
endless dust.'—*Georges Sadoul*
'Unrelieved by the ghost of a smile . . . but
its relentlessness is gripping . . . a fine and
dignified achievement.'—*Pictureplay*

Wind across the Everglades
US 1958   93m   Technicolor
(Warner) Schulberg Productions (Stuart
Schulberg)

Florida 1900: a young schoolteacher tracks
down those responsible for hunting rare birds
for their feathers, and becomes a game
warden.
Dull, meandering adventure story with a
purpose, relying heavily on violence and
eccentric characters.

w Budd Schulberg *d* Nicholas Ray *ph* Joseph
Brun

Christopher Plummer, Burl Ives, Gypsy Rose
Lee, Emmett Kelly, George Voskovec, Tony
Galento, Mackinlay Kantor

The Wind and the Lion
US 1975   119m   Metrocolor   Panavision
Columbia / MGM (Herb Jaffe, Phil Rawlins)

In 1904 Tangier, an American widow and her
children are kidnapped by a Riffian chief, and
the eyes of the world are focused on the
incident.
Basing itself very lightly on an actual event,

this adventure story is both confused as a
narrative and unexciting as an action piece:
the camera stops too often to look at sunsets,
the plot stops too often for philosophizing, and
there are too many underexplained characters
and incidents fitting into the international
jigsaw.

wd John Milius *ph* Billy Williams *m* Jerry
Goldsmith

Sean Connery, Candice Bergen, Brian Keith,
John Huston, Geoffrey Lewis, Steve Kanaly,
Vladek Sheybal

AAN: Jerry Goldsmith

The Wind Cannot Read
GB 1958   115m   Eastmancolor
Rank (Betty E. Box)

In India and Burma during World War II, a
flying officer falls in love with a Japanese
language instructor suffering from a brain
disease.
Or, love is a many-splendoured dark victory.
Old-fashioned romance for addicts, well
enough produced.

w Richard Mason, from his novel *d* Ralph
Thomas *ph* Ernest Steward *m* Angelo
Lavagnino

Dirk Bogarde, Yoko Tani, Ronald Lewis,
John Fraser, Anthony Bushell, Michael
Medwin

Windbag the Sailor
GB 1936   85m   bw
Gainsborough (Edward Black)

An incompetent seaman is washed away on an
old ketch and lands on a South Sea isle.
Rather uninventive star comedy with
inevitable pleasing moments.

w Marriott Edgar, Stafford Dickens, Will
Hay *d* William Beaudine *ph* Jack Cox
md Louis Levy

Will Hay, Moore Marriott, Graham Moffatt,
Norma Varden

Windom's Way*
GB 1957   108m   Technicolor
Rank (John Bryan)

A doctor on a Far Eastern island tries to quell
a native uprising.
Tolerably well intentioned action melodrama,
topical because of Malaya; dramatically rather
sober and predictable.

w Jill Craigie, *novel* James Ramsay Ullman
d Ronald Neame *ph* Christopher Challis
m James Bernard

Peter Finch, Mary Ure, Natasha Parry, Robert
Flemyng, Michael Hordern

The Window***
US 1949   73m   bw
RKO

A New York slum boy is always telling tall
tales, so no one believes him when he actually
witnesses a murder . . . except the murderer.
Classic little second feature, entertaining and
suspenseful; unfortunately it had few
successful imitators.

w Mel Dinelli *d* Ted Tetzlaff *ph* William
Steiner *m* Roy Webb

Bobby Driscoll, Barbara Hale, Arthur
Kennedy, Paul Stewart, Ruth Roman
'Logical, well-shaped, cohesive, admirably
acted, beautifully photographed and cut to a
nicety.'—*Richard Winnington*

A Window in London
GB 1939   77m   bw

A *crime passionel* is witnessed from a passing
train. Modest Anglo-Saxon remake of the
French film *Metropolitan*. Michael Redgrave,
Sally Gray, Paul Lukas, Hartley Power,
Patricia Roc. Written by Ian Dalrymple and
Brigid Cooper; directed by Herbert Mason;
for G and S / GFD. (US title: *Lady in
Distress*.)

Wing and a Prayer*
US 1944   97m   bw
TCF (William Becker, William Morosco)

Life aboard an aircraft carrier.
Standard action flagwaver.

w Jerome Cady *d* Henry Hathaway *ph* Glen
MacWilliams *m* Hugo Friedhofer

Don Ameche, Cedric Hardwicke, Dana
Andrews, Charles Bickford, Richard Jaeckel,
Henry Morgan

AAN: Jerome Cady

Winged Victory**
US 1944   130m   bw
TCF (Darryl F. Zanuck)

During World War II, pilots are inducted,
trained and sent on dangerous missions.
Solid, competent, best-foot-forward flagwaver
of the highest inspirational intention.

w Moss Hart, from his play *d* George Cukor
ph Glen MacWilliams *m* David Rose

Lon McCallister, Jeanne Crain, Edmond
O'Brien, Jane Ball, Mark Daniels, Don
Taylor, Lee J. Cobb, Judy Holliday, Peter
Lind Hayes, Alan Baxter, Red Buttons, Barry
Nelson, Gary Merrill, Karl Malden, Martin
Ritt, Jo-Carroll Dennison
'I suppose it is all right, but I don't enjoy

having anyone tell me, so cheerfully and energetically, that the Air Force personnel is without exception composed of boy scouts old enough to shave.'—*James Agee*

'There is no question that Mr Hart captured much of the gallantry and pathos of youth rushing towards dangerous adventures with surface enthusiasm and inner dread.'—*Bosley Crowther, New York Times*

Wings*
US 1927   136m (24 fps)   bw   silent
Paramount (B. P. Schulberg)

Two young men join the Air Service during World War I, and one eventually shoots down the other by accident.

An epic of early aviation, still stirring in its action sequences.

w Hope Loring, Harry D. Lighton   *d William Wellman   ph* Harry Perry

Clara Bow, Charles Buddy Rogers, Richard Arlen, Gary Cooper, Jobyna Ralston, El Brendel

'Air battles are photographed from every conceivable angle, producing many bold cinematic effects . . . so much in fact happens in the air that it is impossible to take it all in.'—*National Board of Review*

AA: best picture; best engineering effects (Roy Pomeroy)

Wings for the Eagle
US 1942   85m   bw
Warner (Robert Lord)

Aircraft workers do their bit during World War II.

Home Front propaganda, well enough produced.

w Byron Morgan, Harrison Orkow   *d* Lloyd Bacon   *ph* Tony Gaudio   *m* Frederick Hollander

Ann Sheridan, Dennis Morgan, Jack Carson, George Tobias, Don Defore

Wings in the Dark*
US 1935   75m   bw
Paramount (Arthur Hornblow Jnr)

Embittered after being blinded in an accident, a research flier finally leaps into action when his stranded girl friend needs help.

Satisfactory romantic melodrama.

w Jack Kirkland, Frank Partos   *d* James Flood   *ph* William C. Mellor

Cary Grant, Myrna Loy, Roscoe Karns, Hobart Cavanaugh, Dean Jagger, Bert Hanlon, Samuel S. Hinds

The Wings of Eagles*
US 1957   110m   Metrocolor
Cinemascope
MGM (Charles Schnee)

A navy flier breaks his neck in an accident and on recovery becomes a Hollywood writer.

Sentimental biopic of Frank 'Spig' Wead, a routine, easy-going assignment for its director (who is caricatured by Ward Bond as John Dodge).

w Frank Fenton, William Wister Haines   *d* John Ford   *ph* Paul C. Vogel   *m* Jeff Alexander

John Wayne, Maureen O'Hara, Ward Bond, Dan Dailey, Ken Curtis, Edmund Lowe, Kenneth Tobey, Sig Rumann, Henry O'Neill

Wings of the Hawk
US 1953   81m   Technicolor   3-D
U-I (Aaron Rosenberg)

Mexico 1911: a gold miner falls into the hands of revolutionaries.

Routine bang-bang, rather sloppily produced.

w James E. Moser   *d* Budd Boetticher   *ph* Clifford Stine   *m* Frank Skinner

Van Heflin, Julie Adams, George Dolenz, Pedro Gonzales-Gonzales, Rodolfo Acosta, Antonio Moreno, Abbe Lane

Wings of the Morning*
GB 1937   89m   Technicolor
TCF (Robert T. Kane)

In 1899, a gypsy princess marries an Irish nobleman; in 1937, romance again blooms between their descendants.

Britain's first Technicolor film was great to look at and quite charming, though slight; its major attractions being horse races, songs from John McCormack, and a heroine dressed for plot purposes as a boy.

w Tom Geraghty, *story* Donn Byrne   *d* Harold Schuster   *ph* Ray Rennahan, Jack Cardiff   *m* Arthur Benjamin

Henry Fonda, *Annabella*, Stewart Rome, John McCormack, Leslie Banks, Irene Vanbrugh, Harry Tate, Edward Underdown, Helen Haye

'A wholesome, refreshing and altogether likeable little romance.'—*Frank S. Nugent*

Wings of the Navy
US 1939   89m   bw
Warner (Lou Edelman)

The loves and careers of navy pilots.

Competent animated recruiting poster.

w Michael Fessier   *d* Lloyd Bacon   *ph* Arthur Edeson, Elmer Dyer

George Brent, Olivia de Havilland, John
Payne, Frank McHugh, John Litel, Victor
Jory, Henry O'Neill, John Ridgely

Winning*
US 1969   123m   Technicolor
Panavision 70
Universal / Newman–Foreman (John
Foreman)

A racing driver's professional problems strain
his relationship with his wife.
Cliché track melodrama with pretensions, well
but needlessly made.

w Howard Rodman d James Goldstone
ph Richard Moore m Dave Grusin

Paul Newman, Joanne Woodward, Richard
Thomas, Robert Wagner, David Sheiner, Clu
Gulager

The Winning Team
US 1952   98m   bw
Warner (Bryan Foy)

A telephone linesman becomes a great
baseball player despite trouble with his vision
after an accident.
Standard biopic of Grover Cleveland
Alexander; all very pleasant but no surprises.

w Ted Sherdeman, Seeleg Lester, Merwin
Gerard d Lewis Seiler ph Sid Hickox
m David Buttolph

Doris Day, Ronald Reagan, Frank Lovejoy,
Eve Miller, James Millican, Russ Tamblyn

The Winslow Boy***
GB 1948   117m   bw
British Lion / London Films (Anatole de
Grunwald)

A naval cadet is expelled for stealing a postal
order; his father spends all he had on proving
his innocence.
Highly enjoyable middle-class British
entertainment based on an actual case;
performances and period settings are alike
excellent, though the film is a trifle overlong.

w Terence Rattigan, Anatole de Grunwald,
play Terence Rattigan d Anthony Asquith
ph Frederick Young m William Alwyn

Robert Donat, Cedric Hardwicke, Margaret
Leighton, Frank Lawton, Jack Watling, Basil
Radford, Kathleen Harrison, Francis L.
Sullivan, Marie Lohr, Neil North, Wilfrid
Hyde White, Ernest Thesiger

Winter Carnival
US 1939   89m   bw
UA

College romances over a holiday weekend.
Nondescript romantic comedy.

w Lester Cole, Budd Schulberg d Charles
Riesner ph Merrit Gerstad m Werner
Janssen

Ann Sheridan, Richard Carlson, Helen
Parrish, Virginia Gilmore, Robert Walker

Winter Light*
Sweden 1962   80m   bw
Svensk Filmindustri (Allan Ekelund)
original title: Nattvardsgasterna

A widowed village pastor loses his vocation.
In a sense almost parody Bergman; in another,
one of his clearest statements of despair. The
middle section of a pessimistic trilogy which
also included Through a Glass Darkly and The
Silence.

wd Ingmar Bergman ph Sven Nykvist
m none

Max Von Sydow, Ingrid Thulin, Gunnar
Bjornstrand, Gunnel Lindblom
   'The film-maker's mastery alone does not
guarantee a great film. Winter Light is scarcely
even a good one.'—John Simon, 1967

Winter Meeting
US 1948   104m   bw
Warner (Henry Blanke)

A repressed spinster falls for a naval hero
intent on becoming a priest.
Dreary talk marathon which did its star's
career no good at all.

w Catherine Turney, novel Ethel Vance
d Bretaigne Windust ph Ernest Haller
m Max Steiner

Bette Davis, James Davis, Janis Paige, John
Hoyt, Florence Bates, Walter Baldwin

Winterset**
US 1936   78m   bw
RKO

On the New York waterfront, a drifter
determines to avenge his father's death.
Very dated poetic melodrama, here given a
talky, artificial production which at the time
impressed many critics but is now fairly
difficult to endure.

w Anthony Veiller, play Maxwell Anderson
d Alfred Santell ph Peverell Marley
md Nathaniel Shilkret

Burgess Meredith, Eduardo Ciannelli, Margo,
Paul Guilfoyle, John Carradine, Edward Ellis,
Stanley Ridges, Maurice Moscovitch, Myron
McCormick, Mischa Auer
   'Still in a grand manner that just won't do

on the screen . . . but there are fine moments in the performances, and there's something childishly touching in the florid dramatic effects.'—*New Yorker, 1978*

AAN: Nathaniel Shilkret

Wintertime

US 1943 82m bw
TCF (William Le Baron)

A Norwegian skating star comes to Canada where her uncle's winter resort is on its uppers.
The last of the star's Fox musicals is pure routine.

w Edward Moran, Jack Jevne, Lynn Starling *d* John Brahm *ph* Glen MacWilliams *m* Alfred Newman *md* Charles Henderson

Sonja Henie, Jack Oakie, Cesar Romero, S. Z. Sakall, Carole Landis, Cornel Wilde, Woody Herman and his Band

The Wistful Widow of Wagon Gap*

US 1947 78m bw
U-I (Robert Arthur)

In old Montana, an accident-prone wayfarer accidentally kills a man and has to look after his family.
Tame and disappointing comedy vehicle.

w D. D. Beauchamp, William Bowers *d* Charles T. Barton, Robert Lees, Frederic I. Rinaldo, John Grant *ph* Charles Van Enger *m* Walter Shumann

Bud Abbott, Lou Costello, Marjorie Main, Audrey Young, George Cleveland

Witchcraft*

GB 1964 79m bw
TCF / Lippert (Robert Lippert, Jack Parsons)

A family of witches take revenge on their longtime enemies.
Spasmodically arresting horror film spoiled by too complex a plot line and some variable acting.

w Harry Spaulding *d Don Sharp* *ph* Arthur Lavis *m* Carlo Martelli

Jack Hedley, Lon Chaney Jnr, Marie Ney, Jill Dixon, David Weston
'Unpretentious and uncommonly gripping.'—*MFB*

Witchcraft through the Ages**

Sweden 1922 83m approx (24 fps) bw silent
Svensk Filmindustri
original title: *Haxan*

A 'documentary' investigation of the history of witchcraft, with acted examples.

Fascinating reconstruction of ancient rituals, still maintaining its power to frighten.

wd Benjamin Christensen ph Johan Ankarstjerne

Oscar Stribolt, Clara Pontoppidan, Karen Winther

The Witches

GB 1966 90m Technicolor
Hammer (Anthony Nelson Keys)
US title: *The Devil's Own*

A schoolmistress finds witchcraft in an English village.
Chintzy horror with predictable development and risible climax.

w Nigel Kneale, *novel* The Devil's Own by Peter Curtis *d* Cyril Frankel *ph* Arthur Grant *m* Richard Rodney Bennett

Joan Fontaine, Kay Walsh, Alec McCowen, Gwen Ffrangcon Davies, Ingrid Brett, John Collin, Michèle Dotrice, Leonard Rossiter, Martin Stephens, Carmel McSharry

The Witches of Salem*

France / East Germany 1957 143m bw
Borderie / CICC / DEFA / Pathé (Raymond Borderie)
original title: *Les Sorcieres de Salem*

In 1692 Massachussetts, jealousies lead to accusations of witchcraft and multiple trials and executions.
An account of a horrifying historical fact which was also intended to reflect on the McCarthy witch hunts of the fifties; but the film, despite splendid acting, is too literal and slow-moving.

w Jean-Paul Sartre, *play* The Crucible by Arthur Miller *d* Raymond Rouleau *ph* Claude Renoir *m* Georges Auric

Simone Signoret, Yves Montand, Mylène Demongeot, Jean Debucourt

Witchfinder General*

GB 1968 87m Eastmancolor
Tigon (Arnold Miller)
US title: *The Conqueror Worm*

In 1645 a villainous lawyer finds it profitable to travel the country instigating witch hunts.
Savage, stylish minor horror melodrama with a growing reputation as the best work of its young director. Not for the squeamish despite its pleasing countryside photography.

w Michael Reeves, Tom Baker, *novel* Ronald Bassett *d Michael Reeves ph* John Coquillon *m* Paul Ferris, Jim Morahan

Vincent Price, Rupert Davies, Ian Ogilvy, Patrick Wymark, Hilary Dwyer

'Keep the children home! And if you're squeamish, stay home with them!'—*publicity*

With a Song in My Heart*
US 1952   117m   Technicolor
TCF (Lamar Trotti)

Singer Jane Froman is crippled in a plane crash but finally makes a comeback.
Romanticized showbiz biopic with the singer providing voice only. Adequate production and plenty of familiar tunes made this a successful mass appeal sob story.

w Lamar Trotti *d* Walter Lang *ph* Leon Shamroy *md* Alfred Newman

Susan Hayward, David Wayne, Rory Calhoun, Thelma Ritter, Una Merkel, Robert Wagner, Helen Westcott

AA: Alfred Newman
AAN: Susan Hayward; Thelma Ritter

With Six You Get Egg Roll
US 1968   99m   De Luxe   Panavision
Cinema Center / Arwin (Martin Melcher)

A widow with three sons marries a widower with one daughter.
Quite a bright and inventive family comedy.

w Gwen Bagni, Paul Dubov *d* Howard Morris *ph* Ellsworth Fredericks, Harry Stradling Jnr *m* Robert Mersey

Doris Day, Brian Keith, Pat Carroll, Barbara Hershey

Without Love*
US 1945   111m   bw
MGM (Lawrence Weingarten)

The housing shortage in wartime Washington causes a widow to allow a scientist to move in with her, quite platonically.
Altered version of a popular play; rather long-drawn-out and disappointing considering the talent on hand.

w Donald Ogden Stewart, *play* Philip Barry *d* Harold S. Bucquet *ph* Karl Freund *m* Bronislau Kaper

Spencer Tracy, Katharine Hepburn, Lucille Ball, Keenan Wynn, Carl Esmond, Patricia Morison, Felix Bressart, Gloria Grahame

'One of those glossy conversation pieces that MGM does up so handsomely.'—*Rose Pelswick*

Without Reservations
US 1946   101m   bw
RKO / Jesse L. Lasky

A famous woman writer heads for Hollywood by train and meets a marine who seems ideal for her male lead.

Would-be zany romantic comedy à la *It Happened One Night*; doesn't quite come off.

w Andrew Solt *d* Mervyn Le Roy *ph* Milton Krasner *m* Roy Webb

Claudette Colbert, John Wayne, Don Defore, Phil Brown, Frank Puglia

Without Warning
US 1952   70m   bw
UA / Allart

A sex maniac murders a succession of blondes.
Semi-documentary, low-budget police thriller with all elements adequate for their purpose.

w Bill Raynor *d* Arnold Laven *ph* Joseph Biroc *m* Herschel Burke Gilbert

Adam Williams, Edward Binns, Meg Randall

Witness for the Prosecution***
US 1957   114m   bw
UA / Theme / Edward Small (Arthur Hornblow Jnr)

A convalescent QC takes on a murder defence and finds himself in a web of trickery.
Thoroughly likeable though relentlessly over-expanded movie version of a clever stage thriller. Some miscasting and artificiality is condoned by smart dialogue and handling, one celebrated performance, and a handful of surprises.

w Billy Wilder, Harry Kurnitz, *play* Agatha Christie *d* Billy Wilder *ph* Russell Harlan *m* Matty Melneck

Charles Laughton, Tyrone Power, Marlene Dietrich, John Williams, Henry Daniell, Elsa Lanchester, Norma Varden, Una O'Connor, Ian Wolfe

AAN: best picture; Billy Wilder; Charles Laughton; Elsa Lanchester

Witness to Murder*
US 1954   81m   bw
UA / Chester Erskine

A lonely woman sees a strangling in the flat across the street; the police don't believe her but the murderer does.
Predictable but quite effective screamer with a nick-of-time dénouement.

w Chester Erskine *d* Roy Rowland *ph* John Alton *m* Herschel Burke Gilbert

Barbara Stanwyck, George Sanders, Gary Merrill, Jesse White, Harry Shannon, Claire Carleton

Wives and Lovers
US 1963   103m   bw
(Paramount) Hal B. Wallis

A successful author moves his family into Connecticut, where sex rears its ugly head. Would-be sophisticated comedy with insufficient bubbles.

w Edward Anhalt, *play* The First Wife by Jay Presson Allen *d* John Rich *ph* Lucien Ballard *m* Lyn Murray

Van Johnson, Janet Leigh, Ray Walston, Shelley Winters, Martha Hyer, Jeremy Slate

Wives under Suspicion
US 1938 68m bw

A district attorney involved in a love-triangle murder discovers a similar situation developing in his own life. Flat remake of the same director's *The Kiss Before the Mirror*; of little interest. Warren William, Gail Patrick, Ralph Morgan, William Lundigan, Constance Moore. Written by Myles Connelly; directed by James Whale; for Universal.

The Wiz*
US 1978 134m Technicolor
Universal / Motown (Robert Cohen)

A black version of *The Wizard of Oz*, set in New York.

Glossy version of the Broadway musical hit; it offers some rewards, but on the whole the first is the best.

w Joel Schumacher, from play with ly / m by Charlie Smith, book by William Brown *d* Sidney Lumet *ph* Oswald Morris *pd* Tony Walton *m* Quincy Jones *md* Quincy Jones *songs* Charlie Smales

Diana Ross, Michael Jackson, Nipsey Russell, Ted Ross, Lena Horne, Richard Pryor, Mabel King, Theresa Merritt

AAN: Oswald Morris; Quincy Jones

The Wizard of Oz***
US 1939 102m Technicolor
MGM (Mervyn Le Roy)

Unhappy Dorothy runs away from home, has adventures in a fantasy land, but finally decides that happiness was in her own back yard all the time.

Classic fairy tale given vigorous straightforward treatment, made memorable by performances, art direction and hummable tunes.

w Noel Langley, Florence Ryerson, Edgar Allan Wolfe, *book* Frank L. Baum *d* Victor Fleming *ph* Harold Rosson *songs* E. Y. Harburg, Harold Arlen *md* Herbert Stothart *ad* Cedric Gibbons, William A. Horning

Judy Garland, Frank Morgan, Ray Bolger, Jack Haley, Bert Lahr, Margaret Hamilton, Billie Burke, Charley Grapewin, Clara Blandick

'I don't see why children shouldn't like it, but for adults there isn't very much except Bert Lahr.'—*Richard Mallett, Punch*

'As for the light touch of fantasy, it weighs like a pound of fruitcake soaking wet.'—*Otis Ferguson*

† Ray Bolger was originally cast as the tin man but swapped roles with Buddy Ebsen who was to have been the scarecrow. Ebsen then got sick from the metal paint and was replaced by Jack Haley. Edna May Oliver was originally cast as the wicked witch. For Dorothy MGM wanted Shirley Temple, but Twentieth Century Fox wouldn't loan her.

†† The sepia scenes at beginning and end were directed by King Vidor.

AA: song 'Over the Rainbow'; Herbert Stothart
AAN: best picture

Wolf Larsen
US 1958 83m bw
AA (Lindsley Parsons)

Serviceable remake of *The Sea Wolf* (qv) without the Nietzschean overtones.

w Jack de Witt, Turnley Walker *d* Harlan Jones *ph* Floyd Crosby *m* Paul Dunlap

Barry Sullivan, Peter Graves, Thayer David, Gita Hall

The Wolf Man**
US 1940 70m bw
Universal (George Waggner)

The son of an English squire comes home, is bitten by a gypsy werewolf, and becomes one himself.

Dazzlingly cast, moderately well staged, but dramatically very disappointing horror piece which established a new Universal monster who later met Frankenstein, Abbott and Costello, and several other eccentrics.

w Curt Siodmak *d* George Waggner *ph* Joseph Valentine *m* Hans Salter, Frank Skinner *md* Charles Previn

Lon Chaney Jnr, Claude Rains, Warren William, Ralph Bellamy, Bela Lugosi, *Maria Ouspenskaya*, Patric Knowles, Evelyn Ankers, Fay Helm

Woman Accused*
US 1933 73m bw
Paramount

A woman kills her ex-lover in a struggle and goes on the run.

Intriguing rigmarole written as a magazine serial by ten well-known authors contributing a chapter each. The result confirms the method.

w Bayard Veiller, *serial* Rupert Hughes, Vicki Baum, Zane Grey, Vina Delmar, Irvin S. Cobb, Gertrude Atherton, J. P. McEvoy, Ursula Parrott, Polan Banks, Sophie Kerr d Paul Sloane m Karl Struss

Nancy Carroll, Cary Grant, John Halliday, Irving Pichel, Louis Calhern, Jack La Rue, John Lodge

A Woman Alone
GB 1936 78m bw

In nineteenth-century Russia, a captain falls for a peasant girl. Uninteresting melodrama with stilted actors. Anna Sten, Henry Wilcoxon, Viola Keats, John Garrick, Rimilly Lunge. Written by Leo Lania and Warren Chetham Strode, from a novel by Fedor Ozep; directed by Eugene Frenke; for Garrett-Klement. (US title: *Two Who Dared*.)

The Woman from Monte Carlo
US 1932 68m bw

The wife of a naval officer is suspected of adultery. Stiff marital melodrama based on a silent film *The Night Watch*; it worked no wonders for its German star. Lil Dagover, Walter Huston, Warren William, Robert Warwick, John Wray. Written by Harvey Thew; directed by Michael Curtiz; for Warner.

Woman Hater
GB 1948 105m bw
GFD / Two Cities

An English nobleman tries to disprove a film star's statement that she hates men and loves solitude.
Incredibly slight material is interminably stretched out, well beyond an excellent cast's ability to help.

w Robert Westerby, Nicholas Phipps d Terence Young ph André Thomas m Lambert Williamson

Stewart Granger, Edwige Feuillère, Ronald Squire, Mary Jerrold, Jeanne de Casalis

The Woman I Love*
US 1937 85m bw
RKO (Albert Lewis)
GB title: *The Woman Between*

In World War I France, a pilot loves his superior officer's wife.
Well-made romantic action melodrama from a well-praised original.

w Mary Borden, French film L'Equipage and novel of same name by Joseph Kessel d Anatole Litvak ph Charles Rosher m Arthur Honegger, Maurice Thiriet

Paul Muni, Miriam Hopkins, Louis Hayward, Colin Clive, Minor Watson, Elizabeth Risdon, Paul Guilfoyle, Mady Christians

Woman in a Dressing Gown*
GB 1957 94m bw
Godwin / Willis / J. Lee-Thompson

After twenty years of marriage, a wife's slatternly ways alienate her once devoted husband, and he asks for a divorce.
Classic British TV play adequately filmed but now rather dated and irritating.

w Ted Willis, from his play d J. Lee-Thompson ph Gilbert Taylor m Louis Levy

Yvonne Mitchell, Anthony Quayle, Sylvia Syms, Andrew Ray, Carole Lesley

Woman in Hiding
US 1949 92m bw
U-I (Michael Kraike)

After escaping her husband's attempts to murder her, a woman goes into hiding while evidence is being accumulated against him. Modest suspenser with too many near escapes and not much else.

w Oscar Saul d Michael Gordon ph William Daniels m Frank Skinner

Ida Lupino, Howard Duff, Stephen McNally, John Litel, Taylor Holmes, Irving Bacon, Peggy Dow, Joe Besser, Don Beddoe

'The detail is full of things interesting and amusing at the time and pleasant to remember afterwards.'—*Richard Mallett, Punch*

The Woman in Question*
GB 1949 88m bw
GFD / Javelin (Teddy Baird)
US title: *Five Angles on Murder*

Police investigating a woman's death build up several different impressions of her.
Multi-flashback melodrama which somehow doesn't quite come off despite effort all round.

w John Cresswell d Anthony Asquith ph Desmond Dickinson m John Wooldridge

Jean Kent, Dirk Bogarde, Susan Shaw, John McCallum, Hermione Baddeley, Charles Victor, Duncan Macrae, Lana Morris, Vida Hope

The Woman in Red
US 1935 68m bw

A professional horsewoman marries into society and is ill received. Stiff class melodrama partly redeemed by its star.

Barbara Stanwyck, Genevieve Tobin, John Eldredge, Gene Raymond, Philip Reed. Written by Mary McCall Jnr and Peter Milne, from the novel *North Shore* by Wallace Irwin; directed by Robert Florey; for Warner.

The Woman in the Hall
GB 1947 93m bw
GFD / IP / Wessex (Ian Dalrymple)

A well-intentioned woman takes to begging and becomes a bad influence on her daughter. Finger-wagging novelette makes an unrewarding film.

w G. B. Stern, Ian Dalrymple, Jack Lee *novel* G. B. Stern *d* Jack Lee *ph* C. Pennington-Richards and H. E. Fowle *m* Temple Abady

Ursula Jeans, Cecil Parker, Jean Simmons, Jill Raymond, Edward Underdown, Joan Miller

The Woman in the Window***
US 1944 95m bw
International (Nunnally Johnson)

A grass widow professor befriends a girl who gets him involved with murder.
A refreshingly intelligent little thriller which was criticized at the time for a cop-out ending; this can now be seen as a decorative extra to a story which had already ended satisfactorily. Good middlebrow entertainment.

w *Nunnally Johnson, novel* Once Off Guard by J. H. Wallis *d Fritz Lang ph Milton Krasner m* Arthur Lang, Hugo Friedhofer

Edward G. Robinson, Joan Bennett, *Raymond Massey, Dan Duryea*, Edmund Breon, Thomas Jackson, Dorothy Peterson, Arthur Loft

'A perfect example of its kind, and a very good kind too.'—*James Shelley Hamilton*
'The accumulation of tiny details enlarged as though under a district attorney's magnifying glass gives reality a fantastic and anguishing appearance.'—*Jacques Bourgeois*
'In its rather artificial, club library style an effective and well made piece, absorbing, diverting and full of often painful suspense.'—*Richard Mallett, Punch*
'It was the look in her eyes that did it. How could he resist? How could he know it meant murder?'—*publicity*

AAN: Arthur Lang, Hugo Friedhofer

The Woman in White**
US 1948 109m bw
Warner (Henry Blanke)

The new tutor of a strange household finds himself among eccentrics, villains and ill-used ladies.
A Victorian thriller which is long on atmosphere but not so hot on suspense or plot development. The cast helps a lot.

w Stephen Morehouse Avery, *novel* Wilkie Collins *d* Peter Godfrey *ph* Carl Guthrie *m* Max Steiner

Gig Young, Eleanor Parker, *Sidney Greenstreet*, Alexis Smith, Agnes Moorehead, John Emery, *John Abbott*, Curt Bois
'The Wilkie Collins novel is given the studious, stolid treatment ordinarily reserved for the ritual assassination of a great classic. This is not intended as a recommendation.'—*James Agee*
'Greenstreet and others move through the murky passages of the story like visitors in some massive Gothic museum, and they move, on the whole, with stately discretion, and do not scribble on the objects or show anything but the greatest veneration for them.'—*C. A. Lejeune*

Woman Obsessed
US 1959 102m De Luxe Cinemascope
TCF (Sidney Boehm)

In the Canadian Rockies, a pioneer woman's small son does not take to his new stepfather. Antediluvian pulp fiction with quicksand and a forest fire for highlights. Shades of D. W. Griffith, and badly done into the bargain.

w Sidney Boehm, *novel* John Mantley *d* Henry Hathaway *ph* William C. Mellor *m* Hugo Friedhofer

Susan Hayward, Stephen Boyd, Dennis Holmes, Theodore Bikel, Barbara Nichols, Ken Scott, Arthur Franz

A Woman of Affairs
US 1928 90m (24 fps) bw silent
MGM

A wild rich girl goes from man to man and finally kills herself in a car crash.
Romantic star tosh from a fashionable novel of the time.

w Bess Meredyth, *novel* The Green Hat by Michael Arlen *d* Clarence Brown *ph* William Daniels

Greta Garbo, Lewis Stone, John Gilbert, John Mack Brown, Douglas Fairbanks Jnr, Hobart Bosworth

A Woman of Distinction
US 1950 85m bw
Columbia (Buddy Adler)

The lady dean of a New England school falls for a British astronomer.
Pratfall farce for ageing stars. No go.

w Charles Hoffman d Edward Buzzell
ph Joseph Walker m Werner Heymann
md Morris Stoloff

Rosalind Russell, Ray Milland, Edmund Gwenn, Janis Carter, Mary Jane Saunders, Francis Lederer, Jerome Courtland

A Woman of Paris**
US 1923 85m (24 fps) bw silent (music track added 1976)
Charles Chaplin

A country girl goes to the city, becomes a demi-mondaine, and inadvertently causes the death of the one man she loves.
Remarkably simply-handled 'road to ruin' melodrama; its subtleties of treatment make it still very watchable for those so inclined.

wd Charles Chaplin m Rollie Totheroh, Jack Wilson

Edna Purviance, Adolphe Menjou, Carl Miller, Lydia Knott
'After five minutes of watching the sparkling new print, the spell begins to work. Chaplin is neatly turning the clichés inside out, like a glove.'—*Alan Brien, Sunday Times, 1980*
'Mr Chaplin as writer and director has not done anything radical or anything esoteric; he has merely used his intelligence to the highest degree, an act which for many years has ceased to be expected of motion picture people.'—*Robert E. Sherwood*
† Chaplin appeared unbilled as a railway porter. The film was not a commercial success and he withdrew it for fifty years.

Woman of Straw*
GB 1964 114m Eastmancolor
UA / Novus (Michael Relph)

A rich old man's nurse conspires with his nephew in a murder plot.
Rather half-hearted but good-looking star melodrama which ventures into Hitchcock territory.

w Robert Muller, Stanley Mann, Michael Relph, *novel* Catherine Arley d Basil Dearden ph Otto Heller m Muir Mathieson
pd Ken Adam

Gina Lollobrigida, Sean Connery, *Ralph Richardson,* Johnny Sekka, Laurence Hardy, Alexander Knox

Woman of the Dunes*
Japan 1964 127m bw
Teshigahara (Kiichi Ichikawa)
original title: *Suna no Onna*

An entomologist on a deserted beach finds an attractive young widow living in a shack at the bottom of a huge sand pit, spends the night with her, can't escape, and finally doesn't want to.
Unique sex melodrama, all shifting sand and picturesque angles, with a clear meaning; but far too long.

w Kobo Abe d *Hiroshi Teshigahara*
ph Hiroshi Segawa

Eiji Okada, Kyoko Kishoda
'Teasingly opaque, broodingly erotic.'—*MFB*

AAN: Hiroshi Teshigahara

Woman of the North Country
US 1952 90m Trucolor
Republic (Joseph Kane)

Minnesota 1890: rivalry over an iron ore mine erupts between a young engineer and an ambitious woman.
Standard western.

w Norman Reilly Raine d Joseph Kane
ph Jack Marta m R. Dale Butts

Ruth Hussey, Rod Cameron, John Agar, Gale Storm, Jim Davis, J. Carrol Naish

Woman of the Year***
US 1942 114m bw
MGM (Joseph L. Mankiewicz)

A sports columnist marries a lady politician; they have nothing in common but love.
Simple, effective, mildly sophisticated comedy which allows two splendid stars, in harness for the first time, to do their thing to the general benefit.

w Ring Lardner Jnr, Michael Kanin d George Stevens ph Joseph Ruttenberg m Franz Waxman

Spencer Tracy, Katharine Hepburn, Fay Bainter, Reginald Owen, William Bendix, Dan Tobin, Minor Watson, Roscoe Karns
'Between them they have enough charm to keep any ball rolling.'—*William Whitebait*

AA: script
AAN: Katharine Hepburn

The Woman on Pier 13
US 1949 73m bw
RKO (Jack J. Gross)
aka: *I Married a Communist*

A shipping executive is blackmailed by communists, who know of a youthful crime, into helping them spy.
Laboured witch-hunt melodrama.

w Charles Grayson, Robert Hardy Andrews
d Robert Stevenson ph Nicholas Musuraca
m Leigh Harline

Laraine Day, Robert Ryan, John Agar,
Thomas Gomez, Janis Carter, Richard Rober,
William Talman

Woman on the Beach
US 1947   71m   bw
RKO (Jack J. Gross)

A mentally ailing coastguard meets a *femme
fatale* and comes between her and her sadistic
husband.
Nuthouse melodrama which neither convinces
nor compels for a moment.

w Frank Davis, Jean Renoir, *novel* None So
Blind by Mitchell Wilson d Jean Renoir
ph Leo Tover, Harry Wild *m* Hanns Eisler

Joan Bennett, Robert Ryan, Charles Bickford,
Nan Leslie, Walter Sande

A Woman Rebels*
US 1936   88m   bw
RKO (Pandro S. Berman)

A Victorian miss fights for women's rights and
has an illegitimate baby.
Interesting, half-forgotten star drama.

w Anthony Veiller, Ernest Vajda,
novel Portrait of a Rebel by Netta Syrett
d Mark Sandrich *ph* Robert de Grasse
m Roy Webb *ad* Van Nest Polglase

Katharine Hepburn, Herbert Marshall,
Elizabeth Allan, Donald Crisp, Doris Dudley,
David Manners, Van Heflin, Lucile Watson,
Eily Malyon

'Delving into the fascinating ugliness of
Victorian England, RKO Radio have found
material that is picturesque, humorous and
tragic.'—*Frank Nugent, New York Times*

The Woman They Almost Lynched
US 1952   90m   bw

An innocent girl out west is blamed for a
crime wave and almost executed as a spy.
Incredible, random-plotted western with a few
entertaining moments. Joan Leslie, Audrey
Totter, John Lund, Brian Donlevy, Ben
Cooper. Written by Steve Fisher, from a story
by Michael Fessier; directed by Allan Dwan;
for Republic.

Woman Times Seven
US / France 1967   99m   De Luxe
TCF / Embassy (Arthur Cohn)

Seven sketches, in each of which a woman
behaves typically of her sex.
Humourless after-dinner entertainment.

w Cesare Zavattini d Vittorio de Sica
ph Christian Matras *m* Riz Ortolani

Shirley Maclaine, Peter Sellers, Rossano
Brazzi, Vittorio Gassman, Lex Barker, Elsa
Martinelli, Robert Morley, Adrienne Corri,
Patrick Wymark, Alan Arkin, Michael Caine,
Anita Ekberg, Philippe Noiret

Woman to Woman
GB 1923   83m at 24 fps   bw   silent

A shell-shocked officer marries into Society
and later adopts his son by a French ballerina.
Far-fetched melodrama in what later became
the *Random Harvest* style; a great box-office
hit of its time. Betty Compson, Clive Brook,
Josephine Earle, Marie Ault. Written by
Alfred Hitchcock, from the play by Michael
Morton; directed by Graham Cutts; for
Balcon, Freedman and Saville. (Victor Saville
directed a sound remake in 1929, with Betty
Compson and George Barraud; and in 1946
Maclean Rogers had another shot with Adele
Dixon and Douglass Montgomery.)

A Woman under the Influence*
US 1974   146m   colour
Faces International (Sam Shaw)

A white collar worker's marriage goes sour.
Insanely long case history in close up, with all
parties constantly on the brink of hysteria.
Often sharply observed, but hard to sit
through.

wd John Cassavetes *ph* Mitch Breit *m* Bo
Harwood

Peter Falk, Gena Rowlands

AAN: John Cassavetes (as director); Gena
Rowlands

The Woman with No Name
GB 1950   83m   bw

An amnesiac wife finds herself threatened
from all sides. Hoary melodrama with some
unintentional laughs. Phyllis Calvert, Edward
Underdown, Helen Cherry, Richard Burton,
Anthony Nicholls, James Hayter, Betty Ann
Davies. Written by Ladislas Vajda and Guy
Morgan, from the novel *Happy Now I Go* by
Theresa Charles; directed by Ladislas Vajda
and George More O'Ferrall; for IFP / ABP.
(US title: *Her Panelled Door*.)

The Woman's Angle
GB 1952   86m   bw
ABP / Leslie Arliss / Bow Belles (Walter
   Mycroft)

In a divorce court three flashbacks tell of the
life of a composer.
Damp little formula drama for matinee
audiences, refashioned from a successful silent
film.

wd Leslie Arliss, *novel* Three Cups of Coffee by Ruth Feiner *ph* Erwin Hillier *m* Robert Gill; the Mansell Concerto by Kenneth Leslie Smith

Edward Underdown, Cathy O'Donnell, Lois Maxwell, Claude Farrell, Peter Reynolds, Marjorie Fielding

A Woman's Face**
US 1941   105m   bw
MGM (Victor Saville)

A scarred and embittered woman turns to crime but jibs at murder.

Curious, unexpected but very entertaining melodrama with a courtroom frame, Swedish settings, an excellent cast and some bravura sequences.

w Donald Ogden Stewart, *play* Il Était une Fois by Francis de Croisset *d George Cukor ph Robert Planck m* Bronislau Kaper

Joan Crawford, Melvyn Douglas, *Conrad Veidt,* Osa Massen, Reginald Owen, Albert Basserman, Marjorie Main, Donald Meek, Connie Gilchrist

† Also involved in the script were Elliott Paul and Christopher Isherwood.

A Woman's Secret
US 1949   85m   bw
RKO (Herman J. Mankiewicz)

An ex-singer grooms a girl as her successor but lives to regret it.

Downright peculiar little *film noir* by the co-author of *Citizen Kane* (though not so that you'd notice).

w Herman J. Mankiewicz, *novel* Mortgage on Life by Vicki Baum *d* Nicholas Ray *ph* George Diskant *m* Frederick Hollander *md* Constantin Bakaleinikoff

Maureen O'Hara, Gloria Grahame, Melvyn Douglas, Bill Williams, Victor Jory, Mary Phillips

A Woman's Vengeance*
US 1948   96m   bw
U-I

A man is convicted for the murder of his invalid wife, actually committed by a jealous woman in love with him but later spurned. Interesting but very stagey melodrama from one of its author's more commercial ventures.

w Aldous Huxley, from his story and play The Gioconda Smile *d* Zoltan Korda *ph* Russell Metty *m* Miklas Rozsa

Charles Boyer, Jessica Tandy, Ann Blyth, Cedric Hardwicke, Mildred Natwick

'A rather literary movie, but most movies aren't even that; much less are they real movies.'—*James Agee*

Woman's World**
US 1954   94m   Technicolor
   Cinemascope
TCF (Charles Brackett)

Three top salesmen and their wives are summoned to New York by the boss, who seeks to choose a new general manager. Amusing, superficial pattern comedy-drama for an all-star cast, backed by all-round technical competence.

w Claude Binyon, Mary Loos, Richard Sale *d Jean Negulesco ph* Joe MacDonald *m* Cyril Mockridge

Clifton Webb, Lauren Bacall, Van Heflin, June Allyson, Fred MacMurray, Arlene Dahl, Cornel Wilde, Elliott Reid, Margalo Gillmore

Wombling Free
GB 1977   96m   Eastmancolor
Rank / Ian Shand

The furry creatures who live under Wimbledon Common at last make contact with humans.

Disastrous attempt to film a popular TV series for children. The series came in five-minute chunks; this elephantine transcription leaves several talents high and dry.

wd Lionel Jeffries, from characters created by Elizabeth Beresford *ph* Alan Hume *m* Mike Batt

David Tomlinson, Frances de la Tour, Bonnie Langford, Bernard Spear

'A fiasco. If you really must take your kids, it would be less of a pain to go shopping at the same time.'—*Derek Malcolm, Guardian*

The Women***
US 1939   132m   bw (Technicolor
   sequence)
MGM (Hunt Stromberg)

A New York socialite gets a divorce but later thinks better of it.

Bitchy comedy drama distinguished by an all-girl cast ('135 women with men on their minds'). An over-generous slice of real theatre, skilfully adapted, with rich sets, plenty of laughs, and some memorable scenes between the fighting ladies.

w Anita Loos, Jane Murfin, play Clare Boothe d George Cukor ph Oliver T. Marsh, Joseph Ruttenberg *m* Edward Ward, David Snell

Norma Shearer, Joan Crawford, *Rosalind Russell,* Mary Boland, Paulette Goddard, Joan Fontaine, Lucile Watson, Phyllis Povah, Virginia Weidler, Ruth Hussey, Margaret Dumont, Marjorie Main, Hedda Hopper

'Whether you go or not depends on whether you can stand Miss Shearer with tears flowing steadily in all directions at once, and such an endless damn back fence of cats.'—*Otis Ferguson*

'135 women with men on their minds!'—*publicity*

Women in Love•••
GB 1969 130m De Luxe
UA / Brandywine (Larry Kramer)

Two girls have their first sexual encounters in the Midlands during the twenties.
Satisfactory rendering of a celebrated novel, with excellent period detail atoning for rather irritating characters. The nude wrestling scene was a famous first.

w Larry Kramer, *novel D. H. Lawrence*
d Ken Russell *ph* Billy Williams *m* Georges Delerue

Glenda Jackson, Jennie Linden, Alan Bates, Oliver Reed, Michael Gough, Alan Webb

'They should take all the pretentious dialogue off the soundtrack and call it Women in Heat.'—*Rex Reed*

'Two-thirds success, one-third ambitious failure.'—*Michael Billington, Illustrated London News*

AA: Glenda Jackson
AAN: Larry Kramer; Ken Russell; Billy Williams

Women of All Nations
US 1931 72m bw
Fox

Flagg and Quirt, back in the Marines, have amorous adventures in Sweden, Nicaragua and Egypt.
Routine fun and games with the heroes of *What Price Glory.*

w Barry Connors *d* Raoul Walsh *ph* Lucien Andriot *m* Reginald H. Bassett

Edmund Lowe, Victor McLaglen, Greta Nissen, El Brendel, Fifi D'Orsay, Bela Lugosi, Humphrey Bogart

Women of Twilight
GB 1952 89m bw
Romulus (Daniel M. Angel)

Unmarried mothers are victimized by a professional baby farmer.
Sordid, claustrophobic and ham-handed

version of an exploitation play designed to provide another monstrous part for its star.

w Anatole de Grunwald, *novel* Sylvia Rayman *d* Gordon Parry *ph* Jack Asher *m* Alan Gray

Freda Jackson, René Ray, Lois Maxwell, Joan Dowling, Dora Bryan, Vida Hope, Mary Germaine, Laurence Harvey

Won Ton Ton, the Dog Who Saved Hollywood
US 1976 92m colour
Paramount / David V. Picker, Arnold Schulman, Michael Winner

In twenties Hollywood, a lost Alsatian dog becomes a movie star but later suffers some ups and downs before being reunited with his mistress.
Scatty, unlikeable comedy with too frantic a pace, apparently in desperation at the dearth of funny lines and situations. The sixty 'guest stars' barely get a look in; the director seems to think (erroneously) that their appearance makes some kind of point even though they have nothing to do. Altogether, an embarrassment.

w Arnold Schulman, Cy Howard *d* Michael Winner *ph* Richard H. Kline *m* Neal Hefti

Madeleine Kahn, Art Carney, Bruce Dern, Ron Leibman; and Dennis Morgan, William Demarest, Virginia Mayo, Rory Calhoun, Henry Wilcoxon, Ricardo Montalban, Jackie Coogan, Johnny Weissmuller, Aldo Ray, Ethel Merman, Joan Blondell, Yvonne de Carlo, Andy Devine, Broderick Crawford, Richard Arlen, Jack La Rue, Dorothy Lamour, Phil Silvers, Gloria de Haven, Stepin Fetchit, Rudy Vallee, George Jessel, Ann Miller, Janet Blair, the Ritz Brothers, Victor Mature, Fernando Lamas, Cyd Charisse, Huntz Hall, Edgar Bergen, Peter Lawford, Regis Toomey, Alice Faye, Milton Berle, John Carradine, Walter Pidgeon, etc.

'The film tries to conceal its deficiences in comic ideas and comic skill by doing everything at the pace of a clockwork toy with a too-tight spring.'—*Dave Robinson, Times*

Wonder Bar••
US 1934 84m bw
Warner (Robert Lord)

Love and hate backstage at a Paris night club.
Curious musical drama with an interesting cast and fairly stunning numbers.

w Earl Baldwin, *play* Geza Herczeg, Karl Farkas, Robert Katscher *d* Lloyd Bacon *ph* Sol Polito *ch* Busby Berkeley *songs* Harry Warren, Al Dubin *ad* Jack Okey

Al Jolson, Kay Francis, Dolores del Rio, Ricardo Cortez, Dick Powell, Guy Kibbee, Ruth Donnelly, Hugh Herbert, Louise Fazenda, Fifi D'Orsay

Wonder Man***
US 1945   97m   Technicolor
Samuel Goldwyn

A mild-mannered student is persuaded by the ghost of his dead twin to avenge his murder.
Smooth, successful mixture of *Topper*, a nightclub musical, a gangster drama and the star's own brand of fooling; this is possibly his best vehicle.

w Don Hartman, Melville Shavelson, Philip Rapp, story Arthur Sheekman *d Bruce Humberstone ph* Victor Milner, William Snyder *md* Louis Forbes, Ray Heindorf *sp* John Fulton

Danny Kaye, Vera-Ellen, Virginia Mayo, Steve Cochran, S. Z. Sakall, Allen Jenkins, Ed Brophy, Donald Woods, Otto Kruger, Richard Lane, Natalie Schaefer

AAN: Louis Forbes, Ray Heindorf; song 'So in Love' (*m* David Rose, *ly* Leo Robin)

The Wonderful Country
US 1959   96m   Technicolor
UA / DRM (Chester Erskine)

A wandering gunman is offered a job by the Texas Rangers.
Complexly plotted western offering a range of familiar exploits.

w Robert Ardrey, *novel* Tom Lea *d* Robert Parrish *ph* Floyd Crosby, Alex Phillips *m* Alex North

Robert Mitchum, Julie London, Pedro Armendariz, Gary Merrill, Jack Oakie, Albert Dekker, Charles McGraw, John Banner, Jay Novello

Wonderful Life*
GB 1964   113m   Techniscope
EMI / Elstree Distributors / Ivy (Kenneth Harper)

Four entertainers on a luxury liner are hired by a film crew in Africa.
Slight but zestful youth musical with highly illogical detail; the highlight is a ten-minute spoof history of the movies.

w Peter Myers, Ronald Cass *d* Sidney J. Furie *ph* Ken Higgins *pd* Stanley Dorfman

Cliff Richard, Walter Slezak, Susan Hampshire, Melvyn Hayes, Richard O'Sullivan, Una Stubbs, Derek Bond, Gerald Harper, the Shadows

The Wonderful World of the Brothers Grimm*
US 1962   134m   Technicolor   Cinerama
MGM / Cinerama / George Pal

An account of the lives of the German fairy tale writers is supplemented by three of their stories, *The Dancing Princess*, *The Cobbler and the Elves* and *The Singing Bone*.
Saccharine, heavy-handed pantomime with insufficient comedy, menace or spectacle.

w David P. Harmon, Charles Beaumont, William Roberts *d* Henry Levin, George Pal *ph* Paul C. Vogel *m* Leigh Harline *songs* Bob Merrill *ad* George W. Davis, Edward Carfagno

Laurence Harvey, Karl Boehm, Claire Bloom, Barbara Eden, Walter Slezak, Oscar Homolka, *Martita Hunt,* Russ Tamblyn, Yvette Mimieux, *Jim Backus,* Beulah Bondi, Terry-Thomas, Buddy Hackett, Otto Kruger

AAN: Paul C. Vogel; Leigh Harline

The Wonders of Aladdin
Italy 1961   92m   Technicolor
  Cinemascope
Embassy / Lux

With the help of a genie, Aladdin defeats a usurper and wins the princess's hand.
Flat and disappointing pantomime with virtually no charm.

w Luther Davis *d* Henry Levin, Mario Bava *ph* Tonino Delli Colli *m* Angelo Lavagnino

Donald O'Connor, Vittorio de Sica, Aldo Fabrizi, Michèle Mercier

The Wooden Horse**
GB 1950   101m   bw
British Lion / Wessex / London Films (Ian Dalrymple)

During World War II, British prisoners escape from Stalag Luft III by tunnelling under a vaulting horse.
Standard, solid POW drama with predictable but exciting and occasionally moving developments.

w Eric Williams, from his novel *d* Jack Lee *ph* C. Pennington-Richards *m* Clifton Parker

Leo Genn, David Tomlinson, Anthony Steele, David Greene, Michael Goodliffe, Bryan Forbes, Jacques Brunius

Words and Music**
US 1948   121m   Technicolor
MGM *(Arthur Freed)*

The songwriting collaboration of Richard Rodgers and Lorenz Hart.

Musical biopic which packs in a lot of good numbers and manages a script which is neither too offensive nor too prominent.

w *Fred Finklehoffe* d Norman Taurog
ph Charles Rosher, Harry Stradling
md Lennie Hayton ch Robert Alton, Gene Kelly

Tom Drake, Mickey Rooney, Perry Como, *Mel Tormé,* Betty Garrett, *June Allyson,* Lena Horne, Ann Sothern, Allyn McLerie, *Gene Kelly,* Vera-Ellen, Cyd Charisse, Janet Leigh, Marshall Thompson

Work Is a Four-Letter Word
GB 1968 93m Technicolor
Universal / Cavalcade (Thomas Clyde)

A power station attendant is interested only in growing mushrooms, which have a chaotic effect on his private life.
Weakly futuristic industrial fantasy which the author would probably claim to be about lack of communication. Bored audiences might have a similar view.

w Jeremy Brooks, *play* Eh? by Henry Livings d Peter Hall ph Gilbert Taylor m Guy Woolfenden

David Warner, Cilla Black, Elizabeth Spriggs, Zia Mohyeddin, Joe Gladwin

The Working Man
US 1933 78m bw

A wealthy shoe manufacturer hands over his business, goes on holiday, and finds himself helping his bitterest rival. Palatable star parable. George Arliss, Bette Davis, Theodore Newton, J. Farrell MacDonald. Written by Maude T. Howell and Charles Kenyon, from the novel by Edgar Franklin; directed by John Adolfi; for Warner.

The World Changes*
US 1933 91m bw
Warner (Robert Lord)

A simple farmer becomes a powerful executive, and success goes to his head.
Adequate moral drama of its time, well staged and acted.

w Edward Chodorov d Mervyn Le Roy ph Tony Gaudio

Paul Muni, Aline MacMahon, Mary Astor, Donald Cook, Patricia Ellis, Jean Muir, Margaret Lindsay, Guy Kibbee, Alan Dinehart

The World in His Arms*
US 1952 104m Technicolor
Universal (Aaron Rosenberg)

In old San Francisco, a seal-poaching sea captain meets a Russian countess.
Romantic melodrama with plushy period backgrounds and a fair measure of action, climaxing in a boat race.

w Borden Chase d Raoul Walsh ph Russell Metty m Frank Skinner

Gregory Peck, Ann Blyth, Anthony Quinn, John McIntire, Andrea King, Carl Esmond, Eugenie Leontovitch

World in My Corner*
US 1955 85m bw
U-I (Aaron Rosenberg)

A penniless would-be prizefighter becomes the protégé of a millionaire and wins his daughter but not the crucial fight.
Well-done minor melodrama.

w Jack Sher d Jesse Hibbs ph Maury Gertsman m Joseph Gershenson

Audie Murphy, Barbara Rush, Jeff Morrow, John McIntire, Tommy Rall, Howard St John

The World Is Full of Married Men
GB 1979 106m Eastmancolor
New Realm / Married Men Productions (Adrienne Fancey)

The wife of an advertising executive tries to pay him out in kind for his infidelity.
Tedious jet-setting morality play which shows in great detail all the vices it wags a finger at.

w Jackie Collins, from her novel d Robert Young ph Ray Parslow m Frank Musker, Dominic Bugatti

Carroll Baker, Anthony Franciosa, Sherrie Cronn, Paul Nicholas, Gareth Hunt, Georgina Hale, Anthony Steel

The World Moves On*
US 1934 90m bw
Fox (Winfield Sheehan)

The saga of a Louisiana family up to World War I.
Careful, good-looking general entertainment.

w Reginald C. Berkeley d John Ford ph George Schneiderman m Max Steiner

Madeleine Carroll, Franchot Tone, Reginald Denny, Stepin Fetchit, Lumsden Hare, Louise Dresser, Sig Rumann

The World of Henry Orient**
US 1964 106m De Luxe Panavision
UA / Pan Arts (Jerome Hellman)

Two rich 14-year-old New York girls build fantasies around a concert pianist.
Charming, immaculately mounted, refreshingly unusual but overlong comedy.

w Nora and Nunnally Johnson, novel Nora
Johnson *d George Roy Hill ph* Boris
Kaufman, Arthur J. Ornitz *m* Elmer
Bernstein *pd James Sullivan*

Tippy Walker, Merri Spaeth, Peter Sellers,
Angela Lansbury, Paula Prentiss, Phyllis
Thaxter, Tom Bosley, Bibi Osterwald

The World of Suzie Wong
GB 1960   129m   Technicolor
Paramount / Ray Stark (Hugh Perceval)

A Hong Kong prostitute falls in love with the
artist for whom she poses.
Dull, set-bound romantic melodrama without
much gusto.

w John Patrick, *play* Paul Osborn *d* Richard
Quine *ph* Geoffrey Unsworth *m* George
Duning

William Holden, *Nancy Kwan*, Sylvia Syms,
Michael Wilding, Laurence Naismith, Jackie
Chan
   'Maybe one day it will all make the grade as
a musical.'—*MFB*

The World Owes Me a Living
GB 1944   91m   bw

A man gets his memory back and recalls his
air force career. Pointless flagwaving farrago.
David Farrar, Judy Campbell, Sonia Dresdel,
Jack Livesey, John Laurie, Wylie Watson.
Written by Vernon Sewell and Erwin Reiner,
from the novel by John Llewellyn Rhys;
directed by Vernon Sewell; for British
National.

World Premiere*
US 1940   70m   bw
Paramount

A zany film producer thinks up some wild
publicity schemes for his new film and
accidentally traps some Nazi spies.
Occasionally amusing farce mainly notable for
its star.

w Earl Felton *d* Ted Tetzlaff *ph* Daniel Fapp

John Barrymore, Ricardo Cortez, Frances
Farmer, Sig Rumann, Fritz Feld, Eugene
Pallette, Luis Alberni, Virginia Dale, Don
Castle

The World Ten Times Over
GB 1963   93m   bw
Cyclops (Michael Luke)
US title: *Pussycat Alley*

Two semi-prostitutes try to improve their lot.
Dreary, derivative low-life drama with flashy
technique.

wd Wolf Rilla *ph* Larry Pizer *m* Edwin
Astley

Sylvia Syms, June Ritchie, Edward Judd,
William Hartnell, Francis de Wolff

The World, the Flesh and the Devil*
US 1959   95m   bw   Cinemascope
MGM / Sol C. Siegel / Harbel

Trapped for five days in a mine cave-in, a man
struggles to the surface to find a dead world
devastated by atomic war; but still alive are
the elements of an eternal triangle . . .
Enterprising but rather disappointing fantasy
which tends to become merely glum and rather
self-consciously carries a panic button
message.

wd Ranald MacDougall *ph* Harold J.
Marzorati *m* Miklos Rozsa *ad* William A.
Horning, Paul Groesse

Harry Belafonte, Inger Stevens, Mel Ferrer

World without End
US 1956   80m   Technicolor
   Cinemascope
AA (Richard Heermance)

A space ship breaks the time barrier and
returns to earth in 2508, to find that intelligent
humans have been driven underground by
mutants.
Reasonably lively sci-fi with horror elements,
and a plot borrowed from H. G. Wells.

wd Edward Bernds *ph* Ellsworth Fredericks
m Leith Stevens

Hugh Marlowe, Nancy Gates, Rod Taylor

The World's Greatest Athlete
US 1973   92m   Technicolor
Walt Disney (Bill Walsh)

An American sports coach on an African
holiday finds a young Tarzan with amazing
powers.
Simple-minded comedy with lame tomfoolery
and trickwork.

w Gerald Gardiner, Dee Caruso *d* Robert
Scheerer *ph* Frank Phillips *m* Marvin
Hamlisch

Tim Conway, Jan-Michael Vincent, John
Amos, Roscoe Lee Browne

The World's Greatest Lover
US 1977   89m   De Luxe
TCF (Gene Wilder)

In the twenties, a rival studio starts a search
for a man to surpass Valentino.
Imitative slapstick extravaganza in which
anything goes but hardly anything pleases.

wd Gene Wilder *ph* Gerald Hirschfeld
m John Morris

Gene Wilder, Carol Kane, Dom DeLuise,
Fritz Feld

Worm's Eye View
GB 1951   77m   bw
ABFD / Byron (Henry Halsted)

Incidents in the lives of a group of RAF billetees.

Plotless comedy from a highly successful stage romp; plainly made and empty-headed but not disagreeable.

w R. F. Delderfield, from his play d Jack Raymond ph James Wilson m Tony Lowry, Tony Fones

Ronald Shiner, Garry Marsh, Diana Dors, Eric Davis, John Blythe

The Wrath of God
US 1972   111m   Metrocolor   Panavision
MGM / Rainbow / Cineman (William S. Gilmore Jnr)

During a twenties Central American revolution, a bootlegger joins forces with a defrocked priest.

Noisy, violent adventure yarn which works up to a gory climax but does not take itself too seriously.

wd Ralph Nelson, novel James Graham
ph Alex Phillips Jnr m Lalo Schifrin

Robert Mitchum, Frank Langella, Rita Hayworth, Victor Buono, John Colicos

The Wreck of the Mary Deare*
US 1959   108m   Metrocolor   Cinemascope
MGM / Blaustein–Baroda (David Blaustein)

An insurance fraud comes to light when a salvage boat is rescued from high seas.

Curious, star-studded amalgam of seafaring action and courtroom melodrama, originally intended for Hitchcock.

w Eric Ambler, novel Hammond Innes
d Michael Anderson ph Joseph Ruttenberg, F. A. Young m George Duning

Charlton Heston, Gary Cooper, Michael Redgrave, Emlyn Williams, Cecil Parker, Alexander Knox, Virginia McKenna, Richard Harris

The Wrecking Crew
US 1968   104m   Technicolor
Columbia / Meadway / Claude (Irving Allen)

Special agent Matt Helm recovers bullion stolen from a Danish train.

Camped-up spy buffoonery with the usual nubile ladies and a production which seeks to be flashy but succeeds only in being tatty.

w William McGivern, novel Donald Hamilton
d Phil Karlson ph Sam Leavitt m Hugo Montenegro

Dean Martin, Elke Sommer, Sharon Tate, Nancy Kwan, Nigel Green, Tina Louise

Written on the Wind**
US 1956   99m   Technicolor
U-I (Albert Zugsmith)

A secretary marries her oil tycoon boss and finds herself the steadying force in a very rocky family.

The sheerest Hollywood moonshine: high-flying melodramatic hokum which moves fast enough to be very entertaining.

w George Zuckerman, novel Robert Wilder
d Douglas Sirk ph Russell Metty m Frank Skinner

Lauren Bacall, Robert Stack, Dorothy Malone, Rock Hudson, Robert Keith, Grant Williams

'The story of a family's ugly secret and the stark moment that thrust their private lives into public view!'—publicity

AA: Dorothy Malone
AAN: title song (m Victor Young, ly Sammy Cahn); Robert Stack

Wrong Again
US 1929   20m   bw   silent

A horse instead of a painting is delivered to a rich man's house. Pleasing but not very inventive star comedy. Laurel and Hardy, Del Henderson. Written by Lewis R. Foster, Leo McCarey and H. M. Walker; directed by Leo McCarey; for Hal Roach.

The Wrong Arm of the Law*
GB 1962   94m   bw
Romulus / Robert Verlaise (Aubrey Baring, E. M. Smedley Aston)

London gangsters plan retaliation against Australian interlopers, and offer Scotland Yard a temporary truce.

Forgettable but pretty funny crook comedy in the British vein, with pacy script and excellent comedy timing.

w John Warren, Len Heath d Cliff Owen
ph Ernest Steward m Richard Rodney Bennett

Peter Sellers, Lionel Jeffries, Bernard Cribbins, Davy Kaye, Nanette Newman, Bill Kerr, John Le Mesurier

The Wrong Box*
GB 1966   110m   Technicolor
Columbia / Salamander (Bryan Forbes)

Two elderly Victorian brothers are the last survivors of a tontine (an involved form of lottery) and try to murder each other.

Well-intentioned and star-studded black farce

in which the excellent period trappings and stray jokes completely overwhelm the plot.

w Larry Gelbart, Burt Shevelove, *novel* Robert Louis Stevenson, Lloyd Osbourne *d* Bryan Forbes *ph* Gerry Turpin *m* John Barry *ad* Ray Simm

Ralph Richardson, John Mills, Michael Caine, *Wilfrid Lawson*, Nanette Newman, Peter Cook, Dudley Moore, Peter Sellers, Tony Hancock, Thorley Walters, Cicely Courtneidge, Irene Handl, John Le Mesurier, Gerald Sim, Norman Bird, Tutte Lemkow
'A slapdash affair in which anything goes, irrespective of whether or not it fits.'—*Tom Milne*

The Wrong Man*
US 1957   105m   bw
Warner (Herbert Coleman)

A New York musician is mistaken by police for an armed bandit, and both witnesses and circumstances prevent the truth from emerging.
True but downbeat story from the headlines, filmed with remarkably little persuasion; not its director's *métier* despite evidence of his usual thoroughness.

w Maxwell Anderson, Angus MacPhail *d* Alfred Hitchcock *ph* Robert Burks *m* Bernard Herrmann

Henry Fonda, Vera Miles, Anthony Quayle, Harold J. Stone, Esther Minciotti

WUSA*
US 1970   117m   Technicolor
   Panavision
Paramount / Mirror / Coleytown / Stuart
   Rosenberg (Paul Newman, John
   Foreman)

A penniless wanderer causes chaos when he becomes the announcer for a right-wing radio station.
A farcical melodrama for the intelligentsia, and for the most part a thoroughgoing bore. The last part offers a compensation or two.

w Robert Stone, from his novel Hall of Mirrors *d* Stuart Rosenberg *ph* Richard Moore *m* Lalo Schifrin

Paul Newman, Joanne Woodward, Laurence Harvey, Anthony Perkins, Pat Hingle, Cloris Leachman, Don Gordon, Robert Quarry, Bruce Cabot, Moses Gunn, Wayne Rogers
'The most significant film I've ever made and the best.'—*Paul Newman*

Wuthering Heights****
US 1939   104m   bw
Samuel Goldwyn

The daughter of an unhappy middle-class Yorkshire family falls passionately in love with a gypsy who has been brought up with her. Despite American script and settings, this wildly romantic film makes a pretty fair stab at capturing the power of at least the first half of a classic Victorian novel, and in all respects it's a superb Hollywood production of its day and a typical one, complete with ghostly finale and a first-rate cast.

w Ben Hecht, *Charles MacArthur, novel Emily Brontë d William Wyler ph Gregg Toland m Alfred Newman*

Laurence Olivier, Merle Oberon, David Niven, Hugh Williams, Flora Robson, Geraldine Fitzgerald, Donald Crisp, Leo G. Carroll, Cecil Kellaway, *Miles Mander*
'Unquestionably one of the most distinguished pictures of the year.'—*Frank S. Nugent, New York Times*
'A pattern of constant forward motion, with overtones maintained throughout the rise of interest and suspense.'—*Otis Ferguson*
'A strong and sombre film, poetically written as the novel not always was, sinister and wild as it was meant to be, far more compact dramatically than Miss Brontë had made it.'—*Richard Mallett, Punch*

AA: Gregg Toland
AAN: best picture; script; William Wyler; Alfred Newman; Laurence Olivier; Geraldine Fitzgerald

Wuthering Heights*
GB 1970   105m   Movielab
AIP (John Pellatt)

Somewhat rewritten and overkeen to find a 1970 mood and interpretation for what can only be a period piece, this disappointing version marks a Z-film company's first determined effort to enter the big-time.

w Patrick Tilley *d* Robert Fuest *ph* John Coquillon *m* Michel Legrand

Anna Calder-Marshall, Timothy Dalton, Harry Andrews, Pamela Brown, Judy Cornwell, James Cossins, Rosalie Crutchley, Julian Glover, Hugh Griffith, Ian Ogilvy, Aubrey Woods

Wyoming
US 1940   88m   bw

A Missouri badman is persuaded to try an honest life. Well-liked minor western responsible for the first teaming of its

inelegant stars. Wallace Beery, Marjorie
Main, Leo Carrillo, Ann Rutherford, Joseph
Calleia, Lee Bowman, Henry Travers. Written
by Jack Jevne and Hugo Butler; directed by
Richard Thorpe; for MGM. (GB title: *Bad
Man of Wyoming*.)

Wyoming
US 1947 84m bw

Early settlers in the west meet trouble from
government squatters. Minor western for
undemanding audiences. Bill Elliott, Vera
Ralston, John Carroll, George 'Gabby' Hayes,
Albert Dekker. Written by Lawrence Hazard
and Gerald Geraghty; directed by Joe Kane;
for Republic.

X

X—The Man with X-Ray Eyes
US 1963   80m   Pathecolor
'Spectarama'
AIP (Roger Corman)
GB title: *The Man with the X-Ray Eyes*

A scientist gives himself X-ray vision and goes mad.
Interesting but rather unpleasant horror story with moments of cleverness but a general air of disappointment.

w Robert Dillon, Ray Russell *d* Roger Corman *ph* Floyd Crosby *m* Les Baxter

Ray Milland, Diana Van Der Vlis, Harold J. Stone, John Hoyt, Don Rickles, John Dierkes

'When the dialogue suggests that Xavier is being driven insane by strange and satanic visions, what one actually sees is rather a comedown.'—*MFB*

'Concise, confident, and not an ounce overweight.'—*NFT, 1967*

X the Unknown*
GB 1956   81m   bw
Hammer (Anthony Hinds)

A mysterious force feeds on radiation from a research station on a Scottish moor, and becomes a seeping mass.
Minor sci-fi horror with a monster like liquid lino, rushed into release to cash in on *The Quatermass Experiment.*

w Jimmy Sangster *d* Leslie Norman *ph* Gerald Gibbs *m* James Bernard

Dean Jagger, Edward Chapman, Leo McKern, William Lucas, John Harvey, Peter Hammond, Michael Ripper, Anthony Newley

Xanadu
US 1980   93m   Technicolor
Universal / Lawrence Gordon

The muse Terpsichore comes to earth and becomes involved in the opening of a roller-derby disco.
Misguided attempt at a clean nostalgic musical, apparently conceived in a nightmare after somebody saw *Down to Earth* on the late show.

w Richard Christian Danus, Marc Reid Rubel *d* Robert Greenwald *ph* Victor J. Kemper *m* Barry de Vorzon *songs* Jeff Lynne, John Farrar *pd* John W. Corso

Olivia Newton-John, Gene Kelly, Michael Beck

'Truly a stupendously bad film whose only salvage is the music.'—*Variety*
† Gene Kelly uses the same character name, Danny McGuire, as he did in *Cover Girl.*

Y

Yangtse Incident*
GB 1957 113m bw
British Lion / Wilcox/Neagle (Herbert
  Wilcox)
US title: *Battle Hell*; aka: *Escape of the
Amethyst*

In 1949 a British frigate is shelled and held
captive by communist shore batteries in the
Yangtse.
Stalwart but not very exciting British war
heroics.

w Eric Ambler, *book* Franklin Gollings
d Michael Anderson *ph* Gordon Dines
m Leighton Lucas

Richard Todd, William Hartnell, Akim
Tamiroff, Donald Houston, Keye Luke,
Sophie Stewart, Robert Urquhart, James
Kenney, Barry Foster

The Yakuza
US 1975 112m Technicolor
  Panavision
Warner (Sydney Pollack, Michael
  Hamilburg)

Japanese gangsters kidnap the daughter of a
Los Angeles shipping magnate.
Violent thriller roughly exploiting an ancient
Japanese genre.

w Paul Schrader, Robert Towne *d* Sydney
Pollack *ph* Okazaki Kozo, Duke Callaghan
m Dave Grusin

Robert Mitchum, Takakura Ken, Brian Keith,
Kishi Keilo, Okada Eiji
  'No more than a curious footnote to the
western exploitation of oriental action
movies.'—*Tony Rayns*

A Yank at Eton
US 1942 88m bw
MGM (John Considine Jnr)

A rich, wild American boy is sent to Eton to
cool down.
Tame, tasteless imitation of *A Yank at Oxford*
with younger participants.

w George Oppenheimer, Lionel Houser,
Thomas Phipps *d* Norman Taurog *ph* Karl
Freund, Charles Lawton *m* Bromisla Kaper

Mickey Rooney, Freddie Bartholemew, Ian
Hunter, Edmund Gwenn, Alan Mowbray,
Tina Thayer, Marta Linden, Alan Napier,
Terry Kilburn

A Yank at Oxford**
GB 1938 105m bw
MGM (Michael Balcon)

A cocky young American student comes to
Oxford and meets all kinds of trouble.
A huge pre-war success which now seems
naïve, this was the first big Anglo-American
production from a team which went on to
make *The Citadel* and *Goodbye Mr Chips*
before war stymied them.

w Malcolm Stuart Boylan, Walter Ferris,
George Oppenheimer, Leon Gordon, Roland
Pertwee, John Monk Saunders, Sidney Gilliat,
Michael Hogan *d* Jack Conway *ph* Harold
Rosson Edward Ward

Robert Taylor, Vivien Leigh, Maureen
O'Sullivan, Lionel Barrymore, Robert Coote,
Edmund Gwenn, C. V. France, Griffith Jones,
Morton Selten

A Yank in the RAF*
US 1941 98m bw
TCF (Lou Edelman)

An American chorine stranded in London falls
for the titular gentleman.
Silly but entertaining wartime flagwaver.

w Karl Tunberg, Darrell Ware, *story* Melville
Crossman (Zanuck) *d* Henry King *ph* Leon
Shamroy *m* Alfred Newman

Tyrone Power, Betty Grable, John Sutton,
Reginald Gardiner, Donald Stuart, Morton
Lowry, Richard Fraser, Bruce Lester

A Yank on the Burma Road
US 1942 66m bw
MGM (Samuel Marx)
GB title: *China Caravan*

A tough truck driver in the Far East abandons
profit for heroism when he hears of Pearl
Harbor.
Crass action flagwaver.

w George Kahn, Hugo Butler, David Lang
d George B. Seitz *ph* Lester White

Barry Nelson, Laraine Day, Stuart Crawford, Keye Luke, Sen Yung

'Glib humbug, playing tiddleywinks with high stakes.'—*Theodore Strauss*

Yankee Doodle Dandy****
US 1942 126m bw
Warner (Hal B. Wallis, William Cagney)

The life story of dancing vaudevillian George M. Cohan.

Outstanding showbiz biopic, with unassuming but effective production, deft patriotic backdrops and a marvellous, strutting, magnetic star performance.

w Robert Buckner, Edmund Joseph *d* Michael Curtiz *ph* James Wong Howe *m* Heinz Roemheld *md* Heinz Roemheld, Ray Heindorf *songs George M. Cohan*

James Cagney, Joan Leslie, *Walter Huston*, Rosemary de Camp, Richard Whorf, George Tobias, Jeanne Cagney, Irene Manning, S. Z. Sakall, George Barbier, Frances Langford, Walter Catlett, Eddie Foy Jnr

AA: music direction; James Cagney
AAN: best picture; original story (Robert Buckner); Michael Curtiz; Walter Huston

Yankee Pasha
US 1954 84m Technicolor

An American adventurer in nineteenth-century Marseilles saves his girl friend from pirates. Studio-bound hokum for double-featuring. Jeff Chandler, Rhonda Fleming, Mamie Van Doren, Lee J. Cobb, Bart Roberts, Hal March. Written by Joseph Hoffman, from the novel by Edison Marshall; directed by Joseph Pevney; for Universal-International.

Yanks**
GB 1979 141m Technicolor
United Artists / Joe Janni-Lester Persky / CIP

Romances of American GIs billeted on a Lancashire town during World War II.
Not an entirely promising subject, this overlong piece maintains its interest by sheer skill of dramaturgy and cinematic narrative.

w Colin Welland, Walter Bernstein *d John Schlesinger ph* Dick Bush *m* Richard Rodney Bennett *pd* Brian Morris

Vanessa Redgrave, Richard Gere, William Devane, Lisa Eichhorn, Rachel Roberts, Chick Vennera

The Yearling**
US 1946 134m Technicolor
MGM (Sidney Franklin)

The son of an old-time country farmer is attached to a stray deer.
Excellent family film for four-handkerchief patrons.

w Paul Osborn, *novel* Marjorie Kinnan Rawlings *d Clarence Brown ph* Charles Rosher, Leonard Smith *m* Herbert Stothart

Gregory Peck, Jane Wyman, Claude Jarman Jnr, Chill Wills, Clem Bevans, Margaret Wycherly, Henry Travers, Forrest Tucker

AA: Charles Rosher, Leonard Smith (and Arthur Arling)
AAN: best picture; Clarence Brown; Gregory Peck; Jane Wyman

The Years Between
GB 1946 100m bw
GFD / Sydney Box

An MP returns after being presumed dead in the war and finds his wife has been elected in his place.
Stilted variation on the Enoch Arden theme; plot and performances alike unpersuasive.

w Muriel and Sydney Box, *play* Daphne du Maurier *d* Compton Bennett *ph* Reg Wyer

Michael Redgrave, Valerie Hobson, Flora Robson, Felix Aylmer, James McKechnie, Dulcie Gray, Edward Rigby

The Yellow Balloon
GB 1952 80m bw
ABP (Victor Skuzetsky)

A small boy who thinks he has killed his friend is terrorized by a murderer.
Tense but not especially rewarding suspenser, clearly borrowed from *The Window*.

w Anne Burnaby, J. Lee-Thompson *d* J. Lee-Thompson *ph* Gilbert Taylor *m* Philip Green

Kenneth More, William Sylvester, Kathleen Ryan, Andrew Ray, Bernard Lee, Veronica Hurst

The Yellow Cab Man
US 1950 84m bw
MGM (Richard Goldstone)

A taxi-driving inventor is pursued by crooks after his secret formula.
Moderate star comedy.

w Devery Freeman, Albert Beich *d* Jack Donohue *ph* Harry Stradling *m* Scott Bradley

Red Skelton, Gloria de Haven, Walter Slezak, Edward Arnold, James Gleason, Paul Harvey, Jay C. Flippen

Yellow Canary*
GB 1943 98m bw
RKO / Imperator (Herbert Wilcox)

A socialite suspected of being a Nazi sympathizer is really a British spy.
Mild wartime melodrama chiefly notable for allotting an apparently unsympathetic part to the beloved Miss Neagle.

w De Witt Bodeen, Miles Malleson, *story* Pamela Bower d Herbert Wilcox ph Max Greene

Anna Neagle, Richard Greene, Nova Pilbeam, Lucie Mannheim, Cyril Fletcher, Albert Lieven, Margaret Rutherford, Marjorie Fielding

Yellow Canary
US 1963 93m bw Cinemascope
TCF / Cooga Mooga (Maury Dexter)

The baby son of a singing idol is kidnapped.
Rather dreary suspenser with too much dialogue.

w Rod Serling, *novel* Easy Come Easy Go by Whit Masterson d Buzz Kulik ph Floyd Crosby m Kenyon Hopkins

Pat Boone, Barbara Eden, Steve Forrest, Jack Klugman, Jesse White, John Banner, Jeff Corey

Yellow Dog
GB 1973 101m Eastmancolor
Scotia–Barber / Akari (Terence Donovan)

A Japanese agent in London keeps watch on a mysterious scientist.
Incoherent spy thriller with a few hybrid oddities.

w Shinobu Hashimoto d Terence Donovan ph David Watkin m Ron Grainer

Jiro Tamiya, Robert Hardy, Carolyn Seymour, Joseph O'Conor

Yellow Jack*
US 1938 83m bw
MGM (Jack Cummings)

In 1899 Cuba a marine offers himself as a guinea pig to combat yellow fever.
Solid, unsurprising, period medical melodrama with conventional romantic sidelights.

w Edward Chodorov, *play* Sidney Howard, Paul de Kruif d George B. Seitz ph Lester White m William Axt

Robert Montgomery, Virginia Bruce, Lewis Stone, Andy Devine, Henry Hull, Charles Coburn, Buddy Ebsen, Henry O'Neill, Janet Beecher

The Yellow Rolls Royce*
GB 1964 122m Metrocolor Panavision
MGM (Anatole de Grunwald)

Three stories about the owners of an expensive car; an aristocrat, a gangster, and a wandering millionairess.
Lukewarm all-star concoction lacking either good stories or a connecting thread.

w Terence Rattigan d Anthony Asquith ph Jack Hildyard m Riz Ortolani pd Vincent Korda

Rex Harrison, Jeanne Moreau, Edmund Purdom, Moira Lister, Roland Culver, Shirley Maclaine, George C. Scott, Alain Delon, Art Carney, Ingrid Bergman, Omar Sharif, Joyce Grenfell

'Tame, bloodless, smothered in elegance and the worst kind of discreetly daring good taste.'—*Peter John Dyer*

Yellow Sands
GB 1938 68m bw

A Cornish family sets to bickering over a will.
Reliable comedy from a popular stage original. Marie Tempest, Wilfrid Lawson, Belle Chrystall, Robert Newton, Patrick Barr, Edward Rigby. Written by Michael Barringer and Rodney Ackland, from the play by Eden and Adelaide Phillpotts; directed by Herbert Brenon; for ABPC.

Yellow Sky**
US 1948 98m bw
TCF (Lamar Trotti)

Outlaws on the run take over a desert ghost town.
Gleaming, stylish western melodrama which benefits from its unusual and confined setting.

w Lamar Trotti, *story* W. R. Burnett d William Wellman ph Joe MacDonald m Alfred Newman

Gregory Peck, Anne Baxter, Richard Widmark, Robert Arthur, John Russell, Henry Morgan, James Barton

Yellow Submarine*
GB 1968 87m De Luxe
King Features / Apple (Al Brodax)

The happy kingdom of Pepperland is attacked by the Blue Meanies.
Way-out cartoon fantasia influenced by Beatlemania and the swinging sixties; hard to watch for non-addicts.

w Lee Minoff, Al Brodax, Jack Mendelsohn, Erich Segal d George Duning m John Lennon, Paul McCartney

The Yellow Ticket*
US 1931 76m bw
Fox
GB title: *The Yellow Passport*

In Russia during the pogroms, a Jewish girl pretends to be a prostitute in order to get a travel permit to see her dying father. Curious anti-Russian melodrama deriving its plot from *La Tosca*.

w Jules Furthman, Guy Bolton, play Michael Morton *d* Raoul Walsh *ph* James Wong Howe

Elissa Landi, Laurence Olivier, Lionel Barrymore, Walter Byron, Sarah Padden, Mischa Auer, Boris Karloff

Yellowstone Kelly
US 1959   91m   Technicolor
Warner

A fur trapper prevents war between Indians and whites.
Standard western with routine excitements and a cast of TV faces.

w Burt Kennedy *d* Gordon Douglas *ph* Carl Guthrie *m* Howard Jackson

Clint Walker, Edd Byrnes, John Russell, Ray Danton, Claude Akins

Yes, Madam
GB 1938   77m   bw

Heirs to a fortune are obliged to act as servants for three months. Agreeable minor comedy. Bobby Howes, Diana Churchill, Billy Milton, Fred Emney, Bertha Belmore, Wylie Watson, Vera Pearce. Written by Clifford Grey, Bert Lee and William Freshman, from the novel by K. R. G. Browne; directed by Norman Lee; for ABPC. (Previously filmed in 1933 with Frank Pettingell and Kay Hammond.)

Yes My Darling Daughter
US 1939   86m   bw
Warner (Ben Glazer)

Lovers elope and are pursued by her family. Mildly amusing domestic comedy.

w Casey Robinson, *play* Mark Reed *d* William Keighley *ph* Charles Rosher

Priscilla Lane, Jeffrey Lynn, Roland Young, Fay Bainter, May Robson, Genevieve Tobin, Ian Hunter

Yes Sir, That's My Baby
US 1949   82m   Technicolor
U-I (Leonard Goldstein)

Ex-service undergraduates and their wives have trouble settling down to studies.
Witless and exhausting college comedy.

w Oscar Brodney *d* George Sherman *ph* Irving Glassberg *m* Walter Scharf

Donald O'Connor, Gloria de Haven, Charles Coburn, Barbara Brown, Joshua Shelley

Yesterday, Today and Tomorrow
Italy / France 1963   119m   Techniscope
CCC / Concordia / Joseph E. Levin (Carlo Ponti)

Three stories of naughty ladies.
A relentlessly boring compendium with everybody shouting at once.

w Eduardo de Filippo, Cesare Zavattini, others *d* Vittorio de Sica *ph* Giuseppe Rotunno *m* Armando Trovajoli

Marcello Mastroianni, Sophia Loren
  'A sad intimation of the sort of rainy day the Italian cinema is currently having.'—*MFB*

AA: best foreign film

Yesterday's Enemy
GB 1959   95m   bw   Megascope
Columbia / Hammer (T. S. Lyndon-Haynes)

In 1942 Burma, a British unit violently takes over a village and finds an unsolved puzzle.
Would-be ironic war suspenser, economically made but quite effective in putting its message across.

w Peter R. Newman, from his TV play *d* Val Guest *ph* Arthur Grant *m* none

Stanley Baker, Guy Rolfe, Leo McKern, Philip Ahn, Gordon Jackson, David Oxley, Richard Pasco, Russell Waters, Bryan Forbes, David Lodge, Percy Herbert

Yesterday's Hero
GB 1979   95m   colour
Columbia / CinemaSeven (Elliott Kastner)

A successful footballer goes to the bad but redeems himself.
Totally uninteresting sporting version of the Road to Ruin.

w Jackie Collins *d* Neil Leifer *ph* Brian West *md* Stanley Myers *pd* Keith Wilson

Ian McShane, Suzanne Somers, Adam Faith, Paul Nicholas, Sam Kydd

Yield to the Night*
GB 1956   99m   bw
ABP (Kenneth Harper)
US title: *Blonde Sinner*

A condemned murderess relives the events which led to her arrest.
Gloomy prison melodrama vaguely based on the Ruth Ellis case and making an emotional plea against capital punishment.

w John Cresswell, Joan Henry, *novel* Joan Henry *d* J. Lee-Thompson *ph* Gilbert Taylor *m* Ray Martin

Diana Dors, Yvonne Mitchell, Michael Craig, Marie Ney, Athene Seyler, Geoffrey Keen

Yolanda and the Thief*

US 1945 108m Technicolor
MGM (Arthur Freed)

A con man poses as the guardian angel of a
naïve heiress.
Laboured musical fantasy with arty Mexican
settings; not a success in any way, but with a
few effective moments.

w Irving Brecher, *story* Ludwig Bemelmans,
Jacques Théry *d* Vincente Minnelli
ph Charles Rosher *m* Lennie Hayton
songs Harry Warren, Arthur Freed

Fred Astaire, Lucille Bremer, Frank Morgan,
Leon Ames, Mildred Natwick
'The most extreme of the big musical
mistakes.'—*New Yorker, 1979*

You and Me

US 1938 90m bw
Paramount (Fritz Lang)

A department store owner employs ex-
convicts, one of whom has not quite reformed.
Curious comedy drama which never has a
hope of coming off.

w Virginia Van Upp, *story* Norman Krasna
d Fritz Lang *ph* Charles Lang Jnr *m* Kurt
Weill

Sylvia Sidney, George Raft, Harry Carey,
Barton MacLane, Warren Hymer, Roscoe
Karns, George E. Stone, Adrian Morris
'Lang's individual touch is visible
everywhere . . . but for the ordinary George
Raft fan it will not only be unappreciated, it
will be actually confusing.'—*National Board of
Review*

You Belong to Me*

US 1941 94m bw
Columbia (Wesley Ruggles)
GB title: *Good Morning, Doctor*

A playboy becomes jealous of the male
patients of his doctor wife.
Mild comedy for two stars who are well
capable of keeping it afloat.

w Claude Binyon, Dalton Trumbo *d* Wesley
Ruggles *ph* Joseph Walker *m* Frederick
Hollander

Barbara Stanwyck, Henry Fonda, Edgar
Buchanan, Roger Clark, Ruth Donnelly,
Melville Cooper, Maude Eburne

You Came Along

US 1945 103m bw
Paramount (Hal B. Wallis)

A girl from the treasury department falls in
love with one of three GIs she takes on a war
bond tour, but he dies of leukemia.

Weird mishmash of farce and sentimentality;
quite watchable in its way, but an odd
showcase for a new female star.

w Robert Smith, Ayn Rand *d* John Farrow
ph Daniel L. Fapp *m* Victor Young

Lizabeth Scott, Robert Cummings, Don
Defore, Charles Drake, Julie Bishop, Kim
Hunter, Rhys Williams, Franklin Pangborn,
Minor Watson

You Can't Cheat an Honest Man*

US 1939 79m bw
Universal (Lester Cowan)

Trials and tribulations of a circus owner.
Flat, desultory and generally disappointing
comedy vehicle for an irresistible star
combination.

w George Marion Jnr, Richard Mack, Everett
Freeman, *story* Charles Bogle (W. C. Fields)
d George Marshall *ph* Milton Krasner
m Charles Previn

W. C. Fields, Edgar Bergen (with Charlie
McCarthy and Mortimer Snerd), Constance
Moore, Mary Forbes, Thurston Hall, Charles
Coleman, Edward Brophy

You Can't Get Away with Murder

US 1939 78m bw
Warner (Sam Bischoff)

A juvenile delinquent teams up with a
gangster and takes a prison rap for him.
Standard post-Dead End crime melodrama
with no surprises.

w Robert Buckner, Don Ryan, Kenneth
Gamet, *play* Chalked Out by Lewis Lawes,
Jonathan Finn *d* Lewis Seiler *ph* Sol Polito
m Heinz Roemheld

Humphrey Bogart, Billy Halop, Gale Page,
John Litel, Henry Travers, Harvey Stephens,
Harold Huber

You Can't Have Everything*

US 1937 99m bw
TCF (Lawrence Schwab)

A failed play is turned into a musical.
Lively backstage comedy with good moments.

w Harry Tugend, Jack Yellen, Karl Tunberg
d Norman Taurog *ph* Lucien Andriot
md David Buttolph

Alice Faye, *the Ritz Brothers*, Don Ameche,
Charles Winninger, Gypsy Rose Lee, Tony
Martin, Arthur Treacher, Louis Prima, Tip
Tap and Toe, Wally Vernon

You Can't Have Everything

US 1970 90m Eastmancolor
Koala (Lou Brandt)
aka: *Cactus in the Snow*

An 18-year-old virgin GI is about to leave for Vietnam when he picks up a girl and spends a happy but platonic twenty-four hours.
An agreeably understated little love story for those absorbed by teenage sex problems.

wd Martin Zweibach *ph* David M. Walsh *m* Joe Parnello

Richard Thomas, Mary Layne, Lucille Benson, Oscar Beregi

You Can't Run Away from It
US 1956 96m Technicolor
Cinemascope
Columbia (Dick Powell)

An heiress runs away from a marriage arranged by her father, and falls for an amiable reporter.
Flat remake of *It Happened One Night,* with practically no comic sense or talent.

w Claude Binyon, Robert Riskin *d* Dick Powell *ph* Charles Lawton Jnr *m* George Duning *md* Morris Stoloff

June Allyson, Jack Lemmon, Charles Bickford, Jim Backus, Stubby Kaye, Paul Gilbert, Allyn Joslyn

You Can't Take It with You**
US 1938 127m bw
Columbia (Frank Capra)

The daughter of a highly eccentric New York family falls for a rich man's son.
A hilarious, warm and witty play is largely changed into a tirade against big business, but the Capra expertise is here in good measure and the stars all pull their weight.

w Robert Riskin, *play* George S. Kaufman, Moss Hart *d* Frank Capra *ph* Joseph Walker *m* Dmitri Tiomkin

Jean Arthur, Lionel Barrymore, James Stewart, Edward Arnold, Spring Byington, Mischa Auer, Ann Miller, Samuel S. Hinds, Donald Meek, H. B. Warner, Halliwell Hobbes, Mary Forbes, Dub Taylor, Lillian Yarbo, Eddie Anderson, *Harry Davenport*
'Shangri-La in a frame house.'—*Otis Ferguson*

AA: best picture; Frank Capra
AAN: Robert Riskin; Joseph Walker; Spring Byington

You Can't Win 'em All
GB 1970 99m Technicolor Panavision
Columbia / SRO (Gene Corman)

In 1922, two rival American mercenaries have adventures in the Mediterranean.
Hectic, overplotted comedy actioner.

w Leo V. Gordon *d* Peter Collinson *ph* Ken Higgins *m* Bert Kaempfert

Tony Curtis, Charles Bronson, Michèle Mercier, Grégoire Aslan, Patrick Magee

You for Me
US 1952 71m bw
MGM (Henry Berman)

A millionaire patient is courted by a needy hospital and falls for a popular nurse.
Cheerful but thin little programme-filler.

w William Roberts *d* Don Weis *ph* Paul Vogel *m* Alberto Columbo

Peter Lawford, Jane Greer, Gig Young, Paula Corday, Elaine Stewart

You Gotta Stay Happy
US 1948 100m bw
Universal (Karl Tunberg)

A runaway heiress joins cargo pilots on a transcontinental hop with some very queer passengers.
Ho-hum imitation of a Capra comedy; the effort shows.

w Karl Tunberg, *story* Robert Carson *d* H. C. Potter *ph* Russell Metty *m* Daniele Amfitheatrof

Joan Fontaine, James Stewart, Eddie Albert, Roland Young, Willard Parker, Percy Kilbride, Porter Hall, Paul Cavanagh, Halliwell Hobbes

You Must Be Joking*
GB 1965 100m bw
Columbia / Ameran (Charles H. Schneer)

Assorted army personnel vie in an extended initiative test.
Slam-bang location comedy with more hits than misses: cheerful entertainment.

w Alan Hackney *d* Michael Winner *ph* Geoffrey Unsworth *m* Laurie Johnson

Terry-Thomas, Lionel Jeffries, Michael Callan, Gabriella Licudi, *Denholm Elliott,* Lee Montague, Bernard Cribbins, Wilfrid Hyde White, James Robertson Justice, Richard Wattis, James Villiers

You Never Can Tell*
US 1951 78m bw
U-I (Leonard Goldstein)
GB title: *You Never Know*

An Alsatian dog is murdered and is sent back from heaven in the guise of a private detective to expose his killer.
Self-confidently outrageous comedy fantasy in the wake of *Here Comes Mr Jordan;* not badly done if you accept the premise.

w Lou Breslow, David Chandler *d* Lou Breslow *ph* Maury Gertsman *m* Hans Salter

Dick Powell, Peggy Dow, Charles Drake, Joyce Holden, Albert Sharpe, Sara Taft

You Only Live Once**
US 1937 85m bw
Walter Wanger

A petty crook framed for murder breaks out of prison and tries to escape to Canada with his wife.
Gloomy melodrama partly based on Bonnie and Clyde and incorporating a plea for justice; very well made and acted.

w Graham Baker, *story* Gene Towne *d* Fritz Lang *ph* Leon Shamroy *m* Alfred Newman

Sylvia Sidney, Henry Fonda, Barton MacLane, Jean Dixon, William Gargan, Jerome Cowan, Chic Sale, Margaret Hamilton, Warren Hymer

'Again and again in this film we find what can only be described as camera style, the use of the pictorial image to narrate with the maximum of emotional impact.'—*Dilys Powell*

You Only Live Twice**
GB 1967 117m Technicolor Panavision
UA / Eon (Harry Saltzman, Albert R. Broccoli)

James Bond goes to Japan.
The Bond saga at its most expensive and expansive, full of local colour and in-jokes, with an enormously impressive set for the climactic action.

w Roald Dahl, *novel* Ian Fleming *d* Lewis Gilbert *ph* Freddie Young, Bob Huke *m* John Barry *pd* Ken Adam

Sean Connery, Tetsuro Tamba, Akiko Wakabayashi, Mie Hama, Karin Dor, Bernard Lee, Lois Maxwell, Desmond Llewellyn, *Charles Gray, Donald Pleasence*

You Were Meant for Me
US 1948 92m bw
TCF (Fred Kohlmar)

A small-town girl marries a bandleader.
Mildly pleasing, muted, musical romance, with good twenties atmosphere.

w Elick Moll, Valentine Davies *d* Lloyd Bacon *ph* Victor Milner *md* Lionel Newman *songs* various

Jeanne Crain, Dan Dailey, Oscar Levant, Barbara Lawrence, Selena Royle, Percy Kilbride, Herbert Anderson

You Were Never Lovelier*
US 1942 97m bw
Columbia (Louis F. Edelman)

An Argentinian hotel tycoon tries to interest his daughter in marriage by creating a mysterious admirer.
Pleasing musical, a follow up for the stars of *You'll Never Get Rich*.

w Michael Fessier, Ernest Pagano, Delmer Daves *d* William A. Seiter *ph* Ted Tetzlaff *songs* Jerome Kern, Johnny Mercer *m* Leigh Harline

Fred Astaire, Rita Hayworth, Adolphe Menjou, Leslie Brooks, Adele Mara, Isobel Elsom, Gus Schilling, Xavier Cugat and his Orchestra, Larry Parks

AAN: Leigh Harline; song 'Dearly Beloved'

You Will Remember
GB 1940 86m bw

The life of the late Victorian songwriter Leslie Stuart. Pleasant, rather surprising, minor British biopic. Robert Morley, Emlyn Williams, Dorothy Hyson, Tom E. Finglass, Nicholas Phipps, Allan Jeayes. Written by Lydia Hayward; directed by Jack Raymond; for Jack Raymond Productions.

You'll Find Out*
US 1940 97m bw
RKO

Kay Kyser's band is hired to play for a 21st birthday party at a gloomy mansion; they help save the life of the girl concerned.
Cheerful if slow-starting spooky house send-up with a splendid trio of villains.

w James V. Kern, David Butler *d* David Butler *ph* Frank Redman *m* Roy Webb *songs* James McHugh, Johnny Mercer

Kay Kyser, Boris Karloff, Peter Lorre, Bela Lugosi, Dennis O'Keefe, Ginny Simms, Helen Parrish, Alma Kruger, Ish Kabibble

AAN: song, 'I'd Know You Anywhere'

You'll Like My Mother
US 1972 92m Technicolor
Universal / Bing Crosby Productions (Mort Briskin)

Pregnant widow visits neurotic mother-in-law in a snowbound mansion.
Predictable frightened lady shocker aiming somewhere between *Psycho* and *Fanatic*; of strictly routine interest.

w Jo Heims, *novel* Naomi Hintze *d* Lamont Johnson *ph* Jack Marta *m* Gil Melle

Rosemary Murphy, Patty Duke, Richard Thomas, Sian Barbara Allen

You'll Never Get Rich*
US 1941 88m bw
Columbia (Sam Bischoff)

A Broadway dance director helps his philandering producer by taking a romantically-inclined showgirl off his hands.
Smart comedy-musical which set its female lead as a top star.

w Michael Fessier, Ernest Pagano d Sidney Lanfield ph Philip Tannura ch Robert Alton songs Cole Porter m Morris Stoloff

Fred Astaire, Rita Hayworth, Robert Benchley, John Hubbard, Osa Massen, Frieda Inescort, Guinn Williams, Donald MacBride

AAN: Morris Stoloff; song 'Since I Kissed My Baby Goodbye'

Young America
US 1932 74m bw
GB title: *We Humans*

Two young boys get into trouble with the law.
Dog-eared domestic flagwaver.

w William Conselman, *play* John Frederick Ballard d Frank Borzage ph George Schneiderman

Spencer Tracy, Doris Kenyon, Tommy Conlon, Ralph Bellamy, Beryl Mercer, Sarah Padden

Young and Innocent***
GB 1937 80m bw
GFD / Gainsborough (Edward Black)
US title: *A Girl Was Young*

A girl goes on the run with her boy friend when he is suspected of murder.
Pleasant, unassuming chase melodrama with a rather weak cast but plenty of its director's touches.

w Charles Bennett, Alma Reville, *novel* A Shilling for Candles by Josephine Tey d Alfred Hitchcock ph Bernard Knowles m Louis Levy

Nova Pilbeam, Derrick de Marney, Mary Clare, Edward Rigby, Basil Radford, George Curzon, Percy Marmont, John Longden

Young and Willing
US 1942 83m bw
UA (made by Paramount) (Edward H. Griffith)

Impecunious actors in a New York boarding house hit on a great play.
Very mild, innocuous comedy which passed quickly from the public memory.

w Virginia Van Upp, *play* Francis Swann d Edward H. Griffith ph Leo Tover m Victor Young

William Holden, Susan Hayward, Eddie Bracken, Robert Benchley, Martha O'Driscoll, Barbara Britton, James Brown, Mabel Paige

Young at Heart**
US 1954 117m Warnercolor
(Warner) Arwin (Henry Blanke)

The daughters of a small-town music teacher have romantic problems.
Softened, musicalized remake of *Four Daughters* (qv), an old-fashioned treat with roses round the door and a high standard of proficiency in all departments.

w Julius J. Epstein, Lenore Coffee, *novel* Fannie Hurst d Gordon Douglas ph Ted McCord md Ray Heindorff

Doris Day, Frank Sinatra, Ethel Barrymore, Gig Young, Dorothy Malone, Robert Keith, Elizabeth Fraser, Alan Hale Jnr

Young Bess*
US 1953 112m Technicolor
MGM (Sidney Franklin)

The early years of Elizabeth I and her romance with Tom Seymour.
Historical fiction, wildly unreliable as to fact and dramatically not very rewarding. The character actors have the best of it.

w Arthur Wimperis, Jan Lustig, *novel* Margaret Irwin d George Sidney ph Charles Rosher m Miklos Rozsa

Jean Simmons, Stewart Granger, Charles Laughton (as Henry VIII), Kay Walsh, Deborah Kerr, Guy Rolfe, Kathleen Byron, Cecil Kellaway, Robert Arthur, Leo G. Carroll, Elaine Stewart, Dawn Addams, Rex Thompson

Young Billy Young
US 1969 89m De Luxe
UA / Talbot–Youngstein (Max Youngstein)

A young western gunman is helped out of scrapes by a mysterious stranger bent on revenge.
Good-looking but rather ineffective western which throws away good production values.

wd Burt Kennedy, *novel* Who Rides with Wyatt by Will Henry ph Harry Stradling Jnr m Shelly Manne

Robert Mitchum, Angie Dickinson, Robert Walker Jnr, David Carradine, John Anderson, Paul Fix

Young Cassidy*
GB 1964 110m Technicolor
MGM / Sextant (Robert D. Graff, Robert Emmett Ginna)

A romantic view of the early Dublin life of writer Sean O'Casey.
Ambling, unconvincing but generally interesting picture of a past time.

w John Whiting, from the writings of Sean O'Casey d Jack Cardiff, John Ford ph Ted Scaife m Sean O'Riada

Rod Taylor, Maggie Smith, Edith Evans, Flora Robson, Michael Redgrave, Julie Christie, Jack MacGowran, Sian Phillips, T. P. McKenna

Young Dillinger
US 1964 102m bw
Alfred Zimbalist

An embittered young convict becomes Public Enemy Number One.
Fantasized, forgettable biopic with violent moments.

w Arthur Hoerl, Don Zimbalist d Terry Morse ph Stanley Cortez m Shorty Rogers

Nick Adams, John Ashley, Robert Conrad, Mary Ann Mobley, Victor Buono, John Hoyt, Reed Hadley

The Young Doctors*
US 1961 102m bw
UA / Drexel / Stuart Millar / Laurence Turman

Old Dr Pearson resents his modern young assistant and almost causes a tragedy.
Routine medical melo of the Kildare / Gillespie kind, given a Grade A production and cast.

w Joseph Hayes, novel The Final Diagnosis by Arthur Hailey d Phil Karlson ph Arthur J. Ornitz m Elmer Bernstein

Fredric March, Ben Gazzara, Dick Clark, Eddie Albert, Ina Balin, Aline MacMahon, Edward Andrews, Arthur Hill, George Segal, Rosemary Murphy

Young Eagles*
US 1930 71m bw
Paramount

The adventures of American aviators in World War I.
Spirited early sound actioner.

w William McNutt, Grover Jones d William Wellman ph Archie Stout

Charles Rogers, Jean Arthur, Paul Lukas, Stuart Erwin, Virginia Bruce, James Finlayson

Young Frankenstein**
US 1974 108m bw
TCF / Gruskoff / Venture / Jouer / Crossbow (Michael Gruskoff)

Young Frederick Frankenstein, a brain surgeon, goes back to Transylvania and pores over his grandfather's notebooks.
The most successful of Mel Brooks' parodies, Mad Magazine style; the gleamingly reminiscent photography is the best of it, the script being far from consistently funny, but there are splendid moments.

w Gene Wilder, Mel Brooks d Mel Brooks ph Gerald Hirschfeld m John Morris ad Dale Hennesy

Gene Wilder, Marty Feldman, Madeleine Kahn, Peter Boyle, Cloris Leachman, Kenneth Mars, Gene Hackman, Richard Haydn

AAN: script

The Young Girls of Rochefort
France 1967 126m Eastmancolor Franscope
Parc Film / Madeleine / Seven Arts (Mag Bodard, Gilbert de Goldschmidt)
original title: Les Demoiselles de Rochefort

Two country girls join a travelling dancing troupe, and find love on the day of the fair.
Flat, empty tribute to the Hollywood musical, which never inspires despite the presence of one of its greatest stars.

wd Jacques Demy ph Ghislain Cloquet m Michel Legrand

Catherine Deneuve, François Dorléac, George Chakiris, Gene Kelly, Danielle Darrieux, Grover Dale, Michel Piccoli

AAN: Michel Legrand

The Young in Heart***
US 1938 91m bw
David O. Selznick

A family of charming confidence tricksters move in on a rich old lady but she brings out the best in them.
Delightful, roguish romantic comedy, perfectly cast and pacily handled.

w Paul Osborn, Charles Bennett, novel The Gay Banditti by I. A. R. Wylie d Richard Wallace ph Leon Shamroy m Franz Waxman

Douglas Fairbanks Jnr, Janet Gaynor, Roland Young, Billie Burke, Minnie Dupree, Paulette Goddard, Richard Carlson, Henry Stephenson

AAN: Leon Shamroy; Franz Waxman

The Young Land
US 1957 89m Technicolor (Columbia) C. V. Whitney (Patrick Ford)

A young sheriff arrests a gunman and after the trial has to save him from lynching.
Rather stiff attempt at a youth western.

w Norman Shannon Hall d Ted Tetzlaff ph Winton C. Hoch, Henry Sharp

Dan O'Herlihy, Patrick Wayne, Yvonne Craig, Dennis Hopper

AAN: song 'Strange Are the Ways of Love' (*m* Dmitri Tiomkin, *ly* Ned Washington)

The Young Lions**

US 1958 167m bw Cinemascope
TCF (Al Lichtman)

World War II adventures of two Americans and a German skiing instructor.

Three strands are loosely interwoven into a would-be modern epic; the result is well mounted and generally absorbing but uneven and decidedly overlong.

w Edward Anhalt, *novel* Irwin Shaw
d Edward Dmytryk *ph* Joe MacDonald
m Hugo Friedhofer

Marlon Brando, Montgomery Clift, Dean Martin, Hope Lange, Barbara Rush, May Britt, Maximilian Schell, Lee Van Cleef

AAN: Joe MacDonald; Hugo Friedhofer

The Young Lovers*

GB 1954 96m bw
GFD / Group Films (Anthony Havelock-Allan)
US title: *Chance Meeting*

A US Embassy man in London falls in love with the daughter of an Iron Curtain minister. Romeo and Juliet, cold war style, quite nicely put together with a thriller climax.

w Robin Estridge, *story* George Tabori
d Anthony Asquith *ph* Jack Asher
m Tchaikovsky

Odile Versois, David Knight, David Kossoff, Joseph Tomelty, Paul Carpenter, Theodore Bikel, Jill Adams

Young Man with a Horn*

US 1950 112m bw
Warner (Jerry Wald)
GB title: *Young Man of Music*

The professional and romantic tribulations of a trumpet player.

Overwrought character melodrama based on the life of Bix Beiderbecke; quite absorbing though occasionally risible.

w Carl Foreman, Edmund H. North, *novel* Dorothy Baker *d* Michael Curtiz *ph* Ted McCord *m* Ray Heindorf

Kirk Douglas, Lauren Bacall, Doris Day, Hoagy Carmichael, Juano Hernandez, Jerome Cowan, Mary Beth Hughes, Nestor Paiva

Young Man with Ideas*

US 1952 84m bw
MGM (Gottfried Reinhardt, William H. Wright)

A small-town lawyer tries to better himself in Los Angeles.

Modestly likeable comedy which doesn't add up to much.

w Arthur Sheekman *d* Mitchell Leisen
ph Joseph Ruttenberg *m* David Rose

Glenn Ford, Ruth Roman, Nina Foch, Denise Darcel, Donna Corcoran, Mary Wickes, Sheldon Leonard

Young Man's Fancy

GB 1940 77m bw

A young Victorian lord avoids an unsuitable match by eloping to Paris. Rather pallid romantic comedy with likeable period detail. Griffith Jones, Anna Lee, Seymour Hicks, Billy Bennett, Edward Rigby, Francis L. Sullivan. Written by Roland Pertwee, Rodney Ackland and E. V. H. Emmett; directed by Robert Stevenson; for Ealing.

Young Mr Lincoln***

US 1939 100m bw
TCF (Kenneth MacGowan)

Abraham Lincoln as a young country lawyer stops a lynching and proves a young man innocent of murder.

Splendid performances and period atmosphere are rather nipped in the bud by second-feature courtroom twists, but this is a marvellous old-fashioned entertainment with its heart in the right place.

w Lamar Trotti *d* John Ford *ph* Bert Glennon *w* Alfred Newman

Henry Fonda, Alice Brady, Marjorie Weaver, Arleen Whelan, Eddie Collins, Richard Cromwell, Donald Meek, Eddie Quillan, Spencer Charters

'Its simple good faith and understanding are an expression of the country's best life that says as much as forty epics.'—*Otis Ferguson*

'Period details are lovingly sketched in—a log splitting contest, a tug of war, a tar barrel rolling match . . .'—*Charles Higham*

'Its source is a womb of popular and national spirit. This could account for its unity, its artistry, its genuine beauty.'—*Sergei Eisenstein*

AAN: Lamar Trotti

The Young Mr Pitt*

GB 1942 118m bw
TCF (Edward Black)

Britain's youngest prime minister quells the threat of invasion by Napoleon.

Shapeless and overlong but generally diverting historical pastiche timed as wartime propaganda against Hitler.

w Frank Launder, Sidney Gilliat *d* Carol
Reed *ph* Frederick A. Young *m* Charles
Williams *ad* Vetchinsky

Robert Donat, Robert Morley, Phyllis Calvert,
John Mills, Raymond Lovell, Max Adrian,
Felix Aylmer, Albert Lieven

The Young Ones*
GB 1961 108m Technicolor
  Cinemascope
ABP (Kenneth Harper)
US title: *Wonderful to be Young*

The son of a tycoon starts a youth club and
puts on a musical to raise funds.
A shopworn idea is the springboard for a
brave try in a field where Britain was
presumed to have failed; despite the
enthusiasm with which it was greeted at the
time, it has dated badly.

w Peter Myers, Ronald Cass *d* Sidney J.
Furie *ph* Douglas Slocombe *m* Stanley Black

Cliff Richard, Robert Morley, Carole Grey,
Richard O'Sullivan, Melvyn Hayes, Gerald
Harper, Robertson Hare

Young People
US 1940 78m bw
TCF (Harry Joe Brown)

Vaudevillians retire to give their daughter a
proper upbringing, but find that showbiz is in
her blood.
Pleasant but unremarkable comedy-drama
with music, marking the end of its star's
association with the studio.

w Edwin Blum, Don Ettlinger *d* Allan Dwan
ph Edward Cronjager *md* Alfred Newman

Shirley Temple, Jack Oakie, Charlotte
Greenwood, Arleen Whelan, George
Montgomery, Kathleen Howard, Mae Marsh

The Young Philadelphians*
US 1959 136m bw
Warner (producer not credited)
GB title: *The City Jungle*

A forceful young lawyer pushes his way to the
top of the snobbish Philadelphia heap despite
threats to expose his illegitimacy.
Novel on film, gleamingly done and acted with
assurance.

w James Gunn, *novel* The Philadelphian by
Richard Powell *d* Vincent Sherman *ph* Harry
Stradling *m* Ernest Gold

Paul Newman, Barbara Rush, Alexis Smith,
Brian Keith, Billie Burke, John Williams,
Otto Kruger, Diane Brewster, Robert
Vaughn, Paul Picerni, Robert Douglas

AAN: Harry Stradling; Robert Vaughn

The Young Savages*
US 1961 103m bw
UA / Contemporary (Pat Duggan)

An assistant DA prosecutes three hoodlums
for murder but begins to feel that one is not
guilty.
Tough, realistic melodrama of the New York
slums, with roughhouse climaxes and a
political conscience.

w Edward Anhalt, J. P. Miller, *novel* A
Matter of Conviction by Evan Hunter *d* John
Frankenheimer *ph* Lionel Lindon *m* David
Amram

Burt Lancaster, Shelley Winters, John David
Chandler, Dina Merrill, Edward Andrews,
Telly Savalas

The Young Stranger*
US 1957 84m bw
RKO (Stuart Millar)

The 16-year-old son of a film executive gets
into trouble with the police.
Reasonably stimulating film of a TV play
about the kind of causeless rebel who quickly
became a cliché.

w Robert Dozier *d* John Frankenheimer
ph Robert Planck *m* Leonard Rosenman

James MacArthur, Kim Hunter, James Daly,
James Gregory, Whit Bissell

Young Tom Edison*
US 1940 82m bw
MGM (John Considine Jnr)

First of a two-parter (see *Edison the Man*)
tracing Edison's first experiments.
Reasonably factual and absorbing junior
biopic.

w Bradbury Foote, Dore Schary, Hugo
Butler *d* Norman Taurog *ph* Sidney Wagner
m Edward Ward

Mickey Rooney, Eugene Pallette, George
Bancroft, Fay Bainter, Virginia Weidler,
Victor Kilian, Lloyd Corrigan

The Young Widow
US 1946 100m bw
UA / Hunt Stromberg

The widow of a World War II flier returns to
the Virginia farm where they had spent happy
hours.
Glum sudser with talent all at sea.

w Richard Macaulay, Margaret Buell Wilder,
novel Clarissa Fairchild Cushman *d* Edwin L.
Marin *ph* Lee Garmes *m* Carmen Dragon
pd Nicolai Remisoff

Jane Russell, Louis Hayward, Faith Domergue, Marie Wilson, Kent Taylor, Penny Singleton, Connie Gilchrist, Cora Witherspoon

Young Winston**
GB 1972   157m   Eastmancolor
Panavision
Columbia / Open Road / Hugh French (Carl Foreman)

The adventurous life of Winston Churchill up to his becoming an MP.

Generally engaging if lumpy film which switches too frequently from action to family drama to politics to character study and is not helped by irritating directorial tricks.

w Carl Foreman, book My Early Life by Winston Churchill d Richard Attenborough ph Gerry Turpin m Alfred Ralston pd Don Ashton, Geoffrey Drake

Simon Ward, Robert Shaw, Anne Bancroft, Jack Hawkins, Ian Holm, Anthony Hopkins, John Mills, Patrick Magee, Edward Woodward

AAN: Carl Foreman

Young Wives' Tale
GB 1951   79m   bw

A playwright and his slaphappy wife share a house with a super-efficient couple. Very mild but palatable comedy set 'at the wrong end of St John's Wood'. Joan Greenwood, Nigel Patrick, Derek Farr, Guy Middleton, Athene Seyler, Helen Cherry, Audrey Hepburn, Irene Handl. Written by Anne Burnaby, from the play by Ronald Jeans; directed by Henry Cass; for ABPC.

Young Woodley
GB 1929   79m   bw

A schoolboy falls in love with his teacher's wife. Modest early talkie version of a play thought mildly shocking at the time. Madeleine Carroll, Frank Lawton, Sam Livesey, Gerald Rawlinson, Billy Milton. Written by John Van Druten and Victor Kendall, from the play by John Van Druten; directed by Thomas Bentley; for BIP. (A silent version made earlier in the same year, with Marjorie Hume and Robin Irvine, was never released.)

Youngblood Hawke
US 1964   137m   bw
Warner (Delmer Daves)

A Kentucky truck driver becomes a successful novelist and is spoiled by New York success.

Absurdly archetypal soap opera from a bestseller, spilling over with every imaginable cliché; some of its excesses are glossily entertaining.

w Delmer Daves, novel Herman Wouk d Delmer Daves ph Charles Lawton m Max Steiner

James Franciscus, Genevieve Page, Suzanne Pleshette, Eva Gabor, Mary Astor, Lee Bowman, Edward Andrews, John Emery, Don Porter

The Youngest Profession
US 1943   82m   bw
MGM (B. F. Ziedman)

Teenage autograph hounds cause trouble at the MGM studio.

Innocuous comedy with guest stars.

w George Oppenheimer, Charles Lederer, Leonard Spiegelgass, book Lillian Day d Edward Buzzell ph Charles Lawton m David Snell

Virginia Weidler, Jean Porter, Edward Arnold, John Carroll, Agnes Moorehead, Greer Garson, William Powell, Lana Turner, Walter Pidgeon, Robert Taylor

Your Witness*
GB 1950   100m   bw
Warner / Coronado (Joan Harrison)
US title: Eye Witness

An American lawyer comes to an English village to defend a war buddy on a murder charge.

Interesting but ineffective blend of comedy and courtroom procedure intended to contrast English and American ways.

w Hugo Butler, Ian Hunter, William Douglas Home d Robert Montgomery ph Gerald Gibbs m Malcolm Arnold

Robert Montgomery, Leslie Banks, Patricia Cutts, Felix Aylmer, Andrew Cruickshank, Harcourt Williams, Jenny Laird, Michael Ripper

You're a Big Boy Now*
US 1967   96m   Eastmancolor
Warner Seven Arts (William Fadiman)

A young assistant librarian discovers girls. Freewheeling semi-surrealist comedy with exhilarating moments and the inevitable letdowns associated with this kind of campy high style.

wd Francis Ford Coppola, novel David Benedictus ph Andy Laszlo m Bob Prince

Peter Kastner, Elizabeth Hartman, Geraldine Page, Julie Harris, Rip Torn, Tony Bill, Karen Black, Michael Dunn

AAN: Geraldine Page

You're a Sweetheart
US 1937 96m bw
Universal (B. G. De Sylva)

A Broadway star suffers from her press agent's bright ideas.

Muffed musical with all concerned ill at ease with below par material.

w Monte Brice, Charles Grayson d David Butler ph George Robinson md Charles Previn songs various

Alice Faye, George Murphy, Ken Murray, William Gargan, Frances Hunt, Frank Jenks, Andy Devine, Charles Winninger, Donald Meek

You're Darn Tootin'•••
US 1929 20m bw silent

Two musicians get into trouble at work, in their digs and in the street. Star comedy which though early in their teaming shows Stan and Ollie at their best in a salt shaker routine and in a surreal pants-ripping contest. Laurel and Hardy, Agnes Steele. Written by H. M. Walker; directed by Edgar Kennedy; for Hal Roach.

You're in the Army Now••
US 1941 79m bw
Warner (Ben Stoloff)

Two incompetent vacuum cleaner salesmen accidentally join the army.

An excellent vehicle for two star comedians who have often suffered from poor material, with a silent-comedy-style climax involving a house on wheels.

w Paul Gerard Smith, George Beatty d Lewis Seiler ph James Van Trees

Jimmy Durante, Phil Silvers, Donald MacBride, Jane Wyman, Regis Toomey

You're in the Navy Now•
US 1951 93m bw
TCF (Fred Kohlmar)
aka: *USS Teakettle*

Trouble results when the navy instals steam turbines in an experimental patrol craft.

Amusing service comedy with good script touches and capable performances.

w Richard Murphy d Henry Hathaway
ph Joe MacDonald m Cyril Mockridge

Gary Cooper, Millard Mitchell, Jane Greer, Eddie Albert, John McIntire, Ray Collins, Harry Von Zell, Jack Webb, Richard Erdman

You're My Everything•
US 1949 94m Technicolor
TCF (Lamar Trotti)

A Boston socialite marries a hoofer and becomes a movie star.

Pleasant twenties comedy with good period detail and lively performances.

w Lamar Trotti, Will Hays Jnr d Walter Lang ph Arthur E. Arling m Alfred Newman

Anne Baxter, Dan Dailey, Anne Revere, Stanley Ridges, Shari Robinson, Henry O'Neill, Selena Royle, Alan Mowbray, Buster ' Keaton

You're Never Too Young
US 1955 103m Technicolor
      Vistavision
Paramount / Hal B. Wallis (Paul Jones)

An apprentice barber on the run from a murderer poses as a 12-year-old child to travel half fare.

Unattractive revamping of *The Major and the Minor* (qv), with the star team trying too obviously to make bricks with inferior straw.

w Sidney Sheldon d Norman Taurog
ph Daniel L. Fapp m Arthur Schwarz

Dean Martin, Jerry Lewis, Diana Lynn, Nina Foch, Raymond Burr, Veda Ann Borg

You're Only Young Once see The Hardy Family

You're Only Young Twice
GB 1952 81m bw
Group Three (Terry Bishop)

The puritanical head of a Scottish university is laid low by circumstance and his own folly.

Misfire eccentric comedy which deserves marks for trying but fails to amuse.

w Reginald Beckwith, Lindsay Galloway, Terry Bishop, *play* What Say They by James Bridie d Terry Gilbert ph Jo Jago

Duncan Macrae, Charles Hawtrey, Joseph Tomelty, Patrick Barr, Diane Hart, Robert Urquhart

You're Telling Me•
US 1934 66m bw
Paramount

A small-town inventor meets a princess and makes the social grade.

Meaninglessly-titled star vehicle which is often defiantly unamusing but does include the famous golf routine.

w Walter de Leon, Paul M. Jones *d* Erle C. Kenton *ph* Alfred Gilks *m* Arthur Johnston

W. C. Fields, Larry 'Buster' Crabbe, Joan Marsh, Adrienne Ames, Louise Carter

Yours Mine and Ours*
US 1968   111m   Technicolor
UA / Desilu / Walden (Robert F. Blumofe)

A widower with nine children marries a widow with eight, and they settle in an old San Francisco house.
Generally appealing comedy, based on fact and well suited to its stars.

w Mel Shavelson, Mort Lachman *d* Mel Shavelson *ph* Charles Wheeler *m* Fred Karlin

Lucille Ball, Henry Fonda, Van Johnson

Z

Z***

France / Algeria 1968 125m
  Eastmancolor
Reggane / ONCIC / Jacques Pérrin

A leading opposition MP is murdered at a
rally. The police are anxious to establish the
event as an accident, but the examining
magistrate proves otherwise.
An exciting police suspense drama which also
recalls events under the Greek colonels and
was therefore highly fashionable for a while
both as entertainment and as a political *roman
à clef*.

w *Costa-Gavras, Jorge Semprun, novel* Vassili
Vassilikos d *Costa-Gavras ph* Raoul
Coutard m Mikis Theodorakis

Jean-Louis Trintignant, Jacques Pérrin, Yves
Montand, François Périer, Irene Papas,
Charles Denner

AAN: best picture; direction

Zabriskie Point

US 1969 112m Metrocolor Panavision
MGM / Carlo Ponti

A rebellious Los Angeles student steals a
private airplane, meets an aimless girl, and
finds a revelation in Death Valley . . .
Highly self-indulgent and unattractive fantasy
about escape from the crudities of our over-
civilized world. An expensive failure and an
awful warning of what happens if you give an
arty director carte blanche.

wd Michelangelo Antonioni ph Alfio Contini
m pop songs

Mark Frechette, Daria Halprin, Rod Taylor,
Paul Fix

  'Not even a good tourist's notebook . . .
from the choice of Death Valley as a symbol
of American civilization to the inclusion of gag
signs on bar-room walls to the shots of garish
billboards, this film sticks to the surface,
stranded.'—*Stanley Kauffman*

Zandy's Bride

US 1974 116m Technicolor
  Panavision
Warner (Harry Matofsky)

Life for a frontier family.
Dour semi-western.

w Marc Norman, *novel* The Stranger by
Lillian Bos Ross d Joan Troell ph Jordan
Cronenweth m Fred Karlin

Gene Hackman, Liv Ullmann, Eileen
Heckart, Harry Dean Stanton, Joe Santos,
Frank Cady

Zarak*

GB 1956 99m Technicolor
  Cinemascope
Columbia / Warwick (Phil C. Samuel)

An Afghan outlaw finally saves a British
officer at the cost of his own life.
Box-office actioner, shot in Morocco with a
weird cast and the help of old movie clips.

w Richard Maibaum d Terence Young 2nd
unit Yakima Canutt ph John Wilcox, Ted
Moore, Cyril Knowles m William Alwyn
ad John Box

Victor Mature, Michael Wilding, Anita
Ekberg, Bonar Colleano, Finlay Currie,
Bernard Miles, Eunice Gayson, Peter Illing,
Frederick Valk, André Morell

Zardoz

GB 1973 105m De Luxe Panavision
TCF / John Boorman

Life in 2293, when the earth has become
wasteland and a mass of Brutals are ruled by a
few Exterminators who have both memory
and intelligence.
Pompous, boring fantasy for the so-called
intelligentsia.

wd John Boorman ph Geoffrey Unsworth
m David Munrow pd Anthony Pratt

Sean Connery, Charlotte Rampling, John
Alderton

  'A glittering cultural trash pile . . the most
gloriously fatuous movie since *The Oscar*.'—
New Yorker

Zazie dans le Metro**

France 1960 88m Eastmancolor
Nouvelles Editions (Irène Leriche)

A naughty little girl has a day in Paris and
causes chaos.

Inventive little comedy which almost turns into a French *Hellzapoppin*, with everybody chasing or fighting everybody else.

wd Louis Malle, *novel* Raymond Queneau *ph* Henri Raichi

Catherine Demongeot, Philippe Noiret, Vittorio Caprioli

Zebra in the Kitchen

US 1965   93m   Metrocolor
MGM / Ivan Tors

A young boy tries to improve the lot of zoo animals.
Pleasing family film.

w Art Arthur   *d* Ivan Tors   *ph* Lamar Boren

Jay North, Martin Milner, Andy Devine, Joyce Meadows, Jim Davis

Zee and Co.*

GB 1971   109m   colour
Columbia / Zee Films (Kastner–Ladd– Kanter)
US title: *X, Y and Zee*

A successful architect battles with his termagant wife and seeks an affair.
Overwritten but entertaining sexual melodrama about an absolute bitch. The flow of bad language was new at the time.

w Edna O'Brien   *d* Brian G. Hutton   *ph* Billy Williams   *m* Stanley Myers   *ad* Peter Mullins

Elizabeth Taylor, Michael Caine, Susannah York, Margaret Leighton, John Standing
'Miss Taylor is rapidly turning into a latterday Marie Dressler.'—*Tom Milne*
'A slice-of-jet-set-life nightmare far beyond the dreams of the piggiest male chauvinist . . . the distinction of this film is that its characters are repulsive, its style vulgar, its situations beyond belief and its dialogue moronic.'—*Judith Crist*

Zeppelin*

GB 1971   97m   Technicolor   Panavision
Warner / Getty and Fromkess (Owen Crump)

In 1915, the British need to steal secrets from the zeppelin works at Friedrichshafen.
Undistinguished but entertaining period actioner with adequate spectacle but wooden performances.

w Arthur Rowe, Donald Churchill   *d* Etienne Périer   *ph* Alan Hume   *m* Roy Budd
sp Wally Veevers

Michael York, Elke Sommer, Peter Carsten, Marius Goring, Anton Diffring, Andrew Keir, Rupert Davies

Zéro de Conduite**

France 1933   45m approx   bw
Gaumont / Franco Film / Aubert

Boys return from the holiday to a nasty little boarding school, where the headmaster is an unpleasant dwarf and all the staff are hateful.
A revolution breaks out . . .
A clear forerunner of *If* . . . and one of the most famous of surrealist films, though it pales beside Bunuel and is chiefly valuable for being funny.

w Jean Vigo   *ph* Boris Kaufman   *m* Maurice Jaubert

Jean Dasté, Louis Lefébvre, Gilbert Pruchon, le nain Delphin
'One of the most influential films ever made.'—*New Yorker, 1978*

Zero Hour!

US 1957   83m   bw
(Paramount) Bartlett / Champion (John Champion)

Half the passengers and all the crew of a jet plane are stricken with food poisoning and a shell-shocked ex-fighter pilot has to land the plane.
Adequate air melodrama with a premise which later served for *Terror in the Sky* (TV) and *Airport 75*.

w Arthur Hailey, John Champion, Hall Bartlett, *teleplay* Flight into Danger by Arthur Hailey   *d* Hall Bartlett   *ph* John F. Warren   *m* Ted Dale

Dana Andrews, Linda Darnell, Sterling Hayden, Elroy Hirsch, Jerry Paris

Zero Population Growth

US 1971   96m   Eastmancolor
Sagittarius (Thomas F. Madigan)

In the 21st century there is a death penalty for having children, but a young couple defy the authorities.
Good sci-fi quickly develops into sticky sentimentality.

w Max Ehrlich, Frank de Felita   *d* Michael Campus   *ph* Michael Reed   *m* Jonathan Hodge   *pd* Tony Masters

Oliver Reed, Geraldine Chaplin, Diane Cilento, Don Gordon, Bill Nagy, Aubrey Woods

Ziegfeld Follies**

US 1944 (released 1946)   110m   Technicolor
MGM (Arthur Freed)

In heaven, Florenz Ziegfeld dreams up one last spectacular revue.

A rather airless all-star entertainment in which the comedy suffers from the lack of an audience but some of the production numbers are magnificently stylish.

w various *d Vincente Minnelli ph George Folsey, Charles Rosher m* various *ad* Cedric Gibbons, Merrill Pye, Jack Martin Smith

Fred Astaire, Lucille Ball, Bunin's Puppets, William Powell, Jimmy Durante, Edward Arnold, *Fannie Brice*, Lena Horne, Lucille Bremer, Esther Williams, Judy Garland, *Red Skelton, Gene Kelly*, James Melton, Hume Cronyn, Victor Moore, Marion Bell

'Between opening and closing is packed a prodigious amount of material, some of which is frankly not deserving of the lavish treatment accorded it.'—*Film Daily*

Ziegfeld Girl*
US 1941   131m   bw
MGM (Pandro S. Berman)

The professional and romantic problems of Ziegfeld chorus girls.
Adequate big-budget drama with music.

w Marguerite Roberts, Sonya Levien
d Robert Z. Leonard *ph* Ray June
m Herbert Stothart *ch* Busby Berkeley *songs* various

James Stewart, Judy Garland, Hedy Lamarr, Lana Turner, Tony Martin, Jackie Cooper, Ian Hunter, *Charles Winninger, Al Shean*, Edward Everett Horton, Philip Dorn, Paul Kelly, Eve Arden, Dan Dailey, Fay Holden, Felix Bressart

'Heaping portions of show life in the opulent days of Flo Ziegfeld, the man who wanted bigger and better staircases.'—*C. A. Lejeune*

Zigzag*
US 1970   104m   Metrocolor   Panavision
MGM / Freeman–Enders
GB title: *False Witness*

A dying man frames himself for an unsolved murder so that the reward money, claimed under another name, will go to his wife.
Complex thriller which sustains itself pretty well most of the way, but lacks humour and character.

w John T. Kelley *d* Richard A. Colla
ph James A. Crabe *m* Oliver Nelson

George Kennedy, Anne Jackson, Eli Wallach, Steve Ihnat, William Marshall, Joe Maross

Zoo in Budapest*
US 1933   83m   bw
Fox (Jesse Lasky)

An orphan waif runs away to live with a zookeeper.
Curious little romance remembered for its luminescent photography.

w Dan Totheroh, Louise Long, Rowland V. Lee *d* Rowland V. Lee *ph Lee Garmes*

Loretta Young, Gene Raymond, O. P. Heggie, Wally Albright, Paul Fix

'Richly composed impressionistic images, assisted by highly imaginative use of sound and background music, create a poem that Murnau himself would have envied.'—*NFT, 1971*

Zorba the Greek**
GB 1964   142m   bw
TCF / Rockley / Cacoyannis

A young English writer in Crete is befriended by a huge gregarious Greek who comes to dominate his life.
A mainly enjoyable character study of a larger-than-life character, this film made famous by its music does not really hang together dramatically and has several melodramatic excrescences.

wd Michael Cacoyannis, novel Nikos Kazantzakis *ph Walter Lassally m* Mikis *Theodorakis*

Anthony Quinn, Alan Bates, Lila Kedrova, Irene Papas

'For all its immense length, the film never gets down to a clear statement of its theme, or comes within measuring distance of its vast pretensions.'—*Brenda Davies*

AA: Walter Lassally; Lila Kedrova
AAN: best picture; Michael Cacoyannis (as writer and director); Anthony Quinn

Zotz!
US 1962   87m   bw
Columbia / William Castle

A professor finds a rare coin with occult powers.
Footling farce patterned after *The Absent-Minded Professor*. Poor, to say the least.

w Ray Russell, *novel* Walter Karig *d* William Castle *ph* Gordon Avil *m* Bernard Green

Tom Poston, Fred Clark, Jim Backus, Cecil Kellaway, Margaret Dumont

Zulu*
GB 1964   135m   Technirama
Paramount / Diamond (Stanley Baker, Cyril Endfield)

In 1879 British soldiers stand fast against the Zulus at Rorke's Drift.

Standard period heroics, well presented and acted.

w John Prebble, Cy Endfield *d* Cy Endfield *ph* Stephen Dade *m* John Barry

Stanley Baker, Jack Hawkins, *Michael Caine*, Ulla Jacobsson, James Booth, Nigel Green, Ivor Emmanuel, Paul Danceman

Zulu Dawn

US / Netherlands 1979   117m
  Technicolor   Panavision
Samarkand / Zulu Dawn NV (Barrie Saint
  Clair)

In 1878, 1,300 British troops are massacred at Ulundi.

Confusing historical action adventure, very similar to *Zulu* but failing in its cross-cut attempt to show both sides.

w Cy Enfield, Anthony Storey *d* Douglas Hickox *ph* Ousama Rawi *m* Elmer Bernstein *pd* John Rosewarne

Burt Lancaster, Denholm Elliott, Peter O'Toole, John Mills, Simon Ward, Nigel Davenport, Michael Jayston, Ronald Lacey, Freddie Jones, Christopher Cazenove, Ronald Pickup, Anna Calder-Marshall

The Decline and Fall of the Movie

It is only fair that the author of a book which categorizes fifty years of films should give some account of his own prejudices. I have spent more than forty years seeing, talking about and writing about films, so my affection for the medium in its 'golden age' can hardly be doubted. Even then, however, the worthwhile movies were the tip of the iceberg: probably eighty per cent of what was produced was ghastly rubbish, which is why this book deals with ten thousand movies, not all of them good, out of a total output of four times that number. The best kind of film buff loves the movie business for what it can be at its best, not for its journeyman 'B' features, its crackpot experiments, its cheapjack exploitation screamies or those relentlessly boring bottom-of-the-bill fillers.

Jonathan Swift said in 1725: 'I hate and detest that animal called man, although I heartily love John, Peter, Thomas and so forth.' This book encapsulates my Johns, my Peters and my Thomases: this essay complains bitterly that they have lately been so few in number, and attempts, admittedly by some slight use of exaggeration, to throw light on a confused and unhappy segment of cinema history.

When Sam Peckinpah made *Straw Dogs* from a novel called *The Siege of Trencher's Farm* he thought it unnecessary to explain to his audience the significance of his new title which, his publicists informed us on request, was taken from an old Chinese proverb. And when Stanley Kubrick made *A Clockwork Orange* he did not bother to retain the section of the Anthony Burgess novel which explained why it was so called. These almost identical incidents exemplify the kind of arrogance which besets film-makers in the seventies. Steeped in the history of Hollywood's golden age, they have no idea what made it work so well, and as soon as they become successful they begin to despise their audiences and are concerned only to over-spend enormous budgets while putting across some garbled self-satisfying message which is usually anti-establishment, anti-law-and-order and anti-entertainment.

In this they are assisted by such long-haired publications as *Sight and Sound* and a variety of earnest critics who bend over backwards to see 'significance' where none exists and to ascribe all the film's virtues and faults to the director, or in the current jargon the *auteur*. (Would any theatrical critic dream of judging a play solely on the director's contribution, or a literary critic of reviewing a book solely on the basis of its layout on the printed page?) If cinema, which is the creation of so many people, can be an art at all, it must be a folk art which appeals to innocent and sophisticate alike, and can be easily appreciated by both. This happy state of affairs was reached thirty-five years ago by unpretentious and slick productions of the studio system such as *The Maltese Falcon* and *Stagecoach*, which used every camera trick in the book without blinding the audience to the characters and the plot. Nowadays one has to fight one's way through the thick showy surface in order to get to a story which all too often is not worth following.

One problem is that modern films are largely made by people with no sense of humour, people who do not realize that they must please the mass audience if the industry in which they work is to survive. Old-time screenwriters such as Ben Hecht, Dudley Nichols and Lamar Trotti would no doubt be viewed by these young men as cynical hacks, but at least they took pains to please their audience with all the expertise at their command, and they still expressed their own views in a vein of sardonic humour which ran through most of the scripts of the thirties and forties and was there to please and satisfy the minority of film-goers who sought it out.

The absurd pretensions of some modern film-makers certainly cause amusement wherever sensible people congregate, but the advocates of sanity are in no position to have the last word. The present set-up of the film industry encourages wilder and wickeder sensations, from homicidal sharks to diabolical babies, as these are the only subjects which lure large audiences. The successes, however, are all one-offs: no one is much interested in sequels, preferring to wait for horrors of some other variety. The result is that only one film in twenty or thirty makes a profit, but the custodians of the cash have no option but to go on investing in the hope that the occasional fluke will make a fortune, which will then be quickly dissipated by a string of failures. Universal's phenomenally successful *Jaws*, for instance, was immediately followed by such commercial duds as *Gable and Lombard*, *W. C. Fields and Me*, *The Great Waldo Pepper* and *The Hindenberg*, and the studio is still looking for another hit. The sad fact is that no policy can be devised because the people in charge of the money have no idea what is likely to appeal, and they are forced to put their faith in reputedly brilliant directors who have no idea either but are quite prepared to spend large sums of other people's money in flying their own flimsy kites. The flimsiness is sometimes astonishing. The director of an abysmal 1976 comedy called *Harry and Walter go to New York* announced to the press, as a selling point, that it was 'Laurel and Hardy with real people.' Had he inquired of his mass audience, he would surely have been told that Stan and Ollie had more reality in their little fingers than was to be found in the entire crew of *Harry and Walter go to New York*, whether before or behind the camera.

One should of course add that many films these days are not supposed to make money. The adage which used to run 'you're only as good as your last picture' has been changed to 'you're only as big as your last budget', and it is no trick to get a big budget when many films are conceived by industrialists as tax losses: all you have to do is get in the news by holding outlandish views or even making pornography, and Hollywood these days opens its doors to you because at least you must have learnt how to point a camera or arrest public attention. The ones to suffer are the audiences, who have foisted upon them material which they have every right to expect to be professional, and which all too often is not, just the result of untalented exhibitionists spending someone else's money in whatever way happens to divert them most. Even if there is a profit, their habit is to take the money and run, not to invest it in better production facilities as used to happen in the good old days.

Work is thus produced for a small group of jet-setters; meanwhile that patient paying audience discovers that not only the films but the standards of physical cinema comfort are far worse than they were thirty years ago; since then the cost of admission has risen at a phenomenal rate, the average cost in Britain now being twenty times more than in 1956. What other commodity has risen in price to this extent? Television is infinitely cheaper and can be viewed in the comfort of one's own home: no wonder so many people prefer it.

So the movie industry hastens on its way to perdition and catastrophe, a fate which surely cannot be delayed more than another few years, and for which simple-minded greed, lack of foresight and a large measure of incompetence are chiefly responsible. Those of us who are old enough and who still care about the movies sigh frequently for the halcyon days when Harry Cohn and Louis B. Mayer sat in their front offices, for their intellectual limitations were far less harmful and sometimes far more stimulating to the medium than the excesses of the present incumbents, who seldom stay long enough to make their presences felt and certainly not long enough for any sense of continuity to develop. There is for instance no continuity of employment, which makes the unions tougher and tougher to deal with in an industry which was always volatile in its labour relations: every film is a fresh project for which cast and crew have to be accumulated, and the way things are there is no bank of trained talent to fall back on. As Billy Wilder said, you spend eighty per cent of your time making deals and twenty per cent making pictures. The old moguls had enough common sense and business acumen to keep the system working so that costs were comparatively low and one could afford the occasional interesting failure to please the intellectuals.

How did the movie world go so wrong? You can trace it to the restlessness after World War II, when the regular audience declined and television was a coming threat and the bosses knew that new trends had to be found but no one knew what they might be in a glum and depressed world. When actors began to want a say in production and seemed willing to risk their own money, the bosses were delighted to share the possible losses; instead they found themselves being eased out and their profits halved, their studios no longer vast employment centres with a constant production line but simply enclosed space and facilities which could be rented out to the highest bidder.

The old moguls were getting older and couldn't fight the developing situation, the new young ones were businessmen who often backed the wrong horse because they didn't understand the industry. Meanwhile the old showmen had one last irrelevant fling. If television was the enemy, they reasoned, then give the paying public what television cannot provide. Technology now allowed films to be shot on real locations, which was splendid but had two handicaps. First, the units were away from central control for a long time, and the costs were phenomenal; second, the magic was lost, for the real Paris was by no means so romantic or mysterious as Paramount's backlot which had served as Paris for so many years, nor could the lighting of it be so carefully controlled. The new realistic films were slower, because the travel costs had to be justified and travelogue largely took the place of drama. (Did anyone complain about the lack of shots of San Francisco in *The Maltese Falcon*?)

The other way to combat television was to change the shape and effect of the entertainment screen. 3-D was tried, but audiences hated wearing polaroid glasses in order to get a three-dimensional image which producers largely utilized by hurling knives, tennis balls, spiders and even grubby redskins into the audience's lap: this was fairground stuff. Cinemascope was then seized upon by Hollywood: twice as wide as the ordinary image and capable of the most spectacular effects. There is no record that the paying audience ever especially liked Cinemascope, or could even remember whether or not a film was in the process, but once the expensive equipment was installed in theatres there was no turning back. Unfortunately the technique involved a reversion in many cinematic effects to the days of D. W. Griffith. The compression of the wide image on to the film and its subsequent expansion in the projector made the photography grainy, especially in black and white, which was henceforth virtually abandoned. (At about the same time a transference to safety stock lost us the glamorous luminescent 'Feel' which had been possible with nitrate and which can still be seen in old prints.) The new shape was impossible to compose for; as Fritz Lang said, it was fine for funerals but what painter through the ages had ever selected it unless to cut up into a triptych? Editing was cut to a minimum because on an image so large each cut made the audience jump. Instead, and cheaper, the camera stayed still while the cast roved around the empty spaces in front of it, and there was an absurd number of shots in which the leading actors reclined so as better to fit the frame. Close-ups and subtle nuances were forgotten: no longer did the camera direct you to the drama, you had to look around and find it yourself. It is rather astonishing that directors with an eye to their reputations still persist in using the scope format, for after initial release the future of any film these days is on television, and no scope film, will satisfactorily adapt to the TV screen.

In many cinemas Cinemascope was even a fraud, for it had to be on a screen smaller in area than the old image, which was now being referred to sneeringly as 'postage stamp'. This happened when the old screen had already occupied all the width allowed by the cinema's structure: to get the Cinemascope shape, if you could not go any wider, height had to be sacrificed, and audiences wondered why suddenly they were looking at a ribbon of picture across the middle of the space which the fine old screen had occupied.

Cinemascope was patented by Fox, so the other companies all hastened to produce their own variations: Warnerscope, Metroscope, Techniscope, Superscope, Megascope, Camerascope, Panavision, each with its own cheap colour process. Projectionists all over the world were confused by these new names, and seldom knew whether they were projecting a film as they were supposed to. The results were often truly appalling, with lack of focus, too much brightness and wrong screen masking among the most common faults. Paramount's Vistavision, a non-anamorphic process, used the full frame ratio but was intended for projection at anything between 1.33:1 and 2:1, so that the essential action had to take place in a strip along the centre of the picture: consequently, to see a Vistavision print on a 1.33:1 screen was painful indeed, as all the action seemed to take place in the middle distance with great areas of unused space at the top and bottom of the image, and composition, which any painter knows to be all-important, was no longer possible. By the mid-fifties, however, 1.33:1 was no longer generally available, as 'wide screen' had become *de rigueur* even for non-anamorphic films: these cut off the top and bottom of the frame and magnified the rest. This meant that revivals were impossible unless one was prepared to suffer dancers without feet and actors without heads!

The result of all this technical uncertainty was that by the mid-fifties movies were in danger of becoming mere expensive sideshows, uninteresting to anyone of sensitivity. At the same time, an element of sophistication crept away from the popular arts: whereas in the thirties and forties smooth and educated idols had been set up for general approbation, the fifties and sixties showed an alarming tendency not merely to make heroes of 'people like us' but to rub our noses firmly in the gutter by devising stories whose leading characters had few redeeming features. Censorship had been absurdly tight and must obviously relax, but it was unwise and unexpected that the floodgates should open as they did, to admit movies which would previously have been considered anti-social rubbish. It was right, for instance, for Otto Preminger to fight the idiocies of the Production Code with his *The Moon Is Blue* and *The Man with the Golden Arm*, but it was a pity he won his battle with a leaden piece of schoolboy smut and an absurdly melodramatic updating of The Road to Ruin. Such films simply made one yearn to go back to the days of *Trouble in Paradise* and *The Palm Beach Story*, or for the true social concern expressed in the considered, powerful and moving masterpieces of Frank Capra, John Ford, or the early Chaplin.

The talents which had made Hollywood great were certainly nearing retirement by now, but it was perhaps unwise as well as churlish for the new wave to pension them off quite as hurriedly as they did, because there was no comparable talent to take their place. Great art directors like Anton Grot and Hans Dreier, great cameramen like Arthur Miller and James Wong Howe, great directors like Michael Curtiz and William Dieterle were either tossed aside or forced to work on material totally unsuited to their talents and not at all comparable to the films which had made their names. The results were big-budget disasters such as *The Egyptian* and *Omar Khayyam*; meanwhile the young directors were copying low-budget television techniques which for every *Marty* produced a dozen flatly realistic bores.

By the early sixties Hollywood had decided on a new image, but it had lost its old loyalties – the golden age audiences as well as the talents were getting older – and had to appeal deliberately to the 'emancipated' young generation. This meant a virtual abolition of censorship, and from the release of *Who's Afraid of Virginia Woolf?* in 1966 to that of *The Texas Chainsaw Massacre* and *The Devil in Miss Jones* ten years later is but a short step. The film is no longer an art, or even a craft: after a brief 'swinging' period it became an exploitation industry designed to take quick money from suckers, led by maverick Ken Russells rather than conscientious Irving Thalbergs, to plaudits from irresponsible critics whenever some totally untalented new director 'does his thing'. There is no justification except box office for films like *The Exorcist* or *Mandingo*, none except self-indulgence for a $12 million coffee-table film like *Barry Lyndon*, while the popularity even in sophisticated circles of shoddy pornography like *Deep Throat* and *Death Weekend* should stand as an awful warning to the leaders of our society that a vivid young art form has overreached itself and is well and truly on the verge of disaster. It is all very well to say in defence of such films that large numbers of people flock to see them: so they did once to bear-baiting and public executions and witch hunts, but the human race long ago prided itself on having passed that stage.

The movies will be lucky if, in their search for sensationalism, they do not check themselves out altogether. Audiences have dwindled rapidly and are still dwindling; so is the number of cinemas. The lush old two-thousand seaters have turned into supermarkets, and instead each city has its ineptly-run boxes of mini-cinemas, the effect of which is rather like sitting in cheaply decorated funeral parlours and paying through the nose for the privilege. The family outing to the cinema is a thing of the past: few families can afford it or can find a suitable film, except once or twice a year when the Disney organization stirs itself; and *their* standards are by no means as high as they were, as a comparison of *Robin Hood* with *Bambi* or *Pinocchio* will immediately show. (The fact that such an uninventive computerized cartoon as *Robin Hood* can do well at the box office is an instance of how starved the public is for the older, gentler forms of entertainment.)

Another problem besetting the cinema in the sixties was its adoption by verbose and pompous critics who were determined to turn it into serious art. True art is the work of one man, or at least his personal vision: each film is the work of several hundred people. Of these, admittedly the director has the most control, but to assign to him the role of *auteur* and to ignore the contribution of producer, writer, photographer, composer and editor is arrant nonsense, except possibly in the cases of such as Hitchcock and Kubrick who do control almost every aspect of their output. The new cinema journalism simply encouraged the worst motives of the new breed of film-maker, who came to know that whatever idiocy he perpetrated would be staunchly defended, researched and psychoanalysed by one of these mercenaries in search of a cause. If a character spat on the pavement this would be taken as his final shedding of his working-class upbringing; if he went to bed with a girl it would symbolize his treachery to his own beliefs and his giving in to the snares of Mammon. Listen to a modern critic in the British Film Institute's *Monthly Film Bulletin*, once a terse and reliable guide to film trends, on *Alice Doesn't Live Here Any More*: 'What Scorsese has done, however, is to rescue an American cliché from the bland, flat but much more portentous naturalism of such as *Harry and Tonto* and restore it to an emotional and intellectual complexity through his particular brand of baroque realism.' Or on Rafelson's *Stay Hungry*: 'What distinguishes him from other film-makers of the "head" generation is both the poetic sureness of his fragmentary, allusive style, and the elliptical observation which prevents his social themes from being spiked too easily on the cultural antitheses of that bygone era.' Spare us.

Some of the elements missing from modern cinema are to be found in television, certainly in the UK with its brilliant documentaries, sharp comedies, serious art programmes and single plays; Americans are less lucky except on their public broadcasting system. But television is a private enjoyment, and one inevitably misses the sense of comradeship, of sharing a pleasure, that the cinema used to fulfil. Who having experienced them can forget the feeling of a full house being pleasurably chilled by *The Cat and the Canary*, or rolling in the aisles at Laurel and Hardy, or hoping against hope that Colman will find his *Lost Horizon*? What modern films can produce the sheer entertainment value and unforgettable, vivid scenes of such as *The Philadelphia Story, Stagecoach, Rebecca, Camille, Casablanca, Citizen Kane, Singin' in the Rain, A Night at the Opera, The Lady Vanishes,* and *The Third Man?* These were all intelligent films, all made for the despised mass audience, and they all made money because they were produced with impeccable professionalism and star talent, and because to these qualities they added heart and good humour. Where is the good humour in *Jaws?* Where is the heart in *The Exorcist?* These are rides on fairground ghost trains: one pays for the thrill, but one comes out more depressed than uplifted.

Of course there are some genuine talents at work in films today. One respects the likes of Jack Nicholson and Ellen Burstyn and Al Pacino and Glenda Jackson, but they are all depressingly committed to their own self-expression and to the depiction of mankind with warts and all, not to pleasing, stimulating or improving the public. They need control; but where are the likes of Lubitsch to control them? Of Sturges? Of Ben Hecht? Of James Whale? Of Donald Ogden Stewart? Of S. J. Perelman? Of Robert Benchley and Dorothy Parker? The films produced by Altman and Scorsese and Ashby are doubtless stimulating in their violent, abrasive way but they are not the whole of life. David Lean and John Schlesinger and Arthur Penn are meticulous craftsmen, but they are driven by commerce into the excesses of *Ryan's Daughter* and *Marathon Man* and *The Missouri Breaks.* In the acting league, where are our up-and-coming replacements for David Niven, Cary Grant, Melvyn Douglas, Katharine Hepburn, Ronald Colman? When again will it be the turn of grace and elegance? When indeed will actors want to work? Marlon Brando, Elizabeth Taylor and their like prefer to demand an impossibly high fee, and if they do not get it to sit comfortably at home on the proceeds of their previous hits.

Hollywood at its best — and for Hollywood also read Ealing and Tobis Klangfilm and Svenske Filmindustri — was the purveyor of an expensive and elegant craft which at times touched art, though seldom throughout a whole film. Reality was seldom sought, but why should it be? Real life is not dramatic anyway: even *Taxi Driver* is a heightening, a selection, an emphasis. So are all the great realist films from *The Battleship Potemkin* to *The Grapes of Wrath.* And so are the great works of Beethoven, of Rembrandt, of Michelangelo. Film stands to life as poetry to prose, and its comments were at their most apt and stylish when movies were confined to the sound stage and the backlot. Freedom from that confinement has not made them any better: it has only made them diffuse and patchy and overlong, and colour has made things worse because it apes reality whereas black and white conjured up its own mood and its own comment. Today's screens are too large for the eye to take in. Sound tracks are so 'realistic' as to be incoherent. Big budgets are wasted on movies which would have been ten times as effective if a little imagination had been used or required. Kaleidoscopic effects dazzle the eye and befuddle the brain; immensely long precredits sequences make one think the film is nearly over before it actually starts; characterization flies out the window because sex and violence must be fitted in somehow. Plot doesn't matter; since swinging London was invented every film has become a 'happening': which is another way of saying that anything goes and lack of professionalism cannot be criticized.

All right, this essay is a deliberate hatchet job by a disappointed fan who has turned devil's advocate. Some of the new films clearly have virtues which the old ones didn't possess: one is grateful for *The Graduate* and *Charlie Bubbles* and *Cabaret* and *One Flew over the Cuckoo's Nest,* which for various reasons could never have been made in the old Hollywood. But if my thesis were not largely true, how would one explain the enormous popularity of old movies on television, or the recent deluge of books about them? Why, out of more than sixty films on British television over the Christmas of 1976, were *White Heat* (1948), *A Night at the Opera* (1935) and *Yankee Doodle Dandy* (1942) the most discussed and appreciated? Nostalgia is only a trendy word to describe something which people have at last learned to appreciate because it has been taken away from them. No one in his right mind would be nostalgic for PRC second features or for much of the pure assembly line product which inevitably poured out of the studios when they were working at full pitch. And one must progress. But surely not to the wasteful ineptitude which confronts us at the cinema these days. Not to *lucky Lady*, *Mother Jugs and Speed*, *At Long Last Love* or *Harry and Walter go to New York*. Must modern audiences really put up with inane or violent rubbish and appear to enjoy it simply because they are supposed not to know any better? We may not be able to get the golden age back, but we can cry for it. If 'they' fail to respond we can at least appreciate the best of it, and learn from that best. This book, I hope, may help a few people to do that.